The Broadview Anthology of

LITERATURE OF THE
REVOLUTIONARY PERIOD
1770 – 1832

In Memoriam

D.L. Macdonald, 1955–2010

The Broadview Anthology of

LITERATURE OF THE REVOLUTIONARY PERIOD
1770 – 1832

EDITED BY

D.L. MACDONALD AND ANNE McWHIR

broadview press

© 2010 D.L. Macdonald and Anne McWhir

All rights reserved. The use of any part of this publication reproduced, transmitted in any form or by any means, electronic, mechanical, photocopying, recording, or otherwise, or stored in a retrieval system, without prior written consent of the publisher—or in the case of photocopying, a license from Access Copyright (Canadian Copyright Licensing Agency), One Yonge Street, Suite 1900, Toronto, Ontario M5E 1E5—is an infringement of the copyright law.

LIBRARY AND ARCHIVES CANADA CATALOGUING IN PUBLICATION

   The Broadview anthology of literature of the Revolutionary period, 1770-1832 / edited by D.L. Macdonald and Anne McWhir.

Includes bibliographical references and index.
ISBN 978-1-55111-051-6

   1. English literature—18th century. 2. English literature—19th century.
I. Macdonald, D.L. (David Lorne), 1955- II. McWhir, Anne, 1947-

PS533.B76   2009   820.8'006   C2009-903546-4

Broadview Press is an independent, international publishing house, incorporated in 1985. Broadview believes in shared ownership, both with its employees and with the general public; since the year 2000 Broadview shares have traded publicly on the Toronto Venture Exchange under the symbol BDP.

We welcome comments and suggestions regarding any aspect of our publications—please feel free to contact us at the addresses below or at broadview@broadviewpress.com.

North America
PO Box 1243
Peterborough, Ontario
Canada K9J 7H5

2215 Kenmore Avenue
Buffalo, NY, USA 14207
TEL: (705) 743-8990
FAX: (705) 743-8353
customerservice@broadviewpress.com

UK, Europe, Central Asia, Middle East, Africa, India, and Southeast Asia
Eurospan Group
3 Henrietta St.,
London WC2E 8LU, UK
TEL: 44 (0) 1767 604972
FAX: 44 (0) 1767 601640
eurospan@turpin-distribution.com

Australia and New Zealand
NewSouth Books
c/o TL Distribution
15-23 Helles Avenue
Moorebank, NSW, Australia 2170
TEL: (02) 8778 9999
FAX: (02) 8778 9944
orders@tldistribution.com.au

www.broadviewpress.com
Broadview Press acknowledges the financial support of the Government of Canada through the Book Publishing Industry Development Program (BPIDP) for our publishing activities.

Cover design George Kirkpatrick

PRINTED IN CANADA

Contents

EDITORIAL PREFACE XXXII

BENJAMIN FRANKLIN (1706 – 1790) 1
   from *Two Tracts: Information to Those Who Would Remove to America. And, Remarks Concerning the Savages of North America* (1784)
      Remarks Concerning the Savages of North-America 1

RICHARD PRICE (1723 – 1791) 5
   from *A Discourse on the Love of our Country, delivered on Nov. 4, 1789, at the Meeting-House in the Old Jewry, to the Society for Commemorating the Revolution in Great Britain* (1789) 5

SIR JOSHUA REYNOLDS (1723 – 1792) 11
   from *Seven Discourses Delivered in the Royal Academy by the President* (1778)
      from A Discourse, Delivered to the Students of the Royal Academy, on the Distribution of the Prizes, December 10, 1776, by the President [DISCOURSE 7] 11

CLARA REEVE (1729 – 1807) 16
   from *The Progress of Romance, through Times, Countries, and Manners; with Remarks on the Good and Bad Effects of It, on Them Respectively; in a Course of Evening Conversations* (1785)
      from Evening 7 17

EDMUND BURKE (1729? – 1797) 22
   from *Reflections on the Revolution in France, and on the Proceedings in Certain Societies in London Relative to That Event. In a Letter Intended to Have Been Sent to a Gentleman in Paris* (1790) 22
   A Letter from the Right Honourable Edmund Burke to a Noble Lord, on the Attacks Made Upon Him and His Pension, in the House of Lords, by the Duke of Bedford and the Earl of Lauderdale, Early in the Present Sessions of Parliament (1796) 33

IGNATIUS SANCHO (1729? – 1780) 43
   from *Letters of the Late Ignatius Sancho, an African. To Which are Prefixed Memoirs of his Life, by Joseph Jekyll, Esq. M.P.* 5th ed. (1803)
      LETTER 36, To Mr. Sterne 43

JOHN SCOTT (1730 – 1783) 45
   from *Poetical Works* (1782)
      Ode 13 ["I hate that drum's discordant sound"] 45

OLIVER GOLDSMITH (1730? – 1774) 46
   The Deserted Village, A Poem (1770) 46

Contents

CATHARINE MACAULAY (1731 – 1791) 52
   from *Letters on Education, with Observations on Religious and Metaphysical Subjects* (1790)
      PART 1, LETTER 24 52

WILLIAM COWPER (1731 – 1800) 55
   from *The Task, A Poem, in Six Books* (1785)
      from BOOK 2, The Time-Piece 55
   from *The Works of William Cowper, Esq. comprising his Poems, Correspondence, and Translations*, ed. Robert Southey (1837)
      The Negro's Complaint 56
      Sweet Meat Has Sour Sauce: or, The Slave-Trader in the Dumps 57
   from *Life, and Posthumous Writings of William Cowper*, ed. William Hayley (1803)
      Sonnet, to William Wilberforce, Esq. 57
      The Cast-Away 58

ERASMUS DARWIN (1731 – 1802) 59
   from *The Temple of Nature; or, The Origin of Society: A Poem. With Philosophical Notes* (1803)
      from CANTO 4, Of Good and Evil 59

JOHN ADAMS (1734 – 1826) and ABIGAIL ADAMS (1744 – 1818) 61
   Letters
      Abigail Adams to John Adams, 31 March 1776 61
      John Adams to Abigail Adams, 14 April 1776 62

J. HECTOR ST. JOHN DE CRÈVECOEUR (1735 – 1813) 64
   from *Letters from an American Farmer* (1782)
      from LETTER 12, Distresses of a Frontier Man 64

THOMAS PAINE (1737 – 1809) 72
   from *The Age of Reason; Being an Investigation of True and Fabulous Theology* (1794) 72

CHARLOTTE BROOKE (1740 – 1793) 77
   from *Reliques of Irish Poetry: Consisting of Heroic Poems, Odes, Elegies, and Songs, Translated into English Verse: with Notes Explanatory and Historical; and the Originals in the Irish Character. To Which is Subjoined an Irish Tale* (1789)
      The Lamentation of Cucullin, over the Body of his Son Conloch 77
      Song. For Mable Kelly. By Carolan 79

ANNA SEWARD (1742 – 1809) 82
   from *Llangollen Vale, with Other Poems* (1796)
      Eyam 83
      To Time Past. Written Dec. 1772 84
   from *Original Sonnets on Various Subjects; and Odes Paraphrased from Horace* (1799)
      Sonnet 10. To Honora Sneyd 84
      Sonnet 71. To the Poppy 84

Contents

HANNAH COWLEY (1743 – 1809) ... 85
    from the *World, Fashionable Advertiser* (10 July 1787)
        To Della Crusca. The Pen ... 85
    from the *World* (22 December 1787)
        To Della Crusca ... 85

THOMAS JEFFERSON (1743 – 1826) ... 87
    In Congress, July 4, 1776, *A Declaration by the Representatives of the United States of America, in Congress Assembled* ... 87

ANNA LAETITIA BARBAULD (1743 – 1825) ... 90
    from *Poems* (1773)
        The Mouse's Petition, Found in the Trap Where He Had Been Confin'd All Night ... 91
        A Summer Evening's Meditation ... 92
    An Address to the Opposers of the Repeal of the Corporation and Test Acts (1790) ... 93
    Epistle to William Wilberforce, Esq. on the Rejection of the Bill for Abolishing the Slave-Trade (1791) ... 102
    from the *Monthly Magazine* 4 (July–December 1797)
        Washing-Day ... 103
    from the *Monthly Magazine* 7 (January–June 1799)
        To Mr. C———ge ... 105
    Eighteen Hundred and Eleven, A Poem (1812) ... 105
    from *The Works of Anna Laetitia Barbauld. With A Memoir by Lucy Aikin* (1825)
        The Rights of Woman ... 111
        Inscription for an Ice-House ... 112
        To the Poor ... 113
        To a Little Invisible Being Who Is Expected Soon to Become Visible ... 113
        The First Fire. October 1st, 1815 ... 114

HANNAH MORE (1745 – 1833) ... 115
    Slavery, A Poem (1788) ... 116
    Village Politics. Addressed to All the Mechanics, Journeymen, and Day Labourers, in Great Britain. By Will Chip, a Country Carpenter (1792)
        A Dialogue between Jack Anvil the Blacksmith, and Tom Hod the Mason ... 120
    from *Cheap Repository Tracts* (1795)
        Patient Joe; or, the Newcastle Collier ... 125
    from *Strictures on the Modern System of Female Education. With a View of the Principles and Conduct Prevalent among Women of Rank and Fortune* (1799)
        CHAPTER 4 ... 127

THOMAS BELLAMY (1745 – 1800) ... 130
    The Benevolent Planters: A Dramatic Piece as performed at the Theatre Royal, Haymarket (1789) ... 130

Contents

SAMUEL HEARNE (1745 – 1792) 135
    from *A Journey from Prince of Wales's Fort in Hudson's Bay to the Northern Ocean* (1795)
        from CHAPTER 4 135
        from CHAPTER 5 137
        from CHAPTER 9 138

OLAUDAH EQUIANO (1745? – 1797) 140
    from *The Interesting Narrative of the Life of Olaudah Equiano, or Gustavus Vassa, the African. Written by Himself* (1789)
        CHAPTER 2 140

ELIZABETH HANDS (1746? – 1815) 149
    from *The Death of Amnon. A Poem. With an Appendix: Containing Pastorals, and Other Poetical Pieces* (1789)
        A Poem, On the Supposition of an Advertisement Appearing in a Morning Paper, of the Publication of a Volume of Poems, by a Servant Maid 149
        A Poem, On the Supposition of the Book Having Been Published and Read 150
        Written, Originally Extempore, on Seeing a Mad Heifer Run through the Village Where the Author Lives 151

SUSANNA BLAMIRE (1747 – 1794) 152
    from *The Poetical Works of Miss Susanna Blamire, "The Muse of Cumberland"* (1842)
        from Stoklewath Or, The Cumbrian Village 152

CHARLOTTE SMITH (1749 – 1806) 161
    from *Elegiac Sonnets. Third Edition, with Twenty Additional Sonnets* (1786)
        1. ["The partial Muse, has from my earliest hours"] 162
        3. To a nightingale 162
        4. To the moon 162
        7. On the departure of the nightingale 162
        17. From the thirteenth cantata of Metastasio 163
        21. Supposed to be written by Werter 163
        24. By the same 163
        25. By the same. Just before his death 163
        27. ["Sighing I see yon little troop at play"] 164
        32. To Melancholy. Written on the banks of the Arun, October, 1785 164
        35. To fortitude 164
    from *Elegiac Sonnets, by Charlotte Smith. The Fifth Edition, with Additional Sonnets and Other Poems* (1789)
        44. Written in the Church Yard at Middleton in Sussex 165
    from *Elegiac Sonnets. The Sixth Edition, with Additional Sonnets and Other Poems* (1792)
        Thirty-Eight. Address'd to Mrs. H——Y 165
    The Emigrants, A Poem, in Two Books (1793) 166
        To William Cowper, Esq. 166

Contents

    BOOK 1 167
    BOOK 2 173

PRISCILLA WAKEFIELD (1750 – 1832) 180
    from *Excursions in North America, Described in Letters from a Gentleman and his Young Companion, to Their Friends in England* (1806)
        LETTER 32, Mr. Henry Franklin to Edwin Middleton 180

LADY ANNE LINDSAY (1750 – 1825) 186
    Auld Robin Gray; A Ballad, ed. Sir Walter Scott (1825) 187

CATHERINE ANN DORSET (1750? – 1817?) 190
    from *The Peacock at Home; and Other Poems* (1809)
        The Spider 190

THOMAS CARY (1751 – 1823) 192
    from *Abram's Plains: A Poem* (1789) 192

PHILIP FRENEAU (1752 – 1832) 198
    from *Poems Written between the Years 1768 & 1794* (1795)
        The Indian Burying-Ground 198
        The Wild Honey Suckle 199
        George the Third's Soliloquy 199
        To Sir Toby, a Sugar-Planter in the Interior Parts of Jamaica ... 200

FRANCES BURNEY (1752 – 1840) 202
    from *The Journals and Letters of Fanny Burney (Madame d'Arblay)*, ed. Joyce Hemlow et al. (1975)
        from Letter to Esther Burney, 22 March–June 1812 202

THOMAS CHATTERTON (1752 – 1770) 208
    from *Poems, Supposed to Have Been Written at Bristol, by Thomas Rowley, and Others, in the Fifteenth Century; The Greatest Part Now First Published from the Most Authentic Copies, with an Engraved Specimen of One of the MSS.* (1777)
        The Storie of William Canynge 209
        On Happienesse, by William Canynge 212
    from *A Supplement to the Miscellanies of Thomas Chatterton* (1784)
        Heccar and Gaira. An African Eclogue Jan. 3, 1770 212
    from William Barrett, *The History and Antiquities of the City of Bristol* (1789)
        The Warre 214

ELIZABETH INCHBALD (1753 – 1821) 215
    from *The British Theatre* (1806–09)
        On De Monfort; a Tragedy, in Five Acts; by Joanna Baillie, as Performed at the Theatre Royal, Drury Lane 215

Contents

On Lovers' Vows; A Play in Five Acts; Altered from the German of Kotzebue, by Mrs. Inchbald.
As Performed at the Theatre Royal, Covent-Garden 216

PHILLIS WHEATLEY (c. 1753 – 1784) 218
    from *Poems on Various Subjects, Religious and Moral. By Phillis Wheatley, Negro Servant to Mr. John Wheatley of Boston, in New England* (1773)
        On Being Brought from Africa to America 218
        On the Death of the Rev. Mr. George Whitefield. 1770 218
        To the Right Honourable William, Earl of Dartmouth, His Majesty's Principal Secretary of State
          for North America, &c. 219
        To S.M. a Young African Painter, on Seeing His Works 220

ANN YEARSLEY (c. 1753 – 1806) 221
    from *Poems, on Several Occasions. By Ann Yearsley, a Milkwoman of Bristol* (1785)
        To the Same [Stella]; on Her Accusing the Author of Flattery, and of Ascribing to the Creature
          That Praise Which Is Due Only to the Creator 221
        On Mrs. Montagu 222
    Reflections on the Death of Louis XVI (1793) 223
    from *The Rural Lyre; A Volume of Poems: Dedicated to the Right Honourable the Earl of Bristol, Lord Bishop of Derry* (1796)
        To Mira, on the Care of Her Infant 224

JOEL BARLOW (1754 – 1812) 227
    from *The Hasty-Pudding: A Poem, in Three Cantos. Written at Chambery, in Savoy, Jan. 1793* (1793)
        CANTO 1 227
    from the *Huntington Library Quarterly* 2 (1938–39)
        Advice to a Raven in Russia. December, 1812 229

GEORGE CRABBE (1754 – 1832) 231
    from *The Borough: A Poem in Twenty-four Letters* (1810)
        LETTER 22, The Poor of the Borough. Peter Grimes 231

ANNE GRANT (1755 – 1838) 237
    from *The Highlanders, and Other Poems*, 2nd ed. (1808)
        A Familiar Epistle to a Friend. Written in 1795 237

ROBERT MERRY (1755 – 1798) 241
    from the *British Album* (1790)
        The Adieu and Recall to Love 241
        To Anna Matilda 242
        The Interview 243

WILLIAM GODWIN (1756 – 1836) 245
    from *An Enquiry Concerning Political Justice, and Its Influence on General Virtue and Happiness* (1793)
    from BOOK 2, *Principles of Society*, from CHAPTER 2, Of Justice 246

CONTENTS

    from BOOK 8, *Of Property*, *from* CHAPTER 8, Of the Means of Introducing the Genuine
        System of Property 248
    from *Memoirs of the Author of* A Vindication of the Rights of Woman (1798)
        from CHAPTER 6, 1790–1792 250
        from CHAPTER 9, 1796, 1797 253
        from CHAPTER 10 257

GEORGIANA CAVENDISH (1757 – 1806) 261
    The Passage of the Mountain of Saint Gothard. A Poem (1802) 261

WILLIAM BLAKE (1757 – 1827) 264
    from *Songs of Innocence* (1789)
        Introduction 265
        The Ecchoing Green 265
        The Lamb 265
        The Little Black Boy 266
        A Dream 266
        The Chimney Sweeper 266
        The Divine Image 267
        Holy Thursday 267
        Nurse's Song 268
        Infant Joy 268
    The Marriage of Heaven and Hell (1793) 268
    Visions of the Daughters of Albion (1793) 277
    America a Prophecy (1793) 284
    from *Songs of Innocence and of Experience, Shewing the Two Contrary States of the Human Soul* (1794)
        from Songs of Experience 293
            Introduction 293
            Earth's Answer 293
            The Clod & the Pebble 293
            Holy Thursday 294
            The Little Girl Lost 294
            The Little Girl Found 295
            The Chimney Sweeper 295
            The Sick Rose 296
            The Fly 296
            The Tyger 296
            My Pretty Rose Tree 296
            Ah! Sun-Flower 297
            The Garden of Love 297
            London 297
            The Human Abstract 297
            Infant Sorrow 298
            A Poison Tree 298

Contents

from *Milton* (1800–08)
    Preface 298
from *The Pickering Manuscript*
    The Mental Traveller 299
    The Crystal Cabinet 300
    Auguries of Innocence 301
Marginalia
    from Annotations to the *Works of Sir Joshua Reynolds* (1798) 302
    Annotations to Wordsworth's Preface to *The Excursion, being a portion of The Recluse, A Poem* (1814) 304
    from Annotations to Thornton's *The Lord's Prayer, Newly Translated* (1827) 305
Letters
    [To] Rev^d Dr Trusler, 23 August 1799 305
    To Thomas Butts, 22 November 1802 307

HARRIET LEE (1757 – 1851) 309
    from *Canterbury Tales* (1795–1805)
        The Old Woman's Tale. Lothaire: A Legend 309

OTTOBAH CUGOANO (c. 1757 – c. 1801) 322
    from *Thoughts and Sentiments on the Evil and Wicked Traffic of the Slavery and Commerce of the Human Species, Humbly Submitted to the Inhabitants of Great-Britain* (1787) 322

MARY ROBINSON (1758 – 1800) 325
    from *Poems* (1791)
        Ode to Beauty 326
    from the *Morning Post* (29 January 1795)
        January, 1795 327
    Sappho and Phaon. In a Series of Legitimate Sonnets, with Thoughts on Poetical Subjects, and Anecdotes of the Grecian Poetess (1796) 328
    from *Lyrical Tales* (1800)
        The Haunted Beach 343
        The Negro Girl 344
        The Alien Boy 346
    from the *Morning Post* (1 August 1800)
        The Camp 348
    from *The Wild Wreath* (1804)
        A London Summer Morning 349
        The Poet's Garret 349
    from *The Poetical Works of the Late Mrs. Mary Robinson* (1806)
        To the Poet Coleridge 351
        The Savage of Aveyron 352
        The Birth-Day 354
        The Wintry Day 355
        The Old Beggar 355

Contents

HENRIETTA O'NEILL (1758 – 1793) 358
    from *Desmond. A Novel.* By Charlotte Smith (1792)
        Ode to the Poppy 358

ROBERT BURNS (1759 – 1796) 360
    from *Poems, Chiefly in the Scottish Dialect* (1786)
        To a Mouse, On turning her up in her Nest, with the Plough, November, 1785 360
        To A Mountain-Daisy, On turning one down, with the Plough, in April—1786 361
        To A Louse, On Seeing one on a Lady's Bonnet, at Church 362
    from *Poems, Chiefly in the Scottish Dialect* (1787)
        John Barleycorn. A Ballad 363
    from Francis Grose, *The Antiquities of Scotland* (1791)
        Tam O'Shanter. A Tale 364
    from *Holy Willie's Prayer, Letter to John Goudie, Kilmarnock, and Six Favourite Songs* (1799)
        Holy Willie's Prayer 368
        A Man's a Man, for a' That: A Song 369
    from *The Scots Musical Museum* (1787–1803)
        Ae Fond Kiss, And Then We Sever 370
        A Red, Red Rose 370
        Comin' thro' the Rye 371
    from *The Poems and Songs of Robert Burns*, ed. James Kinsley (1968)
        Auld Lang Syne 371
        The Rights of Woman—Spoken by Miss Fontenelle on her benefit night,
            November 26, 1792 371
        Robert Bruce's March to Bannockburn 372

MARY WOLLSTONECRAFT (1759 –1797) 374
    from *A Vindication of the Rights of Men, in a Letter to the Right Honourable Edmund Burke;*
    Occasioned by his Reflections on the Revolution in France (1790) 375
    from *A Vindication of the Rights of Woman* (1792)
        Dedication, To M. Talleyrand-Périgord, Late Bishop Of Autun 385
        Introduction 387
        CHAPTER 2, The Prevailing Opinion of a Sexual Character Discussed 390
        CHAPTER 3, The Same Subject Continued 401
        CHAPTER 4, Observations on the State of Degradation to Which Woman Is Reduced by
            Various Causes 410
        from CHAPTER 13, Some Instances of the Folly Which the Ignorance of Women Generates;
            with Concluding Reflections on the Moral Improvement That a Revolution in Female
            Manners Might Naturally Be Expected to Produce, Section 2 426
    from *Letters Written During a Short Residence in Sweden, Norway, and Denmark* (1796)
        ADVERTISEMENT 428
        LETTER 1 429
        LETTER 6 433
        LETTER 7 436

Contents

    LETTER 8 440
    LETTER 15 444
from *Posthumous Works of the Author of* A Vindication of the Rights of Woman (1798)
    from The Wrongs of Woman: or Maria. A Fragment, CHAPTER 5 446
    On Poetry, and Our Relish for the Beauties of Nature 455
Letters
    To Joseph Johnson, 26 December 1792 458
    To Gilbert Imlay, 19 August 1794 458
    To Gilbert Imlay, 9 February 1795 459
    To Gilbert Imlay, c. March 1796 460
    To William Godwin, 17 August 1796 460
    To William Godwin, 17 August 1796 461

HELEN LEIGH (fl. 1788) 462
    from *Miscellaneous Poems* (1788)
        The Natural Child 462

MARIA LOGAN (fl. 1793) 463
    from *Poems on Several Occasions*. 2nd ed. (1793)
        To Opium 463
        Verses On Hearing That an Airy and Pleasant Situation, near a Populous and Commercial
        Town, Was Surrounded with New Buildings 464

JANET LITTLE (1759 – 1813) 465
    from *The Poetical Works of Janet Little, the Scotch Milkmaid* (1792)
        Given to a Lady Who Asked Me to Write A Poem 465

RICHARD POLWHELE (1760 – 1838) 467
    The Unsex'd Females: A Poem (1798) 467

THOMAS CLARKSON (1760 – 1846) 472
    from *An Essay on the Slavery and Commerce of the Human Species, particularly the African, translated from a Latin Dissertation, which was honoured with the First Prize in the University of Cambridge for the Year 1785* (1786)
        from PART 3, The Slavery of the Africans in the European Colonies, CHAPTER 1 472
    from *The History of the Rise, Progress and Accomplishment of the Abolition of the African Slave-trade, by the British Parliament* (1808)
        Illustration of a Slave Ship 475

MARY HAYS (1760 – 1843) 476
    from *Appeal to the Men of Great Britain in Behalf of Women* (1798)
        What Women Are 476

Contents

HELEN MARIA WILLIAMS (1761 – 1827) 483
    from *Letters Written in France, in the Summer 1790, to a Friend in England; Containing, Various Anecdotes Relative to the French Revolution; and Memoirs of Mons. and Madame du F——* (1790)
        LETTER 4 483
        LETTER 11 486
    A Farewell, for Two Years, to England. A Poem (1791) 487
    from *Poems on Various Subjects. With Introductory Remarks on the Present State of Science and Literature in France* (1823)
        To Sensibility 490
        Sonnet: To the Torrid Zone 492

JOANNA BAILLIE (1762 – 1851) 493
    from *Poems; Wherein It Is Attempted to Describe Certain Views of Nature and of Rustic Manners; and also, To Point Out, in Some Instances, the Different Influence Which the Same Circumstances Produce on Different Characters* (1790)
        A Winter Day 493
        Thunder 497
        A Mother to Her Waking Infant 499
        A Child to his Sick Grand-Father 500
    from *A Series of Plays: In Which it Is Attempted to Delineate the Stronger Passions of the Mind. Each Passion being the Subject of a Tragedy and a Comedy* (1798)
        from Introductory Discourse 500
        De Monfort 515
    from *Fugitive Verses* (1840)
        Thunder 552
        Song, Woo'd and Married and A' 553

WILLIAM LISLE BOWLES (1762 – 1850) 555
    from *Fourteen Sonnets, Elegiac and Descriptive. Written During a Tour* (1789)
        To the River Itchin, Near Winton 555
        On Dover Cliffs. July 20, 1787 555

WILLIAM COBBETT (1763 – 1835) 556
    from *Political Register* (11 December 1813)
        from To Mr. Alderman Wood, On the Subject of Teaching the Children of the Poor to Read
            LETTER 1 556
    from *Cobbett's Weekly Register* (5 January 1822)
        from Kentish Journal 558

SAMUEL ROGERS (1763 – 1855) 561
    from *Poems* (1812)
        The Boy of Egremond 561
    from *Poems* (1814)
        To —— 562

Contents

ANN RADCLIFFE (1764 – 1823) 563
    from *The Mysteries of Udolpho, A Romance; Interspersed with Some Pieces of Poetry* (1794)
        Storied Sonnet 564
        Rondeau 564
        To Autumn 564
        To Melancholy 565
    from *Gaston de Blondeville* (1826)
        Scene on the Northern Shore of Sicily 565
    from *New Monthly Magazine and Literary Journal* 16, Part 1 (1826)
        from On the Supernatural in Poetry. By the Late Mrs. Radcliffe 566

JOHN THELWALL (1764 – 1834) 570
    from *Poems Written in Close Confinement at the Tower and Newgate, under a Charge of High Treason* (1795)
        Stanzas On Hearing for Certainty That We Were to be Tried for High Treason 570
    from *Poems Chiefly Written in Retirement* (1801)
        To the Infant Hampden.—Written during a Sleepless Night. Derby. Oct. 1797 571

CATHERINE MARIA FANSHAWE (1765 – 1834) 572
    from *A Collection of Poems, Chiefly Manuscript, and from Living Authors*, ed. Joanna Baillie (1823)
        A Riddle 572

ROBERT BLOOMFIELD (1766 – 1823) 573
    from *The Farmer's Boy; A Rural Poem* (1800)
        from Spring 573

THOMAS ROBERT MALTHUS (1766 – 1834) 577
    from *An Essay on the Principle of Population, as It Affects the Future Improvement of Society. With Remarks on the Speculations of Mr. Godwin, M. Condorcet, and Other Writers* (1798)
        from CHAPTER 10 577

CAROLINA OLIPHANT, LADY NAIRNE (1766 – 1845) 583
    from *The Scottish Minstrel* (1821–24)
        The Land o' the Leal 583
        Caller Herrin' 584
        The Laird o' Cockpen 584

MARIA EDGEWORTH (1768 – 1849) 586
    from *Popular Tales in Two Volumes* (1804)
        The Grateful Negro 586

ANN BATTEN CRISTALL (c. 1768 – after 1816) 597
    from *Poetical Sketches, in Irregular Verse* (1795)
        Before Twilight. Eyezion 597
        Morning. Rosamonde 599

Contents

  Noon. Lysander 599
  Evening. Gertrude 601
  Night 603

JANE MARCET (1769 – 1858) 604
 from *Conversations on Political Economy; in Which the Elements of that Science are Familiarly Explained* (1816)
  from CONVERSATION 10, On the Condition of the Poor 604

AMELIA OPIE (1769 – 1853) 608
 from *Poems* (1802)
  Song of a Hindustani Girl 608
 from *The Warrior's Return, and Other Poems* (1808)
  To A Maniac 609

GEORGE CANNING (1770 – 1827) and JOHN HOOKHAM FRERE (1769 – 1846) 610
 from *The Anti-Jacobin; or, Weekly Examiner* (27 November 1797)
  Sapphics: The Friend of Humanity and the Knife-Grinder 610
 from *The New Morality* 611

WILLIAM WORDSWORTH (1770 – 1850) 617
 from *Lyrical Ballads, with A Few Other Poems* (1798)
  Advertisement 618
  Goody Blake, and Harry Gill, a true story 619
  Simon Lee, the old Huntsman, with an incident in which he was concerned ... 621
  Anecdote for Fathers, shewing how the art of lying may be taught ... 622
  We are Seven 623
  Lines Written in Early Spring 624
  The Thorn 625
  The Idiot Boy 629
  Expostulation and Reply 635
  The Tables Turned; an Evening Scene, on the same subject 636
  Old Man Travelling; animal tranquility and decay, a sketch 636
  The Complaint of a Forsaken Indian Woman 637
  Lines Written a Few Miles Above Tintern Abbey, on revisiting the banks of the Wye during a tour, July 13, 1798 638
 from *Lyrical Ballads, with Other Poems. In Two Volumes* (1800)
  Preface 640
  There was a Boy 651
  Strange fits of passion I have known 652
  Song ["She dwelt among th' untrodden ways"] 652
  A slumber did my spirit seal 652
  Lucy Gray 653
  The Two April Mornings 654
  Nutting 655

Contents

Three years she grew in sun and shower 655
Michael, A Pastoral Poem 656

from *Poems in Two Volumes* (1807)
    I travell'd among unknown Men 662
    Beggars 663
    Resolution and Independence 663
    Composed upon Westminster Bridge, Sept. 3, 1802 665
    The world is too much with us; late and soon 666
    It is a beauteous Evening, calm and free 666
    To Toussaint L'Ouverture 666
    London, 1802 666
    The Solitary Reaper 667
    To a Butterfly ["Stay near me—do not take thy flight!"] 667
    My heart leaps up when I behold 667
    I wandered lonely as a Cloud 668
    To a Butterfly ["I've watch'd you now a full half hour"] 668
    To Thomas Clarkson, On the final passing of the Bill for the Abolition of the Slave Trade,
        March 1807 668
    Elegiac Stanzas, Suggested by a Picture of Peele Castle, in a Storm, painted by Sir George
        Beaumont 669
    Ode 670

from the *Friend*, 11 (26 October 1809)
    Oh! pleasant exercise of hope and joy! 673

from *The Excursion, Being a Portion of The Recluse, A Poem* (1814)
    from Home at Grasmere 673
        BOOK FIRST, The Wanderer 675

from *Poems by William Wordsworth: including Lyrical Ballads, and the Miscellaneous Pieces
of the Author. With Additional Poems, a New Preface, and a Supplementary Essay* (1815)
    Surprized by joy—impatient as the Wind 687

from *The River Duddon, a Series of Sonnets: Vaudracour and Julia: and Other Poems. To Which Is
Annexed, a Topographical Description of the Country of the Lakes, in the North of England* (1820)
    Vaudracour and Julia 688

from *The Poetical Works of William Wordsworth. In Five Volumes* (1827)
    Scorn not the Sonnet; Critic, you have frowned 691

from the *Athenæum* (12 December 1835)
    The Ettrick Shepherd. Extempore Effusion, upon reading, in the Newcastle Journal,
        the notice of the Death of the Poet, James Hogg 692

from *Poems, Chiefly of Early and Late Years; including The Borderers, A Tragedy* (1842)
    The unremitting voice of nightly streams 693

from *The Prelude 1799, 1805, 1850*, ed. Jonathan Wordsworth, M.H. Abrams,
and Stephen Gill (1979)
    The Two-Part Prelude of 1799 693
        FIRST PART 693
        SECOND PART 699

Contents

Letters
    To Charles James Fox, 14 January 1801 706
    To Mary Wordsworth, 11 August 1810 708

JAMES HOGG (1770 – 1835) 711
    from *The Queen's Wake: A Legendary Poem*, 3rd ed. (1814)
        Kilmeny 711

CHARLES BROCKDEN BROWN (1771 – 1810) 717
    from the *Literary Magazine and American Register* 6.35 (1806)
        On the Standard of Taste 717

SIR WALTER SCOTT (1771 – 1832) 722
    from *Minstrelsy of the Scottish Border: Consisting of Historical and Romantic Ballads, Collected in the Southern Counties of Scotland; with a Few of Modern Date, Founded upon Local Tradition* (1802–03)
        Lord Randal 723
    from *Marmion; A Tale of Flodden Field* (1808)
        Song ["Where shall the lover rest"] 723
        Lochinvar. Lady Heron's Song 724
    from *Miscellaneous Poems* (1820)
        The Sun upon the Weirdlaw Hill 725

DOROTHY WORDSWORTH (1771 – 1855) 726
    from William Wordsworth, *Poems* (1815)
        Address to a Child During a Boisterous Winter Evening 726
    from William Wordsworth, *Poems* (1842)
        Floating Island 727
    from Susan Levin, *Dorothy Wordsworth and Romanticism* (1987)
        Grasmere—A Fragment 728
        Thoughts on my Sick-bed 729
    from *Grasmere Journal*
        from Tuesday 10 June 1800 730
        from Friday 3 October 1800 731
        Sunday Morning 14 March 1802 731
        15 April 1802 731
        Tuesday 26 July 1802 732

MARY TIGHE (1772 – 1810) 735
    from *Psyche, with Other Poems. By the Late Mrs. Henry Tighe* (1811)
        from Psyche; or, The Legend of Love 735
            CANTO 1 736
        On Receiving a Branch of Mezereon Which Flowered at Woodstock.—Dec. 1809 744

Contents

SAMUEL TAYLOR COLERIDGE (1772 – 1834) 746
    from *Poems on Various Subjects* (1796)
        Effusion 35. Composed August 20th, 1795, at Clevedon, Somersetshire 747
    from the *Morning Post* (8 January 1798)
        Fire, Famine, and Slaughter. A War Eclogue 748
    Fears in Solitude, Written in 1798 (1798)
        Fears in Solitude 749
        France. An Ode 752
        Frost at Midnight 754
    from *Lyrical Ballads, with a Few Other Poems* (1798)
        The Rime of the Ancyent Marinere, in Seven Parts 756
    from *Sibylline Leaves: A Collection of Poems* (1817)
        The Rime of the Ancient Mariner. In Seven Parts 757
    from *Lyrical Ballads* (1798)
        The Nightingale; A Conversational Poem, Written in April, 1798 778
        The Dungeon 779
    from the *Annual Anthology* (1800)
        This Lime-Tree Bower My Prison, A Poem, Addressed to Charles Lamb, of the India-House,
            London 780
    from *Memoirs of the Late Mrs. Robinson* (1801)
        A Stranger Minstrel. By S.T. Coleridge, Esq. Written to Mrs. Robinson a Few Weeks before
            Her Death 781
    Christabel: Kubla Khan, a Vision; The Pains of Sleep (1816)
        Christabel 782
        Kubla Khan: or A Vision in a Dream 792
        The Pains of Sleep 793
    from *Sibylline Leaves: A Collection of Poems* (1817)
        To a Gentleman Composed on the night after his recitation of a Poem on the Growth of
            an Individual Mind 794
        Dejection: An Ode 796
    from *Biographia Literaria; or Biographical Sketches of My Literary Life and Opinions* (1817)
        from CHAPTER 4 798
        from CHAPTER 13 801
        CHAPTER 14 803
        from CHAPTER 17 807
        from CHAPTER 18 812
        from CHAPTER 23 817
    from *The Poetical Works of S.T. Coleridge: including the dramas of Wallenstein, Remorse, and
    Zapolya* (1828)
        Constancy to an Ideal Object 820
    Letter
        To Joseph Cottle, 26 April 1814 820

Contents

Raja Rammohun Roy (1772? – 1833) 822
    from *Petitions Against the Press Regulation* (1823)
        Memorial to the Supreme Court 822
    Abstract of the Arguments regarding the Burning of Widows, Considered as a Religious Rite (1830) 826

Christian Milne (1772? – after 1816) 829
    from *Simple Poems, on Simple Subjects. By Christian Milne, Wife of a Journeyman Ship-Carpenter in Footdee, Aberdeen* (1805)
        To a Lady, Who Said It Was Sinful to Read Novels 829
        Sent with a Flower Pot, Begging a Slip of Geranium 829

Francis Jeffrey (1773 – 1850) 830
    from the *Edinburgh Review, or Critical Journal* 24 (Nov. 1814)
        from ART. 1 The Excursion, being a portion of the Recluse, A Poem. By William Wordsworth 830

Robert Southey (1774 – 1843) 835
    from *Poems* (1797)
        To Mary Wollstonecraft 835
        The Widow. Sapphics 836
        The Soldier's Wife. Dactylics 836
    from the *Morning Post* (30 June 1798)
        The Idiot 836
    from *Poems* (1799)
        The Sailor, Who Had Served in the Slave-Trade 837
    from the *Annual Anthology* (1800)
        The Battle of Blenheim 839
    from *Letters from England: by Don Manuel Alvarez Espriella. Translated from the Spanish* (1807)
        LETTER 55 840
    from *A Collection of Poems, Chiefly Manuscript, and from Living Authors*, ed. Joanna Baillie (1823)
        The Cataract of Lodore, Described in Rhymes for the Nursery, by One of the Lake Poets 842
    from *The Poetical Works of Robert Southey* (1853)
        Bishop Bruno 843
        My Days Among the Dead Are Passed 845

Walter Savage Landor (1775 – 1864) 846
    from *Simonidea* (1806)
        [Rose Aylmer] 846
        Mother, I Cannot Mind My Wheel 846
    from *Gebir, Count Julian, and Other Poems* (1831)
        Past ruin'd Ilion Helen lives 847

Mary Lamb (1764 – 1847) and Charles Lamb (1775 – 1834) 848
    from *Blank Verse by Charles Lloyd and Charles Lamb* (1798)
        The Old Familiar Faces 849

Contents

from Charles Lamb and Mary Lamb, *Poetry for Children* (1809)
    The Reaper's Child 849
    Choosing a Profession 849
    Breakfast 850
    The Two Boys 850
    Conquest of Prejudice 851
from Charles Lamb, *Elia* (1823)
    Dream-Children; A Reverie 851
Letters
    To S.T. Coleridge, 27 September 1796 854
    To William Wordsworth, 30 January 1801 854
    from To Thomas Manning, 15 February 1801 856

CHARLES LLOYD (1775 – 1839) 858
  from *Blank Verse by Charles Lloyd and Charles Lamb* (1798)
    Lines to Mary Wollstonecraft Godwin 858

CHARLOTTE RICHARDSON (1775 – 1825) 861
  from *Harvest, A Poem, in Two Parts; with Other Poetical Pieces* (1818)
    The Redbreast 861
    The Rainbow 861

MATTHEW GREGORY LEWIS (1775 – 1818) 863
  from *The Monk: A Romance* (1796)
    Alonzo the Brave and Fair Imogine 863
  from *The Life and Correspondence of M.G. Lewis, author of "The Monk," "Castle Spectre," &c.*
  with Many Pieces in Prose and Verse, Never Before Published (1839)
    The Captive 865

JANE AUSTEN (1775 – 1817) 867
  Love and Freindship 867
  from *Northanger Abbey* (1818)
    from CHAPTER 5 883

THOMAS CAMPBELL (1777 – 1844) 884
  from *New Monthly Magazine and Literary Journal* 8, original papers (March 1823)
    The Last Man 884

WILLIAM HAZLITT (1778 – 1830) 886
  from *The Round Table, Examiner* (Sunday, 26 May 1816)
    NO. 40, On Gusto 886
  from *The Liberal. Verse and Prose from the South* 2 (1823)
    My First Acquaintance with Poets 889
  from *The Plain Speaker: Opinions on Books, Men, and Things* (1826)
    from On the Prose-Style of Poets 901

Contents

SYDNEY OWENSON, LADY MORGAN (c. 1778 – 1859) 904
    from *The Lay of an Irish Harp; or Metrical Fragments* (1807)
        The Irish Harp 905
    from *Italy* (1821)
        from CHAPTER 2, Passage of the Alps 906

THOMAS MOORE (1779 – 1852) 912
    from *The Works of Thomas Moore, Esq., Comprehending All His Melodies, Ballads, etc. Never Before Published Without the Accompanying Music* (1819)
        A Canadian Boat-Song. Written on the River St.-Lawrence 913
        Written on Passing Deadman's Island, in the Gulf of St. Lawrence,
            Late in the Evening, September, 1804 913
    from *Melodies, by Thomas Moore, Esq.* (1821)
        Oh! Breathe Not His Name 914
        The Harp that once through Tara's Halls 914
        Believe Me if all those Endearing Young Charms 914
        The Minstrel Boy 915
        The Time I've Lost in Wooing 915

HORACE SMITH (1779 – 1849) 916
    from *Amarynthus, the Nympholept: A Pastoral Drama, in Three Acts. With Other Poems* (1821)
        On a Stupendous Leg of Granite, Discovered Standing by Itself in the Deserts of Egypt,
            with the Inscription Inserted Below 916
        On the Spanish Revolution 916

WILLIAM HONE (1780 – 1842) 917
    The Political House That Jack Built (1819) 918

JOHN WILSON CROKER (1780 – 1857) 935
    from the *Quarterly Review* 7 (March and June 1812)
        Review of Barbauld's *Eighteen Hundred and Eleven* 935
    from the *Quarterly Review* 19 (April 1818)
        Review of Keats's *Endymion: A Poetic Romance* 938

EBENEZER ELLIOTT (1781 – 1849) 942
    from *Corn Law Rhymes*, 3rd ed. (1831)
        Song 942
        Caged Rats 943

LUCY AIKIN (1781 – 1864) 944
    from *Epistles on women, exemplifying their character and condition in various ages and nations. With miscellaneous poems* (1810)
        INTRODUCTION 944
        EPISTLE 1 946
        EPISTLE 2 948

Contents

CHARLOTTE DACRE (1782? – 1825) 953
    from *Hours of Solitude. A Collection of Original Poems, now first published* (1805)
        The Poor Negro Sadi 953
        The Female Philosopher 954
        The Apparition 955
        Drinking Song 955

JANE TAYLOR (1783 – 1824) 956
    from *Rhymes for the Nursery* (1806)
        The Star 956
    from *Essays in Rhyme, on Morals and Manners*, 3rd ed. (1817)
        Recreation 956

WASHINGTON IRVING (1783 – 1859) 959
    from *The Sketch Book of Geoffrey Crayon, Gent.* (1819)
        Rip Van Winkle. A Posthumous Writing of Diedrich Knickerbocker 959

LEIGH HUNT (1784 – 1859) 968
    from *The Story of Rimini* (1816)
        from CANTO 3 968
    from the *Examiner* (21 September 1817)
        Green little vaulter in the sunny grass 970
    from *Foliage* (1818)
        To Percy Shelley, on the Degrading Notions of Deity 970
    from S.C. Hall, *Book of Gems* (1838)
        Abou Ben Adhem and the Angel 970
    from the *Morning Chronicle* 2 (November 1838)
        Rondeau 970

THOMAS DE QUINCEY (1785 – 1859) 971
    from the *London Magazine* 4 (September 1821)
        from Confessions of an English Opium-Eater: Being an Extract from the Life of a Scholar 971
    from the *London Magazine* 4 (October 1821)
        from Introduction to the Pains of Opium 975
        from The Pains of Opium 977
    from the *London Magazine* 8 (October 1823)
        On the Knocking at the Gate in Macbeth 982

THOMAS LOVE PEACOCK (1785 – 1866) 985
    from *Ollier's Literary Miscellany* (1820)
        from The Four Ages of Poetry 985

Contents

CAROLINE LAMB (1785 – 1828) 992
    A New Canto (1819) 992
    from *Ada Reis, A Tale* (1823)
        Duet 996
    from I[saac] Nathan, *Fugitive Pieces and Reminiscences of Lord Byron: containing an entire new edition of the Hebrew Melodies, with the addition of several never before published; ... also some Original Poetry, Letters and Recollections of Lady Caroline Lamb* (1829)
        Would I had seen thee dead and cold 997

BARRON FIELD (1786 – 1846) 998
    from *First Fruits of Australian Poetry* (1819)
        The Kangaroo 998

MARY RUSSELL MITFORD (1787 – 1855) 1000
    from *Our Village: Sketches of Rural Character and Scenery* (1824)
        Nutting 1000

GEORGE GORDON, LORD BYRON (1788 – 1824) 1004
    The Giaour. A Fragment of a Turkish Tale (1813) 1005
    from *Hebrew Melodies* (1815)
        She Walks in Beauty 1024
    from *Poems* (1816)
        Fare Thee Well! 1024
    from *The Prisoner of Chillon and Other Poems* (1816)
        Darkness 1025
        Prometheus 1027
    from *Childe Harold's Pilgrimage* (1816)
        from CANTO THE THIRD 1028
    Manfred, A Dramatic Poem (1817) 1041
    from *Don Juan* (1819)
        DEDICATION 1063
        CANTO 1 1066
        CANTO 2 1095
    Letters 1121
        To Lady Byron, 8 February 1816 1121
        To Augusta Leigh, 18–29 September 1816 1122
        from To John Murray, 12 August 1819 1127
        from To Douglas Kinnaird, 26 October 1819 1129
        from To John Murray, 16 February 1821 1129
        To Percy Bysshe Shelley, 26 April 1821 1130

MARY PRINCE (c. 1788 – after 1833) 1131
    from *The History of Mary Prince, a West Indian Slave. Related by Herself* (1831) 1131

Contents

THOMAS PRINGLE (1789 – 1834) 1143
    from George Thompson, *Travels and Adventures in Southern Africa, comprising a View of the Present State of the Cape Colony, with Observations on the Progress and Prospects of the British Emigrants* (1827)
        Afar in the Desert 1144

JAMES FENIMORE COOPER (1789 – 1851) 1146
    from *Notions of the Americans, Picked Up by a Travelling Bachelor* (1828) 1146

PERCY BYSSHE SHELLEY (1792 – 1822) 1152
    from *Alastor; or, The Spirit of Solitude: and Other Poems* (1816)
        Preface 1153
        Alastor: Or, The Spirit of Solitude 1154
        To Wordsworth 1163
    from *History of a Six Weeks' Tour through a Part of France, Switzerland, Germany, and Holland: with Letters Descriptive of a Sail round the Lake of Geneva, and of the Glaciers of Chamouni* (1817)
        Mont Blanc 1164
    from the *Examiner* (19 January 1817)
        Hymn to Intellectual Beauty 1166
    from the *Examiner* (11 January 1818)
        Ozymandias 1167
    from *Prometheus Unbound: A Lyrical Drama in Four Acts with Other Poems* (1820)
        Prometheus Unbound 1167
        Ode to the West Wind 1207
        To a Skylark 1208
    The Cenci: A Tragedy, in Five Acts (1820) 1210
    Adonais: An Elegy on the Death of John Keats (1821) 1248
    from *Posthumous Poems*, ed. M.W. Shelley (1824)
        SONNET IV 1256
        The Triumph of Life 1256
    The Masque of Anarchy. A Poem (1832) 1266
    from the *Athenæum* 260 (20 October 1832)
        With a Guitar 1274
    from *The Poetical Works of Percy Bysshe Shelley*, ed. M.W. Shelley (1839)
        England in 1819 1275
    from *Essays, Letters from Abroad, Translations and Fragments*, ed. M.W. Shelley (1840)
        from A Defence of Poetry 1275
    Letters
        To Thomas Love Peacock, 22 December 1818 1281
        To Mary Wollstonecraft Shelley, Bagni di Pisa, 9 August 1821 1285

EDWARD JOHN TRELAWNY (1792 – 1881) 1289
    from *Recollections of the Last Days of Shelley and Byron* (1858)
        from CHAPTER 12 1289

Contents

JOHN CLARE (1793 – 1864) 1293
    from *The Rural Muse. Poems by John Clare* (1835)
        The Nightingale's Nest 1293
    from Frederick Martin, *The Life of John Clare* (1865)
        [I Am] 1295
    from *John Clare: Poems Chiefly from Manuscript*, ed. Edmund Blunden and Alan Porter (1920)
        Badger 1295
        Quail's Nest 1296
        Invitation to Eternity 1296
        Clock-a-Clay 1296
    from *The Poems of John Clare*, ed. J.W. Tibble (1935)
        Enclosure [The Mores] 1297
        The Skylark Leaving Her Nest 1298

FELICIA HEMANS (1793 – 1835) 1299
    from *Tales, and Historic Scenes, in Verse* (1819)
        The Wife of Asdrubal 1299
    from *The League of the Alps, The Siege of Valencia, the Vespers of Palermo, and Other Poems* (1826)
        Casabianca 1301
        Evening Prayer at a Girls' School 1301
    from *Records of Woman: with Other Poems* (1828)
        The Bride of the Greek Isle 1302
        Properzia Rossi 1306
        The Indian City 1308
        Indian Woman's Death-Song 1311
        Joan of Arc, in Rheims 1312
        Madeline. A Domestic Tale 1314
        The Grave of a Poetess 1315
        The Homes of England 1316
        To Wordsworth 1317
        The Landing of the Pilgrim Fathers in New England 1317
        The Graves of a Household 1318
        The Image in Lava 1319
    from *Songs of the Affections* (1830)
        The Return 1320
        Woman on the Field of Battle 1320
        The Mirror in the Deserted Hall 1321

JOSEPH SEVERN (1793 – 1879) 1322
    Letter
        To John Taylor, 6 March 1821 1322

JOHN LOCKHART (1794 – 1854) 1324
    from *Blackwood's Edinburgh Magazine* 3 (August 1818)
        Cockney School of Poetry. NO. 4 1324

Contents

OLIVER GOLDSMITH (1794 – 1861) 1327
    from *The Rising Village. A Poem. By Oliver Goldsmith, a Collateral Descendant of the Author of the "Deserted Village"* (1825) 1327

WILLIAM CULLEN BRYANT (1794 – 1878) 1334
    from the *North American Review and Miscellaneous Journal* (March 1818)
        To a Waterfowl 1334
    from *Poems* (1821)
        Thanatopsis 1335

JOHN KEATS (1795 – 1821) 1337
    from the *Examiner* (1 December 1816)
        On First Looking into Chapman's Homer 1338
    from the *Examiner* (9 March 1817)
        On Seeing the Elgin Marbles 1338
    from the *Examiner* (21 September 1817)
        The poetry of earth is never dead 1338
    from *Endymion* (1818)
        from BOOK 1 1339
    from the *Indicator* (10 May 1820)
        La Belle Dame Sans Mercy 1340
    from *Lamia, Isabella, Eve of St. Agnes, and Other Poems. By John Keats, author of* Endymion (1820)
        Lamia 1341
        The Eve of St. Agnes 1351
        Ode to a Nightingale 1357
        Ode on a Grecian Urn 1359
        Ode to Psyche 1360
        To Autumn 1361
        Ode on Melancholy 1361
        Hyperion 1362
    from the *Indicator* (28 June 1820)
        A Dream After Reading Dante's Episode of Paulo and Francesca 1373
    from the *Plymouth and Devonport Weekly Journal* (1838)
        On Sitting Down to Read King Lear Once Again 1373
        Bright star, would I were stedfast as thou art 1374
    from *Life, Letters, and Literary Remains of John Keats*, ed. Richard Monkton Milnes (1848)
        Ode on Indolence 1374
        When I Have Fears That I May Cease To Be 1375
    from *Miscellanies of the Philobiblon Society* (1856)
        Hyperion, A Vision 1375
    from *Poetical Works of John Keats* (1898)
        This living hand, now warm and capable 1382
    Letters
        To Benjamin Bailey, 22 November 1817 1382
        To J.H. Reynolds, 22 November 1817 1384

Contents

    To George and Tom Keats, 21, 27 (?) December 1817 1386
    To J.H. Reynolds, 3 February 1818 1387
    To J.H. Reynolds, 3 May 1818 1388
    To Richard Woodhouse, 27 October 1818 1392
    To Percy Bysshe Shelley, 16 August 1820 1393

JOHN RICHARDSON (1796 – 1852) 1394
    from *Tecumseh; or, The Warrior of the West: A Poem, in Four Cantos, with Notes* (1828) 1395

MARY WOLLSTONECRAFT SHELLEY (1797 – 1851) 1403
    from *The Liberal: Verse and Prose from the South* 4 (1823)
        from Giovanni Villani 1404
    from *London Magazine* 9 (March 1824)
        On Ghosts 1407
    from *The Keepsake* (1831)
        Transformation 1411
        Absence 1420
        A Dirge 1420
    from *The Keepsake* (1839)
        Stanzas ["How like a star you rose upon my life"] 1421
        Stanzas ["O, come to me in dreams, my love!"] 1421
    Letter
        To Maria Gisborne, 15 August 1822 1421
    Journal
        May 14th [1824] 1427
        May 15th 1428

WILLIAM APESS (1798 – 1839) 1429
    from *A Son of the Forest* (1829)
        CHAPTER 3 1429
        CHAPTER 4 1433

THOMAS HOOD (1799 – 1845) 1435
    from *Whims and Oddities*, 3rd ed. (1828)
        The Last Man 1435
        Faithless Nelly Gray 1438

PETER JONES (1802 – 1856) 1440
    from *History of the Ojebway Indians; with Especial Reference to Their Conversion to Christianity* (1861)
        LETTER to John Jones 1440

CATHERINE PARR TRAILL (1802 – 1899) 1442
    from *The Young Emigrants; or, Pictures of Canada, Calculated to Amuse and Instruct the Minds of Youth* (1826)
        LETTER 5. *Agnes to Ellen* 1442

Contents

LETITIA ELIZABETH LANDON (1802 – 1838) 1445
    from *The Improvisatrice and Other Poems* (1824)
        The Improvisatrice 1445
        Home 1466
    from *The Troubadour, Catalogue of Pictures, and Historical Sketches* (1825)
        The Proud Ladye 1466
    from *The Golden Violet, with its tales of Romance and Chivalry: and Other Poems* (1827)
        Love's Last Lesson 1467
        Erinna 1469
    from *The Venetian Bracelet, The Lost Pleiad, A History of the Lyre, and Other Poems* (1829)
        Revenge 1474
        Lines of Life 1475
    from the *New Monthly Magazine* 35 (1832)
        On the Ancient and Modern Influence of Poetry 1477
    from *Fisher's Drawing Room Scrap Book* (1836)
        Immolation of a Hindoo Widow 1482
    from *The Zenana and Minor Poems of L.E.L.* (1839)
        Felicia Hemans 1482
        On Wordsworth's Cottage, near Grasmere Lake 1483
    from *Life and Literary Remains of L.E.L.*, ed. Laman Blanchard (1841)
        A Poet's Love 1485
        Influence of Poetry 1485
        Changes in London 1486

THOMAS LOVELL BEDDOES (1803 – 1849) 1487
    from *Poems Chiefly from Outidana* (composed 1823–25)
        Lines Written in a Blank Leaf of the "Prometheus Unbound" 1487
    from *Torrismond* (composed 1824)
        Song ["How many times do I love thee, dear?"] 1487
    from *Death's Jest-Book* (1825–28)
        Dirge 1488
        Song ["A cypress-bough, and a rose-wreath sweet"] 1488
        Song ["Old Adam, the carrion crow"] 1488
    from *Death's Jest Book* (revised, 1829–49)
        Song from the Waters 1489
        Dream-Pedlary 1489

SUSANNA MOODIE (1803 – 1885) 1490
    from *Enthusiasm; and Other Poems* (1831)
        The Dream 1490

NATHANIEL HAWTHORNE (1804 – 1864) 1492
    from *Mosses from an Old Manse* (1846)
        Roger Malvin's Burial 1492

Contents

HENRY WADSWORTH LONGFELLOW (1807 – 1882) 1503
    from *Ballads and Other Poems* (1842)
        The Wreck of the Hesperus 1503
        The Village Blacksmith 1504
        Excelsior 1505
    from *Poems on Slavery* (1842)
        The Slave's Dream 1506

EDGAR ALLAN POE (1809 – 1849) 1507
    from *Tamerlane and Other Poems* (1827)
        Visit of the Dead 1507
    from *Al Aaraaf, Tamerlane, and Minor Poems* (1829)
        Sonnet—To Science 1508
    from *Poems by Edgar A. Poe*, 2nd ed. (1831)
        Letter to Mr. — —— 1508
        To Helen 1513
        The Doomed City 1513
    from the *Saturday Courier* (14 January 1832)
        Metzengerstein 1514

HENRY LOUIS VIVIAN DEROZIO (1809 – 1831) 1519
    from *Poems* (1827)
        The Harp of India 1519
    from *The Fakeer of Jungheera: A Metrical Tale and Other Poems* (1828)
        My country! in thy days of glory past 1519
        from The Fakeer of Jungheera
            The Legend of the Shushan 1520
            The Spirit's Song 1522
    from *The Poetical Works of Henry Louis Vivian Derozio*, ed. B.B. Shah (1907)
        To the Pupils of the Hindu College 1523

Bibliography 1525

Index of Authors, Titles, and First Lines 1559

Editorial Preface

In *Cultural Capital* (1993), his magisterial survey of the culture wars, John Guillory argues that the canon, so hotly debated, does not exist: it is only the ideological shadow cast by the syllabus, the list of texts actually chosen to be taught (29–30). Behind the syllabus, one might add, lies the anthology, the material object enabling the syllabus choices teachers (and sometimes students) make. You're holding one now.

Since the (comparatively recent) foundation of English as an academic discipline,[1] syllabi and anthologies for the period including the late eighteenth and early nineteenth centuries have been dominated by four white, male, English poets—William Wordsworth, Coleridge, P.B. Shelley, and Keats—with two others, Blake and Byron, occupying slightly less secure positions. A representative example would be David Perkin's *English Romantic Writers* (1st ed. 1967), which devotes about nine hundred pages to these six writers and about three hundred to twenty-four more, including exactly two to a woman, Dorothy Wordsworth. Harold Bloom's and Lionel Trilling's *Romantic Poetry and Prose* (1973) and Duncan Wu's *Romanticism* (1st ed. 1994) are similar examples. The main advantage of such an approach is obvious: extensive coverage of six of the greatest poets who ever lived. The main disadvantage is equally obvious: a narrowness that not only neglects many other fine writers but also flattens the study of the six great ones by depriving them of their context. It is hard fully to understand P.B. Shelley's *The Masque of Anarchy* without William Hone's *The Political House that Jack Built*, or Keats's "Ode to Psyche" without Mary Tighe's *Psyche*.

Consequently, the recent trend in anthology-making has been towards a broadening of the canon—that is, of the texts available to choose from for teaching and studying. Perkins added more women authors to his second edition (1994), though the rationale for his selection remained fundamentally unchanged. Jerome J. McGann, who had revolutionized critical thinking about the period in *The Romantic Ideology* (1983), first challenged the status quo in *The New Oxford Book of Romantic Period Verse* (1994), a comparatively short book which devoted only about four hundred pages to the big six and almost as many to seventy-three others. Not many of these others were women. Anne K. Mellor, whose *Romanticism and Gender* (1993) had been as influential as McGann's earlier book, took the next step with her co-editor, Richard E. Matlak: in their *British Literature 1780–1830* (1996), almost half the writing is by women, so that major figures like Joanna Baillie, Felicia Hemans, and Mary Wollstonecraft received due attention for the first time.

The inclusion of Joanna Baillie, a Scot living in London (and the leading playwright of her day), reminds us that British Romanticism includes writers from Ireland, Scotland, and Wales as well as from England. Whereas earlier anthologies had represented Scottish literature of this period almost entirely by selections from Robert Burns and Walter Scott (and a handful of—mostly castigated—reviewers), anthologies like Wu's *Romantic Women Writers* (1997) and Feldman's *British Women Poets of the Romantic Era* (1997) recovered a range of poetry that included the work of Scottish labouring-class women. James Hogg (a Scot) and Thomas Moore (an Irishman) regained their place in the canon alongside Janet Little (a Scot) and Charlotte Brooke (an Irishwoman). Extending the geographical range to include all of the British Isles was a first step towards including a wider world of exploration, migration, linguistic and cultural difference, and imperial adventure. Lance Newman, Joel Pace, and Chris Koenig-Woodyard edited *Transatlantic Romanticism* (2006), which not only extended the traditional bounds of the period from 1767 to 1867 but included American and Canadian as well as British writing. In this anthology, we have tried

---

[1] A good account of the history of the discipline is Graff, *Professing Literature* (1987).

Editorial Preface

to take the next step, presenting the literature in English of the period as, for the first time in history, a world literature, including writings from Africa, India, and Australia.[1]

The obvious advantage of such an approach is breadth. The obvious disadvantages are not only a lack of depth (there's not as much Keats here as there is in Perkins) but also a lack of focus. The latter, however, may not be a real disadvantage. Even in 1967, Perkins conceded that "The term 'Romantic' ... is far from adequate" (1), and though he then went on to generalize confidently (and insightfully) about "The Romantic Mode" (8), "British Empiricism" (12), "Transcendentalism" (14), "Time, History, and Nostalgia" (14), "Organicism" (15), "The Imagination" (17), and "The Figure of the Poet" (191), by 1994 McGann would state flatly (and correctly) that "much of the writing during the period—including some of the best work—is not properly speaking 'romantic'" (xx). The literary ideology so lucidly explicated by Perkins in 1967 and so incisively critiqued by McGann in 1983 was dominant but not universal. The awkward titles both of McGann's own anthology and of Mellor and Matlak's are acknowledgements of this new critical understanding.

What the writers of the period did have in common was unprecedented—and still unparalleled—historical change. The Seven Years' War (1756–63) and Britain's acquisition of a global empire, the American and French Revolutions (Edmund Burke famously called the latter the most astonishing event in the history of the world), the Agricultural and Industrial Revolutions, the movements for the emancipation of women and slaves, the drop in infant mortality (due largely to Lady Mary Wortley Montague's introduction of inoculation and Edward Jenner's invention of vaccination), the rise of a new family structure based on what Lawrence Stone has called "affectionate individualism," and (perhaps most critically for writers) the advent of nearly universal literacy profoundly affected every writer—and everyone else. The insistence of working people on acquiring a political voice, numerous reactionary responses to revolutionary ideas and institutions following the defeat of Napoleon, and the debate leading up to the passage of the First Reform Act all contributed to a period of economic, political, and ideological turmoil.

Some welcomed these changes; some resisted them; some, like Burke and Wordsworth, did a bit of both. Consequently we have decided, in this anthology, to refer to the period as the Age of Revolution. It is not, of course, the only such age, but this age of revolution seems to us clearly defined in terms both of politics—from the Boston Massacre (1770) to the First Reform Act (1832)—and of literature—from the death of Chatterton (1770) to the death of Scott (1832). Our choice of texts is therefore somewhat more political (in the narrow sense) than in most of the other available anthologies, but we hope that readers will not find this choice unduly constraining. Like all other anthologists, we have included all the works that everyone always teaches (and like all other anthologists, we have omitted some works that some people always teach); beyond that, we hope that we have enabled teachers and students to make their own syllabic choices.

Our decision to represent the period as inclusively as possible in terms of genre, gender, social class, geographical, racial and national origin, political affiliation, and other markers of difference—and, at the same time, to avoid an anthology of brief and tendentious excerpts—has resulted in some difficult choices. Like all other anthologists, we have been constrained by considerations of space. We have not been able to include all the works we wanted, and although we began with the intention of including only whole works, or at least whole chapters or books or cantos, or at least whole paragraphs, we have not been able to do this either. We have done our best to respect the integrity of the works we have included, but we have made some compromises with our initial intentions.

We include the complete text of William Wordsworth's *Two-Part Prelude* of 1798–99; but we refer students and teachers to one of the several excellent and affordable variorum texts of *The Prelude* (1805 and 1850) for the

---

[1] Our percentage of writing by women is somewhat lower than Mellor and Matlak's, since writing in the colonies seems to have been more heavily dominated by men than in the metropolis.

Editorial Preface

later versions of the poem. In some other cases, however, we have sometimes been forced to cut and select shorter passages. When we do so, we try to provide contextual notes so that students can find their own way to the complete works. In general, however, notes and other apparatus have been kept to a minimum to make room for texts. Thus, the reader will find that our biographical headnotes and annotations are almost exclusively factual. We have left the task of interpretation to teachers and students, hoping to promote a more active classroom. (Readers may wish to compare our approach with the more directive one of Mellor and Matlak.) Similarly, we have saved space by limiting our intertextual references to specifying the intertext, rather than quoting it: we want to encourage, or even compel, students to go to the library and pick up a book.

Curiously, our inclusive editorial practice in some ways reclaims a broad canon that might have been more familiar to writers of the Revolutionary Period than the clearly focused canon represented by such scholars as Perkins. Byron, for example, in a journal entry for Wednesday 24 November 1813, places Scott, "the Monarch of Parnassus," at the top of a pyramid of contemporary greats, supported in descending order by Rogers, Moore, and Campbell. Southey, William Wordsworth, and Coleridge occupy the next level, above "THE MANY" at the base of the pyramid.[1] Byron (foreshadowing twentieth-century developments) makes Parnassus a British possession, not a narrowly English one. Sixteen years later, in a review of the very popular poet Felicia Hemans in the *Edinburgh Review*, Francis Jeffrey puts Rogers and Campbell at the head of his list of those who have withstood the test of time, commenting that "[t]he tuneful quartos of Southey are already little better than lumber:—And the rich melodies of Keats and [P.B.] Shelley,—and the fantastical emphasis of [W.] Wordsworth,—and the plebian pathos of Crabbe, are melting fast from the field of our vision. [...] Even the splendid strains of Moore are fading into distance and dimness [...] and the blazing star of Byron himself is receding from its place of pride."[2] There is little sense here that writers of our period agreed with one another—or with modern editors—about who the best writers were. Recognizing the vagaries of literary reputation, we are inclined to represent the period as broadly as possible and then let our readers decide for themselves.

William Blake appears in neither Byron's list of luminaries nor Jeffrey's list of fading stars. Unknown during his lifetime beyond a narrow circle of contemporaries, he became famous following Alexander Gilchrist's 1863 biography. In a reversal of such an accident of fame, many women writers of the period, neglected in mid-twentieth-century anthologies, were well respected during the nineteenth century. Sixteen women poets are represented without fanfare in William Stanley Braithwaite's *Book of Georgian Verse* (1909), which includes poetry written from the coronation of George I in 1714 until the end of the period covered by our anthology. Palgrave's *Golden Treasury* represents twenty-seven poets born from 1743–1800; Quiller-Couch's *Oxford Book of English Verse* (1918) devotes 216 pages to writers from the same period, of which only 111 pages are by the big six. While only nine pages of poems in Quiller-Couch's anthology are by women writers, those pages do represent eight different writers. In this anthology, our task has been in part the rediscovery of what our predecessors valued and then forgot.

Poetry—especially lyric poetry—had special value in anthologies focused on the big six. The dominance of the New Criticism gave special prominence to lyric poetry: "Romantic literature" used to mean almost exclusively "Romantic poetry." In addition to the philosophical and rhapsodic lyric poetry of the period, however, we include much narrative poetry, some explicitly political poetry, didactic poetry, and poetry aimed at labouring-class readers, women, potential advocates, and activists. We also attempt to include a wide variety of genres apart from poetry, since this was also an age of polemical prose, of journalism, of criticism, and of prose fiction. Complete novels are usually beyond the scope of an anthology; but this anthology nevertheless includes selections by Austen (never a "Romantic" writer), Burney, Peacock, Scott, Mary Shelley, Lewis, Radcliffe, Maria Edgeworth, Godwin, Hays, and

---

[1] "Alas! The Love of Women," vol. 3 of *Byron's Letters and Journals*, ed. Leslie A. Marchand (London: John Murray, 1974), 220.

[2] *Edinburgh Review* 50 (October 1829), rpt. *Jeffrey's Criticism: A Selection*, ed. Peter F. Morgan (Edinburgh: Scottish Academic P, 1983), 102.

Editorial Preface

many others. We have not, however, presumed, as Mellor and Matlak do, to state: "This anthology is [...] *designed to be used in conjunction with at least two novels*: Mary Shelley's *Frankenstein* (1818) and a novel by Jane Austen" (3–4: they go on to suggest *Mansfield Park* in particular). We leave it up to instructors and students to decide on supplementary texts, if any, recognizing that these might include almost any novel of the period—or, just as plausibly, one of the narrative poems of Southey or the complete 1805 and/or 1850 *Prelude*. The canon of non-fictional prose (a genre resistant to disciplinary categories) is represented by political, educational, literary, and philosophical writings by some of the writers already mentioned and by such others as Burke, Cobbett, Coleridge, De Quincey, Hazlitt, Charles Lamb, Paine, and Wollstonecraft.

Our principle of broad inclusion may not lead to choices that satisfy everyone; but there should be enough here to introduce students to this period in much of its richness and diversity and to provide material for more than one syllabus and more than one course. Our project invites readers to explore the Revolutionary Period from the perspective of our post-colonial, global world, in which revolutionary thinking is still very much alive. It also invites them to experience the literature of this period within its own historical contexts. Consequently we have followed Jerome J. McGann's practice of reprinting, as much as possible, the first printed version of each text. Here is what a contemporary reader might have read, even if a writer chose to revise later (and we do include significant revisions in the footnotes or—in the case of "The Rime of the Ancient Mariner"—in parallel-text format). The occasional unfamiliarity of wording in a previously familiar text may be sufficient to administer "a gentle shock of mild surprise" even to those who have taught some of these works for years.

To enhance the contextualization of all our authors, in our annotations we have marked cross-references to authors and texts included in this anthology with asterisks. In the interest of clarity and consistency, we have used Arabic numerals for lines, stanzas, cantos, chapters, books, etc. While we have corrected obvious typographical errors in the texts, we have emended very conservatively: occasional irregularities of metre, for example, have not been smoothed over. Punctuation and spelling are, almost always, as in the original texts.

The editors wish to acknowledge the following scholars, whose editorial work they have found invaluable in making their own decisions about texts and annotations: D.M.R. Bentley (Cary), Jennifer Breen (Baillie), Vincent Carretta (Wheatley), R.W. Chapman (Austen), E.H. Coleridge (Byron, Coleridge), Stuart Curran (C. Smith), Margaret Anne Doody and Douglas Murray (Austen), D.W. Dörrbecker (Blake, *The Continental Prophecies*), Peter Duthie (Baillie), Kay Parkhurst Easson and Roger R. Easson (Blake, *Milton*), Morris Eaves, Robert N. Essick, and Joseph Viscomi (Blake, *The Early Illuminated Books*), Gavin Edwards (Crabbe), James Engell and W. Jackson Bate (Coleridge), David Erdman (Blake), Michael Gnarowski (Cary), Kyle Grimes (Hone), David A. Kent and D.R. Ewen (Hone), Andrew Lincoln (Blake, *Songs of Innocence and of Experience*), Gerald Lynch (Goldsmith), Julian D. Mason, Jr. (Wheatley), J.C.C. Mays (Coleridge), William McCarthy and Elizabeth Kraft (Barbauld), Jerome J. McGann (Byron), Jerome J. McGann and Daniel Riess (Landon), Barry O'Connell (Apess), Judith Pascoe (Robinson), Donald H. Reiman and Sharon B. Powers (P.B. Shelley), T.G. Steffan, E. Steffan, and W.W. Pratt (Byron), Jack Stillinger (Keats), Donald S. Taylor and Benjamin B. Hooper (Chatterton), George Watson (Coleridge), and Susan F. Wolfson (Hemans).

We are also grateful for the work of previous anthologists, all of whom have contributed to our respect for the task at hand and, we hope, to the character and distinctiveness of our own work: M.H. Abrams and Stephen Greenblatt, Paula R. Feldman, Thomas W. Krise, Jerome J. McGann, Anne K. Mellor and Richard E. Matlak, David Perkins, Jack Stillinger and Deirdre Shauna Lynch, Susan Wolfson and Peter Manning, and Duncan Wu.

In addition, we would like to thank the many friends, colleagues, and students who have helped with this project over the years since its inception. For research assistance, we thank Maia Bhojwani, Marilyn Dann, Jay Gamble, Teresa Green, Mical Moser, June Scudeler, Nikki Sheppy, David Sherwin, Kristen Warder, and the students of English 510.09 ("Refurbishing the Revolutionary Canon") at the University of Calgary in the Fall term, 2000: Jessica Barkwell, Shauna Carson, Marilyn Dann, Jillian Garrett, Sandra Ham, Scott Hames, Shawn Hoult,

EDITORIAL PREFACE

Roisin Hutchinson, David Mercier, Jodi O'Neil, Nikki Reimer, Krista Sandusky, Kathy Schaerer, and Jana Towler. We would also like to thank the students of English 440, "Literature of the Romantic Period," at the University of Calgary, who, from 2000–2006, used various early versions of this anthology as their textbook and offered us their suggestions.

    For other help and support at various stages, thanks to Brigitte Clarke, Roberta Jackson, Gary Kelly, David Latane, Cynthia Lawford, Ron Neufeldt, David Oakleaf, Morton Paley, Emma Spooner, Dan White, Susan J. Wolfson, and Laura Zerilli. For invaluable assistance in processing and producing a complex manuscript, we are indebted to Kathryn Brownsey, Judith Earnshaw, Julia Gaunce, Don LePan, Tara Lowes, Paul Papin, Carol Richardson, and Tara Trueman at Broadview Press. Special thanks are due to Susan Chamberlain, typist, production assistant, and designer for the Press, whose patience, good humour, and commitment to the project survived two household moves and more years of hard work than any of us could have imagined at the outset.

Benjamin Franklin
1706 – 1790

Benjamin Franklin was born in Boston on 17 January 1706, the youngest son of Josiah Franklin, a tallow chandler and soap boiler, and his second wife, Abigail Folger Franklin. He had only two years of formal education, but he was a voracious reader. At the age of twelve, he was apprenticed to his half-brother James, a printer. He published his first essays in James's newspaper at the age of sixteen. In 1723, he quarrelled with James, moved to Philadelphia—arriving there with "three great puffy rolls" under his arm—and began working as a journeyman printer. After a trip to England, during which, at the age of nineteen, he published his first book, he returned to Philadelphia, opened a print shop, and took over a newspaper. In September 1730, Franklin, who already had a son, married Deborah Read; they had two more children. He published the first of the *Poor Richard* almanacs in 1732; he continued to publish them until 1757, and they sold ten thousand copies a year. *The Way to Wealth* (1757), a compendium of wisdom from the almanacs, has been called "probably the most printed and translated work in all American literature."

Franklin was so successful that by 1748 he was able largely to retire from printing, entering public life and beginning the experiments in electricity that earned him a membership in the Royal Society and honorary degrees from Harvard, Yale, William and Mary, St. Andrews, and Oxford. From 1757 to 1762 he was in England as the representative of the Pennsylvania Assembly in a dispute with the descendants of William Penn, who wanted to retain their exemption from taxes. He was in England again from 1764 to 1775, representing not only Pennsylvania but Georgia, Massachusetts, and New Jersey. Deborah, who was afraid of sea travel, did not accompany him; when she died in 1774, he had not seen her for ten years. During this sojourn, he became increasingly disillusioned about the relations between Britain and the colonies; on his return, he helped to draft the Declaration of Independence. From 1776 to 1785 he was in France, negotiating the treaty that brought France into the Revolutionary War on the American side. Always a prolific writer, he began his *Autobiography* in 1771 and worked on it, off and on, until his death in Philadelphia on 17 April 1790. (D.L.M.)

☙❧

from *Two Tracts: Information to Those Who Would Remove to America. And, Remarks Concerning the Savages of North America* (1784)

Remarks Concerning the Savages of North-America

Savages we call them, because their manners differ from ours, which we think the perfection of civility; they think the same of theirs.

Perhaps if we could examine the manners of different nations with impartiality, we should find no people so rude as to be without any rules of politeness; nor any so polite as not to have some remains of rudeness.

The Indian men, when young, are hunters and warriors; when old, counsellors; for all their government is by the counsel or advice of the sages; there is no force, there are no prisons, no officers to compel obedience, or inflict punishment. Hence they generally study oratory; the best speaker having the most influence. The Indian women till the ground, dress the food, nurse and bring up the children, and preserve and hand down to posterity the memory of public transactions. These employments of men and women are accounted natural and honourable. Having few artificial wants, they have abundance of leisure for improvement by conversation. Our laborious manner of life compared with theirs, they esteem slavish and base; and the learning on which we value ourselves, they regard as frivolous and useless. An instance of this occurred at the Treaty of Lancaster in Pennsilvania, anno 1744, between the Government of Virginia and the Six Nations.[1] After the principal business was settled, the Commissioners from Virginia acquainted the Indians by a speech, that there was at Williamsburg a college[2] with a fund, for educating Indian youth; and that if the Chiefs of the Six Nations would send down half a dozen of their sons to that college, the Government would take care that they should be well provided for, and instructed in all the learning of the white people. It is one of the Indian rules of politeness not to answer a public proposition the same day that it is made; they think it would be treating it as a light matter; and that they shew it respect by taking time to consider it, as of a matter important. They therefore deferred their answer till the day following; when their Speaker began, by expressing their deep sense of the kindness of the Virginia Government, in making them that offer; "for we know," says he, "that you highly esteem the kind of learning taught in those colleges, and that the maintenance of our young men, while with you, would be very expensive to you. We are convinced, therefore, that you mean to do us good by your proposal, and we thank you heartily. But you who are wise must know, the different nations have different conceptions of things; and you will therefore not take it amiss, if our ideas of this kind of education happen not to be the same with yours. We have had some experience of it: Several of our young people were formerly brought up at the colleges of the Northern Provinces; they were instructed in all your sciences; but when they came back to us, they were bad runners; ignorant of every means of living in the woods; unable to bear either cold or hunger; knew neither how to build a cabin, take a deer, or kill an enemy; spoke our language imperfectly; were therefore neither fit for hunters, warriors, or counsellors; they were totally good for nothing. We are however not the less obliged by your kind offer, though we decline accepting it: And to shew our grateful sense of it, if the Gentlemen of Virginia will send us a dozen of their sons, we will take great care of their education, instruct them in all we know, and make *men* of them."

Having frequent occasions to hold public Councils, they have acquired great order and decency in conducting them. The Old Men sit in the foremost ranks, the Warriors in the next, and the Women and Children in the hindmost. The business of the women is to take exact notice of what passes, imprint it in their memories, for they have no writing, and communicate it to their Children. They are the Records of the Council, and they preserve tradition of the stipulations in Treaties a hundred years back; which, when we compare with our writings, we always find exact. He that would speak, rises. The rest observe a profound silence. When he has finished, and sits down, they leave him five or six minutes to recollect, that if he has omitted any thing he intended to say, or has any thing to add, he may rise again, and deliver it. To interrupt another, even in common conversation, is reckoned highly indecent. How different this is from the conduct of a polite British House of Commons, where scarce a day passes without some confusion, that makes the Speaker hoarse in calling *to order*; and how different from the mode of conversation in many polite companies of Europe, where, if you do not deliver your sentence with great rapidity, you are cut off in the middle of it by the impatient loquacity of those you converse with, and never suffered to finish it.

The politeness of these Savages in conversation, is indeed, carried to excess; since it does not permit them to contradict, or deny the truth of what is asserted in their presence. By this means they indeed avoid disputes; but then it becomes difficult to know their minds, or what impression you make upon them. The Missionaries who have attempted to convert them to Christianity, all complain of this as one of the great difficulties of their Mission. The Indians hear with patience the Truths of the Gospel explained to them, and give their usual tokens of assent and approbation: You would think they were convinced. No such matter. It is mere civility.

A Swedish Minister having assembled the Chiefs of the Sasquehanah Indians, made a Sermon to them,

---

[1] the Iroquois confederation comprising the Cayuga, Mohawk, Oneida, Onondaga, Seneca, and Tuscarora.

[2] William and Mary College, founded in 1694.

acquainting them with the principal historical facts on which our Religion is founded; such as the fall of our First Parents by eating an Apple; the coming of Christ to repair the mischief; his miracles and suffering, &c.—When he had finished, an Indian Orator stood up to thank him. "What you have told us," says he, "is all very good. It is indeed bad to eat apples. It is better to make them all into cyder. We are much obliged by your kindness in coming so far, to tell us those things which you have heard from your Mothers. In return, I will tell you some of those we have heard from ours.

"In the beginning, our Fathers had only the flesh of animals to subsist on; and if their hunting was unsuccessful, they were starving. Two of our young hunters having killed a deer, made a fire in the woods to broil some parts of it. When they were about to satisfy their hunger, they beheld a beautiful young woman descend from the clouds, and seat herself on that hill which you see yonder among the Blue Mountains. They said to each other, it is a Spirit that perhaps has smelt our broiling venison, and wishes to eat of it: Let us offer some to her. They presented her with the tongue: She was pleased with the taste of it, and said, your kindness shall be rewarded. Come to this place after thirteen moons, and you shall find something that will be of great benefit in nourishing you and your children to the latest generations. They did so, and to their surprise, found plants they had never seen before; but which, from that ancient time have been constantly cultivated among us, to our great advantage. Where her right hand had touched the ground, they found maize; where her left hand had touched it, they found kidney-beans; and where her backside had sat on it, they found tobacco." The good Missionary, disgusted with this idle tale, said, "What I delivered to you were sacred truths; but what you tell me is mere fable, fiction, and falsehood." The Indian, offended, replied, "My Brother, it seems your friends have not done you justice in your education; they have not well instructed you in the rules of common civility. You saw, that we who understand and practise those rules, believed all your stories, why do you refuse to believe ours?"

When any of them come into our towns, our people are apt to croud round them, gaze upon them, and incommode them where they desire to be private; this they esteem great rudeness, and the effect of the want of instruction in the rules of civility and good manners. "We have," say they, "as much curiosity as you, and when you come into our towns, we wish for opportunities of looking at you; but for this purpose we hide ourselves behind bushes where you are to pass, and never intrude ourselves into your company."

Their manner of entering one anothers villages has likewise its rules. It is reckoned uncivil in travelling strangers to enter a village abruptly, without giving notice of their approach. Therefore, as soon as they arrive within hearing, they stop and hollow, remaining there till invited to enter. Two old men usually come out to them, and lead them in. There is in every village a vacant dwelling, called the strangers house. Here they are placed, while the old men go round from hut to hut, acquainting the inhabitants that strangers are arrived, who are probably hungry and weary; and every one sends them what he can spare of victuals and skins to repose on. When the strangers are refreshed, pipes and tobacco are brought; and then, but not before, conversation begins, with enquiries who they are, whither bound, what news, &c. and it usually ends with offers of service; if the strangers have occasion of guides, or any necessaries for continuing their journey; and nothing is exacted for the entertainment.

The same hospitality, esteemed among them as a principal virtue, is practised by private persons; of which *Conrad Weiser*,[1] our Interpreter, gave me the following instance. He had been naturalized among the Six Nations, and spoke well the Mohock language. In going through the Indian Country, to carry a message from our Governor to the Council at *Onondaga*, he called at the habitation of *Canassetego*, an old acquaintance, who embraced him, spread furs for him to sit on, placed before him some boiled beans and venison, and mixed some rum and water for his drink. When he was well refreshed, and had lit his pipe, Canassetego began to converse with him: Asked how he had fared the many years since they had seen each other, whence he then

---

[1] German-born pioneer, interpreter, and mediator between Natives and European colonists (1696–1760).

came, what occasioned the journey, &c. Conrad answered all his questions; and when the discourse began to flag, the Indian, to continue it, said, "Conrad, you have lived long among the White People, and know something of their customs; I have been sometimes at Albany, and have observed, that once in seven days they shut up their shops, and assemble all in the great house; tell me, what it is for? What do they do there?" "They meet there," says Conrad, "to hear and learn *good things*." "I do not doubt," says the Indian, "that they tell you so; they have told me the same: But I doubt the truth of what they say, and I will tell you my reasons. I went lately to Albany to sell my skins, and buy blankets, knives, powder, rum, &c. You know I used generally to deal with Hans Hanson, but I was a little inclined this time to try some other Merchants. However, I called first upon Hans, and asked him what he would give for beaver. He said he could not give more than four shillings a pound: But, says he, I cannot talk on business now; this is the day when we meet together to learn *good things*, and I am going to the meeting. So I thought to myself, since I cannot do any business today, I may as well go to the meeting too, and I went with him. There stood up a man in black; and began to talk to the people very angrily. I did not understand what he said; but perceiving that he looked much at me, and at Hanson, I imagined he was angry at seeing me there; so I went out, sat down near the house, struck fire, and lit my pipe, waiting till the meeting should break up. I thought too, that the man had mentioned something of Beaver, and I suspected it might be the subject of their meeting. So when they came out, I accosted my Merchant. 'Well, Hans,' says I, 'I hope you have agreed to give more than four shillings a pound.' 'No,' says he, 'I cannot give so much. I cannot give more than three shillings and sixpence.' I then spoke to several other dealers, but they all sung the same song, three and sixpence. This made it clear to me that my suspicion was right; and that whatever they pretended of meeting to learn *good things*, the real purpose was to consult how to cheat Indians in the price of Beaver. Consider but a little, Conrad, and you must be of my opinion. If they met so often to learn *good things*, they would certainly have learned some before this time. But they are still ignorant. You know our practice. If a white man in travelling through our country, enters one of our cabins, we all treat him as I treat you; we dry him if he is wet, we warm him if he is cold, and give him meat and drink, that he may allay his thirst and hunger; and we spread soft furs for him to rest and sleep on: We demand nothing in return.[1] But, if I go into a white man's house at Albany, and ask for victuals and drink, they say, where is your money; and if I have none, they say, get out, you Indian Dog. You see they have not yet learned those little *good things*, that we need no meetings to be instructed in, because our mothers taught them to us when we were children; and therefore it is impossible their meetings should be, as they say, for any such purpose, or have any such effect; they are only to contrive *the cheating of Indians in the price of Beaver.*"

---

[1] "It is remarkable, that in all ages and countries, hospitality has been allowed as the virtue of those, whom the Civilized were pleased to call Barbarians; the Greeks celebrated the Scythians for it. The Saracens possessed it eminently; and it is to this day the reigning virtue of the wild Arabs. St. Paul too, in the relation of his voyage and shipwreck, on the Island of Melita, says, 'The barbarous people shewed us no little kindness; for they kindled a fire, and received us every one, because of the present rain, and because of the cold.'" (B.F.) The Scythians were a nomadic people who in classical times dominated the region between the Danube and the western border of China. "Saracens" is a medieval term for Arabs. For St. Paul on Melita, see Acts 28.1–10.

Richard Price
1723 – 1791

Richard Price was born on 23 February 1723 at Llangeinor, Glamorgan, Wales, the son of Rice Price, a Presbyterian minister, and his second wife Catherine. Educated at various dissenting academies, he eventually rebelled against his father's orthodox Trinitarian Christianity. In 1744 he became chaplain to a businessman in Stoke Newington, later settling as a minister in Newington Green.

Price's writing covers a wide range of subjects, from ethics, to demographics, to economics, to politics. A member of the Royal Society, he wrote *An Essay on the Population*, condemning the rapid growth of urban centres. Like such contemporaries as Oliver Goldsmith,* he was concerned about what he perceived to be the depopulation of England: this affected his focus on the "yeomanry" as the strength of both Britain and America. As a member of the Club of Honest Whigs from about 1770, Price met Benjamin Franklin;* he befriended fellow-Unitarian Joseph Priestley, with whom he corresponded—and sometimes disagreed. Price's *Observations on the Nature of Civil Liberty* (1776) and *Observations on the American Revolution* (1784) demonstrated his sympathy with the Americans.

In 1787, Price moved to Hackney, where he preached at the Gravel Pit Chapel and helped to found the Unitarian New College. His most famous work, *A Discourse on the Love of Our Country*, appeared in 1789. Price's *Discourse* provoked Edmund Burke's attack in *Reflections on the Revolution in France*,* though Price continued to maintain that he did not support the violence of the French Revolution. Price died on 19 April 1791 and was buried at Bunhill Fields burial-ground, London. (A.M.)

✌✌✌

from *A Discourse on the Love of our Country, delivered on Nov. 4, 1789, at the Meeting-House in the Old Jewry, to the Society for Commemorating the Revolution in Great Britain* (1789)[1]

PSALM cxxii. 2[d], and following verses.[2]

Our feet shall stand within thy gates, O Jerusalem, whither the tribes go up; the tribes of the Lord unto the testimony of Israel. To give thanks to the name of the Lord, for there sit the thrones of judgment; the throne of the House of David. Pray for the peace of JERUSALEM. *They shall prosper that love thee. Peace be within thy walls, and prosperity within thy palaces. For my brethren and companions sake I will now say peace be within thee. Because of the House of the Lord our God, I will seek thy good.* ....

The love of our country has in all times been a subject of warm commendations; and it is certainly a noble passion; but, like all other passions, it requires regulation and direction. There are mistakes and prejudices by which, in this instance, we are in particular danger of being misled.——I will briefly mention some of these to you, and observe,

First, That by our country is meant, in this case, not the soil or the spot of earth on which we happen to have been born; not the forests and fields, but that community of which we are members; or that body of companions and friends and kindred who are associated with us under the same constitution of government, protected

---

[1] Price's *Discourse* was delivered as a sermon in London on 4 November 1789, the 101st anniversary of the Glorious Revolution of 1688, which deposed the Catholic King James II in favour of William and Mary and imposed some limitations on the power of the monarchy. Edmund Burke's *Reflections on the Revolution in France** is a rebuttal; Thomas Paine's* *Rights of Man* (1791–92) develops some of Price's views.

[2] Psalm 122.2–9.

by the same laws, and bound together by the same civil polity.

Secondly, It is proper to observe, that even in this sense of our country, that love of it which is our duty, does not imply any conviction of the superior value of it to other countries, or any particular preference of its laws and constitution of government. Were this implied, the love of their country would be the duty of only a very small part of mankind; for there are few countries that enjoy the advantage of laws and governments which deserve to be preferred. To found, therefore, this duty on such a preference, would be to found it on error and delusion. It is, however, a common delusion. There is the same partiality in countries, to themselves, that there is in individuals. All our attachments should be accompanied, as far as possible, with right opinions.——We are too apt to confine wisdom and virtue within the circle of our own acquaintance and party. Our friends, our country, and in short every thing related to us, we are disposed to overvalue. A wise man will guard himself against this delusion. He will study to think of all things as they are, and not suffer any partial affections to blind his understanding. In other families there may be as much worth as in our own. In other circles of friends there may be as much wisdom; and in other countries as much of all that deserves esteem; but, notwithstanding this, our obligation to love our own families, friends, and country, and to seek, in the first place, their good, will remain the same.

Thirdly, It is proper I should desire you particularly to distinguish between the love of our country and that spirit of rivalship and ambition which has been common among nations.——What has the love of their country hitherto been among mankind? What has it been but a love of domination; a desire of conquest, and a thirst for grandeur and glory, by extending territory, and enslaving surrounding countries? What has it been but a blind and narrow principle, producing in every country a contempt of other countries, and forming men into combinations and factions against their common rights and liberties? This is the principle that has been too often cried up as a virtue of the first rank: a principle of the same kind with that which governs clans of *Indians* or tribes of *Arabs*, and leads them out to plunder and massacre. As most of the evils which have taken place in private life, and among individuals, have been occasioned by the desire of private interest overcoming the public affections; so most of the evils which have taken place among bodies of men have been occasioned by the desire of their own interest overcoming the principle of universal benevolence....

But I am digressing from what I had chiefly in view; which was, after noticing that love of our country which is false and spurious, to explain the nature and effects of that which is just and reasonable. With this view I must desire you to recollect that we are so constituted that our affections are more drawn to some among mankind than to others, in proportion to their degrees of nearness to us, and our power of being useful to them. It is obvious that this is a circumstance in the constitution of our natures which proves the wisdom and goodness of our Maker; for had our affections been determined alike to all our fellow-creatures, human life would have been a scene of embarrassment and distraction. Our regards, according to the order of nature, begin with ourselves; and every man is charged primarily with the care of himself. Next come our families, and benefactors, and friends; and after them our country. We can do little for the interest of mankind at large. To this interest, however, all other interests are subordinate. The noblest principle in our nature is the regard to general justice, and that good-will which embraces all the world.——I have already observed this; but it cannot be too often repeated. Though our immediate attention must be employed in promoting our own interest and that of our nearest connexions; yet we must remember, that a narrower interest ought always to give way to a more extensive interest. In pursuing particularly the interest of our country, we ought to carry our views beyond it. We should love it ardently, but not exclusively. We ought to seek its good, by all the means that our different circumstances and abilities will allow; but at the same time we ought to consider ourselves as citizens of the world, and take care to maintain a just regard to the rights of other countries....

Our first concern, as lovers of our country, must be to *enlighten* it.—Why are the nations of the world so patient under despotism?—Why do they crouch to tyrants, and submit to be treated as if they were a herd of cattle? Is it not because they are kept in darkness, and want knowledge? Enlighten them and you will elevate them. Shew them they are *men*, and they will act like *men*. Give them just ideas of civil government, and let them know that it is an expedient for gaining protection against injury and defending their rights,[1] and it will be impossible for them to submit to governments which, like most of those now in the world, are usurpations on the rights of men, and little better than contrivances for enabling the *few* to oppress the *many*. Convince them that the Deity is a righteous and benevolent as well as omnipotent being, who regards with equal eye all his creatures, and connects his favour with nothing but an honest desire to know and to do his will; and that zeal for mystical doctrines which has led men to hate and harass one another will be exterminated. Set religion before them as a rational service, consisting not in any rites and ceremonies, but in worshipping God with a pure heart and practising righteousness from the fear of his displeasure and the apprehension of a future righteous judgment, and that gloomy and cruel superstition will be abolished which has hitherto gone under the name of religion, and to the support of which civil government has been perverted.——Ignorance is the parent of bigotry, intolerance, persecution and slavery. Inform and instruct mankind; and these evils will be excluded.——Happy is the person who, himself raised above vulgar errors, is conscious of having aimed at giving mankind this instruction. Happy is the Scholar or Philosopher who at the close of life can reflect that he has made this use of his learning and abilities: but happier far must he be, if at the same time he has reason to believe he has been successful, and actually contributed, by his instructions, to disseminate among his fellow-creatures just notions of themselves, of their rights, of religion, and the nature and end of civil government....

The next great blessing of human nature [...] is VIRTUE. This ought to follow knowledge, and to be directed by it. Virtue without knowledge makes enthusiasts; and knowledge without virtue makes devils; but both united elevates to the top of human dignity and perfection.——We must, therefore, if we would serve our country, make both these the objects of our zeal. We must discourage vice in all its forms; and our endeavours to enlighten must have ultimately in view a reformation of manners and virtuous practice.

I must add here, that in the practice of virtue I include the discharge of the public duties of religion....

If there is a Governor of the world, who directs all events, he ought to be invoked and worshipped; and those who dislike that mode of worship which is prescribed by public authority, ought (if they can find no worship *out* of the church which they approve) to set up a separate worship for themselves; and by doing this, and giving an example of a rational and manly worship, men of weight, from their rank or literature, may do the greatest service to society and the world. They may bear a testimony against that application of civil power to the support of particular modes of faith, which obstructs human improvement, and perpetuates error; and they may hold out an instruction which will discountenance superstition, and at the same time recommend religion, by making it appear to be (what it certainly is when rightly understood) the strongest incentive to all that is generous and worthy, and consequently the best friend to public order and happiness.

LIBERTY is the next great blessing which I have mentioned as the object of patriotic zeal. It is inseparable from knowledge and virtue, and together with them completes the glory of a community. An enlightened and virtuous country must be a free country. It cannot suffer invasions of its rights, or bend to tyrants.——I need not, on this occasion, take any pains to shew you how great a blessing liberty is. The smallest attention to the history of past ages, and the present state of mankind, will make you sensible of its importance. Look round the world, and you will find almost every country, respectable or contemptible, happy or miserable, a fruitful field or a frightful waste, according as it possesses or wants this blessing. Think of *Greece*, formerly the seat of arts and science, and the most distinguished spot under heaven; but now, having lost liberty, a vile and

---

[1] "See the Declaration of Rights by the National Assembly of *France*, in the Appendix." (R.P.)

wretched spot, a region of darkness, poverty, and barbarity.——Such reflexions must convince you that, if you love your country, you cannot be zealous enough in promoting the cause of liberty in it. But it will come in my way to say more to this purpose presently.

The observations I have made include our whole duty to our country; for by endeavouring to liberalize and enlighten it, to discourage vice and to promote virtue in it, and to assert and support its liberties, we shall endeavour to do all that is necessary to make it great and happy.——But it is proper that, on this occasion, I should be more explicit, and exemplify our duty to our country by observing farther, that it requires us to obey its laws, and to respect its magistrates.…

Civil governors are properly the servants of the public; and a King is no more than the first servant of the public, created by it, maintained by it, and responsible to it: and all the homage paid him, is due to him on no other account than his relation to the public. His sacredness is the sacredness of the community. His authority is the authority of the community; and the term MAJESTY, which it is usual to apply to him, is by no means *his own* majesty, but the MAJESTY OF THE PEOPLE. For this reason, whatever he may be in his private capacity; and though, in respect of personal qualities, not equal to, or even far below many among ourselves—For this reason, I say, (that is, as representing the community and its first magistrate), he is entitled to our reverence and obedience. The words MOST EXCELLENT MAJESTY are rightly applied to him; and there is a respect which it would be criminal to withhold from him.…

Had I been to address the King on a late occasion,[1] I should have been inclined to do it in a style very different from that of most of the addressers, and to use some such language as the following:——I rejoice, Sir, in your recovery. I thank God for his goodness to you. I honour you not only as my King, but as almost the only lawful King in the world, because the only one who owes his crown to the choice of his people. May you enjoy all possible happiness. May God shew you the folly of those effusions of adulation which you are now receiving, and guard you against their effects. May you be led to such a just sense of the nature of your situation, and endowed with such wisdom, as shall render your restoration to the government of these kingdoms a blessing to it, and engage you to consider yourself as more properly the *Servant* than the *Sovereign* of your people."…

Another expression of our love to our country is defending it against enemies. These enemies are of two sorts, internal and external; or domestic and foreign. The former are the most dangerous, and they have generally been the most successful. I have just observed, that there is a submission due to the executive officers of government, which is our duty; but you must not forget what I have also observed, that it must not be a blind and slavish submission. Men in power (unless better disposed than is common) are always endeavouring to extend their power. They hate the doctrine, that it is a TRUST derived from the people, and not a *right* vested in themselves. For this reason, the tendency of every government is to despotism; and in this the best constituted governments must end, if the people are not vigilant, ready to take alarms, and determined to resist abuses as soon as they begin. This vigilance, therefore, it is our duty to maintain. Whenever it is withdrawn, and a people cease to reason about their rights and to be awake to encroachments, they are in danger of being enslaved, and their *servants* will soon become their *masters*.

I need not say how much it is our duty to defend our country against foreign enemies. When a country is attacked in any of its rights by another country, or when any attempts are made by ambitious foreign powers to injure it, a war in its defence becomes necessary: and, in such circumstances, to die for our country is meritorious and noble.[2] These *defensive* wars are, in my opinion, the only just wars. *Offensive* wars are always unlawful; and to seek the aggrandizement of our country by them, that is, by attacking other countries, in order to extend dominion, or to gratify avarice, is wicked and detestable.

---

[1] George III had been declared insane in November 1788, but he recovered. He would be declared permanently insane in 1811.

[2] Cf. Horace, *Odes* 3.2.13.

Such, however, have been most of the wars which have taken place in the world; but the time is, I hope, coming, when a conviction will prevail, of the folly[1] as well as the iniquity of wars; and when the nations of the earth, happy under just governments, and no longer in danger from the passions of Kings, will find out better ways of settling their disputes; and beat (as Isaiah prophecies) *their swords into ploughshares, and their spears into pruning-hooks....*[2]

But the most important instance of the imperfect state in which the Revolution left our constitution, is the INEQUALITY OF OUR REPRESENTATION. I think, indeed, this defect in our constitution so gross and so palpable, as to make it excellent chiefly in form and theory. You should remember that a representation in the legislature of a kingdom is the *basis* of constitutional liberty in it, and of all legitimate government; and that without it a government is nothing but an usurpation.[3] When the representation is fair and equal, and at the same time vested with such powers as our House of Commons possesses, a kingdom may be said to govern itself, and consequently to possess true liberty. When the representation is partial, a kingdom possesses liberty only partially; and if extremely partial, it only gives a *semblance* of liberty; but if not only extremely partial, but corruptly chosen, and under corrupt influence after being chosen, it becomes a *nuisance*, and produces the worst of all forms of government—a government by corruption—a government carried on and supported by spreading venality and profligacy through a kingdom.

May heaven preserve this kingdom from a calamity so dreadful! It is the point of depravity to which abuses under such a government as ours naturally tend, and the last stage of national unhappiness. We are, at present, I hope, at a great distance from it. But it cannot be pretended that there are no advances towards it, or that there is no reason for apprehension and alarm.

The inadequateness of our representation has been long a subject of complaint. This is, in truth, our fundamental grievance; and I do not think that any thing is much more our duty, as men who love their country, and are grateful for the Revolution, than to unite our zeal in endeavouring to get it redressed. At the time of the American war, associations were formed for this purpose in LONDON, and other parts of the kingdom; and our present Minister[4] himself has, since that war, directed to it an effort which made him a favourite with many of us. But all attention to it seems now lost, and the probability is, that this inattention will continue, and that nothing will be done towards gaining for us this essential blessing, till some great calamity again alarms our fears, or till some great abuse of power again provokes our resentment; or, perhaps, till the acquisition of a pure and equal representation by other countries (while we are mocked with the shadow)[5] kindles our shame.

Such is the conduct by which we ought to express our gratitude for the Revolution.—We should always bear in mind the principles that justify it. We should contribute all we can towards supplying what it left deficient; and shew ourselves anxious about transmitting the blessings obtained by it to our posterity, unimpaired and improved.—But, brethren, while we thus shew our patriotic zeal, let us take care not to disgrace the cause of patriotism, by any licentious, or immoral conduct.—— Oh! how earnestly do I wish that all who profess zeal in this cause, were as distinguished by the purity of their morals, as some of them are by their abilities; and that I could make them sensible of the advantages they

---

[1] "See a striking representation of the folly of wars, in the last sections of Mr. Necker's Treatise on the *Administration of the Finances of* FRANCE. There is reason to believe that the sentiments on this subject in that treatise, are now the prevailing sentiments in the court and legislature of FRANCE; and, consequently, that one of the happy effects of the revolution in that country may be, if not our own fault, such a harmony between the two first kingdoms in the world, strengthened by a common participation in the blessings of liberty, as shall not only prevent their engaging in any future wars with one another, but dispose them to unite in preventing wars every where, and in making the world free and happy." (R.P.) Jacques Necker (1732–1804) wrote *De l'Administration des finances de France* (1784).

[2] Isaiah 2.4.

[3] "Except in states so small as to admit of a Legislative Assembly, consisting of all the members of the state." (R.P.)

[4] William Pitt the Younger (1759–1806), prime minister 1783–1801, 1804–06.

[5] "A representation chosen principally by the Treasury, and a few thousands of the dregs of the people, who are generally paid for their votes." (R.P.)

would derive from a virtuous character, and of the suspicions they incur and the loss of consequence they suffer by wanting it.——Oh! that I could see in men who oppose tyranny in the state, a disdain of the tyranny of low passions in themselves; or, at least, such a sense of shame, and regard to public order and decency as would induce them to *hide* their irregularities, and to avoid insulting the virtuous part of the community by an open exhibition of vice!—I cannot reconcile myself to the idea of an immoral patriot, or to that separation of private from public virtue, which some think to be possible. Is it to be expected that——But I must forbear. I am afraid of applications, which many are too ready to make, and for which I should be sorry to give any just occasion....

You may reasonably expect that I should now close this address to you. But I cannot yet dismiss you. I must not conclude without recalling, particularly, to your recollection, a consideration to which I have more than once alluded, and which, probably, your thoughts have been all along anticipating: A consideration with which my mind is impressed more than I can express. I mean, the consideration of the favourableness of the present times to all exertions in the cause of public liberty.

What an eventful period is this! I am thankful that I have lived to it; and I could almost say, *Lord, now lettest thou thy servant depart in peace, for mine eyes have seen thy salvation.*[1] I have lived to see a diffusion of knowledge, which has undermined superstition and error—I have lived to see the rights of men better understood than ever; and nations panting for liberty, which seemed to have lost the idea of it.——I have lived to see THIRTY MILLIONS of people, indignant and resolute, spurning at slavery, and demanding liberty with an irresistible voice; their king led in triumph, and an arbitrary monarch surrendering himself to his subjects.——After sharing in the benefits of one Revolution, I have been spared to be a witness to two other Revolutions, both glorious.——And now, methinks, I see the ardor for liberty catching and spreading; a general amendment beginning in human affairs; the dominion of kings changed for the dominion of laws, and the dominion of priests giving way to the dominion of reason and conscience.

Be encouraged, all ye friends of freedom, and writers in its defence! The times are auspicious. Your labours have not been in vain. Behold kingdoms, admonished by you, starting from sleep, breaking their fetters, and claiming justice from their oppressors![2] Behold, the light you have struck out, after setting AMERICA free, reflected to FRANCE, and there kindled into a blaze that lays despotism in ashes, and warms and illuminates EUROPE!

Tremble all ye oppressors of the world! Take warning all ye supporters of slavish governments, and slavish hierarchies! Call no more (absurdly and wickedly) REFORMATION, innovation. You cannot now hold the world in darkness. Struggle no longer against increasing light and liberality. Restore to mankind their rights; and consent to the correction of abuses, before they and you are destroyed together.

---

[1] Luke 2.29–30.

[2] Cf. Milton's description of England in *Areopagitica* (1644), "rousing herself like a strong man after sleep and shaking her invincible locks."

Sir Joshua Reynolds
1723 – 1792

Joshua Reynolds was born on 16 July 1723, the seventh child of Samuel Reynolds, a schoolteacher in Plympton, near Plymouth, and Theophila Potter Reynolds. Instead of becoming a country apothecary, as his parents intended, Reynolds moved to London at seventeen as apprentice to the portrait painter Thomas Hudson. When his apprenticeship ended in 1743, he began to establish a career in Plymouth and London; from 1749 until 1752 he studied in Italy, befriended by Augustus Keppel, a naval officer whose portrait he later painted. In Rome, Florence, Venice, Bologna, and Naples, he became familiar with the work of such artists as Michelangelo, Raphael, Titian, and Guido Reni.

Back in London, Reynolds met Samuel Johnson and such other prominent figures as Burke,* the actor David Garrick (whom he painted between the muses of comedy and tragedy), and Goldsmith.* With Johnson, he was a founding member of the Literary Club, whose members included the historian Edward Gibbon, the musicologist Charles Burney (father of Frances Burney),* the Whig statesman Charles James Fox, and the playwright Richard Brinsley Sheridan. In acknowledgement of his stature as a painter, Reynolds was also appointed the first president of the new Royal Academy in 1768.

His fifteen *Discourses* (1769–90), first written as addresses to academy students and other members of the artistic and literary communities, were each subsequently published as a pamphlet. They set down principles of taste and art criticism, advocate for the cultural centrality of the visual arts, and advise students about professional education, training, and discipline. When the Royal Academy moved into Somerset House in 1780, Reynolds' role in the Academy was reflected in his ceiling painting representing "Theory." Reynolds' eyesight failed in 1789, and his last years were solitary and unhappy. He died on 23 February 1792, recognized for his achievements both as a painter and as a man of letters. (A.M.)

✦✦✦

from *Seven Discourses Delivered in the Royal Academy by the President* (1778)

from *A Discourse, Delivered to the Students of the Royal Academy, on the Distribution of the Prizes, December 10, 1776, by the President* [DISCOURSE 7]

Gentlemen,

It has been my uniform endeavour, since I first addressed you from this place, to impress you strongly with one ruling idea. I wished you to be persuaded, that success in your Art depends almost entirely on your own industry; but the industry which I principally recommended, is not the industry of the *hands*, but of the *mind*.

As our art is not a divine *gift*, so neither is it a mechanical *trade*. Its foundations are laid in solid science. And practice, though essential to perfection, can never attain that to which it aims, unless it works under the direction of principle.

Some writers upon art carry this point too far, and suppose that such a body of universal and profound learning is requisite, that the very enumeration of its kinds is enough to frighten a beginner. Vitruvius,[1] after going through the many accomplishments of nature, and the many acquirements of learning, necessary to an architect, proceeds with great gravity to assert, that he ought to be well skilled in the civil law, that he may not be cheated in the title of the ground he builds on.

But without such exaggeration, we may go so far as to assert, that a painter stands in need of more knowledge than is to be picked off his pallet, or collected by looking on his model, whether it be in life or in picture.

---

[1] Vitruvius Pollo (fl. 40 BC), author of the only classical treatise on architecture, *De Architectura*.

He can never be a great artist, who is grossly illiterate.

Every man whose business is description ought to be tolerably conversant with the poets, in some language or other; that he may imbibe a poetical spirit, and enlarge his stock of ideas. He ought to acquire an habit of comparing and digesting his notions. He ought not to be wholly unacquainted with that part of philosophy which gives him an insight into human nature, and relates to the manners, characters, passions and affections. He ought to know *something* concerning the mind, as well as *a great deal* concerning the body of man.

For this purpose, it is not necessary that he should go into such a compass of reading, as must, by distracting his attention, disqualify him for the practical part of his profession, and make him sink the performer in the critic. Reading, if it can be made the favourite recreation of his leisure hours, will improve and enlarge his mind, without retarding his actual industry.

What such partial and desultory reading cannot afford, may be supplied by the conversation of learned and ingenious men, which is the best of all substitutes for those who have not the means or opportunities of deep study. There are many such men in this age; and they will be pleased with communicating their ideas to artists, when they see them curious and docile, if they are treated with that respect and deference which is so justly their due. Into such society, young artists, if they make it the point of their ambition, will by degrees be admitted. There, without formal teaching, they will insensibly come to feel and reason like those they live with, and find a rational and systematic taste imperceptibly formed in their minds, which they will know how to reduce to a standard, by applying general truth to their own purposes, better perhaps than those to whom they owed the original sentiment.

Of these studies and this conversation, the desired and legitimate offspring is a power of distinguishing right from wrong, which power applied to works of art, is denominated *Taste*. Let me then, without further introduction, enter upon an examination, whether Taste be so far beyond our reach, as to be unattainable by care; or be so very vague and capricious, that no care ought to be employed about it....

Genius and taste, in their common acceptation, appear to be very nearly related; the difference lies only in this, that genius has superadded to it a habit or power of execution. Or we may say, that taste, when this power is added, changes its name, and is called genius. They both, in the popular opinion, pretend to an entire exemption from the restraint of rules. It is supposed that their powers are intuitive; that under the name of genius great works are produced, and under the name of taste an exact judgment is given, without our knowing why, and without being under the least obligation to reason, precept, or experience.

One can scarce state these opinions without exposing their absurdity, yet they are constantly in the mouths of men, and particularly of artists. They who have thought seriously on this subject, do not carry the point so far; yet I am persuaded, that even among those few who may be called thinkers, the prevalent opinion gives less than it ought to the powers of reason; and considers the principles of taste, which give all their authority to the rules of art, as more fluctuating, and as having less solid foundations, than we shall find, upon examination, they really have.

The common saying, that *tastes are not to be disputed*,[1] owes its influence, and its general reception, to the same error which leads us to imagine it of too high original to submit to the authority of an earthly tribunal. It will likewise correspond with the notions of those who consider it as a mere phantom of the imagination, so devoid of substance as to elude all criticism.

We often appear to differ in sentiments from each other, merely from the inaccuracy of terms, as we are not obliged to speak always with critical exactness. Something of this too may arise from want of words in the language to express the more nice discriminations which a deep investigation discovers. A great deal however of this difference vanishes, when each opinion is tolerably explained and understood by constancy and precision in the use of terms.

We apply the term *Taste* to that act of the mind by which we like or dislike, whatever be the subject. Our

---

[1] a literal translation of *de gustibus non est disputandum* (L.), "there's no accounting for taste."

judgment upon an airy nothing,[1] a fancy which has no foundation, is called by the same name which we give to our determination concerning those truths which refer to the most general and most unalterable principles of human nature, to works which are only to be produced by the greatest efforts of the human understanding. However inconvenient this may be, we are obliged to take words as we find them; all we can do is to distinguish the *things* to which they are applied.

We may let pass those things which are at once subjects of taste and sense, and which having as much certainty as the senses themselves, give no occasion to enquiry or dispute. The natural appetite or taste of the human mind is for *Truth*; whether that truth results from the real agreement or equality of original ideas among themselves; from the agreement of the representation of any object with the thing represented; or from the correspondence of the several parts of any arrangement with each other. It is the very same taste which relishes a demonstration in geometry, that is pleased with the resemblance of a picture to an original, and touched with the harmony of music.

All these have unalterable and fixed foundations in nature, and are therefore equally investigated by reason, and known by study; some with more, some with less clearness, but all exactly in the same way....

Of the judgment which we make on the works of art, and the preference that we give to one class of art over another, if a reason be demanded, the question is perhaps evaded by answering, I judge from my taste; but it does not follow that a better answer cannot be given, though, for common gazers, this may be sufficient. Every man is not obliged to investigate the causes of his approbation or dislike.

The arts would lie open for ever to caprice and casualty, if those who are to judge of their excellencies had no settled principles by which they are to regulate their decisions, and the merit or defect of performances were to be determined by unguided fancy. And indeed we may venture to assert, that whatever speculative knowledge is necessary to the artist, is equally and indispensably necessary to the connoisseur.

The first idea that occurs in the consideration of what is fixed in art, or in taste, is that presiding principle of which I have so frequently spoken in former discourses, the general idea of nature. The beginning, the middle, and the end of every thing that is valuable in taste, is comprized in the knowledge of what is truly nature; for whatever ideas are not conformable to those of nature, or universal opinion, must be considered as more or less capricious.

The idea of nature comprehends not only the forms which nature produces, but also the nature and internal fabric and organization, as I may call it, of the human mind and imagination. General ideas, beauty, or nature, are but different ways of expressing the same thing, whether we apply these terms to statues, poetry, or picture. Deformity is not nature, but an accidental deviation from her accustomed practice. This general idea therefore ought to be called Nature,[2] and nothing else, correctly speaking, has a right to that name. But we are so far from speaking, in common conversation, with any such accuracy, that, on the contrary, when we criticise Rembrandt and other Dutch painters,[3] who introduced into their historical pictures exact representations of individual objects with all their imperfections, we say, though it is not in a good taste, yet it is nature.

This misapplication of terms must be very often perplexing to the young student. Is not, he may say, art an imitation of nature? Must he not therefore who imitates her with the greatest fidelity, be the best artist? By this mode of reasoning Rembrandt has a higher place than Raffaelle.[4] But a very little reflection will serve to shew us that these particularities cannot be nature: for how can that be the nature of man, in which no two individuals are the same?

It plainly appears, that as a work is conducted under the influence of general ideas, or partial, it is principally to be considered as the effect of a good or a bad taste....

---

[1] Cf. Shakespeare, *A Midsummer Night's Dream* 5.1.16.

[2] Cf., for example, Samuel Johnson, *Rasselas* (1759), chap. 10, and his Preface to *The Plays of William Shakespeare* (1765): "Nothing can please many, and please long, but just representations of general nature."

[3] Rembrandt Harmenszoon van Rijn (1606–69), painter and etcher.

[4] the Italian painter Raphael or Raffaello Sanzio (1483–1520).

I shall now say something on that part of *taste*, which, as I have hinted to you before, does not belong so much to the external form of things, but is addressed to the mind, and depends on its original frame, or, to use the expression, the organization of the soul, I mean the imagination and the passions. The principles of these are as invariable as the former, and are to be known and reasoned upon in the same manner, by an appeal to common sense deciding upon the common feelings of mankind. This sense, and these feelings, appear to me of equal authority, and equally conclusive.

Now this appeal implies a general uniformity and agreement in the minds of men. It would be else an idle and vain endeavour to establish rules of art; it would be pursuing a phantom to attempt to move affections with which we were entirely unacquainted. We have no reason to suspect there is a greater difference between our minds than between our forms, of which, though there are no two alike, yet there is a general similitude that goes through the whole race of mankind; and those who have cultivated their taste can distinguish what is beautiful or deformed, or, in other words, what agrees or what deviates from the general idea of nature, in one case, as well as in the other.

The internal fabric of our mind, as well as the external form of our bodies, being nearly uniform; it seems then to follow of course, that as the imagination is incapable of producing any thing originally of itself, and can only vary and combine these ideas with which it is furnished by means of the senses, there will be of course an agreement in the imaginations as in the senses of men. There being this agreement, it follows, that in all cases, in our lightest amusements, as well as in our most serious actions and engagements of life, we must regulate our affections of every kind by that of others. The well-disciplined mind acknowledges this authority, and submits its own opinion to the public voice.

It is from knowing what are the general feelings and passions of mankind, that we acquire a true idea of what imagination is; though it appears as if we had nothing to do but to consult our own particular sensations, and these were sufficient to ensure us from all error and mistake.

A knowledge of the disposition and character of the human mind can be acquired only by experience: a great deal will be learned, I admit, by a habit of examining what passes in our bosoms, what are our own motives of action, and of what kind of sentiments we are conscious on any occasion. We may suppose an uniformity, and conclude that the same effect will be produced by the same cause in the minds of others. This examination will contribute to suggest to us matters of enquiry; but we can never be sure that our own sensations are true and right, till they are confirmed by more extensive observation....

What distinguishes oratory from a cold narration, is a more liberal, though chaste use of those ornaments which go under the name of figurative and metaphorical expressions; and poetry distinguishes itself from oratory by words and expressions still more ardent and glowing. What separates and distinguishes poetry, is more particularly the ornament of *verse*: it is this which gives it its character, and is an essential without which it cannot exist. Custom has appropriated different metre to different kinds of composition, in which the world is not perfectly agreed. In England the dispute is not yet settled, which is to be preferred, rhyme or blank verse.[1] But however we disagree about what these metrical ornaments shall be, that some metre is essentially necessary is universally acknowledged.

In poetry or eloquence, to determine how far figurative or metaphorical language may proceed, and when it begins to be affectation or beside the truth, must be determined by taste, though this taste we must never forget is regulated and formed by the presiding feelings of mankind, by those works which have approved themselves to all times and all persons.

Thus, though eloquence has undoubtedly an essential and intrinsic excellence, and immoveable principles common to all languages, founded in the nature of our passions and affections; yet it has its ornaments and modes of address, which are merely arbitrary. What is approved in the eastern nations as grand and majestic,

---

[1] The Restoration and eighteenth-century poets generally preferred rhyme to blank verse: Dryden, for example, adapted *Paradise Lost* as a play in heroic couplets in *The State of Innocence and the Fall of Man* (1667).

would be considered by the Greeks and Romans as turgid and inflated; and they, in return, would be thought by the Orientals to express themselves in a cold and insipid manner.

We may add likewise to the credit of ornaments, that it is by their means that art itself accomplishes its purpose. Fresnoy[1] calls colouring, which is one of the chief ornaments of painting, *lena sororis*,[2] that which procures lovers and admirers to the more valuable excellencies of the art.

It appears to be the same right turn of mind which enables a man to acquire the *truth*, or the just idea of what is right in the ornaments, as in the more stable principles of art. It has still the same centre of perfection, though it is the centre of a smaller circle.

To illustrate this by the fashion of dress, in which there is allowed to be a good or bad taste. The component parts of dress are continually changing from great to little, from short to long; but the general form still remains; it is still the same general dress which is comparatively fixed, though on a very slender foundation; but it is on this which fashion must rest. He who invents with the most success, or dresses in the best taste, would probably, from the same sagacity employed to greater purposes, have discovered equal skill, or have formed the same correct taste in the highest labours of art.

I have mentioned taste in dress, which is certainly one of the lowest subjects to which this word is applied; yet, as I have before observed, there is a right even here, however narrow its foundation respecting the fashion of any particular nation. But we have still more slender means of determining, in regard to the different customs of different ages or countries, to which to give the preference, since they seem to be all equally removed from nature.

If an European, when he has cut off his beard, and put false hair on his head, or bound up his own natural hair in regular hard knots, as unlike nature as he can possibly make it; and having rendered them immoveable by the help of the fat of hogs, has covered the whole with flour, laid on by a machine with the utmost regularity; if, when thus attired he issues forth, he meets a Cherokee Indian, who has bestowed as much time at his toilet, and laid on with equal care and attention his yellow and red oker on particular parts of his forehead or cheeks, as he judges most becoming; whoever despises the other for this attention to the fashion of his country; which ever of these two first feels himself provoked to laugh, is the barbarian.

All these fashions are very innocent, neither worth disquisition, nor any endeavour to alter them, as the change would, in all probability, be equally distant from nature. The only circumstances against which indignation may reasonably be moved, is where the operation is painful or destructive of health, such as is practised at Otahaiti,[3] and the strait lacing of the English ladies; of the last of which, how destructive it must be to health and long life, the professor of anatomy took an opportunity of providing a few days since in this Academy....

---

[1] Charles-Alphonse Du Fresnoy (1611–65), French painter and author of a poem, *De arte graphica* [*Of the Art of Drawing*] (1656), which was translated into English by Dryden.

[2] literally, "the procuress of a sister" (L.); i.e., the quality that attracts one to qualities other than—but in a sibling relation to—colouring alone.

[3] Tahiti; Reynolds is probably referring to the practices of tattooing, body-piercing, and slitting practised by the Natives of Hawaii and described by James Cook (1728–79) in *A Compendious History of Captain Cook's Last Voyage* (1784).

Clara Reeve
1729 – 1807

Clara Reeve was born in Ipswich on 23 January 1729, one of the eight children of William Reeve, a clergyman, and Hannah Smithies Reeve, whose father was goldsmith to George I. She never married, moving with her mother to nearby Colchester after her father's death in 1755. Her early education was wide-ranging, including the study of French, German, and Latin: her first book, *Original Poems on Several Occasions* (1769), demonstrates the range of her abilities and interests; her second, a translation of John Barclay's Latin romance *Argenis* (1621), appeared as *The Phoenix; or, The History of Polyarchus and Argenis* in 1772.

Politically conservative, Reeve was also an advocate for women as thinkers, writers, and teachers. Her first and best-known novel, *The Old English Baron* (1778), was first published the previous year as *The Champion of Virtue*, but revised for republication allegedly according to the suggestions of Richardson's daughter, Martha Brigden. Reeve's attempt to rework the material of Horace Walpole's *Castle of Otranto* without the supernatural elements was well received by contemporaries: *The Old English Baron* was adapted for the stage, abridged, translated into French and German, and frequently reprinted in the eighteenth century.

Reeve attempted to use fiction as a pedagogical tool in *The Two Mentors* (1783), *The Exiles* (1788), *The School for Widows* (1791), and *Plans of Education* (1792)—didactic epistolary works focusing on Frances Darnford, who leaves her profligate husband to live a life of virtue, discipline, and benevolence; *Memoirs of Sir Roger de Clarendon* (1793), which makes medieval history relevant to contemporary events in which, Reeve believed, the overthrow of ranks led to social and political chaos; and *Destination* (1799), which attacks Rousseau's principles of education. Her theoretical work *The Progress of Romance* (1785) is better known today: here, Reeve surveys the development of prose romance in a series of fictional conversations, distinguishing between the imaginary, fantastic qualities of romance and the familiar, believable world of the novel, and offering judgments on past and contemporary writers. Clara Reeve died at Ipswich on 3 December 1807. (A.M.)

from *The Progress of Romance, through Times, Countries, and Manners; with Remarks on the Good and Bad Effects of It, on Them Respectively; in a Course of Evening Conversations* (1785)

from *Evening 7*

Hortensius, Sophronia, Euphrasia[1]

HORTENSIUS: We have now, I presume, done with the Romances, and are expecting your investigation of Novels.

EUPHRASIA: It is now that I begin to be sensible in how arduous an undertaking I have engaged, and to fear I shall leave it unfinished.

HORTENSIUS: Have no fears, Madam; we shall not suffer you to leave off presently. We expect the completion of the plan you have given us.

SOPHRONIA: If I judge rightly, the conclusion is yet a great way off.

EUPHRASIA: This is one of the circumstances that frighten me. If I skim over the subject lightly it will be doing nothing; and if I am too minute I may grow dull and tedious, and tire my hearers.

HORTENSIUS: You must aim at the medium you recommended to us.

EUPHRASIA: What Goddess, or what Muse must I invoke to guide me through these vast, unexplored regions of fancy?—regions inhabited by wisdom and folly,—by wit and stupidity,—by religion and profaneness,—by morality and licentiousness.—How shall I separate and distinguish the various and opposite qualities of these strange concomitants?—point out some as the objects of admiration and respect, and others of abhorrence and contempt?

HORTENSIUS: The subject warms you already, and when that is the case, you will never be heard coldly.—Go on and prosper.

EUPHRASIA: In this fairy land are many Castles of various Architecture.—Some are built in the air, and have no foundation at all,—others are composed of such heavy materials, that their own weight sinks them into the earth, where they lie buried under their own ruins, and leave not a trace behind,—a third sort are built upon a real and solid foundation, and remain impregnable against all the attacks of Criticism, and perhaps even of time itself.

SOPHRONIA: So so!—we are indeed got into Fairyland; it is here that I expect to meet with many of my acquaintance, and I shall challenge them whenever I do.

EUPHRASIA: I hope that you will assist my labours.—I will drop the metaphor, and tell you that I mean to take notice only of the most eminent works of this kind:—to pass over others slightly and leave the worst in the depths of Oblivion.

The word *Novel* in all languages signifies something new. It was first used to distinguish these works from Romance, though they have lately been confounded together and are frequently mistaken for each other.

SOPHRONIA: But how will you draw the line of distinction, so as to separate them effectually, and prevent future mistakes?

EUPHRASIA: I will attempt this distinction, and I presume if it is properly done it will be followed,—If not, you are but where you were before. The Romance is an heroic fable, which treats of fabulous persons and things.—The Novel is a picture of real life and manners, and of the times in which it is written. The Romance in lofty and elevated language, describes what never happened nor is likely to happen.—The Novel gives a familiar relation of such things, as pass every day before our eyes, such as may happen to our friend, or to ourselves; and the perfection of it, is to represent every scene, in so easy and natural a manner, and to make them appear so probable, as to deceive us into a persuasion (at least while we are reading) that all is real, until we are affected by the joys or distresses, of the persons in the story, as if they were our own.

---

[1] Reeve presents her ideas through a series of colloquies among three friends, two women, Sophronia ["wise," "foresighted"] and Euphrasia ["cheerful mind"], and a man, Hortensius ["garden lover"]. Euphrasia is Reeve's spokeswoman. "Evening 7" distinguishes between "novel" and "romance," and focusses on early fiction, including novels by Behn, Haywood, Manley, and Defoe. Cf. Macaulay's use of the name Hortensia in her *Letters on Education*.*

HORTENSIUS: You have well distinguished, and it is necessary to make this distinction.—I clearly perceive the difference between the Romance and Novel, and am surprized they should be confounded together.

EUPHRASIA: I have sometimes thought it has been done insidiously, by those who endeavour to render all writings of both kinds contemptible.

SOPHRONIA: I have generally observed that men of learning have spoken of them with the greatest disdain, especially collegians.

EUPHRASIA: Take care what you say my friend, they are a set of men who are not to be offended with impunity. Yet they deal in Romances, though of a different kind.—Some have taken up an opinion upon trust in others whose judgment they prefer to their own.—Others having seen a few of the worst or dullest among them, have judged of all the rest by them;—just as some men affect to despise our sex, because they have only conversed with the worst part of it.

HORTENSIUS: Your sex knows how to retort upon ours, and to punish us for our offences against you.—Proceed however....[1]

EUPHRASIA: ... Let us next consider some of the early Novels of our own country.

We had early translations of the best Novels of all other Countries, but for a long time produced very few of our own. One of the earliest I know of is the *Cyprian Academy*, by *Robert Baron*[2] in the reign of *Charles* the First.—Among our early Novel-writers we must reckon Mrs. *Behn*.[3]—There are strong marks of Genius in all this lady's works, but unhappily, there are some parts of them, very improper to be read by, or recommended to virtuous minds, and especially to youth.—She wrote in an age, and to a court of licentious manners, and perhaps we ought to ascribe to these causes the loose turn of her stories.—Let us do justice to her merits, and cast the veil of compassion over her faults.—She died in the year 1689, and lies buried in the cloisters of Westminster Abbey.—The inscription will shew how high she stood in estimation at that time.

HORTENSIUS: Are you not partial to the sex of this Genius?—when you excuse in her, what you would not to a man?

EUPHRASIA: Perhaps I may, and you must excuse me if I am so, especially as this lady had many fine and amiable qualities, besides her genius for writing.

SOPHRONIA: Pray let her rest in peace,—you were speaking of the inscription on her monument, I do not remember it.

EUPHRASIA: It is as follows:
Mrs. APHRA BEHN, 1689.
Here lies a proof that wit can never be
Defence enough against mortality.

Let me add that Mrs. *Behn* will not be forgotten, so long as the Tragedy of *Oroonoko* is acted, it was from her story of that illustrious African, that Mr. *Southern* wrote that play, and the most affecting parts of it are taken almost literally from her.[4]

HORTENSIUS: Peace be to her *manes*![5]—I shall not disturb her, or her works.

EUPHRASIA: I shall not recommend them to your perusal *Hortensius*.

The next female writer of this class is Mrs. *Manley*,[6] whose works are still more exceptionable than Mrs. *Behn*'s, and as much inferior to them in point of merit.—She hoarded up all the public and private scandal within her reach, and poured it forth, in a work too well known in the last age, though almost forgotten

---

[1] The discussion moves to a survey of early fiction: Giovanni Boccaccio (1313–75) in Italy, Cervantes (Miguel de Cervantes Saavedra, 1547–1616) in Spain, and Paul Scarron (1610–60) and Jean Renaud de Segrais (1624–1701) in France. Euphrasia condemns the novels of Madeleine de Scudéry (1607–1701), and *La Princesse de Clèves* (1678) by Marie-Madeleine de Lafayette (1634–93), and praises Alain-René Le Sage (1668–1747), especially *Gil Blas* (1715–35).

[2] Robert Baron (c. 1630–58), *Erotopaignion: or the Cyprian Academy* (1647).

[3] Aphra Behn (1640–89), an actor and the first professional woman writer in English, wrote plays (including *The Rover; or, The Banish'd Cavaliers*, 1677), poems, and short works of fiction (most notably *Oroonoko; or, The Royal Slave*, 1688).

[4] Thomas Southerne's play *Oroonoko* (1695) was based on Aphra Behn's novel about the suffering and heroism of an African prince sold into slavery in Surinam.

[5] "spirit of the dead" (L.).

[6] Mary Delarivière Manley (c. 1663–1724), novelist and playwright, whose scandal chronicles (especially her popular *Secret Memoirs and Manners of Several Persons of Quality, of Both Sexes from the New Atalantis*, 1709) offered sensational "news" about the rich and famous.

in the present; a work that partakes of the style of the Romance, and the Novel. I forbear the name, and further observations on it, as Mrs. *Manley*'s works are sinking gradually into oblivion. I am sorry to say they were once in fashion, which obliges me to mention them, otherwise I had rather be spared the pain of disgracing an Author of my own sex.

SOPHRONIA: It must be confessed that these books of the last age, were of worse tendency than any of those of the present.

EUPHRASIA: My dear friend, there were bad books at all times, for those who sought for them.—Let us pass them over in silence.

HORTENSIUS: No not yet.—Let me help your memory to one more Lady-Author of the same class.—Mrs. *Heywood*.[1]—She has the same claim upon you as those you have last mentioned.

EUPHRASIA: I had intended to have mentioned Mrs. *Heywood* though in a different way, but I find you will not suffer any part of her character to escape you.

HORTENSIUS: Why should she be spared any more than the others?

EUPHRASIA: Because she repented of her faults, and employed the latter part of her life in expiating the offences of the former.[2]—There is reason to believe that the examples of the two ladies we have spoken of, seduced Mrs. *Heywood* into the same track; she certainly wrote some amorous novels in her youth,[3] and also two books of the same kind as Mrs. *Manley*'s capital work,[4] all of which I hope are forgotten.

HORTENSIUS: I fear they will not be so fortunate, they will be known to posterity by the infamous immortality, conferred upon them by *Pope* in his Dunciad.[5]

EUPHRASIA: Mr. *Pope* was severe in his castigations, but let us be just to merit of every kind. Mrs. *Heywood* had the singular good fortune to recover a lost reputation, and the yet greater honour to atone for her errors.—She devoted the remainder of her life and labours to the service of virtue. Mrs. *Heywood* was one of the most voluminous female writers that ever England produced, none of her latter works are destitute of merit, though they do not rise to the highest pitch of excellence.—*Betsey Thoughtless* is reckoned her best Novel; but those works by which she is most likely to be known to posterity, are the *Female Spectator*, and the *Invisible Spy*.[6]—this lady died so lately as the year 1758.

SOPHRONIA: I have heard it often said that Mr. *Pope* was too severe in his treatment of this lady, it was supposed that she had given some private offence,[7] which he resented publicly as was too much his way.

HORTENSIUS: That is very likely, for he was not of a forgiving disposition.—If I have been too severe also, you ladies must forgive me in behalf of your sex.

EUPHRASIA: Truth is sometimes severe.—Mrs. *Heywood*'s wit and ingenuity were never denied. I would be the last to vindicate her faults, but the first to celebrate her return to virtue, and her atonement for them.

SOPHRONIA: May her first writings be forgotten, and the last survive to do her honour!

EUPHRASIA: Let us proceed to other writers.—As I purpose in future to take notice only of such Novels as are originals, or else of extraordinary merit, I must beg your allowance for all trifling slips of memory, for errors in chronology, and all other mistakes of equal consequence.—I must also have leave to mention English and Foreign books indifferently, just as they happen to rise to my memory, and observation.

HORTENSIUS: It is but just that you should have these, and every other allowance you can require, we have already laid a heavy tax upon you.

---

[1] the novelist, actor, and playwright Eliza Haywood (1693?–1756).

[2] Haywood's later work is much more decorous and conservative than the early novels Euphrasia goes on to criticize.

[3] such as *Love in Excess* (1719–20) and *The Fatal Secret, or Constancy in Distress* (1724).

[4] *The New Atalantis* (1709).

[5] For Haywood, see *Dunciad* 2.157–60 (1728); the only other woman writer mentioned in the *Dunciad* is not Manley, but Elizabeth Thomas (2.69–73).

[6] three works out of about seventy published by Haywood: *Betsy Thoughtless* (1751), a novel; the *Female Spectator* (1744–46), a periodical; and a linked series of short narratives and observations, *The Invisible Spy. By Explorabilis* (1754).

[7] Haywood was attacked by Henry Fielding, Jonathan Swift, and Richard Savage, as well as by Pope: it is unlikely that she offended Pope personally.

EUPHRASIA: You see I have many helps from my notes, and I hope to receive further assistance from you both.—I will proceed with my progress. The life of *Cleveland*, natural son of *Oliver Cromwell*,[1] is one of the *old Novels*, if I may be allowed the expression, I do not certainly know the Author, nor yet the date of the first edition.—When a Novel came out but seldom, it was eagerly received and generally read, this was at the time called a work of uncommon merit, but it will not bear a comparison with those that have been written since. There is originality and regularity in it. The incidents are too much of the marvellous kind, but some of the scenes are very pathetic, and there is business enough to keep the reader's attention constantly awake, and above all other merit, it has a moral tendency.

HORTENSIUS: I have heard this book ascribed to *Daniel de Foe*, who as I think was also the Author of *Robinson Crusoe*.[2]

EUPHRASIA: His title to the last mentioned is not quite clear.—It is said that he was trusted with a manuscript of *Alexander Selkirk*'s, who met with an adventure of the same kind as *Crusoe*'s, and that he stole his materials from thence, and then returned the manuscript to the Author—When *Selkirk*'s book was published, it was taken but little notice of; it had more truth, but less Romance, and beside, the curiosity of the public was gratified, and they looked on *Crusoe* as the Original, and *Selkirk* as the copy only.

HORTENSIUS: That was hard indeed, but I fear not unprecedented; you will give us your opinion of the book, exclusive of this circumstance.

EUPHRASIA: *Robinson Crusoe* was published in the year 1720.—*Gaudentio di Lucca* in 1725. I shall speak of these two books together, because there is a strong resemblance between them, the same marks of Originality appear in both.—They both give account of unknown or rather of *Ideal* countries, but in so natural and probable a manner, that they carry the reader with them wherever they please, in the midst of the most extraordinary occurrences. *Gaudentio di Lucca* is written by the pen of a master, it is imputed to Bishop *Berkely*,[3] and is not unworthy of that truly venerable man.—There is a greatness of design, and a depth of penetration into the causes of the health and prosperity of a state, and of the moral evils that first weaken and undermine, and finally cause the ruin of it.—The vast consequence of the good or bad education of youth, on which depends the health, vigour, and happiness of a nation. —These circumstances give this book a manifest superiority to the other, in many other respects they are both equally entitled to our plaudit.—But what gives a still higher value to these two books, they are evidently written to promote the cause of religion and virtue, and may safely be put into the hands of youth.—Such books cannot be too strongly recommended, as under the disguise of fiction, warm the heart with the love of virtue, and by that means, excite the reader to the practice of it.

HORTENSIUS: A warm plaudit you have given them,—I remember to have read *Robinson Crusoe* when very young, but I have forgot it, and ever since I have looked upon it as a book for children only; but I will read it again upon your recommendation, and judge of its merits.

EUPHRASIA: That is the certain consequence of putting these books too soon into the hands of children.—I will be bold to say a youth who reads them at a proper age, will never forget them.—Let me also beg you will read *Gaudentio di Lucca*.

HORTENSIUS: I will certainly read them both at my best leisure.

SOPHRONIA: But let me beg you to get the old Edition of *Crusoe*, for this is one of the books, which *Fanaticism* has laid her paw upon, and altered it to her own tenets, and she has added some of her own reveries at the end

---

[1] by Antoine François Prévost (1696–1763); translated into English as *The English Philosopher, or History of Mr. Cleveland, Natural Son of Cromwell* (1731). Oliver Cromwell (1599–1658) was a key figure during the Civil War and Lord Protector from 1653 until his death.

[2] Daniel Defoe's highly successful novel *Robinson Crusoe* (1719) is partly based on the adventures of Alexander Selkirk (1676–1721), who spent five years on a desert island.

[3] Simon Berington (not George Berkeley, 1685–1753), wrote *The Memoirs of Sigr Gaudentio di Lucca, taken from his confession and examination before the Fathers of the Inquisition at Bologna in Italy* (1737).

of it, called *Visions of the Angelical World*.[1]—If *Hortensius* should once dip into that part of it, it would entirely discredit our recommendation.

EUPHRASIA: You say true, I will get him the old Edition, which is the best.

HORTENSIUS: Pray do you call these Books Romances or Novels?

EUPHRASIA: They partake of the nature of both, but I consider them as of a different species from either, as works singular and Original.—I shall have occasion to place some later works under this class. But it is time for us to adjourn till next Thursday.

HORTENSIUS: I shall not fail to meet you.

SOPHRONIA: At my house.—No other engagement shall prevent it.

HORTENSIUS: Agreed,—none could give me equal pleasure.

EUPHRASIA: You are always my kind and indulgent friends, and your approbation is the crown of my labours.

---

[1] Daniel Defoe, *Serious Reflections during the Life and Surprising Adventures of Robinson Crusoe: With his Vision of the Angelick World* (1720). Defoe wrote both parts, which were published together in the eighteenth century.

Edmund Burke
1729? – 1797

Edmund Burke was born on 12 January 1729 (or possibly 1730) in Dublin, second son of Richard Burke, an attorney and government official, and Mary Nagle Burke. He was educated at a Quaker school in Ballitore and at Trinity College, Dublin. He graduated in 1748, and in 1750 he went to London to study law at the Middle Temple. After a few years, to his father's displeasure, he abandoned the law for literature. His first book, *A Vindication of Natural Society* (1756), was a philosophical satire; his second, *A Philosophical Enquiry into the Origin of our Ideas of the Sublime and Beautiful* (1757), was one of the major eighteenth-century treatises on aesthetics. In June 1757, he married Jane Nugent; they had two sons, one of whom died as a child. In 1758, Burke became editor of the *Annual Register*. In 1766, after serving as secretary to two prominent Whig politicians, he became a Member of Parliament. His parliamentary career was devoted largely to four causes. The first was reconciliation with the American colonists, who were then being provoked into revolution. The second was relief for Ireland, especially a relaxation of the Penal Laws against Catholics. The third was justice for India, which Burke considered oppressed by the East India Company and particularly by Warren Hastings, Governor-General of Bengal; he was largely responsible for the impeachment of Hastings by the House of Commons, which began in 1787 and lasted for seven years. The fourth was the French Revolution, of which Burke was an early and implacable opponent. On 4 November 1789, he received a letter from Charles Jean-François Depont, asking his opinion of the Revolution; the same day, Richard Price preached his sermon "On the Love of our Country"* at the Old Jewry chapel in London. Burke's masterpiece, *Reflections on the Revolution in France*, was his response. Godwin,* Paine,* and Wollstonecraft,* among others, wrote responses to it in turn. On 20 June 1794, the Commons sent the Hastings case to the Lords for judgment; the following day, Burke resigned his seat. (The next year, Hastings was acquitted.) Burke's retirement was darkened by the deaths of his brother and his surviving son, and by a public attack on his pension, which provoked his *Letter to a Noble Lord*. He died of stomach cancer at Beaconsfield, his country estate, on 9 July 1797. (D.L.M.)

☙☙

from *Reflections on the Revolution in France, and on the Proceedings in Certain Societies in London Relative to That Event. In a Letter Intended to Have Been Sent to a Gentleman in Paris* (1790)[1]

Solicitous chiefly for the peace of my own country, but by no means unconcerned for your's, I wish to communicate more largely, what was at first intended only for your private satisfaction. I shall still keep your affairs in my eye, and continue to address myself to you. Indulging myself in the freedom of epistolary intercourse, I beg leave to throw out my thoughts, and express my feelings, just as they arise in my mind, with very little attention to formal method. I set out with the proceedings of the Revolution Society;[2] but I shall not confine myself to them. Is it possible I should? It looks to me as if I were in a great crisis, not of the affairs of France alone, but of all Europe, perhaps of more than Europe. All circumstances taken together, the French revolution

---

[1] In 1789 a young Frenchman, Charles-Jean-François Depont (1767–96), had asked Burke's opinion about current events in France. In *Reflections*, Burke responds to this request, spurred by his distaste for Richard Price's pro-revolutionary sermon, published as *A Discourse on the Love of Our Country*.*

[2] Founded in 1788, the Revolution Society celebrated the so-called "Glorious Revolution" (1688), which established limited monarchy under King William III and Queen Mary II. Their reign, widely unpopular in Ireland and Scotland, was celebrated by English Whigs as a victory of Parliament over arbitrary monarchy. Richard Price's sermon on patriotism,* based on Psalm 122.6–7, had been delivered prior to the annual dinner of this Society, 4 November 1789.

is the most astonishing that has hitherto happened in the world. The most wonderful things are brought about in many instances by means the most absurd and ridiculous; in the most ridiculous modes; and, apparently, by the most contemptible instruments. Every thing seems out of nature in this strange chaos of levity and ferocity, and of all sorts of crimes jumbled together with all sorts of follies. In viewing this monstrous tragi-comic scene, the most opposite passions necessarily succeed, and sometimes mix with each other in the mind; alternate contempt and indignation; alternate laughter and tears; alternate scorn and horror.

…

On the forenoon of the 4th of November last, Doctor Richard Price, a non-conforming minister of eminence, preached at the dissenting meeting-house of the Old Jewry, to his club or society, a very extraordinary miscellaneous sermon, in which there are some good moral and religious sentiments, and not ill expressed, mixed up in a sort of porridge of various political opinions and reflections: but the revolution in France is the grand ingredient in the cauldron. I consider the address transmitted by the Revolution Society to the National Assembly, through Earl Stanhope,[1] as originating in the principles of the sermon, and as a corollary from them. It was moved by the preacher of that discourse. It was passed by those who came reeking from the effect of the sermon, without any censure or qualification, expressed or implied. If, however, any of the gentlemen concerned shall wish to separate the sermon from the resolution, they know how to acknowledge the one, and to disavow the other. They may do it: I cannot.

For my part, I looked on that sermon as the public declaration of a man much connected with literary caballers, and intriguing philosophers; with political theologians, and theological politicians, both at home and abroad. I know they set him up as a sort of oracle; because, with the best intentions in the world, he naturally *philippizes*,[2] and chaunts his prophetic song in exact unison with their designs.

…

…His doctrines affect our constitution in its vital parts. He tells the Revolution Society, in this political sermon, that his majesty "is almost the *only* lawful king in the world, because the *only* one who owes his crown to the *choice of his people.*" As to the kings of *the world*, all of whom (except one) this archpontiff of the *rights of men*, with all the plenitude, and with more than the boldness of the papal deposing power in its meridian fervour of the twelfth century, puts into one sweeping clause of ban and anathema, and proclaims usurpers by circles of longitude and latitude, over the whole globe, it behoves them to consider how they admit into their territories these apostolic missionaries, who are to tell their subjects they are not lawful kings. That is their concern. It is ours, as a domestic interest of some moment, seriously to consider the solidity of the *only* principle upon which these gentlemen acknowledge a king of Great Britain to be entitled to their allegiance.

This doctrine, as applied to the prince now on the British throne,[3] either is nonsense, and therefore neither true nor false, or it affirms a most unfounded, dangerous, illegal, and unconstitutional position. According to this spiritual doctor of politics, if his majesty does not owe his crown to the choice of his people, he is no *lawful* king. Now nothing can be more untrue than that the crown of this kingdom is so held by his majesty. Therefore if you follow their rule, the king of Great Britain, who most certainly does not owe his high office to any form of popular election, is in no respect better than the rest of the gang of usurpers, who reign, or rather rob, all over the face of this our miserable world, without any sort of right or title to the allegiance of their people. The policy of this general doctrine, so qualified, is evident enough. The propagators of this political gospel are in hopes their abstract principle (their principle that a popular choice is necessary to the legal existence of the sovereign magistracy) would be overlooked whilst the king of Great Britain was not affected by it. In the mean time the ears of their congregations would be gradually habituated to it, as if it were a first principle

---

[1] Charles, 3rd Earl Stanhope (1753–1816), who took a radically sympathetic view of the Revolution in France.

[2] declaims against.

[3] King George III.

admitted without dispute. For the present it would only operate as a theory, pickled in the preserving juices of pulpit eloquence, and laid by for future use. *Condo et compono quæ mox depromere possim.*[1] By this policy, whilst our government is soothed with a reservation in its favour, to which it has no claim, the security, which it has in common with all governments, so far as opinion is security, is taken away.

Thus these politicians proceed, whilst little notice is taken of their doctrines; but when they come to be examined upon the plain meaning of their words and the direct tendency of their doctrines, then equivocations and slippery constructions come into play. When they say the king owes his crown to the choice of his people and is therefore the only lawful sovereign in the world, they will perhaps tell us they mean to say no more than that some of the king's predecessors have been called to the throne by some sort of choice; and therefore he owes his crown to the choice of his people. Thus, by a miserable subterfuge, they hope to render their proposition safe, by rendering it nugatory. They are welcome to the asylum they seek for their offence; since they take refuge in their folly. For, if you admit this interpretation, how does their idea of election differ from our idea of inheritance?

...

You will observe, that from Magna Charta to the Declaration of Right,[2] it has been the uniform policy of our constitution to claim and assert our liberties, as an *entailed inheritance*[3] derived to us from our forefathers, and to be transmitted to our posterity; as an estate specially belonging to the people of this kingdom without any reference whatever to any other more general or prior right. By this means our constitution preserves an unity in so great a diversity of its parts. We have an inheritable crown; an inheritable peerage; and an house of commons and a people inheriting privileges, franchises, and liberties, from a long line of ancestors.

This policy appears to me to be the result of profound reflection; or rather the happy effect of following nature, which is wisdom without reflection, and above it. A spirit of innovation is generally the result of a selfish temper and confined views. People will not look forward to posterity, who never look backward to their ancestors. Besides, the people of England well know, that the idea of inheritance furnishes a sure principle of conservation, and a sure principle of transmission; without at all excluding a principle of improvement. It leaves acquisition free; but it secures what it acquires. Whatever advantages are obtained by a state proceeding on these maxims, are locked fast as in a sort of family settlement; grasped as in a kind of mortmain for ever. By a constitutional policy, working after the pattern of nature, we receive, we hold, we transmit our government and our privileges, in the same manner in which we enjoy and transmit our property and our lives. The institutions of policy, the goods of fortune, the gifts of Providence, are handed down, to us and from us, in the same course and order. Our political system is placed in a just correspondence and symmetry with the order of the world, and with the mode of existence decreed to a permanent body composed of transitory parts; wherein, by the disposition of a stupendous wisdom, moulding together the great mysterious incorporation of the human race, the whole, at one time, is never old, or middle-aged, or young, but in a condition of unchangeable constancy, moves on through the varied tenour of perpetual decay, fall, renovation, and progression. Thus, by preserving the method of nature in the conduct of the state, in what we improve we are never wholly new; in what we retain we are never wholly obsolete. By adhering in this manner and on those principles to our forefathers, we are guided not by the superstition of antiquarians, but by the spirit of philosophic analogy. In this choice of inheritance we have given to our frame of polity the image of a relation in blood; binding up the constitution of our country with our dearest domestic ties; adopting our fundamental laws into the bosom of our family affections; keeping inseparable, and cherish-

---

[1] "I put together and collect things which I will soon be able to draw upon" (Horace, *Epistles* 1.1.12).

[2] Magna Carta was the "great charter" of 1215, by which the English barons forced King John to clarify their feudal relationship and accept the principle of consultation. The Declaration of Right of 1689, also known as the Bill of Rights, protected civil liberties and subjected monarchs to the law.

[3] an inheritance limited to a certain line of descent (usually the male heirs) so that it can never be transferred.

ing with the warmth of all their combined and mutually reflected charities, our state, our hearths, our sepulchres, and our altars.

Through the same plan of a conformity to nature in our artificial institutions, and by calling in the aid of her unerring and powerful instincts, to fortify the fallible and feeble contrivances of our reason, we have derived several other, and those no small benefits, from considering our liberties in the light of an inheritance. Always acting as if in the presence of canonized forefathers, the spirit of freedom, leading in itself to misrule and excess, is tempered with an awful gravity. This idea of a liberal descent inspires us with a sense of habitual native dignity, which prevents that upstart insolence almost inevitably adhering to and disgracing those who are the first acquirers of any distinction. By this means our liberty becomes a noble freedom. It carries an imposing and majestic aspect. It has a pedigree, and illustrating ancestors. It has its bearings, and its ensigns armorial. It has its gallery of portraits; its monumental inscriptions; its records, evidences, and titles. We procure reverence to our civil institutions on the principle upon which nature teaches us to revere individual men; on account of their age; and on account of those from whom they are descended. All your sophisters cannot produce any thing better adapted to preserve a rational and manly freedom than the course that we have pursued, who have chosen our nature rather than our speculations, our breasts rather than our inventions, for the great conservatories and magazines of our rights and privileges.

You might, if you pleased, have profited of our example, and have given to your recovered freedom a correspondent dignity. Your privileges, though discontinued, were not lost to memory. Your constitution, it is true, whilst you were out of possession, suffered waste and dilapidation; but you possessed in some parts the walls, and in all the foundations of a noble and venerable castle. You might have repaired those walls; you might have built on those old foundations. Your constitution was suspended before it was perfected; but you had the elements of a constitution very nearly as good as could be wished. In your old states you possessed that variety of parts corresponding with the various descriptions of which your community was happily composed; you had all that combination, and all that opposition of interests, you had that action and counteraction which, in the natural and in the political world, from the reciprocal struggle of discordant powers, draws out the harmony of the universe. These opposed and conflicting interests, which you considered as so great a blemish in your old and in our present constitution, interpose a salutary check to all precipitate resolutions; They render deliberation a matter not of choice, but of necessity; they make all change a subject of *compromise*; which naturally begets moderation; they produce *temperaments*, preventing the sore evil of harsh, crude, unqualified reformations; and rendering all the headlong exertions of arbitrary power, in the few or in the many, for ever impracticable. Through that diversity of members and interests, general liberty had as many securities as there were separate views in the several orders; whilst by pressing down the whole by the weight of a real monarchy, the separate parts would have been prevented from warping and starting from their allotted places.

…

I find a preacher of the gospel prophaning the beautiful and prophetic ejaculation, commonly called "*nunc dimittis*,"[1] made on the first presentation of our Saviour in the Temple, and applying it, with an inhuman and unnatural rapture, to the most horrid, atrocious, and afflicting spectacle, that perhaps ever was exhibited to the pity and indignation of mankind. This "leading in triumph,"[2] a thing in its best form unmanly and irreligious, which fills our Preacher with such unhallowed transports, must shock, I believe, the moral taste of every well-born mind. Several English were the stupified and indignant spectators of that triumph. It was (unless we have been strangely deceived) a spectacle more resembling a procession of American savages, entering into Onondaga,[3] after some of their murders called victories, and leading into hovels hung round with scalps, their captives, overpowered with the scoffs

---

[1] The opening words, in Latin, of Luke 2.29–30, which Price quotes towards the end of his *Discourse** (10).

[2] Price describes the French "king led in triumph, and an arbitrary monarch surrendering himself to his subjects."

[3] a Native village near the modern city of Syracuse, New York.

and buffets of women as ferocious as themselves, much more than it resembled the triumphal pomp of a civilized martial nation;—if a civilized nation, or any men who had a sense of generosity, were capable of a personal triumph over the fallen and afflicted.
...

Yielding to reasons, at least as forcible as those which were so delicately urged in the compliment on the new year, the king of France will probably endeavour to forget these events, and that compliment. But history, who keeps a durable record of all our acts, and exercises her awful censure over the proceedings of all sorts of sovereigns, will not forget, either those events, or the æra of this liberal refinement in the intercourse of mankind. History will record, that on the morning of the 6th of October 1789,[1] the king and queen of France, after a day of confusion, alarm, dismay, and slaughter, lay down, under the pledged security of public faith, to indulge nature in a few hours of respite, and troubled melancholy repose. From this sleep the queen was first startled by the voice of the centinel at her door, who cried out to her, to save herself by flight—that this was the last proof of fidelity he could give—that they were upon him, and he was dead. Instantly he was cut down. A band of cruel ruffians and assassins, reeking with his blood, rushed into the chamber of the queen, and pierced with an hundred strokes of bayonets and poniards the bed, from whence this persecuted woman had but just time to fly almost naked, and through ways unknown to the murderers had escaped to seek refuge at the feet of a king and husband, not secure of his own life for a moment.

This king, to say no more of him, and this queen, and their infant children (who once would have been the pride and hope of a great and generous people) were then forced to abandon the sanctuary of the most splendid palace in the world, which they left swimming in blood, polluted by massacre, and strewed with scattered limbs and mutilated carcases. Thence they were conducted into the capital of their kingdom. Two had been selected from the unprovoked, unresisted, promiscuous slaughter, which was made of the gentlemen of birth and family who composed the king's body guard. These two gentlemen, with all the parade of an execution of justice, were cruelly and publickly dragged to the block, and beheaded in the great court of the palace. Their heads were stuck upon spears, and led the procession; whilst the royal captives who followed in the train were slowly moved along, amidst the horrid yells, and shrilling screams, and frantic dances, and infamous contumelies, and all the unutterable abominations of the furies of hell, in the abused shape of the vilest of women. After they had been made to taste, drop by drop, more than the bitterness of death, in the slow torture of a journey of twelve miles, protracted to six hours, they were, under a guard, composed of those very soldiers who had thus conducted them through this famous triumph, lodged in one of the old palaces of Paris, now converted into a Bastile for kings.

Is this a triumph to be consecrated at altars? to be commemorated with grateful thanksgiving? to be offered to the divine humanity with fervent prayer and enthusiastick ejaculation?—These Theban and Thracian Orgies,[2] acted in France, and applauded only in the Old Jewry, I assure you, kindle prophetic enthusiasm in the minds but of very few people in this kingdom; although a saint and apostle, who may have revelations of his own, and who has so completely vanquished all the mean superstitions of the heart, may incline to think it pious and decorous to compare it with the entrance into the world of the Prince of Peace, proclaimed in an holy temple by a venerable sage, and not long before not worse announced by the voice of angels to the quiet innocence of shepherds.

At first I was at a loss to account for this fit of unguarded transport. I knew, indeed, that the sufferings of monarchs make a delicious repast to some sort of palates. There were reflexions which might serve to keep this appetite within some bounds of temperance. But when I took one circumstance into my consideration, I

---

[1] On 6 October 1789, King Louis XVI and Queen Marie Antoinette were conducted under guard from the palace at Versailles to the Tuileries in Paris. Burke's account of these events (to which Mary Wollstonecraft alludes in *A Vindication of the Rights of Men*),* was much criticized for factual inaccuracy.

[2] ancient religious rituals associated with Dionysus (at Thebes) and with Artemis (at Samothrace).

was obliged to confess, that much allowance ought to be made for the Society, and that the temptation was too strong for common discretion; I mean, the circumstance of the Io Pæan[1] of the triumph, the animating cry which called "for *all* the BISHOPS to be hanged on the lampposts,"[2] might well have brought forth a burst of enthusiasm on the foreseen consequences of this happy day. I allow to so much enthusiasm some little deviation from prudence. I allow this prophet to break forth into hymns of joy and thanksgiving on an event which appears like the precursor of the Millenium, and the projected fifth monarchy,[3] in the destruction of all church establishments. There was, however (as in all human affairs there is) in the midst of this joy something to exercise the patience of these worthy gentlemen, and to try the long-suffering of their faith. The actual murder of the king and queen, and their child, was wanting to the other auspicious circumstances of this "*beautiful day.*" The actual murder of the bishops, though called for by so many holy ejaculations, was also wanting. A groupe of regicide and sacrilegious slaughter, was indeed boldly sketched, but it was only sketched. It unhappily was left unfinished, in this great history-piece of the massacre of innocents. What hardy pencil of a great master, from the school of the rights of men, will finish it, is to be seen hereafter. The age has not yet the compleat benefit of that diffusion of knowledge that has undermined superstition and error; and the king of France wants another object or two, to consign to oblivion, in consideration of all the good which is to arise from his own sufferings, and the patriotic crimes of an enlightened age.[4]

Although this work of our new light and knowledge, did not go to the length, that in all probability it was intended it should be carried; yet I must think, that such treatment of any human creatures must be shocking to any but those who are made for accomplishing Revolutions. But I cannot stop here. Influenced by the inborn feelings of my nature, and not being illuminated by a single ray of this new-sprung modern light, I confess to you, Sir, that the exalted rank of the persons suffering, and particularly the sex, the beauty, and the amiable qualities of the descendant of so many kings and emperors, with the tender age of royal infants, insensible only through infancy and innocence of the cruel outrages to which their parents were exposed, instead of being a subject of exultation, adds not a little to my sensibility on that most melancholy occasion.

I hear that the august person, who was the principal object of our preacher's triumph, though he supported himself, felt much on that shameful occasion. As a man, it became him to feel for his wife and his children, and the faithful guards of his person, that were massacred in cold blood about him; as a prince, it became him to feel for the strange and frightful transformation of his civilized subjects, and to be more grieved for them, than solicitous for himself. It derogates little from his fortitude, while it adds infinitely to the honour of his humanity. I am very sorry to say it, very sorry indeed, that such personages are in a situation in which it is not unbecoming to praise the virtues of the great.

I hear, and I rejoice to hear, that the great lady,[5] the other object of the triumph, has borne that day (one is interested that beings made for suffering should suffer well) and that she bears all the succeeding days, that she bears the imprisonment of her husband, and her own captivity, and the exile of her friends, and the insulting adulation of addresses, and the whole weight of her accumulated wrongs, with a serene patience, in a manner suited to her rank and race, and becoming the offspring of a sovereign distinguished for her piety and her courage; that like her she has lofty sentiments; that she feels with the dignity of a Roman matron; that in the last extremity she will save herself from the last disgrace, and that if she must fall, she will fall by no ignoble hand.

---

[1] a hymn of praise to Apollo.

[2] "Tous les Eveques à la lanterne." (E.B.)

[3] The millennium is the often-heralded thousand years of peace preceding the Second Coming of Christ; the fifth monarchists of the 17th century believed that the four great empires of Assyria, Persia, Greece, and Rome would be succeeded by the fifth monarchy of Christ. See also Daniel 2.36–45.

[4] We have omitted a long footnote in which Burke quotes, in French, an eyewitness account of the events of 6 October 1789, by Trophime-Gérard de Lally-Tollendal (1751–1830).

[5] I.e., Queen Marie-Antoinette.

It is now sixteen or seventeen years since I saw the queen of France, then the dauphiness, at Versailles; and surely never lighted on this orb, which she hardly seemed to touch, a more delightful vision. I saw her just above the horizon, decorating and cheering the elevated sphere she just began to move in,—glittering like the morning-star, full of life, and splendor, and joy. Oh! what a revolution! and what an heart must I have, to contemplate without emotion that elevation and that fall! Little did I dream that, when she added titles of veneration to those of enthusiastic, distant, respectful love, that she should ever be obliged to carry the sharp antidote against disgrace concealed in that bosom; little did I dream that I should have lived to see such disasters fallen upon her in a nation of gallant men, in a nation of men of honour and of cavaliers. I thought ten thousand swords must have leaped from their scabbards to avenge even a look that threatened her with insult.—But the age of chivalry is gone.—That of sophisters, œconomists, and calculators, has succeeded; and the glory of Europe is extinguished for ever. Never, never more, shall we behold that generous loyalty to rank and sex, that proud submission, that dignified obedience, that subordination of the heart, which kept alive, even in servitude itself, the spirit of an exalted freedom. The unbought grace of life, the cheap defence of nations, the nurse of manly sentiment and heroic enterprize is gone! It is gone, that sensibility of principle, that chastity of honour, which felt a stain like a wound, which inspired courage whilst it mitigated ferocity, which ennobled whatever it touched, and under which vice itself lost half its evil, by losing all its grossness.

This mixed system of opinion and sentiment had its origin in the antient chivalry; and the principle, though varied in its appearance by the varying state of human affairs, subsisted and influenced through a long succession of generations, even to the time we live in. If it should ever be totally extinguished, the loss I fear will be great. It is this which has given its character to modern Europe. It is this which has distinguished it under all its forms of government, and distinguished it to its advantage, from the states of Asia, and possibly from those states which flourished in the most brilliant periods of the antique world. It was this, which, without confounding ranks, had produced a noble equality, and handed it down through all the gradations of social life. It was this opinion which mitigated kings into companions, and raised private men to be fellows with kings. Without force, or opposition, it subdued the fierceness of pride and power; it obliged sovereigns to submit to the soft collar of social esteem, compelled stern authority to submit to elegance, and gave a domination vanquisher of laws, to be subdued by manners.

But now all is to be changed. All the pleasing illusions, which made power gentle, and obedience liberal, which harmonized the different shades of life, and which, by a bland assimilation, incorporated into politics the sentiments which beautify and soften private society, are to be dissolved by this new conquering empire of light and reason. All the decent drapery of life is to be rudely torn off. All the superadded ideas, furnished from the wardrobe of a moral imagination, which the heart owns, and the understanding ratifies, as necessary to cover the defects of our naked shivering nature, and to raise it to dignity in our own estimation, are to be exploded as a ridiculous, absurd, and antiquated fashion.

On this scheme of things, a king is but a man; a queen is but a woman; a woman is but an animal; and an animal not of the highest order. All homage paid to the sex in general as such, and without distinct views, is to be regarded as romance and folly. Regicide, and parricide, and sacrilege, are but fictions of superstition, corrupting jurisprudence by destroying its simplicity. The murder of a king, or a queen, or a bishop, or a father, are only common homicide; and if the people are by any chance, or in any way gainers by it, a sort of homicide much the most pardonable, and into which we ought not to make too severe a scrutiny.

On the scheme of this barbarous philosophy, which is the offspring of cold hearts and muddy understandings, and which is as void of solid wisdom, as it is destitute of all taste and elegance, laws are to be supported only by their own terrors, and by the concern, which each individual may find in them, from his own private speculations, or can spare to them from his own private interests. In the groves of *their* academy, at the end of every visto, you see nothing but the gallows. Nothing is left which engages the affections on the part of the commonwealth. On the principles of this mechanic philosophy, our institutions can never be embodied, if I may use the expression, in persons; so as to create in us love, veneration, admiration, or attachment. But that sort of reason which banishes the affections is incapable of filling their place. These public affections, combined with manners, are required sometimes as supplements, sometimes as correctives, always as aids to law. The precept given by a wise man, as well as a great critic, for the construction of poems, is equally true as to states. *Non satis est pulchra esse poemata, dulcia sunto*.[1] There ought to be a system of manners in every nation which a well-formed mind would be disposed to relish. To make us love our country, our country ought to be lovely.

But power, of some kind or other, will survive the shock in which manners and opinions perish; and it will find other and worse means for its support. The usurpation which, in order to subvert antient institutions, has destroyed antient principles, will hold power by arts similar to those by which it has acquired it. When the old feudal and chivalrous spirit of *Fealty*, which, by freeing kings from fear, freed both kings and subjects from the precautions of tyranny, shall be extinct in the minds of men, plots and assassinations will be anticipated by preventive murder and preventive confiscation, and that long roll of grim and bloody maxims, which form the political code of all power, not standing on its own honour, and the honour of those who are to obey it. Kings will be tyrants from policy when subjects are rebels from principle.

When antient opinions and rules of life are taken away, the loss cannot possibly be estimated. From that moment we have no compass to govern us; nor can we know distinctly to what port we steer. Europe undoubtedly, taken in a mass, was in a flourishing condition the day on which your Revolution was compleated. How much of that prosperous state was owing to the spirit of our old manners and opinions is not easy to say; but as such causes cannot be indifferent in their operation, we must presume, that, on the whole, their operation was beneficial.

We are but too apt to consider things in the state in which we find them, without sufficiently adverting to the causes by which they have been produced, and possibly may be upheld. Nothing is more certain, than that our manners, our civilization, and all the good things which are connected with manners, and with civilization, have, in this European world of ours, depended for ages upon two principles; and were indeed the result of both combined; I mean the spirit of a gentleman, and the spirit of religion. The nobility and the clergy, the one by profession, the other by patronage, kept learning in existence, even in the midst of arms and confusions, and whilst governments were rather in their causes than formed. Learning paid back what it received to nobility and to priesthood; and paid it with usury, by enlarging their ideas, and by furnishing their minds. Happy if they had all continued to know their indissoluble union, and their proper place! Happy if learning, not debauched by ambition, had been satisfied to continue the instructor, and not aspired to be the master! Along with its natural protectors and guardians, learning will be cast into the mire, and trodden down under the hoofs of a swinish multitude.

...

Why do I feel so differently from the Reverend Dr. Price, and those of his lay flock, who will choose to adopt the sentiments of his discourse?—For this plain reason—because it is *natural* I should; because we are so made as to be affected at such spectacles with melancholy sentiments upon the unstable condition of mortal prosperity, and the tremendous uncertainty of human greatness; because in those natural feelings we learn great lessons; because in events like these our passions instruct our reason; because when kings are hurl'd from their thrones by the Supreme Director of this great drama, and become the objects of insult to the base, and of pity to the good, we behold such disasters in the moral, as we should behold a miracle in the physical order of things. We are alarmed into reflexion; our minds (as it has long since been observed) are purified by terror and pity; our weak unthinking pride is hum-

---

[1] "It is not enough for poems to be beautiful; they must also be delightful" (Horace, *Ars Poetica* 99–100).

bled, under the dispensations of a mysterious wisdom.—Some tears might be drawn from me, if such a spectacle were exhibited on the stage. I should be truly ashamed of finding in myself that superficial, theatric sense of painted distress, whilst I could exult over it in real life. With such a perverted mind, I could never venture to shew my face at a tragedy. People would think the tears that Garrick formerly, or that Siddons[1] not long since, have extorted from me, were the tears of hypocrisy; I should know them to be the tears of folly.

Indeed the theatre is a better school of moral sentiments than churches, where the feelings of humanity are thus outraged. Poets, who have to deal with an audience not yet graduated in the school of the rights of men, and who must apply themselves to the moral constitution of the heart, would not dare to produce such a triumph as a matter of exultation. There, where men follow their natural impulses, they would not bear the odious maxims of a Machiavelian policy,[2] whether applied to the attainment of monarchical or democratic tyranny. They would reject them on the modern, as they once did on the antient stage, where they could not bear even the hypothetical proposition of such wickedness in the mouth of a personated tyrant, though suitable to the character he sustained. No theatric audience in Athens would bear what has been borne, in the midst of the real tragedy of this triumphal day; a principal actor weighing, as it were in scales hung in a shop of horrors,—so much actual crime against so much contingent advantage,—and after putting in and out weights, declaring that the balance was on the side of the advantages. They would not bear to see the crimes of new democracy posted as in a ledger against the crimes of old despotism, and the book-keepers of politics finding democracy still in debt, but by no means unable or unwilling to pay the balance. In the theatre, the first intuitive glance, without any elaborate process of reasoning, would shew, that this method of political computation, would justify every extent of crime. They would see, that on these principles, even where the very worst acts were not perpetrated, it was owing rather to the fortune of the conspirators than to their parsimony in the expenditure of treachery and blood. They would soon see, that criminal means once tolerated are soon preferred. They present a shorter cut to the object than through the highway of the moral virtues. Justifying perfidy and murder for public benefit, public benefit would soon become the pretext, and perfidy and murder the end; until rapacity, malice, revenge, and fear more dreadful than revenge, could satiate their insatiable appetites. Such must be the consequences of losing in the splendour of these triumphs of the rights of men, all natural sense of wrong and right.

…

I almost venture to affirm, that not one in a hundred amongst us participates in the "triumph" of the Revolution Society. If the king and queen of France, and their children, were to fall into our hands by the chance of war, in the most acrimonious of all hostilities (I deprecate such an event, I deprecate such hostility) they would be treated with another sort of triumphal entry into London. We formerly have had a king of France in that situation; you have read how he was treated by the victor in the field; and in what manner he was afterwards received in England.[3] Four hundred years have gone over us; but I believe we are not materially changed since that period. Thanks to our sullen resistance to innovation, thanks to the cold sluggishness of our national character, we still bear the stamp of our forefathers. We have not (as I conceive) lost the generosity and dignity of thinking of the fourteenth century; nor as yet have we subtilized ourselves into savages. We are not the converts of Rousseau; we are not the disciples of Voltaire; Helvetius[4] has made no progress amongst us. Atheists are not our preachers; madmen are not our lawgivers. We know that *we* have made no discoveries; and we think that no discoveries are to be

---

[1] the actors David Garrick (1717–79) and Sarah Siddons (1755–1831). Siddons retired temporarily in 1789.

[2] a policy based on intrigue, cynicism and cunning, qualities thought to characterize the writings of Niccolò Machiavelli (1469–1527).

[3] Jean II of France (1319–64) was imprisoned in London following the Battle of Poitiers (1356) during the Hundred Years' War.

[4] three of the *philosophes* whose faith in reason and opposition to established power inspired the next generation of revolutionaries: Jean-Jacques Rousseau (1712–78); François-Marie Arouet (Voltaire) (1694–1778); and Claude Adrien Helvétius (1715–71).

made, in morality; nor many in the great principles of government, nor in the ideas of liberty, which were understood long before we were born, altogether as well as they will be after the grave has heaped its mould upon our presumption, and the silent tomb shall have imposed its law on our pert loquacity. In England we have not yet been completely embowelled of our natural entrails; we still feel within us, and we cherish and cultivate, those inbred sentiments which are the faithful guardians, the active monitors of our duty, the true supporters of all liberal and manly morals. We have not been drawn and trussed, in order that we may be filled, like stuffed birds in a museum, with chaff and rags, and paltry, blurred shreds of paper about the rights of man. We preserve the whole of our feelings still native and entire, unsophisticated by pedantry and infidelity. We have real hearts of flesh and blood beating in our bosoms. We fear God; we look up with awe to kings; with affection to parliaments; with duty to magistrates; with reverence to priests; and with respect to nobility.[1] Why? Because when such ideas are brought before our minds, it is *natural* to be so affected; because all other feelings are false and spurious, and tend to corrupt our minds, to vitiate our primary morals, to render us unfit for rational liberty; and by teaching us a servile, licentious, and abandoned insolence, to be our low sport for a few holidays, to make us perfectly fit for, and justly deserving of slavery, through the whole course of our lives.

You see, Sir, that in this enlightened age I am bold enough to confess, that we are generally men of untaught feelings; that instead of casting away all our old prejudices, we cherish them to a very considerable degree, and, to take more shame to ourselves, we cherish them because they are prejudices; and the longer they have lasted, and the more generally they have prevailed, the more we cherish them. We are afraid to put men to live and trade each on his own private stock of reason; because we suspect that this stock in each man is small, and that the individuals would do better to avail themselves of the general bank and capital of nations, and of ages. Many of our men of speculation, instead of exploding general prejudices, employ their sagacity to discover the latent wisdom which prevails in them. If they find what they seek, and they seldom fail, they think it more wise to continue the prejudice, with the reason involved, than to cast away the coat of prejudice, and to leave nothing but the naked reason; because prejudice, with its reason, has a motive to give action to that reason, and an affection which will give it permanence. Prejudice is of ready application in the emergency; it previously engages the mind in a steady course of wisdom and virtue, and does not leave the man hesitating in the moment of decision, sceptical, puzzled, and unresolved. Prejudice renders a man's virtue his habit; and not a series of unconnected acts. Through just prejudice, his duty becomes a part of his nature.

Your literary men, and your politicians, and so do the whole clan of the enlightened among us, essentially differ in these points. They have no respect for the wisdom of others; but they pay it off by a very full measure of confidence in their own. With them it is a sufficient motive to destroy an old scheme of things, because it is an old one. As to the new, they are in no sort of fear with regard to the duration of a building run up in haste; because duration is no object to those who think little or nothing has been done before their time, and who place all their hopes in discovery. They conceive, very systematically, that all things which give perpetuity are mischievous, and therefore they are at inexpiable war with all establishments. They think that government may vary like modes of dress, and with as little ill effect. That there needs no principle of attachment, except a sense of present conveniency, to any constitution of the state. They always speak as if they were of opinion that there is a singular species of compact between them and their magistrates, which binds the magistrate, but which has nothing reciprocal in it, but that the majesty of the people has a right to dissolve

---

[1] "The English are, I conceive, misrepresented in a Letter published in one of the papers, by a gentleman thought to be a dissenting minister.—When writing to Dr. Price, of the spirit which prevails at Paris, he says, 'The spirit of the people in this place has abolished all the proud *distinctions* which the *king* and *nobles* had usurped in their minds; whether they talk of *the king, the noble, or the priest*, their whole language is that of the most *enlightened and liberal amongst the English.*' If this gentleman means to confine the terms *enlightened and liberal* to one set of men in England, it may be true. It is not generally so." (E.B.)

it without any reason, but its will. Their attachment to their country itself, is only so far as it agrees with some of their fleeting projects; it begins and ends with that scheme of polity which falls in with their momentary opinion.

...

But one of the first and most leading principles on which the commonwealth and the laws are consecrated, is lest the temporary possessors and life-renters in it, unmindful of what they have received from their ancestors, or of what is due to their posterity, should act as if they were the entire masters; that they should not think it amongst their rights to cut off the entail, or commit waste on the inheritance, by destroying at their pleasure the whole original fabric of their society; hazarding to leave to those who come after them, a ruin instead of an habitation—and teaching these successors as little to respect their contrivances, as they had themselves respected the institutions of their forefathers. By this unprincipled facility of changing the state as often, and as much, and in as many ways as there are floating fancies or fashions, the whole chain and continuity of the commonwealth would be broken. No one generation could link with the other. Men would become little better than the flies of a summer....

I do not know under what description to class the present ruling authority in France. It affects to be a pure democracy, though I think it in a direct train of becoming shortly a mischievous and ignoble oligarchy. But for the present I admit it to be a contrivance of the nature and effect of what it pretends to. I reprobate no form of government merely upon abstract principles. There may be situations in which the purely democratic form will become necessary. There may be some (very few, and very particularly circumstanced) where it would be clearly desirable. This I do not take to be the case of France, or of any other great country. Until now, we have seen no examples of considerable democracies. The antients were better acquainted with them. Not being wholly unread in the authors, who had seen the most of those constitutions, and who best understood them, I cannot help concurring with their opinion, that an absolute democracy, no more than absolute monarchy, is to be reckoned among the legitimate forms of government. They think it rather the corruption and degeneracy, than the sound constitution of a republic. If I recollect rightly, Aristotle observes, that a democracy has many striking points of resemblance with a tyranny.[1] Of this I am certain, that in a democracy, the majority of the citizens is capable of exercising the most cruel oppressions upon the minority, whenever strong divisions prevail in that kind of polity, as they often must; and that oppression of the minority will extend to far greater numbers, and will be carried on with much greater fury, than can almost ever be apprehended from the dominion of a single sceptre. In such a popular persecution, individual sufferers are in a much more deplorable condition than in any other. Under a cruel prince they have the balmy compassion of mankind to assuage the smart of their wounds; they have the plaudits of the people to animate their generous constancy under their sufferings: but those who are subjected to wrong under multitudes, are deprived of all external consolation. They seem deserted by mankind; overpowered by a conspiracy of their whole species....

---

[1] "When I wrote this I quoted from memory, after many years had elapsed from my reading the passage. A learned friend has found it, and it is as follows:

"'The ethical character is the same; both exercise despotism over the better class of citizens; and decrees are in the one, what ordinances and arrêts are in the other: the demagogue too, and the court favourite, are not unfrequently the same identical men, and always bear a close analogy; and these have the principal power, each in their respective forms of government, favourites with the absolute monarch, and demagogues with a people such as I have described.' Arist. Politic. lib. iv. cap. 4." (E.B.)

A Letter from the Right Honourable Edmund Burke to a Noble Lord, on the Attacks Made Upon Him and His Pension, in the House of Lords, by the Duke of Bedford and the Earl of Lauderdale, Early in the Present Sessions of Parliament (1796)[1]

MY LORD,

I could hardly flatter myself with the hope, that so very early in the season I should have to acknowledge obligations to the Duke of Bedford and to the Earl of Lauderdale. These noble persons have lost no time in conferring upon me, that sort of honour, which it is alone within their competence, and which it is certainly most congenial to their nature and their manners to bestow.

To be ill spoken of, in whatever language they speak, by the zealots of the new sect in philosophy and politics, of which these noble persons think so charitably, and of which others think so justly, to me, is no matter of uneasiness or surprise. To have incurred the displeasure of the Duke of Orleans or the Duke of Bedford, to fall under the censure of Citizen Brissot or of his friend the Earl of Lauderdale,[2] I ought to consider as proofs, not the least satisfactory, that I have produced some part of the effect I proposed by my endeavours. I have laboured hard to earn, what the noble lords are generous enough to pay. Personal offense I have given them none. The part they take against me is from zeal to the cause. It is well! It is perfectly well! I have to do homage to their justice. I have to thank the Bedfords and the Lauderdales for having so faithfully and so fully acquitted towards me whatever arrear of debt was left undischarged by the Priestleys and the Paines.[3]

...

I knew that there is a manifest marked distinction, which ill men, with ill designs, or weak men incapable of any design, will constantly be confounding, that is, a marked distinction between Change and Reformation. The former alters the substance of the objects themselves; and gets rid of all their essential good, as well as of all the accidental evil annexed to them. Change is novelty; and whether it is to operate any one of the effects of reformation at all, or whether it may not contradict the very principle upon which reformation is desired, cannot be certainly known beforehand. Reform is, not a change in the substance, or in the primary modification of the object, but a direct application of a remedy to the grievance complained of. So far as that is removed, all is sure. It stops there; and if it fails, the substance which underwent the operation, at the very worst, is but where it was.

All this, in effect, I think, but am not sure, I have said elsewhere. It cannot at this time be too often repeated; line upon line; precept upon precept; until it comes into the currency of a proverb, *To innovate is not to reform.* The French revolutionists complained of every thing; they refused to reform any thing; and they left nothing, no, nothing at all *unchanged*. The consequences are *before* us,—not in remote history; not in future prognostication: they are about us; they are upon us. They shake the publick security; they menace private enjoyment. They dwarf the growth of the young; they break the quiet of the old. If we travel, they stop our way. They infest us in town; they pursue us to the country. Our business is interrupted; our repose is troubled; our pleasures are saddened; our very studies are poisoned and perverted, and knowledge is rendered worse than ignorance, by the enormous evils of this

---

[1] Burke addresses his *Letter* to William FitzWilliam, 4th Earl FitzWilliam (1748–1833), nephew and heir to Charles Watson-Wentworth, 2nd Marquess of Rockingham (1730–82), who had been Burke's political patron as leader of the "Rockingham Whigs." In the *Letter* Burke defends himself against Francis Russell, 5th Duke of Bedford (1765–1802), and James Maitland, 8th Earl of Lauderdale (1759–1839), who had opposed a pension of £3,700 a year granted to Burke by William Pitt the Younger, the Prime Minister.

[2] Burke associates Bedford and Lauderdale with two French revolutionary figures. Louis Phillippe Joseph, Duke of Orléans (1747–93), well known in England as a close friend of the Prince of Wales, was caught up in the intrigues of the early 1790s in France, accepting the title of Citoyen Egalité from the Paris Commune, and dying in the Reign of Terror. Jacques Pierre Brissot de Warville (1754–93), a revolutionary and journalist, was also guillotined following the defeat of the moderate Girondins by the radical Jacobins.

[3] Joseph Priestley (1733–1804), scientist, clergyman, and radical writer, and Thomas Paine,* whose *Rights of Man* (1791–92) is a reply to Burke's *Reflections on the Revolution in France.**

dreadful innovation. The revolution harpies of France, sprung from night and hell, or from that chaotick anarchy, which generates equivocally "all monstrous, all prodigious things,"[1] cuckoo-like, adulterously lay their eggs, and brood over, and hatch them in the nest of every neighbouring State. These obscene harpies, who deck themselves, in I know not what divine attributes, but who in reality are foul and ravenous birds of prey (both mothers and daughters) flutter over our heads, and souse down upon our tables, and leave nothing unrent, unrifled, unravaged, or unpolluted with the slime of their filthy offal.[2]

If his Grace can contemplate the result of this compleat innovation, or, as some friends of his will call it *reform*, in the whole body of it's solidity and compound mass, at which, as Hamlet says, the face of Heaven glows with horror and indignation,[3] and which, in truth, makes every reflecting mind, and every feeling heart, perfectly thought-sick, without a thorough abhorrence of every thing they say, and every thing they do, I am amazed at the morbid strength, or the natural infirmity of his mind.

…

The awful state of the time, and not myself or my own justification, is my true object in what I now write; or in what I shall ever write or say. It little signifies to the world what becomes of such things as me, or even as the Duke of Bedford. What I say about either of us is nothing more than a vehicle, as you, my Lord, will easily perceive, to convey my sentiments on matters far more worthy of your attention. It is when I stick to my apparent first subject that I ought to apologize, not when I depart from it. I therefore must beg your Lordship's pardon for again resuming it after this very short digression; assuring you that I shall never altogether lose sight of such matter as persons abler than I am may turn to some profit.

The Duke of Bedford conceives, that he is obliged to call the attention of the House of Peers to his Majesty's grant to me, which he considers as excessive and out of all bounds.

I know not how it has happened, but it really seems, that, whilst his Grace was meditating his well considered censure upon me, he fell into a sort of sleep. Homer nods;[4] and the Duke of Bedford may dream; and as dreams (even his golden dreams) are apt to be ill-pieced and incongruously put together, his Grace preserved his idea of reproach to *me*, but took the subject-matter from the Crown-grants *to his own family*. This is "the stuff of which his dreams are made."[5] In that way of putting things together his Grace is perfectly in the right. The grants to the House of Russel were so enormous, as not only to outrage œconomy, but even to stagger credibility. The Duke of Bedford is the Leviathan among all the creatures of the Crown. He tumbles about his unwieldy bulk; he plays and frolicks in the ocean of the Royal bounty. Huge as he is, and whilst "he lies floating many a rood,"[6] he is still a creature. His ribs, his fins, his whalebone, his blubber, the very spiracles through which he spouts a torrent of brine against his origin, and covers me all over with the spray,—every thing of him and about him is from the Throne. Is it for *him* to question the dispensation of the Royal favour?

---

[1] Milton, *Paradise Lost* 2.625.

[2] "Tristius haud illis monstrum, nec sævior ulla
Pestis, & ira Deûm Stygiis sese extulit undis
Virginei volucrum vultus; fædissima ventris
Proluvies; uncæque manus; & pallida semper
Ora fame—
[Virgil, *Æneid* 3.214–18: "There is no monster harsher than these; no fiercer plague nor wrath of the gods has risen from the Stygian waves. These birds have the faces of young women; their droppings are disgusting; they have clawed hands and faces forever gaunt with hunger."]
"Here the Poet breaks the line, because he (and that He is Virgil) had not verse or language to describe that monster even as he had conceived her. Had he lived to our time, he would have been more overpowered with the reality than he was with the imagination. Virgil only knew the horror of the times before him. Had he lived to see the Revolutionists and Constitutionalists of France, he would have had more horrid and disgusting features of his harpies to describe, and more frequent failures in the attempt to describe them." (E.B.)

[3] Cf. Shakespeare, *Hamlet* 3.4.48–50.

[4] according to Horace, *Ars Poetica*, who goes on to excuse such inevitable lapses: "when a poem is long, sleep inevitably creeps over it" (359–60).

[5] Cf. Shakespeare, *The Tempest* 4.1.155–56.

[6] Milton, *Paradise Lost* 1.196.

I really am at a loss to draw any sort of parallel between the public merits of his Grace, by which he justifies the grants he holds, and these services of mine, on the favourable construction of which I have obtained what his Grace so much disapproves. In private life, I have not at all the honour of acquaintance with the noble Duke. But I ought to presume, and it costs me nothing to do so, that he abundantly deserves the esteem and love of all who live with him. But as to public service, why truly it would not be more ridiculous for me to compare myself in rank, in fortune, in splendid descent, in youth, strength, or figure, with the Duke of Bedford, than to make a parallel between his services, and my attempts to be useful to my country. It would not be gross adulation, but uncivil irony, to say, that he has any publick merit of his own to keep alive the idea of the services by which his vast landed Pensions were obtained. My merits, whatever they are, are original and personal; his are derivative. It is his ancestor, the original pensioner, that has laid up this inexhaustible fund of merit, which makes his Grace so very delicate and exceptious about the merit of all other grantees of the Crown. Had he permitted me to remain in quiet, I should have said, 'tis his estate; that's enough. It is his by law; what have I to do with it or it's history? He would naturally have said on his side, 'tis this man's fortune.—He is as good now, as my ancestor was two hundred and fifty years ago. I am a young man with very old pensions; he is an old man with very young pensions,—that's all?

Why will his Grace, by attacking me, force me reluctantly to compare my little merit with that which obtained from the Crown those prodigies of profuse donation by which he tramples on the mediocrity of humble and laborious individuals? I would willingly leave him to the Herald's College, which the philosophy of the Sans culottes, (prouder by far than all the Garters, and Norroys and Clarencieux, and Rouge Dragons[1] that ever pranced in a procession of what his friends call aristocrates and despots) will abolish with contumely and scorn. These historians, recorders, and blazoners of virtues and arms, differ wholly from that other description of historians, who never assign any act of politicians to a good motive. These gentle historians, on the contrary, dip their pens in nothing but the milk of human kindness. They seek no further for merit than the preamble of a patent, or the inscription on a tomb. With them every man created a peer is first an hero ready made. They judge of every man's capacity for office by the offices he has filled; and the more offices the more ability. Every General-officer with them is a Marlborough; every Statesman a Burleigh; every Judge a Murray or a Yorke. They, who alive, were laughed at or pitied by all their acquaintance, make as good a figure as the best of them in the pages of Guillim, Edmondson, and Collins.[2]

To these recorders, so full of good nature to the great and prosperous, I would willingly leave the first Baron Russel, and Earl of Bedford, and the merits of his grants. But the aulnager, the weigher, the meter of grants, will not suffer us to acquiesce in the judgment of the Prince reigning at the time when they were made. They were never good to those who earn them. Well then; since the new grantees have war made on them by the old, and that the word of the Sovereign is not to be taken, let us turn our eyes to history, in which great men have always a pleasure in contemplating the heroic origin of their house.

The first peer of the name, the first purchaser of the grants, was a Mr. Russel, a person of an ancient gentleman's family raised by being a minion of Henry the Eighth. As there generally is some resemblance of character to create these relations, the favourite was in all likelihood much such another as his master. The first of those immoderate grants was not taken from the antient demesne of the Crown, but from the recent confiscation of the ancient nobility of the land. The lion having sucked the blood of his prey, threw the offal carcase to the jackall in waiting. Having tasted once the food of confiscation, the favourites became fierce and ravenous. This worthy favourite's first grant was from the lay nobility. The second, infinitely improving on the enormity of the first, was from the plunder of the church. In truth his Grace is somewhat excusable for his

---

[1] officers in the College of Heralds, in charge of coats of arms.

[2] authorities on heraldry and aristocratic genealogy.

dislike to a grant like mine, not only in its quantity, but in it's kind so different from his own.

Mine was from a mild and benevolent sovereign; his from Henry the Eighth.

Mine had not it's fund in the murder of any innocent person of illustrious rank,[1] or in the pillage of any body of unoffending men. His grants were from the aggregate and consolidated funds of judgments iniquitously legal, and from possessions voluntarily surrendered by the lawful proprietors with the gibbet at their door.

The merit of the grantee whom he derives from, was that of being a prompt and greedy instrument of a *levelling* tyrant, who oppressed all descriptions of his people, but who fell with particular fury on every thing that was *great and noble*. Mine has been, in endeavouring to screen every man, in every class, from oppression, and particularly in defending the high and eminent, who in the bad times of confiscating Princes, confiscating chief Governors, or confiscating Demagogues, are the most exposed to jealousy, avarice and envy.

The merit of the original grantee of his Grace's pensions, was in giving his hand to the work, and partaking the spoil with a Prince, who plundered a part of his national church of his time and country. Mine was in defending the whole of the national church of my own time and my own country, and the whole of the national churches of all countries, from the principles and the examples which lead to ecclesiastical pillage, thence to a contempt of *all* prescriptive titles, thence to the pillage of *all* property, and thence to universal desolation.

The merit of the origin of his Grace's fortune was in being a favourite and chief adviser to a Prince, who left no liberty to their native country. My endeavour was to obtain liberty for the municipal country in which I was born, and for all descriptions and denominations in it.— Mine was to support with unrelaxing vigilance every right, every privilege, every franchise, in this my adopted, my dearer and more comprehensive country; and not only to preserve those rights in this chief seat of empire, but in every nation, in every land, in every climate, language and religion, in the vast domain that still is under the protection, and the larger that was once under the protection, of the British Crown.

His founder's merits were, by arts in which he served his master and made his fortune, to bring poverty, wretchedness and depopulation on his country. Mine were under a benevolent Prince, in promoting the commerce, manufactures and agriculture of his kingdom; in which his Majesty shews an eminent example, who even in his amusements is a patriot, and in hours of leisure an improver of his native soil.

His founder's merit, was the merit of a gentleman raised by the arts of a Court, and the protection of a Wolsey,[2] to the eminence of a great and potent Lord. His merit in that eminence was by instigating a tyrant to injustice, to provoke a people to rebellion.—My merit was, to awaken the sober part of the country, that they might put themselves on their guard against any one potent Lord, or any greater number of potent Lords, or any combination of great leading men of any sort, if ever they should attempt to proceed in the same courses, but in the reverse order, that is, by instigating a corrupted populace to rebellion, and, through that rebellion, should introduce a tyranny yet worse than the tyranny which his Grace's ancestor supported, and of which he profited in the manner we behold in the despotism of Henry the Eighth.

The political merit of the first pensioner of his Grace's house, was that of being concerned as a counsellor of state in advising, and in his person executing the conditions of a dishonourable peace with France; the surrendering the fortress of Boulogne, then our out guard on the Continent. By that surrender, Calais, the key of France, and the bridle in the mouth of that power, was, not many years afterwards, finally lost.[3] My merit has been in resisting the power and pride of France, under any form of it's rule; but in opposing it

---

[1] "See the history of the melancholy catastrophe of the Duke of Buckingham. Temp. [in the time of] Hen. 8." (E.B.) Edward Stafford, 3rd Duke of Buckingham (1478–1521) was executed by Henry VIII on a treason charge.

[2] Thomas Wolsey (c. 1475–1530), Cardinal and Lord Chancellor under Henry VIII, dismissed for his failure to persuade the Pope to grant Henry's divorce from Catherine of Aragon.

[3] The French town of Calais, across the Strait of Dover from southeast England, was under English rule from 1347 until 1558.

with the greatest zeal and earnestness, when that rule appeared in the worst form it could assume; the worst indeed which the prime cause and principle of all evil could possibly give it. It was my endeavour by every means to excite a spirit in the house, where I had the honour of a seat, for carrying on with early vigour and decision, the most clearly just and necessary war, that this or any nation ever carried on; in order to save my country from the iron yoke of it's power, and from the more dreadful contagion of its principles; to preserve, while they can be preserved pure and untainted, the ancient, inbred integrity, piety, good nature, and good humour of the people of England, from the dreadful pestilence which beginning in France, threatens to lay waste the whole moral, and in a great degree the whole physical world, having done both in the focus of it's most intense malignity.

The labours of his Grace's founder merited the curses, not loud but deep, of the Commons of England, on whom *he* and his master had effected a *complete Parliamentary Reform*, in making them in their slavery and humiliation, the true and adequate representatives of a debased, degraded, and undone people. My merits were, in having had an active, though not always an ostentatious share, in every one act, without exception, of undisputed constitutional utility in my time, and in having supported on all occasions, the authority, the efficiency, and the privileges of the Commons of Great Britain. I ended my services by a recorded and fully reasoned assertion on their own journals of their constitutional rights, and a vindication of their constitutional conduct. I laboured in all things to merit their inward approbation, and (along with the assistance of the largest, the greatest, and best of my endeavours) I received their free, unbiassed, publick, and solemn thanks.

Thus stands the account of the comparative merits of the Crown grants which compose the Duke of Bedford's fortune as balanced against mine. In the name of common sense, why should the Duke of Bedford think, that none but of the House of Russel are entitled to the favour of the Crown? Why should he imagine that no King of England has been capable of judging of merit but King Henry the Eighth? Indeed, he will pardon me; he is a little mistaken; all virtue did not end in the first Earl of Bedford. All discernment did not lose it's vision when his Creator closed his eyes. Let him remit his rigour on the disproportion between merit and reward in others, and they will make no enquiry into the origin of his fortune. They will regard with much more satisfaction, as he will contemplate with infinitely more advantage, whatever in his pedigree has been dulcified by an exposure to the influence of heaven in a long flow of generations, from the hard, acidulous, metallic tincture of the spring. It is little to be doubted, that several of his forefathers in that long series, have degenerated into honour and virtue. Let the Duke of Bedford (I am sure he will) reject with scorn and horror, the counsels of the lecturers, those wicked panders to avarice and ambition, who would tempt him in the troubles of his country, to seek another enormous fortune from the forfeitures of another nobility, and the plunder of another church. Let him (and I trust that yet he will) employ all the energy of his youth, and all the resources of his wealth, to crush rebellious principles which have no foundation in morals, and rebellious movements, that have no provocation in tyranny.

Then will be forgot the rebellions, which, by a doubtful priority in crime, his ancestor had provoked and extinguished. On such a conduct in the noble Duke, many of his countrymen might, and with some excuse might, give way to the enthusiasm of their gratitude, and in the dashing style of some of the old declaimers, cry out, that if the fates had found no other way in which they could give a Duke of Bedford[1] and his opulence as props to a tottering world, then the butchery of the Duke of Buckingham might be tolerated; it might be regarded even with complacency, whilst in the heir of confiscation they saw the sympathizing comforter of the martyrs, who suffer under the cruel confiscation of this day; whilst they beheld with admiration his zealous protection of the virtuous and

---

[1] "At si non aliam venturo fata Neroni, &c." (E.B.) The gist of this passage is that there is no point in complaining if the fates cause suffering in order to bring to power such a wonderful emperor as Nero (Lucan, *Pharsalia* 1.35). Lucan, an opponent of Nero, is probably being ironic; so is Burke, in his implicit comparison between Nero and the Duke of Bedford.

loyal nobility of France, and his manly support of his brethren, the yet standing nobility and gentry of his native land. Then his Grace's merit would be pure and new, and sharp, as fresh from the mint of honour. As he pleased he might reflect honour on his predecessors, or throw it forward on those who were to succeed him. He might be the propagator of the stock of honour, or the root of it, as he thought proper.

Had it pleased God to continue to me the hopes of succession, I should have been, according to my mediocrity, and the mediocrity of the age I live in, a sort of founder of a family; I should have left a son, who, in all the points in which personal merit can be viewed, in science, in erudition, in genius, in taste, in honour, in generosity, in humanity, in every liberal sentiment, and every liberal accomplishment, would not have shewn himself inferior to the Duke of Bedford, or to any of those whom he traces in his line. His Grace very soon would have wanted all plausibility in his attack upon that provision which belonged more to mine than to me. He would soon have supplied every deficiency, and symmetrized every disproportion. It would not have been for that successor to resort to any stagnant wasting reservoir of merit in me, or in any ancestry. He had in himself a salient, living spring, of generous and manly action. Every day he lived he would have re-purchased the bounty of the crown, and ten times more, if ten times more he had received. He was made a public creature; and had no enjoyment whatever, but in the performance of some duty. At this exigent moment, the loss of a finished man is not easily supplied.

But a disposer whose power we are little able to resist, and whose wisdom it behoves us not at all to dispute; has ordained it in another manner, and (whatever my querulous weakness might suggest) a far better. The storm has gone over me; and I lie like one of those old oaks which the late hurricane has scattered about me. I am stripped of all my honours; I am torn up by the roots, and lie prostrate on the earth! There, and prostrate there, I most unfeignedly recognize the divine justice, and in some degree submit to it. But whilst I humble myself before God, I do not know that it is forbidden to repel the attacks of unjust and inconsiderate men. The patience of Job is proverbial. After some of the convulsive struggles of our irritable nature, he submitted himself, and repented in dust and ashes. But even so, I do not find him blamed for reprehending, and with a considerable degree of verbal asperity, those ill-natured neighbours of his, who visited his dunghill to read moral, political, and œconomical lectures on his misery. I am alone. I have none to meet my enemies in the gate. Indeed, my Lord, I greatly deceive myself, if in this hard season I would give a peck of refuse wheat for all that is called fame and honour in the world. This is the appetite but of a few. It is a luxury; it is a privilege; it is an indulgence for those who are at their ease. But we are all of us made to shun disgrace, as we are made to shrink from pain, and poverty, and disease. It is an instinct; and under the direction of reason, instinct is always in the right. I live in an inverted order. They who ought to have succeeded me are gone before me. They who should have been to me as posterity are in the place of ancestors. I owe to the dearest relation (which ever must subsist in memory) that act of piety, which he would have performed to me; I owe it to him to shew that he was not descended, as the Duke of Bedford would have it, from an unworthy parent.

The Crown has considered me after long service: the Crown has paid the Duke of Bedford by advance. He has had a long credit for any service which he may perform hereafter. He is secure, and long may he be secure, in his advance, whether he performs any services or not. But let him take care how he endangers the safety of that Constitution which secures his own utility or his own insignificance; or how he discourages those, who take up, even puny arms, to defend an order of things, which, like the Sun of Heaven, shines alike on the useful and the worthless. His grants are engrafted on the public law of Europe, covered with the awful hoar of innumerable ages. They are guarded by the sacred rules of prescription, found in that full treasury of jurisprudence from which the jejuneness and penury of our municipal law has, by degrees, been enriched and strengthened. This prescription I had my share (a very full share) in bringing to it's perfection.[1] The Duke of Bedford will stand as long as prescriptive law endures; as

---

[1] "Sir George Savile's Act, called the *Nullum Tempus* Act." (E.B.)

long as the great stable laws of property, common to us with all civilized nations, are kept in their integrity, and without the smallest intermixture of the laws, maxims, principles, or precedents of the Grand Revolution. They are secure against all changes but one. The whole revolutionary system, institutes, digest, code, novels, text, gloss, comment, are, not only not the same, but they are the very reverse, and the reverse fundamentally, of all the laws, on which civil life has hitherto been upheld in all the governments of the world. The learned professors of the Rights of Man regard prescription, not as a title to bar all claim, set up against old possession—but they look on prescription as itself a bar against the possessor and proprietor. They hold an immemorial possession to be no more than a long continued, and therefore an aggravated injustice.

Such are *their* ideas; such *their* religion, and such *their* law. But as to *our* country and *our* race, as long as the well compacted structure of our church and state, the sanctuary, the holy of holies of that ancient law, defended by reverence, defended by power, a fortress at once and a temple,[1] shall stand inviolate on the brow of the British Sion—as long as the British Monarchy, not more limited than fenced by the orders of the State, shall, like the proud Keep of Windsor, rising in the majesty of proportion, and girt with the double belt of it's kindred and coeval towers, as long as this awful structure shall oversee and guard the subjected land—so long the mounds and dykes of the low, fat, Bedford level will have nothing to fear from all the pickaxes of all the levellers of France. As long as our Sovereign Lord the King, and his faithful subjects, the Lords and Commons of this realm,—the triple cord, which no man can break; the solemn, sworn, constitutional frank-pledge of this nation; the firm guarantees of each others being, and each others rights; the joint and several securities, each in it's place and order, for every kind and every quality, of property and of dignity—As long as these endure, so long the Duke of Bedford is safe: and we are all safe together—the high from the blights of envy and the spoliations of rapacity; the low from the iron hand of oppression and the insolent spurn of contempt. Amen! and so be it: and so it will be,

> Dum domus Æneae Capitoli immobile saxum
> Accolet; imperiumque pater Romanus habebit.—[2]

But if the rude inroad of Gallick tumult, with it's sophistical Rights of Man, to falsify the account, and it's sword as a makeweight to throw into the scale, shall be introduced into our city by a misguided populace, set on by proud great men, themselves blinded and intoxicated by a frantick ambition, we shall, all of us, perish and be overwhelmed in a common ruin. If a great storm blow on our coast, it will cast the whales on the strand as well as the periwinkles. His Grace will not survive the poor grantee he despises, no not for a twelvemonth. If the great look for safety in the services they render to this Gallick cause, it is to be foolish, even above the weight of privilege allowed to wealth. If his Grace be one of these whom they endeavour to proselytize, he ought to be aware of the character of the sect, whose doctrines he is invited to embrace. With them, insurrection is the most sacred of revolutionary duties to the state. Ingratitude to benefactors is the first of revolutionary virtues. Ingratitude is indeed their four cardinal virtues compacted and amalgamated into one; and he will find it in every thing that has happened since the commencement of the philosophic revolution to this hour. If he pleads the merit of having performed the duty of insurrection against the order he lives in (God forbid he ever should), the merit of others will be to perform the duty of insurrection against him. If he pleads (again God forbid he should, and I do not suspect he will) his ingratitude to the Crown for it's creation of his family, others will plead their right and duty to pay him in kind. They will laugh, indeed they will laugh, at his parchment and his wax. His deeds will be drawn out with the rest of the lumber of his evidence room, and burnt to the tune of *ça ira*[3] in the courts of Bedford (then Equality) house.

Am I to blame, if I attempt to pay his Grace's hostile reproaches to me with a friendly admonition to himself?

---

[1] "Templum in modum arcis. ['A temple in the form of a fortress.'] Tacitus of the Temple of Jerusalem." (E.B.)

[2] "So long as the house of Aeneas shall dwell on the Capitol's unshaken rock, and the Father of Rome hold sovereign sway" (Virgil, *Æneid* 9.448–49).

[3] "That shall go on" (Fr.): the refrain of a song from the period of the French Revolution.

Can I be blamed, to point out to him in what manner he is like to be affected, if the sect of the cannibal philosophers of France should proselytize any considerable part of this people, and, by their joint proselytizing arms, should conquer that Government, to which his Grace does not seem to me to give all the support his own security demands? Surely it is proper, that he, and that others like him, should know the true genius of this sect, what their opinions are; what they have done: and to whom; and what, (if a prognostick is to be formed from the dispositions and actions of men) it is certain they will do hereafter. He ought to know, that they have sworn assistance, the only engagement they ever will keep, to all in this country, who bear a resemblance to themselves, and who think as such, that *The whole duty of man* consists in destruction.[1] They are a misallied and disparaged branch of the house of Nimrod.[2] They are the Duke of Bedford's natural hunters; and he is their natural game. Because he is not very profoundly reflecting, he sleeps in profound security: they, on the contrary, are always vigilant, active, enterprizing, and though far removed from any knowledge, which makes men estimable or useful, in all the instruments and resources of evil, their leaders are not meanly instructed, or insufficiently furnished. In the French Revolution every thing is new; and, from want of preparation to meet so unlooked for an evil, every thing is dangerous. Never, before this time, was a set of literary men, converted into a gang of robbers and assassins. Never before, did a den of bravoes and banditti, assume the garb and tone of an academy of philosophers.

Let me tell his Grace, that an union of such characters, monstrous as it seems, is not made for producing despicable enemies. But if they are formidable as foes, as friends they are dreadful indeed. The men of property in France confiding in a force, which seemed to be irresistible, because it had never been tried, neglected to prepare for a conflict with their enemies at their own weapons. They were found in such a situation as the Mexicans[3] were, when they were attacked by the dogs, the cavalry, the iron, and the gunpowder of an handful of bearded men, whom they did not know to exist in nature. This is a comparison that some, I think, have made; and it is just. In France they had their enemies within their houses. They were even in the bosoms of many of them. But they had not sagacity to discern their savage character. They seemed tame, and even caressing. They had nothing but *douce humanité*[4] in their mouth. They could not bear the punishment of the mildest laws on the greatest criminals. The slightest severity of justice made their flesh creep. The very idea that war existed in the world disturbed their repose. Military glory was no more than, with them, a splendid infamy. Hardly would they hear of self defence, which they reduced within such bounds, as to leave it no defence at all. All this while they meditated the confiscations and massacres we have seen. Had any one told these unfortunate Noblemen and Gentlemen, how, and by whom, the grand fabrick of the French monarchy under which they flourished would be subverted, they would not have pitied him as a visionary, but would have turned from him as what they call a *mauvais plaisant*.[5] Yet we have seen what has happened. The persons who have suffered from the cannibal philosophy of France, are so like the Duke of Bedford, that nothing but his Grace's probably not speaking quite so good French, could enable us to find out any difference. A great many of them had as pompous titles as he, and were of full as illustrious a race: some few of them had fortunes as ample; several of them, without meaning the least disparagement to the Duke of Bedford, were as wise, and as virtuous, and as valiant, and as well educated, and as compleat in all the lineaments of men of honour as he is: And to all this they had added the powerful outguard of a military profession, which, in it's nature, renders men somewhat more cautious than those, who have nothing to attend to but the lazy enjoyment of undisturbed possessions. But security was their ruin. They are dashed to pieces in

---

[1] Ecclesiastes 12.13; also the title of a popular devotional book (1658).

[2] Nimrod, a "mighty hunter before the Lord" (Genesis 10.9), conventionally signifies cruelty and violence.

[3] I.e. the Aztecs.

[4] "sweet humanity" (Fr.).

[5] "mischievous joker" (Fr.).

the storm, and our shores are covered with the wrecks. If they had been aware that such a thing might happen, such a thing never could have happened.

I assure his Grace, that if I state to him the designs of his enemies, in a manner which may appear to him ludicrous and impossible, I tell him nothing that has not exactly happened, point by point, but twenty-four mile from our own shore. I assure him that the Frenchified faction, more encouraged, than others are warned, by what has happened in France, look at him and his landed possessions, as an object at once of curiosity and rapacity. He is made for them in every part of their double character. As robbers, to them he is a noble booty: as speculatists, he is a glorious subject for their experimental philosophy. He affords matter for an extensive analysis, in all the branches of their science, geometrical, physical, civil and political. These philosophers are fanaticks; independent of any interest, which if it operated alone would make them much more tractable, they are carried with such an headlong rage towards every desperate trial, that they would sacrifice the whole human race to the slightest of their experiments. I am better able to enter into the character of this description of men than the noble Duke can be. I have lived long and variously in the World. Without any considerable pretensions to literature in myself, I have aspired to the love of letters. I have lived for a great many years in habitudes with those who professed them. I can form a tolerable estimate of what is likely to happen from a character, chiefly dependent for fame and fortune, on knowledge and talent, as well in it's morbid and perverted state, as in that which is sound and natural. Naturally men so formed and finished are the first gifts of Providence to the World. But when they have once thrown off the fear of God, which was in all ages too often the case, and the fear of man, which is now the case, and when in that state they come to understand one another, and to act in corps, a more dreadful calamity cannot arise out of Hell to scourge mankind. Nothing can be conceived more hard than the heart of a thorough bred metaphysician. It comes nearer to the cold malignity of a wicked spirit than to the frailty and passion of a man. It is like that of the principle of Evil himself, incorporeal, pure, unmixed, dephlegmated, defecated evil. It is no easy operation to eradicate humanity from the human breast. What Shakespeare calls "the compunctious visitings of nature,"[1] will sometimes knock at their hearts, and protest against their murderous speculations. But they have a means of commanding with their nature. Their humanity is not dissolved. They only give it a long prorogation. They are ready to declare, that they do not think two thousand years too long a period for the good that they pursue. It is remarkable, that they never see any way to their projected good but by the road of some evil. Their imagination is not fatigued, with the contemplation of human suffering thro' the wild waste of centuries added to centuries, of misery and desolation. Their humanity is at their horizon—and, like the horizon, it always flies before them. The geometricians, and the chymists bring, the one from the dry bones of their diagrams, and the other from the soot of their furnaces, dispositions that make them worse than indifferent about those feelings and habitudes, which are the supports of the moral world. Ambition is come upon them suddenly; they are intoxicated with it, and it has rendered them fearless of the danger, which may from thence arise to others or to themselves. These philosophers, consider men in their experiments, no more than they do mice in an air pump, or in a recipient of mephitic gas. Whatever his Grace may think of himself, they look upon him, and every thing that belongs to him, with no more regard than they do upon the whiskers of that little long-tailed animal, that has been long the game of the grave, demure, insidious, spring-nailed, velvet-pawed, green-eyed philosophers, whether going upon two legs, or upon four.

…

It would be a most arrogant presumption in me to assume to myself the glory of what belongs to his Majesty, and to his Ministers, and to his Parliament, and to the far greater majority of his faithful people:

---

[1] Shakespeare, *Macbeth* 1.5.42.

But had I stood alone to counsel, and that all were determined to be guided by my advice, and to follow it implicitly—then I should have been the sole author of a war. But it should have been a war on my ideas and my principles. Whatever his Grace may think of my demerits with regard to the war with Regicide, he will find my guilt confined to that alone. He never shall, with the smallest colour of reason, accuse me of being the author of a peace with Regicide. But that is high matter; and ought not to be mixed with any thing of so little moment, as what may belong to me, or even to the Duke of Bedford.

    I have the honour to be, &c.

EDMUND BURKE.

Ignatius Sancho
1729? – 1780

Charles Ignatius Sancho (he would later drop his first name) was born on a slave ship headed from Guinea to the Spanish West-Indies; on arrival in New Grenada, he was baptized by the Roman Catholic bishop. His mother died of disease; his father committed suicide. At the age of two, he was taken as a slave to England, where he was named Sancho after the squire of Cervantes' *Don Quixote*.

The Duke and Duchess of Montagu befriended him as a child; but his mistresses (three sisters) refused to educate him. He ran away; and eventually the Duchess of Montagu employed him as her butler. In her will she left him £70 and an annuity of £30. He frequented the London theatre and wrote books on the theory of music and of painting. Financial problems, apparently related to gambling, meant that he was forced to return as a servant to Montagu House. He married Anne Osborne, "a young woman of West-Indian origin" (Joseph Jekyll's *Life*, 1782), and they managed a grocery shop and raised a large family. Having suffered for many years from gout, Sancho died on 14 December 1780, the first person of African ancestry to be given an obituary in a British newspaper. (A.M.)

---

from *Letters of the Late Ignatius Sancho, an African. To Which are Prefixed Memoirs of his Life, by Joseph Jekyll,*[1] *Esq. M.P.* 5th ed. (1803)

LETTER 36
To Mr. Sterne[2]

July, 17[6]6.

Reverend Sir,
It would be an insult on your humanity (or perhaps look like it) to apologize for the liberty I am taking.—I am one of those people whom the vulgar and illiberal call "*Negurs*."[3]—The first part of my life was rather unlucky, as I was placed in a family who judged ignorance the best and only security for obedience.—A little reading and writing I got by unwearied application.—The latter part of my life has been—thro' God's blessing, truly fortunate, having spent it in the service of one of the best families in the kingdom.[4]—My chief pleasure has been books.—Philanthropy I adore.—How very much, good Sir, am I (amongst millions) indebted to you for the character of your amiable uncle Toby![5]—I declare, I would walk ten miles in the dog-days, to shake hands with the honest corporal.—Your Sermons[6] have touch'd me to the heart, and I hope have amended it, which brings me to the point.—In your tenth discourse, page seventy-eight, in the second volume—is this very affecting passage—"Consider how great a part of our species—in all ages down to this—have been trod under the feet of cruel and capricious tyrants, who would neither hear their cries, nor pity their distresses.—Consider slavery—what it is—how bitter a draught—

---

[1] Sancho's editor Joseph Jekyll (1754–1837), lawyer and politician, appended an anonymous "Memoir" to the *Letters of the Late Ignatius Sancho* (1782), acknowledging his authorship only in 1803.

[2] Laurence Sterne (1713–68), writer and clergyman.

[3] I.e., blacks, from "niger" (L.).

[4] the family of John Montagu, 2nd Duke of Montagu (1690–1749) and his wife Mary (1689–1751), Duchess of Montagu.

[5] a character in Sterne's *The Life and Opinions of Tristram Shandy, Gentleman* (1759–67); for Sterne's anti-racist views see vol. 9, chap. 6. Sterne wrote to Sancho, 27 July 1766, as he was writing this part of the novel: "but 'tis no uncommon thing, my good Sancho, for one half of the world to use the other half of it like brutes, & then endeavour to make 'em so."

[6] published in numerous editions from 1760 on (sometimes as *The Sermons of Mr. Yorick*, a character in Sterne's *A Sentimental Journey*, 1768).

and how many millions are made to drink it!"[1]—Of all my favorite authors, not one has drawn a tear in favor of my miserable black brethren—excepting yourself, and the humane author of Sir George Ellison.[2]—I think you will forgive me;—I am sure you will applaud me for beseeching you to give one half-hour's attention to slavery, as it is at this day practiced in our West Indies.—That subject, handled in your striking manner, would ease the yoke (perhaps) of many—but if only of one—Gracious God!—what a feast to a benevolent heart!—and, sure I am, you are an epicurean in acts of charity.—You, who are universally read, and as universally admired—you could not fail—Dear Sir, think in me you behold the uplifted hands of thousands of my brother Moors.[3]—Grief (you pathetically observe) is eloquent;—figure to yourself their attitudes;—hear their supplicating addresses!—alas!—you cannot refuse.—Humanity must comply—in which hope I beg permission to subscribe myself,

Reverend Sir, &c.
IGN. SANCHO

---

[1] Sterne's Sermon 10, "Job's Account of the Shortness and Troubles of Life, Considered" (published in 1761), is based on Job 14.1–2.

[2] Sarah Scott (1720–95), whose novel *The History of Sir George Ellison* (1766) advocates reform (not abolition) of slavery.

[3] I.e., Africans.

John Scott
1730 – 1783

John Scott was born at Bermondsey, London, on 9 January 1730, the younger son of Samuel Scott, a linen draper and Quaker preacher, and his wife, Martha Wilkins. To avoid an outbreak of smallpox, the family moved to Amwell, Hertfordshire, about 1740. There, Scott studied English poetry and, between 1753 and 1758, contributed verses to the *Gentleman's Magazine*. Edward Young, Elizabeth Carter, and Catherine Talbot praised his *Four Elegies Descriptive and Moral* (1760). After being successfully inoculated against smallpox in 1766 he began visiting London, where he met Samuel Johnson, James Beattie, William Jones, Lord Lyttelton, and Catharine Macaulay.*

Scott's mother died in 1766, his father early in 1768. His wife Sarah died in childbirth the following June; their child died in August. Following his marriage to Maria De Horne on 1 November 1770, Scott moved back to the family house at Amwell, where Johnson visited him in 1773. His *Observations on the Present State of the Parochial and Vagrant Poor* was followed in 1776 by *A Prospect of Ware and the Country Adjacent* and by *Amwell, a Descriptive Poem*, a long poem in blank verse drawing on autobiographical reference, knowledge of local landscape and history, and the literary tradition of the place poem.

Scott participated in the debate about Chatterton's* Rowley poems, defending Chatterton's genius while deploring his fraud. Maintaining a house at Ratcliff, he participated in the London-based literary world, the local affairs of Amwell and Hertfordshire, and broader political issues. Scott died of fever at Ratcliff, on 12 December 1783, and was buried in the Quaker burial-ground there on 18 December. He was survived by his wife and his six-year-old daughter. (A.M.)

❧❧❧

from *Poetical Works* (1782)

Ode 13

    I hate that drum's discordant sound,
Parading round, and round, and round:
To thoughtless youth it pleasure yields,
And lures from cities and from fields,
5   To sell their liberty for charms
Of tawdry lace, and glittering arms;
And when Ambition's voice commands,
To march, and fight, and fall, in foreign lands.

10   I hate that drum's discordant sound,
Parading round, and round, and round:
To me it talks of ravag'd plains,
And burning towns, and ruin'd swains,
And mangled limbs, and dying groans,
15   And widows tears, and orphans moans;
And all that Misery's hand bestows,
To fill the catalogue of human woes.

Oliver Goldsmith
1730? – 1774

Oliver Goldsmith was born on 10 November 1730 (or 1731), probably in Pallas, County Longford, Ireland. His father, Charles Goldsmith, was an Anglican priest; his mother was Ann Jones Goldsmith. He was educated at a series of village and parochial schools and then at Trinity College, Dublin. He went on to study medicine in Edinburgh, Leyden, and Paris, but he never practised successfully and it is not even certain that he qualified. Instead, he became a journalist and author, publishing a wide range of work: history, biography, natural history, poetry, and prose essays. His most important works are probably *The Citizen of the World*, a look at English society through the eyes of a Chinese traveller (1762); *The Vicar of Wakefield* (1766), a sentimental novel; *The Deserted Village* (1770), a poem which would be answered by his Canadian great-nephew Oliver Goldsmith in *The Rising Village* (1825);* and *She Stoops to Conquer* (1773), a comedy. He never married, but he befriended Burke,* Samuel Johnson, and Reynolds.* He died in London, probably from a kidney infection, on 4 April 1774. (D.L.M.)

The Deserted Village, A Poem (1770)[1]

Sweet AUBURN,[2] loveliest village of the plain,
Where health and plenty cheared the labouring swain,
Where smiling spring its earliest visit paid,
And parting summer's lingering blooms delayed,
5 Dear lovely bowers of innocence and ease,
Seats of my youth, when every sport could please,
How often have I loitered o'er thy green,
Where humble happiness endeared each scene;
How often have I paused on every charm,
10 The sheltered cot, the cultivated farm,
The never failing brook, the busy mill,
The decent church that topt the neighbouring hill,
The hawthorn bush, with seats beneath the shade,
For talking age and whispering lovers made.
15 How often have I blest the coming day,
When toil remitting lent its turn to play,
And all the village train from labour free
Led up their sports beneath the spreading tree,
While many a pastime circled in the shade,
20 The young contending as the old surveyed;
And many a gambol frolicked o'er the ground,
And slights of art and feats of strength went round.
And still as each repeated pleasure tired,
Succeeding sports the mirthful band inspired;
25 The dancing pair that simply sought renown
By holding out to tire each other down,
The swain mistrustless of his smutted face,
While secret laughter tittered round the place,
The bashful virgin's side-long looks of love,
30 The matron's glance that would those looks reprove.
These were thy charms, sweet village; sports like these,
With sweet succession, taught even toil to please;
These round thy bowers their chearful influence shed,
These were thy charms—But all these charms are fled.

35 Sweet smiling village, loveliest of the lawn,
Thy sports are fled, and all thy charms withdrawn;
Amidst thy bowers the tyrant's hand is seen,
And desolation saddens all thy green:
One only master grasps the whole domain,[3]
40 And half a tillage stints thy smiling plain;
No more thy glassy brook reflects the day,
But choaked with sedges, works its weedy way.

---

[1] We have omitted the prefatory Dedication to Sir Joshua Reynolds.*

[2] based on Goldsmith's childhood home, Lissoy, County Westmeath.

[3] In the late eighteenth and early nineteenth centuries, Parliament passed thousands of acts of enclosure, taking land out of common use—usually for the benefit of large landowners and at the expense of small farmers.

Along thy glades, a solitary guest,
The hollow sounding bittern guards its nest;
45 Amidst thy desert walks the lapwing flies,
And tires their ecchoes with unvaried cries.
Sunk are thy bowers in shapeless ruin all,
And the long grass o'ertops the mouldering wall,
And trembling, shrinking from the spoiler's hand,
50 Far, far away thy children leave the land.

Ill fares the land, to hastening ills a prey,
Where wealth accumulates, and men decay;
Princes and lords may flourish, or may fade;
A breath can make them, as a breath has made.
55 But a bold peasantry, their country's pride,
When once destroyed, can never be supplied.

A time there was, ere England's griefs began,
When every rood[1] of ground maintained its man;
For him light labour spread her wholesome store,
60 Just gave what life required, but gave no more.
His best companions, innocence and health;
And his best riches, ignorance of wealth.

But times are altered; trade's unfeeling train
Usurp the land and dispossess the swain;
65 Along the lawn, where scattered hamlets rose,
Unwieldy wealth, and cumbrous pomp repose;
And every want to luxury allied,
And every pang that folly pays to pride.
These gentle hours that plenty bade to bloom,
70 Those calm desires that asked but little room,
Those healthful sports that graced the peaceful scene,
Lived in each look, and brightened all the green;
These far departing seek a kinder shore,
And rural mirth and manners are no more.

75 Sweet AUBURN! parent of the blissful hour,
Thy glades forlorn confess the tyrant's power.
Here as I take my solitary rounds,
Amidst thy tangling walks, and ruined grounds,
And, many a year elapsed, return to view
80 Where once the cottage stood, the hawthorn grew,

Here, as with doubtful, pensive steps I range,
Trace every scene, and wonder at the change,
Remembrance wakes with all her busy train,
Swells at my breast, and turns the past to pain.

85 In all my wanderings round this world of care,
In all my griefs—and GOD has given my share—
I still had hopes my latest hours to crown,
Amidst these humble bowers to lay me down;
My anxious day to husband near the close,
90 And keep life's flame from wasting by repose.
I still had hopes, for pride attends us still,
Amidst the swains to shew my book-learned skill,
Around my fire an evening groupe to draw,
And tell of all I felt, and all I saw;
95 And, as an hare whom hounds and horns pursue,
Pants to the place from whence at first she flew,
I still had hopes, my long vexations past,
Here to return—and die at home at last.

O blest retirement, friend to life's decline,
100 Retreats from care that never must be mine,
How blest is he who crowns in shades like these,
A youth of labour with an age of ease;
Who quits a world where strong temptations try,
And, since 'tis hard to combat, learns to fly.
105 For him no wretches, born to work and weep,
Explore the mine, or tempt the dangerous deep;
No surly porter stands in guilty state
To spurn imploring famine from his gate,
But on he moves to meet his latter end,
110 Angels around befriending virtue's friend;
Sinks to the grave with unperceived decay,
While resignation gently slopes the way;
And, all his prospects brightening to the last,
His Heaven commences ere the world be past!

115 Sweet was the sound when oft at evening's close,
Up yonder hill the village murmur rose;
There as I past with careless steps and slow,
The mingling notes came softened from below;
The swain responsive as the milk-maid sung,
120 The sober herd that lowed to meet their young;
The noisy geese that gabbled o'er the pool,

---

[1] a quarter of an acre, or tenth of a hectare.

The playful children just let loose from school;
The watch-dog's voice that bayed the whispering wind,
And the loud laugh that spoke the vacant mind,
125 These all in soft confusion sought the shade,
And filled each pause the nightingale had made.
But now the sounds of population fail,
No chearful murmurs fluctuate in the gale,
No busy steps the grass-grown foot-way tread,
130 But all the bloomy flush of life is fled.
All but yon widowed, solitary thing
That feebly bends beside the plashy spring;
She, wretched matron, forced, in age, for bread,
To strip the brook with mantling cresses spread,
135 To pick her wintry faggot from the thorn,
To seek her nightly shed, and weep till morn;
She only left of all the harmless train,
The sad historian of the pensive plain.

    Near yonder copse, where once the garden smil'd,
140 And still where many a garden flower grows wild;
There, where a few torn shrubs the place disclose,
The village preacher's modest mansion rose.
A man he was, to all the country dear,
And passing rich with forty pounds a year;
145 Remote from towns he ran his godly race,
Nor ere had changed, nor wish'd to change his place;
Unskilful he to fawn, or seek for power,
By doctrines fashioned to the varying hour;
Far other aims his heart had learned to prize,
150 More bent to raise the wretched than to rise.
His house was known to all the vagrant train,
He chid their wanderings, but relieved their pain;
The long remembered beggar was his guest,
Whose beard descending swept his aged breast;
155 The ruined spendthrift, now no longer proud,
Claimed kindred there, and had his claims allowed;
The broken soldier, kindly bade to stay,
Sate by his fire, and talked the night away;
Wept o'er his wounds, or tales of sorrow done,
160 Shouldered his crutch, and shewed how fields were won.
Pleased with his guests, the good man learned to glow,
And quite forgot their vices in their woe;
Careless their merits, or their faults to scan,
His pity gave ere charity began.

    Thus to relieve the wretched was his pride,
165 And even his failings leaned to Virtue's side;
But in his duty prompt at every call,
He watched and wept, he prayed and felt, for all.
And, as a bird each fond endearment tries,
170 To tempt its new fledged offspring to the skies;
He tried each art, reproved each dull delay,
Allured to brighter worlds, and led the way.

    Beside the bed where parting life was layed,
And sorrow, guilt, and pain, by turns dismayed,
175 The reverend champion stood. At his control,
Despair and anguish fled the struggling soul;
Comfort came down the trembling wretch to raise,
And his last faultering accents whispered praise.

    At church, with meek and unaffected grace,
180 His looks adorned the venerable place;
Truth from his lips prevailed with double sway,
And fools, who came to scoff, remained to pray.
The service past, around the pious man,
With ready zeal each honest rustic ran;
185 Even children followed with endearing wile,
And plucked his gown, to share the good man's smile.
His ready smile a parent's warmth exprest,
Their welfare pleased him, and their cares distrest;
To them his heart, his love, his griefs were given,
190 But all his serious thoughts had rest in Heaven.
As some tall cliff that lifts its awful form
Swells from the vale, and midway leaves the storm,
Tho' round its breast the rolling clouds are spread,
Eternal sunshine settles on its head.

195   Beside yon straggling fence that skirts the way,
With blossomed furze unprofitably gay,
There, in his noisy mansion, skill'd to rule,
The village master taught his little school;
A man severe he was, and stern to view,
200 I knew him well, and every truant knew;
Well had the boding tremblers learned to trace

The day's disasters in his morning face;
Full well they laugh'd with counterfeited glee,
At all his jokes, for many a joke had he;
205 Full well the busy whisper circling round,
Conveyed the dismal tidings when he frowned;
Yet he was kind, or if severe in aught,
The love he bore to learning was in fault;
The village all declared how much he knew;
210 'Twas certain he could write, and cypher too;
Lands he could measure, terms and tides presage,[1]
And even the story ran that he could gauge.[2]
In arguing too, the parson owned his skill,
For e'en tho' vanquished, he could argue still;
215 While words of learned length, and thundering sound,
Amazed the gazing rustics ranged around,
And still they gazed, and still the wonder grew,
That one small head could carry all he knew.

But past is all his fame. The very spot
220 Where many a time he triumphed, is forgot.
Near yonder thorn, that lifts its head on high,
Where once the sign-post caught the passing eye,
Low lies that house where nut-brown draughts inspired,
Where grey-beard mirth and smiling toil retired,
225 Where village statesmen talked with looks profound,
And news much older than their ale went round.
Imagination fondly stoops to trace
The parlour splendours of that festive place;
The white-washed wall, the nicely sanded floor,
230 The varnished clock that clicked behind the door;
The chest contrived a double debt to pay,
A bed by night, a chest of drawers by day;
The pictures placed for ornament and use,
The twelve good rules, the royal game of goose;[3]
235 The hearth, except when winter chill'd the day,
With aspen boughs, and flowers, and fennel gay,

While broken tea-cups, wisely kept for shew,
Ranged o'er the chimney, glistened in a row.

Vain transitory splendours! Could not all
240 Reprieve the tottering mansion from its fall!
Obscure it sinks, nor shall it more impart
An hour's importance to the poor man's heart;
Thither no more the peasant shall repair
To sweet oblivion of his daily care;
245 No more the farmer's news, the barber's tale,
No more the wood-man's ballad shall prevail;
No more the smith his dusky brow shall clear,
Relax his ponderous strength, and lean to hear;
The host himself no longer shall be found
250 Careful to see the mantling bliss go round;
Nor the coy maid, half willing to be prest,
Shall kiss the cup to pass it to the rest.

Yes! let the rich deride, the proud disdain,
These simple blessings of the lowly train,
255 To me more dear, congenial to my heart,
One native charm, than all the gloss of art;
Spontaneous joys, where Nature has its play,
The soul adopts, and owns their first born sway,
Lightly they frolic o'er the vacant mind,
260 Unenvied, unmolested, unconfined.
But the long pomp, the midnight masquerade,
With all the freaks of wanton wealth arrayed,
In these, ere triflers half their wish obtain,
The toiling pleasure sickens into pain;
265 And, even while fashion's brightest arts decoy,
The heart distrusting asks, if this be joy.

Ye friends to truth, ye statesmen who survey
The rich man's joys encrease, the poor's decay,
'Tis yours to judge, how wide the limits stand
270 Between a splendid and an happy land.
Proud swells the tide with loads of freighted ore,
And shouting Folly hails them from her shore;
Hoards, even beyond the miser's wish abound,
And rich men flock from all the world around.
275 Yet count our gains. This wealth is but a name
That leaves our useful products still the same.
Not so the loss. The man of wealth and pride,

---

[1] Terms were the days when rents and wages were due; tides were festivals.

[2] estimate volumes.

[3] The twelve good rules were proverbs attributed to Charles I and often hung up in inns; goose was a board game played with dice.

Takes up a space that many poor supplied;
Space for his lake, his park's extended bounds,
280 Space for his horses, equipage, and hounds;
The robe that wraps his limbs in silken sloth,
Has robbed the neighbouring fields of half their growth;
His seat, where solitary sports are seen,
Indignant spurns the cottage from the green;
285 Around the world each needful product flies,
For all the luxuries the world supplies.
While thus the land adorned for pleasure all
In barren splendour feebly waits the fall.

As some fair female unadorned and plain,
290 Secure to please while youth confirms her reign,
Slights every borrowed charm that dress supplies,
Nor shares with art the triumph of her eyes.
But when those charms are past, for charms are frail,
When time advances, and when lovers fail,
295 She then shines forth sollicitous to bless,
In all the glaring impotence of dress.
Thus fares the land, by luxury betrayed,
In nature's simplest charms at first arrayed,
But verging to decline, its splendours rise,
300 Its vistas strike, its palaces surprize;
While scourged by famine from the smiling land,
The mournful peasant leads his humble band;
And while he sinks without one arm to save,
The country blooms—a garden, and a grave.

305 Where then, ah, where shall poverty reside,
To scape the pressure of contiguous pride;
If to some common's fenceless limits strayed,
He drives his flock to pick the scanty blade,
Those fenceless fields the sons of wealth divide,
310 And even the bare-worn common is denied.

If to the city sped—What waits him there?
To see profusion that he must not share;
To see ten thousand baneful arts combined
To pamper luxury, and thin mankind;
315 To see each joy the sons of pleasure know,
Extorted from his fellow-creature's woe.
Here, while the courtier glitters in brocade,
There the pale artist plies the sickly trade;
Here, while the proud their long drawn pomps display,
320 There the black gibbet glooms beside the way.
The dome where pleasure holds her midnight reign,
Here richly deckt admits the gorgeous train,
Tumultuous grandeur crowds the blazing square,
The rattling chariots clash, the torches glare;
325 Sure scenes like these no troubles ere annoy!
Sure these denote one universal joy!
Are these thy serious thoughts—Ah, turn thine eyes
Where the poor houseless shivering female lies.
She once, perhaps, in village plenty blest,
330 Has wept at tales of innocence distrest;
Her modest looks the cottage might adorn,
Sweet as the primrose peeps beneath the thorn;
Now lost to all; her friends, her virtue fled,
Near her betrayer's door she lays her head,
335 And pinch'd with cold, and shrinking from the shower,
With heavy heart deplores that luckless hour,
When idly first, ambitious of the town,
She left her wheel and robes of country brown.

Do thine, sweet AUBURN, thine, the loveliest train,
340 Do thy fair tribes participate her pain?
Even now, perhaps, by cold and hunger led,
At proud men's doors they ask a little bread!

Ah, no. To distant climes, a dreary scene,
Where half the convex world intrudes between,
345 To torrid tracts with fainting steps they go,
Where wild Altama[1] murmurs to their woe.
Far different there from all that charm'd before,
The various terrors of that horrid shore.
Those blazing suns that dart a downward ray,
350 And fiercely shed intolerable day;
Those matted woods where birds forget to sing,
But silent bats in drowsy clusters cling,
Those poisonous fields with rank luxuriance crowned
Where the dark scorpion gathers death around;

---

[1] the Altamaha river in Georgia.

355 Where at each step the stranger fears to wake
The rattling terrors of the vengeful snake;
Where crouching tigers wait their hapless prey,
And savage men more murderous still than they;
While oft in whirls the mad tornado flies,
360 Mingling the ravaged landscape with the skies.
Far different these from every former scene,
The cooling brook, the grassy vested green,
The breezy covert of the warbling grove,
That only sheltered thefts of harmless love.

365 Good Heaven! what sorrows gloom'd that parting day,
That called them from their native walks away;
When the poor exiles, every pleasure past,
Hung round their bowers, and fondly looked their last,
And took a long farewell, and wished in vain
370 For seats like these beyond the western main;
And shuddering still to face the distant deep,
Returned and wept, and still returned to weep.
The good old sire, the first prepared to go
To new found worlds, and wept for other's woe.
375 But for himself, in conscious virtue brave,
He only wished for worlds beyond the grave.
His lovely daughter, lovelier in her tears,
The fond companion of his helpless years,
Silent went next, neglectful of her charms,
380 And left a lover's for her father's arms.
With louder plaints the mother spoke her woes,
And blest the cot where every pleasure rose;
And kist her thoughtless babes with many a tear,
And claspt them close in sorrow doubly dear;
385 Whilst her fond husband strove to lend relief
In all the decent manliness of grief.

O luxury! Thou curst by heaven's decree,
How ill exchanged are things like these for thee!
How do thy potions with insidious joy,
390 Diffuse their pleasures only to destroy!
Kingdoms by thee, to sickly greatness grown,
Boast of a florid vigour not their own.
At every draught more large and large they grow,
A bloated mass of rank unwieldy woe;
395 Till sapped their strength, and every part unsound,
Down, down they sink, and spread a ruin round.

Even now the devastation is begun,
And half the business of destruction done;
Even now, methinks, as pondering here I stand,
400 I see the rural virtues leave the land.
Down where yon anchoring vessel spreads the sail
That idly waiting flaps with every gale,
Downward they move a melancholy band,
Pass from the shore, and darken all the strand.
405 Contented toil, and hospitable care,
And kind connubial tenderness, are there;
And piety with wishes placed above,
And steady loyalty, and faithful love.
And thou, sweet Poetry, thou loveliest maid,
410 Still first to fly where sensual joys invade;
Unfit in these degenerate times of shame,
To catch the heart, or strike for honest fame;
Dear charming nymph, neglected and decried,
My shame in crowds my solitary pride.
415 Thou source of all my bliss, and all my woe,
That found'st me poor at first, and keep'st me so;
Thou guide by which the nobler arts excell,
Thou nurse of every virtue, fare thee well.
Farewell, and O where'er thy voice be tried,
420 On Torno's cliffs, or Pambamarca's side,[1]
Whether where equinoctial fervours glow,
Or winter wraps the polar world in snow,
Still let thy voice prevailing over time,
Redress the rigours of the inclement clime;
425 Aid slighted truth, with thy persuasive strain
Teach erring man to spurn the rage of gain;
Teach him that states of native strength possest,
Tho' very poor, may still be very blest;
That trade's proud empire hastes to swift decay,
430 As ocean sweeps the labour'd mole away;
While self dependent power can time defy,
As rocks resist the billows and the sky.[2]

---

[1] The Tornio is a river in Sweden; Parambarca is a mountain near Quito, in Peru (now in Ecuador).

[2] The last four lines were written by Samuel Johnson.

Catharine Macaulay
1731 – 1791

Catharine Sawbridge was born in 1731 at Olantigh, Kent, one of four children of John Sawbridge and Elizabeth Wanley Sawbridge. Educated at home, in 1760 she married a Scottish physician, Dr. George Macaulay, and moved to London, where she moved in Whig and Scottish circles, meeting the novelist Tobias Smollett, the surgeon William Hunter, and Thomas Hollis.

The eight volumes of Macaulay's *History of England* were published between 1763 and 1783, based largely on primary materials and seventeenth-century ideals of liberty, reason, perfectibility, and anti-monarchism (as opposed to the Tory views of David Hume's *History of England*, 1754–62). Unlike such contemporaries as Richard Price,* Macaulay was no defender of the Glorious Revolution of 1688: she believed that its limitation of monarchical power had failed to give genuine sovereignty to the people.

She was meanwhile involved in contemporary affairs. John Wilkes had been expelled from Parliament in 1763, charged with seditious libel for criticizing King George III's speech from the throne. Macaulay, one of his supporters, met him after his return in 1768 from exile in France. In her reply to Burke's* *Thoughts on the Cause of the Present Discontents* (1770), she argued for frequent elections and for extending the franchise. Her *Address to the People of England, Ireland, and Scotland, on the Present Important Crisis of Affairs* (1775) argued against Britain's oppression of the American colonies.

Macaulay's husband died in 1766. In 1774 she settled in Bath, moving into the house of her friend Thomas Wilson. A one-volume continuation of her *History*, entitled *The History of England from the Revolution to the Present Time in a Series of Letters to the Reverend Doctor Wilson* (1778), was not well received. In 1778, already the subject of gossip, she eloped with the twenty-one-year-old brother of the quack physician James Graham, giving rise to still more speculation about her personal life.

The Grahams travelled to the United States in 1784, where they met George and Martha Washington, and to France in 1787. They then returned to England and settled in Berkshire, where Macaulay published *A Treatise on the Immutability of Moral Truth* (1783) and, in 1790, *Letters on Education*. In her last publication, *Observations on the Reflections of the Right Hon. Edmund Burke*, Macaulay Graham replied to Burke's attack on the French revolutionaries in his *Reflections on the Revolution in France*.* She died on 22 June 1791. (A.M.)

༺༻

from *Letters on Education, with Observations on Religious and Metaphysical Subjects* (1790)

PART 1, LETTER 24

Flattery—Chastity—Male Rakes

After all that has been advanced, Hortensia,[1] the happiness and perfection of the two sexes are so reciprocally dependent on one another that, till both are reformed, there is no expecting excellence in either. The candid Addison has confessed, that in order to embellish the mistress, you must give a new education to the lover, and teach the men not to be any longer dazzled by false charms and unreal beauty.[2] Till this is the case, we must endeavour to palliate the evil we cannot remedy; and, in the education of our females, raise as many barriers to the corruptions of the world, as our understanding and sense of things will permit.

---

[1] Macaulay's letters are addressed by an unsigned correspondent to her pupil, Hortensia. Cf. Clara Reeve's use of the name Hortensius ("garden lover") in *The Progress of Romance*.*

[2] See, for example, Juba's speech about Marcia in Joseph Addison (1672–1719) *Cato* (1713) 1.382–90.

As I give no credit to the opinion of a sexual excellence, I have made no variation in the fundamental principles of the education of the two sexes; but it will be necessary to admit of such a difference in the plan as shall in some degree form the female mind to the particularity of its situation.

The fruits of true philosophy are modesty and humility; for as we advance in knowledge, our deficiencies become more conspicuous; and by learning to set a just estimate on what we possess, we find little gratification for the passion of pride. This is so just an observation, that we may venture to pronounce, without any exception to the rule, that a vain or proud man is, in a positive sense, an ignorant man. However if it should be our lot to have one of the fair sex, distinguished for any eminent degree of personal charms, committed to our care, we must not attempt by a premature cultivation to gather the fruits of philosophy before their season, nor expect to find the qualities of true modesty and humility make their appearance till the blaze of beauty has in some measure been subdued by time. For should we exhaust all the powers of oratory, and all the strength of sound argument, in the endeavour to convince our pupil that beauty is of small weight in the scale of real excellence, the enflamed praises she will continually hear bestowed on this quality will fix her in the opinion, that we *mean* to keep her in ignorance of her true worth. She will think herself deceived, and she will resent the injury by giving little credit to our precepts, and placing her confidence in those who tickle her ears with lavish panegyric on the captivating graces of her person.

Thus vanity steals on the mind, and thus a daughter, kept under by the ill exerted power of parental authority, gives a full ear to the flattery of a coxcomb. Happy would it be for the sex did the mischief end here; but the soothings of flattery never fail to operate on the affections of the heart; and when love creeps into the bosom, the empire of reason is at an end. To prevent our fair pupils therefore from becoming the prey of coxcombs, and serving either to swell their triumph, or repair their ruined fortunes, it will be necessary to give them a full idea of the magnitude of their beauty, and the power this quality has over the frail mind of man. Nor have we in this case so much to fear from the intimations of a judicious friend, as from the insidious adulation of a designing admirer. The haughty beauty is too proud to regard the admiration of fops and triflers; she will never condescend to the base, the treacherous, the dangerous arts of coquettry; and by keeping her heart free from the snares of love, she will have time to cultivate that philosophy which, if well understood, is a never failing remedy to human pride.

But the most difficult part of female education, is to give girls such an idea of chastity, as shall arm their reason and their sentiments on the side of this useful virtue. For I believe there are more women of understanding led into acts of imprudence by the ignorance, the prejudices, and the false craft of those by whom they are educated, than from any other cause founded either in nature or in chance. You may train up a docile idiot to any mode of thinking or acting, as may best suit the intended purpose; but a reasoning being will scan over your propositions, and if they find them grounded in falsehood, they will reject them with disdain. When you tell a girl of spirit and reflection that chastity is a sexual virtue,[1] and the want of it a sexual vice, she will be apt to examine into the principles of religion, morals, and the reason of things, in order to satisfy herself on the truth of your proposition. And when, after the strictest enquiries, she finds nothing that will warrant the confining the proposition to a particular sense, she will entertain doubts either of your wisdom or your sincerity; and regarding you either as a deceiver or a fool, she will transfer her confidence to the companion of the easy vacant hour, whose compliance with her opinions can flatter her vanity. Thus left to Nature, with an unfortunate biass on her mind, she will fall a victim to the first plausible being who has formed a design on her person. Rousseau[2] is so sensible of this truth, that he quarrels with human reason, and would put her out of the question in all considerations of duty. But this is being as great a fanatic in morals, as some are in religion; and I should much doubt the reality of that duty which

---

[1] I.e., a gender-specific virtue. Cf. Wollstonecraft, *A Vindication of the Rights of Woman* 386.*

[2] Jean-Jacques Rousseau (1712–78); cf. Wollstonecraft's attack in *A Vindication of the Rights of Woman** on Rousseau's opinions of women and how they should be educated.

would not stand the test of fair enquiry; beside, as I intend to breed my pupils up to act a rational part in the world, and not to fill up a niche in the seraglio of a sultan,[1] I shall certainly give them leave to use their reason in all matters which concern their duty and happiness, and shall spare no pains in the cultivation of this only sure guide to virtue. I shall inform them of the great utility of chastity and continence; that the one preserves the body in health and vigor, and the other, the purity and independence of the mind, without which it is impossible to possess virtue or happiness. I shall intimate, that the great difference now beheld in the external consequences which follow the deviations from chastity in the two sexes, did in all probability arise from women having been considered as the mere property of the men; and, on this account had no right to dispose of their own persons: that policy adopted this difference, when the plea of property had been given up; and it was still preserved in society from the unruly licentiousness of the men, who, finding no obstacles in the delicacy of the other sex, continue to set at defiance both divine and moral law, and by mutual support and general opinion to use their natural freedom with impunity. I shall observe, that this state of things renders the situation of females, in their individual capacity very precarious; for the strength which Nature has given to the passion of love, in order to serve her purposes, has made it the most ungovernal propensity of any which attends us. The snares therefore, that are continually laid for women, by persons who run no risk in compassing their seduction, exposes them to continual danger; whilst the implacability of their own sex, who fear to give up any advantages which a superior prudence, or even its appearances, give them, renders one false step an irretrievable misfortune. That, for these reasons, coquettry in women is as dangerous as it is dishonorable. That a coquet commonly finds her own perdition, in the very flames which she raises to consume others; and that if any thing can excuse the baseness of female seduction, it is the baits which are flung out by women to entangle the affections, and excite the passions of men.

I know not what you may think of my method, Hortensia, which I must acknowledge to carry the stamp of singularity; but for my part, I am sanguine enough to expect to turn out of my hands a careless, modest beauty, grave, manly, noble, full of strength and majesty; and carrying about her an ægis[2] sufficiently powerful to defend her against the sharpest arrow that ever was shot from Cupid's bow. A woman, whose virtue will not be of the kind to wrankle into an inveterate malignity against her own sex for faults which she even encourages in the men, but who, understanding the principles of true religion and morality, will regard chastity and truth as indispensible qualities in virtuous characters of either sex; whose justice will incline her to extend her benevolence to the frailties of the fair as circumstances invite, and to manifest her resentment against the underminers of female happiness; in short, a woman who will not take a male rake either for a husband or a friend. And let me tell you, Hortensia, if women had as much regard for the virtue of chastity as in some cases they pretend to have, a reformation would long since have taken place in the world; but whilst they continue to cherish immodesty in the men, their bitter persecution of their own sex will not save them from the imputation of those concealed propensities with which they are accused by Pope,[3] and other severe satirists on the sex.

---

[1] Cf. Wollstonecraft, *A Vindication of the Rights of Woman* 389.*

[2] the shield or breastplate of Athena.

[3] Pope satirized women in such poems as "Of the Characters of Women" (*Moral Essays* 2, 1735).

William Cowper
1731 – 1800

William Cowper was born in Berkhamsted, Hertfordshire, on 15 November 1731, the fourth (but first surviving) child of John Cowper, a clergyman, and Ann Donne Cowper, a descendant of Henry III and John Donne. He was educated at a series of local schools and then at Westminster. The death of his mother in 1737, after the birth of her seventh (but only the second surviving) child, and bullying at school may have contributed to the depression that plagued him throughout his life. In 1750, he went to study law in London, but though he was called to the bar in 1754, he was never interested in the profession. He experienced his first major depressive episode in 1753; the second, in 1763, was so severe that he attempted suicide and had to be hospitalized for two years in Nathaniel Cotton's Collegium Insanorum. As he recovered, he became a convert to Evangelicalism; unfortunately, his depression would later feed on his religious beliefs, inspiring the conviction that he was eternally damned. On his release he settled in the country, as the lodger of Morley and Mary Unwin; after the death of her husband, Mary became Cowper's life companion, a kind of second mother. They moved to Olney, Buckinghamshire, in 1767; there Cowper collaborated with John Newton, a former slave trader turned abolitionist and Evangelical curate, on his first book, *Olney Hymns* (1779), including Cowper's "God Moves in a Mysterious Way" and Newton's "Amazing Grace." Despite recurrent attacks of depression, Cowper finished his masterpiece, *The Task* (1785)—the first long autobiographical poem in English, and a significant influence on Coleridge* and W. Wordsworth*—and then dedicated himself to a translation of Homer (1791) and an (ultimately abortive) edition of Milton. He also wrote several propaganda songs for the Committee for the Abolition of the Slave Trade, despite finding the subject unbearably distressing. His last years make painful reading. Mary suffered a stroke in 1791 and died in 1796; for the next four years, Cowper heard voices, had terrible hallucinations, and felt the despair expressed in "The Cast-Away." He died on 25 April 1800. (D.L.M.)

❧❧

from *The Task, A Poem, in Six Books* (1785)

from BOOK 2
The Time-Piece

Oh for a lodge in some vast wilderness,
Some boundless contiguity of shade,
Where rumour of oppression and deceit,
Of unsuccessful or successful war
5   Might never reach me more. My ear is pain'd,
My soul is sick with ev'ry day's report
Of wrong and outrage with which earth is fill'd.
There is no flesh in man's obdurate heart,
It does not feel for man. The nat'ral bond
10 Of brotherhood is sever'd as the flax
That falls asunder at the touch of fire.
He finds his fellow guilty of a skin
Not colour'd like his own, and having pow'r
T' inforce the wrong, for such a worthy cause
15 Dooms and devotes him as his lawful prey.
Lands intersected by a narrow frith
Abhor each other. Mountains interposed,
Make enemies of nations who had else
Like kindred drops been mingled into one.
20 Thus man devotes his brother, and destroys;
And worse than all, and most to be deplored
As human nature's broadest, foulest blot,
Chains him, and tasks him, and exacts his sweat
With stripes, that mercy with a bleeding heart
25 Weeps when she sees inflicted on a beast.
Then what is man? And what man seeing this,
And having human feelings, does not blush
And hang his head, to think himself a man?
I would not have a slave to till my ground,
30 To carry me, to fan me while I sleep,
And tremble when I wake, for all the wealth

That sinews bought and sold have ever earn'd.
No: dear as freedom is, and in my heart's
Just estimation priz'd above all price,
35 I had much rather be myself the slave
And wear the bonds, than fasten them on him.
We have no slaves at home.—Then why abroad?
And they themselves once ferried o'er the wave
That parts us, are emancipate and loos'd.
40 Slaves cannot breathe in England; if their lungs
Receive our air, that moment they are free,
They touch our country and their shackles fall.[1]
That's noble, and bespeaks a nation proud
And jealous of the blessing. Spread it then,
45 And let it circulate through ev'ry vein
Of all your empire. That where Britain's power
Is felt, mankind may feel her mercy too.

from *The Works of William Cowper, Esq. comprising his Poems, Correspondence, and Translations*, ed. Robert Southey (1837)

The Negro's Complaint

Forced from home and all its pleasures,
    Afric's coast I left forlorn,
To increase the stranger's treasures,
    O'er the raging billows borne.
5 Men from England bought and sold me,
    Paid my price in paltry gold;
But, though slave they have enroll'd me,
    Minds are never to be sold.

Still in thought as free as ever,
10   What are England's rights, I ask,
Me from my delights to sever,
    Me to torture, me to task?
Fleecy locks and black complexion
    Cannot forfeit Nature's claim;
15 Skins may differ, but affection
    Dwells in white and black the same.

Why did all creating Nature
    Make the plant for which we toil?
Sighs must fan it, tears must water,
20   Sweat of ours must dress the soil.
Think, ye masters, iron-hearted,
    Lolling at your jovial boards,
Think how many backs have smarted
    For the sweets your cane affords.

25 Is there, as ye sometimes tell us,
    Is there One who reigns on high?
Has He bid you buy and sell us,
    Speaking from his throne, the sky?
Ask Him, if your knotted scourges,
30   Matches, blood-extorting screws,
Are the means that duty urges
    Agents of his will to use?

Hark! He answers!—Wild tornadoes
    Strewing yonder sea with wrecks,
35 Wasting towns, plantations, meadows,
    Are the voice with which he speaks.
He, foreseeing what vexations
    Afric's sons should undergo,
Fix'd their tyrants' habitations
40   Where his whirlwinds answer—No.

By our blood in Afric wasted,
    Ere our necks received the chain;
By the miseries that we tasted,
    Crossing in your barks the main;
45 By our sufferings, since ye brought us
    To the man-degrading mart,
All sustain'd by patience, taught us
    Only by a broken heart!

Deem our nation brutes no longer,
50   Till some reason ye shall find
Worthier of regard and stronger
    Than the colour of our kind.
Slaves of gold, whose sordid dealings
    Tarnish all your boasted powers,
55 Prove that you have human feelings
    Ere you proudly question ours!

---

[1] According to the Mansfield decision of 1772, a slave brought to England could not be compelled to return to the colonies. Like many abolitionists, Cowper assumes this meant they were actually free.

Sweet Meat Has Sour Sauce:
or,
The Slave-Trader in the Dumps

A trader I am to the African shore,
But since that my trading is like to be o'er,[1]
I'll sing you a song that you ne'er heard before,
    Which nobody can deny, deny,
    Which nobody can deny.

When I first heard the news it gave me a shock,
Much like what they call an electrical knock,
And now I am going to sell off my stock,
    Which nobody can deny.

'Tis a curious assortment of dainty regales,
To tickle the Negroes with when the ship sails,
Fine chains for the neck, and a cat with nine tails,[2]
    Which nobody can deny.

Here's supple-jack plenty, and store of rat-tan,[3]
That will wind itself round the sides of a man,
As close as a hoop round a bucket or can,
    Which nobody can deny.

Here's padlocks and bolts, and screws for the thumbs,
That squeeze them so lovingly till the blood comes;
They sweeten the temper like comfits or plums,
    Which nobody can deny.

When a Negro his head from his victuals withdraws,
And clenches his teeth and thrusts out his paws,
Here's a notable engine to open his jaws,
    Which nobody can deny.

Thus going to market, we kindly prepare
A pretty black cargo of African ware,
For what they must meet with when they get there,
    Which nobody can deny.

'Twould do your heart good to see 'em below
Lie flat on their backs all the way as we go,
Like sprats on a gridiron, scores in a row,[4]
    Which nobody can deny.

But ah! if in vain I have studied an art
So gainful to me, all boasting apart,
I think it will break my compassionate heart,
    Which nobody can deny.

For oh! how it enters my soul like an awl!
This pity, which some people self-pity call,
Is sure the most heart-piercing pity of all,
    Which nobody can deny.

So this is my song, as I told you before;
Come, buy off my stock, for I must no more
Carry Cæsars and Pompeys[5] to Sugar-cane shore,
    Which nobody can deny, deny,
    Which nobody can deny.

from *Life, and Posthumous Writings of William Cowper*, ed. William Hayley (1803)

Sonnet, to William Wilberforce, Esq.[6]

Thy country, Wilberforce, with just disdain,
Hears thee, by cruel men and impious, call'd
Fanatic, for thy zeal to loose th'enthrall'd
From exile, public sale, and slav'ry's chain.
Friend of the poor, the wrong'd, the fetter-gall'd,
Fear not lest labour such as thine be vain!
Thou hast achiev'd a part; hast gain'd the ear
Of Britain's Senate to thy glorious cause;

---

[1] In May 1788, Parliament passed a bill imposing some humane restrictions on the slave trade; traders and their parliamentary representatives argued that it would make the trade unprofitable.

[2] a cat-o'-nine-tails, a nine-lashed whip.

[3] Supple-jack, a kind of vine, was used to make whips or ropes for restraint; rattan, a kind of palm, was used to make canes, also good for whipping.

[4] See the diagram of a slave ship in Clarkson's *History*.*

[5] Slaves were regularly renamed, to help obliterate their African identities; often, they were given the names of classical heroes, in jest.

[6] Wilberforce (1759–1833) was the parliamentary leader of the abolition movement.

Hope smiles, joy springs, and though cold caution pause
And weave delay, the better hour is near,
That shall remunerate thy toils severe
By peace for Afric, fenc'd with British laws.
    Enjoy what thou hast won, esteem and love
From all the just on earth, and all the blest above!

The Cast-Away[1]

Obscurest night involv'd the sky;
    Th' Atlantic billows roar'd;
When such a destin'd wretch as I,
    Wash'd headlong from on board,
Of friends, of hope, of all bereft,
His floating home for ever left.

No braver chief could Albion boast
    Than he, with whom he went,
Nor ever ship left Albion's coast,
    With warmer wishes sent.
He lov'd them both, but both in vain,
Nor him beheld, nor her again.

Not long beneath the 'whelming brine,
    Expert to swim he lay;
Nor soon he felt his strength decline,
    Or courage die away;
But wag'd with death a lasting strife,
Supported by despair of life.

He shouted: nor his friends had fail'd
    To check the vessel's course,
But so the furious blast prevail'd,
    That, pitiless perforce,
They left their out-cast mate behind,
And scudded still before the wind.

Some succour yet they could afford:
    And, such as storms allow,
The cask, the coop, the floated cord
    Delay'd not to bestow.
But he (they knew) nor ship, nor shore,
Whate'er they gave should visit more.

Nor, cruel as it seem'd, could he,
    Their haste himself condemn,
Aware that flight, in such a sea,
    Alone could rescue them:
Yet bitter felt it still to die
Deserted, and his friends so nigh.

He long survives, who lives an hour
    In ocean, self-upheld:
And so long he, with unspent power,
    His destiny repell'd:
And ever, as the minutes flew,
Entreated help, or cry'd—"Adieu!"

At length, his transient respite past,
    His comrades, who before
Had heard his voice in ev'ry blast,
    Could catch the sound no more.
For then, by toil subdu'd, he drank
The stifling wave, and then he sank.

No poet wept him: but the page
    Of narrative sincere,
That tells his name, his worth, his age,
    Is wet with Anson's tear.
And tears by bards or heroes shed,
Alike immortalize the dead.

I therefore purpose not, or dream,
    Descanting on his fate,
To give the melancholy theme
    A more enduring date.
But misery still delights to trace
Its 'semblance in another's case.

No voice divine the storm allay'd,
    No light propitious shone;
When, snatch'd from all effectual aid,
    We perish'd, each alone;
But I beneath a rougher sea,
And whelm'd in deeper gulfs than he.

---

[1] The poem is based on an incident in *Voyage round the World* (1748), by Admiral George, Baron Anson (1697–1762), and his chaplain, Richard Walter.

Erasmus Darwin
1731 – 1802

Erasmus Darwin was born on 12 December 1731 in Elston, Nottinghamshire, the youngest son of a retired lawyer. He was educated at Chesterfield School, Cambridge University, and the Edinburgh Medical School, and established a successful medical practice at Lichfield, near Birmingham. He married twice, had one important extra-marital relationship in between, and fathered fourteen children. An inventor as well as a doctor, he created a speaking machine, a copying machine, a horizontal windmill, and new steering and shock-absorbing apparatus for carriages. He was also a member of the Birmingham Lunar Society, of which the other members included Josiah Wedgwood and James Watt, and which made an important intellectual contribution to the Industrial Revolution. In the 1780s, he translated the botanical works of Carolus Linnæus, the Swedish taxonomist, into English; this task inspired his first long poem, *The Botanic Garden* (1789–91). It was a bestseller and earned the praise of Coleridge,* Cowper,* and Walpole. Darwin went on to publish treatises on zoology, botany, and female education. He died of a heart attack on 18 April 1802, leaving another long poem, entitled *The Origin of Society*; his publisher changed the title to *The Temple of Nature*. Darwin's work was an important influence on Blake,* Coleridge,* Goethe, Keats,* M.W. Shelley,* P.B. Shelley,* W. Wordsworth,*—and on his grandson Charles, whose theory of evolution strongly resembles that outlined in *The Temple of Nature*. (D.L.M.)

❧❧❧

from *The Temple of Nature; or, The Origin of Society: A Poem. With Philosophical Notes* (1803)

from CANTO 4
Of Good and Evil

"The wolf, escorted by his milk-drawn dam,[1]
Unknown to mercy, tears the guiltless lamb;
The towering eagle,[2] darting from above,
20 Unfeeling rends the inoffensive dove;
The lamb and dove on living nature feed,
Crop the young herb, or crush the embryon seed.
Nor spares the loud owl in her dusky flight,
Smit with sweet notes, the minstrel of the night;
25 Nor spares, enamour'd of his radiant form,
The hungry nightingale the glowing worm;
Who with bright lamp alarms the midnight hour,
Climbs the green stem, and slays the sleeping flower.
"Fell Oestrus buries[3] in her rapid course
30 Her countless brood in stag, or bull, or horse;
Whose hungry larva eats its living way,
Hatch'd by the warmth, and issues into day.
The wing'd Ichneumon[4] for her embryon young

---

[1] The speaker is the Muse.

[2] "Torva leæna lupum sequitur, lupus ipse capellam, / Florentem cytisum sequitur lasciva capella. Virg." (E.D.) "The grim lioness follows the wolf, the wolf himself the goat, the wanton goat the flowering clover" (Virgil, *Eclogues* 2.63–64, tr. H. Rushton Fairclough). In the original, these are all similes for male-male desire.

[3] "The gadfly, bot-fly, or sheep-fly: the larva lives in the bodies of cattle throughout the whole winter; it is extracted from their backs by an African bird called Buphaga. Adhering to the anus it artfully introduces itself into the intestines of horses, and becomes so numerous in their stomachs, as sometimes to destroy them; it climbs into the nostrils of sheep and calves, and producing a nest of young in a transparent hydatide in the frontal sinus, occasions the vertigo or turn of those animals. In Lapland it so attacks the rein deer that the natives annually travel with the herds from the woods to the mountains. Lin. Syst. Nat." (E.D.) Carolus Linnæus (1707–78), *Systema Naturæ* (1735), the foundation of the modern taxonomy of animals, vegetables, and minerals. Darwin's first epic, *The Botanic Garden* (1789–91), is an exposition and celebration of Linnæus.

[4] "Linneus describes seventy-seven species of the ichneumon fly, some of which have a sting as long and some twice as long as their bodies. Many of them insert their eggs into various caterpillars, which when they are hatched seem for a time to prey on the reservoir of silk in the backs of those animals designed for their own use to   (Continued)

Gores with sharp horn the caterpillar throng.
The cruel larva mines its silky course,
And tears the vitals of its fostering nurse.
While fierce Libellula[1] with jaws of steel
Ingulfs an insect-province at a meal;
Contending bee-swarms[2] rise on rustling wings,
And slay their thousands with envenom'd stings.

   "Yes! smiling Flora[3] drives her armed car
Through the thick ranks of vegetable war;
Herb, shrub, and tree, with strong emotions rise
For light and air, and battle in the skies;
Whose roots diverging with opposing toil
Contend below for moisture and for soil;
Round the tall Elm the flattering Ivies bend,
And strangle, as they clasp, their struggling friend;
Envenom'd dews from Mancinella[4] flow,
And scald with caustic touch the tribes below;
Dense shadowy leaves on stems aspiring borne
With blight and mildew thin the realms of corn;
And insect hordes with restless tooth devour
The unfolded bud, and pierce the ravell'd flower.

"In ocean's pearly haunts, the waves beneath
Sits the grim monarch of insatiate Death;
The shark rapacious[5] with descending blow
Darts on the scaly brood, that swims below;
The crawling crocodiles,[6] beneath that move,
Arrest with rising jaw the tribes above;
With monstrous gape sepulchral whales devour
Shoals at a gulp, a million in an hour.
—Air, earth, and ocean, to astonish'd day
One scene of blood, one mighty tomb display!
From Hunger's arm the shafts of Death are hurl'd,
And one great Slaughter-house[7] the warring world!["]

---

spin a cord to support them, or a bag to contain them, while they change from their larva form to a butterfly; as I have seen in above fifty cabbage-caterpillars. The ichneumon larva then makes its way out of the caterpillar, and spins itself a small cocoon like a silk worm; these cocoons are about the size of a small pin's head, and I have seen about ten of them on each cabbage caterpillar, which soon dies after their exclusion.

   "Other species of ichneumon insert their eggs into the aphis, and into the larva of the aphidivorous fly: others into the bedeguar of rose trees, and the gall-nuts of oaks; whence those excrescences seem to be produced, as well as the hydatides in the frontal sinus of sheep and calves by the stimulus of the larvæ deposited in them." (E.D.)

[1] "The Libellula or Dragon-fly is said to be a most voracious animal; Linneus says in their perfect state they are the hawks to naked winged flies; in their larva state they run beneath the water, and are the cruel crocodiles of aquatic insects. Syst. Nat." (E.D.)

[2] "Stronger bee-swarms frequently attack weak hives, and in two or three days destroy them and carry away their honey; this I once prevented by removing the attacked hive after the first day's battle to a distinct part of the garden. See Phytologia, Sect. XIV. 3. 7." (E.D.) Darwin, *Phytologia; or, The Philosophy of Agriculture and Gardening* (1800).

[3] classical goddess of vegetation.

[4] the manchineel, a West-Indian tree with caustic, poisonous sap.

[5] "The shark has three rows of sharp teeth within each other, which he can bend downwards internally to admit larger prey, and raise to prevent its return; his snout hangs so far over his mouth, that he is necessitated to turn upon his back, when he takes fish that swim over him, and hence seems peculiarly formed to catch those that swim under him." (E.D.)

[6] "As this animal lives chiefly at the bottom of the rivers, which he frequents, he has the power of opening the upper jaw as well as the under one, and thus with greater facility catches the fish or water-fowl which swim over him." (E.D.)

[7] "As vegetables are an inferior order of animals fixed to the soil; and as the locomotive animals prey upon them, or upon each other; the world may indeed be said to be one great slaughter-house. As the digested food of vegetables consists principally of sugar, and from this is produced again their mucilage, starch, and oil, and since animals are sustained by these vegetable productions, it would seem that the sugar-making process carried on in vegetable vessels was the great source of life to all organized beings. And that if our improved chemistry should ever discover the art of making sugar from fossile or aerial matter without the assistance of vegetation, food for animals would then become as plentiful as water, and they might live upon the earth without preying on each other, as thick as blades of grass, with no restraint to their numbers but the want of local room.

   "It would seem that roots fixed in the earth and leaves innumerable waving in the air were necessary for the decomposition of water and air, and the conversion of them into saccharine matter, which would have been not only cumberous but totally incompatible with the locomotion of animal bodies. For how could a man or quadruped have carried on his head or back a forest of leaves, or have had long branching lacteal or absorbent vessels terminating in the earth? Animals therefore subsist on vegetables; that is they take the matter so prepared, and have organs to prepare it further for the purposes of higher animation and greater sensibility." (E.D.)

John Adams
1734 – 1826
Abigail Adams
1744 – 1818

John Adams was born on 30 October 1734, in Braintree, Massachusetts, the son of John Adams, a farmer, and Susanna Boylston Adams, a direct descendant of the Plymouth Rock pilgrims. He was educated at home and at local schools. In 1751, he entered Harvard College, where he graduated in 1755. Between 1756 and 1758 he taught school and studied law. In October 1764, he married Abigail Smith, the home-educated, nineteen-year-old daughter of a Congregational minister. They had five children, one of whom, John Quincy, would follow his father as President. John became politically active after the imposition of the Stamp Act (1765), and in August 1774, he was chosen as one of the Massachusetts representatives to the Continental Congress in Philadelphia. He later drafted the Massachusetts constitution and served as a diplomat in France, Holland, and Britain. During his absences, Abigail managed their farm in Braintree, raised their children, and wrote to him. She joined him in Britain in 1784, thus bringing their correspondence to an end. In 1789, John was elected the first Vice-President and in 1797 the second President of the United States. His published works include *Thoughts on Government* (1776) and *A Defence of the Constitutions of Government of the United States of America* (1787–88). Abigail died on 28 October 1818 and John (like Jefferson*) on 4 July 1826—the fiftieth anniversary of the Declaration of Independence. (D.L.M.)

❧❧❧

Letters

Abigail Adams to John Adams

Braintree March 31, 1776[1]

I wish you would ever write me a Letter half as long as I write you; and tell me if you may where your Fleet are gone? What sort of Defence Virginia can make against our common Enemy?[2] Whether it is so situated as to make an able Defence? Are not the Gentery Lords and the common people vassals, are they not like the uncivilized Natives Brittain represents us to be? I hope their Riffel Men who have shewen themselves very savage and even Blood thirsty; are not a specimen of the Generality of the people.

I [illegible] am willing to allow the Colony great merrit for having produced a Washington but they have been shamefully duped by a Dunmore.[3]

I have sometimes been ready to think that the passion for Liberty cannot be Eaqually Strong in the Breasts of those who have been accustomed to deprive their fellow Creatures of theirs. Of this I am certain that it is not founded upon that generous and christian principal of doing to others as we would that others should do unto us. Do not you want to see Boston; I am fearfull of the small pox,[4] or I should have been in

---

[1] text from the Adams Electronic Archive, <http://www.masshist.org/digitaladams/aea/letter/>.

[2] The British burned Norfolk in January 1776, but they did not attempt a full-scale invasion of Virginia until 1779.

[3] George Washington (1732–99), Commander-in-Chief of the Continental Army and later first President, was a Virginian; John Murray, 4th Earl Dunmore (1732–1809), the colonial governor of Virginia, took vigorous action against the Revolution until he had to return to Britain in July 1776.

[4] Washington besieged Boston in July 1775; the British evacuated it on 17 March 1776, so it was only recently possible for Abigail to visit it. The smallpox epidemic of 1775–82 first broke out in Boston. It ravaged both the British and the Continental armies (Washington's decision to have his troops inoculated is said to have contributed to his final victory) and decimated the Native Americans.

before this time. I got Mr. Crane to go to our House and see what state it was in. I find it has been occupied by one of the Doctors of a Regiment, very dirty, but no other damage has been done to it. The few things which were left in it are all gone. Cranch has the key which he never deliverd up. I have wrote to him for it and am determined to get it cleand as soon as possible and shut it up. I look upon it a new acquisition of property, a property which one month ago I did not value at a single Shilling, and could with pleasure have seen it in flames.

The Town in General is left in a better state than we expected, more oweing to a percipitate flight than any Regard to the inhabitants, tho some individuals discoverd a sense of honour and justice and have left the rent of the Houses in which they were, for the owners and the furniture unhurt, or if damaged sufficent to make it good.

Others have committed abominable Ravages. The Mansion House of your President is safe and the furniture unhurt whilst both the House and Furniture of the Solisiter General have fallen a prey to their own merciless party.[1] Surely the very Fiends feel a Reverential awe for Virtue and patriotism, whilst they Detest the paricide and traitor.

I feel very differently at the approach of spring to what I did a month ago. We knew not then whether we could plant or sow with safety, whether when we had toild we could reap the fruits of our own industry, whether we could rest in our own Cottages, or whether we should not be driven from the sea coasts to seek shelter in the wilderness, but now we feel as if we might sit under our own vine and eat the good of the land.

I feel a gaieti de Coar[2] to which before I was a stranger. I think the Sun looks brighter, the Birds sing more melodiously, and Nature puts on a more chearfull countanance. We feel a temporary peace, and the poor fugitives are returning to their deserted habitations.

Tho we felicitate ourselves, we sympathize with those who are trembling least the Lot of Boston should be theirs. But they cannot be in similar circumstances unless pusilanimity and cowardise should take possession of them. They have time and warning given them to see the Evil and shun it.—I long to hear that you have declared an independency [3]—and by the way in the new Code of Laws which I suppose it will be necessary for you to make I desire you would Remember the Ladies, and be more generous and favourable to them than your ancestors. Do not put such unlimited power into the hands of the Husbands. Remember all Men would be tyrants if they could. If perticuliar care and attention is not paid to the Laidies we are determined to foment a Rebelion, and will not hold ourselves bound by any Laws in which we have no voice, or Representation.

That your Sex are Naturally Tyrannical is a Truth so thoroughly established as to admit of no dispute, but such of you as wish to be happy willingly give up the harsh title of Master for the more tender and endearing one of Friend. Why then, not put it out of the power of the vicious and the Lawless to use us with cruelty and indignity with impunity. Men of Sense in all Ages abhor those customs which treat us only as the vassals of your Sex. Regard us then as Beings placed by providence under your protection and in immitation of the Supreem Being make use of that power only for our happiness.

John Adams to Abigail Adams

Ap. 14, 1776

You justly complain of my short Letters, but the critical State of Things and the Multiplicity of Avocations must plead my Excuse. You ask where the Fleet is. The inclosed Papers will inform you. You ask what Sort of Defence Virginia can make. I believe they will make an able Defence. Their Militia and minute Men have been some time employed in training them selves, and they have Nine Battallions of regulars as they call them, maintained among them, under good Officers, at the Continental Expence. They have set up a Number of Manufactories of Fire Arms, which are busily employed. They are tolerably supplied with Powder, and are

---

[1] John Hancock (1737–93), president of the second Continental Congress, was a Bostonian. Samuel Quincy (1735–89), Solicitor General of Massachusetts, was a British Loyalist.

[2] "*gaieté de Coeur*," "happiness of heart" (Fr.).

[3] The Continental Congress approved the Declaration of Independence* on 4 July 1776.

successfull and assiduous, in making Salt Petre.[1] Their neighbouring Sister or rather Daughter Colony of North Carolina, which is a warlike Colony, and has several Battallions at the Continental Expence, as well as a pretty good Militia, are ready to assist them, and they are in very good Spirits, and seem determined to make a brave Resistance.—The Gentry are very rich, and the common People very poor. This Inequality of Property, gives an Aristocratical Turn to all their Proceedings, and occasions a strong Aversion in their Patricians, to Common Sense.[2] But the Spirit of these Barons, is coming down, and it must submit.

It is very true, as you observe they have been duped by Dunmore. But this is a Common Case. All the Colonies are duped, more or less, at one Time and another. A more egregious Bubble was never blown up, than the Story of Commissioners coming to treat with the Congress. Yet it has gained Credit like a Charm, not only without but against the clearest Evidence. I never shall forget the Delusion, which seized our best and most sagacious Friends the dear Inhabitants of Boston, the Winter before last. Credulity and the Want of Foresight, are Imperfections in the human Character, that no Politician can sufficiently guard against.

You have given me some Pleasure, by your Account of a certain House in Queen Street. I had burned it, long ago, in Imagination. It rises now to my View like a Phoenix.—What shall I say of the Solicitor General? I pity his pretty Children, I pity his Father, and his sisters. I wish I could be clear that it is no moral Evil to pity him and his Lady. Upon Repentance they will certainly have a large Share in the Compassions of many. But [illegible] let Us take Warning and give it to our Children. Whenever Vanity, and Gaiety, a Love of Pomp and Dress, Furniture, Equipage, Buildings, great Company, expensive Diversions, and elegant Entertainments get the better of the Principles and Judgments of Men or Women there is no knowing where they will stop, nor into what Evils, natural, moral, or political, they will lead us.

Your Description of your own Gaiety de Coeur, charms me. Thanks be to God you have just Cause to rejoice—and may the bright Prospect be obscured by no Cloud.

As to Declarations of Independency, be patient. Read our Privateering Laws, and our Commercial Laws.[3] What signifies a Word.

As to your extraordinary Code of Laws, I cannot but laugh. We have been told that our Struggle has loosened the bands of Government every where. That Children and Apprentices were disobedient—that schools and Colledges were grown turbulent—that Indians slighted their Guardians and Negroes grew insolent to their Masters. But your Letter was the first Intimation that another Tribe more numerous and powerfull than all the rest were grown discontented.—This is rather too coarse a Compliment but you are so saucy, I wont blot it out.

Depend upon it, We know better than to repeal our Masculine systems. Altho they are in full Force, you know they are little more than Theory. We dare not exert our Power in its full Latitude. We are obliged to go fair, and softly, and in Practice you know We are the subjects. We have only the Name of Masters, and rather than give up this, which would compleatly subject Us to the Despotism of the Peticoat, I hope General Washington, and all our brave Heroes would fight. I am sure every good Politician would plot, as long as he would against Despotism, Empire, Monarchy, Aristocracy, Oligarchy, or Ochlocracy.—A fine Story indeed. I begin to think the Ministry[4] as deep as they are wicked. After stirring up Tories, Landjobbers, Trimmers, Bigots, Canadians, Indians, Negroes, Hanoverians, Hessians, Russians, Irish Roman Catholicks, Scotch Renegadoes, at last they have stimulated the [word missing] to demand new Priviledges and threaten to rebell.

---

[1] potassium nitrate, the principal ingredient of gunpowder.

[2] the Revolutionary pamphlet (January 1776) by Thomas Paine.*

[3] The Continental Congress authorized privateers—privately owned warships—to capture British ships for profit. It also defied the British mercantilist trade policy, which strictly regulated imports and exports.

[4] the government of George III. Following is a list of his supporters and mercenaries: landjobbers were proprietors of pocket boroughs, parliamentary constituencies that were bought and sold rather than won in elections; trimmers were people who changed their political convictions as their personal interests dictated; George III was a descendant of the House of Hanover; the principality of Hesse (also in Germany) was a notorious source of mercenaries.

J. Hector St. John de Crèvecoeur
1735 – 1813

Michel Guillaume Jean de Crèvecoeur was born in Caen, Normandy, on 31 January 1735, the son of a minor aristocrat and a banker's daughter. He was educated at Caen's Jesuit college. When he was nineteen, he went first to England and then to Lower Canada, where he worked as a surveyor and cartographer. In 1758, he joined the French army; he was wounded at the battle of the Plains of Abraham in 1759. Shortly afterwards, he went to live in New York; he became a citizen of the colony in 1765. He married Mehitable Tippet in 1769; they had three children. He bought some land in Orange County and farmed it until 1780, when, because his neutrality during the Revolutionary War had brought him trouble from both sides (he was briefly imprisoned by the British), he returned to Europe, taking with him his older son and leaving his wife to look after the farm and the other two children. When he arrived in England, he arranged for the publication of *Letters from an American Farmer*, the first American novel, under the pseudonym J. Hector St. John; he is now, confusingly, known by a combination of his two names. After two years in France, Crèvecoeur returned to the United States as consul to Connecticut, New Jersey, and New York. His wife was dead, his farm had been destroyed by fire, and his two children had vanished; he later found them in Boston. He served as consul until 1790 and then returned to France. He died at his daughter's home in Sarcelles on 12 November 1813. (D.L.M.)

❧❧❧

from *Letters from an American Farmer* (1782)

from LETTER 12
Distresses of a Frontier Man[1]

Must I then bid farewell to Britain, to that renowned country? Must I renounce a name so ancient and so venerable? Alas, she herself, that once indulgent parent, forces me to take up arms against her. She herself, first inspired the most unhappy citizens of our remote districts, with the thoughts of shedding the blood of those whom they used to call by the name of friends and brethren. That great nation which now convulses the world; which hardly knows the extent of her Indian kingdoms; which looks toward the universal monarchy of trade, of industry, of riches, of power: why must she strew our poor frontiers with the carcasses of her friends, with the wrecks of our insignificant villages, in which there is no gold? When, oppressed by painful recollection, I revolve all these scattered ideas in my mind; when I contemplate my situation, and the thousand streams of evil with which I am surrounded; when I descend into the particular tendency even of the remedy I have proposed, I am convulsed—convulsed sometimes to that degree, as to be tempted to exclaim— Why has the master of the world permitted so much indiscriminate evil throughout every part of this poor planet, at all times, and among all kinds of people? It ought surely to be the punishment of the wicked only. I bring that cup to my lips, of which I must soon taste, and shudder at its bitterness.[2] What then is life, I ask myself, is it a gracious gift? No, it is too bitter; a gift means something valuable conferred, but life appears to be a mere accident, and of the worst kind: we are born to be victims of diseases and passions, of mischances and death: better not to be than to be miserable.—Thus impiously I roam, I fly from one erratic thought to another, and my mind, irritated by these acrimonious reflections, is ready sometimes to lead me to dangerous extremes of violence. When I recollect that I am a father, and a husband, the return of these endearing ideas strikes deep into my heart. Alas! they once made it to glow with pleasure and with every ravishing exultation; but now they fill it with sorrow. At other times, my wife industriously rouses me out of these dreadful meditations, and soothes me by all the reasoning she is mistress of; but her endeavours only serve to make me more miserable, by reflecting that she

---

[1] The opening of the letter describes the distresses the Farmer has suffered during the Revolutionary War.

[2] Cf. Matthew 26.39, Mark 14.36, Luke 22.42.

must share with me all these calamities, the bare apprehensions of which I am afraid will subvert her reason. Nor can I with patience think that a beloved wife, my faithful help-mate throughout all my rural schemes, the principal hand which has assisted me in rearing the prosperous fabric of ease and independence I lately possessed, as well as my children, those tenants of my heart, should daily and nightly be exposed to such a cruel fate. Self-preservation is above all political precepts and rules, and even superior to the dearest opinions of our minds; a reasonable accommodation of ourselves to the various exigencies of the times in which we live, is the most irresistible precept. To this great evil I must seek some sort of remedy adapted to remove or to palliate it; situated as I am, what steps should I take that will neither injure nor insult any of the parties, and at the same time save my family from that certain destruction which awaits it, if I remain here much longer. Could I insure them bread, safety, and subsistence, not the bread of idleness, but that earned by proper labour as heretofore; could this be accomplished by the sacrifice of my life, I would willingly give it up. I attest before heaven, that it is only for these I would wish to live and to toil: for these whom I have brought into this miserable existence. I resemble, methinks, one of the stones of a ruined arch, still retaining that pristine form which anciently fitted the place I occupied, but the centre is tumbled down; I can be nothing until I am replaced, either in the former circle, or in some stronger one. I see one on a smaller scale, and at a considerable distance, but it is within my power to reach it: and since I have ceased to consider myself as a member of the ancient state now convulsed, I willingly descend into an inferior one. I will revert into a state approaching nearer to that of nature, unincumbered either with voluminous laws, or contradictory codes, often galling the very necks, of those whom they protect; and at the same time sufficiently remote from the brutality of unconnected savage nature. Do you, my friend, perceive the path I have found out? it is that which leads to the tenants of the great —— village of ——,[1] where, far removed from the accursed neighbourhood of Europeans, its inhabitants live with more ease, decency, and peace, than you imagine: where, though governed by no laws, yet find, in uncontaminated simple manners all that laws can afford. Their system is sufficiently compleat to answer all the primary wants of man, and to constitute him a social being, such as he ought to be in the great forest of nature. There it is that I have resolved at any rate to transport myself and family: an eccentric thought, you may say, thus to cut asunder all former connections, and to form new ones with a people whom nature has stamped with such different characteristics! But as the happiness of my family is the only object of my wishes, I care very little where we be, or where we go, provided that we are safe, and all united together. Our new calamities being shared equally by all, will become lighter; our mutual affection for each other, will in this great transmutation become the strongest link of our new society, will afford us every joy we can receive on a foreign soil, and preserve us in unity, as the gravity and coherency of matter prevents the world from dissolution. Blame me not, it would be cruel in you, it would beside be entirely useless; for when you receive this we shall be on the wing. When we think all hopes are gone, must we, like poor pusillanimous wretches, despair and die? No; I perceive before me a few resources, though through many dangers, which I will explain to you hereafter. It is not, believe me, a disappointed ambition which leads me to take this step, it is the bitterness of my situation, it is the impossibility of knowing what better measure to adopt: my education fitted me for nothing more than the most simple occupations of life; I am but a feller of trees, a cultivator of land, the most honourable title an American can have. I have no exploits, no discoveries, no inventions to boast of; I have cleared about 370 acres of land, some for the plough, some for the scythe; and this has occupied many years of my life. I have never possessed, or wish to possess any thing more than what could be earned or produced by the united industry of my family. I wanted nothing more than to live at home independent and tranquil, and to teach my children how to provide the means of a future ample subsistence, founded on labour, like that of their father. This is the career of life I have pursued,

---

[1] The Farmer does not reveal which First Nation he plans to join, but the narrator of one of Crèvecoeur's later books has been adopted by the Oneida.

and that which I had marked out for them and for which they seemed to be so well calculated by their inclinations, and by their constitutions. But now these pleasing expectations are gone, we must abandon the accumulated industry of nineteen years, we must fly we hardly know whither, through the most impervious paths, and become members of a new and strange community. Oh, virtue! is this all the reward thou hast to confer on thy votaries?[1] Either thou art only a chimera, or thou art a timid useless being; soon affrighted, when ambition, thy great adversary, dictates, when war re-echoes the dreadful sounds, and poor helpless individuals are mowed down by its cruel reapers like useless grass. I have at all times generously relieved what few distressed people I have met with; I have encouraged the industrious; my house has always been opened to travellers; I have not lost a month in illness since I have been a man; I have caused upwards of an hundred and twenty families to remove hither. Many of them I have led by the hand in the days of their first trial; distant as I am from any places of worship or school of education, I have been the pastor of my family, and the teacher of many of my neighbours. I have learnt them as well as I could, the gratitude they owe to God, the father of harvests; and their duties to man: I have been as useful a subject; ever obedient to the laws, ever vigilant to see them respected and observed. My wife hath faithfully followed the same line within her province; no woman was ever a better œconomist, or spun or wove better linen; yet we must perish, perish like wild beasts, included within a ring of fire!

Yes, I will chearfully embrace that resource, it is an holy inspiration: by night and by day, it presents itself to my mind: I have carefully revolved the scheme; I have considered in all its future effects and tendencies, the new mode of living we must pursue, without salt, without spices, without linen and with little other cloathing; the art of hunting, we must acquire, the new manners we must adopt, the new language we must speak; the dangers attending the education of my children we must endure. These changes may appear more terrific at a distance perhaps than when grown familiar by practice: what is it to us, whether we eat well made pastry, or pounded àlagrichés; well roasted beef, or smoked venison; cabbages, or squashes? Whether we wear neat home-spun, or good beaver; whether we sleep on featherbeds, or on bear-skins? The difference is not worth attending to. The difficulty of the language, the fear of some great intoxication among the Indians; finally, the apprehension lest my younger children should be caught by that singular charm, so dangerous at their tender years; are the only considerations that startle me. By what power does it come to pass, that children who have been adopted when young among these people, can never be prevailed on to re-adopt European manners? Many an anxious parent have I seen last war,[2] who at the return of the peace, went to the Indian villages where they knew their children had been carried in captivity; when to their inexpressible sorrow, they found them so perfectly Indianised, that many knew them no longer, and those whose more advanced ages permitted them to recollect their fathers and mothers, absolutely refused to follow them, and ran to their adoptive parents for protection against the effusions of love their unhappy real parents lavished on them! Incredible as this may appear, I have heard it asserted in a thousand instances, among persons of credit. In the village of——, where I purpose to go, there lived, about fifteen years ago, an Englishman and a Swede, whose history would appear moving, had I time to relate it. They were grown to the age of men when they were taken; they happily escaped the great punishment of war captives, and were obliged to marry the *Squaws* who had saved their lives by adoption. By the force of habit, they became at last thoroughly naturalised to this wild course of life. While I was there, their friends sent them a considerable sum of money to ransom themselves with. The Indians, their old masters, gave them their choice, and without requiring any consideration, told them, that they had been long as free as themselves. They chose to remain; and the reasons they gave me would greatly surprise you: the most perfect freedom, the ease of living, the absence of those

---

[1] Cf. the despairing exclamation of Marcus Junius Brutus (85?–42 BC), the assassin of Julius Cæsar: "O virtue, thou art but an empty name!"

[2] the Seven Years' War (1756–63), in which Crèvecoeur had served.

cares and corroding solicitudes which so often prevail with us; the peculiar goodness of the soil they cultivated, for they did not trust altogether to hunting; all these, and many more motives, which I have forgot, made them prefer that life, of which we entertain such dreadful opinions. It cannot be, therefore, so bad as we generally conceive it to be; there must be in their social bond something singularly captivating, and far superior to any thing to be boasted of among us; for thousands of Europeans are Indians, and we have no examples of even one of those Aborigines having from choice become Europeans! There must be something more congenial to our native dispositions, than the fictitious society in which we live; or else why should children, and even grown persons, become in a short time so invincibly attached to it? There must be something very bewitching in their manners, something very indelible and marked by the very hands of nature. For, take a young Indian lad, give him the best education you possibly can, load him with your bounty, with presents, nay with riches; yet he will secretly long for his native woods, which you would imagine he must have long since forgot; and on the first opportunity he can possibly find, you will see him voluntarily leave behind him all you have given him, and return with inexpressible joy to lie on the mats of his fathers. Mr.——, some years ago, received from a good old Indian, who died in his house, a young lad, of nine years of age, his grandson. He kindly educated him with his children, and bestowed on him the same care and attention in respect to the memory of his venerable grandfather, who was a worthy man. He intended to give him a genteel trade, but in the spring season when all the family went to the woods to make their maple sugar, he suddenly disappeared; and it was not until seventeen months after, that his benefactor heard he had reached the village of Bald Eagle,[1] where he still dwelt. Let us say what we will of them, of their inferior organs, of their want of bread, &c. they are as stout and well made as the Europeans. Without temples, without priests, without kings, and without laws, they are in many instances superior to us; and the proofs of what I advance, are, that they live without care, sleep without inquietude, take life as it comes, bearing all its asperities with unparalleled patience, and die without any kind of apprehension for what they have done, or for what they expect to meet with hereafter. What system of philosophy can give us so many necessary qualifications for happiness? They most certainly are much more closely connected with nature than we are; they are her immediate children, the inhabitants of the woods are her undefiled offspring: those of the plains are her degenerated breed, far, very far removed from her primitive laws, from her original design. It is therefore resolved on. I will either die in the attempt or succeed; better perish all together in one fatal hour, than to suffer what we daily endure. I do not expect to enjoy in the village of ——, an uninterrupted happiness; it cannot be our lot, let us live where we will; I am not founding my future prosperity on golden dreams. Place mankind where you will, they must always have adverse circumstances to struggle with; from nature, accidents, constitution; from seasons, from that great combination of mischances which perpetually lead us to diseases, to poverty, &c. Who knows but I may meet in this new situation, some accident from whence may spring up new sources of unexpected prosperity? Who can be presumptuous enough to predict all the good? Who can foresee all the evils, which strew the paths of our lives? But after all, I cannot but recollect what sacrifice I am going to make, what amputation I am going to suffer, what transition I am going to experience. Pardon my repetitions, my wild, my trifling reflections, they proceed from the agitations of my mind, and the fulness of my heart; the action of thus retracing them seems to lighten the burthen, and to exhilarate my spirits; this is besides the last letter you will receive from me; I would fain tell you all, though I hardly know how. Oh! in the hours, in the moments of my greatest anguish, could I intuitively represent to you that variety of thought which crouds on my mind, you would have reason to be surprised, and to doubt of their possibility. Shall we ever meet again? If we should, where will it be? On the wild shores of ——. If it be my doom to end my days there, I will greatly improve them; and perhaps make room for a few more families, who will choose to retire from the fury of a storm, the

---

[1] evidently a fictional chief.

agitated billows of which will yet roar for many years on our extended shores. Perhaps I may repossess my house, if it be not burnt down; but how will my improvements look? why half defaced, bearing the strong marks of abandonment, and of the ravages of war. However, at present I give every thing over for lost; I will bid a long farewell to what I leave behind. If ever I repossess it, I shall receive it as a gift, as a reward for my conduct and fortitude. Do not imagine, however, that I am a stoic—by no means: I must, on the contrary, confess to you, that I feel the keenest regret, at abandoning an house which I have in some measure reared with my own hands. Yes, perhaps I may never revisit those fields which I have cleared, those trees which I have planted, those meadows which, in my youth, were a hideous wilderness, now converted by my industry into rich pastures and pleasant lawns. If in Europe it is praiseworthy to be attached to paternal inheritances, how much more natural, how much more powerful must the tie be with us, who, if I may be permitted the expression, are the founders, the creators of our own farms! When I see my table surrounded with my blooming offspring, all united in the bonds of the strongest affection, it kindles in my paternal heart a variety of tumultuous sentiments, which none but a father and a husband in my situation can feel or describe. Perhaps I may see my wife, my children, often distressed, involuntarily recalling to their minds the ease and abundance which they enjoyed under the paternal roof. Perhaps I may see them want that bread which I now leave behind; overtaken by diseases and penury, rendered more bitter by the recollection of former days of opulence and plenty. Perhaps I may be assailed on every side by unforseen accidents, which I shall not be able to prevent or to alleviate. Can I contemplate such images without the most unutterable emotions? My fate is determined; but I have not determined it, you may assure yourself, without having undergone the most painful conflicts of a variety of passions;—interest, love of ease, disappointed views, and pleasing expectations frustrated;—I shuddered at the review! Would to God I was master of the stoical tranquillity of that magnanimous sect; oh, that I were possessed of those sublime lessons which Apollonius of Chalcis gave to the Emperor Antoninus![1] I could then with much more propriety guide the helm of my little bark, which is soon to be freighted with all that I possess most dear on earth, through this stormy passage to a safe harbour; and when there, become to my fellow passengers, a surer guide, a brighter example, a pattern more worthy of imitation, throughout all the new scenes they must pass, and the new career they must traverse. I have observed notwithstanding, the means, hitherto made use of, to arm the principal nations against our frontiers: Yet they have not, they will not take up the hatchet against a people who have done them no harm. The passions necessary to urge these people to war, cannot be roused, they cannot feel the stings of vengeance, the thirst of which alone can impel them to shed blood: far superior in their motives of action to the Europeans, who for sixpence per day, may be engaged to shed that of any people on earth. They know nothing of the nature of our disputes, they have no ideas of such revolutions as this; a civil division of a village or tribe, are events which have never been recorded in their traditions: many of them know very well that they have too long been the dupes and the victims of both parties; foolishly arming for our sakes, sometimes against each other, sometimes against our white enemies. They consider us as born on the same land, and, though they have no reasons to love us, yet they seem carefully to avoid entering into this quarrel, from whatever motives. I am speaking of those nations with which I am best acquainted, a few hundreds of the worst kind mixed with whites, worse than themselves, are now hired by Great Britain, to perpetrate those dreadful incursions. In my youth I traded with the ——, under the conduct of my uncle, and always traded justly and equitably; some of them remember it to this day. Happily their village is far removed from the dangerous neighbourhood of the whites; I sent a man, last spring to it, who understands the woods extremely well, and who speaks their language; he is just returned, after several weeks absence, and has brought me, as I had

---

[1] Crèvecoeur may be thinking of Apollonius of Tyana (fl. AD 100), a Pythagorean (Chalcis is another Greek city), and of the Emperor Marcus Aurelius (AD 121–80), a Stoic, the successor of Antoninus Pius (AD 86–161).

flattered myself, a string of thirty purple wampum,[1] as a token that their honest chief will spare us half of his wigwham until we have time to erect one. He has sent me word that they have land in plenty, of which they are not so covetous as the whites; that we may plant for ourselves, and that in the mean time he will procure us some corn and some meat; that fish is plenty in the waters of ——, and that the village to which he had laid open my proposals, have no objection to our becoming dwellers with them. I have not yet communicated these glad tidings to my wife, nor do I know how to do it; I tremble lest she should refuse to follow me; lest the sudden idea of this removal rushing on her mind, might be too powerful. I flatter myself I shall be able to accomplish it, and to prevail on her; I fear nothing but the effects of her strong attachment to her relations. I would willingly let you know how I purpose to remove my family to so great a distance, but it would become unintelligible to you, because you are not acquainted with the geographical situation of this part of the country. Suffice it for you to know, that with about twenty-three miles land carriage, I am enabled to perform the rest by water; and when once afloat, I care not whether it be two or three hundred miles. I propose to send all our provisions, furniture, and clothes to my wife's father, who approves of the scheme, and to reserve nothing but a few necessary articles of covering; trusting to the furs of the chase, for our future apparel. Were we imprudently to incumber ourselves too much with baggage, we should never reach to the waters of ——, which is the most dangerous as well as the most difficult part of our journey; and yet but a trifle in point of distance. I intend to say to my negroes—In the name of God, be free, my honest lads, I thank you for your past services; go, from henceforth, and work for yourselves; look on me as your old friend and fellow labourer; be sober, frugal, and industrious, and you need not fear earning a comfortable subsistence.—Lest my countrymen should think that I am gone to join the incendiaries of our frontiers, I intend to write a letter to Mr —, to inform him of our retreat, and of the reasons that have urged me to it. The man whom I sent to—— village, is to accompany us also, and a very useful companion he will be on every account.

You may therefore, by means of anticipation, behold me under the Wigwham; I am so well acquainted with the principal manners of these people, that I entertain not the least apprehension from them. I rely more securely on their strong hospitality, than on the witnessed compacts of many Europeans. As soon as possible after my arrival, I design to build myself a wigwham, after the same manner and size with the rest, in order to avoid being thought singular, or giving occasion for any railleries; though these people are seldom guilty of such European follies. I shall erect it hard by the lands which they propose to allot me, and will endeavour that my wife, my children, and myself may be adopted soon after our arrival. Thus becoming truly inhabitants of their village, we shall immediately occupy that rank within the pale of their society, which will afford us all the amends we can possibly expect for the loss we have met with by the convulsions of our own. According to their customs we shall likewise receive names from them, by which we shall always be known. My youngest children shall learn to swim, and to shoot with the bow, that they may acquire such talents as will necessarily raise them into some degree of esteem among the Indian lads of their own age; the rest of us must hunt with the hunters. I have been for several years an expert marksman; but I dread lest the imperceptible charm of Indian education, may seize my younger children, and give them such a propensity to that mode of life, as may preclude their returning to the manners and customs of their parents. I have but one remedy to prevent this great evil; and that is, to employ them in the labour of the fields, as much as I can; I am even resolved to make their daily subsistence depend altogether on it. As long as we keep ourselves busy in tilling the earth, there is no fear of any of us becoming wild; it is the chase and the food it procures, that have this strange effect. Excuse a simile—those hogs which range in the woods, and to whom grain is given once a week, preserve their former degree of tameness; but if, on the contrary, they are reduced to live on ground nuts, and on what they can get, they soon become wild and fierce. For my part, I can plough,

---

[1] beads used by Native Americans for jewelry, money, or other purposes.

sow, and hunt, as occasion may require; but my wife, deprived of wool, and flax, will have no room for industry; what is she then to do? like the other squaws, she must cook for us the nasaump,[1] the ninchickè, and such other preparations of corn as are customary among these people. She must learn to bake squashes and pumkins under the ashes; to slice and smoke the meat of our own killing, in order to preserve it; she must chearfully adopt the manners and customs of her neighbours, in their dress, deportment, conduct, and internal œconomy, in all respects. Surely if we can have fortitude enough to quit all we have, to remove so far, and to associate with people so different from us; these necessary compliances are but subordinate parts of the scheme. The change of garments, when those they carry with them are worne out, will not be the least of my wife's and daughter's concerns: though I am in hopes that self-love will invent some sort of reparation. Perhaps you would not believe that there are in the woods looking-glasses, and paint of every colour; and that the inhabitants take as much pains to adorn their faces and their bodies, to fix their bracelets of silver, and plait their hair, as our forefathers the Picts[2] used to do in the time of the Romans. Not that I would wish to see either my wife or daughter adopt those savage customs; we can live in great peace and harmony with them without descending to every article; the interruption of trade hath, I hope, suspended this mode of dress. My wife understands inoculation[3] perfectly well, she inoculated all our children one after another, and has successfully performed the operation on several scores of people, who, scattered here and there through our woods, were too far removed from all medical assistance. If we can persuade but one family to submit to it, and it succeeds, we shall then be as happy as our situation will admit of; it will raise her into some degree of consideration, for whoever is useful in any society will always be respected. If we are so fortunate as to carry one family through a disorder, which is the plague among these people, I trust to the force of example, we shall then become truly necessary, valued, and beloved: we indeed owe every kind office to a society of men who so readily offer to admit us into their social partnership, and to extend to my family the shelter of their village, the strength of their adoption, and even the dignity of their names. God grant us a prosperous beginning, we may then hope to be of more service to them than even missionaries who have been sent to preach to them a Gospel they cannot understand.

As to religion, our mode of worship will not suffer much by this removal from a cultivated country, into the bosom of the woods; for it cannot be much simpler than that which we have followed here these many years: and I will with as much care as I can, redouble my attention, and twice a week, retrace to them the great outlines of their duty to God and to man. I will read and expound to them some part of the decalogue, which is the method I have pursued ever since I married.

Half a dozen of acres on the shores of ——, the soil of which I know well, will yield us a great abundance of all we want; I will make it a point to give the overplus to such Indians as shall be most unfortunate in their huntings; I will persuade them, if I can, to till a little more land than they do, and not to trust so much to the produce of the chase. To encourage them still farther, I will give a quirn[4] to every six families; I have built many for our poor back settlers, it being often the want of mills which prevents them from raising grain. As I am a carpenter, I can build my own plough, and can be of great service to many of them; my example alone, may rouse the industry of some, and serve to direct others in their labours. The difficulties of the language will soon be removed; in my evening conversations, I will endeavour to make them regulate the trade of their village in such a manner as that those pests of the continent, those Indian traders, may not come within a certain distance; and there they shall be obliged to transact their business before the old people. I am in hopes that the constant respect which is paid to the elders, and shame, may

---

[1] hominy.

[2] the aboriginal inhabitants of Scotland.

[3] The smallpox epidemic of 1775–82 first broke out in Boston. It ravaged both the British and the Continental armies (Washington's decision to have his troops inoculated is said to have contributed to his final victory) and decimated the Native Americans.

[4] or quern, a device for grinding corn.

prevent the young hunters from infringing this regulation. The son of ———, will soon be made acquainted with our schemes, and I trust that the power of love, and the strong attachment he professes for my daughter, may bring him along with us: he will make an excellent hunter; young and vigorous, he will equal in dexterity the stoutest man in the village. Had it not been for this fortunate circumstance, there would have been the greatest danger; for however I respect the simple, the inoffensive society of these people in their villages, the strongest prejudices would make me abhor any alliance with them in blood: disagreeable no doubt, to nature's intentions which have strongly divided us by so many indelible characters. In the days of our sickness, we shall have recourse to their medical knowledge, which is well calculated for the simple diseases to which they are subject. Thus shall we metamorphose ourselves, from neat, decent, opulent planters, surrounded with every conveniency which our external labour and internal industry could give, into a still simpler people divested of every thing beside hope, food, and the raiment of the woods: abandoning the large framed house, to dwell under the wigwham; and the featherbed, to lie on the matt, or bear's skin. There shall we sleep undisturbed by fruitful dreams and apprehensions; rest and peace of mind will make us the most ample amends for what we shall leave behind. These blessings cannot be purchased too dear; too long have we been deprived of them. I would chearfully go even to the Mississippi,[1] to find that repose to which we have been so long strangers. My heart sometimes seems tired with beating, it wants rest like my eye-lids, which feel oppressed with so many watchings.[2] ...

---

[1] then far west of the frontier.

[2] In the rest of the letter, the Farmer describes his plans for educating his children and asks for God's blessing.

Thomas Paine
1737 – 1809

Thomas Paine was born on 29 January in Thetford, Norfolk, the son of an Anglican mother, Frances Cocke Paine, and Joseph Paine, a Quaker corset-maker. After a basic education, he worked for his father; then at nineteen he went to sea. He briefly worked as a corset-maker, in 1759 marrying Mary Lambert, who died the following year. He became an exciseman (tax collector) in the early 1760s, a job from which he was fired for writing a pamphlet linking corruption to low pay. He married for a second time in 1771, but the marriage ended in legal separation. In 1774, he met Benjamin Franklin, who advised him to emigrate to America.

In Philadelphia, he turned to journalism as an editor for the *Pennsylvania Magazine*. In January 1776, he published a popular pamphlet, *Common Sense*, which advocated for American independence from England. 120,000 copies of Paine's pamphlet circulated in the three months following publication.

As aide-de-camp to Gen. Nathaniel Greene during the American Revolution, Paine wrote sixteen papers, *The American Crisis* (1776–83), which improved morale in the Continental Army. In 1777 he became Secretary of the foreign-affairs committee of Congress. However, when he undertook to expose the activities of members of Congress who were privately buying arms from the French government, Paine was forced to resign from his post in 1779. He then worked as a clerk at the Pennsylvania Assembly until his return to Europe in 1787.

Initially, Paine hoped to raise funds in England for developing his method of building iron bridges. But after the outbreak of the French Revolution he became deeply involved in European affairs. Between March 1791 and February 1792 he published numerous editions of his two-part *Rights of Man*, in which he defended the French Revolution against Edmund Burke's attack in his *Reflections on the Revolution in France*.* Paine's book was banned in England, but Paine avoided arrest by leaving for France, where he was elected to the National Convention. He was imprisoned in 1793 under Robespierre, for opposing the execution of Louis XVI. In prison, he wrote the deist work *The Age of Reason*, which provoked charges of atheism in both England and America.

After his release, which he owed in part to the intervention of James Monroe, U. S. Minister to France, Paine stayed in France until 1802, when he returned to America at Thomas Jefferson's invitation. Back in the United States, however, he was regarded as an atheist, and his contributions to the American Revolution seemed to have been forgotten. He continued his critical writings, attacking the Federalists and continuing to oppose what he considered religious superstition. Paine died in poverty in New York City on 8 June 1809. The radical reformer William Cobbett* wished to return Paine's bones to England for burial ten years after his death, but he lost the remains after they were exhumed. (A.M.)

༺༻

from *The Age of Reason; Being an Investigation of True and Fabulous Theology* (1794)

The circumstance that has now taken place in France of the total abolition of the whole national order of priesthood, and of every thing appertaining to compulsive systems of religion, and compulsive articles of faith,[1] has not only precipitated my intention, but rendered a work of this kind exceedingly necessary; lest, in the general wreck of superstition, of false systems of government, and false theology, we lose sight of morality, of humanity, and of the theology that is true.

---

[1] The French revolutionaries made the official religion the Cult of the Supreme Being, closing monasteries and persecuting priests and other members of religious orders.

As several of my colleagues, and others of my fellow-citizens of France, have given me the example of making their voluntary and individual profession of faith, I also will make mine; and I do this with all that sincerity and frankness with which the mind of man communicates with itself.

I believe in one God, and no more; and I hope for happiness beyond this life.

I believe in the equality of man, and I believe that religious duties consist in doing justice, loving mercy,[1] and endeavouring to make our fellow-creatures happy.

But lest it should be supposed that I believe many other things in addition to these, I shall, in the progress of this work, declare the things I do not believe, and my reasons for not believing them. I do not believe in the creed professed by the Jewish church, by the Roman church, by the Greek church, by the Turkish church,[2] by the Protestant church, nor by any church that I know of. My own mind is my own church.

All national institutions of churches, whether Jewish, Christian, or Turkish, appear to me no other than human inventions set up to terrify and enslave mankind, and monopolize power and profit.

I do not mean by this declaration to condemn those who believe otherwise. They have the same right to their belief as I have to mine. But it is necessary to the happiness of man, that he be mentally faithful to himself. Infidelity does not consist in believing, or in disbelieving: it consists in professing to believe what he does not believe.

It is impossible to calculate the moral mischief, if I may so express it, that mental lying has produced in society. When a man has so far corrupted and prostituted the chastity of his mind, as to subscribe his professional belief to things he does not believe, he has prepared himself for the commission of every other crime. He takes up the trade of a priest for the sake of gain, and in order to *qualify* himself for that trade, he begins with a perjury. Can we conceive any thing more destructive to morality than this? ...

Every national church or religion has established itself by pretending some special mission from God communicated to certain individuals. The Jews have their Moses; the Christians their Jesus Christ, their apostles and saints; and the Turks their Mahomet; as if the way to God was not open to every man alike.

Each of those churches show certain books which they call *revelation*, or the word of God. The Jews say, that their word of God was given by God to Moses face to face;[3] the Christians say, that their word of God came by divine inspiration; and the Turks say, that their word of God (the Koran) was brought by an angel from Heaven. Each of those churches accuses the other of unbelief; and, for my own part, I disbelieve them all.

As it is necessary to affix right ideas to words, I will, before I proceed further into the subject, offer some observations on the word *revelation*. Revelation, when applied to religion, means something communicated *immediately* from God to man....

It is a contradiction in terms and ideas to call any thing a revelation that comes to us at second hand, either verbally or in writing. Revelation is necessarily limited to the first communication. After this, it is only an account of something which that person says was a revelation made to him; and though he may find himself obliged to believe it, it cannot be incumbent on me to believe it in the same manner, for it was not a revelation made to *me*, and I have only his word for it that it was made to *him*.

When Moses told the children of Israel that he received the two tables of the commandments from the hand of God, they were not obliged to believe him, because they had no other authority for it than his telling them so; and I have no other authority for it than some historian telling me so. The commandments carry no internal evidence of divinity with them. They contain some good moral precepts, such as any man qualified to be a law-giver or a legislator could produce himself, without having recourse to supernatural intervention.[4]

---

[1] Cf. Micah 6.8.

[2] Judaism, Roman Catholicism, Greek Orthodoxy, and Islam.

[3] See Exodus 33.11.

[4] "It is, however, necessary to except the declaration, which says, that God *visits the sins of the fathers upon the children* [Exodus 34.6–7]. It is contrary to every principle of moral justice." (T.P.)

When I am told that the Koran was written in Heaven, and brought to Mahomet by an angel, the account comes to near the same kind of hearsay evidence, and second hand authority, as the former. I did not see the angel myself, and therefore I have a right not to believe it.

When also I am told that a woman, called the Virgin Mary, said, or gave out, that she was with child without any cohabitation with a man, and that her betrothed husband, Joseph, said, that an angel told him so, I have a right to believe them or not: such a circumstance required a much stronger evidence than their bare word for it: but we have not even this: for neither Joseph nor Mary wrote any such matter themselves. It is only reported by others that *they said so*. It is hearsay upon hearsay, and I do not chuse to rest my belief upon such evidence.

It is, however, not difficult to account for the credit that was given to the story of Jesus Christ being the Son of God. He was born when the Heathen mythology had still some fashion and repute in the world, and that mythology had prepared the people for the belief of such a story. Almost all the extraordinary men that lived under the Heathen mythology were reputed to be the sons of some of their gods. It was not a new thing at that time to believe a man to have been celestially begotten: the intercourse of gods with women was then a matter of familiar opinion. Their Jupiter, according to their accounts, had cohabited with hundreds: the story, therefore, had nothing in it either new, wonderful, or obscene: it was conformable to the opinions that then prevailed among the people called Gentiles, or mythologists,[1] and it was those people only that believed it. The Jews who had kept strictly to the belief of one God, and no more, and who had always rejected the Heathen mythology, never credited the story.

It is curious to observe how the theory of what is called the Christian church, sprung out of the tail of the Heathen mythology. A direct incorporation took place in the first instance, by making the reputed founder to be celestially begotten. The trinity of gods[2] that then followed was no other than a reduction of the former plurality, which was about twenty or thirty thousand. The statue of Mary succeeded the statue of Diana of Ephesus.[3] The deification of heroes, changed into the canonization of saints. The mythologists had gods for every thing; the Christian mythologists had saints for every thing. The church became as crouded with the one, as the pantheon had been with the other;[4] and Rome was the place of both. The Christian theory is little else than the idolatry of the ancient mythologists, accommodated to the purposes of power and revenue; and it yet remains to reason and philosophy to abolish the amphibious fraud.

Nothing that is here said can apply, even with the most distant disrespect, to the *real* character of Jesus Christ. He was a virtuous and an amiable man. The morality that he preached and practised was of the most benevolent kind; and though similar systems of morality had been preached by Confucius,[5] and by some of the Greek philosophers, many years before; by the Quakers since; and by many good men in all ages; it has not been exceeded by any.

Jesus Christ wrote no account of himself, of his birth, parentage, or any thing else. Not a line of what is called the New Testament is of his own writing. The history of him is altogether the work of other people; and as to the account given of his resurrection and ascension, it was the necessary counterpart to the story of his birth. His historians, having brought him into the world in a supernatural manner, were obliged to take him out again in the same manner, or the first part of the story must have fallen to the ground.

The wretched contrivance with which this latter part is told, exceeds every thing that went before it. The first

---

[1] myth-makers outside the Jewish tradition.

[2] Paine's version of the orthodox Christian doctrine that the unity of God is known through the trinity of Father, Son, and Holy Spirit.

[3] In AD 431, the Virgin Mary was declared the Mother of God in the city of Ephesus, displacing the pagan goddess Diana, worshipped there as divine virgin and mother goddess.

[4] The Pantheon in Rome, the temple of all the gods, was transformed into a Christian church with altars dedicated to the saints.

[5] the Chinese philosopher and moral teacher K'ung fu-tzu (551–479 BC).

part, that of the miraculous conception, was not a thing that admitted of publicity; and therefore the tellers of this part of the story had this advantage, that though they might not be credited, they could not be detected. They could not be expected to prove it, because it was not one of those things that admitted of proof, and it was impossible that the person of whom it was told could prove it himself.

But the resurrection of a dead person from the grave, and his ascension through the air, is a thing very different as to the evidence it admits of, to the invisible conception of a child in the womb. The resurrection and ascension, supposing them to have taken place, admitted of public and occular demonstration, like that of the ascension of a balloon, or the sun at noon day, to all Jerusalem at least. A thing which every body is required to believe, requires that the proof and evidence of it should be equal to all and universal; and as the public visibility of this last related act was the only evidence that could give sanction to the former part, the whole of it falls to the ground, because that evidence never was given. Instead of this, a small number of persons, not more than eight or nine, are introduced as proxies for the whole world, to say, they *saw it*, and all the rest of the world are called upon to believe it. But it appears that Thomas[1] did not believe the resurrection; and, as they say, would not believe, without having occular and manual demonstration himself. *So neither will I*; and the reason is equally as good for me and every other person, as for Thomas.

It is in vain to attempt to palliate or disguise this matter. The story, so far as relates to the supernatural part has every mark of fraud and imposition stamped upon the face of it....

That such a person as Jesus Christ existed, and that he was crucified, which was the mode of execution at that day, are historical relations strictly within the limits of probability. He preached most excellent morality, and the equality of man; but he preached also against the corruptions and avarice of the Jewish priests, and this brought upon him the hatred and vengeance of the whole order of priesthood. The accusation which those priests brought against him, was that of sedition and conspiracy against the Roman government, to which the Jews were then subject and tributary; and it is not improbable that the Roman government might have some secret apprehension of the effects of his doctrine as well as the Jewish priests; neither is it improbable that Jesus Christ had in contemplation the delivery of the Jewish nation from the bondage of the Romans. Between the two, however, this virtuous reformer and revolutionist lost his life.

It is upon this plain narrative of facts, together with another case I am going to mention, that the Christian mythologists, calling themselves the Christian Church, have erected their fable, which for absurdity and extravagance is not exceeded by any thing that is to be found in the mythology of the ancients.

The ancient mythologists tell that the race of Giants made war against Jupiter, and that one of them threw an hundred rocks against him at one throw; that Jupiter defeated him with thunder, and confined him afterwards under Mount Etna; and that every time the giant turns himself, Mount Etna belches fire.[2] It is here easy to see that the circumstance of the mountain, that of its being a volcano, suggested the idea of the fable; and that the fable is made to fit and wind itself up with that circumstance.

The Christian mythologists tell that their Satan made war against the Almighty, who defeated him, and confined him afterwards, not under a mountain, but in a pit.[3] It is here easy to see that the first fable suggested the idea of the second; for the fable of Jupiter and the Giants was told many hundred years before that of Satan.

Thus far the ancient and the Christian mythologists differ very little from each other. But the latter have contrived to carry the matter much farther. They have contrived to connect the fabulous part of the story of Jesus Christ, with the fable originating from Mount Etna: and in order to make all the parts of the story tye together, they have taken to their aid the traditions of the Jews; for the Christian mythology is made up partly

---

[1] See John 20.24–29.

[2] Cf. Hesiod, *Theogony* and Virgil, *Aeneid* 4.

[3] Revelation 12.7–12, 20.1–3.

from the ancient mythology, and partly from the Jewish traditions.

The Christian mythologists, after having confined Satan in a pit, were obliged to let him out again, to bring on the sequel of the fable. He is then introduced into the Garden of Eden in the shape of a snake, or a serpent, and in that shape he enters into familiar conversation with Eve, who is no ways surprised to hear a snake talk; and the issue of this tête-à-tête is, that he persuades her to eat an apple, and the eating of that apple damns all mankind.[1] ...

Having thus made an insurrection and a battle in Heaven, in which none of the combatants could be either killed or wounded—put Satan into the pit—let him out again—given him a triumph over the whole creation—damned all mankind by the eating of an apple, these Christian mythologists bring the two ends of their fable together. They represent this virtuous and amiable man, Jesus Christ, to be at once both God and man, and also the Son of God, celestially begotten on purpose to be sacrificed, because, they say, that Eve in her longing had eaten an apple.

Putting aside every thing that might excite laughter by its absurdity, or detestation by its profaneness, and confining ourselves merely to an examination of the parts, it is impossible to conceive a story more derogatory to the Almighty, more inconsistent with his wisdom, more contradictory to his power, than this story is. ...

Not content with this deification of Satan, they represent him as defeating by stratagem, in the shape of an animal of the creation, all the power and wisdom of the Almighty. They represent him as having compelled the Almighty to the *direct necessity* either of surrendering the whole of the creation to the government and sovereignty of this Satan, or of capitulating for its redemption by coming down upon earth and exhibiting himself upon a cross in the shape of a man.

Had the inventors of this story told it the contrary way, that is, had they represented the Almighty as compelling Satan to exhibit *himself* on a cross in the shape of a snake, as a punishment for his new transgression, the story would have been less absurd, less contradictory. But instead of this, they make the transgressor triumph, and the Almighty fall.

That many good men have believed this strange fable, and lived very good lives under that belief (for credulity is not a crime) is what I have no doubt of. In the first place, they were educated to believe it, and they would have believed any thing else in the same manner. There are also many who have been so enthusiastically enraptured by what they conceived to be the infinite love of God to man, in making a sacrifice of himself, that the vehemence of the idea has forbidden and deterred them from examining into the absurdity and profaneness of the story. The more unnatural any thing is, the more is it capable of becoming the object of dismal admiration.

But if objects for gratitude and admiration are our desire, do they not present themselves every hour to our eyes? Do we not see a fair creation prepared to receive us the instant we are born—a world furnished to our hands that cost us nothing? Is it we that light up the sun; that pour down the rain; and fill the earth with abundance? Whether we sleep or wake, the vast machinery of the universe still goes on. Are these things, and the blessings they indicate in future, nothing to us? Can our gross feelings be excited by no other subjects than tragedy and suicide? Or is the gloomy pride of man become so intolerable, that nothing can flatter it but a sacrifice of the Creator?

I know that this bold investigation will alarm many, but it would be paying too great a compliment to their credulity to forbear it upon that account. The times and the subject demand it to be done. The suspicion that the theory of what is called the Christian Church is fabulous, is becoming very extensive in all countries; and it will be a consolation to men staggering under that suspicion, and doubting what to believe and what to disbelieve, to see the subject freely investigated. I therefore pass on to an examination of the books called the Old and the New Testament. ...

---

[1] Genesis 3.

Charlotte Brooke
1740 – 1793

Charlotte Brooke was born in about 1740 at Rantavan, County Cavan, Ireland, among the youngest of the twenty-two children of Henry Brooke, a novelist, and Lettice Digby Brooke. Her father educated her and encouraged her to study Irish and history. She never married. After the deaths of her mother and her last surviving sister in 1772, she devoted herself to caring for her grief-stricken father until he died in 1783. She was left in poverty, but the success of *Reliques of Irish Poetry* (1789) enabled her to recover her social position. She intended *Reliques* to correct the distortions perpetrated by James Macpherson's *Ossian* and to establish Irish poetry as the "elder sister" of "the British muse." Brooke also wrote a tragedy, *Belisarius*, which she sent to Charles Kemble, who lost it; published a children's book, *School for Christians* (1791); and edited a selection of her father's works (1792). She died of "malignant fever" at Longford on 29 March 1793, leaving a novel, *Emma; or, The Foundling of the Wood*, which was published in 1803. (D.L.M.)

❦❦❦

from *Reliques of Irish Poetry: Consisting of Heroic Poems, Odes, Elegies, and Songs, Translated into English Verse: with Notes Explanatory and Historical; and the Originals in the Irish Character. To Which is Subjoined an Irish Tale* (1789)

The Lamentation of Cucullin, over the Body of his Son Conloch[1]

    Alas, alas for thee,
        O Aife's hapless son!
    And oh, of sires the most undone,
My child! my child! woe, tenfold woe to me!
5   Alas! that e'er these fatal plains
        Thy valiant steps receiv'd!
    And oh, for Cualnia's[2] wretched chief
        What now, alas, remains!

    What, but to gaze upon his grief!
10 Of his sole son, by his own arm bereav'd!

    O had I died before this hour!—
        My lost, my lovely child!
Before this arm my Conloch's arm oppos'd;
Before this spear against him was addrest;
15 Before these eyes beheld his eye-lids clos'd,
    And life's warm stream thus issuing from his breast!
Then, Death, how calmly had I met thy power!
Then, at thy worst of terrors, had I smil'd!

    Could fate no other grief devise?—
20   No other foe provide?—
    Oh!—could no arm but mine suffice
        To pierce my darling's side!—
My Conloch! 'tis denied thy father's woe
Even the sad comfort of revenge to know!—
25 To rush upon thy murderer's cruel breast,
Scatter his limbs, and rend his haughty crest!—
While his whole tribe in blood should quench my rage,
And the dire fever of my soul assuage![3]
The debt of vengeance, then, should well be paid,
30 And thousands fall the victims of thy shade!

---

[1] Cucullin (properly Cú Chulainn) is the hero of the Ulster cycle of tales and of the 8th-century Irish epic *Táin Bó Cuailnge*. After he defeated Aife, a Scottish warrior maiden, she bore him a son, Connle. When Connle came to Ireland, Cú Chulainn unknowingly killed him in single combat.

[2] "Cucullin was called, by way of pre-eminence, the HERO OF CUALNIA, that being the name of his patrimony, which it still retains, in the county of Louth." (C.B.)

[3] "What a picture of a heart torn with sorrow is here exhibited, in these wild startings of passion!—the soul of a hero, pressed down with a weight of woe,—stung to madness by complicated aggravations of the most poignant grief, and struggling between reason, and the impatient frenzy of despair!—How naturally does it rave around for some object whereon to vent the burstings of anguish, and the irritations of a wounded spirit!" (C.B.)

Ultonian knights![1] Ye glory of our age!
Well have ye scap'd a frantic father's rage!
That not by *you* this fatal field is won!
That not by *you* I lose my lovely son!—
35 Oh, dearly, else, should all your lives abide
The trophies from my Conloch's valour torn;
And your RED-BRANCH, in deeper crimson dy'd,
The vengeance of a father's arm should mourn!

O thou lost hope of my declining years!
40 O cruel winds that drove thee to this coast!
    Alas! could Destiny afford
      No other arm, no other sword,
    In Leinster of the pointed spears,
On Munster's plains, or in fierce Cruachan's[2] host,
45   To quench in blood my filial light,
And spare my arm the deed, my eyes the sight!

    O had proud India's splendid plain
      Beneath thy prowess bled,
    There, sunk on heaps of hostile slain,
50   Had thy brave spirit fled,
That then EMANIA[3] might the deed pursue,
And, for thy fate, exact the vengeance due!
Expiring millions had thy ransom paid,
And the wild frenzy of my grief allay'd!

55 O that to Lochlin's land of snows[4]
    My son had steer'd his course!
Or Grecian[5] shores, or Persian foes,
    Or Spain, or Britain's force!

There had he fallen, amidst his fame,
60   I yet the loss could bear;
Nor horror thus would shake my frame,
    Nor sorrow be—Despair!—

Why was it not in Sora's barbarous lands
    My lovely Conloch fell?
65 Or by fierce Pictish chiefs,[6] whose ruthless bands
    Would joy the cruel tale to tell;

---

[1] "These were the famous heroes of the RED-BRANCH." (C.B.) The order was created by Conchobor mac Nessa, legendary king of Ulster.

[2] "In Connaught." (C.B.)

[3] "By EMANIA he means the knights of the RED-BRANCH, as a considerable part of that palace was occupied by this celebrated body. The part appointed for their residence was called *Teagh na Craoibhe-ruadh* (i.e., the palace of the RED-BRANCH), where there was also an academy instituted for the instruction of the young knights, and a large hospital for their sick and wounded, called *Bron-bhearg*, or the House of the Warriors' Sorrow. See O'HALL. *Int. to the Hist. of Ireland*, p. 40. See also KEATING.

"The Palace of Emania, or Eamania, stood near Armagh. Some ruins of it were remaining so late as the time of Colgan. Vide *Collect. de Reb. Hib.* vol. III. p. 341." (C.B.) Sylvester O'Halloran (1728–1820), surgeon and historian, author of *An Introduction to the Study of the History and Antiquities of Ireland* (1772); Geoffrey Keating (c. 1580–1644?), Gaelic historian.

[4] Scandinavia.

[5] "The anti-hibernian critic will here exclaim—'What knowledge could Cucullin possibly be supposed to have had of Greece, or Persia, or of proud India's splendid plain?—Does not the very mention banish every idea of the antiquity of this poem, and mark it out at once as a modern production?' It is granted that this would indeed be the case, had our early ancestors been *really* such as modern writers represent them:—*Barbarians, descended from barbarians, and ever continuing the same*; but their Phoenician origin of itself sufficiently accounts for their knowledge of the situation, inhabitants, manners, &c. of the various nations of the earth; since the Phoenicians, a maritime and commercial people, traded to every port, and were acquainted with every country.

"Besides this, the literary and intellectual turn of the ancient Irish, frequently sent them, in quest of knowledge, to different parts of the globe. 'Our early writers (says Mr. O'HALLORAN) tell us, (and Archbishop USHER affirms the same,) that the celebrated champion Conall Cearnach, Master of the Ulster Knights, was actually at Jerusalem at the time of the crucifixion of our Saviour, and related the story to the King of Ulster on his return.' He also adds that one of our great poets, in the fifth century, traversed the east, and dedicated a book to the Emperor Theodosius. Many similar instances and proofs could also be here subjoined; but the limits of my design oblige me to refer my readers to the learned works of O'CONOR, O'HALLORAN and VALANCEY, names dear to every spirit of liberality and science, but by *Irishmen* peculiarly to be revered." (C.B.) James Ussher (1581–1656), Protestant archbishop and historian; Dermod O'Connor (fl. 1720), translator of Keating; Charles Vallancey (1721–1812), military engineer and antiquarian.

[6] "The period, when the Picts first invaded North-Britain, has not (I believe) been exactly ascertained.—We *here* find that country divided between the PICTS and the ALBANIANS, and the former mentioned as a bloody and cruel people.—It was not till two centuries after this that a *third* colony from Ireland, under Carbry Riada, was established there." (C.B.)

Whose souls are train'd all pity to subdue;
Whose savage eyes unmov'd that form could view!

Rejoice, ye heroes of Albania's plains![1]
70 (While yet I live, my conquering troops to lead,)
    Rejoice, that guiltless of the deed
        Your happy earth remains!
And you, ye chiefs of Galia's[2] numerous host;
Bless the kind fate that spar'd your favour'd coast![3]

75   But what for me—for me is left!
Of more, and dearer far than life, bereft!
        Doom'd to yet unheard of woe!
A father, doom'd to pierce his darling's side,
    And,—oh! with blasted eyes abide
80 To see the last dear drops of filial crimson flow!

    Alas!—my trembling limbs!—my fainting frame!—[4]
        Grief!—is it thou?—
    O conquering Grief!—I know thee now!
Well do thy sad effects my woes proclaim!
85   Poor Victor!—see thy trophies, where they lie!—
Wash them with tears!—then lay thee down and die!

    Why, why, O Aifè! Was thy child
        Thus cruelly beguil'd!
Why to my Conloch did'st thou not impart
90 The fatal secret of his father's art?

To warn him to avoid the deadly snare,
And of a combat on the waves beware.[5]

    Alas, I sink!—my failing sight
        Is gone!—'tis lost in night!
95   Clouds and darkness round me dwell!
    Horrors more than tongue can tell!
See where my son, my murdered Conloch lies!
What further sufferings now can fate devise!
O my heart's wounds! Well may your anguish flow,
100 And drop life's tears on this surpassing woe!

Lo, the sad remnant of my slaughter'd race,
Like some lone trunk, I wither in my place!—
No more the sons of USNOTH to my sight
Give manly charms, and to my soul delight!
105 No more my Conloch shall I hope to see;
Nor son, nor kinsman now survives for me!
O my lost son!—my precious child, adieu!
No more these eyes that lovely form shall view!
No more his dark-red spear shall Ainle[6] wield!
110 No more shall Naoise thunder o'er the field!
No more shall Ardan sweep the hostile plains!—
Lost are they all, and nought but woe remains!—
Now, chearless earth, adieu thy every care:
Adieu to all, but Horror and Despair!

Song. For Mable Kelly. By Carolan[7]

The youth whom fav'ring Heaven's decree
To join his fate, my Fair! with thee;

---

[1] Scotland.

[2] France's.

[3] "I had nearly forgotten to acknowledge, that some stanzas of the original of this poem are omitted in the translation; Cucullin, before this, enumerates the heroes of the RED-BRANCH; viz. Conal Cearnach, Loire Buahach, Cormac Conluingeas, Dubthach, Forbuidh, &c. &c. and tells them, one by one, that they happily escaped being guilty of the death of his son, and the vengeance that he would have exacted. In some other copies of the poem I do not find these stanzas; I therefore took the liberty of leaving them out, as I thought they broke the pathos of the composition; and, besides, they were (in point of poetry) rather inferior to the rest of the piece." (C.B.)

[4] "The beautiful lines, in my original, from which the three following stanzas are translated, were not in Mr. O'HALLORAN's copy." (C.B.)

[5] "Some of our romances and poems ascribe to Cucullin the property of being invulnerable in water, and in relating this circumstance of his life, say, that (when hard pressed by Conloch) he took the refuge of a ford, and *then* threw the fatal GATH-BOLG, with which he was sure of killing his antagonist. The preceding poem makes no mention of this fable, perhaps through tenderness for the honor of Cucullin; and from this, and some other circumstances, I am tempted to think they were not written by the same hand." (C.B.) The *gae bulga* was a barbed spear.

[6] "Ainle, Naoise, and Ardan, were the three sons of Usnoth, whose tragical story is related in the notes to the preceding poem." (C.B.)

[7] Toirdhealbhach Ó Cearbhalláin (1670–1738), harper, composer, and poet, blinded by smallpox at eighteen.

And see that lovely head of thine
With fondness on his arm recline:

5   No thought but joy can fill his mind,
Nor any care can entrance find,
Nor sickness hurt, nor terror shake,—
And Death will spare him, for thy sake!

For the bright flowing of thy hair,
10 That decks a face so heavenly fair;
And a fair form, to match that face,
The rival of the Cygnet's grace.

When with calm dignity she moves,
Where the clear stream her hue improves;
15 Where she her snowy bosom laves,
And floats, majestic, on the waves.

Grace gave thy form, in beauty gay,
And rang'd thy teeth in bright array;
All tongues with joy thy praises tell,
20 And love delights with thee to dwell.

To thee harmonious powers belong,
That add to verse the charms of song;
Soft melody to numbers join,
And make the Poet half divine.

25 As when the softly blushing rose
Close by some neighbouring lilly grows;
Such is the glow thy cheeks diffuse,
And such their bright and blended hues!

The timid luster of thine eye[1]
30 With Nature's purest tints can vie;
With the sweet blue-bell's azure gem,
That droops upon its modest stem!

The Poets of Ierne's[2] plains
To thee devote their choicest strains;
35 And oft their harps for thee are strung,
And oft thy matchless charms are sung:

Thy voice, that binds the list'ning soul,—
That can the wildest rage controul;
Bid the fierce Crane its powers obey,
40 And charm him from his finney prey.

Nor doubt I of its wond'rous art;
Nor hear with unimpassion'd heart;
Thy health, thy beauties,—ever dear!
Oft crown my glass with sweetest cheer!

45 Since the fam'd Fair of ancient days,
Whom Bards and Worlds conspir'd to praise,[3]
Not one like thee has since appear'd,
Like thee, to every heart endear'd.

How blest the Bard, O lovely Maid!
50 To find thee in thy charms array'd!—
Thy pearly teeth,—thy flowing hair,—
Thy neck, beyond the Cygnet, fair!—

As when the simple birds, at night,
Fly round the torch's fatal light,—
55 Wild, and with extacy elate,
Unconscious of approaching fate.

So the soft splendours of thy face,
And thy fair form's enchanting grace,
Allure to death unwary Love,
60 And thousands the bright ruin prove!

---

[1] "It is generally believed that Carolan, (as his Biographer tells us) 'remembered no impression of colours.'—But I cannot acquiesce in this opinion: I think it must have been formed without sufficient grounds, for how was it possible that his description could be thus glowing, without he retained the clearest recollection, and the most animated ideas, of every beauty that sight can convey to the mind?" (C.B.)

[2] Ireland's.

[3] Helen of Troy (see note to line 57 of "The Lamentation of Cucullin").

Ev'n he whose hapless eyes[1] no ray
Admit from Beauty's cheering day;
Yet, though he cannot *see* the light,
He feels it warm, and knows it bright.

65 In beauty, talents, taste refin'd,
And all the graces of the mind,
In *all* unmatch'd thy charms remain,
Nor meet a rival on the plain.

Thy slender foot,—thine azure eye,—
70 Thy smiling lip, of scarlet dye,—
Thy tapering hand, so soft and fair,—
The bright redundance of thy hair!—

O blest be the auspicious day
That gave them to thy Poet's lay!
75 O'er rival Bards[2] to lift his name,
Inspire his verse, and swell his fame!—

---

[1] "Every Reader of taste or feeling must surely be struck with the beauty of this passage.—Can any thing be more elegant, or more pathetic, than the manner in which Carolan alludes to his want of sight!—but, indeed, his little pieces abound in all the riches of natural genius." (C.B.)

[2] "How modestly the Poet here introduces a prophecy of his future reputation for genius!" (C.B.)

Anna Seward
1742 – 1809

Anna Seward, known as the "Swan of Lichfield," was born in Eyam, Derbyshire on 12 December 1742, the daughter of Thomas Seward, a clergyman, and Elizabeth Hunter Seward. Her grandfather, John Hunter, had been headmaster of Lichfield Grammar School and had taught Samuel Johnson. Her father taught her to read Shakespeare, Milton, and Pope at the age of three; she could recite the first three books of *Paradise Lost* by age nine. When her father became canon of Lichfield Cathedral in 1750 Seward went to live in the Bishop's palace, where she stayed until her death. Her friends included Samuel Johnson, Thomas Day, and Erasmus Darwin* (who set up a medical practice in Lichfield in 1746). Following the sudden death of Seward's sister Sarah in 1764, the friendship between Seward and Honora Sneyd, her adopted sister, became especially intense. During the 1770s the Seward circle included Darwin, Day, and Richard Lovell Edgeworth (Maria Edgeworth's* father). Seward was deeply distressed when in 1773 Sneyd married Edgeworth and moved to Ireland, where she died of consumption in 1780.

Among Seward's early publications were *Elegy on Captain Cook* (1780) and *Monody on Major André* (1781). The latter is about John André, who had courted Honora Sneyd and who was hanged in 1780 as a British spy in the American Revolution; Seward claimed that he had joined the army because of a broken heart. In 1784 she published *Louisa: a Poetical Novel, in Four Epistles*, which went through four editions in 1784 and a fifth edition in 1785. When her father died in 1790, he left her an annual income of £400. Her *Original Sonnets on Various Subjects; and Odes Paraphrased from Horace* (1799) reprints poems written from the 1770s to 1799.

Seward's poem *Colebrookdale* followed in 1785. She contributed to the *Gentleman's Magazine* the following year under the name of Benvolio, attacking Johnson's posthumous reputation. Unusually outspoken, she attacked supporters of the French Revolution and criticized such writers as More* and Charlotte Smith;* however, in personal letters she expressed admiration for Wollstonecraft's *A Vindication of the Rights of Woman.** In 1804, she published *Memoirs of the Life of Dr. Darwin*, a biography of Darwin's early life in Lichfield (from 1756 to 1781).

In 1768, Seward had fractured her kneecap; as she grew older, she suffered from rheumatism and other illnesses. She died on 25 March 1809 and was buried in the choir of Lichfield Cathedral on 2 April (but not in the tomb of her father or of her friend, John Saville, as she had requested). Walter Scott,* her executor, edited her *Poetical Works* (3 vols.) after her death, but refused to edit her correspondence, which contained outspoken disagreements with such figures as James Boswell and Samuel Johnson. A selection of the letters was published by Constable in 1811. (A.M.)

from *Llangollen Vale, with Other Poems* (1796)

Eyam[1]

For one short week I leave, with anxious heart,
Source of my filial cares, the FULL OF DAYS;[2]
Lur'd by the promise of harmonic Art
To breathe her Handel's[3] soul-exalting lays.
5 Pensive I trace the Derwent's amber wave,[4]
Foaming thro' sylvan banks, or view it lave
The soft romantic vallies, high o'er-peer'd
By hills, and rocks, in savage grandeur rear'd.

Not two short miles from thee,—can I refrain
10 Thy haunts, my native EYAM, long unseen?
Thou, and thy lov'd Inhabitants again
Shall meet my transient gaze.—Thy rocky screen,
Thy airy cliffs I mount; and seek thy shade,
Thy roofs, that brow the steep, romantic glade;
15 But, while on me the eyes of Friendship glow,
Swell my pain'd sighs, my tears spontaneous flow.

In Scenes paternal, not beheld thro' years,
Nor view'd, till *now*, but by a Father's side,
Well might the tender tributary tears,
20 From keen regrets of duteous fondness, glide.
Its Pastor, to this Human-Flock no more
Shall the long flight of future days restore;
Distant he droops—and that once-gladdening eye
Now languid gleams, e'en when his Friends are nigh.

25 Thro' this known walk, where weedy gravel lies,
Rough, and unsightly;—by the long coarse grass
Of the once smooth, and vivid Green, with sighs,
To the deserted Rectory I pass;—
Stray thro' the darken'd chambers naked bound,
30 Where Childhood's earliest, liveliest bliss I found.
How chang'd, since erst, the lightsome walls beneath,
The social joys did their warm comforts breathe!

Ere yet I go, who may return no more,
That sacred Pile, 'mid yonder shadowy trees,
35 Let me revisit!—ancient, massy door,
Thou gratest hoarse!—my vital spirits freeze
Passing the vacant Pulpit to the space
Where humble rails the decent Altar grace,
And where my infant sister's ashes sleep,[5]
40 Whose loss I left the childish sport to weep.

Now the low beams, with paper garlands hung,[6]
In memory of some village Youth, or Maid,
Draw the soft tear, from thrill'd remembrance sprung,
How oft my childhood mark'd that tribute paid.
45 The gloves suspended by the garland's side,
White as its snowy flowers, with ribbands tied;
Dear Village! long these wreaths funereal spread,
Simple memorials of thy early Dead!

But, O! thou blank, and silent Pulpit!—thou
50 That with a Father's precepts, just, and bland,[7]
Did'st win my ear, as Reason's strengthening glow
Show'd their full value—now thou seem'st to stand
Before my sad, suffus'd, and trembling gaze,
The dreariest relic of departed days;
55 Of eloquence paternal, nervous,[8] clear,
DIM APPARITION THOU,—and bitter is my tear.

---

[1] "This Poem was written August 1788, on a journey through Derbyshire, to a music-meeting at Sheffield. The Author's Father was Rector of EYAM, an extensive Village, that runs along a mountainous terrace, in one of the highest parts of the Peak. She was born there, and there passed the first seven years of her life, visiting the Place often with her Father in future periods. The middle part of this Village is built on the edge of a deep Dell, which has very picturesque, and beautiful features." (A.S.) The Peak is a district in Derbyshire known for its scenic beauty. The occasion for this poem was a visit to Lady Eleanor Butler and Sarah Ponsonby, known as the ladies of Llangollen.

[2] Seward's elderly father: cf. Job 42.16–17.

[3] George Frederick Handel (1685–1759), German-born composer.

[4] "From the peculiar nature of the clay on the mountains, from which it descends, the River Derwent has a yellow tint, that well becomes the dark foliage on its banks, and the perpetual foam produced by a narrow, and rocky channel." (A.S.) The Derwent is a river in the Lake District; cf. W. Wordsworth, *The Two-Part Prelude* 1.1–26.*

[5] Only one of Seward's siblings, her sister Sarah, survived childhood; even Sarah died young, at the age of twenty.

[6] "The ancient custom of hanging a garland of white roses, made of writing-paper, and a pair of white gloves, over the pew of the unmarried Villagers, who die in the flower of their age, is observed to this day, in the Village of EYAM, and in most other Villages, and little Towns in the Peak." (A.S.)

[7] agreeable, temperate.

[8] strong, vigorous (archaic).

To Time Past. Written Dec. 1772

Return, blest years!—when not the jocund Spring,
Luxuriant Summer, nor the amber hours
Calm Autumn gives, my heart invok'd to bring
Joys, whose rich balm o'er all the bosom pours;
5 When ne'er I wish'd might grace the closing day
One tint purpureal, or one golden ray;
When the loud Storms, that desolate the bowers,
Found dearer welcome than Favonian[1] gales,
And Winter's bare, bleak fields, than Summer's
   flowery Vales!

10 Yet, not to deck pale hours with vain parade
Beneath the blaze of wide-illumin'd Dome;
Not for the bounding Dance;—not to pervade,
And charm the sense with Music;—nor, as roam
The mimic Passions o'er theatric scene,
15 To laugh, or weep;—O! not for these, I ween,
But for delights that made the *heart* their home,
Was the grey night-frost on the sounding plain
More than the Sun invok'd, that gilds the grassy lane.

Yes, for the joys that trivial joys excell,
20 My lov'd HONORA,[2] did we hail the gloom
Of dim November's eve;—and as it fell,
And the bright fires shone cheerful round the room,
Dropt the warm curtains with no tardy hand;
And felt our spirits, and our hearts expand,
25 Listening their steps, who still, where'er they come,
Make the keen stars, that glaze the settled snows,
More than the Sun invok'd, when first he tints the rose.

Affection,—Friendship,—Sympathy,—your throne
Is Winter's glowing hearth;—and ye were ours,
30 Thy smile, HONORA, made them all our own.—
Where are they *now*?—alas! their choicest powers
Faded at thy retreat;—for thou art gone,
And many a dark, long Eve I sigh alone,
In thrill'd remembrance of the vanish'd hours,
35 When storms were dearer than the balmy gales,
And Winter's bare bleak fields than green luxuriant vales.

from *Original Sonnets on Various Subjects; and Odes Paraphrased from Horace* (1799)

Sonnet 10. To Honora Sneyd

Honora, shou'd that cruel time arrive
   When 'gainst my truth thou should'st my errors poize,
   Scorning remembrance of our vanish'd joys;
   When for the love-warm looks, in which I live,
But cold respect must greet me, that shall give
   No tender glance, no kind regretful sighs;
   When thou shalt pass me with averted eyes,
   Feigning thou see'st me not, to sting, and grieve,
And sicken my sad heart, I cou'd not bear
10   Such dire eclipse of thy soul-cheering rays;
   I cou'd not learn my struggling heart to tear
From thy lov'd form, that thro' my memory strays;
   Nor in the pale horizon of Despair
   Endure the wintry and the darken'd days.

Sonnet 71. To the Poppy

While Summer Roses all their glory yield
   To crown the Votary of Love and Joy,
   Misfortune's Victim hails, with many a sigh,
   Thee, scarlet POPPY of the pathless field,
5 Gaudy, yet wild and lone; no leaf to shield
   Thy flaccid vest, that, as the gale blows high,
   Flaps, and alternate folds around thy head.—
   So stands in the long grass a love-craz'd Maid,
Smiling aghast; while stream to every wind
10   Her gairish ribbons, smear'd with dust and rain;
   But brain-sick visions cheat her tortur'd mind,
And bring false peace. Thus, lulling grief and pain,
   Kind dreams oblivious[3] from thy juice proceed,
   THOU FLIMSY, SHEWY, MELANCHOLY WEED.

---

[1] gentle like Favonius, the west wind in Roman mythology.

[2] "MISS HONORA SNEYD, to whom the gallant, and unfortunate MAJOR ANDRE, was so unalienably attached. See the Author's MONODY on that Gentleman." (A.S.) Seward's *Monody on Major André* (1781) is about John André, who courted Seward's foster-sister Honora Sneyd and who was hanged by the Americans in 1780 as a British spy.

[3] dreams of forgetfulness induced by opium, a drug made from poppies.

Hannah Cowley
1743 – 1809

Hannah Parkhouse was born on 14 March 1743 in Tiverton, Devonshire. Her father, Philip Parkhouse, a bookseller and scholar, educated and encouraged her. In 1772, she married Thomas Cowley, a journalist and Stamp Office clerk, and they moved to London. They had four children. In 1776, Cowley wrote the first of her thirteen plays, mainly comedies distinguished for their realistic dialogue and their witty, independent, resourceful female characters; the most successful was *The Belle's Stratagem* (1780). In 1783, Thomas joined the East India Company and moved to India, where he died in 1797. In 1787, Cowley and Robert Merry* began exchanging love poems in the *World*, under the pen names "Anna Matilda" and "Della Crusca"; the exchange helped popularize the Della Cruscan style of sentimental poetry. When they actually met, in 1789, they were disappointed and the poems stopped. In 1801, Cowley retired to Tiverton, where she died on 11 March 1809. (D.L.M.)

---

from the *World, Fashionable Advertiser*
(10 July 1787)

To Della Crusca. The Pen

O! seize again thy golden quill,
And with its point my bosom thrill;
With magic touch explore my heart,
And bid the tear of passion start.
5 Thy golden quill APOLLO[1] gave—
Drench'd first in bright Aonia's wave:[2]
He snatch'd it flutt'ring thro' the sky,
Borne on the vapour of a sigh;
It fell from *Cupid*'s[3] burnish'd wing
10 As forcefully he drew the string;
Which sent his keenest, surest dart
Thro' a rebellious frozen heart,
That had till then defy'd his pow'r,
And vacant beat thro' each dull hour.

15   Be worthy then the sacred loan!
Seated on Fancy's air-built throne;
Immerse it in her rainbow hues,
Nor, what the Godheads bid, refuse.
APOLLO, CUPID shall inspire,
20 And aid thee with their blended fire.
The *one*, poetic language give,
The *other* bid thy passion live;
With soft ideas fill thy lays,
And crown with LOVE thy wintry days!

from the *World* (22 December 1787)[4]

To Della Crusca

I hate the Elegiac lay—
Chuse me a measure jocund as the day!
Such days as near the ides of June
Meet the Lark's elab'rate tune,
5 When his downy fringed breast
Ambitious on a cloud to rest
He soars aloft; and from his gurgling throat
Darts to the earth the piercing note—
Which softly falling with the dews of morn
10 (That bless the scented pink, and snowy thorn)
Expands upon the Zephyr's wing,

---

[1] the classical god of poetry.

[2] Aonia was the region of Greece including Mount Helicon, sacred to the Muses. Cowley seems to be thinking of the Castalian spring, also sacred to the Muses, which is actually on Mount Parnassus.

[3] the classical god of love.

[4] The title changes as follows: the *World, Fashionable Advertiser* (through issue no. 271, 26 November 1787) to the *World* (from issue no. 272, 27 November 1787 through issue no. 2342, 30 June 1794).

 And wakes the burnish'd finch, and linnet sweet to sing.

 And be thy lines irregular, and free!
Poetic chains should fall, before such bards as thee.
15 Scorn the dull laws that pinch thee round,
Raising about thy verse a mound,
O'er which thy Muse so lofty! dares not bound.
Bid her in verse meandring sport;
Her footsteps quick, or long, or short
20 Just as her various impulse wills—
Scorning the frigid square, which her fine fervor chills.

 And in thy verse meand'ring wild,
Thou, who art FANCY'S *favourite Child*,
May'st sweetly paint the long past hour,
25 When, the slave of Cupid's power,
Thou couldst the tear of rapture weep,
And feed on agony, and banish sleep.

 Hah! and *didst* thou favour'd mortal taste
All that adorns our life's dull waste?
30 *Hast* thou known love's enchanting pain—
Its hopes, its woes, *and yet complain*?
Thy senses, at a voice, been lost,
Thy mad'ning soul in tumults tost?
Extatic wishes fire thy brain—
35 These, hast thou known, *and yet complain*?
Thou then deserv'st ne'er more to feel;—
Thy nerves be rigid, hence, as steel!
Their fine vibrations all destroy'd,
Thy future days a tasteless void!
40 Ne'er shalt thou know again to sigh,
Or, on a soft idea dye;
Ne'er on a *recollection* gasp;
Thy arms, the air-drawn charmer, never grasp.

 Vapid content her poppies round thee shew,
45 Whilst to the bliss of TASTE thou bidst adieu!
To vulgar *comforts* be thou hence confin'd,
And the shrunk bays be from thy brow untwin'd.
Thy statue torn from Cupid's hallow'd nitch,
But in return thou shalt be dull, and rich;
50 The Muses hence disown thy rebel lay—
But thou in *Aldermanic* gown, their scorn repay;
Crimson'd, and furr'd, the highest honours dare,
And on thy laurels tread—a PLUMP LORD MAYOR!

Thomas Jefferson
1743 – 1826

Thomas Jefferson was born on 13 April 1743 in Shadwell, Virginia, the third child of Peter Jefferson, a surveyor, plantation owner, and judge, and Jane Randolph Jefferson, a descendant of Virginia's most prominent family. He was educated by private tutors and at William and Mary College. After studying law, he was admitted to the bar in 1767 and elected to the Virginia Assembly in 1768. On New Year's Day, 1772, he married Martha Wayles Skelton; they had six children, only two of whom would grow up. Martha died in September 1782. Later, Jefferson had a long relationship with one of his slaves, Sally Hemings (Martha's half-sister, whom he had inherited from his father-in-law); they had six children. Jefferson freed the four who grew up, and Sally eventually went to live with them in Ohio.

In 1774, Jefferson published *A Summary View of the Rights of British America*, which lays out the arguments later summarized in the Declaration of Independence. In 1775 he was elected to the Continental Congress, and in 1776 he was asked to write the first draft of the Declaration. In 1779, he was elected governor of Virginia and drafted the *Act for Establishing Religious Freedom*, an important step towards the American separation of Church and State. He published his only book, *Notes on the State of Virginia*, in 1785.

In 1784, Jefferson was appointed one of the Commissioners in Paris, to negotiate economic and political treaties with European nations. He remained in Europe for five years; then he served as Secretary of State (1789–93), Vice President (1797–1801), and President (1801–1809). In 1817, he founded the University of Virginia. He died on the same day as his old friend and rival John Adams,* 4 July 1826. (D.L.M.)

෴

In Congress, July 4, 1776

A Declaration by the Representatives of the United States of America, in Congress Assembled[1]

When in the course of human events, it becomes necessary for one people to dissolve the political bands which have connected them with another, and to assume among the powers of the earth, the separate and equal station to which the laws of nature and of nature's God entitle them, a decent respect to the opinions of mankind requires that they should declare the causes which impel them to the separation.

We hold these truths to be self-evident, that all men are created equal; that they are endowed by their Creator with certain unalienable rights; that among these are life, liberty and the pursuit of happiness;[2] that to secure these rights, governments are instituted among men, deriving their just powers from the consent of the governed; that whenever any form of government becomes destructive of these ends, it is the right of the people to alter or to abolish it, and to institute new government, laying its foundation on such principles, and organizing its powers in such form, as to them shall seem most likely to effect their safety and happiness. Prudence, indeed, will dictate, that governments long established should not be changed for light and transient causes; and accordingly all experience hath shewn, that mankind are more disposed to suffer, while evils are sufferable, than to right themselves by abolishing the forms to which they are accustomed. But when a long train of abuses and usurpations, pursuing invariably the

---

[1] Our copy-text is from *The Constitutions of the Sixteen States Which Compose the Confederated Republic of America* (Boston, 1797). There are no substantive revisions from the 1776 publication.

[2] adapted from the assertion in John Locke (1632–1704), *The Second Treatise of Government* (1689), that the fundamental rights are to life, liberty, and property.

same object, evinces a design to reduce them under absolute despotism, it is their right, it is their duty, to throw off such government, and to provide new guards for their future security. Such has been the patient sufferance of these Colonies; and such is now the necessity which constrains them to alter their former systems of government. The history of the present King of Great-Britain[1] is a history of repeated injuries and usurpations, all having in direct object the establishment of an absolute tyranny over these States. To prove this, let facts be submitted to a candid world.

He has refused his assent to laws, the most wholesome and necessary for the public good.

He has forbidden his Governors to pass laws of immediate and pressing importance, unless suspended in their operation till his assent should be obtained; and when so suspended, he has utterly neglected to attend to them.

He has refused to pass other laws for the accommodation of large districts of people, unless those people would relinquish the right of representation in the legislature, a right inestimable to them, and formidable to tyrants only.

He has called together legislative bodies at places unusual, uncomfortable, and distant from the depository of their public records, for the sole purpose of fatiguing them into compliance with his measures.

He has dissolved Representative Houses repeatedly, for opposing with manly firmness his invasions on the rights of the people.

He has refused for a long time, after such dissolutions, to cause others to be elected; whereby the legislative powers, incapable of annihilation, have returned to the people at large for their exercise; the State remaining in the mean time exposed to all the danger of invasion from without, and convulsions within.

He has endeavoured to prevent the population of these States; for that purpose obstructing the laws for naturalization of foreigners; refusing to pass others to encourage their migrations hither, and raising the conditions of new appropriations of lands.

He has obstructed the administration of justice, by refusing his assent to laws for establishing judiciary powers.

He has made Judges dependent on his will alone, for the tenure of their offices, and the amount and payment of their salaries.

He has erected a multitude of new offices, and sent hither swarms of officers to harrass our people, and eat out their substance.

He has kept among us, in times of peace, standing armies, without the consent of our legislatures.

He has affected to render the military independent of and superior to the civil power.

He has combined with others to subject us to a jurisdiction foreign to our constitution, and unacknowledged by our laws; giving his assent to their acts of pretended legislation:

For quartering large bodies of armed troops among us:

For protecting them, by a mock trial, from punishment for any murders which they should commit on the inhabitants of these States:

For cutting off our trade with all parts of the world:

For imposing taxes on us without our consent:

For depriving us, in many cases, of the benefits of trial by jury:

For transporting us beyond seas to be tried for pretended offences:

For abolishing the free system of English laws in a neighbouring Province,[2] establishing therein an arbitrary government, and enlarging its boundaries, so as to render it at once an example and fit instrument for introducing the same absolute rule into these Colonies:

For taking away our charters, abolishing our most valuable laws, and altering fundamentally the forms of our governments:

For suspending our own legislatures, and declaring themselves invested with power to legislate for us in all cases whatsoever.

He has abdicated government here, by declaring us out of his protection, and waging war against us.

He has plundered our seas, ravaged our coasts, burnt

---

[1] George III (r. 1760–1820).

[2] The Québec Act (1774) restored French civil law in Québec.

our towns, and destroyed the lives of our people.

He is at this time, transporting large armies of foreign mercenaries[1] to complete the works of death, desolation and tyranny, already begun with circumstances of cruelty and perfidy, scarcely paralleled in the most barbarous ages, and totally unworthy the head of a civilized nation.

He has constrained our fellow citizens, taken captive on the high seas, to bear arms against their country, to become the executioners of their friends and brethren, or to fall themselves by their hands.

He has excited domestic insurrections amongst us, and has endeavoured to bring on the inhabitants of our frontiers, the merciless Indian savages, whose known rule of warfare is an undistinguished destruction of all ages, sexes and conditions.[2]

In every stage of these oppressions we have petitioned for redress, in the most humble terms: Our repeated petitions have been answered only by repeated injury. A prince, whose character is thus marked by every act which may define a tyrant, is unfit to be the ruler of a free people.

Nor have we been wanting in attention to our British brethren. We have warned them from time to time, of attempts by their legislature to extend an unwarrantable jurisdiction over us. We have reminded them of the circumstances of our emigration and settlement here. We have appealed to their native justice and magnanimity, and we have conjured them by the ties of our common kindred, to disavow these usurpations, which would inevitably interrupt our connexions and correspondence. They, too, have been deaf to the voice of justice and of consanguinity. We must, therefore, acquiesce in the necessity which denounces our separation, and hold them, as we hold the rest of mankind, enemies in war; in peace, friends.

We, therefore, the Representatives of the UNITED STATES OF AMERICA, in GENERAL CONGRESS assembled, appealing to the Supreme Judge of the world for the rectitude of our intentions, Do, in the name, and by the authority of the good People of these Colonies, solemnly publish and declare, That these United Colonies are, and of right ought to be, *Free and Independent States*; that they are absolved from all allegiance to the *British Crown*, and that all political connexion between them and the State of *Great-Britain*, is, and ought to be totally dissolved; and that as *Free and Independent States*, they have full power to levy war, conclude peace, contract alliances, establish commerce, and to do all other acts and things which *Independent States* may of right do. And for the support of this Declaration, with a firm reliance on the protection of Divine Providence, we mutually pledge to each other, our lives, our fortunes, and our sacred honour.

Signed by order and in behalf of the CONGRESS.
JOHN HANCOCK, President.
Attested.
CHARLES THOMSON, Secretary.

---

[1] The British army included many German (especially Hessian) mercenaries.

[2] Jefferson's original draft included the following clause: "He has waged cruel war against human nature itself, violating it's most sacred rights of life and liberty in the persons of a distant people who never offended him, captivating and carrying them into slavery in another hemisphere, or to incure miserable death in their transportation hither. This piratical warfare, the opprobium of infidel powers, is the warfare of the Christian king of Great Britain. Determined to keep open a market where MEN should be bought and sold, he has prostituted his negative for suppressing every legislative attempt to prohibit or to restrain this execrable commerce ... and that this assemblage of horrors might want no fact of distinguished die, he is now exciting those very people to rise in arms among us, and to purchase that liberty of which he had deprived them, by murdering the people upon whom he also obtruded them: thus paying off former crimes committed against the liberties of one people, with crimes which he urges them to commit against the lives of another."

Anna Laetitia Barbauld
1743 – 1825

Anna Laetitia Aikin was born on 20 June 1743 in Kibworth Harcourt, Leicestershire, the first child of Jane Jennings Aikin and John Aikin, D.D., a Unitarian minister and schoolmaster. She learned to read by the age of three; her father also taught her Latin and Greek. In 1758, the Aikins moved to Warrington, Lancashire, where her father had been appointed classical tutor at the famous Dissenting Academy (an academy for non-Anglican Protestants, who were not allowed to attend Oxford or Cambridge). There she remained until May 1774, when she married Rochemont Barbauld, a former student at the Academy. The Barbaulds moved to Palgrave, Sussex, where Rochemont served as a Dissenting minister and opened a boys' school, which was successful for eleven years, largely thanks to Barbauld's exertions. In 1785 the Barbaulds closed the school, travelled for a year, and then settled in Hampstead. In 1802, they moved to Stoke Newington, to be near her brother. Barbauld lived there until her death. Unfortunately, Rochemont, who was mentally ill, became increasingly violent; Barbauld cared for him as long as she could, but in 1808 he was confined in London. He escaped and was found drowned on 11 November.

One of the most prominent intellectuals of her day, Barbauld knew Baillie,* Burney,* Hester Chapone, Coleridge,* Edgeworth,* Elizabeth Montagu, More,* Opie,* Joseph Priestley, Scott,* and William and Dorothy Wordsworth.* She published in a wide variety of genres. Her first collection, *Poems* (1773), published at her brother's encouragement, was a critical and commercial success. Her first works for children, *Hymns in Prose for Children* (1781) and *Lessons for Children* (1787–88), were equally successful, being translated into a number of European languages and remaining in print for over a hundred years. *An Address to the Opposers of the Repeal of the Corporation and Test Acts* (1790) was the first of several influential political pamphlets. Around the turn of the century, Barbauld turned to editorial work, notably in her 50-volume edition of *The British Novelists* (1810), for which she wrote a substantial introductory essay and biographical/critical prefaces for all 28 novelists (12 of whom were women). Her apocalyptic satire *Eighteen Hundred and Eleven* (1812) was not well received in wartime Britain, and Croker's* vicious review in the *Quarterly* so discouraged her that she published almost nothing for the rest of her life. She died in Stoke Newington on 9 March 1825. (D.L.M.)

from *Poems* (1773)

The Mouse's Petition,[1] *Found in the Trap Where He Had Been Confin'd All Night*

Parcere subjectis, & debellare superbos.
                                    Virgil.[2]

Oh! hear a pensive captive's prayer,
For liberty that sighs;
And never let thine heart be shut
Against the prisoner's cries.

5 For here forlorn and sad I sit,
Within the wiry grate;
And tremble at th' approaching morn,
Which brings impending fate.

If e'er thy breast with freedom glow'd,[3]
10 And spurn'd a tyrant's chain,
Let not thy strong oppressive force
A free-born mouse[4] detain.

Oh! do not stain with guiltless blood
Thy hospitable hearth;
15 Nor triumph that thy wiles betray'd
A prize so little worth.

The scatter'd gleanings of a feast
My scanty meals supply;
But if thine unrelenting heart
20 That slender boon deny,

The chearful light, the vital air,
Are blessings widely given;
Let nature's commoners enjoy
The common gifts of heaven.

25 The well taught philosophic mind
To all compassion gives;
Casts round the world an equal eye,
And feels for all that lives.

If mind, as ancient sages taught,
30 A never dying flame,
Still shifts thro' matter's varying forms,
In every form the same,[5]

Beware, lest in the worm you crush
A brother's soul you find;
35 And tremble lest thy luckless hand
Dislodge a kindred mind.

Or, if this transient gleam of day
Be *all* of life we share,
Let pity plead within thy breast,
40 That little *all* to spare.

So may thy hospitable board
With health and peace be crown'd;
And every charm of heartfelt ease
Beneath thy roof be found.

---

[1] "To Doctor PRIESTLEY." (A.B.) Barbauld's friend Joseph Priestley (1733–1804) was a Presbyterian (later Unitarian) minister, political theorist, and scientist; his research into gases led to his discovery of oxygen in 1774. According to William Turner, "In the course of these investigations, the suffocating nature of various gases required to be determined, and no more easy or unexceptionable way of making such experiments could be devised, than the reserving of these little victims of domestic economy, which were thus at least as easily and as speedily put out of existence, as by any of the more usual modes. It happened that a captive was brought in after supper, too late for any experiment to be made with it that night, and the servant was desired to set it by till next morning. Next morning it was brought in after breakfast, with its petition twisted among the wires of its cage. It scarcely need be added, that the petition was successful" ("Mrs. Barbauld" 184; qtd in McCarthy and Kraft 244). McCarthy and Kraft argue that the poem was probably written in 1771.

[2] "To spare the humble, and war down the proud" (*Aeneid* 6.853).

[3] Priestley was well known for his radical political views. In 1791, his house, church, and laboratory would be destroyed by a counter-Revolutionary mob.

[4] a play on such common expressions as "a free-born Briton" and "a free-born Englishman."

[5] an allusion to the Pythagorean idea of the transmigration of souls, or reincarnation, which had previously seemed plausible to Priestley (McCarthy and Kraft 246).

45　So when unseen destruction lurks,
　　Which men like mice may share,
　　May some kind angel clear thy path,
　　And break the hidden snare.

A Summer Evening's Meditation

> One sun by day, by night ten thousand shine.
> 　　　　　　　　　　　　　　Young.[1]

　　'Tis past! The sultry tyrant of the south
　　Has spent his short-liv'd rage; more grateful hours
　　Move silent on; the skies no more repel
　　The dazzled sight, but with mild maiden beams
5　Of temper'd light, invite the cherish'd eye
　　To wander o'er their sphere; where hung aloft
　　DIAN's bright crescent, like a silver bow
　　New strung in heaven, lifts high its beamy horns
　　Impatient for the night, and seems to push
10　Her brother down the sky. Fair VENUS shines
　　Even in the eye of day; with sweetest beam
　　Propitious shines, and shakes a trembling flood
　　Of soften'd radiance from her dewy locks.
　　The shadows spread apace; while meeken'd Eve
15　Her cheek yet warm with blushes, slow retires
　　Thro' the Hesperian gardens of the west,
　　And shuts the gates of day. 'Tis now the hour
　　When Contemplation, from her sunless haunts,
　　The cool damp grotto, or the lonely depth
20　Of unpierc'd woods, where wrapt in solid shade
　　She mused away the gaudy hours of noon,
　　And fed on thoughts unripen'd by the sun,
　　Moves forward; and with radiant finger points
　　To yon blue concave swell'd by breath divine,
25　Where, one by one, the living eyes of heaven
　　Awake, quick kindling o'er the face of ether
　　One boundless blaze;[2] ten thousand trembling fires,
　　And dancing lustres, where th' unsteady eye
　　Restless, and dazzled wanders unconfin'd
30　O'er all this field of glories: spacious field!

---

[1] Edward Young (1683–1765), *The Complaint: or Night Thoughts* (1742–45) 9.748.

[2] Cf. James Thomson (1700–48), *Liberty* (1735–36) 3.41.

　　And worthy of the master: he, whose hand
　　With hieroglyphics older than the Nile,
　　Inscrib'd the mystic tablet; hung on high
　　To public gaze, and said, adore, O man!
35　The finger of thy GOD. From what pure wells
　　Of milky light, what soft o'erflowing urn,
　　Are all these lamps so fill'd? these friendly lamps,
　　For ever streaming o'er the azure deep
　　To point our path, and light us to our home.
40　How soft they slide along their lucid spheres!
　　And silent as the foot of time, fulfil
　　Their destin'd courses: Nature's self is hush'd,
　　And, but a scatter'd leaf, which rustles thro'
　　The thick-wove foliage, not a sound is heard
45　To break the midnight air; tho' the rais'd ear,
　　Intensely listening, drinks in every breath.
　　How deep the silence, yet how loud the praise!
　　But are they silent all? or is there not
　　A tongue in every star that talks with man,
50　And wooes him to be wise; nor wooes in vain:
　　This dead of midnight is the noon of thought,
　　And wisdom mounts her zenith with the stars.
　　At this still hour the self-collected soul
　　Turns inward, and beholds a stranger there
55　Of high descent, and more than mortal rank;
　　An embryo GOD; a spark of fire divine,
　　Which must burn on for ages, when the sun,
　　(Fair transitory creature of a day!)
　　Has clos'd his golden eye, and wrapt in shades
60　Forgets his wonted journey thro' the east.

　　Ye citadels of light, and seats of GODS!
　　Perhaps my future home, from whence the soul
　　Revolving periods past, may oft look back
　　With recollected tenderness, on all
65　The various busy scenes she left below,
　　Its deep laid projects and its strange events,
　　As on some fond and doating tale that sooth'd
　　Her infant hours; O be it lawful now
　　To tread the hallow'd circles of your courts,
70　And with mute wonder and delighted awe
　　Approach your burning confines. Seiz'd in thought
　　On fancy's wild and roving wing I sail,
　　From the green borders of the peopled earth,

And the pale moon, her duteous fair attendant;
From solitary Mars; from the vast orb
Of Jupiter, whose huge gigantic bulk
Dances in ether like the lightest leaf;
To the dim verge, the suburbs of the system,
Where chearless Saturn 'midst her watry moons
Girt with a lucid zone, majestic sits
In gloomy grandeur; like an exil'd queen
Amongst her weeping handmaids:[1] fearless thence
I launch into the trackless deeps of space,
Where, burning round, ten thousand suns appear,
Of elder beam; which ask no leave to shine
Of our terrestrial star, nor borrow light
From the proud regent of our scanty day;
Sons of the morning,[2] first born of creation,
And only less than him who marks their track,
And guides their fiery wheels. Here must I stop,
Or is there aught beyond? What hand unseen
Impels me onward thro' the glowing orbs
Of habitable nature; far remote,
To the dread confines of eternal night,
To solitudes of vast unpeopled space,
The desarts of creation, wide and wild;
Where embryo systems and unkindled suns
Sleep in the womb of chaos; fancy droops,
And thought astonish'd stops her bold career.
But oh thou mighty mind! whose powerful word
Said, thus let all things be, and thus they were,[3]
Where shall I seek thy presence? how unblam'd[4]
Invoke thy dread perfection?
Have the broad eye-lids of the morn[5] beheld thee?
Or does the beamy shoulder of Orion
Support thy throne? O look with pity down
On erring guilty man; not in thy names
Of terrour clad; not with those thunders arm'd

That conscious Sinai felt, when fear appall'd
The scatter'd tribes;[6] thou hast a gentler voice,
That whispers comfort to the swelling heart,
Abash'd, yet longing to behold her Maker.

But now my soul unus'd to stretch her powers
In flight so daring, drops her weary wing,
And seeks again the known accustom'd spot,
Drest up with sun, and shade, and lawns, and streams,
A mansion fair and spacious for its guest,
And full replete with wonders. Let me here
Content and grateful, wait th' appointed time
And ripen for the skies: the hour will come
When all these splendours bursting on my sight
Shall stand unveil'd, and to my ravished sense
Unlock the glories of the world unknown.

An Address to the Opposers of the Repeal of the Corporation and Test Acts (1790)[7]

A System of Toleration, attended with humiliating Distinctions, is so vicious in itself, that the Man who is forced to tolerate is as much dissatisfied with the Law as he that obtains such a Toleration.
Speech of Count Clermont Tonnere[8]

GENTLEMEN,
Had the question of yesterday[9] been decided in a manner more favourable to our wishes, which however

---

[1] Apparently in response to a reviewer's criticism (McCarthy and Kraft 270–71), Barbauld changed lines 79–82 to read: "Where cheerless Saturn 'midst *his* watery moons/ Girt with a lucid zone, in gloomy pomp/ Sits like an exiled *monarch*: fearless thence …" (emphasis added).

[2] Cf. Isaiah 14.12.

[3] Cf. Genesis 1.

[4] Milton, *Paradise Lost* 3.3.

[5] Cf. Job 41.18.

[6] Exodus 19.16–20.

[7] Our copy-text is the 4th edition (1790). The Corporation Act (1661), directed mainly against Presbyterians, and the Test Act (1673), directed mainly against Catholics, effectively excluded all non-Anglicans from holding public office. They were not repealed until the Catholic Emancipation of 1828–29.

[8] Stanislas, comte de Clermont-Tonnerre (1757–92), *Translation of a Speech, Spoken by the Count Clermont Tonnerre … on the Subject of admitting Non-Catholics, Comedians, and Jews, to all the Privileges of Citizens* (1790). Clermont-Tonnerre, a moderate early leader of the French Revolution, was killed during the overthrow of the monarchy on 10 August 1792.

[9] On 2 March 1790, a motion to repeal the Corporation and Test Acts was defeated in the House of Commons by 189 votes.

the previous intimations of your temper in the business left us little room to expect, we should have addressed our thanks to you on the occasion. As it is, we address to you our thanks for much casual light thrown upon the subject, and for many incidental testimonies of your esteem (whether voluntary or involuntary we will not stop to examine) which in the course of this discussion you have favoured us with. We thank you for the compliment paid the Dissenters,[1] when you suppose that the moment they are eligible to places of power and profit, all such places will at once be filled with them. Not content with confounding, by an artful sophism, the right of eligibility with the right to offices, you again confound that right with the probable fact, and then argue accordingly. Is then the Test Act, your boasted bulwark, of equal necessity with the dykes in Holland; and do we wait, like an impetuous sea, to rush in and overwhelm the land? Our pretensions, Gentlemen, are far humbler. *We* had not the presumption to imagine that, inconsiderable as we are in numbers, compared to the established Church; inferior too in fortune and influence; labouring, as we do, under the frown of the Court, and the anathema of the orthodox; we should make our way so readily into the secret recesses of royal favour; and, of a sudden, like the frogs of Egypt,[2] swarm about your barns, and under your canopies, and in your kneading troughs, and in the chamber of the King. We rather wished this act as a removal of a stigma than the possession of a certain advantage, and we might have been cheaply pleased with the acknowledgment of the right, though we had never been fortunate enough to enjoy the emolument.

Another compliment for which we offer our acknowledgements may be extracted from the great ferment, which has been raised by this business all over the country. What stir and movement has it occasioned among the different orders of men! How quick the alarm has been taken, and sounded from the Church to the Senate,[3] and from the press to the people; while fears and forebodings were communicated like an electric shock! The old cry of, *the Church is in danger*, has again been made to vibrate in our ears. Here too if we gave way to impressions of vanity, we might suppose ourselves of much greater importance in the political scale than our numbers and situation seem to indicate. It shews at least we are feared, which to some minds would be the next grateful thing to being beloved. We, indeed, should only wish for the latter; nor should we have ventured to suppose, but from the information you have given us, that your Church *was* so weak. What! fenced and guarded as she is with her exclusive privileges and rich emoluments, stately with her learned halls and endowed colleges, with all the attraction of her wealth, and the thunder of her censures; all that the orator calls *the majesty of the Church* about her, and does she, resting in security under the broad buckler of the State, does she tremble at the naked and unarmed sectary? he, whose early connections, and phrase uncouth, and unpopular opinions set him at a distance from the means of advancement; he, who in the intercourses of neighbourhood and common life, like new settlers, finds it necessary to clear the ground before him, and is ever obliged to root up a prejudice before he can plant affection. He is not of the world, Gentlemen, and the world loveth her own.[4] All that distinguishes him from other men to common observation, operates in his disfavour. His very advocates, while they plead his cause, are ready to blush for their client; and in justice to their own character think it necessary to disclaim all knowledge of his obscure tenets. And is it from his hand you expect the demolition of so massy an edifice? Does the simple removal of the Test Act involve its destruction? These were not *our* thoughts. *We* had too much reverence for your establishment to imagine that the structure was so loosely put together, or so much shaken by years, as that the removal of so slight a pin should endanger the whole fabric[5]—or is the Test Act the *talisman* which holds it together, that, when it is broken, the whole must fall to pieces like the magic palace of an enchanter? Surely no species of regular architecture can

---

[1] non-Anglican Protestants—e.g., Unitarians like Barbauld.

[2] Cf. Exodus 8.1–14.

[3] The House of Lords.

[4] Cf. John 8.23 and 15.19.

[5] Cf. Jonathan Swift (1667–1745), "An Argument against Abolishing Christianity" (1711).

depend upon so slight a support.———After all what is it we have asked?———to share in the rich benefices of the established church? to have the gates of her schools and universities thrown open to us? No, let her keep her golden prebends, her scarfs, her lawn, her mitres. Let her dignitaries be still associated to the honours of legislation; and, in our courts of executive justice, let her inquisitorial tribunals continue to thwart the spirit of a free constitution by a heterogeneous mixture of priestly jurisdiction. Let her still gather into barns, though she neither sows nor reaps.[1] We desire not to share in her good things. We know it is the children's bread, which must not be given to dogs.[2] But *having* these good things, we *could* wish to hear her say with the generous spirit of Esau, *I have enough, my brother.*[3] We could wish to be considered as children of the State, though we are not so of the Church. She must excuse us if we look upon the alliance between her and the State as an ill sorted union, and herself as a mother-in-law who, with the too frequent arts of that relation, is ever endeavouring to prejudice the State, the common parent of us all, against a part of his offspring, for the sake of appropriating a larger portion to her own children. We claim no share in the dowry of her who is not our mother, but we may be pardoned for thinking it hard to be deprived of the inheritance of our father.

But it is objected to us that we have sinned in the manner of making our request; we have brought it forward as a claim instead of asking it as a favour. We should have sued, and crept, and humbled ourselves. Our preachers and our writers should not have dared to express the warm glow of honest sentiment, or, even in a foreign country glance at the downfall of a haughty aristocracy.[4] As we were suppliants, we should have behaved like suppliants, and then perhaps———No, Gentlemen, we wish to have it understood, that we *do* claim it as a right. It loses otherwise half its value. We claim it as men, we claim it as citizens, we claim it as good subjects. We are not conscious of having brought the disqualification upon ourselves by a failure in any of these characters.

But we already enjoy a complete toleration———It is time, so near the end of the eighteenth century, it is surely time to speak with precision, and to call things by their proper names. What you call toleration, we call the exercise of a natural and unalienable right. We do not conceive it to be toleration, first to strip a man of all his dearest rights, and then to give him back a part; or even if it were the whole. You tolerate us in worshipping God according to our consciences———and why not tolerate a man in the use of his limbs, in the disposal of his private property, the contracting his domestic engagements, or any other the most acknowledged privileges of humanity? It is not to these things that the word toleration is applied with propriety. It is applied, where from lenity or prudence we forbear doing all which in justice we might do. It is the bearing with what is confessedly an evil, for the sake of some good with which it is connected. It is the Christian virtue of long suffering; it is the political virtue of adapting measures to times and seasons and situations. *Abuses* are tolerated, when they are so interwoven with the texture of the piece, that the operation of removing them becomes too delicate and hazardous. *Unjust claims* are tolerated, when they are complied with for the sake of peace and conscience. The failings and imperfections of those characters in which there appears an evident preponderancy of virtue, are tolerated. These are the proper objects of toleration, these exercise the patience of the Christian and the prudence of the Statesman; but if there be a power that advances pretences which we think unfounded in reason or scripture, that exercises an empire within an empire, and claims submission from those naturally her equals; and if we, from a spirit of brotherly charity, and just deference to public opinion, and a salutary dread of innovation, acquiesce in these pretensions; let her at least be told that the virtue of forbearance should be transferred, and that it is we who tolerate her, not she who tolerates us.

Complete Toleration, though an expression often adverted to by both parties, is in truth a solecism in terms; for all that is tolerated ought to be done away

---

[1] Cf. Matthew 6.26.

[2] Cf. Matthew 15.26.

[3] Genesis 33.9.

[4] The French National Assembly abolished all feudal privileges on 4 August 1789.

whenever it is found practicable and expedient. Complete Convalescence is no longer Convalescence, but Health; and complete Toleration is no longer Toleration, but Liberty. Let the term therefore be discarded, which, however softened, involves in it an insult with regard to us, and however extended, an absurdity with regard to yourselves. Sensible that a spirit of liberality requires the indulgence to be *complete*, and desirous at the same time to retain the idea of our holding it through sufferance and not of right, you have been betrayed into this incongruity of expression. Those are always liable to be betrayed into such, who have not the courage to embrace a system in its full extent, and to follow a principle wherever it may lead them. Hence the *progress* from Error to Truth, and from Bigotry to the most enlarged freedom of sentiment, is marked with greater *inconsistencies* than that state in which the mind quietly rests in the former position. It is only when we view objects by a dubious and uncertain twilight that we are apt to mistake their figure and distances, and to be disturbed by groundless terrors; in perfect darkness we form no judgment about them.—It has ever been the untoward fate of your Church to partake largely of these inconsistencies. Placed between the Catholics on one side, and the Dissenters on the other, she has not been able to defend either her resistance or her restraints, and lies equally open to censure for her persecution and her dissent. Pressed by the difficulties of her peculiar situation, she is continually obliged in the course of her polemic warfare to change her ground, and alter her mode of defence; and like the poor Bat in the fable,[1] to tell a different story upon every new attack; and thus it must be, till she shall have the magnanimity to make use of all her light, and follow her reason without reserve.

For Truth is of a nature strangely encroaching, and ought to be kept out entirely if we are not disposed to admit her with perfect freedom. You cannot say to her, Thus far shalt thou go, and no further.[2] Give her the least entrance, and she will never be satisfied till she has gained entire possession. Allow her but a few plain axioms to work with, and step by step, syllogism after syllogism, she insensibly mines her way into the very heart of her enemy's entrenchments. Truth is of a very intolerant spirit. She will not make any compromise with Error, and if she be obliged to hold any fellowship with her, it is such fellowship as light has with darkness, a perpetual warfare and opposition. Every concession made by her antagonist is turned into a fresh weapon against her, and being herself invulnerable, she is sure to gain by each successive contest, till her adversary is driven from every shelter and lurking-hole, and fairly obliged to quit possession of the field.

But this, it is again imputed to us, is no contest for religious liberty, but a contest for power, and place, and influence. We want civil offices—And why should citizens *not* aspire to civil offices? Why should not the fair field of generous competition be freely opened to every one!——A contention for power——It is not a contention for power between Churchmen and Dissenters, nor is it as Dissenters we wish to enter the lists; we wish to bury every name of distinction in the common appellation of Citizen. We wish not the name of Dissenter to be pronounced, except in our theological researches and religious assemblies. It is you, who by considering us as Aliens, make us so. It is you who force us to make our dissent a prominent feature in our character. It is you who give relief, and cause to come out upon the canvas what we modestly wished to have shaded over, and thrown into the back ground. If we are a party, remember it is you who force us to be so.—— We should have sought places of trust—By no unfair, unconstitutional methods should we have sought them, but in the open and honourable rivalship of virtuous emulation; by trying to deserve well of our King and our Country. Our attachment to both is well known.

Perhaps however we have all this while mistaken the matter, and what we have taken for bigotry and a narrow-minded spirit is after all only an affair of calcula-

---

[1] Aesop, "The Bat and the Weasels" (fable 364). Attacked by a weasel who takes it for a mouse, the bat claims to be a bird; attacked by another weasel who takes it for a bird, it makes the opposite claim.

[2] Cf. Job 38.11.

tion and arithmetic. Our fellow-subjects remember the homely proverb, "the fewer the better cheer,"[1] and, very naturally, are glad to see the number of candidates lessened for the advantages they are themselves striving after. If so, we ask their excuse, their conduct is quite simple, and if, from the number of concurrents, Government were to strike out all above or under five feet high, or all whose birth-days happened before the Summer Solstice, or, by any other mode of distinction equally arbitrary and whimsical were to reduce the number of their rivals, *they* would be equally pleased, and equally unwilling to admit an alteration. We are a mercantile people, accustomed to consider chances, and we can easily perceive that in the lottery of life, if a certain proportion are by some means or other excluded from a prize, the adventure is exactly so much the better for the remainder. If this indeed be the case, as I suspect it may, we have been accusing you wrongfully. Your conduct is founded upon principles as sure and unvarying as mathematical truths; and all further discussion is needless. We drop the argument at once. Men have now and then been reasoned out of their prejudices, but it were a hopeless attempt to reason them out of their interest.

We likewise beg leave to apologize to those of the clergy, whom we have unwittingly offended by endeavouring to include *them* as parties in our cause. "Pricked to it by foolish honesty and love,"[2] we thought that what appeared so grievous to us could not be very pleasant to them: but we are convinced of our mistake, and sorry for our officiousness. We own it, Sirs, it was a fond imagination that because *we* should have felt uneasy under the obligation imposed upon you, it should have the same effect upon yourselves. It was weak to impute to you an idle delicacy of conscience, which perhaps can only be preserved at a distance from the splendid scenes which you have continually in prospect. But you will pardon us. We did not consider the force of early discipline over the mind. *We* are not accustomed to those salvos, and glosses, and accommodating modes of reasoning with which you have been long familiarized. You have the happy art of making easy to yourselves greater things than this. You are regularly disciplined troops, and understand every nice manœuvre and dextrous evolution which the nature of the ground may require. We are like an unbroken horse; hard mouthed, and apt to start at shadows. Our conduct towards you in this particular we acknowledge may fairly provoke a smile at our simplicity. Besides, upon reflection what should you startle at? The mixture of secular and religious concerns cannot to you appear extraordinary; and in truth nothing is more reasonable than that, as the State has been drawn in to the aggrandizement of your Church, your Church should in return make itself subservient to the convenience of the State. If we are wise, we shall never again make ourselves uneasy about your share of the grievance.

But we were enumerating our obligations to you, Gentlemen, who have thwarted our request, and we must take the liberty to inform you that if it be any object of our ambition to exist and attract notice as a separate body, you have done us the greatest service in the world. What we desired, by blending us with the common mass of citizens, would have sunk our relative importance, and consigned our discussions to oblivion. You have refused us; and by so doing, you keep us under the eye of the public, in the interesting point of view of men who suffer under a deprivation of their rights. You have set a mark of separation upon us, and it is not in our power to take it off, but it is in our power to determine whether it shall be a disgraceful stigma or an honourable distinction. If, by the continued peaceableness of our demeanour, and the superior sobriety of our conversation, a sobriety for which we have not yet quite ceased to be distinguished; if, by our attention to literature, and that ardent love of liberty which you are pretty ready to allow us, we deserve esteem, we shall enjoy it. If our rising seminaries should excel in wholesome discipline and regularity, if *they* should be schools of morality, and yours, unhappily, should be corrupted into schools of immorality, you will entrust us with the education of your youth, when the parent, trembling at the profligacy of the times, wishes to preserve the blooming and ingenuous child from the

---

[1] originally interpolated by Peter Anthony Motteux (1660–1718) in his translation of Rabelais (1693–94).

[2] Shakespeare, *Othello* 3.3.412.

degrading taint of early licentiousness. If our writers are solid, elegant, or nervous, you will read our books and imbibe our sentiments, and even your Preachers will not disdain, occasionally, to *illustrate* our morality. If we enlighten the world by philosophical discoveries,[1] you will pay the involuntary homage due to genius, and boast of our names when, amongst foreign societies, you are inclined to do credit to your country. If your restraints operate towards keeping us in that middle rank of life where industry and virtue most abound, we shall have the honour to count ourselves among that class of the community which has ever been the source of manners, of population and of wealth. If we seek for fortune in the track which you have left most open to us, we shall increase your commercial importance. If, in short, we render ourselves worthy of respect, you cannot hinder us from being respected—you cannot help respecting us—and in spite of all names of opprobrious separation, we shall be bound together by mutual esteem and the mutual reciprocation of good offices.

One good office we shall most probably do you is rather an invidious one, and seldom meets with thanks. By laying us under such a marked disqualification, you have rendered us—we hope not uncandid—we hope not disaffected—May the God of love and charity preserve us from all such acrimonious dispositions! But you certainly have, as far as in you lies, rendered us quick sighted to encroachment and abuses of all kinds. We have the feelings of men; and though we should be very blameable to suffer ourselves to be biassed by any private hardships, and hope that, as a body, we never shall, yet this you will consider, that we have at least no bias on the other side. We have no favours to blind us, no golden padlock on our tongues, and therefore it is probable enough, that, if cause is given, we shall cry aloud and spare not.[2] But in this you have done yourselves no disservice. It is perfectly agreeable to the jealous spirit of a free constitution that there should be some who will season the mass with the wholesome spirit of opposition. Without a little of that bitter leaven there is great danger of its being corrupted.

With regard to ourselves, you have by your late determination given perhaps a salutary, perhaps a seasonable check to that spirit of worldliness, which of late has gained but too much ground amongst us. Before you—before the world—we have a right to bear the brow erect, to talk of rights and services; but there is a place and a presence where it will become us to make no boast. We, as well as you, are infected. We, as well as you, have breathed in the universal contagion—a contagion more noxious, and more difficult to escape, than that which on the plains of Cherson[3] has just swept from the world the martyr of humanity; the contagion of selfish indifference, and fashionable manners has seized us: and our languishing virtue feels the debilitating influence.—If you were more conversant in our assemblies than your prejudices will permit you to be, you would see indifference, where you fancy there is an over proportion of zeal: you would see principles giving way, and families melting into the bosom of the church under the warm influence of prosperity. You would see that establishments, without calling coercive measures to their aid, possess attraction enough severely to try the virtue and steadiness of those who separate from them. You need not strew thorns, or put bars across our path; your golden apples[4] are sufficient to make us turn out of the way. Believe me, Gentlemen, you do not *know* us sufficiently to aim your censure where we should be most vulnerable.

Nor need you apprehend from us the slightest danger to your own establishment. If you will needs have it that it *is* in danger, we wish you to be aware that the danger arises from among yourselves. If ever your creeds and formularies become as grievous to the generality of your Clergy as they already are to many delicate and thinking minds amongst them; if ever any material articles of your professed belief should be

---

[1] a reference to the scientific work of Barbauld's friend Joseph Priestley.

[2] Isaiah 58.1.

[3] a Greek colony on the Black Sea, on the site of modern-day Sevastopol. John Howard (1726–90), philanthropist and prison reformer, had just died there.

[4] The Greek princess Atalanta would only marry a man who could beat her in a foot-race. Her suitor Hippomenes succeeded by dropping three golden apples Venus had given him: Atalanta paused to pick them up, so he was able to beat her. See Ovid, *Metamorphoses* 10.

generally disbelieved, or that order which has been accustomed to supply faithful pastors and learned enquirers after truth should become a burden upon a generous public; and if her dignities and emoluments, instead of being graced by merit or genius, and thus in some measure balancing the weight of hereditary honour and influence, should be considered as appendages to them, the cry for reformation would then be loud and prevailing. It *would* be heard. Doctrines which will not stand the test of argument and reason will not always be believed, and when they have ceased to be generally believed they will not long be articles of belief. If therefore there is any weak place in your system, any thing which you are obliged to gloss over, and touch with a tender hand, any thing which shrinks at investigation—Look ye to it, its extinction is not far off. Doubts and difficulties, that arise first amongst the learned, will not stop there; they inevitably spread downwards from class to class; and if the people should ever find that your articles are generally subscribed as articles of peace, they will be apt to remember that they are articles of expence too. If all the Dissenters in the kingdom, still believing as Dissenters do, were this moment, in order to avoid the reproach of schism, to enter the pale of your church, they would do you mischief; they would hasten its decline; and if all who in their hearts dissent from your professions of faith were to cease making them, and throw themselves amongst the Dissenters, you would stand the firmer for it. Your church is in no danger because we are of a different church; they might stand together to the end of time without interference; but it will be in great danger whenever it has within itself many who have thrown aside its doctrines, or even, who do not embrace them in the simple and obvious sense. All the power and policy of man cannot continue a system *long* after its truth has ceased to be acknowledged, or an establishment *long* after it has ceased to contribute to utility. It is equally vain, as to expect to preserve a tree, whose roots are cut away. It may look as green and flourishing as before for a short time, but its sentence is passed, its principle of life is gone, and death is already within it. If then you think the church in danger, be not backward to preserve the sound by sacrificing the decayed.

To return to ourselves, and our feelings on the business lately in agitation——You will excuse us if we do not appear with the air of men baffled and disappointed. Neither do we blush at our defeat; we may blush, indeed, but it is for our country; but we lay hold on the consoling persuasion, that reason, truth and liberality must finally prevail. We appeal from Philip intoxicated to Philip sober.[1] We know you will refuse us while you are narrow minded, but you will not always be narrow minded. You have too much light and candour not to have more. We will no more attempt to pluck the green unripe fruit. We see in you our future friends and brethren, eager to confound and blend with ours your interests and your affections. You will grant us all we ask. The only question between us is, whether you will do it to-day—To-morrow you certainly will. You will even intreat us, if need were, to allow you to remove from your country the stigma of illiberality. We appeal to the certain, sure operation of increasing light and knowledge, which it is no more in your power to stop, than to repel the tide with your naked hand, or to wither with your breath the genial influence of vegetation. The spread of that light is in general gradual and imperceptible; but there are periods when its progress is accelerated, when it seems with a sudden flash to open the firmament, and pour in day at once. Can ye not discern the signs of the times?[2] The minds of men are in movement from the Borysthenes[3] to the Atlantic. Agitated with new and strong emotions, they swell and heave beneath oppression, as the seas within the Polar Circle, when, at the approach of Spring, they grow impatient to burst their icy chains; when what, but an instant before, seemed so firm, spread for many a dreary league like a floor of solid marble, at once with a tremendous noise gives way, long fissures spread in every direction, and the air resounds with the clash of floating fragments, which every hour are broken from the mass. The genius of Philosophy is walking abroad, and with

---

[1] According to Valerius Maximus, Philip II of Macedon (382–336 BC) once passed down an unjust sentence while he was drunk. The woman sentenced said she would appeal when he was sober.

[2] Matthew 16.3.

[3] the river Dnieper, which flows from near Moscow to the Black Sea.

the touch of Ithuriel's spear[1] is trying the establishments of the earth. The various forms of Prejudice, Superstition and Servility start up in their true shapes, which had long imposed upon the world under the revered semblances of Honour, Faith, and Loyalty. Whatever is loose must be shaken, whatever is corrupted must be lopt away; whatever is not built on the broad basis of public utility must be thrown to the ground. Obscure murmurs gather, and swell into a tempest; the spirit of Enquiry, like a severe and searching wind, penetrates every part of the great body politic; and whatever is unsound, whatever is infirm, shrinks at the visitation. Liberty, here with the lifted crosier in her hand, and the crucifix conspicuous on her breast; there led by Philosophy, and crowned with the civic wreath, animates men to assert their long forgotten rights. With a policy, far more liberal and comprehensive than the boasted establishments of Greece and Rome, she diffuses her blessings to every class of men; and even extends a smile of hope and promise to the poor African, the victim of hard, impenetrable avarice. Man, *as* man, becomes an object of respect. Tenets are transferred from theory to practice. The glowing sentiment and the lofty speculation no longer serve "but to adorn the pages of a book";[2] they are brought home to men's business and bosoms;[3] and, what some centuries ago it was daring but to think, and dangerous to express, is now realized, and carried into effect. Systems are analysed into their first principles, and principles are fairly pursued to their legitimate consequences. The enemies of reformation, who palliate what they cannot defend, and defer what they dare not refuse; who, with Festus,[4] put off to a more convenient season what, only because it is the present season is inconvenient, stand aghast; and find they have no power to put back the important hour, when nature is labouring with the birth of great events. Can ye not discern—But you do discern these signs; you discern them well, and your alarm is apparent. You see a mighty empire breaking from bondage, and exerting the energies of recovered freedom:[5] and England——which was used to glory in being the assertor of liberty, and refuge of the oppressed——England, who with generous and respectful sympathy, in times not far remote from our own memory, has afforded an asylum to so many of the subjects of that very empire, when crushed beneath the iron rod of persecution; and, by so doing, circulated a livelier abhorrence of tyranny within her own veins ——England, who has long reproached her with being a slave now censures her for daring to be free. England, who has held the torch to her, is mortified to see it blaze brighter in her hands. England, for whom, and for whose manners and habits of thinking, that empire has, for some time past, felt even an enthuiastic predilection; and to whom, as a model of laws and government, she looks up with affectionate reverence——England, nursed at the breast of liberty, and breathing the purest spirit of enlightened philosophy, views a sister nation with affected scorn and real jealousy, and presumes to ask whether she yet exists—— Yes, all of her exists that is worthy to do so. Her dungeons indeed exist no longer, the iron doors are forced, the massy walls are thrown down; and the liberated spectres, trembling between joy and horror, may now blazon the infernal secrets of their prison house.[6] Her cloistered Monks no longer exist, nor does the soft heart of sensibility beat behind the grate of a convent,[7] but the best affections of the human mind permitted to flow in their natural channel, diffuse their friendly influence over the brightening prospect of domestic happiness. Nobles, the creatures of Kings, exist there no longer; but Man, the

---

[1] The spear of the angel Ithuriel could expose any falsehood: Milton, *Paradise Lost* 4.810–14.

[2] Cf. Samuel Johnson (1709–84), *The Vanity of Human Wishes* (1749) 222.

[3] Francis Bacon (1561–1626), Dedication to *Essays* (1625).

[4] It was Felix, the Roman governor of Palestine, who put off the release of St. Paul (Acts 24.25): Porcius Festus comes into the story a little later.

[5] another reference to the French Revolution.

[6] a reference to the fall of the Bastille, 14 July 1789.

[7] The French National Assembly abolished all cloistered monastic orders on 13 February 1790; Revolutionary sympathizers saw this as the liberation of the monks and nuns.

creature of God, exists there. Millions of men exist there who, only now, truly begin to exist, and hail with shouts of grateful acclamation the better birth-day of their country. Go on, generous nation, set the world an example of virtues as you have of talents. Be our model, as we have been yours. May the spirit of wisdom, the spirit of moderation, the spirit of firmness, guide and bless your counsels. With intelligence to discern the best possible, may you have prudence to be content with the best practicable. Overcome our wayward perverseness by your steadiness and temper. Silence the scoff of your enemies, and the misgiving fears of your timorous well-wishers. Go on to destroy the empire of prejudices, that empire of gigantic shadows, which are only formidable while they are not attacked. Cause to succeed to the mad ambition of conquest the pacific industry of commerce, and the simple, useful toils of agriculture. While your corn springs up under the shade of your Olives, may bread and peace be the portion of the Husbandman; and when beneath your ardent sun, his brow is bathed in honest sweat, let no one dare any longer with hard and vexatious exactions to wring from him the bitter drop of anguish. Instructed by the experience of past centuries, and by many a sad and sanguine page in your own histories, may you no more attempt to blend what God has made separate; but may religion and civil polity, like the two necessary but opposite elements of fire and water, each in its province do service to mankind, but never again be forced into discordant union. Let the wandering pilgrims of every tribe and complexion, who in other lands find only an asylum, find with you a country, and may you never seek other proof of the purity of your faith than the largeness of your charity. In your manners, your language, and habits of life, let a manly simplicity, becoming the intercourse of equals with equals, take the place of overstrained refinement and adulation. Let public reformation prepare the way for private. May the abolition of domestic tyranny introduce the modest train of houshold virtues, and purer incense be burned upon the hallowed altar of conjugal fidelity. Exhibit to the world the rare phœnomenon of a patriot minister, of a philosophic senate. May a pure and perfect system of legislation proceed from their forming hands, free from those irregularities and abuses, the wear and tear of a constitution, which in a course of years are necessarily accumulated in the best formed States; and like the new creation in its first gloss and freshness, yet free from any taint of corruption, when its Maker blest and called it good.[1] May you never lose sight of the great principle you have held forth, the natural equality of men. May you never forget that without public spirit there can be no liberty; that without virtue there may be a confederacy, but cannot be a community. May you, and may we, consigning to oblivion every less generous competition, only contest who shall set the brightest example to the nations, and may its healing influence be diffused, till the reign of Peace shall spread

— — — "from shore to shore,
Till *Wars* shall cease, and *Slavery* be no more."[2]

Amidst causes of such mighty operation, what are we, and what are our petty, peculiar interests! Triumph, or despondency, at the success or failure of our plans, would be treason to the large, expanded, comprehensive wish which embraces the general interests of humanity. Here then we fix our foot with undoubting confidence, sure that all events are in the hands of him, who from seeming evil

— — — "is still educing good;
And better thence again, and better still,
In infinite progression."[3]

In this hope we look forward to the period when the name of *Dissenter* shall no more be heard of, than that of *Romanist* or *Episcopalian*, when nothing shall be venerable but truth, and nothing valued but utility.

---

[1] Genesis 1.4, 1.10, 1.12, and so on.

[2] Pope, *Windsor-Forest* (1713) 407–08.

[3] James Thomson (1700–48), "A Hymn on the Seasons" (1746) 114–16.

Epistle to William Wilberforce, Esq. on the Rejection of the Bill for Abolishing the Slave-Trade[1] (1791)

Cease, Wilberforce, to urge thy generous aim!
Thy Country knows the sin, and stands the shame!
The Preacher, Poet, Senator[2] in vain
Has rattled in her sight the Negro's chain;
5 With his deep groans assail'd her startled ear,
And rent the veil that hid his constant tear;
Forc'd her averted eyes his stripes to scan,
Beneath the bloody scourge laid bare the man,
Claim'd Pity's tear, urg'd Conscience's strong controul,
10 And flash'd conviction on her shrinking soul.
The Muse, too soon awak'd, with ready tongue
At Mercy's shrine applausive peans rung;
And Freedom's eager sons, in vain foretold
A new Astrean reign, an age of gold:[3]
15 She knows and she persists—Still Afric bleeds,
Uncheck'd, the human traffic still proceeds;
She stamps her infamy to future time,
And on her harden'd forehead seals the crime.

In vain, to thy white standard gathering round,
20 Wit, Worth, and Parts and Eloquence are found:
In vain, to push to birth thy great design,
Contending chiefs, and hostile virtues join;[4]
All, from conflicting ranks, of power possest
To rouse, to melt, or to inform the breast.
25 Where seasoned tools of Avarice prevail,
A Nation's eloquence, combined, must fail:
Each flimsy sophistry by turns they try;
The plausive argument, the daring lye,
The artful gloss, that moral sense confounds,
30 Th' acknowledged thirst of gain that honour wounds:
Bane of ingenuous minds, th' unfeeling sneer,
Which, sudden, turns to stone the falling tear:
They search assiduous, with inverted skill,
For forms of wrong, and precedents of ill;
35 With impious mockery wrest the sacred page,[5]
And glean up crimes from each remoter age:
Wrung Nature's tortures, shuddering, while you tell,
From scoffing fiends bursts forth the laugh of hell;
In Britain's senate, Misery's pangs give birth
40 To jests unseemly, and to horrid mirth——[6]
Forbear!—thy virtues but provoke our doom,
And swell th' account of vengeance yet to come;
For, not unmark'd in Heaven's impartial plan,
Shall man, proud worm, contemn his fellow-man?
45 And injur'd Afric, by herself redrest,
Darts her own serpents at her Tyrant's breast.
Each vice, to minds deprav'd by bondage known,
With sure contagion fastens on his own;
In sickly languors melts his nerveless frame,
50 And blows to rage impetuous Passion's flame:
Fermenting swift, the fiery venom gains
The milky innocence of infant veins;
There swells the stubborn will, damps learning's fire,
The whirlwind wakes of uncontroul'd desire,
55 Sears the young heart to images of woe,
And blasts the buds of Virtue as they blow.

Lo! where reclin'd, pale Beauty courts the breeze,
Diffus'd on sofas of voluptuous ease;
With anxious awe, her menial train around,
60 Catch her faint whispers of half-utter'd sound;
See her, in monstrous fellowship, unite

---

[1] Wilberforce (1759–1833) was the parliamentary leader of the abolition movement. He introduced a motion in favour of abolition in the House of Commons on 18 April 1791; it was defeated on 19 April, by a vote of 163 to 88.

[2] By 1791, advocates of abolition included preachers like Priestley and poets like Cowper,* More,* Wheatley,* and Yearsley* as well as "senators" (parliamentarians) like Wilberforce.

[3] Astræa, the classical goddess of justice, lived on earth during the Golden Age; she has since retreated to the skies, outraged by the crimes of humanity.

[4] The cause of abolition was supported both by radicals like Charles James Fox and by conservatives like Edmund Burke,* William Pitt the Younger, and Wilberforce himself.

[5] Opponents of abolition cited a number of passages from the Bible, notably Noah's curse on Canaan (Genesis 9.25) and Paul's epistle to Philemon.

[6] Some MPs laughed at the speech of William Smith, which recounted how a slave mother had been forced to throw her murdered child overboard (McCarthy and Kraft 286).

At once the Scythian, and the Sybarite;[1]
Blending repugnant vices, misally'd,
Which *frugal* nature purpos'd to divide;
65 See her, with indolence to fierceness join'd,
Of body delicate, infirm of mind,
With languid tones imperious mandates urge;
With arm recumbent wield the household scourge;
And with unruffled mien, and placid sounds,
70 Contriving torture, and inflicting wounds.[2]

Nor, in their palmy walks and spicy groves,
The form benign of rural Pleasure roves;
No milk-maids' song, or hum of village talk,
Sooths the lone Poet in his evening walk:
75 No willing arm the flail unweary'd plies,
Where the mix'd sounds of cheerful labour rise;
No blooming maids, and frolic swains are seen
To pay gay homage to their harvest queen:
No heart-expanding scenes their eyes must prove
80 Of thriving industry, and faithful love:
But shrieks and yells disturb the balmy air,
Dumb sullen looks of woe announce despair,
And angry eyes thro' dusky features glare.
Far from the sounding lash the Muses fly,
85 And sensual riot drowns each finer joy.

Nor less from the gay East, on essenc'd wings,
Breathing unnam'd perfumes, Contagion springs;
The soft luxurious plague alike pervades
The marble palaces, and rural shades;
90 Hence, throng'd Augusta[3] builds her rosy bowers,
And decks in summer wreaths her smoky towers;
And hence, in summer bow'rs, Art's costly hand
Pours courtly splendours o'er the dazzled land:
The manners melt—One undistinguish'd blaze
95 O'erwhelms the sober pomp of elder days;
Corruption follows with gigantic stride,
And scarce vouchsafes his shameless front to hide:

The spreading leprosy taints ev'ry part,
Infects each limb, and sickens at the heart.
100 Simplicity! most dear of rural maids,
Weeping resigns her violated shades:
Stern Independance from his glebe retires,
And anxious Freedom eyes her drooping fires;
By foreign wealth are British morals chang'd,
105 And Afric's sons, and India's, smile aveng'd.

For you, whose temper'd ardour long has borne
Untir'd the labour, and unmov'd the scorn;
In Virtue's fasti[4] be inscrib'd your fame,
And utter'd your's with Howard's[5] honour'd name,
110 Friends of the friendless—Hail, ye generous band!
Whose efforts yet arrest Heav'n's lifted hand,
Around whose steady brows, in union bright,
The civic wreath, and Christian's palm unite:
Your merit stands, no greater and no less,
115 Without, or with the varnish of success;
But seek no more to break a Nation's fall,
For ye have sav'd yourselves—and that is all.
Succeeding times your struggles, and their fate,
With mingled shame and triumph shall relate,
120 While faithful History, in her various page,
Marking the features of this motley age,
To shed a glory, and to fix a stain,
Tells how you strove, and that you strove in vain.

from the *Monthly Magazine* 4 (July–December 1797)

Washing-Day

——————and their voice,
Turning again towards childish treble, pipes
And whistles in its sound.——[6]

---

[1] In classical times, the Scythians were proverbial for savagery; the Sybarites, for decadence.

[2] Cf. Wollstonecraft's description of plantation ladies in *A Vindication of the Rights of Men** (381).

[3] London.

[4] "annals" (L.).

[5] John Howard (1726–90), prison reformer.

[6] Shakespeare, *As You Like It* 2.7.161–63.

The Muses are turned gossips; they have lost
The buskin'd[1] step, and clear high-sounding phrase,
Language of gods. Come, then, domestic Muse,
In slip-shod[2] measure loosely prattling on
5 Of farm or orchard, pleasant curds and cream,
Or drowning flies, or shoe lost in the mire
By little whimpering boy, with rueful face;
Come, Muse, and sing the dreaded *Washing-Day*.
—Ye who beneath the yoke of wedlock bend,
10 With bowed soul, full well ye ken the day
Which week, smooth sliding after week, brings on
Too soon; for to that day nor peace belongs
Nor comfort; e'er the first grey streak of dawn,
The red-arm'd washers come and chase repose.
15 Nor pleasant smile, nor quaint device of mirth,
E'er visited that day; the very cat,
From the wet kitchen scared, and reeking hearth,
Visits the parlour, an unwonted guest.
The silent breakfast-meal is soon dispatch'd
20 Uninterrupted, save by anxious looks
Cast at the lowering sky, if sky should lower.
From that last evil, oh preserve us, heavens!
For should the skies pour down, adieu to all
Remains of quiet; then expect to hear
25 Of sad disasters—dirt and gravel stains
Hard to efface, and loaded lines at once
Snapped short—and linen-horse by dog thrown down,
And all the petty miseries of life.
Saints have been calm while stretched upon the rack,
30 And Montezuma[3] smil'd on burning coals;
But never yet did housewife notable
Greet with a smile a rainy washing-day.
—But grant the welkin fair, require not thou
Who call'st thyself perchance the master there,
35 Or study swept, or nicely dusted coat,
Or usual 'tendance; ask not, indiscreet,
Thy stockings mended, tho' the yawning rents
Gape wide as Erebus,[4] nor hope to find
Some snug recess impervious; should'st thou try
40 The customed garden walks, thine eye shall rue
The budding fragrance of thy tender shrubs,
Myrtle or rose, all crushed beneath the weight
Of coarse check'd apron, with impatient hand
Twitch'd off when showers impend: or crossing lines
45 Shall mar thy musings, as the wet cold sheet
Flaps in thy face abrupt. Woe to the friend
Whose evil stars have urged him forth to claim
On such a day the hospitable rites;
Looks, blank at best, and stinted courtesy,
50 Shall he receive; vainly he feeds his hopes
With dinner of roast chicken, savoury pie,
Or tart or pudding:—pudding he nor tart
That day shall eat; nor, tho' the husband try,
Mending what can't be help'd, to kindle mirth
55 From cheer deficient, shall his consort's brow
Clear up propitious; the unlucky guest
In silence dines, and early slinks away.
    I well remember, when a child, the awe
This day struck into me; for then the maids,
60 I scarce knew why, looked cross, and drove me from
    them;
Nor soft caress could I obtain, nor hope
Usual indulgencies; jelly or creams,
Relique of costly suppers, and set by
For me their petted one; or butter'd toast,
65 When butter was forbid; or thrilling tale
Of ghost, or witch, or murder—so I went
And shelter'd me beside the parlour fire,
There my dear grandmother, eldest of forms,
Tended the little ones, and watched from harm,
70 Anxiously fond, tho' oft her spectacles
With elfin cunning hid, and oft the pins
Drawn from her ravell'd stocking, might have sour'd
One less indulgent.——
At intervals my mother's voice was heard,
75 Urging dispatch; briskly the work went on,
All hands employed to wash, to rinse, to wring,
To fold, and starch, and clap, and iron, and plait.
Then would I sit me down, and ponder much
Why washings were. Sometimes thro' hollow bole
80 Of pipe amused we blew, and sent aloft
The floating bubbles, little dreaming then

---

[1] tragic. (Buskins were the high shoes worn by Greek tragic actors.)

[2] Cf. Pope, *The Dunciad* (1743) 3.15–16.

[3] or Cuauhtemoc (1497–1522), the last emperor of Mexico, tortured and put to death by Cortés.

[4] the dark cavern through which souls passed on their way to Hades.

To see, Mongolfier,[1] thy silken ball
Ride buoyant thro' the clouds—so near approach
The sports of children and the toils of men.
85 Earth, air, and sky, and ocean, hath its bubbles,[2]
And verse is one of them——this most of all.

from the *Monthly Magazine* 7 (January–June 1799)

To Mr. C———ge[3]

Midway the hill of science,[4] after steep
And rugged paths that tire the unpractised feet,
A *grove* extends; in tangled mazes wrought,
And filled with strange enchantment:—dubious shapes
5 Flit through dim glades, and lure the eager foot
Of youthful ardour to eternal chase.
Dreams hang on every leaf: unearthly forms
Glide through the gloom; and mystic visions swim
Before the cheated sense. Athwart the mists,
10 Far into vacant space, huge shadows stretch
And seem realities; while things of life,
Obvious to sight and touch, all glowing round,
Fade to the hue of shadows——*Scruples* here,
With filmy net, most like the autumnal webs
15 Of floating gossamer, arrest the foot
Of generous enterprise; and palsy hope
And fair ambition with the chilling touch
Of sickly hesitation and blank fear.
Nor seldom *Indolence*, these lawns among,
20 Fixes her turf-built seat; and wears the garb
Of deep philosophy, and museful sits,
In dreamy twilight of the vacant mind,
Soothed by the whispering shade; for soothing soft
The shades; and vistas lengthening into air,
25 With moon-beam rainbows tinted——Here each mind
Of finer mould, acute and delicate,
In its high progress to eternal truth
Rests for a space, in fairy bowers entranced;
And loves the softened light and tender gloom;
30 And, pampered with most unsubstantial food,
Looks down indignant on the grosser world,
And matter's cumbrous shapings. Youth beloved
Of science——of the muse beloved, not here,
Not in the maze of metaphysic lore,
35 Build thou thy place of resting! lightly tread
The dangerous ground, on noble aims intent;
And be this Circe[5] of the studious cell
Enjoyed, but still subservient. Active scenes
Shall soon with healthful spirit brace thy mind:
40 And fair exertion, for bright fame sustained,
For friends, for country, chase each spleen-fed fog
That blots the wide creation—
Now heaven conduct thee with a parent's love!

Eighteen Hundred and Eleven, A Poem (1812)

Still the loud death drum, thundering from afar,
O'er the vext nations pours the storm of war:[6]
To the stern call still Britain bends her ear,
Feeds the fierce strife, the alternate hope and fear;
5 Bravely, though vainly, dares to strive with Fate,
And seeks by turns to prop each sinking state.[7]
Colossal Power[8] with overwhelming force
Bears down each fort of Freedom in its course;

---

[1] Joseph-Michel Montgolfier (1740–1810) and Jacques-Etienne Montgolfier (1745–99) made the first ascent in a hot air balloon in 1783.

[2] Cf. Shakespeare, *Macbeth* 1.3.79.

[3] McCarthy and Kraft suggest (296) that Barbauld wrote this poem at about the time she first met Coleridge,* in August 1797.

[4] Cf. the description of the Hill Difficulty, with the "pleasant Arbour" halfway up, in John Bunyan (1628–88), *The Pilgrim's Progress* (1678–84).

[5] an enchantress, who changed Odysseus's companions into swine. Odysseus slept with her after making her swear an oath not to harm him. See Homer, *Odyssey* 10.

[6] Britain had been at war with France almost continuously since 1793.

[7] Russia had surrendered to France in 1807, Spain in 1808, and Austria in 1809. By 1811, all of continental Europe, except Portugal, was under French domination.

[8] Napoléon.

Prostrate she lies beneath the Despot's sway,
While the hushed nations curse him—and obey.

    Bounteous in vain, with frantic man at strife,
Glad Nature pours the means—the joys of life;
In vain with orange blossoms scents the gale,
The hills with olives clothes, with corn the vale;
Man calls to Famine, nor invokes in vain,
Disease and Rapine follow in her train;
The tramp of marching hosts disturbs the plough,
The sword, not sickle, reaps the harvest now,
And where the Soldier gleans the scant supply,
The helpless Peasant but retires to die;
No laws his hut from licensed outrage shield,
And war's least horror is the ensanguined field.

    Fruitful in vain, the matron counts with pride
The blooming youths that grace her honoured side;
No son returns to press her widow'd hand,
Her fallen blossoms strew a foreign strand.
—Fruitful in vain, she boasts her virgin race,
Whom cultured arts adorn and gentlest grace;
Defrauded of its homage, Beauty mourns,
And the rose withers on its virgin thorns.
Frequent, some stream obscure, some uncouth name
By deeds of blood is lifted into fame;
Oft o'er the daily page some soft-one bends
To learn the fate of husband, brothers, friends,
Or the spread map with anxious eye explores,
Its dotted boundaries and penciled shores,
Asks *where* the spot that wrecked her bliss is found,
And learns its name but to detest the sound.

    And think'st thou, Britain, still to sit at ease,
An island Queen amidst thy subject seas,
While the vext billows, in their distant roar,
But soothe thy slumbers, and but kiss thy shore?
To sport in wars, while danger keeps aloof,
Thy grassy turf unbruised by hostile hoof?
So sing thy flatterers; but, Britain, know,
Thou who hast shared the guilt must share the woe.
Nor distant is the hour; low murmurs spread,
And whispered fears, creating what they dread;

Ruin, as with an earthquake shock, is here,[1]
There, the heart-witherings of unuttered fear,
And that sad death, whence most affection bleeds,
Which sickness, only of the soul, precedes.[2]
Thy baseless wealth dissolves in air away,[3]
Like mists that melt before the morning ray:
No more on crowded mart or busy street
Friends, meeting friends, with cheerful hurry greet;
Sad, on the ground thy princely merchants bend
Their altered looks, and evil days portend,
And fold their arms, and watch with anxious breast
The tempest blackening in the distant West.[4]

    Yes, thou must droop; thy Midas[5] dream is o'er;
The golden tide of Commerce leaves thy shore,
Leaves thee to prove the alternate ills that haunt
Enfeebling Luxury and ghastly Want;
Leaves thee, perhaps, to visit distant lands,
And deal the gifts of Heaven with equal hands.

    Yet, O my Country, name beloved, revered,
By every tie that binds the soul endeared,
Whose image to my infant senses came
Mixt with Religion's light and Freedom's holy flame!
If prayers may not avert, if 'tis thy fate
To rank amongst the names that once were great,
Not like the dim cold Crescent[6] shalt thou fade,
Thy debt to Science and the Muse unpaid;
Thine are the laws surrounding states revere,
Thine the full harvest of the mental year,
Thine the bright stars in Glory's sky that shine,
And arts that make it life to live are thine.

---

[1] 1810 had seen an unusually high number of bankruptcies.

[2] Abraham Goldsmid, a London banker, committed suicide in September 1810. (Barbauld's husband, Rochemont, who was mentally ill, had drowned himself in 1808.) Barbauld may also be referring to George III, who became permanently insane in 1811.

[3] In May 1811, a Commons committee issued a report on the depreciation of Britain's paper money.

[4] War would break out with the United States in June 1812.

[5] Everything that King Midas touched turned into gold. See Ovid, *Metamorphoses* 11.

[6] the Ottoman Empire.

If westward streams the light that leaves thy shores,
80 Still from thy lamp the streaming radiance pours.
Wide spreads thy race from Ganges to the pole,
O'er half the western world thy accents roll:
Nations beyond the Apalachian hills[1]
Thy hand has planted and thy spirit fills:
85 Soon as their gradual progress shall impart
The finer sense of morals and of art,
Thy stores of knowledge the new states shall know,
And think thy thoughts, and with thy fancy glow;
Thy Lockes,[2] thy Paleys[3] shall instruct their youth,
90 Thy leading star direct their search for truth;
Beneath the spreading Platan's[4] tent-like shade,
Or by Missouri's rushing waters laid,
"Old father Thames"[5] shall be the Poets' theme,
Of Hagley's woods[6] the enamoured virgin dream,
95 And Milton's tones the raptured ear enthrall,
Mixt with the roar of Niagara's fall;
In Thomson's glass[7] the ingenuous youth shall learn
A fairer face of Nature to discern;
Nor of the Bards that swept the British lyre
100 Shall fade one laurel, or one note expire.
Then, loved Joanna,[8] to admiring eyes
Thy storied groups in scenic pomp shall rise;
Their high soul'd strains and Shakespear's noble rage
Shall with alternate passion shake the stage.
105 Some youthful Basil[9] from thy moral lay
With stricter hand his fond desires shall sway;

Some Ethwald,[10] as the fleeting shadows pass,
Start at his likeness in the mystic glass;
The tragic Muse resume her just controul,
110 With pity and with terror purge the soul,[11]
While wide o'er transatlantic realms thy name
Shall live in light, and gather *all* its fame.

Where wanders Fancy down the lapse of years
Shedding o'er imaged woes untimely tears?
115 Fond moody Power! as hopes—as fears prevail,
She longs, or dreads, to lift the awful veil,
On visions of delight now loves to dwell,
Now hears the shriek of woe or Freedom's knell:
Perhaps, she says, long ages past away,
120 And set in western waves our closing day,
Night, Gothic night, again may shade the plains
Where Power is seated, and where Science reigns;
England, the seat of arts, be only known
By the gray ruin and the mouldering stone;
125 That Time may tear the garland from her brow,
And Europe sit in dust, as Asia now.

Yet then the ingenuous youth whom Fancy fires
With pictured glories of illustrious sires,
With duteous zeal their pilgrimage shall take
130 From the blue mountains,[12] or Ontario's lake,
With fond adoring steps to press the sod
By statesmen, sages, poets, heroes trod;
On Isis'[13] banks to draw inspiring air,
From Runnymede[14] to send the patriot's prayer;
135 In pensive thought, where Cam's[15] slow waters wind,
To meet those shades that ruled the realms of mind;
In silent halls to sculptured marbles bow,

---

[1] The United States acquired its first western territories with the Louisiana Purchase of 1803.

[2] John Locke (1632–1704), author of *An Essay Concerning Human Understanding* (1690).

[3] William Paley (1743–1805), author of *Natural Theology* (1802).

[4] Oriental plane-tree, *Platanus orientalis*.

[5] John Dryden (1631–1700), *Annus Mirabilis, The Year of Wonders* (1667) 925.

[6] Hagley Park was the Worcestershire estate of George, Lord Lyttleton (1709–73), described in Thomson, *Spring* (1728) 904–62.

[7] Thomson, *The Seasons* (1726–30).

[8] Joanna Baillie.* Walter Scott* and other contemporaries compared her to Shakespeare.

[9] the hero of *Count Basil*, the tragedy on love in the first volume of *Plays on the Passions*.

[10] the eponymous hero of the tragedy on ambition, in the second volume of *Plays on the Passions*.

[11] Cf. Aristotle, *Poetics* chap. 6.

[12] a range in Pennsylvania.

[13] the name given to the Thames at Oxford.

[14] in Surrey, where King John was forced to sign the Magna Carta, the first British declaration of rights, in 1215.

[15] Cambridge University is on the banks of the river Cam.

And hang fresh wreaths round Newton's[1] awful brow.
Oft shall they seek some peasant's homely shed,
140 Who toils, unconscious of the mighty dead,
To ask where Avon's[2] winding waters stray,
And thence a knot of wild flowers bear away;
Anxious enquire where Clarkson,[3] friend of man,
Or all-accomplished Jones[4] his race began;
145 If of the modest mansion aught remains
Where Heaven and Nature prompted Cowper's[5] strains;
Where Roscoe,[6] to whose patriot breast belong
The Roman virtue and the Tuscan song,
Led Ceres[7] to the black and barren moor
150 Where Ceres never gained a wreath before:[8]
With curious search their pilgrim steps shall rove
By many a ruined tower and proud alcove,
Shall listen for those strains that soothed of yore
Thy rock, stern Skiddaw,[9] and thy fall, Lodore;[10]

155 Feast with Dun Edin's[11] classic brow their sight,
And visit "Melross by the pale moonlight."[12]

But who their mingled feelings shall pursue
When London's faded glories rise to view?
The mighty city, which by every road,
160 In floods of people poured itself abroad;
Ungirt by walls, irregularly great,
No jealous drawbridge, and no closing gate;
Whose merchants (such the state which commerce brings)
Sent forth their mandates to dependant kings;
165 Streets, where the turban'd Moslem, bearded Jew,
And woolly Afric, met the brown Hindu;
Where through each vein spontaneous plenty flowed,
Where Wealth enjoyed, and Charity bestowed.
Pensive and thoughtful shall the wanderers greet
170 Each splendid square, and still, untrodden street;
Or of some crumbling turret, mined by time,
The broken stair with perilous step shall climb,
Thence stretch their view the wide horizon round,
By scattered hamlets trace its antient bound,
175 And, choked no more with fleets, fair Thames survey
Through reeds and sedge pursue his idle way.

With throbbing bosoms shall the wanderers tread
The hallowed mansions of the silent dead,
Shall enter the long isle and vaulted dome[13]
180 Where Genius and where Valour find a home;
Awe-struck, midst chill sepulchral marbles breathe,
Where all above is still, as all beneath;
Bend at each antique shrine, and frequent turn
To clasp with fond delight some sculptured urn,
185 The ponderous mass of Johnson's form to greet,
Or breathe the prayer at Howard's sainted feet.[14]

---

[1] Sir Isaac Newton (1642–1727) was a fellow of Trinity College and Lucasian Professor of Mathematics at Cambridge. Like Barbauld, W. Wordsworth* was impressed by the statue of Newton in Trinity Chapel (*The Prelude* [1805] 3.58–59; [1850] 60–63).

[2] The Avon flows through Stratford, Warwickshire, birthplace of Shakespeare.

[3] Thomas Clarkson,* the abolitionist, was born in Wisbech, Cambridgeshire.

[4] Sir William Jones (1746–94), linguist and Orientalist, was born in London.

[5] William Cowper's* *Olney Hymns* (1779) are named after the Buckinghamshire town in which he wrote them.

[6] William Roscoe (1753–1831), historian, poet, agriculturalist, and political radical.

[7] the Latin name for Demeter, the goddess of agriculture.

[8] "The Historian of the age of Leo has brought into cultivation the extensive tract of Chatmoss." (A.B.) Roscoe published *The Life and Pontificate of Leo the Tenth* in 1805. He practised experimental agriculture at Chat Moss, Lancashire.

[9] a mountain in the Lake District, described by Coleridge in "A Stranger Minstrel"* and W. Wordsworth in "The Childless Father" (1800) and *The Prelude* (1805) 1.299.

[10] a waterfall in the Lake District, described by W. Wordsworth in *An Evening Walk* (1793) 3–4 and Southey in "The Cataract of Lodore."*

---

[11] Edinburgh's.

[12] Walter Scott,* *The Lay of the Last Minstrel* (1805) 2.1.1–2.

[13] St. Paul's Cathedral.

[14] There are statues of Samuel Johnson (1709–84), poet, essayist, and lexicographer, and John Howard (1726–90), prison reformer, in St. Paul's.

          Perhaps some Briton, in whose musing mind
          Those ages live which Time has cast behind,
          To every spot shall lead his wondering guests
          On whose known site the beam of glory rests:
190   Here Chatham's[1] eloquence in thunder broke,
          Here Fox[2] persuaded, or here Garrick[3] spoke;
          Shall boast how Nelson,[4] fame and death in view,
          To wonted victory led his ardent crew,
195   In England's name enforced, with loftiest tone,[5]
          Their duty,—and too well fulfilled his own:
          How gallant Moore,[6] as ebbing life dissolved,
          But hoped his country had his fame absolved.
          Or call up sages whose capacious mind
200   Left in its course a track of light behind;
          Point where mute crowds on Davy's[7] lips reposed,
          And Nature's coyest secrets were disclosed;
          Join with their Franklin,[8] Priestley's[9] injured name,
          Whom, then, each continent[10] shall proudly claim.

205   Oft shall the strangers turn their eager feet
          The rich remains of antient art to greet,
          The pictured walls with critic eye explore,
          And Reynolds[11] be what Raphael[12] was before.
          On spoils from every clime their eyes shall gaze,[13]
210   Ægyptian granites and the Etruscan vase;
          And when midst fallen London, they survey
          The stone where Alexander's ashes[14] lay,
          Shall own with humbled pride the lesson just
          By Time's slow finger written in the dust.

215   There walks a Spirit o'er the peopled earth,
          Secret his progress is, unknown his birth;
          Moody and viewless as the changing wind,
          No force arrests his foot, no chains can bind;
          Where'er he turns, the human brute awakes,
220   And, roused to better life, his sordid hut forsakes:
          He thinks, he reasons, glows with purer fires,
          Feels finer wants, and burns with new desires:
          Obedient Nature follows where he leads;
          The steaming marsh is changed to fruitful meads;
225   The beasts retire from man's asserted reign,
          And prove his kingdom was not given in vain.
          Then from its bed is drawn the ponderous ore,
          Then Commerce pours her gifts on every shore,
          Then Babel's towers and terrassed gardens[15] rise,
230   And pointed obelisks invade the skies;
          The prince commands, in Tyrian purple[16] drest,
          And Ægypt's virgins weave the linen vest.
          Then spans the graceful arch the roaring tide,
          And stricter bounds the cultured fields divide.
235   Then kindles Fancy, then expands the heart,
          Then blow the flowers of Genius and of Art;
          Saints, Heroes, Sages, who the land adorn,
          Seem rather to descend than to be born;

---

[1] William Pitt the Elder, first Earl of Chatham (1708–78), Prime Minister.

[2] Charles James Fox (1749–1806), Whig leader and steadfast opponent of the war with France.

[3] David Garrick (1717–79), actor and playwright.

[4] Admiral Horatio Lord Nelson (1758–1805).

[5] "Every reader will recollect the sublime telegraphic dispatch, 'England expects every man to do his duty.'" (A.B.) Nelson sent this message to the ships in his fleet before the battle of Trafalgar (21 October 1805), in which he was killed.

[6] "'I hope England will be satisfied,' were the last words of General Moore." (A.B.) General Sir John Moore (1761–1809) was killed on 16 January 1809, during the evacuation of British troops from Corunna, Spain.

[7] Sir Humphry Davy (1778–1829), chemist, offered popular lectures at the Royal Institution.

[8] Benjamin Franklin,* American scientist, writer, and politician.

[9] See "The Mouse's Petition."* Franklin and Priestley were friends.

[10] Franklin had spent considerable time in France; Priestley went into exile in America in 1794.

[11] Sir Joshua Reynolds,* painter and President of the Royal Academy.

[12] Raffaello Sanzio of Urbino (1483–1520), Italian Renaissance painter.

[13] in the British Museum, which had opened in 1759.

[14] The British Museum acquired a granite sarcophagus, believed to be that of Alexander the Great, in 1802.

[15] "Babel" is probably not the Biblical Babel (Genesis 11.1–9), but Babylon; the gardens are the hanging gardens of Babylon, one of the seven wonders of the classical world.

[16] The purple dye made from the murex, a shellfish harvested from the Mediterranean near Tyre, was traditionally associated with royalty.

Whilst History, midst the rolls consigned to fame,
With pen of adamant inscribes their name.

The Genius now forsakes the favoured shore,
And hates, capricious, what he loved before;
Then empires fall to dust, then arts decay,
And wasted realms enfeebled despots sway;
Even Nature's changed; without his fostering smile
Ophir[1] no gold, no plenty yields the Nile;[2]
The thirsty sand absorbs the useless rill,
And spotted plagues from putrid fens distill.
In desert solitudes then Tadmor[3] sleeps,
Stern Marius[4] then o'er fallen Carthage weeps;
Then with enthusiast love the pilgrim roves
To seek his footsteps in forsaken groves,
Explores the fractured arch, the ruined tower,
Those limbs disjointed of gigantic power;
Still at each step he dreads the adder's sting,
The Arab's javelin, or the tiger's spring;
With doubtful caution treads the echoing ground,
And asks where Troy or Babylon is found.

And now the vagrant Power no more detains
The vale of Tempe,[5] or Ausonian[6] plains;
Northward he throws the animating ray,
O'er Celtic nations bursts the mental day:
And, as some playful child the mirror turns,
Now here now there the moving lustre burns;
Now o'er his changeful fancy more prevail
Batavia's[7] dykes than Arno's[8] purple vale,
And stinted suns, and rivers bound with frost,
Than Enna's[9] plains or Baia's[10] viny coast;
Venice the Adriatic weds[11] in vain,
And Death sits brooding o'er Campania's[12] plain;
O'er Baltic shores and through Hercynian groves,[13]
Stirring the soul, the mighty impulse moves;
Art plies his tools, and Commerce spreads her sail,
And wealth is wafted in each shifting gale.
The sons of Odin[14] tread on Persian looms,
And Odin's daughters breathe distilled perfumes;
Loud minstrel Bards, in Gothic halls, rehearse
The Runic[15] rhyme, and "build the lofty verse":[16]
The Muse, whose liquid notes were wont to swell
To the soft breathings of th' Æolian[17] shell,
Submits, reluctant, to the harsher tone,
And scarce believes the altered voice her own.[18]
And now, where Cæsar saw with proud disdain
The wattled hut and skin of azure stain,[19]

---

[1] in Arabia, a source of gold for King Samuel: see 1 Kings 9.28.

[2] The annual flooding of the Nile provided the fertile soil on which the civilization of Egypt depended.

[3] Palmyra, an oasis city in Syria, destroyed by the Romans in AD 273; see 1 Kings 9.18 and 2 Chronicles 8.4.

[4] Caius Marius (c. 157–86 BC), exiled from Rome and refused entry into Africa in 88 BC, took refuge in the ruins of Carthage, destroyed by the Romans in 146 BC. See Plutarch, *Parallel Lives*.

[5] the vale of Tempe in Thessaly, Greece.

[6] Italian.

[7] Holland.

[8] river in Northern Italy.

[9] a valley in Sicily, site of the abduction of Persephone by Hades. Cf. Ovid, *Metamorphoses* 5, and Milton, *Paradise Lost* 4.268–72.

[10] a Roman resort town on the Bay of Naples.

[11] Annually, on Ascension Day, the Doge of Venice used to drop a ring into the Adriatic Sea, thus wedding it (celebrating Venice's status as a maritime power). By 1811, Venice was no longer even an independent state.

[12] a region in central Italy.

[13] the Black Forest, Germany.

[14] the most important god in Norse mythology; his sons and daughters are Scandinavians.

[15] Runes were the earliest Germanic alphabet, used both by the Scandinavians and by the Anglo-Saxons; "The Runic rhyme" is northern European poetry.

[16] Milton, "Lycidas" 11.

[17] a musical mode, described by Charles Burney as "grand and pompous though sometimes soothing" (qtd in *OED*). Since a shell is a lyre (according to legend, Hermes made the first one from a tortoise shell), Barbauld's reference is to the effect of Greek poetry.

[18] Barbauld's point is the contrast between the Romance languages of the Mediterranean basin and the supposedly harsher Germanic languages of northern Europe; cf. Jean-Jacques Rousseau, *Essay on the Origin of Languages;* and Byron,* *Beppo* (1818) 44, *Childe Harold's Pilgrimage* (1812–18) 4.58.

[19] Julius Cæsar (102–44 BC) commented on the Britons' practice of painting themselves with woad in *De Bello Gallico* 5.14.

285   Corinthian columns rear their graceful forms,
     And light varandas brave the wintry storms,
     While British tongues the fading fame prolong
     Of Tully's[1] eloquence and Maro's[2] song.
     Where once Bonduca[3] whirled the scythed car,
290   And the fierce matrons raised the shriek of war,
     Light forms beneath transparent muslins float,
     And tutored voices swell the artful note.
     Light-leaved acacias and the shady plane
     And spreading cedar grace the woodland reign;
295   While crystal walls the tenderer plants confine,
     The fragrant orange and the nectared pine;
     The Syrian grape there hangs her rich festoons,
     Nor asks for purer air, or brighter noons:
     Science and Art urge on the useful toil,
300   New mould a climate and create the soil,
     Subdue the rigour of the northern Bear,[4]
     O'er polar climes shed aromatic air,
     On yielding Nature urge their new demands,
     And ask not gifts but tribute at her hands.

305   London exults:—on London Art bestows
     Her summer ices and her winter rose;
     Gems of the East her mural crown[5] adorn,
     And Plenty at her feet pours forth her horn;
     While even the exiles her just laws disclaim,[6]
310   People a continent, and build a name:
     August she sits, and with extended hands
     Holds forth the book of life to distant lands.[7]

     But fairest flowers expand but to decay;
     The worm is in thy core, thy glories pass away;
315   Arts, arms and wealth destroy the fruits they bring;
     Commerce, like beauty, knows no second spring.
     Crime walks thy streets, Fraud earns her unblest bread,
     O'er want and woe thy gorgeous robe is spread,
     And angel charities in vain oppose:
320   With grandeur's growth the mass of misery grows.
     For see,—to other climes the Genius soars,
     He turns from Europe's desolated shores;
     And lo, even now, midst mountains wrapt in storm,
     On Andes' heights he shrouds his awful form;
325   On Chimborazo's[8] summits treads sublime,
     Measuring in lofty thought the march of Time;
     Sudden he calls:—"'Tis now the hour!" he cries,
     Spreads his broad hand, and bids the nations rise.
     La Plata[9] hears amidst her torrents' roar,
330   Potosi[10] hears it, as she digs the ore:
     Ardent, the Genius fans the noble strife,
     And pours through feeble souls a higher life,
     Shouts to the mingled tribes from sea to sea,
     And swears—Thy world, Columbus, shall be free.[11]

from *The Works of Anna Laetitia Barbauld. With A Memoir by Lucy Aikin* (1825)

The Rights of Woman[12]

Yes, injured Woman! rise, assert thy right!
Woman! too long degraded, scorned, opprest;
O born to rule in partial Law's despite,
Resume thy native empire o'er the breast!

---

[1] Cicero (Marcus Tullius Cicero, 106–43 BC), Roman orator.

[2] Virgil (Publius Vergilius Maro, 70–19 BC), Roman poet.

[3] Boadicea, a British queen who led an uprising against the Romans. When she was defeated, she committed suicide (AD 61).

[4] the Little Bear or Ursa Minor, the constellation including the Northern Star.

[5] A mural crown is an embattled or crenellated crown, traditionally given by the Romans to the first soldier to scale the walls of a besieged city; the reference is to the British Crown Jewels, many of which are of Asian (especially Indian) provenance.

[6] "Laws" is the subject of the verb; "exiles" is the object. Barbauld is referring to the convicts transported to Australia.

[7] The British and Foreign Bible Society was founded in 1804.

[8] the highest peak in the Andes, a volcano in Ecuador.

[9] a river in Argentina.

[10] a city in Bolivia, famous for silver mines.

[11] Venezuela declared independence in 1811; other Spanish colonies would soon follow.

[12] Wollstonecraft criticized Barbauld's "To A Lady, with Some Painted Flowers" in *A Vindication of the Rights of Woman* (411);* this is Barbauld's reply.

5   Go forth arrayed in panoply divine;
    That angel pureness which admits no stain;
    Go, bid proud Man his boasted rule resign,
    And kiss the golden sceptre of thy reign.

    Go,[1] gird thyself with grace; collect thy store
10 Of bright artillery glancing from afar;
    Soft melting tones thy thundering cannon's roar,
    Blushes and fears thy magazine[2] of war.

    Thy rights are empire: urge no meaner claim,—
    Felt, not defined, and if debated, lost;
15 Like sacred mysteries, which withheld from fame,
    Shunning discussion, are revered the most.

    Try all that wit and art suggest to bend
    Of thy imperial foe the stubborn knee;
    Make treacherous Man thy subject, not thy friend;
20 Thou mayst command, but never canst be free.

    Awe the licentious, and restrain the rude;
    Soften the sullen, clear the cloudy brow:
    Be, more than princes' gifts, thy favours sued;—
    She hazards all, who will the least allow.

25 But hope not, courted idol of mankind,
    On this proud eminence secure to stay;
    Subduing and subdued, thou soon shalt find
    Thy coldness soften, and thy pride give way.

    Then, then, abandon each ambitious thought,
30 Conquest or rule thy heart shall feebly move,
    In Nature's school, by her soft maxims taught,
    That separate rights are lost in mutual love.

Inscription for an Ice-House[3]

    Stranger, approach! within this iron door
    Thrice locked and bolted, this rude arch beneath
    That vaults with ponderous stone the cell; confined
    By man, the great magician, who controuls
5   Fire, earth and air, and genii of the storm,
    And bends the most remote and opposite things
    To do him service and perform his will,—
    A giant sits; stern Winter; here he piles,
    While summer glows around, and southern gales
10 Dissolve the fainting world, his treasured snows
    Within the rugged cave.—Stranger, approach!
    He will not cramp thy limbs with sudden age,
    Nor wither with his touch the coyest flower
    That decks thy scented hair. Indignant here,
15 Like fettered Sampson[4] when his might was spent
    In puny feats to glad the festive halls
    Of Gaza's wealthy sons; or he[5] who sat
    Midst laughing girls submiss, and patient twirled
    The slender spindle in his sinewy grasp;
20 The rugged power, fair Pleasure's minister,
    Exerts his art to deck the genial board;
    Congeals the melting peach, the nectarine smooth,
    Burnished and glowing from the sunny wall:
    Darts sudden frost into the crimson veins
25 Of the moist berry; moulds the sugared hail:
    Cools with his icy breath our flowing cups;
    Or gives to the fresh dairy's nectared bowls
    A quicker zest. Sullen he plies his task,
    And on his shaking fingers counts the weeks
30 Of lingering Summer, mindful of his hour
    To rush in whirlwinds forth, and rule the year.

---

[1] Cf. Alexander Pope (1688–1744), *An Essay on Man* (1733–34) 2.19–30.

[2] where munitions are stored.

[3] McCarthy and Kraft suggest (293) that this poem was written c. 1793.

[4] Judges 16.15–30; cf. Milton, *Samson Agonistes* (1671).

[5] Hercules, enslaved by Omphale, had to wear women's clothes and do women's work. See Ovid, *Heroides*, "Deianira to Hercules."

ANNA LAETITIA BARBAULD

To the Poor

Child of distress, who meet'st the bitter scorn
Of fellow-men to happier prospects born,
Doomed Art and Nature's various stores to see
Flow in full cups of joy—and not for thee;
5 Who seest the rich, to heaven and fate resigned,
Bear *thy* afflictions with a patient mind;
Whose bursting heart disdains unjust controul,
Who feel'st oppression's iron in thy soul,[1]
Who dragg'st the load of faint and feeble years,
10 Whose bread is anguish, and whose water tears;[2]
Bear, bear thy wrongs—fulfill thy destined hour,
Bend thy meek neck beneath the foot of Power;
But when thou feel'st the great deliverer nigh,
And thy freed spirit mounting seeks the sky,
15 Let no vain fears thy parting hour molest,
No whispered terrors shake thy quiet breast:
Think not their threats can work thy future woe,
Nor deem the Lord above like lords below;—
Safe in the bosom of that love repose
20 By whom the sun gives light, the ocean flows;
Prepare to meet a Father undismayed,
Nor fear the God whom priests and kings have made.[3]

To a Little Invisible Being
Who Is Expected Soon to Become Visible[4]

Germ of new life, whose powers expanding slow
For many a moon their full perfection wait,—
Haste, precious pledge of happy love, to go
Auspicious borne through life's mysterious gate.

5 What powers lie folded in thy curious frame,—
Senses from objects locked, and mind from thought!
How little canst thou guess thy lofty claim
To grasp at all the worlds the Almighty wrought!

And see, the genial season's warmth to share,
10 Fresh younglings shoot, and opening roses glow!
Swarms of new life exulting fill the air,—
Haste, infant bud of being, haste to blow!

For thee the nurse prepares her lulling songs,
The eager matrons count the lingering day;
15 But far the most thy anxious parent longs
On thy soft cheek a mother's kiss to lay.

She only asks to lay her burden down,
That her glad arms that burden may resume;
And nature's sharpest pangs her wishes crown,
20 That free thee living from thy living tomb.

She longs to fold to her maternal breast
Part of herself, yet to herself unknown;
To see and to salute the stranger guest,
Fed with her life through many a tedious moon.

25 Come, reap thy rich inheritance of love!
Bask in the fondness of a Mother's eye!
Nor wit nor eloquence her heart shall move
Like the first accents of thy feeble cry.

Haste, little captive, burst thy prison doors!
30 Launch on the living world, and spring to light!
Nature for thee displays her various stores,
Opens her thousand inlets of delight.

If charmed verse or muttered prayers had power,
With favouring spells to speed thee on thy way,
35 Anxious I'd bid my beads[5] each passing hour,
Till thy wished smile thy mother's pangs o'erpay.

---

[1] Cf. Psalm 105.18, as translated in *The Book of Common Prayer*: "the iron entered his soul."

[2] Isaiah 30.20.

[3] "These lines, written in 1795, were described by Mrs. B., on sending them to a friend, as 'inspired by indignation on hearing sermons in which the poor are addressed in a manner which evidently shows the design of making religion an engine of government'" (Lucy Aikin).*

[4] McCarthy and Kraft suggest (296) that this poem was written c. 1795.

[5] pray, using a rosary.

The First Fire. October 1st, 1815

Ha, old acquaintance! many a month has past
Since last I viewed thy ruddy face; and I,
Shame on me! had mean time well nigh forgot
That such a friend existed. Welcome now!—
When summer suns ride high, and tepid airs
Dissolve in pleasing languor; then indeed
We think thee needless, and in wanton pride
Mock at thy grim attire and sooty jaws,
And breath sulphureous, generating spleen,—
As Frenchmen say; Frenchmen, who never knew
The sober comforts of a good coal fire.[1]
—Let me imbibe thy warmth, and spread myself
Before thy shrine adoring:—magnet thou
Of strong attraction, daily gathering in
Friends, brethren, kinsmen, variously dispersed,
All the dear charities of social life,
To thy close circle. Here a man might stand,
And say, This is my world! Who would not bleed
Rather than see thy violated hearth
Prest by a hostile foot? The winds sing shrill;
Heap on the fuel! Not the costly board,
Nor sparkling glass, nor wit, nor music, cheer
Without thy aid. If thrifty thou dispense
Thy gladdening influence, in the chill saloon
The silent shrug declares the' unpleased guest.
—How grateful to belated traveller
Homeward returning, to behold the blaze
From cottage window, rendering visible
The cheerful scene within! There sits the sire,
Whose wicker chair, in sunniest nook enshrined,
His age's privilege,—a privilege for which
Age gladly yields up all precedence else
In gay and bustling scenes,—supports his limbs.
Cherished by thee, he feels the grateful warmth
Creep through his feeble frame and thaw the ice
Of fourscore years, and thoughts of youth arise.
—Nor less the young ones press within, to see
Thy face delighted, and with husk of nuts,
Or crackling holly, or the gummy pine,
Feed thy immortal hunger: cheaply pleased
They gaze delighted, while the leaping flames
Dart like an adder's tongue upon their prey;
Or touch with lighted reed thy wreaths of smoke;
Or listen, while the matron sage remarks
Thy bright blue scorching flame and aspect clear,
Denoting frosty skies. Thus pass the hours,
While Winter spends without his idle rage.
—Companion of the solitary man,
From gayer scenes withheld! With thee he sits,
Converses, moralizes; musing asks
How many æras of uncounted time
Have rolled away since thy black unctuous food
Was green with vegetative life, and what
This planet then: or marks, in sprightlier mood,
Thy flickering smiles play round the' illumined room,
And fancies gay discourse, life, motion, mirth,
And half forgets he is a lonely creature.
—Nor less the bashful poet loves to sit
Snug, at the midnight hour, with only thee
Of his lone musings conscious.[2] Oft he writes,
And blots, and writes again; and oft, by fits,
Gazes intent with eyes of vacancy
On thy bright face; and still at intervals,
Dreading the critic's scorn, to thee commits,
Sole confidant and safe, his fancies crude.

—O wretched he, with bolts and massy bars
In narrow cell immured, whose green damp walls,
That weep unwholesome dews, have never felt
Thy purifying influence! Sad he sits
Day after day, till in his youthful limbs
Life stagnates, and the hue of hope is fled
From his wan cheek.—And scarce less wretched he—
When wintry winds blow loud and frosts bite keen,—
The dweller of the clay-built tenement,
Poverty-struck, who, heartless, strives to raise
From sullen turf, or stick plucked from the hedge,
The short-lived blaze; while chill around him spreads
The dreary fen, and Ague, sallow-faced,
Stares through the broken pane;—Assist him, ye
On whose warm roofs the sun of plenty shines,
And feel a glow beyond material fire!

---

[1] Apparently the French preferred wood fires.

[2] Cf. Coleridge, "Frost at Midnight" 4–23.*

Hannah More
1745 – 1833

Hannah More was born in Fishponds, Gloucestershire, the fourth of the five daughters of Jacob More, a schoolmaster, and Mary Grace More, a farmer's daughter. Her father had lost a lawsuit over an inheritance; subsequently he had worked as an excise officer and then, from 1743, as a schoolteacher. The family lived in a cottage on a small income. When More's older sisters opened a girls' school in Bristol in 1758, More went there as a pupil and later as a teacher. Her first play, *The Search after Happiness*, was written for the girls at the school. She became engaged to a local landowner, William Turner, but after six years of indecision on Turner's part she broke off the engagement in 1773; thereafter, Turner paid her an annuity of £200, which enabled her to abandon teaching for writing.

In the spring of 1774 More and two of her sisters moved to London, where they met the actor-manager David Garrick and many other well-known members of London society, including Samuel Johnson, Edmund Burke,* and Elizabeth Montagu and Elizabeth Carter, members of the Bluestocking Circle, an informal group of women who hosted evenings of conversation. More's tragedy *Percy* was staged at the Covent Garden Theatre in 1777; but following the failure of another play, *The Fatal Falsehood*, she gave up writing for the stage. Her poem *The Bas Bleu; or Conversation* was a light-hearted account of the Bluestocking Circle.

More had been the mentor and patron of the poet Ann Yearsley.* When their relationship came to an acrimonious end, she bought a house in Somerset and gave up London society. During this period she underwent a religious conversion, befriending the Evangelical clergyman and hymn-writer John Newton and the abolitionist Member of Parliament William Wilberforce. Her poem *Slavery* coincided with the first parliamentary debate on the slave trade. In 1789, she and one of her sisters founded a Sunday school at Cheddar, Somerset, and two women's benefit clubs.

Conservative in her response to the French Revolution, in 1792 she published *Village Politics* to counter the effect of Paine's* *The Rights of Man*. In *Thoughts on the Speech of M. Dupont* (1793), she attacked French-revolutionary anti-clericalism, hoping to raise funds for the French émigré clergy living in Britain. In the *Cheap Repository Tracts* (1795–97), she addressed the labouring poor with a combination of conservative politics and moral exhortation. As well as working among the poor, Hannah More produced a series of conduct books aimed at women in polite society, of which the most famous was *Strictures on the Modern System of Female Education*. She argued that women's education prepared them very poorly for their roles as companionable wives, rational mothers, and moral examples. Her most ambitious conduct book, *Hints Towards Forming the Character of a Young Princess* (1805), was written anonymously for the young Princess Charlotte; her only novel, *Coelebs in Search of a Wife* (1809), developed similar themes and attitudes.

More's visitors in her later years included the historian Thomas Babington Macaulay, the Liberal statesman William Gladstone, De Quincey,* Coleridge,* Elizabeth Fry, and the actor Sarah Siddons. She earned nearly £30,000 from her books, contributed generously to charity, and was emulated by charitable Evangelical women in the Victorian age. (A.M.)

Slavery, A Poem (1788)

> O great design!
> Ye Sons of Mercy! O complete your work;
> Wrench from Oppression's hand the iron rod,
> And bid the cruel feel the pains they give.
> *Thompson's Liberty*[1]

If Heaven has into being deign'd to call
Thy light, O LIBERTY! to shine on all;
Bright intellectual Sun! why does thy ray
To earth distribute only partial day?
5   Since no resisting cause from spirit flows
Thy penetrating essence to oppose;
No obstacles by Nature's hand imprest,
Thy subtle and ethereal beams arrest;
Nor motion's laws can speed thy active course,
10 Nor strong repulsion's pow'rs obstruct thy force;
Since there is no convexity in MIND,
Why are thy genial beams to parts confin'd?
While the chill North with thy bright ray is blest,
Why should fell darkness half the South invest?
15 Was it decreed, fair Freedom! at thy birth,
That thou shou'dst ne'er irradiate *all* the earth?
While Britain basks in thy full blaze of light,
Why lies sad Afric quench'd in total night?
   Thee only, sober Goddess! I attest,
20 In smiles chastis'd, and decent graces drest.
Not that unlicenc'd monster of the crowd,
Whose roar terrific bursts in peals so loud,
Deaf'ning the ear of Peace: fierce Faction's tool;
Of rash Sedition born, and mad Misrule;
25 Whose stubborn mouth, rejecting Reason's rein,
No strength can govern, and no skill restrain;
Whose magic cries the frantic vulgar draw
To spurn at Order, and to outrage Law;
To tread on grave Authority and Pow'r,
30 And shake the work of ages in an hour:
Convuls'd her voice, and pestilent her breath,
She raves of mercy, while she deals out death:
Each blast is fate; she darts from either hand
Red conflagration o'er th' astonish'd land;
35 Clamouring for peace, she rends the air with noise,
And to reform a part, the whole destroys.
   O, plaintive Southerne![2] whose impassion'd strain
So oft has wak'd my languid Muse in vain!
Now, when congenial themes her cares engage,
40 She burns to emulate thy glowing page;
Her failing efforts mock her fond desires,
She shares thy feelings, not partakes thy fires.
Strange pow'r of song! the strain that warms the heart
Seems the same inspiration to impart;
45 Touch'd by the kindling energy alone,
We think the flame which melts us is our own;
Deceiv'd, for genius we mistake delight,
Charm'd as we read, we fancy we can write.
   Tho' not to me, sweet Bard, thy pow'rs belong
50 Fair Truth, a hallow'd guide! inspires my song.
Here Art wou'd weave her gayest flow'rs in vain,
For Truth the bright invention wou'd disdain.
For no fictitious ills these numbers flow,
But living anguish, and substantial woe;
55 No individual griefs my bosom melt,
For millions feel what Oronoko felt:
Fir'd by no single wrongs, the countless host
I mourn, by rapine dragg'd from Afric's coast.
   Perish th' illiberal thought which wou'd debase
60 The native genius of the sable race!
Perish the proud philosophy, which sought
To rob them of the pow'rs of equal thought!
Does then th' immortal principle within
Change with the casual colour of a skin?
65 Does matter govern spirit? or is mind
Degraded by the form to which 'tis join'd?

---

[1] These lines are not from James Thomson, *Liberty* (1735–36), but from his *Winter* (*The Seasons*, 1744) 376–81. The reference is not to slavery, but to the reform of British prisons:
   O great design! If executed well,
   With patient care and wisdom-tempered zeal.
   Ye sons of mercy! yet resume the search;
   Drag forth the legal monsters into light,
   Wrench from their hands Oppression's iron rod,
   And bid the cruel feel the pains they give.

[2] "Author of the Tragedy of Oronoko." (H.M.) Thomas Southerne (1659–1746) based his play, *Oroonoko* (1695), on a novel by Aphra Behn (1640–89), *Oroonoko, or The Royal Slave* (1688), about the suffering and heroism of an African prince sold into slavery in Surinam. See line 56.

No: they have heads to think, and hearts to feel,
And souls to act, with firm, tho' erring zeal;
For they have keen affections, kind desires,
70 Love strong as death,¹ and active patriot fires;
All the rude energy, the fervid flame,
Of high-soul'd passion, and ingenuous shame:
Strong, but luxuriant virtues boldly shoot
From the wild vigour of a savage root.
75   Nor weak their sense of honour's proud control,
For pride is virtue in a Pagan soul;
A sense of worth, a conscience of desert,
A high, unbroken haughtiness of heart;
That self-same stuff which erst proud empires sway'd,
80 Of which the conquerors of the world were made.
Capricious fate of man! that very pride
In Afric scourg'd, in Rome was deify'd.
  No Muse, O Qua-shi!² shall thy deeds relate,
No statue snatch thee from oblivious fate!
85 For thou wast born where never gentle Muse
On Valour's grave the flow'rs of Genius strews;
And thou wast born where no recording page
Plucks the fair deed from Time's devouring rage.
Had Fortune plac'd thee on some happier coast,
90 Where polish'd souls heroic virtue boast,
To thee, who sought'st a voluntary grave,
Th' uninjur'd honours of thy name to save,
Whose generous arm thy barbarous Master spar'd,
Altars had smok'd, and temples had been rear'd.
95   Whene'er to Afric's shores I turn my eyes,
Horrors of deepest, deadliest guilt arise;
I see, by more than Fancy's mirror shewn,
The burning village, and the blazing town:
See the dire victim torn from social life,
100 The shrieking babe, the agonizing wife!
She, wretch forlorn! is dragg'd by hostile hands,
To distant tyrants sold, in distant lands!
Transmitted miseries, and successive chains,
The sole sad heritage her child obtains!
105 Ev'n this last wretched boon their foes deny,
To weep together, or together die.
By felon hands, by one relentless stroke,
See the fond links of feeling Nature broke!
The fibres twisting round a parent's heart,
110 Torn from their grasp, and bleeding as they part.
  Hold, murderers, hold! nor aggravate distress;
Respect the passions you yourselves possess;
Ev'n you, of ruffian heart, and ruthless hand,
Love your own offspring, love your native land.
115 Ah! leave them holy Freedom's cheering smile,
The heav'n-taught fondness for the parent soil;
Revere affections mingled with our frame,
In every nature, every clime the same;
In all, these feelings equal sway maintain;
120 In all the love of HOME and FREEDOM reign:
And Tempe's vale,³ and parch'd Angola's sand,
One equal fondness of their sons command.
Th' unconquer'd Savage laughs at pain and toil,
Basking in Freedom's beams which gild his native soil.
125   Does thirst of empire, does desire of fame,
(For these are specious crimes) our rage inflame?
No: sordid lust of gold their fate controls,
The basest appetite of basest souls;
Gold, better gain'd, by what their ripening sky,
130 Their fertile fields, their arts⁴ and mines supply.
  What wrongs, what injuries does Oppression plead
To smooth the horror of th' unnatural deed?
What strange offence, what aggravated sin?
They stand convicted—of a darker skin!
135 Barbarians, hold! th' opprobrious commerce spare,

---

¹ Cf. Song of Songs 8.6.

² "It is a point of honour among negroes of a high spirit to die rather than to suffer their glossy skin to bear the mark of the whip. Qua-shi had somehow offended his master, a young planter with whom he had been bred up in the endearing intimacy of a play-fellow. His services had been faithful; his attachment affectionate. The master resolved to punish him, and pursued him for that purpose. In trying to escape Qua-shi stumbled and fell; the master fell upon him: they wrestled long with doubtful victory; at length Qua-shi got uppermost, and, being firmly seated on his master's breast, he secured his legs with one hand, and with the other drew a sharp knife; then said, 'Master, I have been bred up with you from a child; I have loved you as myself: in return, you have condemned me to a punishment of which I must ever have borne the marks; thus only I can avoid them'; so saying, he drew the knife with all his strength across his own throat, and fell down dead, without a groan, on his master's body. Ramsay's Essay on the Treatment of African Slaves." (H.M.) Qua-shi is a generic slave name.

³ a narrow gorge in northern Thessaly, the site of battles because of its strategic importance.

⁴ "Besides many valuable productions of the soil, cloths and carpets of exquisite manufacture are brought from the coast of Guinea." (H.M.)

Respect *his* sacred image which they bear:
Tho' dark and savage, ignorant and blind,
They claim the common privilege of kind;
Let Malice strip them of each other plea,
140 They still are men, and men shou'd still be free.
Insulted Reason loaths th' inverted trade—
Dire change! the agent is the purchase made!
Perplex'd, the baffled Muse involves the tale;
Nature confounded, well may language fail!
145 The outrag'd Goddess with abhorrent eyes
Sees MAN the traffic, SOULS the merchandize!
    Plead not, in reason's palpable abuse,
Their sense of feeling callous and obtuse:[1]
From heads to hearts lies Nature's plain appeal,
150 Tho' few can reason, all mankind can feel.
Tho' wit may boast a livelier dread of shame,
A loftier sense of wrong refinement claim;
Tho' polish'd manners may fresh wants invent,
And nice distinctions nicer souls torment;
155 Tho' these on finer spirits heavier fall,
Yet natural evils are the same to all.
Tho' wounds there are which reason's force may heal,
There needs no logic sure to make us feel.
The nerve, howe'er untutor'd, can sustain
160 A sharp, unutterable sense of pain;
As exquisitely fashion'd in a slave,
As where unequal fate a sceptre gave.
Sense is as keen where Congo's sons preside,
As where proud Tiber[2] rolls his classic tide.
165 Rhetoric or verse may point the feeling line,
They do not whet sensation, but define.
Did ever slave less feel the galling chain,
When Zeno[3] prov'd there was no ill in pain?
Their miseries philosophic quirks deride,
170 Slaves groan in pangs disown'd by Stoic pride.
    When the fierce Sun darts vertical his beams,
And thirst and hunger mix their wild extremes;
When the sharp iron wounds his inmost soul,[4]
And his strain'd eyes in burning anguish roll;
175 Will the parch'd negro find, ere he expire,
No pain in hunger, and no heat in fire?
    For him, when fate his tortur'd frame destroys,
What hope of present fame, or future joys?
For *this*, have heroes shorten'd nature's date;
180 For *that*, have martyrs gladly met their fate;
But him, forlorn, no hero's pride sustains,
No martyr's blissful visions sooth his pains;
Sullen, he mingles with his kindred dust,
For he has learn'd to dread the Christian's trust;
185 To him what mercy can that Pow'r display,
Whose servants murder, and whose sons betray?
Savage! thy venial error I deplore,
They are *not* Christians who infest thy shore.
    O thou sad spirit, whose preposterous yoke
190 The great deliverer Death, at length, has broke!
Releas'd from misery, and escap'd from care,
Go, meet that mercy man deny'd thee here.
In thy dark home, sure refuge of th' oppress'd,
The wicked vex not, and the weary rest.
195 And, if some notions, vague and undefin'd,
Of future terrors have assail'd thy mind;
If such thy masters have presum'd to teach,
As terrors only they are prone to preach;
(For shou'd they paint eternal Mercy's reign,
200 Where were th' oppressor's rod, the captive's chain?)
If, then, thy troubled soul has learn'd to dread
The dark unknown thy trembling footsteps tread;
On HIM, who made thee what thou art, depend;
HE, who withholds the means, accepts the end.
205 Not *thine* the reckoning dire of LIGHT abus'd,
KNOWLEDGE disgrac'd, and LIBERTY misus'd;
On *thee* no awful judge incens'd shall sit
For parts perverted, and dishonour'd wit.
Where ignorance will be found the surest plea,
210 How many learn'd and wise shall envy *thee*!

---

[1] "Nothing is more frequent than this cruel and stupid argument, that they do not *feel* the miseries inflicted on them as Europeans would do." (H.M.)

[2] the river that runs through Rome.

[3] Zeno of Citium founded the Stoic school of philosophy c. 315 BC, advocating a life of virtue, reason, endurance, and self-discipline, detached from the outside world and free of pain, pleasure, desire, or fear.

[4] "This is not said figuratively. The writer of these lines has seen a complete set of chains, fitted to every separate limb of these unhappy, innocent men; together with instruments for wrenching open the jaws, contrived with such ingenious cruelty as would shock the humanity of an inquisitor." (H.M.)

    And thou, WHITE SAVAGE! whether lust of gold,
Or lust of conquest, rule thee uncontrol'd!
Hero, or robber!—by whatever name
Thou plead thy impious claim to wealth or fame;
215 Whether inferior mischiefs be thy boast,
A petty tyrant rifling Gambia's[1] coast:
Or bolder carnage track thy crimson way,
Kings dispossess'd, and Provinces thy prey;
Panting to tame wide earth's remotest bound;
220 All Cortez[2] murder'd, all Columbus found;
O'er plunder'd realms to reign, detested Lord,
Make millions wretched, and thyself abhorr'd;——
In Reason's eye, in Wisdom's fair account,
Your sum of glory boasts a like amount;
225 The means may differ, but the end's the same;
Conquest is pillage with a nobler name.
Who makes the sum of human blessings less,
Or sinks the stock of general happiness,
No solid fame shall grace, no true renown,
230 His life shall blazon, or his memory crown.
    Had those advent'rous spirits who explore
Thro' ocean's trackless wastes, the far-sought shore;
Whether of wealth insatiate, or of pow'r,
Conquerors who waste, or ruffians who devour:
235 Had these possess'd, O COOK![3] thy gentle mind,
Thy love of arts, thy love of humankind;
Had these pursued thy mild and liberal plan,
DISCOVERERS had not been a curse to man!
Then, bless'd Philanthropy! thy social hands
240 Had link'd dissever'd worlds in brothers' bands;
Careless, if colour, or if clime divide;
Then, lov'd, and loving, man had liv'd, and died.
    The purest wreaths which hang on glory's shrine,
For empires founded, peaceful PENN![4] are thine;
245 No blood-stain'd laurels crown'd thy virtuous toil,
No slaughter'd natives drench'd thy fair-earn'd soil.
Still thy meek spirit in thy flock survives,[5]
Consistent still, *their* doctrines rule their lives;
Thy followers only have effac'd the shame
250 Inscrib'd by SLAVERY on the Christian name.
    Shall Britain, where the soul of Freedom reigns,
Forge chains for others she herself disdains?
Forbid it, Heaven! O let the nations know
The liberty she loves she will bestow;
255 Not to herself the glorious gift confin'd,
She spreads the blessing wide as humankind;
And, scorning narrow views of time and place,
Bids all be free in earth's extended space.
    What page of human annals can record
260 A deed so bright as human rights restor'd?
O may that god-like deed, that shining page,
Redeem OUR fame, and consecrate OUR age!
    And see, the cherub Mercy from above,
Descending softly, quits the sphere of love!
265 On feeling hearts she sheds celestial dew,
And breathes her spirit o'er th' enlighten'd few;
From soul to soul the spreading influence steals,
Till every breast the soft contagion feels.
She bears, exulting, to the burning shore
270 The loveliest office Angel ever bore;
To vindicate the pow'r in Heaven ador'd,
To still the clank of chains, and sheathe the sword;
To cheer the mourner, and with soothing hands
From bursting hearts unbind th' Oppressor's bands;
275 To raise the lustre of the Christian name,
And clear the foulest blot that dims its fame.
    As the mild Spirit hovers o'er the coast,
A fresher hue the wither'd landscapes boast;
Her healing smiles the ruin'd scenes repair,
280 And blasted Nature wears a joyous air.
She spreads her blest commission from above,
Stamp'd with the sacred characters of love;
She tears the banner stain'd with blood and tears,
And, LIBERTY! thy shining standard rears!
285 As the bright ensign's glory she displays,
See pale OPPRESSION faints beneath the blaze!
The giant dies! no more his frown appals,

---

[1] Situated on the West-African coast, Gambia was a British trading colony until 1843.

[2] Hernando Cortés (1485–1547), who defeated the Aztecs and established Spanish rule in Mexico.

[3] James Cook (1728–79), who sailed around the world and whose voyages of discovery ended with his death in Hawaii.

[4] William Penn (1644–1718), who founded Pennsylvania in 1681 as a Quaker colony with freedom of religion and a prohibition against slavery.

[5] "The Quakers have emancipated all their slaves throughout America." (H.M.)

The chain untouch'd, drops off; the fetter falls.
Astonish'd echo tells the vocal shore,
290 Oppression's fall'n, and Slavery is no more!
The dusky myriads crowd the sultry plain,
And hail that mercy long invok'd in vain.
Victorious Pow'r! she bursts their two-fold bands,
And FAITH and FREEDOM spring from Mercy's hands.

Village Politics. Addressed to All the Mechanics, Journeymen, and Day Labourers, in Great Britain. By Will Chip, a Country Carpenter (1792)[1]

A Dialogue between Jack Anvil the Blacksmith, and Tom Hod the Mason

JACK: What's the matter, Tom? Why dost look so dismal?
TOM: Dismal indeed! Well enough I may.
JACK: What's the old mare dead? or work scarce?
TOM: No, no, work's plenty enough, if a man had but the heart to go to it.
JACK: What book art reading? Why dost look so like a hang dog?
TOM: (*looking on his book*.) Cause enough. Why I find here that I'm very unhappy, and very miserable; which I should never have known if I had not had the good luck to meet with this book. O 'tis a precious book!
JACK: A good sign tho'; that you can't find out you're unhappy without looking into a book for it. What is the matter?
TOM: Matter? Why I want liberty.
JACK: Liberty! What has any one fetched a warrant for thee? Come man, cheer up, I'll be bound for thee.— Thou art an honest fellow in the main, tho' thou dost tipple and prate a little too much at the Rose and Crown.
TOM: No, no, I want a new constitution.
JACK: Indeed! Why I thought thou hadst been a desperate healthy fellow. Send for the doctor then.
TOM: I'm not sick; I want Liberty and Equality, and the Rights of Man.
JACK: O now I understand thee. What thou art a leveller[2] and a republican I warrant.
TOM: I'm a friend to the people. I want a reform.
JACK: Then the shortest way is to mend thyself.
TOM: But I want a *general reform*.
JACK: Then let every one mend one.
TOM: Pooh! I want freedom and happiness, the same as they have got in France.
JACK: What, Tom, we imitate them? We follow the French! Why they only begun all this mischief at first, in order to be just what *we* are already. Why I'd sooner go to the Negers[3] to get learning, or to the Turks to get religion, than to the French for freedom and happiness.
TOM: What do you mean by that? ar'n't the French free?
JACK: Free, Tom! aye, free with a witness. They are all so free, that there's nobody safe. They make free to rob whom they will, and kill whom they will. If they don't like a man's looks, they make free to hang him without judge or jury, and the next lamp-post does for the gallows;[4] so then they call themselves free, because you see they have no king to take them up and hang them for it.
TOM: Ah, but Jack, didn't their KING formerly hang people for nothing too? and besides, wer'n't they all papists[5] before the Revolution?
JACK: Why, true enough, they had but a poor sort of religion, but bad is better than none, Tom. And so was the government bad enough too, for they could clap an innocent man into prison, and keep him there too as long as they would, and never say with your leave or by your leave, Gentlemen of the Jury. But what's all that to us?
TOM: To us! Why don't our governors put many of our poor folks in prison against their will? What are all

---

[1] a short tract, ascribed to the fictitious Will Chip, intended to counter the effects of such revolutionary texts as Thomas Paine's* *Rights of Man* (1791) among the English poor.

[2] The Levellers were radical republican democrats at the time of the English Civil War (1642–48).

[3] i.e., Negroes (from *niger*, the Latin word for "black").

[4] Cf. Edmund Burke, *Reflections on the Revolution in France** (27).

[5] Roman Catholics.

the jails for? Down with the jails, I say; all men should be free.

JACK: Harkee,[1] Tom, a few rogues in prison keep the rest in order, and then honest men go about their business, afraid of nobody; that's the way to be free. And let me tell thee, Tom, thou and I are tried by our peers as much as a lord is. Why the *king* can't send me to prison if I do no harm, and if I do, there's reason good why I should go there. I may go to law with Sir John, at the great castle yonder, and he no more dares lift his little finger against me than if I were his equal. A lord is hanged for hanging matter, as thou or I shou'd be; and if it will be any comfort to thee, I myself remember a Peer of the Realm being hanged for killing his man, just the same as the man wou'd have been for killing *him*.[2]

TOM: Well, that is some comfort.—But have you read the Rights of Man?

JACK: No, not I. I had rather by half read the *Whole Duty of Man*.[3] I have but little time for reading, and such as I should therefore only read a bit of the best.

TOM: Don't tell me of those old fashioned notions. Why should not we have the same fine things they have got in France? I'm for a *Constitution*, and *Organization*, and *Equalization*.

JACK: Do be quiet. Now, Tom, only suppose this nonsensical equality was to take place; why it wou'd not last while one cou'd say Jack Robinson; or suppose it cou'd—suppose, in the general division, our new rulers were to give us half an acre of ground a-piece; we cou'd to be sure raise potatoes on it for the use of our families; but as every other man would be equally busy in raising potatoes for *his* family, why then you see if thou wast to break thy spade, I should not be able to mend it. Neighbour Snip wou'd have no time to make us a suit of cloaths, nor the clothier to weave the cloth, for all the world would be gone a digging. And as to boots and shoes, the want of some one to make them for us, wou'd be a greater grievance than the tax on leather. If we shou'd be sick, there wou'd be no doctor's stuff for us;

for doctor wou'd be digging too. We cou'd not get a chimney swept, or a load of coal from pit, for love or money.

TOM: But still I shou'd have no one over my head.

JACK: That's a mistake: I'm stronger than thou; and Standish, the exciseman,[4] is a better scholar; so we should not remain equal a minute. I shou'd out-*fight* thee, and he'd out-*wit* thee. And if such a sturdy fellow as I am, was to come and break down thy hedge for a little firing, or to take away the crop from thy ground, I'm not so sure that these new-fangled laws wou'd see thee righted. I tell thee, Tom, we have a fine constitution already, and our fore-fathers thought so.

TOM: They were a pack of fools, and had never read the Rights of Man.

JACK: I'll tell thee a story. When Sir John married, my Lady, who is a little fantastical, and likes to do every thing like the French, begged him to pull down yonder fine old castle, and build it up in her frippery way. No, says Sir John; what shall I pull down this noble building, raised by the wisdom of my brave ancestors; which outstood the civil wars, and only underwent a little needful repair at the Revolution; and which all my neighbours come to take a pattern by—shall I pull it all down, I say, only because there may be a dark closet or an inconvenient room or two in it? My Lady mumpt and grumbled; but the castle was let stand, and a glorious building it is, though there may be a trifling fault or two, and tho' a few decays may want stopping; so now and then they mend a little thing, and they'll go on mending, I dare say, as they have leisure, to the end of the chapter, if they are let alone. But no pull-me-down works. What is it you are crying out for, Tom?

TOM: Why for a perfect government.

JACK: You might as well cry for the moon. There's nothing perfect in this world, take my word for it.

TOM: I don't see why we are to work like slaves, while others roll about in their coaches, feed on the fat of the land, and do nothing.

JACK: My little maid brought home a story-book from the Charity-School t'other day, in which was a bit of a fable about the Belly and the Limbs. The hands said, I

---

[1] Listen.

[2] "Lord Ferrers was hanged in 1760, for killing his steward." (H.M.)

[3] a popular devotional book (published anonymously in 1658) discussing one's duty to other people and to God.

[4] tax collector.

won't work any longer to feed this lazy belly, who sits in state like a lord, and does nothing. Said the feet, I won't walk and tire myself to carry him about; let him shift for himself; so said all the members; just as your levellers and republicans do now. And what was the consequence? Why the belly was pinched to be sure; but the hands and the feet, and the rest of the members suffered so much for want of their old nourishment, that they fell sick, pined away, and wou'd have died, if they had not come to their senses just in time to save their lives, as I hope all you will do.[1]

TOM: But the times—but the taxes, Jack.

JACK: Things are dear, to be sure: but riot and murder is not the way to make them cheap. And taxes are high; but I'm told there's a deal of old scores paying off, and by them who did not contract the debt neither, Tom. Besides things are mending, I hope, and what little is done, is for us poor people; our candles are somewhat cheaper, and I dare say, if the honest gentleman is not disturbed by you levellers, things will mend every day. But bear one thing in mind: the more we riot, the more we shall have to pay. Mind another thing too, that in France the poor paid all the taxes, as I have heard 'em say, and the quality paid nothing.

TOM: Well, I know what's what, as well as another; and I'm as fit to govern—

JACK: No, Tom, no. You are indeed as good as another man, seeing you have hands to work, and a soul to be saved. But are all men fit for all kinds of things? Solomon says, "How can he be wise whose talk is of oxen?"[2] Every one in his way. I am a better judge of a horse-shoe than Sir John; but he has a deal better notion of state affairs than I; and I can no more do without him than he can do without me. And few are so poor but they may get a vote for a parliament-man, and so you see the poor have as much share in the government as they well know how to manage.

TOM: But I say all men are equal. Why should one be above another?

JACK: If that's thy talk, Tom, thou dost quarrel with Providence and not with government. For the woman is below her husband, and the children are below their mother, and the servant is below his master.

TOM: But the subject is not below the king; all kings are "crowned ruffians":[3] and all governments are wicked. For my part, I'm resolved I'll pay no more taxes to any of them.

JACK: Tom, Tom, this is thy nonsense; if thou didst go oftner to church, thou wou'dst know where it is said, "Render unto Cesar the things that are Cesar's"; and also, "Fear God, honour the king."[4] Your book tells you that we need obey no government but that of the people, and that we may fashion and alter the government according to our whimsies; but mine tells me, "Let every one be subject to the higher powers, for all power is of God, the powers that be are ordained of God; whosoever therefore resisteth the power, resisteth the ordinance of God."[5] Thou sayst, thou wilt pay no taxes to any of them. Dost thou know who it was that work'd a miracle, that he might have money to pay tribute with,[6] rather than set you and me an example of disobedience to government?

TOM: I say we shall never be happy, till we do as the French have done.

JACK: The French and we contending for liberty, Tom, is just as if thou and I were to pretend to run a race; thou to set out from the starting post, when I am in already: why we've got it man; we've no race to run. We're there already. Our constitution is no more like what the French one was, than a mug of our Taunton[7] beer is like a platter of their soup-maigre.[8]

TOM: I know we shall be undone, if we don't get a new *constitution*—that's all.

JACK: And I know we shall be undone if we *do*. I don't know much about politicks, but I can see by a little, what a great deal means. Now only to shew thee the

---

[1] Cf. Shakespeare, *Coriolanus* 1.1.91–150.

[2] Ecclesiasticus 38.26.

[3] "Of more worth is one honest man to society and in the sight of God, than all the crowned ruffians that ever lived" (Thomas Paine, *Common Sense*, 1776).

[4] Matthew 22.21, Luke 20.25; 1 Peter 2.17.

[5] Romans 13.1.

[6] See Matthew 17.24–27.

[7] a town in south-west England, south of the Bristol Channel.

[8] "thin soup" (Fr.).

state of public credit, as I think Tim Standish calls it. There's Farmer Furrow: a few years ago he had an odd 50l.[1] by him; so to keep it out of harm's way, he put it out to use, on government security I think he calls it. Well; t'other day he married one of his daughters, so he thought he'd give her that 50l. for a bit of a portion. Tom, as I'm a living man, when he went to take it out, if his fifty pounds was not grown almost to an hundred! and wou'd have been a full hundred, they say, by this time, if the gentleman had been let alone.

TOM: Well, still, as the old saying is—I shou'd like to do as they do in France.

JACK: What shou'dst like to be murder'd with as little ceremony as Hackabout, the butcher, knocks down a calf? Then for every little bit of tiff, a man gets rid of his wife. And as to liberty of *conscience*, which they brag so much about, why they have driven away their parsons, (aye and murdered many of 'em) because they wou'd not swear as they would have them. And then they talk of liberty of the press; why, Tom, only t'other day they hang'd a man for printing a book against this pretty government of theirs.

TOM: But you said yourself it was sad times in France, before they pull'd down the old government.

JACK: Well, and suppose the French were as much in the right as I know them to be in the wrong; what does that argue for *us*? Because neighbour Furrow t'other day pulled down a crazy, old barn, is that a reason why I must set fire to my tight cottage?

TOM: I don't see why one man is to ride in his coach and six, while another mends the highway for him.

JACK: I don't see why the man in the coach is to *drive over* the man on foot, or hurt a hair of his head. And as to our great folks, that you levellers have such a spite against; I don't pretend to say they are a bit better than they should be; but that's no affair of mine; let them look to that; they'll answer for that in another place. To be sure, I wish they'd set us a better example about going to church, and those things; but still *hoarding's* not the sin of the age; they don't lock up their *money*—away it goes, and every body's the better for it. They do spend too much, to be sure, in feastings and fandangoes,[2] and if I was a parson I'd go to work with 'em in another kind of a way; but as I am only a poor tradesman, why 'tis but bringing more grist to my mill. It all comes among the people—Their coaches and their furniture, and their buildings, and their planting, employ a power of tradespeople and labourers.—Now in this village; what shou'd we do without the castle? Tho' my Lady is too rantipolish,[3] and flies about all summer to hot water and cold water, and fresh water and salt water, when she ought to stay at home with Sir John; yet when she does come down, she brings such a deal of gentry that I have more horses than I can shoe, and my wife more linen than she can wash. Then all our grown children are servants in the family, and rare wages they have got. Our little boys get something every day by weeding their gardens, and the girls learn to sew and knit at Sir John's expence; who sends them all to school of a Sunday.

TOM: Aye, but there's not Sir Johns in every village.

JACK: The more's the pity. But there's other help. 'Twas but last year you broke your leg, and was nine weeks in the Bristol 'Firmary,[4] where you was taken as much care of as a lord, and your family was maintained all the while by the parish. No poor-rates[5] in France, Tom; and here there's a matter of two million and a half paid for them, if 'twas but a little better managed.

TOM: Two million and a half!

JACK: Aye, indeed. Not translated into ten-pences, as your French millions are, but twenty good shillings to the pound. But, when this levelling comes about, there will be no 'firmaries, no hospitals, no charity-schools, no Sunday-schools, where so many hundred thousand poor souls learn to read the word of God for nothing. For who is to pay for them? *equality* can't afford it; and those that may be willing won't be able.

TOM: But we shall be one as good as another, for all that.

JACK: Aye, and bad will be the best. But we must work as we do now, and with this difference, that no one will

---

[1] fifty pounds.

[2] "foolish actions"; from the name of a wild Spanish dance.

[3] resembling a rude, wild person.

[4] founded as a charity hospital in 1737.

[5] levies imposed for relieving destitute people within a parish.

be able to pay us. Tom! I have got the use of my limbs, of my liberty, of the laws, and of my Bible. The two first, I take to be my *natural* rights; the two last my *civil* and *religious*; these, I take it, are the *true Rights of Man*, and all the rest is nothing but nonsense and madness and wickedness. My cottage is my castle; I sit down in it at night in peace and thankfulness, and "no man maketh me afraid."[1] Instead of indulging discontent, because another is richer than I in this world, (for envy is at the bottom of your equality works,) I read my bible, go to church, and think of a treasure in heaven.[2]

TOM: Aye; but the French have got it in *this* world.

JACK: 'Tis all a lye, Tom. Sir John's butler says his master gets letters which *say* 'tis all a lye. 'Tis all murder, and nakedness, and hunger; many of the poor soldiers fight without victuals, and march without clothes. These are your *democrats*! Tom.

TOM: What then, dost think all the men on our side wicked?

JACK: No—not so neither—they've made fools of the most of you, as I believe. I judge no man, Tom; I hate no man. Even republicans and levellers, I hope, will always enjoy the protection of our laws; though I hope they will never be our law-*makers*. There's many true dissenters,[3] and there's hollow churchmen; and a good man is a good man, whether his church has got a steeple to it or not. The new fashioned way of proving one's religion is to *hate* somebody. Now, tho' some folks pretend that a man's hating a Papist, or a Presbyterian, proves him to be a good *Churchman*,[4] it don't prove him to be a good *Christian*, Tom. As much as I hate republican works, I'd scorn to *live* in a country where there was not liberty of conscience; and where every man might not worship God his own way. Now that they had not in France: the Bible was shut up in an unknown heathenish tongue.[5] While here, thou and I can make as free use of our's as a bishop; can no more be sent to prison unjustly than a judge; and are as much taken care of by the laws as the parliament man who makes them. And this leveling makes people so dismal. These poor French fellows used to be the merriest dogs in the world; but since equality come in, I don't believe a Frenchman has ever laughed.

TOM: What then dost thou take French *liberty* to be?

JACK: To murder more men in one night, than ever their poor king did in his whole life.

TOM: And what dost thou take a *Democrat* to be?

JACK: One who likes to be governed by a thousand tyrants, and yet can't bear a king.

TOM: What is *Equality*?

JACK: For every man to pull down every one that is above him, till they're all as low as the lowest.

TOM: What is *the new Rights of Man*?

JACK: Battle, murder, and sudden death.

TOM: What is it to be an *enlightened people*?

JACK: To put out the light of the gospel, confound right and wrong, and grope about in pitch darkness.

TOM: What is *Philosophy*, that Tim Standish talks so much about?

JACK: To believe that there's neither God, nor devil, nor heaven, nor hell.—To dig up a wicked old fellow's rotten bones, whose books, Sir John says, have been the ruin of thousands; and to set his figure up in a church and worship him.[6]

TOM: And what mean the other hard words that Tim talks about—Organization and *function*, and *civism*, and *incivism*, and *equalization*, and *inviolability*, and *imperscriptible*?

JACK: Nonsense, gibberish, downright hocus-pocus. I know 'tis not English; Sir John says 'tis not Latin; and his valet de sham[7] says 'tis not French neither.

TOM: And yet Tim says he shall never be happy till all these fine things are brought over to England.

---

[1] Cf. Ezekiel 34.28.

[2] Cf. Matthew 19.21, Mark 10.21, Luke 18.22.

[3] sincere Christians who did not observe the rites of the Church of England.

[4] i.e., member of the established Church of England.

[5] Roman Catholics heard the Bible read in Latin rather than in their own language.

[6] "Voltaire." (H.M.) The body of the French philosopher and freethinker Voltaire (1694–1778) was moved in 1791 to the recently finished Church of St. Geneviève in Paris, renamed the Panthéon and used as a mausoleum for revolutionary heroes.

[7] i.e., *valet de chambre* or personal servant (Fr.).

JACK: What into this Christian country, Tom? Why dost know they have no *sabbath*? Their mob parliament meets of a Sunday to do their wicked work, as naturally as we do to go to church. They have renounced God's word and God's day, and they don't even date in the year of our Lord. Why dost turn pale man? And the rogues are always making such a noise, Tom, in the midst of their parliament-house, that their speaker rings a bell, like our penny-postman, because he can't keep them in order.

TOM: And dost thou think our Rights of Man will lead to all this wickedness?

JACK: As sure as eggs are eggs.

TOM: I begin to think we're better off as we are.

JACK: I'm sure on't. This is only a scheme to make us go back in every thing. 'Tis making ourselves poor when we are getting rich.

TOM: I begin to think I'm not so very unhappy as I had got to fancy.

JACK: Tom, I don't care for drink myself, but thou dost, and I'll argue with thee in thy own way; when there's all equality there will be no *superfluity*; when there's no wages there'll be no drink; and levelling will rob thee of thy ale more than the malt-tax does.

TOM: But Standish says if we had a good government there'd be no want of any thing.

JACK: He is like many others, who take the king's money and betray him. Tho' I'm no scholar, I know that a good government is a good thing. But don't go to make me believe that *any* government can make a bad man good, or a discontented man happy.—What art musing upon man?

TOM: Let me sum up the evidence, as they say at 'sizes—Hem! To cut every man's throat who does not think as I do, or hang him up at a lamp-post!—Pretend liberty of conscience, and then banish the parsons only for being conscientious!—Cry out liberty of the press, and hang up the first man who writes his mind!—Lose our poor laws!—Lose one's wife perhaps upon every little tiff!—March without clothes, and fight without victuals!—No trade!—No bible!—No sabbath nor day of rest!—No safety, no comfort, no peace in this world—and no world to come!—Jack, I never knew thee tell a lie in my life.

JACK: Nor wou'd I now, not even against the French.

TOM: And thou art very sure we are not ruined.

JACK: I'll tell thee how we are ruined. We have a king so loving, that he wou'd not hurt the people if he cou'd; and so kept in, that he cou'd not hurt the people if he wou'd. We have as much liberty as can make us happy, and more trade and riches than allows us to be good. We have the best laws in the world, if they were more strictly enforced; and the best religion in the world, if it was but better followed. While Old England is safe, I'll glory in her and pray for her, and when she is in danger, I'll fight for her and die for her.

TOM: And so will I too, Jack, that's what I will. [*sings*] "O the roast beef of Old England!"[1]

JACK: Thou art an honest fellow, Tom.

TOM. This is Rose and Crown night, and Tim Standish is now at his mischief; but we'll go and put an end to that fellow's work.

JACK: Come along.

TOM: No; first I'll stay to burn my book, and then I'll go and make a bonfire and——

JACK: Hold, Tom. There is but one thing worse than a bitter enemy, and that is an imprudent friend. If thou woud'st shew thy love to thy King and country, let's have no drinking, no riot, no bonfires; but put in practice this text, which our parson preached on last Sunday, "Study to be quiet, work with your own hands, and mind your own business."[2]

TOM: And so I will, Jack—Come on.

from *Cheap Repository Tracts* (1795)

Patient Joe; or, the Newcastle Collier

Have you heard of a Collier[3] of honest renown,
Who dwelt on the borders of Newcastle Town?
His name it was Joseph—you better may know
If I tell you he always was call'd patient JOE.

---

[1] a line from an eighteenth-century patriotic ballad set to music by Richard Leveridge in 1735.

[2] 1 Thessalonians 4.11.

[3] coal-miner.

5   Whatever betided he thought it was right,
    And Providence still he kept ever in sight;
    To those who love GOD, let things turn as they wou'd
    He was certain that all work'd together for good.[1]

    He prais'd his Creator whatever befel;
10 How thankful was Joseph when matters went well!
    How sincere were his carols of praise for good health,
    And how grateful for any increase in his wealth!

    In trouble he bow'd him to GOD's holy will;
    How contented was Joseph when matters went ill!
15 When rich and when poor he alike understood
    That all things together were working for good.

    If the Land was afflicted with war, he declar'd
    'Twas a needful correction for sins which *he* shar'd
    And when merciful Heaven bid slaughter to cease
20 How thankful was Joe for the blessing of peace!

    When Taxes ran high, and provisions were dear,
    Still Joseph declar'd he had nothing to fear;
    It was but a trial he well understood,
    From HIM who made all work together for good.

25 Tho' his wife was but sickly, his gettings but small,
    A mind so submissive prepar'd him for all;
    He liv'd on his gains were they greater or less,
    And the GIVER he ceas'd not each moment to bless.

    When another child came he receiv'd him with joy,
30 And Providence bless'd who had sent him a boy;
    But when the child dy'd—said poor Joe I'm content
    For GOD had a right to recal what he lent.

    It was Joseph's ill-fortune to work in a pit
    With some who believ'd that profaneness was wit;
35 When disasters befel him much pleasure they shew'd,
    And laugh'd and said—Joseph, will this work for good?

    But ever when these wou'd prophanely advance
    That *this* happen'd by luck, and *that* happen'd by chance,

    Still Joseph insisted no chance cou'd be found,
40 Not a sparrow by accident falls to the ground.[2]

    Among his companions who work'd in the pit,
    And made him the butt of their profligate wit,
    Was idle Tim Jenkins, who drank and who gam'd,
    Who mock'd at his Bible, and was not asham'd.

45 One day at the pit his old comrades be found,
    And they chatted, preparing to go under ground;
    Tim Jenkins as usual was turning to jest
    Joe's notion—that all things which happen'd were best.

    As Joe on the ground had unthinkingly laid
50 His provision for dinner of bacon and bread,
    A dog on the watch seiz'd the bread and the meat,
    And off with his prey run with footsteps so fleet.

    Now to see the delight that Tim Jenkins exprest!
    "Is the loss of thy dinner too, Joe, for the best?"
55 "No doubt on't," said Joe, "but as I must eat,
    'Tis my duty to try to recover my meat."

    So saying he follow'd the dog a long round,
    While Tim laughing and swearing, went down under ground.
    Poor Joe soon return'd, tho' his bacon was lost,
60 For the dog a good dinner had made at his cost.

    When Joseph came back, he expected a sneer,
    But the face of each Collier spoke horror and fear;
    What a narrow escape hast thou had, they all said,
    The pit is fall'n in, and Tim Jenkins is dead!

65 How sincere was the gratitude Joseph express'd!
    How warm the compassion which glow'd in his breast!
    Thus events great and small if aright understood
    Will be found to be working together for good.

    "When my meat," Joseph cry'd, "was just now stol'n away,

---

[1] Cf. Romans 8.28.

[2] Cf. Matthew 10.29.

And I had no prospect of eating to-day,
How cou'd it appear to a short-sighted sinner,
That my life wou'd be sav'd by the loss of my dinner?"

from *Strictures on the Modern System of Female Education. With a View of the Principles and Conduct Prevalent among Women of Rank and Fortune* (1799)

CHAPTER 4

Comparison of the mode of female education in the last age with the present.

To return, however, to the subject of general education. A young lady may excel in speaking French and Italian, may repeat a few passages from a volume of extracts; play like a professor, and sing like a syren; have her dressing-room decorated with her own drawings, tables, stands, screens, and cabinets; nay, she may dance like Sempronia[1] herself, and yet may have been very badly educated. I am far from meaning to set no value whatever on any or all of these qualifications; they are all of them elegant, and many of them properly tend to the perfecting of a polite education. These things, in their measure and degree, may be done, but there are others which should not be left undone. Many things are becoming, but "one thing is needful."[2] Besides, as the world seems to be fully apprized of the value of whatever tends to embellish life, there is less occasion here to insist on its importance.

But, though a well bred young lady may lawfully learn most of the fashionable arts, yet it does not seem to be the true end of education to make women of fashion *dancers, singers, players, painters, actresses, sculptors, gilders, varnishers, engravers,* and *embroiderers.* Most *men* are commonly destined to some profession, and their minds are consequently turned each to its respective object. Would it not be strange if they were called out to exercise their profession, or to set up their trade, with only a little general knowledge of the trades of all other men, and without any previous definite application to their own peculiar calling? The profession of ladies, to which the bent of *their* instruction should be turned, is that of daughters, wives, mothers, and mistresses of families. They should be therefore trained with a view to these several conditions, and be furnished with a stock of ideas and principles, and qualifications ready to be applied and appropriated, as occasion may demand, to each of these respective situations: for though the arts which merely embellish life must claim admiration; yet when a man of sense comes to marry, it is a companion whom he wants, and not an artist. It is not merely a creature who can paint, and play, and dress, and dance; it is a being who can comfort and counsel him; one who can reason and reflect, and feel, and judge, and discourse, and discriminate; one who can assist him in his affairs, lighten his cares, sooth his sorrows, strengthen his principles, and educate his children.

Almost any ornamental talent is a good thing, when it is not the best thing a woman has. And the writer of this page is intimately acquainted with several ladies who, excelling most of their sex in the art of music, but excelling them also in prudence and piety, find little leisure or temptation, amidst the delights and duties of a large and lovely family, for the exercise of this talent, and regret that so much of their own youth was wasted in acquiring an art which can be turned to so little account in married life; and are now conscientiously restricting their daughters in the portion of time allotted to its acquisition.

Far be it from me to discourage the cultivation of any existing talent; but may it not be suggested to the fond believing mother, that talents, like the spirit of Owen Glendower, though conjured with ever so loud a voice,

Yet will not come when you do call for them.[3]

---

[1] "See Cataline's Conspiracy." (H.M.) Sempronia was a highly accomplished and beautiful Roman woman, who allegedly took part in Cataline's conspiracy to take over the state in 63 BC, an event recounted by the Roman historian Gaius Sallustius Crispus (Sallust).

[2] Cf. Luke 10.42.

[3] The rebel Welsh leader Owen Glendower (1359?–1416?) appears as a character in Shakespeare's *1 Henry IV*; cf. 3.1.55.

That injudicious practice, therefore, cannot be too much discouraged, of endeavouring to create talents which do not exist in nature. *That their daughters shall learn every thing*, is so general a maternal maxim, that even unborn daughters, of whose expected abilities and conjectured faculties, it is presumed, no very accurate judgment can previously be formed, are yet predestined to this universality of accomplishments. This comprehensive maxim, thus almost universally brought into practice, at once weakens the general powers of the mind, by drawing off its strength into too great a variety of directions; and cuts up time into too many portions, by splitting it into such an endless multiplicity of employments. I know that I am treading on tender ground; but I cannot help thinking that the restless pains we take to cram up every little vacuity of life, by crowding one new thing upon another, rather creates a thirst for novelty than knowledge; and is but a well-disguised contrivance to keep us in after-life more effectually from conversing with ourselves. The care taken to prevent *ennui*[1] is but a creditable plan for promoting self-ignorance. We run from one occupation to another (I speak of those arts to which little intellect is applied) with a view to lighten the pressure of time; above all to save us from our own thoughts; whereas, were we thrown a little more on our own hands, we might at last be driven, by way of something to do, to try to get acquainted with our own hearts; and though our being less absorbed by this busy trifling and frivolous hurry, might render us somewhat more sensible of the tædium of life, might not this very sensation tend to quicken our pursuit of a better? For an awful thought here suggests itself. If life be so long that we are driven to set at work every engine to pass away the tediousness of time; how shall we do to get rid of the tediousness of eternity? an eternity in which not one of these acquisitions will be of the least use. Let not then the soul be starved by feeding it on these husks, for it can be no more nourished by them than the body can be fed with ideas and principles.

Among the boasted improvements of the present age, none affords more frequent matter of peculiar exultation, than the manifest superiority in the employments of the young ladies of our time over those of the good housewives of the last century. The present are employed in learning the polite arts, or in acquiring liberal accomplishments; while the others wore out their days in adorning the mansion-house with hangings of hideous tapestry and disfiguring tent-stitch.[2] Most chearfully do I allow to the reigning modes their boasted superiority; for certainly there is no piety in bad taste. Still, granting all the deformity of the exploded ornaments, one advantage attended them: the walls and floors were not vain of their decorations; and it is to be feared, that the little person sometimes is. The flattery bestowed on the old employments, for probably even *they* had their flatterers, furnished less aliment and less gratification to vanity, and was less likely to impair the delicacy of modesty, than the exquisite cultivation of *personal* accomplishments or personal decorations; and every mode which keeps down vanity and keeps back *self*, has at least a moral use: and while one admires the elegant fingers of a young lady, busied in working or painting her ball dress, one cannot help suspecting that her alacrity may be a little stimulated by the animating idea *how very well she shall look in it*. Might not this propensity be a little checked, and an interesting feeling combined with her industry, were the fair artist habituated to exercise her skill in adorning some one else rather than herself? For it will add no lightness to the lightest head, nor vanity to the vainest heart, to take pleasure in reflecting how exceedingly the gown she is working will become her mother. This suggestion, trifling as it may seem, of habituating young ladies to exercise their taste and devote their leisure, not to the decoration of their own persons, but to the service of those to whom they are bound by every tender tie, would not only help to repress vanity, but by thus associating the idea of industry with that of filial affection, would promote, while it gratified, some of the best affections of the heart. The Romans (and it is mortifying, on the subject of Christian education to be driven so often to refer to the superiority of Pagans) were so well aware of the importance of keeping up a sense of

---

[1] "boredom," "world-weariness" (Fr.).

[2] a needlepoint stitch.

family fondness and attachment by the same means which promoted simple and domestic employment, that no citizen of note ever appeared in public in any garb but what was spun by his wife and daughter; and this virtuous fashion was not confined to the days of republican severity, but even in all the pomp and luxury of imperial power, Augustus preserved this simplicity of manners.

Let me be allowed to repeat, that I mean not with preposterous praise to descant on the ignorance or the prejudices of past times, nor absurdly to regret that vulgar system of education which rounded the little circle of female acquirements within the limits of the sampler and the receipt book. Yet if a preference almost exclusive was then given to what was merely useful, a preference almost exclusive also is now assigned to what is merely ornamental. And it must be owned, that if the life of a young lady, formerly, too much resembled the life of a confectioner, it now too much resembles that of an actress; the morning is all rehearsal, and the evening is all performance: and those who are trained in this regular routine, who are instructed in order to be exhibited, soon learn to feel a sort of impatience in those societies in which their kind of talents are not likely to be brought into play: the task of an auditor becomes dull to her, who has been used to be a performer. And the excessive commendation which the visitor is expected to pay for his entertainment, not only keeps alive the flame of vanity in the artist by constant fuel, but is not seldom exacted at a price which a veracity at all strict would grudge; but when a whole circle are obliged to be competitors who shall flatter most, it is not easy to be at once very sincere and very civil.[1] And unluckily, while the age is become so knowing and so fastidious, that if a young lady does not play like a public performer, no one thinks her worth attending to, yet if she does so excel, some of the soberest of the admiring circle feel a strong alloy to their pleasure, on reflecting at what a vast expence of time this perfection must probably have been acquired.

May I venture, without being accused of pedantry, to conclude this chapter with another reference to Pagan examples? The Hebrews, Egyptians, and Greeks, believed that they could more effectually teach their youth maxims of virtue, by calling in the aid of music and poetry; these maxims, therefore, they put into verses, and these again were set to the most popular and simple tunes, which the children sang; thus was their love of goodness excited by the very instruments of their pleasure; and the senses, the taste, and the imagination, as it were, pressed into the service of religion and morals. Dare I appeal to Christian parents, if these arts are commonly used by *them*, as subsidiary to religion and to a system of morals much more worthy of every ingenious aid and association, which might tend to recommend them to the youthful mind? Dare I appeal to Christian parents, whether music, which fills up no trifling portion of their daughters' time, does not fill it without any moral end, or even specific object? whether some of the favourite songs of polished societies are not amatory, are not Anacreontic, more than quite become the modest lips of innocent youth and delicate beauty?

---

[1] "That accurate judge of the human heart, Madame de Maintenon, was so well aware of the danger resulting from some kinds of excellence, that, after the young ladies of the Court of Louis Quatorze had distinguished themselves by the performance of some dramatic pieces of Racine, when her friends told her how admirably they had played their parts; 'Yes,' answered this wise woman, 'so admirably that they shall never play again.'" (H.M.) Françoise d'Aubigné, marquise de Maintenon (1635–1719) was the mistress and second wife of Louis XIV.

Thomas Bellamy
1745 – 1800

Thomas Bellamy was born in 1745 at Kingston-on-Thames. He was apprenticed to a hosier and followed that trade for twenty years. He later worked as a bookseller's clerk, started several unsuccessful periodicals, and ran a circulating library. From his youth he had been a writer, and when in 1800 he inherited property from his mother, he decided to devote himself to writing full time. But he died on 29 August 1800, after a short illness. His novel, *The Beggar Boy*, was published in 1801. (D.L.M.)

The Benevolent Planters: A Dramatic Piece as performed at the Theatre Royal, Haymarket (1789)

Prologue, (by a Friend) Spoken by Mr. Kemble, in the Character of an African Sailor

To Afric's torrid clime, where every day
The sun oppresses with his scorching ray,
My birth I owe; and there for many a year,
I tasted pleasure free from every care
5   There 'twas my happy fortune long to prove
The fond endearments of parental love.
'Twas there my Adela, my favourite maid,
Return'd my passion, love with love repaid.
Oft on the banks where golden rivers flow,
10 And aromatic woods enchanting grow,
With my lov'd Adela I pass'd the day,
While suns on suns roll'd unperceiv'd away.
But ah! this happiness was not to last,
Clouds now the brightness of my fate o'ercast;
15 For the white savage fierce upon me sprung,
Wrath in his eye, and fury on his tongue,
And dragg'd me to a loathsome vessel near,
Dragg'd me from every thing I held most dear,
And plung'd me in the horrors of despair.
20 Insensible to all that pass'd around,
Till, in a foreign clime, myself I found,
And sold to slavery!—There with constant toil,
Condemn'd in burning suns to turn the soil.
Oh! if I told you what I suffer'd there,
25 From cruel masters, and the lash severe,
Eyes most unus'd to melt, would drop the tear.

But fortune soon a kinder master gave,
Who made me soon forget I was a slave,
And brought me to this land, this generous land,
30 Where they inform me, that an hallow'd band,
Impell'd by soft humanity's kind laws,
Take up with fervent zeal the Negroe's cause,
And at this very moment, anxious try,
To stop the widespread woes of slavery.
35 But of this hallow'd band a part appears,
Exult my heart, and flow my grateful tears.
Oh sons of mercy! whose extensive mind
Takes in at once the whole of human kind,
Who know the various nations of the earth,
40 To whatsoever clime they owe their birth,
Or of whatever colour they appear,
All children of one gracious Parent are.
And thus united by paternal love,
To all mankind, of all the friend you prove.
45 With fervent zeal pursue your godlike plan,
And man deliver from the tyrant man!
What tho' at first you miss the wish'd-for end,
Success at last your labours will attend.
Then shall your worth, extoll'd in grateful strains,
50 Resound through Gambia's and Angola's plains.[1]
Nations unborn your righteous zeal shall bless,
To them the source of peace and happiness.
Oh mighty Kannoah, thou most holy power,
Whom humbly we thy sable race adore!
55 Prosper the great design—thy children free
From the oppressor's hand, and give them liberty!

---

[1] Gambia (in northwestern Africa) and Angola (in the Southwest) were prominent sources of slaves.

SCENE: JAMAICA

CHARACTERS

PLANTERS

GOODWIN   MR. CHAPMAN
STEADY   MR. USHER
HEARTFREE   MR. GARDNER

SLAVES

ORAN   MR. KEMBLE
SELIMA   MRS. KEMBLE

ARCHERS, &C. &C.

SCENE 1

A Room in GOODWIN's House.
ENTER GOODWIN, *meeting* STEADY *and* HEARTFREE.

GOODWIN: Good morrow, neighbours, friend Steady,[1] is your jetty tribe ready for the diversions?

STEADY: My tribe is prepared and ready to meet thine, and my heart exults on beholding so many happy countenances. But an added joy is come home to my bosom. This English friend, who, sometime since, came to settle among us, in order that he might exhibit to his brother Planters, the happy effects of humanity, in the treatment of those who, in the course of human chance, are destined to the bonds of slavery, has honoured my dwelling with his presence, and gladdened my heart with his friendship.

HEARTFREE: A cause like the present, makes brothers of us all, and may heaven increase the brothers of humanity—Friend Steady informs me, that we are to preside as directors of the different diversions.

GOODWIN: It is our wish to prevent a repetition of disorders, that last year disturbed the general happiness. They were occasioned by the admission of one of those games, which, but too often, begin in sport, and end in passion. The offenders, however, were soon made sensible of the folly of attacking each other without provocation, and with no other view than to shew their superior skill, in an art, which white men have introduced among them.[2]

HEARTFREE: If that art was only made use of as a defence against the attacks of an unprincipled and vulgar violence, no man could with propriety form a wish of checking its progress. But while it opens another field where the gambler fills his pocket at the expence of the credulous and unsuspecting, whose families too often mourn in poverty and distress the effects of their folly; every member of society will hold up his hand against it, if his heart feels as it ought. I am sorry likewise to add, that too many recent instances of its fatal effects among my own countrymen, have convinced me of the guilt and folly of venturing *a life* to display *a skill*.

GOODWIN: We are happy to find our union strengthened by corresponding sentiments.

HEARTFREE: The sports, I find, are to continue six days; repeat your design, respecting the successful archers.

STEADY: The archers, friend, to the number of twelve, consist of selected slaves, whose honest industry and attachment have rendered them deserving of reward. They are to advance in pairs, and the youth who speeds the arrow surest, is to be proclaimed victor.

HEARTFREE: And what is his reward?

STEADY: A portion of land for himself, and his posterity—freedom for his life, and the maiden of his heart.

HEARTFREE: Generous men! humanity confers dignity upon authority. The grateful Africans have hearts as large as ours, and shame on the degrading lash, when it can be spared—Reasonable obedience is what we expect, and let those who look for more, feel and severely feel the sting of disappointment.

STEADY: Will your poor fellow attend the festival?

HEARTFREE: He will. I respect your feelings for the sorrows of the worthy Oran.

GOODWIN: Oran, did you say? What know you of him; pardon my abruptness, but relate his story, it may prove a task of pleasure.

---

[1] The original title of the play was *The Friends*; Bellamy may be implying that his benevolent planters are Quakers—members of the Society of Friends. (Quakers were, in fact, among the leaders of the abolition movement.)

[2] evidently boxing.

HEARTFREE: By the fate of war, Oran had been torn from his beloved Selima. The conquerors were on the point of setting fire to the consuming pile to which he was bound, while the partner of his heart, who was devoted to the arms of the chief of the adverse party, was rending the air with her cries; at this instant a troop of Europeans broke in upon them, and bore away a considerable party to their ships; among the rest was the rescued Oran, who was happily brought to our mart, where I had the good fortune to become his master—he has since served me well and affectionately. But sorrow for his Selima is so deeply rooted in his feeling bosom, that I fear I shall soon lose an excellent domestic and as valuable a friend, whose only consolation springs from a sense of dying in the possession of Christian principles, from whence he acknowledges to have drawn comforts inexpressible.

GOODWIN: And comfort he shall still draw from a worldly as well as a heavenly source. For know, I can produce the Selima he mourns. She has told me her story, which is indeed a tale of woe. Inward grief has preyed upon her mind, and like her faithful Oran, she is bending to her grave. But happiness, love, and liberty shall again restore them.

HEARTFREE: When the mind has made itself up to misery—discoveries admitting of more than hope, ought ever to be made with caution. But you have a heart to feel for the distress of another, and conduct to guide you in giving relief to sorrow; leave me to my poor fellow, and do you prepare his disconsolate partner.

GOODWIN: I'll see her immediately, and when we take our seats on the plain of sports, we will communicate to each other the result of our considerations.

STEADY: Till then, my worthy associates, farewell.

[EXEUNT.]

SCENE 2

Another Apartment in GOODWIN's House.
ENTER GOODWIN and SELIMA.

GOODWIN: Come, my poor disconsolate, be composed, and prepare to meet your friends on those plains, where you never shall experience sorrow; but on the contrary, enjoy every happiness within the power of thy grateful master to bestow; you once told me, Selima, that my participation of your griefs abated their force; will you then indulge me with that pleasing tho' mournful Song you have made, on the loss of him, who, perhaps, may one day be restored?

SELIMA: Good and generous Master! ever consoling me with hope, can I deny you who have given me mind, taught me your language, comforted me with the knowledge of books, and made me every thing I am? Prepared too, my soul for joys, which you say are to succeed the patient bearing of human misery. Oh, Sir, with what inward satisfaction do I answer a request in every way so grateful to my feelings!

SONG

Set to Music by Mr. Reeve.[1]

How vain to me the hours of ease,
    When every daily toil is o'er;
In my sad heart no hope I find,
    For Oran is, alas! no more.

Not sunny Africa could please,
    Nor friends upon my native shore,
To me the dreary world's a cave,
    For Oran is, alas! no more.

In bowers of bliss beyond the moon,
    The white man says, his sorrow's o'er,
And comforts me with soothing hope,
    Tho' Oran is, alas! no more.

O come then, messenger of death,
    Convey me to yon starry shore,
Where I may meet with my true love,
    And never part with Oran more.

GOODWIN: There's my kind Selima! and now attend to a discovery, on which depends your future happiness; not only liberty, but love awaits you.

---

[1] William Reeve (1757–1815), composer and actor.

SELIMA: The first I want not—the last can never be! for where shall I find another Oran?
GOODWIN: O my good girl, your song of sorrow shall be changed into that of gladness. For know—the hours of anguish are gone by, your Oran lives, and lives but to bless his faithful Selima.
SELIMA: [*After a pause.*] To that invisible Being who has sustained my suffering heart, I kneel, overwhelmed with an awful sense of his protecting power. But how?
GOODWIN: As we walk on, I will explain every thing. You soon will embrace your faithful Oran, and his beloved Selima shall mourn no more.

[*EXEUNT.*]

SCENE 3

An open Plain.

On one side a range of men-slaves; on the other a range of women-slaves—at some distance, seated on decorated chairs, HEARTFREE, GOODWIN, and STEADY—twelve archers close the line on the men-side, meeting the audience with ORAN at their head, distinguished from the rest by a rich dress—ORAN advancing to the front of the stage, stands in a dejected posture.

HEARTFREE: Now let the air echo to the sound of the enlivening instruments, and beat the ground to their tuneful melody; while myself and my two worthy friends, who since our last festival have reaped the benefit of your honest labours, in full goblets drink to your happiness.
[*Flourish of music, and a dance.*]
HEARTFREE: Now let the archers advance in pairs, and again, in replenished cups, health and domestic peace to those who surest speed the arrow.
[*Flourish.*]

[*Here the archers advance in pairs to the middle of the Stage, and discharge their arrows through the side wings—the victor is saluted by two female slaves, who present to him the maiden of his choice—then a flourish of music, and the parties fall back to the side. After the ceremony has been repeated five times to as many pair of archers, and ORAN and ALMABOE only remain to advance as the sixth pair, ORAN appears absorbed in grief, which is observed with evident concern by HEARTFREE.*]

HEARTFREE: Why Oran, with looks divided between earth and heaven, dost thou appear an alien among those who are encompassed with joy and gladness? Though your beloved Selima is torn from your widowed arms, yet it is a duty you owe yourself, as a man, an obligation due to me, as your friend, to take to your bosom one whom I have provided for you. A contest with Almaboe is needless; he has fixed on his partner, to whom, according to your request, he is now presented. [*A flourish of music—two female slaves advance with a third, who is presented to ALMABOE—the parties embrace.*] It remains, therefore, for you to comply with the wishes of those who honour your virtues, and have respected your sorrows.
ORAN: Kind and benevolent masters, I indeed came hither unwillingly, to draw the bow, with a heart already pierced with the arrow of hopeless anguish. You have done generously by my friend, to whom I meant to have relinquished the victor's right, had the chance been mine. For alas, Sirs! Selima was my first and only love; and when I lost her, joy fled from a bosom it will never again revisit. The short date of my existence is therefore devoted alone to that Power whom you have taught me to revere. Sacred to gratitude, and sacred to her whose beckoning spirit seems at this moment to call on me from yonder sky—
GOODWIN: What say you, Oran, if I should produce a maiden whose virtues will bring you comfort, and whose affection you will find as strong as hers, whose loss you so feelingly deplore?
ORAN: O Sirs! had you but known my Selima, you would not attempt to produce her equal! Poor lost excellence! Yes, thy spirit, released from all its sufferings, is now looking down upon its Oran! But let not imagination too far transport me: perhaps she yet lives, a prey to brutal lust. [*Turns to* ALMABOE.] Brother of my choice, and friend of my adverse hour, long may your Coanzi be happy in the endearments of her faithful Almaboe. And O my friend! when thy poor Oran is no more, if chance that Selima yet lives, if blessed Providence *should* lead her to these happy shores, if she

should escape the cruel enemy, and be brought hither with honour unsullied; tell her how much she owes to these generous men; comfort her afflicted spirit, and teach her to adore the God of truth and mercy.

ALMABOE: Oran must himself endeavour to live for that day, and not by encouraging despair, sink self-devoted to the grave. The same Providence, my friend, which has turned the terrors of slavery into willing bondage, may yet restore thy Selima.

ORAN: The words of Almaboe come charged with the force of truth, and erring Oran bends to offended Heaven! Yet erring Oran must still feel his loss, and erring Oran must for ever lament it.

GOODWIN: It is true, Oran, our arguments to urge thee to be happy, have hitherto proved fruitless. But know, thou man of sorrow, we are possessed of the means which will restore thee to thyself and to thy friends. Hear, then, the important secret, and know, that thy Selima yet lives!

ORAN: [*After a pause.*] Yet lives! Selima yet lives! what my Selima! my own dear angel! O speak again, your words have visited my heart, and it is lost in rapture.

HEARTFREE: Nay, Oran, but be calm.

ORAN: I am calm—Heaven will permit me to support my joy, but do you relieve me from suspence.

GOODWIN: Let the instruments breathe forth the most pleasing strains—Advance, my happy virgins, with your charge, and restore to Oran his long-lost Selima. You receive her pure as when you parted, with a mind released from the errors of darkness, and refined by its afflictions.

[*Soft music*—SELIMA *comes down the stage, attended by six virgins in fancied dresses, who present her to* ORAN—*the lovers embrace—flourish of music, and a shout.*]

ORAN: Lost in admiration, gratitude, and love, Oran has no words, but can only in silence own the hand of Heaven; while to his beating heart he clasps its restored treasure. And O my masters! for such, though free, suffer me still to call you; let my restored partner and myself bend to such exalted worth; while for ourselves, and for our surrounding brethren, we declare, that you have proved yourselves *The Benevolent Planters*, and that under subjection like yours,

SLAVERY IS BUT A NAME.

SONG

To the Tune of "*Rule Britannia.*"[1]

In honour of this happy day,
   Let Afric's sable sons rejoice;
To mercy we devote the lay,
   To heaven-born mercy raise the voice.
Long may she reign, and call each heart her own,
And nations guard her sacred throne.

Fair child of heaven, our rites approve,
   With smiles attend the votive song,
Inspire with universal love,
   For joy and peace to thee belong.
Long may'st thou reign, and call each heart thy own,
While nations guard thy sacred throne.

---

[1] a patriotic song (1740), by Thomas Arne (1710–78); the original words were by James Thomson (1700–48).

Samuel Hearne
1745 – 1792

Born in 1745 in London, England to Samuel and Diana Hearne, Samuel Hearne joined the British navy when he was eleven years old and saw action in naval battles during the Seven Years' War (1756–63). In 1766 he began work for the Hudson's Bay Company at Prince of Wales Fort (now Churchill, Manitoba). Native reports of copper mines in the north convinced the company to explore there. In 1769, Hearne was appointed to head the land expedition to find the mines and the great river that was close by. However, his first attempts failed.

In December 1770, with Matonabbee, his Chippewyan guide, Hearne set off on his third expedition, which met with some success. He reached the Coppermine River on 14 July 1771. The mines proved to be a disappointment. However, during this expedition, Hearne followed the river and reached the Arctic Ocean, making him the first European to reach it by land. There is some difficulty in tracing Hearne's exact route because Hearne used the Native names of rivers and lakes, while later explorers tended to rename features in English.

After his travels, he briefly served as a ship's mate. He requested a post on land and in 1773 founded the Hudson's Bay Company's first western inland post at Fort Cumberland, Saskatchewan. He was appointed governor of Prince of Wales Fort, which was attacked by French ships on 8 August 1782. Recognizing the impossible odds, Hearne surrendered without firing a shot. He was allowed to sail back to England, but he returned to Churchill in September 1783. Almost four years later, in failing health, Hearne resigned his command at Churchill and returned to England. He died in London in November 1792. (J.G.)

∽∽∽

from *A Journey from Prince of Wales's Fort in Hudson's Bay to the Northern Ocean* (1795)

from CHAPTER 4

18 April 1771

Having a good stock of dried provisions, and most of the necessary work for canoes all ready, on the eighteenth we moved about nine or ten miles to the North North West, and then came to a tent of Northern Indians who were tenting on the North side of Thelewey-aza River. From these Indians Matonabbee[1] purchased another wife; so that he had now no less than seven, most of whom would for size have made good grenadiers. He prided himself much in the height and strength of his wives, and would frequently say, few women would carry or haul heavier loads; and though they had, in general, a very masculine appearance, yet he preferred them to those of a more delicate form and moderate stature. In a country like this, where a partner in excessive hard labour is the chief motive for the union, and the softer endearments of a conjugal life are only considered as a secondary object, there seems to be great propriety in such a choice; but if all the men were of this way of thinking, what would become of the greater part of the women, who in general are but of low stature, and many of them of a most delicate make, though not of the exactest proportion, or most beautiful mould? Take them in a body, the women are as destitute of real beauty as any nation I ever saw, though there are some few of them, when young, who are tolerable; but the care of a family, added to their constant hard labour, soon make the most beautiful among them look old and wrinkled, even before they are thirty; and several of the more ordinary ones at that age are perfect antidotes to love and gallantry. This, however, does not render them less dear and valuable to their owners, which is a lucky circumstance for those women, and a certain proof that there is no such thing as any rule or standard for beauty. Ask a Northern Indian, what is beauty? he will answer, a broad flat face, small eyes, high cheek-bones, three or four broad black lines a-cross each

---

[1] Hearne's Native guide.

cheek, a low forehead, a large broad chin, a clumsy hook-nose, a tawney hide, and breasts hanging down to the belt. Those beauties are greatly heightened, or at least rendered more valuable, when the possessor is capable of dressing all kinds of skins, converting them into the different parts of their clothing, and able to carry eight or ten stone[1] in Summer, or haul a much greater weight in Winter. These, and other similar accomplishments, are all that are sought after, or expected, of a Northern Indian woman. As to their temper, it is of little consequence; for the men have a wonderful facility in making the most stubborn comply with as much alacrity as could possibly be expected from those of the mildest and most obliging turn of mind; so that the only real difference is, the one obeys through fear, and the other complies cheerfully from a willing mind; both knowing that what is commanded must be done. They are, in fact, all kept at a great distance, and the rank they hold in the opinion of the men cannot be better expressed or explained, than by observing the method of treating or serving them at meals, which would appear very humiliating, to an European woman, though custom makes it sit light on those whose lot it is to bear it. It is necessary to observe, that when the men kill any large beast, the women are always sent to bring it to the tent: when it is brought there, every operation it undergoes, such as splitting, drying, pounding, &c. is performed by the women. When any thing is to be prepared for eating, it is the women who cook it; and when it is done, the wives and daughters of the greatest Captains in the country are never served, till all the males, even those who are in the capacity of servants, have eaten what they think proper; and in times of scarcity it is frequently their lot to be left without a single morsel. It is, however, natural to think they take the liberty of helping themselves in secret; but this must be done with great prudence, as capital embezzlements of provisions in such times are looked on as affairs of real consequence, and frequently subject them to a very severe beating. If they are practiced by a woman whose youth and inattention to domestic concerns cannot plead in her favour, they will for ever be a blot in her character, and few men will chuse to have her for a wife....

Having finished such wood-work as the Indians thought would be necessary, and having augmented our stock of dried meat and fat, the twenty-first was appointed for moving; but one of the women having been taken in labour, and it being rather an extraordinary case, we were detained more than two days. The instant, however, the poor woman was delivered, which was not until she had suffered all the pains usually felt on those occasions for near fifty-two hours, the signal was made for moving when the poor creature took her infant on her back and set out with the rest of the company; and though another person had the humanity to haul her sledge for her, (for one day only,) she was obliged to carry a considerable load beside her little charge, and was frequently obliged to wade knee-deep in water and wet snow. Her very looks, exclusive of her moans, were a sufficient proof of the great pain she endured, insomuch that although she was a person I greatly disliked, her distress at this time so overcame my prejudice, that I never felt more for any of her sex in my life; indeed her sighs pierced me to the soul, and rendered me very miserable, as it was not in my power to relieve her.

When a Northern Indian woman is taken in labour, a small tent is erected for her, at such a distance from the other tents that her cries cannot easily be heard, and the other women and young girls are her constant visitants: no male, except children in arms, ever offers to approach her. It is a circumstance perhaps to be lamented, that these people never attempt to assist each other on those occasions, even in the most critical cases. This is in some measure owing to delicacy, but more probably to an opinion they entertain that nature is abundantly sufficient to perform every thing required, without any external help whatever. When I informed them of the assistance which European women derive from the skill and attention of our midwives, they treated it with the utmost contempt; ironically observing, "that the many hump-backs, bandy-legs, and other deformities, so frequent among the English, were undoubtedly owing to the great skill of the persons who assisted in bringing them into the world, and to the extraordinary care of their nurses afterward."

---

[1] "The stone here meant is fourteen pounds." (S.H.)

A Northern Indian woman after child-birth is reckoned unclean for a month or five weeks; during which time she always remains in a small tent placed at a little distance from the others, with only a female acquaintance or two; and during the whole time the father never sees the child. Their reason for this practice is, that children when first born are sometimes not very sightly, having in general large heads, and but little hair, and are, moreover, often discoloured by the force of the labour; so that were the father to see them to such great disadvantage, he might probably take a dislike to them, which never afterward could be removed.

The names of the children are always given to them by the parents, or some person near of kin. Those of the boys are various, and generally derived from some place, season, or animal; the names of the girls are chiefly taken from some part or property of a Martin; such as, the White Martin, the Black Martin, the Summer Martin, the Martin's Head, the Martin's Foot, the Martin's Heart, the Martin's Tail, &c. ...[1]

from CHAPTER 5

June 1771

Much does it redound to the honour of the Northern Indian women when I affirm, that they are the mildest and most virtuous females I have seen in any part of North America; though some think this is more owing to habit, custom, and the fear of their husbands, than from real inclination. It is undoubtedly well known that none can manage a Northern Indian woman so well as a Northern Indian man; and when any of them have been permitted to remain at the Fort, they have, for the sake of gain, been easily prevailed on to deviate from that character; and a few have, by degrees, become as abandoned as the Southern Indians, who are remarkable throughout all their tribes for being the most debauched wretches under the Sun. So far from laying any restraint on their sensual appetites, as long as youth and inclination last, they give themselves up to all manner of even incestuous debauchery; and that in so beastly a manner when they are intoxicated, a state to which they are peculiarly addicted, that the brute creation are not less regardless of decency. I know that some few Europeans, who have had little opportunity of seeing them, and of enquiring into their manners, have been very lavish in their praise: but every one who has had much intercourse with them, and penetration and industry enough to study their dispositions, will agree, that no accomplishments whatever in a man, is sufficient to conciliate the affections, or preserve the chastity of a Southern Indian woman.[2]

The Northern Indian women are in general so far from being like those I have above described, that it is very uncommon to hear of their ever being guilty of incontinency, not even those who are confined to the sixth or even eighth part of a man.

It is true, that were I to form my opinion of those women from the behaviour of such as I have been more particularly acquainted with, I should have little reason to say much in their favour; but impartiality will not permit me to make a few of the worst characters a standard for the general conduct of all of them. Indeed it is but reasonable to think that travellers and interlopers will be always served with the worst commodities, though perhaps they pay the best price for what they have.

It may appear strange, that while I am extolling the chastity of the Northern Indian women, I should acknowledge that it is a very common custom among the men of this country to exchange a night's lodging with each other's wives. But this is so far from being considered as an act which is criminal, that it is esteemed by them as one of the strongest ties of friendship between two families; and in case of the death of either man, the other considers himself bound to support the children of the deceased. Those people are so far from viewing this engagement as a mere ceremony, like most of our Christian god-fathers and god-mothers, who, notwithstanding their vows are made in the most solemn manner, and in the presence of both God and man, scarcely ever afterward remember what they have promised, that there is not an instance of a Northern Indian having once neglected the duty which he is

---

[1] "Matonabee had eight wives, and they were all called Martins." (S.H.)

[2] We have omitted a long authorial note.

supposed to have taken upon himself to perform. The Southern Indians, with all their bad qualities, are remarkably humane and charitable to the widows and children of departed friends; and as their situation and manner of life enable them to do more acts of charity with less trouble than falls to the lot of a Northern Indian, few widows or orphans are ever unprovided for among them….

from CHAPTER 9

Their marriages are not attended with any ceremony; all matches are made by the parents, or next of kin. On those occasions the women seem to have no choice, but implicitly obey the will of their parents, who always endeavour to marry their daughters to those that seem most likely to be capable of maintaining them, let their age, person, or disposition be ever so despicable.

The girls are always betrothed when children, but never to those of equal age, which is doubtless sound policy with people in their situation, where the existence of a family depends entirely on the abilities and industry of a single man. Children, as they justly observe, are so liable to alter in their manners and disposition, that it is impossible to judge from the actions of early youth what abilities they may possess when they arrive at puberty. For this reason the girls are often so disproportionably matched for age, that it is very common to see men of thirty-five or forty years old have young girls of no more than ten or twelve, and sometimes much younger. From the early age of eight or nine years, they are prohibited by custom from joining in the most innocent amusements with children of the opposite sex; so that when sitting in their tents, or even when travelling, they are watched and guarded with such an unremitting attention as cannot be exceeded by the most rigid discipline of an English boarding-school. Custom, however, and constant example, make such uncommon restraint and confinement sit light and easy even on children, whose tender ages seem better adapted to innocent and cheerful amusements, than to be cooped up by the side of old women, and constantly employed in scraping skins, mending shoes, and learning other domestic duties necessary in the care of a family.

Notwithstanding those uncommon restraints on the young girls, the conduct of their parents is by no means uniform or consistent with this plan; as they set no bounds to their conversation, but talk before them, and even to them, on the most indelicate subjects. As their ears are accustomed to such language from their earliest youth, this has by no means the same effect on them, it would have on girls born and educated in a civilized country, where every care is taken to prevent their morals from being contaminated by obscene conversation. The Southern Indians are still less delicate in conversation, in the presence of their children.

The women among the Northern Indians are in general more backward than the Southern Indian women; and though it is well known that neither tribe lose any time, those early connections are seldom productive of children for some years.

Divorces are pretty common among the Northern Indians; sometimes for incontinency, but more frequently for want of what they deem necessary accomplishments, or for bad behaviour. This ceremony, in either case, consists of neither more nor less than a good drubbing, and turning the woman out of doors; telling her to go to her paramour, or relations, according to the nature of her crime.

Providence is very kind in causing these people to be less prolific than the inhabitants of civilized nations; it is very uncommon to see one woman have more than five or six children; and these are always born at such a distance from one another, that the youngest is generally two or three years old before another is brought into the world. Their easy births, and the ceremonies which take place on those occasions, have already been mentioned; I shall therefore only observe here, that they make no use of cradles, like the Southern Indians, but only tie a lump of moss between their legs; and always carry their children at their backs, next the skin, till they are able to walk. Though their method of treating young children is in this respect the most uncouth and awkward I ever saw, there are few among them that can be called deformed, and not one in fifty who is bow-legged.

There are certain periods at which they never permit the women to abide in the same tent with their husbands. At such times they are obliged to make a small hovel for themselves at some distance from the other tents. As this is an universal custom among all the tribes, it is also a piece of policy with the women, upon any difference with their husbands, to make that an excuse for a temporary separation, when, without any ceremony, they creep out (as is their usual custom on those occasions) under the eves of that side of the tent at which they happen to be sitting; for at those times they are not permitted to go in or out through the door. This custom is so generally prevalent among the women, that I have frequently known some of the sulky dames leave their husbands and tent for four or five days at a time, and repeat the farce twice or thrice in a month, while the poor men have never suspected the deceit, or if they have, delicacy on their part has not permitted them to enquire into the matter. I have known Matonabbee's handsome wife, who eloped from him in May one thousand seven hundred and seventy-one, live thunnardy, as they call it, (that is, alone,) for several weeks together, under this pretence; but as a proof he had some suspicion, she was always carefully watched, to prevent her from giving her company to any other man. The Southern Indians are also very delicate in this point; for though they do not force their wives to build a separate tent, they never lie under the same clothes during this period. It is, however, equally true, that the young girls, when those symptoms make their first appearance, generally go a little distance from the other tents for four or five days, and at their return wear a kind of veil or curtain, made of beads, for some time after, as a mark of modesty; as they are then considered marriageable, and of course are called women, though some at those periods are not more than thirteen, while others at the age of fifteen or sixteen have been reckoned as children, though apparently arrived at nearly their full growth.

On those occasions a remarkable piece of superstition prevails among them; women in this situation are never permitted to walk on the ice of rivers or lakes, or near the part where the men are hunting beaver, or where a fishing-net is set, for fear of averting their success. They are also prohibited at those times from partaking of the head of any animal, and even from walking in, or crossing the track where the head of a deer, moose, beaver, and many other animals, have lately been carried, either on a sledge or on the back. To be guilty of a violation of this custom is considered as of the greatest importance; because they firmly believe that it would be a means of preventing the hunter from having an equal success in his future excursions.

Olaudah Equiano
1745? – 1797

Olaudah Equiano's origins are controversial: the opening chapters of his *Interesting Narrative* tell us that he was born in about 1745 in the Essaka region of what is now Nigeria, and that he was kidnapped and enslaved when he was eleven; but his baptismal register, and the muster book of one of his ships, say that he was born a slave in South Carolina. If the latter is true, then Equiano must have learned the information in the *Narrative*—which is consistent with everything we know of eighteenth-century African life and the slave trade—through the oral tradition. His first recorded master was a Mr. Campbell, of Virginia; by 1757, he was the property of Henry Pascal, a lieutenant in the Royal Navy, who was on leave to command a merchant vessel, the *Industrious Bee*. By 1759, Equiano had learned to speak and read English and had acquired a Bible; he was baptized that February. He served Pascal (who was called up to command a warship) throughout the Seven Years' War; in 1763, although he had expected to be given his freedom, Pascal sold him to a slave-ship captain who was returning to the West Indies. There he became the property of Robert King, a Quaker merchant, who allowed him to ship some of his own cargo on trading voyages. Starting with a tumbler that he bought for threepence and sold for sixpence, by 11 July 1766 he had earned the £70 he needed to buy his freedom. Afterwards, he worked (mostly on board ship) as a clerk, cook, crewman, hairdresser, smith, and steward; he went on voyages not only to the North American colonies but to Britain, France, Grenada, Italy, Jamaica, the Miskito coast, and Turkey; in 1773, he was even part of an Arctic expedition. In 1786, he was appointed commissary for Stores for the Black Poor, an association hoping to repatriate freed slaves to Sierra Leone, but he was fired for being too outspoken in his criticism of his superiors. He became active in the abolition movement and, as his main contribution to it, published the *Interesting Narrative*, the first English-language autobiography by an African, in 1789; it was a critical and popular success, going through eight editions in his lifetime. In April 1792, he married Susanna Cullen; they had two daughters. He died on 31 March 1797. (D.L.M.)

☙☙☙

from *The Interesting Narrative of the Life of Olaudah Equiano, or Gustavus Vassa, the African. Written by Himself* (1789)

CHAPTER 2

The author's birth and parentage—His being kidnapped with his sister—Their separation—Surprise at meeting again—Are finally separated—Account of the different places and incidents the author met with till his arrival on the coast—The effect the sight of a slave ship had on him—He sails for the West Indies—Horrors of a slave ship—Arrives at Barbadoes, where the cargo is sold and dispersed.

I hope the reader will not think I have trespassed on his patience in introducing myself to him with some account of the manners and customs of my country. They had been implanted in me with great care, and made an impression on my mind, which time could not erase, and which all the adversity and variety of fortune I have since experienced served only to rivet and record; for, whether the love of one's country be real or imaginary, or a lesson of reason, or an instinct of nature, I still look back with pleasure on the first scenes of my life, though that pleasure has been for the most part mingled with sorrow.

I have already acquainted the reader with the time and place of my birth. My father, besides many slaves, had a numerous family, of which seven lived to grow up, including myself and a sister, who was the only daughter. As I was the youngest of the sons, I became, of course, the greatest favourite with my mother, and was always with her; and she used to take particular pains to form my mind. I was trained up from my earliest years in the art of war; my daily exercise was shooting and throwing javelins; and my mother adorned me with emblems, after the manner of our greatest warriors. In this way I grew up till I was turned the age of eleven, when an end was put to my happiness in the following manner:—Generally when the grown people in the neighbourhood were gone far in the fields to labour, the children assembled together in some of the neighbours' premises to play; and commonly some of us used to get up a tree to look out for any assailant, or kidnapper, that might come upon us; for they sometimes took those opportunities of our parents' absence to attack and carry off as many as they could seize. One day, as I was watching at the top of a tree in our yard, I saw one of those people come into the yard of our next neighbour but one, to kidnap, there being many stout young people in it. Immediately on this I gave the alarm of the rogue, and he was surrounded by the stoutest of them, who entangled him with cords, so that he could not escape till some of the grown people came and secured him. But alas! ere long it was my fate to be thus attacked, and to be carried off, when none of the grown people were nigh. One day, when all our people were gone out to their works as usual, and only I and my dear sister were left to mind the house, two men and a woman got over our walls, and in a moment seized us both, and, without giving us time to cry out, or make resistance, they stopped our mouths, and ran off with us into the nearest wood. Here they tied our hands, and continued to carry us as far as they could, till night came on, when we reached a small house, where the robbers halted for refreshment, and spent the night. We were then unbound, but were unable to take any food; and, being quite overpowered by fatigue and grief, our only relief was some sleep, which allayed our misfortune for a short time. The next morning we left the house, and continued travelling all the day. For a long time we had kept the woods, but at last we came into a road which I believed I knew. I had now some hopes of being delivered; for we had advanced but a little way before I discovered some people at a distance, on which I began to cry out for their assistance: but my cries had no other effect than to make them tie me faster and stop my mouth, and then they put me into a large sack. They also stopped my sister's mouth, and tied her hands; and in this manner we proceeded till we were out of the sight of these people. When we went to rest the following night they offered us some victuals; but we refused it; and the only comfort we had was in being in one another's arms all that night, and bathing each other with our tears. But alas! we were soon deprived of even the small comfort of weeping together. The next day proved a day of greater sorrow than I had yet experienced; for my sister and I were then separated, while we lay clasped in each other's arms. It was in vain that we besought them not to part us; she was torn from me, and immediately carried away, while I was left in a state of distraction not to be described. I cried and grieved continually; and for several days I did not eat any thing but what they forced into my mouth. At length, after many days travelling, during which I had often changed masters, I got into the hands of a chieftain, in a very pleasant country. This man had two wives and some children, and they all used me extremely well, and did all they could to comfort me; particularly the first wife, who was something like my mother. Although I was a great many days journey from my father's house, yet these people spoke exactly the same language with us. This first master of mine, as I may call him, was a smith, and my principal employment was working his bellows, which were the same kind as I had seen in my vicinity. They were in some respects not unlike the stoves here in gentlemen's kitchens; and were covered over with leather; and in the middle of that leather a stick was fixed, and a person stood up, and worked it, in the same manner as is done to pump water out of a cask with a hand pump. I believe it was gold he worked, for it was of a lovely bright yellow colour, and was worn by the women on their wrists and ancles. I was there I suppose about a month, and they at last used to trust me some little distance from the house. This liberty I used in embracing every opportunity to inquire the way to my own home: and I also sometimes, for the same purpose, went with the maidens, in the cool of the evenings, to bring pitchers of water from the springs for the use of the house. I had also remarked where the sun rose in the morning, and set in the evening, as I had travelled along; and I had observed that my father's house was towards the rising of the sun. I therefore determined to seize the first opportunity of making my escape, and to shape my course for that quarter; for I was quite oppressed and weighed down by grief after my mother and friends; and my love of liberty, ever great, was strengthened by the mortifying circumstance of not daring to eat with the free-born children, although I was mostly their companion. While I was projecting my escape, one day an unlucky event happened, which quite disconcerted my plan, and put an end to my hopes. I used to be sometimes employed in assisting an elderly woman slave to cook and take care of the poultry; and one morning, while I was feeding some chickens, I happened to toss a small pebble at one of them, which hit it on the middle and directly killed it. The old slave, having soon after missed the chicken, inquired after it; and on my relating the accident (for I told her the truth, because my mother would never suffer me to tell a lie) she flew into a violent passion, threatened that I should suffer for it; and, my master being out, she immediately went and told her mistress what I had done. This alarmed me very much, and I expected an instant flogging, which to me was uncommonly dreadful; for I had seldom been beaten at home. I therefore resolved to fly; and accordingly I ran into a thicket that was hard by, and hid myself in the bushes. Soon afterwards my mistress and the slave returned, and, not seeing me, they searched all the house, but not finding me, and I not making answer when they called to me, they thought I had run away, and the whole neighbourhood was raised in the pursuit of me. In that part of the country (as in ours) the houses and villages were skirted with woods, or shrubberies, and the bushes were so thick that a man could readily conceal himself in them, so as to elude the strictest search. The neighbours continued the whole day looking for me, and several times many of them came within a few yards of the place where I lay hid. I then gave myself up for lost entirely, and expected every moment, when I heard a rustling among the trees, to be found out, and punished by my master: but they never discovered me, though they were often so near that I even heard their conjectures as they were looking about for me; and I now learned from them, that any attempt to return home would be hopeless. Most of them supposed I had fled towards home; but the distance was so great, and the way so intricate, that they thought I could never reach it, and that I should be lost in the woods. When I heard this I was seized with a violent panic, and abandoned myself to despair. Night too began to approach, and aggravated all my fears. I had before entertained hopes of getting home, and I had determined when it should be dark to make the attempt; but I was now convinced it was fruitless, and I began to consider that, if possibly I could escape all other animals, I could not those of the human kind; and that, not knowing the way, I must perish in the woods. Thus was I like the hunted deer:

—"Ev'ry leaf and ev'ry whisp'ring breath
Convey'd a foe, and ev'ry foe a death."[1]

I heard frequent rustlings among the leaves; and being pretty sure they were snakes I expected every instant to be stung by them. This increased my anguish, and the horror of my situation became now quite insupportable. I at length quitted the thicket, very faint and hungry, for I had not eaten or drank any thing all the day; and crept to my master's kitchen, from whence I set out at first, and which was an open shed, and laid myself down in the ashes with an anxious wish for death to relieve me from all my pains. I was scarcely awake in the morning when the old woman slave, who was the first up, came to light the fire, and saw me in the fire place. She was very much surprised to see me, and could scarcely believe her own eyes. She now promised to intercede for me, and went for her master, who soon after came, and, having slightly reprimanded me, ordered me to be taken care of, and not to be ill-treated.

Soon after this my master's only daughter, and child by his first wife, sickened and died, which affected him so much that for some time he was almost frantic, and really would have killed himself, had he not been watched and prevented. However, in a small time afterwards he recovered, and I was again sold. I was now carried to the left of the sun's rising, through many different countries, and a number of large woods. The people I was sold to used to carry me very often, when I was tired, either on their shoulders or on their backs.

---

[1] Cf. John Denham (1615–69), *Cooper's Hill* (1642) 287–88.

I saw many convenient well-built sheds along the roads, at proper distances, to accommodate the merchants and travellers, who lay in those buildings along with their wives, who often accompany them; and they always go well armed.

From the time I left my own nation I always found somebody that understood me till I came to the sea coast. The languages of different nations did not totally differ, nor were they so copious as those of the Europeans, particularly the English. They were therefore easily learned; and, while I was journeying thus through Africa, I acquired two or three different tongues. In this manner I had been travelling for a considerable time, when one evening, to my great surprise, whom should I see brought to the house where I was but my dear sister! As soon as she saw me she gave a loud shriek, and ran into my arms—I was quite overpowered: neither of us could speak; but, for a considerable time, clung to each other in mutual embraces, unable to do any thing but weep. Our meeting affected all who saw us; and indeed I must acknowledge, in honour of those sable destroyers of human rights, that I never met with any ill treatment, or saw any offered to their slaves, except tying them, when necessary, to keep them from running away. When these people knew we were brother and sister they indulged us together; and the man, to whom I supposed we belonged, lay with us, he in the middle, while she and I held one another by the hands across his breast all night; and thus for a while we forgot our misfortunes in the joy of being together: but even this small comfort was soon to have an end; for scarcely had the fatal morning appeared, when she was again torn from me for ever! I was now more miserable, if possible, than before. The small relief which her presence gave me from pain was gone, and the wretchedness of my situation was redoubled by my anxiety after her fate, and my apprehensions lest her sufferings should be greater than mine, when I could not be with her to alleviate them. Yes, thou dear partner of all my childish sports! thou sharer of my joys and sorrows! happy should I have ever esteemed myself to encounter every misery for you, and to procure your freedom by the sacrifice of my own. Though you were early forced from my arms, your image has been always rivetted in my heart, from which neither *time nor fortune*[1] have been able to remove it; so that, while the thoughts of your sufferings have damped my prosperity, they have mingled with adversity and increased its bitterness. To that Heaven which protects the weak from the strong, I commit the care of your innocence and virtues, if they have not already received their full reward, and if your youth and delicacy have not long since fallen victims to the violence of the African trader, the pestilential stench of a Guinea ship, the seasoning in the European colonies, or the lash and lust of a brutal and unrelenting overseer.

I did not long remain after my sister. I was again sold, and carried through a number of places, till, after travelling a considerable time, I came to a town called Tinmah, in the most beautiful country I had yet seen in Africa. It was extremely rich, and there were many rivulets which flowed through it, and supplied a large pond in the centre of the town, where the people washed. Here I first saw and tasted cocoa-nuts, which I thought superior to any nuts I had ever tasted before; and the trees, which were loaded, were also interspersed amongst the houses, which had commodious shades adjoining, and were in the same manner as ours, the insides being neatly plastered and whitewashed. Here I also saw and tasted for the first time sugar-cane. Their money consisted of little white shells, the size of the finger nail. I was sold here for one hundred and seventy-two of them by a merchant who lived and brought me there. I had been about two or three days at his house, when a wealthy widow, a neighbour of his, came there one evening, and brought with her an only son, a young gentleman about my own age and size. Here they saw me; and, having taken a fancy to me, I was bought of the merchant, and went home with them. Her house and premises were situated close to one of those rivulets I have mentioned, and were the finest I ever saw in Africa: they were very extensive, and she had a number of slaves to attend her. The next day I was washed and perfumed, and when meal-time came I was led into the presence of my mistress, and ate and drank before her with her son. This filled me with astonishment; and I could scarce help expressing my surprise that the young

---

[1] Michael Drayton (1563–1631), *Ideas Mirrour* (1594), sonnet 38; cf. Ecclesiastes 9.11.

gentleman should suffer me, who was bound, to eat with him who was free; and not only so, but that he would not at any time either eat or drink till I had taken first, because I was the eldest, which was agreeable to our custom. Indeed every thing here, and all their treatment of me, made me forget that I was a slave. The language of these people resembled ours so nearly, that we understood each other perfectly. They had also the very same customs as we. There were likewise slaves daily to attend us, while my young master and I with other boys sported with our darts and bows and arrows, as I had been used to do at home. In this resemblance to my former happy state I passed about two months; and I now began to think I was to be adopted into the family, and was beginning to be reconciled to my situation, and to forget by degrees my misfortunes, when all at once the delusion vanished; for, without the least previous knowledge, one morning early, while my dear master and companion was still asleep, I was wakened out of my reverie to fresh sorrow, and hurried away even amongst the uncircumcised.[1]

Thus, at the very moment I dreamed of the greatest happiness, I found myself most miserable; and it seemed as if fortune wished to give me this taste of joy, only to render the reverse more poignant. The change I now experienced was as painful as it was sudden and unexpected. It was a change indeed from a state of bliss to a scene which is inexpressible by me, as it discovered to me an element I had never before beheld, and till then had no idea of, and wherein such instances of hardship and cruelty continually occurred as I can never reflect on but with horror.

All the nations and people I had hitherto passed through resembled our own in their manners, customs, and language: but I came at length to a country, the inhabitants of which differed from us in all those particulars. I was very much struck with this difference, especially when I came among a people who did not circumcise, and ate without washing their hands. They cooked also in iron pots, and had European cutlasses and cross bows, which were unknown to us, and fought with their fists amongst themselves. Their women were not so modest as ours, for they ate, and drank, and slept, with their men. But, above all, I was amazed to see no sacrifices or offerings among them. In some of those places the people ornamented themselves with scars, and likewise filed their teeth very sharp. They wanted sometimes to ornament me in the same manner, but I would not suffer them; hoping that I might some time be among a people who did not thus disfigure themselves, as I thought they did. At last I came to the banks of a large river, which was covered with canoes, in which the people appeared to live with their household utensils and provisions of all kinds. I was beyond measure astonished at this, as I had never before seen any water larger than a pond or a rivulet: and my surprise was mingled with no small fear when I was put into one of these canoes, and we began to paddle and move along the river. We continued going on thus till night; and when we came to land, and made fires on the banks, each family by themselves, some dragged their canoes on shore, others stayed and cooked in theirs, and laid in them all night. Those on the land had mats, of which they made tents, some in the shape of little houses: in these we slept; and after the morning meal we embarked again and proceeded as before. I was often very much astonished to see some of the women, as well as the men, jump into the water, dive to the bottom, come up again, and swim about. Thus I continued to travel, sometimes by land, sometimes by water, through different countries and various nations, till, at the end of six or seven months after I had been kidnapped, I arrived at the sea coast. It would be tedious and uninteresting to relate all the incidents which befell me during this journey, and which I have not yet forgotten; of the various hands I passed through, and the manners and customs of all the different people among whom I lived: I shall therefore only observe, that in all the places where I was the soil was exceedingly rich; the pomkins, eadas, plantains, yams, &c. &c. were in great abundance, and of incredible size. There were also vast quantities of different gums, though not used for any purpose; and every where a great deal of tobacco. The cotton even grew quite wild; and there was plenty of red-wood. I saw no mechanics whatever in all the way, except such as I have mentioned. The chief employment in all these countries was agriculture, and both the males and

---

[1] Cf. Judges 15.18, Ezekiel 32.32.

females, as with us, were brought up to it, and trained in the arts of war.

The first object which saluted my eyes when I arrived on the coast was the sea, and a slave ship, which was then riding at anchor, and waiting for its cargo. These filled me with astonishment, which was soon converted into terror when I was carried on board. I was immediately handled and tossed up to see if I were sound by some of the crew; and I was now persuaded that I had gotten into a world of bad spirits, and that they were going to kill me. Their complexions too differing so much from ours, their long hair, and the language they spoke, (which was very different from any I had ever heard) united to confirm me in this belief. Indeed such were the horrors of my views and fears at the moment, that, if ten thousand worlds had been my own, I would have freely parted with them all to have exchanged my condition with that of the meanest slave in my own country. When I looked round the ship too and saw a large furnace or copper boiling, and a multitude of black people of every description chained together, every one of their countenances expressing dejection and sorrow, I no longer doubted of my fate; and, quite overpowered with horror and anguish, I fell motionless on the deck and fainted. When I recovered a little I found some black people about me, who I believed were some of those who brought me on board, and had been receiving their pay; they talked to me in order to cheer me, but all in vain. I asked them if we were not to be eaten by those white men with horrible looks, red faces, and loose hair. They told me I was not; and one of the crew brought me a small portion of spirituous liquor in a wine glass; but, being afraid of him, I would not take it out of his hand. One of the blacks therefore took it from him and gave it to me, and I took a little down my palate, which, instead of reviving me, as they thought it would, threw me into the greatest consternation at the strange feeling it produced, having never tasted any such liquor before. Soon after this the blacks who brought me on board went off, and left me abandoned to despair. I now saw myself deprived of all chance of returning to my native country, or even the least glimpse of hope of gaining the shore, which I now considered as friendly; and I even wished for my former slavery in preference to my present situation, which was filled with horrors of every kind, still heightened by my ignorance of what I was to undergo. I was not long suffered to indulge my grief; I was soon put down under the decks, and there I received such a salutation in my nostrils as I had never experienced in my life: so that, with the loathsomeness of the stench, and crying together, I became so sick and low that I was not able to eat, nor had I the least desire to taste any thing. I now wished for the last friend, death, to relieve me; but soon, to my grief, two of the white men offered me eatables; and, on my refusing to eat, one of them held me fast by the hands, and laid me across I think the windlass, and tied my feet, while the other flogged me severely. I had never experienced any thing of this kind before; and although, not being used to the water, I naturally feared that element the first time I saw it, yet nevertheless, could I have got over the nettings, I would have jumped over the side, but I could not; and, besides, the crew used to watch us very closely who were not chained down to the decks, lest we should leap into the water: and I have seen some of these poor African prisoners most severely cut for attempting to do so, and hourly whipped for not eating. This indeed was often the case with myself. In a little time after, amongst the poor chained men, I found some of my own nation, which in a small degree gave ease to my mind. I inquired of these what was to be done with us; they gave me to understand we were to be carried to these white people's country to work for them. I then was a little revived, and thought, if it were no worse than working, my situation was not so desperate: but still I feared I should be put to death, the white people looked and acted, as I thought, in so savage a manner; for I had never seen among any people such instances of brutal cruelty; and this not only shewn towards us blacks, but also to some of the whites themselves. One white man in particular I saw, when we were permitted to be on deck, flogged so unmercifully with a large rope near the foremast, that he died in consequence of it; and they tossed him over the side as they would have done a brute. This made me fear these people the more; and I expected nothing less than to be treated in the same manner. I could not help expressing my fears and apprehensions to some of my countrymen: I asked them if these people had no country, but lived in this hollow place (the ship): they told me they did not, but came from a distant one. "Then," said I, "how comes it in all our country we never heard of them?" They told me because they lived so very far off. I then asked where were their women? had they any like themselves? I was told they had: "and why," said I, "do we not see them?" they answered, because they were left behind. I asked how the vessel could go? they told me they could not tell; but that there were cloths put upon the masts by the help of the ropes I saw, and then the vessel went on; and the white men had some spell or magic they put in the water when they liked in order to stop the vessel. I was exceedingly amazed at this account, and really thought they were spirits. I therefore wished much to be from amongst them, for I expected they would sacrifice me: but my wishes were vain; for we were so quartered that it was impossible for any of us to make our escape. While we stayed on the coast I was mostly on deck; and one day, to my great astonishment, I saw one of these vessels coming in with the sails up. As soon as the whites saw it, they gave a great shout, at which we were amazed; and the more so as the vessel appeared larger by approaching nearer. At last she came to an anchor in my sight, and when the anchor was let go I and my countrymen who saw it were lost in astonishment to observe the vessel stop; and were now convinced it was done by magic. Soon after this the other ship got her boats out, and they came on board of us, and the people of both ships seemed very glad to see each other. Several of the strangers also shook hands with us black people, and made motions with their hands, signifying I suppose we were to go to their country; but we did not understand them. At last, when the ship we were in had got in all her cargo, they made ready with many fearful noises, and we were all put under deck, so that we could not see how they managed the vessel. But this disappointment was the least of my sorrow. The stench of the hold while we were on the coast was so intolerably loathsome, that it was dangerous to remain there for any time, and some of us had been permitted to stay on the deck for the fresh air; but now that the whole ship's cargo were confined together, it became absolutely pestilential. The closeness of the place, and the heat of the climate, added to the number in the ship, which was so crowded that each had scarcely room to turn himself, almost suffocated us. This produced copious perspirations, so that the air soon became unfit for respiration, from a variety of loathsome smells, and brought on a sickness among the slaves, of which many died, thus falling victims to the improvident avarice, as I may call it, of their purchasers. This wretched situation was again aggravated by the galling of the chains, now become insupportable; and the filth of the necessary tubs, into which the children often fell, and were almost suffocated. The shrieks of the women, and the groans of the dying, rendered the whole a scene of horror almost inconceivable. Happily perhaps for myself I was soon reduced so low here that it was thought necessary to keep me almost always on deck; and from my extreme youth I was not put in fetters. In this situation I expected every hour to share the fate of my companions, some of whom were almost daily brought upon deck at the point of death, which I began to hope would soon put an end to my miseries. Often did I think many of the inhabitants of the deep much more happy than myself. I envied them the freedom they enjoyed, and as often wished I could change my condition for theirs. Every circumstance I met with served only to render my state more painful, and heighten my apprehensions, and my opinion of the cruelty of the whites. One day they had taken a number of fishes; and when they had killed and satisfied themselves with as many as they thought fit, to our astonishment who were on the deck, rather than give any of them to us to eat as we expected, they tossed the remaining fish into the sea again, although we begged and prayed for some as well as we could, but in vain; and some of my countrymen, being pressed by hunger, took an opportunity, when they thought no one saw them, of trying to get a little privately; but they were discovered, and the attempt procured them some very severe floggings. One day, when we had a smooth sea and moderate wind, two of my wearied countrymen who were chained together (I was near them at the time), preferring death to such a life of misery, somehow made through the nettings and jumped into the sea: immediately another quite dejected fellow, who, on account of his illness, was suffered to be out of irons, also followed their example; and I believe many more would very soon have done the same if they had not been prevented by the ship's crew, who were instantly alarmed. Those of us that were the most active were in a moment put down under the deck, and there was such a noise and confusion amongst the people of the ship as I never heard before, to stop her, and get the boat out to go after the slaves. However two of the wretches were drowned, but they got the other, and afterwards flogged him unmercifully for thus attempting to prefer death to slavery. In this manner we continued to undergo more hardships than I can now relate, hardships which are inseparable from this accursed trade. Many a time we were near suffocation from the want of fresh air, which we were often without for whole days together. This, and the stench of the necessary tubs, carried off many. During our passage I first saw flying fishes, which surprised me very much: they used frequently to fly across the ship, and many of them fell on the deck. I also now first saw the use of the quadrant; I had often with astonishment seen the mariners make observations with it, and I could not think what it meant. They at last took notice of my surprise; and one of them, willing to increase it, as well as to gratify my curiosity, made me one day look through it. The clouds appeared to me to be land, which disappeared as they passed along. This heightened my wonder; and I was now more persuaded than ever that I was in another world, and that every thing about me was magic. At last we came in sight of the island of Barbadoes, at which the whites on board gave a great shout, and made many signs of joy to us. We did not know what to think of this; but as the vessel drew nearer we plainly saw the harbour, and other ships of different kinds and sizes; and we soon anchored amongst them off Bridge Town. Many merchants and planters now came on board, though it was in the evening. They put us in separate parcels, and examined us attentively. They also made us jump, and pointed to the land, signifying we were to go there. We thought by this we should be eaten by these ugly men, as they appeared to us; and, when soon after we were all put down under the deck again, there was much dread and trembling among us, and nothing but bitter cries to be heard all the night from these apprehensions, insomuch that at last the white people got some old slaves from the land to pacify us. They told us we were not to be eaten, but to work, and were soon to go on land, where we should see many of our country people. This report eased us much; and sure enough, soon after we were landed, there came to us Africans of all languages. We were conducted immediately to the merchant's yard, where we were all pent up together like so many sheep in a fold, without regard to sex or age. As every object was new to me every thing I saw filled me with surprise. What struck me first was that the houses were built with stories, and in every other respect different from those in Africa: but I was still more astonished on seeing people on horseback. I did not know what this could mean; and indeed I thought these people were full of nothing but magical arts. While I was in this astonishment one of my fellow prisoners spoke to a countryman of his about the horses, who said they were the same kind they had in their country. I understood them, though they were from a distant part of Africa, and I thought it odd I had not seen any horses there; but afterwards, when I came to converse with different Africans, I found they had many horses amongst them, and much larger than those I then saw. We were not many days in the merchant's custody before we were sold after their usual manner, which is this:—On a signal given, (as the beat of a drum) the buyers rush at once into the yard where the slaves are confined, and make choice of that parcel they like best. The noise and clamour with which this is attended, and the eagerness visible in the countenances of the buyers, serve not a little to increase the apprehensions of the terrified Africans, who may well be supposed to consider them as the ministers of that destruction to which they think themselves devoted. In this manner, without scruple, are relations and friends separated, most of them never to see each other again. I remember in the vessel in which I was brought over, in the men's apartment, there were several brothers, who, in the sale, were sold in different lots; and it was very moving on this occasion to see and hear their cries at parting. O, ye nominal Christians! might not an African ask you, learned you this from your God, who says unto you, Do unto all men as you would men should do unto you?[1] Is it not enough that we are torn from our country and friends to toil for your luxury and lust of gain? Must every tender feeling be likewise sacrificed to your avarice? Are the dearest friends and relations, now rendered more dear by their separation from their kindred, still to be parted from each other, and thus prevented from cheering the gloom of slavery with the small comfort of being together and mingling their sufferings and sorrows? Why are parents to lose their children, brothers their sisters, or husbands their wives? Surely this is a new refinement in cruelty, which, while it has no advantage to atone for it, thus aggravates distress, and adds fresh horrors even to the wretchedness of slavery.

---

[1] Matthew 7.12; Luke 6.31.

Elizabeth Hands
1746? – 1815

Elizabeth Herbert was born in Harbury, Warwickshire, probably on 5 June 1746, the daughter of Henry and Ann Herbert. She worked as a domestic servant for a family that evidently allowed her to educate herself. By 1785, she was married to William Hands, a blacksmith in Bourton-on-Dunsmore, near Rugby; they had two daughters. She published some poems in *Jopson's Coventry Mercury*, and these so impressed Thomas James, the headmaster of Rugby School, that he arranged for *The Death of Amnon* to be published by subscription; among the many subscribers were Sir Joseph Banks, Burke,* Charles James Fox, and Seward.* It was her only book. She died in Frankton on 28 June 1815. When her husband died in Coventry in 1825, he was buried next to her, in the churchyard at Bourton. (D.L.M.)

from *The Death of Amnon. A Poem. With an Appendix: Containing Pastorals, and Other Poetical Pieces* (1789)

A Poem, On the Supposition of an Advertisement Appearing in a Morning Paper, of the Publication of a Volume of Poems, by a Servant Maid

The tea-kettle bubbled, the tea things were set,
The candles were lighted, the ladies were met;
The how d'ye's were over, and entering bustle,
The company seated, and silks ceas'd to rustle:
5 The great Mrs. Consequence open'd her fan;
And thus the discourse in an instant began:
(All affected reserve, and formality scorning,)
I suppose you all saw in the paper this morning,
A Volume of Poems advertis'd—'tis said
10 They're produc'd by the pen of a poor Servant Maid.
A servant write verses! says Madam Du Bloom;
Pray what is the subject?—a Mop, or a Broom?
He, he, he,—says Miss Flounce; I suppose we shall see
An Ode on a Dishclout—what else can it be?
15 Says Miss Coquettilla, why ladies so tart?
Perhaps Tom the Footman has fired her heart;
And she'll tell us how charming he looks in new clothes,
And how nimble his hand moves in brushing the shoes;
Or how the last time that he went to May-Fair,
20 He bought her some sweethearts of ginger-bread ware.
For my part I think, says old lady Marr-joy,
A servant might find herself other employ:
Was she mine I'd employ her as long as 'twas light,
And send her to bed without candle at night.
25 Why so? says Miss Rhymer, displeas'd; I protest
'Tis pity a genius should be so deprest!
What ideas can such low-bred creatures conceive,
Says Mrs. Noworthy, and laugh'd in her sleeve.
Says old Miss Prudella, if servants can tell
30 How to write to their mothers, to say they are well,
And read of a Sunday the Duty of Man;[1]
Which is more I believe than one half of them can;
I think 'tis much *properer* they should rest there,
Than be reaching at things so much out of their sphere.
35 Says old Mrs. Candour, I've now got a maid
That's the plague of my life—a young gossipping jade;
There's no end of the people that after her come,
And whenever I'm out, she is never at home;
I'd rather ten times she would sit down and write,
40 Than gossip all over the town ev'ry night.
Some whimsical trollop most like, says Miss Prim,
Has been scribbling of nonsense, just out of a whim,
And conscious it neither is witty or pretty,
Conceals her true name, and ascribes it to Betty.
45 I once had a servant myself, says Miss Pines,
That wrote on a Wedding, some very good lines:
Says Mrs. Domestic, and when they were done,
I can't see for my part, what use they were *on*;
Had she wrote a receipt, to've instructed you how
50 To warm a cold breast of veal, like a ragou,
Or to make cowslip wine, that would pass for Champain;

---

[1] *The Whole Duty of Man* (1658), a very popular devotional book, possibly by Richard Allestree (1621/2–81).

It might have been useful, again and again.
On the sofa was old lady Pedigree plac'd,
She own'd that for poetry she had no taste,
55 That the study of heraldry was more in fashion,
And boasted she knew all the crests in the nation.
Says Mrs. Routella,—Tom, take out the urn,
And stir up the fire, you see it don't burn.
The tea things remov'd, and the tea-table gone,
60 The card-tables brought, and the cards laid thereon,
The ladies ambitious for each others crown,
Like courtiers contending for honours sat down.

A Poem, On the Supposition of the Book Having Been Published and Read

The dinner was over, the table-cloth gone,
    The bottles of wine and the glasses brought on,
The gentlemen fill'd up the sparkling glasses,
To drink to their king, to their country and lasses:
5 The ladies a glass or two only requir'd,
To th' drawing-room then in due order retir'd;
The gentlemen likewise that chose to drink tea;
And, after discussing the news of the day,
What wife was suspected, what daughter elop'd,
10 What thief was detected, that 'twas to be hop'd,
The rascals would all be convicted, and rop'd;
What chambermaid kiss'd when her lady was out;
Who won, and who lost, the last night at the rout;
What lord gone to France, and what tradesman unpaid,
15 And who and who danc'd at the last masquerade;
What banker stopt payment with evil intention,
And twenty more things much too tedious to mention.
Miss Rhymer says, Mrs. Routella, ma'am, pray
Have you seen the new book (that we talk'd of that day,
20 At your house you remember) of Poems, 'twas said
Produc'd by the pen of a poor Servant Maid?
The company silent, the answer expected;
Says Mrs. Routella, when she'd recollected;
Why, ma'am, I have bought it for Charlotte; the child
25 Is so fond of a book, I'm afraid it is spoil'd:
I thought to have read it myself, but forgat it;
In short, I have never had time to look at it.
Perhaps I may look it o'er some other day;
Is there any thing in it worth reading, I pray?
30 For your nice attention, there's nothing can 'scape.
She answer'd,—There's one piece, whose subject's a Rape.
A Rape! interrupted the Captain Bonair,
A delicate theme for a female I swear;
Then smerk'd at the ladies, they simper'd all round,
35 Touch'd their lips with their fans,—Mrs. Consequence frown'd.
The simper subsided, for she with her nods,
Awes these lower assemblies, as Jove awes the gods.
She smil'd on Miss Rhymer, and bad her proceed—
Says she, there are various subjects indeed:
40 With some little pleasure I read all the rest,
But the Murder of Amnon's the longest and best.[1]
Of Amnon, of Amnon, Miss Rhymer, who's he?
His name, says Miss Gaiety's quite new to me:—
'Tis a Scripture tale, ma'am,—he's the son of King David,
45 Says a Reverend old Rector: quoth madam, I have it;
A Scripture tale?—ay—I remember it—true;
Pray is it i' th' old Testament or the new?
If I thought I could readily find it, I'd borrow
My house-keeper's Bible, and read it to-morrow.
50 'Tis in Samuel, ma'am, says the Rector:—Miss Gaiety
Bow'd, and the Reverend blush'd for the laity.
You've read it, I find, says Miss Harriot Anderson;
Pray, sir, is it any thing like Sir Charles Grandison?[2]
How you talk, says Miss Belle, how should such a girl write
55 A novel, or any thing else that's polite?
You'll know better in time, Miss:—She was but fifteen:
Her mamma was confus'd—with a little chagrin,
Says,—Where's your attention, child? did not you hear
Miss Rhymer say, that it was poems, my dear?
60 Says Sir Timothy Turtle, my daughters ne'er look
In any thing else but a cookery book:
The properest study for women design'd;[3]

---

[1] Amnon, son of King David, raped his half-sister Tamar, so his half-brother Absalom (Tamar's full brother) had him murdered: see 2 Samuel 13.

[2] the third and last novel (1753–54) by Samuel Richardson (1689–1761).

[3] Cf. Pope, *An Essay on Man* (1733–34) 2.2.

Says Mrs. Domestic, I'm quite of your mind.
Your haricoes, ma'am, are the best I e'er eat,
65 Says the Knight, may I venture to beg a receipt.
'Tis much at your service, says madam, and bow'd,
Then flutter'd her fan, of the compliment proud.
Says Lady Jane Rational, the bill of fare
Is th' utmost extent of my cookery care:
70 Most servants can cook for the palate I find,
But very few of them can cook for the mind.
Who, says Lady Pedigree, can this girl be;
Perhaps she's descended of some family:—
Of family, doubtless, says Captain Bonair,
75 She's descended from Adam, I'd venture to swear.
Her Ladyship drew herself up in her chair,
And twitching her fan-sticks, affected a sneer.
I know something of her, says Mrs. Devoir,
She liv'd with my friend, Jacky Faddle, Esq.
80 'Tis sometime ago though; her mistress said then,
The girl was excessively fond of a pen;
I saw her, but never convers'd with her—*though*
One can't make acquaintance with servants, you know.
'Tis pity the girl was not bred in high life,
85 Says Mr. Fribbello:—yes,—then, says his wife,
She doubtless might have wrote something worth
    notice:
'Tis pity, says one,—says another, and so 'tis.
O law! says young Seagram, I've seen the book, now
I remember, there's something about a mad cow.
90 A mad cow!—ha, ha, ha, ha, return'd half the room;
What can y' expect better, says Madam Du Bloom?
They look at each other,—a general pause—
And Miss Coquettella adjusted her gauze.
The Rector reclin'd himself back in his chair,
95 And open'd his snuff-box with indolent air;
This book, says he, (snift, snift) has in the beginning,
(The ladies give audience to hear his opinion)
Some pieces, I think, that are pretty correct;
A stile elevated you cannot expect:
100 To some of her equals they may be a treasure,
And country lasses may read 'em with pleasure.
That Amnon, you can't call it poetry neither,
There's no flights of fancy, or imagery either;
You may stile it prosaic, blank-verse at the best;
105 Some pointed reflections, indeed, are exprest;
The narrative lines are exceedingly poor:
Her Jonadab[1] is a——the drawing-room door
Was open'd, the gentlemen came from below,
And gave the discourse a definitive blow.

*Written, Originally Extempore,
on Seeing a Mad Heifer Run through
the Village Where the Author Lives*

When summer smil'd, and birds on ev'ry spray,
In joyous warblings tun'd their vocal lay,
Nature on all sides shew'd a lovely scene,
And people's minds were, like the air, serene;
5 Sudden from th' herd we saw an heifer stray,
And to our peaceful village bend her way.
She spurns the ground with madness as she flies,
And clouds of dust, like autumn mists, arise;
Then bellows loud: the villagers alarm'd,
10 Come rushing forth, with various weapons arm'd:
Some run with pieces of old broken rakes,
And some from hedges pluck the rotten stakes;
Here one in haste, with hand-staff of his flail,
And there another comes with half a rail:
15 Whips, without lashes, sturdy plough-boys bring,
While clods of dirt and pebbles others fling:
Voices tumultuous rend the listening ear;
Stop her—one cries; another—turn her there:
But furiously she rushes by them all,
20 And some huzza, and some to cursing fall:
A mother snatch'd her infant off the road,
Close to the spot of ground where next she trod;
Camilla walking, trembled and turn'd pale;
See o'er her gentle heart what fears prevail!
25 At last the beast, unable to withstand
Such force united, leapt into a pond:
The water quickly cool'd her madden'd rage;
No more she'll fright our village, I presage.

---

[1] Amnon's friend Jonadab suggested the rape: 2 Samuel 13.3–5.

Susanna Blamire
1747 – 1794

Susanna Blamire was born on 12 January 1747 at Cardew Hall, Cumberland; she was the youngest child of William Blamire, a farmer, and Isabella Simpson Blamire. When Blamire was seven, her mother died; when she was eight, her father remarried and Blamire, along with her brothers and sister, went to live with their widowed aunt, Mary Stevenson Simpson, at Thackwood, a manor house near the village of Stokdalewath. She was educated by her aunt and at a village school in Raughton Head. She learned to play the guitar and the flageolet (many of her songs are set to traditional airs) and was fond of dancing. On a visit to the Earl of Tankerville, whose family greatly enjoyed her songs, she and the Earl's son fell in love and the Earl sent his son abroad to avoid a misalliance; this unhappy love affair may have suggested the story of the Hermit and Ethelinde in "Stoklewath." Blamire never married. In 1767, her sister Sarah married a Colonel Graham, and Blamire lived with them for six years in the Scottish Highlands, where she took to writing in Scots. The family also visited Ireland and London and wintered in Carlisle, where Blamire met and collaborated with another poet, Catherine Gilpin. In 1773, Graham died and Blamire and Sarah returned to Thackwood. Blamire, who had suffered from ill health since her mid-twenties, was confined to her bed for her last months; she died on 5 April 1794 and was buried at Raughton Head Chapel, Carlisle, near her Aunt Mary.

Blamire wrote most of her poems for the entertainment of her family and friends—though she also pinned some of them to tree-branches, so passing strangers could read them. She published very few of them, and they were not collected until long after her death, but for decades they remained a prominent part of the oral tradition of Cumberland. (D.L.M.)

☙☙

from *The Poetical Works of Miss Susanna Blamire, "The Muse of Cumberland"* (1842)

from *Stoklewath*[1]
Or,
The Cumbrian Village

In this gay village hangs a wonderous sign,[2]
The Hounds and Hare are the immense design.
There hunters crack their whips, and seem to bound
460 O'er every hedge, nor touch the mimic ground;
The huntsman winds[3] his horn, his big cheeks swell,
And whippers-in make lagging terriers yell;
The sportive scene tempts many a wight to stay,
As to the school he drags th' unwilling way.
465 Around the front inviting benches wait,
Conscious of many a glass and sage debate;
The great man of the village cracks his joke,
Reads o'er the news, and whiffs the curling smoke;
Tells tales of old, and nods, and heaves the can,[4]
470 Makes fixed decrees, and seems much more than man.
"Come, Jack, sit down. Thy father, man, and me,
Broke many a glass, and many a freak had we.
'Twas when he sought thy mother, at Carel Fair[5]
(I mind the corn was very bad that year)
475 We met thy mother and my wife i' the street,
And took them into Beck's to get a treat;
Blind Joseph played, and I took out thy mother,
Thy father, he was shy, he got another;
And when I took her back, as you may see,
480 I whipp'd her blushing on thy father's knee.

---

[1] "The provincial pronunciation of Stokdalewath." Patrick Maxwell of Edinburgh wrote the notes to Blamire's *Poetical Works*. Stokdalewath is in Cumberland, near Carlisle.

[2] The poem recounts a typical day in Stoklewath. In the evening, the scene shifts to the village pub.

[3] blows.

[4] beer mug.

[5] Carlisle Fair, always held on 26 August.

Then in came Robin Bell, who lik'd her too,
And bit his lip, and turn'd both red and blue,
Teas'd her to dance, as you may see, and then
Kept her himself, nor brought her back again.
I fir'd at this, while up thy father rose,
Gave him a kick, and tweak'd him by the nose.
They stripped to fight, as you may see, and I
In seeing fair play got a blacken'd eye;
I durst not shew my face at home next day,
But bade my mother say I went away,
But kept my bed, i'fegs,[1] as you may see;
Who is it now fights for their lasses? eh!"
The blacksmith laugh'd, the cobbler gave a smile,
And the pleas'd tailor scratch'd his head the while.
But hark! what sounds of mingl'd joy and woe
From yon poor cottage bursting seem to flow.
'Tis honest Sarah. Sixpence-Harry's come,
And, after all his toils, got safely home.
"Welcome, old soldier, welcome from the wars![2]
Honour the man, my lads, seam'd o'er with scars!
Come give's thy hand, and bring the t'other can,
And tell us all thou'st done, and seen, my man."
Now expectation stares in every eye,
The jaw falls down, and every soul draws nigh,
With ear turn'd up, and head held all awry.
"Why, sir, the papers tell you all that's done,
What battle's lost, and what is hardly won.
But when the eye looks into private woes,
And sees the grief that from one battle flows,
Small cause of triumph can the bravest feel,
For never yet were brave hearts made of steel.
It happen'd once, in storming of a town,
When our bold men had push'd the ramparts down,
We found them starving, the last loaf was gone,
Beef was exhausted, and they flour had none;
Their springs we drain, to ditches yet they fly—
The stagnant ditch lent treacherous supply;
For soon the putrid source their blood distains,
And the quick fever hastens through their veins.
In the same room the dying and the dead—
Nay, sometimes, even in the self-same bed,—
You saw the mother with her children lie,
None but the father left to close the sunken eye.
"In a dark corner, once myself I found
A youth whose blood was pouring through the wound;
No sister's hand, no tender mother's eye
To stanch that wound was fondly watching by;
Famine had done her work, and low were laid
The loving mother and the blooming maid.
He rais'd his eyes, and bade me strike the blow,
I've nought to lose, he cried, so fear no foe;
No foe is near, I softly made reply,
A soldier, friend, would save and not destroy.
A drop of cordial in my flask I found;
(And I myself am sovereign for a wound;
I'll bleed you all, lads! if you should be ill,
And in the toothache I've no little skill.
Our drummer too, poor man, dealt much in horns,
And I've his very knack of cutting corns.)
Well; as I dress'd the youth, I found 'twas he
That oft had charm'd the sentinels and me;
From post to post like lightning he would fly,
And pour down thunder from his red-hot sky;
We prais'd him for't,—so I my captain told,
For well I knew he lik'd the foe that's bold;
So then the surgeon took him in his charge,
And the captain made him prisoner at large."
"Was he a Spanishman, or Frenchman, whether?[3]
But it's no matter; they're all rogues together!"
"You're much mistaken: Goodness I have found
Spring like the grass that clothes the common ground;
Some more, some less, you know, grows every where;
Some soils are fertile, and some are but bare.
Nay, 'mongst the Indians I've found kindly cheer,
And as much pity as I could do here!
Once in their woods I stray'd a length of way,
And thought I'd known the path that homeward lay;
We'd gone to forage, but I lost the rest,
Which, till quite out of hearing, never guess'd.
I hollow'd loud, some voices made reply,
But not my comrades; not one friend was nigh.
Some men appear'd, their faces painted o'er,

---

[1] "in faith" (dialect oath).

[2] probably the Seven Years' War (1756–63).

[3] The Spanish and French were allied against the British.

The wampum-belt,[1] and tomahawk they bore;
Their ears were hung with beads, that largely spread
565 A breadth of wing, and cover'd half the head.
I kiss'd the ground; one older than the rest
Stepp'd forth, and laid his hand upon my breast,
Then seiz'd my arms, and sign'd that I should go,
And learn with them to bend the sturdy bow:
570 I bow'd and follow'd; sadly did I mourn,
And never more expected to return."
Here Sarah sobb'd, and stepp'd behind the door,
And with her tears bedew'd the dusty floor.
"We travell'd on some days through woods alone,
575 At length we reach'd their happy silent home.
A few green acres the whole plot compose,
Which woods surround, and fencing rocks enclose,
Skirting whose banks, a river fond of play
Sometimes stood still, and sometimes ran away;
580 The branching deer would drink the dimpl'd tide,
And crop the wild herbs on its flowery side,—
Around the silent hut would sometimes stray,
Then, at the sight of man, bound swift away;
But all in vain; the hunter's flying dart
585 Springs from the bow, and quivers in the heart.
A mother and four daughters here we found,
With shells encircled, and with feathers crown'd,
Bright pebbles shone amidst the plaited hair,
While lesser shells surround the moon-like ear.
590 With screams at sight of me away they flew
(For fear or pleasure springs from what is new);
Then, to their brothers, screaming still they ran,
Thinking my clothes and me the self-same man;
When bolder grown, they ventur'd something near,
595 Light touch'd my coat, but started back with fear.
When time and use had chas'd their fears away,
And I had learned some few short words to say,
They oft would tell me, would I but allow
The rampant lion to o'erhang my brow,
600 And on my cheek the spotted leopard wear,
Stretch out my ears, and let my arms go bare."
"O mercy on us!" cried the listeners round,
Their gaping wonder bursting into sound.

"Tho' different in their manners, yet their heart
605 Was equal mine in every better part.
Brave to a fault, if courage fault can be;
Kind to their fellows, doubly kind to me.
Some little arts my travell'd judgment taught,
Which, tho' a prize to them, seem'd greater than they ought.
610 "Needless with bows for me the woods to roam,
I therefore tried to do some good at home.
The birds, or deer, or boars, were all their food,
Save the swift salmon of the silver flood;
And when long storms the winter-stores would drain,
615 Hunger might ask the stinted meal in vain.
Some goats I saw that brows'd the rocks among,
And oft I thought to trap their playful young;
But not till first a fencing hedge surrounds
Their future fields, and the enclosure bounds;
620 For many a father owns a hatchet here,
Which falls descending to his wealthy heir.
The playful kid we from the pitfall bring,
O'erspread with earth, and many a tempting thing;
Light lay the branches o'er the treacherous deep,
625 And favourite herbs among the long grass creep.
The little prisoner soon is taught to stand,
And crop the food from the betrayer's hand.
A winter-store now rose up to their view,
And in another field the clover grew;
630 But, without scythes or hooks, how could we lay
The ridgy swathe and turn it into hay;
At last, of stone we form'd a sort of spade,
Broad at the end, and sharp, for cutting made;
We push'd along, the tender grass gave way,
635 And soon the sun turn'd every pile to hay.
It was not long before the flocks increased,
And I first gave the unknown milky feast.
Some clay I found, and useful bowls I made,
Tho', I must own, I marr'd the potter's trade;
640 Yet use is every thing—they did the same
As if from China the rude vessels came.
The curdling cheese I taught them next to press;
And twirl'd on strings the roasting meat to dress.
In all the woods the Indian corn was found,
645 Whose grains I scatter'd in the faithful ground;
The willing soil leaves little here to do,

---

[1] a beaded belt used by Native Americans for jewelry, money, or other purposes (see line 672).

Or asks the furrows of the searching plough;
Yet something like one with delight I made,
For tedious are the labours of the spade,
650 The coulter and the sock were pointed stone,
The eager brothers drew the traces on,
I stalk'd behind, and threw the faithful grain,
And wooden harrows closed the earth again:
Soon sprung the seed, and soon 'twas in the ear,
655 Nor wait the golden sheaves the falling year;
In this vast clime two harvests load the field,
And fifty crops th' exhaustless soil can yield.
    "Some bricks I burnt, and now a house arose,
Finer than aught the Indian chieftain knows;
660 A wicker door, with clay-like plaster lin'd,
Serv'd to exclude the piercing wintry wind;
A horn-glaz'd window gave a scanty light,
But lamps cheer'd up the gloom of lengthen'd night;
The cotton shrub through all the woods had run,
665 And plenteous wicks our rocks and spindles spun.
Around their fields the yam I taught to grow,
With all the fruits they either love or know.
The bed I rais'd from the damp earth, and now
Some little comfort walk'd our dwelling through.
670 My fame was spread: the neighbouring Indians came,
View'd all our works, and strove to do the same.
The wampum-belt my growing fame records,
That tells great actions without help of words.
I gain'd much honour, and each friend would bring
675 'Mong various presents many a high-priz'd thing.
And when, with many a prayer, I ask once more
To seek my friends, and wander to the shore,
They all consent,—but drop a sorrowing tear,
While many a friend his load of skins would bear.
680 Riches were mine; but fate will'd it not so,—
They grew the treasure of the Spanish foe;
My Indian friends threw down their fleecy load,
And, like the bounding elk, leap'd back into the wood.
    "What though a prisoner! countrymen I found,
685 Heard my own tongue, and bless'd the cheerful sound;
It seem'd to me as if my home was there,
And every dearest friend would soon appear.
At length a cartel gave us back to share
The wounds and dangers of a bloody war.

690 Peace dawn'd at last, and now the sails were spread,
Some climb the ship unhurt, some few half dead.
Not this afflicts the gallant soldier's mind,
What is't to him tho' limbs are left behind!
Chelsea a crutch and bench will yet supply,[1]
695 And be the veteran's dear lost limb and eye!
    "When English ground first struck the sailor's view,
Huzza! for England, roar'd the jovial crew.
The waving crutch leaped up in every hand,
While one poor leg was left alone to stand;
700 The very name another limb bestows,
And through the artery the blood now flows.
We reach'd the shore, and kiss'd the much-lov'd ground,
And fondly fancied friends would crowd around;
But few with wretchedness acquaintance claim,
705 And little pride is every where the same.
    "In coming down, the seeing eye of day
Darken'd around me, and I lost my way.
Where'er a light shot glimmering through the trees,
I thither urg'd my weary trembling knees,
710 Tapp'd at the door, and begg'd, in piteous tone,
They'd let a wandering soldier find his home;
They barr'd the door, and bade me beg elsewhere,
They'd no spare beds for vagabonds to share.
This was the tale where'er I made a halt,
715 And greater houses grew upon the fault;
The dog was loos'd to keep me far at bay,
And saucy footmen bade me walk away,
Or else a constable should find a home
For wandering captains from the wars new come.
720 Alas! thought I, is this the soldier's praise
For loss of health, of limb, and length of days?
And is this England?—England, my delight!
For whom I thought it glory but to fight—
That has no covert for the soldier's night!
725 I turn'd half fainting, led through all the gloom
By the faint glimmerings of the clouded moon.
One path I kept, that seem'd at times to end,
And oft refus'd the guiding clew to lend;
The thread unhop'd as oft again I found,

---
[1] The Royal Hospital in Chelsea was a rest home for old and disabled soldiers.

730 Till it forsook the open fields around;
By slow degrees, to towering woods it crept,
As if beneath their shade it nightly slept.
I here had halted, lest some beasts of prey,
In midnight theft, had pac'd the treacherous way,
735 But that a twinkling light sometimes appear'd,
Sometimes grew dim, and sometimes brightly clear'd;
This could not be the lure of beasts of prey;
They know no art of imitating day,
Much pleas'd I thought. The mazy path yet led
740 Through shrubby copse, by taller trees o'erspread;
A wimpling rill ran on, and wreath'd its way
Through tufts of flowers, that made its borders gay;
And now a rock the parting leaves unfold,
On which a withering oak had long grown old,
745 The curling ivy oft attempts to hide
Its sad decay, with robes of verdant pride,
Yet through her leafy garb the eye can peer,
And see it buys the youthful dress too dear.
A hollow cavern now methought I spied,
750 Where clustering grapes came wandering down its side,
Between whose leaves a ray of light would dart,
That both rejoic'd and terrified my heart.
I ventur'd in,—my breath I scarcely drew,
Nought save a taper met my wondering view;
755 An inner cavern beamed with fuller light,
And gave a holy hermit to my sight;
Himself and Piety seem'd but the same,
And Wisdom for grey hairs another name;
Some traces yet of sorrow might be found,
760 That o'er his features walk'd their pensive round;
Devotion seem'd to bid them not to stray,
But human feelings gave the wanderers way.
His eye he rais'd from the instructive page,
An eye more sunk by wearing grief than age;
765 Surprise a moment o'er his features spread,
And gave them back their once accustom'd red.
"Welcome my son—a hermit's welcome share,
And let the welcome mend the scanty fare.
A soldier's toils the softest couch requires,
770 The strengthening food, and renovating fires;
Not such the hermit's needy cell bestows,
Pamper'd alone by luxury of woes,

The falling tears bedew the crusty bread,
And the moss pillow props the weary head;
775 The limpid brook the heats of thirst allay,
And gather'd fruits the toilsome search repay;
When hunger calls, these are a feastful store,
And languid Sorrow asks for nothing more;
Sufficient that her eye unseen can weep,
780 Stream while awake, and flow yet more in sleep.
'Tis now twelve years since Solitude first drew
Her closing curtain round my opening view,
Since first I left my once delightful home,
Along with Grief and Solitude to roam."
785 Much I express'd my wonder, how a mind
So stor'd as his could herd from all mankind.
"You speak," he said, "like one whose soul is free,
Slave to no wish, nor chain'd to misery.
When ceaseless anguish clouds the summer's sky,
790 And fairest prospects tarnish in the eye;
When cheerful scenes spread every lure in vain,
And sweet Society but adds to pain;
When weeping Memory incessant brings
The sad reversion of all former things,
795 And show-like Fancy all her colouring lends,
To gild those views that opened with our friends:
When joyful days through the whole year would run,
And Mirth set out and travel with the sun;
When Youth and Pleasure hand in hand would stray,
800 And every month was little less than May;
When changing Fortune shifts th' incessant scene,
And only points to where our joys have been,
Is it a wonder from the world we run,
And all its fleeting empty pageants shun?
805 "There is a something in a well known view,
That seems to shew our long past pleasures through;
Sure in the eye a fairy land is found,
When former scenes bring former friends around.
Let but the woods, the rocks, the streams appear,
810 And every friend you see and think you hear;
Their words, their dress, their every look, you find
Swell to the sight, and burst upon the mind;
Though many a spring has lent the blossom gay,
And many an autumn blown the leaf away,
815 Unchang'd the lasting images remain,
Of which Remembrance ever holds the chain.

E'en the mind's eye a glassy mirror shews,
And far too deeply her bold pencil draws;
The life-like pictures rise before the sight,
820   Glow through the day, and sparkle through the night.
Ah! sure e'en now my Ethelind appears,
Though dimly seen through this sad vale of tears.
That winning form, where elegance has wove
The thousand softnesses of gentlest love;
825 That meaning eye, that artless blushing cheek,
Which leaves so little for the tongue to speak;
The nameless graces of her polish'd mind;
That laughing wit, and serious sense refined;
That altogether which no art can reach,
830 And which 'tis nature's very rare to teach;
That nameless something which pervades the soul,
Wins not by halves, but captivates the whole;
Yet, if one feature shone before the rest,
'Twas surely Pity by Religion drest.
835 Have I not seen the softly stealing tear,
Hung in her eye, like gem in Ethiop's ear![1]
Whilst the dark orb the glittering diamond shed,
From her fair cheek the frighten'd roses fled,
Asham'd that, such a gem so sweetly clear,
840 Aught, save the lily, should presume to wear.
    "Sure there's a pleasure in recounting woes!
And some relief in every tear that flows!
Else why call back those days for ever flown,
And with them every joy this heart can own?
845 Pleasure and pain is the sad mixture still,
Taste but the good, and you must taste the ill;
Dear Recollection is a sorceress fair
That brings up pleasures livelier than they were;
Delighted Fancy dwells upon the view,
850 Compares old scenes with what she meets with new;
The present hour grows dull, her charms decay,
And, one by one, drop silently away.
Neglect succeeds—Neglect, the worst of foes,
That married love or single friendship knows,
855 Whose torpid soul congeal'd in stupor lies,
Nor sees one charm, nor hears the smothering sighs;
Sees not the hourly load of comforts brought
By fond affection, watching every thought,

Nor the heart beating with the wish to please,—
860 Cold, cold Neglect, nor hears, nor feels, nor sees!
    "Thus, in the present hour too, oft slides by
The many a charm that might detain the eye;
But just as if from woes we could not part,
We veil the sight, and close shut up the heart;
865 So I myself would ne'er forget the day
When Ethelinda vowed her heart away.
Our births were equal, but exalted views
For the fair daughter bade the sire refuse.
O'er seas I roam, in quest of much-priz'd wealth,
870 Though, after all, the greatest good is health!
Where'er I roam'd, my Ethelind was there,
My soul's companion join'd me every where;
Whatever scenes entrapped my travelling eye,
My fancied Ethelind stood smiling by,
875 Her just opinion met my listening ear,
And her remarks on men, and climes, I hear.
This was not absence, or it was a dream,
Which, though unreal, yet would real seem.
Each day the tongue-like pen some story told,
880 Of growing love, or less increasing gold;
Yet fortune frown'd not; and, in lengthening time,
One day I saw that mark'd her to be mine.
Hail! heaven-taught letters, that through years convey
The deathless thought, as if just breath'd to-day!
885 That gives the converse of an absent friend,
And, for a moment, makes that absence end;
For, while the eager eyes the lines run o'er,
Distance steps back, and drags the chain no more;
For one short moment the dear friends we see
890 Close by our side, just as they used to be.
Such sweet delusions are not form'd to last,
And Fancy's visions far too soon are past.
No such delights my heart-wrote lines attend,
They met the hand of a deceitful friend;
895 Her brother, anxious for a lord's success,
Thought it no sin to blast my happiness,
Kept up my letters, and base stories told,
That I had sold myself to age, and gold.
Her good opinion baffled long the tale,
900 And love for long kept down the struggling scale.

---

[1] Cf. Shakespeare, *Romeo and Juliet* 1.5.46.

But when, from year to year, Hope pointed on,
And the last hope with the last year was gone,
She tried to think I must be base, and strove
To scorn the man who could give up her love;
905 Yet her soft heart no other flame confessed,
It lodged the tenant of her faithful breast.
    "Home I return'd, much wearied out with woes,
And every fear that fretful silence knows.
Fear for her death was far my greatest dread;
910 How could I bear to think her with the dead!
Did she but live, methought my griefs might end,
When the warm lover cool'd into the friend.
I reach'd my home, and quick inquiries made,
Found her unmarried—found she was not dead.
915 And now, to know the cause of all my woe,
With hope and fear, and joy, and grief, I go;
A thousand fears would stop me in my way,
A thousand hopes forbid one moment's stay.
As nigh the house with anxious step I drew,
920 Fond recollections crowded all the view;
I felt a tear creep round and round my eye,
That shame of man, and yet I know not why.
While at the door her faithful maid I saw,
The short quick breath I scarce had power to draw;
925 Where—is—your la—my lips no more would move."
"She's in the arbour, sir, you us'd to love."
"Something like hope a cordial drop bestow'd,
The heart grew warm, and the pale cheek now glow'd.
Near to the arbour silently I drew,
930 And trembling look'd the leafy lattice through;
The sprightly air which once lit up her face,
To pensive softness long had given place;
Its gentle charms around her features crowd,
And tenderest feeling her fine figure bow'd;
935 More dear she seem'd, more interesting far,
Than when her eye was call'd the evening star;
On her fair hand she lean'd her drooping head,
And many a tear bedew'd the page she read;
'Twas Milton's Paradise—the book I knew,
940 Once my own profile on the leaf I drew,
And wrote beneath this truth-dictated line—
'With thee conversing I forget all time';[1]

Her eye I saw ran every feature o'er,
And scann'd the line where truth seem'd writ no more;
945 She shook her head, its meaning well I knew:
"'Twas even thus, ye once lov'd lines adieu";
The book she shut—so softly was it clos'd,
As if life's joys alone were there repos'd.
    "I walk'd around, the crimping grass would say,—
950 Some heavy foot has brush'd our dews away;
She started up, and, shaking off the tear,
Strove hard to make the pearl-set eye more clear;
But when my form the parting leaves betray'd,
And fuller light around my features play'd,
955 She grows a statue, wrought by Michael's art,[2]
A marble figure, with a human heart,
More pale, more cold, than Medici[3] can seem,
Or all the forms that from the quarry teem.
I bow'd, but spoke not, injur'd as I thought,
960 And wishing much to show the sense I ought;
I durst not trust th' impatient tongue to move,
For, ah! I felt it would but talk of love.
I silent stand." "What art thou, vision, say,
Why dost thou cross a wretched wanderer's way?
965 Sure 'tis the whimsy of a feverish mind
That fancies forms none but itself can find!"
"I bow'd again." "Oh! speak if thou art he
That once was dear—so very dear to me?"
"Yes, Ethelind, most sure—too sure I'm he
970 That once was dear, so very dear to thee;
Why has thy heart its fondness all forborne
To swell my sails, and ask my quick return?"
"A married man!"—she sharply made reply,
With much resentment sparkling in her eye,—
975 "A married man has every right to hear
What thoughts pursue us through the changing year!
Yes, I will tell you: happy was the day
In which you gave your heart and hand away.
I gave not mine, yet free from every vow
980 That would have tied me to a wretch like you.
I feel as blissful in my single state,
As you, no doubt, feel in your wealthy mate!"

---

[1] Milton, *Paradise Lost* 4.639.

[2] Michelangelo Buonarotti (1475–1564), Italian artist.

[3] the Venus de' Medici, in Blamire's time one of the most admired of classical statues.

She rose to go: "My Ethelind, forbear!
Some cruel monster has abus'd your ear;
985 Your faithful lover see before you stand,
Your faithful lover dares to claim your hand;
No other vows that plighted faith could stain,
No other loves melt o'er this heart again!
Let easy fortune nameless comforts spread,
990 And slope for life the soft descending tread.
No needful cares, to study how the year
Shall rule its squares, and run its circles clear;
The generous hand no close restraint shall know,
But opening bounty from the fingers flow.
995 The saddest sight the pitying eyes receive,
Is to see wretchedness with nought to give;
The heart-wrung tear, though e'er so fully shed,
Brings no warm clothing, and affords no bread.
On you shall pleasure wait with ready call,
1000 Speed to the play, or hasten to the ball;
Where safest ease her flowery carpet throws,
And gilded domes their rainbow-lights dispose;
Where splendour turns e'en common things to show,
And plain good comforts ornamental grow.
1005 'Midst scenes like these would Ethelinda blaze,
While wreathing diamonds lend their mingling rays;
Wealth is her own, for it is mine to give,
As it is hers, to bid me how to live.
But should domestic peace her soul allure,
1010 For splendour but hides grief, it cannot cure,—
If in sweet converse hours should steal away,
While we still wander at the close of day;
If every wish preventing love should see,
And all the world we to ourselves should be,
1015 I only wait the soft assenting smile,
To be whate'er her heart would ask the while;
O yes, dear friend! I yet can read the line,
'With thee conversing I forget all time';
Domestic peace has every charm for me,
1020 How doubly charming when enjoy'd with thee!
    "Now honour pleaded that my fame should bleed,
And life is rul'd by her detested creed;
This idol, honour, at whose shrine appears
The heart-broke friend, dissolv'd in endless tears.
1025 He, fiery youth, impatient of control,
And the grey veteran sorry from his soul,
Th' injuring and the injur'd both repair,
And both expect her laurel wreath to wear;
It matters not where right or wrong began,
1030 The man who fights must be an honest man,
Though every baseness that the heart can know
Should damp his soul, and keep his sword in awe;
Sole proof of excellence such warriors give—
Wretches who die, because they dare not live!
1035 The guilty breast is ever up in arms,
And the least look the conscious soul alarms!
Should your quick eye the shuffling card detect,
Or should the gamester think you but suspect,
His injur'd honour dares you to the fight,
1040 And all the world admits the challenge right!
Not to accept it blasts a virtuous fame,
And links your memory with eternal shame;
It matters not though pure your life appears
On the long record of revolving years;
1045 Though heaven you fear, and heaven's forbidding law,
That stamps him criminal who dares to draw,
Yet man, vain man, breaks through the laws of
    heaven,
Dies by the sword, and hopes to be forgiven;
For what we duels from high fashion call,
1050 Is Suicide, or Murder, after all!
    "Sometimes the heart almost approves the deed,
When barbarous wounds make reputation bleed;
Of all the crimes of any shape or dye,
That looks the blackest in true feeling's eye,
1055 If a dear sister's purity we feel,
Nature cries out—where is th' avenging steel?
Avenging steel! how impotent the word,
And all the threats and cures that tend the sword!
    "Sweet Reputation, like a lily fair,
1060 Scents every breath that winnows through the air;
The colouring sunbeam on its whiteness plays,
And dances round and round with gilding rays;
Anon dark clouds these gilding rays withhold,
And the leaf shrivels with the sudden cold;
1065 A blighting vapour sails along the skies,
And the meek lily droops its head, and dies:
Nor can a sword, or the depending pen,
Clear the lost female character again;
The vindication better never hear,—

1070 That fame is safest that has nought to clear;
And female fame is such a tender flower,
It cannot even bear a pitying shower;
Courage in man is something near as nice,
Which life must buy, and wear at any price.
1075   "Much 'gainst my conscience, and against heaven's law,
My destin'd brother to account I draw;
Against his life I meant no hand to rear,—
I meant but with the world to settle clear;
A self-defense, e'en in th' appointed field,
1080 Was all the sword I ever thought to wield.
Hard was the onset; in the fatal strife
His hand I saw aim'd only at my life;
I wav'd its point, still hoping to disarm,
And guard both lives secure from every harm.
1085 I parried long; he made a lounging stroke,
And my sad weapon in his bosom broke."
"'Tis past he said—much injur'd man, adieu!
I've done you wrong—but you'll forgive it now."
"In that sad moment every pang I found
1090 That darts through father's, brother's, sister's, wound!
In what new lights I then saw Honour's creed,
How sunk in sin seem'd the detested deed;
The world's applause was stripped of all its charms,
And the whole Conscience met the Man in arms,
1095 Guilt, sorrow, pity, warr'd within the breast,
With sad remorse, that never can have rest.
My weeping Ethelind now, too, I saw,
Lost in the floods of never ending woe!
For, ah! what woes can ever hope an end
1100 That mourn a brother slaughter'd by a friend!"
Then from his breast some brief, brief lines he drew,—
The blots were many, though the words were few:
"Fly me, for ever, it is time we part,
You've kill'd a brother, and you've broke a heart."
1105 "Tortur'd in soul from place to place I flew,
But swift-wing'd thought as swiftly would pursue;
Unless from memory our thoughts can run,
How vain to journey round and round the sun.
At last this solitude my sorrow sought,
1110 For cities leave no bar for entering thought;
I here have liv'd, in hopes the time will come,
That makes my cell my wish'd-for silent tomb."
"His tears fresh flow'd, and mine ran down my cheek,
Our griefs were such as neither tongue could speak;
1115 At last we parted—he to endless woe,
While happy I to wife and children go."
    Now scolding Nancy to the ale-house flies—
"What are you doing—hearing Harry's lies!
Thomas, get in, and do not sit to drink,
There's work enough at home, if you would think!"[1]

---

[1] The remaining lines describe Stoklewath at night and praise the village.

Charlotte Smith
1749 – 1806

Charlotte Turner was born on 4 May 1749 in London, the oldest child of Nicholas Turner, a landowner and amateur poet, and Anna Towers Turner. When she was three, her mother died in childbirth and she was consigned to the care of her aunt Lucy Towers. Her formal education was devoted largely to polite feminine accomplishments, but she read voraciously and began writing poetry early. (Her sister, Catherine Dorset, would also become a poet.) When she was fifteen, she was married off to Benjamin Smith, the son of a merchant with interests in both the East and the West Indies. Benjamin was abusive, adulterous, drunken, and improvident, but Smith put up with him for twenty-two years. Her father-in-law, who knew his son, left her and her children about £36,000, a sum that would have provided them a comfortable upper-middle-class life, but legal complications tied it up until over thirty years after his death, and six years after Smith's own death. In 1783–84, Smith spent seven months with her husband in debtors' prison. In 1784–85, to avoid being imprisoned again, they spent a winter in exile in Normandy. Smith had twelve children. Her first son died in 1767, at the age of one. Her second son died in 1777, at the age of ten. In 1786, her oldest surviving son left for a job in Bengal, and the next oldest died of a fever. Another had his leg amputated at the battle of Dunkirk, in 1793. Her favourite daughter, Anna Augusta, died from complications of childbirth in 1795. In 1801, another son died in Barbados, and in 1806, yet another, in Surinam; only six of her children outlived her. Her writing has sometimes been criticized for its excessive melancholy.

Smith published her first book, *Elegiac Sonnets*, in 1784. It was a critical and commercial success: the *Gentleman's Magazine* declared, "A very trifling compliment is paid Mrs. Smith, when it is observed how much her Sonnets exceed those of *Shakespeare* and *Milton*," and the book sold out ten editions, expanding to two volumes by 1797. It was a significant contribution to the Romantic revival of the sonnet, influencing Wordsworth,* Coleridge,* and Keats,* among others. In 1787, Smith left her husband, moved with her remaining children to near Chichester, and began writing *Emmeline, the Orphan of the Castle* (1788), the first of her eleven novels. It was another critical and commercial success, going through three editions in two years. Between 1791 and 1793, Smith visited Brighton, where she met a number of French émigrés; both her fourth novel, *Desmond* (1792), and her second book of poetry, *The Emigrants* (1793), are about the Revolution. *The Old Manor House* (1793), written partly at William Hayley's country house in Eartham, where she met Cowper* and the painter George Romney, is sometimes called her best novel. Smith preferred writing poetry to fiction, but she had a family to support. By 1792, she was suffering from arthritis and neuritis, which made writing difficult and painful for her, but she soldiered on. In 1794, she complained of "the mortifying circumstance of being a dependent on booksellers; of procuring by mental labour a precarious subsistence"; and said: "long anxiety has ruined my health, and long oppression broken my spirits—at the end of more than ten years … during which I have been compelled to provide for the necessities of a numerous family, almost entirely by my own labour—and … I am yet to look forward to no other prospect for the future but a repetition of exertions on my part." She published her last novel, *The Letters of a Solitary Wanderer*, in two installments in 1800–02. On 23 February 1806, Benjamin died in a debtors' prison in Scotland. Smith died in Tilford on 28 October. *Beachy Head*, her third book of poetry, and *The Natural History of Birds*, her sixth children's book, were published posthumously in 1807. Her father-in-law's will was finally settled in 1813. (D.L.M.)

from *Elegiac Sonnets. Third Edition, with Twenty Additional Sonnets* (1786)

1

The partial Muse, has from my earliest hours
Smil'd on the rugged path I'm doom'd to tread,
And still with sportive hand has snatch'd wild flowers,
    To weave fantastic garlands for my head:
5 But far, far happier is the lot of those
    Who never learn'd her dear delusive art,
Which while it decks the head with many a rose,
    Reserves the thorn, to fester in the heart.[1]
For still she bids soft Pity's melting eye
10   Stream o'er the ills she knows not to remove,
Points every pang, and deepens every sigh
    Of mourning friendship, or unhappy love.
Ah! then, how dear the Muse's favors cost,
If those paint sorrow best—who feel it most![2]

3. *To a nightingale*[3]

Poor melancholy bird—that all night long
Tell'st to the Moon, thy tale of tender woe;
    From what sad cause can such sweet sorrow flow,
And whence this mournful melody of song?

5 Thy poet's musing fancy would translate
    What mean the sounds that swell thy little breast,
    When still at dewy eve thou leav'st thy nest,
Thus to the listening night to sing thy fate.

Pale Sorrow's victims wert thou once among,
10   Tho' now releas'd in woodlands wild to rove,
Say—hast thou felt from friends some cruel wrong,
    Or diedst thou—martyr of disastrous love?
Ah! songstress sad!—that such my lot might be,
To sigh and sing at liberty—like thee!

4. *To the moon*

Queen of the silver bow![4]—by thy pale beam,
    Alone and pensive, I delight to stray,
And watch thy shadow trembling in the stream,
    Or mark the floating clouds that cross thy way.
5 And while I gaze, thy mild and placid light
    Sheds a soft calm upon my troubled breast;
And oft I think,—fair planet of the night,
    That in thy orb, the wretched may have rest:
The sufferers of the earth perhaps may go,
10   Releas'd by death—to thy benignant sphere,
And the sad children of despair and woe
    Forget in thee, their cup of sorrow here.
Oh! that I soon may reach thy world serene,
Poor wearied pilgrim—in this toiling scene!

7. *On the departure of the nightingale*

Sweet poet of the woods—a long adieu!
    Farewel, soft minstrel of the early year!
Ah! 'twill be long ere thou shalt sing anew,
    And pour thy music on the "night's dull ear."[5]
5 Whether on spring thy wandering flights await,[6]
    Or whether silent in our groves you dwell,
The pensive muse shall own thee for her mate,[7]

---

[1] a reference to the belief that the nightingale's song is provoked by a thorn piercing its heart.

[2] "'The well sung woes shall soothe my pensive ghost;
   He best can paint them, who shall feel them most.'
          Pope's Eloisa to Abelard, 366th line." (C.S.)

[3] "The idea from the 43d Sonnet of Petrarch. Secondo parte. Quel rosigniuol, che si soave piagne." (C.S.) "That nightingale who so tenderly weeps" (trans. Anna Maria Armi). Francesco Petrarca (1304–74), Italian poet and humanist, is known especially for his sonnets expressing his love for Laura (d. 1348); cf. Landon, "The Improvisatrice" 41–80.*

[4] Diana (L.) or Artemis (Gr.), goddess of the moon.

[5] "*Shakespeare*." (C.S.) *Henry V* 4.Cho.11.

[6] "Alludes to the supposed migration of the Nightingale." (C.S.) Nightingales do migrate, wintering in Africa and returning to Britain in April.

[7] "'Whether the Muse or Love call thee his mate,
   Both them I serve, and of their train am I.'
          Milton's First Sonnet." (C.S.) 13–14.
See Robinson, *Sappho and Phaon* (1796) Preface.*

And still protect the song, she loves so well.
With cautious step, the love-lorn youth shall glide
    Thro' the lone brake that shades thy mossy nest;
And shepherd girls, from eyes profane shall hide
    The gentle bird, who sings of pity best.
For still thy voice shall soft affections move,
And still be dear to sorrow, and to love!

17. *From the thirteenth cantata of Metastasio*[1]

On thy grey bark, in witness of my flame,
    I carve Miranda's cypher—Beauteous tree!
Grac'd with the lovely letters of thy name,
    Henceforth be sacred, to my love and me.
Tho' the tall elm, the oak, and sombre pine,
    With broader arms, may noon's fierce ardors break,
To shelter me, and her I love, be thine;
    And thine to see her smile, and hear her speak.
No bird, ill omen'd, round thy graceful head
    Shall clamour harsh, or wave his heavy wing,
But fern and flowers arise beneath thy shade,
    Where the wild bees, their lullabys shall sing.
And in thy boughs the murmuring Ring-dove rest;
And there the Nightingale shall build her nest.

21. *Supposed to be written by Werter*[2]

Go, cruel tyrant of the human breast!
    To other hearts, thy burning arrows bear;
Go, where fond hope, and fair illusion rest;
    Ah! why should love inhabit with despair!
Like the poor maniac[3] I linger here,
    Still haunt the scene, where all my treasure lies;
Still seek for flowers, where only thorns appear,
    And drink delicious poison from her eyes![4]
Towards the deep gulph that opens on my sight
    I hurry forward, passion's helpless slave!
And scorning reason's mild and sober light,
    Pursue the path, that leads me to the grave.
So round the flame the giddy insect flies,
And courts the fatal fire, by which it dies.

24. *By the same*

Make there my tomb; beneath the lime-trees' shade,[5]
    Where grass and flowers in wild luxuriance wave;
Let no memorial mark where I am laid,
    Or point to common eyes the lover's grave!
But oft at twilight morn, or closing day,
    The faithful friend with fault'ring step shall glide,
Tributes of fond regret by stealth to pay,
    And sigh o'er the unhappy suicide.
And sometimes, when the Sun with parting rays
    Gilds the long grass that hides my silent bed,
The tear shall tremble in my CHARLOTTE's eyes;
    Dear, precious drops!—they shall enbalm the dead.
Yes!—CHARLOTTE o'er the mournful spot shall weep,
Where her poor WERTER—and his sorrows sleep.

25. *By the same. Just before his death*

Why should I wish to hold in this low sphere[6]
    "A frail and feverish being?"[7] wherefore try

---

[1] Pietro Metastasio (1698–1782), Italian poet.

[2] the hero of Johann Wolfgang von Goethe (1749–1832), *Die Leiden des Jungen Werthers* (1774), translated by Daniel Malthus as *The Sorrows of [Young] Werter* (1779, new ed. 1789). Werther's sorrows are occasioned by his falling in love with Charlotte, who is already engaged to Albert.

[3] "See the Story of the Lunatic. 'Is this the destiny of Man? Is he only happy before he possesses his reason, or after he has lost it?—Full of hope you go to gather flowers in Winter, and are grieved not to find any—and do not know why they cannot be found.' *Sorrows of Werter. Volume Second*." (C.S.) Letter 71; 30 November (169–70).

[4] Pope, *Eloisa to Abelard* 122.

[5] "'At the corner of the church yard which looks towards the fields, there are two lime trees—it is there I wish to rest.' *Sorrows of Werter. Volume Second*." (C.S.) From the suicide note of 21–22 December (214).

[6] "'May my death remove every obstacle to your happiness.—Be at peace, I intreat you be at peace.' *Sorrows of Werter. Volume Second*." (C.S.) The first sentence is from a note to Albert, also written on 22 December (212); the second is from the end of the suicide note to Charlotte (216).

[7] Cf. the description of women as a "Frail, fev'rish sex!" in Pope, "Sylvia, a fragment" (1727) 17.

Poorly from day to day to linger here,
    Against the powerful hand of destiny?
5 By those who know the force of hopeless care,
    On the worn heart—I sure shall be forgiven,
If to elude dark guilt, and dire despair,
    I go uncall'd—to mercy and to heaven!
Oh thou! to save whose peace I now depart,
10   Will thy soft mind, thy poor lost friend deplore,
When worms shall feed on this devoted heart,
    Where even thy image shall be found no more![1]
Yet may thy pity mingle not with pain,
For then thy hapless lover—dies in vain.

27

Sighing I see yon little troop at play;
    By sorrow yet untouch'd; unhurt by care;
While free and sportive they enjoy to-day,
    "Content, and careless of to-morrow's fare!"[2]
5 O happy age! when Hope's unclouded ray
    Lights their green path, and prompts their simple mirth,
E'er yet they feel the thorns that lurking lay
    To wound the wretched pilgrims of the earth;
Making them rue the hour that gave them birth,
10   And threw them on a world so full of pain,
Where prosperous folly treads on patient worth,
    And to deaf pride, misfortune pleads in vain.
Ah!—for their future fate how many fears
Oppress my heart—and fill mine eyes with tears!

32. *To Melancholy. Written on the banks of the Arun, October, 1785*[3]

When latest Autumn spreads her evening veil,
    And the grey mists from these dim waves arise,
    I love to listen to the hollow sighs,
Thro' the half leafless wood that breathes the gale.
5 For at such hours the shadowy phantom, pale,
    Oft seems to fleet before the poet's eyes;
    Strange sounds are heard, and mournful melodies,
As of night wanderers, who their woes bewail.
Here, by his native stream, at such an hour,
10   Pity's own Otway,[4] I methinks could meet,
    And hear his deep sighs swell the sadden'd wind.
Oh melancholy!—such thy magic power,
    That to the soul these dreams are often sweet,
    And soothe the pensive visionary mind!

35. *To fortitude*

Nymph of the rock! whose dauntless spirit braves
    The beating storm, and bitter winds that howl
Round thy cold breast; and hear'st the bursting waves,
    And the deep thunder with unshaken soul;
5 Oh come!—and shew how vain the cares that press
    On my weak bosom—and how little worth
Is the false fleeting meteor happiness,
    That still misleads the wanderers of the earth!
Strengthen'd by thee, this heart shall cease to melt
10   O'er ills that poor humanity must bear;
Nor friends estrang'd, or ties dissolv'd be felt
    To leave regret, and fruitless anguish there:
And when at length it heaves its latest sigh,
Thou and mild hope, shall teach me how to die!

---

[1] "*From a line in Rousseau's Eloisa.*" (C.S.) Cf. Jean-Jacques Rousseau (1712–78), *Julie; ou, la nouvelle Héloïse* (1761) Part 1, Letter 51: "puisse à l'instant l'image de ma Julie sortir pour jamais de mon cœur, et l'abandonner à l'indifférence et au désespoir" ("At that instant may the image of my Julie forsake my heart forever and abandon it to indifference and to despair" [trans. Judith H. McDowell]).

[2] "*Thomson.*" (C.S.) James Thomson (1700-48), *Autumn* (1730) 191.

[3] The river Arun flows through West Sussex.

[4] Thomas Otway (1652–85), author of *Venice Preserv'd* (1682), was born in Trotten, Sussex.

from *Elegiac Sonnets, by Charlotte Smith. The Fifth Edition, with Additional Sonnets and Other Poems* (1789)

44. *Written in the Church Yard at Middleton in Sussex*

Press'd by the Moon, mute arbitress of tides,
    While the loud equinox its power combines,
    The sea no more its swelling surge confines,
But o'er the shrinking land sublimely rides.
5 The wild blast, rising from the Western cave,
    Drives the huge billows from their heaving bed;
    Tears from their grassy tombs the village dead,[1]
And breaks the silent sabbath of the grave!
With shells and sea-weed mingled, on the shore
10   Lo! their bones whiten in the frequent wave;
    But vain to them the winds and waters rave;
They hear the warring elements no more:
While I am doom'd—by life's long storm opprest,
To gaze with envy, on their gloomy rest.

from *Elegiac Sonnets. The Sixth Edition, with Additional Sonnets and Other Poems* (1792)

Thirty-Eight. Address'd to Mrs. H——Y[2]

In early youth's unclouded scene,
The brilliant morning of eighteen,
With health and sprightly joy elate
    We gaz'd on life's enchanting spring,
5   Nor thought how quickly time would bring
The mournful period——Thirty-eight.

Then the starch maid, or matron sage,
Already of that sober age,
We view'd with mingled scorn and hate;
10   In whose sharp words, or sharper face,
    With thoughtless mirth we lov'd to trace
The sad effects of——Thirty-eight.

Till saddening, sickening at the view,
We learn'd to dread what time might do;
15 And then preferr'd a prayer to Fate
    To end our days ere that arriv'd;
    When (pow'r and pleasure long surviv'd)
We met neglect and——Thirty-eight.

But Time, in spite of wishes flies,
20 And Fate our simple prayer denies,
And bids us Death's own hour await:
    The auburn locks are mix'd with grey,
    The transient roses fade away,
But Reason comes at——Thirty-eight.

25 Her voice the anguish contradicts
That dying vanity inflicts;
Her hand new pleasures can create,
    For us she opens to the view
    Prospects less bright,—but far more true,
30 And bids us smile at——Thirty-eight.

No more shall *Scandal's* breath destroy
The social converse we enjoy
With bard or critic tête a tête;
    O'er Youth's bright blooms her blights shall pour,
35   But spare the improving friendly hour
That Science gives to——Thirty-eight.

Stripp'd of their gaudy hues by truth,
We view the glitt'ring toys of youth,
And blush to think how poor the bait
40   For which to public scenes we ran
    And scorn'd of sober sense the plan
Which gives content at——Thirty-eight.

---

[1] "Middleton is a village on the margin of the sea in Sussex, containing only two or three houses. There were formerly several acres of ground between its small church and the sea; which now, by its continual encroachments, approaches within a few feet of this half-ruined and humble edifice. The wall, which once surrounded the church yard, is entirely swept away, many of the graves broken up, and the remains of bodies interred washed into the sea; whence human bones are found among the sand and shingles on the shore." (C.S.)

[2] Eliza Hayley (1750–97), wife of William Hayley (1745–1820), of Eartham, Sussex, the dedicatee of *Elegiac Sonnets*.

Tho' Time's inexorable sway
Has torn the myrtle[1] bands away,
45 For other wreaths 'tis not too late,
　　The amaranth's[2] purple glow survives,
　　And still Minerva's olive[3] lives
On the calm brow of——Thirty-eight.

With eye more steady we engage
50 To contemplate approaching age,
And life more justly estimate;
　　With firmer souls, and stronger powers,
　　With reason, faith, and friendship ours
We'll not regret the stealing hours
55 That lead from Thirty——even to Forty-eight.

The Emigrants, A Poem, in Two Books (1793)

To William Cowper, Esq.

DEAR SIR,
There is, I hope, some propriety in my addressing a Composition to you, which would never perhaps have existed, had I not, amid the heavy pressure of many sorrows, derived infinite consolation from your Poetry, and some degree of animation and of confidence from your esteem.[4]

　The following performance is far from aspiring to be considered as an imitation of your inimitable Poem, "THE TASK"; I am perfectly sensible, that it belongs not to a feeble and feminine hand to draw the Bow of Ulysses.[5]

The force, clearness, and sublimity of your admirable Poem; the felicity, almost peculiar to your genius, of giving to the most familiar objects dignity and effect, I could never hope to reach; yet, having read "The Task" almost incessantly from its first publication to the present time, I felt that kind of enchantment described by Milton, when he says,
　"The Angel ended, and in Adam's ear
　So charming left his voice, that he awhile
　Thought him still speaking."——[6]
And from the force of this impression, I was gradually led to attempt, in Blank Verse, a delineation of those interesting objects which happened to excite my attention, and which even pressed upon an heart, that has learned, perhaps from its own sufferings, to feel with acute, though unavailing compassion, the calamity of others.

　A Dedication usually consists of praises and of apologies; *my* praise can add nothing to the unanimous and loud applause of your country. She regards you with pride, as one of the few, who, at the present period, rescue her from the imputation of having degenerated in Poetical talents; but in the form of Apology, I should have much to say, if I again dared to plead the pressure of evils, aggravated by their long continuance, as an excuse for the defects of this attempt.

　Whatever may be the faults of its execution, let me vindicate myself from those, that may be imputed to the design.—In speaking of the Emigrant Clergy,[7] I beg to be understood as feeling the utmost respect for the integrity of their principles; and it is with pleasure I add my suffrage to that of those, who have had a similar opportunity of witnessing the conduct of the Emigrants of all descriptions during their exile in England; which has been such as does honour to *their* nation, and ought to secure to them in ours the esteem of every liberal mind.

　Your philanthropy, dear Sir, will induce you, I am persuaded, to join with me in hoping, that this painful exile may finally lead to the extirpation of that reciprocal

---

[1] sacred to Venus, goddess of love.

[2] a mythical unfading flower.

[3] The olive (symbolizing peace) was the gift of Minerva (Gr. Athena, goddess of wisdom) to the city of Athens.

[4] Smith had been introduced to Cowper* by her friend William Hayley in August 1792.

[5] Penelope, besieged by suitors during the absence of her husband Odysseus (L. Ulysses), agrees to marry whichever of them can string his bow and shoot an arrow through twelve axes (Homer, *Odyssey* 19); only Odysseus, who has returned home in disguise, is able to do so (21).

[6] Milton, *Paradise Lost* 8.1–3.

[7] Many French priests refused to accept the Revolutionary government's dissolution of the monasteries, its confiscation of Church property, and the Civil Constitution of the Clergy, which in effect made priests into civil servants. A decree of 26 May 1792 forced them into exile.

hatred so unworthy of great and enlightened nations; that it may tend to humanize both countries, by convincing each, that good qualities exist in the other; and at length annihilate the prejudices that have so long existed to the injury of both.

Yet it is unfortunately but too true, that with the body of the English, this national aversion has acquired new force by the dreadful scenes which have been acted in France during the last summer[1]—even those who are the victims of the Revolution, have not escaped the odium, which the undistinguishing multitude annex to all the natives of a country where such horrors have been acted: nor is this the worst effect those events have had on the minds of the English; by confounding the original cause with the wretched catastrophes that have followed its ill management; the attempts of public virtue, with the outrages that guilt and folly have committed in its disguise, the very name of Liberty has not only lost the charm it used to have in British ears, but many, who have written, or spoken, in its defence, have been stigmatized as promoters of Anarchy, and enemies to the prosperity of their country. Perhaps even the Author of "The Task," with all his goodness and tenderness of heart, is in the catalogue of those, who are reckoned to have been too warm in a cause, which it was once the glory of Englishmen to avow and defend—The exquisite Poem, indeed, in which you have honoured Liberty, by a tribute highly gratifying to her sincerest friends, was published some years before the demolition of regal despotism in France, which, in the fifth book, it seems to foretell[2]—All the truth and energy of the passage to which I allude, must have been strongly felt, when, in the Parliament of England, the greatest Orator of our time quoted the sublimest of our Poets—when the eloquence of Fox[3] did justice to the genius of Cowper.

I am, dear SIR,
　　With the most perfect esteem,
　　　　Your obliged and obedient servant,
　　　　　　CHARLOTTE SMITH.
Brighthelmstone, May 10, 1793.

BOOK 1

SCENE, *on the Cliffs to the Eastward of the Town of Brighthelmstone*[4] *in Sussex.*

TIME, *a Morning in November, 1792.*

Slow in the Wintry Morn, the struggling light
Throws a faint gleam upon the troubled waves;
Their foaming tops, as they approach the shore
And the broad surf that never ceasing breaks
5　On the innumerous pebbles, catch the beams
Of the pale Sun, that with reluctance gives
To this cold northern Isle, its shorten'd day.
Alas! how few the morning wakes to joy!
How many murmur at oblivious night
10　For leaving them so soon; for bearing thus
Their fancied bliss (the only bliss they taste!),
On her black wings away!—Changing the dreams
That sooth'd their sorrows, for calamities
(And every day brings its own sad proportion)
15　For doubts, diseases, abject dread of Death,
And faithless friends, and fame and fortune lost;
Fancied or real wants; and wounded pride,
That views the day star, but to curse his beams.
　　Yet He, whose Spirit into being call'd
20　This wond'rous World of Waters; He who bids
The wild wind lift them till they dash the clouds,
And speaks to them in thunder; or whose breath,
Low murmuring o'er the gently heaving tides,
When the fair Moon, in summer night serene,
25　Irradiates with long trembling lines of light
Their undulating surface; that great Power,
Who, governing the Planets, also knows

---

[1] the storming of the Tuileries and the deposition of Louis XVI (10 August 1792) and the September Massacres (3–4 September 1792). By May 1793 (the date of Smith's dedication), France was at war with Britain and the Reign of Terror had begun.

[2] *The Task* 5.331–62, 446ff.

[3] Charles James Fox (1749–1806), Whig leader and opponent of the war with France. His parliamentary quotation from Cowper has not been identified, but on 26 December 1793, in a letter to his nephew, he would quote *The Task* 2.3–4,* which expresses the desire no longer to be troubled by "rumour of oppression and deceit, / Of unsuccessful or successful war" (Fox, *Letters* 3:59; cf. *The Emigrants* 1.43–44).

[4] Brighton.

If but a Sea-Mew falls,[1] whose nest is hid
In these incumbent cliffs; He surely means
30 To us, his reasoning Creatures, whom He bids
Acknowledge and revere his awful hand,
Nothing but good: Yet Man, misguided Man,
Mars the fair work that he was bid enjoy,
And makes himself the evil he deplores.
35 How often, when my weary soul recoils
From proud oppression, and from legal crimes
(For such are in this Land, where the vain boast
Of equal Law is mockery, while the cost
Of seeking for redress is sure to plunge
40 Th' already injur'd to more certain ruin
And the wretch starves, before his Counsel pleads)[2]
How often do I half abjure Society,
And sigh for some lone Cottage, deep embower'd
In the green woods,[3] that these steep chalky Hills
45 Guard from the strong South West; where round
    their base
The Beach[4] wide flourishes, and the light Ash
With slender leaf half hides the thymy turf!—
There do I wish to hide me; well content
If on the short grass, strewn with fairy flowers,
50 I might repose thus shelter'd;[5] or when Eve
In Orient crimson lingers in the west,
Gain the high mound, and mark these waves remote
(Lucid tho' distant), blushing with the rays
Of the far-flaming Orb, that sinks beneath them;
55 For I have thought, that I should then behold
The beauteous works of God, unspoil'd by Man
And less affected then, by human woes
I witness'd not; might better learn to bear
Those that injustice, and duplicity
60 And faithlessness and folly, fix on me:

For never yet could I derive relief,
When my swol'n heart was bursting with its sorrows,
From the sad thought, that others like myself
Live but to swell affliction's countless tribes!
65 —Tranquil seclusion I have vainly sought;
Peace, who delights in solitary shade,
No more will spread for me her downy wings,
But, like the fabled Danaïds[6]—or the wretch,
Who ceaseless, up the steep acclivity,
70 Was doom'd to heave the still rebounding rock,
Onward I labour; as the baffled wave,
Which yon rough beach repulses, that returns
With the next breath of wind, to fail again.—
Ah! Mourner—cease these wailings: cease and learn,
75 That not the Cot sequester'd, where the briar
And wood-bine wild, embrace the mossy thatch,
(Scarce seen amid the forest gloom obscure!)
Or more substantial farm, well fenced and warm,
Where the full barn, and cattle fodder'd round
80 Speak rustic plenty; nor the statelier dome
By dark firs shaded, or the aspiring pine,
Close by the village Church (with care conceal'd
By verdant foliage, lest the poor man's grave
Should mar the smiling prospect of his Lord),
85 Where offices[7] well rang'd, or dove-cote stock'd,
Declare manorial residence; not these
Or any of the buildings, new and trim[8]
With windows circling towards the restless Sea,
Which ranged in rows, now terminate my walk,
90 Can shut out for an hour the spectre Care,
That from the dawn of reason, follows still
Unhappy Mortals, 'till the friendly grave

---

[1] Cf. Matthew 10.29.

[2] a reference to the protracted and still-unsuccessful lawsuit by which Smith was trying to gain access to a trust fund set up in her father-in-law's will for the benefit of her children.

[3] Cf. Cowper, *The Task* 2.1.*

[4] evidently a beech tree, *Fagus sylvatica*.

[5] Cf. Virgil, *Georgics*, 2.488–89: "O for one to set me in the cool glens of Hæmus, and shield me under the branches' mighty shade!" (trans. H. Rushton Fairclough).

[6] The fifty daughters of King Danaus of Argus all killed their husbands on their wedding night; their punishment after death was to spend eternity drawing water in leaky pots. The "wretch" is Sisyphus, who tried to cheat death; his punishment was to spend eternity rolling a rock up a hill over and over, only to have the rock roll back down as soon as he reached the top. See Ovid, *Metamorphoses* 4.

[7] outbuildings.

[8] After the Prince of Wales made Brighton his principal residence, in the 1780s, the city became a fashionable resort for the upper classes and underwent rapid development.

(Our sole secure asylum) "ends the chace."[1]
　Behold, in witness of this mournful truth,
95 A group approach me, whose dejected looks,
Sad Heralds of distress! proclaim them Men
Banish'd for ever and for conscience sake
From their distracted Country, whence the name
Of Freedom misapplied, and much abus'd
100 By lawless Anarchy, has driven them far
To wander; with the prejudice they learn'd
From Bigotry[2] (the Tut'ress of the blind),
Thro' the wide World unshelter'd; their sole hope,
That German spoilers, thro' that pleasant land
105 May carry wide the desolating scourge
Of War and Vengeance;[3] yet unhappy Men,
Whate'er your errors, I lament your fate:
And, as disconsolate and sad ye hang
Upon the barrier of the rock, and seem
110 To murmur your despondence, waiting long
Some fortunate reverse that never comes;
Methinks in each expressive face, I see
Discriminated anguish; there droops one,
Who in a moping cloister long consum'd
115 This life inactive, to obtain a better,
And thought that meagre abstinence, to wake
From his hard pallet with the midnight bell,
To live on eleemosynary bread,
And to renounce God's works, would please that God.
120 And now the poor pale wretch receives, amaz'd,
The pity, strangers give to his distress,
Because these strangers are, by his dark creed,
Condemn'd as Heretics—and with sick heart
Regrets his pious prison, and his beads.—[4]

125 Another, of more haughty port, declines
The aid he needs not; while in mute despair
His high indignant thoughts go back to France,
Dwelling on all he lost—the Gothic dome,
That vied with splendid palaces;[5] the beds
130 Of silk and down, the silver chalices,
Vestments with gold enwrought for blazing altars;
Where, amid clouds of incense, he held forth
To kneeling crowds the imaginary bones
Of Saints suppos'd, in pearl and gold enchas'd,
135 And still with more than living Monarchs' pomp
Surrounded; was believ'd by mumbling bigots
To hold the keys of Heaven, and to admit
Whom he thought good to share it—Now alas!
He, to whose daring soul and high ambition
140 The World seem'd circumscrib'd; who, wont to dream
Of Fleuri, Richelieu, Alberoni,[6] men
Who trod on Empire, and whose politics
Were not beyond the grasp of his vast mind,
Is, in a Land once hostile, still prophan'd
145 By disbelief, and rites un-orthodox,
The object of compassion—At his side,
Lighter of heart than these, but heavier far
Than he was wont, another victim comes,
An Abbé—who with less contracted brow
150 Still smiles and flatters, and still talks of Hope;
Which, sanguine as he is, he does not feel,
And so he cheats the sad and weighty pressure
Of evils present;——Still, as Men misled
By early prejudice (so hard to break),

---

[1] "I have a confused notion, that this expression, with nearly the same application, is to be found in Young: but I cannot refer to it." (C.S.) The phrase is from Samuel Jackson Pratt's "Cards; Pro and Con," in Dodsley's *Miscellanies* (1785).

[2] probably a pejorative term for Catholicism.

[3] Austria and Prussia were at war with France, and many of the émigrés had joined their armies. (Marie Antoinette was the sister of Joseph II of Austria.)

[4] "Lest the same attempts at misrepresentation should now be made, as have been made on former occasions, it is necessary to repeat, that nothing is farther from my thoughts, than to reflect invidiously on the Emigrant Clergy, whose steadiness of principle excites veneration, as much as their sufferings compassion. Adversity has now taught them the charity and humility they perhaps wanted, when they made it a part of their faith, that salvation could be obtained in no other religion than their own." (C.S.)

[5] "Let it not be considered as an insult to men in fallen fortune, if these luxuries (undoubtedly inconsistent with their profession) be here enumerated—France is not the only country, where the splendour and indulgences of the higher, and the poverty and depression of the inferior Clergy, have alike proved injurious to the cause of Religion." (C.S.)

[6] Cardinal André Hercule de Fleury (1653–1742), Louis XV's tutor and de facto French prime minister (1723–42); Cardinal Armand Jean du Plessis, duc de Richelieu (1585–1642), Louis XIII's principal minister; and Cardinal Giulio Alberoni (1664–1752), de facto Spanish prime minister (1716–19).

155 I mourn your sorrows; for I too have known
Involuntary exile;[1] and while yet
England had charms for me, have felt how sad
It is to look across the dim cold sea,
That melancholy rolls its refluent tides
160 Between us and the dear regretted land
We call our own—as now ye pensive wait
On this bleak morning, gazing on the waves
That seem to leave your shore; from whence the wind
Is loaded to your ears, with the deep groans
165 Of martyr'd Saints and suffering Royalty,[2]
While to your eyes the avenging power of Heaven
Appears in aweful anger to prepare
The storm of vengeance, fraught with plagues and
    death.
Even he of milder heart, who was indeed
170 The simple shepherd in a rustic scene,
And, 'mid the vine-clad hills of Languedoc,[3]
Taught to the bare-foot peasant, whose hard hands
Produc'd[4] the nectar he could seldom taste,
Submission to the Lord for whom he toil'd;
175 He, or his brethren, who to Neustria's[5] sons
Enforc'd religious patience, when, at times,
On their indignant hearts Power's iron hand
Too strongly struck; eliciting some sparks
Of the bold spirit of their native North;
180 Even these Parochial Priests, these humbled men,
Whose lowly undistinguish'd cottages
Witness'd a life of purest piety,
While the meek tenants were, perhaps, unknown
Each to the haughty Lord of his domain,
185 Who mark'd them not; the Noble scorning still
The poor and pious Priest, as with slow pace
He glided thro' the dim arch'd avenue
Which to the Castle led; hoping to cheer
The last sad hour of some laborious life
190 That hasten'd to its close—even such a Man
Becomes an exile; staying not to try
By temperate zeal to check his madd'ning flock,
Who, at the novel sound of Liberty
(Ah! most intoxicating sound to slaves!),
195 Start into licence—Lo! dejected now,
The wandering Pastor mourns, with bleeding heart,
His erring people, weeps and prays for them,
And trembles for the account that he must give
To Heaven for souls entrusted to his care.—
200 Where the cliff, hollow'd by the wintry storm,
Affords a seat with matted sea-weed strewn,
A softer form reclines; around her run,
On the rough shingles, or the chalky bourn,
Her gay unconscious children, soon amus'd;
205 Who pick the fretted stone, or glossy shell,
Or crimson plant marine: or they contrive
The fairy vessel, with its ribband sail
And gilded paper pennant: in the pool,
Left by the salt wave on the yielding sands,
210 They launch the mimic navy—Happy age!
Unmindful of the miseries of Man!—
Alas! too long a victim to distress,
Their Mother, lost in melancholy thought,
Lull'd for a moment by the murmurs low
215 Of sullen billows, wearied by the task
Of having here, with swol'n and aching eyes
Fix'd on the grey horizon, since the dawn
Solicitously watch'd the weekly sail
From her dear native land, now yields awhile
220 To kind forgetfulness, while Fancy brings,
In waking dreams, that native land again!
Versailles[6] appears—its painted galleries,
And rooms of regal splendour, rich with gold,
Where, by long mirrors multiply'd, the crowd
225 Paid willing homage—and, united there,
Beauty gave charms to empire—Ah! too soon
From the gay visionary pageant rous'd,
See the sad mourner start!—and, drooping, look
With tearful eyes and heaving bosom round

---

[1] Smith and her family had had to flee to Normandy in 1784–85, to avoid her husband's creditors.

[2] Louis XVI and his family had been imprisoned in the Temple since August 1792.

[3] in southern France.

[4] "See the finely descriptive Verses written at Montauban in France in 1750, by Dr. Joseph Warton. Printed in Dodsley's Miscellanies, Vol. IV, page 203." (C.S.)

[5] Normandy's.

[6] the palace outside Paris built by Louis XIV.

230 On drear reality—where dark'ning waves,
Urg'd by the rising wind, unheeded foam
Near her cold rugged seat:—To call her thence
A fellow-sufferer comes: dejection deep
Checks, but conceals not quite, the martial air,
235 And that high consciousness of noble blood,
Which he has learn'd from infancy to think
Exalts him o'er the race of common men:
Nurs'd in the velvet lap of luxury,
And fed by adulation—could *he* learn,
240 That worth alone is true Nobility?
And that *the peasant* who, "amid the sons
Of Reason, Valour, Liberty, and Virtue,
Displays distinguish'd merit, is a Noble
Of Nature's own creation!"[1]—If even here,
245 If in this land of highly vaunted Freedom,
Even Britons controvert the unwelcome truth,
Can it be relish'd by the sons of France?
Men, who derive their boasted ancestry
From the fierce leaders of religious wars,
250 The first in Chivalry's emblazon'd page;
Who reckon Gueslin, Bayard, or De Foix,[2]
Among their brave Progenitors? *Their* eyes,
Accustom'd to regard the splendid trophies
Of Heraldry (that with fantastic hand
255 Mingles, like images in feverish dreams,
"Gorgons and Hydras, and Chimeras dire,"[3]
With painted puns, and visionary shapes),
See not the simple dignity of Virtue,
But hold all base, whom honours such as these
260 Exalt not from the crowd[4]—As one, who long
Has dwelt amid the artificial scenes
Of populous City,[5] deems that splendid shows,
The Theatre, and pageant pomp of Courts,
Are only worth regard; forgets all taste
265 For Nature's genuine beauty; in the lapse
Of gushing waters hears no soothing sound,
Nor listens with delight to sighing winds,
That, on their fragrant pinions, waft the notes
Of birds rejoicing in the tangled copse;
270 Nor gazes pleas'd on Ocean's silver breast,
While lightly o'er it sails the summer clouds
Reflected in the wave, that, hardly heard,
Flows on the yellow sands: so to *his* mind,
That long has liv'd where Despotism hides
275 His features harsh, beneath the diadem
Of worldly grandeur, abject Slavery seems,
If by that power impos'd, slavery no more:
For luxury wreathes with silk the iron bonds,
And hides the ugly rivets with her flowers,
280 Till the degenerate triflers, while they love
The glitter of the chains, forget their weight.
But more the Men, whose ill acquir'd wealth[6]
Was wrung from plunder'd myriads, by the means
Too often legaliz'd by power abus'd,
285 Feel all the horrors of the fatal change,
When their ephemeral greatness, marr'd at once
(As a vain toy that Fortune's childish hand
Equally joy'd to fashion or to crush),

---

[1] "These lines are Thomson's, and are among those sentiments which are now called (when used by living writers), not common-place declamation, but sentiments of dangerous tendency." (C.S.) James Thomson (1700-48), *Coriolanus* (1749) 3.3.154–57.

[2] Bertrand de Guesdin (c. 1320–80), Constable of France; Pierre Bayard (c. 1473–1524), "le chevalier sans peur et sans reproche," the knight without fear and above reproach; and Gaston de Foix, duc de Nemours (1489–1512), the "Thunderbolt of Italy."

[3] Milton, *Paradise Lost* 2.628. All three are hideous monsters.

[4] "It has been said, and with great appearance of truth, that the contempt in which the Nobility of France held the common people, was remembered, and with all that vindictive asperity which long endurance of oppression naturally excites, when, by a wonderful concurrence of circumstances, the people acquired the power of retaliation. Yet let me here add, what seems to be in some degree inconsistent with the former charge, that the French are good masters to their servants, and that in their treatment of their Negro slaves, they are allowed to be more mild and merciful than other Europeans." (C.S.)

[5] Cf. Milton, *Paradise Lost* 9.445.

[6] "The Financiers and Fermiers Generaux are here intended. In the present moment of clamour against all those who have spoken or written in favour of the first Revolution of France, the declaimers seem to have forgotten, that under the reign of a mild and easy tempered Monarch, in the most voluptuous Court in the world, the abuses by which men of this description were enriched, had arisen to such height, that their prodigality exhausted the immense resources of France: and, unable to supply the exigencies of Government, the Ministry were compelled to call Le Tiers Etat; a meeting that gave birth to the Revolution, which has since been so ruinously conducted." (C.S.)

Leaves them expos'd to universal scorn
290 For having nothing else; not even the claim
To honour, which respect for Heroes past
Allows to ancient titles; Men, like these,
Sink even beneath the level, whence base arts
Alone had rais'd them;—unlamented sink,
295 And know that they deserve the woes they feel.
    Poor wand'ring wretches! whosoe'er ye are,[1]
That hopeless, houseless, friendless, travel wide
O'er these bleak russet downs; where, dimly seen,
The solitary Shepherd shiv'ring tends
300 His dun discolour'd flock (Shepherd, unlike
Him, whom in song the Poet's fancy crowns
With garlands, and his crook with vi'lets binds);
Poor vagrant wretches! outcasts of the world!
Whom no abode receives, no parish owns;
305 Roving, like Nature's commoners, the land
That boasts such general plenty: if the sight
Of wide-extended misery softens yours
Awhile, suspend your murmurs!—here behold
The strange vicissitudes of fate—while thus
310 The exil'd Nobles, from their country driven,
Whose richest luxuries were their's, must feel
More poignant anguish, than the lowest poor,
Who, born to indigence, have learn'd to brave
Rigid Adversity's depressing breath!—
315 Ah! rather Fortune's worthless favourites!
Who feed on England's vitals—Pensioners
Of base corruption, who, in quick ascent
To opulence unmerited, become
Giddy with pride, and as ye rise, forgetting
320 The dust ye lately left, with scorn look down
On those beneath ye (tho' your *equals* once
In fortune, and *in worth superior still*,
They view the eminence, on which ye stand,
With wonder, not with envy; for they know
325 The means, by which ye reach'd it, have been such
As, in all honest eyes, degrade ye far
Beneath the poor dependent, whose sad heart
Reluctant pleads for what your pride denies);
Ye venal, worthless hirelings of a Court!
330 Ye pamper'd Parasites! whom Britons pay

For forging fetters for them; rather here
Study a lesson that concerns ye much;
And, trembling, learn, that if oppress'd too long,
The raging multitude, to madness stung,
335 Will turn on their oppressors; and, no more
By sounding titles and parading forms
Bound like tame victims, will redress themselves!
Then swept away by the resistless torrent,
Not only all your pomp may disappear,
340 But, in the tempest lost, fair Order sink
Her decent head, and lawless Anarchy
O'erturn celestial Freedom's radiant throne;—
As now in Gallia; where Confusion, born
Of party rage and selfish love of rule,
345 Sully the noblest cause that ever warm'd
The heart of Patriot Virtue.[2]—There arise
The infernal passions; Vengeance, seeking blood,
And Avarice; and Envy's harpy fangs
Pollute the immortal shrine of Liberty,
350 Dismay her votaries, and disgrace her name.
Respect is due to principle; and they,
Who suffer for their conscience, have a claim,
Whate'er that principle may be, to praise.
These ill-starr'd Exiles then, who, bound by ties,
355 To them the bonds of honour; who resign'd
Their country to preserve them, and now seek
In England an asylum—well deserve
To find that (every prejudice forgot,
Which pride and ignorance teaches), we for them
360 Feel as our brethren; and that English hearts,
Of just compassion ever own the sway,
As truly as our element, the deep,
Obeys the mild dominion of the Moon—
This they *have* found; and may they find it still!
365 Thus may'st thou, Britain, triumph!—May thy foes,
By Reason's gen'rous potency subdued,
Learn, that the God thou worshippest, delights
In acts of pure humanity!—May thine
Be still such bloodless laurels! nobler far

---

[1] Cf. Shakespeare, *King Lear* 3.4.28.

[2] "This sentiment will probably *renew* against me the indignation of those, who have an interest in asserting that no such virtue any where exists." (C.S.)

370 Than those acquir'd at Cressy or Poictiers,[1]
Or of more recent growth, those well bestow'd
On him[2] who stood on Calpe's blazing height
Amid the thunder of a warring world,
Illustrious rather from the crowds he sav'd
375 From flood and fire, than from the ranks who fell
Beneath his valour!—Actions such as these,
Like incense rising to the Throne of Heaven,
Far better justify the pride, that swells
In British bosoms, than the deafening roar
380 Of Victory from a thousand brazen throats,
That tell with what success wide-wasting War
Has by our brave Compatriots thinned the world.

BOOK 2

Quippe ubi fas versum atque nefas: tot bella per orbem
Tam multæ scelerum facies; non ullus aratro
Dignus honos: squalent abductis arva colonis,
Et curva rigidum falces conflantur in ensem
Hinc movet Euphrates, illinc Germania bellum;
Vicinæ ruptis inter se legibus urbes
Arma ferunt: sævit toto Mars impius orbe.[3]

SCENE, *on an Eminence on one of those Downs, which afford to the South a View of the Sea; to the North of the Weald of Sussex.*

TIME, *an Afternoon in April, 1793.*

Long wintry months are past; the Moon that now
Lights her pale crescent even at noon, has made
Four times her revolution; since with step,
Mournful and slow,[4] along the wave-worn cliff,
5 Pensive I took my solitary way,[5]
Lost in despondence, while contemplating
Not my own wayward destiny alone,
(Hard as it is, and difficult to bear!)
But in beholding the unhappy lot
10 Of the lorn Exiles; who, amid the storms
Of wild disastrous Anarchy, are thrown,
Like shipwreck'd sufferers, on England's coast,
To see, perhaps, no more their native land,
Where Desolation riots:[6] They, like me,
15 From fairer hopes and happier prospects driven,
Shrink from the future, and regret the past.
But on this Upland scene, while April comes,
With fragrant airs, to fan my throbbing breast,
Fain would I snatch an interval from Care,
20 That weighs my wearied spirit down to earth;
Courting, once more, the influence of Hope
(For "Hope" still waits upon the flowery prime)[7]
As here I mark Spring's humid hand unfold
The early leaves that fear capricious winds,
25 While, even on shelter'd banks, the timid flowers
Give, half reluctantly, their warmer hues
To mingle with the primroses' pale stars.
No shade the leafless copses yet afford,
Nor hide the mossy labours of the Thrush,
30 That, startled, darts across the narrow path;
But quickly re-assur'd, resumes his task,
Or adds his louder notes to those that rise
From yonder tufted brake; where the white buds
Of the first thorn are mingled with the leaves
35 Of that which blossoms on the brow of May.
　　Ah! 'twill not be:——So many years have pass'd,
Since, on my native hills, I learn'd to gaze
On these delightful landscapes; and those years
Have taught me so much sorrow, that my soul
40 Feels not the joy reviving Nature brings;

---

[1] English victories (1346, 1356) over France.

[2] George Augustus Eliott (1717–90), knighted for his services as commander of Gibraltar ("Calpe") under siege by the Spanish (1779–83).

[3] Virgil, *Georgics*, 1.505–11: "For here are right and wrong inverted; so many wars overrun the world, so many are the shapes of sin; the plough meets not its honour due; our lands, robbed of the tillers, lie waste, and the crooked pruning-hooks are forged into stiff swords. Here Euphrates, there Germany, awakes war; neighbour cities break the leagues that bound them and draw the sword; throughout the world rages the god of unholy strife" (trans. H. Ruston Fairclough).

[4] Cf. Sir Philip Sidney (1554–86), *Astrophel and Stella* (1590) 31.1–2.

[5] Cf. Milton, *Paradise Lost* 12.648–49.

[6] a reference to the Reign of Terror (1793–94) or perhaps to the uprising in the region of La Vendée (1793–94).

[7] "Shakspeare." (C.S.) Edmund Waller (1606–87), "To my Young Lady Lucy Sidney" (1645) 13.

But, in dark retrospect, dejected dwells
On human follies, and on human woes.——
What is the promise of the infant year,
The lively verdure, or the bursting blooms,
45 To those, who shrink from horrors such as War
Spreads o'er the affrighted world? With swimming eye,
Back on the past they throw their mournful looks,
And see the Temple, which they fondly hop'd
Reason would raise to Liberty, destroy'd
50 By ruffian hands; while, on the ruin'd mass,
Flush'd with hot blood, the Fiend of Discord sits
In savage triumph; mocking every plea
Of policy and justice, as she shews
The headless corse of one,[1] whose only crime
55 Was being born a Monarch—Mercy turns,
From spectacle so dire, her swol'n eyes;
And Liberty, with calm, unruffled brow
Magnanimous, as conscious of her strength
In Reason's panoply, scorns to distain
60 Her righteous cause with carnage, and resigns
To Fraud and Anarchy the infuriate crowd.——
   What is the promise of the infant year
To those, who (while the poor but peaceful hind
Pens, unmolested, the encreasing flock
65 Of his rich master in this sea-fenc'd isle)
Survey, in neighbouring countries, scenes that make
The sick heart shudder; and the Man, who thinks,
Blush for his species? *There* the trumpet's voice
Drowns the soft warbling of the woodland choir;
70 And violets, lurking in their turfy beds
Beneath the flow'ring thorn, are stain'd with blood.
There fall, at once, the spoiler and the spoil'd;
While War, wide-ravaging, annihilates
The hope of cultivation; gives to Fiends,
75 The meagre, ghastly Fiends of Want and Woe,
The blasted land—There, taunting in the van
Of vengeance-breathing armies, Insult stalks;
And, in the ranks, "Famine, and Sword, and Fire,
Crouch for employment."[2]—Lo! the suffering world,
80 Torn by the fearful conflict, shrinks, amaz'd,

From Freedom's name, usurp'd and misapplied,
And, cow'ring to the purple[3] Tyrant's rod,
Deems *that* the lesser ill—Deluded Men!
Ere ye prophane her ever-glorious name,
85 Or catalogue the thousands that have bled
Resisting her; or those, who greatly died
Martyrs to *Liberty*—revert awhile
To the black scroll, that tells of regal crimes
Committed to destroy her; rather count
90 The hecatombs of victims, who have fallen
Beneath a single despot; or who gave
Their wasted lives for some disputed claim
Between anointed robbers: Monsters both![4]
"Oh! Polish'd perturbation—golden care!"[5]
95 So strangely coveted by feeble Man
To lift him o'er his fellows;—Toy, for which
Such showers of blood have drench'd th' affrighted
   earth—
Unfortunate *his* lot, whose luckless head
Thy jewel'd circlet, lin'd with thorns,[6] has bound;
100 And who, by custom's laws, obtains from thee
Hereditary right to rule, unchec'd,
Submissive myriads: for untemper'd power,
Like steel ill form'd, injures the hand
It promis'd to protect—Unhappy France!
105 If e'er thy lilies,[7] trampled now in dust,
And blood-bespotted, shall again revive
In silver splendour, may the wreath be wov'n
By voluntary hands; and Freemen, such
As England's self might boast, unite to place
110 The guarded diadem on *his* fair brow,
Where Loyalty may join with Liberty
To fix it firmly.—In the rugged school
Of stern Adversity so early train'd,
His future life, perchance, may emulate

---

[1] Louis XVI, guillotined on 21 January 1793.

[2] "Shakspeare." (C.S.) *Henry V* Pro. 7–8; cf. Coleridge, "Fire, Famine, and Slaughter."*

[3] The purple dye made from the murex, a shellfish harvested from the Mediterranean near Tyre, was traditionally associated with royalty.

[4] "Such was the cause of quarrel between the Houses of York and Lancaster; and of too many others, with which the page of History reproaches the reason of man." (C.S.)

[5] "Shakspeare." (C.S.) *2 Henry IV* 4.5.22.

[6] Cf. Matthew 27.29, Mark 15.17, John 19.5.

[7] the emblem of the French monarchy.

115 That of the brave Bernois,[1] so justly call'd
The darling of his people; who rever'd
The Warrior less, than they ador'd the Man!
But ne'er may Party Rage, perverse and blind,
And base Venality, prevail to raise
120 To public trust, a wretch,[2] whose private vice
Makes even the wildest profligate recoil;
And who, with hireling ruffians leagu'd, has burst
The laws of Nature and Humanity!
Wading, beneath the Patriot's specious mask,
125 And in Equality's illusive name,
To empire thro' a stream of kindred blood—
Innocent prisoner!—most unhappy heir[3]
Of fatal greatness, who art suffering now
For all the crimes and follies of thy race;
130 Better for thee, if o'er thy baby brow
The regal mischief never had been held:
Then, in an humble sphere, perhaps content,
Thou hadst been free and joyous on the heights
Of Pyrennean mountains, shagg'd with woods
135 Of chesnut, pine, and oak: as on these hills
Is yonder little thoughtless shepherd lad,
Who, on the slope abrupt of downy turf
Reclin'd in playful indolence, sends off
The chalky ball, quick bounding far below;
140 While, half forgetful of his simple task,
Hardly his length'ning shadow, or the bells'
Slow tinkling of his flock, that supping tend
To the brown fallows in the vale beneath,
Where nightly it is folded, from his sport
145 Recal the happy idler.—While I gaze
On his gay vacant countenance, my thoughts
Compare with his obscure, laborious lot,

Thine, most unfortunate, imperial Boy!
Who round thy sullen prison daily hear'st
150 The savage howl of Murder, as it seeks
Thy unoffending life: while sad within
Thy wretched Mother,[4] petrified with grief,
Views thee with stony eyes, and cannot weep!—
Ah! much I mourn thy sorrows, hapless Queen!
155 And deem thy expiation made to Heaven
For every fault, to which Prosperity
Betray'd thee, when it plac'd thee on a throne
Where boundless power was thine, and thou wert rais'd
High (as it seem'd) above the envious reach
160 Of destiny! Whate'er thy errors[5] were,
Be they no more remember'd; tho' the rage
Of Party swell'd them to such crimes, as bade
Compassion stifle every sigh that rose
For thy disastrous lot—More than enough
165 Thou hast endur'd; and every English heart,
Ev'n those, that highest beat in Freedom's cause,
Disclaim as base, and of that cause unworthy,
The Vengeance, or the Fear, that makes thee still
A miserable prisoner!—Ah! who knows,
170 From sad experience, more than I, to feel
For thy desponding spirit, as it sinks
Beneath procrastinated fears for those
More dear to thee than life! But eminence
Of misery is thine, as once of joy;
175 And, as we view the strange vicissitude,
We ask anew, where happiness is found?——
Alas! in rural life, where youthful dreams
See the Arcadia[6] that Romance describes,
Not even Content resides!—In yon low hut
180 Of clay and thatch, where rises the grey smoke
Of smold'ring turf, cut from the adjoining moor,
The labourer, its inhabitant, who toils
From the first dawn of twilight, till the Sun
Sinks in the rosy waters of the West,
185 Finds that with poverty it cannot dwell;

---

[1] "Henry the Fourth of France. It may be said of this monarch, that had all the French sovereigns resembled him, despotism would have lost its horrors; yet he had considerable failings, and his greatest virtues may be chiefly imputed to his education in the School of Adversity." (C.S.) Henri IV, the first king in the Bourbon dynasty that also included Louis XVI, had tried throughout his reign (1589–1610) to promote harmony between Catholics and Protestants. He was assassinated by François Ravaillac, a Catholic extremist.

[2] apparently Jean-Paul Marat (1743–93), Jacobin leader.

[3] The Dauphin, Louis XVII, was imprisoned with the rest of the royal family. He would die in June 1795.

[4] Marie Antoinette. She would be executed on 16 October 1793.

[5] Marie Antoinette had been accused of extravagance, of associating with dissolute courtiers, and, in the Diamond Necklace Affair (1785–86), of an improper relationship with a cardinal.

[6] a pastoral land described in romances like Sidney's *Arcadia* (1590).

For bread, and scanty bread, is all he earns
For him and for his household—Should Disease,
Born of chill wintry rains, arrest his arm,
Then, thro' his patch'd and straw-stuff'd casement, peeps
190 The squalid figure of extremest Want;
And from the Parish the reluctant dole,[1]
Dealt by th' unfeeling farmer, hardly saves
The ling'ring spark of life from cold extinction:
Then the bright Sun of Spring, that smiling bids
195 All other animals rejoice, beholds,
Crept from his pallet, the emaciate wretch
Attempt, with feeble effort, to resume
Some heavy task, above his wasted strength,
Turning his wistful looks (how much in vain!)
200 To the deserted mansion, where no more
The owner (gone to gayer scenes) resides,
Who made even luxury, Virtue; while he gave
The scatter'd crumbs to honest Poverty.—
But, tho' the landscape be too oft deform'd
205 By figures such as these, yet Peace is here,
And o'er our vallies, cloath'd with springing corn,
No hostile hoof shall trample, nor fierce flames
Wither the wood's young verdure, ere it form
Gradual the laughing May's luxuriant shade;
210 For, by the rude sea guarded, we are safe,
And feel not evils such as with deep sighs
The Emigrants deplore, as they recal
The Summer past, when Nature seem'd to lose
Her course in wild distemperature, and aid,
215 With seasons all revers'd, destructive War.

Shuddering, I view the pictures they have drawn
Of desolated countries, where the ground,
Stripp'd of its unripe produce, was thick strewn
With various Death—the war-horse falling there
220 By famine, and his rider by the sword.
The moping clouds sail'd heavy charg'd with rain,
And bursting o'er the mountains misty brow,
Deluged, as with an inland sea, the vales;[2]
Where, thro' the sullen evening's lurid gloom,
225 Rising, like columns of volcanic fire,
The flames of burning villages illum'd
The waste of water; and the wind, that howl'd
Along its troubled surface, brought the groans
Of plunder'd peasants, and the frantic shrieks
230 Of mothers for their children; while the brave,
To pity still alive, listen'd aghast
To these dire echoes, hopeless to prevent
The evils they beheld, or check the rage,
Which ever, as the people of one land
235 Meet in contention, fires the human heart
With savage thirst of kindred blood, and makes
Man lose his nature; rendering him more fierce
Than the gaunt monsters of the howling waste.
    Oft have I heard the melancholy tale,
240 Which, all their native gaiety forgot,
These Exiles tell—How Hope impell'd them on,
Reckless of tempest, hunger, or the sword,
Till order'd to retreat, they knew not why,
From all their flattering prospects, they became
245 The prey of dark suspicion and regret:[3]
Then, in despondence, sunk the unnerv'd arm
Of gallant Loyalty—At every turn
Shame and disgrace appear'd, and seem'd to mock
Their scatter'd squadrons; which the warlike youth,
250 Unable to endure, often implor'd,
As the last act of friendship, from the hand
Of some brave comrade, to receive the blow
That freed the indignant spirit from its pain.
To a wild mountain, whose bare summit hides
255 Its broken eminence in clouds; whose steeps

---

[1] The Poor Laws required each parish (the territory and population appertaining to a church) to take care of its poor.

[2] "From the heavy and incessant rains during the last campaign, the armies were often compelled to march for many miles through marshes overflowed; suffering the extremities of cold and fatigue. The peasants frequently misled them; and, after having passed these inundations at the hazard of their lives, they were sometimes under the necessity of crossing them a second and a third time; their evening quarters after such a day of exertion were often in a wood without shelter; and their repast, instead of bread, unripe corn, without any other preparation than being mashed into a sort of paste." (C.S.)

[3] "It is remarkable, that notwithstanding the excessive hardships to which the army of the Emigrants was exposed, very few in it suffered from disease till they began to retreat; then it was that despondence consigned to the most miserable death many brave men who deserved a better fate; and then despair impelled some to suicide, while others fell by mutual wounds, unable to survive disappointment and humiliation." (C.S.)

Are dark with woods; where the receding rocks
Are worn by torrents of dissolving snow,
A wretched Woman, pale and breathless, flies!
And, gazing round her, listens to the sound
260 Of hostile footsteps——No! it dies away:
Nor noise remains, but of the cataract,
Or surly breeze of night, that mutters low
Among the thickets, where she trembling seeks
A temporary shelter—clasping close
265 To her hard-heaving heart her sleeping child,
All she could rescue of the innocent groupe
That yesterday surrounded her—Escap'd
Almost by miracle! Fear, frantic Fear,
Wing'd her weak feet: yet, half repentant now
270 Her headlong haste, she wishes she had staid
To die with those affrighted Fancy paints
The lawless soldier's victims—Hark! again
The driving tempest bears the cry of Death,
And, with deep sudden thunder, the dread sound
275 Of cannon vibrates on the tremulous earth;
While, bursting in the air, the murderous bomb
Glares o'er her mansion. Where the splinters fall,
Like scatter'd comets, its destructive path
Is mark'd by wreaths of flame!—Then, overwhelm'd
280 Beneath accumulated horror, sinks
The desolate mourner; yet, in Death itself,
True to maternal tenderness, she tries
To save the unconscious infant from the storm
In which she perishes; and to protect
285 This last dear object of her ruin'd hopes
From prowling monsters, that from other hills,
More inaccessible, and wilder wastes,
Lur'd by the scent of slaughter, follow fierce
Contending hosts, and to polluted fields
290 Add dire increase of horrors—But alas!
The Mother and the Infant perish both!—
    The feudal Chief, whose Gothic battlements
Frown on the plain beneath, returning home
From distant lands, alone and in disguise,
295 Gains at the fall of night his Castle walls,
But, at the vacant gate, no Porter sits
To wait his Lord's admittance!—In the courts
All is drear silence!—Guessing but too well

The fatal truth, he shudders as he goes
300 Thro' the mute hall; where, by the blunted light
That the dim moon thro' painted casements lends,
He sees that devastation has been there:
Then, while each hideous image to his mind
Rises terrific, o'er a bleeding corse
305 Stumbling he falls; another interrupts
His staggering feet—all, all who us'd to rush
With joy to meet him—all his family
Lie murder'd in his way!—And the day dawns
On a wild raving Maniac, whom a fate
310 So sudden and calamitous has robb'd
Of reason; and who round his vacant walls
Screams unregarded, and reproaches Heaven!—
Such are thy dreadful trophies, savage War!
And evils such as these, or yet more dire,
315 Which the pain'd mind recoils from, all are thine—
The purple Pestilence, that to the grave
Sends whom the sword has spar'd, is thine; and thine
The Widow's anguish and the Orphan's tears!—
Woes such as these does Man inflict on Man;
320 And by the closet murderers, whom we style
Wise Politicians, are the schemes prepar'd,
Which, to keep Europe's wavering balance even,
Depopulate her kingdoms, and consign
To tears and anguish half a bleeding world!—
325   Oh! could the time return, when thoughts like these
Spoil'd not that gay delight, which vernal Suns,
Illuminating hills, and woods, and fields,
Gave to my infant spirits—Memory come!
And from distracting cares, that now deprive
330 Such scenes of all their beauty, kindly bear
My fancy to those hours of simple joy,
When, on the banks of Arun, which I see
Make its irriguous course thro' yonder meads,
I play'd; unconscious then of future ill!
335 There (where, from hollows fring'd with yellow broom,
The birch with silver rind, and fairy leaf,
Aslant the low stream trembles) I have stood,
And meditated how to venture best
Into the shallow current, to procure
340 The willow herb of glowing purple spikes,

Or flags,[1] whose sword-like leaves conceal'd the tide,
Startling the timid reed-bird from her nest,
As with aquatic flowers I wove the wreath,
Such as, collected by the shepherd girls,
345 Deck in the villages the turfy shrine,
And mark the arrival of propitious May.—
How little dream'd I then the time would come,
When the bright Sun of that delicious month
Should, from disturb'd and artificial sleep,
350 Awaken me to never-ending toil,
To terror and to tears!—Attempting still,
With feeble hands and cold desponding heart,
To save my children from the o'erwhelming wrongs,
That have for ten long years been heap'd on me!—[2]
355 The fearful spectres of chicane and fraud
Have, Proteus[3] like, still chang'd their hideous forms
(As the Law lent its plausible disguise),
Pursuing my faint steps; and I have seen
Friendship's sweet bonds (which were so early form'd,
360 And once I fondly thought of amaranth[4]
Inwove with silver seven times tried)[5] give way,
And fail; as these green fan-like leaves of fern
Will wither at the touch of Autumn's frost.
Yet there *are those*, whose patient pity still
365 Hears my long murmurs; who, unwearied, try
With lenient hands to bind up every wound
My wearied spirit feels, and bid me go
"Right onward"[6]—a calm votary of the Nymph,
Who, from her adamantine rock,[7] points out
370 To conscious rectitude the rugged path,
That leads at length to Peace!—Ah! yes, my friends
Peace will at last be mine; for in the Grave
Is Peace—and pass a few short years, perchance
A few short months, and all the various pain

375 I now endure shall be forgotten there,
And no memorial shall remain of me,
Save in your bosoms; while even *your* regret
Shall lose its poignancy, as ye reflect
What complicated woes that grave conceals!
380 But, if the little praise, that may await
The Mother's efforts, should provoke the spleen
Of Priest or Levite;[8] and they then arraign
The dust that cannot hear them; be it yours
To vindicate my humble fame; to say,
385 That, not in selfish sufferings absorb'd,
"I gave to misery all I had, my tears."[9]
And if, where regulated sanctity
Pours her long orisons to Heaven, my voice
Was seldom heard, that yet *my prayer* was made
390 To him who hears even silence; not in domes
Of human architecture, fill'd with crowds,
But on these hills, where boundless, yet distinct,
Even as a map, beneath are spread the fields
His bounty cloaths; divided here by woods,
395 And there by commons rude, or winding brooks,
While I might breathe the air perfum'd with flowers,
Or the fresh odours of the mountain turf;
And gaze on clouds above me, as they sail'd
Majestic: or remark the reddening north,
400 When bickering arrows of electric fire
Flash on the evening sky—I made my prayer
In unison with murmuring waves that now
Swell with dark tempests, now are mild and blue,
As the bright arch above; for all to me
405 Declare omniscient goodness; nor need I
Declamatory essays to incite
My wonder or my praise, when every leaf
That Spring unfolds, and every simple bud,
More forcibly impresses on my heart
410 His power and wisdom—Ah! while I adore
That goodness, which design'd to all that lives
Some taste of happiness, my soul is pain'd
By the variety of woes that Man
For Man creates—his blessings often turn'd

---

[1] irises.

[2] another reference to Smith's lawsuit.

[3] a sea-god who could change his shape. See Homer, *Odyssey* 4.450–59.

[4] a mythical unfading flower.

[5] Cf. Psalms 12.6.

[6] "MILTON, Sonnet 22d." (C.S.) Line 9.

[7] Cf. Smith, *Elegiac Sonnets* 35, "To fortitude."*

[8] Cf. John 1.19.

[9] "GRAY." (C.S.) Thomas Gray (1716–71), *Elegy Written in a Country Church-Yard* (1750) 123.

415 To plagues and curses: Saint-like Piety,
Misled by Superstition,[1] has destroy'd
More than Ambition; and the sacred flame
Of Liberty becomes a raging fire,
When Licence and Confusion bid it blaze.
420 From thy high throne, above yon radiant stars,
O Power Omnipotent! with mercy view
This suffering globe, and cause thy creatures cease,
With savage fangs, to tear her bleeding breast:
Restrain that rage for power, that bids a Man,
425 Himself a worm, desire unbounded rule
O'er beings like himself: Teach the hard hearts
Of rulers, that the poorest hind, who dies
For their unrighteous quarrels, in thy sight
Is equal to the imperious Lord, that leads
430 His disciplin'd destroyers to the field.—
May lovely Freedom, in her genuine charms,
Aided by stern but equal Justice, drive
From the ensanguin'd earth the hell-born fiends
Of Pride, Oppression, Avarice, and Revenge,
435 That ruin what thy mercy made so fair!
Then shall these ill-starr'd wanderers, whose sad fate
These desultory lines lament, regain
Their native country; private vengeance then
To public virtue yield; and the fierce feuds,
440 That long have torn their desolated land,
May (even as storms, that agitate the air,
Drive noxious vapours from the blighted earth)
Serve, all tremendous as they are, to fix
The reign of Reason, Liberty, and Peace!

---

[1] another pejorative term for Catholicism.

Priscilla Wakefield
1750 – 1832

Priscilla Bell was born on 20 November 1750, the oldest daughter of Daniel Bell and Catherine Barclay Bell. She was educated at home near London and helped her mother educate her younger sisters. In January 1771, she married Edward Wakefield, a merchant; they had two surviving sons and one daughter. A Quaker, Wakefield was a noted philanthropist, founding a maternity hospital and a "frugality bank" in which the poor could save their money. She is best known as a children's author; she wrote only one book for adults, the feminist *Reflections on the Present Condition of the Female Sex* (1798). Despite never leaving Britain, she wrote a number of travel books, including *Excursions in North America* (1806) and *The Traveller in Africa* (1814), basing them on extensive research. She died at her daughter's house in Ipswich on 12 September 1832. (D.L.M.)

---

from *Excursions in North America, Described in Letters from a Gentleman and his Young Companion, to Their Friends in England* (1806)

LETTER 32

Mr. Henry Franklin to Edwin Middleton

St. John's, on Lake Champlain[1]

My dear Edwin,

There is no occasion to have recourse to novels or feigned tales, in order to amuse and interest, whilst the occurrences of real life are often so full of extraordinary accidents, and contain more instruction than the fictions of the imagination.[2] Arthur mentioned, in his last, a white man that we met with amongst a party of Indians. It proved to be a merchant, who resided at Richmond in Virginia, but, from a train of unfortunate circumstances, had fallen into their hands as a prisoner. A settled distress was marked on his face, till he perceived I gained the confidence of the chief who commanded the expedition, when something like hope began to animate his listless frame. His master did not watch him with such jealousy as to prevent him from telling me his unhappy story, and interesting me in his fate. It happened, some time ago, that he was obliged to go to Kentucky, to receive some money that was due to him. He was accompanied by a friend who was a landholder in Kentucky. They proceeded together to the banks of the Great Kenhaway,[3] where they met with several other persons, who were also going to Kentucky. They joined company, and purchased between them one of those slight, large, flat-bottomed vessels, without any deck, that are used merely to descend the Ohio, but are not sufficiently substantial to remount the stream. Having embarked with their merchandise and stores, they proceeded on the voyage, working the vessels themselves. Their company consisted of six persons: four men, and two young women, who were sisters, and going to settle, under the protection of a relation, at Kentucky. They were all fully aware that the navigation of the Ohio is not free from danger from the Indians; but they also knew that an attack on a vessel in the midst of the stream is very rare, and that such an attempt, with so many on board, had not been heard of for many years. Confiding in their numbers, they proceeded, without anxiety, an hundred and six miles, when, about day-break, they were alarmed by the most

---

[1] Lake Champlain extends from Québec down between New York and Vermont. St. John's is at the north end.

[2] "The principal circumstances of this narrative are facts related by the Duke de Rochefoucault Liancourt." (P.W.) François Alexandre, duc de La Rochefoucauld (1747–1827), *Travels through the United States of North America, the Country of the Iroquois, and Upper Canada, in the years 1795, 1796, and 1797, with an authentic account of Lower Canada* (1799).

[3] the Kanawha, a tributary of the Ohio in West Virginia.

dreadful shrieks, proceeding from two white men on the shore, who told them, with the most affecting tone of grief, that they had been taken prisoners by the Indians, and had made their escape, but feared again to fall into their hands. They said they had not eaten any thing for the last four days, and entreated, if they could not be taken on board, to be at least supplied with some provision, and saved from perishing by hunger. That humanity, which is implanted in every breast, pleaded in their favour with all on board; till a little further consideration induced those of most experience to apprehend that they should expose themselves to danger, by stopping to assist these unfortunate persons. Their arguments were, however, overruled by the rest; and the women, especially, declared it would be an act of the most barbarous cruelty to refuse assistance to two fellow-creatures in such deplorable circumstances. Whilst this contest between prudence and compassion was carrying on, the two men followed the vessel along the shore. Their mournful lamentations, their screams and expressions of agonizing anguish and despair, still increasing, one of the passengers offered to go alone, and carry bread to these miserable sufferers, if his companions would put him on the land; alledging, that he should discern the Indians from afar, if they made their appearance; that in this case, the vessel might easily regain the middle of the stream; and that he should be able to reach Limestone[1] on foot, where they might wait for him. Who could resist this proposal, so noble, so generous, so full of humanity? Those who feared the consequences were obliged to yield. They steered towards the shore, where the two sufferers were dragging themselves along, as if tormented by the most excruciating pains. How lamentable, that generous compassion should ever be abused! The apprehensions of the two gentlemen who opposed the measure were too well founded. The men were two traitors, under the direction of the Indians, and appointed by them to decoy the vessel to the shore. The Indians followed them at some distance, constantly concealing themselves behind trees. The moment the vessel reached the shore, they burst forth, about twenty-five or thirty in number, raised a dreadful howl, and fired on the affrighted passengers. Two of them were killed by the first firing, and the rest, in equal terror and astonishment, endeavoured to regain the middle of the stream; but being too near the shore, and their dexterity checked by a sense of danger, they made but little way. The Indians continued to fire. A man and one of the young women had already fallen victims; another man was wounded, and two horses were killed. Mr. Martin, (the name of my new acquaintance,) and two others only, were left to use their exertions to save themselves. The fury of the savages increased with their hopes of success. Some threw themselves into the river, and swam towards the ship; those who remained on shore threatened to repeat their fire, if the passengers made the least resistance, and levelled their pieces at them. The swimmers succeeded in bringing the ship on shore, and my unfortunate friend and his companions were obliged to land, under the continued howls of the Indians; which, however, were no longer the accents of rage, but shouts of joy, on account of the seizure of their prey. The Indians offered them their hands, which in some measure allayed their apprehensions. Whilst some of their new masters were saluting their prisoners, and leading them to the shore, the rest were employed in landing the merchandise and stores. Some cut wood, and a fire was presently made. The articles found in the ship were carried to the fire, as well as the bodies of the two unfortunate persons who had been shot: these they completely stripped of their clothes, scalped them, and threw them into the river. The scalps were dried by the fire, to increase the trophies of the tribe. To express the horror of the surviving sister, or of Mr. Martin, (whose particular friend had been one of the victims,) at this dreadful sight, is impossible. Mr. Martin and his two male companions were next partly stripped, according to the caprice of those who were near them. The young woman was not touched, perhaps from respect to the female sex. Mr. Martin's coat and waistcoat were already pulled off, and half his shirt; when one of the Indians, with an air of authority, gave him back his shirt, and reproved him who was taking it off: he gave him also a blanket, instead of his coat and waistcoat. They provided him with Indian shoes, made of deer-skins, in exchange for

---

[1] a settlement on the Ohio, in Kentucky.

his own, which, with the rest of the clothes, were added to the booty. The Indians were now about seventy in number, amongst whom were several women. Their leader assembled them around the fire, and, holding the tomahawk in his hand, addressed them in a long speech, which he delivered with great fluency, with gestures and a tone of enthusiasm; looking frequently up to heaven, or casting his eyes down to the ground; and pointing, now to the prisoners—now to the river. The Indians, who listened to him with the utmost attention, expressed their applause with accents of deep, mournful exclamation. The booty was divided among the different tribes which shared in this enterprise. The tribe of the Shawanese[1] received three prisoners, Mr. Martin, the young woman, and another of the passengers: the other fell to the lot of the Cherokees, and was afterwards burnt by them. Every prisoner was given to the charge of an Indian, who was answerable for his person. They were not prevented from the solace of conversing with each other.

The two men who had decoyed them on shore now rejoined the Indians, and were severely reproached by those who had been the wretched victims of their dissimulation. They pleaded that they had been compelled to act so, on pain of death. They said that they had been surprised by the Indians six months before, and had been several times employed on these treacherous expeditions. The stores found on board the vessel served the Indians for their meals, in which they generally allowed the prisoners to partake.

Night coming on, every one lay down to rest under the trees. The prisoners were surrounded by the tribes to which they were each allotted, and singly guarded by the Indians who had the charge of them. Mr. Martin was tied by the elbows, and the ends of the ropes were fastened to trees, which stood far asunder, so that it was impossible for him to lie down; yet they did not think this a sufficient security. Another rope, fastened to a tree, was tied round his neck, from which a rattle was suspended, that on the least motion would have awakened the whole troop. The rest were treated nearly in the same manner. The two white spies enjoyed the most perfect liberty. Some Indians were stationed on the outside, to observe what was passing in the surrounding country.

The next morning, the Indians who were posted along the banks of the Ohio, reported that a vessel was dropping down the river. The prisoners were ordered to join the other two, who only yesterday beguiled them, in exerting their utmost endeavours to decoy the passengers in the ship on shore. How powerful is the fear of instant death!—a punishment with which they were threatened in case of refusal or disobedience. They complied, and joined their hardened companions in a crime their souls abhorred. Mr. Martin, however, though compelled for the preservation of his own life, to accompany the rest, firmly determined not to be guilty of occasioning the slavery, or probable death, of the unsuspecting passengers on board, by any voluntary action; and consequently, neither to make the smallest gesture, nor to speak a word. Nor was there occasion for his efforts. His companions, less refined in their feelings, exerted themselves to the utmost to excite the compassion of those on board, who, without the least hesitation, stood in towards the shore, to succour and rescue from slavery those whom they thought unfortunate captives. Scarcely had they approached within a small distance from the shore, when the Indians, who had stolen along behind the bushes, hastened up, fired, and shot the six persons on board. Shouts of victory succeeded to the howls of barbarous rage. The vessel was hauled on shore; and two of the ill-fated victims, who were not quite dead, were immediately dispatched by the tomahawk. The six scalps were torn off and dried, and the booty divided as before, but with fewer formalities.

The scouts soon after made signals that three other vessels were in sight. The same stratagem was attempted, but in vain. The passengers were too wary to be decoyed out of their course. They were, however, so much panic-struck as to abandon one of their vessels, which was laden with stores and other valuable articles, belonging to several families who had emigrated, in company, from Virginia, to settle in Kentucky. This was a rich booty. Without distributing the whole, the Indians fixed

---

[1] the Shawnee, an Algonkian people then living in Ohio, the main obstacle to the western expansion of European settlements. The Cherokee lived mainly in the South, but they made frequent northern incursions; they sided with the British in the Revolutionary War and had difficult relations with the Americans afterwards.

eagerly on some casks of whiskey. They drank so largely, that most of them were soon intoxicated. Six or seven, to whom were committed the charge of guarding the booty, had been ordered, at the beginning of these Bacchanalian revels, to drink with moderation; and they alone retained the use of their senses. All the rest lay buried in a profound sleep; and among them, the leader of the party and the guards of the prisoners. Mr. Martin's mind was too deeply affected by his dreadful situation to partake of this disgusting banquet. Totally absorbed in reflecting upon the dangers and miseries that threatened him, and anxiously desirous of avoiding them, if possible, he conceived, that whilst the Indians were overpowered by the effects of the liquor, he might contrive a means of escape. This idea he communicated to one of his fellow sufferers, who was lying by his side. The vessels were fastened to stakes along the shore, at a small distance from them. The success of their attempt depended upon their stealing thither unobserved, throwing themselves into the first vessel they should find, (the night being very dark,) and abandoning her to the stream. If they reached the vessel in safety, success seemed as certain, as instant death if they should be discovered. The hopes that this scheme had kindled were soon destroyed; for though they spoke in such a low tone of voice, as seemed hardly possible to have been overheard by an Indian who lay at a considerable distance, had he had a thorough knowledge of English, yet he arose, and tied them in the same manner as the night before, without showing, however, any sign of passion, or even speaking a word. Separated from each other, and convinced that they were closely watched, even in moments when they had imagined themselves to be totally unguarded, they abandoned themselves to the dreadful idea that they were doomed to a state of hopeless misery. The remembrance of all they had heard of the cruelty of the Indians towards their prisoners, oppressed them with constant horror. They expected to be yielded up to the grossest insults, and to suffer a lingering, cruel death. They considered the Indians, who were lying around them in a state of senseless, brutish intoxication, as the instruments of their future tortures. Haunted by these painful ideas, they passed the remainder of the night in despair. At break of day the surrounding troop awoke, untied their prisoners, and renewed their revels with the remainder of the whiskey. On the fourth day the leader of the band proclaimed his will that the expedition should be ended, and that each tribe should return to their respective homes, which were all situated in the neighbourhood of the Lakes Ontario and Erie. Mr. Martin, his wounded companion, and the young woman, had fallen to the lot of the Shawanese. On the first day's journey, Mr. Martin was ordered to lead a cow, which they had taken from on board one of the plundered vessels. The vast booty which formed the share of this tribe, was in part conveyed on horses found in the vessels, and carried by the Indians, who often loaded Mr. Martin with part of their burden. The Shawanese halted in a beautiful vale, where, under straggling trees, about forty horses were grazing, which in the course of the expedition had been taken from the different travellers, and sent to this spot. The cow was killed the first day, roasted, and devoured: what was not eaten was left behind the next morning, when they set out to renew their journey.

The chief, with eight or ten Indians, mounted the best horses, and placing the young woman upon one of them, left the troop, in order to reach their village before the arrival of the rest.

Mr. Martin and his companion were left with the remainder of the troop, to follow more slowly. About twelve the troop halted. The game killed by the huntsmen was dressed; and the time of their halting was frequently determined by the success of the chace. They smoked their pipes before and after dinner, and then set out again to pursue their journey, until about an hour before night-fall. At this time they stopped to eat their evening meal; then usually smoked a pipe, in profound silence; and afterwards lay down to rest on hides. During the march, some Indians, generally the huntsmen, formed a kind of van-guard, and others brought up the rear, at some distance, to watch whether the troop was pursued; for the Indians are as mistrustful as they are vigilant. The main body marched without any regularity. The van-guard seemed charged, in particular, with the care of looking for game; no more of which they killed than was required for the next meal. The women cook the food; having cut it in large pieces, they put it on stakes driven into the ground; but on lighting their fires they are careful not to endanger the neighbouring trees.

The prisoners took the advantage of the liberty of keeping constantly together. Their melancholy conversation breathed despair, in consequence of having missed the last favourable opportunity of escape; though not wholly unmixed with hope, that some unlooked-for accident would present them with another. Some mistrust was at length entertained at their keeping so close to each other, which was increased by Mr. Martin's inadvertently drawing from his pocket a knife, which he had carefully preserved, for the purpose of cutting the ropes with which he was tied at night, if any favourable opportunity should offer. This occasioned their being again searched, and finally stripped of their breeches, to prevent them from secreting any thing that might facilitate their escape. Instead of the clothes that had been taken from them, they were supplied with short aprons, tied round their hips, and reaching half way down their thighs. But in order effectually to deprive them of the power of concerting measures for regaining their liberty, the chief ordered the troop to separate into two divisions, and one of the two prisoners to accompany each. Fellowship in misfortune had endeared them to each other, and the separation was inexpressibly painful to both. Mr. Martin felt that his companion in adversity was his support, his hope, and the only being with whom he could associate; yet he was deprived of this last resource, and for a time gave himself up to grief and apprehension. But a wise man does not long remain in this situation. Being blessed with an innate firmness, self-possession, and cheerfulness of temper, he determined to overcome his feelings, and beguile the mistrust of his masters by an appearance of serenity. Though the hideous image of a painful death often distressed his mind, he consoled himself with the thought, that not every prisoner is irrevocably doomed by the Indians to suffer death; but that sometimes they employ their captives to assist them in hunting, or adopt them as members of their tribes.

The sameness of the remaining journey was not chequered by any remarkable events. The marches were longer or shorter, in proportion to the game they killed, to the duration of their sleep at noon, and to the delight they found in their pipes. But their length especially depended on the will of the chief, and the advice of the conjurors. Their dreams frequently alter the direction of their journeys. Ignorance and superstition go hand in hand, amongst the people of all countries.

Mr. Martin was treated very capriciously, and sometimes beaten without any cause. On one of these occasions his patience forsook him, and he returned the blows, with the approbation of the whole troop. They said he had proved himself a man, and that none but women submitted to such treatment, without opposition. From that time he thought he was treated with more respect.

In the course of their journey they met a negro laden with whiskey. He was the slave of an Indian, who was hunting in the woods, and had commissioned him to sell the liquor. The negro soon sold his whole stock, and followed the troop, waiting for his master. The Indians halted soon after to enjoy their whiskey with more ease, and to prepare for their entrance into Sandusky,[1] which was distant but a few days' journey, by touching up their colours; each being at liberty to paint himself according to his fancy, except that they all, men and women, wear a certain mark, the badge of their tribe, on their breast or arms: that of the Shawanese is a wolf. The troop was soon joined by the negro's master, and shortly after by two other Indians, who took Mr. Martin by the hand, and conducted him to the chief, whom they seemed to address in a suppliant manner. After an hour's conversation, of which Mr. Martin was evidently the subject, and after the petitioners had presented two gallons of whiskey, Mr. Martin was presented to them, and carried off. Every ray of hope now vanished: he gave himself up to certain destruction: he dared not, for some time, ask his fate of the negro, who understood English, lest he should betray him. He moved on in silent and secret despair: but being no longer able to support the torturing idea of uncertainty, he at last, with great timidity, applied to the negro, who told him, that one of the two Indians to whom he now belonged, had some time ago killed one of the Mingo tribe,[2] and by their laws he was

---

[1] a port in Ohio, on the shore of Lake Erie.

[2] an Iroquoian people then living in western Pennsylvania and Ohio.

bound to furnish a person instead of the one he had slain, or be himself surrendered to the vengeance of his family; that being too poor to buy a prisoner, he had prevailed on the Shawanese, by entreaties and the whiskey, to make him a present of their newly-taken prisoner; and that, therefore, he now belonged to the Mingoes, to whom he would be delivered up in a few days. The prospect of slavery was pleasing, compared with the dread of torture and death, which he had had constantly before his eyes.

He journeyed on with his new masters for several days, in the same manner as with the former, except that he was not tied at night. Unfortunately, they fell in with the Shawanese again; and the chief, become sober, regretted his former generosity; and being the stronger, from the numbers that accompanied him, compelled the Mingoes to resign Mr. Martin to his former misery and anxiety. Some days after they met an Indian driving a horse laden with whiskey, belonging to a tribe residing further to the eastward. The desire of another revel induced the chief to exchange his prisoner for a cask of that intoxicating liquor. He was once more consigned to a new master, who employed him in assisting in the chace; and after hunting some time in the woods, carried him to his town, that bordered on the eastern side of Lake Ontario. Here he had passed several months in captivity, occupied in menial offices, though he was not treated with severity. Having gained the confidence of his masters, by his docility and industry, he had prevailed on them to suffer him to accompany them on a trading expedition to St. John's, in hopes that he might meet with some person who would sympathise with his misfortunes, and redeem him from the slavery under which he groaned. I could not hear this affecting recital without attempting to deliver him; but he had rendered himself so useful to his employers, that, after many proposals that were rejected, I almost despaired of success. At length I prevailed, by the influence of a box of paints, several hundred silver buttons, with other silver trinkets, and two casks of rum. To express the gratitude and satisfaction that were shown by Mr. Martin is impossible. I advanced him a sum of money to enable him to make the best of his way to Philadelphia, where he has relations who are persons of the first respectability; and as he appears to be a man of worth, I have no doubt of receiving remittances from him, to reimburse me for what I have expended on his account. The days which afford such opportunities of succouring the distressed, should be reckoned amongst the happiest of our lives. May you enjoy many of them, and suffer none to escape, without tasting the exquisite pleasure they afford.

Yours, &c.
HENRY FRANKLIN.

Lady Anne Lindsay
1750 – 1825

Lady Anne Lindsay, the eldest child of Anne Dalrymple and Sir James Lindsay, fifth earl of Balcarras, was born on 8 December 1750 and grew up in Fife, Scotland. In 1772 she wrote new words for a traditional Scottish melody with "improper words," "The Bridegroom Greits [Weeps] When the Sun Gaes Doun," sung by an eccentric family friend, Sophy Johnstone. The resulting ballad, "Auld Robin Gray," was printed anonymously in anthologies of Scottish verse, becoming well known not only in Scotland and England but even in France, and provoking a debate about whether it was of ancient or modern origin. Mary Wollstonecraft refers to the ballad in *The Wrongs of Woman*,* where the heroine Maria, imprisoned in a madhouse, hears a "lovely maniac" singing "the pathetic ballad" (chapter 1).

Lady Anne Lindsay moved to Edinburgh with her widowed mother and in 1773 hosted Samuel Johnson. Later she went to London to live with her sister, where she acted as intermediary in the Prince of Wales's affair with Mrs. Fitzherbert, was courted by Henry Dundas, Secretary of State for War and the Colonies, and was emotionally entangled with another government minister, William Windham. In 1793, she married Andrew Barnard, son of the bishop of Limerick, and in 1797 moved with him to the Cape of Good Hope (southern Africa), where—thanks to Dundas—Barnard took up the position of colonial secretary. There, Lady Anne wrote letters to Dundas about her observations and experiences. Together with extracts from her journal, those letters were published in 1924, the same year as her letters to Lord Macartney, Governor of the Cape Colony.

Following her husband's death in Africa in 1807, Lady Anne once again lived with her sister in London, where she entertained a wide literary circle and wrote family history (a journal of her early family life, published in *The Lives of the Lindsays*, 1849) and poetry (published in the *Lays of the Lindsays*, a volume of poetry by Lady Anne and her sisters). She died on 6 May 1825.

When Sir Walter Scott wrote a Preface to "Auld Robin Gray" and its later additions in 1825, he formally recognized Lady Anne Lindsay's authorship. He quotes from a letter of 8 July 1823, in which Lindsay explained to him, "At our fire-side and amongst our neighbours, 'Auld Robin Gray' was always called for. I was pleased in secret with the approbation it met with; but such was my dread of being suspected of writing *anything*, perceiving the shyness it created in those who could write *nothing*, that I carefully kept my own secret." Lindsay claimed to have written the second part at her mother's request, many years after the first. The name Robin Gray was that of an old herdsman on the family estate in Scotland. (A.M.)

Lady Anne Lindsay

Auld Robin Gray; A Ballad, ed. Sir Walter Scott (1825)

Auld Robin Gray

1

When the sheep are in the fauld, when the cows come hame,
When a' the weary world to quiet rest are gane,
The woes of my heart fa' in showers frae my ee,
Unken'd[1] by my gudeman,[2] who soundly sleeps by me.

2

5 Young Jamie loo'd[3] me weel, and sought me for his bride;
But saving ae crown-piece, he'd naething else beside,
To make the crown a pound, my Jamie gaed[4] to sea;
And the crown and the pound, oh! they were baith for me!

3

Before he had been gane a twelvemonth and a day,
10 My father brak his arm, our cow was stown[5] away;
My mother she fell sick—my Jamie was at sea—
And Auld Robin Gray, oh! he came a-courting me.

4

My father cou'dna work—my mother cou'dna spin;
I toil'd day and night, but their bread I cou'dna win;
15 Auld Rob maintain'd them baith, and, wi' tears in his ee,
Said, "Jenny, oh! for their sakes, will you marry me?"

5

My heart it said na, and I look'd for Jamie back;
But hard blew the winds, and his ship was a wrack:
His ship it was a wrack! Why didna Jenny dee?[6]
20 Or, wherefore am I spared to cry out, Woe is me!

6

My father argued sair[7]—my mother didna speak,
But she look'd in my face till my heart was like to break:
They gied[8] him my hand, but my heart was in the sea;
And so Auld Robin Gray, he was gudeman to me.

7

25 I hadna been his wife, a week but only four
When mournfu' as I sat on the stane at my door,
I saw my Jamie's ghaist[9]—I cou'dna think it he,
Till he said, "I'm come hame, my love, to marry thee!"

8

O sair, sair did we greet,[10] and mickle[11] say of a';
30 Ae[12] kiss we took, nae mair[13]—I bad him gang awa.[14]
I wish that I were dead, but I'm no like to dee;
For O, I am but young to cry out, Woe is me!

9

I gang like a ghaist, and I carena much to spin;
I darena think o' Jamie, for that wad be a sin.
35 But I will do my best a gude wife aye to be,
For auld Robin Gray, oh! he is sae kind to me.

CONTINUATION of *Auld Robin Gray*

1

The spring had pass'd over, 'twas summer nae mair,
And trembling were scatter'd the leaves in the air:
"Oh, winter!" said Jenny, "we kindly agree,
For wae[15] looks the sun when he shines upon me."

---

[1] "unknown" (Sc.).
[2] "husband."
[3] "loved."
[4] "went."
[5] "stolen."
[6] "die."
[7] "sorely."
[8] "gave."
[9] "ghost."
[10] "weep."
[11] "much."
[12] "one."
[13] "no more."
[14] "go away."
[15] "sad."

2

5   Nae langer she wept, her tears were a' spent—
    Despair it had come, and she thought it content;
    She thought it content, but her cheek was grown pale,
    And she droop'd like a lily bent down by the hail.

3

    Her father was sad, and her mother was wae,
10 But silent and thoughtfu' was Auld Robin Gray;
    He wander'd his lane, and his face look'd as lean
    As the side of a brae[1] where the torrents have been.

4

    He gaed to his bed, but nae physic wou'd take,
    And often he said, "It is best, for her sake."
15 While Jenny supported his head as he lay,
    Her tears trickled down upon Auld Robin Gray.

5

    "O, greet nae mair, Jenny," said he, wi' a groan;
    "I'm no worth your sorrow—the truth maun[2] be
        known!
    Send round for our neighbours; my hour it draws
        near,
20 And I've that to tell that it's fit a' should hear.

6

    "I've wrong'd her," he said, "but I kent[3] it o'er late;
    I've wrong'd her, and sorrow is speeding my date.
    But a's for the best, since my death will soon free
    A faithfu' young heart, that was ill match'd wi' me.

7

25 "I loved and I courted her mony a day;
    The auld folks were for me, but still she said nae.
    I kentna o' Jamie, nor yet of her vow;
    In mercy forgive me!—'twas I stole the cow!

8

    "I cared not for Crummie; I thought but o' thee!
30 I thought it was Crummie stood 'twixt you and me.

    While she fed your parents, oh! did you not say,
    You never would marry wi' Auld Robin Gray?

9

    "But sickness at hame, and want at the door,
    You gied me your hand, while your heart it was sore.
35 I saw it was sore—why took I her hand?
    Oh! that was a deed to cry shame o'er the land.

10

    "But truth, soon or late, it comes ever to light;
    For Jamie came back, and your cheek it grew white.
    White, white grew your cheek, but aye true unto me;
40 Oh, Jenny, I'm thankfu'—I'm thankfu' to dee!

11

    "Is Jamie come here yet?" and Jamie they saw.
    "I've injured you sair, lad, so leave you my a';
    Be kind to my Jenny, and soon may it be!
    Waste nae time, my dauties,[4] in mourning for me."

12

45 They kiss'd his cauld hands; and a smile o'er his face
    Seem'd hopefu' of being accepted by grace:
    "Oh, doubtna," said Jamie, "forgi'en he will be;
    Wha wou'dna be tempted, my love, to win thee?"

. . . .

13

    The first days were dowie[5] while time slipp'd awa;
50 Though saddest and sairest to Jenny of a',
    Was fearing she cou'dna be honest and right,
    Wi' tears in her ee, while her heart was sae light.

14

    But nae guile had she, and her sorrows away,
    The wife of her Jamie—the tears cou'dna stay.
55 A bonnie wee bairn[6]—the auld folks by the fire;—
    O now she has a' that her heart can desire.

---

[1] "a riverbank."

[2] "must."

[3] "knew."

[4] "darlings, special favourites."

[5] "sad, melancholy."

[6] "child."

SECOND CONTINUATION of *Auld Robin Gray*
Sung by Jenny, softly, at her wheel.

1

The wintry days grew lang, my tears they were a' spent;
May be it was despair I fancied was content.
They said my cheek was wan; I cou'dna look to see—
For, oh! the wee bit glass, my Jamie gaed[1] it me.

2

My father he was sad, my mother dull and wae;
But that which grieved me maist, it was Auld Robin Gray;
Though ne'er a word he said, his cheek said mair than a',
It wasted like a brae o'er which the torrents fa'.

3

He gaed into his bed—nae physic wad he take;
And oft he moan'd, and said, "It's better, for her sake."
At length he look'd upon me, and call'd me his "ain[2] dear,"
And beckon'd round the neighbours, as if his hour drew near.

4

"I've wrong'd her sair," he said, "but kent the truth o'er late;
It's grief for that alone that hastens now my date.
But a' is for the best, since death will shortly free
A young and faithful heart that was ill match'd wi' me.

5

"I loo'd, and sought to win her for mony a lang day;
I had her parents' favour, but still she said me nay.
I knew na Jamie's luve; and oh! it's sair to tell—
To force her to be mine, I steal'd her cow mysel!

6

"O what cared I for Crummie! I thought of nought but thee.
I thought it was the cow stood 'twixt my luve and me.

[1] "gave."
[2] "own."

While she maintain'd ye a', was you not heard to say,
That you wad never marry wi' Auld Robin Gray?

7

"But sickness in the house, and hunger at the door
My bairn gied me her hand, although her heart was sore
I saw her heart was sore—why did I take her hand?
That was a sinfu' deed! to blast a bonnie land.

8

"It wasna very lang ere a' did come to light;
For Jamie he came back, and Jenny's cheek grew white.
My spouse's cheek grew white, but true she was to me;
Jenny! I saw it a'—and oh, I'm glad to dee!

9

"Is Jamie come?" he said; and Jamie by us stood—
"Ye loo each other weel—Oh, let me do some good!
I gie you a', young man—my houses, cattle, kyne,[3]
And the dear wife hersel, that ne'er should hae been mine."

10

We kiss'd his clay-cold hands—a smile came o'er his face:
"He's pardon'd," Jamie said, "before the throne o' grace.
Oh, Jenny! see that smile—forgi'en I'm sure is he,
Wha could withstand temptation when hoping to win thee!"

11

The days at first were dowie; but what was sad and sair,
While tears were in my ee, I kent mysel nae mair;
For, oh! my heart was light as ony bird that flew,
And, wae as a' thing was, it had a kindly hue.

12

But sweeter shines the sun than e'er he shone before,
For now I'm Jamie's wife, and what need I say more?
We hae a wee bit bairn—the auld folks by the fire—
And Jamie, oh! he loo's me up to my heart's desire.

[3] "Cattle" refers to livestock in general, "kyne" to cows.

Catherine Ann Dorset
1750? – 1817?

Catherine Ann Turner was born about 1750, the daughter of Nicholas Turner, a landed gentleman and poet, and Anna Towers Turner. A year or so later, her mother died in childbirth, and she was raised and educated by her aunt Lucy Towers. In about 1770, she married Captain Michael Dorset; they had a son, who followed his father into the army—and also followed his mother in writing poetry. Dorset's first poetic efforts were encouraged by her older sister, Charlotte Smith,* who included about a dozen of her poems in *Conversations Introducing Poetry: Chiefly on Subjects of Natural History. For the Use of Children and Young Persons* (1804). After Dorset's husband died in about 1805, she turned to writing full time. In 1807, she published, anonymously, *The Peacock at Home*, a sequel to *The Butterfly's Ball and the Grasshopper's Feast*, by William Roscoe. Both poems were successful, selling about forty thousand copies between them in a year; some critics thought Dorset's was the better of the two, because of her wit and expertise in natural history. In 1809, she published an expanded version under her own name (it went through twenty-six editions by 1812); she also wrote four further sequels. In addition, she wrote other children's books, poems for adults, and at least one tragedy, two comedies, and four novels. She was still alive in 1816. (D.L.M.)

☙☙☙

from *The Peacock at Home; and Other Poems* (1809)

The Spider[1]

Arachne![2] poor degraded maid!
Doom'd to obscurity's cold shade,
The price your vanity has paid
    Excites my pity.
5 No wonder you should take alarm,
Lest vengeance in a housewife's form,
Your fortress should attack by storm,
    And raze your city.

In truth you are not much befriended,
10 For since with wisdom you contended,
And the stern Goddess so offended,
    Each earthly Pallas
Views you with horror and affright,
Shrinks with abhorrence from your sight,
15 Signing your death-warrant in spite,
    To pity callous.

You were not cast in Beauty's mould,
You have no shard of burnish'd gold,
No painted wing can you unfold
20   With gems bespotted.
Your form disgusting to all eyes,
The Toad in ugliness outvies,
And nature has her homeliest guise
    To you allotted.

25 Yet, if with philosophic eye,
The Young would but observe you ply
Your patient toil, and fortify
    Your habitation;
Spreading your net of slenderest twine,
30 Each artful mesh contriv'd to join,
Strengthening with doubled thread the line
    Of circumvallation.

Methinks your curious progress would
Give them a lecture full as good
35 As some; so little understood,
    So much affected.
And as you dart upon your prey,

---

[1] Cf. Burns, "To a Mouse."*

[2] Arachne challenged Pallas Athena, goddess of wisdom, to a spinning contest. She lost, and to punish her for her presumption, Athena turned her into a spider. See Ovid, *Metamorphoses* 6.

Might they not moralize and say,
Spiders and Men alike betray
    The unprotected?

Might you not tell the light coquette,
Who spreads for some poor youth her net,
Entangling thus without regret
    Her simple lover;
That such ensnarers of the heart,
Might in contemplating your art,
Her own unworthy counterpart
    In you discover?

Your sober habits then compare,
With those bright insects who repair
To sport and frolick thro' the air,
    All gay and winning;
While you your household cares attend,
Your toils no vain pursuits suspend,
But carefully your nets you mend,
    And mind your spinning.

The Butterfly, while life is new,
As he has nothing else to do,
May like a Bond-street beau[1] pursue
    His vagrant courses;
But nature to her creatures kind,
You to an humbler fate consign'd,
Yet taught you in yourself to find
    Your own resources.

---

[1] Bond Street was (and is) a fashionable street in London. A beau ("handsome": Fr.) was a dandy or man-about-town.

Thomas Cary
1751 – 1823

Thomas Cary was born near Bristol in 1751. As a young man, he worked as a journalist and for the East India Company. By 1775, he had immigrated to Montréal, where he worked as a merchant; in 1797, he was appointed secretary to Governor Robert Prescott. Cary made an important contribution to the infrastructure of Canadian letters, opening a circulating library, reading room, and bookstore in Montréal in 1797 and founding the *Quebec Mercury* in 1805. But he is known to have published only one poem other than *Abram's Plains*. He died in Québec City on 29 January 1823. (D.L.M.)

☙☙☙

from *Abram's Plains: A Poem* (1789)[1]

Thy Plains, O *Abram!*[2] and thy pleasing views,
Where, hid in shades, I sit and court the muse,
Grateful I sing.[3] For there, from care and noise,
Oft have I fled to taste thy silent joys:
5   There, lost in thought, my musing passion fed,
Or held blest converse with the learned dead.[4]
Else, like a steed, unbroke to bit or rein,
Courting fair health, I drive across the plain;[5]
The balmy breeze of Zephyrus[6] inhale,
10 Or bare my breast to the bleak northern gale.[7]
Oft, on the green sod lolling as I lay,
Heedless, the grazing herds around me stray:
Close by my side shy songsters fearless hop,
And shyer squirrels the young verdure crop:
15 All take me for some native of the wood,
Or else some senseless block[8] thrown from the flood.
Thy flood Saint Lawrence, in whose copious wave
The Naiades[9] of a thousand riv'lets lave:
Through whom, fresh seas, from mighty urns descend,
20 And, in one stream, their many waters blend.
Thee, first of lakes![10] as *Asia's Caspian* great,
Where congregated streams hold icy state.[11]
Huron, distinguish'd by its thund'ring bay,
Where full-charg'd clouds heav'ns ord'nance ceaseless play.
25 Thee *Michigan*, where learned beavers lave,
And two great tribes[12] divided hold thy wave.
Erie for serpents fam'd, whose noisome breath,
By man inhal'd, conveys the venom'd death.[13]
The streams thence rushing with tremendous roar,
30 Down thy dread fall, *Niagara*, prone pour;
Back foaming, in thick hoary mists, they bound,
The thund'ring noise deafens the country round,
Whilst echo, from her caves, redoubling sends the sound.[14]

---

[1] In his Preface, Cary explains his ideas of descriptive poetry, expresses his preference for that of James Thomson (1700–48) over that of Pope, and says that he studied Pope's *Windsor-Forest* (1713) and Goldsmith's *The Deserted Village** in preparation for writing his own poem.

[2] the Plains of Abraham, south of Québec City, site of the victory of the British, commanded by General James Wolfe (1726–59), over the French, commanded by Louis-Joseph, marquis de Montcalm (1712–59), on 13 September 1759. Both Wolfe and Montcalm were killed.

[3] Cf. Virgil, *Æneid* 1.1; Milton, *Paradise Lost* 1.1–6.

[4] Cf. James Thomson, *Winter* (1726) 432.

[5] Cf. Pope, *An Essay on Man* (1733–34) 1.61–62.

[6] the West Wind.

[7] Cf. Thomson, *Autumn* (1730) 60.

[8] Cf. Shakespeare, *Julius Cæsar* 1.1.35.

[9] water-nymphs.

[10] "Lake *Superior.* One quality of whose waters is to be remarkably cold under the surface." (T.C.)

[11] Cf. Jonathon Carver, *Travels through the Interior Parts of North America in the Years 1766, 1767, and 1768* (1781) 132–33.

[12] the Chippewa and the Ottawa.

[13] Cf. Carver, *Travels* 167–68.

[14] Cf. Thomson, *Spring* (1728) 911–12, and *Winter* 97–99.

'Twixt awe and pleasure, rapt in wild suspense,
35 Giddy, the gazer yields up ev'ry sense.
So have I felt when Handel's heavenly strains,
Choral, announce the great Messiah reigns:[1]
Caught up by sound, I leave my earthly part,
And into something more than mortal start.
40 Now, in *Ontario's* urn, spacious they spread,
By added waters, from *Oswego* fed;
Thence down the *Cataraqui* rolling on,[2]
Or gliding gently to the Naiades' song;
Who, in full chorus, vocal, join their lays,
45 To chant, in chearful carols, Ceres' praise:[3]
Whose yellow harvests, nodding, glad the shore,
Where Dryades,[4] midst wild deserts, reign'd before.
Where prowl'd the wolf, the bear and fox obscene,[5]
Now grateful kine, loud lowing, graze the green.
50 Such are thy blessings peace! superior far
To specious conquests of wild-wasting war.
Destructive war![6] at best the good of few,
Its dire effects whilst millions dearly rue.
How blest the task, to tame the savage soil,
55 And, from the waters, bid the woods recoil!
But oh! a task of more exalted kind,
To arts of peace,[7] to tame the savage mind;
The thirst of blood, in human breasts, to shame,
To wrest, from barb'rous vice, fair virtue's name;
60 Bid tomahawks to ploughshares yield the sway,
And skalping-knives to pruning hooks give way;[8]
In *Circe's* glass bid moderation reign,[9]
And moral virtues humanize the plain!
Here, shelter'd from the storm of civil broils,
65 The loyal sufferer renews his toils:[10]
Again, from the unclog'd responsive earth,
Calls a new patrimony into birth.
By British magnanimity repaid,
The foe triumphant dare no more upbraid:
70 But wish he had so lost so to have gain'd,
Pleas'd with the *now*, the *past* no more had pain'd.
Thus mariners wreck'd on some distant shore
Their homes, their all, sunk in the deep, deplore;
'Till with sad step, they inland bend their way
75 Where mines of gold their loss amply repay.
   Now, o'er rude rocks, rapidly rushing hoarse,
Or through some pent-up pass they speed their course:
Then to the *Utawas* in wedlock bound,[11]
Thy city *Montreal*, the streams surround.
80 Great mart![12] where center all the forest's spoils,
The furry treasures of the hunter's toils:
Within thy walls the painted nations pour,
And smiling wealth on thy blest traders show'r.
And now the wedded streams, with blended force,
85 First canoniz'd,[13] downward direct their course.
Thy waters *Champlain*, next augment the floods,
Champlain, renown'd for high aspiring woods—
Down thy wide stream the naked sylvans glide,
And, in tall masts, of navies swell the pride:
90 Thy navies *Britain*, who bid discord cease,[14]
And awe ambitious monarchs into peace.
Next *Masquinongi* tyrant pikes[15] rolls down,
To please the *haut-gout*[16] of the high-fed town.
Now, spreading to a lake, they drown the soil,
95 Then to their wonted deep-worn bed recoil.

---

[1] the "Hallelujah Chorus" from *Messiah* (1742), the oratorio by George Frederick Handel (1685–1759).

[2] Cf. Carver, *Travels* 170–71. The part of the St. Lawrence west of Montréal was then called the Cataraqui.

[3] Ceres was the Roman goddess of agriculture.

[4] wood-nymphs.

[5] Cf. Pope, *Windsor-Forest* 71.

[6] Cf. Pope, *An Essay on Criticism* (1711) 184.

[7] Cf. Thomson, *Summer* (1727) 875.

[8] Cf. Isaiah 2.4, Micah 4.3.

[9] By giving Odysseus's men a drugged drink ("glass"), Circe transformed them into swine; later, she turned them back into men: Homer, *Odyssey* 10.

[10] After the Revolutionary War, the United Empire Loyalists came to settle in Canada. The British government gave them financial assistance.

[11] The Ottawa flows into the St. Lawrence just above Montréal.

[12] Cf. Carver, *Travels* 99.

[13] That is, the river is now called the St. Lawrence.

[14] Cf. Pope, *Windsor-Forest* 327.

[15] Cf. Pope, *Windsor-Forest* 146.

[16] "fastidious taste" (Fr.).

With added streams, still gath'ring as they run,
Their course directing to the rising sun,
'Till thy strong base, *Quebec*, they rapid lave,
Where British spirits, bold, oppose the wave:
100 For here the swelling far-projected quay,
Gains daily on the wave's extended way:
Such is the ardour of the British breast,
If of that liberty it loves possess'd,
At their command floods back their billows heave,
105 And a bold shore their oozy bottom leave:[1]
High flinty rocks descend to level plains,
Whence, on both sides, commerce a footing gains.
Tall forests their high-waving branches bow,
And yield, submiss, to lay their honors low;
110 The plowing keel the builder artist lays,
Her ribs of oak[2] the rising ship displays;
Now, grown mature, she glides with forward pace,
And eager rushes to the saint's[3] embrace.
Then rising, Venus[4] like, with gay parade,
115 Strait turns kept-mistress to the god of trade.
Thick-matted woods, where rank luxuriance[5] shoots,
Where branch entwines with branch and roots with roots;
Where flies, in myriads,[6] borne on filmy wings,
Unceasing teaze, with tumifying stings.
120 Where the dark adder and envenom'd snake,
In curling folds, lurk in the shelt'ring brake.
There, guileful, charm with facinating eyes,
Or, fir'd to wrathful vengeance, rattling rise;
With crest erect, quick darting on the prey,
125 Swift as through ether speeds the solar ray.[7]
Shocking to thought! but nature good and wise,
Where poison shoots its antidote[8] supplies.
Deep hid in mists, eternal glooms where reign,
Nor once light enters but with utmost pain:
130 Tho' hard the task, yet bare the soil shall lay,
And, unobstructed, shine the lamp of day.
Here sleepy *Saint Charles*, scarcely seen to flow,
His mazy current solemn yields and slow;
Whilst, a strong contrast strikingly to form,
135 His stream *Montmorenci* sends down in storm:
From the dread precipice foaming it pours,
High smoking round in clouds of silver show'rs.
Here might secure *Britannia*'s navy ride,
Nor danger dread from wind or swelling tide:
140 Here, like the ant, commerce, with pregnant sails,
Busy, of summer-months herself avails;
For long, too long, here dreary winter reigns,
And bars the liquid way with icy chains.
Hence, as they flow, they stretch their spacious bed,
145 And, here and there, an isle uplifts its head;
Whilst from *Malbay*, the mill's remorseless sound,
And piteous groans of rending firrs, resound;[9]
Within whose rind, I shudder while I tell,
Spirits of warriors close imprison'd dwell,
150 Who in cold blood, butcher'd a valiant foe,
For which, transform'd to weeping firrs, they grow:[10]
Down their tall trunks trickling the tears distill,
'Till last the ax and saw groaning they feel.
Next the rough *Saguenay*, 'tween rosy[11] shores,
155 From plenteous urns, his waters roaring pours;
The current of the master flood impedes,
Whilst *Taddusac*'s rich spoils he grateful cedes.

---

[1] Cf. Exodus 14.21; Pope, *Windsor-Forest* 329.

[2] Cf. Thomson, *Autumn* 131.

[3] "Saint Lawrence." (T.C.)

[4] Roman goddess of love.

[5] Cf. Goldsmith, *The Deserted Village* 353.*

[6] Cf. Thomson, *Spring* 121.

[7] Cf. Carver, *Travels* 479–85; Milton, *Paradise Lost* 9.499–502.

[8] "A striking instance of this, is the Rattle-snake plaintain; which grows where those reptiles abound. When the bite of the snake is most venomous, which is in the dog-days, the plant is in its greatest perfection. The person bit has but to chew the leaf and apply it to the wound, at the same time swallowing some of the juice. This seldom fails of preventing every dangerous symptom." (T.C.) Cf. Carver, *Travels* 517–18.

[9] The sawmill at Malbaie, about 130 km (80 miles) downstream from Québec City, was one of the oldest in Québec (1687).

[10] No such Native Canadian legend has been identified. Cf. the daughters of Clymene in Ovid, *Metamorphoses* 2; the wood of the suicides in Dante, *Inferno* 13; and Spenser, *The Faerie Queen* 1.1.9.

[11] "A great number of wild roses grow on its banks." (T.C.)

Where rules, gainsay it envy, if you can,
The best of nature's works—an honest man.[1]
160 Thence coursing on, the wide-spread Gulph they gain,
'Till lost, at length, they swell the distant main.
First laving on their way the fatten'd shore,
That butchery of seals, bleak *Labradore*;
Where dwarfish *Esquimaux*, with small pig's eyes,
165 At cook'ry sick, raw seal and rank oil prize.
Let city epicures their sauces boast,
And fancy excellence in boil'd and roast:
His culinary art let Dillon[2] try,
In soupes and jellies with fam'd Horton vie;
170 Let, on the board, Le Moine's[3] *ragouts* high smoke,
Believe me friends, at best, 'tis all a joke.
Judgment in eating! where's the standard plac'd?
Where but in each man's fickle froward taste.
What then is luxury, ye lib'ral say,
175 What but to pamper each his sep'rate way?
Let cits on turtle gormandize and cloy,
The courtier ortolans and creams enjoy;
The first with heavy port crown his repast,
Whilst light champagne exhilirates the last:
180 Not with more *gout* dines citizen or beau,
Than on his seal and oil, our *Esquimaux*;
Nor less his stomach at their dainties turns,
Than each, with loathing, his strong viands spurns.
Habit forms all, taste, gesture, action, thought,
185 The man ripe rises as the stripling's taught;
Ductile as soften'd wax the human soul,
Twig-like, insensibly stoops to controul:
By rules, but more by great example, led,
He rises Jew, Turk, Christian, as he's bred.
190 Since then, we own, man is but moulded clay,
Life's journey let each travel his own way.
And since heaven's roofs beyond all limits rise,
And a free passage opens through the skies;
Why not suppose there's ample room for all,
195 Be life resign'd with or without a call?

What tho' no mines their gold pour through thy stream,
Nor shining silver from thy waters gleam;
Equal to these, the forests yield their spoils,
And richly pay the skilful hunter's toils.
200 The beaver's silken fur to grace the head,
And, on the soldier's front assurance spread;
The martin's sables to adorn the fair,
And aid the silk-worm to set off her air.
Gems of *Golconda* or *Potosi*'s mines,[4]
205 Than these not more assist her eyes' designs.
The jetty fox to majesty adds grace,
And of grave justice dignifies the place;
The bulky buffalo, tall elk, the shaggy bear,
Huge carriboo, fleet moose, the swift-foot deer,
210 Gaunt wolf, amphibious otter, have their use,
And to thy worth, O first of floods! conduce.
For thee the sylvans of the forest bleed,
And, to the ax, their long-worn honors cede.
The sturdy oak, the lofty mountain-pine,
215 Their branching limbs and trunks mature resign;
Whilst Ceres, bounteous, from her gran'ries pours,
On craving realms, her grain in golden showers.
Nor is it want of climate or of soil
Thy shores not more the Muscovite's yet foil:
220 Our infant world asks but time's fost'ring hand,
It's faculties must by degrees expand.
Nor must thy own resources be past by,
Resources that within thy bosom lie;
The heavy porpus and the silly seal,
225 Their forfeit lives yield to the club or steel;
Soon of their skins and fat, reduc'd to oil,
The skilful fishers the dead victims spoil.
Here too the whale rolls his unwieldy form,
Laughs at the blust'ring winds and mocks the storm;
230 Gamesome, the billows far behind him throws,
And from his nostrils, a salt tempest blows:
Till, close beset, swift flies the barbed dart,
Down prone the monster dives to shun the smart;
The fishers, active, yield the smoking line,
235 The boats, like light'ning, cut the liquid brine;

---

[1] Cf. Pope, *An Essay on Man* 4.248.

[2] Richard Dillon, proprietor of the Québec Hotel.

[3] Jacques Lemoine, a tavern-keeper. (Horton has not been identified.)

[4] Cf. Thomson, *Summer* 871. Golconda, India, was noted for diamonds; Potosi, Bolivia, for silver.

Oft-times borne down beneath the briny wave,
Both boats and men share one wide watry grave:
His onward way, his doubles they pursue,
'Till, spent his strength, he panting floats in view;
240 Midst seas of blood wrathful his nostrils smoke,
An isle, his bare broad back lies to the stroke.
Now strong harpooners dart the iron death,
The monster force to yield his forfeit breath:
E'en while the waves he lashes into storm,
245 A monstrous mass floats motionless his form.
The grampus, of less bulk, stays his swift course,
Arrested on his way by iron force.
The fierce sea-cow, tho' cloth'd in stoutest mail,
Finds, 'gainst man's arts, his strength of small avail.
250 The salmon, cod, thy wave in myriads pours,
And, on far worlds, plenty redundant show'rs.
Next these the Naiades yield, for home supply,
Numbers, of various name and various dye.
The bass, rich flavor'd, high to pamper lust,
255 The pout or cat of no less luscious gust;
The speckled trout choice native of the lake,
'Tis thine the skilful angler's art to wake.
Thee silver white,[1] and thou bedropt with gold,
The dusky eel, in circling volumes roll'd;[2]
260 The bony shad, the poor man's bounteous friend,
E'er summer-suns dry roads and plenty send.
The weighty sturgeon, rank with native oil,
High fed from the fat river's slimy soil;
The autumn smelt, whose constant bite, tho' small,
265 E'er fix'd the ice, relief affords to all;
The winter tomi-cod—when with feeble blaze,
From the bleak archer, Sol shoots oblique rays;[3]
Then, from the ice-cot, on the frozen stream,
Through murky night, like meteors, fires gleam;
270 There, gather'd crouds, from the pierc'd solid flood,
With fleshy baits, attract the finny brood.[4]

Here hill and dale diversify the scene,[5]
There pensile woods[6] cloth'd with eternal green;
The russet plain[7] with thorny brambles spread,
275 Where clust'ring haws deep blush a ruddy red;
The distant wood, wide-waving to the breeze,
Where shining villas peep through crowded trees;
Here babbling brooks gurgle adown the glade,
There rise mementos of the soldier's spade;
280 Where on the green-sward oft incamp'd they lay,
Seen by the rising and the setting ray.
Here, in life's vigour, *Wolfe* resign'd his breath,
And, conqu'ring sunk to the dark shades of death:
When threatning *Gallia*, with incroaching sway,
285 With frowning forts, dar'd bar th' *Ohio*'s way;[8]
Hoping, alone, the chrystal nymphs to share,
And from their smiles the sons of *Britain* tear.
Presumptuous *Gallia!* rash was the design,
Britons not easily the fair[9] resign.
290 This truth, Lake *George*, loudly thy shores resound,
Where the brave *Johnson*[10] was with laurels crown'd;
When smiling conquest hail'd him not less great
In fighting fields than in his peaceful seat:
That seat where *Eden*, tranplanted arose,
295 Scene of the hero's glorious repose.[11]
His fame, in arms, let *Dieskau*'s ghost tell,
Who, to his sword, a bleeding captive fell.
Is worth hereditary? ask his heir—
Soft, muse—the cheek of conscious virtue spare.
300 But chiefly here presumption's price she paid,
And, in the dust, her faded honors laid;

---

[1] "The White-fish, and what the Canadians call the *Poison-doré* or Gold-fish." (T.C.)

[2] Cf. Pope, *Windsor-Forest* 143–44.

[3] The "bleak archer" is Sagittarius, the sign of the Zodiac for 22 November–21 December. For "oblique rays," cf. Thomson, *Winter* 43–47.

[4] Cf. Pope, *Windsor-Forest* 139; Thomson, *Spring* 395.

[5] Cf. Pope, *Windsor-Forest* 11–16.

[6] Cf. William Shenstone (1714–63), "Ruined Abbey" 6.

[7] Cf. Pope, *Windsor-Forest* 23.

[8] To maintain control over the Ohio basin, the French had built a series of forts between their possessions in Canada and Louisiana.

[9] "Besides the allusion to the water-nymphs the reader will recollect that the Ohio is called in English the *Fair River*." (T.C.)

[10] "Sir William Johnson." (T.C.) In 1755, the British, commanded by Johnson (c.1715–74), defeated the French, commanded by Jean-Armand, Baron Dieskau (1701–67), near Lake George. Dieskau was captured.

[11] not his grave but his estate, Johnson Hall, near Johnston, New York.

When up the heights, great *Wolfe* his vet'rans led,[1]
Panting, the level lawn they dauntless tread:
As bold they rise the broad battalion forms,
The gain'd ascent, for fight, their bosom warms;
When soon, in view, appears the num'rous foe,
With arms bright-flashing from the plains below:
With ardour glowing in his country's cause,
His hostile sword the chief intrepid draws;
The troops, to conquest, now inspiring cheers,
High beat their breasts, strangers to abject fears:
A chief no more he leads on foot the line,—
Thus, with his soldiers' fate, his hopes combine.
The deaf'ning drums the charge loud rattling sound,
The charge th' opposing cliffs thund'ring rebound.
The battle rages, bullets, charg'd with fate,
The hungry soil, with human victims, sate.
Attending fate, grim death, with hasty stride,
Triumphs a victor over either side.
Too sure, alas! the leaden vengeance flies,
And on the chief its force repeated tries.
Heedless of wounds, he hides the purple flood,
His courage kindling with the loss of blood;
'Till spent, at length, nature's oblig'd to yield,
He falls ere fix'd the fortune of the field.
Whilst, o'er his sight, spreads the thick veil of death,
And life suspended stays the struggling breath,
Anxious, he hears the shout—"they fly, they fly,"
"Who fly?" "The foe"—"contented then I die."—
Whilst death exulting triumphs o'er his clay,
His name fame echoes through the realms of day.
If so much praise to conquest then be due,
Can man less honor saving wisdom shew?
When here his tatter'd troops *Montgom'ry* led,[2]
Of glorious spoils by hopes delusive fed;
Whose prudence, without rashness, wise maintain'd
What *Wolfe*, with loss of life, so bravely gain'd?
Praise, double praise, surely to him is due,
Who, tender saves man's blood and conquers too.
O never more may hostile arms distain,
With human gore, the verdure of the plain!
False is the fame on man's destruction rais'd,
As well might famines, plagues, or storms be prais'd.
Not that I wish the patriot to restrain
The noble ardour of his boiling vein,
When rash ambition, soaring with high flight,
Studious alone of greatness, not of right;
By artifice, big threats, or thund'ring arm,
His bosom for his country, dares alarm:
Far, far be from me the degrading thought,
'Twere virtue, principle, to set at naught.
No, be of heav'n, of man, the wretch accurs'd,
Of grov'ling reptiles, void of soul, the worst,
Who his best blood, defensive, would not show'r,
To stay the torrent of incroaching pow'r![3]
…

[1] In 1759 the British scaled the Heights of Abraham to take the French by surprise.

[2] On 31 December 1775, General Richard Montgomery (1738–75) led the American forces in an attack on Québec. They were repulsed by the British, commanded by Major-General Sir Guy Carleton, later Lord Dorchester (1724–1808), and Montgomery was killed.

[3] The remaining 232 lines criticize the Catholic church, describe Québec City and the surrounding countryside, assure the inhabitants that they are lucky to have been conquered by Britain, reminisce further about the Revolutionary War, describe a Québec winter and then, to conclude, a sunset and night.

Philip Freneau
1752 – 1832

Philip Freneau was born in New York City on 2 January 1752, the son of Pierre Fresneau, an importer, and Agnes Watson Fresneau. He was educated at a New Jersey grammar school and the College of New Jersey (later Princeton), where he allegedly roomed with James Madison. His first publication was *A Poem, on the Rising Glory of America* (1772), written in collaboration with another college friend. As tensions between Britain and the colonies increased, he wrote a series of patriotic poems; but in early 1776, he left for a two-year stay in the Caribbean, as secretary to a planter on Santa Cruz. On his return, he joined the New Jersey militia, serving as a sailor. In May 1780, he was captured by the British and suffered a serious illness in prison; the experience inspired a long poem, *The British Prison-Ship* (1781). After his recovery, and the end of the war, he worked as a merchant captain, sailing the East Coast and the Caribbean. In April 1790, he married Eleanor Forman; they had four daughters. For most of the 1790s, he worked as a journalist, attaining such prominence as editor of the *National Gazette* that Washington denounced him as "that rascal Freneau" and Jefferson credited him with "sav[ing] our Constitution, which was galloping fast into Monarchy." Except for another period at sea (1802–07), he spent the rest of his life on his mother's estate, Mount Pleasant, New Jersey, and, after it burned down in 1818, in neighbouring Freehold. He was always a prolific poet and published his last collection in 1815. On 18 December 1832, at the age of eighty, he was caught in a snowstorm and died of exposure. (D.L.M.)

---

from *Poems Written between the Years 1768 & 1794* (1795)

The Indian Burying-Ground

In spite of all the learn'd have said,
I still my old opinion keep;
The *posture*, that *we* give the dead,
Points out the soul's eternal sleep.

5 Not so the ancients of these lands—
The Indian, when from life releas'd,
Again is seated with his friends,
And shares again the joyous feast.[1]

His imag'd birds, and painted bowl,
10 And ven'son, for a journey dress'd,
Bespeak the nature of the soul,
ACTIVITY, that knows no rest.

His bow, for action ready bent,
And arrows, with a head of stone,
15 Can only mean that life is spent,
And not the finer essence gone.

Thou, stranger, that shalt come this way,
No fraud upon the dead commit—
Observe the swelling turf, and say
20 They do not *lie*, but here they *sit*.

Here still a lofty rock remains,
On which the curious eye may trace
(Now wasted, half, by wearing rains)
The fancies of a ruder race.

25 Here still an aged elm aspires,
Beneath whose far-projecting shade
(And which the shepherd still admires)
The children of the forest play'd!

---

[1] "The North American Indians bury their dead in a sitting posture; decorating the corpse with wampum, the images of birds, quadrupeds, &c: And (if that of a warrior) with bows, arrows, tomhawks, and other military weapons." (P.F.)

There oft a restless Indian queen
(Pale *Shebah*,[1] with her braided hair)
And many a barbarous form is seen
To chide the man that lingers there.

By midnight moons, o'er moistening dews,
In vestments for the chace array'd,
The hunter still the deer pursues,
The hunter and the deer, a shade!

And long shall timorous fancy see
The painted chief, and pointed spear,
And Reason's self shall bow the knee
To shadows and delusions here.

The Wild Honey Suckle[2]

Fair flower, that dost so comely grow,
Hid in this silent, dull retreat,
Untouch'd thy honey'd blossoms blow,
Unseen thy little branches greet:
    No roving foot shall find thee here,
    No busy hand provoke a tear.

By Nature's self in white array'd,
She bade thee shun the vulgar eye,
And planted here the guardian shade,
And sent soft waters murmuring by;
    Thus quietly thy summer goes,
    Thy days declining to repose.

Smit with those charms, that must decay,
I grieve to see your future doom;
They died—nor were those flowers less gay,
The flowers that did in Eden bloom;
    Unpitying frosts, and Autumn's power
    Shall leave no vestige of this flower.

From morning suns and evening dews
At first thy little being came:
If nothing once, you nothing lose,
For when you die you are the same;
    The space between, is but an hour,
    The frail duration of a flower.

George the Third's Soliloquy[3]

What mean these dreams, and hideous forms that rise
Night after night, tormenting to my eyes—
No real foes these horrid shapes can be,
But thrice as much they vex and torture me.
    How curs'd is he,—how doubly curs'd am I—
Who lives in pain, and yet who dares not die;
To him no joy this world of Nature brings,
In vain the wild rose blooms, the daisy springs.
Is this a prelude to some new disgrace,
Some baleful omen to my name and race—!
It may be so—ere mighty Cesar died
Presaging Nature felt his doom, and sigh'd;[4]
A bellowing voice through midnight groves was heard,
And threatening ghosts at dusk of eve appear'd—
Ere Brutus fell, to adverse fates a prey,
His evil genius met him on the way,[5]
And so may mine!—but who would yield so soon
A prize, some luckier hour may make my own?—
Shame seize my crown, ere such a deed be mine—
No—to the last my squadrons shall combine,
And slay my foes, while foes remain to slay,
Or *heaven* shall grant me one successful day.
    Is there a robber close in Newgate[6] hemm'd,
Is there a cut-throat, fetter'd and condemn'd?
Haste, loyal slaves, to George's standard come,
Attend his lectures when you hear the drum;
Your chains I break—for better days prepare,
Come out, my friends, from prison and from care,
Far to the west I plan your desperate sway,
There 'tis no sin to ravage, burn, and slay
There, without fear, your bloody aims pursue,
And show mankind what English thieves can do.

---

[1] See 1 Kings 10.1–10; 2 Chronicles 9.1–9.

[2] *Azalea viscosa*, also known as the swamp honeysuckle.

[3] George III (1738–1820) reigned from 1760.

[4] Cf. Shakespeare, *Julius Cæsar* 2.2.1–82; *Hamlet* 1.1.113–25.

[5] Cf. Shakespeare, *Julius Cæsar* 5.5.17–20.

[6] prison in London.

That day, when first I mounted to the throne,
I swore to let all foreign foes alone.
35 Through love of peace to terms did I advance,
And made, they say, a shameful league with France.¹
But different scenes rise horrid to my view,
I charg'd my hosts to plunder and subdue—
At first, indeed, I thought short wars to wage
40 And sent some jail-birds to be led by *Gage*,²
For 'twas but right, that those we mark'd for slaves
Should be reduc'd by cowards, fools, and knaves:
Awhile, directed by his feeble hand,
Those *troops* were kick'd and pelted through the land,
45 Or starv'd in Boston, curs'd the unlucky hour
They left their dungeons for that fatal shore.³

France aids them now, a desperate game I play,
And hostile Spain will do the same, they say;
My armies vanquish'd, and my heroes fled,
50 My people murmuring, and my commerce dead,
My shatter'd navy pelted, bruis'd, and clubb'd,
By Dutchmen bullied, and by Frenchmen drubb'd,
My name abhorr'd, my nation in disgrace,
How should I act in such a mournful case!
55 My hopes and joys are vanish'd with my coin,
My ruin'd army, and my lost Burgoyne!⁴
What shall I do—confess my labours vain,
Or whet my tusks, and to the charge again!
But where's my force—my choicest troops are fled,
60 Some thousands crippled, and a myriad dead—
If I were own'd the boldest of mankind,
And hell with all her flames inspir'd my mind,
Could I at once with Spain and France contend,
And fight the *rebels*, on the world's green end?—
65 The pangs of *parting* I can ne'er endure,
Yet *part* we must, and part to meet no more!

Oh, blast this *Congress*, blast each upstart STATE,
On whose commands ten thousand captains wait;
From various climes that dire *Assembly* came,
70 True to their trust, as hostile to my fame;
'Tis these, ah these, have ruin'd half my sway,
Disgrac'd my arms, and led my slaves astray—
Curs'd be the day, when first I saw the sun,
Curs'd be the hour, when I these wars begun:
75 The fiends of darkness then possess'd my mind,
And powers unfriendly to the human kind.
To wasting grief, and sullen rage a prey,
To *Scotland's* utmost verge I'll take my way,
There with eternal storms due concert keep,
80 And while the billows rage, as fiercely weep—
Ye highland lads, my rugged fate bemoan,
Assist me with one sympathizing groan;
For late I find the nations are my foes,
I must submit, and that with bloody nose,
85 Or, like our James, fly basely from the state,
Or share, what still is worse—old *Charles's* fate.⁵

To Sir Toby, a Sugar-Planter in the Interior Parts of Jamaica

If there exists a HELL—the case is clear—
Sir Toby's slaves enjoy that portion here:
Here are no blazing brimstone lakes—'tis true,
But kindled RUM full often burns as blue,⁶
5 In which some fiend (whom NATURE must detest)
Steeps TOBY's name, and brands poor CUDJOE's⁷ breast.

Here, whips on whips excite a thousand fears,
And mingled howlings vibrate on my ears:
Here Nature's plagues abound, of all degrees,
10 Snakes, scorpions, despots, lizards, centipees—
No art, no care escapes the busy lash,
All have their dues, and all are paid in cash:
The lengthy cart-whip guards this tyrant's reign,

---

¹ The Treaty of Paris (1763) ended the Seven Years' War.

² Thomas Gage (1719/20–87), English general, whose attempt to seize military supplies at Concord led to the battles of Lexington and Concord, 19 April 1775; he resigned his command that October. Freneau satirized him in *General Gage's Soliloquy* and *General Gage's Confession* (1775).

³ Washington besieged Boston in July 1775; the British evacuated it on 17 March 1776.

⁴ John Burgoyne (1722–92), English general, surrendered to the Americans at Saratoga, 17 October 1777.

⁵ James II (1633–1701) fled to France in 1688; his father, Charles I (1600–49), had been beheaded for treason.

⁶ "This passage has a reference to the custom of branding the slaves in the islands, as a mark of property.—" (P.F.)

⁷ a stereotypical name for a slave.

And cracks like pistols from the fields of CANE.
15   Ye POWERS that form'd these wretched tribes, relate,
What had they done, to merit such a fate?
Why were they brought from EBOE's sultry waste[1]
To see the plenty which they must not taste—
Food, which they cannot buy, and dare not steal,
20 Yams and potatoes!—many a scanty meal!
One, with a jibbet wakes his negro's fears,
One, to the wind-mill nails him by the ears;
One keeps his slave in dismal dens, unfed,
One puts the wretch in pickle, ere he's dead;
25 This, from a tree suspends him by the thumbs,
That, from his table grudges even the crumbs!
   O'er yon' rough hills a tribe of females go,
Each with her gourd, her infant, and her hoe,
Scorch'd by a sun, that has no mercy here,
30 Driven by a devil, that men call Overseer:
In chains twelve wretches to their labour haste,
Twice twelve I see with iron collars grac'd:—

Are these the joys that flow from vast domains!
Is wealth thus got, Sir Toby, worth your pains—
35 Who would that wealth, on terms like these, possess,
Where all we see is pregnant with distress;
ANGOLA's[2] natives scourg'd by hireling hands,
And toil's hard earnings shipp'd to foreign lands?
   Talk not of blossoms, and your endless spring—
40 No joys, no smiles, such scenes of misery bring!
Though Nature here has every blessing spread,
Poor is the labourer—and how meanly fed!
Here, Stygian paintings all their shades renew,
Pictures of woe, that VIRGIL's pencil drew:[3]
45 Here, surly Charons make their annual trip,
And souls arrive in every Guinea ship[4]
To find what hells this western world affords,
Plutonian scourges, and Tartarian lords;—[5]
Where they who pine, and languish to be free
50 Must climb the tall cliffs of the LIGUANEE,[6]
Beyond the clouds in sculking haste repair,
And hardly safe from brother butchers there![7]

---

[1] It is now part of Nigeria.

[2] a Portuguese colony in West Africa, a common source of slaves.

[3] In Virgil's *Æneid* 6, Aeneas visits the underworld. *Télémaque* (*The Adventures of Telemachus*, 1699), by François de Salignac de la Mothe Fénelon (1651–1715), tells the story of Telemachus's search for his father, Ulysses (Odysseus). "Stygian" (43): pertaining to the Styx, one of the rivers of the underworld. Charon (45) is the ferryman of the dead.

[4] slave ship from West Africa.

[5] Pluto (L.) or Hades (Gr.) is the lord of the underworld; Tartarus is the lowest part of the underworld, reserved for the exceptionally wicked.

[6] a mountain range north of Kingston.

[7] "Alluding to the independent Negroes in the Blue-Mountains; who, for a stipulated reward deliver up every fugitive that falls into their hands." (P.F.)

Frances Burney
1752 – 1840

Frances Burney was born in King's Lynn, Norfolk, on 13 June 1752, fourth of the six children of Charles Burney, an organist and pioneering musicologist, and Esther Sleepe Burney. When she was ten, her mother died. At about the same age, she began "scribbling ... in private," but on her fifteenth birthday, apparently because her father disapproved of the activity, she burned everything she had written. She published her first novel, *Evelina* (1778), in secret, with the help of her brother Charles; she was paid twenty guineas for it. Six months after publication, she revealed her authorship to her father; pleased, he introduced her to Samuel Johnson. Her second novel, *Cecilia*, appeared in 1782. In 1786, at the urging of her father, she became second keeper of the robes to Queen Charlotte, but the life of a lady-in-waiting made her so depressed that she became ill, and she was allowed to resign in 1791. Burney took an interest in the plight of the émigrés from Revolutionary France; she met several, including Talleyrand and Madame de Staël, and in July 1793, she married one, Alexandre Jean-Baptiste Piochard d'Arblay. Alexander, their only child, was born in December 1794. Since d'Arblay was impoverished, the family depended on Burney's writing; she published her third novel, *Camilla*, in 1796, earning two thousand pounds (d'Arblay had worked as her copyist). In addition to her fiction, Burney was a prolific and brilliant writer of letters and journals. She also wrote a number of plays, but was unable to overcome her father's conviction that it was improper for her to have a comedy produced; one tragedy, *Edwy and Elgiva*, was produced (1795), but it was a failure. In 1801, d'Arblay returned to France; Burney joined him in 1802, and they lived there until 1815. While there, she was diagnosed with breast cancer and underwent a mastectomy, without anæsthetic, in 1811. Burney published her last novel, *The Wanderer*, in 1814, earning fifteen hundred pounds. After Waterloo, the d'Arblays returned to England and settled in Bath. D'Arblay died of an obstruction of the bowels in 1818, and Alexander, to his mother's great distress, died of influenza in 1837. Burney herself died on 6 January 1840—the fortieth anniversary of the death of her beloved sister Susanna. (D.L.M.)

from *The Journals and Letters of Fanny Burney (Madame d'Arblay),* ed. Joyce Hemlow et al. (1975)

from *Letter to Esther Burney,*[1] 22 March–June 1812

Separated as I have now so long—long been from my dearest Father—BROTHERS—SISTERS—NIECES, & NATIVE FRIENDS, I would spare, at least, their kind hearts any grief for me but what they must inevitably feel in reflecting upon the sorrow of such an absence to one so tenderly attached to all her first and for-ever so dear & regretted ties—nevertheless, if they should hear that I have been dangerously ill from any hand but my own, they might have doubts of my perfect recovery which my own alone can obviate. And how can I hope they will escape hearing what has reached Seville to the South, and Constantinople to the East? from both I have had messages—yet nothing could urge me to this communication till I heard that M. de Boinville[2] had written it to his Wife, without any precaution, because in ignorance of my plan of silence. Still I must hope it may never travel to my dearest Father—But to You, my beloved Esther, who, living more in the World, will surely hear it ere long, to you I will write the whole history, certain that, from the moment you know any evil has befallen me your kind kind heart will be constantly anxious to learn its extent, & its circumstances, as well as its termination.

About August, in the year 1810, I began to be annoyed by a small pain in my breast, which went on augmenting from week to week, yet, being rather heavy

---

[1] Burney's sister (1749–1832).

[2] Jean-Baptiste Chastel de Boinville (1756–1813).

than acute, without causing me any uneasiness with respect to consequences: Alas, '*what was the ignorance?*' The most sympathising of Partners, however, was more disturbed: not a start, not a wry face, not a movement that indicated pain was unobserved, & he early conceived apprehensions to which I was a stranger. He pressed me to see some Surgeon; I revolted from the idea, & hoped, by care & warmth, to make all succour unnecessary.... M. Dubois,[1] the most celebrated surgeon of France, was then appointed accoucheur to the Empress, & already lodged in the Tuilleries, & in constant attendance: but nothing could slacken the ardour of M. d'A. to obtain the first advice. Fortunately for his kind wishes, M. Dubois had retained a partial regard for me from the time of his former attendance, &, when applied to through a third person, he took the first moment of liberty, granted by a *promenade* taken by the Empress, to come to me. It was now I began to perceive my real danger, M. Dubois gave me a prescription to be pursued for a month, during which time he could not undertake to see me again, & pronounced nothing—but uttered so many charges to me to be tranquil, & to suffer no uneasiness, that I could not but suspect there was room for terrible inquietude. My alarm was encreased by the non-appearance of M. d'A. after his departure. They had remained together some time in the Book room, & M. d'A. did not return—till, unable to bear the suspence, I begged him to come back. He, also, sought then to tranquilize me—but in words only; his looks were shocking! his features, his whole face displayed the bitterest woe. I had not, therefore, much difficulty in telling myself what he endeavoured not to tell me—that a small operation would be necessary to avert evil consequences!—Ah, my dearest Esther, for this I felt no courage—my dread & repugnance, from a thousand reasons *besides* the pain, almost shook all my faculties, &, for some time, I was rather confounded & stupified than affrighted.—Direful, however, was the effect of this interview; the pains become quicker & more violent, & the hardness of the spot affected encreased. I took, but vainly, my proscription,

& every symtom grew more serious.... A formal consultation now was held, of Larrey, Ribe, & Moreau[2]—&, in fine, I was formally condemned to an operation by all Three. I was as much astonished as disappointed—for the poor breast was no where discoloured, & not much larger than its healthy neighbour. Yet I felt the evil to be deep, so deep, that I often thought if it could not be dissolved, it could only with life be extirpated. I called up, however, all the reason I possessed, or could assume, & told them—that if they saw no other alternative, I would not resist their opinion & experience:—the good Dr. Larrey, who, during his long attendance had conceived for me the warmest friendship, had now tears in his Eyes; from my dread he had expected resistance. He proposed again calling in M. Dubois. No, I told him, if I could not by himself be saved, I had no sort of hope elsewhere, &, if it must be, what I wanted in courage should be supplied by Confidence. The good man was now dissatisfied with himself, and declared I ought to have the First & most eminent advice his Country could afford; ...

All hope of escaping this evil being now at an end, I could only console or employ my Mind in considering how to render it less dreadful to M. d'A. M. Dubois had pronounced 'il faut s'attendre à souffrir, Je ne veux pas vous trompez—Vous Souffrirez—vous souffrirez *beaucoup*!—'[3] M. Ribe had *charged* me to cry! to withhold or restrain myself might have seriously bad consequences, he said. M. Moreau, in ecchoing this injunction, enquired whether I had cried or screamed at the birth of Alexander—Alas, I told him, it had not been possible to do otherwise; Oh then, he answered, there is no fear!— What terrible inferences were here to be drawn! I desired, therefore, that M. d'A. might be kept in ignorance of the day till the operation should be over. To this they agreed, except M. Larrey, with high approbation: M. Larrey looked dissentient, but was silent. M. Dubois protested he would not undertake to act, after what he had seen of the agitated spirits of M. d'A. if he

---

[1] Antoine Dubois (1756–1837), obstetrician to Marie-Louise (1791–1847), consort of Napoleon.

[2] Dominique-Jean Larrey (1766–1842), surgeon; François Ribes (1765–1845), physician and anatomist; and Jacques-Louis Moreau de la Sarthe (1771–1826), physician.

[3] "You must expect to suffer. I do not wish to deceive you—you will suffer—you will suffer *greatly*!"

were present: nor would he suffer me to know the time myself over night; I obtained with difficulty a promise of 4 hours warning, which were essential to me for sundry regulations....

... One morning—the last of September, 1811, while I was still in Bed, & M. d'A. was arranging some papers for his office, I received a Letter written by M. de Lally[1] to a Journalist, in vindication of the honoured memory of his Father against the assertions of Mad^e du Deffand. I read it aloud to My Alexanders, with tears of admiration & sympathy, & then sent it by Alex: to its excellent Author, as I had promised the preceding evening. I then dressed, aided, as usual for many months, by my maid, my right arm being condemned to total inaction; but not yet was the grand business over, when another Letter was delivered to me—another, indeed!—'twas from M. Larrey, to acquaint me that at 10 o'clock he should be with me, properly accompanied, & to exhort me to rely as much upon his sensibility & his prudence, as upon his dexterity & his experience; he charged to secure the absence of M. d'A: & told me that the young Physician who would deliver me this *announce*, would prepare for the operation, in which he must lend his aid: & also that it had been the decision of the consultation to allow me but two hours notice.—Judge, my Esther, if I read this unmoved!—yet I had to disguise my sensations & intentions from M. d'A.!—Dr. Aumont,[2] the Messenger & terrible Herald, was in waiting; M. d'A stood by my bed side; I affected to be long reading the Note, to gain time for forming some plan, & such was my terror of involving M. d'A. in the unavailing wretchedness of witnessing what I must go through, that it conquered every other, & gave me the force to act as if I were directing some third person. The detail would be too *Wordy*, as James[3] says, but the *wholesale* is—I called Alex. to my Bed side, & sent him to inform M. Barbier Neuville,[4] chef du division du Bureau de M. d'A. that *the moment was come*, & I entreated him to write a summons upon urgent business for M. d'A. & to detain him till all should be over. Speechless & appalled, off went Alex, &, as I have since heard, was forced to sit down & sob in executing his commission. I then, by the Maid, sent word to the young Dr. Aumont that I could not be ready till one o'clock: & I finished my breakfast, &—not with much appetite, you will believe! forced down a crust of bread, & hurried off, under various pretences, M. d'A. He was scarcely gone, when M. Du Bois arrived: I renewed my request for one o'clock: the rest came; all were fain to consent to the delay, for I had an apartment to prepare for my banished Mate. This arrangement, & those for myself, occupied me completely. Two engaged nurses were out of the way—I had a bed, Curtains, & heaven knows what to prepare—but business was good for my nerves. I was obliged to quit my room to have it put in order:—Dr. Aumont would not leave the house; he remained in the Sallon, folding linen!—He had demanded 4 or 5 old & fine left off under Garments—I glided to our Book Cabinet: sundry necessary works & orders filled up my time entirely till One O'clock, When all was ready— —but Dr. Moreau then arrived, with news that M. Dubois could not attend till three. Dr. Aumont went away—& the Coast was clear. This, indeed, was a dreadful interval. I had no longer any thing to do—I had only to think—TWO HOURS thus spent seemed never-ending. I would fain have written to my dearest Father—to You, my Esther—to Charlotte James—Charles—Amelia Lock[5]— but my arm prohibited me: I strolled to the Sallon—I saw it fitted with preparations, & I recoiled—But I soon returned; to what effect disguise from myself what I must so soon know?—yet the sight of the immense quantity of bandages, compresses, spunges, Lint— — Made me a little sick:—I walked backwards & forwards till I quieted all emotion, & became, by degrees, nearly stupid—torpid, without sentiment or conscious-

---

[1] Thomas Arthur Lally, baron de Tolendal (1702–66). Marie du Deffand de la Lande (1696–1780) was a voluminous and famous letter-writer.

[2] Philippe-Éléonor-Godefroy Aumond (1775–1825), surgeon.

[3] Burney's brother (1750–1821), a Rear Admiral.

[4] Jean-Pierre Barbier de Neuville (1754–1822), bureaucrat.

[5] Charlotte Ann Broome (1761–1838), Burney's sister; Charles Burney (1757–1817), her brother, a clergyman and schoolmaster; and her friend Amelia Locke Angerstein (1776–1848).

ness;—& thus I remained till the Clock struck three. A sudden spirit of exertion then returned,—I defied my poor arm, no longer worth sparing, & took my long banished pen to write a few words to M. d'A—& a few more for Alex, in case of a fatal result. These short billets I could only deposit safely, when the Cabriolets[1]—one—two—three—four—succeeded rapidly to each other in stopping at the door. Dr. Moreau instantly entered my room, to see if I were alive. He gave me a wine cordial, & went to the Sallon. I rang for my Maid & Nurses,—but before I could speak to them, my room, without previous message, was entered by 7 Men in black, Dr. Larry, M. Dubois, Dr. Moreau, Dr. Aumont, Dr. Ribe, & a pupil of Dr. Larry, & another of M. Dubois. I was now awakened from my stupor—& by a sort of indignation—Why so many? & without leave?—But I could not utter a syllable. M. Dubois acted as Commander in Chief. Dr. Larry kept out of sight; M. Dubois ordered a Bed stead into the middle of the room. Astonished, I turned to Dr. Larry, who had promised that an Arm Chair would suffice; but he hung his head, & would not look at me. Two *old mattrasses* M. Dubois then demanded, & an old Sheet. I now began to tremble violently, more with distaste & horrour of the preparations even than of the pain. These arranged to his liking, he desired me to mount the Bed stead. I stood suspended, for a moment, whether I should not abruptly escape—I looked at the door, the windows—I felt desperate—but it was only for a moment, my reason then took the command, & my fears & feelings struggled vainly against it. I called to my maid—she was crying, & the two Nurses stood, transfixed, at the door. Let those women all go! cried M. Dubois. This order recovered me my Voice—No, I cried, let them stay! *qu'elles restent!* This occasioned a little dispute, that re-animated me—The Maid, however, & one of the nurses ran off—I charged the other to approach, & she obeyed. M. Dubois now tried to issue his commands *en militaire*, but I resisted all that were resistable—I was compelled, however, to submit to taking off my long robe de Chambre, which I had meant to retain—Ah, then, how did I think of My Sisters!—not one, at so dreadful an instant, at hand, to protect—adjust—guard me—I regretted that I had refused Me de Maisonneuve—Me Chastel[2]—no one upon whom I could rely—my departed Angel![3]—how did I think of her!—how did I long—long for my Esther—my Charlotte!—My distress was, I suppose, apparent, though not my Wishes, for M. Dubois himself now softened, & spoke soothingly. Can *You*, I cried, feel for an operation that, to *You*, must seem so trivial?—Trivial? he repeated—taking up a bit of paper, which he tore, unconsciously, into a million of pieces, '*oui—c'est peu de chose—mais—*'[4] he stammered, & could not go on. No one else attempted to speak, but I was softened myself, when I saw even M. Dubois grow agitated, while Dr. Larry kept always aloof, yet a glance shewed me he was pale as ashes. I knew not, positively, then, the immediate danger, but every thing convinced me danger was hovering about me, & that this experiment could alone save me from its jaws. I mounted, therefore, unbidden, the Bed stead—& M. Dubois placed me upon the Mattress, & spread a cambric handkerchief upon my face. It was transparent, however, & I saw, through it, that the Bed stead was instantly surrounded by the 7 men & my nurse. I refused to be held; but when, Bright through the cambric, I saw the glitter of polished Steel—I closed my Eyes. I would not trust to convulsive fear the sight of the terrible incision. A silence the most profound ensued, which lasted for some minutes, during which, I imagine, they took their orders by signs, & made their examination—Oh what a horrible suspension!—I did not breathe—& M. Dubois tried vainly to find any pulse. This pause, at length, was broken by Dr. Larry, who, in a voice of solemn melancholy, said '*Qui me tiendra ce sein?—*'[5]

No one answered; at least not verbally; but this aroused me from my passively submissive state, for I feared they imagined the whole breast infected—feared

---

[1] light, one-horse, two-wheeled carriages.

[2] Marie-Françoise-Élisabeth Bidault de Maisonneuve (1770–1850) and Catherine-Françoise Chastel de Moyenpal (b. 1763), Burney's friends.

[3] Susanna Phillips (1755–1800), Burney's sister.

[4] "yes—it's a little thing—but—" (Fr.).

[5] "Who will hold this breast for me?—" (Fr.).

it too justly,—for, again through the Cambric, I saw the hand of M. Dubois held up, while his fore finger first described a straight line from top to bottom of the breast, secondly a Cross, & thirdly a circle; intimating that the WHOLE was to be taken off. Excited by this idea, I started up, threw off my veil, &, in answer to the demand '*Qui me tiendra ce sein?,*' cried '*C'est moi, Monsieur!*' & I held My hand under it, & explained the nature of my sufferings, which all sprang from one point, though they darted into every part. I was heard attentively, but in utter silence, & M. Dubois then replaced me as before, &, as before, spread my veil over my face. How vain, alas, my representation! immediately again I saw the fatal finger describe the Cross—& the circle—Hopeless, then, desperate, & self-given up, I closed once more my Eyes, relinquishing all watching, all resistance, all interference, & sadly resolute to be wholly resigned.

My dearest Esther,—& all my dears to whom she communicates this doleful ditty, will rejoice to hear that this resolution once taken, was firmly adhered to, in defiance of a terror that surpasses all description, & the most torturing pain. Yet—when the dreadful steel was plunged into the breast—cutting through veins—arteries—flesh—nerves—I needed no injunctions not to restrain my cries. I began a scream that lasted unintermittingly during the whole time of the incision—& I almost marvel that it rings not in my Ears still! so excruciating was the agony. When the wound was made, & the instrument was withdrawn, the pain seemed undiminished, for the air that suddenly rushed into those delicate parts felt like a mass of minute but sharp & forked poniards, that were tearing the edges of the wound—but when again I felt the instrument—describing a curve—cutting against the grain, if I may so say, while the flesh resisted in a manner so forcible as to oppose & tire the hand of the operator, who was forced to change from the right to the left—then, indeed, I thought I must have expired. I attempted no more to open my Eyes,—they felt as if hermetically shut, & so firmly closed, that the Eyelids seemed indented into the Cheeks. The instrument this second time withdrawn, I concluded the operation over—Oh no! presently the terrible cutting was renewed—& worse than ever, to separate the bottom, the foundation of this dreadful gland from the parts to which it adhered—Again all description would be baffled—yet again all was not over,—Dr Larry rested but his own hand, &—Oh Heaven!—I then felt the Knife <rack>ling against the breast bone—scraping it!—This performed, while I yet remained in utterly speechless torture, I heard the Voice of Mr. Larry,—(all others guarded a dead silence) in a tone nearly tragic, desire every one present to pronounce if any thing more remained to be done; The general voice was Yes,—but the finger of Mr. Dubois—which I literally *felt* elevated over the wound, though I saw nothing, & though he touched nothing, so indescribably sensitive was the spot—pointed to some further requisition—& again began the scraping!—and, after this, Dr. Moreau thought he discerned a peccant attom—and still, & still, M. Dubois demanded attom after attom—My dearest Esther, not for days, not for Weeks, but for Months I could not speak of this terrible business without nearly again going through it! I could not *think* of it with impunity! I was sick, I was disordered by a single question—even now, 9 months after it is over, I have a head ache from going on with the account! & this miserable account, which I began 3 Months ago, at least, I dare not revise, nor read, the recollection is still so painful.

To conclude, the evil was so profound, the case so delicate, & the precautions necessary for preventing a return so numerous, that the operation, including the treatment & the dressing, lasted 20 minutes! a time, for sufferings so acute, that was hardly supportable—However, I bore it with all the courage I could exert, & never moved, nor stopt them, nor resisted, nor remonstrated, nor spoke—except once or twice, during the dressings, to say '*Ah Messieurs! que je vous plains!*—'[1] for indeed I was sensible to the feeling concern with which they all saw what I endured, though my speech was principally—*very* principally meant for Dr. Larry. Except this, I uttered not a syllable, save, when so often they re-commenced, calling out '*Avertissez moi, Messieurs! avertissez moi!*—'[2] Twice, I believe, I fainted; at

---

[1] "Ah Gentlemen! how sorry I am for you!—" (Fr.).

[2] "Warn me, Gentlemen! warn me!—" (Fr.).

least, I have two total chasms in my memory of this transaction, that impede my tying together what passed. When all was done, & they lifted me up that I might be put to bed, my strength was so totally annihilated, that I was obliged to be carried, & could not even sustain my hands & arms, which hung as if I had been lifeless; while my face, as the Nurse has told me, was utterly colourless. This removal made me open my Eyes—& I then saw my good Dr. Larry, pale nearly as myself, his face streaked with blood, & its expression depicting grief, apprehension, & almost horrour....

Thomas Chatterton
1752 – 1770

Thomas Chatterton was born in Bristol on 10 November 1752. His father, Thomas Chatterton, a schoolmaster, had already died; his mother, Sarah Young Chatterton, supported her family (including her daughter and infant son and her mother-in-law) by needlework. Chatterton was educated at a charity school and then apprenticed to a lawyer as a copyist; when his master discovered that he wrote poetry in his off hours, he beat him, tore it up, and forbade him to write any more. Chatterton disobeyed. The reading of Macpherson's *Ossian*, Percy's *Reliques of Ancient English Poetry*, and other works, and his family's chance possession of some ancient manuscripts from the church of St. Mary Redcliffe inspired him to create a fifteenth-century poet-priest, Thomas Rowley, and to forge works to attribute to him. (There really was a Thomas Rowley, but he was not a poet or priest.) He managed to interest two local antiquarians and gave them many of his Rowley manuscripts, and then tried to obtain the patronage of Horace Walpole, but Walpole, who had been deceived by Macpherson, was not fooled a second time. Chatterton then largely gave up on Rowley and began writing modern poetry, in a wide variety of genres, especially political satire. In April 1770, he was released from his apprenticeship and went to London to make his fortune. He managed to place his poems in a number of periodicals, but not to make a living. On 24 August, he tried to beg a loaf from a baker. His landlady, who knew he had not been eating, asked him to share a meal with her, but he declined. That night, he poisoned himself with opium and arsenic. He was seventeen.

Thomas Tyrwhitt, a Chaucer scholar, published the Rowley poems in 1777. He realized that they were forgeries, but the debate over their authenticity continued for fifteen years. Chatterton's extraordinary achievement and his tragic life were an inspiration for many later Romantic poets. Blake* passionately believed that his account of Rowley was true. Coleridge* wrote a poem on his death (1790). Southey* co-edited his complete works (1803) to raise money for his sister and niece. W. Wordsworth* called him "the marvellous boy" and compared him to Burns* in "Resolution and Independence" (1807);* P. B. Shelley compared him to Sidney in *Adonais* (1821).* Keats called him "the purest writer in the English Language" and dedicated *Endymion* (1818),* his first major work, to his memory. Later, D.G. Rossetti called him "the *true* day-spring of modern romantic poetry," and Meredith posed for Wallis's painting of his suicide. (D.L.M.)

Thomas Chatterton

from *Poems, Supposed to Have Been Written at Bristol, by Thomas Rowley, and Others, in the Fifteenth Century; The Greatest Part Now First Published from the Most Authentic Copies, with an Engraved Specimen of One of the MSS. To Which are Added, a Preface, an Introductory Account of the Several Pieces, and a Glossary* (1777)

The Storie of William Canynge[1]

Anent[2] a brooklette as I laie reclynd,
Listeynge to heare the water glyde alonge,
Myndeynge how thorowe the grene mees[3] yt twynd,
Awhilst the cavys respons'd yts mottring songe,
5 At dystaunt rysyng Avonne[4] to he sped,
Amenged[5] wyth rysyng hylles dyd shewe yts head;
Engarlanded wyth crownes of osyer weedes
And wraytes of alders of a bercie scent,
And stickeynge out wyth clowde agested[6] reedes,
10 The hoarie Avonne show'd dyre semblamente,[7]
Whylest blataunt Severne, from Sabryna clepde,[8]
Rores flemie[9] o'er the sandes that she hepde.

These eynegears swythyn[10] bringethe to mie thowghte
Of hardie champyons knowen to the floude,
15 How onne the bankes thereof brave Ælle[11] foughte,
Ælle descended from Merce[12] kynglie bloude,
Warden of Brystowe towne and castel stede,
Who ever and anon made Danes to blede.

Methoughte such doughtie menn must have a sprighte
20 Dote[13] yn the armour brace that Mychael bore,
Whan he wyth Satan kynge of helle dyd fyghte,
And earthe was drented yn a mere of gore;
Orr, soone as theie dyd see the worldis lyghte,
Fate had wrott downe, thys mann ys borne to fyghte.

25 Ælle, I sayd, or els my mynde dyd saie,
Whie ys thy actyons left so spare yn storie?
Were I toe dispone,[14] there should lyvven aie
In erthe and hevenis rolles thie tale of glorie;
Thie actes soe doughtie should for aie abyde,
30 And bie theyre teste all after actes be tryde.

Next holie Wareburghus[15] fylld mie mynde,
As fayre a sayncte as anie towne can boaste,
Or bee the erthe wyth lyghte or merke ywrynde,[16]
I see hys ymage waulkeyng throwe the coaste:
35 Fitz Hardynge, Bithrickus, and twentie moe[17]
Ynn visyonn fore mie phantasie dyd goe.

---

[1] William Canynges (1399?–1474), a merchant, served Bristol as sheriff, member of parliament, and (five times) as mayor. Chatterton imagines him as Rowley's patron.

[2] "beside."

[3] "meads, meadows."

[4] the Lower or Bristol Avon.

[5] "mingled."

[6] "heaped-up."

[7] "appearance."

[8] "called." Sabrina is the ancient name of the river Severn. The Avon is one of its tributaries.

[9] "frightened."

[10] "These objects quickly."

[11] a fictitious character, the most important hero of the Rowley poems.

[12] Mercia, an Anglo-Saxon kingdom much troubled by Danish invasions.

[13] "dressed." The archangel Michael led the angelic host that defeated Satan: see Milton, *Paradise Lost* 6.

[14] "dispose."

[15] possibly St. Werburga (d. c. 700), the daughter of a king of Mercia. Chatterton/Rowley uses the name in a variety of feminine and masculine forms.

[16] "covered."

[17] Robert Fitzharding (d. 1170), reeve of Bristol, built the abbey of St. Augustine. Earl Brightric or Bithric was ruler of Bristol in the time of William the Conqueror.

Thus all mie wandrynge faytour[1] thynkeynge strayde,
And eche dygne[2] buylder dequac'd[3] onn mie mynde,
Whan from the distaunt streeme arose a mayde,
40 Whose gentle tresses mov'd not to the wynde;
Lyche to the sylver moone yn frostie neete,
The damoiselle dyd come soe blythe and sweete.

Ne browded mantell of a scarlette hue,
Ne shonne pykes[4] plaited o'er wyth ribbande geere,
45 Ne costlie paraments of woden blue,[5]
Noughte of a dresse, but bewtie dyd shee weere;
Naked shee was, and loked swete of youthe,
All dyd bewryen[6] that her name was Trouthe.

The ethie[7] ringletts of her notte-browne hayre
50 What ne a manne should see dyd swotelie hyde,
Whych on her milk-white bodykin so fayre
Dyd showe lyke browne streemes fowlyng the white tyde,
Or veynes of brown hue yn a marble cuarr,
Whyche by the traveller ys kenn'd[8] from farr.

55 Astouned mickle[9] there I sylente laie,
Still scauncing[10] wondrous at the walkynge syghte;
Mie senses forgarde[11] ne coulde reyn awaie;
But was ne forstraughte[12] whan shee dyd alyghte
Anie to mee, dreste up yn naked viewe,
60 Whych mote yn some ewbrycious thoughtes abrewe.

But I ne dyd once thynke of wanton thoughte;
For well I mynded what bie vowe I hete,[13]
And yn mie pockate han a crouchee[14] broughte,
Whych yn the blosom woulde such sins anete;[15]
65 I lok'd wyth eyne as pure as angelles doe,
And dyd the everie thoughte of foule eschewe.

Wyth sweet semblate and an angel's grace
Shee gan to lecture from her gentle breste;
For Trouthis wordes ys her myndes face,
70 False oratoryes she dyd aie deteste:
Sweetnesse was yn eche worde she dyd ywreene,[16]
Tho shee strove not to make that sweetnesse sheene.

Shee sayd; mie manner of appereynge here
Mie name and sleyghted myndbruch[17] maie thee telle;
75 I'm Trouthe, that dyd descende fromm heavenwere,
Goulers[18] and courtiers doe not kenne mee welle;
Thie inmoste thoughtes, thie labrynge brayne I sawe,
And from thie gentle dreeme will thee adawe.[19]

Full manie champyons and menne of lore,
80 Paynters and carvellers have gaind good name,
But there's a Canynge, to encrease the store,
A Canynge, who shall buie uppe all theyre fame.
Take thou mie power, and see yn chylde and manne
What troulie noblenesse yn Canynge ranne.

85 As when a bordelier[20] onn ethie bedde,
Tyr'd wyth the laboures maynt[21] of sweltrie daie,
Yn slepeis bosom laieth hys deft[22] headde,
So, senses sonke to reste, mie boddie laie;

---

[1] "treacherous."
[2] "worthy."
[3] "dashed, rushed."
[4] "picked shoes."
[5] "garments dyed blue with woad."
[6] "reveal."
[7] "easy."
[8] "known."
[9] "greatly astounded."
[10] "looking askance."
[11] "lost."
[12] "distracted."

[13] "promised."
[14] "crucifix."
[15] "annihilate."
[16] "disclose."
[17] "offense against honour": "sleyghted mindbruch" is redundant.
[18] "usurers, moneylenders."
[19] "awaken."
[20] "cottager."
[21] "many."
[22] "neat."

Thomas Chatterton

Eftsoons mie sprighte, from erthlie bandes untyde,
90 Immengde yn flanched[1] ayre wyth Trouthe asyde.

Strayte was I carryd back to tymes of yore,[2]
Whylst Canynge swathed yet yn fleshlie bedde,
And saw all actyons whych han been before,
And all the scroll of Fate unravelled;
95 And when the fate-mark'd babe acome to syghte,
I saw hym eager gaspynge after lyghte.

In all hys shepen[3] gambols and chyldes plaie,
In everie merriemakeyng, fayre or wake,
I kenn'd a perpled[4] lyghte of Wysdom's raie;
100 He eate downe learnynge wyth the wastle cake.
As wise as anie of the eldermenne,
He'd wytte enowe toe make a mayre at tenne.

As the dulce[5] downie barbe beganne to gre,
So was the well thyghte[6] texture of hys lore;
105 Eche daie enhedeynge mockler for to bee,[7]
Greete yn hys councel for the daies he bore.
All tongues, all carrols dyd unto hym synge,
Wondryng at one soe wyse, and yet soe yinge.

Encreaseynge yn the yeares of mortal lyfe,
110 And hasteynge to hys journie ynto heaven,
Hee thoughte ytt proper for to cheese a wyfe,
And use the sexes for the purpose gevene.
Hee then was yothe of comelie semelikeede,
And hee had made a mayden's herte to blede.

115 He had a fader, (Jesus rest hys soule!)
Who loved money, as hys charie[8] joie;

Hee had a broder (happie manne be's dole!)
Yn mynde and boddie, hys owne fadre's boie;
What then could Canynge wissen[9] as a parte
120 To gyve to her whoe had made chop[10] of hearte?

But landes and castle tenures, golde and bighes,[11]
And hoardes of sylver rousted yn the ent,[12]
Canynge and hys fayre sweete dyd that despyse,
To change of troulie love was theyr content;
125 Theie lyv'd togeder yn a house adygne,[13]
Of goode sendaument[14] commilie and fyne.

But soone hys broder and hys syre dyd die,
And lefte to Willyam states and renteynge rolles,
And at hys wyll hys broder Johne supplie.
130 Hee gave a chauntrie to redeeme theyre soules;
And put hys broder ynto syke a trade,
That he lorde mayor of Londonne towne was made.

Eftsoons hys mornynge tournd to gloomie nyghte;
Hys dame, hys seconde selfe, gyve upp her brethe,[15]
135 Seekeynge for eterne lyfe and endless lyghte,
And sleed[16] good Canynge; sad mystake of dethe!
Soe have I seen a flower ynn Sommer tyme
Trodde downe and broke and widder ynn ytts pryme.

Next Radcleeve chyrche[17] (oh worke of hande of heav'n,
140 Whare Canynge sheweth as an instrumente,)
Was to my bismarde[18] eyne-syghte newlie giv'n;
'Tis past to blazonne ytt to good contente,

---

[1] "mingled in arching."

[2] a possibly unconscious admission that this is not really a fifteenth-century poem.

[3] "sheep-like, innocent."

[4] "scattered."

[5] "soft."

[6] "well-knit."

[7] "taking care to be greater (or stronger) every day."

[8] "cherished."

[9] "wish."

[10] "exchange."

[11] "jewels."

[12] "rusted in the purse."

[13] "worthy."

[14] "appearance."

[15] Canynges' wife, Joanna, died in 1460.

[16] "fled."

[17] Canynges rebuilt the church of St. Mary Redcliffe, Bristol.

[18] "astonished."

You that woulde faygn the fetyve[1] buyldynge see
  Repayre to Radcleve, and contented bee.

145 I sawe the myndbruch of hys nobille soule
  Whan Edwarde meniced a seconde wyfe;[2]
  I saw what Pheryons[3] yn hys mynde dyd rolle;
  Nowe fyx'd fromm seconde dames a preeste for lyfe.
  Thys ys the manne of menne, the vision spoke;
150 Then belle for even-songe mie senses woke.

On Happienesse, by William Canynge

  Maie Selynesse[4] on erthes boundes bee hadde?
  Maie yt adyghte[5] yn human shape bee founde?
  Wote yee, ytt was wyth Edin's bower bestadde,[6]
  Or quite eraced from the scaunce-layd[7] grounde,
5 Whan from the secret fontes the waterres dyd
       abounde?
  Does yt agrosed[8] shun the bodyed waulke,
  Lyve to ytself and to yttes ecchoe taulke?

  All hayle, Contente, thou mayde of turtle-eyne,
  As thie behoulders thynke thou arte iwreene,[9]
10 To ope the dore to Selynesse ys thyne,
  And Chrystis glorie doth upponne thee sheene.
  Doer of the foule thynge ne hath thee seene;
  In caves, ynn wodes, ynn woe, and dole distresse,
  Whoere hath thee hath gotten Selynesse.

---

[1] probably "festive."
[2] Edward IV is said to have pressured Canynges to remarry; he became a priest instead.
[3] "arrows," or perhaps "(potential) mates."
[4] "happiness."
[5] "dressed."
[6] "lost."
[7] "uneven."
[8] "frightened."
[9] "displayed."

from *A Supplement to the Miscellanies of Thomas Chatterton* (1784)

Heccar and Gaira. An African Eclogue
Jan. 3, 1770

  Where the rough Caigra rolls the surgy wave,
  Urging his thunders thro the echoing cave;
  Where the sharp rocks, in distant horror seen,
  Drive the white currents thro' the spreading green;
5 Where the loud Tyger, pawing in his rage,
  Bids the black Archers of the wilds engage;
  Stretch'd on the sand, two panting Warriors lay,
  In all the burning torments of the day;
  Their bloody jav'lins reek'd a living steem
10 Their bows were broken at the roaring stream;
  Heccar the Chief of Jarra's fruitful Hill,
  Where the dark vapours nightly dews distill,
  Saw Gaira the companion of his soul,
  Extended where loud Caigra's billows roll;
15 Gaira, the King of warring Archers found,
  Where daily lightnings plow the sandy ground,
  Where brooding tempests howl along the sky,
  Where rising desarts whirl'd in circles fly.

Heccar

  Gaira, 'tis useless to attempt the chace,
20 Swifter than hunted Wolves they urge the race;
  Their lessening forms elude the straining eye,
  Upon the plumage of Macaws they fly.
  Let us return, and strip the reeking slain
  Leaving the bodies on the burning plain.

Gaira

25 Heccar, my vengeance still exclaims for blood,
  'Twould drink a wider stream than Caigra's flood.
  This jav'lin, oft in nobler quarrels try'd,
  Put the loud thunder of their arms aside.
  Fast as the streaming rain, I pour'd the dart,
30 Hurling a whirlwind thro' the trembling heart:
  But now my lingring feet revenge denies,
  O could I throw my javlin from my eyes!

Heccar

When Gaira the united armies broke,
Death wing'd the arrow; Death impell'd the stroke.
35 See, pil'd in mountains, on the sanguine sand
The blasted of the lightnings of thy hand.
Search the brown desart, and the glossy green;
There are the trophies of thy valour seen.
The scatter'd bones mantled in silver white,
40 Once animated, dared thy force in fight.
The Children of the Wave, whose palid race
Views the faint sun, display a languid face,
From the red fury of thy justice fled,
Swifter than torrents from their rocky bed.
45 Fear with a sicken'd silver ting'd their hue:
The guilty fear, when vengeance is their due.

Gaira

Rouse not Remembrance from her shad'wy cell,
Nor of those bloody sons of mischief tell.
Cawna, O Cawna! deck'd in sable charms,
50 What distant region holds thee from my arms?
Cawna, the pride of Afric's sultry vales,
Soft as the cooling murmur of the gales,
Majestic as the many colour'd Snake,
Trailing his glories thro' the blossom'd brake;
55 Black as the glossy rocks, where Eascal roars,
Foaming thro' sandy wastes to Jaghirs shores;
Swift as the arrow, hasting to the breast,
Was Cawna the companion of my rest.

The sun sat low'ring in the Western sky,
60 The swelling tempest spread around the eye;
Upon my Cawna's bosom I reclind,
Catching the breathing whispers of the wind:
Swift from the wood a prowling Tiger came;
Dreadful his voice, his eyes a glowing flame;
65 I bent the bow, the never-erring dart
Pierc'd his rough armour, but escap'd his heart;
He fled, tho' wounded, to a distant waste,
I urg'd the furious flight with fatal haste;
He fell, he dy'd—spent in the fiery toil,
70 I strip'd his carcase of the furry spoil
And as the varied spangles met my eye,
On this, I cried, shall my lov'd Cawna lie.
The dusky midnight hung the skies in grey;
Impell'd by Love, I wing'd the airy way;
75 In the deep valley and the mossy plain,
I sought my Cawna, but I sought in vain.
The pallid shadows of the azure waves
Had made my Cawna and my children slaves.
Reflection maddens, to recall the hour,
80 The Gods had giv'n me to the Dæmon's power.
The dusk slow vanish'd from the hated lawn,
I gain'd a mountain glaring with the dawn.
There the full sails, expanded to the wind,
Struck horror and distraction in my mind,
85 There Cawna mingled with a worthless train,
In common slav'ry drags the hated chain.
Now judge my Heccar, have I cause for rage?
Should aught the thunder of my arm assuage?
In ever-reeking blood this jav'lin dy'd
90 With vengeance shall be never satisfied:
I'll strew the beaches with the mighty dead
And tinge the lily of their features red.

Heccar

When the loud shriekings of the hostile cry
Roughly salute my ear, enrag'd I'll fly;
95 Send the sharp arrow quivering thro' the heart
Chill the hot vitals with the venom'd dart;
Nor heed the shining steel or noisy smoke,
Gaira and Vengeance shall inspire the stroke.

from William Barrett, *The History and Antiquities of the City of Bristol* (1789)

The Warre

Of warres glumm pleasaunce doe I chaunte mie laie,
Trouthe tips the poynctelle wysdomme skemps the lyne,[1]
Whylste hoare experiaunce telleth what toe saie,
And forwyned[2] hosbandrie wyth blearie eyne,
Stondeth and woe bements;[3] the trecklynge bryne
Rounnynge adone hys cheekes which doethe shewe,
Lyke hys unfrutefulle fieldes, longe straungers to the ploughe.
Saie, Glowster,[4] whanne besprenged[5] on evrich syde,
The gentle hyndlette and the vylleyn felle;[6]
Whanne smetheynge sange[7] dyd flowe lyke to a tyde,
And sprytes were damned for the lacke of knelle,
Diddest thou kenne ne lykeness to an helle,
Where all were misdeedes doeynge lyche unwise,
Where hope unbarred and deathe eftsoones dyd shote theyre eies.
Ye shepster swaynes who the ribibble[8] kenne,
Ende the thyghte[9] daunce, ne loke uponne the spere:
In ugsommnesse[10] ware moste bee dyghte toe menne,
Unseliness attendethe hounourewere;[11]
Quaffe your swote vernage and atreeted beere.[12]

---

[1] "poynctelle": "pencil or pen"; "skemps": "marks."
[2] "blasted or burnt."
[3] "laments."
[4] the Earl of Gloucester.
[5] "scattered."
[6] "The noble, servant, and peasant fell."
[7] "smoking blood."
[8] "shepster swaynes": "shepherds"; "ribibble": "fiddle."
[9] "orderly."
[10] "frightfulness."
[11] "Unseliness": "unhappiness"; "hounourwere": "the way of honour."
[12] "swote vernage": "sweet wine"; "attreeted beere": "beer made from grain."

Elizabeth Inchbald
1753 – 1821

Elizabeth Simpson was born in Stanningfield, Suffolk, on 15 October 1753. Her father, John Simpson, was a farmer; her brother George was an actor in Norwich. She was self-educated. In June 1772, she married Joseph Inchbald, an actor. The same year, in Bristol, she first appeared on stage, as Cordelia, with her husband as Lear. She had a prosperous career in the provinces, but a stammer limited her success on the London stage, and after her husband died in 1779, she turned to writing. Her first play, *A Mogul Tale*, was performed in 1784. It was a success, as were most of her eighteen later plays (many of them adapted from French originals); some of them were still being performed in the 1860s. Perhaps her greatest dramatic success was *Lovers' Vows* (1798), adapted from Kotzebue's *Das Kind der Liebe* ("The Child of Love"). She also wrote two novels, *A Simple Story* (1791) and *Nature and Art* (1796). She befriended Godwin* and Wollstonecraft* but broke off relations when their marriage revealed that Wollstonecraft had not been married to Gilbert Imlay. In 1805, Longman asked her to write the introductions for a 25-volume, 125-play collection called *The British Theatre*. She spent her last years in Kensington House, a residence for Catholics, and died there on 1 August 1821. (D.L.M.)

☙❧

from *The British Theatre* (1806–09)

On De Monfort; a Tragedy, in Five Acts; by Joanna Baillie, as Performed at the Theatre Royal, Drury Lane

Amongst the many female writers of this and other nations, how few have arrived at the elevated character of a woman of genius!

The authoress of "De Monfort" received that rare distinction, upon this her first publication.

There was genius in the novelty of her conception, in the strength of her execution; and though her play falls short of dramatic excellence, it will ever be rated as a work of genius.

Joanna Baillie, in her preface to her first publication, displays knowledge, taste, and judgment, upon the subject of the drama, to a very high degree: still, as she observes, "theory and practice are very different things"; and, perhaps, so distinct is the art of criticism, from the art of producing plays, that no one critic so good as herself, has ever written a play half so good as the following tragedy.

Authors may think too profoundly, as well as too superficially—and if a dramatic author, with the most accurate knowledge of the heart of man, probe it too far, the smaller, more curious, and new created passions, which he may find there, will be too delicate for the observation of those who hear and see in a mixed, and, sometimes riotous, company.

The spirit, the soul, the every thought and sensation of the first character in this piece, De Monfort, is clearly discerned by the reader, and he can account for all the events to which they progressively lead: but the most attentive auditor, whilst he plainly beholds effects, asks after causes; and not perceiving those diminutive seeds of hatred, here described, till, swollen, they extend to murder, he conceives the hero of the tragedy to be more a pitiable maniac, than a man acting under the dominion of natural propensity.

Even to the admiring reader of this work, who sees the delineation of nature in every page, it may perchance occur, that disease must have certain influence with hate so rancorous; for rooted antipathy, without some more considerable provocation than is here adduced, is very like the first unhappy token of insanity.

Strike not upon one particular chord in all De Monfort's feelings, and he is a noble creature; but from this individual string vibrates all that is mean and despicable in man. Thus is the mind of the lunatic generally tyrannized by one obstinate idea.

Though hatred be the passion described in this tragedy, pride was its origin, and envy its promoter.—The schoolboy, who, by his ridicule, wounded the self importance of his playfellow, might, we find, have been forgiven, had not good fortune bestowed, on this Rezenvelt, unexpected riches, social qualities, and friends; to rival those possessed by Monfort, his former superior.

From hence is derived this most admirable moral—The proud man, yielding to every vice which pride engenders, descends, in the sequel of his arrogance, to be the sport of his enemy, the pity of his friends, to receive his life a gift from the man he abhors, and to do a midnight murder!

Still the author's talents invest with dignity this cowardly assassin, and he inspires a sublime horror to the last moment of his existence—and even when extended as a corse.

The character of Rezenvelt is well drawn; and, in one scene, gives an excellent sample of the writer's powers in comedy; in that comic dialogue, at least, which has most pleasant effect, when dispersed through a tragedy.

On Jane De Monfort she has bestowed some of her very best poetic descriptions; and, from the young Page's first account of the "queenly" stranger, has given such a striking resemblance of both the person and mien of Mrs. Siddons, that it would almost raise a suspicion she was, at the time of the writing, designed for the representation of this noble female.

This drama, of original and very peculiar formation, plainly denotes that the authoress has studied theatrical productions as a reader more than as a spectator; and it may be necessary to remind her—that Shakspeare gained his knowledge of the effect produced from plays upon an audience, and profited, through such attainment, by his constant attendance on dramatic representations, even with the assiduity of a performer.

Of this tragedy, which she certainly possessed the genius to have made of the highest importance in theatric exhibition, she may now exclaim, in De Monfort's words—more impressive than any the whole composition contains—

"'Tis done, 'tis number'd with the things o'erpast;
'Would! 'would it were to come!"[1]

But let her also reflect, that other dramas may yet proceed from her pen, to gratify every expectation which this production has excited.

On Lovers' Vows; A Play in Five Acts; Altered from the German of Kotzebue, by Mrs. Inchbald. As Performed at the Theatre Royal, Covent-Garden

Plays, founded on German dramas, have long been a subject both of ridicule and of serious animadversion. Ridicule is a jocund slanderer; and who does not love to be merry? but the detraction that is dull, is inexcusable calumny.

The grand moral of this play is to set forth the miserable consequences which arise from the neglect, and to enforce the watchful care, of illegitimate offspring; and surely, as the pulpit has not had eloquence to eradicate the crime of seduction, the stage may be allowed an humble endeavour to prevent its most fatal effects.

But there are some pious declaimers against theatrical exhibitions; so zealous to do good, they grudge the poor dramatist his share in the virtuous concern.

Not furnished with one plea throughout four acts of "Lovers' Vows" for accusation, those critics arraign its catastrophe, and say,—"the wicked should be punished."—They forget there is a punishment called *conscience*, which, though it seldom troubles the defamer's peace, may weigh heavy on the fallen female and her libertine seducer.

But as a probationary prelude to the supposed happiness of the frail personages of this drama, the author has plunged the offender, Agatha, in bitterest poverty and wo; which she receives as a contrite penitent, atoning for her sins. The Baron Wildenhaim, living in power and splendour, is still more rigorously visited by remorse; and, in the reproaches uttered by his outcast son, (become, by the father's criminal disregard of his necessities, a culprit, subject to death by the law,) the Baron's guilt has sure exemplary chastisement. But

---

[1] Baillie, *De Monfort* 4.3.71–72* (544).

yet, after all the varied anguish of his mind, should tranquillity promise, at length, to crown his future days, where is the immorality? If holy books teach that the wicked too often prosper, why are plays to be withheld from inculcating the self-same doctrine? Not that a worldly man would class it amongst the prosperous events of life, to be (like the Baron) compelled to marry his cast-off mistress, after twenty years absence.

It may not here be wholly useless to observe, that, in the scene in the fourth act, just mentioned, between the Baron and his son, the actor who plays Frederick, too frequently forms his notion of the passion he is to pourtray through the interview, from the following lines at the end of one of his speeches:

"And, when he dies, a funeral sermon will praise his great benevolence, his Christian charities."

The sarcasm here to be expressed, should be evinced in no one sentence else. Where, in a preceding speech, he says, the Baron is "a man, kind, generous, beloved by his tenants";[1] he certainly means *this* to be his character. Frederick is not ironical, except by accident. Irony and sarcasm do not appertain to youth: open, plain, downright habits, are the endearing qualities of the young. Moreover, a son, urged by cruel injuries, may upbraid his father even to rage, and the audience will yet feel interest for them both; but if he contemn or deride him, all respect is lost, both for the one and the other.

The passions which take possession of this young soldier's heart, when admitted to the presence of the Baron, knowing him to be his father, are various; but scorn is not amongst the number. Awe gives the first sensation, and is subdued by pride; filial tenderness would next force its way, and is overwhelmed by anger. These passions strive in his breast, till grief for his mother's wrongs, and his own ignominious state, burst all restraint; and as fury drives him to the point of distraction, he changes his accents to a tone of irony, in the lines just quoted.

"Oh! there be actors I have seen, and heard others praise, who (not to speak it profanely) have"[2] scornfully sneered at their father through this whole scene, and yet been highly applauded.

While it is the fashion to see German plays, both the German and the English author will patiently bear the displeasure of a small party of critics, as the absolute conditions on which they enjoy popularity. Nor, till the historian is forbid to tell how tyrants have success in vanquishing nations, or the artist be compelled to paint the beauteous courtezan with hideous features, as the emblem of her mind shall the free dramatist be untrue to his science; which, like theirs, is to follow nature through all her rightful course. Deception, beyond the result of genuine imitative art, he will disclaim, and say with Shakspeare to the self-approving zealot,

"Virtue itself turns vice, being misapplied,
And vice sometimes by action dignified."[3]

---

[1] Both speeches are from Inchbald, *Lovers' Vows* 4.2.

[2] Cf. Shakespeare, *Hamlet* 3.2.31–33.

[3] Shakespeare, *Romeo and Juliet* 2.3.21–22.

Phillis Wheatley
c. 1753 – 1784

Phillis Wheatley was born somewhere in West Africa, sometime around 1753. In 1761, she was abducted, enslaved, and brought to Boston, where John Wheatley, a merchant and ship-owner, bought her as a present for his wife, Susanna; they named her Phillis after the ship that she arrived in. The Wheatleys were indulgent to their new slave, and her mistress took charge of her education; according to her master, she became literate in English within sixteen months. She began writing in 1765 and published her first poem in 1767. Her elegy for George Whitefield, an Evangelical minister (1770), made her famous on both sides of the Atlantic. In 1773, she accompanied her master's son to England, partly for her health and partly to arrange for the publication of a book of poems under the patronage of the Countess of Huntingdon, who had also been Whitefield's patron. She was made much of and met such celebrities as Franklin* and the abolitionist Granville Sharp, who took her to see the lions in the Tower of London. But before she could meet Huntingdon or see her book published, she had to return to Boston because of the illness of her mistress, who died in March 1774. At about this time, her master freed her. Unfortunately, the upheavals of the Revolutionary War deprived her of most of her local patrons, who were British loyalists (Wheatley was an American patriot), and she did not succeed in publishing a second volume of poems. John Wheatley died in March 1778, and two weeks later, Wheatley married John Peters, a free African-American grocer and apparently a rather feckless person; they had three children, all of whom died in infancy. Wheatley had to find work as a scullery maid in a boarding house—harder work than she had to do as a slave. She and her third child died on 5 December 1784; John Peters was not present. (D.L.M.)

ତ୨ଓ

from *Poems on Various Subjects, Religious and Moral. By Phillis Wheatley, Negro Servant to Mr. John Wheatley of Boston, in New England* (1773)

On Being Brought from Africa to America[1]

'Twas mercy brought me from my *Pagan* land,
Taught my benighted soul to understand
That there's a God, that there's a *Saviour* too:
Once I redemption neither sought nor knew.
5 Some view our sable race with scornful eye,
"Their colour is a diabolic die."
Remember, *Christians*, *Negros*, black as *Cain*,[2]
May be refin'd, and join th' angelic train.

---

[1] written in 1768.

[2] Africans were sometimes believed to be the descendants of Cain (see Genesis 4.1–15), possibly because of a confused recollection of the curse of Canaan (Genesis 9.25), which was invoked as a justification for slavery.

On the Death of the Rev. Mr. George Whitefield. 1770[3]

Hail, happy saint, on thine immortal throne,
Possest of glory, life, and bliss unknown;
We hear no more the music of thy tongue,
Thy wonted auditories cease to throng.
5 Thy sermons in unequall'd accents flow'd,
And ev'ry bosom with devotion glow'd;
Thou didst in strains of eloquence refin'd
Inflame the heart, and captivate the mind.
Unhappy we the setting sun deplore,
10 So glorious once, but ah! it shines no more.

---

[3] written and first published in 1770. Whitefield (1714–70) was one of the founders and leaders of the Methodist movement, which (among other reforms) was noted for welcoming slaves and other oppressed groups. He visited America seven times, and died there on 30 September 1770. Wheatley may have met him. Her patron, Selina Hastings, Countess of Huntingdon (1707–91), also supported his work.

Behold the prophet in his tow'ring flight!
He leaves the earth for heav'n's unmeasur'd height,
And worlds unknown receive him from our sight.
There *Whitefield* wings with rapid course his way,
15 And sails to *Zion*[1] through vast seas of day.
Thy pray'rs, great saint, and thine incessant cries
Have pierc'd the bosom of thy native skies.
Thou moon hast seen, and all the stars of light,
How he has wrestled with his God by night.[2]
20 He pray'd that grace in ev'ry heart might dwell,
He long'd to see *America* excel;
He charg'd its youth that ev'ry grace divine
Should with full lustre in their conduct shine;
That Saviour, which his soul did first receive,
25 The greatest gift that ev'n a God can give,
He freely offer'd to the num'rous throng,
That on his lips with list'ning pleasure hung.

"Take him, ye wretched, for your only good,
Take him ye starving sinners, for your food;
30 Ye thirsty, come to this life-giving stream,
Ye preachers, take him for your joyful theme;
Take him my dear *Americans*, he said,
Be your complaints on his kind bosom laid:
Take him, ye *Africans*, he longs for you,
35 *Impartial Saviour* is his title due:
Wash'd in the fountain of redeeming blood,
You shall be sons, and kings, and priests to God."

Great *Countess*,[3] we *Americans* revere
Thy name, and mingle in thy grief sincere;
40 *New England* deeply feels, the *Orphans* mourn,
Their more than father will no more return.

But, though arrested by the hand of death,
Whitefield no more exerts his lab'ring breath,
Yet let us view him in th' eternal skies,
45 Let ev'ry heart to this bright vision rise;
While the tomb safe retains its sacred trust,
Till life divine re-animates his dust.

---

[1] the Promised Land, Heaven.

[2] Cf. Genesis 32.24–30.

[3] "The Countess of *Huntingdon*, to whom Mr. *Whitefield* was Chaplain." (Original editor's note.)

To the Right Honourable William, Earl of Dartmouth, His Majesty's Principal Secretary of State for North America, &c.[4]

Hail, happy day, when, smiling like the morn,
Fair *Freedom* rose *New-England* to adorn:
The northern clime beneath her genial ray,
Dartmouth, congratulates thy blissful sway:
5 Elate with hope her race no longer mourns,
Each soul expands, each grateful bosom burns,
While in thine hand with pleasure we behold
The silken reins, and *Freedom's* charms unfold.
Long lost to realms beneath the northern skies
10 She shines supreme, while hated *faction* dies:
Soon as appear'd the *Goddess* long desir'd,
Sick at the view, she languish'd and expir'd;
Thus from the splendors of the morning light
The owl in sadness seeks the caves of night.

15 No more, *America*, in mournful strain
Of wrongs, and grievance unredress'd complain,
No longer shall thou dread the iron chain,
Which wanton *Tyranny* with lawless hand
Had made, and with it meant t' enslave the land.

20 Should you, my lord, while you peruse my song,
Wonder from whence my love of *Freedom* sprung,
Whence flow these wishes for the common good,
By feeling hearts alone best understood,
I, young in life, by seeming cruel fate
25 Was snatch'd from *Afric's* fancy'd happy seat:
What pangs excruciating must molest,
What sorrows labour in my parent's breast?
Steel'd was that soul and by no misery mov'd
That from a father seiz'd his babe belov'd:
30 Such, such my case. And can I then but pray
Others may never feel tyrannic sway?

---

[4] William Legge, 2nd Earl of Dartmouth (1731–1801), was appointed secretary of state for the North American colonies in August 1772. He was a friend of the Countess of Huntingdon. The subject was proposed to Wheatley by Thomas Wooldridge, to see if she could really write. She later met Dartmouth in England, and he gave her money to buy books.

For favours past, great Sir, our thanks are due,
And thee we ask thy favours to renew,
Since in thy pow'r, as in thy will before,
35 To sooth the griefs, which thou did'st once deplore.
May heav'nly grace the sacred sanction give
To all thy works, and thou for ever live
Not only on the wings of fleeting *Fame*,
Though praise immortal crowns the patriot's name,
40 But to conduct to heav'ns refulgent fane,
May fiery coursers sweep th' ethereal plain,
And bear thee upwards to that blest abode,
Where, like the prophet, thou shalt find thy God.

To S.M. a Young African Painter, on Seeing His Works[1]

To show the lab'ring bosom's deep intent,
And thought in living characters to paint,
When first thy pencil did those beauties give,
And breathing figures learnt from thee to live,
5 How did those prospects give my soul delight,
A new creation rushing on my sight?
Still, wond'rous youth! each noble path pursue,
On deathless glories fix thine ardent view:
Still may the painter's and the poet's fire
10 To aid thy pencil, and thy verse conspire!

And may the charms of each seraphic theme
Conduct thy footsteps to immortal fame!
High to the blissful wonders of the skies
Elate thy soul, and raise thy wishful eyes.
15 Thrice happy, when exalted to survey
That splendid city, crown'd with endless day,
Whose twice six gates on radiant hinges ring:
Celestial *Salem*[2] blooms in endless spring.

Calm and serene thy moments glide along,
20 And may the muse inspire each future song!
Still, with the sweets of contemplation bless'd,
May peace with balmy wings your soul invest!
But when these shades of time are chas'd away,
And darkness ends in everlasting day,
25 On what seraphic pinions shall we move,
And view the landscapes in the realms above?
There shall thy tongue in heav'nly murmurs flow,
And there my muse with heav'nly transport glow:
No more to tell of *Damon's* tender sighs,[3]
30 Or rising radiance of *Aurora's* eyes,
For nobler themes demand a nobler strain,
And purer language on th' ethereal plain.
Cease, gentle muse! the solemn gloom of night
Now seals the fair creation from my sight.

---

[1] Scipio Moorhead is believed to have drawn the portrait of Wheatley on which the frontispiece for her book was based.

[2] the new Jerusalem: see Revelation 21.10–27.

[3] Damon is a stereotypical pastoral name; cf. Virgil, *Eclogues* 8 and Pope, "Spring" (1709). Aurora (30) is the classical goddess of the dawn.

Ann Yearsley
c. 1753 – 1806

Ann Cromartie was baptized at Clifton, near Bristol, in July 1753, the daughter of John Cromartie, a labourer, and Ann Cromartie, who kept cows and sold milk. She followed in her mother's footsteps as a milkwoman, but developed literary interests not common in the labouring classes. Her brother William taught her to read; her mother borrowed books from ladies willing to lend them. In 1774 Ann married John Yearsley; but the marriage appears not to have been happy. In the next ten years Yearsley had seven children; the poverty-stricken family would have starved without help. When Yearsley's poems were brought to the attention of Hannah More* in 1784, More became Yearsley's patron.

More promoted Yearsley's poems (published as the highly successful *Poems, on Several Occasions*, 1785); but Yearsley (known to her readers as "Lactilla") was not content to play the role of labouring-class poet for consumption by her social superiors. As Yearsley came to find More condescending, More charged Yearsley with ingratitude. When Yearsley insisted on controlling her own capital (the substantial sum of about £600, some of which she invested in a circulating library), More withdrew her patronage. The fourth edition of *Poems, on Several Occasions* (1786) and *Poems on Various Subjects* (1787) included Yearsley's version of her relationship with More. Yearsley's new patron, Frederick Augustus Hervey, Earl of Bristol and bishop of Derry, practised a more detached benevolence.

Yearsley's views are liberal rather than radical. Her play, *Earl Goodwin* (1791, written in 1789) praises the early stages of the French Revolution; she sympathizes with the oppressed in *A Poem on the Inhumanity of the Slave Trade* (1788). *Reflections on the Death of Louis XVI* (1793) draws the line at the French king's execution, regarding it as a betrayal of liberty. Her last collection of poems, *The Rural Lyre* (1796), unites political and domestic themes. Yearsley appears to have spent her final years struggling financially; she died on 6 May 1806. (A.M.)

∽∽∽

from *Poems, on Several Occasions. By Ann Yearsley, a Milkwoman of Bristol* (1785)

To the Same [Stella];[1] on Her Accusing the Author of Flattery, and of Ascribing to the Creature That Praise Which Is Due Only to the Creator

Excuse me, STELLA, sunk in humble state,
With more than needful awe I view the great;
No glossy diction e'er can aid the thought,
First stamp'd in ignorance, with error fraught.
5 My friends I've prais'd—they stood in heavenly guise
When first I saw them, and my mental eyes
Shall in that heavenly rapture view them still,
For mine's a stubborn and a savage will;
No customs, manners, or soft arts I boast,
10 On my rough soul your nicest rules are lost;
Yet shall unpolish'd gratitude be mine,
While STELLA deigns to nurse the spark divine.
A savage pleads—let e'en her errors move,
And your forgiving spirit melt in love.
15 O, cherish gentle Pity's lambent flame,
From Heaven's own bosom the soft pleader came!
Then deign to bless a soul, who'll ne'er degrade
Your gift, tho' sharpest miseries invade!
You I acknowledge, next to bounteous Heaven,
20 Like his, your influence chears where'er 'tis given;
Blest in dispensing! gentle STELLA, hear
My only, short, but pity-moving prayer,
That thy great soul may spare the rustic Muse,
Whom Science ever scorn'd, and errors still abuse.

---

[1] Hannah More,* Yearsley's patron.

On Mrs. Montagu[1]

Why boast, O arrogant, imperious man,
Perfection so exclusive? are thy powers
Nearer approaching Deity? can'st thou solve
Questions which high Infinity propounds,
5 Soar nobler flights, or dare immortal deeds,
Unknown to woman, if she greatly dares
To use the powers assign'd her? Active strength,
The boast of animals, is clearly thine;
By this upheld, thou think'st the lesson rare
10 That female virtues teach; and poor the height
Which female wit obtains. The theme unfolds
Its ample maze, for MONTAGU befriends
The puzzled thought, and, blazing in the eye
Of boldest Opposition, strait presents
15 The soul's best energies, her keenest powers,
Clear, vigorous, enlighten'd; with firm wing
Swift she o'ertakes *his* Muse, which spread afar
Its brightest glories in the days of yore;
Lo! where she, mounting, spurns the stedfast earth,
20 And, sailing on the cloud of science, bears
The banner of Perfection.——
Ask GALLIA's mimic sons[2] how strong her powers,
Whom, flush'd with plunder from her SHAKESPEARE's page,
She swift detects amid their dark retreats;
25 (Horrid as CACUS[3] in their thievish dens)
Regains the trophies, bears in triumph back
The pilfer'd glories to a wond'ring world.
So STELLA[4] boasts, from her the tale I learn'd;
With pride she told it, I with rapture heard.

30 O, MONTAGU! forgive me, if I sing
Thy wisdom temper'd with the milder ray
Of soft humanity, and kindness bland:
So wide its influence, that the bright beams
Reach the low vale where mists of ignorance lodge,
35 Strike on the innate spark which lay immers'd,
Thick clogg'd, and almost quench'd in total night—
On me it fell, and cheer'd my joyless heart.

Unwelcome is the first bright dawn of light
To the dark soul; impatient, she rejects,
40 And fain wou'd push the heavenly stranger back;
She loaths the cranny which admits the day;
Confus'd, afraid of the intruding guest;
Disturb'd, unwilling to receive the beam,
Which to herself her native darkness shews.
45 The effort rude to quench the cheering flame
Was mine, and e'en on STELLA cou'd I gaze
With sullen envy, and admiring pride,
Till, doubly rous'd by MONTAGU, the pair
Conspire to clear my dull, imprison'd sense,
50 And chase the mists which dimm'd my visual beam.

Oft as I trod my native wilds alone,
Strong gusts of thought wou'd rise, but rise to die;
The portals of the swelling soul, ne'er op'd
By liberal converse, rude ideas strove
55 Awhile for vent, but found it not, and died.
Thus rust the Mind's best powers. Yon starry orbs,
Majestic ocean, flowery vales, gay groves,
Eye-wasting lawns, and Heaven-attempting hills,
Which bound th' horizon, and which curb the view;
60 All those, with beauteous imagery, awak'd
My ravish'd soul to extacy untaught,
To all the transport the rapt sense can bear;
But all expir'd, for want of powers to speak;
All perish'd in the mind as soon as born,
65 Eras'd more quick than cyphers on the shore,
O'er which the cruel waves, unheedful, roll.

Such timid rapture as young EDWIN[5] seiz'd,
When his lone footsteps on the Sage obtrude,
Whose noble precept charm'd his wond'ring ear,

---

[1] Elizabeth Montagu, a leader in the Blue Stocking Circle, an informal group of literary women to which Yearsley's patron Hannah More* also belonged. More prefaced Yearsley's *Poems, on Several Occasions* with a letter to Montagu recounting Yearsley's life.

[2] Montagu's *Essay on the Writings and Genius of Shakespeare* (1769) defended Shakespeare against criticism and plagiarism by French writers ("Gallia's mimic sons").

[3] in classical mythology, a monster killed by Heracles.

[4] Hannah More.*

[5] "See the Minstrel." (A.Y.) *The Minstrel* (1771–74), a poem in two books by James Beattie (1735–1803), traces the development of a poet-hero named Edwin.

70 Such rapture fill'd LACTILLA's[1] vacant soul,
　　When the bright Moralist, in softness drest,
　Opes all the glories of the mental world,
　　Deigns to direct the infant thought, to prune
　The budding sentiment, uprear the stalk
75 Of feeble fancy, bid idea live,
　　Woo the abstracted spirit from its cares,
　And gently guide her to the scenes of peace.
　Mine was that balm, and mine the grateful heart,
　Which breathes its thanks in rough, but timid strains.

Reflections on the Death of Louis XVI[2]
(1793)

　　　　　　——————Is it good
　For Man to drain the sacred Stream of Life
　From his sad Brother's Heart? O tis a Deed
　Unworthy an immortal Spirit! where
　Shall meek neglected Mercy find a Spot
　To weep in Silence o'er her slaughter'd Sons![3]

　A Pause of Sorrow hangs upon the World,
　　While heav'nly Pity, sighs thro' all the Air,
　Too late she mourns! Fury her Torch hath hurl'd,
　　Man, sickens with her Heat, his wildest Passions
　　　　　glare!

5 Yet, gentle Pity, stay! tho' thy soft Charms,
　　Are dim'd awhile, thy Lustre shall return;
　Murder shall tremble mid the Din of Arms,
　　And o'er his Victim the fierce Soldier mourn.

　Melted by Thee, thro' many a lonely Hour,
10　E'en Stoic Pride shall weep a murder'd King:
　Such Tears are sacred to thy soft'ning Pow'r,
　　Then bathe in honest Grief thy rosy Wing;

　And shake the healing Drops on ev'ry Shore,
　　Where mad BELLONA,[4] stings the troubled Mind;
15 Where feeble Mortals blindly would adore
　　That airy Vision, Wisdom ne'er could find.

　Where fancied Liberty, with rude Excess,
　　Courts Man from sober Joy, and lures him on
　To frantic War, struck by her gaudy Dress,
20　His ardent Soul is in the Chace undone.

　The *Ignis fatuus*[5] follow'd by the Clown,
　　Deceives not more than Liberty, her Arms
　Were never round the weary Warriour thrown,
　　He dies a Victim to fallacious Charms.

25 Ask, ye! where joyous Liberty resorts,
　　In *France*, in *Spain*, or in *Britannia*'s Vale?
　O no!—She only with poor Fancy sports
　　Her richest Dwelling is the passing Gale.

　Like Echo, she exists in airy Sound,
30　Never possess'd, ne'er to one Rule confin'd,
　Fix but one Hair to mark her fairy Ground,
　　She vanishes! nor leaves a Trace behind.

　Yet for this Vapour, gen'rous Man must die,
　　For this, he ventures on a World unknown;
35 For this, he braves the Crime of sanguine Dye;
　　For this, he drags a Monarch from his Throne.

　Ill-fated LOUIS!—all thy Pangs are o'er!
　　Nature's keen Agony hath left thy Heart;
　Thy Children's Groans by thee are heard no more,
40　To hold thee back, when Murder cries "depart!"

　O deep! deep Struggle!—surely thou wert made
　　To break the strongest Ligament of Woe;
　To feel ere Death could thy full Veins invade,
　　The finest Torture Human-kind can know.

45 Yes, Millions fall, but few so high are wrought
　　By Nature's working in the awful Hour,
　Few Taste the Cup with Pain so deeply fraught:

---

[1] "The Author." (A.Y.) Yearsley's pseudonym Lactilla (from Latin *lac*, "milk") refers to her occupation as a dairywoman.

[2] King Louis XVI of France was condemned to death by the National Convention on 20 January 1793 and was guillotined the following day.

[3] unidentified; possibly written by Yearsley herself.

[4] the Roman goddess of war.

[5] "foolish fire" (L.); the will o' the wisp, phosphorescence caused by marsh gases which could lead unwary travellers to their deaths.

Ah LOUIS! thou hast prov'd the Soul's sublimest
   Pow'r!

Thy Murd'rers live,—what friendly Arm shall ease
50   The Pillow which supports a guilty Head?
When Conscience nourishes the Mind's Disease,
   And Mem'ry brings the Shadow of the Dead?

In that dread Hour, much injur'd Spirit rise!
   And breathe Forgiveness thro' thy Murd'rer's Soul:
55 Ah! bid him save thy Children ere he dies,
   Then guide him to thy GOD, where Worlds
      eternal roll.

from *The Rural Lyre; A Volume of Poems: Dedicated to the Right Honourable the Earl of Bristol, Lord Bishop of Derry*[1] (1796)

To Mira, on the Care of Her Infant

Whilst war, destruction, crimes that fiends delight,
Burst on the globe, and millions sink in night;
Whilst here a monarch, there a subject dies,
Equally dear to him who rules the skies;
5 Whilst man to man oppos'd wou'd shake the world,
And see vast systems into chaos hurl'd,
Rather than turn his face from yon dread field,
Or, by forgiving, teach his foe to yield:
Let us, whose sweet employ the Gods admire,
10 Serenely blest, to softer joys retire!
Spite of those wars, we will mild pleasure know—
Pleasure, that, long as woman lives, shall flow!
We are not made for Mars;[2] we ne'er could bear
His pond'rous helmet and his burning spear;
15 Nor in fierce combat prostrate lay that form
That breathes affection whilst the heart is warm:—
No: whilst our heroes from their homes retire,
We'll nurse the infant, and lament the sire.
   I am no Amazon;[3] nor would I give
20 One silver groat[4] by iron laws to live.
Nay, if, like hers, my heart were iron-bound,
My warmth would melt the fetters to the ground.
   Ah, weep not, Mira! In this cradle view
Thy lovely charge—Amyntor's[5] copy true;
25 Think, by this pledge the absent sire ensures
Thy constant memory, and thy heart secures.
And, whilst we read, reflect, by turns converse,
Comment on wars in prose or mimic verse,
Permit me, pensive friend, who long have known
30 A mother's duty, pleasing cares to own,
Teach thee to gently nurse thy beauteous boy—
Lest Custom gentle Nature's pow'r destroy:[6]
So young an infant should reposing lie,
Unswath'd and loose,[7] that the fair limbs may ply
35 To every motion happy Nature tries,
Whilst life seems fluid, and from pressure flies.
Clothe him with easy warmth. Of ills the worst
Are cruel swathes, of infant griefs the first.
Think what the stomach feels when hardly press'd!—
40 The breath confin'd swells high the snowy chest:
The pulses throb, the heart with flutt'ring beats;
The eyes roll ghastly; wind the nurture meets;
And, ere the new-born appetite hath din'd,
The food's rejected, and the head reclin'd.
45   Be tender, Mira!—Downy beds prepare;
To thy own bosom clasp Amyntor's heir!
See not thy babe pining with speechless grief,
His thirsty lip craving thy kind relief:
Relief that Nature bids the infant claim;
50 Withheld by healthy mothers, to their shame.
   Behold gay Circe[8] in her gig![9]—Old Night
Hath from one moon receiv'd her valu'd light,

---

[1] Frederick Augustus Hervey, 4th Earl of Bristol (1730–1803), Bishop of Derry, Yearsley's patron after 1786.

[2] the Roman god of war.

[3] legendary woman warrior.

[4] fourpence.

[5] In accordance with convention, Yearsley gives both Mira and her husband classical names.

[6] Like Wollstonecraft, Yearsley believes that women should nurse their own babies; cf. *A Vindication of the Rights of Woman,** chap. 12.

[7] i.e., free to move the body without constraint; with this, contrast Blake, "Infant Sorrow" 6.*

[8] in mythology the name of the daughter of the Sun, a sorceress who turns men into animals; see Homer, *Odyssey* 10.

[9] a light two-wheeled carriage pulled by one horse.

Since Circe's heir was with his grandsire laid;
And all her grief on yon rich tomb display'd.
55   Her child was lovely, strong, and promis'd fair;
His looks transporting, his complexion clear;
Ardent to seek her bosom, and recline
Where dear affection makes the gift divine!
But no:—could Circe dress renounce, the ball—
60 For a child's humour suffer TASTE to fall?
"*Immensely monstrous! singular!*" she cried—
A boist'rous nurse her wish'd-for love supplied.
And soon her babe's wan look proclaim'd the cheat:
He loath'd the bosom he was forc'd to meet;
65 Refus'd in silence, starv'd in robes of lace,
And oft imploring view'd his mother's face.
Too proud to nurse, maternal fevers came—
Her burthen'd bosom caught th' invited flame;
Too late she woo'd her infant to her breast,
70 He only sigh'd, and sunk to lasting rest.
   Do thou not, Mira, follow Circe's line—
In thee, let soft maternal pleasure shine;
Pleasure that virtuous mothers highly taste,
When gen'rous Hymen¹ makes them more than chaste.
75 Benign and social, new affections grow;
Their minds enlarg'd, their noblest spirits flow;
Friendship, compassion, sympathy, and love,
Such as the self-corrected mind may prove,
Stamp ev'ry act.——These gen'rous joys are thine—
80 Wouldst thou exchange them for Golconda's mine?²
   I own such is the force of social law,
The unmarried ****** loves her babe with awe:
Nurs'd far from public view in yon lone wild,
She sometimes strays to tremble o'er her child.
85 There coarse rusticity, vice, vulgar sound—
All that can sentiment or wisdom wound,
Breaks on the eye and ear—Unhappy fair!
Yet not condemn'd, if thy sweet pledge be dear—
Leave thy fond soul with him, to him return:
90 O let his FUTURE on thy fancy burn!
Quick bear him thence! Instruct him, point to Fame—
Neglected, he will mourn; ay, seal thy shame!

   Mira, as thy dear Edward's senses grow,
Be sure they all will seek this point—TO KNOW:
95 Woo to enquiry—strictures long avoid,
By force the thirst of weakly sense is cloy'd:
Silent attend the frown, the gaze, the smile,
To grasp far objects the incessant toil;
So play life's springs with energy, and try
100 The unceasing thirst of knowledge to supply.
   I saw the beauteous Caleb t'other day
Stretch forth his little hand to touch a spray,
Whilst on the grass his drowsy nurse inhal'd
The sweets of Nature as her sweets exhal'd:
105 But, ere the infant reach'd the playful leaf,
She pull'd him back—His eyes o'erflow'd with grief;
He check'd his tears—Her fiercer passions strove,
She look'd a vulture cow'ring o'er a dove!
"I'll teach you, brat!" The pretty trembler sigh'd—
110 When, with a cruel shake, she hoarsely cried—
"Your Mother spoils you—every thing you see
You covet. It shall ne'er be so with me!
Here, eat this cake, sit still, and don't you rise—
Why don't you pluck the sun down from the skies?
115 I'll spoil your sport—Come, laugh me in the face—
And henceforth learn to keep your proper place.
You rule me in the house!—To hush your noise
I, like a spaniel, must run for toys:
But here, Sir, let the trees alone, nor cry—
120 Pluck, if you dare—Who's master? you, or I?"
   O brutal force, to check th' enquiring mind,
When it would pleasure in a rose-bud find!
Whose wondrous strength was never yet discern'd,
By millions gone, by all we yet have learn'd.
125 True to the senses, systematic man
Conceives himself a mighty, finish'd plan;
To see, to touch, to taste, and smell and hear,
He strives to prove, make full existence here:
These to the brain exquisite forms convey;
130 On these she works, these keep her life in play.
   And is this all, Mira, we boast below?
Does not the soul spring forward still to KNOW;
Pant for the future as her pow'rs expand,
And pine for more than sense can understand?
135 Does she not, when the senses weary lie,
Paint brighter visions on some unknown sky;

¹ the Roman god of marriage.

² an ancient and fabled diamond mine near the city of Hyderabad, India.

Again forego her visionary joy,
To guide the senses in their strong employ;
With life's affections share their gentle flow,
But still, unsated, onward rove TO KNOW?
In infancy, when all her force is young,
She patient waits behind the useless tongue;
Silent attunes her senses, silent sees
Objects thro' mists, plainer by swift degrees.
SOUND strikes at first on her new-organ'd ear
As if far off; monotonous comes near.
Her taste yet sleeps, no melody she owns,
Nor wakes to joyous, or to thrilling tones:
Dull indiscrimination blinds her views;
But still, the sound once caught, the ear pursues;
Till cadence whispers o'er the eager thought,
And human accents strike, with MEANING fraught;
Then gentle breathings in the babe inspire
Joy, pleasure, sympathy, new-born desire.
He feels instinctive happiness, and tries
To grasp her fully as she onward flies.
Hence Mira's soft endearments shall excite
In her dear Edward exquisite delight.
    Wouldst thou Amyntor should adore his child;
Nurse him thyself, for thou canst make him mild;
Grant him the toy that suits his young desire,
Nor, when he pensive moans, his temper tire;
Keep froward passions from his tranquil breast—
By irritation, who were ever blest?—
Distorting frowns delirious fear create;
And blows, a sense of injury and hate.
Long—very long, should surly chiding sleep—
Nay, it were best thy babe should never weep.
No cure, no medicine fills the tear—the eye
Whose owner ne'er offended should be dry.
    I grant, when he the distant toy would reach,
Stern self-denial maiden aunts would preach:
But, contrary to this cold maxim tried,
Bestow the gift, Indulgence be thy guide;
Ay, give unask'd; example has its kind,
Pouring its image on the ductile mind.
Hence nobler spirits shall their likeness breed,

And ONE great virtue take the mental lead:
Hence vice and ignorance (What ills are worse?)
Arise contagious in the artful nurse;
For Virtue's self she ne'er could virtue prize,
O'er THOUGHT deform'd she throws the fair disguise;
Coarse in idea—furious in her ire,
Her passions grow amid their smother'd fire.
O trust not Edward to so warm a breast,
Lest she infuse the evils you detest.
    Early instruction does the infant need—
On pictured lessons we are prone to feed:
Thro' ev'ry stage, what strikes the eye bestrides
Attention, judgment follows and decides.
With mental vision deck th' instructive show.
Say what we will, we wish ourselves to know;
For this the child of seventy eager tries—
Explores his inward world—exploring dies!
However, early teach him mind to scan:
And when he's weary, tell him, "SUCH IS MAN."
    Next, try thy soothing skill—A challenge make—
An apple, orange, or some gew-gaw[1] stake.
Which shall read best the alphabetic line,
Be his the wish'd reward—the sorrow thine.
This rule perhaps is contrary to those
Who on the failing babe some task impose:
Ah, too severe! they chill the struggling mind—
'Tis hard to learn—the tutor should be kind.
When Edward fails, console him—let him see
Thou mourn'st his loss, and he will mourn with thee:
Not long he will thy mimic sorrow view;
Thy point once seen, he will that point pursue.
A rival for perfection, generous shame
Will touch the soul's best spark, and blaze it into fame.
    Thus far I've lightly tripp'd the infant stage:
Truths bold and strong await the second age.
To ancient fathers be thy boy consign'd,
But plant thyself true virtue in his mind.
Watch his belief, his doubts, his fruitless fears;
Convince him, The frail babe of seventy years
Will unresisting slumber on the sod,
The sole undoubted property of GOD!

---

[1] a decorative trinket.

Joel Barlow
1754 – 1812

Joel Barlow was born on 24 March 1754 in Redding, Connecticut, eighth of the nine children of Samuel Barlow, a farmer, and Esther Hull Barlow. He was educated at a village school, at Moor's Indian School in Hanover NH, and then at Dartmouth and Yale. The latter stages of his education were interrupted by the Revolutionary War, in which he served first as a volunteer and then as an army chaplain. He became secretly engaged to Ruth Baldwin in 1779, and they married secretly in January 1781. After the war, he worked as a bookseller, editor, and lawyer, while writing his epic poem *The Vision of Columbus* (1787, revised and expanded as *The Columbiad*, 1807); it was a bestseller. In 1788, he travelled to France as the representative of an Ohio real-estate company, which (unknown to Barlow) was a scam and soon collapsed; but Barlow made his fortune as an importer. He also became a radical supporter of the French Revolution, befriending Paine,* Joseph Priestley, Price,* and Wollstonecraft,* and publishing *Advice to the Privileged Orders in the Several States of Europe* (1792–93), an answer to Burke,* and other pro-Revolutionary poems and pamphlets. He returned to America in 1804. In 1811, President Madison and Secretary of State Monroe sent him to Europe to negotiate a treaty with Napoleon, then about to embark on his disastrous invasion of Russia. The horrors Barlow saw as he travelled towards the French front lines inspired "Advice to a Raven in Russia" (1812). Barlow died of pneumonia in Zarnowiec, Poland, on 24 December 1812. (D.L.M.)

※

from *The Hasty-Pudding: A Poem, in Three Cantos. Written at Chambery, in Savoy, Jan. 1793* (1793)

Omne tulit punctum qui miscuit utile dulci.[1]
He makes a good breakfast who mixes pudding with molasses.

CANTO 1

Ye Alps audacious, thro' the Heavens that rise,
To cramp the day and hide me from the skies;
Ye Gallic flags, that o'er their heights unfurl'd,
Bear death to kings, and freedom to the world,[2]
5 I sing not you. A softer theme I chuse,
A virgin theme, unconscious of the Muse,
But fruitful, rich, well suited to inspire

The purest frenzy of poetic fire.
  Despise it not, ye Bards to terror steel'd,
10 Who hurl'd your thunders round the epic field;
Nor ye who strain your midnight throats to sing
Joys that the vineyard and the still-house bring;
Or on some distant fair your notes employ,
And speak of raptures that you ne'er enjoy.
15 I sing the sweets I know, the charms I feel,
My morning incense, and my evening meal,
The sweets of Hasty-Pudding. Come, dear bowl,
Glide o'er my palate, and inspire my soul.
The milk beside thee, smoking from the kine,
20 Its substance mingled, married in with thine,
Shall cool and temper thy superior heat,
And save the pains of blowing while I eat.
  Oh! could the smooth, the emblematic song
Flow like thy genial juices o'er my tongue,
25 Could those mild morsels in my numbers chime,
And, as they roll in substance, roll in rhyme,
No more thy aukward unpoetic name
Should shun the Muse, or prejudice thy fame;
But rising grateful to the accustom'd ear,
30 All Bards should catch it, and all realms revere!
  Assist me first with pious toil to trace

---

[1] "He has won every vote who has blended profit with pleasure": Horace, *Ars Poetica* 343 (tr. H. Rushton Fairclough).

[2] So far, the French Revolutionary armies had been successful in resisting the forces of reaction. In 1792, they conquered Savoy, where Barlow wrote the poem in January 1793, after some friends served him a dish he remembered from his childhood.

Thro' wrecks of time thy lineage and thy race;
Declare what lovely squaw, in days of yore,
(Ere great Columbus sought thy native shore)
35 First gave thee to the world; her works of fame
Have liv'd indeed, but liv'd without a name.
Some tawny Ceres,[1] goddess of her days,
First learn'd with stones to crack the well-dry'd maize,
Thro' the rough sieve to shake the golden show'r,
40 In boiling water stir the yellow flour.
The yellow flour, bestrew'd and stir'd with haste,
Swells in the flood and thickens to a paste,
Then puffs and wallops, rises to the brim,
Drinks the dry knobs that on the surface swim:
45 The knobs at last the busy ladle breaks,
And the whole mass its true consistence takes.

    Could but her sacred name, unknown so long,
Rise like her labors, to the sons of song,
To her, to them, I'd consecrate my lays,
50 And blow her pudding with the breath of praise.
If 'twas Oella, whom I sang before,[2]
I here ascribe her one great virtue more.
Not thro' the rich Peruvian realms alone
The fame of Sol's sweet daughter should be known,
55 But o'er the world's wide climes should live secure,
Far as his rays extend, as long as they endure.

    Dear Hasty-Pudding, what unpromis'd joy
Expands my heart, to meet thee in Savoy!
Doom'd o'er the world thro' devious paths to roam,
60 Each clime my country, and each house my home,
My soul is sooth'd, my cares have found an end,
I greet my long-lost, unforgotten friend.

    For thee thro' Paris, that corrupted town,
How long in vain I wandered up and down,
65 Where shameless Bacchus,[3] with his drenching hoard
Cold from his cave usurps the morning board.
London is lost in smoke and steep'd in tea;
No Yankey there can lisp the name of thee:
The uncouth word, a libel on the town,
70 Would call a proclamation from the crown.[4]
For climes oblique, that fear the sun's full rays,
Chill'd in their fogs, exclude the generous maize;
A grain whose rich luxuriant growth requires
Short gentle showers, and bright etherial fires.
75 But here tho' distant from our native shore,
With mutual glee we meet and laugh once more,
The same! I know thee by that yellow face,
That strong complexion of true Indian race,
Which time can never change, nor soil impair,
80 Nor Alpine snows, nor Turkey's morbid air;
For endless years, thro' every mild domain,
Where grows the maize, there thou art sure to reign.

    But man, more fickle, the bold licence claims,
In different realms to give thee different names.
85 Thee the soft nations round the warm Levant[5]
Palanta call, the French of course *Polante*;
E'en in thy native regions, how I blush
To hear the Pennsylvanians call thee *Mush*!
On Hudson's banks, while men of Belgic spawn
90 Insult and eat thee by the name *suppawn*.[6]
All spurious appellations, void of truth:
I've better known thee from my earliest youth,
Thy name is *Hasty-Pudding*! thus our sires
Were wont to greet thee fuming from their fires;
95 And while they argu'd in thy just defence
With logic clear, they thus explained the sense:—
"In *haste* the boiling cauldron o'er the blaze,
Receives and cooks the ready-powder'd maize;
In *haste* 'tis serv'd, and then in equal *haste*,
100 With cooling milk, we make the sweet repast.
No carving to be done, no knife to grate
The tender ear, and wound the stony plate;
But the smooth spoon, just fitted to the lip,
And taught with art the yielding mass to dip,
105 By frequent journies to the bowl well stor'd,
Performs the hasty honors of the board."
Such is thy name, significant and clear,

---

[1] Roman goddess of the harvest.

[2] Barlow had written of the Inca Oella, daughter of the sun (line 54) and inventor of spinning, in *The Vision of Columbus* (1787).

[3] Roman god of wine.

[4] "A certain king, at the time when this was written, was publishing proclamations to prevent American principles from being propagated in his country." (J.B.)

[5] the Mediterranean.

[6] a Dutch corruption of the Algonkian word for cornmeal porridge.

A name, a sound to every Yankey dear,
But most to me, whose heart and palate chaste
110 Preserve my pure hereditary taste.
    There are who strive to stamp with disrepute
The luscious food, because it feeds the brute;
In tropes of high-strain'd wit, while gaudy prigs
Compare thy nursling man to pamper'd pigs;
115 With sovereign scorn I treat the vulgar jest,
Nor fear to share thy bounties with the beast.
What though the generous cow gives me to quaff
The milk nutritious; am I then a calf?
Or can the genius of the noisy swine,
120 Tho' nurs'd on pudding, thence lay claim to mine?
Sure the sweet song, I fashion to thy praise,
Runs more melodious than the notes they raise.
    My song resounding in its grateful glee,
No merit claims; I praise myself in thee.
125 My father lov'd thee through his length of days:
For thee his fields were shaded o'er with maize;
From thee what health, what vigour he possest,
Ten sturdy freemen sprung from him attest;
Thy constellation rul'd my natal morn,
130 And all my bones were made of Indian corn.
Delicious grain! whatever form it take,
To roast or boil, to smother or to bake,
In every dish 'tis welcome still to me,
But most, my Hasty-Pudding, most in thee.
135   Let the green Succatash with thee contend,
Let beans and corn their sweetest juices blend,
Let butter drench them in its yellow tide,
And a long slice of bacon grace their side;
Not all the plate, how fam'd soe'er it be,
140 Can please my palate like a bowl of thee.
    Some talk of Hoe-cake, fair Virginia's pride,
Rich Johnny-cake[1] this mouth has often tri'd;
Both please me well, their virtues much the same;
Alike their fabric, as allied their fame,
145 Except in dear New-England, where the last
Receives a dash of pumpkin in the paste,
To give it sweetness and improve the taste.
But place them all before me, smoking hot,
The big round dumplin rolling from the pot;
150 The pudding of the bag, whose quivering breast,
With suet lin'd leads on the Yankey feast;
The Charlotte brown,[2] within whose crusty sides
A belly soft the pulpy apple hides;
The yellow bread, whose face like amber glows,
155 And all of Indian that the bake-pan knows—
You tempt me not—my fav'rite greets my eyes,
To that lov'd bowl my spoon by instinct flies.[3]

from the *Huntington Library Quarterly* 2 (1938–39)

Advice to a Raven in Russia. December, 1812[4]

Black fool, why winter here? These frozen skies,
Worn by your wings and deafen'd by your cries,
Should warn you hence, where milder suns invite,
And day alternates with his mother night.[5]
5   You fear perhaps your food will fail you there,
Your human carnage, that delicious fare
That lured you hither, following still your friend
The great Napoleon to the world's bleak end.
You fear, because the southern climes pour'd forth
10 Their clustering nations to infest the north,
Bavarians, Austrians, those who Drink the Po[6]
And those who skirt the Tuscan seas below,
With all Germania, Neustria, Belgia, Gaul,[7]

---

[1] types of cornmeal cake popular in the South.

[2] a kind of pudding.

[3] The second canto describes the growing of the corn; the third describes the husking and cooking and gives advice on how to eat the hasty-pudding.

[4] edited from manuscript by Leon Howard for his article "Joel Barlow and Napoleon." This poem was published earlier in the Erie (Pennsylvania) *Chronicle* (10 October 1843), but with numerous emendations. Napoleon invaded Russia in June 1812. He captured Moscow in September and, after the city was burned down, began his disastrous retreat in October. Most of his troops perished from the cold, disease, starvation, or guerrilla attacks.

[5] Cf. Johann Wolfgang von Goethe (1749–1832), *Faust* Part 1 (1808), scene 3.

[6] a river that flows through Tuscany (line 12), in the north of Italy.

[7] classical names for Germany, Normandy, the Netherlands, and France.

Doom'd here to wade thro slaughter to their fall,
You fear he left behind no wars, to feed
His feather'd canibals and nurse the breed.

 Fear not, my screamer, call your greedy train,
Sweep over Europe, hurry back to Spain,[1]
You'll find his legions there; the valliant crew
Please best their master when they toil for you.
Abundant there they spread the country o'er
And taint the breeze with every nation's gore,
Iberian, Lussian,[2] British widely strown,
But still more wide and copious flows their own.

 Go where you will; Calabria,[3] Malta, Greece,
Egypt and Syria still his fame increase,
Domingo's fatten'd isle[4] and India's plains
Glow deep with purple drawn from Gallic veins.
No Raven's wing can stretch the flight so far
As the torn bandrols of Napoleon's war.
Choose then your climate, fix your best abode,
He'll make you deserts and he'll bring you blood.

 How could you fear a dearth? have not mankind,
Tho slain by millions, millions left behind?
Has not CONSCRIPTION still the power to weild
Her annual faulchion o'er the human field?
A faithful harvester! or if a man
Escape that gleaner, shall he scape the BAN?
The triple BAN,[5] that like the hound of hell
Gripes with three joles, to hold his victim well.

 Fear nothing then, hatch fast your ravenous brood,
Teach them to cry to Bonaparte for food;
They'll be like you, of all his supplicant train,
The only class that never cries in vain.

For see what mutual benefits you lend!
(The surest way to fix the mutual friend)
While on his slaughter'd troops your tribes are fed,
You cleanse his camp and carry off his dead.
Imperial Scavenger! but now you know
Your work is vain amid these hills of snow.
His tentless troops are marbled thro with frost
And change to crystal when the breath is lost.
Mere trunks of ice, tho limb'd like human frames
And lately warm'd with life's endearing flames,
They cannot taint the air, the world impest,
Nor can you tear one fiber from their breast.
No! from their visual sockets, as they lie,
With beak and claws you cannot pluck an eye.
The frozen orb, preserving still its form,
Defies your talons as it braves the storm,
But stands and stares to God, as if to know
In what curst hands he leaves his world below.

 Fly then, or starve; tho all the dreadful road
From Minsk[6] to Moskow with their bodies strow'd
May count some Myriads, yet they can't suffice
To feed you more beneath these dreary skies.
Go back, and winter in the wilds of Spain;
Feast there awhile, and in the next campaign
Rejoin your master; for you'll find him then,
With his new million of the race of men,
Clothed in his thunders, all his flags unfurl'd,
Raging and storming o'er the prostrate world.

 War after war his hungry soul requires,
State after State shall sink beneath his fires,
Yet other Spains in victim smoke shall rise
And other Moskows suffocate the skies,
Each land lie reeking with its people's slain
And not a stream run bloodless to the main.
Till men resume their souls, and dare to shed
Earth's total vengeance on the monster's head,
Hurl from his blood-built throne this king of woes,
Dash him to dust, and let the world repose.

---

[1] At the same time as his invasion of Russia, Napoleon's armies were engaged in the Peninsular War, which lasted from 1808 to 1814.

[2] classical names for Spanish and Portuguese.

[3] in southern Italy.

[4] Santo Domingo, the island comprising Haiti and the Dominican Republic, the scene of a slave revolution in the 1790s.

[5] The third ban, or conscription list, named the youngest conscripts for Napoleon's army. Barlow compares it to Cerberus, the three-headed dog that guarded the gates of the classical Hades.

[6] a city about 640 km (400 miles) southwest of Moscow.

George Crabbe
1754 – 1832

George Crabbe was born in Aldeburgh, Suffolk, on 24 December 1754, the son of George Crabbe, a customs official, and Mary Lodwick Crabbe. He was educated at local schools and then apprenticed, first to an apothecary and then to a surgeon, completing his medical training in London in 1777. Crabbe then returned to Aldeburgh, but his practice there was not a success. In 1775, he had published his first book, *Inebriety*, a satire; and in 1780, he went to London to try his luck as an author. He was not successful until, in 1781, he appealed to Edmund Burke,* who helped him publish *The Library* (1781) and *The Village* (1783). He also arranged for him to become a clergyman, and Crabbe served in a number of rural parishes for the rest of his life. In December 1783, he married Sarah Elmy; they had been engaged for eleven years. They had seven children, but only two lived to adulthood; after the death of their son Edmund in 1796, Sarah became depressed, and remained so for the rest of her life. She died in 1813. After publishing another satire, *The News-Paper*, in 1785, Crabbe was silent for twenty-two years. He wrote a botanical treatise and three novels but burned them all, with the delighted assistance of his children. He returned to print with *Poems* (1807), *The Borough* (1810), *Tales* (1812), and *Tales of the Hall* (1819), for which he was offered £3,000. His most characteristic works are narratives in heroic couplets, offering an unflinchingly realistic portrayal of rural life. He died in his rectory in Trowbridge, Wiltshire, on 3 February 1832. (D.L.M.)

---

from *The Borough: A Poem in Twenty-four Letters* (1810)

LETTER 22
The Poor of the Borough.
Peter Grimes[1]

   Was a sordid soul,
Such as does murder for a meed;
Who but for fear knows no controul,
Because his conscience, sear'd and foul,
 Feels not the import of the deed;
One whose brute feeling ne'er aspires
Beyond his own more brute desires.
     Scott. Marmion.[2]

Methought the souls of all that I had murder'd
Came to my tent, and every one did threat—
    Shakspeare. Richard III.[3]

The time hath been,
That when the brains were out the man would die,
And there an end; but now they rise again,
With twenty mortal murders on their crowns,
And push us from our stools.
    Macbeth.[4]

The Father of *Peter* a Fisherman.—*Peter*'s early Conduct.—His Grief for the old Man.—He takes an Apprentice.—The Boy's Suffering and Fate.—A second Boy: how he died.—*Peter* acquitted.—A third Apprentice.—A Voyage by Sea: the Boy does not return.—Evil Report on *Peter*: he is tried and threatened.—Lives alone.—His Melancholy and insipient Madness.—Is observed and visited.—He escapes and is taken; is lodged in a Parish-House: Women attend and watch him.—He speaks in a Delirium: grows more collected.—His Account of his Feelings and visionary Terrors previous to his Death.

---

[1] The poem is based on a true story Crabbe heard in Aldeburgh. It has inspired an opera (1945) by Benjamin Britten.

[2] Scott, *Marmion** 2.22.1–7.

[3] Shakespeare, *Richard III* 5.3.205–6.

[4] Shakespeare, *Macbeth* 3.4.78–82.

Old *Peter Grimes* made Fishing his employ,[1]
His Wife he cabin'd[2] with him and his Boy,
And seem'd that Life laborious to enjoy:
To Town came quiet *Peter* with his Fish,
5 And had of all a civil word and wish.
He left his Trade upon the Sabbath-Day,
And took young *Peter* in his hand to pray;
But soon the stubborn Boy from care broke loose,
At first refus'd, then added his abuse:
10 His Father's Love he scorn'd, his Power defied,
But being drunk, wept sorely when he died.

Yes! then he wept, and to his Mind there came
Much of his Conduct, and he felt the Shame,—
How he had oft the good old Man revil'd,
15 And never paid the Duty of a Child;
How, when the Father in his Bible read,
He in contempt and anger left the Shed:
"It is the Word of Life," the Parent cried;
—"This is the Life itself," the Boy replied,
20 And while Old *Peter* in amazement stood,
Gave the hot Spirit to his boiling Blood:—
How he, with Oath and furious Speech, began
To prove his Freedom and assert the Man;
And when the Parent check'd his impious Rage,
25 How he had curs'd the Tyranny of Age,—
Nay, once had dealt the sacrilegious Blow[3]
On his bare Head and laid his Parent low:
The Father groan'd—"If thou art old," said he,
"And hast a Son—thou wilt remember me:
30 Thy Mother left me in an happy Time,
Thou kill'dst not her—Heav'n spares the double Crime."

On an Inn-Settle,[4] in his maudlin Grief,
This he revolv'd and drank for his Relief.

Now liv'd the Youth in freedom, but debar'd
35 From constant Pleasure, and he thought it hard;

Hard that he could not every wish obey,
But must awhile relinquish Ale and Play;
Hard! that he could not to his Cards attend,
But must acquire the Money he would spend.

40 With greedy eye he look'd on all he saw,
He knew not Justice and he laugh'd at Law;
On all he mark'd he stretch'd his ready Hand,
He fish'd by Water and he filch'd by Land:
Oft in the Night has *Peter* dropt his Oar,
45 Fled from his Boat and saught for Prey on shore;
Oft up the Hedge-row glided, on his Back
Bearing the Orchard's Produce in a Sack,
Or Farm-yard Load, tug'd fiercely from the Stack;
And as these Wrongs to greater numbers rose,
50 The more he look'd on all Men as his Foes.

He built a mud-wall'd Hovel, where he kept
His various Wealth, and there he oft-times slept;
But no Success could please his cruel Soul,
He wish'd for one to trouble and controul;
55 He wanted some obedient Boy to stand
And bear the blow of his outrageous hand;
And hop'd to find in some propitious hour
A feeling Creature subject to his Power.

Peter had heard there were in London then,—
60 Still have they being?—Workhouse-clearing Men,
Who, undisturb'd by Feelings just or kind,
Would Parish-Boys to needy Tradesmen bind:
They in their want a trifling Sum would take,
And toiling Slaves of piteous Orphans make.

65 Such *Peter* sought, and when a Lad was found,
The Sum was dealt him and the Slave was bound.
Some few in Town observ'd in *Peter*'s Trap[5]
A Boy, with Jacket blue and woollen Cap;
But none enquir'd how *Peter* us'd the Rope,
70 Or what the Bruise, that made the Stripling stoop;
None could the Ridges on his Back behold,
None sought him shiv'ring in the Winter's Cold;
None put the question,—"*Peter*, dost thou give
The Boy his Food?—What, Man! the Lad must live:
75 Consider, *Peter*, let the Child have Bread,

---

[1] The pious old Peter is named after Christ's disciple St. Peter, a fisher.

[2] possibly an echo of Macbeth 3.4.24.

[3] Cf. Exodus 20.12.

[4] a settee or sofa in a pub.

[5] a light horse-drawn carriage.

He'll serve thee better if he's strok'd and fed."
None reason'd thus—and some, on hearing Cries,
Said calmly, "*Grimes* is at his Exercise."

    Pin'd, beaten, cold, pinch'd, threaten'd, and
        abused,—
80 His Efforts punish'd and his Food refus'd,—
Awake tormented,—soon arous'd from sleep,—
Struck if he wept, and yet compell'd to weep,
The trembling Boy dropt down and strove to pray,
Receiv'd a Blow and trembling turn'd away,
85 Or sob'd and hid his piteous face;—while he,
The savage Master, grin'd in horrid glee;
He'd now the power he ever lov'd to show,
A feeling Being subject to his Blow.

    Thus liv'd the Lad in Hunger, Peril, Pain,
90 His Tears despis'd, his Supplications vain:
Compell'd by fear to lie, by need to steal,
His Bed uneasy and unblest his Meal,
For three sad Years the Boy his Tortures bore,
And then his Pains and Trials were no more.

95   "How died he, *Peter*?" when the People said,
He growl'd—"I found him lifeless in his Bed";
Then try'd for softer tone, and sigh'd, "Poor *Sam* is dead."
Yet murmurs were there and some questions ask'd,—
How he was fed, how punish'd, and how task'd?
100 Much they suspected, but they little prov'd,
And *Peter* past untroubled and unmov'd.

    Another Boy with equal ease was found,
The Money granted and the Victim bound;
And what his Fate?—One night it chanc'd he fell
105 From the Boat's Mast and perish'd in her Well,
Where Fish were living kept, and where the Boy
(So reason'd Men) could not himself destroy:—

    "Yes! so it was," said *Peter*, "in his play,
For he was idle both by night and day;
110 He climb'd the Main-mast and then fell below";—
Then show'd his Corpse and pointed to the Blow:
"What said the Jury?"—they were long in doubt,
But sturdy *Peter* faced the matter out:
So they dismiss'd him, saying at the time,

115 "Keep fast your Hatchway when you've Boys who
    climb."
This hit the Conscience, and he colour'd more
Than for the closest questions put before.

    Thus all his fears the Verdict set aside,
And at the Slave-shop *Peter* still applied.

120   Then came a Boy, of Manners soft and mild,—
Our Seamen's Wives with grief beheld the Child;
All thought (the Poor themselves) that he was one
Of gentle Blood, some noble Sinner's Son,
Who had, belike, deceiv'd some humble Maid,
125 Whom he had first seduc'd and then betray'd:—
However this, he seem'd a gracious Lad,
In Grief submissive and with Patience sad.

    Passive he labour'd, till his slender Frame
Bent with his Loads, and he at length was lame:
130 Strange that a frame so weak could bear so long
The grossest Insult and the foulest Wrong;
But there were causes—in the Town they gave
Fire, Food, and Comfort, to the gentle Slave;
And though stern *Peter*, with a cruel Hand,
135 And knotted Rope, enforc'd the rude Command,
Yet he consider'd what he'd lately felt,
And his vile Blows with selfish Pity dealt.

    One day such Draughts the cruel Fisher made,
He could not vend them in his Borough-Trade,
140 But sail'd for London-Mart: the Boy was ill,
But ever humbled to his Master's will;
And on the River, where they smoothly sail'd,
He strove with terror and awhile prevail'd;
But new to Danger on the angry Sea,
145 He clung affrighten'd to his Master's knee:
The Boat grew leaky and the Wind was strong,
Rough was the Passage and the Time was long;
His Liquor fail'd, and *Peter*'s Wrath arose,—
No more is known—the rest we must suppose,
150 Or learn of *Peter;*—*Peter*, says he, "spied
The Stripling's danger and for Harbour tried;
Meantime the Fish and then th'Apprentice died."
    The pitying Women rais'd a Clamour round,
And weeping said, "Thou hast thy 'Prentice drown'd."

155   Now the stern Man was summon'd to the Hall,
To tell his Tale before the Burghers all:
He gave th'Account, profess'd the Lad he lov'd,
And kept his brazen Features all unmov'd.

     The Mayor himself with tone severe replied,
160 "Henceforth with thee shall never Boy abide;
Hire thee a Freeman, whom thou durst not beat,
But who, in thy despite, will sleep and eat:
Free thou art now!—again shouldst thou appear,
Thou'lt find thy Sentence, like thy Soul, severe."

165   Alas! for *Peter* not an helping Hand,
So was he hated, could he now command;
Alone he row'd his Boat, alone he cast
His Nets beside, or made his Anchor fast;
To hold a Rope or hear a Curse was none,—
170 He toil'd and rail'd; he groan'd and swore alone.

     Thus by himself compell'd to live each day,
To wait for certain hours the Tide's delay;
At the same times the same dull views to see,
The bounding Marsh-bank and the blighted Tree;
175 The Water only, when the Tides were high,
When low, the Mud half-cover'd and half-dry;
The Sun-burn'd Tar that blisters on the Planks,
And Bank-side Stakes in their uneven ranks;
Heaps of entangled Weeds that slowly float,
180 As the Tide rolls by the impeded Boat.

     When Tides were neap, and, in the sultry day,
Through the tall bounding Mud-banks made their way,
Which on each side rose swelling, and below
The dark warm Flood ran silently and slow;
185 There anchoring, *Peter* chose from Man to hide,
There hang his Head, and view the lazy Tide
In its hot slimy Channel slowly glide;
Where the small Eels that left the deeper way
For the warm Shore, within the Shallows play;
190 Where gaping Muscles, left upon the Mud,
Slope their slow passage to the fallen Flood;—
Here dull and hopeless he'd lie down and trace
How side-long Crabs had scrawl'd their crooked race;
Or sadly listen to the tuneless cry

195 Of fishing *Gull* or clanging *Golden-Eye*;[1]
What time the Sea-Birds to the Marsh would come,
And the loud *Bittern*, from the Bull-rush home,
Gave from the Salt-ditch side the bellowing Boom:
He nurst the Feelings these dull Scenes produce,
200 And lov'd to stop beside the opening Sluice;
Where the small Stream, confin'd in narrow bound,
Ran with a dull, unvaried, sad'ning sound;
Where all presented to the Eye or Ear,
Oppress'd the Soul! with Misery, Grief, and Fear.

205   Besides these objects, there were places three,
Which *Peter* seem'd with certain dread to see;
When he drew near them he would turn from each,
And loudly whistle till he past the *Reach*.[2]

     A change of Scene to him brought no relief,
210 In Town, 'twas plain, Men took him for a Thief:
The Sailors' Wives would stop him in the Street,
And say, "Now, *Peter*, thou'st no Boy to beat":
Infants at play, when they perceiv'd him, ran,
Warning each other—"That's the wicked Man":
215 He growl'd an oath, and in an angry tone
Curs'd the whole Place and wish'd to be alone.

     Alone he was, the same dull Scenes in view,
And still more gloomy in his sight they grew:
Though Man he hated, yet employ'd alone
220 At bootless labour, would swear and groan,
Cursing the Shoals that glided by the spot,
And *Gulls* that caught them when his arts could not.

     Cold nervous Tremblings shook his sturdy Frame,
And strange Disease—he couldn't say the name;
225 Wild were his Dreams, and oft he rose in fright,
Wak'd by his view of Horrors in the Night,—
Horrors that would the sternest Minds amaze,
Horrors that Dæmons might be proud to raise:

---

[1] a kind of salt-water duck.

[2] "The reaches in a river are those parts which extend from point to point. *Johnson* has not the word precisely in this sense, but it is very common, and I believe used wheresoever a navigable river can be found in this country." (G.C.) Samuel Johnson (1709–84), *A Dictionary of the English Language* (1755).

And though he felt forsaken, griev'd at heart,
To think he liv'd from all Mankind apart;
Yet, if a Man approach'd, in terrors he would start.

A Winter past since *Peter* saw the Town,
And Summer Lodgers were again come down;
These, idly-curious, with their glasses spied
The Ships in Bay as anchor'd for the Tide,—
The River's Craft,—the bustle of the Quay,—
And Sea-port views, which Landmen love to see.

One, up the River, had a Man and Boat
Seen day by day, now anchor'd, now afloat;
Fisher he seem'd, yet us'd no Net nor Hook,
Of Sea-fowl swimming by, no heed he took,
But on the gliding Waves still fix'd his lazy look:
At certain stations he would view the Stream,
As if he stood bewilder'd in a Dream,
Or that some Power had chain'd him for a time,
To feel a Curse or meditate on Crime.

This known, some curious, some in pity went,
And others question'd—"Wretch, dost thou repent?"
He heard, he trembled, and in fear resign'd
His Boat: new terror fill'd his restless Mind;
Furious he grew and up the Country ran,
And there they seiz'd him—a distemper'd Man:—
Him we receiv'd, and to a Parish-bed,
Follow'd and curs'd, the groaning Man was led.

Here when they saw him, whom they us'd to shun,
A lost, lone Man, so harass'd and undone;
Our gentle Females, ever prompt to feel,
Perceiv'd Compassion on their Anger steal;
His Crimes they couldn't from their Memories blot,
But they were griev'd and trembled at his Lot.

A Priest too came, to whom his words are told,
And all the signs they shudder'd to behold.

"Look! look!" they cried; "his Limbs with horror shake,
And as he grinds his Teeth, what noise they make!
How glare his angry Eyes, and yet he's not awake:
See! what cold drops upon his Forehead stand,
And how he clenches that broad bony Hand."

The Priest attending, found he spoke at times
As one alluding to his Fears and Crimes:
"It was the fall," he mutter'd, "I can show
The manner how—I never struck a blow":—
And then aloud—"Unhand me, free my Chain;
On Oath, he fell—it struck him to the Brain:—
Why ask my Father?—that old Man will swear
Against my Life; besides, he wasn't there:—
What, all agreed?—Am I to die to-day?—
My Lord, in Mercy, give me time to pray."

Then as they watch'd him, calmer he became,
And grew so weak he couldn't move his Frame,
But murmuring spake,—while they could see and hear
The start of Terror and the groan of Fear;
See the large Dew-beads on his Forehead rise,
And the cold Death-drop glaze his sunken Eyes;
Nor yet he died, but with unwonted force,
Seem'd with some fancied Being to discourse:
He knew not us, or with accustom'd art
He hid the knowledge, yet expos'd his Heart:
'Twas part Confession and the rest Defence,
A Madman's Tale, with gleams of waking Sense.

"I'll tell you all," he said, "the very day
When the old Man first plac'd them in my way:
My Father's Spirit—he who always tried
To give me trouble, when he liv'd and died—
When he was gone, he could not be content
To see my Days in painful Labour spent,
But would appoint his Meetings, and he made
Me watch at these, and so neglect my Trade.

"'Twas one hot Noon, all silent, still, serene,
No living Being had I lately seen;
I paddled up and down and dipt my Net,
But (such his pleasure) I could nothing get,—
A Father's pleasure! when his Toil was done,
To plague and torture thus an only Son;
And so I sat and look'd upon the Stream,

305　How it ran on, and felt as in a Dream:
　　　But Dream it was not; No!—I fix'd my Eyes
　　　On the mid Stream and saw the Spirits rise;
　　　I saw my Father on the Water stand,
　　　And hold a thin pale Boy in either hand;
310　And there they glided ghastly on the top
　　　Of the salt Flood and never touch'd a drop:
　　　I would have struck them, but they knew th'intent,
　　　And smil'd upon the Oar, and down they went.

　　　　"Now, from that day, whenever I began
315　To dip my Net, there stood the hard old Man—
　　　He and those Boys: I humbled me and pray'd
　　　They would be gone;—they heeded not, but stay'd:
　　　Nor could I turn, nor would the Boat go by,
　　　But gazing on the Spirits, there was I;
320　They bade me leap to death, but I was loth to die:
　　　And every day, as sure as day arose,
　　　Would these three Spirits meet me 'eer the close;
　　　To hear and mark them daily was my doom,
　　　And 'Come,' they said, with weak, sad voices, 'come.'
325　To row away with all my strength I try'd,
　　　But there were they, hard by me in the Tide,
　　　The three unbodied Forms—and 'Come,' still 'come,'
　　　　　they cried.

　　　　"Fathers should pity—but this old Man shook
　　　His hoary Locks and froze me by a Look:
330　Thrice, when I struck them, through the water came
　　　An hollow Groan, that weaken'd all my Frame:
　　　'Father!' said I, ' have Mercy':—He replied,
　　　I know not what—the angry Spirit lied,—
　　　'Didst thou not draw thy Knife?' said he:—'Twas true,
335　But I had Pity and my Arm withdrew:
　　　He cried for Mercy, which I kindly gave,
　　　But he has no Compassion in his Grave.

　　　　"There were three places, where they ever rose,—
　　　The whole long River has not such as those,—
340　Places accurs'd, where, if a Man remain,
　　　He'll see the things which strike him to the Brain;
　　　And there they made me on my Paddle lean,
　　　And look at them for hours;—accursed Scene!
　　　When they would glide to that smooth Eddy-space,
345　Then bid me leap and join them in the place;
　　　And at my Groans each little villain Sprite
　　　Enjoy'd my Pains and vanish'd in delight.

　　　　"In one fierce Summer-day, when my poor Brain
　　　Was burning-hot and cruel was my Pain,
350　Then came this Father-foe, and there he stood
　　　With his two Boys again upon the Flood;
　　　There was more Mischief in their Eyes, more Glee
　　　In their pale Faces when they glar'd at me:
　　　Still did they force me on the Oar to rest,
355　And when they saw me fainting and opprest,
　　　He, with his Hand, the old Man, scoop'd the Flood,
　　　And there came Flame about him mix'd with Blood;
　　　He bade me stoop and look upon the place,
　　　Then flung the hot-red Liquor in my Face;
360　Burning it blaz'd, and then I roar'd for Pain,
　　　I thought the Dæmons would have turn'd my Brain.

　　　　"Still there they stood, and forc'd me to behold
　　　A place of Horrors—they cannot be told—
　　　Where the Flood open'd, there I heard the Shriek
365　Of tortur'd Guilt—no earthly Tongue can speak:
　　　'All Days alike! for ever!' did they say,
　　　'And unremitted Torments every Day'—
　　　Yes, so they said":—But here he ceas'd and gaz'd
　　　On all around, affrighten'd and amaz'd;
370　And still he try'd to speak and look'd in dread
　　　Of frighten'd Females gathering round his Bed;
　　　Then dropt exhausted and appeared at rest,
　　　Till the strong Foe the vital Powers possest;
　　　Then with an inward, broken voice he cried,
375　"Again they come," and mutter'd as he died.

Anne Grant
1755 – 1838

Anne MacVicar was born in Glasgow on 21 February 1755, the daughter of Duncan MacVicar, an army officer, and Catherine MacKenzie MacVicar. In 1757, her father was posted to America to serve in the Seven Years' War, and the next year, Anne and her mother followed him, settling near Albany. She was educated by her mother and by a neighbour, Margaretta Schuyler. The family returned to Scotland in 1768. In 1779, Anne married a minister, James Grant, and went to live with him in Laggan, a village fifty miles from Inverness. They had twelve children, only one of whom survived their mother. James died in 1801, leaving his widow with eight children to support and debts to pay; she turned to writing, publishing *Poems on Various Subjects* in 1803 (the second edition, entitled *The Highlanders, and Other Poems*, appeared in 1808). She also published *Letters from the Mountains* (1806), an account of Highland society; *Memoirs of an American Lady* (1808), a tribute to Schuyler; *Essays on the Superstitions of the Highlanders* (1811); and *Eighteen Hundred and Thirteen* (1814), a long poetic response to Barbauld's pessimistic *Eighteen Hundred and Eleven*.* Living in Edinburgh, she came to know Baillie,* Byron,* Campbell,* De Quincey,* Hemans,* Hogg,* Irving,* Jeffrey,* Henry Mackenzie, Scott,* Southey,* and W. Wordsworth.* She died of influenza on 7 November 1838. (D.L.M.)

ぞうぞ

from *The Highlanders, and Other Poems*, 2nd ed. (1808)

A Familiar Epistle to a Friend.
Written in 1795

> The hours that we have spent,
> When we have chid the hasty-footed time
> For parting us.
>   SHAKSPEARE.[1]

Dear Beatrice, with pleasure I read your kind letter;
On the subject, methinks, there could scarce be a better:
How vivid the scenes it recall'd to my view,
And how lively it waken'd remembrance anew!
5 Yet our souls are so crusted with housewifely moss,
That Fancy's bright furnace yields nothing but dross;
Surrounded with balling, and squalling, and prattle,
With handmaids unhandy, and gossipping tattle,
Cut fingers to bandage, and stockings to darn,
10 And labyrinths endless of ill-manag'd yarn,
Through whose windings *Daedalean*[2] bewilder'd we wander,
Like draggle-tail'd nymphs of the mazy *Meander*,[3]
Till at length, like the *Hero of Macedon*,[4] tir'd
Of the slow perseverance untwisting required,
15 We brandish out scissars, resolved on the spot,
Since we cannot unravel, to cut through the knot.
Blest vicars of England! how happy your wives!
Though devoted to pudding and plain work their lives,
Though quotations and homilies forced to endure,
20 While fumes of tobacco their graces obscure;
Though their quiet be disturb'd with the nursery's noise,
Though their girls should be hoydens, or dunces their boys,
With the tangling of yarn they are never perplex'd,
More difficult to clear than his Reverence's text.

---

[1] Shakespeare, *A Midsummer Night's Dream* 3.2.199–201.

[2] Dædalus designed the labyrinth in which King Minos of Crete confined the Minotaur: see Ovid, *Metamorphoses* 8.

[3] a river in ancient Phrygia (modern Turkey) proverbial for its winding course.

[4] Alexander the Great (356–323 BC). Challenged to untie the Gordian Knot, he cut through it with his sword instead.

While with labour incessant our toils we renew,
To furnish fine linen, and purple and blue,
Such a series of self-same minute occupation
Yields nothing, you'll own, to enliven narration;
And as for the friend of all poets, *Invention*,
'Tis a thing, of late years, I scarce think of or mention:
Or of useful inventions alone make my boast,
Such as saving potatoes and turnips from frost;
Or repulsing whole armies of mice from my cheese;
Or plucking the quills without paining the geese.
    What a change on the scene and the actors appears?
'Tis now but a dozen and odd of short years,
Since when we, and the season, and fancy were young,
On *Tarfe's*[1] flowery banks our gay whimsies we sung,
Regardless of profit, and hopeless of fame,
Yet heedless of censure, and fearless of blame,
We travers'd the vale, or we haunted the grove,
As free as the birds that were chanting above;
Where the fair face of Nature was bright with a smile,
Enraptur'd in silence we gaz'd for a while;
Then as clear and as artless resounded our lays,
As the sky or the stream we endeavour'd to praise;
While strains of delight the pure pleasures impart
That thrill'd through each bosom, and glow'd in each heart;
But when from the east, with dun vapours o'ercast,
Came horrors bestriding the bleak howling blast;
When rude echoing rocks with brown cataracts foam'd,
And bewilder'd in mist the sad traveller roam'd;
When to part us, loud storms and deep gullies conspir'd,
And sublime meditation to garrats retir'd;
To the workings of fancy to give a relief,
We sat ourselves down to imagine some grief,
Till we conjur'd up phantoms so solemn and sad,
As, if they had lasted, would make us half mad;
Then in strains so affecting we pour'd the soft ditty,
As mov'd both the rocks and their echoes to pity:
And to prove it, each note of the soul-moving strain
In more sonorous sounds was return'd back again;
And we, silly souls, were so proud of our parts,
When we thought that our pathos had reach'd their hard hearts!
But when grave looking HYMEN[2] had kindl'd his torch,
With a pure lambent flame that would glow but not scorch,
The Muses, who plain humble virtues revere,
Were affrighted to look on his brow so austere;
The cottage so humble, or sanctified dome,
For the revels of fancy afforded no room;
And the lyre and the garland, were forc'd to give place
To duties domestic, and records of grace:
Then farewell *Illysus*, adieu *Hippocrene*,
The vales of *Arcadia* and *Tempe* so green;[3]
To the hills of *Judea* we now must draw near,
King LEMUEL's good mother's wise maxims to hear,[4]
And strive to leave none of the duties undone
Which the matron prescrib'd for the spouse of her son;
For my own part, I labour'd and strove with my might
To do all that the proverbs applauded as right:
Fine coverings I made that with tapestry vied,
And with heather and madder my fleeces I dy'd,
While the sun shone I still made the most of his light,
And my candle most faithfully burnt through the night;
And while that and large fires through the winter did glow,
Not a farthing my household would care for the snow:
Their plaids, hose, and garters, with scarlet adorn'd,
Chill December they braved, and its rigours they scorn'd;
Yet these were not all my pretensions to claim
Of a matron industrious and virtuous the name;
My mate (can you doubt it?) was known in the gates,
Among seniors, and elders, and men of estates:
I made him a coat of a grave solemn hue,
Two threads they were black, and the other two blue;

---

[1] "*Tarfe* is a beautiful little river which descends from the *Corryaric*; and, after winding among rocky caverns, through a narrow wooded glen of the same name, discharges itself into *Lochness* at *Fort-Augustus*." [A.G.]

[2] the classical god of marriage. A torch was his traditional attribute.

[3] The Ilissus is a stream on the plain of Athens, celebrated by Plato in the *Phædrus*. The Hippocrene is a spring on Mount Helicon, supposedly started by a blow from the hoof of Pegasus and sacred to the Muses. Arcadia is a pastoral region in the central Peloponnese. Tempe is a beautiful valley between Mount Olympus and Mount Ossa.

[4] Proverbs 31.1.

So warm, and so clerical, comely and cheap, [95]
'Twas a proof both of thrift and contrivance so deep;
His cravats of muslin were spun by my hands,
I knit all his stockings and stitch'd all his bands;
Till the neighbours all swore by St. BRIDGET herself,[1]
Such a wife was worth titles, and beauty, and pelf.[2] [100]
Quite dead and extinct all poetical fire,
At the foot of the cradle conceal'd lay my lyre;
What witchcraft had alter'd its form I ne'er knew,
But by some means or other a whistle it grew;
The brats in succession all jingled its bells, [105]
While its music to them the piano excels:
But when slowly and surely the cold hand of time
Had stole my complexion, and wither'd my prime,
Resolv'd for a while to respire at my ease,
In *Clydesdale*[3] I courted the soft western breeze; [110]
Whose fresh breathing whispers my languor could soothe,
With visions of fancy, and dreams of my youth.
While slowly retracing my dear native *Clyde*,
And reviewing my visage, so chang'd, in its tide,
As sad and reluctant I strove to retire, [115]
To my grasp was presented my trusty old lyre,—
I snatch'd it, I strumm'd it, and thrumm'd it again,
But strove to awaken its music in vain;
So rusty the wire, so enfeebled my hand,
A while in suspence and dumb wonder I stand: [120]
Thus it happen'd they say, to ULYSSES of old,[4]
When twenty long years of sad absence had roll'd,
To his ITHACA forc'd in disguise to resort,
When the suitors with uproar were filling his court;
He set his foot forward, and bending his brow, [125]
With a dignified air he demanded his bow;
With joy-mingled sorrow review'd his old friend,
And three times essay'd the tough crescent to bend,
Till the string to his efforts resounded so sharp,
Some thought it a swallow and some an old harp.[5]— [130]
Thus awkward and faint were my efforts at first,
But I rais'd the note higher whenever I durst:
To Friendship and Truth I exalted the lay,
And homewards with music beguil'd the long way;
And now since beyond any doubt it appears, [135]
From duties discharg'd through a series of years,
That nor peace nor industry are banish'd the cell
Where in ease and retirement the Muse loves to dwell;
Once more let us try to awaken the strain,
So friendly to sorrow, so soothing to pain! [140]
The blessings we've tasted let's carefully rate,
And be just to kind Nature, and grateful to Fate;
Thus wisely employing the last closing strain,
We shall not have liv'd or have warbled in vain.
Were the foot-path of life to be travell'd anew, [145]
When we calmly look back with a serious review,
For noisy applause or for tinsel parade,
Would we part with sweet Peace that delights in the shade?
Or blame the kind harbour, remote and obscure,
Where our minds were kept tranquil, our hearts were kept pure? [150]
While with streamers all flying, and wide-swelling sails,
Toss'd high on the billows, the sport of the gales,
The Muse's fair daughters triumphant were borne
Till the public applause was converted to scorn;
For by vanity guided, so wildly they steer'd, [155]
Or by caprice directed, so frequently veer'd;
Creation's proud Masters observ'd with a sneer,
That like comets eccentric forsaking their sphere,
Their brightness so gaz'd at, would never produce,
Or pleasure, or profit, or comfort, or use. [160]
****** and ****** thus shone for a day,
How prais'd was each period! how flatter'd each lay!
Till a crop so luxuriant arising of pride,
Affectation, and fifty new follies beside,
The duties and joys of the mother and wife, [165]
The nameless soft comforts of calm private life,
Fell victims together at Vanity's shrine,
For who could endure to exist and not shine!

---

[1] an Irish saint (453?–523?) popular all over Britain and associated especially with charity and justice.

[2] Cf. Proverbs 31.10.

[3] the valley of the river Clyde, which flows through Glasgow, where Grant was born.

[4] When Odysseus (Ulysses) returned to Ithaca after his long absence, he was able to identify himself because no-one else could string his bow: see Homer, *Odyssey* 21.

[5] Homer, *Odyssey* 21.404–11.

MACAULAY, of STUARTS had tore up the graves,[1]
170 To prove half of them fools, and the other half knaves,
And sully'd the mitre and spatter'd the gown,
And flatter'd the mob and insulted the Crown;
Then insensibly shrunk to a faction's blind tool,
And discover'd too late they had made her their fool.
175 With virtues, and graces, and beauties beside,
The delight of her friends, of her country the pride,
Say, who could to ******* [2] their suffrage refuse,
Or who not be charm'd with her chaste classic Muse?
To the passion for liberty giving loose rein,
180 At length she flew off to carouse on the *Seine*;[3]
And growing inebriate while quaffing the draught,
Equality's new-fangled doctrines she taught;
And murder and sacrilege calmly survey'd;
In the new *Pandemonium*[4] those demons had made;
185 *Seine's* blood-crimson'd waters with apathy ey'd,
While the glories of old father *Thames*[5] she decried.
Now with equals in misery hid in some hole,
Her body a prison confining her soul,
From the freedom of *Gallia*[6] how fain would she fly,
190 To the freedom which genius shall taste in the sky!
No longer pursue those fond lovers of fame,
Nor envy the honours and trophies they claim;
No further excursive to speculate roam,
But fix our attention and pleasure at home:
195 Why regret, when celebrity proves such a curse,
The cares of the mother and toils of the nurse:
While the nurse finds delight in sweet infancy's smiles,
And hope the fond mother's long trouble beguiles.
"But why these quick feelings, or why this nice ear,
200 Or musical accents, if no one must hear?
Why blossoms of fancy all scatter'd to waste,
The glow sympathetic, or pleasures of taste?—"

Ask why in the mountains the flow'ret should blow,
Which none but the hermit is destin'd to know?
205 Why the wild woods re-echo with melody clear,
Which none but the hunter is destined to hear?
When often enjoyed and but seldom they're shewn,
Our riches and pleasures are truly our own:
The milk-maid that carols her wild native airs
210 To solace her labours, and lighten her cares,
Feels a pleasure more genuine and free from alloy,
Than CATLEY or MARA could ever enjoy:[7]
Who, while their divisions they warbled aloud,
Depended for joy on the praise of the crowd;
215 Then blest be the lyre, ever sacred its strain,
In the regions of bliss let it waken again:
When the kind hand of Nature has fitted its strings,
And the dictates of truth and of virtue it sings,
As softly and sweetly it touches the mind,
220 As AEOLUS' harp when 'tis mov'd by the wind;[8]
Untainted by art were the notes it has sung,
It has cheer'd our decline, and has charm'd us when
    young;
And when useful employments demanded our prime,
Our leisure it soothed without wasting our time:
225 And when all our sorrows and toils shall be o'er,
Its music perhaps may delight us once more;
When swelling to concords more rich and sublime,
It may rise beyond earth, and may live beyond time.
The blossoms I once so admir'd and caress'd,
230 That cheer'd my fond heart till they dy'd on my
    breast,
Which my tears that fell frequent, like soft silent rain,
Could not waken to life and new fragrance again:
There, again, in new sweetness and beauty shall bloom,
And the evergreen plain with fresh odours perfume;
235 Perhaps while exalted their graces shall rise,
Again their dear verdure shall gladden my eyes!
When the season of fear and of sorrow is o'er,
And our tears and our songs are remember'd no more!

---

[1] Catharine Macaulay's* *History of England* (1763–83) takes a Whig view of the Stuarts that displeased Grant.

[2] Helen Maria Williams,* who went to France during the Revolution. She was imprisoned during the Reign of Terror.

[3] the river flowing through Paris.

[4] the habitation of all the devils: see Milton, *Paradise Lost* 1.670–792.

[5] Cf. John Dryden (1631–1700), *Annus Mirabilis, The Year of Wonders* (1667) 925.

[6] "France" (L.).

---

[7] Ann Catley (1745–89) and Gertrude Elizabeth Mara (1749–1833), singers.

[8] Aeolus was the classical god of the winds. An Aeolian harp is played by the winds: see Coleridge, "Effusion 35"* and "Dejection,"* and Wollstonecraft, *Letters* (435).*

Robert Merry
1755 – 1798

Robert Merry was born in April 1755, the son of Robert Merry, governor of the Hudson's Bay Company. Following his education at Harrow and at Christ's College, Cambridge, Merry became a lieutenant in the horse guards and spent his youth travelling and gambling. In 1784 he arrived in Florence, Italy, where he adopted "Della Crusca" as his poetic pseudonym and started the Della Cruscan movement (named after an academy founded in Florence in the sixteenth century). Following publication of *The Florence Miscellany* in 1785, poems by members of the group circulated in England and were printed in such periodicals as the *Oracle* and the *World*.

Returning to England in 1787, Merry published other works, including plays. In response to one of his poems, "The Adieu and Recall to Love," the playwright Hannah Cowley* (who adopted the pseudonym Anna Matilda) began a poetic love affair with Merry. Cowley was married, but her husband had deserted her. She was nevertheless criticized for entering into an adulterous relationship, though she and Merry did not meet until 1789, just before the end of their poetic exchange. The poems of "Della Crusca" and "Anna Matilda," published in the *World*, made the Della Cruscans famous. Merry, Cowley, and others, including Mary Robinson* ("Laura Maria") contributed to the *British Album*, which went through several editions between 1788 and 1794. The ideals of the group included personal liberty and support for revolutionary goals. William Gifford, who opposed them on political as well as literary and moral grounds, satirized the group in *The Baviad* (1791) and *The Maeviad* (1795). In spite of the claim in the Preface to the *British Album* that Merry and Cowley's relationship was purely poetic, the women in the group were attacked in such works as Richard Polwhele's *The Unsex'd Females*.*

In 1791 Merry married the actress Ann Brunton. The next year she retired from the stage, but by 1796 Merry's extravagance made it necessary for her to accept an offer from a Philadelphia theatre manager. The same year, the Merrys moved to the United States, where Ann Merry made her American debut in *Romeo and Juliet*. After Robert Merry's death in 1798, she continued to live and work in America. (A.M.)

*****

from the *British Album* (1790)[1]

The Adieu and Recall to Love

Go, idle Boy! I quit thy pow'r;
Thy couch of many a thorn, and flow'r;
Thy twanging bow, thine arrow keen,
Deceitful Beauty's timid mien;
5 The feign'd surprise, the roguish leer,
The tender smile, the thrilling tear,
Have now no pangs, no joys for me,
So fare thee well, for I am free!

Then flutter hence on wanton wing,
10 Or lave thee in yon lucid spring,
Or take thy bev'rage from the rose,
Or on *Louisa*'s breast repose:
I wish thee well for pleasures past,
Yet bless the hour, I'm free at last.

15 But sure, methinks, the alter'd day
Scatters around a mournful ray;
And chilling ev'ry zephyr blows,
And ev'ry stream untuneful flows;
No rapture swells the linnet's voice,
20 No more the vocal groves rejoice;
And e'en thy song, *sweet Bird of Eve*![2]
With whom I lov'd so oft to grieve,

---

[1] first published in the *World* (29 June 1787), and reprinted as the first poem in the *British Album*, an anthology of "Della Cruscan" verse (Merry's pseudonym was "Della Crusca.") "The Adieu and Recall to Love" is the first poem in the collection, followed by Hannah Cowley, "To Della Crusca: The Pen."*

[2] the nightingale.

Now scarce regarded meets my ear,
Unanswer'd by a sigh or tear.
25 No more with devious step I choose
To brush the mountain's morning dews;
"To drink the spirit of the breeze,"[1]
Or wander midst o'er-arching trees;
Or woo with undisturb'd delight,
30 The pale-cheek'd Virgin of the Night,[2]
That piercing thro' the leafy bow'r,
Throws on the ground a silv'ry show'r,
Alas! is all this boasted ease,
To lose each warm desire to please,
35 No sweet solicitude to know
For others bliss, for others woe,
A frozen apathy to find,
A sad vacuity of mind?
O hasten back, then, heav'nly Boy,
40 And with thine anguish bring thy joy!
Return with all thy torments here,
And let me hope, and doubt, and fear.
O rend my heart with ev'ry pain!
But let me, let me love again.

To Anna Matilda[3]

I know thee well, enchanting Maid
I've mark'd thee in the silent glade,
I've seen thee on the mountain's height,
I've met thee in the storms of night;
5 I've view'd thee on the wild beach run
To gaze upon the setting sun;
Then stop aghast, his ray no more,
To hear th' impetuous surge's roar.
Hast thou not stood with rapt'rous eye
10 To trace the starry worlds on high,
T' observe the moon's weak crescent throw
O'er hills, and woods, a glimm'ring glow:
Or, all beside some wizard stream,
To watch its undulating beam?
15 O well thy form divine I know—
When youthful errors brought me woe;
When all was dreary to behold,
And many a bosom-friend grew cold;
Thou, thou unlike the summer crew
20 That from my adverse fortune flew,
Cam'st with melodious voice, to cheer
My throbbing heart, and check the tear.
From thee I learnt, 'twas vain to scan
The low ingratitude of Man
25 Thou bad'st me Fancy's wilds to rove,
And seek th' ecstatic bow'r of Love.
When on his couch I threw me down,
I saw thee weave a myrtle crown,
And blend it with the shining hair
30 Of *her*, the Fairest of the Fair.
For this, may ev'ry wand'ring gale
The essence of the rose exhale,
And pour the fragrance on thy breast,
And gently fan thy charms to rest.
35 Soon as the purple slumbers fly
The op'ning radiance of thine eye,
Strike, strike again the magic lyre,
With all thy pathos, all thy fire;
With all that sweetly-warbled grace,
40 Which proves thee of celestial race.
O then, in varying colours drest,
And living glory stand confest,
Shake from thy locks ambrosial dew,
And thrill each pulse of joy a-new;
45 With glowing ardours rouse my soul,
And bid the tides of Passion roll.
But think no longer in disguise,
To screen thy beauty from mine eyes;
Nor deign a borrow'd name to use,
50 For well I know——thou art *the* MUSE!

---

[1] unidentified.

[2] Diana, goddess of the moon.

[3] the pseudonym of Hannah Cowley,* who exchanged love poems with Merry in the *World* in 1787 and 1788. "To Anna Matilda" first appeared on 31 July 1787.

The Interview[1]

O WE HAVE MET, and now I call
On yon dark clouds that as they fall,
Sweep their long show'rs across the plain,
Or mingle with the clam'rous main.
5 Alas! I call them, here to pour
Around my head their gather'd store,
While the loud gales which speed away
To the far edge of weeping day,
Mid the tumultuous gloom shall bear
10 On their wet wings my sigh'd despair.

OF LATE—where confluent torrents crash,
I paused to view the mazy dash
Of waters, shattering in the twilight beam;
While oft my wand'ring eye would trace
15 The distant forest's solemn grace,
As o'er its black robe hung the tawny gleam.
Nor *then* on joys gone by, my Mem'ry dwelt,
Nor all the pangs which wounded Friendship felt;
But ANNA, tho' *unknown*, usurp'd my mind,
20 *Alone* she claim'd the tributary tear,
For ev'ry solace, ev'ry charm combin'd
In the sweet madd'nings of her song sincere.

Sudden I turn—for from a young grove's shade,
Whose infant boughs but mock th' expecting glade,
25 Sweet sounds stole forth—upborne upon the gale,
Press'd thro' the air, and broke amidst the vale.
Then *silent* walk'd the breezes of the plain,
Or lightly wanton'd where the corn-flow'r blows,
Or 'mongst the od'rous wild-thyme sought repose,
30 Or soar'd aloft and seized the hov'ring strain.

As the fond Lark, whose clear and piercing shake
Bids Morning on her crimson bed awake,
Hears from the greensward seat his fav'rite's cry,
Drops thro' the heavens, and scorns the glowing sky:
35 So *I*, soul-touch'd, th' impetuous Cat'ract leave,
And almost seem th' etherial waste to cleave;

Allured, entranc'd, I rush amidst the wood,
AND THERE THE SOFT MUSICIAN CONSCIOUS
    STOOD.
Ah! 'twas no visionary Fair,
40 Imagination's bodied air,
That now with strong illusion caught,
Mental *creations* fled my thought,
A *living* Angel bless'd my sight,
Strung ev'ry nerve to new delight,
45 With joy's full tide bedew'd my cheek,
'Twas ANNA's self I saw, NOR HAD I POW'R TO SPEAK.
O then I led her to the woven bow'r,
Where slept the Woodbine's shelter'd flow'r,
Where bending o'er the Violet's bed
50 The Rose its liquid blushes shed;
While near the feather'd Mourner flung
Such plaints from his enamour'd tongue,
That all subdued at my MATILDA's feet
I sunk, but with an agony more sweet,
55 Than favour'd mortal e'er before had proved,
Or ever yet *conceiv'd*, unless like *me* he loved.

SHE SPOKE but O! no sound was heard
Of the wanton, rapt'rous bird,
That climbs the morning's upmost sky,
60 When first the golden vapours fly;
But fainter was the moving measure,
Than the Linnet's noontide leisure
Lets the sultry breezes steal—
Dar'st thou, my tongue! the tale reveal?

65 "ILL-FATED BARD!" she cried, "whose length'ning
    grief
Had won the pathos of my lyre's relief,
For whom, full oft, I've loiter'd to rehearse
In phrenzied mood the deep impassion'd verse,
Ill-fated Bard! from each frail hope remove,
70 And shun the certain Suicide of Love:
Lean not to me, *th' impassion'd verse is o'er*,
Which chain'd thy heart, and forced thee to adore:
For O! observe where haughty DUTY stands,
    Her form in radiance drest, her eye severe,
75 Eternal Scorpions writhing in her hands,
    To urge th' offender's *unavailing* tear!

---

[1] Hannah Cowley and Merry met in April 1788; shortly thereafter their exchange of love poems came to an end. "The Interview" is signed "DELLA CRUSCA."

Dread Goddess, I obey!—
Ah! smooth thy awful terror-striking brow,
Hear and record MATILDA's sacred vow!
80 Ne'er will I quit th' undeviating LINE,
   Whose SOURCE THOU art, and THOU the LAW DIVINE.
The Sun shall be subdued, his system fade,
Ere I forsake the path thy FIAT[1] made;
Yet grant one soft regretful tear to flow,
85 Prompted by pity for a Lover's woe,
   O grant *without* REVENGE, one bursting sigh,
Ere from his desolating grief I fly.——
'Tis past,—Farewell! ANOTHER claims my heart,
Then wing thy sinking steps, for here we part,
90 WE PART! and listen, for the word is MINE,
   ANNA MATILDA NEVER CAN BE THINE!"

   She ceas'd, and sudden, like an evening wind
Rushing, some prison'd tempest to unbind,
And all regardless of the scenes it leaves,
95 Skimming o'er bending blooms, and russet sheaves,
MATILDA fled! the closing Night pursued,
And the cold INGRATE scarce I longer view'd;
Her form grew indistinct—each step more dim,
And now a distant vapour seems to swim,
100 Her white robe glistens on my eye no more,
   Its strainings all are vain—THE FOND DELUSION's O'ER.

   MY SONG SUBSIDES, yet ere I close
The ling'ring lay that feeds my woes,
Ere yet forgotten DELLA CRUSCA runs
105 To torrid gales, or petrifying suns,

Ere bow'd to earth my latest feeling flies,
And the big passion settles on my eyes;
O may this sacred sentiment be known,
That my adoring heart is ANNA's OWN;
110 YES, ALL HER OWN, and tho' ANOTHER claim
Her mind's rich treasure, still *I* love the same;
And tho' ANOTHER, O how blest! has felt
Her soften'd soul in dear delirium melt,
While from her gaze the welcome meaning sprung,
115 As on her neck in frantic joy he hung,
Yet I *will* bear it, and tho' Hell deride,
My pangs shall *soothe*, my curse shall be my pride.
Nor can HE boast like me; O no, HE found
The tranquilizing balm that cures the wound;
120 He never knew the loftier bliss, to rave,
Without a pow'r to aid, a chance to save;
HE never bath'd him in the Nightshade's dew,
Nor drank the pois'nous meteors as they flew,
Nor told his rending story to the Moon,
125 Link'd with the demons of her direst noon;
HE never *smiled* Distraction's ills to share,
Nor gain'd th' exalted glory of despair.

   Then be it HIS, for many a year t' enfold
Those charms, and wanton in her curls of gold,
130 Drain the sweet fountain of her eye's fond stream,
And fancy suff'rance but the wretch's *dream*;
While *I* will prove that I deserve my fate,
Was born for anguish, and was form'd for hate,
With such transcendent woe will breathe my sigh,
135 That envying fiends shall think it EXTACY,
And with fierce taunts my cherish'd griefs invade,
Till on my pow'rless tongue the last "MATILDA" fade.

---

[1] "Let there be" (L.), as in the divine command, "Let there be light" (Genesis 1.3); used here as a noun meaning "command."

William Godwin
1756–1836

William Godwin was born in Wisbech, Cambridgeshire, on 3 March 1756, seventh of the thirteen children of John Godwin, a Calvinist minister, and Ann Hull Godwin, a ship-owner's daughter. He was educated at schools in his father's parishes and at Hoxton College, a Dissenting academy. He began preaching in 1777, but his faith, and his Tory politics, were shaken by his reading of Helvétius, Holbach, Priestley, and Rousseau, and, later, by his friendship with the radical novelist and playwright Thomas Holcroft. In 1783 he settled in London and published the first three of his more than forty books. In 1784, he began writing the historical portions of the *New Annual Register*, a job he would hold for seven years. He was present in the Old Jewry chapel when Richard Price delivered *A Discourse on the Love of Our Country*,* and when Edmund Burke attacked Price in *Reflections on the Revolution in France*,* Godwin began preparing a reply. He published *Political Justice*, the classic statement of philosophical anarchism, in February 1793; despite its forbidding price of 36 shillings, it was a bestseller. The next year, he published his fictional masterpiece, a novelization of the doctrines of *Political Justice* entitled *Things as they Are; or, The Adventures of Caleb Williams*; it was another bestseller. In 1796, he fell in love with Mary Wollstonecraft,* and in March 1797, after she had become pregnant, they married. She died on 10 September 1797, after giving birth to the baby who would become Mary Shelley;* to memorialize her, Godwin edited her *Posthumous Works* and wrote a *Memoir* of her life. Unfortunately, the frankness of the *Memoir*, and the inclusion in the *Posthumous Works* of her letters to her former lover, Gilbert Imlay, contributed to the eclipse of her reputation for fifty years. His second novel, *St. Leon* (1799), in part a tribute to Wollstonecraft, failed to repair the damage.

In 1801, desperate for a mother to care for the infant Mary and his stepdaughter, Fanny Imlay, Godwin married Mary Jane Clairmont, who had a son and daughter of her own; the next year, they had a son. Together, they founded the Juvenile Library, a publishing house and bookstore for children. They made a significant contribution to the development of children's literature, not only as publishers (they published the Lambs'* *Tales from Shakespeare*) but also as writer (Godwin) and editor/translator (Mary Jane); but the project was a financial disaster from the beginning; Godwin's financial problems—especially his constant borrowing—destroyed his morale and reputation, and he went bankrupt in 1825.

Godwin's personal life was also in disarray. His difficult marriage alienated friends like Coleridge,* Hazlitt,* and Charles Lamb.* In 1814, his daughter Mary eloped with a married man, his disciple Percy Bysshe Shelley,* taking her stepsister, Claire Clairmont, with her. In October 1816, his stepdaughter Fanny committed suicide in Swansea, and in December, Harriet Shelley was found drowned in the Serpentine—which at least meant that Bysshe and Mary could marry.

After Bysshe's death in 1822, Mary returned to live with her father. After the bankruptcy, Godwin returned to scholarship, philosophy, and fiction, publishing a total of six novels. He died on 7 April 1836 and was buried in the Old St. Pancras Churchyard, beside Wollstonecraft. (D.L.M.)

from *An Enquiry Concerning Political Justice, and Its Influence on General Virtue and Happiness* (1793)

from BOOK 2, *Principles of Society*

from CHAPTER 2

Of Justice

From what has been said it appears, that the subject of the present enquiry is strictly speaking a department of the science of morals. Morality is the source from which its fundamental axioms must be drawn, and they will be made somewhat clearer in the present instance, if we assume the term justice as a general appellation for all moral duty.

That this appellation is sufficiently expressive of the subject will appear, if we consider for a moment mercy, gratitude, temperance, or any of those duties which in looser speaking are contradistinguished from justice. Why should I pardon this criminal, remunerate this favour, abstain from this indulgence? If it partake of the nature of morality, it must be either right or wrong, just or unjust. It must tend to the benefit of the individual, either without intrenching upon, or with actual advantage to the mass of individuals. Either way it benefits the whole, because individuals are parts of the whole. Therefore to do it is just, and to forbear it is unjust. If justice have any meaning, it is just that I should contribute every thing in my power to the benefit of the whole.

Considerable light will probably be thrown upon our investigation, if, quitting for the present the political view, we examine justice merely as it exists among individuals. Justice is a rule of conduct originating in the connection of one percipient being with another. A comprehensive maxim which has been laid down upon the subject is, "that we should love our neighbour as ourselves."[1] But this maxim, though possessing considerable merit as a popular principle, is not modelled with the strictness of philosophical accuracy.

In a loose and general view I and my neighbour are both of us men; and of consequence entitled to equal attention. But in reality it is probable that one of us is a being of more worth and importance than the other. A man is of more worth than a beast; because, being possessed of higher faculties, he is capable of a more refined and genuine happiness. In the same manner the illustrious archbishop of Cambray[2] was of more worth than his chambermaid, and there are few of us that would hesitate to pronounce, if his palace were in flames, and the life of only one of them could be preserved, which of the two ought to be preferred.

But there is another ground of preference, beside the private consideration of one of them being farther removed from the state of a mere animal. We are not connected with one or two percipient beings, but with a society, a nation, and in some sense with the whole family of mankind. Of consequence that life ought to be preferred which will be most conducive to the general good. In saving the life of Fenelon, suppose at the moment when he was conceiving the project of his immortal Telemachus, I should be promoting the benefit of thousands, who have been cured by the perusal of it of some error, vice and consequent unhappiness. Nay, my benefit would extend farther than this, for every individual thus cured has become a better member of society, and has contributed in his turn to the happiness, the information and improvement of others.

Supposing I had been myself the chambermaid, I ought to have chosen to die, rather than that Fenelon should have died. The life of Fenelon was really preferable to that of the chambermaid. But understanding is the faculty that perceives the truth of this and similar propositions; and justice is the principle that regulates my conduct accordingly. It would have been just in the chambermaid to have preferred the archbishop to herself. To have done otherwise would have been a breach of justice.

Supposing the chambermaid had been my wife, my mother or my benefactor. This would not alter the truth

---

[1] Cf. Romans 13.9.

[2] François de Selignac de la Mothe Fénelon (1651–1715), author of *The Adventures of Telemachus* (1699), an attack on the French monarchy.

of the proposition. The life of Fenelon would still be more valuable than that of the chambermaid; and justice, pure, unadulterated justice, would still have preferred that which was most valuable. Justice would have taught me to save the life of Fenelon at the expence of the other. What magic is there in the pronoun "my," to overturn the decisions of everlasting truth? My wife or my mother may be a fool or a prostitute, malicious, lying or dishonest. If they be, of what consequence is it that they are mine?

"But my mother endured for me the pains of child bearing, and nourished me in the helplessness of infancy." When she first subjected herself to the necessity of these cares, she was probably influenced by no particular motives of benevolence to her future offspring. Every voluntary benefit however entitles the bestower to some kindness and retribution. But why so? Because a voluntary benefit is an evidence of benevolent intention, that is, of virtue. It is the disposition of the mind, not the external action, that entitles to respect. But the merit of this disposition is equal, whether the benefit was conferred upon me or upon another. I and another man cannot both be right in preferring our own individual benefactor, for no man can be at the same time both better and worse than his neighbour. My benefactor ought to be esteemed, not because he bestowed a benefit upon me, but because he bestowed it upon a human being. His desert will be in exact proportion to the degree, in which that human being was worthy of the distinction conferred. Thus every view of the subject brings us back to the consideration of my neighbour's moral worth and his importance to the general weal, as the only standard to determine the treatment to which he is entitled. Gratitude therefore, a principle which has so often been the theme of the moralist and the poet, is no part either of justice or virtue. By gratitude I understand a sentiment, which would lead me to prefer one man to another, from some other consideration than that of his superior usefulness or worth: that is, which would make something true to me (for example this preferableness), which cannot be true to another man, and is not true in itself.[1]

It may be objected, "that my relation, my companion, or my benefactor will of course in many instances obtain an uncommon portion of my regard: for, not being universally capable of discriminating the comparative worth of different men, I shall inevitably judge most favourably of him, of whose virtues I have received the most unquestionable proofs; and thus shall be compelled to prefer the man of moral worth whom I know, to another who may possess, unknown to me, an essential superiority."

This compulsion however is founded only in the present imperfection of human nature. It may serve as an apology for my error, but can never turn error into truth. It will always remain contrary to the strict and inflexible decisions of justice. The difficulty of conceiving this is owing merely to our confounding the disposition from which an action is chosen, with the action itself. The disposition, that would prefer virtue to vice and a greater degree of virtue to a less, is undoubtedly a subject of approbation; the erroneous exercise of this disposition by which a wrong object is selected, if unavoidable, is to be deplored, but can by no colouring and under no denomination be converted into right.[2]

It may in the second place be objected, "that a mutual commerce of benefits tends to increase the mass of benevolent action, and that to increase the mass of benevolent action is to contribute to the general good." Indeed! Is the general good promoted by falshood, by treating a man of one degree of worth, as if he had ten times that worth? or as if he were in any degree different from what he really is? Would not the most beneficial consequences result from a different plan; from my constantly and carefully enquiring into the deserts of all those with whom I am connected, and from their being sure, after a certain allowance for the fallibility of human judgment, of being treated by me exactly as they de-

---

[1] "This argument respecting gratitude is stated with great clearness in an Essay on the Nature of True Virtue, by the Rev. Jonathan Edwards. 12mo. Dilly." (W.G.) This essay by the American theologian Jonathan Edwards (1703–58) was first published posthumously in 1765; Charles Dilly was one of the English booksellers for the 1778 edition.

[2] "See this subject more copiously treated in the following chapter." (W.G.)

served? Who can tell what would be the effects of such a plan of conduct universally adopted?

There seems to be more truth in the argument, derived chiefly from the unequal distribution of property, in favour of my providing in ordinary cases for my wife and children, my brothers and relations, before I provide for strangers. As long as providing for individuals belongs to individuals, it seems as if there must be a certain distribution of the class needing superintendence and supply among the class affording it, that each man may have his claim and resource. But this argument, if admitted at all, is to be admitted with great caution. It belongs only to ordinary cases; and cases of a higher order or a more urgent necessity will perpetually occur, in competition with which these will be altogether impotent. We must be severely scrupulous in measuring out the quantity of supply; and, with respect to money in particular, must remember how little is yet understood of the true mode of employing it for the public benefit....

from BOOK 8, *Of Property*

from CHAPTER 8[1]

Of the Means of Introducing the Genuine System of Property

Having thus stated explicitly and without reserve the great branches of this illustrious picture, there is but one subject that remains. In what manner shall this interesting improvement of human society be carried into execution? Are there not certain steps that are desirable for this purpose? Are there not certain steps that are inevitable? Will not the period that must first elapse, necessarily be stained with a certain infusion of evil?

No idea has excited greater horror in the minds of a multitude of persons, than that of the mischiefs that are to ensue from the dissemination of what they call levelling principles. They believe "that these principles will inevitably ferment in the minds of the vulgar, and that the attempt to carry them into execution will be attended with every species of calamity." They represent to themselves "the uninformed and uncivilised part of mankind, as let loose from all restraint, and hurried into every kind of excess. Knowledge and taste, the improvements of intellect, the discoveries of sages, the beauties of poetry and art, are trampled under foot and extinguished by barbarians. It is another inundation of Goths and Vandals, with this bitter aggravation, that the viper that stings us to death was warmed in our own bosoms."

They conceive of the scene as "beginning in massacre." They suppose "all that is great, preeminent and illustrious as ranking among the first victims. Such as are distinguished by peculiar elegance of manners or energy of diction and composition, will be the inevitable objects of envy and jealousy. Such as intrepidly exert themselves to succour the persecuted, or to declare to the public those truths which they are least inclined, but which are most necessary for them to hear, will be marked out for assassination."

Let us not, from any partiality to the system of equality delineated in this book, shrink from the picture here exhibited. Massacre is the too possible attendant upon revolution, and massacre is perhaps the most hateful scene, allowing for its momentary duration, that any imagination can suggest. The fearful, hopeless expectation of the defeated, and the bloodhound fury of their conquerors, is a complication of mischief that all which has been told of infernal regions cannot surpass. The cold-blooded massacres that are perpetrated under the name of criminal justice fall short of these in their most frightful aggravations. The ministers and instruments of law have by custom reconciled their minds to the dreadful task they perform, and bear their respective parts in the most shocking enormities, without being sensible to the passions allied to those enormities. But the instruments of massacre are actuated with all the sentiments of fiends. Their eyes emit flashes of cruelty and rage. They pursue their victims from street to street and from house to house. They tear them from the arms of their fathers and their wives. They glut themselves with barbarity and insult, and utter shouts of horrid joy at the spectacle of their tortures.

---

[1] Godwin omitted some chapters from the revised editions of 1796 and 1798; the material in this chapter was reworked as Book 8, chapter 10, "Reflections."

We have now contemplated the tremendous picture; what is the conclusion it behoves us to draw? Must we shrink from reason, from justice, from virtue and happiness? Suppose that the inevitable consequence of communicating truth were the temporary introduction of such a scene as has just been described, must we on that account refuse to communicate it? The crimes that were perpetrated would in no just estimate appear to be the result of truth, but of the error which had previously been infused. The impartial enquirer would behold them as the last struggles of expiring despotism, which, if it had survived, would have produced mischiefs, scarcely less atrocious in the hour of their commission, and infinitely more calamitous by the length of their duration. If we would judge truly, even admitting the unfavourable supposition above stated, we must contrast a moment of horror and distress with ages of felicity. No imagination can sufficiently conceive the mental improvement and the tranquil virtue that would succeed, were property once permitted to rest upon its genuine basis.

And by what means suppress truth, and keep alive the salutary intoxication, the tranquillising insanity of mind which some men desire? Such has been too generally the policy of government through every age of the world. Have we slaves? We must assiduously retain them in ignorance. Have we colonies and dependencies? The great effort of our care is to keep them from being too populous and prosperous. Have we subjects? It is "by impotence and misery that we endeavour to render them supple: plenty is fit for nothing but to make them unmanageable, disobedient and mutinous."[1] If this were the true philosophy of social institutions, well might we shrink from it with horror. How tremendous an abortion would the human species be found, if all that tended to make them wise, tended to make them unprincipled and profligate? But this it is impossible for any one to believe, who will lend the subject a moment's impartial consideration. Can truth, the perception of justice and a desire to execute it, be the source of irretrievable ruin to mankind? It may be conceived that the first opening and illumination of mind will be attended with disorder. But every just reasoner must confess that regularity and happiness will succeed to this confusion. To refuse the remedy, were this picture of its operation ever so true, would be as if a man who had dislocated a limb, should refuse to undergo the pain of having it replaced. If mankind have hitherto lost the road of virtue and happiness, that can be no just reason why they should be suffered to go wrong for ever. We must not refuse a conviction of error, or even the treading over again some of the steps that were the result of it.

Another question suggests itself under this head. Can we suppress truth? Can we arrest the progress of the enquiring mind? If we can, it will only be done by the most unmitigated despotism. Mind has a perpetual tendency to rise. It cannot be held down but by a power that counteracts its genuine tendency through every moment of its existence. Tyrannical and sanguinary must be the measures employed for this purpose. Miserable and disgustful must be the scene they produce. Their result will be thick darkness of the mind, timidity, servility, hypocrisy. This is the alternative, so far as there is any alternative in their power, between the opposite measures of which the princes and governments of the earth have now to choose: they must either suppress enquiry by the most arbitrary stretches of power, or preserve a clear and tranquil field in which every man shall be at liberty to discover and vindicate his opinion.

No doubt it is the duty of governments to maintain the most unalterable neutrality in this important transaction. No doubt it is the duty of individuals to publish truth without diffidence or reserve, to publish it in its genuine form without seeking aid from the meretricious arts of publication. The more it is told, the more it is known in its true dimensions, and not in parts, the less is it possible that it should coalesce with or leave room for the pernicious effects of error. The true philanthropist will be eager, instead of suppressing discussion, to take an active share in the scene, to exert the full strength of his faculties in discovery, and to contribute by his exertions to render the operation of thought at once perspicuous and profound.

It being then sufficiently evident that truth must be told at whatever expence, let us proceed to consider the

---

[1] "Book V, Chap. III, p. 405." (W.G.) The title of Book 5 is "Of Legislative and Executive Power"; chap. 3 is called "Private Life of a Prince." Godwin is paraphrasing rather than quoting directly.

precise amount of that expence, to enquire how much of confusion and violence is inseparable from the transit which mind has to accomplish. And here it plainly appears that mischief is by no means inseparable from the progress. In the mere circumstance of our acquiring knowledge and accumulating one truth after another there is no direct tendency to disorder. Evil can only spring from the clash of mind with mind, from one body of men in the community outstripping another in their ideas of improvement, and becoming impatient of the opposition they have to encounter....

To the general mass of the adherents of the cause of justice it may be proper to say a few words. "If there be any force in the arguments of this work, thus much at least we are authorised to deduce from them, that truth is irresistible. If man be endowed with a rational nature, then whatever is clearly demonstrated to his understanding to have the most powerful recommendations, so long as that clearness is present to his mind, will inevitably engage his choice. It is to no purpose to say that mind is fluctuating and fickle; for it is so only in proportion as evidence is imperfect. Let the evidence be increased, and the persuasion will be made firmer, and the choice more uniform. It is the nature of individual mind to be perpetually adding to the stock of its ideas and knowledge. Similar to this is the nature of general mind, exclusively of casualties which, arising from a more comprehensive order of things, appear to disturb the order of limited systems. This is confirmed to us, if a truth of this universal nature can derive confirmation from partial experiments, by the regular advances of the human mind from century to century, since the invention of printing.

"Let then this axiom of the omnipotence of truth be the rudder of our undertakings. Let us not precipitately endeavour to accomplish that to-day, which the dissemination of truth will make unavoidable to-morrow. Let us not anxiously watch for occasions and events: the ascendancy of truth is independent of events. Let us anxiously refrain from violence: force is not conviction, and is extremely unworthy of the cause of justice. Let us admit into our bosoms neither contempt, animosity, resentment nor revenge. The cause of justice is the cause of humanity. Its advocates should overflow with universal good will. We should love this cause, for it conduces to the general happiness of mankind. We should love it, for there is not a man that lives, who in the natural and tranquil progress of things will not be made happier by its approach. The most powerful cause by which it has been retarded, is the mistake of its adherents, the air of ruggedness, brutishness and inflexibility which they have given to that which in itself is all benignity. Nothing less than this could have prevented the great mass of enquirers from bestowing upon it a patient examination. Be it the care of the now increasing advocates of equality to remove this obstacle to the success of their cause. We have but two plain duties, which, if we set out right, it is not easy to mistake. The first is an unwearied attention to the great instrument of justice, reason. We must divulge our sentiments with the utmost frankness. We must endeavour to impress them upon the minds of others. In this attempt we must give way to no discouragement. We must sharpen our intellectual weapons; add to the stock of our knowledge; be pervaded with a sense of the magnitude of our cause; and perpetually increase that calm presence of mind and self possession which must enable us to do justice to our principles. Our second duty is tranquillity."...

from *Memoirs of the Author of* A Vindication of the Rights of Woman (1798)

from CHAPTER 6

1790–1792

The event, immediately introductory to the rank which from this time she held in the lists of literature, was the publication of Burke's Reflections[1] on the Revolution in France. This book, after having been long promised to the world, finally made its appearance on the first of November 1790; and Mary, full of sentiments of liberty, and impressed with a warm interest in the struggle that

---

[1] In *Reflections on the Revolution in France,** Edmund Burke attacked the principles of the French Revolution and the notion of the "rights of man."

was now going on, seized her pen in the first burst of indignation, an emotion of which she was strongly susceptible. She was in the habit of composing with rapidity, and her answer, which was the first of the numerous ones that appeared, obtained extraordinary notice. Marked as it is with the vehemence and impetuousness of its eloquence, it is certainly chargeable with a too contemptuous and intemperate treatment of the great man against whom its attack is directed. But this circumstance was not injurious to the success of the publication. Burke had been warmly loved by the most liberal and enlightened friends of freedom, and they were proportionably inflamed and disgusted by the fury of his assault, upon what they deemed to be its sacred cause.

Short as was the time in which Mary composed her Answer to Burke's Reflections,[1] there was one anecdote she told me concerning it, which seems worth recording in this place. It was sent to the press, as is the general practice when the early publication of a piece is deemed a matter of importance, before the composition was finished. When Mary had arrived at about the middle of her work, she was seized with a temporary fit of torpor and indolence, and began to repent of her undertaking. In this state of mind, she called, one evening, as she was in the practice of doing, upon her publisher,[2] for the purpose of relieving herself by an hour or two's conversation. Here, the habitual ingenuousness of her nature, led her to describe what had just past in her thoughts. Mr. Johnson immediately, in a kind and friendly way, intreated her not to put any constraint upon her inclination, and to give herself no uneasiness about the sheets already printed, which he would cheerfully throw aside, if it would contribute to her happiness. Mary had wanted stimulus. She had not expected to be encouraged, in what she well knew to be an unreasonable access of idleness. Her friend's so readily falling in with her ill-humour, and seeming to expect that she would lay aside her undertaking, piqued her pride. She immediately went home; and proceeded to the end of her work, with no other interruptions but what were absolutely indispensible.

It is probable that the applause which attended her Answer to Burke, elevated the tone of her mind. She had always felt much confidence in her own powers; but it cannot be doubted, that the actual perception of a similar feeling respecting us in a multitude of others, must increase the confidence, and stimulate the adventure of any human being. Mary accordingly proceeded, in a short time after, to the composition of her most celebrated production, the Vindication of the Rights of Woman.[3]

Never did any author enter into a cause, with a more ardent desire to be found, not a flourishing and empty declaimer, but an effectual champion. She considered herself as standing forth in defence of one half of the human species, labouring under a yoke which, through all the records of time, had degraded them from the station of rational beings, and almost sunk them to the level of the brutes. She saw indeed, that they were often attempted to be held in silken fetters, and bribed into the love of slavery; but the disguise and the treachery served only the more fully to confirm her opposition. She regarded her sex, in the language of Calista, as

"In every state of life the slaves of men":[4]
the rich as alternately under the despotism of a father, a brother, and a husband; and the middling and the poorer classes shut out from the acquisition of bread with independence, when they are not shut out from the very means of an industrious subsistence. Such were the views she entertained of the subject; and such the feelings with which she warmed her mind.

The work is certainly a very bold and original production. The strength and firmness with which the author repels the opinions of Rousseau, Dr. Gregory,

---

[1] *A Vindication of the Rights of Men,* published anonymously in 1790 and under Wollstonecraft's name in 1791.

[2] Joseph Johnson, publisher and bookseller, distributed Unitarian and other dissenting literature and was at the centre of reforming and radical society during the revolutionary period. His circle at St. Paul's Churchyard included Barbauld,* Blake,* Coleridge,* Cowper,* Maria Edgeworth,* Godwin,* Thomas Holcroft, Paine,* Joseph Priestley, Wollstonecraft,* and William Wordsworth.*

[3] published early in 1792.

[4] In Nicholas Rowe's tragedy, *The Fair Penitent* (1703), the heroine, Calista, is seduced and abandoned by Lothario and forced into marriage with another man. Cf. 3.1.41.

and Dr. James Fordyce,[1] respecting the condition of women, cannot but make a strong impression upon every ingenuous reader. The public at large formed very different opinions respecting the character of the performance. Many of the sentiments are undoubtedly of a rather masculine description. The spirited and decisive way in which the author explodes the system of gallantry, and the species of homage with which the sex is usually treated, shocked the majority. Novelty produced a sentiment in their mind, which they mistook for a sense of injustice. The pretty, soft creatures that are so often to be found in the female sex, and that class of men who believe they could not exist without such pretty, soft creatures to resort to, were in arms against the author of so heretical and blasphemous a doctrine. There are also, it must be confessed, occasional passages of a stern and rugged feature, incompatible with the true stamina of the writer's character. But, if they did not belong to her fixed and permanent character, they belonged to her character *pro tempore*;[2] and what she thought, she scorned to qualify.

Yet, along with this rigid, and somewhat amazonian temper, which characterised some parts of the book, it is impossible not to remark a luxuriance of imagination, and a trembling delicacy of sentiment, which would have done honour to a poet, bursting with all the visions of an Armida and a Dido.[3]

The contradiction, to the public apprehension, was equally great, as to the person of the author, as it was when they considered the temper of the book. In the champion of her sex, who was described as endeavouring to invest them with all the rights of man, those whom curiosity prompted to seek the occasion of beholding her, expected to find a sturdy, muscular, raw-boned virago; and they were not a little surprised, when, instead of all this, they found a woman, lovely in her person, and, in the best and most engaging sense, feminine in her manners.

The Vindication of the Rights of Woman is undoubtedly a very unequal performance, and eminently deficient in method and arrangement. When tried by the hoary and long-established laws of literary composition, it can scarcely maintain its claim to be placed in the first class of human productions. But when we consider the importance of its doctrines, and the eminence of genius it displays, it seems not very improbable that it will be read as long as the English language endures. The publication of this book forms an epocha in the subject to which it belongs; and Mary Wollstonecraft will perhaps hereafter be found to have performed more substantial service for the cause of her sex, than all the other writers, male or female, that ever felt themselves animated in the behalf of oppressed and injured beauty.

The censure of the liberal critic as to the defects of this performance, will be changed into astonishment, when I tell him, that a work of this inestimable moment, was begun, carried on, and finished in the state in which it now appears, in a period of no more than six weeks. ...

It was in the month of November in the same year (1791), that the writer of this narrative was first in company with the person to whom it relates. He dined with her at a friend's, together with Mr. Thomas Paine[4] and one or two other persons. The invitation was of his own seeking, his object being to see the author of the Rights of Man, with whom he had never before conversed.

The interview was not fortunate. Mary and myself parted, mutually displeased with each other. I had not read her Rights of Woman. I had barely looked into her Answer to Burke, and been displeased, as literary men are apt to be, with a few offences, against grammar and other minute points of composition. I had therefore little curiosity to see Mrs. Wollstonecraft, and a very

---

[1] Jean-Jacques Rousseau (1712–78), political, social, and educational writer, autobiographer, and novelist; John Gregory (1724–73), author of *A Father's Legacy to his Daughters* (1774); and James Fordyce (1726–96), author of *Sermons to Young Women* (1765). Wollstonecraft critiques all three writers in her *Vindication of the Rights of Woman*.*

[2] "according to the occasion" (L.).

[3] In Torquato Tasso (1544–95) *Jerusalem Delivered* (1580–81), the magician Armida lures Christian knights into a magical garden of indolence. In Virgil's *Æneid*, Dido, queen of Carthage, kills herself when her lover, Aeneas, abandons her in pursuit of his quest to found Rome.

[4] Thomas Paine* spent the years from 1772–87 in America. He published *The Rights of Man* in two parts (1791 and 1792); fled to France where he risked his life in opposing the execution of Louis XVI; published *The Age of Reason*,* a defence of deism against both Christianity and atheism; and returned to America in 1802.

great curiosity to see Thomas Paine. Paine, in his general habits, is no great talker; and, though he threw in occasionally some shrewd and striking remarks; the conversation lay principally between me and Mary. I, of consequence, heard her, very frequently when I wished to hear Paine.

We touched on a considerable variety of topics, and particularly on the characters and habits of certain eminent men. Mary, as has already been observed, had acquired, in a very blameable degree, the practice of seeing every thing on the gloomy side, and bestowing censure with a plentiful hand, where circumstances were in any respect doubtful. I, on the contrary, had a strong propensity, to favourable construction, and particularly, where I found unequivocal marks of genius, strongly to incline to the supposition of generous and manly virtue. We ventilated in this way the characters of Voltaire and others,[1] who have obtained from some individuals an ardent admiration, while the greater number have treated them with extreme moral severity. Mary was at last provoked to tell me, that praise, lavished in the way that I lavished it, could do no credit either to the commended or the commender. We discussed some questions on the subject of religion, in which her opinions approached much nearer to the received ones, than mine. As the conversation proceeded, I became dissatisfied with the tone of my own share in it. We touched upon all topics, without treating forcibly and connectedly upon any. Meanwhile, I did her the justice, in giving an account of the conversation to a party in which I supped, though I was not sparing of my blame, to yield her the praise of a person of active and independent thinking. On her side, she did me no part of what perhaps I considered as justice.

We met two or three times in the course of the following year, but made a very small degree of progress towards a cordial acquaintance....

from CHAPTER 9

1796, 1797

I am now led, by the progress of the story, to the last branch of her history, the connection between Mary and myself. And this I shall relate with the same simplicity that has pervaded every other part of my narrative. If there ever were any motives of prudence or delicacy, that could impose a qualification upon the story, they are now over. They could have no relation but to factitious rules of decorum. There are no circumstances of her life, that, in the judgment of honour and reason, could brand her with disgrace. Never did there exist a human being, that needed, with less fear, expose all their actions, and call upon the universe to judge them. An event of the most deplorable sort, has awfully imposed silence upon the gabble of frivolity.

We renewed our acquaintance in January 1796, but with no particular effect, except so far as sympathy in her anguish, added in my mind to the respect I had always entertained for her talents. It was in the close of that month that I read her Letters from Norway;[2] and the impression that book produced upon me has been already related.

It was on the fourteenth of April that I first saw her after her excursion into Berkshire. On that day she called upon me in Somers Town, she having, since her return, taken a lodging in Cumming-street, Pentonville, at no great distance from the place of my habitation. From that time our intimacy increased, by regular, but almost imperceptible degrees.

The partiality we conceived for each other, was in that mode, which I have always regarded as the purest and most refined style of love. It grew with equal advances in the mind of each. It would have been impossible for the most minute observer to have said who was before, and who was after. One sex did not take the priority which long established custom has awarded it, nor the other overstep that delicacy which is so severely imposed. I am not conscious that either party can

---

[1] The French writer Voltaire (1694–1778) condemned dogmatism and superstition, critiquing institutional authority of all kinds. As a radical himself, Godwin aligns himself with Voltaire and the other *philosophes*.

[2] Wollstonecraft's *Letters Written during a Short Residence in Sweden, Norway, and Denmark*,* published by Joseph Johnson in 1796. Godwin elsewhere calls this book *Travels in Norway*.

assume to have been the agent or the patient, the toil-spreader or the prey, in the affair. When, in the course of things, the disclosure came, there was nothing, in a manner, for either party to disclose to the other.

In July 1796 I made an excursion into the county of Norfolk, which occupied nearly the whole of that month. During this period Mary removed, from Cumming-street, Pentonville, to Judd place West, which may be considered as the extremity of Somers Town. In the former situation she had occupied a furnished lodging. She had meditated a tour to Italy or Switzerland, and knew not how soon she should set out with that view. Now however she felt herself reconciled to a longer abode in England, probably without exactly knowing why this change had taken place in her mind. She had a quantity of furniture locked up at a broker's ever since her residence in Store-street, and she now found it adviseable to bring it into use. This circumstance occasioned her present removal.

The temporary separation attendant on my little journey, had its effect on the mind of both parties. It gave a space for the maturing of inclination. I believe that, during this interval, each furnished to the other the principal topic of solitary and daily contemplation. Absence bestows a refined and aërial delicacy upon affection, which it with difficulty acquires in any other way. It seems to resemble the communication of spirits, without the medium, or the impediment, of this earthly frame.

When we met again, we met with new pleasure, and, I may add, with a more decisive preference for each other. It was however three weeks longer, before the sentiment which trembled upon the tongue, burst from the lips of either. There was, as I have already said, no period of throes and resolute explanation attendant on the tale. It was friendship melting into love. Previously to our mutual declaration, each felt half-assured, yet each felt a certain trembling anxiety to have assurance complete.

Mary rested her head upon the shoulder of her lover, hoping to find a heart with which she might safely treasure her world of affection; fearing to commit a mistake, yet, in spite of her melancholy experience, fraught with that generous confidence, which, in a great soul, is never extinguished. I had never loved till now; or, at least, had never nourished a passion to the same growth, or met with an object so consummately worthy.

We did not marry. It is difficult to recommend any thing to indiscriminate adoption, contrary to the established rules and prejudices of mankind; but certainly nothing can be so ridiculous upon the face of it, or so contrary to the genuine march of sentiment, as to require the overflowing of the soul to wait upon a ceremony, and that which, wherever delicacy and imagination exist, is of all things most sacredly private, to blow a trumpet before it, and to record the moment when it has arrived at its climax.

There were however other reasons why we did not immediately marry. Mary felt an entire conviction of the propriety of her conduct. It would be absurd to suppose that, with a heart withered by desertion, she was not right to give way to the emotions of kindness which our intimacy produced, and to seek for that support in friendship and affection, which could alone give pleasure to her heart, and peace to her meditations. It was only about six months since she had resolutely banished every thought of Mr. Imlay;[1] but it was at least eighteen that he ought to have been banished, and would have been banished, had it not been for her scrupulous pertinacity in determining to leave no measure untried to regain him. Add to this, that the laws of etiquette ordinarily laid down in these cases, are essentially absurd, and that the sentiments of the heart cannot submit to be directed by the rule and the square. But Mary had an extreme aversion to be made the topic of vulgar discussion; and, if there be any weakness in this, the dreadful trials through which she had recently passed, may well plead in its excuse. She felt that she had been too much, and too rudely spoken of, in the former instance; and she could not resolve to do any thing that should immediately revive that painful topic.

For myself, it is certain that I had for many years regarded marriage with so well-grounded an apprehension, that, notwithstanding the partiality for Mary that had taken possession of my soul, I should have felt it

---

[1] Gilbert Imlay (c. 1754–1828?), whom Wollstonecraft met in Paris in 1793 and who became her lover and the father of her daughter Fanny (b. 14 May 1794 in Le Havre).

very difficult, at least in the present stage of our intercourse, to have resolved on such a measure. Thus, partly from similar, and partly from different motives, we felt alike in this, as we did perhaps in every other circumstance that related to our intercourse.

I have nothing further that I find it necessary to record, till the commencement of April 1797. We then judged it proper to declare our marriage, which had taken place a little before. The principal motive for complying with this ceremony, was the circumstance of Mary's being in a state of pregnancy. She was unwilling, and perhaps with reason, to incur that exclusion from the society of many valuable and excellent individuals, which custom awards in cases of this sort. I should have felt an extreme repugnance to the having caused her such an inconvenience. And, after the experiment of seven months of as intimate an intercourse as our respective modes of living would admit, there was certainly less hazard to either, in the subjecting ourselves to those consequences which the laws of England annex to the relations of husband and wife. On the sixth of April we entered into possession of a house, which had been taken by us in concert.

In this place I have a very curious circumstance to notice, which I am happy to have occasion to mention, as it tends to expose certain regulations of polished society, of which the absurdity vies with the odiousness. Mary had long possessed the advantage of an acquaintance with many persons of genius, and with others whom the effects of an intercourse with elegant society, combined with a certain portion of information and good sense, sufficed to render amusing companions. She had lately extended the circle of her acquaintance in this respect; and her mind, trembling between the opposite impressions of past anguish and renovating tranquillity, found ease in this species of recreation. Wherever Mary appeared, admiration attended upon her. She had always displayed talents for conversation; but maturity of understanding, her travels, her long residence in France, the discipline of affliction, and the smiling, new-born peace which awaked a corresponding smile in her animated countenance, inexpressibly increased them. The way in which the story of Mr. Imlay was treated in these polite circles, was probably the result of the partiality she excited. These elegant personages were divided between their cautious adherence to forms, and the desire to seek their own gratification. Mary made no secret of the nature of her connection with Mr. Imlay; and in one instance, I well know, she put herself to the trouble of explaining it to a person totally indifferent to her, because he never failed to publish every thing he knew, and, she was sure, would repeat her explanation to his numerous acquaintance. She was of too proud and generous a spirit to stoop to hypocrisy. These persons however, in spite of all that could be said, persisted in shutting their eyes, and pretending they took her for a married woman.

Observe the consequence of this! While she was, and constantly professed to be, an unmarried mother; she was fit society for the squeamish and the formal. The moment she acknowledged herself a wife, and that by a marriage perhaps unexceptionable, the case was altered. Mary and myself, ignorant as we were of these elevated refinements, supposed that our marriage would place her upon a surer footing in the calendar of polished society, than ever. But it forced these people to see the truth, and to confess their belief of what they had carefully been told; and this they could not forgive. Be it remarked, that the date of our marriage had nothing to do with this, that question being never once mentioned during this period. Mary indeed had, till now, retained the name of Imlay which had first been assumed from necessity in France;[1] but its being retained thus long, was purely from the aukwardness that attends the introduction of a change, and not from an apprehension of consequences of this sort. Her scrupulous explicitness as to the nature of her situation, surely sufficed to make the name she bore perfectly immaterial....

Mary felt a transitory pang, when the conviction reached her of so unexpected a circumstance, that was rather exquisite. But she disdained to sink under the injustice (as this ultimately was) of the supercilious and the foolish, and presently shook off the impression of the

---

[1] In 1793 England and France were at war, the Terror was under way, and the English in Paris (including Helen Maria Williams),* were being imprisoned. Imlay registered Wollstonecraft as his wife at the American embassy so that she could claim the benefits of American citizenship.

first surprize. That once subsided, I well know that the event was thought of, with no emotions, but those of superiority to the injustice she sustained; and was not of force enough, to diminish a happiness, which seemed hourly to become more vigorous and firm.

I think I may venture to say, that no two persons ever found in each other's society, a satisfaction more pure and refined. What it was in itself, can now only be known, in its full extent, to the survivor. But, I believe, the serenity of her countenance, the increasing sweetness of her manners, and that consciousness of enjoyment that seemed ambitious that every one she saw should be happy as well as herself, were matters of general observation to all her acquaintance. She had always possessed, in an unparalleled degree, the art of communicating happiness, and she was now in the constant and unlimited exercise of it. She seemed to have attained that situation, which her disposition and character imperiously demanded, but which she had never before attained; and her understanding and her heart felt the benefit of it.

While we lived as near neighbours only, and before our last removal, her mind had attained considerable tranquillity, and was visited but seldom with those emotions of anguish, which had been but too familiar to her. But the improvement in this respect, which accrued upon our removal and establishment, was extremely obvious. She was a worshipper of domestic life. She loved to observe the growth of affection between me and her daughter, then three years of age, as well as my anxiety respecting the child not yet born. Pregnancy itself, unequal as the decree of nature seems to be in this respect, is the source of a thousand endearments. No one knew better than Mary how to extract sentiments of exquisite delight, from trifles, which a suspicious and formal wisdom would scarcely deign to remark. A little ride into the country with myself and the child, has sometimes produced a sort of opening of the heart, a general expression of confidence and affectionate soul, a sort of infantine, yet dignified endearment, which those who have felt may understand, but which I should in vain attempt to pourtray.

In addition to our domestic pleasures, I was fortunate enough to introduce her to some of my acquaintance of both sexes, to whom she attached herself with all the ardour of approbation and friendship.

Ours was not an idle happiness, a paradise of selfish and transitory pleasures. It is perhaps scarcely necessary to mention, that, influenced by the ideas I had long entertained upon the subject of cohabitation, I engaged an apartment, about twenty doors from our house in the Polygon, Somers Town, which I designed for the purpose of my study and literary occupations. Trifles however will be interesting to some readers, when they relate to the last period of the life of such a person as Mary. I will add therefore, that we were both of us of opinion, that it was possible for two persons to be too uniformly in each other's society. Influenced by that opinion, it was my practice to repair to the apartment I have mentioned as soon as I rose, and frequently not to make my appearance in the Polygon, till the hour of dinner. We agreed in condemning the notion, prevalent in many situations in life, that a man and his wife cannot visit in mixed society, but in company with each other; and we rather sought occasions of deviating from, than of complying with, this rule. By these means, though, for the most part, we spent the latter half of each day in one another's society, yet we were in no danger of satiety. We seemed to combine, in a considerable degree, the novelty and lively sensation of a visit, with the more delicious and heart-felt pleasures of domestic life.

Whatever may be thought, in other respects, of the plan we laid down to ourselves, we probably derived a real advantage from it, as to the constancy and uninterruptedness of our literary pursuits. Mary had a variety of projects of this sort, for the exercise of her talents, and the benefit of society; and, if she had lived, I believe the world would have had very little reason to complain of any remission of her industry. One of her projects, which has been already mentioned, was of a series of Letters on the Management of Infants. Though she had been for some time digesting her ideas on this subject with a view to the press, I have found comparatively nothing that she had committed to paper respecting it. Another project, of longer standing, was of a series of books for the instruction of children. A fragment she left in execution of this project, is inserted in her Posthumous Works.[1]

But the principal work, in which she was engaged for more than twelve months before her decease, was a novel, entitled, The Wrongs of Woman.[2] I shall not stop here to explain the nature of the work, as so much of it as was already written, is now given to the public. I shall only observe that, impressed, as she could not fail to be, with the consciousness of her talents, she was desirous, in this instance, that they should effect what they were capable of effecting. She was sensible how arduous a task it is to produce a truly excellent novel; and she roused her faculties to grapple with it. All her other works were produced with a rapidity, that did not give her powers time fully to expand. But this was written slowly and with mature consideration. She began it in several forms, which she successively rejected, after they were considerably advanced. She wrote many parts of the work again and again, and, when she had finished what she intended for the first part, she felt herself more urgently stimulated to revise and improve what she had written, than to proceed, with constancy of application, in the parts that were to follow.

from CHAPTER 10

I am now led, by the course of my narrative, to the last fatal scene of her life. She was taken in labour on Wednesday, the thirtieth of August. She had been somewhat indisposed on the preceding Friday, the consequence, I believe, of a sudden alarm. But from that time she was in perfect health. She was so far from being under any apprehension as to the difficulties of childbirth, as frequently to ridicule the fashion of ladies in England, who keep their chamber for one full month after delivery. For herself, she proposed coming down to dinner on the day immediately following. She had already had some experience on the subject in the case of Fanny; and I cheerfully submitted in every point to her judgment and her wisdom. She hired no nurse. Influenced by ideas of decorum, which certainly ought to have no place, at least in cases of danger, she determined to have a woman to attend her in the capacity of midwife. She was sensible that the proper business of a midwife, in the instance of a natural labour, is to sit by and wait for the operations of nature, which seldom, in these affairs, demand the interposition of art.

At five o'clock in the morning of the day of delivery, she felt what she conceived to be some notices of the approaching labour. Mrs. Blenkinsop, matron and midwife to the Westminster Lying in Hospital, who had seen Mary several times previous to her delivery, was soon after sent for, and arrived about nine. During the whole day Mary was perfectly cheerful. Her pains came on slowly; and, in the morning, she wrote several notes, three addressed to me, who had gone, as usual, to my apartments, for the purpose of study. About two o'clock in the afternoon, she went up to her chamber,—never more to descend.

The child was born at twenty minutes after eleven at night. Mary had requested that I would not come into the chamber till all was over, and signified her intention of then performing the interesting office of presenting the new-born child to its father. I was sitting in a parlour; and it was not till after two o'clock on Thursday morning, that I received the alarming intelligence, that the placenta was not yet removed, and that the midwife dared not proceed any further, and gave her opinion for calling in a male practitioner. I accordingly went for Dr. Poignand,[3] physician and man-midwife to the same hospital, who arrrived between three and four hours after the birth of the child. He immediately proceeded to the extraction of the placenta, which he brought away in pieces, till he was satisfied that the whole was removed. In that point however it afterwards appeared that he was mistaken.

The period from the birth of the child till about eight o'clock the next morning, was a period full of peril and alarm. The loss of blood was considerable, and produced an almost uninterrupted series of fainting fits. I went to the chamber soon after four in the morning,

---

[1] probably written in 1795, when Wollstonecraft, a single mother, was desperate for money; published as the unfinished "Lessons for Children" in Posthumous Works.

[2] published, unfinished, in Posthumous Works (1798) as Maria, or the Wrongs of Woman.*

[3] Louis Poignand, chief obstetrician at the Westminster Lying-In Hospital.

and found her in this state. She told me some time on Thursday, "that she should have died the preceding night, but that she was determined not to leave me." She added, with one of those smiles which so eminently illuminated her countenance, "that I should not be like Porson,"[1] alluding to the circumstance of that great man having lost his wife, after being only a few months married. Speaking of what she had already passed through, she declared, "that she had never known what bodily pain was before."

On Thursday morning Dr. Poignand repeated his visit. Mary had just before expressed some inclination to see Dr. George Fordyce,[2] a man probably of more science than any other medical professor in England, and between whom and herself there had long subsisted a mutual friendship. I mentioned this to Dr. Poignand, but he rather discountenanced the idea, observing that he saw no necessity for it, and that he supposed Dr. Fordyce was not particularly conversant with obstetrical cases; but that I would do as I pleased. After Dr. Poignand was gone, I determined to send for Dr. Fordyce. He accordingly saw the patient about three o'clock on Thursday afternoon. He however perceived no particular cause of alarm; and, on that or the next day, quoted, as I am told, Mary's case, in a mixed company, as a corroboration of a favourite idea of his, of the propriety of employing females in the capacity of midwives. Mary "had had a woman, and was doing extremely well."

What had passed however in the night between Wednesday and Thursday, had so far alarmed me, that I did not quit the house, and scarcely the chamber, during the following day. But my alarms wore off, as time advanced. Appearances were more favourable, than the exhausted state of the patient would almost have permitted me to expect. Friday morning therefore I devoted to a business of some urgency, which called me to different parts of the town, and which, before dinner, I happily completed. On my return, and during the evening, I received the most pleasurable sensations from the promising state of the patient. I was now perfectly satisfied that every thing was safe, and that, if she did not take cold, or suffer from any external accident, her speedy recovery was certain.

Saturday was a day less auspicious than Friday, but not absolutely alarming.

Sunday, the third of September, I now regard as the day, that finally decided on the fate of the object dearest to my heart that the universe contained. Encouraged by what I considered as the progress of her recovery, I accompanied a friend in the morning in several calls, one of them as far as Kensington, and did not return till dinner-time. On my return I found a degree of anxiety in every face, and was told that she had had a sort of shivering fit, and had expressed some anxiety at the length of my absence. My sister and a friend of hers, had been engaged to dine below stairs, but a message was sent to put them off, and Mary ordered that the cloth should not be laid, as usual, in the room immediately under her on the first floor, but in the ground-floor parlour. I felt a pang at having been so long and so unseasonably absent, and determined that I would not repeat the fault.

In the evening she had a second shivering fit, the symptoms of which were in the highest degree alarming. Every muscle of the body trembled, the teeth chattered, and the bed shook under her. This continued probably for five minutes. She told me, after it was over, that it had been a struggle between life and death, and that she had been more than once, in the course of it, at the point of expiring. I now apprehend these to have been the symptoms of a decided mortification, occasioned by the part of the placenta that remained in the womb. At the time however I was far from considering it in that light. When I went for Dr. Poignand, between two and three o'clock on the morning of Thursday,[3] despair was in my heart. The fact of the adhesion of the placenta was stated to me; and, ignorant as I was of obstetrical science, I felt as if the death of Mary was in a manner decided. But hope had re-visited my bosom; and her chearings were so delightful, that I hugged her obstinately to my heart. I was only mortified at what appeared to me a new delay in the recovery I so earnestly

---

[1] Richard Porson (1759–1808), Regius Professor of Greek at Cambridge and editor of the plays of Euripides.

[2] Scottish lecturer-physician, a member of the circle Wollstonecraft had met through Joseph Johnson, her publisher.

[3] actually Monday—an uncharacteristic error.

longed for. I immediately sent for Dr. Fordyce, who had been with her in the morning, as well as on the three preceding days. Dr. Poignand had also called this morning, but declined paying any further visits, as we had thought proper to call in Dr. Fordyce.

The progress of the disease was now uninterrupted. On Tuesday I found it necessary again to call in Dr. Fordyce in the afternoon, who brought with him Dr. Clarke of New Burlington-street,[1] under the idea that some operation might be necessary. I have already said, that I pertinaciously persisted in viewing the fair side of things; and therefore the interval between Sunday and Tuesday evening, did not pass without some mixture of cheerfulness. On Monday, Dr. Fordyce forbad the child's having the breast, and we therefore procured puppies to draw off the milk. This occasioned some pleasantry of Mary with me and the other attendants. Nothing could exceed the equanimity, the patience and affectionateness of the poor sufferer. I intreated her to recover; I dwelt with trembling fondness on every favourable circumstance; and, as far it was possible in so dreadful a situation, she, by her smiles and kind speeches, rewarded my affection.

Wednesday was to me the day of greatest torture in the melancholy series. It was now decided that the only chance of supporting her through what she had to suffer, was by supplying her rather freely with wine. This task was devolved upon me. I began about four o'clock in the afternoon. But for me, totally ignorant of the nature of diseases and of the human frame, thus to play with a life that now seemed all that was dear to me in the universe, was too dreadful a task. I knew neither what was too much, nor what was too little. Having begun, I felt compelled, under every disadvantage, to go on. This lasted for three hours. Towards the end of that time, I happened foolishly to ask the servant who came out of the room, "What she thought of her mistress?" she replied, "that, in her judgment, she was going as fast as possible." There are moments, when any creature that lives, has power to drive one into madness. I seemed to know the absurdity of this reply; but that was of no consequence. It added to the measure of my distraction. A little after seven I intreated a friend to go for Mr. Carlisle,[2] and bring him instantly wherever he was to be found. He had voluntarily called on the patient on the preceding Saturday, and two or three times since. He had seen her that morning, and had been earnest in recommending the wine-diet. That day he dined four miles out of town, on the side of the metropolis, which was furthest from us. Notwithstanding this, my friend returned with him after three-quarters of an hour's absence. No one who knows my friend, will wonder either at his eagerness or success, when I name Mr. Basil Montagu.[3] The sight of Mr. Carlisle thus unexpectedly, gave me a stronger alleviating sensation, than I thought it possible to experience.

Mr. Carlisle left us no more from Wednesday evening, to the hour of her death. It was impossible to exceed his kindness and affectionate attention. It excited in every spectator a sentiment like adoration. His conduct was uniformly tender and anxious, ever upon the watch, observing every symptom, and eager to improve every favourable appearance. If skill or attention could have saved her, Mary would still live. In addition to Mr. Carlisle's constant presence, she had Dr. Fordyce and Dr. Clarke every day. She had for nurses, or rather for friends, watching every occasion to serve her, Mrs. Fenwick,[4] author of an excellent novel, entitled Secrecy, another very kind and judicious lady, and a favourite female servant. I was scarcely ever out of the room. Four friends, Mr. Fenwick, Mr. Basil Montagu, Mr. Marshal, and Mr. Dyson,[5] sat up nearly the whole of the last week of her existence in the house, to be

---

[1] John Clarke (bap. 1760, d. 1815), physician and lecturer on midwifery, and author of several books on obstetrics and the diseases of children.

[2] Anthony Carlisle (1768–1840), a doctor and friend of Godwin and of the playwright and novelist Thomas Holcroft. Carlisle later tried, unsuccessfully, to cure Coleridge* of his opium addiction.

[3] Basil Montagu (1770–1851), illegitimate son of the Earl of Sandwich, friend of W. Wordsworth,* and a London lawyer.

[4] Eliza Fenwick (1766–1840), author of *Secresy* (1795), a novel about an idealistic young woman who rejects the institution of marriage and is consequently betrayed. Fenwick looked after the baby for a few days after Wollstonecraft's death.

[5] John Fenwick, Irish patriot, political writer, and husband of Eliza Fenwick; James Marshal, a friend since school-days and, at times, Godwin's literary agent; George Dyson, who had weaned Godwin from Calvinism.

dispatched, on any errand, to any part of the metropolis, at a moment's warning.

Mr. Carlisle being in the chamber, I retired to bed for a few hours on Wednesday night. Towards morning he came into my room with an account that the patient was surprisingly better. I went instantly into the chamber. But I now sought to suppress every idea of hope. The greatest anguish I have any conception of, consists in that crushing of a new-born hope which I had already two or three times experienced. If Mary recovered, it was well, and I should see it time enough. But it was too mighty a thought to bear being trifled with, and turned out and admitted in this abrupt way.

I had reason to rejoice in the firmness of my gloomy thoughts, when, about ten o'clock on Thursday evening, Mr. Carlisle told us to prepare ourselves, for we had reason to expect the fatal event every moment. To my thinking, she did not appear to be in that state of total exhaustion, which I supposed to precede death; but it is probable that death does not always take place by that gradual process I had pictured to myself; a sudden pang may accelerate his arrival. She did not die on Thursday night.

Till now it does not appear that she had any serious thoughts of dying; but on Friday and Saturday, the two last days of her life, she occasionally spoke as if she expected it. This was however only at intervals; the thought did not seem to dwell upon her mind. Mr. Carlisle rejoiced in this. He observed, and there is great force in the suggestion, that there is no more pitiable object, than a sick man, that knows he is dying. The thought must be expected to destroy his courage, to cooperate with the disease, and to counteract every favourable effort of nature.

On these two days her faculties were in too decayed a state, to be able to follow any train of ideas with force or any accuracy of connection. Her religion, as I have already shown, was not calculated to be the torment of a sick bed; and, in fact, during her whole illness, not one word of a religious cast fell from her lips.

She was affectionate and compliant to the last. I observed on Friday and Saturday nights, that, whenever her attendants recommended to her to sleep, she discovered her willingness to yield, by breathing, perhaps for the space of a minute, in the manner of a person that sleeps, though the effort, from the state of her disorder, usually proved ineffectual.

She was not tormented by useless contradiction. One night the servant, from an error in judgment, teazed her with idle expostulations, but she complained of it grievously, and it was corrected. "Pray, pray, do not let her reason with me," was her expression. Death itself is scarcely so dreadful to the enfeebled frame, as the monotonous importunity of nurses everlastingly repeated.

Seeing that every hope was extinct, I was very desirous of obtaining from her any directions, that she might wish to have followed after her decease. Accordingly, on Saturday morning, I talked to her for a good while of the two children. In conformity to Mr. Carlisle's maxim of not impressing the idea of death, I was obliged to manage my expressions. I therefore affected to proceed wholly upon the ground of her having been very ill, and that it would be some time before she could expect to be well; wishing her to tell me any thing that she would choose to have done respecting the children, as they would now be principally under my care. After having repeated this idea to her in a great variety of forms, she at length said, with a significant tone of voice, "I know what you are thinking of," but added, that she had nothing to communicate to me upon the subject.

The shivering fits had ceased entirely for the two last days. Mr. Carlisle observed that her continuance was almost miraculous, and he was on the watch for favourable appearances, believing it highly improper to give up all hope, and remarking, that perhaps one in a million, of persons in her state might possibly recover. I conceive that not one in a million, unites so good a constitution of body and of mind.

There were the amusements of persons in the very gulph of despair. At six o'clock on Sunday morning, September the tenth, Mr. Carlisle called me from my bed to which I had retired at one, in conformity to my request, that I might not be left to receive all at once the intelligence that she was no more. She expired at twenty minutes before eight....

Georgiana Cavendish
1757 – 1806

Georgiana Spencer was born on 9 June 1757, the oldest daughter of John, Earl Spencer and Georgiana Poyntz, Countess Spencer. She was educated by her mother. She published her first novel, *Emma; or, The Unfortunate Attachment,* in 1773, and a second novel, *The Sylph,* in 1779. In 1774, she married William Cavendish, Duke of Newcastle. A famous beauty, she became a leader of society. She became politically active, canvassing on behalf of her friend Charles James Fox. She also became addicted to gambling and at one point was almost £60,000 in debt. In 1782, the Duke and Duchess became involved with Lady Elizabeth Foster. Both women had the Duke's children; they were also passionately fond of each other. In 1791, the Duchess became pregnant as the result of an affair with Charles Grey (later Prime Minister); the Duke objected to this extramural attachment and sent her and Lady Foster on the tour of Europe that inspired *The Passage of the Mountain of Saint Gothard.* On her return, the Duchess briefly took care of her nine-year-old niece, Caroline Ponsonby (later Lady Caroline Lamb).* She died in London on 30 March 1806. The Duke married Lady Foster in 1809, but he died in 1811. (D.L.M.)

※

The Passage of the Mountain of Saint Gothard. A Poem[1] (1802)

To My Children

Ye plains, where three fold harvests press the ground,
    Ye climes, where genial gales incessant swell,
Where art and nature shed profusely round
    Their rival wonders—*Italy* farewell.

5 Still may thy year in fullest splendor shine!
    Its icy darts in vain may winter throw!
To thee, a parent, sister, I consign,[2]
    And wing'd with health, I woo thy gales to blow.

Yet, pleas'd, *Helvetia*'s[3] rugged brows I see,
10   And thro' their craggy steeps delighted roam;
Pleas'd with a people, honest, brave and free,
    Whilst every step conducts me nearer home.

I wander where *Tesino*[4] madly flows,
    From cliff to cliff in foaming eddies tost;
15 On the rude mountain's barren breast he rose,
    In *Po*'s broad wave now hurries to be lost.

His shores, neat huts and verdant pastures fill,
    And hills where woods of pine the storm defy;
While, scorning vegetation, higher still,
20   Rise the bare rocks coeval with the sky.

Upon his banks a favor'd spot I found,
    Where shade and beauty tempted to repose;
Within a grove, by mountains circled round,
    By rocks o'erhung, my rustic seat I chose.

25 Advancing thence, by gentle pace and slow,
    Unconscious of the way my footsteps prest,
Sudden, supported by the hills below,
    ST. GOTHARD's summits rose above the rest.

'Midst tow'ring cliffs and tracts of endless cold
30   Th' industrious path pervades the rugged stone,
And seems—*Helvetia* let thy toils be told—
    A granite girdle o'er the mountain thrown.

---

[1] The poem records a journey across the Alps undertaken in August 1793. We have omitted Cavendish's copious notes.

[2] Cavendish's mother, Georgiana, Countess Spencer, and her sister, Henrietta Ponsonby, Countess Bessborough, were planning to spend the winter in Naples.

[3] Switzerland's.

[4] The Tesino, a tributary of the Po, has its source near the summit of St. Gothard.

No haunt of man the weary traveller greets,
    No vegetation smiles upon the moor,
35 Save where the flow'ret breathes uncultur'd sweets,
    Save where the patient monk receives the poor.[1]

Yet let not these rude paths be coldly trac'd,
    Let not these wilds with listless steps be trod,
Here fragrance scorns not to perfume the waste,
40   Here charity uplifts the mind to God.[2]

His humble board the holy man prepares,
    And simple food, and wholesome lore bestows,
Extols the treasures that his mountain bears,
    And paints the perils of impending snows.

45 For whilst bleak Winter numbs with chilling hand—
    Where frequent crosses mark the traveller's fate—
In slow procession moves the merchant band,
    And silent bends, where tottering ruins wait.

Yet 'midst those ridges, 'midst that drifted snow,
50   Can nature deign her wonders to display;
Here Adularia[3] shines with vivid glow,
    And gems of crystal sparkle to the day.

Here too, the hoary mountain's brow to grace,
    Five silver lakes, in tranquil state are seen;
55 While from their waters, many a stream we trace,[4]
    That, scap'd from bondage, rolls the rocks
        between.

Hence flows the *Reuss* to seek her wedded love,[5]
    And, with the *Rhine*, *Germanic* climes explore;
Her stream I mark'd, and saw her wildly move
60   Down the bleak mountain, thro' her craggy shore.

My weary footsteps hop'd for rest in vain,
    For steep on steep, in rude confusion rose;
At length I paus'd above a fertile plain
    That promis'd shelter and foretold repose.

65 Fair runs the streamlet o'er the pasture green,
    Its margin gay, with flocks and cattle spread;
Embowering trees the peaceful village screen,
    And guard from snow each dwelling's jutting shed.

Sweet vale! whose bosom wastes and cliffs surround,
70   Let me awhile thy friendly shelter share!
Emblem of life! where some bright hours are found
    Amidst the darkest, dreariest years of care.

Delv'd thro' the rock, the secret passage bends;
    And beauteous horror strikes the dazzled sight;
75 Beneath the pendent bridge the stream descends
    Calm—till it tumbles o'er the frowning height.

We view the fearful pass—we wind along
    The path that marks the terrors of our way—
'Midst beetling rocks, and hanging woods among,
80   The torrent pours, and breathes its glitt'ring
        spray.

Weary at length, serener scenes we hail—
    More cultur'd groves o'ershade the grassy meads,
The neat, tho' wooden hamlets, deck the vale,
    And *Altorf*'s spires recall heroic deeds.[6]

85 But tho' no more amidst those scenes I roam,
    My fancy long each image shall retain—
The flock returning to its welcome home—
    And the wild carrol of the cowherd's strain.

Lucernia's lake its glassy surface shews,
90   Whilst nature's varied beauties deck its side;
Here, rocks and woods its narrow waves inclose,
    And there, its spreading bosom opens wide.

---

[1] At the top of the mountain there was a small convent, where the monks offered food and shelter to poor travellers.

[2] Cf. Thomas Gray (1716–71), *Elegy Written in a Country Church-Yard* (1750) 55–56, 128.

[3] a kind of feldspar.

[4] The Aar, the Reuss, the Rhine, the Rhone, and the Tesino all have their sources on Mont St. Gothard.

[5] The Reuss joins the Aar past Lake Lucerne.

[6] Altdorf is the setting for the legendary exploit of William Tell (see lines 93–96).

And hail the chapel! hail the platform wild!
    Where Tell directed the avenging dart,
95 With well strung arm, that first preserv'd his child,
    Then wing'd the arrow to the tyrant's heart.[1]

Across the lake, and deep embower'd in wood,
    Behold another hallow'd chapel stand,
Where three Swiss heroes, lawless force withstood,
100   And stamp'd the freedom of their native land.[2]

Their liberty requir'd no rites uncouth,
    No blood demanded, and no slaves enchain'd;
Her rule was gentle and her voice was truth,
    By social order form'd, by laws restrain'd.

105 We quit the lake—and cultivation's toil,
    With nature's charms combin'd, adorns the way,
And well earn'd wealth improves the ready soil,
    And simple manners still maintain their sway.

Farewell *Helvetia*! from whose lofty breast,
110   Proud *Alps* arise, and copious rivers flow;
Where, source of streams, eternal glaciers rest,
    And peaceful science gilds the plains below.

Oft on thy rocks the wondering eye shall gaze,
    Thy vallies oft the raptur'd bosom seek—
115 There, nature's hand her boldest work displays,
    Here, bliss domestic beams on every cheek.

Hope of my life! dear CHILDREN of my heart!
    That anxious heart, to each fond feeling true,
To YOU still pants each pleasure to impart,
120   And more—oh transport—reach its HOME and YOU.

---

[1] According to legend, William Tell refused to pay homage to the bailiff Gessler and was ordered to shoot an apple off his son's head. He succeeded, and later shot Gessler. A chapel was erected at the spot.

[2] According to legend, the Swiss independence movement began with the Rütli Oath, sworn on the shore of Lake Lucerne in 1307 by Walter Fürst of the canton of Uri, Arnold von Melchtal of Unterwalden, and Werner Stauffacher of Schwyz.

William Blake
1757 – 1827

William Blake was born in London on 28 November 1757, the third son of James Blake, a hosier, and Catherine Harmitage Blake. He had no formal education; his mother taught him to read and write. At ten, he entered a drawing school, and at fourteen, he was apprenticed to James Basire, a master engraver. In 1779–80, after completing his apprenticeship, he briefly attended the Royal Academy; the aesthetic ideas of its president, Sir Joshua Reynolds,* were later anathema to him. He worked for the rest of his life as an engraver and artist, illustrating the Bible and works by Dante, Gray, Milton, and Virgil, along with more commercial assignments. Among his most important employers was the radical publisher Joseph Johnson, at whose house he met Barbauld* (possibly), Godwin,* Paine,* Priestley, and Wollstonecraft* (whose children's book, *Original Stories*, he illustrated in 1791). In August 1782, he married Catherine Boucher; she was illiterate, but Blake taught her to read, write, and draw, and she assisted him in his work. Their marriage was happy, though they had no children.

From his childhood, Blake was a visionary. At four, he saw God "put his head to the window," and on a walk as a boy he saw "a tree filled with angels, bright angelic wings bespangling every bough like stars." His parents, who were Baptists, did not appreciate these visions, and Catherine later remarked, "I have very little of Mr. Blake's company; he is always in Paradise."

These visionary experiences not only inspired all his work after *Poetical Sketches* (1783), they provided its medium: his brother Robert (1767–87), whom Blake had nursed tenderly through his last illness, appeared to him in a dream and revealed the secret of relief etching, or "illuminated printing," combining text and illustration, which Blake used to print such works as *Songs of Innocence and of Experience* (1789–94). Throughout the 1790s, Blake continued to compose and print visionary works like *The Marriage of Heaven and Hell* (1793?), *Visions of the Daughters of Albion* (1793), *America. A Prophecy* (1793), and *Europe a Prophecy* (1794). He also worked on a full-length epic called *Vala* or *The Four Zoas*, which he never finished.

In 1800 a patron, William Hayley, persuaded Blake to move to Felpham, Sussex. The patronage of Hayley, who considered Blake impractical, was not a success, and Blake's time in Felpham was disturbed by a soldier, who, after Blake had evicted him from his property, accused him of sedition (he was acquitted). By the time he returned to London in 1803, however, he had written his epic *Milton*, which he began to engrave in 1804. He also began to write and engrave another epic, *Jerusalem*, in 1804; work on the two poems (which incorporate some of the material from *Vala*) seems to have taken him until about 1820. In 1809–10, Blake held a public exhibition of his watercolours. It was not a success; Charles Lamb* found the pictures "marvelous," but Southey* found some of them "hideous" and others evidence of "madness." Blake spent his last years in poverty, despite the efforts of his friend John Linnell, who arranged commissions for him and, when all else failed, commissioned work himself. Blake died on 12 August 1827. His friend George Richmond reported: "Just before he died His countenance became fair—His eyes Brighten'd and He burst out in Singing of the things he saw in Heaven."

Almost unknown as a poet in his own time, Blake was rediscovered in the mid-nineteenth century and has been an important inspiration for such later visionary poets as Swinburne, Yeats, and Ginsberg. (D.L.M.)

from *Songs of Innocence* (1789)

Introduction

Piping down the valleys wild
Piping songs of pleasant glee
On a cloud I saw a child.
And he laughing said to me.

5 Pipe a song about a Lamb;
So I piped with merry chear,
Piper pipe that song again—
So I piped, he wept to hear.

Drop thy pipe thy happy pipe
10 Sing thy songs of happy chear,
So I sung the same again
While he wept with joy to hear

Piper sit thee down and write
In a book that all may read—
15 So he vanish'd from my sight.
And I pluck'd a hollow reed.

And I made a rural pen,
And I stain'd the water clear,
And I wrote my happy songs
20 Every child may joy to hear

The Ecchoing Green

The Sun does arise,
And make happy the skies.
The merry bells ring
To welcome the Spring.
5 The sky-lark and thrush,
The birds of the bush,
Sing louder around,
To the bells chearful sound.
While our sports shall be seen
10 On the Ecchoing Green.

Old John with white hair
Does laugh away care,
Sitting under the oak,
Among the old folk,
15 They laugh at our play,
And soon they all say.
Such such were the joys.
When we all girls & boys,
In our youth-time were seen,
20 On the Ecchoing Green.

Till the little ones weary
No more can be merry
The sun does descend,
And our sports have an end:
25 Round the laps of their mothers,
Many sisters and brothers,
Like birds in their nest,
Are ready for rest;
And sport no more seen,
30 On the darkening Green.

The Lamb

Little Lamb who made thee
Dost thou know who made thee
Gave thee life & bid thee feed.
By the stream & o'er the mead;
5 Gave thee clothing of delight,
Softest clothing wooly bright;
Gave thee such a tender voice,
Making all the vales rejoice!
Little Lamb who made thee
10 Dost thou know who made thee

Little Lamb I'll tell thee,
Little Lamb I'll tell thee!
He is called by thy name,
For he calls himself a Lamb:[1]
15 He is meek & he is mild,[2]
He became a little child:
I a child & thou a lamb,

---

[1] John 1.29, 36; 1 Peter 1.19; Revelation 5.6, 8, 12, 13, and many other passages.

[2] Cf. Charles Wesley (1707–88), "Gentle Jesus, meek and mild."

We are called by his name.
    Little Lamb God bless thee.
20   Little Lamb God bless thee.

The Little Black Boy

My mother bore me in the southern wild,
And I am black, but O! my soul is white;
White as an angel is the English child:
But I am black as if bereav'd of light.

5 My mother taught me underneath a tree
And sitting down before the heat of day,
She took me on her lap and kissed me,
And pointing to the east began to say.

Look on the rising sun:[1] there God does live
10 And gives his light, and gives his heat away.
And flowers and trees and beasts and men recieve
Comfort in morning joy in the noon day.

And we are put on earth a little space,
That we may learn to bear the beams of love,
15 And these black bodies and this sun-burnt face
Is but a cloud, and like a shady grove.

For when our souls have learn'd the heat to bear
The cloud will vanish we shall hear his voice.
Saying: come out from the grove my love & care,
20 And round my golden tent like lambs rejoice.

Thus did my mother say and kissed me,
And thus I say to little English boy.
When I from black and he from white cloud free,
And round the tent of God like lambs we joy:

25 Ill shade him from the heat till he can bear,
To lean in joy upon our fathers knee.
And then I'll stand and stroke his silver hair,
And be like him and he will then love me.

---

[1] Cf. Isaiah 45.6, 59.19.

A Dream

Once a dream did weave a shade,
O'er my Angel-guarded bed,
That an Emmet lost it's way
Where on grass methought I lay.

5 Troubled wilderd and forlorn
Dark benighted travel-worn,
Over many a tangled spray
All heart-broke I heard her say.

O my children! do they cry
10 Do they hear their father sigh.
Now they look abroad to see,
Now return and weep for me.

Pitying I drop'd a tear:
But I saw a glow-worm near:
15 Who replied. What wailing wight
Calls the watchman of the night.[2]

I am set to light the ground,
While the beetle goes his round:
Follow now the beetles hum,
20 Little wanderer hie thee home.

The Chimney Sweeper[3]

When my mother died I was very young,
And my father sold me while yet my tongue,
Could scarcely cry weep weep weep weep.[4]
So your chimneys I sweep & in soot I sleep.[5]

---

[2] The dor-beetle, a nocturnal insect, was called "the watchman."

[3] Children had to climb up chimneys to clean them, a filthy, dangerous, and unhealthy job. A law ameliorating their working conditions was passed in 1788 but never enforced.

[4] The child is attempting to say "sweep," the chimney-sweeper's street-cry. The act of 1788 should have prevented the apprenticing of children younger than eight.

[5] The sweeps used their bags of soot as blankets.

5   Theres little Tom Dacre,[1] who cried when his head
    That curl'd like a lambs back, was shav'd, so I said.
    Hush Tom never mind it, for when your head's bare,
    You know that the soot cannot spoil your white hair.

    And so he was quiet, & that very night,
10 As Tom was a sleeping he had such a sight,
    That thousands of sweepers Dick, Joe, Ned & Jack
    Were all of them lock'd up in coffins of black,

    And by came an Angel who had a bright key,
    And he open'd the coffins & set them all free.
15 Then down a green plain leaping laughing they run
    And wash in a river and shine in the Sun.[2]

    Then naked & white, all their bags left behind,
    They rise upon clouds, and sport in the wind.
    And the Angel told Tom if he'd be a good boy,
20 He'd have God for his father & never want joy.

    And so Tom awoke and we rose in the dark
    And got with our bags & our brushes to work.
    Tho' the morning was cold, Tom was happy & warm,
    So if all do their duty, they need not fear harm.

The Divine Image

    To Mercy Pity Peace and Love,
    All pray in their distress:
    And to these virtues of delight
    Return their thankfulness.

5   For Mercy Pity Peace and Love,
    Is God our father dear:
    And Mercy Pity Peace and Love,
    Is Man his child and care.

    For Mercy has a human heart
10 Pity, a human face:
    And Love, the human form divine,
    And Peace, the human dress.

    Then every man of every clime,
    That prays in his distress,
15 Prays to the human form divine
    Love Mercy Pity Peace.

    And all must love the human form,
    In heathen, turk or jew.[3]
    Where Mercy, Love & Pity dwell,
20 There God is dwelling too[4]

Holy Thursday[5]

    Twas on a Holy Thursday their innocent faces clean
    The children walking two & two in red & blue & green[6]
    Grey headed beadles[7] walkd before with wands as white as snow
    Till into the high dome of Pauls they like Thames waters flow

5   O what a multitude they seemd these flowers of London town
    Seated in companies they sit with radiance all their own
    The hum of multitudes was there but multitudes of lambs
    Thousands of little boys & girls raising their innocent hands

    Now like a mighty wind they raise to heaven the voice of song

---

[1] presumably a foundling from the almshouse established by Lady Ann Dacre.

[2] The act of 1788 called for weekly washings for sweeps.

[3] Cf. Isaac Watts, "Praise for the Gospel": "Lord, I ascribe it to thy Grace / And not to Chance, as others do, / That I was born of *Christian* Race, / And not a *Heathen*, or a *Jew*."

[4] Cf. 1 John 4.16.

[5] Each year since 1782, the 6,000 children in London's charity schools had been brought to St. Paul's Cathedral for a thanksgiving service. It was always on a Thursday, but apparently never on either Maundy Thursday or Ascension Day (forty days after Easter), the two most obvious "holy Thursdays." See M.G. Jones, *The Charity School Movement* (1938).

[6] the school uniforms.

[7] church officials.

10   Or like harmonious thunderings[1] the seats of heaven among
     Beneath them sit the aged men wise guardians of the poor
     Then cherish pity, lest you drive an angel from your door[2]

Nurse's Song

When the voices of children are heard on the green
And laughing is heard on the hill,
My heart is at rest within my breast
And every thing else is still

5 Then come home my children, the sun is gone down
   And the dews of night arise
   Come come leave off play, and let us away
   Till the morning appears in the skies

   No no let us play, for it is yet day
10 And we cannot go to sleep
   Besides in the sky, the little birds fly
   And the hills are all coverd with sheep

   Well well go & play till the light fades away
   And then go home to bed
15 The little ones leaped & shouted & laugh'd
   And all the hills ecchoed

Infant Joy

I have no name
I am but two days old.—
What shall I call thee?
I happy am
5 Joy is my name,—
   Sweet joy befall thee!

Pretty joy!
Sweet joy but two days old,
Sweet joy I call thee;
10 Thou dost smile.

---

[1] Cf. Revelation 19.6.

[2] Cf. Hebrews 13.2.

I sing the while
Sweet joy befall thee.

The Marriage of Heaven and Hell (1793)[3]

[Plate 2]
The Argument.[4]

Rintrah roars[5] & shakes his fires in the burdend air;
Hungry clouds swag on the deep

Once meek, and in a perilous path,
The just man kept his course along
5 The vale of death.[6]
   Roses are planted where thorns grow.
   And on the barren heath
   Sing the honey bees.

Then the perilous path was planted:
10 And a river, and a spring[7]
   On every cliff and tomb;
   And on the bleached bones[8]
   Red clay[9] brought forth.

Till the villain left the paths of ease,
15 To walk in perilous paths, and drive
   The just man into barren climes.[10]

---

[3] Blake combines the title of two works by the Swedish visionary Emanuel Swedenborg (1688–1772), *A Treatise Concerning Heaven and Hell, and of the Wonderful Things Therein, as Heard and Seen, by Emanuel Swedenborg* (1758, trans. 1784) and *Conjugal Love* (1768, trans. 1790).

[4] For the imagery of "The Argument," Cf. Isaiah 5.1–7, 7.23–25, 35.1–10.

[5] Cf. Amos 1.2, 3.8. The character of Rintrah reappears in Blake's *Europe a Prophecy* (1794).

[6] The just man and his adventures are reminiscent of Christian, in John Bunyan (1628–88), *The Pilgrim's Progress* (1678–84).

[7] Cf. Exodus 17.1–7.

[8] Cf. Ezekiel 37.1–11.

[9] Since God created Adam from "the dust of the ground" (Genesis 2.8), "Adam" is sometimes said to mean "red clay" in Hebrew.

[10] Cf. Milton, *Paradise Lost* 11.808–18.

Now the sneaking serpent[1] walks
In mild humility.
And the just man rages in the wilds[2]
20 Where lions roam.

Rintrah roars & shakes his fires in the burdend air;
Hungry clouds swag on the deep.

[Plate 3]

As a new heaven is begun, and it is now thirty-three years since its advent: the Eternal Hell revives.[3] And lo! Swedenborg is the Angel sitting at the tomb; his writings are the linen clothes folded up.[4] Now is the dominion of Edom,[5] & the return of Adam into Paradise; see Isaiah XXXIV & XXXV Chap:[6]

Without Contraries is no progression. Attraction and Repulsion, Reason and Energy, Love and Hate, are necessary to Human existence.

From these contraries spring what the religious call Good & Evil. Good is the passive that obeys Reason[.] Evil is the active springing from Energy.

Good is Heaven. Evil is Hell.

[Plate 4]
The voice of the Devil

All Bibles or sacred codes. have been the causes of the following Errors.

1. That Man has two real existing principles Viz: a Body & a Soul.

2. That Energy. calld Evil. is alone from the Body. & that Reason. calld Good. is alone from the Soul.

3. That God will torment Man in Eternity for following his Energies.

But the following Contraries to these are True

1. Man has no Body distinct from his Soul[7] for that calld Body is a portion of Soul discernd by the five Senses. the chief inlets of Soul in this age

2. Energy is the only life and is from the Body and Reason is the bound or outward circumference of Energy.

3. Energy is Eternal Delight

[Plate 5]

Those who restrain desire, do so because theirs is weak enough to be restrained; and the restrainer or reason usurps its place & governs the unwilling.

And being restrained it by degrees becomes passive till it is only the shadow of desire.

The history of this is written in Paradise Lost. & the Governor or Reason is call'd Messiah.

And the original Archangel or possessor of the command of the heavenly host, is calld the Devil or Satan and his children are call'd Sin & Death[8]

But in the Book of Job Miltons Messiah is call'd Satan.

For this history has been adopted by both parties

It indeed appear'd to Reason as if Desire was cast out. but the Devils account is, that the Messi[Plate 6]ah fell. & formed a heaven of what he stole from the Abyss

This is shewn in the Gospel, where he prays to the Father to send the comforter[9] or Desire that Reason may have Ideas to build on, the Jehovah of the Bible being no other than he,[10] who dwells in flaming fire.

Know that after Christs death, he became Jehovah.

But in Milton; the Father is Destiny, the Son, a Ratio of the five senses. & the Holy-ghost, Vacuum!

Note. The reason Milton wrote in fetters when he wrote of Angels & God, and at liberty when of Devils & Hell, is because he was a true Poet and of the Devils party without knowing it[11]

---

[1] Cf. Genesis 3.1–5, 13–15.

[2] Cf. Isaiah 40.3, Matthew 3.3, John 1.23.

[3] Swedenborg had predicted that the Last Judgment would occur in 1757 (*Last Judgment* [trans. 1788] n.45), coincidentally the year of Blake's birth. In 1790, the "now" of the poem, Blake is 33, Christ's age when he was crucified and rose again.

[4] See Matthew 28.1–8, Mark 16.1–8, Luke 24.1–9, John 20.1–8.

[5] Esau: see Genesis 25.30, 27.40, Isaiah 63.1–4. Like "Adam," "Edom" suggests redness.

[6] prophecies of divine vengeance and restoration.

[7] Cf. Joseph Priestley (1733–1804), *Disquisitions Relating to Matter and Spirit* (1777, 1782).

[8] Milton, *Paradise Lost* 2.746–814.

[9] John 14.16–17, 26, 16.7.

[10] One letter before and one word after "he" were deleted from the plate. Erdman suggests (801) that the passage originally read "the Devil" (or, less probably, "the Angel").

[11] Cf. the discussion of *Paradise Lost* in P.B. Shelley, "A Defense of Poetry" (1840).*

A Memorable Fancy.[1]

As I was walking among the fires of hell, delighted with the enjoyments of Genius; which to Angels look like torment and insanity. I collected some of their Proverbs: thinking that as the sayings used in a nation, mark its character, so the Proverbs of Hell, shew the nature of Infernal wisdom better than any description of buildings or garments.

When I came home; on the abyss of the five senses, where a flat sided steep frowns over the present world. I saw a mighty Devil folded in black clouds, hovering on the sides of the rock, with cor[Plate 7]roding fires[2] he wrote the following sentence now percieved by the minds of men, & read by them on earth.

  How do you know but ev'ry Bird that cuts the
   airy way,
  Is an immense world of delight, clos'd by your
   senses five?[3]

Proverbs of Hell.

In seed time learn, in harvest teach, in winter enjoy.
Drive your cart and your plow over the bones of the dead.
The road of excess leads to the palace of wisdom.
Prudence is a rich ugly old maid courted by Incapacity.
5 He who desires but acts not, breeds pestilence.
The cut worm forgives the plow.
Dip him in the river who loves water.
A fool sees not the same tree that a wise man sees.
He whose face gives no light, shall never become a star.
10 Eternity is in love with the productions of time.
The busy bee has no time for sorrow.
The hours of folly are measur'd by the clock, but of
  wisdom: no clock can measure.

---

[1] Blake's "Memorable Fancies" are modelled on the "Memorable Relations" in which Swedenborg recounts his visionary experiences.

[2] a reference to Blake's use of acids to etch the copper plates from which he printed his poems. More extended accounts of the printing process occur on plates 14 and 15.

[3] Cf. Chatterton,* "Bristowe Tragedie or the Dethe of Syr Charles Bawdin" (1768): "How dydd I knowe thatt ev'ry darte / That cutte the airie waie / Myghte notte fynde passage toe my harte / And close myne eyes for aie?" (133–36).

All wholsom food is caught without a net or a trap.
Bring out number weight & measure in a year of dearth.
15 No bird soars too high. if he soars with his own wings.
A dead body. revenges not injuries.
The most sublime act is to set another before you.
If the fool would persist in his folly he would become wise
Folly is the cloke of knavery.
20 Shame is Prides cloke.

[Plate 8]

Prisons are built with stones of Law, Brothels with
  bricks of Religion.
The pride of the peacock is the glory of God.
The lust of the goat is the bounty of God.
The wrath of the lion is the wisdom of God.
25 The nakedness of woman is the work of God.
Excess of sorrow laughs. Excess of joy weeps.
The roaring of lions, the howling of wolves, the raging
  of the stormy sea, and the destructive sword. are
  portions of eternity too great for the eye of man.
The fox condemns the trap, not himself.
Joys impregnate. Sorrows bring forth.
30 Let man wear the fell of the lion. woman the fleece of
  the sheep.
The bird a nest, the spider a web, man friendship.
The selfish smiling fool. & the sullen frowning fool.
  shall be both thought wise. that they may be a rod.
What is now proved was once, only imagin'd.
The rat, the mouse, the fox, the rabbet; watch the
  roots, the lion, the tyger, the horse, the elephant,
  watch the fruits.
35 The cistern contains: the fountain overflows
One thought. fills immensity.
Always be ready to speak your mind, and a base man
  will avoid you.
Every thing possible to be believ'd is an image of truth.
The eagle never lost so much time. as when he
  submitted to learn of the crow.

[Plate 9]

40 The fox provides for himself. but God provides for the
  lion.
Think in the morning, Act in the noon, Eat in the
  evening, Sleep in the night.
He who has sufferd you to impose on him knows you.

As the plow follows words, so God rewards prayers.
The tygers of wrath are wiser than the horses of instruction
45 Expect poison from the standing water.
You never know what is enough unless you know
    what is more than enough.
Listen to the fools reproach! it is a kingly title!
The eyes of fire, the nostrils of air, the mouth of water,
    the beard of earth.
The weak in courage is strong in cunning.
50 The apple tree never asks the beech how he shall grow,
    nor the lion. the horse; how he shall take his prey.
The thankful receiver bears a plentiful harvest.
If others had not been foolish. we should be so.
The soul of sweet delight. can never be defil'd,[1]
When thou seest an Eagle, thou seest a portion of
    Genius. lift up thy head!
55 As the catterpiller chooses the fairest leaves to lay her
    eggs on, so the priest lays his curse on the fairest joys.
To create a little flower is the labour of ages.
Damn. braces: Bless relaxes.
The best wine is the oldest. the best water the newest.
Prayers plow not! Praises reap not!
60 Joys laugh not! Sorrows weep not!

[Plate 10]

The head Sublime, the heart Pathos, the genitals
    Beauty, the hands & feet Proportion.
As the air to a bird or the sea to a fish, so is contempt to
    the contemptible.
The crow wish'd every thing was black, the owl, that
    every thing was white.
Exuberance is Beauty.
65 If the lion was advised by the fox. he would be cunning.
Improvement makes strait roads, but the crooked roads
    without Improvement, are roads of Genius.
Sooner murder an infant in its cradle than nurse
    unacted desires
Where man is not nature is barren.
Truth can never be told so as to be understood, and not
    be believ'd.
70   Enough! or Too much

---

[1] The proverb is repeated in *America* (1793) 8.14.*

[Plate 11]

The ancient Poets animated all sensible objects with Gods or Geniuses, calling them by the names and adorning them with the properties of woods, rivers, mountains, lakes, cities, nations, and whatever their enlarged & numerous senses could percieve.

And particularly they studied the genius of each city & country. placing it under its mental deity.

Till a system was formed, which some took advantage of & enslav'd the vulgar by attempting to realize or abstract the mental deities from their objects: thus began Priesthood.

Choosing forms of worship from poetic tales.

And at length they pronounced that the Gods had orderd such things.

Thus men forgot that All deities reside in the human breast.

[Plate 12]
A Memorable Fancy.

The Prophets Isaiah and Ezekiel dined with me, and I asked them how they dared so roundly to assert. that God spake to them;[2] and whether they did not think at the time, that they would be misunderstood, & so be the cause of imposition.

Isaiah answer'd. I saw no God. nor heard any, in a finite organical perception; but my senses discover'd the infinite in every thing, and as I was then perswaded. & remain confirm'd; that the voice of honest indignation[3] is the voice of God, I cared not for consequences but wrote.

Then I asked: does a firm perswasion that a thing is so, make it so?

He replied. All poets believe that it does, & in ages of imagination this firm perswasion removed mountains;[4] but many are not capable of a firm perswasion of any thing.

Then Ezekiel said. The philosophy of the east taught the first principles of human perception some nations held one principle for the origin & some another, we of Israel taught that the Poetic Genius (as you now call it) was the first principle and all the others merely deriva-

---

[2] e.g., Isaiah 8.1, Ezekiel 2.2.

[3] Cf. Isaiah 30.27.

[4] Matthew 21.21.

tive, which was the cause of our despising the Priests & Philosophers of other countries, and prophecying that all Gods [Plate 13] would at last be proved. to originate in ours & to be the tributaries of the Poetic Genius, it was this. that our great poet King David desired so fervently & invokes so patheticly, saying by this he conquers enemies & governs kingdoms; and we so loved our God. that we cursed in his name all the deities of surrounding nations,[1] and asserted that they had rebelled; from these opinions the vulgar came to think that all nations would at last be subject to the jews.

This said he, like all firm perswasions, is come to pass, for all nations believe the jews code and worship the jews god, and what greater subjection can be

I heard this with some wonder, & must confess my own conviction. After dinner I ask'd Isaiah to favour the world with his lost works, he said none of equal value was lost. Ezekiel said the same of his.

I also asked Isaiah what made him go naked and barefoot three years?[2] he answerd, the same that made our friend Diogenes the Grecian.[3]

I then asked Ezekiel. why he eat dung, & lay so long on his right & left side?[4] he answerd. the desire of raising other men into a perception of the infinite   this the North American tribes practise. & is he honest who resists his genius or conscience. only for the sake of present ease or gratification?

[Plate 14]

The ancient tradition that the world will be consumed in fire at the end of six thousand years[5] is true. as I have heard from Hell.

For the cherub with his flaming sword is hereby commanded to leave his guard at the tree of life,[6] and when he does, the whole creation will be consumed, and appear infinite. and holy whereas it now appears finite & corrupt.

This will come to pass by an improvement of sensual enjoyment.

But first the notion that man has a body distinct from his soul, is to be expunged; this I shall do, by printing in the infernal method, by corrosives, which in Hell are salutary and medicinal, melting apparent surfaces away, and displaying the infinite which was hid.[7]

If the doors of perception were cleansed every thing would appear to man as it is: infinite.

For man has closed himself up, till he sees all things thro' narrow chinks of his cavern.[8]

[Plate 15]
A Memorable Fancy

I was in a Printing house in Hell[9] & saw the method in which knowledge is transmitted from generation to generation.

In the first chamber was a Dragon-Man, clearing away the rubbish from a caves mouth; within, a number of Dragons were hollowing the cave,

In the second chamber was a Viper folding round the rock & the cave, and others adorning it with gold silver and precious stones.

In the third chamber was an Eagle with wings and feathers of air, he caused the inside of the cave to be infinite, around were numbers of Eagle like men, who built palaces in the immense cliffs.

In the fourth chamber were Lions of flaming fire raging around & melting the metals into living fluids.

---

[1] Isaiah 19, Ezekiel 29–32.

[2] Isaiah 20.2–3.

[3] founder (d. 320 BC) of the Cynic school of philosophers, who advocated and practised a lifestyle of extreme simplicity.

[4] Ezekiel 4.4–6, 12, 15.

[5] In Genesis 8.21, just after the Flood, God promises not to destroy the world again. The New Testament, however, contains several prophecies that it will be destroyed again, this time by fire (Luke 12.49, 2 Peter 3.5–7). The traditional figure of six thousand years seems to have been obtained by combining the six days it took to make the world (Genesis 1) and the idea "that one day is with the Lord as a thousand years" (2 Peter 3.8).

[6] Genesis 3.24; Cf. Milton, *Paradise Lost* 12.632–36.

[7] In conventional etching, only the lines of the design are burned away by the acid, the rest of the plate being protected by an acid-proof substance such as wax. In Blake's relief etching process, however, almost the whole surface of the plate is burned away, leaving the lines in relief.

[8] Cf. the allegory of the cave in Plato, *Republic* 7.514a–517a, and the image of the camera obscura in John Locke (1632–1704), *An Essay Concerning Human Understanding* (1690) 2.11.162–63.

[9] Cf. the account of printing in heaven in Swedenborg, *Heaven and Hell* nn.258–64.

In the fifth chamber were Unnam'd forms, which cast the metals into the expanse.

There they were reciev'd by Men who occupied the sixth chamber, and took the forms of books & were arranged in libraries.

[Plate 16]

The Giants who formed this world into its sensual existence and now seem to live in it in chains; are in truth. the causes of its life & the sources of all activity, but the chains are, the cunning of weak and tame minds. which have power to resist energy. according to the proverb, the weak in courage is strong in cunning.

Thus one portion of being, is the Prolific. the other, the Devouring: to the devourer it seems as if the producer was in his chains, but it is not so, he only takes portions of existence and fancies that the whole.

But the Prolific would cease to be Prolific unless the Devourer as a sea recieved the excess of his delights.[1]

Some will say, Is not God alone the Prolific? I answer, God only Acts & Is, in existing beings or Men.

These two classes of men are always upon earth, & they should be enemies; whoever tries [Plate 17] to reconcile them seeks to destroy existence.

Religion is an endeavour to reconcile the two.

Note. Jesus Christ did not wish to unite but to seperate them, as in the Parable of sheep and goats![2] & he says I came not to send Peace but a Sword.[3]

Messiah or Satan or Tempter was formerly thought to be one of the Antediluvians who are our Energies.

A Memorable Fancy

An Angel came to me and said. O pitiable foolish young man! O horrible! O dreadful state! consider the hot burning dungeon thou art preparing for thyself to all eternity, to which thou art going in such career.

I said. perhaps you will be willing to shew me my eternal lot & we will contemplate together upon it and see whether your lot or mine is most desirable

So he took me thro' a stable & thro' a church & down into the church vault at the end of which was a mill: thro' the mill we went, and came to a cave. down the winding cavern we groped our tedious way till a void boundless as a nether sky appeard beneath us & we held by the roots of trees and hung over this immensity; but I said, if you please we will commit ourselves to this void, and see whether providence is here also, if you will not I will? but he answerd. do not presume O youngman but as we here remain behold thy lot which will soon appear when the darkness passes away

So I remaind with him sitting in the twisted [Plate 18] root of an oak. he was suspended in a fungus which hung with the head downward into the deep:

By degrees we beheld the infinite Abyss, fiery as the smoke of a burning city; beneath us at an immense distance was the sun, black but shining[;] round it were fiery tracks on which revolv'd vast spiders, crawling after their prey; which flew or rather swum in the infinite deep, in the most terrific shapes of animals sprung from corruption. & the air was full of them, & seemd composed of them; these are Devils. and are called Powers of the air, I now asked my companion which was my eternal lot? he said, between the black & white spiders

But now, from between the black & white spiders a cloud and fire burst and rolled thro the deep blackning all beneath, so that the nether deep grew black as a sea & rolled with a terrible noise: beneath us was nothing now to be seen but a black tempest, till looking east between the clouds & the waves, we saw a cataract of blood mixed with fire and not many stones throw from us appeard and sunk again the scaly fold of a monstrous serpent. at last to the east, distant about three degrees[4] appeard a fiery crest above the waves slowly it reared like a ridge of golden rocks till we discoverd two globes of crimson fire. from which the sea fled away in clouds of smoke, and now we saw, it was the head of Leviathan.[5]

---

[1] Cf. the account of sexual relations in Swedenborg, *Conjugial Love* nn. 115, 172. The word "Devourer" is not from Swedenborg; it recalls 1 Peter 5.8 and Revelation 20.9.

[2] Matthew 25.32–33.

[3] Matthew 10.34; cf. Luke 12.51.

[4] Paris is three degrees east of London.

[5] Cf. Job 4.1, Psalms 104.26, Isaiah 27.1, Revelation 11.7, 12.9, 13.2, 20.1-3. Blake may also be thinking of Thomas Hobbes (1588–1679), *Leviathan; or, The Matter, Form, and Power of a Commonwealth, Ecclesiastical and Civil* (1651).

his forehead was divided into streaks of green & purple like those on a tygers forehead: soon we saw his mouth & red gills hang just above the raging foam tinging the black deep with beams of blood, advancing toward [Plate 19] us with all the fury of a spiritual existence.

My friend the Angel climb'd up from his station into the mill; I remain'd alone, & then this appearance was no more, but I found myself sitting on a pleasant bank beside a river by moon light hearing a harper who sung to the harp.[1] & his theme was, The man who never alters his opinion is like standing water, & breeds reptiles of the mind.

But I arose, and sought for the mill, & there I found my Angel, who surprised asked me, how I escaped?

I answer. All that we saw was owing to your metaphysics: for when you ran away, I found myself on a bank by moonlight hearing a harper, But now we have seen my eternal lot, shall I shew you yours? he laughd at my proposal: but I by force suddenly caught him in my arms, & flew westerly thro' the night, till we were elevated above the earths shadow: then I flung myself with him directly into the body of the sun, here I clothed myself in white,[2] & taking in my hand Swedenborgs volumes sunk from the glorious clime, and passed all the planets till we came to saturn, here I staid to rest & then leap'd into the void, between saturn & the fixed stars.

Here said I! is your lot, in this space, if space it may be calld,[3] Soon we saw the stable and the church, & I took him to the altar[4] and open'd the Bible, and lo! it was a deep pit, into which I descended driving the Angel before me, soon we saw seven houses of brick,[5] one we enterd; in it were a [Plate 20] number of monkeys, baboons, & all of that species chaind by the middle, grinning and snatching at one another, but witheld by the shortness of their chains: however I saw that they sometimes grew numerous, and then the weak were caught by the strong and with a grinning aspect, first coupled with & then devourd, by plucking off first one limb and then another till the body was left a helpless trunk. this after grinning & kissing it with seeming fondness they devourd too; and here & there I saw one savourily picking the flesh off of his own tail; as the stench terribly annoyd us both we went into the mill, & I in my hand brought the skeleton of a body, which in the mill was Aristotles Analytics.[6]

So the Angel said: thy phantasy has imposed upon me & thou oughtest to be ashamed.

I answered: we impose on one another, & it is but lost time to converse with you whose works are only Analytics.

Opposition is true Friendship.

[Plate 21]

I have always found that Angels have the vanity to speak of themselves as the only wise; this they do with a confident insolence sprouting from systematic reasoning:

Thus Swedenborg boasts that what he writes is new; tho' it is only the Contents or Index of already publish'd books

A man carried a monkey about for a shew, & because he was a little wiser than the monkey, grew vain, and conciev'd himself as much wiser than seven men. It is so with Swedenborg; he shews the folly of churches & exposes hypocrites, till he imagines that all are religious. & himself the single [Plate 22] one on earth that ever broke a net.

Now hear a plain fact: Swedenborg has not written one new truth: Now hear another: he has written all the old falshoods.

And now hear the reason. He conversed with Angels who are all religious, & conversed not with Devils who all hate religion, for he was incapable thro' his conceited notions.

Thus Swedenborgs writings are a recapitulation of all superficial opinions, and an analysis of the more sublime, but no further.

Have now another plain fact: Any man of mechanical talents may from the writings of Paracelsus or Jacob

---

[1] Cf. Revelation 14.2–3.

[2] Cf. Revelation 7.9.

[3] Cf. Milton, *Paradise Lost* 2.667.

[4] Cf. Ezekiel 8.5–13.

[5] Cf. Revelation 1.4.

[6] Aristotle's two treatises on logic.

Behmen,[1] produce ten thousand volumes of equal value with Swedenborg's. and from those of Dante or Shakespear, an infinite number.

But when he has done this, let him not say that he knows better than his master, for he only holds a candle in sunshine.

A Memorable Fancy

Once I saw a Devil in a flame of fire. who arose before an Angel that sat on a cloud. and the Devil utterd these words.

The worship of God is. Honouring his gifts in other men each according to his genius. and loving the [Plate 23] greatest men best, those who envy or calumniate great men hate God, for there is no other God.

The Angel hearing this became almost blue but mastering himself he grew yellow, & at last white pink & smiling, and then replied,

Thou Idolater, is not God One? & is not he visible in Jesus Christ? and has not Jesus Christ given his sanction to the law of ten commandments and are not all other men fools, sinners, & nothings?

The Devil answer'd; bray a fool in a morter with wheat. yet shall not his folly be beaten out of him:[2] if Jesus Christ is the greatest man, you ought to love him in the greatest degree; now hear how he has given his sanction to the law of ten commandments: did he not mock at the sabbath,[3] and so mock the sabbaths God? murder those who were murderd because of him?[4] turn away the law from the woman taken in adultery?[5] steal the labor of others to support him?[6] bear false witness when he omitted making a defence before Pilate?[7] covet when he pray'd for his disciples, and when he bid them shake off the dust of their feet against such as refused to lodge them?[8] I tell you, no virtue can exist without breaking these ten commandments: Jesus was all virtue, and acted from im[Plate 24]pulse: not from rules.

When he had so spoken: I beheld the Angel who stretched out his arms embracing the flame of fire & he was consumed and arose as Elijah.[9]

Note. This Angel, who is now become a Devil, is my particular friend: we often read the Bible together in its infernal or diabolical sense which the world shall have if they behave well.

I have also: The Bible of Hell:[10] which the world shall have whether they will or no.

One Law for the Lion & Ox is Oppression[11]

[Plate 25]
A Song of Liberty

1. The Eternal Female groand! it was heard over all the Earth:
2. Albions[12] coast is sick silent; the American meadows faint!
3 Shadows of Prophecy shiver along by the lakes and the rivers and mutter across the ocean! France rend down thy dungeon;[13]
4. Golden Spain burst the barriers of old Rome;

---

[1] Paracelsus (Philippus Aureolus, Theophrastus Bombastus von Hohenheim, 1493–1541), Swiss alchemist, and Jakob Boehme (1575–1624), German mystic.

[2] Proverbs 27.22. This Devil can quote scripture to his purpose.

[3] Exodus 20.8-11; Matthew 12.8–12, Mark 2.27, 3.2–4, Luke 14.3–5, John 5.16.

[4] Exodus 20.13; see the martyrdom of Stephen (Acts 7.58–60).

[5] Exodus 20.14; John 8.3–11.

[6] Exodus 20.15; Matthew 26.6–13.

[7] Exodus 20.16; Matthew 27.11–14, Mark 15.2–5.

[8] Exodus 20.17; Matthew 10.14, Luke 9.5. The Devil has skipped the commandments against having other gods (Exodus 20.3), making graven images (4), and taking the lord's name in vain (7), and in favour of honouring fathers and mothers (12).

[9] Cf. 2 Kings 2.11.

[10] possibly a reference to an ongoing poetic project. In addition to the Proverbs of Hell (plates 7–10), this bible is sometimes said to include such later works as *The [First] Book of Urizen*, *The Book of Ahania*, and *The Book of Los* (1794–95).

[11] Cf. *Visions of the Daughters of Albion* 4.22.*

[12] a poetic name for England; it may derive from *albus* (L. "white"), in reference to the chalk cliffs.

[13] a reference to the fall of the Bastille, 14 July 1789.

5. Cast thy keys O Rome[1] into the deep down falling, even to eternity down falling,
6. And weep!
7. In her trembling hands she took the new born terror[2] howling;
8. On those infinite mountains of light now barr'd out by the atlantic sea, the new born fire stood before the starry king![3]
9. Flag'd with grey brow'd snows and thunderous visages the jealous wings wav'd over the deep.
10. The speary hand burned aloft, unbuckled was the shield, forth went the hand of jealousy among the flaming hair, and [Plate 26] hurl'd the new born wonder thro' the starry night.
11. The fire, the fire, is falling!
12. Look up! look up! O citizen of London. enlarge thy countenance; O Jew, leave counting gold! return to thy oil and wine; O African! black African! (go. winged thought widen his forehead.)
13. The fiery limbs, the flaming hair, shot like the sinking sun into the western sea.
14. Wak'd from his eternal sleep, the hoary element roaring fled away:[4]
15. Down rushd beating his wings in vain the jealous king: his grey brow'd councellors, thunderous warriors, curl'd veterans, among helms, and shields, and chariots horses, elephants: banners, castles, slings and rocks,
16. Falling, rushing, ruining! buried in the ruins, on Urthona's dens.[5]
17. All night beneath the ruins, then their sullen flames faded emerge round the gloomy king,
18. With thunder and fire: leading his starry hosts thro' the waste wilderness [Plate 27] he promulgates his ten commands,[6] glancing his beamy eyelids over the deep in dark dismay,
19. Where the son of fire in his eastern cloud, while the morning plumes her golden breast,
20. Spurning the clouds written with curses, stamps the stony law to dust, loosing the eternal horses from the dens of night, crying

Empire is no more! and now the lion & wolf shall cease.[7]

Chorus

Let the Priests of the Raven of dawn, no longer in deadly black, with hoarse note curse the sons of joy. Nor his accepted brethren whom, tyrant, he calls free; lay the bound or build the roof. Nor pale religious letchery call that virginity, that wishes but acts not!

For every thing that lives is Holy[8]

---

[1] The keys of St. Peter (Matthew 16.19) are a symbol of the power of the Roman Catholic church.

[2] In later works, such as *America** and *Milton* (1804), this figure becomes the character named Orc, a spirit of revolution.

[3] This (also the "jealous king" of line 15) is an early version of the character named Urizen in *Visions of the Daughters of Albion** and *Milton*.

[4] Cf. Revelation 21.1.

[5] In later works like *Milton*,* Urthona (whose name may mean "Earth-Owner") is the unfallen form of Los, the figure of the imagination. This is the first appearance of the name in Blake's work.

[6] Cf. Exodus 20.

[7] Cf. Isaiah 65.25. The words are repeated in *America* 6.15.*

[8] Cf. Revelation 15.4. The words are repeated in *Visions of the Daughters of Albion* 8.10,* *America* 8.13,* and *The Four Zoas* (1797) 2.34.80. For a modern response, see Allen Ginsberg, "Footnote to Howl" (1955).

WILLIAM BLAKE

Visions of the Daughters of Albion (1793)[1]

The Eye sees more than the Heart knows.

[Plate iii]

The Argument

I loved Theotormon[2]
And I was not ashamed
I trembled in my virgin fears
And I hid in Leutha's vale![3]

5   I plucked Leutha's flower,
And I rose up from the vale;
But the terrible thunders tore
My virgin mantle in twain.

[Plate 1]

Visions

ENSLAV'D, the Daughters of Albion weep: a trembling lamentation
Upon their mountains; in their valleys. sighs toward America.

For the soft soul of America, Oothoon[4] wanderd in woe,
Along the vales of Leutha seeking flowers to comfort her;
5   And thus she spoke to the bright Marygold of Leutha's vale

    Art thou a flower! art thou a nymph! I see thee now a flower;
    Now a nymph! I dare not pluck thee from thy dewy bed!

---

[1] In this poem, Blake combines the feminism of Wollstonecraft, *A Vindication of the Rights of Woman** and the abolitionism of John Gabriel Stedman, *A Narrative, of a Five Years' Expedition, against the Revolted Negroes of Surinam* (1796). Blake had engraved illustrations for at least one of Wollstonecraft's books; and as he was composing *Visions*, he was engraving the illustrations for Stedman's *Narrative*. Some of his designs for *Visions* resemble the illustrations to Stedman. The Daughters of Albion recall the Daughters of Jerusalem in the Song of Solomon (e.g., 1.5, 2.7), to which *Visions* makes several allusions. Albion is a character in *The Four Zoas* and *Milton*; Albion and his daughters are major characters in *Jerusalem*.

[2] apparently from *theos* (Gr., "god") and *torment*: the god-tormented man. The names in this poem also recall names in "Oithona" (1762), a prose poem by James Macpherson, which Blake and some of his contemporaries believed to be a translation of an epic by an ancient Scottish bard named Ossian (it is now known to be a forgery). Oothoon's name recalls that of Oithona, Macpherson's heroine ("the virgin of the wave"); Theotormon's recalls Tromáthon, the desert island to which Oithona is abducted. The combination of disparate mythological sources is characteristic of Blake's method in this poem.

[3] There is a stream called Lutha in "Berrathon," another prose poem by Macpherson, and a "maid of Lutha" in "Oina-Morul," yet another. Blake may also be thinking of Leucothea, the Greek goddess of the dawn. Leutha reappears in *Europe* and in *Milton* 11.28–12.7.

[4] Oothoon reappears (or is mentioned) in *Europe*, *The Song of Los*, *The Four Zoas*, *Milton*, and *Jerusalem*.

The Golden nymph replied; pluck thou my flower Oothoon the mild
Another flower shall spring, because the soul of sweet delight
10   Can never pass away.[1] she ceas'd & closd her golden shrine.

Then Oothoon pluck'd the flower saying, I pluck thee from thy bed
Sweet flower. and put thee here to glow between my breasts
And thus I turn my face to where my whole soul seeks.

Over the waves she went in wing'd exulting swift delight;
15   And over Theotormons reign, took her impetuous course.

Bromion[2] rent her with his thunders. on his stormy bed
Lay the faint maid, and soon her woes appalld his thunders hoarse

Bromion spoke. behold this harlot here on Bromions bed,
And let the jealous dolphins sport around the lovely maid;
20   Thy soft American plains are mine, and mine thy north & south:
Stampt with my signet are the swarthy children of the sun:
They are obedient, they resist not, they obey the scourge:
Their daughters worship terrors and obey the violent:[3]

[Plate 2]
Now thou maist marry Bromions harlot, and protect the child
Of Bromions rage, that Oothoon shall put forth in nine moons time

Then storms rent Theotormons limbs; he rolld his waves around.
And folded his black jealous waters round the adulterate pair
5   Bound back to back in Bromions caves terror & meekness dwell

At entrance Theotormon sits wearing the threshold hard
With secret tears; beneath him sound like waves on a desart shore
The voice of slaves beneath the sun, and children bought with money.
That shiver in religious caves beneath the burning fires
10   Of lust, that belch incessant from the summits of the earth

Oothoon weeps not: she cannot weep! her tears are locked up;
But she can howl incessant writhing her soft snowy limbs.
And calling Theotormons Eagles to prey upon her flesh.

I call with holy voice! kings of the sounding air,
15   Rend away this defiled bosom that I may reflect.
The image of Theotormon on my pure transparent breast.

---

[1] repeated from *The Marriage of Heaven and Hell*, pl. 9.

[2] The name is apparently derived from *Bromios* ("the Thunderer"), an epithet of Dionysus, or Bacchus, the classical god of wine, perhaps combined with Boreas, the north wind (who commits a rape in Ovid, *Metamorphoses* 6) and with Macpherson's "Berrathon."

[3] Cf. *The Four Zoas* 6.68.26.

The Eagles at her call descend & rend their bleeding prey;[1]
Theotormon severely smiles. her soul reflects the smile;
As the clear spring mudded with feet of beasts grows pure & smiles.

20   The Daughters of Albion hear her woes. & eccho back her sighs.

Why does my Theotormon sit weeping upon the threshold;
And Oothoon hovers by his side, perswading him in vain:
I cry arise O Theotormon for the village dog
Barks at the breaking day. the nightingale has done lamenting.
25   The lark does rustle in the ripe corn, and the Eagle returns
From nightly prey, and lifts his golden beak to the pure east;[2]
Shaking the dust from his immortal pinions to awake
The sun that sleeps too long. Arise my Theotormon I am pure.
Because the night is gone that clos'd me in its deadly black.
30   They told me that the night & day were all that I could see;
They told me that I had five senses to inclose me up.
And they inclos'd my infinite brain into a narrow circle.
And sunk my heart into the Abyss, a red round globe hot burning[3]
Till all from life I was obliterated and erased.
35   Instead of morn arises a bright shadow, like an eye
In the eastern cloud: instead of night a sickly charnel house;
That Theotormon hears me not! to him the night and morn
Are both alike: a night of sighs, a morning of fresh tears;
[Plate 3]
And none but Bromion can hear my lamentations.

With what sense is it that the chicken shuns the ravenous hawk?
With what sense does the tame pigeon measure out the expanse?
With what sense does the bee form cells? have not the mouse & frog
5   Eyes and ears and sense of touch? yet are their habitations.
And their pursuits, as different as their forms and as their joys:
Ask the wild ass why he refuses burdens: and the meek camel
Why he loves man: is it because of eye ear mouth or skin
Or breathing nostrils? No. for these the wolf and tyger have.
10   Ask the blind worm the secrets of the grave, and why her spires
Love to curl round the bones of death; and ask the rav'nous snake
Where she gets poison: & the wing'd eagle why he loves the sun
And then tell me the thoughts of man, that have been hid of old.

---

[1] Oothoon's torture recalls that of Prometheus.

[2] Cf. Song of Solomon 2.10–12.

[3] repeated in *The Book of Urizen*, pl. 11.1–4.

Silent I hover all the night, and all day could be silent.
15 If Theotormon once would turn his loved eyes upon me;
How can I be defild when I reflect thy image pure?
Sweetest the fruit that the worm feeds on. & the soul prey'd on by woe
The new wash'd lamb ting'd with the village smoke & the bright swan
By the red earth of our immortal river:[1] I bathe my wings.
20 And I am white and pure to hover round Theotormons breast.

Then Theotormon broke his silence. and he answered.

Tell me what is the night or day to one o'erflowd with woe?
Tell me what is a thought? & of what substance is it made?
Tell me what is a joy? & in what gardens do joys grow?
25 And in what rivers swim the sorrows? and upon what mountains
[Plate 4]
Wave shadows of discontent? and in what houses dwell the wretched
Drunken with woe forgotten. and shut up from cold despair.

Tell me where dwell the thoughts forgotten till thou call them forth
Tell me where dwell the joys of old! & where the ancient loves?
5 And when will they renew again & the night of oblivion past?
That I might traverse times & spaces far remote and bring
Comforts into a present sorrow and a night of pain
Where goest thou O thought? to what remote land is thy flight?
If thou returnest to the present moment of affliction
10 Wilt thou bring comforts on thy wings. and dews and honey and balm;
Or poison from the desart wilds, from the eyes of the envier.

Then Bromion said: and shook the cavern with his lamentation

Thou knowest that the ancient trees seen by thine eyes have fruit;
But knowest thou that trees and fruits flourish upon the earth
15 To gratify senses unknown? trees beasts and birds unknown:
Unknown, not unpercievd, spread in the infinite microscope,
In places yet unvisited by the voyager. and in worlds
Over another kind of seas, and in atmospheres unknown:
Ah! are there other wars, beside the wars of sword and fire!
20 And are there other sorrows, beside the sorrows of poverty?
And are there other joys, beside the joys of riches and ease?
And is there not one law for both the lion and the ox?[2]
And is there not eternal fire, and eternal chains?
To bind the phantoms of existence from eternal life?

---

[1] Since "red earth" is the literal Hebrew meaning of Adam, the river may be the one that "went out of Eden" (Genesis 2.10).

[2] Cf. the last line of *The Marriage of Heaven and Hell*, pl. 24.*

25   Then Oothoon waited silent all the day. and all the night,
[Plate 5]
But when the morn arose, her lamentation renewd,
The Daughters of Albion hear her woes, & eccho back her sighs.

O Urizen![1] Creator of men! mistaken Demon of heaven:
Thy joys are tears! thy labour vain, to form men to thine image.
5   How can one joy absorb another? are not different joys
Holy, eternal, infinite! and each joy is a Love.

Does not the great mouth laugh at a gift? & the narrow eyelids mock
At the labour that is above payment, and wilt thou take the ape
For thy councellor? or the dog, for a schoolmaster to thy children?[2]
10   Does he who contemns poverty, and he who turns with abhorrence
From usury: feel the same passion or are they moved alike?
How can the giver of gifts experience the delights of the merchant?
How the industrious citizen the pains of the husbandman.
How different far the fat fed hireling with hollow drum;
15   Who buys whole corn fields into wastes, and sings upon the heath:
How different their eye and ear! how different the world to them!
With what sense does the parson claim the labour of the farmer?
What are his nets & gins & traps. & how does he surround him
With cold floods of abstraction, and with forests of solitude,
20   To build him castles and high spires. where kings & priests may dwell.
Till she who burns with youth. and knows no fixed lot; is bound
In spells of law to one she loaths: and must she drag the chain
Of life, in weary lust! must chilling murderous thoughts. obscure
The clear heaven of her eternal spring? to bear the wintry rage
25   Of a harsh terror driv'n to madness, bound to hold a rod
Over her shrinking shoulders all the day; & all the night
To turn the wheel of false desire: and longings that wake her womb
To the abhorred birth of cherubs in the human form
That live a pestilence & die a meteor & are no more.
30   Till the child dwell with one he hates. and do the deed he loaths
And the impure scourge force his seed into its unripe birth
E'er yet his eyelids can behold the arrows of the day.

Does the whale worship at thy footsteps as the hungry dog?
Or does he scent the mountain prey, because his nostrils wide
35   Draw in the ocean? does his eye discern the flying cloud
As the ravens eye? or does he measure the expanse like the vulture?

---

[1] Blake's first use of this name, possibly a punning combination of "your reason" and "horizon." The character, developed from the unnamed "starry king" in "A Song of Liberty,"* is also the "father of jealousy" in 7.12. He plays a very prominent role in such later works as *The Book of Urizen* and *Milton*.

[2] Cf. *The Four Zoas* 2.35.3–4.

Does the still spider view the cliffs where eagles hide their young?
Or does the fly rejoice. because the harvest is brought in?
Does not the eagle scorn the earth & despise the treasures beneath?
40   But the mole knoweth what is there, & the worm shall tell it thee.[1]
Does not the worm erect a pillar in the mouldering church yard?
[Plate 6]
And a palace of eternity in the jaws of the hungry grave[2]
Over his porch these words are written. Take thy bliss O Man!
And sweet shall be thy taste & sweet thy infant joys renew!

Infancy, fearless, lustful, happy! nestling for delight
5   In laps of pleasure; Innocence! honest, open, seeking
The vigorous joys of morning light; open to virgin bliss.
Who taught thee modesty, subtil modesty! child of night & sleep
When thou awakest. wilt thou dissemble all thy secret joys
Or wert thou not awake when all this mystery was disclos'd!
10   Then com'st thou forth a modest virgin knowing to dissemble
With nets found under thy night pillow, to catch virgin joy,
And brand it with the name of whore; & sell it in the night,
In silence. ev'n without a whisper, and in seeming sleep:
Religious dreams and holy vespers, light thy smoky fires:
15   Once were thy fires lighted by the eyes of honest morn
And does my Theotormon seek this hypocrite modesty!
This knowing, artful, secret, fearful, cautious, trembling hypocrite.
Then is Oothoon a whore indeed! and all the virgin joys
Of life are harlots: and Theotormon is a sick mans dream
20   And Oothoon is the crafty slave of selfish holiness.

But Oothoon is not so, a virgin fill'd with virgin fancies
Open to joy and to delight where ever beauty appears
If in the morning sun I find it: there my eyes are fix'd
[Plate 7]
In happy copulation; if in evening mild. wearied with work;
Sit on a bank and draw the pleasures of this free born joy.

The moment of desire! the moment of desire! The virgin
That pines for man; shall awaken her womb to enormous joys
5   In the secret shadows of her chamber; the youth shut up from
The lustful joy. shall forget to generate. & create an amorous image
In the shadows of his curtains and in the folds of his silent pillow.
Are not these the places of religion? the rewards of continence?
The self enjoyings of self denial? Why dost thou seek religion?

---

[1] Cf. *The Book of Thel* (1789), pl. i.1–2, 4.1–6.

[2] Cf. *The Four Zoas* 8.108.11–12.

10   Is it because acts are not lovely, that thou seekest solitude,
      Where the horrible darkness is impressed with reflections of desire.

      Father of Jealousy. be thou accursed from the earth!
      Why hast thou taught my Theotormon this accursed thing?
      Till beauty fades from off my shoulders darken'd and cast out,
15   A solitary shadow wailing on the margin of non-entity.

      I cry, Love! Love! Love! happy happy Love! free as the mountain wind![1]
      Can that be Love, that drinks another as a sponge drinks water?
      That clouds with jealousy his nights, with weepings all the day:
      To spin a web of age around him. grey and hoary! dark!
20   Till his eyes sicken at the fruit that hangs before his sight.[2]
      Such is self-love that envies all! a creeping skeleton
      With lamplike eyes watching around the frozen marriage bed.

      But silken nets and traps of adamant will Oothoon spread,
      And catch for thee girls of mild silver, or of furious gold;
25   I'll lie beside thee on a bank & view their wanton play
      In lovely copulation bliss on bliss with Theotormon:
      Red as the rosy morning, lustful as the first born beam,
      Oothoon shall view his dear delight, nor e'er with jealous cloud
      Come in the heaven of generous love; nor selfish blightings bring.

30   Does the sun walk in glorious raiment. on the secret floor
      [Plate 8]
      Where the cold miser spreads his gold? or does the bright cloud drop
      On his stone threshold? does his eye behold the beam that brings
      Expansion to the eye of pity? or will he bind himself
      Beside the ox to thy hard furrow? does not that mild beam blot
5   The bat, the owl, the glowing tyger, and the king of night.
      The sea fowl takes the wintry blast. for a cov'ring to her limbs:
      And the wild snake, the pestilence to adorn him with gems & gold.
      And trees. & birds. & beasts. & men. behold their eternal joy.
      Arise you little glancing wings, and sing your infant joy![3]
10   Arise and drink your bliss, for every thing that lives is holy![4]

      Thus every morning wails Oothoon. but Theotormon sits
      Upon the margind ocean conversing with shadows dire.

      The Daughters of Albion hear her woes, & eccho back her sighs.

---

[1] Cf. Song of Solomon 2.8.

[2] possibly a reference to Tantalus, who was tormented with the sight of fruit he couldn't eat and water he couldn't drink.

[3] Cf. "Infant Joy," in *Songs of Innocence.**

[4] repeated from the last line of "A Song of Liberty";* cf. *The Four Zoas* 2.34.78–80.

William Blake

America a Prophecy (1793)

[Plate 1]

Preludium

The shadowy daughter of Urthona[1] stood before red Orc.[2]
When fourteen suns[3] had faintly journeyed o'er his dark abode;
His food she brought in iron baskets, his drink in cups of iron;
Crown'd with a helmet & dark hair the nameless female stood;
5 A quiver with its burning stores, a bow like that of night,
When pestilence is shot from heaven; no other arms she need:
Invulnerable tho' naked, save where clouds roll round her loins,
Their awful folds in the dark air; silent she stood as night;
For never from her iron tongue could voice or sound arise;
10 But dumb till that dread day when Orc assay'd his fierce embrace.

Dark virgin; said the hairy youth, thy father stern abhorr'd;
Rivets my tenfold chains while still on high my spirit soars;
Sometimes an eagle screaming in the sky, sometimes a lion,
Stalking upon the mountains, & sometimes a whale I lash
15 The raging fathomless abyss, anon a serpent[4] folding
Around the pillars of Urthona, and round thy dark limbs,
On the Canadian wilds[5] I fold, feeble my spirit folds.
For chaind beneath I rend these caverns; when thou bringest food
I howl my joy! and my red eyes seek to behold thy face
20 In vain! these clouds roll to & fro, & hide thee from my sight.

[Plate 2]
Silent as despairing love, and strong as jealousy,
The hairy shoulders rend the links, free are the wrists of fire;
Round the terrific loins he siez'd the panting struggling womb;

---

[1] In this context, her father's name ("Earth-Owner"), which also appears in "A Song of Liberty" (16),* probably refers to George III (1738–1820), king of England.

[2] the spirit of revolution. He is developed from the "new born terror" of "A Song of Liberty" (7);* this is the first time Blake refers to him by his name, which may be an anagram of *cor* (L., "heart"), or an allusion to Orcus, god of the underworld. Since he is red and hairy (1.11, 2.2), he recalls Esau (Genesis 25.25).

[3] possibly the fourteen years between the publication of Rousseau, *Du Contrat social* (1762) and the Declaration of Independence (1776), or between the accession of George III (1760) and the Coercive Acts against Boston (1774).

[4] Blake often associates the serpent with fire, so these four animal forms of Orc's spirit correspond to the four elements.

[5] Blake may be interested in Canada (see also 2.12) because the legislature of Upper Canada had recently passed a bill that in effect abolished slavery.

It joy'd: she put aside her clouds & smiled her first-born smile;
As when a black cloud shews its light'nings to the silent deep.

Soon as she saw the terrible boy then burst the virgin cry.

I know thee, I have found thee, & I will not let thee go;[1]
Thou art the image of God who dwells in darkness of Africa;
And thou art fall'n to give me life in regions of dark death.
On my American plains I feel the struggling afflictions
Endur'd by roots that writhe their arms into the nether deep:
I see a serpent in Canada, who courts me to his love;
In Mexico an Eagle, and a Lion in Peru;
I see a Whale in the South-sea, drinking my soul away.
O what limb rending pains I feel. thy fire & my frost
Mingle in howling pains, in furrows by thy lightnings rent;
This is eternal death; and this the torment long foretold.[2]

[Plate 3]

A Prophecy

The Guardian Prince of Albion[3] burns in his nightly tent,[4]
Sullen fires across the Atlantic glow to America's shore:
Piercing the souls of warlike men, who rise in silent night,
Washington, Franklin, Paine & Warren, Gates, Hancock & Green;[5]
Meet on the coast glowing with blood from Albions fiery Prince.[6]

Washington spoke; Friends of America look over the Atlantic sea;
A bended bow is lifted in heaven, & a heavy iron chain

---

[1] Cf. Song of Solomon 3.4.

[2] the curse on Eve (Genesis 3.16). Blake etched four further lines for his "Preludium" but deleted them while printing all but two copies of the poem:
"The stern Bard ceas'd, asham'd of his own song; enrag'd he swung
His harp aloft sounding, then dash'd its shining frame against
A ruin'd pillar in glittring fragments; silent he turn'd away,
And wander'd down the vales of Kent in sick & drear lamentings."

[3] George III, here imagined as commander-in-chief of the British troops.

[4] Cf. Isaiah 40.22.

[5] George Washington (1732–99), commander-in-chief of the Revolutionary forces and later first president of the United States (he had just been re-elected when Blake wrote the poem); Benjamin Franklin,* scientist, diplomat, and pamphleteer; Thomas Paine,* author of *Common Sense* (1776), *The Rights of Man* (1791), and other pro-Revolutionary works; Joseph Warren (1741–75), the "True Patriot," major general of the Massachusetts troops, killed at the battle of Bunker Hill (June 1775); Horatio Gates (1727–1806), adjutant general; John Hancock (1737–93), member of the provincial and Continental congresses and first signatory of the Declaration of Independence; Nathanael Greene (1742–86), commander of Boston in 1776.

[6] possibly a reference to the Boston Massacre (5 March 1770).

Descends link by link from Albions cliffs across the sea to bind
Brothers & sons of America, till our faces pale and yellow;
10 Heads deprest, voices weak, eyes downcast, hands work-bruis'd,
Feet bleeding on the sultry sands, and the furrows of the whip
Descend to generations that in future times forget.——

The strong voice ceas'd; for a terrible blast swept over the heaving sea;
The eastern cloud rent; on his cliffs stood Albions wrathful Prince
15 A dragon form clashing his scales at midnight he arose,[1]
And flam'd red meteors round the land of Albion beneath[.][2]
His voice, his locks, his awful shoulders, and his glowing eyes,
[Plate 4]
Appear to the Americans upon the cloudy night.

Solemn heave the Atlantic waves between the gloomy nations,
Swelling, belching from its deeps red clouds & raging Fires!
Albion is sick. America faints! enrag'd the Zenith grew.
5 As human blood shooting its veins all round the orbed heaven
Red rose the clouds from the Atlantic in vast wheels of blood
And in the red clouds rose a Wonder o'er the Atlantic sea;
Intense! naked! a Human fire fierce glowing, as the wedge
Of iron heated in the furnace; his terrible limbs were fire
10 With myriads of cloudy terrors banners dark & towers
Surrounded; heat but not light[3] went thro' the murky atmosphere

The King of England looking westward trembles at the vision

[Plate 5]
Albions Angel[4] stood beside the Stone of night, and saw
The terror like a comet,[5] or more like the planet red
That once inclos'd the terrible wandering comets in its sphere.
Then Mars thou wast our center, & the planets three flew round
5 Thy crimson disk; so e'er the Sun was rent from thy red sphere;
The Spectre glowd his horrid length staining the temple long
With beams of blood; & thus a voice came forth, and shook the temple

[Plate 6]
The morning comes, the night decays, the watchmen leave their stations;

---

[1] Cf. the comparison of Pharaoh to a dragon in Ezekiel 29.3.

[2] Cf. Isaiah 34.4, 9–10, and Shakespeare, *Richard II* 2.4.7–15.

[3] Cf. Milton, *Paradise Lost* 1.62–63.

[4] It is not clear whether the Guardian Prince and Albion's Angel are the same character. Perhaps they represent the British state and the Anglican Church respectively. (King George was the head of both.)

[5] Cf. Shakespeare, *1 Henry VI* 1.1.2, and Milton, *Paradise Lost* 2.707–11.

The grave is burst, the spices shed, the linen wrapped up;[1]
The bones of death, the cov'ring clay, the sinews shrunk & dry'd.
Reviving shake, inspiring move, breathing! awakening![2]
Spring like redeemed captives when their bonds & bars are burst;
Let the slave grinding at the mill,[3] run out into the field:
Let him look up into the heavens & laugh in the bright air;
Let the inchained soul shut up in darkness and in sighing,
Whose face has never seen a smile in thirty weary years;
Rise and look out, his chains are loose, his dungeon doors are open.
And let his wife and children return from the opressors scourge;
They look behind at every step & believe it is a dream.
Singing. The Sun has left his blackness, & has found a fresher morning
And the fair Moon rejoices in the clear & cloudless night;
For Empire is no more, and now the Lion & Wolf shall cease.[4]

[Plate 7]
In thunders ends the voice. Then Albions Angel wrathful burnt
Beside the Stone of Night; and like the Eternal Lions howl
In famine & war, reply'd. Art thou not Orc, who serpent-form'd[5]
Stands at the gate of Enitharmon[6] to devour her children;[7]
Blasphemous Demon, Antichrist, hater of Dignities;
Lover of wild rebellion, and transgresser of Gods Law;
Why dost thou come to Angels eyes in this terrific form?

[Plate 8]
The terror answer'd: I am Orc, wreath'd round the accursed tree:
The times are ended; shadows pass the morning gins to break;
The fiery joy, that Urizen perverted to ten commands,[8]
What night he led the starry hosts thro' the wide wilderness:
That stony law I stamp to dust:[9] and scatter religion abroad

---

[1] The imagery of morning is recalled from *Visions of the Daughters of Albion* 2.23–26;* of resurrection, from *The Marriage of Heaven and Hell*, pl. 3.* Cf. Isaiah 35, John 20.5–7.

[2] Cf. Ezekiel 37.1–10.

[3] Cf. Judges 16.21, Matthew 24.41.

[4] repeated from "A Song of Liberty" 20.*

[5] The image of the serpent associates Orc not only with Satan, but also with the emblem of a rattlesnake (and the accompanying motto, "Don't tread on me") adopted by the Revolutionaries.

[6] Spiritual Beauty or the Eternal Female; her name may be derived from *anarithmon* (Gr., "numberless") or a combination of "[z]enith" and "[h]armon[y]."

[7] Cf. Revelation 12.4.

[8] Cf. "A Song of Liberty" 18.*

[9] Cf. "A Song of Liberty" 20.*

To the four winds as a torn book, & none shall gather the leaves;
But they shall rot on desart sands, & consume in bottomless deeps;
To make the desarts blossom, & the deeps shrink to their fountains,[1]
And to renew the fiery joy, and burst the stony roof.
10 That pale religious letchery, seeking Virginity,
May find it in a harlot, and in coarse-clad honesty
The undefil'd tho' ravish'd in her cradle night and morn:
For every thing that lives is holy, life delights in life;
Because the soul of sweet delight can never be defil'd.
15 Fires inwrap the earthly globe, yet man is not consumd;
Amidst the lustful fires he walks:[2] his feet become like brass,
His knees and thighs like silver, & his breast and head like gold.[3]

[Plate 9]
Sound! sound! my loud war-trumpets & alarm my Thirteen Angels![4]
Loud howls the eternal Wolf! the eternal Lion lashes his tail!
America is darkned; and my punishing Demons terrified
Crouch howling before their caverns deep like skins dry'd in the wind.
5 They cannot smite the wheat, nor quench the fatness of the earth.
They cannot smite with sorrows, nor subdue the plow and spade.
They cannot wall the city, nor moat round the castle of princes.
They cannot bring the stubbed oak to overgrow the hills.
For terrible men stand on the shores, & in their robes I see
10 Children take shelter from the lightnings, there stands Washington
And Paine and Warren with their foreheads reard toward the east
But clouds obscure my aged sight. A vision from afar!
Sound! sound! my loud war-trumpets & alarm my thirteen Angels:
Ah vision from afar! Ah rebel form that rent the ancient
15 Heavens; Eternal Viper self-renew'd, rolling in clouds
I see thee in thick clouds and darkness on America's shore.
Writhing in pangs of abhorred birth; red flames the crest rebellious
And eyes of death; the harlot womb oft opened in vain
Heaves in enormous circles, now the times are return'd upon thee,
20 Devourer of thy parent, now thy unutterable torment renews.
Sound! sound! my loud war trumpets & alarm my thirteen Angels!
Ah terrible birth! a young one bursting! where is the weeping mouth?
And where the mothers milk? instead those ever-hissing jaws
And parched lips drop with fresh gore; now roll thou in the clouds
25 Thy mother lays her length outstretch'd upon the shore beneath.

---

[1] Cf. Isaiah 35.1.

[2] Cf. Daniel 3.25.

[3] Cf. Daniel 2.31–45.

[4] the governors of the thirteen colonies.

WILLIAM BLAKE

Sound! sound! my loud war-trumpets & alarm my thirteen Angels!
Loud howls the eternal Wolf: the eternal Lion lashes his tail!

[Plate 10]
Thus wept the Angel voice & as he wept the terrible blasts
Of trumpets, blew a loud alarm across the Atlantic deep.
No trumpets answer; no reply of clarions or of fifes,[1]
Silent the Colonies remain and refuse the loud alarm.

5   On those vast shady hills between America & Albions shore;
Now barr'd out by the Atlantic sea: call'd Atlantean hills:
Because from their bright summits you may pass to the Golden world
An ancient palace, archetype of mighty Emperies,
Rears its immortal pinnacles, built in the forest of God
10 By Ariston[2] the king of beauty for his stolen bride,

Here on their magic seats the thirteen Angels sat perturb'd
For clouds from the Atlantic hover o'er the solemn roof.

[Plate 11]
Fiery the Angels rose, & as they rose deep thunder roll'd
Around their shores: indignant burning with the fires of Orc
And Bostons Angel cried aloud as they flew thro' the dark night.

He cried: Why trembles honesty and like a murderer,
5   Why seeks he refuge from the frowns of his immortal station!
Must the generous tremble & leave his joy, to the idle: to the pestilence!
That mock him? who commanded this? what God? what Angel!
To keep the gen'rous from experience till the ungenerous
Are unrestraind performers of the energies of nature;
10 Till pity is become a trade, and generosity a science,
That men get rich by, & the sandy desart is giv'n to the strong
What God is he, writes laws of peace, & clothes him in a tempest
What pitying Angel lusts for tears, and fans himself with sighs
What crawling villain preaches abstinence & wraps himself
15 In fat of lambs? no more I follow, no more obedience pay.

[Plate 12]
So cried he, rending off his robe & throwing down his scepter.
In sight of Albions Guardian, and all the thirteen Angels
Rent off their robes to the hungry wind, & threw their golden scepters
Down on the land of America. indignant they descended

---

[1] Cf. Milton, *Paradise Lost* 1.531–32.

[2] This king of Atlantis seems to be Blake's own invention. His name, which means "best," may be borrowed from Herodotus, *The Persian War* 6.61–66.

WILLIAM BLAKE

5   Headlong from out their heav'nly heights, descending swift as fires
Over the land; naked & flaming are their lineaments seen
In the deep gloom, by Washington & Paine & Warren they stood
And the flame folded roaring fierce within the pitchy night
Before the Demon red, who burnt towards America,
10   In black smoke thunders and loud winds rejoicing in its terror
Breaking in smoky wreaths from the wild deep, & gath'ring thick
In flames as of a furnace on the land from North to South

[Plate 13]
What time the thirteen Governors that England sent convene
In Bernards house;[1] the flames coverd the land, they rouze they cry
Shaking their mental chains they rush in fury to the sea
To quench their anguish; at the feet of Washington down fall'n
5   They grovel on the sand and writhing lie, while all
The British soldiers thro' the thirteen states sent up a howl
Of anguish: threw their swords & muskets to the earth & ran
From their encampments and dark castles seeking where to hide
From the grim flames; and from the visions of Orc; in sight
10   Of Albions Angel; who enrag'd his secret clouds open'd
From north to south, and burnt outstretchd on wings of wrath[2] cov'ring
The eastern sky, spreading his awful wings across the heavens;
Beneath him roll'd his num'rous hosts, all Albions Angels camp'd
Darkend the Atlantic mountains & their trumpets shook the valleys
15   Arm'd with diseases of the earth to cast upon the Abyss,
Their numbers forty millions, must'ring in the eastern sky.

[Plate 14]
In the flames stood & view'd the armies drawn out in the sky
Washington Franklin Paine & Warren Allen Gates & Lee:[3]
And heard the voice of Albions Angel give the thunderous command:
His plagues obedient to his voice flew forth out of their clouds
5   Falling upon America, as a storm to cut them off
As a blight cuts the tender corn when it begins to appear.[4]
Dark is the heaven above, & cold & hard the earth beneath;
And as a plague wind fill'd with insects cuts off man & beast;
And as a sea o'erwhelms a land in the day of an earthquake;

---

[1] Blake imagines the thirteen governors meeting at the house of Sir Francis Bernard (1712–79), governor of Massachusetts from 1760 to 1769.

[2] Cf. 2 Esdras 11.39–44.

[3] Ethan Allen (1737–89), military leader; and (probably) Richard Henry Lee (1732–94), author of "Address to the Inhabitants of Britain" (1775) and proposer of the Declaration of Independence in Congress.

[4] The siege of Boston (1775–76) was marked by food shortages and outbreaks of dysentery, smallpox, and (apparently) diphtheria. Cf. Exodus 7–10.

10　　Fury! rage! madness! in a wind swept through America
　　　And the red flames of Orc that folded roaring fierce around
　　　The angry shores, and the fierce rushing of th'inhabitants together:
　　　The citizens of New-York close their books & lock their chests;
　　　The mariners of Boston drop their anchors and unlade;[1]
15　　The scribe of Pensylvania[2] casts his pen upon the earth;
　　　The builder of Virginia throws his hammer down in fear.

　　　Then had America been lost, o'erwhelm'd by the Atlantic,
　　　And Earth had lost another portion of the infinite,
　　　But all rush together in the night in wrath and raging fire
20　　The red fires rag'd! the plagues recoil'd! then rolld they back with fury[3]
　　　[Plate 15]
　　　On Albions Angels; then the Pestilence began in streaks of red
　　　Across the limbs of Albions Guardian, the spotted plague smote Bristols
　　　And the Leprosy Londons Spirit, sickening all their bands:
　　　The millions sent up a howl of anguish and throw off their hammerd mail,
5　　 And cast their swords & spears to earth, & stood a naked multitude.[4]
　　　Albions Guardian writhed in torment on the eastern sky
　　　Pale quivring toward the brain his glimmering eyes, teeth chattering
　　　Howling & shuddering his legs quivering; convuls'd each muscle & sinew
　　　Sick'ning lay Londons Guardian, and the ancient miter'd York[5]
10　　Their heads on snowy hills, their ensigns sick'ning in the sky
　　　The plagues creep on the burning winds driven by flames of Orc,
　　　And by the fierce Americans rushing together in the night
　　　Driven o'er the Guardians of Ireland and Scotland and Wales
　　　They spotted with plagues forsook the frontiers & their banners seard
15　　With fires of hell, deform their ancient heavens with shame & woe.
　　　Hid in his caves the Bard of Albion[6] felt the enormous plagues.
　　　And a cowl of flesh grew o'er his head & scales on his back & ribs;
　　　And rough with black scales all his Angels fright their ancient heavens
　　　The doors of marriage are open, and the Priests in rustling scales
20　　Rush into reptile coverts, hiding from the fires of Orc,
　　　That play around the golden roofs in wreaths of fierce desire,
　　　Leaving the females naked and glowing with the lusts of youth

---

[1] a reference to the Boston Tea Party (1773).

[2] possibly Thomas Paine: *Common Sense* was published in Philadelphia.

[3] Cf. Proverbs 10.24, Ezekiel 22.31.

[4] The British troops have deserted en masse.

[5] York is "miter'd" because it is the seat of an archbishop.

[6] the Poet Laureate, William Whitehead (1715–85) at the time of the Revolution and Henry James Pye (1745–1813) at the time of writing.

>   For the female spirits of the dead pining in bonds of religion;
>   Run from their fetters reddening, & in long drawn arches sitting:
> 25 They feel the nerves of youth renew, and desires of ancient times,
>   Over their pale limbs as a vine when the tender grape appears[1]
>
> [Plate 16]
>   Over the hills, the vales, the cities, rage the red flames fierce;
>   The Heavens melted from north to south; and Urizen who sat
>   Above all heavens in thunders wrap'd, emerg'd his leprous head
>   From out his holy shrine, his tears in deluge piteous
> 5   Falling into the deep sublime! flag'd with grey-brow'd snows
>   And thunderous visages, his jealous wings wav'd over the deep;
>   Weeping in dismal howling woe he dark descended howling
>   Around the smitten bands, clothed in tears & trembling shudd'ring cold.
>   His stored snows he poured forth, and his icy magazines
> 10 He open'd on the deep, and on the Atlantic sea white shiv'ring.
>   Leprous his limbs, all over white, and hoary was his visage.
>   Weeping in dismal howlings before the stern Americans
>   Hiding the Demon red with clouds & cold mists from the earth;
>   Till Angels & weak men twelve years[2] should govern o'er the strong:
> 15 And then their end should come, when France reciev'd the Demons light.
>
>   Stiff shudderings shook the heav'nly thrones! France Spain & Italy,
>   In terror view'd the bands of Albion, and the ancient Guardians
>   Fainting upon the elements, smitten with their own plagues
>   They slow advance to shut the five gates of their law-built heaven
> 20 Filled with blasting fancies and with mildews of despair[3]
>   With fierce disease and lust, unable to stem the fires of Orc;
>   But the five gates were consum'd, & their bolts and hinges melted
>   And the fierce flames burnt round the heavens, & round the abodes of men

---

[1] Cf. Song of Solomon 2.13.

[2] perhaps the twelve years between the battle of Saratoga (1777) and the outbreak of the French Revolution (1789), perhaps those between the capture of Yorktown (1781) and the execution of Louis XVI (1793).

[3] Cf. Deuteronomy 28.15, 22.

from *Songs of Innocence and of Experience, Shewing the Two Contrary States of the Human Soul* (1794)

from *Songs of Experience*

Introduction

Hear the voice of the Bard!
Who Present, Past, & Future sees
Whose ears have heard,
The Holy Word,
5   That walk'd among the ancient trees.[1]

Calling the lapsed Soul
And weeping in the evening dew:
That might controll,
The starry pole;
10 And fallen fallen light renew!

O Earth O Earth return![2]
Arise from out the dewy grass;
Night is worn,
And the morn
15 Rises from the slumberous mass.

Turn away no more:
Why wilt thou turn away
The starry floor
The watry shore
20 Is giv'n thee till the break of day.

Earth's Answer

Earth rais'd up her head,
From the darkness dread & drear.
Her light fled:
Stony dread!
5   And her locks cover'd with grey despair.

Prison'd on watry shore
Starry Jealousy[3] does keep my den
Cold and hoar
Weeping o'er
10 I hear the Father of the ancient men

Selfish father of men
Cruel jealous selfish fear
Can delight
Chain'd in night
15 The virgins of youth and morning bear.

Does spring hide its joy
When buds and blossoms grow?
Does the sower?
Sow by night?
20 Or the plowman in darkness plow?

Break this heavy chain,
That does freeze my bones around
Selfish! vain!
Eternal bane!
25 That free Love with bondage bound.

The Clod & the Pebble

Love seeketh not Itself to please,
Nor for itself hath any care;
But for another gives its ease,
And builds a Heaven in Hells despair.[4]

5   So sang a little Clod of Clay,
    Trodden with the cattles feet:
    But a Pebble of the brook,
    Warbled out these metres meet.

Love seeketh only Self to please,
10 To bind another to Its delight:
Joys in anothers loss of ease,
And builds a Hell in Heavens despite.[5]

---

[1] Cf. Genesis 3.8, John 1.1.

[2] Cf. Deuteronomy 32.1, Jeremiah 22.29.

[3] Cf. Exodus 20.5, 34.14, Deuteronomy 4.24.

[4] Cf. 1 Corinthians 13.

[5] Cf. Milton, *Paradise Lost* 1.254–55.

Holy Thursday

Is this a holy thing to see,
In a rich and fruitful land,
Babes reducd to misery,
Fed with cold and usurous hand?

5   Is that trembling cry a song?
Can it be a song of joy?
And so many children poor?
It is a land of poverty!

And their sun does never shine.
10 And their fields are bleak & bare.
And their ways are fill'd with thorns.
It is eternal winter there.

For where-e'er the sun does shine,
And where-e'er the rain does fall:
15 Babe can never hunger there,[1]
Nor poverty the mind appall.

The Little Girl Lost[2]

In futurity
I prophetic see,
That the earth from sleep,
(Grave the sentence deep)

5   Shall arise and seek
For her maker meek:
And the desert wild
Become a garden mild.

In the southern clime,
10 Where the summers prime,
Never fades away;
Lovely Lyca lay.

Seven summers old
Lovely Lyca told,
15 She had wanderd long,
Hearing wild birds song.

Sweet sleep come to me
Underneath this tree;
Do father, mother weep.—
20 Where can Lyca sleep.

Lost in desart wild
Is your little child.
How can Lyca sleep,
If her mother weep.

25 If her heart does ake,
Then let Lyca wake;
If my mother sleep,
Lyca shall not weep.

Frowning frowning night,
30 O'er this desart bright,
Let thy moon arise,
While I close my eyes.

Sleeping Lyca lay;
While the beasts of prey,
35 Come from caverns deep,
View'd the maid asleep

The kingly lion stood
And the virgin view'd,
Then he gambold round
40 O'er the hallowd ground;

Leopards, tygers play,
Round her as she lay;
While the lion old,
Bow'd his mane of gold.

45 And her bosom lick,
And upon her neck,
From his eyes of flame,
Ruby tears there came;

---

[1] Cf. Revelation 7.16.

[2] Blake originally published this poem and "The Little Girl Found" in *Songs of Innocence*; in 1794, he transferred them to *Songs of Experience*.

    While the lioness,
50   Loos'd her slender dress,
    And naked they convey'd
    To caves the sleeping maid.[1]

The Little Girl Found

    All the night in woe,
    Lyca's parents go:
    Over vallies deep,
    While the desarts weep.

5   Tired and woe-begone,
    Hoarse with making moan:
    Arm in arm seven days,[2]
    They trac'd the desart ways.

    Seven nights they sleep,
10   Among shadows deep:
    And dream they see their child
    Starv'd in desart wild.

    Pale thro' pathless ways
    The fancied image strays,
15   Famish'd, weeping, weak
    With hollow piteous shriek

    Rising from unrest,
    The trembling woman prest,
    With feet of weary woe;
20   She could no further go.

    In his arms he bore,
    Her arm'd with sorrow sore;
    Till before their way,
    A couching lion lay.

25   Turning back was vain,
    Soon his heavy mane,
    Bore them to the ground;
    Then he stalk'd around.

---

[1] Cf. Isaiah 11.6, Daniel 6.12–22, Hebrews 11.33.

[2] Cf. Daniel 4.32.

    Smelling to his prey.
30   But their fears allay,
    When he licks their hands;
    And silent by them stands.

    They look upon his eyes
    Fill'd with deep surprise:
35   And wondering behold,
    A spirit arm'd in gold.

    On his head a crown
    On his shoulders down,
    Flow'd his golden hair.
40   Gone was all their care.

    Follow me he said,
    Weep not for the maid;
    In my palace deep,
    Lyca lies asleep.

45   Then they followed,
    Where the vision led:
    And saw their sleeping child,
    Among tygers wild.

    To this day they dwell
50   In a lonely dell
    Nor fear the wolvish howl,
    Nor the lions growl.

The Chimney Sweeper

    A little black thing among the snow:
    Crying weep, weep, in notes of woe!
    Where are thy father & mother? say?
    They are both gone up to the church to pray.

5   Because I was happy upon the heath,
    And smil'd among the winters snow:
    They clothed me in the clothes of death,
    And taught me to sing the notes of woe.

    And because I am happy, & dance & sing,
10   They think they have done me no injury:

And are gone to praise God & his Priest & King
Who make up a heaven of our misery.

The Sick Rose

O Rose thou art sick.
The invisible worm,
That flies in the night
In the howling storm:

5 Has found out thy bed
Of crimson joy:
And his dark secret love
Does thy life destroy.

The Fly

Little Fly
Thy summers play,[1]
My thoughtless hand
Has brush'd away.

5 Am not I
A fly like thee?[2]
Or art not thou
A man like me?

For I dance
10 And drink & sing:[3]
Till some blind hand
Shall brush my wing.

If thought is life
And strength & breath:[4]
15 And the want
Of thought is death;

Then am I
A happy fly,
If I live,
20 Or if I die.

The Tyger

Tyger Tyger, burning bright,
In the forests of the night;
What immortal hand or eye,
Could frame thy fearful symmetry?

5 In what distant deeps or skies.
Burnt the fire of thine eyes?
On what wings dare he aspire?
What the hand, dare sieze the fire?

And what shoulder, & what art,
10 Could twist the sinews of thy heart?
And when thy heart began to beat,
What dread hand? & what dread feet?

What the hammer? what the chain,
In what furnace was thy brain?
15 What the anvil? what dread grasp,
Dare its deadly terrors clasp!

When the stars threw down their spears
And water'd heaven with their tears:
Did he smile his work to see?
20 Did he who made the Lamb make thee?[5]

Tyger Tyger burning bright,
In the forests of the night:
What immortal hand or eye,
Dare frame thy fearful symmetry?

My Pretty Rose Tree

A flower was offerd to me;
Such a flower as May never bore.

---

[1] Cf. Burke, *Reflections* 32.*

[2] Cf. Shakespeare, *King Lear* 4.1.36–37.

[3] Cf. Abraham Cowley (1618–67), "The Grasshopper": "Thou dost drink, and dance, and sing; / Happier then the happiest *King*!" (9–10).

[4] Cf. René Descartes (1596–1650), *Discourse on Method* (1637): "cogito, ergo sum" ("I think, therefore I am").

[5] Tigers are not mentioned in the Bible.

But I said I've a Pretty Rose-tree:
And I passed the sweet flower o'er.

5 Then I went to my Pretty Rose-tree;
To tend her by day and by night.
But my Rose turnd away with jealousy:
And her thorns were my only delight.

Ah! Sun-Flower

Ah Sun-flower! weary of time,
Who countest the steps of the Sun:
Seeking after that sweet golden clime
Where the travellers journey is done.

5 Where the Youth pined away with desire,
And the pale Virgin shrouded in snow:
Arise from their graves and aspire,
Where my Sun-flower wishes to go.

The Garden of Love

I went to the Garden of Love,
And saw what I never had seen:
A Chapel was built in the midst,
Where I used to play on the green.[1]

5 And the gates of this Chapel were shut,
And Thou shalt not.[2] writ over the door;
So I turn'd to the Garden of Love,
That so many sweet flowers bore.

And I saw it was filled with graves,
10 And tomb-stones where flowers should be:
And Priests in black gowns, were walking their rounds,
And binding with briars, my joys & desires.

---

[1] possibly a reference to the erection of a chapel on South Lambeth Green in 1793.

[2] the phrase that introduces most of the ten commandments (Exodus 20.3–17).

London

I wander thro' each charter'd street,
Near where the charter'd Thames does flow.
And mark in every face I meet
Marks of weakness, marks of woe.

5 In every cry of every Man,
In every Infants cry of fear,
In every voice: in every ban,
The mind-forg'd manacles I hear

How the Chimney-sweepers cry
10 Every blackning Church appalls,
And the hapless Soldiers sigh
Runs in blood down Palace walls

But most thro' midnight streets I hear
How the youthful Harlots curse
15 Blasts the new-born Infants tear
And blights with plagues the Marriage hearse

The Human Abstract

Pity would be no more,
If we did not make somebody Poor:
And Mercy no more could be,
If all were as happy as we;

5 And mutual fear brings peace;
Till the selfish loves increase.
Then Cruelty knits a snare,
And spreads his baits with care.

He sits down with holy fears,
10 And waters the ground with tears:
Then Humility takes its root
Underneath his foot.

Soon spreads the dismal shade
Of Mystery over his head;
15 And the Catterpiller and Fly,
Feed on the Mystery.

And it bears the fruit of Deceit,
Ruddy and sweet to eat;
And the Raven his nest has made
20 In its thickest shade.

The Gods of the earth and sea,
Sought thro' Nature to find this Tree
But their search was all in vain:
There grows one in the Human Brain

Infant Sorrow

My mother groand! my father wept.
Into the dangerous world I leapt:
Helpless, naked, piping loud;
Like a fiend hid in a cloud.[1]

5 Struggling in my fathers hands:
Striving against my swaddling bands:
Bound and weary I thought best
To sulk upon my mothers breast.

A Poison Tree[2]

I was angry with my friend;
I told my wrath, my wrath did end.
I was angry with my foe:
I told it not, my wrath did grow.

5 And I waterd it in fears,
Night & morning with my tears:
And I sunned it with smiles,
And with soft deceitful wiles.

And it grew both day and night.
10 Till it bore an apple bright.[3]
And my foe beheld it shine,
And he knew that it was mine.

---

[1] Cf. Exodus 16.10.

[2] Another version of this poem is entitled "Christian forebearance."

[3] Cf. Genesis 3.

And into my garden stole,
When the night had veild the pole;
15 In the morning glad I see;
My foe outstretchd beneath the tree.

from *Milton* (1800–08)

PLATE I

Preface

The Stolen and Perverted Writings of Homer & Ovid: of Plato & Cicero. which all Men ought to contemn: are set up by artifice against the Sublime of the Bible. but when the New Age is at leisure to Pronounce: all will be set right: & those Grand Works of the more ancient & consciously & professedly Inspired Men, will hold their proper rank, & the Daughters of Memory shall become the Daughters of Inspiration. Shakespeare & Milton were both curbed by the general malady & infection from the silly Greek & Latin slaves of the Sword.

   Rouze up O Young Men of the New Age! set your foreheads against the ignorant Hirelings! For we have Hirelings in the Camp, the Court & the University: who would if they could, for every depress Mental & prolong Corporeal War. Painters! on you I call! Sculptors! Architects! Suffer not the fash[i]onable Fools to depress your powers by the prices they pretend to give for contemptible works or the expensive advertizing boasts that they make of such works; believe Christ & his Apostles that there is a Class of Men whose whole delight is in Destroying. We do not want either Greek or Roman Models if we are but just & true to our own Imaginations, those Worlds of Eternity in which we shall live for ever; in Jesus our Lord.

And did those feet in ancient time.
Walk upon Englands mountains green:
And was the holy Lamb of God,
On Englands pleasant pastures seen!

5 And did the Countenance Divine,
Shine forth upon our clouded hills?

And was Jerusalem builded here,
Among these dark Satanic Mills?

Bring me my Bow of burning gold:
10 Bring me my Arrows of desire:
Bring me my Spear: O clouds unfold!
Bring me my Chariot of fire!

I will not cease from Mental Fight,
Nor shall my Sword sleep in my hand:
15 Till we have built Jerusalem,
In Englands green & pleasant Land.

Would to God that all the Lords people were Prophets.
Numbers XI. ch 29 v.

from *The Pickering Manuscript*[1]

The Mental Traveller

I traveld thro' a Land of Men
A Land of Men & Women too
And heard & saw such dreadful things
As cold Earth wanderers never knew

5 For there the Babe is born in joy
That was begotten in dire woe
Just as we Reap in joy the fruit
Which we in bitter tears did sow

And if the Babe is born a Boy
10 He's given to a Woman Old
Who nails him down upon a rock
Catches his Shrieks in Cups of gold

She binds iron thorns around his head
She pierces both his hands & feet
15 She cuts his heart out at his side
To make it feel both cold & heat

Her fingers number every Nerve
Just as a Miser counts his gold
She lives upon his shrieks & cries
20 And She grows young as he grows old

Till he becomes a bleeding youth
And she becomes a Virgin bright
Then he rends up his Manacles
And binds her down for his delight

25 He plants himself in all her Nerves
Just as a Husbandman his mould
And She becomes his dwelling place
And Garden fruitful seventy fold

An aged Shadow soon he fades
30 Wandring round an Earthly Cot
Full filled all with gems & gold
Which he by industry had got

And these are the gems of the Human Soul
The rubies & pearls of a lovesick eye
35 The countless gold of the akeing heart
The martyrs groan & the lovers sigh

They are his meat they are his drink
He feeds the Beggar & the Poor
And the way faring Traveller
40 For ever open is his door

His grief is their eternal joy
They make the roofs & walls to ring
Till from the fire on the hearth
A little Female Babe does spring

45 And she is all of solid fire
And gems & gold that none his hand
Dares stretch to touch her Baby form
Or wrap her in his swaddling-band

But She comes to the Man she loves
50 If young or old or rich or poor
They soon drive out the aged Host
A Beggar at anothers door

---

[1] The ten poems in the Pickering Manuscript, inscribed by Blake for a friend but never engraved, were not published during his lifetime. They were probably composed between 1800 and 1804.

He wanders weeping far away
Untill some other take him in
55 Oft blind & age-bent sore distrest
Untill he can a Maiden win

And to allay his freezing Age
The Poor Man takes her in his arms
The Cottage fades before his Sight
60 The Garden & its lovely Charms

The Guests are scatterd thro' the land
For the Eye altering alters all
The Senses roll themselves in fear
And the flat Earth becomes a Ball

65 The Stars Sun Moon all shrink away
A desert vast without a bound
And nothing left to eat or drink
And a dark desert all around

The honey of her Infant lips
70 The bread & wine of her sweet smile
The wild game of her roving Eye
Does him to Infancy beguile

For as he eats & drinks he grows
Younger & younger every day
75 And on the desert wild they both
Wander in terror & dismay

Like the wild Stag she flees away
Her fear plants many a thicket wild
While he pursues her night & day
80 By various arts of Love beguild

By various arts of Love & Hate
Till the wide desert planted oer
With Labyrinths of wayward Love
Where roams the Lion Wolf & Boar

85 Till he becomes a wayward Babe
And she a weeping Woman Old
Then many a Lover wanders here
The Sun & Stars are nearer rolld

The trees bring forth sweet Extacy
90 To all who in the desart roam
Till many a City there is Built
And many a pleasant Shepherds home

But when they find the frowning Babe
Terror strikes thro the region wide
95 They cry the Babe the Babe is Born
And flee away on Every side

For who dare touch the frowning form
His arm is witherd to its root
Lions Boars Wolves all howling flee
100 And every Tree does shed its fruit

And none can touch that frowning form
Except it be a Woman Old
She nails him down upon the Rock
And all is done as I have told

The Crystal Cabinet

The Maiden caught me in the Wild
Where I was dancing merrily
She put me into her Cabinet
And Lockd me up with a golden Key

5 This Cabinet is formd of Gold
And Pearl & Crystal shining bright
And within it opens into a World
And a little lovely Moony Night

Another England there I saw
10 Another London with its Tower
Another Thames & other Hills
And another pleasant Surrey Bower

Another Maiden like herself
Translucent lovely shining clear
15 Threefold each in the other closd
O what a pleasant trembling fear

O what a smile a threefold Smile
Filld me that like a flame I burnd

I bent to Kiss the lovely Maid
20   And found a Threefold Kiss returnd

I strove to sieze the inmost Form
With ardor fierce & hands of flame
But burst the Crystal Cabinet
And like a Weeping Babe became

25   A weeping Babe upon the wild
And Weeping Woman pale reclind
And in the outward air again
I filld with woes the passing Wind

Auguries of Innocence

To see a World in a Grain of Sand
And a Heaven in a Wild Flower
Hold Infinity in the palm of your hand
And Eternity in an hour
5   A Robin Red breast in a Cage
Puts all Heaven in a Rage
A dove house filld with doves & Pigeons
Shudders Hell thro all its regions
A dog starvd at his Masters Gate
10   Predicts the ruin of the State
A Horse misusd upon the Road
Calls to Heaven for Human blood
Each outcry of the hunted Hare
A fibre from the Brain does tear
15   A Skylark wounded in the wing
A Cherubim does cease to sing
The Game Cock clipd & armd for fight
Does the Rising Sun affright
Every Wolfs & Lions howl
20   Raises from Hell a Human Soul
The wild deer wandring here & there
Keeps the Human Soul from Care
The Lamb misusd breeds Public strife
And yet forgives the Butchers Knife
25   The Bat that flits at close of Eve
Has left the Brain that wont Believe
The Owl that calls upon the Night
Speaks the Unbelievers fright
He who shall hurt the little Wren

30   Shall never be belovd by Men
He who the Ox to wrath has movd
Shall never be by Woman lovd
The wanton Boy that kills the Fly
Shall feel the Spiders enmity
35   He who torments the Chafers[1] sprite
Weaves a Bower in endless Night
The Catterpiller on the Leaf
Repeats to thee thy Mothers grief
Kill not the Moth nor Butterfly
40   For the Last judgment draweth nigh
He who shall train the Horse to War
Shall never pass the Polar Bar
The Beggers Dog & Widows Cat
Feed them & thou wilt grow fat
45   The Gnat that sings his Summers song
Poison gets from Slanders tongue
The poison of the Snake & Newt
Is the sweat of Envys Foot
The Poison of the Honey Bee
50   Is the Artists Jealousy
The Princes Robes & Beggars Rags
Are Toadstools on the Misers Bags
A truth thats told with bad intent
Beats all the Lies you can invent
55   It is right it should be so
Man was made for Joy & Woe
And when this we rightly know
Thro the World we safely go
Joy & Woe are woven fine
60   A Clothing for the soul divine
Under every grief & pine
Runs a joy with silken twine
The Babe is more than swadling Bands
Throughout all these Human Lands
65   Tools were made & Born were hands
Every Farmer Understands
Every Tear from Every Eye
Becomes a Babe in Eternity
This is caught by Females bright
70   And returnd to its own delight
The Bleat the Bark Bellow & Roar
Are Waves that Beat on Heavens Shore

---

[1] beetle's.

The Babe that weeps the Rod beneath
Writes Revenge in realms of death
75 The Beggars Rags fluttering in Air
Does to Rags the Heavens tear
The Soldier armd with Sword & Gun
Palsied strikes the Summers Sun
The poor Mans Farthing is worth more
80 Than all the Gold on Africs Shore
One Mite wrung from the Labrers hands
Shall buy & sell the Misers Lands
Or if protected from on high
Does that whole Nation sell & buy
85 He who mocks the Infants Faith
Shall be mock'd in Age & Death
He who shall teach the Child to Doubt
The rotting Grave shall neer get out
He who respects the Infants faith
90 Triumphs over Hell & Death
The Childs Toys & the Old Mans Reasons
Are the Fruits of the Two seasons
The Questioner who sits so sly
Shall never know how to Reply
95 He who replies to words of Doubt
Doth put the Light of Knowledge out
The Strongest Poison ever known
Came from Caesars Laurel Crown
Nought can deform the Human Race
100 Like to the Armours iron brace
When Gold & Gems adorn the Plow
To peaceful Arts shall Envy Bow
A Riddle or the Crickets Cry
Is to Doubt a fit Reply
105 The Emmets Inch & Eagles Mile
Make Lame Philosophy to smile
He who Doubts from what he sees
Will neer Believe do what you Please
If the Sun & Moon should doubt
110 Theyd immediately Go out
To be in a Passion you Good may do
But no Good if a Passion is in you
The Whore & Gambler by the State
Licencd build that Nations Fate
115 The Harlots cry from Street to Street
Shall weave Old Englands winding Sheet
The Winners Shout the Losers Curse
Dance before dead Englands Hearse
Every Night & every Morn
120 Some to Misery are Born
Every Morn & every Night
Some are Born to sweet delight
Some are Born to sweet delight
Some are Born to Endless Night
125 We are led to Believe a Lie
When we see not Thro the Eye
Which was Born in a Night to perish in a Night
When the Soul Slept in Beams of Light
God Appears & God is Light[1]
130 To those poor Souls who dwell in Night
But does a Human Form Display
To those who Dwell in Realms of day

Marginalia

from Annotations to the *Works of Sir Joshua Reynolds* (1798)[2]

[p 188, back of title]
<The Purpose of the following Discourse[3] is to Prove That Taste & Genius are not of Heavenly Origin & that all who have Supposed that they Are so. Are to be Considered as Weak headed Fanatics

The obligations Reynolds has laid on Bad Artists of all Classes will at all times make them his Admirers but most especially for this Discourse in which it is proved that the Stupid are born with Faculties Equal to other Men Only they have not Cultivated them because they thought it not worth the trouble>

[p 194] ... obscurity ... is one source of the sublime.
<Obscurity is Neither the Source of the Sublime nor of any Thing Else>

[That] liberty of imagination is cramped by ... rules; ... smothered ... by too much judgment; ... [are] notions not

---

[1] Cf. 1 John 1.5.

[2] Cf. Reynolds, *Seven Disclosures Delivered in the Royal Academy by the President* (1778).*

[3] Reynolds, Discourse 7.*

only groundless, but pernicious.

<The Ancients & the wisest of the Moderns were of the opinion that Reynolds Condemns & laughs at>

[p 195] ... scarce a poet is to be found, ... whose latter works are not as replete with ... imagination, as those [of] his more youthful days.

<As Replete but Not More Replete>

To understand literally these metaphors ... seems ... absurd....

<The Ancients did not mean to Impose when they affirmd their belief in Vision & Revelation Plato was in Earnest. Milton was in Earnest. They believed that God did Visit Man Really & Truly & not as Reynolds pretends

[p 196] [idea absurd that a winged genius] did really inform him in a whisper what he was to write; ...

How very Anxious Reynolds is to Disprove & Contemn Spiritual Perception

[p 197] It is supposed that ... under the name of genius great works are produced, ... without our being under the least obligation to reason, precept, or experience.[1]

<Who Ever said this>

... scarce state these opinions without exposing their absurdity; yet ... constantly in the mouths of ... artists.[2]

<He states Absurdities in Company with Truths & calls both Absurd>

[p 198] ... prevalent opinion ... considers the principles of taste ... as having less solid foundations, than ... they really have. ... [and imagines taste of too high origin] to submit to the authority of an earthly tribunal.[3]

<The Artifice of the Epicurean Philosophers is to Call all other Opinions Unsolid & Unsubstantial than those which are Derived from Earth>

We often appear to differ in sentiments ... merely from the inaccuracy of terms, ...[4]

It is not in Terms that Reynolds & I disagree Two Contrary Opinions can never by any Language be made alike. I say Taste & Genius are Not Teachable or Acquirable but are born with us Reynolds says the Contrary

[p 199] ... take words as we find them; ... distinguish the THINGS to which they are applied.[5]

<This is False the Fault is not in Words. but in Things Lockes Opinions of Words & their Fallaciousness are Artful Opinions & Fallacious also>

[p 200] It is the very same taste which relishes a demonstration in geometry, that is pleased with the resemblance of a picture to an original, and touched with the harmony of musick.[6]

<Demonstration Similitude & Harmony are Objects of Reasoning Invention Identity & Melody are Objects of Intuition>

[p 201] ... as true as mathematical demonstration; ...

<God forbid that Truth should be Confined to Mathematical Demonstration>

But beside real, there is also apparent truth, ...

<He who does not Know Truth at Sight is unworthy of Her Notice>

... taste ... approaches ... a sort of resemblance to real science, even where opinions are ... no better than prejudices.

<Here is a great deal to do to Prove that All Truth is Prejudice for All that is Valuable in Knowledge[s] is Superior to Demonstrative Science such as is Weighed or Measured>

[p 202] As these prejudices become more narrow, ... this secondary taste becomes more and more fantastical; ...

<And so he thinks he has proved that Genius & Inspiration are All a Hum>

... I shall [now] proceed with less method, ...

<He calls the Above proceeding with Method>

We will take it for granted, that reason is something invariable ...

---

[1] See Reynolds, 12.*

[2] See Reynolds, 12.*

[3] See Reynolds, 12.*

[4] See Reynolds, 12.*

[5] See Reynolds, 13.*

[6] See Reynolds, 13.*

<Reason or A Ratio of All We have Known is not the Same it shall be when we know More. he therefore takes a Falshood for granted to set out with>

[p 203] [Whatever of taste we can] fairly bring under the dominion of reason, must be considered as equally exempt from change.

<Now this is Supreme Fooling>

The arts would lie open for ever to caprice ... if those who ... judge ... had no settled principles....[1]

<He may as well say that if Man does not. lay down settled Principles. The Sun will not rise in a Morning>

[p 204] My notion of nature comprehends ... also the ... human mind and imagination.

<Here is a Plain Confession that he Thinks Mind & Imagination not to be above the Mortal & Perishing Nature. Such is the End of Epicurean or Newtonian Philosophy it is Atheism>

[p 208] [Poussin's Perseus and Medusa's head] ... I remember turning from it with disgust, ...

<Reynolds's Eye. could not bear Characteristic Colouring or Light & Shade>

A picture should please at first sight, ...

Please! Whom? Some Men Cannot See a Picture except in a Dark Corner

[p 209] No one can deny, that violent passions will naturally emit harsh and disagreeable tones: ...

<Violent Passions Emit the Real Good & Perfect Tones>

[p 214] ... Rubens ... thinking it necessary to make his work so very ornamental, ...

<Here it is calld Ornamental that the Roman & Bolognian Schools may be Insinuated not to be Ornamental>

[p 215] Nobody will dispute but some of the best of the Roman or Bolognian schools would have produced a more learned and more noble work [than that of Rubens].

---

[1] See Reynolds, 13.*

<Learned & Noble is Ornamental>

... weighing the value of the different classes of the art, ...

<A Fools Balance is no Criterion because tho it goes down on the heaviest side we ought to look what he puts into it.>

[p 228] Thus it is the ornaments, rather than the proportions of architecture, which at the first glance distinguish the different orders from each other; the Dorick is known by its triglyphs, the Ionick by its volutes, and the Corinthian by its acanthus.

[*He could not tell Ionick from the Corinthian or Dorick or one column from another.*]

[p 232] [European meeting Cherokee Indian] ... which ever first feels himself to laugh, is the barbarian.[2]

<Excellent>

[p 242] [In the highest] flights of ... imagination, reason ought to preside from first to last, ...

<If this is True it is a Devilish Foolish Thing to be An Artist>

Annotations to Wordsworth's Preface to *The Excursion, being a portion of The Recluse, A Poem* (1814)

[LINES 31–35] All strength, all terror, single or in bands
    That ever was put forth in personal Form
    Jehovah—with his thunder & the choir
    Of shouting Angels & the empyreal thrones—
    I pass them unalarmed, ...[3]

Solomon when he Married Pharohs daughter & became a Convert to the Heathen Mythology Talked exactly in this way of Jehovah as a Very inferior object of Mans Contemplations he also passed him by unalarmd & was permitted. Jehovah dropped a tear & followd him by his Spirit into the Abstract Void it is called the Divine Mercy Satan dwells in it but Mercy does not dwell in him he knows not to Forgive

---

[2] See Reynolds, 15.*

[3] Blake quotes from "On Man, on Nature, and on Human Life,"* W. Wordsworth's excerpt from his poem "Home at Grasmere," which he printed at the end of the Preface to *The Excursion* (1814).

[LINES 63–68]
    How exquisitely the individual Mind
    (And the progressive powers perhaps no less
    Of the whole species) to the external World
    Is fitted.—& how exquisitely too,
    Theme this but little heard of among Men
    The external World is fitted to the Mind.

You shall not bring me down to believe such fitting & fitted I know better & Please your Lordship

[LINES 71–82]
    —Such Grateful haunts forgoing. if I oft
    Must turn elsewhere—to travel near the tribes
    And fellowships of men, and see ill sights
    Of madding passions mutually inflamed
    Must hear *Humanity in fields and groves*
    Pipe solitary anguish; or must hang
    Brooding above the fierce confederate storm
    Of Sorrow barricadoed evermore
    Within the walls of cities; may these sounds
    Have their authentic comment—that even these
    Hearing I be not downcast nor forlorn

does not this Fit & is it not Fitting most Exquisitely too but to what not to Mind but to the Vile Body only & to its Laws of Good & Evil & its Enmities against Mind

from Annotations to Thornton's *The Lord's Prayer, Newly Translated* (1827)[1]

[PAGE 10, blank]
This is Saying the Lords Prayer Backwards which they say Raises the Devil

Doctor Thorntons <Tory> Translation Translated out of its disguise in the <Classical &> Scotch language into [*plain*] <the vulgar> English

Our Father Augustus Caesar who art in these thy <Substantial Astronomical Telescopic> Heavens Holiness to thy Name <or Title & reverence to thy Shadow> Thy Kingship come upon Earth first & thence in Heaven Give us day by day our Real Taxed <Substantial Money bought> Bread [& *take*] <deliver from the Holy Ghost <so we call Nature> whatever cannot be Taxed> [*debt that was owing to him*] <for all is debts & Taxes between Caesar & us & one another> lead us not to read the Bible <but let our Bible be Virgil & Shakspeare> & deliver us from Poverty in Jesus <that Evil one> For thine is the Kingship <or Allegoric Godship> & the Power or War & the Glory or Law Ages after Ages in thy Descendants <for God is only an Allegory of Kings & nothing Else> Amen....

Letters

[To] Rev[d] Dr Trusler, Englefield Green, Egham, Surrey[2]

13 Hercules Buildings, Lambeth, August 23, 1799
[Postmark: 28 August]

Rev[d] Sir

I really am sorry that you are falln out with the Spiritual World Especially if I should have to answer for it I feel very sorry that your Ideas & Mine on Moral Painting differ so much as to have made you angry with my method of Study. If I am wrong I am wrong in good company. I had hoped your plan comprehend All Species of this Art & Especially that you would not reject that Species which gives Existence to Every other. namely Visions of Eternity You say that I want some-

---

[1] For the Lord's Prayer, see Matthew 6.9–13, Luke 11.2–4. In his pamphlet, *The Lord's Prayer, Newly Translated with Notes*, Robert John Thornton (1768–1837), physician and writer on botany, translated the prayer as follows:
    "O, Father of Mankind, Thou, who dwellest in the highest of the Heavens, Reverenc'd be Thy Name!
    "May Thy Reign be, every where, proclaim'd so that Thy Will may be done upon the Earth, as it is in the mansions of Heaven.
    "Grant unto me, and the whole world, day by day, an abundant supply of spiritual and corporeal Food.
    "Forgive us our transgressions against Thee, as we extend our Kindness, and Forgiveness, to all.
    "O God! Abandon us not, when surrounded by trials.
    "But preserve us from the Dominion of Satan: For Thine only, is the Sovereignty, the power, and the glory, throughout Eternity!!!
                "Amen."

[2] John Trusler (1735–1820) was a clergyman and the author of such books as *The Way to Be Rich and Respectable*. Blake had been recommended to him as a possible illustrator, but Trusler found his imagination too otherworldly.

body to Elucidate my Ideas. But you ought to know that What is Grand is necessarily obscure to Weak men. That which can be made Explicit to the Idiot is not worth my care. The wisest of the Ancients considerd what is not too Explicit as the fittest for Instruction because it rouzes the faculties to act. I name Moses Solomon Esop Homer Plato

But as you have favord me with your remarks on my Design permit me in return to defend it against a mistaken one, which is. That I have supposed Malevolence without a Cause.[1]—Is not Merit in one a Cause of Envy in another & Serenity & Happiness & Beauty a Cause of Malevolence. But Want of Money & the Distress of A Thief can never be alledged as the Cause of his Thievery. for many honest people endure greater hard ships with Fortitude We must therefore seek the Cause elsewhere than in want of Money for that is the Misers passion, not the Thiefs

I have therefore proved your Reasonings Ill proportiond which you can never prove my figures to be. They are those of Michael Angelo Rafael & the Antique & of the best living Models. I percieve that your Eye[s] is perverted by Caricature Prints, which ought not to abound so much as they do. Fun I love but too much Fun is of all things the most loathsom. Mirth is better than Fun & Happiness is better than Mirth—I feel that a Man may be happy in This World. And I know that This World Is a World of Imagination & Vision I see Every thing I paint In This World, but Every body does not see alike. To the Eyes of a Miser a Guinea is more beautiful than the Sun & a bag worn with the use of Money has more beautiful proportions than a Vine filled with Grapes. The tree which moves some to tears of joy is in the Eyes of others only a Green thing that stands in the way. Some See Nature all Ridicule & Deformity & by these I shall not regulate my proportions, & Some Scarce see Nature at all But to the Eyes of the Man of Imagination Nature is Imagination itself. As a man is So he Sees. As the Eye is formed such are its Powers You certainly Mistake when you say that the Visions of Fancy are not be found in This World.

To Me This World is all One continued Vision of Fancy or Imagination & I feel Flatterd when I am told So. What is it sets Homer Virgil & Milton in so high a rank of Art. Why is the Bible more Entertaining & Instructive than any other book. Is it not because they are addressed to the Imagination which is Spiritual Sensation & but mediately to the Understanding or Reason Such is True Painting and such <was> alone valued by the Greeks & the best modern Artists. Consider what Lord Bacon says "Sense sends over to Imagination before Reason have judged & Reason sends over to Imagination before the Decree can be acted." See Advancem^t of Learning Part 2 P 47 of first Edition[2]

But I am happy to find a Great Majority of Fellow Mortals who can Elucidate My Visions & Particularly they have been Elucidated by Children who have taken a greater delight in contemplating my Pictures than I even hoped. Neither Youth nor Childhood is Folly or Incapacity Some Children are Fools & so are some Old Men. But There is a vast Majority on the side of Imagination or Spiritual Sensation

To Engrave after another Painter is infinitely more laborious than to Engrave ones own Inventions. And of the Size you require my price has been Thirty Guineas & I cannot afford to do it for less. I had Twelve for the Head I sent you as a Specimen, but after my own designs I could do at least Six times the quantity of labour in the same time which will account for the difference of price as also that Chalk Engraving is at least six times as laborious as Aqua tinta. I have no objection to Engraving after another Artist. Engraving is the profession I was apprenticed to, & should never have attempted to live by any thing else If orders had not come in for my Designs & Paintings, which I have the pleasure to tell you are Increasing Every Day. Thus If I am a Painter it is not to be attributed to Seeking after. But I am contented whether I live by Painting or Engraving

I am Revd Sir Your very obedient servant
WILLIAM BLAKE

---

[1] a reference to a picture, entitled *Malevolence*, which Blake had shown to Trusler.

[2] Sir Francis Bacon, Baron Verulam (1561–1626), *Of the Advancement of Learning* (1605).

WILLIAM BLAKE

To Thomas Butts [22 November 1802][1]

Dear Sir
After I had finishd my Letter I found that I had not said half what I intended to say & in particular I wish to ask you what subject you choose to be painted on the remaining Canvas which I brought down with me (for there were three) and to tell you that several of the Drawings were in great forwardness you will see by the Inclosed Account that the remaining Number of Drawings which you gave me orders for is Eighteen I will finish these with all possible Expedition if indeed I have not tired you or as it is politely calld Bored you too much already or if you would rather cry out Enough Off Off! tell me in a Letter of forgiveness if you were offended & of accustomd friendship if you were not. But I will bore you more with some Verses which My Wife desires me to Copy out & send you with her kind love & Respect they were Composed <above> a twelvemonth ago [in a] <while> Walk<ing> from Felpham to Lavant to meet my Sister

With happiness stretchd across the hills
In a cloud that dewy sweetness distills
With a blue sky spread over with wings
And a mild sun that mounts & sings
5   With trees & fields full of Fairy elves
And little devils who fight for themselves
Remembring the Verses that Hayley sung[2]
When my heart knockd against the root of my
      tongue
With Angels planted in Hawthorn bowers
10 And God himself in the passing hours
With Silver Angels across my way
And Golden Demons that none can stay
With my Father hovering upon the wind
And my Brother Robert just behind

15 And my Brother John the evil one[3]
In a black cloud making his mone
Tho dead they appear upon my path
Notwithstanding my terrible wrath
They beg they intreat they drop their tears
20 Filld full of hopes filld full of fears
With a thousand Angels upon the Wind
Pouring disconsolate from behind
To drive them off & before my way
A frowning Thistle implores my stay
25 What to others a trifle appears
Fills me full of smiles or tears
For double the vision my Eyes do see
And a double vision is always with me
With my inward Eye 'tis an old Man grey
30 With my outward a Thistle across my way
"If thou goest back the thistle said
Thou art to endless woe betrayd
For here does Theotormon lower
And here is Enitharmons bower
35 And Los[4] the terrible thus hath sworn
Because thou backward dost return
Poverty Envy old age & fear
Shall bring thy Wife upon a bier
And Butts shall give what Fuseli[5] gave
40 A dark black Rock & a gloomy Cave."

I struck the Thistle with my foot
And broke him up from his delving root
"Must the duties of life each other cross
Must every joy be dung & dross
45 Must my dear Butts feel cold neglect
Because I give Hayley his due respect
Must Flaxman[6] look upon me as wild

---

[1] Butts (1757–1845), Chief Clerk of the Commissary General of Musters, was Blake's most important patron, commissioning over two hundred pictures from him between 1800 and 1810, and buying ten of his illuminated books.

[2] poems by Blake's patron William Hayley (1745–1820), possibly his translation of Tasso's *Seven Days of the Created World*.

[3] Blake's father (d. 1784) and his brothers, Robert (1767–87), who died of tuberculosis and who Blake believed continued to communicate with him and inspire him; and John (b. 1760), a soldier, who died young of complications of alcoholism.

[4] For Theotormon, see note to *Visions of the Daughters of Albion* iii.1; for Enitharmon, see note to *America* 7.4; for Los, see note to *The Marriage of Heaven and Hell* 25.16.

[5] Henry Fuseli (1741–1825), painter, a friend of Blake.

[6] John Flaxman (1755–1826), sculptor, a friend of Blake.

And all my friends be with doubts beguild
Must my Wife live in my Sisters bane[1]
50 Or my sister survive on my Loves pain
The curses of Los the terrible shade
And his dismal terrors make me afraid
So I spoke & struck in my wrath
The old man weltering upon my path
55 Then Los appeard in all his power
In the Sun he appeard descending before
My face in fierce flames in my double sight
Twas outward a Sun: inward Los in his might

"My hands are labour day & night
60 And Ease comes never in my sight
My Wife has no indulgence given
Except what comes to her from heaven
We eat little we drink less
This Earth breeds not our happiness
65 Another Sun feeds our lifes streams
We are not warmed with thy beams
Thou measurest not the Time to me
Nor yet the Space that I do see
My Mind is not with thy light arrayd
70 Thy terrors shall not make me afraid"

When I had my Defiance given
The Sun stood trembling in heaven
The Moon that glowd remote below
Became leprous & white as snow

75 And every Soul of men on the Earth
Felt affliction & sorrow & sickness & dearth
Los flamd in my path & the Sun was hot
With the bows of my Mind & the Arrows of Thought
My bowstring fierce with Ardour breathes
80 My arrows glow in their golden sheaves
My brothers & father march before
The heavens drop with human gore

Now I a fourfold vision see
And a fourfold vision is given to me
85 Tis fourfold in my supreme delight
And three fold in soft Beulahs night[2]
And twofold Always. May God us keep
From Single vision & Newtons sleep[3]

I also inclose you some Ballads by Mr Hayley with prints to them by Your H^{ble}. Servt.[4] I should have sent them before now but could not get any thing done for You to please myself for I do assure you that I have truly studied the two little pictures I now send & do not repent of the time I have spent upon them
    God bless you

                         Yours
                          W B

P.S. I have taken the liberty to trouble you with a letter to my Brother which you will be so kind as to send or give him & oblige yours W B

---

[1] Blake's sister was living with him and his wife at Felpham.

[2] Cf. Isaiah 62.4.

[3] Blake disapproved of the physics of Sir Isaac Newton (1642–1727) for its materialism and mechanism.

[4] Blake had done 14 engravings for *Designs to a Series of Ballads Written by William Hayley* (1820).

Harriet Lee
1757 – 1851

Harriet Lee was born in London in 1757. Her father, John Lee, was a playwright and actor. Her mother, also an actor, died young, and her older sister Sophia took on responsibility for her five younger siblings; Harriet later remembered gratefully her role as an "after-guide." Sophia had her first play, *The Chapter of Accidents*, produced in 1780. It was so successful that Sophia was able to found a girls' school in Bath, where she and her sisters Harriet and Ann taught until 1803. Harriet's first novel, *The Errors of Innocence*, was published in 1786; her first play, *The New Peerage; or, Our Eyes May Deceive Us*, was produced in 1787. Between them, the Lees produced twelve works of fiction, poetry, and drama. The five-volume *Canterbury Tales* (1797–1805) is their most substantial collaboration: Sophia wrote the Introduction and Harriet most of the tales. It was another success, enjoying new editions throughout the nineteenth century (our text is taken from the 1832 edition in the significantly titled "Standard Novels" series). Some of the tales were dramatized—both Byron* and Harriet herself wrote dramatizations of "The German's Tale. Kruitzner," and both were successfully staged. Neither Sophia nor Harriet ever married; in 1798, the recently widowed Godwin* proposed to Harriet, but she turned him down because he was an unbeliever. Sophia died in Clifton, near Bath, on 13 March 1824. Harriet died there on 1 August 1851. (D.L.M.)

✺✺✺

from *Canterbury Tales* (1795–1805)[1]

from *The Old Woman's Tale. Lothaire: A Legend*[2]

    The laurels wither on your brow;
    Then boast no more your mighty deeds;
        For on Death's purple altar now
    Lo, where the victor, victim bleeds!
           All heads must come
           To the cold tomb:
    Only the actions of the just
    Smell sweet, and blossom in the dust.
                  SHIRLEY[3]

It drew towards evening, ere the Prior and his guest returned from visiting the ruin; masses of which, irregularly fallen, and overgrown with moss and weeds, had rendered their progress tedious and uncertain. "To shorten our way, we will, if you please, pass through that part of the abbey which still stands," said the Prior, as, drawing a bunch of keys from his pocket, he opened the Gothic and heavy door. Bareheaded, and with a silent sense of devotion, the Baron entered: he was struck with the venerable grandeur of the scene; and while his footsteps rang through the massy pillars and decaying arches, he looked upon the *Ci-gît*[4]—the little history of man, profusely scattered around, with a sentiment that partook at once of sadness and sublimity.

"The building, even as it now stands," said the Prior, "does not ill accord with the ideas you may have formed of it during our walk. The spot which fronts us was once the high altar: observe how magnificently it has been decorated. Tradition tells us of numberless miracles performed here! the saints have, indeed, fallen from their niches; and, like their worshippers, are possibly mingled with the dust: but the rich Gothic fretwork is every where visible. Examine the steps too! for, though worn, as you perceive, with acts of devotion, the curious in marble still speak of them with rapture. What compli-

---

[1] Sophia's Introduction explains that seven travellers find themselves snowbound in Canterbury and decide to pass the time by telling stories. Cf. Geoffrey Chaucer (1343?–1400), *The Canterbury Tales* (1387–1400).

[2] In the Introduction, the frame narrator, noticing the "old gentlewoman a little alarmed at a coffin [an oblong cinder, supposed to be an omen of death] that had popped from the fire," concludes that "superstition [is] her weak side."

[3] James Shirley (1596–1666), "Dirge" (1659) 17–24.

[4] "Here lies." (H.L.)

cated ideas here obtrude themselves upon the mind! It is but a few moments since our feet, my dear Baron, passed over the graves of the noble, the valiant, and the beautiful. How many human sighs have they breathed on the very spot where we now stand! how many human tears have they dropped! Of all they solicited in this world we have seen the end!—Pardon an old man's freedom, when he bids you lift your thoughts to a better!"

The Baron looked in silence on his venerable friend. He had faith; but the habits of his mind were not those of devotion; and the sentiment that impressed, overawed him.

"A soldier," continued the Prior, "should not, methinks, quit the abbey without visiting the tomb of a soldier. It is not yet so dark but we may take a cursory view of it. Come a little to the left; and be not afraid of passing through the low arch, which, I observe, however, wears a more threatening appearance than when I saw it last. This recess was formerly a chapel dedicated to the blessed Virgin, and once contained a tomb of black marble, of which we have a very singular tradition lodged in the records of the convent. The chapel, though frequently rebuilt, is now again in ruins. Of the tomb, all vestiges have long since vanished; but, as the site is ascertained, it doubtless stood opposite that you now look at."

"And to whom was *that* inscribed?" said the Baron.

"It is rather the memorial of a family, than an individual," replied the Prior. "The illustrious house, that, from the thirteenth to the sixteenth century, bore the titles and honours of St. Aubert,[1] owed much of its distinction to a young man, whose valour and fidelity are here commemorated."

As he spoke, the Baron, who at the first glance had seen nothing to attract his attention but mutilated figures, drew near, and began to examine more curiously.

"Lothaire," continued the Prior, "was the trusty and well-beloved page of Louis IX.[2] The dangers that pious monarch encountered before he was taken prisoner by the Infidels at Damietta, you will see rudely delineated in the *relievo*[3] that time has yet spared. The twilight is rather unfavourable, but I believe you will have no great difficulty in distinguishing knights, horses, and all the *insignia* of a battle. Here you plainly perceive the red-cross shield—and here, the lilies of France triumphant over the prostrate crescent.[4] It should seem that our national characteristic has been the same in all ages," added he, smiling; "for the sculptor has taken more pleasure in describing the monarch's first victorious sallies, than his subsequent defeat: that was probably represented on the other side, though now wholly defaced. Were I to choose my time and place for re-counting to you the legend annexed to the name of Lothaire, it should be by this very light, and on this very spot. But the brave are generally superstitious, and I should be sorry to cast a shade over the valour of a soldier. Or, to speak seriously, my good friend, I begin already to feel the cold and damp air incident to the building. Let us, therefore, put up a short prayer to the Virgin, for the souls of the deceased, and get home." The convent-bell, for evening service, chimed as he spoke. The Baron started, and thoughtfully followed his friend along the aisles of the abbey.

A blazing fire, some light wines, and a plentiful, though simple, repast, soon restored their natural warmth to the limbs of the good Prior. His conversation, which, while it breathed sincere piety, partook of the cheerfulness that is generally its companion, would doubtless have entertained the Baron, had not the mind of the latter been otherwise engrossed. His friend, at length, perceived that he was unusually silent, and began to rally him on the subject.

"Blame yourself, Monsieur *le Prieur*," said the Baron smiling. "In the world we meet with so little that is not in the beaten track, that our very ideas seem mechanical. In getting out of it, with folks like you, we blunder upon a new one now and then; and nothing makes a man worse company than being in love with his own

---

[1] the surname of Emily, heroine of Radcliffe's* *The Mysteries of Udolpho*.

[2] St. Louis (1214–70).

[3] a relief sculpture, one carved on the side of the tomb.

[4] The red cross is a symbol of Christianity; lilies, of France; the crescent, of Islam.

thoughts."

"And whither may yours now be wandering?"

"A long pilgrimage, I assure you! Beyond the limits of Christendom!—In plain terms, I have had nothing before my eyes but knights, and bloody banners, since we left the abbey. Tell me somewhat more of the family of St. Aubert."

"That it flourished till the sixteenth century, I have already told you," said the Prior: "its last representative, on whose tomb you saw commemorated the actions of his predecessors, was, like them, a soldier; and, doubtless, a brave one!—He perished young, at the battle of Pavia;[1] and it was in consequence of his donation, for he was childless, that the abbey was founded. It was raised on the very spot on which the family château had long stood. Time had rendered the château itself little better than a ruin; but the gratitude of the church took that method of consecrating its memory. The chapel of the Virgin adjoined to the house: it then became a part of the abbey, and was long an object of peculiar veneration, as well for the legend annexed to it, as for containing the monument of the founder. The legend itself I can show you," said he, opening his small, but neat, library: "it is curious for its antiquity; though I will not pledge my faith for it in any other light." The Baron, who saw several small rolls of vellum, or parchment, covered with black characters,[2] that appeared to him wholly unintelligible, looked at it with an air of surprise and disappointment, that made the other smile.

"You, my good friend, should have lived in the age of the *Troubadours* and *Jongleurs*,"[3] said the Prior, "by the curiosity you seem to feel for our *preux Chevaliers*.[4] However, if it was not so near the hour of rest, I could easily gratify it. What I am now displaying is as unintelligible to me as to you; and, though it has been carefully preserved, is worm-eaten, and imperfect; as you will perceive in the very first pages. The language has been modernised, however, in every succeeding century, down to the present. One of our order has constantly undertaken the office, which I am myself now performing. You have here," continued he, opening another drawer, "both my copy and that of my predecessor. Mine is yet imperfect; but to-morrow you may read either at your leisure; and compare them, if you will, with the original."

"I had rather read one of them to-night," interrupted the Baron.

"It will be time ill spent!"

"It will be curiosity gratified."

The good Prior was not without a certain share of superstition. He looked at the old-fashioned dial that stood over the chimney, and perceived the hand already pointed towards midnight.

"You may repent!" said he mysteriously, and after a pause.

"At my peril," returned the other, possessing himself of the papers, and drawing his chair nearer the fire. The Prior again remonstrated—the Baron was obstinate; and, like most obstinate people, gained his point. On finding himself alone, he threw fresh wood on the fire, snuffed the candles, and, having made his little establishment, prepared, amidst the profound stillness of the convent, to examine the manuscripts. Here, however, imagination was soon bewildered, and memory confused. The scroll that fell under his hand had not yet been modernised by his friend; and, if not wholly unintelligible, yet quickly defied his patience in a regular perusal. In the second he was not more lucky: but, though the Baron was no scholar, he was a man both of valour and birth. The arms of France, curiously blazoned according to the fashion of the times, attracted his eyes in the first scroll; and, from examining those, with other rich and singular devices that adorned it, he insensibly learned that it was a testimonial of knighthood, bestowed by the King, while prisoner within the walls of Cairo, upon one of his followers.

The second was more interesting: it contained a minute detail of all the ceremonies of a single combat, in which honour and fortune were the stake, and death the sole admitted umpire. It was sanctioned by the Queen Dowager, regent of the kingdom, and held by her in

---

[1] At the battle of Pavia (1525), Francis I, king of France, was defeated and taken prisoner by Charles V, emperor of the Holy Roman Empire.

[2] Gothic script.

[3] Troubadours were aristocratic poets and composers of medieval Provence; jongleurs were lower-ranked performers.

[4] "gallant knights" (Fr.).

person, in the name of "the most puissant and sovereign lord, Louis IX."

To the victor, or the vanquished, the Baron was indifferent; but his imagination insensibly grew heated,

"As lengths of far-fam'd ages rolled away
In unsubstantial images of air";[1]

and, while reading the long catalogue of illustrious names, he seemed indeed to behold—

"The melancholy ghosts of dead renown,
With penitential aspect, as they pass'd,
All point at earth, and smile at human pride."[2]

A superstitious veneration crept over his frame; and, breaking abruptly from papers which he could but half decipher, he entered at once upon those of his friend.

The Prior's Manuscript

——The King, whose great heart swelled within him as his page continued to speak, was some moments ere he could reply.

"Brave Lothaire!" said he at length, "hast thou well weighed the perils of the enterprise thou wouldst undertake? Nay, more—examine thy bosom, and tell me whether thou hast also weighed the uncertainty of the event. To the soldier who falls in battle for his prince, a wreath of glory is indeed allotted; but to the solitary and devoted heart, that bleeds in secret for his friend, where shall be the recompense?"

"It will be found in that heart," eagerly replied Lothaire. "Oh that mine were at this moment laid bare before its sovereign, that he might know how deeply he penetrated it, when he bestowed the sacred name of friend!"

"Generous youth!" said Louis, with emotion; "the prince is but too fortunate who can substitute that term for the less valuable one of subject. But let us wave a discourse that presses so painfully upon my feelings. In me thou no longer beholdest the monarch of a generous and a loyal nation; but a captive, betrayed by his flatterers, and oppressed by his enemies: one on whom the wrath of Heaven has been poured, doubtless for his own crimes or those of his ancestors.[3] Explain to me, however, more at full, the means by which thou wouldst return to France; and, should a miraculous interposition conduct thee thither, (and surely little less than a miraculous interposition *can* do it,) fear not but our mother[4] will supply such forces and such treasures as may at once facilitate our ransom, and extend the arm of justice over those recreants, whom we suspect so basely to have betrayed the cause of Christendom."

Lothaire, who in various sallies had acquired a superior knowledge of the country through which he must necessarily pass, now imparted his scheme at full length to the King, and again earnestly supplicated him to rely on the zeal and ingenuity of the commander of the galley.

Louis still hesitated. That pious prince, daring and intrepid in his own person, yet knew how to fear for his friends: but, as destruction pressed closely, not only on himself, but on that part of the flower of his army whose lives the avarice of the infidels induced them yet to spare, the monarch subdued the feelings of the man, and he consented that his young favourite should depart.

The evening of the ensuing day was fixed upon for the execution of the plan.—"Yet ere thou goest," said the King, "let us complete those ceremonies, that alone can entitle thee to enter the lists against our proudest vassals; and may He whose cross we bear prosper thy arms in the service of thy country and thy king!" That night, like the preceding ones, was spent in vigils and in prayer; and, after the solemn observance of such rites as the time and place admitted, Lothaire received from the sword of the brave Louis the honours and the claims of knighthood. Testimonials of this, together with the secret mandate and instructions of the King, and a small quantity of gold, he carefully concealed in his garments. The darkness of the season favoured his flight; and,

---

[1] Cf. Edward Young (1683–1765), *Night Thoughts* (1742–45) 9.116–18.

[2] Cf. Young, *Night Thoughts* 9.119–22.

[3] In 1250, while on crusade, Louis was defeated and captured in Egypt. He was ransomed but did not return to France until 1254. (He died in Tunisia, on another crusade, in 1270.)

[4] Blanche of Castile (1185?–1252), who served as regent during Louis's minority, and again after his departure on his crusade.

committing himself to the fidelity of the Arab,[1] paddling by night down the Nile, and concealed among its reeds by day, after hazards and hardships innumerable, he at length found himself on board the Christian galley.

The commander instantly crowded sail, and favourable winds seemed for some time to promise them a speedy navigation—but the face of the heavens suddenly changed. The weather grew lowering and tempestuous—black and accumulating vapours obscured the sun, and the sea assumed its most threatening aspect. A heavy gale succeeded; and, as they drove before it, the sharp promontories and rocky shores of Greece menaced the vessel hourly with destruction. After having escaped this danger, another still more formidable seemed to present itself: for the sailors, most of them French, and desirous to return to their native country, dreaded, above all other evils, that of being thrown upon the coast of Africa, where certain captivity or death awaited them.— Eager to run the ship into any port of Sicily or Italy, they found themselves, with rapture, in sight of the latter—the rude and barren shore was pronounced by some of the most experienced to be part of the coast of Calabria.[2] Vainly did the master remonstrate on the danger of approaching it; his authority was drowned in their clamour: and while their shouts yet rent the air, the vessel struck upon a rock, and was soon discovered to admit the water with irresistible rapidity. Those who before had hoped, now abandoned every care but that of life: and Lothaire, who perceived that the boat they had hoisted out must quickly sink, with the numbers that crowded into her, hastily threw off his garments, and, binding them in a small parcel round his head, plunged fearlessly into the waves.

Vigorous in health and youth, to him the water had long been an element almost as familiar and as natural as air; the storm had considerably abated, though the sea yet ran high. Often repelled, bruised, and disappointed in his efforts, he nevertheless made good his landing; and breathing a sigh of commiseration for his companions, whom he perceived driven down the coast, and nearly out of sight, he directed his eyes from them to the trackless and wild solitude that surrounded him. It was, indeed, a cheerless horizon, in which no traces of human habitation, food or succour, were to be discerned; yet nature loudly demanded all; and he continued to walk in search of them till the storm, which had been for some hours suspended, once more began to brood. The sultry atmosphere grew heavy and lurid around, forked lightning broke over the sea, and low reverberations of deep and distant thunder were heard from the hills. A rocky hollow in the bosom of one of them offered him temporary shelter: hastily he entered it; and, as his feet were blistered, and his strength exhausted, gladly accepted that repose which a bank of earth at the extremity seemed to promise; throwing from him, without examination, some hard substance that incommoded him as he fell.

The tumultuous winds, that shook the very bosom of nature, at length slowly died away; and profound slumber began to seal up the eyes of Lothaire, when a wild and fearful vision, that seemed to pass like supernatural influence across his senses, at once unclosed them. Starting, he found his pulse beat high, his lips dry and clammy, and his whole frame suffused with a cold dew, that denoted internal convulsion. Instinctively grasping his dagger, he half-raised himself, and looked round the cavern: the light, though imperfect, was yet sufficient to convince him, that nothing *human* was within it but himself. He listened—no sound, no motion, was to be distinguished, save the low and monotonous roaring of the waves, as they broke upon the distant beach.

Lothaire was unaccustomed to fear. With disdain he now repelled the involuntary sensation, and earnestly directed his attention to recall the imperfect ideas that had escaped him ere he well awoke. But the mysterious visitation was past; and, as all desire to sleep had vanished with it, he arose, and advanced towards the mouth of the cave, where the returning sun now shot a bright and slanting ray. On approaching it, he perceived his garments to be spotted in many places with a dusky red; which, as it easily shook off, he concluded to be the soil of the country, that had been attracted only by the damp: a nearer examination, however, discovered to him that it was tufts of human hair, adhering together with

---

[1] The hospitality of Arabs was proverbial; cf. Byron, *Don Juan* 2.196.*

[2] a region in the South of Italy—the toe of the boot.

a substance, which, though it pulverised at his touch, he had no difficulty to assure himself had been blood.

Impelled by curiosity, he drew his poniard and re-entered the cave; searching every corner of it, to discover whether, by an outlet yet unobserved, some being had not obtruded upon his repose. His search, however, was fruitless. In returning, he mused for a moment over the bank of earth—it did not appear to have been lately thrown up; but it struck him to be just the length of a human figure, and he wondered he had not before observed that he must have slept upon a grave. A waking dream of horror, not unlike that which had disturbed his sleep, seemed to shiver his senses; and in turning from the spot, something like reality assailed them, as he struck his foot against the same hard substance that he had before thrown from him, and, on picking it up, perceived that it was the handle of a battle-axe, from which time or violence had loosened the steel.—Abruptly he quitted the cavern, and its gloomy environs; directing his course, as night drew on, by the stars; and listening in every gale for the sound of some distant bell, that might guide him to a monastery; his only hope of relief amidst the solitude with which he was surrounded. As the east reddened before him, he perceived it to be stained with rising smoke. Eagerly he directed his steps towards the spot; but, though he exerted all the speed that fatigue would allow, it was yet some time ere he reached it. He found traces of a fire that had been kindled on the turf, probably to prepare a rustic repast; but the persons who had partaken of it were gone; and the heart of Lothaire sunk beneath the prospect of an evil, from which, he had reason to fear, no exertion of courage or fortitude could rescue him. Pensively he continued to gaze, when his eye suddenly rested on a small bag left on the ground through negligence or haste, and which had the appearance of containing the provisions of a hunter. He opened it, and saw that he was not deceived: the scanty store it held afforded indeed no gratification to luxury; but a pious and abstemious spirit taught him to discern in the gift the hand of a supreme Giver, who thus indeed protected the absent monarch in the person of his knight.[1]

With invigorated spirits he now continued his journey. The road as he advanced grew more wild, and sometimes almost impervious, so that it was difficult to know what direction he pursued. Forcing his way, however, through every obstacle, he flattered himself that he had proceeded many leagues to the north; when on the sunset of the second day he suddenly emerged from a glen into the bosom of a rocky valley, and, looking round, perceived with astonishment that he had only taken a wearisome circuit, which had brought him once more within sight of the detestable cavern. He stopped with an emotion of anger and regret, when his eyes were struck for the first time with the appearance of a human being in this vast solitude.

On a low stone, not many yards distant from the mouth of the cave, sat a monk. His hood fell over his head, which inclined pensively downwards; his arms rested on his knees, and his hands were clasped, in the attitude of one who meditates deeply. A bold point of rock projected above him, and the wild and tangled branches that hung from it cast a sombre shade over the spot.

Lothaire advanced. At the sound of his footsteps the monk gently raised his head, and civilly, though solemnly, returned his greeting. His accent denoted him to be French; and from the little that escaped him, Lothaire learned that he was, like himself, a wanderer, travelling homewards, in order to lay his bones in their native earth.

They continued to journey on together. The religieux[2] seemed perfectly acquainted with the country, and often, by leading his companion through narrow and obscure passes, spared him the fatigue that must otherwise have been encountered. The suspicion which his appearance, and the reserve of his manners, first excited in Lothaire, insensibly died away as he perceived neither treachery nor ambush. To open violence, as man to man, he could not but be indifferent, as he was himself armed with a powerful and massy poniard, as well as with a short dagger, which he wore concealed in his bosom. The monk, on the contrary, *appeared* to have no weapon: yet his close-drawn garments gave a mysteri-

---

[1] Cf. M.W. Shelley,* *Frankenstein* (1818) 3.7.

[2] "monk" (Fr.).

ous air to his person and deportment. But though distrust subsided, there were some strange peculiarities observable in the conduct of the latter, that involuntarily tinctured the mind of his companion with suspicious and black ideas. No excess of fasting, no extremity of fatigue, ever induced him to partake of the food, however simple, bestowed by the charity of the good Christians they encountered; but, plunging daily into some thicket, he found his whole sustenance in water and berries: the rudest crag, always two or three hundred paces distant, served him to repose upon; and Lothaire often dwelt with secret and inexplicable horror on the extent of crimes that could demand a penance so severe. It was at those moments that the recollection of the cavern in Calabria obtruded itself upon him; till, by much thinking, the ideas became intimately connected, and he rarely fixed his eyes on his fellow-traveller without feeling a succession of gloomy and indefinable images float before his fancy.

They now once more beheld the broad bosom of the ocean, and approaching a small port, still within the Neapolitan territories, where lay a few trading vessels, one of which bore the French flag, Lothaire, with a portion of the gold which he had treasured in his garments, easily obtained a passage for himself and his companion.

The gay and pleasant shores of Provence, as they saluted his eyes, conveyed an enlivening sensation to his heart. Already in imagination he beheld the magnanimous, and still beautiful, *Blanche of Castile*, grasping with steady hand the reins of empire during the absence of her son. He revolved carefully in his mind all the instructions of the King, and the names of those knights, or barons, whom he had a discretional power to challenge as disloyal. He recollected with exultation the honour so lately conferred upon him, at an age yet immature; and when he considered himself as the champion of the cross, and the avenger of his prince, his young heart beat proudly with valour and with hope.

The turrets of a magnificent castle, visible at the distance of some leagues, now attracted his eyes; and the gallant name of St. Aubert assured him of hospitality within its walls. The sun was yet blazing in the meridian; but Lothaire, forgetful of its scorching influence, continued for some hours to press forward.

"We will rest here," said the monk, as they skirted the side of a thick wood. "For thee, who art vested with the mission of thy God and King, repose will be necessary. Well thus far, brave Lothaire, hast thou performed thy task. *Be constant, and be valiant!*"

Lothaire, whose mind was pre-occupied, and whose spirits were already enlivened, without attending minutely to the personal knowledge of him, implied in the words of his companion, readily assented to his proposal; and, throwing himself on the turf, indulged a pleasing reverie; which, lulling his senses, at length sealed up his eyes.

His slumbers were long and balmy; and when he awoke he was surprised to find that day was wholly closed. He started up, and looked around. The moon in full splendour silvered the wood on one side, while, on the other, the towers of the castle, gaily and superbly illuminated, blazed their friendly invitation to the forlorn and houseless stranger. Lothaire cast his eyes about in search of his fellow-traveller, who in yet unbroken slumbers lay stretched at the foot of a large oak. In the moment of advancing to wake him, he was suddenly urged by a secret, and irresistible curiosity, to lift the mantle and the cowl, in order to view the features and person of one, whom, during their long intercourse, he had never yet distinctly seen—nor ever *distinctly was* to see:—the garments covered only a human skeleton. He started back— suspended for some instants between incredulity and horror; then, with curious eye surveyed the dry and mouldering frame, till he was fully convinced all vital moisture had long since escaped; and while deeply considering the intents of Providence in this miraculous intervention, it suddenly occurred to him that the monk, at their first meeting, had announced an intention to lay his bones in the bosom of his native land.

With grateful and pious awe, Lothaire proceeded to fulfil this ceremony, in which the strong poniard he was provided with assisted him. In the act of interment he had occasion particularly to notice the skull, which he discerned to have been cleft in many places by some violent weapon; and where it had entered deepest, it had carried with it tufts of hair, resembling in colour that which had formerly adhered to his garments in the cave.

The gay spirits of Lothaire had now received a sudden revulsion; and, as he pensively advanced towards the castle, he continued to meditate upon the strange concurrence of events by which he had been hitherto pursued.

The gates readily opened to receive him. To Lothaire the lord of St. Aubert was personally unknown; but he found him a man yet unbroken by years, of a gay and graceful demeanour, and who, to the valour by which he was reported to have distinguished himself amidst the crusaders, added the courtesy of a true and loyal knight. A slender repast was immediately served; after which they conversed familiarly together; and the mind of Lothaire, which at first had been thoughtful and abstracted, insensibly opened itself to the pleasures of society.

It was already late, when a sprightly strain of music resounded through the castle. St. Aubert, starting up, motioned to his guest to follow, and the attendants at the same moment threw open the doors of a magnificent saloon, of which the sparkling and brilliant appearance fixed the eyes of the young knight, while the superb banquet he saw prepared in the apartment beyond filled him with an astonishment he attempted not to conceal.

"You are deceived," said St. Aubert with a smile, "if you suppose our evening was to conclude with the sober cheer of which you have already partaken! It is not thus I am accustomed to treat my guests: neither, to say truth, am I inclined so poorly to treat myself."

Lothaire quickly perceived his host to be sincere; and that whatever pleasure he might find in exercising the rites of hospitality, the enjoyments of the table in his own person were no inconsiderable addition to it.

But though art and expense had been lavished to produce gaiety, they seemed unhappily to fail of their effect. As the hours wore on, the spirits of St. Aubert visibly flagged; the most animating strains of music were lost upon his ear, and the richest viands upon his taste. His conversation, though broken into snatches of artificial merriment, was yet cold and disjointed: and Lothaire, who began to conclude that he entertained a secret weariness which complaisance did not permit him to show, at length proposed retiring.

Two attendants conducted him through a range of superb apartments; but he started on perceiving the magnificence of that intended for his repose.

"Thy lord," said he, turning to one of the domestics, "has mistaken the rank of the guest whom he thus honours. Accommodation so splendid I know not that I should desire were I a prince—as a soldier, I must be permitted to decline it."

"The apartment you behold," said the man respectfully, "is indeed the best in the castle:—it is invariably allotted by my lord to every guest: he is himself contented with a more humble one."

Lothaire, whose pure and temperate habits made him look on luxury with disgust, again remonstrated; but, as the domestic seemed earnest in his answers, he waved further debate; and taking from him a small lamp, which he placed upon a marble table, he closed the door.

Night was far advanced, and the fatigued traveller had no difficulty to believe that he should sleep. Hastily he threw himself into bed, and had already slept some hours, when he suddenly started with the same horrible impression that had visited him in the cavern of Calabria. A phantom, of which he could ascertain no form, no feature, no distinct outline, seemed again to shiver his senses, and unnerve his frame: vainly he strove to recollect it;—vainly he cast his eyes around the wide and solitary chamber, feebly illuminated by a lamp: they presented him nothing but vacuity and gloom, and with disdain he perceived an unusual pulsation continue to beat through his veins. With the first beams of the sun he arose, and descended. His host, with a smiling countenance, already attended his coming: and as they walked together on the ramparts of the castle, the dreams of weakness and superstition fled before the gallant themes that engrossed them; while the soft breath of morning, the bright sparkling of the dew, and the song of the birds, combined to call forth every energy of mind and constitution.

The character of the lord of St. Aubert, sprightly, bold, and ardent, embellished by the acquirements of society, and enlivened by its enjoyments, contrasted with the unassuming and simple dignity of Lothaire, produced an effect that was altogether new, and gratifying to both. Familiar with courts, as well as camps, St.

Aubert spoke with energy and information upon either. Lothaire listened with interest; nor was it till the moments of confidence and enthusiasm were past, that he perceived he had inadvertently intrusted to his host some of those secrets which the prudence of his prince had recommended to the sanctuary of his own bosom. Aware of indiscretion, though fearless of any ill effects from it, save that of being urged to further communication, he now prepared for his departure: but St. Aubert, who seemed to have found in his young guest that charm which original and simple manners ever diffuse, so strenuously urged his stay, that he found himself, for the first time, entangled by courtesies he was yet too young in life boldly to reject; and, if to reject them had been in his will, yet was it not in his power to deny the arguments by which they were enforced. But though it was true that hardships and fatigue had made some alteration in his person, he felt a secret confusion on recollecting that the rose of health had faded less from the actual sufferings he had encountered, than from the pressure of a silent and superstitious weight within.

"The repose to which you invite me," said he thoughtfully, and after a pause, "I might, perhaps, be tempted to indulge in—could I find it." The Baron stopped, and looked earnestly at him.

"Your surprise is just," continued Lothaire with the same unaffected candour. "You will, perhaps, mingle with it somewhat of that contempt which arises in my own bosom, when I add, that the soldier of his king, though fearless in the field, is yet a coward in his dreams." He then related the extraordinary impression which his fancy had received from the vision of the preceding night, and his fruitless efforts to ascertain its nature.

St. Aubert, whose curiosity had been awakened by the opening of his discourse, listened to its conclusion with a smiling and incredulous air.

"An accidental malady of constitution!" said he as it finished.—"Fancies like these, brave Lothaire, engendered by much thinking and fatigue, good cheer and ease alone can remedy."

"On the effects of fatigue," said Lothaire, "I will not pronounce: but, trust me, this supernatural visitation (for such I cannot but term it) has no connection with previous thought; and I will frankly own that the internal conviction of my soul denies it to be chance. Once, and once only, in a cavern of Calabria——" He stopped; for St. Aubert, who, while earnestly listening, had walked too near the edge of the rampart, was seized with dizziness; and, but for the timely assistance of his companion, would suddenly have plunged over the low parapet, perhaps into eternity. Lothaire abruptly seized him by the arm, and perceiving, by the paleness of his countenance, that he was extremely ill, signed to a sentinel, who instantly quitted his post to give assistance to his lord. The temporary malady was soon subdued. The pleasures of the table once more invited; and Lothaire was not proof against solicitation, enforced by raillery, that piqued at once his courage and his pride. The recital he was about to make remained unfinished, and the rest of the day was passed in a festivity that was yet only preparatory to that of the evening; when the gaily illuminated rooms, the superb banquet, and the sprightly band, were again called in, as auxiliaries to pleasure. Lothaire, however, no longer beheld them as such. In the countenance of St. Aubert he thought he discerned something watchful and sinister. While reposing in the bosom of luxury, he treated the ministers of his amusement with the fierceness and petulance of a man who is ill at peace with himself. The domestics, on their part, had an air of servility and constraint. The eyes of one of them, like those of a picture, were constantly upon Lothaire; and the latter became convinced, from all he observed, that it is possible to bask in the full blaze of prosperity without receiving warmth from the ray.

While plunged, he hardly knew why, in a train of *sombre* and unpleasant recollections, the hours wore fast away, and he retired, as before, to his spacious and princely chamber; where, banishing every idea that should impede his rest, he threw himself into bed—again to start from it with horror and aversion. Instinctively, as before in the cavern, he grasped his poniard with a recollection of some confused sound, that jarred upon his ear, and seemed to die away with his awakening faculties. The night had been rough and stormy; and, as the lamp swayed with the blast, its wavering and uncertain blaze gave temporary light and animation to the figures wrought on the tapestry. He fixed his eyes earnestly upon them, and smiled on finding he could almost persuade himself they moved. While continuing to pause and meditate, he heard the tinkling of a bell, as it was borne strongly to him upon the wind; and, rising, perceived that, though the morning was gloomy and overcast, it was already the grey dawn. The bell he discerned to be that of the chapel belonging to the castle, which rang for the first mass; and in the bosom of that Redeemer whose cause he served, Lothaire resolved to seek the firmness which no mortal effort seemed able to bestow.

Rising, he explored his way to a chapel dedicated to the Virgin.[1] It was yet obscurely lighted by the growing beams of the morning, while the few old domestics whom devotion had collected were shivering in its raw and autumnal air. Lothaire threw himself at the foot of the altar, and silently invoked the Deity, either to illuminate his mind with some great and useful truth, or to banish from it the visions by which it was distempered.

He arose refreshed, invigorated, purified. Such is the sacred force of prayer!—The light was now clearer; and curiosity directed his eyes round the chapel, which was magnificently decorated. They rested, with singular exultation, upon the spoils torn from the Infidels by the valour of the house of St. Aubert; and while the image of his king and suffering fellow-soldiers pressed upon his memory, he did not immediately notice the monument those banners seemed to consecrate. It was of black marble.

The art of the sculptor had displayed itself in emblematical and warlike ornaments. The helm, the corslet, and the spear, curiously carved and intermingled, appeared grouped behind the half-recumbent shield, of which Lothaire drew near to examine the device:—

"*Valiant and constant!*"

He started as though one had spoken to him from the grave; and involuntarily casting his eyes towards heaven, the beams of the morning, at the same moment, broke full upon them, through a rich window of stained glass above the tomb, where heraldry, yet in its infancy, was blended with the figures of saints and martyrs.—"Valiant and constant!" exclaimed he aloud, as the oft-repeated words appeared inscribed amidst the armorial bearings in various hues and in various directions.

"It was the chosen device of my late lord," said a silver-headed domestic who stood near.

"He perished in the field?" cried Lothaire with a tone of eager inquiry.

"Alas, no! he was not so fortunate. He died of a fever."

"Within the castle walls?"

"Beyond sea—in Italy. But, blessed be God! he wanted not succour. His kinsman, our present lord, and Bertram, both were with him."

Lothaire grew pale; but the garrulous old man perceived it not. He continued to recount various marvellous tales with which his memory was stored, concerning the wars in Palestine, till the luckless hour when the two noble kinsmen, the Lord of St. Aubert, and Sir Hugh de Mercie, thrown by shipwreck on a barbarous coast, had traversed the greatest part of Italy, *concealing their arms under the habits of religieux.* "There," added the old man, "hangs the trophy of our present lord: he offered it to our patron saint immediately on his return."

"The armour is perfect," said Lothaire, considering it—"save that I see no weapon."

"My lord had none," said a voice on the other side.

"No, surely, Bertram," added the first speaker, "or, doubtless, he would have offered it with the rest."

"Thy lord would, methinks, have found little security in his armour," continued Lothaire, still musing, "without some instrument of defence."

"He had a battle-axe," said the same voice; "but it was lost as we journeyed through Calabria."

Lothaire now started in despite of caution, and fixed his attention to the speaker: his eye told him it was the same man whose gaze before oppressed him. His other senses carried conviction to his heart that it was Bertram, and perhaps a murderer. In throwing himself before the altar of the Supreme Being, he had at length, then, touched the point of truth; since hardly could the immediate voice of Heaven have announced more forcibly the guilt of St. Aubert. Recollection, too, now

---

[1] the chapel in which the baron will be shown Lothaire's family tomb.

told him that the man to whom, under the security of that favoured and gallant name, he had intrusted the secrets of his sovereign, by the appellation of Sir Hugh de Mercie, stood foremost in the list of suspected treason and disloyalty.

Slowly, and wrapped in thought, he returned to the castle. As he passed, the noise of workmen busied in repairs roused his attention. His eye silently rested on the scene—the height of the walls, the well-provided state of the ramparts, and the labour he saw evidently bestowed to render both perfect wherever time or accident had introduced decay, discovered at once, to his now enlightened judgment, a powerful vassal, more ready to dispute than to obey the mandate of his sovereign.

To dissemble was a science new to Lothaire: he strove, however, to smooth his brow, and calmly announced to his host the necessity of his immediate departure.

The courtesy of St. Aubert, not yet exhausted, however, furnished him with various and plausible reasons by which to urge a further stay. The country around, often pillaged by freebooters, who, during the absence of their monarch, acknowledged no law but violence, was now, he assured his guest, particularly dangerous.

"Let us, then, devote this night," added he, "to mirth. Fear no ill dreams! I will promise you a sweet and sound repose, and a guard, ere the morrow, that shall safely guide you to your journey's end."

Lothaire became now sensible that he was taken in the toils; and that to depart against the consent of his host was as difficult as to obtain it. Too late did he regret having so indiscreetly confided the important trust he was invested with; and too evidently perceive he risked both that and life, if he betrayed the smallest suspicion.

Secretly resolving to quit the castle at the hour of morning prayer, as one in which his steps were unobserved, he consented to pass a third night within its hateful walls.

Night came; but brought with it no inclination to sleep. Disposed to find food for observation in every thing that presented itself, his eyes wandered, as he passed the gallery that led to his apartment, over the various portraits with which it was enriched. He stopped opposite a full length of the Lord of St. Aubert; but it was that next it which chiefly engaged his attention. He suspected it to be his kinsman, and found, on inquiry, that he was not mistaken. After long pausing on the features, he retired to his chamber, where, considering the bed, he found in himself an invincible repugnance to encounter again those feverish chimeras that had disturbed him. Thoughtfully he continued to walk about the room, though it was already late, till the most profound silence reigned throughout the castle. The very winds, which the night before had been so stormy, were sunk to stillness. All nature appeared to repose in the lap of midnight. Lulled by her influence, he had thrown himself into a chair, and the first dews of a beginning slumber were stealing over his senses.

"*Lothaire!*" said a piercing voice not far distant. Sleep fled before the sound. He raised his eyes; and, exactly opposite to him, not many yards removed, once more beheld the buried monk.

"Speak once again!" said the intrepid Lothaire, starting forward.

The phantom spoke not, however; but seemed slowly to retreat towards the extremity of the chamber, while, by a gentle motion of its head, the cowl fell backwards; and Lothaire perceived a countenance similar to that which he had seen in the picture, save that it was *very* pale, and "its bright hair dabbled in blood":[1] a groan at the same moment burst from the corner of the apartment; and Bertram, rushing from behind the tapestry, white with horror, and his eyes starting from their sockets, was at the feet of Lothaire.

"What brought thee hither? and of what art thou afraid?" said the latter, grasping him firmly with one hand, while his dagger was suspended over him with the other, and his looks earnestly, though incredulously, directed to the spot where the phantom had vanished.

"Do not *you* see him, then?" said Bertram, without venturing to look up.

"See whom?" repeated Lothaire.

"St. Aubert—my lord—my murdered lord!" again incoherently cried Bertram. "These were his apart-

---

[1] "Shakspeare." (H.L.) *Richard III* 1.4.53–54.

ments!—Oh God! I shall never forget him!—It was at the very moment when I was stepping forth to point my dagger at your throat——Doubtless you saw him before—*for you started in the same manner last night*!"

"Thou wert present, then, in the cave of Calabria?" said Lothaire, recollecting himself.

"Too surely I was," returned Bertram; "and so were God and his angels, or you would never have known it. All the reparation, however, I can make, I will. Your life is not safe here an hour, nor can you quit the castle without my aid. My lord knows that you bear about you papers of importance, which I was to have rifled from your bosom. He is aware that you will impeach him. He even suspects you of knowing all—though *how* he is at a loss to guess. You have here," he added, offering a small, but exquisitely tempered poinard, "my only weapon. Blessed be Heaven, it is not in your heart! But as you would shun destruction, fly ere it is daylight!"

Lothaire felt that the moment was critical. Taking, therefore, from his bosom a crucifix of peculiar sanctity which he had brought with him out of Egypt, he extorted from Bertram a hasty oath of fidelity; after which, trusting to Heaven, and his own native valour, he prepared to follow him.

His guide proved faithful; and, after winding through many obscure and subterraneous passages, they at length emerged to starlight and the open country.

Retracing, with rapid step, the path he had trod when advancing to the castle, he was soon several miles from it. Already he beheld the wood where he had reposed with his supernatural conductor; and the east, already flaming with the approach of the sun, looked red through the broad branches of the oak, at the foot of which he had interred the skeleton. Riveting his eyes upon it, and immersed in thought, Lothaire became insensible to every other recollection, when Bertram, who, as day advanced, had continued to look with increasing anxiety behind, suddenly exclaimed "that they were pursued." Lothaire paused to listen. Footsteps and voices struck at once upon his ear; and ere he had leisure to consider whence they might proceed, he found that he was deserted; for his companion, treacherous or cowardly, plunged into the wood, and was in a moment lost within its shades.

But Lothaire was not alone. Faith, innocence, and valour, at once asserted all their energies within him; and, grasping his poniard, he stood firm to abide the event.

The domestics of St. Aubert, who were now in full sight, paused as they beheld the countenance and attitude of the young man. But their zeal was presently enlivened, when their lord himself, advancing, reproached their tardy obedience, and commanded them to lay hands upon Lothaire.

"Ere you obey the mandate of a despot," said the latter, motioning them from him, "beware, my friends, of the event! You perceive I wear a dagger that may prove dangerous; but I have yet a surer and more inviolable guard than that. Which of you," he added, stripping away his upper garment, and displaying the badge of knighthood upon his shoulder, "which of you will dare to injure the champion of the cross?"[1]

"Rather say, the traitor who violates the rites of hospitality," said St. Aubert fiercely; "he who, conscious of guilt, meanly flies from the roof that has sheltered him."

"That I fled from *thy* roof to avoid assassination, is most true," said Lothaire calmly. "Happy would it have been if all on whom thou hast smiled with deceitful regard had been equally cautious. My *flight*, however, I presume thou wilt not term a crime—and of what other am I accused?"

"It is sufficient that I know thy guilt," replied St. Aubert, "and my vassals know my pleasure. If," added he, turning to the latter, whose countenances he perceived did not yield a ready assent to this decision—"if, on examining, ye find not that he bears, concealed in his garments, papers with which my confidence too readily intrusted him, and that touch the honour and fortunes of my house, I consent that he shall depart unmolested."

Lothaire at once perceived the snare into which his own indiscretion had betrayed him; and that St. Aubert, who well knew how to calculate the ignorance of his vassals, would, by a master-stroke, possess himself of the most confidential mandates of the King, while the mere sight of them, confirming his assertion, would enable

---

[1] "It was thus worn by the knights crusaders." (H.L.)

him to impose on the credulous vulgar any fiction by which he might be empowered to sacrifice the bearer. The perplexity that struck upon his mind became instantly visible in his countenance. The momentary change was mistaken for that of guilt; and those who before had favoured him, now prepared to strike the weapon from his hand.

"Let him be secured," said St. Aubert, who exultingly watched the moment of success; "and take from him papers whose import ought only to be known to myself."

Lothaire, with the most determined presence of mind, again stepped back.

"That which it most imports thee to know," said he, mysteriously, "I have buried at the foot of yonder oak. See you not, my friends," he added, pointing towards it, "that the earth has been newly turned?—Dig boldly, and I will abide by the event."

They waited no second mandate; but, impressed with the idea of some important discovery, each strove who should be foremost to show his alacrity. St. Aubert, meantime, who, though he expected not any fruit from their labour, had no ostensible motive for forbidding it, gazed on the spot with a sullen expression of disdain and incredulity; when suddenly the whole group fell back, and the criminal himself, thunderstruck with what he beheld, sunk pale and speechless into the arms of those nearest.

"Lord of St. Aubert!" said Lothaire, in a voice of thunder; "beneath that sacred garment thou seest the bones of thy kinsman and thy friend! Lay thine hand upon them, if thou darest, and swear, by every hope of salvation, that thou wert not his murderer!"

St. Aubert shrunk back—and as he fearfully raised his eyes to scan the impression of the scene on the bystanders, they encountered those of Bertram, whom his own servants had met with, and secured. The haggard, pale, and downcast look of the latter at once assured him that all was avowed.

In the tumult of his soul he advanced a few steps towards the skeleton; but when he would have touched it, nature prevailed, and he shrunk back.

"By what other test, than the hideous one thou hast proposed," said he, shuddering, "shall I assert my innocence?"

Lothaire was young in arms, and burnt to signalise himself.

"Swear to me," said he, after a pause, "upon the faith of a soldier and a knight, to abide my charge before our queen, in single combat. Let thy vassals be witness to the oath; and be they free to renounce or do thee wrong by night or day, in castle or in field, if thou neglect or violate thy plighted faith."

"*I swear!*" said St. Aubert, reluctantly, and not without indignation.

"Enough!" said Lothaire; "to God and my own right arm I trust the rest!"

The Baron, who had with difficulty kept awake so long over the extravagant story he had been reading, and who was already apprised of the event of a combat, which transferred to Lothaire the titles and honours of the vanquished St. Aubert, now found his curiosity yield to the lateness of the hour. He paused—leaned back in his easy chair—took a pinch of snuff, and determined to indulge himself with ruminating for a few moments. They were very few: for his eyes insensibly closed; he relaxed his hold—the manuscript dropped from his hand—and he fell into a profound sleep, from which he was roused—not by a ghost—but by a plump friar of the convent.

Ottobah Cugoano
c. 1757 – c. 1801

Ottobah Cugoano was born near what is now Adjumako, Ghana, in about 1757. In 1770, he was enslaved and taken to the West Indies. His master, Alexander Campbell, brought him to Britain in 1772. Campbell had changed his name to Stuart (it was usual to change slaves' names, to help obliterate their African identities); when Cugoano was baptized in 1773, he added the Christian name John. By the late 1780s, he was free, married to an English woman, and working as a personal servant for Richard Cosway, painter to the Prince of Wales. He was also in contact with Granville Sharp and other abolitionists, and in 1787 he published *Thoughts and Sentiments*, his contribution to the cause, pointedly using his African name. In a note to the (much shorter) second edition of the book in 1791, he announced his intention "*to open a* School, *for all such of his* Complexion *as are desirous of being acquainted with the Knowledge of the* Christian Religion *and the Laws of* Civilization." We do not know whether he succeeded in opening his school, or anything else about him. (D.L.M.)

☙☙☙

from *Thoughts and Sentiments on the Evil and Wicked Traffic of the Slavery and Commerce of the Human Species, Humbly Submitted to the Inhabitants of Great-Britain* (1787)

And now that blessings may come instead of a curse, and that many beneficent purposes of good might speedily arise and flow from it, and be more readily promoted: I would hereby presume to offer the following considerations, as some outlines of a general reformation which ought to be established and carried on. And first, I would propose, that there ought to be days of mourning and fasting appointed, to make enquiry into that great and pre-eminent evil for many years past carried on against the Heathen nations, and the horrible iniquity of making merchandize of us, and cruelly enslaving the poor Africans: and that you might seek grace and repentance, and find mercy and forgiveness before God Omnipotent; and that he may give you wisdom and understanding to devise what ought to be done.

Secondly, I would propose that a total abolition of slavery should be made and proclaimed; and that an universal emancipation of slaves should begin from the date thereof, and be carried on in the following manner: That a proclamation should be caused to be made, setting forth the Antichristian unlawfulness of the slavery and commerce of the human species; and that it should be sent to all the courts and nations in Europe, to require their advice and assistance, and as they may find it unlawful to carry it on, let them whosoever will join to prohibit it. And if such a proclamation be found advisable to the British legislature, let them publish it, and cause it to be published, throughout all the British empire, to hinder and prohibit all men under their government to traffic either in buying or selling men; and, to prevent it, a penalty might be made against it of one thousand pounds, for any man either to buy or sell another man. And that it should require all slave-holders, upon the immediate information thereof, to mitigate the labour of their slaves to that of a lawful servitude, without tortures or oppression; and that they should not hinder, but cause and procure some suitable means of instruction for them in the knowledge of the Christian religion. And agreeable to the late *royal Proclamation, for the Encouragement of Piety and Virtue, and for the preventing and punishing of Vice, Profaneness and Immorality*;[1] that by no means, under any pretence whatsoever, either for themselves or their masters, the slaves under their subjection should not be suffered to work on the Sabbath days, unless it be such

---

[1] Issued by George III on 1 June 1787, and promoted by the Proclamation Society, this proclamation was an important step in the development of Victorian values. William Wilberforce (1759–1833) was a member both of the Abolition Committee and of the Proclamation Society.

works as necessity and mercy may require. But that those days, as well as some other hours selected for the purpose, should be appropriated for the time of their instruction; and that if any of their owners should not provide such suitable instructors for them, that those slaves should be taken away from them and given to others who would maintain and instruct them for their labour. And that it should be made known to the slaves, that those who had been above seven years in the islands or elsewhere, if they had obtained any competent degree of knowledge of the Christian religion, and the laws of civilization, and had behaved themselves honestly and decently, that they should immediately become free; and that their owners should give them reasonable wages and maintenance for their labour, and not cause them to go away unless they could find some suitable employment elsewhere. And accordingly, from the date of their arrival to seven years, as they arrive at some suitable progress in knowledge, and behaved themselves honestly, that they should be getting free in the course of that time, and at the end of seven years to let every honest man and woman become free; for in the course of that time, they would have sufficiently paid their owners by their labour, both for their first purpose,[1] and for the expences attending their education. By being thus instructed in the course of seven years, they would become tractable and obedient, useful labourers, dutiful servants and good subjects; and Christian men might have the honor and happiness to see many of them vieing with themselves to praise the God of their salvation. And it might be another necessary duty for Christians, in the course of that time, to make enquiry concerning some of their friends and relations in Africa: and if they found any intelligent persons amongst them, to give them as good education as they could, and find out a way of recourse to their friends; that as soon as they had made any progress in useful learning and the knowledge of the Christian religion, they might be sent back to Africa, to be made useful there as soon, and as many of them as could be made fit for instructing others. The rest would become useful residentors in the colonies; where there might be employment enough given to all free people, with suitable wages according to their usefulness, in the improvement of land; and the more encouragement that could be given to agriculture, and every other branch of useful industry, would thereby encrease the number of the inhabitants; without which any country, however blessed by nature, must continue poor.

And, thirdly, I would propose, that a fleet of some ships of war should be immediately sent to the coast of Africa, and particularly where the slave trade is carried on, with faithful men to direct that none should be brought from the coast of Africa without their own consent and the approbation of their friends, and to intercept all merchant ships that were bringing them away, until such a scrutiny was made, whatever nation they belonged to. And, I would suppose, if Great-Britain was to do any thing of this kind, that it would meet with the general approbation and assistance of other Christian nations; but whether it did or not, it could be very lawfully done at all the British forts and settlements on the coast of Africa; and particular remonstrances could be given to all the rest, to warn them of the consequences of such an evil and enormous wicked traffic as is now carried on. The Dutch have some crocodile settlers at the Cape,[2] that should be called to a particular account for their murders and inhuman barbarities. But all the present governors of the British forts and factories[3] should be dismissed, and faithful and good men appointed in their room; and those forts and factories, which at present are a den of thieves, might be turned into shepherd's tents, and have good shepherds sent to call the flocks to feed beside them. Then would doors of hospitality in abundance be opened in Africa to supply the weary travellers, and that immense abundance which they are enriched with, might be diffused afar; but the character of the inhabitants on the west coast of Africa, and the rich produce of their country, have been too long misrepresented by avaricious plunderers and merchants who deal in slaves; and if that country was not annually ravished and laid waste, there might be a very considerable and profitable trade carried on with the Africans. And, should the noble Britons, who have often supported their own liberties with their

---

[1] possibly an error for "purchase."

[2] the Cape of Good Hope, now in South Africa.

[3] trading-posts.

lives and fortunes, extend their philanthropy to abolish the slavery and oppression of the Africans, they might have settlements and many kingdoms united in a friendly alliance with themselves, which might be made greatly to their own advantage, as well as they might have the happiness of being useful to promoting the prosperity and felicity of others, who have been cruelly injured and wrongfully dealt with. Were the Africans to be dealt with in a friendly manner, and kind instruction to be administered unto them, as by degrees they became to love learning, there would be nothing in their power, but what they would wish to render their service in return for the means of improving their understanding; and the present British factories, and other settlements, might be enlarged to a very great extent. And as Great-Britain has been remarkable for ages past, for encouraging arts and sciences, and may now be put in competition with any nation in the known world, if they would take compassion on the inhabitants of the coast of Guinea, and to make use of such means as would be needful to enlighten their minds in the knowledge of Christianity, their virtue, in this respect, would have its own reward. And as the Africans became refined and established in light and knowledge, they would imitate their noble British friends, to improve their lands, and make use of that industry as the nature of their country might require, and to supply those that would trade with them, with such productions as the nature of their climate would produce; and, in every respect, the fair Britons would have the preference with them to a very great extent; and, in another respect, they would become a kind of first ornament to Great-Britain for her tender and compassionate care of such a set of distressed poor ignorant people. And were the noble Britons, and their august Sovereign, to cause protection and encouragement to be given to those Africans, they might expect in a short time, if need required it, to receive from thence great supplies of men in a lawful way, either for industry or defence; and of other things in abundance, from so great a source, where every thing is luxurious and plenty, if not laid waste by barbarity and gross ignorance. Due encouragement being given to so great, so just, and such a noble undertaking, would soon bring more revenue in a righteous way to the British nation, than ten times its share in all the profits that slavery can produce;[1] and such a laudable example would inspire every generous and enterprizing mind to imitate so great and worthy a nation, for establishing religion, justice, and equity to the Africans, and, in doing this, would be held in the highest esteem by all men, and be admired by all the world.

---

[1] "A gentleman of my acquaintance told me that, if ever he hears tell of any thing of this kind taking place, he has a plan in contemplation, which would, in some equitable manner, produce from one million to fifteen millions sterling to the British government annually, as it might be required; of which a due proportion of that revenue would be paid by the Africans; and that it would prevent all smuggling and illicit traffic; in a great measure, prevent running into debt, long imprisonment, and all unlawful bankruptcies; effectually prevent all dishonesty and swindling, and almost put an end to all robbery, fraud and theft." (O.C.)

Mary Robinson
1758 – 1800

Mary Darby was born in Bristol in 1758, the daughter of John Darby, an American-born merchant, and Hester Seys. She attended the boarding school run by Hannah More's* sisters, where she developed interests in music and poetry. When she was nine, her father left home to establish a whale fishery in Labrador, taking his mistress with him.

This was the first of many family upheavals. When his business failed, John Darby returned to England and placed Mary first in Meribah Lorrington's school at Chelsea (which closed because of the owner's alcoholism), and then in a school in Battersea. She briefly taught grammar and literature to the younger girls at a boarding school established by her mother. Having closed down that school (as he had a right to do in spite of having left the marriage), John Darby sent Mary to a London finishing school. At age 15, already a frequent theatre-goer, she was introduced to the actor David Garrick, who encouraged her to go on the stage. However, in 1774, with her mother's encouragement, she married Thomas Robinson, who lied to her and her family about his background and prospects. Their daughter, Maria Elizabeth, was born the same year at Thomas Robinson's father's house in Wales, where the Robinsons were already hiding from creditors.

Robinson's *Poems* (1775) could not bring in enough money to keep the Robinsons out of debtor's prison. After almost ten months of imprisonment, Mary was rescued by Georgiana, Duchess of Devonshire, who invited her to stay at Devonshire House. When Thomas Robinson got out of prison five months later, the actor William Brereton introduced Mary to Richard Brinsley Sheridan, manager of the Theatre Royal, Drury Lane. Mary made her debut there in December 1776 as Juliet in *Romeo and Juliet*; she rapidly became a star. *Captivity, A Poem, and Celadon and Lydia, a Tale*, was published in 1777, dedicated to Robinson's patron the Duchess of Devonshire.

In 1778, Robinson gave birth to a second daughter, who died. Separated from her husband, Robinson entertained lavishly at her house near Covent Garden. In 1779 the seventeen-year-old Prince of Wales (later the Prince Regent and George IV) saw her as Perdita in *The Winter's Tale* and courted her as "Florizel." She agreed to meet him after receiving a bond for £20,000 payable on the prince's coming-of-age in 1783. In May 1780 she gave up acting to become the prince's acknowledged mistress—but the relationship lasted only until the end of the year. Robinson received £5000 for returning the prince's letters, and she gave up his bond in exchange for an annuity of £500 for herself and an additional £200 annuity for her daughter.

Robinson's portrait was painted by such famous artists as Gainsborough, Reynolds,* and Romney; her lovers included Lord Malden and possibly Charles James Fox. In 1782, she met Colonel Banastre Tarleton, a veteran of the American War of Independence, who seduced her to win a bet against Lord Malden. When Tarleton went to France to evade his debts in 1783, Robinson, pregnant again, followed him; but she went into labour on the Dover road, miscarried, and suffered permanent paralysis. Tarleton came back to her; but he continued to live extravagantly and to gamble: the couple was forced to live in France from 1784 to 1788.

Back in London, Robinson began a poetic correspondence with Robert Merry* ("Della Crusca") in the *World* (1788), signing her work "Laura" or "Laura Maria"; these poems were published under her own name in her *Poems* of 1791. Other work of this period included *Monody to the Memory of Sir Joshua Reynolds* (1792) and *Monody to the Memory of the Late Queen of France* (1793): Robinson's earlier enthusiasm for the French Revolution had been dampened by the execution of the King and Queen. Alternately separated from and reunited with Tarleton from 1791 to 1797, Robinson also turned to novel-writing, which was more lucrative than writing verse; her novels include *Vancenza; or the Dangers of Credulity* (1792), *Angelina* (1796) and *Walsingham; or, the Pupil of Nature* (1797). Her sonnet sequence *Sappho and Phaon* appeared in 1796.

Robinson and Tarleton separated for the last time in 1797; he had refused to assist her financially after inheriting his mother's money. When Tarleton married a young heiress the following year, Robinson exposed his betrayal in *The False Friend* (1799) and his new wife's illegitimacy in *The Natural Daughter* (1799). In *Thoughts on the Condition of Women, and On the Injustice of Mental Subordination* (1799), Robinson criticized marriage as an institution oppressive to women. Until the end of her life she published poems in the *Morning Post* under the pseudonyms Julia, Laura, Laura Maria, and Tabitha Bramble; she followed Southey* as poetry editor of the *Post* in 1799 and 1800. Her final book, *Lyrical Tales*, appeared just eight days before her death on 26 Dec. 1800. Her daughter completed and published (in 1801) the memoirs she left in draft. Robinson was buried at Old Windsor Churchyard. (A.M.)

❧❧❧

from *Poems* (1791)

Ode to Beauty[1]

Exulting BEAUTY,—phantom of an hour,
Whose magic spells enchain the heart,
Ah! what avails thy fascinating pow'r,
    Thy thrilling smile, thy witching art?
5   Thy lip, where balmy nectar glows;
      Thy cheek, where round the damask rose
    A thousand nameless Graces move,
    Thy mildly speaking azure eyes,
    Thy golden hair, where cunning Love
10   In many a mazy ringlet lies?
    Soon as thy radiant form is seen,
    Thy native blush, thy timid mien,
Thy hour is past! thy charms are vain!
ILL-NATURE haunts thee with her sallow train,
15 Mean JEALOUSY deceives thy list'ning ear,
And SLANDER stains thy cheek with many a bitter tear.

In calm retirement form'd to dwell,
    NATURE, thy handmaid fair and kind,
    For thee, a beauteous garland twin'd;
20 The vale-nurs'd Lily's downcast bell
    Thy modest mien display'd,
The snow-drop, April's meekest child,
    With myrtle blossoms undefil'd,
    Thy mild and spotless mind pourtray'd;
25 Dear blushing maid, of cottage birth,
    'Twas thine, o'er dewy meads to stray,

While sparkling health, and frolic mirth,
    Led on thy laughing Day.

Lur'd by the babbling tongue of FAME,
30 Too soon, insidious FLATT'RY came;
    Flush'd VANITY her footsteps led,
      To charm thee from thy blest repose,
    While Fashion twin'd about thy head
      A wreath of wounding woes;
35 See Dissipation smoothly glide,
Cold Apathy, and puny Pride,
Capricious Fortune, dull, and blind,
O'er splendid Folly throws her veil,
While Envy's meagre tribe assail
40 Thy gentle form, and spotless mind.

Their spells prevail! no more those eyes
    Shoot undulating fires;
On thy wan cheek, the young rose dies,
    Thy lip's deep tint expires;
45 Dark Melancholy chills thy mind;
    Thy silent tear reveals thy woe;
TIME strews with thorns thy mazy way,
Where'er thy giddy footsteps stray,
    Thy thoughtless heart is doom'd to find
50   An unrelenting foe.

'Tis thus, the infant Forest flow'r
    Bespangled o'er with glitt'ring dew,
    At breezy morn's refreshing hour,
    Glows with pure tints of varying hue,
55 Beneath an aged oak's wide spreading shade,
Where no rude winds, or beating storms invade.
    Transplanted from its lonely bed,

---

[1] first published in the *Oracle* (24 June 1789), signed "Laura Maria."

No more it scatters perfumes round,
No more it rears its gentle head,
   Or brightly paints the mossy ground;
For ah! the beauteous bud, too soon,
   Scorch'd by the burning eye of day;
Shrinks from the sultry glare of noon,
   Droops its enamell'd brow, and blushing, dies away.

from the *Morning Post* (29 January 1795)

January, 1795 [1]

1
Pavement slip'ry; People sneezing;
Lords in ermine, beggars freezing;
Nobles,[2] scarce the Wretched heeding;
Gallant Soldiers—fighting!—bleeding!

2
Lofty Mansions, warm and spacious;
Courtiers, cringing and voracious:
Titled Gluttons, dainties carving;
Genius, in a garret, starving!

3
Wives, who laugh at passive Spouses;
Theatres, and Meeting-houses;
Balls, where simpring Misses languish;
Hospitals, and groans of anguish.

4
Arts and Sciences bewailing;
Commerce drooping, Credit failing!
Placement, mocking subjects loyal;
Separations; Weddings Royal!

5
Authors, who can't earn a dinner;
Many a subtle rogue, a winner!
Fugitives, for shelter seeking,
Misers hoarding, Tradesmen breaking!

6
Ladies gambling, night and mornings;
Fools, the works of Genius scorning!
Ancient Dames for Girls mistaken,
Youthful Damsels—quite forsaken!

7
Some in luxury delighting;
More in talking than in fighting;
Lovers old, and Beaux decrepid;
Lordlings, empty and insipid.

8
Poets, Painters, and Musicians;
Lawyers, Doctors, Politicians;
Pamphlets, Newspapers, and Odes,
Seeking Fame, by diff'rent roads.

9
Taste and Talents quite deserted;
All the laws of Truth perverted;
Arrogance o'er Merit soaring!
Merit, silently deploring!

10
Gallant Souls with empty purses;
Gen'rals, only fit for Nurses!
Schoolboys, smit with Martial spirit,
Taking place of vet'ran merit!

11
Honest men, who can't get places;
Knaves, who shew unblushing faces;
Ruin hasten'd, Peace retarded!
Candour spurn'd, and Art rewarded!

---

[1] signed "Portia."

[2] In Robinson's *Poetical Works* (1806), this word is replaced with "Misers."

Sappho and Phaon. In a Series of Legitimate Sonnets, with Thoughts on Poetical Subjects, and Anecdotes of the Grecian Poetess (1796)

Sappho and Phaon[1]

PREFACE

It must strike every admirer of poetical compositions, that the modern sonnet, concluding with two lines, winding up the sentiment of the whole, confines the poet's fancy, and frequently occasions an abrupt termination of a beautiful and interesting picture; and that the ancient, or what is generally denominated, the LEGITIMATE SONNET, may be carried on in a series of sketches, composing, in parts, one historical or imaginary subject, and forming in the whole a complete and connected story.

With this idea, I have ventured to compose the following collection; not presuming to offer them as imitations of PETRARCH, but as specimens of that species of sonnet writing, so seldom attempted in the English language; though adopted by that sublime Bard, whose Muse produced the grand epic of Paradise Lost, and the humbler effusion, which I produce as an example of the measure to which I allude, and which is termed by the most classical writers, the *legitimate sonnet*.

"O Nightingale, that on yon bloomy spray
　　Warblest at eve, when all the woods are still,
　　Thou with fresh hope the lover's heart dost fill,
While the jolly hours lead on propitious May.
Thy liquid notes that close the eye of day
First heard before the shallow cuccoo's bill,
Portend success in love; O if Jove's will
Have link'd that amorous power to thy soft lay,
　　Now timely sing, ere the rude bird of hate
Foretel my hopeless doom in some grove nigh,
　　As thou from year to year hast sung too late
For my relief, yet hadst no reason why:
　　Whether the Muse, or Love call thee his mate,
Both them I serve, and of their train am I."[2]

To enumerate the variety of authors who have written sonnets of all descriptions, would be endless; indeed few of them deserve notice: and where, among the heterogeneous mass of insipid and laboured efforts, sometimes a bright gem sheds lustre on the page of poesy, it scarcely excites attention, owing to the disrepute into which sonnets are fallen. So little is rule attended to by many, who profess the art of poetry, that I have seen a composition of more than thirty lines, ushered into the world under the name of Sonnet, and that, from the pen of a writer, whose classical taste ought to have avoided such a misnomer.

Doctor Johnson describes a Sonnet, as "a short poem, consisting of fourteen lines, of which the rhymes are adjusted by a particular rule." He further adds, "It has not been used by any man of eminence since MILTON."[3]

---

[1] Sappho was a Greek poet, who lived on the island of Lesbos (7th century BC). According to legend, she killed herself for love of Phaon, a ferryman, by throwing herself from the rock of Leucata, a promontory on the coast of Epirus; cf. Landon, "Sappho's Song," in "The Improvisatrice."* Robinson herself was known as "the English Sappho" and used "Sappho" as one of her pseudonyms.

A "legitimate" sonnet is an Italian or Petrarchan one, divided into an octave (rhyming ABBAABBA) and a sestet (rhyming CDECDE or some variation). It is a more demanding form than the English or Shakespearean sonnet (divided into three quatrains and a couplet), because it allows only five rhymes (rather than seven); Robinson's version is more demanding still, allowing only four rhymes for each sonnet (ABBAABBA CDCDCD).

[2] Milton, "Sonnet 1" (1630?) uses the demanding four-rhyme scheme favoured by Robinson.

[3] "Since the death of Doctor Johnson a few ingenious and elegant writers have composed sonnets, according to the rules described by him: of their merits the public will judge, and the *literati* decide. The following quotations are given as the opinions of living authors, respecting the legitimate sonnet.

"'The little poems which are here called Sonnets, have, I believe, no very just claim to that title: but they consist of fourteen lines, and appear to me no improper vehicle for a single sentiment. I am told, and I read it as the opinion of very good judges, that the legitimate sonnet is ill calculated for our language. The specimens Mr. Hayley has given, though they form a strong exception, prove no more, than that the difficulties of the attempt vanish before uncommon powers.' Mrs. C. Smith's *Preface to her Elegiac Sonnets*.

"Likewise in the preface to a volume of very charming poems, (among which are many *legitimate sonnets*) by Mr. William Kendall, of Exeter, the following opinion is given of the Italian rhythm, which constitutes the legitimate sonnet: he describes it as—

"'A chaste and elegant model, which the most enlightened poet of our own country disdained not to contemplate. Amidst the degeneracy

Sensible of the extreme difficulty I shall have to encounter, in offering to the world a little wreath, gathered in that path, which, even the best poets have thought it dangerous to tread; and knowing that the English language is, of all others, the least congenial to such an undertaking, (for, I believe, that the construction of this kind of sonnet was originally in the Italian, where the vowels are used almost every other letter,) I only point out the track where more able pens may follow with success; and where the most classical beauties may be adopted, and drawn forth with peculiar advantage.

Sophisticated sonnets are so common, for every rhapsody of rhyme, from six lines to sixty comes under that denomination, that the eye frequently turns from this species of poem with disgust. Every school-boy, every romantic scribbler, thinks a sonnet a task of little difficulty. From this ignorance in some, and vanity in others, we see the monthly and diurnal publications abounding with ballads, odes, elegies, epitaphs, and allegories, the non-descript ephemera from the heated brains of self-important poetasters, all ushered into notice under the appellation of SONNET!

I confess myself such an enthusiastic votary of the Muse, that any innovation which seems to threaten even the least of her established rights, makes me tremble, lest that chaos of dissipated pursuits which has too long been growing like an overwhelming shadow, and menacing the lustre of intellectual light, should, aided by the idleness of some, and the profligacy of others, at last obscure the finer mental powers, and reduce the dignity of talents to the lowest degradation.

As poetry has the power to raise, so has it also the magic to refine. The ancients considered the art of such importance, that before they led forth their heroes to the most glorious enterprizes, they animated them by the recital of grand and harmonious compositions. The wisest scrupled not to reverence the invocations of minds, graced with the charm of numbers: so mystically fraught are powers said to be, which look beyond the surface of events, that an admired and classical writer,[1] describing the inspirations of the MUSE, thus expresses his opinion:

"So when remote futurity is brought
Before the keen inquiry of her thought,
A terrible sagacity informs
The Poet's heart, he looks to distant storms,
He hears the thunder ere the tempest low'rs,
And, arm'd with strength surpassing human pow'rs,
Seizes events as yet unknown to man,
And darts his soul into the dawning plan.
Hence in a Roman mouth the graceful name
Of Prophet and of Poet was the same,
Hence British poets too the priesthood shar'd,
And ev'ry hallow'd druid—was a bard."

That poetry ought to be cherished as a national ornament, cannot be more strongly exemplified than in the simple fact, that, in those centuries when the poets' laurels have been most generously fostered in Britain, the minds and manners of the natives have been most polished and enlightened. Even the language of a country refines into purity by the elegance of numbers: the strains of WALLER[2] have done more to effect that, than all the labours of monkish pedantry, since the days of druidical mystery and superstition.

Though different minds are variously affected by the infinite diversity of harmonious effusions, there are, I believe, very few that are wholly insensible to the powers of poetic compositions. Cold must that bosom be, which can resist the magical versification of Eloisa to Abelard;[3] and torpid to all the more exalted sensations of the soul is that being, whose ear is not delighted by the grand and sublime effusions of the divine Milton!

---

of modern taste, if the studies of a Milton have lost their attraction, legitimate sonnets, enriched by varying pauses, and an elaborate recurrence of rhyme, still assert their superiority over those tasteless and inartificial productions, which assume the name, without evincing a single characteristic of distinguishing modulation.'" (M.R.) Johnson's definition is from his *Dictionary of the English Language* (1755). Nine editions of Charlotte Smith's *Elegiac Sonnets and Other Poems* appeared between 1784 and 1800; they are dedicated to William Hayley (1745–1820). A number of them are "legitimate," though Smith experimented extensively with the sonnet form.

[1] "Cowper." (M.R.) *Table Talk* (1781) 492–503.

[2] Edmund Waller (1606–87).

[3] Alexander Pope, "Eloisa to Abelard" (1717).

The romantic chivalry of Spencer[1] vivifies the imagination; while the plaintive sweetness of Collins[2] soothes and penetrates the heart. How much would Britain have been deficient in a comparison with other countries on the scale of intellectual grace, had these poets never existed! yet it is a melancholy truth, that here, where the attributes of genius have been diffused by the liberal hand of nature, almost to prodigality, there has not been, during a long series of years, the smallest mark of public distinction bestowed on literary talents. Many individuals, whose works are held in the highest estimation, now that their ashes sleep in the sepulchre, were, when living, suffered to languish, and even to perish, in obscure poverty: as if it were the peculiar fate of genius, to be neglected while existing, and only honoured when the consciousness of inspiration is vanished for ever.

The ingenious mechanic has the gratification of seeing his labours patronized, and is rewarded for his invention while he has the powers of enjoying its produce. But the Poet's life is one perpetual scene of warfare: he is assailed by envy, stung by malice, and wounded by the fastidious comments of concealed assassins. The more eminently beautiful his compositions are, the larger is the phalanx he has to encounter; for the enemies of genius are multitudinous.

It is the interest of the ignorant and powerful, to suppress the effusions of enlightened minds: when only monks could write, and nobles read, authority rose triumphant over right; and the slave, spell-bound in ignorance, hugged his fetters without repining. It was then that the best powers of reason lay buried like the gem in the dark mine; by a slow and tedious progress they have been drawn forth, and must, ere long, diffuse an universal lustre: for that era is rapidly advancing, when talents will tower like an unperishable column, while the globe will be strewed with the wrecks of superstition.

As it was the opinion of the ancients, that poets possessed the powers of prophecy, the name was consequently held in the most unbounded veneration. In less remote periods the bard has been publicly distinguished; princes and priests have bowed before the majesty of genius: Petrarch was crowned with laurels, the noblest diadem, in the Capitol of Rome: his admirers were liberal, his cotemporaries were just; and his name will stand upon record, with the united and honourable testimony of his own talents, and the generosity of his country.

It is at once a melancholy truth, and a national disgrace, that this Island, so profusely favoured by nature, should be marked, of all enlightened countries, as the most neglectful of literary merit! and I will venture to believe, that there are both POETS and PHILOSOPHERS, now living in Britain, who, had they been born in any *other* clime, would have been honoured with the proudest distinctions, and immortalized to the latest posterity.

I cannot conclude these opinions without paying tribute to the talents of my illustrious country-women; who, unpatronized by the courts, and unprotected by the powerful, persevere in the paths of literature, and ennoble themselves by the unperishable lustre of MENTAL PRE-EMINENCE!

To the Reader

THE story of the LESBIAN MUSE, though not new to the classical reader, presented to my imagination such a lively example of the human mind, enlightened by the most exquisite talents, yet yielding to the destructive controul of ungovernable passions, that I felt an irresistible impulse to attempt the delineation of their progress; mingling with the glowing picture of her soul, such moral reflections, as may serve to excite that pity, which, while it proves the susceptibility of the heart, arms it against the danger of indulging a too luxuriant fancy.

The unfortunate lovers, Heloise and Abeilard;[3] and, the supposed platonic, Petrarch and Laura,[4] have found

---

[1] Edmund Spenser (c. 1552–99).

[2] William Collins (1721–59).

[3] Pierre Abélard (1079–1142/4), French philosopher, secretly married his pupil Héloïse. Her uncle had Abélard castrated and sent Héloïse to a nunnery. The story is told in Abélard's *Historia Calamitatum*; it is the subject of Pope's *Eloisa to Abelard* (1717).

[4] Francesco Petrarca (1304–74), Italian poet and humanist, is known especially for his sonnets expressing his love for Laura (d. 1348); cf. Landon, "The Improvisatrice" 41–80.*

panegyrists in many distinguished authors. OVID *and* POPE *have celebrated the passion of Sappho for Phaon;*[1] *but their portraits, however beautifully finished, are replete with shades, tending rather to depreciate than to adorn the Grecian Poetess.*

I have endeavoured to collect, in the succeeding pages, the most liberal accounts of that illustrious woman, whose fame has transmitted to us some fragments of her works, through many dark ages, and for the space of more than two thousand years. The merit of her compositions must have been indisputable, to have left all cotemporary female writers in obscurity; for it is known, that poetry was, at the period in which she lived, held in the most sacred veneration; and that those who were gifted with that divine inspiration, were ranked as the first class of human beings.

Among the many Grecian writers, Sappho was the unrivalled poetess of her time: the envy she excited, the public honours she received, and the fatal passion which terminated her existence, will, I trust, create that sympathy in the mind of the susceptible reader, which may render the following poetical trifles not wholly uninteresting.

MARY ROBINSON.

St. James's Place,
1796.

ACCOUNT OF SAPPHO

SAPPHO, whom the ancients distinguished by the title of the TENTH MUSE,[2] was born at Mytilene in the island of Lesbos, six hundred years before the Christian era. As no particulars have been transmitted to posterity, respecting the origin of her family, it is most likely she derived but little consequence from birth or connections. At an early period of her life she was wedded to Cercolus, a native of the isle of Andros; he was possessed of considerable wealth, and though the Lesbian Muse is said to have been sparingly gifted with beauty, he became enamoured of her, more perhaps on account of mental, than personal charms. By this union she is said to have given birth to a daughter; but Cercolus leaving her, while young, in a state of widowhood, she never after could be prevailed on to marry.

The Fame which her genius spread even to the remotest parts of the earth, excited the envy of some writers who endeavoured to throw over her private character, a shade, which shrunk before the brilliancy of her poetical talents. Her soul was replete with harmony; that harmony which neither art nor study can acquire; she felt the intuitive superiority, and to the Muses she paid unbounded adoration.

The Mytilenians held her poetry in such high veneration, and were so sensible of the honour conferred on the country which gave her birth, that they coined money with the impression of her head; and at the time of her death, paid tribute to her memory, such as was offered to sovereigns only.

The story of Antiochus has been related as an unequivocal proof of Sappho's skill in discovering, and powers of describing the passions of the human mind. That prince is said to have entertained a fatal affection for his mother-in-law Stratonice; which, though he endeavoured to subdue it's influence, preyed upon his frame, and after many ineffectual struggles, at length reduced him to extreme danger. His physicians marked the symptoms attending his malady, and found them so exactly correspond with Sappho's delineation of the tender passion, that they did not hesitate to form a decisive opinion on the cause, which had produced so perilous an effect.

That Sappho was not insensible to the feelings she so well described, is evident in her writings: but it was scarcely possible, that a mind so exquisitely tender, so sublimely gifted, should escape those fascinations which even apathy itself has been awakened to acknowledge.

The scarce specimens now extant,[3] from the pen of the Grecian Muse, have by the most competent judges been esteemed as the standard for the pathetic, the glowing, and the amatory. The ode, which has been so highly estimated, is written in a measure distinguished

---

[1] "Sappho to Phaon" is the fifteenth of the *Heroides* ("Heroines"), a collection of verse epistles by Ovid (43 BC – AD 17). Pope's translation, "Sapho to Phaon," was published in 1712.

[2] In classical mythology, the nine muses were sisters, the daughters of Zeus and Mnemosyne (Memory). Each was the patron of one of the arts.

[3] In Robinson's time, only two complete poems, two epigrams, and six fragments by Sappho were known to exist.

by the title of the Sapphic.[1] POPE made it his model in his juvenile production, beginning—

"Happy the man—whose wish and care"—[2]

Addison was of opinion, that the writings of Sappho were replete with such fascinating beauties, and adorned with such a vivid glow of sensibility, that, probably, had they been preserved entire, it would have been dangerous to have perused them.[3] They possessed none of the artificial decorations of a feigned passion; they were the genuine effusions of a supremely enlightened soul, labouring to subdue a fatal enchantment; and vainly opposing the conscious pride of illustrious fame, against the warm susceptibility of a generous bosom.

Though few stanzas from the pen of the Lesbian poetess have darted through the shades of oblivion: yet, those that remain are so exquisitely touching and beautiful, that they prove beyond dispute the taste, feeling, and inspiration of the mind which produced them. In examining the curiosities of antiquity, we look to the perfections, and not the magnitude of those reliques, which have been preserved amidst the wrecks of time: as the smallest gem that bears the fine touches of a master, surpasses the loftiest fabric reared by the labours of false taste, so the precious fragments of the immortal Sappho, will be admired, when the voluminous productions of inferior poets are mouldered into dust.

When it is considered, that the few specimens we have of the poems of the Grecian Muse, have passed through three and twenty centuries, and consequently through the hands of innumerable translators: and when it is known that Envy frequently delights in the base occupation of depreciating merit which it cannot aspire to emulate; it may be conjectured, that some passages are erroneously given to posterity, either by ignorance or design. Sappho, whose fame beamed round her with the superior effulgence which her works had created, knew that she was writing for future ages: it is not therefore natural that she should produce any composition which might tend to tarnish her reputation, or to lessen that celebrity which it was the labour of her life to consecrate.

The delicacy of her sentiments cannot find a more eloquent advocate than in her own effusions; she is said to have commended in the most animated panegyric, the virtues of her brother Lanychus; and with the most pointed and severe censure, to have contemned the passion which her brother Charaxus entertained for the beautiful Rhodope. If her writings were, in some instances, too glowing for the fastidious refinement of modern times; let it be her excuse, and the honour of her country, that the liberal education of the Greeks was such, as inspired them with an unprejudiced enthusiasm for the works of genius: and that when they paid adoration to Sappho, they idolized the MUSE, and not the WOMAN.

I shall conclude this account with an extract from the works of the learned and enlightened ABBÉ BARTHELEMI;[4] at once the vindication and eulogy of the Grecian Poetess.

"SAPPHO undertook to inspire the Lesbian women with a taste for literature; many of them received instructions from her, and foreign women increased the number of her disciples. She loved them to excess, because it was impossible for her to love otherwise; and she expressed her tenderness in all the violence of passion: your surprize at this will cease, when you are acquainted with the extreme sensibility of the Greeks; and discover, that amongst them the most innocent connections often borrow the impassioned language of love.

"A certain facility of manners, she possessed; and the warmth of her expressions were but too well calculated to expose her to the hatred of some women of distinction, humbled by her superiority; and the jealousy of some of her disciples, who happened not to be the objects of her preference. To this hatred she replied by truths and irony, which completely exasperated her enemies. She repaired to Sicily, where a statue was erected to her; it was sculptured by SILANION, one of the most celebrated staturists of his time. The sensibility of SAPPHO was extreme! she loved PHAON, who forsook her; after various efforts to bring him back, she took the

---

[1] a four-line stanza in a syllabic metre, named after Sappho.

[2] Pope, "Ode on Solitude" (1717) 1.

[3] Joseph Addison (1672–1719), *Spectator* 223 (1711).

[4] Jean-Jacques Barthélemy (1716–95), *Le Voyage du jeune Anacharse en Grèce* (1788), trans. W. Beaumont (1794) 2:63–65.

leap of Leucata,[1] and perished in the waves!

"Death has not obliterated the stain imprinted on her character; for ENVY, which fastens on ILLUSTRIOUS NAMES, does not expire; but bequeaths her aspersions to that calumny which NEVER DIES.

"Several Grecian women have cultivated POETRY, with success, but none have hitherto attained to the excellence of SAPPHO. And among other poets, there are few, indeed, who have surpassed her."

THE SUBJECT OF EACH SONNET

1. INTRODUCTORY
2. The Temple of Chastity
3. The Bower of Pleasure
4. Sappho discovers her Passion
5. Contemns its Power
6. Describes the characteristics of Love
7. Invokes Reason
8. Her Passion increases
9. Laments the volatility of Phaon
10. Describes Phaon
11. Rejects the Influence of Reason
12. Previous to her Interview with Phaon
13. She endeavours to fascinate him
14. To the Æolian Harp
15. Phaon awakes
16. Sappho rejects Hope
17. The Tyranny of Love
18. To Phaon
19. Suspects his constancy
20. To Phaon
21. Laments her early Misfortunes
22. Phaon forsakes her
23. Sappho's Conjectures
24. Her Address to the Moon
25. To Phaon
26. Contemns Philosophy
27. Sappho's Address to the Stars
28. Describes the fascinations of Love
29. Determines to follow Phaon
30. Bids farewell to Lesbos
31. Describes her Bark
32. Dreams of a Rival
33. Reaches Sicily
34. Sappho's Prayer to Venus
35. Reproaches Phaon
36. Her confirmed Despair
37. Foresees her Death
38. To a Sigh
39. To the Muses
40. Visions appear to her in a dream
41. Resolves to take the Leap of Leucata
42. Her last Appeal to Phaon
43. Her Reflections on the Leucadian Rock before she perishes
44. Sonnet Conclusive

"FLENDUS AMOR MEUS EST; ELEGEÏA FLEBILE CARMEN; NON FACIT AD LACRYMAS BARBITOS ULLA MEAS."
Ovid.[2]

"Love taught my tears in sadder notes to flow,
And tun'd my heart to elegies of woe."
Pope.[3]

Sonnet Introductory

Favour'd by Heav'n are those, ordain'd to taste
    The bliss supreme that kindles fancy's fire;
    Whose magic fingers sweep the muses' lyre,
In varying cadence, eloquently chaste!
5 Well may the mind, with tuneful numbers grac'd,
    To Fame's immortal attributes aspire,
    Above the treach'rous spells of low desire,
That wound the sense, by vulgar joys debas'd.
    For thou, blest POESY! with godlike pow'rs

---

[1] "Leucata was a promontory of Epirus, on the top of which stood a temple dedicated to Apollo. From this promontory despairing lovers threw themselves into the sea, with an idea, that, if they survived, they should be cured of their hopeless passions. The Abbé Barthelemi says, that, 'many escaped, but others having perished, the custom fell into disrepute; and at length was wholly abolished.'—*Vide Travels of Anacharsis the Younger.*" (M.R.)

[2] "I must weep, for my love—and elegy is the weeping strain; no lyre is suited to my tears." *Heroides* 15.7–8 (trans. Grant Showerman): Ovid's poem is in elegiac couplets rather than the lyric metre used by the historical Sappho.

[3] "Sapho to Phaon" (1712) 7–8.

10 To calm the miseries of man wert giv'n;
    When passion rends, and hopeless love devours,
By mem'ry goaded, and by frenzy driv'n,
'Tis thine to guide him 'midst Elysian bow'rs,[1]
And shew his fainting soul,—a glimpse of Heav'n.

2

High on a rock, coæval with the skies,
    A Temple stands, rear'd by immortal pow'rs
    To Chastity divine! ambrosial flow'rs
Twining round icicles, in columns rise
5 Mingling with pendent gems of orient dyes!
    Piercing the air, a golden crescent tow'rs,
    Veil'd by transparent clouds; while smiling hours[2]
Shake from their varying wings—celestial joys!
    The steps of spotless marble, scatter'd o'er
10 With deathless roses arm'd with many a thorn,
    Lead to the altar. On the frozen floor,
Studded with tear-drops petrified by scorn,
    Pale vestals[3] kneel the Goddess to adore,
While Love, his arrows broke, retires forlorn.

3

Turn to yon vale beneath, whose tangled shade
    Excludes the blazing torch of noon-day light,
    Where sportive Fawns, and dimpled Loves invite,
The bow'r of Pleasure[4] opens to the glade:
5 Lull'd by soft flutes, on leaves of violets laid,
    There witching beauty greets the ravish'd sight,
    More gentle than the arbitress of night
In all her silv'ry panoply array'd!
    The birds breathe bliss! light zephyrs kiss the ground,
10 Stealing the hyacinth's divine perfume;
    While from pellucid fountains glitt'ring round,
Small tinkling rills bid rival flow'rets bloom!

HERE, laughing Cupids bathe the bosom's wound;
THERE, tyrant passion finds a glorious tomb!

4

Why, when I gaze on Phaon's beauteous eyes,
    Why does each thought in wild disorder stray?
    Why does each fainting faculty decay,
And my chill'd breast[5] in throbbing tumults rise?
5 Mute, on the ground my Lyre neglected lies,
    The Muse forgot,[6] and lost the melting lay;
    My down-cast looks, my faultering lips betray,
That stung by hopeless passion,—Sappho dies!
    Now, on a bank of Cypress[7] let me rest;
10 Come, tuneful maids, ye pupils of my care,
    Come, with your dulcet numbers soothe my breast;
And, as the soft vibrations float on air,
    Let pity waft my spirit to the blest,
To mock the barb'rous triumphs of despair!

5

O! How can LOVE exulting Reason quell!
    How fades each nobler passion from his gaze!
    E'en Fame, that cherishes the Poet's lays,
That fame, ill-fated Sappho lov'd so well.
5 Lost is the wretch, who in his fatal spell
    Wastes the short Summer of delicious days,
    And from the tranquil path of wisdom strays,
In passion's thorny wild, forlorn to dwell.
    O ye! who in that sacred Temple smile
10 Where holy Innocence resides enshrin'd;
    Who fear not sorrow, and who know not guile,
Each thought compos'd, and ev'ry wish resign'd;
    Tempt not the path where pleasure's flow'ry wile
In sweet, but pois'nous fetters, holds the mind.

6

Is it to love, to fix the tender gaze,
    To hide the timid blush, and steal away;
    To shun the busy world, and waste the day

---

[1] In classical eschatology, the Elysian fields are the abode of the blessed.

[2] Horæ (L.): the Seasons, daughters of Jupiter and Themis.

[3] virgins. The Vestal virgins maintained the fire in the temple of Vesta (the goddess of the hearth) in Rome.

[4] Cf. the Bower of Bliss in Edmund Spenser, *The Faerie Queene* 2.1.51, 2.12.69–87.

[5] Cf. Pope, "Sapho to Phaon" 126.

[6] Cf. Pope, "Sapho to Phaon" 6.

[7] symbolic of mourning.

    In some rude mountain's solitary maze?
5 Is it to chant *one* name in ceaseless lays,
      To hear no words that other tongues can say,
      To watch the pale moon's melancholy ray,
    To chide in fondness, and in folly praise?
      Is it to pour th'involuntary sigh,
10 To dream of bliss, and wake new pangs to prove;
      To talk, in fancy, with the speaking eye,
    Then start with jealousy, and wildly rove;
    Is it to loath the light, and wish to die?
    For these I feel,—and feel that they are Love.

7

    Come, Reason, come! each nerve rebellious bind,
      Lull the fierce tempest of my fev'rish soul;
      Come, with the magic of thy meek controul,
    And check the wayward wand'rings of my mind:
5 Estrang'd from thee, no solace can I find,
      O'er my rapt brain, where pensive visions stole,
      Now passion reigns and stormy tumults roll—
    So the smooth Sea obeys the furious wind!
      In vain Philosophy unfolds his store,
10 O'erwhelm'd is ev'ry source of pure delight;
      Dim is the golden page of wisdom's lore;
    All nature fades before my sick'ning sight:
      For what bright scene can fancy's eye explore,
    'Midst dreary labyrinths of mental night?

8

    Why, through each aching vein, with lazy pace
      Thus steals the languid fountain of my heart,
      While, from its source, each wild convulsive start
    Tears the scorch'd roses from my burning face?
5 In vain, O Lesbian Vales! your charms I trace;
      Vain is the poet's theme, the sculptor's art;
      No more the Lyre its magic can impart,
    Though wak'd to sound, with more than mortal grace!
      Go, tuneful maids, go bid my Phaon prove
10 That passion mocks the empty boast of fame;
      Tell him no joys are sweet, but joys of love,
    Melting the soul, and thrilling all the frame!
      Oh! may th'ecstatic thought his bosom move,
    And sighs of rapture, fan the blush of shame!

9

    Ye, who in alleys green and leafy bow'rs,
      Sport, the rude children of fantastic birth;
      Where frolic nymphs, and shaggy tribes of mirth,
    In clam'rous revels waste the midnight hours;
5 Who, link'd in flaunting bands of mountain flow'rs,
      Weave your wild mazes o'er the dewy earth,
      Ere the fierce Lord of Lustre rushes forth,
    And o'er the world his beamy radiance pours!
      Oft has your clanking cymbal's madd'ning strain,
10 Loud ringing through the torch-illumin'd grove,
      Lur'd my lov'd Phaon from the youthful train,
    Through rugged dells, o'er craggy rocks to rove;
      Then how can she his vagrant heart detain,
    Whose Lyre throbs only to the touch of Love?

10

    Dang'rous to hear, is that melodious tongue,
      And fatal to the sense those murd'rous eyes,[1]
      Where in a sapphire sheath, Love's arrow lies,
    Himself conceal'd the crystal haunts among!
5 Oft o'er that form, enamour'd have I hung,[2]
      On that smooth cheek to mark the deep'ning dyes,
      While from that lip the fragrant breath would rise,
    That lip, like Cupid's bow with rubies strung!
      Still let me gaze upon that polish'd brow,
10 O'er which the golden hair luxuriant plays;
      So, on the modest lily's leaves of snow
    The proud Sun revels in resplendent rays!
      Warm as his beams this sensate heart shall glow,
    Till life's last hour, with Phaon's self decays!

11

    O! Reason! vaunted Sov'reign of the mind!
      Thou pompous vision with a sounding name!
      Can'st thou, the soul's rebellious passions tame?
    Can'st thou in spells the vagrant fancy bind?
5 Ah, no! capricious as the wav'ring wind
      Are sighs of Love that dim thy boasted flame,
      While Folly's torch consumes the wreath of fame,
    And Pleasure's hands the sheaves of Truth unbind.

---

[1] Cf. Pope, *The Rape of the Lock* (1714) 5.145.

[2] Cf. Milton, *Paradise Lost* 5.13.

Press'd by the storms of Fate, hope shrinks and
        dies;
10 Frenzy darts forth in mightiest ills array'd;
        Around thy throne destructive tumults rise,
    And hell-fraught jealousies, thy rights invade!
        Then, what art thou? O! Idol of the wise!
    A visionary theme!—a gorgeous shade!

12

Now, o'er the tessellated pavement strew
    Fresh saffron, steep'd in essence of the rose,
    While down yon agate column gently flows
A glitt'ring streamlet of ambrosial[1] dew!
5 My Phaon smiles! the rich carnation's hue,
    On his flush'd cheek in conscious lustre glows,
    While o'er his breast enamour'd Venus throws
Her starry mantle of celestial blue!
    Breathe soft, ye dulcet flutes, among the trees
10 Where clust'ring boughs with golden citron twine;
    While slow vibrations, dying on the breeze,
Shall soothe his soul with harmony divine!
    Then let my form his yielding fancy seize,
And all his fondest wishes, blend with mine.

13

Bring, bring to deck my brow, ye Sylvan girls,
    A roseate wreathe; nor for my waving hair
    The costly band of studded gems prepare,
Of sparkling crysolite or orient pearls:
5 Love, o'er my head his canopy unfurls,
    His purple pinions fan the whisp'ring air;
    Mocking the golden sandal, rich and rare,
Beneath my feet the fragrant woodbine curls.
    Bring the thin robe; to fold about my breast,
10 White as the downy swan; while round my waist
    Let leaves of glossy myrtle[2] bind the vest,
Not idly gay, but elegantly chaste!
    Love scorns the nymph in wanton trappings drest;
And charms the most conceal'd, are doubly grac'd.

14

Come, soft Æolian harp,[3] while zephyr plays
    Along the meek vibration of thy strings,
    As twilight's hand her modest mantle brings,
Blending with sober grey, the western blaze!
5 O! prompt my Phaon's dreams with tend'rest lays,
    Ere night o'ershade thee with its humid wings,
    While the lorn Philomel[4] his sorrow sings
In leafy cradle, red with parting rays!
    Slow let thy dulcet tones on ether[5] glide,
10 So steals the murmur of the am'rous dove;
    The mazy legions swarm on ev'ry side,
To lulling sounds the sunny people move!
    Let not the wise their little world deride,
The smallest sting can wound the breast of Love.

15

Now, round my favour'd grot let roses rise,
    To strew the bank where Phaon wakes from rest;
    O! happy buds! to kiss his burning breast,
And die, beneath the lustre of his eyes!
5 Now, let the timbrels echo to the skies,
    Now damsels sprinkle cassia on his vest,
    With od'rous wreaths of constant myrtle drest,
And flow'rs, deep tinted with the rainbow's dyes!
    From cups of porphyry let nectar[6] flow,
10 Rich as the perfume of Phœnicia's vine!
    Now let his dimpling cheek with rapture glow,
While round his heart love's mystic fetters twine,
    And let the Grecian Lyre its aid bestow,
In songs of triumph, to proclaim him mine!

16

Delusive Hope! more transient than the ray
    That leads pale twilight to her dusky bed,
    O'er woodland glen, or breezy mountain's head,

---

[1] Ambrosia was the food of the gods.

[2] sacred to Venus.

[3] a stringed instrument that is not played but placed in a window, where the wind can cause its strings to vibrate; cf. Coleridge, "Effusion 35"* and "Dejection."*

[4] nightingale. For the story of Philomela and Tereus, see Ovid, *Metamorphoses* 6.

[5] the air breathed by the gods.

[6] the drink of the gods.

Ling'ring to catch the parting sigh of day.
Hence with thy visionary charms, away!
   Nor o'er my path the flow'rs of fancy spread;
   Thy airy dreams on peaceful pillows shed,
And weave for thoughtless brows, a garland gay.
   Farewell low vallies; dizzy cliffs, farewell!
Small vagrant rills that murmur as ye flow:
   Dark bosom'd labyrinth and thorny dell;
The task be mine all pleasures to forego;
   To hide, where meditation loves to dwell,
And feed my soul, with luxury of woe!

17

Love steals unheeded o'er the tranquil mind,
   As Summer breezes fan the sleeping main,
   Slow through each fibre creeps the subtle pain,
'Till closely round the yielding bosom twin'd.
Vain is the hope the magic to unbind,
   The potent mischief riots in the brain,
   Grasps ev'ry thought, and burns in ev'ry vein,
'Till in the heart the Tyrant lives enshrin'd.
   Oh! Victor strong! bending the vanquish'd frame;
Sweet is the thraldom that thou bid'st us prove!
   And sacred is the tear thy victims claim,
For blest are those whom sighs of sorrow move!
   Then nymphs beware how ye profane my name,
Nor blame my weakness, till like me ye love!

18

Why art thou chang'd? O Phaon! tell me why?
   Love flies reproach, when passion feels decay;
   Or, I would paint the raptures of that day,
When, in sweet converse,[1] mingling sigh with sigh,
I mark'd the graceful languor of thine eye
   As on a shady bank entranc'd we lay:
   O! Eyes! whose beamy radiance stole away
As stars fade trembling from the burning sky!
   Why art thou chang'd? dear source of all my woes?
Though dark my bosom's tint,[2] through ev'ry vein
   A ruby tide of purest lustre flows,
Warm'd by thy love, or chill'd by thy disdain;

And yet no bliss this sensate Being knows;
Ah! why is rapture so allied to pain?

19

Farewell, ye coral caves, ye pearly sands,
   Ye waving woods that crown yon lofty steep;
   Farewell, ye Nereides[3] of the glitt'ring deep,
Ye mountain tribes, ye fawns, ye sylvan bands:
On the bleak rock your frantic minstrel stands,
   Each task forgot, save that, to sigh and weep;
   In vain the strings her burning fingers sweep,
No more her touch, the Grecian Lyre commands!
   In Circe's[4] cave my faithless Phaon's laid,
Her dæmons dress his brow with opiate flow'rs;
   Or, loit'ring in the brown pomgranate shade,
Beguile with am'rous strains the fateful hours;
   While Sappho's lips, to paly ashes fade,
And sorrow's cank'ring worm her heart devours!

20

Oh! I could toil for thee o'er burning plains;
   Could smile at poverty's disastrous blow;
   With thee, could wander 'midst a world of snow,
Where one long night o'er frozen Scythia[5] reigns.
Sever'd from thee, my sick'ning soul disdains
   The thrilling thought, the blissful dream to know,
   And can'st thou give my days to endless woe,
Requiting sweetest bliss with cureless pains?
   Away, false fear! nor think capricious fate
Would lodge a dæmon in a form divine!
   Sooner the dove shall seek a tyger mate,
Or the soft snow-drop round the thistle twine;
   Yet, yet, I dread to hope, nor dare to hate,
Too proud to sue! too tender to resign!

21

Why do I live to loath the cheerful day,
   To shun the smiles of Fame, and mark the hours

---

[1] Milton, *Paradise Lost* 9.909.

[2] Cf. Pope, "Sapho to Phaon" 41–42.

[3] sea-nymphs, the daughters of Nereus and Doria.

[4] An enchantress, who changed Odysseus's companions into swine. See Homer, *Odyssey* 10.133–397.

[5] the region including the Caucasus and the Russian coast of the Black Sea.

On tardy pinions move, while ceaseless show'rs
Down my wan cheek in lucid currents stray?
5   My tresses all unbound, nor gems display,
     Nor scents Arabian! on my path no flow'rs
     Imbibe the morn's resuscitating pow'rs,
For one blank sorrow, saddens all my way!
   As slow the radiant Sun of reason rose,[1]
10 Through tears my dying parents saw it shine;
     A brother's frailties,[2] swell'd the tide of woes,—
     And, keener far, maternal griefs[3] were mine!
   Phaon! if soon these weary eyes shall close,
Oh! must that task, that mournful task, be thine!

22

Wild is the foaming Sea! The surges roar!
     And nimbly dart the livid lightnings round!
     On the rent rock the angry waves rebound;
Ah me! the less'ning bark is seen no more!
5   Along the margin of the trembling shore,
     Loud as the blast my frantic cries shall sound,
     My storm-drench'd limbs the flinty fragments
         wound,
And o'er my bleeding breast the billows pour!
   Phaon! return! ye winds, O! waft the strain
10 To his swift bark; ye barb'rous waves forbear!
     Taunt not the anguish of a lover's brain,
     Nor feebly emulate the soul's despair!
   For howling winds, and foaming seas, in vain
Assail the breast, when passion rages there!

23

To Ætna's scorching sands my Phaon flies![4]
     False Youth! can other charms attractive prove?
     Say, can Sicilian loves thy passions move,
Play round thy heart, and fix thy fickle eyes,
5 While in despair the Lesbian Sappho dies?
     Has Spring for thee a crown of poppies wove,
     Or dost thou languish in th'Idalian grove,[5]
Whose altar kindles, fann'd by Lovers' sighs?
   Ah! think, that while on Ætna's shores you stray,
10 A fire, more fierce than Ætna's, fills my breast;[6]
     Nor deck Sicilian nymphs with garlands gay,
While Sappho's brows with cypress wreaths are drest;
   Let one kind word my weary woes repay,
Or, in eternal slumbers bid them rest.

24

O thou! meek Orb! that stealing o'er the dale
     Cheer'st with thy modest beams the noon of night!
     On the smooth lake diffusing silv'ry light,
Sublimely still, and beautifully pale!
5 What can thy cool and placid eye avail,
     Where fierce despair absorbs the mental sight,
     While inbred glooms the vagrant thoughts invite,
To tempt the gulph where howling fiends assail?
   O, Night! all nature owns thy temper'd pow'r;
10 Thy solemn pause, thy dews, thy pensive beam;
     Thy sweet breath whisp'ring in the moonlight
         bow'r,
     While fainting flow'rets kiss the wand'ring stream!
   Yet, vain is ev'ry charm! and vain the hour,
That brings to madd'ning love, no soothing dream!

25

Can'st thou forget, O! Idol of my Soul!
     Thy Sappho's voice, her form, her dulcet Lyre!
     That melting ev'ry thought to fond desire,
Bade sweet delirium o'er thy senses roll?
5 Can'st thou, so soon, renounce the blest control
     That calm'd with pity's tears love's raging fire,

---

[1] "Sex mihi natales ierant, cum lecta parentis
   Ante diem lacrymas ossa bibere meas.
Arsit inops frater, victus meretricis amore;
   Mistaque cum turpi damna pudore tulit.
              Ovid." (M.R.)
"Six natal days had passed for me, when I gathered the bones of my father, dead before his time, and let them drink my tears. My untaught brother was caught in the flame of harlot love, and suffered loss together with foul shame …" *Heroides* 15.61–64 (trans. Grant Showerman).

[2] Sappho's brother, Charaxos, allegedly wasted his money on Rhodope, a courtesan.

[3] Sappho allegedly had a daughter, Cleis, but nothing bad is known to have happened to her.

[4] "Arva Phaon celebrat diversa Typhoidos Ætnæ." (M.R.)

[5] Mount Idalus is in Cyprus, the birthplace of Venus (Gr. Aphrodite).

[6] "Me calor Ætnæo non minor igne coquit. *Ovid.*" (M.R.)

    While Hope, slow breathing on the trembling wire,
  In every note with soft persuasion stole?
      Oh! Sov'reign of my heart! return! return!
10 For me no spring appears, no summers bloom,
      No Sun-beams glitter, and no altars burn!
  The mind's dark winter of eternal gloom,
      Shews 'midst the waste a solitary urn,
  A blighted laurel, and a mould'ring tomb!

26

Where antique woods o'er-hang the mountain's crest,
    And mid-day glooms in solemn silence lour;
      Philosophy, go seek a lonely bow'r,
And waste life's fervid noon in fancied rest.
5 Go, where the bird of sorrow weaves her nest,
    Cooing, in sadness sweet, through night's dim hour;
      Go, cull the dew-drops from each potent flow'r
That med'cines to the cold and reas'ning breast!
    Go, where the brook in liquid lapse steals by,
10 Scarce heard amid'st the mingling echoes round,
    What time, the moon fades slowly down the sky,
And slumb'ring zephyrs moan, in caverns bound:
      Be these thy pleasures, dull Philosophy!
  Nor vaunt the balm, to heal a lover's wound.

27

Oh! ye bright Stars! that on the Ebon fields
    Of Heav'n's vast empire, trembling seem to stand;
      'Till rosy morn unlocks her portal bland,
Where the proud Sun his fiery banner wields!
5 To flames, less fierce than mine, your lustre yields,
    And pow'rs more strong my countless tears command;
      Love strikes the feeling heart with ruthless hand,
    And only spares the breast which dullness shields.
    Since, then, capricious nature but bestows
10 The fine affections of the soul, to prove
      A keener sense of desolating woes,
Far, far from me the empty boast remove;
    If bliss from coldness, pain from passion flows,
  Ah! who would wish to feel, or learn to love?

28

Weak is the sophistry, and vain the art
  That whispers patience to the mind's despair!
    That bids reflection bathe the wounds of care,
While Hope, with pleasing phantoms, soothes their smart;
5 For mem'ry still, reluctant to depart
    From the dear spot, once rich in prospects fair,
      Bids the fond soul enamour'd linger there,
And its least charm is grateful to the heart!
    He never lov'd, who could not muse and sigh,
10 Spangling the sacred turf with frequent tears,
    Where the small rivulet, that ripples by,
Recalls the scenes of past and happier years,
    When, on its banks he watch'd the speaking eye,
And one sweet smile o'erpaid an age of fears!

29

Farewell, ye tow'ring Cedars, in whose shade,
    Lull'd by the Nightingale, I sunk to rest,
      While spicy breezes hover'd o'er my breast
To fan my cheek, in deep'ning tints array'd;
5 While am'rous insects, humming round me, play'd,
    Each flow'r forsook, of prouder sweets in quest;
      Of glowing lips, in humid fragrance drest,
That mock'd the Sunny Hybla's[1] vaunted aid!
    Farewell, ye limpid rivers! Oh! farewell!
10 No more shall Sappho to your grots repair;
    No more your white waves to her bosom swell,
Or your dank weeds, entwine her floating hair;
    As erst, when Venus in her sparry cell
Wept, to behold a brighter goddess there!

30

O'er the tall cliff that bounds the billowy main
    Shad'wing the surge that sweeps the lonely strand,
      While the thin vapours break along the sand,
Day's harbinger unfolds the liquid plain.
5 The rude Sea murmurs, mournful as the strain

---

[1] a mountain in Sicily, renowned for its honey.

That love-lorn minstrels strike with trembling hand,
   While from their green beds rise the Syren band[1]
With tongues aërial to repeat my pain!
   The vessel rocks beside the pebbly shore,
10 The foamy curls its gaudy trappings lave;
   Oh! Bark propitious! bear me gently o'er,
Breathe soft, ye winds; rise slow, O! swelling wave!
   Lesbos; these eyes shall meet thy sands no more:
I fly, to seek my Lover, or my Grave!

31

Far o'er the waves my lofty Bark shall glide,
   Love's frequent sighs the flutt'ring sails shall swell,[2]
While to my native home I bid farewell,
   Hope's snowy hand the burnish'd helm shall guide!
5 Tritons[3] shall sport amidst the yielding tide,
   Myriads of Cupids round the prow shall dwell,
   And Venus, thron'd within her opal shell,[4]
Shall proudly o'er the glitt'ring billows ride!
   Young Dolphins, dashing in the golden spray,
10 Shall with their scaly forms illume the deep
   Ting'd with the purple flush of sinking day,
Whose flaming wreath shall crown the distant steep:
   While on the breezy deck soft minstrels play,
And songs of love, the lover soothe to sleep!

32

Blest as the Gods! Sicilian Maid is he,[5]
   The youth whose soul thy yielding graces charm;
Who bound, O! thraldom sweet! by beauty's arm,
In idle dalliance fondly sports with thee!
5 Blest as the Gods! that iv'ry throne to see,
   Throbbing with transports, tender, timid, warm!
   While round thy fragrant lips light zephyrs swarm,
As op'ning buds attract the wand'ring Bee!
   Yet, short is youthful passion's fervid hour;
10 Soon, shall another clasp the beauteous boy;
   Soon, shall a rival prove, in that gay bow'r,
The pleasing torture of excessive joy!
   The Bee flies sicken'd from the sweetest flow'r;
The lightning's shaft, but dazzles to destroy!

33

I wake! delusive phantoms hence, away!
   Tempt not the weakness of a lover's breast;
   The softest breeze can shake the halcyon's nest,[6]
And lightest clouds o'er cast the dawning ray!
5 'Twas but a vision! Now, the star of day
   Peers, like a gem on Ætna's burning crest!
   Wellcome, ye Hills, with golden vintage drest;
Sicilian forests brown, and vallies gay!
   A mournful stranger, from the Lesbian Isle,
10 Not strange, in loftiest eulogy of Song!

---

[1] The sirens were sea-nymphs who lured sailors to their death through the beauty of their singing; see Homer, *Odyssey* 12.

[2] Cf. Pope, "Sapho to Phaon" 253.

[3] sea-gods.

[4] Venus is often described or painted standing on a shell, as in *The Birth of Venus*, by Botticelli.

[5] "Vide Sappho's Ode." (M.R.) This is Sappho's most famous surviving poem. Addison published a translation by Ambrose Philips (1674–1749) in *Spectator* 229 (1711):

1.
Blest as th'Immortal Gods is he,
The Youth who fondly sits by thee,
And hears and sees thee all the while
Softly speak and sweetly smile.

2.
'Twas this depriv'd my Soul of Rest,
And rais'd such Tumults in my Breast;
For while I gaz'd, in Transport tost,
My Breath was gone, my Voice was lost:

3.
My Bosom glow'd; the subtle Flame
Ran quick thro' all my vital Frame;
O'er my dim Eyes a Darkness hung;
My Ears with hollow Murmurs rung:

4.
In dewy Damps my Limbs were chill'd;
My Blood with gentle Horrours thrill'd;
My feeble Pulse forgot to play;
I fainted, sunk, and dy'd away.

[6] The halcyon is a seabird that was believed to make its nest on the surface of the sea during periods of perfectly calm weather ("halcyon days"). For the story of Alcyone and Ceyx, see Ovid, *Metamorphoses* 11.

She, who could teach the Stoic's cheek to smile,[1]
Thaw the cold heart, and chain the wond'ring throng,
   Can find no balm, love's sorrows to beguile;
Ah! Sorrows known too soon! and felt too long!

34

Venus! to thee, the Lesbian Muse shall sing,
   The song, which Myttellenian youths admir'd,[2]
   When Echo, am'rous of the strain inspir'd,
Bade the wild rocks with madd'ning plaudits ring!
5 Attend my pray'r! O! Queen of rapture! bring
   To these fond arms, he, whom my soul has fir'd;
   From these fond arms remov'd, yet, still desir'd,
Though love, exulting, spreads his varying wing!
   Oh! source of ev'ry joy! of ev'ry care!
10 Blest Venus! Goddess of the zone divine!
   To Phaon's bosom, Phaon's victim bear;
   So shall her warmest, tend'rest vows be thine!
   For Venus, Sappho shall a wreath prepare,
And Love be crown'd, immortal as the Nine![3]

35

What means the mist opake that veils these eyes;
   Why does yon threat'ning tempest shroud the day?
   Why does thy altar, Venus, fade away,
And on my breast the dews of horror rise?
5 Phaon is false! be dim, ye orient Skies,
   And let black Erebus[4] succeed your ray;
   Let clashing thunders roll, and lightnings play;
Phaon is false! and hopeless Sappho dies!
   "Farewell! my Lesbian love, you might have said,"[5]
10 Such sweet remembrance had some pity prov'd,

---

[1] Stoic philosophers such as Epictetus (b.c. AD 50) and Marcus Aurelius (AD 121–80) advised the overcoming of emotion.

[2] Sappho was allegedly born in Mytilene, on Lesbos.

[3] the Muses.

[4] the dark cavern through which souls passed on their way to Hades.

[5] "Pope.
Si tam certus eras hinc ire, modestius isses,
Et modo dixisses Lesbi puella, vale. *Ovid.*" (M.R.) "If you were so resolved to leave my side, you could have gone in more becoming wise. You might at least have said to me: 'O Lesbian mistress, fare you well!'" Ovid, *Heroides* 15.99–100 (trans. Grant Showerman). Robinson's quotation is from Pope, "Sapho to Phaon" 113–14.

   "Or coldly thus, farewell, Oh! Lesbian maid!"
No task severe, for one so fondly lov'd!
   The gentle thought had sooth'd my wand'ring shade,
From life's dark valley, and its thorns remov'd!

36

Lead me, Sicilian Maids, to haunted bow'rs,
   While yon pale moon displays her faintest beams
   O'er blasted woodlands, and enchanted streams,
Whose banks infect the breeze with pois'nous flow'rs.
5 Ah! lead me, where the barren mountain tow'rs,
   Where no sounds echo, but the night-owl's screams,
   Where some lone spirit of the desert gleams,
And lurid horrors wing the fateful hours!
   Now goaded frenzy grasps my shrinking brain,
10 Her touch absorbs the crystal fount of woe!
   My blood rolls burning through each gasping vein;
Away, lost Lyre! unless thou can'st bestow
   A charm, to lull that agonizing pain,
Which those who never lov'd, can never know!

37

When, in the gloomy mansion of the dead,
   This with'ring heart, this faded form shall sleep:
   When these fond eyes, at length shall cease to weep,
And earth's cold lap receive this fev'rish head:
5 Envy shall turn away, a tear to shed,
   And Time's obliterating pinions sweep
   The spot, where poets shall their vigils keep,
To mourn and wander near my freezing bed!
   Then, my pale ghost, upon th'Elysian shore,
10 Shall smile, releas'd from ev'ry mortal care;
   While, doom'd love's victim to repine no more,
My breast shall bathe in endless rapture there!
   Ah! no! my restless shade would still deplore,
Nor taste that bliss, which Phaon did not share.

38

Oh Sigh! thou steal'st, the herald of the breast,
   The lover's fears, the lover's pangs to tell;
   Thou bid'st with timid grace the bosom swell,

    Cheating the day of joy, the night of rest!
5 Oh! lucid Tears! with eloquence confest,
        Why on my fading cheek unheeded dwell,
        Meek, as the dew-drops on the flowret's bell
    By ruthless tempests to the green-sod prest.
        Fond sigh be hush'd! congeal, O! slighted tear!
10 Thy feeble pow'rs the busy Fates[1] control!
        Or if thy crystal streams again appear,
    Let them, like Lethe's,[2] to oblivion roll:
        For Love the tyrant plays, when hope is near,
    And she who flies the lover,—chains the soul!

39

    Prepare your wreaths, Aonian maids divine,[3]
        To strew the tranquil bed where I shall sleep;
        In tears, the myrtle and the laurel steep,
    And let Erato's[4] hand the trophies twine.
5 No parian marble,[5] there, with labour'd line,
        Shall bid the wand'ring lover stay to weep;
        There holy silence shall her vigils keep,
    Save, when the nightingale such woes as mine
        Shall sadly sing; as twilight's curtains spread,
10 There shall the branching lotos[6] widely wave,
        Sprinkling soft show'rs upon the lily's head,
        Sweet drooping emblem for a lover's grave!
    And there shall Phaon pearls of pity shed,
    To gem the vanquish'd heart he scorn'd to save!

40

    On the low margin of a murm'ring stream,
        As rapt in meditation's arms I lay;
        Each aching sense in slumbers stole away,
    While potent fancy form'd a soothing dream;
5 O'er the Leucadian deep, a dazzling beam
        Shed the bland light of empyrean[7] day!
        But soon transparent shadows veil'd each ray,
    While mystic visions sprang athwart the gleam!
        Now to the heaving gulf they seem'd to bend,
10 And now across the sphery regions glide;
        Now in mid-air, their dulcet voices blend,
        "Awake! awake!" the restless phalanx cried,
    "See ocean yawns the lover's woes to end,
    Plunge the green wave, and bid thy griefs subside."

41

    Yes, I will go, where circling whirlwinds rise,
        Where threat'ning clouds in sable grandeur lour;
        Where the blast yells, the liquid columns pour,
    And madd'ning billows combat with the skies!
5 There, while the Dæmon of the tempest flies
        On growing pinions through the troublous hour,
        The wild waves gasp impatient to devour,
    And on the rock the waken'd Vulture cries!
        Oh! dreadful solace to the stormy mind!
10 To me, more pleasing than the valley's rest,
        The woodland songsters, or the sportive kind,
    That nip the turf, or prune the painted crest;
        For in despair alone, the wretched find
    That unction sweet, which lulls the bleeding breast!

42

    Oh! can'st thou bear to see this faded frame,
        Deform'd and mangled by the rocky deep?
        Wilt thou remember, and forbear to weep,
    My fatal fondness, and my peerless fame?
5 Soon o'er this heart, now warm with passion's flame,
        The howling winds and foamy waves shall sweep;
        Those eyes be ever clos'd in death's cold sleep,
    And all of Sappho perish, but her name!
        Yet, if the Fates suspend their barb'rous ire,
10 If days less mournful, Heav'n designs for me!
        If rocks grow kind, and winds and waves conspire,
    To bear me softly on the swelling sea;

---

[1] Fatæ or Parcæ (L.), three sister-goddesses who presided over human birth, life, and death.

[2] a river in the underworld, whose waters cause forgetfulness.

[3] Mount Helicon, sacred to the Muses, is in Aonia, a part of Bœotia.

[4] the Muse of lyric poetry.

[5] kind of fine white marble, from the island of Paros. The *Parian Chronicle*, an inscription on marble, is one of the sources for the story of Sappho.

[6] Cf. Homer, *Odyssey* 9.82–104; Alfred, Lord Tennyson, "The Lotos-Eaters" (1832).

[7] The Empyrean is the highest of the heavens.

To Phœbus[1] only will I tune my Lyre,
"What suits with Sappho, Phœbus suits with thee!"[2]

43

While from the dizzy precipice I gaze,
   The world receding from my pensive eyes,
   High o'er my head the tyrant eagle flies,
Cloth'd in the sinking sun's transcendent blaze!
5 The meek-ey'd moon, 'midst clouds of amber plays
   As o'er the purpling plains of light she hies,
   Till the last stream of living lustre dies,
And the cool concave owns her temper'd rays!
   So shall this glowing, palpitating soul,
10 Welcome returning Reason's placid beam,
   While o'er my breast the waves Lethean roll,
To calm rebellious Fancy's fev'rish dream;
   Then shall my Lyre disdain love's dread control,
And loftier passions, prompt the loftier theme!

Sonnet 44 Conclusive

Here droops the muse! while from her glowing mind,
   Celestial Sympathy, with humid eye,
   Bids the light Sylph[3] capricious Fancy fly,
Time's restless wings with transient flow'rs to bind!
5 For now, with folded arms and head inclin'd,
   Reflection pours the deep and frequent sigh,
   O'er the dark scroll of human destiny,
Where gaudy buds and wounding thorns are twin'd.
   O! Sky-born VIRTUE! sacred is thy name!
10 And though mysterious Fate, with frown severe,
   Oft decorates thy brows with wreaths of Fame,
Bespangled o'er with sorrow's chilling tear!

Yet shalt thou more than mortal raptures claim,
The brightest planet of th'ETERNAL SPHERE!

from *Lyrical Tales* (1800)

The Haunted Beach[4]

Upon a lonely desert Beach
   Where the white foam was scatter'd,
A little shed uprear'd its head
   Though lofty Barks were shatter'd.
5 The Sea-weeds gath'ring near the door,
   A sombre path display'd;
And, all around, the deaf'ning roar,
Re-echo'd on the chalky shore,
   By the green billows made.

10 Above, a jutting cliff was seen
   Where Sea Birds hover'd, craving;
And all around, the craggs were bound
   With weeds—for ever waving.
And here and there, a cavern wide
15 Its shad'wy jaws display'd;
And near the sands, at ebb of tide,
A shiver'd mast was seen to ride
   Where the green billows stray'd.

And often, while the morning wind
20 Stole o'er the Summer Ocean;
The moonlight scene, was all serene,
   The waters scarce in motion:
Then, while the smoothly slanting sand
   The tall cliff wrapp'd in shade,
25 The Fisherman beheld a band
Of Spectres, gliding hand in hand—
   Where the green billows play'd.

And pale their faces were, as snow,
   And sullenly they wander'd:
30 And to the skies with hollow eyes

---

[1] Apollo, the god of poetry.

[2] "Pope.
Grata lyram posui tibi Phœbe, poëtria Sappho:
Convenit illa mihi, convenit illa tibi. *Ovid.*" (M.R.) "SAPPHO THE SINGER, O PHOEBUS, HATH GRATEFULLY BROUGHT THEE A ZITHER [i.e. lyre]:/TOKEN WELL SUITED TO ME, TOKEN WELL SUITED TO THEE." Ovid, *Heroides* 14.183–84 (trans. Grant Showerman); in capitals because it is supposedly an inscription. Robinson's quotation is from Pope, "Sapho to Phaon" 216.

[3] a creature of the air. "The Sylphid" was one of Robinson's pseudonyms.

[4] first published in the *Morning Post* (26 February 1800). For an account of the composition of the poem, see *Memoirs of the Late Mrs. Robinson* (1801) 2:121–24.

    They look'd as though they ponder'd.
And sometimes, from their hammock shroud,
    They dismal howlings made,
And while the blast blew strong and loud
35 The clear moon mark'd the ghastly croud,
    Where the green billows play'd!

And then, above the haunted hut
    The Curlews screaming hover'd;
And the low door with furious roar
40   The frothy breakers cover'd.
For, in the Fisherman's lone shed
    A MURDER'D MAN was laid,
With ten wide gashes in his head
And deep was made his sandy bed
45   Where the green billows play'd.

A Shipwreck'd Mariner was he,
    Doom'd from his home to sever;
Who swore to be thro' wind and sea
    Firm and undaunted ever!
50 And when the wave resistless roll'd,
    About his arm he made
A packet rich of Spanish gold,
And, like a British sailor, bold,
    Plung'd, where the billows play'd!

55 The Spectre band, his messmates brave
    Sunk in the yawning ocean,
While to the mast he lash'd him fast
    And brav'd the storm's commotion.
The winter moon upon the sand,
60   A silv'ry carpet[1] made,
And mark'd the Sailor reach the land,
And mark'd his murd'rer wash his hand
    Where the green billows play'd.

And since that hour the Fisherman
65   Has toil'd and toil'd in vain!
For all the night, the moony light

    Gleams on the specter'd main!
And when the skies are veil'd in gloom,
    The Murd'rer's liquid way
70 Bounds o'er the deeply yawning tomb,
And flashing fires the sands illume,
    Where the green billows play!

Full thirty years his task has been,
    Day after day more weary;
75 For Heav'n design'd, his guilty mind
    Should dwell on prospects dreary.
Bound by a strong and mystic chain,
    He has not pow'r to stray;
But, destin'd mis'ry to sustain,
80 He wastes, in Solitude and Pain—
    A loathsome life away.

The Negro Girl[2]

1

Dark was the dawn, and o'er the deep
    The boist'rous whirlwinds blew;
The Sea-bird wheel'd its circling sweep,
    And all was drear to view—
5 When on the beach that binds the western shore
The love-lorn ZELMA stood, list'ning the tempest's roar.

2

Her eager Eyes beheld the main,
    While on her DRACO dear
She madly call'd, but call'd in vain,
10   No sound could DRACO hear,
Save the shrill yelling of the fateful blast,
While ev'ry Seaman's heart, quick shudder'd as it past.

3

White were the billows, wide display'd
    The clouds were black and low;
15 The Bittern shriek'd, a gliding shade
    Seem'd o'er the waves to go!
The livid flash illum'd the clam'rous main,
While ZELMA pour'd, unmark'd, her melancholy strain.

---

[1] Of this line, Coleridge remarked: "that 'silvery carpet' is so *just* that it is unfortunate it should *seem* so bad, for it is *really* good." He also enjoyed the metre of the poem: "aye, that woman has an ear!" (*Letters* 1:576).

[2] first published in *Ladies Magazine* (1 February 1796).

4

"Be still!" she cries, "loud tempest cease!
    O! spare the gallant souls:
The thunder rolls—the winds increase—
    The Sea like mountains rolls!
While, from the deck, the storm-worn victims leap,
And o'er their struggling limbs, the furious billows sweep.

5

"O! barb'rous Pow'r! relentless Fate!
    Does Heav'n's high will decree
That some should sleep on beds of state,—
    Some, in the roaring Sea?
Some, nurs'd in splendour, deal Oppression's blow,
While worth and DRACO pine—in Slavery and woe!

6

"Yon Vessel oft has plough'd the main
    With human traffic fraught;
Its cargo,—our dark Sons of pain—
    For worldly treasure bought!
What had they done?—O Nature tell me why—
Is taunting scorn the lot, of thy dark progeny?

7

"Thou gav'st, in thy caprice, the Soul
    Peculiarly enshrin'd;
Nor from the ebon Casket stole
    The Jewel of the mind!
Then wherefore let the suff'ring Negro's breast
Bow to his fellow, MAN, in brighter colours drest.

8

"Is it the dim and glossy hue
    That marks him for despair?—
While men with blood their hands embrue,
    And mock the wretch's pray'r?
Shall guiltless Slaves the Scourge of tyrants feel,
And, e'en before their GOD! unheard, unpitied kneel.

9

"Could the proud rulers of the land
    Our Sable race behold;
Some bow'd by torture's giant hand
    And others, basely sold!
Then would they pity Slaves, and cry, with shame,
Whate'er their TINTS may be, their SOULS are still the same!

10

"Why seek to mock the Ethiop's face?
    Why goad our hapless kind?
Can features alienate the race—
    Is there no kindred mind?
Does not the cheek which vaunts the roseate hue
Oft blush for crimes, that Ethiops never knew?

11

"Behold! the angry waves conspire
    To check the barb'rous toil!
While wounded Nature's vengeful ire—
    Roars, round this trembling Isle!
And hark! her voice re-echoes in the wind—
Man was not form'd by Heav'n, to trample on his kind!

12

"Torn from my Mother's aching breast,
    My Tyrant sought my love—
But, in the Grave shall ZELMA rest,
    E'er she will faithless prove—
No DRACO!—Thy companion I will be
To that celestial realm, where Negros shall be free!

13

"The Tyrant WHITE MAN taught my mind—
    The letter'd page to trace;—
He taught me in the Soul to find
    No tint, as in the face:
He bade my Reason blossom like the tree—
But fond affection gave, the ripen'd fruits to thee.

14

"With jealous rage he mark'd my love;
    He sent thee far away;—
And prison'd in the plaintain grove—
    Poor ZELMA pass'd the day—

But ere the moon rose high above the main,
ZELMA, and Love contriv'd to break the Tyrant's
   chain.

15

85 "Swift, o'er the plain of burning Sand
      My course I bent to thee;
   And soon I reach'd the billowy strand
      Which bounds the stormy Sea.—
   DRACO! my Love! Oh yet, thy ZELMA's soul
90 Springs ardently to thee,—impatient of controul.

16

"Again the lightning flashes white—
      The rattling cords among!
   Now, by the transient vivid light,
      I mark the frantic throng!
95 Now up the tatter'd shrouds my DRACO flies—
   While o'er the plunging prow, the curling billows
      rise.

17

"The topmast falls—three shackled slaves—
      Cling to the Vessel's side!
   Now lost amid the madd'ning waves—
100   Now on the mast they ride—
   See! on the forecastle my DRACO stands
   And now he waves his chain, now clasps his bleeding
      hands.

18

"Why, cruel WHITE-MAN! when away
      My sable Love was torn,
105 Why did you let poor ZELMA stay,
      On Afric's sands to mourn?
   No! ZELMA is not left, for she will prove
   In the deep troubled main, her fond—her faithful
      LOVE."

19

   The lab'ring Ship was now a wreck,
110   The shrouds were flutt'ring wide!
   The rudder gone, the lofty deck
      Was rock'd from side to side—
   Poor ZELMA's eyes now dropp'd their last big tear,
   While, from her tawny cheek, the blood recoil'd with
      fear.

20

115 Now frantic, on the sands she roam'd,
      Now shrieking stop'd to view
   Where high the liquid mountains foam'd,
      Around the exhausted crew—
   'Till, from the deck, her DRACO's well known form
120 Sprung mid the yawning waves, and buffetted the
      Storm.

21

   Long, on the swelling surge sustain'd
      Brave DRACO sought the shore,
   Watch'd the dark Maid, but ne'er complain'd,
      Then sunk, to gaze no more!
125 Poor ZELMA saw him buried by the wave—
   And, with her heart's true Love, plung'd in a wat'ry
      grave.

The Alien Boy

'Twas on a Mountain, near the Western Main
An ALIEN dwelt. A solitary Hut
Built on a jutting crag, o'erhung with weeds,
Mark'd the poor Exile's home. Full ten long years
5 The melancholy wretch had liv'd unseen
By all, save HENRY, a lov'd, little Son
The partner of his sorrows. On the day
When Persecution, in the sainted guise
Of Liberty, spread wide its venom'd pow'r,[1]
10 The brave, Saint HUBERT, fled his Lordly home,
And, with his baby Son, the mountain sought.
Resolv'd to cherish in his bleeding breast
The secret of his birth, Ah! birth too high
For his now humbled state, from infancy
15 He taught him, labour's task: He bade him chear
The dreary day of cold adversity
By patience and by toil. The Summer morn

---

[1] probably a reference to one of the periods of repression during the French Revolution.

Shone on the pillow of his rushy bed;
The noontide, sultry hour, he fearless past
On the shagg'd eminence; while the young Kid
Skipp'd, to the cadence of his minstrelsy.

At night young HENRY trimm'd the faggot fire
While oft, Saint HUBERT wove the ample net
To snare the finny victim. Oft they sang
And talk'd, while sullenly the waves would sound
Dashing the sandy shore. Saint HUBERT's eyes
Would swim in tears of fondness, mix'd with joy,
When he observ'd the op'ning harvest rich
Of promis'd intellect, which HENRY's soul,
Whate'er the subject of their talk, display'd.

Oft, the bold Youth, in question intricate,
Would seek to know the story of his birth;
Oft ask, who bore him: and with curious skill
Enquire, why he, and only one beside,
Peopled the desart mountain? Still his Sire
Was slow of answer, and, in words obscure,
Varied the conversation. Still the mind
Of HENRY ponder'd; for, in their lone hut,
A daily journal would Saint HUBERT make
Of his long banishment: and sometimes speak
Of Friends forsaken, Kindred massacred;—
Proud mansions, rich domains, and joyous scenes
For ever faded,—lost!
                     One winter time,
'Twas on the Eve of Christmas, the shrill blast
Swept o'er the stormy main. The boiling foam
Rose to an altitude so fierce and strong
That their low hovel totter'd. Oft they stole
To the rock's margin, and with fearful eyes
Mark'd the vex'd deep, as the slow rising moon
Gleam'd on the world of waters. 'Twas a scene
Would make a Stoic[1] shudder! For, amid
The wavy mountains, they beheld, *alone*,
A LITTLE BOAT, now scarcely visible;
And now not seen at all; or, like a buoy,
Bounding, and buffeting, to reach the shore!

---

[1] Stoic philosophers such as Epictetus (b.c. AD 50) and Marcus Aurelius (AD 121–80) advised the overcoming of emotion.

Now the full Moon, in crimson lustre shone
Upon the outstretch'd Ocean. The black clouds
Flew swiftly on, the wild blast following,
And, as they flew, dimming the angry main
With shadows horrible! Still, the small boat
Struggled amid the waves, a sombre speck
Upon the wide domain of howling Death!
Saint HUBERT sigh'd! while HENRY's speaking eye
Alternately the stormy scene survey'd
And his low hovel's safety. So past on
The hour of midnight,—and, since first they knew
The solitary scene, no midnight hour
E'er seem'd so long and weary.
                           While they stood,
Their hands fast link'd together, and their eyes
Fix'd on the troublous Ocean, suddenly
The breakers, bounding on the rocky shore,
Left the small wreck; and crawling on the side
Of the rude crag,—a HUMAN FORM was seen!
And now he climb'd the foam-wash'd precipice,
And now the slipp'ry weeds gave way, while he
Descended to the sands: The moon rose high—
The wild blast paus'd, and the poor shipwreck'd Man
Look'd round aghast, when on the frowning steep
He marked the lonely exiles. Now he call'd
But he was feeble, and his voice was lost
Amid the din of mingling sounds that rose
From the wild scene of clamour.
                               Down the steep
Saint HUBERT hurried, boldly venturous,
Catching the slimy weeds, from point to point,
And unappall'd by peril. At the foot
Of the rude rock, the fainting mariner
Seiz'd on his outstretch'd arm, impatient, wild,
With transport exquisite! But ere they heard
The blest exchange of sounds articulate,
A furious billow, rolling on the steep,
Engulph'd them in Oblivion!
                                   On the rock
Young HENRY stood; with palpitating heart,
And fear-struck, e'en to madness! Now he call'd,
Louder and louder, as the shrill blast blew;
But, mid the elemental strife of sounds,
No human voice gave answer! The clear moon

No longer quiver'd on the curling main,
But, mist-encircled, shed a blunted light,
Enough to shew all things that mov'd around,
100 Dreadful, but indistinctly! The black weeds
Wav'd, as the night-blast swept them; and along
The rocky shore the breakers, sounding low
Seem'd like the whisp'ring of a million souls
Beneath the green-deep mourning.
                              Four long hours
105 The lorn Boy listen'd! four long tedious hours
Pass'd wearily away, when, in the East
The grey beam coldly glimmer'd. All alone
Young HENRY stood aghast: his eye wide fix'd;
While his dark locks, uplifted by the storm
110 Uncover'd met its fury. On his cheek
Despair sate terrible! For, mid the woes,
Of poverty and toil, he had not known,
Till then, the horror-giving chearless hour
Of TOTAL SOLITUDE!
                           He spoke—he groan'd,
115 But no responsive voice, no kindred tone
Broke the dread pause: For now the storm had ceas'd,
And the bright Sun-beams glitter'd on the breast
Of the green placid Ocean. To his Hut
The lorn Boy hasten'd; there the rushy couch,
120 The pillow still indented, met his gaze
And fix'd his eye in madness.—From that hour
A maniac wild, the Alien Boy has been;
His garb with sea-weeds fring'd, and his wan cheek
The tablet of his mind, disorder'd, chang'd,
125 Fading, and worn with care. And if, by chance,
A Sea-beat wand'rer from the outstretch'd main
Views the lone Exile, and with gen'rous zeal
Hastes to the sandy beach, he suddenly
Darts 'mid the cavern'd cliffs, and leaves pursuit
130 To track him, where no footsteps but his own,
Have e'er been known to venture! YET HE LIVES
A melancholy proof that Man may bear
All the rude storms of Fate, and still suspire
By the wide world forgotten!

from the *Morning Post* (1 August 1800)

The Camp[1]

Tents, *marquees*, and baggage waggons;
Suttling houses, beer in flaggons;
Drums and trumpets, singing, firing;
Girls seducing, *beaux* admiring;
5 Country lasses gay and smiling,
City lads their hearts beguiling;
Dusty roads, and horses frisky;
Many an *Eton boy*[2] in whisky;
Tax'd carts full of farmer's daughters;
10 Brutes condemn'd, and man—who slaughters!
Public-houses, booths, and castles;
Belles of fashion, serving vassals;
Lordly Gen'rals fiercely staring,
Weary soldiers, sighing, swearing!
15 *Petit maitres*[3] always dressing—
In the glass themselves caressing;
Perfum'd, painted, patch'd and blooming
Ladies—manly airs assuming!
Dowagers of fifty, simp'ring
20 Misses, for a lover whimp'ring—
Husbands drill'd to household tameness;
Dames heart sick of wedded sameness.
Princes setting girls a-madding—
Wives for ever fond of gadding—
25 Princesses with lovely faces,
Beauteous children of the Graces![4]
Britain's pride and Virtue's treasure,
Fair and gracious, beyond measure!
Aid de Camps,[5] and youthful pages—

---

[1] signed "Oberon." For an account of military camps at this time, see Gillian Russell, *The Theatres of War: Performance, Politics, and Society, 1793–1815* (1995).

[2] students at Eton College, in Windsor. A "whisky" is a kind of carriage.

[3] "little masters" (Fr.): dandies, fops.

[4] goddesses attendant on Venus.

[5] assistants to staff officers.

30 Prudes, and vestals[1] of all ages!—
Old coquets, and matrons surly,
Sounds of distant *hurly burly*!
Mingled voices uncouth singing;
Carts, full laden, forage bringing;
35 Sociables,[2] and horses weary;
Houses warm, and dresses airy;
Loads of fatten'd poultry; pleasure
Serv'd (TO NOBLES) without measure.
Doxies, who the waggons follow;
40 Beer, for thirsty hinds to swallow;
Washerwomen, fruit-girls chearful,
ANTIENT LADIES—*chaste* and *fearful*!
Tradesmen, leaving shops, and seeming
More of *war* than profit dreaming;
45 Martial sounds, and braying asses;
Noise, that ev'ry noise surpasses!
All confusion, din, and riot—
NOTHING CLEAN—and NOTHING QUIET.—

from *The Wild Wreath* (1804)

A London Summer Morning[3]

Who has not wak'd to list the busy sounds
Of SUMMER MORNING, in the sultry smoke
Of noisy LONDON?—On the pavement hot
The sooty Chimney-boy, with dingy face
5 And tatter'd covering, shrilly bawls his trade,
Rousing the sleepy House-maid. At the door
The Milk-pail rattles, and the tinkling bell
Proclaims the Dustman's office; while the street
Is lost in clouds imperious. Now begins
10 The din of Hackney-coaches, Waggons, Carts;
While Tin-men's shops, and noisy Trunk-makers,
Knife-grinders, Coopers, squeaking Cork-cutters,
Fruit-barrows, and the hunger-giving cries
Of Vegetable-venders, fill the air.
15 Now ev'ry Shop displays its varied trade;
And the fresh-sprinkled pavement cools the feet
Of early walkers. At the private door
The ruddy House-maid twirls the busy mop,
Annoying the smart 'prentice, or neat girl
20 Tripping with band-box lightly. Now the Sun
Darts burning splendor on the glitt'ring pane,
Save where the canvas awning throws a shade
On the gay merchandise. Now spruce and trim
In shops, where beauty smiles with industry,
25 Sits the smart damsel, while the passenger
Peeps through the window, watching ev'ry charm.
Now Pastry dainties catch the eyes minute
Of hummy insects, while the slimy snare[4]
Waits to enthral them. Now the Lamp-lighter
30 Mounts the slight ladder, nimbly venturous,
To trim the half-fill'd lamp; while at his feet
The Pot-boy yells discordant. All along
The sultry pavement, the Old Clothes-man cries
In tone monotonous, and sidelong views
35 The area for his traffic: now the bag
Is slily open'd, and the half-worn suit
(Sometimes the pilfer'd treasure of the base
Domestic spoiler) for one half its worth
Sinks in the green abyss. The Porter now
40 Bears his huge load along the burning way:
And the poor POET wakes from busy dreams,
To paint THE SUMMER MORNING.

The Poet's Garret[5]

Come, sportive Fancy! Come with me, and trace
The POET's Attic home! The lofty seat
Of th'Heaven-tutor'd Nine![6] The airy throne
Of bold Imagination, rapture-fraught,

---

[1] virgins. The Vestal Virgins maintained the fire in the temple of Vesta (the goddess of the hearth) in Rome.

[2] open carriages.

[3] first published under the title, "London's Summer Morning," in the *Morning Post* (23 August 1800). Cf. Jonathan Swift (1667–1745), "A Description of the Morning" (1709).

[4] In *Poetical Works* (1806), this reads "limy snare": the insects are being caught with bird-lime, a sticky substance spread on sticks or paper.

[5] first published in the *Morning Post* (6 September 1800), signed "M.R."

[6] the Muses.

5   Above the herd of mortals!—All around,
    A solemn stillness seems to guard the scene,
    Nursing the brood of thought; a thriving brood,
    In the rich mazes of the cultur'd brain.
    Upon thy altar, an old worm-eat board,
10 The pannel of a broken door, or lid
    Of a strong coffer, plac'd on three-legg'd stool,
    Stand quires of paper, white and beautiful;
    Paper, by Destiny ordain'd to be
    Scrawl'd o'er and blotted, dash'd and scratch'd, and torn,
15 Or mark'd with lines severe, or scatter'd wide
    In rage impetuous! Sonnet, Song, and Ode;
    Satire, and Epigram, and smart *Charade*;
    Neat Paragraph, or legendary Tale
    Of short and simple metre; each by turns
20 Will there delight the reader.

                    On the bed
    Lies an old rusty "suit of solemn black,"[1]
    Brush'd thread-bare, and with brown unglossy hue
    Grown rather ancient. On the floor is seen
    A pair of silken hose, whose footing bad
25 Shews they are travellers, but who still bear
    Marks somewhat *holy*. At the scanty fire
    A chop turns round, by packthread strongly held;
    And on the blackened bar a vessel shines
    Of batter'd pewter, just half-fill'd, and warm,
30 With *Whitbread*'s beverage[2] pure. The kitten purs,
    Anticipating dinner; while the wind
    Whistles through broken panes, and drifted snow
    Carpets the parapet with spotless garb
    Of vestal[3] coldness.—Now the sullen hour
35 (The fifth hour after noon) with dusky hand
    Closes the lids of day. The farthing[4] light
    Gleams through the cobweb'd chamber, and THE BARD
    Concludes his pen's hard labour. Now he eats
    With appetite voracious! Nothing sad

40 That the costly plate, nor the napkin fine,
    Nor china rich nor sav'ry viands greet
    His eye, or palate. On his lyric board
    A sheet of paper serves for table-cloth;
    A heap of salt is serv'd (Oh! heav'nly treat),
45 On Ode *Pindaric*![5] while his tuneful Puss
    Scratches his slipper, for her fragment sweet,
    And sings her love-song, soft, yet mournfully.

        Mocking the pillar Doric, or the roof
    Of architecture Gothic, all around
50 The well-known ballads flit, of Grub-street[6] fame!
    The casement broke gives breath celestial
    To the long "*Dying Speech*," or gently fans
    The love-enflaming Sonnet. 'Round about
    Small scraps of paper lie, torn vestiges
55 Of an unquiet fancy: here a page
    Of flights poetic; here a Dedication;
    A list of *Dramatis Personae* bold,
    Of heroes yet unborn, and lofty dames,
    Of perishable compound "light as air,"[7]
60 But sentenc'd to oblivion!

                    On a shelf,
    Yclept a mantle-piece, a phial stands,
    Half-fill'd with potent spirits, clear and strong,
    Which sometimes haunt the Poet's restless brain,
    And fill his mind with fancies whimsical.

65   Poor Poet! happy art thou, thus remov'd
    From pride and folly! For, in thy domain
    Thou cans't command thy subjects, fill thy lines
    With the all-conqu'ring weapon *Heav'n* bestows
    In the grey-goose's wing![8] which, tow'ring high,
70 Bears thy rich fancy to immortal fame!

---

[1] Shakespeare, *Hamlet* 1.2.78.

[2] beer. The brewery founded by Samuel Whitbread (d. 1796) is still in business.

[3] virginal, pure.

[4] a coin worth one quarter of a penny. A farthing light is a cheap candle.

[5] an ode in the manner of Pindar (c. 522–443 BC), Greek poet.

[6] "originally the name of a street near Moorfields in London, much inhabited by writers of small histories, dictionaries, and temporary poems, whence any mean production is called *grubstreet*." Samuel Johnson (1709–84), *A Dictionary of the English Language* (1755).

[7] Shakespeare, *Othello* 3.3.319.

[8] a quill pen.

from *The Poetical Works of the Late Mrs. Mary Robinson* (1806)

To the Poet Coleridge[1]

Rapt in the visionary theme!
    SPIRIT DIVINE! with THEE I'll wander,
Where the blue, wavy, lucid stream,
    'Mid forest glooms, shall slow meander!
With THEE I'll trace the circling bounds
    Of thy NEW PARADISE extended;
And listen to the varying sounds
    Of winds, and foamy torrents blended.

Now by the source which lab'ring heaves
    The mystic fountain, bubbling, panting,
While Gossamer its net-work weaves,
    Adown the blue lawn slanting!
I'll mark thy *sunny dome*, and view
Thy *Caves of Ice*, thy fields of dew!
Thy ever-blooming mead, whose flow'r
Waves to the cold breath of the moonlight hour!
Or when the day-star, peering bright
On the grey wing of parting night;
While more than vegetating pow'r
Throbs grateful to the burning hour,
As summer's whisper'd sighs unfold
Her million, million buds of gold;
Then will I climb the breezy bounds,
    Of thy NEW PARADISE extended,
And listen to the distant sounds
    Of winds, and foamy torrents blended!

SPIRIT DIVINE! with THEE I'll trace
Imagination's boundless space!
With thee, beneath thy *sunny dome*,
    I'll listen to the minstrel's lay,
    Hymning the gradual close of day;
In *Caves of Ice* enchanted roam,
Where on the glitt'ring entrance plays
The moon's-beam with its silv'ry rays;
    Or, when glassy stream,
        That thro' the deep dell flows,
    Flashes the noon's hot beam;
        The noon's hot beam, that midway shows
Thy flaming Temple, studded o'er
With all PERUVIA's lustrous store![2]
There will I trace the circling bounds
    Of thy NEW PARADISE extended!
And listen to the awful sounds,
    Of winds, and foamy torrents blended!

And now I'll pause to catch the moan
    Of distant breezes, cavern-pent;
Now, ere the twilight tints are flown,
Purpling the landscape, far and wide,
On the dark promontory's side
    I'll gather wild flow'rs, dew besprent,
And weave a crown for THEE,
GENIUS OF HEAV'N-TAUGHT POESY!
While, op'ning to my wond'ring eyes,
Thou bidst a new creation rise,
I'll raptur'd trace the circling bounds
    Of thy RICH PARADISE extended,
And listen to the varying sounds
    Of winds, and foaming torrents blended.

And now, with lofty tones inviting,
Thy NYMPH, her dulcimer swift smiting,
Shall wake me in ecstatic measures!
Far, far remov'd from mortal pleasures!
    In cadence rich, in cadence strong,
Proving the wondrous witcheries of song!
    I hear her voice! thy *sunny dome*,
    Thy *caves of ice*, loud repeat,
    Vibrations, madd'ning sweet,
    Calling the visionary wand'rer home.
She sings of THEE, O favour'd child
Of Minstrelsy, SUBLIMELY WILD!
Of thee, whose soul can feel the tone
Which gives to airy dreams *a magic* ALL THY OWN!

---

[1] first published in *Memoirs of the Late Mrs. Robinson, Written by Herself* (1801), signed "Sappho." Cf. Coleridge, "Kubla Khan,"* which Robinson had seen in manuscript.

[2] silver from Peru.

The Savage of Aveyron[1]

'Twas in the mazes of a wood,
The lonely wood of AVEYRON,
I heard a melancholy tone:—
   It seem'd to freeze my blood!
5 A torrent near was flowing fast,
And hollow was the midnight blast
As o'er the leafless woods it past,
   While terror-fraught I stood!
O! mazy woods of AVEYRON!
10   O! wilds of dreary solitude!
   Amid thy thorny alleys rude
I thought myself alone!
   I thought no living thing could be
   So weary of the world as me,—
15 While on my winding path the pale moon shone.

   Sometimes the tone was loud and sad,
And sometimes dulcet, faint, and slow;
And then a tone of frantic woe:
   It almost made me mad.
20 The burthen was "Alone! alone!"
And then the heart did feebly groan;—
Then suddenly a cheerful tone
   Proclaim'd a spirit glad!
O! mazy woods of AVEYRON!
25   O! wilds of dreary solitude!
   Amid your thorny alleys rude
I wish'd myself—a traveller alone.

"*Alone!*" I heard the wild boy say,—
And swift he climb'd a blasted oak;
30 And there, while morning's herald woke,
   He watch'd the opening day.
Yet dark and sunken was his eye,
Like a lorn maniac's, wild and shy,
And scowling like a winter sky,
35   Without one beaming ray!
Then, mazy woods of AVEYRON!
   Then, wilds of dreary solitude!
   Amid thy thorny alleys rude
I sigh'd to be—a traveller alone.

40 "*Alone, alone!*" I heard him shriek,
'Twas like the shriek of dying man!
And then to mutter he began,—
   But, O! *he could not speak*!
I saw him point to Heav'n, and sigh,
45 The big drop trembl'd in his eye;
And slowly from the yellow sky,
   I saw the pale morn break.
I saw the woods of AVEYRON,
   Their wilds of dreary solitude:
50   I mark'd their thorny alleys rude,
And wish'd to be—a traveller alone!

   His hair was long and black, and he
From infancy *alone* had been:
For since his fifth year he had seen
55   None mark'd his destiny!
No mortal ear had heard his groan,
For him no beam of Hope had shone:
While sad he sigh'd—"*alone, alone!*"
   Beneath the blasted tree.
60 And then, O! woods of AVEYRON,
   O! wilds of dreary solitude,
   Amid your thorny alleys rude
I thought myself a traveller—alone.

   And now upon the blasted tree
65 He carv'd *three* notches, broad and long,
And all the while he sang a song—
   Of nature's melody!
And though of words he nothing knew,

---

[1] first published in *Memoirs of the Late Mrs. Robinson, Written by Herself* (1801). A naked and mute ten-year-old boy was first seen in the forests of Aveyron (a department in south-central France) in 1797. After several unsuccessful attempts, he was captured in 1799 and observed for several months by Father Pierre-Joseph Bonnaterre; Robinson probably saw the account of Bonnaterre's observations in the *Morning Post* on 3 October 1800. Later, the boy was transferred to the Institute for Deaf-Mutes in Paris, where Dr. Jean-Marc-Gaspard Itard (1775-1838) studied and tried to educate him, and named him Victor. After Itard finished his study in 1805 (he published *Rapports sur le sauvage d'Aveyron* in 1807), Victor lived with the Institute's housekeeper, Mme. Guérin, until his death in 1828. The story is the subject of *L'Enfant sauvage* (1970), a film by François Truffaut, and of *The Wild Boy of Aveyron* (1976), by Harlan Lane.

And, though his dulcet tones were few,
70 Across the yielding bark he drew,
 Deep sighing, notches THREE.
 O! mazy woods of AVEYRON,
  O! wilds of dreary solitude,
  Amid your thorny alleys rude
75 Upon this BLASTED OAK no sun beam shone!

 And now he pointed one, two, three;
 Again he shriek'd with wild dismay;
 And now he paced the thorny way,
  Quitting the blasted tree.
80 It was a dark December morn,
 The dew was frozen on the thorn:
 But to a wretch so sad, so lorn,
  All days alike would be!
 Yet, mazy woods of AVEYRON,
85 Yet, wilds of dreary solitude,
  Amid your frosty alleys rude
 I wish'd to be—a traveller alone.

 He follow'd me along the wood
 To a small grot his hands had made,
90 Deep in a black rock's sullen shade,
  Beside a tumbling flood.
 Upon the earth I saw him spread
 Of wither'd leaves a narrow bed,
 Yellow as gold, and streak'd with red,
95 They look'd like streaks of blood!
 Pull'd from the woods of AVEYRON,
  And scatter'd o'er the solitude
 By midnight whirlwinds strong and rude,
 To pillow the scorch'd brain that throbb'd alone.

100 Wild berries were his winter food,
 With them his sallow lip was dy'd;
 On chesnuts wild he fed beside,
  Steep'd in the foamy flood.
 Chequer'd with scars his breast was seen,[1]

105 Wounds streaming fresh with anguish keen,
 And marks where other wounds had been
  Torn by the brambles rude.
 Such was the boy of AVEYRON,
  The tenant of that solitude,
110 Where still, by misery unsubdued,
 He wander'd *nine long winters*, all alone.

 Before the step of his rude throne,
 The *squirrel* sported, tame and gay;
 The *dormouse* slept its life away,
115 Nor heard his midnight groan.
 About his form a garb he wore,
 Ragged it was, and mark'd with gore,
 And yet, where'er 'twas folded o'er,
  Full many a spangle shone!
120 Like little stars, O! AVEYRON,
  They gleam'd amid thy solitude;
  Or like, along thy alleys rude,
 The summer dew-drops sparkling in the sun.

 It once had been a lady's vest,
125 White as the whitest mountain's snow,
 Till ruffian hands had taught to flow
  The fountain of her breast!
 Remembrance bade the WILD BOY trace
 Her beauteous form, her angel face,
130 Her eye that beam'd with Heavenly grace,
  Her fainting voice that blest,—
 When in the woods of AVEYRON,
  Deep in their deepest solitude,
 Three barb'rous ruffians shed her blood,
135 And mock'd, with cruel taunts, her dying groan.

 Remembrance trac'd the summer bright,
 When all the trees were fresh and green,
 When lost, the alleys long between,
  The lady past the night:
140 She past the night, bewilder'd wild,
 She past it with her fearless child,
 Who raised his little arms, and smil'd
  To see the morning light.
 While in the woods of AVEYRON,
145 Beneath the broad oak's canopy,

---

[1] The *Morning Post* reported: "He lived on potatoes, chestnuts, and acorns ... every part of his body is covered with scars; these scars attest the cruelty of the persons by whom, it is presumed, he has been abandoned; or perhaps they are attributable only to the dangers of a solitary existence at a tender age, and in a rude tract of country."

She mark'd aghast the RUFFIANS THREE,
Waiting to seize the traveller alone!

    Beneath the broad oak's canopy
The lovely lady's bones were laid;
150 But since that hour no breeze has play'd
    About the blasted tree!
The leaves all wither'd ere the sun
His next day's rapid course had run,
And ere the summer day was done
155   It winter seem'd to be:
And still, O! woods of AVEYRON,
    Amid thy dreary solitude
    The oak a sapless trunk has stood,
To mark the spot where MURDER foul was done!

160   From HER the WILD BOY learn'd "ALONE,"
She tried to say, *my babe will die*!
But angels caught her parting sigh,
    The BABE her *dying tone*.
And from that hour the BOY has been
165 Lord of the solitary scene,
Wand'ring the dreary shades between,
    Making his dismal moan!
Till, mazy woods of AVEYRON,
    Dark wilds of dreary solitude,
170   Amid your thorny alleys rude
I thought myself alone.
    And could a wretch more wretched be,
    More wild, or fancy-fraught than he,
Whose melancholy tale would pierce AN HEART OF
    STONE.

The Birth-Day[1]

Here bounds the gaudy gilded chair,
    Bedeck'd with fringe, and tassels gay;
The melancholy Mourner there
    Pursues her sad and painful way.

5 Here, guarded by a motley train,
    The pamper'd Countess glares along;
There, wrung by poverty and pain,
    Pale Mis'ry mingles with the throng.

Here, as the blazon'd chariot rolls,
10   And prancing horses scare the crowd,
Great names, adorning little souls,
    Announce the empty, vain, and proud.

Here four tall lacquies slow precede
    A painted dame, in rich array;
15 There the sad shiv'ring child of need
    Steals barefoot o'er the flinty way.

"Room, room! stand back!" they loudly cry,
    The wretched poor are driv'n around
On ev'ry side, they scatter'd fly,
20   And shrink before the threat'ning sound.

Here, amidst jewels, feathers, flow'rs,
    The senseless Duchess sits demure;
Heedless of all the anguish'd hours
    The sons of modest worth endure.

25 All silver'd, and embroider'd o'er,
    She neither knows nor pities pain;
The Beggar freezing at her door
    She overlooks with nice disdain.

The wretch whom poverty subdues
30   Scarce dares to raise his tearful eye;
Or if by chance the throng he views,
    His loudest murmur is a sigh!

The poor wan mother, at whose breast
    The pining infant craves relief,
35 In one thin tatter'd garment drest,
    Creeps forth to pour the plaint of grief.

But ah! how little heeded here
    The fault'ring tongue reveals its woe;
For high-born fools, with frown austere,
40   Contemn the pangs they never know.

---

[1] first published in the *Morning Post* (21 January 1795), signed "Portia." The birthday is that of Queen Charlotte (18 January).

"Take physic, Pomp!"[1] let Reason say,
 "What can avail thy trappings rare?
The tomb shall close thy glitt'ring day,
 The BEGGAR prove thy equal there!"

The Wintry Day[2]

Is it in mansions rich and gay,
 On downy beds, or couches warm,
That Nature owns the wintry day,
 And shrinks to hear the howling storm?
5   Ah! No!

'Tis on the bleak and barren heath,
 Where Mis'ry feels the ice of death,
As to the dark and freezing grave
 Her children, not a friend to save,
10   Unheeded go!

Is it in chambers silken drest,
 At tables which profusions heap,
Is it on pillows soft to rest,
 In dreams of long and balmy sleep?
15   Ah! No!

'Tis in the rushy hut obscure,
 Where Poverty's low sons endure,
And, scarcely daring to repine,
 On a straw pallet, mute, recline,
20   O'erwhelm'd with woe!

Is it to flaunt in warm attire,
 To laugh, to feast, and dance, and sing;
To crowd around the blazing fire,
 And make the roof with revels ring?
25   Ah! No!

'Tis on the prison's flinty floor,
 'Tis where the deaf'ning whirlwinds roar;
'Tis when the Sea-boy, on the mast,
 Hears the wave bounding to the blast,
30   And looks below!

'Tis in a cheerless naked room,
 Where Mis'ry's victims wait their doom,
Where a fond mother famish'd dies,
 While forth a frantic father flies,
35   Man's desp'rate foe!

Is it where gamesters thronging round,
 Their shining heaps of wealth display?
Where fashion's giddy tribes are found,
 Sporting their senseless hours away?
40   Ah! No!

'Tis in the silent spot obscure,
 Where, forc'd all sorrows to endure,
Pale Genius learns—oh! lesson sad!
 To court the vain, and on the bad
45   False praise bestow!

Where the neglected Hero sighs,
 Where Hope, exhausted, silent dies,
Where Virtue starves, by Pride oppress'd,
 'Till ev'ry stream that warms the breast
50   Forbears to flow!

The Old Beggar[3]

1

Do you see the OLD BEGGAR who sits at yon gate,
 With his beard silver'd over like snow?
Tho' he smiles as he meets the keen arrows of fate,
 Still his bosom is wearied with woe.

2

5 Many years has he sat at the foot of the hill,
 Many days seen the summer sun rise;
And at evening the traveller passes him still,
 While the shadows steal over the skies.

---

[1] Shakespeare, *King Lear* 3.4.33

[2] first published in the *Morning Post* (4 January 1800). Robinson's *Poetical Works* also includes a companion poem, "The Summer Day," first published in the *Morning Post* (7 August 1800), signed "T.B." (for "Tabitha Bramble").

[3] first published in the *Morning Post* (25 July 1800), signed "M.R."

3

In the bleak blast of winter he hobbles along
    O'er the heath, at the dawning of day;
And the *dew-drops* that freeze the rude thistles among,
    Are the *stars* that illumine his way.

4

How mild is his aspect, how modest his eye,
    How meekly his soul bears each wrong!
How much does he speak by his eloquent sigh,
    Tho' no accent is heard from his tongue.

5

Time was, when this BEGGAR, in martial trim dight,
    Was as bold as the chief of his throng;
When he march'd thro' the storms of the day or the night,
    And still smil'd as he journey'd along.

6

Then his form was athletic, his eyes' vivid glance
    Spoke the lustre of youth's glowing day!
And the village all mark'd, in the combat and dance,
    The brave younker[1] still valiant as gay.

7

When the prize was propos'd, how his footsteps wou'd bound,
    While the MAID *of his heart* led the throng,
While the ribands that circled the May-pole around,
    Wav'd the trophies of garlands among!

8

But love o'er his bosom triumphantly reign'd,
    Love taught him in secret to pine;
Love wasted his youth, yet he never complain'd,
    For the silence of love—is divine!

9

The dulcet ton'd word, and the plaint of despair,
    Are no signs of the soul-wasting smart;
'Tis the pride of affection to cherish its care,
    And to count the quick throbs of the heart.

10

Amidst the loud din of the battle he stood,
    Like a lion, undaunted and strong;
But the tear of compassion was mingled with blood,
    When his sword was the first in the throng.

11

When the bullet whizz'd by, and his arm bore away,
    Still he shrunk not, with anguish oppress'd;
And when victory shouted the fate of the day,
    Not a groan check'd the joy of his breast.

12

To his dear native shore the poor wand'rer hied;
    But he came to complete his despair:
For the maid of his soul was that morning *a bride*!
    And a gay *lordly rival* was there!

13

From that hour, o'er the world he has wander'd forlorn;
    But still LOVE his companion would go;
And tho' deeply fond memory planted its thorn,
    Still he silently cherish'd his woe.

14

See him now, while with age and with sorrow oppress'd,
    He the gate opens slowly, and sighs!
See him drop the big tears on his woe-wither'd breast,
    The big tears that fall fast from his eyes!

15

See his habit all tatter'd, his shrivell'd cheek pale;
    See his locks, waving thin in the air;
See his lip is half froze with the sharp cutting gale,
    And his head, o'er the temples, all bare!

---

[1] youngster.

16

His eye-beam no longer in lustre displays
   The warm sunshine that visits his breast;
For deep sunk is its orbit, and darken'd its rays,
   And he sighs for the grave's silent rest.

17

And his voice is grown feeble, his accent is slow,
   And he sees not the distant hill's side;
And he hears not the breezes of morn as they blow,
   Nor the streams that soft murmuring glide.

18

To him all is silent, and mournful, and dim,
   E'en the seasons pass dreary and slow;
For affliction has plac'd its cold fetters on him,
   And his soul is enamour'd of woe.

19

See the TEAR, which, imploring, is fearful to roll,
   Tho' in silence he bows as you stray;
'Tis the eloquent silence which speaks to the soul,
   'Tis the *star* of his *slow-setting day*!

20

Perchance, ere the *May-blossoms* cheerfully wave,
   Ere the *zephyrs* of SUMMER soft sigh;
The sun-beams shall dance on the grass o'er his GRAVE,
   And his *journey* be mark'd—TO THE SKY.

Henrietta O'Neill
1758 – 1793

Henrietta Boyle O'Neill was the only child of Charles Boyle, Lord Dungarvon, and Susannah Hoare Boyle, daughter of the banker Henry Hoare. In 1777, she married the Irish politician John O'Neill, with whom she set up a private theatre at Shane's Castle, Antrim, Ireland. An amateur actor, she performed with Sir Edward Fitzgerald and befriended Sarah Siddons. On a visit to London she also met Charlotte Smith,* in whose novel *Desmond* (1792), O'Neill's much-anthologized poem "Ode to a Poppy" was first published. She and her husband had two sons, to whom she addressed a poem, "Written on Seeing her Two Sons at Play," published in Smith's *Sonnets* in 1797. Suffering from poor health, O'Neill visited Portugal, where she died in 1793. Her husband, created Baron O'Neill shortly after her death, was killed trying to suppress the Irish Rebellion of 1798. (A.M.)

෴

from *Desmond. A Novel.* By Charlotte Smith
(1792)

Ode to the Poppy

Not for the promise of the labor'd field,
Not for the good the yellow harvests yield,
    I bend at Ceres'[1] shrine;
    For dull, to humid eyes appear,
5   The golden glories of the year;
Alas!—A melancholy worship's mine!

I hail the Goddess for her scarlet flower!
    Thou brilliant weed,
    That dost so far exceed,
10 The richest gifts gay Flora[2] can bestow;
Heedless I pass'd thee, in life's morning hour,
    (Thou comforter of woe,)
'Till sorrow taught me to confess thy power.

    In early days, when Fancy cheats,
15   A various wreath I wove;
    Of laughing springs luxuriant sweets,
    To deck ungrateful love:
The rose, or thorn, my numbers crown'd,
    As Venus smil'd, or Venus frown'd;
20 But Love, and Joy, and all their train, are flown;
    E'en languid Hope no more is mine,
    And I will sing of thee alone;
Unless, perchance, the attributes of grief,
    The cypress bud, and willow leaf,[3]
25 Their pale, funereal foliage, blend with thine.

    Hail, lovely blossom!—thou can'st ease,
    The wretched victims of disease;
Can'st close those weary eyes, in gentle sleep,
    Which never open but to weep;
30   For, oh! thy potent charm,
    Can agonizing pain disarm;
Expel imperious memory from her seat,
And bid the throbbing heart forget to beat.

Soul-soothing plant!—that can such blessings give,
35   By thee the mourner bears to live!
    By thee the hopeless die!
Oh! ever "friendly to despair,"[4]
    Might sorrow's palid votary dare,
Without a crime, that remedy implore,
40 Which bids the spirit from its bondage fly,
I'd court thy palliative aid no more;

---

[1] the Roman name for the goddess of plants and grain.

[2] the Roman goddess of flowers.

[3] The cypress and willow both signify mourning.

[4] John Dryden (1631–1700), "Sigismonda and Guiscardo" (1700) 624.

No more I'd sue, that thou shouldst spread,
Thy spell around my aching head,
But would conjure thee to impart,
Thy balsam for a broken heart;

And by thy soft Lethean power,[1]
(Inestimable flower)
Burst these terrestrial bonds, and other regions try.

---

[1] associated with Lethe, the river of forgetfulness in the underworld.

Robert Burns
1759 – 1796

The "Scotch Bard," as Robert Burns is also known, was born in Alloway, Scotland, in 1759, on 25 January, a date still marked to celebrate Scotland's national poet. Although he was better educated than many tenant farmers at the time, he nevertheless easily adopted the role of peasant poet, a role that was greatly admired, particularly since the poetry of the commoner was alleged to be "natural," devoid of the artifice that educated poets employed.

He began his career as a local poet, but the 1786 publication of his first collection, *Poems, Chiefly in the Scottish Dialect*, made him famous almost immediately. He was particularly well-received in Edinburgh, where he relocated shortly after the first edition of *Poems*. There, he moved in the social circle of the wealthy, and soon another edition of his *Poems*, slightly expanded, was published. While in Edinburgh, he met James Johnson, whose project was to collect all the songs of Scotland. Burns, in part because of his support of Scottish cultural nationalism, greatly admired Johnson's work and began to help him collect these songs. Soon, Burns turned to the song as his primary form of poetic expression.

In 1788, he moved to a farm near Dumfries, where he married Jean Armour. He was able to leave farming entirely in order to become an excise collector in 1791. However, his health deteriorated, and he died near Dumfries in 1796, at the age of 35.

His life is as much celebrated as his poetry, which was written primarily in the Scottish dialect, in part so that Scottish cultural traditions could be preserved in the face of English hegemony. He has been called the last truly Scottish poet, since after his death, standard English was so widespread that the Scots vernacular was virtually unintelligible to the majority of readers. (J.G.)

☙❧

from *Poems, Chiefly in the Scottish Dialect*
(1786)

To a Mouse, On turning her up in her Nest, with the Plough, November, 1785

Wee, sleekit,[1] cowrin, tim'rous *beastie*,
O, what a panic's in thy breastie!
Thou need na start awa sae hasty,
    Wi' bickering brattle![2]
5 I wad be laith to rin an' chase thee,
    Wi' murd'ring *pattle*![3]

I'm truly sorry Man's dominion
Has broken Nature's social union,
An' justifies that ill opinion,
10   Which makes thee startle,
At me, thy poor, earth-born companion,
    An' *fellow-mortal*!

I doubt na, whyles,[4] but thou may thieve;
What then? poor beastie, thou maun[5] live!
15 A *daimen-icker* in a *thrave*[6]
    'S a sma' request:
I'll get a blessin wi' the lave,[7]
    An' never miss't!

---

[1] "sleek" (Sc.).

[2] "with a scurrying hurry."

[3] a spade used for cleaning the plough.

[4] "sometimes."

[5] "must."

[6] "an occasional ear of corn in twenty-four sheaves."

[7] "rest."

    Thy wee-bit *housie*, too, in ruin!
20 It's silly[1] wa's the win's are strewin!
An' naething, now, to big[2] a new ane,
        O' foggage[3] green!
An' bleak *December's winds* ensuin,
        Baith snell[4] an' keen!

25   Thou saw the fields laid bare an' wast,
An' weary *Winter* comin fast,
An' cozie here, beneath the blast,
        Thou thought to dwell,
Till crash! the cruel *coulter* past
30   Out thro' thy cell.

    That wee-bit heap o' leaves an' stibble,[5]
Has cost thee monie a weary nibble!
Now thou's turn'd out, for a' thy trouble,
        But house or hald,
35 To thole[6] the Winter's *sleety dribble*,
        An' *cranreuch*[7] cauld!

    But, Mousie, thou art no thy-lane,[8]
In proving *foresight* may be vain:
The best laid schemes o' *Mice* an' *Men*
40   Gang aft agley,[9]
An' lea'e us nought but grief an' pain,
        For promis'd joy!

    Still, thou art blest, compar'd wi' *me*!
The *present* only toucheth thee:
45 But, Och! I *backward* cast my e'e
        On prospects drear!

---

[1] "frail."

[2] "build."

[3] "rank grass."

[4] "bitter, biting."

[5] "stubble."

[6] "to suffer, to endure."

[7] "hoar frost."

[8] "alone."

[9] "often go awry."

An' *forward*, tho' I canna *see*,
    I *guess* an' fear!

To A Mountain-Daisy,
*On turning one down, with the Plough,
in April—1786*

    Wee, modest, crimson-tipped flow'r,
Thou's met me in an evil hour;
For I maun crush amang the stoure[10]
        Thy slender stem:
5 To spare thee now is past my pow'r,
        Thou bonie gem.

    Alas! It's no thy neebor sweet,
The bonie *Lark*, companion meet!
Bending thee 'mang the dewy weet!
10   Wi's spreckl'd breast,
When upward-springing, blythe, to greet
        The purpling East.

    Cauld blew the bitter-biting *North*
Upon thy early, humble birth;
15 Yet chearfully thou glinted forth
        Amid the storm,
Scarce rear'd above the *Parent-earth*
        Thy tender form.

    The flaunting *flow'rs* our Gardens yield,
20 High-shelt'ring woods and wa's maun[11] shield,
But thou, beneath the random bield[12]
        O' clod or stane,
Adorns the histie[13] *stibble-field*,
        Unseen, alane.

25   There, in thy scanty mantle clad,
Thy snawie bosom sun-ward spread,
Thou lifts thy unassuming head

---

[10] "dust."

[11] "walls must."

[12] "shelter."

[13] "dry, barren."

   In humble guise;
But now the *share* uptears thy bed,
   And low thou lies!

Such is the fate of artless Maid,
Sweet *flow'ret* of the rural shade!
By Love's simplicity betray'd,
   And guileless trust,
Till she, like thee, all soil'd, is laid
   Low i' the dust.

Such is the fate of simple Bard,
On Life's rough ocean luckless starr'd!
Unskilful he to note the card
   Of *prudent Lore*,
Till billows rage, and gales blow hard,
   And whelm him o'er!

Such fate to *suffering worth* is giv'n,
Who long with wants and woes has striv'n,
By human pride or cunning driv'n
   To Mis'ry's brink,
Till wrench'd of ev'ry stay but HEAV'N,
   He, ruin'd, sink!

Ev'n thou who mourn'st the *Daisy's* fate,
That fate is thine—no distant date;
Stern Ruin's *plough-share* drives, elate,
   Full on thy bloom,
Till crush'd beneath the *furrow's* weight,
   Shall be thy doom!

To A Louse, On Seeing one on a Lady's Bonnet, at Church

Ha! whaur ye gaun, ye crowlin ferlie![1]
Your impudence protects you sairly:[2]
I canna say but ye strunt[3] rarely,
   Owre *gauze* and *lace*;
Tho' faith, I fear ye dine but sparely,
   On sic a place.

Ye ugly, creepin, blastit wonner,[4]
Detested, shunn'd, by saunt[5] an' sinner,
How daur ye set your fit upon her,
   Sae fine a *Lady*!
Gae somewhere else and seek your dinner,
   On some poor body.

Swith, in some beggar's haffet squattle;[6]
There ye may creep, and sprawl, and sprattle,[7]
Wi' ither kindred, jumping cattle,
   In shoals and nations;
Whaur *horn* nor *bane* ne'er daur unsettle,
   Your thick plantations.

Now haud you there, ye're out o' sight,
Below the fatt'rels,[8] snug and tight,
Na, faith ye yet! ye'll no be right,
   Till ye've got on it,
The verra tapmost, tow'rin height
   O' *Miss's* bonnet.

My sooth! right bauld ye set your nose out,
As plump an' grey as onie grozet:[9]
O for some rank, mercurial rozet,[10]
   Or fell, red smeddum,[11]
I'd gie you sic a hearty dose o't,
   Wad dress your droddum![12]

---

[1] "wonder."

[2] "sorely."

[3] "strut."

[4] "wonder."

[5] "saint."

[6] "suddenly sprawl in some beggar's temple."

[7] "struggle."

[8] "ribbon ends."

[9] "gooseberry."

[10] "rosin."

[11] "dust."

[12] "breach."

I wad na been surpriz'd to spy
You on an auld wife's *flainen toy*;[1]
Or *aiblins*[2] some bit *duddie*[3] boy,
    On's *wylecoat*,[4]
35 But Miss's fine *Lunardi*,[5] fye!
    How daur ye do't?

O *Jenny*, dinna toss your head,
An' set your beauties a' abread!
Ye little ken what cursed speed
40   The blastie's makin!
Thae *winks* and *finger-ends*, I dread,
    Are notice takin!

O wad some Pow'r the giftie[6] gie us
To see oursels as others see us!
45 It wad frae mony a blunder free us
    An' foolish notion:
What airs in dress an' gait wad lea'e us,
    An' ev'n Devotion!

from *Poems, Chiefly in the Scottish Dialect* (1787)

John Barleycorn. A Ballad

1

There was three kings into the east,
Three kings both great and high,
And they hae sworn a solemn oath
John Barleycorn should die.

2

5 They took a plough and plough'd him down,
Put clods upon his head,

---

[1] "a woman's hat."
[2] "perhaps."
[3] "ragged."
[4] "flannel vest."
[5] a hat.
[6] "gift."

And they hae sworn a solemn oath
John Barleycorn was dead.

3

But the chearful Spring came kindly on,
10 And show'rs began to fall;
John Barleycorn got up again,
And sore surpris'd them all.

4

The sultry suns of Summer came,
And he grew thick and strong,
15 His head weel arm'd wi' pointed spears,
That no one should him wrong.

5

The sober Autumn enter'd mild,
When he grew wan and pale;
His bending joints and drooping head
20 Show'd he began to fail.

6

His colour sicken'd more and more,
He faded into age;
And then his enemies began
To show their deadly rage.

7

25 They've taen a weapon, long and sharp,
And cut him by the knee;
Then ty'd him fast upon a cart,
Like a rogue for forgerie.

8

They laid him down upon his back,
30 And cudgell'd him full sore;
They hung him up before the storm,
And turn'd him o'er and o'er.

9

They filled up a darksome pit
With water to the brim,
35 They heaved in John Barleycorn,
There let him sink or swim.

10

They laid him out upon the floor,
To work him farther woe,
And still, as signs of life appear'd,
They toss'd him to and fro.

11

They wasted, o'er a scorching flame,
The marrow of his bones;
But a Miller us'd him worst of all,
For he crush'd him between two stones.

12

And they hae taen his very heart's blood,
And drank it round and round;
And still the more and more they drank,
Their joy did more abound.

13

John Barleycorn was a hero bold,
Of noble enterprise,
For if you do but taste his blood,
'Twill make your courage rise.

14

'Twill make a man forget his woe;
'Twill heighten all his joy:
'Twill make the widow's heart to sing,
Tho' the tear were in her eye.

15

Then let us toast John Barleycorn,
Each man a glass in hand;
And may his great posterity
Ne'er fail in old Scotland!

from Francis Grose, *The Antiquities of Scotland* (1791)[1]

Tam O'Shanter. A Tale

When chapmen billies[2] leave the street,
And drouthy neebors, neebors meet,
As market-days are wearing late,
And folk begin to tak the gate;
While we sit bowsing[3] at the nappy,[4]
And gettin fou,[5] and unco[6] happy,
We think na on the long Scots miles,
The waters, mosses, slaps and styles,
That lie between us and our hame,
Where sits our sulky, sullen dame,
Gathering her brows, like gathering storm,
Nursing her wrath to keep it warm.

This truth fand honest Tom o'Shanter,
As he frae Ayr ae night did canter;
(Auld Ayr, whom ne'er a town surpasses
For honest men and bonnie lasses.)

O Tam! hadst thou but been sae wise
As taen thy ain wife Kate's advice!
She tauld thee weel, thou was a skellum,[7]
A bletherin, blusterin, drunken blellum;[8]
That frae November till October,
Ae market-day thou was na sober;
That ilka melder, wi' the miller,
Thou sat as long as thou had siller[9]

---

[1] "Tam O'Shanter" was also published in the *Edinburgh Magazine* (March 1791), and in *Poems, Chiefly in the Scottish Dialect* (1800).

[2] "friends."

[3] "drinking, boozing."

[4] "strong beer."

[5] "full, drunk."

[6] "very."

[7] "a worthless person."

[8] "one who talks idly."

[9] "silver, money."

25　That every naig was ca'd[1] a shoe on,
　　The smith and thee gat roarin fou on;
　　That at the L—d's house, even on Sunday,
　　Thou drank wi' Kirkton Jean till Monday.—
　　She prophesied that, late or soon,
30　Thou wad be found deep-drown'd in Doon;
　　Or catch'd wi' warlocks in the mirk
　　By Aloway's old haunted kirk.

　　　Ah, gentle dames! it gars me greet,[2]
　　To think how mony counsels sweet,
35　How mony lengthen'd sage advices,
　　The husband frae the wife despises!

　　　But to our tale:—Ae market-night,
　　Tam had got planted unco right,
　　Fast by an ingle[3] bleezing finely,
40　Wi' reamin swats that drank divinely;
　　And at his elbow, souter Johnie,
　　His ancient, trusty, drouthy cronie;
　　Tam lo'ed him like a vera brither,
　　They had been fou for weeks tegither.—
45　The night drave on wi' sangs and clatter,
　　And ay the ale was growing better:
　　The landlady and Tam grew gracious,
　　With favors secret, sweet, and precious:
　　The souter tauld his queerest stories;
50　The landlord's laugh was ready chorus:
　　The storm without might rair and rustle,
　　Tam did na mind the storm a whistle.—
　　Care, mad to see a man sae happy,
　　E'en drown'd himself amang the nappy:
55　As bees flee hame, wi' lades o' treasure,
　　The minutes wing'd their way wi' pleasure:
　　Kings may be blest, but Tam was glorious,
　　O'er a' the ills o' life victorious!

　　　But pleasures are like poppies spread,
60　You seize the flower, its bloom is shed;
　　Or like the snow falls in the river,

---

[1] "nag was called."

[2] "makes me weep."

[3] "fire."

　　A moment white—then melts for ever;
　　Or like the borealis race,
　　That flit ere you can point their place;
65　Or like the rainbow's lovely form,
　　Evanishing amid the storm.—
　　Nae man can tether time or tide,
　　The hour approaches Tam maun ride;
　　That hour o' night's black arch the key-stane,
70　That dreary hour he mounts his beast in;
　　And fie a night he taks the road in
　　As ne'er poor sinner was abroad in.

　　　The wind blew, as 'twad blawn its last;
　　The rattling showers rose on the blast;
75　The speedy gleams the darkness swallow'd
　　Loud, deep, and lang, the thunder bellow'd:
　　That night, a child might understand
　　The deil[4] had business on his hand.

　　　Weel mounted on his grey meare, Meg,
80　A better never lifted leg,
　　Tam skelpit[5] on thro' dub and mire,
　　Despising wind, and rain, and fire:
　　Whyles holding fast his gude blue bonnet;
　　Whyles crooning o'er an auld Scots sonnet;
85　Whyles glowring round wi' prudent cares,
　　Lest bogles[6] catch him unawares;
　　Kirk-Aloway was drawing nigh,
　　Where ghaists and houlets[7] nightly cry.

　　　By this time he was cross the ford,
90　Where in the snaw the chapman smoor'd;
　　And past the birks and meikle[8] stane,
　　Where drunken Charlie brak's neck-bane;
　　And thro' the whins, and by the cairn,
　　Where hunters fand the murder'd bairn;
95　And near the tree, aboon the well,

---

[4] "devil."

[5] "hastened."

[6] "goblins."

[7] "owls."

[8] "great."

Where Mungo's mither hang'd hersel:
Before him, Doon pours all his floods;
The doubling storm roars thro' the woods;
The light'nings flash from pole to pole;
100 Near, and more near, the thunders roll;
When, glimmering thro' groaning trees,
Kirk-Aloway seem'd in a bleeze;[1]
Thro' ilka bore the beams were glancing,
And loud resounded mirth and dancing.

105   Inspiring, bold John Barleycorn!
What dangers thou canst make us scorn:
Wi' tippeny, we fear nae evil;
Wi' usquebae,[2] we'll face the devil!
The swats sae ream'd in Tammie's noddle,
110 Fair-play, he car'd na deils a boddle:[3]
But Maggy stood, right fair astonish'd,
Till by the heel and hand admonish'd,
She ventur'd forward on the light,
And, wow! Tam saw an unco sight!

115   Warlocks and witches in a dance,
Nae cotillon[4] brent new frae France,
But hornpipes, jigs, strathspeys and reels,
Put life and mettle in their heels.—
A winnock-bunker[5] in the East,
120 There sat auld Nick[6] in shape o' beast;
A towzie[7] tyke, black, grim, and large;
To gie them music was his charge:
He screw'd the pipes and gart them skirl,[8]
Till roof and rafters a' did dirl.[9]—
125 Coffins stood round, like open presses,
That shaw'd the dead in their last dresses;
And (by some deevilish cantraip[10] slight)
Each in its cauld hand held a light;
By which heroic Tam was able
130 To note upon the haly table,
A murderer's banes, in gibbet-airns;
Twa span-lang, wee, unchirsten'd bairns;
A thief, new cutted frae a rape,
Wi' his last gasp his gab did gape;
135 Five tomahawks, wi' blood red-rusted;
Five scymitars, wi' murder crusted;
A garter which a babe had strangled;
A knife a father's throat had mangled,
Whom his ain son of life bereft,
140 The grey hairs yet stack[11] to the heft:
Wi' mair of horrible and awefu',
That even to name wad be unlawfu':—
Three lawyers' tongues, turn'd inside out,
Wi' lies seam'd like a beggar's clout;
145 Three priests' hearts, rotten, black as muck,
Lay stinking, vile, in every neuk.

    As Tammie glowr'd, amaz'd and curious,
The mirth and fun grew fast and furious:
The piper loud and louder blew;
150 The dancers quick and quicker flew;
They reel'd, they set, they cross'd, they cleekit,[12]
Till ilka Carlin swat and reekit,[13]
And coost her duddies[14] on the wark,[15]
And linket[16] at it in her sark.[17]—

155   Now Tam! O Tam! had thae been queans,[18]
A' plump and strappin in their teens!

---

[1] "blaze."

[2] "whisky."

[3] "a half-penny."

[4] "a formal French dance."

[5] "a window seat."

[6] "Satan."

[7] "shaggy dog."

[8] "shriek—the characteristic sound of the bagpipe."

[9] "blow, rattle."

[10] "magic."

[11] "stuck."

[12] "linked themselves."

[13] "reeked."

[14] "clothes."

[15] "work."

[16] "tripped."

[17] "shift."

[18] "young women."

Their sarks, instead o' creeshie flainen,[1]
Been snaw-white, seventeen-hunder linen;
Thir breeks o' mine, my only pair,
160 That ance were plush o' gude blue hair,
I wad hae gien them off my hurdies[2]
For ae blink o' the bonie burdies![3]
But withered beldams, auld and droll,
Rigwoodie[4] hags wad spean[5] a foal,
165 Loupin and flingin on a crumock,[6]
I wonder did na turn thy stomach.—

But Tam kend what was what fu' brawlie;[7]
There was ae winsome wench and walie,[8]
That night enlisted in the core,
170 (Lang after kend on Carrick shore;
For mony a beast to dead she shot,
And perish'd mony a bonnie boat,
And shook baith meikle corn and bear
And kept the country-side in fear)—
175 Her cutty-sark[9] o' Paisley harn,[10]
That while a lassie she had worn,
In longitude tho' sorely scanty,
It was her best, and she was vauntie.[11]—
Ah! little thought thy reverend graunie,
180 That sark she cost for her wee Nannie
Wi' twa pund Scots ('twas a' her riches)
Should ever grac'd a dance o' witches!

But here my Muse her wing maun cour,[12]
Sic flights are far beyond her power;
185 To sing how Nannie lap and flang,
(A souple jad[13] she was and strang,)
And how Tam stood like ane bewitch'd,
And thought his very een enrich'd;
Even Satan glowr'd, and fidg'd fu' fain,[14]
190 And hotch'd, and blew wi' might and main;
Till first ae caper—syne anither—
Tam lost his reason a'thegither,
And roars out—"Weel done, cutty-sark!"
And in an instant all was dark;
195 And scarcely had he Maggie rallied,
When out the hellish legion sallied.—

As bees bizz out wi' angry fyke,[15]
When plundering herds assail their byke;[16]
As open puffie's mortal foes,
200 When, pop, she starts before their nose;
As eager rins the market-croud,
When "catch the thief!" resounds aloud;
So Maggy rins, the witches follow,
Wi' mony an eldritch[17] shout and hollo.—

205 Ah Tam! ah Tam! thou'll get thy fairin!
In hell they'll roast thee like a herrin!
In vain thy Kate awaits thy comin,
Kate soon will be a woefu' woman!
Now, do thy speedy utmost, Meg!
210 And win the key-stane o' the brig;
There at them thou thy tail may toss,
A running stream they dare na cross!
But ere the key-stane she could make,
The fient[18] a tale she had to shake;
215 For Nannie, far before the rest,

---

[1] "greasy flannel."
[2] "hips."
[3] "women."
[4] "withered."
[5] "wean."
[6] "a crooked staff."
[7] "perfectly."
[8] "handsome."
[9] "short shift."
[10] "coarse linen."
[11] "proud."
[12] "cower."
[13] "wild young woman."
[14] "fidgeted with amusement."
[15] "fuss."
[16] "beehive."
[17] "elvish; strange or wild."
[18] "fiend."

Hard upon noble Maggy prest,
And flew at Tam with furious ettle,[1]
But little kend she Maggy's mettle!
Ae spring brought off her master hale,
220 But left behind her ain gray tail:
The carlin[2] claught her by the rump,
And left poor Maggy scarce a stump.

Now wha this Tale o' truth shall read,
Ilk man and mother's son, take heed:
225 Whene'er to drink you are inclin'd,
Or cutty-sarks rin in your mind,
Think, ye may buy the joys o'er dear;
Remember TAM O' SHANTER'S MEARE![3]

from *Holy Willie's Prayer, Letter to John Goudie, Kilmarnock, and Six Favourite Songs* (1799)

Holy Willie's Prayer[4]

O THOU, wha in the heavens dost dwell,
Wha, as it pleases best thysel',
Sends ane to heaven and ten to hell,
    A' for Thy glory,
5 And no for ony guid or ill
    They've done afore Thee!

---

[1] "intent."

[2] "old woman."

[3] "mare."

[4] In *Poems Ascribed to Robert Burns*, ed. Thomas Stewart (1801), the poem is introduced by the following Argument:
    "Holy Willie was a rather oldish bachelor elder, in the parish of Mauchline, and much and justly famed for that polemical chattering, which ends in tippling orthodoxy, and for that spiritualized bawdry which refines to liquorish devotion. In a sessional process with a gentleman in Mauchline—a Mr. Gavin Hamilton—Holy Willie and his priest, Father Auld, after full hearing in the presbytery of Ayr, came off but second best; owing partly to the oratorical powers of Mr. Robert Aiken, Mr. Hamilton's counsel; but chiefly to Mr. Hamilton's being one of the most irreproachable and truly respectable characters in the county. On losing the process, the muse overheard him [Holy Willie] at his devotions, as follows:—"

I bless and praise thy matchless might,
Whan thousands thou hast left in night,
That I am here afore thy sight,
10   For gifts an' grace
A burnin' an' a shinin' light,
    To a' this place.

What was I, or my generation,
That I should get sic exaltation,
15 I wha deserve sic just damnation,
    For broken laws,
Five thousand years 'fore my creation,
    Thro' Adam's cause.

When frae my mither's womb I fell,
20 Thou might hae plunged me in hell,
To gnash my gums, to weep and wail,
    In burnin' lake,
Whar damned devils roar and yell,
    Chain'd to a stake.

25 Yet I am here a chosen sample,
To show thy grace is great an' ample;
I'm here a pillar in thy temple,
    Strong as a rock,
A guide, a buckler an' example
30   To a' thy flock.

O L— d! yestreen, thou kens, wi' Meg,
Thy pardon I sincerely beg,
O! may't ne'er be a livin' plague
    To my dishonour,
35 An' I'll ne'er lift a lawless leg
    Again upon her.

Besides, I farther maun allow,
Wi' Lizie's lass, three times I trow;
But L— d, that Friday I was fow,
40   When I cam near her;
Or else, thou kens, thy *servant true*,
    Wad ne'er hae steer'd her.

Maybe thou lets this *fleshly thorn*
Beset thy servant e'en and morn,

45 Lest he owre high and proud shou'd turn,
        'Cause he's sae *gifted*;
If sae, thy han' maun e'en be born,
        Until Thou lift it.

L— d bless thy chosen in this place,
50 For *here* thou hast a *chosen race*;
But G— d confound their stubborn face,
        And blast their name,
Wha bring thy elders to disgrace
        An' public shame.

55 L— d, mind G— n H— n's deserts,
He drinks, an' swears, an' plays at carts,
Yet has sae mony takin' arts,
        Wi' grit an' sma',
Frae G— d's ain priest the people's hearts
60   He steals awa'.

An' when we chasten'd him therefore,
Thou kens how he bred sic a splore,[1]
As set the warld in a roar
        O' laughing at us;
65 Curse thou his basket and his store,
        Kail[2] an' potatoes.

L— d, hear my earnest cry an' pray'r,
Against that presbyt'ry o' Ayr;
Thy strong right hand, L— d, make it bare,
70   Upo' their heads,
L— d weigh it down, and dinna spare,
        For their misdeeds.

O L— d, my G— d, that glib-tongu'd A— n,
My very heart an' saul are quakin',
75 To think how we stood sweatin' shakin',
        An' p—d wi' dread,
While he wi' hingin' lips an' snakin'
        Held up his head.

L— d in the day of vengeance try him,
80 L— d visit them wha did employ him,
An' pass not in thy mercy by 'em,
        Nor hear their pray'r;
But for thy people's sake destroy 'em,
        And dinna spare.

85 But, L— d remember me and mine
Wi' mercies temp'ral and divine,
That I for gear and grace may shine,
        Extoll'd by name,
An' a' the glory shall be thine,
90   Amen, Amen!

A Man's a Man, for a' That: A Song[3]

Is there, for honest poverty,
    Wha hangs his head an' a' that?
The coward slave we pass him by,
    And dare be poor for a' that.
5 For a' that, and a' that,
    Our toils obscure, and a' that,
The rank is but the guinea stamp,
    The man's the gowd[4] for a' that.

What though on hamely fare we dine,
10   Wear hodden[5] gray, and a' that:
Gie fools their silks, and knaves their wine,
    A man's a man, for a' that.
For a' that, and a' that,
    Their tinsel shew, an' a' that;
15 An honest man, though ne'er sae poor,
    Is chief o' men, for a' that.

Ye see yon birkie,[6] ca'd a lord,
    Wha struts and stares, and a' that,
Tho' hundreds worship at his word,

---

[1] "frolic."

[2] "kale, a kind of cabbage."

[3] originally published in the *Glasgow Magazine* (August 1795).

[4] "gold."

[5] "grey cloth."

[6] "a forward, lively man."

He's but a cuif[1] for a' that.
    For a' that, and a' that,
        His ribband, star, and a' that;
    A man of independent mind,
        Can look, and laugh at a' that.

The king can mak' a belted knight,
        A marquis, duke, and a' that;
An honest man's aboon[2] his might,
        Guid faith he manna fa' that!
    For a' that, and a' that,
        His dignities, and a' that;
The pith o' sense, and pride o' worth,
        Are grander far than a' that.

Then let us pray that come it may,
        As come it shall for a' that;
That sense and worth o'er a' the earth,
        Shall bear the gree, and a' that;
    For a' that, an' a' that,
        Its coming yet, for a' that,
Whan man and man, the world o'er,
        Shall brothers be, and a' that.

from *The Scots Musical Museum* (1787–1803)

Ae Fond Kiss, And Then We Sever

TUNE—"RORY DALL'S PORT."

Ae fond kiss, and then we sever;
Ae farewell, and then for ever!
Deep in heart-wrung tears I'll pledge thee,
Warring sighs and groans I'll wage thee.
Who shall say that fortune grieves him
While the star of hope she leaves him?
Me, nae chearfu' twinkle lights me;
Dark despair around benights me.

I'll ne'er blame my partial fancy,
Naething could resist my Nancy:
But to see her, was to love her;
Love but her, and love for ever.
Had we never lov'd sae kindly,
Had we never lov'd sae blindly,
Never met—or never parted,
We had ne'er been broken-hearted.

Fare thee weel, thou first and fairest!
Fare thee weel, thou best and dearest!
Thine be ilka joy and treasure,
Peace, Enjoyment, Love and Pleasure!
Ae fond kiss, and then we sever!
Ae fareweel, Alas, for ever!
Deep in heart-wrung tears I'll pledge thee,
Warring sighs and groans I'll wage thee.

A Red, Red Rose

O my Luve's like a red, red rose,
    That's newly sprung in June;
O My Luve's like the melodie
    That's sweetly play'd in tune.

As fair art thou, my bonie lass,
    So deep in luve am I;
And I will luve thee still, my Dear,
    Till a' the seas gang dry.

Till a' the seas gang dry, my Dear,
    And the rocks melt wi' the sun;
I will love thee still, my Dear,
    While the sands o' life shall run.

And fare thee weel, my only Luve!
    And fare thee weel, a while!
And I will come again, my Luve,
    Tho' it ware ten thousand mile!

---

[1] "fool."

[2] "above."

Comin' thro' the Rye

Comin thro' the rye, poor body,
    Comin thro the rye,
She draigl't[1] a' her petticoatie,
    Comin thro the rye!

Chorus:
5 Oh Jenny's a' weet[2] poor body,
    Jenny's seldom dry
She draigl't a' her petticoatie
    Comin thro the rye.

Gin a body meet a body
10   Comin thro' the rye,
Gin a body kiss a body
    Need a body cry

Gin a body meet a body
    Comin thro' the glen;
15 Gin a body kiss a body
    Need the warld ken![3]

from *The Poems and Songs of Robert Burns*, ed. James Kinsley (1968)

Auld Lang Syne

Should auld acquaintance be forgot
    And never brought to mind?
Should auld acquaintance be forgot,
    And auld lang syne![4]

5 *Chorus.*—For auld lang syne, my jo,
    For auld lang syne,
We'll tak a cup o' kindness yet
    For auld lang syne.

And surely ye'll be your pint stowp![5]
10   And surely I'll be mine!
And we'll tak a cup o' kindness yet,
    For auld lang syne.
    For auld, &c.

We twa hae run about the braes,[6]
15   And pou'd the gowans[7] fine;
But we've wander'd mony a weary fitt,[8]
    Sin' auld lang syne.
    For auld, &c.

We twa hae paidl'd in the burn,[9]
20   Frae morning sun till dine;
But seas between us braid[10] hae roar'd,
    Sin' auld lang syne.
    For auld, &c.

And there's a hand, my trusty fiere![11]
25   And gie's a hand o' thine!
And we'll tak a right gude-willie-waught,
    For auld lang syne.
    For auld, &c.

The Rights Of Woman—Spoken by Miss Fontenelle on her benefit night, November 26, 1792[12]

While Europe's eye is fixed on mighty things,
The fate of Empires, and the fall of Kings;
While quacks of State must each produce his plan,

---

[1] "draggled."

[2] "all wet."

[3] "know."

[4] "old long since," or old time's sake.

[5] "cup."

[6] "slopes of hills."

[7] "daisies."

[8] "foot."

[9] "stream."

[10] "broad."

[11] "friend."

[12] Kinsley's text collates MS versions of Nov. 1792–Jan. 1793. Louisa Fontenelle (1769–1799) was a London actress and singer who toured Scotland and performed in Edinburgh in 1789.

And even children lisp The Rights of Man;
Amid this mighty fuss, just let me mention,
The Rights of Woman merit some attention.—First, in
the Sexes' intermixed connection,
One sacred Right of Woman is, Protection.
The tender flower that lifts its head, elate,
Helpless, must fall before the blasts of Fate,
Sunk on the earth, defaced its lovely form,
Unless *your Shelter* ward th' impending storm.

    Our second Right—but needless here is caution,
To keep that Right inviolate's the fashion.
Each man of sense has it so full before him
He'd die before he'd wrong it—'tis Decorum.—
There was, indeed, in far less polished days,
A time when rough rude man had naughty ways:
Would swagger, swear, get drunk, kick up a riot,
Nay even thus invade a lady's quiet.—
Now, thank our Stars! these Gothic times are fled,
Now well-bred men (and you are all well-bred)
Most justly think (and we are much the gainers)
Such conduct neither spirit, wit, nor manners.—

    For Right the third, our last, our best, our dearest,
That Right to fluttering Female hearts the nearest,
Which even the Rights of Kings, in low prostration,
Most humbly own—'tis dear, dear Admiration!
[In that blest sphere alone we live and move;
There taste that life of life—immortal love.—]
Smiles, glances, sighs, tears, fits, flirtations, airs;
'Gainst such an host, what flinty savage dares.—
When aweful Beauty joins with all her charms
Who is so rash as rise in rebel arms?

    But truce with kings, and truce with Constitutions,
With bloody armaments, and Revolutions;
Let MAJESTY your first attention summon,
Ah! ca ira![1] THE MAJESTY OF WOMAN!!!

---

[1] "There it goes" (Fr.), the chorus of a French Revolutionary song.

Robert Bruce's March to Bannockburn[2]

Scots, wha hae wi' WALLACE[3] bled,
Scots, wham BRUCE has aften led,
Welcome to your gory bed,—
    Or to victorie.—

Now's the day, and now's the hour;
See the front o'battle lour;[4]

---

[2] Robert Bruce was King Robert I of Scotland (r. 1306–1329). Bannockburn, near Stirling, is the site of a battle on 24 June 1314. The Scots, though outnumbered three to one, defeated the English army and achieved a major victory that eventually led to Scotland's freedom from English rule. Kinsley prints a text from the Dalhousie MS, c. 30 August 1793. A printed version in the *Morning Chronicle* (8 May 1794) is adapted to a different tune:

Scots, wha hae wi' Wallace bled,
Scots, wham BRUCE has aften led,
Welcome to your gory bed,
Or to glorious Victorie!

Now's the day, and now's the hour!
See the front o' battle lour!
See approach proud EDWARD's pow'r!
Chains and slaverie!

Wha will be a traitor knave?
Wha can fill a coward's grave!
Wha sae base as be a slave?
Traitor, coward, turn and flee!

Wha, for Scotland's King and Law,
FREEDOM's sword will strongly draw,
Freeman stand, or Freeman fa'!
CALEDONIAN! on wi' me!

By Oppression's woes and pains!
By your sons in servile chains!
We will drain our dearest veins —
But —they SHALL be free!

Lay the proud usurpers low;
Tyrants fall in every foe;
LIBERTY's in every blow!—
Forward Let us Do or Die!

[3] Sir William Wallace (1270–1305), legendary Scottish national hero.

[4] approach.

See approach proud EDWARD's[1] power,
    Chains and Slaverie.—

Wha will be a traitor-knave?
Wha can fill a coward's grave?
Wha sae base as be a Slave?
    —Let him turn and flie:—

Wha for SCOTLAND's king and law,
Freedom's sword will strongly draw,
FREE-MAN stand, or FREE-MAN fa',
    Let him follow me.—

By Oppressions' woes and pains!
By your Sons in servile chains!
We will drain our dearest veins,
    But they *shall* be free!

Lay the proud Usurpers low!
Tyrants fall in every foe!
LIBERTY's in every blow!
    Let us DO—or DIE!!!

---

[1] King Edward II of England (r. 1307–1327).

Mary Wollstonecraft
1759 – 1797

Mary Wollstonecraft was born in London on 27 April 1759, second of the seven children (one died young) of Edward John Wollstonecraft, a weaver, and Elizabeth Dickson Wollstonecraft. When she was young, her father attempted to climb the social ladder by becoming a farmer. The attempt was unsuccessful. He became an abusive alcoholic, and Wollstonecraft sometimes slept on the landing outside her mother's room, to intercept the blows intended for her. The family moved repeatedly, and Wollstonecraft received only a few months' formal schooling, in Beverley, Yorkshire. In 1778, she left home to work as a lady's companion in Windsor and Bath, but she returned in 1780 to care for her mother, who died in 1782. The next year, she cared for her married sister Eliza during her first pregnancy. After the delivery, Eliza became depressed; convinced that the husband was responsible, Wollstonecraft helped her to escape from his house. (The baby died in infancy.) Together with Eliza, their sister Everina, and her friend Fanny Blood, Wollstonecraft founded a school in Islington. Later, they moved it to Newington Green, and there Wollstonecraft met a number of Dissenting intellectuals, including her mentor, Richard Price.* In 1785, she travelled to Lisbon, to be with Fanny, who had married an English businessman there, during the birth of her child; Fanny and the child both died, and when Wollstonecraft returned to England, the school was failing. Next, she became governess to the daughters of Viscount Kingsborough, in Ireland, but in August 1787, she was fired because the girls had become too fond of her.

There was nothing to do except to become what she called "the first of a new genus," supporting herself and several members of her family through her writing. In 1787, she published her first book, *Thoughts on the Education of Daughters*, with the radical London publisher Joseph Johnson. The next year, she published *Mary*, a novel based partly on her journey to Lisbon, and *Original Stories, from Real Life*, a children's book. She translated three children's books for Johnson and undertook reviewing and editorial tasks for his *Analytical Review*. Through Johnson, she met a number of radical London intellectuals, Barbauld,* Godwin,* Paine,* and probably Blake,* who illustrated the second edition of *Original Stories*. In 1790, she published *A Vindication of the Rights of Men*, the first answer to Burke's *Reflections on the Revolution in France*;* a little more than a year later, she followed it up with her most important book, *A Vindication of the Rights of Woman* (1792).

Around this time, Wollstonecraft became involved with the painter Henry Fuseli (best known for *The Nightmare*); she proposed coming to live with him platonically. The proposal was not well received by his wife, and Wollstonecraft went to Revolutionary Paris. There she met a number of Girondin (moderate) political figures and such Anglophone writers as Barlow* and Williams.* She also met Gilbert Imlay, an American author and businessman, who after war broke out between Britain and France registered her as his wife. Their daughter, Fanny, was born in May 1794, and Wollstonecraft published a book on the Revolution later that year. Imlay was unfaithful to her; after a suicide attempt, she undertook a daring journey to Scandinavia to protect his business interests there. The journey inspired her best book, *Letters Written during a Short Residence in Sweden, Norway, and Denmark* (1796): "If ever there was a book calculated to make a man in love with its author," the normally unimpassioned Godwin declared, "this appears to me to be the book." After her return to England, after a second suicide attempt, and after her final rupture with Imlay, Wollstonecraft and Godwin did fall in love, and when she became pregnant, they married. During her pregnancy, she worked on her second novel, *The Wrongs of Woman*, a fictional treatment of issues she had discussed in the second *Vindication*. She gave birth to the future Mary Shelley on 30 August 1797: there were complications during the delivery; specialists were called in; and after eleven days of agony, Wollstonecraft died of puerperal fever on 10 September. (D.L.M.)

from *A Vindication of the Rights of Men, in a Letter to the Right Honourable Edmund Burke; Occasioned by his Reflections on the Revolution in France* (1790)[1]

Sir,
It is not necessary, with courtly insincerity, to apologise to you for thus intruding on your precious time, nor to profess that I think it an honour to discuss an important subject with a man whose literary abilities have raised him to notice in the state. I have not yet learned to twist my periods, nor, in the equivocal idiom of politeness, to disguise my sentiments, and imply what I should be afraid to utter: if, therefore, in the course of this epistle, I chance to express contempt, and even indignation, with some emphasis, I beseech you to believe that it is not a flight of fancy; for truth, in morals, has ever appeared to me the essence of the sublime; and, in taste, simplicity the only criterion of the beautiful.[2] But I war not with an individual when I contend for the *rights of men* and the liberty of reason. You see I do not condescend to cull my words to avoid the invidious phrase, nor shall I be prevented from giving a manly definition of it, by the flimsy ridicule which a lively fancy has interwoven with the present acceptation of the term. Reverencing the rights of humanity, I shall dare to assert them; not intimidated by the horse laugh that you have raised, or waiting till time has wiped away the compassionate tears which you have elaborately laboured to excite....

The birthright of man, to give you, Sir, a short definition of this disputed right, is such a degree of liberty, civil and religious, as is compatible with the liberty of every other individual with whom he is united in a social compact, and the continued existence of that compact.[3]

Liberty, in this simple, unsophisticated sense, I acknowledge, is a fair idea that has never yet received a form in the various governments that have been established on our beauteous globe; the demon of property has ever been at hand to encroach on the sacred rights of men, and to fence round with awful pomp laws that war with justice. But that it results from the eternal foundation of right—from immutable truth—who will presume to deny, that pretends to rationality—if reason has led them to build their morality and religion on an everlasting foundation—the attributes of God? ...

The civilization which has taken place in Europe has been very partial, and, like every custom that an arbitrary point of honour has established, refines the manners at the expence of morals, by making sentiments and opinions current in conversation that have no root in the heart, or weight in the cooler resolves of the mind. —And what has stopped its progress?—hereditary property—hereditary honours. The man has been changed into an artificial monster by the station in which he was born, and the consequent homage that benumbed his faculties like the torpedo's touch;[4]—or a being, with a capacity of reasoning, would not have failed to discover, as his faculties unfolded, that true happiness arose from the friendship and intimacy which can only be enjoyed by equals; and that charity is not a condescending distribution of alms, but an intercourse of good offices and mutual benefits, founded on respect for justice and humanity.

Governed by these principles, the poor wretch, whose *inelegant* distress extorted from a mixed feeling of disgust and animal sympathy present relief, would have been considered as a man, whose misery demanded a part of his birthright, supposing him to be industrious; but should his vices have reduced him to poverty, he could only have addressed his fellow-men as weak beings, subject to like passions, who ought to forgive,

---

[1] The text is that of the 2nd edition.

[2] Throughout, Wollstonecraft is concerned not only with Burke's *Reflections on the Revolution in France* (1790),* but with his *A Philosophical Enquiry into the Origin of our Ideas of the Sublime and the Beautiful* (1757).

[3] "As religion is included in my idea of morality, I should not have mentioned the term without specifying all the simple ideas which that comprehensive word generalizes; but as the charge of atheism has been very freely banded about in the letter I am considering, I wish to guard against misrepresentation." (M.W.)

[4] A torpedo is a stinging fish (an electric ray).

because they expect to be forgiven, for suffering the impulse of the moment to silence the suggestions of conscience, or reason, which you will; for, in my view of things, they are synonymous terms.

Will Mr. Burke be at the trouble to inform us, how far we are to go back to discover the rights of men, since the light of reason is such a fallacious guide that none but fools trust to its cold investigation?

In the infancy of society, confining our view to our own country, customs were established by the lawless power of an ambitious individual; or a weak prince was obliged to comply with every demand of the licentious barbarous insurgents, who disputed his authority with irrefragable arguments at the point of their swords; or the more specious requests of the Parliament, who only allowed him conditional supplies.

Are these the venerable pillars of our constitution? And is Magna Charta to rest for its chief support on a former grant, which reverts to another, till chaos becomes the base of the mighty structure—or we cannot tell what?—for coherence, without some pervading principle of order, is a solecism....[1]

It is necessary emphatically to repeat, that there are rights which men inherit at their birth, as rational creatures, who were raised above the brute creation by their improvable faculties; and that, in receiving these, not from their forefathers but, from God, prescription can never undermine natural rights.

A father may dissipate his property without his child having any right to complain;—but should he attempt to sell him for a slave, or fetter him with laws contrary to reason; nature, in enabling him to discern good from evil, teaches him to break the ignoble chain, and not to believe that bread becomes flesh, and wine blood, because his parents swallowed the Eucharist with this blind persuasion.

There is no end to this implicit submission to authority—some where it must stop, or we return to barbarism; and the capacity of improvement, which gives us a natural sceptre on earth, is a cheat, an ignis-fatuus,[2] that leads us from inviting meadows into bogs and dunghills. And if it be allowed that many of the precautions, with which any alteration was made, in our government, were prudent, it rather proves its weakness than substantiates an opinion of the soundness of the stamina, or the excellence of the constitution.

But on what principle Mr. Burke could defend American independence,[3] I cannot conceive; for the whole tenor of his plausible arguments settles slavery on an everlasting foundation. Allowing his servile reverence for antiquity, and prudent attention to self-interest, to have the force which he insists on, the slave trade ought never to be abolished; and, because our ignorant forefathers, not understanding the native dignity of man, sanctioned a traffic that outrages every suggestion of reason and religion, we are to submit to the inhuman custom, and term an atrocious insult to humanity the love of our country, and a proper submission to the laws by which our property is secured.—Security of property! Behold, in a few words, the definition of English liberty. And to this selfish principle every nobler one is sacrificed.—The Briton takes place of the man, and the image of God is lost in the citizen! But it is not that enthusiastic flame which in Greece and Rome consumed every sordid passion: no, self is the focus; and the disparting rays rise not above our foggy atmosphere. But softly—it is only the property of the rich that is secure; the man who lives by the sweat of his brow has no asylum from oppression; the strong man may enter—when was the castle of the poor sacred? and the base informer steal him from the family that depend on his industry for subsistence.

Fully sensible as you must be of the baneful consequences that inevitably follow this notorious infringement on the dearest rights of men, and that it is an infernal blot on the very face of our immaculate constitution, I cannot avoid expressing my surprise that when you recommended our form of government as a model, you did not caution the French against the arbitrary

---

[1] Cf. Burke, *Reflections*.* Magna Charta, signed (reluctantly) by King John in 1215, had come to be interpreted as limiting the absolute power of the Crown and protecting its subjects from oppression.

[2] literally, "foolish fire" (L.); phosphorescent light on marshy ground, signifying delusive hope.

[3] Burke, *Speech on ... Conciliation with America* (22 March 1775).

custom of pressing men for the sea service.[1] You should have hinted to them, that property in England is much more secure than liberty, and not have concealed that the liberty of an honest mechanic—his all—is often sacrificed to secure the property of the rich. For it is a farce to pretend that a man fights *for his country, his hearth, or his altars,* when he has neither liberty nor property.—His property is in his nervous arms—and they are compelled to pull a strange rope at the surly command of a tyrannic boy, who probably obtained his rank on account of his family connections, or the prostituted vote of his father, whose interest in a borough, or voice as a senator, was acceptable to the minister.

Our penal laws punish with death the thief who steals a few pounds; but to take by violence, or trepan, a man, is no such heinous offence.—For who shall dare to complain of the venerable vestige of the law that rendered the life of a deer more sacred than that of a man? But it was the poor man with only his native dignity who was thus oppressed—and only metaphysical sophists and cold mathematicians can discern this insubstantial form; it is a work of abstraction—and a *gentleman* of lively imagination must borrow some drapery from fancy before he can love or pity a *man*.—Misery, to reach your heart, I perceive, must have its cap and bells; your tears are reserved, very *naturally* considering your character, for the declamation of the theatre, or for the downfall of queens, whose rank alters the nature of folly, and throws a graceful veil over vices that degrade humanity; whilst the distress of many industrious mothers, whose *helpmates* have been torn from them, and the hungry cry of helpless babes, were vulgar sorrows that could not move your commiseration, though they might extort an alms. "The tears that are shed for fictitious sorrow are admirably adapted," says Rousseau, "to make us proud of all the virtues which we do not possess."...[2]

Blackstone,[3] to whom Mr. Burke pays great deference,[4] seems to agree with Dr. Price, that the succession of the King of Great Britain depends on the choice of the people, or that they have a power to cut it off; but this power, as you have fully proved, has been cautiously exerted, and might with more propriety be termed a *right* than a power. Be it so!—yet when you elaborately cited precedents to shew that our forefathers paid great respect to hereditary claims, you might have gone back to your favourite epoch, and shewn their respect for a church that fulminating laws have since loaded with opprobrium. The preponderance of inconsistencies, when weighed with precedents, should lessen the most bigotted veneration for antiquity, and force men of the eighteenth century to acknowledge, that our *canonized forefathers*[5] were unable, or afraid, to revert to reason, without resting on the crutch of authority; and should not be brought as a proof that their children are never to be allowed to walk alone....

Man has been termed, with strict propriety, a microcosm, a little world in himself.—He is so;—yet

---

[1] Impressment, a form of forcible conscription into the navy, lasted until 1815.

[2] Jean-Jacques Rousseau, *Politics and the Arts: Letter to M. d'Alembert on the Theatre* (1758).

[3] "'The doctrine of *hereditary* right does by no means imply an *indefeasible* right to the throne. No man will, I think, assert this, that has considered our laws, constitution, and history, without prejudice, and with any degree of attention. It is unquestionably in the breast of the supreme legislative authority of this kingdom, the King and both Houses of Parliament, to defeat this hereditary right; and, by particular entails, limitations, and provisions, to exclude the immediate heir, and vest the inheritance in any one else. This is strictly consonant to our laws and constitution; as may be gathered from the expression so frequently used in our statute books, of "the King's Majesty, his heirs, and successors." In which we may observe that, as the word "heirs" necessarily implies an inheritance, or hereditary right, generally subsisting in "the royal person"; so the word successors, distinctly taken, must imply that this inheritance may sometimes be broken through; or, that there may be a successor, without being the heir of the king.'

"I shall not, however, rest in something like a subterfuge, and quote, as partially as you have done, from Aristotle. Blackstone has so cautiously fenced round his opinion with provisos, that it is obvious he thought the letter of the law leaned towards your side of the question—but a blind respect for the law is not a part of my creed." (M.W.) William Blackstone (1723–80), *Commentaries on the Laws of England* (1765–69) 1.3. Burke, *Reflections** cites Aristotle, *Politics* 4.4.1.

[4] Burke, *Reflections.**

[5] Burke, *Reflections** (25).

must, however, be reckoned an ephemera, or, to adopt your figure of rhetoric, a summer's fly.[1] The perpetuation of property in our families is one of the privileges you most warmly contend for; yet it would not be very difficult to prove that the mind must have a very limited range that thus confines its benevolence to such a narrow circle, which, with great propriety, may be included in the sordid calculations of blind self-love.

A brutal attachment to children has appeared most conspicuous in parents who have treated them like slaves, and demanded due homage for all the property they transferred to them, during their lives. It has led them to force their children to break the most sacred ties; to do violence to a natural impulse, and run into legal prostitution to increase wealth or shun poverty; and, still worse, the dread of parental malediction has made many weak characters violate truth in the face of Heaven; and, to avoid a father's angry curse, the most sacred promises have been broken. It appears to be a natural suggestion of reason, that a man should be freed from implicit obedience to parents and private punishments, when he is of an age to be subject to the jurisdiction of the laws of his country; and that the barbarous cruelty of allowing parents to imprison their children, to prevent their contaminating their noble blood by following the dictates of nature when they chose to marry, or for any misdemeanor that does not come under the cognizance of public justice, is one of the most arbitrary violations of liberty.[2]

Who can recount all the unnatural crimes which the *laudable, interesting* desire of perpetuating a name has produced?[3] The younger children have been sacrificed to the eldest son; sent into exile, or confined in convents, that they might not encroach on what was called, with shameful falsehood, the *family* estate. Will Mr. Burke call this parental affection reasonable or virtuous?—No; it is the spurious offspring of over-weening, mistaken pride—and not that first source of civilization, natural parental affection, that makes no difference between child and child, but what reason justifies by pointing out superior merit....

The only security of property that nature authorizes and reason sanctions is, the right a man has to enjoy the acquisitions which his talents and industry have acquired; and to bequeath them to whom he chooses. Happy would it be for the world if there were no other road to wealth or honour; if pride, in the shape of parental affection, did not absorb the man, and prevent friendship from having the same weight as relationship. Luxury and effeminacy would not then introduce so much idiotism into the noble families which form one of the pillars of our state: the ground would not lie fallow, nor would undirected activity of mind spread the contagion of restless idleness, and its concomitant, vice, through the whole mass of society.

Instead of gaming they might nourish a virtuous ambition, and love might take place of the gallantry which you, with knightly fealty, venerate. Women would probably then act like mothers, and the fine lady, become a rational woman, might think it necessary to superintend her family and suckle her children, in order to fulfil her part of the social compact. But vain is the hope, whilst great masses of property are hedged round by hereditary honours; for numberless vices, forced in the hot-bed of wealth, assume a sightly form to dazzle the senses and cloud the understanding. The respect paid to rank and fortune damps every generous purpose of the soul, and stifles the natural affections on which human contentment ought to be built. Who will venturously ascend the steeps of virtue, or explore the great deep for knowledge, when *the one thing needful*,[4] attained by less arduous exertions, if not inherited, procures the attention man naturally pants after, and vice "loses half its evil by losing all its grossness."[5] —What a sentiment to come from a moral pen!

A surgeon would tell you that by skinning over a wound you spread disease through the whole frame;

---

[1] Burke, *Reflections** (32).

[2] Under the *ancien régime*, persons could be imprisoned without trial through the use of *lettres de cachets*. Parents sometimes obtained them to prevent their children from making unsuitable marriages; see W. Wordsworth,* *The Prelude* (1805) 9.555–934 and "Vaudracour and Julia" 120–31.*

[3] Burke, *Reflections*.

[4] Cf. Luke 10.42.

[5] "Page 113." (M.W.) Burke, *Reflections** (28).

and, surely, they indirectly aim at destroying all purity of morals, who poison the very source of virtue, by smearing a sentimental varnish over vice, to hide its natural deformity. Stealing, whoring, and drunkenness, are gross vices, I presume, though they may not obliterate every moral sentiment, and have a vulgar brand that makes them appear with all their native deformity; but overreaching, adultery, and coquetry, are venial offences, though they reduce virtue to an empty name, and make wisdom consist in saving appearances.

"On this scheme of things[1] a king *is* but a man; a queen *is* but a woman; a woman *is* but an animal, and an animal not of the highest order."—All true, Sir; if she is not more attentive to the duties of humanity than queens and fashionable ladies in general are. I will still further accede to the opinion you have so justly conceived of the spirit which begins to animate this age.—"All homage paid to the sex in general, as such, and without distinct views, is to be regarded as *romance* and folly." Undoubtedly; because such homage vitiates them, prevents their endeavouring to obtain solid personal merit; and, in short, makes those beings vain inconsiderate dolls, who ought to be prudent mothers and useful members of society. "Regicide and sacrilege are but fictions of superstition corrupting jurisprudence, by destroying its simplicity. The murder of a king, or a queen, or a bishop, are only common homicide."[2]—Again I agree with you; but you perceive, Sir, that by leaving out the word *father*, I think the whole extent of the comparison invidious....

Whether the glory of Europe is set, I shall not now enquire; but probably the spirit of romance and chivalry is in the wane; and reason will gain by its extinction.

From observing several cold romantic characters I have been led to confine the term romantic to one definition—false, or rather artificial, feelings. Works of genius are read with a prepossession in their favour, and sentiments imitated, because they were fashionable and pretty, and not because they were forcibly felt.

In modern poetry the understanding and memory often fabricate the pretended effusions of the heart, and romance destroys all simplicity; which, in works of taste, is but a synonymous word for truth. This romantic spirit has extended to our prose, and scattered artificial flowers over the most barren heath; or a mixture of verse and prose producing the strangest incongruities. The turgid bombast of some of your periods fully proves these assertions; for when the heart speaks we are seldom shocked by hyperbole, or dry raptures....

A sentiment of this kind glanced across my mind when I read the following exclamation. "Whilst the royal captives, who followed in the train, were slowly moved along, amidst the horrid yells, and shrilling screams, and frantic dances, and infamous contumelies, and all the unutterable abominations of the furies of hell, in the abused shape of the vilest of women."[3] Probably you mean women who gained a livelihood by selling vegetables or fish, who never had had any advantages of education; or their vices might have lost part of their abominable deformity, by losing part of their grossness. The queen of France—the great and small vulgar, claim our pity; they have almost insuperable obstacles to surmount in their progress towards true dignity of character; still I have such a plain downright understanding that I do not like to make a distinction without a difference. But it is not very extraordinary that *you* should, for throughout your letter you frequently advert to a sentimental jargon, which has long been current in conversation, and even in books of morals, though it never received the *regal* stamp of reason. A kind of mysterious instinct is *supposed* to reside in the soul, that instantaneously discerns truth, without the tedious labour of ratiocination. This instinct, for I know not what other name to give it, has been termed *common sense*, and more frequently *sensibility*; and, by a kind of *indefeasible* right, it has been *supposed*, for rights of this kind are not easily proved, to reign paramount over the other faculties of the mind, and to be an authority from which there is no appeal....

If virtue be an instinct, I renounce all hope of immortality; and with it all the sublime reveries and

---

[1] "As you ironically observe, p. 114." Burke, *Reflections** (28).

[2] Burke, *Reflections** (28). The italics are Wollstonecraft's; and, as she implies, Burke includes parricide in his list of uncommon homicide.

[3] "Page 106." (M.W.). Burke, *Reflections** (26).

dignified sentiments that have smoothed the rugged path of life: it is all a cheat, a lying vision; I have disquieted myself in vain;[1] for in my eye all feelings are false and spurious, that do not rest on justice as their foundation, and are not concentred by universal love.

I reverence the rights of men.—Sacred rights! for which I acquire a more profound respect, the more I look into my own mind; and, professing these heterodox opinions, I still preserve my bowels; my heart is human, beats quick with human sympathies—and I FEAR God!

I bend with awful reverence when I enquire on what my fear is built.—I fear that sublime power, whose motive for creating me must have been wise and good; and I submit to the moral laws which my reason deduces from this view of my dependence on him.—It is not his power that I fear—it is not to an arbitrary will, but to unerring *reason* I submit.—Submit—yes; I disregard the charge of arrogance, to the law that regulates his just resolves; and the happiness I pant after must be the same in kind, and produced by the same exertions as his—though unfeigned humility overwhelms every idea that would presume to compare the goodness which the most exalted created being could acquire, with the grand source of life and bliss.

This fear of God makes me reverence myself.—Yes, Sir, the regard I have for honest fame, and the friendship of the virtuous, falls far short of the respect which I have for myself. And this, enlightened self-love, if an epithet the meaning of which has been grossly perverted will convey my idea, forces me to see; and, if I may venture to borrow a prostituted term, to *feel*, that happiness is reflected, and that, in communicating good, my soul receives its noble aliment.—I do not trouble myself, therefore, to enquire whether this is the fear the *people* of England feel:—and, if it be *natural* to include all the modifications which you have annexed—it is not.[2] ...

That civilization, that the cultivation of the understanding, and refinement of the affections, naturally make a man religious, I am proud to acknowledge.—What else can fill the aching void in the heart, that human pleasures, human friendships can never fill? What else can render us resigned to live, though condemned to ignorance?—What but a profound reverence for the model of all perfection, and the mysterious tie which arises from a love of goodness? What can make us reverence ourselves, but a reverence for that Being, of whom we are a faint image? That mighty Spirit moves on the waters—confusion hears his voice, and the troubled heart ceases to beat with anguish, for trust in Him bade it be still.[3] Conscious dignity may make us rise superior to calumny, and sternly brave the winds of adverse fortune,—raised in our own esteem by the very storms of which we are the sport[4]—but when friends are unkind, and the heart has not the prop on which it fondly leaned, where can a tender suffering being fly but to the Searcher of hearts? and, when death has desolated the present scene, and torn from us the friend of our youth—when we walk along the accustomed path, and, almost fancying nature dead, ask, Where art thou who gave life to these well-known scenes? when memory heightens former pleasures to contrast our present prospects—there is but one source of comfort within our reach;—and in this sublime solitude the world appears to contain only the Creator and the creature, of whose happiness he is the source.—These are human feelings; but I know not of any common nature or common relation amongst men but what results from reason. The common affections and passions equally bind brutes together; and it is only the continuity of those relations that entitles us to the denomination of rational creatures; and this continuity arises from reflection—from the operations of that reason which you contemn with flippant disrespect....

That the British House of Commons is filled with every thing illustrious in rank, in descent, in hereditary, and acquired opulence, may be true,—but that it contains every thing respectable in talents, in military, civil, naval, and political distinction, is very problematical. Arguing from natural causes, the very contrary

---

[1] Cf. Psalms 39.6.

[2] "*Vide* Reflections, p.128. 'We fear God; we look up with *awe* to kings; with *affection* to parliaments; with *duty* to magistrates; with *reverence* to priests; and with *respect* to nobility.'" (M.W.) Burke, *Reflections* (31); Wollstonecraft's italics.

[3] Genesis 1.2; Mark 4.39; Milton, *Paradise Lost* 7.210–17.

[4] Cf. Shakespeare, *King Lear* 3.2.1–24, 4.1.36–37.

would appear to the speculatist to be the fact; and let experience say whether these speculations are built on sure ground.

It is true you lay great stress on the effects produced by the bare idea of a liberal descent;[1] but from the conduct of men of rank, men of discernment would rather be led to conclude, that this idea obliterated instead of inspiring native dignity, and substituted a factitious pride that disemboweled the man. The liberty of the rich has its ensigns armorial[2] to puff the individual out with insubstantial honours; but where are blazoned the struggles of virtuous poverty? Who, indeed, would dare to blazon what would blur the pompous monumental inscription you boast of, and make us view with horror, as monsters in human shape, the superb gallery of portraits proudly set in battle array?

But to examine the subject more closely. Is it among the list of possibilities that a man of rank and fortune *can* have received a good education? How can he discover that he is a man, when all his wants are instantly supplied, and invention is never sharpened by necessity? Will he labour, for every thing valuable must be the fruit of laborious exertions, to attain knowledge and virtue, in order to merit the affection of his equals, when the flattering attention of sycophants is a more luscious cordial?

Health can only be secured by temperance; but is it easy to persuade a man to live on plain food even to recover his health, who has been accustomed to fare sumptuously every day? Can a man relish the simple food of friendship, who has been habitually pampered by flattery? And when the blood boils, and the senses meet allurements on every side, will knowledge be pursued on account of its abstract beauty? No; it is well known that talents are only to be unfolded by industry, and that we must have made some advances, led by an inferior motive, before we discover that they are their own reward.

But *full blown* talents *may*, according to your system, be hereditary, and as independent of ripening judgment, as the inbred feelings that, rising above reason, naturally guard Englishmen from error. Noble franchises! what a grovelling mind must that man have, who can pardon his step-dame Nature for not having made him at least a lord?

And who will, after your description of senatorial virtues, dare to say that our House of Commons has often resembled a bear-garden; and appeared rather like a committee of *ways and means* than a dignified legislative body, though the concentrated wisdom and virtue of the whole nation blazed in one superb constellation? That it contains a dead weight of benumbing opulence I readily allow, and of ignoble ambition; nor is there any thing surpassing belief in a supposition that the raw recruits, when properly drilled by the minister, would gladly march to the Upper House to unite hereditary honours to fortune. But talents, knowledge, and virtue, must be a part of the man, and cannot be put, as robes of state often are, on a servant or a block, to render a pageant more magnificent....

...[W]ithout fixed principles even goodness of heart is no security from inconsistency, and mild affectionate sensibility only renders a man more ingeniously cruel, when the pangs of hurt vanity are mistaken for virtuous indignation, and the gall of bitterness for the milk of Christian charity.

Where is the dignity, the infallibility of sensibility, in the fair ladies, whom, if the voice of rumour is to be credited, the captive negroes curse in all the agony of bodily pain, for the unheard of tortures they invent? It is probable that some of them, after the sight of a flagellation, compose their ruffled spirits and exercise their tender feelings by the perusal of the last imported novel.—How true these tears are to nature, I leave you to determine. But these ladies may have read your Enquiry concerning the origin of our ideas of the Sublime and Beautiful, and, convinced by your arguments, may have laboured to be pretty, by counterfeiting weakness.[3]

---

[1] "Page 49. 'Always acting as if in the presence of canonized forefathers, the spirit of freedom, leading in itself to misrule and excess, is tempered with an awful gravity. This idea of a liberal descent inspires us with a sense of habitual native dignity, which prevents that upstart insolence almost inevitably adhering to and disgracing those who are the first acquirers of any distinction!'" (M.W.) Burke, *Reflections* (25).

[2] heraldic symbols carried on flags or shields.

[3] Burke, *Philosophical Enquiry* 3.9, 3.16.

You may have convinced them that *littleness* and *weakness* are the very essence of beauty; and that the Supreme Being, in giving women beauty in the most supereminent degree, seemed to command them, by the powerful voice of Nature, not to cultivate the moral virtues that might chance to excite respect, and interfere with the pleasing sensations they were created to inspire. Thus confining truth, fortitude, and humanity, within the rigid pale of manly morals, they might justly argue, that to be loved, woman's high end and great distinction! they should "learn to lisp, to totter in their walk, and nick-name God's creatures."[1] Never, they might repeat after you, was any man, much less a woman, rendered amiable by the force of those exalted qualities, fortitude, justice, wisdom, and truth; and thus forewarned of the sacrifice they must make to those austere, unnatural virtues, they would be authorized to turn all their attention to their persons, systematically neglecting morals to secure beauty.—Some rational old woman indeed might chance to stumble at this doctrine, and hint, that in avoiding atheism you had not steered clear of the mussulman's creed;[2] but you could readily exculpate yourself by turning the charge on Nature, who made our idea of beauty independent of reason. Nor would it be necessary for you to recollect, that if virtue has any other foundation than worldly utility, you have clearly proved that one half of the human species, at least, have not souls; and that Nature, by making women *little, smooth, delicate, fair* creatures,[3] never designed that they should exercise their reason to acquire the virtues that produce opposite, if not contradictory, feelings. The affection they excite, to be uniform and perfect, should not be tinctured with the respect which moral virtues inspire, lest pain should be blended with pleasure, and admiration disturb the soft intimacy of love. This laxity of morals in the female world is certainly more captivating to a libertine imagination than the cold arguments of reason, that give no sex to virtue. If beautiful weakness be interwoven in a woman's frame, if the chief business of her life be (as you insinuate) to inspire love, and Nature has made an eternal distinction between the qualities that dignify a rational being and this animal perfection, her duty and happiness in this life must clash with any preparation for a more exalted state. So that Plato and Milton were grossly mistaken in asserting that human love led to heavenly, and was only an exaltation of the same affection;[4] for the love of the Deity, which is mixed with the most profound reverence, must be love of perfection, and not compassion for weakness.

To say the truth, I not only tremble for the souls of women, but for the good natured man, whom every one loves. The *amiable* weakness of his mind is a strong argument against its immateriality, and seems to prove that beauty relaxes the *solids* of the soul as well as the body.

It follows then immediately, from your own reasoning, that respect and love are antagonist principles; and that, if we really wish to render men more virtuous, we must endeavour to banish all enervating modifications of beauty from civil society. We must, to carry your argument a little further, return to the Spartan regulations, and settle the virtues of men on the stern foundation of mortification and self-denial; for any attempt to civilize the heart, to make it humane by implanting reasonable principles, is a mere philosophic dream. If refinement inevitably lessens respect for virtue, by rendering beauty, the grand tempter, more seductive; if these relaxing feelings are incompatible with the nervous exertions of morality, the sun of Europe is not set; it begins to dawn, when cold metaphysicians try to make the head give laws to the heart.

But should experience prove that there is a beauty in virtue, a charm in order, which necessarily implies exertion, a depraved sensual taste may give way to a more manly one—and *melting* feelings to rational satisfactions. Both may be equally natural to man; the test is their moral difference, and that point reason alone can decide.

---

[1] an amalgam of Shakespeare, *Hamlet* 3,1.144–45; and Burke, *Philosophical Enquiry* 3.9.

[2] Wollstonecraft shared the common Enlightenment misconception that Islam denied women souls.

[3] Burke, *Philosophical Enquiry* 3.13–16.

[4] Plato, *Symposium* 210a–211c; Milton, *Paradise Lost* 8.589–92.

Such a glorious change can only be produced by liberty. Inequality of rank must ever impede the growth of virtue, by vitiating the mind that submits or domineers; that is ever employed to procure nourishment for the body, or amusement for the mind. And if this grand example be set by an assembly of unlettered clowns, if they can produce a crisis that may involve the fate of Europe, and "more than Europe,"[1] you must allow us to respect unsophisticated reason, and reverence the active exertions that were not relaxed by a fastidious respect for the beauty of rank, or a dread of the deformity produced by any *void* in the social structure....

...[A]mong all your plausible arguments, and witty illustrations, your contempt for the poor always appears conspicuous, and rouses my indignation. The following paragraph in particular struck me, as breathing the most tyrannic spirit, and displaying the most factitious feelings. "Good order is the foundation of all good things. To be enabled to acquire, the people, without being servile, must be tractable and obedient. The magistrate must have his reverence, the laws their authority. The body of the people must not find the principles of natural subordination by art rooted out of their minds. They *must* respect that property of which they *cannot* partake. *They must labour to obtain what by labour can be obtained; and when they find, as they commonly do, the success disproportioned to the endeavour, they must be taught their consolation in the final proportions of eternal justice.* Of this consolation, whoever deprives them, deadens their industry, and strikes at the root of all acquisition as of all conservation. He that does this, is the cruel oppressor, the merciless enemy, of the poor and wretched; at the same time that, by his wicked speculations, he exposes the fruits of successful industry, and the accumulations of fortune," (ah! there's the rub)[2] "to the plunder of the negligent, the disappointed, and the unprosperous."[3]

This is contemptible hard-hearted sophistry, in the specious form of humility, and submission to the will of Heaven.—It is, Sir, *possible* to render the poor happier in this world, without depriving them of the consolation which you gratuitously grant them in the next. They have a right to more comfort than they at present enjoy; and more comfort might be afforded them, without encroaching on the pleasures of the rich: not now waiting to enquire whether the rich have any right to exclusive pleasures. What do I say?—encroaching! No; if an intercourse were established between them, it would impart the only true pleasure that can be snatched in this land of shadows, this hard school of moral discipline.

I know, indeed, that there is often something disgusting in the distresses of poverty, at which the imagination revolts, and starts back to exercise itself in the more attractive Arcadia of fiction. The rich man builds a house, art and taste give it the highest finish. His gardens are planted, and the trees grow to recreate the fancy of the planter, though the temperature of the climate may rather force him to avoid the dangerous damps they exhale, than seek the umbrageous retreat. Every thing on the estate is cherished but man;—yet, to contribute to the happiness of man, is the most sublime of all enjoyments. But if, instead of sweeping pleasure-grounds, obelisks, temples, and elegant cottages, as *objects* for the eye, the heart was allowed to beat true to nature, decent farms would be scattered over the estate, and plenty smile around. Instead of the poor being subject to the griping hand of an avaricious steward, they would be watched over with fatherly solicitude, by the man whose duty and pleasure it was to guard their happiness, and shield from rapacity the beings who, by the sweat of their brow, exalted him above his fellows.

I could almost imagine I see a man thus gathering blessings as he mounted the hill of life; or consolation, in those days when the spirits lag, and the tired heart finds no pleasure in them. It is not by squandering alms that the poor can be relieved, or improved—it is the fostering sun of kindness, the wisdom that finds them employments calculated to give them habits of virtue, that meliorates their condition. Love is only the fruit of love; condescension and authority may produce the

---

[1] "Page 11. 'It looks to me as if I were in a great crisis, not of the affairs of France alone but of all Europe, perhaps of more than Europe. All circumstances taken together, the French revolution is the most astonishing that has hitherto happened in the world.'" (M.W.) Burke, *Reflections** (22–23).

[2] Shakespeare, *Hamlet* 3.1.65.

[3] "Page 351." (M.W.) Burke, *Reflections**.

obedience you applaud; but he has lost his heart of flesh who can see a fellow-creature humbled before him, and trembling at the frown of a being, whose heart is supplied by the same vital current, and whose pride ought to be checked by a consciousness of having the same infirmities.

What salutary dews might not be shed to refresh this thirsty land, if men were more *enlightened*! Smiles and premiums might encourage cleanliness, industry, and emulation.—A garden more inviting than Eden would then meet the eye, and springs of joy murmur on every side. The clergyman would superintend his own flock, the shepherd would then love the sheep he daily tended; the school might rear its decent head, and the buzzing tribe, let loose to play, impart a portion of their vivacious spirits to the heart that longed to open their minds, and lead them to taste the pleasures of men. Domestic comfort, the civilizing relations of husband, brother, and father, would soften labour, and render life contented.

Returning once from a despotic country[1] to a part of England well cultivated, but not very picturesque—with what delight did I not observe the poor man's garden!—The homely palings and twining woodbine, with all the rustic contrivances of simple, unlettered taste, was a sight which relieved the eye that had wandered indignant from the stately palace to the pestiferous hovel, and turned from the awful contrast into itself to mourn the fate of man, and curse the arts of civilization!...

Surveying civilized life, and seeing, with undazzled eye, the polished vices of the rich, their insincerity, want of natural affections, with all the specious train that luxury introduces, I have turned impatiently to the poor, to look for man undebauched by riches or power —but, alas! what did I see? a being scarcely above the brutes, over which he tyrannized; a broken spirit, worn-out body, and all those gross vices which the example of the rich, rudely copied, could produce. Envy built a wall of separation, that made the poor hate, whilst they bent to their superiors; who, on their part, stepped aside to avoid the loathsome sight of human misery.

What were the outrages of a day[2] to these continual miseries? Let those sorrows hide their diminished head before the tremendous mountain of woe that thus defaces our globe! Man preys on man; and you mourn for the idle tapestry that decorated a gothic pile, and the dronish bell that summoned the fat priest to prayer. You mourn for the empty pageant of a name, when slavery flaps her wing, and the sick heart retires to die in lonely wilds, far from the abodes of men. Did the pangs you felt for insulted nobility, the anguish that rent your heart when the gorgeous robes were torn off the idol human weakness had set up, deserve to be compared with the long-drawn sigh of melancholy reflection, when misery and vice are thus seen to haunt our steps, and swim on the top of every cheering prospect? Why is our fancy to be appalled by terrific perspectives of a hell beyond the grave?—Hell stalks abroad;—the lash resounds on the slave's naked sides; and the sick wretch, who can no longer earn the sour bread of unremitting labour, steals to a ditch to bid the world a long good night—or, neglected in some ostentatious hospital, breathes his last amidst the laugh of mercenary attendants.

Such misery demands more than tears—I pause to recollect myself; and smother the contempt I feel rising for your rhetorical flourishes and infantine sensibility....

---

[1] Portugal, which Wollstonecraft visited in 1785.

[2] "The 6th of October." (M.W.) On 6 Oct. 1789, the French King and Queen were conducted under guard from Versailles to Paris; Burke describes the events of this day in his *Reflections*.

from *A Vindication of the Rights of Woman* (1792)

DEDICATION

To M. Talleyrand-Périgord, Late Bishop Of Autun[1]

Sir,

Having read with great pleasure a pamphlet which you have lately published,[2] I dedicate this volume to you; to induce you to reconsider the subject, and maturely weigh what I have advanced respecting the rights of woman and national education: and I call with the firm tone of humanity; for my arguments, Sir, are dictated by a disinterested spirit—I plead for my sex—not for myself. Independence I have long considered as the grand blessing of life, the basis of every virtue—and independence I will ever secure by contracting my wants, though I were to live on a barren heath.

It is then an affection for the whole human race that makes my pen dart rapidly along to support what I believe to be the cause of virtue: and the same motive leads me earnestly to wish to see woman placed in a station in which she would advance, instead of retarding, the progress of those glorious principles that give a substance to morality. My opinion, indeed, respecting the rights and duties of woman, seems to flow so naturally from these simple principles, that I think it scarcely possible, but that some of the enlarged minds who formed your admirable constitution, will coincide with me.

In France there is undoubtedly a more general diffusion of knowledge than in any part of the European world, and I attribute it, in a great measure, to the social intercourse which has long subsisted between the sexes.

It is true, I utter my sentiments with freedom, that in France the very essence of sensuality has been extracted to regale the voluptuary, and a kind of sentimental lust has prevailed, which, together with the system of duplicity that the whole tenour of their political and civil government taught, have given a sinister sort of sagacity to the French character, properly termed finesse; from which naturally flow a polish of manners that injures the substance, by hunting sincerity out of society.—And, modesty, the fairest garb of virtue! has been more grossly insulted in France than even in England, till their women have treated as *prudish* that attention to decency, which brutes instinctively observe.

Manners and morals are so nearly allied that they have often been confounded; but, though the former should only be the natural reflection of the latter, yet, when various causes have produced factitious and corrupt manners, which are very early caught, morality becomes an empty name. The personal reserve, and sacred respect for cleanliness and delicacy in domestic life, which French women almost despise, are the graceful pillars of modesty; but, far from despising them, if the pure flame of patriotism have reached their bosoms, they should labour to improve the morals of their fellow-citizens, by teaching men, not only to respect modesty in women, but to acquire it themselves, as the only way to merit their esteem.

Contending for the rights of woman, my main argument is built on this simple principle, that if she be not prepared by education to become the companion of man, she will stop the progress of knowledge and virtue; for truth must be common to all, or it will be inefficacious with respect to its influence on general practice. And how can woman be expected to co-operate unless she know why she ought to be virtuous? unless freedom strengthen her reason till she comprehend her duty, and see in what manner it is connected with her real good? If children are to be educated to understand the true principle of patriotism, their mother must be a patriot; and the love of mankind, from which an orderly train of virtues spring, can only be produced by considering the moral and civil interest of mankind; but the education and situation of woman, at present, shuts her out from such investigations.

---

[1] Charles-Maurice de Talleyrand-Périgord (1754–1838), was made Bishop of Autun in 1788. As minister of finance in the French revolutionary government, he initiated the confiscation of church property that so exercised Edmund Burke.* He resigned his bishopric in January 1791 and was excommunicated that April.

[2] *Rapport sur l'instruction publique, fait au nom du Comité de Constitution à l'Assemblée Nationale, les 10, 11, et 19 Septembre 1791, par M. de Talleyrand-Périgord, Ancien Évêque d'Autun.* Talleyrand prepared the report with the help of such distinguished thinkers as Condorcet and Laplace.

In this work I have produced many arguments, which to me were conclusive, to prove that the prevailing notion respecting a sexual[1] character was subversive of morality, and I have contended, that to render the human body and mind more perfect, chastity must more universally prevail, and that chastity will never be respected in the male world till the person of a woman is not, as it were, idolized, when little virtue or sense embellish it with the grand traces of mental beauty, or the interesting simplicity of affection.

Consider, Sir, dispassionately, these observations—for a glimpse of this truth seemed to open before you when you observed, "that to see one half of the human race excluded by the other from all participation of government, was a political phaenomenon that, according to abstract principles, it was impossible to explain."[2] If so, on what does your constitution rest? If the abstract rights of man[3] will bear discussion and explanation, those of woman, by a parity of reasoning, will not shrink from the same test: though a different opinion prevails in this country, built on the very arguments which you use to justify the oppression of woman—prescription.

Consider, I address you as a legislator, whether, when men contend for their freedom, and to be allowed to judge for themselves respecting their own happiness, it be not inconsistent and unjust to subjugate women, even though you firmly believe that you are acting in the manner best calculated to promote their happiness? Who made man the exclusive judge, if woman partake with him the gift of reason?

In this style, argue tyrants of every denomination, from the weak king to the weak father of a family; they are all eager to crush reason; yet always assert that they usurp its throne only to be useful. Do you not act a similar part, when you *force* all women, by denying them civil and political rights, to remain immured in their families groping in the dark? for surely, Sir, you will not assert, that a duty can be binding which is not founded on reason? If indeed this be their destination, arguments may be drawn from reason: and thus augustly supported, the more understanding women acquire, the more they will be attached to their duty—comprehending it—for unless they comprehend it, unless their morals be fixed on the same immutable principle as those of man, no authority can make them discharge it in a virtuous manner. They may be convenient slaves, but slavery will have its constant effect, degrading the master and the abject dependent.

But, if women are to be excluded, without having a voice, from a participation of the natural rights of mankind, prove first, to ward off the charge of injustice and inconsistency, that they want reason—else this flaw in your NEW CONSTITUTION will ever shew that man must, in some shape, act like a tyrant, and tyranny, in whatever part of society it rears its brazen front, will ever undermine morality.

I have repeatedly asserted, and produced what appeared to me irrefragable arguments drawn from matters of fact, to prove my assertion, that women cannot, by force, be confined to domestic concerns; for they will, however ignorant, intermeddle with more weighty affairs, neglecting private duties only to disturb, by cunning tricks, the orderly plans of reason which rise above their comprehension.

Besides, whilst they are only made to acquire personal accomplishments, men will seek for pleasure in variety, and faithless husbands will make faithless wives; such ignorant beings, indeed, will be very excusable when, not taught to respect public good, nor allowed any civil rights, they attempt to do themselves justice by retaliation.

The box of mischief thus opened in society, what is to preserve private virtue, the only security of public freedom[4] and universal happiness?

---

[1] Wollstonecraft almost always uses this word to mean "gender-specific."

[2] The French constitution of 1791 recognized only men over 25 as citizens; French women did not get the vote until 1944.

[3] as defined, for example, in the *Declaration of the Rights of Men and of Citizens, by the National Assembly of France* (1789).

[4] Wollstonecraft often seems to allude, and always ironically, to the subtitle of Bernard Mandeville (1670–1733), *The Fable of the Bees; or, Private Vices, Public Benefits* (1714). In disparaging him, she follows Catharine Macaulay, *Letters on Education.*ˣ Wollstonecraft reviewed Macaulay's book enthusiastically in the *Analytical Review* and she recommends it later in the *Vindication* (chap. 5, section 4).

Let there be then no coercion *established* in society, and the common law of gravity prevailing, the sexes will fall into their proper places. And, now that more equitable laws are forming your citizens, marriage may become more sacred: your young men may choose wives from motives of affection, and your maidens allow love to root out vanity.

The father of a family will not then weaken his constitution and debase his sentiments, by visiting the harlot, nor forget, in obeying the call of appetite, the purpose for which it was implanted.[1] And, the mother will not neglect her children to practise the arts of coquetry, when sense and modesty secure her the friendship of her husband.

But, till men become attentive to the duty of a father, it is vain to expect women to spend that time in their nursery which they, "wise in their generation,"[2] choose to spend at their glass; for this exertion of cunning is only an instinct of nature to enable them to obtain indirectly a little of that power of which they are unjustly denied a share: for, if women are not permitted to enjoy legitimate rights, they will render both men and themselves vicious, to obtain illicit privileges.

I wish, Sir, to set some investigations of this kind afloat in France; and should they lead to a confirmation of my principles, when your constitution is revised the Rights of Woman may be respected, if it be fully proved that reason calls for this respect, and loudly demands JUSTICE for one half of the human race.

I am, SIR,
Your's respectfully,
M.W.

Introduction

After considering the historic page, and viewing the living world with anxious solicitude, the most melancholy emotions of sorrowful indignation have depressed my spirits, and I have sighed when obliged to confess, that either nature has made a great difference between man and man, or that the civilization which has hitherto taken place in the world has been very partial. I have turned over various books written on the subject of education, and patiently observed the conduct of parents and the management of schools; but what has been the result?—a profound conviction that the neglected education of my fellow-creatures is the grand source of the misery I deplore; and that women, in particular, are rendered weak and wretched by a variety of concurring causes, originating from one hasty conclusion. The conduct and manners of women, in fact, evidently prove that their minds are not in a healthy state; for, like the flowers which are planted in too rich a soil, strength and usefulness are sacrificed to beauty; and the flaunting leaves, after having pleased a fastidious eye, fade, disregarded on the stalk, long before the season when they ought to have arrived at maturity.—One cause of this barren blooming I attribute to a false system of education, gathered from the books written on this subject by men who, considering females rather as women than human creatures, have been more anxious to make them alluring mistresses than affectionate wives and rational mothers; and the understanding of the sex has been so bubbled by this specious homage, that the civilized women of the present century, with a few exceptions, are only anxious to inspire love, when they ought to cherish a nobler ambition, and by their abilities and virtues exact respect.

In a treatise, therefore, on female rights and manners, the works which have been particularly written for their improvement must not be overlooked; especially when it is asserted, in direct terms, that the minds of women are enfeebled by false refinement; that the books of instruction, written by men of genius, have had the same tendency as more frivolous productions; and that, in the true style of Mahometanism, they are treated as a kind of subordinate beings, and not as a part of the human species, when improveable reason is allowed to be the dignified distinction which raises men above the brute creation, and puts a natural sceptre in a feeble hand.

Yet, because I am a woman, I would not lead my readers to suppose that I mean violently to agitate the contested question respecting the equality or inferiority

---

[1] This is the first of several warnings that sensual overindulgence is bad for the health.

[2] Luke 16.8.

of the sex; but as the subject lies in my way, and I cannot pass it over without subjecting the main tendency of my reasoning to misconstruction, I shall stop a moment to deliver, in a few words, my opinion.—In the government of the physical world it is observable that the female in point of strength is, in general, inferior to the male. This is the law of nature; and it does not appear to be suspended or abrogated in favour of woman. A degree of physical superiority cannot, therefore, be denied—and it is a noble prerogative! But not content with this natural pre-eminence, men endeavour to sink us still lower, merely to render us alluring objects for a moment; and women, intoxicated by the adoration which men, under the influence of their senses, pay them, do not seek to obtain a durable interest in their hearts, or to become the friends of the fellow creatures who find amusement in their society.

I am aware of an obvious inference:—from every quarter have I heard exclamations against masculine women; but where are they to be found? If by this appellation men mean to inveigh against their ardour in hunting, shooting, and gaming, I shall most cordially join in the cry; but if it be against the imitation of manly virtues, or, more properly speaking, the attainment of those talents and virtues, the exercise of which ennobles the human character, and which raise females in the scale of animal being, when they are comprehensively termed mankind;—all those who view them with a philosophic eye must, I should think, wish with me, that they may every day grow more and more masculine.

This discussion naturally divides the subject. I shall first consider women in the grand light of human creatures, who, in common with men, are placed on this earth to unfold their faculties; and afterwards I shall more particularly point out their peculiar designation.

I wish also to steer clear of an error which many respectable writers have fallen into; for the instruction which has hitherto been addressed to women, has rather been applicable to *ladies*, if the little indirect advice, that is scattered through Sandford and Merton,[1] be excepted; but, addressing my sex in a firmer tone, I pay particular attention to those in the middle class, because they appear to be in the most natural state. Perhaps the seeds of false-refinement, immorality, and vanity, have ever been shed by the great. Weak, artificial beings, raised above the common wants and affections of their race, in a premature unnatural manner, undermine the very foundation of virtue, and spread corruption through the whole mass of society! As a class of mankind they have the strongest claim to pity; the education of the rich tends to render them vain and helpless, and the unfolding mind is not strengthened by the practice of those duties which dignify the human character.—They only live to amuse themselves, and by the same law which in nature invariably produces certain effects, they soon only afford barren amusement.

But as I purpose taking a separate view of the different ranks of society, and of the moral character of women, in each, this hint is, for the present, sufficient; and I have only alluded to the subject, because it appears to me to be the very essence of an introduction to give a cursory account of the contents of the work it introduces.

My own sex, I hope, will excuse me, if I treat them like rational creatures, instead of flattering their *fascinating* graces, and viewing them as if they were in a state of perpetual childhood, unable to stand alone. I earnestly wish to point out in what true dignity and human happiness consists—I wish to persuade women to endeavour to acquire strength, both of mind and body, and to convince them that the soft phrases, susceptibility of heart, delicacy of sentiment, and refinement of taste, are almost synonymous with epithets of weakness, and that those beings who are only the objects of pity and that kind of love, which has been termed its sister, will soon become objects of contempt.

Dismissing then those pretty feminine phrases, which the men condescendingly use to soften our slavish dependence, and despising that weak elegancy of mind, exquisite sensibility, and sweet docility of manners, supposed to be the sexual characteristics of the weaker vessel, I wish to shew that elegance is inferior to virtue, that the first object of laudable ambition is to obtain a character as a human being, regardless of the distinction of sex; and that secondary views should be brought to this simple touchstone.

---

[1] Thomas Day (1748–89), *The History of Sandford and Merton* (1783–89). Wollstonecraft reviewed the third volume for the *Analytical Review*.

This is a rough sketch of my plan; and should I express my conviction with the energetic emotions that I feel whenever I think of the subject, the dictates of experience and reflection will be felt by some of my readers. Animated by this important object, I shall disdain to cull my phrases or polish my style;—I aim at being useful, and sincerity will render me unaffected; for, wishing rather to persuade by the force of my arguments, than dazzle by the elegance of my language, I shall not waste my time in rounding periods, or in fabricating the turgid bombast of artificial feelings, which, coming from the head, never reach the heart.—I shall be employed about things, not words!—and, anxious to render my sex more respectable members of society, I shall try to avoid that flowery diction which has slided from essays into novels, and from novels into familiar letters and conversation.

These pretty superlatives, dropping glibly from the tongue, vitiate the taste, and create a kind of sickly delicacy that turns away from simple unadorned truth; and a deluge of false sentiments and overstretched feelings, stifling the natural emotions of the heart, render the domestic pleasures insipid, that ought to sweeten the exercise of those severe duties, which educate a rational and immortal being for a nobler field of action.

The education of women has, of late, been more attended to than formerly; yet they are still reckoned a frivolous sex, and ridiculed or pitied by the writers who endeavour by satire or instruction to improve them. It is acknowledged that they spend many of the first years of their lives in acquiring a smattering of accomplishments; meanwhile strength of body and mind are sacrificed to libertine notions of beauty, to the desire of establishing themselves,—the only way women can rise in the world,—by marriage. And this desire making mere animals of them, when they marry they act as such children may be expected to act:—they dress; they paint, and nickname God's creatures.[1]— Surely these weak beings are only fit for a seraglio!—Can they be expected to govern a family with judgment, or take care of the poor babes whom they bring into the world?

If then it can be fairly deduced from the present conduct of the sex, from the prevalent fondness for pleasure which takes place of ambition and those nobler passions that open and enlarge the soul; that the instruction which women have hitherto received has only tended, with the constitution of civil society, to render them insignificant objects of desire—mere propagators of fools!—if it can be proved that in aiming to accomplish them, without cultivating their understandings, they are taken out of their sphere of duties, and made ridiculous and useless when the short-lived bloom of beauty is over,[2] I presume that *rational* men will excuse me for endeavouring to persuade them to become more masculine and respectable.

Indeed the word masculine is only a bugbear: there is little reason to fear that women will acquire too much courage or fortitude; for their apparent inferiority with respect to bodily strength, must render them, in some degree, dependent on men in the various relations of life; but why should it be increased by prejudices that give a sex to virtue, and confound simple truths with sensual reveries?

Women are, in fact, so much degraded by mistaken notions of female excellence, that I do not mean to add a paradox when I assert, that this artificial weakness produces a propensity to tyrannize, and gives birth to cunning, the natural opponent of strength, which leads them to play off those contemptible infantine airs that undermine esteem even whilst they excite desire. Let men become more chaste and modest, and if women do not grow wiser in the same ratio, it will be clear that they have weaker understandings. It seems scarcely necessary to say, that I now speak of the sex in general. Many individuals have more sense than their male relatives; and, as nothing preponderates where there is a constant struggle for an equilibrium, without it has naturally more gravity, some women govern their husbands without degrading themselves, because intellect will always govern.

---

[1] Shakespeare, *Hamlet* 3.1.142–46. Cf. Burke, *Philosophical Enquiry* 3.9.

[2] "A lively writer, I cannot recollect his name, asks what business women turned of forty have to do in the world?" (M.W.) Wollstonecraft may be thinking of a remark made by Lord Merton, a character in Frances Burney,* *Evelina; or The History of a Young Lady's Entrance into the World* (1778), vol. 3, letter 1.

CHAPTER 2
The Prevailing Opinion of a Sexual Character Discussed

To account for, and excuse the tyranny of man, many ingenious arguments have been brought forward to prove, that the two sexes, in the acquirement of virtue, ought to aim at attaining a very different character: or, to speak explicitly, women are not allowed to have sufficient strength of mind to acquire what really deserves the name of virtue. Yet it should seem, allowing them to have souls, that there is but one way appointed by Providence to lead *mankind* to either virtue or happiness.

If then women are not a swarm of ephemeron triflers, why should they be kept in ignorance under the specious name of innocence? Men complain, and with reason, of the follies and caprices of our sex, when they do not keenly satirize our headstrong passions and groveling vices.—Behold, I should answer, the natural effect of ignorance! The mind will ever be unstable that has only prejudices to rest on, and the current will run with destructive fury when there are no barriers to break its force. Women are told from their infancy, and taught by the example of their mothers, that a little knowledge of human weakness, justly termed cunning, softness of temper, *outward* obedience, and a scrupulous attention to a puerile kind of propriety, will obtain for them the protection of man; and should they be beautiful, every thing else is needless, for, at least, twenty years of their lives.

Thus Milton describes our first frail mother; though when he tells us that women are formed for softness and sweet attractive grace,[1] I cannot comprehend his meaning, unless, in the true Mahometan strain, he meant to deprive us of souls, and insinuate that we were beings only designed by sweet attractive grace, and docile blind obedience, to gratify the senses of man when he can no longer soar on the wing of contemplation.

How grossly do they insult us who thus advise us only to render ourselves gentle, domestic brutes! For instance, the winning softness so warmly, and frequently, recommended, that governs by obeying. What childish expressions, and how insignificant is the being—can it be an immortal one? who will condescend to govern by such sinister methods! "Certainly," says Lord Bacon, "man is of kin to the beasts by his body; and if he be not of kin to God by his spirit, he is a base and ignoble creature!"[2] Men, indeed, appear to me to act in a very unphilosophical manner when they try to secure the good conduct of women by attempting to keep them always in a state of childhood. Rousseau was more consistent when he wished to stop the progress of reason in both sexes, for if men eat of the tree of knowledge, women will come in for a taste;[3] but, from the imperfect cultivation which their understandings now receive, they only attain a knowledge of evil.

Children, I grant, should be innocent; but when the epithet is applied to men, or women, it is but a civil term for weakness. For if it be allowed that women were destined by Providence to acquire human virtues, and by the exercise of their understandings, that stability of character which is the firmest ground to rest our future hopes upon, they must be permitted to turn to the fountain of light, and not forced to shape their course by the twinkling of a mere satellite. Milton, I grant, was of a very different opinion; for he only bends to the indefeasible right of beauty, though it would be difficult to render two passages which I now mean to contrast, consistent. But into similar inconsistencies are great men often led by their senses.

"To whom thus Eve with *perfect beauty* adorn'd.
My Author and Disposer, what thou bidst
Unargued I obey; so God ordains;
God is *thy law, thou mine*: to know no more
Is Woman's *happiest* knowledge and her *praise*."[4]

These are exactly the arguments that I have used to children; but I have added, your reason is now gaining strength, and, till it arrives at some degree of maturity, you must look up to me for advice—then you ought to *think*, and only rely on God.

---

[1] Milton, *Paradise Lost* 4.297–98.

[2] Francis Bacon (1561–1626), *Essays or Councils Civil and Moral* (1625), Essay 16, "Of Atheism."

[3] See Genesis 2–3.

[4] Milton, *Paradise Lost* 4.634–38.

Yet in the following lines Milton seems to coincide with me; when he makes Adam thus expostulate with his Maker.

> "Hast thou not made me here thy substitute,
> And these inferior far beneath me set?
> Among *unequals* what society
> Can sort, what harmony or true delight?
> Which must be mutual, in proportion due
> Giv'n and receiv'd; but in *disparity*
> The one intense, the other still remiss
> Cannot well suit with either, but soon prove
> Tedious alike: of *fellowship* I speak
> Such as I seek, fit to participate
> All rational delight—"[1]

In treating, therefore, of the manners of women, let us, disregarding sensual arguments, trace what we should endeavour to make them in order to co-operate, if the expression be not too bold, with the supreme Being.

By individual education, I mean, for the sense of the word is not precisely defined, such an attention to a child as will slowly sharpen the senses, form the temper, regulate the passions as they begin to ferment, and set the understanding to work before the body arrives at maturity; so that the man may only have to proceed, not to begin, the important task of learning to think and reason.

To prevent any misconstruction, I must add, that I do not believe that a private education can work the wonders which some sanguine writers have attributed to it. Men and women must be educated, in a great degree, by the opinions and manners of the society they live in. In every age there has been a stream of popular opinion that has carried all before it, and given a family character, as it were, to the century. It may then fairly be inferred, that, till society be differently constituted, much cannot be expected from education. It is, however, sufficient for my present purpose to assert, that, whatever effect circumstances have on the abilities, every being may become virtuous by the exercise of its own reason; for if but one being was created with vicious inclinations, that is positively bad, what can save us from atheism? or if we worship a God, is not that God a devil?

Consequently, the most perfect education, in my opinion, is such an exercise of the understanding as is best calculated to strengthen the body and form the heart. Or, in other words, to enable the individual to attain such habits of virtue as will render it independent. In fact, it is a farce to call any being virtuous whose virtues do not result from the exercise of its own reason. This was Rousseau's opinion respecting men: I extend it to women, and confidently assert that they have been drawn out of their sphere by false refinement, and not by an endeavour to acquire masculine qualities. Still the regal homage which they receive is so intoxicating, that till the manners of the times are changed, and formed on more reasonable principles, it may be impossible to convince them that the illegitimate power, which they obtain, by degrading themselves, is a curse, and that they must return to nature and equality, if they wish to secure the placid satisfaction that unsophisticated affections impart. But for this epoch we must wait—wait, perhaps, till kings and nobles, enlightened by reason, and, preferring the real dignity of man to childish state, throw off their gaudy hereditary trappings: and if then women do not resign the arbitrary power of beauty—they will prove that they have *less* mind than man.

I may be accused of arrogance; still I must declare what I firmly believe, that all the writers who have written on the subject of female education and manners from Rousseau to Dr. Gregory,[2] have contributed to render women more artificial, weak characters, than they would otherwise have been; and, consequently, more useless members of society. I might have expressed this conviction in a lower key; but I am afraid it would have been the whine of affectation, and not the faithful expression of my feelings, of the clear result, which experience and reflection have led me to draw. When I come to that division of the subject, I shall advert to the passages that I more particularly disapprove of, in the works of the authors I have just alluded to; but it is first necessary to observe, that my objection extends to the whole purport of those books, which tend, in my opinion, to degrade

---

[1] Milton, *Paradise Lost* 8.381–91.

[2] Rousseau, *Emile* Book 5; John Gregory (1724–73), *A Father's Legacy to his Daughters* (1774). Wollstonecraft included substantial excerpts from Gregory in *The Female Reader* (1789).

one half of the human species, and render women pleasing at the expence of every solid virtue.

Though, to reason on Rousseau's ground, if man did attain a degree of perfection of mind when his body arrived at maturity, it might be proper, in order to make a man and his wife *one*, that she should rely entirely on his understanding; and the graceful ivy, clasping the oak that supported it, would form a whole in which strength and beauty would be equally conspicuous. But, alas! husbands, as well as their helpmates, are often only overgrown children; nay, thanks to early debauchery, scarcely men in their outward form—and if the blind lead the blind, one need not come from heaven to tell us the consequence.[1]

Many are the causes that, in the present corrupt state of society, contribute to enslave women by cramping their understandings and sharpening their senses. One, perhaps, that silently does more mischief than all the rest, is their disregard of order.

To do every thing in an orderly manner, is a most important precept, which women, who, generally speaking, receive only a disorderly kind of education, seldom attend to with that degree of exactness that men, who from their infancy are broken into method, observe. This negligent kind of guess-work, for what other epithet can be used to point out the random exertions of a sort of instinctive common sense, never brought to the test of reason? prevents their generalizing matters of fact—so they do to-day, what they did yesterday, merely because they did it yesterday.

This contempt of the understanding in early life has more baneful consequences than is commonly supposed; for the little knowledge which women of strong minds attain, is, from various circumstances, of a more desultory kind than the knowledge of men, and it is acquired more by sheer observations on real life, than from comparing what has been individually observed with the results of experience generalized by speculation. Led by their dependent situation and domestic employments more into society, what they learn is rather by snatches; and as learning is with them, in general, only a secondary thing, they do not pursue any one branch with that persevering ardour necessary to give vigour to the faculties, and clearness to the judgment. In the present state of society, a little learning[2] is required to support the character of a gentleman; and boys are obliged to submit to a few years of discipline. But in the education of women, the cultivation of the understanding is always subordinate to the acquirement of some corporeal accomplishment; even while enervated by confinement and false notions of modesty, the body is prevented from attaining that grace and beauty which relaxed half-formed limbs never exhibit. Besides, in youth their faculties are not brought forward by emulation; and having no serious scientific study, if they have natural sagacity it is turned too soon on life and manners. They dwell on effects, and modifications, without tracing them back to causes; and complicated rules to adjust behaviour are a weak substitute for simple principles.

As a proof that education gives this appearance of weakness to females, we may instance the example of military men, who are, like them, sent into the world before their minds have been stored with knowledge or fortified by principles. The consequences are similar; soldiers acquire a little superficial knowledge, snatched from the muddy current of conversation, and, from continually mixing with society, they gain, what is termed a knowledge of the world; and this acquaintance with manners and customs has frequently been confounded with a knowledge of the human heart. But can the crude fruit of casual observation, never brought to the test of judgment, formed by comparing speculation and experience, deserve such a distinction? Soldiers, as well as women, practice the minor virtues with punctilious politeness. Where is then the sexual difference, when the education has been the same? All the difference that I can discern, arises from the superior advantage of liberty, which enables the former to see more of life.

It is wandering from my present subject, perhaps, to make a political remark; but, as it was produced naturally by the train of my reflections, I shall not pass it silently over.

Standing armies can never consist of resolute, robust men; they may be well disciplined machines, but they

---

[1] Matthew 15.14. The speaker is Jesus, who has "come from heaven."

[2] Cf. Alexander Pope, *An Essay on Criticism* (1711) 215.

will seldom contain men under the influence of strong passions, or with very vigorous faculties. And as for any depth of understanding, I will venture to affirm, that it is as rarely to be found in the army as amongst women; and the cause, I maintain, is the same. It may be further observed, that officers are also particularly attentive to their persons, fond of dancing, crowded rooms, adventures, and ridicule.[1] Like the *fair* sex, the business of their lives is gallantry.—They were taught to please, and they only live to please. Yet they do not lose their rank in the distinction of sexes, for they are still reckoned superior to women, though in what their superiority consists, beyond what I have just mentioned, it is difficult to discover.

The great misfortune is this, that they both acquire manners before morals, and a knowledge of life before they have, from reflection, any acquaintance with the grand ideal outline of human nature. The consequence is natural; satisfied with common nature, they become a prey to prejudices, and taking all their opinions on credit, they blindly submit to authority. So that, if they have any sense, it is a kind of instinctive glance, that catches proportions, and decides with respect to manners; but fails when arguments are to be pursued below the surface, or opinions analyzed.

May not the same remark be applied to women? Nay, the argument may be carried still further, for they are both thrown out of a useful station by the unnatural distinctions established in civilized life. Riches and hereditary honours have made cyphers of women to give consequence to the numerical figure; and idleness has produced a mixture of gallantry and despotism into society, which leads the very men who are the slaves of their mistresses to tyrannize over their sisters, wives, and daughters. This is only keeping them in rank and file, it is true. Strengthen the female mind by enlarging it, and there will be an end to blind obedience; but, as blind obedience is ever sought for by power, tyrants and sensualists are in the right when they endeavour to keep women in the dark, because the former only want slaves,

and the latter a play-thing. The sensualist, indeed, has been the most dangerous of tyrants, and women have been duped by their lovers, as princes by their ministers, whilst dreaming that they reigned over them.

I now principally allude to Rousseau, for his character of Sophia is, undoubtedly, a captivating one, though it appears to me grossly unnatural; however it is not the superstructure, but the foundation of her character, the principles on which her education was built, that I mean to attack; nay, warmly as I admire the genius of that able writer, whose opinions I shall often have occasion to cite, indignation always takes place of admiration, and the rigid frown of insulted virtue effaces the smile of complacency, which his eloquent periods are wont to raise, when I read his voluptuous reveries. Is this the man, who, in his ardour for virtue, would banish all the soft arts of peace, and almost carry us back to Spartan discipline? Is this the man who delights to paint the useful struggles of passion, the triumphs of good dispositions, and the heroic flights which carry the glowing soul out of itself?—How are these mighty sentiments lowered when he describes the pretty foot and enticing airs of his little favourite! But, for the present, I wave the subject, and, instead of severely reprehending the transient effusions of overweening sensibility, I shall only observe, that whoever has cast a benevolent eye on society, must often have been gratified by the sight of humble mutual love, not dignified by sentiment, or strengthened by a union in intellectual pursuits. The domestic trifles of the day have afforded matters for cheerful converse, and innocent caresses have softened toils which did not require great exercise of mind or stretch of thought: yet, has not the sight of this moderate felicity excited more tenderness than respect? An emotion similar to what we feel when children are playing, or animals sporting,[2] whilst the contemplation

---

[1] "Why should women be censured with petulant acrimony, because they seem to have a passion for a scarlet coat? Has not education placed them more on a level with soldiers than any other class of men?" (M.W.)

[2] "Similar feelings has Milton's pleasing picture of paradisiacal happiness ever raised in my mind; yet, instead of envying the lovely pair, I have, with conscious dignity, or Satanic pride, turned to hell for sublimer objects. In the same style, when viewing some noble monument of human art, I have traced the emanation of the Deity in the order I admired, till, descending from that giddy height, I have caught myself contemplating the grandest of all human sights;—for fancy quickly placed, in some solitary recess, an outcast of fortune, rising superior to passion and discontent." (M.W.)

of the noble struggles of suffering merit has raised admiration, and carried our thoughts to that world where sensation will give place to reason.

Women are, therefore, to be considered either as moral beings, or so weak that they must be entirely subjected to the superior faculties of men.

Let us examine this question. Rousseau declares that a woman should never, for a moment, feel herself independent, that she should be governed by fear to exercise her *natural* cunning, and made a coquetish slave in order to render her a more alluring object of desire, a *sweeter* companion to man, whenever he chooses to relax himself. He carries the arguments, which he pretends to draw from the indications of nature, still further, and insinuates that truth and fortitude, the corner stones of all human virtue, should be cultivated with certain restrictions, because, with respect to the female character, obedience is the grand lesson which ought to be impressed with unrelenting rigour.

What nonsense! when will a great man arise with sufficient strength of mind to puff away the fumes which pride and sensuality have thus spread over the subject! If women are by nature inferior to men, their virtues must be the same in quality, if not in degree, or virtue is a relative idea; consequently, their conduct should be founded on the same principles, and have the same aim.[1]

Connected with man as daughters, wives, and mothers, their moral character may be estimated by their manner of fulfilling those simple duties; but the end, the grand end of their exertions should be to unfold their own faculties and acquire the dignity of conscious virtue. They may try to render their road pleasant; but ought never to forget, in common with man, that life yields not the felicity which can satisfy an immortal soul. I do not mean to insinuate, that either sex should be so lost in abstract reflections or distant views, as to forget the affections and duties that lie before them, and are, in truth, the means appointed to produce the fruit of life; on the contrary, I would warmly recommend them, even while I assert, that they afford most satisfaction when they are considered in their true, sober light.

Probably the prevailing opinion, that woman was created for man, may have taken its rise from Moses's poetical story;[2] yet, as very few, it is presumed, who have bestowed any serious thought on the subject, ever supposed that Eve was, literally speaking, one of Adam's ribs, the deduction must be allowed to fall to the ground; or, only be so far admitted as it proves that man, from the remotest antiquity, found it convenient to exert his strength to subjugate his companion, and his invention to shew that she ought to have her neck bent under the yoke, because the whole creation was only created for his convenience or pleasure.

Let it not be concluded that I wish to invert the order of things; I have already granted, that, from the constitution of their bodies, men seem to be designed by Providence to attain a greater degree of virtue. I speak collectively of the whole sex; but I see not the shadow of a reason to conclude that their virtues should differ in respect to their nature. In fact, how can they, if virtue has only one eternal standard? I must therefore, if I reason consequentially, as strenuously maintain that they have the same simple direction, as that there is a God.

It follows then that cunning should not be opposed to wisdom, little cares to great exertions, or insipid softness, varnished over with the name of gentleness, to that fortitude which grand views alone can inspire.

I shall be told that woman would then lose many of her peculiar graces, and the opinion of a well known poet might be quoted to refute my unqualified assertion. For Pope has said, in the name of the whole male sex,

"Yet ne'er so sure our passion to create,
As when she touch'd the brink of all we hate."[3]

In what light this sally places men and women, I shall leave to the judicious to determine; meanwhile I shall content myself with observing, that I cannot discover why, unless they are mortal, females should always be degraded by being made subservient to love or lust.

To speak disrespectfully of love is, I know, high treason against sentiment and fine feelings; but I wish to

---

[1] Rousseau argues in *Emile* that men's and women's virtues are essentially different.

[2] Genesis 2.18–25. Moses was believed to be the author of Genesis.

[3] Alexander Pope, "Of the Characters of Women" 51–52.

speak the simple language of truth, and rather to address the head than the heart. To endeavour to reason love out of the world, would be to out Quixote Cervantes,[1] and equally offend against common sense; but an endeavour to restrain this tumultuous passion, and to prove that it should not be allowed to dethrone superior powers, or to usurp the sceptre which the understanding should ever coolly wield, appears less wild.

Youth is the season for love in both sexes; but in those days of thoughtless enjoyment provision should be made for the more important years of life, when reflection takes place of sensation. But Rousseau, and most of the male writers who have followed his steps, have warmly inculcated that the whole tendency of female education ought to be directed to one point:—to render them pleasing.

Let me reason with the supporters of this opinion who have any knowledge of human nature, do they imagine that marriage can eradicate the habitude of life? The woman who has only been taught to please will soon find that her charms are oblique sunbeams, and that they cannot have much effect on her husband's heart when they are seen every day, when the summer is passed and gone. Will she then have sufficient native energy to look into herself for comfort, and cultivate her dormant faculties? or, is it not more rational to expect that she will try to please other men; and, in the emotions raised by the expectation of new conquests, endeavour to forget the mortification her love or pride has received? When the husband ceases to be a lover—and the time will inevitably come, her desire of pleasing will then grow languid, or become a spring of bitterness; and love, perhaps, the most evanescent of all passions, gives place to jealousy or vanity.

I now speak of women who are restrained by principle or prejudice; such women, though they would shrink from an intrigue with real abhorrence, yet, nevertheless, wish to be convinced by the homage of gallantry that they are cruelly neglected by their husbands; or, days and weeks are spent in dreaming of the happiness enjoyed by congenial souls till their health is undermined and their spirits broken by discontent. How then can the great art of pleasing be such a necessary study? it is only useful to a mistress; the chaste wife, and serious mother, should only consider her power to please as the polish of her virtues, and the affection of her husband as one of the comforts that render her task less difficult and her life happier.—But, whether she be loved or neglected, her first wish should be to make herself respectable, and not to rely for all her happiness on a being subject to like infirmities with herself.

The worthy Dr. Gregory fell into a similar error. I respect his heart; but entirely disapprove of his celebrated Legacy to his Daughters.

He advises them to cultivate a fondness for dress, because a fondness for dress, he asserts, is natural to them. I am unable to comprehend what either he or Rousseau mean, when they frequently use this indefinite term. If they told us that in a pre-existent state the soul was fond of dress, and brought this inclination with it into a new body, I should listen to them with a half smile, as I often do when I hear a rant about innate elegance.—But if he only meant to say that the exercise of the faculties will produce this fondness—I deny it.—It is not natural; but arises, like false ambition in men, from a love of power.

Dr. Gregory goes much further; he actually recommends dissimulation, and advises an innocent girl to give the lie to her feelings, and not dance with spirit, when gaiety of heart would make her feet eloquent without making her gestures immodest. In the name of truth and common sense, why should not one woman acknowledge that she can take more exercise than another? or, in other words, that she has a sound constitution; and why, to damp innocent vivacity, is she darkly to be told that men will draw conclusions which she little thinks of?—Let the libertine draw what inference he pleases; but, I hope, that no sensible mother will restrain the natural frankness of youth by instilling such indecent cautions. Out of the abundance of the heart the mouth speaketh;[2] and a wiser than Solomon hath said,

---

[1] an allusion to the impossibly idealistic hero of Miguel de Cervantes Saavedra (1547–1615), *Don Quixote* (1604–14). Edmund Burke compared Richard Price to Don Quixote (*Reflections**); in turn, radical writers and cartoonists applied the comparison to Burke, because of his lament for the age of chivalry.

[2] Matthew 12.34, Luke 6.45.

that the heart should be made clean, and not trivial ceremonies observed, which it is not very difficult to fulfil with scrupulous exactness when vice reigns in the heart.[1]

Women ought to endeavour to purify their heart;[2] but can they do so when their uncultivated understandings make them entirely dependent on their senses for employment and amusement, when no noble pursuit sets them above the little vanities of the day, or enables them to curb the wild emotions that agitate a reed over which every passing breeze has power? To gain the affections of a virtuous man is affectation necessary? Nature has given woman a weaker frame than man; but, to ensure her husband's affections, must a wife, who by the exercise of her mind and body whilst she was discharging the duties of a daughter, wife, and mother, has allowed her constitution to retain its natural strength, and her nerves a healthy tone, is she, I say, to condescend to use art and feign a sickly delicacy in order to secure her husband's affection? Weakness may excite tenderness, and gratify the arrogant pride of man; but the lordly caresses of a protector will not gratify a noble mind that pants for, and deserves to be respected. Fondness is a poor substitute for friendship!

In a seraglio, I grant, that all these arts are necessary; the epicure must have his palate tickled, or he will sink into apathy; but have women so little ambition as to be satisfied with such a condition? Can they supinely dream life away in the lap of pleasure, or the languor of weariness, rather than assert their claim to pursue reasonable pleasures and render themselves conspicuous by practising the virtues which dignify mankind? Surely she has not an immortal soul who can loiter life away merely employed to adorn her person, that she may amuse the languid hours, and soften the cares of a fellow-creature who is willing to be enlivened by her smiles and tricks, when the serious business of life is over.

Besides, the woman who strengthens her body and exercises her mind will, by managing her family and practising various virtues, become the friend, and not the humble dependent of her husband; and if she, by possessing such substantial qualities, merit his regard, she will not find it necessary to conceal her affection, nor to pretend to an unnatural coldness of constitution to excite her husband's passions. In fact, if we revert to history, we shall find that the women who have distinguished themselves have neither been the most beautiful nor the most gentle of their sex.

Nature, or, to speak with strict propriety, God, has made all things right; but man has sought him out many inventions to mar the work. I now allude to that part of Dr. Gregory's treatise, where he advises a wife never to let her husband know the extent of her sensibility or affection. Voluptuous precaution, and as ineffectual as absurd.—Love, from its very nature, must be transitory. To seek for a secret that would render it constant, would be as wild a search as for the philosopher's stone, or the grand panacea:[3] and the discovery would be equally useless, or rather pernicious, to mankind. The most holy band of society is friendship. It has been well said, by a shrewd satirist, "that rare as true love is, true friendship is still rarer."[4]

This is an obvious truth, and the cause not lying deep, will not elude a slight glance of inquiry.

Love, the common passion, in which chance and sensation take place of choice and reason, is, in some degree, felt by the mass of mankind; for it is not necessary to speak, at present, of the emotions that rise above or sink below love. This passion, naturally increased by suspense and difficulties, draws the mind out of its accustomed state, and exalts the affections; but the security of marriage, allowing the fever of love to subside, a healthy temperature is thought insipid, only by those who have not sufficient intellect to substitute the calm tenderness of friendship, the confidence of respect, instead of blind admiration, and the sensual emotions of fondness.

This is, must be, the course of nature.—Friendship or indifference inevitably succeeds love.—And this

---

[1] Matthew 23.25–28; Luke 11.31–44. The speaker is Christ, wiser than Solomon (cf. Milton, *Paradise Regained* 2.205–06).

[2] Matthew 5.8.

[3] Alchemists sought for two substances (or a substance with two properties): the philosopher's stone, which could transmute base metals into gold; and the elixir or panacea, which could prolong life indefinitely.

[4] François, duc de La Rochefoucauld (1613–80), *Reflexions; ou, Sentences et maxims morales* (1678) no. 473.

constitution seems perfectly to harmonize with the system of government which prevails in the moral world. Passions are spurs to action, and open the mind; but they sink into mere appetites, become a personal and momentary gratification, when the object is gained, and the satisfied mind rests in enjoyment. The man who had some virtue whilst he was struggling for a crown, often becomes a voluptuous tyrant when it graces his brow; and, when the lover is not lost in the husband, the dotard, a prey to childish caprices, and fond jealousies, neglects the serious duties of life, and the caresses which should excite confidence in his children are lavished on the overgrown child, his wife.

In order to fulfil the duties of life, and to be able to pursue with vigour the various employments which form the moral character, a master and mistress of a family ought not to continue to love each other with passion. I mean to say, that they ought not to indulge those emotions which disturb the order of society, and engross the thoughts that should be otherwise employed. The mind that has never been engrossed by one object wants vigour—if it can long be so, it is weak.

A mistaken education, a narrow, uncultivated mind, and many sexual prejudices, tend to make women more constant than men; but, for the present, I shall not touch on this branch of the subject. I will go still further, and advance, without dreaming of a paradox, that an unhappy marriage is often very advantageous to a family, and that the neglected wife is, in general, the best mother. And this would almost always be the consequence if the female mind were more enlarged: for, it seems to be the common dispensation of Providence, that what we gain in present enjoyment should be deducted from the treasure of life, experience; and that when we are gathering the flowers of the day and revelling in pleasure, the solid fruit of toil and wisdom should not be caught at the same time. The way lies before us, we must turn to the right or left; and he who will pass life away in bounding from one pleasure to another, must not complain if he acquire neither wisdom nor respectability of character.

Supposing, for a moment, that the soul is not immortal, and that man was only created for the present scene,—I think we should have reason to complain that love, infantine fondness, ever grew insipid and palled upon the sense. Let us eat, drink, and love, for tomorrow we die,[1] would be, in fact, the language of reason, the morality of life; and who but a fool would part with a reality for a fleeting shadow? But, if awed by observing the improbable powers of the mind, we disdain to confine our wishes or thoughts to such a comparatively mean field of action; that only appears grand and important, as it is connected with a boundless prospect and sublime hopes, what necessity is there for falsehood in conduct, and why must the sacred majesty of truth be violated to detain a deceitful good that saps the very foundation of virtue? Why must the female mind be tainted by coquetish arts to gratify the sensualist, and prevent love from subsiding into friendship, or compassionate tenderness, when there are not qualities on which friendship can be built? Let the honest heart shew itself, and *reason* teach passion to submit to necessity; or, let the dignified pursuit of virtue and knowledge raise the mind above those emotions which rather imbitter than sweeten the cup of life, when they are not restrained within due bounds.

I do not mean to allude to the romantic passion, which is the concomitant of genius.—Who can clip its wing? But that grand passion not proportioned to the puny enjoyments of life, is only true to the sentiment, and feeds on itself. The passions which have been celebrated for their durability have always been unfortunate. They have acquired strength by absence and constitutional melancholy.—The fancy has hovered round a form of beauty dimly seen—but familiarity might have turned admiration into disgust; or, at least, into indifference, and allowed the imagination leisure to start fresh game. With perfect propriety, according to this view of things, does Rousseau make the mistress of his soul, Eloisa, love St. Preux, when life was fading before her; but this is no proof of the immortality of the passion.[2]

---

[1] Isaiah 22.13.

[2] The heroine of Rousseau's *Julie; ou, La Nouvelle Héloïse* (1761), faithfully married to Wolmar, confesses her love for St. Preux on her deathbed.

Of the same complexion is Dr. Gregory's advice respecting delicacy of sentiment, which he advises a woman not to acquire, if she have determined to marry. This determination, however, perfectly consistent with his former advice, he calls *indelicate*, and earnestly persuades his daughters to conceal it, though it may govern their conduct:—as if it were indelicate to have the common appetites of human nature.

Noble morality! and consistent with the cautious prudence of a little soul that cannot extend its views beyond the present minute division of existence. If all the faculties of woman's mind are only to be cultivated as they respect her dependence on man; if, when a husband be obtained, she have arrived at her goal, and meanly proud rests satisfied with such a paltry crown, let her grovel contentedly, scarcely raised by her employments above the animal kingdom; but, if, struggling for the prize of her high calling, she look beyond the present scene, let her cultivate her understanding without stopping to consider what character the husband may have whom she is destined to marry. Let her only determine, without being too anxious about present happiness, to acquire the qualities that ennoble a rational being, and a rough inelegant husband may shock her taste without destroying her peace of mind. She will not model her soul to suit the frailties of her companion, but to bear with them: his character may be a trial, but not an impediment to virtue.

If Dr. Gregory confined his remark to romantic expectations of constant love and congenial feelings, he should have recollected that experience will banish what advice can never make us cease to wish for, when the imagination is kept alive at the expence of reason.

I own it frequently happens that women who have fostered a romantic unnatural delicacy of feeling, waste their[1] lives in *imagining* how happy they should have been with a husband who could love them with a fervid increasing affection every day, and all day. But they might as well pine married as single—and would not be a jot more unhappy with a bad husband than longing for a good one. That a proper education; or, to speak with more precision, a well stored mind, would enable a woman to support a single life with dignity, I grant; but that she should avoid cultivating her taste, lest her husband should occasionally shock it, is quitting a substance for a shadow. To say the truth, I do not know of what use is an improved taste, if the individual be not rendered more independent of the casualties of life; if new sources of enjoyment, only dependent on the solitary operations of the mind, are not opened. People of taste, married or single, without distinction, will ever be disgusted by various things that touch not less observing minds. On this conclusion the argument must not be allowed to hinge; but in the whole sum of enjoyment is taste to be denominated a blessing?

The question is, whether it procures most pain or pleasure? The answer will decide the propriety of Dr. Gregory's advice, and shew how absurd and tyrannic it is thus to lay down a system of slavery; or to attempt to educate moral beings by any other rules than those deduced from pure reason, which apply to the whole species.

Gentleness of manners, forbearance and long-suffering, are such amiable Godlike qualities,[2] that in sublime poetic strains the Deity has been invested with them; and, perhaps, no representation of his goodness so strongly fastens on the human affections as those that represent him abundant in mercy and willing to pardon.[3] Gentleness, considered in this point of view, bears on its front all the characteristics of grandeur, combined with the winning graces of condescension; but what a different aspect it assumes when it is the submissive demeanour of dependence, the support of weakness that loves, because it wants protection; and is forbearing, because it must silently endure injuries; smiling under the lash at which it dare not snarl. Abject as this picture appears, it is the portrait of an accomplished woman, according to the received opinion of female excellence, separated by specious reasoners from human excellence. Or, they[4] kindly restore the rib, and

---

[1] "For example, the herd of Novelists." (M.W.)

[2] Galatians 5.22, Ephesians 4.2.

[3] Isaiah 55.7.

[4] "Vide Rousseau, and Swedenborg." (M.W.) Rousseau, *Emile*; Emmanuel Swedenborg (1688–1772), *Conjugal Love* (trans. 1789), which Wollstonecraft reviewed.

make one moral being of a man and woman; not forgetting to give her all the "submissive charms."[1]

How women are to exist in that state where there is to be neither marrying nor giving in marriage,[2] we are not told. For though moralists have agreed that the tenor of life seems to prove that *man* is prepared by various circumstances for a future state, they constantly concur in advising *woman* only to provide for the present. Gentleness, docility, and a spaniel-like affection are, on this ground, consistently recommended as the cardinal virtues of the sex; and, disregarding the arbitrary economy of nature, one writer has declared that it is masculine for a woman to be melancholy. She was created to be the toy of man, his rattle, and it must jingle in his ears whenever, dismissing reason, he chooses to be amused.

To recommend gentleness, indeed, on a broad basis is strictly philosophical. A frail being should labour to be gentle. But when forbearance confounds right and wrong, it ceases to be a virtue; and, however convenient it may be found in a companion—that companion will ever be considered as an inferior, and only inspire a vapid tenderness, which easily degenerates into contempt. Still, if advice could really make a being gentle, whose natural disposition admitted not of such a fine polish, something towards the advancement of order would be attained; but if, as might quickly be demonstrated, only affectation be produced by this indiscriminate counsel, which throws a stumbling-block in the way of gradual improvement, and true melioration of temper, the sex is not much benefited by sacrificing solid virtues to the attainment of superficial graces, though for a few years they may procure the individuals regal sway.

As a philosopher, I read with indignation the plausible epithets which men use to soften their insults; and, as a moralist, I ask what is meant by such heterogeneous associations, as fair defects, amiable weaknesses, &c.?[3] If there be but one criterion of morals, but one archetype for man, women appear to be suspended by destiny, according to the vulgar tale of Mahomet's coffin;[4] they have neither the unerring instinct of brutes, nor are allowed to fix the eye of reason on a perfect model. They were made to be loved, and must not aim at respect, lest they should be hunted out of society as masculine.

But to view the subject in another point of view. Do passive indolent women make the best wives? Confining our discussion to the present moment of existence, let us see how such weak creatures perform their part? Do the women who, by the attainment of a few superficial accomplishments, have strengthened the prevailing prejudice, merely contribute to the happiness of their husbands? Do they display their charms merely to amuse them? And have women, who have early imbibed notions of passive obedience, sufficient character to manage a family or educate children? So far from it, that, after surveying the history of woman, I cannot help, agreeing with the severest satirist, considering the sex as the weakest as well as the most oppressed half of the species. What does history disclose but marks of inferiority, and how few women have emancipated themselves from the galling yoke of sovereign man?—So few, that the exceptions remind me of an ingenious conjecture respecting Newton: that he was probably a being of a superior order, accidentally caged in a human body.[5] Following the same train of thinking, I have been led to imagine that the few extraordinary women who have rushed in eccentrical directions out of the orbit prescribed to their sex, were *male* spirits, confined by mistake in female frames. But if it be not philosophical to think of sex when the soul is mentioned, the inferiority must depend on the organs; or the heavenly fire, which is to ferment the clay, is not given in equal portions.

---

[1] Milton, *Paradise Lost* 4.498.

[2] Matthew 22.30; Mark 12.25; Luke 20.35.

[3] Milton, *Paradise Lost* 10.891; Pope, "Of the Characters of Women" 44 (misquoted).

[4] According to the legend, Muhammad's coffin was suspended in midair by magnets. See Milton, *Eikonoklastes* (1649); Samuel Butler (1613–80), *Hudibras* (1663–78) 2.3.442, 3.2.605; Matthew Prior (1664–1721), *Alma; or, The Progress of the Mind* (1718) 2: 198–99.

[5] See James Thomson (1700–48), *A Poem Sacred to the Memory of Sir Isaac Newton* (1727); Pope, *An Essay on Man* (1733–34) 2: 31–34; "Epitaph. Intended for Sir Isaac Newton, In Westminster–Abbey" (1730).

But avoiding, as I have hitherto done, any direct comparison of the two sexes collectively, or frankly acknowledging the inferiority of woman, according to the present appearance of things, I shall only insist that men have increased that inferiority till women are almost sunk below the standard of rational creatures. Let their faculties have room to unfold, and their virtues to gain strength, and then determine where the whole sex must stand in the intellectual scale. Yet let it be remembered, that for a small number of distinguished women I do not ask a place.

It is difficult for us purblind mortals to say to what height human discoveries and improvements may arrive when the gloom of despotism subsides, which makes us stumble at every step; but, when morality shall be settled on a more solid basis, then, without being gifted with a prophetic spirit, I will venture to predict that woman will be either the friend or slave of man. We shall not, as at present, doubt whether she is a moral agent, or the link which unites man with brutes. But, should it then appear, that like the brutes they were principally created for the use of man, he will let them patiently bite the bridle, and not mock them with empty praise; or, should their rationality be proved, he will not impede their improvement merely to gratify his sensual appetites. He will not, with all the graces of rhetoric, advise them to submit implicitly their understanding to the guidance of man. He will not, when he treats of the education of women, assert that they ought never to have the free use of reason, nor would he recommend cunning and dissimulation to beings who are acquiring, in like manner as himself, the virtues of humanity.

Surely there can be but one rule of right, if morality has an eternal foundation, and whoever sacrifices virtue, strictly so called, to present convenience, or whose *duty* it is to act in such a manner, lives only for the passing day, and cannot be an accountable creature.

The poet then should have dropped his sneer when he says,

"If weak women go astray,
The stars are more in fault than they."[1]

For that they are bound by the adamantine chain of destiny is most certain, if it be proved that they are never to exercise their own reason, never to be independent, never to rise above opinion, or to feel the dignity of a rational will that only bows to God, and often forgets that the universe contains any being but itself and the model of perfection to which its ardent gaze is turned, to adore attributes that, softened into virtues, may be imitated in kind, though the degree overwhelms the enraptured mind.

If, I say, for I would not impress by declamation when Reason offers her sober light, if they be really capable of acting like rational creatures, let them not be treated like slaves; or, like the brutes who are dependent on the reason of man, when they associate with him; but cultivate their minds, give them the salutary, sublime curb of principle, and let them attain conscious dignity by feeling themselves only dependent on God. Teach them, in common with man, to submit to necessity, instead of giving, to render them more pleasing, a sex to morals.

Further, should experience prove that they cannot attain the same degree of strength of mind, perseverance, and fortitude, let their virtues be the same in kind, though they may vainly struggle for the same degree; and the superiority of man will be equally clear, if not clearer; and truth, as it is a simple principle, which admits of no modification, would be common to both. Nay, the order of society as it is at present regulated would not be inverted, for woman would then only have the rank that reason assigned her, and arts could not be practised to bring the balance even, much less to turn it.

These may be termed Utopian dreams.—Thanks to that Being who impressed them on my soul, and gave me sufficient strength of mind to dare to exert my own reason, till, becoming dependent only on him for the support of my virtue, I view, with indignation, the mistaken notions that enslave my sex.

I love man as my fellow; but his scepter, real, or usurped, extends not to me, unless the reason of an individual demands my homage; and even then the submission is to reason, and not to man. In fact, the conduct of an accountable being must be regulated by the operations of its own reason; or on what foundation rests the throne of God?

---

[1] Matthew Prior, "Hans Carvel" (1700) 11–12.

It appears to me necessary to dwell on these obvious truths, because females have been insulated, as it were; and, while they have been stripped of the virtues that should clothe humanity, they have been decked with artificial graces that enable them to exercise a short-lived tyranny. Love, in their bosoms, taking place of every nobler passion, their sole ambition is to be fair, to raise emotion instead of inspiring respect; and this ignoble desire, like the servility in absolute monarchies, destroys all strength of character. Liberty is the mother of virtue, and if women be, by their very constitution, slaves, and not allowed to breathe the sharp invigorating air of freedom, they must ever languish like exotics, and be reckoned beautiful flaws in nature.

As to the argument respecting the subjection in which the sex has ever been held, it retorts on man. The many have always been enthralled by the few; and monsters, who scarcely have shewn any discernment of human excellence, have tyrannized over thousands of their fellow-creatures. Why have men of superiour endowments submitted to such degradation? For, is it not universally acknowledged that kings, viewed collectively, have ever been inferior, in abilities and virtue, to the same number of men taken from the common mass of mankind—yet, have they not, and are they not still treated with a degree of reverence that is an insult to reason? China is not the only country where a living man has been made a God. *Men* have submitted to superior strength to enjoy with impunity the pleasure of the moment—*women* have only done the same, and therefore till it is proved that the courtier, who servilely resigns the birthright of a man, is not a moral agent, it cannot be demonstrated that woman is essentially inferior to man because she has always been subjugated.

Brutal force has hitherto governed the world, and that the science of politics is in its infancy, is evident from philosophers scrupling to give the knowledge most useful to man that determinate distinction.

I shall not pursue this argument any further than to establish an obvious inference, that as sound politics diffuse liberty, mankind, including woman, will become more wise and virtuous.

CHAPTER 3
The Same Subject Continued[1]

Bodily strength from being the distinction of heroes is now sunk into such unmerited contempt that men, as well as women, seem to think it unnecessary: the latter, as it takes from their feminine graces, and from that lovely weakness the source of their undue power; and the former, because it appears inimical to the character of a gentleman.

That they have both by departing from one extreme run into another, may easily be proved; but first it may be proper to observe, that a vulgar error has obtained a degree of credit, which has given force to a false conclusion, in which an effect has been mistaken for a cause.

People of genius have, very frequently, impaired their constitutions by study or careless inattention to their health, and the violence of their passions bearing a proportion to the vigour of their intellects, the sword's destroying the scabbard has become almost proverbial,[2] and superficial observers have inferred from thence, that men of genius have commonly weak, or, to use a more fashionable phrase, delicate constitutions. Yet the contrary, I believe, will appear to be the fact; for, on diligent inquiry, I find that strength of mind has, in most cases, been accompanied by superior strength of body,—natural soundness of constitution,—not that robust tone of nerves and vigour of muscles, which arise from bodily labour, when the mind is quiescent, or only directs the hands.

Dr. Priestley has remarked, in the preface to his biographical chart,[3] that the majority of great men have lived beyond forty-five. And, considering the thoughtless manner in which they have lavished their strength, when investigating a favourite science they have wasted the lamp of life, forgetful of the midnight hour; or, when, lost in poetic dreams, fancy has peopled the scene, and the soul has been disturbed, till it shook the constitution, by the passions that meditation had raised;

---

[1] This is the title of nine of Macaulay's *Letters on Education.**

[2] Rousseau, *Confessions* Book 5.

[3] Joseph Priestley (1733–1804), *A Description of a Chart of Biography* (1765).

whose objects, the baseless fabric of a vision,[1] faded before the exhausted eye, they must have had iron frames. Shakspeare never grasped the airy dagger with a nerveless hand,[2] nor did Milton tremble when he led Satan far from the confines of his dreary prison.[3]—These were not the ravings of imbecility, the sickly effusions of distempered brains; but the exuberance of fancy, that "in a fine phrenzy" wandering,[4] was not continually reminded of its material shackles.

I am aware that this argument would carry me further than it may be supposed I wish to go; but I follow truth, and, still adhering to my first position, I will allow that bodily strength seems to give man a natural superiority over woman; and this is the only solid basis on which the superiority of the sex can be built. But I still insist, that not only the virtue, but the *knowledge* of the two sexes should be the same in nature, if not in degree, and that women, considered not only as moral, but rational creatures, ought to endeavour to acquire human virtues (or perfections) by the *same* means as men, instead of being educated like a fanciful kind of *half* being—one of Rousseau's wild chimeras.[5]

But, if strength of body be, with some shew of reason, the boast of men, why are women so infatuated as to be proud of a defect? Rousseau has furnished them with a plausible excuse, which could only have occurred to a man, whose imagination had been allowed to run wild, and refine on the impressions made by exquisite senses;—that they might, forsooth, have a pretext for yielding to a natural appetite without violating a romantic species of modesty, which gratifies the pride and libertinism of man.

Women, deluded by these sentiments, sometimes boast of their weakness, cunningly obtaining power by playing on the *weakness* of men; and they may well glory in their illicit sway, for, like Turkish bashaws,[6] they have more real power than their masters: but virtue is sacrificed to temporary gratifications, and the respectability of life to the triumph of an hour.

Women, as well as despots, have now, perhaps, more power than they would have if the world, divided and subdivided into kingdoms and families, were governed

---

[1] Shakespeare, *The Tempest* 4.1.151.

[2] Shakespeare, *Macbeth* 2.1.33–49.

[3] Milton, *Paradise Lost* 2.629–1055.

[4] Shakespeare, *A Midsummer Night's Dream* 5.1.12.

[5] "'Researches into abstract and speculative truths, the principles and axioms of sciences, in short, every thing which tends to generalize our ideas, is not the proper province of women; their studies should be relative to points of practice; it belongs to them to apply those principles which men have discovered; and it is their part to make observations, which direct men to the establishment of general principles. All the ideas of women, which have not the immediate tendency to points of duty, should be directed to the study of men, and to the attainment of those agreeable accomplishments which have taste for their object; for as to works of genius, they are beyond their capacity; neither have they sufficient precision or power of attention to succeed in sciences which require accuracy: and as to physical knowledge, it belongs to those only who are most active, most inquisitive; who comprehend the greatest variety of objects: in short, it belongs to those who have the strongest powers, and who exercise them most, to judge of the relations between sensible beings and the laws of nature. A woman who is naturally weak, and does not carry her ideas to any great extent, knows how to judge and make a proper estimate of those movements which she sets to work, in order to aid her weakness; and these movements are the passions of men. The mechanism she employs is much more powerful than ours; for all her levers move the human heart. She must have the skill to incline us to do every thing which her sex will not enable her to do herself, and which is necessary or agreeable to her; therefore she ought to study the mind of man thoroughly, not the mind of man in general, abstractedly, but the dispositions of those men to whom she is subject, either by the laws of her country or by the force of opinion. She should learn to penetrate into their real sentiments from their conversation, their actions, their looks, and gestures. She should also have the art, by her own conversation, actions, looks, and gestures, to communicate those sentiments which are agreeable to them, without seeming to intend it. Men will argue more philosophically about the human heart; but women will read the heart of man better than they. It belongs to women, if I may be allowed the expression, to form an experimental morality, and to reduce the study of man to a system. Women have most wit, men have most genius; women observe, men reason: from the concurrence of both we derive the clearest light and the most perfect knowledge, which the human mind is, of itself, capable of attaining. In one word, from hence we acquire the most intimate acquaintance, both with ourselves and others, of which our nature is capable; and it is thus that art has a constant tendency to perfect those endowments which nature has bestowed.—The world is the book of women.' *Rousseau's Emilius.* I hope my readers still remember the comparison, which I have brought forward, between women and officers." (M.W.) Wollstonecraft quotes from *Emilius and Sophia; or, A New System of Education,* a translation of Rousseau's *Emile* by William Kenrick (1763).

[6] or pashas, high-ranking officers of the Ottoman Empire.

by laws deduced from the exercise of reason; but in obtaining it, to carry on the comparison, their character is degraded, and licentiousness spread through the whole aggregate of society. The many become pedestal to the few. I, therefore, will venture to assert, that till women are more rationally educated, the progress of human virtue and improvement in knowledge must receive continual checks. And if it be granted that woman was not created merely to gratify the appetite of man, or to be the upper servant, who provides his meals and takes care of his linen, it must follow, that the first care of those mothers or fathers, who really attend to the education of females, should be, if not to strengthen the body, at least, not to destroy the constitution by mistaken notions of beauty and female excellence; nor should girls ever be allowed to imbibe the pernicious notion that a defect can, by any chemical process of reasoning, become an excellence. In this respect, I am happy to find, that the author of one of the most instructive books, that our country has produced for children, coincides with me in opinion; I shall quote his pertinent remarks to give the force of his respectable authority to reason.[1]

But should it be proved that woman is naturally weaker than man, whence does it follow that it is natural for her to labour to become still weaker than nature intended her to be? Arguments of this cast are an insult to common sense, and savour of passion. The *divine right* of husbands, like the divine right of kings, may, it is to be hoped, in this enlightened age, be contested without danger, and, though conviction may not silence many boisterous disputants, yet, when any prevailing prejudice is attacked, the wise will consider, and leave the narrow-minded to rail with thoughtless vehemence at innovation.

The mother, who wishes to give true dignity of character to her daughter, must, regardless of the sneers of ignorance, proceed on a plan diametrically opposite to that which Rousseau has recommended with all the deluding charms of eloquence and philosophical sophistry: for his eloquence renders absurdities plausible, and his dogmatic conclusions puzzle, without convincing, those who have not ability to refute them.

Throughout the whole animal kingdom every young creature requires almost continual exercise, and the infancy of children, conformable to this intimation, should be passed in harmless gambols, that exercise the feet and hands, without requiring very minute direction from the head, or the constant attention of a nurse. In fact, the care necessary for self-preservation is the first natural exercise of the understanding, as little inventions to amuse the present moment unfold the imagination. But these wise designs of nature are counteracted by mistaken fondness or blind zeal. The child is not left a moment to its own direction, particularly a girl, and thus rendered dependent—dependence is called natural.

To preserve personal beauty, woman's glory! the limbs and faculties are cramped with worse than Chi-

---

[1] "A respectable old man gives the following sensible account of the method he pursued when educating his daughter. 'I endeavoured to give both to her mind and body a degree of vigour, which is seldom found in the female sex. As soon as she was sufficiently advanced in strength to be capable of the lighter labours of husbandry and gardening, I employed her as my constant companion. Selene, for that was her name, soon acquired a dexterity in all these rustic employments, which I considered with equal pleasure and admiration. If women are in general feeble both in body and mind, it arises less from nature than from education. We encourage a vicious indolence and inactivity, which we falsely call delicacy; instead of hardening their minds by the severer principles of reason and philosophy, we breed them to useless arts, which terminate in vanity and sensuality. In most of the countries which I had visited, they are taught nothing of an higher nature than a few modulations of the voice, or useless postures of the body; their time is consumed in sloth or trifles, and trifles become the only pursuits capable of interesting them. We seem to forget, that it is upon the qualities of the female sex that our own domestic comforts and the education of our children must depend. And what are the comforts or the education which a race of beings, corrupted from their infancy, and unacquainted with all the duties of life, are fitted to bestow? To touch a musical instrument with useless skill, to exhibit their natural or affected graces to the eyes of indolent and debauched young men, to dissipate their husband's patrimony in riotous and unnecessary expences, these are the only arts cultivated by women in most of the polished nations I had seen. And the consequences are uniformly such as may be expected to proceed from such polluted sources, private misery and public servitude.

"'But Selene's education was regulated by different views, and conducted upon severer principles; if that can be called severity which opens the mind to a sense of moral and religious duties, and most effectually arms it against the inevitable evils of life.' *Mr. Day's Sandford and Merton*, Vol. III." (M.W.)

nese bands,[1] and the sedentary life which they are condemned to live, whilst boys frolic in the open air, weakens the muscles and relaxes the nerves.—As for Rousseau's remarks, which have since been echoed by several writers, that they have naturally, that is from their birth, independent of education, a fondness for dolls, dressing, and talking—they are so puerile as not to merit a serious refutation. That a girl, condemned to sit for hours together listening to the idle chat of weak nurses, or to attend at her mother's toilet, will endeavour to join the conversation, is, indeed, very natural; and that she will imitate her mother or aunts, and amuse herself by adorning her lifeless doll, as they do in dressing her, poor innocent babe! is undoubtedly a most natural consequence. For men of the greatest abilities have seldom had sufficient strength to rise above the surrounding atmosphere; and, if the page of genius have always been blurred by the prejudices of the age, some allowance should be made for a sex, who, like kings, always see things through a false medium.

Pursuing these reflections, the fondness for dress, conspicuous in women, may be easily accounted for, without supposing it the result of a desire to please the sex on which they are dependent. The absurdity, in short, of supposing that a girl is naturally a coquette, and that a desire connected with the impulse of nature to propagate the species, should appear even before an improper education has, by heating the imagination, called it forth prematurely, is so unphilosophical, that such a sagacious observer as Rousseau would not have adopted it, if he had not been accustomed to make reason give way to his desire of singularity, and truth to a favourite paradox.[2]

Yet thus to give a sex to mind was not very consistent with the principles of a man who argued so warmly, and so well, for the immortality of the soul.—But what a weak barrier is truth when it stands in the way of an hypothesis! Rousseau respected—almost adored virtue—and yet he allowed himself to love with sensual fondness. His imagination constantly prepared inflammable fewel for his inflammable senses; but, in order to reconcile his respect for self-denial, fortitude, and those heroic virtues, which a mind like his could not coolly admire, he labours to invert the law of nature, and broaches a doctrine pregnant with mischief and derogatory to the character of supreme wisdom.

His ridiculous stories, which tend to prove that girls are *naturally* attentive to their persons, without laying any stress on daily example, are below contempt.—And that a little miss should have such a correct taste as to neglect the pleasing amusement of making O's, merely because she perceived that it was an ungraceful attitude, should be selected with the anecdotes of the learned pig.[3]

I have, probably, had an opportunity of observing more girls in their infancy than J.J. Rousseau—I can recollect my own feelings, and I have looked steadily around me; yet, so far from coinciding with him in opinion respecting the first dawn of the female character, I will venture to affirm, that a girl, whose spirits have not been damped by inactivity, or innocence tainted by false shame, will always be a romp, and the doll will never excite attention unless confinement allows her no alternative.[4] Girls and boys, in short, would play harmlessly together, if the distinction of sex was not inculcated long before nature makes any difference.—I will go further, and affirm, as an indisputable fact, that most of the women, in the circle of my observation, who have acted like rational creatures, or

---

[1] an allusion to the practice of foot-binding. Cf. John Locke (1632–1704), *Some Thoughts concerning Education* (1693) para. 12.

[2] Rousseau, *Emile*; he does, however, warn against a premature education. Macaulay also accuses Rousseau of a taste for paradoxes (*Letters* 205), which he concedes.

[3] "'I once knew a young person who learned to write before she learned to read, and began to write with her needle before she could use a pen. At first, indeed, she took it into her head to make no other letter than the O: this letter she was constantly making of all sizes, and always the wrong way. Unluckily, one day, as she was intent on this employment, she happened to see herself in the looking-glass; when, taking a dislike to the constrained attitude in which she sat while writing, she threw away her pen, like another Pallas, and determined against making the O any more. Her brother was also equally averse to writing: it was the confinement, however, and not the constrained attitude, that most disgusted him.' *Rousseau's Emilius*." (M.W.) For the learned pig, see Sarah Trimmer (1741–1810), *Fabulous Histories* (1786) chap. 9; James Boswell (1740–1795), *Life of Johnson* (1791) Nov. 1784; Robert Southey, *Letters from England* (840).*

[4] In fact, Rousseau approves of exercise (within limits) for girls.

shewn any vigour of intellect, have accidentally been allowed to run wild—as some of the elegant formers of the fair sex would insinuate.

The baneful consequences which flow from inattention to health during infancy, and youth, extend further than is supposed—dependence of body naturally produces dependence of mind; and how can she be a good wife or mother, the greater part of whose time is employed to guard against or endure sickness? Nor can it be expected that a woman will resolutely endeavour to strengthen her constitution and abstain from enervating indulgencies, if artificial notions of beauty, and false descriptions of sensibility, have been early entangled with her motives of action. Most men are sometimes obliged to bear with bodily inconveniencies, and to endure, occasionally, the inclemency of the elements; but genteel women are, literally speaking, slaves to their bodies, and glory in their subjection.

I once knew a weak woman of fashion, who was more than commonly proud of her delicacy and sensibility. She thought a distinguishing taste and puny appetite the height of all human perfection, and acted accordingly.—I have seen this weak sophisticated being neglect all the duties of life, yet recline with self-complacency on a sofa, and boast of her want of appetite as a proof of delicacy that extended to, or, perhaps, arose from, her exquisite sensibility: for it is difficult to render intelligible such ridiculous jargon.—Yet, at the moment, I have seen her insult a worthy old gentlewoman, whom unexpected misfortunes had made dependent on her ostentatious bounty, and who, in better days, had claims on her gratitude. Is it possible that a human creature could have become such a weak and depraved being, if, like the Sybarites,[1] dissolved in luxury, every thing like virtue had not been worn away, or never impressed by precept, a poor substitute, it is true, for cultivation of mind, though it serves as a fence against vice?

Such a woman is not a more irrational monster than some of the Roman emperors, who were depraved by lawless power. Yet, since kings have been more under the restraint of law, and the curb, however weak, of honour, the records of history are not filled with such unnatural instances of folly and cruelty, nor does the despotism that kills virtue and genius in the bud, hover over Europe with that destructive blast which desolates Turkey, and renders the men, as well as the soil, unfruitful.[2]

Women are every where in this deplorable state; for, in order to preserve their innocence, as ignorance is courteously termed, truth is hidden from them, and they are made to assume an artificial character before their faculties have acquired any strength. Taught from their infancy that beauty is woman's sceptre, the mind shapes itself to the body, and, roaming round its gilt cage, only seeks to adorn its prison. Men have various employments and pursuits which engage their attention, and give a character to the opening mind; but women, confined to one, and having their thoughts constantly directed to the most insignificant part of themselves, seldom extend their views beyond the triumph of the hour. But were their understanding once emancipated from the slavery to which the pride and sensuality of man and their short-sighted desire, like that of dominion in tyrants, of present sway, has subjected them, we should probably read of their weaknesses with surprise. I must be allowed to pursue the argument a little farther.

Perhaps, if the existence of an evil being were allowed, who, in the allegorical language of scripture, went about seeking whom he should devour,[3] he could not more effectually degrade the human character than by giving a man absolute power.

This argument branches into various ramifications.—Birth, riches, and every extrinsic advantage that exalt a man above his fellows, without any mental exertion, sink him in reality below them. In proportion to his weakness, he is played upon by designing men, till the bloated monster has lost all traces of humanity. And that tribes of men, like flocks of sheep, should quietly follow such a leader, is a solecism that only a desire of

---

[1] The citizens of Sybaris, a Greek colony in Southern Italy, were proverbial for self-indulgence.

[2] the simoom or samiel, a hot and allegedly unwholesome wind, here used as a symbol of despotism.

[3] 1 Peter 5.8.

present enjoyment and narrowness of understanding can solve. Educated in slavish dependence, and enervated by luxury and sloth, where shall we find men who will stand forth to assert the rights of man;—or claim the privilege of moral beings, who should have but one road to excellence? Slavery to monarchs and ministers, which the world will be long in freeing itself from, and whose deadly grasp stops the progress of the human mind, is not yet abolished.

Let not men then in the pride of power, use the same arguments that tyrannic kings and venal ministers have used, and fallaciously assert that woman ought to be subjected because she has always been so.—But, when man, governed by reasonable laws, enjoys his natural freedom, let him despise woman, if she do not share it with him; and, till that glorious period arrives, in descanting on the folly of the sex, let him not overlook his own.

Women, it is true, obtaining power by unjust means, by practising or fostering vice, evidently lose the rank which reason would assign them, and they become either abject slaves or capricious tyrants. They lose all simplicity, all dignity of mind, in acquiring power, and act as men are observed to act when they have been exalted by the same means.

It is time to effect a revolution in female manners—time to restore to them their lost dignity—and make them, as a part of the human species, labour by reforming themselves to reform the world. It is time to separate unchangeable morals from local manners.—If men be demi-gods—why let us serve them! And if the dignity of the female soul be as disputable as that of animals—if their reason does not afford sufficient light to direct their conduct whilst unerring instinct is denied—they are surely of all creatures the most miserable! and, bent beneath the iron hand of destiny, must submit to be a *fair defect* in creation. But to justify the ways of Providence respecting them,[1] by pointing out some irrefragable reason for thus making such a large portion of mankind accountable and not accountable, would puzzle the subtilest casuist.

The only solid foundation for morality appears to be the character of the supreme Being; the harmony of which arises from a balance of attributes;—and, to speak with reverence, one attribute seems to imply the *necessity* of another. He must be just, because he is wise, he must be good, because he is omnipotent. For to exalt one attribute at the expence of another equally noble and necessary, bears the stamp of the warped reason of man—the homage of passion. Man, accustomed to bow down to power in his savage state, can seldom divest himself of this barbarous prejudice, even when civilization determines how much superior mental is to bodily strength; and his reason is clouded by these crude opinions, even when he thinks of the Deity.—His omnipotence is made to swallow up, or preside over his other attributes, and those mortals are supposed to limit his power irreverently, who think that it must be regulated by his wisdom.

I disclaim that specious humility which, after investigating nature, stops at the author.—The High and Lofty One, who inhabiteth eternity, doubtless possesses many attributes of which we can form no conception; but reason tells me that they cannot clash with those I adore—and I am compelled to listen to her voice.

It seems natural for man to search for excellence, and either to trace it in the object that he worships, or blindly to invest it with perfection, as a garment. But what good effect can the latter mode of worship have on the moral conduct of a rational being? He bends to power; he adores a dark cloud, which may open a bright prospect to him, or burst in angry, lawless fury, on his devoted head—he knows not why. And, supposing that the Deity acts from the vague impulse of an undirected will, man must also follow his own, or act according to rules, deduced from principles which he disclaims as irreverent. Into this dilemma have both enthusiasts and cooler thinkers fallen, when they laboured to free men from the wholesome restraints which a just conception of the character of God imposes.

It is not impious thus to scan the attributes of the Almighty: in fact, who can avoid it that exercises his faculties? For to love God as the fountain of wisdom, goodness, and power, appears to be the only worship

---

[1] Milton, *Paradise Lost* 10.891–92, 1.25–26.

useful to a being who wishes to acquire either virtue or knowledge. A blind unsettled affection may, like human passions, occupy the mind and warm the heart, whilst, to do justice, love mercy, and walk humbly with our God,[1] is forgotten. I shall pursue this subject still further, when I consider religion in a light opposite to that recommended by Dr. Gregory, who treats it as a matter of sentiment or taste.

To return from this apparent digression. It were to be wished that women would cherish an affection for their husbands, founded on the same principle that devotion ought to rest upon. No other firm base is there under heaven—for let them beware of the fallacious light of sentiment; too often used as a softer phrase for sensuality. It follows then, I think, that from their infancy women should either be shut up like eastern princes, or educated in such a manner as to be able to think and act for themselves.

Why do men halt between two opinions, and expect impossibilities? Why do they expect virtue from a slave, from a being whom the constitution of civil society has rendered weak, if not vicious?

Still I know that it will require a considerable length of time to eradicate the firmly rooted prejudices which sensualists have planted; it will also require some time to convince women that they act contrary to their real interest on an enlarged scale, when they cherish or affect weakness under the name of delicacy, and to convince the world that the poisoned source of female vices and follies, if it be necessary, in compliance with custom, to use synonymous terms in a lax sense, has been the sensual homage paid to beauty:—to beauty of features; for it has been shrewdly observed by a German writer, that a pretty woman, as an object of desire, is generally allowed to be so by men of all descriptions; whilst a fine woman, who inspires more sublime emotions by displaying intellectual beauty, may be overlooked or observed with indifference, by those men who find their happiness in the gratification of their appetites.[2] I foresee an obvious retort—whilst man remains such an imperfect being as he appears hitherto to have been, he will, more or less, be the slave of his appetites; and those women obtaining most power who gratify a predominant one, the sex is degraded by a physical, if not by a moral necessity.

This objection has, I grant, some force; but while such a sublime precept exists, as, "be pure as your heavenly Father is pure";[3] it would seem that the virtues of man are not limited by the Being who alone could limit them; and that he may press forward without considering whether he steps out of his sphere by indulging such a noble ambition. To the wild billows it has been said, "thus far shalt thou go, and no further; and here shall thy proud waves be stayed."[4] Vainly then do they beat and foam, restrained by the power that confines the struggling planets in their orbits, matter yields to the great governing Spirit.—But an immortal soul, not restrained by mechanical laws and struggling to free itself from the shackles of matter, contributes to, instead of disturbing, the order of creation, when, cooperating with the Father of spirits, it tries to govern itself by the invariable rule that, in a degree, before which our imagination faints, regulates the universe.

Besides, if women be educated for dependence; that is, to act according to the will of another fallible being, and submit, right or wrong, to power, where are we to stop? Are they to be considered as viceregents allowed to reign over a small domain, and answerable for their conduct to a higher tribunal, liable to error?

It will not be difficult to prove that such delegates will act like men subjected by fear, and make their children and servants endure their tyrannical oppression. As they submit without reason, they will, having no fixed rules to square their conduct by, be kind, or cruel, just as the whim of the moment directs; and we ought not to wonder if sometimes, galled by their heavy yoke, they take a malignant pleasure in resting it on weaker shoulders.

But, supposing a woman, trained up to obedience, be married to a sensible man, who directs her judgment without making her feel the servility of her subjection,

---

[1] Micah 6.8.

[2] Immanuel Kant, *Observations on the Feeling of the Beautiful and Sublime* (1764).

[3] Matthew 5.48; 1 John 3.3.

[4] Job 38.11.

to act with as much propriety by this reflected light as can be expected when reason is taken at second hand, yet she cannot ensure the life of her protector; he may die and leave her with a large family.

A double duty devolves on her; to educate them in the character of both father and mother; to form their principles and secure their property. But, alas! she has never thought, much less acted for herself. She has only learned to please[1] men, to depend gracefully on them; yet, encumbered with children, how is she to obtain another protector—a husband to supply the place of reason? A rational man, for we are not treading on romantic ground, though he may think her a pleasing docile creature, will not choose to marry a *family* for love, when the world contains many more pretty creatures. What is then to become of her? She either falls an easy prey to some mean fortune-hunter, who defrauds her children of their paternal inheritance, and renders her miserable; or becomes the victim of discontent and blind indulgence. Unable to educate her sons, or impress them with respect; for it is not a play on words to assert, that people are never respected, though filling an important station, who are not respectable; she pines under the anguish of unavailing impotent regret. The serpent's tooth enters into her very soul,[2] and the vices of licentious youth bring her with sorrow, if not with poverty also, to the grave.

This is not an overcharged picture; on the contrary, it is a very possible case, and something similar must have fallen under every attentive eye.

I have, however, taken it for granted, that she was well-disposed, though experience shews, that the blind may as easily be led into a ditch as along the beaten road.[3] But supposing, no very improbable conjecture, that a being only taught to please must still find her happiness in pleasing;—what an example of folly, not to say vice, will she be to her innocent daughters! The mother will be lost in the coquette, and, instead of making friends of her daughters, view them with eyes askance, for they are rivals—rivals more cruel than any other, because they invite a comparison, and drive her from the throne of beauty, who has never thought of a seat on the bench of reason.

It does not require a lively pencil, or the discriminating outline of a caricature, to sketch the domestic miseries and petty vices which such a mistress of a family diffuses. Still she only acts as a woman ought to act, brought up according to Rousseau's system. She can never be reproached for being masculine, or turning out of her sphere; nay, she may observe another of his grand rules, and, cautiously preserving her reputation free from spot, be reckoned a good kind of woman. Yet in what respect can she be termed good? She abstains, it is true, without any great struggle, from committing gross crimes; but how does she fulfil her duties? Duties!—in truth she has enough to think of to adorn her body and nurse a weak constitution.

With respect to religion, she never presumed to judge for herself; but conformed, as a dependent creature should, to the ceremonies of the church which she was brought up in, piously believing that wiser heads than her own have settled that business:—and not to doubt is her point of perfection. She therefore pays her

---

[1] "'In the union of the sexes, both pursue one common object, but not in the same manner. From their diversity in this particular, arises the first determinate difference between the moral relations of each. The one should be active and strong, the other passive and weak: it is necessary the one should have both the power and the will, and that the other should make little resistance.

"'This principle being established, it follows that woman is expressly formed to please the man: if the obligation be reciprocal also, and the man ought to please in his turn, it is not so immediately necessary: his great merit is in his power, and he pleases merely because he is strong. This, I must confess, is not one of the refined maxims of love; it is, however, one of the laws of nature, prior to love itself.

"'If woman be formed to please and be subjected to man, it is her place, doubtless, to render herself agreeable to him, instead of challenging his passion. The violence of his desires depends on her charms; it is by means of these she should urge him to the exertion of those powers which nature hath given him. The most successful method of exciting them, is, to render such exertion necessary by resistance; as, in that case, self-love is added to desire, and the one triumphs in the victory which the other obliged to acquire. Hence arise the various modes of attack and defence between the sexes; the boldness of one sex and the timidity of the other; and, in a word, that bashfulness and modesty with which nature hath armed the weak, in order to subdue the strong.' *Rousseau's Emilius.*

"I shall make no other comment on this ingenious passage, than just to observe, that it is the philosophy of lasciviousness." (M.W.)

[2] Shakespeare, *King Lear* 1.4.297–98.

[3] Matthew 15.14.

tythe of mint and cummin—and thanks her God that she is not as other women are.[1] These are the blessed effects of a good education! These the virtues of man's help-mate![2]

I must relieve myself by drawing a different picture.

Let fancy now present a woman with a tolerable understanding, for I do not wish to leave the line of mediocrity, whose constitution, strengthened by exercise, has allowed her body to acquire its full vigour; her mind, at the same time, gradually expanding itself to comprehend the moral duties of life, and in what human virtue and dignity consist.

Formed thus by the discharge of the relative duties of her station, she marries from affection, without losing sight of prudence, and looking beyond matrimonial felicity, she secures her husband's respect before it is necessary to exert mean arts to please him and feed a dying flame, which nature doomed to expire when the object became familiar, when friendship and forbearance take place of a more ardent affection.—This is the natural death of love, and domestic peace is not destroyed by struggles to prevent its extinction. I also suppose the husband to be virtuous; or she is still more in want of independent principles.

Fate, however, breaks this tie.—She is left a widow, perhaps, without a sufficient provision; but she is not desolate! The pang of nature is felt; but after time has softened sorrow into melancholy resignation, her heart turns to her children with redoubled fondness, and anxious to provide for them, affection gives a sacred heroic cast to her maternal duties. She thinks that not only the eye sees her virtuous efforts from whom all her comfort now must flow, and whose approbation is life; but her imagination, a little abstracted and exalted by grief, dwells on the fond hope that the eyes which her trembling hand closed, may still see how she subdues every wayward passion to fulfil the double duty of being the father as well as the mother of her children. Raised to heroism by misfortunes, she represses the first faint dawning of a natural inclination, before it ripens into love, and in the bloom of life forgets her sex—forgets the pleasure of an awakening passion, which might again have been inspired and returned. She no longer thinks of pleasing, and conscious dignity prevents her from priding herself on account of the praise which her conduct demands. Her children have her love, and her brightest hopes are beyond the grave, where her imagination often strays.

I think I see her surrounded by her children, reaping the reward of her care. The intelligent eye meets hers, whilst health and innocence smile on their chubby cheeks, and as they grow up the cares of life are lessened by their grateful attention. She lives to see the virtues which she endeavoured to plant on principles, fixed into habits, to see her children attain a strength of character sufficient to enable them to endure adversity without forgetting their mother's example.

The task of life thus fulfilled, she calmly waits for the sleep of death, and rising from the grave, may say—Behold, thou gavest me a talent—and here are five talents.[3]

I wish to sum up what I have said in a few words, for I here throw down my gauntlet, and deny the existence of sexual virtues, not excepting modesty. For man and woman, truth, if I understand the meaning of the word, must be the same; yet the fanciful female character, so prettily drawn by poets and novelists, demanding the sacrifice of truth and sincerity, virtue becomes a relative idea, having no other foundation than utility, and of that utility men pretend arbitrarily to judge, shaping it to their own convenience.

Women, I allow, may have different duties to fulfil; but they are *human* duties, and the principles that should regulate the discharge of them, I sturdily maintain, must be the same.

---

[1] Matthew 23.23; Luke 18.11.

[2] "'O how lovely,' exclaims Rousseau, speaking of Sophia, 'is her ignorance! Happy is he who is destined to instruct her! She will never pretend to be the tutor of her husband, but will be content to be his pupil. Far from attempting to subject him to her taste, she will accommodate herself to his. She will be more estimable to him, than if she was learned: he will have a pleasure in instructing her.' *Rousseau's Emilius.*

"I shall content myself with simply asking, how friendship can subsist, when love expires, between the master and his pupil?" (M.W.)

[3] Matthew 25.14–30; Luke 19.12–26.

To become respectable, the exercise of their understanding is necessary, there is no other foundation for independence of character; I mean explicitly to say that they must only bow to the authority of reason, instead of being the *modest* slaves of opinion.

In the superior ranks of life how seldom do we meet with a man of superior abilities, or even common acquirements? The reason appears to me clear, the state they are born in was an unnatural one. The human character has ever been formed by the employments the individual, or class, pursues; and if the faculties are not sharpened by necessity, they must remain obtuse. The argument may fairly be extended to women; for, seldom occupied by serious business, the pursuit of pleasure gives that insignificancy to their character which renders the society of the *great* so insipid. The same want of firmness, produced by a similar cause, forces them both to fly from themselves to noisy pleasures, and artificial passions, till vanity takes place of every social affection, and the characteristics of humanity can scarcely be discerned. Such are the blessings of civil governments, as they are at present organized, that wealth and female softness equally tend to debase mankind, and are produced by the same cause; but allowing women to be rational creatures, they should be incited to acquire virtues which they may call their own, for how can a rational being be ennobled by any thing that is not obtained by its *own* exertions?

CHAPTER 4
Observations on the State of Degradation to Which Woman Is Reduced by Various Causes

That woman is naturally weak, or degraded by a concurrence of circumstances, is, I think, clear. But this position I shall simply contrast with a conclusion, which I have frequently heard fall from sensible men in favour of an aristocracy: that the mass of mankind cannot be any thing, or the obsequious slaves, who patiently allow themselves to be driven forward, would feel their own consequence, and spurn their chains. Men, they further observe, submit every where to oppression, when they have only to lift up their heads to throw off the yoke; yet, instead of asserting their birthright, they quietly lick the dust, and say, let us eat and drink, for to-morrow we die.[1] Women, I argue from analogy, are degraded by the same propensity to enjoy the present moment; and, at last, despise the freedom which they have not sufficient virtue to struggle to attain. But I must be more explicit.

With respect to the culture of the heart, it is unanimously allowed that sex is out of the question; but the line of subordination in the mental powers is never to be passed over.[2] Only "absolute in loveliness,"[3] the portion of rationality granted to woman, is, indeed, very scanty; for, denying her genius and judgment, it is scarcely possible to divine what remains to characterize intellect.

The stamen of immortality, if I may be allowed the phrase, is the perfectibility of human reason; for, were man created perfect, or did a flood of knowledge break in upon him, when he arrived at maturity, that precluded error, I should doubt whether his existence would be continued after the dissolution of the body. But, in the present state of things, every difficulty in morals that escapes from human discussion, and equally baffles the investigation of profound thinking, and the lightning glance of genius, is an argument on which I build my belief of the immortality of the soul. Reason is, consequentially, the simple power of improvement; or, more properly speaking, of discerning truth. Every individual is in this respect a world in itself. More or less may be conspicuous in one being than another; but the nature of reason must be the same in all, if it be an emanation of divinity, the tie that connects the creature with the Creator; for, can that soul be stamped with the heavenly image, that is not perfected by the exercise of

---

[1] Psalms 72.9; Isaiah 22.13; Corinthians 15.32.

[2] "Into what inconsistencies do men fall when they argue without the compass of principles. Women, weak women, are compared with angels; yet, a superiour order of beings should be supposed to possess more intellect than man; or, in what does their superiority consist? In the same strain, to drop the sneer, they are allowed to possess more goodness of heart, piety, and benevolence.—I doubt the fact, though it be courteously brought forward, unless ignorance be allowed to be the mother of devotion; for I am firmly persuaded that, on an average, the proportion between virtue and knowledge, is more upon a par than is commonly granted." (M.W.)

[3] Milton, *Paradise Lost* 8.547.

its own reason?[1] Yet outwardly ornamented with elaborate care, and so adorned to delight man, "that with honour he may love,"[2] the soul of woman is not allowed to have this distinction, and man, ever placed between her and reason, she is always represented as only created to see through a gross medium, and to take things on trust. But dismissing these fanciful theories, and considering woman as a whole, let it be what it will, instead of a part of man, the inquiry is whether she have reason or not. If she have, which, for a moment, I will take for granted, she was not created merely to be the solace of man, and the sexual should not destroy the human character.

Into this error men have, probably, been led by viewing education in a false light; not considering it as the first step to form a being advancing gradually towards perfection;[3] but only as a preparation for life. On this sensual error, for I must call it so, has the false system of female manners been reared, which robs the whole sex of its dignity, and classes the brown and fair with the smiling flowers that only adorn the land. This has ever been the language of men, and the fear of departing from a supposed sexual character, has made even women of superior sense adopt the same sentiments.[4] Thus understanding, strictly speaking, has been denied to woman; and instinct, sublimated into wit and cunning, for the purposes of life, has been substituted in its stead.

The power of generalizing ideas, of drawing comprehensive conclusions from individual observations, is the only acquirement, for an immortal being, that really deserves the name of knowledge.[5] Merely to observe, without endeavouring to account for any thing, may (in a very incomplete manner) serve as the common sense of life; but where is the store laid up that is to clothe the soul when it leaves the body?

This power has not only been denied to women; but writers have insisted that it is inconsistent, with a few exceptions, with their sexual character. Let men prove this, and I shall grant that woman only exists for man. I must, however, previously remark, that the power of generalizing ideas, to any great extent, is not very common amongst men or women. But this exercise is the true cultivation of the understanding; and every thing conspires to render the cultivation of the understanding more difficult in the female than the male world.

I am naturally led by this assertion to the main subject of the present chapter, and shall now attempt to point out some of the causes that degrade the sex, and prevent women from generalizing their observations.

---

[1] "'The brutes,' says Lord Monboddo, 'remain in the state in which nature has placed them, except in so far as their natural instinct is improved by the culture we bestow upon them.'" (M.W.) James Burnett, Lord Monboddo (1714–99), *Of the Origin and Progress of Language* (1773–92) 1: 137.

[2] "Vide Milton." (M.W.) *Paradise Lost* 8.577.

[3] "This word is not strictly just, but I cannot find a better." (M.W.)

[4] "'Pleasure's the portion of th' *inferior* kind;
But glory, virtue, Heaven for *man* design'd.'
"After writing these lines, how could Mrs. Barbauld write the following ignoble comparison?

'To a Lady, with some painted flowers.'

'Flowers to the fair: to you these flowers I bring,
And strive to greet you with an earlier spring.
Flowers SWEET, *and gay, and* DELICATE LIKE YOU;
Emblems of innocence, and beauty too.
With flowers the Graces bind their yellow hair,
And flowery wreaths consenting lovers wear.
Flowers, the sole luxury which nature knew,
In Eden's pure and guiltless garden grew.
*To loftier forms are rougher tasks assign'd;
The sheltering oak resists the stormy wind,
The tougher yew repels invading foes,
And the tall pine for future navies grows;
But this soft family, to cares unknown,
Were born for pleasure and delight* ALONE.
Gay without toil, and lovely without art,
They spring to CHEER *the sense, and* GLAD *the heart.*
Nor blush, my fair, to own you copy these;
Your BEST *your* SWEETEST *empire is—to* PLEASE.'
"So the men tell us; but virtue, says reason, must be acquired by *rough* toils, and useful struggles with worldly *cares.*" (M.W.) Both quotations are from Barbauld,* *Poems* (1792). The first is from "To Mrs. P[riestley], with some Drawings of Birds and Insects" 101–02; note that "man" includes women; "th' *inferior* kind" is birds and insects. The second is quoted in its entirety. In both, the italics and block capitals are Wollstonecraft's. Wollstonecraft included several excerpts from Barbauld in *The Female Reader* (1789).

[5] John Locke, *An Essay Concerning Human Understanding* (1689).

I shall not go back to the remote annals of antiquity to trace the history of woman; it is sufficient to allow that she has always been either a slave, or a despot, and to remark, that each of these situations equally retards the progress of reason. The grand source of female folly and vice has ever appeared to me to arise from narrowness of mind; and the very constitution of civil governments has put almost insuperable obstacles in the way to prevent the cultivation of the female understanding:—yet virtue can be built on no other foundation! The same obstacles are thrown in the way of the rich, and the same consequences ensue.

Necessity has been proverbially termed the mother of invention—the aphorism may be extended to virtue. It is an acquirement, and an acquirement to which pleasure must be sacrificed—and who sacrifices pleasure when it is within the grasp, whose mind has not been opened and strengthened by adversity, or the pursuit of knowledge goaded on by necessity?—Happy is it when people have the cares of life to struggle with; for these struggles prevent their becoming a prey to enervating vices, merely from idleness! But, if from their birth men and women be placed in a torrid zone, with the meridian sun of pleasure darting directly upon them, how can they sufficiently brace their minds to discharge the duties of life, or even to relish the affections that carry them out of themselves?

Pleasure is the business of woman's life, according to the present modification of society, and while it continues to be so, little can be expected from such weak beings. Inheriting, in a lineal descent from the first fair defect in nature,[1] the sovereignty of beauty, they have, to maintain their power, resigned the natural rights, which the exercise of reason might have procured them, and chosen rather to be short-lived queens than labour to obtain the sober pleasures that arise from equality. Exalted by their inferiority (this sounds like a contradiction), they constantly demand homage as women, though experience should teach them that the men who pride themselves upon paying this arbitrary insolent respect to the sex, with the most scrupulous exactness, are most inclined to tyrannize over, and despise, the very weakness they cherish. Often do they repeat Mr. Hume's sentiments; when, comparing the French and Athenian character, he alludes to women. "But what is more singular in this whimsical nation, say I to the Athenians, is, that a frolick of yours during the Saturnalia, when the slaves are served by their masters, is seriously continued by them through the whole year, and through the whole course of their lives; accompanied too with some circumstances, which still further augment the absurdity and ridicule. Your sport only elevates for a few days those whom fortune has thrown down, and whom she too, in sport, may really elevate for ever above you. But this nation gravely exalts those, whom nature has subjected to them, and whose inferiority and infirmities are absolutely incurable. The women, though without virtue, are their masters and sovereigns."[2]

Ah! why do women, I write with affectionate solicitude, condescend to receive a degree of attention and respect from strangers, different from that reciprocation of civility which the dictates of humanity and the politeness of civilization authorise between man and man? And, why do they not discover, when "in the noon of beauty's power,"[3] that they are treated like queens only to be deluded by hollow respect, till they are led to resign, or not assume, their natural prerogatives? Confined then in cages like the feathered race, they have nothing to do but to plume themselves, and stalk with mock majesty from perch to perch. It is true they are provided with food and raiment, for which they neither toil nor spin;[4] but health, liberty, and virtue, are given in exchange. But, where, amongst mankind, has been found sufficient strength of mind to enable a being to resign these adventitious prerogatives; one who, rising with the calm dignity of reason above opinion, dared to be proud of the privileges inherent in man? And it is vain to expect it whilst hereditary power chokes the

---

[1] Milton, *Paradise Lost* 10.891–92.

[2] David Hume (1711–76), "A Dialogue" (1777). The Saturnalia was the feast of Saturn (in Greek, Kronos), celebrated in midwinter; it involved a temporary suspension of social distinctions.

[3] Wollstonecraft quotes her review of Christoph Martin Wieland (1733–1813), *Henrietta of Gerstenfeld* (trans. 1787–88). The reference is probably to Wieland 2:24.

[4] Matthew 6.28; Luke 12.27–28.

affections and nips reason in the bud.

The passions of men have thus placed women on thrones, and, till mankind become more reasonable, it is to be feared that women will avail themselves of the power which they attain with the least exertion, and which is the most indisputable. They will smile,—yes, they will smile, though told that—

> "In beauty's empire is no mean,
> And woman, either slave or queen,
> Is quickly scorn'd when not ador'd."[1]

But the adoration comes first, and the scorn is not anticipated.

Lewis the XIVth, in particular, spread factitious manners, and caught, in a specious way, the whole nation in his toils; for, establishing an artful chain of despotism, he made it the interest of the people at large, individually to respect his station and support his power. And women, whom he flattered by a puerile attention to the whole sex, obtained in his reign that prince-like distinction so fatal to reason and virtue.

A king is always a king—and a woman always a woman:[2] his authority and her sex, ever stand between them and rational converse. With a lover, I grant, she should be so, and her sensibility will naturally lead her to endeavour to excite emotion, not to gratify her vanity, but her heart. This I do not allow to be coquetry, it is the artless impulse of nature, I only exclaim against the sexual desire of conquest when the heart is out of the question.

This desire is not confined to women; "I have endeavoured," says Lord Chesterfield, "to gain the hearts of twenty women, whose persons I would not have given a fig for."[3] The libertine, who, in a gust of passion, takes advantage of unsuspecting tenderness, is a saint when compared with this cold-hearted rascal; for I like to use significant words. Yet only taught to please, women are always on the watch to please, and with true heroic ardour endeavour to gain hearts merely to resign or spurn them, when the victory is decided, and conspicuous.

I must descend to the minutiae of the subject.

I lament that women are systematically degraded by receiving the trivial attentions, which men think it manly to pay to the sex, when, in fact, they are insultingly supporting their own superiority. It is not condescension to bow to an inferior. So ludicrous, in fact, do these ceremonies appear to me, that I scarcely am able to govern my muscles, when I see a man start with eager, and serious solicitude, to lift a handkerchief, or shut a door, when the *lady* could have done it herself, had she only moved a pace or two.

A wild wish has just flown from my heart to my head, and I will not stifle it though it may excite a horse-laugh.—I do earnestly wish to see the distinction of sex confounded in society, unless where love animates the behaviour. For this distinction is, I am firmly persuaded, the foundation of the weakness of character ascribed to woman; is the cause why the understanding is neglected, whilst accomplishments are acquired with sedulous care: and the same cause accounts for their preferring the graceful before the heroic virtues.

Mankind, including every description, wish to be loved and respected by *something*; and the common herd will always take the nearest road to the completion of their wishes. The respect paid to wealth and beauty is the most certain, and unequivocal; and, of course, will always attract the vulgar eye of common minds. Abilities and virtues are absolutely necessary to raise men from the middle rank of life into notice; and the natural consequence is notorious, the middle rank contains most virtue and abilities. Men have thus, in one station, at least an opportunity of exerting themselves with dignity, and of rising by the exertions which really improve a rational creature; but the whole female sex are, till their character is formed, in the same condition as the rich: for they are born, I now speak of a state of civilization, with certain sexual privileges, and whilst they are gratuitously granted them, few will ever think of works of supererogation, to obtain the esteem of a small number of superiour people.

---

[1] Barbauld,* "Song V" (1772) 16–18.

[2] "And a wit, always a wit, might be added; for the vain fooleries of wits and beauties to obtain attention, and make conquests, are much upon a par." (M.W.)

[3] paraphrased from Philip Dormer Stanhope, 4th Earl of Chesterfield (1694–1773), *Letters to his Son* (1774) no. 294 (16 Nov. 1752). Wollstonecraft included an excerpt from Chesterfield in *The Female Reader* (1789).

When do we hear of women who, starting out of obscurity, boldly claim respect on account of their great abilities or daring virtues? Where are they to be found?—"To be observed, to be attended to, to be taken notice of with sympathy, complacency, and approbation, are all the advantages which they seek."[1]—True! my male readers will probably exclaim; but let them, before they draw any conclusion, recollect that this was not written originally as descriptive of women, but of the rich. In Dr. Smith's Theory of Moral Sentiments, I have found a general character of people of rank and fortune, that, in my opinion, might with the greatest propriety be applied to the female sex. I refer the sagacious reader to the whole comparison; but must be allowed to quote a passage to enforce an argument that I mean to insist on, as the one most conclusive against a sexual character. For if, excepting warriors, no great men, of any denomination, have ever appeared amongst the nobility, may it not be fairly inferred that their local situation swallowed up the man, and produced a character similar to that of women, who are *localized*, if I may be allowed the word, by the rank they are placed in, by *courtesy*? Women, commonly called Ladies, are not to be contradicted in company, are not allowed to exert any manual strength; and from them the negative virtues only are expected, when any virtues are expected, patience, docility, good-humour, and flexibility; virtues incompatible with any vigorous exertion of intellect. Besides, by living more with each other, and being seldom absolutely alone, they are more under the influence of sentiments than passions. Solitude and reflection are necessary to give to wishes the force of passions, and to enable the imagination to enlarge the object, and make it the most desirable. The same may be said of the rich; they do not sufficiently deal in general ideas, collected by impassioned thinking, or calm investigation, to acquire that strength of character on which great resolves are built. But hear what an acute observer says of the great.

"Do the great seem insensible of the easy price at which they may acquire the publick admiration; or do they seem to imagine that to them, as to other men, it must be the purchase either of sweat or of blood? By what important accomplishments is the young nobleman instructed to support the dignity of his rank, and to render himself worthy of that superiority over his fellow-citizens, to which the virtue of his ancestors had raised them? Is it by knowledge, by industry, by patience, by self-denial, or by virtue of any kind? As all his words, as all his motions are attended to, he learns an habitual regard to every circumstance of ordinary behaviour, and studies to perform all those small duties with the most exact propriety. As he is conscious how much he is observed, and how much mankind are disposed to favour all his inclinations, he acts, upon the most indifferent occasions, with that freedom and elevation which the thought of this naturally inspires. His air, his manner, his deportment, all mark that elegant and graceful sense of his own superiority, which those who are born to inferior station can hardly ever arrive at. These are the arts by which he proposes to make mankind more easily submit to his authority, and to govern their inclinations according to his own pleasure: and in this he is seldom disappointed. These arts, supported by rank and pre-eminence, are, upon ordinary occasions, sufficient to govern the world. Lewis XIV. during the greater part of his reign, was regarded, not only in France, but over all Europe, as the most perfect model of a great prince. But what were the talents and virtues by which he acquired this great reputation? Was it by the scrupulous and inflexible justice of all his undertakings, by the immense dangers and difficulties with which they were attended, or by the unwearied and unrelenting application with which he pursued them? Was it by his extensive knowledge, by his exquisite judgment, or by his heroic valour? It was by none of these qualities. But he was, first of all, the most powerful prince in Europe, and consequently held the highest rank among kings; and then, says his historian, 'he surpassed all his courtiers in the gracefulness of his shape, and the majestic beauty of his features. The sound of his voice, noble and affecting, gained those hearts which his presence intimidated. He had a step and a deportment which could suit only him and his rank, and which would have been ridiculous in any

---

[1] adapted from Adam Smith (1723–90), *The Theory of Moral Sentiments* (1759) 1.3.2.1.

other person. The embarrassment which he occasioned to those who spoke to him, flattered that secret satisfaction with which he felt his own superiority.' These frivolous accomplishments, supported by his rank, and, no doubt too, by a degree of other talents and virtues, which seems, however, not to have been much above mediocrity, established this prince in the esteem of his own age, and have drawn, even from posterity, a good deal of respect for his memory. Compared with these, in his own times, and in his own presence, no other virtue, it seems, appeared to have any merit. Knowledge, industry, valour, and beneficence, trembled, were abashed, and lost all dignity before them."[1]

Woman also thus "in herself complete," by possessing all these *frivolous* accomplishments, so changes the nature of things

> ——"That what she wills to do or say
> Seems wisest, virtuousest, discreetest, best;
> All higher knowledge in *her presence* falls
> Degraded. Wisdom in discourse with her
> Loses discountenanc'd, and, like Folly, shows;
> Authority and Reason on her wait."—[2]

And all this is built on her loveliness!

In the middle rank of life, to continue the comparison, men, in their youth, are prepared for professions, and marriage is not considered as the grand feature in their lives; whilst women, on the contrary, have no other scheme to sharpen their faculties. It is not business, extensive plans, or any of the excursive flights of ambition, that engross their attention; no, their thoughts are not employed in rearing such noble structures. To rise in the world, and have the liberty of running from pleasure to pleasure, they must marry advantageously, and to this object their time is sacrificed, and their persons often legally prostituted.[3] A man when he enters any profession has his eye steadily fixed on some future advantage (and the mind gains great strength by having all its efforts directed to one point), and, full of his business, pleasure is considered as mere relaxation; whilst women seek for pleasure as the main purpose of existence. In fact, from the education, which they receive from society, the love of pleasure may be said to govern them all; but does this prove that there is a sex in souls? It would be just as rational to declare that the courtiers in France, when a destructive system of despotism had formed their character, were not men, because liberty, virtue, and humanity, were sacrificed to pleasure and vanity.—Fatal passions, which have ever domineered over the *whole* race!

The same love of pleasure, fostered by the whole tendency of their education, gives a trifling turn to the conduct of women in most circumstances: for instance, they are ever anxious about secondary things; and on the watch for adventures, instead of being occupied by duties.

A man, when he undertakes a journey, has, in general, the end in view; a woman thinks more of the incidental occurrences, the strange things that may possibly occur on the road; the impression that she may make on her fellow-travellers; and, above all, she is anxiously intent on the care of the finery that she carries with her, which is more than ever a part of herself, when going to figure on a new scene; when, to use an apt French turn of expression, she is going to produce a sensation.—Can dignity of mind exist with such trivial cares?

In short, women, in general, as well as the rich of both sexes, have acquired all the follies and vices of civilization, and missed the useful fruit. It is not necessary for me always to premise, that I speak of the condition of the whole sex, leaving exceptions out of the question. Their senses are inflamed, and their understandings neglected, consequently they become the prey of their senses, delicately termed sensibility, and are blown about by every momentary gust of feeling. Civilized women are, therefore, so weakened by false refinement, that, respecting morals, their condition is much below what it would be were they left in a state nearer to nature. Ever restless and anxious, their over exercised sensibility not only renders them uncomfortable themselves, but troublesome, to use a soft phrase, to others. All their thoughts turn on things calculated to

---

[1] Smith, *The Theory of Moral Sentiments* 1.3.2.4 (abridged). The "historian" is Voltaire (1694–1778).

[2] Milton, *Paradise Lost* 8.548–54; Wollstonecraft's italics.

[3] Daniel Defoe (1660–1731) uses the phrase "legal prostitution" in *Conjugal Lewdness; or, Matrimonial Whoredom* (1727).

excite emotion; and feeling, when they should reason, their conduct is unstable, and their opinions are wavering—not the wavering produced by deliberation or progressive views, but by contradictory emotions. By fits and starts they are warm in many pursuits; yet this warmth, never concentrated into perseverance, soon exhausts itself; exhaled by its own heat, or meeting with some other fleeting passion, to which reason has never given any specific gravity, neutrality ensues. Miserable, indeed, must be that being whose cultivation of mind has only tended to inflame its passions! A distinction should be made between inflaming and strengthening them. The passions thus pampered, whilst the judgment is left unformed, what can be expected to ensue?—Undoubtedly, a mixture of madness and folly!

This observation should not be confined to the *fair* sex; however, at present, I only mean to apply it to them.

Novels, music, poetry, and gallantry, all tend to make women the creatures of sensation, and their character is thus formed in the mould of folly during the time they are acquiring accomplishments, the only improvement they are excited, by their station in society, to acquire. This overstretched sensibility naturally relaxes the other powers of the mind, and prevents intellect from attaining that sovereignty which it ought to attain to render a rational creature useful to others, and content with its own station: for the exercise of the understanding, as life advances, is the only method pointed out by nature to calm the passions.

Satiety has a very different effect, and I have often been forcibly struck by an emphatical description of damnation:—when the spirit is represented as continually hovering with abortive eagerness round the defiled body, unable to enjoy any thing without the organs of sense. Yet, to their senses, are women made slaves, because it is by their sensibility that they obtain present power.

And will moralists pretend to assert, that this is the condition in which one half of the human race should be encouraged to remain with listless inactivity and stupid acquiescence? Kind instructors! what were we created for? To remain, it may be said, innocent; they mean in a state of childhood.—We might as well never have been born, unless it were necessary that we should be created to enable man to acquire the noble privilege of reason, the power of discerning good from evil, whilst we lie down in the dust from whence we were taken, never to rise again.—

It would be an endless task to trace the variety of meannesses, cares, and sorrows, into which women are plunged by the prevailing opinion, that they were created rather to feel than reason, and that all the power they obtain, must be obtained by their charms and weakness:

"Fine by defect, and amiably weak!"[1]

And, made by this amiable weakness entirely dependent, excepting what they gain by illicit sway, on man, not only for protection, but advice, is it surprising that, neglecting the duties that reason alone points out, and shrinking from trials calculated to strengthen their minds, they only exert themselves to give their defects a graceful covering, which may serve to heighten their charms in the eye of the voluptuary, though it sink them below the scale of moral excellence?

Fragile in every sense of the word, they are obliged to look up to man for every comfort. In the most trifling dangers they cling to their support, with parasitical tenacity, piteously demanding succour; and their *natural* protector extends his arm, or lifts up his voice, to guard the lovely trembler—from what? Perhaps the frown of an old cow, or the jump of a mouse; a rat, would be a serious danger. In the name of reason, and even common sense, what can save such beings from contempt; even though they be soft and fair?

These fears, when not affected, may produce some pretty attitudes; but they shew a degree of imbecility which degrades a rational creature in a way women are not aware of—for love and esteem are very distinct things.

I am fully persuaded that we should hear of none of these infantine airs, if girls were allowed to take sufficient exercise, and not confined in close rooms till their muscles are relaxed, and their powers of digestion destroyed. To carry the remark still further, if fear in girls, instead of being cherished, perhaps, created, were

---

[1] Pope, "Of the Characters of Women" 44.

treated in the same manner as cowardice in boys, we should quickly see women with more dignified aspects. It is true, they could not then with equal propriety be termed the sweet flowers that smile in the walk of man; but they would be more respectable members of society, and discharge the important duties of life by the light of their own reason. "Educate women like men," says Rousseau, "and the more they resemble our sex the less power will they have over us."[1] This is the very point I aim at. I do not wish them to have power over men; but over themselves.

In the same strain have I heard men argue against instructing the poor; for many are the forms that aristocracy assumes. "Teach them to read and write," say they, "and you take them out of the station assigned them by nature." An eloquent Frenchman has answered them, I will borrow his sentiments. But they know not, when they make man a brute, that they may expect every instant to see him transformed into a ferocious beast.[2] Without knowledge there can be no morality!

Ignorance is a frail base for virtue! Yet, that it is the condition for which woman was organized, has been insisted upon by the writers who have most vehemently argued in favour of the superiority of man; a superiority not in degree, but essence; though, to soften the argument, they have laboured to prove, with chivalrous generosity, that the sexes ought not to be compared; man was made to reason, woman to feel: and that together, flesh and spirit, they make the most perfect whole, by blending happily reason and sensibility into one character.

And what is sensibility? "Quickness of sensation; quickness of perception; delicacy." Thus is it defined by Dr. Johnson;[3] and the definition gives me no other idea than of the most exquisitely polished instinct. I discern not a trace of the image of God in either sensation or matter. Refined seventy times seven,[4] they are still material; intellect dwells not there; nor will fire ever make lead gold!

I come round to my old argument; if woman be allowed to have an immortal soul, she must have, as the employment of life, an understanding to improve. And when, to render the present state more complete, though every thing proves it to be but a fraction of a mighty sum, she is incited by present gratification to forget her grand destination, nature is counteracted, or she was born only to procreate and rot. Or, granting brutes, of every description, a soul, though not a reasonable one, the exercise of instinct and sensibility may be the step, which they are to take, in this life, towards the attainment of reason in the next; so that through all eternity they will lag behind man, who, why we cannot tell, had the power given him of attaining reason in his first mode of existence.

When I treat of the peculiar duties of women, as I should treat of the peculiar duties of a citizen or father, it will be found that I do not mean to insinuate that they should be taken out of their families, speaking of the majority. "He that hath wife and children," says Lord Bacon, "hath given hostages to fortune; for they are impediments to great enterprises, either of virtue or mischief. Certainly the best works, and of greatest merit for the public, have proceeded from the unmarried or childless men."[5] I say the same of women. But, the welfare of society is not built on extraordinary exertions; and were it more reasonably organized, there would be still less need of great abilities, or heroic virtues.

In the regulation of a family, in the education of children, understanding, in an unsophisticated sense, is particularly required: strength both of body and mind; yet the men who, by their writings, have most earnestly laboured to domesticate women, have endeavoured, by arguments dictated by a gross appetite, which satiety had rendered fastidious, to weaken their bodies and cramp their minds. But, if even by these sinister methods they really *persuaded* women, by working on their feelings, to stay at home, and fulfil the duties of a mother and

---

[1] from Rousseau, *Emile*, chap. 5; the sentence ends "and then men will truly be the masters."

[2] possibly Honoré Riqueti, comte de Mirabeau (1749–91), who said, in the Constituent Assembly in 1790, "You have loosed the bull—do you expect he will not use his horns?"

[3] in his *Dictionary* (1755).

[4] Matthew 18.22.

[5] Bacon, Essay 8, "Of Marriage and Single Life."

mistress of a family, I should cautiously oppose opinions that led women to right conduct, by prevailing on them to make the discharge of such important duties the main business of life, though reason were insulted. Yet, and I appeal to experience, if by neglecting the understanding they be as much, nay, more detached from these domestic employments, than they could be by the most serious intellectual pursuit, though it may be observed, that the mass of mankind will never vigorously pursue an intellectual object,[1] I may be allowed to infer that reason is absolutely necessary to enable a woman to perform any duty properly, and I must again repeat, that sensibility is not reason.

The comparison with the rich still occurs to me; for, when men neglect the duties of humanity, women will follow their example; a common stream hurries them both along with thoughtless celerity. Riches and honours prevent a man from enlarging his understanding, and enervate all his powers by reversing the order of nature, which has ever made true pleasure the reward of labour. Pleasure—enervating pleasure is, likewise, within women's reach without earning it. But, till hereditary possessions are spread abroad, how can we expect men to be proud of virtue? And, till they are, women will govern them by the most direct means, neglecting their dull domestic duties to catch the pleasure that sits lightly on the wing of time.

"The power of the woman," says some author, "is her sensibility"; and men, not aware of the consequence, do all they can to make this power swallow up every other. Those who constantly employ their sensibility will have most: for example; poets, painters, and composers.[2] Yet, when the sensibility is thus increased at the expence of reason, and even the imagination, why do philosophical men complain of their fickleness? The sexual attention of man particularly acts on female sensibility, and this sympathy has been exercised from their youth up. A husband cannot long pay those attentions with the passion necessary to excite lively emotions, and the heart, accustomed to lively emotions, turns to a new lover, or pines in secret, the prey of virtue or prudence. I mean when the heart has really been rendered susceptible, and the taste formed; for I am apt to conclude, from what I have seen in fashionable life, that vanity is oftener fostered than sensibility by the mode of education, and the intercourse between the sexes, which I have reprobated; and that coquetry more frequently proceeds from vanity than from that inconstancy, which overstrained sensibility naturally produces.

Another argument that has had great weight with me, must, I think, have some force with every considerate benevolent heart. Girls who have been thus weakly educated, are often cruelly left by their parents without any provision; and, of course, are dependent on, not only the reason, but the bounty of their brothers. These brothers are, to view the fairest side of the question, good sort of men, and give as a favour, what children of the same parents had an equal right to. In this equivocal humiliating situation, a docile female may remain some time, with a tolerable degree of comfort. But, when the brother marries, a probable circumstance, from being considered as the mistress of the family, she is viewed with averted looks as an intruder, an unnecessary burden on the benevolence of the master of the house, and his new partner.

Who can recount the misery, which many unfortunate beings, whose minds and bodies are equally weak, suffer in such situations—unable to work, and ashamed to beg? The wife, a cold-hearted, narrow-minded, woman, and this is not an unfair supposition; for the present mode of education does not tend to enlarge the heart any more than the understanding, is jealous of the little kindness which her husband shews to his relations; and her sensibility not rising to humanity, she is displeased at seeing the property of *her* children lavished on an helpless sister.

These are matters of fact, which have come under my eye again and again. The consequence is obvious, the wife has recourse to cunning to undermine the habitual affection, which she is afraid openly to oppose; and neither tears nor caresses are spared till the spy is worked out of her home, and thrown on the world,

---

[1] "The mass of mankind are rather the slaves of their appetites than of their passions." (M.W.)

[2] "Men of these descriptions pour it into their compositions, to amalgamate the gross materials; and, moulding them with passion, give to the inert body a soul; but, in woman's imagination, love alone concentrates these ethereal beams." (M.W.)

unprepared for its difficulties; or sent, as a great effort of generosity, or from some regard to propriety, with a small stipend, and an uncultivated mind, into joyless solitude.

These two women may be much upon a par, with respect to reason and humanity; and changing situations, might have acted just the same selfish part; but had they been differently educated, the case would also have been very different. The wife would not have had that sensibility, of which self is the centre, and reason might have taught her not to expect, and not even to be flattered by, the affection of her husband, if it led him to violate prior duties. She would wish not to love him merely because he loved her, but on account of his virtues; and the sister might have been able to struggle for herself instead of eating the bitter bread of dependence.

I am, indeed, persuaded that the heart, as well as the understanding, is opened by cultivation; and by, which may not appear so clear, strengthening the organs; I am not now talking of momentary flashes of sensibility, but of affections. And, perhaps, in the education of both sexes, the most difficult task is so to adjust instruction as not to narrow the understanding, whilst the heart is warmed by the generous juices of spring, just raised by the electric fermentation of the season; nor to dry up the feelings by employing the mind in investigations remote from life.

With respect to women, when they receive a careful education, they are either made fine ladies, brimful of sensibility, and teeming with capricious fancies; or mere notable women. The latter are often friendly, honest creatures, and have a shrewd kind of good sense joined with worldly prudence, that often render them more useful members of society than the fine sentimental lady, though they possess neither greatness of mind nor taste. The intellectual world is shut against them; take them out of their family or neighbourhood, and they stand still; the mind finding no employment, for literature affords a fund of amusement which they have never sought to relish, but frequently to despise. The sentiments and taste of more cultivated minds appear ridiculous, even in those whom chance and family connections have led them to love; but in mere acquaintance they think it all affectation.

A man of sense can only love such a woman on account of her sex, and respect her, because she is a trusty servant. He lets her, to preserve his own peace, scold the servants, and go to church in clothes made of the very best materials. A man of her own size of understanding would, probably, not agree so well with her; for he might wish to encroach on her prerogative, and manage some domestic concerns himself. Yet women, whose minds are not enlarged by cultivation, or the natural selfishness of sensibility expanded by reflection, are very unfit to manage a family; for, by an undue stretch of power, they are always tyrannizing to support a superiority that only rests on the arbitrary distinction of fortune. The evil is sometimes more serious, and domestics are deprived of innocent indulgences, and made to work beyond their strength, in order to enable the notable woman to keep a better table, and outshine her neighbours in finery and parade. If she attend to her children, it is, in general, to dress them in a costly manner—and, whether this attention arise from vanity or fondness, it is equally pernicious.

Besides, how many women of this description pass their days; or, at least, their evenings, discontentedly. Their husbands acknowledge that they are good managers, and chaste wives; but leave home to seek for more agreeable, may I be allowed to use a significant French word, *piquant* society; and the patient drudge, who fulfils her task, like a blind horse in a mill, is defrauded of her just reward; for the wages due to her are the caresses of her husband; and women who have so few resources in themselves, do not very patiently bear this privation of a natural right.

A fine lady, on the contrary, has been taught to look down with contempt on the vulgar employments of life; though she has only been incited to acquire accomplishments that rise a degree above sense; for even corporeal accomplishments cannot be acquired with any degree of precision unless the understanding has been strengthened by exercise. Without a foundation of principles taste is superficial, grace must arise from something deeper than imitation. The imagination, however, is heated, and the feelings rendered fastidious, if not sophisticated; or, a counterpoise of judgment is not acquired, when the heart still remains artless, though it becomes too tender.

These women are often amiable; and their hearts are really more sensible to general benevolence, more alive to the sentiments that civilize life, than the square-elbowed family drudge; but, wanting a due proportion of reflection and self-government, they only inspire love; and are the mistresses of their husbands, whilst they have any hold on their affections; and the platonic friends of his male acquaintance. These are the fair defects in nature;[1] the women who appear to be created not to enjoy the fellowship of man, but to save him from sinking into absolute brutality, by rubbing off the rough angles of his character; and by playful dalliance to give some dignity to the appetite that draws him to them.—Gracious Creator of the whole human race! hast thou created such a being as woman, who can trace thy wisdom in thy works, and feel that thou alone art by thy nature exalted above her,—for no better purpose?—Can she believe that she was only made to submit to man, her equal, a being, who, like her, was sent into the world to acquire virtue?—Can she consent to be occupied merely to please him; merely to adorn the earth, when her soul is capable of rising to thee?—And can she rest supinely dependent on man for reason, when she ought to mount with him the arduous steeps of knowledge?—

Yet, if love be the supreme good, let women be only educated to inspire it, and let every charm be polished to intoxicate the senses; but, if they be moral beings, let them have a chance to become intelligent; and let love to man be only a part of that glowing flame of universal love, which, after encircling humanity, mounts in grateful incense to God.

To fulfil domestic duties much resolution is necessary, and a serious kind of perseverance that requires a more firm support than emotions, however lively and true to nature. To give an example of order, the soul of virtue, some austerity of behaviour must be adopted, scarcely to be expected from a being who, from its infancy, has been made the weathercock of its own sensations. Whoever rationally means to be useful must have a plan of conduct; and, in the discharge of the simplest duty, we are often obliged to act contrary to the present impulse of tenderness or compassion. Severity is frequently the most certain, as well as the most sublime proof of affection; and the want of this power over the feelings, and of that lofty, dignified affection, which makes a person prefer the future good of the beloved object to a present gratification, is the reason why so many fond mothers spoil their children, and has made it questionable whether negligence or indulgence be most hurtful: but I am inclined to think, that the latter has done most harm.

Mankind seem to agree that children should be left under the management of women during their childhood. Now, from all the observation that I have been able to make, women of sensibility are the most unfit for this task, because they will infallibly, carried away by their feelings, spoil a child's temper. The management of the temper, the first, and most important branch of education, requires the sober steady eye of reason; a plan of conduct equally distant from tyranny and indulgence: yet these are the extremes that people of sensibility alternately fall into; always shooting beyond the mark. I have followed this train of reasoning much further, till I have concluded, that a person of genius is the most improper person to be employed in education, public or private. Minds of this rare species see things too much in masses, and seldom, if ever, have a good temper. That habitual cheerfulness, termed good-humour, is, perhaps, as seldom united with great mental powers, as with strong feelings. And those people who follow, with interest and admiration, the flights of genius; or, with cooler approbation suck in the instruction which has been elaborately prepared for them by the profound thinker, ought not to be disgusted, if they find the former choleric, and the latter morose; because liveliness of fancy, and a tenacious comprehension of mind, are scarcely compatible with that pliant urbanity which leads a man, at least, to bend to the opinions and prejudices of others, instead of roughly confronting them.

But, treating of education or manners, minds of a superior class are not to be considered, they may be left to chance; it is the multitude, with moderate abilities, who call for instruction, and catch the colour of the atmosphere they breathe. This respectable concourse, I

---

[1] Milton, *Paradise Lost* 10.891–92.

contend, men and women, should not have their sensations heightened in the hot-bed of luxurious indolence, at the expence of their understanding; for, unless there be a ballast of understanding, they will never become either virtuous or free: an aristocracy, founded on property, or sterling talents, will ever sweep before it, the alternately timid, and ferocious, slaves of feeling.

Numberless are the arguments, to take another view of the subject, brought forward with a shew of reason, because supposed to be deduced from nature, that men have used morally and physically, to degrade the sex. I must notice a few.

The female understanding has often been spoken of with contempt, as arriving sooner at maturity than the male. I shall not answer this argument by alluding to the early proofs of reason, as well as genius, in Cowley, Milton, and Pope,[1] but only appeal to experience to decide whether young men, who are early introduced into company (and examples now abound), do not acquire the same precocity. So notorious is this fact, that the bare mentioning of it must bring before people, who at all mix in the world, the idea of a number of swaggering apes of men, whose understandings are narrowed by being brought into the society of men when they ought to have been spinning a top or twirling a hoop.

It has also been asserted, by some naturalists, that men do not attain their full growth and strength till thirty; but that women arrive at maturity by twenty.[2] I apprehend that they reason on false ground, led astray by the male prejudice, which deems beauty the perfection of woman—mere beauty of features and complexion, the vulgar acceptation of the word, whilst male beauty is allowed to have some connection with the mind. Strength of body, and that character of countenance, which the French term a *physionomie*, women do not acquire before thirty, any more than men. The little artless tricks of children, it is true, are particularly pleasing and attractive; yet, when the pretty freshness of youth is worn off, these artless graces become studied airs, and disgust every person of taste. In the countenance of girls we only look for vivacity and bashful modesty; but, the spring-tide of life over, we look for soberer sense in the face, and for traces of passion, instead of the dimples of animal spirits; expecting to see individuality of character, the only fastener of the affections.[3] We then wish to converse, not to fondle; to give scope to our imaginations as well as to the sensations of our hearts.

At twenty the beauty of both sexes is equal; but the libertinism of man leads him to make the distinction, and superannuated coquettes are commonly of the same opinion; for, when they can no longer inspire love, they pay for the vigour and vivacity of youth. The French, who admit more of mind into their notions of beauty, give the preference to women of thirty. I mean to say that they allow women to be in their most perfect state, when vivacity gives place to reason, and to that majestic seriousness of character, which marks maturity;—or, the resting point. In youth, till twenty, the body shoots out, till thirty the solids are attaining a degree of density; and the flexible muscles, growing daily more rigid, give character to the countenance; that is, they trace the operations of the mind with the iron pen of fate, and tell us not only what powers are within, but how they have been employed.

It is proper to observe, that animals who arrive slowly at maturity, are the longest lived, and of the noblest species. Men cannot, however, claim any natural superiority from the grandeur of longevity; for in this respect nature has not distinguished the male.

Polygamy is another physical degradation; and a plausible argument for a custom, that blasts every domestic virtue, is drawn from the well-attested fact, that in the countries where it is established, more females are born than males. This appears to be an indication of nature, and to nature, apparently reasonable speculations must yield. A further conclusion

---

[1] "Many other names might be added." (M.W.) Abraham Cowley (1618–67) published *Poetical Blossoms* when he was only fifteen; John Milton (1608–74) composed verse in both English and Latin when he was sixteen; Alexander Pope (1688–1744) refers to his own poetic precocity in "An Epistle to Dr. Arbuthnot" (1735) 127–28.

[2] Georges, comte de Buffon, *Natural History*, trans. William Smellie (1780) 2: 436.

[3] "The strength of an affection is, generally, in the same proportion as the character of the species in the object beloved, is lost in that of the individual." (M.W.)

obviously presented itself; if polygamy be necessary, woman must be inferior to man, and made for him.

With respect to the formation of the fetus in the womb, we are very ignorant; but it appears to me probable, that an accidental physical cause may account for this phenomenon, and prove it not to be a law of nature. I have met with some pertinent observations on the subject in Forster's Account of the Isles of the South-Sea, that will explain my meaning. After observing that of the two sexes amongst animals, the most vigorous and hottest constitution always prevails, and produces its kind; he adds,—"If this be applied to the inhabitants of Africa, it is evident that the men there, accustomed to polygamy, are enervated by the use of so many women, and therefore less vigorous; the women, on the contrary, are of a hotter constitution, not only on account of their more irritable nerves, more sensible organization, and more lively fancy; but likewise because they are deprived in their matrimony of that share of physical love which, in a monogamous condition, would all be theirs; and thus, for the above reasons, the generality of children are born females."[1]

"In the greater part of Europe it has been proved by the most accurate lists of mortality, that the proportion of men to women is nearly equal, or, if any difference takes place, the males born are more numerous, in the proportion of 105 to 100."

The necessity of polygamy, therefore, does not appear; yet when a man seduces a woman, it should, I think, be termed a *left-handed* marriage, and the man should be *legally* obliged to maintain the woman and her children, unless adultery, a natural divorcement, abrogated the law. And this law should remain in force as long as the weakness of women caused the word seduction to be used as an excuse for their frailty and want of principle; nay, while they depend on man for a subsistence, instead of earning it by the exertion of their own hands or heads. But these women should not, in the full meaning of the relationship, be termed wives, or the very purpose of marriage would be subverted, and all those endearing charities that flow from personal fidelity, and give a sanctity to the tie, when neither love nor friendship unites the hearts, would melt into selfishness. The woman who is faithful to the father of her children demands respect, and should not be treated like a prostitute; though I readily grant that if it be necessary for a man and woman to live together in order to bring up their offspring, nature never intended that a man should have more than one wife.

Still, highly as I respect marriage, as the foundation of almost every social virtue, I cannot avoid feeling the most lively compassion for those unfortunate females who are broken off from society, and by one error torn from all those affections and relationships that improve the heart and mind. It does not frequently even deserve the name of error; for many innocent girls become the dupes of a sincere, affectionate heart, and still more are, as it may emphatically be termed, *ruined* before they know the difference between virtue and vice:—and thus prepared by their education for infamy, they become infamous. Asylums and Magdalens are not the proper remedies for these abuses.[2] It is justice, not charity, that is wanting in the world!

A woman who has lost her honour, imagines that she cannot fall lower, and as for recovering her former station, it is impossible; no exertion can wash this stain away. Losing thus every spur, and having no other means of support, prostitution becomes her only refuge, and the character is quickly depraved by circumstances over which the poor wretch has little power, unless she possesses an uncommon portion of sense and loftiness of spirit. Necessity never makes prostitution the business of men's lives; though numberless are the women who are thus rendered systematically vicious. This, however, arises, in a great degree, from the state of idleness in which women are educated, who are always taught to look up to man for a maintenance, and to consider their persons as the proper return for his exertions to support them. Meretricious airs, and the whole science of wantonness, have then a more powerful stimulus than either appetite or vanity; and this remark gives force to

---

[1] John Reinhold Forster (1729–98), *Observations Made during a Voyage round the World* (1778). Forster had circumnavigated the globe with Cook in the *Resolution*, in 1772–75. The second paragraph in quotation marks is not by Forster; it is unidentified.

[2] London's Magdalen Hospital, a reformatory for prostitutes, was founded in 1758. It was named after St. Mary Magdalene, the type of the redeemed harlot (Luke 7.37–50, 8.2).

the prevailing opinion, that with chastity all is lost that is respectable in woman. Her character depends on the observance of one virtue, though the only passion fostered in her heart—is love. Nay, the honour of a woman is not made even to depend on her will.

When Richardson[1] makes Clarissa tell Lovelace that he had robbed her of her honour, he must have had strange notions of honour and virtue. For, miserable beyond all names of misery is the condition of a being, who could be degraded without its own consent! This excess of strictness I have heard vindicated as a salutary error. I shall answer in the words of Leibnitz—"Errors are often useful; but it is commonly to remedy other errors."[2]

Most of the evils of life arise from a desire of present enjoyment that outruns itself. The obedience required of women in the marriage state comes under this description; the mind, naturally weakened by depending on authority, never exerts its own powers, and the obedient wife is thus rendered a weak indolent mother. Or, supposing that this is not always the consequence, a future state of existence is scarcely taken into the reckoning when only negative virtues are cultivated. For, in treating of morals, particularly when women are alluded to, writers have too often considered virtue in a very limited sense, and made the foundation of it *solely* worldly utility; nay, a still more fragile base has been given to this stupendous fabric, and the wayward fluctuating feelings of men have been made the standard of virtue. Yes, virtue as well as religion, has been subjected to the decisions of taste.

It would almost provoke a smile of contempt, if the vain absurdities of man did not strike us on all sides, to observe, how eager men are to degrade the sex from whom they pretend to receive the chief pleasure of life; and I have frequently with full conviction retorted Pope's sarcasm on them;[3] or, to speak explicitly, it has appeared to me applicable to the whole human race. A love of pleasure or sway seems to divide mankind, and the husband who lords it in his little haram thinks only of his pleasure or his convenience. To such lengths, indeed, does an intemperate love of pleasure carry some prudent men, or worn out libertines, who marry to have a safe bedfellow, that they seduce their own wives.—Hymen banishes modesty, and chaste love takes its flight.

Love, considered as an animal appetite, cannot long feed on itself without expiring. And this extinction in its own flame, may be termed the violent death of love. But the wife who has thus been rendered licentious, will probably endeavour to fill the void left by the loss of her husband's attentions; for she cannot contentedly become merely an upper servant after having been treated like a goddess. She is still handsome, and, instead of transferring her fondness to her children, she only dreams of enjoying the sunshine of life. Besides, there are many husbands so devoid of sense and parental affection, that during the first effervescence of voluptuous fondness they refuse to let their wives suckle their children.[4] They are only to dress and live to please them: and love—even innocent love, soon sinks into lasciviousness when the exercise of a duty is sacrificed to its indulgence.

Personal attachment is a very happy foundation for friendship; yet, when even two virtuous young people marry, it would, perhaps, be happy if some circumstances checked their passion; if the recollection of some prior attachment, or disappointed affection, made it on one side, at least, rather a match founded on esteem. In that case they would look beyond the present moment, and try to render the whole of life respectable, by forming a plan to regulate a friendship which only death ought to dissolve.

---

[1] "Dr. Young supports the same opinion, in his plays, when he talks of the misfortune that shunned the light of day." (M.W.) Samuel Richardson (1689–1761), *Clarissa* (1747–48) Mr. Lovelace to John Belford, Esq. (Friday, June 16) Paper 8; since Clarissa is still in shock after being raped by Lovelace, the note may not express her considered opinion. Edward Young (1683–1765), *Busiris, King of Egypt* (1719) 1.1.158; the "black ... story" that "well might shun the day" actually concerns how Myris persuaded Busiris to kill her brother, the rightful king of Egypt, and then married the murderer. Wollstonecraft included several excerpts from Young in *The Female Reader* (1789).

[2] Gottfried Wilhelm von Leibniz (1646–1716), *Theodicy* (1710), preface.

[3] Pope, "Of the Characters of Women" 207–10.

[4] At this time, it was still common for women of the upper classes to employ wet-nurses. Cf. Rousseau's advocacy of breastfeeding in *Emile*.

Friendship is a serious affection; the most sublime of all affections, because it is founded on principle, and cemented by time. The very reverse may be said of love. In a great degree, love and friendship cannot subsist in the same bosom; even when inspired by different objects they weaken or destroy each other, and for the same object can only be felt in succession. The vain fears and fond jealousies, the winds which fan the flame of love, when judiciously or artfully tempered, are both incompatible with the tender confidence and sincere respect of friendship.

Love, such as the glowing pen of genius has traced, exists not on earth, or only resides in those exalted, fervid imaginations that have sketched such dangerous pictures. Dangerous, because they not only afford a plausible excuse, to the voluptuary who disguises sheer sensuality under a sentimental veil; but as they spread affectation, and take from the dignity of virtue. Virtue, as the very word imports, should have an appearance of seriousness, if not of austerity; and to endeavour to trick her out in the garb of pleasure, because the epithet has been used as another name for beauty, is to exalt her on a quicksand; a most insidious attempt to hasten her fall by apparent respect. Virtue and pleasure are not, in fact, so nearly allied in this life as some eloquent writers have laboured to prove. Pleasure prepares the fading wreath, and mixes the intoxicating cup; but the fruit which virtue gives, is the recompence of toil: and, gradually seen as it ripens, only affords calm satisfaction; nay, appearing to be the result of the natural tendency of things, it is scarcely observed. Bread, the common food of life, seldom thought of as a blessing, supports the constitution and preserves health; still feasts delight the heart of man, though disease and even death lurk in the cup or dainty that elevates the spirits or tickles the palate. The lively heated imagination likewise, to apply the comparison, draws the picture of love, as it draws every other picture, with those glowing colours, which the daring hand will steal from the rainbow that is directed by a mind, condemned in a world like this, to prove its noble origin by panting after unattainable perfection; ever pursuing what it acknowledges to be a fleeting dream. An imagination of this vigorous cast can give existence to insubstantial forms, and stability to the shadowy reveries which the mind naturally falls into when realities are found vapid. It can then depict love with celestial charms, and dote on the grand ideal object—it can imagine a degree of mutual affection that shall refine the soul, and not expire when it has served as a "scale to heavenly";[1] and, like devotion, make it absorb every meaner affection and desire. In each others arms, as in a temple, with its summit lost in the clouds, the world is to be shut out, and every thought and wish, that do not nurture pure affection and permanent virtue.—Permanent virtue! alas! Rousseau, respectable visionary! thy paradise would soon be violated by the entrance of some unexpected guest. Like Milton's it would only contain angels, or men sunk below the dignity of rational creatures. Happiness is not material, it cannot be seen or felt! Yet the eager pursuit of the good which every one shapes to his own fancy, proclaims man the lord of this lower world, and to be an intelligential creature, who is not to receive, but acquire happiness. They, therefore, who complain of the delusions of passion, do not recollect that they are exclaiming against a strong proof of the immortality of the soul.

But leaving superior minds to correct themselves, and pay dearly for their experience, it is necessary to observe, that it is not against strong, persevering passions; but romantic wavering feelings that I wish to guard the female heart by exercising the understanding: for these paradisiacal reveries are oftener the effect of idleness than of a lively fancy.

Women have seldom sufficient serious employment to silence their feelings; a round of little cares, or vain pursuits frittering away all strength of mind and organs, they become naturally only objects of sense.—In short, the whole tenour of female education (the education of society) tends to render the best disposed romantic and inconstant; and the remainder vain and mean. In the present state of society this evil can scarcely be remedied, I am afraid, in the slightest degree; should a more laudable ambition ever gain ground they may be brought nearer to nature and reason, and become more virtuous and useful as they grow more respectable.

---

[1] Milton, *Paradise Lost* 8.591–92.

But, I will venture to assert that their reason will never acquire sufficient strength to enable it to regulate their conduct, whilst the making an appearance in the world is the first wish of the majority of mankind. To this weak wish the natural affections, and the most useful virtues are sacrificed. Girls marry merely to *better themselves*, to borrow a significant vulgar phrase, and have such perfect power over their hearts as not to permit themselves to *fall in love* till a man with a superior fortune offers. On this subject I mean to enlarge in a future chapter; it is only necessary to drop a hint at present, because women are so often degraded by suffering the selfish prudence of age to chill the ardour of youth.

From the same source flows an opinion that young girls ought to dedicate great part of their time to needlework; yet, this employment contracts their faculties more than any other that could have been chosen for them, by confining their thoughts to their persons.[1] Men order their clothes to be made, and have done with the subject; women make their own clothes, necessary or ornamental, and are continually talking about them; and their thoughts follow their hands. It is not indeed the making of necessaries that weakens the mind; but the frippery of dress. For when a woman in the lower rank of life makes her husband's and children's clothes, she does her duty, this is her part of the family business; but when women work only to dress better than they could otherwise afford, it is worse than sheer loss of time. To render the poor virtuous they must be employed, and women in the middle rank of life, did they not ape the fashions of the nobility, without catching their ease, might employ them, whilst they themselves managed their families, instructed their children, and exercised their own minds. Gardening, experimental philosophy,[2] and literature, would afford them subjects to think of and matter for conversation, that in some degree would exercise their understandings. The conversation of French women, who are not so rigidly nailed to their chairs to twist lappets, and knot ribands, is frequently superficial; but, I contend, that it is not half so insipid as that of those English women whose time is spent in making caps, bonnets, and the whole mischief of trimmings, not to mention shopping, bargain-hunting, &c. &c.: and it is the decent, prudent women, who are most degraded by these practices; for their motive is simply vanity. The wanton who exercises her taste to render her passion alluring, has something more in view.

These observations all branch out of a general one, which I have before made, and which cannot be too often insisted upon, for, speaking of men, women, or professions, it will be found that the employment of the thoughts shapes the character both generally and individually. The thoughts of women ever hover round their persons, and is it surprising that their persons are reckoned most valuable? Yet some degree of liberty of mind is necessary even to form the person; and this may be one reason why some gentle wives have so few attractions beside that of sex. Add to this, sedentary employments render the majority of women sickly—and false notions of female excellence make them proud of this delicacy, though it be another fetter, that by calling the attention continually to the body, cramps the activity of the mind.

Women of quality seldom do any of the manual part of their dress, consequently only their taste is exercised, and they acquire, by thinking less of the finery, when the business of their toilet is over, that ease, which seldom appears in the deportment of women, who dress merely for the sake of dressing. In fact, the observation with respect to the middle rank, the one in which talents thrive best, extends not to women; for those of the superior class, by catching, at least, a smattering of literature, and conversing more with men, on general topics, acquire more knowledge than the women who ape their fashions and faults without sharing their advantages. With respect to virtue, to use the word in a comprehensive sense, I have seen most in low life. Many poor women maintain their children by the sweat of their brow,[3] and keep together families that the vices of

---

[1] Rousseau disapproves of needle-work, but only for men; Macaulay* defends it for women. For a later view, see also Mary Lamb,* "On Needle-work" (1815).

[2] natural science.

[3] Genesis 3.19. Wollstonecraft transfers to "poor women" the curse placed on Adam, not on Eve.

the fathers[1] would have scattered abroad; but gentlewomen are too indolent to be actively virtuous, and are softened rather than refined by civilization. Indeed, the good sense which I have met with, among the poor women who have had few advantages of education, and yet have acted heroically, strongly confirmed me in the opinion that trifling employments have rendered woman a trifler. Man, taking her[2] body, the mind is left to rust; so that while physical love enervates man, as being his favourite recreation, he will endeavour to enslave woman:—and, who can tell, how many generations may be necessary to give vigour to the virtue and talents of the freed posterity of abject slaves?[3]

In tracing the causes that, in my opinion, have degraded woman, I have confined my observations to such as universally act upon the morals and manners of the whole sex, and to me it appears clear that they all spring from want of understanding. Whether this arise from a physical or accidental weakness of faculties, time alone can determine; for I shall not lay any great stress on the example of a few women[4] who, from having received a masculine education, have acquired courage and resolution; I only contend that the men who have been placed in similar situations, have acquired a similar character—I speak of bodies of men, and that men of genius and talents have started out of a class, in which women have never yet been placed.

from CHAPTER 13
Some Instances of the Folly Which the Ignorance of Women Generates; with Concluding Reflections on the Moral Improvement That a Revolution in Female Manners Might Naturally Be Expected to Produce

SECTION 2

Another instance of that feminine weakness of character, often produced by a confined education, is a romantic twist of the mind, which has been very properly termed *sentimental*.

Women subjected by ignorance to their sensations, and only taught to look for happiness in love, refine on sensual feelings, and adopt metaphysical notions respecting that passion, which lead them shamefully to neglect the duties of life, and frequently in the midst of these sublime refinements they plump into actual vice.

These are the women who are amused by the reveries of the stupid novelists, who, knowing little of human nature, work up stale tales, and describe meretricious scenes, all retailed in a sentimental jargon, which equally tend to corrupt the taste, and draw the heart aside from its daily duties. I do not mention the understanding, because never having been exercised, its slumbering energies rest inactive, like the lurking particles of fire which are supposed universally to pervade matter.[5]

Females, in fact, denied all political privileges, and not allowed, as married women, excepting in criminal

---

[1] Cf. Exodus 20.5.

[2] "'I take her body,' says Ranger." (M.W.) When Ranger, a rakish character in *The Suspicious Husband* (1747) by Benjamin Hoadly (1706–57), delivers this line (1.1), he is actually reading William Congreve (1670–1729), "Song" 13–14.

[3] "'Supposing that women are voluntary slaves—slavery of any kind is unfavourable to human happiness and improvement.' *Knox's Essays*." (M.W.) Vicesimus Knox (1752–1821), Essay 5, "On the Fear of Appearing Singular," *Essays, Moral and Literary* (1778). Wollstonecraft misquotes Knox, who is not referring specifically to women.

[4] "Sappho, Eloisa, Mrs. Macaulay, the Empress of Russia, Madame d'Eon, &c. These, and many more, may be reckoned exceptions; and, are not all heroes, as well as heroines, exceptions to general rules? I wish to see women neither heroines nor brutes; but reasonable creatures." (M.W.) Sappho (c. 600 BC) was a distinguished poet. Héloïse (c. 1101–64), secretly married to the philosopher Peter Abelard (1079–1142), was herself a scholar; their love letters inspired Pope's "Eloisa to Abelard" (1717) and Rousseau's *Julie; ou, La Nouvelle Héloïse*. Catharine Macaulay* was the author of an eight-volume *History of England* (1763–83) and other works including *Observations on the Reflections of the Right Honourable Edmund Burke on the Revolution in France* (1790) and *Letters on Education* (1790). Catherine II of Russia (1729–96) displayed her "courage and resolution" by deposing and murdering her husband; but she also introduced inoculation for smallpox and promoted religious toleration and the education of women. Charles de Beaumont, Chevalier d'Eon (1728–1810), a distinguished French diplomat, dressed as a woman for much of his life, and (in consequence of litigation over wagers about his sex) had been legally declared one in 1777. In *Emile*, Rousseau repeatedly accuses feminists of basing their arguments on exceptions.

[5] phlogiston, an imaginary element thought to cause combustion.

cases, a civil existence, have their attention naturally drawn from the interest of the whole community to that of the minute parts, though the private duty of any member of society must be very imperfectly performed when not connected with the general good. The mighty business of female life is to please, and restrained from entering into more important concerns by political and civil oppression, sentiments become events, and reflection deepens what it should, and would have effaced, if the understanding had been allowed to take a wider range.

But, confined to trifling employments, they naturally imbibe opinions which the only kind of reading calculated to interest an innocent frivolous mind, inspires. Unable to grasp any thing great, is it surprising that they find the reading of history a very dry task, and disquisitions addressed to the understanding intolerably tedious, and almost unintelligible? Thus are they necessarily dependent on the novelist for amusement. Yet, when I exclaim against novels, I mean when contrasted with those works which exercise the understanding and regulate the imagination.—For any kind of reading I think better than leaving a blank still a blank, because the mind must receive a degree of enlargement and obtain a little strength by a slight exertion of its thinking powers; besides, even the productions that are only addressed to the imagination, raise the reader a little above the gross gratification of appetites, to which the mind has not given a shade of delicacy.

This observation is the result of experience; for I have known several notable women, and one in particular, who was a very good woman—as good as such a narrow mind would allow her to be, who took care that her daughters (three in number) should never see a novel. As she was a woman of fortune and fashion, they had various masters to attend them, and a sort of menial governess to watch their footsteps. From their masters they learned how tables, chairs, &c. were called in French and Italian; but as the few books thrown in their way were far above their capacities, or devotional, they neither acquired ideas nor sentiments, and passed their time, when not compelled to repeat *words*, in dressing, quarrelling with each other, or conversing with their maids by stealth, till they were brought into company as marriageable.

Their mother, a widow, was busy in the mean time in keeping up her connections, as she termed a numerous acquaintance, lest her girls should want a proper introduction into the great world. And these young ladies, with minds vulgar in every sense of the word, and spoiled tempers, entered life puffed up with notions of their own consequence, and looking down with contempt on those who could not vie with them in dress and parade.

With respect to love, nature, or their nurses, had taken care to teach them the physical meaning of the word; and, as they had few topics of conversation, and fewer refinements of sentiment, they expressed their gross wishes not in very delicate phrases, when they spoke freely, talking of matrimony.

Could these girls have been injured by the perusal of novels? I almost forgot a shade in the character of one of them; she affected a simplicity bordering on folly, and with a simper would utter the most immodest remarks and questions, the full meaning of which she had learned whilst secluded from the world, and afraid to speak in her mother's presence, who governed with a high hand: they were all educated, as she prided herself, in a most exemplary manner; and read their chapters and psalms before breakfast, never touching a silly novel.

This is only one instance; but I recollect many other women who, not led by degrees to proper studies, and not permitted to choose for themselves, have indeed been overgrown children; or have obtained, by mixing in the world, a little of what is termed common sense: that is, a distinct manner of seeing common occurrences, as they stand detached: but what deserves the name of intellect, the power of gaining general or abstract ideas, or even intermediate ones, was out of the question. Their minds were quiescent, and when they were not roused by sensible objects and employments of that kind, they were low-spirited, would cry, or go to sleep.

When, therefore, I advise my sex not to read such flimsy works, it is to induce them to read something superiour; for I coincide in opinion with a sagacious man, who, having a daughter and niece under his care, pursued a very different plan with each.

The niece, who had considerable abilities, had, before she was left to his guardianship, been indulged in desultory reading. Her he endeavoured to lead, and did lead to history and moral essays; but his daughter, whom a fond weak mother had indulged, and who consequently was averse to every thing like application, he allowed to read novels: and used to justify his conduct by saying, that if she ever attained a relish for reading them, he should have some foundation to work upon; and that erroneous opinions were better than none at all.

In fact the female mind has been so totally neglected, that knowledge was only to be acquired from this muddy source, till from reading novels some women of superiour talents learned to despise them.

The best method, I believe, that can be adopted to correct a fondness for novels is to ridicule them: not indiscriminately, for then it would have little effect; but, if a judicious person, with some turn for humour, would read several to a young girl, and point out both by tones, and apt comparisons with pathetic incidents and heroic characters in history, how foolishly and ridiculously they caricatured human nature, just opinions might be substituted instead of romantic sentiments.

In one respect, however, the majority of both sexes resemble, and equally shew a want of taste and modesty. Ignorant women, forced to be chaste to preserve their reputation, allow their imagination to revel in the unnatural and meretricious scenes sketched by the novel writers of the day, slighting as insipid the sober dignity, and matron graces of history,[1] whilst men carry the same vitiated taste into life, and fly for amusement to the wanton, from the unsophisticated charms of virtue, and the grave respectability of sense.

Besides, the reading of novels makes women, and particularly ladies of fashion, very fond of using strong expressions and superlatives in conversation; and, though the dissipated artificial life which they lead prevents their cherishing any strong legitimate passion, the language of passion in affected tones slips for ever from their glib tongues, and every trifle produces those phosphoric bursts which only mimick in the dark the flame of passion.

from Letters Written During a Short Residence in Sweden, Norway, and Denmark (1796)[2]

ADVERTISEMENT

The writing travels, or memoirs, has ever been a pleasant employment; for vanity or sensibility always renders it interesting. In writing these desultory letters, I found I could not avoid being continually the first person—"the little hero of each tale." I tried to correct this fault, if it be one, for they were designed for publication; but in proportion as I arranged my thoughts, my letter, I found, became stiff and affected: I, therefore, determined to let my remarks and reflections flow unrestrained, as I perceived that I could not give a just description of what I saw, but by relating the effect different objects had produced on my mind and feelings, whilst the impression was still fresh.

A person has a right, I have sometimes thought, when amused by a witty or interesting egotist, to talk of himself when he can win on our attention by acquiring our affection. Whether I deserve to rank amongst this privileged number, my readers alone can judge—and I give them leave to shut the book, if they do not wish to

---

[1] "I am not now alluding to that superiority of mind which leads to the creation of ideal beauty, when he, surveyed with a penetrating eye, appears a tragi-comedy, in which little can be seen to satisfy the heart without the help of fancy." (M.W.) The first edition reads "life," not "he."

[2] In 1795, Wollstonecraft followed her lover, Gilbert Imlay, from France to England, where she discovered his infidelity. A week after her first suicide attempt, she set off with her one-year-old daughter, Fanny Imlay, and the child's French nurse, Marguerite, on the journey described in these *Letters*. She was acting as Imlay's agent, attempting to track down a ship containing funds and resources intended for the purchase of goods to be smuggled past the English blockade of France. Wollstonecraft was empowered to represent Imlay's business interests—but her motives for undertaking such a challenging journey must have been partly to regain Imlay's wavering affection. The *Letters* were published in 1796, by which time Imlay had clearly lost interest in resuming the relationship. Addressed to Imlay, they occasionally hint at the emotional pain of their writer while focusing on the landscape and culture of what was then, for most people in England, a little-known part of Europe.

become better acquainted with me.

My plan was simply to endeavour to give a just view of the present state of the countries I have passed through, as far as I could obtain information during so short a residence; avoiding those details which, without being very useful to travellers who follow the same route, appear very insipid to those who only accompany you in their chair.

LETTER 1

Eleven days of weariness on board a vessel not intended for the accommodation of passengers have so exhausted my spirits, to say nothing of the other causes, with which you are already sufficiently acquainted,[1] that it is with some difficulty I adhere to my determination of giving you my observations, as I travel through new scenes, whilst warmed with the impression they have made on me.

The captain, as I mentioned to you, promised to put me on shore at Arendall,[2] or Gothenburg, in his way to Elsineur;[3] but contrary winds obliged us to pass both places during the night. In the morning, however, after we had lost sight of the entrance of the latter bay, the vessel was becalmed; and the captain, to oblige me, hanging out a signal for a pilot, bore down towards the shore.

My attention was particularly directed to the light-house; and you can scarcely imagine with what anxiety I watched two long hours for a boat to emancipate me—still no one appeared. Every cloud that flitted on the horizon was hailed as a liberator, till approaching nearer, like most of the prospects sketched by hope, it dissolved under the eye into disappointment.

Weary of expectation, I then began to converse with the captain on the subject; and, from the tenour of the information my questions drew forth, I soon concluded, that, if I waited for a boat, I had little chance of getting on shore at this place. Despotism, as is usually the case, I found had here cramped the industry of man. The pilots being paid by the king, and scantily, they will not run into any danger, or even quit their hovels, if they can possibly avoid it, only to fulfil what is termed their duty. How different is it on the english coast, where, in the most stormy weather, boats immediately hail you, brought out by the expectation of extraordinary profit.

Disliking to sail for Elsineur, and still more to lie at anchor, or cruise about the coast for several days, I exerted all my rhetoric to prevail on the captain to let me have the ship's boat; and though I added the most forcible of arguments, I for a long time addressed him in vain.

It is a kind of rule at sea, not to send out a boat. The captain was a good-natured man; but men with common minds seldom break through general rules. Prudence is ever the resort of weakness; and they rarely go as far as they may in any undertaking, who are determined not to go beyond it on any account. If, however, I had some trouble with the captain, I did not lose much time with the sailors; for they, all alacrity, hoisted out the boat, the moment I obtained permission, and promised to row me to the light-house.

I did not once allow myself to doubt of obtaining a conveyance from thence round the rocks—and then away for Gothenburg—confinement is so unpleasant.

The day was fine; and I enjoyed the water till, approaching the little island, poor Marguerite,[4] whose timidity always acts as a feeler before her adventuring spirit, began to wonder at our not seeing any inhabitants. I did not listen to her. But when, on landing, the same silence prevailed, I caught the alarm, which was not lessened by the sight of two old men, whom we forced out of their wretched hut. Scarcely human in their appearance, we with difficulty obtained an intelligible reply to our questions—the result of which was, that they had no boat, and were not allowed to quit their post, on any pretence. But, they informed us, that

---

[1] Wollstonecraft alludes to her personal relationship with Imlay.

[2] "In Norway." (M.W.) Arendal, built on seven islands and an important eighteenth-century port, is on the south coast of Norway.

[3] Göteborg (Wollstonecraft's Gothenburg, founded in 1621) is on the west coast of Sweden on the banks of the River Göta and its estuary; Elsinore (Helsingør) is a sea-port in eastern Denmark, north of Copenhagen, known to readers of Shakespeare as the setting of *Hamlet*.

[4] Fanny Imlay's nurse.

there was at the other side, eight or ten miles over, a pilot's dwelling; two guineas tempted the sailors to risk the captain's displeasure, and once more embark to row me over.

The weather was pleasant, and the appearance of the shore so grand, that I should have enjoyed the two hours it took to reach it, but for the fatigue which was too visible in the countenances of the sailors who, instead of uttering a complaint, were, with the thoughtless hilarity peculiar to them, joking about the possibility of the captain's taking advantage of a slight westerly breeze, which was springing up, to sail without them. Yet, in spite of their good humour, I could not help growing uneasy when the shore, receding, as it were, as we advanced, seemed to promise no end to their toil. This anxiety increased when, turning into the most picturesque bay I ever saw, my eyes sought in vain for the vestige of a human habitation. Before I could determine what step to take in such a dilemma, for I could not bear to think of returning to the ship, the sight of a barge relieved me, and we hastened towards it for information. We were immediately directed to pass some jutting rocks when we should see a pilot's hut.

There was a solemn silence in this scene, which made itself be felt. The sun-beams that played on the ocean, scarcely ruffled by the lightest breeze, contrasted with the huge, dark rocks, that looked like the rude materials of creation forming the barrier of unwrought space, forcibly struck me; but I should not have been sorry if the cottage had not appeared equally tranquil. Approaching a retreat where strangers, especially women, so seldom appeared, I wondered that curiosity did not bring the beings who inhabited it to the windows or door. I did not immediately recollect that men who remain so near the brute creation, as only to exert themselves to find the food necessary to sustain life, have little or no imagination to call forth the curiosity necessary to fructify the faint glimmerings of mind which entitles them to rank as lords of the creation.—Had they either, they could not contentedly remain rooted in the clods they so indolently cultivate.

Whilst the sailors went to seek for the sluggish inhabitants, these conclusions occurred to me; and, recollecting the extreme fondness which the parisians ever testify for novelty, their very curiosity appeared to me a proof of the progress they had made in refinement. Yes; in the art of living—in the art of escaping from the cares which embarrass the first steps towards the attainment of the pleasures of social life.

The pilots informed the sailors that they were under the direction of a lieutenant retired from the service, who spoke english; adding, that they could do nothing without his orders; and even the offer of money could hardly conquer their laziness, and prevail on them to accompany us to his dwelling. They would not go with me alone which I wanted them to have done, because I wished to dismiss the sailors as soon as possible. Once more we rowed off, they following tardily, till, turning round another bold protuberance of the rocks, we saw a boat making towards us, and soon learnt that it was the lieutenant himself, coming with some earnestness to see who we were.

To save the sailors any further toil, I had my baggage instantly removed into his boat; for, as he could speak english, a previous parley was not necessary; though Marguerite's respect for me could hardly keep her from expressing the fear, strongly marked on her countenance, which my putting ourselves into the power of a strange man excited. He pointed out his cottage; and, drawing near to it, I was not sorry to see a female figure, though I had not, like Marguerite, been thinking of robberies, murders, or the other evil which instantly, as the sailors would have said, runs foul of a woman's imagination.

On entering, I was still better pleased to find a clean house, with some degree of rural elegance. The beds were of muslin, coarse it is true, but dazzlingly white; and the floor was strewed over with little sprigs of juniper (the custom, as I afterwards found, of the country), which formed a contrast with the curtains and produced an agreeable sensation of freshness, to soften the ardour of noon. Still nothing was so pleasing as the alacrity of hospitality—all that the house afforded was quickly spread on the whitest linen.—Remember I had just left the vessel, where, without being fastidious, I had continually been disgusted. Fish, milk, butter, and cheese, and I am sorry to add, brandy, the bane of this country, were spread on the board. After we had dined, hospitality made them, with some degree of mystery, bring us some excellent coffee. I did not then know that it was prohibited.[1]

The good man of the house apologized for coming in continually, but declared that he was so glad to speak english, he could not stay out. He need not have apologized; I was equally glad of his company. With the wife I could only exchange smiles; and she was employed observing the make of our clothes. My hands, I found, had first led her to discover that I was the lady. I had, of course, my quantum of reverences; for the politeness of the north seems to partake of the coldness of the climate, and the rigidity of its iron sinewed rocks. Amongst the peasantry, there is, however, so much of the simplicity of the golden age in this land of flint—so much overflowing of heart, and fellow-feeling, that only benevolence, and the honest sympathy of nature, diffused smiles over my countenance when they kept me standing, regardless of my fatigue, whilst they dropt courtesy after courtesy.

The situation of this house was beautiful, though chosen for convenience. The master being the officer who commanded all the pilots on the coast, and the person appointed to guard wrecks, it was necessary for him to fix on a spot that would overlook the whole bay. As he had seen some service, he wore, not without a pride I thought becoming, a badge to prove that he had merited well of his country. It was happy, I thought, that he had been paid in honour; for the stipend he received was little more than twelve pounds a year.— I do not trouble myself or you with the calculation of swedish ducats. Thus, my friend, you perceive the necessity of *perquisites*. This same narrow policy runs through every thing. I shall have occasion further to animadvert on it.

Though my host amused me with an account of himself, which gave me an idea of the manners of the people I was about to visit, I was eager to climb the rocks to view the country, and see whether the honest tars had regained their ship. With the help of the lieutenant's telescope I saw the vessel underway with a fair though gentle gale. The sea was calm, playful even as the most shallow stream, and on the vast bason I did not see a dark speck to indicate the boat. My conductors were consequently arrived.

Straying further, my eye was attracted by the sight of some heart's-ease[2] that peeped through the rocks. I caught at it as a good omen, and going to preserve it in a letter that had not conveyed balm to my heart, a cruel remembrance suffused my eyes; but it passed away like an April shower. If you are deep read in Shakspeare, you will recollect that this was the little western flower tinged by love's dart, which "maidens call love in idleness."[3] The gaiety of my babe was unmixed; regardless of omens or sentiments, she found a few wild strawberries more grateful than flowers or fancies.

The lieutenant informed me that this was a commodious bay. Of that I could not judge, though I felt its picturesque beauty. Rocks were piled on rocks, forming a suitable bulwark to the ocean. Come no further, they emphatically said, turning their dark sides to the waves to augment the idle roar. The view was sterile: still little patches of earth, of the most exquisite verdure, enamelled with the sweetest wild flowers, seemed to promise the goats and a few straggling cows luxurious herbage. How silent and peaceful was the scene. I gazed around with rapture, and felt more of that spontaneous pleasure which gives credibility to our expectation of happiness, than I had for a long, long time before. I forgot the horrors I had witnessed in France,[4] which had cast a gloom over all nature, and suffering the enthusiasm of my character, too often, gracious God! damped by the tears of disappointed affection, to be lighted up afresh, care took wing while simple fellow feeling expanded my heart.

To prolong this enjoyment, I readily assented to the proposal of our host to pay a visit to a family, the master of which spoke english, who was the drollest dog in the country, he added, repeating some of his stories, with a hearty laugh.

---

[1] because of sumptuary laws forbidding its import or use.

[2] a flower, probably a wild pansy or viola.

[3] Cf. Shakespeare, *A Midsummer Night's Dream* 2.1.168.

[4] during her residence there from Dec. 1792 until Apr. 1795. Her account of events there, *An Historical and Moral View of the Origin and Progress of the French Revolution*, was published in 1794.

I walked on, still delighted with the rude beauties of the scene; for the sublime often gave place imperceptibly to the beautiful, dilating the emotions which were painfully concentrated.

When we entered this abode, the largest I had yet seen, I was introduced to a numerous family; but the father, from whom I was led to expect so much entertainment, was absent. The lieutenant consequently was obliged to be the interpreter of our reciprocal compliments. The phrases were awkwardly transmitted, it is true; but looks and gestures were sufficient to make them intelligible and interesting. The girls were all vivacity, and respect for me could scarcely keep them from romping with my host, who, asking for a pinch of snuff, was presented with a box, out of which an artificial mouse, fastened to the bottom, sprung. Though this trick had doubtless been played time out of mind, yet the laughter it excited was not less genuine.

They were overflowing with civility; but to prevent their almost killing my babe with kindness, I was obliged to shorten my visit; and two or three of the girls accompanied us, bringing with them a part of whatever the house afforded to contribute towards rendering my supper more plentiful; and plentiful in fact it was, though I with difficulty did honour to some of the dishes, not relishing the quantity of sugar and spices put into every thing. At supper my host told me bluntly that I was a woman of observation, for I asked him *men's questions*.

The arrangements for my journey were quickly made; I could only have a car with post-horses, as I did not chuse to wait till a carriage could be sent for to Gothenburg. The expense of my journey, about one or two and twenty english miles, I found would not amount to more than eleven or twelve shillings, paying, he assured me, generously. I gave him a guinea and a half. But it was with the greatest difficulty that I could make him take so much, indeed any thing for my lodging and fare. He declared that it was next to robbing me, explaining how much I ought to pay on the road. However, as I was positive, he took the guinea for himself; but, as a condition, insisted on accompanying me, to prevent my meeting with any trouble or imposition on the way.

I then retired to my apartment with regret. The night was so fine, that I would gladly have rambled about much longer; yet recollecting that I must rise very early, I reluctantly went to bed: but my senses had been so awake, and my imagination still continued so busy, that I sought for rest in vain. Rising before six, I scented the sweet morning air; I had long before heard the birds twittering to hail the dawning day, though it could scarcely have been allowed to have departed.

Nothing, in fact, can equal the beauty of the northern summer's evening and night; if night it may be called that only wants the glare of day, the full light, which frequently seems so impertinent; for I could write at midnight very well without a candle. I contemplated all nature at rest; the rocks, even grown darker in their appearance, looked as if they partook of the general repose, and reclined more heavily on their foundation.—What, I exclaimed, is this active principle which keeps me still awake?—Why fly my thoughts abroad when every thing around me appears at home? My child was sleeping with equal calmness—innocent and sweet as the closing flowers.—Some recollections, attached to the idea of home, mingled with reflections respecting the state of society I had been contemplating that evening, made a tear drop on the rosy cheek I had just kissed; and emotions that trembled on the brink of extacy and agony gave a poignancy to my sensations, which made me feel more alive than usual.

What are these imperious sympathies? How frequently has melancholy and even mysanthropy taken possession of me, when the world has disgusted me, and friends have proved unkind. I have then considered myself as a particle broken off from the grand mass of mankind;—I was alone, till some involuntary sympathetic emotion, like the attraction of adhesion, made me feel that I was still a part of a mighty whole, from which I could not sever myself—not, perhaps, for the reflection has been carried very far, by snapping the thread of an existence which loses its charms in proportion as the cruel experience of life stops or poisons the current of the heart. Futurity, what hast thou not to give to those who know that there is such as thing as happiness! I speak not of philosophical contentment, though pain has afforded them the strongest conviction of it.

After our coffee and milk, for the mistress of the house had been roused long before us by her hospitality, my baggage was taken forward in a boat by my host, because the car could not safely have been brought to the house.

The road at first was very rocky and troublesome; but our driver was careful, and the horses accustomed to the frequent and sudden acclivities and descents; so that not apprehending any danger, I played with my girl, whom I would not leave to Marguerite's care, on account of her timidity.

Stopping at a little inn to bait the horses, I saw the first countenance in Sweden that displeased me, though the man was better dressed than any one who had as yet fallen in my way. An altercation took place between him and my host, the purport of which I could not guess, excepting that I was the occasion of it, be it what it would. The sequel was his leaving the house angrily; and I was immediately informed that he was the custom-house officer. The professional had indeed effaced the national character, for living as he did with these frank hospitable people, still only the exciseman appeared,— the counterpart of some I had met with in England and France. I was unprovided with a passport, not having entered any great town. At Gothenburg I knew I could immediately obtain one, and only the trouble made me object to the searching my trunks. He blustered for money; but the lieutenant was determined to guard me, according to promise, from imposition.

To avoid being interrogated at the town-gate, and obliged to go in the rain to give an account of myself, merely a form, before we could get the refreshment we stood in need of, he requested us to descend, I might have said step, from our car, and walk into town.

I expected to have found a tolerable inn, but was ushered into a most comfortless one; and, because it was about five o'clock, three or four hours after their dining hour, I could not prevail on them to give me any thing warm to eat.

The appearance of the accommodations obliged me to deliver one of my recommendatory letters, and the gentleman, to whom it was addressed, sent to look out for a lodging for me whilst I partook of his supper. As nothing passed at this supper to characterize the country, I shall here close my letter.

Your's truly,

LETTER 6

The sea was boisterous; but, as I had an experienced pilot, I did not apprehend any danger. Sometimes I was told, boats are driven far out and lost. However, I seldom calculate chances so nicely—sufficient for the day is the obvious evil![1]

We had to steer amongst islands and huge rocks, rarely losing sight of the shore, though it now and then appeared only a mist that bordered the water's edge. The pilot assured me that the numerous harbours on the Norway coast were very safe, and the pilot-boats were always on the watch. The Swedish side is very dangerous, I am also informed; and the help of experience is not often at hand, to enable strange vessels to steer clear of the rocks, which lurk below the water, close to the shore.

There are no tides here, nor in the cattegate;[2] and, what appeared to me a consequence, no sandy beach. Perhaps this observation has been made before; but it did not occur to me till I saw the waves continually beating against the bare rocks, without ever receding to leave a sediment to harden.

The wind was fair, till we had to tack about in order to enter Laurvig,[3] where we arrived towards three o'clock in the afternoon. It is a clean, pleasant town, with a considerable iron-work, which gives life to it.

As the norwegians do not frequently see travellers, they are very curious to know their business, and who they are—so curious that I was half tempted to adopt Dr. Franklin's plan, when travelling in America, where they are equally prying, which was to write on a paper, for public inspection, my name, from whence I came, where I was going, and what was my business.[4] But if I were importuned by their curiosity, their friendly gestures gratified me. A woman, coming alone, interested them. And I know not whether my weariness gave

---

[1] Cf. Matthew 6.34.

[2] the Kattegat, the channel between Sweden and Denmark.

[3] or Larvik, in Norway, south-west of the capital, Christiania (now Oslo).

[4] A similar anecdote is told of Franklin* by his untrustworthy biographer Mason Locke Weems (1818). Where Wollstonecraft heard or read the story is unknown.

me a look of peculiar delicacy; but they approached to assist me, and enquire after my wants, as if they were afraid to hurt, and wished to protect me. The sympathy I inspired, thus dropping down from the clouds in a strange land, affected me more than it would have done, had not my spirits been harassed by various causes—by much thinking—musing almost to madness—and even by a sort of weak melancholy that hung about my heart at parting with my daughter for the first time.

You know that as a female I am particularly attached to her—I feel more than a mother's fondness and anxiety, when I reflect on the dependent and oppressed state of her sex. I dread lest she should be forced to sacrifice her heart to her principles, or principles to her heart. With trembling hand I shall cultivate sensibility, and cherish delicacy of sentiment, lest, whilst I lend fresh blushes to the rose, I sharpen the thorns that will wound the breast I would fain guard—I dread to unfold her mind, lest it should render her unfit for the world she is to inhabit—Hapless woman! what a fate is thine!

But whither am I wandering? I only meant to tell you that the impression the kindness of the simple people made visible on my countenance increased my sensibility to a painful degree. I wished to have had a room to myself; for their attention, and rather distressing observation, embarrassed me extremely. Yet, as they would bring me eggs, and make my coffee, I found I could not leave them without hurting their feelings of hospitality.

It is customary here for the host and hostess to welcome their guests as master and mistress of the house.

My clothes, in their turn, attracted the attention of the females; and I could not help thinking of the foolish vanity which makes many women so proud of the observation of strangers as to take wonder very gratuitously for admiration. This error they are very apt to fall into; when arrived in a foreign country, the populace stare at them as they pass: yet the make of a cap, or the singularity of a gown, is often the cause of the flattering attention, which afterwards supports a fantastic superstructure of self-conceit.

Not having brought a carriage over with me, expecting to have met a person where I landed, who was immediately to have procured me one, I was detained whilst the good people of the inn sent round to all their acquaintance to search for a vehicle. A rude sort of *cabriole*[1] was at last found, and a driver half drunk, who was not less eager to make a good bargain on that account. I had a danish captain of a ship and his mate with me: the former was to ride on horseback, at which he was not very expert, and the latter to partake of my seat. The driver mounted behind to guide the horses, and flourish the whip over our shoulders; he would not suffer the reins out of his own hands. There was something so grotesque in our appearance, that I could not avoid shrinking into myself when I saw a gentleman-like man in the group which crowded round the door to observe us. I could have broken the driver's whip for cracking to call the women and children together; but seeing a significant smile on the face, I had before remarked, I burst into a laugh, to allow him to do so too,—and away we flew. This is not a flourish of the pen; for we actually went on full gallop a long time, the horses being very good; indeed I have never met with better, if so good, post-horses, as in Norway; they are of a stouter make than the english horses, appear to be well fed, and are not easily tired.

I had to pass over, I was informed, the most fertile and best cultivated tract of country in Norway. The distance was three norwegian miles, which are longer than the swedish. The roads were very good; the farmers are obliged to repair them; and we scampered through a great extent of country in a more improved state than any I had viewed since I left England. Still there was sufficient of hills, dales, and rocks, to prevent the idea of a plain from entering the head, or even of such scenery as England and France afford. The prospects were also embellished by water, rivers, and lakes, before the sea proudly claimed my regard; and the road running frequently through lofty groves, rendered the landscapes beautiful, though they were not so romantic as those I had lately seen with such delight.

It was late when I reached Tonsberg;[2] and I was glad to go to bed at a decent inn. The next morning, the

---

[1] a two-wheeled carriage drawn by a single horse.

[2] Tønsberg, the oldest town in Norway, a port about 40 miles south of Oslo.

17th of July, conversing with the gentleman with whom I had business to transact, I found that I should be detained at Tonsberg three weeks; and I lamented that I had not brought my child with me.

The inn was quiet, and my room so pleasant, commanding a view of the sea, confined by an amphitheatre of hanging woods, that I wished to remain there, though no one in the house could speak english or french. The mayor, my friend, however, sent a young woman to me who spoke a little english, and she agreed to call on me twice a day, to receive my orders, and translate them to my hostess.

My not understanding the language was an excellent pretext for dining alone, which I prevailed on them to let me do at a late hour; for the early dinners in Sweden had entirely deranged my day. I could not alter it there, without disturbing the economy of a family where I was as a visitor; necessity having forced me to accept of an invitation from a private family, the lodgings were so incommodious.

Amongst the norwegians I had the arrangement of my own time; and I determined to regulate it in such a manner, that I might enjoy as much of their sweet summer as I possibly could;—short, it is true; but "passing sweet."[1]

I never endured a winter in this rude clime; consequently it was not the contrast, but the real beauty of the season which made the present summer appear to me the finest I had ever seen. Sheltered from the north and eastern winds, nothing can exceed the salubrity, the soft freshness of the western gales. In the evening they also die away; the aspen leaves tremble into stillness, and reposing nature seems to be warmed by the moon, which here assumes a genial aspect: and if a light shower has chanced to fall with the sun, the juniper the underwood of the forest, exhales a wild perfume, mixed with a thousand nameless sweets, that, soothing the heart, leave images in the memory which the imagination will ever hold dear.

Nature is the nurse of sentiment,—the true source of taste;—yet what misery, as well as rapture, is produced by a quick perception of the beautiful and sublime, when it is exercised in observing animated nature, when every beauteous feeling and emotion excites responsive sympathy, and the harmonized soul sinks into melancholy, or rises to extasy, just as the chords are touched, like the æolian harp[2] agitated by the changing wind. But how dangerous is it to foster these sentiments in such an imperfect state of existence; and how difficult to eradicate them when an affection for mankind, a passion for an individual, is but the unfolding of that love which embraces all that is great and beautiful.

When a warm heart has received strong impressions, they are not to be effaced. Emotions become sentiments; and the imagination renders even transient sensations permanent, by fondly retracing them. I cannot, without a thrill of delight, recollect views I have seen, which are not to be forgotten,—nor looks I have felt in every nerve which I shall never more meet. The grave has closed over a dear friend, the friend of my youth;[3] still she is present with me, and I hear her soft voice warbling as I stray over the heath. Fate has separated me from another,[4] the fire of whose eyes, tempered by infantine tenderness, still warms my breast; even when gazing on these tremendous cliffs, sublime emotions absorb my soul. And, smile not, if I add, that the rosy tint of morning reminds me of a suffusion, which will never more charm my senses, unless it reappears on the cheeks of my child. Her sweet blushes I may yet hide in my bosom, and she is still too young to ask why starts the tear, so near akin to pleasure and pain?

I cannot write any more at present. Tomorrow we will talk of Tonsberg.

---

[1] William Cowper,* "Retirement" 740.

[2] an instrument placed in a window, so its strings can vibrate in the wind (and named after Æolus, the god of the winds). Cf. Coleridge, "Effusion 35"* and "Dejection."*

[3] Fanny Blood, who died in Portugal in 1785 while Wollstonecraft was visiting her there.

[4] In pursuit of business, Wollstonecraft had left her daughter, Fanny, behind in Sweden.

LETTER 7

Though the king of Denmark be an absolute monarch,[1] yet the norwegians appear to enjoy all the blessings of freedom. Norway may be termed a sister kingdom; but the people have no viceroy to lord it over them, and fatten his dependants with the fruit of their labour.

There are only two counts in the whole country, who have estates, and exact some feudal observances from their tenantry. All the rest of the country is divided into small farms, which belong to the cultivator. It is true, some few, appertaining to the church, are let; but always on a lease for life, generally renewed in favour of the eldest son, who has this advantage, as well as a right to a double portion of the property. But the value of the farm is estimated; and after his portion is assigned to him, he must be answerable for the residue to the remaining part of the family.

Every farmer, for ten years, is obliged to attend annually about twelve days, to learn the military exercise; but it is always at a small distance from his dwelling, and does not lead him into any new habits of life.

There are about six thousand regulars also, garrisoned at Christiania and Fredericshall,[2] which are equally reserved, with the militia, for the defence of their own country. So that when the prince royal[3] passed into Sweden, in 1788, he was obliged to request, not command, them to accompany him on this expedition.

These corps are mostly composed of the sons of the cottagers, who being labourers on the farms, are allowed a few acres to cultivate for themselves. These men voluntarily enlist; but it is only for a limited period, (six years) at the expiration of which they have the liberty of retiring. The pay is only two-pence a day, and bread; still, considering the cheapness of the country, it is more than sixpence in England.

The distribution of landed property into small farms, produces a degree of equality which I have seldom seen elsewhere; and the rich being all merchants, who are obliged to divide their personal fortune amongst their children, the boys always receiving twice as much as the girls, property has not a chance of accumulating till overgrown wealth destroys the balance of liberty.

You will be surprised to hear me talk of liberty; yet the norwegians appear to me to be the most free community I have ever observed.

The mayor of each town or district, and the judges in the country, exercise an authority almost patriarchal. They can do much good, but little harm, as every individual can appeal from their judgment: and as they may always be forced to give a reason for their conduct, it is generally regulated by prudence. "They have not time to learn to be tyrants," said a gentleman to me, with whom I discussed the subject.

The farmers not fearing to be turned out of their farms, should they displease a man in power, and having no vote to be commanded at an election for a mock representative, are a manly race; for not being obliged to submit to any debasing tenure, in order to live, or advance themselves in the world, they act with an independent spirit. I never yet have heard of any thing like domineering, or oppression, excepting such as has arisen from natural causes. The freedom the people enjoy may, perhaps, render them a little litigious, and subject them to the impositions of cunning practitioners of the law; but the authority of office is bounded, and the emoluments of it do not destroy its utility.

Last year a man, who had abused his power, was cashiered, on the representation of the people to the bailiff of the district.

There are four in Norway, who might with propriety be termed sheriffs; and, from their sentence, an appeal, by either party, may be made to Copenhagen.

Near most of the towns are commons, on which the cows of all the inhabitants, indiscriminately, are allowed to graze. The poor, to whom a cow is necessary, are

---

[1] Christian VII (1766–1808). Constitutional monarchy was not established in Denmark until 1849; Norway was at this time under Danish rule.

[2] Oslo, rebuilt after a fire by King Christian IV of Norway in 1624 and named Christiania in his honour, regained its original Viking name in 1925. Fredericshall (also called Frederikshald and Halden) was besieged by Russian, Danish, and Norwegian forces in 1718; the Swedish king, Charles XII, was killed there.

[3] The future Frederick VI (who ruled from 1808–39 but was regent from 1784) passed through Norway during a brief war with Sweden in 1788.

almost supported by it. Besides, to render living more easy, they all go out to fish in their own boats; and fish is their principal food.

The lower class of people in the towns are in general sailors; and the industrious have usually little ventures of their own that serve to render the winter comfortable.

With respect to the country at large, the importation is considerably in favour of Norway.

They are forbidden, at present, to export corn or rye, on account of the advanced price.

The restriction which most resembles the painful subordination of Ireland,[1] is that vessels, trading to the West Indies, are obliged to pass by their own ports, and unload their cargoes at Copenhagen, which they afterwards re-ship. The duty is indeed inconsiderable; but the navigation being dangerous, they run a double risk.

There is an excise on all articles of consumption brought to the towns; but the officers are not strict; and it would be reckoned invidious to enter a house to search, as in England.

The norwegians appear to me a sensible, shrewd people, with little scientific knowledge, and still less taste for literature: but they are arriving at the epoch which precedes the introduction of the arts and sciences.

Most of the towns are sea-ports, and sea-ports are not favourable to improvement. The captains acquire a little superficial knowledge by travelling, which their indefatigable attention to the making of money prevents their digesting; and the fortune that they thus laboriously acquire, is spent, as it usually is in towns of this description, in shew and good living. They love their country, but have not much public spirit.[2] Their exertions are, generally speaking, only for their families; which I conceive will always be the case, till politics, becoming a subject of discussion, enlarges the heart by opening the understanding. The french revolution will have this effect. They sing at present, with great glee, many republican songs, and seem earnestly to wish that the republic may stand; yet they appear very much attached to their prince royal; and, as far as rumour can give an idea of a character, he appears to merit their attachment. When I am at Copenhagen, I shall be able to ascertain on what foundation their good opinion is built; at present I am only the echo of it.

In the year 1788 he travelled through Norway; and acts of mercy gave dignity to the parade, and interest to the joy, his presence inspired. At this town he pardoned a girl condemned to die for murdering an illegitimate child, a crime seldom committed in this country. She is since married, and become the careful mother of a family. This might be given as an instance, that a desperate act is not always a proof of an incorrigible depravity of character; the only plausible excuse that has been brought forward to justify the infliction of capital punishments.

I will relate two or three other anecdotes to you; for the truth of which I will not vouch, because the facts were not of sufficient consequence for me to take much pains to ascertain them; and, true or false, they evince that the people like to make a kind of mistress of their prince.

An officer, mortally wounded at the ill-advised battle of Quistram,[3] desired to speak with the prince; and, with his dying breath, earnestly recommended to his care a young woman of Christiania, to whom he was engaged. When the prince returned there, a ball was given by the chief inhabitants. He inquired whether this unfortunate girl was invited, and requested that she might, though of the second class. The girl came; she was pretty; and finding herself amongst her superiors, bashfully sat down as near the door as possible, nobody taking notice of her. Shortly after, the prince entering, immediately inquired for her, and asked her to dance, to the mortification of the rich dames. After it was over he handed her to the top of the room, and placing himself by her, spoke of the loss she had sustained, with tenderness, promising to provide for any one she should marry,—as the story goes. She is since married, and he has not forgotten his promise.

---

[1] Irish wool and linen had to be exported through England.

[2] "The grand virtues of the heart particularly the enlarged humanity which extends to the whole human race, depend more on the understanding, I believe, than is generally imagined." (M.W.)

[3] Quistram, north of Göteborg, Sweden, was the site of a battle at which the Danes defeated the Swedes in 1788. See Letter 5 (not in this selection).

A little girl, during the same expedition, in Sweden, who informed him that the logs of a bridge were cut underneath, was taken by his orders to Christiania, and put to school at his expence.

Before I retail other beneficial effects of his journey, it is necessary to inform you that the laws here are mild, and do not punish capitally for any crime but murder, which seldom occurs. Every other offence merely subjects the delinquent to imprisonment and labour in the castle, or rather arsenal, at Christiania, and the fortress at Fredericshall. The first and second conviction produces a sentence for a limited number of years,— two, three, five, or seven, proportioned to the atrocity of the crime. After the third he is whipped, branded in the forehead, and condemned to perpetual slavery. This is the ordinary march of justice. For some flagrant breaches of trust, or acts of wanton cruelty, criminals have been condemned to slavery for life, the first time of conviction, but not frequently. The number of these slaves do not, I am informed, amount to more than an hundred, which is not considerable, compared with the population, upwards of eight hundred thousand. Should I pass through Christiania, on my return to Gothenburg, I shall probably have an opportunity of learning other particulars.

There is also a house of correction at Christiania for trifling misdemeanors, where the women are confined to labour and imprisonment even for life. The state of the prisoners was represented to the prince; in consequence of which, he visited the arsenal and house of correction. The slaves at the arsenal were loaded with irons of a great weight; he ordered them to be lightened as much as possible.

The people in the house of correction were commanded not to speak to him; but four women, condemned to remain there for life, got into the passage, and fell at his feet. He granted them a pardon; and inquiring respecting the treatment of the prisoners, he was informed that they were frequently whipt going in, and coming out; and for any fault, at the discretion of the inspectors. This custom he humanely abolished; though some of the principal inhabitants, whose situation in life had raised them above the temptation of stealing, were of opinion that these chastisements were necessary and wholesome.

In short, every thing seems to announce that the prince really cherishes the laudable ambition of fulfilling the duties of his station. This ambition is cherished and directed by the count Bernstof,[1] the prime minister of Denmark, who is universally celebrated for his abilities and virtue. The happiness of the people is a substantial eulogium; and, from all I can gather, the inhabitants of Denmark and Norway are the least oppressed people of Europe. The press is free. They translate any of the french publications of the day, deliver their opinion on the subject, and discuss those it leads to with great freedom, and without fearing to displease the government.

On the subject of religion they are likewise becoming tolerant, at least, and perhaps have advanced a step further in free-thinking. One writer has ventured to deny the divinity of Jesus Christ, and to question the necessity or utility of the christian system, without being considered universally as a monster, which would have been the case a few years ago. They have translated many german works on education; and though they have not adopted any of their plans, it is become a subject of discussion. There are some grammar and free schools; but, from what I hear, not very good ones. All the children learn to read, write, and cast accounts, for the purposes of common life. They have no university; and nothing that deserves the name of science is taught; nor do individuals, by pursuing any branch of knowledge, excite a degree of curiosity which is the forerunner of improvement. Knowledge is not absolutely necessary to enable a considerable portion of the community to live; and, till it is, I fear, it never becomes general.

In this country, where minerals abound, there is not one collection: and, in all probability, I venture a conjecture, the want of mechanical and chemical knowledge renders the silver mines unproductive; for the quantity of silver obtained every year is not sufficient to defray the expences. It has been urged, that the employment of such a number of hands is very beneficial. But a positive loss is never to be done away; and the

---

[1] Andreas Peter, Count von Bernstorff til Sartow (1735–97), was the Minister of State at the time of Wollstonecraft's visit.

men, thus employed, would naturally find some other means of living, instead of being thus a dead weight on government, or rather on the community from whom its revenue is drawn.

About three english miles from Tonsberg there is a salt work, belonging, like all their establishments, to government, in which they employ above an hundred and fifty men, and maintain nearly five hundred people, who earn their living. The clear profit, and increasing one, amounts to two thousand pounds sterling. And as the eldest son of the inspector, an ingenious young man, has been sent by the government to travel, and acquire some mathematical and chemical knowledge in Germany, it has a chance of being improved. He is the only person I have met with here, who appears to have a scientific turn of mind. I do not mean to assert that I have not met with others, who have a spirit of inquiry.

The salt-works at St. Ubes[1] are basons in the sand, and the sun produces the evaporation: but here there is no beach. Besides, the heat of summer is so short-lived, that it would be idle to contrive machines for such an inconsiderable portion of the year. They therefore always use fires; and the whole establishment appears to be regulated with judgment.

The situation is well chosen and beautiful. I do not find, from the observation of a person who has resided here for forty years, that the sea advances or recedes on this coast.

I have already remarked, that little attention is paid to education, excepting reading, writing, and the rudiments of arithmetic; I ought to have added, that a catechism is carefully taught, and the children obliged to read in the churches, before the congregation, to prove that they are not neglected.

Degrees, to enable any one to practise any profession, must be taken at Copenhagen; and the people of this country, having the good sense to perceive that men who are to live in a community should at least acquire the elements of their knowledge, and form their youthful attachments there, are seriously endeavouring to establish an university in Norway. And Tonsberg, as a centrical place in the best part of the country, had the most suffrages; for, experiencing the bad effects of a metropolis, they have determined not to have it in or near Christiania. Should such an establishment take place, it will promote inquiry throughout the country, and give a new face to society. Premiums have been offered, and prize questions written, which I am told have merit. The building college-halls, and other appendages of the seat of science, might enable Tonsberg to recover its pristine consequence; for it is one of the most ancient towns of Norway, and once contained nine churches. At present there are only two. One is a very old structure, and has a gothic respectability about it, which scarcely amounts to grandeur, because, to render a gothic pile grand, it must have a huge unwieldiness of appearance. The chapel of Windsor[2] may be an exception to this rule; I mean before it was in its present *nice, clean* state. When I first saw it, the pillars within had acquired, by time, a sombre hue, which accorded with the architecture; and the gloom increased its dimensions to the eye by hiding its parts; but now it all bursts on the view at once; and the sublimity has vanished before the brush and broom; for it has been white-washed and scraped till it is become as bright and neat as the pots and pans in a notable house-wife's kitchen—yes; the very spurs on the recumbent knights were deprived of their venerable rust, to give a striking proof that a love of order in trifles, and taste for proportion and arrangement, are very distinct. The glare of light thus introduced, entirely destroys the sentiment these piles are calculated to inspire; so that, when I heard something like a jig from the organ-loft, I thought it an excellent hall for dancing or feasting. The measured pace of thought with which I had entered the cathedral, changed into a trip; and I bounded on the terrace, to see the royal family, with a number of ridiculous images in my head, that I shall not now recall.

---

[1] a town near Lisbon, Portugal, now called Setubal.

[2] St. George's Chapel at Windsor Castle, recently restored by King George III.

The norwegians are fond of music; and every little church has an organ. In the church I have mentioned, there is an inscription importing that a king,[1] James the sixth, of Scotland, and first of England, who came with more than princely gallantry, to escort his bride home, stood there, and heard divine service.

There is a little recess full of coffins, which contains bodies embalmed long since—so long, that there is not even a tradition to lead to a guess at their names.

A desire of preserving the body seems to have prevailed in most countries of the world, futile as it is to term it a preservation, when the noblest parts are immediately sacrificed merely to save the muscles, skin and bone from rottenness. When I was shewn these human petrifactions, I shrunk back with disgust and horror. "Ashes to ashes!" thought I—"Dust to dust!"[2]— If this be not dissolution, it is something worse than natural decay—It is treason against humanity, thus to lift up the awful veil which would fain hide its weakness. The grandeur of the active principle is never more strongly felt than at such a sight; for nothing is so ugly as the human form when deprived of life, and thus dried into stone, merely to preserve the most disgusting image of death. The contemplation of noble ruins produces a melancholy that exalts the mind.—We take a retrospect of the exertions of man, the fate of empires and their rulers; and marking the grand destruction of ages, it seems the necessary change of time leading to improvement.—Our very soul expands, and we forget our littleness; how painfully brought to our recollection by such vain attempts to snatch from decay what is destined so soon to perish. Life, what art thou? Where goes this breath? this *I*, so much alive? In what element will it mix, giving or receiving fresh energy?—What will break the enchantment of animation?—For worlds, I would not see a form I loved—embalmed in my heart—thus sacrilegiously handled!—Pugh! my stomach turns.—Is this all the distinction of the rich in the grave?—They had better quietly allow the scythe of equality to mow them down with the common mass, than struggle to become a monument of the instability of human greatness.

The teeth, nails and skin were whole, without appearing black like the Egyptian mummies; and some silk, in which they had been wrapt, still preserved its colour, pink, with tolerable freshness.

I could not learn how long the bodies had been in this state, in which they bid fair to remain till the day of judgment, if there is to be such a day; and before that time, it will require some trouble to make them fit to appear in company with angels, without disgracing humanity.—God bless you! I feel a conviction that we have some perfectible principle in our present vestment, which will not be destroyed just as we begin to be sensible of improvement; and I care not what habit it next puts on, sure that it will be wisely formed to suit a higher state of existence. Thinking of death makes us tenderly cling to our affections—with more than usual tenderness, I therefore assure you that I am your's, wishing that the temporary death of absence may not endure longer than is absolutely necessary.

LETTER 8

Tonsberg was formerly the residence of one of the little sovereigns of Norway; and on an adjacent mountain the vestiges of a fort remain, which was battered down by the swedes; the entrance of the bay lying close to it.

Here I have frequently strayed, sovereign of the waste, I seldom met any human creature; and sometimes, reclining on the mossy down, under the shelter of a rock, the prattling of the sea amongst the pebbles has

---

[1] "'Anno 1589, St. Martin's Day, which was the 11th Day of November, on a Tuesday, came the highborn Prince and Lord Jacob Stuart, King in Scotland, to this Town, and the 25th Sunday after Trinity (Sunday:) which was the 16th Day of November, stood his Grace in this Pew, and heard Scotch Preaching from the 23d Psalm, "The Lord is my Shepherd," &c. which M. David Lentz, Preacher in Lith, then preached between 10 and 12.'

"The above is an inscription which stands in St. Mary's church, in Tonsberg.

"It is known that king James the sixth went to Norway, to marry princess Anna, the daughter of Frederick the second, and sister to Christian the fourth; and that the wedding was performed at Opslo (now Christiania), where the princess, by contrary winds, was detained; but that the king, during this voyage, was at Tonsberg, nobody would have known, if an inscription, in remembrance of it, had not been placed in this church." (M.W.)

[2] Cf. Genesis 3.19, Ecclesiastes 3.20.

lulled me to sleep—no fear of any rude satyr's approaching to interrupt my repose. Balmy were the slumbers, and soft the gales, that refreshed me, when I awoke to follow, with an eye vaguely curious, the white sails, as they turned the cliffs, or seemed to take shelter under the pines which covered the little islands that so gracefully rose to render the terrific ocean beautiful. The fishermen were calmly casting their nets; whilst the seagulls hovered over the unruffled deep. Every thing seemed to harmonize into tranquillity—even the mournful call of the bittern was in cadence with the tinkling bells on the necks of the cows, that, pacing slowly one after the other, along an inviting path in the vale below, were repairing to the cottages to be milked. With what ineffable pleasure have I not gazed—and gazed again, losing my breath through my eyes—my very soul diffused itself in the scene—and, seeming to become all senses, glided in the scarcely agitated waves, melted in the freshening breeze, or, taking its flight with fairy wing, to the misty mountains which bounded the prospect, fancy tript over new lawns, more beautiful even than the lovely slopes on the winding shore before me.——I pause, again breathless, to trace, with renewed delight, sentiments which entranced me, when, turning my humid eyes from the expanse below to the vault above, my sight pierced the fleecy clouds that softened the azure brightness; and, imperceptibly recalling the reveries of childhood, I bowed before the awful throne of my Creator, whilst I rested on its footstool.

You have sometimes wondered, my dear friend, at the extreme affection of my nature—But such is the temperature of my soul—It is not the vivacity of youth, the hey-day of existence. For years have I endeavoured to calm an impetuous tide—labouring to make my feelings take an orderly course.—It was striving against the stream.—I must love and admire with warmth, or I sink into sadness. Tokens of love which I have received have rapt me in elysium—purifying the heart they enchanted.—My bosom still glows.—Do not saucily ask, repeating Sterne's question, "Maria, is it still so warm?"[1] Sufficiently, O my God! has it been chilled by sorrow and unkindness—still nature will prevail—and if I blush at recollecting past enjoyment, it is the rosy hue of pleasure heightened by modesty; for the blush of modesty and shame are as distinct as the emotions by which they are produced.

I need scarcely inform you, after telling you of my walks, that my constitution has been renovated here; and that I have recovered my activity, even whilst attaining a little *embonpoint*.[2] My imprudence last winter, and some untoward accidents just at the time I was weaning my child, had reduced me to a state of weakness which I never before experienced. A slow fever preyed on me every night, during my residence in Sweden, and after I arrived at Tonsberg. By chance I found a fine rivulet filtered through the rocks, and confined in a bason for the cattle. It tasted to me like a chalybeat;[3] at any rate it was pure; and the good effect of the various waters which invalids are sent to drink, depends, I believe, more on the air, exercise and change of scene, than on their medicinal qualities. I therefore determined to turn my morning walks towards it, and seek for health from the nymph of the fountain; partaking of the beverage offered to the tenants of the shade.

Chance likewise led me to discover a new pleasure, equally beneficial to my health. I wished to avail myself of my vicinity to the sea, and bathe; but it was not possible near the town; there was no convenience. The young woman whom I mentioned to you, proposed rowing me across the water, amongst the rocks; but as she was pregnant, I insisted on taking one of the oars, and learning to row. It was not difficult; and I do not know a pleasanter exercise. I soon became expert, and my train of thinking kept time, as it were, with the oars, or I suffered the boat to be carried along by the current, indulging a pleasing forgetfulness, or fallacious hopes.—How fallacious! yet, without hope, what is to sustain life, but the fear of annihilation—the only thing of which I have ever felt a dread—I cannot bear to think of being no more—of losing myself—though existence is often but a painful consciousness of misery; nay, it appears to me impossible that I should cease to exist, or

---

[1] Cf. Yorick's question to Maria, a figure of sensibility in Laurence Sterne's *A Sentimental Journey* (1768).

[2] "plumpness"; literally, "in good condition" (Fr.).

[3] chalybeate; mineral water containing iron, taken as a tonic.

that this active, restless spirit, equally alive to joy and sorrow, should only be organized dust—ready to fly abroad the moment the spring snaps, or the spark goes out, which kept it together. Surely something resides in this heart that is not perishable—and life is more than a dream.

Sometimes, to take up my oar, once more, when the sea was calm, I was amused by disturbing the innumerable young star fish which floated just below the surface: I had never observed them before; for they have not a hard shell, like those which I have seen on the sea-shore. They look like thickened water, with a white edge; and four purple circles, of different forms, were in the middle, over an incredible number of fibres, or white lines. Touching them, the cloudy substance would turn or close, first on one side, then on the other, very gracefully; but when I took one of them up in the ladle with which I heaved the water out of the boat, it appeared only a colourless jelly.

I did not see any of the seals, numbers of which followed our boat when we landed in Sweden; for though I like to sport in the water, I should have had no desire to join in their gambols.

Enough, you will say, of inanimate nature, and of brutes, to use the lordly phrase of man; let me hear something of the inhabitants.

The gentleman with whom I had business, is the mayor of Tonsberg; he speaks english intelligibly; and, having a sound understanding, I was sorry that his numerous occupations prevented my gaining as much information from him as I could have drawn forth, had we frequently conversed. The people of the town, as far as I had an opportunity of knowing their sentiments, are extremely well satisfied with his manner of discharging his office. He has a degree of information and good sense which excites respect, whilst a chearfulness, almost amounting to gaiety, enables him to reconcile differences, and keep his neighbours in good humour.—

"I lost my horse," said a woman to me; "but ever since, when I want to send to the mill, or go out, the mayor lends me one.—He scolds if I do not come for it."

A criminal was branded, during my stay here, for the third offence; but the relief he received made him declare that the judge was one of the best men in the world.

I sent this wretch a trifle, at different times, to take with him into slavery. As it was more than he expected, he wished very much to see me; and this wish brought to my remembrance an anecdote I heard when I was in Lisbon.[1]

A wretch who had been imprisoned several years, during which period lamps had been put up, was at last condemned to a cruel death; yet, in his way to execution, he only wished for one night's respite, to see the city lighted.

Having dined in company at the mayor's, I was invited with his family to spend the day at one of the richest merchant's houses.—Though I could not speak danish, I knew that I could see a great deal: yes; I am persuaded that I have formed a very just opinion of the character of the norwegians, without being able to hold converse with them.

I had expected to meet some company; yet was a little disconcerted at being ushered into an apartment full of well-dressed people; and, glancing my eyes round, they rested on several very pretty faces. Rosy cheeks, sparkling eyes, and light brown or golden locks; for I never saw so much hair with a yellow cast; and, with their fine complexions, it looked very becoming.

These women seem a mixture of indolence and vivacity; they scarcely ever walk out, and were astonished that I should, for pleasure; yet they are immoderately fond of dancing. Unaffected in their manners, if they have no pretensions to elegance, simplicity often produces a gracefulness of deportment, when they are animated by a particular desire to please—which was the case at present. The solitariness of my situation, which they thought terrible, interested them very much in my favour. They gathered round me—sung to me—and one of the prettiest, to whom I gave my hand, with some degree of cordiality, to meet the glance of her eyes, kissed me very affectionately.

At dinner, which was conducted with great hospitality, though we remained at table too long, they sung several songs, and, amongst the rest, translations of some patriotic french ones. As the evening advanced, they

---

[1] Wollstonecraft had visited her dying friend, Fanny Blood, in Lisbon, Portugal, in 1785.

became playful, and we kept up a sort of conversation of gestures. As their minds were totally uncultivated, I did not lose much, perhaps gained, by not being able to understand them; for fancy probably filled up, more to their advantage, the void in the picture. Be that as it may, they excited my sympathy; and I was very much flattered when I was told, the next day, that they said it was a pleasure to look at me, I appeared so good-natured.

The men were generally captains of ships. Several spoke english very tolerably; but they were merely matter of fact men, confined to a very narrow circle of observation. I found it difficult to obtain from them any information respecting their own country, when the fumes of tobacco did not keep me at a distance.

I was invited to partake of some other feasts, and always had to complain of the quantity of provision, and the length of time taken to consume it; for it would not have been proper to have said devour, all went on so fair and softly. The servants wait as slowly as their mistresses carve.

The young women here, as well as in Sweden, have commonly bad teeth, which I attribute to the same causes. They are fond of finery, but do not pay the necessary attention to their persons, to render beauty less transient than a flower; and that interesting expression which sentiment and accomplishments give, seldom supplies its place.

The servants have likewise an inferior sort of food here; but their masters are not allowed to strike them with impunity. I might have added mistresses; for it was a complaint of this kind, brought before the mayor, which led me to a knowledge of the fact.

The wages are low, which is particularly unjust, because the price of clothes is much higher than provisions. A young woman, who is wet nurse to the mistress of the inn where I lodge, receives only twelve dollars a year, and pays ten for the nursing of her own child; the father had run away to get clear of the expence. There was something in this most painful state of widowhood which excited my compassion, and led me to reflections on the instability of the most flattering plans of happiness, that were painful in the extreme, till I was ready to ask whether this world was not created to exhibit every possible combination of wretchedness. I asked these questions of a heart writhing with anguish, whilst I listened to a melancholy ditty sung by this poor girl. It was too early for thee to be abandoned, thought I, and I hastened out of the house, to take my solitary evening's walk—And here I am again, to talk of any thing, but the pangs arising from the discovery of estranged affection, and the lonely sadness of a deserted heart.

The father and mother, if the father can be ascertained, are obliged to maintain an illegitimate child at their joint expence; but, should the father disappear, go up the country or to sea, the mother must maintain it herself. However, accidents of this kind do not prevent their marrying; and then it is not unusual to take the child or children home; and they are brought up very amicably with the marriage progeny.

I took some pains to learn what books were written originally in their language; but for any certain information respecting the state of danish literature, I must wait till I arrive at Copenhagen.

The sound of the language is soft, a great proportion of the words ending in vowels; and there is a simplicity in the turn of some of the phrases which have been translated to me, that pleased and interested me. In the country, the farmers use the *thou* and *thee*; and they do not acquire the polite plurals of the towns by meeting at market. The not having markets established in the large towns appears to me a great inconvenience. When the farmers have any thing to sell, they bring it to the neighbouring town, and take it from house to house. I am surprised that the inhabitants do not feel how very incommodious this usage is to both parties, and redress it. They indeed perceive it; for when I have introduced the subject, they acknowledged that they were often in want of necessaries, there being no butchers, and they were often obliged to buy what they did not want; yet it was the *custom*; and the changing of customs of a long standing requires more energy than they yet possess. I received a similar reply, when I attempted to persuade the women that they injured their children by keeping them too warm. The only way of parrying off my reasoning was, that they must do as other people did. In short, reason on any subject of change, and they stop you by saying that "the town would talk." A person of sense, with a large fortune, to insure respect, might be very useful here, by inducing them to treat their children, and manage their sick properly, and eat food dressed in a simpler manner: the example, for instance, of a count's lady.

Reflecting on these prejudices made me revert to the wisdom of those legislators who established institutions for the good of the body, under the pretext of serving heaven for the salvation of the soul. These might with strict propriety be termed pious frauds; and I admire the peruvian pair for asserting that they came from the sun,[1] when their conduct proved that they meant to enlighten a benighted country, whose obedience, or even attention, could only be secured by awe.

Thus much for conquering the *inertia* of reason; but, when it is once in motion, fables, once held sacred, may be ridiculed; and sacred they were, when useful to mankind.—Prometheus alone stole fire to animate the first man;[2] his posterity need not supernatural aid to preserve the species, though love is generally termed a flame; and it may not be necessary much longer to suppose men inspired by heaven to inculcate the duties which demand special grace, when reason convinces them that they are the happiest who are the most nobly employed.

In a few days I am to set out for the western part of Norway, and then shall return by land to Gothenburg. I cannot think of leaving this place without regret. I speak of the place before the inhabitants, though there is a tenderness in their artless kindness which attaches me to them; but it is an attachment that inspires a regret very different from that I felt at leaving Hull,[3] in my way to Sweden. The domestic happiness, and good-humoured gaity, of the amiable family where I and my Frances were so hospitably received, would have been sufficient to insure the tenderest remembrance, without the recollection of the social evenings to stimulate it,

when good-breeding gave dignity to sympathy, and wit, zest to reason.

Adieu!—I am just informed that my horse has been waiting this quarter of an hour. I now venture to ride out alone. The steeple serves as a land-mark. I once or twice lost my way, walking alone, without being able to inquire after a path. I was therefore obliged to make to the steeple, or wind-mill, over hedge and ditch.

Your's truly.

LETTER 15

I left Christiania yesterday. The weather was not very fine; and having been a little delayed on the road, I found that it was too late to go round, a couple of miles, to see the cascade near Fredericstadt,[4] which I had determined to visit. Besides, as Fredericstadt is a fortress, it was necessary to arrive there before they shut the gate.

The road along the river is very romantic, though the views are not grand; and the riches of Norway, its timber, floats silently down the stream, often impeded in its course by islands and little cataracts, the offspring, as it were, of the great one I had frequently heard described.

I found an excellent inn at Fredericstadt, and was gratified by the kind attention of the hostess, who, perceiving that my clothes were wet, took great pains to procure me, as a stranger, every comfort for the night.

It had rained very hard; and we passed the ferry in the dark, without getting out of our carriage, which I think wrong, as the horses are sometimes unruly. Fatigue and melancholy, however, had made me regardless whether I went down or across the stream; and I did not know that I was wet before the hostess remarked it. My imagination has never yet severed me from my griefs—and my mind has seldom been so free as to allow my body to be delicate.[5]

---

[1] See Helen Maria Williams,* *Peru: A Poem in Six Cantos* (1784).

[2] Wollstonecraft conflates two stories about the mythical Prometheus: his creation of human beings out of clay and his theft of fire from the gods to benefit humanity.

[3] the port in northeast England where Wollstonecraft began her journey.

---

[4] Fredrikstad, Norway, a town on the eastern shore of the Oslofjord, 100 km (60 miles) south of Oslo.

[5] "'When the mind's free,
   The body's delicate.'
      "Vid. *King Lear*." (M.W.) *King Lear* 3.4.11–12.

How I am altered by disappointment!—When going to Lisbon, the elasticity of my mind was sufficient to ward off weariness, and my imagination still could dip her brush in the rainbow of fancy, and sketch futurity in glowing colours. Now—but let me talk of something else—will you go with me to the cascade?

The cross road to it was rugged and dreary; and though a considerable extent of land was cultivated on all sides, yet the rocks were entirely bare, which surprised me, as they were more on a level with the surface than any I had yet seen. On inquiry, however, I learnt that some years since a forest had been burnt. This appearance of desolation was beyond measure gloomy, inspiring emotions that sterility had never produced. Fires of this kind are occasioned by the wind suddenly rising when the farmers are burning roots of trees, stalks of beans, &c. with which they manure the ground. The devastation must, indeed, be terrible, when this, literally speaking, wild fire, runs along the forest, flying from top to top, and crackling amongst the branches. The soil, as well as the trees, is swept away by the destructive torrent; and the country, despoiled of beauty and riches, is left to mourn for ages.

Admiring, as I do, these noble forests, which seem to bid defiance to time, I looked with pain on the ridge of rocks that stretched far beyond my eye, formerly crowned with the most beautiful verdure.

I have often mentioned the grandeur, but I feel myself unequal to the task of conveying an idea of the beauty and elegance of the scene when the spiral tops of the pines are loaded with ripening seed, and the sun gives a glow to their light green tinge, which is changing into purple, one tree more or less advanced, contrasting with another. The profusion with which nature has decked them, with pendant honours, prevents all surprise at seeing, in every crevice, some sapling struggling for existence. Vast masses of stone are thus encircled; and roots, torn up by the storms, become a shelter for a young generation. The pine and fir woods, left entirely to nature, display an endless variety; and the paths in the wood are not entangled with fallen leaves, which are only interesting whilst they are fluttering between life and death. The grey cobweb-like appearance of the aged pines is a much finer image of decay; the fibres whitening as they lose their moisture, imprisoned life seems to be stealing away. I cannot tell why—but death, under every form, appears to me like something getting free—to expand in I know not what element; nay I feel that this conscious being must be as unfettered, have the wings of thought, before it can be happy.

Reaching the cascade, or rather cataract, the roaring of which had a long time announced its vicinity, my soul was hurried by the falls into a new train of reflections. The impetuous dashing of the rebounding torrent from the dark cavities which mocked the exploring eye, produced an equal activity in my mind: my thoughts darted from earth to heaven, and I asked myself why I was chained to life and its misery? Still the tumultous emotions this sublime object excited, were pleasurable; and, viewing it, my soul rose, with renewed dignity, above its cares—grasping at immortality—it seemed as impossible to stop the current of my thoughts, as of the always varying, still the same, torrent before me—I stretched out my hand to eternity, bounding over the dark speck of life to come.

We turned with regret from the cascade. On a little hill, which commands the best view of it, several obelisks are erected to commemorate the visits of different kings. The appearance of the river above and below the falls is very picturesque, the ruggedness of the scenery disappearing as the torrent subsides into a peaceful stream. But I did not like to see a number of saw-mills crowded together close to the cataracts; they destroyed the harmony of the prospect.

The sight of a bridge erected across a deep valley, at a little distance, inspired very dissimilar sensations. It was most ingeniously supported by mast-like trunks, just stript of their branches; and logs, placed one across the other, produced an appearance equally light and firm, seeming almost to be built in the air when we were below it; the height taking from the magnitude of the supporting trees give them a slender, graceful look.

There are two noble estates in this neighbourhood, the proprietors of which seem to have caught more than their portion of the enterprising spirit that is gone abroad. Many agricultural experiments have been made; and the country appears better enclosed and cultivated;

yet the cottages had not the comfortable aspect of those I had observed near Moss,[1] and to the westward. Man is always debased by servitude, of any description; and here the peasantry are not entirely free.

Adieu!

I almost forgot to tell you, that I did not leave Norway without making some inquiries after the monsters said to have been seen in the northern sea; but though I conversed with several captains, I could not meet with one who had ever heard any traditional description of them, much less had any ocular demonstration of their existence. Till the fact be better ascertained, I should think the account of them ought to be torn out of our Geographical Grammars.

from *Posthumous Works of the Author of* A Vindication of the Rights of Woman (1798)

from *The Wrongs of Woman: or Maria. A Fragment*[2]

CHAPTER 5

"My father," said Jemima, "seduced my mother, a pretty girl, with whom he lived fellow-servant; and she no sooner perceived the natural, the dreaded consequence, than the terrible conviction flashed on her— that she was ruined. Honesty, and a regard for her reputation, had been the only principles inculcated by her mother; and they had been so forcibly impressed, that she feared shame, more than the poverty to which it would lead. Her incessant importunities to prevail upon my father to screen her from reproach by marrying her, as he had promised in the fervour of seduction, estranged him from her so completely, that her very person became distasteful to him; and he began to hate, as well as despise me, before I was born.

"My mother, grieved to the soul by his neglect, and unkind treatment, actually resolved to famish herself; and injured her health by the attempt; though she had not sufficient resolution to adhere to her project, or renounce it entirely. Death came not at her call; yet sorrow, and the methods she adopted to conceal her condition, still doing the work of a house-maid, had such an effect on her constitution, that she died in the wretched garret, where her virtuous mistress had forced her to take refuge in the very pangs of labour, though my father, after a slight reproof, was allowed to remain in his place—allowed by the mother of six children, who, scarcely permitting a footstep to be heard, during her month's indulgence, felt no sympathy for the poor wretch, denied every comfort required by her situation.

"The day my mother died, the ninth after my birth, I was consigned to the care of the cheapest nurse my father could find; who suckled her own child at the same time, and lodged as many more as she could get, in two cellar-like apartments.

"Poverty, and the habit of seeing children die off her hands, had so hardened her heart, that the office of a mother did not awaken the tenderness of a woman; nor were the feminine caresses which seem a part of the rearing of a child, ever bestowed on me. The chicken has a wing to shelter under; but I had no bosom to nestle in, no kindred warmth to foster me. Left in dirt, to cry with cold and hunger till I was weary, and sleep without ever being prepared by exercise, or lulled by kindness to rest; could I be expected to become any thing but a weak and rickety babe? Still, in spite of neglect, I continued to exist, to learn to curse existence," [her countenance grew ferocious as she spoke,] "and the treatment that rendered me miserable, seemed to sharpen my wits. Confined then in a damp hovel, to rock the cradle of the succeeding tribe, I looked like a little old woman, or a hag shrivelling into nothing. The furrows of reflection and care contracted the youthful cheek, and gave a sort of supernatural wildness to the

---

[1] a coastal town on the eastern shore of the Oslofjord near Oslo, Norway.

[2] Wollstonecraft's unfinished novel about the oppression of women, both middle-class and socially marginal, was published posthumously (1798) with editorial interpolations by William Godwin. It tells the story of Maria, a woman separated from her infant daughter and imprisoned in a madhouse by her avaricious and cruel husband. There she writes her story so that her daughter may someday know the truth. Jemima, who guards Maria in the asylum, comes to pity her, and eventually relates the story of her own life to Maria and to Henry Darnford, another inmate and, later, Maria's lover.

ever watchful eye. During this period, my father had married another fellow-servant, who loved him less, and knew better how to manage his passion, than my mother. She likewise proving with child, they agreed to keep a shop: my step-mother, if, being an illegitimate offspring, I may venture thus to characterize her, having obtained a sum of a rich relation, for that purpose.

"Soon after her lying-in, she prevailed on my father to take me home, to save the expence of maintaining me, and of hiring a girl to assist her in the care of the child. I was young, it was true, but appeared a knowing little thing, and might be made handy. Accordingly I was brought to her house; but not to a home—for a home I never knew. Of this child, a daughter, she was extravagantly fond; and it was a part of my employment, to assist to spoil her, by humouring all her whims, and bearing all her caprices. Feeling her own consequence, before she could speak, she had learned the art of tormenting me, and if I ever dared to resist, I received blows, laid on with no compunctious hand, or was sent to bed dinnerless, as well as supperless. I said that it was a part of my daily labour to attend this child, with the servility of a slave; still it was but a part. I was sent out in all seasons, and from place to place, to carry burdens far above my strength, without being allowed to draw near the fire, or ever being cheered by encouragement or kindness. No wonder then, treated like a creature of another species, that I began to envy, and at length to hate, the darling of the house. Yet, I perfectly remember, that it was the caresses, and kind expressions of my step-mother, which first excited my jealous discontent. Once, I cannot forget it, when she was calling in vain her wayward child to kiss her, I ran to her, saying, 'I will kiss you, ma'am!' and how did my heart, which was in my mouth, sink, what was my debasement of soul, when pushed away with—'I do not want you, pert thing!' Another day, when a new gown had excited the highest good humour, and she uttered the appropriate *dear*, addressed unexpectedly to me, I thought I could never do enough to please her; I was all alacrity, and rose proportionably in my own estimation.

"As her daughter grew up, she was pampered with cakes and fruit, while I was, literally speaking, fed with the refuse of the table, with her leavings. A liquorish tooth[1] is, I believe, common to children, and I used to steal any thing sweet, that I could catch up with a chance of concealment. When detected, she was not content to chastize me herself at the moment, but, on my father's return in the evening (he was a shopman), the principal discourse was to recount my faults, and attribute them to the wicked disposition which I had brought into the world with me, inherited from my mother. He did not fail to leave the marks of his resentment on my body, and then solaced himself by playing with my sister.—I could have murdered her at those moments. To save myself from these unmerciful corrections, I resorted to falshood, and the untruths which I sturdily maintained, were brought in judgment against me, to support my tyrant's inhuman charge of my natural propensity to vice. Seeing me treated with contempt, and always being fed and dressed better, my sister conceived a contemptuous opinion of me, that proved an obstacle to all affection; and my father, hearing continually of my faults, began to consider me as a curse entailed on him for his sins: he was therefore easily prevailed on to bind me apprentice to one of my step-mother's friends, who kept a slop-shop in Wapping.[2] I was represented (as it was said) in my true colours; but she, 'warranted,' snapping her fingers, 'that she should break my spirit or heart.'

"My mother replied, with a whine, 'that if any body could make me better, it was such a clever woman as herself; though, for her own part, she had tried in vain; but good-nature was her fault.'

"I shudder with horror, when I recollect the treatment I had now to endure. Not only under the lash of my task-mistress, but the drudge of the maid, apprentices and children, I never had a taste of human kindness to soften the rigour of perpetual labour. I had been introduced as an object of abhorrence into the family; as a creature of whom my step-mother, though she had been kind enough to let me live in the house with her own child, could make nothing. I was described as a

---

[1] sweet tooth.

[2] a shop selling cheap clothes to lower-class people and sailors, in the dock-side area of London, on the north side of the Thames east of the Tower.

wretch, whose nose must be kept to the grinding stone—and it was held there with an iron grasp. It seemed indeed the privilege of their superior nature to kick me about, like the dog or cat. If I were attentive, I was called fawning, if refractory, an obstinate mule, and like a mule I received their censure on my loaded back. Often has my mistress, for some instance of forgetfulness, thrown me from one side of the kitchen to the other, knocked my head against the wall, spit in my face, with various refinements on barbarity that I forbear to enumerate, though they were all acted over again by the servant, with additional insults, to which the appellation of *bastard*, was commonly added, with taunts or sneers. But I will not attempt to give you an adequate idea of my situation, lest you, who probably have never been drenched with the dregs of human misery, should think I exaggerate.

"I stole now, from absolute necessity,—bread; yet whatever else was taken, which I had it not in my power to take, was ascribed to me. I was the filching cat, the ravenous dog, the dumb brute, who must bear all; for if I endeavoured to exculpate myself, I was silenced, without any enquiries being made, with 'Hold your tongue, you never tell truth.' Even the very air I breathed was tainted with scorn; for I was sent to the neighbouring shops with Glutton, Liar, or Thief, written on my forehead. This was, at first, the most bitter punishment; but sullen pride, or a kind of stupid desperation, made me, at length, almost regardless of the contempt, which had wrung from me so many solitary tears at the only moments when I was allowed to rest.

"Thus was I the mark of cruelty till my sixteenth year; and then I have only to point out a change of misery; for a period I never knew. Allow me first to make one observation. Now I look back, I cannot help attributing the greater part of my misery, to the misfortune of having been thrown into the world without the grand support of life—a mother's affection. I had no one to love me; or to make me respected, to enable me to acquire respect. I was an egg dropped on the sand; a pauper by nature, hunted from family to family, who belonged to nobody—and nobody cared for me. I was despised from my birth, and denied the chance of obtaining a footing for myself in society. Yes; I had not even the chance of being considered as a fellow-creature—yet all the people with whom I lived, brutalized as they were by the low cunning of trade, and the despicable shifts of poverty, were not without bowels, though they never yearned for me. I was, in fact, born a slave, and chained by infamy to slavery during the whole of existence, without having any companions to alleviate it by sympathy, or teach me how to rise above it by their example. But, to resume the thread of my tale—

"At sixteen, I suddenly grew tall, and something like comeliness appeared on a Sunday, when I had time to wash my face, and put on clean clothes. My master had once or twice caught hold of me in the passage; but I instinctively avoided his disgusting caresses. One day however, when the family were at a methodist meeting,[1] he contrived to be alone in the house with me, and by blows—yes; blows and menaces, compelled me to submit to his ferocious desire; and, to avoid my mistress's fury, I was obliged in future to comply, and skulk to my loft at his command, in spite of increasing loathing.

"The anguish which was now pent up in my bosom, seemed to open a new world to me: I began to extend my thoughts beyond myself, and grieve for human misery, till I discovered, with horror—ah! what horror!—that I was with child. I know not why I felt a mixed sensation of despair and tenderness, excepting that, ever called a bastard, a bastard appeared to me an object of the greatest compassion in creation.

"I communicated this dreadful circumstance to my master, who was almost equally alarmed at the intelligence; for he feared his wife, and public censure at the meeting. After some weeks of deliberation had elapsed, I in continual fear that my altered shape would be noticed, my master gave me a medicine in a phial, which he desired me to take, telling me, without any circumlocution, for what purpose it was designed.[2] I burst into tears, I thought it was killing myself—yet was such a self as I worth preserving? He cursed me for a

---

[1] an evangelical religious meeting of the kind that attracted large numbers of working people. In this context, Wollstonecraft perhaps implies that religion has no necessary effect on morality.

[2] to induce miscarriage.

fool, and left me to my own reflections. I could not resolve to take this infernal potion; but I wrapped it up in an old gown, and hid it in a corner of my box.

"Nobody yet suspected me, because they had been accustomed to view me as a creature of another species. But the threatening storm at last broke over my devoted head—never shall I forget it! One Sunday evening when I was left, as usual, to take care of the house, my master came home intoxicated, and I became the prey of his brutal appetite. His extreme intoxication made him forget his customary caution, and my mistress entered and found us in a situation that could not have been more hateful to her than me. Her husband was 'pot-valiant,'[1] he feared her not at the moment, nor had he then much reason, for she instantly turned the whole force of her anger another way. She tore off my cap, scratched, kicked, and buffetted me, till she had exhausted her strength, declaring, as she rested her arm, 'that I had wheedled her husband from her.—But, could any thing better be expected from a wretch, whom she had taken into her house out of pure charity?' What a torrent of abuse rushed out? till, almost breathless, she concluded with saying, 'that I was born a strumpet; it ran in my blood, and nothing good could come to those who harboured me.'

"My situation was, of course, discovered, and she declared that I should not stay another night under the same roof with an honest family. I was therefore pushed out of doors, and my trumpery thrown after me, when it had been contemptuously examined in the passage, lest I should have stolen any thing.

"Behold me then in the street, utterly destitute! Whither could I creep for shelter? To my father's roof I had no claim, when not pursued by shame—now I shrunk back as from death, from my mother's cruel reproaches, my father's execrations. I could not endure to hear him curse the day I was born, though life had been a curse to me. Of death I thought, but with a confused emotion of terror, as I stood leaning my head on a post, and starting at every footstep, lest it should be my mistress coming to tear my heart out. One of the boys of the shop passing by, heard my tale, and immediately repaired to his master, to give him a description of my situation; and he touched the right key—the scandal it would give rise to, if I were left to repeat my tale to every enquirer. This plea came home to his reason, who had been sobered by his wife's rage, the fury of which fell on him when I was out of her reach, and he sent the boy to me with half-a-guinea, desiring him to conduct me to a house, where beggars, and other wretches, the refuse of society, nightly lodged.

"This night was spent in a state of stupefaction, or desperation. I detested mankind, and abhorred myself.

"In the morning I ventured out, to throw myself in my master's way, at his usual hour of going abroad. I approached him, he 'damned me for a b———, declared I had disturbed the peace of the family, and that he had sworn to his wife, never to take any more notice of me.' He left me; but, instantly returning, he told me that he should speak to his friend, a parish-officer,[2] to get a nurse for the brat I laid to him; and advised me, if I wished to keep out of the house of correction, not to make free with his name.

"I hurried back to my hole, and, rage giving place to despair, sought for the potion that was to procure abortion, and swallowed it, with a wish that it might destroy me, at the same time that it stopped the sensations of new-born life, which I felt with indescribable emotion. My head turned round, my heart grew sick, and in the horrors of approaching dissolution, mental anguish was swallowed up. The effect of the medicine was violent, and I was confined to my bed several days; but, youth and a strong constitution prevailing, I once more crawled out, to ask myself the cruel question, 'Whither I should go?' I had but two shillings left in my pocket, the rest had been expended, by a poor woman who slept in the same room, to pay for my lodging, and purchase the necessaries of which she partook.

"With this wretch I went into the neighbouring streets to beg, and my disconsolate appearance drew a few pence from the idle, enabling me still to command a bed; till, recovering from my illness, and taught to put on my rags to the best advantage, I was accosted from

---

[1] made courageous by liquor.

[2] an official who exercised the parish's responsibility to provide for the poor. A "poor tax" was imposed on parishioners for this purpose; however, many ended up in the workhouse or house of correction.

different motives, and yielded to the desire of the brutes I met, with the same detestation that I had felt for my still more brutal master. I have since read in novels of the blandishments of seduction, but I had not even the pleasure of being enticed into vice.

"I shall not," interrupted Jemima, "lead your imagination into all the scenes of wretchedness and depravity, which I was condemned to view; or mark the different stages of my debasing misery. Fate dragged me through the very kennels of society; I was still a slave, a bastard, a common property. Become familiar with vice, for I wish to conceal nothing from you, I picked the pockets of the drunkards who abused me; and proved by my conduct, that I deserved the epithets, with which they loaded me at moments when distrust ought to cease.

"Detesting my nightly occupation, though valuing, if I may so use the word, my independence, which only consisted in choosing the street in which I should wander, or the roof, when I had money, in which I should hide my head, I was some time before I could prevail on myself to accept of a place in a house of ill fame, to which a girl, with whom I had accidentally conversed in the street, had recommended me. I had been hunted almost into a fever, by the watchmen of the quarter of the town I frequented; one, whom I had unwittingly offended, giving the word to the whole pack. You can scarcely conceive the tyranny exercised by these wretches: considering themselves as the instruments of the very laws they violate, the pretext which steels their conscience, hardens their heart. Not content with receiving from us, outlaws of society (let other women talk of favours), a brutal gratification gratuitously as a privilege of office, they extort a tithe of prostitution, and harrass with threats the poor creatures whose occupation affords not the means to silence the growl of avarice. To escape from this persecution, I once more entered into servitude.

"A life of comparative regularity restored my health; and—do not start—my manners were improved, in a situation where vice sought to render itself alluring, and taste was cultivated to fashion the person, if not to refine the mind. Besides, the common civility of speech, contrasted with the gross vulgarity to which I had been accustomed, was something like the polish of civilization. I was not shut out from all intercourse of humanity. Still I was galled by the yoke of service, and my mistress often flying into violent fits of passion, made me dread a sudden dismission, which I understood was always the case. I was therefore prevailed on, though I felt a horror of men, to accept the offer of a gentleman, rather in the decline of years, to keep his house, pleasantly situated in a little village near Hampstead.[1]

"He was a man of great talents, and of brilliant wit; but, a worn-out votary of voluptuousness, his desires became fastidious in proportion as they grew weak, and the native tenderness of his heart was undermined by a vitiated imagination. A thoughtless career of libertinism and social enjoyment, had injured his health to such a degree, that, whatever pleasure his conversation afforded me (and my esteem was ensured by proofs of the generous humanity of his disposition), the being his mistress was purchasing it at a very dear rate. With such a keen perception of the delicacies of sentiment, with an imagination invigorated by the exercise of genius, how could he sink into the grossness of sensuality!

"But, to pass over a subject which I recollect with pain, I must remark to you, as an answer to your often-repeated question, 'Why my sentiments and language were superior to my station?' that I now began to read, to beguile the tediousness of solitude, and to gratify an inquisitive, active mind. I had often, in my childhood, followed a ballad-singer, to hear the sequel of a dismal story, though sure of being severely punished for delaying to return with whatever I was sent to purchase. I could just spell and put a sentence together, and I listened to the various arguments, though often mingled with obscenity, which occurred at the table where I was allowed to preside: for a literary friend or two frequently came home with my master, to dine and pass the night. Having lost the privileged respect of my sex, my presence, instead of restraining, perhaps gave the reins to their tongues; still I had the advantage of hearing discussions, from which, in the common course of life, women are excluded.

"You may easily imagine, that it was only by degrees that I could comprehend some of the subjects they

---

[1] at that time, a northern suburb of London.

investigated, or acquire from their reasoning what might be termed a moral sense. But my fondness of reading increasing, and my master occasionally shutting himself up in this retreat, for weeks together, to write, I had many opportunities of improvement. At first, considering money (I was right!" exclaimed Jemima, altering her tone of voice) "as the only means, after my loss of reputation, of obtaining respect, or even the toleration of humanity, I had not the least scruple to secrete a part of the sums intrusted to me, and to screen myself from detection by a system of falshood. But, acquiring new principles, I began to have the ambition of returning to the respectable part of society, and was weak enough to suppose it possible. The attention of my unassuming instructor, who, without being ignorant of his own powers, possessed great simplicity of manners, strengthened the illusion. Having sometimes caught up hints for thought, from my untutored remarks, he often led me to discuss the subjects he was treating, and would read to me his productions, previous to their publication, wishing to profit by the criticism of unsophisticated feeling. The aim of his writings was to touch the simple springs of the heart; for he despised the would-be oracles, the self-elected philosophers, who fright away fancy, while sifting each grain of thought to prove that slowness of comprehension is wisdom.

"I should have distinguished this as a moment of sunshine, a happy period in my life, had not the repugnance the disgusting libertinism of my protector inspired, daily become more painful.—And, indeed, I soon did recollect it as such with agony, when his sudden death (for he had recourse to the most exhilarating cordials to keep up the convivial tone of his spirits) again threw me into the desert of human society. Had he had any time for reflection, I am certain he would have left the little property in his power to me: but, attacked by the fatal apoplexy[1] in town, his heir, a man of rigid morals, brought his wife with him to take possession of the house and effects, before I was even informed of his death,—'to prevent,' as she took care indirectly to tell me, 'such a creature as she supposed me to be, from purloining any of them, had I been apprized of the event in time.'

"The grief I felt at the sudden shock the information gave me, which at first had nothing selfish in it, was treated with contempt, and I was ordered to pack up my clothes; and a few trinkets and books, given me by the generous deceased, were contested, while they piously hoped, with a reprobating shake of the head, 'that God would have mercy on his sinful soul!' With some difficulty, I obtained my arrears of wages; but asking—such is the spirit-grinding consequence of poverty and infamy—for a character for honesty and economy, which God knows I merited, I was told by this—why must I call her a woman?—'that it would go against her conscience to recommend a kept mistress.' Tears started in my eyes, burning tears; for there are situations in which a wretch is humbled by the contempt they are conscious they do not deserve.

"I returned to the metropolis; but the solitude of a poor lodging was inconceivably dreary, after the society I had enjoyed. To be cut off from human converse, now I had been taught to relish it, was to wander a ghost among the living. Besides, I foresaw, to aggravate the severity of my fate, that my little pittance would soon melt away. I endeavoured to obtain needlework; but, not having been taught early, and my hands being rendered clumsy by hard work, I did not sufficiently excel to be employed by the ready-made linen shops, when so many women, better qualified, were suing for it. The want of a character prevented my getting a place; for, irksome as servitude would have been to me, I should have made another trial, had it been feasible. Not that I disliked employment, but the inequality of condition to which I must have submitted. I had acquired a taste for literature, during the five years I had lived with a literary man, occasionally conversing with men of the first abilities of the age; and now to descend to the lowest vulgarity, was a degree of wretchedness not to be imagined unfelt. I had not, it is true, tasted the charms of affection, but I had been familiar with the graces of humanity.

"One of the gentlemen, whom I had frequently dined in company with, while I was treated like a companion, met me in the street, and enquired after my health. I seized the occasion, and began to describe my

---

[1] a stroke.

situation; but he was in haste to join, at dinner, a select party of choice spirits; therefore, without waiting to hear me, he impatiently put a guinea into my hand, saying, 'It was a pity such a sensible woman should be in distress—he wished me well from his soul.'

"To another I wrote, stating my case, and requesting advice. He was an advocate for unequivocal sincerity; and had often, in my presence, descanted on the evils which arise in society from the despotism of rank and riches.

"In reply, I received a long essay on the energy of the human mind, with continual allusions to his own force of character. He added, 'That the woman who could write such a letter as I had sent him, could never be in want of resources, were she to look into herself, and exert her powers; misery was the consequence of indolence, and, as to my being shut out from society, it was the lot of man to submit to certain privations.'

"How often have I heard," said Jemima, interrupting her narrative, "in conversation, and read in books, that every person willing to work may find employment? It is the vague assertion, I believe, of insensible indolence, when it relates to men; but, with respect to women, I am sure of its fallacy, unless they will submit to the most menial bodily labour; and even to be employed at hard labour is out of the reach of many, whose reputation misfortune or folly has tainted.

"How writers, professing to be friends to freedom, and the improvement of morals, can assert that poverty is no evil, I cannot imagine."

"No more can I," interrupted Maria; "yet they even expatiate on the peculiar happiness of indigence, though in what it can consist, excepting in brutal rest, when a man can barely earn a subsistence, I cannot imagine. The mind is necessarily imprisoned in its own little tenement; and, fully occupied by keeping it in repair, has not time to rove abroad for improvement. The book of knowledge is closely clasped, against those who must fulfil their daily task of severe manual labour or die; and curiosity, rarely excited by thought or information, seldom moves on the stagnate lake of ignorance."

"As far as I have been able to observe," replied Jemima, "prejudices, caught up by chance, are obstinately maintained by the poor, to the exclusion of improvement; they have not time to reason or reflect to any extent, or minds sufficiently exercised to adopt the principles of action, which form perhaps the only basis of contentment in every station."[1]

"And independence," said Darnford, "they are necessarily strangers to, even the independence of despising their persecutors. If the poor are happy, or can be happy, *things are very well as they are*.[2] And I cannot conceive on what principle those writers contend for a change of system, who support this opinion. The authors on the other side of the question are much more consistent, who grant the fact; yet, insisting that it is the lot of the majority to be oppressed in this life, kindly turn them over to another, to rectify the false weights and measures of this, as the only way to justify the dispensations of Providence. I have not," continued Darnford, "an opinion more firmly fixed by observation in my mind, than that, though riches may fail to produce proportionate happiness, poverty most commonly excludes it, by shutting up all the avenues to improvement."

"And as for the affections," added Maria, with a sigh, "how gross, and even tormenting do they become, unless regulated by an improving mind! The culture of the heart ever, I believe, keeps pace with that of the mind. But pray go on," addressing Jemima, "though your narrative gives rise to the most painful reflections on the present state of society."

"Not to trouble you," continued she, "with a detailed description of all the painful feelings of unavailing exertion, I have only to tell you, that at last I got recommended to wash in a few families, who did me the favour to admit me into their houses, without the most strict enquiry, to wash from one in the morning till eight at night, for eighteen or twenty-pence a day. On the happiness to be enjoyed over a washing-tub I need

---

[1] "The copy which appears to have received the author's last corrections, ends at this place." (W.G.)

[2] a notion vehemently opposed by William Godwin and other radicals of the 1790s who advocated for change. The full title of Godwin's first novel (1794) was *Things As They Are; or, The Adventures of Caleb Williams*.

not comment; yet you will allow me to observe, that this was a wretchedness of situation peculiar to my sex. A man with half my industry, and, I may say, abilities, could have procured a decent livelihood, and discharged some of the duties which knit mankind together; whilst I, who had acquired a taste for the rational, nay, in honest pride let me assert it, the virtuous enjoyments of life, was cast aside as the filth of society. Condemned to labour, like a machine, only to earn bread, and scarcely that, I became melancholy and desperate.

"I have now to mention a circumstance which fills me with remorse, and fear it will entirely deprive me of your esteem. A tradesman became attached to me, and visited me frequently,—and I at last obtained such a power over him, that he offered to take me home to his house.—Consider, dear madam, I was famishing: wonder not that I became a wolf!—The only reason for not taking me home immediately, was the having a girl in the house, with child by him—and this girl—I advised him—yes, I did! would I could forget it!—to turn out of doors: and one night he determined to follow my advice. Poor wretch! she fell upon her knees, reminded him that he had promised to marry her, that her parents were honest!—What did it avail?—She was turned out.

"She approached her father's door, in the skirts of London,—listened at the shutters,—but could not knock. A watchman had observed her go and return several times—Poor wretch!"—[The remorse Jemima spoke of, seemed to be stinging her to the soul, as she proceeded.]

"She left it, and, approaching a tub where horses were watered, she sat down in it, and, with desperate resolution, remained in that attitude—till resolution was no longer necessary!

"I happened that morning to be going out to wash, anticipating the moment when I should escape from such hard labour. I passed by, just as some men, going to work, drew out the stiff, cold corpse—Let me not recal the horrid moment!—I recognized her pale visage; I listened to the tale told by the spectators, and my heart did not burst. I thought of my own state, and wondered how I could be such a monster!—I worked hard; and, returning home, I was attacked by a fever. I suffered both in body and mind. I determined not to live with the wretch. But he did not try me; he left the neighbourhood. I once more returned to the wash-tub.

"Still this state, miserable as it was, admitted of aggravation. Lifting one day a heavy load, a tub fell against my shin, and gave me great pain. I did not pay much attention to the hurt, till it became a serious wound; being obliged to work as usual, or starve. But, finding myself at length unable to stand for any time, I thought of getting into an hospital. Hospitals, it should seem (for they are comfortless abodes for the sick) were expressly endowed for the reception of the friendless; yet I, who had on that plea a right to assistance, wanted the recommendation of the rich and respectable, and was several weeks languishing for admittance; fees were demanded on entering; and, what was still more unreasonable, security for burying me, that expence not coming into the letter of the charity. A guinea was the stipulated sum—I could as soon have raised a million; and I was afraid to apply to the parish for an order, lest they should have passed me, I knew not whither. The poor woman at whose house I lodged, compassionating my state, got me into the hospital; and the family where I received the hurt, sent me five shillings, three and six-pence of which I gave at my admittance—I know not for what.

"My leg grew quickly better; but I was dismissed before my cure was completed, because I could not afford to have my linen washed to appear decently, as the virago of a nurse said, when the gentlemen (the surgeons) came. I cannot give you an adequate idea of the wretchedness of an hospital; every thing is left to the care of people intent on gain. The attendants seem to have lost all feeling of compassion in the bustling discharge of their offices; death is so familiar to them, that they are not anxious to ward it off. Every thing appeared to be conducted for the accommodation of the medical men and their pupils, who came to make experiments on the poor, for the benefit of the rich. One of the physicians, I must not forget to mention, gave me half-a-crown, and ordered me some wine, when I was at the lowest ebb. I thought of making my case known to the lady-like matron; but her forbidding countenance prevented me. She condescended to look on the patients, and make general enquiries, two or three times a week; but the nurses knew the hour when the visit of ceremony would commence, and every thing was as it should be.

"After my dismission, I was more at a loss than ever for a subsistence, and, not to weary you with a repetition of the same unavailing attempts, unable to stand at the washing-tub, I began to consider the rich and poor as natural enemies, and became a thief from principle. I could not now cease to reason, but I hated mankind. I despised myself, yet I justified my conduct. I was taken, tried, and condemned to six months' imprisonment in a house of correction. My soul recoils with horror from the remembrance of the insults I had to endure, till, branded with shame, I was turned loose in the street, pennyless. I wandered from street to street, till, exhausted by hunger and fatigue, I sunk down senseless at a door, where I had vainly demanded a morsel of bread. I was sent by the inhabitant to the work-house, to which he had surlily bid me go, saying, he 'paid enough in conscience to the poor,' when, with parched tongue, I implored his charity. If those well-meaning people who exclaim against beggars, were acquainted with the treatment the poor receive in many of these wretched asylums, they would not stifle so easily involuntary sympathy, by saying that they have all parishes to go to, or wonder that the poor dread to enter the gloomy walls. What are the common run of work-houses, but prisons, in which many respectable old people, worn out by immoderate labour, sink into the grave in sorrow, to which they are carried like dogs!"

Alarmed by some indistinct noise, Jemima rose hastily to listen, and Maria, turning to Darnford, said, "I have indeed been shocked beyond expression when I have met a pauper's funeral. A coffin carried on the shoulders of three or four ill-looking wretches, whom the imagination might easily convert into a band of assassins, hastening to conceal the corpse, and quarrelling about the prey on their way. I know it is of little consequence how we are consigned to the earth; but I am led by this brutal insensibility, to what even the animal creation appears forcibly to feel, to advert to the wretched, deserted manner in which they died."

"True," rejoined Darnford, "and, till the rich will give more than a part of their wealth, till they will give time and attention to the wants of the distressed, never let them boast of charity. Let them open their hearts, and not their purses, and employ their minds in the service, if they are really actuated by humanity; or charitable institutions will always be the prey of the lowest order of knaves."

Jemima returning, seemed in haste to finish her tale. "The overseer farmed the poor of different parishes, and out of the bowels of poverty was wrung the money with which he purchased this dwelling, as a private receptacle for madness. He had been a keeper at a house of the same description, and conceived that he could make money much more readily in his old occupation. He is a shrewd—shall I say it?—villain. He observed something resolute in my manner, and offered to take me with him, and instruct me how to treat the disturbed minds he meant to intrust to my care. The offer of forty pounds a year, and to quit a workhouse, was not to be despised, though the condition of shutting my eyes and hardening my heart was annexed to it.

"I agreed to accompany him; and four years have I been attendant on many wretches, and"—she lowered her voice,—"the witness of many enormities. In solitude my mind seemed to recover its force, and many of the sentiments which I imbibed in the only tolerable period of my life, returned with their full force. Still what should induce me to be the champion for suffering humanity?—Who ever risked any thing for me?—Who ever acknowledged me to be a fellow-creature?"—

Maria took her hand, and Jemima, more overcome by kindness than she had ever been by cruelty, hastened out of the room to conceal her emotions.

Darnford soon after heard his summons, and, taking leave of him, Maria promised to gratify his curiosity, with respect to herself, the first opportunity.

On Poetry, and Our Relish for the Beauties of Nature

A taste for rural scenes, in the present state of society, appears to be very often an artificial sentiment, rather inspired by poetry and romances, than a real perception of the beauties of nature. But, as it is reckoned a proof of refined taste to praise the calm pleasures which the country affords, the theme is never exhausted. Yet it may be made a question, whether this romantic kind of declamation, has much effect on the conduct of those, who leave, for a season, the crowded cities in which they were bred.

I have been led to these reflections, by observing, when I have resided for any length of time in the country, how few people seem to contemplate nature with their own eyes. I have "brushed the dew away" in the morning; but, pacing over the printless grass, I have wondered that, in such delightful situations, the sun was allowed to rise in solitary majesty, whilst my eyes alone hailed its beautifying beams. The webs of the evening have still been spread across the hedged path, unless some labouring man, trudging to work, disturbed the fairy structure; yet, in spite of this supineness, when I joined the social circle, every tongue rang changes on the pleasures of the country.

Having frequently had occasion to make the same observation, I was led to endeavour, in one of my solitary rambles, to trace the cause, and likewise to enquire why the poetry written in the infancy of society, is most natural: which, strictly speaking (for *natural* is a very indefinite expression) is merely to say, that it is the transcript of immediate sensations, in all their native wildness and simplicity, when fancy, awakened by the sight of interesting objects, was most actively at work. At such moments, sensibility quickly furnishes similes, and the sublimated spirits combine images, which rising spontaneously, it is not necessary coldly to ransack the understanding or memory, till the laborious efforts of judgment exclude present sensations, and damp the fire of enthusiasm.

The effusions of a vigorous mind, will ever tell us how far the understanding has been enlarged by thought, and stored with knowledge. The richness of the soil even appears on the surface; and the result of profound thinking, often mixing, with playful grace, in the reveries of the poet, smoothly incorporates with the ebullitions of animal spirits, when the finely fashioned nerve vibrates acutely with rapture, or when, relaxed by soft melancholy, a pleasing languor prompts the long-drawn sigh, and feeds the slowly falling tear.

The poet, the man of strong feelings, gives us only an image of his mind, when he was actually alone, conversing with himself, and marking the impression which nature had made on his own heart.—If, at this sacred moment, the idea of some departed friend, some tender recollection when the soul was most alive to tenderness, intruded unawares into his thoughts, the sorrow which it produced is artlessly, yet poetically expressed—and who can avoid sympathizing?

Love to man leads to devotion—grand and sublime images strike the imagination—God is seen in every floating cloud, and comes from the misty mountain to receive the noblest homage of an intelligent creature—praise. How solemn is the moment, when all affections and remembrances fade before the sublime admiration which the wisdom and goodness of God inspires, when he is worshipped in a *temple not made with hands*,[1] and the world seems to contain only the mind that formed, and the mind that contemplates it! These are not the weak responses of ceremonial devotion; nor, to express them, would the poet need another poet's aid: his heart burns within him, and he speaks the language of truth and nature with resistless energy.

Inequalities, of course, are observable in his effusions; and a less vigorous fancy, with more taste, would have produced more elegance and uniformity; but, as passages are softened or expunged during the cooler moments of reflection, the understanding is gratified at the expence of those involuntary sensations, which, like the beauteous tints of an evening sky, are so evanescent, that they melt into new forms before they can be analyzed. For however eloquently we may boast of our reason, man must often be delighted he cannot tell why, or his blunt feelings are not made to relish the beauties which nature, poetry, or any of the imitative arts, afford.

---

[1] Cf. Mark 14.58.

The imagery of the ancients seems naturally to have been borrowed from surrounding objects and their mythology. When a hero is to be transported from one place to another, across pathless wastes, is any vehicle so natural, as one of the fleecy clouds on which the poet has often gazed, scarcely conscious that he wished to make it his chariot? Again, when nature seems to present obstacles to his progress at almost every step, when the tangled forest and steep mountain stand as barriers, to pass over which the mind longs for supernatural aid; an interposing deity, who walks on the waves, and rules the storm,[1] severely felt in the first attempts to cultivate a country, will receive from the impassioned fancy "a local habitation and a name."[2]

It would be a philosophical enquiry, and throw some light on the history of the human mind, to trace, as far as our information will allow us to trace, the spontaneous feelings and ideas which have produced the images that now frequently appear unnatural, because they are remote; and disgusting, because they have been servilely copied by poets, whose habits of thinking, and views of nature must have been different; for, though the understanding seldom disturbs the current of our present feelings, without dissipating the gay clouds which fancy has been embracing, yet it silently gives the colour to the whole tenour of them, and the dream is over, when truth is grossly violated, or images introduced, selected from books, and not from local manners or popular prejudices.

In a more advanced state of civilization, a poet is rather the creature of art, than of nature. The books that he reads in his youth, become a hot-bed in which artificial fruits are produced, beautiful to the common eye, though they want the true hue and flavour. His images do not arise from sensations; they are copies; and, like the works of the painters who copy ancient statues when they draw men and women of their own times, we acknowledge that the features are fine, and the proportions just; yet they are men of stone; insipid figures, that never convey to the mind the idea of a portrait taken from life, where the soul gives spirit and homogeneity to the whole. The silken wings of fancy are shrivelled by rules; and a desire of attaining elegance of diction, occasions an attention to words, incompatible with sublime, impassioned thoughts.

A boy of abilities, who has been taught the structure of verse at school, and been roused by emulation to compose rhymes whilst he was reading works of genius, may, by practice, produce pretty verses, and even become what is often termed an elegant poet: yet his readers, without knowing what to find fault with, do not find themselves warmly interested. In the works of the poets who fasten on their affections, they see grosser faults, and the very images which shock their taste in the modern; still they do not appear as puerile or extrinsic in one as the other.—Why?—because they did not appear so to the author.

It may sound paradoxical, after observing that those productions want vigour, that are merely the work of imitation, in which the understanding has violently directed, if not extinguished, the blaze of fancy, to assert, that, though genius be only another word for exquisite sensibility, the first observers of nature, the true poets, exercised their understanding much more than their imitators. But they exercised it to discriminate things, whilst their followers were busy to borrow sentiments and arrange words.

Boys who have received a classical education, load their memory with words, and the correspondent ideas are perhaps never distinctly comprehended. As a proof of this assertion, I must observe, that I have known many young people who could write tolerably smooth verses, and string epithets prettily together, when their prose themes showed the barrenness of their minds, and how superficial the cultivation must have been, which their understanding had received.

Dr. Johnson, I know, has given a definition of genius, which would overturn my reasoning, if I were to admit it.—He imagines, that *a strong mind, accidentally led to some particular study* in which it excels is a genius.—Not to stop to investigate the causes which produced this happy *strength* of mind, experience seems to prove, that those minds have appeared most vigorous, that have pursued a study, after nature had discovered a bent; for it would be absurd to suppose, that a slight

---

[1] Cf. William Cowper,* "Light Shining out of Darkness" (1779) 3–4.

[2] Shakespeare, *A Midsummer Night's Dream* 5.1.17

impression made on the weak faculties of a boy, is the fiat of fate, and not to be effaced by any succeeding impression, or unexpected difficulty. Dr. Johnson in fact, appears sometimes to be of the same opinion (how consistently I shall not now enquire), especially when he observes, "that Thomson looked on nature with the eye which she only gives to a poet."[1]

But, though it should be allowed that books may produce some poets, I fear they will never be the poets who charm our cares to sleep, or extort admiration. They may diffuse taste, and polish the language; but I am inclined to conclude that they will seldom rouse the passions, or amend the heart.

And, to return to the first subject of discussion, the reason why most people are more interested by a scene described by a poet, than by a view of nature, probably arises from the want of a lively imagination. The poet contracts the prospect, and, selecting the most picturesque part in his *camera*, the judgment is directed, and the whole force of the languid faculty turned towards the objects which excited the most forcible emotions in the poet's heart; the reader consequently feels the enlivened description, though he was not able to receive a first impression from the operations of his own mind.

Besides, it may be further observed, that gross minds are only to be moved by forcible representations. To rouse the thoughtless, objects must be presented, calculated to produce tumultuous emotions; the unsubstantial, picturesque forms which a contemplative man gazes on, and often follows with ardour till he is mocked by a glimpse of unattainable excellence, appear to them the light vapours of a dreaming enthusiast, who gives up the substance for the shadow. It is not within that they seek amusement; their eyes are seldom turned on themselves; consequently their emotions, though sometimes fervid, are always transient, and the nicer perceptions which distinguish the man of genuine taste, are not felt, or make such a slight impression as scarcely to excite any pleasurable sensations. Is it surprising then that they are often overlooked, even by those who are delighted by the same images concentrated by the poet?

But even this numerous class is exceeded, by witlings, who, anxious to appear to have wit and taste, do not allow their understandings or feelings any liberty; for, instead of cultivating their faculties and reflecting on their operations, they are busy collecting prejudices; and are predetermined to admire what the suffrage of time announces as excellent, not to store up a fund of amusement for themselves, but to enable them to talk.

These hints will assist the reader to trace some of the causes why the beauties of nature are not forcibly felt, when civilization, or rather luxury, has made considerable advances—those calm sensations are not sufficiently lively to serve as a relaxation to the voluptuary, or even to the moderate pursuer of artificial pleasures. In the present state of society, the understanding must bring back the feelings to nature, or the sensibility must have such native strength, as rather to be whetted than destroyed by the strong exercises of passion.

That the most valuable things are liable to the greatest perversion, is however as trite as true:—for the same sensibility, or quickness of senses, which makes a man relish the tranquil scenes of nature, when sensation, rather than reason, imparts delight, frequently makes a libertine of him, by leading him to prefer the sensual tumult of love a little refined by sentiment, to the calm pleasures of affectionate friendship, in whose sober satisfactions, reason, mixing her tranquillizing convictions, whispers, that content, not happiness, is the reward of virtue in this world.

---

[1] See Samuel Johnson's life of James Thomson in *Lives of the English Poets* (1781). Thomson (1700–48) was author of *The Seasons* (1726–44).

Letters[1]

To Joseph Johnson[2]

Paris, December 26, 1792

I should immediately on the receipt of your letter, my dear friend, have thanked you for your punctuality, for it highly gratified me, had I not wished to wait till I could tell you that this day was not stained with blood. Indeed the prudent precautions taken by the National Convention[3] to prevent a tumult, made me suppose that the dogs of faction would not dare to bark, much less to bite, however true to their scent; and I was not mistaken; for the citizens, who were all called out, are returning home with composed countenances, shouldering their arms. About nine o'clock this morning, the king passed by my window, moving silently along (excepting now and then a few strokes on the drum, which rendered the stillness more awful) through empty streets, surrounded by the national guards, who, clustering round the carriage, seemed to deserve their name. The inhabitants flocked to their windows, but the casements were all shut, not a voice was heard, nor did I see any thing like an insulting gesture.—For the first time since I entered France, I bowed to the majesty of the people, and respected the propriety of behaviour so perfectly in unison with my own feelings. I can scarcely tell you why, but an association of ideas made the tears flow insensibly from my eyes, when I saw Louis[4] sitting, with more dignity than I expected from his character, in a hackney coach, going to meet death, where so many of his race have triumphed. My fancy instantly brought Louis XIV before me, entering the capital with all his pomp, after one of the victories most flattering to his pride, only to see the sunshine of prosperity overshadowed by the sublime gloom of misery. I have been alone ever since; and, though my mind is calm, I cannot dismiss the lively images that have filled my imagination all the day.—Nay, do not smile, but pity me; for, once or twice, lifting my eyes from the paper, I have seen eyes glare through a glass-door opposite my chair, and bloody hands shook at me. Not the distant sound of a footstep can I hear.—My apartments are remote from those of the servants, the only persons who sleep with me in an immense hotel, one folding door opening after another.—I wish I had even kept the cat with me!—I want to see something alive; death in so many frightful shapes has taken hold of my fancy.—I am going to bed—and, for the first time in my life, I cannot put out the candle.

M.W.

To Gilbert Imlay[5]

H[avre], August 19, Tuesday. [1794]

I received both your letters to-day—I had reckoned on hearing from you yesterday, therefore was disappointed, though I imputed your silence to the right cause. I intended answering your kind letter immediately, that you might have felt the pleasure it gave me; but—— came in, and some other things interrupted me; so that the fine vapour has evaporated—yet, leaving a sweet scent behind, I have only to tell you, what is sufficiently obvious, that the earnest desire I have shown to keep my place, or gain more ground in your heart, is a sure proof how necessary your affection is to my happiness.—Still I do not think it false delicacy, or foolish pride, to wish that your attention to my happiness should arise *as much* from love, which is always rather a selfish passion, as reason— that is, I want you to promote my felicity, by seeking your own.—For, whatever pleasure it may give me to discover your generosity of soul, I would not be dependent for your affection on the very quality I most admire. No; there are qualities in your heart, which demand my affection; but, unless the attachment

---

[1] from *Collected Letters of Mary Wollstonecraft*, ed. Ralph M. Wardle (1979).

[2] The bookseller Joseph Johnson (1738–1809) was Wollstonecraft's publisher and friend.

[3] the French constitutional and legislative assembly from 20 September 1792 to 26 October 1795.

[4] The French king, Louis XVI, was deposed in August 1792 and guillotined on 21 January 1793. His trial began on 26 December 1792.

[5] Wollstonecraft's lover, who had returned to England in July 1794, leaving Wollstonecraft and their baby daughter in France.

appears to me clearly mutual, I shall labour only to esteem your character, instead of cherishing a tenderness for your person.

I write in a hurry, because the little one,[1] who has been sleeping a long time, begins to call for me. Poor thing! when I am sad, I lament that all my affections grow on me, till they become too strong for my peace, though they all afford me snatches of exquisite enjoyment—This for our little girl was at first very reasonable—more the effect of reason, a sense of duty, than feeling—now, she has got into my heart and imagination, and when I walk out without her, her little figure is ever dancing before me.

You too have somehow clung round my heart—I found I could not eat my dinner in the great room—and, when I took up the large knife to carve for myself, tears rushed into my eyes.—Do not however suppose that I am melancholy—for, when you are from me, I not only wonder how I can find fault with you—but how I can doubt your affection.

I will not mix any comments on the inclosed (it roused my indignation) with the effusion of tenderness, with which I assure you, that you are the friend of my bosom, and the prop of my heart.

            MARY

To Gilbert Imlay

[Paris] February 9 [1795]

The melancholy presentiment has for some time hung on my spirits, that we were parted for ever; and the letters I received this day, by Mr.——, convince me that it was not without foundation. You allude to some other letters, which I suppose have miscarried; for most of those I have got, were only a few hasty lines, calculated to wound the tenderness the sight of the superscriptions excited.

I mean not however to complain; yet so many feelings are struggling for utterance, and agitating a heart almost bursting with anguish, that I find it very difficult to write with any degree of coherence.

You left me indisposed, though you have taken no notice of it; and the most fatiguing journey I ever had, contributed to continue it. However, I recovered my health; but a neglected cold, and continual inquietude during the last two months, have reduced me to a state of weakness I never before experienced. Those who did not know that the canker-worm was at work at the core, cautioned me about suckling my child too long.—God preserve this poor child, and render her happier than her mother!

But I am wandering from my subject: indeed my head turns giddy, when I think that all the confidence I have had in the affection of others is come to this.—I did not expect this blow from you. I have done my duty to you and my child; and if I am not to have any return of affection to reward me, I have the sad consolation of knowing that I deserved a better fate. My soul is weary—I am sick at heart; and, but for this little darling, I would cease to care about a life, which is now stripped of every charm.

You see how stupid I am, uttering declamation, when I meant simply to tell you, that I consider your requesting me to come to you, as merely dictated by honour.—Indeed, I scarcely understand you.—You request me to come, and then tell me, that you have not given up all thoughts of returning to this place.

When I determined to live with you, I was only governed by affection.—I would share poverty with you, but I turn with affright from the sea of trouble on which you are entering.—I have certain principles of action: I know what I look for to found my happiness on.—It is not money.—With you I wished for sufficient to procure the comforts of life—as it is, less will do.—I can still exert myself to obtain the necessaries of life for my child, and she does not want more at present.—I have two or three plans in my head to earn our subsistence; for do not suppose that, neglected by you, I will lie under obligations of a pecuniary kind to you!—No; I would sooner submit to menial service.—I wanted the support of your affection—that gone, all is over!—I did not think, when I complained of ——'s contemptible avidity to accumulate money, that he would have dragged you into his schemes.

---

[1] Imlay and Wollstonecraft's daughter Frances (Fanny) Imlay, b. May 1794.

I cannot write.—I inclose a fragment of a letter, written soon after your departure, and another which tenderness made me keep back when it was written.—You will see then the sentiments of a calmer, though not a more determined, moment.—Do not insult me by saying, that "our being together is paramount to every other consideration!" Were it, you would not be running after a bubble, at the expence of my peace of mind.

Perhaps this is the last letter you will ever receive from me.

MARY

To Gilbert Imlay

[London, c. March 1796]
You must do as you please with respect to the child.—I could wish that it might be done soon, that my name may be no more mentioned to you. It is now finished.—Convinced that you have neither regard nor friendship, I disdain to utter a reproach, though I have had reason to think, that the "forbearance" talked of, has not been very delicate.—It is however of no consequence.—I am glad you are satisfied with your own conduct.

I now solemnly assure you, that this is an eternal farewell.—Yet I flinch not from the duties which tie me to life.

That there is "sophistry" on one side or other, is certain; but now it matters not on which. On my part it has not been a question of words. Yet your understanding or mine must be strangely warped—for what you term "delicacy," appears to me to be exactly the contrary. I have no criterion for morality, and have thought in vain, if the sensations which lead you to follow an ancle or step, be the sacred foundation of principle and affection. Mine has been of a very different nature, or it would not have stood the brunt of your sarcasms.

The sentiment in me is still sacred. If there be any part of me that will survive the sense of my misfortunes, it is the purity of my affections. The impetuosity of your senses, may have led you to term mere animal desire, the source of principle; and it may give zest to some years to come.—Whether you will always think so, I shall never know.

It is strange that, in spite of all you do, something like conviction forces me to believe, that you are not what you appear to be.

I part with you in peace.

To William Godwin

[London] Wednesday morning [17 August 1796]
I have not lately passed so painful a night as the last. I feel that I cannot speak clearly on the subject to you, let me then briefly explain myself now I am alone. Yet, struggling as I have been a long time to attain peace of mind (or apathy) I am afraid to trace emotions to their source, which border on agony.

Is it not sufficient to tell you that I am thoroughly out of humour with myself? Mortified and humbled, I scarcely know why—still, despising false delicacy I almost fear that I have lost sight of the true. Could a wish have transported me to France or Italy, last night, I should have caught up my Fanny and been off in a twinkle, though convinced that it is my mind, not the place, which requires changing. My imagination is for ever betraying me into fresh misery, and I perceive that I shall be a child to the end of the chapter. You talk of the roses which grow profusely in every path of life—I catch at them; but only encounter the thorns.—

I would not be unjust for the world—I can only say that you appear to me to have acted injudiciously; and that full of your own feelings, little as I comprehend them, you forgot mine—or do not understand my character. It is my turn to have a fever to day—I am not well—I am hurt—But I mean not to hurt you. Consider what has passed as a fever of your imagination; one of the slight mortal shakes to which you are liable—and I—will become again a *Solitary Walker*.[1] Adieu! I was going to add God bless you!—

Wednesday Morning[2]

---

[1] a reference to Rousseau's autobiographical *Les Rêveries du Promeneur Solitaire* (1782).

[2] Godwin immediately responded to this letter, as follows:
How shall I answer you? In one point we sympathize; I had rather

Mary Wollstonecraft

To William Godwin

[London, August 17, 1796]

I like your last—may I call it *love* letter? better than the first—and can I give you a higher proof of my esteem than to tell you, the style of my letter will whether I will or no, that it has calmed my mind—a mind that had been painfully active all the morning, haunted by old sorrows that seemed to come forward with new force to sharpen the present anguish—Well! well—it is almost gone—I mean all my unreasonable fears—and a whole train of tormentors, which you have routed—I can scarcely describe to you their ugly shapes so quickly do they vanish—and let them go, we will not bring them back by talking of them. You may see me when you please. I shall take this letter, just before dinner time, to ask you to come and dine with me, and Fanny, whom I have shut out to day. Should you be engaged come in the evening. Miss H—seldom stays late, never to supper—or to morrow—as you wish—I shall be content—You say you want soothing—will it sooth you to tell you the truth? I cannot hate you—I do not think you deserve it. Nay, more I cannot withhold my friendship from you, and will try to merit yours, that *necessity* may bind you to me.

One word of my ONLY fault—our imaginations have been rather differently employed—I am more of a painter than you—I like to tell the truth, my taste for the picturesque has been more cultivated—I delight to view the grand scenes of nature and the various changes of the human countenance—Beautiful as they are animated by intelligence or sympathy—My affections have been more exercised than yours, I believe, and my senses are quick, without the aid of fancy—yet tenderness always prevails, which inclines me to be angry with myself, when I do not animate and please those I [love?].

Now will you not be a good boy, and smile upon me, I dine at half past four—you ought to come and give me an appetite for my dinner, as you deprived me of one for my breakfast.

MARY

Two O'Clock

at this moment talk to you on paper than in any other mode. I should feel ashamed in seeing you.

You do not know how honest I am. I swear to you that I told you nothing but the strict & literal truth, when I described to you the manner in which you set my imagination on fire on Saturday. For six & thirty hours I could think of nothing else. I longed inexpressibly to have you in my arms. Why did not I come to you? I am a fool. I feared still that I might be deceiving myself as to your feelings, & that I was feeding my mind with groundless presumptions. I determined to suffer the point to arrive at its own denouement. I was not aware that the fervour of my imagination was exhausting itself. Yet this, I believe, is no uncommon case.

Like any other man, I can speak only of what I know. But this I can boldly affirm, that nothing that I have seen in you would in the slightest degree authorise the opinion, that, *in despising the false delicacy, you have lost sight of the true.* I see nothing in you but what I respect & adore.

I know the acuteness of your feelings, & there is perhaps nothing upon earth that would give me so pungent a remorse, as to add to your unhappiness.

Do not hate me. Indeed I do not deserve it. Do not cast me off. Do not become again a *solitary walker*. Be just to me, & then, though you will discover in me much that is foolish and censurable, yet a woman of your understanding will still regard me with some partiality.

Upon consideration I find in you one fault, & but one. You have the feelings of nature, & you have the honesty to avow them. In all this you do well. I am sure you do. But do not let them tyrannise over you. Estimate every thing at its just value. It is best that we should be friends in every sense of the word; but in the mean time let us be friends.

Suffer me to see you. Let us leave every thing else to its own course. My imagination is not dead, I suppose, though it sleeps. But, be it as it will, I will torment you no more. I will be your friend, the friend of your mind, the admirer of your excellencies. All else I commit to the disposition of futurity, glad, if completely happy; passive & silent in this respect, while I am not so.

Be happy. Resolve to be happy. You deserve to be so. Every thing that interferes with it, is weakness & wandering; & a woman, like you, can, must, shall, shake it off. Afford, for instance, no food for the morbid madness, & no triumph to the misanthropical gloom, of your afternoon visitor. Call up, with firmness, the energies, which, I am sure, you so eminently possess.

Send me word that I may call on you in a day or two. Do you not see, while I exhort you to be a philosopher, how painfully acute are my own feelings? I need some soothing, though I cannot ask it from you. Wednesday.

461

Helen Leigh
fl. 1788

Almost all we know about Helen Leigh comes from the Preface to her only book, in which she describes herself as "the Wife of a Country Curate, and Mother of seven Children." She must have been dead by 1795, the date of her husband's second marriage. (D.L.M.)

―――

from *Miscellaneous Poems* (1788)

The Natural Child

Let not the title of my verse offend,
    Nor let the Prude contract her rigid brow;
That helpless Innocence demands a friend,
    Virtue herself will cheerfully allow:

5 And shou'd my pencil[1] prove too weak to paint,
    The ills attendant on the babe ere born;
Whose parents swerv'd from Virtue's mild restraint,
    Forgive th'attempt, nor treat the Muse with scorn.

Yon rural farm, where Mirth was wont to dwell,
10   Of Melancholy, now appears the seat;
Solemn and silent as the hermit's cell—
    Say what, my muse, has caus'd a change so great?

This hapless morn, an Infant first saw light,
    Whose innocence a better fate might claim,
15 Than to be shunn'd as hateful to the sight,
    And banish'd soon as it receives a name.

No joy attends its entrance into life,
    No smile upon its mother's face appears,
She cannot smile, alas! she is no wife;
20   But vents the sorrows of her heart in tears.

No father flies to clasp it to his breast,
    And bless the pow'r that gave it to his arms;
To see his form, in miniature, express'd,
    Or trace, with ecstacy, its mother's charms.

25 Unhappy babe! thy father is thy foe!
    Oft shall he wish thee number'd with the dead;
His crime entails on thee a load of woe,
    And sorrow heaps on thy devoted head.

Torn from its mother's breast, by shame or pride,
30   No matter which—to hireling hands assign'd;
A parent's tenderness, when thus deny'd,
    Can it be thought its nurse is over-kind?

Too many, like this infant may we see,
    Expos'd, abandon'd, helpless and forlorn;
35 'Till death, misfortune's friend, has set them free,
    From a rude world, which gave them nought but scorn.

Too many mothers—horrid to relate!
    Soon as their infants breathe the vital air,
Deaf to their plaintive cries, their helpless state,
40   Led on by shame, and driv'n by despair,

Fell murderers become——Here cease, my pen,
    And leave these wretched victims of despair;
But ah! what punishments await the men,
    Who, in such depths of mis'ry, plunge the fair.

---

[1] the word pencil then meant "paintbrush."

Maria Logan
fl. 1793

Little is known about Maria Logan's life. We know only that she published her *Poems on Several Occasions* in York in 1793, that a second edition was published the same year, and that the subscription list includes the names of Anna Lætitia Barbauld,* Barbauld's brother John Aikin (Lucy Aikin's* father), and the novelist Henry Mackenzie. Logan refers in her inscription to "seven tedious years of uninterrupted sickness"; we can conclude from her poem "To Opium" that she relied on the drug to relieve pain. She is remembered primarily for "To Opium." (A.M.)

಄಄

from *Poems on Several Occasions*. 2nd ed. (1793)[1]

To Opium

Let others boast the golden spoil,
    Which Indian climes afford;
And still, with unavailing toil,
    Increase the shining hoard:—

5 Still let Golconda's[2] dazzling pride
    On Beauty's forehead glow,
And round the fair, on ev'ry side,
    Sabean odours[3] flow:—

Be mine the balm, whose sov'reign pow'r
10   Can still the throb of Pain;
The produce of the scentless flow'r,
    That strews Hindostan's plain.[4]

No gaudy hue its form displays,
    To catch the roving eye;
15 And Ignorance, with vacant gaze,
    May pass regardless by.

But shall the Muse with cold disdain,
    Its simple charms behold!
Shall she devote the tuneful strain
20   To incense, gems, or gold!

When latent ills the frame pervade,
    And mock the healing art;
Thy friendly balm shall lend its aid,
    And transient ease impart;

25 Shall charm the restless hour of day,
    And cheer the midnight gloom;
Shall blunt each thorn, which strews the way
    That leads us to the tomb.

And oft, when Reason vainly tries
30   To calm the troubled breast,
Thy pow'r can seal our streaming eyes,
    And bid our sorrows rest.

What tho' this calm must quickly cease,
    And Grief resume its pow'r,
35 The heart that long has sigh'd for ease,
    Will prize the tranquil hour!

---

[1] Logan's dedication to this volume reads as follows: "To those friends whose tender and unremitted attentions have enlivened seven tedious years of uninterrupted sickness, the following trifles are inscribed by their sincerely grateful and affectionate friend, Maria Logan."

[2] the site of an ancient diamond mine in India; hence, a place of great riches.

[3] the scent of spices from Saba or Sheba (modern Yemen): cf. Jeremiah 6.20.

[4] "The best Opium is procured from the white poppy of Hindostan." (M.L.) Hindustan is in northern India.

A short oblivion of its care
    Relieves the weary'd mind,
Till suff'ring nature learns to bear
40   The weight by Heav'n assign'd.

Reviv'd by thee, my drooping Muse
    Now pours the grateful strain,
And Fancy's hand sweet flow'rets strews
    Around the bed of Pain.

45 At her command gay scenes arise
    To charm my raptur'd sight,
While Memory's faithful hand supplies
    Past objects of delight.

Yet Memory's soothing charms were vain,
50   Without thy friendly aid;
And sportive Fancy's smiling train,
    Would fly Disease's shade—

Did not thy magic pow'r supply,
    A mild, tho' transient ray;
55 As meteors in a northern sky,
    Shed artificial day.

And shall my humble Muse alone
    Thy peerless worth declare!
A Muse to all the world unknown,
60   Whose songs are lost in air.

O! may the bard, whose tuneful strain
    Resounds thro' Derwent's vale,[1]
At whose command the hosts of Pain,
    Disease and Sickness, fail—

65 That Sage, to whom the God of Day[2]
    His various gifts imparts,
Whose healing pow'r, whose melting lay,
    United, charm our hearts—

May he devote one tuneful page,
70   To thee, neglected Flow'r!
Then Fame shall bid each future age,
    Admiring, own thy pow'r![3]

Verses On Hearing That an Airy and Pleasant Situation, near a Populous and Commercial Town, Was Surrounded with New Buildings

There was a time! that time the Muse bewails,
When Sunny-Hill enjoy'd refreshing gales;
When Flora[4] sported in its fragrant bow'rs,
And strew'd with lib'ral hand her sweetest flow'rs!
5 Now sable vapours, pregnant with disease,
Clog the light pinions of the southern breeze;
Each verdant plant assumes a dusky hue,
And sooty atoms taint the morning dew.
No more the lily rears her spotless head,
10 Health, verdure, beauty, fragrance, all are fled:
Sulphureous clouds deform the rising day,
Nor own the pow'r of Sol's[5] meridian ray;
While sickly damps, from Aire's[6] polluted stream,
Quench the pure radiance of his parting beam.
15 These are thy triumphs, Commerce!—these thy spoils!
Yet sordid mortals glory in their toils,
Spurn the pure joys which simple Nature yields,
Her breezy hills, dark groves, and verdant fields,
With cold indiff'rence, view her blooming charms,
20 And give youth, ease, and health to thy enfeebling arms.

---

[1] The bard is Erasmus Darwin,* who published his botanical poem *The Loves of the Plants* in 1789. Derwent's Vale is a valley in the Lake District of northwest England, also associated with the Wordsworths.*

[2] Apollo, the god of medicine as well as of the sun and of poetry.

[3] "This was written just before the publication of 'The Loves of the Plants'; a work which had been long impatiently expected by every one who had been so fortunate as to see any specimen of the Author's poetical abilities." (M.L.) Darwin's *Loves of the Plants*, vol. 2 of *The Botanic Garden* (1789–91), was published in 1789. Darwin introduces "Papaver," "poppy" (L.), in 2.270 and note.

[4] the Roman goddess of flowers.

[5] "Sol" is the sun (L.).

[6] a river running through the city of Leeds; the second edition of Logan's poems was published in York and Leeds as well as in London.

Janet Little
1759 – 1813

The daughter of George Little of Nether Bogside, Ecclefechan, Dumfries, Scotland, Janet Little from a young age worked as a servant and chambermaid. In 1788 she went to work for Frances Dunlop, Robert Burns's* patron, who took an interest in her writing. The following year, she moved to Loudoun Castle to manage the dairy for Dunlop's daughter and her husband, James Henri, a French émigré. The eighteenth-century fashion for labouring-class poets (such as Stephen Duck, the "thresher poet," and Mary Collier, "the Petersfield washerwoman") encouraged Little's ambition. With Frances Dunlop's support, she wrote to Burns in 1789, enclosing one of her poems; it is not known whether he replied or not. Initially skeptical about the proliferation of working-class poets attempting to follow in his footsteps, Burns eventually helped to raise a subscription for the publication of *The Poetical Works of Janet Little, the Scotch Milkmaid* (1792), which includes several poems addressed to him.

Little had wanted to dedicate her book to James Boswell, a fellow Scot and the biographer of Samuel Johnson. However, recognizing the politics of publication for a book of poems by a woman of Little's social station, Boswell advised her to dedicate it instead to a woman of rank. The book was dedicated to Flora, Countess of Loudoun, a young ward of the Countess of Dumfries. Little married James Richmond, a labourer at Loudoun Castle and the father of five children; thereafter she lived a busy life of which few details are known. She died on 15 March 1813. (A.M.)

❧❧

from *The Poetical Works of Janet Little, the Scotch Milkmaid* (1792)

Given to a Lady Who Asked Me to Write A Poem

In royal Anna's golden days,[1]
Hard was the task to gain the bays:
Hard was it then the hill to climb;
Some broke a neck, some lost a limb.
5   The vot'ries for poetic fame,
Got aff[2] decrepit, blind, an' lame:
Except that little fellow Pope,[3]
Few ever then got near its top:
An' Homer's crutches[4] he may thank,
10 Or down the brae[5] he'd got a clank.

Swift, Thomson, Addison, an' Young[6]
Made Pindus[7] echo to their tongue,
In hopes to please a learned age;
But Doctor Johnston,[8] in a rage,
15 Unto posterity did shew
Their blunders great, their beauties few.
But now he's dead, we weel may ken;[9]

---

[1] Queen Anne reigned from 1702 to 1714. Cf. "The Vicar of Bray" (anon., 18th century).

[2] "off" (Sc.).

[3] the poet Pope, whose growth was stunted by a childhood illness.

[4] Pope regarded Homer as the source of and model for poetry; see *An Essay on Criticism* (1711) 124–27 and Preface to the *Iliad* (1715).

[5] "hillside."

[6] the writers Jonathan Swift (1667–1745), James Thomson (1700–48), Joseph Addison (1672–1719), and Edward Young (1683–1765).

[7] the ancient name of the mountain range between Thessaly and Epirus.

[8] Samuel Johnson (1709–84), who wrote lives of the writers named in line 11 (published in *Lives of the English Poets*, 1779–81).

[9] "we well may know."

For ilka[1] dunce maun[2] hae a pen,
To write in hamely, uncouth rhymes;
An' yet forsooth they please the times.

    A ploughman chiel,[3] Rab Burns[4] his name,
Pretends[5] to write; an' thinks nae shame
To souse[6] his sonnets on the court;
An' what is strange, they praise him for't.
Even folks, wha're of the highest station,
Ca' him the glory of our nation.

    But what is more surprising still,
A milkmaid[7] must tak up her quill;
An' she will write, shame fa'[8] the rabble!
That think to please wi' ilka bawble.[9]
They may thank heav'n, auld Sam's[10] asleep:
For could he ance[11] but get a peep,
He, wi' a vengeance wad them sen'
A' headlong to the dunces' den.

    Yet Burns, I'm tauld, can write wi' ease,
An' a' denominations please;
Can wi' uncommon glee impart
A usefu' lesson to the heart;
Can ilka latent thought expose,
An' Nature trace whare'er she goes:
Of politics can talk wi' skill,
Nor dare the critics blame his quill.

    But then a rustic country quean[12]
To write—was e'er the like o't seen?
A milk maid poem-books to print;
Mair fit she wad her dairy tent;[13]
Or labour at her spinning wheel,
An' do her wark baith swift an' weel.
Frae that she may some profit share,
But winna frae her rhyming ware.
Does she, poor silly thing, pretend
The manners of our age to mend?
Mad as we are, we're wise enough
Still to despise sic paultry stuff.[14]

    "May she wha writes, of wit get mair,
An' a' that read an ample share
Of candour ev'ry fault to screen,
That in her dogg'ral scrawls are seen."

    All this and more, a critic said;
I heard and slunk behind the shade:
So much I dread their cruel spite,
My hand still trembles when I write.

---

[1] "each, every."

[2] "must."

[3] "fellow."

[4] the Scottish poet Robert Burns.*

[5] in the sense of "claims" or "professes."

[6] "immerse, drench": the meaning is probably "to drench the court with his poems."

[7] Little herself.

[8] "befall."

[9] "toy, trifling thing."

[10] i.e., Samuel Johnson.

[11] "once."

[12] "young unmarried woman."

[13] "It's more fitting for her to tend her dairy."

[14] "such silly trivia."

Richard Polwhele
1760 – 1838

Richard Polwhele was born in Truro, Cornwall, on 6 January 1760, the son of Thomas and Mary Thomas Polwhele. One of his teachers, the poet and satirist John Wolcot ("Peter Pindar"), encouraged Polwhele's literary ambition; however, years later, in *A Sketch of Peter Pindar* (1800), Polwhele attacked Wolcot. Other friends of the family included Catharine Macaulay* and Hannah More,* whom Polwhele first met in 1777. He wrote an ode for Macaulay, which was published along with five other poems in April 1777; his next volume of poetry, *The Fate of Llewellyn* (1778), was a failure. In 1778 he entered Christ Church, Oxford; from there he was ordained as a clergyman, serving as curate of Kenton, Devonshire, from 1782 to 1793. He participated in an anthology, *Poems, Chiefly by Gentlemen of Devonshire and Cornwall*, in 1792. He also translated the Greek pastoral poets Theocritus, Bion, and Moschus (1786), and published his topographical works, *Historical Views of Devonshire* (1793) and *The History of Devonshire* (1793–1806). Following the death of his first wife, he remarried in 1794 and moved to Manaccan, near Helston, Cornwall. There he corresponded with such writers as Macaulay, William Cowper,* Erasmus Darwin,* and Anna Seward,* and wrote his three-volume *History of Cornwall* (1803), essays and satires on religious matters, and several poems, including *The Old English Gentleman* (1797) and *The Unsex'd Females*. He was a contributor to the *Anti-Jacobin Review*.* His work as a clergyman occupied most of his time in later years. He died at Truro on 12 March 1838. (A.M.)

The Unsex'd Females: A Poem (1798)

"Our unsex'd female writers now instruct, or confuse, us and themselves, in the labyrinth of politics, or turn us wild with Gallic frenzy."
— *Pursuits of Literature*, Edit. 7. p. 238.[1]

Thou, who with all the poet's genuine rage,
Thy "fine eye rolling" o'er "this aweful age,"[2]
Where polish'd life unfolds its various views,
Hast mark'd the magic influence of the muse;
5 Where witlings wildly think, or madly dare,
With Honor, Virtue, Truth, announcing war;
Survey with me, what ne'er our fathers saw,
A female band despising NATURE's law,
As "proud defiance"[3] flashes from their arms,
10 And vengeance smothers all their softer charms.
    I shudder at the new unpictur'd scene,
Where unsex'd woman vaunts the imperious mien;
Where girls, affecting to dismiss the heart,
Invoke the Proteus of petrific art;[4]
15 With equal ease, in body or in mind,
To Gallic freaks or Gallic faith[5] resign'd,
The crane-like neck, as Fashion bids, lay bare,
Or frizzle, bold in front, their borrow'd hair;
Scarce by a gossamery film carest,
20 Sport, in full view, the meretricious breast;[6]
Loose the chaste cincture, where the graces shone,
And languish'd all the Loves, the ambrosial zone;
As lordly domes inspire dramatic rage,

---

[1] from the Preface to Dialogue 4 of Thomas James Mathias's satirical poem *The Pursuits of Literature* (1794–97), which went through 16 editions; Polwhele addresses his opening lines to Mathias, from whom he borrows his title and many of his examples. Except for some brief quotations, we have omitted Polwhele's extensive notes on this and other references in *The Unsex'd Females*.

[2] *The Pursuits of Literature*, Dialogue 1.7.

[3] Pope, "The Temple of Fame" (1715) 343.

[4] Proteus is the shape-changing god of classical myth; see *Odyssey* 4; "petrific art" is sculpture.

[5] French fashions—including atheism.

[6] Polwhele's note blames this on the influence of French fashion; the high-waisted fashionable chemise dress, often worn without a corset, could be very revealing unless worn with a neckerchief.

Court prurient Fancy to the private stage;[1]
25 With bliss botanic[2] as their bosoms heave,
Still pluck forbidden fruit, with mother Eve,
For puberty in sighing florets pant,
Or point the prostitution of a plant;
Dissect its organ of unhallow'd lust,
30 And fondly gaze the titillating dust;
With liberty's sublimer views expand,
And o'er the wreck of kingdoms sternly stand;
And, frantic, midst the democratic storm,
Pursue, Philosophy! thy phantom-form.
35   Far other is the female shape and mind,
By modest luxury heighten'd and refin'd;
Those limbs, that figure, tho' by Fashion grac'd,
By Beauty polish'd, and adorn'd by Taste;
That soul, whose harmony perennial flows,
40 In Music trembles, and in Color glows;
Which bids sweet Poesy reclaim the praise
With faery light to gild fastidious days,
From sullen clouds relieve domestic care,
And melt in smiles the withering frown of war.
45 Ah! once the female Muse, to NATURE true,
The unvalued store from FANCY, FEELING drew;
Won, from the grasp of woe, the roseate hours,
Cheer'd life's dim vale, and strew'd the grave with
        flowers.
    But lo! where, pale amidst the wild, she draws
50 Each precept cold from sceptic Reason's vase;
Pours with rash arm the turbid stream along,
And in the foaming torrent whelms the throng.
    Alas! her pride sophistic flings a gloom,
To chase, sweet Innocence! thy vernal bloom,
55 Of each light joy to damp the genial glow,
And with new terrors clothe the groupe of woe,
Quench the pure daystar in oblivion deep,
And, Death! restore thy "long, unbroken sleep."[3]
    See Wollstonecraft, whom no decorum checks,
60 Arise, the intrepid champion of her sex;
O'er humbled man assert the sovereign claim,
And slight the timid blush of virgin fame.
    "Go, go (she cries) ye tribes of melting maids,[4]
Go, screen your softness in sequester'd shades;
65 With plaintive whispers woo the unconscious grove,
And feebly perish, as despis'd ye love.
What tho' the fine Romances of Rousseau[5]
Bid the frame flutter, and the bosom glow;
Tho' the rapt Bard, your empire fond to own,
70 Fall prostrate and adore your living throne,
The living throne his hands presum'd to rear,
Its seat a simper, and its base a tear;
Soon shall the sex disdain the illusive sway,
And wield the sceptre in yon blaze of day;
75 Ere long, each little artifice discard,
No more by weakness winning fond regard;
Nor eyes, that sparkle from their blushes, roll,
Nor catch the languors of the sick'ning soul,
Nor the quick flutter, nor the coy reserve,
80 But nobly boast the firm gymnastic nerve;[6]
Nor more affect with Delicacy's fan
To hide the emotion from congenial man;
To the bold heights where glory beams, aspire,
Blend mental energy with Passion's fire,
85 Surpass their rivals in the powers of mind
And vindicate *the Rights of womankind.*"[7]

---

[1] Theatrical performances in private houses were controversial because they gave respectable women opportunities to act on the stage. Cf. headnote to O'Neill* and the debate about private theatricals in Austen,* *Mansfield Park* (1814). Mathias disapprovingly calls the private stage "a convenient chapel of ease to *Hymen*" (note to *The Pursuits of Literature*, Dialogue 2).

[2] Polwhele cites Erasmus Darwin, *The Loves of the Plants*, as an influence on the fashion for botany, adding: "how the sexual system of plants can accord with female modesty, I am not able to comprehend." For a different view, see Wollstonecraft, *A Vindication of the Rights of Woman*,* chapters 7 and 12.

[3] Polwhele quotes the pastoral poet Moschus (fl. c. 150 BC), "Idyllium the Third. Epitaph on Bion," from his own translation, *The Idyllia, Epigrams, and Fragments, of Theocritus, Bion, and Moschus, with the Elegies of Tyrtæus* (1786).

[4] Pope, *The Rape of the Lock* (1714) 1.71.

[5] especially Jean-Jacques Rousseau, *Julie, ou La Nouvelle Héloïse* (1761).

[6] Wollstonecraft advocated regular exercise for girls as well as boys: see *A Vindication of the Rights of Woman*, chapter 3.*

[7] like Wollstonecraft herself in *A Vindication of the Rights of Woman** (403).

She spoke: and veteran BARBAULD[1] caught the strain,
And deem'd her songs of Love, her Lyrics vain;
And ROBINSON to Gaul her Fancy gave,[2]
90 And trac'd the picture of a Deist's grave!
And charming SMITH[3] resign'd her power to please,
Poetic feeling and poetic ease;
And HELEN, fir'd by Freedom, bade adieu
To all the broken visions of Peru;[4]
95 And YEARSELEY,[5] who had warbled, Nature's child,
Midst twilight dews, her minstrel ditties wild,
(Tho' soon a wanderer from her meads and milk,
She long'd to rustle, like her sex, in silk)
Now stole the modish grin, the sapient sneer,
100 And flippant HAYS[6] assum'd a cynic leer;
While classic KAUFFMAN[7] her Priapus drew,
And linger'd a sweet blush with EMMA CREWE.[8]
    Yet, say, ye Fair, with man's tyrannic host,
Say, where the battles ye so proudly boast,
105 While, urg'd to triumph by the Spartan fife,[9]
Corporeal struggles mix'd with mental strife?
Where, the plum'd chieftain of your chosen train,
To fabricate your laws, and fix your reign?
Say, hath her eye its lightnings flash'd, to scath
110 The bloom young Pleasure sheds on Glory's path;
Her ear, indignant as she march'd along,
Scorn'd every charm of soft lascivious song?
Say, hath she view'd, if pass'd the mourner by,
The drooping form, nor heav'd one female sigh;
115 Arm'd with proud intellect, at fortune laugh'd,
Mock'd the vain threat, and brav'd the envenom'd shaft?
Say, hath your chief the ideal depths explor'd,
Amid the flaming tracts of spirit soar'd,
And from base earth, by Reason's vigor borne,
120 Hail'd the fair beams of Mind's expanding morn?
    Alas! in every aspiration bold,
I saw the creature of a mortal mould:
Yes! not untrembling (tho' I half ador'd
A mind by Genius fraught, by Science stor'd)
125 I saw the Heroine mount the dazzling dome
Where Shakspeare's spirit kindled, to illume
His favourite FUSELI,[10] and with magic might
To earthly sense unlock'd a world of light!
    Full soon, amid the high pictorial blaze,
130 I saw a Sibyl-transport in her gaze:
To the great Artist, from his wondrous Art,
I saw transferr'd the whole enraptur'd Heart;
Till, mingling soul with soul, in airy trance,
Enlighten'd and inspir'd at every glance,
135 And from the dross of appetite refin'd,
And, grasping at angelic food, all mind,
Down from the empyreal heights she sunk, betray'd
To poor Philosophy—a love-sick maid!
——But hark! lascivious murmurs melt around;
140 And pleasure trembles in each dying sound.
A myrtle bower, in fairest bloom array'd,
To laughing Venus streams the silver shade:
Thrill'd with fine ardors *Collinsonias*[11] glow,

---

[1] the poet Anna Lætitia Barbauld.*

[2] the poet, actor, and novelist Mary Robinson.* For her attitude to France ("Gaul"), see, for example, "Ainsi Va le Monde" in *Poems* (1791).

[3] the poet and novelist Charlotte Smith.*

[4] the poet Helen Maria Williams, author of *Peru* (1784), whom Polwhele condemns for her later revolutionary sympathies. See her *Letters from France*.*

[5] the poet Ann Yearsley,* known as the "Bristol milkmaid." Polwhele goes on to mock her for acting above her social station in opposing her patroness Hannah More,* who tried to control Yearsley's access to the money she earned from her writing.

[6] the novelist Mary Hays.* Polwhele, who explains in a note that he has read her *Letters and Essays, Moral, and Miscellaneous* (1793), identifies her as a "Wollstonecraftian."

[7] the Swiss-born painter Angelica Kauffmann (1741–1807), a founding member of the Royal Academy of Arts. Priapus is an ancient Greek fertility god.

[8] painter and etcher (fl. c. 1783); Polwhele condemns her "Flora at Play with Cupid," the frontispiece to Darwin's* *The Botanic Garden*, Part 2.

[9] In his note, Polwhele cites the example of the ancient Spartan women to make the case that female modesty is the only safeguard against libertinism.

[10] Henry Fuseli (1741–1825), the Swiss-born artist with whom Wollstonecraft fell in love before her departure for France in 1792. See Godwin, *Memoirs*, chap. 6.*

[11] Polwhele quotes a note from Darwin's *The Botanic Garden*, Part 1, which describes "the manifest adultery of several females of the plant Collinsonias, who had bent themselves into contact with the males of other flowers of the same plant, in their vicinity, regardless of their own."

And, bending, breathe their loose desires below.
Each gentle air a swelling anther heaves,
Wafts its full sweets, and shivers thro' the leaves.
    Bath'd in new bliss, the Fair-one greets the bower,
And ravishes a flame from every flower;
Low at her feet inhales the master's sighs,
And darts voluptuous poison from her eyes.
Yet, while each heart-pulse, in the Paphian grove,[1]
Beats quick to IMLAY[2] and licentious love,
A sudden gloom the gathering tempest spreads;
The floral arch-work withers o'er their heads;
Whirlwinds the paramours asunder tear;[3]
And wisdom falls, the victim of despair.
    And dost thou rove, with no internal light,
Poor maniac! thro' the stormy waste of night?
Hast thou no sense of guilt to be forgiv'n,
No comforter on earth, no hope in Heaven?
Stay, stay—thine impious arrogance restrain—
What tho' the flood may quench thy burning brain,
Rash woman! can its whelming wave bestow
Oblivion, to blot out eternal woe?
    "O come (a voice seraphic seems to say)
Fly that pale form—come sisters! come away.
Come, from those livid limbs withdraw your gaze,
Those limbs which Virtue views in mute amaze;
Nor deem, that Genius lends a veil, to hide
The dire apostate, the fell suicide.[4]——
Come, join, with wonted smiles, a kindred train,
Who court, like you, the Muse; nor court in vain.
Mark, where the sex have oft, in ancient days,
To modest Virtue, claim'd a nation's praise;
Chas'd from the public scene the fiend of strife,
And shed a radiance o'er luxurious life;
In silken fetters bound the obedient throng,
And soften'd despots by the power of song.
    "Yet woman owns a more extensive sway
Where Heaven's own graces pour the living ray:
And vast its influence o'er the social ties,
By Heaven inform'd, if female genius rise—
Its power how vast, in critic wisdom sage,
If MONTAGUE[5] refine a letter'd age;
And CARTER,[6] with a milder air, diffuse
The moral precepts of the Grecian Muse;
And listening girls perceive a charm unknown
In grave advice, as utter'd by CHAPONE;[7]
If SEWARD[8] sting with rapture every vein,
Or gay PIOZZI[9] sport in lighter strain;
If BURNEY[10] mix with sparkling humour chaste
Delicious feelings and the purest taste,
Or RADCLIFFE[11] wrap in necromantic gloom
The impervious forest and the mystic dome;
If BEAUCLERK paint Lenora's spectre-horse,[12]
The uplifted lance of death, the grisly corse;

---

[1] the grove of Venus, goddess of love; Paphos, a city in Cyprus, was an important site of her worship.

[2] Gilbert Imlay (c. 1754–1828?), Wollstonecraft's lover and the father of her first child, Fanny; see Godwin, *Memoirs*,* chap. 7.

[3] Cf. the fate of the lovers Paolo and Francesca in Dante, *Inferno*, canto 5.

[4] Polwhele alludes to Wollstonecraft's* marriage to Godwin* in spite of his opposition to marriage as an institution; to her lack of religious feeling on her deathbed; and to her suicide attempts: all are chronicled in Godwin, *Memoirs of the Author of* A Vindication of the Rights of Woman (1798), chapters 9,* 10,* and 8, respectively.

[5] Elizabeth Montagu (1720–1800), according to Polwhele "the best female critic ever produced in any country." Like Carter, Chapone, and More,* mentioned below, she was a member of the Blue Stocking Circle of literary women.

[6] Elizabeth Carter (1717–1806), who translated Epictetus (1758); Polwhele compares her poetry to Barbauld's,* preferring the latter.

[7] See Hester Chapone (1721–1801), *Letters on the Improvement of the Mind* (1773).

[8] the poet Anna Seward,* for whom Polwhele's note expresses unqualified admiration.

[9] the writer Hester Thrale, later Piozzi (1741–1821).

[10] the novelist Frances Burney.* Polwhele's note praises her novels *Evelina* (1778), *Cecilia* (1782), and *Camilla* (1796).

[11] the novelist Ann Radcliffe;* Polwhele's note praises her Gothic novel *The Mysteries of Udolpho* (1794).

[12] Lady Diana Beauclerk (1734–1808) illustrated a translation of G. A. Burger's supernatural ballad *Leonora* (pub. in German in 1773 and in several English translations in the 1790s, including one illustrated by Blake).*

And e'en a Princess[1] lend poetic grace
The pencil's charm, and breathe in every trace."
   She ceas'd; and round their MORE[2] the sisters sigh'd!

200 Soft on each tongue repentant murmurs died;
And sweetly scatter'd (as they glanc'd away)
Their conscious "blushes spoke a brighter day."[3]

---

[1] probably a compliment to Princess Caroline, who married the Prince Regent (later George IV) in 1795.

[2] the writer Hannah More,* according to Polwhele "a character … diametrically opposite to Miss Wollstonecraft."

[3] Polwhele's last note reads: "That Mrs. Godwin herself, may be numbered among the penitent, and he, also [Godwin], who 'drew her frailties from their dread abode,' is the sincere and fervent wish of a heart in charity with all men." This last quotation is adapted from Thomas Gray, "Elegy Written in a Country Churchyard" (1750) 126; the one in the text is unidentified.

Thomas Clarkson
1760 – 1846

Thomas Clarkson was born in Wisbech, Cambridgeshire, on 28 March 1760. His father, John Clarkson, was a schoolmaster and clergyman; his mother was "a woman of great energy of character." He was educated at his father's school, at St. Paul's School, London, and at St. John's College, Cambridge, receiving his B.A. in 1783. In 1785, he entered a contest for the best Latin essay on the topic "Is it right to make slaves of others against their will?" He won first prize. He seems to have undertaken the essay as an academic exercise, but the writing of it was a conversion experience: "if the contents of the Essay were true," he reflected, "it was time some person should see these calamities to their end." He decided to be that person. He began by translating his essay into English as *An Essay on the Slavery and Commerce of the Human Species* (1786); it was the first of his nineteen books on the subject. He helped found the Society for the Abolition of the Slave Trade in 1787 and immediately became its chief investigator, regularly travelling thousands of miles and visiting hundreds of ships to collect evidence for the abolitionist cause. After the abolition of the trade in 1807, he published the celebratory *History of the Rise, Progress, and Accomplishment of the Abolition of the African Slave-Trade by the British Parliament* (1808). In 1840, after the final emancipation of the slaves in British colonies, the eighty-year-old Clarkson was awakened in the night by a voice saying, "You have not done all your work. There is America." He got up in the morning and started writing another polemic, in support of the American abolitionists. He fought the good fight until he died on 26 September 1846. (D.L.M.)

❧❧❧

from *An Essay on the Slavery and Commerce of the Human Species, particularly the African, translated from a Latin Dissertation, which was honoured with the First Prize in the University of Cambridge for the Year 1785* (1786)

from PART 3,
The Slavery of the Africans in the European Colonies

CHAPTER 1

Having confined ourselves wholly, in the second part of this Essay, to the consideration of the *commerce*, we shall now proceed to the consideration of the *slavery* that is founded upon it. As this slavery will be conspicuous in the *treatment*, which the unfortunate Africans uniformly undergo, when they are put in the hands of the *receivers*, we shall describe the manner in which they are accustomed to be used from this period.

To place this in the clearest, and most conspicuous point of view, we shall throw a considerable part of our information on this head into the form of a narrative: we shall suppose ourselves, in short, on the continent of Africa, and relate a scene, which, from its agreement with unquestionable facts, might not unreasonably be presumed to have been presented to our view, had we been really there.

And first, let us turn our eyes to the cloud of dust that is before us. It seems to advance rapidly, and, accompanied with dismal shrieks and yellings, to make the very air, that is above it, tremble as it rolls along. What can possibly be the cause? Let us inquire of that melancholy African, who seems to walk dejected near the shore; whose eyes are stedfastly fixed on the approaching object, and whose heart, if we can judge from the appearance of his countenance, must be greatly agitated.

"Alas!" says the unhappy African, "the cloud that you see approaching, is a train of wretched slaves. They are going to the ships behind you. They are destined for the English colonies, and, if you will stay here but for a little time, you will see them pass. They were last night drawn up upon the plain which you see before you, where they were branded upon the breast with an *hot iron*; and when they had undergone the whole of the treatment which is customary on these occasions, and which I am informed that you Englishmen at home use to the *cattle* which you buy, they were returned to their prison. As I have some dealings with the members of the factory[1] which you see at a little distance, (though thanks to the Great Spirit, I never dealt in the *liberty* of my fellow creatures) I gained admittance there. I learned the history of some of the unfortunate people, whom I saw confined, and will explain to you, if my eye should catch them as they pass, the real causes of their servitude."

Scarcely were these words spoken, when they came distinctly into sight. They appeared to advance in a long column, but in a very irregular manner. There were three only in the front, and these were chained together. The rest that followed seemed to be chained by pairs, but by pressing forward, to avoid the lash of the drivers, the breadth of the column began to be greatly extended, and ten or more were observed abreast.

While we were making these remarks, the intelligent African thus resumed his discourse. "The first three whom you observe, at the head of the train, to be chained together, are prisoners of war. As soon as the ships that are behind you arrived, the news was dispatched into the inland country; when one of the petty kings immediately assembled his subjects, and attacked a neighbouring tribe. The wretched people, though they were surprized, made a formidable resistance, as they resolved, almost all of them, rather to lose their lives, than survive their liberty. The person whom you see in the middle, is the father of the two young men, who are chained to him on each side. His wife and two of his children were killed in the attack, and his father being wounded, and, on account of his age, *incapable of servitude*, was left bleeding on the spot where this transaction happened.

"With respect to those who are now passing us, and are immediately behind the former, I can give you no other intelligence, than that some of them, to about the number of thirty, were taken in the same skirmish. Their tribe was said to have been numerous before the attack; these however are *all that are left alive*. But with respect to the unhappy man, who is now opposite to us, and whom you may distinguish, as he is now looking back and wringing his hands in despair, I can inform you with more precision. He is an unfortunate convict. He lived only about five days journey from the factory. He went out with his king to hunt, and was one of his train; but, through too great an anxiety to afford his royal master diversion, he roused the game from the covert rather sooner than was expected. The king, exasperated at this circumstance, sentenced him to slavery. His wife and children, fearing lest the tyrant should extend the punishment to themselves, *which is not unusual,* fled directly to the woods, where they were all devoured.

"The people, whom you see close behind the unhappy convict, form a numerous body, and reach a considerable way. They speak a language, which no person in this part of Africa can understand, and their features, as you perceive, are so different from those of the rest, that they almost appear a distinct race of men. From this circumstance I recollect them. They are the subjects of a very distant prince, who agreed with the *slave merchants, for a quantity of spirituous liquors,* to furnish him with a stipulated number of slaves. He accordingly surrounded, and set fire to one of his own villages in the night, and seized these people, who were unfortunately the inhabitants, as they were escaping from the flames. I first saw them as the merchants were driving them in, about two days ago. They came in a large body, and were tied together at the neck with leather thongs, which permitted them to walk at the distance of about a yard from one another. Many of them were loaden with elephants teeth, which had been purchased at the same time. All of them had bags, made of skin, upon their shoulders; for as they were to travel, in their way from the great mountains, through barren sands and inhospitable woods for many days together, they were obliged to carry water and provisions with them. Notwithstanding this, many of them perished, some by hunger, but the greatest number by fatigue, as the place from whence they came, is at such an amazing distance from this, and the obstacles, from the nature of the country, so great, that the journey could scarcely be completed in seven moons."

When this relation was finished, and we had been looking stedfastly for some time on the croud that was going by, we lost sight of that peculiarity of feature,

---

[1] slave-trading outpost.

which we had before remarked. We then discovered that the inhabitants of the depopulated village had all of them passed us, and that the part of the train, to which we were now opposite, was a numerous body of kidnapped people. Here we indulged our imagination. We thought we beheld in one of them a father, in another an husband, and in another a son, each of whom was forced from his various and tender connections, and without even the opportunity of bidding them adieu. While we were engaged in these and other melancholy reflections, the whole body of slaves had entirely passed us. We turned almost insensibly to look at them again, when we discovered an unhappy man at the end of the train, who could scarcely keep pace with the rest. His feet seemed to have suffered much from long and constant travelling, for he was limping painfully along.

"This man" resumes the African, "has travelled a considerable way. He lived at a great distance from hence, and had a large family, for whom he was daily to provide. As he went out one night to a neighbouring spring, to procure water for his thirsty children, he was kidnapped by two *slave hunters*, who sold him in the morning to some country merchants for a *bar of iron*. These drove him with other slaves, procured almost in the same manner, to the nearest market, where the English merchants, to whom the train that has just now passed us belongs, purchased him and two others, by means of their travelling agents, for a *pistol*. His wife and children have been long waiting for his return. But he is gone for ever from their sight: and they must be now disconsolate, as they must be certain by his delay, that he has fallen into the hands of the *Christians*.

"And now, as I have mentioned the name of *Christians*, a name, by which the Europeans distinguish themselves from us, I could wish to be informed of the meaning which such an appellation may convey. They consider themselves as *men*, but us unfortunate Africans, whom they term *Heathens*, as the *beasts* that serve us. But ah! how different is the fact! What is *Christianity*, but a system of *murder* and *oppression*? The cries and yells of the unfortunate people, who are now soon to embark for the regions of servitude, have already pierced my heart. Have you not heard me sigh, while we have been talking? Do you not see the tears that now trickle down my cheeks? and yet these hardened *Christians* are unable to be moved at all: nay, they will scourge them amidst their groans, and even smile, while they are torturing them to death. Happy, happy Heathenism? which can detest the vices of Christianity, and feel for the distresses of mankind."

"But" we reply, "You are totally mistaken: *Christianity* is the most perfect and lovely of moral systems. It blesses even the hand of persecution itself, and returns good for evil. But the people against whom you so justly declaim, are not *Christians*. They are *infidels*. They are *monsters*. They are out of the common course of nature. Their countrymen at home are generous and brave. They support the sick, the lame, and the blind. They fly to the succour of the distressed. They have noble and stately buildings for the sole purpose of benevolence. They are in short, of all nations, the most remarkable for humanity and justice."

"But why then," replies the honest African, "do they suffer this? Why is Africa a scene of blood and desolation? Why are her children wrested from her, to administer to the luxuries and greatness of those whom they never offended? And why are these dismal cries in vain?"

"Alas!" we reply again, "can the cries and groans, with which the air now trembles, be heard across this extensive continent? Can the southern winds convey them to the ear of Britain? If they could reach the generous Englishman at home, they would pierce his heart, as they have already pierced your own. He would sympathize with you in your distress. He would be enraged at the conduct of his countrymen, and resist their tyranny."—

But here a shriek unusually loud, accompanied with a dreadful rattling of chains, interrupted the discourse. The wretched Africans were just about to embark: they had turned their face to their country, as if to take a last adieu, and, with arms uplifted to the sky, were making the very atmosphere resound with their prayers and imprecations.

Thomas Clarkson

from *The History of the Rise, Progress and Accomplishment of the Abolition of the African Slave-trade, by the British Parliament* (1808)

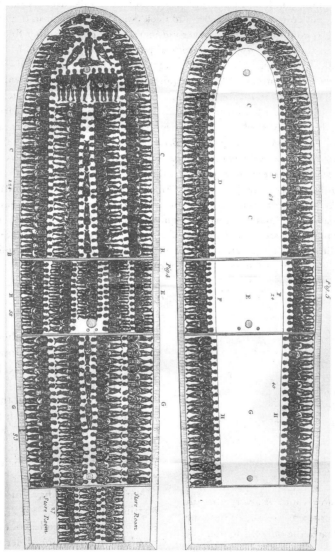

Illustration of a Slave Ship

Mary Hays
1760 – 1843

Mary Hays was born on 4 May 1760 in the London suburb of Southwark. Her father, John Hays, a merchant sailor, died in 1774, and her mother, Elizabeth, went into the wine business. Hays was largely self-educated. In about 1777, she fell in love with John Eccles, whom she had met at a Baptist chapel. Both families disapproved of their relationship, but they corresponded secretly and Eccles was her first mentor. In 1780, the families relented, but Eccles died before they could marry. Hays never did marry. She published her first poem in 1781, her first story in 1786, and her first book, a pamphlet in favour of public worship, in 1791. Meanwhile, she was coming to know a number of radical intellectuals, including George Dyer, William Frend, Godwin,* Joseph Priestley, and, perhaps most importantly, Wollstonecraft.* Her unrequited love for Frend, and Godwin's supportive friendship, inspired her first novel, *Memoirs of Emma Courtney* (1796). Also in 1796, she reintroduced Godwin and Wollstonecraft, who had not liked each other in 1791; they fell in love and were married the next year. After Wollstonecraft's death, Hays published two obituaries of her and an anonymous work very much in the Wollstonecraft tradition, *Appeal to the Men of Great Britain in Behalf of Women* (1798). Her second novel, *The Victim of Prejudice* (1799) is also radically feminist. Next she embarked on an ambitious six-volume work, *Female Biography* (1803), which took her three years to complete. The nearly three hundred biographies cover such eminent women as Sappho, Boadicea, Cleopatra, Joan of Arc, Anne Boleyn, Elizabeth I and Mary Queen of Scots, and Catherine the Great. As Hays grew older she became more conservative, and increasingly influenced by the evangelicalism of Hannah More,* but she never relinquished her belief in the moral and intellectual equality of women and men. She taught at a school and published three children's books, two more novels, and, despite her concern about her "declining ... physical strength and mental activity," another biographical dictionary, *Memoirs of Queens* (1821). She died in Lower Clapton on 22 February 1843. (D.L.M.)

༄༅༄

from *Appeal to the Men of Great Britain in Behalf of Women* (1798)

> ————Reason we resign;
> Against our senses we adopt the plan
> Which reverence, fear, and folly think divine.
>   YEARSLEY[1]

What Women Are

To say what women *really* are, would be a very difficult task indeed; we must therefore endeavour, to describe them by negatives. As, perhaps, the only thing that can be advanced with certainty on the subject, is,—what they are *not*. For it is very clear, that they are not what they ought to be, that they are not what men would have them to be, and to finish the portrait, that they are not what they appear to be. Indeed, indeed, they cannot say with honest Hamlet, that they "know not what seem is."[2] I hope however that these observations will not be considered as a libel upon the sex; for as this inconsistency and uncertainty of character is a matter of necessity and not of choice, they are rather objects of pity than of blame. And as their defects are generally speaking, I presume, those of education, rather than of nature, the men have more subject for remorse than triumph.

That I may endeavour to establish in some degree what I have advanced, let us examine a little on what footing women are placed in this, or indeed in any other country; and if laying aside prejudice, it is obvious to

---
[1] Ann Yearsley,* "To the Honourable H.W., on Reading *The Castle of Otranto*" (1785) 54–56.

[2] Cf. Shakespeare, *Hamlet* 1.2.76.

common sense, that their situation is against them in more points than in their favour; and if it is particularly against that candor and honest simplicity of heart and manner, without which no character can be really and intrinsically valuable;—if upon examination all this appear to be true, I hope it will help to extenuate the imputed faults of the sex. And it ought certainly to induce men to give up some of those high pretensions, which are as little calculated to produce real happiness in domestic life, to the one party as the other. Indeed I most firmly believe,—and it cannot be too often repeated,—that the greatest difficulty is to bring men to consider the subject with attention; which if they once did, there is every reason to hope, that they would of themselves be inclined to do justice.

In the first place then, I hold it as an infallible truth, and a truth that few will attempt to deny; that any race of people, or I should rather say any class of rational beings,—though by no means inferior originally in intellectual endowments,—may be held in a state of subjection and dependence from generation to generation, by another party, who, by a variety of circumstances, none of them depending on actual, original superiority of mind, may have established an authority over them. And it must be acknowledged a truth equally infallible, that any class so held in a state of subjection and dependence, will degenerate both in body and mind.

We have for examples of this, only to contemplate the characters and conduct of the descendants of the Egyptians, the Greeks, the Romans, and other nations, living under the same climates, and upon the very same soil, where their renowned ancestors flourished in arts, and triumphed in arms; and to consider to what a state of degradation and humiliation they are now reduced! On these reflections, however, it is unnecessary here to enlarge; we have only to bring home the application to the state of women in general, who, degraded and humiliated in society, and held in a constant state of dependence,—can it be wondered, that they have lost even the idea of what they might have been, or what they still might be? For they are confined, not only within those bounds, which nature and reason unite in prescribing for the real happiness and good of mankind; and in which every virtuous and well informed mind acquiesces, as much from choice as necessity; but they are likewise bound by chains, of such enormous weight and complicated form, that the more they are considered, the less hope remains of being able to unloose them by perseverance, or break through them by force. Or if some impelled by an ardent love of liberty, by genius, or by despair, "burst their bonds asunder, and cast their cords away"[1]—Alas! the consequences too often are—Ruin to the individual, without benefit to the whole.

Women therefore, generally speaking, act a wiser and a better part as individuals, to keep within that boundary prescribed for them by their lawgivers. Within it they often contrive to do mischief enough; without it who can pretend to say where the mischief might end? For, candidly speaking, perhaps it would be dangerous to trust women all at once, with liberty in that extent which is their due.

But it is to be regretted, that the temperance and good sense shewn by women, in submitting with so good a grace to injuries, which though they cannot redress, they nevertheless feel very severely; it is much to be regretted, that this temperance and good sense, is not attended with better consequences to themselves.

Indeed their fate in this respect is extremely hard; for every method they can attempt, to improve their situation, is equally inefficacious. Silence and submission are looked upon as proofs of acquiescence and content; and men will hardly of themselves, seek to improve a situation, with which many are apparently satisfied. On the other hand any marks of spirit, or sense of injury, or desire to better their situation either as individuals or in society; is treated not only with contempt, but abhorrence; and so far from gaining any thing by proposing reasonable and equitable terms for themselves in either case, the generality of men are enraged at the attempt; and would upon these occasions think it no crime to rob the poor culprits, of the wretched, ill understood, and worse inforced rights that remain to them.

The following little story, illustrates well the progress of lawless authority; and is applicable enough to our subject.

---

[1] Cf. Psalms 2.3.

A Brother and Sister were one day going to market with some eggs, and other country provisions to sell. "Dear Jacky," said the sister, after a good deal of consideration, and not a little proud of her powers of calculation,—"Dear Jacky, you have somehow made a very unfair division of our eggs, of which you know it was intended that we should have equal shares; so pray give me two dozen of yours, and I shall then have as many as you have." "No," says John,—John Bull[1] as likely as any John,—"that would never do; but dear, sweet, pretty sister Peg, give me one dozen of yours, and then I shall have five times as many as you have; which you know will be quite the same as if you had them yourself, or indeed better; as I shall save you the trouble of carrying them, shall protect you and the rest of your property, and shall besides give you many fine things when we get to the fair—Bless me, Margaret! what is the matter with you? How frightful you always are when in a passion! And how horribly ugly you look whenever you contradict me! I wish poor Ralph the miller saw you just now, I'm sure he'd never look at you again. Besides, sister of mine, since you force me to it, and provoke me beyond all bearing, I must tell you, that as I am stronger than you, I can take them whether you will or no." The thing was no sooner said than done, and poor Peg, found herself obliged to submit to something much more convincing than her brother's logic.

On they jogged however together, Peg pouting all the way, and John not a bit the civiler for having got what he knew in his heart he had no title to; and when they got to the fair, poor Peg's property, of which he was to have been the faithful guardian, and careful steward; went with his own, to purchase baubles and gin for his worthless favorite. But then, had not Peg pretended to put herself upon a footing of equality with him, or had she even after all, but calmly and quietly given up her own rights without murmuring,—nothing so easy as that, till it comes home to a man's own case,—he swore manfully that there should not have been a word between them.

Thus goes the world! And a pretty farce it is!—And such are the weighty arguments used to deprive women of rights, of which, were they on the contrary put in full possession, and taught the right use, would not only encrease their own stock of happiness; but, however it might affect individuals, which can never be guarded against in any system, or any plan of reformation whatever, would certainly meliorate the mass of humanity upon the whole. And, affected as this phrase may appear, it is the only idea I have, or definition I can give, of rational reformation, or possible perfection, in our present state.

But to return to our subject, let me ask; is it wonderful since women cannot be in reality what men would have them to be, though they must often endeavour to appear so; since they dare not be what they really ought to be, because it clashes with the pretensions and prejudices of the stronger party; since they are compelled upon the one hand and restrained upon the other;—is it wonderful I say if they pursue a trifling, a dissipated, and often a hypocritical and vicious conduct? Or in other words, is it wonderful if they are what they are? I believe I may readily answer the question. It is not wonderful. It is perfectly in the course of nature. It is an effect, resulting of necessity from a cause.

The seeds of pride and vanity, are originally planted in the breast of every human being, man and woman; for in fact they differ but little. Or shall we say the seeds of ambition; for the same things are often called by different names; and men are ashamed of even acknowledging under one, that which they boast of under another. By whatever name we chuse however, to distinguish the passion to which we allude, it is a certain tendency, a certain inexplicable impulse in the mind to rise, which prompts us to excel by some means or other. The seeds of this, like those of all the other passions, are planted by a wise and unerring hand; and reason and experience prove to us, that according to the management of these, the consequences are. They are evidently calculated to produce pleasure and utility on the whole, when kept within due bounds, and directed to proper objects; but if these rules are neglected, they as evidently tend to destruction. Now this passion to distinguish themselves,—this rage to excel,—women are admitted to possess in as great perfection, if not perhaps in a stronger degree than men. With this difference only,

---

[1] the stereotypical Englishman.

that when applied to woman it commonly receives the denomination of vanity, or at best of pride; but I think seldom or never of ambition. No—that high sounding term, is too sublime for woman; and is reserved to varnish over the passions, and crimes of man; while those of the other sex, called by their proper names, and seen in their natural colours, impose not on mankind.

The different objects however on which the vanity, or the pride, or the ambition of the sexes is employed, give a distinction and superiority to the men, to which they are by no means entitled in reality; because it is not yet clearly proven, that the choice of every thing that is most consequential, decorous, pleasant, and profitable for their own sphere of action, is not an usurpation; and for other powerful reasons, which would lead into too large a field of controversy if here touched upon. I repeat however, that men are by no means entitled to superior respect and consideration upon such grounds, when we reflect; that women are compelled on the one hand to adopt a conduct they cannot approve of, nor feel easy and natural; and are restrained on the other, from the exercise of one more congenial to the rights of human nature; and therefore it is very difficult to say if they were not thus limited, how far it might not appear that they are equal to any sphere of action however great or good.

But taking women on the footing they now are, and on which they will probably remain for some time at least, the tide of their passions must waste itself upon something; and thus being forced into wrong channels, there it flows; but for the honour of the sex I trust

"Still it murmurs as it flows,
Panting for its native home."[1]

Thus many a good head is stuffed with ribbons, gauze, fringes, flounces, and furbelows, that might have received and communicated, far other and more noble impressions. And many a fine imagination has been exhausted upon these, which had they been turned to the study of nature, or initiated into the dignified embellishments of the fine arts, might have adorned, delighted, and improved society. For oh! what patience and industry, what time and trouble, what acute observation, what intense thought, what ceaseless anxiety, what hopes and fears, alternately elate and depress thy trembling spirit, thou busy priestess of vanity! The half of the talents, the perseverance, the resolution and attention, hadst thou been but a man; might have placed thee on the woolsack,[2] or have put a mitre on thy head, or a long robe on thy back, or a truncheon in thy hand. Or, being even what thou art, the fiftieth part of thy misemployed talents if turned into proper channels, might have made thee what is tantamount, to a Chancellor, a Bishop, a Judge, or a General—An useful, an amiable, and an interesting woman.

The mind, as we have before said, must be occupied one way or other, well or ill; and therefore after the first merely animal duties are performed, the remaining void must be filled up; and indeed much time remains that cannot be occupied well, by people whose situation places them above the necessity of habits of industry. For, to be accomplished even in the elegant arts, requires habits of industry and attention, and to be accomplished in these is therefore not the lot of every one; and though most women of the middling and higher classes, aim at this in the course of their education, yet few in comparison acquire them, or acquiring retain them in a sufficient degree, to render them amusing, or interesting in after life.

Domestic duties have ever been recommended to women, as the most useful and meritorious occupation in which they can pass their time; and against them, who shall dare to lift their voice? for in the right exercise of these, are best laid the foundations of all the virtues and charities. In the sweet circle of domestic life we may venture to affirm, that the seeds of every virtue publick and private, and in both sexes, are planted and nourished to best advantage.

There are however reasons, which I shall perhaps hereafter touch upon, that prevent these from being held in estimation among women of the higher classes; and falling into disuse among them, the middle ranks of course follow their example. Alas! what can women be expected to do? Driven and excluded from what are

---

[1] "Water parted from the sea," an anonymous lyric set by Thomas Arne (1710–78) 7–8.

[2] the ceremonial throne of the Lord Chancellor.

commonly esteemed the consequential offices of life;—denied, and perhaps with reason and propriety too, any political existence;—and literary talents and acquirements, nay genius itself, being in them generally regarded rather with contempt or jealousy, than meeting with encouragement and applause;—nothing in short being left for them, but domestic duties, and superficial accomplishments and vanities—Is it surprising, that instead of doing as men bid them, they in some degree, and as far as particular circumstances permit, do as men do;—that laying aside dull precept, they follow the more animating power of example;—that spoiled by prosperity and goaded on by temptation and the allurements of pleasure, they give a loose rein to their passions, and plunge headlong into folly and dissipation; regardless in an eminent degree of their family, their fame, and their fortune, if they can but indulge in the idle vagaries of the present moment; to the utter extinction of thought, moderation, or strict morality? And, if they but shun that, which when fully proven against them, banishes them from society; they think they sacrifice sufficiently to decency and duty. And indeed when compared with the conduct of the men, they do so.

If this sentence, which I presume to pronounce on a considerable portion of my own sex, be deemed severe; let me be permitted to appeal to the votaries of fashion themselves; and let their own hearts tell, whether or not I judge harshly of their conduct.

Certainly I mean not this as a censure adapted without exception to one particular class; for in no class, in no rank whatever, are there women of more exalted virtue, or more exemplary conduct than many in high life; and whose merit is magnified, and multiplied ten thousand fold, by the consideration of their resistance to bad example, to temptation, and to the most dangerous of all privileges;—that of committing folly with impunity. But still I revert to my argument, and appeal again to their own hearts, for the general truth of my assertions.

Is this to be ascribed to their mode of education; or is it not? In part perhaps it is; and yet a great portion of their education is good. The theoretical part at least is excellent; for I believe there are few teachers public or private, who would not be ashamed and afraid, independent of conscientious feelings, to inculcate any thing directly against religion or morality. The practical part too, as far as it goes, is much of it good; as it tends to the habits of order, discipline, and application; though that these are often misplaced and misemployed cannot well be denied, and especially by one who of course rests much of the necessity of a new system of education, on the faults and blemishes of the present.

The fact is that education properly speaking, that is, the foundation of character, is begun and ended at home; before children go to, and after they leave schools; and to these periods perhaps, reformation should be applied with most vigor and least hesitation. But the consideration of this part of our subject, belongs to another division of this sketch. In the mean time we may observe here that the general conduct of the sexes to each other, before any particular or lasting engagements are made, is very unfavorable to the virtue and good conduct of both. Women do not find it their interest to tell men the truth before marriage, and afterwards alas! they dare not. Men it is true compound the matter with them for a season, and while youth and beauty is on their side; by the grossest, the most general, and unmeaning flattery; and this sort of mutual imposition, is reduced into a system of licensed hypocrisy on both sides, till the day of inquisition arrives; and when men become husbands and fathers,—that day is near at hand. Then it is,—a few solitary instances excepted,—that the romance of life, the enchanted prospect vanishes, as if by the touch of magic; and then it is generally speaking that the reality of life commences.

So far however all is fair and equal on both sides; and reason must at times have anticipated, that the enthusiasm of love was of a nature too volatile to last for ever. No reasonable woman, no woman with a spark of common sense, dreams that a husband is to continue a lover, in the romantic sense of the word; or if she does so she is soon undeceived, and very properly forced to submit to reason. But what is infinitely absurd and unfair, though undeniably true; men coming under the same description, men otherwise wise enough, and reasonable enough, to outward appearance; do seriously suppose that their wives are to turn out, the angels, their imaginations had painted. Or if they do not seriously suppose it, which after all is possible, they act precisely as if they did. They either expect, or affect to expect, that the same sweetness of temper, the same equality and flow of spirits, the same eagerness to please, shall uniformly prevail in the wife; when the amiable, the devoted lover, is metamorphosed into the sullen and tyrannical husband. Such expectations however, are above the reach of almost any human being to fulfil; and from such unreasonable and unfair expectations may often therefore be traced, the many disagreements and disappointments which but too frequently occur in that state, which is certainly, however, of all others in this sublunary world; that most capable of promoting and preserving,—pure, lasting, and interesting attachments.

Alas! were men but half as anxious, to fulfil their own share of the engagements entered into in the most important concern in life, as they are to press home matrimonial duties upon women, all might be well; but unfortunately for themselves, as well as those connected with them, they place their happiness, and what they seem to value more,—their consequence,—in being indulged and humored beyond all reasonable bounds, in whatever mode their fancy or passions suggest.

In matters of great and important concern, women are generally soon taught to understand, that they ought to have, and can claim, no weight whatever. They then naturally think that the lesser ones, mere family matters, those of taste, of ornament, or fashion, may be left to them; but even here they are mistaken and misinformed; for their share in the management of home, and domestic concerns, lies entirely at the mercy of the husbands, who except they are more than human, will rather be guided by their own caprice, than by the exact rules of equity. Except therefore, when the station and fortune are so great, that each can afford to live in their own way without the interference of the other; as is the case in high life, where men are in a manner compelled to share with their wives in some degree that liberty which they so amply take to themselves; in every other case, the wife is acknowledged to be, even in domestic concerns, the upper servant of her husband only; and he must be very good-natured indeed, if he does not make her sensible of it. In every other case, the iron hand of authority lies desperately heavy, on even the trifles of life. And if it were not that the men, are often addicted to vanity, to shew, and to all the fopperies of fashion as much as the other sex; women would not be indulged even in these so much as they are.

The authority then of the men, is far from being merely nominal, as they would sometimes have it believed in their good-natured moments, and when they wish to be extremely condescending; for women find to their cost, that it is positive, in the utmost extent of the word. And though it is often alleged, that the public influence of the men, is balanced by the private influence of the women; yet if there is truth in this remark at all, it is that kind of back stair influence, which is enjoyed rather by the unworthy, than the virtuous part of the sex. For commonly speaking this is so far from being the case, that it is in the private and domestic scenes of life, above all others, where women are supposed to be obliged to act with the greatest humility and circumspection; and where indeed it often happens, that if they are not willing to give up every feeling that interests humanity, they are accused of want of temper and prudence, and consequently are considered as very indifferent wives.

In fine, it seems to be expected that women should in a manner cease to exist, in a rational and mental point of view, before they resign life; by giving up along with their name every title to judge or act for themselves, but when their masters chuse to bestow such privileges upon them. Were it possible however for women to fulfil such implicit articles of slavery, it were, perhaps, wrong to oppose any thing, which not being of itself absolutely immoral, might contribute to the peace of society. But women being formed by the power of the Almighty, so nearly to resemble man in their desire after happiness, they must be supposed equally selfish in their pursuit of it; and having upon the same principles with men, wills and opinions of their own, they will of course ever be promoting the attainments of their own ends, either directly or indirectly. That the latter system is the one that women find themselves under the necessity of adopting, is but too evident; but if men persist in thinking it the only one suitable to their characters and situation, they have no right to expect that beings so unfortunately circumstanced, and so unfairly treated, should under such disadvantages act up to the perfection of their nature, nor do I pretend to allege that they do so. If they did, all attempts at reformation were vain and unnecessary.

The substance of what the writer has already presumed to recommend to men,—and that which follows will be to the same purpose,—is shortly this;—generously, and in conformity with sound politicks to allow women such privileges, such degrees of liberty and equality as they will otherwise, as they ever have done, take in a worse way, and in a greater degree. And if indeed, women do avail themselves of the only weapons they are permitted to wield, can they be blamed? Undoubtedly not; since they are compelled to it by the injustice and impolicy of men. Petty treacheries—mean subterfuge—whining and flattery—feigned submission—and all the dirty little attendants, which compose the endless train of low cunning; if not commendable, cannot with justice be very severely censured, when practised by women. Since alas!—THE WEAK HAVE NO OTHER ARMS AGAINST THE STRONG! Since alas!—NECESSITY ACKNOWLEDGES NO LAW, BUT HER OWN!

Helen Maria Williams
1761 – 1827

Helen Maria Williams was born on 17 June 1761 in London, the younger daughter of a Welsh army officer, Charles Williams, and of Helen Hay Williams. When her father died in 1769, her mother, who was Scottish, took her daughters to Berwick and educated them there. Williams went back to London in 1781; she published her anti-war poem, *Edwin and Eltruda: A Legendary Tale*, in 1782; it was the first of a series of poems in support of radical causes. She began to move in literary circles, meeting Burke,* Dr. Charles Burney and his daughter Frances,* Franklin,* Godwin,* Samuel Johnson, Merry,* Elizabeth Montagu, Rogers,* George Romney, Seward,* Sarah Siddons, and Smith,* and corresponding with Burns.* In 1790, she travelled to France and published *Letters Written in France*, the first of her eight eyewitness accounts of the French Revolution. She returned to France in 1791 (the occasion of her poem *A Farewell, for Two Years, to England*); there she began a relationship with a pro-Revolutionary—and married—English businessman, John Hurford Stone, that would last until Stone's death in 1818. Returning to France yet again in 1792, she became acquainted not only with pro-Revolutionary foreigners like Paine* and Wollstonecraft,* but also with members of the Girondin (moderate) faction, including Jean-Marie Roland de la Platière, Minister of the Interior, and his influential wife, Manon. In October 1793, after the outbreak of war with Britain and the advent of the Reign of Terror, Williams was imprisoned; she passed the time translating Jacques-Henri Bernardin de Saint-Pierre's *Paul et Virginie* (1788), and the translation became her most popular book. In 1794, after her release, Stone was arrested. Fearing that he would be arrested again, they went to Switzerland, where they stayed until the fall of Robespierre. Then they went back to Paris. When her sister died in 1798, Williams adopted her sons. Her initial admiration for Napoléon soon turned to disillusionment, and in 1801 she published "Ode on the Peace of Amiens," which so displeased him that he had her imprisoned again. Williams's varying attempts to defend or to explain the Revolution became less and less popular with English readers; she came under attack from critics like Polwhele* and Horace Walpole. After Stone's death, she lived in Amsterdam with one of her nephews. She published a collected edition of her poetry in 1823. She died on 15 December 1827, in Paris, and was buried in the Père Lachaise cemetery, next to Stone. (D.L.M.)

෴

from *Letters Written in France, in the Summer 1790, to a Friend in England; Containing, Various Anecdotes Relative to the French Revolution; and Memoirs of Mons. and Madame du F——* (1790)

LETTER 4

Before I suffered my friends at Paris to conduct me through the usual routine of convents, churches, and palaces, I requested to visit the Bastille;[1] feeling a much stronger desire to contemplate the ruins of that building than the most perfect edifices of Paris. When we got into the carriage, our French servant called to the coachman, with an air of triumph, "A la Bastille—mais nous n'y resterons pas."[2] We drove under that porch which so many wretches have entered never to repass, and alighting from the carriage descended with difficulty into the dungeons, which were too low to admit of our standing upright, and so dark that we were obliged at noon-day to visit them with the light of a candle. We saw the hooks of those chains by which the prisoners were fastened round the neck, to the walls of their cells; many of which being below the level of the water, are in a constant state of humidity; and a noxious vapour issued from them, which more than once extinguished

---

[1] See note to *A Farewell, for Two Years* 69.

[2] "To the Bastille,—but we shall not remain there." (H.M.W.)

the candle, and was so insufferable that it required a strong spirit of curiosity to tempt one to enter. Good God! and to these regions of horror were human creatures dragged at the caprice of despotic power. What a melancholy consideration, that

>———"Man! proud man,
>Drest in a little brief authority,
>Plays such fantastic tricks before high heaven,
>As make the angels weep."———[1]

There appears to be a greater number of these dungeons than one could have imagined the hard heart of tyranny itself would contrive; for, since the destruction of the building, many subterraneous cells have been discovered underneath a piece of ground which was inclosed within the walls of the Bastille, but which seemed a bank of solid earth before the horrid secrets of this prison-house were disclosed. Some skeletons were found in these recesses, with irons still fastened on their decaying bones.

After having visited the Bastille, we may indeed be surprised, that a nation so enlightened as the French, submitted so long to the oppressions of their government; but we must cease to wonder that their indignant spirits at length shook off the galling yoke.

Those who have contemplated the dungeons of the Bastille, without rejoicing in the French revolution, may, for aught I know, be very respectable persons, and very agreeable companions in the hours of prosperity; but, if my heart were sinking with anguish, I should not fly to those persons for consolation. Sterne says, that a man is incapable of loving one woman as he ought, who has not a sort of an affection for the whole sex;[2] and as little should I look for particular sympathy from those who have no feelings of general philanthropy. If the splendour of a despotic throne can only shine like the radiance of lightning, while all around is involved in gloom and horror, in the name of heaven let its baleful lustre be extinguished for ever. May no such strong contrast of light and shade again exist in the political system of France! but may the beams of liberty, like the beams of day, shed their benign influence on the cottage of the peasant, as well as on the palace of the monarch! May liberty, which for so many ages past has taken pleasure in softening the evils of the bleak and rugged climates of the north, in fertilizing a barren soil, in clearing the swamp, in lifting mounds against the inundations of the tempest, diffuse her blessings also on the genial land of France, and bid the husbandman rejoice under the shade of the olive and the vine!

The Bastille, which Henry the Fourth[3] and his veteran troops assailed in vain, the citizens of Paris had the glory of taking in a few hours. The avarice of Mons. de Launay[4] had tempted him to guard this fortress with only half the complement of men ordered by government; and a letter which he received the morning of the 14th of July, commanding him to sustain the siege till the evening, when succour would arrive, joined to his own treachery towards the assailants, cost him his life.

The courage of the besiegers was inflamed by the horrors of famine, there being at this time only twenty-four hours provision of bread in Paris. For some days the people had assembled in crouds round the shops of the bakers, who were obliged to have a guard of soldiers to protect them from the famished multitude; while the women, rendered furious by want, cried, in the resolute tone of despair, "Il nous faut du pain pour nos enfans."[5] Such was the scarcity of bread, that a French gentleman told me, that, the day preceding the taking of the Bastille, he was invited to dine with a Negotiant, and, when he went, was informed that a servant had been out five hours in search of bread, and had at last been able to purchase only one loaf.

It was at this crisis, it was to save themselves the shocking spectacle of their wives and infants perishing before their eyes, that the citizens of Paris flew to arms, and, impelled by such causes, fought with the daring intrepidity of men who had all that renders life of any

---

[1] Cf. Shakespeare, *Measure for Measure* 2.2.117–22.

[2] Sterne says this in his short novel *A Sentimental Journey through France and Italy* (1768), "The Passport: Versailles."

[3] Henry IV (1553–1610) had to abandon the siege of Paris, which was held by the Catholic League, during the War of the Three Henrys (1590).

[4] Bernard-René Jordan, marquis de Launay, the governor of the Bastille, was killed after it fell. He had actually asked for reinforcements shortly beforehand.

[5] "We must have bread for our children." (H.M.W.)

value at stake, and who determined to die or conquer. The women too, far from indulging the fears incident to our feeble sex, in defiance of the cannon of the Bastille, ventured to bring victuals to their sons and husbands; and, with a spirit worthy of Roman matrons, encouraged them to go on. Women mounted guard in the streets, and, when any person passed, called out boldly, "Qui va la?"[1]

A gentleman, who had the command of fifty men in this enterprize, told me, that one of his soldiers being killed by a cannon-ball, the people, with great marks of indignation, removed the corpse, and then, snatching up the dead man's hat, begged money of the bystanders for his interment, in a manner characteristic enough of that gaiety, which never forsakes the French, even on such occasions as would make any other people on earth serious. "Madame, pour ce pauvre diable qui ce fait tué pour la Nation!—Mons. pour ce pauvre chien qui se fait tué pour la nation!"[2] This mode of supplication, though not very pathetic, obtained the end desired; no person being sufficiently obdurate to resist the powerful plea, "qu'il se fait tué pour la Nation."[3]

When the Bastille was taken, and the old man, of whom you have no doubt heard, and who had been confined in a dungeon thirty-five years, was brought into day-light, which had not for so long a space of time visited his eyes, he staggered, shook his white beard, and cried faintly, "Messieurs, vous m'avez rendu un grand service, rendez m'en un autre, tuez moi! je ne sais pas où aller."—"Allons, allons," the croud answered with one voice, "la Nation te nourrira."[4]

As the heroes of the Bastille passed along the streets after its surrender, the citizens stood at the doors of their houses loaded with wine, brandy, and other refreshments, which they offered to these deliverers of their country. But they unanimously refused to taste any strong liquors, considering the great work they had undertaken as not yet accomplished, and being determined to watch the whole night, in case of any surprize.

All those who had assisted in taking the Bastille, were presented by the municipality of Paris with a ribbon of the national colours, on which is stamped, inclosed in a circle of brass, an impression of the Bastille, and which is worn as a military order.

The municipality of Paris also proposed a solemn funeral procession in memory of those who lost their lives in this enterprize; but, on making application to the National Assembly for a deputation of its members to assist at this solemnity, the assembly were of opinion that these funeral honours should be postponed till a more favourable moment, as they might at present have a tendency to inflame the minds of the people.

I have heard several persons mention a young man, of a little insignificant figure, who, the day before the Bastille was taken, got up on a chair in the Palais Royal, and harangued the multitude, conjuring them to make a struggle for their liberty, and asserting, that now the moment was arrived. They listened to his eloquence with the most eager attention; and, when he had instructed as many as could hear him at one time, he requested them to depart, and repeated his harangue to a new set of auditors.

Among the dungeons of the Bastille are placed, upon a heap of stones, the figures of the two men who contrived the plan of this fortress, where they were afterwards confined for life. These men are represented chained to the wall, and are beheld without any emotion of sympathy.

The person employed to remove the ruins of the Bastille, has framed of the stones eighty-three complete models of this building, which, with a true patriotic spirit, he has presented to the eighty-three departments of the kingdom, by way of hint to his countrymen to take care of their liberties in future.[5]

---

[1] "Who goes there?" (H.M.W.)

[2] "Madam, for this poor devil, who has been killed for the Nation!—Sir, for this unfortunate dog, who has been killed for the Nation!" (H.M.W.)

[3] "Had been killed for the Nation." (H.M.W.)

[4] "Gentlemen, you have rendered me one great service; render me another, kill me! for I know not where to go.—Come along, come along, the Nation will provide for you." (H.M.W.)

---

[5] The ruins of the Bastille were made into a variety of patriotic souvenirs, including these scale models.

LETTER 11

We are just returned from Versailles, where I could not help fancying I saw, in the back ground of that magnificent abode of a despot, the gloomy dungeons of the Bastille, which still haunt my imagination, and prevented my being much dazzled by the splendour of this superb palace.

We were shewn the passages through which the Queen escaped from her own apartment to the King's, on the memorable night when the *Poissardes*[1] visited Versailles, and also the balcony at which she stood with the Dauphin in her arms, when, after having remained a few hours concealed in some secret recess of the palace, it was thought proper to comply with the desire of the croud, who repeatedly demanded her presence. I could not help moralizing a little, on being told that the apartment to which this balcony belongs, is the very room in which Louis the Fourteenth died;[2] little suspecting what a scene would, in the course of a few years, be acted on that spot.

All the bread which could be procured in the town of Versailles, was distributed among the *Poissardes*; who, with savage ferocity, held up their morsels of bread on their bloody pikes, towards the balcony where the Queen stood, crying, in a tone of defiance, "Nous avons du pain!"[3]

During the whole of the journey from Versailles to Paris, the Queen held the Dauphin in her arms, who had been previously taught to put his infant hands together, and attempt to soften the enraged multitude by repeating, "Grace pour maman!"[4]

Mons. de la Fayette[5] prevented the whole Gardes du Corps from being massacred at Versailles, by calling to the incensed people, "Le Roi vous demande grace pour ses Gardes du Corps."[6] The voice of Mons. de la Fayette was listened to, and obeyed. The Gardes du Corps were spared; with whom, before they set out for Paris, the people exchanged clothes, giving them also national cockades;[7] and, as a farther protection from danger, part of the croud mounted on the horses of the Gardes du Corps, each man taking an officer behind him. Before the King came out of La Maison du Ville, Mons. de la Fayette appeared, and told the multitude, who had preserved an indignant silence the whole way from Versailles to Paris, that the King had expressed sentiments of the strongest affection for his people, and had accepted the national cockade; and that he (Mons. de la Fayette) hoped, when his Majesty came out of la Maison du Ville, they would testify their gratitude. In a few minutes the King appeared, and was received with the loudest acclamations.

When the Queen was lately asked to give her deposition on the attempt which, it is said, was made to assassinate her, by the *Poissardes* at Versailles, she answered, with great prudence, "Jai tout vu, tout entendu, et tout oublié!"[8]

The King is now extremely popular, and the people sing in the streets to the old tune of "Vive Henri quatre! &c." "Vive Louis seize!"[9]

The Queen is, I am told, much altered lately in her appearance, but she is still a fine woman. Madame is a beautiful girl; and the Dauphin, who is about seven years of age, is the idol of the people.[10] They expect that he will be educated in the principles of the new constitution, and will be taught to consider himself less a king

---

[1] "fishwives" (Fr.). Parisian women marched on Versailles on 5 October 1789, demanding bread; for a different account of the incident, see Burke, *Reflections.*

[2] on 1 September 1715.

[3] "We now have bread." (H.M.W.)

[4] "Spare mama!" (H.M.W.)

[5] Marie Jean-Paul Yves Roche Gilbert du Motier, marquis de Lafayette (1757–1834), a hero of the American Revolution and a voice for moderation in the French Revolution.

[6] "The King begs of you to spare his body-guards." (H.M.W.)

[7] ribbon ornaments for hats, in red, white, and blue, the colours of the Revolution.

[8] "I saw every thing, heard every thing, and have forgot every thing." (H.M.W.)

[9] "Long live Henry the Fourth. Long live Lewis the Sixteenth." (H.M.W.)

[10] Marie Antoinette (b. 1755), whose hair is said to have turned grey with the advent of the Revolution and who would be guillotined on 16 October 1793; her daughter, Marie Thérèse (b. 1778); and her son, the Dauphin or crown prince Louis (b. 1785), who would die in prison in 1795.

than a citizen. He appears to be a sweet engaging child, and I have just heard one of his sayings repeated. He has a collection of animals, which he feeds with his own hand. A few days ago, an ungrateful rabbit, who was his first favourite, bit his finger when he was giving him food. The Prince, while smarting with the pain, called out to his petit lapin, "Tu ès Aristocrate." One of the attendants enquired, "Eh! Monseigneur, qu'est-ce que c'est qu'un Aristocrate." "Ce sont ceux," answered the Prince, "qui font de la peine à Papa."[1]

The King lately called the Queen, en badinage,[2] Madame Capet; to which she retorted very readily, by giving his Majesty the appellation of "Monsieur *Capot*."[3]

When Les gardes Francoises laid down their arms at Versailles, their officers endeavoured to persuade them to take them up. An officer of my acquaintance told me, that he said to his soldiers, "Mes enfans, vous allez donc me quitter, vous ne m'aimez plus?" "Mon officier," they answered, "nous vous aimons tous, si il s'agit d'aller contre nos ennemis, nous sommes tous prets à vous suivre, mais nous ne tirerons jamais contre nos compatriotes."[4] Since that period, whenever any of les gardes Francoises appear, they are followed by the acclamations of the people, and "Vive les Gardes Francoises!"[5] resounds from every quarter.

While we were sitting, after dinner, at the inn at Versailles, the door was suddenly opened, and a Franciscan friar entered the room. He had so strong a resemblance to Sterne's monk,[6] that I am persuaded he must be a descendant of the same family. We could not, like Sterne, bestow immortality; but we gave some alms: and the venerable old monk, after thanking us with affecting simplicity, added, spreading out his hands with a slow and solemn movement, "Que la paix soit avec vous,"[7] and then departed. I have been frequently put in mind of Sterne since my arrival in France; and the first post-boy I saw in jack-boots, appeared to me a very classical figure, by recalling the idea of La Fleur mounted on his bidet.[8]

A Farewell, for Two Years, to England. A Poem (1791)

Sweet Spring! while others hail thy op'ning flowers,
The first young hope of Summer's blushing hours;
Me they remind, that when her ardent ray
Shall reach the summit of our lengthen'd day,
5   Then, ALBION![9] far from Thee, my cherish'd home,
To foreign climes my pensive steps must roam;
And twice shall Spring, dispelling Winter's gloom,
Shed o'er thy lovely vales her vernal bloom;
Twice shall thy village-maids, with chaplets gay,
10 And simple carols, hail returning May;[10]
And twice shall Autumn, o'er thy cultur'd plain,
Pour the rich treasures of his yellow grain;
Twice shall thy happy peasants bear along
The lavish store, and wake the harvest-song;
15 Ere from the bounded deep my searching eye,
Ah! land belov'd, shall thy white cliffs descry.—
Where the slow Loire,[11] on borders ever gay,
Delights to linger, in his sunny way,
Oft, while I seem to count, with musing glance,
20 The murm'ring waves that near his brink advance,
My wand'ring thoughts shall seek the grassy side,

---

[1] "Little rabbit, Thou art an Aristocrate.—And pray, my Lord, what is an Aristocrate?—Those who make my papa uneasy." (H.M.W.)

[2] "playfully" (Fr.). Capet was the surname of the French royal family; to address the King and Queen as M. and Mme. Capet was to deny their royal status.

[3] "Capot is the French term at picquet, when the game is lost." (H.M.W.) Picquet is a card game.

[4] "My friends, you are going then to forsake me; I possess none of your affection.—Captain, they answered, we all love you; and, if you will lead us against our enemies, we are all ready to follow you: but we will never fire at our fellow citizens." (H.M.W.)

[5] "Long live the French guards." (H.M.W.)

[6] Sterne describes this "poor monk of the order of St. Francis" in the opening pages of *A Sentimental Journey* (1768).

[7] "Peace be with you." (H.M.W.)

[8] La Fleur, Yorick's servant in Sterne's *A Sentimental Journey*, rides—and is thrown by—a post-horse ("bidet," Fr.).

[9] a poetic name for England.

[10] Mayday was traditionally celebrated in English villages.

[11] the longest river in France.

Parental Thames!¹ where rolls thy ample tide;
Where, on thy willow'd bank, methinks, appears
Engrav'd the record of my passing years;
25 Ah! not like thine, their course is gently led,
By zephyrs² fann'd, thro' paths with verdure spread;
They flow, as urg'd by storms the mountain rill
Falls o'er the fragments of the rocky hill.
　　My native scenes! can aught in time, or space,
30 From this fond heart your lov'd remembrance chase?
Link'd to that heart by ties for ever dear,
By Joy's light smile, and Sorrow's tender tear;
By all that ere my anxious hopes employ'd,
By all my soul has suffer'd, or enjoy'd!
35 Still blended with those well-known scenes, arise
The varying images the past supplies;
The childish sports that fond attention drew,
And charm'd my vacant heart when life was new;
The harmless mirth, the sadness robb'd of power
40 To cast its shade beyond the present hour—
And that dear hope which sooth'd my youthful breast,
And show'd the op'ning world in beauty drest;
That hope which seem'd with bright unfolding rays
(Ah, vainly seem'd!) to gild my future days;
45 That hope which, early wrapp'd in lasting gloom,
Sunk in the cold inexorable tomb!—
And Friendship, ever powerful to controul
The keen emotions of the wounded soul,
To lift the suff'ring spirit from despair,
50 And bid it feel that life deserves a care.
Still each impression that my heart retains
Is link'd, dear Land! to thee by lasting chains.
　　She too, sweet soother of my lonely hours!
Who gilds my thorny path with fancy's flowers,
55 The Muse, who early taught my willing heart
To feel with transport her prevailing art;
Who deign'd before my infant eyes to spread
Those dazzling visions she alone can shed;
She, who will still be found where'er I stray,
60 The lov'd companion of my distant way;
'Midst foreign sounds, her voice, that charms my ear,
Breath'd in my native tongue, I still shall hear;
'Midst foreign sounds, endear'd will flow the song
Whose tones, my ALBION, will to thee belong!
65 　　And when with wonder thrill'd, with mind elate,
I mark the change sublime in GALLIA's³ state!
Where new-born Freedom treads the banks of Seine,⁴
Hope in her eye, and Virtue in her train!
Pours day upon the dungeon's central gloom,⁵
70 And leads the captive from his living tomb;
Tears the sharp iron from his loaded breast,
And bids the renovated land be blest—
My thoughts shall fondly turn to that lov'd Isle,
Where Freedom long has shed her genial smile.
75 Less safe in other lands the triple wall,
And massy portal, of the Gothic hall,
Than in that favour'd Isle the straw-built thatch,
Where Freedom sits, and guards the simple latch.
　　Yet, ALBION! while my heart to thee shall spring,
80 To thee its first, its best affections bring;
Yet, when I hear exulting millions pour
The shout of triumph on the GALLIC shore;
Not without sympathy my pensive mind
The bounds of human bliss enlarg'd, shall find;
85 Not without sympathy my glowing breast
Shall hear, on any shore, of millions blest!
Scorning those narrow souls, whate'er their clime,
Who meanly think that sympathy a crime;
Who, if one wish for human good expand
90 Beyond the limits of their native land,
And from the worst of ills would others free,
Deem that warm wish, my Country! guilt to thee.
Ah! why those blessings to one spot confine,
Which, when diffus'd, will not the less be thine?
95 Ah! why repine if far those blessings spread
For which so oft thy gen'rous sons have bled?
Shall ALBION mark with scorn the lofty thought,
The love of Liberty, herself has taught?
Shall *her* brave sons, in this enlighten'd age,
100 Assume the bigot-frown of papal rage,

---

¹ river flowing through London.

² western breezes, traditionally considered soothing.

³ "France's" (L.).

⁴ river flowing through Paris.

⁵ The fall of the Bastille, the state prison in Paris, on 14 July 1789, is usually taken to mark the start of the Revolution. It was later demolished.

Nor tolerate the vow to Freedom paid,
If diff'ring from the ritual *they* have made?
Freedom! who oft on ALBION's fost'ring breast
Has found *her* friends in stars and ermine drest,[1]
105 Allows that some among her chosen race
Should there the claim to partial honours trace,
And in the long-reflected lustre shine
That beams thro' Ancestry's ennobled line;
While she, with guardian wing, can well secure
110 From each proud wrong the undistinguish'd poor.
On GALLIA's coast, where oft the robe of state
Was trail'd by those whom Freedom's soul must hate;
Where, like a comet, rank appear'd to glow
With dangerous blaze, that threaten'd all below;
115 There Freedom now, with gladden'd eye, beholds
The simple vest that flows in equal folds.
   And tho' on Seine's fair banks a transient storm[2]
Flung o'er the darken'd wave its angry form;
That purifying tempest now has past,
120 No more the trembling waters feel the blast;
The bord'ring images, confus'dly trac'd
Along the ruffled stream, to order haste;
The vernal day-spring bursts the partial gloom,
And all the landscape glows with fresher bloom.
125 When, far around that bright'ning scene, I view
Objects of gen'ral bliss, to GALLIA new;
Then, ALBION! shall my soul reflect with pride
Thou wert her leading star, her honour'd guide;
That, long in slav'ry sunk, when taught by thee,
130 She broke her fetters, and has dar'd be free;
In new-born majesty she seems to rise,
While sudden from the land oppression flies.
So, at the solemn hour of Nature's birth,
When brooding darkness[3] veil'd the beauteous earth,
135 Heaven's awful mandate pierc'd the solid night,
"Let there be light," it said, "and there was light!"[4]
   Ah! when shall Reason's intellectual ray
Shed o'er the moral world more perfect day?
When shall that gloomy world appear no more
140 A waste, where desolating tempests roar?
Where savage Discord howls in threat'ning form,
And wild Ambition leads the mad'ning storm;
Where hideous Carnage marks his dang'rous way,
And where the screaming vulture scents his prey?—
145 Ah! come, blest Concord! chase, with smile serene,
The hostile passions from the human scene!
May Glory's lofty path be found afar
From agonizing groans and crimson war;
And may the ardent mind, that seeks renown,
150 Claim, not the martial, but the civic crown!
While pure Benevolence, with happier views
Of bright success, the gen'ral good pursues;
Ah! why, my Country! with indignant pain,
Why in thy senate did she plead in vain?
155 Ah! why in vain enforce the Captives' cause,
And urge Humanity's eternal laws?
With fruitless zeal the tale of horror trace,
And ask redress for AFRIC's injur'd race?[5]
Unhappy race! ah! what to them avail'd,
160 That touching eloquence, whose efforts fail'd?
Tho' in the senate Mercy found combin'd
All who possess the noblest pow'rs of mind,
On other themes, pre-eminently bright,
They shine, like single stars, with sep'rate light;
165 *Here*, only *here*, with intermingled rays,
In one resplendent constellation blaze;
Yes, Captive race! if all the force display'd
By glowing Genius, in Compassion's aid,
When, with that energy she boasts alone,
170 She made your wrongs, your ling'ring tortures known;
Bade full in view the bloody visions roll,
Shook the firm nerves, and froze the shudd'ring soul!—
As when the sun, in piercing radiance bright,
Dispelling the low mists of doubtful light,
175 Its lustre on some hideous object throws,
And all its hateful horror clearly shows—
If Genius could in Mercy's cause prevail,

---

[1] wearing the insignia of nobility: the members of Britain's House of Lords, unlike the French aristocracy, are friendly to Freedom.

[2] the storming of the Bastille. Since then the progress of the Revolution had been mostly non-violent.

[3] Cf. Milton, *L'Allegro* 6.

[4] Genesis 1.3.

[5] Williams had celebrated a recent reform in *A Poem on the Bill Lately Passed for Regulating the Slave Trade* (1788); but the trade was not abolished until 1807, and the slaves were not emancipated until 1833.

  When Interest presses the opposing scale,
  How swift had BRITONS torn your galling chain,
180 And from their country wip'd its foulest stain!—
  But oh, since mis'ry, in its last excess,
  In vain from BRITISH honour hopes redress;
  May other Lands the bright example show,
  May other regions lessen human woe!
185 Yes, GALLIA, haste! tho' BRITAIN's sons decline
  The glorious power to save, that power is thine;
  Haste! since, while BRITAIN courts that dear-bought gold,
  For which her virtue and her fame are sold,
  And calmly calculates her trade of death,
190 Her groaning victims yield in pangs their breath;
  Then save some portion of that suff'ring race
  From ills the mind can scarce endure to trace!
  Oh! whilst with mien august thy Leaders scan,
  And guard with jealous zeal the rights of man,[1]
195 Forget not that to all kind Nature gives
  Those common rights, the claim of all that lives.—
  But yet my filial heart its wish must breathe
  That BRITAIN first may snatch this deathless wreath;
  First to the earth this act divine proclaim,
200 And wear the freshest palm of virtuous fame;
  May I, in foreign realms, her glories hear,
  Catch the lov'd sounds, and pour th' exulting tear!
    And when, the destin'd hour of exile past,
  My willing feet shall reach their home at last;
205 When, with the trembling hope Affection proves,
  My eager heart shall search for those it loves,
  May no sharp pang that cherish'd hope destroy,
  And from my bosom tear the promis'd joy;
  Shroud every object, every scene in gloom,
210 And lead my bleeding soul to Friendship's tomb!
  But may that moment to my eyes restore
  The friends whose love endears my native shore!
  Ah! long may Friendship, like the western ray,
  Chear the sad evening of a stormy day;
215 And gild my shadowy path with ling'ring light,
  The last dear beam that slowly sinks in night.

---

[1] The Constituent Assembly passed the Declaration of the Rights of Man and the Citizen on 26 August 1789 and incorporated it as a preamble into the Constitution of 1791.

from *Poems on Various Subjects. With Introductory Remarks on the Present State of Science and Literature in France* (1823)

To Sensibility

In SENSIBILITY's lov'd praise
 I tune my trembling reed,
And seek to deck her shrine with bays,
 On which my heart must bleed!

5 No cold exemption from her pain
 I ever wish to know;
Cheer'd with her transport, I sustain
 Without complaint her woe.

Above whate'er content can give,
10 Above the charm of ease,
The restless hopes and fears, that live
 With her, have power to please.

Where, but for her, were Friendship's power
 To heal the wounded heart,
15 To shorten sorrow's ling'ring hour,
 And bid its gloom depart?

'Tis she that lights the melting eye
 With looks to anguish dear;
She knows the price of every sigh,
20 The value of a tear.

She prompts the tender marks of love,
 Which words can scarce express;
The heart alone their force can prove,
 And feel how much they bless.

25 Of every finer bliss the source!
 'Tis she on love bestows
The softer grace, the boundless force,
 Confiding passion knows;

  When to another, the fond breast
30   Each thought for ever gives;
  When on another leans for rest,
   And in another lives!

  Quick, as the trembling metal flies
   When heat or cold impels,
35 Her anxious heart to joy can rise,
   Or sink where anguish dwells!

  Yet though her soul must griefs sustain
   Which she alone can know,
  And feel that keener sense of pain
40   Which sharpens every woe;

  Though she, the mourners' grief to calm,
   Still shares each pang they feel,
  And, like the tree distilling balm,
   Bleeds others' wounds to heal;[1]

45 Though she, whose bosom, fondly true,
   Has never wish'd to range,
  One alter'd look will trembling view,
   And scarce can bear the change;

  Though she, if death the bands should tear
50   She vainly thought secure,
  Through life must languish in despair,
   That never hopes a cure;

  Though wounded by some vulgar mind,
   Unconscious of the deed,
55 Who never seeks those wounds to bind,
   But wonders why they bleed;—

  She oft will heave a secret sigh,
   Will shed a lonely tear,
  O'er feelings nature wrought so high,
60   And gave on terms so dear.

  Yet who would hard INDIFFERENCE choose,
   Whose breast no tears can steep?
  Who, for her apathy, would lose
   The sacred power to weep?

65 Though in a thousand objects pain
   And pleasure tremble nigh,
  Those objects strive to reach in vain
   The circle of her eye.

  Cold as the fabled god appears
70   To the poor suppliant's grief,
  Who bathes the marble form in tears,
   And vainly hopes relief.

  Ah, GREVILLE![2] why the gifts refuse
   To souls like thine allied?
75 No more thy nature seem to lose,
   No more thy softness hide.

  No more invoke the playful sprite
   To chill, with magic spell,
  The tender feelings of delight,
80   And anguish sung so well;

  That envied ease thy heart would prove
   Were sure too dearly bought
  With friendship, sympathy, and love,
   And every finer thought.

---

[1] The resin of balm of Gilead (*Commiphora opobalsam*), a small evergreen, has medicinal properties; cf. Jeremiah 8.22.

[2] perhaps Charles Cavendish Fulke Greville (1794–1865), Clerk of the Privy Council, a cynic whose "diary is full of pathetic lamentations over his wasted opportunities and educational shortcomings" (*DNB* 8: 601).

Sonnet: To the Torrid Zone [1]

Pathway of light! o'er thy empurpled zone,
With lavish charms, perennial summer strays;
Soft 'midst thy spicy groves the zephyr plays,
   While far around the rich perfumes are thrown;
   The Amadavid-bird[2] for thee alone
Spreads his gay plumes, that catch thy vivid rays;
For thee the gems with liquid lustre blaze,
   And Nature's various wealth is all thy own.
But ah! not thine is Twilight's doubtful gloom,
   Those mild gradations, mingling day with night;
Here instant darkness shrouds thy genial bloom,
   Nor leaves my pensive soul that ling'ring light,
When musing Mem'ry would each trace resume
   Of fading pleasures in successive flight.

---

[1] previously published in the 2nd ed. (1796) of Williams' translation of Bernardin de St. Pierre's novel *Paul et Virginie* (1771), and in *Poems Moral, Elegant, and Pathetic* (1802).

[2] the amadavat, *Estrilda amandava*, a brown-and-white songbird of India.

Joanna Baillie
1762 – 1851

Joanna Baillie was born on 11 September 1762, in the manse at Bothwell, Lanarkshire; a twin sister died a few hours later. Her parents were the Reverend James Baillie and Dorothea Hunter Baillie. Her father educated her and her older sister, Agnes; and in about 1772, he sent them to boarding school in Glasgow, where her literary interests first developed. In 1776, James Baillie was appointed Professor of Divinity at the University of Glasgow, but in 1778, he died. Dorothea Baillie's brother, William Hunter, a famous London doctor, patronized Joanna's brother Matthew, and when Hunter died in 1783, Matthew inherited his house and Joanna, Agnes, and Dorothea moved to London to keep it for him. When he married in 1791, they moved to Hampstead, where they lived for the rest of their lives. Baillie never married, but she became friends with Anna Lætitia Barbauld,* Mary Berry, Henry MacKenzie, Samuel Rogers, William Sotheby, and, most importantly, Sir Walter Scott.* She published a volume of poems in 1790, and in 1798 she inaugurated her life's work with the publication of the first volume of *A Series of Plays: in which it is attempted to delineate the stronger passions of the mind—each passion being the subject of a tragedy and a comedy*. This volume included a tragedy and a comedy on love; *De Monfort*, her tragedy on hate; and a substantial Introductory Discourse, in which she explained and justified her ambitious project, and which has been compared to Wordsworth's Preface to *Lyrical Ballads*.* In later volumes, she published plays on ambition, fear, hope, jealousy, and remorse, in addition to miscellaneous plays and poems and *A View of the General Tenour of the New Testament regarding the nature and dignity of Jesus Christ* (1831). *De Monfort*, the most successful of her plays, was produced in London in 1800, starring John Philip Kemble and Sarah Siddons; several other of her plays also received productions. Shortly before her death on 23 February 1851, she compiled her "great monster book," *The Dramatic and Poetical Works of Joanna Baillie, complete in one volume* (1851). (D.L.M.)

☙❧

from *Poems; Wherein It Is Attempted to Describe Certain Views of Nature and of Rustic Manners; and also, To Point Out, in Some Instances, the Different Influence Which the Same Circumstances Produce on Different Characters* (1790)

A Winter Day [1]

The cock, warm roosting 'midst his feather'd dames
Now lifts his beak and snuffs the morning air,
Stretches his neck and claps his heavy wings,
Gives three hoarse crows, and glad his task is done;
5 Low, chuckling, turns himself upon the roost,
Then nestles down again amongst his mates.
The lab'ring hind,[2] who on his bed of straw,
Beneath his home-made coverings, coarse, but warm,
Lock'd in the kindly arms of her who spun them,
10 Dreams of the gain that next year's crop should bring;
Or at some fair disposing of his wool,
Or by some lucky and unlook'd-for bargain,
Fills his skin purse with heaps of tempting gold,
Now wakes from sleep at the unwelcome call,
15 And finds himself but just the same poor man
As when he went to rest.——
He hears the blast against his window beat,

---

[1] *Poems* (1790) also includes a companion poem, "A Summer Day."

[2] In *Fugitive Verses* (1840), Baillie added a note: "Hind does not perfectly express the condition of the person here intended, who is somewhat above a common labourer,—the tenant of a very small farm, which he cultivates with his own hands; a few cows, perhaps a horse, and some six or seven sheep, being all the wealth he possessed. A class of men very common in the west of Scotland, ere political economy was thought of."

  And wishes to himself he were a lord,
  That he might lie a-bed.——
20 He rubs his eyes, and stretches out his arms;
  Heigh ho! heigh ho! he drawls with gaping mouth,
  Then most unwillingly creeps out of bed,
  And without looking-glass puts on his clothes.
  With rueful face he blows the smother'd fire,
25 And lights his candle at the red'ning coal;
  First sees that all be right amongst his cattle,
  Then hies him to the barn with heavy tread,
  Printing his footsteps on the new fall'n snow.
  From out the heap of corn he pulls his sheaves,
30 Dislodging the poor red-breast from his shelter,
  Where all the live-long night he slept secure;
  But now afrighted, with uncertain flight
  He flutters round the walls, to seek some hole,
  At which he may escape out to the frost.
35 And now the flail, high whirling o'er his head,
  Descends with force upon the jumping sheave,
  Whilst every rugged wall, and neighb'ring cot[1]
  Re-echoes back the noise of his strokes.

   The fam'ly cares call next upon the wife
40 To quit her mean but comfortable bed.
  And first she stirs the fire, and blows the flame,
  Then from her heap of sticks, for winter stor'd,
  An armful brings; loud crackling as they burn,
  Thick fly the red sparks upward to the roof,
45 While slowly mounts the smoke in wreathy clouds.
  On goes the seething pot with morning cheer,
  For which some little wishful hearts await,
  Who, peeping from the bed-clothes, spy, well pleas'd,
  The cheery light that blazes on the wall,
50 And bawl for leave to rise.——
  Their busy mother knows not where to turn,
  Her morning work comes now so thick upon her.
  One she must help to tye his little coat,
  Unpin his cap, and seek another's shoe.
55 When all is o'er, out to the door they run,
  With new comb'd sleeky hair, and glist'ning cheeks,
  Each with some little project in his head.
  One on the ice must try his new sol'd shoes:

  To view his well-set trap another hies,
60 In hopes to find some poor unwary bird
  (No worthless prize) entangled in his snare;
  Whilst one, less active, with round rosy face,
  Spreads out his purple fingers to the fire,
  And peeps, most wishfully, into the pot.

65 But let us leave the warm and cheerful house,
  To view the bleak and dreary scene without,
  And mark the dawning of a winter day.
  For now the morning vapour, red and grumly,[2]
  Rests heavy on the hills; and o'er the heav'ns
70 Wide spreading forth in lighter gradual shades,
  Just faintly colours the pale muddy sky.
  Then slowly from behind the southern hills,
  Inlarg'd and ruddy looks the rising sun,
  Shooting his beams askance the hoary waste,
75 Which gild the brow of ev'ry swelling height,
  And deepen every valley with a shade.
  The crusted window of each scatter'd cot,
  The icicles that fringe the thatched roof,
  The new swept slide upon the frozen pool,
80 All lightly glance, new kindled with his rays;
  And e'en the rugged face of scowling Winter
  Looks somewhat gay. But for a little while
  He lifts his glory o'er the bright'ning earth,
  Then hides his head behind a misty cloud.

85 The birds now quit their holes and lurking sheds,
  Most mute and melancholy, where thro' night
  All nestling close to keep each other warm,
  In downy sleep they had forgot their hardships;
  But not to chant and carol in the air,
90 Or lightly swing upon some waving bough,
  And merrily return each other's notes;
  No; silently they hop from bush to bush,
  Yet find no seeds to stop their craving want,
  Then bend their flight to the low smoking cot,
95 Chirp on the roof, or at the window peck,
  To tell their wants to those who lodge within.
  The poor lank hare flies homeward to his den,
  But little burthen'd with his nightly meal

---

[1] cottage.

[2] "muddy," "turbid" (Sc.).

Of wither'd greens grubb'd from the farmer's garden;
A poor and scanty portion snatch'd in fear;
And fearful creatures, forc'd abroad by want,
Are now to ev'ry enemy a prey.

The husbandman lays bye his heavy flail,
And to the house returns, where on him wait
His smoking breakfast and impatient children;
Who, spoon in hand, and longing to begin,
Towards the door cast many a weary look
To see their dad come in.——
Then round they sit, a chearful company,
All eagerly begin, and with heap'd spoons
Besmear from ear to ear their rosy cheeks.
The faithful dog stands by his master's side
Wagging his tail, and looking in his face;
While humble puss pays court to all around,
And purs and rubs them with her furry sides;
Nor goes this little flattery unrewarded.
But the laborious sit not long at table;
The grateful father lifts his eyes to heav'n
To bless his God, whose ever bounteous hand
Him and his little ones doth daily feed;
Then rises satisfied to work again.

The chearful rousing noise of industry
Is heard, with varied sounds, thro' all the village.
The humming wheel, the thrifty housewife's tongue,
Who scolds to keep her maidens at their work,
Rough grating cards, and voice of squaling children
Issue from every house.——
But, hark!—the sportsman from the neighb'ring hedge
His thunder sends!—loud bark each village cur;
Up from her wheel each curious maiden starts,
And hastens to the door, whilst matrons chide,
Yet run to look themselves, in spite of thrift,
And all the little town is in a stir.

Strutting before, the cock leads forth his train,
And, chuckling near the barn among the straw,
Reminds the farmer of his morning's service;
His grateful master throws a lib'ral handful;
They flock about it, whilst the hungry sparrows
Perch'd on the roof, look down with envious eye,
Then, aiming well, amidst the feeders light,
And seize upon the feast with greedy bill,
Till angry partlets[1] peck them off the field.
But at a distance, on the leafless tree,
All woe be gone, the lonely blackbird sits;
The cold north wind ruffles his glossy feathers;
Full oft' he looks, but dare not make approach;
Then turns his yellow bill to peck his side,
And claps his wings close to his sharpen'd breast.
The wand'ring fowler, from behind the hedge,
Fastens his eye upon him, points his gun,
And firing wantonly as at a mark,
E'en lays him low in that same cheerful spot
Which oft' hath echo'd with his ev'ning's song.

The day now at its height, the pent-up kine[2]
Are driven from their stalls to take the air.
How stupidly they stare! and feel how strange!
They open wide their smoking mouths to low,
But scarcely can their feeble sound be heard;
Then turn and lick themselves, and step by step
Move dull and heavy to their stalls again.
In scatter'd groups the little idle boys
With purple fingers, moulding in the snow
Their icy ammunition, pant for war;
And, drawing up in opposite array,
Send forth a mighty shower of well aim'd balls,
Whilst little hero's try their growing strength,
And burn to beat the en'my off the field.
Or on the well worn ice in eager throngs,
Aiming their race, shoot rapidly along,
Trip up each other's heels, and on the surface
With knotted shoes, draw many a chalky line.
Untir'd of play, they never cease their sport
Till the faint sun has almost run his course,
And threat'ning clouds, slow rising from the north,
Spread grumly darkness o'er the face of heav'n;
Then, by degrees, they scatter to their homes,
With many a broken head and bloody nose,

---

[1] "hens."

[2] "cattle."

To claim their mothers' pity, who, most skilful,
Cures all their troubles with a bit of bread.
　　　The night comes on a pace——
Chill blows the blast, and drives the snow in wreaths.
Now ev'ry creature looks around for shelter,
And, whether man or beast, all move alike
Towards their several homes; and happy they
Who have a house to screen them from the cold!
Lo, o'er the frost a rev'rend form advances!
His hair white as the snow on which he treads,
His forehead mark'd with many a care-worn furrow,
Whose feeble body, bending o'er a staff,
Still shews that once it was the seat of strength,
Tho' now it shakes like some old ruin'd tow'r.
Cloth'd indeed, but not disgrac'd with rags,
He still maintains that decent dignity
Which well becomes those who have serv'd their
　　country.
With tott'ring steps he to the cottage moves:
The wife within, who hears his hollow cough,
And patt'ring of his stick upon the threshold,
Sends out her little boy to see who's there.
The child looks up to view the stranger's face,
And seeing it enlighten'd with a smile,
Holds out his little hand to lead him in.
Rous'd from her work, the mother turns her head,
And sees them, not ill-pleas'd.——
The stranger whines not with a piteous tale,
But only asks a little, to relieve
A poor old soldier's wants.——
The gentle matron brings the ready chair,
And bids him sit, to rest his wearied limbs,
And warm himself before her blazing fire.
The children, full of curiosity,
Flock round, and with their fingers in their mouths,
Stand staring at him; whilst the stranger, pleas'd,
Takes up the youngest boy upon his knee.
Proud of its seat, it wags its little feet,
And prates, and laughs, and plays with his white
　　locks.
But soon the soldier's face lays off its smiles;

His thoughtful mind is turn'd on other days,
When his own boys were wont to play around him,
Who now lie distant from their native land
In honourable, but untimely graves.
He feels how helpless and forlorn he is,
And bitter tears gush from his dim-worn eyes.
His toilsome daily labour at an end,
In comes the wearied master of the house,
And marks with satisfaction his old guest,
With all his children round.——
His honest heart is fill'd with manly kindness;
He bids him stay, and share their homely meal,
And take with them his quarters for the night.
The weary wanderer thankfully accepts,
And, seated with the cheerful family,
Around the plain but hospitable board,
Forgets the many hardships he has pass'd.

　　　When all are satisfied, about the fire
They draw their seats, and form a cheerful ring.
The thrifty housewife turns her spinning wheel;
The husband, useful even in his rest,
A little basket weaves of willow twigs,
To bear her eggs to town on market days;
And work but serves t'enliven conversation.
Some idle neighbours now come straggling in,
Draw round their chairs, and widen out the circle.
Without a glass the tale and jest go round;
And every one, in his own native way,
Does what he can to cheer the merry group.
Each tells some little story of himself,
That constant subject upon which mankind,
Whether in court or country, love to dwell.
How at a fair he sav'd a simple clown[1]
From being trick'd in buying of a cow;
Or laid a bet upon his horse's head
Against his neighbour's, bought for twice his price,
Which fail'd not to repay his better skill:
Or on a harvest day, bound in an hour
More sheaves of corn than any of his fellows,

---
[1] "peasant."

Tho' ne'er so keen, could do in twice the time.[1]
But chief the landlord, at his own fire-side,
Doth claim the right of being listen'd to;
Nor dares a little bawling tongue be heard,
Tho' but in play, to break upon his story.
The children sit and listen with the rest;
And should the youngest raise its little voice,
The careful mother, ever on the watch,
And always pleas'd with what her husband says,
Gives it a gentle tap upon the fingers,
Or stops its ill tim'd prattle with a kiss.
The soldier next, but not unask'd, begins,
And tells in better speech what he has seen;
Making his simple audience to shrink
With tales of war and blood. They gaze upon him,
And almost weep to see the man so poor,
So bent and feeble, helpless and forlorn,
That oft' has stood undaunted in the battle
Whilst thund'ring cannons shook the quaking earth,
And showering bullets hiss'd around his head.
With little care they pass away the night,
Till time draws on when they should go to bed;
Then all break up, and each retires to rest
With peaceful mind, nor torn with vexing cares,
Nor dancing with the unequal beat of pleasure.[2]

But long accustom'd to observe the weather,
The labourer cannot lay him down in peace
Till he has look'd to mark what bodes the night.
He turns the heavy door, thrusts out his head,
Sees wreathes of snow heap'd up on ev'ry side,
And black and grumly all above his head,
Save when a red gleam shoots along the waste
To make the gloomy night more terrible.
Loud blows the northern blast——
He hears it hollow grumbling from afar,
Then, gath'ring strength, roll on with doubl'd might,
And break in dreadful bellowings o'er his head;
Like pithless saplings bend the vexed trees,
And their wide branches crack. He shuts the door,
And, thankful for the roof that covers him,
Hies him to bed.

Thunder[3]

Spirit of strength, to whom in wrath 'tis given
To mar the earth, and shake the vasty heaven:
Behold the gloomy robes, that spreading hide
Thy secret majesty, lo! slow and wide,
Thy heavy skirts sail in the middle air,
Thy sultry shroud is o'er the noonday glare:
Th'advancing clouds sublimely roll'd on high,
Deep in their pitchy volumes clothe the sky:

---

[1] In *Fugitive Verses*, Baillie added four lines describing the foot races traditionally run at Scottish country weddings:
 "Or won the bridal rose with savoury bruise
 And first kiss of the bonny bride, though all
 The fleetest youngsters of the parish strove
 In rivalry against him."
Savoury: "pleasant"; bruise (broose): "race" (Sc.).

[2] In *Fugitive Verses*, Baillie replaced lines 276–80 with the following lines and note:
 "Thus passes quickly on the evening hour,
 Till sober folks must needs retire to rest.
 Then all break up, and, by their several paths,
 Hie homeward, with the evening pastime cheered
 Far more, belike, than those who issue forth
 From city theatre's gay scenic show,
 Or crowded ball-room's splendid moving maze.
 But where the song and story, joke and gibe
 So lately circled, what a solemn change
 In little time takes place!
 The sound of psalms, by mingled voices raised
 Of young and old, upon the night-air borne,
 Haply to some benighted traveller,
 Or the late parted neighbours on their way,
 A pleasing notice gives that, those whose sires
 In former days on the bare mountain's side,
 In deserts, heaths, and caverns, praise and prayer,
 At peril of their lives, in their own form
 Of covenanted worship offered up,
 In peace and safety in their own quiet home
 Are—(as in quaint and modest phrase is termed)
 Are now engaged in *evening exercise*.
 "In the first edition of the *Winter Day*, nothing regarding family worship was mentioned: a great omission, for which I justly take shame to myself. 'The Evening exercise,' as it was called, prevailed in every house over the simple country parts of the West of Scotland; and I have often heard the sound of it passing through the twilight air, in returning from a late walk." (J.B.) For another account of the "evening exercise," see Burns,* "The Cotter's Saturday Night" (1786) 12–17.

[3] *Poems* also includes a companion poem, "Wind." Cf. the revised version of the poem in *Fugitive Verses* (560).

    Like hosts of gath'ring foes array'd in death,
10 Dread hangs their gloom upon the earth beneath.
    It is thy hour: the awful deep is still,
    And laid to rest the wind of ev'ry hill.
    Wild creatures of the forest homeward scour,
    And in their dens with fear unwonted cow'r.
15 Pride in the lordly palace is forgot,
    And in the lowly shelter of the cot
    The poor man sits, with all his fam'ly round,
    In awful expectation of thy sound.
    Lone on his way the trav'ller stands aghast;
20 The fearful looks of man to heav'n are cast,
    When, lo! thy lightning gleams on high,
    As swiftly turns his startled eye;
    And swiftly as thy shooting blaze
    Each half performed motion stays,
25 Deep awe, all human strife and labour stills,
    And thy dread voice alone, the earth and heaven fills.

      Bright bursts the lightning from the cloud's dark
          womb,
    As quickly swallow'd in the closing gloom.
    The distant streamy flashes, spread askance
30 In paler sheetings, skirt the wide expanse.
    Dread flaming from aloft, the cat'ract dire
    Oft meets in middle space the nether fire.
    Fierce, red, and ragged, shiv'ring in the air,
    Athwart mid-darkness shoots the lengthen'd glare.
35 Wild glancing round, the feebler lightning plays;
    The rifted center pours the gen'ral blaze;
    And from the warring clouds in fury driven,[1]
    Red writhing falls the keen embodied bolt of heaven.

      From the dark bowels of the burthen'd cloud
40 Dread swells the rolling peal, full, deep'ning, loud.
    Wide ratt'ling claps the heavens scatter'd o'er,
    In gather'd strength lift the tremendous roar;
    With weaning force it rumbles over head,
    Then, growling, wears away to silence dread.
45 Now waking from afar in doubled might,

    Slow rolling onward to the middle height;
    Like crash of mighty mountains downward hurl'd,
    Like the upbreaking of a wrecking world,
    In dreadful majesty, th'explosion grand
50 Bursts wide, and awful, o'er the trembling land.
    The lofty mountains echo back the roar,
    Deep from afar rebounds earth's rocky shore;
    All else existing in the senses bound
    Is lost in the immensity of sound.
55 Wide jarring sounds by turns in strength convene,
    And deep, and terrible, the solemn pause between.

      Aloft upon the mountain's side
    The kindled forest blazes wide.
    Huge fragments[2] of the rugged steep
60 Are tumbled to the lashing deep.
    Firm rooted in the cloven rock,
    Loud crashing falls the stubborn oak.
    The lightning keen, in wasteful ire,
    Fierce darting on the lofty spire,
65 Wide rends in twain the ir'n-knit stone,
    And stately tow'rs are lowly thrown.
    Wild flames o'erscour the wide campaign,
    And plough askance the hissing main.
    Nor strength of man may brave the storm,
70 Nor shelter skreen the shrinking form;
    Nor castle wall its fury stay,
    Nor massy gate may bar its way.
    It visits those of low estate,
    It shakes the dwellings of the great,
75 It looks athwart the secret tomb,
    And glares upon the prison's gloom;
    While dungeons deep, in unknown light,
    Flash hidious on the wretches' sight,
    And lowly groans the downward cell,
80 Where deadly silence wont to dwell.

      Now upcast eyes to heav'n adore,
    And knees that never bow'd before.
    In stupid wonder stares the child;
    The maiden turns her glances wild,
85 And lists to hear the coming roar:

---

[1] "In poetry we have only to do with appearances; and the zig-zag lightning, commonly thought to be the thunder-bolt, is certainly firm and embodied, compared to the ordinary lightning, which takes no distinct shape at all." (J.B.)

[2] Cf. Coleridge, "Kubla Khan" 21.*

The aged shake their locks so hoar:
And stoutest hearts begin to fail,
And many a manly cheek is pale;
Till nearer closing peals astound,
90 And crashing ruin mingles round;
Then 'numbing fear awhile up-binds
The pausing action of their minds,
Till wak'd to dreadful sense, they lift their eyes,
And round the stricken corse, shrill shrieks of horror
    rise.

95   Now thinly spreads the falling hail
A motly winter o'er the vale,
The hailstones bounding as they fall
On hardy rock, or storm-beat' wall.
The loud beginning peal its fury checks,
100 Now full, now fainter, with irreg'lar breaks,
The weak in force, unites the scatter'd sound;
And rolls its lengthen'd grumblings to the distant
    bound.
A thick and muddy whiteness clothes the sky.
In paler flashes gleams the lightning by;
105 And thro' the rent cloud, silver'd with his ray,
The sun looks down on all this wild affray;
As high enthron'd above all mortal ken,
A greater Pow'r beholds the strife of men:
Yet o'er the distant hills the darkness scowls,
110 And deep, and long, the parting tempest growls.

A Mother to Her Waking Infant

Now in thy dazzling half-op'd eye,
Thy curled nose, and lip awry,
Thy up-hoist arms, and noddling head,
And little chin with crystal spread,
5 Poor helpless thing! what do I see,
    That I should sing of thee?

From thy poor tongue no accents come,
Which can but rub thy toothless gum:
Small understanding boast thy face,
10 Thy shapeless limbs nor step, nor grace:
A few short words thy feats may tell,
    And yet I love thee well.

When sudden wakes the bitter shriek,
And redder swells thy little cheek;
15 When rattled keys thy woe beguile,
And thro' the wet eye gleams the smile,
Still for thy weakly self is spent
    Thy little silly plaint.

But when thy friends are in distress,
20 Thou'lt laugh and chuckle ne'er the less;
Nor e'en with sympathy be smitten,
Tho' all are sad but thee and kitten;
Yet little varlet that thou art,
    Thou twitchest at the heart.

25 Thy rosy cheek so soft and warm;
Thy pinky hand, and dimpled arm;
Thy silken locks that scantly peep,
With gold-tip'd ends, where circle deep
Around thy neck in harmless grace
30 So soft and sleekly hold their place,
Might harder hearts with kindness fill,
    And gain our right good will.

Each passing clown[1] bestows his blessing,
Thy mouth is worn with old wives' kissing:
35 E'en lighter looks the gloomy eye
Of surly sense, when thou art by;
And yet I think whoe'er they be,
    They love thee not like me.

Perhaps when time shall add a few
40 Short years to thee, thou'lt love me too.
Then wilt thou thro' life's weary way
Become my sure and cheering stay:
Wilt care for me, and be my hold,
    When I am weak and old.

---

[1] "peasant."

> Thou'lt listen to my lengthen'd tale,
> And pity me when I am frail———[1]
> But see, the sweepy spinning fly
> Upon the window takes thine eye.
> Go to thy little senseless play———
>   Thou doest not heed my lay.[2]

A Child to his Sick Grand-Father

> Grand-dad, they say your old and frail,
> Your stocked[3] legs begin to fail:
> Your knobbed stick (that was my horse)
> Can scarce support your bended corse;[4]
> While back to wall, you lean so sad,
>   I'm vex'd to see you, dad.
>
> You us'd to smile, and stroke my head,
> And tell me how good children did;
> But now I wot[5] not how it be,
> You take me seldom on your knee;
> Yet ne'ertheless I am right glad
>   To sit beside you, dad.
>
> How lank and thin your beard hangs down!
> Scant are the white hairs on your crown:
> How wan and hollow are your cheeks!
> Your brow is rough with crossing breaks;
> But yet, for all his strength is fled,
>   I love my own old dad.
>
> The housewives round their potions brew,
> And gossips[6] come to ask for you:
> And for your weal[7] each neighbour cares,
> And good men kneel, and say their pray'rs:
> And ev'ry body looks so sad,
>   When you are ailing, dad.
>
> You will not die, and leave us then?
> Rouse up and be our dad again.
> When you are quiet and laid in bed,
> We'll doff our shoes and softly tread;
> And when you wake we'll aye be near,
>   To fill old dad his cheer.
>
> When thro' the house you shift your stand,
> I'll lead you kindly by the hand:
> When dinner's set, I'll with you bide,
> And aye be serving by your side:
> And when the weary fire burns blue,
>   I'll sit and talk with you.
>
> I have a tale both long and good,
> About a partlet and her brood;
> And cunning greedy fox, that stole,
> By dead of midnight thro' a hole,
> Which slyly to the hen-roost led———
>   You love a story, dad?
>
> And then I have a wond'rous tale
> Of men all clad in coats of mail,
> With glitt'ring swords—you nod, I think?
> Your fixed eyes begin to wink:
> Down on your bosom sinks your head:
>   You do not hear me, dad.

---

[1] In *Fugitive Verses*, Baillie added a note: "In this sense the word is often applied in Scotland."
[2] "song."
[3] "wearing stockings" (the grandfather's clothes are old-fashioned).
[4] "(living) body."
[5] "know."
[6] "friends."
[7] "welfare."

from *A Series of Plays: In Which it Is Attempted to Delineate the Stronger Passions of the Mind. Each Passion being the Subject of a Tragedy and a Comedy* (1798)

from *Introductory Discourse*

From that strong sympathy which most creatures, but the human above all, feel for others of their kind, nothing has become so much an object of man's curiosity as man himself. We are all conscious of this within ourselves, and so constantly do we meet with it in others, that like every circumstance of continually repeated occurrence, it thereby escapes observation. Every person, who is not deficient in intellect, is more or less occupied in tracing, amongst the individuals he converses with, the varieties of understanding and temper which constitute the characters of men; and receives great pleasure from every stroke of nature that points out to him those varieties. This is, much more than we are aware of, the occupation of children, and of grown people also, whose penetration is but lightly esteemed; and that conversation which degenerates with them into trivial and mischievous tattling, takes its rise not unfrequently from the same source that supplies the rich vein of the satirist and the wit. That eagerness so universally shewn for the conversation of the latter, plainly enough indicates how many people have been occupied in the same way with themselves. Let any one, in a large company, do or say what is strongly expressive of his peculiar character, or of some passion or humour of the moment, and it will be detected by almost every person present. How often may we see a very stupid countenance animated with a smile, when the learned and the wise have betrayed some native feature of their own minds! and how often will this be the case when they have supposed it to be concealed under a very sufficient disguise! From this constant employment of their minds, most people, I believe, without being conscious of it, have stored up in idea the greater part of those strong marked varieties of human character, which may be said to divide it into classes; and in one of those classes they involuntarily place every new person they become acquainted with.

I will readily allow that the dress and the manners of men, rather than their characters and disposition are the subjects of our common conversation, and seem chiefly to occupy the multitude. But let it be remembered that it is much easier to express our observations upon these. It is easier to communicate to another how a man wears his wig and cane, what kind of house he inhabits, and what kind of table he keeps, than from what slight traits in his words and actions we have been led to conceive certain impressions of his character: traits that will often escape the memory, when the opinions that were founded upon them remain. Besides, in communicating our ideas of the characters of others, we are often called upon to support them with more expence of reasoning than we can well afford, but our observations on the dress and appearance of men, seldom involve us in such difficulties. For these, and other reasons too tedious to mention, the generality of people appear to us more trifling than they are: and I may venture to say that, but for this sympathetick curiosity[1] towards others of our kind, which is so strongly implanted within us, the attention we pay to the dress and the manners of men would dwindle into an employment as insipid, as examining the varieties of plants and minerals, is to one who understands not natural history.

In our ordinary intercourse with society, this sympathetick propensity of our minds is exercised upon men, under the common occurrences of life, in which we have often observed them. Here vanity and weakness put themselves forward to view, more conspicuously than the virtues: here men encounter those smaller trials, from which they are not apt to come off victorious; and here, consequently, that which is marked with the whimsical and ludicrous will strike us most forcibly, and make the strongest impression on our memory. To this sympathetick propensity of our minds, so exercised, the genuine and pure comick of every composition, whether drama, fable, story, or satire is addressed.

If man is an object of so much attention to man, engaged in the ordinary occurrences of life, how much more does he excite his curiosity and interest when placed in extraordinary situations of difficulty and distress? It cannot be any pleasure we receive from the sufferings of a fellow-creature which attracts such multitudes of people to a publick execution,[2] though it is the horrour we conceive for such a spectacle that keeps so many more away. To see a human being bearing himself up under such circumstances, or struggling with the terrible apprehensions which such a

---

[1] Cf. Edmund Burke,* *A Philosophical Enquiry into the Origin of our Ideas of the Sublime and Beautiful* (1757) chap. 1.13; Adam Smith, *The Theory of Moral Sentiments* (1759) chap. 1.2.1.

[2] Cf. Burke, *A Philosophical Enquiry* chap. 1.15.

situation impresses, must be the powerful incentive, which makes us press forward to behold what we shrink from, and wait with trembling expectation for what we dread.[1] For though few at such a spectacle can get near enough to distinguish the expression of face, or the minuter parts of a criminal's behaviour, yet from a considerable distance will they eagerly mark whether he steps firmly; whether the motions of his body denote agitation or calmness; and if the wind does but ruffle his garment, they will, even from that change upon the outline of his distant figure, read some expression connected with his dreadful situation. Though there is a greater proportion of people in whom this strong curiosity will be overcome by other dispositions and motives; though there are many more who will stay away from such a sight than will go to it; yet there are very few who will not be eager to converse with a person who has beheld it; and to learn, very minutely, every circumstance connected with it, except the very act itself of inflicting death. To lift up the roof of his dungeon, like the *Diable boiteux*,[2] and look upon a criminal the night before he suffers, in his still hours of privacy, when all that disguise, which respect for the opinion of others, the strong motive by which even the lowest and wickedest of men still continue to be moved, would present an object to the mind of every person, not withheld from it by great timidity of character, more powerfully attractive than almost any other.

Revenge, no doubt, first began amongst the savages of America that dreadful custom of sacrificing their prisoners of war. But the perpetration of such hideous cruelty could never have become a permanent national custom, but for this universal desire in the human mind to behold man in every situation, putting forth his strength against the current of adversity, scorning all bodily anguish, or struggling with those feelings of nature, which, like a beating stream, will oft'times burst through the artificial barriers of pride. Before they begin those terrible rites they treat their prisoner kindly; and it cannot be supposed that men, alternately enemies and friends to so many neighbouring tribes, in manners and appearance like themselves, should so strongly be actuated by a spirit of publick revenge. This custom, therefore, must be considered as a grand and terrible game, which every tribe plays against another; where they try not the strength of the arm, the swiftness of the feet, nor the acuteness of the eye, but the fortitude of the soul. Considered in this light, the excess of cruelty exercised upon their miserable victim, in which every hand is described as ready to inflict its portion of pain, and every head ingenious in the contrivance of it, is no longer to be wondered at. To put into his measure of misery one agony less, would be, in some degree, betraying the honour of their nation: would be doing a species of injustice to every hero of their own tribe who had already sustained it, and to those who might be called upon to do so; amongst whom each of these savage tormentors has his chance of being one, and has prepared himself for it from his childhood. Nay, it would be a species of injustice to the haughty victim himself, who would scorn to purchase his place amongst the heroes of his nation, at an easier price than his undaunted predecessors.

Amongst the many trials to which the human mind is subjected, that of holding intercourse, real or imaginary, with the world of spirits: of finding itself alone with a being terrifick and awful, whose nature and power are unknown, has been justly considered as one of the most severe. The workings of nature in this situation, we all know, have ever been the object of our most eager enquiry. No man wishes to see the Ghost himself, which would certainly procure him the best information on the subject, but every man wishes to see one who believes that he sees it, in all the agitation and wildness of that species of terrour. To gratify this curiosity how many people have dressed up hideous apparitions to frighten the timid and superstitious! and

---

[1] "In confirmation of this opinion I may venture to say, that of the great numbers who go to see a publick execution, there are but very few who would not run away from, and avoid it, if they happened to meet with it unexpectedly. We find people stopping to look at a procession, or any other uncommon sight, they may have fallen in with accidentally, but almost never an execution. No one goes there who has not made up his mind for the occasion; which would not be the case, if any natural love of cruelty were the cause of such assemblies." (J.B.)

[2] "Limping devil" (Fr.). In *Le Diable boiteux* (1707), by Alain-René Lesage (1668–1747), the devil Asmodée lifts off the roofs of the houses in order to reveal the human frailties concealed beneath them.

have done it at the risk of destroying their happiness or understanding for ever. For the instances of intellect being destroyed by this kind of trial are more numerous, perhaps, in proportion to the few who have undergone it than by any other.

How sensible are we of this strong propensity within us, when we behold any person under the pressure of great and uncommon calamity! Delicacy and respect for the afflicted will, indeed, make us turn ourselves aside from observing him, and cast down our eyes in his presence; but the first glance we direct to him will involuntarily be one of the keenest observation, how hastily soever it may be checked; and often will a returning look of enquiry mix itself by stealth with our sympathy and reserve.

But it is not in situations of difficulty and distress alone, that man becomes the object of this sympathetick curiosity; he is no less so when the evil he contends with arises in his own breast, and no outward circumstance connected with him either awakens our attention or our pity. What human creature is there, who can behold a being like himself under the violent agitation of those passions which all have, in some degree, experienced, without feeling himself most powerfully excited by the sight? I say, all have experienced; for the bravest man on earth knows what fear is as well as the coward; and will not refuse to be interested for one under the dominion of this passion, provided there be nothing in the circumstances attending it to create contempt. Anger is a passion that attracts less sympathy than any other, yet the unpleasing and distorted features of an angry man will be more eagerly gazed upon, by those who are no wise concerned with his fury or the objects of it, than the most amiable placid countenance in the world. Every eye is directed to him; every voice hushed to silence in his presence; even children will leave off their gambols as he passes, and gaze after him more eagerly than the gaudiest equipage. The wild tossings of despair; the gnashing of hatred and revenge; the yearnings of affection, and the softened mien of love; all that language of the agitated soul, which every age and nation understands, is never addressed to the dull nor inattentive.

It is not merely under the violent agitations of passion, that man so rouses and interests us; even the smallest indications of an unquiet mind, the restless eye, the muttering lip, the half-checked exclamation, and the hasty start, will set our attention as anxiously upon the watch, as the first distant flashes of a gathering storm. When some great explosion of passion bursts forth, and some consequent catastrophe happens, if we are at all acquainted with the unhappy perpetrator, how minutely will we endeavour to remember every circumstance of his past behaviour! and with what avidity will we seize upon every recollected word or gesture, that is in the smallest degree indicative of the supposed state of his mind, at the time when they took place. If we are not acquainted with him, how eagerly will we listen to similar recollections from another! Let us understand, from observation or report, that any person harbours in his breast, concealed from the world's eye, some powerful rankling passion of what kind soever it may be, we will observe every word, every motion, every look, even the distant gait of such a man, with a constancy and attention bestowed upon no other. Nay, should we meet him unexpectedly on our way, a feeling will pass across our minds as though we found ourselves in the neighbourhood of some secret and fearful thing. If invisible, would we not follow him into his lonely haunts, into his closet, into the midnight silence of his chamber? There is, perhaps, no employment which the human mind will with so much avidity pursue, as the discovery of concealed passion, as the tracing the varieties and progress of a perturbed soul.

It is to this sympathetick curiosity of our nature, exercised upon mankind in great and trying occasions, and under the influence of the stronger passions, when the grand, the generous, the terrible attract our attention far more than the base and depraved, that the high and powerfully tragick, of every composition, is addressed. ...[1]

In proportion as moral writers of every class have exercised within themselves this sympathetick propensity of our nature, and have attended to it in others,

---

[1] Baillie goes on to discuss the importance of sympathetic curiosity in making people better human beings.

their works have been interesting and instructive. They have struck the imagination more forcibly, convinced the understanding more clearly, and more lastingly impressed the memory. If unseasoned with any reference to this, the fairy bowers of the poet, with all his gay images of delight, will be admired and forgotten; the important relations of the historian, and even the reasonings of the philosopher will make a less permanent impression....[1]

Our desire to know what men are in the closet[2] as well as the field, by the blazing hearth, and at the social board, as well as in the council and the throne, is very imperfectly gratified by real history; romance writers, therefore, stepped boldly forth to supply the deficiency; and tale writers, and novel writers, of many descriptions, followed after. If they have not been very skilful in their delineations of nature; if they have represented men and women speaking and acting as men and women never did speak or act; if they have caricatured both our virtues and our vices; if they have given us such pure and unmixed, or such heterogeneous combinations of character as real life never presented, and yet have pleased and interested us, let it not be imputed to the dulness of man in discerning what is genuinely natural in himself. There are many inclinations belonging to us, besides this great master-propensity of which I am treating. Our love of the grand, the beautiful, the novel, and above all of the marvellous, is very strong; and if we are richly fed with what we have a good relish for, we may be weaned to forget our native and favourite aliment. Yet we can never so far forget it, but that we will cling to, and acknowledge it again, whenever it is presented before us. In a work abounding with the marvellous and unnatural, if the author has any how stumbled upon an unsophisticated genuine stroke of nature, we will immediately perceive and be delighted with it, though we are foolish enough to admire at the same time, all the nonsense with which it is surrounded. After all the wonderful incidents, dark mysteries, and secrets revealed, which eventful novel so liberally presents to us; after the beautiful fairy ground, and even the grand and sublime scenes of nature with which descriptive novel so often enchants us; those works which most strongly characterize human nature in the middling and lower classes of society,[3] where it is to be discovered by stronger and more unequivocal marks, will ever be the most popular. For though great pains have been taken in our higher sentimental novels to interest us in the delicacies, embarrassments, and artificial distresses of the more refined part of society, they have never been able to cope in the publick opinion with these. The one is a dressed and beautiful pleasure-ground, in which we are enchanted for a while, amongst the delicate and unknown plants of artful cultivation; the other is a rough forest of our native land; the oak, the elm, the hazle, and the bramble are there; and amidst the endless varieties of its paths we can wander for ever. Into whatever scenes the novelist may conduct us, what objects soever he may present to our view, still is our attention most sensibly awake to every touch faithful to nature; still are we upon the watch for every thing that speaks to us of ourselves....[4]

If the study of human nature then, is so useful to the poet, the novelist, the historian, and the philosopher, of how much greater importance must it be to the dramatick writer? To them it is a powerful auxiliary, to him it is the centre and strength of the battle. If characteristick views of human nature enliven not their pages, there are many excellencies with which they can, in some degree, make up for the deficiency, it is what we receive from them with pleasure rather than demand. But in his works no richness of invention, harmony of language, nor grandeur of sentiment will supply the place of faithfully delineated nature. The poet and the novelist may represent to you their great characters from the cradle to the tomb. They may represent them in any mood or temper, and under the influence of any passion which they see proper, without being obliged to put words into their mouths, those great betrayers of the feigned and adopted. They may relate every circum-

---

[1] Baillie goes on to discuss the importance of the study of human nature in historical and philosophical writing.

[2] not a closet in the modern sense but a small, private room.

[3] Cf. W. Wordsworth, Preface to *Lyrical Ballads* (641).*

[4] Baillie goes on to discuss the importance of the study of human nature in poetry.

stance however trifling and minute, that serves to develope their tempers and dispositions. They tell us what kind of people they intend their men and women to be, and as such we receive them. If they are to move us with any scene of distress, every circumstance regarding the parties concerned in it, how they looked, how they moved, how they sighed, how the tears gushed from their eyes, how the very light and shadow fell upon them, is carefully described, and the few things that are given them to say along with all this assistance, must be very unnatural indeed if we refuse to sympathize with them. But the characters of the drama must speak directly for themselves. Under the influence of every passion, humour, and impression; in the artificial veilings of hypocrisy and ceremony, in the openness of freedom and confidence, and in the lonely hour of meditation they speak. He who made us hath placed within our breast a judge that judges instantaneously of every thing they say. We expect to find them creatures like ourselves; and if they are untrue to nature, we feel that we are imposed upon; as though the poet had introduced to us for brethren, creatures of a different race, beings of another world.

As in other works deficiency in characteristick truth may be compensated by excellencies of a different kind, in the drama characteristick truth will compensate every other defect. Nay, it will do what appears a contradiction; one strong genuine stroke of nature will cover a multitude of sins[1] even against nature herself. When we meet in some scene of a good play a very fine stroke of this kind, we are apt to become so intoxicated with it, and so perfectly convinced of the author's great knowledge of the human heart, that we are unwilling to suppose that the whole of it has not been suggested by the same penetrating spirit. Many well-meaning enthusiastick criticks have given themselves a great deal of trouble in this way; and have shut their eyes most ingeniously against the fair light of nature for the very love of it. They have converted, in their great zeal, sentiments palpably false, both in regard to the character and situation of the persons who utter them, sentiments which a child or a clown would detect, into the most skilful depictments of the heart. I can think of no stronger instance to shew how powerfully this love of nature dwells within us.[2]

Formed as we are with these sympathetick propensities in regard to our own species, it is not at all wonderful that theatrical exhibition has become the grand and favourite amusement of every nation into which it has been introduced. Savages will, in the wild contortions of a dance, shape out some rude story expressive of character or passion, and such a dance will give more delight to his companions than the most artful exertions of agility. Children in their gambols will make out a mimick representation of the manners, characters, and passions of grown men and women, and such a pastime will animate and delight them much more than a treat of the daintiest sweetmeats, or the handling of the gaudiest toys. Eagerly as it is enjoyed by the rude and the young, to the polished and the ripe in years it is still the most interesting amusement. Our taste for it is durable as it is universal. Independently of those circumstances which first introduced it, the world would not have long been without it. The progress of society would soon have brought it forth; and men in the whimsical decorations of fancy would have displayed the characters and actions of their heroes, the folly and aburdity of their fellow-citizens, had no Priests of Bacchus[3] ever existed.[4]

---

[1] Cf. 1 Peter 4.8.

[2] "It appears to me a very strong testimony of the excellence of our great national Dramatist, that so many people have been employed in finding out obscure and refined beauties, in what appear to ordinary observation his very defects. Men, it may be said, do so merely to shew their own superior penetration and ingenuity. But granting this; what could make other men listen to them, and listen so greedily too, if it were not that they have received from the works of Shakspeare, pleasure far beyond what the most perfect poetical compositions of a different character can afford." (J.B.)

[3] Dionysus, the classical god of wine. The Greek tragedies were first presented as part of a festival in his honour.

[4] "Though the progress of society would have given us the Drama, independently of the particular cause of its first commencement, the peculiar circumstances connected with its origin, have had considerable influence upon its character and style, in the ages through which it has passed even to our days, and still will continue to affect it. Homer had long preceded the dramatick poets of Greece; poetry was in a high state of cultivation when they began to write; and their style, the construction of their pieces, and the characters of their heroes were different from what they would have been, had theatrical exhibi- (Continued)

In whatever age or country the Drama might have taken its rise, tragedy would have been the first-born of its children. For every nation has its great men, and its great events upon record; and to represent their own forefathers struggling with those difficulties, and braving those dangers, of which they have heard with admiration, and the effects of which they still, perhaps, experience, would certainly have been the most animating subject for the poet, and the most interesting for his audience, even independently of the natural inclination we all so universally shew for scenes of horrour and distress, of passion and heroick exertion. Tragedy would have been the first child of the Drama, for the same reasons that have made heroick ballad, with all its battles, murders, and disasters, the earliest poetical compositions of every country.

tions been the invention of an earlier age or a ruder people. Their works were represented to an audience, already accustomed to hear long poems rehearsed at their publick games, and the feasts of their gods. A play, with the principal characters of which they were previously acquainted; in which their great men and heroes, in the most beautiful language, complained of their rigorous fate, but piously submitted to the will of the Gods; in which sympathy was chiefly excited by tender and affecting sentiments; in which strong bursts of passion were few; and in which whole scenes frequently passed, without giving the actors any thing to do but to speak, was not too insipid for them. Had the Drama been the invention of a less cultivated nation, more of action and of passion would have been introduced into it. It would have been more irregular, more imperfect, more varied, more interesting. From poor beginnings it would have advanced in a progressive state; and succeeding poets, not having those polished and admired originals to look back upon, would have presented their respective contemporaries with the produce of a free and unbridled imagination. A different class of poets would most likely have been called into existence. The latent powers of men are called forth by contemplating those works in which they find any thing congenial to their own peculiar talents; and if the field, wherein they could have worked, is already enriched with a produce unsuited to their cultivation, they think not of entering it at all. Men, therefore, whose natural turn of mind led them to labour, to reason, to refine and exalt, have caught their animation from the beauties of the Grecian Drama, and they who, perhaps, ought only to have been our Criticks have become our Poets. I mean not, however, in any degree to depreciate the works of the ancients; a great deal we have gained by those beautiful compositions; and what we have lost by them it is impossible to compute. Very strong genius will sometimes break through every disadvantage of circumstances: Shakspeare has arisen in this country, and we ought not to complain." (J.B.)

We behold heroes and great men at a distance, unmarked by those small but distinguishing features of the mind, which give a certain individuality to such an infinite variety of similar beings, in the near and familiar intercourse of life. They appear to us from this view like distant mountains, whose dark outlines we trace in the clear horizon, but the varieties of whose roughened sides, shaded with heath and brushwood, and seamed with many a cleft, we perceive not. When accidental anecdote reveals to us any weakness or peculiarity belonging to them, we start upon it like a discovery. They are made known to us in history only, by the great events they are connected with, and the part they have taken in extraordinary or important transactions. Even in poetry and romance, with the exception of some love story interwoven with the main events of their lives, they are seldom more intimately made known to us. To Tragedy it belongs to lead them forward to our nearer regard, in all the distinguishing varieties which nearer inspection discovers; with the passions, the humours, the weaknesses, the prejudices of men. It is for her to present to us the great and magnanimous hero, who appears to our distant view as a superior being, as a God, softened down with those smaller frailties and imperfections which enable us to glory in, and claim kindred to his virtues. It is for her to exhibit to us the daring and ambitious man, planning his dark designs, and executing his bloody purposes, mark'd with those appropriate characteristicks, which distinguish him as an individual of that class; and agitated with those varied passions, which disturb the mind of man when he is engaged in the commission of such deeds. It is for her to point out to us the brave and impetuous warrior struck with those visitations of nature, which, in certain situations, will unnerve the strongest arm, and make the boldest heart tremble. It is for her to shew the tender, gentle, and unassuming mind animated with that fire which, by the provocation of circumstances, will give to the kindest heart the ferocity and keenness of a tiger. It is for her to present to us the great and striking characters that are to be found amongst men, in a way which the poet, the novelist, and the historian can but imperfectly attempt. But above all, to her, and to her only it belongs to unveil us the human mind under the dominion of those strong and fixed passions, which, seemingly unprovoked by outward circumstances, will from small beginnings brood within the breast, till all the better dispositions, all the fair gifts of nature are borne down before them. Those passions which conceal themselves from the observation of men; which cannot unbosom themselves even to the dearest friend; and can, often times, only give their fulness vent in the lonely desert, or in the darkness of midnight. For who hath followed the great man into his secret closet, or stood by the side of his nightly couch, and heard those exclamations of the soul which heaven alone may hear, that the historian should be able to inform us? and what form of story, what mode of rehearsed speech will communicate to us those feelings, whose irregular bursts, abrupt transitions, sudden pauses, and half-uttered suggestions, scorn all harmony of measured verse, all method and order of relation?

On the first part of this task her Bards have eagerly exerted their abilities: and some amongst them, taught by strong original genius to deal immediately with human nature and their own hearts, have laboured in it successfully. But in presenting to us those views of great characters, and of the human mind in difficult and trying situations which peculiarly belong to Tragedy, the far greater proportion, even of those who may be considered as respectable dramatick poets, have very much failed. From the beauty of those original dramas to which they have ever looked back with admiration, they have been tempted to prefer the embellishments of poetry to faithfully delineated nature. They have been more occupied in considering the works of the great Dramatists who have gone before them, and the effects produced by their writings, than the varieties of human character which first furnished materials for those works, or those principles in the mind of man by means of which such effects were produced. Neglecting the boundless variety of nature, certain strong outlines of character, certain bold features of passion, certain grand vicissitudes, and striking dramatick situations have been repeated from one generation to another; whilst a pompous and solemn gravity, which they have supposed to be necessary for the dignity of tragedy, has excluded almost entirely from their works those smaller touches of nature, which so well develope the mind; and by showing men in their hours of state and exertion only, they have consequently shewn them imperfectly. Thus, great and magnanimous heroes, who bear with majestick equanimity every vicissitude of fortune; who in every temptation and trial stand forth in unshaken virtue, like a rock buffeted by the waves; who encompast with the most terrible evils, in calm possession of their souls, reason upon the difficulties of their state; and, even upon the brink of destruction, pronounce long eulogiums on virtue, in the most eloquent and beautiful language, have been held forth to our view as objects of imitation and interest; as though they had entirely forgotten that it is only from creatures like ourselves that we feel, and therefore, only from creatures like ourselves that we receive the instruction of example.[1] Thus, passionate and impetuous warriors, who are proud, irritable, and vindictive, but generous, daring, and disinterested; setting their lives at a pin's fee[2] for the good of others, but incapable of curbing their own humour of a moment to gain the whole world for themselves; who will pluck the orbs of heaven from their places, and crush the whole universe in one grasp, are called forth to kindle in our souls the generous contempt of every thing abject and base; but with an effect proportionably feeble, as the hero is made to exceed in

---

[1] "To a being perfectly free from all human infirmity our sympathy refuses to extend. Our Saviour himself, whose character is so beautiful, and so harmoniously consistent; in whom, with outward proofs of his mission less strong than those that are offered to us, I should still be compelled to believe, from being utterly unable to conceive how the idea of such a character could enter into the imagination of man, never touches the heart more nearly than when he says, 'Father, let this cup pass from me.' Had he been represented to us in all the unshaken strength of these tragick heroes, his disciples would have made fewer converts, and his precepts would have been listened to coldly. Plays in which heroes of this kind are held forth, and whose aim is, indeed, honourable and praise-worthy, have been admired by the cultivated and refined, but the tears of the simple, the applauses of the young and untaught have been wanting." (J.B.) See Matthew 26.39.

[2] Cf. Shakespeare, *Hamlet* 1.4.65.

courage and fire what the standard of humanity will agree to.[1] Thus, tender and pathetick lovers, full of the most gentle affections, the most amiable dispositions, and the most exquisite feelings; who present their defenceless bosoms to the storms of this rude world in all the graceful weakness of sensibility, are made to sigh out their sorrows in one unvaried strain of studied pathos, whilst this constant demand upon our feelings makes us absolutely incapable of answering it.[2] Thus, also, tyrants are represented as monsters of cruelty, unmixed with any feelings of humanity; and villains as delighting in all manner of treachery and deceit, and acting upon many occasions for the very love of villainy itself; though the perfectly wicked are as ill fitted for the purposes of warning, as the perfectly virtuous are for those of example.[3] This spirit of imitation, and attention to effect, has likewise confined them very much in their choice of situations and events to bring their great characters into action; rebellions, conspiracies, contentions for empire, and rivalships in love have alone been thought worthy of trying those heroes; and palaces and dungeons the only places magnificent or solemn enough for them to appear in.

They have, indeed, from this regard to the works of preceding authors, and great attention to the beauties of composition, and to dignity of design, enriched their plays with much striking, and sometimes sublime imagery, lofty thoughts, and virtuous sentiments; but in striving so eagerly to excel in those things that belong to tragedy in common with many other compositions, they have very much neglected those that are peculiarly her own. As far as they have been led aside from the first labours of a tragick poet by a desire to communicate more perfect moral instruction, their motive has been respectable, and they merit our esteem. But this praiseworthy end has been injured instead of promoted by their mode of pursuing it. Every species of moral writing has its own way of conveying instruction, which it can never, but with disadvantage, exchange for any other. The Drama improves us by the knowledge we acquire of our own minds, from the natural desire we have to look into the thoughts, and observe the behaviour of others. Tragedy brings to our view men placed in those elevated situations, exposed to those great trials, and engaged in

---

[1] "In all burlesque imitations of tragedy, those plays in which this hero is pre-eminent, are always exposed to bear the great brunt of the ridicule; which proves how popular they have been, and how many poets, and good ones too, have been employed upon them. That they have been so popular, however, is not owing to the intrinsick merit of the characters they represent, but their opposition to those mean and contemptible qualities belonging to human nature, of which we are most ashamed. Besides, there is something in the human mind, independently of its love of applause, which inclines it to boast. This is ever the attendant of that elasticity of soul, which makes us bound up from the touch of oppression; and if there is nothing in the accompanying circumstances to create disgust, or suggest suspicions of their sincerity, (as in real life is commonly the case,) we are very apt to be carried along with the boasting of others. Let us in good earnest believe that a man is capable of achieving all that human courage can achieve, and we will suffer him to talk of impossibilities. Amidst all their pomp of words, therefore, our admiration of such heroes is readily excited, (for the understanding is more easily deceived than the heart,) but how stands our sympathy affected? As no caution nor foresight, on their own account, is ever suffered to occupy the thoughts of such bold disinterested beings, we are the more inclined to care for them, and take an interest in their fortune through the course of the play; yet, as their souls are unappalled by any thing; as pain and death are not at all regarded by them; and as we have seen them very ready to plunge their own swords into their own bosoms, on no very weighty occasion, perhaps, their death distresses us but little, and they commonly fall unwept." (J.B.)

[2] "Were it not, that in tragedies where these heroes preside, the same soft tones of sorrow are so often repeated in our ears, till we are perfectly tired of it, they are more fitted to interest us than any other: both because in seeing them, we own the ties of kindred between ourselves and the frail mortals we lament; and sympathize with the weakness of mortality unmixed with any thing to degrade or disgust; and also, because the misfortunes, which form the story of the play, are frequently of the more familiar and domestick kind. A king driven from his throne, will not move our sympathy so strongly, as a private man torn from the bosom of his family." (J.B.)

[3] "I have said nothing here in regard to female character, though in many tragedies it is brought forward as the principal one of the piece, because what I have said of the above characters is likewise applicable to it. I believe there is no man that ever lived, who has behaved in a certain manner, on a certain occasion, who has not had amongst women some corresponding spirit, who on the like occasion, and every way similarly circumstanced, would have behaved in the like manner. With some degree of softening and refinement, each class of the tragick heroes I have mentioned has its corresponding one amongst the heroines. The tender and pathetick no doubt has the most numerous, but the great and magnanimous is not without it, and the passionate and impetuous boasts of one by no means inconsiderable in numbers, and drawn sometimes to the full as passionate and impetuous as itself." (J.B.)

those extraordinary transactions, in which few of us are called upon to act. As examples applicable to ourselves, therefore, they can but feebly affect us; it is only from the enlargement of our ideas in regard to human nature, from that admiration of virtue, and abhorrence of vice which they excite, that we can expect to be improved by them. But if they are not represented to us as real and natural characters, the lessons we are taught from their conduct and their sentiments will be no more to us than those which we receive from the pages of the poet or the moralist.

But the last part of the task which I have mentioned as peculiarly belonging to tragedy, unveiling the human mind under the dominion of those strong and fixed passions, which seemingly unprovoked by outward circumstances, will from small beginnings brood within the breast, till all the better dispositions, all the fair gifts of nature are borne down before them, her poets in general have entirely neglected, and even her first and greatest have but imperfectly attempted. They have made use of the passions to mark their several characters, and animate their scenes, rather than to open to our view the nature and portraitures of those great disturbers of the human breast, with whom we are all, more or less, called upon to contend. With their strong and obvious features, therefore, they have been presented to us, stripped almost entirely of those less obtrusive, but not less discriminating traits, which mark them in their actual operation. To trace them in their rise and progress in the heart, seems but rarely to have been the object of any dramatist. We commonly find the characters of a tragedy affected by the passions in a transient, loose, unconnected manner; or if they are represented as under the permanent influence of the more powerful ones, they are generally introduced to our notice in the very height of their fury, when all that timidity, irresolution, distrust, and a thousand delicate traits, which make the infancy of every great passion more interesting, perhaps, than its full-blown strength, are fled. The impassioned character is generally brought into view under those irresistible attacks of their power, which it is impossible to repel; whilst those gradual steps that led him into this state, in some of which a stand might have been made against the foe, are left entirely in the shade. These passions that may be suddenly excited, and are of short duration, as anger, fear, and oftentimes jealousy, may in this manner be fully represented; but those great masters of the soul, ambition, hatred, love, every passion that is permanent in its nature, and varied in progress, if represented to us but in one stage of its course, is represented imperfectly. It is a characteristick of the more powerful passions that they will encrease and nourish themselves on very slender aliment; it is from within that they are chiefly supplied with what they feed on; and it is in contending with opposite passions and affections of the mind that we best discover their strength, not with events. But in tragedy it is events more frequently than opposite affections which are opposed to them; and those often of such force and magnitude that the passions themselves are almost obscured by the splendour and importance of the transactions to which they are attached.[1] But besides being thus confined and mutilated, the passions have been, in the greater part of our tragedies, deprived of the very power of making themselves known. Bold and figurative language belongs peculiarly to them. Poets, admiring those bold expressions which a mind, labouring with ideas too strong to be conveyed in the ordinary forms of speech, wildly throws out, taking earth, sea, and sky, every thing great and terrible in nature to image forth the violence of its feelings, borrowed them gladly, to adorn the calm sentiments of their premeditated song. It has therefore been thought that the less animated parts of tragedy might be so embellished and enriched. In doing this, however, the passions have been robbed of their native prerogative; and in adorning with their strong figures and lofty expressions the calm speeches of the unruffled, it is found that, when they are called upon to raise their voice, the power of distinguishing themselves has been taken away. This is an injury by no means compensated, but very greatly aggravated by embellishing, in return, the speeches of passion with the ingenious conceits, and

---

[1] Cf. W. Wordsworth, Preface to *Lyrical Ballads* (642–43).*

compleat similies of premeditated thought.[1] There are many other things regarding the manner in which dramatick poets have generally brought forward the passions in tragedy, to the great prejudice of that effect they are naturally fitted to produce upon the mind, which I forbear to mention, lest they should too much increase the length of this discourse; and leave an impression on the mind of my reader, that I write more on the spirit of criticism, than becomes one who is about to bring before the publick a work, with, doubtless, many faults and imperfections on its head.[2]

From this general view, which I have endeavoured to communicate to my reader, of tragedy, and those principles in the human mind upon which the success of her efforts depends, I have been led to believe, that an attempt to write a series of tragedies, of simpler construction, less embellished with poetical decorations, less constrained by that lofty seriousness which has so generally been considered as necessary for the support of tragick dignity, and in which the chief object should be to delineate the progress of the higher passions in the human breast, each play exhibiting a particular passion, might not be unacceptable to the publick. And I have been the more readily induced to act upon this idea, because I am confident, that tragedy, written upon this plan, is fitted to produce stronger moral effect than upon any other. I have said that tragedy in representing to us great characters struggling with difficulties, and placed in situations of eminence and danger, in which few of us have any chance of being called upon to act, conveys its moral efficacy to our minds by the enlarged views which it gives to us of human nature, by the admiration of virtue, and execration of vice which it excites, and not by the examples it holds up for our immediate application. But in opening to us the heart of man under the influence of those passions to which all are liable, this is not the case. Those strong passions that, with small assistance from outward circumstances, work their way in the heart, till they become the tyrannical masters of it, carry on a similar operation in the breast of the Monarch, and the man of low degree. It exhibits to us the mind of man in that state when we are most curious to look into it, and is equally interesting to all. Discrimination of character is a turn of mind, tho' more common than we are aware of, which every body does not possess; but to the expressions of passion, particularly strong passion, the dullest mind is awake; and its true unsophisticated language the dullest understanding will not misinterpret. To hold up for our example those peculiarities in disposition, and modes of thinking which nature has fixed upon us, or which long and early habit has incorporated with our original selves, is almost desiring us to remove the everlasting mountains, to take away the native land-marks of the soul; but representing the passions brings before us the operation of a tempest that rages out its time and passes away. We cannot, it is true, amidst its wild uproar, listen to the voice of reason, and save ourselves from destruction; but we can foresee its coming, we can mark its rising signs, we can know the situations that will most expose us to its rage, and we can shelter our heads from the coming blast. To change a certain disposition of mind which makes us view objects in a particular light, and thereby, oftentimes, unknown to ourselves, influences our conduct and manners, is almost impossible; but in checking and subduing those visitations of the soul, whose causes and effects we are aware of, every one may make considerable progress, if he proves not entirely successful. Above all, looking back to the first rise, and tracing the progress of passion, points out to us those stages in the approach of the enemy, when he might have been combated most successfully; and where the suffering him to pass may be considered as occasioning all the misery that ensues....[3]

It was the saying of a sagacious Scotchman, "let who will make the laws of a nation, if I have the writing of its ballads."[4] Something similar to this may be said in

---

[1] "This, perhaps, more than any thing else has injured the higher scenes of tragedy. For having made such free use of bold hyperbolical language in the inferior parts, the poet when he arrives at the highly impassioned sinks into total inability: or if he will force himself to rise still higher on the wing, he flies beyond nature altogether, into the regions of bombast and nonsense." (J.B.)

[2] Cf. Shakespeare, *Hamlet* 1.5.79.

[3] Baillie goes on to discuss the different types of comedy.

[4] Andrew Fletcher, *An Account of a Conversation concerning a Right Regulation of Governments for the Common Good of Mankind* (1704).

regard to the Drama. Its lessons reach not, indeed, to the lowest classes of the labouring people, who are the broad foundation of society, which can never be generally moved without endangering every thing that is constructed upon it, and who are our potent and formidable ballad readers; but they reach to the classes next in order to them, and who will always have over them no inconsiderable influence. The impressions made by it are communicated, at the same instant of time, to a greater number of individuals, than those made by any other species of writing; and they are strengthened in every spectator, by observing their effects upon those who surround him. From this observation, the mind of my reader will suggest of itself, what it would be unnecessary, and, perhaps, improper in me here to enlarge upon. The theatre is a school in which much good or evil may be learned. At the beginning of its career the Drama was employed to mislead and excite; and were I not unwilling to refer to transactions of the present times, I might abundantly confirm what I have said by recent examples. The authour, therefore, who aims in any degree to improve the mode of its instruction, and point to more useful lessons than it is generally employed to dispense, is certainly praiseworthy, though want of abilities may unhappily prevent him from being successful in his efforts.

This idea has prompted me to begin a work in which I am aware of many difficulties. In plays of this nature the passions must be depicted not only with their bold and prominent features, but also with those minute and delicate traits which distinguish them in an infant, growing, and repressed state; which are the most difficult of all to counterfeit, and one of which falsely imagined, will destroy the effect of a whole scene. The characters over whom they are made to usurp dominion, must be powerful and interesting, exercising them with their full measure of opposition and struggle; for the chief antagonists they contend with must be the other passions and propensities of the heart, not outward circumstances and events. Though belonging to such characters, they must still be held to view in their most baleful and unseductive light; and those qualities in the impassioned which are necessary to interest us in their fate, must not be allowed, by any lustre borrowed from them, to diminish our abhorrence of guilt. The second and even the inferiour persons of each play, as they must be kept perfectly distinct from the great impassioned one, should generally be represented in a calm unagitated state, and therefore more pains is necessary than in other dramatick works, to mark them by appropriate distinctions of character, lest they should appear altogether insipid and insignificant. As the great object here is to trace passion through all its varieties, and in every stage, many of which are marked by shades so delicate, that in much bustle of events they would be little attended to, or entirely overlooked, simplicity of plot is more necessary, than in those plays where only occasional bursts of passion are introduced, to distinguish a character, or animate a scene. But where simplicity of plot is necessary, there is very great danger of making a piece appear bare and unvaried, and nothing but great force and truth in the delineations of nature will prevent it from being tiresome.[1] Soliloquy, or those overflowings of the perturbed soul, in which it unburthens itself of those thoughts which it cannot communicate to others, and which in certain situations is the only mode that a Dramatist can employ to open up to us the mind he would display, must necessarily be often, and to considerable length, introduced. Here, indeed, as it naturally belongs to passion, it will not be so offensive as it generally is in other plays, when a calm unagitated person tells over to himself all that has befallen him, and

---

[1] "To make up for this simplicity of plot, the shew and decorations of the theatre ought to be allowed, to plays written upon this plan, in their full extent. How fastidious soever some poets may be in regard to these matters, it is much better to relieve our tired-out attention with a battle, a banquet, or a procession, than an accumulation of incidents. In the latter case the mind is harassed and confused with those doubts, conjectures, and disappointments which multiplied events occasion, and in a great measure unfitted for attending to the worthier parts of the piece; but in the former it enjoys a rest, a pleasing pause in its more serious occupation, from which it can return again, without any incumberance of foreign intruding ideas. The shew of a splendid procession will afford to a person of the best understanding, a pleasure in kind, though not in degree, with that which a child would receive from it. But when it is past he thinks no more of it; whereas some confusion of circumstances, some half-explained mistake, which gives him no pleasure at all when it takes place, may take off his attention afterwards from the refined beauties of a natural and characteristick dialogue." (J.B.)

all his future schemes of intrigue or advancement; yet to make speeches of this kind sufficiently natural and impressive, to excite no degree of weariness nor distaste, will be found to be no easy task. There are, besides these, many other difficulties peculiarly belonging to this undertaking, too minute and tedious to mention. If, fully aware of them, I have not shrunk back from the attempt, it is not from any idea that my own powers or discernment will at all times enable me to overcome them; but I am emboldened by the confidence I feel in that candour and indulgence, with which the good and enlightened do ever regard the experimental efforts of those, who wish in any degree to enlarge the sources of pleasure and instruction amongst men.

It will now be proper to say something of the particular plays which compose this volume....[1]

... The last play, the subject of which is hatred, will more clearly discover the nature and intention of my design. The rise and progress of this passion I have been obliged to give in retrospect, instead of representing it all along in its actual operation, as I could have wished to have done. But hatred is a passion of slow growth; and to have exhibited it from its beginnings would have included a longer period, than even those who are least scrupulous about the limitation of dramatick time, would have thought allowable. I could not have introduced my chief characters upon the stage as boys, and then as men. For this passion must be kept distinct from that dislike which we conceive for another when he has greatly offended us, and which is almost the constant companion of anger; and also from that eager desire to crush, and inflict suffering on him who has injured us, which constitutes revenge. This passion, as I have conceived it, is that rooted and settled aversion, which from opposition of character, aided by circumstances of little importance, grows at last into such antipathy and personal disgust as makes him who entertains it, feel, in the presence of him who is the object of it, a degree of torment and restlessness which is insufferable. It is a passion, I believe less frequent than any other of the stronger passions, but in the breast where it does exist, it creates, perhaps, more misery than any other. To endeavour to interest the mind for a man under the dominion of a passion so baleful, so unamiable, may seem, perhaps, reprehensible. I therefore beg it may be considered that it is the passion and not the man which is held up to our execration; and that this and every other bad passion does more strongly evince its pernicious and dangerous nature, when we see it thus counteracting and destroying the good gifts of heaven, than when it is represented as the suitable associate in the breast of inmates as dark as itself. This remark will likewise be applicable to many of the other plays belonging to my work, that are intended to follow. A decidedly wicked character can never be interesting; and to employ such for the display of any strong passion would very much injure instead of improving the moral effect. In the breast of a bad man passion has comparatively little to combat, how then can it shew its strength? I shall say no more upon this subject, but submit myself to the judgment of my reader.

It may, perhaps, be supposed from my publishing these plays, that I have written them for the closet rather than the stage.[2] If upon perusing them with attention, the reader is disposed to think they are better calculated for the first than the last, let him impute it to want of skill in the authour, and not to any previous design. A play, but of small poetical merit, that is suited to strike and interest the spectator, to catch the attention of him who will not, and of him who cannot read, is a more valuable and useful production than one whose elegant and harmonious pages are admired in the libraries of the tasteful and refined. To have received approbation from an audience of my countrymen, would have been more pleasing to me than any other praise. A few tears from the simple and young would have been, in my eyes, pearls of great price;[3] and the spontaneous, untutored plaudits of the rude and uncultivated would have come to my heart as offerings of no mean value. I should, therefore, have been better pleased to have introduced them to the world from the stage than from the press. I possess, however, no likely channel to the former mode

---

[1] Baillie goes on to discuss *Count Basil* and *The Tryal*, the tragedy and comedy on love which begin the volume.

[2] for private reading rather than for public performance.

[3] Cf. Matthew 13.46.

of publick introduction; and upon further reflection it appeared to me that by publishing them in this way, I have an opportunity afforded me of explaining the design of my work, and enabling the publick to judge, not only of each play by itself, but as making a part likewise of the whole; an advantage which, perhaps, does more than over-balance the splendour and effect of theatrical representation.

It may be thought that with this extensive plan before me, I should not have been in a hurry to publish, but have waited to give a larger portion of it to the publick, which would have enabled them to make a truer estimate of its merit. To bring forth only three plays of the whole, and the last without its intended companion, may seem like the haste of those vain people, who as soon as they have written a few pages of a discourse, or a few couplets of a poem, cannot be easy till every body has seen them. I do protest, in honest simplicity! it is distrust and not confidence, that has led me at this early stage of the undertaking, to bring it before the publick. To labour in uncertainty is at all times unpleasant; but to proceed in a long and difficult work with any impression upon your mind that your labour may be in vain; that the opinion you have conceived of your ability to perform it may be a delusion, a false suggestion of self-love, the fantasy of an aspiring temper, is most discouraging and cheerless. I have not proceeded so far, indeed, merely upon the strength of my own judgment; but the friends to whom I have shewn my manuscripts are partial to me, and their approbation which in the case of any indifferent person would be in my mind completely decisive, goes but a little way in relieving me from these apprehensions. To step beyond the circle of my own immediate friends in quest of opinion, from the particular temper of my mind I feel an uncommon repugnance: I can with less pain to myself bring them before the publick at once, and submit to its decision.[1] It is to my countrymen at large that I call for assistance. If this work is fortunate enough to attract their attention, let their strictures as well as their praise come to my aid: the one will encourage me in a long and arduous undertaking, the other will teach me to improve it as I advance. For there are many errours that may be detected, and improvements that may be suggested in the prosecution of this work, which from the observations of a great variety of readers are more likely to be pointed out to me, than from those of a small number of persons, even of the best judgment. I am not possessed of that confidence in mine own powers, which enables the concealed genius, under the pressure of present discouragement, to pursue his labours in security, looking firmly forward to other more enlightened times for his reward. If my own countrymen with whom I live and converse, who look upon the same race of men, the same state of society, the same passing events with myself, receive not my offering, I presume not to look to posterity.

Before I close this discourse, let me crave the forbearance of my reader, if he has discovered in the course of it any unacknowledged use of the thoughts of other authours, which he thinks ought to have been noticed; and let me beg the same favour, if in reading the following plays, any similar neglect seems to occur. There are few writers who have sufficient originality of thought to strike out for themselves new ideas upon every occasion. When a thought presents itself to me, as suited to the purpose I am aiming at, I would neither be thought proud enough to reject it, on finding that another has used it before me, nor mean enough to make use of it without acknowledging the obligation, when I can at all guess to whom such acknowledgments are due. But I am situated where I have no library to consult; my reading through the whole of my life has been of a loose, scattered, unmethodical kind, with no determined direction, and I have not been blessed by nature with the advantages of a retentive or accurate memory. Do not, however, imagine from this, I at all wish to insinuate that I ought to be acquitted of every obligation to preceding authours; and that when a palpable similarity of thought and expression is observable between us, it is a similarity produced by accident alone, and with perfect unconsciousness on my part. I am frequently sensible, from the manner in which an idea arises to my

---

[1] "The first of these plays, indeed, has been shewn to two or three Gentlemen whom I have not the honour of reckoning amongst my friends. One of them, who is a man of distinguished talents, has honoured it with very flattering approbation; and, at his suggestion, one or two slight alterations in it have been made." (J.B.)

imagination, and the readiness with which words, also, present themselves to clothe it in, that I am only making use of some dormant part of that hoard of ideas which the most indifferent memories lay up, and not the native suggestions of mine own mind. Whenever I have suspected myself of doing so, in the course of this work, I have felt a strong inclination to mark that suspicion in a note. But, besides that it might have appeared like an affectation of scrupulousness which I would avoid, there being likewise, most assuredly, many other places in it where I have done the same thing without being conscious of it, a suspicion of wishing to slur them over, and claim all the rest as unreservedly my own, would unavoidably have attached to me. If this volume should appear, to any candid and liberal critic, to merit that he should take the trouble of pointing out to me in what parts of it I seem to have made that use of other authours' writings, which according to the fair laws of literature[1] ought to have been acknowledged, I shall think myself obliged to him. I shall examine the sources he points out as having supplied my own lack of ideas; and if this book should have the good fortune to go through a second edition, I shall not fail to own my obligations to him, and the authours from whom I may have borrowed.

How little credit soever, upon perusing these plays, the reader may think me entitled to in regard to the execution of the work, he will not, I flatter myself, deny me some credit in regard to the plan. I know of no series of plays, in any language, expressly descriptive of the different passions; and I believe there are few plays existing in which the display of one strong passion is the chief business of the drama, so written that they could properly make part of such a series. I do not think that we should, from the works of various authours, be able to make a collection which would give us any thing exactly of the nature of that which is here proposed. If the reader, in perusing it, perceives that the abilities of the authour are not proportioned to the task which is imposed upon them, he will wish in the spirit of kindness rather than of censure, as I most sincerely do, that they had been more adequate to it. However, if I perform it ill, I am still confident that this (pardon me if I call it, noble) design will not be suffered to fall to the ground; some one will arise after me who will do it justice; and there is no poet, possessing genius for such a work, who will not at the same time possess that spirit of justice and of candour, which will lead him to remember me with respect.

I have now only to thank my reader, whoever he may be, who has followed me through the pages of this discourse, for having had the patience to do so. May he, in going through what follows (a wish the sincerity of which he cannot doubt) find more to reward his trouble than I dare venture to promise him; and for the pains he has already taken, and that which he intends to take for me, I request that he will accept of my grateful acknowledgments.[2]

---

[1] Baillie was a supporter of a copyright reform, which did not come about until 1844.

[2] "Shakspeare, more than any of our poets, gives peculiar and appropriate distinction to the characters of his tragedies. The remarks I have made, in regard to the little variety of character to be met with in tragedy, apply not to him. Neither has he, as other Dramatists generally do, bestowed pains on the chief persons of his drama only, leaving the second and inferiour ones insignificant and spiritless. He never wears out our capacity to feel, by eternally pressing upon it. His tragedies are agreeably chequered with variety of scenes, enriched with good sense, nature, and vivacity, which relieve our minds from the fatigue of continued distress. If he sometimes carries this so far as to break in upon that serious tone of mind, which disposes us to listen with effect to the higher scenes of tragedy, he has done so chiefly in his historical plays, where the distresses set forth are commonly of that publick kind, which does not, at any rate, make much impression upon the feelings." (J.B.)

De Monfort

PERSONS OF THE DRAMA

MEN

DE MONFORT
REZENVELT
COUNT FREBERG, *friend to De Monfort and Rezenvelt*
MANUEL, *servant to De Monfort*
JEROME, *De Monfort's old Landlord*
GRIMBALD, *an artful knave*
BERNARD, *a Monk*

MONKS, GENTLEMEN, OFFICERS, PAGE &C. &C.

WOMEN

JANE DE MONFORT, *sister to De Monfort*
COUNTESS FREBERG, *wife to Freberg*
THERESA, *servant to the Countess*

ABBESS, NUNS, AND A LAY SISTER, LADIES, &C.

SCENE, *a town in Germany.*

ACT 1

SCENE 1

Jerome's House. A large old fashioned Chamber.

JEROME: [*Speaking without.*] This way good masters.
[*ENTER JEROME, bearing a light, and followed by MANUEL, and SERVANTS carrying luggage.*]
                  Rest your burdens here.
This spacious room will please the Marquis best.
He takes me unawares; but ill prepar'd:
If he had sent, e'en tho' a hasty notice,
I had been glad.
5 MANUEL: Be not disturb'd, good Jerome;
Thy house is in most admirable order;
And they who travel o'cold winter nights
Think homeliest quarters good.
JEROME: He is not far behind?
MANUEL: A little way.
10 [*To the servants.*] Go you and wait below till he arrives.
JEROME: [*Shaking MANUEL by the hand.*] Indeed, my friend, I'm glad to see you here,
Yet marvel wherefore.
MANUEL: I marvel wherefore too, my honest Jerome:
But here we are, pri'thee be kind to us.
15 JEROME: Most heartily I will. I love your master:
He is a quiet and a lib'ral man:
A better inmate never cross'd my door.
MANUEL: Ah! but he is not now the man he was.
Lib'ral he will, God grant he may be quiet.
20 JEROME: What has befallen him?
MANUEL: I cannot tell thee;
But faith, there is no living with him now.
JEROME: And yet, methinks, if I remember well,
You were about to quit his service, Manuel,
When last he left this house. You grumbled then.
25 MANUEL: I've been upon the eve of leaving him
These ten long years; for many times is he
So difficult, capricious, and distrustful,
He galls my nature—yet, I know not how,
A secret kindness binds me to him still.
30 JEROME: Some, who offend from a suspicious nature,
Will afterwards such fair confession make
As turns e'en the offence into a favour.
MANUEL: Yes, some indeed do so: so will not he;
He'd rather die than such confession make.
35 JEROME: Ay, thou art right, for now I call to mind
That once he wrong'd me with unjust suspicion,
When first he came to lodge beneath my roof;
And when it so fell out that I was proved
Most guiltless of the fault, I truly thought
40 He would have made profession of regret;
But silent, haughty, and ungraciously
He bore himself as one offended still.
Yet shortly after, when unwittingly
I did him some slight service, o'the sudden
45 He overpower'd me with his grateful thanks;
And would not be restrain'd from pressing on me

A noble recompense. I understood
His o'erstrain'd gratitude and bounty well,
And took it as he meant.
MANUEL: 'Tis often thus.
50 I would have left him many years ago,
But that with all his faults there sometimes come
Such bursts of natural goodness from his heart,
As might engage a harder churl than I
To serve him still.—And then his sister too,
55 A noble dame, who should have been a queen:
The meanest of her hinds, at her command,
Had fought like lions for her, and the poor,
E'en o'er their bread of poverty had bless'd her——
She would have griev'd if I had left my Lord.
60 JEROME: Comes she along with him?
MANUEL: No, he departed all unknown to her,
Meaning to keep conceal'd his secret route;
But well I knew it would afflict her much,
And therefore left a little nameless billet,
65 Which after our departure, as I guess,
Would fall into her hands, and tell her all.
What could I do? O 'tis a noble lady!
JEROME: All this is strange—something disturbs his
mind——
Belike he is in love.
MANUEL: No, Jerome, no.
70 Once on a time I serv'd a noble master,
Whose youth was blasted with untoward love,
And he with hope and fear and jealousy
For ever toss'd, led an unquiet life:
Yet, when unruffled by the passing fit,
75 His pale wan face such gentle sadness wore
As mov'd a kindly heart to pity him;
But Monfort, even in his calmest hour,
Still bears that gloomy sternness in his eye
Which sullenly repells all sympathy.
80 O no! good Jerome, no, it is not love.
JEROME: Hear I not horses trampling at the gate?
[*Listening.*]
He is arriv'd—stay thou—I had forgot——
A plague upon't! my head is so confus'd——
I will return i'the instant to receive him.
[*EXIT hastily.*]

[*A great bustle without.* EXIT MANUEL *with lights, and returns again lighting in* DE MONFORT, *as if just alighted from his journey.*]
85 MANUEL: Your ancient host, my lord, receives you
gladly,
And your apartment will be soon prepar'd.
DE MONFORT: 'Tis well.
MANUEL: Where shall I place the chest you gave in
charge?
So please you, say my lord.
DE MONFORT: [*Throwing himself into a chair.*]
Where-e'er thou wilt.
90 MANUEL: I would not move that luggage till you
came. [*Pointing to certain things.*]
DE MONFORT: Move what thou wilt, and trouble
me no more.
[MANUEL, *with the assistance of other* SERVANTS, *sets about putting the things in order, and* DE MONFORT *remains sitting in a thoughtful posture.*
ENTER JEROME, *bearing wine, &c. on a salver. As he approaches* DE MONFORT, MANUEL *pulls him by the sleeve.*]
MANUEL: [*Aside to* JEROME.] No, do not now; he
will not be disturb'd.
JEROME: What not to bid him welcome to my house,
And offer some refreshment?
MANUEL: No, good Jerome.
95 Softly, a little while: I pri'thee do.
[JEROME *walks softly on tip-toes, till he gets near* DE MONFORT, *behind backs, then peeping on one side to see his face.*]
JEROME: [*Aside to* MANUEL.] Ah, Manuel, what an
alter'd man is here!
His eyes are hollow, and his cheeks are pale——
He left this house a comely gentleman.
DE MONFORT: Who whispers there?
MANUEL: 'Tis your old landlord, sir.
100 JEROME: I joy to see you here—I crave your
pardon——
I fear I do intrude.——
DE MONFORT: No, my kind host, I am oblig'd to
thee.
JEROME: How fares it with your honour?
DE MONFORT: Well enough.

JEROME: Here is a little of the fav'rite wine
105 That you were wont to praise. Pray honour me.
[*Fills a glass.*]
DE MONFORT: [*After drinking.*] I thank you, Jerome,
'tis delicious.
JEROME: Ay, my dear wife did ever make it so.
DE MONFORT: And how does she?
JEROME: Alas, my lord! she's
dead.
DE MONFORT: Well, then she is at rest.
JEROME: How well, my
lord?
110 DE MONFORT: Is she not with the dead, the quiet
dead,
Where all is peace. Not e'en the impious wretch,
Who tears the coffin from its earthy vault,
And strews the mould'ring ashes to the wind
Can break their rest.
115 JEROME: Woe's me! I thought you would have
griev'd for her.
She was a kindly soul! Before she died,
When pining sickness bent her cheerless head,
She set my house in order——
And but the morning ere she breath'd her last,
120 Bade me preserve some flaskets of this wine,
That should the Lord De Monfort come again
His cup might sparkle still.
[*DE MONFORT walks across the stage, and wipes his eyes.*]
Indeed I fear I have distress'd you, sir:
I surely thought you would be griev'd for her.
125 DE MONFORT: [*Taking JEROME'S hand.*] I am, my
friend. How long has she been dead?
JEROME: Two sad long years.
DE MONFORT: Would she were living still!
I was too troublesome, too heedless of her.
JEROME: O no! she lov'd to serve you.
[*Loud knocking without.*]
DE MONFORT: What fool comes here, at such
untimely hours,
130 To make this cursed noise. [*To MANUEL.*] Go to
the gate. [*EXIT MANUEL.*]
All sober citizens are gone to bed;
It is some drunkards on their nightly rounds,
Who mean it but in sport.
JEROME: I hear unusual voices—here they come.
[*RE-ENTER MANUEL, shewing in COUNT FREBERG and his
LADY.*]
FREBERG: [*Running to embrace DE MONFORT.*]
135 My dearest Monfort! most unlook'd-for pleasure.
Do I indeed embrace thee here again?
I saw thy servant standing by the gate,
His face recall'd, and learnt the joyful tidings.
Welcome, thrice welcome here!
140 DE MONFORT: I thank thee, Freberg, for this
friendly visit,
And this fair Lady too. [*Bowing to the LADY.*]
LADY: I fear, my Lord,
We do intrude at an untimely hour:
But now returning from a midnight mask,[1]
My husband did insist that we should enter.
145 FREBERG: No, say not so; no hour untimely call,
Which doth together bring long absent friends.
Dear Monfort, wherefore hast thou play'd so sly,
To come upon us thus all suddenly?
DE MONFORT: O! many varied thoughts do cross
our brain,
150 Which touch the will, but leave the memory trackless;
And yet a strange compounded motive make
Wherefore a man should bend his evening walk
To th'east or west, the forest or the field.
Is it not often so?
155 FREBERG: I ask no more, happy to see you here
From any motive. There is one behind,
Whose presence would have been a double bliss:
Ah! how is she? The noble Jane de Monfort.
DE MONFORT: [*Confused.*] She is—I have—I have
left my sister well.
160 LADY: [*To FREBERG.*] My Freberg, you are heedless
of respect:
You surely meant to say the Lady Jane.
FREBERG: Respect! No, Madam; Princess, Empress,
Queen,
Could not denote a creature so exalted
As this plain native appellation doth,
165 The noble Jane de Monfort.

---

[1] a masquerade, a form of festivity popular in the eighteenth century.

LADY: [*Turning from him displeased to* DE MONFORT.]
  You are fatigued, my Lord; you want repose;
  Say, should we not retire?
FREBERG: Ha! is it so?
  My friend, your face is pale, have you been ill?
DE MONFORT: No, Freberg, no; I think I have been
    well.
170 FREBERG: [*Shaking his head.*] I fear thou hast not,
    Monfort—Let it pass.
  We'll re-establish thee: we'll banish pain.
  I will collect some rare, some cheerful friends,
  And we shall spend together glorious hours,
  That gods might envy. Little time so spent
175 Doth far outvalue all our life beside.
  This is indeed our life, our waking life,
  The rest dull breathing sleep.
DE MONFORT: Thus, it is true, from the sad years
    of life
  We sometimes do short hours, yea minutes strike,
180 Keen, blissful, bright, never to be forgotten;
  Which thro' the dreary gloom of time o'erpast
  Shine like fair sunny spots on a wild waste.
  But few they are, as few the heaven-fir'd souls
  Whose magick power creates them. Bless'd art thou,
185 If in the ample circle of thy friends
  Thou canst but boast a few.
FREBERG: Judge for thyself: in truth I do not boast.
  There is amongst my friends, my later friends,
  A most accomplish'd stranger. New to Amberg,[1]
190 But just arriv'd; and will ere long depart.
  I met him in Franconia[2] two years since.
  He is so full of pleasant anecdote,
  So rich, so gay, so poignant is his wit,
  Time vanishes before him as he speaks,
195 And ruddy morning thro' the lattice peeps
  Ere night seems well begun.
DE MONFORT: How is he call'd?
FREBERG: I will surprise thee with a welcome face:
  I will not tell thee now.
LADY: [*To* DE MONFORT.] I have, my Lord, a small
    request to make,

200 And must not be denied. I too may boast
  Of some good friends, and beauteous country-women:
  To-morrow night I open wide my doors
  To all the fair and gay; beneath my roof
  Musick, and dance, and revelry shall reign.
205 I pray you come and grace it with your presence.
DE MONFORT: You honour me too much to be
    denied.
LADY: I thank you, Sir; and in return for this,
  We shall withdraw, and leave you to repose.
FREBERG: Must it be so? Good night—sweet sleep
    to thee. [*To* DE MONFORT.]
210 DE MONFORT: [*To* FREBERG.] Good night. [*To*
    LADY.] Good-night, fair Lady.
LADY: Farewell!
        [EXEUNT FREBERG *and* LADY.]
DE MONFORT: [*To* JEROME.] I thought Count
    Freberg had been now in France.
JEROME: He meant to go, as I have been inform'd.
DE MONFORT: Well, well, prepare my bed; I will
    to rest.   [EXIT JEROME.]
DE MONFORT: [*Alone.*] I know not how it is, my
    heart stands back,
215 And meets not this man's love.—Friends! rarest
    friends!
  Rather than share his undiscerning praise
  With every table wit, and book-form'd sage,
  And paltry poet puling to the moon,
  I'd court from him proscription; yea abuse,
220 And think it proud distinction.   [EXIT.]

SCENE 2

A Small Apartment in JEROME'S *House: a table and breakfast set out.* ENTER DE MONFORT, *followed by* MANUEL, *and sets himself down by the table, with a cheerful face.*

DE MONFORT: Manuel, this morning's sun shines
    pleasantly:
  These old apartments too are light and cheerful.
  Our landlord's kindness has reviv'd me much;
  He serves as though he lov'd me. This pure air

---

[1] a city near Nuremberg.

[2] part of Bavaria.

Braces the listless nerves, and warms the blood:
I feel in freedom here.
[*Filling a cup of coffee, and drinking.*]
MANUEL: Ah! sure, my Lord,
No air is purer than the air at home.
DE MONFORT: Here can I wander with assured steps,
Nor dread, at every winding of the path,
Lest an abhorred serpent cross my way,
And move—[*Stopping short.*]
MANUEL: What says your honour?
There are no serpents in our pleasant fields.
DE MONFORT: Think'st thou there are no serpents
   in the world
But those who slide along the grassy sod,
And sting the luckless foot that presses them?
There are who in the path of social life
Do bask their spotted skins in Fortune's sun,
And sting the soul—Ay, till its healthful frame
Is chang'd to secret, fest'ring, sore disease,
So deadly is the wound.
MANUEL: Heaven guard your honour from such
   horrid skathe:
They are but rare, I hope?
DE MONFORT: [*Shaking his head.*] We mark the
   hollow eye, the wasted frame,
The gait disturb'd of wealthy honour'd men,
But do not know the cause.
MANUEL: 'Tis very true. God keep you well, my
   Lord!
DE MONFORT: I thank thee, Manuel, I am very well.
I shall be gay too, by the setting sun.
I go to revel it with sprightly dames,
And drive the night away.
[*Filling another cup, and drinking.*]
MANUEL: I should be glad to see your honour gay.
DE MONFORT: And thou too shalt be gay. There,
   honest Manuel,
Put these broad pieces in thy leathern purse,
And take at night a cheerful jovial glass.
Here is one too, for Bremer; he loves wine;
And one for Jacques: be joyful all together.
[*ENTER SERVANT.*]
SERVANT: My Lord, I met e'en now, a short way off,
Your countryman the Marquis Rezenvelt.
DE MONFORT: [*Starting from his seat, and letting
   the cup fall from his hand.*] Who, say'st thou?
SERVANT: Marquis Rezenvelt, an' please you.
DE MONFORT: Thou ly'st—it is not so—it is
   impossible.
SERVANT: I saw him with these eyes, plain as
   yourself.
DE MONFORT: Fool! 'tis some passing stranger thou
   hast seen,
And with a hideous likeness been deceiv'd.
SERVANT: No other stranger could deceive my sight.
DE MONFORT: [*Dashing his clenched hand violently
   upon the table, and overturning every thing.*]
Heaven blast thy sight! it lights on nothing good.
SERVANT: I surely thought no harm to look upon
   him.
DE MONFORT: What, dost thou still insist? Him
   must it be?
Does it so please thee well? [*SERVANT endeavours to
   speak.*] hold thy damn'd tongue.
By heaven I'll kill thee. [*Going furiously up to him.*]
MANUEL: [*In a soothing voice.*] Nay harm him not,
   my Lord; he speaks the truth;
I've met his groom, who told me certainly
His Lord is here.   I should have told you so,
But thought, perhaps, it might displease your honour.
DE MONFORT: [*Becoming all at once calm, and
   turning sternly to MANUEL.*] And how dar'st thou to
   think it would displease me?
What is't it to me who leaves or enters Amberg?
But it displeases me, yea ev'n to frenzy,
That every idle fool must hither come
To break my leisure with the paltry tidings
Of all the cursed things he stares upon.
[*SERVANT attempts to speak—DE MONFORT stamps
with his foot.*]
Take thine ill-favour'd visage from my sight,
And speak of it no more.   [*EXIT SERVANT.*]
DE MONFORT: And go thou too; I choose to be
   alone.   [*EXIT MANUEL.*]
[*DE MONFORT goes to the door by which they went out;
opens it, and looks.*]
But is he gone indeed? Yes, he is gone.
[*Goes to the opposite door, opens it, and looks: then gives

loose to all the fury of gesture, and walks up and down in great agitation.]
It is too much: by heaven it is too much!
He haunts me—stings me—like a devil haunts——
He'll make a raving maniack of me—Villain!
The air wherein thou draw'st thy fulsome breath
Is poison to me—Oceans shall divide!   [*Pauses.*]
But no; thou think'st I fear thee, cursed reptile!
And hast a pleasure in the damned thought.
Though my heart's blood should curdle at thy sight,
I'll stay and face thee still.
[*Knocking at the chamber door.*]
                    Ha! Who knocks there?
FREBERG: [*Without.*] It is thy friend, De Monfort.
DE MONFORT: [*Opening the door.*]   Enter, then.
[ENTER FREBERG.]
FREBERG: [*Taking his hand kindly.*] How art thou now? How hast thou past the night?
Has kindly sleep refresh'd thee?
DE MONFORT: Yes, I have lost an hour or two in sleep,
And so should be refresh'd.
FREBERG: And art thou not?
Thy looks speak not of rest. Thou art disturb'd.
DE MONFORT: No, somewhat ruffled from a foolish cause,
Which soon will pass away.
FREBERG: [*Shaking his head.*] Ah no, De Monfort! something in thy face
Tells me another tale. Then wrong me not:
If any secret grief distracts thy soul,
Here am I all devoted to thy love;
Open thy heart to me. What troubles thee?
DE MONFORT: I have no grief: distress me not, my friend.
FREBERG: Nay, do not call me so. Wert thou my friend,
Woulds't thou not open all thine inmost soul,
And bid me share its every consciousness?
DE MONFORT: Freberg, thou know'st not man; not nature's man,
But only him who, in smooth studied works
Of polish'd sages, shines deceitfully
In all the splendid foppery of virtue.

That man was never born whose secret soul
With all its motley treasure of dark thoughts,
Foul fantasies, vain musings, and wild dreams,
Was ever open'd to another's scan.
Away, away! it is delusion all.
FREBERG: Well, be reserved then: perhaps I'm wrong.
DE MONFORT: How goes the hour?
FREBERG: 'Tis early: a long day is still before us,
Let us enjoy it. Come along with me;
I'll introduce you to my pleasant friend.
DE MONFORT: Your pleasant friend?
FREBERG: Yes, he of whom I spake.
[*Taking his hand.*]
There is no good I would not share with thee,
And this man's company, to minds like thine,
Is the best banquet-feast I could bestow.
But I will speak in mystery no more,
It is thy townsman, noble Rezenvelt.
[DE MONFORT *pulls his hand hastily from* FREBERG, *and shrinks back.*] Ha! what is this?
Art thou pain-stricken, Monfort?
Nay, on my life, thou rather seem'st offended:
Does it displease thee that I call him friend?
DE MONFORT: No, all men are thy friends.
FREBERG: No, say not all men. But thou art offended.
I see it well. I thought to do thee pleasure.
But if his presence is not welcome here,
He shall not join our company to-day.
DE MONFORT: What dost thou mean to say? What is't to me
Whether I meet with such a thing as Rezenvelt
To-day, to-morrow, every day, or never.
FREBERG: In truth, I thought you had been well with him.
He prais'd you much.
DE MONFORT: I thank him for his praise—Come, let us move:
This chamber is confin'd and airless grown.
[*Starting.*]
I hear a stranger's voice!
FREBERG: 'Tis Rezenvelt.
Let him be told that we are gone abroad.

DE MONFORT: [*Proudly.*] No; let him enter. Who
    waits there? Ho! Manuel!
[ENTER MANUEL.]
    What stranger speaks below?
MANUEL: The Marquis Rezenvelt.
    I have not told him that you are within.
130 DE MONFORT: [*Angrily.*] And wherefore dids't thou
    not? Let him ascend.
[*A long pause. DE MONFORT walking up and down with a quick pace.*
    ENTER REZENVELT, *and runs freely up to* DE MONFORT.]
REZENVELT: [*To DE MONFORT.*] My noble
    Marquis, welcome.
DE MONFORT: Sir, I thank you.
REZENVELT: [*To FREBERG.*] My gentle friend, well
    met. Abroad so early?
FREBERG: It is indeed an early hour for me.
    How sits thy last night's revel on thy spirits?
135 REZENVELT: O, light as ever. On my way to you
    E'en now I learnt De Monfort was arriv'd,
    And turn'd my steps aside; so here I am.
[*Bowing gaily to DE MONFORT.*]
DE MONFORT: I thank you, Sir; you do me too
    much honour.   [*Proudly.*]
REZENVELT: Nay, say not so; not too much
    honour, Marquis,
140 Unless, indeed, 'tis more than pleases you.
DE MONFORT: [*Confused.*] Having no previous
    notice of your coming,
    I look'd not for it.
REZENVELT: Ay, true indeed; when I approach
    you next,
    I'll send a herald to proclaim my coming,
145 And make my bow to you by sound of trumpet.
DE MONFORT: [*To FREBERG.*] [*Turning haughtily from REZENVELT with affected indifference.*] How
    does your cheerful friend, that good old man?
FREBERG: My cheerful friend? I know not whom
    you mean.
DE MONFORT: Count Waterlan.
FREBERG: I know not one so named.

DE MONFORT: [*Very confused.*] O pardon me—it
    was at Bâle[1] I knew him.
150 FREBERG: You have not yet enquired for honest
    Reisdale.
    I met him as I came, and mention'd you.
    He seem'd amaz'd; and fain he would have learnt
    What cause procur'd us so much happiness.
    He question'd hard, and hardly would believe
155 I could not satisfy his strong desire.
REZENVELT: And know you not what brings
    De Monfort here?
FREBERG: Truly, I do not.
REZENVELT: O! 'tis love of me.
    I have but two short days in Amberg been,
    And here with postman's speed he follows me,
160 Finding his home so dull and tiresome grown.
FREBERG: [*To DE MONFORT.*] Is Rezenvelt so sadly
    miss'd with you?
    Your town so chang'd?
DE MONFORT: Not altogether so:
    Some witlings and jest-mongers still remain
    For fools to laugh at.
165 REZENVELT: But he laughs not, and therefore he
    is wise.
    He ever frowns on them with sullen brow
    Contemptuous; therefore he is very wise.
    Nay, daily frets his most refined soul
    With their poor folly, to its inmost core;
170 Therefore he is most eminently wise.
FREBERG: Fy, Rezenvelt! You are too early gay;
    Such spirits rise but with the ev'ning glass.
    They suit not placid morn.
[*To DE MONFORT, who after walking impatiently up and down, comes close to his ear, and lays hold of his arm.*]
    What would you, Monfort?
DE MONFORT: Nothing—Yet, what is't it o'clock?
175 No, no—I had forgot—'tis early still.
[*Turns away again.*]
FREBERG: [*To REZENVELT.*] Waltser informs me
    that you have agreed
    To read his verses o'er, and tell the truth.
    It is a dangerous task.

---

[1] or Basel, a city in northern Switzerland.

REZENVELT: Yet I'll be honest:
I can but lose his favour and a feast.
[*Whilst they speak,* DE MONFORT *walks up and down impatiently and irresolute; at last, pulls the bell violently.* ENTER SERVANT.]
DE MONFORT: [*To* SERVANT.] What dost thou
180   want?—
SERVANT: I thought your honour rung.
DE MONFORT: I have forgot—Stay; are my horses
    saddled?
SERVANT: I thought, my Lord, you would not ride
    to-day,
After so long a journey.
DE MONFORT: [*Impatiently.*] Well—'tis good.
Begone!—I want thee not.   [EXIT SERVANT.]
185 REZENVELT: [*Smiling significantly.*] I humbly crave
    your pardon, gentle Marquis.
It grieves me that I cannot stay with you,
And make my visit of a friendly length.
I trust your goodness will excuse me now;
Another time I shall be less unkind.
190 [*To* FREBERG.] Will you not go with me?
FREBERG: Excuse me, Monfort, I'll return again.
    [EXEUNT REZENVELT *and* FREBERG.]
DE MONFORT: [*Alone, tossing his arms distractedly.*]
Hell hath no greater torment for th'accurs'd
Than this man's presence gives—
Abhorred fiend! he hath a pleasure too,
195 A damned pleasure in the pain he gives!
Oh! the side glance of that detested eye!
That conscious smile! that full insulting lip!
It touches every nerve: it makes me mad.
What, does it please thee? Dost thou woo my hate?
Hate shalt thou have! determin'd, deadly hate,
200 Which shall awake no smile. Malignant villain!
The venom of thy mind is rank and devilish,
And thin the film that hides it.
Thy hateful visage ever spoke thy worth:
205 I loath'd thee when a boy.
That ——[1] should be besotted with him thus!
And Freberg likewise so bewitched is,
That like a hireling flatt'rer, at his heels
He meanly paces, off'ring brutish praise.
210 O! I could curse him too.
                            [EXIT.]

ACT 2

SCENE 1

A very splendid apartment in COUNT FREBERG's *house, fancifully decorated. A wide folding door opened, shews another magnificent room lighted up to receive company.* ENTER *through the folding doors the* COUNT *and* COUNTESS, *richly dressed.*

FREBERG: [*Looking round.*] In truth, I like those
    decorations well:
They suit those lofty walls. And here, my love,
The gay profusion of a woman's fancy
Is well display'd. Noble simplicity
5 Becomes us less on such a night as this
Than gaudy show.
LADY: Is it not noble, then? [*He shakes his head.*] I
    thought it so,
And as I know you love simplicity,
I did intend it should be simple too.
10 FREBERG: Be satisfy'd, I pray; we want to-night
A cheerful banquet-house, and not a temple.
How runs the hour?
LADY: It is not late, but soon we shall be rous'd
With the loud entry of our frolick guests.
[ENTER *a* PAGE, *richly dressed.*]
15 PAGE: Madam, there is a Lady in your hall,
Who begs to be admitted to your presence.
LADY: Is it not one of our invited friends?
PAGE: No, far unlike to them; it is a stranger.
LADY: How looks her countenance?
20 PAGE: So queenly, so commanding, and so noble,
I shrunk at first in awe; but when she smil'd,
For so she did to see me thus abash'd,
Methought I could have compass'd sea and land
To do her bidding.
LADY: Is she young or old?

---

[1] In the later editions, Baillie replaced the blank with the word "men."

25 PAGE: Neither, if right I guess, but she is fair;
For time hath laid his hand so gently on her,
As he too had been aw'd.
LADY: The foolish stripling!
She has bewitch'd thee. Is she large in stature?
PAGE: So stately and so graceful is her form,
30 I thought at first her stature was gigantick,
But on a near approach I found, in truth,
She scarcely does surpass the middle size.
LADY: What is her garb?
PAGE: I cannot well describe the fashion of it.
35 She is not deck'd in any gallant trim,
But seems to me clad in the usual weeds
Of high habitual state; for as she moves
Wide flows her robe in many a waving fold,
As I have seen unfurled banners play
40 With the soft breese.
LADY: Thine eyes deceive thee, boy,
It is an apparition thou hast seen.
FREBERG: [*Starting from his seat, where he has been sitting during the conversation between the* LADY *and the* PAGE.] It is an apparition he has seen,
Or it is Jane De Monfort.   [EXIT, *hastily.*]
LADY: [*Displeased.*] No; such description surely suits not her.
45 Did she enquire for me?
PAGE: She ask'd to see the lady of Count Freberg.
LADY: Perhaps it is not she—I fear it is—
Ha! here they come. He has but guess'd too well.
[ENTER FREBERG, *leading in* JANE DE MONFORT.]
FREBERG: [*Presenting her to* LADY.] Here, madam, welcome a most worthy guest.
50 LADY: Madam, a thousand welcomes. Pardon me;
I could not guess who honour'd me so far;
I should not else have waited coldly here.
JANE: I thank you for this welcome, gentle Countess,
But take those kind excuses back again;
55 I am a bold intruder on this hour,
And am entitled to no ceremony.
I came in quest of a dear truant friend,
But Freberg has inform'd me—
[*To* FREBERG.] And he is well you say?
FREBERG: Yes, well, but joyless.

60 JANE: It is the usual temper of his mind:
It opens not, but with the thrilling touch
Of some strong heart-string o'the sudden press'd.
FREBERG: It may be so, I've known him otherwise.
He is suspicious grown.
65 JANE: Not so, Count Freberg, Monfort is too noble.
Say rather, that he is a man in grief,
Wearing at times a strange and scowling eye;
And thou, less generous than beseems a friend,
Hast thought too hardly of him.
FREBERG: [*Bowing with great respect.*] So will I say
70 I'll own nor word, nor will, that can offend you.
LADY: De Monfort is engag'd to grace our feast,
Ere long you'll see him here.
JANE: I thank you truly, but this homely dress
Suits not the splendour of such scenes as these.
75 FREBERG: [*Pointing to her dress.*] Such artless and majestick elegance,
So exquisitely just, so nobly simple,
Will make the gorgeous blush.
JANE: [*Smiling.*] Nay, nay, be more consistent, courteous knight,
And do not praise a plain and simple guise
80 With such profusion of unsimple words.
I cannot join your company to-night.
LADY: Not stay to see your brother?
JANE: Therefore it is I would not, gentle hostess.
Here he will find all that can woo the heart
85 To joy and sweet forgetfulness of pain;
The sight of me would wake his feeling mind
To other thoughts. I am no doting mistress,
No fond distracted wife, who must forthwith
Rush to his arms and weep. I am his sister:
90 The eldest daughter of his father's house:
Calm and unwearied is my love for him;
And having found him, patiently I'll wait,
Nor greet him in the hour of social joy,
To dash his mirth with tears.—
95 The night wears on; permit me to withdraw.
FREBERG: Nay, do not, do not injure us so far!
Disguise thyself, and join our friendly train.
JANE: You wear not masks to-night?
LADY: We wear not masks, but you may be conceal'd

100   Behind the double foldings of a veil.
    JANE: [*After pausing to consider.*] In truth, I feel a
        little so inclin'd.
    Methinks unknown, I e'en might speak to him,
    And gently prove the temper of his mind:
    But for the means I must become your debtor.
    [*To LADY.*]
105   LADY: Who waits? [*ENTER her WOMAN.*] Attend this
        lady to my wardrobe,
    And do what she commands you.
                [*EXEUNT JANE and WAITING-WOMAN.*]
    FREBERG: [*Looking after JANE, as she goes out, with
        admiration.*] Oh! what a soul she bears! see how she
        steps!
    Nought but the native dignity of worth
    E'er taught the moving form such noble grace.
110   LADY: Such lofty mien, and high assumed gait
    I've seen ere now, and men have call'd it pride.
    FREBERG: No, 'faith! thou never dids't, but oft
        indeed
    The paltry imitation thou hast seen.
    [*Looking at her.*] How hang those trappings on thy
        motley gown?
115   They seem like garlands on a May-day queen,
    Which hinds have dress'd in sport.
    LADY: I'll doff it, then, since it displeases you.
    FREBERG: [*Softening.*] No, no, thou art lovely still
        in every garb.
    But see the guests assemble.
    [*ENTER groups of well dressed people, who pay their compliments to FREBERG and his LADY; and followed by her pass into the inner apartment, where more company appear assembling, as if by another entry.*]
    FREBERG: [*Who remains on the front of the stage,
120   with a friend or two.*] How loud the hum of this gay
        meeting croud!
    'Tis like a bee-swarm in the noonday sun.
    Musick will quell the sound. Who waits without?
    Musick strike up.
    [*A grand piece of musick is playing, and when it ceases, ENTER from the inner apartment REZENVELT, with several gentlemen, all richly dressed.*]
    FREBERG: [*To those just entered.*] What lively gallants
        quit the field so soon?

125   Are there no beauties in that moving crowd
    To fix your fancy?
    REZENVELT: Ay, marry, are there! men of ev'ry mind
    May in that moving croud some fair one find,
    To suit their taste, tho' whimsical and strange,
130   As ever fancy own'd.
    Beauty of every cast and shade is there,
    From the perfection of a faultless form,
    Down to the common, brown, unnoted maid,
    Who looks but pretty in her Sunday gown.
135   1ST GENTLEMAN: There is, indeed, a gay variety.
    REZENVELT: And if the liberality of nature
    Suffices not, there's store of grafted charms
    Blending in one the sweets of many plants
    So obstinately, strangely opposite,
140   As would have well defy'd all other art
    But female cultivation. Aged youth,
    With borrow'd locks in rosy chaplets bound,
    Cloaths her dim eye, parch'd lip, and skinny cheek
    In most unlovely softness.
145   And youthful age, with fat round trackless face,
    The down-cast look of contemplation deep,
    Most pensively assumes.
    Is it not even so? The native prude,
    With forced laugh, and merriment uncouth,
150   Plays off the wild coquet's successful charms
    With most unskilful pains; and the coquet,
    In temporary crust of cold reserve,
    Fixes her studied looks upon the ground
    Forbiddingly demure.
155   FREBERG: Fy! thou art too severe.
    REZENVELT: Say, rather, gentle.
    I' faith! the very dwarfs attempt to charm
    With lofty airs of puny majesty,
    Whilst potent damsels, of a portly make,
    Totter like nurselings, and demand the aid
160   Of gentle sympathy.
    From all those diverse modes of dire assault,
    He owns a heart of hardest adamant,
    Who shall escape to-night.
    FREBERG: [*To DE MONFORT, who has entered during REZENVELT's speech, and heard the greatest part of it.*]
        Ha, ha, ha, ha!
    How pleasantly he gives his wit the rein,

165   Yet guides its wild career!
[DE MONFORT is silent.]
REZENVELT: [Smiling archly.] What, think you,
    Freberg, the same powerful spell
Of transformation reigns o'er all to-night?
Or that De Monfort is a woman turn'd,
So widely from his native self to swerve,
170 As grace my gai'ty with a smile of his?
DE MONFORT: Nay, think not, Rezenvelt, there is no smile
I can bestow on thee. There is a smile,
A smile of nature too, which I can spare,
And yet, perhaps, thou wilt not thank me for it.
[Smiles contemptuously.]
175 REZENVELT: Not thank thee! It were surely most ungrateful
No thanks to pay for nobly giving me
What, well we see, has cost thee so much pain.
For nature hath her smiles, of birth more painful
Than bitt'rest execrations.
180 FREBERG: These idle words will lead us to disquiet:
Forbear, forbear, my friends. Go, Rezenvelt,
Accept the challenge of those lovely dames,
Who thro' the portal come with bolder steps
To claim your notice.
[ENTER a group of LADIES from the other apartment. REZENVELT shrugs up his shoulders, as if unwilling to go.]
1ST GENTLEMAN: [To REZENVELT.] Behold in sable
185   veil a lady comes,
Whose noble air doth challange fancy's skill
To suit it with a countenance as goodly.
[Pointing to JANE DE MONFORT, who now ENTERS in a thick black veil.]
REZENVELT: Yes, this way lies attraction. [To FREBERG.] With permission,
[Going up to JANE.]
Fair lady, tho' within that envious shroud
190 Your beauty deigns not to enlighten us,
We bid you welcome, and our beauties here
Will welcome you the more for such concealment.
With the permission of our noble host—
[Taking her hand, and leading her to the front of the stage.]
JANE: [To FREBERG.] Pardon me this presumption, courteous sir:
195 I thus appear, [Pointing to her veil.] not careless of respect
Unto the gen'rous lady of the feast.
Beneath this veil no beauty shrouded is,
That, now, or pain, or pleasure can bestow.
Within the friendly cover of its shade
200 I only wish unknown, again to see
One who, alas! is heedless of my pain.
DE MONFORT: Yet, it is ever thus. Undo that veil,
And give thy count'nance to the cheerful light.
Men now all soft, and female beauty scorn,
205 And mock the gentle cares which aim to please.
It is most damnable! undo thy veil,
And think of him no more.
JANE: I know it well, even to a proverb grown,
Is lovers' faith, and I had borne such slight:
210 But he who has, alas! forsaken me
Was the companion of my early days,
My cradle's mate, mine infant play-fellow.
Within our op'ning minds with riper years
The love of praise and gen'rous virtue sprung:
215 Thro' varied life our pride, our joys, were one;
At the same tale we wept: he is my brother.
DE MONFORT: And he forsook thee?—No, I dare not curse him:
My heart upbraids me with a crime like his.
JANE: Ah! do not thus distress a feeling heart.
220 All sisters are not to the soul entwin'd
With equal bands; thine has not watch'd for thee,
Weep'd for thee, cheer'd thee, shar'd thy weal and woe,
As I have done for him.
DE MONFORT: [Eagerly.] Ha! has she not?
By heaven! the sum of all thy kindly deeds
225 Were but as chaff pois'd against the massy gold,
Compar'd to that which I do owe her love.
Oh pardon me! I mean not to offend—
I am too warm—But she of whom I speak
Is the dear sister of my earliest love;
230 In noble virtuous worth to none a second:
And tho' behind those sable folds were hid
As fair a face as ever woman own'd,
Still would I say she is as fair as thee.
How oft amidst the beauty-blazing throng,
235 I've proudly to th'inquiring stranger told

    Her name and lineage! yet within her house,
    The virgin mother of an orphan race
    Her dying parents left, this noble woman
    Did, like a Roman matron, proudly sit,
240 Despising all the blandishments of love;
    Whilst many a youth his hopeless love conceal'd,
    Or, humbly distant, woo'd her like a queen.
    Forgive, I pray you! O forgive this boasting!
    In faith! I mean you no discourtesy.
  JANE: [*Off her guard, in a soft natural tone of voice.*]
245   Oh no! nor do me any.
  DE MONFORT: What voice speaks now?
    Withdraw, withdraw this shade!
    For if thy face bear semblance to thy voice,
    I'll fall and worship thee. Pray! pray undo!
    [*Puts forth his hand eagerly to snatch away the veil, whilst she shrinks back, and REZENVELT steps between to prevent him.*]
  REZENVELT: Stand off: no hand shall lift this sacred veil.
250 DE MONFORT: What, dost thou think De Monfort
     fall'n so low,
    That there may live a man beneath heav'n's roof
    Who dares to say he shall not?
  REZENVELT: He lives who dares to say—
  JANE: [*Throwing back her veil, very much alarmed, and rushing between them.*] Forbear, forbear!
    [*REZENVELT, very much struck, steps back respectfully, and makes her a very low bow. DE MONFORT stands for a while motionless, gazing upon her, till she, looking expressively to him, extends her arms, and he, rushing into them, bursts into tears. FREBERG seems very much pleased. The company then gather about them, and the Scene closes.*]

SCENE 2

DE MONFORT's apartments. ENTER DE MONFORT, with a disordered air, and his hand pressed upon his forehead, followed by JANE.

  DE MONFORT: No more, my sister, urge me not again:
    My secret troubles cannot be revealed.
    From all participation of its thoughts
    My heart recoils: I pray thee be contented.
5 JANE: What, must I, like a distant humble friend,
    Observe thy restless eye, and gait disturb'd,
    In timid silence, whilst with yearning heart
    I turn aside to weep? O no! De Monfort!
    A nobler task thy noble mind will give;
10 Thy true intrusted friend I still shall be.
  DE MONFORT: Ah, Jane, forbear! I cannot e'en to thee.
  JANE: Then fy upon it! fy upon it, Monfort!
    There was a time when e'en with murder stain'd,
    Had it been possible that such dire deed
15 Could e'er have been the crime of one so piteous,
    Thou would'st have told it me.
  DE MONFORT: So would I now—but ask of this
     no more.
    All other trouble but the one I feel
    I had disclos'd to thee. I pray thee spare me.
20 It is the secret weakness of my nature.
  JANE: Then secret let it be; I urge no farther.
    The eldest of our valiant father's hopes,
    So sadly orphan'd, side by side we stood,
    Like two young trees, whose boughs, in early strength,
25 Screen the weak saplings of the rising grove,
    And brave the storm together—
    I have so long, as if by nature's right,
    Thy bosom's inmate and adviser been,
    I thought thro' life I should have so remain'd,
30 Nor ever known a change. Forgive me, Monfort,
    A humbler station will I take by thee:
    The close attendant of thy wand'ring steps;
    The cheerer of this home, by strangers sought;
    The soother of those griefs I must not know,
35 This is mine office now: I ask no more.
  DE MONFORT: Oh Jane! thou dost constrain me
     with thy love!
    Would I could tell it thee!
  JANE: Thou shalt not tell me. Nay, I'll stop mine ears,
    Nor from the yearnings of affection wring
40 What shrinks from utt'rance. Let it pass, my brother.
    I'll stay by thee; I'll cheer thee, comfort thee:
    Pursue with thee the study of some art,
    Or nobler science, that compels the mind
    To steady thought progressive, driving forth
45 All floating, wild, unhappy fantasies;
    Till thou, with brow unclouded, smil'st again,

Like one who from dark visions of the night,
When th'active soul within its lifeless cell
Holds its own world, with dreadful fancy press'd
50 Of some dire, terrible, or murd'rous deed,
Wakes to the dawning morn, and blesses heaven.
DE MONFORT: It will not pass away: 'twill haunt me still.
JANE: Ah! say not so, for I will haunt thee too;
And be to it so close an adversary,
55 That, tho' I wrestle darkling with the fiend,
I shall o'ercome it.
DE MONFORT: Thou most gen'rous woman!
Why do I treat thee thus? It should not be—
And yet I cannot—O that cursed villain!
He will not let me be the man I would.
60 JANE: What say'st thou, Monfort? Oh! what words are these?
They have awak'd my soul to dreadful thoughts.
I do beseech thee speak!
[*He shakes his head and turns from her; she following him.*]
By the affection thou didst ever bear me,
By the dear mem'ry of our infant days;
65 By kindred living ties, ay, and by those
Who sleep i'the tomb, and cannot call to thee,
I do conjure thee speak.
[*He waves her off with his hand, and covers his face with the other, still turning from her.*]
Ha! wilt thou not?
[*Assuming dignity.*] Then, if affection, most unwearied love,
Tried early, long, and never wanting found,
70 O'er gen'rous man hath more authority,
More rightful power than crown and sceptre give,
I do command thee.
[*He throws himself into a chair greatly agitated.*]
De Monfort, do not thus resist my love.
Here I entreat thee on my bended knees.
[*Kneeling.*]
75 Alas! my brother!
[*DE MONFORT starts up, and, catching her in his arms, raises her up, then placing her in the chair, kneels at her feet.*]
DE MONFORT: Thus let him kneel who should the abased be,
And at thine honour'd feet confession make.
I'll tell thee all—but oh! thou wilt despise me.
For in my breast a raging passion burns,
80 To which thy soul no sympathy will own.
A passion which hath made my nightly couch
A place of torment; and the light of day,
With the gay intercourse of social man,
Feel like th'oppressive airless pestilence.
85 O Jane! thou wilt despise me.
JANE: Say not so:
I never can despise thee, gentle brother.
A lover's jealousy and hopeless pangs
No kindly heart contemns.
DE MONFORT: A lover, say'st thou?
No, it is hate! black, lasting, deadly hate;
90 Which thus hath driv'n me forth from kindred peace,
From social pleasure, from my native home,
To be a sullen wand'rer on the earth,
Avoiding all men, cursing and accurs'd.
JANE: De Monfort, this is fiend-like, frightful, terrible!
95 What being, by th'Almighty Father form'd,
Of flesh and blood, created even as thou,
Could in thy breast such horrid tempest wake,
Who art thyself his fellow?
Unknit thy brows, and spread those wrath-clench'd hands:
100 Some sprite accurst within thy bosom mates
To work thy ruin. Strive with it, my brother!
Strive bravely with it; drive it from thy breast:
'Tis the degrader of a noble heart;
Curse it, and bid it part.
105 DE MONFORT: It will not part. [*His hand on his breast.*] I've lodged it here too long;
With my first cares I felt its rankling touch,
I loath'd him when a boy.
JANE: Who did'st thou say?
DE MONFORT: Oh! that detested Rezenvelt!
E'en in our early sports, like two young whelps
110 Of hostile breed, instinctively reverse,
Each 'gainst the other pitch'd his ready pledge,
And frown'd defiance. As we onward pass'd
From youth to man's estate, his narrow art,
And envious gibing malice, poorly veil'd

   In the affected carelessness of mirth, [115]
   Still more detestable and odious grew.
   There is no living being on this earth
   Who can conceive the malice of his soul,
   With all his gay and damned merriment,
   To those, by fortune or by merit plac'd [120]
   Above his paltry self. When, low in fortune,
   He look'd upon the state of prosp'rous men,
   As nightly birds, rous'd from their murky holes,
   Do scowl and chatter at the light of day,
   I could endure it; even as we bear [125]
   Th'impotent bite of some half-trodden worm,
   I could endure it. But when honours came,
   And wealth and new-got titles fed his pride;
   Whilst flatt'ring knaves did trumpet forth his praise,
   And grov'ling idiots grinn'd applauses on him; [130]
   Oh! then I could no longer suffer it!
   It drove me frantick.——What! what would I give!
   What would I give to crush the bloated toad,
   So rankly do I loath him!
JANE: And would thy hatred crush the very man [135]
   Who gave to thee that life he might have ta'en?
   That life which thou so rashly did'st expose
   To aim at his! Oh! this is horrible!
DE MONFORT: Ha! thou hast heard it, then? From all the world,
   But most of all from thee, I thought it hid. [140]
JANE: I heard a secret whisper, and resolv'd
   Upon the instant to return to thee.
   Dids't thou receive my letter?
DE MONFORT: I did! I did! 'twas that which drove me hither.
   I could not bear to meet thine eye again. [145]
JANE: Alas! that, tempted by a sister's tears,
   I ever left thy house! these few past months,
   These absent months, have brought us all this woe.
   Had I remain'd with thee it had not been.
   And yet, methinks, it should not move you thus. [150]
   You dar'd him to the field; both bravely fought;
   He more adroit disarm'd you; courteously
   Return'd the forfeit sword, which, so return'd,
   You did refuse to use against him more;
   And then, as says report, you parted friends. [155]
DE MONFORT: When he disarm'd this curs'd, this worthless hand
   Of its most worthless weapon, he but spar'd
   From dev'lish pride, which now derives a bliss
   In seeing me thus fetter'd, sham'd, subjected
   With the vile favour of his poor forbearance; [160]
   Whilst he securely sits with gibing brow
   And basely bates me, like a muzzled cur
   Who cannot turn again.——
   Until that day, till that accursed day,
   I knew not half the torment of this hell, [165]
   Which burns within my breast. Heaven's lightning blast him!
JANE: O this is horrible! Forbear, forbear!
   Lest heaven's vengeance light upon thy head,
   For this most impious wish.
DE MONFORT: Then let it light.
   Torments more fell than I have felt already [170]
   It cannot send. To be annihilated;
   What all men shrink from; to be dust, be nothing,
   Were bliss to me, compar'd to what I am.
JANE: Oh! would'st thou kill me with these dreadful words?
DE MONFORT: [*Raising his arms to heaven.*] Let me [175]
   but once upon his ruin look,
   Then close mine eyes for ever!
[*JANE, in great distress, staggers back, and supports herself upon the side scene. DE MONFORT, alarm'd, runs up to her with a soften'd voice.*]
   Ha! how is this? thou'rt ill; thou'rt very pale.
   What have I done to thee? Alas, alas!
   I meant not to distress thee.—O my sister!
JANE: [*Shaking her head.*] I cannot speak to thee. [180]
DE MONFORT: I have kill'd thee.
   Turn, turn thee not away! look on me still!
   Oh! droop not thus, my life, my pride, my sister!
   Look on me yet again.
JANE: Thou too, De Monfort,
   In better days, wert wont to be my pride.
DE MONFORT: I am a wretch, most wretched in myself, [185]
   And still more wretched in the pain I give.
   O curse that villain! that detested villain!

　　　　He hath spread mis'ry o'er my fated life:
　　　　He will undo us all.
190　JANE:　　I've held my warfare through a troubled world,
　　　　And borne with steady mind my share of ill;
　　　　For then the helpmate of my toil wert thou.
　　　　But now the wane of life comes darkly on,
　　　　And hideous passion tears thee from my heart,
195　Blasting thy worth.—I cannot strive with this.
　　DE MONFORT:　　[*Affectionately.*]　　What shall I do?
　　JANE:　　　　　　　　　　　Call up thy noble spirit,
　　　　Rouse all the gen'rous energy of virtue;
　　　　And with the strength of heaven-endued man,
　　　　Repel the hideous foe. Be great; be valiant.
200　O, if thou could'st! E'en shrouded as thou art
　　　　In all the sad infirmities of nature,
　　　　What a most noble creature would'st thou be!
　　DE MONFORT:　　Ay, if I could: alas! alas! I cannot.
　　JANE:　　Thou can'st, thou may'st, thou wilt.
205　We shall not part till I have turn'd thy soul.
　　　　[ENTER MANUEL.]
　　DE MONFORT:　　Ha! some one enters. Wherefore
　　　　com'st thou here?
　　MANUEL:　　Count Freberg waits your leisure.
　　DE MONFORT:　　[*Angrily.*] Be gone, be gone.—I
　　　　cannot see him now.　　　　　　[EXIT MANUEL.]
　　JANE:　　Come to my closet; free from all intrusion,
210　I'll school thee there; and thou again shalt be
　　　　My willing pupil, and my gen'rous friend;
　　　　The noble Monfort I have lov'd so long,
　　　　And must not, will not lose.
　　DE MONFORT:　　Do as thou wilt; I will not grieve
　　　　thee more.　　　　　　　　　　　　[EXEUNT.]

　　　　　　　　　　SCENE 3

　　　　COUNT FREBERG's *House*. ENTER *the* COUNTESS, *followed by the* PAGE, *and speaking as she enters*.

　　LADY:　　Take this and this. [*Giving two packets.*]
　　　　And tell my gentle friend,
　　　　I hope to see her ere the day be done.
　　PAGE:　　Is there no message for the Lady Jane?
　　LADY:　　No, foolish boy, that would too far extend
5　　Your morning's route, and keep you absent long.
　　PAGE:　　O no, dear Madam! I'll the swifter run.
　　　　The summer's light'ning moves not as I'll move,
　　　　If you will send me to the Lady Jane.
　　LADY:　　No, not so slow, I ween. The summer's
　　　　light'ning!
10　Thou art a lad of taste and letters grown:
　　　　Would'st poetry admire, and ape thy master.
　　　　Go, go; my little spaniels are unkempt;
　　　　My cards unwritten, and my china broke:
　　　　Thou art too learned for a lady's page.
15　Did I not bid thee call Theresa here?
　　PAGE:　　Madam, she comes.
　　　　[ENTER THERESA, *carrying a robe over her arm.*]
　　LADY:　　[*To* THERESA.] What has employ'd you all
　　　　this dreary while?
　　　　I've waited long.
　　THERESA:　　　　　　　　Madam, the robe is finish'd.
　　LADY:　　Well, let me see it.
　　　　[THERESA *spreads out the robe.*]
20　[*Impatiently to the* PAGE.] Boy, hast thou ne'er a
　　　　hand to lift that fold?
　　　　See where it hangs.
　　　　[PAGE *takes the other side of the robe, and spreads it out to its full extent before her, whilst she sits down and looks at it with much dissatisfaction.*]
　　THERESA:　　Does not my lady like this easy form?
　　LADY:　　That sleeve is all awry.
　　THERESA:　　　　　　　　　Your pardon, madam;
　　　　'Tis but the empty fold that shades it thus.
25　I took the pattern from a graceful shape;
　　　　The Lady Jane De Monfort wears it so.
　　LADY:　　Yes, yes, I see 'tis thus with all of you.
　　　　Whate'er she wears is elegance and grace,
　　　　Whilst ev'ry ornament of mine, forsooth,
30　Must hang like trappings on a May-day queen.
　　　　[*Angrily to the* PAGE, *who is smiling to himself.*] Youngster
　　　　be gone. Why do you loiter here?
　　　　　　　　　　　　　　　　　　　　[EXIT PAGE.]
　　THERESA:　　What would you, madam, chuse to wear
　　　　to-night?
　　　　One of your newest robes?
　　LADY:　　　　　　　　　　　　I hate them all.

THERESA: Surely, that purple scarf became you well,
35   With all those wreaths of richly hanging flowers.
     Did I not overhear them say, last night,
     As from the crouded ball-room ladies past,
     How gay and handsome, in her costly dress,
     The Countess Freberg look'd.
LADY: Did'st thou o'erhear it?
40 THERESA: I did, and more than this.
LADY: Well, all are not so greatly prejudic'd;
     All do not think me like a May-day queen,
     Which peasants deck in sport.
THERESA: And who said this?
LADY: [*Putting her handkerchief to her eyes.*] E'en
     my good lord, Theresa.
45 THERESA: He said it but in jest. He loves you well.
LADY: I know as well as thee he loves me well;
     But what of that? he takes no pride in me.
     Elsewhere his praise and admiration go,
     And Jane De Monfort is not mortal woman.
50 THERESA: The wond'rous character this lady bears
     For worth and excellence; from early youth
     The friend and mother of her younger sisters
     Now greatly married, as I have been told,
     From her most prudent care, may well excuse
55   The admiration of so good a man
     As my good master is. And then, dear madam,
     I must confess, when I myself did hear
     How she was come thro' the rough winter's storm,
     To seek and comfort an unhappy brother,
60   My heart beat kindly to her.
LADY: Ay, ay, there is a charm in this I find:
     But wherefore may she not have come as well
     Through wintry storms to seek a lover too?
THERESA: No, madam, no, I could not think of this.
65 LADY: That would reduce her in your eyes, mayhap,
     To woman's level.—Now I see my vengeance!
     I'll tell it round that she is hither come,
     Under pretence of finding out De Monfort,
     To meet with Rezenvelt. When Freberg hears it
70   'Twill help, I ween, to break this magick charm.
THERESA: And say what is not, madam?
LADY: How can'st thou know that I shall say what
     is not?
     'Tis like enough I shall but speak the truth.

THERESA: Ah no! there is—
LADY: Well, hold thy foolish tongue.
75   Carry that robe into my chamber, do:
     I'll try it there myself.
                                           [*EXEUNT.*]

ACT 3

SCENE 1

DE MONFORT discovered sitting by a table reading.
After a little time he lays down his book, and continues in
a thoughtful posture. ENTER *to him JANE DE MONFORT.*

JANE: Thanks, gentle brother.—
     [*Pointing to the book.*]
     Thy willing mind has been right well employ'd.
     Did not thy heart warm at the fair display
     Of peace and concord and forgiving love?
5 DE MONFORT: I know resentment may to love be
          turn'd;
     Tho' keen and lasting, into love as strong:
     And fiercest rivals in th'ensanguin'd field
     Have cast their brandish'd weapons to the ground,
     Joining their mailed breasts in close embrace,
10   With gen'rous impulse fir'd. I know right well
     The darkest, fellest wrongs have been forgiven
     Seventy times o'er from blessed heavenly love:
     I've heard of things like these; I've heard and wept.
     But what is this to me?
JANE: All, all, my brother!
15   It bids thee too that noble precept learn,
     To love thine enemy.
DE MONFORT: Th'uplifted stroke that would a
          wretch destroy
     Gorg'd with my richest spoil, stain'd with my blood,
     I would arrest and cry, hold! hold! have mercy:
20   But when the man most adverse to my nature;
     Who e'en from childhood hath, with rude
          malevolence,
     Withheld the fair respect all paid beside,
     Turning my very praise into derision;
     Who galls and presses me where'er I go,

25   Would claim the gen'rous feelings of my heart,
       Nature herself doth lift her voice aloud,
       And cries, it is impossible.
       JANE: [*Shaking her head.*]—Ah Monfort, Monfort!
       DE MONFORT: I can forgive th'envenom'd reptile's sting,
30   But hate his loathsome self.
       JANE: And canst thou do no more for love of heaven?
       DE MONFORT: Alas! I cannot now so school my mind
       As holy men have taught, nor search it truly:
       But this, my Jane, I'll do for love of thee;
35   And more it is than crowns could win me to,
       Or any power but thine. I'll see the man.
       Th'indignant risings of abhorrent nature;
       The stern contraction of my scowling brows,
       That, like the plant,[1] whose closing leaves do shrink
40   At hostile touch, still knit at his approach;
       The crooked curving lip, by instinct taught,
       In imitation of disgustful things
       To pout and swell, I strictly will repress;
       And meet him with a tamed countenance,
45   E'en as a townsman, who would live at peace,
       And pay him the respect his station claims.
       I'll crave his pardon too for all offence
       My dark and wayward temper may have done;
       Nay more, I will confess myself his debtor
50   For the forbearance I have curs'd so oft.
       Life spar'd by him, more horrid than the grave
       With all its dark corruption! This I'll do.
       Will it suffice thee? More than this I cannot.
       JANE: No more than this do I require of thee
55   In outward act, tho' in thy heart, my friend,
       I hop'd a better change, and still will hope.
       I told thee Freberg had propos'd a meeting.
       DE MONFORT: I know it well.
       JANE: And Rezenvelt consents.
       He meets you here; so far he shews respect.
60   DE MONFORT: Well, let it be; the sooner past the better.
       JANE: I'm glad to hear you say so, for, in truth,
       He has propos'd it for an early hour.

---

[1] the sensitive plant, *Mimosa pudica*.

       'Tis almost near his time; I came to tell you.
       DE MONFORT: What, comes he here so soon? shame on his speed!
65   It is not decent thus to rush upon me.
       He loves the secret pleasure he will feel
       To see me thus subdued.
       JANE: O say not so! he comes with heart sincere.
       DE MONFORT: Could we not meet elsewhere? from home—i' the fields,
70   Where other men—must I alone receive him?
       Where is your agent, Freberg, and his friends,
       That I must meet him here?
       [*Walks up and down very much disturbed.*]
       Now did'st thou say?—how goes the hour?—e'en now?
       I would some other friend were first arriv'd.
75   JANE: See, to thy wish comes Freberg and his dame.
       DE MONFORT: His lady too! why comes he not alone?
       Must all the world stare upon our meeting?
       [ENTER COUNT FREBERG *and his* COUNTESS.]
       FREBERG: A happy morrow to my noble marquis
       And his most noble sister.
       JANE: Gen'rous Freberg,
80   Your face, methinks, forbodes a happy morn
       Open and cheerful. What of Rezenvelt?
       FREBERG: I left him at his home, prepar'd to follow:
       He'll soon appear. [*To* DE MONFORT.] And now, my worthy friend,
       Give me your hand; this happy change delights me.
       [DE MONFORT *gives him his hand coldly, and they walk to the bottom of the stage together, in earnest discourse, whilst* JANE *and the* COUNTESS *remain in the front.*]
85   LADY: My dearest madam, will you pardon me?
       I know Count Freberg's bus'ness with De Monfort,
       And had a strong desire to visit you,
       So much I wish the honour of your friendship.
       For he retains no secret from mine ear.
90   JANE: [*Archly.*] Knowing your prudence.—You are welcome, madam,
       So shall Count Freberg's lady ever be.
       [DE MONFORT *and* FREBERG *returning towards the front of the stage, still engaged in discourse.*]
       FREBERG: He is indeed a man, within whose breast,
       Firm rectitude and honour hold their seat,

Tho' unadorned with that dignity
95 Which were their fittest garb. Now, on my life!
I know no truer heart than Rezenvelt.
DE MONFORT: Well, Freberg, well, there needs not all this pains
To garnish out his worth; let it suffice.
I am resolv'd I will respect the man,
100 As his fair station and repute demand.
Methinks I see not at your jolly feasts
The youthful knight, who sung so pleasantly.
FREBERG: A pleasant circumstance detains him hence;
Pleasant to those who love high gen'rous deeds
105 Above the middle pitch of common minds;
And, tho' I have been sworn to secrecy,
Yet must I tell it thee.
This knight is near a kin to Rezenvelt
To whom an old relation, short while dead,
110 Bequeath'd a good estate, some leagues distant.
But Rezenvelt, now rich in fortune's store,
Disdain'd the sordid love of further gain,
And gen'rously the rich bequest resign'd
To this young man, blood of the same degree
115 To the deceas'd, and low in fortune's gifts,
Who is from hence to take possession of it.
Was it not nobly done?
DE MONFORT: 'Twas right, and honourable.
This morning is oppressive, warm, and heavy:
There hangs a foggy closeness in the air;
120 Dost thou not feel it?
FREBERG: O no! to think upon a gen'rous deed
Expands my soul, and makes me lightly breathe.
DE MONFORT: Who gives the feast to night? His name escapes me.
You say I am invited.
FREBERG: Old Count Waterlan.
125 In honour of your townsman's gen'rous gift
He spreads the board.
DE MONFORT: He is too old to revel with the gay.
FREBERG: But not too old is he to honour virtue.
I shall partake of it with open soul;
130 For, on my honest faith, of living men
I know not one, for talents, honour, worth,
That I should rank superiour to Rezenvelt.

DE MONFORT: How virtuous he hath been in three short days!
FREBERG: Nay, longer, Marquis, but my friendship rests
135 Upon the good report of other men;
And that has told me much.
[DE MONFORT aside, going some steps hastily from FREBERG, and rending his cloak with agitation as he goes.]
Would he were come! by heaven I would he were!
This fool besets me so.
[Suddenly correcting himself, and joining the LADIES, who have retired to the bottom of the stage, he speaks to COUNTESS FREBERG with affected cheerfulness.]
The sprightly dames of Amberg rise by times
140 Untarnish'd with the vigils of the night.
LADY: Praise us not rashly, 'tis not always so.
DE MONFORT: He does not rashly praise who praises you;
For he were dull indeed—
[Stopping short, as if he heard something.]
LADY: How dull indeed?
DE MONFORT: I should have said—It has escap'd me now—
[Listening again, as if he heard something.]
145 JANE: [To DE MONFORT.] What, hear you ought?
DE MONFORT: [Hastily.]   'Tis nothing.
LADY: [To DE MONFORT.] Nay, do not let me lose it so, my lord.
Some fair one has bewitch'd your memory,
And robs me of the half-form'd compliment.
JANE: Half-utter'd praise is to the curious mind,
150 As to the eye half-veiled beauty is,
More precious than the whole. Pray pardon him.
Some one approaches. [Listening.]
FREBERG: No, no, it is a servant who ascends;
He will not come so soon.
155 DE MONFORT: [Off his guard.] 'Tis Rezenvelt: I heard his well-known foot!
From the first stair-case, mounting step by step.
FREBERG: How quick an ear thou hast for distant sound!
I heard him not.

[DE MONFORT *looks embarrassed, and is silent.*
ENTER REZENVELT. DE MONFORT, *recovering himself, goes up to receive* REZENVELT, *who meets him with a cheerful countenance.*]
DE MONFORT: [*To* REZENVELT.] I am, my lord,
    beholden to you greatly.
160 This ready visit makes me much your debtor.
REZENVELT: Then may such debts between us, noble
    marquis,
Be oft incurr'd, and often paid again.
[*To* JANE.] Madam, I am devoted to your service,
And ev'ry wish of yours commands my will.
165 [*To* COUNTESS.] Lady, good morning. [*To* FREBERG.]
    Well, my gentle friend,
You see I have not linger'd long behind.
FREBERG: No, thou art sooner than I look'd for thee.
REZENVELT: A willing heart adds feather to the heel,
And makes the clown a winged mercury.
170 DE MONFORT: Then let me say, that with a grateful
    mind
I do receive these tokens of good will;
And must regret that, in my wayward moods,
I have too oft forgot the due regard
Your rank and talents claim.
REZENVELT: No, no, De Monfort,
175 You have but rightly curb'd a wanton spirit,
Which makes me too, neglectful of respect.
Let us be friends, and think of this no more.
FREBERG: Ay, let it rest with the departed shades
Of things which are no more; whilst lovely concord,
180 Follow'd by friendship sweet, and firm esteem,
Your future days enrich. O heavenly friendship!
Thou dost exalt the sluggish souls of men,
By thee conjoin'd, to great and glorious deeds;
As two dark clouds, when mix'd in middle air,
185 The vivid lightning's flash, and roar sublime.
Talk not of what is past, but future love.
DE MONFORT: [*With dignity.*] No, Freberg, no, it
    must not. [*To* REZENVELT.] No, my lord.
I will not offer you an hand of concord
And poorly hide the motives which constrain me.
190 I would that, not alone these present friends,
But ev'ry soul in Amberg were assembled,
That I, before them all, might here declare
I owe my spared life to your forbearance.
[*Holding out his hand.*] Take this from one who boasts
    no feeling warmth,
195 But never will deceive.
[JANE *smiles upon* DE MONFORT *with great approbation, and* REZENVELT *runs up to him with open arms.*]
REZENVELT: Away with hands! I'll have thee to my
    breast.
Thou art, upon my faith, a noble spirit!
DE MONFORT: [*Shrinking back from him.*] Nay, if you
    please, I am not so prepar'd—
My nature is of temp'rature too cold—
200 I pray you pardon me. [JANE's *countenance changes.*]
But take this hand, the token of respect;
The token of a will inclin'd to concord;
The token of a mind that bears within
A sense impressive of the debt it owes you;
205 And cursed be its power, unnerv'd its strength,
If e'er again it shall be lifted up
To do you any harm.
REZENVELT: Well, be it so, De Monfort, I'm contented;
I'll take thy hand since I can have no more.
210 [*Carelessly.*] I take of worthy men whate'er they give.
Their heart I gladly take; if not, their hand:
If that too is withheld, a courteous word,
Or the civility of placid looks;
And, if e'en these are too great favours deem'd,
215 'Faith, I can set me down contentedly
With plain and homely greeting, or, God save ye!
DE MONFORT: [*Aside, starting away from him some paces.*] By the good light, he makes a jest of it!
[JANE *seems greatly distressed, and* FREBERG *endeavours to cheer her.*]
FREBERG: [*To* JANE.] Cheer up, my noble friend; all
    will go well;
For friendship is no plant of hasty growth.
220 Tho' planted in esteem's deep-fixed soil,
The gradual culture of kind intercourse
Must bring it to perfection.
[*To the* COUNTESS.] My love, the morning, now, is
    far advanced;
Our friends elsewhere expect us; take your leave.
225 LADY: [*To* JANE.] Farewell! dear madam, till the
    ev'ning hour.

FREBERG: [*To DE MONFORT.*] Good day, De
    Monfort. [*To JANE.*] Most devoutly yours.
REZENVELT: [*To FREBERG.*] Go not too fast, for I will
    follow you.
            [*EXEUNT FREBERG and his LADY.*]
[*To JANE.*] The Lady Jane is yet a stranger here:
She might, perhaps, in the purlieus of Amberg
230 Find somewhat worth her notice.
JANE: I thank you, Marquis, I am much engaged; I go
    not out to-day.
REZENVELT: Then fare ye well! I see I cannot now
Be the proud man who shall escort you forth,
235 And shew to all the world my proudest boast,
The notice and respect of Jane De Monfort.
DE MONFORT: [*Aside, impatiently.*] He says farewell,
    and goes not!
JANE: [*To REZENVELT.*] You do me honour.
REZENVELT: Madam, adieu! [*To JANE.*] Good
    morning, noble marquis.   [*EXIT.*]
[*JANE and DE MONFORT look expressively to one another,
without speaking, and then EXEUNT, severally.*]

                SCENE 2

    A splendid Banquetting Room. DE MONFORT,
    REZENVELT, FREBERG, MASTER OF THE HOUSE, *and*
    GUESTS, *are discovered sitting at table, with wine, &c.
              before them.*

            SONG—A GLEE.
        Pleasant is the mantling bowl,
        And the song of merry soul;
        And the red lamp's cheery light,
        And the goblet glancing bright;
5   Whilst many a cheerful face, around,
        Listens to the jovial sound.
        Social spirits, join with me;
        Bless the God of jollity.

FREBERG: [*To DE MONFORT, who rises to go away.*]
    Thou wilt not leave us, Monfort? wherefore so?
10 DE MONFORT: [*Aside to FREBERG.*] I pray thee take
    no notice of me now.

Mine ears are stunned with these noisy fools;
Let me escape.   [*EXIT, hastily.*]
MASTER OF THE HOUSE: What, is De Monfort gone?
FREBERG: Time presses him.
REZENVELT: It seem'd to sit right heavily upon him,
15 We must confess.
MASTER OF THE HOUSE: [*To FREBERG.*] How is your
    friend? he wears a noble mien,
But most averse, methinks, from social pleasure.
Is this his nature?
FREBERG: No, I've seen him cheerful,
And at the board, with soul-enliven'd face,
20 Push the gay goblet round.—But it wears late.
We shall seem topers more than social friends,
If the returning sun surprise us here.
[*To MASTER.*] Good rest, my gen'rous host; we will
    retire.
You wrestle with your age most manfully,
25 But brave it not too far. Retire to sleep.
MASTER OF THE HOUSE: I will, my friend, but do
    you still remain,
With noble Rezenvelt, and all my guests.
Ye have not fourscore years upon your head;
Do not depart so soon. God save you all!
            [*EXIT MASTER, leaning upon a SERVANT.*]
30 FREBERG: [*To the GUESTS.*] Shall we resume?
GUESTS: The night is too far spent.
FREBERG: Well then, good rest to you.
REZENVELT: [*To GUESTS.*]   Good rest, my friends.
            [*EXEUNT all but FREBERG and REZENVELT.*]
FREBERG: Alas! my Rezenvelt!
I vainly hop'd the hand of gentle peace,
From this day's reconciliation sprung,
35 These rude unseemly jarrings had subdu'd:
But I have mark'd, e'en at the social board,
Such looks, such words, such tones, such untold things,
Too plainly told, 'twixt you and Monfort pass,
That I must now despair.
40 Yet who could think, two minds so much refin'd,
So near in excellence, should be remov'd,
So far remov'd, in gen'rous sympathy.
REZENVELT: Ay, far remov'd indeed.
FREBERG: And yet, methought, he made a noble
    effort,

45 　And with a manly plainness bravely told
　　The galling debt he owes to your forbearance.
　REZENVELT: 'Faith! so he did, and so did I receive it;
　　When, with spread arms, and heart e'en mov'd to tears,
　　I frankly proffer'd him a friend's embrace:
50 　And, I declare, had he as such receiv'd it,
　　I from that very moment had forborne
　　All opposition, pride-provoking jest,
　　Contemning carelessness, and all offence;
　　And had caress'd him as a worthy heart,
55 　From native weakness such indulgence claiming:
　　But since he proudly thinks that cold respect,
　　The formal tokens of his lordly favour,
　　So precious are, that I would sue for them
　　As fair distinction in the world's eye,
60 　Forgetting former wrongs, I spurn it all;
　　And but that I do bear the noble woman,
　　His worthy, his incomparable sister,
　　Such fix'd profound regard, I would expose him;
　　And as a mighty bull, in senseless rage,
65 　Rous'd at the baiter's will, with wretched rags
　　Of ire-provoking scarlet, chaffs and bellows,
　　I'd make him at small cost of paltry wit,
　　With all his deep and manly faculties,
　　The scorn and laugh of fools.
70 　FREBERG: For heaven's sake, my friend! restrain your wrath;
　　For what has Monfort done of wrong to you,
　　Or you to him, bating one foolish quarrel,
　　Which you confess from slight occasion rose,
　　That in your breasts such dark resentment dwells,
75 　So fix'd, so hopeless?
　REZENVELT: O! from our youth he has distinguish'd me
　　With ev'ry mark of hatred and disgust.
　　For e'en in boyish sports I still oppos'd
　　His proud pretensions to pre-eminence;
80 　Nor would I to his ripen'd greatness give
　　That fulsome adulation of applause
　　A senseless croud bestow'd. Tho' poor in fortune,
　　I still would smile at vain-assuming wealth:
　　But when unlook'd-for fate on me bestow'd
85 　Riches and splendour equal to his own,
　　Tho' I, in truth, despise such poor distinction,
　　Feeling inclin'd to be at peace with him,
　　And with all men beside, I curb'd my spirit,
　　And sought to soothe him. Then, with spiteful rage,
90 　From small offence he rear'd a quarrel with me,
　　And dar'd me to the field. The rest you know.
　　In short, I still have been th'opposing rock,
　　O'er which the stream of his o'erflowing pride
　　Hath foam'd and bellow'd. See'st thou how it is?
95 　FREBERG: Too well I see, and warn thee to beware.
　　Such streams have oft, by swelling floods surcharg'd,
　　Borne down with sudden and impetuous force
　　The yet unshaken stone of opposition,
　　Which had for ages stopp'd their flowing course.
100 　I pray thee, friend, beware.
　REZENVELT: Thou canst not mean—he will not murder me?
　FREBERG: What a proud heart, with such dark passion toss'd,
　　May, in the anguish of its thoughts, conceive,
　　I will not dare to say.
　REZENVELT: Ha, ha! thou knows't him not.
105 　Full often have I mark'd it in his youth,
　　And could have almost lov'd him for the weakness;
　　He's form'd with such antipathy, by nature,
　　To all infliction of corporeal pain,
　　To wounding life, e'en to the sight of blood,
110 　He cannot if he would.
　FREBERG: Then fy upon thee!
　　It is not gen'rous to provoke him thus.
　　But let us part; we'll talk of this again.
　　Something approaches.—We are here too long.
　REZENVELT: Well, then, to-morrow I'll attend your call.
115 　Here lies my way. Good night. [EXIT.]
　[ENTER GRIMBALD.]
　GRIMBALD: Forgive, I pray, my lord, a stranger's boldness.
　　I have presum'd to wait your leisure here,
　　Though at so late an hour.
　FREBERG: But who art thou?
　GRIMBALD: My name is Grimbald, sir,
120 　A humble suitor to your honour's goodness,
　　Who is the more embolden'd to presume,
　　In that the noble Marquis of De Monfort

Is so much fam'd for good and gen'rous deeds.
FREBERG: You are mistaken, I am not the man.
125 GRIMBALD: Then, pardon me; I thought I could not err.
That mien so dignified, that piercing eye
Assur'd me it was he.
FREBERG: My name is not De Monfort, courteous stranger;
But, if you have a favour to request,
130 I may, perhaps, with him befriend your suit.
GRIMBALD: I thank your honour, but I have a friend
Who will commend me to De Monfort's favour:
The Marquis Rezenvelt has known me long,
Who, says report, will soon become his brother.
135 FREBERG: If thou would'st seek thy ruin from De Monfort,
The name of Rezenvelt employ, and prosper;
But, if ought good, use any name but his.
GRIMBALD: How may this be?
FREBERG: I cannot now explain.
Early to-morrow call upon Count Freberg;
140 So am I call'd, each burgher knows my house,
And there instruct me how to do you service.
Good-night.   [*EXIT.*]
GRIMBALD: [*Alone.*] Well, this mistake may be of service to me;
And yet my bus'ness I will not unfold
To this mild, ready, promise-making courtier;
145 I've been by such too oft deceiv'd already:
But if such violent enmity exists
Between De Monfort and this Rezenvelt,
He'll prove my advocate by opposition.
For, if De Monfort would reject my suit,
150 Being the man whom Rezenvelt esteems,
Being the man he hates, a cord as strong,
Will he not favour me? I'll think of this.
                                            [*EXIT.*]

SCENE 3

A lower Apartment in JEROME's *House, with a wide folding glass door, looking into a garden, where the trees and shrubs are brown and leafless.* ENTER DE MONFORT *with his arms crossed, with a thoughtful frowning aspect, and paces slowly across the stage,* JEROME *following behind him with a timid step.*
DE MONFORT *hearing him, turns suddenly about.*

DE MONFORT: [*Angrily.*] Who follows me to this sequester'd room?
JEROME: I have presum'd, my lord. 'Tis somewhat late:
I am inform'd you eat at home to-night;
Here is a list of all the dainty fare
5 My busy search has found; please to peruse it.
DE MONFORT: Leave me: begone! Put hemlock in thy soup,
Or deadly night-shade, or rank hellebore,
And I will mess upon it.
JEROME: Heaven forbid!
Your honour's life is all too precious, sure—
10 DE MONFORT: [*Sternly.*] Did I not say begone?
JEROME: Pardon, my lord, I'm old, and oft forget.
                                            [*EXIT.*]
DE MONFORT: [*Looking after him, as if his heart smote him.*] Why will they thus mistime their foolish zeal,
That I must be so stern?
O! that I were upon some desert coast!
15 Where howling tempests and the lashing tide
Would stun me into deep and senseless quiet;
As the storm-beaten trav'ller droops his head,
In heavy, dull, lethargick weariness,
And, midst the roar of jarring elements,
20 Sleeps to awake no more.
What am I grown? All things are hateful to me.

[*ENTER MANUEL.*]
[*Stamping with his foot.*] Who bids thee break upon
   my privacy?
MANUEL: Nay, good, my lord! I heard you speak
   aloud,
And dreamt not, surely, that you were alone.
DE MONFORT: What, dost thou watch, and pin thine
   ear to holes,
To catch those exclamations of the soul,
Which heaven alone should hear? Who hir'd thee,
   pray?
Who basely hir'd thee for a task like this?
MANUEL: My lord, I cannot hold. For fifteen years,
Long-troubled years, I have your servant been,
Nor hath the proudest lord in all the realm,
With firmer, with more honourable faith
His sov'reign serv'd, than I have served you;
But, if my honesty is doubted now,
Let him who is more faithful take my place,
And serve you better.
DE MONFORT: Well, be it as thou wilt. Away with
   thee.
Thy loud-mouth'd boasting is no rule for me
To judge thy merit by.
[*ENTER JEROME hastily, and pulls MANUEL away.*]
JEROME: Come, Manuel, come away; thou art not
   wise.
The stranger must depart and come again,
For now his honour will not be disturb'd.
                              [*EXIT MANUEL sulkily.*]
DE MONFORT: A stranger said'st thou.
[*Drops his handkerchief.*][1]
JEROME: I did, good sir, but he shall go away;
You shall not be disturb'd.
[*Stooping to lift the handkerchief.*]
                        You have dropp'd somewhat.
DE MONFORT: [*Preventing him.*] Nay, do not stoop,
   my friend! I pray thee not!
Thou art too old to stoop.—
I am much indebted to thee.—Take this ring—
I love thee better than I seem to do.
I pray thee do it—thank me not.—What stranger?

---

[1] possibly a reminiscence of Shakespeare, *Othello* 3.3.291sd.

JEROME: A man who does most earnestly entreat
To see your honour, but I know him not.
DE MONFORT: Then let him enter.   [*EXIT JEROME.*]
[*A pause. ENTER GRIMBALD.*]
DE MONFORT: You are the stranger who would
   speak with me?
GRIMBALD: I am so far unfortunate, my lord,
That, though my fortune on your favour hangs,
I am to you a stranger.
DE MONFORT: How may this be? What can I do for
   you?
GRIMBALD: Since thus your lordship does so frankly
   ask,
The tiresome preface of apology
I will forbear, and tell my tale at once.—
In plodding drudgery I've spent my youth,
A careful penman in another's office;
And now, my master and employer dead,
They seek to set a stripling o'er my head,
And leave me on to drudge, e'en to old age,
Because I have no friend to take my part.
It is an office in your native town,
For I am come from thence, and I am told
You can procure it for me. Thus, my lord,
From the repute of goodness which you bear,
I have presum'd to beg.
DE MONFORT: They have befool'd thee with a false
   report.
GRIMBALD: Alas! I see it is in vain to plead.
Your mind is pre-possess'd against a wretch,
Who has, unfortunately for his weal,
Offended the revengeful Rezenvelt.
DE MONFORT: What dost thou say?
GRIMBALD: What I, perhaps, had better leave unsaid.
Who will believe my wrongs if I complain?
I am a stranger, Rezenvelt my foe,
Who will believe my wrongs?
DE MONFORT: [*Eagerly catching him by the coat.*]
                        I will believe them!
Though they were base as basest, vilest deeds,
In ancient record told, I would believe them.
Let not the smallest atom of unworthiness
That he has put upon thee be conceal'd.
Speak boldly, tell it all; for, by the light!

    I'll be thy friend, I'll be thy warmest friend,
    If he has done thee wrong.
90 GRIMBALD: Nay, pardon me, it were not well advis'd,
    If I should speak so freely of the man,
    Who will so soon your nearest kinsman be.
DE MONFORT: What canst thou mean by this?
GRIMBALD: That Marquis Rezenvelt
    Has pledg'd his faith unto your noble sister,
95 And soon will be the husband of her choice.
    So, I am told, and so the world believes.
DE MONFORT: 'Tis false! 'tis basely false!
    What wretch could drop from his envenom'd tongue
    A tale so damn'd?—It chokes my breath—
100 [*Stamping with his foot.*] What wretch did tell it thee?
GRIMBALD: Nay, every one with whom I have
       convers'd
    Has held the same discourse. I judge it not.
    But you, my lord, who with the lady dwell,
    You best can tell what her deportment speaks;
105 Whether her conduct and unguarded words
    Belie such rumour.
    [*DE MONFORT pauses, staggers backwards, and sinks into a chair; then starting up hastily.*]
DE MONFORT: Where am I now? 'midst all the
       cursed thoughts
    That on my soul like stinging scorpions prey'd,
    This never came before——Oh, if it be!
110 The thought will drive me mad.—Was it for this
    She urged her warm request on bended knee?
    Alas! I wept, and thought of sister's love,
    No damned love like this.
    Fell devil! 'tis hell itself has lent thee aid
115 To work such sorcery! [*Pauses.*] I'll not believe it.
    I must have proof clear as the noon-day sun[1]
    For such foul charge as this! Who waits without!
    [*Paces up and down furiously agitated.*]
GRIMBALD: [*Aside.*] What have I done? I've carried
       this too far.
    I've rous'd a fierce ungovernable madman.
    [ENTER JEROME.]
120 DE MONFORT: [*In a loud angry voice.*] Where did she
       go, at such an early hour,
    And with such slight attendance?
JEROME: Of whom inquires your honour?
DE MONFORT: Why, of your lady. Said I not my
       sister?
125 JEROME: The Lady Jane, your sister?
DE MONFORT: [*In a faultering voice.*] Yes, I did call
       her so.
JEROME: In truth, I cannot tell you where she went.
    E'en now, from the short-beechen walk hard-by,
    I saw her through the garden-gate return.
130 The Marquis Rezenvelt, and Freberg's Countess
    Are in her company. This way they come,
    As being nearer to the back apartments;
    But I shall stop them, if it be your will,
    And bid them enter here.
135 DE MONFORT: No, stop them not. I will remain
       unseen,[2]
    And mark them as they pass. Draw back a little.
    [*GRIMBALD seems alarm'd, and steals off unnoticed. DE MONFORT grasps JEROME tightly by the hand, and drawing back with him two or three steps, not to be seen from the garden, waits in silence with his eyes fixed on the glass-door.*]
DE MONFORT: I hear their footsteps on the grating
       sand.
    How like the croaking of a carrion bird,
    That hateful voice sounds to the distant ear!
140 And now she speaks—her voice sounds cheerly too—
    O curse their mirth!—
    Now, now, they come, keep closer still! keep steady!
    [*Taking hold of JEROME with both hands.*]
JEROME: My lord, you tremble much.
DE MONFORT: What, do I shake?
JEROME: You do, in truth, and your teeth chatter too.
145 DE MONFORT: See! see they come! he strutting by
       her side.
    [*JANE, REZENVELT, and COUNTESS FREBERG appear through the glass-door, pursuing their way up a short walk leading to the other wing of the house.*]
    See how he turns his odious face to her's!
    Utt'ring with confidence some nauseous jest.
    And she endures it too—Oh! this looks vilely!

---

[1] Cf. Shakespeare, *Othello* 3.3.194–5, 366.

[2] Cf. Shakespeare, *Othello* 4.1.74–166.

Ha! mark that courteous motion of his arm—
150 What does he mean?—He dares not take her hand!
[*Pauses and looks eagerly.*] By heaven and hell he does!
[*Letting go his hold of* JEROME, *he throws out his hands vehemently, and thereby pushes him against the scene.*]
JEROME: Oh! I am stunn'd! my head is crack'd in twain:
Your honour does forget how old I am.
DE MONFORT: Well, well, the wall is harder than I wist.
155 Begone! and whine within.
     [*EXIT JEROME, with a sad rueful countenance.*]
[*DE MONFORT comes forward to the front of the stage, and makes a long pause, expressive of great agony of mind.*]
It must be so; each passing circumstance;
Her hasty journey here; her keen distress
Whene'er my soul's abhorrence I express'd;
Ay, and that damned reconciliation,
160 With tears extorted from me: Oh, too well!
All, all too well bespeak the shameful tale.
I should have thought of heav'n and hell conjoin'd,
The morning star mix'd with infernal fire,
Ere I had thought of this—
165 Hell's blackest magick, in the midnight hour,
With horrid spells and incantation dire,
Such combination opposite, unseemly,
Of fair and loathsome, excellent and base,
Did ne'er produce.—But every thing is possible,
170 So as it may my misery enhance!
Oh! I did love her with such pride of soul!
When other men, in gayest pursuit of love,
Each beauty follow'd, by her side I stay'd;
Far prouder of a brother's station there,
175 Than all the favours favour'd lovers boast.
We quarrel'd once, and when I could no more
The alter'd coldness of her eye endure,
I slipp'd o' tip-toe to her chamber door;
And when she ask'd who gently knock'd—Oh! oh!
180 Who could have thought of this?
[*Throws himself into a chair, covers his face with his hand, and bursts into tears. After some time he starts up from his seat furiously.*]

Hell's direst torment seize th'infernal villain!
Detested of my soul! I will have vengeance![1]
I'll crush thy swelling pride—I'll still thy vaunting—
I'll do a deed of blood—Why shrink I thus?
185 If, by some spell or magick sympathy,
Piercing the lifeless figure on that wall
Could pierce his bosom too, would I not cast it?
[*Throwing a dagger against the wall.*]
Shall groans and blood affright me? No, I'll do it.
Tho' gasping life beneath my pressure heav'd,
190 And my soul shudder'd at the horrid brink,
I would not flinch.—Fy, this recoiling nature!
O that his sever'd limbs were strew'd in air,
So as I saw him not!
[*ENTER REZENVELT behind, from the glass door.* DE MONFORT *turns round, and on seeing him starts back, then drawing his sword, rushes furiously upon him.*]
Detested robber; now all forms are over:
195 Now open villainy, now open hate!
Defend thy life.
REZENVELT: De Monfort, thou art mad.
DE MONFORT: Speak not, but draw. Now for thy hated life!
[*They fight:* REZENVELT *parries his thrusts with great skill, and at last disarms him.*] Then take my life, black fiend, for hell assists thee.
REZENVELT: No, Monfort, but I'll take away your sword.
200 Not as a mark of disrespect to you,
But for your safety. By to-morrow's eve
I'll call on you myself and give it back;
And then, if I am charg'd with any wrong,
I'll justify myself. Farewell, strange man!
               [*EXIT.*]
[*DE MONFORT stands for some time quite motionless, like one stupified.* ENTER *to him a* SERVANT: *he starts.*]
205 DE MONFORT: Ha! who art thou?
SERVANT: 'Tis I, an' please your honour.
DE MONFORT: [*Staring wildly at him.*] Who art thou?
SERVANT: Your servant Jacques.
DE MONFORT: Indeed I know thee not.

---

[1] Cf. Shakespeare, *Othello* 3.3.449–69.

Leave me, and when Rezenvelt is gone,
Return and let me know.
SERVANT: He's gone already, sir.
210 DE MONFORT: How, gone so soon?
SERVANT: Yes, as his servant told me,
He was in haste to go, for night comes on,
And at the ev'ning hour he must take horse,
To visit some old friend whose lonely mansion
Stands a short mile beyond the farther wood;
215 And, as he loves to wander thro' those wilds
Whilst yet the early moon may light his way,
He sends his horses round the usual road,
And crosses it alone.
I would not walk thro' those wild dens alone
220 For all his wealth. For there, as I have heard,
Foul murders have been done, and ravens scream;
And things unearthly, stalking thro' the night,
Have scar'd the lonely trav'ller from his wits.
[*DE MONFORT stands fixed in thought.*]
I've ta'en your mare, an please you, from her field,
225 And wait your farther orders.
[*DE MONFORT heeds him not.*]
Her hoofs are sound, and where the saddle gall'd
Begins to mend. What further must be done?
[*DE MONFORT still heeds him not.*]
His honour heeds me not. Why should I stay?
DE MONFORT: [*Eagerly, as he is going.*] He goes alone
saidst thou?
230 SERVANT: His servant told me so.
DE MONFORT: And at what hour?
SERVANT: He parts from Amberg by the fall of eve.
Save you, my lord? how chang'd your count'nance is!
Are you not well?
DE MONFORT: Yes, I am well, begone!
And wait my orders by the city wall:
235 I'll that way bend, and speak to thee again.
[*EXIT SERVANT.*]
[*DE MONFORT walks rapidly two or three times across the stage; then siezes his dagger from the wall; looks steadfastly at its point, and EXIT, hastily.*]

ACT 4

SCENE 1

Moon-light. A wild path in a wood, shaded with trees.
ENTER DE MONFORT, *with a strong expression of disquiet, mixed with fear, upon his face, looking behind him, and bending his ear to the ground, as if he listened to something.*

DE MONFORT: How hollow groans the earth beneath
my tread!
Is there an echo here? Methinks it sounds
As tho' some heavy footstep follow'd me.
I will advance no farther.
5 Deep settled shadows rest across the path,
And thickly-tangled boughs o'er-hang this spot.
O that a tenfold gloom did cover it!
That 'midst the murky darkness I might strike;
As in the wild confusion of a dream,
10 Things horrid, bloody, terrible, do pass,
As tho' they pass'd not; nor impress the mind
With the fix'd clearness of reality.
[*An owl is heard screaming near him.*]
[*Starting.*] What sound is that?
[*Listens, and the owl cries again.*]
         It is the screech-owl's cry.
Foul bird of night! what spirit guides thee here?
15 Art thou instinctive drawn to scenes of horrour?
I've heard of this. [*Pauses and listens.*]
How those fall'n leaves so rustle on the path,
With whisp'ring noise, as tho' the earth around me
Did utter secret things!
20 The distant river, too, bears to mine ear
A dismal wailing. O mysterious night!
Thou art not silent; many tongues hast thou.
A distant gath'ring blast sounds thro' the wood,
And dark clouds fleetly hasten o'er the sky:
25 O! that a storm would rise, a raging storm;
Amidst the roar of warring elements

I'd lift my hand and strike: but this pale light,
The calm distinctness of each stilly thing,
Is terrible.   [*Starting.*]   Footsteps are near—
30 He comes, he comes! I'll watch him farther on—
I cannot do it here.   [*EXIT.*]
[*ENTER REZENVELT, and continues his way slowly across the stage, but just as he is going off the owl screams, he stops and listens, and the owl screams again.*]
REZENVELT: Ha! does the night bird greet me on my way?
How much his hooting is in harmony
With such a scene as this! I like it well.
35 Oft when a boy,[1] at the still twilight hour,
I've leant my back against some knotted oak,
And loudly mimick'd him, till to my call
He answer would return, and thro' the gloom
We friendly converse held.
40 Between me and the star-bespangl'd sky
Those aged oaks their crossing branches wave,
And thro' them looks the pale and placid moon.
How like a crocodile, or winged snake,
Yon sailing cloud bears on its dusky length!
45 And now transformed by the passing wind,
Methinks it seems a flying Pegasus.
Ay, but a shapeless band of blacker hue
Come swiftly after.—
A hollow murm'ring wind comes thro' the trees;
50 I hear it from afar; this bodes a storm.
I must not linger here—
[*A bell heard at some distance.*]
                What bell is this?
It sends a solemn sound upon the breeze.
Now, to a fearful superstitious mind,
In such a scene, 'twould like a death-knell come:
55 For me it tells but of a shelter near,
And so I bid it welcome.   [*EXIT.*]

---

[1] Cf. W. Wordsworth, "There was a boy"* and *The Prelude* (1805) 5.389–413.

SCENE 2

The inside of a Convent Chapel, of old Gothick architecture, almost dark; two torches only are seen at a distance, burning over a new-made grave.[2] The noise of loud wind, beating upon the windows and roof, is heard.
ENTER two MONKS.

1ST MONK: The storm increases: hark how dismally
It howls along the cloisters. How goes time?
2ND MONK: It is the hour: I hear them near at hand;
And when the solemn requiem has been sung
5 For the departed sister, we'll retire.
Yet, should this tempest still more violent grow,
We'll beg a friendly shelter till the morn.
1ST MONK: See, the procession enters: let us join.
[*The organ strikes up a solemn prelude. ENTER a procession of NUNS, with the ABBESS, bearing torches. After compassing the grave twice, and remaining there some time, whilst the organ plays a grand dirge, they advance to the front of the stage.*]

SONG, BY THE NUNS

Departed soul, whose poor remains
10 This hallow'd lowly grave contains;
Whose passing storm of life is o'er,
Whose pains and sorrows are no more!
Bless'd be thou with the bless'd above!
Where all is joy, and purity, and love.

15 Let him, in might and mercy dread,
Lord of the living and the dead;
In whom the stars of heav'n rejoice,
To whom the ocean lifts his voice,
Thy spirit purified to glory raise,
20 To sing with holy saints his everlasting praise.
Departed soul, who in this earthly scene
Hast our lowly sister been.

---

[2] In the fourth edition (1802), Baillie changed "new-made" to "newly-covered" and added a note: "I have put above *newly-covered* instead of *new-made* grave, as it stands in the former editions, because I wish not to give the idea of a funeral procession, but merely that of a hymn or requiem sung over the grave of a person who has been recently buried."

Swift be thy way to where the blessed dwell!
Until we meet thee there, farewell! farewell!

[ENTER a LAY SISTER, *with a wild terrified look, her hair and dress all scattered, and rushes forward amongst them.*]

25 ABBESS: Why com'st thou here, with such disorder'd looks,
To break upon our sad solemnity?
SISTER: Oh! I did hear, thro' the receding blast,
Such horrid cries! it made my blood run chill.
ABBESS: 'Tis but the varied voices of the storm,
30 Which many times will sound like distant screams:
It has deceiv'd thee.
1ST SISTER: O no, for twice it call'd, so loudly call'd,
With horrid strength, beyond the pitch of nature.
And murder! murder! was the dreadful cry.
35 A third time it return'd with feeble strength,
But o'the sudden ceas'd, as tho' the words
Were rudely smother'd in the grasped throat;
And all was still again, save the wild blast
Which at a distance growl'd—
40 Oh! it will never from my mind depart!
That dreadful cry all i'the instant still'd,
For then, so near, some horrid deed was done,
And none to rescue.
ABBESS: Where didst thou hear it?
SISTER: In the higher cells,
45 As now a window, open'd by the storm,
I did attempt to close.
1ST MONK: I wish our brother Bernard were arriv'd;
He is upon his way.
ABBESS: Be not alarm'd; it still may be deception.
50 'Tis meet we finish our solemnity,
Nor shew neglect unto the honour'd dead.
[*Gives a sign, and the organ plays again: just as it ceases a loud knocking is heard without.*]
ABBESS: Ha! who may this be? hush!
[*Knocking heard again.*]
2ND MONK: It is the knock of one in furious haste.
Hush, hush! What footsteps come? Ha! brother Bernard.
[ENTER BERNARD *bearing a lantern.*]
55 1ST MONK: See, what a look he wears of stiffen'd fear!
Where hast thou been, good brother?
BERNARD: I've seen a horrid sight!
ALL: [*Gathering round him and speaking at once.*]
What hast thou seen?
BERNARD: As on I hasten'd, bearing thus my light,
Across the path, not fifty paces off,
60 I saw a murther'd corse stretch'd on its back,
Smear'd with new blood, as tho' but freshly slain.
ABBESS: A man or woman?
BERNARD: A man, a man!
ABBESS: Did'st thou examine if within its breast
There yet is lodg'd some small remains of life?
65 Was it quite dead?
BERNARD: Nought in the grave is deader.
I look'd but once, yet life did never lodge
In any form so laid.—
A chilly horrour seiz'd me, and I fled.
1ST MONK: And does the face seem all unknown to thee?
70 BERNARD: The face! I would not on the face have look'd
For e'en a kingdom's wealth, for all the world.
O no! the bloody neck, the bloody neck!
[*Shaking his head, and shuddering with horrour. Loud knocking heard without.*]
SISTER: Good mercy! who comes next?
BERNARD: Not far behind
I left our brother Thomas on the road;
75 But then he did repent him as he went,
And threaten'd to return.
2ND MONK: See, here he comes.
[ENTER *brother* THOMAS, *with a wild terrified look.*]
1ST MONK: How wild he looks!
BERNARD: [*Going up to him eagerly.*] What, hast thou seen it too?
THOMAS: Yes, yes! it glar'd upon me as it pass'd.
80 BERNARD: What glar'd upon thee?
[*All gathering round* THOMAS *and speaking at once.*]
O! what hast thou seen?
THOMAS: As, striving with the blast, I onward came,
Turning my feeble lantern from the wind,
Its light upon a dreadful visage gleam'd,
Which paus'd, and look'd upon me as it pass'd.
85 But such a look, such wildness of despair,
Such horrour-strain'd features never yet

Did earthly visage show. I shrunk and shudder'd.
If damned spirits may to earth return
I've seen it.
BERNARD: 　　　　　Was there blood upon it?
THOMAS: Nay, as it pass'd, I did not see its form;
Nought but the horrid face.
BERNARD: 　　It is the murderer.
1ST MONK: 　　　　　　　What way went it?
THOMAS: 　I durst not look till I had pass'd it far,
Then turning round, upon the rising bank,
I saw, between me and the paly sky,
A dusky form, tossing and agitated.
I stopp'd to mark it, but, in truth, I found
'Twas but a sapling bending to the wind,
And so I onward hied, and look'd no more.
1ST MONK: 　But we must look to't; we must follow it:
Our duty so commands. [*To* 2ND MONK.] Will you go, brother?
[*To* BERNARD.] And you, good Bernard?
BERNARD: 　　　　　　If I needs must go.
1ST MONK: 　Come, we must all go.
ABBESS: 　　　　　Heaven be with you, then!
　　　　　　　　　　　[EXEUNT MONKS.]
SISTER: 　Amen, amen! Good heaven be with us all!
O what a dreadful night!
ABBESS: 　Daughters retire; peace to the peaceful dead!
Our solemn ceremony now is finish'd.

SCENE 3

A large room in the Convent, very dark. ENTER *the* AB-
BESS, LAY SISTER *bearing a light, and several* NUNS.
SISTER *sets down the light on a table at the bottom of the stage, so that the room is still very gloomy.*

ABBESS: 　They have been longer absent than I thought;
I fear he has escap'd them.
1ST NUN: 　　　　　　Heaven forbid!
SISTER: 　No no, found out foul murder ever is,
And the foul murd'rer too.
2ND NUN: 　The good Saint Francis will direct their search;

The blood so near his holy convent shed
For threefold vengeance calls.
ABBESS: 　I hear a noise within the inner court,
They are return'd; [*Listening.*] And Bernard's voice
I hear:
They are return'd.
SISTER: 　　　　　Why do I tremble so?
It is not I who ought to tremble thus.
2ND NUN: 　　I hear them at the door.
BERNARD: 　[*Without.*] Open the door, I pray thee, brother Thomas;
I cannot now unhand the prisoner.
ALL: 　[*Speak together, shrinking back from the door, and staring upon one another.*] He is with them.
[*A folding door at the bottom of the stage is opened, and* ENTER BERNARD, THOMAS, *and the other two* MONKS, *carrying lanterns in their hands, and bringing in* DE MONFORT. *They are likewise followed by other* MONKS. *As they lead forward* DE MONFORT *the light is turned away, so that he is seen obscurely; but when they come to the front of the stage they all turn the light side of their lanterns on him at once, and his face is seen in all the strengthened horrour of despair, with his hands and cloaths bloody.*]
ABBESS *and* NUNS: 　[*Speak at once, and starting back.*]
　　　　　　　　　　　Holy saints be with us!
BERNARD: 　[*To* ABBESS.] Behold the man of blood!
ABBESS: 　Of misery too; I cannot look upon him.
BERNARD: 　[*To* NUNS.] Nay, holy sisters, turn not thus away.
Speak to him, if, perchance, he will regard you:
For from his mouth we have no utt'rance heard,
Save one deep and smother'd exclamation,
When first we seiz'd him.
ABBESS: 　[*To* DE MONFORT.] Most miserable man, how art thou thus? [*Pauses.*]
Thy tongue is silent, but those bloody hands
Do witness horrid things. What is thy name?
DE MONFORT: 　[*Roused; looks steadfastly at the* ABBESS *for some time, then speaking in a short hurried voice.*] I have no name.
ABBESS: 　[*To* BERNARD.] Do it thyself: I'll speak to him no more.
SISTER: 　O holy saints! that this should be the man,
Who did against his fellow lift the stroke,

30   Whilst he so loudly call'd.—
Still in mine ear it sounds: O murder! murder!
DE MONFORT: [*Starting.*] He calls again!
SISTER: No, he did call, but now his voice is still'd.
'Tis past.
DE MONFORT: [*In great anguish.*] 'Tis past!
35   SISTER: Yes it is past, art thou not he who did it?
[*DE MONFORT utters a deep groan, and is supported from falling by the MONKS. A noise is heard without.*]
ABBESS: What noise is this of heavy lumb'ring steps,
Like men who with a weighty burden come?
BERNARD: It is the body: I have orders given
That here it should be laid.
[*ENTER men bearing the body of REZENVELT, covered with a white cloth, and set it down in the middle of the room: they then uncover it. DE MONFORT stands fixed and motionless with horrour, only that a sudden shivering seems to pass over him when they uncover the corps. The ABBESS and NUNS shrink back and retire to some distance; all the rest fixing their eyes steadfastly upon DE MONFORT. A long pause.*]
40   BERNARD: [*To DE MONFORT.*] See'st thou that lifeless corps, those bloody wounds,
See how he lies, who but so shortly since
A living creature was, with all the powers
Of sense, and motion, and humanity?
Oh! what a heart had he who did this deed!
45   1ST MONK: [*Looking at the body.*] How hard those teeth against the lips are press'd,
As tho' he struggled still!
2ND MONK: The hands, too, clench'd: the last efforts of nature.
[*DE MONFORT still stands motionless. Brother THOMAS then goes to the body, and raising up the head a little, turns it towards DE MONFORT.*]
THOMAS: Know'st thou this gastly face?
DE MONFORT: [*Putting his hands before his face in violent perturbation.*] Oh do not! do not! veil it from my sight!
50   Put me to any agony but this!
THOMAS: Ha! dost thou then confess the dreadful deed?
Hast thou against the laws of awful heav'n
Such horrid murder done? What fiend could tempt thee?
[*Pauses and looks steadfastly at DE MONFORT.*]
DE MONFORT: I hear thy words but do not hear their sense—
55   Hast thou not cover'd it?
BERNARD: [*To THOMAS.*] Forbear, my brother, for thou see'st right well
He is not in a state to answer thee.
Let us retire and leave him for a while.
These windows are with iron grated o'er;
60   He cannot 'scape, and other duty calls.
THOMAS: Then let it be.
BERNARD: [*To MONKS, &c.*] Come, let us all depart.
[*EXEUNT ABBESS and NUNS, followed by the MONKS. One MONK lingering a little behind.*]
DE MONFORT: All gone! [*Perceiving the MONK.*] O stay thou here!
MONK: It must not be.
DE MONFORT: I'll give thee gold; I'll make thee rich in gold,
If thou wilt stay e'en but a little while.
65   MONK: I must not, must not stay.
DE MONFORT: I do conjure thee!
MONK: I dare not stay with thee. [*Going.*]
DE MONFORT: And wilt thou go?
[*Catching hold of him eagerly.*]
O! throw thy cloak upon this grizly form!
The unclos'd eyes do stare upon me still.
O do not leave me thus!
[*MONK covers the body, and EXIT.*]
70   DE MONFORT: [*Alone, looking at the covered body, but at a distance.*] Alone with thee! but thou art nothing now,
'Tis done, 'tis number'd with the things o'erpast,
Would! would it were to come!
What fated end, what darkly gath'ring cloud
Will close on all this horrour?
75   O that dire madness would unloose my thoughts,
And fill my mind with wildest fantasies,
Dark, restless, terrible! ought, ought but this!
[*Pauses and shudders.*]
How with convulsive life he heav'd beneath me,

E'en with the death's wound gor'd. O horrid, horrid!
Methinks I feel him still.—What sound is that?
I heard a smother'd groan.—It is impossible!
[*Looking steadfastly at the body.*]
It moves! it moves! the cloth doth heave and swell.
It moves again.—I cannot suffer this—
Whate'er it be I will uncover it.
[*Runs to the corps and tears off the cloth in despair.*]
All still beneath.
Nought is there here but fix'd and grizly death.
How sternly fixed! Oh! those glazed eyes!
They look me still.
[*Shrinks back with horrour.*]
Come, madness! come unto me senseless death!
I cannot suffer this! Here, rocky wall,
Scatter these brains, or dull them.
[*Runs furiously, and, dashing his head against the wall, falls upon the floor.*
ENTER *two* MONKS, *hastily.*]
1ST MONK: See; wretched man, he hath destroy'd himself.
2ND MONK: He does but faint. Let us remove him hence.
1ST MONK: We did not well to leave him here alone.
2ND MONK: Come, let us bear him to the open air.
[EXEUNT, *bearing out* DE MONFORT.]

ACT 5

SCENE 1

Before the gates of the Convent. ENTER JANE DE MONFORT, FREBERG *and* MANUEL. *As they are proceeding towards the gate,* JANE *stops short and shrinks back.*

FREBERG: Ha! wherefore? has a sudden illness seiz'd thee?
JANE: No, no, my friend.—And yet I am very faint—
I dread to enter here!
MANUEL: Ay, so I thought!
For, when between the trees, that abbey tower
First shew'd its top, I saw your count'nance change.
But breathe a little here; I'll go before,
And make enquiry at the nearest gate.
FREBERG: Do so, good Manuel.
[MANUEL *goes and knocks at the gate.*]
Courage, dear madam: all may yet be well.
Rezenvelt's servant, frighten'd with the storm,
And seeing that his master join'd him not,
As by appointment, at the forest's edge,
Might be alarm'd, and give too ready ear
To an unfounded rumour.
He saw it not; he came not here himself.
JANE: [*Looking eagerly to the gate, where* MANUEL *talks with the Porter.*] Ha! see, he talks with some one earnestly.
And sees't thou not that motion of his hands?
He stands like one who hears a horrid tale.
Almighty God!
[MANUEL *goes into the convent.*]
          He comes not back; he enters.
FREBERG: Bear up, my noble friend.
JANE: I will, I will! But this suspence is dreadful.
[*A long pause.* MANUEL RE-ENTERS *from the convent, and comes forward slowly, with a sad countenance.*]
Is this the pace of one who bears good tidings?
O God! his face doth tell the horrid fact;
There is nought doubtful here.
FREBERG: How is it, Manuel?
MANUEL: I've seen him through a crevice in his door:
It is indeed my master. [*Bursting into tears.*]
[*Jane faints, and is supported by* FREBERG.—ENTER ABBESS *and several* NUNS *from the convent, who gather about her, and apply remedies. She recovers.*]
1ST NUN: The life returns again.
2ND NUN: Yes, she revives.
ABBESS: [*To* FREBERG.] Let me entreat this noble lady's leave
To lead her in. She seems in great distress:
We would with holy kindness soothe her woe,
And do by her the deeds of christian love.
FREBERG: Madam, your goodness has my grateful thanks.
[EXEUNT, *supporting* JANE *into the convent.*]

SCENE 2

DE MONFORT is discovered sitting in a thoughtful posture. He remains so for some time. His face afterwards begins to appear agitated, like one whose mind is harrowed with the severest thoughts; then, starting from his seat, he clasps his hands together, and holds them up to heaven.

DE MONFORT: O that I had ne'er known the light of day!
That filmy darkness on mine eyes had hung,
And clos'd me out from the fair face of nature!
O that my mind, in mental darkness pent,
5 Had no perception, no distinction known,
Of fair or foul, perfection nor defect;
Nor thought conceiv'd of proud pre-eminence!
O that it had! O that I had been form'd
An idiot from the birth! a senseless changeling,[1]
10 Who eats his glutton's meal with greedy haste,
Nor knows the hand who feeds him.—
[*Pauses; then, in a calmer sorrowful voice.*]
What am I now? how ends the day of life?
For end it must; and terrible this gloom,
The storm of horrours that surround it close.
15 This little term of nature's agony
Will soon be o'er, and what is past is past:
But shall I then, on the dark lap of earth
Lay me to rest, in still unconsciousness,
Like senseless clod that doth no pressure feel
20 From wearing foot of daily passenger;
Like steeped rock o'er which the breaking waves
Bellow and foam unheard? O would I could!
[*ENTER MANUEL, who springs forward to his master, but is checked upon perceiving DE MONFORT draw back and look sternly at him.*]
MANUEL: My lord, my master! O my dearest master!
[*DE MONFORT still looks at him without speaking.*]
Nay, do not thus regard me; good my lord!
25 Speak to me: am I not your faithful Manuel?
DE MONFORT: [*In a hasty broken voice.*] Art thou alone?

MANUEL: No, sir, the lady Jane is on her way;
She is not far behind.
DE MONFORT: [*Tossing his arm over his head in an agony.*] This is too much! All I can bear but this!
30 It must not be.—Run and prevent her coming.
Say, he who is detain'd a pris'ner here
Is one to her unknown. I now am nothing.
I am a man, of holy claims bereft;
Out from the pale of social kindred cast;
35 Nameless and horrible.—
Tell her De Monfort far from hence is gone
Into a desolate, and distant land,
Ne'er to return again. Fly, tell her this;
For we must meet no more.
[*ENTER JANE DE MONFORT, bursting into the chamber, and followed by FREBERG, ABBESS, and several NUNS.*]
40 JANE: We must! we must! My brother, O my brother!
[*DE MONFORT turns away his head and hides his face with his arm. JANE stops short, and, making a great effort, turns to FREBERG, and the others who followed her; and with an air of dignity stretches out her hand, beckoning them to retire. All retire but FREBERG, who seems to hesitate.*]
And thou too, Freberg: call it not unkind.
[*EXIT FREBERG, JANE and DE MONFORT only remain.*]
JANE: My hapless Monfort!
[*DE MONFORT turns round and looks sorrowfully upon her; she opens her arms to him, and he, rushing into them, hides his face upon her breast and weeps.*]
JANE: Ay, give thy sorrow vent: here may'st thou weep.
DE MONFORT: [*In broken accents.*] Oh! this, my sister, makes me feel again
45 The kindness of affection.
My mind has in a dreadful storm been tost;
Horrid and dark.—I thought to weep no more.—
I've done a deed—But I am human still.
JANE: I know thy suff'rings: leave thy sorrow free:
50 Thou art with one who never did upbraid;
Who mourns, who loves thee still.
DE MONFORT: Ah! say'st thou so? no, no; it should not be.
[*Shrinking from her.*] I am a foul and bloody murderer,
For such embrace unmeet. O leave me! leave me!
55 Disgrace and publick shame abide me now;
And all, alas! who do my kindred own

---

[1] According to superstition, mentally disabled children were "changelings"; that is, they had been exchanged for other children by the fairies.

The direful portion share.—Away, away!
Shall a disgrac'd and publick criminal
Degrade thy name, and claim affinity
60 To noble worth like thine?—I have no name—
I am nothing, now, not e'en to thee; depart.
[*She takes his hand, and grasping it firmly, speaks with a determined voice.*]
JANE: De Monfort, hand in hand we have enjoy'd
The playful term of infancy together;
And in the rougher path of ripen'd years
65 We've been each other's stay. Dark lowers our fate,
And terrible the storm that gathers over us;
But nothing, till that latest agony
Which severs thee from nature, shall unloose
This fix'd and sacred hold. In thy dark prison-house;
70 In the terrifick face of armed law;
Yea, on the scaffold, if it needs must be,
I never will forsake thee.
DE MONFORT: [*Looking at her with admiration.*]
Heav'n bless thy gen'rous soul, my noble Jane!
I thought to sink beneath this load of ill,
75 Depress'd with infamy and open shame;
I thought to sink in abject wretchedness:
But for thy sake I'll rouse my manhood up,
And meet it bravely; no unseemly weakness,
I feel my rising strength, shall blot my end,
80 To clothe thy cheek with shame.
JANE: Yes, thou art noble still.
DE MONFORT: With thee I am; who were not so with thee?
But, ah, my sister! short will be the term:
Death's stroke will come, and in that state beyond,
85 Where things unutterable wait the soul,
New from its earthly tenement discharg'd,
We shall be sever'd far.
Far as the spotless purity of virtue
Is from the murd'rer's guilt, far shall we be.
90 This is the gulf of dread uncertainty
From which the soul recoils.
JANE: The God who made thee is a God of mercy;
Think upon this.
DE MONFORT: [*Shaking his head.*] No, no! this blood! this blood!
JANE: Yea, e'en the sin of blood may be forgiv'n,
95 When humble penitence hath once aton'd.
DE MONFORT: [*Eagerly.*] What, after terms of lengthen'd misery,
Imprison'd anguish of tormented spirits,
Shall I again, a renovated soul,
Into the blessed family of the good
100 Admittance have? Thinks't thou that this may be?
Speak if thou canst: O speak me comfort here!
For dreadful fancies, like an armed host,
Have push'd me to despair. It is most horrible—
O speak of hope! if any hope there be.
[*JANE is silent and looks sorrowfully upon him; then clasping her hands, and turning her eyes to heaven, seems to mutter a prayer.*]
105 DE MONFORT: Ha! dost thou pray for me? heav'n hear thy prayer!
I fain would kneel—Alas! I dare not do it.
JANE: Not so; all by th'Almighty Father form'd
May in their deepest mis'ry call on him.
Come kneel with me, my brother.
[*She kneels and prays to herself; he kneels by her, and clasps his hands fervently, but speaks not. A noise of chains clanking is heard without, and they both rise.*]
110 DE MONFORT: Hear'st thou that noise? They come to interrupt us.
JANE: [*Moving towards a side door.*] Then let us enter here.
DE MONFORT: [*Catching hold of her with a look of horrour.*] Not there—not there—the corps—the bloody corps.
JANE: What, lies he there?—Unhappy Rezenvelt!
DE MONFORT: A sudden thought has come across my mind;
115 How came it not before? Unhappy Rezenvelt!
Say'st thou but this?
JANE: What should I say? he was an honest man;
I still have thought him such, as such lament him.
[*DE MONFORT utters a deep groan.*]
What means this heavy groan?
DE MONFORT: It hath a meaning.
[*ENTER ABBESS and MONKS, with two OFFICERS of justice carrying fetters in their hands to put upon DE MONFORT.*]
120 JANE: [*Starting.*] What men are these?
1ST OFFICER: Lady, we are the servants of the law,

And bear with us a power, which doth constrain
To bind with fetters this our prisoner.
[*Pointing to* DE MONFORT.]
JANE: A stranger uncondemn'd? this cannot be.
125 1ST OFFICER: As yet, indeed, he is by law unjudg'd,
But is so far condemn'd by circumstance,
That law, or custom sacred held as law,
Doth fully warrant us, and it must be.
JANE: Nay, say not so; he has no power to escape:
130 Distress hath bound him with a heavy chain;
There is no need of yours.
1ST OFFICER: We must perform our office.
JANE: O! do not offer this indignity!
1ST OFFICER: Is it indignity in sacred law
135 To bind a murderer? [*To* 2ND OFFICER.] Come, do thy work.
JANE: Harsh are thy words, and stern thy harden'd brow;
Dark is thine eye; but all some pity have
Unto the last extreme of misery.
I do beseech thee! if thou art a man—[*Kneeling to him.*]
[DE MONFORT *roused at this, runs up to* JANE, *and raises her hastily from the ground; then stretches himself up proudly.*]
DE MONFORT: [*To Jane.*] Stand thou erect in native
140 dignity;
And bend to none on earth the suppliant knee,
Though cloath'd in power imperial. To my heart
It gives a feller gripe than many irons.
[*Holding out his hands.*] Here, officers of law, bind on
those shackles,
145 And if they are too light bring heavier chains.
Add iron to iron, load, crush me to the ground;
Nay, heap ten thousand weight upon my breast,
For that were best of all.
[*A long pause, whilst they put irons upon him. After they are on,* JANE *looks at him sorrowfully, and lets her head sink on her breast.* DE MONFORT *stretches out his hands, looks at them, and then at* JANE; *crosses them over his breast, and endeavours to suppress his feelings.*][1]

1ST OFFICER: I have it, too, in charge to move you
hence, [*To* DE MONFORT.]
150 Into another chamber, more secure.
DE MONFORT: Well, I am ready, sir.
[*Approaching* JANE, *whom the* ABBESS *is endeavouring to comfort, but to no purpose.*]
Ah! wherefore thus! most honour'd and most dear?
Shrink not at the accoutrements of ill,
Daring the thing itself.
[*Endeavouring to look cheerful.*]
155 Wilt thou permit me with a gyved hand?
[*She gives him her hand, which he raises to his lips.*]
This was my proudest office.
[EXEUNT, DE MONFORT *leading out* JANE.]

SCENE 3

A long narrow gallery in the convent, with the doors of the cells on each side. The stage darkened. A NUN *is discovered at a distance listening.* ENTER *another* NUN *at the front of the stage, and starts back.*

1ST NUN: Ha! who is this not yet retir'd to rest?
My sister, is it you? [*To the other who advances.*]
2ND NUN: Returning from the sister Nina's cell,
Passing yon door where the poor pris'ner lies,
5 The sound of one who struggl'd with despair
Struck on me as I went: I stopp'd and listen'd;
O God! such piteous groans!
1ST NUN: Yes, since the ev'ning sun it hath been so.
The voice of mis'ry oft hath reach'd mine ear,
10 E'en in the cell above.
2ND NUN: How is it thus?
Methought he brav'd it with a manly spirit,
And led, with shackl'd hands, his sister forth,
Like one resolv'd to bear misfortune boldly.
1ST NUN: Yes, with heroick courage, for a while
15 He seem'd inspir'd; but, soon depress'd again,
Remorse and dark despair o'erwhelm'd his soul,
And so he hath remain'd.

---

[1] In the later editions, Baillie added a note: "Should this play ever again be acted, perhaps it would be better that the curtain should drop here; since here the story may be considered as completed, and what comes after, prolongs the piece too much when our interest for the fate of De Monfort is at an end."

[ENTER Father BERNARD, *advancing from the further end of the gallery, bearing a crucifix.*]
1ST NUN: How goes it, father, with your penitent?
We've heard his heavy groans.
BERNARD: Retire, my daughters; many a bed of death,
With all its pangs and horrour I have seen,
But never ought like this.
2ND NUN: He's dying, then?
BERNARD: Yes, death is dealing with him.
From violent agitation of the mind,
Some stream of life within his breast has burst;
For many times, within a little space,
The ruddy-tide has rush'd into his mouth.
God, grant his pains be short!
1ST NUN: Amen, amen!
2ND NUN: How does the lady?
BERNARD: She sits and bears his head upon her lap;
And like a heaven-inspir'd angel, speaks
The word of comfort to his troubled soul:
Then does she wipe the cold drops from his brow,
With such a look of tender wretchedness,
It wrings the heart to see her.
1ST NUN: Ha! hear ye nothing?
2ND NUN: [*Alarmed.*] Yes, I heard a noise.
1ST NUN: And see'st thou nothing?
[*Creeping close to her sister.*]
BERNARD: 'Tis a nun in white.
[ENTER LAY SISTER *in her night cloaths, advancing from the dark end of the gallery.*]
[*To* SISTER.] Wherefore, my daughter, hast thou left thy cell?
It is not meet at this untimely hour.
SISTER: I cannot rest. I hear such dismal sounds,
Such wailings in the air, such shrilly shrieks,
As though the cry of murder rose again
From the deep gloom of night. I cannot rest:
I pray you let me stay with you, good sisters!
[*Bell tolls.*]
NUNS: [*Starting.*] What bell is that?
BERNARD: It is the bell of death.
A holy sister was upon the watch
To give this notice. [*Bell tolls again.*] Hark! another knell!
The wretched struggler hath his warfare clos'd;
May heaven have mercy on him.

[*Bell tolls again.*]
Retire, my daughters; let us all retire,
For scenes like this to meditation call.
[EXEUNT, *bell tolling again.*]

SCENE 4

A hall or large room in the convent. The bodies of DE MONFORT *and* REZENVELT *are discovered laid out upon a low table or platform, covered with black.* FREBERG, BERNARD, ABBESS, MONKS, *and* NUNS *attending.*

ABBESS: [*To* FREBERG.] Here must they lie, my lord, until we know
Respecting this the order of the law.
FREBERG: And you have wisely done, my rev'rend mother.
[*Goes to the table, and looks at the bodies, but without uncovering them.*]
Unhappy men! ye, both in nature rich,
With talents and with virtues were endu'd.
Ye should have lov'd, yet deadly rancour came,
And in the prime and manhood of your days
Ye sleep in horrid death. O direful hate!
What shame and wretchedness his portion is
Who, for a secret inmate, harbours thee!
And who shall call him blameless who excites,
Ungen'rously excites, with careless scorn,
Such baleful passion in a brother's breast,
Whom heav'n commands to love. Low are ye laid:
Still all contention now.—Low are ye laid.
I lov'd you both, and mourn your hapless fall.
ABBESS: They were your friends, my lord?
FREBERG: I lov'd them both. How does the Lady Jane?
ABBESS: She bears misfortune with intrepid soul.
I never saw in woman bow'd with grief
Such moving dignity.
FREBERG: Ay, still the same.
I've known her long; of worth most excellent;
But, in the day of woe, she ever rose
Upon the mind with added majesty,
As the dark mountain more sublimely tow'rs
Mantled in clouds and storm.

[ENTER MANUEL and JEROME.]
MANUEL: [*Pointing.*] Here, my good Jerome, there's a
    piteous sight.
JEROME: A piteous sight! yet I will look upon him:
I'll see his face in death. Alas, alas!
30 I've seen him move a noble gentleman;
And when with vexing passion undisturb'd,
He look'd most graciously.
[*Lifts up in mistake the cloth from the body of REZENVELT, and starts back with horrour.*]
Oh! this was bloody work! Oh, oh! oh, oh!
That human hands could do it!
[*Drops the cloth again.*]
35 MANUEL: That is the murder'd corps; here lies
    De Monfort.
[*Going to uncover the other body.*]
JEROME: [*Turning away his head.*] No, no! I cannot
    look upon him now.
MANUEL: Didst thou not come to see him?
JEROME: Fy! cover him—inter him in the dark—
Let no one look upon him.
40 BERNARD: [*To JEROME.*] Well dost thou show the
    abhorrence nature feels
For deeds of blood, and I commend thee well.
In the most ruthless heart compassion wakes
For one who, from the hand of fellow man,
Hath felt such cruelty.
[*Uncovering the body of REZENVELT.*]
45 This is the murder'd corse.
[*Uncovering the body of DE MONFORT.*]
                      But see, I pray!
Here lies the murderer. What think'st thou here?
Look on those features, thou hast seen them oft,
With the last dreadful conflict of despair,
So fix'd in horrid strength.
50 See those knit brows, those hollow sunken eyes;
The sharpen'd nose, with nostrils all distent;
That writhed mouth, where yet the teeth appear,
In agony, to gnash the nether lip.
Think'st thou, less painful than the murd'rer's knife
55 Was such a death as this?
Ay, and how changed too those matted locks!
JEROME: Merciful heaven! his hair is grisly grown,
Chang'd to white age, what was, but two days since,
Black as the raven's plume. How may this be?
60 BERNARD: Such change, from violent conflict of the
    mind,
Will sometimes come.
JEROME: Alas, alas! most wretched!
Thou wert too good to do a cruel deed,
And so it kill'd thee. Thou hast suffer'd for it.
God rest thy soul! I needs must touch thy hand,
65 And bid thee long farewell.
[*Laying his hand on DE MONFORT.*]
BERNARD: Draw back, draw back! see where the lady
    comes.
[*ENTER JANE DE MONFORT. FREBERG, who has been for sometime retired by himself to the bottom of the stage, now steps forward to lead her in, but checks himself on seeing the fixed sorrow of her countenance, and draws back respectfully. JANE advances to the table, and looks attentively at the covered bodies. MANUEL points out the body of DE MONFORT, and she gives a gentle inclination of the head, to signify that she understands him. She then bends tenderly over it, without speaking.*]
MANUEL: [*To JANE, as she raises her head.*] Oh,
    madam! my good lord.
JANE: Well says thy love, my good and faithful Manuel;
But we must mourn in silence.
70 MANUEL: Alas! the times that I have follow'd him!
JANE: Forbear, my faithful Manuel. For this love
Thou hast my grateful thanks; and here's my hand:
Thou hast lov'd him, and I'll remember thee:
Where'er I am; in whate'er spot of earth
75 I linger out the remnant of my days,
I'll remember thee.
MANUEL: Nay, by the living God! where'er you are,
There will I be. I'll prove a trusty servant:
I'll follow you, e'en to the world's end.
80 My master's gone, and I, indeed, am mean,
Yet will I show the strength of nobler men,
Should any dare upon your honour'd worth
To put the slightest wrong. Leave you, dear lady!
Kill me, but say not this!
[*Throwing himself at her feet.*]
85 JANE: [*Raising him.*] Well, then! be thou my
    servant, and my friend.
Art thou, good Jerome, too, in kindness come?

I see thou art. How goes it with thine age?
JEROME: Ah, madam! woe and weakness dwell with
    age:
Would I could serve you with a young man's strength!
I'd spend my life for you.
JANE: Thanks, worthy Jerome.
O! who hath said, the wretched have no friends![1]
FREBERG: In every sensible and gen'rous breast
Affliction finds a friend; but unto thee,
Thou most exalted and most honourable,
The heart in warmest adoration bows,
And even a worship pays.
JANE: Nay, Freberg, Freberg! grieve me not, my friend.
He to whose ear my praise most welcome was,
Hears it no more; and, oh our piteous lot!
What tongue will talk of him? Alas, alas!
This more than all will bow me to the earth;
I feel my misery here.
The voice of praise was wont to name us both:
I had no greater pride.
[*Covers her face with her hands, and bursts into tears. Here they all hang about her:* FREBERG *supporting her tenderly;* MANUEL *embracing her knees, and old* JEROME *catching hold of her robe affectionately.* BERNARD, ABBESS, MONKS, *and* NUNS, *likewise, gather round her, with looks of sympathy.*
    ENTER *two* OFFICERS *of law.*]
1ST OFFICER: Where is the prisoner?
Into our hands he straight must be consign'd.
BERNARD: He is not subject now to human laws;
The prison that awaits him is the grave.
1ST OFFICER: Ha! sayst thou so? there is foul play in
    this.
MANUEL: [*To* OFFICER.] Hold thy unrighteous
    tongue, or hie thee hence,
Nor, in the presence of this honour'd dame,
Utter the slightest meaning of reproach.
1ST OFFICER: I am an officer on duty call'd,
And have authority to say, how died?
[*Here* JANE *shakes off the weakness of grief, and repressing* MANUEL, *who is about to reply to the* OFFICER, *steps forward with dignity.*]
JANE: Tell them by whose authority you come,
He died that death which most becomes a man
Who is with keenest sense of conscious ill
And deep remorse assail'd, a wounded spirit.
A death that kills the noble and the brave,
And only them. He had no other wound.
1ST OFFICER: And shall I trust to this.
JANE: Do as thou wilt:
To one who can suspect my simple word
I have no more reply. Fulfill thine office.
1ST OFFICER: No, lady, I believe your honour'd word,
And will no farther search.
JANE: I thank your courtesy: thanks, thanks to all!
My rev'rend mother, and ye honour'd maids;
Ye holy men; and you, my faithful friends,
The blessing of the afflicted rest with you:
And he, who to the wretched is most piteous,
Will recompense you.—Freberg, thou art good,
Remove the body of the friend you lov'd,
'Tis Rezenvelt I mean. Take thou this charge:
'Tis meet that, with his noble ancestors,
He lie entomb'd in honourable state.
And now, I have a sad request to make,
Nor will these holy sisters scorn my boon;
That I, within these sacred cloister walls
May raise a humble, nameless tomb to him,
Who, but for one dark passion, one dire deed,
Had claim'd a record of as noble worth,
As e'er enrich'd the sculptur'd pedestal.[2]

[*EXEUNT.*]

---

[1] Cf. John Dryden (1631–1700), *All for Love* (1678) 3.1.83.

[2] In the later editions, Baillie added two notes: "The last three lines of the last speech are not intended to give the reader a true character of *De Monfort*, whom I have endeavoured to represent throughout the play as, notwithstanding his other good qualities, proud, suspicious, and susceptible of envy, but only to express the partial sentiments of an affectionate sister, naturally more inclined to praise him from the misfortune into which he has fallen.

"The Tragedy of *De Monfort* has been brought out at Drury-Lane Theatre, adapted to the stage by *Mr. Kemble*. I am infinitely obliged to that gentleman for the excellent powers he has exerted, assisted by the incomparable talents of his sister, *Mrs. Siddons*, in endeavouring to obtain for it that public favour, which I sincerely wish it had been found more worth of receiving." *De Monfort* was produced at Drury Lane, starring John Philip Kemble (1757–1823) and Sarah Siddons (1755–1831), in April-May 1800; as Baillie implies, it was not favourably received, but it had a respectable run of eight performances.

from *Fugitive Verses* (1840)

Thunder[1]

Spirit of strength! to whom in wrath 'tis given,
To mar the earth and shake its vasty dome,
Behold the somber robes whose gathering folds,
Thy secret majesty conceal. Their skirts
5 Spread on mid air move slow and silently,
O'er noon-day's beam thy sultry shroud is cast,
Advancing clouds from every point of heaven,
Like hosts of gathering foes in pitchy volumes,
Grandly dilated, clothe the fields of air,
10 And brood aloft o'er the empurpled earth.
Spirit of strength! It is thy awful hour;
The wind of every hill is laid to rest,
And far o'er sea and land deep silence reigns.

   Wild creatures of the forest homeward hie,
15 And in their dens with fear unwonted cower;
Pride in the lordly palace is put down,
While in his humble cot the poor man sits
With all his family round him hushed and still,
In awful expectation. On his way
20 The traveller stands aghast and looks to heaven.
On the horizon's verge thy lightning gleams,
And the first utterance of thy deep voice
Is heard in reverence and holy fear.

   From nearer clouds bright burst more vivid gleams,
25 As instantly in closing darkness lost;
Pale sheeted flashes cross the wide expanse
While over boggy moor or swampy plain,
A steaming cataract of flame appears,
To meet a nether fire from earth cast up,
30 Commingling terribly; appalling gloom
Succeeds, and lo! the rifted centre pours
A general blaze, and from the war of clouds,
Red, writhing falls the embodied bolt of heaven.
Then swells the rolling peal, full, deep'ning, grand,
35 And in its strength lifts the tremendous roar,
With mingled discord, rattling, hissing, growling;
Crashing like rocky fragments downward hurled,
Like the upbreaking of a ruined world,
In awful majesty the explosion bursts
40 Wide and astounding o'er the trembling land.
Mountain, and cliff, repeat the dread turmoil,
And all to man's distinctive senses known,
Is lost in the immensity of sound.
Peal after peal, succeeds with waning strength,
45 And hushed and deep each solemn pause between.

   Upon the lofty mountain's side
The kindled forest blazes wide;
Huge fragments of the rugged steep
Are tumbled to the lashing deep;
50 Firm rooted in his cloven rock,
Crashing falls the stubborn oak.
The lightning keen in wasteful ire
Darts fiercely on the pointed spire,
Rending in twain the iron-knit stone,
55 And stately towers to earth are thrown.
No human strength may brave the storm,
Nor shelter skreen the shrinking form,
Nor castle wall its fury stay,
Nor massy gate impede its way:
60 It visits those of low estate,
It shakes the dwellings of the great,
It looks athwart the vaulted tomb,
And glares upon the prison's gloom.
Then dungeons black in unknown light,
65 Flash hideous on the wretches' sight,
And strangely groans the downward cell,
Where silence deep is wont to dwell.

   Now eyes, to heaven up-cast, adore,
Knees bend that never bent before,
70 The stoutest hearts begin to fail,
And many a manly face is pale;
Benumbing fear awhile up-binds,
The palsied action of their minds,
Till waked to dreadful sense they lift their eyes,
75 And round the stricken corse shrill shrieks of horror rise.

   Now rattling hailstones, bounding as they fall
To earth, spread motley winter o'er the plain,

---

[1] Cf. the version in *Poems* (1790), (505).

Receding peals sound fainter on the ear,
And roll their distant grumbling far away:
The lightning doth in paler flashes gleam,
And through the rent cloud, silvered with his rays,
The sun on all this wild affray looks down,
As, high enthroned above all mortal ken,
A higher Power beholds the strife of men.

Song,
Woo'd and Married and A'

(Version taken from an old song of that name.)

The bride she is winsome and bonny,
  Her hair it is snooded[1] sae sleek,
And faithfu' and kind is her Johnny,
  Yet fast fa' the tears on her cheek.
New pearlins[2] are cause of her sorrow,
  New pearlins and plenishing[3] too,
The bride that has a' to borrow,
  Has e'en right mickle[4] ado.
    Woo'd and married and a'!
    Woo'd and married and a'!
    Is na' she very weel aff
    To be woo'd and married at a'?

Her mither then hastily spak,
  "The lassie is glakit[5] wi' pride;
In my pouch I had never a plack[6]
  On the day when I was a bride.
E'en tak' to your wheel,[7] and be clever,
  And draw out your thread in the sun;
The gear[8] that is gifted, it never
  Will last like the gear that is won.

    Woo'd and married and a'!
    Wi' havins[9] and tocher[10] sae sma'!
    I think ye are very weel aff,
    To be woo'd and married at a'!"

"Toot, toot!" quo' her grey-headed faither,
  "She's less o' a bride than a bairn,[11]
She's ta'en like a cout[12] frae the heather,
  Wi' sense and discretion to learn.
Half husband, I trow,[13] and half daddy,
  As humour inconstantly leans,
The chiel[14] maun[15] be patient and steady,
  That yokes wi' a mate in her teens.
    A kerchief sae douce[16] and sae neat,
    O'er her locks that the winds used to blaw!
    I'm baith like to laugh and to greet,[17]
    When I think o' her married at a'!"

Then out spak' the wily bridegroom,
  Weel waled[18] were his wordies, I ween,
"I'm rich, though my coffer be toom,[19]
  Wi' the blinks o' your bonny blue een.[20]
I'm prouder o' thee by my side,
  Though thy ruffles or ribbons be few,
Than Kate o' the Croft were my bride,
  Wi' purfles[21] and pearlins enow.
    Dear, and dearest of ony!

---

[1] "tied with a ribbon" (Sc.): the hairstyle is a symbol of virginity.
[2] "lace."
[3] "household furnishings."
[4] "much."
[5] "foolish, silly."
[6] low-denomination copper coin.
[7] spinning-wheel.
[8] "goods, possessions."
[9] "possessions."
[10] "dowry."
[11] "child."
[12] "colt, filly."
[13] "believe, suppose."
[14] "fellow."
[15] "must."
[16] "proper, respectable."
[17] "weep."
[18] "chosen."
[19] "empty."
[20] "eyes."
[21] "embroidery."

Ye're woo'd and buikit[1] and a'!
And do ye think scorn o' your Johnny,
And grieve to be married at a'?"

She turned, and she blushed, and she smiled,
And she looket sae bashfully down;
The pride o' her heart was beguiled,
And she played wi' the sleeves o' her gown;
She twirled the tag o' her lace,
And she nippet[2] her boddice sae blue,
Sine[3] blinket[4] sae sweet in his face,
And aff like a maukin[5] she flew.
Woo'd and married and a'!
Wi' Johnny to roose[6] her and a'!
She thinks hersel very weel aff,
To be woo'd and married at a'.

---

[1] "booked" (i.e., the marriage has been entered in the parish registry).
[2] "nipped, bit."
[3] "afterwards."
[4] "glanced."
[5] "hare."
[6] "flatter, praise."

William Lisle Bowles
1762 – 1850

William Lisle Bowles was born on 24 September 1762 at King's Sutton, Northamptonshire, the oldest of the seven children of William Thomas Bowles, a clergyman (and the son and grandson of clergymen) and of Bridget Grey Bowles. He was educated at Winchester School and Trinity College, Oxford. After graduating, he became a clergyman and settled in Wiltshire, where he lived for the rest of his life. In 1797, he married Magdalen Wake. An indefatigable poet, he published about sixty books, but he is remembered mainly for his first, *Fourteen Sonnets, Elegiac and Descriptive* (1789), which was inspired by a tour he undertook to recover from a romantic disappointment, and which so impressed the sixteen-year-old Coleridge* that (unable to afford multiple copies) he copied out forty copies by hand to give to friends. A second claim to fame is Bowles's edition of Pope (1806), in which his disparaging remarks about the poet provoked the wrath of Byron.* Bowles died on 7 April 1850. (D.L.M.)

☙☙☙

from *Fourteen Sonnets, Elegiac and Descriptive. Written During a Tour* (1789)

To the River Itchin, Near Winton[1]

Itchin, when I behold thy banks again,
Thy crumbling margin, and thy silver breast,
   On which the self-same tints still seem to rest,
Why feels my heart the shiv'ring sense of pain?
5 Is it, that many a summer's day has past
Since, in life's morn, I carol'd on thy side?
Is it, that oft, since then, my heart has sigh'd,
   As Youth, and Hope's delusive gleams, flew fast?
Is it that those, who circled on thy shore,
10 Companions of my youth, now meet no more?
   Whate'er the cause, upon thy banks I bend
Sorrowing, yet feel such solace at my heart,
   As at the meeting of some long-lost friend,
From whom, in happier hours, we wept to part.

On Dover Cliffs. July 20, 1787

On these white cliffs, that calm above the flood
Uplift their shadowing heads, and, at their feet,
   Scarce hear the surge that has for ages beat,
Sure many a lonely wanderer has stood;
5 And, whilst the lifted murmur met his ear,
And o'er the distant billows the still Eve
   Sail'd slow, has thought of all his heart must leave
To-morrow,—of the friends he lov'd most dear,—
   Of social scenes, from which he wept to part:—
10 But if, like me, he knew how fruitless all
   The thoughts that would full fain the past recall,
Soon would he quell the risings of his heart,
   And brave the wild winds and unhearing tide,
The World his country, and his GOD his guide.

---

[1] The Itchin flows through Winchester ("Wintoncester"), where Bowles had been a schoolboy.

William Cobbett
1763 – 1835

William Cobbett was born in Farnham, Surrey, on 9 March 1763, the third son of George Cobbett, a farmer and innkeeper, and of Ann Vincent Cobbett. He was educated by his father and at a dame school. After working as a farm boy, gardener, and lawyer's clerk, he enlisted in the army and served in Nova Scotia and New Brunswick from 1785 to 1791. In 1792, he married Anne Reid; they would have seven children. After a brief visit to Revolutionary France, the Cobbetts sailed for America, where they remained until 1800 and where Cobbett began his career as a fearless and indefatigable reformist journalist; according to one estimate, he wrote and published some twenty million words in his career. In Philadelphia, he founded first the *Political Censor* (1796–97) and then *Porcupine's Gazette* (1797–99); on returning to England, he founded the *Porcupine* (1800–1801) and then, in 1802, *Cobbett's Weekly Political Register*, which he continued to write and publish for the rest of his life. It attained a circulation of fifty thousand. In 1804, he bought a farm in Hampshire. During a second sojourn in America (1817–19), he wrote *A Grammar of the English Language*, intended to bring the power of the written word to the working classes. When he returned to England this time, he brought with him the bones of Thomas Paine,* intending to give them a burial befitting a hero of freedom; unfortunately, he seems to have misplaced them. Between 1822 and 1826, he published in the *Political Register* the essays that he would later collect as *Rural Rides* (1830), his masterpiece. In 1832, he was elected member of parliament for Oldham. He died on 18 June 1835. (D.L.M.)

༺༻

from *Political Register* (11 December 1813)

from *To Mr. Alderman Wood,*[1] *On the Subject of Teaching the Children of the Poor to Read*

LETTER 1

Sir,

I see, from accounts published in the news-papers, that you are taking great pains to establish a school upon the Lancasterian plan,[2] the main object of which appears to be to teach poor children to *read*, and particularly to *read the Bible*. I have, for some months, had an intention to address you upon this subject, and to state to you my reasons for believing, that an act, arising solely from your benevolent disposition, is not, with sufficient clearness, founded in reason, and that it is not likely to produce the good which you certainly have in view.

The subject naturally divides itself into two parts; or, rather, presents two questions for discussion: 1st. Whether, under the present circumstances, in this country, the teaching of poor children *to read generally* be likely to do good; and, 2nd, whether it be likely to do good to teach them *to read the Bible*.

Whatever men may think about reading the Bible; however their opinions may differ as to the utility of reading this particular Book, the number is very small, indeed, who think that the teaching of poor children to *read generally* is not a good past all dispute. To that very small number, however, I belong; and my opinion decidedly is, that, under the present circumstances of this country, the teaching of poor children to read generally is calculated to produce *evil* rather than *good*; for which opinion I will now proceed to offer you my reasons, and not without some hope of being able to convince you, that your money, laid out in pots of beer to the parents, would be full as likely to benefit the community.

---

[1] Sir Matthew Wood (1768–1843), alderman and later Lord Mayor of London.

[2] Joseph Lancaster (1778–1838) tried to promote universal, secular, free education through a system in which older students taught younger ones.

The *utility* of reading consists in the imparting knowledge to those who read; knowledge dispels ignorance. Reading, therefore, naturally tends to enlighten mankind. As mankind become enlightened, they become less exposed to the arts of those who would enslave them. Whence reading naturally tends to promote and ensure the liberties of mankind. "How, then," you will ask, "can you object to the teaching of the children of the ignorant to read?" But, Sir, when we thus describe the effects of reading, we must always be understood as meaning, the reading of works which convey *truth* to the mind; for, I am sure, that you will not deny, that it is possible for a person to become by reading more ignorant than he was before. For instance, a child has *no knowledge* of the source whence coals are drawn; but, if, in consequence of what he reads, he believes coals to be made out of clay, he is more ignorant than he was before he read; because falsehood is farther from truth than is the absence of knowledge. A child, in the neighbourhood of Loretto,[1] who had been happy enough to escape the lies of the priests, would know nothing at all of the origin of the Virgin Mary's House at that famous resort of pilgrims; but, if he had read the history of the Bees' House, he would believe that it came thither, flying across the sea from Palestine; and he would, of course, be a great deal *more ignorant* than if he had never read the said history.

Thus, then, reading does not tend to enlighten men, unless what they read convey *truth* to their minds. The next question is, therefore, whether, under the present circumstances of this country, the children of the poor are likely to come at truth by reading; which question, I think, we must decide in the negative.

You will please to observe, that I am not now speaking of the Bible, or of works upon religion. Those I shall notice by-and-by. I am now speaking of *reading in general*. To those who object to the teaching of children to read the Bible, as being above their capacity to comprehend, it is usually answered, that if children learn to read the Bible, they will inevitably read *other things*; and that out of *reading* will proceed *light*, and the means of giving the people true notions of their *rights* in society. But, here again it is taken for granted, that what they will read, after they have been taught to read the Bible, will be calculated to give them *true notions*, and will inculcate the principles upon which men ought to be governed.

Now, Sir, is this the fact? Does the press in this country send forth works calculated to produce such an effect? That is to say, are its productions *generally* of this description? Or, to put the question more closely, is the *major part* of its productions of this description? Because, if it send forth more productions which are calculated to give *false* notions, than of productions which are calculated to give *true* notions, it follows, of course, that reading, generally, must tend to the increase of a belief in falsehood, which no one will deny to be the worst species of ignorance.

Let us see, then, what is the real state of this *press*; this vaunted press, which, in ninety-nine hundredths of the publications which issue from it, is represented as being FREE. Let us see what is the real state of this press.

In the first place, a man is liable, if he write, or print, or publish any thing, which the Attorney General (an officer *appointed by the Crown* and *removable at pleasure*), chooses to prosecute him for; any man who does this is liable to be prosecuted, and to be punished in a manner much more severe than a great part of the persons convicted of felony. You yourself remember (and I shall always retain a grateful recollection of your goodness upon the occasion), that I, for writing an article, respecting the treatment of the Local Militia at the town of Ely, was sent to pass two years of my life in a place where there were felons, and men actually found guilty of unnatural crimes.[2] Many of the felons, at that time in Newgate, were punished with a shorter term of imprisonment than I was; to say nothing of the *fine*, a sum equal to what may be fairly deemed a fourth part of the average earnings of any literary man's whole life.

And, who will say, that, if he venture to utter what is calculated to displease men in power, he will escape such punishment? There are no laws, which set bounds

---

[1] in Italy, a famous shrine of the Virgin Mary, whose house was supposed to have been transported there from Nazareth by angels.

[2] In 1810, Cobbett had been sentenced to two years' imprisonment and a fine of £1000 for an article protesting the flogging of five soldiers.

to his pen; there is no settled rule of law which enables him to know what is criminal and what is not criminal. He is prosecuted if the King's officer chooses to prosecute him; and the Jury, by whom he is tried, is specially nominated by another officer of the Crown, the accused party having the privilege of objecting to twelve out of forty-eight of the persons so nominated. The Attorney General may, if he please, commence a prosecution and *not proceed in it*. He may keep a criminal charge hanging over the head of any writer as long as he chooses; and, with the consent of a Judge, he may hold the party to bail for his appearance for as long a time as he chooses to keep the charge suspended over his head. So that such writer, during his whole life time, may have a criminal charge kept suspended over his head, and, without forfeiting his recognizances and those of his sureties, he cannot, during his whole life time, quit the country, or be absent at any one term; for, at any term, whenever his accuser pleases, though, perhaps, after his witnesses are dead, he may be commanded to come and take his trial.

On the *other hand*, the Attorney General may, if he chooses, drop the prosecution, and that, too, at whatever time he may please to drop it. After having charged a writer with a crime, he may keep the charge suspended over his head for months or years; and then, without even leave of the Court, and *without assigning any reason at all*, he may *wholly withdraw the charge*, and relieve the poor creature and his family from their fears.

This is the state of our press as it is affected by the *law*. And, under such circumstances, is it to be expected, that the press will convey, freely convey, *truths* to the people? For, you will be particular in bearing in mind, that the *truth* of any writing, so far from being a *justification* of the author, is not permitted to be *pleaded* in his defence. To utter *truth*, therefore, respecting the measures of the government, the administration of the laws, the weight or the mode of collecting the taxes, the treatment of the army or the navy, the conduct of the clergy, the creeds of the Church; to utter *truth* respecting any of these may, in the eye of the law, be a greatly criminal act, and may subject the utterer to a punishment more severe than that inflicted on a great part of the felons.

We are not inquiring here, whether this law of the press be good or bad. There are those who assert it to be full of justice and wisdom. We will not, therefore, raise a dispute upon that point. We will content ourselves with observing that such *is* the law; and, then, we have only to determine, whether, under such a law, the press is likely to be the vehicle of *truth*. There are those, who say, that it ought not to be permitted to convey, in an undisguised manner, truths, upon all public matters and concerning all public men, to the people. Very well; but, if this be the case, can the reading of the productions of this press tend to dispel ignorance; can it tend to *enlighten* the people? Can it be any public benefit, can it further the cause of public liberty, to teach the children of the poor to *read*? ...

from *Cobbett's Weekly Register* (5 January 1822)

from *Kentish Journal*[1]

Tuesday, Dec. 4, 1821. *Elverton Farm, near Faversham, Kent.*—This is the first time, since I went to France, in 1792, that I have been on this side of *Shooters' Hill*. The land, generally speaking, from Deptford to Dartford is poor, and the surface ugly by nature, to which *ugliness* there has been made, just before we came to the latter place, a considerable addition by the *inclosure of a common*, and by the sticking up of some shabby-genteel houses, surrounded with dead fences and things called gardens, in all manner of ridiculous forms, making, all together, the bricks, hurdle-rods and earth say, as plainly as they can speak, "Here dwell *vanity* and *poverty*." This is a little excrescence that has grown out of the immense sums, which have been drawn from other parts of the kingdom to be expended on Barracks, Magazines, Martello-Towers, Catamarans, and all the excuses for lavish expenditure, which the *war for the Bourbons*[2] gave rise to. All things will return; these rubbishy flimsy things, on this common, will first be deserted, then

---

[1] reprinted in *Rural Rides* (1830).

[2] the war against Revolutionary France, which resulted in the restoration of the Bourbon dynasty in 1815.

crumble down, then be swept away, and the cattle, sheep, pigs and geese will once more graze upon the common, which will again furnish heath, furze and turf for the labourers on the neighbouring lands.—After you leave Dartford the land becomes excellent. You come to a bottom of *chalk*, many feet from the surface, and when that is the case the land is sure to be good; no *wet* at bottom; no deep ditches, no water furrows, necessary; sufficiently moist in dry weather, and no water lying about upon it in wet weather for any length of time. The chalk acts as a *filtering-stone*, not as a *sieve*, like gravel, and not as a *dish*, like clay. The chalk acts as the soft stone in Herefordshire does; but it is not so congenial to trees that have tap-roots.—Along through Gravesend towards Rochester the country presents a sort of gardening scene. *Rochester* (the Bishop of which is, or lately was, *tax Collector for London and Middlesex*) is a small but crowded place, lying on the south bank of the beautiful Medway, with a rising ground on the other side of the city. *Stroud*, which you pass through before you come to the bridge, over which you go to enter Rochester; *Rochester* itself, and *Chatham*, form, in fact, one main street of about two miles and a half in length. —Here I was got into the scenes of my cap-and-feather days! Here, at between sixteen and seventeen, I enlisted for a soldier. Upon looking up towards the fortifications and the barracks, how many recollections crowded into my mind! The girls in these towns do not seem to be *so pretty* as they were thirty-eight years ago; or, am I not so quick in discovering beauties as I was then? Have thirty-eight years corrected my taste, or made me a hyper critic in these matters? Is it that I now look at them with the solemness of a "professional man," and not with the enthusiasm and eagerness of an "amateur?" I leave these questions for philosophers to solve. One thing I will say for the young women of these towns, and that is, that I always found those of them that I had the great happiness to be acquainted with, evince a sincere desire to do their best to smooth the inequalities of life, and to give us, "*brave fellows*," as often as they could, strong beer, when their churlish masters or fathers or husbands would have drenched us to death with small. This, at the out-set of life, gave me a high opinion of the judgment and justice of the female sex; an opinion which has been confirmed by the observations of my whole life.—This Chatham has had some monstrous *wens* stuck on to it by the lavish expenditure of the war. These will moulder away. It is curious enough that I should meet with a gentleman in an inn at Chatham to give me a picture of the *house-distress* in that enormous *wen*, which, during the war, was stuck on to *Portsmouth*. Not less than *fifty thousand people* had been drawn together there! These are now *dispersing*. The coagulated blood is diluting and flowing back through the veins. Whole streets are deserted, and the eyes of the houses knocked out by the boys that remain. The jack-daws, as much as to say, "Our turn to *be inspired and to teach* is come," are beginning to take possession of the Methodist chapels. The gentleman told me, that he had been down to Portsea to *sell* half a street of houses, left him by a relation; and that nobody would give him *any* thing for them further than as very cheap *fuel* and *rubbish*! Good God! And is this "*prosperity*?" Is this the "*prosperity of the war*?" Have I not, for twenty long years, been regretting the existence of these unnatural embossments; these white-swellings, these odious wens, produced by *Corruption* and engendering crime and misery and slavery? We shall see the whole of these wens abandoned by the inhabitants, and, at last, the cannons on the fortifications may be of *some use* in battering down the buildings.—But, what is to be the fate of the *great wen* of all? The monster, called, by the silly coxcombs of the press, "the *metropolis of the empire*?" What is to become of that multitude of towns that has been stuck up around it? The *village of Kingston* was smothered in the *town of Portsea;* and why? Because taxes, drained from other parts of the kingdom, were brought thither. Who, except such people as "Walter the base," does not see, that it is taxes, which have swelled out London? Who does not see, that these taxes must cease to be carried thither in such quantities? And, must not the *wen* be dispersed? Yes, and I shall see the eyes out of thousands of houses, if I live but a very few years. Let builders and owners of houses take warning; for such scenes are going to take place, as never yet entered into their speculations. This *dispersion of the wen* is the only *real difficulty* that I see in settling the affairs of the nation and restoring it to a happy state. But, dispersed it *must* be; and, if there be half a million, or more, of people to suffer, the consolation is, that the suffering will be divided into *half a million of parts*. As if the swelling out of London, naturally produced by the Funding system, were not sufficient; as if the evil were not sufficiently great from the inevitable tendency of the system of loans and funds, our *pretty gentlemen* must resort to positive institutions to augment the population of the Wen. They found that the increase of the Wen produced an increase of thieves and prostitutes, an increase of all sorts of diseases, an increase of miseries of all sorts; they saw, that taxes drawn up to one point produced these effects; they must have a "*penitentiary*," for instance, to check the evil, and that they must needs have *in the Wen*! So that here were a million of pounds, drawn up in taxes, employed not only to *keep the thieves and prostitutes still in the Wen*, but to bring up to the Wen *workmen to build the penitentiary*, who and whose families, amounting, perhaps, to *thousands*, make an addition to the cause of that crime and misery, to *check* which is the *object of the Penitentiary*! People would follow, they *must* follow, the million of money. However, this is of a piece with all the rest of their goings on. They and their predecessors, ministers and *House*, have been collecting together all the materials for a dreadful explosion; and, if the explosion be not dreadful, *other heads* must point out the means of prevention....

Samuel Rogers
1763 – 1855

Samuel Rogers was born on 30 July 1763 at The Hill, Newington Green, Middlesex, the third son of Thomas Rogers, son of a glass manufacturer, and Mary Rogers, daughter of Daniel Radford, treasurer of the Presbyterian congregation at Stoke Newington. Rogers attended dissenting schools in Hackney and Stoke Newington. He wanted to be a Presbyterian minister, but his father persuaded him to be a banker; Rogers became very rich through business while simultaneously pursuing his literary ambitions.

In 1781 he contributed several essays to the *Gentleman's Magazine*. His first book of poetry, *An Ode to Superstition, with some other Poems*, appeared in 1786. When his brother Thomas died in 1788, Rogers' share in the bank's management and profits increased. In 1789 he visited Scotland, where he met such writers as Adam Smith, Henry Mackenzie, and Walter Scott;* in 1791 he visited France, where he saw the art collections in the Palais Royal. His poem *The Pleasures of Memory* (1792) went through fifteen editions by 1806.

Rogers' father died in June 1793 and left him a fortune of £5000 a year. Rogers formed a London salon, making the acquaintance of Charles Fox, Richard Brinsley Sheridan, and Horne Tooke. In 1795 he wrote an epilogue for the actor Sarah Siddons; the following year he became a fellow of the Royal Society.

During the Peace of Amiens in 1802 Rogers visited Paris, where he met such English artists as Henry Fuseli, John Flaxman, Benjamin West, and John Opie. The next year he built himself a house in London and filled it with his growing art collection. Rogers befriended writers as well as artists: he reconciled Moore* with Jeffrey* and with Byron;* he helped to arrange W. Wordsworth's* position as distributor of stamps for Westmoreland. Byron regarded his poetry highly, seeing Rogers as a much better poet than those in the "Lake School." However, Rogers' fragmentary epic, *Columbus* (privately printed in 1808), was not highly successful. His poem *Jacqueline*, in the style of Scott* and Byron, appeared in 1814 in the same volume as Byron's *Lara*. *Human Life* followed in 1819. Rogers visited Italy in 1815 and wrote an anonymous poem, *Italy*, published in two parts in 1822 and 1828 and, more successfully, in an illustrated version in 1834. On his next visit to Italy in 1822, Rogers visited Byron and P.B. Shelley* at Pisa. After Wordsworth's death in 1850 Rogers declined the poet laureateship in favour of Tennyson. On 18 December 1855, he died at his home in London; he was buried in Hornsey churchyard. (A.M.)

༒

from *Poems* (1812)

The Boy of Egremond[1]

"Say, what remains when Hope is fled?"
She answered, "Endless weeping!"
For in the herdsman's eye she read
Who in his shroud lay sleeping.
5   At Embsay[2] rung the matin-bell,

The stag was roused on Barden-fell;[3]
The mingled sounds were swelling, dying,
And down the Wharfe a hern was flying;
When near the cabin in the wood,
10   In tartan clad and forest-green,
With hound in leash and hawk in hood,
The Boy of Egremond was seen.[4]

---

[1] or Egremont, a town and castle in Cumbria; the boy of Egremond is visiting Yorkshire when the accident described in the poem occurs.

[2] a village in north Yorkshire.

[3] A fell is a moor or upland stretch of open country.

[4] "In the twelfth century William Fitz-Duncan laid waste the valleys of Craven with fire and sword; and was afterwards established there by his uncle, David King of Scotland.

"He was the last of the race; his son, commonly called the Boy of Egremond, dying before him in the manner here related; when a Priory was removed from Embsay to Bolton, that it might be   (Continued)

Blithe was his song, a song of yore;
But where the rock is rent in two,
15 And the river rushes through,
His voice was heard no more!
'Twas but a step! the gulf he passed;
But that step—it was his last!
As through the mist he winged his way,
20 (A cloud that hovers night and day,)
The hound hung back, and back he drew
The Master and his merlin[1] too.
That narrow place of noise and strife
Received their little all of Life!
25   There now the matin-bell is rung;
The "Miserere!"[2] duly sung;
And holy men in cowl and hood
Are wandering up and down the wood.
But what avail they? Ruthless Lord,
30 Thou didst not shudder when the sword
Here on the young its fury spent,
The helpless and the innocent.
Sit now and answer groan for groan.
The child before thee is thy own.
35 And she who wildly wanders there,

The mother in her long despair,
Shall oft remind thee, waking, sleeping,
Of those who by the Wharfe were weeping;
Of those who would not be consoled
40 When red with blood the river rolled.

from *Poems* (1814)

To ——

Go—you may call it madness, folly;
You shall not chase my gloom away.
There's such a charm in melancholy,
I would not, if I could, be gay.

5 Oh, if you knew the pensive pleasure
That fills my bosom when I sigh,
You would not rob me of a treasure
Monarchs are too poor to buy.

---

as near as possible to the place where the accident happened. That place is still known by the name of the *Strid*; and the mother's answer, as given in the first stanza, is to this day often repeated in Wharfedale.— See Whitaker's Hist. of Craven." (S.R.) The "strid" or striding place is a narrow channel of the river Wharfe near Bolton Abbey which, according to legend, was built as a memorial by the boy of Egremond's parents. The historian T.D. Whitaker's *History of Craven* (2nd ed. 1812) gives the history of each parish in Craven, a deanery in the old West Riding of Yorkshire. W. Wordsworth* has a poem on the same subject as "The Boy of Egremond": "The Force of Prayer; or, The Founding of Bolton Priory" (1815).

[1] a hunting hawk.

[2] "Have mercy," a prayer from the Latin mass.

Ann Radcliffe
1764 – 1823

Ann Ward was born at Holborn, London, on 9 July 1764, the only child of William and Ann Oates Ward. Her father was a shopkeeper, but the family was well connected: through her uncle, Thomas Bentley, partner of the potter Josiah Wedgwood, Ann met such prominent literary figures as the Bluestocking Elizabeth Montagu and Anna Lætitia Barbauld.* The Wards moved to Bath when Ann was eight; there she met and in 1787 married William Radcliffe, an Oxford graduate who took up a career as a journalist in London.

Ann and William Radcliffe travelled within England at least annually until about 1813. Only once did they visit the Continent, on a trip to Holland and Germany in 1794; in spite of the settings of some of her novels, Radcliffe never saw Italy. Influenced by her reading of English authors (including Edmund Burke's* 1757 essay on the sublime and the beautiful), her interest in antiquarianism, and her knowledge of the paintings of Claude Lorrain, Nicolas Poussin, Guido Reni, and Salvator Rosa, over nine years Radcliffe wrote a series of psychologically compelling "Gothic" novels set in sublime or picturesque landscapes, evoking emotions of terror, and exploring the sensibility of their heroines.

The first two novels, *The Castles of Athlin and Dunbayne* (1789) and *A Sicilian Romance* (1790), establish some of Radcliffe's characteristic devices and qualities: distrust of Catholicism, suspense and coincidence in the plot, themes of pursuit, and an atmosphere of the supernatural. However, not until her third novel, *The Romance of the Forest* (1791), did Radcliffe achieve popular success. *The Mysteries of Udolpho* (1794), in which the heroine, Emily, separated from her lover, is imprisoned by her evil uncle, Montoni, in his mountain castle, was wildly popular—and, like other Radcliffe novels, was adapted for the stage. In her Gothic parody, *Northanger Abbey*,* Jane Austen seems to assume that her readers are familiar with the plot and atmosphere of *Udolpho*. Here, as in most of Radcliffe's other novels, the supernatural is evoked only to be explained away at the end of the novel. *The Italian* (1797), for which Radcliffe received the huge sum of £800, was partly a response to Matthew Gregory Lewis's *The Monk*.* Her last novel, *Gaston de Blondeville*, written in 1802, was published posthumously in 1826.

Suffering from asthma, Radcliffe lived in seclusion for the last ten years of her life. She died on 7 February 1823. Her posthumously published essay, "On the Supernatural in Poetry,"* was originally intended as the introduction to *Gaston de Blondeville*. (A.M.)

from *The Mysteries of Udolpho, A Romance; Interspersed with Some Pieces of Poetry* (1794)[1]

Storied Sonnet[2]

The weary traveller, who, all night long,
Has climb'd among the Alps' tremendous steeps,
Skirting the pathless precipice, where throng
Wild forms of danger; as he onward creeps
5 If, chance, his anxious eye at distance sees
The mountain-shepherd's solitary home,
Peeping from forth the moon-illumin'd trees,
What sudden transports to his bosom come!
But, if between some hideous chasm yawn,
10 Where the cleft pine a doubtful bridge displays,
In dreadful silence, on the brink, forlorn
He stands, and views in the faint rays
Far, far below, the torrent's rising surge,
And listens to the wild impetuous roar;
15 Still eyes the depth, still shudders on the verge,
Fears to return, nor dares to venture o'er.
Desperate, at length the tottering plank he tries,
His weak steps slide, he shrieks, he sinks—he dies!

Rondeau[3]

Soft as yon silver ray, that sleeps
Upon the ocean's trembling tide;

Soft as the air, that lightly sweeps
Yon sail, that swells in stately pride:

5 Soft as the surge's stealing note,
That dies along the distant shores,
Or warbled strain, that sinks remote—
So soft the sigh my bosom pours!

True as the wave to Cynthia's ray,
10 True as the vessel to the breeze,
True as the soul to music's sway,
Or music to Venetian seas:

Soft as yon silver beams, that sleep
Upon the ocean's trembling breast;
15 So soft, so true, fond Love shall weep,
So soft, so true, with *thee* shall rest.

To Autumn

Sweet Autumn! how thy melancholy grace
Steals on my heart, as through these shades I wind!
Sooth'd by thy breathing sigh, I fondly trace
Each lonely image of the pensive mind!
5 Lov'd scenes, lov'd friends—long lost! around me rise,
And wake the melting thought, the tender tear!
That tear, that thought, which more than mirth I prize—
Sweet as the gradual tint, that paints thy year!
Thy farewel smile, with fond regret, I view,
10 Thy beaming lights, soft gliding o'er the woods;
Thy distant landscape, touch'd with yellow hue
While falls the lengthen'd gleam; thy winding floods,
Now veil'd in shade, save where the skiff's white sails
Swell to the breeze, and catch thy streaming ray.
15 But now, e'en now!—the partial vision fails,
And the wave smiles, as sweeps the cloud away!
Emblem of life!—Thus checquer'd is its plan,
Thus joy succeeds to grief—thus smiles the varied man!

---

[1] Following her parents' death, Radcliffe's heroine Emily de St. Aubert is separated from her lover, Valancourt, by Madame Cheron, her aunt and guardian. Madame Charon's Italian husband, the sinister Montoni, imprisons her in his Gothic castle in the Appenines. Eventually she escapes, returns to the south of France, and is reunited with Valancourt. Descriptions of landscape and moods of terror, mystery, superstition, and sensibility are heightened by the poems and songs that punctuate Radcliffe's narrative.

[2] Radcliffe has her heroine, Emily St. Aubert, compose this sonnet as she descends the Alps into Italy.

[3] Count Morano, one of Emily's admirers in Venice, sings this song, accompanying himself on the lute; a "rondeau" is a form making use of refrains repeated according to a certain stylized pattern: this poem is not a conventional example of the form.

To Melancholy

Spirit of love and sorrow—hail!
Thy solemn voice from far I hear,
Mingling with ev'ning's dying gale:
Hail, with this sadly-pleasing tear!

5 O! at this still, this lonely hour,
Thine own sweet hour of closing day,
Awake thy lute, whose charmful pow'r
Shall call up Fancy to obey:

To paint the wild romantic dream,
10 That meets the poet's musing eye,
As, on the bank of shadowy stream,
He breathes to her the fervid sigh.

O lonely spirit! let thy song
Lead me through all thy sacred haunt;
15 The minster's moon-light aisles along,
Where spectres raise the midnight chaunt.

I hear their dirges faintly swell!
Then, sink at once in silence drear,
While, from the pillar'd cloister's cell,
20 Dimly their gliding forms appear!

Lead where the pine-woods wave on high,
Whose pathless sod is darkly seen,
As the cold moon, with trembling eye,
Darts her long beams the leaves between.

25 Lead to the mountain's dusky head,
Where, far below, in shade profound,
Wide forests, plains and hamlets spread,
And sad the chimes of vesper sound.

Or guide me, where the dashing oar
30 Just breaks the stillness of the vale,
As slow it tracks the winding shore,
To meet the ocean's distant sail:

To pebbly banks, that Neptune laves,
With measur'd surges, loud and deep,
35 Where the dark cliff bends o'er the waves,
And wild the winds of autumn sweep.

There pause at midnight's spectred hour,
And list the long-resounding gale;
And catch the fleeting moon-light's pow'r,
40 O'er foaming seas and distant sail.

from *Gaston de Blondeville* (1826)[1]

Scene on the Northern Shore of Sicily

Here, from the Castle's terraced site,
   I view, once more, the varied scene
   Of hamlets, woods, and pastures green,
And vales far stretching from the sight
5 Beneath the tints of coming night;
   And there is misty ocean seen,
   With glancing oars and waves serene,
And stealing sail of shifting light.
Now, let me hear the shepherd's lay,
10   As on some bank he sits alone;
   That oaten reed, of tender tone,
He loves, at setting sun, to play.
It speaks in Joy's delightful glee;
   Then Pity's strains its breath obey—
15 Or Love's soft voice it seems to be—
   And steals at last the soul away!
And now, the village bells afar
   Their melancholy music sound
Mournfully o'er the waters round,
20   Till Twilight sends her trembling star.
Oft shall my pensive heart attend,
   As swell the notes along the breeze,
And weep anew the buried friend,
   In tears, that sadly, softly please;
25 And, when pale moonlight tips the trees,
   On the dark Castle's tower ascends,
Throws o'er it's walls a silvery gleam,

---

[1] *Gaston de Blondeville: or, The Court of Henry III Keeping Festival in Ardennes* (1826) is a posthumously published antiquarian novel in the style of Sir Walter Scott.*

  And in one soft confusion blends
 Forest and mountain, plain and stream,
30 I list the drowsy sounds, that creep
  On night's still air, to soothe the soul;
  The hollow moan of Ocean's roll,
 The bleat and bell of wandering sheep,
  The distant watch-dog's feeble bark,
35 The voice of herdsman pacing home
  Along the leafy labyrinth dark,
 And sounds, that from the Castle come
  Of closing door, that sullen falls,
 And murmurs, through the chambers high
40 Of half-sung strains from ancient halls,
 That through the long, long galleries die.
  And now the taper's flame I spy
  In antique casement, glimmering pale;
  And now 'tis vanished from my eye,
45 And all but gloom and silence fail.

 Once more, I stand in pensive mood,
  And gaze on forms, that Truth delude;
 And still, 'mid Fancy's flitting scene,
  I catch the streaming cottage-light,
50 Twinkling the restless leaves between,
  And Ocean's flood, in moonbeams bright.

from *New Monthly Magazine and Literary Journal* 16, Part 1 (1826)

from *On the Supernatural in Poetry.* By the Late Mrs. Radcliffe[1]

One of our travellers began a grave dissertation on the illusions of the imagination. "And not only on frivolous occasions," said he, "but in the most important pursuits of life, an object often flatters and charms at a distance, which vanishes into nothing as we approach it; and 'tis well if it leave only disappointment in our hearts. Sometimes a severer monitor is left there."

 These truisms, delivered with an air of discovery by Mr. S——, who seldom troubled himself to think upon any subject, except that of a good dinner, were lost upon his companion, who, pursuing the airy conjectures which the present scene, however humbled, had called up, was following Shakspeare into unknown regions.... "Macbeth shows [continues the second speaker, Mr. S——'s companion W——], by many instances, how much Shakspeare delighted to heighten the effect of his characters and his story by correspondent scenery: there the desolate heath, the troubled elements, assist the mischief of his malignant beings. But who, after hearing Macbeth's thrilling question—

  ——'What are these,
 So withered and so wild in their attire,
 That look not like the inhabitants o' the earth,
 And yet are on't?'——[2]

who would have thought of reducing them to mere human beings, by attiring them not only like the

---

[1] "Having been permitted to extract the above eloquent passages from the manuscripts of the author of the 'Mysteries of Udolpho,' we have given this title to them, though certainly they were not intended by the writer to be offered as a formal or deliberate essay, under this, or any other denomination. They were, originally, part of an INTRODUCTION to the Romance, or Phantasie, which is about to appear. The discussion is supposed to be carried on by two travellers in Shakspeare's native country, Warwickshire." (*New Monthly Magazine* editor's note.) Thomas Campbell* was editor of the New Monthly Magazine from 1820–26.

[2] Shakespeare, *Macbeth* 1.3.39–42; the question is actually Banquo's.

inhabitants of the earth, but in the dress of a particular country, and making them downright Scotch-women? thus not only contradicting the very words of Macbeth, but withdrawing from these cruel agents of the passions all that strange and supernatural air which had made them so affecting to the imagination, and which was entirely suitable to the solemn and important events they were foretelling and accomplishing. Another *improvement* on Shakspeare is the introducing a crowd of witches[1] thus arrayed, instead of the three beings 'so withered and so wild in their attire.'"

About the latter part of this sentence, W——, as he was apt to do, thought aloud, and Mr. S—— said, "*I*, now, have sometimes considered, that it was quite suitable to make Scotch witches on the stage, appear like Scotch women. You must recollect that, in the superstition concerning witches, they lived familiarly upon the earth, mortal sorcerers, and were not always known from mere old women; consequently they must have appeared in the dress of the country where they happened to live, or they would have been more than suspected of witchcraft, which we find was not always the case."

"You are speaking of old women, and not of witches," said W—— laughing, "and I must more than suspect you of crediting that obsolete superstition which destroyed so many wretched, yet guiltless persons,[2] if I allow your argument to have any force. I am speaking of the only real witch—the witch of the poet; and all our notions and feelings connected with terror accord with his. The wild attire, the look *not of this earth*, are essential traits of supernatural agents, working evil in the darkness of mystery. Whenever the poet's witch condescends, according to the vulgar notion, to mingle mere ordinary mischief with her malignity, and to become familiar, she is ludicrous, and loses her power over the imagination; the illusion vanishes. So vexatious is the effect of the stage-witches upon my mind, that I should probably have left the theatre when they appeared, had not the fascination of Mrs. Siddons's[3] influence so spread itself over the whole play, as to overcome my disgust, and to make me forget even Shakspeare himself; while all consciousness of fiction was lost, and his thoughts lived and breathed before me in the very form of truth. Mrs. Siddons, like Shakspeare, always disappears in the character she represents, and throws an illusion over the whole scene around her, that conceals many defects in the arrangements of the theatre...."

"I still think," said Mr. S——, without attending to these remarks, "that, in a popular superstition, it is right to go with the popular notions, and dress your witches like the old women of the place where they are supposed to have appeared."

"As far as these notions prepare us for the awe which the poet designs to excite, I agree with you that he is right in availing himself of them; but, for this purpose, every thing familiar and common should be carefully avoided. In nothing has Shakspeare been more successful than in this; and in another case somewhat more difficult—that of selecting circumstances of manners and appearance for his supernatural beings, which, though wild and remote, in the highest degree, from common apprehension, never shock the understanding by incompatibility with themselves— never compel us, for an instant, to recollect that he has a licence for extravagance. Above every ideal being is the ghost of Hamlet, with all its attendant incidents of time and place. The dark watch upon the remote platform, the dreary aspect of the night, the very expression of the officer on guard, 'the air bites shrewdly; it is very cold';[4] the recollection of a star, an unknown world, are all circumstances which excite forlorn, melancholy, and solemn feelings, and dispose us to welcome, with trembling curiosity, the awful being that draws near; and to indulge in that strange mixture of horror, pity,

---

[1] Replacing Shakespeare's three witches with a whole coven was common in contemporary productions.

[2] the belief in witchcraft, which resulted in the persecution and judicial murder of many innocent people, most of them women. The last execution in England for witchcraft was in 1684; the last conviction was in 1712.

[3] the actor Sarah Siddons (1755–1831), whose performance of the role of Lady Macbeth was legendary.

[4] Shakespeare, *Hamlet* 1.4.1; the speaker is actually Hamlet himself.

and indignation, produced by the tale it reveals. Every minute circumstance of the scene between those watching on the platform, and of that between them and Horatio, preceding the entrance of the apparition, contributes to excite some feeling of dreariness, or melancholy, or solemnity, or expectation, in unison with, and leading on toward that high curiosity and thrilling awe with which we witness the conclusion of the scene. So the first question of Bernardo, and the words in reply, 'Stand and unfold yourself.'[1] But there is not a single circumstance in either dialogue, not even in this short one, with which the play opens, that does not take its secret effect upon the imagination...."

"Certainly you must be very superstitious," said Mr. S——, "or such things could not interest you thus."

"There are few people less so than I am," replied W——, "or I understand myself and the meaning of superstition very ill."

"That is quite paradoxical."

"It appears so, but so it is not. If I cannot explain this, take it as a mystery of the human mind."

"If it were possible for me to believe the appearance of ghosts at all," replied Mr. S——, "it would certainly be the ghost of Hamlet; but I never can suppose such things; they are out of all reason and probability."

"You would believe the immortality of the soul," said W——, with solemnity, "even without the aid of revelation; yet our confined faculties cannot comprehend *how* the soul may exist after separation from the body. I do not absolutely know that spirits are permitted to become visible to us on earth; yet that they may be permitted to appear for very rare and important purposes, such as could scarcely have been accomplished without an equal suspension, or a momentary change, of the laws prescribed to what we call NATURE—that is, without one more exercise of the same CREATIVE POWER of which we must acknowledge so many millions of existing instances, and by which alone we ourselves at this moment breathe, think, or disquisite at all, cannot be impossible, and, I think, is probable. Now, probability is enough for the poet's justification, the ghost being supposed to have come for an important purpose. Oh, I should never be weary of dwelling on the perfection of Shakspeare, in his management of every scene connected with that most solemn and mysterious being, which takes such entire possession of the imagination, that we hardly seem conscious we are beings of this world while we contemplate 'the extravagant and erring spirit.'...[2] There is, however, no little vexation in seeing the ghost of Hamlet *played*. The finest imagination is requisite to give the due colouring to such a character on the stage; and yet almost any actor is thought capable of performing it. In the scene where Horatio breaks his secret to Hamlet, Shakspeare, still true to the touch of circumstances, makes the time evening, and marks it by the very words of Hamlet, 'Good even, sir,' which Hanmer and Warburton changed, without any reason, to 'good morning,'[3] thus making Horatio relate his most interesting and solemn story by the clear light of the cheerfullest part of the day; when busy sounds are stirring, and the sun itself seems to contradict every doubtful tale, and lessen every feeling of terror. The discord of this must immediately be understood by those who have bowed the willing soul to the poet."

"How happens it then," said Mr. S——, "that objects of terror sometimes strike us very forcibly, when introduced into scenes of gaiety and splendour, as, for instance, in the Banquet scene in Macbeth?"[4]

"They strike, then, chiefly by the force of contrast," replied W——; "but the effect, though sudden and strong, is also transient; it is the thrill of horror and surprise, which they then communicate, rather than the deep and solemn feelings excited under more accordant circumstances, and left long upon the mind. Who ever suffered for the ghost of Banquo, the gloomy and

---

[1] Shakespeare, *Hamlet* 1.1.2.

[2] Shakespeare, *Hamlet* 1.1.169.

[3] The scene is Shakespeare, *Hamlet* 1.2: the quotation is from 1.2.167. Such eighteenth-century editors as Thomas Hanmer (*The Works of Mr. William Shakespeare*, 1743–44) and William Warburton (*The Works of Shakespear*, 1747) emended Shakespeare in accordance with contemporary taste.

[4] Shakespeare, *Macbeth* 3.4.

sublime kind of terror, which that of Hamlet calls forth? though the appearance of Banquo, at the high festival of Macbeth, not only tells us that he is murdered, but recalls to our minds the fate of the gracious Duncan, laid in silence and death by those who, in this very scene, are revelling in his spoils. There, though deep pity mingles with our surprise and horror, we experience a far less degree of interest, and that interest too of an inferior kind. The union of grandeur and obscurity, which Mr. Burke describes as a sort of tranquillity tinged with terror, and which causes the sublime,[1] is to be found only in Hamlet; or in scenes where circumstances of the same kind prevail."

"That may be," said Mr. S——, "and I perceive you are not one of those who contend that obscurity does not make any part of the sublime." "They must be men of very cold imaginations," said W——, "with whom certainty is more terrible than surmise. Terror and horror are so far opposite, that the first expands the soul, and awakens the faculties to a high degree of life; the other contracts, freezes, and nearly annihilates them. I apprehend, that neither Shakspeare not Milton by their fictions, nor Mr. Burke by his reasoning, anywhere looked to positive horror as a source of the sublime, though they all agree that terror is a very high one; and where lies the great difference between horror and terror, but in the uncertainty and obscurity that accompany the first, respecting the dreaded evil?"

"But what say you to Milton's image—
  'On his brow sat horror plumed.'"[2]

"As an image, it certainly is sublime; it fills the mind with an idea of power, but it does not follow that Milton intended to declare the feeling of horror to be sublime; and after all, his image imparts more of terror than of horror; for it is not distinctly pictured forth, but is seen in glimpses through obscuring shades, the great outlines only appearing which excite the imagination to complete the rest; he only says, 'sat horror plumed'; you will observe, that the look of horror and the other characteristics are left to the imagination of the reader; and according to the strength of that, he will feel Milton's image to be either sublime or otherwise. Milton, when he sketched it, probably felt, that not even his art could fill up the outline, and present to other eyes the countenance which his 'mind's eye' gave to him. Now, if obscurity has so much effect on fiction, what must it have in real life, when to ascertain the object of our terror, is frequently to acquire the means of escaping it. You will observe, that this image, though indistinct or obscure, is not confused."

"How can any thing be indistinct and not confused?" said Mr. S——.

"Ay, that question is from the new school," replied W.; "but recollect, that obscurity, or indistinctness, is only a negative, which leaves the imagination to act upon the few hints that truth reveals to it; confusion is a thing as positive as distinctness, though not necessarily so palpable; and it may, by mingling and confounding one image with another, absolutely counteract the imagination, instead of exciting it. Obscurity leaves something for the imagination to exaggerate; confusion, by blurring one image into another, leaves only a chaos in which the mind can find nothing to be magnificent, nothing to nourish its fears or doubts, or to act upon in any way; yet confusion and obscurity are terms used indiscriminately by those, who would prove, that Shakspeare and Milton were wrong when they employed obscurity as a cause of the sublime, that Mr. Burke was equally mistaken in his reasoning upon the subject, and that mankind have been equally in error, as to the nature of their own feelings, when they were acted upon by the illusions of those great masters of the imagination, at whose so potent bidding, the passions have been awakened from their sleep, and by whose magic a crowded Theatre has been changed to a lonely shore, to a witch's cave, to an enchanted island, to a murderer's castle, to the ramparts of an usurper, to the battle, to the midnight carousal of the camp or the tavern, to every various scene of the living world."…

---

[1] Edmund Burke,* *A Philosophical Enquiry into the Origin of Our Ideas Concerning the Sublime and Beautiful* (1757), especially 2: 3–5.

[2] Cf. Milton, *Paradise Lost* 4.988–89.

John Thelwall
1764 – 1834

John Thelwall was born on 27 July 1764 in London, the son of Joseph Thelwall, a silk mercer, who died when he was nine. He was taken out of school at fourteen to work in the family shop; later, he was apprenticed to a tailor, studied to be a priest, and was articled to a lawyer. Only a few months before he was to be called to the bar, he gave up the law and devoted himself to literature. He published his first book, *Poems on Various Subjects*, in 1787, and his first novel, *The Peripatetic; or, Sketches of the Heart, of Nature and Society*, in 1793. On 27 July 1791, he married Susan Vellum; they had four children. At about this time, he met the radical Horne Tooke and became the most famous radical speaker and journalist in London, active in the Society for Free Debate, the Friends of the People, and the London Corresponding Society. In May 1794, he was arrested along with Horne Tooke and other radical leaders and charged with high treason—a capital offense. They were acquitted, largely because of a cogent critique of the charge against them by Thelwall's friend Godwin.* Soon afterwards Godwin became alienated from him because of his political agitating, and government repression made it impossible for him to earn a living as a speaker and writer. He retired to a farm in Wales, stopping to introduce himself to Coleridge* and the Wordsworths* on the way. But the farm was a failure and he returned to London, this time as a teacher of oratory and speech therapist, curing stammerers by having them recite Milton and other classics. Susan died in 1816, and in 1819, Thelwall married Cecil Boyle; they had one more child. In his later years, Thelwall returned to political activism. He died in Bath on 17 February 1834, having lived long enough to see the passage of the First Reform Act. (D.L.M.)

⁂

from *Poems Written in Close Confinement at the Tower and Newgate, under a Charge of High Treason* (1795)[1]

Stanzas
On Hearing for Certainty That We Were to be Tried for High Treason

Short is perhaps our date of life,
    But let us while we live be gay—
To those be thought and anxious care
    Who build upon the distant day.

5 Tho' in our cup tyrannic Power
    Would dash the bitter dregs of fear,
We'll gaily quaff the mantling draught,
    While patriot toasts the fancy cheer.

Sings not the seaman, tempest-tost,
10   When surges wash the rivven shroud—
Scorning the threat'ning voice of Fate,
    That pipes in rocking winds aloud?

Yes;—he can take his cheerful glass,
    And toast his mistress[2] in the storm,
15 While duty and remember'd joys
    By turns his honest bosom warm.

And shall not we, in storms of state,
    At base Oppression's fury laugh,
And while the vital spirits flow,
20   To Freedom fill, and fearless quaff?

---

[1] The Tower of London was the main place of confinement for accused traitors; Newgate was London's main criminal prison.

[2] beloved; the word did not then suggest an improper sexual involvement.

Short is perhaps our date of life,
    But let us while we live be gay—
To those be thought and anxious care
    Who build upon the distant day.
                          Tower, Sept. 28, 1794

from *Poems Chiefly Written in Retirement* (1801)

To the Infant Hampden.—Written during a Sleepless Night. Derby. Oct. 1797 [1]

Sweet Babe! that, on thy mother's guardian breast,
Slumberest, unheedful of the autumnal blast
That rocks our lowly dwelling,[2] nor dost dream
Of woes, or cares, or persecuting rage,
5   Or rending passions, or the pangs that wait
On ill-requited services, sleep on;
Sleep, and be happy!—'Tis the sole relief
This anxious mind can hope, from the dire pangs
Of deep corroding wrong, that thou, my babe!
10 And the sweet twain—the firstlings of my love![3]
As yet are blest; and that my heart's best pride,
Who, with maternal fondness, pillows thee
Beside thy Life's warm fountain,[4] is not quite
Hopeless, or joyless; but, with matron cares,
15 And calm domestic Virtues, can avert

The melancholy fiend, and in your smiles
Read nameless consolations. Ah! sleep on—
As yet unconscious of The Patriot's name,
Or of a patriot's sorrows—of the cares
20 For which thy name-sire bled;[5] and, more unblest,
Thy natural father, in his native land,
Wanders an exile; and, of all that land,
Can find no spot his home. Ill-omen'd babe!
Conceiv'd in tempests, and in tempests born!
25 What destiny awaits thee?—Reckless thou.
Oh! blest inapprehension!——Let it last.
Sleep on, my Babe! now while the rocking wind
Pipes, mournful, lengthning my nocturnal plaint
With troubled symphony!—Ah! sleep secure:
30 And may thy dream of Life be ne'er disturb'd
With visions such as mar thy father's peace—
Visions (Ah! that they were but such indeed!)
That shew this world a wilderness of wrongs—
A waste of troubled waters: whelming floods
35 Of tyrannous injustice, canopy'd
With clouds dark louring; whence the pelting storms
Of cold unkindness the rough torrents swell,
On every side resistless. There my Ark—
The scanty remnant of my delug'd joys!
40 Floats anchorless; while thro' the dreary round,
Fluttering on anxious pinion, the tired foot
Of persecuted Virtue cannot find
One spray on which to rest; or scarce one leaf
To cheer with promise of subsiding woe.

---

[1] Cf. Coleridge, "Frost at Midnight."*

[2] a cottage in Derby.

[3] Thelwall's first two children, Algernon Sydney and Maria.

[4] Susan Thelwall nursed her children herself.

[5] Hampden is named after John Hampden (1594–1643), hero of the Parliamentary side in the Civil War, who was killed at the battle of Chalgrove Field.

Catherine Maria Fanshawe
1765 – 1834

Catherine Maria Fanshawe was born on 6 July 1765 in Shabden, Chipstead, Surrey, the second daughter of John Fanshawe, First Clerk of the Board of Green Cloth to George III, and of Penelope Dredge Fanshawe. She never married; after her father's death in 1816, she lived in London with her two sisters. All three were talented graphic artists, but only Catherine wrote poetry—which, however, she rarely published. They became friends with Baillie,* Grant,* Mitford,* and Scott.* "A Riddle," Fanshawe's most famous poem, was sometimes attributed to Byron* and even included in editions of his poetry. Disabled and "very delicate," Fanshawe often travelled to Italy for the sake of her health. She died on 17 April 1834. (D.L.M.)

from *A Collection of Poems, Chiefly Manuscript, and from Living Authors*, ed. Joanna Baillie (1823)

A Riddle

'Twas in heaven pronounced, and 'twas muttered in hell,
And echo caught faintly the sound as it fell:
On the confines of earth 'twas permitted to rest,
And the depths of the ocean its presence confest;
5 'Twill be found in the sphere when 'tis riven
    asunder,
Be seen in the lightning, and heard in the thunder.
'Twas allotted to man with his earliest breath,
Attends at his birth, and awaits him in death,
Presides o'er his happiness, honor, and health,
10 Is the prop of his house, and the end of his wealth.
In the heaps of the miser 'tis hoarded with care,
But is sure to be lost on his prodigal heir.
It begins every hope, every wish it must bound,
With the husbandman toils, and with monarchs is
    crown'd.
15 Without it the soldier, the seaman may roam,
But wo to the wretch who expels it from home!
In the whispers of conscience its voice will be
    found,
Nor e'en in the whirlwind of passion be drown'd.
'Twill not soften the heart; but though deaf be the ear,
20 It will make it acutely and instantly hear.
Yet in shade let it rest like a delicate flower,
Ah breathe on it softly—it dies in an hour.

Robert Bloomfield
1766 – 1823

Robert Bloomfield was born on 3 December 1766 in Honington, Suffolk, the sixth and youngest child of George Bloomfield, a tailor, and Elizabeth Manly Bloomfield, the village schoolmistress. His father died of smallpox before he was one, leaving his mother to support her family by spinning wool and teaching school. She taught Bloomfield herself, and, shortly before he turned seven, sent him to a tutor for a few months: this was his only formal education. At eleven, he went to work as a farmer's boy for his mother's brother-in-law. He enjoyed the work but was not strong enough for it, so in 1781, his brother George, a shoemaker, offered to teach him his trade, and the fourteen-year-old Bloomfield went to London. George was one of five shoemakers who worked together; since Bloomfield was the least skilled of them, he was initially asked to entertain the others by reading aloud, a task which greatly contributed to his education. By the mid-1780s he was a journeyman shoemaker; he also learned to make æolian harps and began submitting poems to the newspapers. In December 1790, he married Mary-Anne Church; they had four children. He began to write *The Farmer's Boy*, a season-by-season celebration of rural life, in 1796, composing it in his head as he worked. He finished it in 1798, but it was not until 1800 that, with the help of a wealthy barrister, Capel Lofft, he managed to publish it. It was a spectacular success, going through fourteen editions and selling twenty-six thousand copies in his lifetime, and being translated into French, Italian, and (in part) Latin. Soon Bloomfield was meeting Clare,* Crabbe,* George Dyer, Dr. Edward Jenner, Charles Lamb,* Samuel Rogers,* Southey,* and William Wordsworth,* while continuing to make shoes and wind-harps to support his growing family, and to write poetry. He published a book every few years, including *Good Tidings; or, News from the Farm* (1804), a poem in support of vaccination (then still a controversial procedure) inspired by the death of his father and the friendship of Jenner. His later years were plagued by financial troubles, ill health, failing eyesight, and depression, but he continued to write, publishing his last book of poetry, *May Day with the Muses*, in 1822, and *Hazelwood Hall: A Village Drama*, in 1823. He died on 19 August 1823. (D.L.M.)

☙☙☙

from *The Farmer's Boy; A Rural Poem* (1800)

from *Spring*

O come, blest Spirit! Whatsoe'er thou art,
Thou rushing warmth that hover'st round my heart,
Sweet inmate, hail! thou source of sterling joy,
That poverty itself cannot destroy,
5   Be thou my Muse; and faithful still to me,
Retrace the paths of wild obscurity.
No deeds of arms my humble lines rehearse,
No *Alpine* wonders thunder through my verse,
The roaring cataract, the snow-topt hill,
10 Inspiring awe, till breath itself stands still:
Nature's sublimer scenes ne'er charm'd mine eyes,
Nor Science led me through the boundless skies;
From meaner objects far my raptures flow:
O point these raptures! bid my bosom glow!
15 And lead my soul to ecstasies of praise
For all the blessings of my infant days!
Bear me through regions where gay Fancy dwells;
But mould to Truth's fair form what Memory tells.

Live, trifling incidents, and grace my song,
20 That to the humblest menial belong:
To him whose drudgery unheeded goes,
His joys unreckon'd as his cares or woes;
Though joys and cares in every path are sown,
And youthful minds have feelings of their own,
25 Quick springing sorrows, transient as the dew,
Delights from trifles, trifles ever new.
'Twas thus with GILES: meek, fatherless, and poor:
Labour his portion, but he felt no more;
No stripes, no tyranny his steps pursu'd;

30 His life was constant, cheerful, servitude:
　　Strange to the world, he wore a bashful look,
　　The fields his study, Nature was his book;
　　And, as revolving SEASONS chang'd the scene
　　From heat to cold, tempestuous to serene,
35 Though every change still varied his employ,
　　Yet each new duty brought its share of joy.

　　Where noble GRAFTON spreads his rich domains,[1]
　　Round *Euston's* water'd vale, and sloping plains,
　　Where woods and groves in solemn grandeur rise,
40 Where the kite[2] brooding unmolested flies;
　　The woodcock and the painted pheasant race,
　　And sculking foxes, destin'd for the chace;
　　There Giles, untaught and unrepining, stray'd
　　Thro' every copse, and grove, and winding glade;
45 There his first thoughts to Nature's charms inclin'd,
　　That stamps devotion on th' inquiring mind.
　　A little farm his generous Master till'd,
　　Who with peculiar grace his station fill'd;
　　By deeds of hospitality endear'd,
50 Serv'd from affection, for his worth rever'd;
　　A happy offspring blest his plenteous board,
　　His fields were fruitful, and his barns well stor'd,
　　And fourscore ewes he fed, a sturdy team,
　　And lowing kine that grazed beside the stream:
55 Unceasing industry he kept in view;
　　And never lack'd a job for Giles to do.

　　Fled now the sullen murmurs of the North,
　　The splendid raiment of the SPRING peeps forth;
　　Her universal green, and the clear sky,
60 Delight still more and more the gazing eye.
　　Wide o'er the fields, in rising moisture strong,
　　Shoots up the simple flower, or creeps along
　　The mellow'd soil; imbibing fairer hues
　　Or sweets from frequent showers and evening dews;
65 That summon from its shed the slumb'ring ploughs,
　　While health impregnates every breeze that blows.
　　No wheels support the diving pointed share;
　　No groaning ox is doom'd to labour there;
　　No helpmates teach the docile steed his road;
70 (Alike unknown the plow-boy and the goad;)
　　But, unassisted through each toilsome day,
　　With smiling brow the plowman cleaves his way,
　　Draws his fresh parallels, and wid'ning still,
　　Treads slow the heavy dale, or climbs the hill:
75 Strong on the wing his busy followers play,
　　Where writhing earth-worms meet th' unwelcome day;
　　Till all is chang'd, and hill and level down
　　Assume a livery of sober brown:
　　Again disturb'd, when Giles with wearying strides
80 From ridge to ridge the ponderous harrow guides;
　　His heels deep sinking every step he goes,
　　Till dirt usurp the empire of his shoes.
　　Welcome green headland! firm beneath his feet;
　　Welcome the friendly bank's refreshing seat;
85 There, warm with toil, his panting horses browse
　　Their shelt'ring canopy of pendent boughs;
　　Till rest, delicious, chase each transient pain,
　　And new-born vigour swell in every vein.
　　Hour after hour, and day to day succeeds;
90 Till every clod and deep-drawn furrow spreads
　　To crumbling mould; a level surface clear,
　　And strew'd with corn to crown the rising year;
　　And o'er the whole Giles once transverse again,
　　In earth's moist bosom buries up the grain.
95 The work is done; no more to man is given;
　　The grateful farmer trusts the rest to Heaven.
　　Yet oft with anxious heart he looks around,
　　And marks the first green blade that breaks the ground;
　　In fancy sees his trembling oats uprun,
100 His tufted barley yellow with the sun;
　　Sees clouds propitious shed their timely store,
　　And all his harvest gather'd round his door.
　　But still unsafe the big swoln grain below,
　　A fav'rite morsel with the Rook and Crow;
105 From field to field the flock increasing goes;
　　To level crops most formidable foes:
　　Their danger well the wary plunderers know,
　　And place a watch on some conspicuous bough;
　　Yet oft the sculking gunner by surprise
110 Will scatter death amongst them as they rise.
　　These, hung in triumph round the spacious field,

---

[1] Augustus Henry Fitzroy, 3rd Duke of Grafton (1735–1811), had his country seat at Euston Hall, Suffolk.

[2] a kind of hawk.

At best will but a short-lived terror yield:
Nor guards of property; (not penal law,
But harmless riflemen of rags and straw);
115 Familiariz'd to these, they boldly rove,
Nor heed such centinels that never move.
Let then your birds lie prostrate on the earth,
In dying posture, and with wings stretch'd forth;
Shift them at eve or morn from place to place,
120 And death shall terrify the pilfering race;
In the mid air, while circling round and round,
They call their lifeless comrades from the ground;
With quick'ning wing, and notes of loud alarm,
Warn the whole flock to shun the' impending harm.

125   This task had *Giles*, in fields remote from home:
Oft has he wish'd the rosy morn to come.
Yet never fam'd was he nor foremost found
To break the seal of sleep; his sleep was sound:
But when at day-break summon'd from his bed,
130 Light as the lark that carol'd o'er his head,
His sandy way deep-worn by hasty showers,
O'er-arch'd with oaks that form'd fantastic bow'rs,
Waving aloft their tow'ring branches proud,
In borrow'd tinges from the eastern cloud,
135 (Whence inspiration, pure as ever flow'd,
And genuine transport in his bosom glow'd)
His own shrill matin join'd the various notes
Of Nature's music, from a thousand throats:
The blackbird strove with emulation sweet,
140 And Echo answer'd from her close retreat;
The sporting white-throat on some twig's end borne,
Pour'd hymns to freedom and the rising morn;
Stopt in her song perchance the starting thrush
Shook a white shower from the black-thorn bush,
145 Where dew-drops thick as early blossoms hung,
And trembled as the minstrel sweetly sung.
Across his path, in either grove to hide,
The timid rabbit scouted by his side;
Or bold cock-pheasant stalk'd along the road,
150 Whose gold and purple tints alternate glow'd.
But groves no farther fenc'd the devious way;
A wide-extended heath before him lay,
Where on the grass the stagnant shower had run,
And shone a mirror to the rising sun,
155 (Thus doubly seen) lighting a distant wood,
Giving new life to each expanding bud;
Effacing quick the dewy foot-marks found,
Where prowling Reynard trod his nightly round;
To shun whose thefts 'twas Giles's evening care,
160 His feather'd victims to suspend in air,
High on the bough that nodded o'er his head,
And thus each morn to strew the field with dead.

    His simple errand done, he homeward hies;
Another instantly its place supplies.
165 The clatt'ring dairy-maid immers'd in steam,
Singing and scrubbing midst her milk and cream,
Bawls out, "*Go fetch the cows*: ..." he hears no more;
For pigs, and ducks, and turkies, throng the door,
And sitting hens, for constant war prepar'd;
170 A concert strange to that which late he heard.
Straight to the meadow then he whistling goes;
With well-known halloo calls his lazy cows:
Down the rich pasture heedlessly they graze,
Or hear the summon with an idle gaze;
175 For well they know the cow-yard yields no more
Its tempting fragrance, nor its wint'ry store.
Reluctance marks their steps, sedate and slow;
The right of conquest all the law they know:
Subordinate they one by one succeed;
180 And one among them always takes the lead,
Is ever foremost, wheresoe'er they stray;
Allow'd precedence, undisputed sway;
With jealous pride her station is maintain'd,
For many a broil that post of honour gain'd.
185 At home, the yard affords a grateful scene;
For Spring makes e'en a miry cow-yard clean.
Thence from its chalky bed behold convey'd
The rich manure that drenching winter made,
Which pil'd near home, grows green with many a weed,
190 A promis'd nutriment for Autumn's seed.
Forth comes the Maid, and like the morning smiles;
The Mistress too, and follow'd close by Giles.
A friendly tripod forms their humble seat,
With pails bright scour'd, and delicately sweet.
195 Where shadowing elms obstruct the morning ray,
Begins their work, begins the simple lay;
The full-charg'd udder yields its willing streams,

    While *Mary* sings some lover's amorous dreams;
    And crouching *Giles* beneath a neighbouring tree
200 Tugs o'er his pail, and chants with equal glee;
    Whose hat with tatter'd brim, of nap so bare,
    From the cow's side purloins a coat of hair,
    A mottled ensign of his harmless trade,
    An unambitious, peaceable cockade.[1]
205 As unambitious too that cheerful aid
    The mistress yields beside her rosy maid;
    With joy she views her plenteous reeking store,
    And bears a brimmer to the dairy door;
    Her cows dismiss'd, the luscious mead to roam,
210 Till eve again recall them loaded home.
    And now the DAIRY claims her choicest care,
    And half her household find employment there:
    Slow rolls the churn, its load of clogging cream
    At once foregoes its quality and name;
215 From knotty particles first floating wide
    Congealing butter's dash'd from side to side;
    Streams of new milk thro' flowing coolers stray,
    And snow-white curd abounds, and wholesome whey.
    Due north th' unglazed windows, cold and clear,
220 For warming sunbeams are unwelcome here.
    Brisk goes the work beneath each busy hand,
    And *Giles* must trudge, whoever gives command;
    A *Gibeonite*, that serves them all by turns:[2]
    He drains the pump, from him the faggot burns;
225 From him the noisy hogs demand their food;
    While at his heels run many a chirping brood,
    Or down his path in expectation stand,
    With equal claims upon his strewing hand.
    Thus wastes the morn, till each with pleasure sees
230 The bustle o'er, and press'd the new-made cheese.[3]

...

    Down, indignation! hence, ideas foul!
360 Away the shocking image from my soul!
    Let kindlier visitants attend my way,
    Beneath approaching *Summer's* fervid ray;
    Nor thankless glooms obtrude, nor cares annoy,
    Whilst the sweet theme is *universal joy*.

---

[1] a rosette or other ornament worn on the hat, often as a sign of party allegiance. (Bloomfield may be thinking of the tricolour rosettes worn by the French Revolutionaries.)

[2] Joshua and the Israelites enslaved the inhabitants of Gibeon, a city northwest of Jerusalem: see Joshua 9.

[3] The rest of "Spring" describes Suffolk cheese, spring flowers, Giles's duties as a shepherd, the antics of the spring lambs—and their fate at the hands of the butcher.

Thomas Robert Malthus
1766 – 1834

Thomas Robert Malthus was born on 13 February 1766 in Dorking, Surrey, the sixth child of Daniel and Henrietta Graham Malthus. His father, an admirer of Rousseau, sent him to a boarding school at Claverton run by the clergyman and writer Richard Graves. Later, he studied with the Unitarian Gilbert Wakefield at the Dissenting Academy at Warrington. After this schooling, unusual for a non-dissenter, Malthus attended Jesus College, Cambridge, where his tutor was William Frend, one of the Cambridge Unitarians. Opposed to the Thirty-Nine Articles, which defined the religious orthodoxy of the Church of England, Frend resigned in 1787. Malthus avoided the surrounding controversy, graduating with high honours in mathematics in 1788; he went on to become a clergyman in the Church of England, working as a rural curate in Surrey.

*An Essay on the Principle of Population** was published anonymously in 1798, attacking theories of "the perfectibility of man and society" promulgated by Godwin and Condorcet; a second, much expanded, edition of his *Essay* appeared in 1803. Attacks and rebuttals followed, by such writers as Hazlitt* (*Reply to the Essay on Population*, 1807), Southey,* Godwin* (*On Population*, 1820, answered by Malthus in 1821) and De Quincey,* all of whom advocated for reform and feared the effect of Malthus's conservatism.

In 1803, he became rector of the church at Walesby, Lincolnshire, and married Harriet Eckersall. Two years later he was appointed professor at the East India College, Haileybury, newly founded for training civil servants. He continued to write widely on economics, arguing in his *Letter to Samuel Whitbread* (1807) that building cottages for poor families would encourage early marriages, large families, and lower wages for workers perceived to have the advantage of free housing. Malthus worked within the laissez-faire tradition of Adam Smith; his three pamphlets on the Corn Laws (1814, 1815) qualify this position by supporting the need for protective legislation and tariffs on imported grain to support agriculture when prices drop below a certain level.

Malthus's *Principles of Political Economy* (1820) argued (against David Ricardo) that economics was moral, political, and empirical, and should not be based on purely abstract ideas. In debating amendments to the Poor Laws in 1834, proponents of restrictions on relief invoked Malthus as their champion; opponents called him callous and unfeeling. He died on 29 December 1834 and is buried in Bath Abbey. (A.M.)

from *An Essay on the Principle of Population, as It Affects the Future Improvement of Society. With Remarks on the Speculations of Mr. Godwin, M. Condorcet, and Other Writers* (1798)[1]

from CHAPTER 10

Mr. Godwin's system of equality.—Error of attributing all the vices of mankind to human institutions.—Mr. Godwin's first answer to the difficulty arising from population totally insufficient.—Mr. Godwin's beautiful system of equality supposed to be realized.—It's utter destruction simply from the principle of population in so short a time as thirty years.

Mr. Godwin, at the conclusion of the third chapter of his eighth book, speaking of population, says, "There is a principle in human society, by which population is perpetually kept down to the level of the means of subsistence. Thus among the wandering tribes of America and Asia, we never find through the lapse of ages that population has so increased as to render necessary the cultivation of the earth."[2] This principle, which Mr. Godwin thus mentions as some mysterious and occult cause, and which he does not attempt to investigate, will be found to be the grinding law of necessity; misery, and the fear of misery.

The great error under which Mr. Godwin labours throughout his whole work, is, the attributing almost all the vices and misery that are seen in civil society to human institutions. Political regulations, and the established administration of property, are with him the fruitful sources of all evil, the hotbeds of all the crimes that degrade mankind. Were this really a true state of the case, it would not seem a hopeless task to remove evil completely from the world; and reason seems to be the proper and adequate instrument for effecting so great a purpose. But the truth is, that though human institutions appear to be the obvious and obtrusive causes of much mischief to mankind; yet, in reality, they are light and superficial, they are mere feathers that float on the surface, in comparison with those deeper seated causes of impurity that corrupt the springs, and render turbid the whole stream of human life....

Man cannot live in the midst of plenty. All cannot share alike the bounties of nature. Were there no established administration of property, every man would be obliged to guard with force his little store. Selfishness would be triumphant. The subjects of contention would be perpetual. Every individual mind would be under a constant anxiety about corporal support; and not a single intellect would be left free to expatiate in the field of thought.

How little Mr. Godwin has turned the attention of his penetrating mind to the real state of man on earth, will sufficiently appear from the manner in which he endeavours to remove the difficulty of an overcharged population. He says, "The obvious answer to this objection, is, that to reason thus is to foresee difficulties at a great distance. Three fourths of the habitable globe is now uncultivated. The parts already cultivated are capable of immeasurable improvement. Myriads of centuries of still increasing population may pass away, and the earth be still found sufficient for the subsistence of its inhabitants."[3]

I have already pointed out the error of supposing that no distress and difficulty would arise from an overcharged population before the earth absolutely refused to produce any more. But let us imagine for a moment Mr. Godwin's beautiful system of equality realized in its utmost purity, and see how soon this difficulty might be expected to press under so perfect a form of society. A theory that will not admit of application cannot possibly be just.

Let us suppose all the causes of misery and vice in this island removed. War and contention cease. Unwholesome trades and manufactures do not exist.

---

[1] Malthus argues against the views expressed in such works as William Godwin, *Political Justice** and Jean Antoine Nicolas Caritat, marquis de Condorcet, *Sketch for a Historical Picture of the Progress of the Human Mind* (1794). This selection from Malthus focuses in particular on Book 8 of Political Justice, "Of Property."

[2] *Political Justice*, Book 8, chap. 3, "Benefits Attendant on a System of Equality," 3rd ed. (1798), 2: 466–67.

[3] *Political Justice*, Book 8, chap. 9, "Objection to this System from the Principle of Population," 3rd ed. (1798), 2: 518.

Crowds no longer collect together in great and pestilent cities for purposes of court intrigue, of commerce, and vicious gratifications. Simple, healthy, and rational amusements take place of drinking, gaming and debauchery. There are no towns sufficiently large to have any prejudicial effects on the human constitution. The greater part of the happy inhabitants of this terrestrial paradise live in hamlets and farm-houses scattered over the face of the country. Every house is clean, airy, sufficiently roomy, and in a healthy situation. All men are equal. The labours of luxury are at end. And the necessary labours of agriculture are shared amicably among all. The number of persons, and the produce of the island, we suppose to be the same as at present. The spirit of benevolence, guided by impartial justice, will divide this produce among all the members of the society according to their wants. Though it would be impossible that they should all have animal food every day, yet vegetable food, with meat occasionally, would satisfy the desires of a frugal people, and would be sufficient to preserve them in health, strength, and spirits.

Mr. Godwin considers marriage as a fraud and a monopoly. Let us suppose the commerce of the sexes established upon principles of the most perfect freedom. Mr. Godwin does not think himself that this freedom would lead to a promiscuous intercourse; and in this I perfectly agree with him. The love of variety is a vicious, corrupt, and unnatural taste, and could not prevail in any great degree in a simple and virtuous state of society. Each man would probably select himself a partner, to whom he would adhere as long as that adherence continued to be the choice of both parties. It would be of little consequence, according to Mr. Godwin, how many children a woman had, or to whom they belonged. Provisions and assistance would spontaneously flow from the quarter in which they abounded, to the quarter that was deficient.[1] And every man would be ready to furnish instruction to the rising generation according to his capacity.

I cannot conceive a form of society so favourable upon the whole to population. The irremediableness of marriage, as it is at present constituted, undoubtedly deters many from entering into that state. An unshackled intercourse on the contrary, would be a most powerful incitement to early attachments: and as we are supposing no anxiety about the future support of children to exist, I do not conceive that there would be one woman in a hundred, of twenty three, without a family.

With these extraordinary encouragements to population, and every cause of depopulation, as we have supposed, removed, the numbers would necessarily increase faster than in any society that has ever yet been known. I have mentioned, on the authority of a pamphlet published by a Dr. Styles, and referred to by Dr. Price,[2] that the inhabitants of the back settlements of America doubled their numbers in fifteen years. England is certainly a more healthy country than the back settlements of America; and as we have supposed every house in the island to be airy and wholesome, and the encouragements to have a family greater even than with the back settlers, no probable reason can be assigned, why the population should not double itself in less, if possible, than fifteen years. But to be quite sure that we do not go beyond the truth, we will only suppose the period of doubling to be twenty-five years, a ratio of increase, which is well known to have taken place throughout all the Northern States of America.

There can be little doubt, that the equalization of property which we have supposed, added to the circumstance of the labour of the whole community being directed chiefly to agriculture, would tend greatly to augment the produce of the country. But to answer the demands of a population increasing so rapidly, Mr. Godwin's calculation of half an hour a day for each man, would certainly not be sufficient. It is probable that the half of every man's time must be employed for this purpose. Yet with such, or much greater exertions, a person who is acquainted with the nature of the soil in this country, and who reflects on the fertility of the lands already in cultivation, and the barrenness of those

---

[1] "See B. 8. Chap. 8. P. 504." (T.M.) *Political Justice*, Book 8, Appendix to chap. 8, "Of Cooperation, Cohabitation, and Marriage," 3rd ed. (1798), 2: 512.

[2] See the postscript to Richard Price,* *Observations on Reversionary Payment* (1780).

that are not cultivated, will be very much disposed to doubt, whether the whole average produce could possibly be doubled in twenty-five years from the present period. The only chance of success would be the ploughing up all the grazing countries, and putting an end almost entirely to the use of animal food. Yet a part of this scheme might defeat itself. The soil of England will not produce much without dressing; and cattle seem to be necessary to make that species of manure, which best suits the land. In China, it is said, that the soil in some of the provinces is so fertile, as to produce two crops of rice in the year without dressing. None of the lands in England will answer to this description.

Difficult, however, as it might be, to double the average produce of the island in twenty-five years, let us suppose it effected. At the expiration of the first period therefore, the food, though almost entirely vegetable, would be sufficient to support in health, the doubled population of fourteen millions.

During the next period of doubling, where will the food be found to satisfy the importunate demands of the increasing numbers? Where is the fresh land to turn up? where is the dressing necessary to improve that which is already in cultivation? There is no person with the smallest knowledge of land, but would say, that it was impossible that the average produce of the country could be increased during the second twenty-five years by a quantity equal to what it at present yields. Yet we will suppose this increase, however improbable, to take place. The exuberant strength of the argument allows of almost any concession. Even with this concession, however, there would be seven millions at the expiration of the second term, unprovided for. A quantity of food equal to the frugal support of twenty-one millions, would be to be divided among twenty-eight millions.

Alas! what becomes of the picture where men lived in the midst of plenty: where no man was obliged to provide with anxiety and pain for his restless wants: where the narrow principle of selfishness did not exist: where Mind was delivered from her perpetual anxiety about corporal support, and free to expatiate in the field of thought which is congenial to her. This beautiful fabric of imagination vanishes at the severe touch of truth. The spirit of benevolence, cherished and invigorated by plenty, is repressed by the chilling breath of want. The hateful passions that had vanished, reappear. The mighty law of self-preservation, expels all the softer and more exalted emotions of the soul. The temptations to evil are too strong for human nature to resist. The corn is plucked before it is ripe, or secreted in unfair proportions; and the whole black train of vices that belong to falsehood are immediately generated. Provisions no longer flow in for the support of the mother with a large family. The children are sickly from insufficient food. The rosy flush of health gives place to the pallid cheek and hollow eye of misery. Benevolence yet lingering in a few bosoms, makes some faint expiring struggles, till at length self-love resumes his wonted empire, and lords it triumphant over the world....

If we are not yet too well convinced of the reality of this melancholy picture, let us but look for a moment into the next period of twenty-five years; and we shall see twenty-eight millions of human beings without the means of support; and before the conclusion of the first century, the population would be one hundred and twelve millions, and the food only sufficient for thirty-five millions, leaving seventy-seven millions unprovided for. In these ages want would be indeed triumphant, and rapine and murder must reign at large: and yet all this time we are supposing the produce of the earth absolutely unlimited, and the yearly increase greater than the boldest speculator can imagine.

This is undoubtedly a very different view of the difficulty arising from population, from that which Mr. Godwin gives, when he says, "Myriads of centuries of still increasing population may pass away, and the earth be still found sufficient for the subsistence of its inhabitants."[1]...

It might be urged perhaps by some objectors, that, as the fertility of the land increased, and various accidents occurred, the share of some men might be much more than sufficient for their support, and that when the reign of self-love was once established, they would not distribute their surplus produce without some compensation in return. It would be observed, in

---

[1] *Political Justice*, Book 8, chap. 9, "Objection to this System from the Principle of Population," 2: 518.

answer, that this was an inconvenience greatly to be lamented; but that it was an evil which bore no comparison to the black train of distresses, that would inevitably be occasioned by the insecurity of property: that the quantity of food which one man could consume, was necessarily limited by the narrow capacity of the human stomach: that it was not certainly probable that he should throw away the rest; but that even if he exchanged his surplus food for the labour of others, and made them in some degree dependent on him, this would still be better than that these others should absolutely starve.

It seems highly probable, therefore, that an administration of property, not very different from that which prevails in civilized States at present, would be established, as the best, though inadequate, remedy, for the evils which were pressing on the society.

The next subject that would come under discussion, intimately connected with the preceding, is, the commerce between the sexes. It would be urged by those who had turned their attention to the true cause of the difficulties under which the community laboured, that while every man felt secure that all his children would be well provided for by general benevolence, the powers of the earth would be absolutely inadequate to produce food for the population which would inevitably ensue: that even, if the whole attention and labour of the society were directed to this sole point, and if, by the most perfect security of property, and every other encouragement that could be thought of, the greatest possible increase of produce were yearly obtained; yet still, that the increase of food would by no means keep pace with the much more rapid increase of population: that some check to population therefore was imperiously called for: that the most natural and obvious check seemed to be, to make every man provide for his own children: that this would operate in some respect, as a measure and guide, in the increase of population; as it might be expected that no man would bring beings into the world, for whom he could not find the means of support: that where this notwithstanding was the case, it seemed necessary, for the example of others, that the disgrace and inconvenience attending such a conduct, should fall upon that individual, who had thus inconsiderately plunged himself and innocent children in misery and want.

The institution of marriage, or at least, of some express or implied obligation on every man to support his own children, seems to be the natural result of these reasonings in a community under the difficulties that we have supposed.

The view of these difficulties, presents us with a very natural origin of the superior disgrace which attends a breach of chastity in the woman, than in the man. It could not be expected that women should have resources sufficient to support their own children. When therefore a woman was connected with a man, who had entered into no compact to maintain her children; and aware of the inconveniences that he might bring upon himself, had deserted her, these children must necessarily fall for support upon the society, or starve. And to prevent the frequent recurrence of such an inconvenience, as it would be highly unjust to punish so natural a fault by personal restraint or infliction, the men might agree to punish it with disgrace. The offence is besides more obvious and conspicuous in the woman, and less liable to any mistake. The father of a child may not always be known, but the same uncertainty cannot easily exist with regard to the mother. Where the evidence of the offence was most complete, and the inconvenience to the society at the same time the greatest, there, it was agreed, that the largest share of blame should fall. The obligation on every man to maintain his children, the society would enforce, if there were occasion; and the greater degree of inconvenience or labour, to which a family would necessarily subject him, added to some portion of disgrace which every human being must incur, who leads another into unhappiness, might be considered as a sufficient punishment for the man.

That a woman should at present be almost driven from society, for an offence, which men commit nearly with impunity, seems to be undoubtedly a breach of natural justice. But the origin of the custom, as the most obvious and effectual method of preventing the frequent recurrence of a serious inconvenience to a community, appears to be natural, though not perhaps perfectly justifiable. This origin, however, is now lost in the new train of ideas which the custom has since generated.

What at first might be dictated by state necessity, is now supported by female delicacy; and operates with the greatest force on that part of society, where, if the original intention of the custom were preserved, there is the least real occasion for it.

When these two fundamental laws of society, the security of property, and the institution of marriage, were once established, inequality of conditions must necessarily follow. Those who were born after the division of property, would come into a world already possessed. If their parents, from having too large a family, could not give them sufficient for their support, what are they to do in a world where every thing is appropriated? We have seen the fatal effects that would result to a society, if every man had a valid claim to an equal share of the produce of the earth. The members of a family which was grown too large for the original division of land appropriated to it, could not then demand a part of the surplus produce of others, as a debt of justice. It has appeared, that from the inevitable laws of our nature, some human beings must suffer from want. These are the unhappy persons who, in the great lottery of life, have drawn a blank. The number of these claimants would soon exceed the ability of the surplus produce to supply. Moral merit is a very difficult distinguishing criterion, except in extreme cases. The owners of surplus produce would in general seek some more obvious mark of distinction. And it seems both natural and just, that except upon particular occasions, their choice should fall upon those, who were able, and professed themselves willing, to exert their strength in procuring a further surplus produce; and thus at once benefiting the community, and enabling these proprietors to afford assistance to greater numbers. All who were in want of food would be urged by imperious necessity to offer their labour in exchange for this article so absolutely essential to existence. The fund appropriated to the maintenance of labour, would be, the aggregate quantity of food possessed by the owners of land beyond their own consumption. When the demands upon this fund were great and numerous, it would naturally be divided in very small shares. Labour would be ill paid. Men would offer to work for a bare subsistence, and the rearing of families would be checked by sickness and misery. On the contrary, when this fund was increasing fast; when it was great in proportion to the number of claimants; it would be divided in much larger shares. No man would exchange his labour without receiving an ample quantity of food in return. Labourers would live in ease and comfort; and would consequently be able to rear a numerous and vigorous offspring.

On the state of this fund, the happiness, or the degree of misery, prevailing among the lower classes of people in every known State, at present chiefly depends. And on this happiness, or degree of misery, depends the increase, stationariness, or decrease of population....

Carolina Oliphant, Lady Nairne
1766 – 1845

Carolina Oliphant was born in Gask, Perthshire, Scotland on 16 August 1766, one of the six children of Laurence Oliphant, a leading Jacobite (or defender of the Scottish royal family descended from the Stuarts), and Margaret Robertson Oliphant. Her father believed in equal education for women, so she was educated along with her brothers. Both her father and her grandfather had had to leave Scotland after the battle of Culloden, returning only in 1763; following this exile her father's health was poor, and Carolina tried to entertain him by writing Jacobite words for traditional tunes. She admired Burns's* work in Johnson's *Musical Museum* and Thomson's *Songs of Scotland*; in 1786 she persuaded her brother Laurence to subscribe to Burns's poems.

In 1806, she married her cousin William Murray Nairne; they lived in Edinburgh until his death in 1830. There, following Burns's example, Nairne collected traditional melodies for which she wrote appropriate words. Without telling even her husband about her project, Nairne published her work anonymously, or under the pseudonym Mrs. Bogan of Bogan. She contributed to Robert Purdie's *The Scottish Minstrel*, published in Edinburgh in six volumes, 1821–24, with music edited by R.A. Smith. Some of her nearly one hundred songs and poems illustrate the characters and manners of the Scottish gentry (such as "The Laird o' Cockpen,"* written for a melody or "air" with original lyrics too crude for polite society). Others were Jacobite songs, including the well known "Charlie is my darling," "He's owre the Hills," and "Will ye no come back again?" Some of her songs were mistakenly attributed to Burns, Hogg,* or Sir Walter Scott.*

In 1824, following George IV's visit to Edinburgh in 1822 and Scott's petitioning, Parliament restored the forfeited Jacobite peerages; Carolina Nairne and her husband became Baron and Baroness Nairne. After her husband's death, Lady Nairne and her ailing son travelled, living in Bristol, in Ireland, and on the Continent. Her son died in Brussels in 1837, and Nairne's relatives persuaded her to return to Scotland in 1845. Back home in Gask, she died on 26 October 1845. In 1846 her sister published a posthumous collection of verse, *Lays of Strathearn*, with Lady Nairne's name on the title-page. (A.M.)

☙☙☙

from *The Scottish Minstrel* (1821–24)

The Land o' the Leal[1]

AIR–"HEY TUTTI TAITI."[2]

I'm wearin' awa', John,
Like snaw-wreaths in thaw, John,
I'm wearin' awa'
   To the land o' the leal.
5 There's nae sorrow there, John,
There's neither cauld nor care, John,
The day is aye fair
   In the land o' the leal.

Our bonnie bairn's there, John,
10 She was baith gude and fair, John,
And oh! we grudged her sair
   To the land o' the leal.
But sorrow's sel' wears past, John,
And joy's a-comin' fast, John,
15 The joy that's aye to last
   In the land o' the leal.

Sae dear's that joy was bought, John,
Sae free the battle fought, John,
That sinfu' man e'er brought
20   To the land o' the leal.
Oh! dry your glist'ning e'e, John,
My saul langs to be free, John,
And angels beckon me
   To the land o' the leal.

---

[1] "loyal" (Sc.)

[2] also the tune of Burns,* "Hey Tuti Tatey, or Landlady Count the Lawin" (1788).

25 Oh! haud ye leal and true, John,
Your day it's wearin' through, John,
And I'll welcome you
    To the land o' the leal.
Now fare-ye-weel, my ain John,
30 This warld's cares are vain, John,
We'll meet, and we'll be fain,
    In the land o' the leal.

Caller Herrin'[1]

AIR BY NEIL GOW.[2]

Wha'll buy my caller herrin'?
They're bonnie fish and halesome farin';[3]
Wha'll buy my caller herrin',
    New drawn frae the Forth?[4]

5 When ye were sleepin' on your pillows,
Dream'd ye aught o' our puir fellows,
Darkling as they faced the billows,
A' to fill the woven willows?

    Buy my caller herrin',
10   New drawn frae the Forth.

Wha'll buy my caller herrin'?
They're no brought here without brave daring;
Buy my caller herrin',
Haul'd through wind and rain.

15   Wha'll buy my caller herrin'? &c.

Wha'll buy my caller herrin'?
Oh, ye may ca' them vulgar farin',
Wives and mithers maist despairing,
Ca' them lives o' men.

20   Wha'll buy my caller herrin'? &c.

When the creel[5] o' herrin' passes,
Ladies, clad in silks and laces,
Gather in their braw pelisses,[6]
Cast their heads and screw their faces.

25   Wha'll buy my caller herrin'? &c.

Caller herrin's no got lightlie,
Ye can trip the spring fu' tightlie,
Spite o' tauntin', flauntin', flingin',
Gow has set you a' a-singin'.

30   Wha'll buy my caller herrin'? &c.

Neebour wives, now tent[7] my tellin':
When the bonny fish ye're sellin',
At ae word be in yere dealin'—
Truth will stand when a' thing's failin'.

35   Wha'll buy my caller herrin'?
They're bonnie fish and halesome farin';
Wha'll buy my caller herrin',
    New drawn frae the Forth?

The Laird o' Cockpen

AIR—"WHEN SHE CAM' BEN, SHE BOBBIT."[8]

The laird o' Cockpen, he's proud an' he's great,
His mind is ta'en up wi' things o' the State;
He wanted a wife, his braw house to keep,
But favour wi' wooin' was fashious[9] to seek.

---

[1] "freshly caught herring."

[2] a famous Scottish fiddler and composer (1727–1807).

[3] "wholesome food."

[4] the Firth of Forth, a river estuary in south-east Scotland.

[5] "basket."

[6] "beautiful mantles."

[7] "heed."

[8] the title of a poem by Burns (1792): "When she came through, she curtsied."

[9] "troublesome."

Carolina Oliphant, Lady Nairne

5 Down by the dyke-side a lady did dwell,
   At his table head he thought she'd look well,
   McClish's ae daughter o' Clavers-ha' Lee,
   A penniless lass wi' a lang pedigree.

   His wig was weel pouther'd[1] and as gude as new,
10 His waistcoat was white, his coat it was blue;
   He put on a ring, a sword, and cock'd hat,
   And wha could refuse the laird wi' a' that?

   He took the grey mare, and rade cannily,
   An' rapp'd at the yett[2] o' Clavers-ha' Lee;
15 "Gae tell Mistress Jean to come speedily ben,—
   She's wanted to speak to the Laird o' Cockpen."

   Mistress Jean was makin' the elder-flower wine;
   "An' what brings the laird at sic[3] a like time?"
   She put aff her apron, and on her silk gown,
20 Her mutch[4] wi' red ribbons, and gaed awa' down.

   An' when she cam' ben[5] he bowed fu' low,
   An' what was his errand he soon let her know;
   Amazed was the laird when the lady said "Na,"
   And wi' a laigh[6] curtsie she turned awa'.

25 Dumfounder'd was he, nae sigh did he gie,
   He mounted his mare—he rade cannily;
   An' aften he thought, as he gaed through the glen,
   She's daft to refuse the laird o' Cockpen.

   And now that the laird his exit had made,
30 Mistress Jean she reflected on what she had said;
   "Oh, for ane I'll get better, its waur[7] I'll get ten,
   I was daft to refuse the Laird o' Cockpen."

   Next time that the laird and the lady were seen,
   They were gaun arm-in-arm to the kirk on the green;
35 Now she sits in the ha' like a weel-tappit[8] hen,
   But as yet there's nae chickens appear'd at Cockpen.

---

[1] "powdered."

[2] "gate."

[3] "such."

[4] "close-fitting cap."

[5] "through."

[6] "low."

[7] "worse."

[8] "well-tufted."

Maria Edgeworth
1768 – 1849

The third child of Richard Lovell Edgeworth and Anna Maria Elers Edgeworth, Maria Edgeworth was born on 1 January 1768 in Black Bourton, Oxfordshire. Her parents had an unhappy marriage, and her mother died when Maria was five: only four months later, her father married Honora Sneyd, a friend of Anna Seward.* Honora considered Maria a difficult child, and in 1775 she was sent to a boarding school in Derby; she did not see her family for three years. Richard Edgeworth's friend Thomas Day took an interest in Maria and assisted with her education. In 1780, she was sent to another school in London and, in 1782, she moved to Edgeworthston, her father's Irish estate.

Following Honora Sneyd's death in 1780, Richard Edgeworth married her sister Elizabeth: Maria may well have felt neglected. Her desire to gain her father's approval is often considered the driving force behind her aspirations; her children's stories, which she began to write in 1791, followed her father's educational theory, which proposed that children should have literature suited to their ages. *The Parent's Assistant; or, Stories for Children* appeared in 1796. Edgeworth tested many of the stories in this and subsequent collections on her stepbrothers and stepsisters. In 1798, she and her father published *Practical Education*, a collection of essays and tales. The same year, Elizabeth died and Richard married Frances Anna Beaufort. A year older than her new stepmother, Maria was not pleased. Nevertheless, Maria and "Fanny" became close friends.

Edgeworth's first and most successful novel, *Castle Rackrent*, appeared anonymously—and, unusually, without her father's approval—in 1800. Her other fiction for adults included *Belinda* (1801), *Tales of Fashionable Life* (1809–12), and *Patronage* (1814). She also continued to write for children: *Moral Tales for Young People* appeared in 1801, and *Popular Tales* in 1804. Edgeworth's father took the family on visits to England and the Continent: Edgeworth became a literary celebrity in London, where she met Byron,* who admired her but was not impressed by her father. She also befriended Joanna Baillie* and Sydney Smith.

Richard Edgeworth died on 13 June 1817, and thereafter, with the exception of her final novel *Helen: A Tale* (1834) and stories for children, Maria found it difficult to write. She often turned to Sir Walter Scott,* one of her few rivals as a popular writer, for literary guidance. She influenced many writers, including Austen,* Cooper,* and later, William Butler Yeats (1865–1939). On 22 May 1849, at the age of eighty-one, Edgeworth died in the arms of her stepmother, Fanny, in their home in Edgeworthston. (J.G.)

❦

from *Popular Tales in Two Volumes* (1804)[1]

The Grateful Negro

In the island of Jamaica there lived two planters, whose methods of managing their slaves were as different as possible. Mr. Jefferies considered the negroes as an inferior species, incapable of gratitude, disposed to treachery, and to be roused from their natural indolence only by force; he treated his slaves, or rather suffered his overseer to treat them, with the greatest severity.

Jefferies was not a man of a cruel, but of a thoughtless and extravagant temper. He was of such a sanguine disposition, that he always calculated upon having a fine season, and fine crops on his plantation; and never had the prudence to make allowance for unfortunate accidents: he required, as he said, from his overseer produce and not excuses.

---

[1] Our text is from the 1832 edition.

Durant, the overseer, did not scruple to use the most[1] cruel and barbarous methods of forcing the slaves to exertions beyond their strength. Complaints of his brutality, from time to time, reached his master's ears; but though Mr. Jefferies was moved to momentary compassion, he shut his heart against conviction: he hurried away to the jovial banquet, and drowned all painful reflections in wine.

He was this year much in debt; and, therefore, being more than usually anxious about his crop, he pressed his overseer to exert himself to the utmost.

The wretched slaves upon his plantation thought themselves still more unfortunate when they compared their condition with that of the negroes on the estate of Mr. Edwards. This gentleman treated his slaves with all possible humanity and kindness. He wished that there was no such thing as slavery in the world; but he was convinced, by the arguments of those who have the best means of obtaining information, that the sudden emancipation of the negroes would rather increase than diminish their miseries. His benevolence, therefore, confined itself within the bounds of reason. He adopted those plans for the amelioration of the state of the slaves which appeared to him the most likely to succeed without producing any violent agitation or revolution.[2] For instance, his negroes had reasonable and fixed daily tasks; and when these were finished, they were permitted to employ their time for their own advantage or amusement. If they chose to employ themselves longer for their master, they were paid regular wages for their extra work. This reward, for as such it was considered, operated most powerfully upon the slaves. Those who are animated by hope can perform what would seem impossibilities to those who are under the depressing influence of fear. The wages which Mr. Edwards promised, he took care to see punctually paid.

He had an excellent overseer, of the name of Abraham Bayley, a man of a mild but steady temper, who was attached not only to his master's interests but to his virtues; and who, therefore, was more intent upon seconding his humane views than upon squeezing from the labour of the negroes the utmost produce. Each negro had, near his cottage, a portion of land, called his provision-ground; and one day in the week was allowed for its cultivation.

It is common in Jamaica for the slaves to have provision-grounds, which they cultivate for their own advantage; but it too often happens that, when a good negro has successfully improved his little spot of ground, when he has built himself a house, and begins to enjoy the fruits of his industry, his acquired property is seized upon by the sheriff's officer for the payment of his master's debts;[3] he is forcibly separated from his wife and children, dragged to public auction, purchased by a stranger, and perhaps sent to terminate his miserable existence in the mines of Mexico; excluded for ever from the light of heaven; and all this without any crime or imprudence on his part, real or pretended. He is punished because his master is unfortunate!

To this barbarous injustice the negroes on Mr. Edward's plantation were never exposed. He never exceeded his income; he engaged in no wild speculations; he contracted no debts; and his slaves, therefore, were in no danger of being seized by a sheriff's officer: their property was secured to them by the prudence as well as by the generosity of their master.

One morning, as Mr. Edwards was walking in that part of his plantation which joined to Mr. Jefferies' estate, he thought he heard the voice of distress at some distance. The lamentations grew louder and louder as he approached a cottage, which stood upon the borders of Jefferies' plantation.

This cottage belonged to a slave of the name of

---

[1] "THE NEGRO SLAVES—A fine drama, by Kotzebue. It is to be hoped that such horrible instances of cruelty are not now to be found in nature. Bryan Edwards, in his History of Jamaica, says that most of the planters are humane; but he allows that some facts can be cited in contradiction of this assertion." (M.E.) *The Negro Slaves* (1796), by August Friedrich Ferdinand von Kotzebue (1761–1819); *The History, Civil and Commercial, of the British Colonies in the West Indies* (1793), by Bryan Edwards (1743–1800).

[2] "History of the West Indies, from which these ideas are adopted—not stolen." (M.E.)

[3] "See an eloquent and pathetic passage on this subject in the History of the West Indies, vol. ii p. 153, second edition." (M.E.)

Cæsar, the best negro in Mr. Jefferies' possession. Such had been his industry and exertion that, notwithstanding the severe tasks imposed by Durant, the overseer, Cæsar found means to cultivate his provision-ground to a degree of perfection nowhere else to be seen on this estate. Mr. Edwards had often admired this poor fellow's industry, and now hastened to inquire what misfortune had befallen him.

When he came to the cottage, he found Cæsar standing with his arms folded, and eyes fixed upon the ground. A young and beautiful female negro was weeping bitterly, as she knelt at the feet of Durant, the overseer, who, regarding her with a sullen aspect, repeated, "He must go. I tell you, woman, he must go. What signifies all this nonsense?"

At the sight of Mr. Edwards, the overseer's countenance suddenly changed, and assumed an air of obsequious civility. The poor woman retired to the farther corner of the cottage, and continued to weep. Cæsar never moved. "Nothing is the matter, sir," said Durant, "but that Cæsar is going to be sold. That is what the woman is crying for. They were to be married; but we'll find Clara another husband, I tell her; and she'll get the better of her grief, you know, sir, as I tell her, in time."

"Never! never!" said Clara.

"To whom is Cæsar going to be sold; and for what sum?"

"For what can be got for him," replied Durant, laughing; "and to whoever will buy him. The sheriff's officer is here, who has seized him for debt, and must make the most of him at market."

"Poor fellow!" said Mr. Edwards; "and must he leave this cottage which he has built, and these bananas which he has planted?"

Cæsar now for the first time looked up, and fixing his eyes upon Mr. Edwards for a moment, advanced with an intrepid rather than an imploring countenance, and said, "Will you be my master? Will you be her master? Buy both of us. You shall not repent of it. Cæsar will serve you faithfully."

On hearing these words, Clara sprang forward, and clasping her hands together, repeated, "Cæsar will serve you faithfully."

Mr. Edwards was moved by their entreaties, but he left them without declaring his intentions. He went immediately to Mr. Jefferies, whom he found stretched on a sofa, drinking coffee. As soon as Mr. Edwards mentioned the occasion of his visit, and expressed his sorrow for Cæsar, Jefferies exclaimed, "Yes, poor devil! I pity him from the bottom of my soul. But what can I do? I leave all those things to Durant. He says the sheriff's officer has seized him; and there's an end of the matter. You know, money must be had. Besides, Cæsar is not worse off than any other slave sold for debt. What signifies talking about the matter, as if it were something that never happened before! Is not it a case that occurs every day in Jamaica?"

"So much the worse," replied Mr. Edwards.

"The worse for them, to be sure," said Jefferies. "But, after all, they are slaves, and used to be treated as such; and they tell me the negroes are a thousand times happier here, with us, than they ever were in their own country."

"Did the negroes tell you so themselves?"

"No; but people better informed than negroes have told me so; and, after all, slaves there must be; for indigo,[1] and rum, and sugar, we must have."

"Granting it to be physically impossible that the world should exist without rum, sugar, and indigo, why could they not be produced by freemen as well as by slaves? If we hired negroes for labourers, instead of purchasing them for slaves, do you think they would not work as well as they do now? Does any negro, under the fear of the overseer, work harder than a Birmingham journeyman, or a Newcastle collier, who toil for themselves and their families?"

"Of that I don't pretend to judge. All I know is that the West India planters would be ruined if they had no slaves, and I am a West India planter."

"So am I: yet I do not think they are the only people whose interests ought to be considered in this business."

"Their interests, luckily, are protected by the laws of the land; and though they are rich men, and white men, and freemen, they have as good a claim to their rights as the poorest black slave on any of our plantations."

---

[1] a blue dye made from plants.

"The law, in our case, seems to make the right; and the very reverse ought to be done—the right should make the law."

"Fortunately for us planters, we need not enter into such nice distinctions. You could not, if you would, abolish the trade. Slaves would be smuggled into the islands."

"What, if nobody would buy them! You know that you cannot smuggle slaves into England. The instant a slave touches English ground he becomes free. Glorious privilege! Why should it not be extended to all her dominions? If the future importation of slaves into these islands were forbidden by law, the trade must cease. No man can either sell or possess slaves without its being known: they cannot be smuggled like lace or brandy."

"Well, well!" retorted Jefferies, a little impatiently, "as yet the law is on our side. I can do nothing in this business, nor you neither."

"Yes, we can do something; we can endeavour to make our negroes as happy as possible."

"I leave the management of these people to Durant."

"That is the very thing of which they complain; forgive me for speaking to you with the frankness of an old acquaintance."

"Oh! you can't oblige me more: I love frankness of all things! To tell you the truth, I have heard complaints of Durant's severity; but I make it a principle to turn a deaf ear to them, for I know nothing can be done with these fellows without it. You are partial to negroes; but even you must allow they are a race of beings naturally inferior to us. You may in vain think of managing a black as you would a white. Do what you please for a negro, he will cheat you the first opportunity he finds. You know what their maxim is: 'God gives black men what white men forget.'"

To these common-place desultory observations Mr. Edwards made no reply; but recurred to poor Cæsar, and offered to purchase both him and Clara, at the highest price the sheriff's officer could obtain for them at market. Mr. Jefferies, with the utmost politeness to his neighbour, but with the most perfect indifference to the happiness of those whom he considered of a different species from himself, acceded to this proposal. Nothing could be more reasonable, he said; and he was happy to have it in his power to oblige a gentleman for whom he had such a high esteem.

The bargain was quickly concluded with the sheriff's officer; for Mr. Edwards willingly paid several dollars more than the market price for the two slaves. When Cæsar and Clara heard that they were not to be separated, their joy and gratitude were expressed with all the ardour and tenderness peculiar to their different characters. Clara was an Eboe, Cæsar a Koromantyn[1] negro: the Eboes are soft, languishing, and timid; the Koromantyns are frank, fearless, martial, and heroic.

Mr. Edwards carried his new slaves home with him, desired Bayley, his overseer, to mark out a provision-ground for Cæsar, and to give him a cottage, which happened at this time to be vacant.

"Now, my good friend," said he to Cæsar, "you may work for yourself, without fear that what you earn may be taken from you; or that you should ever be sold, to pay your master's debts. If he does not understand what I am saying," continued Mr. Edwards, turning to his overseer, "you will explain it to him."

Cæsar perfectly understood all that Mr. Edwards said; but his feelings were at this instant so strong that he could not find expression for his gratitude: he stood like one stupified! Kindness was new to him; it overpowered his manly heart; and, at hearing the words "my good friend," the tears gushed from his eyes: tears which no torture could have extorted! Gratitude swelled in his bosom; and he longed to be alone, that he might freely yield to his emotions.

He was glad when the conch-shell sounded to call the negroes to their daily labour, that he might relieve the sensations of his soul by bodily exertion. He performed his task in silence; and an inattentive observer might have thought him sullen.

In fact, he was impatient for the day to be over, that he might get rid of a heavy load which weighed upon his mind.

The cruelties practised by Durant, the overseer of Jefferies' plantation, had exasperated the slaves under his

---

[1] Eboes were from Benin (now southern Nigeria); Koromantyns or Coromantins, from the Gold Coast (now Ghana).

dominion.

They were all leagued together in a conspiracy, which was kept profoundly secret. Their object was to extirpate every white man, woman, and child, in the island. Their plans were laid with consummate art; and the negroes were urged to execute them by all the courage of despair.

The confederacy extended to all the negroes in the island of Jamaica, excepting those on the plantation of Mr. Edwards. To them no hint of the dreadful secret had yet been given; their countrymen, knowing the attachment they felt to their master, dared not trust them with these projects of vengeance. Hector, the negro who was at the head of the conspirators, was the particular friend of Cæsar, and had imparted to him all his designs. These friends were bound to each other by the strongest ties. Their slavery and their sufferings began in the same hour: they were both brought from their own country in the same ship. This circumstance alone forms, amongst the negroes, a bond of connexion not easily to be dissolved. But the friendship of Cæsar and Hector commenced even before they were united by the sympathy of misfortune; they were both of the same nation, both Koromantyns. In Africa they had both been accustomed to command; for they had signalized themselves by superior fortitude and courage. They respected each other for excelling in all which they had been taught to consider as virtuous; and with them revenge was a virtue!

Revenge was the ruling passion of Hector: in Cæsar's mind it was rather a principle instilled by education. The one considered it as a duty, the other felt it as a pleasure. Hector's sense of injury was acute in the extreme; he knew not how to forgive. Cæsar's sensibility was yet more alive to kindness than to insult. Hector would sacrifice his life to extirpate an enemy. Cæsar would devote himself for the defence of a friend; and Cæsar now considered a white man as his friend.

He was now placed in a painful situation. All his former friendships, all the solemn promises by which he was bound to his companions in misfortune, forbade him to indulge that delightful feeling of gratitude and affection, which, for the first time, he experienced for one of that race of beings whom he had hitherto considered as detestable tyrants—objects of implacable and just revenge!

Cæsar was most impatient to have an interview with Hector, that he might communicate his new sentiments, and dissuade him from those schemes of destruction which he meditated. At midnight, when all the slaves except himself were asleep, he left his cottage, and went to Jefferies' plantation, to the hut in which Hector slept. Even in his dreams Hector breathed vengeance. "Spare none! Sons of Africa, spare none!" were the words he uttered in his sleep, as Cæsar approached the mat on which he lay. The moon shone full upon him. Cæsar contemplated the countenance of his friend, fierce even in sleep. "Spare none! Oh, yes! There is one that must be spared. There is one for whose sake all must be spared."

He awakened Hector by this exclamation. "Of what were you dreaming?" said Cæsar.

"Of that which, sleeping or waking, fills my soul—revenge! Why did you waken me from my dream? It was delightful. The whites were weltering in their blood! But silence! we may be overheard."

"No; every one sleeps but ourselves," replied Cæsar. "I could not sleep, without speaking to you on—a subject that weighs upon my mind. You have seen Mr. Edwards?"

"Yes. He that is now your master."

"He that is now my benefactor—my friend!"

"Friend! Can you call a white man friend?" cried Hector, starting up with a look of astonishment and indignation.

"Yes," replied Cæsar, with firmness. "And you would speak, ay, and would feel, as I do, Hector, if you knew this white man. Oh, how unlike he is to all of his race, that we have ever seen! Do not turn from me with so much disdain. Hear me with patience, my friend."

"I cannot," replied Hector, "listen with patience to one who between the rising and the setting sun can forget all his resolutions, all his promises; who by a few soft words can be so wrought upon as to forget all the insults, all the injuries he has received from this accursed race; and can even call a white man friend!"

Cæsar, unmoved by Hector's anger, continued to speak of Mr. Edwards with the warmest expressions of gratitude; and finished by declaring he would sooner forfeit his life than rebel against such a master. He conjured Hector to desist from executing his designs; but all was in vain. Hector sat with his elbows fixed upon his knees, leaning his head upon his hands, in gloomy silence.

Cæsar's mind was divided between love for his friend and gratitude to his master: the conflict was violent and painful. Gratitude at last prevailed: he repeated his declaration, that he would rather die than continue in a conspiracy against his benefactor!

Hector refused to except him from the general doom. "Betray us if you will!" cried he. "Betray our secrets to him whom you call your benefactor; to him whom a few hours have made your friend! To him sacrifice the friend of your youth, the companion of your better days, of your better self! Yes, Cæsar, deliver me over to the tormentors: I can endure no more than they can inflict. I shall expire without a sigh, without a groan. Why do you linger here, Cæsar? Why do you hesitate? Hasten this moment to your master; claim your reward for delivering into his power hundreds of your countrymen! Why do you hesitate? Away! The coward's friendship can be of use to none. Who can value his gratitude? Who can fear his revenge?"

Hector raised his voice so high, as he pronounced these words, that he wakened Durant, the overseer, who slept in the next house. They heard him call out suddenly, to inquire who was there: and Cæsar had but just time to make his escape, before Durant appeared. He searched Hector's cottage; but finding no one, again retired to rest. This man's tyranny made him constantly suspicious: he dreaded that the slaves should combine against him; and he endeavoured to prevent them by every threat and every stratagem he could devise, from conversing with each other.

They had, however, taken their measures, hitherto, so secretly, that he had not the slightest idea of the conspiracy which was forming in the island. Their schemes were not yet ripe for execution; but the appointed time approached. Hector, when he coolly reflected on what had passed between him and Cæsar, could not help admiring the frankness and courage with which he had avowed his change of sentiments. By this avowal, Cæsar had in fact exposed his own life to the most imminent danger, from the vengeance of the conspirators; who might be tempted to assassinate him who had their lives in his power. Notwithstanding the contempt with which, in the first moment of passion, he had treated his friend, he was extremely anxious that he should not break off all connexion with the conspirators. He knew that Cæsar possessed both intrepidity and eloquence; and that his opposition to their schemes would perhaps entirely frustrate their whole design. He therefore determined to use every possible means to bend him to their purposes.

He resolved to have recourse to one of those persons[1]

---

[1] "The enlightened inhabitants of Europe may, perhaps, smile at the superstitious credulity of the negroes, who regard those ignorant beings called *Obeah* people with the most profound respect and dread; who believe that they hold in their hands the power of good and evil fortune, of health and sickness, of life and death. The instances which are related of their power over the minds of their countrymen are so wonderful that none but the most unquestionable authority could make us think them credible. The following passage from Edwards' History of the West Indies, is inserted, to give an idea of this strange infatuation.

"'In the year 1760, when a very formidable insurrection of the Koromantyn or Gold Coast negroes broke out, in the parish of St. Mary, and spread through almost every other district of the island, an old Koromantyn negro, the chief instigator and oracle of the insurgents in that parish, who had administered the fetish, or solemn oath, to the conspirators, and furnished them with a magical preparation, which was to render them invulnerable, was fortunately apprehended, convicted, and hung up, with all his feathers and trumperies about him; and his execution struck the insurgents with a general panic, from which they never afterwards recovered. The examinations, which were taken at that period, first opened the eyes of the public to the very dangerous tendency of the *Obeah* practices; and gave birth to the law, which was then enacted, for their suppression and punishment; but neither the terror of this law, the strict investigation which has since been made after the professors of *Obi*, nor the many examples of those, who from time to time have been hanged or transported, have hitherto produced the desired effect. A gentleman, on his returning to Jamaica, in the year 1775, found that a great many of his negroes had died during his absence; and that, of such as remained alive, at least one half were debilitated, bloated, and in a very deplorable condition. The mortality continued after his arrival; and two or three were frequently buried in one day; others were taken ill, and began to decline under the same symptoms. Every means were tried, by medicine and the most careful nursing, to preserve the lives of the feeblest; but, in spite of all his endeavours, this depopulation went on for a twelve- (Continued)

who, amongst the negroes, are considered as sorceresses. Esther, an old Koromantyn negress, had obtained by her skill in poisonous herbs, and her knowledge of venomous reptiles, a high reputation amongst her countrymen. She soon taught them to believe her to be possessed of supernatural powers; and she then worked their imagination to what pitch and purpose she pleased.

She was the chief instigator of this intended rebellion. It was she who had stimulated the revengeful temper of Hector almost to phrensy. She now promised him that her arts should be exerted over his friend; and it was not long before he felt their influence. Cæsar soon perceived an extraordinary change in the countenance and manner of his beloved Clara. A melancholy hung over her, and she refused to impart to him the cause of her dejection. Cæsar was indefatigable in his exertions to

---

month longer, with more or less intermission, and without his being able to ascertain the real cause, though the *Obeah* practice was strongly suspected, as well by himself as by the doctor, and other white persons upon the plantation; as it was known to have been very common in that part of the island, and particularly among the negroes of the *Popaw* or *Popo* country. Still he was unable to verify his suspicions; because the patients constantly denied their having any thing to do with persons of that order, or any knowledge of them. At length, a negress, who had been ill for some time, came and informed him that, feeling it was impossible for her to live much longer, she thought herself bound in duty, before she died, to impart a very great secret, and acquaint him with the true cause of her disorder; in hopes that the disclosure might prove the means of stopping that mischief, which had already swept away such a number of her fellow-slaves. She proceeded to say that her step-mother, a woman of the *Popo* country, above eighty years old, but still hale and active, had *put Obi upon her*; as she had upon those who had lately died; and that the old woman had practiced *Obi* for as many years past as she could remember. The other negroes of the plantation no sooner heard of this impeachment than they ran in a body to their master, and confirmed the truth of it. * * * * Upon this he repaired directly, with six white servants, to the old woman's house; and, forcing open the door, observed the whole inside of the roof, which was of thatch, and every crevice of the wall, stuck with the implements of her trade, consisting of rags, feathers, bones of cats, and a thousand other articles. * * * * The house was instantly pulled down; and, with the whole of its contents, committed to the flames, amidst the general acclamations of all his other negroes. * * * * From the moment of her departure, his negroes seemed all to be animated with new spirits; and the malady spread no farther among them. The total of his losses, in the course of about fifteen years preceding the discovery, and imputable solely to the *Obeah practice*, he estimates, at least, at one hundred negroes.'" (M.E.)

---

cultivate and embellish the ground near his cottage, in hopes of making it an agreeable habitation for her; but she seemed to take no interest in any thing. She would stand beside him immoveable, in a deep reverie; and when he inquired whether she was ill, she would answer no, and endeavour to assume an air of gaiety: but this cheerfulness was transient; she soon relapsed into despondency. At length, she endeavoured to avoid her lover, as if she feared his farther inquiries.

Unable to endure this state of suspense, he one evening resolved to bring her to an explanation. "Clara," said he, "you once loved me: I have done nothing, have I, to forfeit your confidence?"

"I once loved you!" said she, raising her languid eyes, and looking at him with reproachful tenderness; "and can you doubt my constancy? Oh, Cæsar, you little know what is passing in my heart! You are the cause of my melancholy!"

She paused, and hesitated, as if afraid that she had said too much: but Cæsar urged her with so much vehemence, and so much tenderness, to open to him her whole soul, that, at last, she could not resist his eloquence. She reluctantly revealed to him that secret of which she could not think without horror. She informed him that, unless he complied with what was required of him by the sorceress Esther, he was devoted[1] to die. What it was that Esther required of him, Clara knew not: she knew nothing of the conspiracy. The timidity of her character was ill-suited to such a project; and every thing relating to it had been concealed from her with the utmost care.

When she explained to Cæsar the cause of her dejection, his natural courage resisted these superstitious fears; and he endeavoured to raise Clara's spirits. He endeavoured in vain: she fell at his feet, and with tears, and the most tender supplications, conjured him to avert the wrath of the sorceress by obeying her commands whatever they might be!

"Clara," replied he, "you know not what you ask!"

"I ask you to save your life!" said she. "I ask you, for my sake, to save your life, while yet it is in your power!"

---

[1] doomed.

"But would you to save my life, Clara, make me the worst of criminals? Would you make me the murderer of my benefactor?"

Clara started with horror!

"Do you recollect the day, the moment, when we were on the point of being separated for ever, Clara? Do you remember the white man's coming to my cottage? Do you remember his look of benevolence—his voice of compassion? Do you remember his generosity? Oh! Clara, would you make me the murderer of this man?"

"Heaven forbid!" said Clara. "This cannot be the will of the sorceress!"

"It is," said Cæsar. "But she shall not succeed; even though she speaks with the voice of Clara. Urge me no farther; my resolution is fixed. I should be unworthy of your love if I were capable of treachery and ingratitude."

"But, is there no means of averting the wrath of Esther?" said Clara. "Your life——"

"Think, first, of my honour," interrupted Cæsar. "Your fears deprive you of reason. Return to this sorceress, and tell her that I dread not her wrath. My hands shall never be imbrued in the blood of my benefactor. Clara! can you forget his look when he told us that we should never more be separated?"

"It went to my heart," said Clara, bursting into tears. "Cruel, cruel Esther! Why do you command us to destroy such a generous master?"

The conch sounded to summon the negroes to their morning's work. It happened this day, that Mr. Edwards, who was continually intent upon increasing the comforts and happiness of his slaves, sent his carpenter, while Cæsar was absent, to fit up the inside of his cottage; and when Cæsar returned from work, he found his master pruning the branches of a tamarind tree that overhung the thatch. "How comes it, Cæsar," said he, "that you have not pruned these branches?"

Cæsar had no knife. "Here is mine for you," said Mr. Edwards. "It is very sharp," added he, smiling; "but I am not one of those masters who are afraid to trust their negroes with sharp knives."

These words were spoken with perfect simplicity: Mr. Edwards had no suspicion, at this time, of what was passing in the negro's mind. Cæsar received the knife without uttering a syllable; but no sooner was Mr. Edwards out of sight than he knelt down, and, in a transport of gratitude, swore that, with this knife, he would stab himself to the heart sooner than betray his master!

The principle of gratitude conquered every other sensation. The mind of Cæsar was not insensible to the charms of freedom: he knew the negro conspirators had so taken their measures, that there was the greatest probability of their success. His heart beat high at the idea of recovering his liberty: but he was not to be seduced from his duty, not even by this delightful hope; nor was he to be intimidated by the dreadful certainty that his former friends and countrymen, considering him as a deserter from their cause, would become his bitterest enemies. The loss of Hector's esteem and affection was deeply felt by Cæsar. Since the night that the decisive conversation relative to Mr. Edwards passed, Hector and he had never exchanged a syllable.

This visit proved the cause of much suffering to Hector, and to several of the slaves on Jefferies' plantation. We mentioned that Durant had been awakened by the raised voice of Hector. Though he could not find any one in the cottage, yet his suspicions were not dissipated; and an accident nearly brought the whole conspiracy to light. Durant had ordered one of the negroes to watch a boiler of sugar: the slave was overcome by the heat, and fainted. He had scarcely recovered his senses when the overseer came up, and found that the sugar had fermented, by having remained a few minutes too long in the boiler. He flew into a violent passion, and ordered that the negro should receive fifty lashes. His victim bore them without uttering a groan; but, when his punishment was over, and when he thought the overseer was gone, he exclaimed, "It will soon be our turn!"

Durant was not out of hearing. He turned suddenly, and observed that the negro looked at Hector when he pronounced these words, and this confirmed the suspicion that Hector was carrying on some conspiracy. He immediately had recourse to that brutality which he considered as the only means of governing black men: Hector and three other negroes were lashed unmercifully; but no confessions could be extorted.

Mr. Jefferies might perhaps have forbidden such

violence to be used, if he had not been at the time carousing with a party of jovial West Indians, who thought of nothing but indulging their appetites in all the luxuries that art and nature could supply. The sufferings which had been endured by many of the wretched negroes to furnish out this magnificent entertainment were never once thought of by these selfish epicures. Yet so false are the general estimates of character, that all these gentlemen passed for men of great feeling and generosity! The human mind, in certain situations, becomes so accustomed to ideas of tyranny and cruelty, that they no longer appear extraordinary or detestable: they rather seem part of the necessary and immutable order of things.

Mr. Jefferies was stopped, as he passed from his dining-room into his drawing-room, by a little negro child, of about five years old, who was crying bitterly. He was the son of one of the slaves who were at this moment under the torturer's hand. "Poor little devil!" said Mr. Jefferies, who was more than half intoxicated. "Take him away; and tell Durant, some of ye, to pardon his father—if he can."

The child ran, eagerly, to announce his father's pardon; but he soon returned, crying more violently than before. Durant would not hear the boy; and it was now no longer possible to appeal to Mr. Jefferies, for he was in the midst of an assembly of fair ladies; and no servant belonging to the house dared to interrupt the festivities of the evening. The three men, who were so severely flogged to extort from them confessions, were perfectly innocent: they knew nothing of the confederacy; but the rebels seized the moment when their minds were exasperated by this cruelty and injustice, and they easily persuaded them to join the league. The hope of revenging themselves upon the overseer was a motive sufficient to make them brave death in any shape.

Another incident, which happened a few days before the time destined for the revolt of the slaves, determined numbers who had been undecided. Mrs. Jefferies was a languid beauty, or rather a languid fine lady who had been a beauty, and who spent all that part of the day which was not devoted to the pleasures of the table, or to reclining on a couch, in dress. She was one day extended on a sofa, fanned by four slaves, two at her head and two at her feet, when news was brought that a large chest, directed to her, was just arrived from London.

This chest contained various articles of dress of the newest fashions. The Jamaica ladies carry their ideas of magnificence to a high pitch: they willingly give a hundred guineas for a gown, which they perhaps wear but once or twice. In the elegance and variety of her ornaments, Mrs. Jefferies was not exceeded by any lady in the island, except by one who had lately received a cargo from England. She now expected to outshine her competitor, and desired that the chest should be unpacked in her presence.

In taking out one of the gowns, it caught on a nail in the lid, and was torn. The lady, roused from her natural indolence by this disappointment to her vanity, instantly ordered that the unfortunate female slave should be severely chastised. The woman was the wife of Hector; and this fresh injury worked up his temper, naturally vindictive, to the highest point. He ardently longed for the moment when he might satiate his vengeance.

The plan the negroes had laid was to set fire to the canes, at one and the same time, on every plantation; and when the white inhabitants of the island should run to put out the fire, the blacks were to seize this moment of confusion and consternation to fall upon them, and make a general massacre. The time when this scheme was to be carried into execution was not known to Cæsar; for the conspirators had changed their day, as soon as Hector told them that his friend was no longer one of the confederacy. They dreaded he should betray them; and it was determined that he and Clara should both be destroyed, unless they could be prevailed upon to join the conspiracy.

Hector wished to save his friend; but the desire of vengeance overcame every other feeling. He resolved, however, to make an attempt, for the last time, to change Cæsar's resolution.

For this purpose, Esther was the person he employed: she was to work upon his mind by means of Clara. On returning to her cottage one night, she found suspended from the thatch one of those strange fantastic charms with which the Indian sorceresses terrify those whom they have proscribed. Clara, unable to conquer her terror, repaired again to Esther, who received her first in mysterious silence; but, after she had implored her forgiveness for the past, and with all possible humility conjured her to grant her future protection, the sorceress deigned to speak. Her commands were that Clara should prevail upon her lover to meet her, on this awful spot, the ensuing night.

Little suspecting what was going forward on the plantation of Jefferies, Mr. Edwards that evening gave his slaves a holiday. He and his family came out at sunset, when the fresh breeze had sprung up, and seated themselves under a spreading palm-tree, to enjoy the pleasing spectacle of this negro festival. His negroes were all well clad, and in the gayest colours, and their merry countenances suited the gaiety of their dress. While some were dancing, and some playing on the tambourine, others appeared amongst the distant trees, bringing baskets of avocado pears, grapes, and pine-apples, the produce of their own provision-grounds; and others were employed in spreading their clean trenchers, or the calabashes,[1] which served for plates and dishes. The negroes continued to dance and divert themselves till late in the evening. When they separated and retired to rest, Cæsar, recollecting his promise to Clara, repaired secretly to the habitation of the sorceress. It was situated in the recess of a thick wood. When he arrived there, he found the door fastened; and he was obliged to wait some time before it was opened by Esther.

The first object he beheld was his beloved Clara, stretched on the ground, apparently a corpse! The sorceress had thrown her into a trance by a preparation of deadly nightshade. The hag burst into an infernal laugh, when she beheld the despair that was painted in Cæsar's countenance. "Wretch!" cried she, "you have defied my power: behold its victim!"

Cæsar, in a transport of rage, seized her by the throat: but his fury was soon checked.

"Destroy me," said the fiend, "and you destroy your Clara. She is not dead: but she lies in the sleep of death, into which she has been thrown by magic art, and from which no power but mine can restore her to the light of life. Yes! look at her, pale and motionless! Never will she rise from the earth, unless, within one hour, you obey my commands. I have administered to Hector and his companions the solemn fetish oath, at the sound of which every negro in Africa trembles! You know my object."

"Fiend, I do!" replied Cæsar, eyeing her sternly; "but, while I have life, it shall never be accomplished."

"Look yonder!" cried she, pointing to the moon; "in a few minutes that moon will set: at that hour Hector and his friends will appear. They come armed—armed with weapons which I shall steep in poison for their enemies. Themselves I will render invulnerable. Look again!" continued she; "if my dim eyes mistake not, yonder they come. Rash man, you die if they cross my threshold."

"I wish for death," said Cæsar. "Clara is dead!"

"But you can restore her to life by a single word."

Cæsar, at this moment, seemed to hesitate.

"Consider! Your heroism is vain," continued Esther. "You will have the knives of fifty of the conspirators in your bosom, if you do not join them; and, after you have fallen, the death of your master is inevitable. Here is the bowl of poison, in which the negro knives are to be steeped. Your friends, your former friends, your countrymen, will be in arms in a few minutes; and they will bear down every thing before them—Victory, Wealth, Freedom, and Revenge, will be theirs."

Cæsar appeared to be more and more agitated. His eyes were fixed upon Clara. The conflict in his mind was violent; but his sense of gratitude and duty could not be shaken by hope, fear, or ambition; nor could it be vanquished by love. He determined, however, to appear to yield. As if struck with panic, at the approach of the confederate negroes, he suddenly turned to the sorceress, and said, in a tone of feigned submission, "It is in vain to struggle with fate. Let my knife, too, be dipt in your magic poison."

The sorceress clapped her hands with infernal joy in her countenance. She bade him instantly give her his knife, that she might plunge it to the hilt in the bowl of poison, to which she turned with savage impatience. His knife was left in his cottage; and, under pretence of going in search of it, he escaped. Esther promised to

---

[1] fruit from the calabash tree, often used for utensils.

prepare Hector and all his companions to receive him with their ancient cordiality on his return. Cæsar ran with the utmost speed along a by-path out of the wood, met none of the rebels, reached his master's house, scaled the wall of his bedchamber, got in at the window, and wakened him, exclaiming, "Arm—arm yourself, my dear master! Arm all your slaves! They will fight for you, and die for you; as I will the first. The Koromantyn yell of war will be heard in Jefferies' plantation this night! Arm—arm yourself, my dear master, and let us surround the rebel leaders while it is yet time. I will lead you to the place where they are all assembled, on condition that their chief, who is my friend, shall be pardoned."

Mr. Edwards armed himself and the negroes on his plantation, as well as the whites: they were all equally attached to him. He followed Cæsar into the recesses of the wood.

They proceeded with all possible rapidity, but in perfect silence, till they reached Esther's habitation: which they surrounded completely, before they were perceived by the conspirators.

Mr. Edwards looked through a hole in the wall; and, by the blue flame of a caldron, over which the sorceress was stretching her shrivelled hands, he saw Hector and five stout negroes standing, intent upon her incantations. These negroes held their knives in their hands, ready to dip them into the bowl of poison. It was proposed, by one of the whites, to set fire immediately to the hut; and thus to force the rebels to surrender. The advice was followed; but Mr. Edwards charged his people to spare their prisoners. The moment the rebels saw that the thatch of the hut was in flames, they set up the Koromantyn yell of war, and rushed out with frantic desperation.

"Yield! you are pardoned, Hector," cried Mr. Edwards, in a loud voice.

"You are pardoned, my friend!" repeated Cæsar.

Hector, incapable at this instant of listening to any thing but revenge, sprang forwards, and plunged his knife into the bosom of Cæsar. The faithful servant staggered back a few paces: his master caught him in his arms. "I die content," said he. "Bury me with Clara."

He swooned from loss of blood as they were carrying him home; but when his wound was examined, it was found not to be mortal. As he recovered from his swoon, he stared wildly round him, trying to recollect where he was, and what had happened. He thought that he was still in a dream, when he saw his beloved Clara standing beside him. The opiate, which the pretended sorceress had administered to her, had ceased to operate; she wakened from her trance just at the time the Koromantyn yell commenced. Cæsar's joy!—We must leave that to the imagination.

In the mean time, what became of the rebel negroes, and Mr. Edwards?

The taking the chief conspirators prisoners did not prevent the negroes upon Jefferies' plantation from insurrection. The moment they heard the war-whoop, the signal agreed upon, they rose in a body; and, before they could be prevented, either by the whites on the estate, or by Mr. Edwards' adherents, they had set fire to the overseer's house, and to the canes. The overseer was the principal object of their vengeance—he died in tortures, inflicted by the hands of those who had suffered most by his cruelties. Mr. Edwards, however, quelled the insurgents before rebellion spread to any other estates in the island. The influence of his character, and the effect of his eloquence upon the minds of the people, were astonishing: nothing but his interference could have prevented the total destruction of Mr. Jefferies and his family, who, as it was computed, lost this night upwards of fifty thousand pounds. He was never afterwards able to recover his losses, or to shake off his constant fear of a fresh insurrection among his slaves. At length, he and his lady returned to England, where they were obliged to live in obscurity and indigence. They had no consolation in their misfortunes but that of railing at the treachery of the whole race of slaves. Our readers, we hope, will think that at least one exception may be made, in favour of THE GRATEFUL NEGRO.

March, 1802.

Ann Batten Cristall
c. 1768 – after 1816

Ann Batten Cristall was baptized in Penzance, Cornwall, on 7 December 1769. Her father, Joseph Alexander Cristall, a ship- and shipyard-owner, was said to be a jealous and violent man. She was educated by her mother, Elizabeth Batten Cristall. In 1788, she became a teacher. She published *Poetical Sketches*, her only book, by subscription in 1795; the subscribers included John Aikin, Amelia Alderson (later Opie),* Barbauld,* George Dyer, Mary Hays,* Samuel Rogers,* and her friends Everina and Mary Wollstonecraft.* It received generally favourable reviews, except for some criticisms of the irregularity of her verse. In 1797, Southey* met her and was impressed by her "genius." We can infer from remarks in Wollstonecraft's letters that she had an unhappy life. And that is almost all we know. In 1816, a biographical dictionary listed her, under her maiden name, as still alive; she may have lived with her brother, Joshua (1767–1847), a watercolourist. (D.L.M.)

---

from *Poetical Sketches, in Irregular Verse* (1795)

Before Twilight. Eyezion

Dawn had not streak'd the spacious veil of night,
When EYEZION, the light poet of the spring,
Hied from his restless bed, to sing,
Impatient for the promis'd beams of light:
5 Sweetly his voice through woods and vallies rang,
While fleeting o'er the hills, these anxious notes he sang:

Swift, swift, ye lingering hours,
    And wake the morning star;
Rouse from the dew-fraught flowers
10   The shades, and drive them far.

Quick on the wings of morning,
    Dart the young glimmering light,
Th'horizon's verge adorning,
    With blushing radiance dight.

15 Rise, Phoebus,[1] from yon mountain,
    Your saffron robes display;
Warm every lake and fountain,
    And kindle up the day.

My soul, fledg'd with desires,
20   Flutters, and pants for morn,

To catch the orient fires
    Light trembling o'er the lawn.

When rays, o'er meadows blushing,
    Illumine VIZA'S eyes,
25 Her lily-bosom flushing
    Reflects the glowing skies.

O soul! that dart'st through ages,
    And wing'st with subtile power,
Why weak, when ardour rages,
30   To speed one slumbering hour?

Its beams when morning glances,
    VIZA unfolds her charms,
Spangled with dews advances,
    And glows within my arms.

35 Midst rills she laves her tresses,
    And blooming beams delight;
Swift-love my soul oppresses—
    Why's thought more quick than light?

All hung with stars, as scorning,
40   Night lingers 'mid the skies;
O! when will rise the morning?
    O! when will VIZA rise?

---

[1] Apollo, classical god of the sun.

These notes a sportive zephyr gently blew;
    The lovely VIZA op'd her star-like eyes:
45 Her dreams dissolving 'mid night's shadows flew,
    While sweet sensations in her bosom rise.
Her ears th'enchanting strains with pleasure greet,
She asks, who sang so early, and so sweet?

EYEZION.

    From VIZA'S memory then is EYEZION flown?
50 And is the music she inspires unknown?
If still no trait on thy remembrance pours,
Listen, whilst I describe my mental powers.

A current of creative mind,
Wild as the wandering gusts of wind,
55 'Mid fertile fancy's visions train'd,
Unzon'd[1] I shot, and o'er each limit strain'd;
Around in airy circles whirl'd
    By a genius infinite;
While Love in wanton ringlets curl'd
60   My tresses, passion to excite.

Music waited on my birth,
    And call'd itself the soul of verse;
And wildly, through the mazy earth,
    My lips its melodies rehearse.

65 Thus skimming o'er the tracts of life,
Borne on light elements, I bound;
Free from rage, and coarser strife,
I catch new beauties all around;
From Love's light wings I steal the tender down,
70 While each gay Muse my aspiring temples crown.

When Grief pursues with harpy wing,
To whirl me to dark realms of Care,
    Upon poetic spells I fly,
Wafted afar from black Despair;
75   And, as I sing,
    Am rais'd on high:
Young Joy with pleasure smoothes the scene,
Of mortal eyes unseen;

---

[1] unbound: a zone is a girdle or belt.

With these I fleet,
80 Amid the Loves and Smiles sweet flowrets wreathe;
And every sigh I waft, and every joy I breathe,
Mix'd with seraphic airs, fly on poetic feet.

VIZA.

Thou sweet enthusiast! say, what brings thee here,
Ere mounting larks have hail'd the morning star?
85 Involving shades, with cruel care,
    Now wrap thee in their womb;
Though here and there a glittering star
Shoots through blank night, and breaks the gloom.

EYEZION.

Drawn by what irresistless power,
90 Shall I with trembling notes recite,
Why, glowing like an opening flower,
I fleet before the morning light?

Yet fancy paints a conscious blush
O'er thy fair cheeks; nor need my tongue
95 With deeper die thy beauties flush—
Thou know'st I'm drawn by thee alone.

From distant tracts I bound along,
Nor hills nor streams my course delay,
Whilst oft reverb'rating my song,
100 Sweet echo with the Muses play.

VIZA.

Methinks the fading night decays,
And morning breezes fan the air.

EYEZION.

Distinct I view the silvering rays
O'er yonder mountain tops appear.

VIZA.

105 Soon as young light shall clear the heaven,
Urg'd by the glowing rays of morn;

When circling mists are distant driven,
Expect me on the dewy lawn.

Morning. Rosamonde[1]

Wild midst the teeming buds of opening May,
Breaking large branches from the flow'ry thorn,
O'er the fern'd hills see ROSAMONDA stray,
Scattering the pearls which the gay leaves adorn!
5   Her ringlets o'er her temples play,
Flush'd with the orient splendour of the morn.
The sun broke forth—and wide its glories threw,
Blushing along the sky, and sparkling in the dew.
The plains gay-glitter'd with ethereal light;
10   And the field-melody,
        Nature's wild harmony,
Breath'd love, and sang delight!

Fresh ROSAMONDE the glowing scene surveys,
Her youthful bosom inly stung with pain;
15 Early amid the shadowy trees she strays,
Her shining eyes the starting tears restrain;
While tyrant Love within her pulses plays,
O'er the wet grass she flew with wild disdain.
She flew from thought, and far
20 She sang, and hail'd the morning star.
Her voice was pinion'd on[2] the wind,
Which wafts her notes around;
Encircling zephyrs caught each sound,
And bore them echoing through the wood,
25 Where pleas'd offended URBAN stood,
With archest smile, yet musical and kind:
Conquering the sigh, she gayly sung,
And scorn loud-trembled on her wiery tongue.

While URBAN stood, and held her in his eyes,
30 He to his lips applies
    The soft-breath'd flute;

Whose notes, when touch'd with art,
Steal to the inmost heart,
And throw the tyrannizing spirit down—
35 While vanity and pride are charm'd and mute.

Those lays reach'd ROSAMONDA'S ear,
She fluttering, like a bird whom fear
Has drawn within the fascinating serpent's fangs,
Unable to conceal the pangs
40 Of pride, conflicting with returning love,
To hide her blushes, darts amid the grove:
Sweet showers fast sprinkle from her lovely eyes,
Which drown her short-liv'd scorn;
But as she moves the young musician flies,
45 Leaves her all wild, sad, weeping, and forlorn!

Noon. Lysander[3]

The sun had thrown its noontide ray
Amid the flowers, and scorch'd the plains,
Which panted for refreshing rains;
While gaudy flies their golden wings display,
5   And bees cull'd sweets to chear a wintry day:
Each beam that darted down
Chas'd lingering shades,
Through the thick umbrage of the trees pervades,
And universal splendour shed around:
10 The slippery grass, burnt brown with heat,
Unkindly scorch'd the traveller's feet.

And now, oppress'd,
While every creature languid hied to rest,
Amid the blaze LYSANDER bounds along,
15 Bold as a lion, scorch'd by many a clime;
Far off was heard the echoes of his song,
Responsive to his clear and artless rhyme:
He seeks no shade, nor grotto's cool retreat,
But on, amidst the furzy heath, he press'd;
20 The heart's warm passions through his pulses beat,
And native fire inspires his manly breast.
He seeks the craggy shore which ocean laves,

---

[1] possibly named after the Fair Rosamond (Clifford, d. c. 1176), allegedly the mistress of Henry II, and the subject of "The Complaint of Rosamond" (1592), by Samuel Daniel (1563–1619); *Rosamond* (1707), by Joseph Addison (1672–1719); and a ballad in *Reliques of Ancient English Poetry* (1765), by Thomas Percy (1729–1811).

[2] given wings by.

[3] Lysander is named after one of the young lovers in Shakespeare, *A Midsummer Night's Dream*.

And, seated on a rock, surveys the swelling waves:
The eminence th'horizon's scope commands,
25 The plains surrounding, and the burning strands.
O'er the wild scene he threw a happy look,
Compares the present pleasure with the past;
Gladly he turns each page of Nature's book,
And prays the freedom of his soul may last.
30   He roll'd his eyes
     Across the seas;
Now glancing o'er the glassy waves,
   Now mounting to the skies,
   Th'immortal prize
35 Of valiant souls who find deep watery graves.

Thus as he sat, by strong reflection bound,
Up the rough rock ascends a sound,
   Which piercingly pervades his ears;
It seem'd the frantic cry of woe,
40   Which struggling groan'd, without the aid of tears.
The sounds like lightening reach'd his heart; and
     flush'd
With quick alarm he made no longer stay,
Ardently down the craggy steep he rush'd,
Rough heights he leap'd, impatient of delay,
45 And tow'rds the sufferer bent his eager way;
Till by the sea he reach'd some rocky caves,
Lash'd by the loud-resounding waves.

There a wild female rent her golden hair,
   With raging passions blind;
50   Her sad young bosom bare,
And frantic seem'd her stormy mind.
Swift tow'rds the sea she flies,
   With direful cries;
Driven on by fierce despair,
55 Mid oozy waves to drown remaining sense of care.

Touch'd by each generous thought,
By strong humanity impress'd,
The damsel in his arms he caught,
And held her, struggling, to his breast.
60 "Why trembles thus thy soul, O wretched maid!
O agony! too piercing agony!
Is through thy miserable frame pourtray'd.
O could my breast relieve thy misery!

Just heaven! if thou hast pity, ease her pain!
65 Her heart will burst! she faints within my arms!—
Upon my bosom she reclines her charms;
My falling tears bedew her cheeks in vain!"
He stretch'd her on the shore—
He fetch'd cool water from the seas,
70 And sprinkled her all o'er,
And fanning her with leaves collects the breeze:
Till on the heavens she op'd her azure eyes,
And, with returning thought and grief, look'd up—
"Ah, wretched me!" she cry'd, with bursting sighs,
75 "I've plenteous drank at sorrow's bitter cup!
To GOD I fly; no help on earth I find,
And from my soul would tear the mortal part;
Such sad disorders fill the human mind,
Such deep afflictions rive my guilty heart.

80 "I far in vice have stray'd;
And, too severe,
The parents who ador'd the maid,
No sighs from my repentant heart would hear:
Till, raging in despair,
85 I franticly resolv'd to die—
Rather than (sad alternative!) to lie
Amid the streets, and common insults share."

Stung to the heart, she rose;
Tears stream'd from her fair eyes;
90 Shame in her cheeks reviv'd the damask rose,
And poignant sorrow burst in bitter sighs:
She wept all silently:
LYSANDER scarce could speak,
Though sometimes, "Cruelty! O cruelty!"
95 Forth from his lips would break.

With generous passions swell'd his noble breast;
Passions too strong and deep to be express'd;
Pity and rage with equal strivings beat,
And sympathy, wrought high by nat'ral heat:
100 "By my true soul!" at length he cried,
"As Nature's my director and my guide,
My heart, chain'd by thy woe,
Shall neither joy nor comfort know,
Till I've reveng'd thy wrongs, and giv'n thee ease,
105 And, by my love, have set thy troubled soul at peace.

O! let not misery o'erwhelm thy heart,
    Nor the fair path of life and joy decline;
Vengeance shall find the authors of thy smart—
    O! fearless rest thy drooping soul on mine,
110 Which, like the oak, round which the ivy strays,
With blessings yet may store thy future days."

The damsel's sorrow, like a furious storm,
    Rack'd her celestial system with its rage;
Dire elements in her bosom war did wage,
115 And the mild radiance of her charms deform.
At length the vivid fires rush'd to her heart,
    Tingled in ev'ry vein, blaz'd from her eyes,
    While sudden joys before her spirits rise,
And o'er her cheeks warm transient colours dart:
120 Fir'd by his zeal,
    Extatic feelings tinge her frame;
Whose glow the passions of her breast reveal
Bright blossom of a future ripening flame!

Evening. Gertrude

In clouds drew on the evening's close,
Which cross the west in ranges stood,
As pensive GERTRUDE sought the wood,
And there the darkest thicket chose;
5 While from her eyes amid the wild briar flows
A sad and briny flood.
    Dark o'er her head
Roll'd heavy clouds, while showers,
Perfum'd by summer's wild and spicy flowers,
10 Their ample torrents shed.

Why does she mourn?
Why droop, like flowret nipp'd in early spring?
Alas! her tenderness meets no return!
Love hovers round her with his airy wing,
15 And warms her youthful heart with vain delight:
While URBAN'S graceful form enchants her sight,
And from his eyes shoots forth the poisonous sting,
Another's charms th' impassion'd youth inspir'd,
The sportive ROSAMONDE his genius fir'd.

20 The drops which glide down GERTRUDE'S cheeks,
Mid bitter agonies did flow;
And though awhile her pallid lips might glow,
'Twas as a blossom blighted soon with woe:
Her disregarded tresses, wet with tears,
25 Hung o'er her panting bosom straight and sleek;
Her faithful heart was all despondency and fears.

The skies disgorg'd, their last large drops refrain,
The cloudy hemisphere's no more perturb'd;
The leafy boughs, that had receiv'd the rain,
30 With gusts of wind disturb'd,
Shake wild their scattering drops o'er glade and plain;
They fall on GERTRUDE'S breast, and her white
    garments stain.
Sighing, she threw her mantle o'er her head,
And through the brakes towards her mansion sped;
35 Unheedingly her vestments drew along,
Sweeping the tears that to the branches hung:
    And as she pass'd
O'er the soak'd road, from off the shining grass,
In clods around her feet the moist earth clung.

40 The clouds dispers'd, again to sight
The evening sun glow'd lambent bright;
And forcing back the lowering shades,
Spread its enlivening beams, and kindled mid the glades:
With high-wrought verdure every object glow'd,
45 And purple hills their glittering mansions show'd.
The universal gleam invites to sport,
    For toil and care cease with the ebbing day;
Th' industrious youths to plains or groves resort,
Dance on the lawn, or o'er the hillocks stray.

50 GERTRUDE, wandering up a lane,
From among the winding trees,
Fann'd by a refreshing breeze,
Ascends upon the glistening plain.
Across gay Iris[1] flung her bow,
55 Reflecting each celestial ray;
As if the flowers that deck'd the May
Were there exhal'd, and through its watery pores did glow.

---

[1] the rainbow, also the messenger of the classical gods.

From a fair covert, URBAN'S gay resort,
A whistling pipe in warbling notes respir'd;
60 The well-known sound invites each youth to sport,
And every heart its harmony inspir'd;
While from each mead,
So thick with daisies spread,
The bounding nymphs with fairy lightness sprung,
65 And gayly wild their sportive sonnets sung;
The air was scented by the odorous flowers,
Bright sprinkled with the dew of fresh-fall'n show'rs.

Of lively grace, and dimpled smiles,
Slim CYNTHIA, the refin'd,
70 Came, with neat PHILLIS, full of tricksome wiles;
While SILVIUS stroll'd behind,
Chas'd by the marble-hearted ROSALIND:
The loud and witty large-mouth'd MADGE,
With her obsequious servant HODGE.[1]

75 Blythe from the mill, which briskly turning round
Made the young zephyrs breathe a rural sound,
Leap'd CHARLES, gay glowing with industrious heat,
Active to lead in every rustic feat:
Back from his brows he shook his wavy locks,
80 And turning quick his lively eyes,
His lovely, modest PEGGY spies,
Returning with her aged father's flocks.
Straight with his hand he gave his heart sincere,
Devoid of order danc'd, and whistled loud and clear.

85 HEBE,[2] a blooming, sprightly fair,
With shallow NED, an ill-match'd pair;
Simple DAPHNE,[3] rosy JOHN,
And ever-blundering HELESON:
From a large mansion, gloom'd by shading trees,
90 Forth sprung the star-ey'd LUISSE;
Graceful her tresses flow'd around,
Like scatter'd clouds, that catch the moon's pale beams;
Scarcely she seem'd to touch the verdant ground,

---

[1] typical pastoral names; Rosalind is the heroine of Shakespeare, *As You Like It*.

[2] named after the classical goddess of youth.

[3] named after a nymph who was pursued by Apollo and who turned into a laurel: see Ovid, *Metamorphoses* 1.

But, as inspired, along the plain she streams.
95 More join the flock;—they spring in air,
Light as wing'd doves, and like to doves they pair;
The sun's last ray now linger'd o'er their head,
And sweets delectable around were spread.
Poor GERTRUDE, hid amongst the trees, survey'd
100 Each ardent youth, each blooming maid;
And as she gaz'd,
Pleasure by slow degrees within her senses steals:
Her eyes, with tears impearl'd, she rais'd,
Her heart each sweet sensation feels;
105 Lightly her feet the grassy meadows tread,
While music's power deludes her from her cares;
Among the nymphs, by its soft influence led,
Her sympathetic breast their raptures shares.

Thus while she felt, and join'd the lively throng,
110 Lo! quick ascends the plain
The glory of each swain,
URBAN, with sportive song,
Whose chearful notes in frolic measures fled;
    While ROSAMONDE,
115 Fleet-footed, glowing ROSAMONDE, he led:
The rapture of the lark her voice sent forth,
Too well, ah! GERTRUDE knew its worth;
Dire tremblings soon her spirits seize:
Could she, vain untaught nymph, aspire to please?
120 Her body owns no grace,
No smiles, no dimples, deck her eyes or face:
She feels that she has nought to prize;
Yet, totally devoid of art,
Expression's charm was her's, with beaming eyes,
125 A voice far-reaching, and a feeling heart.

She turn'd around—
The flying breezes loosen'd to the air
Her ill-beseeming vests, her scatter'd hair:
So sad she look'd, so artless was her woe,
130 As from a thinking mind had drawn a tear;
But joy through every vein had stole,
And mirth shut out the sympathetic glow.
The heart's gay dance admits of no controul,
Sweet joys but seldom through our senses steal;
135 'Tis pity then we should forget to feel.

Gay wicked wit amid the circles spread,
And wanton round the lively sallies sped;
Each neat-trimm'd maiden laugh'd with playful glee,
Whom whispering swains divert with mimickry.
140 Fair ROSAMONDE, whose rival bosom burn'd,
With taunting mirth directs young URBAN'S eyes;
He, with mischievous archness, smiles return'd,
Amid whose circles wounding satires rise;
Their sportive feet still beat the flowery ground,
145 While wicked looks, and jests, and jeers went round.

Pierc'd by their insults, stung with bitter smart,
Sad fell poor GERTRUDE'S tears, high heav'd her heart.
Distant she flew, and sitting on a stone,
Conceal'd, gave sorrow vent, and wept alone:
150 Till 'mid her grief, a virtuous just disdain
    Came to her aid, and made her bosom glow;
    With shame she burns, she blushes at her woe,
And wonders at her weakness and her pain.
"Unhappy maid!" she cry'd, "thou art to blame,
155 Thus to expose thy virtuous breast to shame:
Poor heart! thy love is laugh'd at for its truth;
Yet 'tis a holy treasure, though disdain'd,
And wantonly by thoughtlessness profan'd;
Ah! why then waste the blessings of thy youth?
160 No more fair reason's sacred light despise;
Thy heart may blessings find
That dwell not in the eyes,
But in the virtues of the feeling mind."

Night

Solemn is night, when Silence holds her reign,
And the hush'd winds die on the heaving main;
When no short gleam of scatter'd light appears,
Nor lunar beams make faint the nobler stars;
5 Then those whom inward cares deprive of rest
Pour forth the secret sorrows of the breast.

Such was the night—smooth glides the bark along,
From whence young HENRY breath'd his thoughtful song;
Pacing the deck, he threw his eyes around
10 The thick-starr'd firmament, and vast profound;
The patient winds scarce whistled o'er the waste,
The burning waves the vessel's prow embrac'd;
The nitrous[1] air unclouded glow'd on high,
With northern meteors trembling through the sky.
15 "Eternal Power!" he cried, "with justice fraught,
O! teach a wretch to curb each stubborn thought,
Whose passions reason's powers no more restrain,
Grown wanton midst intolerable pain.

"Pierc'd by ingratitude, I rove forlorn,
20 My faithful heart from strong affection's torn;
A willing exile on the dangerous main,
Unshook by storms, while calms breathe peace in vain.
Oft with unmanly tenderness I mourn;
And, tortur'd by imagination, burn;
25 Sighs in a natural cadence close each song,
And tones of anguish vibrate on my tongue.

"All is now hush'd, still as the silent grave,
The breeze scarce swells the smooth unruffled wave,
Which glittering with celestial lustre bright,
30 Reflects the spangled heaven's ethereal light:
O! how sublime this tract, for man design'd!
Vast the perceptions of his rapid mind!
Strongly to earth his young affections cling,
While Fancy waves her bright and various wing;
35 But soon each hope of earthly bliss is cross'd,
Nipt in the bud, or in possession lost;
Blushing, our empty wishes we survey,
When we our passions with their motives weigh.

"Deeply I feel this still and solemn hour,
40 Impress'd with GOD'S immeasurable power;
While worlds unnumber'd 'mid yon ether burn,
And thoughts immense pour in where'er I turn.
How much man errs, whose soul, with thought sublime,
Looks on tow'rds endless bliss thro' boundless time!
45 When he to earthly passions gives dire sway,
Or mourns those joys which of themselves decay!["]

---

[1] explosive, because of the meteors in line 14.

Jane Marcet
1769 – 1858

Born in London in 1769 to a wealthy Swiss banker, Anthony Francis Haldimand, and his wife, Jane Haldimand, Jane Haldimand was educated at home alongside her brothers. After her marriage in 1799 to Alexander Marcet, a Swiss-born physician and chemist, she became interested in his scientific research, studying chemistry and attending Sir Humphry Davy's lectures at the Royal Institution. In 1805 she published her *Conversations on Chemistry, Intended More Especially for the Female Sex*. Taking the form of a dialogue between a teacher, Mrs. B—, and two pupils, the book became widely popular, influencing, among others, Michael Faraday. During Marcet's lifetime there were sixteen British editions, twenty-three American editions, and two French editions.

Marcet went on to write *Conversations* on many other subjects: *On Political Economy* (1816), *On Natural Philosophy* (1819), *On Evidences of Christianity* (1826), *On Vegetable Physiology* (1829), *On Mineralogy* (1829), *On the History of England* (1842), and *On Language for Children* (1844). Having raised four children, the Marcets moved to Geneva in 1820. But following Alexander's death in 1822, Jane Marcet settled in London, where she lived in a circle that included the writer Harriet Martineau. There she wrote children's books, notably *Mary's Grammar* (1835). She died at her daughter's house in London on 28 June 1858. (A.M.)

❧❧

from *Conversations on Political Economy; in Which the Elements of that Science are Familiarly Explained* (1816)

from CONVERSATION 10
On the Condition of the Poor

Of the cultivation of commons and waste lands.—Of emigration.—Education of the lower classes.—Benefit clubs.—Saving banks.—Parochial relief.—Alms and private charities.—Rewards.

CAROLINE: I have been reflecting ever since [our last conversation] whether there might be any means of averting [the evils arising from overpopulation],[1] and of raising subsistence to the level of population, rather than suffering population to sink to the level of subsistence. Though we have not the same resource in land as America; yet we have large tracts of waste land, which by being brought into cultivation would produce an additional stock of subsistence.

MRS. B: You forget that industry is limited by the extent of capital, and that no more labourers can be employed than we have the means of maintaining; they work for their daily bread, and without obtaining it, they neither could nor would work. All the labourers which the capital of the country can maintain being disposed of, the only question is, whether it be better to employ them on land already in a state of cultivation, or in breaking up and bringing into culture new lands; and this point may safely be trusted to the decision of the landed proprietors, as it is no less their interest than that of the labouring classes that the greatest possible quantity of produce should be raised. To a certain extent it has been found more advantageous to lay out capital in improving the culture of old land, rather than to employ it in bringing new land into tillage; because the soil of the waste land is extremely poor and ungrateful, and requires a great deal to be laid out on it before it brings in a return. But there is often capital sufficient for both these purposes, and of late years we have seen not only prodigious improvements in the processes of agriculture throughout the country, but a great number of commons inclosed and cultivated.

---

[1] the subject of Thomas Malthus's *Essay on the Principle of Population.**

CAROLINE: I fear you will think me inconsistent, but I cannot help regretting the inclosure of commons;[1] they are the only resource of the cottagers for the maintenance of a few lean cattle. Let me once more quote my favourite Goldsmith:

> "Where then, ah where shall poverty reside,
> To 'scape the pressure of contiguous pride?
> If to some common's fenceless limits stray'd,
> He drives his flock to pick the scanty blade,
> Those fenceless fields the sons of wealth deride,
> And e'en the bare-worn common is deny'd."[2]

MRS. B: You should recollect that we do not admit poets to be very good authority in political economy. If, instead of feeding a few lean cattle, a common can, by being inclosed, fatten a much greater number of fine cattle, you must allow that the quantity of subsistence will be increased, and the poor, though in a less direct manner, will fare the better for it. Labourers are required to inclose and cultivate those commons, the neighbouring cottagers are employed for that purpose, and this additional demand for labour turns to their immediate advantage. They not only receive an indemnity for their loss of right of common, but they find purchasers for the cattle they can no longer maintain, in the proprietors of the new inclosures....

CAROLINE: But if we have it not in our power to provide for a redundant population by the cultivation of our waste lands, what objection is there to sending those who cannot find employment at home, to seek a maintenance in countries where it is more easily obtained, where there is a greater demand for labour? Or why should they not found new colonies in the yet unsettled parts of America?

MRS. B: Emigration is undoubtedly a resource for an overstocked population; but one that is adopted in general with great reluctance by individuals; and is commonly discouraged by governments, from an apprehension of its diminishing the strength of the country.

CAROLINE: It might be wrong to encourage emigration to a very great extent; I meant only to provide abroad for those whom we cannot maintain at home.

MRS. B: Under an equitable government there is little danger of emigration ever exceeding that point. The attachment to our native land is naturally so strong, and there are so many ties of kindred and association to break through before we can quit it, that no slight motive will induce a man to expatriate himself. An author deeply versed in the knowledge of the human mind says, "La seule bonne loi contre les emigrations, est celle que la nature a gravé dans nos cœurs."[3] On this subject I am very willing to quote the Deserted Village:

> "Good heaven! what sorrows gloom'd that parting day
> That call'd them from their native walks away."[4]

Besides, the difficulties with which a colony of emigrants have to struggle before they can effect a settlement; and the hardships they must undergo, until they have raised food for their subsistence, are so discouraging, that no motive less strong than that of necessity is likely to induce them to settle in an uncultivated land. Some capital too is required for this as well as for all undertakings; the colonists must be provided with implements of husbandry and of art; and supplied with food and clothing until they shall have succeeded in producing such necessaries for themselves.

Were emigration therefore allowed, instead of being checked, scarcely any would abandon their country but those who could not find a maintenance in it. But should emigration ever become so great as to leave the means of subsistence easy and plentiful to those who remain, it would naturally cease, and the facility of rearing children, and maintaining families, would soon fill the vacancy in population.

There are some emigrations which are extremely detrimental to the wealth and prosperity of a country; these, however, are not occasioned by poverty, but result from the severity and hardships imposed by arbitrary governments on particular classes of men. Want of toleration in religion has caused the most considerable

---

[1] The private enclosure of lands formerly open to common use was deplored by such writers as Oliver Goldsmith, in *The Deserted Village,** as one cause of rural depopulation and emigration.

[2] *The Deserted Village* 303–08.*

[3] "The only good law against emigration is the one that nature has engraved on our hearts" (Fr.) [source unidentified].

[4] *The Deserted Village* 363–64.*

and numerous emigrations of this description. Such was that of the Huguenots from France at the revocation of the edict of Nantz.[1] They were a skilful and industrious people, who carried their arts and manufactures into Germany, Prussia, Holland, and England, and deprived France of some of her most valuable subjects. Spain has never recovered the blow which her industry received by the expulsion of the Moors, under Ferdinand and Isabella;[2] not all the wealth of America has repaid her for this loss.

But to return to the population of England; the more we find ourselves unable to provide for an overgrown population, the more desirous we should be to avail ourselves of those means which tend to prevent the evil;—such, for instance, as a general diffusion of knowledge, which would excite greater attention in the lower classes to their future interests.

CAROLINE: Surely you would not teach political economy to the labouring classes, Mrs. B.?

MRS. B: No; but I would endeavour to give the rising generation such an education as would render them not only moral and religious, but industrious, frugal, and provident. In proportion as the mind is informed, we are able to calculate the consequences of our actions: it is the infant and the savage who live only for the present moment; those whom instruction has taught to think, reflect upon the past and look forward to the future. Education gives rise to prudence, not only by enlarging our understandings, but by softening our feelings, by humanizing the heart, and promoting amiable affections. The rude and inconsiderate peasant marries without either foreseeing or caring for the miseries he may entail on his wife and children; but he who has been taught to value the comforts and decencies of life, will not heedlessly involve himself and all that is dear to him in poverty, and its long train of miseries.

CAROLINE: I am very happy to hear that you think instruction may produce this desirable end, since the zeal for the education of the poor that has been displayed of late years gives every prospect of success; and in a few years more, it may perhaps be impossible to meet with a child who cannot read and write.

MRS. B: The highest advantages, both religious, moral, and political, may be expected to result from this general ardour for the instruction of the poor. No great or decided improvement can be effected in the manners of the people but by the education of the rising generation.... But independently of schools and the various institutions for the education of youth, there is an establishment among the lower classes which is peculiarly calculated to inculcate lessons of prudence and economy. I mean the Benefit Clubs, or Friendly Societies;[3] the members of which, by contributing a small stipend monthly, accumulate a fund which furnishes them relief and aid in times of sickness or distress. These associations have spread throughout the country, and their good effects are rendered evident by comparing the condition of such of the labouring classes as belong to them with those of the same district who have no resource in times of distress, but parochial relief or private charity. The former are comparatively cleanly, industrious, sober, frugal, respecting themselves, and respected by others; depending in times of casual sickness or accident on funds created by their own industry, they maintain an honourable pride and independance of character: whilst the latter, in a season of distress, become a prey to dirt and wretchedness; and being dissatisfied with the scantiness of parish relief,[4] they are often driven to the commission of crimes. It is above a century since these clubs were first instituted; they have received encouragement both from government and individuals, and have spread throughout the country. I dare say that your prudent gardener Thomas is a member of one of them.

CAROLINE: Yes; and he belongs to one which can boast of peculiar advantages, as most of the gentlemen in the neighbourhood subscribe to it; in order by increasing the fund, and consequently the amount of

---

[1] French Protestants, known as Huguenots, were granted a degree of religious freedom by the Edict of Nantes (1598); its revocation in 1685 resulted in mass emigration.

[2] Under King Ferdinand II and Queen Isabella of Spain, the Moors (or Muslims) were compelled in 1502 to convert to Christianity or leave the country.

[3] such as those established by Hannah More* in 1789.

[4] Parishes were responsible for relieving the poor within their boundaries.

the relief which the distressed members can receive, to encourage the poor to belong to it....

MRS. B: The certainty that the parish is bound to succour their wants, renders the poor less apprehensive of indigence than if they were convinced that they must suffer all the wretchedness it entails. When a young man marries without having the means of supporting his family by his labour, and without having saved some little provision against accidents or sickness, he depends upon the parish as a never-failing resource. A profligate man knows that if he spend his wages at the public-house instead of providing for his family, his wife and children can at worst but go to the poor-house. Parish relief thus becomes the very cause of the mischief which it professes to remedy....

CAROLINE: But what is to be done, the poor cannot be allowed to starve, even when idle and vicious?

MRS. B: Certainly not; and besides the wife and children of a profligate man are often the innocent victims of his misconduct. Then there are frequently cases of casual distress, which no prudence could foresee nor guard against; under these circumstances the poor rates[1] could not be abolished without occasioning the most cruel distress. I know therefore of no other remedy to this evil than the slow and gradual effect of education; by enlightening the minds of the lower classes their moral habits are improved, and they rise above that state of degradation in which all feelings of dignity and independance are extinguished.

CAROLINE: But, alas! how many years will elapse before these happy results can take place. I am impatient that benefits should be immediately and universally diffused; their progress is in general so slow and partial, that there is but a small chance of our living to see their effects.

MRS. B: There is some gratification in looking forward to an improved state of society, even if we should not live to witness it.

CAROLINE: Since it is so little in our power to accelerate its progress, we must endeavour to be contented: but I confess that I cannot help regretting the want of sovereign power to forward measures so conducive to the happiness of mankind....

MRS. B: I cannot blame any one for indulging feelings of humanity; to pity and relieve the sufferings of our fellow creatures is one of the first lessons which nature teaches us: but our actions should be regulated by good sense, not blindly directed by undistinguishing compassion. We should certainly consider it as a duty to ascertain whether the object whom we relieve is in real want, and we should proportion our charity not only to his distress, but also to his merits. We ought to do much more for an industrious family, whom unforeseen or unavoidable accidents have reduced to poverty, than for one who has brought on distress through want of a well-regulated conduct. When we relieve objects of this latter description, it would be well at the same time to bestow a trifling reward on some individual among the labouring classes of the neighbourhood distinguished for his industry and good conduct. This would counteract the pernicious effect which cannot fail to be produced by assisting the indolent, whilst we suffer the industrious to remain without reward....

---

[1] levies imposed for relieving the destitute in a parish.

Amelia Opie
1769 – 1853

Amelia Alderson Opie, the only child of James Alderson, a physician and dissenter, and Amelia Briggs Alderson, was born in Norwich on 12 November 1769. Her mother died in 1784; thereafter, Opie acted as hostess for her father, meeting such intellectuals and writers as Godwin,* Harriet Martineau, Thomas Holcroft, and John Aikin. She published her first novel, *Dangers of Coquetry*, in 1790.

In the mid-90s, Amelia Alderson made annual trips to London, where she moved in literary and theatrical circles, becoming friends with the Kembles, Godwin,* Wollstonecraft,* and Inchbald.* In 1797 she met the recently divorced painter, John Opie, whom she married the following year and with whom she travelled to Paris during the Peace of Amiens in 1802. He encouraged her to write. In 1801 she dedicated her "simple, moral tale," *Father and Daughter*, to her father. Her *Poems* followed in 1802. Her most popular novel, *Adeline Mowbray* (1805), told the story of a heroine (loosely modelled on Mary Wollstonecraft) who rejects marriage. *Simple Tales*, a collection of short fiction, followed in 1806.

John Opie died in April 1807, and Opie returned to Norwich to care for her father. There her social circle included W. Wordsworth,* Walter Scott,* and the actor Sarah Siddons. *The Warrior's Return, and Other Poems* appeared in 1808. In 1809 she published a biography of her husband, *Memoir of John Opie*. During the next years, she published a considerable body of fiction, making a good income from her writing: *Temper, or Domestic Scenes* (1812); a second collection of stories, *Tales of Real Life* (1813); *Valentine's Eve* (1816); *Tales of the Heart* (1820); and her last novel, *Madeline* (1822). Her father died in October 1825. Her 1826 poem, *The Black Man's Lament, or, How to Make Sugar*, expresses her strong anti-slavery beliefs.

Opie's lifelong friend Joseph John Gurney had taken her to Quaker (Society of Friends) meetings since 1814. She became a Quaker shortly before her father died and subsequently gave up writing fiction. For the rest of her life she did charity work and wrote didactic works. She travelled, corresponded widely, contributed to periodicals, and was active in the anti-slavery movement, attending the London convention in 1840 as the delegate from Norwich. She died at Norwich on 2 December 1853. (A.M.)

ഔഔ

from *Poems* (1802)

Song of a Hindustani Girl[1]

'Tis thy will, and I must leave thee:
O! then, best-beloved, farewell!
I forbear, lest I should grieve thee,
  Half my heartfelt pangs to tell.
5 Soon a British fair will charm thee,
  Thou her smiles wilt fondly woo;
But though she to rapture warm thee,
  Don't forget THY POOR HINDOO.

Well I know this happy beauty
10   Soon thine envied bride will shine;
But will she by anxious duty
  Prove a passion warm as mine?
If to rule be her ambition,
  And her own desires pursue,
15 Thou'lt recall my fond submission,
  And regret THY POOR HINDOO.

---

[1] "This Song was occasioned by the following circumstance: ... Mr. Biggs, the composer and editor of many beautiful Airs, gave me, some time ago, a plaintive melody, said to have been composed and sung by a Hindustàni girl on being separated from the man she loved.

"She had lived several years in India with an English gentleman to whom she was tenderly attached; but he, when about to marry, sent his Indian favourite up the country; and, as she was borne along in her palanquin, she was heard to sing the above-mentioned melody. To this melody I write the following words; and they have been already given to the public, with the original music, in a second set of Hindoo airs, arranged and harmonized by Mr. Biggs." (A.O.)

Born herself to rank and splendour,
    Will she deign to wait on thee,
And those soft attentions render
20   Thou so oft hast praised in me?
Yet, why doubt her care to please thee?
    Thou must every heart subdue;
I am sure each maid that sees thee
    Loves thee like THY POOR HINDOO.

25 No, ah! no! ... though from thee parted,
    Other maids will peace obtain;
But thy Lolà, broken-hearted,
    Ne'er, oh! ne'er, will smile again.
Oh! How fast from thee they tear me!
30   Faster still shall death pursue:
But 'tis well ... death will endear me,
    And thou'lt mourn THY POOR HINDOO.

from *The Warrior's Return, and Other Poems* (1808)

To A Maniac

There was a time, poor phrensied maid,
When I could o'er thy grief have mourned,
And still with tears the tale repaid
Of sense by sorrow's sway o'erturned.

5 But now thy state my envy moves:
For thou art woe's unconscious prize;
Thy heart no sense of suffering proves,
No fruitless tears bedew thine eyes.

Excess of sorrow, kind to thee,
10 At once destroyed thy reason's power;
But reason still remains to me,
And only bids me grieve the more.

George Canning
1770 – 1827
John Hookham Frere
1769 – 1846

George Canning was born on 11 April 1770 in London, the son of George Canning, a lawyer, and Mary Anne Costello Canning; in 1771, his father died and his mother became an actor, to support her family. He was educated at Eton College, where he met Frere, and at Christ Church College, Oxford. In 1793, he was elected to Parliament. A brilliant orator, he served as Under-secretary of State, Secretary of the Navy, and Foreign Minister. He married Joan Scott in 1800. He died in Chiswick on 8 August 1827, three months after becoming Prime Minister.

John Hookham Frere was born on 21 May 1769 in London, the eldest son of John Frere, an antiquarian, and Jane Hookham Frere. He was educated at Eton and at Caius College, Cambridge. He was a Member of Parliament for one term (1796–1802) and then followed Canning as Under-secretary of State and eventually became a diplomat, representing Britain in Portugal, Spain, and Prussia. In 1809, he retired from public life. In 1816, he married Elizabeth Erroll; in 1818, she became ill, and they moved to Malta for her health. Literary history owes Frere a debt of gratitude for his poem *Prospectus and Specimen of an Intended National Work* (1817–18), published under the pseudonyms William and Robert Whistlecraft, which first suggested to Byron the comic possibilities of the *ottava rima* stanza he used in *Beppo*, "The Vision of Judgment," and *Don Juan*.* Frere died in Malta on 7 January 1846.

Canning and Frere founded a magazine, the *Microcosm*, while they were still at Eton. It ran through forty issues, sold as many as seven hundred copies, and counted George III among its readers. They founded the *Anti-Jacobin* in November 1797, intending it to be "full of sound reasoning, good principles and good jokes to set the mind of the people right upon every subject." It soon became known for the violence of its satire on supporters of the French Revolution and other reform causes. Its last issue appeared on 9 July 1798. (D.L.M.)

❧

from *The Anti-Jacobin; or, Weekly Examiner*
(27 November 1797)

Sapphics
The Friend of Humanity and the Knife-Grinder[1]

FRIEND OF HUMANITY.
"Needy Knife-grinder! whither are you going?
Rough is the road, your Wheel is out of order—
Bleak blows the blast;—your hat has got a hole in't,
        So have your breeches!

5 "Weary Knife-grinder! little think the proud ones,
Who in their coaches roll along the turnpike-
road, what hard work 'tis crying all day "Knives and
        Scissars to grind O!"

"Tell me, Knife-grinder, how you came to grind
    knives?
10 Did some rich man tyrannically use you?
Was it the 'Squire, or Parson of the Parish?
        Or the Attorney?

"Was it the 'Squire, for killing of his Game? or
Covetous Parson, for his Tythes distraining?
15 Or roguish Lawyer made you lose your little
        All in a law-suit?

---

[1] a parody of Southey, "The Widow."* "Sapphics" refers to their common metre, supposedly invented by the Greek poet Sappho (c. 600 BC).

"(Have you not read the Rights of Man, by TOM
    PAINE?)
Drops of compassion tremble on my eye-lids,
Ready to fall, as soon as you have told your
                    Pitiful story."

            KNIFE-GRINDER.
"Story! God bless you! I have none to tell, Sir,
Only last night a-drinking at the Chequers,
This poor old hat and breeches, as you see, were
                    Torn in a scuffle.

"Constables came up for to take me into
Custody; they took me before the Justice;
Justice OLDMIXON put me in the Parish-
                    Stocks for a Vagrant.

"I should be glad to drink your Honour's health in
A Pot of Beer, if you will give me Sixpence;
But for my part, I never love to meddle
                    With Politics, Sir."

            FRIEND OF HUMANITY.
"*I* give thee Sixpence! I will see thee damn'd first—
Wretch! whom no sense of wrongs can rouse to
    vengeance;
Sordid, unfeeling, reprobate, degraded,
                    Spiritless outcast!"

(*Kicks the Knife-grinder, overturns his Wheel, and exit in
a transport of republican enthusiasm and universal philanthropy.*)
—9 *July 1798*

from *The New Morality*

If Vice appal thee,—if thou view with awe[1]
Insults that brave, and Crimes that 'scape the Law;—
Yet may the specious bastard brood, which claim
A spurious homage under Virtue's name,
Sprung from that Parent of ten thousand crimes,
The *New Philosophy* of modern times,—
Yet, these may rouse thee!—With unsparing hand
Oh, lash the vile impostures from the land!

    First, stern PHILANTHROPY:—not she, who dries
The orphan's tears, and wipes the widow's eyes;
Not She, who, sainted Charity her guide,
Of British bounty pours the annual tide:—
But *French* PHILANTHROPY;—whose boundless mind
Glows with the general love of all mankind;—
PHILANTHROPY,—beneath whose baneful sway
Each patriot passion sinks, and dies away.

    Taught in her school to' imbibe thy mawkish
        strain,
CONDORCET, filter'd through the dregs of PAINE,[2]
Each pert Adept disowns a Briton's part,
And plucks the name of ENGLAND from his heart.

    What shall a name, a word, a sound controul
The' aspiring thought, and cramp the' expansive soul?
Shall one half-peopled Island's rocky round
A love, that glows for all Creation, bound?
And social charities contract the plan
Fram'd for thy Freedom, UNIVERSAL MAN?
—No—through the' extended globe his feelings run
As broad and general as the' unbounded Sun!
No narrow bigot *he*;—*his* reason'd view
Thy interests, *England*, ranks with thine *Peru*!
France at our doors, *he* sees no danger nigh,

---

[1] The opening lines call for a satirist like Pope to arise and punish the wickedness and folly of the times.

[2] Marie-Jean-Antoine-Nicolas Caritat, marquis de Condorcet (1743–94), mathematician, philosopher, and Revolutionary; and Thomas Paine.*

But heaves for *Turkey's* woes the' impartial sigh;
A steady Patriot of the World alone,
The Friend of every Country—but his own.

    Next comes a gentler Virtue.—Ah! beware
115 Lest the harsh verse her shrinking softness scare.
Visit her not too roughly;—the warm sigh
Breathes on her lips;—the tear-drop gems her eye.
Sweet SENSIBILITY, who dwells enshrin'd
In the fine foldings of the feeling mind;—
120 With delicate *Mimosa's*[1] sense endu'd,
Who, shrinks instinctive from a hand too rude;
Or, like the *Anagallis*, prescient flow'r,
Shuts her soft petals at the' approaching show'r.

    Sweet Child of sickly FANCY!—Her of yore
125 From her lov'd *France* ROUSSEAU to exile bore;[2]
And, while midst lakes and mountains wild he ran
Full of himself, and shunn'd the haunts of Man,
Taught her o'er each lone vale and Alpine steep
To lisp the story of his wrongs, and weep;
130 Taught her to cherish still in either eye,
Of tender tears a plentiful supply,
And pour them in the brooks that babbled by;—
—Taught by nice scale to meet her feelings strong,
False by degrees, and exquisitely wrong;—
135 —For the crush'd Beetle, *first*.—the widow'd Dove,
And all the warbled sorrows of the grove;—
Next for poor suff'ring *Guilt*;—and, *last* of all,
For Parents, Friends, a King and Country's fall.

    Mark her fair Votaries, prodigal of grief,
140 With cureless pangs, and woes that mock relief,
Droop in soft sorrow o'er a faded flow'r;
O'er a dead Jack-Ass pour the pearly show'r:—[3]

But hear, unmov'd, of *Loire's* ensanguin'd flood,[4]
Choak'd up with slain;—of *Lyons* drench'd in blood;[5]
145 Of crimes that blot the Age, the World with shame,
Foul crimes, but sicklied o'er with Freedom's name;
Altars and Thrones subverted, social life
Trampled to earth,—the Husband from the Wife,
Parent from Child, with ruthless fury torn,—
150 Of Talents, Honour, Virtue, Wit, forlorn,
In friendless exile,—of the wise and good
Staining the daily Scaffold with their blood,—
Of savage cruelties, that scare the mind,
The rage of madness with Hell's lusts combin'd—
155 Of Hearts torn reeking from the mangled breast,—
They hear—and hope, that ALL IS FOR THE BEST.

    Fond hope!—but JUSTICE sanctifies the pray'r—
JUSTICE!—Here Satire strike! 'twere sin to spare!
Not She in British Courts that takes her stand,
160 The dawdling balance dangling in her hand,
Adjusting punishments to Fraud and Vice,
With scrupulous quirks, and disquisition nice:—
But firm, erect, with keen reverted glance
The' avenging Angel of regenerate *France*,
165 Who visits antient sins on modern times,
And punishes the POPE for CÆSAR's crimes.[6]

---

[1] *Mimosa pudica*, the sensitive plant. *Anagallis* (line 123) is another genus of plant.

[2] Jean-Jacques Rousseau (1712–78), author of *Julie* (1761), a novel of sensibility, and *Du Contrat social* (1762), a treatise often credited with helping to inspire the Revolution, went into exile in England in 1765.

[3] Cf. Laurence Sterne (1713–68), *A Sentimental Journey* (1768), "Nampont: The Dead Ass."

[4] In suppressing the Catholic/Royalist uprising in the Vendée region of France (March–December 1793), the Revolutionary government was responsible for mass drownings (known as "vertical deportations") in the Loire.

[5] The Reign of Terror in Lyons was so terrible that even the executioner was executed.

[6] "The Manes of VERCENGETORIX are supposed to have been very much gratified by the Invasion of Italy and the Plunder of the Roman Territory. The defeat of the Burgundians is to be revenged on the modern inhabitants of Switzerland.—But the Swiss were a free People, defending their Liberties against a Tyrant. Moreover, they happened to be in Alliance with France at the time. No matter, *Burgundy* is since become a Province of France, and the French have acquired a property in all the injuries and defeats which the People of that Country may have sustained, together with a title to revenge and retaliation to be exercised in the present, or any future centuries, as may be found most glorious and convenient." (G.C./J.H.F.) Vercingetorix led a revolt of the Gauls against Julius Cæsar, who defeated him, brought him to Rome in triumph, and had him put to death in 46 BC. Napoleon invaded Switzerland and Italy in 1798. The Swiss had defeated the Burgundians at the battle of Morat on 14 June 1476. Byron* celebrates the battle in *Childe Harold* 3.63–64 (not included here).

Such is the liberal JUSTICE which presides
In these our days, and modern Patriots guides;—
JUSTICE, whose blood-stain'd Book one sole Decree,
One Statute fills—"The People shall be Free."
Free by what means?—by folly, madness, guilt,
By boundless rapines, blood in oceans spilt;
By confiscation, in whose sweeping toils
The poor Man's pittance with the rich Man's spoils,
Mix'd in one common mass, are swept away,
To glut the short-liv'd Tyrant of the day;—
By Laws, Religion, Morals all o'erthrown:—
—Rouse then, ye Sovereign People, claim your own;—
The License that enthrals, the Truth that blinds,
The Wealth that starves you, and the Pow'r that grinds.
—So JUSTICE bids.—'Twas her enlighten'd doom,
LOUIS, thy holy head devoted to the tomb![1]
'Twas JUSTICE claim'd, in that accursed hour,
The fatal forfeit of too lenient pow'r.
—Mourn for the Man we may;—but for the King,—
Freedom, oh! Freedom's such a charming thing!

"Much may be said on both sides."—Hark! I hear
A well-known voice that murmurs in my ear,—
The voice of CANDOUR.—Hail! most solemn Sage,
Thou driveling Virtue of this moral Age,
CANDOUR, which softens Party's headlong rage.
CANDOUR,—which spares its foes;—nor e'er descends
With bigot zeal to combat for its friends.
CANDOUR,—which loves in see-saw strain to tell
Of *acting foolishly*, but *meaning well*;
Too nice to praise by wholesale, or to blame,
Convinc'd that *all* men's *motives* are the same;—
And finds, with keen discriminating sight,
BLACK's not *so* black;—nor WHITE *so very* white.

"FOX, to be sure, was vehement and wrong:—
But then PITT's words, you'll own, were *rather* strong.
Both must be blamed, both pardon'd;—'twas just so

With FOX and PITT full forty years ago;[2]
So WALPOLE, PULTENEY;—Factions in all times
Have had their follies, Ministers their crimes."

Give me the' avow'd, the' erect, the manly Foe
Bold I can meet,—perhaps may turn his blow;
But of all plagues, good Heav'n, thy wrath can send,
Save, save, oh! save me from the *Candid Friend*![3]
...
Ere long, perhaps, to this astonish'd Isle,
Fresh from the Shores of subjugated *Nile*,[4]
Shall *Buonaparte*'s victor Fleet protect
The genuine THEO-PHILANTHROPIC Sect,—
The Sect of MARAT, MIRABEAU, VOLTAIRE,—
Led by their Pontiff, good LA REVEILLERE.[5]
—Rejoic'd our CLUBS[6] shall greet him, and install
The holy Hunch-back in thy Dome, *St. Paul*!
While countless votaries thronging in his train
Wave their Red Caps,[7] and hymn this jocund strain:

"*Couriers* and *Stars*, Sedition's Evening Host,
Thou *Morning Chronicle*, and *Morning Post*,
Whether ye make the Rights of Man your theme,
Your Country libel, and your God blaspheme,
Or dirt on private worth and virtue throw,
Still blasphemous or blackguard, praise LEPAUX.

---

[1] Louis XVI was guillotined on 21 January 1793.

[2] Charles James Fox (1749–1806) had not in fact been an opponent of William Pitt the Elder (1708–78), who retired from politics in 1768, the year Fox entered Parliament; but he was certainly an opponent of William Pitt the Younger (1759–1806), especially about the war with France. Robert Walpole, 1st Earl of Orford (1676–1745), and William Pulteney, 1st Earl of Bath (1684–1764), were political opponents of an earlier generation.

[3] The omitted lines satirize various French Revolutionaries and their British supporters.

[4] In the event, Nelson would defeat Napoleon's fleet in the battle of the Nile on 1 August 1798.

[5] François-Marie Arouet de Voltaire (1694–1778), a writer often considered to have helped inspire the Revolution; and three Revolutionaries: Jean-Paul Marat (1743–93); Honoré-Gabriel Riquetti, comte de Mirabeau (1749–91); and Louis-Marie de La Révellière-Lépaux (1753–1824), noted for his hostility towards Christianity. Canning and Frere usually call him "Lepaux."

[6] reformist political organizations.

[7] Phrygian caps, symbols of Revolutionary allegiance.

"And ye five other wandering Bards that move
335 In sweet accord of harmony and love,
C——DGE and S——TH——Y, L——D, and L——BE[1]
 and Co.
"Tune all your mystic harps to praise LEPAUX!

 "PR——TL——Y and W——F——LD, humble, holy
  men,[2]
Give praises to his name with tongue and pen!

340 "TH——LW——L, and ye that lecture as ye go,[3]
And for your pains get pelted, praise LEPAUX!

 "Praise him each Jacobin, or Fool, or Knave,
And your cropp'd heads in sign of worship wave!

 "All creeping creatures, venomous and low,
345 PAINE, W——LL——MS, G——DW——N, H——L——CR——FT[4]
 ——praise LEPAUX!

 "And thou *Leviathan*![5] on Ocean's brim
Hugest of living things that sleep and swim;
Thou in whose nose by BURKE's gigantic hand
The hook was fix'd to drag thee to the land
350 With ———, ———, and ——— in thy train,[6]

And ———, wallowing in the yeasty main—[7]
Still as ye snort, and puff, and spout, and blow,
In puffing, and in spouting, praise LEPAUX!"

 BRITAIN beware; nor let the' insidious Foe,
355 Of force despairing, aim a deadlier blow.
Thy Peace, thy Strength, with devilish wiles assail,
And when her Arms are vain, by Arts prevail.
True, thou art rich, art powerful!—thro' thine Isle
Industrious skill, contented labour, smile;
360 Far Seas are studded with thy countless Sails;
What wind but wafts them, and what shore but hails!
True, thou art brave!—o'er all the busy land
In patriot ranks embattled myriads stand;
Thy Foes behold with impotent amaze,
365 And drop the lifted weapon as they gaze!

 But what avails to guard each outward part,
If subtlest poison, circling at thy heart,
Spite of thy courage, of thy pow'r, and wealth,
Mine the sound fabric of thy vital health?

370 So thine own Oak,[8] by some fair streamlet's side
Waves its broad arms, and spreads its leafy pride,
Tow'rs from the Earth, and rearing to the Skies
It's conscious strength, the Tempest's wrath defies.
It's ample branches shield the fowls of air,
375 To its cool shade the panting Herds repair.—
The treacherous Current works its noiseless way,—
The fibres loosen, and the roots decay;
Prostrate the beauteous Ruin lies; and all
That shared its shelter, perish in its fall.

380 O thou!—lamented Sage!—whose prescient scan
Pierced thro' foul Anarchy's gigantic plan,
Prompt to incredulous hearers to disclose
The guilt of *France*, and Europe's world of woes;—
Thou, on whose Name Posterity shall gaze,
385 The mighty Sea-mark of these troubled days!

---

[1] Coleridge (see "Effusion 35"),* Southey,* Lloyd,* and Charles Lamb.* Gillray's cartoon illustrating this poem gives Coleridge long ears because of his poem "To a Young Ass" (1794).

[2] Joseph Priestley (1733–1804) and Gilbert Wakefield (1756–1801), both Unitarians and political radicals.

[3] John Thelwall,* author of *The Peripatetic* (1793), was tried for treason in 1794.

[4] Paine,* Williams,* Godwin,* and Thomas Holcroft (1745–1809), playwright and novelist, who was also tried for treason in 1794.

[5] Burke's characterization of Francis Russell, 5th Duke of Bedford (1765–1802), in his *Letter to a Noble Lord.** See Job 41.1–2.

[6] "The Reader is at liberty to fill up the blanks according to his own opinion, and after the chances and changes of the times. It would be highly unfair to hand down to posterity as followers of *Leviathan*, the names of men who may, and probably will soon, grow ashamed of their leader."(G.C./J.H.F.)

[7] "Though the *yeasty* sea
  Consume and swallow navigation up.   MACBETH." (G.C./J.H.F.)
Shakespeare, *Macbeth* 4.1.54.

[8] a traditional symbol of Britain.

O large of soul, of genius unconfin'd,
Born to delight, instruct, and mend Mankind![1]—
BURKE! in whose breast a Roman ardour glow'd;
Whose copious tongue with Grecian richness flow'd;
390 Well hast thou found (if such thy Country's doom)
A timely refuge in the sheltering tomb![2]

As, in far Realms, where Eastern Kings are laid,
In pomp of death, beneath the cypress shade,
The perfum'd lamp with unextinguish'd light
395 Flames thro' the vault, and cheers the gloom of night:—
So, mighty BURKE! in thy sepulchral urn,
To Fancy's view, the lamp of Truth shall burn.
Thither late times shall turn their reverent eyes,
Led by thy light, and by thy wisdom wise.

400 There *are*, to whom (*their* taste such pleasures cloy)
No light thy wisdom yields, thy wit no joy.
Peace to their heavy heads, and callous hearts,
Peace—such as Sloth, as Ignorance imparts!—
Pleas'd may they live to plan their Country's good,
405 And crop with calm Content their flow'ry food!

What tho' thy venturous Spirit lov'd to urge
The labouring theme to Reason's utmost verge,
Kindling and mounting from th' enraptur'd sight;—
Still anxious Wonder watch'd thy daring flight!
410 —While vulgar souls, with mean malignant stare
Gaz'd up, the triumph of thy fall to share!
Poor triumph! price of that extorted praise,
Which still to daring Genius envy pays.

Oh! for thy playful smile,—thy potent frown,—
415 To' abash bold Vice, and laugh pert Folly down!
So should the Muse, in Humour's happiest vein,
With verse that flow'd in metaphoric strain,
And apt allusions to the rural trade,
Tell, of *what wood young* JACOBINS *are made*;[3]
420 How the skill'd Gardener grafts with nicest rule
The *slip* of COXCOMB, on the *stock* of FOOL;—
Forth in bright blossom bursts the tender sprig,
A thing to wonder at—perhaps a *Whig*.—[4]
Should tell, how wise each half-fledg'd Pedant prates
425 Of weightiest matters, grave distinctions states—
—That rules of Policy, and Public Good,
In Saxon times were rightly understood;
—That Kings are proper, *may be* useful things,
But then some Gentlemen object to Kings;
430 —That in all times the Minister's to blame;
—That British Liberty's an empty name,
Till each fair Burgh, numerically free,
Shall chuse its Members by *the Rule of Three*.[5]

So should the Muse, with verse in thunder cloath'd,
435 Proclaim the Crimes by God and Nature loath'd,
Which—when fell poison revels in the veins—
(That poison fell, which frantic *Gallia*[6] drains
From the crude Fruit of Freedom's blasted Tree)
Blot the fair Records of Humanity.

---

[1] Cf. Horace, *Ars Poetica* 333–46; and Pope, *The Temple of Fame* 300.

[2] Burke died on 9 July 1797. He was buried at St. Mary's All Saints, Beaconsfield.

[3] The Jacobins were the most radical faction in the French Revolution, so called because they met in a Jacobin monastery. The term "English Jacobin" was used to refer to almost any supporter of the Revolution or of domestic reform—hence the title of Canning and Frere's periodical.

[4] "i.e., perhaps *a Member of the* WHIG CLUB—a Society that has presumed to monopolize to itself a title to which it never had any claim, but from the character of those who have now withdrawn themselves from it.—'Perhaps' signifies that *even the* WHIG CLUB *sometimes* rejects a candidate, whose PRINCIPLES (*visum teneatis*) it affects to disapprove." (G.C./J.H.F.) In his *Appeal from the New to the Old Whigs* (1791), Burke had accused his fellow Whigs (such as Fox) of having abandoned their principles. For the Latin in parentheses, cf. Horace, *Ars Poetica* 5: "could you … refrain from laughing?" (tr. H. Rushton Fairclough).

[5] a mathematical rule for finding the fourth term in a proportion when the first three are known. In *Reflections on the Revolution in France* (passage not included here), Burke had mocked the French Constitution's complicated and mathematical rules for the election of members to the National Assembly.

[6] "France" (L.).

440   To feebler Nations let proud *France* afford
Her damning choice,—the Chalice or the Sword,—
To drink or die;—oh fraud! oh specious lie!
Delusive choice! for *if* they drink, they die.

    The Sword we dread not:—of ourselves secure,
445 Firm were our Strength, our Peace and Freedom sure.—
Let all the World confederate all its pow'rs,
"Be they not back'd by those that should be ours."[1]
High on his Rock shall BRITAIN's GENIUS stand,
Scatter the crowded Hosts, and vindicate the land.

450   Guard We but our own Hearts: with constant view
To antient Morals, antient Manners true,
True to the manlier virtues, such as nerv'd
Our Father's breasts, and this proud Isle preserv'd
For many a rugged age:—and scorn the while,—
455 Each philosophic Atheist's specious guile.—
The soft seductions, the refinements nice,
Of gay Morality, and easy Vice:—
So shall we brave the storm;—our 'stablish'd pow'r
Thy refuge, EUROPE, in some happier hour.—
460 —But, FRENCH *in heart*—tho' Victory crown our brow,
Low at our feet tho' prostrate Nations bow,
Wealth gild our Cities, Commerce croud our shore,—
LONDON may shine, but ENGLAND is no more.

---

[1] Shakespeare, *Macbeth* 5.5.5.

William Wordsworth
1770 – 1850

William Wordsworth was born on 7 April 1770 in Cockermouth, Cumberland, the second of the five children of John Wordsworth and Ann Cookson Wordsworth. His father was a legal agent for local landowners, the Lowthers; William's early life was comfortable and stable. In 1778, however, Ann Wordsworth died; John Wordsworth followed her late in 1783. The household was broken up: Dorothy Wordsworth,* the only girl in the family, went to live with relatives; and the four boys boarded with Ann Tyson and attended Hawkshead Grammar School.

Wordsworth began writing poetry in 1784; in his last year at Hawkshead School he composed "The Vale of Esthwaite" and published his "Sonnet, On Seeing Miss Helen Maria Williams* Weep at a Tale of Distress" (1787). The same year he went to St. John's College, Cambridge to study modern languages. From July to October 1790 he and his friend Robert Jones went on a walking tour of the Alps; Wordsworth returned to the university and graduated in January 1791. Rather than immediately taking up a profession, he set out for France, where he sympathized with the Girondins (or moderate revolutionaries), befriended Michel Beaupuy (who would later figure in *The Prelude*), and had a love affair with a young woman called Annette Vallon. Their child, Anne-Caroline, was born after Wordsworth returned to England in 1792.

He continued to travel on foot within Britain, as he would for most of his life. In 1793 he published *An Evening Walk* and *Descriptive Sketches*, both with the radical publisher Joseph Johnson. During this period Wordsworth admired the work and shared the pro-revolutionary sympathies of William Godwin.* Without the financial independence to be a poet, he remained uncertain about the course his life should take. When in 1795 he inherited £900 from Raisley Calvert, whom he had nursed through his final illness, he and his sister Dorothy settled at Racedown Lodge, Dorset, near Coleridge,* whom Wordsworth had met earlier in the year.

During 1796, Wordsworth worked on his tragedy, *The Borderers*, and on "The Ruined Cottage." The following year he and Dorothy moved to Alfoxden House, near Nether Stowey, Somerset, where Coleridge now lived. There he and Coleridge worked on their contributions to *Lyrical Ballads* (1798). Proceeds from the first edition of *Lyrical Ballads* enabled William and Dorothy Wordsworth to go to Germany with Coleridge, where, in the winter of 1798–99, William wrote fragments of poetry that would later become parts of *The Prelude*. Returning to England he finished the "Two-Part Prelude" of 1799, unpublished during his lifetime.

In December 1799, William and Dorothy rented a cottage at Grasmere in the Lake District; there Wordsworth wrote "Home at Grasmere,"* intended as Book 1 of *The Recluse*, a massive unfinished project. The second edition of *Lyrical Ballads* appeared in 1800 (including thirty-seven additional poems and the famous Preface); a third edition, including an "Appendix on Poetic Diction," appeared in 1802. Wanting to marry Mary Hutchinson, Wordsworth first travelled to Calais to see Annette Vallon and their daughter: Dorothy Wordsworth, who accompanied him, recounts the journey in her 1802 Journals. William and Mary were married in October 1802.

In 1804, Wordsworth returned to *The Prelude*, which he called the "poem to Coleridge"; he had finished a thirteen-book version by May 1805, which he did not publish. In February 1805 his brother John was drowned at sea; Wordsworth wrote about his grief in "Elegiac Stanzas" (1806). Meanwhile, the friendship between Coleridge and Wordsworth was deteriorating: Coleridge, in poor health and addicted to opium, was unhappily married and in love with Mary Wordsworth's sister, Sara Hutchinson.

Wordsworth's *Poems, in two Volumes* appeared in 1807 (and was harshly reviewed by Francis Jeffrey* in the *Edinburgh Review*). Jeffrey allied Wordsworth with Coleridge and Southey* as the "Lake Poets"—an association that Byron would exploit in the Dedication to *Don Juan* (1818–24).* In 1808, Wordsworth worked on *The White Doe of Rylstone* (pub. 1815) and also returned to his major project, *The Recluse*. "The Ruined Cottage" was revised as "The Pedlar" and became Book 1 of the nine-book poem *The Excursion* (pub. 1814). Jeffrey began his review* of *The Excursion* (November 1814) by protesting, "This will never do!"

Two of the Wordsworths' children, Catherine and Thomas, died in 1812: of the remaining three, Wordsworth was closest to Dora. (She acted as his amanuensis and he only reluctantly agreed to her marriage when she was thirty-seven years old.) In March 1813, Lord Lonsdale (a member of the Lowther family) appointed Wordsworth Distributor of Stamps for Westmoreland and part of Cumberland; the Wordsworths were able to move to Rydal Mount, a comfortable house near Grasmere. Wordsworth was criticized for accepting such an official position by those—including Percy Bysshe Shelley in *Peter Bell the Third* (1819, pub. 1839) and Robert Browning in "The Lost Leader" (1845)—who felt he had betrayed his earlier ideals for material gain. The publications of these prosperous years include *Poems By William Wordsworth, Including Lyrical Ballads, and the Miscellaneous Pieces of the Author* (1815), which includes a significant Preface; *Peter Bell* (written in 1798 but first published in 1819); *The Waggoner* (written in 1806, published in 1819 with a dedication to Charles Lamb);* *The River Duddon, A Series of Sonnets: Vaudracour and Julia: and Other Poems* (1820); *Ecclesiastical Sketches* (a collection of sonnets, 1822); and *Yarrow Revisited, And Other Poems* (1835). Collected editions of Wordsworth's poetry appeared from 1820 on; in 1842–43 he dictated to his friend Isabella Fenwick notes included in most subsequent editions.

On Shakespeare's birthday, 23 April 1850, Wordsworth died at Rydal Mount of pleurisy. Three months later, Mary Wordsworth published *The Prelude, or Growth of a Poet's Mind, An Autobiographical Poem*; the title is hers. (A.M.)

⁂

from *Lyrical Ballads, with A Few Other Poems* (1798)

Advertisement

It is the honourable characteristic of Poetry that its materials are to be found in every subject which can interest the human mind. The evidence of this fact is to be sought, not in the writings of Critics, but in those of Poets themselves.

The majority of the following poems are to be considered as experiments. They were written chiefly with a view to ascertain how far the language of conversation in the middle and lower classes of society is adapted to the purposes of poetic pleasure. Readers accustomed to the gaudiness and inane phraseology of many modern writers, if they persist in reading this book to its conclusion, will perhaps frequently have to struggle with feelings of strangeness and aukwardness: they will look round for poetry, and will be induced to enquire by what species of courtesy these attempts can be permitted to assume that title. It is desirable that such readers, for their own sakes, should not suffer the solitary word Poetry, a word of very disputed meaning, to stand in the way of their gratification; but that, while they are perusing this book, they should ask themselves if it contains a natural delineation of human passions, human characters, and human incidents; and if the answer be favorable to the author's wishes, that they should consent to be pleased in spite of that most dreadful enemy to our pleasures, our own pre-established codes of decision.

Readers of superior judgment may disapprove of the style in which many of these pieces are executed; it must be expected that many lines and phrases will not exactly suit their taste. It will perhaps appear to them, that wishing to avoid the prevalent fault of the day, the author has sometimes descended too low, and that many of his expressions are too familiar, and not of sufficient dignity. It is apprehended, that the more conversant the reader is with our elder writers, and with those in modern times who have been the most successful in painting manners and passions, the fewer complaints of this kind will he have to make.

An accurate taste in poetry, and in all the other arts, Sir Joshua Reynolds has observed,[1] is an acquired talent, which can only be produced by severe thought, and a long continued intercourse with the best models of composition. This is mentioned not with so ridiculous a purpose as to prevent the most inexperienced reader from judging for himself; but merely to temper the rashness of decision, and to suggest that if poetry be a subject on which much time has not been bestowed, the judgment may be erroneous, and that in many cases it necessarily will be so.

The tale of Goody Blake and Harry Gill is founded on a well-authenticated fact which happened in Warwickshire. Of the other poems in the collection, it may be proper to say that they are either absolute inventions of the author, or facts which took place within his personal observation or that of his friends. The poem of the Thorn, as the reader will soon discover, is not supposed to be spoken in the author's own person: the character of the loquacious narrator will sufficiently shew itself in the course of the story. The Rime of the Ancyent Marinere was professedly written in imitation of the *style*, as well as of the spirit of the elder poets; but with a few exceptions, the Author believes that the language adopted in it has been equally intelligible for these three last centuries. The lines entitled Expostulation and Reply, and those which follow, arose out of conversation with a friend who was somewhat unreasonably attached to modern books of moral philosophy.[2]

Goody Blake, and Harry Gill, a true story

Oh! what's the matter? what's the matter?
What is't that ails young Harry Gill?
That evermore his teeth they chatter,
Chatter, chatter, chatter still.
5 Of waistcoats Harry has no lack,
Good duffle grey, and flannel fine;
He has a blanket on his back,
And coats enough to smother nine.

In March, December, and in July,
10 'Tis all the same with Harry Gill;
The neighbours tell, and tell you truly,
His teeth they chatter, chatter still.
At night, at morning, and at noon,
'Tis all the same with Harry Gill;
15 Beneath the sun, beneath the moon,
His teeth they chatter, chatter still.

Young Harry was a lusty drover,
And who so stout of limb as he?
His cheeks were red as ruddy clover,
20 His voice was like the voice of three.
Auld Goody Blake was old and poor,
Ill fed she was, and thinly clad;
And any man who pass'd her door,
Might see how poor a hut she had.

25 All day she spun in her poor dwelling,
And then her three hours' work at night!
Alas! 'twas hardly worth the telling,
It would not pay for candle-light.
—This woman dwelt in Dorsetshire,
30 Her hut was on a cold hill-side,
And in that country coals are dear,
For they come far by wind and tide.

By the same fire to boil their pottage,
Two poor old dames, as I have known,
35 Will often live in one small cottage,
But she, poor woman, dwelt alone.
'Twas well enough when summer came,
The long, warm, lightsome summer-day,
Then at her door the *canty*[3] dame
40 Would sit, as any linnet gay.

But when the ice our streams did fetter,
Oh! then how her old bones would shake!

---

[1] for example in *Discourse* 12: "The habit of contemplating and brooding over the ideas of great geniuses, till you find yourself warmed by the contact, is the true method of forming an artist-like mind ... the taste [is formed] by such an intercourse."

[2] probably William Hazlitt,* who visited Wordsworth at Alfoxden in May–June 1798.

[3] "lively," "brisk," "active" (northern dialect).

You would have said, if you had met her,
'Twas a hard time for Goody Blake.
Her evenings then were dull and dead;
Sad case it was, as you may think,
For very cold to go to bed,
And then for cold not sleep a wink.

Oh joy for her! when e'er in winter
The winds at night had made a rout,
And scatter'd many a lusty splinter,
And many a rotten bough about.
Yet never had she, well or sick,
As every man who knew her says,
A pile before-hand, wood or stick,
Enough to warm her for three days.

Now, when the frost was past enduring,
And made her poor old bones to ache,
Could any thing be more alluring,
Than an old hedge to Goody Blake?
And now and then, it must be said,
When her old bones were cold and chill,
She left her fire, or left her bed,
To seek the hedge of Harry Gill.

Now Harry he had long suspected
This trespass of old Goody Blake,
And vow'd that she should be detected,
And he on her would vengeance take.
And oft from his warm fire he'd go,
And to the fields his road would take,
And there, at night, in frost and snow,
He watch'd to seize old Goody Blake.

And once; behind a rick of barley,
Thus looking out did Harry stand;
The moon was full and shining clearly,
And crisp with frost the stubble-land.
—He hears a noise—he's all awake—
Again?—on tip-toe down the hill
He softly creeps—'Tis Goody Blake,
She's at the hedge of Harry Gill.

Right glad was he when he beheld her:
Stick after stick did Goody pull,
He stood behind a bush of elder,
Till she had filled her apron full.
When with her load she turned about,
The bye-road back again to take,
He started forward with a shout,
And sprang upon poor Goody Blake.

And fiercely by the arm he took her,
And by the arm he held her fast,
And fiercely by the arm he shook her,
And cried, "I've caught you then at last!"
Then Goody, who had nothing said,
Her bundle from her lap let fall;
And kneeling on the sticks, she pray'd
To God that is the judge of all.

She pray'd, her wither'd hand uprearing,
While Harry held her by the arm—
"God! who art never out of hearing,
O may he never more be warm!"
The cold, cold moon above her head,
Thus on her knees did Goody pray,
Young Harry heard what she had said,
And icy-cold he turned away.

He went complaining all the morrow
That he was cold and very chill:
His face was gloom, his heart was sorrow,
Alas! that day for Harry Gill!
That day he wore a riding-coat,
But not a whit the warmer he:
Another was on Thursday brought,
And ere the Sabbath he had three.

'Twas all in vain, a useless matter,
And blankets were about him pinn'd;
Yet still his jaws and teeth they clatter,
Like a loose casement in the wind.
And Harry's flesh it fell away;
And all who see him say 'tis plain,
That, live as long as live he may,
He never will be warm again.

No word to any man he utters,
A-bed or up, to young or old;
But ever to himself he mutters,
"Poor Harry Gill is very cold."
125 A-bed or up, by night or day;
His teeth they chatter, chatter still.
Now think, ye farmers all, I pray,
Of Goody Blake and Harry Gill.

*Simon Lee, the old Huntsman,
with an incident in which he was
concerned*

In the sweet shire of Cardigan,
Not far from pleasant Ivor-hall,[1]
An old man dwells, a little man,
I've heard he once was tall.
5 Of years he has upon his back,
No doubt, a burthen weighty;
He says he is three score and ten,
But others say he's eighty.

A long blue livery-coat has he,
10 That's fair behind, and fair before;
Yet, meet him where you will, you see
At once that he is poor.
Full five and twenty years he lived
A running huntsman merry;
15 And, though he has but one eye left,
His cheek is like a cherry.

No man like him the horn could sound,
And no man was so full of glee;
To say the least, four counties round
20 Had heard of Simon Lee;
His master's dead, and no one now

Dwells in the hall of Ivor;
Men, dogs, and horses, all are dead;
He is the sole survivor.

25 His hunting feats have him bereft
Of his right eye, as you may see:
And then, what limbs those feats have left
To poor old Simon Lee!
He has no son, he has no child,
30 His wife, an aged woman,
Lives with him, near the waterfall,
Upon the village common.

And he is lean and he is sick,
His little body's half awry
35 His ancles they are swoln and thick;
His legs are thin and dry.
When he was young he little knew
Of husbandry or tillage;
And now he's forced to work, though weak,
40 —The weakest in the village.

He all the country could outrun,
Could leave both man and horse behind;
And often, ere the race was done,
He reeled and was stone-blind.
45 And still there's something in the world
At which his heart rejoices;
For when the chiming hounds are out,
He dearly loves their voices!

Old Ruth works out of doors with him,
50 And does what Simon cannot do;
For she, not over stout of limb,
Is stouter of the two.
And though you with your utmost skill
From labour could not wean them,
55 Alas! 'tis very little, all
Which they can do between them.

Beside their moss-grown hut of clay,
Not twenty paces from the door,
A scrap of land they have, but they
60 Are poorest of the poor.

---

[1] "This old man had been huntsman to the Squires of Alfoxden, which, at the time we occupied it, belonged to a minor. The old man's cottage stood upon the common, a little way from the entrance to Alfoxden Park. But it had disappeared ... I have, after an interval of 45 years, the image of the old man as fresh before my eyes as if I had seen him yesterday. The expression when the hounds were out, 'I dearly love their voices' was word for word from his own lips." (W.W., as dictated to Isabella Fenwick, 1843.)

This scrap of land he from the heath
Enclosed when he was stronger;
But what avails the land to them,
Which they can till no longer?

65 Few months of life has he in store,
As he to you will tell,
For still, the more he works, the more
His poor old ancles swell.
My gentle reader, I perceive
70 How patiently you've waited,
And I'm afraid that you expect
Some tale will be related.

O reader! had you in your mind
Such stores as silent thought can bring,
75 O gentle reader! you would find
A tale in every thing.
What more I have to say is short,
I hope you'll kindly take it;
It is no tale; but should you think,
80 Perhaps a tale you'll make it.

One summer-day I chanced to see
This old man doing all he could
About the root of an old tree,
A stump of rotten wood.
85 The mattock totter'd in his hand;
So vain was his endeavour
That at the root of the old tree
He might have worked for ever.

"You're overtasked, good Simon Lee,
90 Give me your tool" to him I said;
And at the word right gladly he
Received my proffer'd aid.
I struck, and with a single blow
The tangled root I sever'd,
95 At which the poor old man so long
And vainly had endeavour'd.

The tears into his eyes were brought,
And thanks and praises seemed to run
So fast out of his heart, I thought
100 They never would have done.
—I've heard of hearts unkind, kind deeds
With coldness still returning.
Alas! the gratitude of men
Has oftner left me mourning.

Anecdote for Fathers, shewing how the art of lying may be taught[1]

I have a boy of five years old,
His face is fair and fresh to see;
His limbs are cast in beauty's mold,
And dearly he loves me.

5 One morn we stroll'd on our dry walk,
Our quiet house all full in view,
And held such intermitted talk
As we are wont to do.

My thoughts on former pleasures ran;
10 I thought of Kilve's delightful shore,
My pleasant home, when spring began,
A long, long year before.

A day it was when I could bear
To think, and think, and think again;
15 With so much happiness to spare,
I could not feel a pain.

My boy was by my side, so slim
And graceful in his rustic dress!
And oftentimes I talked to him,
20 In very idleness.

The young lambs ran a pretty race;
The morning sun shone bright and warm;

---

[1] "The Boy was a son of my friend Basil Montagu, who had been two or three years under our care. The name of Kilve is from a village on the Bristol Channel, about a mile from Alfoxden; and the name of Liswin Farm was taken from a beautiful spot on the Wye." (W.W., as dictated to Isabella Fenwick, 1843.)

"Kilve," said I, "was a pleasant place,
And so is Liswyn farm.

25 "My little boy, which like you more,"
I said and took him by the arm—
"Our home by Kilve's delightful shore,
Or here at Liswyn farm?

"And tell me, had you rather be,"
30 I said and held him by the arm,
"At Kilve's smooth shore by the green sea,
Or here at Liswyn farm?"

In careless mood he looked at me,
While still I held him by the arm,
35 And said, "At Kilve I'd rather be
Than here at Liswyn farm."

"Now, little Edward, say why so;
My little Edward, tell me why";
"I cannot tell, I do not know."
40 "Why this is strange," said I.

"For, here are woods and green-hills warm;
There surely must some reason be
Why you would change sweet Liswyn farm
For Kilve by the green sea."

45 At this, my boy, so fair and slim,
Hung down his head, nor made reply;
And five times did I say to him,
"Why? Edward, tell me why?"

His head he raised—there was in sight,
50 It caught his eye, he saw it plain—
Upon the house-top, glittering bright,
A broad and gilded vane.

Then did the boy his tongue unlock,
And thus to me he made reply;
55 "At Kilve there was no weather-cock,
And that's the reason why."

Oh dearest, dearest boy! my heart
For better lore would seldom yearn,
Could I but teach the hundredth part
60 Of what from thee I learn.

We are Seven[1]

A simple child, dear brother Jim,
That lightly draws its breath,
And feels its life in every limb,
What should it know of death?

5 I met a little cottage girl,
She was eight years old, she said;
Her hair was thick with many a curl
That cluster'd round her head.

She had a rustic, woodland air,
10 And she was wildly clad;
Her eyes were fair, and very fair,
—Her beauty made me glad.

"Sisters and brothers, little maid,
How many may you be?"
15 "How many? seven in all," she said,
And wondering looked at me.

"And where are they, I pray you tell?"
She answered, "Seven are we,
And two of us at Conway dwell,
20 And two are gone to sea.

---

[1] In 1843, Wordsworth told Isabella Fenwick, "When ['We are Seven'] was all but finished, I came in and recited it to Mr. Coleridge and my Sister, and said, 'A prefatory stanza must be added, and I should sit down to our little tea-meal with greater pleasure if my task was finished.' I mentioned in substance what I wished to be expressed, and Coleridge immediately threw off the stanza thus:
  A little child, dear brother Jem,—
I objected to the rhyme, dear brother Jem, as being ludicrous, but we all enjoyed the joke of hitching in our friend James Tobin's name, who was familiarly called Jem." Wordsworth removed the "ludicrous" rhyme in 1815 and all subsequent printings of the poem. In the 1800 Preface,* W.W. says that the poem deals with "the perplexity and obscurity which in childhood attend our notion of death, or rather our utter inability to admit that notion."

"Two of us in the church-yard lie,
My sister and my brother,
And in the church-yard cottage, I
Dwell near them with my mother."

25 "You say that two at Conway dwell,
And two are gone to sea,
Yet you are seven; I pray you tell
Sweet Maid, how this may be?"

Then did the little Maid reply,
30 "Seven boys and girls are we;
Two of us in the church-yard lie,
Beneath the church-yard tree."

"You run about, my little maid,
Your limbs they are alive;
35 If two are in the church-yard laid,
Then ye are only five."

"Their graves are green, they may be seen,"
The little Maid replied,
"Twelve steps or more from my mother's door,
40 And they are side by side.

"My stockings there I often knit,
My 'kerchief there I hem;
And there upon the ground I sit—
I sit and sing to them.

45 "And often after sunset, Sir,
When it is light and fair,
I take my little porringer,
And eat my supper there.

"The first that died was little Jane;
50 In bed she moaning lay,
Till God released her of her pain,
And then she went away.

"So in the church-yard she was laid,
And all the summer dry,
55 Together round her grave we played,
My brother John and I.

"And when the ground was white with snow,
And I could run and slide,
My brother John was forced to go,
60 And he lies by her side."

"How many are you then," said I,
"If they two are in Heaven?"
The little Maiden did reply,
"O Master! we are seven."

65 "But they are dead; those two are dead!
Their spirits are in heaven!"
'Twas throwing words away; for still
The little Maid would have her will,
And said, "Nay, we are seven!"

Lines
Written in Early Spring

I heard a thousand blended notes,
While in a grove I sate reclined,
In that sweet mood when pleasant thoughts
Bring sad thoughts to the mind.

5 To her fair works did nature link
The human soul that through me ran;
And much it griev'd my heart to think
What man has made of man.

Through primrose-tufts, in that sweet bower,
10 The periwinkle trail'd its wreathes;
And 'tis my faith that every flower
Enjoys the air it breathes.

The birds around me hopp'd and play'd:
Their thoughts I cannot measure,
15 But the least motion which they made,
It seem'd a thrill of pleasure.

The budding twigs spread out their fan,
To catch the breezy air;
And I must think, do all I can,
20 That there was pleasure there.

William Wordsworth

If I these thoughts may not prevent,
If such be of my creed the plan,
Have I not reason to lament
What man has made of man?

The Thorn[1]

1

There is a thorn; it looks so old,
In truth you'd find it hard to say,
How it could ever have been young,
It looks so old and grey.
5 Not higher than a two-years' child,
It stands erect this aged thorn;
No leaves it has, no thorny points;
It is a mass of knotted joints,
A wretched thing forlorn.
10 It stands erect, and like a stone
With lichens it is overgrown.

2

Like rock or stone, it is o'ergrown
With lichens to the very top,

---

[1] "This Poem ought to have been preceded by an introductory Poem, which I have been prevented from writing by never having felt myself in a mood when it was probable that I should write it well.—The character which I have here introduced speaking is sufficiently common. The Reader will perhaps have a general notion of it, if he has ever known a man, a Captain of a small trading vessel for example, who being past the middle age of life, had retired upon an annuity or small independent income to some village or country town of which he was not a native, or in which he had not been accustomed to live. Such men having little to do become credulous and talkative from indolence; and from the same cause, and other predisposing causes by which it is probable that such men may have been affected, they are prone to superstition. On which account it appeared to me proper to select a character like this to exhibit some of the general laws by which superstition acts upon the mind. Superstitious men are almost always men of slow faculties and deep feelings; their minds are not loose but adhesive; they have a reasonable share of imagination, by which word I mean the faculty which produces impressive effects out of simple elements; but they are utterly destitute of fancy, the power by which pleasure and surprize are excited by sudden varieties of situation and by accumulated imagery.

"It was my wish in this poem to shew the manner in which such men cleave to the same ideas; and to follow the turns of passion, always different, yet not palpably different, by which their conversation is swayed. I had two objects to attain; first, to represent a picture which should not be unimpressive yet consistent with the character that should describe it, secondly, while I adhered to the style in which such persons describe, to take care that words, which in their minds are impregnated with passion, should likewise convey passion to Readers who are not accustomed to sympathize with men feeling in that manner or using such language. It seemed to me that this might be done by calling in the assistance of Lyrical and rapid Metre. It was necessary that the Poem, to be natural, should in reality move slowly; yet I hoped, that, by the aid of the metre, to those who should at all enter into the spirit of the Poem, it would appear to move quickly. The Reader will have the kindness to excuse this note as I am sensible that an introductory Poem is necessary to give this Poem its full effect.

"Upon this occasion I will request permission to add a few words closely connected with THE THORN and many other Poems in these Volumes. There is a numerous class of readers who imagine that the same words cannot be repeated without tautology: this is a great error: virtual tautology is much oftener produced by using different words when the meaning is exactly the same. Words, a Poet's words more particularly, ought to be weighed in the balance of feeling and not measured by the space which they occupy upon paper. For the Reader cannot be too often reminded that Poetry is passion: it is the history or science of feelings: now every man must know that an attempt is rarely made to communicate impassioned feelings without something of an accompanying consciousness of the inadequateness of our own powers, or the deficiencies of language. During such efforts there will be a craving in the mind, and as long as it is unsatisfied the Speaker will cling to the same words, or words of the same character. There are also various other reasons why repetition and apparent tautology are frequently beauties of the highest kind. Among the chief of these reasons is the interest which the mind attaches to words, not only as symbols of the passion, but as *things*, active and efficient, which are of themselves part of the passion. And further, from a spirit of fondness, exultation, and gratitude, the mind luxuriates in the repetition of words which appear successfully to communicate its feelings. The truth of these remarks might be shewn by innumerable passages from the Bible and from the impassioned poetry of every nation.

"'Awake, awake Deborah: awake, awake, utter a song:
Arise Barak, and lead thy captivity captive, thou Son of Abinoam.
At her feet he bowed, he fell, he lay down: at her feet he bowed, he fell; where he bowed there he fell down dead.
Why is his Chariot so long in coming? Why tarry the Wheels of his Chariot?'—Judges, Chap. 5th. Verses 12th, 27th, and part of 28th.—See also the whole of that tumultuous and wonderful Poem."

(W.W., note to *Lyrical Ballads*, 1800.)

In 1843, Wordsworth dictated the following to Isabella Fenwick: "Alfoxden. 1798. Arose out of my observing, on the ridge of Quantock Hill, on a stormy day a thorn which I had often passed in calm and bright weather without noticing it. I said to myself, 'Cannot I by some invention do as much to make this Thorn … an impressive object as the storm has made it to my eyes at this moment.'" A "thorn" here signifies the hawthorn, a spiny shrub with blossoms and red berries.

      And hung with heavy tufts of moss,
15   A melancholy crop:
      Up from the earth these mosses creep,
      And this poor thorn they clasp it round
      So close, you'd say that they were bent
      With plain and manifest intent,
20   To drag it to the ground;
      And all had joined in one endeavour
      To bury this poor thorn for ever.

3

      High on a mountain's highest ridge,
      Where oft the stormy winter gale
25   Cuts like a scythe, while through the clouds
      It sweeps from vale to vale;
      Not five yards from the mountain-path,
      This thorn you on your left espy;
      And to the left, three yards beyond,
30   You see a little muddy pond
      Of water, never dry;
      I've measured it from side to side:
      'Tis three feet long, and two feet wide.

4

      And close beside this aged thorn,
35   There is a fresh and lovely sight,
      A beauteous heap, a hill of moss,
      Just half a foot in height.
      All lovely colours there you see,
      All colours that were ever seen,
40   And mossy network too is there,
      As if by hand of lady fair
      The work had woven been,
      And cups, the darlings of the eye,
      So deep is their vermilion dye.

5

45   Ah me! what lovely tints are there!
      Of olive-green and scarlet bright,
      In spikes, in branches, and in stars,
      Green, red, and pearly white.
      This heap of earth o'ergrown with moss,
50   Which close beside the thorn you see,
      So fresh in all its beauteous dyes,

      Is like an infant's grave in size
      As like as like can be:
      But never, never any where,
55   An infant's grave was half so fair.

6

      Now would you see this aged thorn,
      This pond and beauteous hill of moss,
      You must take care and chuse your time
      The mountain when to cross.
60   For oft there sits, between the heap
      That's like an infant's grave in size,
      And that same pond of which I spoke,
      A woman in a scarlet cloak,
      And to herself she cries,
65   "Oh misery! oh misery!
      Oh woe is me! oh misery!"

7

      At all times of the day and night
      This wretched woman thither goes,
      And she is known to every star,
70   And every wind that blows;
      And there beside the thorn she sits
      When the blue day-light's in the skies,
      And when the whirlwind's on the hill,
      Or frosty air is keen and still,
75   And to herself she cries,
      "Oh misery! oh misery!
      Oh woe is me! oh misery!"

8

      "Now wherefore thus, by day and night,
      In rain, in tempest, and in snow,
80   Thus to the dreary mountain-top
      Does this poor woman go?
      And why sits she beside the thorn
      When the blue day-light's in the sky,
      Or when the whirlwind's on the hill,
85   Or frosty air is keen and still,
      And wherefore does she cry?—
      Oh wherefore? wherefore? tell me why
      Does she repeat that doleful cry?"

9

I cannot tell; I wish I could;
For the true reason no one knows,
But if you'd gladly view the spot,
The spot to which she goes;
The heap that's like an infant's grave,
The pond—and thorn, so old and grey,
Pass by her door—'tis seldom shut—
And if you see her in her hut,
Then to the spot away!—
I never heard of such as dare
Approach the spot when she is there.

10

"But wherefore to the mountain-top
Can this unhappy woman go,
Whatever star is in the skies,
Whatever wind may blow?"
Nay rack your brain—'tis all in vain,
I'll tell you every thing I know;
But to the thorn, and to the pond
Which is a little step beyond,
I wish that you would go:
Perhaps when you are at the place
You something of her tale may trace.

11

I'll give you the best help I can:
Before you up the mountain go,
Up to the dreary mountain-top,
I'll tell you all I know.
'Tis now some two and twenty years,
Since she (her name is Martha Ray)
Gave with a maiden's true good will
Her company to Stephen Hill;
And she was blithe and gay,
And she was happy, happy still
Whene'er she thought of Stephen Hill.

12

And they had fix'd the wedding-day,
The morning that must wed them both;
But Stephen to another maid
Had sworn another oath;
And with this other maid to church
Unthinking Stephen went—
Poor Martha! on that woful day
A cruel, cruel fire, they say,
Into her bones was sent:
It dried her body like a cinder,
And almost turn'd her brain to tinder.

13

They say, full six months after this,
While yet the summer-leaves were green,
She to the mountain-top would go,
And there was often seen.
'Tis said, a child was in her womb,
As now to any eye was plain;
She was with child, and she was mad,
Yet often she was sober sad
From her exceeding pain.
Oh me! ten thousand times I'd rather
That he had died, that cruel father!

14

Sad case for such a brain to hold
Communion with a stirring child!
Sad case, as you may think, for one
Who had a brain so wild!
Last Christmas when we talked of this,
Old Farmer Simpson did maintain,
That in her womb the infant wrought
About its mother's heart, and brought
Her senses back again:
And when at last her time drew near,
Her looks were calm, her senses clear.

15

No more I know, I wish I did,
And I would tell it all to you;
For what became of this poor child
There's none that ever knew:
And if a child was born or no,
There's no one that could ever tell;
And if 'twas born alive or dead,
There's no one knows, as I have said,
But some remember well,

        That Martha Ray about this time
165   Would up the mountain often climb.

16

        And all that winter, when at night
        The wind blew from the mountain-peak,
        'Twas worth your while, though in the dark,
        The church-yard path to seek:
170   For many a time and oft were heard
        Cries coming from the mountain-head,
        Some plainly living voices were,
        And others, I've heard many swear,
        Were voices of the dead:
175   I cannot think, whate'er they say,
        They had to do with Martha Ray.

17

        But that she goes to this old thorn,
        The thorn which I've described to you,
        And there sits in a scarlet cloak,
180   I will be sworn is true.
        For one day with my telescope,
        To view the ocean wide and bright,
        When to this country first I came,
        Ere I had heard of Martha's name,
185   I climbed the mountain's height:
        A storm came on, and I could see
        No object higher than my knee.

18

        'Twas mist and rain, and storm and rain,
        No screen, no fence could I discover,
190   And then the wind! in faith, it was
        A wind full ten times over.
        I looked around, I thought I saw
        A jutting crag, and off I ran,
        Head-foremost, through the driving rain,
195   The shelter of the crag to gain,
        And, as I am a man,
        Instead of jutting crag, I found
        A woman seated on the ground.

19

        I did not speak—I saw her face,

200   Her face it was enough for me;
        I turned about and heard her cry,
        "O misery! O misery!"
        And there she sits, until the moon
        Through half the clear blue sky will go,
205   And when the little breezes make
        The waters of the pond to shake,
        As all the country know,
        She shudders and you hear her cry,
        "Oh misery! oh misery!"

20

210   "But what's the thorn? and what's the pond?
        And what's the hill of moss to her?
        And what's the creeping breeze that comes
        The little pond to stir?"
        I cannot tell; but some will say
215   She hanged her baby on the tree,
        Some say she drowned it in the pond,
        Which is a little step beyond,
        But all and each agree,
        The little babe was buried there,
220   Beneath that hill of moss so fair.

21

        I've heard the scarlet moss is red
        With drops of that poor infant's blood;
        But kill a new-born infant thus!
        I do not think she could.
225   Some say, if to the pond you go,
        And fix on it a steady view,
        The shadow of a babe you trace,
        A baby and a baby's face,
        And that it looks at you;
230   Whene'er you look on it, 'tis plain
        The baby looks at you again.

22

        And some had sworn an oath that she
        Should be to public justice brought;
        And for the little infant's bones
235   With spades they would have sought.
        But then the beauteous hill of moss
        Before their eyes began to stir;

And for full fifty yards around,
The grass it shook upon the ground;
240 But all do still aver
The little babe is buried there,
Beneath that hill of moss so fair.

23

I cannot tell how this may be,
But plain it is, the thorn is bound
245 With heavy tufts of moss, that strive
To drag it to the ground.
And this I know, full many a time,
When she was on the mountain high,
By day, and in the silent night,
250 When all the stars shone clear and bright,
That I have heard her cry,
"Oh misery! oh misery!
O woe is me! oh misery!"

The Idiot Boy[1]

'Tis eight o'clock,—a clear March night,
The moon is up—the sky is blue,
The owlet in the moonlight air,
He shouts from nobody knows where;
5 He lengthens out his lonely shout,
Halloo! halloo! a long halloo!

—Why bustle thus about your door,
What means this bustle, Betty Foy?
Why are you in this mighty fret?
10 And why on horseback have you set
Him whom you love, your idiot boy?

Beneath the moon that shines so bright,
Till she is tired, let Betty Foy
With girt and stirrup fiddle-faddle;
15 But wherefore set upon a saddle
Him whom she loves, her idiot boy?

There's scarce a soul that's out of bed;
Good Betty! put him down again;
His lips with joy they burr at you,
20 But, Betty! what has he to do
With stirrup, saddle, or with rein?

The world will say 'tis very idle,
Bethink you of the time of night;
There's not a mother, no not one,
25 But when she hears what you have done,
Oh! Betty she'll be in a fright.

But Betty's bent on her intent,
For her good neighbour, Susan Gale,
Old Susan, she who dwells alone,
30 Is sick, and makes a piteous moan,
As if her very life would fail.

There's not a house within a mile,
No hand to help them in distress:
Old Susan lies a bed in pain,
35 And sorely puzzled are the twain,
For what she ails they cannot guess.

And Betty's husband's at the wood,
Where by the week he doth abide,
A woodman in the distant vale;
40 There's none to help poor Susan Gale,
What must be done? what will betide?

And Betty from the lane has fetched
Her pony, that is mild and good,
Whether he be in joy or pain,
45 Feeding at will along the lane,
Or bringing faggots from the wood.

And he is all in travelling trim,
And by the moonlight, Betty Foy

---

[1] "Alfoxden, 1798. The last stanza, 'The Cocks did crow to-whoo, to-whoo, And the sun did shine so cold,' was the foundation of the whole. The words were reported to me by my dear friend, Thomas Poole; but I have since heard the same repeated of other Idiots. Let me add that this long poem was composed in the groves of Alfoxden almost extempore; not a word, I believe, being corrected, though one stanza was omitted. I mention this in gratitude to those happy moments, for, in truth, I never wrote anything with so much glee." (W.W., as dictated to Isabella Fenwick, 1843.)

    Has up upon the saddle set,
50 The like was never heard of yet,
    Him whom she loves, her idiot boy.

    And he must post without delay
    Across the bridge that's in the dale,
    And by the church, and o'er the down,
55 To bring a doctor from the town,
    Or she will die, old Susan Gale.

    There is no need of boot or spur,
    There is no need of whip or wand,
    For Johnny has his holly-bough,
60 And with a hurly-burly now
    He shakes the green bough in his hand.

    And Betty o'er and o'er has told
    The boy who is her best delight,
    Both what to follow, what to shun,
65 What do, and what to leave undone,
    How turn to left, and how to right.

    And Betty's most especial charge,
    Was, "Johnny! Johnny! mind that you
    Come home again, nor stop at all,
70 Come home again, whate'er befal,
    My Johnny do, I pray you do."

    To this did Johnny answer make,
    Both with his head, and with his hand,
    And proudly shook the bridle too,
75 And then! his words were not a few,
    Which Betty well could understand.

    And now that Johnny is just going,
    Though Betty's in a mighty flurry,
    She gently pats the pony's side,
80 On which her idiot boy must ride,
    And seems no longer in a hurry.

    But when the pony moved his legs,
    Oh! then for the poor idiot boy!
    For joy he cannot hold the bridle,
85 For joy his head and heels are idle,
    He's idle all for very joy.

    And while the pony moves his legs,
    In Johnny's left-hand you may see,
    The green bough's motionless and dead;
90 The moon that shines above his head
    Is not more still and mute than he.

    His heart it was so full of glee,
    That till full fifty yards were gone,
    He quite forgot his holly whip,
95 And all his skill in horsemanship,
    Oh! happy, happy, happy John.

    And Betty's standing at the door,
    And Betty's face with joy o'erflows,
    Proud of herself, and proud of him,
100 She sees him in his travelling trim;
    How quietly her Johnny goes.

    The silence of her idiot boy,
    What hopes it sends to Betty's heart!
    He's at the guide-post—he turns right,
105 She watches till he's out of sight,
    And Betty will not then depart.

    Burr, burr—now Johnny's lips they burr,
    As loud as any mill, or near it,
    Meek as a lamb the pony moves,
110 And Johnny makes the noise he loves,
    And Betty listens, glad to hear it.

    Away she hies to Susan Gale:
    And Johnny's in a merry tune,
    The owlets hoot, the owlets curr,
115 And Johnny's lips they burr, burr, burr,
    And on he goes beneath the moon.

    His steed and he right well agree,
    For of this pony there's a rumour,
    That should he lose his eyes and ears,
120 And should he live a thousand years,
    He never will be out of humour.

But then he is a horse that thinks!
And when he thinks his pace is slack;
Now, though he knows poor Johnny well,
Yet for his life he cannot tell   125
What he has got upon his back.

So through the moonlight lanes they go,
And far into the moonlight dale,
And by the church, and o'er the down,
To bring a doctor from the town,   130
To comfort poor old Susan Gale.

And Betty, now at Susan's side,
Is in the middle of her story,
What comfort Johnny soon will bring,
With many a most diverting thing,   135
Of Johnny's wit and Johnny's glory.

And Betty's still at Susan's side:
By this time she's not quite so flurried;
Demure with porringer and plate
She sits, as if in Susan's fate   140
Her life and soul were buried.

But Betty, poor good woman! she,
You plainly in her face may read it,
Could lend out of that moment's store
Five years of happiness or more,   145
To any that might need it.

But yet I guess that now and then
With Betty all was not so well,
And to the road she turns her ears,
And thence full many a sound she hears,   150
Which she to Susan will not tell.

Poor Susan moans, poor Susan groans,
"As sure as there's a moon in heaven,"
Cries Betty, "he'll be back again;
They'll both be here, 'tis almost ten,   155
They'll both be here before eleven."

Poor Susan moans, poor Susan groans,
The clock gives warning for eleven;

'Tis on the stroke—"If Johnny's near,"
Quoth Betty "he will soon be here,   160
As sure as there's a moon in heaven."

The clock is on the stroke of twelve,
And Johnny is not yet in sight,
The moon's in heaven, as Betty sees,
But Betty is not quite at ease;   165
And Susan has a dreadful night.

And Betty, half an hour ago,
On Johnny vile reflections cast;
"A little idle sauntering thing!"
With other names, an endless string,   170
But now that time is gone and past.

And Betty's drooping at the heart,
That happy time all past and gone,
"How can it be he is so late?
The doctor he has made him wait,   175
Susan! they'll both be here anon."

And Susan's growing worse and worse,
And Betty's in a sad quandary;
And then there's nobody to say
If she must go or she must stay: 180
—She's in a sad quandary.

The clock is on the stroke of one;
But neither Doctor nor his guide
Appear along the moonlight road,
There's neither horse nor man abroad,   185
And Betty's still at Susan's side.

And Susan she begins to fear
Of sad mischances not a few,
That Johnny may perhaps be drown'd,
Or lost perhaps, and never found;   190
Which they most both for ever rue.

She prefaced half a hint of this
With, "God forbid it should be true!"
At the first word that Susan said

195 Cried Betty, rising from the bed,
"Susan, I'd gladly stay with you.

"I must be gone, I must away,
Consider, Johnny's but half-wise;
Susan, we must take care of him,
200 If he is hurt in life or limb"—
"Oh God forbid!" poor Susan cries.

"What can I do?" says Betty, going,
"What can I do to ease your pain?
Good Susan tell me, and I'll stay;
205 I fear you're in a dreadful way,
But I shall soon be back again."

"Good Betty go, good Betty go,
There's nothing that can ease my pain."
Then off she hies, but with a prayer
210 That God poor Susan's life would spare,
Till she comes back again.

So, through the moonlight lane she goes,
And far into the moonlight dale;
And how she ran, and how she walked,
215 And all that to herself she talked,
Would surely be a tedious tale.

In high and low, above, below,
In great and small, in round and square,
In tree and tower was Johnny seen,
220 In bush and brake, in black and green,
'Twas Johnny, Johnny, every where.

She's past the bridge that's in the dale,
And now the thought torments her sore,
Johnny perhaps his horse forsook,
225 To hunt the moon that's in the brook,
And never will be heard of more.

And now she's high upon the down,
Alone amid a prospect wide;
There's neither Johnny nor his horse,
230 Among the fern or in the gorse;
There's neither doctor nor his guide.

"Oh saints! what is become of him?
Perhaps he's climbed into an oak,
Where he will stay till he is dead;
235 Or sadly he has been misled,
And joined the wandering gypsey-folk.

"Or him that wicked pony's carried
To the dark cave, the goblin's hall,
Or in the castle he's pursuing,
240 Among the ghosts, his own undoing;
Or playing with the waterfall."

At poor old Susan then she railed,
While to the town she posts away;
"If Susan had not been so ill,
245 Alas! I should have had him still,
My Johnny, till my dying day."

Poor Betty! in this sad distemper,
The doctor's self would hardly spare,
Unworthy things she talked and wild,
250 Even he, of cattle the most mild,
The pony had his share.

And now she's got into the town,
And to the doctor's door she hies;
'Tis silence all on every side;
255 The town so long, the town so wide,
Is silent as the skies.

And now she's at the doctor's door,
She lifts the knocker, rap, rap, rap,
The doctor at the casement shews,
260 His glimmering eyes that peep and doze;
And one hand rubs his old night-cap.

"Oh Doctor! Doctor! where's my Johnny?"
"I'm here, what is't you want with me?"
"Oh Sir! you know I'm Betty Foy,
265 And I have lost my poor dear boy,
You know him—him you often see;

"He's not so wise as some folks be,"
"The devil take his wisdom!" said

The Doctor, looking somewhat grim,
270 "What, woman! should I know of him?"
And, grumbling, he went back to bed.

"O woe is me! O woe is me!
Here will I die; here will I die;
I thought to find my Johnny here,
275 But he is neither far nor near,
Oh! what a wretched mother I!"

She stops, she stands, she looks about,
Which way to turn she cannot tell.
Poor Betty! it would ease her pain
280 If she had heart to knock again;
—The clock strikes three—a dismal knell!

Then up along the town she hies,
No wonder if her senses fail,
This piteous news so much it shock'd her,
285 She quite forgot to send the Doctor,
To comfort poor old Susan Gale.

And now she's high upon the down,
And she can see a mile of road,
"Oh cruel! I'm almost three-score;
290 Such night as this was ne'er before,
There's not a single soul abroad."

She listens, but she cannot hear
The foot of horse, the voice of man;
The streams with softest sound are flowing,
295 The grass you almost hear it growing,
You hear it now if e'er you can.

The owlets through the long blue night
Are shouting to each other still:
Fond lovers, yet not quite hob nob,
300 They lengthen out the tremulous sob,
That echoes far from hill to hill.

Poor Betty now has lost all hope,
Her thoughts are bent on deadly sin;
A green-grown pond she just has pass'd,
305 And from the brink she hurries fast,
Lest she should drown herself therein.

And now she sits her down and weeps;
Such tears she never shed before;
"Oh dear, dear pony! my sweet joy!
310 Oh carry back my idiot boy!
And we will ne'er o'erload thee more."

A thought is come into her head;
"The pony he is mild and good,
And we have always used him well;
315 Perhaps he's gone along the dell,
And carried Johnny to the wood."

Then up she springs as if on wings;
She thinks no more of deadly sin;
If Betty fifty ponds should see,
320 The last of all her thoughts would be,
To drown herself therein.

Oh reader! now that I might tell
What Johnny and his horse are doing!
What they've been doing all this time,
325 Oh could I put it into rhyme,
A most delightful tale pursuing!

Perhaps, and no unlikely thought!
He with his pony now doth roam
The cliffs and peaks so high that are,
330 To lay his hands upon a star,
And in his pocket bring it home.

Perhaps he's turned himself about,
His face unto his horse's tail,
And still and mute, in wonder lost,
335 All like a silent horseman-ghost,
He travels on along the vale.

And now, perhaps, he's hunting sheep,
A fierce and dreadful hunter he!
Yon valley, that's so trim and green,
340 In five month's time, should he be seen,
A desert wilderness will be.

Perhaps, with head and heels on fire,
And like the very soul of evil,
He's galloping away, away,
345 And so he'll gallop on for aye,
The bane of all that dread the devil.

I to the muses have been bound,
These fourteen years, by strong indentures;
Oh gentle muses! let me tell
350 But half of what to him befel,
For sure he met with strange adventures.

Oh gentle muses! is this kind?
Why will ye thus my suit repel?
Why of your further aid bereave me?
355 And can ye thus unfriended leave me?
Ye muses! whom I love so well.

Who's yon, that, near the waterfall,
Which thunders down with headlong force,
Beneath the moon, yet shining fair,
360 As careless as if nothing were,
Sits upright on a feeding horse?

Unto his horse, that's feeding free,
He seems, I think, the rein to give;
Of moon or stars he takes no heed;
365 Of such we in romances read,
—'Tis Johnny! Johnny! as I live.

And that's the very pony too.
Where is she, where is Betty Foy?
She hardly can sustain her fears;
370 The roaring water-fall she hears,
And cannot find her idiot boy.

Your pony's worth his weight in gold,
Then calm your terrors, Betty Foy!
She's coming from among the trees,
375 And now, all full in view, she sees
Him whom she loves, her idiot boy.

And Betty sees the pony too:
Why stand you thus Good Betty Foy?
It is no goblin, 'tis no ghost,
380 'Tis he whom you so long have lost,
He whom you love, your idiot boy.

She looks again—her arms are up—
She screams—she cannot move for joy;
She darts as with a torrent's force,
385 She almost has o'erturned the horse,
And fast she holds her idiot boy.

And Johnny burrs and laughs aloud,
Whether in cunning or in joy,
I cannot tell; but while he laughs,
390 Betty a drunken pleasure quaffs,
To hear again her idiot boy.

And now she's at the pony's tail,
And now she's at the pony's head,
On that side now, and now on this,
395 And almost stifled with her bliss,
A few sad tears does Betty shed.

She kisses o'er and o'er again,
Him whom she loves, her idiot boy,
She's happy here, she's happy there,
400 She is uneasy every where;
Her limbs are all alive with joy.

She pats the pony, where or when
She knows not, happy Betty Foy!
The little pony glad may be,
405 But he is milder far than she,
You hardly can perceive his joy.

"Oh! Johnny, never mind the Doctor;
You've done your best, and that is all."
She took the reins, when this was said,
410 And gently turned the pony's head
From the loud water-fall.

By this the stars were almost gone,
The moon was setting on the hill,
So pale you scarely looked at her:

415 The little birds began to stir,
Though yet their tongues were still.

The pony, Betty, and her boy,
Wind slowly through the woody dale:
And who is she, be-times abroad,
420 That hobbles up the steep rough road?
Who is it, but old Susan Gale?

Long Susan lay deep lost in thought,
And many dreadful fears beset her,
Both for her messenger and nurse;
425 And as her mind grew worse and worse,
Her body it grew better.

She turned, she toss'd herself in bed,
On all sides doubts and terrors met her;
Point after point did she discuss;
430 And while her mind was fighting thus,
Her body still grew better.

"Alas! what is become of them?
These fears can never be endured,
I'll to the wood."—The word scarce said,
435 Did Susan rise up from her bed,
As if by magic cured.

Away she posts up hill and down,
And to the wood at length is come,
She spies her friends, she shouts a greeting;
440 Oh me! it is a merry meeting,
As ever was in Christendom.

The owls have hardly sung their last,
While our four travellers homeward wend;
The owls have hooted all night long,
445 And with the owls began my song,
And with the owls must end.

For while they all were travelling home,
Cried Betty, "Tell us Johnny, do,
Where all this long night you have been,
450 What you have heard, what you have seen,
And Johnny, mind you tell us true."

Now Johnny all night long had heard
The owls in tuneful concert strive;
No doubt too he the moon had seen;
455 For in the moonlight he had been
From eight o'clock till five.

And thus to Betty's question, he
Made answer, like a traveller bold,
(His very words I give to you,)
460 "The cocks did crow to-whoo, to-whoo,
And the sun did shine so cold."
—Thus answered Johnny in his glory,
And that was all his travel's story.

Expostulation and Reply[1]

"Why William, on that old grey stone,
Thus for the length of half a day,
Why William, sit you thus alone,
And dream your time away?

5 "Where are your books? that light bequeath'd
To beings else forlorn and blind!
Up! Up! and drink the spirit breath'd
From dead men to their kind.

"You look round on your mother earth,
10 As if she for no purpose bore you;
As if you were her first-born birth,
And none had lived before you!"

One morning thus, by Esthwaite lake,
When life was sweet I knew not why,
15 To me my good friend Matthew spake,
And thus I made reply.

"The eye it cannot chuse but see,
We cannot bid the ear be still;

---

[1] See the last sentence of the Advertisement to the 1798 *Lyrical Ballads*.* Wordsworth later claimed that "this Schoolmaster [Matthew] was made up of several both of his class and men of other occupations." (W.W., as dictated to Isabella Fenwick, 1843.) The following poem, "The Tables Turned," was written at the same time as "Expostulation and Reply."

  Our bodies feel, where'er they be,
20 Against, or with our will.

  "Nor less I deem that there are powers,
  Which of themselves our minds impress,
  That we can feed this mind of ours,
  In a wise passiveness.

25 "Think you, mid all this mighty sum
  Of things for ever speaking,
  That nothing of itself will come,
  But we must still be seeking?

  "—Then ask not wherefore, here, alone,
30 Conversing as I may,
  I sit upon this old grey stone,
  And dream my time away."

The Tables Turned;
an Evening Scene, on the same subject

  Up! up! my friend, and clear your looks,
  Why all this toil and trouble?
  Up! up! my friend, and quit your books,
  Or surely you'll grow double.

5 The sun above the mountain's head,
  A freshening lustre mellow,
  Through all the long green fields has spread,
  His first sweet evening yellow.

  Books! 'tis a dull and endless strife,
  Come, hear the woodland linnet,
  How sweet his music; on my life
  There's more of wisdom in it.

  And hark! how blithe the throstle sings!
  And he is no mean preacher;
  Come forth into the light of things,
  Let Nature be your teacher.

  She has a world of ready wealth,
  Our minds and hearts to bless—

  Spontaneous wisdom breathed by health,
20 Truth breathed by chearfulness.

  One impulse from a vernal wood
  May teach you more of man;
  Of moral evil and of good,
  Than all the sages can.

25 Sweet is the lore which nature brings;
  Our meddling intellect
  Mishapes the beauteous forms of things;
  —We murder to dissect.

  Enough of science and of art;
30 Close up these barren leaves;
  Come forth, and bring with you a heart
  That watches and receives.

Old Man Travelling;
animal tranquility and decay, a sketch[1]

  The little hedge-row birds,
  That peck along the road, regard him not.
  He travels on, and in his face, his step,
  His gait, is one expression; every limb,
5 His look and bending figure, all bespeak
  A man who does not move with pain, but moves
  With thought—He is insensibly subdued
  To settled quiet: he is one by whom
  All effort seems forgotten, one to whom
10 Long patience has such mild composure given,
  That patience now doth seem a thing, of which
  He hath no need. He is by nature led
  To peace so perfect, that the young behold
  With envy, what the old man hardly feels.
15 —I asked him whither he was bound, and what
  The object of his journey; he replied
  "Sir! I am going many miles to take
  A last leave of my son, a mariner,
  Who from a sea-fight has been brought to Falmouth,
20 And there is dying in an hospital."

---

[1] Wordsworth omitted the first three words of the title in the 1800 and later editions; he dropped lines 15–20 in 1815.

William Wordsworth

The Complaint of a Forsaken Indian Woman

[*When a Northern Indian, from sickness, is unable to continue his journey with his companions; he is left behind, covered over with Deer-skins, and is supplied with water, food, and fuel if the situation of the place will afford it. He is informed of the track which his companions intend to pursue, and if he is unable to follow, or overtake them, he perishes alone in the Desert; unless he should have the good fortune to fall in with some other Tribes of Indians. It is unnecessary to add that the females are equally, or still more, exposed to the same fate. See that very interesting work,* Hearne's Journey *from* Hudson's Bay *to the* Northern Ocean.[1] *When the Northern Lights, as the same writer informs us, vary their position in the air, they make a rustling and a crackling noise. This circumstance is alluded to in the first stanza of the following poem.*]

Before I see another day,
Oh let my body die away!
In sleep I heard the northern gleams;
The stars they were among my dreams;
5 In sleep did I behold the skies,
I saw the crackling flashes drive;
And yet they are upon my eyes,
And yet I am alive.
Before I see another day,
10 Oh let my body die away!

My fire is dead: it knew no pain;
Yet is it dead, and I remain.
All stiff with ice the ashes lie;
And they are dead, and I will die.
15 When I was well, I wished to live,
For clothes, for warmth, for food, and fire;
But they to me no joy can give,
No pleasure now, and no desire.
Then here contented will I lie;
20 Alone I cannot fear to die.

Alas! you might have dragged me on
Another day, a single one!

---

[1] Samuel Hearne, *A Journey from Prince of Wales's Fort in Hudson's Bay to the Northern Ocean.**

Too soon despair o'er me prevailed;
Too soon my heartless spirit failed;
25 When you were gone my limbs were stronger,
And Oh how grievously I rue,
That, afterwards, a little longer,
My friends, I did not follow you!
For strong and without pain I lay,
30 My friends, when you were gone away.

My child! they gave thee to another,
A woman who was not thy mother.
When from my arms my babe they took,
On me how strangely did he look!
35 Through his whole body something ran,
A most strange something did I see;
—As if he strove to be a man,
That he might pull the sledge for me.
And then he stretched his arms, how wild!
40 Oh mercy! like a little child.

My little joy! my little pride!
In two days more I must have died.
Then do not weep and grieve for me;
I feel I must have died with thee.
45 Oh wind that o'er my head art flying,
The way my friends their course did bend,
I should not feel the pain of dying,
Could I with thee a message send.
Too soon, my friends, you went away;
50 For I had many things to say.

I'll follow you across the snow,
You travel heavily and slow:
In spite of all my weary pain,
I'll look upon your tents again.
55 My fire is dead, and snowy white
The water which beside it stood;
The wolf has come to me to-night,
And he has stolen away my food.
For ever left alone am I,
60 Then wherefore should I fear to die?

My journey will be shortly run,
I shall not see another sun,

I cannot lift my limbs to know
If they have any life or no.
65 My poor forsaken child! if I
For once could have thee close to me,
With happy heart I then would die,
And my last thoughts would happy be.
I feel my body die away,
70 I shall not see another day.

Lines Written a Few Miles Above Tintern Abbey,
on revisiting the banks of the Wye during a tour, July 13, 1798[1]

Five years have passed; five summers, with the length
Of five long winters! and again I hear
These waters, rolling from their mountain-springs
With a sweet inland murmur.[2]—Once again
5 Do I behold these steep and lofty cliffs,
Which on a wild secluded scene impress
Thoughts of more deep seclusion; and connect
The landscape with the quiet of the sky.
The day is come when I again repose
10 Here, under this dark sycamore, and view
These plots of cottage-ground, these orchard-tufts,
Which, at this season, with their unripe fruits,
Among the woods and copses lose themselves,
Nor, with their green and simple hue, disturb
15 The wild green landscape. Once again I see
These hedge-rows, hardly hedge-rows, little lines
Of sportive wood run wild; these pastoral farms
Green to the very door; and wreathes of smoke

"July 1798. No poem of mine was composed under circumstances
more pleasant for me to remember than this. I began it upon leaving
Tintern, after crossing the Wye, and concluded it just as I was entering
Bristol in the evening, after a ramble of 4 or 5 days, with my sister.
Not a line of it was altered, and not any part of it written down till I
reached Bristol. It was published almost immediately after in the little
volume [*Lyrical Ballads*] of which so much has been said in these
notes." (W.W., as dictated to Isabella Fenwick, 1843.) Wordsworth
visited the Wye Valley in August 1793 and again, with his sister
Dorothy, in July 1798.

[2] The river is not affected by the tides a few miles above Tintern."

Sent up, in silence, from among the trees,
20 With some uncertain notice, as might seem,
Of vagrant dwellers in the houseless woods,
Or of some hermit's cave, where by his fire
The hermit sits alone.
            Though absent long,
These forms of beauty have not been to me,
25 As is a landscape to a blind man's eye:
But oft, in lonely rooms, and mid the din
Of towns and cities, I have owed to them,
In hours of weariness, sensations sweet,
Felt in the blood, and felt along the heart,
30 And passing even into my purer mind
With tranquil restoration:—feelings too
Of unremembered pleasure; such, perhaps,
As may have had no trivial influence
On that best portion of a good man's life;
35 His little, nameless, unremembered acts
Of kindness and of love. Nor less, I trust,
To them I may have owed another gift,
Of aspect more sublime; that blessed mood,
In which the burthen of the mystery,
40 In which the heavy and the weary weight
Of all this unintelligible world
Is lighten'd:—that serene and blessed mood,
In which the affections gently lead us on,
Until, the breath of this corporeal frame,
45 And even the motion of our human blood
Almost suspended, we are laid asleep
In body, and become a living soul:
While with an eye made quiet by the power
Of harmony, and the deep power of joy,
50 We see into the life of things.
            If this
Be but a vain belief, yet, oh! how oft,
In darkness, and amid the many shapes
Of joyless day-light; when the fretful stir
Unprofitable, and the fever of the world,
55 Have hung upon the beatings of my heart,
How oft, in spirit, have I turned to thee
O sylvan Wye! Thou wanderer through the wood
How often has my spirit turned to thee!

And now, with gleams of half-extinguish'd thought,
With many recognitions dim and faint,
And somewhat of a sad perplexity,
The picture of the mind revives again:
While here I stand, not only with the sense
Of present pleasure, but with pleasing thoughts
That in this moment there is life and food
For future years. And so I dare to hope
Though changed, no doubt, from what I was, when first
I came among these hills; when like a roe
I bounded o'er the mountains, by the sides
Of the deep rivers, and the lonely streams,
Wherever nature led; more like a man
Flying from something that he dreads, than one
Who sought the thing he loved. For nature then
(The coarser pleasures of my boyish days,
And their glad animal movements all gone by,)
To me was all in all.—I cannot paint
What then I was. The sounding cataract
Haunted me like a passion: the tall rock,
The mountain, and the deep and gloomy wood,
Their colours and their forms, were then to me
An appetite: a feeling and a love,
That had no need of a remoter charm,
By thought supplied, or any interest
Unborrowed from the eye.—That time is past,
And all its aching joys are now no more,
And all its dizzy raptures. Not for this
Faint I, nor mourn nor murmur: other gifts
Have followed, for such loss, I would believe,
Abundant recompence. For I have learned
To look on nature, not as in the hour
Of thoughtless youth, but hearing oftentimes
The still, sad music of humanity,
Not harsh nor grating, though of ample power
To chasten and subdue. And I have felt
A presence that disturbs me with the joy
Of elevated thoughts; a sense sublime
Of something far more deeply interfused,
Whose dwelling is the light of setting suns,
And the round ocean, and the living air,
And the blue sky, and in the mind of man,
A motion and a spirit, that impels
All thinking things, all objects of all thought,
And rolls through all things. Therefore am I still
A lover of the meadows and the woods,
And mountains; and of all that we behold
From this green earth; of all the mighty world
Of eye and ear, both what they half-create,[1]
And what perceive; well pleased to recognize
In nature and the language of the sense,
The anchor of my purest thoughts, the nurse,
The guide, the guardian of my heart, and soul
Of all my moral being.

              Nor, perchance,
If I were not thus taught, should I the more
Suffer my genial spirits to decay:
For thou art with me, here, upon the banks
Of this fair river; thou, my dearest Friend,[2]
My dear, dear Friend, and in thy voice I catch
The language of my former heart, and read
My former pleasures in the shooting lights
Of thy wild eyes. Oh! yet a little while
May I behold in thee what I was once,
My dear, dear Sister! And this prayer I make,
Knowing that Nature never did betray
The heart that loved her; 'tis her privilege,
Through all the years of this our life, to lead
From joy to joy: for she can so inform
The mind that is within us, so impress
With quietness and beauty, and so feed
With lofty thoughts, that neither evil tongues,
Rash judgments, nor the sneers of selfish men,
Nor greetings where no kindness is, nor all
The dreary intercourse of daily life,
Shall e'er prevail against us, or disturb
Our chearful faith that all which we behold
Is full of blessings. Therefore let the moon
Shine on thee in thy solitary walk;
And let the misty mountain winds be free
To blow against thee: and in after years,

---

[1] "This line has a close resemblance to an admirable line of Young, t' exact expression of which I cannot recollect." (W.W.) See Edw Young, *Night Thoughts* (1742–44) 6.424.

[2] the poet's sister, Dorothy Wordsworth.*

When these wild ecstasies shall be matured
Into a sober pleasure, when thy mind
Shall be a mansion for all lovely forms,
Thy memory be as a dwelling-place
For all sweet sounds and harmonies; Oh! then,
If solitude, or fear, or pain, or grief,
Should be thy portion, with what healing thoughts
Of tender joy wilt thou remember me,
And these my exhortations! Nor, perchance,
If I should be, where I no more can hear
Thy voice, nor catch from thy wild eyes these gleams
Of past existence, wilt thou then forget
That on the banks of this delightful stream
We stood together; and that I, so long
A worshipper of Nature, hither came,
Unwearied in that service: rather say
With warmer love, oh! with far deeper zeal
Of holier love. Nor wilt thou then forget,
That after many wanderings, many years
Of absence, these steep woods and lofty cliffs,
And this green pastoral landscape, were to me
More dear, both for themselves, and for thy sake.

from *Lyrical Ballads, with Other Poems. In Two Volumes* (1800)

Preface[1]

The First Volume of these Poems has already been submitted to general perusal. It was published, as an experiment which, I hoped, might be of some use to ascertain, how far, by fitting to metrical arrangement a selection of the real language of men in a state of vivid sensation, that sort of pleasure and that quantity of pleasure may be imparted, which a Poet may rationally endeavour to impart.

I had formed no very inaccurate estimate of the probable effect of those Poems: I flattered myself that those who should be pleased with them would read them with more than common pleasure: and on the other hand I was well aware that by those who should dislike them they would be read with more than common dislike. The result has differed from my expectation in this only, that I have pleased a greater number, than I ventured to hope I should please.

For the sake of variety and from a consciousness of my own weakness I was induced to request the assistance of a Friend, who furnished me with the Poems of the ANCIENT MARINER, the FOSTER-MOTHER'S TALE, the NIGHTINGALE, the DUNGEON, and the Poem entitled LOVE.[2] I should not, however, have requested this assistance, had I not believed that the poems of my Friend would in a great measure have the same tendency as my own, and that, though there would be found a difference, there would be found no discordance in the colours of our style; as our opinions on the subject of poetry do almost entirely coincide.

Several of my Friends are anxious for the success of these Poems from a belief, that if the views, with which they were composed, were indeed realized, a class of Poetry would be produced, well adapted to interest mankind permanently, and not unimportant in the multiplicity and in the quality of its moral relations: and on this account they have advised me to prefix a systematic defence of the theory, upon which the poems were written. But I was unwilling to undertake the task, because I knew that on this occasion the Reader would look coldly upon my arguments, since I might be suspected of having been principally influenced by the selfish and foolish hope of *reasoning* him into an approbation of these particular Poems: and I was still more unwilling to undertake the task, because adequately to display my opinions and fully to enforce my arguments would require a space wholly disproportionate to the nature of a preface. For to treat the subject with the clearness and coherence, of which I believe it susceptible, it would be necessary to give a full account of the present state of the public taste in this country, and to determine how far this taste is healthy or depraved; which again could not be determined, without pointing out, in what manner language and the human mind act

---

[1] ...revised and added to this Preface for the 1802 edition ...Selected passages from the 1802 Preface are given in...

[2] Of these poems by Wordsworth's friend Samuel Taylor Coleridge,* only "The Rime of the Ancient Mariner" appears in this volume.

and react on each other, and without retracing the revolutions not of literature alone but likewise of society itself. I have therefore altogether declined to enter regularly upon this defence; yet I am sensible, that there would be some impropriety in abruptly obtruding upon the Public, without a few words of introduction, Poems so materially different from those, upon which general approbation is at present bestowed.

It is supposed, that by the act of writing in verse an Author makes a formal engagement that he will gratify certain known habits of association, that he not only thus apprizes the Reader that certain classes of ideas and expressions will be found in his book, but that others will be carefully excluded. This exponent or symbol held forth by metrical language must in different æras of literature have excited very different expectations: for example, in the age of Catullus Terence and Lucretius, and that of Statius or Claudian, and in our own country, in the age of Shakespeare and Beaumont and Fletcher, and that of Donne and Cowley, or Dryden, or Pope.[1] I will not take upon me to determine the exact import of the promise which by the act of writing in verse an Author in the present day makes to his Reader; but I am certain it will appear to many persons that I have not fulfilled the terms of an engagement thus voluntarily contracted.[2] I hope therefore the Reader will not censure me, if I attempt to state what I have proposed to myself to perform, and also, (as far as the limits of a preface will permit) to explain some of the chief reasons which have determined me in the choice of my purpose: that at least he may be spared any unpleasant feeling of disappointment, and that I myself may be protected from the most dishonorable accusation which can be brought against an Author, namely, that of an indolence which prevents him from endeavouring to ascertain what is his duty, or, when his duty is ascertained prevents him from performing it.

The principal object then which I proposed to myself in these Poems was to make the incidents of common life interesting[3] by tracing in them, truly though not ostentatiously, the primary laws of our nature: chiefly as far as regards the manner in which we associate ideas in a state of excitement. Low and rustic life was generally chosen because in that situation the essential passions of the heart find a better soil in which they can attain their maturity, are less under restraint, and speak a plainer and more emphatic language; because in that situation our elementary feelings exist in a state of greater simplicity and consequently may be more accurately contemplated and more forcibly communicated; because the manners of rural life germinate from those elementary feelings; and from the necessary character of rural occupations are more easily comprehended; and are more durable; and lastly, because in that situation the passions of men are incorporated with the beautiful and permanent forms of nature. The language too of these men is adopted (purified indeed from what appear to be its real defects, from all lasting and rational causes of dislike or disgust) because such men hourly communicate with the best objects from which the best part of language is originally derived; and because, from their rank in society and the sameness and narrow circle of their intercourse, being less under the action of social vanity they convey their feelings and notions in simple and unelaborated expressions. Accordingly such a language arising out of repeated experience and regular feelings is a more permanent and a far more

---

[1] Wordsworth's "æras of literature" are as follows: Latin poetry and drama of the century and a half before Christ (represented by Catullus, c. 84–c. 54 BC, Terence, 195 or 185–159 BC, and Lucretius, c. 99–c. 55 BC); poetry of the Augustan and later Roman empire (Statius, c. AD 40–c. 96, and Claudian, 4th C. AD); drama contemporary with Shakespeare (Sir Francis Beaumont, 1584–1616, and John Fletcher, 1579–1625); poetry of the so-called metaphysical school (John Donne, 1572–1631, and Abraham Cowley, 1618–67); and the works of John Dryden (1631–1700) and Alexander Pope (1688–1744).

[2] Wordsworth inserted the following sentence in 1802: "They who have been accustomed to the gaudiness and inane phraseology of many modern writers, if they persist in reading this book to its conclusion, will, no doubt, frequently have to struggle with feelings of strangeness and aukwardness: they will look round for poetry, and will be induced to inquire by what species of courtesy these attempts can be permitted to assume that title."

[3] In 1802, Wordsworth replaced "make the incidents of common life interesting" with the following: "chuse incidents and situations from common life, and to relate or describe them, throughout, as far as was possible, in a selection of language really used by men; and, at the same time, to throw over them a certain colouring of imagination, whereby ordinary things should be presented to the mind in an unusual way; and, further, and above all, to make these incidents and situations interesting."

philosophical language than that which is frequently substituted for it by Poets, who think that they are conferring honour upon themselves and their art in proportion as they separate themselves from the sympathies of men, and indulge in arbitrary and capricious habits of expression in order to furnish food for fickle tastes and fickle appetites of their own creation.[1]

I cannot be insensible of the present outcry against the triviality and meanness both of thought and language, which some of my contemporaries have occasionally introduced into their metrical compositions; and I acknowledge that this defect where it exists, is more dishonorable to the Writer's own character than false refinement or arbitrary innovation, though I should contend at the same time that it is far less pernicious in the sum of its consequences. From such verses the Poems in these volumes will be found distinguished at least by one mark of difference, that each of them has a worthy *purpose*. Not that I mean to say, that I always began to write with a distinct purpose formally conceived; but I believe that my habits of meditation have so formed my feelings, as that my descriptions of such objects as strongly excite those feelings, will be found to carry along with them a *purpose*. If in this opinion I am mistaken I can have little right to the name of a Poet. For all good poetry is the spontaneous overflow of powerful feelings; but though this be true, Poems to which any value can be attached, were never produced on any variety of subjects but by a man who being possessed of more than usual organic sensibility had also thought long and deeply. For our continued influxes of feeling are modified and directed by our thoughts, which are indeed the representatives of all our past feelings; and as by contemplating the relation of these general representatives to each other, we discover what is really important to men, so by the repetition and continuance of this act feelings connected with important subjects will be nourished, till at length, if we be originally possessed of much organic sensibility, such habits of mind will be produced that by obeying blindly and mechanically the impulses of those habits we shall describe objects and utter sentiments of such a nature and in such connection with each other, that the understanding of the being to whom we address ourselves, if he be in a healthful state of association, must necessarily be in some degree enlightened, his taste exalted, and his affections ameliorated.

I have said that each of these poems has a purpose. I have also informed my Reader what this purpose will be found principally to be: namely to illustrate the manner in which our feelings and ideas are associated in a state of excitement. But speaking in less general language, it is to follow the fluxes and refluxes of the mind when agitated by the great and simple affections of our nature. This object I have endeavoured in these short essays to attain by various means; by tracing the maternal passion through many of its more subtle windings, as in the poems of the IDIOT BOY and the MAD MOTHER; by accompanying the last struggles of a human being at the approach of death, cleaving in solitude to life and society, as in the Poem of the FORSAKEN INDIAN; by shewing, as in the Stanzas entitled WE ARE SEVEN, the perplexity and obscurity which in childhood attend our notion of death, or rather our utter inability to admit that notion; or by displaying the strength of fraternal, or to speak more philosophically, of moral attachment when early associated with the great and beautiful objects of nature, as in THE BROTHERS; or, as in the Incident of SIMON LEE, by placing my Reader in the way of receiving from ordinary moral sensations another and more salutary impression than we are accustomed to receive from them. It has also been part of my general purpose to attempt to sketch characters under the influence of less impassioned feelings, as in the OLD MAN TRAVELLING, THE TWO THIEVES, &c. characters of which the elements are simple, belonging rather to nature than to manners, such as exist now and will probably always exist, and which from their constitution may be distinctly and profitably contemplated. I will not abuse the indulgence of my Reader by dwelling longer upon this subject; but it is proper that I should mention one other circumstance which distinguishes these Poems from the popular Poetry of the day; it is this, that the feeling therein developed gives importance to the action and

---

[1] "It is worth while here to observe that the affecting parts of Chaucer are almost always expressed in language pure and universally intelligible even to this day." (W.W.)

situation and not the action and situation to the feeling. My meaning will be rendered perfectly intelligible by referring my Reader to the Poems entitled POOR SUSAN and the CHILDLESS FATHER, particularly to the last Stanza of the latter Poem.

I will not suffer a sense of false modesty to prevent me from asserting, that I point my Reader's attention to this mark of distinction far less for the sake of these particular Poems than from the general importance of the subject. The subject is indeed important! For the human mind is capable of excitement without the application of gross and violent stimulants; and he must have a very faint perception of its beauty and dignity who does not know this, and who does not further know that one being is elevated above another in proportion as he possesses this capability. It has therefore appeared to me that to endeavour to produce or enlarge this capability is one of the best services in which, at any period, a Writer can be engaged; but this service, excellent at all times, is especially so at the present day. For a multitude of causes unknown to former times are now acting with a combined force to blunt the discriminating powers of the mind, and unfitting it for all voluntary exertion to reduce it to a state of almost savage torpor. The most effective of these causes are the great national events which are daily taking place,[1] and the encreasing accumulation of men in cities, where the uniformity of their occupations produces a craving for extraordinary incident which the rapid communication of intelligence hourly gratifies. To this tendency of life and manners the literature and theatrical exhibitions of the country have conformed themselves. The invaluable works of our elder writers, I had almost said the works of Shakespear and Milton, are driven into neglect by frantic novels, sickly and stupid German Tragedies, and deluges of idle and extravagant stories in verse.[2]—When I think upon this degrading thirst after outrageous stimulation I am almost ashamed to have spoken of the feeble effort with which I have endeavoured to counteract it; and reflecting upon the magnitude of the general evil, I should be oppressed with no dishonorable melancholy, had I not a deep impression of certain inherent and indestructible qualities of the human mind, and likewise of certain powers in the great and permanent objects that act upon it which are equally inherent and indestructible; and did I not further add to this impression a belief that the time is approaching when the evil will be systematically opposed by men of greater powers and with far more distinguished success.

Having dwelt thus long on the subjects and aim of these Poems, I shall request the Reader's permission to apprize him of a few circumstances relating to their *style*, in order, among other reasons, that I may not be censured for not having performed what I never attempted. Except in a very few instances the Reader will find no personifications of abstract ideas in these volumes, not that I mean to censure such personifications: they may be well fitted for certain sorts of composition, but in these Poems I propose to myself to imitate, and, as far as possible, to adopt the very language of men, and I do not find that such personifications make any regular or natural part of that language. I wish to keep my Reader in the company of flesh and blood, persuaded that by so doing I shall interest him. Not but that I believe that others who pursue a different track may interest him likewise: I do not interfere with their claim, I only wish to prefer a different claim of my own. There will also be found in these volumes little of what is usually called poetic diction; I have taken as much pains to avoid it as others ordinarily take to produce it; this I have done for the reason already alleged, to bring my language near to the language of men, and further, because the pleasure which I have proposed to myself to impart is of a kind

---

[1] The 1790s had seen—to name only a few critical events—the French Revolution, the execution of Louis XVI, war between Britain and France, treason trials in England, the rise of Napoleon in France, and mutinies, food scarcity, and rebellion in Ireland.

[2] Gothic novels such as Ann Radcliffe's *The Mysteries of Udolpho* (1794)* and *The Italian* (1797), and Matthew Gregory Lewis's *The Monk* (1796)*; plays by such writers as August Friedrich von Kotzebue (1761–1819), who wrote for a popular audience; such verse narratives as the hundreds of gothic and sentimental "tales" listed in J.R. de J. Jackson, *Annals of English Verse 1770–1835*.

very different from that which is supposed by many persons to be the proper object of poetry. I do not know how without being culpably particular I can give my Reader a more exact notion of the style in which I wished these poems to be written than by informing him that I have at all times endeavoured to look steadily at my subject, consequently I hope it will be found that there is in these Poems little falsehood of description, and that my ideas are expressed in language fitted to their respective importance. Something I must have gained by this practice, as it is friendly to one property of all good poetry, namely good sense; but it has necessarily cut me off from a large portion of phrases and figures of speech which from father to son have long been regarded as the common inheritance of Poets. I have also thought it expedient to restrict myself still further, having abstained from the use of many expressions; in themselves proper and beautiful, but which have been foolishly repeated by bad Poets till such feelings of disgust are connected with them as it is scarcely possible by any art of association to overpower.

If in a Poem there should be found a series of lines, or even a single line, in which the language, though naturally arranged and according to the strict laws of metre, does not differ from that of prose, there is a numerous class of critics who, when they stumble upon these prosaisms as they call them, imagine that they have made a notable discovery, and exult over the Poet as over a man ignorant of his own profession. Now these men would establish a canon of criticism which the Reader will conclude he must utterly reject if he wishes to be pleased with these volumes. And it would be a most easy task to prove to him that not only the language of a large portion of every good poem, even of the most elevated character, must necessarily, except with reference to the metre, in no respect differ from that of good prose, but likewise that some of the most interesting parts of the best poems will be found to be strictly the language of prose when prose is well written. The truth of this assertion might be demonstrated by innumerable passages from almost all the poetical writings, even of Milton himself. I have not space for much quotation; but, to illustrate the subject in a general manner, I will here adduce a short composition of Gray, who was at the head of those who by their reasonings have attempted to widen the space of separation betwixt Prose and Metrical composition, and was more than any other man curiously elaborate in the structure of his own poetic diction.

> In vain to me the smiling mornings shine,
> And reddening Phœbus lifts his golden fire:
> The birds in vain their amorous descant join,
> Or chearful fields resume their green attire:
> These ears alas! for other notes repine;
> *A different object do these eyes require;*
> *My lonely anguish melts no heart but mine;*
> *And in my breast the imperfect joys expire;*
> Yet Morning smiles the busy race to cheer,
> And new-born pleasure brings to happier men;
> The fields to all their wonted tribute bear;
> To warm their little loves the birds complain.
> *I fruitless mourn to him that cannot hear*
> *And weep the more because I weep in vain.*[1]

It will easily be perceived that the only part of this Sonnet which is of any value is the lines printed in Italics: it is equally obvious that except in the rhyme, and in the use of the single word "fruitless" for fruitlessly, which is so far a defect, the language of these lines does in no respect differ from that of prose.

Is there then, it will be asked, no essential difference between the language of prose and metrical composition? I answer that there neither is nor can be any essential difference. We are fond of tracing the resemblance between Poetry and Painting, and, accordingly, we call them Sisters: but where shall we find bonds of connection sufficiently strict to typify the affinity betwixt metrical and prose composition? They both speak by and to the same organs; the bodies in which both of them are clothed may be said to be of the same substance, their affections are kindred and almost identical, not necessarily differing even in degree;

---

[1] Thomas Gray, "Sonnet on the Death of Mr. Richard West" (1742).

Poetry[1] sheds no tears "such as Angels weep,"[2] but natural and human tears; she can boast of no celestial Ichor[3] that distinguishes her vital juices from those of prose; the same human blood circulates through the veins of them both.

If it be affirmed that rhyme and metrical arrangement of themselves constitute a distinction which overturns what I have been saying on the strict affinity of metrical language with that of prose, and paves the way for other distinctions which the mind voluntarily admits, I answer that[4] the distinction of rhyme and metre the language outwardly holden by men, a practical faith in the opinions which I am wishing to establish is almost unknown. If my conclusions are admitted, and carried as far as they must be carried if admitted at all, our judgments concerning the works of the greatest Poets both ancient and modern will be far different from what they are at present, both when we praise, and when we censure: and our moral feelings influencing, and influenced by these judgments will, I believe, be corrected and purified.

"Taking up the subject, then, upon general grounds, I ask what is meant by the word Poet? What is a Poet? To whom does he address himself? And what language is to be expected from him? He is a man speaking to men: a man, it is true, endued with more lively sensibility, more enthusiasm and tenderness, who has a greater knowledge of human nature, and a more comprehensive soul, than are supposed to be common among mankind; a man pleased with his own passions and volitions, and who rejoices more than other men in the spirit of life that is in him; delighting to contemplate similar volitions and passions as manifested in the goings-on of the Universe, and habitually impelled to create them where he does not find them. To these qualities he has added a disposition to be affected more than other men by absent things as if they were present; an ability of conjuring up in himself passions, which are indeed far from being the same as those produced by real events, yet (especially in those parts of the general sympathy which are pleasing and delightful) do more nearly resemble the passions produced by real events, than any thing which, from the motions of their own minds merely, other men are accustomed to feel in themselves; whence, and from practice, he has acquired a greater readiness and power in expressing what he thinks and feels, and especially those thoughts and feelings which, by his own choice, or from the structure of his own mind, arise in him without immediate external excitement.

"But, whatever portion of this faculty we may suppose even the greatest Poet to possess, there cannot be a doubt but that the language which it will suggest to him, must, in liveliness and truth, fall far short of that which is uttered by men in real life, under the actual pressure of those passions, certain shadows of which the Poet thus produces, or feels to be produced, in himself. However exalted a notion we would wish to cherish of the character of a Poet, it is obvious, that, while he describes and imitates passions, his situation is altogether slavish and mechanical, compared with the freedom and power of real and substantial action and suffering. So that it will be the wish of the Poet to bring his feelings near to those of the persons whose feelings he describes, nay, for short spaces of time perhaps, to let himself slip into an entire delusion, and even confound and identify his own feelings with theirs; modifying only the language which is thus suggested to him, by a consideration that he describes for a particular purpose, that of giving pleasure. Here, then, he will apply the principle on which I have so much insisted, namely, that of selection; on this he will depend for removing what would otherwise be painful or disgusting in the passion; he will feel that there is no necessity to trick out or to elevate nature: and, the more industriously he applies this principle, the deeper will be his faith that no words, which his fancy or   (Continued)

---

[1] "I here use the word 'Poetry' (though against my own judgment) as opposed to the word Prose, and synonymous with metrical composition. But much confusion has been introduced into criticism by this contradistinction of Poetry and Prose, instead of the more philosophical one of Poetry and Science. The only strict antithesis to Prose is Metre." (W.W.)

[2] Milton, *Paradise Lost* 1.620.

[3] the fluid said by the Greeks to run through the veins of the gods.

[4] At this point, Wordsworth added the following long section in 1802: "I answer that the language of such Poetry as I am recommending is, as far as is possible, a selection of the language really spoken by men; that this selection, wherever it is made with true taste and feeling, will of itself form a distinction far greater than would at first be imagined, and will entirely separate the composition from the vulgarity and meanness of ordinary life; and, if metre be superadded thereto, I believe that a dissimilitude will be produced altogether sufficient for the gratification of a rational mind. What other distinction would we have? Whence is it to come? And where is it to exist? Not, surely, where the Poet speaks through the mouths of his characters: it cannot be necessary here, either for elevation of style, or any of its supposed ornaments: for, if the Poet's subject be judiciously chosen, it will naturally, and upon fit occasion, lead him to passions the language of which, if selected truly and judiciously, must necessarily be dignified and variegated, and alive with metaphors and figures. I forbear to speak of an incongruity which would shock the intelligent Reader, should the Poet interweave any foreign splendour of his own with that which the passion naturally suggests: it is sufficient to say that such addition is unnecessary. And, surely, it is more probable that those passages, which with propriety abound with metaphors and figures, will have their due effect, if, upon other occasions where the passions are of a milder character, the style also be subdued and temperate.

"But, as the pleasure which I hope to give by the Poems I now present to the Reader must depend entirely on just notions upon this subject, and, as it is in itself of the highest importance to our taste and moral feelings, I cannot content myself with these detached remarks. And if, in what I am about to say, it shall appear to some that my labour is unnecessary, and that I am like a man fighting a battle without enemies, I would remind such persons, that, whatever may be imagination can suggest, will be to be compared with those which are the emanations of reality and truth.

"But it may be said by those who do not object to the general spirit of these remarks, that, as it is impossible for the Poet to produce upon all occasions language as exquisitely fitted for the passion as that which the real passion itself suggests, it is proper that he should consider himself as in the situation of a translator, who deems himself justified when he substitutes excellences of another kind for those which are unattainable by him; and endeavours occasionally to surpass his original, in order to make some amends for the general inferiority to which he feels that he must submit. But this would be to encourage idleness and unmanly despair. Further, it is the language of men who speak of what they do not understand; who talk of Poetry as of a matter of amusement and idle pleasure; who will converse with us as gravely about a *taste* for Poetry, as they express it, as if it were a thing as indifferent as a taste for Rope-dancing, or Frontiniac or Sherry. Aristotle, I have been told, hath said, that Poetry is the most philosophic of all writing [cf. *Poetics* 9.3]: it is so: its object is truth, not individual and local, but general, and operative; not standing upon external testimony, but carried alive into the heart by passion; truth which is its own testimony, which gives strength and divinity to the tribunal to which it appeals, and receives them from the same tribunal. Poetry is the image of man and nature. The obstacles which stand in the way of the fidelity of the Biographer and Historian, and of their consequent utility, are incalculably greater than those which are to be encountered by the Poet, who has an adequate notion of the dignity of his art. The Poet writes under one restriction only, namely, that of the necessity of giving immediate pleasure to a human Being possessed of that information which may be expected from him, not as a lawyer, a physician, a mariner, an astronomer or a natural philosopher, but as a Man. Except this one restriction, there is no object standing between the Poet and the image of things; between this, and the Biographer and Historian there are a thousand.

"Nor let this necessity of producing immediate pleasure be considered as a degradation of the Poet's art. It is far otherwise. It is an acknowledgment of the beauty of the universe, an acknowledgment the more sincere because it is not formal, but indirect; it is a task light and easy to him who looks at the world in the spirit of love: further, it is a homage paid to the native and naked dignity of man, to the grand elementary principle of pleasure, by which he knows, and feels, and lives, and moves. We have no sympathy but what is propagated by pleasure: I would not be misunderstood; but wherever we sympathize with pain it will be found that the sympathy is produced and carried on by subtle combinations with pleasure. We have no knowledge, that is, no general principles drawn from the contemplation of particular facts, but what has been built up by pleasure, and exists in us by pleasure alone. The Man of Science, the Chemist and Mathematician, whatever difficulties and disgusts they may have had to struggle with, know and feel this. However painful may be the objects with which the Anatomist's knowledge is connected, he feels that his knowledge is pleasure; and where he has no pleasure he has no knowledge. What then does the Poet? He considers man and the objects that surround him as acting and re-acting upon each other, so as to produce an infinite complexity of pain and pleasure; he considers man in his own nature and in his ordinary life as contemplating this with a certain quantity of immediate knowledge, with certain convictions, intuitions, and deductions which by habit become of the nature of intuitions; he considers him as looking upon this complex scene of ideas and sensations, and finding every where objects that immediately excite in him sympathies which, from the necessities of his nature, are accompanied by an overbalance of enjoyment.

"To this knowledge which all men carry about with them, and to these sympathies in which without any other discipline than that of our daily life we are fitted to take delight, the Poet principally directs his attention. He considers man and nature as essentially adapted to each other, and the mind of man as naturally the mirror of the fairest and most interesting qualities of nature. And thus the Poet, prompted by this feeling of pleasure which accompanies him through the whole course of his studies, converses with general nature with affections akin to those, which, through labour and length of time, the Man of Science has raised up in himself, by conversing with those particular parts of nature which are the objects of his studies. The knowledge both of the Poet and the Man of Science is pleasure; but the knowledge of the one cleaves to us as a necessary part of our existence, our natural and unalienable inheritance; the other is a personal and individual acquisition, slow to come to us, and by no habitual and direct sympathy connecting us with our fellow-beings. The Man of Science seeks truth as a remote and unknown benefactor; he cherishes and loves it in his solitude: the Poet, singing a song in which all human beings join with him, rejoices in the presence of truth as our visible friend and hourly companion. Poetry is the breath and finer spirit of all knowledge; it is the impassioned expression which is in the countenance of all Science. Emphatically may it be said of the Poet, as Shakespeare hath said of man, 'that he looks before and after' [*Hamlet* 4.4.37]. He is the rock of defence of human nature; an upholder and preserver, carrying every where with him relationship and love. In spite of difference of soil and climate, of language and manners, of laws and customs, in spite of things silently gone out of mind and things violently destroyed, the Poet binds together by passion and knowledge the vast empire of human society, as it is spread over the whole earth, and over all time. The objects of the Poet's thoughts are every where; though the eyes and senses of man are, it is true, his favorite guides, yet he will follow wheresoever he can find an atmosphere of sensation in which to move his wings. Poetry is the first and last of all knowledge—it is as immortal as the heart of man. If the labours of men of Science should ever create any material revolution, direct or indirect, in our condition, and in the impressions which we habitually receive, the Poet will sleep then no more than at present, but he will be ready to follow the steps of the Man of Science, not only in those general indirect effects, but he will be at his side, carrying sensation into the midst of the objects of the Science itself. The remotest discoveries of the Chemist, the Botanist, or Mineralogist, will be as proper objects of the Poet's art as any upon which it can be employed, if the time should ever come when these things shall be familiar to us, and the relations under which they are contemplated by the followers of these respective Sciences shall be manifestly and palpably material to us as enjoying and suffering beings. If the time should ever come when what is now called Science, thus familiarized to men, shall be ready to put on, as it were, a form of flesh and blood, the Poet will lend his divine spirit to aid the transfiguration, and will welcome the Being thus produced, as a dear and genuine inmate of the household of man. It is not, then, to be supposed that any one, who holds that sublime notion of Poetry which I have attempted to convey, will break in upon the sanctity and truth of his pictures by transitory and accidental ornaments, and endeavour to excite admiration of himself by arts, the necessity of which must manifestly depend upon the assumed meanness of his subject.

"What I have thus far said applies to Poetry in general; but especially to those parts of composition where the Poet speaks through the mouths of his characters; and upon this point it appears to have such weight that I will conclude, there are few persons, of good sense, who would not allow that the dramatic parts of composition are defective, in proportion as they deviate from the real language of nature, and are coloured by a diction of the Poet's own, either peculiar to him as an individual Poet, or belonging simply to Poets in general, to a body of men who, from the circumstance of their compositions being in metre, it is expected will employ a particular language.

"It is not, then, in the dramatic parts of composition that we look for this distinction of language; but still it may be proper and necessary where the Poet speaks to us in his own person and character. To this I answer: by referring my Reader to the description which I have before given of a Poet. Among the qualities which I have enumerated as principally conducing to form a Poet, is implied nothing differing in kind from other men, but only in degree. The sum of what I have there said is, that the Poet is chiefly distinguished from other men by a greater promptness to think and feel without immediate external excitement, and a greater power in expressing such thoughts and feelings as are produced in him in that manner. But these passions and thoughts and feelings are the general passions and thoughts and feelings of men. And with what are they connected? Undoubtedly with our moral sentiments and animal sensations, and with the causes which excite these; with the operations of the elements and the appearances of the visible universe; with storm and sun-shine, with the revolutions of the seasons, with cold and heat, with loss of friends and kindred, with injuries and resentments, gratitude and hope, with fear and sorrow. These, and the like, are the sensations and objects which the Poet describes, as they are the sensations of other men, and the objects which interest them. The Poet thinks and feels in the spirit of the passions of men. How, then, can his language differ in any material degree from that of all other men who feel vividly and see clearly? It might be *proved* that it is impossible. But supposing that this were not the case, the Poet might then be allowed to use a peculiar language, when expressing his feelings for his own gratification, or that of men like himself. But Poets do not write for Poets alone, but for men. Unless therefore we are advocates for that admiration which depends upon ignorance, and that pleasure which arises from hearing what we do not understand, the Poet must descend from this supposed height,

is regular and uniform, and not, like that which is produced by what is usually called poetic diction, arbitrary and subject to infinite caprices upon which no calculation whatever can be made. In the one case the Reader is utterly at the mercy of the Poet respecting what imagery or diction he may choose to connect with the passion, whereas in the other the metre obeys certain laws, to which the Poet and Reader both willingly submit because they are certain, and because no interference is made by them with the passion but such as the concurring testimony of ages has shewn to heighten and improve the pleasure which co-exists with it.

It will now be proper to answer an obvious question, namely, why, professing these opinions have I written in verse? To this in the first place I reply, because, however I may have restricted myself, there is still left open to me what confessedly constitutes the most valuable object of all writing whether in prose or verse, the great and universal passions of men, the most general and interesting of their occupations, and the entire world of nature, from which I am at liberty to supply myself with endless combinations of forms and imagery. Now, granting for a moment that whatever is interesting in these objects may be as vividly described in prose, why am I to be condemned if to such description I have endeavoured to superadd the charm which by the consent of all nations is acknowledged to exist in metrical language? To this it will be answered, that a very small part of the pleasure given by Poetry depends upon the metre, and that it is injudicious to write in metre unless it be accompanied with the other artificial distinctions of style with which metre is usually accompanied, and that by such deviation more will be lost from the shock which will be thereby given to the Reader's associations than will be counterbalanced by any pleasure which he can derive from the general power of numbers. In answer to those who thus contend for the necessity of accompanying

and, in order to excite rational sympathy, he must express himself as other men express themselves. To this it may be added, that while he is only selecting from the real language of men, or, which amounts to the same thing, composing accurately in the spirit of such selection, he is treading upon safe ground, and we know what we are to expect from him. Our feelings are the same with respect to metre; for, as it may be proper to remind the Reader ... "

metre with certain appropriate colours of style in order to the accomplishment of its appropriate end, and who also, in my opinion, greatly under-rate the power of metre in itself, it might perhaps be almost sufficient to observe that poems are extant, written upon more humble subjects, and in a more naked and simple style than what I have aimed at, which poems have continued to give pleasure from generation to generation. Now, if nakedness and simplicity be a defect, the fact here mentioned affords a strong presumption that poems somewhat less naked and simple are capable of affording pleasure at the present day; and all that I am now attempting is to justify myself for having written under the impression of this belief.

But I might point out various causes why, when the style is manly, and the subject of some importance, words metrically arranged will long continue to impart such a pleasure to mankind as he who is sensible of the extent of that pleasure will be desirous to impart. The end of Poetry is to produce excitement in coexistence with an overbalance of pleasure. Now, by the supposition, excitement is an unusual and irregular state of the mind; ideas and feelings do not in that state succeed each other in accustomed order. But if the words by which this excitement is produced are in themselves powerful, or the images and feelings have an undue proportion of pain connected with them, there is some danger that the excitement may be carried beyond its proper bounds. Now the co-presence of something regular, something to which the mind has been accustomed when in an unexcited or a less excited state, cannot but have great efficacy in tempering and restraining the passion by an intertexture of ordinary feeling. This may be illustrated by appealing to the Reader's own experience of the reluctance with which he comes to the re-perusal of the distressful parts of Clarissa Harlowe, or the Gamester.[1] While Shakespeare's writings, in the most pathetic scenes, never act upon us as pathetic beyond the bounds of pleasure—an effect which is in a great degree to be ascribed to small, but continual and regular impulses of pleasurable surprise from the metrical arrangement.—On the other hand (what it must be allowed will much more frequently happen) if the Poet's words should be incommensurate with the passion, and inadequate to raise the Reader to a height of desirable excitement, then, (unless the Poet's choice of his metre has been grossly injudicious) in the feelings of pleasure which the Reader has been accustomed to connect with metre in general, and in the feeling, whether chearful or melancholy, which he has been accustomed to connect with that particular movement of metre, there will be found something which will greatly contribute to impart passion to the words, and to effect the complex end which the Poet proposes to himself.

If I had undertaken a systematic defence of the theory upon which these poems are written, it would have been my duty to develope the various causes upon which the pleasure received from metrical language depends. Among the chief of these causes is to be reckoned a principle which must be well known to those who have made any of the Arts the object of accurate reflection; I mean the pleasure which the mind derives from the perception of similitude in dissimilitude. This principle is the great spring of the activity of our minds and their chief feeder. From this principle the direction of the sexual appetite, and all the passions connected with it take their origin: It is the life of our ordinary conversation; and upon the accuracy with which similitude in dissimilitude, and dissimilitude in similitude are perceived, depend our taste and our moral feelings. It would not have been a useless employment to have applied this principle to the consideration of metre, and to have shewn that metre is hence enabled to afford much pleasure, and to have pointed out in what manner that pleasure is produced. But my limits will not permit me to enter upon this subject, and I must content myself with a general summary.

I have said that Poetry is the spontaneous overflow of powerful feelings: it takes its origin from emotion recollected in tranquillity: the emotion is contemplated till by a species of reaction the tranquillity gradually disappears, and an emotion, similar to that which was before the subject of contemplation, is gradually pro-

---

[1] Samuel Richardson's *Clarissa* (1747–48) is an epistolary novel recounting the heroine's resistance to an unscrupulous lover, her rape, and its tragic consequences. *The Gamester*, a tragedy by Edward Moore (1753), shows Beverley's destruction by Stukeley at the gambling table.

duced, and does itself actually exist in the mind. In this mood successful composition generally begins, and in a mood similar to this it is carried on; but the emotion, of whatever kind and in whatever degree, from various causes is qualified by various pleasures, so that in describing any passions whatsoever, which are voluntarily described, the mind will upon the whole be in a state of enjoyment. Now if Nature be thus cautious in preserving in a state of enjoyment a being thus employed, the Poet ought to profit by the lesson thus held forth to him, and ought especially to take care, that whatever passions he communicates to his Reader, those passions, if his Reader's mind be sound and vigorous, should always be accompanied with an overbalance of pleasure. Now the music of harmonious metrical language, the sense of difficulty overcome, and the blind association of pleasure which has been previously received from works of rhyme or metre of the same or similar construction, all these imperceptibly make up a complex feeling of delight, which is of the most important use in tempering the painful feeling which will always be found intermingled with powerful descriptions of the deeper passions. This effect is always produced in pathetic and impassioned poetry; while in lighter compositions the ease and gracefulness with which the Poet manages his numbers are themselves confessedly a principal source of the gratification of the Reader. I might perhaps include all which it is *necessary* to say upon this subject by affirming what few persons will deny, that of two descriptions either of passions, manners, or characters, each of them equally well executed, the one in prose and the other in verse, the verse will be read a hundred times where the prose is read once. We see that Pope by the power of verse alone, has contrived to render the plainest common sense interesting, and even frequently to invest it with the appearance of passion. In consequence of these convictions I related in metre the Tale of GOODY BLAKE and HARRY GILL, which is one of the rudest of this collection. I wished to draw attention to the truth that the power of the human imagination is sufficient to produce such changes even in our physical nature as might almost appear miraculous. The truth is an important one; the fact (for it is a *fact*) is a valuable illustration of it. And I have the satisfaction of knowing that it has been communicated to many hundreds of people who would never have heard of it, had it not been narrated as a Ballad, and in a more impressive metre than is usual in Ballads.

Having thus adverted to a few of the reasons why I have written in verse, and why I have chosen subjects from common life, and endeavoured to bring my language near to the real language of men, if I have been too minute in pleading my own cause, I have at the same time been treating a subject of general interest; and it is for this reason that I request the Reader's permission to add a few words with reference solely to these particular poems, and to some defects which will probably be found in them. I am sensible that my associations must have sometimes been particular instead of general, and that, consequently, giving to things a false importance, sometimes from diseased impulses I may have written upon unworthy subjects; but I am less apprehensive on this account, than that my language may frequently have suffered from those arbitrary connections of feelings and ideas with particular words, from which no man can altogether protect himself. Hence I have no doubt that in some instances feelings even of the ludicrous may be given to my Readers by expressions which appeared to me tender and pathetic. Such faulty expressions, were I convinced they were faulty at present, and that they must necessarily continue to be so, I would willingly take all reasonable pains to correct. But it is dangerous to make these alterations on the simple authority of a few individuals, or even of certain classes of men; for where the understanding of an Author is not convinced, or his feelings altered, this cannot be done without great injury to himself: for his own feelings are his stay and support, and if he sets them aside in one instance, he may be induced to repeat this act till his mind loses all confidence in itself and becomes utterly debilitated. To this it may be added, that the Reader ought never to forget that he is himself exposed to the same errors as the Poet, and perhaps in a much greater degree: for there can be no presumption in saying that it is not probable he will be so well acquainted with the various stages of meaning through which words have passed, or with the fickleness or stability of the relations of particular ideas to each other; and above all, since he is so much less interested in the subject, he may decide lightly and carelessly.

Long as I have detained my Reader, I hope he will permit me to caution him against a mode of false criticism which has been applied to Poetry in which the language closely resembles that of life and nature. Such verses have been triumphed over in parodies of which Dr. Johnson's Stanza is a fair specimen.

"I put my hat upon my head,
And walk'd into the Strand,
And there I met another man
Whose hat was in his hand."[1]

Immediately under these lines I will place one of the most justly admired stanzas of the "*Babes* in the Wood."

"These pretty Babes with hand in hand
Went wandering up and down;
But never more they saw the Man
Approaching from the Town."[2]

In both these stanzas the words, and the order of the words, in no respect differ from the most unimpassioned conversation. There are words in both, for example, "the Strand," and "the Town," connected with none but the most familiar ideas; yet the one stanza we admit as admirable, and the other as a fair example of the superlatively contemptible. Whence arises this difference? Not from the metre, not from the language, not from the order of the words; but the *matter* expressed in Dr. Johnson's stanza is contemptible. The proper method of treating trivial and simple verses to which Dr. Johnson's stanza would be a fair parallelism is not to say this is a bad kind of poetry, or this is not poetry, but this wants sense; it is neither interesting in itself, nor can *lead* to any thing interesting; the images neither originate in that sane state of feeling which arises out of thought, nor can excite thought or feeling in the Reader. This is the only sensible manner of dealing with such verses: Why trouble yourself about the species till you have previously decided upon the genus? Why take pains to prove that an Ape is not a Newton when it is self-evident that he is not a man.

I have one request to make of my Reader, which is, that in judging these Poems he would decide by his own feelings genuinely, and not by reflection upon what will probably be the judgment of others. How common is it to hear a person say, "I myself do not object to this style of composition or this or that expression, but to such and such classes of people it will appear mean or ludicrous." This mode of criticism so destructive of all sound unadulterated judgment is almost universal: I have therefore to request that the Reader would abide independently by his own feelings, and that if he finds himself affected he would not suffer such conjectures to interfere with his pleasure.

If an Author by any single composition has impressed us with respect for his talents, it is useful to consider this as affording a presumption, that, on other occasions where we have been displeased, he nevertheless may not have written ill or absurdly; and, further, to give him so much credit for this one composition as may induce us to review what has displeased us with more care than we should otherwise have bestowed upon it. This is not only an act of justice, but in our decisions upon poetry especially, may conduce in a high degree to the improvement of our own taste: for an *accurate* taste in Poetry and in all the other arts, as Sir Joshua Reynolds has observed, is an *acquired* talent, which can only be produced by thought and a long continued intercourse with the best models of composition.[3] This is mentioned not with so ridiculous a purpose as to prevent the most inexperienced Reader from judging for himself, (I have already said that I wish him to judge for himself;) but merely to temper the rashness of decision, and to suggest that if Poetry be a subject on which much time has not been bestowed, the judgment may be erroneous, and that in many cases it necessarily will be so.

I know that nothing would have so effectually contributed to further the end which I have in view as to have shewn of what kind the pleasure is, and how

---

[1] Johnson is parodying Thomas Percy's *The Hermit of Warkworth* (1771).

[2] from a ballad in Thomas Percy's *Reliques of Ancient English Poetry* (1765), in which an evil uncle plots to murder two children for their inheritance.

[3] Reynolds,* *Discourses*: cf. the Advertisement to *Lyrical Ballads* (1798)* and note.

that pleasure is produced which is confessedly produced by metrical composition essentially different from what I have here endeavoured to recommend; for the Reader will say that he has been pleased by such composition and what can I do more for him? The power of any art is limited and he will suspect that if I propose to furnish him with new friends it is only upon condition of his abandoning his old friends. Besides, as I have said, the Reader is himself conscious of the pleasure which he has received from such composition, composition to which he has peculiarly attached the endearing name of Poetry; and all men feel an habitual gratitude, and something of an honorable bigotry for the objects which have long continued to please them: we not only wish to be pleased, but to be pleased in that particular way in which we have been accustomed to be pleased. There is a host of arguments in these feelings; and I should be the less able to combat them successfully, as I am willing to allow, that, in order entirely to enjoy the Poetry which I am recommending, it would be necessary to give up much of what is ordinarily enjoyed. But would my limits have permitted me to point out how this pleasure is produced, I might have removed many obstacles, and assisted my Reader in perceiving that the powers of language are not so limited as he may suppose; and that it is possible that poetry may give other enjoyments, of a purer, more lasting, and more exquisite nature. But this part of my subject I have been obliged altogether to omit: as it has been less my present aim to prove that the interest excited by some other kinds of poetry is less vivid, and less worthy of the nobler powers of the mind, than to offer reasons for presuming, that, if the object which I have proposed to myself were adequately attained, a species of poetry would be produced, which is genuine poetry; in its nature well adapted to interest mankind permanently, and likewise important in the multiplicity and quality of its moral relations.

From what has been said, and from a perusal of the Poems, the Reader will be able clearly to perceive the object which I have proposed to myself: he will determine how far I have attained this object; and, what is a much more important question, whether it be worth attaining; and upon the decision of these two questions will rest my claim to the approbation of the public.

There was a Boy[1]

There was a Boy, ye knew him well, ye Cliffs
And Islands of Winander! many a time,
At evening, when the stars had just begun
To move along the edges of the hills,
Rising or setting, would he stand alone,
Beneath the trees, or by the glimmering lake,
And there, with fingers interwoven, both hands
Press'd closely palm to palm and to his mouth
Uplifted, he, as through an instrument,
Blew mimic hootings to the silent owls
That they might answer him.[2] And they would shout
Across the wat'ry vale and shout again
Responsive to his call, with quivering peals,
And long halloos, and screams, and echoes loud
Redoubled and redoubled, a wild scene
Of mirth and jocund din. And, when it chanced
That pauses of deep silence mock'd his skill,
Then, sometimes, in that silence, while he hung
Listening, a gentle shock of mild surprize
Has carried far into his heart the voice
Of mountain torrents, or the visible scene
Would enter unawares into his mind
With all its solemn imagery, its rocks,
Its woods, and that uncertain heaven, receiv'd
Into the bosom of the steady lake.

Fair are the woods, and beauteous is the spot,
The vale where he was born: the Church-yard hangs
Upon a slope above the village school,
And there along that bank when I have pass'd
At evening, I believe, that near his grave
A full half-hour together I have stood,
Mute—for he died when he was ten years old.

---

[1] Cf. Baillie, *De Monfort* 4.1.32–39.* The poem was included in *The Prelude* (5.389–422 [1805], 5.364–97 [1850]).

[2] "This practice of making an instrument of their own fingers is known to most boys, though some are more skilful at it than others." (W.W., as dictated to Isabella Fenwick, 1843.)

Strange fits of passion I have known[1]

Strange fits of passion I have known,
And I will dare to tell,
But in the lover's ear alone,
What once to me befel.

5 When she I lov'd, was strong and gay
And like a rose in June,
I to her cottage bent my way,
Beneath the evening moon.

Upon the moon I fix'd my eye,
10 All over the wide lea;
My horse trudg'd on, and we drew nigh
Those paths so dear to me.

And now we reach'd the orchard plot,
And, as we climb'd the hill,
15 Towards the roof of Lucy's cot
The moon descended still.

In one of those sweet dreams I slept,
Kind Nature's gentlest boon!
And, all the while, my eyes I kept
20 On the descending moon.

My horse mov'd on; hoof after hoof
He rais'd and never stopp'd:

When down behind the cottage roof
At once the planet dropp'd.

25 What fond and wayward thoughts will slide
Into a Lover's head—

"O mercy!" to myself I cried,
"If Lucy should be dead!"[2]

Song

She dwelt among th' untrodden ways
    Beside the springs of Dove,
A Maid whom there were none to praise
    And very few to love.

5 A Violet by a mossy stone
    Half-hidden from the Eye!
—Fair, as a star when only one
    Is shining in the sky!

She *liv'd* unknown, and few could know
10   When Lucy ceas'd to be;
But she is in her Grave, and Oh!
    The difference to me.

A slumber did my spirit seal

A slumber did my spirit seal,
    I had no human fears:
She seem'd a thing that could not feel
    The touch of earthly years.

5 No motion has she now, no force
    She neither hears nor sees
Roll'd round in earth's diurnal course
    With rocks and stones and trees!

---

[1] This poem, together with "She dwelt among th' untrodden ways,"* "A slumber did my spirit seal,"* "Three years she grew in sun and shower,"* and "I travell'd among unknown Men,"* make up the group known as the Lucy poems. Lucy's identity—if she ever existed outside the poems—is unknown.

[2] Wordsworth sent an additional stanza to Coleridge in 1798–99, not printed in *Lyrical Ballads*:
    I told her this; her laughter light
    Is ringing in my ears;
    And when I think upon that night
    My eyes are dim with tears.

Lucy Gray[1]

Oft I had heard of Lucy Gray,
And when I cross'd the Wild,
I chanc'd to see at break of day
The solitary Child.

5 No Mate, no comrade Lucy knew;
She dwelt on a wide Moor,
The sweetest Thing that ever grew
Beside a human door!

You yet may spy the Fawn at play,
10 The Hare upon the Green;
But the sweet face of Lucy Gray
Will never more be seen.

"To-night will be a stormy night,
You to the Town must go,
15 And take a lantern, Child, to light
Your Mother thro' the snow."

"That, Father! will I gladly do;
'Tis scarcely afternoon—
The Minster-clock has just struck two,
20 And yonder is the Moon."

At this the Father rais'd his hook
And snapp'd a faggot-band;
He plied his work, and Lucy took
The lantern in her hand.

25 Not blither is the mountain roe,
With many a wanton stroke
Her feet disperse the powd'ry snow
That rises up like smoke.

The storm came on before its time,
30 She wander'd up and down,
And many a hill did Lucy climb
But never reach'd the Town.

The wretched Parents all that night
Went shouting far and wide;
35 But there was neither sound nor sight
To serve them for a guide.

At day-break on a hill they stood
That overlook'd the Moor;
And thence they saw the Bridge of Wood
40 A furlong from their door.

And now they homeward turn'd, and cry'd
"In Heaven we all shall meet!"
When in the snow the Mother spied
The print of Lucy's feet.

45 Then downward from the steep hill's edge
They track'd the footmarks small;
And through the broken hawthorn-hedge,
And by the long stone-wall;

And then an open field they cross'd,
50 The marks were still the same;
They track'd them on, nor ever lost,
And to the Bridge they came.

They follow'd from the snowy bank
The footmarks, one by one,
55 Into the middle of the plank,
And further there were none.

Yet some maintain that to this day
She is a living Child,
That you may see sweet Lucy Gray
60 Upon the lonesome Wild.

O'er rough and smooth she trips along,
And never looks behind;

---

[1] later given the title "Lucy Gray, or Solitude." "Written at Goslar in Germany in 1799. It was founded on a circumstance told me by my Sister, of a little girl who, not far from Halifax in Yorkshire, was bewildered in a snow-storm. Her footsteps were traced by her parents to the middle of the lock of a canal, and no other vestige of her, backward or forward, could be traced. The body however was found in the canal. The way in which the incident was treated and the spiritualizing of the character might furnish hints for contrasting the imaginative influences which I have endeavoured to throw over common life with Crabbe's matter of fact style of treating subjects of the same kind." (W.W., as dictated to Isabella Fenwick, 1843.) Cf. Coleridge, "Dejection" 117–25.*

And sings a solitary song
That whistles in the wind.

The Two April Mornings

We walk'd along, while bright and red
Uprose the morning sun,
And Matthew stopp'd, he look'd, and said,
"The will of God be done!"

5 A village Schoolmaster was he,
With hair of glittering grey;
As blithe a man as you could see
On a spring holiday.

And on that morning, through the grass,
10 And by the steaming rills,
We travell'd merrily to pass
A day among the hills.

"Our work," said I, "was well begun;
Then, from thy breast what thought,
15 Beneath so beautiful a sun,
So sad a sigh has brought?"

A second time did Matthew stop,
And fixing still his eye
Upon the eastern mountain-top
20 To me he made reply.

Yon cloud with that long purple cleft
Brings fresh into my mind
A day like this which I have left
Full thirty years behind.

25 And on that slope of springing corn
The self-same crimson hue
Fell from the sky that April morn,
The same which now I view!¹

With rod and line my silent sport
30 I plied by Derwent's wave,
And, coming to the church, stopp'd short
Beside my Daughter's grave.

Nine summers had she scarcely seen
The pride of all the vale;
35 And then she sang!—she would have been
A very nightingale.

Six feet in earth my Emma lay,
And yet I lov'd her more,
For so it seem'd, than till that day
40 I e'er had lov'd before.

And, turning from her grave, I met
Beside the church-yard Yew
A blooming Girl, whose hair was wet
With points of morning dew.

45 A basket on her head she bare,
Her brow was smooth and white,
To see a Child so very fair,
It was a pure delight!

No fountain from its rocky cave
50 E'er tripp'd with foot so free,
She seem'd as happy as a wave
That dances on the sea.

There came from me a sigh of pain
Which I could ill confine;
55 I look'd at her and look'd again;
—And did not wish her mine.

Matthew is in his grave, yet now
Methinks I see him stand,
As at that moment, with his bough
60 Of wilding in his hand.

---

¹ In 1802, Wordsworth replaced this stanza with the following:
    And just above yon slope of corn
    Such colours, and no other
    Were in the sky, that April morn,
    Of this the very brother.

Nutting[1]

————It seems a day,
One of those heavenly days which cannot die,
When forth I sallied from our cottage-door,[2]
And with a wallet o'er my shoulder slung,
5 A nutting crook in hand, I turn'd my steps
Towards the distant woods, a Figure quaint,
Trick'd out in proud disguise of Beggar's weeds
Put on for the occasion, by advice
And exhortation of my frugal Dame.
10 Motley accoutrements! of power to smile
At thorns, and brakes, and brambles, and, in truth,
More ragged than need was. Among the woods,
And o'er the pathless rocks, I forc'd my way
Until, at length, I came to one dear nook
15 Unvisited, where not a broken bough
Droop'd with its wither'd leaves, ungracious sign
Of devastation, but the hazels rose
Tall and erect, with milk-white clusters hung,
A virgin scene!—A little while I stood,
20 Breathing with such suppression of the heart
As joy delights in; and with wise restraint
Voluptuous, fearless of a rival, eyed
The banquet, or beneath the trees I sate
Among the flowers, and with the flowers I play'd;
25 A temper known to those, who, after long
And weary expectation, have been bless'd
With sudden happiness beyond all hope.—
—Perhaps it was a bower beneath whose leaves
The violets of five seasons re-appear
30 And fade, unseen by any human eye,
Where fairy water-breaks do murmur on
For ever, and I saw the sparkling foam,
And with my cheek on one of those green stones
That, fleec'd with moss, beneath the shady trees,
35 Lay round me scatter'd like a flock of sheep,
I heard the murmur and the murmuring sound,
In that sweet mood when pleasure loves to pay
Tribute to ease, and, of its joy secure
The heart luxuriates with indifferent things,
40 Wasting its kindliness on stocks and stones,
And on the vacant air. Then up I rose,

And dragg'd to earth both branch and bough, with crash
And merciless ravage; and the shady nook
Of hazels, and the green and mossy bower
45 Deform'd and sullied, patiently gave up
Their quiet being: and unless I now
Confound my present feelings with the past,
Even then, when from the bower I turn'd away,
Exulting, rich beyond the wealth of kings
50 I felt a sense of pain when I beheld
The silent trees and the intruding sky.—
Then, dearest Maiden![3] move along these shades
In gentleness of heart with gentle hand
Touch,—for there is a Spirit in the woods.

Three years she grew in sun and shower

Three years she grew in sun and shower,
Then Nature said, "A lovelier flower
On earth was never sown;
This Child I to myself will take,
5 She shall be mine, and I will make
A Lady of my own.

"Myself will to my darling be
Both law and impulse, and with me
The Girl in rock and plain,
10 In earth and heaven, in glade and bower,
Shall feel an overseeing power
To kindle or restrain.

---

[1] "Like most of my school-fellows I was an impassioned nutter. For this pleasure, the Vale of Esthwaite, abounding in coppice-wood, furnished a very wide range. These verses arose out of the remembrance of feelings I had often had when a boy, and particularly in the extensive woods that still stretch from the side of Esthwaite Lake towards Graythwaite, the seat of the ancient family of Sandys." (W.W., as dictated to Isabella Fenwick, 1843.) Cf. *The Two-Part Prelude* 1.234–36* and Mary Mitford, "Nutting."*

[2] "The house at which I was boarded during the time I was at School." (W.W.) The "frugal Dame" of line 9 is Ann Tyson, Wordsworth's landlady at Hawkshead during the years 1779–87.

[3] probably Wordsworth's sister, Dorothy.*

"She shall be sportive as the fawn
That wild with glee across the lawn
Or up the mountain springs,
And hers shall be the breathing balm,
And hers the silence and the calm
Of mute insensate things.

"The floating clouds their state shall lend
To her, for her the willow bend,
Nor shall she fail to see
Even in the motions of the storm
A beauty that shall mould her form
By silent sympathy.

"The stars of midnight shall be dear
To her, and she shall lean her ear
In many a secret place
Where rivulets dance their wayward round,
And beauty born of murmuring sound
Shall pass into her face.

"And vital feelings of delight
Shall rear her form to stately height,
Her virgin bosom swell,
Such thoughts to Lucy I will give
While she and I together live
Here in this happy dell."

Thus Nature spake—The work was done—
How soon my Lucy's race was run!
She died and left to me
This heath, this calm and quiet scene,
The memory of what has been,
And never more will be.

Michael, A Pastoral Poem[1]

If from the public way you turn your steps
Up the tumultuous brook of Green-head Gill,[2]
You will suppose that with an upright path
Your feet must struggle; in such bold ascent
The pastoral Mountains front you, face to face.
But, courage! for beside that boisterous Brook
The mountains have all open'd out themselves,
And made a hidden valley of their own.
No habitation there is seen; but such
As journey thither find themselves alone
With a few sheep, with rocks and stones, and kites[3]
That overhead are sailing in the sky.
It is in truth an utter solitude,
Nor should I have made mention of this Dell
But for one object which you might pass by,
Might see and notice not. Beside the brook
There is a straggling heap of unhewn stones!
And to that place a story appertains,
Which, though it be ungarnish'd with events,
Is not unfit, I deem, for the fire-side,
Or for the summer shade. It was the first,
The earliest of those tales that spake to me
Of Shepherds, dwellers in the vallies, men
Whom I already lov'd, not verily
For their own sakes, but for the fields and hills
Where was their occupation and abode.

---

[1] "The Sheepfold, on which so much of the poem turns, remains, or rather the ruins of it. The character and circumstances of Luke were taken from a family to whom had belonged, many years before, the house we lived in at Town-End, along with some fields and woodlands on the eastern shore of Grasmere. The name of the Evening Star was not in fact given to this house but to another on the same side of the valley more to the north." (W.W., as dictated to Isabella Fenwick, 1843.) In a letter to his friend Thomas Poole, 9 April 1801, Wordsworth commented: "I have attempted to give a picture of a man, of strong mind and lively sensibility, agitated by two of the most powerful affections of the human heart; the parental affection, and the love of property, *landed* property, including the feelings of inheritance, home, and personal and family independence." See also letter to Charles James Fox, 14 Jan. 1801.*

[2] a ravine a mile north of the village of Grasmere, where Wordsworth went to live in 1799.

[3] birds of prey.

And hence this Tale, while I was yet a boy
Careless of books, yet having felt the power
Of Nature, by the gentle agency
30 Of natural objects led me on to feel
For passions that were not my own, and think
At random and imperfectly indeed
On man; the heart of man and human life.
Therefore, although it be a history
35 Homely and rude, I will relate the same
For the delight of a few natural hearts,
And with yet fonder feeling, for the sake
Of youthful Poets, who among these Hills
Will be my second self when I am gone.

40 Upon the Forest-side in Grasmere Vale
There dwelt a Shepherd, Michael was his name,
An old man, stout of heart, and strong of limb.
His bodily frame had been from youth to age
Of an unusual strength: his mind was keen
45 Intense and frugal, apt for all affairs,
And in his Shepherd's calling he was prompt
And watchful more than ordinary men.
Hence he had learn'd the meaning of all winds,
Of blasts of every tone, and often-times
50 When others heeded not, He heard the South
Make subterraneous music, like the noise
Of Bagpipers on distant Highland hills;
The Shepherd, at such warning, of his flock
Bethought him, and he to himself would say
55 The winds are now devising work for me!
And truly at all times the storm, that drives
The Traveller to a shelter, summon'd him
Up to the mountains: he had been alone
Amid the heart of many thousand mists
60 That came to him and left him on the heights.
So liv'd he till his eightieth year was pass'd.

And grossly that man errs, who should suppose
That the green Valleys, and the Streams and Rocks
Were things indifferent to the Shepherd's thoughts.
65 Fields, where with chearful spirits he had breath'd
The common air; the hills, which he so oft
Had climb'd with vigorous steps; which had impress'd
So many incidents upon his mind
Of hardship, skill or courage, joy or fear;
70 Which like a book preserv'd the memory
Of the dumb animals, whom he had sav'd,
Had fed or shelter'd, linking to such acts,
So grateful in themselves, the certainty
Of honorable gains; these fields, these hills
75 Which were his living Being, even more
Than his own Blood—what could they less? had laid
Strong hold on his affections, were to him
A pleasurable feeling of blind love,
The pleasure which there is in life itself.

80 He had not passed his days in singleness.
He had a Wife, a comely Matron, old
Though younger than himself full twenty years.
She was a woman of a stirring life
Whose heart was in her house: two wheels she had
85 Of antique form, this large for spinning wool,
That small for flax, and if one wheel had rest,
It was because the other was at work.
The Pair had but one Inmate in their house,
An only Child, who had been born to them
90 When Michael telling o'er his years began
To deem that he was old, in Shepherd's phrase,
With one foot in the grave. This only son,
With two brave sheep dogs tried in many a storm,
The one of an inestimable worth,
95 Made all their Household. I may truly say,
That they were as a proverb in the vale
For endless industry. When day was gone,
And from their occupations out of doors
The Son and Father were come home, even then
100 Their labour did not cease, unless when all
Turn'd to their cleanly supper-board, and there
Each with a mess of pottage and skimm'd milk,
Sate round their basket pil'd with oaten cakes,
And their plain home-made cheese. Yet when their meal
105 Was ended, LUKE (for so the Son was nam'd)
And his old Father, both betook themselves
To such convenient work, as might employ
Their hands by the fire-side; perhaps to card
Wool for the House-wife's spindle, or repair
110 Some injury done to sickle, flail, or scythe,
Or other implement of house or field.

Down from the cieling by the chimney's edge,
Which in our ancient uncouth country style
Did with a huge projection overbrow
115 Large space beneath, as duly as the light
Of day grew dim, the House-wife hung a lamp;
An aged utensil, which had perform'd
Service beyond all others of its kind.
Early at evening did it burn and late,
120 Surviving Comrade of uncounted Hours
Which going by from year to year had found
And left the Couple neither gay perhaps
Nor chearful, yet with objects and with hopes
Living a life of eager industry.
125 And now, when LUKE was in his eighteenth year,
There by the light of this old lamp they sate,
Father and Son, while late into the night
The House-wife plied her own peculiar work,
Making the cottage thro' the silent hours
130 Murmur as with the sound of summer flies.
Not with a waste of words, but for the sake
Of pleasure, which I know that I shall give
To many living now, I of this Lamp
Speak thus minutely: for there are no few
135 Whose memories will bear witness to my tale.[1]
The Light was famous in its neighbourhood,
And was a public Symbol of the life,
The thrifty Pair had liv'd. For, as it chanc'd,
Their Cottage on a plot of rising ground
140 Stood single, with large prospect North and South,
High into Easedale, up to Dunmal-Raise,
And Westward to the village near the Lake.
And from this constant light so regular
And so far seen, the House itself by all
145 Who dwelt within the limits of the vale,
Both old and young, was nam'd The Evening Star.

Thus living on through such a length of years,
The Shepherd, if he lov'd himself, must needs
Have lov'd his Help-mate; but to Michael's heart
150 This Son of his old age was yet more dear—
Effect which might perhaps have been produc'd
By that instinctive tenderness, the same

Blind Spirit, which is in the blood of all,
Or that a child, more than all other gifts,
155 Brings hope with it, and forward-looking thoughts,
And stirrings of inquietude, when they
By tendency of nature needs must fail.
From such, and other causes, to the thoughts
Of the old Man his only Son was now
160 The dearest object that he knew on earth.
Exceeding was the love he bare to him,
His Heart and his Heart's joy! For oftentimes
Old Michael, while he was a babe in arms,
Had done him female service, not alone
165 For dalliance and delight, as is the use
Of Fathers, but with patient mind enforc'd
To acts of tenderness; and he had rock'd
His cradle with a woman's gentle hand.

And in a later time, ere yet the Boy
170 Had put on Boy's attire, did Michael love,
Albeit of a stern unbending mind,
To have the young one in his sight, when he
Had work by his own door, or when he sate
With sheep before him on his Shepherd's stool,
175 Beneath that large old Oak, which near their door
Stood, and from it's enormous breadth of shade
Chosen for the Shearer's covert from the sun,
Thence in our rustic dialect was call'd
The CLIPPING TREE,[2] a name which yet it bears.
180 There, while they two were sitting in the shade,
With others round them, earnest all and blithe,
Would Michael exercise his heart with looks
Of fond correction and reproof bestow'd
Upon the child, if he disturb'd the sheep
185 By catching at their legs, or with his shouts
Scar'd them, while they lay still beneath the shears.

And when by Heaven's good grace the Boy grew up
A healthy Lad, and carried in his cheek
Two steady roses that were five years old,
190 Then Michael from a winter coppice cut
With his own hand a sapling, which he hoop'd

---

[1] Wordsworth deleted lines 131–35 in 1802.

[2] "Clipping is the word used in the North of England for shearing." (W.W.)

With iron, making it throughout in all
Due requisites a perfect Shepherd's Staff,
And gave it to the Boy; wherewith equipp'd
He as a Watchman oftentimes was plac'd
At gate or gap, to stem or turn the flock,
And to his office prematurely call'd
There stood the urchin, as you will divine,
Something between a hindrance and a help,
And for this cause not always, I believe,
Receiving from his Father hire of praise.[1]
Though nought was left undone which staff or voice,
Or looks, or threatening gestures could perform.
But soon as Luke, full ten years old, could stand
Against the mountain blasts, and to the heights,
Not fearing toil, nor length of weary ways,
He with his Father daily went, and they
Were as companions, why should I relate
That objects which the Shepherd loved before
Were dearer now? that from the Boy there came
Feelings and emanations, things which were
Light to the sun and music to the wind;
And that the Old Man's heart seemed born again.
Thus in his Father's sight the Boy grew up:
And now when he had reached his eighteenth year,
He was his comfort and his daily hope.

While this good household thus were living on
From day to day, to Michael's ear there came
Distressful tidings. Long before the time
Of which I speak, the Shepherd had been bound
In surety for his Brother's Son, a man
Of an industrious life, and ample means,
But unforeseen misfortunes suddenly
Had press'd upon him, and old Michael now
Was summon'd to discharge the forfeiture,
A grievous penalty, but little less
Than half his substance. This un-look'd for claim
At the first hearing, for a moment took
More hope out of his life than he supposed
That any old man ever could have lost.
As soon as he had gather'd so much strength
That he could look his trouble in the face,
It seem'd that his sole refuge was to sell
A portion of his patrimonial fields.
Such was his first resolve; he thought again,
And his heart fail'd him. "Isabel," said he,
Two evenings after he had heard the news,
"I have been toiling more than seventy years,
And in the open sun-shine of God's love
Have we all liv'd, yet if these fields of ours
Should pass into a Stranger's hand, I think
That I could not lie quiet in my grave.
Our lot is a hard lot; the Sun itself
Has scarcely been more diligent than I,
And I have liv'd to be a fool at last
To my own family. An evil Man
That was, and made an evil choice, if he
Were false to us; and if he were not false,
There are ten thousand to whom loss like this
Had been no sorrow. I forgive him—but
'Twere better to be dumb than to talk thus.
When I began, my purpose was to speak
Of remedies and of a chearful hope.
Our Luke shall leave us, Isabel; the land
Shall not go from us, and it shall be free,
He shall possess it, free as is the wind
That passes over it. We have, thou knowest,
Another Kinsman, he will be our friend
In this distress. He is a prosperous man,
Thriving in trade, and Luke to him shall go,
And with his Kinsman's help and his own thrift,
He quickly will repair this loss, and then
May come again to us. If here he stay,
What can be done? Where every one is poor
What can be gain'd?" At this, the old man paus'd,
And Isabel sate silent, for her mind
Was busy, looking back into past times.
There's Richard Bateman,[2] thought she to herself,
He was a parish-boy[3]—at the church-door
They made a gathering for him, shillings, pence,

[1] Lines 202–16 were omitted in 1800 because of a printer's error. Here we use the 1802 edition to restore the missing lines.

[2] "The story alluded to here is well known in the country. The chapel is called Ings Chapel; and is on the right hand side of the road leading from Kendal to Ambleside." (W.W.)

[3] a boy supported by the parish under the Poor Law.

And halfpennies, wherewith the Neighbours bought
A Basket, which they fill'd with Pedlar's wares,
And with this Basket on his arm, the Lad
Went up to London, found a Master there,
275 Who out of many chose the trusty Boy
To go and overlook his merchandise
Beyond the seas, where he grew wond'rous rich,
And left estates and monies to the poor,
And at his birth-place built a Chapel, floor'd
280 With Marble, which he sent from foreign lands.
These thoughts, and many others of like sort,
Pass'd quickly thro' the mind of Isabel,
And her face brighten'd. The Old Man was glad,
And thus resum'd. "Well! Isabel, this scheme
285 These two days has been meat and drink to me.
Far more than we have lost is left us yet.
—We have enough—I wish indeed that I
Were younger, but this hope is a good hope.
—Make ready Luke's best garments, of the best
290 Buy for him more, and let us send him forth
To-morrow, or the next day, or to-night:
—If he could go, the Boy should go to-night."

Here Michael ceas'd, and to the fields went forth
With a light heart. The House-wife for five days
295 Was restless morn and night, and all day long
Wrought on with her best fingers to prepare
Things needful for the journey of her Son.
But Isabel was glad when Sunday came
To stop her in her work; for, when she lay
300 By Michael's side, she for the two last nights
Heard him, how he was troubled in his sleep:
And when they rose at morning she could see
That all his hopes were gone. That day at noon
She said to Luke, while they two by themselves
305 Were sitting at the door, "Thou must not go,
We have no other Child but thee to lose,
None to remember—do not go away,
For if thou leave thy Father he will die."
The Lad made answer with a jocund voice,
310 And Isabel, when she had told her fears,
Recover'd heart. That evening her best fare
Did she bring forth, and all together sate
Like happy people round a Christmas fire.

Next morning Isabel resum'd her work,
315 And all the ensuing week the house appear'd
As cheerful as a grove in Spring: at length
The expected letter from their Kinsman came,
With kind assurances that he would do
His utmost for the welfare of the Boy,
320 To which requests were added that forthwith
He might be sent to him. Ten times or more
The letter was read over; Isabel
Went forth to shew it to the neighbours round:
Nor was there at that time on English Land
325 A prouder heart than Luke's. When Isabel
Had to her house return'd, the Old Man said,
"He shall depart to-morrow." To this word
The House-wife answered, talking much of things
Which, if at such short notice he should go,
330 Would surely be forgotten. But at length
She gave consent, and Michael was at ease.

Near the tumultuous brook of Green-head Gill,
In that deep Valley, Michael had design'd
To build a Sheep-fold,[1] and, before he heard
335 The tidings of his melancholy loss,
For this same purpose he had gathered up
A heap of stones, which close to the brook side
Lay thrown together, ready for the work.
With Luke that evening thitherward he walk'd;
340 And soon as they had reach'd the place he stopp'd,
And thus the Old Man spake to him. "My Son,
To-morrow thou wilt leave me; with full heart
I look upon thee, for thou art the same
That wert a promise to me ere thy birth,
345 And all thy life hast been my daily joy.
I will relate to thee some little part
Of our two histories; 'twill do thee good
When thou art from me, even if I should speak
Of things thou canst not know of.—After thou
350 First cam'st into the world, as it befalls

---

[1] "It may be proper to inform some readers, that a sheep-fold in these mountains is an unroofed building of stone walls, with different divisions. It is generally placed by the side of a brook, for the convenience of washing the sheep; but it is also useful as a shelter for them, and as a place to drive them into, to enable the shepherds conveniently to single out one or more for any particular purpose." (W.W.)

To new-born infants, thou didst sleep away
Two days, and blessings from thy Father's tongue
Then fell upon thee. Day by day pass'd on,
And still I lov'd thee with encreasing love.
³⁵⁵ Never to living ear came sweeter sounds
Than when I heard thee by our own fire-side
First uttering without words a natural tune,
When thou, a feeding babe, didst in thy joy
Sing at thy Mother's breast. Month follow'd month,
³⁶⁰ And in the open fields my life was pass'd
And in the mountains, else I think that thou
Hadst been brought up upon thy father's knees.
—But we were playmates, Luke; among these hills,
As well thou know'st, in us the old and young
³⁶⁵ Have play'd together, nor with me didst thou
Lack any pleasure which a boy can know."
Luke had a manly heart; but at these words
He sobb'd aloud; the Old Man grasp'd his hand,
And said, "Nay do not take it so—I see
³⁷⁰ That these are things of which I need not speak.
—Even to the utmost I have been to thee
A kind and a good Father: and herein
I but repay a gift which I myself
Receiv'd at others hands, for, though now old
³⁷⁵ Beyond the common life of man, I still
Remember them who lov'd me in my youth.
Both of them sleep together: here they liv'd
As all their Forefathers had done, and when
At length their time was come, they were not loth
³⁸⁰ To give their bodies to the family mold.
I wish'd that thou should'st live the life they liv'd.
But 'tis a long time to look back, my Son,
And see so little gain from sixty years.
These fields were burthen'd when they came to me;
³⁸⁵ 'Till I was forty years of age, not more
Than half of my inheritance was mine.
I toil'd and toil'd; God bless'd me in my work,
And 'till these three weeks past the land was free.
—It looks as if it never could endure
³⁹⁰ Another Master. Heaven forgive me, Luke,
If I judge ill for thee, but it seems good
That thou should'st go." At this the Old Man paus'd,
Then, pointing to the Stones near which they stood,
Thus, after a short silence, he resum'd:

³⁹⁵ "This was a work for us, and now, my Son,
It is a work for me. But, lay one Stone—
Here, lay it for me, Luke, with thine own hands.
I for the purpose brought thee to this place.
Nay, Boy, be of good hope:—we both may live
⁴⁰⁰ To see a better day. At eighty-four
I still am strong and stout;—do thou thy part,
I will do mine.—I will begin again
With many tasks that were resign'd to thee;
Up to the heights, and in among the storms,
⁴⁰⁵ Will I without thee go again, and do
All works which I was wont to do alone,
Before I knew thy face.—Heaven bless thee, Boy!
Thy heart these two weeks has been beating fast
With many hopes—it should be so—yes—yes—
⁴¹⁰ I knew that thou could'st never have a wish
To leave me, Luke, thou hast been bound to me
Only by links of love, when thou art gone
What will be left to us!—But, I forget
My purposes. Lay now the corner-stone,
⁴¹⁵ As I requested, and hereafter, Luke,
When thou art gone away, should evil men
Be thy companions, let this Sheep-fold be
Thy anchor and thy shield; amid all fear
And all temptation, let it be to thee
⁴²⁰ An emblem of the life thy Fathers liv'd,
Who, being innocent, did for that cause
Bestir them in good deeds. Now, fare thee well—
When thou return'st, thou in this place wilt see
A work which is not here, a covenant
⁴²⁵ 'Twill be between us[1]——but whatever fate
Befall thee, I shall love thee to the last,
And bear thy memory with me to the grave."

The Shepherd ended here; and Luke stoop'd down,
And as his Father had requested, laid
⁴³⁰ The first stone of the Sheep-fold; at the sight
The Old Man's grief broke from him, to his heart
He press'd his Son, he kissed him and wept;
And to the House together they return'd.

---

[1] A covenant is an agreement, contract, or binding promise, particularly the promises made by God to the Israelites in the Bible: cf. Genesis 6.18, 15.18, 17.4.

Next morning, as had been resolv'd, the Boy
435 Began his journey, and when he had reach'd
The public Way, he put on a bold face;
And all the Neighbours as he pass'd their doors
Came forth, with wishes and with farewell pray'rs,
That follow'd him 'till he was out of sight.

440 A good report did from their Kinsman come,
Of Luke and his well-doing; and the Boy
Wrote loving letters, full of wond'rous news,
Which, as the House-wife phrased it, were throughout
The prettiest letters that were ever seen.
445 Both parents read them with rejoicing hearts.
So, many months pass'd on: and once again
The Shepherd went about his daily work
With confident and cheerful thoughts; and now
Sometimes when he could find a leisure hour
450 He to that valley took his way, and there
Wrought at the Sheep-fold. Meantime Luke began
To slacken in his duty, and at length
He in the dissolute city gave himself
To evil courses: ignominy and shame
455 Fell on him, so that he was driven at last
To seek a hiding-place beyond the seas.

There is a comfort in the strength of love;
'Twill make a thing endurable, which else
Would break the heart:—Old Michael found it so.
460 I have convers'd with more than one who well
Remember the Old Man, and what he was
Years after he had heard this heavy news.
His bodily frame had been from youth to age
Of an unusual strength. Among the rocks
465 He went, and still look'd up upon the sun,
And listen'd to the wind; and as before
Perform'd all kinds of labour for his Sheep,
And for the land his small inheritance.
And to that hollow Dell from time to time
470 Did he repair, to build the Fold of which
His flock had need. 'Tis not forgotten yet
The pity which was then in every heart
For the Old Man—and 'tis believ'd by all
That many and many a day he thither went,
475 And never lifted up a single stone.

There, by the Sheep-fold, sometimes was he seen
Sitting alone, with that his faithful Dog,
Then old, beside him, lying at his feet.
The length of full seven years from time to time
480 He at the building of this Sheep-fold wrought,
And left the work unfinished when he died.

Three years, or little more, did Isabel,
Survive her Husband: at her death the estate
Was sold, and went into a Stranger's hand.
485 The Cottage which was nam'd The Evening Star
Is gone, the ploughshare has been through the ground
On which it stood; great changes have been wrought
In all the neighbourhood, yet the Oak is left
That grew beside their Door; and the remains
490 Of the unfinished Sheep-fold may be seen
Beside the boisterous brook of Green-head Gill.

from *Poems in Two Volumes* (1807)

I travell'd among unknown Men

I travell'd among unknown Men,
    In Lands beyond the Sea;
Nor England! did I know till then
    What love I bore to thee.

5 'Tis past, that melancholy dream!
    Nor will I quit thy shore
A second time; for still I seem
    To love thee more and more.

Among thy mountains did I feel
10   The joy of my desire;
And She I cherish'd turn'd her wheel
    Beside an English fire.

Thy mornings shew'd—thy nights conceal'd
    The bowers where Lucy play'd;
15 And thine is, too, the last green field
    Which Lucy's eyes survey'd!

Beggars[1]

She had a tall Man's height, or more;
No bonnet screen'd her from the heat;
A long drab-colour'd Cloak she wore,
A Mantle reaching to her feet:
5   What other dress she had I could not know;
Only she wore a Cap that was as white as snow.

In all my walks, through field or town,
Such Figure had I never seen:
Her face was of Egyptian brown:
10 Fit person was she for a Queen,
To head those ancient Amazonian files:
Or ruling Bandit's Wife, among the Grecian Isles.

Before me begging did she stand,
Pouring out sorrows like a sea;
15 Grief after grief:—on English Land
Such woes I knew could never be;
And yet a boon I gave her; for the Creature
Was beautiful to see; a Weed of glorious feature!

I left her, and pursued my way;
20 And soon before me did espy
A pair of little Boys at play,
Chasing a crimson butterfly;
The Taller follow'd with his hat in hand,
Wreath'd round with yellow flow'rs, the gayest of the land.

25 The Other wore a rimless crown,
With leaves of laurel stuck about:
And they both follow'd up and down,
Each whooping with a merry shout;
Two Brothers seem'd they, eight and ten years old;
30 And like that Woman's face as gold is like to gold.

They bolted on me thus, and lo!
Each ready with a plaintive whine;
Said I, "Not half an hour ago
Your Mother has had alms of mine."
35 "That cannot be," one answer'd, "She is dead."
"Nay but I gave her pence, and she will buy you bread."

"She has been dead, Sir, many a day."
"Sweet Boys, you're telling me a lie;
It was your Mother, as I say—"
40 And in the twinkling of an eye,
"Come, come!" cried one; and, without more ado,
Off to some other play they both together flew.

Resolution and Independence[2]

There was a roaring in the wind all night;
The rain came heavily and fell in floods;
But now the sun is rising calm and bright;
The birds are singing in the distant woods;
5   Over his own sweet voice the Stock-dove broods;
The Jay makes answer as the Magpie chatters;
And all the air is fill'd with pleasant noise of waters.

All things that love the sun are out of doors;
The sky rejoices in the morning's birth;
10 The grass is bright with rain-drops; on the moors
The Hare is running races in her mirth;
And with her feet she from the plashy earth
Raises a mist; which, glittering in the sun,
Runs with her all the way, wherever she doth run.

15 I was a Traveller then upon the moor;
I saw the Hare that rac'd about with joy;
I heard the woods, and distant waters, roar;
Or heard them not, as happy as a Boy:

---

[1] "Written at Town-end, Grasmere. Met, and described to me by my Sister, near the quarry at the head of Rydal lake, a place still a chosen resort of vagrants travelling with their families." (W.W. as dictated to Isabella Fenwick, 1843.) Cf. D. Wordsworth, *Journal*, Tuesday 10 June 1800.*

[2] "This old man I met a few hundred yards from my cottage; and the account of him is taken from his own mouth. I was in the state of feeling described in the beginning of the poem, while crossing over Barton Fell from Mr. Clarkson's, at the foot of Ullswater, towards Askham. The image of the hare [line 11] I then observed on the ridge of the Fell." (W.W., as dictated to Isabella Fenwick, 1843.) See also Dorothy Wordsworth's journal entry for 3 October 1800.* "Mr. Clarkson" is the abolitionist writer Thomas Clarkson.*

The pleasant season did my heart employ:
20   My old remembrances went from me wholly;
And all the ways of men, so vain and melancholy.

But, as it sometimes chanceth, from the might
Of joy in minds that can no farther go,
As high as we have mounted in delight
25   In our dejection do we sink as low,
To me that morning did it happen so;
And fears, and fancies, thick upon me came;
Dim sadness, & blind thoughts I knew not nor could
        name.

I heard the Sky-lark singing in the sky;
30   And I bethought me of the playful Hare:
Even such a happy Child of earth am I;
Even as these blissful Creatures do I fare;
Far from the world I walk, and from all care;
But there may come another day to me,
35   Solitude, pain of heart, distress, and poverty.

My whole life I have liv'd in pleasant thought,
As if life's business were a summer mood;
As if all needful things would come unsought
To genial faith, still rich in genial good;
40   But how can He expect that others should
Build for him, sow for him, and at his call
Love him, who for himself will take no heed at all?

I thought of Chatterton, the marvellous Boy,
The sleepless Soul that perish'd in its pride;[1]
45   Of Him who walk'd in glory and in joy
Behind his plough, upon the mountain-side:[2]
By our own spirits are we deified;
We Poets in our youth begin in gladness;
But thereof comes in the end despondency and
        madness.

---

[1] Thomas Chatterton,* who committed suicide to avoid starvation at the age of seventeen.

[2] Robert Burns,* who achieved fame as a poet, but who had spent his early years as a farm labourer.

50   Now, whether it were by peculiar grace,
A leading from above, a something given,
Yet it befel, that, in this lonely place,
When up and down my fancy thus was driven,
And I with these untoward thoughts had striven,
55   I saw a Man before me unawares:
The oldest Man he seem'd that ever wore grey hairs.

My course I stopped as soon as I espied
The Old Man in that naked wilderness:
Close by a Pond, upon the further side,
60   He stood alone: a minute's space I guess
I watch'd him, he continuing motionless:
To the Pool's further margin then I drew;
He being all the while before me full in view.[3]

As a huge Stone is sometimes seen to lie
65   Couch'd on the bald top of an eminence;
Wonder to all who do the same espy
By what means it could thither come, and whence;
So that it seems a thing endued with sense:
Like a Sea-beast crawl'd forth, which on a shelf
70   Of rock or sand reposeth, there to sun itself.

Such seem'd this Man, not all alive nor dead,
Nor all asleep; in his extreme old age:
His body was bent double, feet and head
Coming together in their pilgrimage;
75   As if some dire constraint of pain, or rage
Of sickness felt by him in times long past,
A more than human weight upon his frame had cast.

Himself he propp'd, his body, limbs, and face,
Upon a long grey Staff of shaven wood:
80   And, still as I drew near with gentle pace,
Beside the little pond or moorish flood
Motionless as a Cloud the Old Man stood;
That heareth not the loud winds when they call;
And moveth altogether, if it move at all.

---

[3] Wordsworth deleted this stanza in 1820. For a possible reason, see *Biographia Literaria,** chap. 22, where Coleridge quotes the last five lines to illustrate alleged incongruity or disharmony in Wordsworth's style.

85 At length, himself unsettling, he the Pond
    Stirred with his Staff, and fixedly did look
    Upon the muddy water, which he conn'd,
    As if he had been reading in a book:
    And now such freedom as I could I took;
90 And, drawing to his side, to him did say,
    "This morning gives us promise of a glorious day."

    A gentle answer did the Old Man make,
    In courteous speech which forth he slowly drew:
    And him with further words I thus bespake,
95 "What kind of work is that which you pursue?
    This is a lonesome place for one like you."
    He answer'd me with pleasure and surprize;
    And there was, while he spake, a fire about his eyes.

    His words came feebly, from a feeble chest,
100 Yet each in solemn order follow'd each,
    With something of a lofty utterance drest;
    Choice word, and measured phrase; above the reach
    Of ordinary men; a stately speech!
    Such as grave Livers do in Scotland use,
105 Religious men, who give to God and Man their dues.

    He told me that he to this pond had come
    To gather Leeches, being old and poor:
    Employment hazardous and wearisome!
    And he had many hardships to endure:
110 From Pond to Pond he roam'd, from moor to moor,
    Housing, with God's good help, by choice or chance:
    And in this way he gain'd an honest maintenance.

    The Old Man still stood talking by my side;
    But now his voice to me was like a stream
115 Scarce heard; nor word from word could I divide;
    And the whole Body of the man did seem
    Like one whom I had met with in a dream;
    Or like a Man from some far region sent;
    To give me human strength, and strong
        admonishment.

120 My former thoughts return'd: the fear that kills;
    The hope that is unwilling to be fed;
    Cold, pain, and labour, and all fleshly ills;
    And mighty Poets in their misery dead.
    And now, not knowing what the Old Man had said,
125 My question eagerly did I renew,
    "How is it that you live, and what is it you do?"

    He with a smile did then his words repeat;
    And said, that, gathering Leeches, far and wide
    He travelled; stirring thus about his feet
130 The waters of the Ponds where they abide.
    "Once I could meet with them on every side;
    But they have dwindled long by slow decay;
    Yet still I persevere, and find them where I may."

    While he was talking thus, the lonely place,
135 The Old Man's shape, and speech, all troubled me:
    In my mind's eye I seem'd to see him pace
    About the weary moors continually,
    Wandering about alone and silently.
    While I these thoughts within myself pursued,
140 He, having made a pause, the same discourse renewed.

    And soon with this he other matter blended,
    Chearfully uttered, with demeanour kind,
    But stately in the main; and, when he ended,
    I could have laugh'd myself to scorn, to find
145 In that decrepit Man so firm a mind.
    "God," said I, "be my help and stay secure;
    I'll think of the Leech-gatherer on the lonely moor."

*Composed upon Westminster Bridge,
Sept. 3, 1802*[1]

Earth has not any thing to shew more fair:
Dull would he be of soul who could pass by
A sight so touching in it's majesty:
This City now doth like a garment wear
5   The beauty of the morning; silent, bare,
Ships, towers, domes, theatres, and temples lie
Open unto the fields, and to the sky;
All bright and glittering in the smokeless air.
Never did sun more beautifully steep
10 In his first splendor valley, rock, or hill;

---

[1] See Dorothy Wordsworth's journal entry for 26 July 1802.*

Ne'er saw I, never felt, a calm so deep!
The river glideth at his own sweet will:
Dear God! the very houses seem asleep;
And all that mighty heart is lying still!

The world is too much with us; late and soon

The world is too much with us; late and soon,
Getting and spending, we lay waste our powers:
Little we see in nature that is ours;
We have given our hearts away, a sordid boon!
5 This Sea that bares her bosom to the moon;
The Winds that will be howling at all hours
And are up-gathered now like sleeping flowers;
For this, for every thing, we are out of tune;
It moves us not—Great God! I'd rather be
10 A Pagan suckled in a creed outworn;
So might I, standing on this pleasant lea,
Have glimpses that would make me less forlorn:
Have sight of Proteus coming from the sea;
Or hear old Triton blow his wreathed horn.

It is a beauteous Evening, calm and free

It is a beauteous Evening, calm and free;
The holy time is quiet as a Nun
Breathless with adoration; the broad sun
Is sinking down in its tranquillity;
5 The gentleness of heaven is on the Sea:
Listen! the mighty Being is awake
And doth with his eternal motion make
A sound like thunder—everlastingly.
Dear Child! dear Girl![1] that walkest with me here,
10 If thou appear'st untouch'd by solemn thought,
Thy nature is not therefore less divine:
Thou liest in Abraham's bosom all the year;[2]
And worshipp'st at the Temple's inner shrine,
God being with thee when we know it not.

To Toussaint L'Ouverture[3]

Toussaint, the most unhappy Man of Men!
Whether the rural Milk-maid by her Cow
Sing in thy hearing, or thou liest now
Alone in some deep dungeon's earless den,
5 O miserable chieftain! where and when
Wilt thou find patience? Yet die not; do thou
Wear rather in thy bonds a chearful brow:
Though fallen Thyself, never to rise again,
Live, and take comfort. Thou hast left behind
10 Powers that will work for thee; air, earth, and skies;
There's not a breathing of the common wind
That will forget thee; thou hast great allies;
Thy friends are exultations, agonies,
And love, and Man's unconquerable mind.

London, 1802

Milton! thou should'st be living at this hour:
England hath need of thee: she is a fen
Of stagnant waters: altar, sword and pen,
Fireside, the heroic wealth of hall and bower,
5 Have forfeited their ancient English dower
Of inward happiness. We are selfish men;
Oh! raise us up, return to us again;
And give us manners, virtue, freedom, power.
Thy soul was like a Star and dwelt apart:
10 Thou hadst a voice whose sound was like the sea;
Pure as the naked heavens, majestic, free,
So didst thou travel on life's common way,
In chearful godliness; and yet thy heart
The lowliest duties on itself did lay.

---

[1] probably Wordsworth's French daughter, Caroline.

[2] Cf. Luke 16.22.

[3] François Dominique Toussaint (1743–1803), son of a slave who became governor of Haiti and was imprisoned for opposing Napoleon's re-establishment of slavery.

William Wordsworth

The Solitary Reaper[1]

Behold her, single in the field,
Yon solitary Highland Lass!
Reaping and singing by herself;
Stop here, or gently pass!
Alone she cuts, and binds the grain,
And sings a melancholy strain;
O listen! for the Vale profound
Is overflowing with the sound.

No Nightingale did ever chaunt
So sweetly to reposing bands
Of Travellers in some shady haunt,
Among Arabian Sands:
No sweeter voice was ever heard
In spring-time from the Cuckoo-bird,
Breaking the silence of the seas
Among the farthest Hebrides.

Will no one tell me what she sings?
Perhaps the plaintive numbers flow
For old, unhappy, far-off things,
And battles long ago:
Or is it some more humble lay,
Familiar matter of today?
Some natural sorrow, loss, or pain,
That has been, and may be again!

Whate'er the theme, the Maiden sung
As if her song could have no ending;
I saw her singing at her work,
And o'er the sickle bending;
I listen'd till I had my fill:
And, as I mounted up the hill,
The music in my heart I bore,
Long after it was heard no more.

To a Butterfly

Stay near me—do not take thy flight!
A little longer stay in sight!
Much converse do I find in Thee,
Historian of my Infancy!
Float near me; do not yet depart!
Dead times revive in thee:
Thou bring'st, gay Creature as thou art!
A solemn image to my heart,
My Father's Family!

Oh! pleasant, pleasant were the days,
The time, when in our childish plays
My Sister Emmeline and I
Together chaced the Butterfly![2]
A very hunter did I rush
Upon the prey:—with leaps and springs
I follow'd on from brake to bush;
But She, God love her! feared to brush
The dust from off its wings.

My heart leaps up when I behold[3]

My heart leaps up when I behold
A Rainbow in the sky:
So was it when my life began;
So is it now I am a Man;
So be it when I shall grow old,
    Or let me die!
The Child is Father of the Man;
And I could wish my days to be
Bound each to each by natural piety.

---

[1] "This Poem was suggested by a beautiful sentence in a MS Tour in Scotland written by a Friend, the last line being taken from it *verbatim*." (W.W.) Wordsworth refers to the following passage from the MS of Thomas Wilkinson's *Tours to the British Mountains* (unpublished until 1824): "Passed a female who was reaping alone: she sung in Erse [Scottish Gælic] as she bended over her sickle; the sweetest human voice I ever heard: her strains were tenderly melancholy, and felt delicious long after they were heard no more."

[2] "My sister and I were parted immediately after the death of our mother, who died in 1778, both being very young." (W.W., as dictated to Isabella Fenwick, 1843.) An early MS reads "Dorothy" instead of "Emmeline" in line 12.

[3] See note to the title of Wordsworth's "Ode," below.*

I wandered lonely as a Cloud[1]

I wandered lonely as a Cloud
That floats on high o'er Vales and Hills,
When all at once I saw a crowd
A host of dancing Daffodils;
5 Along the Lake, beneath the trees,
Ten thousand dancing in the breeze.[2]

The waves beside them danced, but they
Outdid the sparkling waves in glee:—
A Poet could not but be gay
10 In such a laughing company:
I gaz'd—and gaz'd—but little thought
What wealth the shew to me had brought:

For oft when on my couch I lie
In vacant or in pensive mood,
15 They flash upon that inward eye
Which is the bliss of solitude,
And then my heart with pleasure fills,
And dances with the Daffodils.

To a Butterfly

I've watch'd you now a full half hour,
Self-pois'd upon that yellow flower;
And, little Butterfly! indeed
I know not if you sleep, or feed.
5 How motionless! not frozen seas
More motionless! and then
What joy awaits you, when the breeze
Hath found you out among the trees,
And calls you forth again!

10 This plot of Orchard-ground is ours;
My trees they are, my Sister's[3] flowers;
Stop here whenever you are weary,
And rest as in a sanctuary!
Come often to us, fear no wrong;
15 Sit near us on the bough!
We'll talk of sunshine and of song;
And summer days, when we were young,
Sweet childish days, that were as long
    As twenty days are now!

To Thomas Clarkson,[4]
On the final passing of the Bill for the Abolition of the Slave Trade, March 1807

Clarkson! it was an obstinate Hill to climb;
How toilsome, nay how dire it was, by Thee
Is known,—by none, perhaps, so feelingly;
But Thou, who, starting in thy fervent prime,
5 Didst first lead forth this pilgrimage sublime,
Hast heard the constant Voice its charge repeat,
Which, out of thy young heart's oracular seat,
First roused thee.—O true yoke-fellow of Time
With unabating effort, see, the palm
10 Is won, and by all Nations shall be worn!
The bloody Writing is for ever torn,
And Thou henceforth shalt have a good Man's calm,
A great Man's happiness; thy zeal shall find
Repose at length, firm Friend of human kind!

---

[1] "The daffodils grew and still grow on the margin of Ullswater and probably may be seen to this day as beautiful in the month of March, nodding their heads beside the dancing and foaming waves." (W.W., as dictated to Isabella Fenwick, 1843.) See also Dorothy Wordsworth's journal entry for 15 April 1802.*

[2] Wordsworth added the following stanza in 1815:
    Continuous as the stars that shine
    And twinkle on the milky way,
    They stretched in never-ending line
    Along the margin of a bay:
    Ten thousand saw I at a glance,
    Tossing their heads in sprightly dance.

[3] Dorothy Wordsworth;* see note to "To a Butterfly"* ["Stay near me"].

[4] Wordsworth's friend Thomas Clarkson,* a prominent anti-slavery writer and activist.

William Wordsworth

Elegiac Stanzas,
Suggested by a Picture of Peele Castle, in a Storm,
painted by Sir George Beaumont[1]

I was thy Neighbour once, thou rugged Pile!
Four summer weeks I dwelt in sight of thee:
I saw thee every day; and all the while
Thy Form was sleeping on a glassy sea.

5   So pure the sky, so quiet was the air!
So like, so very like, was day to day!
Whene'er I look'd, thy Image still was there;
It trembled, but it never pass'd away.

How perfect was the calm! it seem'd no sleep;
10 No mood, which season takes away, or brings:
I could have fancied that the mighty Deep
Was even the gentlest of all gentle Things.

Ah! THEN, if mine had been the Painter's hand,
To express what then I saw; and add the gleam,
15 The light that never was, on sea or land,
The consecration, and the Poet's dream;

I would have planted thee, thou hoary Pile!
Amid a world how different from this!
Beside a sea that could not cease to smile;
20 On tranquil land, beneath a sky of bliss:

Thou shouldst have seem'd a treasure-house, a mine
Of peaceful years; a chronicle of heaven:—
Of all the sunbeams that did ever shine
The very sweetest had to thee been given.

25 A Picture had it been of lasting ease,
Elysian quiet, without toil or strife;
No motion but the moving tide, a breeze,
Or merely silent Nature's breathing life.

Such, in the fond delusion of my heart,
30 Such Picture would I at that time have made:
And seen the soul of truth in every part;
A faith, a trust, that could not be betray'd.

So once it would have been,—'tis so no more;
I have submitted to a new controul:
35 A power is gone, which nothing can restore;
A deep distress[2] hath humaniz'd my Soul.

Not for a moment could I now behold
A smiling sea and be what I have been:
The feeling of my loss will ne'er be old;
40 This, which I know, I speak with mind serene.

Then, Beaumont, Friend! who would have been the Friend,
If he had lived, of Him whom I deplore,
This Work of thine I blame not, but commend;
This sea in anger, and that dismal shore.

45 Oh 'tis a passionate Work!—yet wise and well;
Well chosen is the spirit that is here;
That Hulk which labours in the deadly swell,
This rueful sky, this pageantry of fear!

And this huge Castle, standing here sublime,
50 I love to see the look with which it braves,
Cased in the unfeeling armour of old time,
The light'ning, the fierce wind, and trampling waves.

Farewell, farewell the Heart that lives alone,
Hous'd in a dream, at distance from the Kind![3]
55 Such happiness, wherever it be known,
Is to be pitied; for 'tis surely blind.

But welcome fortitude, and patient chear,
And frequent sights of what is to be born!
Such sights, or worse, as are before me here.—
60 Not without hope we suffer and we mourn.

---

[1] Peele Castle is in north Lancashire, near Rampside, where Wordsworth visited in 1794; Wordsworth's wife, Mary, owned a painting of the castle by their friend Sir George Beaumont (1753–1827).

[2] the death of Wordsworth's brother, John, lost at sea 6 February 1805.

[3] I.e., humankind.

Ode[1]

Paulo majora canamus[2]

There was a time[3] when meadow, grove, and stream,
The earth, and every common sight,
      To me did seem
      Apparell'd in celestial light,
5 The glory and the freshness of a dream.
It is not now as it has been of yore;—
      Turn wheresoe'er I may,
      By night or day,
The things which I have seen I now can see no more.

      10 The Rainbow comes and goes,
      And lovely is the Rose,
      The Moon doth with delight
Look round her when the heavens are bare;
      Waters on a starry night
15   Are beautiful and fair;
      The sunshine is a glorious birth;
      But yet I know, where'er I go,
That there hath pass'd away a glory from the earth.

Now, while the Birds thus sing a joyous song,
20   And while the young Lambs bound
      As to the tabor's sound,
To me alone there came a thought of grief:
A timely utterance[4] gave that thought relief,
      And I again am strong.
25 The Cataracts blow their trumpets from the steep,
No more shall grief of mine the season wrong;
I hear the Echoes through the mountains throng,
The Winds come to me from the fields of sleep,
      And all the earth is gay,
30   Land and sea
      Give themselves up to jollity,
      And with the heart of May

---

[1] "This was composed during my residence at Town-End, Grasmere; two years at least passed between the writing of the four first stanzas and the remaining part. To the attentive and competent reader the whole sufficiently explains itself; but there may be no harm in adverting here to particular feelings or *experiences* of my own mind on which the structure of the poem partly rests. Nothing was more difficult for me in childhood than to admit the notion of death as a state applicable to my own being. I have said elsewhere—

    'A simple child,
    That lightly draws its breath,
    And feels its life in every limb,
    What should it know of death!'—

But it was not so much from [feelings] of animal vivacity that *my* difficulty came as from a sense of the indomitableness of the spirit within me. I used to brood over the stories of Enoch and Elijah, and almost to persuade myself that, whatever might become of others, I should be translated, in something of the same way, to heaven. With a feeling congenial to this, I was often unable to think of external things as having external existence, and I communed with all that I saw as something not apart from, but inherent in, my own immaterial nature. Many times while going to school have I grasped at a wall or tree to recall myself from this abyss of idealism to the reality. At that time I was afraid of such processes. In later periods of life I have deplored, as we have all reason to do, a subjugation of an opposite character, and have rejoiced over the remembrances, as is expressed in the lines—

    'Obstinate questionings
    Of sense and outward things,
    Fallings from us, vanishings'; etc.

To that dream-like vividness and splendour which invest objects of sight in childhood, every one, I believe, if he would look back, could bear testimony, and I need not dwell upon it here: but having in the Poem regarded it as presumptive evidence of a prior state of existence, I think it right to protest against a conclusion, which has given pain to some good and pious persons, that I meant to inculcate such a belief. It is far too shadowy a notion to be recommended to faith, as more than an element in our instincts of immortality. But let us bear in mind that, though the idea is not advanced in revelation, there is nothing there to contradict it, and the fall of Man presents an analogy in its favor. Accordingly, a pre-existent state has entered into the popular creeds of many nations; and, among all persons acquainted with classic literature, is known as an ingredient in Platonic philosophy. Archimedes said that he could move the world if he had a point whereon to rest his machine. Who has not felt the same aspirations as regards the world of his own mind? Having to wield some of its elements when I was impelled to write this Poem on the 'Immortality of the Soul', I took hold of the notion of pre-existence as having sufficient foundation in humanity for authorizing me to make for my purpose the best use of it I could as a Poet." (W.W., as dictated to Isabella Fenwick, 1843.)

In 1815, Wordsworth changed the title to "Ode: Intimations of Immortality from Recollections of Early Childhood."

[2] "Let us sing a little higher" (Virgil, *Eclogues* 4): Wordsworth is signaling his intention to write a serious kind of pastoral poetry. From 1815 on, he replaced this epigraph with the last three lines of "My heart leaps up when I behold."*

[3] Cf. Coleridge, "Dejection" 76.*

[4] possibly "Resolution and Independence."*

    Doth every Beast keep holiday,
        Thou Child of Joy
35 Shout round me, let me hear thy shouts, thou happy
        Shepherd Boy!

    Ye blessed Creatures, I have heard the call
        Ye to each other make; I see
    The heavens laugh with you in your jubilee;
        My heart is at your festival,
40   My head hath it's coronal,
    The fullness of your bliss, I feel—I feel it all.
        Oh evil day! if I were sullen
        While the Earth herself is adorning,
        This sweet May-morning,
45   And the Children are pulling[1]
        On every side,
    In a thousand vallies far and wide,
    Fresh flowers; while the sun shines warm,
    And the Babe leaps up on his mother's arm:—
50 I hear, I hear, with joy I hear!
    —But there's a Tree, of many one,
    A single Field which I have look'd upon,
    Both of them speak of something that is gone:
        The Pansy at my feet
55   Doth the same tale repeat:
    Whither is fled the visionary gleam?
    Where is it now, the glory and the dream?

    Our birth is but a sleep and a forgetting:
    The Soul that rises with us our life's Star,
60   Hath had elsewhere it's setting,
        And cometh from afar:
        Not in entire forgetfulness,
        And not in utter nakedness,
    But trailing clouds of glory do we come
65   From God, who is our home:
    Heaven lies about us in our infancy!
    Shades of the prison-house begin to close
        Upon the growing Boy,
    But He beholds the light, and whence it flows,
70   He sees it in his joy;
    The Youth, who daily farther from the East
        Must travel, still is Nature's Priest,

[1] Subsequent editions read "culling."

        And by the vision splendid
        Is on his way attended;
75 At length the Man perceives it die away,
    And fade into the light of common day.

    Earth fills her lap with pleasures of her own;
    Yearnings she hath in her own natural kind,
    And, even with something of a Mother's mind,
80   And no unworthy aim,
        The homely Nurse doth all she can
    To make her Foster-child, her Inmate Man,
        Forget the glories he hath known,
    And that imperial palace whence he came.

85 Behold the Child among his new-born blisses,
    A four year's Darling of a pigmy size!
    See, where mid work of his own hand he lies,
    Fretted by sallies of his Mother's kisses,
    With light upon him from his Father's eyes!
90 See, at his feet, some little plan or chart,
    Some fragment from his dream of human life,
    Shap'd by himself with newly-learned art;
        A wedding or a festival,
        A mourning or a funeral;
95   And this hath now his heart,
    And unto this he frames his song:
        Then will he fit his tongue
    To dialogues of business, love, or strife;
        But it will not be long
100   Ere this be thrown aside,
        And with new joy and pride
    The little Actor cons another part,
    Filling from time to time his "humourous stage"[2]
    With all the Persons, down to palsied Age,
105 That Life brings with her in her Equipage;
        As if his whole vocation
        Were endless imitation.

    Thou, whose exterior semblance doth belie
        Thy Soul's immensity;
110 Thou best Philosopher, who yet dost keep

[2] from Samuel Daniel (1562–1619), dedicatory sonnet to *Musophilus* (1599), 1.

Thy heritage, thou Eye among the blind,
That, deaf and silent, read'st the eternal deep,
Haunted for ever by the eternal mind,—
    Mighty Prophet! Seer blest!
    On whom those truths do rest,
Which we are toiling all our lives to find;
Thou, over whom thy Immortality
Broods like the Day, a Master o'er a Slave,
A Presence which is not to be put by;
    To whom the grave
Is but a lonely bed without the sense or sight
    Of day or the warm light,
A place of thought where we in waiting lie;[1]
Thou little Child, yet glorious in the might
Of untam'd pleasures, on thy Being's height,
Why with such earnest pains dost thou provoke
The Years to bring the inevitable yoke,
Thus blindly with thy blessedness at strife?
Full soon thy Soul shall have her earthly freight,
And custom lie upon thee with a weight,
Heavy as frost, and deep almost as life!

    O joy! that in our embers
    Is something that doth live,
    That nature yet remembers
    What was so fugitive!
The thought of our past years in me doth breed
Perpetual benedictions: not indeed
For that which is most worthy to be blest;
Delight and liberty, the simple creed
Of Childhood, whether fluttering or at rest,
With new-born hope for ever in his breast:—
    Not for these I raise
    The song of thanks and praise;
But for those obstinate questionings
Of sense and outward things,
Fallings from us, vanishings;
Blank misgivings of a Creature
Moving about in worlds not realiz'd,
High instincts, before which our mortal Nature
Did tremble like a guilty Thing surpriz'd:
    But for those first affections,
    Those shadowy recollections,
        Which, be they what they may,
Are yet the fountain light of all our day,
Are yet a master light of all our seeing;
    Uphold us, cherish us, and make
Our noisy years seem moments in the being
Of the eternal Silence: truths that wake,
    To perish never;
Which neither listlessness, nor mad endeavour,
    Nor Man nor Boy,
Nor all that is at enmity with joy,
Can utterly abolish or destroy!
    Hence, in a season of calm weather,
    Though inland far we be,
Our Souls have sight of that immortal sea
    Which brought us hither,
    Can in a moment travel thither,
And see the Children sport upon the shore,
And hear the mighty waters rolling evermore.

Then, sing ye Birds, sing, sing a joyous song!
    And let the young Lambs bound
    As to the tabor's sound!
We in thought will join your throng,
    Ye that pipe and ye that play,
    Ye that through your hearts to day
    Feel the gladness of the May!
What though the radiance which was once so bright
Be now for ever taken from my sight,
    Though nothing can bring back the hour
Of splendour in the grass, of glory in the flower;
    We will grieve not, rather find
    Strength in what remains behind,
    In the primal sympathy
    Which having been must ever be,
    In the soothing thoughts that spring
    Out of human suffering,
    In the faith that looks through death,
In years that bring the philosophic mind.

---

[1] Wordsworth removed these last four lines after 1815, probably in response to Coleridge's criticism in *Biographia Literaria*,* chapter 22 that a Christian child would have no such "frightful notion" of death. A single line added after line 116 of our text, "In darkness lost, the darkness of the grave," represents in the revised text the poet's notion of death rather than the child's.

    And oh ye Fountains, Meadows, Hills, and Groves, 190
Think not of any severing of our loves!
Yet in my heart of hearts I feel your might;
I only have relinquish'd one delight
To live beneath your more habitual sway.
I love the Brooks which down their channels fret, 195
Even more than when I tripp'd lightly as they;
The innocent brightness of a new-born Day
    Is lovely yet;
The Clouds that gather round the setting sun
Do take a sober colouring from an eye 200
That hath kept watch o'er man's mortality;
Another race hath been, and other palms are won.
Thanks to the human heart by which we live,
Thanks to its tenderness, its joys, and fears,
To me the meanest flower that blows can give 205
Thoughts that do often lie too deep for tears.

from the *Friend*, 11 (26 October 1809)[1]

Oh! pleasant exercise of hope and joy!

Oh! pleasant exercise of hope and joy!
For mighty were the auxiliars which then stood
Upon our side, we who were strong in love!
Bliss was it in that dawn to be alive,
But to be young was very heaven! oh! times, 5
In which the meagre stale forbidding ways
Of custom, law, and statute, took at once
The attraction of a country in Romance!
When Reason seem'd the most to assert her rights,
When most intent on making of herself 10
A prime Enchanter to assist the work,
Which then was going forward in her name!
Not favour'd spots alone, but the whole earth
The beauty wore of promise—that which sets
(To take an image which was felt no doubt 15
Among the bowers of paradise itself)
The budding rose above the rose full blown.
What temper at the prospect did not wake
To happiness unthought of? The inert
Were rous'd, and lively natures rapt away! 20
They who had fed their childhood upon dreams,
The play-fellows of fancy, who had made
All powers of swiftness, subtilty, and strength
Their ministers, used to stir in lordly wise
Among the grandest objects of the sense 25
And deal with whatsoever they found there
As if they had within some lurking right
To wield it;—they too, who of gentle mood
Had watch'd all gentle motions, and to these
Had fitted their own thoughts, schemers more mild 30
And in the region of their peaceful selves;—
Now was it that both found, the Meek and Lofty,
Did both find helpers to their heart's desire
And stuff at hand, plastic as they could wish!—
Were call'd upon to exercise their skill 35
Not in Utopia, subterraneous Fields,
Or some secreted Island, heaven knows where!
But in the very world, which is the world
Of all of us, the place where in the end
We find our happiness, or not at all! 40

from *The Excursion, Being a Portion of The Recluse, A Poem* (1814)

from *Home at Grasmere*
(written in 1798 and first published at the end of the Preface to The Excursion, 1814)[2]

    On Man, on Nature, and on Human Life
Musing in Solitude, I oft perceive 755
Fair trains of imagery before me rise,
Accompanied by feelings of delight
Pure, or with no unpleasing sadness mixed;

---

[1] These lines, first published in Coleridge's journal the *Friend* (1809–10), eventually became part of *The Prelude*. See *Prelude* 10.689–727 (1805) and 11.105–44 (1850).

[2] Wordsworth planned to write a long three-part philosophical poem called *The Recluse*, "having for its principal subject the sensations and opinions of a poet living in retirement." (W.W., from the Preface to *The Excursion*). He never finished this ambitious project, but the second part became the nine-book poem, *The Excursion*, published separately in 1814. Of the first part, he completed only one book, "Home at Grasmere," largely unpublished during his lifetime.

And I am conscious of affecting thoughts
And dear remembrances, whose presence soothes
Or elevates the Mind, intent to weigh
The good and evil of our mortal state.
—To these emotions, whencesoe'er they come,
Whether from breath of outward circumstance,
Or from the Soul—an impulse to herself,
I would give utterance in numerous Verse.
—Of Truth, of Grandeur, Beauty, Love, and Hope—
And melancholy Fear subdued by Faith;
Of blessed consolations in distress;
Of moral strength, and intellectual power;
Of joy in widest commonalty spread;
Of the individual Mind that keeps her own
Inviolate retirement, subject there
To Conscience only, and the law supreme
Of that Intelligence which governs all;
I sing:—"fit audience let me find though few!"[1]

So prayed, more gaining than he asked, the Bard,
Holiest of Men.—Urania,[2] I shall need
Thy guidance, or a greater Muse, if such
Descend to earth or dwell in highest heaven!
For I must tread on shadowy ground, must sink
Deep—and, aloft ascending, breathe in worlds
To which the heaven of heavens is but a veil.
All strength—all terror, single or in bands,
That ever was put forth in personal form;
Jehovah—with his thunder, and the choir
Of shouting Angels, and the empyreal thrones,
I pass them, unalarmed. Not Chaos, not
The darkest pit of lowest Erebus,[3]
Nor aught of blinder vacancy—scooped out
By help of dreams, can breed such fear and awe
As fall upon us often when we look
Into our Minds, into the Mind of Man,
My haunt, and the main region of my Song.
—Beauty—a living Presence of the earth,
Surpassing the most fair ideal Forms
Which craft of delicate Spirits hath composed
From earth's materials—waits upon my steps;
Pitches her tents before me as I move,
An hourly neighbour. Paradise, and groves
Elysian, Fortunate Fields—like those of old
Sought in the Atlantic Main,[4] why should they be
A history only of departed things,
Or a mere fiction of what never was?
For the discerning intellect of Man,
When wedded to this goodly universe
In love and holy passion, shall find these
A simple produce of the common day.
—I, long before the blissful hour arrives,
Would chaunt, in lonely peace, the spousal verse
Of this great consummation:—and, by words
Which speak of nothing more than what we are,
Would I arouse the sensual from their sleep
Of Death, and win the vacant and the vain
To noble raptures; while my voice proclaims
How exquisitely the individual Mind
(And the progressive powers perhaps no less
Of the whole species) to the external World
Is fitted:—and how exquisitely, too,
Theme this but little heard of among Men,
The external World is fitted to the Mind;[5]
And the creation (by no lower name
Can it be called) which they with blended might
Accomplish:—this is our high argument.
—Such grateful haunts foregoing, if I oft
Must turn elsewhere—to travel near the tribes
And fellowships of men, and see ill sights
Of madding passions mutually inflamed;
Must hear Humanity in fields and groves
Pipe solitary anguish; or must hang
Brooding above the fierce confederate storm
Of sorrow, barricadoed evermore
Within the walls of Cities; may these sounds

---

[1] Milton, *Paradise Lost* 7.30–31.

[2] Milton's "heavenly muse" in *Paradise Lost*.

[3] Chaos is the unformed state before creation; Erebus is the classical underworld.

[4] Elysian groves are the place of the blessed in the classical underworld; Wordsworth sums up all blissful imaginary places by referring to Atlantis, the legendary lost city of antiquity.

[5] William Blake strongly objected to this passage, remarking in his marginal notes to Wordsworth's poem, "You shall not bring me down to believe such fitting & fitted I know better & Please your Lordship."*

<pre>
              Have their authentic comment,—that, even these
835   Hearing, I be not downcast or forlorn!
              —Come thou prophetic Spirit, that inspir'st
              The human Soul of universal earth,
              Dreaming on things to come;¹ and dost possess
              A metropolitan Temple in the hearts
840   Of mighty Poets; upon me bestow
              A gift of genuine insight; that my Song
              With star-like virtue in its place may shine;
              Shedding benignant influence,—and secure,
              Itself, from all malevolent effect
845   Of those mutations that extend their sway
              Throughout the nether sphere!—And if with this
              I mix more lowly matter; with the thing
              Contemplated, describe the Mind and Man
              Contemplating; and who, and what he was,
850   The transitory Being that beheld
              This Vision,—when and where, and how he lived;—
              Be not this labour useless. If such theme
              May sort with highest objects, then, dread Power,
              Whose gracious favour is the primal source
855   Of all illumination, may my Life
              Express the image of a better time,
              More wise desires, and simpler manners;—nurse
              My Heart in genuine freedom:—all pure thoughts
              Be with me;—so shall thy unfailing love
860   Guide, and support, and cheer me to the end!
</pre>

The Excursion

BOOK FIRST
*The Wanderer*²

<pre>
       'Twas summer, and the sun had mounted high:
       Southward, the landscape indistinctly glared
       Through a pale steam; but all the northern downs,
</pre>

---

¹ "Not mine own fears, nor the prophetic Soul / Of the wide world dreaming on things to come. *Shakespeare's Sonnets* [107, 1–2]." (W.W.)

² Wordsworth's early version of "The Wanderer," entitled "The Ruined Cottage," was written between 1795 and 1798. Revised in 1801–02 under a new title, "The Pedlar," it was first published as the first book of *The Excursion* in 1814.

<pre>
              In clearest air ascending, shew'd far off
5   A surface dappled o'er with shadows, flung
              From many a brooding cloud; far as the sight
              Could reach, those many shadows lay in spots
              Determined and unmoved, with steady beams
              Of bright and pleasant sunshine interposed.
10   Pleasant to him who on the soft cool moss
              Extends his careless limbs along the front
              Of some huge cave, whose rocky ceiling casts
              A twilight of its own, an ample shade,
              Where the wren warbles; while the dreaming Man,
15   Half conscious of the soothing melody,
              With side-long eye looks out upon the scene,
              By that impending covert made more soft,
              More low and distant! Other lot was mine;
              Yet with good hope that soon I should obtain
20   As grateful resting-place, and livelier joy.
              Across a bare wide Common I was toiling
              With languid feet, which by the slippery ground
              Were baffled; nor could my weak arm disperse
              The host of insects gathering round my face,
25   And ever with me as I paced along.

                 Upon that open level stood a Grove,
              The wished-for Port to which my steps were bound.
              Thither I came, and there—amid the gloom
              Spread by a brotherhood of lofty elms—
30   Appeared a roofless Hut; four naked walls
              That stared upon each other! I looked round,
              And to my wish and to my hope espied
              Him whom I sought; a Man of reverend age,
              But stout and hale, for travel unimpaired.
35   There was he seen upon the Cottage bench,
              Recumbent in the shade, as if asleep;
              An iron-pointed staff lay at his side.

                 Him had I marked the day before—alone
              And in the middle of the public way
40   Stationed, as if to rest himself, with face
              Turned tow'rds the sun then setting, while that staff
              Afforded to his Figure, as he stood,
              Detained for contemplation or repose,
              Graceful support; the countenance of the Man
45   Was hidden from my view, and he himself
</pre>

Unrecognized; but, stricken by the sight,
With slacken'd footsteps I advanced, and soon
A glad congratulation we exchanged
At such unthought-of meeting.—For the night
50 We parted, nothing willingly; and now
He by appointment waited for me here,
Beneath the shelter of these clustering elms.

    We were tried Friends: I from my Childhood up
Had known him.—In a little Town obscure,
55 A market-village, seated in a tract
Of mountains, where my school-day time was pass'd,
One room he own'd, the fifth part of a house,
A place to which he drew, from time to time,
And found a kind of home or harbour there.
60   He loved me; from a swarm of rosy Boys
Singled out me, as he in sport would say,
For my grave looks—too thoughtful for my years.
As I grew up it was my best delight
To be his chosen Comrade. Many a time,
65 On holidays, we wandered through the woods,
A pair of random travellers; we sate—
We walked; he pleas'd me with his sweet discourse
Of things which he had seen; and often touch'd
Abstrusest matter, reasonings of the mind
70 Turned inward; or at my request he sang
Old songs—the product of his native hills;
A skilful distribution of sweet sounds,
Feeding the soul, and eagerly imbibed
As cool refreshing Water, by the care
75 Of the industrious husbandman, diffused
Through a parched meadow-ground, in time of
    drought.
Still deeper welcome found his pure discourse:
How precious when in riper days I learn'd
To weigh with care his words, and to rejoice
80 In the plain presence of his dignity!

    Oh! many are the Poets that are sown
By Nature; Men endowed with highest gifts,
The vision and the faculty divine,
Yet wanting the accomplishment of Verse,
85 (Which in the docile season of their youth
It was denied them to acquire, through lack
Of culture and the inspiring aid of books,
Or haply by a temper too severe,
Or a nice backwardness afraid of shame),
90 Nor having e'er, as life advanced, been led
By circumstance to take unto the height
The measure of themselves, these favored Beings,
All but a scattered few, live out their time,
Husbanding that which they possess within,
95 And go to the grave, unthought of. Strongest minds
Are often those of whom the noisy world
Hears least; else surely this Man had not left
His graces unrevealed and unproclaimed.
But, as the mind was filled with inward light,
100 So not without distinction had he lived,
Beloved and honoured—far as he was known.
And some small portion of his eloquent speech,
And something that may serve to set in view
The feeling pleasures of his loneliness,
105 The doings, observations, which his mind
Had dealt with—I will here record in verse;
Which, if with truth it correspond, and sink
Or rise, as venerable Nature leads,
The high and tender Muses shall accept
110 With gracious smile, deliberately pleased,
And listening Time reward with sacred praise.

    Among the hills of Athol[2] he was born:
There, on a small hereditary Farm,
An unproductive slip of rugged ground,
115 His Father dwelt; and died in poverty;
While He, whose lowly fortune I retrace,
The youngest of three sons, was yet a babe,
A little One—unconscious of their loss.
But ere he had outgrown his infant days
120 His widowed Mother, for a second Mate,
Espoused the Teacher of the Village School;
Who on her offspring zealously bestowed
Needful instruction; not alone in arts
Which to his humble duties appertained,
125 But in the lore of right and wrong, the rule

---

[1] Hawkshead, where Wordsworth attended school.

[2] in Perthshire, central Scotland.

Of human kindness, in the peaceful ways
Of honesty, and holiness severe.
A virtuous Household though exceeding poor!
Pure Livers were they all, austere and grave,
130 And fearing God; the very Children taught
Stern self-respect, a reverence for God's word,
And an habitual piety, maintained
With strictness scarcely known on English ground.

From his sixth year, the Boy of whom I speak,
135 In summer, tended cattle on the Hills;
But, through the inclement and the perilous days
Of long-continuing winter, he repaired
To his Step-father's School, that stood alone,
Sole Building on a mountain's dreary edge,
140 Far from the sight of City spire, or sound
Of Minster clock! From that bleak Tenement
He, many an evening to his distant home
In solitude returning, saw the Hills
Grow larger in the darkness, all alone
145 Beheld the stars come out above his head,
And travelled through the wood, with no one near
To whom he might confess the things he saw.
So the foundations of his mind were laid.
In such communion, not from terror free,
150 While yet a Child, and long before his time,
He had perceived the presence and the power
Of greatness; and deep feelings had impress'd
Great objects on his mind, with portraiture
And colour so distinct, that on his mind
155 They lay like substances, and almost seemed
To haunt the bodily sense. He had received
(Vigorous in native genius as he was)
A precious gift; for, as he grew in years,
With these impressions would he still compare
160 All his remembrances, thoughts, shapes, and forms;
And, being still unsatisfied with aught
Of dimmer character, he thence attained
An active power to fasten images
Upon his brain; and on their pictured lines
165 Intensely brooded, even till they acquired
The liveliness of dreams. Nor did he fail,
While yet a Child, with a Child's eagerness
Incessantly to turn his ear and eye

On all things which the moving seasons brought
170 To feed such appetite: nor this alone
Appeased his yearning:—in the after day
Of Boyhood, many an hour in caves forlorn,
And 'mid the hollow depths of naked crags
He sate, and even in their fix'd lineaments,
175 Or from the power of a peculiar eye,
Or by creative feeling overborne,
Or by predominance of thought oppress'd,
Even in their fix'd and steady lineaments
He traced an ebbing and a flowing mind,
180 Expression ever varying!
                    Thus informed,
He had small need of books; for many a Tale
Traditionary, round the mountains hung,
And many a Legend, peopling the dark woods,
Nourished Imagination in her growth,
185 And gave the Mind that apprehensive power
By which she is made quick to recognize
The moral properties and scope of things.
But eagerly he read, and read again,
Whate'er the Minister's old Shelf supplied;
190 The life and death of Martyrs, who sustained,
With will inflexible, those fearful pangs
Triumphantly displayed in records left
Of Persecution, and the Covenant-Times
Whose echo rings through Scotland to this hour![1]
195 And there by lucky hap had been preserved
A straggling volume, torn and incomplete,
That left half-told the preternatural tale,
Romance of Giants, chronicle of Fiends
Profuse in garniture of wooden cuts
200 Strange and uncouth; dire faces, figures dire,
Sharp-knee'd, sharp-elbowed, and lean-ankled too,
With long and ghostly shanks—forms which once seen
Could never be forgotten!
                    In his heart,
Where Fear sate thus, a cherished visitant,
205 Was wanting yet the pure delight of love
By sound diffused, or by the breathing air,

---

[1] The Scottish Church was not only Protestant but also anti-episcopalian; the Solemn League and Covenant of 1643 stipulated the protection of the reformed Church in Scotland, the reformation of religion in England, and opposition to the Pope and bishops.

Or by the silent looks of happy things,
Or flowing from the universal face
Of earth and sky. But he had felt the power
210 Of Nature, and already was prepared,
By his intense conceptions, to receive
Deeply the lesson deep of love which he,
Whom Nature, by whatever means, has taught
To feel intensely, cannot but receive.

215 From early childhood, even, as hath been said,
From his sixth year, he had been sent abroad
In summer to tend herds: such was his task
Thenceforward 'till the later day of youth.
O then what soul was his, when, on the tops
220 Of the high mountains, he beheld the sun
Rise up, and bathe the world in light! He looked—
Ocean and earth, the solid frame of earth
And ocean's liquid mass, beneath him lay
In gladness and deep joy. The clouds were touch'd,
225 And in their silent faces did he read
Unutterable love. Sound needed none,
Nor any voice of joy; his spirit drank
The spectacle; sensation, soul, and form
All melted into him; they swallowed up
230 His animal being; in them did he live,
And by them did he live; they were his life.
In such access of mind, in such high hour
Of visitation from the living God,
Thought was not; in enjoyment it expired.
235 No thanks he breathed, he proffered no request;
Rapt into still communion that transcends
The imperfect offices of prayer and praise,
His mind was a thanksgiving to the power
That made him; it was blessedness and love!

240   A Herdsman on the lonely mountain tops,
Such intercourse was his, and in this sort
Was his existence oftentimes *possessed*.
Oh then how beautiful, how bright appeared
The written Promise! He had early learned
245 To reverence the Volume which displays
The mystery, the life which cannot die:
But in the mountains did he *feel* his faith;
There did he see the writing;—all things there

Breathed immortality, revolving life
250 And greatness still revolving; infinite;
There littleness was not; the least of things
Seemed infinite; and there his spirit shaped
Her prospects, nor did he believe,—he *saw*.
What wonder if his being thus became
255 Sublime and comprehensive! Low desires,
Low thoughts had there no place; yet was his heart
Lowly; for he was meek in gratitude,
Oft as he called those extacies to mind,
And whence they flowed: and from them he acquired
260 Wisdom, which works through patience; thence he learned
In many a calmer hour of sober thought
To look on Nature with a humble heart,
Self-questioned where it did not understand,
And with a superstitious eye of love.

265   So passed the time; yet to a neighbouring town
He duly went with what small overplus
His earnings might supply, and brought away
The Book which most had tempted his desires
While at the Stall he read. Among the hills
270 He gazed upon that mighty Orb of Song
The divine Milton. Lore of different kind,
The annual savings of a toilsome life,
His Step-father supplied; books that explain
The purer elements of truth involved
275 In lines and numbers, and, by charm severe,
(Especially perceived where nature droops
And feeling is suppressed,) preserve the mind
Busy in solitude and poverty.
These occupations oftentimes deceived
280 The listless hours, while in the hollow vale,
Hollow and green, he lay on the green turf
In pensive idleness. What could he do
With blind endeavours, in that lonesome life,
Thus thirsting daily? Yet still uppermost
285 Nature was at his heart as if he felt,
Though yet he knew not how, a wasting power
In all things which from her sweet influence
Might tend to wean him. Therefore with her hues,
Her forms, and with the spirit of her forms,
290 He clothed the nakedness of austere truth.

While yet he lingered in the rudiments
Of science, and among her simplest laws,
His triangles—they were the stars of heaven,
The silent stars! Oft did he take delight
295 To measure th' altitude of some tall crag
Which is the eagle's birth-place, or some peak
Familiar with forgotten years, that shews
Inscribed, as with the silence of the thought,
Upon it's bleak and visionary sides,
300 The history of many a winter storm,—
Or obscure records of the path of fire.

    And thus, before his eighteenth year was told,
Accumulated feelings pressed his heart
With an increasing weight; he was o'erpower'd
305 By Nature, by the turbulence subdued
Of his own mind; by mystery and hope,
And the first virgin passion of a soul
Communing with the glorious Universe.
Full often wished he that the winds might rage
310 When they were silent; far more fondly now
Than in his earlier season did he love
Tempestuous nights—the conflict and the sounds
That live in darkness:—from his intellect
And from the stillness of abstracted thought
315 He asked repose; and I have heard him say
That often, failing at this time to gain
The peace required, he scanned the laws of light
Amid the roar of torrents, where they send
From hollow clefts up to the clearer air
320 A cloud of mist, which in the sunshine frames
A lasting tablet—for the observer's eye
Varying it's rainbow hues. But vainly thus,
And vainly by all other means, he strove
To mitigate the fever of his heart.

325   In dreams, in study, and in ardent thought,
Thus, even from Childhood upward, was he reared;
For intellectual progress wanting much,
Doubtless, of needful help—yet gaining more;
And every moral feeling of his soul
330 Strengthened and braced, by breathing in content

The keen, the wholesome air of poverty,
And drinking from the well of homely life.
—But, from past liberty, and tried restraints,
He now was summoned to select the course
335 Of humble industry which promised best
To yield him no unworthy maintenance.
The Mother strove to make her Son perceive
With what advantage he might teach a School
In the adjoining Village; but the Youth,
340 Who of this service made a short essay,
Found that the wanderings of his thought were then
A misery to him; that he must resign
A task he was unable to perform.

    That stern yet kindly spirit, Who constrains
345 The Savoyard[1] to quit his naked rocks,
The free-born Swiss to leave his narrow vales,
(Spirit attached to regions mountainous
Like their own stedfast clouds)—did now impel
His restless Mind to look abroad with hope.
350 —An irksome drudgery seems it to plod on,
Through dusty ways, in storm, from door to door,
A vagrant Merchant bent beneath his load!
Yet do such Travellers find their own delight;
And their hard service, deemed debasing now,
355 Gained merited respect in simpler times;
When Squire, and Priest, and they who round them dwelt
In rustic sequestration, all, dependant
Upon the PEDLAR's toil—supplied their wants,
Or pleased their fancies, with the wares he brought.
360 Not ignorant was the Youth that still no few
Of his adventurous Countrymen were led
By perseverance in this Track of life
To competence and ease;—for him it bore
Attractions manifold;—and this he chose.
365 He asked his Mother's blessing; and, with tears
Thanking his second Father, asked from him
Paternal blessings. The good Pair bestowed
Their farewell benediction, but with hearts
Foreboding evil. From his native hills

---

[1] inhabitant of Savoy, a mountainous region of southeast France, bordering on Switzerland and Italy.

370   He wandered far; much did he see of Men,[1]
    Their manners, their enjoyments, and pursuits,
    Their passions, and their feelings; chiefly those
    Essential and eternal in the heart,
    Which, mid the simpler forms of rural life,
375   Exist more simple in their elements,
    And speak a plainer language. In the woods,
    A lone Enthusiast, and among the fields,
    Itinerant in this labour, he had passed
    The better portion of his time; and there
380   Spontaneously had his affections thriven
    Upon the bounties of the year, and felt
    The liberty of Nature; there he kept
    In solitude and solitary thought
    His mind in a just equipoise of love.
385   Serene it was, unclouded by the cares
    Of ordinary life; unvexed, unwarped
    By partial bondage. In his steady course
    No piteous revolutions had he felt,
    No wild varieties of joy and grief.
390   Unoccupied by sorrow of it's own
    His heart lay open; and, by Nature tuned
    And constant disposition of his thoughts
    To sympathy with Man, he was alive
    To all that was enjoyed where'er he went;
395   And all that was endured; for in himself
    Happy, and quiet in his chearfulness,
    He had no painful pressure from without
    That made him turn aside from wretchedness
    With coward fears. He could *afford* to suffer
400   With those whom he saw suffer. Hence it came
    That in our best experience he was rich,
    And in the wisdom of our daily life.
    For hence, minutely, in his various rounds,
    He had observed the progress and decay
405   Of many minds, of minds and bodies too;
    The History of many Families;
    How they had prospered; how they were o'erthrown
    By passion or mischance; or such misrule
    Among the unthinking masters of the earth
410   As makes the nations groan.—This active course,
    Chosen in youth, through manhood he pursued,
    Till due provision for his modest wants
    Had been obtained;—and, thereupon, resolved
    To pass the remnant of his days—untasked
415   With needless services,—from hardship free.
    His Calling laid aside, he lived at ease:
    But still he loved to pace the public roads
    And the wild paths; and, when the summer's warmth
    Invited him, would often leave his home
420   And journey far, revisiting those scenes
    Which to his memory were most endeared.
    —Vigorous in health, of hopeful spirits, untouched
    By worldly-mindedness or anxious care;
    Observant, studious, thoughtful, and refreshed
425   By knowledge gathered up from day to day;—
    Thus had he lived a long and innocent life.

    The Scottish Church, both on himself and those
    With whom from childhood he grew up, had held
    The strong hand of her purity; and still
430   Had watched him with an unrelenting eye.
    This he remembered in his riper age
    With gratitude, and reverential thoughts.
    But by the native vigour of his mind,
    By his habitual wanderings out of doors,
435   By loneliness, and goodness, and kind works,
    Whate'er in docile childhood or in youth
    He had imbibed of fear or darker thought
    Was melted all away: so true was this
    That sometimes his religion seemed to me
440   Self-taught, as of a dreamer in the woods;
    Who to the model of his own pure heart
    Framed his belief, as grace divine inspired,
    Or human reason dictated with awe.
    —And surely never did there live on earth
445   A Man of kindlier nature. The rough sports
    And teazing ways of Children vexed not him,
    Nor could he bid them from his presence, tired
    With questions and importunate demands:

---

[1] "In Heron's Tour in Scotland is given an intelligent account of the qualities by which this class of men used to be, and still are, in some degree, distinguished, and of the benefits which Society derives from their labours. Among their characteristics, he does not omit to mention that, from being obliged to pass so much of their time in solitary wandering among rural objects, they frequently acquire meditative habits of mind, and are strongly disposed to enthusiasm poetical and religious. I regret that I have not the book at hand to quote the passage, as it is interesting on many accounts." (W.W.)

William Wordsworth

      Indulgent listener was he to the tongue
450 Of garrulous age; nor did the sick man's tale,
      To his fraternal sympathy addressed,
      Obtain reluctant hearing.
                        Plain his garb
      Such as might suit a rustic sire, prepared
      For sabbath duties; yet he was a Man
455 Whom no one could have passed without remark.
      Active and nervous was his gait; his limbs
      And his whole figure breathed intelligence.
      Time had compressed the freshness of his cheek
      Into a narrower circle of deep red
460 But had not tamed his eye; that under brows
      Shaggy and grey had meanings which it brought
      From years of youth; which, like a Being made
      Of many Beings, he had wondrous skill
      To blend with knowledge of the years to come,
465 Human, or such as lie beyond the grave.

      So was He framed; and such his course of life
      Who now, with no Appendage but a Staff,
      The prized memorial of relinquish'd toils,
      Upon that Cottage bench reposed his limbs,
470 Screened from the sun. Supine the Wanderer lay,
      His eyes as if in drowsiness half shut,
      The shadows of the breezy elms above
      Dappling his face. He had not heard my steps
      As I approached; and near him did I stand
475 Unnotic'd in the shade some minutes' space.
      At length I hailed him, seeing that his hat
      Was moist with water-drops, as if the brim
      Had newly scooped a running stream. He rose,
      And ere the pleasant greeting that ensued
480 Was ended, "'Tis," said I, "a burning day;
      My lips are parched with thirst, but you, I guess,
      Have somewhere found relief." He, at the word,
      Pointing towards a sweet-briar, bade me climb
      The fence hard by, where that aspiring shrub
485 Looked out upon the road. It was a plot
      Of garden-ground run wild, it's matted weeds
      Marked with the steps of those, whom, as they pass'd,
      The gooseberry trees that shot in long lank slips,
      Or currants hanging from their leafless stems
490 In scanty strings, had tempted to o'erleap
      The broken wall. I looked around, and there,
      Where two tall hedge-rows of thick alder boughs
      Joined in a cold damp nook, espied a Well
      Shrouded with willow-flowers and plumy fern.
495 My thirst I slaked, and from the cheerless spot
      Withdrawing, straightway to the shade returned
      Where sate the Old Man on the Cottage bench;
      And, while, beside him, with uncovered head,
      I yet was standing, freely to respire,
500 And cool my temples in the fanning air,
      Thus did he speak. "I see around me here
      Things which you cannot see: we die, my Friend,
      Nor we alone, but that which each man loved
      And prized in his peculiar nook of earth
505 Dies with him, or is changed; and very soon
      Even of the good is no memorial left.
      —The Poets, in their elegies and songs
      Lamenting the departed, call the groves,
      They call upon the hills and streams to mourn,
510 And senseless rocks; nor idly; for they speak,
      In these their invocations, with a voice
      Obedient to the strong creative power
      Of human passion. Sympathies there are
      More tranquil, yet perhaps of kindred birth,
515 That steal upon the meditative mind,
      And grow with thought. Beside yon Spring I stood,
      And eyed its waters till we seemed to feel
      One sadness, they and I. For them a bond
      Of brotherhood is broken: time has been
520 When, every day, the touch of human hand
      Dislodged the natural sleep that binds them up
      In mortal stillness; and they minister'd
      To human comfort. As I stooped to drink,
      Upon the slimy foot-stone I espied
525 The useless fragment of a wooden bowl,
      Green with the moss of years; a pensive sight
      That moved my heart!—recalling former days
      When I could never pass that road but She
      Who lived within these walls, at my approach,
530 A daughter's welcome gave me; and I loved her
      As my own child. O, Sir! the good die first,

And they whose hearts are dry as summer dust
　　　Burn to the socket.[1] Many a Passenger
　　　Hath blessed poor Margaret for her gentle looks,
535　When she upheld the cool refreshment drawn
　　　From that forsaken Spring; and no one came
　　　But he was welcome; no one went away
　　　But that it seemed she loved him. She is dead,
　　　The light extinguished of her lonely Hut,
540　The Hut itself abandoned to decay,
　　　And She forgotten in the quiet grave!

　　　　"I speak," continued he, "of One whose stock
　　　Of virtues bloom'd beneath this lowly roof.
　　　She was a Woman of a steady mind,
545　Tender and deep in her excess of love,
　　　Not speaking much, pleased rather with the joy
　　　Of her own thoughts: by some especial care
　　　Her temper had been framed, as if to make
　　　A Being—who by adding love to peace
550　Might live on earth a life of happiness.
　　　Her wedded Partner lacked not on his side
　　　The humble worth that satisfied her heart:
　　　Frugal, affectionate, sober, and withal
　　　Keenly industrious. She with pride would tell
555　That he was often seated at his loom,
　　　In summer, ere the Mower was abroad
　　　Among the dewy grass,—in early spring,
　　　Ere the last Star had vanished.—They who passed
　　　At evening, from behind the garden fence
560　Might hear his busy spade, which he would ply,
　　　After his daily work, until the light
　　　Had failed, and every leaf and flower were lost
　　　In the dark hedges. So their days were spent
　　　In peace and comfort; and a pretty Boy
565　Was their best hope,—next to the God in Heaven.

　　　　"Not twenty years ago, but you I think
　　　Can scarcely bear it now in mind, there came
　　　Two blighting seasons when the fields were left
　　　With half a harvest. It pleased heaven to add
570　A worse affliction in the plague of war;
　　　This happy Land was stricken to the heart!

　　　A Wanderer then among the Cottages
　　　I, with my freight of winter raiment, saw
　　　The hardships of that season; many rich
575　Sank down, as in a dream, among the poor;
　　　And of the poor did many cease to be
　　　And their place knew them not.[2] Meanwhile abridg'd
　　　Of daily comforts, gladly reconciled
　　　To numerous self-denials, Margaret
580　Went struggling on through those calamitous years
　　　With chearful hope: but ere the second autumn
　　　Her life's true Help-mate on a sick-bed lay,
　　　Smitten with perilous fever. In disease
　　　He lingered long; and when his strength return'd,
585　He found the little he had stored, to meet
　　　The hour of accident or crippling age,
　　　Was all consumed. Two children had they now,
　　　One newly born. As I have said, it was
　　　A time of trouble; shoals of Artisans
590　Were from their daily labour turn'd adrift
　　　To seek their bread from public charity,
　　　They, and their wives and children—happier far
　　　Could they have lived as do the little birds
　　　That peck along the hedges, or the Kite
595　That makes his dwelling on the mountain Rocks!

　　　　"A sad reverse it was for Him who long
　　　Had filled with plenty, and possess'd in peace,
　　　This lonely Cottage. At his door he stood,
　　　And whistled many a snatch of merry tunes
600　That had no mirth in them; or with his knife
　　　Carved uncouth figures on the heads of sticks—
　　　Then, not less idly, sought, through every nook
　　　In house or garden, any casual work
　　　Of use or ornament; and with a strange,
605　Amusing, yet uneasy novelty,
　　　He blended, where he might, the various tasks
　　　Of summer, autumn, winter, and of spring.
　　　But this endured not; his good humour soon
　　　Became a weight in which no pleasure was:
610　And poverty brought on a petted mood
　　　And a sore temper: day by day he drooped,
　　　And he would leave his work—and to the Town,

---

[1] P.B. Shelley quotes lines 531–33 in his Preface to *Alastor.*

[2] Cf. Job 7.10.

Without an errand, would direct his steps,
Or wander here and there among the fields.
615 One while he would speak lightly of his Babes,
And with a cruel tongue: at other times
He toss'd them with a false unnatural joy:
And 'twas a rueful thing to see the looks
Of the poor innocent children. 'Every smile,'
620 Said Margaret to me, here beneath these trees,
'Made my heart bleed.'"
                At this the Wanderer paused;
And, looking up to those enormous Elms,
He said, "'Tis now the hour of deepest noon.—
At this still season of repose and peace,
625 This hour, when all things which are not at rest
Are chearful; while this multitude of flies
Is filling all the air with melody;
Why should a tear be in an Old Man's eye?
Why should we thus, with an untoward mind,
630 And in the weakness of humanity,
From natural wisdom turn our hearts away,
To natural comfort shut our eyes and ears,
And, feeding on disquiet, thus disturb
The calm of nature with our restless thoughts?"

---

635 He spake with somewhat of a solemn tone:
But, when he ended, there was in his face
Such easy chearfulness, a look so mild,
That for a little time it stole away
All recollection, and that simple Tale
640 Passed from my mind like a forgotten sound.
A while on trivial things we held discourse,
To me soon tasteless. In my own despite
I thought of that poor Woman as of one
Whom I had known and loved. He had rehearsed
645 Her homely Tale with such familiar power,
With such an active countenance, an eye
So busy, that the things of which he spake
Seemed present; and, attention now relax'd,
There was a heart-felt chillness in my veins.—
650 I rose; and, turning from the breezy shade,
Went forth into the open air, and stood
To drink the comfort of the warmer sun.
Long time I had not staid, ere, looking round
Upon that tranquil Ruin, I return'd,
655 And begged of the Old Man that, for my sake,
He would resume his story.—
                He replied,
"It were a wantonness, and would demand
Severe reproof, if we were Men whose hearts
Could hold vain dalliance with the misery
660 Even of the dead; contented thence to draw
A momentary pleasure, never marked
By reason, barren of all future good.
But we have known that there is often found
In mournful thoughts, and always might be found,
665 A power to virtue friendly; were't not so,
I am a Dreamer among men, indeed
An idle Dreamer! 'Tis a common Tale,
An ordinary sorrow of Man's life,
A tale of silent suffering, hardly clothed
670 In bodily form.—But, without further bidding,
I will proceed.—
            "While thus it fared with them,
To whom this Cottage, till those hapless years,
Had been a blessed home, it was my chance
To travel in a Country far remote.
675 And glad I was, when, halting by yon gate
That leads from the green lane, once more I saw
Those lofty elm-trees. Long I did not rest:
With many pleasant thoughts I chear'd my way
O'er the flat Common.—Having reached the door
680 I knock'd,—and, when I entered with the hope
Of usual greeting, Margaret looked at me
A little while; then turn'd her head away
Speechless,—and sitting down upon a chair
Wept bitterly. I wist not what to do,
685 Or how to speak to her. Poor Wretch! at last
She rose from off her seat, and then,—O Sir!
I cannot *tell* how she pronounced my name.—
With fervent love, and with a face of grief
Unutterably helpless, and a look
690 That seemed to cling upon me, she enquired
If I had seen her Husband. As she spake
A strange surprize and fear came to my heart,
Nor had I power to answer ere she told
That he had disappear'd—not two months gone.
695 He left his House: two wretched days had pass'd,

And on the third, as wistfully she rais'd
Her head from off her pillow, to look forth,
Like one in trouble, for returning light,
Within her chamber-casement she espied
700 A folded paper, lying as if placed
To meet her waking eyes. This tremblingly
She open'd—found no writing, but therein
Pieces of money carefully enclosed,
Silver and gold.—'I shuddered at the sight,'
705 Said Margaret, 'for I knew it was his hand
Which placed it there: and ere that day was ended,
That long and anxious day! I learned from One
Sent hither by my Husband to impart
The heavy news,—that he had joined a Troop
710 Of Soldiers, going to a distant Land.
—He left me thus—he could not gather heart
To take a farewell of me; for he fear'd
That I should follow with my Babes, and sink
Beneath the misery of that wandering Life.'

715 "This Tale did Margaret tell with many tears:
And when she ended I had little power
To give her comfort, and was glad to take
Such words of hope from her own mouth as served
To chear us both:—but long we had not talked
720 Ere we built up a pile of better thoughts,
And with a brighter eye she look'd around
As if she had been shedding tears of joy.
We parted.—'Twas the time of early spring;
I left her busy with her garden tools;
725 And well remember, o'er that fence she looked,
And, while I paced along the foot-way path,
Called out, and sent a blessing after me,
With tender chearfulness; and with a voice
That seem'd the very sound of happy thoughts.

730 "I roved o'er many a hill and many a dale,
With my accustomed load; in heat and cold,
Through many a wood, and many an open ground,
In sunshine and in shade, in wet and fair,
Drooping, or blithe of heart, as might befal;
735 My best companions now the driving winds,
And now the "trotting brooks" and whispering trees,
And now the music of my own sad steps,
With many a short-lived thought that pass'd between,
And disappeared.—I journey'd back this way
740 Towards the wane of Summer; when the wheat
Was yellow; and the soft and bladed grass
Springing afresh had o'er the hay-field spread
Its tender verdure. At the door arrived,
I found that she was absent. In the shade,
745 Where now we sit, I waited her return.
Her Cottage, then a chearful Object, wore
Its customary look,—only, I thought,
The honeysuckle, crowding round the porch,
Hung down in heavier tufts: and that bright weed,
750 The yellow stone-crop, suffered to take root
Along the window's edge, profusely grew,
Blinding the lower panes. I turned aside,
And strolled into her garden. It appeared
To lag behind the season, and had lost
755 Its pride of neatness. From the border lines
Composed of daisy and resplendent thrift,
Flowers straggling forth had on those paths
    encroached
Which they were used to deck:—Carnations, once
Prized for surpassing beauty, and no less
760 For the peculiar pains they had required,
Declined their languid heads—without support.
The cumbrous bind-weed, with its wreaths and bells,
Had twined about her two small rows of pease,
And dragged them to the earth.—Ere this an hour
765 Was wasted.—Back I turned my restless steps,
And, as I walked before the door, it chanced
A Stranger passed; and, guessing whom I sought,
He said that she was used to ramble far.—
The sun was sinking in the west; and now
770 I sate with sad impatience. From within
Her solitary Infant cried aloud;
Then, like a blast that dies away self-stilled,
The voice was silent. From the bench I rose;
But neither could divert nor soothe my thoughts.
775 The spot, though fair, was very desolate—
The longer I remained more desolate.
And, looking round, I saw the corner stones,
Till then unnotic'd, on either side the door
With dull red stains discolour'd, and stuck o'er
780 With tufts and hairs of wool, as if the Sheep,

That fed upon the Common, thither came
Familiarly; and found a couching-place
Even at her threshold. Deeper shadows fell
From these tall elms;—the Cottage-clock struck eight;—
785 I turned, and saw her distant a few steps.
Her face was pale and thin, her figure too
Was changed. As she unlocked the door, she said,
"It grieves me you have waited here so long,
But, in good truth, I've wandered much of late,
790 And, sometimes,—to my shame I speak, have need
Of my best prayers to bring me back again.'
While on the board she spread our evening meal
She told me,—interrupting not the work
Which gave employment to her listless hands,
795 That she had parted with her elder Child;
To a kind Master on a distant farm
Now happily apprenticed—'I perceive
You look at me, and you have cause; to-day
I have been travelling far; and many days
800 About the fields I wander, knowing this
Only, that what I seek I cannot find.
And so I waste my time: for I am changed;
And to myself,' said she, 'have done much wrong
And to this helpless Infant. I have slept
805 Weeping, and weeping have I waked; my tears
Have flowed as if my body were not such
As others are; and I could never die.
But I am now in mind and in my heart
More easy; and I hope,' said she, 'that heaven
810 Will give me patience to endure the things
Which I behold at home.' It would have grieved
Your very soul to see her; Sir, I feel
The story linger in my heart: I fear
'Tis long and tedious; but my spirit clings
815 To that poor Woman:—so familiarly
Do I perceive her manner, and her look,
And presence, and so deeply do I feel
Her goodness, that, not seldom, in my walks
A momentary trance comes over me;
820 And to myself I seem to muse on One
By sorrow laid asleep;—or borne away,
A human being destined to awake
To human life, or something very near

To human life, when he shall come again
825 For whom she suffered. Yes, it would have grieved
Your very soul to see her: evermore
Her eyelids drooped, her eyes were downward cast;
And, when she at her table gave me food,
She did not look at me. Her voice was low,
830 Her body was subdued. In every act
Pertaining to her house affairs, appeared
The careless stillness of a thinking mind
Self-occupied; to which all outward things
Are like an idle matter. Still she sighed,
835 But yet no motion of the breast was seen,
No heaving of the heart. While by the fire
We sate together, sighs came on my ear,
I knew not how, and hardly whence they came.

"Ere my departure to her care I gave,
840 For her Son's use, some tokens of regard,
Which with a look of welcome She received;
And I exhorted her to have her trust
In God's good love, and seek his help by prayer.
I took my staff, and when I kissed her babe
845 The tears stood in her eyes. I left her then
With the best hope and comfort I could give;
She thanked me for my wish;—but for my hope
Methought she did not thank me.
                                                  I returned,
And took my rounds along this road again
850 Ere on its sunny bank the primrose flower
Peeped forth, to give an earnest of the Spring.
I found her sad and drooping; she had learned
No tidings of her Husband; if he lived
She knew not that he lived; if he were dead
855 She knew not he was dead. She seem'd the same
In person and appearance; but her House
Bespake a sleepy hand of negligence.
The floor was neither dry nor neat, the hearth
Was comfortless, and her small lot of books,
860 Which, in the Cottage window, heretofore
Had been piled up against the corner panes
In seemly order, now, with straggling leaves
Lay scattered here and there, open or shut,
As they had chanced to fall. Her Infant Babe
865 Had from its Mother caught the trick of grief,

And sighed among its playthings. Once again
I turned towards the garden gate, and saw,
More plainly still, that poverty and grief
Were now come nearer to her: weeds defaced
870 The harden'd soil, and knots of wither'd grass;
No ridges there appeared of clear black mold,
No winter greenness; of her herbs and flowers,
It seemed the better part were gnawed away
Or trampled into earth; a chain of straw,
875 Which had been twined about the slender stem
Of a young apple-tree, lay at its root;
The bark was nibbled round by truant Sheep.
—Margaret stood near, her Infant in her arms,
And, noting that my eye was on the tree,
880 She said, 'I fear it will be dead and gone
Ere Robert come again.' Towards the House
Together we returned; and she enquired
If I had any hope:—but for her Babe
And for her little orphan Boy, she said,
885 She had no wish to live, that she must die
Of sorrow. Yet I saw the idle loom
Still in its place; his Sunday garments hung
Upon the self-same nail; his very staff
Stood undisturbed behind the door. And when,
890 In bleak December, I retraced this way,
She told me that her little Babe was dead,
And she was left alone. She now, released
From her maternal cares, had taken up
The employment common through these Wilds, and
    gain'd
895 By spinning hemp a pittance for herself;
And for this end had hired a neighbour's Boy
To give her needful help. That very time
Most willingly she put her work aside,
And walked with me along the miry road
900 Heedless how far; and, in such piteous sort
That any heart had ached to hear her, begged
That, wheresoe'er I went, I still would ask
For him whom she had lost. We parted then,
Our final parting; for from that time forth
905 Did many seasons pass ere I return'd
Into this tract again.
                  Nine tedious years;
From their first separation, nine long years,

She lingered in unquiet widowhood;
A Wife and Widow. Needs must it have been
910 A sore heart-wasting! I have heard, my Friend,
That in yon arbour oftentimes she sate
Alone, through half the vacant Sabbath-day,
And if a dog passed by she still would quit
The shade, and look abroad. On this old Bench
915 For hours she sate; and evermore her eye
Was busy in the distance, shaping things
That made her heart beat quick. You see that path,
Now faint,—the grass has crept o'er its grey line;
There, to and fro, she paced through many a day
920 Of the warm summer, from a belt of hemp
That girt her waist, spinning the long drawn thread
With backward steps. Yet ever as there pass'd
A man whose garments shewed the Soldiers red,
Or crippled Mendicant in Sailor's garb,
925 The little Child who sate to turn the wheel
Ceas'd from his task; and she with faultering voice
Made many a fond enquiry; and when they,
Whose presence gave no comfort, were gone by,
Her heart was still more sad. And by yon gate,
930 That bars the Traveller's road, she often stood,
And when a stranger Horseman came the latch
Would lift, and in his face look wistfully;
Most happy, if, from aught discovered there
Of tender feeling, she might dare repeat
935 The same sad question. Meanwhile her poor Hut
Sank to decay: for he was gone—whose hand,
At the first nipping of October frost,
Closed up each chink, and with fresh bands of straw
Chequered the green-grown thatch. And so she lived
940 Through the long winter, reckless and alone;
Until her House by frost, and thaw, and rain,
Was sapped; and while she slept the nightly damps
Did chill her breast; and in the stormy day
Her tattered clothes were ruffled by the wind;
945 Even at the side of her own fire. Yet still
She loved this wretched spot, nor would for worlds
Have parted hence; and still that length of road,
And this rude bench, one torturing hope endeared,
Fast rooted at her heart: and here, my Friend,
950 In sickness she remained; and here she died,
Last human Tenant of these ruined Walls."

The old Man ceased: he saw that I was moved;
From that low Bench, rising instinctively
I turn'd aside in weakness, nor had power
955 To thank him for the Tale which he had told.
I stood, and leaning o'er the Garden wall,
Reviewed that Woman's sufferings; and it seemed
To comfort me while with a Brother's love
I bless'd her—in the impotence of grief.
960 At length towards the Cottage I returned
Fondly,—and traced, with interest more mild,
That secret spirit of humanity
Which, mid the calm oblivious tendencies
Of Nature, mid her plants, and weeds, and flowers,
965 And silent overgrowings, still survived.
The Old Man, noting this, resumed, and said,
"My Friend! enough to sorrow you have given,
The purposes of wisdom ask no more;
Be wise and chearful; and no longer read
970 The forms of things with an unworthy eye.
She sleeps in the calm earth, and peace is here.
I well remember that those very plumes,
Those weeds, and the high spear-grass on that wall,
By mist and silent rain-drops silver'd o'er,
975 As once I passed, did to my heart convey
So still an image of tranquillity,
So calm and still, and looked so beautiful
Amid the uneasy thoughts which filled my mind,
That what we feel of sorrow and despair
980 From ruin and from change, and all the grief
That passing shews of Being leave behind,
Appeared an idle dream, that could not live
Where meditation was. I turned away
And walked along my road in happiness."

985 He ceased. Ere long the sun declining shot
A slant and mellow radiance, which began
To fall upon us, while beneath the trees
We sate on that low Bench: and now we felt,
Admonished thus, the sweet hour coming on.

990 A linnet warbled from those lofty elms,
A thrush sang loud, and other melodies,
At distance heard, peopled the milder air.
The Old Man rose, and, with a sprightly mien
Of hopeful preparation, grasped his Staff:
995 Together casting then a farewell look
Upon those silent walls, we left the Shade;
And, ere the Stars were visible, had reached
A Village Inn,—our Evening resting-place.

from *Poems by William Wordsworth: including Lyrical Ballads, and the Miscellaneous Pieces of the Author. With Additional Poems, a New Preface, and a Supplementary Essay* (1815)

Surprized by joy—impatient as the Wind

Surprized by joy—impatient as the Wind
I wished to share the transport—Oh! with whom
But Thee,[1] long buried in the silent Tomb,
That spot which no vicissitude can find?
5 Love, faithful love recalled thee to my mind—
But how could I forget thee?—Through what power,
Even for the least division of an hour,
Have I been so beguiled as to be blind
To my most grievous loss?—That thought's return
10 Was the worst pang that sorrow ever bore,
Save one, one only, when I stood forlorn,
Knowing my heart's best treasure was no more;
That neither present time, nor years unborn
Could to my sight that heavenly face restore.

---

[1] Wordsworth's daughter Catherine, who died in June 1812 at the age of three.

from *The River Duddon, a Series of Sonnets: Vaudracour and Julia: and Other Poems. To Which Is Annexed, a Topographical Description of the Country of the Lakes, in the North of England* (1820)

Vaudracour and Julia[1]

The following was written as an Episode, in a work from which its length may perhaps exclude it. The facts are true; no invention as to these has been exercised, as none was needed.

O happy time of youthful lovers, (thus
My story may begin) O balmy time,
In which a love-knot on a lady's brow
Is fairer than the fairest star in heaven!
5 To such inheritance of blessed fancy
(Fancy that sports more desperately with minds
Than ever fortune hath been known to do)
The high-born Vaudracour was brought, by years
Whose progress had a little overstepped
10 His stripling prime. A town of small repute,
Among the vine-clad mountains of Auvergne,
Was the Youth's birth-place. There he woo'd a Maid
Who heard the heart-felt music of his suit
With answering vows. Plebeian was the stock,
15 Plebeian, though ingenuous, the stock,
From which her graces and her honours sprung;
And hence the father of the enamoured Youth,
With haughty indignation, spurn'd the thought
Of such alliance.—From their cradles up,
20 With but a step between their several homes,
Twins had they been in pleasure; after strife
And petty quarrels, had grown fond again;
Each other's advocate, each other's stay;
And strangers to content if long apart,
25 Or more divided than a sportive pair
Of sea-fowl, conscious both that they are hovering
Within the eddy of a common blast,
Or hidden only by the concave depth
Of neighbouring billows from each other's sight.
30   Thus, not without concurrence of an age
Unknown to memory, was an earnest given,
By ready nature, for a life of love,
For endless constancy and placid truth;
But whatsoe'er of such rare treasure lay
35 Reserved, had fate permitted, for support
Of their maturer years, his present mind
Was under fascination;—he beheld
A vision, and adored the thing he saw.
Arabian fiction never filled the world
40 With half the wonders that were wrought for him.
Earth breathed in one great presence of the spring;
Life turn'd the meanest of her implements,
Before his eyes, to price above all gold;
The house she dwelt in was a sainted shrine;
45 Her chamber window did surpass in glory
The portals of the dawn; all paradise
Could, by the simple opening of a door,
Let itself in upon him; pathways, walks,
Swarm'd with enchantment, till his spirit sank
50 Surcharged within him,—overblest to move
Beneath a sun that wakes a weary world
To its dull round of ordinary cares;
A man too happy for mortality!
    So passed the time, till, whether through effect
55 Of some unguarded moment that dissolved
Virtuous restraint—ah, speak it, think it not!
Deem rather that the fervent Youth, who saw
So many bars between his present state
And the dear haven where he wished to be
60 In honourable wedlock with his Love,
Was inwardly prepared to turn aside
From law and custom, and entrust his cause
To nature for a happy end of all;
Deem that by such fond hope the Youth was swayed,
65 And bear with their transgression, when I add
That Julia, wanting yet the name of wife,
Carried about her for a secret grief

---

[1] written in 1804 and included as an episode in the 1805 version of *Prelude* 9, which recounts some of Wordsworth's experiences in France in 1791–92. The name of the hero, Vaudracour, was perhaps adapted from that of Lieutenant de Vaudrecourt, who served under Michel Beaupuy (1755–96), a revolutionary officer whom Wordsworth singles out for particular praise in *Prelude* 9. The story also reflects Wordsworth's affair with Annette Vallon and the story of M. du F[ossé] in Williams, *Letters from France** 16–22.

             The promise of a mother.
                         To conceal
     The threatened shame, the parents of the Maid
70   Found means to hurry her away by night
     And unforewarned, that in some distant spot
     She might remain shrouded in privacy,
     Until the babe was born. When morning came
     The Lover, thus bereft, stung with his loss,
75   And all uncertain whither he should turn,
     Chaf'd like a wild beast in the toils; but soon
     Discovering traces of the fugitives,
     Their steps he followed to the Maid's retreat.
     The sequel may be easily divined,—
80   Walks to and fro—watchings at every hour;
     And the fair Captive, who, whene'er she may,
     Is busy at her casement as the swallow
     Fluttering its pinions, almost within reach,
     About the pendant nest; did thus espy
85   Her Lover;—thence a stolen interview,
     Accomplished under friendly shade of night.
           I pass the raptures of the Pair;—such theme
     Is, by innumerable poets, touched
     In more delightful verse than skill of mine
90   Could fashion, chiefly by that darling bard
     Who told of Juliet and her Romeo,
     And of the lark's note heard before its time,
     And of the streaks that laced the severing clouds
     In the unrelenting east.[1]—Through all her courts
95   The vacant City slept; the busy winds,
     That keep no certain intervals of rest,
     Mov'd not; meanwhile the galaxy display'd
     Her fires, that like mysterious pulses beat
     Aloft;—momentous but uneasy bliss!
100 To their full hearts the universe seemed hung
     On that brief meeting's slender filament!
           They parted; and the generous Vaudracour
     Reached speedily the native threshold, bent
     On making (so the Lovers had agreed)
105 A sacrifice of birth-right, to attain
     A final portion from his Father's hand;
     Which granted, Bride and Bridegroom then would flee
     To some remote and solitary place,

---

[1] Cf. Shakespeare, *Romeo and Juliet* 3.5.7–8.

     Shady as night and beautiful as heaven,
110 Where they may live, with no one to behold
     Their happiness, or to disturb their love.
     But *now* of this no whisper; not the less,
     If ever an obtrusive word were dropped
     Touching the matter of his passion, still,
115 In his stern Father's hearing, Vaudracour
     Persisted openly that death alone
     Should abrogate his human privilege
     Divine, of swearing everlasting truth,
     Upon the altar, to the Maid he loved.
120   "You shall be baffled in your mad intent
     If there be justice in the Court of France,"
     Muttered the Father.—From this time the Youth
     Conceived a terror,—and, by night or day,
     Stirred no where without arms. To their rural seat,
125 Meanwhile, his Parents artfully withdrew
     Upon some feigned occasion, and the Son
     Remained with one attendant. At midnight
     When to his chamber he retired, attempt
     Was made to seize him by three armed men,
130 Acting, in furtherance of the Father's will,
     Under a private signet of the State.
     One, did the Youth's ungovernable hand
     Assault and slay;—and to a second gave
     A perilous wound,—he shuddered to behold
135 The breathless corse; then peacefully resigned
     His person to the law, was lodged in prison,
     And wore the fetters of a criminal.
           Have you beheld a tuft of winged seed
     That, from the dandelion's naked stalk
140 Mounted aloft, is suffered not to use
     Its natural gifts for purposes of rest,
     Driven by the autumnal whirlwind to and fro
     Through the wide element? or have you marked
     The heavier substance of a leaf-clad bough,
145 Within the vortex of a foaming flood,
     Tormented? by such aid you may conceive
     The perturbation of each mind;—ah, no!
     Desperate the Maid,—the Youth is stained with blood!
     But as the troubled seed and tortured bough
150 Is man, subjected to despotic sway.
           For him, by private influence with the Court,
     Was pardon gained, and liberty procured;

But not without exaction of a pledge
Which liberty and love dispersed in air.
155 He flew to her from whom they would divide him—
He clove to her who could not give him peace—
Yea, his first word of greeting was,—"All right
Is gone from me; my lately-towering hopes,
To the least fibre of their lowest root,
160 Are withered;—thou no longer canst be mine,
I thine—the conscience-stricken must not woo
The unruffled Innocent,—I see thy face,
Behold thee, and my misery is complete!"
   "One, are we not?" exclaim'd the Maiden—"One,
165 For innocence and youth, for weal and woe?"
Then, with the Father's name she coupled words
Of vehement indignation; but the Youth
Check'd her with filial meekness; for no thought
Uncharitable, no presumptuous rising
170 Of hasty censure, modelled in the eclipse
Of true domestic loyalty, did e'er
Find place within his bosom.—Once again
The persevering wedge of tyranny
Achieved their separation;—and once more
175 Were they united,—to be yet again
Disparted—pitiable lot! But here
A portion of the Tale may well be left
In silence, though my memory could add
Much how the Youth, in scanty space of time,
180 Was traversed from without; much, too, of thoughts
That occupied his days in solitude
Under privation and restraint; and what,
Through dark and shapeless fear of things to come,
And what, through strong compunction for the past,
185 He suffered—breaking down in heart and mind!
   Doomed to a third and last captivity,
His freedom he recovered on the eve
Of Julia's travail. When the babe was born
Its presence tempted him to cherish schemes
190 Of future happiness. "You shall return,
Julia," said he, "and to your Father's house
Go with the Child.—You have been wretched, yet
The silver shower, whose reckless burthen weighs
Too heavily upon the lily's head,
195 Oft leaves a saving moisture at its root.
Malice, beholding you, will melt away.

Go!—'tis a Town where both of us were born;
None will reproach you, for our truth is known;
And if, amid those once-bright bowers, our fate
200 Remain unpitied, pity is not in man.
With ornaments—the prettiest, nature yields
Or art can fashion, shall you deck your Boy,
And feed his countenance with your own sweet looks
Till no one can resist him.—Now, even now,
205 I see him sporting on the sunny lawn;
My Father from the window sees him too;
Startled, as if some new-created Thing
Enriched the earth, or Faery of the woods
Bounded before him;—but the unweeting Child
210 Shall by his beauty win his Grandsire's heart
So that it shall be softened, and our loves
End happily—as they began!" These gleams
Appeared but seldom: oftener was he seen
Propping a pale and melancholy face
215 Upon the Mother's bosom; resting thus
His head upon one breast, while from the other
The Babe was drawing in its quiet food.
—That pillow is no longer to be thine,
Fond Youth! that mournful solace now must pass
220 Into the list of things that cannot be!
Unwedded Julia, terror-smitten, hears
The sentence, by her Mother's lip pronounced,
That dooms her to a Convent.—Who shall tell,
Who dares report, the tidings to the Lord
225 Of her affections? So they blindly asked
Who knew not to what quiet depths a weight
Of agony had press'd the sufferer down;—
The word, by others dreaded, he can hear
Composed and silent, without visible sign
230 Of even the least emotion. Noting this
When the impatient Object of his love
Upbraided him with slackness, he returned
No answer, only took the Mother's hand
And kissed it—seemingly devoid of pain,
235 Or care, that what so tenderly he pressed,
Was a dependant upon the obdurate heart
Of One who came to disunite their lives
For ever—sad alternative! preferred,
By the unbending Parents of the Maid,
240 To secret 'spousals meanly disavowed.—

—So be it!
　　　　In the city he remained
A season after Julia had withdrawn
To those religious walls. He, too, departs—
Who with him?—even the senseless Little-one!
With that sole Charge he pass'd the city-gates
For the last time, attendant by the side
Of a close chair, a litter, or sedan,
In which the Babe was carried. To a hill,
That rose a brief league distant from the town,
The Dwellers in that house where he had lodged
Accompanied his steps, by anxious love
Impell'd:—they parted from him there, and stood
Watching below, till he had disappeared
On the hill-top. His eyes he scarcely took,
Throughout that journey, from the vehicle
(Slow-moving ark of all his hopes!) that veiled
The tender Infant: and at every inn,
And under every hospitable tree
At which the Bearers halted or reposed,
Laid him with timid care upon his knees,
And looked, as mothers ne'er were known to look,
Upon the Nursling which his arms embraced.
—This was the manner in which Vaudracour
Departed with his Infant; and thus reached
His Father's house, where to the innocent Child
Admittance was denied. The young Man spake
No words of indignation or reproof,
But of his Father begged, a last request,
That a retreat might be assigned to him
Where in forgotten quiet he might dwell,
With such allowance as his wants required;
For wishes he had none. To a Lodge that stood
Deep in a forest, with leave given, at the age
Of four-and-twenty summers he withdrew;
And thither took with him his infant Babe,
And one Domestic, for their common needs,
An aged Woman. It consoled him here
To attend upon the Orphan, and perform
Obsequious service to the precious Child,
Which, after a short time, by some mistake,
Or indiscretion of the Father, died.—
The Tale I follow to its last recess
Of suffering or of peace, I know not which;
Theirs be the blame who caused the woe, not mine!
From this time forth he never shared a smile
With mortal creature. An Inhabitant
Of that same Town, in which the Pair had left
So lively a remembrance of their griefs,
By chance of business, coming within reach
Of his retirement, to the spot repaired
With an intent to visit him. He reached
The house, and only found the Matron there,
Who told him that his pains were thrown away,
For that her Master never uttered word
To living Thing—not even to her.—Behold!
While they were speaking, Vaudracour approached;
But, seeing some one near, even as his hand
Was stretched towards the garden gate, he shrunk—
And, like a shadow, glided out of view.
Shocked at his savage aspect, from the place
The Visitor retired.
　　　　Thus lived the Youth
Cut off from all intelligence with man,
And shunning even the light of common day;
Nor could the voice of Freedom, which through France
Full speedily resounded, public hope,
Or personal memory of his own deep wrongs,
Rouse him: but in those solitary shades
His days he wasted, an imbecile mind!

from *The Poetical Works of William Wordsworth. In Five Volumes* (1827)

*Scorn not the Sonnet;
Critic, you have frowned*

Scorn not the Sonnet; Critic, you have frowned,
Mindless of its just honours;—with this Key
Shakspeare unlocked his heart; the melody
Of this small Lute gave ease to Petrarch's wound;
A thousand times this Pipe did Tasso sound;

Camöens soothed with it an Exile's grief;[1]
The Sonnet glittered a gay myrtle Leaf
Amid the cypress with which Dante crowned
His visionary brow: a glow-worm Lamp,
It cheered mild Spenser, called from Faery-land
To struggle through dark ways; and when a damp
Fell round the path of Milton, in his hand
The Thing became a Trumpet, whence he blew
Soul-animating strains—alas, too few!

from the *Athenæum* (12 December 1835)

The Ettrick Shepherd. Extempore Effusion, upon reading, in the Newcastle Journal, the notice of the Death of the Poet, James Hogg[2]

When first, descending from the Moorlands,
I saw the stream of Yarrow glide
Along a bare and open valley,
The Ettrick Shepherd was my guide.

When last along its banks I wandered,
Thro' groves that had begun to shed
Their golden leaves upon the pathways,
My steps the Border Minstrel led.[3]

The mighty Minstrel breathes no longer,
'Mid mouldering ruins low he lies;
And death upon the Braes of Yarrow
Has closed the Shepherd-poet's eyes:

Nor has the rolling year twice measured,
From sign to sign, his stedfast course,
Since every Mortal Power of Coleridge
Was frozen at its marvellous source;[4]

The rapt One of the Godlike forehead,
The heaven-eyed Creature, sleeps in earth;
And Lamb, the frolic and the gentle,
Has vanished from his lonely hearth.[5]

Like clouds that rake the mountain-summits,
Or waves that own no curbing hand,
How fast has Brother followed Brother
From sunshine to the sunless land!

Yet I, whose lids from infant slumbers
Were earlier raised, remain to hear
A timid voice, that asks in whispers,
"Who next will drop and disappear?"

Our haughty life is crowned with darkness,
Like London with its own black wreath,
On which, with thee, O Crabbe, forth-looking
I gazed from Hampstead's breezy heath;

As if but yesterday departed,
Thou too art gone before;[6] yet why
For ripe fruit seasonably gathered
Should frail survivors heave a sigh?[7]

No more of old romantic sorrows
For slaughtered Youth or love-lorn Maid!

---

[1] The Portuguese poet Luis de Camoens (1524–80) and the Italian poet Torquato Tasso (1544–95) are, like most of the poets mentioned in this sonnet, best known for longer works.

[2] signed and dated "Wm. Wordsworth. Rydal Mount, Nov. 30, 1835." At the end of the poem, W.W. adds the following note: "In the above there is an expression borrowed from a Sonnet by Mr. G. Bell, the Author of a small volume of Poems lately printed at Penrith. Speaking of Skiddaw, he says, 'Yon dark cloud rakes and shrouds its noble brow.' These poems, though incorrect often in expression and metre, do honour to their unpretending Author; and may be added to the number of proofs daily occurring, that a finer perception of the appearances of Nature is spreading through the humbler classes of society." Skiddaw, near Keswick in the Lake District, is the fourth highest mountain in England.

[3] Sir Walter Scott* lived in—and wrote about—the border country between England and Scotland; he died in Sept. 1832.

[4] Samuel Taylor Coleridge* died July 1834.

[5] Charles Lamb* died Dec. 1834.

[6] George Crabbe* died Feb. 1832.

[7] Wordsworth later added the following stanza:
   Mourn rather for that holy Spirit,
   Sweet as the spring, as ocean deep;
   For Her who, ere her summer faded,
   Has sunk into a breathless sleep.
The "holy Spirit" is Felicia Hemans,* who died 16 May 1835.

WILLIAM WORDSWORTH

With sharper grief is Yarrow smitten,
40 And Ettrick mourns with her their Shepherd dead!

from Poems, Chiefly of Early and Late Years; including The Borderers, A Tragedy (1842)

The unremitting voice of nightly streams

The unremitting voice of nightly streams
That wastes so oft, we think, its tuneful powers,
If neither soothing to the worm that gleams
Through dewy grass, nor small birds hushed in bowers,
5 Nor unto silent leaves and drowsy flowers,—
That voice of unpretending harmony
(For who what is shall measure by what seems
To be, or not to be,
Or tax high Heaven with prodigality?)
10 Wants not a healing influence that can creep
Into the human breast, and mix with sleep
To regulate the motion of our dreams
For kindly issues—as through every clime
Was felt near murmuring brooks in earliest time;
15 As at this day, the rudest swains who dwell
Where torrents roar, or hear the tinkling knell
Of water-breaks, with grateful heart could tell.

from *The Prelude 1799, 1805, 1850*, ed. Jonathan Wordsworth, M.H. Abrams, and Stephen Gill (1979)

The Two-Part Prelude of 1799[1]

FIRST PART[2]

Was it for this
That one, the fairest of all rivers, loved
To blend his murmurs with my nurse's song,
And from his alder shades and rocky falls,
5 And from his fords and shallows, sent a voice
That flowed along my dreams? For this didst thou,
O Derwent,[3] travelling over the green plains
Near my "sweet birthplace,"[4] didst thou, beauteous stream,
Make ceaseless music through the night and day,
10 Which with its steady cadence tempering
Our human waywardness, composed my thoughts
To more than infant softness, giving me

---

[1] This is the earliest version of the *Prelude*, largely written in Goslar, Germany, in 1798–99; this version of the poem was not published until 1974 (ed. Jonathan Wordsworth and Stephen Gill in *The Norton Anthology of English Literature*, 3rd ed.). Wordsworth then went on to write a five-book version of the *Prelude* in 1804; unfortunately this survives only in fragments. The following year, he completed a thirteen-book poem, including an account of his experience at Cambridge and in France during the revolutionary period, and tracing his intellectual commitments and disillusionments. Wordsworth laid aside this 1805 version of the *Prelude*, which was first published in 1926 (ed. Ernest de Selincourt). The 1850 *Prelude*, published a few weeks after his death, was the result of three major revisions and many minor changes over the intervening years.

Wordsworth envisioned the *Prelude* as a "preparatory poem" for a much larger project, a long three-part philosophical poem called *The Recluse*. He never finished this ambitious project, but the second part became the nine-book poem, *The Excursion*, published separately in 1814. See notes to "Home at Grasmere," above, and Wordsworth's Preface to *The Excursion*. The title, *The Prelude*, was assigned to the 1850 poem by the poet's widow, Mary Wordsworth.

[2] With lines 1–246, cf. 1805 *Prelude* 1.271–524 and 1850 *Prelude* 1.269–498.

[3] The river Derwent flows past the house in Cockermouth where Wordsworth was born.

[4] Coleridge, "Frost at Midnight" 28.*

　　　　Among the fretful dwellings of mankind
　　　　A knowledge, a dim earnest, of the calm
15　　　Which Nature breathes among the fields and groves?
　　　　Beloved Derwent, fairest of all streams,
　　　　Was it for this that I, a four years' child,
　　　　A naked boy, among thy silent pools
　　　　Made one long bathing of a summer's day,
20　　　Basked in the sun, or plunged into thy streams,
　　　　Alternate, all a summer's day, or coursed
　　　　Over the sandy fields, and dashed the flowers
　　　　Of yellow grunsel;[1] or, when crag and hill,
　　　　The woods, and distant Skiddaw's[2] lofty height,
25　　　Were bronzed with a deep radiance, stood alone
　　　　A naked savage in the thunder-shower?

　　　　　　And afterwards ('twas in a later day,
　　　　Though early), when upon the mountain slope
　　　　The frost and breath of frosty wind had snapped
30　　　The last autumnal crocus, 'twas my joy
　　　　To wander half the night among the cliffs
　　　　And the smooth hollows where the woodcocks ran
　　　　Along the moonlight turf. In thought and wish
　　　　That time, my shoulder all with springes[3] hung,
35　　　I was a fell destroyer. Gentle powers,
　　　　Who give us happiness and call it peace,
　　　　When scudding on from snare to snare I plied
　　　　My anxious visitation, hurrying on,
　　　　Still hurrying, hurrying onward, how my heart
40　　　Panted; among the scattered yew-trees and the crags
　　　　That looked upon me, how my bosom beat
　　　　With expectation! Sometimes strong desire
　　　　Resistless overpowered me, and the bird
　　　　Which was the captive of another's toils
45　　　Became my prey; and when the deed was done
　　　　I heard among the solitary hills
　　　　Low breathings coming after me, and sounds
　　　　Of undistinguishable motion, steps
　　　　Almost as silent as the turf they trod.

50　　　　　Nor less in springtime, when on southern banks
　　　　The shining sun had from his knot of leaves
　　　　Decoyed the primrose flower, and when the vales
　　　　And woods were warm, was I a rover then
　　　　In the high places, on the lonesome peaks,
55　　　Among the mountains and the winds. Though mean
　　　　And though inglorious were my views, the end
　　　　Was not ignoble. Oh, when I have hung
　　　　Above the raven's nest, by knots of grass
　　　　Or half-inch fissures in the slipp'ry rock
60　　　But ill sustained, and almost, as it seemed,
　　　　Suspended by the blast which blew amain,
　　　　Shouldering the naked crag, oh, at that time,
　　　　While on the perilous ridge I hung alone,
　　　　With what strange utterance did the loud dry wind
65　　　Blow through my ears; the sky seemed not a sky
　　　　Of earth, and with what motion moved the clouds!

　　　　　　The mind of man is fashioned and built up
　　　　Even as a strain of music. I believe
　　　　That there are spirits which, when they would form
70　　　A favored being, from his very dawn
　　　　Of infancy do open out the clouds
　　　　As at the touch of lightning, seeking him
　　　　With gentle visitation—quiet powers,
　　　　Retired, and seldom recognized, yet kind,
75　　　And to the very meanest not unknown—
　　　　With me, though rarely, in my boyish days
　　　　They communed. Others too there are, who use,
　　　　Yet haply aiming at the self-same end,
　　　　Severer interventions, ministry
80　　　More palpable—and of their school was I.

　　　　　　They guided me: one evening led by them
　　　　I went alone into a shepherd's boat,
　　　　A skiff, that to a willow-tree was tied
　　　　Within a rocky cave, its usual home.
85　　　The moon was up, the lake was shining clear
　　　　Among the hoary mountains; from the shore
　　　　I pushed, and struck the oars, and struck again
　　　　In cadence, and my little boat moved on
　　　　Just like a man who walks with stately step
90　　　Though bent on speed.[4] It was an act of stealth
　　　　And troubled pleasure. Not without the voice
　　　　Of mountain echoes did my boat move on,

---

[1] ragweed.

[2] a mountain in the Lake District, nine miles (14 km) east of Cockermouth.

[3] snares.

[4] Cf. Milton, *Paradise Lost* 12.2.

Leaving behind her still on either side
Small circles glittering idly in the moon,
95 Until they melted all into one track
Of sparkling light.¹ A rocky steep uprose
Above the cavern of the willow-tree,
And now, as suited one who proudly rowed
With his best skill, I fixed a steady view
100 Upon the top of that same craggy ridge,
The bound of the horizon—for behind
Was nothing but the stars and the grey sky.
She was an elfin pinnace; twenty times
I dipped my oars into the silent lake,
105 And as I rose upon the stroke my boat
Went heaving through the water like a swan—
When from behind that rocky steep, till then
The bound of the horizon, a huge cliff,
As if with voluntary power instinct,
110 Upreared its head. I struck, and struck again,
And, growing still in stature, the huge cliff
Rose up between me and the stars, and still,
With measured motion, like a living thing
Strode after me. With trembling hands I turned,
115 And through the silent water stole my way
Back to the cavern of the willow-tree.
There in her mooring-place I left my bark,
And through the meadows homeward went with grave
And serious thoughts; and after I had seen
120 That spectacle, for many days my brain
Worked with a dim and undetermined sense
Of unknown modes of being. In my thoughts
There was a darkness—call it solitude,
Or blank desertion—no familiar shapes
125 Of hourly objects, images of trees,
Of sea or sky, no colours of green fields,
But huge and mighty forms that do not live
Like living men moved slowly through my mind
By day, and were the trouble of my dreams.

130   Ah, not in vain ye beings of the hills,
And ye that walk the woods and open heaths
By moon or star-light, thus, from my first dawn
Of childhood, did ye love to intertwine

The passions that build up our human soul
135 Not with the mean and vulgar works of man,
But with high objects, with eternal things,
With life and Nature, purifying thus
The elements of feeling and of thought,
And sanctifying by such discipline
140 Both pain and fear, until we recognise
A grandeur in the beatings of the heart.
Nor was this fellowship vouchsafed to me
With stinted kindness. In November days,
When vapours rolling down the valleys made
145 A lonely scene more lonesome, among woods
At noon, and 'mid the calm of summer nights
When by the margin of the trembling lake
Beneath the gloomy hills I homeward went
In solitude, such intercourse was mine.

150   And in the frosty season, when the sun
Was set, and visible for many a mile
The cottage windows through the twilight blazed,
I heeded not the summons. Clear and loud
The village clock tolled six; I wheeled about
155 Proud and exulting, like an untired horse
That cares not for its home. All shod with steel
We hissed along the polished ice in games
Confederate, imitative of the chace
And woodland pleasures, the resounding horn,
160 The pack loud bellowing, and the hunted hare.
So through the darkness and the cold we flew,
And not a voice was idle. With the din,
Meanwhile, the precipices rang aloud;
The leafless trees and every icy crag
165 Tinkled like iron; while the distant hills
Into the tumult sent an alien sound
Of melancholy, not unnoticed; while the stars,
Eastward, were sparkling clear, and in the west
The orange sky of evening died away.

170   Not seldom from the uproar I retired
Into a silent bay, or sportively
Glanced sideway, leaving the tumultuous throng,
To cut across the shadow of a star
That gleamed upon the ice. And oftentimes
175 When we had given our bodies to the wind,
And all the shadowy banks on either side

---

¹ Cf. Coleridge, "The Rime of the Ancyent Marinere" (1798) 265–66.*

Came sweeping through the darkness, spinning still
The rapid line of motion, then at once
Have I, reclining back upon my heels
180 Stopped short—yet still the solitary cliffs
Wheeled by me, even as if the earth had rolled
With visible motion her diurnal round.[1]
Behind me did they stretch in solemn train,
Feebler and feebler, and I stood and watched
185 Till all was tranquil as a summer sea.

    Ye powers of earth, ye genii of the springs,
And ye that have your voices in the clouds,
And ye that are familiars of the lakes
And of the standing pools,[2] I may not think
190 A vulgar hope was yours when ye employed
Such ministry—when ye through many a year
Thus, by the agency of boyish sports,
On caves and trees, upon the woods and hills,
Impressed upon all forms the characters
195 Of danger or desire, and thus did make
The surface of the universal earth
With meanings of delight, of hope and fear,
Work like a sea.

           Not uselessly employed,
I might pursue this theme through every change
200 Of exercise and sport to which the year
Did summon us in its delightful round.
We were a noisy crew; the sun in heaven
Beheld not vales more beautiful than ours,
Nor saw a race in happiness and joy
205 More worthy of the fields where they were sown.
I would record with no reluctant voice
Our home amusements by the warm peat fire
At evening, when with pencil and with slate,
In square divisions parcelled out, and all
210 With crosses and with cyphers scribbled o'er,[3]
We schemed and puzzled, head opposed to head,
In strife too humble to be named in verse;
Or round the naked table, snow-white deal,
Cherry, or maple, sate in close array,
215 And to the combat—lu or whist—led on
A thick-ribbed army, not as in the world
Discarded and ungratefully thrown by
Even for the very service they had wrought,
But husbanded through many a long campaign.
220 Oh, with what echoes on the boards they fell—
Ironic diamonds, hearts of sable hue,
Queens gleaming through their splendour's last decay,
Knaves wrapt in one assimilating gloom,
And kings indignant at the shame incurred
225 By royal visages.[4] Meanwhile abroad
The heavy rain was falling, or the frost
Raged bitterly with keen and silent tooth,
And, interrupting the impassioned game,
Oft from the neighbouring lake the splitting ice,
230 While it sank down towards the water, sent
Among the meadows and the hills its long
And frequent yellings, imitative some
Of wolves that howl along the Bothnic main.[5]

    Nor with less willing heart would I rehearse
235 The woods of autumn, and their hidden bowers
With milk-white clusters hung;[6] the rod and line—
True symbol of the foolishness of hope—
Which with its strong enchantment led me on
By rocks and pools, where never summer star
240 Impressed its shadow, to forlorn cascades
Among the windings of the mountain-brooks;
The kite[7] in sultry calms from some high hill
Sent up, ascending thence till it was lost
Among the fleecy clouds—in gusty days
245 Launched from the lower grounds, and suddenly
Dashed headlong and rejected by the storm.
All these, and more, with rival claims demand
Grateful acknowledgement. It were a song
Venial, and such as—if I rightly judge—
250 I might protract unblamed, but I perceive
That much is overlooked, and we should ill
Attain our object if, from delicate fears

---

[1] Cf. "A Slumber Did My Spirit Seal" 7.*

[2] Cf. Shakespeare, *The Tempest* 5.1.33.

[3] Cf. Milton, *Paradise Lost* 8.83.

[4] Cf. Pope, *The Rape of the Lock* (1714) 3.37–100; and Cowper,* *The Task* 4.218–19.

[5] the northern Baltic Sea.

[6] Cf. Wordsworth's poem "Nutting."*

[7] a bird of prey.

Of breaking in upon the unity
Of this my argument, I should omit
255 To speak of such effects as cannot here
Be regularly classed, yet tend no less
To the same point, the growth of mental power
And love of Nature's works.

      Ere I had seen[1]
Eight summers—and 'twas in the very week
260 When I was first transplanted to thy vale,
Beloved Hawkshead;[2] when thy paths, thy shores
And brooks, were like a dream of novelty
To my half-infant mind—I chanced to cross
One of those open fields which, shaped like ears,
265 Make green peninsulas on Esthwaite's lake.
Twilight was coming on, yet through the gloom
I saw distinctly on the opposite shore,
Beneath a tree and close by the lake side,
A heap of garments, as if left by one
270 Who there was bathing. Half an hour I watched
And no one owned them; meanwhile the calm lake
Grew dark with all the shadows on its breast,
And now and then a leaping fish disturbed
The breathless stillness. The succeeding day
275 There came a company, and in their boat
Sounded with iron hooks and with long poles.
At length the dead man, 'mid that beauteous scene
Of trees and hills and water, bolt upright
Rose with his ghastly face.[3] I might advert
280 To numerous accidents in flood or field,[4]
Quarry or moor, or 'mid the winter snows,
Distresses and disasters, tragic facts
Of rural history, that impressed my mind
With images to which in following years
285 Far other feelings were attached—with forms
That yet exist with independent life,
And, like their archetypes, know no decay.

There are in our existence spots of time[5]
Which with distinct preeminence retain
290 A fructifying virtue, whence, depressed
By trivial occupations and the round
Of ordinary intercourse, our minds—
Especially the imaginative power—
Are nourished and invisibly repaired;
295 Such moments chiefly seem to have their date
In our first childhood. I remember well
('Tis of an early season that I speak,
The twilight of rememberable life),
While I was yet an urchin, one who scarce
300 Could hold a bridle, with ambitious hopes
I mounted, and we rode towards the hills.
We were a pair of horsemen: honest James[6]
Was with me, my encourager and guide.
We had not travelled long ere some mischance
305 Disjoined me from my comrade, and, through fear
Dismounting, down the rough and stony moor
I led my horse, and stumbling on, at length
Came to a bottom where in former times
A man, the murderer of his wife, was hung
310 In irons.[7] Mouldered was the gibbet-mast;
The bones were gone, the iron and the wood;
Only a long green ridge of turf remained
Whose shape was like a grave. I left the spot,
And reascending the bare slope I saw
315 A naked pool that lay beneath the hills,
The beacon on the summit, and more near
A girl who bore a pitcher on her head
And seemed with difficult steps to force her way
Against the blowing wind. It was in truth
320 An ordinary sight, but I should need
Colours and words that are unknown to man
To paint the visionary dreariness
Which, while I looked all round for my lost guide,
Did at that time invest the naked pool,

---

[1] With lines 258–87, cf. 1805 *Prelude* 5.450–81 and 1850 *Prelude* 5.426–59.

[2] Wordsworth moved to Hawkshead to attend school there in 1779.

[3] that of a schoolmaster called James Jackson, who drowned in Esthwaite Water on 18 June 1779.

[4] Cf. Shakespeare, *Othello* 1.3.135.

[5] With lines 288–327, cf. 1805 *Prelude* 11.257–315 and 1850 *Prelude* 12.208–61.

[6] probably a servant of Wordsworth's grandparents, who lived in Penrith.

[7] Wordsworth is thinking of two murderers: Thomas Nicholson killed a butcher and was hanged at Penrith in 1767; the wife-murderer, Thomas Lancaster, was hanged at Hawkshead in 1672.

       The beacon on the lonely eminence,
325 The woman and her garments vexed and tossed
       By the strong wind.

               Nor less I recollect—
Long after, though my childhood had not ceased—
Another scene which left a kindred power
330 Implanted in my mind. One Christmas-time,[1]
The day before the holidays began,
Feverish, and tired, and restless, I went forth
Into the fields, impatient for the sight
Of those three horses which should bear us home,
335 My brothers and myself. There was a crag,
An eminence, which from the meeting-point
Of two highways ascending overlooked
At least a long half-mile of those two roads,
By each of which the expected steeds might come—
340 The choice uncertain. Thither I repaired
Up to the highest summit. 'Twas a day
Stormy, and rough, and wild, and on the grass
I sate half sheltered by a naked wall.
Upon my right hand was a single sheep,
345 A whistling hawthorn on my left, and there,
Those two companions at my side, I watched
With eyes intensely straining, as the mist
Gave intermitting prospects of the wood
And plain beneath. Ere I to school returned
350 That dreary time, ere I had been ten days
A dweller in my father's house, he died,
And I and my two brothers, orphans then,[2]
Followed his body to the grave. The event,
With all the sorrow which it brought, appeared
355 A chastisement; and when I called to mind
That day so lately passed, when from the crag
I looked in such anxiety of hope,
With trite reflections of morality,
Yet with the deepest passion, I bowed low
360 To God who thus corrected my desires.
And afterwards the wind and sleety rain,
And all the business of the elements,
The single sheep, and the one blasted tree,
And the bleak music of that old stone wall,
365 The noise of wood and water, and the mist
Which on the line of each of those two roads
Advanced in such indisputable shapes—
All these were spectacles and sounds to which
I often would repair, and thence would drink
370 As at a fountain. And I do not doubt
That in this later time, when storm and rain
Beat on my roof at midnight, or by day
When I am in the woods, unknown to me
The workings of my spirit thence are brought.

375   Nor, sedulous as I have been to trace[3]
How Nature by collateral interest,
And by extrinsic passion, peopled first
My mind with forms or beautiful or grand
And made me love them, may I well forget
380 How other pleasures have been mine, and joys
Of subtler origin—how I have felt
Not seldom, even in that tempestuous time,
Those hallowed and pure motions of the sense[4]
Which seem in their simplicity to own
385 An intellectual charm, that calm delight
Which, if I err not, surely must belong
To those first-born affinities that fit
Our new existence to existing things,
And, in our dawn of being, constitute
390 The bond of union betwixt life and joy.

    Yes, I remember when the changeful earth
And twice five seasons on my mind had stamped
The faces of the moving year, even then,
A child, I held unconscious intercourse
395 With the eternal beauty, drinking in
A pure organic pleasure from the lines
Of curling mist, or from the level plain
Of waters coloured by the steady clouds.
The sands of Westmoreland,[5] the creeks and bays

---

[1] in the year 1783. With lines 330–74, cf. 1805 *Prelude* 11.344–88 and 1850 *Prelude* 12.287–335.

[2] Wordsworth's father John died on 30 December 1783; his mother had died in 1778.

[3] With lines 375–464, cf. 1805 *Prelude* 1.571–663 and 1850 *Prelude* 1.544–636.

[4] Cf. Shakespeare, *Measure for Measure* 1.4.59.

[5] one of the two counties (Cumberland and Westmoreland) that constitute the English Lake District.

400 Of Cumbria's[1] rocky limits, they can tell
     How when the sea threw off his evening shade
     And to the shepherd's hut beneath the crags
     Did send sweet notice of the rising moon,
     How I have stood, to images like these
405 A stranger, linking with the spectacle
     No body of associated forms,
     And bringing with me no peculiar sense
     Of quietness or peace—yet I have stood
     Even while my eye has moved o'er three long leagues[2]
410 Of shining water, gathering, as it seemed,
     Through the wide surface of that field of light
     New pleasure, like a bee among the flowers.

     Thus often in those fits of vulgar joy
     Which through all seasons on a child's pursuits
415 Are prompt attendants, 'mid that giddy bliss
     Which like a tempest works along the blood[3]
     And is forgotten, even then I felt
     Gleams like the flashing of a shield. The earth
     And common face of Nature spake to me
420 Rememberable things—sometimes, 'tis true,
     By quaint associations, yet not vain
     Nor profitless, if haply they impressed
     Collateral objects and appearances,
     Albeit lifeless then, and doomed to sleep
425 Until maturer seasons called them forth
     To impregnate and to elevate the mind.
     And if the vulgar joy by its own weight
     Wearied itself out of the memory,
     The scenes which were a witness of that joy
430 Remained, in their substantial lineaments
     Depicted on the brain, and to the eye
     Were visible, a daily sight. And thus
     By the impressive agency of fear,
     By pleasure and repeated happiness—
435 So frequently repeated—and by force
     Of obscure feelings representative
     Of joys that were forgotten, these same scenes,
     So beauteous and majestic in themselves,
     Though yet the day was distant, did at length

440 Become habitually dear, and all
     Their hues and forms were by invisible links
     Allied to the affections.

                                          I began
     My story early, feeling, as I fear,
     The weakness of a human love for days
445 Disowned by memory—ere the birth of spring
     Planting my snowdrops among winter snows.
     Nor will it seem to thee, my friend, so prompt
     In sympathy, that I have lengthened out
     With fond and feeble tongue a tedious tale.
450 Meanwhile my hope has been that I might fetch
     Reproaches from my former years, whose power
     May spur me on, in manhood now mature,
     To honourable toil. Yet should it be
     That this is but an impotent desire—
455 That I by such inquiry am not taught
     To understand myself, nor thou to know
     With better knowledge how the heart was framed
     Of him thou lovest—need I dread from thee
     Harsh judgements if I am so loth to quit
460 Those recollected hours that have the charm
     Of visionary things, and lovely forms
     And sweet sensations, that throw back our life
     And make our infancy a visible scene
     On which the sun is shining?

                         SECOND PART

     Thus far, my friend, have we retraced the way[4]
     Through which I travelled when I first began
     To love the woods and fields; the passion yet
     Was in its birth, sustained, as might befal,
5   By nourishment that came unsought—for still
     From week to week, from month to month, we lived
     A round of tumult. Duly were our games
     Prolonged in summer till the daylight failed:
     No chair remained before the doors, the bench
10   And threshold steps were empty, fast asleep
     The labourer and the old man who had sate

---

[1] Cumberland's.

[2] A league is about three miles (just under 5 km).

[3] Cf. "Tintern Abbey" 28.*

[4] The "friend" is Coleridge.* With lines 1–139, cf. 1805 *Prelude* 2.1–144 and 1850 *Prelude* 2.1–137.

      A later lingerer, yet the revelry
Continued and the loud uproar. At last,
When all the ground was dark and the huge clouds
15 Were edged with twinkling stars, to bed we went
With weary joints and with a beating mind.
Ah, is there one who ever has been young
And needs a monitory voice to tame
The pride of virtue and of intellect?
20 And is there one, the wisest and the best
Of all mankind, who does not sometimes wish
For things which cannot be, who would not give,
If so he might, to duty and to truth
The eagerness of infantine desire?
25 A tranquillizing spirit presses now
On my corporeal frame,[1] so wide appears
The vacancy between me and those days,
Which yet have such self-presence in my heart
That sometimes when I think of them I seem
30 Two consciousnesses—conscious of myself,
And of some other being.

                A grey stone
Of native rock, left midway in the square
Of our small market-village, was the home
And centre of these joys; and when, returned
35 After long absence thither I repaired,
I found that it was split and gone to build
A smart assembly-room[2] that perked and flared
With wash and rough-cast, elbowing the ground
Which had been ours. But let the fiddle scream,
40 And be ye happy! Yet I know, my friends,
That more than one of you will think with me
Of those soft starry nights, and that old dame
From whom the stone was named, who there had sate
And watched her table with its huckster's wares,
45 Assiduous, for the length of sixty years.

      We ran a boisterous race, the year span round
With giddy motion; but the time approached
That brought with it a regular desire
For calmer pleasures—when the beauteous scenes
50 Of Nature were collaterally attached

To every scheme of holiday delight,
And every boyish sport, less grateful else
And languidly pursued. When summer came
It was the pastime of our afternoons
55 To beat along the plain of Windermere
With rival oars; and the selected bourn
Was now an island musical with birds
That sang for ever, now a sister isle
Beneath the oak's umbrageous covert, sown
60 With lilies-of-the-valley like a field,
And now a third small island[3] where remained
An old stone table and one mouldered cave—
A hermit's history. In such a race,
So ended, disappointment could be none,
65 Uneasiness, or pain, or jealousy;
We rested in the shade, all pleased alike,
Conquered or conqueror. Thus our selfishness
Was mellowed down, and thus the pride of strength
And the vainglory of superior skill
70 Were interfused with objects which subdued
And tempered them, and gradually produced
A quiet independence of the heart.
And to my friend who knows me I may add,
Unapprehensive of reproof, that hence
75 Ensued a diffidence and modesty,
And I was taught to feel—perhaps too much—
The self-sufficing power of solitude.
      No delicate viands sapped our bodily strength:
More than we wished we knew the blessing then
80 Of vigorous hunger, for our daily meals
Were frugal, Sabine[4] fare—and then, exclude
A little weekly stipend, and we lived
Through three divisions of the quartered year
In pennyless poverty. But now, to school
85 Returned from the half-yearly holidays,
We came with purses more profusely filled,
Allowance which abundantly sufficed
To gratify the palate with repasts
More costly than the dame of whom I spake,

---

[1] Cf. "Tintern Abbey" 44–46.*

[2] Hawkshead Town Hall, built in 1790.

[3] Lady Holm, an island in Windermere once the site of a chapel dedicated to the Virgin Mary.

[4] frugal (like the Roman poet Horace, who retired to his "Sabine farm," named for the ancient tribe that had once inhabited that area of Italy).

90　That ancient woman, and her board, supplied.
　　Hence inroads into distant vales, and long
　　Excursions far away among the hills,
　　Hence rustic dinners on the cool green ground—
　　Or in the woods, or by a river-side
95　Or fountain—festive banquets, that provoked
　　The languid action of a natural scene
　　By pleasure of corporeal appetite.
　　　　Nor is my aim neglected if I tell
　　How twice in the long length of those half-years
100　We from our funds perhaps with bolder hand
　　Drew largely, anxious for one day at least
　　To feel the motion of the galloping steed;
　　And with the good old innkeeper, in truth
　　I needs must say, that sometimes we have used
105　Sly subterfuge, for the intended bound
　　Of the day's journey was too distant far
　　For any cautious man: a structure famed
　　Beyond its neighbourhood, the antique walls
　　Of a large abbey,[1] with its fractured arch,
110　Belfry, and images, and living trees—
　　A holy scene. Along the smooth green turf
　　Our horses grazed. In more than inland peace,
　　Left by the winds that overpass the vale,
　　In that sequestered ruin trees and towers—
115　Both silent and both motionless alike—
　　Hear all day long the murmuring sea that beats
　　Incessantly upon a craggy shore.
　　　　Our steeds remounted, and the summons given,
　　With whip and spur we by the chantry flew
120　In uncouth race, and left the cross-legged knight
　　And the stone abbot, and that single wren
　　Which one day sang so sweetly in the nave
　　Of the old church that, though from recent showers
　　The earth was comfortless, and, touched by faint
125　Internal breezes, from the roofless walls
　　The shuddering ivy dripped large drops, yet still
　　So sweetly 'mid the gloom the invisible bird
　　Sang to itself that there I could have made
　　My dwelling-place, and lived for ever there,
130　To hear such music. Through the walls we flew
　　And down the valley, and, a circuit made
　　In wantonness of heart, through rough and smooth
　　We scampered homeward. O, ye rocks and streams,
　　And that still spirit of the evening air,
135　Even in this joyous time I sometimes felt
　　Your presence, when, with slackened step, we breathed
　　Along the sides of the steep hills, or when,
　　Lightened by gleams of moonlight from the sea,
　　We beat with thundering hoofs the level sand.
140　　　There was a row of ancient trees, since fallen,
　　That on the margin of a jutting land
　　Stood near the lake of Coniston, and made,
　　With its long boughs above the water stretched,
　　A gloom through which a boat might sail along
145　As in a cloister. An old hall[2] was near,
　　Grotesque and beautiful, its gavel-end[3]
　　And huge round chimneys to the top o'ergrown
　　With fields of ivy. Thither we repaired—
　　'Twas even a custom with us—to the shore,
150　And to that cool piazza. They who dwelt
　　In the neglected mansion-house supplied
　　Fresh butter, tea-kettle and earthenware,
　　And chafing-dish with smoking coals; and so
　　Beneath the trees we sate in our small boat,
155　And in the covert eat our delicate meal
　　Upon the calm smooth lake. It was a joy
　　Worthy the heart of one who is full grown
　　To rest beneath those horizontal boughs
　　And mark the radiance of the setting sun,
160　Himself unseen, reposing on the top
　　Of the high eastern hills. And there I said,
　　That beauteous sight before me, there I said
　　(Then first beginning in my thoughts to mark
　　That sense of dim similitude which links
165　Our moral feelings with external forms)
　　That in whatever region I should close
　　My mortal life I would remember you,
　　Fair scenes—that dying I would think on you,
　　My soul would send a longing look to you,
170　Even as that setting sun, while all the vale
　　Could nowhere catch one faint memorial gleam,
　　Yet with the last remains of his last light
　　Still lingered, and a farewell lustre threw

---

[1] Furness Abbey, about 20 miles (32 km) south of Hawkshead.

[2] Coniston Hall; the village of Coniston is a few miles west of Hawkshead.

[3] gable-end.

On the dear mountain-tops where first he rose.
175 'Twas then my fourteenth summer, and these words
Were uttered in a casual access
Of sentiment, a momentary trance
That far outran the habit of my mind.
   Upon the eastern shore of Windermere[1]
180 Above the crescent of a pleasant bay
There was an inn,[2] no homely-featured shed,
Brother of the surrounding cottages,
But 'twas a splendid place, the door beset
With chaises, grooms, and liveries, and within
185 Decanters, glasses and the blood-red wine.
In ancient times, or ere the hall was built
On the large island, had the dwelling been
More worthy of a poet's love, a hut
Proud of its one bright fire and sycamore shade;
190 But though the rhymes were gone which once inscribed
The threshold, and large golden characters
On the blue-frosted signboard had usurped
The place of the old lion, in contempt
And mockery of the rustic painter's hand,
195 Yet to this hour the spot to me is dear
With all its foolish pomp. The garden lay
Upon a slope surmounted by the plain
Of a small bowling-green; beneath us stood
A grove, with gleams of water through the trees
200 And over the tree-tops—nor did we want
Refreshment, strawberries and mellow cream—
And there through half an afternoon we played
On the smooth platform, and the shouts we sent
Made all the mountains ring. But ere the fall
205 Of night, when in our pinnace we returned
Over the dusky lake, and to the beach
Of some small island steered our course, with one,
The minstrel of our troop, and left him there,
And rowed off gently, while he blew his flute
210 Alone upon the rock,[3] oh, then the calm
And dead still water lay upon my mind
Even with a weight of pleasure, and the sky,

---

[1] With lines 179–514, cf. 1805 *Prelude* 2.145–484 and 1850 *Prelude* 2.138–471.

[2] the White Lion Inn, Bowness.

[3] Robert Greenwood, the flute-player, later became Senior Fellow of Trinity College, Cambridge.

Never before so beautiful, sank down
Into my heart and held me like a dream.
215   Thus day by day my sympathies increased,
And thus the common range of visible things
Grew dear to me: already I began
To love the sun, a boy I loved the sun
Not as I since have loved him—as a pledge
220 And surety of my earthly life, a light
Which while I view I feel I am alive—
But for this cause, that I had seen him lay
His beauty on the morning hills, had seen
The western mountain touch his setting orb
225 In many a thoughtless hour, when from excess
Of happiness my blood appeared to flow
With its own pleasure, and I breathed with joy.
And from like feelings, humble though intense,
To patriotic and domestic love
230 Analogous, the moon to me was dear:
For I would dream away my purposes
Standing to look upon her, while she hung
Midway between the hills as if she knew
No other region but belonged to thee,
235 Yea, appertained by a peculiar right
To thee and thy grey huts, my native vale.

   Those incidental charms which first attached
My heart to rural objects, day by day
Grew weaker, and I hasten on to tell
240 How Nature, intervenient till this time
And secondary, now at length was sought
For her own sake. But who shall parcel out
His intellect by geometric rules,
Split like a province into round and square?
245 Who knows the individual hour in which
His habits were first sown even as a seed?
Who that shall point as with a wand, and say
"This portion of the river of my mind
Came from yon fountain"? Thou, my friend, art one
250 More deeply read in thy own thoughts, no slave
Of that false secondary power by which
In weakness we create distinctions, then
Believe our puny boundaries are things
Which we perceive, and not which we have made.
255 To thee, unblinded by these outward shews,

The unity of all has been revealed;
And thou wilt doubt with me, less aptly skilled
Than many are to class the cabinet
Of their sensations, and in voluble phrase
²⁶⁰ Run through the history and birth of each
As of a single independent thing.
Hard task[1] to analyse a soul, in which
Not only general habits and desires,
But each most obvious and particular thought—
²⁶⁵ Not in a mystical and idle sense,
But in the words of reason deeply weighed—
Hath no beginning.

                Blessed the infant babe—
For my best conjectures I would trace
The progress of our being—blest the babe
²⁷⁰ Nursed in his mother's arms, the babe who sleeps
Upon his mother's breast, who, when his soul
Claims manifest kindred with an earthly soul,
Doth gather passion from his mother's eye.
Such feelings pass into his torpid life
²⁷⁵ Like an awakening breeze, and hence his mind,
Even in the first trial of its powers,
Is prompt and watchful, eager to combine
In one appearance all the elements
And parts of the same object, else detached
²⁸⁰ And loth to coalesce. Thus day by day
Subjected to the discipline of love,
His organs and recipient faculties
Are quickened, are more vigorous; his mind spreads,
Tenacious of the forms which it receives.
²⁸⁵ In one beloved presence—nay and more,
In that most apprehensive habitude
And those sensations which have been derived
From this beloved presence—there exists
A virtue which irradiates and exalts
²⁹⁰ All objects through all intercourse of sense.[2]
No outcast he, bewildered and depressed;
Along his infant veins are interfused
The gravitation and the filial bond
Of Nature that connect him with the world.
²⁹⁵ Emphatically such a being lives,

---

[1] Cf. Milton, *Paradise Lost* 5.564.

[2] Cf. "Tintern Abbey" 101–02.*

An inmate of this *active* universe.
From Nature largely he receives, nor so
Is satisfied, but largely gives again;
For feeling has to him imparted strength,
³⁰⁰ And—powerful in all sentiments of grief,
Of exultation, fear and joy—his mind,
Even as an agent of the one great mind,
Creates, creator and receiver both,
Working but in alliance with the works
³⁰⁵ Which it beholds. Such, verily, is the first
Poetic spirit of our human life—
By uniform control of after years
In most abated and suppressed, in some
Through every change of growth or of decay
³¹⁰ Preeminent till death.

                From early days,
Beginning not long after that first time
In which, a babe, by intercourse of touch
I held mute dialogues with my mother's heart,
I have endeavoured to display the means
³¹⁵ Whereby this infant sensibility,
Great birthright of our being, was in me
Augmented and sustained. Yet is a path
More difficult before me, and I fear
That in its broken windings we shall need
³²⁰ The chamois' sinews and the eagle's wing.
For now a trouble came into my mind
From obscure causes: I was left alone
Seeking this visible world, nor knowing why.
The props of my affections were removed,
³²⁵ And yet the building stood, as if sustained
By its own spirit. All that I beheld
Was dear to me, and from this cause it came
That now to Nature's finer influxes
My mind lay open—to that more exact
³³⁰ And intimate communion which our hearts
Maintain with the minuter properties
Of objects which already are beloved,
And of those only.

                Many are the joys
Of youth, but oh, what happiness to live
³³⁵ When every hour brings palpable access
Of knowledge, when all knowledge is delight,

And sorrow is not there. The seasons came,
And every season brought a countless store
Of modes and temporary qualities
340 Which but for this most watchful power of love
Had been neglected, left a register
Of permanent relations else unknown.
Hence life, and change, and beauty, solitude
More active even than "best society,"[1]
345 Society made sweet as solitude
By silent inobtrusive sympathies,
And gentle agitations of the mind
From manifold distinctions, difference
Perceived in things where to the common eye
350 No difference is, and hence, from the same source,
Sublimer joy. For I would walk alone
In storm and tempest, or in starlight nights
Beneath the quiet heavens, and at that time
Would feel whate'er there is of power in sound
355 To breathe an elevated mood, by form
Or image unprofaned; and I would stand
Beneath some rock, listening to sounds that are
The ghostly language of the ancient earth,
Or make their dim abode in distant winds.
360 Thence did I drink the visionary power.
I deem not profitless these fleeting moods
Of shadowy exaltations; not for this,
That they are kindred to our purer mind
And intellectual life, but that the soul—
365 Remembering how she felt, but what she felt
Remembering not—retains an obscure sense
Of possible sublimity, to which
With growing faculties she doth aspire,
With faculties still growing, feeling still
370 That whatsoever point they gain they still
Have something to pursue.

       And not alone
In grandeur and in tumult, but no less
In tranquil scenes, that universal power
And fitness in the latent qualities
375 And essences of things, by which the mind
Is moved with feelings of delight, to me
Came strengthened with a superadded soul,

A virtue not its own. My morning walks
Were early: oft before the hours of school
380 I travelled round our little lake, five miles
Of pleasant wandering—happy time, more dear
For this, that one was by my side, a friend
Then passionately loved.[2] With heart how full
Will he peruse these lines, this page—perhaps
385 A blank to other men—for many years
Have since flowed in between us, and, our minds
Both silent to each other, at this time
We live as if those hours had never been.
Nor seldom did I lift our cottage latch
390 Far earlier, and before the vernal thrush
Was audible, among the hills I sate
Alone upon some jutting eminence[3]
At the first hour of morning, when the vale
Lay quiet in an utter solitude.
395 How shall I trace the history, where seek
The origin of what I then have felt?
Oft in those moments such a holy calm
Did overspread my soul that I forgot
The agency of sight, and what I saw
400 Appeared like something in myself, a dream,
A prospect in my mind.

       'Twere long to tell
What spring and autumn, what the winter snows,
And what the summer shade, what day and night,
The evening and the morning, what my dreams
405 And what my waking thoughts, supplied to nurse
That spirit of religious love in which
I walked with Nature. But let this at least
Be not forgotten, that I still retained
My first creative sensibility,
410 That by the regular action of the world
My soul was unsubdued. A plastic[4] power
Abode with me, a forming hand, at times
Rebellious, acting in a devious mood,
A local spirit of its own, at war
415 With general tendency, but for the most

---

[1] Milton, *Paradise Lost* 9.249.

[2] John Fleming; cf. Wordsworth's early poem "The Vale of Esthwaite" (1785–87).

[3] James Thomson (1700–48), *Summer* (1727) 942.

[4] creative, shaping.

      Subservient strictly to the external things
      With which it communed. An auxiliar light
      Came from my mind, which on the setting sun
      Bestowed new splendour; the melodious birds,
420 The gentle breezes, fountains that ran on
      Murmuring so sweetly in themselves, obeyed
      A like dominion, and the midnight storm
      Grew darker in the presence of my eye.
      Hence my obeisance, my devotion hence,
425 And *hence* my transport.

                      Nor should this, perchance,
      Pass unrecorded, that I still had loved
      The exercise and produce of a toil
      Than analytic industry to me
      More pleasing, and whose character I deem
430 Is more poetic, as resembling more
      Creative agency—I mean to speak
      Of that interminable building reared
      By observation of affinities
      In objects where no brotherhood exists
435 To common minds. My seventeenth year was come,
      And, whether from this habit rooted now
      So deeply in my mind, or from excess
      Of the great social principle of life
      Coercing all things into sympathy,
440 To unorganic natures I transferred
      My own enjoyments, or, the power of truth
      Coming in revelation, I conversed
      With things that really are, I at this time
      Saw blessings spread around me like a sea.
445 Thus did my days pass on, and now at length
      From Nature and her overflowing soul
      I had received so much that all my thoughts
      Were steeped in feeling. I was only then
      Contented when with bliss ineffable
450 I felt the sentiment of being spread
      O'er all that moves, and all that seemeth still,
      O'er all that, lost beyond the reach of thought
      And human knowledge, to the human eye
      Invisible, yet liveth to the heart
455 O'er all that leaps, and runs, and shouts, and sings,
      Or beats the gladsome air, o'er all that glides
      Beneath the wave, yea, in the wave itself
      And mighty depth of waters. Wonder not

      If such my transports were, for in all things
460 I saw one life, and felt that it was joy;
      One song they sang and it was audible—
      Most audible then when the fleshly ear,
      O'ercome by grosser prelude of that strain,
      Forgot its functions and slept undisturbed.
465   If this be error, and another faith
      Find easier access to the pious mind,
      Yet were I grossly destitute of all
      Those human sentiments which make this earth
      So dear if I should fail with grateful voice
470 To speak of you, ye mountains, and ye lakes
      And sounding cataracts, ye mists and winds
      That dwell among the hills where I was born.
      If in my youth I have been pure in heart,
      If, mingling with the world, I am content
475 With my own modest pleasures, and have lived
      With God and Nature communing, removed
      From little enmities and low desires,
      The gift is yours; if in these times of fear,
      This melancholy waste of hopes o'erthrown,[1]
480 If, 'mid indifference and apathy
      And wicked exultation, when good men
      On every side fall off we know not how
      To selfishness, disguised in gentle names
      Of peace and quiet and domestic love—
485 Yet mingled, not unwillingly, with sneers
      On visionary minds—if, in this time
      Of dereliction and dismay, I yet
      Despair not of our nature, but retain
      A more than Roman confidence, a faith
490 That fails not, in all sorrow my support,
      The blessing of my life, the gift is yours
      Ye mountains, thine O Nature. Thou hast fed
      My lofty speculations, and in thee
      For this uneasy heart of ours I find
495 A never-failing principle of joy
      And purest passion.

                      Thou, my friend, wast reared
      In the great city, 'mid far other scenes,[2]
      But we by different roads at length have gained

---

[1] Cf. Coleridge, "France: An Ode."*

[2] Cf. Coleridge, "Frost at Midnight" 56–57.*

       The self-same bourne. And from this cause to thee
500   I speak unapprehensive of contempt,
       The insinuated scoff of coward tongues,
       And all that silent language which so oft
       In conversation betwixt man and man
       Blots from the human countenance all trace
505   Of beauty and of love. For thou hast sought
       The truth in solitude, and thou art one
       The most intense of Nature's worshippers,
       In many things my brother, chiefly here
       In this my deep devotion. Fare thee well:
510   Health and the quiet of a healthful mind
       Attend thee, seeking oft the haunts of men—
       But yet more often living with thyself,
       And for thyself—so haply shall thy days
       Be many, and a blessing to mankind.

Letters[1]

To Charles James Fox[2]

Grasmere, Westmoreland January 14th 1801

Sir,

It is not without much difficulty, that I have summoned the courage to request your acceptance of these Volumes.[3] Should I express my real feelings, I am sure that I should seem to make a parade of diffidence and humility.

Several of the poems contained in these Volumes are written upon subjects, which are the common property of all Poets, and which, at some period of your life, must have been interesting to a man of your sensibility, and perhaps may still continue to be so. It would be highly gratifying to me to suppose that even in a single instance the manner in which I have treated these general topics should afford you any pleasure; but such a hope does not influence me upon the present occasion; in truth I do not feel it. Besides, I am convinced that there must be many things in this collection, which may impress you with an unfavorable idea of my intellectual powers. I do not say this with a wish to degrade myself; but I am sensible that this must be the case, from the different circles in which we have moved, and the different objects with which we have been conversant.

Being utterly unknown to you as I am, I am well aware, that if I am justified in writing to you at all, it is necessary, my letter should be short; but I have feelings within me which I hope will so far shew themselves in this letter, as to excuse the trespass which I am afraid I shall make. In common with the whole of the English people I have observed in your public character a constant predominance of sensibility of heart. Necessitated as you have been from your public situation to have much to do with men in bodies, and in classes, and accordingly to contemplate them in that relation, it has been your praise that you have not thereby been prevented from looking upon them as individuals, and that you have habitually left your heart open to be influenced by them in that capacity. This habit cannot but have made you dear to Poets; and I am sure that, if since your first entrance into public life there has been a single true poet living in England, he must have loved you.

But were I assured that I myself had a just claim to the title of a Poet, all the dignity being attached to the word which belongs to it, I do not think that I should have ventured for that reason to offer these volumes to you: at present it is solely on account of two poems in the second volume, the one entitled "The Brothers," and the other "Michael," that I have been emboldened to take this liberty.

It appears to me that the most calamitous effect, which has followed the measures which have lately been pursued in this country, is a rapid decay of the domestic affections among the lower orders of society.[4] This effect the present Rulers of this country are not conscious of, or they disregard it. For many years past, the tendency of society amongst almost all the nations of Europe has been to produce it. But recently by the spreading of manufactures through every part of the country, by the heavy taxes upon postage, by workhouses, Houses of Industry,

---

[1] from *Letters of William Wordsworth: a new selection*, ed. Alan G. Hill (1984).

[2] Whig statesman (1749–1806).

[3] the two volumes of *Lyrical Ballads* (1800).

[4] Wordsworth is deploring the cruelty of charitable institutions that controlled the lives of the poor and disregarded their existing emotional attachments.

and the invention of Soup-shops etc. etc. superadded to the encreasing disproportion between the price of labour and that of the necessaries of life, the bonds of domestic feeling among the poor, as far as the influence of these things has extended, have been weakened, and in innumerable instances entirely destroyed. The evil would be the less to be regretted, if these institutions were regarded only as palliatives to a disease; but the vanity and pride of their promoters are so subtly interwoven with them, that they are deemed great discoveries and blessings to humanity. In the mean time parents are separated from their children, and children from their parents; the wife no longer prepares with her own hands a meal for her husband, the produce of his labour; there is little doing in his house in which his affections can be interested, and but little left in it which he can love. I have two neighbours, a man and his wife, both upwards of eighty years of age; they live alone; the husband has been confined to his bed many months and has never had, nor till within these few weeks has ever needed, any body to attend to him but his wife. She has recently been seized with a lameness which has often prevented her from being able to carry him his food to his bed; the neighbours fetch water for her from the well, and do other kind offices for them both, but her infirmities encrease. She told my Servant two days ago that she was afraid they must both be boarded out among some other Poor of the parish (they have long been supported by the parish) but she said, it was hard, having kept house together so long, to come to this, and she was sure that "it would burst her heart." I mention this fact to shew how deeply the spirit of independence is, even yet, rooted in some parts of the country. These people could not express themselves in this way without an almost sublime conviction of the blessings of independent domestic life. If it is true, as I believe, that this spirit is rapidly disappearing, no greater curse can befal a land.

I earnestly entreat your pardon for having detained you so long. In the two Poems, "The Brothers" and "Michael" I have attempted to draw a picture of the domestic affections as I know they exist amongst a class of men who are now almost confined to the North of England. They are small independent *proprietors* of land here called statesmen, men of respectable education who daily labour on their own little properties. The domestic affections will always be strong amongst men who live in a country not crowded with population, if these men are placed above poverty. But if they are proprietors of small estates, which have descended to them from their ancestors, the power which these affections will acquire amongst such men is inconceivable by those who have only had an opportunity of observing hired labourers, farmers, and the manufacturing Poor. Their little tract of land serves as a kind of permanent rallying point for their domestic feelings, as a tablet upon which they are written which makes them objects of memory in a thousand instances when they would otherwise be forgotten. It is a fountain fitted to the nature of social man from which supplies of affection, as pure as his heart was intended for, are daily drawn. This class of men is rapidly disappearing. You, Sir, have a consciousness, upon which every good man will congratulate you, that the whole of your public conduct has in one way or other been directed to the preservation of this class of men, and those who hold similar situations. You have felt that the most sacred of all property is the property of the Poor. The two poems which I have mentioned were written with a view to shew that men who do not wear fine cloaths can feel deeply. "Pectus enim est quod disertos facit, et vis mentis. Ideoque imperitis quoque, si modo sint aliquo affectu concitati, verba non desunt."[1] The poems are faithful copies from nature; and I hope, whatever effect they may have upon you, you will at least be able to perceive that they may excite profitable sympathies in many kind and good hearts, and may in some small degree enlarge our feelings of reverence for our species, and our knowledge of human nature, by shewing that our best qualities are possessed by men whom we are too apt to consider, not with reference to the points in which they resemble us, but to those in which they manifestly differ from us. I thought, at a time when these feelings are sapped in so many ways that the two poems might co-operate, however feebly, with the illustrious efforts which you have made to stem this and other evils with which the country

---

[1] "It is the heart and the power of the mind that makes us eloquent. This is why even the unskilled, so long as they are stirred by some emotion, are not short of words" (Quintilian, *Institutio Oratoria* 10.7.15, trans. Donald A. Russell).

is labouring, and it is on this account alone that I have taken the liberty of thus addressing you.

Wishing earnestly that the time may come when the country may perceive what it has lost by neglecting your advice, and hoping that your latter days may be attended with health and comfort.

I remain, With the highest respect and admiration
Your most obedient and humble Servt
W Wordsworth

To Mary Wordsworth[1]

Hindwell—Saturday August 11th [1810] I arrived here at 10 this morning; where I found all well, Sara wonderfully improved in look and Joanna[2] quite fat, Sara indeed also. The house is comfortable, and its situation beside the pool, and the pool itself quite charming, and far beyond my expectation. Having said this, let me turn at once to thee my love of loves and to thy dearest of Letters which I found here, and read with a beating heart. O my blessing, how happy was I in learning that my Letter had moved thee so deeply, and thy delight in reading had if possible been more exquisite than mine in writing. You seem to have been surprized at the receipt of my Letter, and surely it is odd that I did not mention to you I should avail myself of some opportunity, and as strange that you did not take for granted that I should. My Letter had been written three or four days before I could find the means of sending it off, which was the reason of its arriving so late; you would notice also that it was somewhat worn, for I had carried it about with me in my pocket.—I was sure that you would be most happy in receiving from me such a gift from the whole undivided heart for your whole and sole possession; and the Letter in answer which I have received from you today I will entrust to your keeping when I return, and they shall be deposited side by side as a bequest for the survivor of us. Every day every hour every moment makes me feel more deeply how blessed we are in each other, how purely how faithfully how ardently, and how tenderly we love each other; I put this last word last because, though I am persuaded that a deep affection is not uncommon in married life, yet I am confident that a lively, gushing, thought-employing, spirit-stirring, passion of love, is very rare even among good people. I will say more upon this when we meet, grounded upon recent observation of the condition of others. We have been parted my sweet Mary too long, but we have not been parted in vain, for wherever I go I am admonished how blessed, and almost peculiar a lot mine is.—

You praised the penmanship of my last; I could wish that this should be legible also, but I fear I shall wish in vain; for I must write in a great hurry having only an hour allotted to me. Let me then first communicate the facts in which you may be interested, relating to my journey etc otherwise if I give way to the emotions of my heart first you will hear nothing of these.—On Monday morn: at 9 o'clock Sir G.B.[3] and I left Ashby in a chaise. Sir G— had a wish to see the Leasowes[4] with me; I had never been there and he had not seen the place these thirty years; I reserve the detail of this journey till we meet. We slept the first night at Hagley returned to Birmingham next day at 4 afternoon, went together to the play, and the next morning walked about the Town, and I accompanied Sir G. back on his way as far as four miles which brought me to within 2 miles a ½ of Castle Bromwich, Mr. Blairs. At Mr Blairs, I found a note from my B^r Chris^[5] who had accidentally heard of my intention of being at Mr Blairs. I was greatly surprised at this, as I had confidently concluded that he was either gone from Birm: or had never come thither from his not having answered the Letter inviting him to

---

[1] from *The Letters of William and Dorothy Wordsworth. VIII: A Supplement of New Letters*, ed. Alan G. Hill (1993). William Wordsworth married Mary Hutchinson in 1802.

[2] Joanna and Sara Hutchinson, Mary Wordsworth's sisters, who were staying with their brother Thomas at Hindwell in Wales. During this period W. Wordsworth's friendship with Coleridge, unhappily in love with Sara Hutchinson, was deteriorating.

[3] the painter Sir George Beaumont, whose estate was at Coleorton, Leicestershire.

[4] the estate in Worcestershire of the poet and landscape gardener William Shenstone (1714–63).

[5] W. Wordsworth's brother Christopher (1774–1846) later became Master of Trinity College, Cambridge.

Coleorton. On Thursday he came over to Mr Blairs, dined with us, and I returned with him, and supped at Lloyds, where I found Priscilla[1] looking I thought not very well. The children were gone to bed and asleep so of course I can have no accurate image of them: their faces were heated and they seemed bloomed, but their natural complexions, are sallow. The eldest is the handsomest, much, the 2nd the stoutest, and the third the plainest; so it appeared as they slept and so, I was told, it is; Christopher looked uncommonly; but I am sorry to say that he is likely to have great trouble (at least I fear so) from the state of his wifes health and the nature of her malady; great expense also which at present he can ill bear,—for his living has entangled him in two law suits; and you will grieve to hear that he has been much deceived as the income of it; it is some hundreds lower than he had reason to expect, so that he will be not a little pinched, unless it should please God to take the Bishop.[2] But not a word of these particulars to any body.

On friday Morning, I was called a little after three, having had two hours feverish sleep, got on the top of the Coach, it began to rain before we were out of Birming: and rained for two hours and a half; my umbrella and coat however protected me pretty well; when we were half way to Worcester the weather cleared up and I had a pleasant ride through a fine Country to that City, which stands charmingly upon the Severn, at no great distance from the Malvern hills. These hills which are a fine object brought Joseph Cottle[3] to my mind, and dearest Dorothy,[4] who had travelled this way when she came from Newcastle to meet me at Bristol whence we journeyd to Racedown;[5] but though much endeared to me on this latter account, I looked at them with a trembling which I cannot describe when I thought that *you* had not seen them, but *might* have seen, if you had but taken the road through Bristol when you left Racedown; in which case I should certainly have accompanied you as far as Bristol; or further, perhaps: and then I thought, that you would not have taken the coach at Bristol, but that you would have walked on Northwards with me at your side, till unable to part from each other we might have come in sight of those hills which skirt the road for so many miles, and thus continuing our journey (for we should have moved on at small expense) I fancied that we should have seen so deeply into each others hearts, and been so fondly locked in each others arms, that we should have braved the worst and parted no more. Under that tree, I thought as I passed along we might have rested, of that stream might have drank, in that thicket we might have hidden ourselves from the sun, and from the eyes of the passenger; and thus did I feed on the thought of bliss that might have been, which would have [been] intolerable from the force of regret had I not felt the happiness which waits me when I see you again. O Mary I love you with a passion of love which grows till I tremble to think of its strength; your children and the care which they require must fortunately steal between you and the solitude and the longings of absence—when I am moving about in travelling I am less unhappy than when stationary, but then I am at every moment, I will not say reminded of you, for you never I think are out of my mind 3 minutes together however I am engaged, but I am every moment seized with a longing wish that you might see the objects which interest me as I pass along, and not having you at my side my pleasure is so imperfect that after a short look I had rather not see the objects at all. But I must return to my journey. I left Worcester at half past ten, reached Leominster at 5, and there was 20 miles to Hindwell, without coach—Luckily two other persons were going part of the same way; so we took chaise for 14 miles, I slept at Presteigne 5 miles from hence, hired a Guide who bore my luggage, and I arrived here before eleven.

---

[1] Priscilla Lloyd, the sister of Charles Lloyd,* was married to Wordsworth's brother Christopher. They had three children, John, Charles, and Christopher.

[2] The Bishop of London had the power to grant the living (or ecclesiastical appointment) for which Christopher Wordsworth was contending.

[3] Cottle, the publisher of *Lyrical Ballads,** had written *Malvern Hills: A Poem* (1798).

[4] W. Wordsworth's sister, Dorothy Wordsworth.*

[5] Mary Wordsworth had stayed in Racedown with William and Dorothy from Nov. 1796–June 1797.

I have read to Sara the parts of your Letter intended for her,[1] and all the rest which I could read; she will reply to these of course herself. How happy am I [to] learn that thou art so well, and untormented with that cruel pain in thy mouth! May it never return! if it does fail not to apply to Dr Dicks[2] remedies: for my account for really I have suffered much in this cruel complaint of thine—I have thought of it ten thousand times since we parted and sometimes I have fancied that I was caressing thee, and thou couldst not meet me with kindred delight and rapture from the interruption of this distressing pain. But far oftener for less selfish reasons has it employed my mind with an anxiety which I cannot describe; for every thing about you that is indicative of weakness or derangement of health affects me when I [am] absent from you, and cannot see how you look, beyond what it is in the power of words to describe. O take care of yourself for all our sakes—but I cannot bear to look that way, and I know you will do nothing to hurt yourself for my sake.—

My stomach failed about a fortnight since from too much talking, or rather from not being sufficiently alone—before I left C— by taking more care I brought it about; and except in my eyelids I look well, and am well; but certainly though not weak far from being so strong as I should have been but for my old enemy: that has troubled me more than ever.—I agree with you that it was unreasonable in the B's to expect me to go to C— again next summer; be assured, I shall not do it on any account nor will I go any where without thee. I cannot but think knowing how the little ones would be taken care of but that we might be happy supremely happy together in a tour of a few weeks if our circumstances would allow; but this will never, I fear be the case, nor am I anxious about this; but I never will part from you for more than a week or a *fort*night at the very utmost, unless when I [am] compelled by a sense of duty that leaves no choice—I cannot and ought not; if I could lay in a stock of health and strength to enable me to work more vigorously when I return there might be some plea for this but the contrary is the case; for my longing day and night to see you again is more powerful far, as I said before than when you were at Middleham; and when I am away from you I seem to have heart for nothing and no body else—But this theme is endless; I must content myself with your Letters for a short time; and oh most dearly shall I prize them, till I consign them to your care to be preserved whatever else we lose.

I have not yet said a word about the time I purpose to stay here; but I came with a resolution not to extend it beyond a fortnight, for a hundred reasons which will crowd in upon your mind. At all events I shall move heaven and earth to be with you by this day three weeks. I shall not stop a moment at Liverpool more than I can help, if I go that way. You may guess how eager I am to be at home, when I tell you that Christophers entreaties and my own wishes, could not prevail upon me to stay half a day at Birmingham.—Certainly I parted from him with great regret, as he and I are likely to be so much divided. I will satisfy Sara's claim upon me and let me add a little too for Joanna and Mary Monkhouse[3] especially, and then I shall take wing and oh for the sight of dear Grasmere, and how I shall pant up the hill, and then for dear little W. and his beloved Mother, and how shall we pour out hearts together in the lonely house, and in the lonely and to *us* thrice dear Season.

Thank you for your pretty tales of Dorothy and strin[g]-loving Thomas bless [him] he shall be contented if possible, I will bring him string from his Godmother, string for his Uncle, for Mr Addison and for myself adieu adieu adieu, for I am told I have not a moment to lose, and that the post will be lost—this must not be again and again farewell—a thousand kisses for you all, yourself first, John Dorothy, Thomas, Catharine, W^m.[4] dear little Catharine I have not mentioned her, but she has often been here in my thoughts again and again farewell—I fear for her[5] Take care.

---

[1] Mary wanted Sara to know about the arrangement their brother John was making to care for their disabled sister, Betsy.

[2] Richard Scambler, the physician in Grasmere.

[3] The daughter of W. Wordsworth's friend and cousin, Thomas Monkhouse.

[4] the Wordsworths' children: John (b. 1803), Dorothy, or Dora (b. 1804), Thomas (b. 1806), Catherine (b. 1808), and William (b. 1810).

[5] Cf. Wordsworth's poem "Surprized by Joy" and note.*

James Hogg
1770 – 1835

Also known as "the Ettrick Shepherd," James Hogg was born at Ettrickhall farm in Selkirkshire, in the Scottish border country, in 1770. In 1777, his father was bankrupt, and Hogg's formal education came to an end. However, in his twenties, Hogg worked as shepherd for the Laidlaw family at Blackhouse farm, where he had access to a library. There, he read and began to write. Eventually, through his connections to the Laidlaw family, he met Walter Scott,* who encouraged him to pursue a literary career.

The publication of "The Mountain Bard" in 1807 gained him some recognition; interestingly, this same year, he published a guide to sheep care. Like Robert Burns,* to whom he is often compared for their "rustic" qualities, he moved to Edinburgh in 1810. For a year, he was the publisher of and main contributor to a weekly magazine, *The Spy*. Soon, he established himself as a critically acclaimed and popular writer with the 1813 publication of *The Queen's Wake*, a long poem in which Scottish poets gather in Holyrood Palace in Edinburgh for a bardic contest to celebrate the return of Mary Queen of Scots. He later became a contributor to *Blackwood's Edinburgh Magazine*, and he made his living partly as a writer and partly through various ill-fated farming ventures.

He wrote mostly poetry until he was in his forties, at which point he wrote a series of novels, including *The Private Memoirs and Confessions of a Justified Sinner* (1824). In 1832, he travelled to London where he was much admired; he was even offered a knighthood, which he declined. On 21 November 1835, he died at the farm at Altrive that had been given to him by the Duke of Buccleuch. (J.G.)

಄಄಄

from *The Queen's Wake: A Legendary Poem*, 3rd ed. (1814)[1]

Kilmeny

THE THIRTEENTH BARD'S SONG

Bonny Kilmeny gaed up the glen;
But it wasna to meet Duneira's men,
Nor the rosy monk of the isle to see,
For Kilmeny was pure as pure could be.
5 It was only to hear the yorlin[2] sing,
And pu' the cress-flower round the spring;
The scarlet hypp[3] and the hindberrye,
And the nut that hang frae the hazel tree;
For Kilmeny was pure as pure could be.

10 But lang may her minny[4] look o'er the wa',
And lang may she seek i' the green-wood shaw;
Lang the laird of Duneira blame,
And lang, lang greet or Kilmeny come hame!

When many a day had come and fled,
15 When grief grew calm, and hope was dead,
When mess for Kilmeny's soul had been sung,
When the bedes-man[5] had prayed, and the dead-bell rung,
Late, late in a gloamin, when all was still,
When the fringe was red on the westlin[6] hill,
20 The wood was sere, the moon i' the wane,
The reek o' the cot hung over the plain,
Like a little wee cloud in the world its lane;

---

[1] first published January 1813.

[2] "yellow-hammer" (Sc.), a kind of bird.

[3] "rose-hip."

[4] "mother."

[5] "beadsman," one hired to pray (tell the beads on his rosary) for others; cf. Keats, "The Eve of St. Agnes."*

[6] "western."

When the ingle[1] lowed with an eiry leme,[2]
Late, late in the gloaming Kilmeny came hame!

  "Kilmeny, Kilmeny, where have you been?
Lang hae we sought baith holt and den;
By linn, by ford, and green-wood tree,
Yet you are halesome and fair to see.
Where gat you that joup[3] o' the lilly scheen?
That bonny snood of the birk sae green?
And these roses, the fairest that ever were seen?
Kilmeny, Kilmeny, where have you been?"—

  Kilmeny looked up with a lovely grace,
But nae smile was seen on Kilmeny's face;
As still was her look, and as still was her ee,
As the stillnes that lay on the emerant lea,
Or the mist that sleeps on a waveless sea.
For Kilmeny had been she knew not where,
And Kilmeny had seen what she could not declare;
Kilmeny had been where the cock never crew,
Where the rain never fell, and the wind never blew.
But it seemed as the harp of the sky had rung,
And the airs of heaven played round her tongue,
When she spake of the lovely forms she had seen,
And a land where sin had never been;
A land of love, and a land of light,
Withouten sun, or moon, or night:
Where the river swa'd[4] a living stream,
And the light a pure celestial beam:
The land of vision it would seem,
A still, an everlasting dream.

  In yon green-wood there is a waik,[5]
And in that waik there is a wene,[6]
  And in that wene there is a maike,[7]
That neither has flesh, blood, nor bane;
  And down in yon green-wood he walks his lane.

  In that green wene Kilmeny lay,
Her bosom happed wi' the flowerits gay;
But the air was soft and the silence deep,
And bonny Kilmeny fell sound asleep.
She kend nae mair, nor opened her ee,
Till waked by the hymns of a far countrye.

  She 'wakened on couch of the silk sae slim,
All striped wi' the bars of the rainbow's rim;
And lovely beings round were rife,
Who erst had travelled mortal life;
And aye they smiled, and 'gan to speer,[8]
"What spirit has brought this mortal here?"—

  "Lang have I journeyed the world wide,"
A meek and reverend fere[9] replied;
"Baith night and day I have watched the fair,
Eident[10] a thousand years and mair.
Yes, I have watched o'er ilk degree,
Wherever blooms femenitye;
But sinless virgin, free of stain
In mind and body, fand I nane.
Never, since the banquet of time,
Found I virgin in her prime,
Till late this bonny maiden I saw
As spotless as the morning snaw:
Full twenty years she has lived as free
As the spirits that sojourn this countrye.
I have brought her away frae the snares of men,
That sin or death she never may ken."—

  They clasped her waiste and her hands sae fair,
They kissed her cheek, and they kemed[11] her hair,
And round came many a blooming fere,
Saying, "Bonny Kilmeny, ye're welcome here!
Women are freed of the littand scorn:

---

[1] "fire."
[2] "eerie gleam."
[3] "mantle."
[4] "swelled."
[5] "plot of deep grass."
[6] "dwelling."
[7] "being" (the primary meaning of the word is "equal" or "mate").
[8] "inquire."
[9] "fellow."
[10] "unintermittently."
[11] "combed."

90   O, blessed be the day Kilmeny was born!
Now shall the land of the spirits see,
Now shall it ken what a woman may be!
Many a lang year in sorrow and pain,
Many a lang year thro' the world we've gane,
95   Commissioned to watch fair womankind,
For its they who nurice th' immortal mind.
We have watched their steps as the dawning shone,
And deep in the green-wood walks alone;
By lilly bower and silken bed,
100   The viewless tears have o'er them shed;
Have soothed their ardent minds to sleep,
Or left the couch of love to weep.
We have seen! we have seen! but the time must come,
And the angels will weep at the day of doom!

105   "O, would the fairest of mortal kind
Aye keep the holy truths in mind,
That kindred spirits their motions see,
Who watch their ways with anxious ee,
And grieve for the guilt of humanitye!
110   O, sweet to heaven the maiden's prayer,
And the sigh that heaves a bosom sae fair!
And dear to heaven the words of truth,
And the praise of virtue frae beauty's mouth!
And dear to the viewless forms of air,
115   The minds that kyth[1] as the body fair!

"O, bonny Kilmeny! free frae stain,
If ever you seek the world again,
That world of sin, of sorrow, and fear,
O, tell of the joys that are waiting here!
120   And tell of the signs you shall shortly see;
Of the times that are now, and the times that shall be."—

They lifted Kilmeny, they led her away,
And she walked in the light of a sunless day:
The sky was a dome of crystal bright,
125   The fountain of vision, and fountain of light:
The emerald fields were of dazzling glow,
And the flowers of everlasting blow.

Then deep in the stream her body they laid,
That her youth and beauty never might fade;
130   And they smiled on heaven, when they saw her lie
In the stream of life that wandered bye.
And she heard a song, she heard it sung,
She kend not where; but sae sweetly it rung,
It fell on her ear like a dream of the morn:
135   "O! blest be the day Kilmeny was born!
Now shall the land of the spirits see,
Now shall it ken what a woman may be!
The sun that shines on the world sae bright,
A borrowed gleid[2] frae the fountain of light;
140   And the moon that sleeks the sky sae dun,
Like a gouden bow, or a beamless sun,
Shall wear away, and be seen nae mair,
And the angels shall miss them travelling the air.
But lang, lang after baith night and day,
145   When the sun and the world have elyed[3] away;
When the sinner has gane to his waesome doom,
Kilmeny shall smile in eternal bloom!"—

They bore her away she wist not how,
For she felt not arm nor rest below;
150   But so swift they wained her through the light,
'Twas like the motion of sound or sight;
They seemed to split the gales of air,
And yet nor gale nor breeze was there.
Unnumbered groves below them grew,
155   They came, they past, and backward flew,
Like floods of blossoms gliding on,
In moment seen, in moment gone.
O, never vales to mortal view
Appeared like those o'er which they flew!
160   That land to human spirits given,
The lowermost vales of the storied heaven;
From thence they can view the world below,
And heaven's blue gates with sapphires glow,
More glory yet unmeet to know.

165   They bore her far to a mountain green,
To see what mortal never had seen;

---

[1] "appear."

[2] "glow."

[3] "disappeared."

And they seated her high on a purple sward,
And bade her heed what she saw and heard,
And note the changes the spirits wrought,
170 For now she lived in the land of thought.
She looked, and she saw nor sun nor skies,
But a crystal dome of a thousand dies.
She looked, and she saw nae land aright,
But an endless whirl of glory and light.
175 And radiant beings went and came
Far swifter than wind, or the linked flame.
She hid her een frae the dazzling view;
She looked again and the scene was new.

    She saw a sun on a summer sky,
180 And clouds of amber sailing bye;
A lovely land beneath her lay,
And that land had glens and mountains gray;
And that land had vallies and hoary piles,
And marled seas, and a thousand isles:
185 Its fields were speckled, its forests green,
And its lakes were all of the dazzling sheen,
Like magic mirrors, where slumbering lay
The sun and the sky and the cloudlet gray;
Which heaved and trembled and gently swung,
190 On every shore they seemed to be hung;
For there they were seen on their downward plain
A thousand times and a thousand again;
In winding lake and placid firth,
Little peaceful heavens in the bosom of earth.

195   Kilmeny sighed and seemed to grieve,
For she found her heart to that land did cleave;
She saw the corn wave on the vale,
She saw the deer run down the dale;
She saw the plaid and the broad claymore,
200 And the brows that the badge of freedom bore;
And she thought she had seen the land before.

    She saw a lady sit on a throne,
The fairest that ever the sun shone on!
A lion licked her hand of milk,
205 And she held him in a leish of silk;
And a leifu'[1] maiden stood at her knee,
With a silver wand and melting ee;
Her sovereign shield till love stole in,
And poisoned all the fount within.

210   Then a gruff untoward bedeman came,
And hundit the lion on his dame;
And the guardian maid wi' the dauntless ee,
She dropped a tear, and left her knee;
And she saw till the queen frae the lion fled,
215 Till the bonniest flower of the world lay dead.
A coffin was set on a distant plain,
And she saw the red blood fall like rain:
Then bonny Kilmeny's heart grew sair,
And she turned away, and could look nae mair.

220   Then the gruff grim carle girned amain,[2]
And they trampled him down, but he rose again;
And he baited the lion to deeds of weir,[3]
Till he lapped the blood to the kingdom dear;
And weening his head was danger-preef,[4]
225 When crowned with the rose and clover leaf,
He gowled[5] at the carle and chased him away,
To feed wi' the deer on the mountain gray.
He gowled at the carle, and he gecked[6] at heaven,
But his mark was set, and his arles[7] given.
230 Kilmeny a while her een withdrew;
She looked again, and the scene was new.

    She saw below her fair unfurled
One half of all the glowing world,
Where oceans rolled, and rivers ran,
235 To bound the aims of sinful man.
She saw a people, fierce and fell,

---

[1] "modest."

[2] "fellow snarled forcibly."

[3] "war."

[4] "danger-proof."

[5] "howled."

[6] "mocked."

[7] figuratively, "a beating" (literally "money paid on making a bargain").

Burst frae their bounds like fiends of hell;
There lilies grew, and the eagle flew,
And she herked on her ravening crew,
240 Till the cities and towers were wrapt in a blaze,
And the thunder it roared o'er the lands and the seas.
The widows they wailed, and the red blood ran,
And she threatned an end to the race of man:
She never lened,[1] nor stood in awe,
245 Till claught by the lion's deadly paw.
Oh! then the eagle swinked[2] for life,
And brainzelled[3] up a mortal strife;
But flew she north, or flew she south,
She met wi' the gowl of the lion's mouth.

250 With a mooted[4] wing and waefu' maen,
The eagle sought her eiry again;
But lang may she cour[5] in her bloody nest,
And lang, lang sleek her wounded breast,
Before she sey another flight,
255 To play wi' the norland lion's might

But to sing the sights Kilmeny saw,
So far surpassing nature's law,
The singer's voice wad sink away,
And the string of his harp wad cease to play.
260 But she saw till the sorrows of man were bye,
And all was love and harmony;
Till the stars of heaven fell calmly away,
Like the flakes of snaw on a winter day.

Then Kilmeny begged again to see
265 The friends she had left in her own country,
To tell of the place where she had been,
And the glories that lay in the land unseen;
To warn the living maidens fair,
The loved of heaven, the spirits' care,
270 That all whose minds unmeled[6] remain
Shall bloom in beauty when time is gane.

With distant music, soft and deep,
They lulled Kilmeny sound asleep;
And when she awakened, she lay her lane,
275 All happed with flowers in the green-wood wene.
When seven lang years had come and fled;
When grief was calm, and hope was dead;
When scarce was remembered Kilmeny's name,
Late, late in a gloamin Kilmeny came hame!

280 And O, her beauty was fair to see,
But still and stedfast was her ee!
Such beauty bard may never declare,
For there was no pride nor passion there;
And the soft desire of maidens een
285 In that mild face could never be seen.
Her seymar[7] was the lilly flower,
And her cheek the moss-rose in the shower;
And her voice like the distant melodye,
That floats along the twilight sea.
290 But she loved to raike[8] the lanely glen,
And keeped afar frae the haunts of men;
Her holy hymns unheard to sing,
To suck the flowers, and drink the spring.
But wherever her peaceful form appeared,
295 The wild beasts of the hill were cheered;
The wolf played blythly round the field,
The lordly byson lowed and kneeled;
The dun deer wooed with manner bland,
And cowered aneath her lilly hand.
300 And when at even the woodlands rung,
When hymns of other worlds she sung,
In extacy of sweet devotion,
O, then the glen was all in motion.
The wild beasts of the forest came,
305 Broke from their bughts[9] and faulds the tame,

---

[1] "bent over, crouched."
[2] "worked."
[3] "beat."
[4] "molted."
[5] "cower."
[6] "without blemish."
[7] "a thin covering."
[8] "wander."
[9] "pens used for milking."

  And goved[1] around, charmed and amazed;
  Even the dull cattle crooned and gazed,
  And murmured and looked with anxious pain
  For something the mystery to explain.
310 The buzzard came with the thristle-cock;
  The corby left her houf[2] in the rock;
  The blackbird alang wi' the eagle flew;
  The hind came tripping o'er the dew;
  The wolf and the kid their raike began,
315 And the tod, and the lamb, and the leveret ran;
  The hawk and the hern attour[3] them hung,
  And the merl and the mavis forhooyed[4] their young;
  And all in a peaceful ring were hurled:
  It was like an eve in a sinless world!

320 When a month and a day had come and gane,
  Kilmeny sought the greenwood wene;
  There laid her down on the leaves sae green,
  And Kilmeny on earth was never mair seen.
  But O, the words that fell from her mouth,
325 Were words of wonder, and words of truth!
  But all the land were in fear and dread,
  For they kendna whether she was living or dead.
  It wasna her hame, and she couldna remain;
  She left this world of sorrow and pain,
330 And returned to the land of thought again.

---

[1] "stared."
[2] "nest."
[3] "out over."
[4] "ignored."

Charles Brockden Brown
1771 – 1810

Charles Brockden Brown was born in Philadelphia on 17 January 1771, fifth of the six children of Elijah Brown, a Quaker merchant, and Mary Armitt Brown. He was educated in the Friends Latin School and later apprenticed to a Philadelphia lawyer, but in 1792 he gave up the law for literature. He published his first book, *Alcuin*, a dialogue on the rights of women, in 1798. That July, he went to live in New York with his best friend, Elihu Hubbard Smith, who shortly afterwards died of yellow fever; Brown also contracted the disease but recovered. After this tragedy, he returned to Philadelphia. Between 1798 and 1801, in a heroic effort to establish himself as a man of letters, he published six novels, including *Wieland; or, The Transformation* (1798) and *Edgar Huntly; or, Memoirs of a Sleep-Walker* (1799). They won the admiration of Godwin,* Keats,* Peacock,* and P.B. Shelley,* and later of Cooper,* Hawthorne,* Longfellow,* Poe,* and Whittier, but they were not commercially successful, and Brown devoted the rest of his career to journalism (he founded, edited, and wrote much of the copy for, three different periodicals) and political pamphleteering. In November 1804, he married Elizabeth Linn, the daughter of a Presbyterian minister. Despite his parents' disapproval, they were happy and had four children. In his last years, Brown worked on but did not complete an ambitious "System of General Geography." He died in Philadelphia of tuberculosis on 22 February 1810. (D.L.M.)

☙☙☙

from the *Literary Magazine and American Register* 6.35 (1806)

On the Standard of Taste

Some are inclined to deny the existence of a standard of taste, from the versatility of fashion, in dress, building, furniture, and the like. But dress and furniture are not, generally speaking, the objects of that mode of judgment or feeling, which we call taste. There is nothing naturally gratifying to the imagination in the shape and workmanship of a chair or a chest of drawers, a pelisse or a petticoat. Ruffs have given way to lawn handkerchiefs, and velvet suits to plain broad cloth; green, blue, and red have succeeded each other scores of times in the approbation of the fashionable.—What then? Are there no real grounds, in such matters as these, for preferring one fashion to another? There are, very frequently; and for the following reasons:

Good sense, which is a necessary ingredient in good taste, prescribes that every work of human art should be calculated to promote its own proper end, whether that be pleasure, as in the fine arts, or the prevention of evil, as in most of the mechanical. Every thing, therefore, in the decorations of dress, building, or furniture, which is repugnant to health, comfort, or convenience, is clearly wrong; and such fashions have seldom been permanent, even with the multitude.

In such of the fine arts themselves as are connected with purposes of utility, eloquence, architecture, and gardening, any palpable deviation from those purposes, even though attended with pleasure to the imagination, is offensive to taste itself. Further, if articles of furniture or dress can be so ordered as to suggest delightful trains of ideas to the cultivated mind; ideas, for example, connected with classical or feudal antiquity; or to present graceful forms and agreeable combinations of colour to the lover of painting, they become, in the strictest sense, objects of taste, because they aim at that end, the pleasure of the imagination, their tendency towards which it is the province of taste to estimate. Fifty years since, this seems to have been little more thought of in Great Britain than ornamental architecture in the days of Alfred;[1] and it is as unreasonable to bring either of these *improvements* as proofs of mutabil-

---

[1] Alfred the Great (849–99), king of Wessex.

ity and caprice in matters of taste, as to infer a like caprice in agriculture and manufactures, from the introduction of the drill-plough and the steam-engine.[1] The high state of practical art in England, and, much more, their increasing attention to the sculpture, great and small, of that marvelous people,[2] from whom their knowledge of excellence, in almost all the objects of taste, has been derived, have wrought an uncommon revolution in their decorations of every kind. But this is rather like a newly-acquired sense than a change of taste: for it should ever be remembered, that neither an individual nor a nation can be said to show a preference, in point of taste, to one thing above another, unless the two have been fairly set before them at the same time. With regard to the notions of female beauty, obvious examples of diversity in human taste are drawn from the repugnant sentiments in these matters of a voluptuary of Congo and one of France or England, but we cannot help thinking that the colour of the Europeans is intrinsically superior to that of their sable rivals. This has been proved in an elegant and satisfactory manner by Uvedale Price, in the third volume of his Essays on the Picturesque.[3]

Varied and harmonious reflections of light and colours are certainly not immaterial in beauty, since beauty of colour consists in nothing else. But, what is far more important, the physiognomical expression, the eloquence of the countenance, the symbols which, by a kind of natural telegraph, indicate the transitory emotions of love, modesty, and delight, or the more permanent glow of healthfulness and youth;

The bloom of young desire, and purple light of love;[4] are intimately allied with that complexion, which could never be praised in a toast of Tombuctoo.[5] As to *form*, it would be difficult to prove the inferiority of the Ethiopian. Many negroes, from their symmetry, strength, and activity, give us the idea of masculine beauty. But in the beauty of women, we are led away by sympathies and associations of a peculiar kind. A woman of a different colour seems at first a creature of a different species; and as our opinion of beauty in that sex is commonly attended with some degree of love or desire, it cannot exist where any circumstances excite associations of disgust. But this cause can never be fairly tried, unless the two races were intermixed in a state of civil and intellectual equality with each other: an experiment which has not yet been made; since, in the East and West Indies, the moral relations of the two are so dissimilar, that full scope has not been given for the determination of physical preference.

After all this, however, has been cleared away, there still remains a prodigious difference in the sentiments of mankind in matters of taste. This will not be found in the decisions of men as to models of acknowledged excellence, where a hardy rebellion against established authority would bring down on their heads the penalties of critical high treason. It is not quite safe to call Handel an indifferent composer; and nobody but Mr. Pinkerton[6] treats Virgil as a poetaster. But, where the public voice has not had time to declare itself, it is not surprising what variety of opinion is sure to be expressed. Let any one, conversant with literary society, go over in his mind the opinions which he has heard from his acquaintance, as to the chief works of poetry that have been published during his time. How frequently he finds, that, of two men, who esteem alike the great masters of the art, one will raise a living poet almost to the level of those masters whom the other treats as quite contemptible. Nor is this confined to poetry. The stage is deservedly accounted an object of elegant criticism. Yet, as to the art of declamation, we have had very recent experience, that men of discriminating and cultivated intellects may discover transcendant excellence, where others, equally gifted, can see nothing but mediocrity. We have been often struck, at an exhibition of the Royal Academy[7] in London, with the various

---

[1] The steam engine, patented by James Watt in 1768, made the Industrial Revolution possible.

[2] the ancient Greeks.

[3] Sir Uvedale Price (1747–1829), *Essay on the Picturesque* (1794).

[4] Thomas Gray (1716–71), *The Progress of Poesy* (1757) 41.

[5] Timbuktu, a city in central Mali.

[6] George Frederick Handel (1685–1759), composer; John Pinkerton (1758–1826), author of *Letters on Literature* (1785), in which he expresses a dismissive view of classical authors.

[7] The Royal Academy, founded in 1768, holds annual exhibitions of Old Masters and of contemporary art.

characters which are conferred on the same pictures by the motley multitude who flock to criticise them; till, after some days, a few pictures obtain, from those who are real judges, a decided character, which cannot afterwards, without the imputation of bad taste, be contravened. Even those, however, who in poetry claim a right *to please themselves*, as their phrase is wont to be, acknowledge the authority of positive rules in painting: and the fact of so great a diversity of opinion as to the latter may lead us to suspect, that there is some way of accounting for that which exists as to the former, without giving up the reality of a right and a wrong in matters of taste.

There are three causes to which we may ascribe most of this contrariety of sentiment, with respect to the productions of the fine arts. The first is want of feeling; that is, inability to enjoy, in any great degree, the pleasures of the imagination. Every body knows, that persons wholly destitute of a musical ear cannot have any relish for the excellencies of that art; and their pretensions to criticism in it, if they are unwise enough to make any, only tend to render themselves ridiculous. But it does not seem to strike every body, though it is equally true, that the souls of a great portion of mankind are just as obtuse, with regard to poetry and other matters of taste, as the most ill-constructed organ can be to the distinctions of tones and semitones. The judgments of such men must be perpetually wrong, because, as they are incapable of receiving pleasure themselves, they can only know by conjecture what will excite it in others. It is true, that there are few candid enough to confess this general insensibility to the works of imagination. But we are persuaded, that those who look narrowly, will find it exceedingly common; and the prevailing manner of the time, the contemptuous apathy, which stops so many pleasures in their source, is at once the proof and the effect of what we have advanced.

Men are often mistaken in points of taste, through want of knowledge. The principles of the fine arts are founded partly on general nature, and partly on arbitrary rules. But to judge of general nature requires much attention and experience.—Whether, for instance, the character of Achilles in Homer[1] is justly and naturally delineated, cannot be decided by every one. We meet with no such men in the streets.—We must previously form notions of human nature, as general as possible, dropping all local and individual characteristics. We must enlarge our views of it, by the study of ancient manners, and of its state in countries remote from our own. Arbitrary rules, it is still more evident, must be understood, before we can know whether they are preserved. But these rules are, in all the arts, numerous and complicated, and very easy to be confounded by unskilful judges.

Men are often misled, through hastiness of decision. It seems to pass for ignorance or dulness, if a man hesitates to give his opinion in a moment on a poem or a picture.—Men of reflection are sometimes astonished at the readiness with which people pass sentence upon works, which it would take them some days to appreciate. For, when we consider the comparison of ideas, the analogies of language, the parallelisms of former poets, which it is often necessary to run over in the mind, before we can ascertain the justness of a single metaphor, we may well think the power of deciding instantaneously on any given passage, a surprising proof of natural genius.—It is some consolation to dull mortals, that Mr. Burke[2] seems to have wanted this faculty, and not given much credit to those who profess to exercise it.

Of these three sources of critical error, want of sensibility most naturally leads men to dispraise what is good; and want of knowledge, to praise what is indifferent. This is, however, nothing like a general rule. Some are afraid to censure what they cannot relish; and a great many condemn what they cannot judge of. Precipitancy is an impartial failing, and scatters smiles and frowns at random.

Women are not often deficient in critical feeling, though it is not often much heightened by exercise. They have rarely, however, observed with sufficient comprehension, and scarce ever reflected with sufficient

---

[1] Achilles is the superhuman hero of Homer's *Iliad*.

[2] Edmund Burke,* *Philosophical Enquiry*, 2nd ed. (1759), "Introduction on Taste."

steadiness, to become knowing in the laws of taste. From these causes, and from having more modesty and good nature than men, they are apt to err on the side of admiration. Among men, on the contrary, among those particularly who aspire to be critics, a tone of fastidiousness seems pretty general.

The remedy for error in criticism is precisely the same as for error of any other kind: a diligent inquiry into truth. Criticism is a science, and taste can only be rendered accurate by much study and attention. As astronomy is not learned by casting our eyes on the heavens, so a taste in poetry cannot be acquired by lightly running over poems.

What is called, sometimes invidiously, metaphysical criticism, is the only real foundation for the principles of taste. For the more superficial style, such, for example, as the Prelections of bishop Lowth on Hebrew, or the Commentaries of sir W. Jones on oriental, poetry,[1] will never satisfy the reader who would search to the bottom, nor afford an answer to those who deny the existence of any positive standard. Something, indeed, has been said by Johnson, whose critical notions, when not warped by personal prejudice, were usually acute and profound, about "the cant of those who judge by principles rather than perception."[2] Without animadverting on the strange phrase of "judging by perception," it is a pity he has lent the sanction of his name to those, who, confiding in their own good taste, despise all philosophical inquiry into principles, as chimerical and unnecessary. Nothing is more truly *cant*, either in morals or criticism, than the language of those, who profess to decide from the impulse of their immediate feelings, without listening to so cold an arbitress as reason.

The laws of taste are partly natural, and partly arbitrary. Under the former class fall, in poetry and eloquence, whatever suggests associations generally delightful and interesting, or awakens sympathies which the constitution of mankind leads them to feel; in painting, truth of imitation, and forcibleness of expression; in music, gratification of the ear, and power over the affections. Under the latter may be reckoned what is called style in writing; and the observance of those rules with which critics are conversant, in the other arts. Architecture, in particular, mainly depends upon such rules; there being scarce any foundations in nature for the exact proportions of columns, limitations of ornaments, and the other *costumi*[3] of the art.

Independently of these principles of approbation and disapprobation in the objects of taste, all men are more or less influenced by circumstances peculiar to themselves. Every one is, in many cases, the slave of accidental associations; and these operate even more powerfully in matters of taste where few are sufficiently used to reason, than in the conduct of life. The most vulgar instance of this, is in our feelings of the beauties of nature. The house where we were born, the village where we have lived, the trees which have sheltered us, the mountains we have wandered over, have a claim on our hearts, more powerful than any which mere taste can create, but which we are apt to confound with the dictates of taste itself. It is the same energy of habitual sentiment that misleads us in many other subjects. In poetry, we often take a casual liking to a passage, for which, if we were to analyze our thoughts, we could give no reason. We repeat lines over, till we cannot get the chime of their sound out of our ears; and though we may gain from them no ideas worth attending to, we make up for it by associations of feeling.

Prejudices of education, so very common in critical decisions, seem to fall under this class. It is a general law indeed of our natures, that wherever ideas are the instruments of suggesting, by way of association,[4] sentiments of pleasure or pain, we consider these sentiments as springing from the ideas themselves, without attending to the intermediate associations. It is plain, therefore, that such persons, as have never formed these associations, will not be affected by the corresponding feelings; and will falsely accuse themselves of

---

[1] Robert Lowth (1710–87), bishop of London and author of *De sacra poesi Hebræorum* ("On the Sacred Poetry of the Hebrews," 1753); Sir William Jones (1746–94), justice in Calcutta, Sanskrit scholar, and founder of modern linguistics.

[2] Samuel Johnson (1709–84), "The Life of Pope" (1781).

[3] "customs" (It.).

[4] Cf. David Hartley (1705–57), *Observations on Man, his Frame, his Duty, and his Expectations* (1749).

want of taste, where taste, in a strict sense, has not been applied. The more hastily men judge, it must be clear, the more liable they will be to mistake their accidental associations for those of reason and comprehensive experience. It is for all men a matter of difficulty to be on their guard against such delusions. The imagination is the source of all error; and it is hard for taste to keep a rein over so restive a faculty. The state of our spirits and temper will make a mighty difference: a new poem is the worse for an east wind;[1] and a good critic may execrate a good actor, when he found nothing but standing-room to hear him.

As there are rules of taste, which are absolute and universal, and founded only on the common nature of human beings; so the rules of ethics are universal, and obligatory on all intelligent creatures who have received the same constitution as ourselves.

As there are rules, which were originally arbitrary, and which are observed in conformity to certain standards, but the authority of which is not recognized in all ages, nor every where; so there are positive enactments, and customs prescribed by usage, in each particular country, by which those who live under them are bound to regulate their actions, though they cannot reasonably condemn others, who have never assented to their authority. Finally, as there are prejudices and associations which lead some individuals to admire and dislike, in points of taste, what would not excite kindred sentiments in others; so there are particular habits of thinking and acting, which every one acquires for himself: such as walking with a stick, or without one; eating mutton rather than beef, or beef rather than mutton; liking pink ribands better than blue, or the contrary; in which he does very well to please himself, and very absurdly if he attempts to impose the same opinions on his neighbour. But as, from the pride and obstinacy of mankind, such intolerance, absurd as it is, is far from unusual in trifling matters, it cannot be wondered at, that many should set down their acquaintance as dull or ignorant, who happen not to have formed the same associations with a tune or a poem as themselves.

---

[1] The east wind was proverbially unpleasant.

Sir Walter Scott
1771 – 1832

W alter Scott was born in Edinburgh on 15 August 1771, the tenth child of Walter Scott, a solicitor, and Anne Rutherford, whose father was professor of physiology in the University of Edinburgh. Following an attack of poliomyelitis, from 1773 until 1778 he lived mainly with his grandfather in the country, where the family told stories and recited poetry from memory. Returning to school in Edinburgh, and later in Kelso, Scott learned Latin and developed his interest in seventeenth-century history. At Kelso grammar school he met James Ballantyne, his future printer and business partner. He read Shakespeare, Milton, Spenser, Richardson, Fielding, Smollett, Macpherson, and Mackenzie; he discovered Thomas Percy's *Reliques of Ancient English Poetry*, which inspired his own interest in collecting traditional ballads. In November 1783 he entered the University of Edinburgh, but withdrew early in 1786 because of poor health.

Indentured to train as a solicitor with his father, he also began to travel within Scotland: at a school-friend's house in 1787, he met Burns.* In 1789 he returned to university and in July 1792 was admitted to the Scottish bar. He married Margaret Charlotte Carpenter in 1797: they would have five children, one of whom, Sophia, would marry John Lockhart.* Scott continued to travel in the Highlands and the Scottish border country, learning about local history and traditional songs and ballads, collecting historical artifacts, and studying historical documents. During this period he encountered German Romanticism through Henry Mackenzie's 1788 lecture on German drama to the Royal Society of Edinburgh and through Alexander Fraser Tytler's translation of Schiller's *Die Räuber* (1792). He translated two poems by Bürger and published them anonymously as *The Chase and William and Helen: Two Ballads from the German of Gottfried Augustus Bürger* (1796). He contributed to Lewis's* *Tales of Wonder* (1801) and worked on *The Minstrelsy of the Scottish Border*, a collection of ballads: the first edition was published by Cadell and Davies and printed by James Ballantyne in 1802.

Scott's work as a literary editor ranged from sixteenth- to eighteenth-century texts. His first long poem, *The Lay of the Last Minstrel*, was published in Edinburgh in 1805, indebted to medieval romance and ballad and to Coleridge's *Christabel*.* It was highly successful, going through twenty-one British editions during his lifetime. His next long poem, *Marmion* (1808), about the defeat of the Scottish army at the battle of Flodden Field in 1513, proved even more popular. *The Lady of the Lake*, another success, appeared in 1810. Two more long poems, *Rokeby* (1813) and *The Lord of the Isles* (1815), and shorter ones such as *The Vision of Don Roderick* (1811), *The Bridal of Triermain* (1813), and *Harold the Dauntless* (1817) were less popular.

Scott entertained Campbell* in 1803 and Southey* in 1805. On a visit to London in 1806 he met Baillie,* dined with the princess of Wales, and met the Tory minister George Canning.* In 1808, following a dispute with Francis Jeffrey,* editor of the *Edinburgh Review*, Scott cancelled his subscription and allied himself with John Murray to found the *Quarterly Review* and with James and John Ballantyne to establish the publishing business John Ballantyne & Co.

In 1811 Scott bought a farm on the bank of the river Tweed near Melrose, which he renamed Abbotsford. His first novel, *Waverley*, appeared anonymously in 1814. Thereafter, he published twenty-three works of historical fiction, known as the Waverley Novels. He contributed reviews to the *Edinburgh Review* from 1802 to 1808, to the *Quarterly* from 1809 on, and to *Blackwood's Edinburgh Magazine* from 1818 on.

Scott was awarded a baronetcy in 1818 for legal rather than literary services. Planning and building of a new house at Abbotsford continued until 1825. He remained opposed to reform movements: following the massacre of protestors at St. Peter's Fields, Manchester, in 1819 ("Peterloo"), he published letters against radicalism. He was elected president of the Royal Society of Edinburgh in December 1820 and organized the king's visit to Scotland in July 1822. When, in 1826, his publishing business crashed, Scott undertook to repay debts amounting to a total of £126,000 largely through his writing—a commitment that eventually destroyed his health. After a trip to the continent in 1832, he returned to Abbotsford on 11 July and died there on 21 September 1832. He was buried with his wife in Dryburgh Abbey, Berwickshire. His son-in-law Lockhart, editor of the *Quarterly Review*, published his *Memoirs of the Life of Sir Walter Scott* in 1837–38. (A.M.)

from *Minstrelsy of the Scottish Border: Consisting of Historical and Romantic Ballads, Collected in the Southern Counties of Scotland; with a Few of Modern Date, Founded upon Local Tradition* (1802–03)[1]

Lord Randal

"O where hae ye been, lord Randal, my son?
O where hae ye been, my handsome young man?"
"I hae been to the wild wood; mother, make my bed
 soon,
For I'm weary wi' hunting, and fain wald lie down."

5 "Where gat ye your dinner, lord Randal, my son?
Where gat ye your dinner, my handsome young man?"
"I din'd wi' my true-love; mother, make my bed
 soon,
For I'm weary wi' hunting, and fain wald lie down."

"What gat ye to your dinner, lord Randal, my son,
10 What gat ye to your dinner, my handsome young
 man?"
"I gat eels boil'd in broo'; mother, make my bed soon,
For I'm weary wi' hunting, and fain wald lie down."

"What became of your bloodhounds, lord Randal,
 my son?
What became of your bloodhounds, my handsome
 young man?"

15 "O they swell'd and they died—mother, make my
 bed soon,
For I'm weary wi' hunting, and fain wald lie down."

"O I fear ye are poison'd, lord Randal, my son!
O I fear ye are poison'd, my handsome young man!"
"O yes! I am poison'd—mother, make my bed soon,
20 For I'm sick at the heart, and I fain wald lie down."

from *Marmion; A Tale of Flodden Field* (1808)[2]

Song

Where shall the lover rest,
 Whom the fates sever
From his true maiden's breast,
 Parted for ever?
5 Where, through groves deep and high,
 Sounds the far billow,
Where early violets die,
 Under the willow.
 CHORUS
Eleu loro, &c. Soft shall be his pillow.

10 There, through the summer day,
 Cool streams are laving;
There, while the tempests sway,
 Scarce are boughs waving;
There, thy rest shalt thou take,
15 Parted for ever,
Never again to wake,
 Never, O never.

---

[1] the volumes of traditional ballads (with some imitations by Scott and others) that Scott collected and published from 1802–1812.

[2] Scott's long poem, *Marmion*, focuses on the battle of Flodden Field (1513), where an English army inflicted heavy losses on the Scots, killing King James IV.

CHORUS
Eleu loro, &c. Never, O never.

Where shall the traitor rest,
    He, the deceiver,
Who could win maiden's breast,
    Ruin, and leave her?
In the lost battle,
    Borne down by the flying,
Where mingles war's rattle,
    With groans of the dying.
CHORUS
Eleu loro, &c. There shall he be lying.

Her wing shall the eagle flap,
    O'er the false-hearted;
His warm blood the wolf shall lap,
    Ere life be parted.
Shame and dishonour sit
    By his grave ever;
Blessing shall hallow it,—
    Never, O never.
CHORUS
Eleu loro, &c. Never, O never.

Lochinvar. Lady Heron's Song[1]

O, young Lochinvar is come out of the west,
Through all the wide Border[2] his steed was the best;
And save his good broad-sword he weapons had none,
He rode all unarmed, and he rode all alone.
So faithful in love, and so dauntless in war,
There never was knight like the young Lochinvar.

He staid not for brake,[3] and he stopped not for stone;
He swam the Eske[4] river where ford there was none;
But, ere he alighted at Netherby gate,
The bride had consented, the gallant came late:
For a laggard in love, and a dastard in war,
Was to wed the fair Ellen of brave Lochinvar.
So boldly he entered the Netherby Hall,
Among bride's-men, and kinsmen, and brothers,
    and all:
Then spoke the bride's father, his hand on his sword,
(For the poor craven bridegroom said never a word,)
"O come ye in peace here, or come ye in war,
Or to dance at our bridal, young Lord Lochinvar?"

"I long wooed your daughter, my suit you denied;—
Love swells like the Solway,[5] but ebbs like its tide—
And now am I come, with this lost love of mine,
To lead but one measure, drink one cup of wine.
There are maidens in Scotland more lovely by far,
That would gladly be bride to the young Lochinvar."

The bride kissed the goblet; the knight took it up,
He quaffed off the wine, and he threw down the cup.
She looked down to blush, and she looked up to sigh,
With a smile on her lips, and a tear in her eye.
He took her soft hand, ere her mother could bar,—
"Now tread we a measure!" said young Lochinvar.

So stately his form, and so lovely her face,
That never a hall such a galliard[6] did grace;
While her mother did fret, and her father did fume,
And the bridegroom stood dangling his bonnet and
    plume;
And the bride-maidens whispered, "'Twere better by far
To have matched our fair cousin with young
    Lochinvar."

One touch to her hand, and one word in her ear,
When they reached the hall-door, and the charger
    stood near;
So light to the croupe the fair lady he swung,
So light to the saddle before her he sprung!—
"She is won! we are gone, over bank, bush, and scaur;

---

[1] from *Marmion*, canto 5, sung by an Englishwoman at the court of King James IV of Scotland.

[2] the country on the border of England and Scotland, which continually changed hands over centuries of warfare.

[3] thicket.

[4] in East Yorkshire.

[5] an inlet of the Irish Sea at the western end of the border between England and Scotland.

[6] a lively French dance.

They'll have fleet steeds that follow," quoth young
    Lochinvar.

There was mounting 'mong Græmes of the Netherby
    clan;
Forsters, Fenwicks, and Musgraves, they rode and
    they ran:
45 There was racing, and chasing, on Cannobie Lee,
But the lost bride of Netherby ne'er did they see.
So daring in love, and so dauntless in war,
Have ye e'er heard of gallant like young Lochinvar?

from *Miscellaneous Poems* (1820)

The Sun upon the Weirdlaw Hill

AIR—*"Rimhin aluin 'stu mo run."*

The air, composed by the Editor of Albyn's Anthology. The words written for Mr GEORGE THOMSON's Scottish Melodies.

The sun upon the Weirdlaw hill,
    In Ettrick's vale,[1] is sinking sweet;
The westland wind is hush and still,
    The lake lies sleeping at my feet.
5 Yet not the landscape to mine eye
    Bears those bright hues that once it bore;
Though evening, with her richest dye,
    Flames o'er the hills of Ettrick's shore.

With listless look, along the plain
10   I see Tweed's[2] silver current glide,
And coldly mark the holy fane
    Of Melrose[3] rise in ruin'd pride.
The quiet lake, the balmy air,
    The hill, the stream, the tower, the tree,—
15 Are they still such as once they were,
    Or is the dreary change in me?

Alas, the warp'd and broken board,
    How can it bear the painter's dye!
The harp of strain'd and tuneless chord,
20   How to the minstrel's skill reply!
To aching eyes each landscape lowers,
    To feverish pulse each gale blows chill;
And Araby's or Eden's bowers
    Were barren as this moorland hill.

---

[1] The Ettrick Valley is in the Scottish borders. James Hogg,* known as the "Ettrick Shepherd," was born there.

[2] the river Tweed, roughly on the English-Scottish border.

[3] Melrose, on the river Tweed near Scott's house, Abbotsford, is the site of a now-ruined Cistercian abbey. Cf. Scott, *The Lay of the Last Minstrel* (1805) 2.1.1–2; and Barbauld, *Eighteen Hundred and Eleven* 156.*

Dorothy Wordsworth
1771 – 1855

Dorothy Wordsworth was born on 25 December 1771 in Cockermouth, Cumberland, the third of five children and the only daughter of John Wordsworth, an attorney, and his wife, Ann, née Cookson. Her mother died in 1778, her father in 1783; she grew up apart from her brothers with relatives at Halifax, Penrith, and Forncett rectory, near Norwich. When her uncle William Cookson was installed as a canon of Windsor in 1792, she went to stay there with the family. She was reunited with her brother William* at Windy Brow, Keswick, in 1794; in 1795, with the help of a legacy from Raisley Calvert, Dorothy and William moved to a house at Racedown Lodge, Dorset. Two years later they moved to Alfoxden House in Somerset, in order to be near Coleridge* at Nether Stowey; there Dorothy met Charles Lamb* and Hazlitt.* Her "Alfoxden journal" (1798) demonstrates the developing creative partnership between brother and sister.

In 1799, after a trip to Germany, the Wordsworths returned to the Lake District, where they were joined by Coleridge* and his wife, Southey* and his wife, and later by De Quincey.* When William married Mary Hutchinson in 1802, Dorothy continued to live with her brother and sister-in-law and their growing family. She worked as transcriber of her brother's poems, as housekeeper, aunt, and writer. Her "Grasmere journal" (1800–03) describes rural society, local characters, and domestic life.

The family moved to Rydal Mount in 1813. Dorothy continued to write letters, staying in touch with such friends as Jane Pollard, who married John Marshall, a Leeds industrialist; Catherine Clarkson, wife of the abolitionist Thomas Clarkson;* and Henry Crabb Robinson. Her journals describe many of Dorothy's travels with her brother: the winter in Germany (1798–99); an excursion to Calais during the peace of Amiens (1802) to visit Annette Vallon and William's daughter Caroline; and a tour to Switzerland and the Italian lakes in 1820. She visited Scotland twice; the first time, in 1803, she met Walter Scott.* She visited the Isle of Man on her own in 1828 and spent holidays with various relatives. William published five of her poems in his own collections of verse; Dorothy herself seems not to have been interested in publication.

In 1835, after several years of illness, she began to suffer from dementia. She spent the rest of her life at Rydal Mount, where she died on 25 January 1855. She was buried beside her brother William in Grasmere churchyard. (A.M.)

☙❧

from William Wordsworth, *Poems* (1815)

Address to a Child During a Boisterous Winter Evening[1]

What way does the Wind come? What way does he go?
He rides over the water, and over the snow,
Through wood, and through vale; and o'er rocky height,
Which the goat cannot climb, takes his sounding flight;
5 He tosses about in every bare tree,
As, if you look up, you plainly may see;
But how he will come, and whither he goes,
There's never a scholar in England knows.

He will suddenly stop in a cunning nook,
10 And rings a sharp 'larum;—but, if you should look,
There's nothing to see but a cushion of snow
Round as a pillow, and whiter than milk,

---

[1] When William Wordsworth* published this poem in his 1815 *Poems* (among his "Poems Referring to the Period of Childhood"), he assigned 1806 as the year of composition and added to the title the words, "by a female friend of the author." Susan Levin, *Dorothy Wordsworth and Romanticism* (1987), prints a slightly different version based on Dorothy Wordsworth's Coleorton Commonplace Book.

And softer than if it were covered with silk.
Sometimes he'll hide in the cave of a rock,
15 Then whistle as shrill as the buzzard cock;
—Yet seek him,—and what shall you find in the place?
Nothing but silence and empty space;
Save, in a corner, a heap of dry leaves,
That he's left, for a bed, to beggars or thieves!

20 As soon as 'tis daylight, to-morrow, with me
You shall go to the orchard, and then you will see
That he has been there, and made a great rout,
And cracked the branches, and strewn them about;
Heaven grant that he spare but that one upright twig
25 That looked up at the sky so proud and big
All last summer, as well you know,
Studded with apples, a beautiful show!

Hark! over the roof he makes a pause,
And growls as if he would fix his claws
30 Right in the slates, and with a huge rattle
Drive them down, like men in a battle:
—But let him range round; he does us no harm,
We build up the fire, we're snug and warm;
Untouched by his breath see the candle shines bright,
35 And burns with a clear and steady light;
Books have we to read,—but that half-stifled knell,
Alas! 'tis the sound of the eight o'clock bell.
—Come, now we'll to bed! and when we are there
He may work his own will, and what shall we care?
40 He may knock at the door,—we'll not let him in;
May drive at the windows,—we'll laugh at his din;
Let him seek his own home wherever it be;
Here's a *cozie* warm house for Edward and me.

from William Wordsworth, *Poems* (1842)

Floating Island[1]

Harmonious Powers with Nature work
On sky, earth, river, lake and sea;
Sunshine and cloud, whirlwind and breeze,
All in one duteous task agree.

5 Once did I see a slip of earth
(By throbbing waves long undermined)
Loosed from its hold; how, no one knew,
But all might see it float, obedient to the wind;

Might see it, from the mossy shore
10 Dissevered, float upon the Lake,
Float with its crest of trees adorned
On which the warbling birds their pastime take.

Food, shelter, safety, there they find;
There berries ripen, flowerets bloom;
15 There insects live their lives, and die;
A peopled world it is; in size a tiny room.

And thus through many seasons' space
This little Island may survive;
But Nature, though we mark her not,
20 Will take away, may cease to give.

Perchance when you are wandering forth
Upon some vacant sunny day,
Without an object, hope, or fear,
Thither your eyes may turn—the Isle is passed away;

25 Buried beneath the glittering Lake,
Its place no longer to be found;
Yet the lost fragments shall remain
To fertilise some other ground.

---

[1] The "floating island" was at Hawkshead; the poem was probably written in the late 1820s. In his *Poems* of 1842, W. Wordsworth included the poem with the following headnote: "These lines are by the Author of the Address to the Wind, &c., published heretofore along with my poems." In 1843 he told Isabella Fenwick, "My poor sister takes a pleasure in repeating these verses, which she composed not long before the beginning of her sad illness."

from Susan Levin, *Dorothy Wordsworth and Romanticism* (1987)

Grasmere—A Fragment[1]

Peaceful our valley, fair and green,
And beautiful her cottages,
Each in its nook, its sheltered hold,
Or underneath its tuft of trees

5 Many and beautiful they are;
But there is *one* that I love best,
A lowly shed, in truth, it is,
A brother of the rest.

Yet when I sit on rock or hill,
10 Down looking on the valley fair,
That Cottage with its clustering trees
Summons my heart; it settles there.

Others there are whose small domain
Of fertile fields and hedgerows green
15 Might more seduce a wanderer's mind
To wish that *there* his home had been.

Such wish be his! I blame him not,
My fancies they perchance are wild
—I love that house because it is
20 The very Mountains' child.

Fields hath it of its own, green fields,
But they are rocky steep and bare;
Their fence is of the mountain stone,
And moss and lichen flourish there.

25 And when the storm comes from the North
It lingers near that pastoral spot,
And, piping through the mossy walls,
It seems delighted with its lot.

And let it take its own delight;
30 And let it range the pastures bare;
Until it reach that group of trees,
—It may not enter there!

A green unfading grove it is,
Skirted with many a lesser tree,
35 Hazel & holly, beech and oak,
A bright and flourishing company.

Precious the shelter of those trees;
They screen the cottage that I love;
The sunshine pierces to the roof,
40 And the tall pine-trees tower above.

When first I saw that dear abode,
It was a lovely winter's day:
After a night of perilous storm
The west wind ruled with gentle sway;

45 A day so mild, it might have been
The first day of the gladsome spring;
The robins warbled, and I heard
One solitary throstle sing.

A Stranger, Grasmere, in thy Vale,
50 All faces then to me unknown,
I left my sole companion-friend[2]
To wander out alone.

Lured by a little winding path,
I quitted soon the public road,
55 A smooth and tempting path it was,
By sheep and shepherds trod.

---

[1] A version of this poem was first published in the *Monthly Packet* (Feb. 1892). Our text is Susan Levin's, based on various fair-copy versions in the Trevenen Album, Wordsworth Collection, Cornell University; in Dorothy's Commonplace Book; and in the Rydal notebook.

[2] probably her brother, William Wordsworth,* with whom she moved to Grasmere, 20 December 1799.

Eastward, toward the lofty hills,
This pathway led me on
Until I reached a stately Rock,
60 With velvet moss o'ergrown.

With russet oak and tufts of fern
Its top was richly garlanded;
Its sides adorned with eglantine
Bedropp'd with hips of glossy red.

65 There, too, in many a sheltered chink
The foxglove's broad leaves flourished fair,
And silver birch whose purple twigs
Bend to the softest breathing air.

Beneath that Rock my course I stayed,
70 And, looking to its summit high,
"Thou wear'st," said I, "a splendid garb,
Here winter keeps his revelry.

"Full long a dweller on the Plains,[1]
I griev'd when summer days were gone;
75 No more I'll grieve; for Winter here
Hath pleasure gardens of his own.

"What need of flowers? The splendid moss
Is gayer than an April mead;
More rich its hues of various green,
80 Orange, and gold, & glittering red."

—Beside that gay and lovely Rock
There came with merry voice
A foaming streamlet glancing by;
It seemed to say "Rejoice!"

85 My youthful wishes all fulfill'd,
Wishes matured by thoughtful choice,
I stood an Inmate of this vale
How *could* I but rejoice?

---

[1] After her parents died, Dorothy lived in Norfolk, a relatively flat part of the country. See also Jeremiah 21.13.

Thoughts on my Sick-bed[2]

And has the remnant of my life
 Been pilfered of this sunny Spring?
And have its own prelusive sounds
 Touched in my heart no echoing string?

5 Ah! say not so—the hidden life
 Couchant[3] within this feeble frame
Hath been enriched by kindred gifts,
 That, undesired, unsought-for, came

With joyful heart in youthful days
10 When fresh each season in its Round
I welcomed the earliest Celandine
 Glittering upon the mossy ground;

With busy eyes I pierced the lane
 In quest of known and *un*known things,
15 —The primrose a lamp on its fortress rock,
 The silent butterfly spreading its wings,

The violet betrayed by its noiseless breath,
 The daffodil dancing in the breeze,
The carolling thrush, on his naked perch,
20 Towering above the budding trees.

Our cottage-hearth no longer our home,
 Companions of Nature were we,
The Stirring, the Still, the Loquacious, the Mute—
 To all we gave our sympathy.

25 Yet never in those careless days
 When spring-time in rock, field, or bower
Was but a fountain of earthly hope
 A promise of fruits & the *splendid* flower.

---

[2] In a letter to Edward Quintilian, 25 May 1832, W. Wordsworth's daughter Dora comments on this poem: "you must excuse limping measure. Aunt cannot write regular metre."

[3] "lying" (Fr.).

No! then I never felt a bliss
That might with *that* compare
Which, piercing to my couch of rest,
Came on the vernal air.

When loving Friends an offering brought,
The first flowers of the year,
Culled from the precincts of our home,
From nooks to Memory dear.

With some sad thoughts the work was done,
Unprompted and unbidden,
But joy it brought to my *hidden* life,
To consciousness no longer hidden.

I felt a Power unfelt before,
Controlling weakness, languor, pain;
It bore me to the Terrace walk[1]
I trod the Hills again;—

No prisoner in this lonely room,
I *saw* the green Banks of the Wye,[2]
Recalling thy prophetic words,
Bard, Brother, Friend from infancy!

No need of motion,[3] or of strength,
Or even the breathing air:
—I thought of Nature's loveliest scenes;
And with Memory I was there.

---

[1] at Rydal Mount, the Wordsworths' home.

[2] See W. Wordsworth, "Lines Written a Few Miles Above Tintern Abbey."*

[3] Cf. W. Wordsworth, "A Slumber Did My Spirit Seal."*

from *Grasmere Journal*[4]

from *Tuesday 10th*. [June 1800]

On Tuesday, May 27th, a very tall woman, tall much beyond the measure of tall women, called at the door.[5] She had on a very long brown cloak, and a very white cap without Bonnet—her face was excessively brown, but it had plainly once been fair. She led a little barefooted child about 2 years old by the hand and said her husband who was a tinker was gone before with the other children. I gave her a piece of Bread. Afterwards on my road to Ambleside, beside the Bridge at Rydale, I saw her husband sitting by the roadside, his two asses feeding beside him and the two young children at play upon the grass. The man did not beg. I passed on and about 1/4 of a mile further I saw two boys before me, one about 10 the other about 8 years old at play chasing a butterfly. They were wild figures, not very ragged, but without shoes and stockings; the hat of the elder was wreathed round with yellow flowers, the younger whose hat was only a rimless crown, had stuck it round with laurel leaves. They continued at play till I drew very near and then they addressed me with the Beggars' cant and the whining voice of sorrow. I said I served your mother this morning. (The Boys were so like the woman who had called at the door that I could not be mistaken.) O! says the elder you could not serve my mother for she's dead and my father's on at the next town—he's a potter. I persisted in my assertion and that I would give them nothing. Says the elder Come, let's away, and away they flew like lightning. They had however sauntered so long in their road that they did not reach Ambleside before me, and I saw them go up to Matthew Harrison's house with their wallet upon the elder's shoulder, and creeping with a Beggar's complaining foot. On my return through Ambleside I met in the street the mother driving her asses; in the two Panniers of one of which were the two little children whom she was chiding and threatening with a wand which she used to drive on her asses, while the little things hung in wantonness over the

---

[4] from *The Journals of Dorothy Wordsworth*, ed. Mary Moorman, 2nd ed. corrected (1973).

[5] Cf. W. Wordsworth, "Beggars."*

Pannier's edge. The woman had told me in the morning that she was of Scotland, which her accent fully proved, but that she had lived (I think at Wigton), that they could not keep a house and so they travelled.

from *Friday 3rd October 1800*

N.B. When Wm and I returned from accompanying Jones we met an old man almost double,[1] he had on a coat thrown over his shoulders above his waistcoat and coat. Under this he carried a bundle and had an apron on and a night cap. His face was interesting. He had dark eyes and a long nose. John who afterwards met him at Wythburn[2] took him for a Jew. He was of Scotch parents but had been born in the army. He had had a wife "and a good woman and it pleased God to bless us with ten children." All these were dead but one of whom he had not heard for many years, a sailor. His trade was to gather leeches, but now leeches are scarce and he had not strength for it. He lived by begging and was making his way to Carlisle[3] where he should buy a few godly books to sell. He said leeches were very scarce partly owing to this dry season, but many years they have been scarce—he supposed it owing to their being much sought after, that they did not breed fast, and were of slow growth. Leeches were formerly 2/6 [per] 100; they are now 30/. He had been hurt in driving a cart, his leg broke his body driven over his skull fractured. He felt no pain till he recovered from his first insensibility. It was then late in the evening, when the light was just going away.

Sunday Morning [*14 March 1802*]

William had slept badly—he got up at 9 o'clock, but before he rose he had finished the Beggar Boys—and while we were at Breakfast that is (for I had breakfasted) he, with his Basin of Broth before him untouched and a little plate of Bread and butter he wrote the Poem to a Butterfly![4] He ate not a morsel, nor put on his stockings but sate with his shirt neck unbuttoned, and his waistcoat open while he did it. The thought first came upon him as we were talking about the pleasure we both always feel at the sight of a Butterfly. I told him that I used to chase them a little but that I was afraid of brushing the dust off their wings, and did not catch them—He told me how they used to kill all the white ones when he went to school because they were frenchmen. Mr Simpson came in just as he was finishing the Poem. After he was gone I wrote it down and the other poems and I read them all over to him....

[*15 April 1802*]

Thursday 15th. It was a threatening misty morning—but mild. We set off after dinner from Eusemere.[5] Mrs Clarkson went a short way with us but turned back. The wind was furious and we thought we must have returned. We first rested in the large Boat-house, then under a furze Bush opposite Mr Clarkson's. Saw the plough going in the field. The wind seized our breath the Lake was rough. There was a Boat by itself floating in the middle of the Bay below Water Millock. We rested again in the Water Millock Lane. The hawthorns are black and green, the birches here and there greenish but there is yet more of purple to be seen on the Twigs. We got over into a field to avoid some cows—people working, a few primroses by the roadside, wood-sorrel flower, the anemone, scentless violets, strawberries, and that starry yellow flower which Mrs C. calls pile wort. When we were in the woods beyond Gowbarrow park we saw a few daffodils close to the water side.[6] We fancied that the lake had floated the seeds ashore and that the little colony had so sprung up. But as we went along there were more and yet more and at last under the boughs of the trees, we saw that there was a long belt of them along the shore, about the breadth of a country turnpike road. I never saw daffodils so beautiful they grew among the mossy stones about and about them, some rested their heads upon these stones as on a pillow for weariness and the rest tossed and reeled and danced and seemed as if they verily laughed with the wind that

---

[1] Cf. W. Wordsworth, "Resolution and Independence"* 66.

[2] a village in Cumbria.

[3] a town in southwest Scotland, across the Cumbrian border.

[4] "Stay near me—do not take thy flight!"*

[5] on the east side of Ullswater, home of Thomas Clarkson* and his wife Catherine, Dorothy Wordsworth's "Mrs. Clarkson."

[6] Cf. W. Wordsworth, "I wandered lonely as a cloud."*

blew upon them over the lake, they looked so gay ever glancing ever changing. This wind blew directly over the lake to them. There was here and there a little knot and a few stragglers a few yards higher up but they were so few as not to disturb the simplicity and unity and life of that one busy highway. We rested again and again. The Bays were stormy, and we heard the waves at different distances and in the middle of the water like the sea. Rain came on—we were wet when we reached Luffs but we called in. Luckily all was chearless and gloomy so we faced the storm—we *must* have been wet if we had waited—put on dry clothes at Dobson's. I was very kindly treated by a young woman, the Landlady looked sour but it is her way. She gave us a goodish supper. Excellent ham and potatoes. We paid 7/ when we came away. William was sitting by a bright fire when I came downstairs. He soon made his way to the Library piled up in a corner of the window. He brought out a volume of Enfield's Speaker,[1] another miscellany, and an odd volume of Congreve's plays.[2] We had a glass of warm rum and water. We enjoyed ourselves and wished for Mary. It rained and blew when we went to bed. N.B. Deer in Gowbarrow park like skeletons.

Tuesday 26th. [*July 1802*][3]
Market day. Streets dirty, very rainy, did not leave Hull till 4 o'clock, and left Barton at about 6—rained all the way almost. A beautiful village at the foot of a hill with trees—a gentleman's house converted into a Lady's Boarding school. We had a woman in bad health in the coach, and took in a Lady and her Daughter—supped at Lincoln. Duck and peas, and cream cheese—paid 2/—. We left Lincoln on Wednesday morning 27th July at six o'clock it rained heavily and we could see nothing but the antientry of some of the Buildings as we passed along. The night before, however, we had seen enough to make us regret this. The minster stands at the edge of a hill, overlooking an immense plain. The country very flat as we went along—the Day mended. We went to see the outside of the Minster while the passengers were dining at Peterborough—the West End very grand. The little girl who was a great scholar, and plainly her Mother's favourite tho' she had a large family at home had bought The Farmer's Boy.[4] She said it was written by a man without education and was very wonderful.

On Thursday morning, 29th, we arrived in London. Wm left me at the Inn—I went to bed. Etc. etc. After various troubles and disasters we left London on Saturday morning at ½ past 5 or 6, the 31st of July (I have forgot which). We mounted the Dover Coach at Charing Cross. It was a beautiful morning. The City, St Paul's, with the River and a multitude of little Boats, made a most beautiful sight as we crossed Westminster Bridge.[5] The houses were not overhung by their cloud of smoke and they were spread out endlessly, yet the sun shone so brightly with such a pure light that there was even something like the purity of one of nature's own grand spectacles. We rode on chearfully now with the Paris Diligence[6] before us, now behind. We walked up the steep hills, beautiful prospects everywhere, till we even reached Dover. At first the rich populous wide spreading woody country about London, then the River Thames, ships sailing, chalk cliffs, trees, little villages. Afterwards Canterbury, situated on a plain, rich and woody, but the City and Cathedral disappointed me. Hop grounds on each side of the road some miles from Canterbury, then we came to a common, the race ground, an elevated plain, villages among trees in the bed of a valley at our right, and rising above this valley, green hills scattered over with wood—neat gentlemen's houses. One white house almost hid with green trees which we longed for and the parson's house as neat a

---

[1] William Enfield, *The Speaker: or, Miscellaneous Pieces, selected from the Best English Writers, and disposed under proper heads, with a view to facilitate the Improvement of Youth in Reading and Speaking. To which is prefixed an Essay on Elocution* (1774).

[2] William Congreve (1670–1729) is best known for his comedy *The Way of the World* (1700).

[3] The excerpt describes Dorothy and William Wordsworth's journey to Calais by way of London and Dover to spend a month with William's nine-year-old daughter Caroline and her mother, Annette Vallon. Following this visit, Dorothy and William returned to England for W. Wordsworth's marriage to Mary Hutchinson, 4 October 1802.

[4] by Robert Bloomfield.*

[5] Cf. W. Wordsworth, "Composed upon Westminster Bridge, Sept. 3, 1802."*

[6] stage-coach.

place as could be which would just have suited Coleridge. No doubt we might have found one for Tom Hutchinson and Sara[1] and a good farm too. We halted at a halfway house—fruit carts under the shade of trees, seats for guests, a tempting place to the weary traveller. Still as we went along the country was beautiful, hilly, with cottages lurking under the hills and their little plots of hop ground like vineyards. It was a bad hop-year. A woman on the top of the coach said to me "It is a sad thing for the poor people for the hop-gathering is the women's harvest, there is employment about the hops both for women and children". We saw the Castle of Dover and the sea beyond 4 or 5 miles before we reached D. We looked at it through a long vale, the castle being upon an eminence, as it seemed at the end of this vale which opened to the Sea. The country now became less fertile but near Dover it seemed more rich again. Many buildings stand on the flat fields, sheltered with tall trees. There is one old chapel that might have been there just in the same state in which it now is, when this vale was as retired and as little known to travellers, as our own Cumberland mountain wilds 30 years ago. There was also a very old Building on the other side of the road which had a strange effect among the many new ones that are springing up everywhere. It seemed odd that it could have kept itself pure in its anciently among so many upstarts. It was near dark when we reached Dover. We were told that the packet was about to sail, so we went down to the Custom-house in half an hour had our luggage examined etc. etc. and then we drank tea, with the honorable Mr Knox and his Tutor. We arrived at Calais at 4 o'clock on Sunday morning, the 31st of July. We stayed in the vessel till ½-past 7, then Wm went for Letters, at about ½ past 8 or 9 we found out Annette and C.[2] chez Madame Avril dans la Rue de la Tête d'or. We lodged opposite two Ladies in tolerably decent-sized rooms but badly furnished, and with large store of bad smells and dirt in the yard, and all about. The weather was very hot. We walked by the sea-shore almost every evening with Annette and Caroline or Wm and I alone. I had a bad cold and could not bathe at first but William did. It was a pretty sight to see as we walked upon the sands when the tide was low perhaps a hundred people bathing about ¼ of a mile distant from us, and we had delightful walks after the heat of the day was passed away—seeing far off in the west the Coast of England like a cloud crested with Dover Castle, which was but like the summit of the cloud. The Evening star and the glory of the sky. The Reflections in the water were more beautiful than the sky itself, purple waves brighter than precious stones for ever melting away upon the sands. The fort, a wooden Building, at the Entrance of the harbour at Calais, when the Evening twilight was coming on, and we could not see anything of the building but its shape which was far more distinct than in perfect daylight, seemed to be reared upon pillars of Ebony, between which pillars the sea was seen in the most beautiful colours that can be conceived. Nothing in Romance was ever half so beautiful. Now came in view as the Evening star sank down and the colours of the west faded away the two lights of England, lighted up by the Englishmen in our Country, to warn vessels of rocks or sands. These we used to see from the Pier when we could see no other distant objects but the Clouds the Sky and the Sea itself. All was dark behind. The town of Calais seemed deserted of the light of heaven, but there was always light, and life, and joy upon the Sea.—One night, though, I shall never forget. The day had been very hot, and William and I walked alone together upon the pier. The sea was gloomy for there was a blackness over all the sky except when it was overspread with lightning which often revealed to us a distant vessel. Near us the waves roared and broke against the pier, and as they broke and a Ray travelled towards us, and they were interfused with greenish fiery light. The more distant sea always black and gloomy. It was also beautiful on the calm hot night to see the little Boats row out of harbour with wings of fire and the sail boats with the fiery track which they cut as they went along and which closed up after them with a hundred thousand sparkles balls shootings, and streams of glowworm light. Caroline was delighted.

---

[1] the brother and sister of W. Wordsworth's fiancée, Mary.

[2] Annette Vallon, W. Wordsworth's former lover, and their daughter Caroline.

On Sunday the 29th of August we left Calais at 12 o'clock in the morning, and landed at Dover at 1 on Monday the 30th. I was sick all the way. It was very pleasant to me when we were in harbour at Dover to breathe the fresh air, and to look up and see the stars among the Ropes of the vessel. The next day was very hot. We both bathed and sate upon the Dover Cliffs and looked upon France with many a melancholy and tender thought. We could see the shores almost as plain as if it were but an English lake—we mounted the coach at ½ past 4 and arrived in London at 6 the 30th August. It was misty and we could see nothing. We stayed in London till Wednesday the 22nd of September, and arrived at Gallow Hill on Friday 24th September. Mary[1] first met us in the avenue. She looked so fat and well that we were made very happy by the sight of her. Then came Sara, and last of all Joanna. Tom was forking corn standing upon the corn cart. We dressed ourselves immediately and got tea—the garden looked gay with asters and sweet peas. I looked at everything with tranquillity and happiness—was ill on Saturday and on Sunday and continued to be during most of the time of our stay. Jack and George came on Friday Evening 1st October. On Saturday 2nd we rode to Hackness, William Jack George and Sara single, I behind Tom. On Sunday 3rd Mary and Sara were busy packing. On Monday 4th October 1802, my Brother William was married to Mary Hutchinson. I slept a good deal of the night and rose fresh and well in the morning. At a little after 8 o'clock I saw them go down the avenue towards the Church. William had parted from me upstairs. I gave him the wedding ring—with how deep a blessing! I took it from my forefinger where I had worn it the whole of the night before—he slipped it again onto my finger and blessed me fervently. When they were absent my dear little Sara prepared the breakfast. I kept myself as quiet as I could, but when I saw the two men running up the walk, coming to tell us it was over, I could stand it no longer and threw myself on the bed where I lay in stillness, neither hearing or seeing any thing, till Sara came upstairs to me and said "They are coming." This forced me from the bed where I lay and I moved I knew not how straight forward, faster than my strength could carry me till I met my beloved William and fell upon his bosom. He and John Hutchinson led me to the house and there I stayed to welcome my dear Mary. As soon as we had breakfasted we departed. It rained when we set off. Poor Mary was much agitated when she parted from her Brothers and Sisters and her home. Nothing particular occurred till we reached Kirby. We had sunshine and showers, pleasant talk, love and chearfulness. We were obliged to stay two hours at K. while the horses were feeding. We wrote a few lines to Sara and then walked out, the sun shone and we went to the Church-yard after we had put a Letter into the Post office for the York Herald. We sauntered about and read the Grave--stones. There was one to the memory of 5 Children, who had all died within 5 years, and the longest lived had only lived 4 years. There was another stone erected to the memory of an unfortunate woman (as we supposed, by a stranger). The verses engraved upon it expressed that she had been neglected by her Relations and counselled the Readers of those words to look within and recollect their own frailties. ...

---

[1] Mary Hutchinson, whom W. Wordsworth was about to marry.

Mary Tighe
1772 – 1810

Mary Blachford was born in Dublin on 9 October 1772, the daughter of Theodosia Tighe, a Methodist leader, and William Blachford, a Church of Ireland clergyman and librarian of St. Patrick's Library, Dublin. Her father died in 1773, and Mary and her brother John were educated by their mother, whose curriculum emphasized literature and religious instruction. In 1793 Mary Blachford married her first cousin, Henry Tighe, a member of the Irish parliament for Inistioge, co. Kilkenny; the marriage seems to have been unhappy. The Tighes moved to London so that Henry could study law, but he failed to complete his training. They returned to Ireland in 1801. Settling at Woodstock, Tighe composed *Psyche* and wrote an unpublished novel, *Selena*. Thomas Moore,* an early admirer of Tighe's work, read *Psyche* in manuscript and responded with his poem, "To Mrs. Henry Tighe on Reading her 'Psyche'" (1802); *Psyche* was published in a limited edition of 50 copies in 1805.

By this time, Tighe was living in Dublin where, sick with consumption, she was visited by Moore, Owenson (later Lady Morgan),* and Sir Arthur Wellesley (later the Duke of Wellington). She died at the estate of her brother-in-law William Tighe at Woodstock, co. Wicklow, Ireland on 24 March 1810; she was buried in Inistioge church. The 1811 edition of *Psyche*, edited by William Tighe, was successful, proving to be a significant influence on the poetry of Keats.* (A.M.)

☙❧

from *Psyche, with Other Poems. By the Late Mrs. Henry Tighe* (1811)[1]

from *Psyche; or, The Legend of Love*

—Castos docet et pios amores.[2]
                MARTIAL

Chi pensa quanto un bel desio d'amore
  Un spirto pellegrin tenga sublime;
  Non vorria non averne acceso il core;
Chi gusta quanto dolce il creder sia
  Solo esser caro a chi sola n'e cara,
  Regna in un stato a cui null' altro e pria.
              ARIOSTO, ELEG. XII.[3]

ARGUMENT

Proem—Psyche introduced—Her royal origin—Envy of Venus—Her instructions to Cupid—The island of Pleasure—The fountains of Joy and of Sorrow—The appearance of Love—Psyche asleep—Mutually wounded—Psyche reveals her dream to her Mother—The Oracle consulted—Psyche abandoned on the Rock by its decree—Carried by Zephyrs to the island of Pleasure—The Palace of Love—Banquet of Love—Marriage of Cupid and Psyche—Psyche's daily solitude—Her request to her Lover—His reluctant consent.

---

[1] The first edition of 1805 consisted of only fifty copies for private circulation. Two editions followed in 1811; according to Earle Vonard Weller, *Keats and Mary Tighe* (New York: MLA, 1927), the third edition "was probably the edition used by Keats."* Our text is that of the second edition (1811). *Psyche* consists of six cantos, only one of which is printed here. The story goes on to describe how Psyche disobeys the command that she not look at her lover's face, how the lovers are separated, and how Venus imposes trials on Psyche. Psyche sets off on an allegorical journey; tested by her encounters with Vanity, Flattery, Credulity, Jealousy, and Indifference. Finally Cupid convinces Jupiter to intervene and reunite him with Psyche. Some readers will recognize in the tale of Cupid and Psyche a version of the Grimm brothers' story "Beauty and the Beast." Keats's "Ode to Psyche"* is, like Tighe's poem, indebted to Lucius Apuleius, whose romance *The Metamorphoses of Lucius, or The Golden Ass* (Books 4–6) contains the first extant version of the story of Cupid and Psyche. The story of Cupid and Psyche has often been interpreted as an allegory of the soul achieving perfection through love: Psyche means "soul" in Greek.

[2] *Epigrams* 10.35.8: "She tells of pure and lawful love."

[3] "He who thinks that a beautiful lover can lift a sad spirit, will want to set his heart on fire; he who knows how sweet it is to know that he is loved only by her, is the sole ruler in this state" (trans. Duncan Wu).

Let not the rugged brow the rhymes accuse,
Which speak of gentle knights and ladies fair,
Nor scorn the lighter labours of the muse,
Who yet, for cruel battles would not dare
The low-strung chords of her weak lyre prepare:
But loves to court repose in slumbery lay,
To tell of goodly bowers and gardens rare,
Of gentle blandishments and amorous play,
And all the lore of love, in courtly verse essay.

And ye whose gentle hearts in thraldom held
The power of mighty Love already own,
When you the pains and dangers have beheld,
Which erst your lord hath for his Psyche known,
For all your sorrows this may well atone,
That he you serve the same hath suffered;
And sure, your fond applause the tale will crown
In which your own distress is pictured,
And all that weary way which you yourselves must tread.

Most sweet would to my soul the hope appear,
That sorrow in my verse a charm might find,
To smooth the brow long bent with bitter cheer,
Some short distraction to the joyless mind
Which grief, with heavy chain, hath fast confined
To sad remembrance of its happier state;
For to myself I ask no boon more kind
Than power another's woes to mitigate,
And that soft soothing art which anguish can abate.

And thou, sweet sprite,[1] whose sway doth far extend,
Smile on the mean historian of thy fame!
My heart in each distress and fear befriend,
Nor ever let it feel a fiercer flame
Than innocence may cherish free from blame,
And hope may nurse, and sympathy may own;
For, as thy rights I never would disclaim,
But true allegiance offered to thy throne,
So may I love but one, by one beloved alone.

That anxious torture may I never feel,
Which, doubtful, watches o'er a wandering heart.
Oh! who that bitter torment can reveal,
Or tell the pining anguish of that smart!
In those affections may I ne'er have part,
Which easily transferred can learn to rove:
No, dearest Cupid! when I feel thy dart,
For thy sweet Psyche's sake may no false love
The tenderness I prize lightly from me remove!

CANTO 1

Much wearied with her long and dreary way,
And now with toil and sorrow well nigh spent,
Of sad regret and wasting grief the prey,
Fair Psyche through untrodden forests went,
To lone shades uttering oft a vain lament.
And oft in hopeless silence sighing deep,
As she her fatal error did repent,
While dear remembrance bade her ever weep,
And her pale cheek in ceaseless showers of sorrow steep.

'Mid the thick covert of that woodland shade,
A flowery bank there lay undressed by art,
But of the mossy turf spontaneous made;
Here the young branches shot their arms athwart,
And wove the bower so thick in every part,
That the fierce beams of Phœbus glancing strong
Could never through the leaves their fury dart;
But the sweet creeping shrubs that round it throng,
Their loving fragrance mix, and trail their flowers along.

And close beside a little fountain played,
Which through the trembling leaves all joyous shone,
And with the cheerful birds sweet music made,
Kissing the surface of each polished stone
As it flowed past: sure as her favourite throne
Tranquillity might well esteem the bower,
The fresh and cool retreat have called her own,
A pleasant shelter in the sultry hour,
A refuge from the blast, and angry tempest's power.

---

[1] I.e., Cupid, god of love.

Wooed by the soothing silence of the scene
Here Psyche stood, and looking round, lest aught
30 Which threatened danger near her might have been,
Awhile to rest her in that quiet spot
She laid her down, and piteously bethought
Herself on the sad changes of her fate,
Which in so short a space so much had wrought,
35 And now had raised her to such high estate,
And now had plunged her low in sorrow desolate.

Oh! how refreshing seemed the breathing wind
To her faint limbs! and while her snowy hands
From her fair brow her golden hair unbind,
40 And of her zone[1] unloose the silken bands,
More passing bright unveiled her beauty stands;
For faultless was her form as beauty's queen,
And every winning grace that Love demands,
With mild attempered dignity was seen
45 Play o'er each lovely limb, and deck her angel mien.

Though solitary now, dismayed, forlorn,
Without attendant through the forest rude,
The peerless maid of royal lineage born
By many a royal youth had oft been wooed;
50 Low at her feet full many a prince had sued,
And homage paid unto her beauty rare;
But all their blandishments her heart withstood;
And well might mortal suitor sure despair,
Since mortal charms were none which might with hers compare.

55 Yet nought of insolence or haughty pride
Found ever in her gentle breast a place;
Though men her wondrous beauty deified,
And rashly deeming such celestial grace
Could never spring from any earthly race,
60 Lo! all forsaking Cytherea's[2] shrine,
Her sacred altars now no more embrace,

But to fair Psyche pay those rites divine,
Which, Goddess! are thy due, and should be only thine.

But envy of her beauty's growing fame
65 Poisoned her sisters' hearts with secret gall,
And oft with seeming piety they blame
The worship which they justly impious call;
And oft, lest evil should their sire befal,
Besought him to forbid the erring crowd
70 Which hourly thronged around the regal hall,
With incense, gifts, and invocations loud,
To her whose guiltless breast, ne'er felt elation proud.

For she was timid as the wintry flower,
That, whiter than the snow it blooms among,
75 Droops its fair head submissive to the power
Of every angry blast which sweeps along
Sparing the lovely trembler, while the strong
Majestic tenants of the leafless wood
It levels low. But, ah! the pitying song
80 Must tell how, than the tempest's self more rude,
Fierce wrath and cruel hate their suppliant prey pursued.

Indignant quitting her deserted fanes,
Now Cytherea sought her favourite isle,[3]
And there from every eye her secret pains
85 'Mid her thick myrtle bowers concealed awhile;
Practised no more the glance, or witching smile,
But nursed the pang she never felt before,
Of mortified disdain; then to beguile
The hours which mortal flattery soothed no more,
90 She various plans revolved her influence to restore.

She called her son with unaccustomed voice;
Not with those thrilling accents of delight
Which bade so oft enchanted Love rejoice,
Soft as the breezes of a summer's night:
95 Now choked with rage its change could Love affright;
As all to sullen discontent a prey,

---

[1] belt or girdle.

[2] Cytherea is Venus, goddess of love, whose jealousy of Psyche initiates the events of the story.

[3] Cyprus.

    Shunning the cheerful day's enlivening light,
    She felt the angry power's malignant sway,
And bade her favourite boy her vengeful will obey.

100   Bathed in those tears which vanquish human hearts,
    "Oh, son beloved!" (the suppliant goddess cries,)
    "If e'er thy too indulgent mother's arts
    Subdued for thee the potent deities
    Who rule my native deep,[1] or haunt the skies;
105   Or if to me the grateful praise be due,
    That to thy sceptre bow the great and wise,
    Now let thy fierce revenge my foe pursue,
And let my rival scorned her vain presumption rue.

    "For what to me avails my former boast
110   That, fairer than the wife of Jove confest,
    I gained the prize thus basely to be lost?
    With me the world's devotion to contest
    Behold a mortal dares; though on my breast
    Still vainly brilliant shines the magic zone.[2]
115   Yet, yet I reign: by you my wrongs redrest,
    The world with humbled Psyche soon shall own
That Venus, beauty's queen, shall be adored alone.

    "Deep let her drink of that dark, bitter spring,
    Which flows so near thy bright and crystal tide;
120   Deep let her heart thy sharpest arrow sting,
    Its tempered barb in that black poison dyed.
    Let her, for whom contending princes sighed,
    Feel all the fury of thy fiercest flame
    For some base wretch to foul disgrace allied,
125   Forgetful of her birth and her fair fame,
Her honours all defiled, and sacrificed to shame."

    Then, with sweet pressure of her rosy lip,
    A kiss she gave bathed in ambrosial dew;
    The thrilling joy he would for ever sip,
130   And his moist eyes in ecstasy imbrue.
    But she whose soul still angry cares pursue,
    Snatched from the soft caress her glowing charms;
    Her vengeful will she then enforced anew,
    As she in haste dismissed him from her arms,
135   The cruel draught to seek of anguish and alarms.

    'Mid the blue waves by circling seas embraced
    A chosen spot of fairest land was seen;
    For there with favouring hand had Nature placed
    All that could lovely make the varied scene:
140   Eternal Spring there spread her mantle green;
    There high surrounding hills deep-wooded rose
    O'er placid lakes; while marble rocks between
    The fragrant shrubs their pointed heads disclose,
And balmy breathes each gale which o'er the island blows.

145   Pleasure had called the fertile lawns her own,
    And thickly strewed them with her choicest flowers;
    Amid the quiet glade her golden throne
    Bright shone with lustre through o'erarching bowers:
    There her fair train, the ever downy Hours,
150   Sport on light wing with the young Joys entwined;
    While Hope delighted from her full lap showers
    Blossoms, whose fragrance can the ravished mind
Inebriate with dreams of rapture unconfined.

    And in the grassy centre of the isle,
155   Where the thick verdure spreads a damper shade,
    Amid their native rocks concealed awhile,
    Then o'er the plains in devious streams displayed,
    Two gushing fountains rise; and thence conveyed,
    Their waters through the woods and vallies play,
160   Visit each green recess and secret glade,
    With still unmingled, still meandering way,
Nor widely wandering far, can each from other stray.

    But of strange contrast are their virtues found,
    And oft the lady of that isle has tried
165   In rocky dens and caverns under ground,
    The black deformed stream in vain to hide;
    Bursting all bounds her labours it defied;
    Yet many a flowery sod its course conceals
    Through plains where deep its silent waters glide,
170   Till secret ruin all corroding steals,
And every treacherous arch the hideous gulph reveals.

---

[1] Venus was said to have emerged fully grown from the sea: see Hesiod, *Theogony* (8th century BC), and the *Homeric Hymns*.

[2] Cf. line 40, above.

Forbidding every kindly prosperous growth,
Where'er it ran, a channel bleak it wore;
The gaping banks receded, as though loth
To touch the poison which disgraced their shore:
There deadly anguish pours unmixed his store
Of all the ills which sting the human breast,
The hopeless tears which past delights deplore,
Heart-gnawing jealousy which knows no rest,
And self-upbraiding shame, by stern remorse opprest.

Oh, how unlike the pure transparent stream,
Which near it bubbles o'er its golden sands!
The impeding stones with pleasant music seem
Its progress to detain from other lands;
And all its banks, inwreathed with flowery bands,
Ambrosial fragrance shed in grateful dew:
There young Desire enchanted ever stands,
Breathing delight and fragrance ever new,
And bathed in constant joys of fond affection true.[1]

But not to mortals is it e'er allowed
To drink unmingled of that current bright;
Scarce can they taste the pleasurable flood,
Defiled by angry Fortune's envious spite;
Who from the cup of amorous delight
Dashes the sparkling draught of brilliant joy,
Till, with dull sorrow's stream despoiled quite,
No more it cheers the soul nor charms the eye,
But 'mid the poisoned bowl distrust and anguish lie.

Here Cupid tempers his unerring darts,
And in the fount of bliss delights to play;
Here mingles balmy sighs and pleasing smarts,
And here the honied draught will oft allay
With that black poison's all-polluting sway,
For wretched man. Hither, as Venus willed,
For Psyche's punishment he bent his way:
From either stream his amber vase he filled,
For her were meant the drops which grief alone distilled.

His quiver, sparkling bright with gems and gold,
From his fair plumed shoulder graceful hung,
And from its top in brilliant chords enrolled
Each little vase resplendently was slung:
Still as he flew, around him sportive clung
His frolic train of winged Zephyrs light,
Wafting the fragrance which his tresses flung:
While odours dropped from every ringlet bright,
And from his blue eyes beamed ineffable delight.

Wrapt in a cloud unseen by mortal eye,
He sought the chamber of the royal maid;
There, lulled by careless soft security,
Of the impending mischief nought afraid,
Upon her purple couch was Psyche laid,
Her radiant eyes a downy slumber sealed;
In light transparent veil alone arrayed,
Her bosom's opening charms were half revealed,
And scarce the lucid folds her polished limbs concealed.

A placid smile plays o'er each roseate lip,
Sweet severed lips! why thus your pearls disclose,
That slumbering thus unconscious she may sip
The cruel presage of her future woes?
Lightly, as fall the dews upon the rose,
Upon the coral gates of that sweet cell
The fatal drops he pours; nor yet he knows,
Nor, though a God, can he presaging tell
How he himself shall mourn the ills of that sad spell!

Nor yet content, he from his quiver drew,
Sharpened with skill divine, a shining dart:
No need had he for bow, since thus too true
His hand might wound her all exposed heart;
Yet her fair side he touched with gentlest art,
And half relenting on her beauties gazed;
Just then awaking with a sudden start
Her opening eye in humid lustre blazed,
Unseen he still remained, enchanted and amazed.

---

[1] Cf. Keats, "Ode on a Grecian Urn" 21–30.*

     The dart which in his hand now trembling stood,
245   As o'er the couch he bent with ravished eye,
     Drew with its daring point celestial blood
     From his smooth neck's unblemished ivory:
     Heedless of this, but with a pitying sigh
     The evil done now anxious to repair,
250   He shed in haste the balmy drops of joy
     O'er all the silky ringlets of her hair;
Then stretched his plumes divine, and breathed celestial air.

     Unhappy Psyche! soon the latent wound
     The fading roses of her cheek confess,
255   Her eyes bright beams, in swimming sorrows drowned,
     Sparkle no more with life and happiness
     Her parents fond exulting heart to bless;
     She shuns adoring crowds, and seeks to hide
     The pining sorrows which her soul oppress,
260   Till to her mother's tears no more denied,
The secret grief she owns, for which she lingering sighed.

     A dream of mingled terror and delight
     Still heavy hangs upon her troubled soul,
     An angry form still swims before her sight,
265   And still the vengeful thunders seem to roll;
     Still crushed to earth she feels the stern control
     Of Venus unrelenting, unappeased:
     The dream returns, she feels the fancied dole;
     Once more the furies on her heart have seized,
270 But still she views the youth who all her sufferings eased.

     Of wonderous beauty did the vision seem,
     And in the freshest prime of youthful years;
     Such at the close of her distressful dream
     A graceful champion to her eyes appears;
275   Her loved deliverer from her foes and fears
     She seems in grateful transport still to press;
     Still his soft voice sounds in her ravished ears;
     Dissolved in fondest tears of tenderness
His form she oft invokes her waking eyes to bless.

280   Nor was it quite a dream,[1] for as she woke,
     Ere heavenly mists concealed him from her eye,
     One sudden transitory view she took
     Of Love's most radiant bright divinity;
     From the fair image never can she fly,
285   As still consumed with vain desire she pines;
     While her fond parents heave the anxious sigh,
     And to avert her fate seek holy shrines
The threatened ills to learn by auguries and signs.

     And now, the royal sacrifice prepared,
290   The milk-white bull they to the altar lead,[2]
     Whose youth the galling yoke as yet had spared,
     Now destined by the sacred knife to bleed:
     When lo! with sudden spring his horns he freed,
     And head-long rushed amid the frighted throng:
295   While from the smoke-veiled shrine such sounds proceed
     As well might strike with awe the soul most strong;
And thus divinely spoke the heaven inspired tongue.

     "On nuptial couch, in nuptial vest arrayed,
     On a tall rock's high summit Psyche place:
300   Let all depart, and leave the fated maid
     Who never must a mortal Hymen[3] grace:
     A winged monster of no earthly race
     Thence soon shall bear his trembling bride away;
     His power extends o'er all the bounds of space,
305   And Jove himself has owned his dreaded sway,
Whose flaming breath sheds fire, whom earth and heaven obey."

     With terror, anguish, and astonishment
     The oracle her wretched father hears;
     Now from his brow the regal honours rent,
310   And now in frantic sorrow wild appears,
     Nor threatened plagues, nor punishment he fears,
     Refusing long the sentence to obey,
     Till Psyche, trembling with submissive tears,

---

[1] Cf. Keats, "The Eve of St. Agnes" 326–28* and "Ode to Psyche" 6.*

[2] Cf. Keats, "Ode on a Grecian Urn" 31–33.*

[3] the Roman god of marriage; here, a bridegroom.

Bids them the sacrifice no more delay,
315 Prepare the funeral couch, and leave the destined prey.

    Pleased by the ambiguous doom the Fates promulge,
    The angry Goddess and enamoured Boy
    Alike content their various hopes indulge;
    He, still exploring with an anxious eye
320 The future prospect of uncertain joy,
    Plans how the tender object of his care
    He may protect from threatened misery;
    Ah sanguine Love! so oft deceived, forbear
With flattering tints to paint illusive hope so fair.

325 But now what lamentations rend the skies!
    In amaracine wreaths the virgin choir
    With Io Hymen[1] mingle funeral cries:
    Lost in the sorrows of the Lydian lyre[2]
    The breathing flutes' melodious notes expire;
330 In sad procession pass the mournful throng
    Extinguishing with tears the torches' fire,
    While the mute victim weeping crowds among,
By unknown fears oppressed, moves silently along.

    But on such scenes of terror and dismay
335 The mournful Muse delights not long to dwell;
    She quits well pleased the melancholy lay,
    Nor vainly seeks the parents' woes to tell:
    But what to wondering Psyche then befel
    When thus abandoned, let her rather say,
340 Who shuddering looks to see some monster fell
    Approach the desert rock to seize his prey,
With cruel fangs devour, or tear her thence away.

    When lo! a gentle breeze began to rise,
    Breathed by obedient Zephyrs[3] round the maid,
345 Fanning her bosom with its softest sighs
    Awhile among her fluttering robes it strayed,
    And boldly sportive latent charms displayed:
    And then, as Cupid willed, with tenderest care
    From the tall rock, where weeping she was laid,
350 With gliding motion through the yielding air
To Pleasure's blooming isle their lovely charge they bear.

    On the green bosom of the turf reclined,
    They lightly now the astonished virgin lay,
    To placid rest they sooth her troubled mind;
355 Around her still with watchful care they stay,
    Around her still in quiet whispers play;
    Till lulling slumbers bid her eyelids close,
    Veiling with silky fringe each brilliant ray,
    While soft tranquillity divinely flows
360 O'er all her soul serene, in visions of repose.

    Refreshed she rose, and all enchanted gazed
    On the rare beauties of the pleasant scene.
    Conspicuous far a lofty palace blazed
    Upon a sloping bank of softest green;
365 A fairer edifice was never seen;
    The high ranged columns own no mortal hand,
    But seem a temple meet for Beauty's queen.
    Like polished snow the marble pillars stand
In grace attempered majesty sublimely grand.

370 Gently ascending from a silvery flood,
    Above the palace rose the shaded hill,
    The lofty eminence was crowned with wood,
    And the rich lawns, adorned by nature's skill,
    The passing breezes with their odours fill;
375 Here ever blooming groves of orange glow,
    And here all flowers which from their leaves distil
    Ambrosial dew in sweet succession blow,
And trees of matchless size a fragrant shade bestow.

    The sun looks glorious mid a sky serene,
380 And bids bright lustre sparkle o'er the tide;
    The clear blue ocean at a distance seen
    Bounds the gay landscape on the western side,
    While closing round it with majestic pride,
    The lofty rocks mid citron groves arise;
385 "Sure some divinity must here reside,"

---

[1] "Hail, Hymen," part of a hymn to Hymen, god of marriage.

[2] The Lydian mode is actually a major scale with a raised fourth; its effect is supposed to be plaintive and pathetic.

[3] west winds.

As tranced in some bright vision, Psyche cries,
And scarce believes the bliss, or trusts her charmed
  eyes.

When lo! a voice divinely sweet she hears,
From unseen lips proceeds the heavenly sound;
"Psyche approach, dismiss thy timid fears,
At length his bride thy longing spouse has found,
And bids for thee immortal joys abound;
For thee the palace rose at his command,
For thee his love a bridal banquet crowned;
He bids attendant nymphs around thee stand
Prompt every wish to serve, a fond obedient band."

Increasing wonder filled her ravished soul,
For now the pompous portals opened wide,
There, pausing oft, with timid foot she stole
Through halls high domed, enriched with
  sculptured pride,
While gay saloons appeared on either side
In splendid vista opening to her sight;
And all with precious gems so beautified,
And furnished with such exquisite delight,
That scarce the beams of heaven emit such lustre
  bright.

The amethyst was there of violet hue,
And there the topaz shed its golden ray,
The chrysoberyl, and the sapphire blue
As the clear azure of a sunny day,
Or the mild eyes where amorous glances play;
The snow white jasper, and the opal's flame,
The blushing ruby, and the agate grey,
And there the gem which bears his luckless name
Whose death by Phœbus mourned ensured him
  deathless fame.[1]

There the green emerald, there cornelians glow,
And rich carbuncles pour eternal light,
With all that India and Peru can shew,
Or Labrador can give so flaming bright
To the charmed mariner's half dazzled sight:[2]
The coral paved baths with diamonds blaze:
And all that can the female heart delight
Of fair attire, the last recess displays,
And all that Luxury can ask, her eye surveys.

Now through the hall melodious music stole,
And self-prepared the splendid banquet stands,
Self-poured the nectar sparkles in the bowl,
The lute and viol touched by unseen hands
Aid the soft voices of the choral bands;
O'er the full board a brighter lustre beams
Than Persia's monarch at his feast commands:
For sweet refreshment all inviting seems
To taste celestial food, and pure ambrosial streams.

But when meek Eve[3] hung out her dewy star,
And gently veiled with gradual hand the sky,
Lo! the bright folding doors retiring far,
Display to Psyche's captivated eye
All that voluptuous ease could e'er supply
To sooth the spirits in serene repose:
Beneath the velvet's purple canopy
Divinely formed a downy couch arose,
While alabaster lamps a milky light disclose.

Once more she hears the hymeneal strain;
Far other voices now attune the lay;
The swelling sounds approach, awhile remain,
And then retiring faint dissolved away:
The expiring lamps emit a feebler ray,
And soon in fragrant death extinguished lie:
Then virgin terrors Psyche's soul dismay,
When through the obscuring gloom she nought
  can spy,
But softly rustling sounds declare some Being nigh.

Oh, you for whom I write! whose hearts can melt
At the soft thrilling voice whose power you prove,

---

[1] possibly a (mistaken) reference to Hyacinthus: see Ovid, *Metamorphoses* 10.

[2] Early explorers thought that Labrador was a land of gold; hence its name, *le bras d'or* ("golden arm," Fr.). The gold turned out to be iron pyrites ("fool's gold").

[3] I.e., the evening.

You know what charm, unutterably felt,
Attends the unexpected voice of Love:
Above the lyre, the lute's soft notes above,
With sweet enchantment to the soul it steals
And bears it to Elysium's happy grove;[1]
You best can tell the rapture Psyche feels
When Love's ambrosial lip the vows of Hymen seals.

"'Tis he, 'tis my deliverer! deep imprest
Upon my heart those sounds I well recal,"
The blushing maid exclaimed, and on his breast
A tear of trembling ecstasy let fall.
But, ere the breezes of the morning call
Aurora[2] from her purple, humid bed,
Psyche in vain explores the vacant hall,
Her tender lover from her arms is fled,
While sleep his downy wings had o'er her eye-lids
  spread.

Again the band invisible attend,
And female voices sooth the mournful bride;
Light hands to braid her hair assistance lend,
By some she sees the glowing bracelet tied,
Others officious hover at her side,
And each bright gem for her acceptance bring,
While some, the balmy air diffusing wide,
Fan softer perfumes from each odorous wing
Than the fresh bosom sheds of earliest, sweetest
  spring.

With songs divine her anxious soul they cheer,
And woo her footsteps to delicious bowers,
They bid the fruit more exquisite appear
Which at her feet its bright profusion showers:
For her they cull unknown, celestial flowers;
The gilded car they bid her fearless guide,
Which at her wish self-moved with wondrous
  powers,
The rapid bird's velocity defied,
While round the blooming isle it rolled with circuit
  wide.

Again they spread the feast, they strike the lyre,
But to her frequent questions nought reply,
Her lips in vain her lover's name require,
Or wherefore thus concealed he shuns her eye.
But when reluctant twilight veils the sky,
And each pale lamp successively expires;
Again she trembling hears the voice of joy,
Her spouse a tender confidence inspires,
But with a fond embrace ere dawn again retires.

To charm the languid hours of solitude
He oft invites her to the Muse's lore,
For none have vainly e'er the Muse pursued,
And those whom she delights, regret no more
The social, joyous hours, while rapt they soar
To worlds unknown, and live in fancy's dream:
Oh Muse divine! thee only I implore,
Shed on my soul thy sweet inspiring beams,
And pleasure's gayest scene insipid folly seems!

Silence and solitude the Muses love,
And whom they charm they can alone suffice;
Nor ever tedious hour their votaries prove:
This solace now the lonely Psyche tries,
Or, while her hand the curious needle plies,
She learns from lips unseen celestial strains;
Responsive now with their soft voice she vies,
Or bids her plaintive harp express the pains
Which absence sore inflicts where Love all potent
  reigns.

But melancholy poisons all her joys,
And secret sorrows all her hopes depress,
Consuming languor every bliss destroys,
And sad she droops repining, comfortless.
Her tender lover well the cause can guess,
And sees too plain inevitable fate
Pursue her to the bowers of happiness.
"Oh Psyche! most beloved, ere yet too late,
Dread the impending ills and prize thy tranquil
  state."

---

[1] the place of the blessed in the classical underworld.

[2] the goddess of dawn.

In vain his weeping love he thus advised;
She longs to meet a parent's sweet embrace,
525 "Oh, were their sorrowing hearts at least apprised
How Psyche's wondrous lot all fears may chase;
For whom thy love prepared so fair a place!
Let but my bliss their fond complaints repress,
Let me but once behold a mother's face,
530 Oh, spouse adored! and in full happiness
This love-contented heart its solitude shall bless.

"Oh, by those beauties I must ne'er behold!
The spicy-scented ringlets of thine hair:
By that soft neck my loving arms enfold,
535 Crown with a kind consent thy Psyche's prayer!
Their dear embrace, their blessing let me share;
So shall I stain our couch with tears no more:
But, blest in thee, resign each other care,
Nor seek again thy secret to explore,
540 Which yet, denied thy sight, I ever must deplore."

Unable to resist her fond request,
Reluctant Cupid thus at last complied,
And sighing clasped her closer to his breast.
"Go then, my Psyche! go, my lovely bride!
545 But let me in thy faith at least confide,
That by no subtle, impious arts betrayed,
Which, ah! too well I know will all be tried,
Thy simply trusting heart shall e'er be swayed
The secret veil to rend which fate thy screen hath made.

550 "For danger hovers o'er thy smiling days,
One only way to shield thee yet I know;
Unseen, I may securely guard thy ways
And save thee from the threatened storm of woe;
But forced, if known, my Psyche to forego,
555 Thou never, never must again be mine!
What mutual sorrows hence must ceaseless flow!
Compelled thy dear embraces to resign,
While thou to anguish doomed for lost delights shalt pine.

"Solace thy mind with hopes of future joy!
560 In a dear infant thou shalt see my face;
Blest mother soon of an immortal boy,
In him his father's features thou shalt trace!
Yet go! for thou art free, the bounds of space
Are none for thee: attendant Zephyrs stay,
565 Speak but thy will, and to the wished for place
Their lovely mistress swift they shall convey:
Yet hither, ah! return, ere fades the festive day."

"Light of my soul, far dearer than the day!"
(Exulting Psyche cries in grateful joy)
570 "Me all the bliss of earth could ill repay
For thy most sweet, divine society;
To thee again with rapture will I fly,
Nor with less pleasure hail the star of eve
Than when in tedious solitude I sigh;
575 My vows of silent confidence believe,
Nor think thy Psyche's faith will e'er thy love deceive."

Her suit obtained, in full contentment blest,
Her eyes at length in placid slumbers close.
Sleep, hapless fair! sleep on thy lover's breast!
580 Ah, not again to taste such pure repose!
Till thy sad heart by long experience knows
How much they err, who to their interest blind,
Slight the calm peace which from retirement flows;
And while they think their fleeting joys to bind,
585 Banish the tranquil bliss which heaven for man designed!

On Receiving a Branch of Mezereon Which Flowered at Woodstock.—Dec. 1809[1]

Odours of Spring, my sense ye charm
    With fragrance premature;
And, mid these days of dark alarm,
    Almost to hope allure.
5 Methinks with purpose soft ye come
    To tell of brighter hours,
Of May's blue skies, abundant bloom,
    The sunny gales and showers.

---

[1] The pink flowers on the mezereon shrub usually bloom between February and April. Tighe died at the family estate at Woodstock on 24 March 1810.

  Alas! for me shall May in vain
10   The powers of life restore;
  These eyes that weep and watch in pain
   Shall see her charms no more.
  No, no, this anguish cannot last!
   Beloved friends, adieu!
15   The bitterness of death were past,
   Could I resign but you.

  But oh! in every mortal pang
   That rends my soul from life,
  That soul, which seems on you to hang
20   Through each convulsive strife,
  Even now, with agonizing grasp
   Of terror and regret,
  To all in life its love would clasp
   Clings close and closer yet.

25   Yet why, immortal, vital spark!
   Thus mortally opprest?
  Look up, my soul, through prospects dark,
   And bid thy terrors rest;

  Forget, forego thy earthly part,
30   Thine heavenly being trust:—
  Ah, vain attempt! my coward heart
   Still shuddering clings to dust.

  Oh ye! who sooth the pangs of death
   With love's own patient care,
35   Still, still retain this fleeting breath,
   Still pour the fervent prayer:—
  And ye, whose smile must greet my eye
   No more, nor voice my ear,
  Who breathe for me the tender sigh,
40   And shed the pitying tear,

  Whose kindness (though far far removed)
   My grateful thoughts perceive,
  Pride of my life, esteemed, beloved,
   My last sad claim receive!
45   Oh! do not quite your friend forget,
   Forget alone her faults;
  And speak of her with fond regret
   Who asks your lingering thoughts.

Samuel Taylor Coleridge
1772 – 1834

Samuel Taylor Coleridge was born in Ottery St. Mary, Devonshire, on 21 October 1772, the tenth child of John Coleridge, a clergyman and teacher, and Ann Bowdon Coleridge. His father died in 1781, and Coleridge was sent as a charity student to Christ's Hospital, London, where the discipline of the headmaster, James Bowyer, was so severe that Coleridge was still having nightmares about it in 1817. There he met Charles Lamb,* who became a lifelong friend. In October 1791, he entered Jesus College, Cambridge, but after a personal crisis, he enlisted in the cavalry in December 1793. His brother George managed to get him discharged as insane, and he returned to Cambridge, but he did not finish his degree.

In June 1794, Coleridge met Southey;* they collaborated on a tragedy, *The Fall of Robespierre*, and concocted a scheme to establish an egalitarian, or "Pantisocratic," commune in Pennsylvania. Since the members of the commune were supposed to be married, Coleridge became engaged to Sara Fricker, the sister of Southey's fiancée, Edith; they were married in October 1795 and settled in Clevedon, Somerset. Meanwhile, Coleridge was lecturing on politics and religion in Bristol and organizing his first periodical, the *Watchman* (March-May 1796), which was intended to "preserve Freedom and her Friends from the attacks of Robbers and Assassins!!" The Pantisocratic dream faded and the Coleridges settled in the village of Nether Stowey. Coleridge had already begun taking opium, which would inspire "Kubla Khan" (1797) and make him miserable for the rest of his life.

In 1797, the most important friendship of Coleridge's life began when William Wordsworth,* whom he had met in 1795, moved with his sister Dorothy* to nearby Alfoxden. Together, they published *Lyrical Ballads* (1798), commonly regarded as one of the defining documents of Romanticism; "The Rime of the Ancyent Marinere" was the lead poem. Soon after publication, Coleridge and the Wordsworths travelled to Germany, where Coleridge remained until June 1799, studying the language and modern philosophy—leaving behind Sara and their two children, one of whom died while he was away. On his return, he moved his family to Keswick, in the Lake District, to be near the Wordsworths in Grasmere. He was becoming increasingly estranged from his wife; he also fell hopelessly in love with Sara Hutchinson, soon to be Wordsworth's sister-in-law. "Dejection" (1802), his last major poem, began as a long verse letter to her. This relationship in turn contributed to his growing estrangement from Wordsworth, who had declined to include "Christabel" in the second edition of *Lyrical Ballads* (1800) and moved the "Rime" from the beginning to the end; the final rupture between them came in 1810, when Wordsworth told a common friend that Coleridge was a drunk and a nuisance. After a trip to Malta and Italy (1804–06), Coleridge returned to Keswick, only to tell Sara that they should separate.

Throughout his career, Coleridge had been a prolific and brilliant journalist, and in 1809–10 he published another periodical, the *Friend*, writing (or, to be precise, dictating to Sara Hutchinson) almost all of it himself. He also became a popular and influential lecturer, speaking (when his addiction allowed it) on Shakespeare, Milton, Cervantes, the history of philosophy, and the principles of poetry to large audiences that included Byron,* De Quincey,* Hazlitt,* Charles Lamb,* and Henry Crabb Robinson.

In 1816, Coleridge went to live with Dr. James Gillman in Highgate, then a village north of London; Gillman helped him to moderate his opium intake, and he lived there for the rest of his life. In 1817, he published both *Sibylline Leaves*, a two-volume collection of his poems, and *Biographia Literaria*, his major statement of literary theory. He devoted his last years to philosophical and theological writings and to entertaining a steady stream of worshipful visitors, including Cooper,* Emerson, Harriet Martineau, and John Stuart Mill. He died on 25 July 1834. (D.L.M.)

from *Poems on Various Subjects* (1796)

*Effusion 35. Composed August 20th,
1795, at Clevedon, Somersetshire*[1]

My pensive SARA![2] thy soft cheek reclin'd
Thus on mine arm, most soothing sweet it is
To sit beside our cot,[3] our cot o'er grown
With white-flower'd Jasmin, and the broad-leav'd
    Myrtle,
5 (Meet emblems they of Innocence and Love!)[4]
And watch the clouds, that late were rich with light,
Slow-sad'ning round, and mark the star of eve
Serenely brilliant (such should Wisdom be)
Shine opposite! How exquisite the scents
10 Snatch'd from yon bean-field![5] and the world *so*
    hush'd!
The stilly murmur of the distant Sea
Tells of us Silence. And that simplest Lute,[6]
Plac'd length-ways in the clasping casement, hark!
How by the desultory breeze caress'd,
15 Like some coy Maid half-yielding to her Lover,
It pours such sweet upbraidings, as must needs
Tempt to repeat the wrong! And now its strings
Boldlier swept, the long sequacious notes
Over delicious surges sink and rise,
20 Such a soft floating witchery of sound
As twilight Elfins make, when they at eve
Voyage on gentle gales from Faery Land,
Where *Melodies* round honey-dropping flowers
Footless and wild, like birds of Paradise,[7]
25 Nor pause nor perch, hov'ring on untam'd wing.[8]

And thus, my Love! as on the midway slope
Of yonder hill I stretch my limbs at noon
Whilst thro' my half-clos'd eyelids I behold
The sunbeams dance, like diamonds, on the main,
30 And tranquil muse upon tranquillity;
Full many a thought uncall'd and undetain'd,
And many idle flitting phantasies,
Traverse my indolent and passive brain
As wild and various, as the random gales
35 That swell or flutter on this subject Lute!
And what if all of animated nature
Be but organic Harps diversly fram'd,
That tremble into thought, as o'er them sweeps,
Plastic and vast, one intellectual Breeze,
40 At once the Soul of each, and God of all?
But thy more serious eye a mild reproof
Darts, O beloved Woman! nor such thoughts
Dim and unhallow'd dost thou not reject,
And biddest me walk humbly with my God.

45 Meek Daughter in the Family of Christ,
Well hast thou said and holily disprais'd
These shapings of the unregenerate mind,
Bubbles that glitter as they rise and break
On vain Philosophy's aye-babbling spring.
50 For never guiltless may I speak of Him,
Th' INCOMPREHENSIBLE! save when with awe

---

[1] In subsequent publications, Coleridge gave this poem the title "The Eolian Harp."

[2] Sara Fricker, whom Coleridge married on 4 October 1795.

[3] here and in 56, not a bed but a cottage—Coleridge's home at 55 Old Church Road, Clevedon.

[4] The myrtle was sacred to Aphrodite (Venus), goddess of love.

[5] Cf. James Thomson (1700–48), *Spring* (1728) 499–500.

[6] an Æolian harp, a musical instrument which was not played but placed in a window so that the wind could vibrate its strings, on the same principle as the wind-chime, though with a very different sound. Cf. Thomson, *The Castle of Indolence* (1748) 1.39–41.

[7] When the skins of these birds were tanned for sale to Europeans, the legs were removed, giving rise to the belief that the birds had no feet and had to spend almost their entire lives in flight.

[8] In later versions, Coleridge added the following eight lines:
    O! the one Life within us and abroad,
    Which meets all motion and becomes its soul,
    A light in sound, a sound-like power in light,
    Rhythm in all thought, and joyance every where—
    Methinks, it should have been impossible
    Not to love all things in a world so fill'd;
    Where the breeze warbles, and the mute still air
    Is Music slumbering on her instrument.

I praise him, and with Faith that inly *feels*;[1]
Who with his saving mercies healed me,
A sinful and most miserable man
55 Wilder'd and dark, and gave me to possess
PEACE, and this COT, and THEE, heart-honor'd Maid!

from the *Morning Post* (8 January 1798)

Fire, Famine, and Slaughter. A War Eclogue[2]

SCENE— *A depopulated tract in La Vendée.*[3]
FAMINE *is discovered stretched on the ground; to her
enter* SLAUGHTER *and* FIRE.

FAMINE:
Sisters! Sisters! who sent you here?
SLAUGHTER:
I will name him in your ear.
FIRE:
   No! No! No!
Spirits hear what spirits tell:
5 'Twill make an holiday in hell.
   No! no! no!
Myself I nam'd him once below,
And all the souls that damned be,
Leap'd up at once in anarchy;
10 Clapp'd their hands and danc'd for glee;
They no longer heeded *me*;

But laugh'd to hear hell's burning rafters
Unwillingly re-echo laughters.
   No! no! no!
15 Spirits hear what spirits tell:
'Twill make an holiday in hell.
FAMINE:
Then sound it not, yet let me know;
Darkly hint it—soft and low!
SLAUGHTER:
Four letters form his name.[4]
20 And who sent you?
FAMINE:
   The same! the same!
SLAUGHTER:
He came by stealth and unlock'd my den,
And I have spill'd the blood since then
Of thrice ten hundred thousand men.
FIRE AND FAMINE:
Who bade you do't?
SLAUGHTER:
   The same! the same!
25 Four letters form his name.
He let me loose, and cry'd Halloo![5]
To him alone the praise is due.
FAMINE:
Thanks, Sisters, thanks! the men have bled,
Their wives and children faint for bread;
30 I stood in a swampy field of battle,
With bones and skulls I made a rattle,
To frighten the wolf and the carrion crow,
And the homeless dog—but they would not go.
So off I flew; for how could I bear
35 To see them gorge their dainty fare.
I heard a groan, and a peevish squall,
And thro' the chink of a cottage wall,
Can you guess what I saw there?
SLAUGHTER AND FIRE:
Whisper it, Sister! in our ear!
FAMINE:
40 A baby beat its dying mother—
I had starv'd the one, and was starving the other!

---

[1] In a note, Coleridge appended a quotation (in French) from the French Revolutionary Mme. Manon Roland (1754–93), *An Appeal to Impartial Posterity* (London, 1795): "The Atheist is not, in my eyes, a man of ill faith: I can live with him as well, nay, better than with the devotee, for he reasons more, but he is deficient in a certain sense, and my soul does not keep pace with his: he is unmoved at a spectacle the most ravishing, and he hunts for a syllogism, where I perform an act of grace."

[2] An eclogue is a poem in dialogue, usually pastoral in content. Coleridge published this poem over the pseudonym "Laberius," after Decimus Laberius (c. 105–43 BC), writer of dramatic sketches and outspoken critic of Julius Caesar. Cf. Shakespeare, *Henry V* Pro. 7–8.

[3] In March-December 1793, there was a Catholic/Royalist uprising in the Vendée region of France. The Revolutionary government suppressed it brutally.

[4] William Pitt the Younger (1759–1806), the Prime Minister.

[5] a huntsman's cry, urging the hounds after the fox.

SLAUGHTER AND FIRE:
Who bade you do't?
FAMINE:
   The same! the same!
Four letters form his name.
He let me loose, and cry'd Halloo!
45 To him alone the praise is due.
FIRE:
Sisters! I from Ireland came—
Huts and corn-fields all on flame,
I triumph'd o'er the setting Sun;
And all the while the work was done.
50 As on I strode with mons'trous strides,
I flung back my head, and held my sides;
It was so rare a piece of fun,
To see the swelter'd cattle run,
With uncouth gallop, all the night,
55 Scar'd by the red and noisy light!
By the light of his own blazing cot,
Was many a naked Rebel shot:[1]
The house-stream met the fire, and hiss'd
While, crash! the roof fell in, I wish
60 On some of those old bed-rid nurses,
That deal in discontent and curses!
SLAUGHTER AND FAMINE:
Who bad you do't?
FIRE:
   The same! The same!
Four letters form his name.
He let me loose, and cry'd Halloo!
65 How shall I give him honour due?
ALL:
He let us loose, and cry'd Halloo!
How shall I give him honour due?
FAMINE:
Wisdom comes with lack of food,
I'll gnaw, I'll gnaw the multitude,
70 Till the cup of rage o'er brim,
They shall seize him of his brood.
SLAUGHTER:
They shall tear him limb from limb!

FIRE:
O thankless Beldames, and untrue!
And is this all that you can do
75 For him that did so much for you!
[*To* SLAUGHTER.]
For *you* he turn'd the dust to mud,
With his fellow creatures' blood!
[*To* FAMINE.]
And hunger scorch'd as many more,
To make *your* cup of joy run o'er.
[*To* BOTH.]
80 Full ninety moons, he by my troth,
Hath richly cater'd for you both;
And in an hour you would repay,
An eight years debt, away! away!
I alone am faithful, I
85 Cling to him everlastingly!

Fears in Solitude, Written in 1798 (1798)

Fears in Solitude
Written, April 1798, during the Alarms of an Invasion[2]

A green and silent spot amid the hills!
A small and silent dell!—O'er stiller place
No singing sky-lark ever pois'd himself!
The hills are heathy, save that swelling slope,
5 Which hath a gay and gorgeous covering on,
All golden with the never-bloomless furze,[3]
Which now blooms most profusely; but the dell,
Bath'd by the mist, is fresh and delicate,
As vernal corn field, or the unripe flax,
10 When thro' its half-transparent stalks, at eve,
The level sunshine glimmers with green light.
O 'tis a quiet spirit-healing nook,
Which all, methinks, would love; but chiefly he,

---

[1] In March 1797, the British army, under General Lake, burned cottages in the North of Ireland.

[2] In February 1797, the French had actually landed an expeditionary force of 1200 at Fishguard, Pembrokeshire, Wales, and fears of an invasion persisted through 1798.

[3] Furze or gorse (*Ulex europæus*), an evergreen shrub, is always in bloom.

The humble man, who in his youthful years
15 Knew just so much of folly as had made
His early manhood more securely wise:
Here he might lie on fern or wither'd heath,
While from the singing lark (that sings unseen
The minstrelsy which solitude loves best)
20 And from the sun, and from the breezy air,
Sweet influences trembled o'er his frame;
And he with many feelings, many thoughts,
Made up a meditative joy, and found
Religious meanings in the forms of nature!
25 And so, his senses gradually wrapp'd
In a half-sleep, he dreams of better worlds,
And dreaming hears thee still, O singing lark!
That singest like an angel in the clouds.

My God! it is a melancholy thing
30 For such a man, who would full fain preserve
His soul in calmness, yet perforce must feel
For all his human brethren—O my God,
It is indeed a melancholy thing,
And weighs upon the heart, that he must think
35 What uproar and what strife may now be stirring
This way or that way o'er these silent hills—
Invasion, and the thunder and the shout,
And all the crash of onset; fear and rage
And undetermined conflict—even now,
40 Ev'n now, perchance, and in his native Isle,
Carnage and screams beneath this blessed sun!
We have offended, O my countrymen!
We have offended very grievously,
And have been tyrannous. From east to west
45 A groan of accusation pierces heaven!
The wretched plead against us, multitudes
Countless and vehement, the sons of God,
Our brethren! like a cloud that travels on,
Steam'd up from Cairo's swamps of pestilence,
50 Ev'n so, my countrymen! have we gone forth
And borne to distant tribes slavery and pangs,
And, deadlier far, our vices, whose deep taint
With slow perdition murders the whole man,
His body and his soul! Meanwhile, at home,
55 We have been drinking with a riotous thirst
Pollutions from the brimming cup of wealth,
A selfish, lewd, effeminated race,
Contemptuous of all honourable rule,
Yet bartering freedom, and the poor man's life,
60 For gold, as at a market! The sweet words
Of christian promise, words that even yet
Might stem destruction, were they wisely preach'd,
Are mutter'd o'er by men, whose tones proclaim,
How flat and wearisome they feel their trade.
65 Rank scoffers some, but most too indolent,
To deem them falsehoods, or to *know* their truth.
O blasphemous! the book of life is made
A superstitious instrument, on which
We gabble o'er the oaths we mean to break,
70 For all must swear[1]—all, and in every place,
College and wharf, council and justice-court,
All, all must swear, the briber and the brib'd,
Merchant and lawyer, senator and priest,
The rich, the poor, the old man, and the young,
75 All, all make up one scheme of perjury,
That faith doth reel; the very name of God
Sounds like a juggler's charm; and bold with joy,
Forth from his dark and lonely hiding-place
(Portentous sight) the owlet, ATHEISM,
80 Sailing on obscene wings athwart the noon,
Drops his blue-fringed lids, and holds them close,
And, hooting at the glorious sun in heaven,
Cries out, "where is it?"
                          Thankless too for peace,
(Peace long preserv'd by fleets and perilous seas)
85 Secure from actual warfare, we have lov'd
To swell the war-whoop, passionate for war!
Alas! for ages ignorant of all
It's ghastlier workings (famine or blue plague,
Battle, or siege, or flight thro' wintry snows)
90 We, this whole people, have been clamorous
For war and bloodshed, animating sports,
The which we pay for, as a thing to talk of,

---

[1] The Test and Corporation Acts discriminated against Catholics and dissenting Protestants by requiring, among other things, that all holders of public office swear the Oaths of Allegiance and Supremacy and take communion in an Anglican church. They were not repealed until 1828.

Spectators and not combatants! no guess
Anticipative of a wrong unfelt,
95 No speculation on contingency,
However dim and vague, too vague and dim
To yield a justifying cause: and forth
(Stuff'd out with big preamble, holy names,
And adjurations of the God in heaven)
100 We send our mandates for the certain death
Of thousands and ten thousands! Boys and girls,
And women that would groan to see a child
Pull off an insect's leg, all read of war,
The best amusement for our morning meal!
105 The poor wretch, who has learnt his only prayers
From curses, who knows scarcely words enough
To ask a blessing of his heavenly Father,
Becomes a fluent phraseman, absolute
And technical in victories and defeats,
110 And all our dainty terms for fratricide,
Terms which we trundle smoothly o'er our tongues
Like mere abstractions, empty sounds to which
We join no feeling and attach no form,
As if the soldier died without a wound;
115 As if the fibres of this godlike frame
Were gor'd without a pang: as if the wretch,
Who fell in battle doing bloody deeds,
Pass'd off to heaven, *translated* and not kill'd;
As tho' he had no wife to pine for him,
120 No God to judge him!—Therefore evil days
Are coming on us, O my countrymen!
And what if all-avenging Providence,
Strong and retributive, should make us know
The meaning of our words, force us to feel
125 The desolation and the agony
Of our fierce doings?—
                    Spare us yet a while,
Father and God! O spare us yet a while!
O let not English women drag their flight
Fainting beneath the burden of their babes,
130 Of the sweet infants, that but yesterday
Laugh'd at the breast! Sons, brothers, husbands, all
Who ever gaz'd with fondness on the forms,
Which grew up with you round the same fire side,

And all who ever heard the sabbath bells
135 Without the infidel's scorn, make yourselves pure!
Stand forth! be men! repel an impious foe,
Impious and false, a light yet cruel race,
That laugh away all virtue, mingling mirth
With deeds of murder; and still promising
140 Freedom, themselves too sensual to be free
Poison life's amities, and cheat the heart
Of Faith and quiet Hope, and all that soothes
And all that lifts the spirit! Stand we forth;
Render them back upon th' insulted ocean,
145 And let them toss as idly on it's waves,
As the vile sea-weeds, which some mountain blast
Swept from our shores! And O! may we return
Not with a drunken triumph, but with fear,
Repenting of the wrongs, with which we stung
150 So fierce a foe to frenzy!
                    I have told,
O Britons! O my brethren! I have told
Most bitter truth, but without bitterness.
Nor deem my zeal or factious or mistim'd;
For never can true courage dwell with them,
155 Who, playing tricks with conscience, dare not look
At their own vices. We have been too long
Dupes of a deep delusion! Some, belike,
Groaning with restless enmity, expect
All change from change of constituted power:
160 As if a government had been a robe,
On which our vice and wretchedness were tagg'd
Like fancy-points and fringes, with the robe
Pull'd off at pleasure. Fondly these attach
A radical causation to a few
165 Poor drudges of chastising Providence,
Who borrow all their hues and qualities
From our own folly and rank wickedness,
Which gave them birth, and nurse them. Others, meanwhile,
Dote with a mad idolatry; and all,
170 Who will not fall before their images,
And yield them worship, they are enemies
Ev'n of their country!—Such have I been deem'd.
But, O dear Britain! O my mother Isle!

Needs must thou prove a name most dear and holy
175 To me, a son, a brother, and a friend,
A husband and a father! who revere
All bonds of natural love, and find them all
Within the limits of thy rocky shores.
O native Britain! O my mother Isle!
180 How should'st thou prove aught else but dear and holy
To me, who from thy lakes and mountain-hills,
Thy clouds, thy quiet dales, thy rocks, and seas,
Have drunk in all my intellectual life,
All sweet sensations, all ennobling thoughts,
185 All adoration of the God in nature,
All lovely and all honourable things,
Whatever makes this mortal spirit feel
The joy and greatness of it's future being?
There lives nor form nor feeling in my soul
190 Unborrow'd from my country! O divine
And beauteous island, thou hast been my sole
And most magnificent temple, in the which
I walk with awe, and sing my stately songs,
Loving the God that made me!—
                                      May my fears,
195 My filial fears, be vain! and may the vaunts
And menace of the vengeful enemy
Pass like the gust, that roar'd and died away
In the distant tree, which heard, and only heard;
In this low dell bow'd not the delicate grass.
200 But now the gentle dew-fall sends abroad
The fruitlike perfume of the golden furze:
The light has left the summit of the hill,
Tho' still a sunny gleam lies beautiful
On the long-ivied beacon.[1]—Now, farewell,
205 Farewell, awhile, O soft and silent spot!
On the green sheep-track, up the heathy hill,
Homeward I wind my way; and lo! recall'd
From bodings, that have well nigh wearied me,
I find myself upon the brow, and pause
210 Startled! And after lonely sojourning
In such a quiet and surrounded scene,
This burst of prospect, here the shadowy main,
Dim-tinted, there the mighty majesty
Of that huge amphitheatre of rich
215 And elmy fields, seems like society,
Conversing with the mind, and giving it
A livelier impulse, and a dance of thought;
And now, beloved STOWEY![2] I behold
Thy church-tower, and (methinks) the four huge elms
220 Clust'ring, which mark the mansion of my friend;[3]
And close behind them, hidden from my view,
Is my own lowly cottage, where my babe[4]
And my babe's mother dwell in peace! With light
And quicken'd footsteps thitherward I tend,
225 Rememb'ring thee, O green and silent dell!
And grateful, that by nature's quietness
And solitary musings all my heart
Is soften'd, and made worthy to indulge
Love, and the thoughts that yearn for human kind.
                                Nether Stowey, April 20th, 1798.

France. An Ode[5]

I

Ye Clouds, that far above me float and pause,
Whose pathless march no mortal may control!
Ye ocean waves, that, wheresoe'er ye roll,
Yield homage only to eternal laws!
5 Ye woods, that listen to the night-bird's singing,
Midway the smooth and perilous steep reclin'd;
Save when your own imperious branches swinging
Have made a solemn music of the wind!
Where, like a man belov'd of God,
10 Thro' glooms, which never woodman trod,
How oft, pursuing fancies holy,
My moonlight way o'er flow'ring weeds I wound,
Inspir'd beyond the guess of folly,

---

[1] Beacons had been erected across the country to give the alarm if the French invaded.

[2] Coleridge and his family moved to the village of Nether Stowey, Somerset, on 31 December 1796.

[3] Coleridge's neighbour Thomas Poole (1765–1806), a leather manufacturer with extensive intellectual interests.

[4] Coleridge's first son, Hartley, was born on 19 September 1796.

[5] When first published in the *Morning Post* (16 April 1798), the poem was entitled "The Recantation." Napoleon's invasion of Switzerland forced many English supporters of the Revolution to recant.

By each rude shape, and wild unconquerable sound!
15 O, ye loud waves, and O, ye forests high,
And O, ye clouds, that far above me soar'd!
Thou rising sun! thou blue rejoicing sky!
Yea, every thing that is and will be free,
Bear witness for me wheresoe'er ye be,
20 With what deep worship I have still ador'd
The spirit of divinest liberty.

2

When France in wrath her giant limbs uprear'd,
And with that oath which smote earth, air, and sea,[1]
Stamp'd her strong foot and said, she would be free,
25 Bear witness for me, how I hop'd and fear'd!
With what a joy my lofty gratulation
Unaw'd I sung amid a slavish band:
And when to whelm the disenchanted nation,
Like fiends embattled by a wizard's wand,
30 The monarchs march'd in evil day,
And Britain join'd the dire array;[2]
Though dear her shores, and circling ocean,
Though many friendships, many youthful loves
Had swoln the patriot emotion,
35 And flung a magic light o'er all her hills and groves;
Yet still my voice unalter'd sang defeat
To all that brav'd the tyrant-quelling lance,
And shame too long delay'd, and vain retreat!
For ne'er, O Liberty! with partial aim
40 I dimm'd thy light, or damp'd thy holy flame;
But blest the pæans of deliver'd France,
And hung my head, and wept at Britain's name!

3

"And what (I said) tho' blasphemy's loud scream
With that sweet music of deliv'rance strove;
45 Tho' all the fierce and drunken passions wove
A dance more wild than ever maniac's dream;

Ye storms, that round the dawning east assembled,
The sun was rising, tho' ye hid his light!"
And when to sooth my soul, that hop'd and trembled,
50 The dissonance ceas'd, and all seem'd calm and bright;
When France, her front deep-scar'd and gory,
Conceal'd with clust'ring wreaths of glory;
When insupportably advancing,
Her arm made mock'ry of the warrior's ramp,[3]
55 While, timid looks of fury glancing,
Domestic treason, crush'd beneath her fatal stamp,
Writh'd, like a wounded dragon in his gore;
Then I reproach'd my fears that would not flee,
"And soon (I said) shall wisdom teach her lore
60 In the low huts of them that toil and groan!
And conqu'ring by her happiness alone,
Shall France compel the nations to be free,
Till love and joy look round, and call the earth their own!"

4

Forgive me, Freedom! O forgive these dreams!
65 I hear thy voice, I hear thy loud lament,
From bleak Helvetia's[4] icy caverns sent—
I hear thy groans upon her blood-stain'd streams!
Heroes, that for your peaceful country perish'd;
And ye, that fleeing spot the mountain snows
70 With bleeding wounds: forgive me, that I cherish'd
One thought, that ever bless'd your cruel foes!
To scatter rage and trait'rous guilt
Where Peace her jealous home had built;
A patriot race to disinherit
75 Of all that made their stormy wilds so dear,
And with inexpiable spirit
To taint the bloodless freedom of the mountaineer.—
O France! that mockest heav'n, adult'rous, blind,
And patriot only in pernicious toils!
80 Are these thy boasts, champion of human kind:
To mix with kings in the low lust of sway,
Yell in the hunt, and share the murd'rous prey;

---

[1] the Tennis Court Oath: on 20 June 1789, the representatives of the Third Estate (the commoners) were prevented from attending a meeting of the Estates General. They assembled instead on an indoor tennis court and vowed to remain in session until they had drafted a new constitution.

[2] Britain declared war on France in February 1793. The "dire array" of allies also included Austria, Prussia, and Holland.

[3] Cf. Milton, *Samson Agonistes* 136, 139.

[4] Switzerland's.

T' insult the shrine of liberty with spoils
From freemen torn; to tempt and to betray!

5

85 　　The sensual and the dark rebel in vain,
Slaves by their own compulsion! In mad game
They burst their manacles, and wear the name
Of freedom graven on a heavier chain!
O Liberty! with profitless endeavour
90 Have I pursued thee many a weary hour:
But thou nor swell'st the victor's strain, nor ever
Didst breathe thy soul in forms of human pow'r.
Alike from all, howe'er they praise thee,
(Nor pray'r, nor boastful name delays thee)
95 Alike from priesthood's harpy minions,
And factious blasphemy's obscener slaves,
Thou speedest on thy subtle pinions,
To live amid the winds, and move upon the waves!
And then I felt thee on that sea-cliff's verge,
100 Whose pines, scarce travell'd by the breeze above,
Had made one murmur with the distant surge!
Yes! while I stood and gaz'd, my temples bare,
And shot my being thro' earth, sea, and air,
Possessing all things with intensest love,
105 O Liberty, my spirit felt thee there!

　　　　　　　　　　　　February 1798.

Frost at Midnight

The Frost performs it's secret ministry,
Unhelp'd by any wind. The owlet's cry
Came loud—and hark, again! loud as before.
The inmates of my cottage, all at rest,
5 Have left me to that solitude, which suits
Abstruser musings: save that at my side
My cradled infant[1] slumbers peacefully.
'Tis calm indeed! so calm, that it disturbs
And vexes meditation with it's strange
10 And extreme silentness. Sea, hill, and wood,
This populous village! Sea, and hill, and wood,
With all the numberless goings on of life,
Inaudible as dreams! The thin blue flame
Lies on my low-burnt fire, and quivers not:
15 Only that film,[2] which flutter'd on the grate,
Still flutters there, the sole unquiet thing,
Methinks, it's motion in this hush of nature
Gives it dim sympathies with me, who live,
Making it a companionable form,
20 With which I can hold commune. Idle thought!
But still the living spirit in our frame,
That loves not to behold a lifeless thing,
Transfuses into all it's own delights
It's own volition, sometimes with deep faith,
25 And sometimes with fantastic playfulness.
Ah me! amus'd by no such curious toys
Of the self-watching subtilizing mind,
How often in my early school-boy days,
With most believing superstitious wish
30 Presageful have I gaz'd upon the bars,
To watch the *stranger* there! and oft belike,
With unclos'd lids, already had I dreamt
Of my sweet birthplace,[3] and the old church-tower,
Whose bells, the poor man's only music, rang
35 From morn to evening, all the hot fair-day,
So sweetly, that they stirr'd and haunted me
With a wild pleasure, falling on mine ear
Most like articulate sounds of things to come!
So gaz'd I, till the soothing things, I dreamt,
40 Lull'd me to sleep, and sleep prolong'd my dreams!
And so I brooded all the following morn,
Aw'd by the stern preceptor's[4] face, mine eye
Fix'd with mock study on my swimming book:
Save if the door half-open'd, and I snatch'd
45 A hasty glance, and still my heart leapt up,
For still I hop'd to see the *stranger's* face,

---

[1] Coleridge's first son, Hartley (1796–1849), then a year and a half old.

[2] "In all parts of the kingdom these films are called *strangers*, and supposed to portend the arrival of some absent friend."(S.T.C.) Cf. Cowper,* *The Task* 4.301–5.

[3] Ottery St. Mary, Devon.

[4] James Bowyer, the headmaster of Christ's Hospital, the charity school in London to which Coleridge was sent after the death of his father in 1781. Coleridge admired him greatly, but his discipline was so harsh that Coleridge had nightmares about it for the rest of his life.

Townsman, or aunt, or sister more belov'd,[1]
My play-mate when we both were cloth'd alike!

    Dear babe, that sleepest cradled by my side,
50 Whose gentle breathings, heard in this dead calm,
Fill up the interspersed vacancies
And momentary pauses of the thought!
My babe so beautiful! it fills my heart
With tender gladness, thus to look at thee,
55 And think, that thou shalt learn far other lore,
And in far other scenes! For I was rear'd
In the great city, pent mid cloisters dim,[2]
And saw nought lovely but the sky and stars.
But *thou*, my babe! Shalt wander, like a breeze,
60 By lakes and sandy shores, beneath the crags
Of ancient mountain, and beneath the clouds,
Which image in their bulk both lakes and shores
And mountain crags: so shalt thou see and hear
The lovely shapes and sounds intelligible
65 Of that eternal language, which thy God
Utters, who from eternity doth teach
Himself in all, and all things in himself.

Great universal Teacher! he shall mould
Thy spirit, and by giving make it ask.

70   Therefore all seasons shall be sweet to thee,
Whether the summer clothe the general earth
With greenness, or the redbreasts sit and sing
Betwixt the tufts of snow on the bare branch
Of mossy apple-tree, while all the thatch
75 Smokes in the sun-thaw: whether the eave-drops fall
Heard only in the trances of the blast,
Or whether the secret ministery of cold
Shall hang them up in silent icicles,
Quietly shining to the quiet moon,[3]
80 Like those, my babe! which, ere to-morrow's warmth
Have capp'd their sharp keen points with pendulous drops,
Will catch thine eye, and with their novelty
Suspend thy little soul; then make thee shout,
And stretch and flutter from thy mother's arms
85 As thou would'st fly for very eagerness.
                                February 1798.

---

[1] Ann Coleridge (1767–91).

[2] Cf. Milton, *Paradise Lost* 9.445–54. Coleridge used to lie on the school roof at night and gaze at the stars (line 58).

[3] Coleridge later deleted the last six lines, so the final version of the poem ends here.

Samuel Taylor Coleridge 1798

from *Lyrical Ballads, with a Few Other Poems* (1798)

The Rime of the Ancyent Marinere, in Seven Parts[1]

ARGUMENT

How a Ship having passed the Line was driven by Storms to the cold Country towards the South Pole; and how from thence she made her course to the tropical Latitude of the Great Pacific Ocean; and of the strange things that befell; and in what manner the Ancyent Marinere came back to his own Country.

1

It is an ancyent Marinere,
    And he stoppeth one of three:
"By thy long grey beard and thy glittering eye
    Now wherefore stoppest me?

5 "The Bridegroom's doors are open'd wide
    And I am next of kin;
The Guests are met, the Feast is set,—
    May'st hear the merry din."

But still he holds the wedding-guest—
10   There was a Ship, quoth he—
"Nay, if thou'st got a laughsome tale,
    Marinere! come with me."

He holds him with his skinny hand,
    Quoth he, there was a Ship—
15 "Now get thee hence, thou grey-beard Loon!
    Or my Staff shall make thee skip."

He holds him with his glittering eye—
    The wedding guest stood still
And listens like a three year's child;
20   The Marinere hath his will.[2]

The wedding-guest sate on a stone,
    He cannot chuse but hear:
And thus spake on that ancyent man,
    The bright-eyed Marinere.

25 The Ship was cheer'd, the Harbour clear'd—
    Merrily did we drop
Below the Kirk,[3] below the Hill,
    Below the Light-house top.

The Sun came up upon the left,
30   Out of the Sea came he:
And he shone bright, and on the right
    Went down into the Sea.

Higher and higher every day,
    Till over the mast at noon—
35 The wedding-guest here beat his breast,
    For he heard the loud bassoon.

The Bride hath pac'd into the Hall,
    Red as a rose is she;
Nodding their heads before her goes
40   The merry Minstralsy.[4]

---

[1] Compare the later version of "The Rime" on the facing pages. This poem, and "Kubla Khan," are the subject of John Livingstone Lowes, *The Road to Xanadu: A Study in the Ways of the Imagination* (1927), one of the great classics in the history of criticism.

[2] W. Wordsworth* later claimed to have contributed lines 19–20.

[3] "church" (Sc.).

[4] Cf. Chaucer, "The Squire's Tale" 268.

from *Sibylline Leaves: A Collection of Poems* (1817)[1]

The Rime of the Ancient Mariner. In Seven Parts

    Facile credo, plures esse Naturas invisibiles quam visibiles in rerum universitate. Sed horum omnium familiam quis nobis enarrabit? et gradus et cognationes et discrimina et singulorum munera? Quid agunt? quæ loca habitant? Harum rerum notitiam semper ambivit ingenium humanum, nunquam attigit. Juvat, interea, non diffiteor, quandoque in animo, tanquam in Tabulâ, majoris et melioris mundi imaginem contemplari: ne mens assuefacta hodierniæ vitæ minutiis se contrahat nimis, & tota subsidat in pusillas cogitationes. Sed veritati interea invigilandum est, modusque servandus, ut certa ab incertis, diem a nocte, distinguamus.
                    T. BURNET:[2] *Archæol. Phil.* p. 68.

It is an ancient Mariner,   *An ancient Mariner*
And he stoppeth one of three.   *meeteth three*
"By thy long grey beard and glittering eye, *Gallants bidden to a*
Now wherefore stopp'st thou me?   *wedding-feast, and*
                                                            detaineth one.

5 "The Bridegroom's doors are open'd wide,
And I am next of kin;
The guests are met, the feast is set:
May'st hear the merry din."

He holds him with his skinny hand,
10 "There was a ship," quoth he.
"Hold off! unhand me, grey-beard loon!"
Eftsoons his hand dropt he.

He holds him with his glittering eye—   *The wedding-guest is*
The wedding-guest stood still,   *spellbound by the eye*
15 And listens like a three years child: *of the old sea-faring*
The Mariner hath his will.   *man, and constrained*
                                 to hear his tale.

The wedding-guest sat on a stone:
He can not chuse but hear;
And thus spake on that ancient man,
20 The bright-eyed mariner.

The ship was cheer'd, the harbour clear'd,
Merrily did we drop
Below the kirk, below the hill,
Below the light-house top.

25 The Sun came up upon the left,   *The Mariner tells how*
Out of the sea came he;   *the ship sailed southward*
And he shone bright, and on the right *with a good wind and fair*
Went down into the sea.   *weather, till it reached*
                                 the line.

Higher and higher every day,
30 Till over the mast at noon—
The Wedding-Guest here beat his breast,
For he heard the loud bassoon.

The bride hath paced into the hall,   *The wedding-guest*
Red as a rose is she;   *heareth the bridal*
35 Nodding their heads before her goes *music; but the*
The merry minstrelsy.   *mariner continueth*
                               his tale.

---

[1] Compare the earlier version of this poem on the opposite page. In classical mythology, the Sibyls were believed to write their prophecies on leaves. When the Cumæan Sibyl, the most famous of them, offered a nine-book collection to Tarquinius Priscus, king of Rome, he refused, because her price was too high. She kept burning them and offering him the remainder at the original price, until he broke down and bought the last three. M.W. Shelley* also makes use of the Sibyl's leaves in *The Last Man* (1826).

[2] Thomas Burnet (1635–1715), *Archæologia Philosophica* (1692): "I can easily believe, that there are more Invisible than Visible Beings in the Universe.... but who will declare to us the Family of all these, and acquaint us with the Agreements, Differences, and peculiar Talents which are to be found among them? It is true, human Wit has always desired a Knowledge of these Things, though it has never yet attained it.... I will own that it is very profitable, sometimes to contemplate in the Mind, as in a Draught, the Image of the greater and better World; lest the Soul being accustomed to the Trifles of this present Life, should contract itself too much, and altogether rest in mean Cogitations; but, in the mean Time, we must take Care to keep to the Truth, and observe Moderation, that we may distinguish certain from uncertain Things, and Day from Night" (trans. Richard Mead and Thomas Foxton [1736], 86–88).

The wedding-guest he beat his breast,
    Yet he cannot chuse but hear:
And thus spake on that ancyent Man,
    The bright-eyed Marinere.

45 Listen, Stranger! Storm and Wind,
    A Wind and Tempest strong!
For days and weeks it play'd us freaks—
    Like Chaff we drove along.

Listen, Stranger! Mist and Snow,
50   And it grew wond'rous cauld:
And Ice mast-high came floating by
    As green as Emerauld.

And thro' the drifts the snowy clifts
    Did send a dismal sheen;
55 Ne shapes of men ne beasts we ken—
    The Ice was all between.

The Ice was here, the Ice was there,
    The Ice was all around:
It crack'd and growl'd, and roar'd and howl'd—
60   Like noises of a swound.

At length did cross an Albatross,
    Thorough the Fog it came;
And an it were a Christian Soul,
    We hail'd it in God's name.

65 The Marineres gave it biscuit-worms,
    And round and round it flew:
The Ice did split with a Thunder-fit;
    The Helmsman steer'd us thro'.

And a good south wind sprung up behind,
70   The Albatross did follow;
And every day for food or play
    Came to the Marinere's hollo!

In mist or cloud on mast or shroud
    It perch'd for vespers nine,
75 Whiles all the night thro' fog smoke-white
    Glimmer'd the white moon-shine.

"God save thee, ancyent Marinere!
    From the fiends that plague thee thus—
Why look'st thou so?"—with my cross bow
80   I shot the Albatross.[1]

2

The Sun came up upon the right,
    Out of the Sea came he;
And broad as a weft[2] upon the left
    Went down into the Sea.

85 And the good south wind still blew behind,
    But no sweet Bird did follow
Ne any day for food or play
    Came to the Marinere's hollo!

And I had done an hellish thing
90   And it would work 'em woe;
For all averr'd, I had kill'd the Bird
    That made the Breeze to blow.

Ne dim ne red, like God's own head,
    The glorious Sun uprist:
95 Then all averr'd, I had kill'd the Bird
    That brought the fog and mist.
'Twas right, said they, such birds to slay
    That bring the fog and mist.

---

[1] This incident is taken from Captain George Shelvocke's *A Voyage Round the World* (1726); W. Wordsworth suggested making it the basis of the poem: "We had continual squals of sleet, snow and rain, and the heavens were perpetually hid from us by gloomy dismal clouds. In short, one would think it impossible that any thing living could subsist in so rigid a climate; and, indeed, we all observed, that we had not had the sight of one fish of any kind, since we were come to the Southward of the streights of *le Mair*, nor one sea-bird, except a disconsolate black *Albitross*, who accompanied us for several days, hovering about us as if he had lost himself, till *Hatley*, (my second Captain) observing, in one of his melancholy fits, that this bird was always hovering near us, imagin'd, from his colour, that it might be some ill omen. That which, I suppose, induced him the more to encourage his superstition, was the continued series of contrary tempestuous winds, which had oppress'd us ever since we had got into this sea. But be that as it would, he, after some fruitless attempts, at length, shot the *Albitross*, not doubting (perhaps) that we should have a fair wind after it" (72–73).

[2] a broad pennant flown as a distress signal.

Samuel Taylor Coleridge 1817

The Wedding-Guest he beat his breast,
Yet he can not chuse but hear;
And thus spake on that ancient man,
40 　The bright-eyed Mariner.

And now the STORM-BLAST came, and he
Was tyrannous and strong: *The ship drawn by a storm toward the south pole.*
He struck with his o'ertaking wings,
And chased us south along.

45 With sloping masts and dipping prow,
As who pursued with yell and blow
Still treads the shadow of his foe
And forward bends his head,
The ship drove fast, loud roar'd the blast,
50 And southward aye we fled.

And now there came both mist and snow,
And it grew wonderous cold:
And ice, mast-high, came floating by,
As green as emerald.

55 And through the drifts the snowy clift   *The land of ice, and of fearful sounds, where no living thing was to be seen.*
Did send a dismal sheen:
Nor shapes of men nor beasts we ken—
The ice was all between.

The ice was here, the ice was there,
60 The ice was all around:
It cracked and growled, and roar'd and howl'd,
Like noises in a swound!

At length did cross an Albatross: *Till a great sea-bird, called the Albatross, came through the snow-fog, and was received with great joy and hospitality.*
Thorough the fog it came;
65 As if it had been a Christian soul,
We hailed it in God's name.

It ate the food it ne'er had eat,
And round and round it flew.
The ice did split with a thunder-fit;
70 The helmsman steer'd us through!

And a good south wind sprung up behind;   *And lo! the Albatross proveth a bird of good omen, and followeth the ship as it returned northward, through fog and floating ice.*
The Albatross did follow,
And every day, for food or play,
Came to the Mariner's hollo!

75 In mist or cloud, on mast or shroud,
It perch'd for vespers nine;
Whiles all the night, through fog-smoke white,
Glimmered the white Moon-shine.

"God save thee, ancient Mariner!   *The ancient Mariner inhospitably killeth the pious bird of good omen.*
80 From the fiends, that plague thee thus!—
Why look'st thou so?"—With my cross-bow
I shot the ALBATROSS!

PART THE SECOND

The Sun now rose upon the right:
Out of the sea came he,
85 Still hid in mist, and on the left
Went down into the sea.

And the good south wind still blew behind,
But no sweet bird did follow,
Nor any day for food or play
90 Came to the mariners' hollo!

And I had done an hellish thing,   *His ship-mates cry out against the ancient Mariner, for killing the bird of good luck.*
And it would work 'em woe:
For all averred, I had killed the bird
That made the breeze to blow.
95 Ah wretch! said they, the bird to slay,
That made the breeze to blow!

Nor dim nor red, like God's own head,   *But when the fog cleared off, they justify the same—and thus make themselves accomplices in the crime.*
The glorious Sun uprist:
Then all averred, I had killed the bird
100 That brought the fog and mist.
'Twas right, said they, such birds to slay,
That bring the fog and mist.

The breezes blew, the white foam flew,
    The furrow follow'd free:
We were the first that ever burst
    Into that silent Sea.[1]

Down dropt the breeze, the Sails dropt down,
    'Twas sad as sad could be
And we did speak only to break
    The silence of the Sea.

All in a hot and copper sky
    The bloody sun at noon,
Right up above the mast did stand,
    No bigger than the moon.

Day after day, day after day,
    We stuck, ne breath ne motion,
As idle as a painted Ship
    Upon a painted Ocean.

Water, water, every where
    And all the boards did shrink;
Water, water, every where,
    Ne any drop to drink.

The very deeps did rot: O Christ!
    That ever this should be!
Yea, slimy things did crawl with legs
    Upon the slimy Sea.

About, about, in reel and rout
    The Death-fires danc'd at night;
The water, like a witch's oils,
    Burnt green and blue and white.[2]

And some in dreams assured were
    Of the Spirit that plagued us so:
Nine fathom deep he had follow'd us
    From the Land of Mist and Snow.

And every tongue thro' utter drouth
    Was wither'd at the root;
We could not speak no more than if
    We had been choked with soot.

Ah wel-a-day! what evil looks
    Had I from old and young;
Instead of the Cross the Albatross
    About my neck was hung.[3]

3

I saw a something in the Sky
    No bigger than my fist;
At first it seem'd a little speck
    And then it seem'd a mist:
It mov'd and mov'd, and took at last
    A certain shape, I wist.[4]

A speck, a mist, a shape, I wist!
    And still it ner'd and ner'd;
And, an it dodg'd a water-sprite,
    It plung'd and tack'd and veer'd.

With throat unslack'd, with black lips bak'd
    Ne could we laugh, ne wail:
Then while thro' drouth all dumb they stood
I bit my arm and suck'd the blood
    And cry'd, A sail! a sail!

With throat unslack'd, with black lips bak'd
    Agape they hear'd me call:
Gramercy![5] they for joy did grin
And all at once their breath drew in
    As they were drinking all.

---

[1] the Pacific ("peaceful") Ocean.

[2] The "Death-fires" are St. Elmo's fire, caused by static electricity in the rigging (traditionally considered an evil omen); the burning water is phosphorescence.

[3] The sooty albatross (*Phoebetria palpebrata antarctica*), unlike the wandering albatross (*Diomeda exulans*), is small enough to hang around a man's neck.

[4] knew.

[5] great thanks (Fr., "grand-merci").

The fair breeze blew, the white foam flew, *The fair breeze continues; the ship enters the Pacific Ocean and sails northward, even till it reaches the Line.*
The furrow[1] stream'd off free:
105   We were the first that ever burst
Into that silent sea.

Down dropt the breeze, the sails dropt down,
'Twas sad as sad could be;
And we did speak only to break   *The ship hath been suddenly becalmed.*
110   The silence of the sea!

All in a hot and copper sky,
The bloody Sun, at noon,
Right up above the mast did stand,
No bigger than the Moon.

115   Day after day, day after day,
We stuck, nor breath nor motion,
As idle as a painted ship
Upon a painted ocean.

Water, water, every where,   *And the Albatross begins to be avenged.*
120   And all the boards did shrink;
Water water, every where,
Nor any drop to drink.

The very deep did rot: O Christ!
That ever this should be!   *A spirit had followed them; one of the invisible inhabitants of this planet, neither departed souls nor angels; concerning whom the learned Jew, Josephus, and the Platonic Constantinopolitan, Michael Psellus,[2] may be consulted. They are very numerous, and there is no climate or element without one or more.*
125   Yea, slimy things did crawl with legs
Upon the slimy sea.

About, about, in reel and rout
The death-fires danced at night;
The water, like a witch's oils,
130   Burnt green, and blue and white.

And some in dreams assured were
Of the spirit that plagued us so:

---

[1] "In the former edition the line was,
    The furrow follow'd free;
but I had not been long on board a ship, before I perceived that this was the image as seen by a spectator from the shore, or from another vessel. From the ship itself the *Wake* appears like a brook flowing off from the stern." (S.T.C.)

[2] Byzantine philosopher (1018–78?).

Nine fathom deep he had followed us
From the land of mist and snow.

135   And every tongue, through utter drought,
Was wither'd at the root;
We could not speak, no more than if
We had been choak'd with soot.   *The ship-mates, in their sore distress, would fain throw the whole guilt on the ancient Mariner: in sign whereof they hang the dead sea-bird round his neck.*

Ah! well a-day! what evil looks
140   Had I from old and young!
Instead of the cross, the Albatross
About my neck was hung.

PART THE THIRD

There passed a weary time. Each throat
Was parched, and glazed each eye.
145   A weary time! a weary time!
How glazed each weary eye!
When looking westward, I beheld   *The ancient Mariner beholdeth a sign in the element afar off.*
A something in the sky.

At first it seem'd a little speck,
150   And then it seem'd a mist:
It moved and moved, and took at last
A certain shape, I wist.

A speck, a mist, a shape, I wist!
And still it near'd and near'd:
155   And as if it dodged a water-sprite,
It plunged and tack'd and veer'd.

With throat unslack'd, with black lips baked, *At its nearer approach, it seemeth him to be a ship; and at a dear ransom he freeth his speech from the bonds of thirst.*
We could nor laugh nor wail;
Through utter drought all dumb we stood!
160   I bit my arm, I sucked the blood,
And cried, A sail! a sail!

With throat unslacked, with black lips baked,
Agape they heard me call:
Gramercy! they for joy did grin,   *A flash of joy.*
165   And all at once their breath drew in,
As they were drinking all.

She doth not tack from side to side—
    Hither to work us weal
Withouten wind, withouten tide
    She steddies with upright keel.

The western wave was all a flame,
    The day was well nigh done!
Almost upon the western wave
    Rested the broad bright Sun;
When that strange shape drove suddenly
    Betwixt us and the Sun.

And strait the Sun was fleck'd with bars
    (Heaven's mother send us grace)
As if thro' a dungeon grate he peer'd
    With broad and burning face.

Alas! (thought I, and my heart beat loud)
    How fast she neres and neres!
Are those *her* Sails that glance in the Sun
    Like restless gossameres?[1]

Are those *her* naked ribs, which fleck'd
    The sun that did behind them peer?
And are those two all, all the crew,
    That woman and her fleshless Pheere?[2]

His bones were black with many a crack,
    All black and bare, I ween;
Jet-black and bare, save where with rust
Of mouldy damps and charnel crust
    They're patch'd with purple and green.

Her lips are red, *her* looks are free,
    Her locks are yellow as gold:
Her skin is as white as leprosy,
And she is far liker Death than he;
    Her flesh makes the still air cold.

The naked Hulk alongside came
    And the Twain were playing dice;

"The Game is done! I've won, I've won!"
    Quoth she, and whistled thrice.

A gust of wind sterte up behind
    And whistled thro' his bones;
Thro' the holes of his eyes and the hole of his mouth
    Half-whistles and half-groans.

With never a whisper in the Sea
    Off darts the Spectre-ship;
While clombe above the Eastern bar
The horned Moon, with one bright Star
    Almost atween the tips.[3]

One after one by the horned Moon
    (Listen, O Stranger! to me)
Each turn'd his face with a ghastly pang
    And curs'd me with his ee.

Four times fifty living men,
    With never a sigh or groan,
With heavy thump, a lifeless lump
    They dropp'd down one by one.

Their souls did from their bodies fly,—
    They fled to bliss or woe;
And every soul it pass'd me by,
    Like the whiz of my Cross-bow.

4

" I fear thee, ancyent Marinere!
    I fear thy skinny hand;
And thou art long and lank and brown
    As is the ribb'd Sea-sand.[4]

"I fear thee and thy glittering eye
    And thy skinny hand so brown—"
Fear not, fear not, thou wedding guest!
    This body dropt not down.

---

[1] cobwebs.

[2] companion.

[3] According to Coleridge, sailors believed this to be an evil omen.

[4] Coleridge later credited W. Wordsworth with the last two lines of this stanza. See facing page, n. 2.

See! see! (I cried) she tacks no more!
Hither to work us weal;
Without a breeze, without a tide,
170 She steddies with upright keel!

The western wave was all a-flame.
The day was well nigh done!
Almost upon the western wave
Rested the broad bright Sun;
175 When that strange shape drove suddenly
Betwixt us and the Sun.

And straight the Sun was flecked with bars,
(Heaven's Mother send us grace!)
As if through a dungeon-grate he peer'd,
180 With broad and burning face.

Alas! (thought I, and my heart beat loud)
How fast she nears and nears!
Are those *her* sails that glance in the Sun,
Like restless gossameres!

185 Are those *her* ribs through which the Sun
Did peer, as through a grate?
And is that Woman all her crew?
Is that a DEATH? and are there two?
Is DEATH that woman's mate?

190 *Her* lips were red, *her* looks were free,
Her locks were yellow as gold:
Her skin was as white as leprosy,
The Night-Mair LIFE-IN-DEATH was she,
Who thicks man's blood with cold.

195 The naked hulk alongside came,
And the twain were casting dice;
"The game is done! I've won, I've won!"
Quoth she, and whistles thrice.

A gust of wind sterte up behind
200 And whistled through his bones;
Through the holes of his eyes and the hole of his mouth,
Half whistles and half groans.

And horror follows. For can it be a ship that comes onward without wind or tide?

It seemeth him but the skeleton of a ship.

And its ribs are seen as bars on the face of the setting Sun. The spectre-woman and her death-mate, and no other on board the skeleton-ship.

Like vessel, like crew!

DEATH, and LIFE-IN-DEATH have diced for the ship's crew, and she (the latter) winneth the ancient Mariner.

The Sun's rim dips; the stars rush out:[1]
At one stride comes the dark;
205 With far-heard whisper, o'er the sea,
Off shot the spectre-bark.

We listen'd and look'd sideways up!
Fear at my heart, as at a cup,
My life-blood seem'd to sip!
210 The stars were dim, and thick the night,
The steerman's face by his lamp gleam'd white;
From the sails the dews did drip—
Till clombe above the eastern bar
The horned Moon, with one bright star
215 Within the nether tip.

One after one, by the star-dogg'd Moon
Too quick for groan or sigh,
Each turn'd his face with a ghastly pang,
And curs'd me with his eye.

220 Four times fifty living men,
(And I heard nor sigh nor groan)
With heavy thump, a lifeless lump,
They dropped down one by one.

The souls did from their bodies fly,—
225 They fled to bliss or woe!
And every soul, it passed me by,
Like the whiz of my CROSS-BOW!

At the rising of the Moon,

One after another,

His ship-mates drop down dead;

But LIFE-IN-DEATH begins her work on the ancient Mariner.

PART THE FOURTH

"I fear thee, ancient Mariner!
I fear thy skinny hand!
230 And thou art long, and lank, and brown,
As is the ribbed sea-sand.[2]

"I fear thee and thy glittering eye,
And thy skinny hand, so brown."—
Fear not, fear not, thou Wedding-Guest!
235 This body dropt not down.

The wedding-guest feareth that a spirit is talking to him;

But the ancient Mariner assureth him of his bodily life, and proceedeth to relate his horrible penance.

---

[1] Coleridge later added a gloss: "No twilight within the courts of the Sun."

[2] "For the two last lines of this stanza, I am indebted to Mr. WORDSWORTH. It was on a delightful walk from Nether Stowey to Dulverton, with him and his sister, in the Autumn of 1797, that this Poem was planned, and in part composed." (S.T.C.)

Alone, alone, all all alone
    Alone on the wide wide Sea;
And Christ would take no pity on
    My soul in agony.

The many men so beautiful,
    And they all dead did lie!
And a million million slimy things
    Liv'd on—and so did I.

I look'd upon the rotting Sea,
    And drew my eyes away;
I look'd upon the eldritch deck,
    And there the dead men lay.

I look'd to Heaven, and try'd to pray;
    But or ever a prayer had gusht,
A wicked whisper came and made
    My heart as dry as dust.

I clos'd my lids and kept them close,
    Till the balls like pulses beat;
For the sky and the sea, and the sea and the sky
Lay like a load on my weary eye,
    And the dead were at my feet.

The cold sweat melted from their limbs,
    Ne rot, ne reek did they;
The look with which they look'd on me,
    Had never pass'd away.

An orphan's curse would drag to Hell
    A spirit from on high:
But O! more horrible than that
    Is the curse in a dead man's eye!
Seven days, seven nights I saw that curse,
    And yet I could not die.

The moving Moon went up the sky
    And no where did abide:
Softly she was going up
    And a star or two beside—

Her beams bemock'd the sultry main
    Like morning frosts yspread;
But where the ship's huge shadow lay,
The charmed water burnt alway
    A still and awful red.

Beyond the shadow of the ship
    I watch'd the water-snakes:
They mov'd in tracks of shining white;
And when they rear'd, the elfish light
    Fell off in hoary flakes.

Within the shadow of the ship
    I watch'd their rich attire:
Blue, glossy green, and velvet black
They coil'd and swam; and every track
    Was a flash of golden fire.

O happy living things! no tongue
    Their beauty might declare:
A spring of love gusht from my heart,
    And I bless'd them unaware!
Sure my kind saint took pity on me,
    And I bless'd them unaware.

The self-same moment I could pray;
    And from my neck so free
The Albatross fell off, and sank
    Like lead into the sea.

5

O sleep, it is a gentle thing
    Belov'd from pole to pole!
To Mary-queen the praise be yeven
She sent the gentle sleep from heaven
    That slid into my soul.

The silly[1] buckets on the deck
    That had so long remain'd,
I dreamt that they were fill'd with dew
    And when I awoke it rain'd.

---

[1] simple, humble.

Alone, alone, all, all alone,
Alone on a wide wide sea!
And never a saint took pity on
My soul in agony.

240 The many men, so beautiful!   *He despiseth the*
And they all dead did lie: *creatures of the*
And a thousand thousand slimy things   *calm,*
Liv'd on; and so did I.

I look'd upon the rotting sea,   *And envieth that*
245 And drew my eyes away;   *they should live, and*
I look'd upon the rotting deck,   *so many lie dead.*
And there the dead men lay.

I look'd to Heaven, and tried to pray;
But or ever a prayer had gusht,
250 A wicked whisper came, and made
My heart as dry as dust.

I closed my lids, and kept them close,
And the balls like pulses beat;
For the sky and the sea, and the sea and the sky
255 Lay, like a cloud, on my weary eye,
And the dead were at my feet.

The cold sweat melted from their limbs,   *But the curse liveth*
Nor rot nor reek did they: *for him in the eye of*
The look with which they look'd on me   *the dead men.*
260 Had never pass'd away.

An orphan's curse would drag to Hell
A spirit from on high;
But oh! more horrible than that
Is the curse in a dead man's eye!
265 Seven days, seven nights, I saw that curse,
And yet I could not die.

                                 In his loneliness and
                                 fixedness, he yearneth
The moving Moon went up the sky,   *towards the journeying*
And no where did abide: *Moon, and the stars that*
Softly she was going up,   *still sojourn, yet still*
270 And a star or two beside—   *move onwards; and*
                                 every where the blue sky
                                 belongs to them, and is
                                 their appointed rest,

Her beams bemock'd the sultry main,   *and their native country,*
Like April hoar-frost spread;   *and their own natural*
But where the ship's huge shadow lay, *homes, which they enter*
The charmed water burnt alway   *unannounced, as lords*
275 A still and awful red.   *that are certainly*
                               expected, and yet there
                               is a silent joy at their
Beyond the shadow of the ship,   *arrival.*
I watch'd the water-snakes:
They moved in tracks of shining white, *By the light of the*
And when they reared, the elfish light   *Moon he beholdeth*
280 Fell off in hoary flakes.   *God's creatures of*
                               the great calm.
Within the shadow of the ship
I watch'd their rich attire:
Blue, glossy green, and velvet black,
They coiled and swam; and every track
285 Was a flash of golden fire.

O happy living things! no tongue   *Their beauty and*
Their beauty might declare: *their happiness.*
A spring of love gusht from my heart,
And I blessed them unaware!   *He blesseth them in*
290 Sure my kind saint took pity on me,   *his heart.*
And I blessed them unaware.

The self same moment I could pray;   *The spell begins*
And from my neck so free   *to break.*
The Albatross fell off, and sank
295 Like lead into the sea.

PART THE FIFTH

Oh sleep! it is a gentle thing,
Belov'd from pole to pole!
To Mary Queen the praise be given!
She sent the gentle sleep from Heaven,
300 That slid into my soul.

The silly buckets on the deck,   *By grace of the holy*
That had so long remained,   *Mother, the ancient*
I dreamt that they were filled with dew; *Mariner is refreshed*
And when I awoke, it rained.   *with rain.*

My lips were wet, my throat was cold,
    My garments all were dank;
Sure I had drunken in my dreams
    And still my body drank.

I mov'd and could not feel my limbs,
    I was so light, almost
I thought that I had died in sleep,
    And was a blessed Ghost.

The roaring wind! it roar'd far off,
    It did not come anear;
But with its sound it shook the sails
    That were so thin and sere.

The upper air bursts into life,
    And a hundred fire-flags sheen[1]
To and fro they are hurried about;
And to and fro, and in and out
    The stars dance on between.

The coming wind doth roar more loud;
    The sails do sigh, like sedge:
The rain pours down from one black cloud
    And the Moon is at its edge.

Hark! hark! the thick black cloud is cleft,
    And the Moon is at its side:
Like waters shot from some high crag,
The lightning falls with never a jag
    A river steep and wide.

The strong wind reach'd the ship: it roar'd
    And dropp'd down, like a stone!
Beneath the lightning and the moon
    The dead men gave a groan.

They groan'd, they stirr'd, they all uprose,
    Ne spake, ne mov'd their eyes:
It had been strange, even in a dream
    To have seen those dead men rise.

The helmsman steerd, the ship mov'd on;
    Yet never a breeze up-blew;
The Marineres all 'gan work the ropes,
    Where they were wont to do:
They rais'd their limbs like lifeless tools—
    We were a ghastly crew.

The body of my brother's son
    Stood by me knee to knee:
The body and I pull'd at one rope,
    But he said nought to me—
And I quak'd to think of my own voice
    How frightful it would be!

The day-light dawn'd—they dropp'd their arms,
    And cluster'd round the mast:
Sweet sounds rose slowly thro' their mouths
    And from their bodies pass'd.

Around, around, flew each sweet sound,
    Then darted to the sun:
Slowly the sounds came back again
    Now mix'd, now one by one.

Sometimes a dropping from the sky
    I heard the Lavrock[2] sing;
Sometimes all little birds that are
How they seem'd to fill the sea and air
    With their sweet jargoning,

And now 'twas like all instruments,
    Now like a lonely flute;
And now it is an angel's song
    That makes the heavens be mute.

It ceas'd: yet still the sails made on
    A pleasant noise till noon,
A noise like of a hidden brook
    In the leafy month of June,
That to the sleeping woods all night
    Singeth a quiet tune.

---

[1] probably St. Elmo's fire (see note to 126, 1798 version).

[2] skylark.

Samuel Taylor Coleridge 1817

305 My lips were wet, my throat was cold,
My garments all were dank;
Sure I had drunken in my dreams,
And still my body drank.

I moved, and could not feel my limbs:
310 I was so light—almost
I thought that I had died in sleep,
And was a blessed ghost.

And soon I heard a roaring wind: *He heareth sounds,*
It did not come anear; *and seeth strange*
315 But with its sound it shook the sails, *sights and*
That were so thin and sere. *commotions in*
the sky and the
element.

The upper air burst into life!
And a hundred fire-flags sheen,
To and fro they were hurried about;
320 And to and fro, and in and out,
The wan stars danced between.

And the coming wind did roar more loud,
And the sails did sigh like sedge;
And the rain pour'd down from one black cloud;
325 The Moon was at its edge.

The thick black cloud was cleft, and still
The Moon was at its side:
Like waters shot from some high crag,
The lightning fell with never a jag,
330 A river steep and wide.

The loud wind never reached the ship, *The bodies of the*
Yet now the ship moved on! *ship's crew are*
Beneath the lightning and the Moon *inspirited, and the*
The dead men gave a groan. *ship moves on.*

335 They groan'd, they stirr'd, they all uprose,
Nor spake, nor moved their eyes;
It had been strange, even in a dream,
To have seen those dead men rise.

The helmsman steered, the ship moved on;
340 Yet never a breeze up blew;

The mariners all 'gan work the ropes,
Where they were wont to do:
They raised their limbs like lifeless tools—
We were a ghastly crew.

345 The body of my brother's son
Stood by me, knee to knee:
The body and I pulled at one rope,
But he said nought to me.

"I fear thee, ancient Mariner!" *But not by the souls*
350 Be calm, thou Wedding-Guest! *of the men, nor by*
'Twas not those souls that fled in pain, *dæmons of earth or*
Which to their corses came again, *middle air, but by a*
But a troop of spirits blest: *blessed troop of*
angelic spirits, sent
For when it dawned—they dropped *down by the*
their arms, *invocation of the*
355 And clustered round the mast; *guardian saint.*
Sweet sounds rose slowly through their mouths,
And from their bodies passed.

Around, around, flew each sweet sound,
Then darted to the Sun;
360 Slowly the sounds came back again,
Now mixed, now one by one.

Sometimes a-dropping from the sky
I heard the sky-lark sing;
Sometimes all little birds that are,
365 How they seem'd to fill the sea and air
With their sweet jargoning!

And now 'twas like all instruments,
Now like a lonely flute;
And now it is an angel's song,
370 That makes the Heavens be mute.

It ceased; yet still the sails made on
A pleasant noise till noon,
A noise like of a hidden brook
In the leafy month of June,
375 That to the sleeping woods all night
Singeth a quiet tune.

Listen, O listen, thou Wedding-guest!
    "Marinere! thou hast thy will:
For that, which comes out of thine eye, doth make
    My body and soul to be still."

Never sadder tale was told
    To a man of woman born:
Sadder and wiser thou wedding-guest!
    Thou'lt rise to morrow morn.

Never sadder tale was heard
    By a man of woman born:
The Marineres all return'd to work
    As silent as beforne.

The Marineres all 'gan pull the ropes,
    But look at me they n'old:
Thought I, I am as thin as air—
    They cannot me behold.

Till noon we silently sail'd on
    Yet never a breeze did breathe:
Slowly and smoothly went the ship
    Mov'd onward from beneath.

Under the keel nine fathom deep
    From the land of mist and snow
The spirit slid: and it was He
    That made the Ship to go.
The sails at noon left off their tune
    And the Ship stood still also.

The sun right up above the mast
    Had fix'd her to the ocean:
But in a minute she 'gan stir
    With a short uneasy motion—
Backwards and forwards half her length
    With a short uneasy motion.

Then, like a pawing horse let go,
    She made a sudden bound:
It flung the blood into my head,
    And I fell into a swound.

How long in that same fit I lay,
    I have not to declare;
But ere my living life return'd,
I heard and in my soul discern'd
    Two voices in the air,

"Is it he?" quoth one, "Is this the man?
    By him who died on cross,
With his cruel bow he lay'd full low
    The harmless Albatross.

"The spirit who bideth by himself
    In the land of mist and snow,
He lov'd the bird that lov'd the man
    Who shot him with his bow."

The other was a softer voice,
    As soft as honey-dew:
Quoth he the man hath penance done,
    And penance more will do.

6

FIRST VOICE

"But tell me, tell me! speak again,
    Thy soft response renewing—
What makes that ship drive on so fast?
    What is the Ocean doing?"

SECOND VOICE

"Still as a Slave before his Lord,
    The Ocean hath no blast:
His great bright eye most silently
    Up to the moon is cast—

"If he may know which way to go,
    For she guides him smooth or grim.
See, brother, see! how graciously
    She looketh down on him."

FIRST VOICE

"But why drives on that ship so fast
    Withouten wave or wind?"

SECOND VOICE

"The air is cut away before,
    And closes from behind.

Till noon we quietly sailed on,
Yet never a breeze did breathe:
Slowly and smoothly went the ship,
380 Moved onward from beneath.

Under the keel nine fathom deep,   *The lonesome spirit*
From the land of mist and snow,   *from the south-pole*
The spirit slid: and it was he   *carries on the ship as*
That made the ship to go.   *far as the line, in*
385 The sails at noon left off their tune,   *obedience to the*
And the ship stood still also.   *angelic troop, but*
   still requireth
   vengeance.

The Sun, right up above the mast,
Had fixt her to the ocean;
But in a minute she 'gan stir,
390 With a short uneasy motion—
Backwards and forwards half her length,
With a short uneasy motion.

Then like a pawing horse let go,
She made a sudden bound:
395 It flung the blood into my head,
And I fell down in a swound.

How long in that same fit I lay,   *The Polar Spirit's*
I have not to declare;   *fellow-dæmons, the*
But ere my living life returned,   *invisible inhabitants*
400 I heard and in my soul discerned   *of the element, take*
Two VOICES in the air.   *part in his wrong;*
   and two of them
"Is it he?" quoth one, "Is this the man?   *relate, one to the*
By him who died on cross,   *other, that penance*
With his cruel bow he laid full low,   *long and heavy for*
405 The harmless Albatross.   *the ancient Mariner*
   hath been accorded
"The spirit who bideth by himself   *to the Polar Spirit,*
In the land of mist and snow,   *who returneth*
   southward.

He loved the bird that loved the man
Who shot him with his bow."

410 The other was a softer voice,
As soft as honey-dew:
Quoth he, "The man hath penance done,
And penance more will do."

PART THE SIXTH

FIRST VOICE

But tell me, tell me! speak again,
415 Thy soft response renewing—
What makes that ship drive on so fast?
What is the OCEAN doing?

SECOND VOICE

Still as a slave before his lord,
The OCEAN hath no blast;
420 His great bright eye most silently
Up to the Moon is cast—

If he may know which way to go;
For she guides him smooth or grim.
See, brother, see! how graciously
425 She looketh down on him.

FIRST VOICE

But why drives on that ship so fast,   *The Mariner hath*
Without or wave or wind?   *been cast into a*
   trance; for the
SECOND VOICE   *angelic power*
   causeth the vessel to
The air is cut away before,   *drive northward,*
And closes from behind.   *faster than human*
   life could endure.

"Fly, brother, fly! more high, more high,
    Or we shall be belated:
For slow and slow that ship will go,
    When the Marinere's trance is abated."

435 I woke, and we were sailing on
    As in a gentle weather:
'Twas night, calm night, the moon was high;
    The dead men stood together.

All stood together on the deck,
440   For a charnel-dungeon fitter:
All fix'd on me their stony eyes
    That in the moon did glitter.

The pang, the curse, with which they died,
    Had never pass'd away:
445 I could not draw my een from theirs
    Ne turn them up to pray.

And in its time the spell was snapt,
    And I could move my een:
I look'd far-forth, but little saw
450   Of what might else be seen.

Like one, that on a lonely road
    Doth walk in fear and dread,
And having once turn'd round, walks on
    And turns no more his head:
455 Because he knows, a frightful fiend
    Doth close behind him tread.

But soon there breath'd a wind on me,
    Ne sound ne motion made:
Its path was not upon the sea
460   In ripple or in shade.

It rais'd my hair, it fann'd my cheek,
    Like a meadow-gale of spring—
It mingled strangely with my fears,
    Yet it felt like a welcoming.

465 Swiftly, swiftly flew the ship,
    Yet she sail'd softly too:
Sweetly, sweetly blew the breeze—
    On me alone it blew.

O dream of joy! is this indeed
470   The light-house top I see?
Is this the Hill? Is this the Kirk?
    Is this mine own countrée?

We drifted o'er the Harbour-bar,
    And I with sobs did pray—
475 "O let me be awake, my God!
    Or let me sleep alway!"

The harbour-bay was clear as glass,
    So smoothly it was strewn!
And on the bay the moon light lay,
480   And the shadow of the moon.

The moonlight bay was white all o'er,
    Till rising from the same,
Full many shapes, that shadows were,
    Like as of torches came.

485 A little distance from the prow
    Those dark-red shadows were;
But soon I saw that my own flesh
    Was red as in a glare.

430 Fly, brother, fly! more high! more high!
Or we shall be belated:
For slow and slow that ship will go,
When the Mariner's trance is abated.

I woke, and we were sailing on
435 As in a gentle weather:
'Twas night, calm night, the Moon was high;
The dead men stood together.

The supernatural motion is retarded; the Mariner awakes, and his penance begins anew.

All stood together on the deck,
For a charnel-dungeon fitter:
440 All fixed on me their stony eyes,
That in the Moon did glitter.

The pang, the curse, with which they died,
Had never passed away:
I could not draw my eyes from theirs,
445 Nor turn them up to pray.

And now this spell was snapt: once more
I viewed the ocean green,
And looked far forth, yet little saw
Of what had else been seen—

The curse is finally expiated.

450 Like one, that on a lonesome road
Doth walk in fear and dread,
And having once turn'd round, walks on,
And turns no more his head;
Because he knows, a frightful fiend
455 Doth close behind him tread.

But soon there breathed a wind on me,
Nor sound nor motion made:
Its path was not upon the sea,
In ripple or in shade.

460 It raised my hair, it fanned my cheek
Like a meadow-gale of spring—
It mingled strangely with my fears,
Yet it felt like a welcoming.

Swiftly, swiftly flew the ship,
465 Yet she sailed softly too:
Sweetly, sweetly blew the breeze—
On me alone it blew.

Oh! dream of joy! is this indeed
The light-house top I see?
470 Is this the hill? is this the kirk?
Is this mine own countree?

And the ancient Mariner beholdeth his native country.

We drifted o'er the harbour-bar,
And I with sobs did pray—
O let me be awake, my God!
475 Or let me sleep alway.

The harbour-bay was clear as glass,
So smoothly was it strewn!
And on the bay the moonlight lay,
And the shadow of the moon.

480 The rock shone bright, the kirk no less,
That stands above the rock:
The moonlight steeped in silentness
The steady weathercock.

And the bay was white with silent light,
485 Till rising from the same,
Full many shapes, that shadows were,
In crimson colours came.

The angelic spirits leave the dead bodies,

A little distance from the prow
Those crimson shadows were:
490 I turned my eyes upon the deck—
Oh, Christ! what saw I there!

And appear in their own forms of light.

I turn'd my head in fear and dread,
    And by the holy rood,
The bodies had advanc'd, and now
    Before the mast they stood.

They lifted up their stiff right arms,
    They held them strait and tight;
And each right-arm burnt like a torch,
    A torch that's borne upright.[1]
Their stony eye-balls glitter'd on
    In the red and smoky light.

I pray'd and turn'd my head away
    Forth looking as before.
There was no breeze upon the bay,
    No wave against the shore.

The rock shone bright, the kirk no less
    That stands above the rock:
The moonlight steep'd in silentness
    The steady weathercock.

And the bay was white with silent light,
    Till rising from the same
Full many shapes, that shadows were,
    In crimson colours came.

A little distance from the prow
    Those crimson shadows were:
I turn'd my eyes upon the deck—
    O Christ! what saw I there?

Each corse lay flat, lifeless and flat;
    And by the Holy rood[2]
A man all light, a seraph-man,
    On every corse there stood.

This seraph-band, each wav'd his hand:
    It was a heavenly sight:
They stood as signals to the land,
    Each one a lovely light:

This seraph-band, each wav'd his hand,
    No voice did they impart—
No voice; but O! the silence sank,
    Like music on my heart.

Eftsones[3] I heard the dash of oars,
    I heard the pilot's cheer:
My head was turn'd perforce away
    And I saw a boat appear.

Then vanish'd all the lovely lights;
    The bodies rose anew:
With silent pace, each to his place,
    Came back the ghastly crew.
The wind, that shade nor motion made,
    On me alone it blew.

The pilot, and the pilot's boy
    I heard them coming fast:
Dear Lord in Heaven! it was a joy,
    The dead men could not blast.

I saw a third—I heard his voice:
    It is the Hermit good!
He singeth loud his godly hymns
    That he makes in the wood.
He'll shrieve my soul,[4] he'll wash away
    The Albatross's blood.

---

[1] This supernatural phenomenon is known as the "Hand of Glory."

[2] cross.

[3] immediately.

[4] grant absolution.

Each corse lay flat, lifeless and flat,
And, by the holy rood!
A man all light, a seraph-man,
On every corse there stood.

This seraph-band, each waved his hand:
It was a heavenly sight!
They stood as signals to the land,
Each one a lovely light:

This seraph-band, each waved his hand,
No voice did they impart—
No voice; but oh! the silence sank
Like music on my heart.

But soon I heard the dash of oars,
I heard the Pilot's cheer;
My head was turn'd perforce away,
And I saw a boat appear.

The Pilot, and the Pilot's boy,
I heard them coming fast:
Dear Lord in Heaven! it was a joy
The dead men could not blast.

I saw a third—I heard his voice:
It is the Hermit good!
He singeth loud his godly hymns
That he makes in the wood.
He'll shrieve my soul, he'll wash away
The Albatross's blood.

7

This Hermit good lives in that wood
    Which slopes down to the Sea.
How loudly his sweet voice he rears!
550 He loves to talk with Marineres
    That come from a far Countrée.

He kneels at morn and noon and eve—
    He hath a cushion plump:
It is the moss, that wholly hides
555   The rotted old Oak-stump.

The Skiff-boat ne'rd: I heard them talk,
    "Why, this is strange, I trow!
Where are those lights so many and fair
    That signal made but now?"

560 "Strange, by my faith!" the Hermit said—
    "And they answer'd not our cheer.
The planks look warp'd, and see those sails,
    How thin they are and sere!
I never saw aught like to them
565   Unless perchance it were

"The skeletons of leaves that lag
    My forest brook along:
When the Ivy-tod is heavy with snow,
And the Owlet whoops to the wolf below
570   That eats the she-wolf's young."

"Dear Lord! it has a fiendish look—
    (The Pilot made reply)
"I am a-fear'd."—"Push on, push on!"
    Said the Hermit cheerily.

575 The Boat came closer to the Ship,
    But I ne spake ne stirr'd!
The Boat came close beneath the Ship,
    And strait a sound was heard!

Under the water it rumbled on,
580   Still louder and more dread:
It reach'd the Ship, it split the bay;
    The Ship went down like lead.

Stunn'd by that loud and dreadful sound,
    Which sky and ocean smote:
585 Like one that hath been seven days drown'd
    My body lay afloat:
But, swift as dreams, myself I found
    Within the Pilot's boat.

Upon the whirl, where sank the Ship,
590   The boat spun round and round:
And all was still, save that the hill
    Was telling of the sound.

I mov'd my lips: the Pilot shriek'd
    And fell down in a fit.
595 The Holy Hermit rais'd his eyes
    And pray'd where he did sit.

I took the oars: the Pilot's boy,
    Who now doth crazy go,
Laugh'd loud and long, and all the while
600   His eyes went to and fro,
"Ha! ha!" quoth he—"full plain I see,
    The devil knows how to row."

And now all in mine own Countrée
    I stood on the firm land!
605 The Hermit stepp'd forth from the boat,
    And scarcely he could stand.

"O shrieve me, shrieve me, holy Man!"
    The Hermit cross'd his brow—
"Say quick," quoth he, "I bid thee say
610   What manner man art thou?"

Forthwith this frame of mine was wrench'd
    With a woeful agony,
Which forc'd me to begin my tale
    And then it left me free.

615 Since then at an uncertain hour,
    Now oftimes and now fewer,
That anguish comes and makes me tell
    My ghastly aventure.

PART THE SEVENTH

This Hermit good lives in that wood   *The Hermit of the*
Which slopes down to the sea.   *Wood,*
520 How loudly his sweet voice he rears!
He loves to talk with marineres
That come from a far countree.

He kneels at morn, and noon and eve—
He hath a cushion plump:
525 It is the moss that wholly hides
The rotted old oak-stump.

The Skiff-boat near'd: I heard them talk,
"Why this is strange, I trow!
Where are those lights so many and fair,
530 That signal made but now?"

"Strange, by my faith!" the Hermit said—   *Approacheth the*
"And they answered not our cheer!   *ship with wonder.*
The planks look warped! and see those sails,
How thin they are and sere!
535 I never saw ought like to them,
Unless perchance it were

"The skeletons of leaves that lag
My forest-brook along:
When the ivy-tod is heavy with snow,
540 And the owlet whoops to the wolf below,
That eats the she-wolf's young.

"Dear Lord! it hath a fiendish look—"
(The Pilot made reply)
"I am a-feared"—"Push on, push on!"
545 Said the Hermit cheerily.

The boat came closer to the ship,
But I nor spake nor stirred;
The boat came close beneath the ship,
And straight a sound was heard.

550 Under the water it rumbled on,   *The ship suddenly*
Still louder and more dread: *sinketh.*
It reach'd the ship, it split the bay;
The ship went down like lead.

Stunned by that loud and dreadful sound,   *The ancient*
555 Which sky and ocean smote,   *Mariner is saved in*
Like one that hath been seven days drown'd, *the Pilot's boat.*
My body lay afloat;
But swift as dreams, myself I found
Within the Pilot's boat.

560 Upon the whirl, where sank the ship,
The boat spun round and round;
And all was still, save that the hill
Was telling of the sound.

I moved my lips—the Pilot shrieked
565 And fell down in a fit;
The holy Hermit raised his eyes,
And prayed where he did sit.

I took the oars: the Pilot's boy,
Who now doth crazy go,
570 Laughed loud and long, and all the while
His eyes went to and fro.
"Ha! ha!" quoth he, "full plain I see,
The Devil knows how to row."

And now, all in my own countree,
575 I stood on the firm land!
The Hermit stepped forth from the boat,
And scarcely he could stand.

"O shrieve me, shrieve me, holy man!"   *The ancient Mariner*
The Hermit cross'd his brow.   *earnestly entreateth*
580 "Say quick," quoth he, "I bid thee say—   *the Hermit to*
What manner of man art thou?"   *shrieve him; and the*
                                                                      penance of life falls
Forthwith this frame of mine was wrench'd   *on him.*
With a woeful agony,
Which forced me to begin my tale;
585 And then it left me free.

Since then, at an uncertain hour,   *And ever and anon*
That agony returns;   *throughout his*
And till my ghastly tale is told,   *future life an agony*
This heart within me burns.   *constraineth him to*
                                                                      travel from land to
                                                                      land,

    I pass, like night, from land to land;
620   I have strange power of speech;
    The moment that his face I see
    I know the man that must hear me;
        To him my tale I teach.

    What loud uproar bursts from that door!
625   The Wedding-guests are there;
    But in the Garden-bower the Bride
        And Bride-maids singing are:
    And hark the little Vesper-bell
        Which biddeth me to prayer.

630   O Wedding-guest! this soul hath been
        Alone on a wide wide sea:
    So lonely 'twas, that God himself
        Scarce seemed there to be.

    O sweeter than the Marriage-feast,
635   'Tis sweeter far to me
    To walk together to the Kirk
        With a goodly company.

    To walk together to the Kirk
        And all together pray,

640   While each to his great father bends,
    Old men, and babes, and loving friends,
        And Youths, and Maidens gay.

    Farewell, farewell! but this I tell
        To thee, thou wedding-guest!
645   He prayeth well who loveth well,
        Both man and bird and beast.

    He prayeth best who loveth best,
        All things both great and small:
    For the dear God, who loveth us,
650   He made and loveth all.

    The Marinere, whose eye is bright,
        Whose beard with age is hoar,
    Is gone; and now the wedding-guest
        Turn'd from the bridegroom's door.

655   He went, like one that hath been stunn'd
        And is of sense forlorn:
    A sadder and a wiser man
        He rose the morrow morn.

590 I pass, like night, from land to land;
I have strange power of speech;
That moment that his face I see,
I know the man that must hear me:
To him my tale I teach.

595 What loud uproar bursts from that door!
The wedding-guests are there;
But in the garden-bower the bride
And bride-maids singing are;
And hark the little vesper bell,
600 Which biddeth me to prayer!

O Wedding-Guest! this soul hath been
Alone on a wide wide sea:
So lonely 'twas, that God himself
Scarce seemed there to be.

605 O sweeter than the marriage-feast,
'Tis sweeter far to me,
To walk together to the kirk
With a goodly company!—

To walk together to the kirk,
610 And all together pray,

While each to his great Father bends,
Old men, and babes, and loving friends,
And youths and maidens gay!

Farewell, farewell! but this I tell
615 To thee, thou Wedding-Guest!
He prayeth well, who loveth well
Both man and bird and beast.

> And to teach by his own example, love and reverence to all things that God made and loveth.

He prayeth best, who loveth best
All things both great and small;
620 For the dear God who loveth us,
He made and loveth all.

The Mariner, whose eye is bright,
Whose beard with age is hoar,
Is gone; and now the Wedding-Guest
625 Turned from the bridegroom's door.

He went like one that hath been stunned,
And is of sense forlorn:
A sadder and a wiser man,
He rose the morrow morn.

from *Lyrical Ballads* (1798)

*The Nightingale;
A Conversational Poem,
Written in April, 1798*

No cloud, no relique of the sunken day
Distinguishes the West, no long thin slip
Of sullen Light, no obscure trembling hues.
Come, we will rest on this old mossy Bridge!
5 You see the glimmer of the stream beneath,
But hear no murmuring: it flows silently
O'er its soft bed of verdure. All is still,
A balmy night! and tho' the stars be dim,
Yet let us think upon the vernal showers
10 That gladden the green earth, and we shall find
A pleasure in the dimness of the stars.
And hark! the Nightingale begins its song,
"Most musical, most melancholy"[1] Bird!
A melancholy Bird? O idle thought!
15 In nature there is nothing melancholy.
—But some night-wandering Man, whose heart was
    pierc'd
With the remembrance of a grievous wrong,
Or slow distemper or neglected love,
(And so, poor Wretch! fill'd all things with himself
20 And made all gentle sounds tell back the tale
Of his own sorrows) he and such as he
First nam'd these notes a melancholy strain;
And many a poet echoes the conceit,
Poet, who hath been building up the rhyme
25 When he had better far have stretch'd his limbs
Beside a brook in mossy forest-dell[2]
By sun or moonlight, to the influxes
Of shapes and sounds and shifting elements

Surrendering his whole spirit, of his song
30 And of his fame forgetful! so his fame
Should share in nature's immortality,
A venerable thing! and so his song
Should make all nature lovelier, and itself
Be lov'd, like nature!—But 'twill not be so;
35 And youths and maidens most poetical
Who lose the deep'ning twilights of the spring
In ball-rooms and hot theatres, they still
Full of meek sympathy must heave their sighs
O'er Philomela's pity-pleading strains.[3]
40 My Friend, and my Friend's Sister![4] we have learnt
A different lore: we may not thus profane
Nature's sweet voices always full of love
And joyance! 'Tis the merry Nightingale
That crowds, and hurries, and precipitates
45 With fast thick warble his delicious notes,
As he were fearful, that an April night
Would be too short for him to utter forth
His love-chant, and disburthen his full soul
Of all its music! And I know a grove
50 Of large extent, hard by a castle huge
Which the great lord inhabits not: and so
This grove is wild with tangling underwood,
And the trim walks are broken up, and grass,
Thin grass and king-cups grow within the paths.
55 But never elsewhere in one place I knew
So many Nightingales: and far and near
In wood and thicket over the wide grove
They answer and provoke each other's songs—
With skirmish and capricious passagings,
60 And murmurs musical and swift jug jug
And one low piping sound more sweet than all—
Stirring the air with such an harmony,
That should you close your eyes, you might almost
Forget it was not day! On moonlight bushes,
65 Whose dewy leafits are but half disclos'd,
You may perchance behold them on the twigs,

---

[1] "This passage in Milton possesses an excellence far superior to that of mere description: it is spoken in the character of the melancholy Man, and has therefore a *dramatic* propriety. The Author makes this remark, to rescue himself from the charge of having alluded with levity to a line in Milton: a charge than which none could be more painful to him, except perhaps that of having ridiculed his Bible." (S.T.C.) Milton, "Il Penseroso" 62.

[2] Cf. Thomas Gray (1716–71), "Elegy Written in a Country Churchyard" (1750) 103–04.

[3] In the classical legend, Philomela's brother-in-law, Tereus, rapes her and cuts out her tongue. At the end of the story, Philomela, her sister Procne, and Tereus are all turned into birds (Philomela into a nightingale). See Virgil, *Georgics* 4.511–15; and Ovid, *Metamorphoses* 6.

[4] William and Dorothy Wordsworth.*

Their bright, bright eyes, their eyes both bright and
   full,
Glistning, while many a glow-worm in the shade
Lights up her love-torch.

                              A most gentle maid
70 Who dwelleth in her hospitable home
Hard by the Castle, and at latest eve,
(Even like a Lady vow'd and dedicate
To something more than nature in the grove)
Glides thro' the pathways; she knows all their notes,
75 That gentle Maid! and oft, a moment's space,
What time the moon was lost behind a cloud,
Hath heard a pause of silence: till the Moon
Emerging, hath awaken'd earth and sky
With one sensation, and those wakeful Birds
80 Have all burst forth in choral minstrelsy,
As if one quick and sudden Gale had swept
An hundred airy harps![1] And she hath watch'd
Many a Nightingale perch giddily
On blosmy twig still swinging from the breeze,
85 And to that motion tune his wanton song,
Like tipsy Joy that reels with tossing head.

Farewell, O Warbler! till to-morrow eve,
And you, my friends! farewell, a short farewell!
We have been loitering long and pleasantly,
90 And now for our dear homes.—That strain again![2]
Full fain it would delay me!—My dear Babe,[3]
Who, capable of no articulate sound,
Mars all things with his imitative lisp,
How he would place his hand beside his ear,
95 His little hand, the small forefinger up,
And bid us listen! And I deem it wise
To make him Nature's playmate. He knows well
The evening star: and once when he awoke
In most distressful mood (some inward pain
100 Had made up that strange thing, an infant's dream)
I hurried with him to our orchard plot,
And he beholds the moon, and hush'd at once
Suspends his sobs, and laughs most silently,
While his fair eyes that swam with undropt tears
105 Did glitter in the yellow moon-beam! Well—
It is a father's tale. But if that Heaven
Should give me life, his childhood shall grow up
Familiar with these songs, that with the night
He may associate Joy! Once more farewell,
110 Sweet Nightingale! once more, my friends! farewell.

The Dungeon[4]

And this place our forefathers made for man!
This is the process of our love and wisdom,
To each poor brother who offends against us—
Most innocent, perhaps—and what if guilty?
5 Is this the only cure? Merciful God!
Each pore and natural outlet shrivell'd up
By ignorance and parching poverty,
His energies roll back upon his heart,
And stagnate and corrupt; till changed to poison,
10 They break out on him, like a loathsome plague-spot;
Then we call in our pamper'd mountebanks—
And this is their best cure! uncomforted
And friendless solitude, groaning and tears,
And savage faces, at the clanking hour
15 Seen through the steams and vapour of his dungeon,
By the lamp's dismal twilight! So he lies
Circled with evil, till his very soul
Unmoulds its essence, hopelessly deformed
By sights of ever more deformity!

20 With other ministrations thou, O nature!
Healest thy wandering and distempered child:
Thou pourest on him thy soft influences,
Thy sunny hues, fair forms, and breathing sweets,
Thy melodies of woods, and winds, and waters,
25 Till he relent, and can no more endure
To be a jarring and a dissonant thing,
Amid this general dance and minstrelsy;

---

[1] Cf. "Effusion 35" 12–25, 36–40.*

[2] Cf. Shakespeare, *Twelfth Night* 1.1.4.

[3] Coleridge's first son, Hartley (1796–1849).

[4] An excerpt from Coleridge's tragedy *Osorio*, 5.2.1–30. In 1813, the play was performed and published as *Remorse*, in which these lines are 5.1.1–30. The speaker is the hero, Albert (later Alvar), who has been unjustly imprisoned.

But, bursting into tears, wins back his way,
His angry spirit healed and harmonized
30 By the benignant touch of love and beauty.

from the *Annual Anthology* (1800)

This Lime-Tree Bower My Prison,
A Poem, Addressed to Charles Lamb, of the
India-House, London

ADVERTISEMENT

In the June of 1797, some long-expected Friends paid a visit to the Author's Cottage; and on the morning of their arrival he met with an accident, which disabled him from walking during the whole time of their stay. One evening, when they had left him for a few hours, he composed the following lines, in the Garden Bower.[1]

Well, they are gone, and here must I remain,[2]
This lime-tree bower my prison! I have lost
Such beauties and such feelings, as had been
Most sweet to have remember'd, even when age
5 Had dimm'd my eyes to blindness! They, meanwhile,
My friends, whom I may never meet again,
On springy heath along the hill-top edge
Wander in gladness, and wind down, perchance
To that still roaring dell, of which I told;
10 The roaring dell, o'erwooded, narrow, deep,
And only speckled by the mid-day sun;
Where its slim trunk the Ash from rock to rock
Flings arching like a bridge; that branchless Ash
Unsunn'd and damp, whose few poor yellow leaves
15 Ne'er tremble in the gale, yet tremble still
Fann'd by the water-fall! And there my friends,
Behold the dark-green file of long lank weeds,[3]
That all at once (a most fantastic sight!)
Still nod and drip beneath the dripping edge
20 Of the dim clay-stone.
　　　　　　　Now my friends emerge
Beneath the wide wide Heaven, and view again
The many-steepled track magnificent
Of hilly fields and meadows, and the sea
With some fair bark perhaps which lightly touches
25 The slip of smooth clear blue betwixt two isles
Of purple shadow! Yes! they wander on
In gladness all; but thou, methinks, most glad
My gentle-hearted CHARLES![4] for thou had'st pin'd
And hunger'd after nature many a year
30 In the great city pent,[5] winning thy way
With sad yet patient soul, thro' evil and pain
And strange calamity![6] Ah slowly sink
Behind the western ridge, thou glorious Sun!
Shine in the slant beams of the sinking orb,
35 Ye purple heath-flowers! richlier burn, ye clouds!
Live in the yellow light, ye distant groves!
And kindle, thou blue ocean!—So my Friend
Struck with deep joy may stand, as I have stood,
Silent with swimming sense; yea, gazing round
40 On the wide landscape, gaze till all doth seem
Less gross than bodily, a living thing
Which *acts* upon the mind—and with such hues
As cloath the Almighty Spirit, when he makes
Spirits perceive his presence.
　　　　　　　　　　　A delight
45 Comes sudden on my heart, and I am glad
As I myself were there! Nor in this bower,
This little lime-tree bower have I not mark'd
Much that has sooth'd me. Pale beneath the blaze

---

[1] In July 1797, William and Dorothy Wordsworth* and Charles Lamb* were visiting the Coleridges in Nether Stowey. Coleridge was unable to go for walks with them because his wife had spilt boiling milk on his foot. The bower belonged to his neighbour Thomas Poole.

[2] Cf. Henry Vaughan (1621–95), "They are all gone into the world of light!" (1655).

[3] "The Asplenium scolopendrium, called in some countries the Adder's tongue, in others the Hart's tongue: but Withering gives the Adder's tongue, as the trivial name of the Ophioalossum only." (S.T.C.) William Withering, *An Arrangement of British Plants* 3: 761, 766.

[4] Lamb objected violently to being described as "gentle-hearted," here and at 68 and 75.

[5] Cf. Milton, *Paradise Lost* 9.445.

[6] In September 1796, Mary Lamb* had killed her mother, and attempted to kill her father, in a fit of insanity.

Hung the transparent foliage; and I watch'd
Some broad and sunny leaf, and lov'd to see
The shadow of the leaf and stem above
Dappling its sunshine! And that Wallnut tree
Was richly ting'd; and a deep radiance lay
Full on the ancient Ivy which *usurps*
Those fronting elms, and now with blackest mass
Makes their dark branches gleam a lighter hue
Thro' the late Twilight: and tho' now the Bat
Wheels silent by, and not a Swallow twitters,
Yet still the solitary humble Bee,
Sings in the bean-flower! Henceforth I shall know
That Nature ne'er deserts the wise and pure,
No scene so narrow but may well employ
Each faculty of sense, and keep the heart
Awake to love and beauty! And sometimes
'Tis well to be bereft of promis'd good,
That we may lift the soul, and contemplate
With lively joy the joys we cannot share.
My gentle-hearted CHARLES! when the last Rook
Beat its straight path along the dusky air
Homewards, I blest it! deeming its black wing
(Now a dim speck, now vanishing in the light)
Had cross'd the mighty orb's dilated glory
While thou stood'st gazing; or when all was still
Flew *creeking*[1] o'er thy head, and had a charm
For thee, my gentle-hearted CHARLES! to whom
No sound is dissonant, which tells of Life.[2]

---

[1] "Some months after I had written this line, it gave me pleasure to observe that Bartram had observed the same circumstance of the Savannah Crane. 'When these birds move their wings in flight, their strokes are slow, moderate and regular; and even when at a considerable distance, or high above us, we plainly hear the quill feathers, their shafts and webs upon one another creek as the joints or working of a vessel in a tempestuous sea.'" (S.T.C.) William Bartram, *Travels through North & South Carolina* (London, 1794) 219.

[2] The poem is signed "ESTEESI"; that is, S.T.C.

---

from *Memoirs of the Late Mrs. Robinson* (1801)

A Stranger Minstrel. By S.T. Coleridge, Esq. Written to Mrs. Robinson a Few Weeks before Her Death

As late on Skiddaw[3] mount I lay supine
Midway th' ascent, in that repose divine,
When the soul, center'd in the heart's recess,
Hath quaff'd its fill of Nature's loveliness,
Yet still beside the fountain's marge will stay,
    And fain would thirst again, again to quaff;—
Then, when the tear, slow travelling on its way,
    Fills up the wrinkle of a silent laugh;
In that sweet mood of sad and humorous thought—
A form within me rose, within me wrought
With such strong magic, that I cry'd aloud,
Thou ancient SKIDDAW! by thy helm of cloud,
And by thy many-colour'd chasms so deep;
And by their shadows, that for ever sleep;
By yon small flaky mists, that love to creep
Along the edges of those spots of light,
Those sunshine islands on thy smooth green height;
    And by yon shepherds with their sheep,
    And dogs and boys, a gladsome crowd,
    That rush even now with clamour loud
    Sudden from forth thy topmost cloud;
    And by this laugh, and by this tear,
    I would, old Skiddaw! SHE were here!
    A Lady of sweet song is she,
    Her soft blue eye was made for thee!
O ancient Skiddaw! by this tear,
I would, I would, that she were here!

Then ancient SKIDDAW, stern and proud,
    In sullen majesty replying,
Thus spake from out his helm of cloud,
    (His voice was like an echo dying!)
"She dwells, belike, by scenes more fair,
And scorns a mount so bleak and bare!"

---

[3] a mountain in the Lake District.

I only sigh'd, when this I heard,
35　Such mournful thoughts within me stirr'd,
That all my heart was faint and weak,
　　So sorely was I troubled!
No laughter wrinkled now my cheek,
　　But O! the tears were doubled.

40　But ancient Skiddaw, green and high,
　　Heard and understood my sigh:
And now in tones less stern and rude,
　　As if he wish'd to end the feud,
Spake he, the proud response renewing:
45　(His voice was like a monarch wooing!)

"Nay, but thou dost not know her might,
　　The pinions of her soul how strong!
But many a stranger in my height
　　Hath sung to me her magic song,
50　　　Sending forth his extacy
　　　In her divinest melody;
And hence I know, her soul is free,
　　She is, where'er she wills to be,
　　　Unfetter'd by mortality!
55　Now to the 'haunted beach' can fly,[1]
　　　Beside the threshold scourg'd with waves,
　　Now to the maniac while he raves,
'Pale moon! thou spectre of the sky!'[2]
No wind that hurries o'er my height
60　Can travel with so swift a flight.
　　　I too, methinks, might merit
　　　The presence of her spirit!
　　　To me too might belong
The honour of her song, and witching melody,
65　　　Which most resembles me,
　　　Soft, various, and sublime,
　　　Exempt from wrongs of Time!"
Thus spake the mighty Mount: and I
Made answer with a deep-drawn sigh,
70　Thou ancient SKIDDAW! by this tear
I would, I would, that she were here!

---

[1] See Mary Robinson, "The Haunted Beach,"* a poem which Coleridge particularly admired.

[2] Robinson, "Jasper" (1806) 2.

Christabel: Kubla Khan, a Vision; The Pains of Sleep (1816)

Christabel

PREFACE

The first part of the following poem was written in the year one thousand seven hundred and ninety seven, at Stowey in the county of Somerset. The second part, after my return from Germany, in the year one thousand eight hundred, at Keswick, Cumberland. Since the latter date, my poetic powers have been, till very lately, in a state of suspended animation. But as, in my very first conception of the tale, I had the whole present to my mind, with the wholeness, no less than with the liveliness of a vision; I trust that I shall be able to embody in verse the three parts yet to come, in the course of the present year.

　　It is probable, that if the poem had been finished at either of the former periods, or if even the first and second part had been published in the year 1800,[3] the impression of its originality would have been much greater than I dare at present expect. But for this, I have only my own indolence to blame. The dates are mentioned for the exclusive purpose of precluding charges of plagiarism or servile imitation from myself. For there is among us a set of critics, who seem to hold, that every possible thought and image is traditional; who have no notion that there are such things as fountains in the world, small as well as great; and who would therefore charitably derive every rill, they behold flowing, from a perforation made in some other man's tank. I am confident however, that as far as the present poem is concerned, the celebrated poets whose writings I might be suspected of having imitated,[4] either in particular passages, or in the tone and the spirit of the whole,

---

[3] Coleridge had intended "Christabel" to be included in the second edition of *Lyrical Ballads* (1800). W. Wordsworth rejected it, writing and including "Michael"* instead.

[4] Scott,* in *The Lay of the Last Minstrel* (1805), and Byron,* in *The Siege of Corinth* (1815), had imitated the accentual metre of "Christabel," which they had read, or heard read, in manuscript.

would be among the first to vindicate me from the charge, and who, on any striking coincidence, would permit me to address them in this doggrel version of two monkish Latin hexameters:

> 'Tis mine and it is likewise your's,
> But an if this will not do;
> Let it be mine, good friend! for I
> Am the poorer of the two.

I have only to add, that the metre of the Christabel is not, properly speaking, irregular, though it may seem so from its being founded on a new principle: namely, that of counting in each line the accents, not the syllables. Though the latter may vary from seven to twelve, yet in each line the accents will be found to be only four. Nevertheless this occasional variation in the number of syllables is not introduced wantonly, or for the mere ends of convenience, but in correspondence with some transition in the nature of the imagery or passion.

PART 1

'Tis the middle of night by the castle clock,
And the owls have awaken'd the crowing cock;
Tu—whit!——Tu—whoo!
And hark, again! the crowing cock,
5 How drowsily it crew.

Sir Leoline, the Baron rich,
Hath a toothless mastiff bitch;
From her kennel beneath the rock
She makes answer to the clock,
10 Four for the quarters, and twelve for the hour;
Ever and aye, moonshine or shower,
Sixteen short howls, not over loud;
Some say, she sees my lady's shroud.

Is the night chilly and dark?
15 The night is chilly, but not dark.
The thin gray cloud is spread on high,
It covers but not hides the sky.
The moon is behind, and at the full;
And yet she looks both small and dull.
20 The night is chill, the cloud is gray:
'Tis a month before the month of May,
And the Spring comes slowly up this way.

The lovely lady, Christabel,[1]
Whom her father loves so well,
25 What makes her in the wood so late,
A furlong from the castle gate?
She had dreams all yesternight
Of her own betrothed knight;
Dreams, that made her moan and leap,
30 As on her bed she lay in sleep;
And she in the midnight wood will pray
For the weal of her lover that's far away.

She stole along, she nothing spoke,
The breezes they were still also;
35 And naught was green upon the oak,
But moss and rarest misletoe:[2]
She kneels beneath the huge oak tree,
And in silence prayeth she.

The lady leaps up suddenly,
40 The lovely lady, Christabel!
It moan'd as near, as near can be,
But what it is, she cannot tell.—
On the other side it seems to be,
Of the huge, broad-breasted, old oak tree.

45 The night is chill; the forest bare;
Is it the wind that moaneth bleak?
There is not wind enough in the air
To move away the ringlet curl
From the lovely lady's cheek—
50 There is not wind enough to twirl
The one red leaf, the last of its clan,
That dances as often as dance it can,
Hanging so light, and hanging so high,
On the topmost twig that looks up at the sky.

---

[1] Coleridge took the name from "Sir Cauline," a ballad in Thomas Percy (1729–1811), *Reliques of Ancient English Poetry* (1765).

[2] The mistletoe, a parasitic plant, only rarely grows on an oak tree. When it did, the Druids considered it sacred.

55 Hush, beating heart of Christabel!
Jesu, Maria, shield her well!
She folded her arms beneath her cloak,
And stole to the other side of the oak.
   What sees she there?

60 There she sees a damsel bright,
Drest in a silken robe of white;
Her neck, her feet, her arms were bare,
And the jewels disorder'd in her hair.[1]
I guess, 'twas frightful there to see
65 A lady so richly clad as she—
Beautiful exceedingly!

Mary mother, save me now!
(Said Christabel,) And who art thou?

The lady strange made answer meet,
70 And her voice was faint and sweet:—
Have pity on my sore distress,
I scarce can speak for weariness.
Stretch forth thy hand, and have no fear,
Said Christabel, How cam'st thou here?
75 And the lady, whose voice was faint and sweet,
Did thus pursue her answer meet:—

My sire is of a noble line,
And my name is Geraldine.
Five warriors seiz'd me yestermorn,
80 Me, even me, a maid forlorn:
They chok'd my cries with force and fright,
And tied me on a palfrey white.
The palfrey was as fleet as wind,
And they rode furiously behind.
85 They spurr'd amain, their steeds were white;
And once we cross'd the shade of night.

As sure as Heaven shall rescue me,
I have no thought what men they be;
Nor do I know how long it is
90 (For I have lain in fits, I wis)[2]
Since one, the tallest of the five,
Took me from the palfrey's back,
A weary woman, scarce alive.
Some mutter'd words his comrades spoke:
95 He plac'd me underneath this oak,
He swore they would return with haste;
Whither they went I cannot tell—
I thought I heard, some minutes past,
Sounds as of a castle bell.
100 Stretch forth thy hand (thus ended she),
And help a wretched maid to flee.

Then Christabel stretch'd forth her hand
And comforted fair Geraldine,
Saying, that she should command
105 The service of Sir Leoline;
And straight be convoy'd, free from thrall,
Back to her noble father's hall.

So up she rose, and forth they pass'd,
With hurrying steps, yet nothing fast;
110 Her lucky stars the lady blest,
And Christabel she sweetly said—
All our household are at rest,
Each one sleeping in his bed;
Sir Leoline is weak in health,
115 And may not well awaken'd be;
So to my room we'll creep in stealth,
And you to-night must sleep with me.

They cross'd the moat, and Christabel
Took the key that fitted well;
120 A little door she open'd straight,
All in the middle of the gate;
The gate that was iron'd within and without,
Where an army in battle array had march'd out.

---

[1] In later versions Coleridge replaced this couplet with the following six lines:
   That shadowy in the moonlight shone:
   The neck that made that white robe wan,
   Her stately neck, and arms were bare;
   Her blue-veined feet unsandal'd were,
   And wildly glitter'd here and there
   The gems entangled in her hair.

[2] certainly.

The lady sank, belike thro' pain,
And Christabel with might and main
Lifted her up, a weary weight,
Over the threshold of the gate:
Then the lady rose again,
And mov'd, as she were not in pain.

So free from danger, free from fear,
They cross'd the court: right glad they were.
And Christabel devoutly cried,
To the lady by her side,
Praise we the Virgin all divine
Who hath rescued thee from thy distress!
Alas, alas! said Geraldine,
I cannot speak for weariness.
So free from danger, free from fear,
They cross'd the court: right glad they were.

Outside her kennel, the mastiff old
Lay fast asleep, in moonshine cold.
The mastiff old did not awake,
Yet she an angry moan did make!
And what can ail the mastiff bitch?
Never till now she utter'd yell
Beneath the eye of Christabel.
Perhaps it is the owlet's scritch:
For what can ail the mastiff bitch?

They pass'd the hall, that echoes still,
Pass as lightly as you will!
The brands were flat, the brands were dying,
Amid their own white ashes lying;
But when the lady pass'd, there came
A tongue of light, a fit of flame;
And Christabel saw the lady's eye,
And nothing else saw she thereby,
Save the boss of the shield of Sir Leoline tall,
Which hung in a murky old nitch in the wall.
O softly tread, said Christabel,
My father seldom sleepeth well.

Sweet Christabel her feet she bares,
And they are creeping up the stairs;
Now in glimmer, and now in gloom,
And now they pass the Baron's room,
As still as death with stifled breath!
And now have reach'd her chamber door;
And now with eager feet press down
The rushes of her chamber floor.

The moon shines dim in the open air,
And not a moonbeam enters here.
But they without its light can see
The chamber carv'd so curiously,
Carv'd with figures strange and sweet,
All made out of the carver's brain,
For a lady's chamber meet:
The lamp with twofold silver chain
Is fasten'd to an angel's feet.

The silver lamp burns dead and dim;
But Christabel the lamp will trim.
She trimm'd the lamp, and made it bright,
And left it swinging to and fro,
While Geraldine, in wretched plight,
Sank down upon the floor below.

O weary lady, Geraldine,
I pray you, drink this cordial wine!
It is a wine of virtuous powers;
My mother made it of wild flowers.

And will your mother pity me,
Who am a maiden most forlorn?
Christabel answer'd—Woe is me!
She died the hour that I was born.
I have heard the gray-hair'd friar tell,
How on her death-bed she did say,
That she should hear the castle bell
Strike twelve upon my wedding day.
O mother dear! that thou wert here!
I would, said Geraldine, she were!

But soon with alter'd voice, said she—
"Off, wandering mother! Peak and pine!
I have power to bid thee flee."
Alas! what ails poor Geraldine?

Why stares she with unsettled eye?
Can she the bodiless dead espy?
And why with hollow voice cries she,
205 "Off, woman, off! this hour is mine—
Though thou her guardian spirit be,
Off, woman, off! 'tis given to me."

Then Christabel knelt by the lady's side,
And rais'd to heaven her eyes so blue—
210 Alas! said she, this ghastly ride—
Dear lady! it hath wilder'd you!
The lady wip'd her moist cold brow,
And faintly said, "'Tis over now!"

Again the wild-flower wine she drank:
215 Her fair large eyes 'gan glitter bright,
And from the floor whereon she sank,
The lofty lady stood upright:
She was most beautiful to see,
Like a lady of a far countrée.

220 And thus the lofty lady spake—
All they, who live in the upper sky,
Do love you, holy Christabel!
And you love them, and for their sake
And for the good which me befel,
225 Even I in my degree will try,
Fair maiden, to requite you well.
But now unrobe yourself; for I
Must pray, ere yet in bed I lie.

Quoth Christabel, so let it be!
230 And as the lady bade, did she.
Her gentle limbs did she undress,
And lay down in her loveliness.
But thro' her brain of weal and woe
So many thoughts moved to and fro,
235 That vain it were her lids to close;
So half-way from the bed she rose,
And on her elbow did recline
To look at the lady Geraldine.

Beneath the lamp the lady bow'd,
240 And slowly roll'd her eyes around;
Then drawing in her breath aloud,
Like one that shudder'd, she unbound
The cincture from beneath her breast:
Her silken robe, and inner vest,
245 Dropt to her feet, and full in view,
Behold! her bosom and half her side——[1]
A sight to dream of, not to tell!
And she is to sleep by Christabel.

She took two paces, and a stride,
250 And lay down by the maiden's side:
And in her arms the maid she took,
 Ah wel-a-day!
And with low voice and doleful look
These words did say:
255 In the touch of this bosom there worketh a spell,
Which is lord of thy utterance, Christabel!
Thou knowest to-night, and wilt know to-morrow
This mark of my shame, this seal of my sorrow;
 But vainly thou warrest,
260 For this is alone in
 Thy power to declare,
  That in the dim forest
   Thou heard'st a low moaning,
And found'st a bright lady, surpassingly fair:
265 And didst bring her home with thee in love and in charity,
To shield her and shelter her from the damp air.

THE CONCLUSION TO PART THE FIRST

It was a lovely sight to see
The lady Christabel, when she
Was praying at the old oak tree.
270 Amid the jagged shadows
  Of mossy leafless boughs,
  Kneeling in the moonlight,
  To make her gentle vows;
Her slender palms together prest,

---

[1] In the manuscript, this line is followed by an explicit description: Geraldine's bosom and side "Are lean and old and foul of hue."

275 Heaving sometimes on her breast;
Her face resign'd to bliss or bale—
Her face, oh call it fair not pale,
And both blue eyes more bright than clear,
Each about to have a tear.

280 With open eyes (ah woe is me!)
Asleep, and dreaming fearfully,
Fearfully dreaming, yet I wis,
Dreaming that alone, which is——
O sorrow and shame! Can this be she,
285 The lady, who knelt at the old oak tree?
And lo! the worker of these harms,
That holds the maiden in her arms,
Seems to slumber still and mild,
As a mother with her child.

290 A star hath set, a star hath risen,
O Geraldine! since arms of thine
Have been the lovely lady's prison.
O Geraldine! one hour was thine—

Thou'st had thy will! By tairn and rill,
295 The night-birds all that hour were still.
But now they are jubilant anew,
From cliff and tower, tu–whoo! tu–whoo!
Tu–whoo! tu–whoo! from wood and fell!

And see! the lady Christabel
300 Gathers herself from out her trance;
Her limbs relax, her countenance
Grows sad and soft; the smooth thin lids
Close o'er her eyes; and tears she sheds—
Large tears that leave the lashes bright!
305 And oft the while she seems to smile
As infants at a sudden light!

Yea, she doth smile, and she doth weep,
Like a youthful hermitess,
Beauteous in a wilderness,
310 Who, praying always, prays in sleep.
And, if she move unquietly,

Perchance, 'tis but the blood so free,
Comes back and tingles in her feet.
No doubt, she hath a vision sweet.
315 What if her guardian spirit 'twere
What if she knew her mother near?
But this she knows, in joys and woes,
That saints will aid if men will call:
For the blue sky bends over all!

PART 2

320 Each matin bell, the Baron saith,
Knells us back to a world of death.
These words Sir Leoline first said,
When he rose and found his lady dead:
These words Sir Leoline will say
325 Many a morn to his dying day.

And hence the custom and law began,
That still at dawn the sacristan,
Who duly pulls the heavy bell,
Five and forty beads must tell
330 Between each stroke—a warning knell,
Which not a soul can choose but hear
From Bratha Head to Wyn'dermere.

Saith Bracy the bard, So let it knell!
And let the drowsy sacristan
335 Still count as slowly as he can!
There is no lack of such, I ween
As well fill up the space between.
In Langdale Pike and Witch's Lair,
And Dungeon-ghyll so foully rent,
340 With ropes of rock and bells of air
Three sinful sextons' ghosts are pent,
Who all give back, one after t'other,
The death-note to their living brother;
And oft too, by the knell offended,
345 Just as their one! two! three! is ended,
The devil mocks the doleful tale
With a merry peal from Borrowdale.[1]

---

[1] The places named in these two paragraphs are all near Coleridge's home, Keswick, in the Lake District.

The air is still! thro' mist and cloud
That merry peal comes ringing loud;
350 And Geraldine shakes off her dread,
And rises lightly from the bed;
Puts on her silken vestments white,
And tricks her hair in lovely plight,
And nothing doubting of her spell
355 Awakens the lady Christabel.
"Sleep you, sweet lady Christabel?
I trust that you have rested well."

And Christabel awoke and spied
The same who lay down by her side—
360 O rather say, the same whom she
Rais'd up beneath the old oak tree!
Nay, fairer yet! and yet more fair!
For she belike hath drunken deep
Of all the blessedness of sleep!
365 And while she spake, her looks, her air
Such gentle thankfulness declare,
That (so it seem'd) her girded vests
Grew tight beneath her heaving breasts.
"Sure I have sinned!" said Christabel,
370 "Now heaven be prais'd if all be well!"
And in low faltering tones, yet sweet,
Did she the lofty lady greet
With such perplexity of mind
As dreams too lively leave behind.

375 So quickly she rose, and quickly array'd
Her maiden limbs, and having pray'd
That He, who on the cross did groan,
Might wash away her sins unknown,
She forthwith led fair Geraldine
380 To meet her sire, Sir Leoline.

The lovely maid and the lady tall
Are pacing both into the hall,
And pacing on thro' page and groom
Enter the Baron's presence room.

385 The Baron rose, and while he prest
His gentle daughter to his breast,
With cheerful wonder in his eyes
The lady Geraldine espies,
And gave such welcome to the same,
390 As might beseem so bright a dame!

But when he heard the lady's tale,
And when she told her father's name,
Why wax'd Sir Leoline so pale,
Murmuring o'er the name again,
395 Lord Roland de Vaux of Tryermaine?

Alas! they had been friends in youth;
But whispering tongues can poison truth;
And constancy lives in realms above;
And life is thorny; and youth is vain;
400 And to be wroth with one we love,
Doth work like madness in the brain.
And thus it chanc'd, as I divine,
With Roland and Sir Leoline.
Each spake words of high disdain
405 And insult to his heart's best brother:
They parted—ne'er to meet again!
But never either found another
To free the hollow heart from paining—
They stood aloof, the scars remaining,
410 Like cliffs which had been rent asunder;
A dreary sea now flows between,
But neither heat, nor frost, nor thunder,
Shall wholly do away, I ween,
The marks of that which once hath been.

415 Sir Leoline, a moment's space,
Stood gazing on the damsel's face;
And the youthful Lord of Tryermaine
Came back upon his heart again.

O then the Baron forgot his age,
420 His noble heart swell'd high with rage;
He swore by the wounds in Jesu's side,
He would proclaim it far and wide
With trump and solemn heraldry,
That they, who thus had wrong'd the dame,
425 Were base as spotted infamy!
"And if they dare deny the same,
My herald shall appoint a week,

And let the recreant traitors seek
My tournay court[1]—that there and then
I may dislodge their reptile souls
From the bodies and forms of men!"
He spake: his eye in lightning rolls!
For the lady was ruthlessly seiz'd; and he kenn'd
In the beautiful lady the child of his friend!

And now the tears were on his face,
And fondly in his arms he took
Fair Geraldine, who met th' embrace,
Prolonging it with joyous look.
Which when she view'd, a vision fell
Upon the soul of Christabel,
The vision of fear, the touch and pain!
She shrunk and shudder'd, and saw again
(Ah, woe is me! Was it for thee,
Thou gentle maid! such sights to see?)
Again she saw that bosom old,
Again she felt that bosom cold,
And drew in her breath with a hissing sound:
Whereat the Knight turn'd wildly round,
And nothing saw, but his own sweet maid
With eyes uprais'd, as one that pray'd.

The touch, the sight, had pass'd away,
And in its stead that vision blest,
Which comforted her after-rest,
While in the lady's arms she lay,
Had put a rapture in her breast,
And on her lips and o'er her eyes
Spread smiles like light!
                    With new surprise,
"What ails then my beloved child?"
The Baron said—His daughter mild
Made answer, "All will yet be well!"
I ween, she had no power to tell
Aught else: so mighty was the spell.
Yet he, who saw this Geraldine,
Had deem'd her sure a thing divine,
Such sorrow with such grace she blended,
As if she fear'd, she had offended

Sweet Christabel, that gentle maid!
And with such lowly tones she pray'd,
She might be sent without delay
Home to her father's mansion.
                              "Nay!
Nay, by my soul!" said Leoline.
"Ho! Bracy the bard, the charge be thine!
Go thou, with music sweet and loud,
And take two steeds with trappings proud,
And take the youth whom thou lov'st best
To bear thy harp, and learn thy song,
And clothe you both in solemn vest,
And over the mountains haste along,
Lest wand'ring folk, that are abroad,
Detain you on the valley road.

"And when he has cross'd the Irthing flood,
My merry bard! he hastes, he hastes
Up Knorren Moor, thro' Halegarth Wood,
And reaches soon that castle good
Which stands and threatens Scotland's wastes.

"Bard Bracy! bard Bracy! your horses are fleet,
Ye must ride up the hall, your music so sweet,
More loud than your horses' echoing feet!
And loud and loud to Lord Roland call,
Thy daughter is safe in Langdale hall!
Thy beautiful daughter is safe and free—
Sir Leoline greets thee thus thro' me.
He bids thee come without delay
With all thy numerous array;
And take thy lovely daughter home,
And he will meet thee on the way
With all his numerous array
White with their panting palfreys' foam,
And, by mine honour! I will say,
That I repent me of the day
When I spake words of fierce disdain
To Roland de Vaux of Tryermaine!—
—For since that evil hour hath flown,
Many a summer's sun have shone;
Yet ne'er found I a friend again
Like Roland de Vaux of Tryermaine."

---

[1] an arena for tournaments.

The lady fell, and clasped his knees,
Her face uprais'd, her eyes o'erflowing;
And Bracy replied, with faltering voice,
510 His gracious hail on all bestowing:—
Thy words, thou sire of Christabel,
Are sweeter than my harp can tell;
Yet might I gain a boon of thee,
This day my journey should not be,
515 So strange a dream hath come to me:
That I had vow'd with music loud
To clear yon wood from thing unblest,
Warn'd by a vision in my rest!
For in my sleep I saw that dove,
520 That gentle bird, whom thou dost love,
And call'st by thy own daughter's name—
Sir Leoline! I saw the same,
Fluttering, and uttering fearful moan,
Among the green herbs in the forest alone.
525 Which when I saw and when I heard,
I wonder'd what might ail the bird:
For nothing near it could I see,
Save the grass and green herbs underneath the old tree.

And in my dream, methought, I went
530 To search out what might there be found;
And what the sweet bird's trouble meant,
That thus lay fluttering on the ground.
I went and peer'd, and could descry
No cause for her distressful cry;
535 But yet for her dear lady's sake
I stoop'd, methought the dove to take,
When lo! I saw a bright green snake
Coil'd around its wings and neck.
Green as the herbs on which it couch'd,
540 Close by the dove's its head it crouch'd;
And with the dove it heaves and stirs,
Swelling its neck as she swell'd hers![1]
I woke; it was the midnight hour,
The clock was echoing in the tower;
545 But tho' my slumber was gone by,
This dream it would not pass away—

---
[1] Cf. William Bartram, *Travels through North & South Carolina* (London, 1794) 216–17.

It seems to live upon my eye!
And thence I vow'd this self-same day,
With music strong and saintly song
550 To wander thro' the forest bare,
Lest aught unholy loiter there.

Thus Bracy said: the Baron, the while,
Half-listening heard him with a smile;
Then turn'd to Lady Geraldine,
555 His eyes made up of wonder and love;
And said in courtly accents fine,
Sweet maid, Lord Roland's beauteous dove,
With arms more strong than harp or song,
Thy sire and I will crush the snake!
560 He kiss'd her forehead as he spake,
And Geraldine in maiden wise,
Casting down her large bright eyes,
With blushing cheek and courtesy fine
She turn'd her from Sir Leoline;
565 Softly gathering up her train,
That o'er her right arm fell again;
And folded her arms across her chest,
And couch'd her head upon her breast,
And look'd askance at Christabel——
570 Jesu, Maria, shield her well!

A snake's small eye blinks dull and shy,
And the lady's eyes they shrunk in her head,
Each shrunk up to a serpent's eye,
And with somewhat of malice, and more of dread
575 At Christabel she look'd askance!——
One moment—and the sight was fled!
But Christabel in dizzy trance,
Stumbling on the unsteady ground—
Shudder'd aloud, with a hissing sound;
580 And Geraldine again turn'd round,
And like a thing, that sought relief,
Full of wonder and full of grief,
She roll'd her large bright eyes divine
Wildly on Sir Leoline.

585 The maid, alas! her thoughts are gone,
She nothing sees—no sight but one!

The maid, devoid of guile and sin,
I know not how, in fearful wise
So deeply had she drunken in
590 That look, those shrunken serpent eyes,
That all her features were resign'd
To this sole image in her mind:
And passively did imitate
That look of dull and treacherous hate.
595 And thus she stood, in dizzy trance,
Still picturing that look askance,
With forc'd unconscious sympathy
Full before her father's view——
As far as such a look could be,
600 In eyes so innocent and blue!

But when the trance was o'er, the maid
Paus'd awhile, and inly pray'd,
Then falling at her father's feet,
"By my mother's soul do I entreat
605 That thou this woman send away!"
She said; and more she could not say,
For what she knew she could not tell,
O'er-master'd by the mighty spell.

Why is thy cheek so wan and wild,
610 Sir Leoline? Thy only child
Lies at thy feet, thy joy, thy pride,
So fair, so innocent, so mild;
The same, for whom thy lady died!
O by the pangs of her dear mother
615 Think thou no evil of thy child!
For her, and thee, and for no other,
She pray'd the moment, ere she died;
Pray'd that the babe for whom she died,
Might prove her dear lord's joy and pride!
620 That prayer her deadly pangs beguil'd,
Sir Leoline!
And would'st thou wrong thy only child,
Her child and thine?
Within the Baron's heart and brain
625 If thoughts, like these, had any share,
They only swell'd his rage and pain,
And did but work confusion there.

His heart was cleft with pain and rage,
His cheeks they quiver'd, his eyes were wild,
630 Dishonour'd thus in his old age;
Dishonour'd by his only child,
And all his hospitality
To th' insulted daughter of his friend
By more than woman's jealousy,
635 Brought thus to a disgraceful end—
He roll'd his eye with stern regard
Upon the gentle minstrel bard,
And said in tones abrupt, austere—
Why, Bracy! dost thou loiter here?
640 I bade thee hence! The bard obey'd;
And turning from his own sweet maid,
The aged knight, Sir Leoline,
Led forth the lady Geraldine!

THE CONCLUSION TO PART THE SECOND

A little child, a limber elf,[1]
645 Singing, dancing to itself,
A fairy thing with red round cheeks
That always finds, and never seeks,
Makes such a vision to the sight
As fills a father's eyes with light;
650 And pleasures flow in so thick and fast
Upon his heart, that he at last
Must needs express his love's excess
With words of unmeant bitterness.
Perhaps 'tis pretty to force together
655 Thoughts so all unlike each other;
To mutter and mock a broken charm,
To dally with wrong that does no harm.
Perhaps 'tis tender too and pretty
At each wild word to feel within,
660 A sweet recoil of love and pity.
And what, if in a world of sin
(O sorrow and shame should this be true!)
Such giddiness of heart and brain
Comes seldom save from rage and pain,
665 So talks as it's most used to do.

---

[1] The Conclusion was originally a description of Coleridge's son Hartley, and of his own fatherly feelings for him (*Letters* 2: 728).

Kubla Khan: or
A Vision in a Dream

Of the Fragment of Kubla Khan

The following fragment is here published at the request of a poet of great and deserved celebrity,[1] and as far as the Author's own opinions are concerned, rather as a psychological curiosity, than on the ground of any supposed *poetic* merits.

In the summer of the year 1797, the Author, then in ill health, had retired to a lonely farm-house between Porlock and Linton, on the Exmoor confines of Somerset and Devonshire. In consequence of a slight indisposition, an anodyne[2] had been prescribed, from the effects of which he fell asleep in his chair at the moment that he was reading the following sentence, or words of the same substance, in "Purchas's Pilgrimage": "Here the Khan Kubla commanded a palace to be built, and a stately garden thereunto. And thus ten miles of fertile ground were inclosed with a wall."[3] The author continued for about three hours in a profound sleep, at least of the external senses, during which time he has the most vivid confidence, that he could not have composed less than from two to three hundred lines; if that indeed can be called composition in which all the images rose up before him as *things*, with a parallel production of the correspondent expressions, without any sensation or consciousness of effort. On awaking he appeared to himself to have a distinct recollection of the whole, and taking his pen, ink, and paper, instantly and eagerly wrote down the lines that are here preserved. At this moment he was unfortunately called out by a person on business from Porlock, and detained by him above an hour, and on his return to his room, found to his no small surprise and mortification, that though he still retained some vague and dim recollection of the general purpose of the vision, yet, with the exception of some eight or ten scattered lines and images, all the rest had passed away like the images on the surface of a stream into which a stone has been cast, but, alas! without the after restoration of the latter:

> Then all the charm
> Is broken—all that phantom-world so fair
> Vanishes, and a thousand circlets spread,
> And each mis-shape the other. Stay awhile,
> Poor youth! who scarcely dar'st lift up thine eyes—
> The stream will soon renew its smoothness, soon
> The visions will return! And lo, he stays,
> And soon the fragments dim of lovely forms
> Come trembling back, unite, and now once more
> The pool becomes a mirror.[4]

Yet from the still surviving recollections in his mind, the Author has frequently purposed to finish for himself what had been originally, as it were, given to him. Σαμερον αδσον ασω[5] but the to-morrow is yet to come.

As a contrast to this vision, I have annexed a fragment of a very different character,[6] describing with equal fidelity the dream of pain and disease.

In Xanadu did KUBLA KHAN
A stately pleasure-dome decree:
Where ALPH,[7] the sacred river, ran
Through caverns measureless to man
    Down to a sunless sea.   5
So twice five miles of fertile ground
With walls and towers were girdled round:

---

[1] Byron,* who admired the poem and encouraged Coleridge to publish it along with "Christabel."

[2] According to Coleridge's manuscript, the indisposition was dysentery and the anodyne was opium.

[3] The complete sentence in Samuel Purchas (1577?–1626), *Purchas his Pilgrimage, or Relations of the World and the Religions Observed in all Ages* (1613–25) reads: "In *Xamdu* did *Cublai Can* build a stately Palace, encompassing sixteene miles of plaine ground with a wall, wherein are fertile Meddowes, pleasant springs, delightfull Streames, and all sorts of beasts of chase and game, and in the middest thereof a sumptuous house of pleasure, which may be remoued from place to place" (472). Kublai Khan (1215?–94), grandson of Genghis, was the Mongol emperor met by Marco Polo (1254?–1324?).

[4] Coleridge, "The Picture; or, The Lover's Resolution" (1802) 91–100.

[5] "Tomorrow I shall sing more sweetly" (Gr.): adapted from Theocritus, *Idyll* 1.145.

[6] "The Pains of Sleep."

[7] possibly named after the river Alpheus, which disappeared underground (see Ovid, *Metamorphoses* 5), or *alpha*, the first letter of the Greek alphabet.

And here were gardens bright with sinuous rills
Where blossom'd many an incense-bearing tree;
10 And here were forests ancient as the hills,
And folding sunny spots of greenery.

But oh that deep romantic chasm which slanted
Down the green hill athwart a cedarn cover!
A savage place! as holy and inchanted
15 As e'er beneath a waning moon was haunted
By woman wailing for her demon-lover!
And from this chasm, with ceaseless turmoil seething,
As if this earth in fast thick pants were breathing,
A mighty fountain momently was forced:
20 Amid whose swift half-intermitted Burst
Huge fragments vaulted like rebounding hail,
Or chaffy grain beneath the thresher's flail:
And mid these dancing rocks at once and ever
It flung up momently the sacred river.
25 Five miles meandering with a mazy motion
Through wood and dale the sacred river ran,
Then reached the caverns measureless to man,
And sank in tumult to a lifeless ocean:
And 'mid this tumult Kubla heard from far
30 Ancestral voices prophesying war!

 The shadow of the dome of pleasure
 Floated midway on the waves;
 Where was heard the mingled measure
 From the fountain and the caves.
35 It was a miracle of rare device,
A sunny pleasure-dome with caves of ice!

 A damsel with a dulcimer
 In a vision once I saw:
 It was an Abyssinian maid
40 And on her dulcimer she play'd,
 Singing of Mount Abora.[1]
 Could I revive within me
 Her symphony and song,
 To such a deep delight 'twould win me,
45 That with music loud and long,
I would build that dome in air,
That sunny dome! those caves of ice!
And all who heard should see them there,
And all should cry, Beware! Beware!
50 His flashing eyes, his floating hair!
Weave a circle round him thrice,
And close your eyes with holy dread:
For he on honey-dew hath fed,
And drank the milk of Paradise.[2]

The Pains of Sleep[3]

Ere on my bed my limbs I lay,
It hath not been my use to pray
With moving lips or bended knees;
But silently, by slow degrees,
5 My spirit I to Love compose,
In humble Trust mine eye-lids close,
With reverential resignation,
No wish conceived, no thought expressed!
Only a *sense* of supplication,
10 A sense o'er all my soul imprest
That I am weak, yet not unblest,
Since in me, round me, every where
Eternal Strength and Wisdom are.

But yester-night I pray'd aloud
15 In anguish and in agony,
Up-starting from the fiendish crowd
Of shapes and thoughts that tortured me:
A lurid light, a trampling throng,
Sense of intolerable wrong,
20 And whom I scorn'd, those only strong!
Thirst of revenge, the powerless will
Still baffled, and yet burning still!
Desire with loathing strangely mixed
On wild or hateful objects fixed.
25 Fantastic passions! mad'ning brawl!
And shame and terror over all!
Deeds to be hid which were not hid,

---

[1] Cf. Milton, *Paradise Lost* 4.280–87.

[2] Cf. Plato, *Ion* 534a.

[3] Coleridge wrote the poem in September 1803, after a desperate attempt (which involved walking over 260 miles in eight days) to break his opium habit.

Which all confused I could not know,
Whether I suffered, or I did:
30 For all seemed guilt, remorse or woe,
My own or others still the same
Life-stifling fear, soul-stifling shame!

So two nights passed: the night's dismay
Sadden'd and stunn'd the coming day.
35 Sleep, the wide blessing, seemed to me
Distemper's worst calamity.
The third night, when my own loud scream
Had waked me from the fiendish dream,
O'ercome with sufferings strange and wild,
40 I wept as I had been a child;
And having thus by tears subdued
My anguish to a milder mood,
Such punishments, I said, were due
To natures deepliest stain'd with sin:
45 For aye entempesting anew
Th'unfathomable hell within
The horror of their deeds to view,
To know and loathe, yet wish and do!
Such griefs with such men well agree,
50 But wherefore, wherefore fall on me?
To be beloved is all I need,
And whom I love, I love indeed.

from *Sibylline Leaves: A Collection of Poems* (1817)

To a Gentleman
Composed on the night after his recitation of a Poem on the Growth of an Individual Mind[1]

Friend of the Wise! and Teacher of the Good!
Into my heart have I received that Lay
More than historic, that prophetic Lay
Wherein (high theme by thee first sung aright)
5 Of the foundations and the building up

Of the Human Spirit,[2] thou hast dared to tell
What may be told, to th'understanding mind
Revealable; and what within the mind
By vital Breathings, like the secret soul
10 Of vernal growth, oft quickens in the Heart
Thoughts all too deep for words![3]—

      Theme hard as high!
Of smiles spontaneous, and mysterious fears
(The first-born they of Reason and twin-birth)
Of tides obedient to external force,
15 And currents self-determined, as might seem,
Or by some inner Power; of moments awful,
Now in thy inner life, and now abroad,
When Power stream'd from thee, and thy soul received
The light reflected, as a light bestow'd—
20 Of Fancies fair, and milder hours of youth,
Hyblean[4] murmurs of Poetic Thought
Industrious in its Joy, in Vales and Glens
Native or outland, Lakes and famous Hills!
Or on the lonely High-road, when the Stars
25 Were rising; or by secret Mountain-streams,
The Guides and the Companions of thy way!

    Of more than Fancy, of the Social Sense
Distending wide, and Man belov'd as Man,
Where France in all her Towns lay vibrating
30 Even as a Bark becalm'd beneath the Burst
Of Heaven's immediate Thunder, when no cloud
Is visible, or shadow on the Main.
For thou wert there,[5] thine own brows garlanded,
Amid the tremor of a realm aglow,
35 Amid a mighty nation jubilant,
When from the general Heart of Human kind
Hope sprang forth like a full-born Deity!

---

[1] The gentleman is W. Wordsworth,* who finished reading *The Prelude* aloud to Coleridge on 7 January 1807.

[2] Cf. *Two-Part Prelude* 1.67–80,* *Prelude* (1805) 1.351–71; Coleridge's passage alludes to Wordsworth's adaptation of Milton in "On Man, on Nature, and on Human Life" (787–93),* written in 1798 but first published at the end of the Preface to the *Excursion* (1814).

[3] Cf. W. Wordsworth, "Ode" 206.*

[4] Sweet or mellifluous, with reference to the Sicilian town of Hybla, celebrated for its honey.

[5] See *Prelude* (1805), Books 9 and 10.

  —Of that dear Hope afflicted and struck down,[1]
  So summon'd homeward, thenceforth calm and sure
40 From the dread Watch-Tower of man's absolute Self,
  With light unwaning on her eyes, to look
  Far on—herself a glory to behold,
  The Angel of the vision! Then (last strain)
  Of Duty, chosen Laws controlling choice,
45 Action and Joy!—An orphic song[2] indeed,
  A song divine of high and passionate thoughts,
  To their own Music chaunted!

        O great Bard!
  Ere yet that last strain dying awed the air,
  With stedfast eye I view'd thee in the choir
50 Of ever-enduring men. The truly Great
  Have all one age, and from one visible space
  Shed influence! They, both in power and act,
  Are permanent, and Time is not with *them*,
  Save as it worketh *for* them, they *in* it.
55 Nor less a sacred Roll, than those of old,
  And to be placed, as they, with gradual fame
  Among the Archives of Mankind, thy work
  Makes audible a linked lay of Truth,
  Of Truth profound a sweet continuous lay,
60 Not learnt, but native, her own natural notes!
  Ah! as I listen'd with a heart forlorn
  The pulses of my Being beat anew:
  And even as Life returns upon the Drown'd,
  Life's joy rekindling rous'd a throng of Pains—
65 Keen Pangs of Love, awakening as a babe
  Turbulent, with an outcry in the heart;
  And Fears self-will'd, that shunn'd the eye of Hope,
  And Hope that scarce would know itself from Fear;
  Sense of past Youth, and Manhood come in vain,
70 And Genius given, and Knowledge won in vain;
  And all which I had cull'd in Wood-walks wild,
  And all which patient toil had rear'd, and all,
  Commune with *thee* had open'd out—but Flowers
  Strew'd on my corse, and borne upon my Bier,
75 In the same Coffin, for the self-same Grave!

  That way no more! and ill beseems it me,
  Who came a welcomer in Herald's Guise,
  Singing of Glory, and Futurity,
  To wander back on such unhealthful road,
80 Plucking the poisons of self-harm! And ill
  Such Intertwine beseems triumphal wreaths
  Strew'd before *thy* advancing!

        Nor do thou,
  Sage Bard! impair the memory of that hour
  Of thy communion with my nobler mind
85 By Pity or Grief, already felt too long!
  Nor let my words import more blame than needs.
  The tumult rose and ceas'd: for Peace is nigh
  Where wisdom's voice has found a listening heart.
  Amid the howl of more than wintry storms,
90 The Halcyon[3] hears the voice of vernal Hours
  Already on the wing!

        Eve following Eve,
  Dear tranquil time, when the sweet sense of Home
  Is sweetest! moments for their own sake hail'd
  And more desired, more precious for thy song,
95 In silence listening, like a devout child,
  My soul lay passive, by thy various strain
  Driven, as in surges now beneath the stars,
  With momentary Stars of my own birth,
  Fair constellated Foam,[4] still darting off
100 Into the darkness; now a tranquil sea,
  Outspread and bright, yet swelling to the Moon.

  And when—O Friend! my comforter and guide!
  Strong in thy self, and powerful to give strength!—
  Thy long sustained Song finally closed,

---

[1] See especially *Prelude* (1805) 9.38–201.

[2] entrancing, like the music of Orpheus, which charmed the inanimate world. Cf. P.B. Shelley, *Prometheus Unbound* 4.415.*

[3] the bird of calm (cf. Milton, "On the Morning of Christ's Nativity" 68) which, according to mythology, laid its eggs in a nest floating on the sea and charmed the wind and waves.

[4] "'A beautiful white cloud of Foam at momentary intervals coursed by the side of the Vessel with a Roar, and little stars of flame danced and sparkled and went out in it: and every now and then light detachments of this white cloud-like foam darted off from the vessel's side, each with its own small constellation, over the Sea, and scoured out of sight like a Tartar Troop over a Wilderness.'—THE FRIEND, p. 220." (S.T.C.) *The Friend* 14 (23 November 1809).

105 And thy deep voice had ceased—yet thou thyself
Wert still before my eyes, and round us both
That happy vision of beloved Faces—
Scarce conscious, and yet conscious of its close
I sate, my being blended in one thought
110 (Thought was it? or Aspiration? or Resolve?)
Absorb'd, yet hanging still upon the sound—
And when I rose, I found myself in prayer.

Dejection: An Ode[1]

> Late, late yestreen I saw the new Moon,
> With the old Moon in her arms;
> And I fear, I fear, my Master dear!
> We shall have a deadly storm.
> Ballad of Sir PATRICK SPENCE.[2]

I

Well! If the Bard was weather-wise, who made
The grand old ballad of Sir Patrick Spence,
    This night, so tranquil now, will not go hence
Unrous'd by winds, that ply a busier trade
5 Than those which mould yon clouds in lazy flakes,
Or the dull sobbing draft, that moans and rakes
        Upon the strings of this Æolian lute,[3]
        Which better far were mute.
    For lo! the New-moon winter-bright!
10   And overspread with phantom-light,
    (With swimming phantom-light o'erspread
        But rimm'd and circled by a silver thread)
I see the old Moon in her lap, foretelling
    The coming on of rain and squally blast.
15 And oh! that even now the gust were swelling,
    And the slant night-shower driving loud and fast!

Those sounds which oft have raised me, whilst they awed,
    And sent my soul abroad,
Might now perhaps their wonted impulse give,
20 Might startle this dull pain, and make it move and live!

2

A grief without a pang, void, dark, and drear,[4]
    A stifled, drowsy, unimpassion'd grief,
    Which finds no natural outlet, no relief,
        In word, or sigh, or tear—
25 O Lady! in this wan and heartless mood,
To other thoughts by yonder throstle woo'd,
    All this long eve, so balmy and serene,
Have I been gazing on the western sky,
    And it's peculiar tint of yellow green:
30 And still I gaze—and with how blank an eye!
And those thin clouds above, in flakes and bars,
    That give away their motion to the stars;
Those stars, that glide behind them or between,
Now sparkling, now bedimm'd, but always seen;
35 Yon crescent Moon, as fix'd as if it grew
In its own cloudless, starless lake of blue;
I see them all so excellently fair,
I see, not feel how beautiful they are![5]

3

    My genial spirits fail,[6]
40   And what can these avail,
To lift the smoth'ring weight from off my breast?
        It were a vain endeavor,
        Though I should gaze for ever
On that green light that lingers in the west:
45 I may not hope from outward forms to win
The passion and the life, whose fountains are within.

---

[1] The poem began as a 340-line "Letter to [Sara Hutchinson]," written in April 1802. It was first published in the *Morning Post* on 4 October 1802 (W. Wordsworth's wedding day, and the seventh anniversary of Coleridge's), with the sixth and seventh stanzas omitted, and addressed to "Edmund," a pseudonym for W. Wordsworth. Cf. W. Wordsworth, "Resolution and Independence"* and "Ode."*

[2] "Sir Patrick Spens," in Thomas Percy (1729–1811), *Reliques of Ancient English Poetry* (1765).

[3] See note to "Effusion 35" 12.*

[4] Cf. Genesis 1.2.

[5] Cf. Shakespeare, *King Lear* 4.1.68–69.

[6] Cf. Milton, *Samson Agonistes* 594; and W. Wordsworth, "Tintern Abbey" 114.*

4

O Lady! we receive but what we give,
And in our life alone does nature live:
Ours is her wedding-garment, ours her shroud!
    And would we aught behold, of higher worth,
Than that inanimate cold world allow'd
To the poor loveless ever-anxious crowd,
    Ah! from the soul itself must issue forth,
A light, a glory,[1] a fair luminous cloud
        Enveloping the Earth—
And from the soul itself must there be sent
    A sweet and potent voice, of its own birth,
Of all sweet sounds the life and element!

5

O pure of heart! thou need'st not ask of me
What this strong music in the soul may be!
What, and wherein it doth exist,
This light, this glory, this fair luminous mist,
This beautiful, and beauty-making power.
    Joy, virtuous Lady! Joy that ne'er was given,
Save to the pure, and in their purest hour,
Life, and Life's Effluence,[2] Cloud at once and Shower.
Joy, Lady! is the spirit and the power,
Which wedding Nature to us gives in dow'r
    A new Earth and new Heaven,[3]
Undreamt of by the sensual and the proud—
Joy is the sweet voice, Joy the luminous cloud—
    We in ourselves rejoice!
And thence flows all that charms or ear or sight,
    All melodies the echoes of that voice,
All colours a suffusion from that light.

6

There was a time[4] when, though my path was rough,
    This joy within me dallied with distress,
And all misfortunes were but as the stuff
    Whence Fancy made me dreams of happiness:
For hope grew round me, like the twining vine,
And fruits, and foliage, not my own, seem'd mine.
But now afflictions bow me down to earth:
Nor care I that they rob me of my mirth,
    But oh! each visitation
Suspends what nature gave me at my birth,
    My shaping spirit of Imagination.
For not to think of what I needs must feel,
    But to be still and patient, all I can;
And haply by abstruse research to steal
    From my own nature all the natural Man—
This was my sole resource, my only plan:
Till that which suits a part infects the whole,
And now is almost grown the habit of my Soul.

7

Hence, viper thoughts, that coil around my mind,
    Reality's dark dream!
I turn from you, and listen to the wind,
    Which long has rav'd unnotic'd. What a scream
Of agony by torture lengthen'd out
That lute sent forth! Thou Wind, that rav'st without,
    Bare crag, or mountain-tairn,[5] or blasted tree,
Or pine-grove whither woodman never clomb,[6]
Or lonely house, long held the witches' home,
    Methinks were fitter instruments for thee,
Mad Lutanist! who in this month of show'rs,
Of dark brown gardens, and of peeping flow'rs,
Mak'st Devils' yule, with worse than wint'ry song,
The blossoms, buds, and tim'rous leaves among.
    Thou Actor, perfect in all tragic sounds!
Thou mighty Poet, e'en to Frenzy bold!
    What tell'st thou now about?
    'Tis of the Rushing of an Host in rout,
    With groans of trampled men, with smarting wounds—
At once they groan with pain, and shudder with the cold!
But hush! there is a pause of deepest silence!
    And all that noise, as of a rushing crowd,

---

[1] Cf. W. Wordsworth, "Ode" 18.*

[2] Cf. Milton, *Paradise Lost* 3.6.

[3] Cf. Revelation 21.1.

[4] Cf. W. Wordsworth, "Ode" 1.*

[5] "Tairn is a small lake, generally if not always applied to the lakes up in the mountains, and which are the feeders of those in the vallies. This address to the wind will not appear extravagant to those who have heard it at night, and in a mountainous country." (S.T.C.)

[6] Cf. Milton, "Il Penseroso" 135–37.

With groans, and tremulous shudderings—all is
    over—
  It tells another tale, with sounds less deep and loud!
    A tale of less affright,
    And temper'd with delight,
120 As Otway's self had fram'd the tender lay—
    'Tis of a little child
    Upon a lonesome wild,
Not far from home, but she hath lost her way:
And now moans low in bitter grief and fear,
125 And now screams loud, and hopes to make her
    mother hear.[1]

8

'Tis midnight, but small thoughts have I of sleep:
Full seldom may my friend such vigils keep!
Visit her, gentle Sleep! with wings of healing,[2]
  And may this storm be but a mountain-birth,[3]
130 May all the stars hang bright above her dwelling,
  Silent as though they watch'd the sleeping Earth!
    With light heart may she rise,
    Gay fancy, cheerful eyes,
  Joy lift her spirit, joy attune her voice:
135 To her may all things live, from Pole to Pole,
Their life the eddying of her living soul!
  O simple spirit, guided from above,
Dear Lady! friend devoutest of my choice,
Thus may'st thou ever, evermore rejoice.

from *Biographia Literaria; or Biographical Sketches of My Literary Life and Opinions* (1817)

from CHAPTER 4

The lyrical ballads with the preface—Mr. Wordsworth's earlier poems—On fancy and imagination—The investigation of the distinction important to the fine arts.

---

[1] Thomas Otway (1652–85; line 120) was the author of *The Orphan* and *Venice Preserv'd* (1682). The reference, however, is clearly to William Wordsworth, "Lucy Gray."*

[2] Cf. Malachi 4.2.

[3] Cf. Horace, *Ars Poetica* 139.

As little do I believe that "Mr. WORDSWORTH's Lyrical Ballads" were in *themselves* the cause. I speak exclusively of the two volumes so entitled. A careful and repeated examination of these confirms me in the belief, that the omission of less than an hundred lines would have precluded nine-tenths of the criticism on this work. I hazard this declaration, however, on the supposition, that the reader had taken it up, as he would have done any other collection of poems purporting to derive their subjects or interests from the incidents of domestic or ordinary life, intermingled with higher strains of meditation which the poet utters in his own person and character; with the proviso, that they were perused without knowledge of, or reference to, the author's peculiar opinions, and that the reader had not had his attention previously directed to those peculiarities. In these, as was actually the case with Mr. Southey's earlier works, the lines and passages which might have offended the general taste, would have been considered as mere inequalities, and attributed to inattention, not to perversity of judgement. The men of business who had passed their lives chiefly in cities, and who might therefore be expected to derive the highest pleasure from acute notices of men and manners conveyed in easy, yet correct and pointed language; and all those who, reading but little poetry, are most stimulated with that species of it, which seems most distant from prose, would probably have passed by the volume altogether. Others more catholic in their taste, and yet habituated to be most pleased when most excited, would have contented themselves with deciding, that the author had been successful in proportion to the elevation of his style and subject. Not a few perhaps, might by their admiration of "the lines written near Tintern Abbey," those "left upon a Seat under a Yew Tree," the "old Cumberland beggar," and "Ruth," have been gradually led to peruse with kindred feeling the "Brothers," the "Hart leap well," and whatever other poems in that collection may be described as holding a middle place between those written in the highest and those in the humblest style; as for instance between the "Tintern Abbey," and "the Thorn," or the "Simon Lee." Should their taste submit to no further change, and still remain unreconciled to the colloquial phrases, or the imitations of them, that are, more or less, scattered through the class last mentioned; yet even from the small number of the latter, they would have deemed them but an inconsiderable subtraction from the merit of the whole work; or, what is sometimes not unpleasing in the publication of a new writer, as serving to ascertain the natural tendency, and consequently the proper direction of the author's genius.

In the critical remarks therefore, prefixed and annexed to the "Lyrical Ballads," I believe, that we may safely rest, as the true origin of the unexampled opposition which Mr. Wordsworth's writings have been since doomed to encounter. The humbler passages in the poems themselves were dwelt on and cited to justify the rejection of the theory. What in and for themselves would have been either forgotten or forgiven as imperfections, or at least comparative failures, provoked direct hostility when announced as intentional, as the result of choice after full deliberation. Thus the poems, admitted by *all* as excellent, joined with those which had pleased the far *greater* number, though they formed two-thirds of the whole work, instead of being deemed (as in all right they should have been, even if we take for granted that the reader judged aright) an atonement for the few exceptions, gave wind and fuel to the animosity against both the poems and the poet. In all perplexity there is a portion of fear, which predisposes the mind to anger. Not able to deny that the author possessed both genius and a powerful intellect, they felt *very positive*, but were not *quite certain*, that he might not be in the right, and they themselves in the wrong; an unquiet state of mind, which seeks alleviation by quarrelling with the occasion of it, and by wondering at the perverseness of the man, who had written a long and argumentative essay to persuade them, that

    Fair is foul, and foul is fair;[1]

in other words, that they had been all their lives admiring without judgement, and were now about to censure without reason.[2]

That this conjecture is not wide from the mark, I am induced to believe from the noticeable fact, which I can state on my own knowledge, that the same general censure should have been grounded almost by each different person on some different poem. Among those, whose candour and judgement I estimate highly, I distinctly remember six who expressed their objections to the "Lyrical Ballads" almost in the same words, and altogether to the same purport, at the same time admitting, that several of the poems had given them great pleasure; and, strange as it might seem, the composition which one had cited as execrable, another had quoted as his favorite. I am indeed convinced in my own mind, that could the same experiment have been tried with these volumes, as was made in the well known story of the picture, the result would have been the same; the parts which had been covered by the number of the *black* spots on the one day, would be found equally *albo lapide notatæ*[3] on the succeeding.

However this may be, it is assuredly hard and unjust to fix the attention on a few separate and insulated poems with as much aversion, as if they had been so many plague-spots on the whole work, instead of passing them over in silence, as so much blank paper, or leaves of bookseller's catalogue; especially, as no one pretends to have found immorality or indelicacy; and the poems therefore, at the worst, could only be regarded as so many light or inferior coins in a roleau of gold, not as so much alloy in a weight of bullion. A friend whose *talents* I hold in the highest respect, but whose *judgement* and strong sound sense I have had almost continued occasion to *revere*, making the usual complaints to me concerning both the style and subjects of Mr. Wordsworth's minor poems; I admitted that there were some few of the tales and incidents, in which I could not myself find a sufficient cause for their having been recorded in metre. I mentioned the "Alice Fell" as an instance; "nay," replied my friend with more than usual quickness of manner, "I cannot agree with you *there!* that I own *does* seem to me a remarkably pleasing poem." In the "Lyrical Ballads" (for my experience does not enable me to extend the remark equally

---

[1] Shakespeare, *Macbeth* 1.1.10.

[2] We have omitted a long authorial note.

[3] "marked with a *white* stone" (L.; cf. Catullus 68.148). It was a Roman custom to use white and black stones to mark auspicious and inauspicious days, and also to cast votes for and against. The "well known story of the picture" is unidentified.

unqualified to the two subsequent volumes) I have heard at different times, and from different individuals every single poem *extolled* and *reprobated*, with the exception of those of loftier kind, which as was before observed, seem to have won universal praise. This fact of itself would have made me diffident in my censures, had not a still stronger ground been furnished by the strange contrast of the heat and long continuance of the opposition, with the nature of the faults stated as justifying it. The seductive faults, the dulcia vitia[1] of Cowley, Marini, or Darwin[2] might reasonably be thought capable of corrupting the public judgement for half a century, and require a twenty years war, campaign after campaign, in order to dethrone the usurper and re-establish the legitimate taste. But that a downright simpleness, under the affectation of simplicity, prosaic words in feeble metre, silly thoughts in childish phrases, and a preference of mean, degrading, or at best trivial associations and characters, should succeed in forming a school of imitators, a company of almost *religious* admirers, and this too among young men of ardent minds, liberal education, and not

           with academic laurels unbestowed;[3]

and that this bare and bald *counterfeit* of poetry, which is characterized as *below* criticism, should for nearly twenty years have well-nigh *engrossed* criticism, as the main, if not the only, *butt* of review, magazine, pamphlets, poem, and paragraph;—this is indeed matter of wonder! …

    ["]In poems, equally as in philosophic disquisitions, genius produces the strongest impressions of novelty, while it rescues the most admitted truths from the impotence caused by the very circumstance of their universal admission. Truths of all others the most awful and mysterious, yet being at the same time of universal interest, are too often considered as *so* true, that they lose all the life and efficiency of truth, and lie bedridden in the dormitory of the soul, side by side, with the most despised and exploded errors." THE FRIEND,[4] page 76, No. 5.

    This excellence, which in all Mr. Wordsworth's writings is more or less predominant, and which constitutes the character of his mind, I no sooner felt, than I sought to understand. Repeated meditations led me first to suspect, (and a more intimate analysis of the human faculties, their appropriate marks, functions, and effects matured my conjecture into full conviction) that fancy and imagination were two distinct and widely different faculties, instead of being, according to the general belief, either two names with one meaning, or at furthest, the lower and higher degree of one and the same power. It is not, I own, easy to conceive a more apposite translation of the Greek *Phantasia*, than the Latin Imaginatio; but it is equally true that in all societies there exists an instinct of growth, a certain collective, unconscious good sense working progressively to desynonymize[5] those words originally of the same

---

[1] "attractive faults" (L.; cf. Quintilian [c. AD 35–95] 10.1.129; Cicero [106–43 BC], *De Senectute* 65).

[2] Abraham Cowley (1618–67), Giambattista Marino or Marini (1569–1625), Erasmus Darwin,* poets noted for ornateness of style.

[3] adapted from Thomas Warton (1728-90), "To the River Lodon" (1777) 14. Coleridge often seems to quote from memory.

[4] "As 'the Friend' was printed on stampt sheets, and sent only by the post to a very limited number of subscribers, the author has felt less objection to quote from it, though a work of his own. To the public at large indeed it is the same as a volume in manuscript." (S.T.C.) *The Friend* was a periodical published, and almost entirely written, by Coleridge in 1809–10.

[5] "This is effected either by giving to the one word a general, and to the other an exclusive use; as 'to put on the back' and 'to indorse'; or by an actual distinction of meanings as 'naturalist,' and 'physician'; or by difference of relation as 'I' and 'Me'; (each of which the rustics of our different provinces still use in all the cases singular of the first personal pronoun). Even the mere difference, or corruption, in the *pronunciation* of the same word, if it have become general, will produce a new word with a distinct signification; thus 'property' and 'propriety'; the latter of which, even to the time of Charles II. was the *written* word for all the senses of both. Thus too 'mister' and 'master' both hasty pronouncings of the same word 'magister,' 'mistress,' and 'miss,' 'if,' and 'give,' &c. &c. There is a sort of *minim immortal* among the animalcula infusoria which has not naturally either birth, or death, absolute beginning, or absolute end: for at a certain period a small point appears on its back, which deepens and lengthens till the creature divides into two, and the same process recommences in each of the halves now become integral. This may be a fanciful, but it is by no means a bad emblem of the formation of words, and may facilitate the conception, how immense a nomenclature may be organized from a few simple sounds by rational beings in a social state. For each new application, or excitement of the same sound, will call forth a different sensation, which cannot but affect the pronunciation. The after

meaning, which the conflux of dialects had supplied to the more homogeneous languages, as the Greek and German: and which the same cause, joined with accidents of translation from original works of different countries, occasion in mixt languages like our own. The first and most important point to be proved is, that two conceptions perfectly distinct are confused under one and the same word, and (this done) to appropriate that word exclusively to one meaning, and the synonyme (should there be one) to the other. But if (as will be often the case in the arts and sciences) no synonyme exists, we must either invent or borrow a word. In the present instance the appropriation had already begun, and been legitimated in the derivative adjective: Milton had a highly *imaginative*, Cowley a very *fanciful* mind. If therefore I should succeed in establishing the actual existences of two faculties generally different, the nomenclature would be at once determined. To the faculty by which I had characterized Milton, we should confine the term *imagination*; while the other would be contra-distinguished as *fancy*. Now were it once fully ascertained, that this division is no less grounded in nature, than that of delirium from mania, or Otway's

Lutes, lobsters, seas of milk, and ships of amber,[1]

from Shakespear's

What! have his daughters brought him to this pass?[2]

or from the preceding apostrophe to the elements;[3] the theory of the fine arts, and of poetry in particular, could not, I thought, but derive some additional and important light. It would in its immediate effects furnish a torch of guidance to the philosophical critic; and ultimately to the poet himself. In energetic minds, truth soon changes by domestication into power; and from directing in the discrimination and appraisal of the product, becomes influencive in the production. To admire on principle, is the only way to imitate without loss of originality....

from CHAPTER 13
On the imagination, or esemplastic[4] power.

Thus far had the work been transcribed for the press, when I received the following letter from a friend,[5] whose practical judgement I have had ample reason to estimate and revere, and whose taste and sensibility preclude all the excuses which my self-love might possibly have prompted me to set up in plea against the decision of advisers of equal good sense, but with less tact and feeling.

"Dear C.

"You ask my opinion concerning your *Chapter on the Imagination*, both as to the impressions it made on *myself*, and as to those which I think it will make on the PUBLIC, *i.e., that part of the public, who from the title of the work and from its forming a sort of introduction to a volume of poems, are likely to constitute the great majority of your readers.*

"As to myself, and stating in the first place the effect on *my* understanding, *your opinions and method of argument were not only so* new *to me, but so directly the reverse of all I had ever been accustomed to consider as truth, that even if I had comprehended your premises sufficiently to have admitted them, and had seen the necessity of your conclusions, I should still have been in that state of mind, which in your note, p. 75, 76, you have so ingeniously evolved, as the antithesis to that in which a man is, when he makes a* bull.[6] *In your own words, I should have felt as if I had been standing on my head.*

"The effect on *my* feelings, *on the other hand, I cannot better represent, than by supposing myself to have known only our light airy modern chapels of ease, and then for the first time to have been placed, and left alone, in one of our largest Gothic cathedrals in a gusty moonlight night of*

---

recollection of the sound, without the same vivid sensation, will modify it still further; till at length all trace of the original likeness is worn away." (S.T.C.)

[1] adapted from Thomas Otway (1652–85), *Venice Preserv'd* (1682) 5.1.369; the lobsters are from Samuel Butler (1613–80), *Hudibras* (1660–80) 2.2.31.

[2] Shakespeare, *King Lear* 3.4.61.

[3] Shakespeare, *King Lear* 3.2.1–24.

[4] "shaping into one," a word coined by Coleridge.

[5] Coleridge wrote the following letter himself.

[6] a logical absurdity.

autumn. 'Now in glimmer, and now in gloom';[1] often in palpable darkness not without a chilly sensation of terror; then suddenly emerging into broad yet visionary lights with coloured shadows, of fantastic shapes yet all decked with holy insignia and mystic symbols; and ever and anon coming out full upon pictures and stone-work images of great men, with whose names I was familiar, but which looked upon me with countenances and an expression, the most dissimilar to all I had been in the habit of connecting with those names. Those whom I had been taught to venerate as almost super-human in magnitude of intellect, I found perched in little fret-work niches, as grotesque dwarfs; while the grotesques, in my hitherto belief, stood guarding the high altar with all the characters of Apotheosis. In short, what I had supposed substances were thinned away into shadows, while every where shadows were deepened into substances:

> If substance may be call'd what shadow seem'd,
> For each seem'd either!
>
> MILTON.[2]

"Yet after all, I could not but repeat the lines which you had quoted from a MS. poem of your own in the FRIEND, and applied to a work of Mr. Wordsworth's though with a few of the words altered:

> ———An orphic tale indeed,
> A tale *obscure* of high and passionate thoughts
> To *a strange* music chaunted![3]

"Be assured, however, that I look forward anxiously to your great book on the CONSTRUCTIVE PHILOSOPHY, which you have promised and announced: and that I will do my best to understand it. Only I will not promise to descend into the dark cave of Trophonius[4] with you, there to rub my own eyes, in order to make the sparks and figured flashes, which I am required to see.

"So much for myself. But as for the PUBLIC, I do not hesitate a moment in advising and urging you to withdraw the Chapter from the present work, and to reserve it for your announced treatises on the Logos[5] or communicative intellect in Man and Deity. First, because imperfectly as I understand the present Chapter, I see clearly that you have done too much, and yet not enough. You have been obliged to omit so many links, from the necessity of compression, that what remains, looks (if I may recur to my former illustration) like the fragments of the winding steps of an old ruined tower. Secondly, a still stronger argument (at least one that I am sure will be more forcible with you) is, that your readers will have both right and reason to complain of you. This Chapter, which cannot, when it is printed, amount to so little as an hundred pages, will of necessity greatly increase the expense of the work; and every reader who, like myself, is neither prepared or perhaps calculated for the study of so abstruse a subject so abstrusely treated, will, as I have before hinted, be almost entitled to accuse you of a sort of imposition on him. For who, he might truly observe, could from your title-page, viz. "𝔐𝔶 𝔏𝔦𝔱𝔢𝔯𝔞𝔯𝔶 𝔏𝔦𝔣𝔢 𝔞𝔫𝔡 𝔒𝔭𝔦𝔫𝔦𝔬𝔫𝔰," published too as introductory to a volume of miscellaneous poems, have anticipated, or even conjectured, a long treatise on ideal Realism, which holds the same relation in abstruseness to Plotinus, as Plotinus does to Plato. It will be well, if already you have not too much of metaphysical disquisition in your work, though as the larger part of the disquisition is historical, it will doubtless be both interesting and instructive to many to whose unprepared minds your speculations on the esemplastic power would be utterly unintelligible. Be assured, if you do publish this Chapter in the present work, you will be reminded of Bishop Berkeley's *Siris*,[6] announced as an Essay on Tar-water, which beginning with Tar ends with the Trinity, the *omne scibile*[7] forming the interspace. I say in the present work. In that greater work to which you have devoted so many years, and study so intense and various, it will be in its proper place. Your prospectus will have described and announced both its contents and their nature; and if any persons purchase it, who feel no interest

---

[1] Coleridge, "Christabel" 167.*

[2] *Paradise Lost* 2.669–70.

[3] adapted from Coleridge, "To a Gentleman" ("To William Wordsworth") 45–47.*

[4] a Greek architect, swallowed up by the earth at the time of his death. There was an oracle sacred to him in a cave; those descending into the cave to consult the oracle heard strange noises and saw strange lights.

[5] "word" (Gr.): Cf. John 1.1–4.

[6] George Berkeley (1685–1753), *Siris: A Chain of Philosophical Reflexions and Inquiries concerning the Virtues of Tar Water, and Divers Other Subjects* (1744).

[7] "everything knowable" (L.).

in the subjects of which it treats, they will have themselves only to blame.

"I could add to these arguments one derived from pecuniary motives, and particularly from the probable effects on the sale *of your present publication; but they would weigh little with you compared with the preceding. Besides, I have long observed, that arguments drawn from your own personal interests more often act on you as narcotics than as stimulants, and that in money concerns you have some small portion of pig-nature in your moral idiosyncracy, and like these amiable creatures, must occasionally be pulled backward from the boat in order to make you enter it. All success attend you, for if hard thinking and hard reading are merits, you have deserved it.*

Your affectionate, &c."

In consequence of this very judicious letter, which produced complete conviction on my mind, I shall content myself for the present with stating the main result of the Chapter, which I have reserved for that future publication, a detailed prospectus of which the reader will find at the close of the second volume.[1]

The IMAGINATION then I consider either as primary, or secondary. The primary IMAGINATION I hold to be the living Power and prime Agent of all human Perception, and as a repetition in the finite mind of the eternal act of creation in the infinite I AM.[2] The secondary I consider as an echo of the former, co-existing with the conscious will, yet still as identical with the primary in the *kind* of its agency, and differing only in *degree*, and in the *mode* of its operation. It dissolves, diffuses, dissipates, in order to re-create; or where this process is rendered impossible, yet still at all events it struggles to idealize and to unify. It is essentially *vital*, even as all objects (*as* objects) are essentially fixed and dead.

FANCY, on the contrary, has no other counters to play with, but fixities and definites. The Fancy is indeed no other than a mode of Memory emancipated from the order of time and space; and blended with, and modified by that empirical phenomenon of the will, which we express by the word CHOICE. But equally with the ordinary memory it must receive all its materials ready made from the law of association.

Whatever more than this, I shall think it fit to declare concerning the powers and privileges of the imagination in the present work, will be found in the critical essay on the uses of the Supernatural in poetry and the principles that regulate its introduction: which the reader will find prefixed to the poem of 𝔈𝔥𝔢 𝔄𝔫𝔠𝔦𝔢𝔫𝔱 𝔐𝔞𝔯𝔦𝔫𝔢𝔯.[3]

CHAPTER 14

Occasion of the Lyrical Ballads, and the objects originally proposed—Preface to the second edition—The ensuing controversy, its causes and acrimony—Philosophic definitions of a poem and poetry with scholia.

During the first year that Mr. Wordsworth and I were neighbours, our conversations turned frequently on the two cardinal points of poetry, the power of exciting the sympathy of the reader by a faithful adherence to the truth of nature, and the power of giving the interest of novelty by the modifying colours of imagination. The sudden charm, which accidents of light and shade, which moon-light or sun-set diffused over a known and familiar landscape, appeared to represent the practicability of combining both. These are the poetry of nature. The thought suggested itself (to which of us I do not recollect) that a series of poems might be composed of two sorts. In the one, the incidents and agents were to be, in part at least, supernatural; and the excellence aimed at was to consist in the interesting of the affections by the dramatic truth of such emotions, as would naturally accompany such situations, supposing them real. And real in *this* sense they have been to every human being who, from whatever source of delusion, has at any time believed himself under supernatural agency. For the second class, subjects were to be chosen from ordinary life; the characters and incidents were to be such, as will be found in every village and its vicinity, where there is a meditative and feeling mind to seek

---

[1] This prospectus was never published.

[2] Cf. Exodus 3.14.

[3] This essay was never published.

after them, or to notice them, when they present themselves.

In this idea originated the plan of the "Lyrical Ballads"; in which it was agreed, that my endeavours should be directed to persons and characters supernatural, or at least romantic; yet so as to transfer from our inward nature a human interest and a semblance of truth sufficient to procure for these shadows of imagination[1] that willing suspension of disbelief for the moment, which constitutes poetic faith. Mr. Wordsworth, on the other hand, was to propose to himself as his object, to give the charm of novelty to things of every day, and to excite a feeling analogous to the supernatural, by awakening the mind's attention from the lethargy of custom, and directing it to the loveliness and the wonders of the world before us; an inexhaustible treasure, but for which in consequence of the film of familiarity and selfish solicitude we have eyes, yet see not, ears that hear not, and hearts that neither feel nor understand.[2]

With this view I wrote the "Ancient Mariner," and was preparing among other poems, the "Dark Ladie," and the "Christabel," in which I should have more nearly realized my ideal, than I had done in my first attempt. But Mr. Wordsworth's industry had proved so much more successful, and the number of his poems so much greater, that my compositions, instead of forming a balance, appeared rather an interpolation of heterogeneous matter.[3] Mr. Wordsworth added two or three poems written in his own character, in the impassioned, lofty, and sustained diction, which is characteristic of his genius.[4] In this form the "Lyrical Ballads" were published; and were presented by him, as an *experiment*,[5] whether subjects, which from their nature rejected the usual ornaments and extra-colloquial style of poems in general, might not be so managed in the language of ordinary life as to produce the pleasurable interest, which it is the peculiar business of poetry to impart. To the second edition he added a preface of considerable length; in which notwithstanding some passages of apparently a contrary import, he was understood to contend for the extension of this style to poetry of all kinds, and to reject as vicious and indefensible all phrases and forms of style that were not included in what he (unfortunately, I think, adopting an equivocal expression) called the language of *real* life.[6] From this preface, prefixed to poems in which it was impossible to deny the presence of original genius, however mistaken its direction might be deemed, arose the whole long continued controversy. For from the conjunction of perceived power with supposed heresy I explain the inveteracy and in some instances, I grieve to say, the acrimonious passions, with which the controversy has been conducted by the assailants.

Had Mr. Wordsworth's poems been the silly, the childish things, which they were for a long time described as being; had they been really distinguished from the compositions of other poets merely by meanness of language and inanity of thought; had they indeed contained nothing more than what is found in the parodies and pretended imitations of them; they must have sunk at once, a dead weight, into the slough of oblivion, and have dragged the preface along with them. But year after year increased the number of Mr. Wordsworth's admirers. They were found too not in the lower classes of the reading public, but chiefly among young men of strong sensibility and meditative minds; and their admiration (inflamed perhaps in some degree by opposition) was distinguished by its intensity, I might almost say, by its *religious* fervour. These facts, and the intellectual energy of the author, which was more or less consciously felt, where it was outwardly and even boisterously denied, meeting with sentiments of aversion to his opinions, and of alarm at their consequences, produced an eddy of criticism, which would of itself have borne up the poems by the violence, with which it whirled them round and round. With many parts of this preface in the sense attributed to them and which the

---

[1] Cf. Shakespeare, *A Midsummer Night's Dream* 5.1.209–10.

[2] Cf. Isaiah 6.10, Jeremiah 5.21.

[3] Coleridge wrote only four of the twenty-three poems in the first edition of *Lyrical Ballads*.

[4] for example, W. Wordsworth, "Expostulation and Reply,"* "The Tables Turned,"* and "Tintern Abbey."*

[5] Cf. W. Wordsworth, Advertisement to *Lyrical Ballads*.*

[6] Cf. W. Wordsworth, Preface to *Lyrical Ballads* (640).*

words undoubtedly seem to authorise, I never concurred; but on the contrary objected to them as erroneous in principle, and as contradictory (in appearance at least) both to other parts of the same preface, and to the author's own practice in the greater number of the poems themselves. Mr. Wordsworth in his recent collection[1] has, I find, degraded this prefatory disquisition to the end of his second volume, to be read or not at the reader's choice. But he has not, as far as I can discover, announced any change in his poetic creed. At all events, considering it as the source of a controversy, in which I have been honored more, than I deserve, by the frequent conjunction of my name with his, I think it expedient to declare once for all, in what points I coincide with his opinions, and in what points I altogether differ. But in order to render myself intelligible I must previously, in as few words as possible, explain my ideas, first, of a POEM; and secondly, of POETRY itself, in *kind*, and in *essence*.

The office of philosophical *disquisition* consists in just *distinction*; while it is the priviledge of the philosopher to preserve himself constantly aware, that distinction is not division. In order to obtain adequate notions of any truth, we must intellectually separate its distinguishable parts; and this is the technical *process* of philosophy. But having so done, we must then restore them in our conceptions to the unity, in which they actually co-exist; and this is the *result* of philosophy. A poem contains the same elements as a prose composition; the difference therefore must consist in a different combination of them, in consequence of a different object proposed. According to the difference of the object will be the difference of the combination. It is possible, that the object may be merely to facilitate the recollection of any given facts or observations by artificial arrangement; and the composition will be a poem, merely because it is distinguished from prose by metre, or by rhyme, or by both conjointly. In this, the lowest sense, a man might attribute the name of a poem to the well known enumeration of the days in the several months;

Thirty days hath September,
April, June, and November, &c.

and others of the same class and purpose. And as a particular pleasure is found in anticipating the recurrence of sounds and quantities, all compositions that have this charm superadded, whatever be their contents, *may* be entitled poems.

So much for the superficial *form*. A difference of object and contents supplies an additional ground of distinction. The immediate purpose may be the communication of truths; either of truth absolute and demonstrable, as in works of science; or of facts experienced and recorded, as in history. Pleasure, and that of the highest and most permanent kind, may *result* from the *attainment* of the end; but it is not itself the immediate end. In other works the communication of pleasure may be the immediate purpose; and though truth, either moral or intellectual, ought to be the *ultimate* end, yet this will distinguish the character of the author, not the class to which the work belongs. Blest indeed is that state of society, in which the immediate purpose would be baffled by the perversion of the proper ultimate end; in which no charm of diction or imagery could exempt the Bathyllus even of an Anacreon, or the Alexis of Virgil, from disgust and aversion![2]

But the communication of pleasure may be the immediate object of a work not metrically composed; and that object may have been in a high degree attained, as in novels and romances. Would then the mere superaddition of metre, with or without rhyme, entitle *these* to the name of poems? The answer is, that nothing can permanently please, which does not contain in itself the reason why it is so, and not otherwise. If metre be superadded, all other parts must be made consonant with it. They must be such, as to justify the perpetual and distinct attention to each part, which an exact correspondent recurrence of accent and sound are calculated to excite. The final definition then, so deduced, may be thus worded. A poem is that species of

---

[1] *Poems by William Wordsworth* (1815).

[2] See the 17th anacreontic ode (no longer attributed to Anacreon), and Virgil, *Eclogues* 2 (both are homoerotic).

composition, which is opposed to works of science, by proposing for its *immediate* object pleasure, not truth; and from all other species (having *this* object in common with it) it is discriminated by proposing to itself such delight from the *whole*, as is compatible with a distinct gratification from each component *part*.

Controversy is not seldom excited in consequence of the disputants attaching each a different meaning to the same word; and in few instances has this been more striking, than in disputes concerning the present subject. If a man chooses to call every composition a poem, which is rhyme, or measure, or both, I must leave his opinion uncontroverted. The distinction is at least competent to characterize the writer's intention. If it were subjoined, that the whole is likewise entertaining or affecting, as a tale, or as a series of interesting reflections, I of course admit this as another fit ingredient of a poem, and an additional merit. But if the definition sought for be that of a *legitimate* poem, I answer, it must be one, the parts of which mutually support and explain each other; all in their proportion harmonizing with, and supporting the purpose and known influences of metrical arrangement. The philosophic critics of all ages coincide with the ultimate judgement of all countries, in equally denying the praises of a just poem, on the one hand, to a series of striking lines or distichs, each of which absorbing the whole attention of the reader to itself disjoins it from its context, and makes it a separate whole, instead of an harmonizing part; and on the other hand, to an unsustained composition, from which the reader collects rapidly the general result unattracted by the component parts. The reader should be carried forward, not merely or chiefly by the mechanical impulse of curiosity, or by a restless desire to arrive at the final solution; but by the pleasurable activity of mind excited by the attractions of the journey itself. Like the motion of a serpent, which the Egyptians made the emblem of intellectual power; or like the path of sound through the air; at every step he pauses and half recedes, and from the retrogressive movement collects the force which again carries him onward. Precipitandus est *liber* spiritus,[1] says Petronius Arbiter most happily. The epithet, *liber*, here balances the preceding verb; and it is not easy to conceive more meaning condensed in fewer words.

But if this should be admitted as a satisfactory character of a poem, we have still to seek for a definition of poetry. The writings of PLATO, and Bishop TAYLOR, and the Theoria Sacra of BURNET,[2] furnish undeniable proofs that poetry of the highest kind may exist without metre, and even without the contradistinguishing objects of a poem. The first chapter of Isaiah (indeed a very large proportion of the whole book) is poetry in the most emphatic sense; yet it would be not less irrational than strange to assert, that pleasure, and not truth, was the immediate object of the prophet. In short, whatever *specific* import we attach to the word, poetry, there will be found involved in it, as a necessary consequence, that a poem of any length neither can be, or ought to be, all poetry. Yet if an harmonious whole is to be produced, the remaining parts must be preserved *in keeping* with the poetry; and this can be no otherwise effected than by such a studied selection and artificial arrangement, as will partake of *one*, though not a *peculiar*, property of poetry. And this again can be no other than the property of exciting a more continuous and equal attention, than the language of prose aims at, whether colloquial or written.

My own conclusions on the nature of poetry, in the strictest use of the word, have been in part anticipated in the preceding disquisition on the fancy and imagination. What is poetry? is so nearly the same question with, what is a poet? that the answer to the one is involved in the solution of the other. For it is a distinction resulting from the poetic genius itself, which sustains and modifies the images, thoughts, and emotions of the poet's own mind.

The poet, described in *ideal* perfection, brings the whole soul of man into activity, with the subordination of its faculties to each other, according to their relative worth and dignity. He diffuses a tone, and spirit of

---

[1] "The *free* spirit [of the poet] must be hurried onward": Petronius (c. AD 27–66) *Satyricon*, 118.

[2] Jeremy Taylor (1613–67), author of *Holy Living and Holy Dying* (1650–51), and Thomas Burnet (1635–1715), author of *Telluris theoria sacra* (1681), translated as *The Sacred Theory of the Earth* (1684–89). Coleridge quotes Burnet in the epigraph to "The Rime of the Ancient Mariner" (1817).*

unity, that blends, and (as it were) *fuses*, each into each, by that synthetic and magical power, to which we have exclusively appropriated the name of imagination. This power, first put in action by the will and understanding, and retained under their irremissive, though gentle and unnoticed, controul (*laxis effertur habenis*)[1] reveals itself in the balance or reconciliation of opposite or discordant qualities: of sameness, with difference; of the general, with the concrete; the idea, with the image; the individual, with the representative; the sense of novelty and freshness, with old and familiar objects; a more than usual state of emotion, with more than usual order; judgement ever awake and steady self-possession, with enthusiasm and feeling profound or vehement; and while it blends and harmonizes the natural and the artificial, still subordinates art to nature; the manner to the matter; and our admiration of the poet to our sympathy with the poetry. "Doubtless," as Sir John Davies observes of the soul (and his words may with slight alteration be applied, and even more appropriately to the poetic IMAGINATION.)

> Doubtless this could not be, but that she turns
> Bodies to spirit by sublimation strange,
> As fire converts to fire the things it burns,
> As we our food into our nature change.
>
> From their gross matter she abstracts their forms,
> And draws a kind of quintessence from things,
> Which to her proper nature she transforms
> To bear them light, on her celestial wings.
>
> Thus does she, when from individual states
> She doth abstract the universal kinds;
> Which then re-clothed in divers names and fates
> Steal access through our senses to our minds.[2]

Finally, GOOD SENSE is the BODY of poetic genius, FANCY its DRAPERY, MOTION its LIFE, and IMAGINATION the SOUL that is every where, and in each; and forms all into one graceful and intelligent whole.

---

[1] "It is carried onwards with loose reins": Virgil, *Georgics* 2.364.

[2] adapted from Sir John Davies (1570–1626), *Nosce Teipsum* [(L.): "*Know Thyself*"]: *Of the Soule of Man and the Immortalitie Thereof* (1599) 4.11–13.

from CHAPTER 17

Examination of the tenets peculiar to Mr. Wordsworth—Rustic life (above all, *low* and rustic life) especially unfavorable to the formation of a human diction—The *best* parts of language the product of philosophers, not clowns or shepherds—Poetry essentially ideal and generic—The language of Milton as much the language of *real* life, yea, incomparably more so than that of the cottager.

As far then as Mr. Wordsworth in his preface contended, and most ably contended, for a reformation in our poetic diction, as far as he has evinced the truth of passion, and the *dramatic* propriety of those figures and metaphors in the original poets, which stript of their justifying reasons and converted into mere artifices of connection or ornament, constitute the characteristic falsity in the poetic style of the moderns; and as far as he has, with equal acuteness and clearness, pointed out the process in which this change was effected, and the resemblances between that state into which the reader's mind is thrown by the pleasureable confusion of thought from an unaccustomed train of words and images; and that state which is induced by the natural language of empassioned feeling; he undertook a useful task, and deserves all praise, both for the attempt and for the execution. The provocations to this remonstrance in behalf of truth and nature were still of perpetual recurrence before and after the publication of this preface. I cannot likewise but add, that the comparison of such poems of merit, as have been given to the public within the last ten or twelve years, with the majority of those produced previously to the appearance of that preface, leave no doubt on my mind, that Mr. Wordsworth is fully justified in believing his efforts to have been by no means ineffectual. Not only in the verses of those who have professed their admiration of his genius, but even of those who have distinguished themselves by hostility to his theory, and depreciation of his writings, are the impressions of his principles plainly visible. It is possible, that with these principles others may have been blended, which are not equally evident; and some which are unsteady and subvertible from the narrowness or imperfection of their basis. But it is more than possible, that these errors of defect or exaggeration, by kindling and feeding the controversy, may have conduced not only to the wider propagation of the accompanying truths, but that by their frequent presentation to the mind in an excited state, they may have won for them a more permanent and practical result. A man will borrow a part from his opponent the more easily, if he feels himself justified in continuing to reject a part. While there remain important points in which he can still feel himself in the right, in which he still finds firm footing for continued resistance, he will gradually adopt those opinions, which were the least remote from his own convictions, as not less congruous with his own theory, than with that which he reprobates. In like manner with a kind of instinctive prudence, he will abandon by little and little his weakest posts, till at length he seems to forget that they had ever belonged to him, or affects to consider them at most as accidental and "petty annexments,"[1] the removal of which leaves the citadel unhurt and unendangered.

My own differences from certain supposed parts of Mr. Wordsworth's theory ground themselves on the assumption, that his words had been rightly interpreted, as purporting that the proper diction for poetry in general consists altogether in a language taken, with due exceptions, from the mouths of men in real life, a language which actually constitutes the natural conversation of men under the influence of natural feelings. My objection is, first, that in *any* sense this rule is applicable only to *certain* classes of poetry; secondly, that even to these classes it is not applicable, except in such a sense, as hath never by any one (as far as I know or have read) been denied or doubted; and lastly, that as far as, and in that degree in which it is *practicable*, yet as a *rule* it is useless, if not injurious, and therefore either need not, or ought not to be practised. The poet informs his reader, that he had generally chosen *low and rustic* life;[2] but not *as* low and rustic, or in order to repeat that pleasure of doubtful moral effect, which persons of elevated rank and of superior refinement oftentimes derive from a happy *imitation* of the rude unpolished manners and discourse of their inferiors. For the pleasure so derived may be traced to three exciting causes. The first is the naturalness, in *fact*, of the things represented. The second is the apparent naturalness of the *representation*, as raised and qualified by an imperceptible infusion of the author's own knowledge and talent, which infusion does, indeed, constitute it an *imitation* as distinguished from a mere *copy*. The third cause may be found in the reader's conscious feeling of his superiority awakened by the contrast presented to him; even as for the same purpose the kings and great barons of yore retained, sometimes *actual* clowns and fools, but more frequently shrewd and witty fellows in that *character*. These, however, were not Mr. Wordsworth's objects. *He* chose low and rustic life, "because in that condition the essential passions of the heart find a better soil, in which they can attain their maturity, are less under restraint, and speak a plainer and more emphatic language; because in that condition of life our elementary feelings co-exist in a state of greater simplicity, and consequently may be more accurately contemplated, and more forcibly communicated; because the manners of rural life germinate from those elementary feelings; and from the necessary character of rural occupations are more easily comprehended, and are more durable; and lastly, because in that condition the passions of men are incorporated with the beautiful and permanent forms of nature."[3]

Now it is clear to me, that in the most interesting of the poems, in which the author is more or less dramatic, as the "Brothers," "Michael," "Ruth," the "Mad Mother," &c. the persons introduced are by no means taken *from low or rustic life* in the common acceptation of those words; and it is not less clear, that the sentiments and language, as far as they can be conceived to have been really transferred from the minds and conversation of such persons, are attributable to causes and circumstances not necessarily connected with "their occupations and abode." The thoughts, feelings, language, and manners of the shepherd-farmers in the vales of Cumberland and Westmoreland, as far as they are actually adopted in those poems, may be accounted for

---

[1] Cf. Shakespeare, *Hamlet* 3.3.21.

[2] Cf. W. Wordsworth, Preface to *Lyrical Ballads* (641).*

[3] W. Wordsworth, Preface to *Lyrical Ballads* (641).*

from causes, which will and do produce the same results in *every* state of life, whether in town or country. As the two principal I rank that INDEPENDENCE, which raises a man above servitude, or daily toil for the profit of others, yet not above the necessity of industry and a frugal simplicity of domestic life; and the accompanying unambitious, but solid and religious EDUCATION, which has rendered few books familiar, but the bible, and the liturgy or hymn book. To this latter cause, indeed, which is so far *accidental*, that it is the blessing of particular countries and a particular age, not the product of particular places or employments, the poet owes the shew of probability, that his personages might really feel, think, and talk with any tolerable resemblance to his representation. It is an excellent remark of Dr. Henry More's (Enthusiasmus triumphatus, Sec. xxxv) that "a man of confined education, but of good parts, by constant reading of the bible will naturally form a more winning and commanding rhetoric than those that are learned; the intermixture of tongues and of artificial phrases debasing *their* style."[1]

It is, moreover, to be considered that to the formation of healthy feelings, and a reflecting mind, *negations* involve impediments not less formidable, than sophistication and vicious intermixture. I am convinced, that for the human soul to prosper in rustic life, a certain vantage-ground is pre-requisite. It is not every man, that is likely to be improved by a country life or by country labours. Education, or original sensibility, or both, must pre-exist, if the changes, forms, and incidents of nature are to prove a sufficient stimulant. And where these are not sufficient, the mind contracts and hardens by want of stimulants; and the man becomes selfish, sensual, gross, and hard-hearted. Let the management of the POOR LAWS in Liverpool, Manchester, or Bristol be compared with the ordinary dispensation of the poor rates in agricultural villages, where the *farmers* are the overseers and guardians of the poor. If my own experience have not been particularly unfortunate, as well as that of the many respectable country clergymen with whom I have conversed on the subject, the result would engender more than scepticism concerning the desirable influences of low and rustic life in and for itself. Whatever may be concluded on the other side, from the stronger local attachments and enterprizing spirit of the Swiss, and other mountaineers, applies to a particular mode of pastoral life, under forms of property, that permit and beget manners truly republican, not to rustic life in general, or to the absence of artificial cultivation. On the contrary the mountaineers, whose manners have been so often eulogized, are in general, better educated and greater readers than men of equal rank elsewhere. But where this is not the case, as among the peasantry of North Wales, the ancient mountains, with all their terrors and all their glories, are pictures to the blind, and music to the deaf.

I should not have entered so much into detail upon this passage, but here seems to be the point, to which all the lines of difference converge as to their source and centre. (I mean, as far as, and in whatever respect, my poetic creed *does* differ from the doctrines promulged in this preface.) I adopt with full faith the principle of Aristotle, that poetry as poetry is essentially[2] *ideal*, that it avoids and excludes all *accident*; that its apparent individualities of rank, character, or occupation must be *representative* of a class; and that the *persons* of poetry must be clothed with *generic* attributes, with the *common* attributes of the class; not with such as one gifted individual might *possibly* possess, but such as from his situation it is most probable before-hand, that he *would* possess.[3] If my premises are right, and my deductions legitimate, it follows that there can be no *poetic* medium between the swains of Theocritus and those of an imaginary golden age....

In the "Thorn," the poet himself acknowledges in a note the necessity of an introductory poem, in which he should have pourtrayed the character of the person from whom the words of the poem are supposed to proceed: a superstitious man moderately imaginative, of slow faculties and deep feelings, "a captain of a small trading vessel, for example, who being past the middle age of life, had retired upon an annuity, or small independent

---

[1] adapted from Henry More (1614–87), *Enthusiasmus Triumphatus*: [(L.): "Enthusism Defeated"]: *A Collection of Several Philosophical Writings* (1662).

[2] We have cut a long authorial note.

[3] Cf. Aristotle, *Poetics* 9.1–4.

income, to some village or country town of which he was not a native, or in which he had not been accustomed to live. Such men having nothing to do become credulous and talkative from indolence." But in a poem, still more in a lyric poem (and the NURSE in Shakspeare's Romeo and Juliet alone prevents me from extending the remark even to dramatic *poetry*, if indeed the Nurse itself can be deemed altogether a case in point) it is not possible to imitate truly a dull and garrulous discourser, without repeating the effects of dulness and garrulity. However this may be, I dare assert, that the parts (and these form the far larger portion of the whole) which might as well or still better have proceeded from the poet's own imagination, and have been spoken in his own character, are those which have given, and which will continue to give universal delight; and that the passages exclusively appropriate to the supposed narrator, such as the last couplet of the third stanza; the seven last lines of the tenth;[1] and the five following stanzas, with the exception of the four admirable lines at the commencement of the fourteenth are felt by many unprejudiced and unsophisticated hearts, as sudden and unpleasant sinkings from the height to which the poet had previously lifted them, and to which he again re-elevates both himself and his reader.

If then I am compelled to doubt the theory, by which the choice of *characters* was to be directed, not only *a priori*, from grounds of reason, but both from the few instances in which the poet himself *need* be supposed to have been governed by it, and from the comparative inferiority of those instances; still more must I hesitate in my assent to the sentence which immediately follows the former citation; and which I can neither admit as particular fact, or as general rule. "The language too of these men is adopted (purified indeed from what appears to be its real defects, from all lasting and rational causes of dislike or disgust) because such men hourly communicate with the best objects from which the best part of language is originally derived; and because, from their rank in society, and the sameness and narrow circle of their intercourse, being less under the action of social vanity, they convey their feelings and notions in simple and unelaborated expressions."[2] To this I reply; that a rustic's language, purified from all provincialism and grossness, and so far re-constructed as to be made consistent with the rules of grammar (which are in essence no other than the laws of universal logic, applied to Psychological materials) will not differ from the language of any other man of common-sense, however learned or refined he may be, except as far as the notions, which the rustic has to convey, are fewer and more indiscriminate. This will become still clearer, if we add the consideration (equally important though less obvious) that the rustic, from the more imperfect developement of his faculties, and from the lower state of their cultivation, aims almost solely to convey *insulated facts*, either those of his scanty experience or his traditional belief; while the educated man chiefly seeks to discover and express those *connections* of things, or those relative *bearings* of fact to fact, from which some more or less general law is deducible. For *facts* are valuable to a wise man, chiefly as they lead to the discovery of the indwelling *law*, which is the true *being* of things, the sole solution of their modes of existence, and in the knowledge of which consists our dignity and our power.

As little can I agree with the assertion, that from the objects with which the rustic hourly communicates, the best part of language is formed. For first, if to communicate with an object implies such an acquaintance with it, as renders it capable of being discriminately reflected on; the distinct knowledge of an uneducated rustic would furnish a very scanty vocabulary. The few things, and modes of action, requisite for his bodily conveniences, would alone be individualized; while all the rest of nature would be expressed by a small number of confused, general terms. Secondly, I deny that the words and combinations of words derived from the objects, with which the rustic is familiar, whether with distinct or confused knowledge, can be justly said to form the *best* part of language. It is more than probable, that many classes of the brute creation possess discriminating

---

[1] W. Wordsworth, "The Thorn" 32–33, 104–65.* Coleridge quotes these passages in his notes. Wordsworth later revised them in response to Coleridge's criticism.

[2] W. Wordsworth, Preface to *Lyrical Ballads* (641).*

sounds, by which they can convey to each other notices of such objects as concern their food, shelter, or safety. Yet we hesitate to call the aggregate of such sounds a language, otherwise than metaphorically. The best part of human language, properly so called, is derived from reflection on the acts of the mind itself. It is formed by a voluntary appropriation of fixed symbols to internal acts, to processes and results of imagination, the greater part of which have no place in the consciousness of uneducated man; though in civilized society, by imitation and passive remembrance of what they hear from their religious instructors and other superiors, the most uneducated share in the harvest which they neither sowed or reaped. If the history of the phrases in hourly currency among our peasants were traced, a person not previously aware of the fact would be surprized at finding so large a number, which three or four centuries ago were the exclusive property of the universities and the schools; and at the commencement of the Reformation had been transferred from the school to the pulpit, and thus gradually passed into common life. The extreme difficulty, and often the impossibility, of finding words for the simplest moral and intellectual processes in the languages of uncivilized tribes has proved perhaps the weightiest obstacle to the progress of our most zealous and adroit missionaries. Yet these tribes are surrounded by the same nature, as our peasants are; but in still more impressive forms; and they are, moreover, obliged to *particularize* many more of them. When therefore Mr. Wordsworth adds, "accordingly such a language" (meaning, as before, the language of rustic life purified from provincialism) "arising out of repeated experience and regular feelings is a more permanent, and a far more philosophical language, than that which is frequently substituted for it by poets, who think they are conferring honor upon themselves and their art in proportion as they indulge in arbitrary and capricious habits of expression";[1] it may be answered, that the language, which he has in view, can be attributed to rustics with no greater right, than the style of Hooker or Bacon to Tom Brown or Sir Roger L'Estrange.[2] Doubtless, if what is peculiar to each were omitted in each, the result must needs be the same. Further, that the poet, who uses an illogical diction, or a style fitted to excite only the low and changeable pleasure of wonder by means of groundless novelty, substitutes a language of *folly* and *vanity*, not for that of the *rustic*, but for that of *good sense* and *natural feeling*.

Here let me be permitted to remind the reader, that the positions, which I controvert, are contained in the sentences—"*a selection of the* REAL *language of men*";—"*the language of these men* (i.e., men in low and rustic life) *I propose to myself to imitate, and as far as possible, to adopt the very language of men.*" "*Between the language of prose and that of metrical composition, there neither is, nor can be any essential difference.*"[3] It is against these exclusively that my opposition is directed.

I object, in the very first instance, to an equivocation in the use of the word "real." Every man's language varies, according to the extent of his knowledge, the activity of his faculties, and the depth or quickness of his feelings. Every man's language has, first, its *individualities*; secondly, the common properties of the *class* to which he belongs; and thirdly, words and phrases of *universal* use. The language of Hooker, Bacon, Bishop Taylor, and Burke, differ from the common language of the learned class only by the superior number and novelty of the thoughts and relations which they had to convey. The language of Algernon Sidney[4] differs not at all from that, which every well educated gentleman would wish to write, and (with due allowances for the undeliberateness, and less connected train, of thinking natural and proper to conversation) such as he would wish to talk. Neither one or the other differ half as much from the general language of cultivated society, as the language of Mr. Wordsworth's homeliest composition differs from that of a common peasant. For "real"

---

[1] W. Wordsworth, Preface to *Lyrical Ballads* (641–42).*

[2] Richard Hooker (1554–1600), author of *Of the Laws of Ecclesiastical Polity* (1593–1600); Sir Francis Bacon, Baron Verulam (1561–1626), essayist; Thomas Brown (1663–1704), satirical poet; Sir Roger l'Estrange (1616–1704), translator, pamphleteer, and journalist.

[3] adapted from W. Wordsworth, Preface to *Lyrical Ballads* (643, 644).*

[4] Algernon Sidney (1622–83), author of *Discourses concerning Government* (1698).

therefore, we must substitute *ordinary*, or *lingua communis*. And this, we have proved, is no more to be found in the phraseology of low and rustic life, than in that of any other class. Omit the peculiarities of each, and the result of course must be common to all. And assuredly the omissions and changes to be made in the language of rustics, before it could be transferred to any species of poem, except the drama or other professed imitation, are at least as numerous and weighty, as would be required in adapting to the same purpose the ordinary language of tradesmen and manufacturers. Not to mention, that the language so highly extolled by Mr. Wordsworth varies in every county, nay in every village, according to the accidental character of the clergyman, the existence or non-existence of schools; or even, perhaps, as the exciseman, publican, or barber happen to be, or not to be, zealous politicians, and readers of the weekly newspaper *pro bono publico*.[1] Anterior to cultivation the lingua communis[2] of every country, as Dante has well observed, exists every where in parts, and no where as a whole.[3]

Neither is the case rendered at all more tenable by the addition of the words, "*in a state of excitement.*" For the nature of a man's words, when he is strongly affected by joy, grief, or anger, must necessarily depend on the number and quality of the general truths, conceptions and images, and of the words expressing them, with which his mind had been previously stored. For the property of passion is not to *create*; but to set in increased activity. At least, whatever new connections of thoughts or images, or (which is equally, if not more than equally, the appropriate effect of strong excitement) whatever generalizations of truth or experience, the heat of passion may produce; yet the terms of their conveyance must have pre-existed in his former conversations, and are only collected and crowded together by the unusual stimulation. It is indeed very possible to adopt in a poem the unmeaning repetitions, habitual phrases, and other blank counters, which an unfurnished or confused understanding interposes at short intervals, in order to keep hold of his subject which is still slipping from him, and to give him time for recollection; or in mere aid of vacancy, as in the scanty companies of a country stage the same player pops backwards and forwards, in order to prevent the appearance of empty spaces, in the procession of Macbeth, or Henry VIIIth. But what assistance to the poet, or ornament to the poem, these can supply, I am at a loss to conjecture. Nothing assuredly can differ either in origin or in mode more widely from the *apparent* tautologies of intense and turbulent feeling, in which the passion is greater and of longer endurance, than to be exhausted or satisfied by a single representation of the image or incident exciting it. Such repetitions I admit to be a beauty of the highest kind; as illustrated by Mr. Wordsworth himself from the song of Deborah. "*At her feet he bowed, he fell, he lay down; at her feet he bowed, he fell; where he bowed, there he fell down dead.*"[4]

from CHAPTER 18

Language of metrical composition, why and wherein essentially different from that of prose—Origin and elements of metre—Its necessary consequences, and the conditions thereby imposed on the metrical writer in the choice of his diction.

I conclude therefore, that the attempt is impracticable; and that, were it not impracticable, it would still be useless. For the very power of making the selection implies the previous possession of the language selected. Or where can the poet have lived? And by what rules could he direct his choice, which would not have enabled him to select and arrange his words by the light of his own judgement? We do not adopt the language of a class by the mere adoption of such words exclusively, as that class would use, or at least understand; but likewise by following the *order*, in which the words of such men are wont to succeed each other. Now this order, in the intercourse of uneducated men, is distin-

---

[1] "for the public good" (L.).

[2] "common language" (L.).

[3] Dante, *De vulgari eloquentia* [L.: "Writing in the Vulgar Tongue"]1.16.

[4] Judges 5.27, quoted by W. Wordsworth in a note on repetition in "The Thorn."*

guished from the diction of their superiors in knowledge and power, by the greater *disjunction* and *separation* in the component parts of that, whatever it be, which they wish to communicate. There is a want of that prospectiveness of mind, that *surview*, which enables a man to foresee the whole of what he is to convey, appertaining to any one point; and by this means so to subordinate and arrange the different parts according to their relative importance, as to convey it at once, and as an organized whole.

Now I will take the first stanza, on which I have chanced to open, in the Lyrical Ballads. It is one the most simple and the least peculiar in its language.

> In distant countries I have been,
> And yet I have not often seen
> A healthy man, a man full grown,
> Weep in the public road alone.
> But such a one, on English ground,
> And in the broad highway I met;
> Along the broad highway he came,
> His cheeks with tears were wet.
> Sturdy he seem'd, though he was sad,
> And in his arms a lamb he had.[1]

The words here are doubtless such as are current in all ranks of life; and of course not less so, in the hamlet and cottage, than in the shop, manufactory, college, or palace. But is this the *order*, in which the rustic would have placed the words? I am grievously deceived, if the following less *compact* mode of commencing the same tale be not a far more faithful copy. "I have been in a many parts far and near, and I don't know that I ever saw before a man crying by himself in the public road; a grown man I mean, that was neither sick nor hurt," &c. &c. But when I turn to the following stanza in "The Thorn":

> At all times of the day and night
> This wretched woman thither goes,
> And she is known to every star
> And every wind that blows:
> And there beside the thorn she sits,
> When the blue day-light's in the skies;
> And when the whirlwind's on the hill,
> Or frosty air is keen and still;
> And to herself she cries,
> Oh misery! Oh misery!
> Oh woe is me! Oh misery![2]

and compare this with the language of ordinary men; or with that which I can conceive at all likely to proceed, in *real* life, from *such* a narrator, as is supposed in the note to the poem; compare it either in the succession of the images or of the sentences, I am reminded of the sublime prayer and hymn of praise, which MILTON, in opposition to an established liturgy, presents as a fair *specimen* of common extemporary devotion, and such as we might expect to hear from every self-inspired minister of a conventicle![3] And I reflect with delight, how little a mere theory, though of his own workmanship, interferes with the processes of genuine imagination in a man of true poetic genius, who possesses, as Mr. Wordsworth, if ever man did, most assuredly does possess,

THE VISION AND THE FACULTY DIVINE.[4]

One point then alone remains, but that the most important; its examination having been, indeed, my chief inducement for the preceding inquisition. "*There neither is or can be any essential difference between the language of prose and metrical composition.*" Such is Mr. Wordsworth's assertion. Now prose itself, at least, in all argumentative and consecutive works differs, and ought to differ, from the language of conversation; even as[5] reading ought to differ from talking. Unless therefore the difference denied be that of the mere *words*, as materials common to all styles of writing, and not of the *style* itself in the universally admitted sense of the term, it might be naturally presumed that there must exist a still greater between the ordonnance of poetic composition and that of prose, than is expected to distinguish prose from ordinary conversation....

Essence, in its primary signification, means the principle of *individuation*, the inmost principle of the *possibility* of any thing, *as* that particular thing. It is

---

[1] Cf. W. Wordsworth,* "The Last of the Flock" (1798).

[2] W. Wordsworth, "The Thorn" 67–77.*

[3] Cf. Milton, *Paradise Lost* 5.144–208 and *Eikonoklastes* (1649) chap. 16.

[4] W. Wordsworth, *The Excursion* 1.79.*

[5] We have cut an authorial note.

equivalent to the *idea* of a thing, whenever we use the word idea, with philosophic precision. Existence, on the other hand, is distinguished from essence, by the superinduction of *reality*. Thus we speak of the essence, and essential properties of a circle; but we do not therefore assert, that any thing, which really *exists*, is mathematically circular. Thus too, without any tautology we contend for the *existence* of the Supreme Being; that is, for a reality correspondent to the idea. There is, next, a *secondary* use of the word essence, in which it signifies the point or ground of contra-distinction between two modifications of the same substance or subject. Thus we should be allowed to say, that the style of architecture of Westminster Abbey is *essentially* different from that of Saint Paul, even though both had been built with blocks cut into the same form, and from the same quarry. Only in this latter sense of the term must it have been *denied* by Mr. Wordsworth (for in this sense alone is it *affirmed* by the general opinion) that the language of poetry (i.e., the formal construction, or architecture, of the words and phrases) is *essentially* different from that of prose. Now the burthen of the proof lies with the oppugner, not with the supporters of the common belief. Mr. Wordsworth, in consequence, assigns as the proof of his position, "that not only the language of a large portion of every good poem, even of the most elevated character, must necessarily, except with reference to the metre, in no respect differ from that of good prose; but likewise that some of the most interesting parts of the best poems will be found to be strictly the language of prose, when prose is well written. The truth of this assertion might be demonstrated by innumerable passages from almost all the poetical writings even of Milton himself." He then quotes Gray's sonnet—

> In vain to me the smiling mornings shine,
> And reddening Phœbus lifts his golden fire;
> The birds in vain their amorous descant join,
> Or cheerful fields resume their green attire;
> These ears alas! for other notes repine;
> *A different object do these eyes require;*
> *My lonely anguish melts no heart but mine,*
> *And in my breast the imperfect joys expire!*
> Yet morning smiles the busy race to cheer,
> And new born pleasure brings to happier men:
> The fields to all their wonted tributes bear,
> To warm their little loves the birds complain.
> *I fruitless mourn to him that cannot hear,*
> *And weep the more because I weep in vain;*

and adds the following remark:—"It will easily be perceived, that the only part of this Sonnet which is of any value, is the lines printed in italics. It is equally obvious, that except in the rhyme, and in the use of the single word 'fruitless' for fruitlessly, which is so far a defect, the language of these lines does in no respect differ from that of prose."[1]

An idealist defending his system by the fact, that when asleep we often believe ourselves awake, was well answered by his plain neighbour, "Ah, but when awake do we ever believe ourselves asleep?"—Things identical must be convertible. The preceding passage seems to rest on a similar sophism. For the question is not, whether there may not occur in prose an order of words, which would be equally proper in a poem; nor whether there are not beautiful lines and sentences of frequent occurrence in good poems, which would be equally becoming as well as beautiful in good prose; for neither the one or the other has ever been either denied or doubted by any one. The true question must be, whether there are not modes of expression, a *construction*, and an *order* of sentences, which are in their fit and natural place in a serious prose composition, but would be disproportionate and heterogeneous in metrical poetry; and, vice versa, whether in the language of a serious poem there may not be an arrangement both of words and sentences, and a use and selection of (what are called) *figures of speech*, both as to their kind, their frequency, and their occasions, which on a subject of equal weight would be vicious and alien in correct and manly prose. I contend, that in both cases this unfitness of each for the place of the other frequently will and ought to exist.

And first from the *origin* of metre. This I would trace to the balance in the mind effected by that spontaneous effort which strives to hold in check the workings of passion.[2] It might be easily explained likewise in what

---

[1] W. Wordsworth, Preface to *Lyrical Ballads* (644).*

[2] Cf. W. Wordsworth, Preface to *Lyrical Ballads* (642).*

manner this salutary antagonism is assisted by the very state, which it counteracts; and how this balance of antagonists became organized into *metre* (in the usual acceptation of that term) by a supervening act of the will and judgement, consciously and for the foreseen purpose of pleasure. Assuming these principles, as the data of our argument, we deduce from them two legitimate conditions, which the critic is entitled to expect in every metrical work. First, that as the *elements* of metre owe their existence to a state of increased excitement, so the metre itself should be accompanied by the natural language of excitement. Secondly, that as these elements are formed into metre *artificially*, by a *voluntary* act, with the design and for the purpose of blending *delight* with emotion, so the traces of present *volition* should throughout the metrical language be proportionally discernible. Now these two conditions must be reconciled and co-present. There must be not only a partnership, but a union; an interpenetration of passion and of will, of *spontaneous* impulse and of *voluntary* purpose. Again, this union can be manifested only in a frequency of forms and figures of speech (originally the offspring of passion, but now the adopted children of power) greater, than would be desired or endured, where the emotion is not voluntarily encouraged, and kept up for the sake of that pleasure, which such emotion so tempered and mastered by the will is found capable of communicating. It not only dictates, but of itself tends to produce, a more frequent employment of picturesque and vivifying language, than would be natural in any other case, in which there did not exist, as there does in the present, a previous and well understood, though tacit, *compact* between the poet and his reader, that the latter is entitled to expect, and the former bound to supply this species and degree of pleasurable excitement. We may in some measure apply to this union the answer of POLIXENES, in the Winter's Tale, to PERDITA'S neglect of the streaked gilly-flowers, because she had heard it said,

> There is an art which in their piedness shares
> With great creating nature.
>   *Pol:*   Say there be:
> Yet nature is made better by no mean,
> But nature makes that mean. So ev'n that art,
> Which you say adds to nature, is an art,
> That nature makes! You see, sweet maid, we marry
> *A gentler scyon to the wildest stock:*
> And make conceive a bark of ruder kind
> By bud of nobler race. This is an art,
> Which does mend nature—change it rather; but
> The art itself is nature.[1]

Secondly, I argue from the EFFECTS of metre. As far as metre acts in and for itself, it tends to increase the vivacity and susceptibility both of the general feelings and of the attention. This effect it produces by the continued excitement of surprize, and by the quick reciprocations of curiosity still gratified and still re-excited, which are too slight indeed to be at any one moment objects of distinct consciousness, yet become considerable in their aggregate influence. As a medicated atmosphere, or as wine during animated conversation; they act powerfully, though themselves unnoticed. Where, therefore, correspondent food and appropriate matter are not provided for the attention and feelings thus roused, there must needs be a disappointment felt; like that of leaping in the dark from the last step of a stair-case, when we had prepared our muscles for a leap of three or four....

Thirdly, I deduce the position from all the causes elsewhere assigned, which render metre the proper form of poetry, and poetry imperfect and defective without metre. Metre therefore having been connected with *poetry* most often and by a peculiar fitness, whatever else is combined with *metre* must, though it be not itself *essentially* poetic, have nevertheless some property in common with poetry, as an intermedium of affinity, a sort (if I may dare borrow a well-known phrase from technical chemistry) of *mordaunt*[2] between it and the superadded metre. Now poetry, Mr. Wordsworth truly affirms, does always imply PASSION;[3] which word must be here understood in its most general sense, as an excited state of the feelings and faculties. And as every passion has its proper pulse,[4] so will it likewise have its

---

[1] Cf. Shakespeare, *The Winter's Tale* 4.4.87–97.

[2] a substance used in dyeing, to fix the colours to the fabric.

[3] Cf. W. Wordsworth, Preface to *Lyrical Ballads* (648).*

[4] Cf. Sir Kenelm Digby (1603–65), *Treatise on Bodies* (1645) 377.

characteristic modes of expression. But where there exists that degree of genius and talent which entitles a writer to aim at the honors of a poet, the very *act* of poetic composition *itself* is, and is *allowed* to imply and to produce, an unusual state of excitement, which of course justifies and demands a correspondent difference of language, as truly, though not perhaps in as marked a degree, as the excitement of love, fear, rage, or jealousy. The vividness of the descriptions or declamations in DONNE, or DRYDEN, is as much and as often derived from the force and fervour of the describer, as from the reflections forms or incidents which constitute their subject and materials. The wheels take fire from the mere rapidity of their motion.[1] To what extent, and under what modifications, this may be admitted to act, I shall attempt to define in an after remark on Mr. Wordsworth's reply to this objection, or rather on his objection to this reply, as already anticipated in his preface.

Fourthly, and as intimately connected with this, if not the same argument in a more general form, I adduce the high spiritual instinct of the human being impelling us to seek unity by harmonious adjustment, and thus establishing the principle, that *all* the parts of an organized whole must be assimilated to the more *important* and *essential* parts. This and the preceding arguments may be strengthened by the reflection, that the composition of a poem is among the *imitative* arts; and that imitation, as opposed to copying, consists either in the interfusion of the SAME throughout the radically DIFFERENT, or of the different throughout a base radically the same.

Lastly, I appeal to the practice of the best poets, of all countries and in all ages, as *authorizing* the opinion, (*deduced* from all the foregoing) that in every import of the word ESSENTIAL, which would not here involve a mere truism, there may be, is, and ought to be, an *essential* difference between the language of prose and of metrical composition.

In Mr. Wordsworth's criticism of GRAY'S Sonnet, the reader's sympathy with his praise or blame of the different parts is taken for granted rather perhaps too easily. He has not, at least, attempted to win or compel it by argumentative analysis. In *my* conception at least, the lines rejected as of no value do, with the exception of the two first, differ as much and as little from the language of common life, as those which he has printed in italics as possessing genuine excellence. Of the five lines thus honorably distinguished, two of them differ from prose even more widely, than the lines which either precede or follow, in the *position* of the words.

A different object do these eyes require;
My lonely anguish melts no heart but mine;
And in my breast the imperfect joys expire.

But were it otherwise, what would this prove, but a truth, of which no man ever doubted? Videlicet, that there are sentences, which would be equally in their place both in verse and prose. Assuredly it does not prove the point, which alone requires proof; namely, that there are not passages, which would suit the one, and not suit the other. The first line of this sonnet is distinguished from the ordinary language of men by the epithet to morning. (For we will set aside, at present, the consideration, that the particular word "*smiling*" is hackneyed, and (as it involves a sort of personification) not quite congruous with the common and material attribute of *shining*.) And, doubtless, this adjunction of epithets for the purpose of additional description, where no particular attention is demanded for the quality of the thing, would be noticed as giving a poetic cast to a man's conversation. Should the sportman exclaim, "*come boys! the rosy morning calls you up*," he will be supposed to have some song in his head. But no one suspects this, when he says, "A wet morning shall not confine us to our beds." This then is either a defect in poetry, or it is not. Whoever should decide in the *affirmative*, I would request him to reperuse any one poem, of any confessedly great poet from Homer to Milton, or from Eschylus to Shakspeare; and to strike out (in thought I mean) every instance of this kind. If the number of these fancied erasures did not startle him; or if he continued to deem the work improved by their total omission; he must advance reasons of no ordinary strength and evidence, reasons grounded in the essence of human nature. Otherwise I should not hesitate to consider him as a man not so much *proof against* all

---

[1] Cf. Ezekiel 1.15–21, 10.1–22.

authority, as *dead to* it.

The second line,
   And reddening Phœbus lifts his golden fire.

has indeed almost as many faults as words. But then it is a bad line, not because the language is distinct from that of prose; but because it conveys incongruous images, because it confounds the cause and the effect, the real *thing* with the personified *representative* of the thing; in short, because it differs from the language of GOOD SENSE! That the "Phœbus" is hacknied, and a school-boy image, is an *accidental* fault, dependent on the age in which the author wrote, and not deduced from the nature of the thing. That it is part of an exploded mythology, is an objection more deeply grounded. Yet when the torch of ancient learning was re-kindled, so cheering were its beams, that our eldest poets, cut off by christianity from all *accredited* machinery, and deprived of all *acknowledged* guardians and symbols of the great objects of nature, were naturally induced to adopt, as a *poetic* language, those fabulous personages, those forms of the supernatural[1] in nature, which had given them such dear delight in the poems of their great masters. Nay, even at this day what scholar of genial taste will not so far sympathize with them, as to read with pleasure in PETRARCH, CHAUCER, or SPENSER, what he would perhaps condemn as puerile in a modern poet? …

… To sum up the whole in one sentence. When a poem, or a part of a poem, shall be adduced, which is evidently vicious in the figures and contexture of its style, yet for the condemnation of which no reason can be assigned, except that it differs from the style in which men actually converse, then, and not till then, can I hold this theory to be either plausible, or practicable, or capable of furnishing either rule, guidance, or precaution, that might not, more easily and more safely, as well as more naturally, have been deduced in the author's own mind from considerations of grammar, logic, and the truth and nature of things, confirmed by the authority of works, whose fame is not of ONE country, nor of ONE age.

from CHAPTER 23[2]

I know nothing that contributes more to a clear insight into the true nature of any literary phenomenon, than the comparison of it with some elder production, the *likeness* of which is *striking*, yet only *apparent*: while the *difference* is *real*. In the present case this opportunity is furnished us, by the old Spanish play, entitled *Atheista Fulminato*,[3] formerly, and perhaps still, acted in the churches and monasteries of Spain, and which, under various names *(Don Juan, the Libertine, &c.)* has had its day of favour in every country throughout Europe. A popularity so extensive, and of a work so grotesque and extravagant, claims and merits philosophical attention and investigation. The first point to be noticed is, that the play is throughout *imaginative*. Nothing of it belongs to the real world, but the names of the places and persons. The comic parts, equally with the tragic; the living, equally with the defunct characters, are creatures of the brain; as little amenable to the rules of ordinary probability, as the *Satan* of *Paradise Lost*, or the *Caliban* of the *Tempest*, and therefore to be understood and judged of as impersonated *abstractions*. Rank, fortune, wit, talent, acquired knowledge, and liberal accomplishments, with beauty of person, vigorous health, and constitutional hardihood,—all these advantages, elevated by the habits and sympathies of noble birth and national character, are supposed to have combined in *Don Juan*, so as to give him the means of carrying into all its *practical* consequences the doctrine of a godless nature, as the sole ground and efficient cause not only of all things, events, and appearances, but likewise of all our thoughts, sensations, impulses, and actions. Obedience to nature is the only virtue: the gratification of the passions and appetites her only dictate: each individual's self-will the sole organ through which nature utters her commands, and

---

[1] "But still more by the mechanical system of philosophy which has needlessly infected our theological opinions, and teaching us to consider the world in its relation to God, as of a building to its mason leaves the idea of omnipresence a mere abstract notion in the stateroom of our reason." (S.T.C.)

[2] Byron may have had this passage in mind when choosing the hero for his epic, *Don Juan.*

[3] No play entitled *Atheista Fulminato* ("The Atheist Struck by Lightning") has been discovered. The Don Juan legend was created by Tirso de Molina (Gabriel Téllez, c.1583–1658) in *El Burlador de Sevilla y convidado di piedra* ("The Trickster of Seville and the Stone Guest," 1616?).

> Self-contradiction is the only wrong!
> For by the laws of spirit, in the right
> Is every individual character
> That acts in strict consistence with itself.[1]

That speculative opinions, however impious and daring they may be, are not always followed by correspondent conduct, is most true, as well as that they can scarcely in any instance be *systematically* realized, on account of their unsuitableness to human nature and to the institutions of society. It can be hell, only where it is *all* hell: and a separate world of devils is necessary for the existence of any one complete devil. But on the other hand it is no less clear, nor, with the biography of Carrier[2] and his fellow-atheists before us, can it be denied without wilful blindness, that the (so called) *system of nature*, (i.e., materialism, with the utter rejection of moral responsibility, of a present providence, and of both present and future retribution) may influence the characters and actions of individuals, and even of communities, to a degree that almost does away the distinction between men and devils, and will make the page of the future historian resemble the narration of a madman's dreams. It is not the *wickedness* of *Don Juan*, therefore, which constitutes the character an *abstraction*, and removes it from the rules of probability; but the rapid succession of the correspondent acts and incidents, his intellectual superiority, and the splendid accumulation of his gifts and desirable qualities, as co-existent with *entire* wickedness in one and the same person. But this likewise is the very circumstance which gives to this strange play its charm and universal interest. *Don Juan* is, from beginning to end, an *intelligible* character: as much so as the *Satan* of Milton. The poet asks only of the reader, what as a poet he is privileged to ask: viz. that sort of negative faith in the existence of such a being, which we willingly give to productions *professedly ideal*, and a disposition to the same state of feeling, as that with which we contemplate the *idealized* figures of the Apollo Belvidere, and the Farnese Hercules.[3] What the Hercules is to the *eye* in *corporeal* strength, Don Juan is to the *mind* in strength of *character*. The ideal consists in the happy balance of the generic with the individual. The former makes the character representative and symbolical, therefore instructive; because, *mutatis mutandis*,[4] it is applicable to whole classes of men. The latter gives it *living* interest; for nothing *lives* or is *real*, but as definite and individual. To understand this compleatly, the reader need only recollect the specific state of his feelings, when in looking at a picture of the historic (more properly of the poetic or heroic) class, he objects to a particular figure as being too much of a *portrait*; and this interruption of his complacency he feels without the least reference to, or the least acquaintance with, any person in real life whom he might recognize in this figure. It is enough that such a figure is not *ideal*: and therefore not ideal, because one of the two factors or elements of the *ideal* is in excess. A similar and more powerful objection he would feel towards a set of figures which were *mere* abstractions, like those of Cipriani,[5] and what have been called Greek forms and faces, i.e., outlines drawn according to a recipe. These again are not *ideal*; because in these the *other* element is in excess. "*Forma formans per formam formatam translucens*,"[6] is the definition and perfection of *ideal* art.

This excellence is so happily achieved in the *Don Juan*, that it is capable of interesting without poetry, nay, even without words, as in our pantomime of that name.[7] We see clearly how the character is formed; and the very extravagance of the incidents, and the superhuman *entireness* of *Don Juan's* agency, prevents the wickedness from shocking our minds to any painful degree. (We do not *believe* it enough for this effect; no, not even with that kind of temporary and negative belief or acquiescence which I have described above.) Meantime the qualities of his character are too desirable, too flattering to our pride and our wishes, not to make up on this side as much additional faith as was lost on the other. There is no danger (thinks the spectator or

---

[1] Cf. Coleridge's translation (1800) of Schiller's *Piccolomini* 4.7.191–94.

[2] Jean-Baptiste Carrier (1756–94), radical French Revolutionary.

[3] classical statues admired for their beauty.

[4] "upon changing what needs to be changed" (L.).

[5] Giovanni Battista Cipriani (1727–85), painter and engraver noted for his elaborate style.

[6] "the forming form shining through the formed form" (L.).

[7] Don Juan pantomimes were common; Byron claims to have seen one in *Don Juan* 1.1.*

reader) of *my* becoming such a monster of iniquity as *Don Juan*! *I* never shall be an atheist! *I* shall never disallow all distinction between right and wrong! *I* have not the least inclination to be so outrageous a drawcansir[1] in my love affairs! But to possess such a power of captivating and enchanting the affections of the other sex! to be capable of inspiring in a charming and even a virtuous woman, a love so deep, and so entirely personal to *me!* that even my worst vices, (if I *were* vicious) even my cruelty and perfidy, (if I *were* cruel and perfidious) could not eradicate the passion! To be so loved for my *own self,* that even with a distinct knowledge of my character, she yet died to save me! this, sir, takes hold of two sides of our nature, the better and the worse. For the heroic disinterestedness, to which love can transport a woman, can not be contemplated without an honourable emotion of reverence towards womanhood: and on the other hand, it is among the miseries, and abides in the dark ground-work of our nature, to crave an outward confirmation of that *something* within us, which is our *very self,* that something, not *made up* of our qualities and relations, but itself the supporter and substantial basis of all these. Love *me,* and not my qualities, may be a vicious and an insane wish, but it is not a wish wholly without a meaning....

In fine the character of *Don John* consists in the union of every thing desirable to human nature, as *means,* and which therefore by the well known law of association become at length desirable on their own account. On their own account, and in their own dignity they are here displayed, as being employed to *ends* so *un*human, that in the effect, they appear almost as *means* without an *end.* The ingredients too are mixed in the happiest proportion, so as to uphold and relieve each other—more especially in that constant interpoise of wit, gaiety, and social generosity, which prevents the criminal, even in his most atrocious moments, from sinking into the mere ruffian, as far at least, as our *imagination* sits in judgment. Above all, the fine suffusion through the whole, with the characteristic manners and feelings, of a highly bred gentleman gives life to the drama. Thus having invited the *statue-ghost* of the governor whom he had murdered, to supper, which invitation the marble ghost accepted by a nod of the head, *Don John* has prepared a banquet.

D. JOHN.—Some wine, sirrah! Here's to Don Pedro's ghost—he should have been welcome.

D. LOP.—The rascal is afraid of you after death.

(*One knocks hard at the door.*)

D. JOHN.—(*to the servant*)—Rise and do your duty.

SERV.—Oh the devil, the devil! (*marble ghost enters.*)

D. JOHN.—Ha! 'tis the ghost! Let's rise and receive him! Come Governor you are welcome, sit there; if we had thought you would have come, we would have staid for you.

. . . .

Here Governor, your health! Friends put it about! Here's excellent meat, taste of this ragout. Come, I'll help you, come eat and let old quarrels be forgotten.

(*The ghost threatens him with vengeance.*)

D. JOHN.—We are too much confirmed—curse on this dry discourse. Come, here's to your mistress, you had one when you were living: not forgetting your sweet sister.

(*devils enter.*)

D. JOHN.—Are these some of your retinue? Devils say you? I'm sorry I have no burnt brandy to treat 'em with, that's drink fit for devils. &c.[2]

Nor is the scene from which we quote interesting, in *dramatic* probability alone; it is susceptible likewise of a sound moral; of a moral that has more than common claims on the notice of a too numerous class, who are ready to receive the qualities of gentlemanly courage, and scrupulous honor (in all the recognized laws of honor,) as the *substitutes* of virtue, instead of its *ornaments*.[3] This, indeed, is the moral value of the play at large, and that which places it at a world's distance from the spirit of modern jacobinism. The latter introduces to us clumsy copies of these showy instrumental qualities, in order to *reconcile* us to vice and want of principle; while the *Atheista Fulminato* presents an exquisite portraiture of the same qualities, in all their gloss and glow, but presents them for the sole purpose of display-

---

[1] an aggressive character in George Villiers (1628–87), *The Rehearsal* (1671).

[2] Cf. Thomas Shadwell (c. 1642–92), *The Libertine* (1676) 4.4.

[3] a reminiscence of a speech made by Burke* to the House of Lords, at the end of the impeachment of Warren Hastings, 16 June 1794.

ing their hollowness, and in order to put us on our guard by demonstrating their utter indifference to vice and virtue, whenever these, and the like accomplishments are contemplated for themselves alone.

Eighteen years ago I observed, that the whole secret of the modern jacobinical drama, (which, and not the German, is its appropriate designation,) and of all its popularity, consists in the confusion and subversion of the natural order of things in their causes and effects: namely, in the excitement of surprise by representing the qualities of liberality, refined feeling, and a nice sense of honour (those things rather which pass amongst us for such) in persons and in classes where experience teaches us least to expect them; and by rewarding with all the sympathies which are the due of virtue, those criminals whom law, reason, and religion have excommunicated from our esteem.

from *The Poetical Works of S.T. Coleridge: including the dramas of Wallenstein, Remorse, and Zapolya* (1828)

Constancy to an Ideal Object

Since all, that beat about in Nature's range,
Or veer or vanish; why should'st thou remain
The only constant in a world of change,
O yearning THOUGHT, that liv'st but in the brain?
5 Call to the HOURS, that in the distance play,
The faery people of the future day——
Fond THOUGHT! not one of all that shining swarm
Will breathe on *thee* with life-enkindling breath,
Till when, like strangers shelt'ring from a storm,
10 Hope and Despair meet in the porch of Death!
Yet still thou haunt'st me: and though well I see,
She is not thou, and only thou art she,
Still, still as though some dear *embodied* Good,
Some *living* Love before my eyes there stood
15 With answering look a ready ear to lend,
I mourn to thee and say—"Ah! loveliest Friend!
That this the meed of all my toils might be,
To have a home, an English home, and thee!
Vain repetition! Home and Thou are one.
20 The peacefull'st cot, the moon shall shine upon,
Lulled by the Thrush and wakened by the Lark
Without thee were but a becalmed Bark,
Whose Helmsman on an Ocean waste and wide
Sits mute and pale his mouldering helm beside."
25 And art thou nothing? Such thou art, as when
The woodman winding westward up the glen
At wintry dawn, where o'er the sheep-track's maze
The viewless snow-mist weaves a glist'ning haze,
Sees full before him, gliding without tread,
30 An image[1] with a glory round its head:
The enamoured rustic worships its fair hues,
Nor knows, he *makes* the shadow, he pursues!

Letter[2]

To Joseph Cottle

26 April 1814

You have poured oil in the raw and festering Wound of an old friend's Conscience, Cottle! but it is oil of Vitriol! I but barely glanced at the middle of the first page of your Letter, & have seen no more of it—not from resentment (God forbid!) but from the state of my bodily & mental sufferings, that scarcely permitted human fortitude to let in a new visitor of affliction. The object of my present reply is to state the case just as it is—first, that for years the anguish of my spirit has been indescribable, the sense of my danger *staring*, but the conscience of my GUILT worse, far far worse than all!—I

---

[1] "This phœnomenon, which the Author has himself experienced, and of which the reader may find a description in one of the earlier volumes of the Manchester Philosophical Transactions, is applied figuratively in the following passage of the AIDS to REFLECTION: "'Pindar's fine remark respecting the different effects of music, on different characters, holds equally true of Genius: as many as are not delighted by it are disturbed, perplexed, irritated. The beholder either recognizes it *as a projected form of his own Being, that moves before him with a Glory round its head,* or recoils from it as a spectre.'—AIDS to REFLECTION, p. 220." (S.T.C.) Coleridge, *Aids to Reflection* (1825); Pindar "Pythian Ode" 1.10–14.

[2] from *Collected Letters of Samuel Taylor Coleridge*, ed. Earl Leslie Griggs (1971).

have prayed with drops of agony on my Brow, trembling not only before the Justice of my Maker, but even before the Mercy of my Redeemer. "I gave thee so many Talents. What hast thou done with them"?[1]—Secondly—that it is false & cruel to say, (overwhelmed as I am with the sense of my direful Infirmity) that I attempt or ever have attempted to *disguise* or conceal the cause. On the contrary, not only to friends have I stated the whole Case with tears & the very bitterness of shame; but in two instances I have warned young men, mere acquaintances who had spoken of having taken Laudanum, of the direful Consequences, by an ample exposition of it's tremendous effects on myself—Thirdly, tho' before God I dare not lift up my eyelids, & only do not despair of his Mercy because to despair would be adding crime to crime; yet to my fellow-men I may say, that I was seduced into the ACCURSED Habit ignorantly.—I had been almost bed-ridden for many months with swellings in my knees—in a medical Journal I unhappily met with an account of a cure performed in a similar case (or what to me appeared so) by rubbing in of Laudanum, at the same time taking a given dose internally—It acted like a charm, like a miracle! I recovered the use of my Limbs, of my appetite, of my Spirits—& this continued for near a fortnight—At length, the unusual Stimulus subsided—the complaint returned—the supposed remedy was recurred to——but I can not go thro' the dreary history—suffice it to say, that effects were produced, which acted on me by *Terror* & *Cowardice* of PAIN & sudden Death, not (so help me God!) by any temptation of Pleasure, or expectation or desire of exciting pleasurable Sensations. On the very contrary, Mrs Morgan & her Sister will bear witness so far, as to say that the longer I abstained, the higher my spirits were, the keener my enjoyments—till the moment, the direful moment, arrived, when my pulse began to fluctuate, my Heart to palpitate, & such a dreadful *falling-abroad*, as it were, of my whole frame, such intolerable Restlessness & incipient Bewilderment, that in the last of my several attempts to abandon the dire poison, I exclaimed in agony, what I now repeat in seriousness & solemnity—"I am too poor to hazard this! Had I but a few hundred Pounds, but 200£, half to send to Mrs Coleridge, & half to place myself in a private madhouse, where I could procure nothing but what a Physician thought proper, & where a medical attendant could be constantly with me for two or three months (in less than that time Life or Death would be determined) then there might be Hope. Now there is none!"—O God! how willingly would I place myself under Dr Fox in his Establishment—for my Case is a species of madness, only that it is a derangement, an utter impotence of the *Volition*, & not of the intellectual Faculties—You bid me rouse myself—go, bid a man paralytic in both arms rub them briskly together, & that will cure him. Alas! (he would reply) that I cannot move my arms is my Complaint & my misery.—

My friend, Wade, is not at home—& I sent off all the little money, I had—or I would with this have inclosed the 10£ received from you.—

May God bless you | & | Your affectionate & | most afflicted

S.T. Coleridge.—

Dr Estlin, I found, is raising the city against me, as far as he & his friends can, for having stated a mere matter of fact, … —viz—that Milton had represented Satan as a sceptical Socinian—which is the case, & I could not have explained the excellence of the sublimest single Passage in all his Writings had I not previously informed the Audience, that Milton had represented Satan as knowing the prophetic & Messianic Character of Christ, but sceptical as to any higher Claims—& what other definition could Dr E. himself give of a sceptical Socinian?—Now that M. has done so, please to consult, Par. Regained, Book IV. from line 196.— & then the same Book from line 500.—

---

[1] See Matthew 25.14–30.

Raja Rammohun Roy
1772? – 1833

Rammohun Roy was born in Radhanagore, West Bengal, the son of Ramkanta Roy, an orthodox Brahmin, and Tarini Devi. Educated in Persian, Arabic, Sanskrit, Bengali, and English, Rammohun became a freethinker: when his disapproving father asked him to leave home, he may have studied Buddhism in Tibet—where his independent views are said to have annoyed his teachers. Following his father's death in 1803, Rammohun worked for the East India Company. His publication of a Persian treatise, *Gift to Monotheists* (*Tuhfat-al-muwahhidin*), offended orthodox Muslims. During this period Rammohun studied Hindu, Muslim, and Jain texts, studied English, and followed European events (including the French Revolution).

In 1815 he moved to Calcutta and the next year founded a society for theological discussion across religions, the Atmiya Sabha. He published the *Upanishads* in a translation and edition that defended monotheism against what he perceived as the corruptions of contemporary Hinduism. Considering himself a Hindu Unitarian, Rammohun supported Unitarian Christian missions in India. He agitated against sati (the practice of burning widows on their husbands' funeral pyres): this custom was officially abolished in 1829, largely because of Rammohun's efforts. In 1825 he founded Vedanta College, for teaching the monotheistic doctrines of the *Upanishads*.

Rammohun left for England in 1830, to appeal for an increase in the income allowed by the East India Company to Akbar II (who gave him the title of Raja or king); to ensure that the Suttee Act of 1829 was not repealed; and to hear parliamentary discussion about the renewal of the East India Company charter. He died in Bristol on 27 September 1833. (A.M.)

༄༅༅

from *Petitions Against the Press Regulation* (1823)

Memorial to the Supreme Court[1]

TO THE HONOURABLE SIR FRANCIS MAGNAUGHTEN,[2] *Sole Acting Judge of the Supreme Court of Judicature at Fort William in Bengal.*

MY LORD,

In consequence of the late Rule and Ordinance passed by His Excellency the Governor-General in Council, regarding the Publication of Periodical Works, your Memorialists[3] consider themselves called upon with due submission, to represent to you their feelings and sentiments on the subject.

Your Memorialists beg leave, in the first place, to bring to the notice of your Lordship, various proofs given by the Natives of this country of their unshaken loyalty to, and unlimited confidence in the British Government of India, which may remove from your mind any apprehension of the Government being brought into hatred and contempt, or of the peace, harmony, and good order of society in this country, being liable to be interrupted and destroyed, as implied in the preamble of the above Rule and Ordinance.

First. Your Lordship is well aware, that the Natives of Calcutta and its vicinity, have voluntarily entrusted

---

[1] This document, signed by Rammohun Roy and five other prominent citizens of Calcutta, protested the Press Ordinance of 1823, which required newspapers to obtain a government licence to publish. When the petition was turned down, Rammohun Roy continued to protest by stopping publication of his Persian-language weekly *Mirat-ul-Akhbar* (*The Mirror of News*), which he had launched in April 1822. The Ordinance was not repealed until 1835.

[2] Sir Francis McNaughton was knighted in 1809 when he became Judge of the Supreme Court at Madras, India; in 1815 he was transferred to the Supreme Court of Bengal, and in 1825 he retired from the bench.

[3] writers of a statement of facts accompanying a petition.

Government with millions of their wealth, without indicating the least suspicion of its stability and good faith, and reposing in the sanguine hope that their property being so secured, their interests will be as permanent as the British Power itself; while on the contrary, their fathers were invariably compelled to conceal their treasures in the bowels of the earth, in order to preserve them from the insatiable rapacity of their oppressive Rulers.

Secondly. Placing entire reliance on the promises made by the British Government at the time of the Perpetual Settlement of the landed property in this part of India, in 1793,[1] the Landholders have since, by constantly improving their estates, been able to increase their produce, in general very considerably; whereas, prior to that period, and under former Governments, their forefathers were obliged to lay waste the greater part of their estates, in order to make them appear of inferior value, that they might not excite the cupidity of Government, and thus cause their rents to be increased or themselves to be dispossessed of their lands,—a pernicious practice which often incapacitated the landholders from discharging even their stipulated revenue to Government, and reduced their families to poverty.

Thirdly. During the last wars which the British Government were obliged to undertake against neighbouring Powers,[2] it is well known, that the great body of Natives of wealth and respectability, as well as the Landholders of consequence, offered up regular prayers to the objects of their worship for the success of the British arms from a deep conviction that under the sway of that nation, their improvement, both mental and social, would be promoted, and their lives, religion, and property be secured. Actuated by such feelings, even in those critical times, which are the best test of the loyalty of the subject, they voluntarily came forward with a large portion of their property to enable the British Government to carry into effect the measures necessary for its own defence, considering the cause of the British as their own, and firmly believing that on its success, their own happiness and prosperity depended.

Fourthly. It is manifest as the light of day, that the general subjects of observation and the constant and the familiar topic of discourse among the Hindu community of Bengal, are the literary and political improvements which are continually going on in the state of the country under the present system of Government, and a comparison between their present auspicious prospects and their hopeless condition under their former Rulers.

Under these circumstances, your Lordship cannot fail to be impressed with a full conviction, that whoever charges the Natives of this country with disloyalty, or insinuates aught to the prejudice of their fidelity and attachment to the British Government, must either be totally ignorant of the affairs of this country and the feelings and sentiments of its inhabitants, as above stated, or, on the contrary, be desirous of misrepresenting the people and misleading the Government, both here and in England, for unworthy purposes of his own.

Your Memorialists must confess, that these feelings of loyalty and attachment, of which the most unequivocal proofs stand on record, have been produced by the wisdom and liberality displayed by the British Government in the means adopted for the gradual improvement of their social and domestic condition, by the establishment of Colleges, Schools, and other beneficial institutions in this city, among which the creation of a British Court of Judicature for the more effectual administration of Justice, deserves to be gratefully remembered.

A proof of the Natives of India being more and more attached to the British Rule in proportion as they experience from it the blessings of just and liberal treatment, is, that the Inhabitants of Calcutta, who enjoy in many respects very superior privileges to those of their fellow-subjects in other parts of the country, are known to be in like measure more warmly devoted to the existing Government; nor is it at all wonderful they should in loyalty be not at all inferior to British-born Subjects, since they feel assured of the possession of the

---

[1] Concluded under Charles Cornwallis, 1st Marquess Cornwallis (Governor-General from 1786–93), the Permanent Settlement of 1793 was a contract between the East India Company and the Bengal landholders whereby the landholders became the absolute proprietors of landed property at a fixed rent in perpetuity.

[2] the war with France and the ensuing Napoleonic Wars (1793–1815).

same civil and religious liberty, which is enjoyed in England, without being subjected to such heavy taxation as presses upon the people there.

Hence the population of Calcutta, as well as the value of land in this City, have rapidly increased of late years, notwithstanding the high rents of houses and the dearness of all the necessaries of life compared with other parts of the country, as well as the Inhabitants being subjected to additional taxes, and also liable to the heavy costs necessarily incurred in case of suits before the Supreme Court.

Your Lordship may have learned from the works of the Christian Missionaries, and also from other sources, that ever since the art of printing has become generally known among the Natives of Calcutta, numerous Publications have been circulated in the Bengalee Language, which by introducing free discussion among the Natives and inducing them to reflect and inquire after knowledge, have already served greatly to improve their minds and ameliorate their condition. This desirable object has been chiefly promoted by the establishment of four Native Newspapers, two in the Bengalee and two in the Persian Language, published for the purpose of communicating to those residing in the interior of the country, accounts of whatever occurs worthy of notice at the Presidency[1] or in the country, and also the interesting and valuable intelligence of what is passing in England and in other parts of the world, conveyed through the English Newspapers or other channels.

Your Memorialists are unable to discover any disturbance of the peace, harmony, and good order of society, that has arisen from the English Press, the influence of which must necessarily be confined to that part of the community who understand the language thoroughly; but they are quite confident, that the publications in the Native Languages, whether in the shape of a Newspaper or any other work, have none of them been calculated to bring the Government of the country into hatred and contempt, and that they have not proved, as far as can be ascertained by the strictest inquiry, in the slightest degree injurious; which has very lately been acknowledged in one of the most respectable English Missionary works. So far from obtruding upon Government groundless representations, Native Authors and Editors have always restrained themselves from publishing even such facts respecting the judicial proceedings in the Interior of the country as they thought were likely at first view to be obnoxious to Government.

While your Memorialists were indulging the hope that Government, from a conviction of the manifold advantages of being put in possession of full and impartial information regarding what is passing in all parts of the Country, would encourage the establishment of Newspapers in the cities and districts under the special patronage and protection of Government, that they might furnish the Supreme Authorities in Calcutta with an accurate account of local occurrences and reports of Judicial proceedings,—they have the misfortune to observe, that on the contrary, his Excellency the Governor-General in Council[2] has lately promulgated a Rule and Ordinance imposing severe restraints on the Press and prohibiting all Periodical Publications even at the Presidency and in the Native Languages, unless sanctioned by a License from Government, which is to be revocable at pleasure whenever it shall appear to Government that a publication has contained anything of an unsuitable character.

Those Natives who are in more favourable circumstances and of respectable character, have such an invincible prejudice against making a voluntary affidavit, or undergoing the solemnities of an oath, that they will never think of establishing a publication which can only be supported by a series of oaths and affidavits, abhorrent to their feelings and derogatory to their reputation amongst their countrymen.

After this Rule and Ordinance shall have been carried into execution, your Memorialists are therefore extremely sorry to observe, that a complete stop will be put to the diffusion of knowledge and the consequent mental improvement now going on, either by translations into the popular dialect of this country from the learned languages of the East, or by the circulation of

---

[1] the Presidency of Fort William in Bengal, of which Calcutta was the capital, covered the entire north-east part of India.

[2] In 1823 the interim Governor General was John Adam, during whose brief term of office the Press Ordinance was issued.

literary intelligence drawn from foreign publications. And the same cause will also prevent those Natives who are better versed in the laws and customs of the British Nation, from communicating to their fellow-subjects a knowledge of the admirable system of Government established by the British, and the peculiar excellencies of the means they have adopted for the strict and impartial administration of justice. Another evil, of equal importance in the eyes of a just Ruler, is, that it will also preclude the Natives from making the Government readily acquainted with the errors and injustice that may be committed by its executive officers in the various parts of this extensive country; and it will also preclude the Natives from communicating frankly and honestly to their Gracious Sovereign in England and his Council, the real condition of his Majesty's faithful subjects in this distant part of his dominions and the treatment they experience from the local Government: since such information cannot in future be conveyed to England, as it has heretofore been, either by the translations from the Native publications inserted in the English Newspapers printed here and sent to Europe, or by the English publications which the Natives themselves had in contemplation to establish, before this Rule and Ordinance was proposed.

After this sudden deprivation of one of the most precious of their rights, which has been freely allowed them since the Establishment of the British Power, a right which they are not, and cannot be charged with having ever abused, the inhabitants of Calcutta would be no longer justified in boasting, that they are fortunately placed by Providence under the protection of the whole British Nation, or that the King of England and his Lords and Commons are their Legislators, and that they are secured in the enjoyment of the same civil and religious privileges that every Briton is entitled to in England.

Your Memorialists are persuaded that the British Government is not disposed to adopt the political maxim so often acted upon by Asiatic Princes, that the more a people are kept in darkness, their Rulers will derive the greater advantages from them; since, by reference to History, it is found that this was but a short-sighted policy which did not ultimately answer the purpose of its authors. On the contrary, it rather proved disadvantageous to them; for we find that as often as an ignorant people, when an opportunity offered, have revolted against their Rulers, all sorts of barbarous excesses and cruelties have been the consequence; whereas a people naturally disposed to peace and ease, when placed under a good Government from which they experience just and liberal treatment, must become the more attached to it, in proportion as they become enlightened and the great body of the people are taught to appreciate the value of the blessings they enjoy under its Rule.

Every good Ruler, who is convinced of the imperfection of human nature, and reverences the Eternal Governor of the world, must be conscious of the great liability to error in managing the affairs of a vast empire; and therefore he will be anxious to afford every individual the readiest means of bringing to his notice whatever may require his interference. To secure this important object, the unrestrained Liberty of Publication, is the only effectual means that can be employed. And should it ever be abused, the established Law of the Land is very properly armed with sufficient powers to punish those who may be found guilty of misrepresenting the conduct or character of Government, which are effectually guarded by the same Laws to which individuals must look for protection of their reputation and good name.

Your memorialists conclude by humbly entreating your Lordship to take this Memorial into your gracious consideration; and that you will be pleased by not registering the above Rule and Ordinance, to permit the Natives of this country to continue in possession of the civil rights and privileges which they and their fathers have so long enjoyed under the auspices of the British nation, whose kindness and confidence, they are not aware of having done anything, to forfeit.

CHUNDER COOMAR TAGORE,
DWARKA NAUTH TAGORE,
RAMMOHUN ROY,
HURCHUNDER GHOSE,
GOWREE CHURN BONNERGEE,
PROSSUNNO COOMAR TAGORE.

Abstract of the Arguments regarding the Burning of Widows, Considered as a Religious Rite (1830)[1]

Several Essays, Tracts, and Letters, written in defence of or against the practice of burning Hindu widows alive have for some years past attracted the attention of the public. The arguments therein adduced by the parties being necessarily scattered, a complete view of the question cannot be easily attained by such readers as are precluded by their immediate avocations from bestowing much labour in acquiring information on the subject. Although the practice itself has now happily ceased to exist under the Government of Bengal,[2] nevertheless it seems still desirable that the substance of those publications should be condensed in a concise but comprehensive manner, so that enquirers may with little difficulty, be able to form a just conclusion, as to the true light in which this practice is viewed in the religion of Hindus. I have, therefore, made an attempt to accomplish this object, hoping that the plan pursued may be found to answer this end.

The first point to be ascertained is, whether or not the practice of burning widows alive on the pile and with the corpse of their husbands, is imperatively enjoined by the Hindu religion? To this question even the staunch advocates for Concremation[3] must reluctantly give a negative reply, and unavoidably concede the practice to the option of widows. This admission on their part is owing to two principal considerations, which it is now too late for them to feign to overlook. First, because Manu[4] in plain terms enjoins a widow to "*continue till death* forgiving all injuries, performing austere duties, avoiding every sensual pleasure, and cheerfully practising the incomparable rules of virtue which have been followed by such women as were devoted to one only husband." (ch. v., v. 158.)[5] So Yajnavalkya inculcates the same doctrine: "A widow shall live under care of her father, mother, son, brother, mother-in-law, father-in-law, or uncle; since, on the contrary, she shall be liable to reproach." (*Vide* Mitakshara, ch. i.)[6] Secondly, because an attempt on the part of the advocates for Concremation to hold out the act as an incumbent duty on widows, would necessarily bring a stigma upon the character of the living widows, who have preferred a virtuous life to Concremation, as charging them with a violation of the duty said to be indispensible. These advocates, therefore, feel deterred from giving undue praise to a few widows, choosing death on the pile, to the disgrace of a vast majority of that class preferring a virtuous life. And in consideration of these obvious circumstances, the celebrated Smartta Raghunandana,[7] the latest commentator on Hindu Law in Bengal, found himself compelled to expound the following passage of Angira, "there is no other course for a widow besides Concremation,"[8] as "conveying exag-

---

[1] In 1829 the British government outlawed suttee (or "sati"; literally, "good woman"), the practice of burning widows alive on their husbands' funeral pyres. Advocates of suttee appealed unsuccessfully to the British Parliament to have the legislation overturned. In this *Abstract*, Rammohun Roy summarizes the arguments against suttee; see also his *Translation of a Conference between an Advocate for, and an Opponent of, the Practice of Burning Widows Alive; from the Original Bungla* (Calcutta, 1818) and *A Second Conference between an Advocate for, and an Opponent of the Practice of Burning Widows Alive* (Calcutta, 1820), both rpt. in *The English Works of Raja Rammohun Roy* (Bahadurganj, Allahabad: Panini Office, 1906).

[2] The practice was outlawed by the government of Lord William Cavendish Bentinck (1774–1839), Governor General from 1828–35; his council included Sir Stapleton Cotton, Viscount Combermere (1772–1865), William Butterworth Bayley (1781–1860), director of the East India Company and acting Governor General in 1828, and Charles Theophilus Metcalfe, 1st Baron Metcalfe (1785–1846), who would serve as acting Governor General in 1835–36.

[3] literally, the act of burning things together.

[4] a Hindu law-giver, author of *Manu Smriti* (*The Laws of Manu*, dating from 200 BC–AD 200).

[5] *Laws of Manu* 5.158.

[6] Yajnavalkya is a Hindu sage (c. 1800 BC), a major figure in the *Upanishads* (commentary on the Vedas). The *Mitakshara* is an 11th-century commentary on the laws of Yajnavalkya (*Yajnavalkya Smriti*).

[7] a legal commentator from Bengal (1510–1580).

[8] *Apararka* on Angiras, from *Apararka Yajnavalkya Dharmasastra*, a commentary on *Mitakshara* by the Apararka or Aparaditya (12th C.); Angiras (R.R. consistently spells the name "Angira") was a Hindu sage and law-giver.

gerated praise of the adoption of that course."[1]

The second point is, that in case the alternative be admitted, that a widow may either live a virtuous life, or burn herself on the pile of her husband, it should next be determined whether both practices are esteemed equally meritorious, or one be declared preferable to the other. To satisfy ourselves on this question, we should first refer to the Vedas,[2] whose authority is considered paramount, and we find in them a passage most pointed and decisive against Concremation, declaring that "From a desire, during life, of future fruition, life ought not to be destroyed." (*Vide* Mitakshara, ch. i.) While the advocates of Concremation quote a passage from the Vedas, of a very abstruse nature, in support of their position, which is as follows: "O fire, let these women, with bodies anointed with clarified butter, eyes coloured with collyrium and void of tears, enter thee, the parent of water, that they may not be separated from their husbands, themselves sinless, and jewels amongst women."[3] This passage (if genuine) does not, in the first place, enjoin widows to offer themselves as sacrifices; secondly, no allusion whatever is made in it to voluntary death by a widow *with the corpse of her husband*; thirdly, the phrase "these women" in the passage, literally implies women then present; fourthly, some commentators consider the passage as conveying an allegorical allusion to the constellations of the moon's path, which are invariably spoken of in Sanskrit in the feminine gender:—butter implying the milky path, collyrium meaning unoccupied space between one star and another, husbands signifying the more splendid of the heavenly bodies, and entering the fire, or, properly speaking, ascending it, indicating the rise of the constellations through the south-east horizon, considered as the abode of fire. Whatever may be the real purport of this passage, no one ever ventured to give it an interpretation as *commanding* widows to burn themselves on the pile and with the corpse of their husbands.

We next direct attention to the Smriti,[4] as next in authority to the Vedas. Manu, whose authority supersedes that of other law-givers, enjoins widows to live a virtuous life, as already quoted. Yajnavalkya and some others have adopted the same mode of exhortation. On the other hand, Angira recommends the practice of Concremation, saying, "That a woman who, on the death of her husband, *ascends the burning pile* with him, is exalted to heaven as equal to Arundhati."[5] So Vyasa says, "A pigeon devoted to her husband, after his death, *entered the flames*, and, ascending to heaven, she there found her husband."[6] "She who follows her husband to another world, shall dwell in a region of glory for so many years as there are hairs in the human body, or thirty-five millions."[7] Vishnu, the saint, lays down this rule, "After the death of her husband, a wife should live as an ascetic or ascend his pile."[8] Harita and others have followed Angira in recommending Concremation.

The above quoted passages, from Angira and others, recommend Concremation on the part of widows, as means to obtain future carnal fruition; and, accordingly, previous to their ascent on the pile, all widows invariably and solemnly declare future fruition as their object in Concremation. But the Bhagavadgita,[9] whose authority is considered the most sacred by Hindus of all persuasions, repeatedly condemns rites performed for fruition. I here quote a few passages of that book. "All those ignorant persons who attach themselves to the words of the Sastras that convey promises of fruition, consider those extravagant and alluring passages as leading to real happiness, and say, besides them there is

---

[1] Raghunandana on Angiras.

[2] Hindu scriptures, also known as the Shruti canon ("what is heard").

[3] Rig Veda 10.18.7; the Rig Veda is the earliest of Hindu scriptures.

[4] a canon of Hindu scriptures ("what deserves to be remembered"; laws), secondary in importance to Shruti (the *Vedas*).

[5] *Mitaksara* on Angiras; Arundhati is the wife of Brahmarsi Vasistha, revered for her devotion to her husband.

[6] *Mitaksara* on Vyasa, the ascribed author of the Sanskrit epic *Mahabharata*.

[7] *Mitaksara* on Angiras.

[8] *Vishnu Dharmasutra* 25.14, quoted in *Mitaksara*. Vishnu, like Harita in the next sentence, is a sage and law-giver.

[9] one of the main scriptures of the Hindus, comprising part of the *Mahabharata* and belonging to the *Upanishads* or philosophical portion of the Vedas.

no other reality. Agitated in their minds by these desires, they believe the abodes of the celestial gods to be the chief object, and they devote themselves to those texts which treat of ceremonies and their fruits, and entice by promises of enjoyment. Such people can have no real confidence in the Supreme Being."[1] "Observers of rites, after the completion of their rewards, return to earth. Therefore they, for the sake of rewards, repeatedly ascend to heaven and return to the world, and cannot obtain eternal bliss."[2]

Manu repeats the same. "Whatever act is performed for the sake of gratification in this world or the next, is called Pravartak, as leading to the temporary enjoyment of the mansions of gods; and those which are performed according to the knowledge respecting God are called Nivartak, as means to procure release from the five elements of this body; that is, they obtain eternal bliss."[3]

The author of the Mitakshara, a work which is considered as a standard of Hindu Law throughout Hindustan, referring on the one hand to the authority of Manu, Yajnavalkya, the Bhagavadgita, and similar sacred writings, and to the passages of Angira, Harita and Vyasa on the other hand, and after having weighed both sides of the question, declares that "The widow who is not desirous of eternal beatitude, but who wishes only for a perishable and small degree of future fruition, is authorized to accompany her husband." So that the Smartta Raghuandana, the modern expounder of Law in Bengal, classes Concremation among the rites holding out promise of fruition; and this author thus inculcates: "Learned men should not endeavour to persuade the ignorant to perform rites holding out promises of fruition." Hence, Concremation, in their opinion, is the least virtuous act that a widow can perform.

The third and the last point to be ascertained is whether or not *the mode* of Concremation prescribed by Harita and others was ever duly observed. The passages recommending Concremation, as quoted by these expounders of law, require that a widow, resolving to die after the demise of her husband, should *voluntarily ascend and enter the flames to destroy her existence*;[4] allowing her, at the same time, an opportunity of retracting her resolution, should her courage fail from the alarming sight or effect of the flames, and of returning to her relatives, performing a penance for abandoning the sacrifice,[5] or bestowing the value of a cow on a Brahman.[6] Hence, as *voluntarily ascending* upon and *entering into the flames* are described as indispensably necessary for a widow in the performance of this rite, the violation of one of these provisions renders the act mere suicide, and implicates, in the guilt of female murder, those that assist in its perpetration, even according to the above quoted authorities, which are themselves of an inferior order. But no one will venture to assert, that the provisions, prescribed in the passages adduced, have ever been observed; that is, no widow ever voluntarily *ascended* on and *entered* into the *flames* in the fulfilment of this rite. The advocates for Concremation have been consequently driven to the necessity of taking refuge in *usage*, as justifying both suicide and female murder, the most heinous of crimes.

We should not omit the present opportunity of offering up thanks to Heaven, whose protecting arm has rescued our weaker sex from cruel murder, under the cloak of religion, and our character, as a people, from the contempt and pity with which it has been regarded, on account of this custom, by all civilized nations on the surface of the globe.

---

[1] *Bhagavad Gita* 2.42–44; sastras (or shastras) are sacred texts.

[2] *Bhagavad Gita* 9.21.

[3] *Laws of Manu* 12.88–90.

[4] *Mitaksara* on Angiras and on Vyasa.

[5] *Apastambha Dharmasutra*, quoted in *Apararka*.

[6] A Brahman or Brahmin is a member of the highest of the Hindu castes.

Christian Milne
1772? – after 1816

Christian Ross was baptized in Inverness, Scotland, on 19 May 1772, the daughter of Mary Gordon and Thomas Ross, a cabinet-maker. Her mother died when she was very young; following her father's remarriage, the family moved to Auchintoul, Banffshire, where Milne learned to read, knit, write, and do arithmetic. At the age of fourteen she went to Aberdeen as a servant, continuing to write in secret. In the Preface to her *Simple Poems on Simple Subjects*, she would remark on the difficulties of writing poetry under such circumstances: "I began to write down my little pieces; though, having no opportunity of shewing them to people of education, I had the mortification to find myself laughed at, and called idle by my fellow servants."

About the same time her father suffered financial disaster and her brother was drowned at sea. She and her widowed father moved to Edinburgh on foot, where she worked as a servant for a lawyer, supporting her father as his only surviving child and continuing to write poetry. Following a severe illness at age nineteen, she returned to Aberdeen, where she worked for various employers including the principal of King's College, who encouraged her to keep writing. At twenty-four, she married Patrick Milne, a ship's carpenter, with whom she had eight surviving children. Her *Simple Poems on Simple Subjects*, written in moments snatched from attending to her children and her domestic work, was published by subscription and dedicated to the duchess of Gordon, her patron.

Not much is known about Milne's later life. In 1816 she was living in the fishing village of Footdee, saving the profits from her book, teaching her children, and barely surviving on her husband's half pay and whatever she could earn from sewing while he was in America. She published no further poetry. (A.M.)

❦

from *Simple Poems, on Simple Subjects. By Christian Milne, Wife of a Journeyman Ship-Carpenter in Footdee, Aberdeen* (1805)

To a Lady, Who Said It Was Sinful to Read Novels

To love these Books, and harmless Tea,
    Has always been my foible,
Yet will I ne'er forgetful be
    To read my Psalms and Bible.

5 Travels I like, and Hist'ry too,
    Or entertaining Fiction;
Novels and Plays I'd have a few,
    If sense and proper diction.

I love a natural harmless Song,
10   But cannot sing like HANDEL;[1]
Depriv'd of such resource, the tongue
    Is sure employ'd——in scandal.

Sent with a Flower Pot, Begging a Slip of Geranium

I've sent my empty pot again,
    To beg another slip;
The last you gave, I'm griev'd to tell,
    December's frost did nip.

5 I love fair FLORA[2] and her train,
    But nurse her children ill;
I tend too little or too much;
    They die from want of skill.

I blush to trouble you again,
10   Who've serv'd me oft before;
But, should this die, I'll break the pot,
    And trouble you no more.

---

[1] George Frederick Handel (1685–1759), German-born composer who settled in England in 1712.

[2] Roman goddess of flowers.

Francis Jeffrey
1773 – 1850

Francis Jeffrey was born in Edinburgh on 23 October 1773, third of the five children of George Jeffrey, Clerk of the Court of Session, and Henrietta Louden Jeffrey, a farmer's daughter. He was educated at the Edinburgh High School, Glasgow University, and Queen's College, Oxford; then he studied law in Edinburgh. He was called to the bar in 1794. He is remembered mainly for his contributions to the Whig *Edinburgh Review*, the most influential journal of the period, which he helped to found in 1802 and of which he soon became the editor.

Jeffrey had married Catherine Wilson in November 1801; they had one child, who died in infancy, and Catherine died in August 1805. Despondent, Jeffrey accepted a challenge from Thomas Moore,* who had taken offense at a review. They met in London on 11 August 1806 but were arrested before the duel could proceed. The police discovered that Jeffrey had not bothered to load his pistol. He and Moore later became friends. In 1810, he fell in love with Charlotte Wilkes, and in 1813—despite the ongoing War of 1812—he followed her to America to marry her. They had one daughter.

In 1829, Jeffrey, who had continued to practice law, was elected Dean of the Faculty of Advocates; he gave up the *Edinburgh Review*. In 1831, he was elected to Parliament, and in 1834 he was made a judge. In his later years he befriended such emerging Victorian writers as the Carlyles, Dickens, and Thomas Babington Macaulay. He died on 26 January 1850. (D.L.M.)

❧❧❧

from the *Edinburgh Review, or Critical Journal* 24 (Nov. 1814)

from ART. 1 *The Excursion, being a portion of the Recluse, a Poem.* By William Wordsworth

This will never do. It bears no doubt the stamp of the author's heart and fancy; but unfortunately not half so visibly as that of his peculiar system. His former poems were intended to recommend that system, and to bespeak favour for it by their individual merit;—but this, we suspect, must be recommended by the system—and can only expect to succeed where it has been previously established. It is longer, weaker, and tamer, than any of Mr Wordsworth's other productions; with less boldness of originality, and less even of that extreme simplicity and lowliness of tone which wavered so prettily, in the Lyrical Ballads, between silliness and pathos. We have imitations of Cowper, and even of Milton here, engrafted on the natural drawl of the Lakers—[1] and all diluted into harmony by that profuse and irrepressible wordiness which deluges all the blank verse of this school of poetry, and lubricates and weakens the whole structure of their style.

Though it fairly fills four hundred and twenty good quarto pages, without note, vignette, or any sort of extraneous assistance, it is stated in the title—with something of an imprudent candour—to be but "a portion" of a larger work; and in the preface, where an attempt is rather unsuccessfully made to explain the whole design, it is still more rashly disclosed, that it is but "a part of the second part of a *long* and laborious work"—which is to consist of three parts.[2]

What Mr Wordsworth's ideas of length are, we have no means of accurately judging; but we cannot help suspecting that they are liberal, to a degree that will alarm the weakness of most modern readers. As far as we can gather from the preface, the entire poem—or one of them, for we really are not sure whether there is to be

---

[1] Coleridge,* Southey,* and W. Wordsworth* were known as the Lake Poets because they lived in the Lake District.

[2] W. Wordsworth actually projected a four-part *The Recluse*, of which he finished only *The Prelude* and *The Excursion*.

one or two—is of a biographical nature; and is to contain the history of the author's mind, and of the origin and progress of his poetical powers, up to the period when they were sufficiently matured to qualify him for the great work on which he has been so long employed. Now, the quarto before us contains an account of one of his youthful rambles in the vales of Cumberland, and occupies precisely the period of three days; so that, by the use of a very powerful *calculus*, some estimate may be formed of the probable extent of the entire biography.

This small specimen, however, and the statements with which it is prefaced, have been sufficient to set our minds at rest in one particular. The case of Mr Wordsworth, we perceive, is now manifestly hopeless; and we give him up as altogether incurable, and beyond the power of criticism. We cannot indeed altogether omit taking precautions now and then against the spreading of the malady;—but for himself, though we shall watch the progress of his symptoms as a matter of professional curiosity and instruction, we really think it right not to harass him any longer with nauseous remedies,—but rather to throw in cordials and lenitives, and wait in patience for the natural termination of the disorder. In order to justify this desertion of our patient, however, it is proper to state why we despair of the success of a more active practice.

A man who has been for twenty years at work on such matter as is now before us, and who comes complacently forward with a whole quarto of it after all the admonitions he has received, cannot reasonably be expected to "change his hand, or check his pride," upon the suggestion of far weightier monitors than we can pretend to be. Inveterate habit must now have given a kind of sanctity to the errors of early taste; and the very powers of which we lament the perversion, have probably become incapable of any other application. The very quantity, too, that he has written, and is at this moment working up for publication upon the old pattern, makes it almost hopeless to look for any change of it. All this is so much capital already sunk in the concern; which must be sacrificed if it be abandoned: and no man likes to give up for lost the time and talent and labour which he has embodied in any permanent production. We were not previously aware of these obstacles to Mr Wordsworth's conversion; and, considering the peculiarities of his former writings merely as the result of certain wanton and capricious experiments on public taste and indulgence, conceived it to be our duty to discourage their repetition by all the means in our power. We now see clearly, however, how the case stands;—and, making up our minds, though with the most sincere pain and reluctance, to consider him as finally lost to the good cause of poetry, shall endeavour to be thankful for the occasional gleams of tenderness and beauty which the natural force of his imagination and affections must still shed over all his productions,—and to which we shall ever turn with delight, in spite of the affectation and mysticism and prolixity, with which they are so abundantly contrasted.

Long habits of seclusion, and an excessive ambition of originality, can alone account for the disproportion which seems to exist between this author's taste and his genius; or for the devotion with which he has sacrificed so many precious gifts at the shrine of those paltry idols which he has set up for himself among his lakes and his mountains. Solitary musings, amidst such scenes, might no doubt be expected to nurse up the mind to the majesty of poetical conception,—(though it is remarkable, that all the greater poets lived, or had lived, in the full current of society):—But the collision of equal minds,—the admonition of prevailing impressions—seems necessary to reduce its redundancies, and repress that tendency to extravagance or puerility, into which the self-indulgence and self-admiration of genius is so apt to be betrayed, when it is allowed to wanton, without awe or restraint, in the triumph and delight of its own intoxication. That its flights should be graceful and glorious in the eyes of men, it seems almost to be necessary that they should be made in the consciousness that men's eyes are to behold them,—and that the inward transport and vigour by which they are inspired, should be tempered by an occasional reference to what will be thought of them by those ultimate dispensers of glory. An habitual and general knowledge of the few settled and permanent maxims, which form the canon of general taste in all large and polished societies—a certain tact, which informs us at once that many things, which we still love and are moved by in secret, must necessarily be despised as childish, or derided as absurd, in all such societies—though it will not stand in the place of genius, seems necessary to the success of its exertions; and though it will never enable any one to produce the higher beauties of art, can alone secure the talent which does produce them, from errors that must render it useless. Those who have most of the talent, however, commonly acquire this knowledge with the greatest facility;—and if Mr Wordsworth, instead of confining himself almost entirely to the society of the dalesmen and cottagers, and little children, who form the subjects of his book, had condescended to mingle a little more with the people that were to read and judge of it, we cannot help thinking, that its texture would have been considerably improved: At least it appears to us to be absolutely impossible, that any one who had lived or mixed familiarly with men of literature and ordinary judgment in poetry, (of course we exclude the coadjutors and disciples of his own school), could ever have fallen into such gross faults, or so long mistaken them for beauties. His first essays we looked upon in a good degree as poetical paradoxes,—maintained experimentally, in order to display talent, and court notoriety;—and so maintained, with no more serious belief in their truth, than is usually generated by an ingenious and animated defence of other paradoxes. But when we find, that he has been for twenty years exclusively employed upon articles of this very fabric, and that he has still enough of raw material on hand to keep him so employed for twenty years to come, we cannot refuse him the justice of believing that he is a sincere convert to his own system, and must ascribe the peculiarities of his composition, not to any transient affectation, or accidental caprice of imagination, but to a settled perversity of taste or understanding, which has been fostered, if not altogether created, by the circumstances to which we have already alluded.

The volume before us, if we were to describe it very shortly, we should characterize as a tissue of moral and devotional ravings, in which innumerable changes are rung upon a few very simple and familiar ideas:—but with such an accompaniment of long words, long sentences, and unwieldy phrases—and such a hubbub of strained raptures and fantastical sublimities, that it is often extremely difficult for the most skilful and attentive student to obtain a glimpse of the author's meaning—and altogether impossible for an ordinary reader to conjecture what he is about. Moral and religious enthusiasm, though undoubtedly poetical emotions, are at the same time but dangerous inspirers of poetry; nothing being so apt to run into interminable dulness or mellifluous extravagance, without giving the unfortunate author the slightest intimation of his danger. His laudable zeal for the efficacy of his preachments, he very naturally mistakes for the ardour of poetical inspiration;—and, while dealing out the high words and glowing phrases which are so readily supplied by themes of this description, can scarcely avoid believing that he is eminently original and impressive:—All sorts of commonplace notions and expressions are sanctified in his eyes, by the sublime ends for which they are employed; and the mystical verbiage of the methodist pulpit is repeated, till the speaker entertains no doubt that he is the elected organ of divine truth and persuasion. But if such be the common hazards of seeking inspiration from those potent fountains, it may easily be conceived what chance Mr Wordsworth had of escaping their enchantment,—with his natural propensities to wordiness, and his unlucky habit of debasing pathos with vulgarity. The fact accordingly is, that in this production he is more obscure than a Pindaric poet of the seventeenth century;[1] and more verbose "than even himself of yore"; while the wilfulness with which he persists in choosing his examples of intellectual dignity and tenderness exclusively from the lowest ranks of society, will be sufficiently apparent, from the circumstance of his having thought fit to make his chief prolocutor in this poetical dialogue, and chief advocate of Providence and Virtue, *an old Scotch Pedlar*—retired indeed from business—but still rambling about in his former haunts, and gossiping among his old customers, without his pack on his shoulders. The other persons of the drama are, a retired military chaplain, who has grown half an atheist and half a misanthrope—the wife

---

[1] Poets like Abraham Cowley (1618–67) and John Dryden (1631–1700) wrote complex and difficult odes in imitation of the Greek poet Pindar (c. 522–443 BC).

of an unprosperous weaver—a servant girl with her infant—a parish pauper, and one or two other personages of equal rank and dignity.

The character of the work is decidedly didactic; and more than nine tenths of it are occupied with a species of dialogue, or rather a series of long sermons or harangues which pass between the pedlar, the author, the old chaplain, and a worthy vicar, who entertains the whole party at dinner on the last day of their excursion. The incidents which occur in the course of it are as few and trifling as can be imagined;—and those which the different speakers narrate in the course of their discourses, are introduced rather to illustrate their arguments or opinions, than for any interest they are supposed to possess of their own.—The doctrine which the work is intended to enforce, we are by no means certain that we have discovered. In so far as we can collect, however, it seems to be neither more nor less than the old familiar one, that a firm belief in the providence of a wise and beneficent Being must be our great stay and support[1] under all afflictions and perplexities upon earth—and that there are indications of his power and goodness in all the aspects of the visible universe, whether living or inanimate—every part of which should therefore be regarded with love and reverence, as exponents of those great attributes. We can testify, at least, that these salutary and important truths are inculcated at far greater length, and with more repetitions, than in any ten volumes of sermons that we ever perused. It is also maintained, with equal conciseness and originality, that there is frequently much good sense, as well as much enjoyment, in the humbler conditions of life; and that, in spite of great vices and abuses, there is a reasonable allowance both of happiness and goodness in society at large. If there be any deeper or more recondite doctrines in Mr Wordsworth's book, we must confess that they have escaped us;—and, convinced as we are of the truth and soundness of those to which we have alluded, we cannot help thinking that they might have been better enforced with less parade and prolixity. His effusions on what may be called the physiognomy of external nature, or its moral and theological expression, are eminently fantastic, obscure, and affected[2]....

These examples, we perceive, are not very well chosen—but we have not leisure to improve the selection; and, such as they are, they may serve to give the reader a notion of the sort of merit which we meant to illustrate by their citation.—When we look back to them, indeed, and to the other passages which we have now extracted, we feel half inclined to rescind the severe sentence which we passed on the work at the beginning:—But when we look into the work itself, we perceive that it cannot be rescinded. Nobody can be more disposed to do justice to the great powers of Mr Wordsworth than we are; and, from the first time that he came before us, down to the present moment, we have uniformly testified in their favour, and assigned indeed our high sense of their value as the chief ground of the bitterness with which we resented their perversion.[3] That perversion, however, is now far more visible than their original dignity; and while we collect the fragments, it is impossible not to lament the ruins from which we are condemned to pick them. If any one should doubt of the existence of such a perversion, or be disposed to dispute about the instances we have hastily brought forward, we would just beg leave to refer him to the general plan and the characters of the poem now before us.—Why should Mr Wordsworth have made his hero a superannuated Pedlar? What but the most wretched and provoking perversity of taste and judgment, could induce any one to place his chosen advocate of wisdom and virtue in so absurd and fantastic a condition? Did Mr Wordsworth really imagine, that his favourite doctrines were likely to gain any thing in point of effect or authority by being put into the mouth of a person accustomed to higgle about tape, or brass sleeve-buttons? Or is it not plain that, independent of the ridicule and disgust which such a personification must give to many of his readers, its adoption exposes his work throughout to the charge of revolting incongruity,

---

[1] Cf. W. Wordsworth, "Resolution and Independence" 146.*

[2] Jeffrey goes on to summarize and assess *The Excursion*, quoting long excerpts from the text to illustrate his points.

[3] In fact, Jeffrey had described *Poems in Two Volumes* (1807) as "trash."

and utter disregard of probability or nature? For, after he has thus willfully debased his moral teacher by a low occupation, is there one word that he puts into his mouth, or one sentiment of which he makes him the organ, that has the most remote reference to that occupation? Is there any thing in his learned, abstracted, and logical harangues, that savours of the calling that is ascribed to him? Are any of their materials such as a pedlar could possibly have dealt in? Are the manners, the diction, the sentiments, in any, the very smallest degree, accommodated to a person in that condition? or are they not eminently and conspicuously such as could not by possibility belong to it? A man who went about selling flannel and pocket-handkerchiefs in this lofty diction, would soon frighten away all his customers; and would infallibly pass either for a madman, or for some learned and affected gentleman, who, in a frolic, had taken up a character which he was peculiarly ill qualified for supporting.

The absurdity in this case, we think, is palpable and glaring; but it is exactly of the same nature with that which infects the whole substance of the work—a puerile ambition of singularity engrafted on an unlucky predilection for truisms; and an affected passion for simplicity and humble life, most awkwardly combined with a taste for mystical refinements, and all the gorgeousness of obscure phraseology. His taste for simplicity is evinced, by sprinkling up and down his interminable declamations, a few descriptions of baby-houses,[1] and of old hats with wet brims;[2] and his amiable partiality for humble life, by assuring us, that a wordy rhetorician, who talks about Thebes,[3] and allegorizes all the heathen mythology, was once a pedlar—and making him break in upon his magnificent orations with two or three awkward notices of something that he had seen when selling winter raiment about the country—or of the changes in the state of society, which had almost annihilated his former calling.

---

[1] W. Wordsworth, *The Excursion* 2.425.

[2] W. Wordsworth, *The Excursion* 1.445.*

[3] the ancient capital of Egypt: W. Wordsworth, *The Excursion* 8.216.

Robert Southey
1774 – 1843

Robert Southey was born in Bristol on 12 August 1774, the oldest surviving child of Robert Southey, a draper, and Margaret Hill Southey. (Only three of his eight siblings lived to grow up.) At the age of two he was consigned to the care of his maternal aunt. He was educated at a boarding school and then at Westminster School, from which he was expelled for publishing a satire on flogging in the school newspaper. He spent only two terms at Balliol College, Oxford, but there he made one of the most important friendships of his life, with Coleridge.* Together they planned to establish a "Pantisocratic" or egalitarian commune in Pennsylvania; to raise money for this plan, they collaborated on the first of his forty-five books, *The Fall of Robespierre: An Historic Drama* (1794), and as part of it, they married Edith and Sarah Fricker. But the plan fell through, and Southey spent 1795–96 travelling in Spain and Portugal instead; he revisited the area in 1800 and would eventually become one of England's greatest experts on Spanish culture. He published the first of his five epics, *Joan of Arc*, in 1796; it was a success. Like Coleridge and W. Wordsworth* (with whom he also became friends), Southey began as a radical but became more conservative as he grew older. In 1803, after the death of his first child (he and Edith had eight children, but only four lived to grow up), he accepted Coleridge's invitation to come and live with him at Greta Hall, Keswick, in the Lake District; he would live there for the next forty years, and in time would assume responsibility for the wife and children of the wayward Coleridge, and for Edith and Sarah's widowed sister Mary. The three poets came to be called the Lake Poets, though they did not think of themselves as a school and Coleridge subsequently spent little time in the area.

In 1813, the Prince Regent made Southey poet laureate; but by then his career as a poet was largely over: he published his last epic, *Roderick, the Last of the Goths*, in 1814, and thereafter dedicated himself mainly to prose, writing criticism for the *Quarterly Review*; histories of Brazil (1810–19) and the Peninsular War (1823–32); biographies of Nelson (1813), Wesley (1820), Cowper* (1835), and the British Admirals (1833–40); and a seven-volume novel, *The Doctor* (1834–47), which is notable for the inclusion of "The Story of the Three Bears."

Edith became mentally ill in 1834 and died in 1837. In 1839, Southey married an old friend, Caroline Bowles, but he began to suffer from dementia soon afterwards. Even after he could no longer read his 14,000 books, his son reported, they "remained a pleasure to him": "he would walk slowly round his library, looking at them and taking them down mechanically." He had a stroke and died on 21 March 1843. (D.L.M.)

☙❧☙

from *Poems* (1797)

To Mary Wollstonecraft

The lilly cheek, the "purple light of love,"[1]
The liquid lustre of the melting eye,—
Mary! of these the Poet sung, for these
Did Woman triumph! with no angry frown
5   View this degrading conquest. At that age
No MAID OF ARC[2] had snatch'd from coward man
The heaven-blest sword of Liberty; thy sex
Could boast no female ROLAND's martyrdom;[3]

---

[1] Thomas Gray (1716–71), *The Progress of Poesy* (1757) 41.

[2] Jeanne d'Arc (c. 1412–31) was inspired by angelic voices to lead the French against the English in the Hundred Years' War. In 1429, she raised the siege of Orléans and arranged for the coronation of Charles VII; later, she was captured by the English, tried for sorcery, and burned at the stake. She was the subject of Southey's first epic poem (1796).

[3] Jeanne Manon Philipon Roland (1754–93), wife of a Girondin (moderate) Revolutionary cabinet minister and an important political figure in her own right. She was guillotined in 1793; on her way to the scaffold, she exclaimed, "O Liberty, what crimes are committed in your name!"

No CORDE's angel and avenging arm[1]
10 Had sanctified again the Murderer's name
As erst when Caesar perish'd:[2] yet some strains
May even adorn this theme, befitting me
To offer, nor unworthy thy regard.

The Widow. Sapphics[3]

Cold was the night wind, drifting fast the snows fell,
Wide were the downs and shelterless and naked,
When a poor Wanderer struggled on her journey
    Weary and way-sore.

5   Drear were the downs, more dreary her reflections;
Cold was the night wind, colder was her bosom!
She had no home, the world was all before her,[4]
    She had no shelter.

Fast o'er the bleak heath rattling drove a chariot,
10 "Pity me!" feebly cried the poor night wanderer.
"Pity me Strangers! lest with cold and hunger
    Here I should perish.

"Once I had friends,—but they have all forsook me!
Once I had parents,—they are now in Heaven!
15 I had a home once—I had once a husband—
    Pity me Strangers!

"I had a home once—I had once a husband—
I am a Widow poor and broken-hearted!"
Loud blew the wind, unheard was her complaining,
20   On drove the chariot.

On the cold snows she laid her down to rest her;
She heard a horseman, "pity me!" she groan'd out;
Loud blew the wind, unheard was her complaining,
    On went the horseman.

25 Worn out with anguish, toil and cold and hunger,
Down sunk the Wanderer, sleep had seiz'd her senses;
There, did the Traveller find her in the morning,
    GOD had releast her.

The Soldier's Wife. Dactylics[5]

Weary way-wanderer languid and sick at heart
Travelling painfully over the rugged road,
Wild-visag'd Wanderer! ah for thy heavy chance!

Sorely thy little one drags by thee bare-footed,
5   Cold is the baby that hangs at thy bending back
Meagre and livid and screaming its wretchedness.

Woe-begone mother, half anger, half agony,
As over thy shoulder thou lookest to hush the babe,
Bleakly the blinding snow beats in thy hagged face.[6]

10 Thy husband will never return from the war again,
Cold is thy hopeless heart even as Charity—
Cold are thy famish'd babes—God help thee,
    widow'd One!

from the *Morning Post* (30 June 1798)

The Idiot[7]

The circumstance related in the following ballad happened some years since in Herefordshire.

It had pleas'd God to form poor Ned,
A thing of idiot mind,

---

[1] Charlotte Corday (1768–93), a sympathizer with the Girondins, assassinated the extremist Revolutionary Jean-Paul Marat on 13 July 1793; she was guillotined shortly afterwards.

[2] In 44 BC, Julius Caesar was assassinated by a group of conspirators including his adopted son Brutus, who feared he was going to proclaim himself king.

[3] The metre of the poem was supposedly invented by the Greek poet Sappho (7th century BC). Cf. the parody by Canning and Frere, "The Friend of Humanity and the Knife-Grinder."*

[4] Cf. Milton, *Paradise Lost* 12.646.

[5] This title also refers to the poem's metre, based on a poetic foot comprising one stressed and two unstressed syllables.

[6] "This stanza was supplied by S.T. COLERIDGE." (R.S.)

[7] Cf. W. Wordsworth, "The Idiot Boy."*

    Yet to the poor, unreas'ning man,
        God had not been unkind.

5 Old Sarah lov'd her helpless child,
        Whom helplessness made dear,
    And life was happiness to him,
        Who had no hope nor fear.

    She knew his wants, she understood
10   Each half-artic'late call,
    And he was ev'ry thing to her,
        And she to him was all.

    And so for many a year they dwelt,
        Nor knew a wish beside,
15 But age at length on Sarah came,
        And she fell sick and died.

    He tried in vain to waken her,
        And call'd her o'er and o'er.
    They told him she was dead—the sound
20   To him no import bore.

    They clos'd her eyes and shrouded her,
        And he stood wond'ring by,
    And when they bore her to the grave,
        He follow'd silently.

25 They laid her in the narrow house,
        They sung the fun'ral stave;
    But when the fun'ral train dispers'd,
        He loiter'd by the grave.

    The rabble boys who us'd to jeer
30   Whene'er they saw poor Ned,
    Now stood and watch'd him at the grave,
        And not a word they said.

    They came and went and came again,
        Till night at last came on,
35 And still he loiter'd by the grave,
        Till all to rest were gone.

    And when he found himself alone,
        He swift remov'd the clay,
    And rais'd the coffin up in haste,
40   And bore it swift away.

    And when he reach'd his hut, he laid
        The coffin on the floor,
    And with the eagerness of joy,
        He barr'd the cottage door.

45 And out he took his mother's corpse,
        And plac'd it in her chair,
    And then he heapt the hearth, and blew
        The kindling fire with care.

    He plac'd his mother in her chair,
50   And in her wonted place,
    And blew the kindling fire, that shone
        Reflected on her face:

    And pausing now, her hand would feel,
        And now her face behold,
55 "Why, mother, do you look so pale,
        And why are you so cold?"

    It had pleas'd God from the poor wretch
        His only friend to call,
    But God was kind to him, and soon
        In death restor'd him all.

from *Poems* (1799)

The Sailor, Who Had Served in the Slave-Trade[1]

    He stopt,—it surely was a groan
        That from the hovel came!
    He stopt and listened anxiously
        Again it sounds the same.

5 It surely from the hovel comes!
        And now he hastens there,
    And thence he hears the name of Christ
        Amidst a broken prayer.

---

[1] first published in the *Morning Post* (9 August 1798).

He entered in the hovel now,
    A sailor there he sees,
His hands were lifted up to Heaven
    And he was on his knees.

Nor did the Sailor so intent
    His entering footsteps heed,
But now the Lord's prayer said, and now
    His half-forgotten creed.[1]

And often on his Saviour call'd
    With many a bitter groan,
In such heart-anguish as could spring
    From deepest guilt alone.

He ask'd the miserable man
    Why he was kneeling there,
And what the crime had been that caus'd
    The anguish of his prayer.

Oh I have done a wicked thing!
    It haunts me night and day,
And I have sought this lonely place
    Here undisturb'd to pray.

I have no place to pray on board
    So I came here alone,
That I might freely kneel and pray,
    And call on Christ and groan.

If to the main-mast head I go,
    The wicked one is there,
From place to place, from rope to rope,
    He follows every where.

I shut my eyes,—it matters not—
    Still still the same I see,—
And when I lie me down at night
    'Tis always day with me.

He follows follows every where,
    And every place is Hell![2]
O God—and I must go with him
    In endless fire to dwell.

He follows follows every where,
    He's still above—below,
Oh tell me where to fly from him!
    Oh tell me where to go!

But tell me, quoth the Stranger then,
    What this thy crime hath been,
So haply I may comfort give
    To one that grieves for sin.

O I have done a cursed deed
    The wretched man replies,
And night and day and every where
    'Tis still before my eyes.

I sail'd on board a Guinea-man[3]
    And to the slave-coast went;
Would that the sea had swallowed me
    When I was innocent!

And we took in our cargo there,
    Three hundred negroe slaves,
And we sail'd homeward merrily
    Over the ocean waves.

But some were sulky of the slaves
    And would not touch their meat,
So therefore we were forced by threats
    And blows to make them eat.

One woman sulkier than the rest
    Would still refuse her food,—
O Jesus God! I hear her cries—
    I see her in her blood!

---

[1] "Our Father" (15): the Lord's Prayer (Matthew 6.9–13); "creed": a statement of faith in Christianity, which the sailor would have learned in Sunday school.

[2] Cf. Milton, *Paradise Lost* 4.75.

[3] a slave ship: "Guinea" was the west coast of Africa.

The Captain made me tie her up
    And flog while he stood by,
And then he curs'd me if I staid
    My hand to hear her cry.

She groan'd, she shriek'd—I could not spare
    For the Captain he stood by—
Dear God! that I might rest one night
    From that poor woman's cry!

She twisted from the blows—her blood
    Her mangled flesh I see—
And still the Captain would not spare—
    Oh he was worse than me!

She could not be more glad than I
    When she was taken down,
A blessed minute—'twas the last
    That I have ever known!

I did not close my eyes all night,
    Thinking what I had done;
I heard her groans and they grew faint
    About the rising sun.

She groan'd and groan'd, but her groans grew
    Fainter at morning tide,
Fainter and fainter still they came
    Till at the noon she died.

They flung her overboard;—poor wretch
    She rested from her pain,—
But when—o Christ! o blessed God!
    Shall I have rest again!

I saw the sea close over her,
    Yet she was still in sight;
I see her twisting every where;
    I see her day and night.

Go where I will, do what I can
    The wicked one I see—
Dear Christ have mercy on my soul,
    O God deliver me!

To morrow I set sail again
    Not to the Negroe shore—
Wretch that I am I will at least
    Commit that sin no more.

O give me comfort if you can—
    Oh tell me where to fly—
And bid me hope, if there be hope,
    For one so lost as I.

Poor wretch, the stranger he replied,
    Put thou thy trust in heaven,
And call on him for whose dear sake
    All sins shall be forgiven.

This night at least is thine, go thou
    And seek the house of prayer,
There shalt thou hear the word of God
    And he will help thee there!

from the *Annual Anthology* (1800)

The Battle of Blenheim[1]

It was a Summer evening,
    Old Kaspar's work was done,
And he before his cottage door
    Was sitting in the sun;
And by him sported on the green
His little grandchild Wilhelmine.

She saw her brother Peterkin
    Roll something large and round,
That he beside the rivulet
    In playing there had found;
He came to know what he had found,
That was so large, and light, and round.

Old Kaspar took it from the boy,
    Who stood expectant by—

---

[1] On 13 August 1704, the English under John Churchill, Duke of Marlborough, and Prince Eugene of Savoy defeated the French at the Battle of Blenheim, part of the War of the Spanish Succession.

15 And then the old man shook his head,
    And with a nat'ral sigh,
'Tis some poor fellow's skull, said he,
Who fell in the great Victory.

I find them in the garden—for
20   There's many here about;
And often when I go to plough,
    The ploughshare turns them out;
For many thousand men, said he,
Were slain in the great Victory.

25 Now tell us what 'twas all about,
    Young Peterkin he cries;
And little Wilhelmine looks up
    With wonder-waiting eyes.
Now tell us all about the war,
30 And what they kill'd each other for?

It was the English, Kaspar cried,
That put the French to rout;
But what they kill'd each other for
    I could not well make out;
35 But ev'ry body said, quoth he,
That 'twas a famous Victory.

My father liv'd at Blenheim then,
    Yon little stream hard by;
They burnt his dwelling to the ground—
40   And he was forc'd to fly:—
So with his wife and child he fled,
Nor had they where to rest their head.

With fire and sword the country round
    Was wasted far and wide,
45 And many a childing mother then,
    And new-born infant died;
But things like these, you know, must be
At ev'ry famous Victory.

They say it was a shocking sight
50   After the field was won,
For many thousand bodies here
    Lay rotting in the sun;

But things like that, you know, must be
After a famous Victory.

55 Great praise the Duke of Marlbro' won,
    And our good Prince Eugene.
Why 'twas a very wicked thing,
    Said little Wilhelmine.
Nay, nay, my little girl, quoth he,
60 It was a famous Victory.

And ev'ry body prais'd the Duke
    Who such a fight did win.
But what good came of it at last?
    Quoth little Peterkin.
65 Why that I cannot tell, quoth he;
But 'twas a famous Victory.

from *Letters from England: by Don Manuel Alvarez Espriella. Translated from the Spanish* (1807)[1]

LETTER 55

Curiosity and Credulity of the English.—The Wild Indian Woman.—The Large Child.—The Wandering Jew.—The Ethiopian Savage.—The Great High German Highter-Flighter.—The Learned Pig.

My morning's walk has supplied me with two instances of English credulity. Passing through St. George's-fields[2] I saw a sort of tent pitched, at the entrance of which a fellow stood holding a board in his hand, on which was painted in large letters "*The Wild Indian Woman.*"— "What," said I to my companion, "do you catch the

---

[1] Like Montesquieu, *Lettres Persanes* (1721) and Oliver Goldsmith,* *The Citizen of the World* (1762), Southey's book only pretends to give a foreigner's viewpoint. Southey adopts the persona of a Catholic Spanish traveller recording often critical observations of English life.

[2] the land between Southwark and Lambeth on the south bank of the Thames, undeveloped in Southey's time.

savages and show them like wild beasts? This is worse than even the slave trade!" "We will go in and see," said he. Accordingly we paid our sixpence each, and, to our no small amusement, found one of the lowest order of the worst kind of women, her face bedaubed with red and yellow, her hair stuck with feathers, drest in cat skins, and singing some unintelligible gibberish in the true cracked voice of vulgar depravity. A few passers-by, as idle and more ignorant than ourselves, who had in like manner been taken in, were gazing at her in astonishment, and listening open-mouthed to the rogue who told a long story how she came from the wilds of America, where the people are heathen folk and eat one another.—We had not gone a mile further before another showman, with a printed paper on his showboard, invited our attention again—"*To be seen here, the surprising Large Child.*" This was a boy who seemed to be about four years old; and because he was stupid, and could only articulate a few words very imperfectly, his parents swore he was only of eighteen months—and were showing him for a prodigy.

A few years ago there was a fellow with a long beard in London, who professed himself to be the Wandering Jew.[1] He did not adhere to the legend, which was of little consequence, as his visitors were not likely to be better informed than himself,—but laid claim to higher antiquity than the Jerusalem shoe-maker, and declared that he had been with Noah in the ark.[2] Noah, he said, had refused to take him in; but he got in secretly, and hid himself among the beasts, which is the reason why his name is not mentioned in the Bible; and while he was there the he-goat had given him a blow on the forehead, the mark of which was visible to this day. Some person asked him which country he liked best of all that he had visited in his long peregrinations: he answered "Spain," as perhaps a man would have done who had really seen all the world. But it was remarked as rather extraordinary that a Jew should prefer the country of the Inquisition.[3] "God bless you, sir!" replied the ready rogue, shaking his head and smiling at the same time, as if at the error of the observations,—"it was long before Christianity that I was last in Spain, and I shall not go there again till long after it is all over!"

Any thing in England will do for a show. At one of the provincial fairs J.[4] saw a shaved monkey exhibited for a Fairy; and a shaved bear in a check waistcoat and trowsers sitting in an armed chair as an Ethiopian savage. The unnatural position to which the poor animal had been tortured, and the accursed brutality of his keeper, a woman, who sate upon his lap, put her arm round his neck, and called him husband and sweet-heart and kissed him, made this, he says, the most hideous and disgusting sight he had ever witnessed. A fellow at one of these fairs once exhibited a large dragon-fly through a magnifying glass, as the Great High German Highter-Flighter. But the most extraordinary instance of witty impudence and blind curiosity which I have ever heard of, occurred at Cirencester in the province of Gloucestershire, where a man showed for a penny apiece, the fork which belonged to the knife with which Margaret Nicholson attempted to kill the King.[5]

Nothing is too absurd to be believed by the people in this country. Some time ago there was a woman who went about showing herself for money, with a story that she had been pregnant three years. There was something extraordinary concerning this impostor; for the house in which she lived, which stood upon the shore in the province, or shire as it is called of Sussex, had no other walls or roof than laths and brown-paper pitched over. It had stood three years without injury, when the person who related this to me saw it. In the last reign[6] the

---

[1] The legend of the Wandering Jew, who insulted Christ on his way to Calvary and so was doomed to wander the Earth until the Second Coming, has been traced to John 18.20–22; it was first elaborated in the 13th century.

[2] See Genesis 6–8.

[3] the Inquisition, an ecclesiastical tribunal intended to suppress heresy in the Roman Catholic Church, was not finally abolished in Spain until 1834.

[4] the narrator's English friend and travelling companion.

[5] Following her stabbing of George III in August 1786, Margaret Nicholson (c.1750–1828) spent the rest of her life in Bedlam Hospital. P.B. Shelley* and Thomas Jefferson Hogg published a volume of poems under the title *Posthumous Fragments of Margaret Nicholson* (1810).

[6] "This circumstance happened in the latter end of the reign of George I [1714–27]." (R.S.)

whole kingdom was astonished by a woman who pretended to breed rabbits, and the king's surgeons were appointed by the state to examine her.—Many persons are living who can remember when the people of London went to see a man get into a quart bottle. This trick was practised for a wager, which some one who knew the world ventured upon its credulity; but as impudent a one was played off by a sharper in the city of Bristol at a later period. He promised to make himself invisible, collected a company of spectators, received their money for admittance, appeared on the stage before them, and saying, "Now, gentlemen and ladies, you see me,"—opened a trap-door and descended, and ran off with his gains.

Any thing that is strange, or that is called strange, a tall man or a short man, a Goitre or an Albino, a white negro or a spotted negro, which may be made at any time with little difficulty and no pain, a great ox or a fat pig, no matter what the wonder be, and no matter how monstrous or how disgusting, it will attract crowds in England. There was a woman born without arms, who made a good livelihood by writing and cutting paper with her toes. One family support themselves by living in a travelling cart, made in the shape of the vessel wherein the English boil water for their tea, the spout of which is the chimney. The learned pig[1] was in his day a far greater object of admiration to the English nation than ever was sir Isaac Newton.[2] I met a person once who had lived next door to the lodgings of this erudite swine, and in a house so situated that he could see him at his rehearsals. He told me he never saw the keeper beat him; but that, if he did not perform his lesson well, he used to threaten to take off his red waistcoat,—for the pig was proud of his dress. Perhaps even Solomon himself did not conceive that vanity was so universal a passion.[3]

Yet from this indiscriminate curiosity some general good arises. Natural history has been considerably improved by the opportunities afforded of examining rare animals, which would not have been brought from remote countries for the mere purposes of science. Posture-makers and stone-eaters have demonstrated strange and anomalous powers in the human body; and the docility of animals, which has thus been practised upon for the sake of immediate gain, may one day be applied to better and more important purposes. Animals have no natural fear of man:—the birds on a desert island are as fearless as they were in Paradise, and suffer him to approach till he knocks them on the head. The power of the Eastern jugglers, who by a song call forth the serpents from their holes, is not more wonderful than that which has been acquired over bees in England. The horse of the Arab is as well domesticated, and as affectionately attached to his master, as the dog of the European. The cattle from one end of Africa to the other are under the most perfect obedience to their keeper; a boy will collect a herd of a thousand by his whistle: by this easy language they are made to attack an armed enemy as readily as to come to their milker; and they have thus overthrown soldiers who had conquered the elephants of the East and the cavalry of Europe. When man shall cease to be the tyrant of inferior beings he may truly become their lord.

from *A Collection of Poems, Chiefly Manuscript, and from Living Authors*, ed. Joanna Baillie (1823)

The Cataract of Lodore, Described in Rhymes for the Nursery, by One of the Lake Poets[4]

How does the water come down at Lodore?
    Here it comes sparkling,
    And there it lies darkling;
    Here smoking and frothing,
    Its tumult and wrath in,
  It hastens along, conflicting strong;

---

[1] See Boswell's *Life of Johnson*, November 1784.

[2] Sir Isaac Newton (1642–1727) was President of the Royal Society and one of the founders of modern science.

[3] Solomon, King of Israel, was renowned for wisdom: see 1 Kings 3 and Ecclesiastes (attributed to Solomon) 1.2, 1.14, 2.1.

[4] The cataract is near Southey's home in Keswick. Southey later revised and added to this first printed version of the poem, written for his children.

           Now striking and raging,
           As if a war waging,
           Its caverns and rocks among.
10   Rising and leaping,
           Sinking and creeping,
           Swelling and flinging,
           Showering and springing,
           Eddying and whisking,
15   Spouting and frisking,
           Turning and twisting
               Around and around,
           Collecting, disjecting
               With endless rebound;
20   Smiting and fighting,
           A sight to delight in,
           Confounding, astounding,
    Dizzying and deafening the ear with its sound.

           Receding and speeding,
25   And shocking and rocking,
           And darting and parting,
           And threading and spreading,
           And whizzing and hissing,
           And dripping and skipping,
30   And whitening and brightening,
           And quivering and shivering,
           And hitting and splitting,
           And shining and twining,
           And rattling and battling,
35   And shaking and quaking,
           And pouring and roaring,
           And waving and raving,
           And tossing and crossing,
           And flowing and growing,
40   And running and stunning,
           And hurrying and skurrying,
           And glittering and frittering,
           And gathering and feathering,
           And dinning and spinning,
45   And foaming and roaming,
           And dropping and hopping,
           And working and jerking,
           And guggling and struggling,
           And heaving and cleaving,

50   And thundering and floundering,
           And falling and brawling and sprawling,
           And driving and riving and striving,
           And sprinkling and twinkling and wrinkling,
           And sounding and bounding and rounding,
55   And bubbling and troubling and doubling,
           Dividing and gliding and sliding,
           And grumbling and rumbling and tumbling,
           And clattering and battering and shattering,
           And gleaming and streaming and steaming and
               beaming,
60   And rushing and flushing and brushing and gushing,
           And flapping and rapping and clapping and slapping,
           And curling and whirling and purling and twirling,
           Retreating and beating and meeting and sheeting,
           Delaying and straying and playing and spraying,
65   Advancing and prancing and glancing and dancing,
           Recoiling, turmoiling and toiling and boiling,
           And thumping and flumping and bumping and
               jumping,
           And dashing and flashing and splashing and clashing,
           And so never ending, but always descending,
70   Sounds and motions for ever and ever are blending,
           All at once and all o'er, with a mighty uproar,
           And this way the water comes down at Lodore.

from *The Poetical Works of Robert Southey* (1853)

Bishop Bruno[1]

"Bruno, the Bishop of Herbipolitanum, sailing in the river of Danubius, with Henry the Third, then Emperor, being not far from a place which the Germanes call *Ben Strudel*, or the devouring gulfe, which is neere into Grinon, a castle in Austria, a spirit was heard clamouring aloud, 'Ho, ho, Bishop Bruno, whither art thou travelling? but dispose of thyselfe how thou pleasest, thou shalt be my prey and spoil.' At the hearing of these words they were all stupified, and the Bishop with the rest crost and blest themselves. The issue was, that within a short time after, the Bishop, feasting with the Emperor in a castle belonging to the Countesse of

---

[1] written in 1798.

Esburch, a rafter fell from the roof of the chamber wherein
they sate, and strooke him dead at the table."
—*Heywood's Hierarchie of the Blessed Angels*[1]

Bishop Bruno awoke in the dead midnight,
And he heard his heart beat loud with affright:
He dreamt he had rung the Palace bell,
And the sound it gave was his passing knell.

5 Bishop Bruno smiled at his fears so vain,
He turn'd to sleep and he dreamt again;
He rang at the Palace gate once more,
And Death was the Porter that open'd the door.

He started up at the fearful dream,
10 And he heard at his window the screech-owl scream;
Bishop Bruno slept no more that night, …
Oh! glad was he when he saw the daylight!

Now he goes forth in proud array,
For he with the Emperor dines to-day;
15 There was not a Baron in Germany
That went with a nobler train than he.

Before and behind his soldiers ride,
The people throng'd to see their pride;
They bow'd the head, and the knee they bent,
20 But nobody blest him as he went.

So he went on stately and proud,
When he heard a voice that cried aloud,
"Ho, ho! Bishop Bruno! you travel with glee, …
But I would have you know, you travel to me!"

25 Behind and before and on either side,
He look'd, but nobody he espied;
And the Bishop at that grew cold with fear,
For he heard the words distinct and clear.

And when he rang at the Palace bell,
30 He almost expected to hear his knell;
And when the Porter turn'd the key,
He almost expected Death to see.

But soon the Bishop recover'd his glee,
For the Emperor welcomed him royally;
35 And now the tables were spread, and there
Were choicest wines and dainty fare.

And now the Bishop had blest the meat,
When a voice was heard as he sat in his seat, …
"With the Emperor now you are dining with glee,
40 But know, Bishop Bruno! you sup with me!"

The Bishop then grew pale with affright,
And suddenly lost his appetite;
All the wine and dainty cheer
Could not comfort his heart that was sick with fear.

45 But by little and little recovered he,
For the wine went flowing merrily,
Till at length he forgot his former dread,
And his cheeks again grew rosy red.

When he sat down to the royal fare
50 Bishop Bruno was the saddest man there;
But when the masquers enter'd the hall,
He was the merriest man of all.

Then from amid the masquers' crowd
There went a voice hollow and loud, …
55 "You have pass'd the day, Bishop Bruno, in glee;
But you must pass the night with me!"

His cheek grows pale, and his eye-balls glare,
And stiff round his tonsure bristled his hair;
With that there came one from the masquers' band,
60 And took the Bishop by the hand.

The bony hand suspended his breath,
His marrow grew cold at the touch of Death;
On saints in vain he attempted to call.
Bishop Bruno fell dead in the Palace hall.

---

[1] Thomas Heywood (1574?–1641), *The Hierarchy of the Blessed Angels* (1635).

My Days Among the Dead Are Passed[1]

1

My days among the Dead are past;
    Around me I behold,
Where'er these casual eyes are cast,
    The mighty minds of old;
My never-failing friends are they,
With whom I converse day by day.

2

With them I take delight in weal,
    And seek relief in woe;
And while I understand and feel
    How much to them I owe,
My cheeks have often been bedew'd
With tears of thoughtful gratitude.

3

My thoughts are with the Dead, with them
    I live in long-past years,
Their virtues love, their faults condemn,
    Partake their hopes and fears,
And from their lessons seek and find
Instruction with an humble mind.

4

My hopes are with the Dead, anon
    My place with them will be,
And I with them shall travel on
    Through all Futurity;
Yet leaving here a name, I trust,
That will not perish in the dust.

---

[1] first published in 1823.

Walter Savage Landor
1775 – 1864

Walter Savage Landor was born on 30 January 1775 at Warwick, the son of Walter Landor, a physician and landowner, and Elizabeth Savage Landor, an heiress. He was educated at Rugby and Trinity College, Oxford, from both of which he was expelled, and then embarked on a life of travel, study, and writing. *The Poems of Walter Savage Landor*, the first of his 50 books and pamphlets of poetry and prose, appeared in 1795. His most successful writings were his series of over 150 *Imaginary Conversations* (1824–29) in prose, in which the speakers include Plato, Hannibal, Cicero, Caesar, Lady Godiva, Fra Filippo Lippi, Henry VIII, Sir Philip Sidney, Milton, Newton, Chesterfield, Franklin, Washington, and Southey.* In 1811, Landor married Julia Thuillier; they had four children, but he never addressed any poems to her, and they separated in 1835. Despite his tempestuous temper and radical politics, over a long life Landor befriended the Brownings, Carlyle, Coleridge,* Dickens, Emerson, the Lambs,* M.W. Shelley,* Southey, Tennyson, Trelawny,* and W. Wordsworth.* He died in Florence on 17 September 1864. (D.L.M.)

❧

from *Simonidea* (1806)[1]

[*Rose Aylmer*][2]

Ah what avails the sceptred race,
    Ah what the form divine!
What, every virtue, every grace!
    For, Aylmer, all were thine.

5 Sweet Aylmer, whom these wakeful eyes
    May weep, but never see,
A night of sorrows and of sighs
    I consecrate to thee.

Mother, I Cannot Mind My Wheel[3]

Mother, I cannot mind my wheel;
    My fingers ache, my lips are dry:
Oh! if you felt the pain I feel!
    But Oh, who ever felt as I?

5 No longer could I doubt him true;
    All other men may use deceit:
He always said my eyes were blue,
    And often swore my lips were sweet.

---

[1] In his Preface, Landor comments, "These poems are called Simonidea, because the first of them commemorate the dead: a species of composition in which Simonideas excelled...." Simonides of Cos (556–468 BC), a Greek lyric poet, was famous for his epitaphs.

[2] Landor met Rose Aylmer, daughter of Baron Aylmer, in Swansea in 1796; he was "not indifferent" to her. In 1799, she sailed to Calcutta to join her uncle, a justice on the Supreme Court there. The next year, only twenty, she died of cholera.

[3] Cf. Goethe (1749–1832), *Faust*, Part 1, scene 15 ("Gretchen's Room"). The scene already occurs in *Faust: Ein Fragment* (1790).

from *Gebir, Count Julian, and Other Poems* (1831)

Past ruin'd Ilion Helen lives

Past ruin'd Ilion[1] Helen lives,
    Alcestis[2] rises from the shades;
Verse calls them forth; 'tis verse that gives
    Immortal youth to mortal maids.

Soon shall Oblivion's deepening veil
    Hide all the peopled hills you see,
The gay, the proud, while lovers hail
    In distant ages you and me.

The tear for fading beauty check,
    For passing glory cease to sigh;
One form shall rise above the wreck,
    One name, Ianthe,[3] shall not die.

---

[1] Troy; Helen's part in its ruin is commemorated in Homer's *Iliad* and *Odyssey*.

[2] Euripides' *Alcestis* tells how Alcestis sacrificed her life to save her husband and was brought back from the grave by Heracles.

[3] "Narcissus" (Gr.): Jane Sophia Swift, the great love of Landor's life. Cf. note to Landon, *The Improvisatrice* 1440.*

Mary Lamb
1764 – 1847
Charles Lamb
1775 – 1834

Mary Lamb was born in London on 3 December 1764; her brother Charles, on 10 February 1775. Their father, John Lamb, was a lawyer's servant; their mother, Elizabeth Field Lamb, was a housekeeper's daughter. Mary, Charles, and their older brother, John, were the only three of the Lambs' seven children to grow up. Mary received some schooling; Charles and John went to Christ's Hospital, where Charles met Coleridge,* who became a lifelong friend. Because his stammer made him unsuitable for the priesthood, Charles was not sent on to university; instead, he became a clerk, first at South Sea House and then at the East India Company, where, though he hated the job, he stayed for thirty-three years. Mary became a dressmaker and assumed responsibility for their aging parents.

Both suffered from mental illness. In 1795, after being rejected by his sweetheart Ann Simmons, Charles had a breakdown. Then, on 22 September 1796, Mary stabbed their mother to death and assaulted their father. The coroner's jury brought in a verdict of lunacy and Mary was never charged with murder, but she was confined in a madhouse. John thought she should be confined for life, but Charles refused. As soon as she was well enough, he found her lodgings; when their father died in 1799, he brought her home, and they lived together for the rest of his life. It wasn't easy: her attacks of insanity recurred regularly and became longer and more severe as she grew older. The social stigma attached to her illness meant that they had to move frequently. "Our love for each other," Mary remarked in 1806, "has been the torment of our lives"; later, Charles complained: "'tis a tedious cut out of a life of sixty-four to lose twelve or thirteen weeks every year or two." But when she was well, they enjoyed an active social life, entertaining writers such as Coleridge, Hazlitt,* Hunt,* and W. Wordsworth.* In 1819, Charles proposed to Fanny Kelly, an actor, who rejected him. In 1823, Charles and Mary informally adopted a teenaged orphan, Emma Isola, who lived with them until her marriage in 1833.

In 1798, Charles published *Rosamund Gray*, a novel based on his relationship with Simmons, and in 1802 *John Woodvil*, a tragedy. His anthology of extracts from the plays of Shakespeare's contemporaries (1808) contributed significantly to the revival of interest in Elizabethan and Jacobean drama. But the Lambs' first great success came when they began to write children's literature for the Godwins'* publishing house. *Tales from Shakespear* (1807) went through five editions in its first ten years and has never gone out of print. *Mrs. Leicester's School* (1809) and *Poetry for Children* (1809) were also successes. Mary wrote most of all three of these books (all the children's poems below are hers); Charles also wrote *The Adventures of Ulysses* (1808). In 1820, he began to publish a series of essays, under the pen-name "Elia," in the *London Magazine*; these are probably his most important contribution to literature.

In 1825, Charles retired and the Lambs moved to Enfield, in the hope that country living would be good for Mary. It was not a success; Charles was bored in the country, and Mary's illness only became worse. They spent their last year together in a sanatorium in Edmonton. In December 1834, Charles fell while out for a walk; he contracted erysipelas and died on the 27th. Mary lived, under the care of a nurse, until 20 May 1847. They are buried together in the Edmonton Churchyard. (D.L.M.)

from *Blank Verse by Charles Lloyd and Charles Lamb* (1798)

The Old Familiar Faces

Where are they gone, the old familiar faces?
I had a mother, but she died, and left me,
Died prematurely in a day of horrors—[1]
All, all are gone, the old familiar faces.

5 I have had playmates, I have had companions,
In my days of childhood, in my joyful school days—
All, all are gone, the old familiar faces.

I have been laughing, I have been carousing,
Drinking late, sitting late, with my bosom cronies—
10 All, all are gone, the old familiar faces.

I lov'd a love once, fairest among women;[2]
Clos'd are her doors on me, I must not see her—
All, all are gone, the old familiar faces.

I have a friend, a kinder friend has no man.
15 Like an ingrate, I left my friend abruptly;[3]
Left him, to muse on the old familiar faces.

Ghost-like, I pac'd round the haunts of my childhood.
Earth seem'd a desert I was bound to traverse,
Seeking to find the old familiar faces.

Friend of my bosom, thou more than a brother![4]
Why wert not thou born in my father's dwelling?
So might we talk of the old familiar faces.

For some they have died, and some they have left me,
And some are taken from me;[5] all are departed;
25 All, all are gone, the old familiar faces.

from Charles Lamb and Mary Lamb, *Poetry for Children* (1809)

The Reaper's Child

If you go to the field where the Reapers now bind
    The sheaves of ripe corn, there a fine little lass,
Only three months of age, by the hedge-row you'll find,
    Left alone by its mother upon the low grass.

5 While the mother is reaping, the infant is sleeping;
    Not the basket that holds the provision is less
By the hard-working Reaper, than this little sleeper,
    Regarded, till hunger does on the babe press.

Then it opens its eyes, and it utters loud cries,
10   Which its hard-working mother afar off will hear;
She comes at its calling, she quiets its squalling,
    And feeds it, and leaves it again without fear.

When you were as young as this field-nursed daughter,
    You were fed in the house, and brought up on the knee;
15 So tenderly watched, thy fond mother thought her
    Whole time well bestow'd in nursing of thee.

Choosing a Profession

A Creole boy from the West Indies brought,
To be in European learning taught,
Some years before to Westminster he went,
To a Preparatory School was sent.[6]

---

[1] Mary had stabbed their mother to death, and injured their father, on 22 September 1796.

[2] Ann Simmons, to whom Charles had proposed marriage.

[3] Lloyd* got on Charles's nerves by playing the piano until Charles had to leave his lodgings.

[4] Coleridge.*

[5] Mary had suffered another episode of madness and had to be confined.

[6] Boys were sent to preparatory schools (essentially primary schools) to prepare them for great public schools (that is, private schools) like Westminster.

5 When from his artless tale the mistress found,
   The child had not one friend on English ground,
   She, ev'n as if she his own mother were,
   Made the dark Indian her peculiar care.
   Oft on her fav'rite's future lot she thought;
10 To know the bent of his young mind she sought,
   For much the kind preceptress wish'd to find
   To what profession he was most inclin'd,
   That where his genius led they might him train;
   For nature's kindly bent she held not vain.
15 But vain her efforts to explore his will;
   The frequent question he evaded still:
   Till on a day at length he to her came,
   Joy sparkling in his eyes; and said, the same
   Trade he would be those boys of colour were,
20 Who danc'd so happy in the open air.
   It was a troop of chimney-sweeping boys,
   With wooden music and obstrep'rous noise,
   In tarnish'd finery and grotesque array,
   Were dancing in the street the first of May.[1]

Breakfast

A dinner party, coffee, tea,
Sandwich, or supper, all may be
In their way pleasant. But to me
Not one of these deserves the praise
5 That welcomer of new-born days,
A breakfast, merits; ever giving
Cheerful notice we are living
Another day refresh'd by sleep,
When its festival we keep.
10 Now although I would not slight
Those kindly words we use "Good night,"
Yet parting words are words of sorrow,
And may not vie with sweet "Good morrow,"
With which again our friends we greet,
15 When in the breakfast-room we meet,
At the social table round,

Listening to the lively sound
Of those notes which never tire,
Of urn, or kettle on the fire.
20 Sleepy Robert never hears
Or urn, or kettle; he appears
When all have finish'd, one by one
Dropping off, and breakfast done.
Yet has he too his own pleasure,
25 His breakfast hour's his hour of leisure;
And, left alone, he reads or muses,
Or else in idle mood he uses
To sit and watch the vent'rous fly,
Where the sugar's piled high,
30 Clambering o'er the lumps so white,
Rocky cliffs of sweet delight.

The Two Boys

I saw a boy with eager eye
Open a book upon a stall,
And read as he'd devour it all:
Which when the stall-man did espy,
5 Soon to the boy I heard him call,
"You, Sir, you never buy a book,
Therefore in one you shall not look."
The boy pass'd slowly on, and with a sigh
He wish'd he never had been taught to read,
10 Then of the old churl's books he should have had no need.

Of sufferings the poor have many,
Which never can the rich annoy.
I soon perceiv'd another boy
Who look'd as if he'd not had any
15 Food for that day at least, enjoy
The sight of cold meat in a tavern larder.
This boy's case, thought I, is surely harder,
Thus hungry longing, thus without a penny,
Beholding choice of dainty dressed meat:
20 No wonder if he wish he ne'er had learn'd to eat.

---

[1] May Day was the chimney-sweepers' festival in London. Cf. Blake, "The Chimney Sweeper" (both versions),* and Charles's "The Praise of Chimney-Sweepers: A May-Day Effusion" (1822).

Conquest of Prejudice

Unto a Yorkshire school was sent
    A Negro youth to learn to write,
And the first day young Juba went
    All gaz'd on him as a rare sight.

But soon with alter'd looks askance
    They view his sable face and form,
When they perceive the scornful glance
    Of the head boy, young Henry Orme.

He in the school was first in fame:
    Said he, "It does to me appear
To be a great disgrace and shame
    A black should be admitted here."

His words were quickly whisper'd round,
    And every boy now looks offended;
The master saw the change, and found
    That Orme a mutiny intended.

Said he to Orme, "This African
    It seems is not by you approv'd;
I'll find a way, young Englishman,
    To have this prejudice remov'd.

"Nearer acquaintance possibly
    May make you tolerate his hue;
At least 'tis my intent to try
    What a short month may chance to do."

Young Orme and Juba then he led
    Into a room, in which there were
For each of the two boys a bed,
    A table, and a wicker chair.

He lock'd them in, secur'd the key,
    That all access to them was stopt;
They from without can nothing see;
    Their food is through a sky-light dropt.

A month in this lone chamber Orme
    Is sentenc'd during all that time
To view no other face or form
    Than Juba's parch'd by Afric clime.

One word they neither of them spoke
    The first three days of the first week;
On the fourth day the ice was broke;
    Orme was the first that deign'd to speak.

The dreary silence o'er, both glad
    To hear of human voice the sound,
The Negro and the English lad
    Comfort in mutual converse found.

Of ships and seas, and foreign coast,
    Juba can speak, for he has been
A voyager: and Orme can boast
    He London's famous town has seen.

In eager talk they pass the day,
    And borrow hours ev'n from the night;
So pleasantly time past away,
    That they have lost their reckoning quite.

And when their master set them free,
    They thought a week was sure remitted,
And thank'd him that their liberty
    Had been before the time permitted.

Now Orme and Juba are good friends;
    The school, by Orme's example won,
Contend who most shall make amends
    For former slights to Afric's son.

from Charles Lamb, *Elia* (1823)

Dream-Children; A Reverie

Children love to listen to stories about their elders, when *they* were children; to stretch their imagination to the conception of a traditionary great-uncle, or grandame, whom they never saw. It was in this spirit that my little ones crept about me the other evening to hear about their great-grandmother Field, who lived in a great house in Norfolk (a hundred times bigger than that in which they and papa lived) which had been the scene—so at least it was generally believed in that part of the country—of the tragic incidents which they had lately become familiar with from the ballad of the Children in the Wood.[1] Certain it is that the whole story of the children and their cruel uncle was to be seen fairly carved out in wood upon the chimney-piece of the great hall, the whole story down to the Robin Redbreasts, till a foolish rich person pulled it down to set up a marble one of modern invention in its stead, with no story upon it. Here Alice put out one of her dear mother's looks, too tender to be called upbraiding. Then I went on to say, how religious and how good their great-grandmother Field was, how beloved and respected by every body, though she was not indeed the mistress of this great house, but had only the charge of it (and yet in some respects she might be said to be the mistress of it too) committed to her by the owner, who preferred living in a newer and more fashionable mansion which he had purchased somewhere in the adjoining county; but still she lived in it in a manner as if it had been her own, and kept up the dignity of the great house in a sort while she lived, which afterwards came to decay, and was nearly pulled down, and all its old ornaments stripped and carried away to the owner's other house, where they were set up, and looked as awkward as if some one were to carry away the old tombs they had seen lately at the Abbey,[2] and stick them up in Lady C.'s tawdry gilt drawing-room. Here John smiled, as much as to say, "that would be foolish indeed." And then I told how, when she came to die, her funeral was attended by a concourse of all the poor, and some of the gentry too, of the neighbourhood for many miles round, to show their respect for her memory, because she had been such a good and religious woman; so good indeed that she knew all the Psaltery by heart, ay, and a great part of the Testament besides. Here little Alice spread her hands. Then I told what a tall, upright, graceful person their great-grandmother Field once was; and how in her youth she was esteemed the best dancer—here Alice's little right foot played an involuntary movement, till, upon my looking grave, it desisted—the best dancer, I was saying, in the county, till a cruel disease, called a cancer, came, and bowed her down with pain; but it could never bend her good spirits, or make them stoop, but they were still upright, because she was so good and religious. Then I told how she was used to sleep by herself in a lone chamber of the great lone house; and how she believed that an apparition of two infants was to be seen at midnight gliding up and down the great staircase near where she slept, but she said "those innocents would do her no harm"; and how frightened I used to be, though in those days I had my maid to sleep with me, because I was never half so good or religious as she—and yet I never saw the infants. Here John expanded all his eye-brows and tried to look courageous. Then I told how good she was to all her grand-children, having us to the great-house in the holydays, where I in particular used to spend many hours by myself, in gazing upon the old busts of the Twelve Cæsars, that had been Emperors of Rome, till the old marble heads would seem to live again, or I to be turned into marble with them; how I never could be tired with roaming about that huge mansion, with its vast empty rooms, with their worn-out hangings, fluttering tapestry, and carved oaken pannels, with the gilding almost rubbed out—sometimes in the spacious old-fashioned gardens, which I had almost to myself, unless when now and then a solitary gardening man would cross me—and how the nectarines and peaches hung upon the walls, without my ever offering to pluck them, because they were forbidden fruit, unless now and then,—and because I had more pleasure in strolling about among the old melancholy-looking yew trees, or the firs, and picking up the red berries, and the fir apples, which were good for nothing but to look at—or in lying about upon the fresh grass, with all the fine garden smells around me—or basking in the orangery, till I could almost fancy myself ripening too along with the oranges and the limes in that grateful warmth—or in watching the dace that darted to and fro in the fish-

---

[1] a ballad collected in Thomas Percy (1729–1811), *Reliques of Ancient English Poetry* (1765). The children die in the wood and a robin covers them with leaves.

[2] Westminster Abbey.

pond, at the bottom of the garden, with here and there a great sulky pike hanging midway down the water in silent state, as if it mocked at their impertinent friskings,—I had more pleasure in these busy-idle diversions than in all the sweet flavours of peaches, nectarines, oranges, and such like common baits of children. Here John slyly deposited back upon the plate a bunch of grapes, which, not unobserved by Alice, he had meditated dividing with her, and both seemed willing to relinquish them for the present as irrelevant. Then in somewhat a more heightened tone, I told how, though their great-grandmother Field loved all her grand-children, yet in an especial manner she might be said to love their uncle, John L———,[1] because he was so handsome and spirited a youth, and a king to the rest of us; and, instead of moping about in solitary corners, like some of us, he would mount the most mettlesome horse he could get, when but an imp no bigger than themselves, and make it carry him half over the county in a morning, and join the hunters when there were any out—and yet he loved the old great house and gardens too, but had too much spirit to be always pent up within their boundaries—and how their uncle grew up to man's estate as brave as he was handsome, to the admiration of every body, but of their great-grandmother Field most especially; and how he used to carry me upon his back when I was a lame-footed boy[2]—for he was a good bit older than me—many a mile when I could not walk for pain;—and how in after life he became lame-footed too, and I did not always (I fear) make allowances enough for him when he was impatient, and in pain, nor remember sufficiently how considerate he had been to me when I was lame-footed; and how when he died, though he had not been dead an hour, it seemed as if he had died a great while ago, such a distance there is betwixt life and death; and how I bore his death as I thought pretty well at first, but afterwards it haunted and haunted me; and though I did not cry or take it to heart as some do, and as I think he would have done if I had died, yet I missed him all day long, and knew not till then how much I had loved him. I missed his kindness, and I missed his crossness, and wished him to be alive again, to be quarrelling with him (for we quarreled sometimes), rather than not have him again, and was as uneasy without him, as he their poor uncle must have been when the doctor took off his limb. Here the children fell a crying, and asked if their little mourning which they had on was not for uncle John, and they looked up, and prayed me not to go on about their uncle, but to tell them some stories about their pretty dead mother. Then I told how for seven long years, in hope sometimes, sometimes in despair, yet persisting ever, I courted the fair Alice W——n;[3] and, as much as children could understand, I explained to them what coyness, and difficulty, and denial meant in maidens—when suddenly, turning to Alice, the soul of the first Alice looked out at her eyes with such a reality of re-presentment, that I became in doubt which of them stood there before me, or whose that bright hair was; and while I stood gazing, both the children gradually grew fainter to my view, receding, and still receding till nothing at last but two mournful features were seen in the uttermost distance, which, without speech, strangely impressed upon me the effects of speech; "We are not of Alice, nor of thee, nor are we children at all. The children of Alice call Bartrum father. We are nothing; less than nothing, and dreams. We are only what might have been, and must wait upon the tedious shores of Lethe[4] millions of ages before we have existence, and a name"———and immediately awaking, I found myself quietly seated in my bachelor arm-chair, where I had fallen asleep, with the faithful Bridget[5] unchanged by my side—but John L. (or James Elia) was gone for ever.

---

[1] Charles and Mary's brother John had died on 26 October 1821. He had previously had to have a foot amputated after an accident.

[2] Charles had been lamed by a childhood illness, possibly polio.

[3] Ann Simmons, to whom Charles had proposed marriage.

[4] They are waiting to be born, by the river of forgetfulness in the classical underworld; see Virgil, *Aeneid* 6.

[5] In his essays, Charles presents his sister as his cousin Bridget.

Letters[1]

To S.T. Coleridge
27 September 1796

My dearest friend—
White or some of my friends or the public papers by this time may have informed you of the terrible calamities that have fallen on our family. I will only give you the outlines. My poor dear dearest sister in a fit of insanity has been the death of her own mother. I was at hand only time enough to snatch the knife out of her grasp. She is at present in a mad house, from whence I fear she must be moved to an hospital. God has preserved to me my senses,—I eat and drink and sleep, and have my judgment I believe very sound. My poor father was slightly wounded, and I am left to take care of him and my aunt. Mr. Norris of the Bluecoat school[2] has been very kind to us, and we have no other friend, but thank God I am very calm and composed, and able to do the best that remains to do. Write,—as religious a letter as possible—but no mention of what is gone and done with—with me the former things are passed away,[3] and I have something more to do that [than] to feel——
   God almighty
            have us all in
            his keeping.——
                          C. Lamb

   mention nothing of poetry. I have destroyed every vestige of past vanities of that kind. Do as you please, but if you publish, publish mine (I give free leave) without name or initial, and never send me a book, I charge you, you[r] own judgment will convince you not to take any notice of this yet to your dear wife.—You look after your family,—I have my reason and strength left to take care of mine. I charge you don't think of coming to see me. Write. I will not see you if you come. God almighty love you and all of us——

To William Wordsworth, 30 January 1801

Thanks for your **Letter** and **Present**.—I had already borrowed your second volume—. What most please me are, the Song of Lucy.... *Simon's sickly daughter* in the Sexton made me *cry*.—Next to these are the description of the continuous **Echoes** in the story of Joanna's laugh, where the mountains and all the scenery absolutely seem alive—and that fine Shakesperian character of the Happy Man, in the Brothers,
    that creeps about the fields,
  Following his fancies by the hour, to bring
  Tears down his cheek, or solitary smiles
  Into his face, **until the Setting Sun**
  Write Fool upon his forehead —
I will mention one more: the delicate and curious feeling in the wish for the Cumberland Beggar, that he may ha[ve] about him the melody of Birds, altho' he hear them not.—Here the mind knowingly passes a fiction upon herself, first substituting her own feelings for the Beggar's, and, in the same breath detecting the fallacy, will not part with the wish.— —The **Poets** Epitaph is disfigured, to my taste by the vulgar satire upon parsons and lawyers in the beginning, and the coarse epithet of pin point in the 6th stanza.[4]—All the rest is eminently good, and your own —. I will just add that it appears to me a fault in the Beggar, that the instructions conveyed in it are too direct and like a lecture: they dont slide into the mind of the reader, while he is imagining no such matter.—An intelligent reader finds a sort of insult in being told, I will teach you how to think upon this subject. This fault, if I am right, is in a ten thousandth worse degree to be found in **Sterne**[5] and many many novelists & modern poets, who

---

[1] from *The Letters of Charles and Mary Lamb*, ed. Edwin W. Marrs, Jr., vol.1 (1975). Boldface indicates words in larger handwriting in the MS.

[2] Christ's Hospital, where Charles and Coleridge were both educated, and where they met. Philip Norris was doing building work for the school.

[3] Revelation 21.4.

[4] Charles has been discussing "Lucy Gray," "To a Sexton," "To Joanna," "The Brothers" (108–12), "The Old Cumberland Beggar," and "A Poet's Epitaph," from the second edition of *Lyrical Ballads*.

[5] Laurence Sterne (1713–68), author of *Tristram Shandy* (1759–67) and *A Sentimental Journey* (1768).

continually put a sign post up to shew **where you are to feel**. They set out with assuming their readers to be stupid. Very different from Robinson Crusoe, the Vicar of Wakefie[l]d, Roderick Random,[1] and other beautiful bare narratives.—There is implied an unwritten compact between Author and reader; I will tell you a story, and I suppose you will understand it.—Modern Novels "St. Leons"[2] and the like are full of such flowers as these "Let not my reader suppose"—"Imagine, **if you can**"—modest!—&c.—I will here have done with praise and blame. I have written so much, only that you may not think I have passed over your book without observation.— —I am sorry that Coleridge has christened his Ancient Marinere "a poet's Reverie"—it is as bad as Bottom the Weaver's declaration that **he is** not a Lion but only the scenical representation of a Lion.[3] What new idea is gained by this Title, but one subversive of all credit, which the Tale should force upon us, of its truth?—For me, I was never so affected with any human Tale. After first reading it, I was totally possessed with it for many days.—I dislike all the miraculous part of it, but the feelings of the man under the operation of such scenery dragged me along like Tom Piper's magic Whistle.—[4] I totally differ from your idea that the Marinere should have had a character and profession.—[5] This is a Beauty in Gulliver's Travels,[6] where the mind is kept in a placid state of little wonderments; but the **Ancient Marinere** undergoes such **Trials**, as overwhelm and bury all individuality or memory of what he was.— Like the state of a man in a **Bad dream**, one terrible peculiarity of which is, that all consciousness of personality is **gone**. —Your other observation is I think as well a little unfounded: the **Marinere** from being conversant in supernatural events *has* acquired a supernatural and strange **cast** of *phrase*, **eye**, appearance &c. which frighten the wedding guest. —You will excuse my remarks, because I am hurt and vexed that you should think it necessary, with a prose apology, to open the eyes of dead men that cannot see — — —. To sum up a general opinion of the second vol.—I do not **feel** any one poem in it so forcibly as the Ancient Marinere, the Mad mother,[7] and the Lines at Tintern Abbey in the **first**.— —I could, too, have wished that The Critical preface had appeared in a separate treatise.— All its dogmas are true and just and most of them new, *as criticism*.— But they associate a *diminishing* idea with the Poems which follow, as having been written for **Experiments** on the public taste, more than having sprung (as they must have done) from living and daily circumstances.——I am prolix, because I am gratified in the opportunity of writing to you, and I dont well know when to leave off.—I ought before this to have reply'd to your very kind invitation into Cumberland.—With you and your Sister I could gang any where. But I am afraid whether I shall ever be able to afford so desperate a Journey.—Separate from the pleasure of your company, I dont mu[ch] care if I never see a mountain in my life.—I have passed all my days in London, until I have formed as many and intense local attachments, as any of you **Mountaineers** can have done with dead nature. The Lighted shops of the Strand and Fleet Street, the innumerable trades, tradesmen and customers, coaches, waggons, play houses, all the bustle and wickedness round about Covent Garden,[8] the very women of the Town, the Watchmen, drunken scenes, rattles;—life awake, if you awake, at all hours of the night, the impossibility of being dull in Fleet Street, the crowds, the very dirt & mud, the Sun shining upon houses and pavements, the print shops, the **old Book** stalls, parsons cheap'ning books, coffee houses, steams of soups from kitchens, the pantomimes, London itself, a

---

[1] Daniel Defoe (1660–1731), *Robinson Crusoe* (1719); Goldsmith,* *The Vicar of Wakefield* (1760); Tobias Smollett (1721–71), *Roderick Random* (1748).

[2] Godwin's* second novel, *St. Leon* (1799).

[3] Shakespeare, *A Midsummer Night's Dream* 3.1.27–41, 5.1.216–23.

[4] The Piper in a Morris dance is known as Tom Piper.

[5] In a note to the second edition of *Lyrical Ballads*, Wordsworth had complained: "The Poem of my Friend has indeed great defects; first, that the principal person has no distinct character, either in his profession of Mariner, or as a human being who having been long under the controul of supernatural impressions might be supposed himself to partake of something supernatural...."

[6] Jonathan Swift (1667–1745), *Gulliver's Travels* (1726).

[7] "Her Eyes Are Wild."

[8] an area frequented by prostitutes.

pantomime and a masquerade, all these things work themselves into my mind and feed me, without a power of satiating me. The wonder of these sights impells me into night-walks about her crowded streets, and I often shed tears in the motley Strand from fullness of joy at so much **Life**——. All these emotions must be strange to you. So are your rural emotions to me.—But consider, what must I have been doing all my life, not to have lent great portions of my heart with usury to such scenes?——

My attachments are all local, purely local —. I have no passion (or have had none since I was in love, and then it was the spurious engendering of poetry & books) to groves and vallies.—The rooms where I was born, the furniture which has been before my eyes all my life, a book case which has followed me about, (like a faithful dog, only exceeding him in knowledge) wherever I have moved—old chairs, old tables, streets, squares, where I have sunned myself, my old school,—these are my mistresses—have I not enough, without your mountains?—I do not envy you. I should pity you, did I not know, that the Mind will make friends of any thing. Your sun & moon and skys and hills & lakes affect me no more, or scarcely come to me in more venerable characters, than as a gilded room with tapestry and tapers, where I might live with handsome visible objects.—I consider the clouds above me but as a **roof** beautifully painted, but unable to satisfy the mind, and at last, like the pictures of the apartment of a Connoisseur, unable to afford him any longer a pleasure. So **fading** upon me from disuse, have been the Beauties of Nature, as they have been confinedly called; so ever fresh & green and warm are all the inventions of men and assemblies of men in this great city—. I should certainly have laughed with dear Joanna.—

Give my kindest love, *and my sister's*, to Dorothy & yourself. And a kiss from me to little Barbara Lewthwaite.— —[1]

C. Lamb

Thank you for Liking my Play ! !—[2]

---

[1] mentioned in Wordsworth's poem "The Pet-Lamb, A Pastoral."

[2] *John Woodvil* (1802).

from *To Thomas Manning*[3]

15 February 1801

I had need be cautious henceforward what opinion I give of the Lyrical Bal[l]ads.—All the North of England are in a turmoil. Cumberland and Westmorland[4] have already declared a state of war.—I lately received from Wordsw. a copy of the second volume, accompanied by an acknowledgment of having received from me many months since a copy of a certain Tragedy, with excuses for not having made any acknowledgment sooner, it being owing to an "almost insurmountable aversion from Letter writing."—This letter I answered in due form and time, and enumerated several of the p[ass]ages which had most affected me, adding, unfortunately, that no single piece had moved me so forcibly as the Ancient Marinere, the Mad Mother, or the Lines at Tintern Abbey. The Post did not sleep a moment. I received almost instantaneously a long letter of four sweating pages from my **reluctant Letterwriter**, the purport of which was, that he was sorry his 2d vol. had not given me more pleasure (Devil a hint did I give that it had *not pleased me*) and "was compelled to wish that my range of **Sensibility** was more extended, being obliged to believe that I should receive large influxes of happiness & happy Thoughts" (I suppose from the L. B.—) With a deal of stuff about a certain "**Union** of **Tenderness & Imagination**, which in the sense he used Imag. was not the characteristic of Shakesp. but which Milton possessed in a degree far exceeding other Poets: which **Union**, as the highest species of Poetry, and chiefly deserving that name, He was most proud to aspire to"—then illustrating the said Union by two quotations from his own 2d vol. (which I had been so unfortunate as to miss)—. 1st Specimen—A father addresses his Son—

When thou
First cams't into the world, as it befalls
To new born Infants, thou didst sleep away
Two days: And *Blessings from thy father's tongue*

---

[3] a close friend (1772–1840), who had met Charles through Lloyd.* He later travelled extensively in China, India, Bhutan, and Tibet.

[4] Coleridge lived in Keswick, Cumberland; the Wordsworths in nearby Grasmere, Westmorland.

Then fell upon thee.[1]
The lines were thus undermark'd & then followed "This Passage as combining in an extraordinary degree that union of Imagination & Tenderness, which I am speaking of, I consider as one of the Best I ever wrote."
———

2d Specimen.—A Youth after years of absence revisits his native place, and thinks (as most people do) that there has been strange alteration in his absence—
———
> And that the rocks
> And Everlasting Hills themselves were chang'd —[2]

You see both these are good Poetry: but after one has been reading Shaksp. twenty of the best years of one's life, to have a fellow start up, and prate about some unknown quality, which Shakspere possess'd in a degree inferior to Milton and somebody else! !— — This was not to be *all* my castigation.—Coleridge, who had not written to me some months before, starts up from his bed of sickness to reprove me for my hardy presumption: four long pages, equally sweaty, and more tedious, came from him: assuring me, that, when the words of a man of true Genius, such as W. undoubtedly was, do not please me at first sight, I should suspect the fault to lie "in me & not in them"—&c. &c.&c. &c. &c.——
What am I to do with such people?—I certainly shall write them a very merry Letter.—.—

Writing to *you*, I may say, that the 2d vol. has no such pieces as the three I enumerated.—It is full of original thinking and an observing mind, but it does not often make you laugh or cry.—It too artfully aims at simplicity of expression. And you sometimes doubt if simplicity be not a cover for Poverty. The best Piece in it I will send you, being *short*—I have grievously offended my friends in the North by declaring my undue preference. But I need not fear you—

> She dwelt among the untrodden ways
>   Beside the Springs of **Dove**,
> A maid whom there were few to praise,
>   And very few to love.—
>
> A Violet, by a mossy stone
>   Half hidden from the eye;
> Fair as a star, when only one
>   Is shining in the sky. —
>
> She lived unknown; & few could know,
>   When **Lucy** ceas'd to be.
> But she is in the grave, and Oh!
>   The difference to me.

This is choice and genuine, and so are many many more. But one does not like to have 'em ramm'd down one's throat —"Pray take it—its very good—let me help you—eat faster."—.—.

---

[1] W. Wordsworth, "Michael" 349–53.*
[2] W. Wordsworth, "The Brothers" 96–97.

Charles Lloyd
1775 – 1839

Born in Birmingham, the eldest son of a Quaker philanthropist, Charles Lloyd was educated at home with the expectation that he become a banker like his father. However, Lloyd published his first book of poetry in 1795, *Poems on Various Subjects*; the following year he met Coleridge,* who became his teacher, landlord, and friend. Lloyd lived with Coleridge at Kingsdown, Bristol and Nether Stowey until the summer of 1796. In January 1797, a few months after Charles Lamb's* sister, Mary Lamb,* had killed their mother in a fit of insanity, Lloyd and Lamb met for the first time: in his essay "The Old Familiar Faces,"* Lamb refers to Lloyd as "a friend." In addition to their work in *Blank Verse* (1798), they also collaborated with Coleridge in the second edition of *Poems* (1797).

In 1799 Lloyd married Sophia Pemberton, moving in 1800 to Ambleside in the Lake District and raising a large family. During this period he worked on a translation of Ovid's *Metamorphoses*. Thomas De Quincey* became a regular daily visitor for several years from 1809. Lloyd was an epileptic; by 1811 he had also developed symptoms of mental instability. His epistolary novel, *Edmund Oliver* (1798), included critical portraits of Godwin,* Wollstonecraft,* and Coleridge. A further novel written at this time, *Isabel*, was not published until 1820. Lloyd was admitted to an asylum near York; when he escaped in 1818, De Quincey looked after him, reuniting him with his wife, Sophia, in London.

In 1819 Lloyd published a collection of poems entitled *Nugæ Canoræ*, dedicated to Sophia. A period of intense productivity followed: Lloyd published his *Poetical Essays on the Character of Pope* (1821), a play (*The Duke D'Ormond*, 1822), *Beritola* (1822), and *Poems* (1823). He moved with his family to France, but his illness recurred. He died in an asylum at Chaillot, near Versailles, on 16 January 1839. (A.M.)

༺༻

from *Blank Verse by Charles Lloyd and Charles Lamb* (1798)

Lines to Mary Wollstonecraft Godwin[1]

I am happy in being able to offer this imperfect tribute to the memory of a woman, whose undeserved sufferings have excited my indignation and pity, and whose virtues, both of heart and mind, my warmest esteem.

This will not be deemed a parasitical profession, when I avow a complete dissent from Mrs. Godwin with regard to almost all her moral speculations.

Her posthumous works, so far from convincing me that "the misery and oppression peculiar to women arise out of the partial laws and institutions of society,"[2] appear little less throughout than an indirect panegyric on the institutions she wishes to abolish. She (with all other great minds) owed her degree of intellectualization to the very restraints on the passions which she was aiming to annihilate; and the source of the miseries she complained of must rather be sought for in the brute turbulencies of human nature, than in the operation of any laws conventional or positive.

However, the heart and upright dignity of this excellent woman have much interested me. I never quarrel with opinions; and I fervently wish that the expression of my admiration were more worthy of its object. "On examining my heart, I find that it is so constituted, I cannot live without some particular affection. I am afraid not without a passion; and I feel the want of it more in society than in solitude."

Mary Wollstonecraft Godwin's Letters, vol. i, p. 178.[3]

---

[1] Mary Wollstonecraft, author of *A Vindication of the Rights of Woman*,* married Godwin* in 1797; Lloyd is responding to her *Posthumous Works*, which Godwin published in four volumes in 1798.

[2] "See Posthumous Works, vol. ii. p. 166." (C.L.) The quotation is from the concluding paragraph of the preface to Wollstonecraft's posthumously published novel, *The Wrongs of Woman.**

[3] Lloyd quotes from a letter from Wollstonecraft to her former lover, Gilbert Imlay, dated 5 August [1795] and published in *Posthumous Works* 3: 177–78.

Mary, I've trod the turf, beneath whose damp
And dark green coverture thou liest![1] 'Twas strange!
And somewhat most like madness shot athwart
The incredulous mind, when I bethought myself
That there so many earnest hopes and fears,
So many warm desires, and lofty thoughts,
Affections imitating, in their wide
And boundless aim, heaven's universal love,
Lay cold and silent! Listening to the breeze,
That scarcely murmur'd thro' the misty air,
And looking on the white and solemn clouds,
(The only things whose motion spake of life)[2]
I almost counted to have heard thy voice,
And seen thy shadowy shape; for my full heart
(Tho' to my mortal sense thou ne'er wert known)
Had bodied all thy mental attributes
In th' unintelligent and vacant space.
MARY, thou sleep'st not there! 'Twas but a trance,
An idle trance, that led my wayward thought
To seek a more especial intercourse
With thy pure spirit on the senseless sod,
Where what was thine, not *thou*, lies sepulchred.
Life is a dream! and death a dream to those
Who gaze upon the dead: to those who die
'Tis the withdrawing of a lower scene
For one more real, pure, and infinite!
Amid the trials of this difficult world,
Surely none press so sorely on the heart
As disappointed loves, and impulses
(Mingling the lonely insulated soul
With all surrounding and external things)
Sever'd from nature's destin'd sympathies!
This was thy lot on earth! Yet think not thou,
Man of the world, to triumph here o'er those,
Whose separate and immortalized spirits
Spoil them for life's pernicious intercourse.
This is the school of minds; and every wish
Drawn from the earthly part shall raise the being,
And fit it for a wider range, whene'er
The twofold ministry of flesh and spirit
Hath done its troubled business. Therefore thou,
Though here tormented, shalt in better worlds
Be greatly comforted!
              I laugh at those
Who blame that upright singleness[3] of soul,
Which ever shap'd the accents of thy tongue!
Look to yourselves, pedantic censurers!
Examine well within; for much, I fear,
Ye would but ill endure the scrutiny
That only gives to her a nobler rank
'Mid beings compos'd of heart and intellect.
In this fantastic scene each one assumes
A borrow'd character, and all agree
To seem a something, which in his secret thought
Each knows he is not; which the God of nature
Ne'er made, or meant a child of his to be!
And if a *Man of Truth* make no pretence
To some *unhuman* virtue, the brute crowd
Pluck off his hair, and plant with bitterness
Thorns of reproach on his devoted head![4]
Heaven knows that we have passions, and have hearts
To love; and they alone embrute or soil
The divine lustre of the better part,
Who love, nor intellectual preference seek,
Eradicating from each sympathy
The holiness of reason, and that pure,
And high imagination, which would lose
The bodily in the spiritual.[5]
              I revere
That simpleness which gave to her pure lips
A ready utterance to each inward thought.
And I revere that *obstinate regard*
Which hung upon its object, e'en till all
The tender semblances, which lingering hope
Loves with such earnestness, were fully gone!
For passion, sanctified, will centre all

---

[1] Wollstonecraft was buried in St. Pancras churchyard, London.

[2] perhaps an echo of Coleridge, "This Lime-Tree Bower My Prison" 76.*

[3] "See the interesting letters in the second and third volumes of Posthumous Works." (C.L.) The letters are actually in volumes 3 and 4.

[4] The "Man of Truth" (56) is Christ; cf. Isaiah 50.6, Mark 15.17, John 19.2.

[5] "My *earthly* by his *heavenly* overpowered. MILTON." (C.L.) Milton, *Paradise Lost* 8.453.

75 Its warm[1] hopes in a *chosen one*! Not dead,
    Nor e'er abolish'd, as some idly talk;
    Impostors, or base carles,[2] who never knew
    Man's dearest charities. And passions ever
    Shake with most potent stirrings the sublime
80 And pregnant minds, which wield with mightiest skill
    The multitudinous elements of life.
    But if *that one* forsake the soul which twin'd
    So many warm endearments round its choice,
    The world will seem a very wilderness!

---

[1] "'The individuality of an attachment constitutes its chastity.' For this remark, to which I implicitly subscribe, I believe I am indebted to the 'Emma Courtney,' of Miss Hays. The chastity which results from no original passion is the mere 'dribble' of an ideot." (C.L.) See Mary Hays, *Memoirs of Emma Courtney* (1796), vol. 2, chap. 7.

[2] ill-bred fellows.

Charlotte Richardson
1775 – 1825

Charlotte Smith was born in York on 5 March 1775. At the age of twelve she was sent to a charity school that taught girls practical skills, Bible-reading, and accounting to prepare them for work as domestic servants. After four years at school she undertook a succession of jobs that left her no time for reading; then she was employed for £4 a year by a widow who gave her access to a small collection of books. Charlotte's mother died in 1790; her disabled brother died in a poorhouse a few years later. In 1802 she married a shoemaker; when he died of consumption in 1804, she and her baby were left friendless, destitute, and ill.

The educational reformer Catherine Cappe was moved by Richardson's plight and impressed by her verse. Cappe arranged to have a volume published by subscription: the *Gentleman's Magazine* published her account of Richardson's life and two poems. *Poems on Different Occasions* appeared in 1806; a second edition appeared in 1806. Richardson opened a school; but she was too ill to keep it going. Her second collection of poems, *Poems Chiefly Composed during the Pressure of Severe Illness*, was published by subscription in 1809. She died in Acomb, Yorkshire, on 26 September 1825. (A.M.)

છબછ

from *Harvest, A Poem, in Two Parts; with Other Poetical Pieces* (1818)

The Redbreast

Cold blew the freezing Northern blast,
    And Winter sternly frown'd;
The flaky snow fell thick and fast,
    And clad the fields around.

5 Forc'd by the storm's relentless pow'r,
    Embolden'd by despair,
A shiv'ring Redbreast sought my door,
    Some friendly warmth to share.

"Welcome, sweet Bird!" I fondly cried,
10   "No danger need'st thou fear,
Secure with me thou may'st abide,
    Till warmer suns appear.

"And when mild Spring comes smiling on,
    And bids the fields look gay,
15 Thou, with thy sweet, thy grateful song,
    My kindness shalt repay."

Mistaken thought!—But, how shall I
    The mournful truth display?
An envious Cat, with jealous eye,
20   Had mark'd him as her prey.

Remorseless wretch!—her cruel jaws
    Soon seal'd her victim's doom,
While I in silence mourn his loss,
    And weep o'er Robin's tomb.

25 So, oft in Life's uneven way,
    Some stroke may intervene;
Sweep all our fancied joys away,
    And change the flatt'ring scene.

The Rainbow

Soft falls the show'r, the thunders cease!
And see, the messenger of peace
    Illumes the eastern skies;
Blest sign of firm unchanging love![1]
5 While others seek the cause to prove,
    That bids thy beauties rise.

---

[1] See Genesis 9.9–16.

My soul, content with humbler views,
Well pleas'd admires thy varied hues,
   And can with joy behold
10 Thy beauteous form, and wond'ring gaze
Enraptur'd on thy mingled rays
   Of purple, green, and gold.

Enough for me to deem divine
The hand that paints each glowing line;
15   To think that thou art giv'n
A transient gleam of that bright place
Where Beauty owns celestial grace,
   A faint display of Heav'n!

Matthew Gregory Lewis
1775 – 1818

Born in London, 9 July 1775, Lewis was the first child of Matthew and Frances Maria Sewell Lewis. Both parents had Jamaican connections: his father, who had been born there, owned sugar plantations and over 500 slaves; his maternal uncle became attorney general of Jamaica. Matthew was educated at Marylebone Seminary and at Westminster School, where he participated in theatrical productions. In 1781, his mother left his father for a music master, with whom she had a child: Lewis managed to remain on good terms with both his parents, until his father, unable to obtain a divorce, took a mistress in 1803.

While a student at Christ Church, Oxford, Lewis travelled to Paris, reading widely in French and German and writing his first play and an unpublished burlesque novel. The following year, 1792, he travelled to Germany, where he met the writers Johann Wolfgang von Goethe and Christoph Martin Wieland and translated German poetry. Having received his degree in 1794, he went to The Hague as a diplomat: there he wrote his novel, *The Monk*, one of the most famous, influential—and sensational—examples of Gothic fiction, mingling satire, sex, legend, violence, moral cynicism, and psychological insight with the conventions made familiar in such works as Horace Walpole's *The Castle of Otranto* (1764) and Radcliffe's* *The Mysteries of Udolpho* (published in 1794). Published anonymously in 1795, *The Monk* proved to be controversial, giving rise to dramatic adaptations and making the story of Agnes and Raymond (an episode in the novel) particularly famous. The book's success gave Lewis his nickname: "Monk" Lewis. A second Gothic work, a play called *The Castle Spectre*, was successfully performed at Drury Lane in 1797. Other plays followed, but Lewis also went on to work collaboratively with Walter Scott* on a collection of ballads, *Tales of Wonder* (1801). A second novel, *The Bravo of Venice*, was translated from a German source in 1805 and adapted successfully for the stage the same year.

Following his father's death in 1812, Lewis made two trips to Jamaica to look after his property there, keeping a journal and writing poetry. In August 1816, he visited Byron* in Switzerland, meeting Mary and Percy Shelley* and other members of their circle and introducing Byron to Goethe's *Faust*. He died of yellow fever on the way home from his second visit to Jamaica and was buried at sea. (A.M.)

❧

from *The Monk: A Romance* (1796)

Alonzo the Brave and Fair Imogine[1]

A warrior so bold and a virgin so bright
    Conversed, as they sat on the green;
They gazed on each other with tender delight:
Alonzo the Brave was the name of the knight,
5   The maid's was the Fair Imogine.

"And, oh!" said the youth, "since to-morrow I go
    To fight in a far distant land,
Your tears for my absence soon leaving to flow,
Some other will court you, and you will bestow
10   On a wealthier suitor your hand."

"Oh! hush these suspicions," Fair Imogine said,
    "Offensive to love and to me!
For, if you be living, or if you be dead,
I swear by the Virgin, that none in your stead
15   Shall husband of Imogine be.

"If e'er I, by lust or by wealth led aside,
    Forget my Alonzo the Brave,
God grant, that to punish my falsehood and pride,
Your ghost at the marriage may sit by my side,

---

[1] In *The Monk*, the heroine, Antonia, reads this poem from a "volume of old Spanish Ballads" she finds in her dead mother's bedchamber; immediately afterwards, the ghost of her mother appears to her.

20 May tax me with perjury, claim me as bride,
        And bear me away to the grave!"

    To Palestine hastened the hero so bold;
        His love, she lamented him sore:
    But scarce had a twelvemonth elapsed, when behold,
25 A Baron all covered with jewels and gold
        Arrived at Fair Imogine's door.

    His treasure, his presents, his spacious domain
        Soon made her untrue to her vows:
    He dazzled her eyes; he bewildered her brain;
30 He caught her affections so light and so vain,
        And carried her home as his spouse.

    And now had the marriage been blest by the priest;
        The revelry now was begun:
    The tables they groaned with the weight of the feast;
35 Nor yet had the laughter and merriment ceased,
        When the bell of the castle told—"one!"

    Then first with amazement Fair Imogine found
        That a stranger was placed by her side:
    His air was terrific; he uttered no sound;
40 He spoke not, he moved not, he looked not around,
        But earnestly gazed on the bride.

    His vizor was closed, and gigantic his height;
        His armour was sable to view:
    All pleasure and laughter were hushed at his sight;
45 The dogs as they eyed him drew back in affright;
        The lights in the chamber burned blue!

    His presence all bosoms appeared to dismay;
        The guests sat in silence and fear.
    At length spoke the bride, while she trembled: "I pray,
50 Sir Knight, that your helmet aside you would lay,
        And deign to partake of our cheer."

    The lady is silent: the stranger complies.
        His vizor he slowly unclosed:
    Oh! God! what a sight met Fair Imogine's eyes!

55 What words can express her dismay and surprise,
        When a skeleton's head was exposed!
    All present then uttered a terrified shout;
        All turned with disgust from the scene.
    The worms they crept in, and the worms they crept out,
60 And sported his eyes and his temples about,
        While the spectre addressed Imogine:

    "Behold me, thou false one! Behold me!" he cried;
        "Remember Alonzo the Brave!
    God grants, that to punish thy falsehood and pride
65 My ghost at thy marriage should sit by thy side,
        Should tax thee with perjury, claim thee as bride,
        And bear thee away to the grave!"

    Thus saying, his arms round the lady he wound,
        While loudly she shrieked in dismay;
70 Then sank with his prey through the wide-yawning ground:
        Nor ever again was Fair Imogine found,
        Or the spectre who bore her away.

    Not long lived the Baron; and none since that time
        To inhabit the castle presume;
75 For chronicles tell that, by order sublime,
    There Imogine suffers the pain of her crime,
        And mourns her deplorable doom.

    At midnight four times in each year does her spright,
        When mortals in slumber are bound,
80 Arrayed in her bridal apparel of white,
    Appear in the hall with the Skeleton-Knight,
        And shriek as he whirls her around.

    While they drink out of skulls newly torn from the grave,
        Dancing round them the spectres are seen:
85 Their liquor is blood, and this horrible stave
    They howl:—"To the health of Alonzo the Brave,
        And his consort, the False Imogine!"

from *The Life and Correspondence of M.G. Lewis, author of "The Monk," "Castle Spectre," &c. with Many Pieces in Prose and Verse, Never Before Published* (1839)

The Captive[1]

The scene represents a dungeon, in which is a grated door, guarded by strong bars and chains. In the upper part is an open gallery, leading to the cells above.

Slow and melancholy music. The Captive is discovered in the attitude of hopeless grief:—she is in chains;—her eyes are fixed, with a vacant stare, and her hands are folded.

After a pause, the Gaoler is seen passing through the upper gallery with a lamp: he appears at the grate, and opens the door. The noise of the bars falling rouses the Captive. She looks round eagerly; but on seeing the Gaoler enter, she waves her hand mournfully, and relapses into her former stupor.

The Gaoler replenishes a jug with water, and places a loaf of bread by her side. He then prepares to leave the dungeon, when the Captive seems to resolve on making an attempt to excite his compassion: she rises from her bed of straw, clasps his hand, and sinks at his feet. The music ceases, and she speaks.

  Stay, gaoler, stay, and hear my woe!
    She is not mad who kneels to thee:
  For what I'm now too well I know,
    And what I was, and what should be.
5   I'll rave no more in proud despair;
    My language shall be calm, though sad;
  But yet I'll firmly, truly swear
    I am not mad! [*then kissing his hand*] I am not mad!
[*He offers to leave her; she detains him, and continues, in a tone of eager persuasion,*]
    A tyrant husband forged the tale
10   Which chains me in this dreary cell;

---

[1] first performed at Covent Garden, London, 22 March 1803 (inducing fainting fits among some ladies in the audience, according to contemporary observers). Lewis adapted the monodrama as a poem in his *Poems* (1812). Some contemporaries thought *The Captive* was based on Wollstonecraft's *Wrongs of Woman*,* where the heroine, Maria, is imprisoned in a madhouse.

  My fate, unknown, my friends bewail—
    Oh! gaoler, haste, that fate to tell.
  Oh! haste, my father's heart to cheer;
    That heart, at once, 'twill grieve and glad
15   To know, though kept a captive here,
    I am not mad! not mad! not mad!
[*Harsh music, while the Gaoler, with a look of contempt and disbelief, forces his hand from her grasp, and leaves her. The bars are heard replacing.*]
    He smiles in scorn!—
    He turns the key!
    He quits the grate!—I knelt in vain!
20   Still—still, his glimmering lamp I see.
[*Music expressing the light growing fainter, as the Gaoler retires through the gallery, and the Captive watches his departure with eager looks.*]
  'Tis lost!—and all is gloom again.
[*She shivers, and wraps her garment more closely round her.*]
    Cold!—bitter cold!—no warmth!—no light!
    Life! all thy comforts once I had;
    Yet, here I'm chain'd this freezing night,
25 [*Eagerly.*] Although not mad! no, no, no, no—not mad!
[*A few bars of melancholy music, which she interrupts, by exclaiming suddenly,*]
  'Tis sure a dream?—some fancy vain!
[*Proudly.*] I—I, the child of rank and wealth!
  Am I the wretch who clanks this chain,
    Deprived of freedom, friends, and health?
30   Oh! while I count those blessings fled,
    Which never more my hours must glad,
  How aches my heart!—how burns my head!—
[*Interrupting herself hastily, and pressing her hands forcibly against her forehead.*]
    But 'tis not mad!—no, 'tis not mad!
[*She remains fixed in this attitude, with a look of fear, till the music, changing, expresses that some tender, melancholy reflection has passed her mind.*]
My child!
    Ah! hast thou not forgot, by this,
35   Thy mother's face—thy mother's tongue?
    She'll ne'er forget your parting kiss,
[*With a smile.*] Nor round her neck how fast you
      clung;

            Nor how you sued with her to stay;
            Nor how that suit your sire forbad!
40   [*With agony.*] Nor how—   [*With a look of terror.*]
                                I'll drive such
        thoughts away;
    [*In a hollow hurried voice.*]
            They'll make me mad! They'll make me mad!
    [*A pause—she then proceeds with a melancholy smile.*]
            His rosy lips, how sweet they smiled!
            His mild blue eyes how bright they shone!
            Was never born a lovelier child,
    [*With a sudden burst of passionate grief, approaching to frenzy.*]
45   And art now thou for ever gone?
            And must I never see thee more?
            My pretty, pretty, pretty lad!
    [*With energy.*] I will be free!
    [*Endeavouring to force the grate.*] Unbar this door!
            I am not mad! I am not mad!
    [*She falls, exhausted, against the grate, by the bars of which she supports herself. She is roused from her stupor by loud shrieks, rattling of chains, &c.*]
50   Hark! hark!—What mean those yells—those cries?
    [*The noise grows louder.*]
            His chain some furious madman breaks!
    [*The madman is seen to rush along the gallery with a blazing firebrand in his hand.*]
            He comes! I see his glaring eyes!
    [*The madman appears at the grate, which he endeavours to force, while she shrinks in an agony of terror.*]
            Now! now! my dungeon bars he shakes!
            Help! help!
    [*Scared by her cries, the madman quits the grate. The madman again appears above, is seized by his keepers, with torches; and after resistance, is dragged away.*]
            He's gone!—
55   Oh! fearful woe,
            Such screams to hear—such sights to see!
            My brain! my brain!—I know, I know
            I am not mad, but soon shall be.
            Yes—soon! for, lo! yon—while I speak—
            Mark yonder demon's eyeballs glare!
60   He sees me!—now, with dreadful shriek,
            He whirls a scorpion high in air!
            Horror!—the reptile strikes his tooth
            Deep in my heart, so crush'd and sad:
            Ay!—laugh, ye fiends!—I feel the truth!
65   'Tis done! 'tis done! [*With a loud shriek.*]
                                I'm mad!—I'm mad!
[*She dashes herself in frenzy upon the ground.*]

    The two Brothers cross the gallery, dragging the Gaoler; then a servant appears with a torch, conducting the Father, who is supported by his youngest daughter. They are followed by servants with torches, part of whom remain in the gallery. The Brothers appear at the grate, which they force the Gaoler to open; they enter, and on seeing the Captive, one is struck with sorrow, while the other expresses violent anger against the Gaoler, who endeavours to excuse himself; the Father and Sister enter, and approach the Captive, offering to raise her, when she starts up suddenly, and eyes them with a look of terror: they endeavour to make themselves known to her, but in vain; she shuns them, with fear and aversion, and taking some straw, begins to twine it into a crown, when her eyes falling on the Gaoler, she shrieks in terror, and hides her face; the Gaoler is ordered to retire, and obeys; the Father again endeavours to awaken her attention, but in vain. He covers his face with his handkerchief, which the Captive draws away with a look of surprise. Their hopes are excited, and they watch her with eagerness. She wipes the old man's eyes with her hair, which she afterwards touches, and finding it wet with tears, bursts into a delirious laugh, resumes her crown of straw, and after working at it eagerly for a moment, suddenly drops it, and remains motionless with a vacant stare. The Father, &c., express their despair of her recovery—the music ceases. An old servant enters, leading her child, who advances with a careless look; but on seeing his mother, breaks from the servant, runs to her, and clasps her hand. She looks at him with a vacant stare, then, with an expression of excessive joy, exclaims "My child!" sinks on her knees, and clasps him to her bosom. The Father, &c., raise their hands to heaven, in gratitude for the return of her reason, and the curtain falls slowly to solemn music.

Jane Austen
1775 – 1817

Jane Austen was born on 16 December 1775, in Steventon, Hampshire, the sixth child of George Austen (1731–1805), the local rector, and Cassandra Leigh Austen (1739–1827), who altogether had six sons and two daughters. She received some training in such accomplishments as dancing, drawing, and music (which was always important to her), and a few years of formal education, but essentially, she was self-educated; luckily, the Austens were all great readers. Austen never married; she had three suitors, but the first was sent back to Ireland by his aunt and the second died suddenly; in the third case, she broke off the engagement after only a day. She began writing, to entertain her family, at an early age; when she completed "Love and Freindship," her parody of the then-fashionable epistolary novel of sentiment, she was only fourteen. By 1799, she had substantially completed *Northanger Abbey* (1817) and written early versions of *Sense and Sensibility* (1810), *Pride and Prejudice* (1813), and possibly *Mansfield Park* (1814). In 1800, however, her father decided to retire and move to Bath, and this move seems to have put a temporary end to Austen's literary activity. After her father's death in 1805, Austen's brother Frank invited her, her sister, and their mother to live with him in Southampton; after the death of her brother Edward's wife in 1808, Edward offered them a house in Chawton, Kent, near Steventon; Austen lived there for the rest of her life. In her hew home, she returned to writing, and masterpiece followed masterpiece rapidly. By 1815, she had attained such eminence that she was asked to dedicate her latest novel, *Emma*, to the Prince Regent. In 1816, Austen became ill, probably with Addison's disease. She completed *Persuasion* and began *Sanditon*, but by March 1817, she was too ill to write. In May, she went to see a surgeon in Winchester, where she stayed in lodgings for the last weeks of her life, accompanied by her sister, Cassandra. She died on 18 July and was buried in Winchester Cathedral. *Northanger Abbey* and *Persuasion* were published at the end of the year. (D.L.M.)

Love and Freindship[1]

> To Madame La Comtesse De Feuillide[2]
> This Novel is inscribed by
> Her obliged Humble Servant
> The Author

"Deceived in Freindship and Betrayed in Love"[3]

LETTER THE FIRST
from Isabel to Laura[4]

How often, in answer to my repeated intreaties that you would give my Daughter a regular detail of the Misfortunes and Adventures of your Life, have you said "No, my freind never will I comply with your request till I may be no longer in Danger of again experiencing such dreadful ones."

Surely that time is now at hand. You are this day 55. If a woman may ever be said to be in safety from the determined Perseverance of disagreable Lovers and the cruel Persecutions of obstinate Fathers, surely it must be at such a time of Life.

Isabel.

LETTER 2ND
Laura to Isabel

Altho' I cannot agree with you in supposing that I shall never again be exposed to Misfortunes as unmerited as those I have already experienced, yet to avoid the

---

[1] Our text is from *The Works of Jane Austen*, ed. R.W. Chapman, vol. 6.

[2] In 1780, Austen's cousin Eliza Hancock (1761–1813) married Jean Gabriel Capotte, Comte de Feuillide. The Comte was guillotined in Paris in 1794; in 1797, Eliza married Austen's brother Henry.

[3] unidentified.

[4] a romantic name, since Laura (d. 1348) was the addressee of the love sonnets of Petrarch (1304–74).

imputation of Obstinacy or ill-nature, I will gratify the curiosity of your daughter; and may the fortitude with which I have suffered the many afflictions of my past Life, prove to her a useful lesson for the support of those which may befall her in her own.

Laura.

LETTER 3RD
Laura to Marianne

As the Daughter of my most intimate freind I think you entitled to that knowledge of my unhappy story, which your Mother has so often solicited me to give you.

My Father was a native of Ireland and an inhabitant of Wales; my Mother was the natural[1] Daughter of a Scotch Peer by an italian Opera-girl—I was born in Spain and received my Education at a Convent in France.

When I had reached my eighteenth Year I was recalled by my Parents to my paternal roof in Wales. Our mansion was situated in one of the most romantic parts of the Vale of Uske. Tho' my Charms are now considerably softened and somewhat impaired by the Misfortunes I have undergone, I was once beautiful. But lovely as I was the Graces of my Person were the least of my Perfections. Of every accomplishment accustomary to my sex, I was Mistress. When in the Convent, my progress had always exceeded my instructions, my Acquirements had been wonderfull for my age, and I had shortly surpassed my Masters.

In my Mind, every Virtue that could adorn it was centered; it was the Rendez-vous of every good Quality and of every noble sentiment.

A sensibility[2] too tremblingly alive to every affliction of my Freinds, my Acquaintance and particularly to every affliction of my own, was my only fault, if a fault it could be called. Alas! how altered now! Tho' indeed my own Misfortunes do not make less impression on me than they ever did, yet now I never feel for those of an other. My accomplishments too, begin to fade—I can neither sing so well nor Dance so gracefully as I once did—and I have entirely forgot the *Minuet Dela Cour*.[3]

Adeiu.
Laura.

LETTER 4TH
Laura to Marianne

Our neighbourhood was small, for it consisted only of your Mother. She may probably have already told you that being left by her Parents in indigent Circumstances she had retired into Wales on eoconomical motives. There it was our freindship first commenced. Isabel was then one and twenty. Tho' pleasing both in her Person and Manners, (between ourselves) she never possessed the hundredth part of my Beauty or Accomplishments. Isabel had seen the World. She had passed 2 Years at one of the first Boarding-schools in London; had spent a fortnight in Bath and had supped one night in Southampton.

"Beware my Laura (she would often say) Beware of the insipid Vanities and idle Dissipations of the Metropolis of England; Beware of the unmeaning Luxuries of Bath and of the stinking fish of Southampton."

"Alas! (exclaimed I) how am I to avoid those evils I shall never be exposed to? What probability is there of my ever tasting the Dissipations of London, the Luxuries of Bath, or the stinking Fish of Southampton? I who am doomed to waste my Days of Youth and Beauty in an humble Cottage in the Vale of Uske."

Ah! little did I then think I was ordained so soon to quit that humble Cottage for the Deceitfull Pleasures of the World.

Adeiu
Laura.

---

[1] illegitimate.

[2] The idea that sensibility—a capacity for heightened emotional response and sympathy with others—is a virtue is the target of Austen's satire here and in *Sense and Sensibility* (1811).

[3] "minuet of the court" (Fr.): a fashionable dance.

LETTER 5TH
Laura to Marianne

One Evening in December, as my Father, my Mother and myself, were arranged in social converse round our Fireside, we were on a sudden, greatly astonished, by hearing a violent knocking on the outward door of our rustic Cot.

My Father started—"What noise is that," (said he.) "It sounds like a loud rapping at the door"—(replied my Mother.) "It does indeed." (cried I.) "I am of your opinion; (said my Father) it certainly does appear to proceed from some uncommon violence exerted against our unoffending door." "Yes (exclaimed I) I cannot help thinking it must be somebody who knocks for admittance."

"That is another point (replied he;) We must not pretend to determine on what motive the person may knock—tho' that someone *does* rap at the door, I am partly convinced."

Here, a 2ᵈ tremendous rap interrupted my Father in his speech, and somewhat alarmed my Mother and me.

"Had we not better go and see who it is? (said she) the servants are out." "I think we had." (replied I.) "Certainly, (added my Father) by all means." "Shall we go now?" (said my Mother,) "The sooner the better." (answered he.) "Oh! let no time be lost" (cried I.)

A third more violent Rap than ever again assaulted our ears. "I am certain there is somebody knocking at the Door." (said my Mother.) "I think there must," (replied my Father) "I fancy the servants are returned; (said I) I think I hear Mary going to the Door." "I'm glad of it (cried my Father) for I long to know who it is."

I was right in my conjecture; for Mary instantly entering the Room, informed us that a young Gentleman and his Servant were at the door, who had lossed their way, were very cold and begged leave to warm themselves by our fire.

"Won't you admit them?" (said I.) "You have no objection, my Dear?" (said my Father.) "None in the World." (replied my Mother.)

Mary, without waiting for any further commands immediately left the room and quickly returned introducing the most beauteous and amiable Youth, I had ever beheld. The servant, she kept to herself.

My natural sensibility had already been greatly affected by the sufferings of the unfortunate stranger and no sooner did I first behold him, than I felt that on him the happiness or Misery of my future Life must depend.

       Adeiu
        Laura.

LETTER 6TH
Laura to Marianne

The noble Youth informed us that his name was Lindsay—for particular reasons however I shall conceal it under that of Talbot. He told us that he was the son of an English Baronet, that his Mother had been many years no more and that he had a Sister of the middle size. "My Father (he continued) is a mean and mercenary wretch—it is only to such particular freinds as this Dear Party that I would thus betray his failings. Your Virtues my amiable Polydore (addressing himself to my father) yours Dear Claudia and yours my Charming Laura call on me to repose in you, my confidence." We bowed. "My Father, seduced by the false glare of Fortune and the Deluding Pomp of Title, insisted on my giving my hand to Lady Dorothea. No never exclaimed I. Lady Dorothea is lovely and Engaging; I prefer no woman to her; but know Sir, that I scorn to marry her in compliance with your Wishes. No! Never shall it be said that I obliged my Father."

We all admired the noble Manliness of his reply. He continued.

"Sir Edward was surprised; he had perhaps little expected to meet with so spirited an opposition to his will. "Where, Edward in the name of wonder (said he) did you pick up this unmeaning gibberish? You have been studying Novels I suspect."[1] I scorned to answer: it would have been beneath my dignity. I mounted my Horse and followed by my faithful William set forwards for my Aunts."

---

[1] Cf. Austen's defense of the novel in *Northanger Abbey*, chap. 5.*

"My Father's house is situated in Bedfordshire, my Aunt's in Middlesex, and tho' I flatter myself with being a tolerable proficient in Geography, I know not how it happened, but I found myself entering this beautifull Vale which I find is in South Wales,[1] when I had expected to have reached my Aunts."

"After having wandered some time on the Banks of the Uske without knowing which way to go, I began to lament my cruel Destiny in the bitterest and most pathetic Manner. It was now perfectly dark, not a single star was there to direct my steps, and I know not what might have befallen me had I not at length discerned thro' the solemn Gloom that surrounded me a distant light, which as I approached it, I discovered to be the chearfull Blaze of your fire. Impelled by the combination of Misfortunes under which I laboured, namely Fear, Cold and Hunger I hesitated not to ask admittance which at length I have gained; and now my Adorable Laura (continued he taking my Hand) when may I hope to receive that reward of all the painfull sufferings I have undergone during the course of my attachment to you, to which I have ever aspired. Oh! when will you reward me with Yourself?"

"This instant, Dear and Amiable Edward." (replied I.) We were immediately united by my Father, who tho' he had never taken orders had been bred to the Church.

Adeiu

Laura.

LETTER 7TH
Laura to Marianne

We remained but a few days after our Marriage, in the Vale of Uske. After taking an affecting Farewell of my Father, my Mother and my Isabel, I accompanied Edward to his Aunt's in Middlesex. Philippa received us both with every expression of affectionate Love. My arrival was indeed a most agreable surprise to her as she had not only been totally ignorant of my Marriage with her Nephew, but had never even had the slightest idea of there being such a person in the World.

Augusta, the sister of Edward was on a visit to her when we arrived. I found her exactly what her Brother had described her to be—of the middle size. She received me with equal surprise though not with equal Cordiality, as Philippa. There was a disagreable coldness and Forbidding Reserve in her reception of me which was equally distressing and Unexpected. None of that interesting Sensibility or amiable simpathy in her manners and Address to me when we first met which should have distinguished our introduction to each other. Her Language was neither warm, nor affectionate, her expressions of regard were neither animated nor cordial; her arms were not opened to receive me to her Heart, tho' my own were extended to press her to mine.

A short Conversation between Augusta and her Brother, which I accidentally overheard encreased my dislike to her, and convinced me that her Heart was no more formed for the soft ties of Love than for the endearing intercourse of Freindship.

"But do you think that my Father will ever be reconciled to this imprudent connection?" (said Augusta.)

"Augusta (replied the noble Youth) I thought you had a better opinion of me, than to imagine I would so abjectly degrade myself as to consider my Father's Concurrence in any of my affairs, either of Consequence or concern to me. Tell me Augusta tell me with sincerity; did you ever know me consult his inclinations or follow his Advice in the least trifling Particular since the age of fifteen?"

"Edward (replied she) you are surely too diffident in your own praise. Since you were fifteen only! My Dear Brother since you were five years old, I entirely acquit you of ever having willingly contributed to the satisfaction of your Father. But still I am not without apprehensions of your being shortly obliged to degrade yourself in your own eyes by seeking a support for your wife in the Generosity of Sir Edward."

"Never, never Augusta will I so demean myself. (said Edward). Support! What support will Laura want which she can receive from him?"

"Only those very insignificant ones of Victuals and Drink." (answered she.)

"Victuals and Drink! (replied my Husband in a most nobly contemptuous Manner) and dost thou then

---

[1] Bedfordshire and Middlesex (London) are only about thirty miles (48 km) apart, in the South-East of England; the Vale of Usk, in South Wales, is over a hundred miles (160 km) away.

imagine that there is no other support for an exalted mind (such as is my Laura's) than the mean and indelicate employment of Eating and Drinking?"

"None that I know of, so efficacious." (returned Augusta).

"And did you then never feel the pleasing Pangs of Love, Augusta? (replied my Edward). Does it appear impossible to your vile and corrupted Palate, to exist on Love? Can you not conceive the Luxury of living in every distress that Poverty can inflict, with the object of your tenderest affection?"

"You are too ridiculous (said Augusta) to argue with; perhaps however you may in time be convinced that...."

Here I was prevented from hearing the remainder of her speech, by the appearance of a very Handsome young Woman, who was ushered into the Room at the Door of which I had been listening. On hearing her announced by the Name of "Lady Dorothea," I instantly quitted my Post and followed her into the Parlour, for I well remembered that she was the Lady, proposed as a Wife for my Edward by the Cruel and Unrelenting Baronet.

Altho' Lady Dorothea's visit was nominally to Philippa and Augusta, yet I have some reason to imagine that (acquainted with the Marriage and arrival of Edward) to see me was a principal motive to it.

I soon perceived that tho' Lovely and Elegant in her Person and tho' Easy and Polite in her Address, she was of that inferior order of Beings with regard to Delicate Feeling, tender Sentiments, and refined Sensibility, of which Augusta was one.

She staid but half an hour and neither in the Course of her Visit, confided to me any of her secret thoughts, nor requested me to confide in her, any of Mine. You will easily imagine therefore my Dear Marianne that I could not feel any ardent affection or very sincere Attachment for Lady Dorothea.

      Adeiu
        Laura.

LETTER 8TH
Laura to Marianne, in continuation

Lady Dorothea had not left us long before another visitor as unexpected a one as her Ladyship, was announced. It was Sir Edward, who informed by Augusta of her Brother's marriage, came doubtless to reproach him for having dared to unite himself to me without his Knowledge. But Edward foreseeing his design, approached him with heroic fortitude as soon as he entered the Room, and addressed him in the following Manner.

"Sir Edward, I know the motive of your Journey here—You come with the base Design of reproaching me for having entered into an indissoluble engagement with my Laura without your Consent. But Sir, I glory in the Act—. It is my greatest boast that I have incurred the displeasure of my Father!"

So saying, he took my hand and whilst Sir Edward, Philippa, and Augusta were doubtless reflecting with admiration on his undaunted Bravery, led me from the Parlour to his Father's Carriage which yet remained at the Door and in which we were instantly conveyed from the pursuit of Sir Edward.

The Postilions had at first received orders only to take the London road; as soon as we had sufficiently reflected However, we ordered them to Drive to M——. the seat of Edward's most particular freind, which was but a few miles distant. At M——. we arrived in a few hours; and on sending in our names were immediately admitted to Sophia,[1] the Wife of Edward's freind. After having been deprived during the course of 3 weeks of a real freind (for such I term your Mother) imagine my transports at beholding one, most truly worthy of the Name. Sophia was rather above the middle size; most elegantly formed. A soft languor spread over her lovely features, but increased their Beauty—. It was the Charectarestic of her Mind—. She was all sensibility and Feeling. We flew into each others arms and after having exchanged vows of mutual Freindship for the rest of our Lives, instantly unfolded to each other the most inward secrets of our Hearts—. We were interrupted in the

---

[1] The name means "wisdom."

delightfull Employment by the entrance of Augustus, (Edward's freind) who was just returned from a solitary ramble.

Never did I see such an affecting Scene as was the meeting of Edward and Augustus.

"My Life! my Soul!" (exclaimed the former) "My adorable angel!" (replied the latter) as they flew into each other's arms. It was too pathetic for the feelings of Sophia and myself —We fainted alternately on a sofa.[1]

Adeiu
Laura.

LETTER THE 9TH
From the same to the same

Towards the close of the day we received the following Letter from Philippa.

"Sir Edward is greatly incensed by your abrupt departure; he has taken back Augusta with him to Bedfordshire. Much as I wish to enjoy again your charming society, I cannot determine to snatch you from that, of such dear and deserving Freinds—When your Visit to them is terminated, I trust you will return to the arms of your"

"Philippa."

We returned a suitable answer to this affectionate Note and after thanking her for her kind invitation assured her that we would certainly avail ourselves of it, whenever we might have no other place to go to. Tho' certainly nothing could to any reasonable Being, have appeared more satisfactory, than so gratefull a reply to her invitation, yet I know not how it was, but she was certainly capricious enough to be displeased with our behaviour and in a few weeks after, either to revenge our Conduct, or releive her own solitude, married a young and illiterate Fortune-hunter. This imprudent step (tho' we were sensible that it would probably deprive us of that fortune which Philippa had ever taught us to expect) could not on our own accounts, excite from our exalted minds a single sigh; yet fearfull lest it might prove a source of endless misery to the deluded Bride, our trembling Sensibility was greatly affected when we were first informed of the Event. The affectionate Entreaties of Augustus and Sophia that we would for ever consider their House as our Home, easily prevailed on us to determine never more to leave them, In the society of my Edward and this Amiable Pair, I passed the happiest moments of my Life; Our time was most delightfully spent, in mutual Protestations of Freindship, and in vows of unalterable Love, in which we were secure from being interrupted, by intruding and disagreable Visitors, as Augustus and Sophia had on their first Entrance in the Neighbourhood, taken due care to inform the surrounding Families, that as their Happiness centered wholly in themselves, they wished for no other society. But alas! my Dear Marianne such Happiness as I then enjoyed was too perfect to be lasting. A most severe and unexpected Blow at once destroyed every sensation of Pleasure. Convinced as you must be from what I have already told you concerning Augustus and Sophia, that there never were a happier Couple, I need not I imagine, inform you that their union had been contrary to the inclinations of their Cruel and Mercenary Parents; who had vainly endeavoured with obstinate Perseverance to force them into a Marriage with those whom they had ever abhorred; but with an Heroic Fortitude worthy to be related and admired, they had both, constantly refused to submit to such despotic Power.

After having so nobly disentangled themselves from the shackles of Parental Authority, by a Clandestine Marriage, they were determined never to forfeit the good opinion they had gained in the World, in so doing, by accepting any proposals of reconciliation that might be offered them by their Fathers—to this farther tryal of their noble independance however they never were exposed.

They had been married but a few months when our visit to them commenced during which time they had been amply supported by a considerable sum of money which Augustus had gracefully purloined from his unworthy father's Escritoire, a few days before his union with Sophia.

By our arrival their Expenses were considerably encreased tho' their means for supplying them were then nearly exhausted. But they, Exalted Creatures!

---

[1] Cf. Richard Brinsley Sheridan (1751–1816), *The Critic* (1779) 3.1.

scorned to reflect a moment on their pecuniary Distresses and would have blushed at the idea of paying their Debts.—Alas! what was their Reward for such disinterested Behaviour! The beautifull Augustus was arrested and we were all undone. Such perfidious Treachery in the merciless perpetrators of the Deed will shock your gentle nature Dearest Marianne as much as it then affected the Delicate sensibility of Edward, Sophia, your Laura, and of Augustus himself. To compleat such unparalelled Barbarity we were informed that an Execution in the House[1] would shortly take place. Ah! what could we do but what we did! We sighed and fainted on the sofa.

Adeiu
Laura.

LETTER 10TH
Laura in continuation

When we were somewhat recovered from the overpowering Effusions of our grief, Edward desired that we would consider what was the most prudent step to be taken in our unhappy situation while he repaired to his imprisoned freind to lament over his misfortunes. We promised that we would, and he set forwards on his journey to Town. During his absence we faithfully complied with his Desire and after the most mature Deliberation, at length agreed that the best thing we could do was to leave the House; of which we every moment expected the officers of Justice to take possession. We waited therefore with the greatest impatience, for the return of Edward in order to impart to him the result of our Deliberations. But no Edward appeared. In vain did we count the tedious moments of his absence—in vain did we weep—in vain even did we sigh—no Edward returned—. This was too cruel, too unexpected a Blow to our Gentle Sensibility—we could not support it—we could only faint. At length collecting all the Resolution I was Mistress of, I arose and after packing up some necessary apparel for Sophia and myself, I dragged her to a Carriage I had ordered and we instantly set out for London. As the Habitation of Augustus was within twelve miles of Town, it was not long e'er we arrived there, and no sooner had we entered Holboun than letting down one of the Front Glasses I enquired of every decent-looking Person that we passed "If they had seen my Edward?"

But as we drove too rapidly to allow them to answer my repeated Enquiries, I gained little, or indeed, no information concerning him. "Where am I to Drive?" said the Postilion. "To Newgate[2] Gentle Youth (replied I), to see Augustus." "Oh! no, no, (exclaimed Sophia) I cannot go to Newgate; I shall not be able to support the sight of my Augustus in so cruel a confinement—my feelings are sufficiently shocked by the *recital,* of his Distress, but to behold it will overpower my Sensibility." As I perfectly agreed with her in the Justice of her Sentiments the Postilion was instantly directed to return into the Country. You may perhaps have been somewhat surprised my Dearest Marianne, that in the Distress I then endured, destitute of any support, and unprovided with any Habitation, I should never once have remembered my Father and Mother or my paternal Cottage in the Vale of Uske. To account for the seeming forgetfullness I must inform you of a trifling circumstance concerning them which I have as yet never mentioned. The death of my Parents a few weeks after my Departure, is the circumstance I allude to. By their decease I became the lawfull Inheritress of their House and Fortune. But alas! the House had never been their own and their Fortune had only been an Annuity on their own Lives. Such is the Depravity of the World! To your Mother I should have returned with Pleasure, should have been happy to have introduced to her, my charming Sophia and should with Chearfullness have passed the remainder of my Life in their dear Society in the Vale of Uske, had not one obstacle to the execution of so agreable a scheme, intervened; which was the Marriage and Removal of your Mother to a distant part of Ireland.

Adeiu.
Laura.

---

[1] That is, bailiffs will be sent to seize Augustus's possessions in partial payment of his debts.

[2] the main prison in London. It was not a debtors' prison: Augustus has been arrested for theft.

LETTER 11TH
Laura in continuation

"I have a Relation in Scotland (said Sophia to me as we left London) who I am certain would not hesitate in receiving me." "Shall I order the Boy to drive there?" said I—but instantly recollecting myself, exclaimed, "Alas I fear it will be too long a Journey for the Horses." Unwilling however to act only from my own inadequate Knowledge of the Strength and Abilities of Horses, I consulted the Postilion, who was entirely of my Opinion concerning the Affair. We therefore determined to change Horses at the next Town and to travel Post[1] the remainder of the Journey—. When we arrived at the last Inn we were to stop at, which was but a few miles from the House of Sophia's Relation, unwilling to intrude our Society on him unexpected and unthought of, we wrote a very elegant and well penned Note to him containing an account of our Destitute and melancholy Situation, and of our intention to spend some months with him in Scotland. As soon as we had dispatched this Letter, we immediately prepared to follow it in person and were stepping into the Carriage for that Purpose when our attention was atracted by the Entrance of a coroneted Coach[2] and 4 into the Inn-yard. A Gentleman considerably advanced in years, descended from it. At his first Appearance my Sensibility was wonderfully affected and e'er I had gazed at him a 2^d time, an instinctive sympathy whispered to my Heart, that he was my Grandfather. Convinced that I could not be mistaken in my conjecture I instantly sprang from the Carriage I had just entered, and following the Venerable Stranger into the Room he had been shewn to, I threw myself on my knees before him and besought him to acknowledge me as his Grand Child. He started, and after having attentively examined my features, raised me from the Ground and throwing his Grand-fatherly arms around my Neck, exclaimed, "Acknowledge thee! Yes dear resemblance of my Laurina and Laurina's Daughter, sweet image of my Claudia and my Claudia's Mother, I do acknowledge thee as the Daughter of the one and the Granddaughter of the other." While he was thus tenderly embracing me, Sophia astonished at my precipitate Departure, entered the Room in search of me. No sooner had she caught the eye of the venerable Peer, than he exclaimed with every mark of astonishment—"Another Granddaughter! Yes, yes, I see you are the Daughter of my Laurina's eldest Girl; Your resemblance to the beauteous Matilda sufficiently proclaims it." "Oh! replied Sophia, when I first beheld you the instinct of Nature whispered me that we were in some degree related—But whether Grandfathers, or Grandmothers, I could not pretend to determine." He folded her in his arms, and whilst they were tenderly embracing, the Door of the Apartment opened and a most beautifull Young Man appeared. On perceiving him Lord St. Clair started and retreating back a few paces, with uplifted Hands, said, "Another Grand-child! What an unexpected Happiness is this! to discover in the space of 3 minutes, as many of my Descendants! This, I am certain is Philander the son of my Laurina's 3^d girl the amiable Bertha; there wants now but the presence of Gustavus to compleat the Union of my Laurina's Grand-Children."

"And here he is; (said a Gracefull Youth who that instant entered the room) here is the Gustavus you desire to see. I am the son of Agatha your Laurina's 4th and youngest Daughter." "I see you are indeed; replied Lord St. Clair—But tell me (continued he looking fearfully towards the Door) tell me, have I any other Grand-children in the House."[3] "None my Lord." "Then I will provide for you all without farther delay—Here are 4 Banknotes of £50 each—Take them and remember I have done the Duty of a Grandfather." He instantly left the Room and immediately afterwards the House.

Adeiu.
Laura.

---

[1] to travel by stopping at posting stations (inns) along the way and changing horses, instead of using one's own horses for the entire length of the journey.

[2] A coronet painted on the panels of a coach indicated that its owner was an aristocrat. A coach and four is a four-wheel carriage drawn by four horses.

[3] Cf. Frances Burney,* *Evelina* (1778) vol. 3, letter 17.

LETTER THE 12TH
Laura in continuation

You may imagine how greatly we were surprised by the sudden departure of Lord St Clair. "Ignoble Grandsire!" exclaimed Sophia. "Unworthy Grandfather!" said I, and instantly fainted in each other's arms. How long we remained in this situation I know not; but when we recovered we found ourselves alone, without either Gustavus, Philander, or the Banknotes. As we were deploring our unhappy fate, the Door of the Apartment opened and "Macdonald" was announced. He was Sophia's cousin. The haste with which he came to our releif so soon after the receipt of our Note, spoke so greatly in his favour that I hesitated not to pronounce him at first sight, a tender and simpathetic Freind. Alas! he little deserved the name—for though he told us that he was much concerned at our Misfortunes, yet by his own account it appeared that the perusal of them, had neither drawn from him a single sigh, nor induced him to bestow one curse on our vindictive stars—. He told Sophia that his Daughter depended on her returning with him to Macdonald-Hall, and that as his Cousin's freind he should be happy to see me there also. To Macdonald-Hall, therefore we went, and were received with great kindness by Janetta the Daughter of Macdonald, and the Mistress of the Mansion. Janetta was then only fifteen; naturally well disposed, endowed with a susceptible Heart, and a simpathetic Disposition, she might, had these amiable qualities been properly encouraged, have been an ornament to human Nature; but unfortunately her Father possessed not a soul sufficiently exalted to admire so promising a Disposition, and had endeavoured by every means in his power to prevent its encreasing with her Years. He had actually so far extinguished the natural noble Sensibility of her Heart, as to prevail on her to accept an offer from a young Man of his Recommendation. They were to be married in a few months, and Graham, was in the House when we arrived. *We* soon saw through his character. He was just such a Man as one might have expected to be the choice of Macdonald. They said he was Sensible, well-informed, and Agreable; we did not pretend to Judge of such trifles, but as we were convinced he had no soul, that he had never read the sorrows of Werter,[1] and that his Hair bore not the least resemblance to auburn, we were certain that Janetta could feel no affection for him, or at least that she ought to feel none. The very circumstance of his being her father's choice too, was so much in his disfavour, that had he been deserving her, in every other respect yet *that* of itself ought to have been a sufficient reason in the Eyes of Janetta for rejecting him. These considerations we were determined to represent to her in their proper light and doubted not of meeting with the desired success from one naturally so well disposed; whose errors in the affair had only arisen from a want of proper confidence in her own opinion, and a suitable contempt of her father's. We found her indeed all that our warmest wishes could have hoped for; we had no difficulty to convince her that it was impossible she could love Graham, or that it was her Duty to disobey her Father; the only thing at which she rather seemed to hesitate was our assertion that she must be attached to some other Person. For some time, she persevered in declaring that she knew no other young man for whom she had the smallest Affection; but upon explaining the impossibility of such a thing she said that she beleived she *did like* Captain M'Kenrie better than any one she knew besides. This confession satisfied us and after having enumerated the good Qualities of M'Kenrie and assured her that she was violently in love with him, we desired to know whether he had ever in any wise declared his affection to her.

"So far from having ever declared it, I have no reason to imagine that he has ever felt any for me." said Janetta. "That he certainly adores you (replied Sophia) there can be no doubt—. The Attachment must be reciprocal. Did he never gaze on you with admiration—tenderly press your hand—drop an involantary tear—and leave the room abruptly?" "Never (replied she) that I remember—he has always left the room indeed when his visit has been ended, but has never gone away particularly abruptly or without making a bow."

---

[1] Johann Wolfgang von Goethe (1749–1832), *The Sorrows of Young Werther* (1774), also in epistolary form.

"Indeed my Love (said I) you must be mistaken—for it is absolutely impossible that he should ever have left you but with Confusion, Despair, and Precipitation. Consider but for a moment Janetta, and you must be convinced how absurd it is to suppose that he could ever make a Bow, or behave like any other Person." Having settled this Point to our satisfaction, the next we took into consideration was, to determine in what manner we should inform M'Kenrie of the favourable Opinion Janetta entertained of him.… We at length agreed to acquaint him with it by an anonymous Letter which Sophia drew up in the following manner.

"Oh! happy Lover of the beautifull Janetta, oh! amiable Possessor of *her* Heart whose hand is destined to another, why do you thus delay a confession of your attachment to the amiable Object of it? Oh! consider that a few weeks will at once put an end to every flattering Hope that you may now entertain, by uniting the unfortunate Victim of her father's Cruelty to the execrable and detested Graham.

"Alas! why do you thus so cruelly connive at the projected Misery of her and of yourself by delaying to communicate that scheme which had doubtless long possessed your imagination? A secret Union will at once secure the felicity of both."

The amiable M'Kenrie, whose modesty as he afterwards assured us had been the only reason of his having so long concealed the violence of his affection for Janetta, on receiving this Billet flew on the wings of Love to Macdonald-Hall, and so powerfully pleaded his Attachment to her who inspired it, that after a few more private interveiws, Sophia and I experienced the satisfaction of seeing them depart for Gretna-Green,[1] which they chose for the celebration of their Nuptials, in preference to any other place although it was at a considerable distance from Macdonald-Hall.

Adeiu
Laura.

---

[1] a town in southern Scotland where couples could be married under the age of 21 and without the permission of their parents, and so a favourite destination of eloping couples. (Compared to England, Scotland had very lenient marriage laws between 1754 and 1856.)

LETTER THE 13TH
Laura in continuation

They had been gone nearly a couple of Hours, before either Macdonald or Graham had entertained any suspicion of the affair. And they might not even then have suspected it, but for the following little Accident. Sophia happening one day to open a private Drawer in Macdonald's Library with one of her own keys, discovered that it was the Place where he kept his Papers of consequence and amongst them some bank notes of considerable amount. This discovery she imparted to me; and having agreed together that it would be a proper treatment of so vile a Wretch as Macdonald to deprive him of money, perhaps dishonestly gained, it was determined that the next time we should either of us happen to go that way, we would take one or more of the Bank notes from the drawer. This well meant Plan we had often successfully put in Execution; but alas! on the very day of Janetta's Escape, as Sophia was majestically removing the 5th Bank-note from the Drawer to her own purse, she was suddenly most impertinently interrupted in her employment by the entrance of Macdonald himself, in a most abrupt and precipitate Manner. Sophia (who though naturally all winning sweetness could when occasions demanded it call forth the Dignity of her sex) instantly put on a most forbiding look, and darting an angry frown on the undaunted culprit, demanded in a haughty tone of voice "Wherefore her retirement was thus insolently broken in on?" The unblushing Macdonald, without even endeavouring to exculpate himself from the crime he was charged with, meanly endeavoured to reproach Sophia with ignobly defrauding him of his money … The dignity of Sophia was wounded; "Wretch (exclaimed she, hastily replacing the Bank-note in the Drawer) how darest thou to accuse me of an Act, of which the bare idea makes me blush?" The base wretch was still unconvinced and continued to upbraid the justly-offended Sophia in such opprobious Language, that at length he so greatly provoked the gentle sweetness of her Nature, as to induce her to revenge herself on him by informing him of Janetta's Elopement, and of the active Part we had both taken in the affair. At this period of their Quarrel

I entered the Library and was as you may imagine equally offended as Sophia at the ill-grounded accusations of the malevolent and contemptible Macdonald. "Base Miscreant! (cried I) how canst thou thus undauntedly endeavour to sully the spotless reputation of such bright Excellence? Why dost thou not suspect *my* innocence as soon?" "Be satisfied Madam (replied he) I *do* suspect it, and therefore must desire that you will both leave this House in less than half an hour."

"We shall go willingly; (answered Sophia) our hearts have long detested thee, and nothing but our freindship for thy Daughter could have induced us to remain so long beneath thy roof."

"Your Freindship for my Daughter has indeed been most powerfully exerted by throwing her into the arms of an unprincipled Fortune-hunter." (replied he.)

"Yes, (exclaimed I) amidst every misfortune, it will afford us some consolation to reflect that by this one act of Freindship to Janetta, we have amply discharged every obligation that we have received from her father."

"It must indeed be a most gratefull reflection, to your exalted minds." (said he.)

As soon as we had packed up our wardrobe and valuables, we left Macdonald Hall, and after having walked about a mile and a half we sate down by the side of a clear limpid stream to refresh our exhausted limbs. The place was suited to meditation. A grove of full-grown Elms sheltered us from the East—. A Bed of full-grown Nettles from the West—. Before us ran the murmuring brook and behind us ran the turn-pike road. We were in a mood for contemplation and in a Disposition to enjoy so beautifull a spot.[1] A mutual silence which had for some time reigned between us, was at length broke by my exclaiming—"What a lovely scene! Alas why are not Edward and Augustus here to enjoy its Beauties with us?"

"Ah! my beloved Laura (cried Sophia) for pity's sake forbear recalling to my remembrance the unhappy situation of my imprisoned Husband. Alas, what would I not give to learn the fate of my Augustus! to know if he is still in Newgate, or if he is yet hung. But never shall I be able so far to conquer my tender sensibility as to enquire after him. Oh! do not I beseech you ever let me again hear you repeat his beloved name—. It affects me too deeply—. I cannot bear to hear him mentioned it wounds my feelings."

"Excuse me my Sophia for having thus unwillingly offended you—" replied I—and then changing the conversation, desired her to admire the noble Grandeur of the Elms which sheltered us from the Eastern Zephyr.[2] "Alas! my Laura (returned she) avoid so melancholy a subject, I intreat you. Do not again wound my Sensibility by observations on those elms. They remind me of Augustus. He was like them, tall, magestic—he possessed that noble grandeur which you admire in them."

I was silent, fearfull lest I might any more unwillingly distress her by fixing on any other subject of conversation which might again remind her of Augustus.

"Why do you not speak my Laura?" (said she after a short pause) "I cannot support this silence you must not leave me to my own reflections; they ever recur to Augustus."

"What a beautifull sky! (said I) How charmingly is the azure varied by those delicate streaks of white!"

"Oh! my Laura (replied she hastily withdrawing her Eyes from a momentary glance at the sky) do not thus distress me by calling my Attention to an object which so cruelly reminds me of my Augustus's blue sattin waistcoat striped with white! In pity to your unhappy freind avoid a subject so distressing." What could I do? The feelings of Sophia were at that time so exquisite, and the tenderness she felt for Augustus so poignant that I had not power to start any other topic, justly fearing that it might in some unforseen manner again awaken all her sensibility by directing her thoughts to her Husband. Yet to be silent would be cruel; she had intreated me to talk.

From this Dilemma I was most fortunately releived by an accident truly apropos; it was the lucky overturning of a Gentleman's Phaeton, on the road which ran murmuring behind us. It was a most fortunate accident as it diverted the attention of Sophia from the melan-

---

[1] Cf. Samuel Johnson (1709–84), *A Journey to the Western Isles of Scotland* (1775) chap. "Anoch."

[2] The Zephyr is the west wind.

choly reflections which she had been before indulging. We instantly quitted our seats and ran to the rescue of those who but a few moments before had been in so elevated a situation as a fashionably high Phaeton, but who were now laid low and sprawling in the Dust. "What an ample subject for reflection on the uncertain Enjoyments of this World, would not that Phaeton and the Life of Cardinal Wolsey[1] afford a thinking Mind!" said I to Sophia as we were hastening to the field of Action.

She had not time to answer me, for every thought was now engaged by the horrid spectacle before us. Two Gentlemen most elegantly attired but weltering in their blood was what first struck our Eyes—we approached—they were Edward and Augustus—. Yes dearest Marianne they were our Husbands. Sophia shreiked and fainted on the ground—I screamed and instantly ran mad—. We remained thus mutually deprived of our senses, some minutes, and on regaining them were deprived of them again. For an Hour and a Quarter did we continue in this unfortunate situation—Sophia fainting every moment and I running mad as often. At length a groan from the hapless Edward (who alone retained any share of life) restored us to ourselves. Had we indeed before imagined that either of them lived, we should have been more sparing of our Greif—but as we had supposed when we first beheld them that they were no more, we knew that nothing could remain to be done but what we were about. No sooner therefore did we hear my Edward's groan than postponing our lamentations for the present, we hastily ran to the Dear Youth and kneeling on each side of him implored him not to die—. "Laura (said He fixing his now languid Eyes on me) I fear I have been overturned."

I was overjoyed to find him yet sensible.

"Oh! tell me Edward (said I) tell me I beseech you before you die, what has befallen you since that unhappy Day in which Augustus was arrested and we were separated—"

"I will" (said he) and instantly fetching a deep sigh, Expired—. Sophia immediately sunk again into a swoon—. *My* greif was more audible. My Voice faltered, My Eyes assumed a vacant stare, my face became as pale as Death, and my senses were considerably impaired—.

"Talk not to me of Phaetons (said I, raving in a frantic, incoherent manner)—Give me a violin—. I'll play to him and sooth him in his melancholy Hours—Beware ye gentle Nymphs of Cupid's Thunderbolts, avoid the piercing shafts of Jupiter—Look at that grove of Firs—I see a Leg of Mutton—They told me Edward was not Dead; but they deceived me—they took him for a cucumber—"[2] Thus I continued wildly exclaiming on my Edward's Death—. For two Hours did I rave thus madly and should not then have left off, as I was not in the least fatigued, had not Sophia who was just recovered from her swoon, intreated me to consider that Night was now approaching and that the Damps began to fall. "And whither shall we go (said I) to shelter us from either."? "To that white Cottage." (replied she pointing to a neat Building which rose up amidst the grove of Elms and which I had not before observed—) I agreed and we instantly walked to it—we knocked at the door—it was opened by an old woman; on being requested to afford us a Night's Lodging, she informed us that her House was but small, that she had only two Bedrooms, but that However we should be wellcome to one of them. We were satisfied and followed the good woman into the House where we were greatly cheered by the sight of a comfortable fire—. She was a Widow and had only one Daughter, who was then just seventeen—One of the best of ages; but alas! she was very plain and her name was Bridget..... Nothing therefore could be expected from her—she could not be supposed to possess either exalted Ideas, Delicate Feelings or refined Sensibilities—. She was nothing more than a mere good-tempered, civil and obliging young woman; as such we could scarcely dislike her—she was only an Object of Contempt—.

Adeiu
Laura.

---

[1] Cardinal Thomas Wolsey (c. 1475–1530), Lord Chancellor to Henry VIII, fell from grace in 1529 for failing to secure Henry a quick divorce from Katharine of Aragon. Cf. Shakespeare, *Henry VIII* 3.2.350–72; and Johnson, *The Vanity of Human Wishes* (1749) 99–120.

[2] Cf. Shakespeare, *Hamlet* 4.5 and *King Lear* 3.4, 3.6, 4.6; and Sheridan, *The Critic* 3.1.

LETTER THE 14TH
Laura in continuation

Arm yourself my amiable young Freind with all the philosophy you are Mistress of; summon up all the fortitude you possess, for alas! in the perusal of the following Pages your sensibility will be most severely tried. Ah! what were the misfortunes I had before experienced and which I have already related to you, to the one I am now going to inform you of. The Death of my Father my Mother and my Husband though almost more than my gentle Nature could support, were trifles in comparison to the misfortune I am now proceeding to relate. The morning after our arrival at the Cottage, Sophia complained of a violent pain in her delicate limbs, accompanied with a disagreable Head-ake She attributed it to a cold caught by her continued faintings in the open air as the Dew was falling the Evening before. This I feared was but too probably the case; since how could it be otherwise accounted for that I should have escaped the same indisposition, but by supposing that the bodily Exertions I had undergone in my repeated fits of frenzy had so effectually circulated and warmed my Blood as to make me proof against the chilling Damps of Night, whereas, Sophia lying totally inactive on the ground must have been exposed to all their severity. I was most seriously alarmed by her illness which trifling as it may appear to you, a certain instinctive sensibility whispered me, would in the End be fatal to her.

Alas! my fears were but too fully justified; she grew gradually worse—and I daily became more alarmed for her. At length she was obliged to confine herself solely to the Bed allotted us by our worthy Landlady—. Her disorder turned to a galloping Consumption[1] and in a few days carried her off. Amidst all my Lamentations for her (and violent you may suppose they were) I yet received some consolation in the reflection of my having paid every attention to her, that could be offered, in her illness. I had wept over her every Day—had bathed her sweet face with my tears and had pressed her fair Hands continually in mine—. "My beloved Laura (said she to me a few Hours before she died) take warning from my unhappy End and avoid the imprudent conduct which had occasioned it ... Beware of fainting-fits ... Though at the time they may be refreshing and agreable yet beleive me they will in the end, if too often repeated and at improper seasons, prove destructive to your Constitution ... My fate will teach you this .. I die a Martyr to my greif for the loss of Augustus. . One fatal swoon has cost me my Life .. Beware of swoons Dear Laura.... A frenzy fit is not one quarter so pernicious; it is an exercise to the Body and if not too violent, is I dare say conducive to Health in its consequences——Run mad as often as you chuse; but do not faint—"

These were the last words she ever addressed to me .. It was her dieing Advice to her afflicted Laura, who has ever most faithfully adhered to it.

After having attended my lamented freind to her Early Grave, I immediately (tho' late at night) left the detested Village in which she died, and near which had expired my Husband and Augustus. I had not walked many yards from it before I was overtaken by a stage-coach,[2] in which I instantly took a place, determined to proceed in it to Edinburgh, where I hoped to find some kind some pitying Freind who would receive and comfort me in my afflictions.

It was so dark when I entered the Coach that I could not distinguish the Number of my Fellow-travellers; I could only perceive that they were many. Regardless however of anything concerning them, I gave myself up to my own sad Reflections. A general silence prevailed—A silence, which was by nothing interrupted but by the loud and repeated snores of one of the Party.

"What an illiterate villain must that man be! (thought I to myself) What a total want of delicate refinement must he have, who can thus shock our senses by such a brutal noise! He must I am certain be capable of every bad action! There is no crime too black for such a Character!"[3] Thus reasoned I within myself, and doubtless such were the reflections of my fellow travellers.

---

[1] tuberculosis.

[2] a coach used for public transport.

[3] Cf. Sheridan, *The School for Scandal* (1777) 4.3.

At length, returning Day enabled me to behold the unprincipled Scoundrel who had so violently disturbed my feelings. It was Sir Edward the father of my Deceased Husband. By his side, sate Augusta, and on the same seat with me were your Mother and Lady Dorothea. Imagine my surprise at finding myself thus seated amongst my old Acquaintance. Great as was my astonishment, it was yet increased, when on looking out of Windows, I beheld the Husband of Philippa, with Philippa by his side, on the Coachbox and when on looking behind I beheld, Philander and Gustavus in the Basket.[1] "Oh! Heavens, (exclaimed I) is it possible that I should so unexpectedly be surrounded by my nearest Relations and Connections"? These words roused the rest of the Party, and every eye was directed to the corner in which I sat. "Oh! my Isabel (continued I throwing myself across Lady Dorothea into her arms) receive once more to your Bosom the unfortunate Laura. Alas! when we last parted in the Vale of Usk, I was happy in being united to the best of Edwards; I had then a Father and a Mother, and had never known misfortunes—But now deprived of every freind but you——"

"What! (interrupted Augusta) is my Brother dead then? Tell us I intreat you what is become of him?" "Yes, cold and insensible Nymph, (replied I) that luckless swain your Brother, is no more, and you may now glory in being the Heiress of Sir Edward's fortune."

Although I had always despised her from the Day I had overheard her conversation with my Edward, yet in civility I complied with hers and Sir Edward's intreaties that I would inform them of the whole melancholy affair. They were greatly shocked—even the obdurate Heart of Sir Edward and the insensible one of Augusta, were touched with sorrow, by the unhappy tale. At the request of your Mother I related to them every other misfortune which had befallen me since we parted. Of the imprisonment of Augustus and the absence of Edward—of our arrival in Scotland—of our unexpected Meeting with our Grand-father and our cousins—of our visit to Macdonald-Hall—of the singular service we there performed towards Janetta—of her Fathers ingratitude for it.... of his inhuman Behaviour, unaccountable suspicions, and barbarous treatment of us, in obliging us to leave the House.... of our lamentations on the loss of Edward and Augustus and finally of the melancholy Death of my beloved Companion.

Pity and surprise were strongly depictured in your Mother's countenance, during the whole of my narration, but I am sorry to say, that to the eternal reproach of her sensibility, the latter infinitely predominated. Nay, faultless as my conduct had certainly been during the whole course of my late misfortunes and adventures, she pretended to find fault with my behaviour in many of the situations in which I had been placed. As I was sensible myself, that I had always behaved in a manner which reflected Honour on my Feelings and Refinement, I paid little attention to what she said, and desired her to satisfy my Curiosity by informing me how she came there, instead of wounding my spotless reputation with unjustifiable Reproaches. As soon as she had complied with my wishes in this particular and had given me an accurate detail of every thing that had befallen her since our separation (the particulars of which if you are not already acquainted with, your Mother will give you) I applied to Augusta for the same information respecting herself, Sir Edward and Lady Dorothea.

She told me that having a considerable taste for the Beauties of Nature, her curiosity to behold the delightful scenes it exhibited in that part of the World had been so much raised by Gilpin's Tour to the Highlands,[2] that she had prevailed on her Father to undertake a Tour to Scotland and had persuaded Lady Dorothea to accompany them. That they had arrived at Edinburgh a few Days before and from thence had made daily Excursions into the Country around in the Stage Coach they were then in, from one of which Excursions they were at that time returning. My next enquiries were concerning Philippa and her Husband, the latter of whom I learned having spent all her fortune, had recourse for subsistance to the talent in which,

---

[1] the compartment hanging at the rear of the carriage, commonly used for luggage.

[2] William Gilpin (1724–1804), *Observations, relative chiefly to Picturesque Beauty, made in the year 1776, on Several Parts of Great Britain; particularly the Highlands of Scotland* (1789).

he had always most excelled, namely, Driving, and that having sold every thing which belonged to them except their Coach, had converted it into a Stage and in order to be removed from any of his former Acquaintance, had driven it to Edinburgh from whence he went to Sterling every other Day. That Philippa still retaining her affection for her ungratefull Husband, had followed him to Scotland and generally accompanied him in his little Excursions to Sterling. "It has only been to throw a little money into their Pockets (continued Augusta) that my Father has always travelled in their Coach to veiw the beauties of the Country since our arrival in Scotland—for it would certainly have been much more agreable to us, to visit the Highlands in a Postchaise than merely to travel from Edinburgh to Sterling and from Sterling to Edinburgh every other Day in a crowded and uncomfortable Stage." I perfectly agreed with her in her sentiments on the affair, and secretly blamed Sir Edward for thus sacrificing his Daughter's Pleasure for the sake of a ridiculous old woman whose folly in marrying so young a man ought to be punished. His Behaviour however was entirely of a peice with his general Character; for what could be expected from a man who possessed not the smallest atom of Sensibility, who scarcely knew the meaning of simpathy, and who actually snored—.

Adeiu
Laura.

LETTER THE 15TH
Laura in continuation

When we arrived at the town where we were to Breakfast, I was determined to speak with Philander and Gustavus, and to that purpose as soon as I left the Carriage, I went to the Basket and tenderly enquired after their Health, expressing my fears of the uneasiness of their situation. At first they seemed rather confused at my appearance dreading no doubt that I might call them to account for the money which our Grandfather had left me and which they had unjustly deprived me of, but finding that I mentioned nothing of the Matter, they desired me to step into the Basket as we might there converse with greater ease. Accordingly I entered and whilst the rest of the party were devouring green tea and buttered toast, we feasted ourselves in a more refined and sentimental Manner by a confidential Conversation. I informed them of every thing which had befallen me during the course of my life, and at my request they related to me every incident of theirs.

"We are the sons as you already know, of the two youngest Daughters which Lord St Clair had by Laurina an italian opera girl. Our mothers could neither of them exactly ascertain who were our Fathers, though it is generally beleived that Philander, is the son of one Philip Jones a Bricklayer and that my Father was Gregory Staves a Staymaker[1] of Edinburgh. This is however of little consequence for as our Mothers were certainly never married to either of them it reflects no Dishonour on our Blood, which is of a most ancient and unpolluted kind. Bertha (the Mother of Philander) and Agatha (my own Mother) always lived together. They were neither of them very rich; their united fortunes had originally amounted to nine thousand Pounds, but as they had always lived upon the principal of it, when we were fifteen it was diminished to nine Hundred. This nine Hundred, they always kept in a Drawer in one of the Tables which stood in our common sitting Parlour, for the convenience of having it always at Hand. Whether it was from this circumstance, of its being easily taken, or from a wish of being independant, or from an excess of sensibility (for which we were always remarkable) I cannot now determine, but certain it is that when we had reached our 15th year, we took the nine Hundred Pounds and ran away. Having obtained this prize we were determined to manage it with eoconomy and not to spend it either with folly or Extravagance. To this purpose we therefore divided it into nine parcels, one of which we devoted to Victuals, the 2^d to Drink, the 3^d to Housekeeping, the 4th to Carriages, the 5th to Horses, the 6th to Servants, the 7th to Amusements the 8th to Cloathes and the 9th to Silver Buckles. Having thus arranged our Expences for two months (for we expected to make the nine Hundred Pounds last as long) we hastened to London and had the good luck to spend it in 7 weeks and a Day which was

---

[1] a corset-maker.

6 Days sooner than we had intended. As soon as we had thus happily disencumbered ourselves from the weight of so much money, we began to think of returning to our Mothers, but accidentally hearing that they were both starved to Death, we gave over the design and determined to engage ourselves to some strolling Company of Players, as we had always a turn for the Stage. Accordingly we offered our services to one and were accepted; our Company was indeed rather small, as it consisted only of the Manager his wife and ourselves, but there were fewer to pay and the only inconvenience attending it was the Scarcity of Plays which for want of People to fill the Characters, we could perform. We did not mind trifles however—. One of our most admired Performances was *Macbeth*, in which we were truly great. The Manager always played *Banquo* himself, his Wife my *Lady Macbeth*. I did the *Three Witches* and Philander acted *all the rest*. To say the truth this tragedy was not only the Best, but the only Play we ever performed; and after having acted it all over England, and Wales, we came to Scotland to exhibit it over the remainder of Great Britain. We happened to be quartered in that very Town, where you came and met your Grandfather—. We were in the Inn-yard when his Carriage entered and perceiving by the arms to whom it belonged, and knowing that Lord St Clair was our Grandfather, we agreed to endeavour to get something from him by discovering the Relationship—. You know how well it succeeded—. Having obtained the two Hundred Pounds, we instantly left the Town, leaving our Manager and his Wife to act *Macbeth* by themselves, and took the road to Sterling, where we spent our little fortune with great *eclat*. We are now returning to Edinburgh in order to get some preferment in the Acting way; and such my Dear Cousin is our History."

I thanked the amiable Youth for his entertaining narration, and after expressing my wishes for their Welfare and Happiness, left them in their little Habitation and returned to my other Freinds who impatiently expected me.

My adventures are now drawing to a close my dearest Marianne; at least for the present.

When we arrived at Edinburgh Sir Edward told me that as the Widow of his son, he desired I would accept from his Hands of four Hundred a year. I graciously promised that I would, but could not help observing that the unsimpathetic Baronet offered it more on account of my being the Widow of Edward than in being the refined and amiable Laura.

I took up my Residence in a romantic Village in the Highlands of Scotland where I have ever since continued, and where I can uninterrupted by unmeaning Visits, indulge in a melancholy solitude, my unceasing Lamentations for the Death of my Father, my Mother, my Husband and my Freind.

Augusta has been for several years united to Graham the Man of all others most suited to her; she became acquainted with him during her stay in Scotland.

Sir Edward in hopes of gaining an Heir to his Title and Estate, at the same time married Lady Dorothea—. His wishes have been answered.

Philander and Gustavus, after having raised their reputation by their Performances in the Theatrical Line at Edinburgh, removed to Covent Garden,[1] where they still Exhibit under the assumed names of *Lewis* and *Quick*.[2] Philippa has long paid the Debt of Nature, Her Husband however still continues to drive the Stage-Coach from Edinburgh to Sterling:—

Adeiu my Dearest Marianne.

Laura.

Finis

June 13th 1790

---

[1] one of only two London theatres licensed to present spoken drama.

[2] Philander and Gustavus borrow their stage names from two real actors, William Thomas "Gentleman" Lewis (1748?–1811) and John Quick (1748–1831).

Jane Austen

from *Northanger Abbey* (1818)

from CHAPTER 5

The progress of the friendship between Catherine and Isabella was quick as its beginning had been warm, and they passed so rapidly through every gradation of increasing tenderness, that there was shortly no fresh proof of it to be given to their friends or themselves. They called each other by their Christian name, were always arm in arm when they walked, pinned up each other's train for the dance, and were not to be divided in the set; and if a rainy morning deprived them of other enjoyments, they were still resolute in meeting in defiance of wet and dirt, and shut themselves up, to read novels together. Yes, novels;— for I will not adopt that ungenerous and impolitic custom so common with novel writers, of degrading by their contemptuous censure the very performances, to the number of which they are themselves adding—joining with their greatest enemies in bestowing the harshest epithets on such works, and scarcely ever permitting them to be read by their own heroine, who, if she accidentally take up a novel, is sure to turn over its insipid pages with disgust. Alas! if the heroine of one novel be not patronized by the heroine of another, from whom can she expect protection and regard? I cannot approve of it. Let us leave it to the Reviewers to abuse such effusions of fancy at their leisure, and over every new novel to talk in threadbare strains of the trash with which the press now groans. Let us not desert one another; we are an injured body. Although our productions have afforded more extensive and unaffected pleasure than those of any other literary corporation in the world, no species of composition has been so much decried. From pride, ignorance, or fashion, our foes are almost as many as our readers. And while the abilities of the nine-hundredth abridger of the History of England, or of the man who collects and publishes in a volume some dozen lines of Milton, Pope, and Prior, with a paper from the Spectator, and a chapter from Sterne,[1] are eulogized by a thousand pens,—there seems almost a general wish of decrying the capacity and undervaluing the labour of the novelist, and of slighting the performances which have only genius, wit, and taste to recommend them. "I am no novel reader—I seldom look into novels—Do not imagine that *I* often read novels—It is really very well for a novel."—Such is the common cant.— "And what are you reading, Miss——?" "Oh! it is only a novel!" replies the young lady; while she lays down her book with affected indifference, or momentary shame.—"It is only Cecilia, or Camilla, or Belinda";[2] or, in short, only some work in which the greatest powers of the mind are displayed, in which the most thorough knowledge of human nature, the happiest delineation of its varieties, the liveliest effusions of wit and humour are conveyed to the world in the best chosen language. Now, had the same young lady been engaged with a volume of the Spectator, instead of such a work, how proudly would she have produced the book, and told its name; though the chances must be against her being occupied by any part of that voluminous publication, of which either the matter or manner would not disgust a young person of taste: the substance of its papers so often consisting in the statement of improbable circumstances, unnatural characters, and topics of conversation, which no longer concern any one living; and their language, too, frequently so coarse as to give no very favourable idea of the age that could endure it.

---

[1] Matthew Prior (1664–1721), poet; the *Spectator*, a journal of essays published daily between Mar. 1711 and Dec. 1712 by Joseph Addison (1672–1719), Sir Richard Steele (1672–1729), and others; Laurence Sterne (1713–68), author of *Tristram Shandy* (1759–67) and *A Sentimental Journey* (1768): all contained material that Austen would have found offensive.

[2] *Cecilia* (1782) and *Camilla* (1796), by Burney;* *Belinda* (1801), by Maria Edgeworth.*

Thomas Campbell
1777 – 1844

Thomas Campbell was born in Glasgow on 27 July 1777, the eleventh and youngest child of Alexander Campbell, a retired businessperson, and Margaret Campbell. He was educated at Glasgow University and then moved to Edinburgh, where he published his most important poem, *The Pleasures of Hope* (1799). In October 1803, he married Matilda Sinclair and they moved to London, where Campbell worked as a writer, lecturer, and editor. They had two sons; unfortunately, one died of scarlet fever and the other became mentally ill. Campbell published his favourite among his poems, *Gertrude of Wyoming*, in 1809. From 1821 to 1830, he edited the *New Monthly Magazine*, in which he published the "Lectures on Poetry" he originally presented at the Royal Institution (1821–26). Starting in 1825, he was involved in the founding of London University, and from 1826 to 1829 he served as Lord Rector of Glasgow University. Matilda, his mainstay, died on 9 May 1828. In the 1830s, Campbell concentrated on scholarly work, publishing biographies of Sarah Siddons, Petrarch, and Frederick the Great, and editing the work of Shakespeare. In 1843, he went for health and financial reasons to Boulogne, where he died on 15 June 1844. He is buried in Poets' Corner, Westminster Abbey. (D.L.M.)

෴

from *New Monthly Magazine and Literary Journal* 8, original papers (March 1823)

The Last Man[1]

All worldly shapes shall melt in gloom,
    The Sun himself must die,
Before this mortal shall assume
    Its Immortality!
5 I saw a vision in my sleep,
That gave my spirit strength to sweep
    Adown the gulf of Time!
I saw the last of human mould,
That shall Creation's death behold,
10   As Adam saw her prime!

The Sun's eye had a sickly glare,
    The Earth with age was wan,
The skeletons of nations were
    Around that lonely man!
15 Some had expir'd in fight,—the brands
Still rusted in their bony hands;

In plague and famine some!
Earth's cities had no sound nor tread;
And ships were drifting with the dead
20   To shores where all was dumb!

Yet, prophet like, that lone one stood,
    With dauntless words and high,
That shook the sere leaves from the wood
    As if a storm pass'd by,
25 Saying, we are twins in death, proud Sun,
Thy face is cold, thy race is run,
    'Tis Mercy bids thee go.
For thou ten thousand thousand years
Hast seen the tide of human tears,
30   That shall no longer flow.

What though beneath thee man put forth
    His pomp, his pride, his skill;
And arts that made fire, flood, and earth,
    The vassals of his will;—
35 Yet mourn I not thy parted sway,
Thou dim discrowned king of day:
    For all those trophied arts
And triumphs that beneath thee sprang,
Heal'd not a passion or a pang
40   Entail'd on human hearts.

---

[1] Campbell claimed to have given Byron the idea for "Darkness."* There is no independent evidence for this claim. See also Hood, "The Last Man."*

> Go, let oblivion's curtain fall
>   Upon the stage of men,
> Nor with thy rising beams recall
>   Life's tragedy again.
> 45 Its piteous pageants bring not back,
> Nor waken flesh, upon the rack
>   Of pain anew to writhe;
> Stretch'd in disease's shapes abhorr'd,
> Or mown in battle by the sword,
> 50   Like grass beneath the scythe.
>
> Ev'n I am weary in yon skies
>   To watch thy fading fire;
> Test of all sumless agonies,
>   Behold not me expire.
> 55 My lips that speak thy dirge of death—
> Their rounded gasp and gurgling breath
>   To see thou shalt not boast.
> The eclipse of Nature spreads my pall,—
> The majesty of Darkness shall
> 60   Receive my parting ghost!
>
> This spirit shall return to Him
>   That gave its heavenly spark;
> Yet think not, Sun, it shall be dim
>   When thou thyself art dark!
> 65 No! it shall live again, and shine
> In bliss unknown to beams of thine,
>   By Him recall'd to breath,
> Who captive led captivity.
> Who robbed the grave of Victory,—
> 70   And took the sting from Death![1]
>
> Go, Sun, while Mercy holds me up
>   On Nature's awful waste
> To drink this last and bitter cup
>   Of grief that man shall taste—[2]
> 75 Go, tell the night that hides thy face,
> Thou saw'st the last of Adam's race,
>   On Earth's sepulchral clod,
> The dark'ning universe defy
> To quench his Immortality,
> 80   Or shake his trust in God!

---

[1] Cf. 1 Corinthians 15.55.

[2] Cf. Luke 22.42.

William Hazlitt
1778 – 1830

William Hazlitt was born on 10 April 1778 in Maidstone, Kent, the third child of William Hazlitt, a Presbyterian minister, and Grace Loftus Hazlitt. In 1780, the peripatetic Rev. Hazlitt moved his family to Ireland, and in 1783 to America, where he was involved in founding the first Unitarian church in Boston. By 1787, the Hazlitts were back in England, and William, intended for the ministry, was educated at the New Unitarian College in Hackney. He came to know such figures of religious Dissent as Coleridge,* Godwin,* Thomas Holcroft, Price,* Joseph Priestley, Horne Tooke,* and Wollstonecraft;* but he decided against the ministry. For a while he studied painting with his brother, John, but then he decided on writing. He published his first book, *An Essay on the Principles of Human Action*, in 1805.

In 1806, Hazlitt met Sarah Stoddard, and they were married in May 1808. They had three children, but two died in infancy. They were divorced in 1822, and Hazlitt suffered an unrequited passion for a domestic servant, Sally Walker, which inspired his *Liber Amoris* ("The Book of Love," 1823). In 1824 he married a widow, Isabella Bridgewater, but they eventually separated.

Meanwhile, Hazlitt was writing industriously, publishing a critique of the war with France (1806), a reply to Malthus* (1807), a grammar book (1810), and a biography of Holcroft (1816). In 1812, he became parliamentary reporter for the *Morning Chronicle*. In 1814, he moved on to write for the *Examiner*, edited by Henry and Leigh Hunt,* and the next year he also began writing for the *Edinburgh Review*, edited by Francis Jeffrey.* All these periodicals were liberal politically. A regular feature in the *Examiner* led to Hazlitt's first important book, *The Round Table* (1817). Hazlitt also became a popular lecturer, publishing *Lectures on the English Poets* (1818), *Lectures on the English Comic Writers* (1819), and *Lectures chiefly on the Dramatic Literature of the Age of Elizabeth* (1820). His best-known work, *The Spirit of the Age* (1825), is a collection of twenty-five character studies of such contemporaries as Canning,* Cobbett,* Coleridge, Jeffrey, Scott,* and W. Wordsworth.* He finished his most ambitious work, a four-volume *Life of Napoleon Bonaparte*, in 1830. He died in London on 18 September 1830. (D.L.M.)

༄༅༄

from *The Round Table, Examiner* (Sunday, 26 May 1816)

NO. 40
On Gusto

Gusto in art is power or passion defining any object.—It is not so difficult to explain this term in what relates to expression (of which it may be said to be the highest degree) as in what relates to things without expression, to the natural appearances of objects, as mere colour or form. The truth is, that there is hardly any object entirely devoid of expression, without some character of power belonging to it, some precise association with pleasure or pain; and it is in giving this truth of character from the truth of feeling, whether in the highest or the lowest degree, but always in the highest degree of which the subject is capable, that gusto consists.

There is a gusto in the colouring of Titian.[1] Not only do his heads seem to think—his bodies seem to feel. This is what the Italians mean by the *morbidezza*[2] of his flesh-colour. It seems sensitive and alive all over; not merely to have the look and texture of flesh, but the feeling in itself. For example, the limbs of his female figures have a luxurious softness and delicacy, which appears conscious of the pleasure of the beholder. As the objects themselves in nature would produce an impression on

---

[1] Tiziano Vecelli (c. 1487–1576), Italian painter.

[2] "softness," "smoothness" (It.).

the sense, distinct from every other object, and having something divine in it, which the heart owns and the imagination consecrates, the objects in the picture preserve the same impression, absolute, unimpaired, stamped with all the truth of passion, the pride of the eye, and the charms of beauty. Rubens[1] makes his flesh-colour like flowers; Albano's[2] is like ivory, Titian's is like flesh, and like nothing else. It is as different from that of other painters, as the skin is from a piece of white or red drapery thrown over it. The blood circulates here and there, the blue veins just appear, the rest is distinguished throughout only by that sort of tingling sensation to the eye, which the body feels within itself. This is gusto.—Vandyke's[3] flesh-colour, though it has great truth and purity, wants gusto. It has not the internal character, the living principle in it. It is a smooth surface, not a warm, moving mass. It is painted without passion, with indifference. The hand only has been concerned. The impression slides off from the eye, and does not, like the tones of Titian's pencil, leave a sting behind it in the mind of the spectator. The eye does not acquire a taste or appetite for what it sees. In a word, gusto in painting is where the impression made on one sense excites by affinity those of another.

Michael Angelo's[4] forms are full of gusto. They everywhere obtrude the sense of power upon the eye. His limbs convey an idea of muscular power, of moral grandeur, and even of intellectual dignity: they are firm, commanding, broad, and massy, capable of executing with ease the determined purposes of the will. His faces have no other expression than his figures, conscious power and capacity. They appear only to think what they shall do, and to know that they can do it. This is what is meant by saying that his style is hard and masculine. It is the reverse of Correggio's,[5] which is effeminate. That is, the gusto of Michael Angelo consists in expressing energy of will without proportionable sensibility, Correggio's in expressing exquisite sensibility without energy of will. In Correggio's faces as well as figures we see neither bones nor muscles, but then what a soul is there, full of sweetness and of grace—pure, playful, soft, angelical! There is sentiment enough in a hand painted by Correggio to set up a school of history-painters. Whenever we look at the hands of Correggio's women or of Raphael's,[6] we always wish to touch them.[7]

Again, Titian's landscapes have a prodigious gusto, both in the colouring and forms. We shall never forget one that we saw many years ago in the Orleans Gallery of Acteon hunting.[8] It had a brown, mellow, autumnal look. The sky was of the colour of stone. The winds seemed to sing through the rustling branches of the trees, and already you might hear the twanging of bows resound through the tangled mazes of the wood. Mr.

---

[1] Peter Paul Rubens (1577–1640), Flemish painter.

[2] Francesco Albani (1578–1660), Italian painter.

[3] Sir Anthony Van Dyck (1599–1641), Flemish portrait painter who settled in England; student of Rubens, also influenced by Titian.

[4] Michelangelo Buonarotti (1475–1564), Italian sculptor, architect, painter, and poet.

[5] Antonio Allegri di Correggio (c.1489–1534), Italian painter.

[6] Raffaello Sanzio of Urbino (1483–1520), Italian painter.

[7] "This may seem obscure. We will therefore avail ourselves of our privilege to explain as Members of Parliament do, when they let fall any thing too paradoxical, novel, or abstruse, to be immediately apprehended by the other side of the House. When the Widow Wadman looked over my Uncle Toby's map of the siege of Namur with him, and as he pointed out the approaches of his battalion in a transverse line across the plain to the gate of St. Nicholas, kept her hand constantly pressed against his, if my Uncle Toby had then 'been an artist and could paint,' (as Mr. Fox wished himself to be, that 'he might draw Bonaparte's conduct to the King of Prussia in the blackest colours') my Uncle Toby would have drawn the hand of his fair enemy in the manner we have above described. We have heard a good story of this same Buonaparte playing off a very ludicrous parody of the Widow Wadman's strategy upon as great a Commander by sea as my Uncle Toby was by land. Now, when Sir Isaac Newton, who was sitting smoking with his mistress's hand in his, took her little finger and made use of it as a tobacco-pipe stopper, there was here a total absence of mind, or a great want of gusto." (W.H.) The Widow Wadman and Uncle Toby are characters in Laurence Sterne, *Tristram Shandy* (1759–67). Charles James Fox (1749–1806), Whig statesman, started out as an admirer of Napoleon but changed his mind. The source of Hazlitt's anecdote about the scientist and mathematician Sir Isaac Newton (1643–1727) is unidentified.

[8] Titian painted "Diana and Actaeon" (1556–59), now in the National Gallery of Scotland and "The Death of Actaeon" (1565–76), now in the National Gallery, London. The Orleans Gallery was an exhibition and sale in 1798–99 of Italian Renaissance painting.

West,[1] we understand, has this landscape. He will know if this description of it is just. The landscape background of the St. Peter Martyr[2] is another well known instance of the power of this great painter to give a romantic interest and an appropriate character to the objects of his pencil, where every circumstance adds to the effect of the scene,—the bold trunks of the tall forest trees, the trailing ground plants, with that tall convent spire rising in the distance, amidst the blue sapphire mountains and the golden sky.

Rubens has a great deal of gusto in his Fauns and Satyrs, and in all that expresses motion, but in nothing else. Rembrandt[3] has it in every thing; every thing in his pictures has a tangible character. If he puts a diamond in the ear of a Burgomaster's wife, it is of the first water; and his furs and stuffs are proof against a Russian winter. Raphael's gusto was only in expression; he had no idea of the character of any thing but the human form. The dryness and poverty of his stile in other respects is a phenomenon in the art. His trees are like sprigs of grass stuck in a book of botanical specimens. Was it that Raphael never had time to go beyond the walls of Rome? That he was always in the streets, at church, or in the bath? He was not one of the Society of Arcadians.[4]

Claude's[5] landscapes, perfect as they are, want gusto. This is not easy to explain. They are perfect abstractions of the visible images of things; they speak the visible language of nature truly. They resemble a mirror or a microscope. They are more perfect to the eye only than any other landscapes that ever were or will be painted; they give more of nature, as cognizable by one sense alone; but they lay an equal stress on all visible impressions; they do not interpret one sense by another; they do not distinguish the character of different objects as we are taught, and can only be taught to distinguish them, by their effect on the different senses. That is, his eye wanted imagination; it did not strongly sympathise with his other faculties. He saw the atmosphere, but he did not feel it. He painted the trunk of a tree or a rock in the foreground as smooth— with as complete an abstraction of the gross, tangible impression, as any other part of the picture; his trees are perfectly beautiful, but quite immoveable. His landscapes are unequalled imitations of nature, released from its subjection to the elements,—as if all objects were become a delightful fairy vision, and the eye had rarefied and refined away the other senses. They have a look of enchantment.

Perhaps the Greek statues want gusto for the same reason. The sense of perfect form occupies the whole mind, and hardly suffers it to dwell on any other feeling. It seems enough for them *to be*, without acting or suffering. Their forms are ideal, spiritual. Their beauty is power. "By their beauty they are raised above the frailties of pain or passion; by their beauty they are deified."[6]

The infinite quantity of dramatic invention in Shakespear takes from his gusto. The power he delights to shew is not intense, but discursive. He never insists on any thing as much as he might, except a quibble. Milton has great gusto. He repeats his blow twice; grapples with and exhausts his subject. His imagination has a double relish of its objects, an inveterate attachment to the things he describes, and to the words describing them.

—"Or where Chineses drive
With sails and wind their *cany* waggons *light*."

* * * * *

---

[1] Benjamin West (1738–1820), an American painter who succeeded Sir Joshua Reynolds* as President of the Royal Academy (1792–1820).

[2] Titian's painting of the death of St. Peter Martyr, a Dominican killed by heretics in 1252, was highly regarded in the nineteenth century but was destroyed by fire in 1867; Hazlitt saw it at the Louvre in 1802.

[3] Rembrandt Harmenszoon Van Rijn (1606–69), Dutch painter.

[4] "Raphael not only could not paint a landscape; he could not paint people in a landscape. He could not have painted the heads or the figures or even the dresses, of the St. Peter Martyr. His figures have always an *in-door* look, that is, a set, determined, voluntary, dramatic character, arising from their own passions or a watchfulness of those of others, and want that wild uncertainty of expression, which is connected with the accidents of nature and the changes of the elements. He has nothing *romantic* about him." (W.H.)

[5] Claude Lorrain (1600–82), French landscape painter.

[6] Cf. W. Wordsworth, "Resolution and Independence" 47.*

"Wild above rule or art, *enormous* bliss."[1] There is a gusto in Pope's compliments, in Dryden's satires, and Prior's tales; and among prose-writers, Boccacio and Rabelais had the most of it.[2] We will only mention one other work which appears to us to be full of gusto, and that is the *Beggar's Opera*.[3] If it is not, we are altogether mistaken in our notions on this delicate subject.

from *The Liberal. Verse and Prose from the South* 2 (1823)

My First Acquaintance with Poets

My father was a Dissenting Minister at W——m in Shropshire;[4] and in the year 1798 (the figures that compose that date are to me like the "dreaded name of Demogorgon"[5]) Mr. Coleridge came to Shrewsbury, to succeed Mr. Rowe in the spiritual charge of a Unitarian Congregation there. He did not come till late on the Saturday afternoon before he was to preach; and Mr. Rowe, who himself went down to the coach in a state of anxiety and expectation, to look for the arrival of his successor, could find no one at all answering the description but a round-faced man in a short black coat (like a shooting-jacket) which hardly seemed to have been made for him, but who seemed to be talking at a great rate to his fellow-passengers. Mr. Rowe had scarce returned to give an account of his disappointment, when the round-faced man in black entered, and dissipated all doubts on the subject, by beginning to talk. He did not cease while he staid; nor has he since, that I know of. He held the good town of Shrewsbury in delightful suspense for three weeks that he remained there, "fluttering the *proud Salopians* like an eagle in a dove-cote";[6] and the Welch mountains that skirt the horizon with their tempestuous confusion, agree to have heard no such mystic sounds since the days of

"High-born Hoel's harp or soft Llewellyn's lay!"[7]

As we passed along between W——m and Shrewsbury, and I eyed their blue tops seen through the wintry branches, or the red rustling leaves of the sturdy oak-trees by the roadside, a sound was in my ears as of a Siren's song;[8] I was stunned, startled with it, as from deep sleep; but I had no notion then that I should ever be able to express my admiration to others in motley imagery or quaint allusion, till the light of his genius shone into my soul, like the sun's rays glittering in the puddles of the road. I was at that time dumb, inarticulate, helpless, like a worm by the way-side, crushed, bleeding, lifeless; but now, bursting from the deadly bands that "bound them,

"With Styx nine times round them,"[9]

my ideas float on winged words, and as they expand their plumes, catch the golden light of other years. My soul has indeed remained in its original bondage, dark, obscure, with longings infinite and unsatisfied; my heart, shut up in the prison-house of this rude clay, has never found, nor will it ever find, a heart to speak to; but that my understanding also did not remain dumb and brutish, or at length found a language to express itself, I owe to Coleridge. But this is not to my purpose.

My father lived ten miles from Shrewsbury, and was in the habit of exchanging visits with Mr. Rowe, and with Mr. Jenkins of Whitchurch (nine miles farther on)

---

[1] John Milton, *Paradise Lost* 3.438–39; 5.297.

[2] the English writers Alexander Pope (1688–1744), John Dryden (1631–1700), and Matthew Prior (1664–1721); the Italian writer Giovanni Boccaccio (1313–75); and the French writer François Rabelais (c. 1494–c. 1553).

[3] a satiric ballad opera (1728) by John Gay (1685–1732).

[4] Hazlitt spent much of his early life in the town of Wem, 10 miles (16 km) north of Shrewsbury in Shropshire.

[5] Milton, *Paradise Lost* 2.964–65.

[6] Hazlitt adapts Shakespeare, *Coriolanus* 5.6.115; Salopians are inhabitants of Shropshire (L. *Salopia*).

[7] Thomas Gray (1716–71), *The Bard: A Pindaric Ode* (1757) 28.

[8] In classical mythology, the Sirens are creatures with the heads of women and the bodies of birds who lure sailors on to the rocks with their beautiful singing. See Homer, *Odyssey* 12.39, Virgil, *Aeneid* 5.846, Ovid, *Metamorphoses* 14.88.

[9] Cf. Alexander Pope, *Ode for Music on St. Cecilia's Day* (1713) 90–91. Souls cross the river Styx into the classical underworld.

according to the custom of Dissenting Ministers[1] in each other's neighbourhood. A line of communication is thus established, by which the flame of civil and religious liberty is kept alive, and nourishes its smouldering fire unquenchable, like the fires in the Agamemnon of Æschylus,[2] placed at different stations, that waited for ten long years to announce with their blazing pyramids the destruction of Troy. Coleridge had agreed to come over to see my father, according to the courtesy of the country, as Mr. Rowe's probable successor; but in the mean time I had gone to hear him preach the Sunday after his arrival. A poet and a philosopher getting up into a Unitarian pulpit to preach the Gospel, was a romance in these degenerate days, a sort of revival of the primitive spirit of Christianity, which was not to be resisted.

It was in January, 1798, that I rose one morning before day-light, to walk ten miles in the mud, and went to hear this celebrated person preach. Never, the longest day I have to live, shall I have such another walk as this cold, raw, comfortless one, in the winter of the year 1798.—*Il y a des impressions que ni le tems ni les circonstances peuvent effacer. Dusse-je vivre des siècles entiers, le doux tems de ma jeunesse ne peut renaitre pour moi, ni s'effacer jamais dans ma mémoire.*[3] When I got there, the organ was playing the 100th psalm, and, when it was done, Mr. Coleridge rose and gave out his text, "And he went up into the mountain to pray, HIMSELF, ALONE."[4] As he gave out this text, his voice "rose like a steam of rich distilled perfumes,"[5] and when he came to the two last words, which he pronounced loud, deep, and distinct, it seemed to me, who was then young, as if the sounds had echoed from the bottom of the human heart, and as if that prayer might have floated in solemn silence through the universe. The idea of St. John came into mind, "of one crying in the wilderness, who had his loins girt about, and whose food was locusts and wild honey."[6] The preacher then launched into his subject, like an eagle dallying with the wind. The sermon was upon peace and war; upon church and state—not their alliance, but their separation—on the spirit of the world and the spirit of Christianity, not as the same, but as opposed to one another. He talked of those who had "inscribed the cross of Christ on banners dripping with human gore." He made a poetical and pastoral excursion,—and to shew the fatal effects of war, drew a striking contrast between the simple shepherd boy, driving his team afield, or sitting under the hawthorn, piping to his flock, "as though he should never be old,"[7] and the same poor country-lad, crimped, kidnapped, brought into town, made drunk at an alehouse, turned into a wretched drummer-boy, with his hair sticking on end with powder and pomatum, a long cue at his back, and tricked out in the loathsome finery of the profession of blood.

"Such were the notes our once-lov'd poet sung."[8] And for myself, I could not have been more delighted if I had heard the music of the spheres. Poetry and Philosophy had met together, Truth and Genius had embraced, under the eye and with the sanction of Religion. This was even beyond my hopes. I returned home well satisfied. The sun that was still labouring pale and wan through the sky, obscured by thick mists, seemed an emblem of the *good cause*; and the cold dank drops of dew that hung half melted on the beard of the thistle, had something genial and refreshing in them; for there was a spirit of hope and youth in all nature, that turned every thing into good. The face of nature had not then the brand of JUS DIVINUM[9] on it:

"Like to that sanguine flower inscribed with woe."[10]

---

[1] Protestant clergymen who did not conform to the established Church of England.

[2] See lines 281–316.

[3] "There are impressions which neither time nor circumstances can efface. Were I to live whole ages, the sweet days of my youth could not return to me, nor ever be effaced from my memory" (Jean-Jacques Rousseau, *Confessions* 2.7).

[4] Cf. John 6.15.

[5] Milton, *Comus* 555.

[6] Cf. Matthew 3.3–4.

[7] from the description of Arcadia in Sir Philip Sidney, *The Countess of Pembroke's Arcadia* (1581).

[8] Cf. Alexander Pope, "Epistle to Robert, Earl of Oxford" (1721) 1.

[9] "divine right or law" (L.).

[10] Milton, "Lycidas" 106.

On the Tuesday following, the half-inspired speaker came. I was called down into the room where he was, and went half-hoping, half-afraid. He received me very graciously, and I listened for a long time without uttering a word. I did not suffer in his opinion by my silence. "For those two hours," he afterwards was pleased to say, "he was conversing with W.H.'s forehead!" His appearance was different from what I had anticipated from seeing him before. At a distance, and in the dim light of the chapel, there was to me a strange wildness in his aspect, a dusky obscurity, and I thought him pitted with the small-pox. His complexion was at that time clear, and even bright—

"As are the children of yon azure sheen."[1]

His forehead was broad and high, light as if built of ivory, with large projecting eyebrows, and his eyes rolling beneath them like a sea with darkened lustre. "A certain tender bloom his face o'erspread,"[2] a purple tinge as we see it in the pale thoughtful complexions of the Spanish portrait-painters, Murillo and Valesquez.[3] His mouth was gross, voluptuous, open, eloquent; his chin good-humoured and round; but his nose, the rudder of the face, the index of the will, was small, feeble, nothing—like what he has done. It might seem that the genius of his face as from a height surveyed and projected him (with sufficient capacity and huge aspiration) into the world unknown of thought and imagination, with nothing to support or guide his veering purpose, as if Columbus had launched his adventurous course for the New World in a scallop, without oars or compass. So at least I comment on it after the event. Coleridge in his person was rather above the common size, inclining to the corpulent, or like Lord Hamlet, "somewhat fat and pursy."[4] His hair (now, alas! grey) was then black and glossy as the raven's, and fell in smooth masses over his forehead. This long pendulous hair is peculiar to enthusiasts, to those whose minds tend heavenward; and is traditionally inseparable (though of a different colour) from the pictures of Christ. It ought to belong, as a character, to all who preach *Christ crucified*, and Coleridge was at that time one of those!

It was curious to observe the contrast between him and my father, who was a veteran in the cause, and then declining into the vale of years. He had been a poor Irish lad, carefully brought up by his parents, and sent to the University of Glasgow (where he studied under Adam Smith)[5] to prepare him for his future destination. It was his mother's proudest wish to see her son a Dissenting Minister. So if we look back to past generations (as far as eye can reach) we see the same hopes, fears, wishes, followed by the same disappointments, throbbing in the human heart; and so we may see them (if we look forward) rising up for ever, and disappearing, like vapourish bubbles, in the human breast! After being tossed about from congregation to congregation in the heats of the Unitarian controversy, and squabbles about the American war, he had been relegated to an obscure village, where he was to spend the last thirty years of his life, far from the only converse that he loved, the talk about disputed texts of Scripture and the cause of civil and religious liberty. Here he passed his days, repining but resigned, in the study of the Bible, and the perusal of the Commentators,—huge folios, not easily got through, one of which would outlast a winter! Why did he pore on these from morn to night (with the exception of a walk in the fields or a turn in the garden to gather brocoli-plants or kidney-beans of his own rearing, with no small degree of pride and pleasure)?—Here were "no figures nor no fantasies,"[6]—neither poetry nor philosophy—nothing to dazzle, nothing to excite modern curiosity; but to his lack-lustre eyes there appeared, within the pages of the ponderous, unwieldy, neglected tomes, the sacred name of JEHOVAH in Hebrew capitals: pressed down by the weight of the style, worn to the last fading thinness of the understanding, there were glimpses, glimmering notions of the patriarchal wander-

---

[1] Cf. James Thomson, *The Castle of Indolence* (1748) 2.295.

[2] Cf. *The Castle of Indolence* 1.507.

[3] Bartolomé Esteban Murillo (1617–82) and Diego Velásquez (1599–1660), Spanish painters.

[4] Cf. Shakespeare, *Hamlet* 3.4.153, 5.2.279.

[5] Adam Smith (1723–90), Scottish rhetorician, philosopher, and economic theorist, author of *The Theory of Moral Sentiments* (1759) and *The Wealth of Nations* (1776).

[6] Shakespeare, *Julius Caesar* 2.1.231.

ings, with palm-trees hovering in the horizon, and processions of camels at the distance of three thousand years; there was Moses with the Burning Bush,[1] the number of the Twelve Tribes, types, shadows,[2] glosses on the law and the prophets; there were discussions (dull enough) on the age of Methuselah,[3] a mighty speculation! there were outlines, rude guesses at the shape of Noah's Ark and of the riches of Solomon's Temple; questions as to the date of the creation, predictions of the end of all things; the great lapses of time, the strange mutations of the globe were unfolded with the voluminous leaf, as it turned over; and though the soul might slumber with an hieroglyphic veil of inscrutable mysteries drawn over it, yet it was in a slumber ill-exchanged for all the sharpened realities of sense, wit, fancy, or reason. My father's life was comparatively a dream; but it was a dream of infinity and eternity, of death, the resurrection, and a judgment to come!

No two individuals were ever more unlike than were the host and his guest. A poet was to my father a sort of nondescript: yet whatever added grace to the Unitarian cause was to him welcome. He could hardly have been more surprised or pleased, if our visitor had worn wings. Indeed, his thoughts had wings; and as the silken sounds rustled round our little wainscoted parlour, my father threw back his spectacles over his forehead, his white hairs mixing with its sanguine hue; and a smile of delight beamed across his rugged cordial face, to think that Truth had found a new ally in Fancy![4] Besides, Coleridge seemed to take considerable notice of me, and that of itself was enough. He talked very familiarly, but agreeably, and glanced over a variety of subjects. At dinner-time he grew more animated, and dilated in a very edifying manner on Mary Wolstonecraft and Mackintosh.[5] The last, he said, he considered (on my father's speaking of his *Vindiciæ Gallicæ* as a capital performance) as a clever scholastic man—a master of the topics,—or as the ready warehouseman of letters, who knew exactly where to lay his hand on what he wanted, though the goods were not his own. He thought him no match for Burke,[6] either in style or matter. Burke was a metaphysician, Mackintosh a mere logician. Burke was an orator (almost a poet) who reasoned in figures, because he had an eye for nature: Mackintosh, on the other hand, was a rhetorician, who had only an eye to common-places. On this I venture to say that I had always entertained a great opinion of Burke, and that (as far as I could find) the speaking of him with contempt might be made the test of a vulgar democratical mind. This was the first observation I ever made to Coleridge, and he said it was a very just and striking one. I remember the leg of Welsh mutton and the turnips on the table that day had the finest flavour imaginable. Coleridge added that Mackintosh and Tom. Wedgwood[7] (of whom, however, he spoke highly) had expressed a very indifferent opinion of his friend Mr. Wordsworth, on which he remarked to them—"He strides on so far before you, that he dwindles in the distance!" Godwin had once boasted to him of having carried on an argument with Mackintosh for three hours with dubious success; Coleridge told him—"If there had been a man of genius in the room, he would have settled the question in five minutes." He asked me if I had ever seen Mary Wolstonecraft, and I said, I had once for a few moments, and that she seemed to me to turn off Godwin's objections to something she advanced with quite a playful, easy air. He replied, that "this was only one instance of the ascendancy which people of imagination exercised over those of mere intellect." He did not

---

[1] Exodus 3.1–6.

[2] for the twelve tribes of Israel, see Genesis 49.1–28. Hazlitt here alludes to a way of reading the Bible in which a person, thing, or event in the Old Testament (a "type" or "shadow" of something not yet understood) was believed to prefigure its fulfillment in the New Testament.

[3] Genesis 5.25–27.

[4] "My father was one of those who mistook his talent after all. He used to be very much dissatisfied that I preferred his Letters to his Sermons. The last were forced and dry; the first came naturally from him. For ease, half-plays on words, and a supine, monkish, indolent pleasantry, I have never seen them equalled." (W.H.)

---

[5] Mary Wollstonecraft* and Sir James Mackintosh (1765–1832) defended the values of the French Revolution in, respectively, *A Vindication of the Rights of Men** and *Vindiciae Gallicae* [L. "Vindication of the French"] (1791). Hazlitt probably met both writers in 1796.

[6] Edmund Burke,* Irish-born statesman and writer.

[7] Thomas Wedgwood (1771–1805), a patron of Coleridge* and the second son of Josiah Wedgwood, founder of the famous pottery factory.

rate Godwin very high[1] (this was caprice or prejudice, real or affected) but he had a great idea of Mrs. Wolstonecraft's powers of conversation, none at all of her talent for book-making. We talked a little about Holcroft.[2] He had been asked if he was not much struck *with* him, and he said, he thought himself in more danger of being struck *by* him. I complained that he would not let me get on at all, for he required a definition of even the commonest word, exclaiming, "What do you mean by a *sensation*, Sir? What do you mean by an *idea*?" This, Coleridge said, was barricadoing the road to truth:—it was setting up a turnpike-gate at every step we took. I forget a great number of things, many more than I remember; but the day passed off pleasantly, and the next morning Mr. Coleridge was to return to Shrewsbury. When I came down to breakfast, I found that he had just received a letter from his friend, T. Wedgwood, making him an offer of £150 a-year if he chose to wave his present pursuit, and devote himself entirely to the study of poetry and philosophy. Coleridge seemed to make up his mind to close with this proposal in the act of tying on one of his shoes. It threw an additional damp on his departure. It took the wayward enthusiast quite from us to cast him into Deva's winding vales,[3] or by the shores of old romance. Instead of living at ten miles distance, of being the pastor of a Dissenting congregation at Shrewsbury, he was henceforth to inhabit the Hill of Parnassus, to be a Shepherd on the Delectable Mountains.[4] Alas! I knew not the way thither, and felt very little gratitude for Mr. Wedgwood's bounty. I was presently relieved from this dilemma; for Mr. Coleridge, asking for a pen and ink, and going to a table to write something on a bit of card, advanced towards me with undulating step, and giving me the precious document, said that that was his address, *Mr. Coleridge, Nether-Stowey, Somersetshire*;[5] and that he should be glad to see me there in a few weeks' time, and, if I chose, would come half-way to meet me. I was not less surprised than the shepherd-boy (this simile is to be found in Cassandra)[6] when he sees a thunder-bolt fall close at his feet. I stammered out my acknowledgments and acceptance of this offer (I thought Mr. Wedgwood's annuity a trifle to it) as well as I could; and this mighty business being settled, the poet-preacher took leave, and I accompanied him six miles on the road. It was a fine morning in the middle of winter, and he talked the whole way. The scholar in Chaucer is described as going

——"Sounding on his way."[7]

So Coleridge went on his. In digressing, in dilating, in passing from subject to subject, he appeared to me to float in air, to slide on ice. He told me in confidence (going along) that he should have preached two sermons before he accepted the situation at Shrewsbury, one on Infant Baptism, the other on the Lord's Supper, shewing that he could not administer either, which would have effectually disqualified him for the object in view. I observed that he continually crossed me on the way by shifting from one side of the foot-path to the other. This struck me as an odd movement; but I did not at that time connect it with any instability of purpose or involuntary change of principle, as I have done since. He seemed unable to keep on in a strait line. He spoke slightingly of Hume[8] (whose Essay on Miracles he said was stolen from an objection started in one of South's

---

[1] "He complained in particular of the presumption of his attempting to establish the future immortality of man, 'without' (as he said) 'knowing what Death was or what Life was'—and the tone in which he pronounced these two words seemed to convey a complete image of both." (W.H.) William Godwin, author of *Political Justice*,* married Mary Wollstonecraft* in 1796.

[2] Thomas Holcroft (1745–1809), actor, novelist, and radical political activist.

[3] Deva was an ancient Roman encampment on the site of the modern city of Chester.

[4] In classical mythology, Mount Parnassus was sacred to Apollo, divine musician-poet, whose oracle, Delphi, was at its base; in John Bunyan (1628–88), *The Pilgrim's Progress* (1678), the Delectable Mountains are within sight of the Celestial City of God.

[5] Coleridge moved to Nether Stowey in 1797.

[6] a heroic romance in 10 vols., by the French novelist Gauthier de Costes de Calprenède (1614–63).

[7] possibly a version of Chaucer's *Prioress's Tale*, 105, where the pious schoolboy goes "singing by the way."

[8] David Hume (1711–76), philosophical skeptic and historian, author of *A Treatise of Human Nature* (1739), *An Enquiry Concerning Human Understanding* (1748), *Dialogues Concerning Natural Religion* (1779), and *History of Great Britain* (1754–62). His essay "On Miracles" was part of the *Enquiry* (1748).

Sermons—*Credat Judæus Apella!*).[1] I was not very much pleased at this account of Hume, for I had just been reading, with infinite relish, that completest of all metaphysical *choke-pears*, his *Treatise on Human Nature*, to which the *Essays*, in point of scholastic subtlety and close reasoning, are mere elegant trifling, light summer-reading. Coleridge even denied the excellence of Hume's general style, which I think betrayed a want of taste or candour. He however made me amends by the manner in which he spoke of Berkeley.[2] He dwelt particularly on his *Essay on Vision* as a masterpiece of analytical reasoning. So it undoubtedly is. He was exceedingly angry with Dr. Johnson for striking the stone with his foot, in allusion to this author's Theory of Matter and Spirit, and saying, "Thus I confute him, Sir."[3] Coleridge drew a parallel (I don't know how he brought about the connection) between Bishop Berkeley and Tom Paine.[4] He said the one was an instance of a subtle, the other of an acute mind, than which no two things could be more distinct. The one was a shop-boy's quality, the other the characteristic of a philosopher. He considered Bishop Butler[5] as a true philosopher, a profound and conscientious thinker, a genuine reader of nature and of his own mind. He did not speak of his *Analogy*, but of his *Sermons at the Rolls' Chapel*, of which I had never heard. Coleridge somehow always contrived to prefer the *unknown* to the *known*. In this instance he was right. The *Analogy* is a tissue of sophistry, of wire-drawn, theological special-pleading; the *Sermons* (with the Preface to them) are in a fine vein of deep, matured reflection, a candid appeal to our observation of human nature, without pedantry and without bias. I told Coleridge I had written a few remarks, and was sometimes foolish enough to believe that I had made a discovery on the same subject (the *Natural Disinterestedness of the Human Mind*)[6]—and I tried to explain my view of it to Coleridge, who listened with great willingness, but I did not succeed in making myself understood. I sat down to the task shortly afterwards for the twentieth time, got new pens and paper, determined to make clear work of it, wrote a few meagre sentences in the skeleton-style of a mathematical demonstration, stopped half-way down the second page; and, after trying in vain to pump up any words, images, notions, apprehensions, facts, or observations, from that gulph of abstraction in which I had plunged myself for four or five years preceding, gave up the attempt as labour in vain, and shed tears of helpless despondency on the blank unfinished paper. I can write fast enough now. Am I better than I was then? Oh no! One truth discovered, one pang of regret at not being able to express it, is better than all the fluency and flippancy in the world. Would that I could go back to what I then was! Why can we not revive past times as we can revisit old places? If I had the quaint Muse of Sir Philip Sidney[7] to assist me, I would write a *Sonnet to the Road between W—m and Shrewsbury*, and immortalise every step of it by some fond enigmatical conceit. I would swear that the very milestones had ears, and that Harmer-hill stooped with all its pines, to listen to a poet, as he passed! I remember but one other topic of discourse in this walk. He mentioned Paley,[8] praised the naturalness and clearness of his style, but condemned his sentiments, thought him a mere time-serving casuist, and said that "the fact of his work on Moral and Political Philosophy being made a text-book in our Universities was a disgrace to the national character." We parted at the six-mile stone; and I returned homeward pensive but much pleased. I had

---

[1] Robert South (1634–1716), preacher and theologian. The Latin phrase means "Let the Jew Apella believe it" (i.e., don't expect *me* to believe it) and is taken from Horace, *Satires* 1.5.

[2] George Berkeley (1685–1753), bishop and philosophical idealist, who maintained that to be is to be perceived (L. *esse est percipi*). Since nothing exists unless it perceives or is perceived, the existence of the world establishes the existence of an infinite perceiving mind, or God.

[3] James Boswell, *The Life of Samuel Johnson* (1791), episode of 1763.

[4] Thomas Paine,* political radical and supporter of the American Revolution.

[5] Joseph Butler (1692–1752), Bishop of Bristol and author of the *Analogy of Religion* (1736), a defence of Christianity against the deists.

[6] subtitle of Hazlitt's *Essay on the Principles of Human Action* (1805).

[7] Sir Philip Sidney (1554–86), courtier, poet, and soldier, wrote a prose-romance, *The Countess of Pembroke's Arcadia* (1581, 1590, 1593) and a sonnet sequence, *Astrophel and Stella* (1591).

[8] William Paley (1743–1805), theologian and philosopher, author of *View of the Evidences of Christianity* (1794).

met with unexpected notice from a person, whom I believed to have been prejudiced against me. "Kind and affable to me had been his condescension, and should be honoured ever with suitable regard."[1] He was the first poet I had known, and he certainly answered to that inspired name. I had heard a great deal of his powers of conversation, and was not disappointed. In fact, I never met with any thing at all like them, either before or since. I could easily credit the accounts which were circulated of his holding forth to a large party of ladies and gentlemen, an evening or two before, on the Berkeleian Theory, when he made the whole material universe look like a transparency of fine words; and another story (which I believe he has somewhere told himself) of his being asked to a party at Birmingham, of his smoking tobacco and going to sleep after dinner on a sofa, where the company found him to their no small surprise, which was increased to wonder when he started up of a sudden, and rubbing his eyes, looked about him, and launched into a three-hours' description of the third heaven, of which he had had a dream, very different from Mr. Southey's Vision of Judgment, and also from that other Vision of Judgment, which Mr. Murray, the secretary of the Bridge-street Junto, has taken into his especial keeping![2]

On my way back, I had a sound in my ears, it was the voice of Fancy: I had a light before me, it was the face of Poetry. The one still lingers there, the other has not quitted my side! Coleridge in truth met me halfway on the ground of philosophy, or I should not have been won over to his imaginative creed. I had an uneasy, pleasurable sensation all the time, till I was to visit him. During those months the chill breath of winter gave me a welcoming; the vernal air was balm and inspiration to me. The golden sun-sets, the silver star of evening, lighted me on my way to new hopes and prospects. *I was to visit Coleridge in the Spring.* This circumstance was never absent from my thoughts, and mingled with all my feelings. I wrote to him at the time proposed, and received an answer postponing my intended visit for a week or two, but very cordially urging me to complete my promise then. This delay did not damp, but rather increased my ardour. In the meantime, I went to Llangollen Vale,[3] by way of initiating myself in the mysteries of natural scenery; and I must say I was enchanted with it. I had been reading Coleridge's description of England, in his fine *Ode on the Departing Year*,[4] and I applied it, *con amore*,[5] to the objects before me. That valley was to me (in a manner) the cradle of a new existence: in the river that winds through it, my spirit was baptised in the waters of Helicon![6]

I returned home, and soon after set out on my journey with unworn heart and untried feet. My way lay through Worcester and Gloucester, and by Upton, where I thought of Tom Jones and the adventure of the muff.[7] I remember getting completely wet through one day, and stopping at an inn (I think it was at Tewkesbury) where I sat up all night to read Paul and Virginia.[8] Sweet were the showers in early youth that drenched my body, and sweet the drops of pity that fell upon the books I read! I recollect a remark of Coleridge's upon this very book, that nothing could shew the gross indelicacy of French manners and the entire corruption of their imagination more strongly than the behaviour of the heroine in the last fatal scene, who turns away from a person on board the sinking vessel, that offers to save her life, because he has thrown off his clothes to assist him in swimming. Was this a time to think of such a circumstance? I once hinted to Wordsworth, as we were sailing in his boat on Grasmere lake, that I thought he

---

[1] Cf. Milton, *Paradise Lost* 8.648–50.

[2] See Coleridge, *Biographia Literaria*,* chap. 10. Charles Murray was the solicitor for the Constitutional Association for Opposing Disloyal and Seditious Principles, which met in an office on Bridge St. and which prosecuted John Hunt for publishing Byron's* *Vision of Judgment* in the *Liberal* 1 (October 1822).

[3] a deep valley in North Wales; see also Anna Seward's *Llangollen Vale*.*

[4] a poem by Coleridge,* published in 1796.

[5] "with love" (It.).

[6] Helicon is a mountain in Boeotia, known to the Greeks as home of the Muses; its fountains signify poetic inspiration.

[7] See Henry Fielding (1707–54), *The History of Tom Jones* (1749) Book 10, chap. 5.

[8] *Paul et Virginie* (1788), a romance by Jacques-Henri Bernardin de Saint-Pierre.

had borrowed the idea of his *Poems on the Naming of Places*,[1] from the local inscriptions of the same kind in *Paul and Virginia*. He did not own the obligation, and stated some distinction without a difference, in defence of his claim to originality. Any the slightest variation would be sufficient for this purpose in his mind; for whatever *he* added or omitted would inevitably be worth all that any one else had done, and contain the marrow of the sentiment.—I was still two days before the time fixed for my arrival, for I had taken care to set out early enough. I stopped these two days at Bridgewater, and when I was tired of sauntering on the banks of its muddy river, returned to the inn, and read *Camilla*.[2] So have I loitered my life away, reading books, looking at pictures, going to plays, hearing, thinking, writing on what pleased me best. I have wanted only one thing to make me happy; but wanting that, have wanted every thing!

I arrived, and was well received. The country about Nether Stowey is beautiful, green and hilly, and near the sea-shore. I saw it but the other day, after an interval of twenty years, from a hill near Taunton. How was the map of my life spread out before me, as the map of the country lay at my feet! In the afternoon, Coleridge took me over to All-Foxden,[3] a romantic old family-mansion of the St. Aubins, where Wordsworth lived. It was then in the possession of a friend of the poet's, who gave him the free use of it. Somehow that period (the time just after the French Revolution) was not a time when *nothing was given for nothing*. The mind opened, and a softness might be perceived coming over the heart of individuals, beneath "the scales that fence"[4] our self-interest. Wordsworth himself was from home, but his sister kept house, and set before us a frugal repast; and we had free access to her brother's poems, the *Lyrical Ballads*, which were still in manuscript, or in the form of *Sybilline Leaves*.[5] I dipped into a few of these with great satisfaction, and with the faith of a novice. I slept that night in an old room with blue hangings, and covered with the round-faced family-portraits of the age of George I. and II. and from the wooded declivity of the adjoining park that overlooked my window, at the dawn of day, could

—"hear the loud stag speak."[6]

In the outset of life (and particularly at this time I felt it so) our imagination has a body to it. We are in a state between sleeping and waking, and have indistinct but glorious glimpses of strange shapes, and there is always something to come better than what we see. As in our dreams the fullness of the blood gives warmth and reality to the coinage of the brain, so in youth our ideas are clothed, and fed, and pampered with our good spirits; we breathe thick with thoughtless happiness, the weight of future years presses on the strong pulses of the heart, and we repose with undisturbed faith in truth and good. As we advance, we exhaust our fund of enjoyment and of hope. We are no longer wrapped in *lamb's-wool*, lulled in Elysium.[7] As we taste the pleasures of life, their spirit evaporates, the sense palls; and nothing is left but the phantoms, the lifeless shadows of what *has been*!

That morning, as soon as breakfast was over, we strolled out into the park, and seating ourselves on the trunk of an old ash-tree that stretched along the ground, Coleridge read aloud with a sonorous and musical voice, the ballad of *Betty Foy*.[8] I was not critically or sceptically inclined. I saw touches of truth and nature, and took the rest for granted. But in the *Thorn*, the *Mad Mother*, and the *Complaint of a Poor Indian Woman*,[9] I felt that deeper power and pathos which have been since acknowledged,

---

[1] a group of poems printed together under this heading from 1815 on, including "To M[ary] H[utchinson]," "It Was an April Morning," "To Joanna," "There Is an Eminence," "A Narrow Girdle of Rough Stones," and "When, to the Attractions of the Busy World."

[2] *Camilla, or a Picture of Youth* (1796), a novel by Frances Burney.*

[3] where the Wordsworths lived in 1797–98, near Coleridge's home at Nether Stowey, Somerset.

[4] unidentified; elsewhere, Hazlitt quotes a fuller version: "we see a softness coming over the heart, and the iron scales of ambition that fenced and guarded it melt and drop off" (*Life of Napoleon*).

[5] loose pages, like fragments of ancient books containing prophecies of the sibyls, women consulted as oracles; Coleridge's 1817 volume of poems is called *Sibylline Leaves*.*

[6] Ben Jonson (1572/3–1637), "To Sir Robert Wroth" (1616) 22.

[7] the place of the blessed in the classical underworld.

[8] Betty Foy is the mother of the central character in W. Wordsworth's poem "The Idiot Boy."*

[9] three poems from *Lyrical Ballads*.*

"In spite of pride, in erring reason's spite,"[1] as the characteristics of this author; and the sense of a new style and a new spirit in poetry came over me. It had to me something of the effect that arises from the turning up of the fresh soil, or of the first welcome breath of Spring,

"While yet the trembling year is unconfirmed."[2]

Coleridge and myself walked back to Stowey that evening, and his voice sounded high

"Of Providence, foreknowledge, will, and fate,
Fix'd fate, free-will, foreknowledge absolute."[3]

as we passed through echoing grove, by fairy stream or waterfall, gleaming in the summer moonlight! He lamented that Wordsworth was not prone enough to belief in the traditional superstitions of the place, and that there was a something corporeal, a *matter-of-fact-ness*, a clinging to the palpable, or often to the petty, in his poetry, in consequence. His genius was not a spirit that descended to him through the air; it sprung out of the ground like a flower, or unfolded itself from a green spray, on which the gold-finch sang. He said, however (if I remember right) that this objection must be confined to his descriptive pieces, that his philosophic poetry had a grand and comprehensive spirit in it, so that his soul seemed to inhabit the universe like a palace, and to discover truth by intuition, rather than by deduction. The next day Wordsworth arrived from Bristol at Coleridge's cottage. I think I see him now. He answered in some degree to his friend's description of him, but was more gaunt and Don Quixote-like.[4] He was quaintly dressed (according to the *costume* of that unconstrained period) in a brown fustian jacket and striped pantaloons. There was something of a roll, a lounge in his gait, not unlike his own Peter Bell.[5] There was a severe, worn pressure of thought about his temples, a fire in his eye (as if he saw something in objects more than the outward appearance) an intense high, narrow forehead, a Roman nose, cheeks furrowed by strong purpose and feeling, and a convulsive inclination to laughter about the mouth, a good deal at variance with the solemn, stately expression of the rest of his face. Chantrey's bust[6] wants the marking traits; but he was teazed into making it regular and heavy: Haydon's head of him, introduced into the *Entrance of Christ into Jerusalem*,[7] is the most like his drooping weight of thought and expression. He sat down and talked very naturally and freely, with a mixture of clear gushing accents in his voice, a deep guttural intonation, and a strong tincture of the northern *burr*, like the crust on wine. He instantly began to make havoc of the half of a Cheshire cheese on the table, and said triumphantly that "his marriage with experience had not been so unproductive as Mr. Southey's[8] in teaching him a knowledge of the good things of this life." He had been to see the *Castle Spectre* by Monk Lewis,[9] while at Bristol, and described it very well. He said "it fitted the taste of the audience like a glove." This *ad captandum*[10] merit was however by no means a recommendation of it, according to the severe principles of the new school, which reject rather than court popular effect. Wordsworth, looking out of the low, latticed window, said, "How beautifully the sun sets on that yellow bank!" I thought within myself, "With what eyes these poets see nature!" and ever after, when I saw the sun-set stream upon the objects facing it, conceived I had made a discovery, or thanked Mr. Wordsworth for having made one for me! We went over to All-Foxden again the day following, and Wordsworth read us the story of Peter Bell in the open air; and the comment made upon it by his face and voice was very different from that of some later critics! Whatever

---

[1] Cf. Pope, *An Essay on Man* (1733–34) 1.293.

[2] Cf. James Thomson, *The Seasons* (1730), "Spring" 18.

[3] Milton, *Paradise Lost* 2.559–60.

[4] like the hero of Miguel de Cervantes Saavedra (1547–1616), *Don Quixote de la Mancha* (1605, 1615), a man self-deluded by tales of chivalry.

[5] a narrative poem by W. Wordsworth* (1798, published 1819).

[6] Sir Francis Legatt Chantrey (1781–1841) sculpted this bust when Wordsworth was 50 years old; the original is now in the Lilly Library, Indiana University.

[7] Benjamin Robert Haydon (1786–1846), painter, autobiographer, and friend of John Keats,* W. Wordsworth,* and Leigh Hunt.* He painted portraits of his friends in *The Entrance of Christ into Jerusalem* (1820).

[8] Robert Southey,* poet and friend of Coleridge and Wordsworth.

[9] a play by Matthew Gregory Lewis.*

[10] "to capture [attention]" or "to suit popular taste" (L.).

might be thought of the poem, "his face was as a book where men might read strange matters,"[1] and he announced the fate of his hero in prophetic tones. There is a *chaunt* in the recitation both of Coleridge and Wordsworth, which acts as a spell upon the hearer, and disarms the judgment. Perhaps they have deceived themselves by making habitual use of this ambiguous accompaniment. Coleridge's manner is more full, animated, and varied; Wordsworth's more equable, sustained, and internal. The one might be termed more *dramatic*, the other more *lyrical*. Coleridge has told me that he himself liked to compose in walking over uneven ground, or breaking through the straggling branches of a copsewood; whereas Wordsworth always wrote (if he could) walking up and down a strait gravel-walk, or in some spot where the continuity of his verse met with no collateral interruption. Returning that same evening, I got into a metaphysical argument with Wordsworth, while Coleridge was explaining the different notes of the nightingale to his sister, in which we neither of us succeeded in making ourselves perfectly clear and intelligible. Thus I passed three weeks at Nether Stowey and in the neighbourhood, generally devoting the afternoons to a delightful chat in an arbour made of bark by the poet's friend Tom Poole,[2] sitting under two fine elm-trees, and listening to the bees humming round us, while we quaffed our *flip*.[3] It was agreed, among other things, that we should make a jaunt down the Bristol-Channel, as far as Linton. We set off together on foot, Coleridge, John Chester, and I. This Chester was a native of Nether Stowey, one of those who were attracted to Coleridge's discourse as flies are to honey, or bees in swarming-time to the sound of a brass pan. He "followed in the chace, like a dog who hunts, not like one that made up the cry."[4] He had on a brown cloth coat, boots, and corduroy breeches, was low in stature, bow-legged, had a drag in his walk like a drover, which he assisted by a hazel switch, and kept on a sort of trot by the side of Coleridge, like a running footman by a state coach, that he might not lose a syllable or sound, that fell from Coleridge's lips. He told me his private opinion, that Coleridge was a wonderful man. He scarcely opened his lips, much less offered an opinion the whole way: yet of the three, had I to chuse during that journey, I would be John Chester. He afterwards followed Coleridge into Germany, where the Kantean philosophers were puzzled how to bring him under any of their categories.[5] When he sat down at table with his idol, John's felicity was complete; Sir Walter Scott's, or Mr. Blackwood's,[6] when they sat down at the same table with the King, was not more so. We passed Dunster on our right, a small town between the brow of a hill and the sea. I remember eying it wistfully as it lay below us: contrasted with the woody scene around, it looked as clear, as pure, as *embrowned* and ideal as any landscape I have seen since, of Gaspar Poussin's or Domenichino's.[7] We had a long day's march—(our feet kept time to the echoes of Coleridge's tongue)—through Mine-head and by the Blue Anchor, and on to Linton, which we did not reach till near midnight, and where we had some difficulty in making a lodgment. We however knocked the people of the house up at last, and we were repaid for our apprehensions and fatigue by some excellent rashers of fried bacon and eggs. The view in coming along had been splendid. We walked for miles and miles on dark brown heaths overlooking the channel, with the Welsh hills beyond, and at times descended into little sheltered valleys close by the sea-side, with a smuggler's face scowling by us, and then had to ascend conical hills with a path winding up through a coppice to a barren top, like a monk's shaven crown, from one of which I pointed out to Coleridge's notice the bare masts of a vessel on the very edge of the horizon and within the red-orbed disk of the setting sun, like his own spectre-ship in the *Ancient*

---

[1] Cf. Shakespeare, *Macbeth* 1.5.62–63.

[2] Thomas Poole (1765–1837), friend of Wordsworth and Coleridge.

[3] a warm drink made of ale, beer, or cider, with spices, milk, and eggs.

[4] Cf. Shakespeare, *Othello* 2.3.370.

[5] Coleridge spent ten months in Germany (1798–99) studying German literature and philosophy.

[6] Walter Scott,* Scottish poet and novelist; William Blackwood (1776–1834), Scottish publisher and editor of *Blackwood's Magazine*.

[7] Gaspar Poussin, French painter (1613–75), brother-in-law of the painter Nicholas Poussin; and Domenico Zampieri (1581–1641), Italian painter.

Mariner.[1] At Linton the character of the sea-coast becomes more marked and rugged. There is a place called the *Valley of Rocks* (I suspect this was only the poetical name for it) bedded among precipices overhanging the sea, with rocky caverns beneath, into which the waves dash, and where the sea-gull for ever wheels its screaming flight. On the tops of these are huge stones thrown transverse, as if an earthquake had tossed them there, and behind these is a fretwork of perpendicular rocks, something like the *Giant's Causeway*.[2] A thunder-storm came on while we were at the inn, and Coleridge was running out bareheaded to enjoy the commotion of the elements in the *Valley of Rocks*, but as if in spite, the clouds only muttered a few angry sounds, and let fall a few refreshing drops. Coleridge told me that he and Wordsworth were to have made this place the scene of a prose-tale, which was to have been in the manner of, but far superior to, the *Death of Abel*,[3] but they had relinquished the design. In the morning of the second day, we breakfasted luxuriously in an old-fashioned parlour, on tea, toast, eggs, and honey, in the very sight of the bee-hives from which it had been taken, and a garden full of thyme and wild flowers that had produced it. On this occasion Coleridge spoke of Virgil's Georgics,[4] but not well. I do not think he had much feeling for the classical or elegant. It was in this room that we found a little worn-out copy of the *Seasons*,[5] lying in a window-seat, on which Coleridge exclaimed, "*That* is true fame!" He said Thomson was a great poet, rather than a good one; his style was as meretricious as his thoughts were natural. He spoke of Cowper[6] as the best modern poet. He said the *Lyrical Ballads* were an experiment about to be tried by him and Wordsworth, to see how far the public taste would endure poetry written in a more natural and simple style than had hitherto been attempted; totally discarding the artifices of poetical diction, and making use only of such words as had probably been common in the most ordinary language since the days of Henry II.[7] Some comparison was introduced between Shakespear and Milton. He said "he hardly knew which to prefer. Shakespear appeared to him a mere stripling in the art; he was as tall and as strong, with infinitely more activity than Milton, but he never appeared to have come to man's estate; or if he had, he would not have been a man, but a monster." He spoke with contempt of Gray, and with intolerance of Pope.[8] He did not like the versification of the latter. He observed that "the ears of these couplet-writers might be charged with having short memories, that could not retain the harmony of whole passages." He thought little of Junius as a writer; he had a dislike of Dr. Johnson; and a much higher opinion of Burke as an orator and politician, than of Fox or Pitt.[9] He however thought him very inferior in richness of style and imagery to some of our elder prose-writers, particularly Jeremy Taylor.[10] He liked Richardson, but not Fielding; nor could I get him to enter in the merits of *Caleb Williams*.[11] In short, he

---

[1] See "The Rime of the Ancient Mariner" (1817) 149–202.*

[2] a formation of black basalt columns along the seacoast of Northern Ireland.

[3] *Tod Abels*, a heroic poem in five books (1758) by the German poet Salomon Gessner (1730–88).

[4] Latin poem in four books (36–29 BC) about the practical aspects of agricultural life.

[5] a blank-verse poem in four parts (1730, revised 1744, 1746) by James Thomson.

[6] the poet William Cowper.*

[7] King of England 1154–89.

[8] the poets Thomas Gray (1716–71) and Alexander Pope (1688–1744), both of whom Hazlitt quotes freely.

[9] Junius was the pseudonym of the author of a series of letters (1769–72) attacking enemies of the Whig party; Samuel Johnson (1709–84) was a professional writer, lexicographer, and poet, author of (among many other works) *A Dictionary of the English Language* (1755) and *Lives of the English Poets* (1779–81); Edmund Burke* was an Irish-born statesman and writer. William Pitt, 1st Earl of Chatham (1708–78) and Charles James Fox (1749–1806) were Whig statesmen and orators.

[10] Jeremy Taylor (1613–67), bishop and author of *The Rule and Exercises of Holy Living* (1650) and *The Rule and Exercises of Holy Dying* (1651).

[11] Hazlitt refers to Samuel Richardson (1689–1761), author of *Pamela* (1740) and *Clarisa* (1747–48); to Henry Fielding (1707–54), author of *Tom Jones* (1749); and to *Caleb Williams* (1794), a novel by William Godwin (1756–1836). He adds the following note: "He [Coleridge] had no idea of pictures, of Claude or Raphael, and at this time I had as little as he. He sometimes gives a striking account at (Continued)

was profound and discriminating with respect to those authors whom he liked, and where he gave his judgment fair play; capricious, perverse, and prejudiced in his antipathies and distastes. We loitered on the "ribbed sea-sands,"[1] in such talk as this, a whole morning, and I recollect met with a curious sea-weed, of which John Chester told us the country name! A fisherman gave Coleridge an account of a boy that had been drowned the day before, and that they had tried to save him at the risk of their own lives. He said "he did not know how it was that they ventured, but, Sir, we have a *nature* towards one another." This expression, Coleridge remarked to me, was a fine illustration of that theory of disinterestedness which I (in common with Butler) had adopted. I broached to him an argument of mine to prove that *likeness* was not mere association of ideas. I said that the mark in the sand put one in mind of a man's foot, not because it was part of a former impression of a man's foot (for it was quite new) but because it was like the shape of a man's foot. He assented to the justness of this distinction (which I have explained at length elsewhere, for the benefit of the curious) and John Chester listened; not from any interest in the subject, but because he was astonished that I should be able to suggest any thing to Coleridge that he did not already know. We returned on the third morning, and Coleridge remarked the silent cottage-smoke curling up the valleys where, a few evenings before, we had seen the lights gleaming through the dark.

In a day or two after we arrived at Stowey, we set out, I on my return home, and he for Germany. It was a Sunday morning, and he was to preach that day for Dr. Toulmin of Taunton. I asked him if he had prepared any thing for the occasion? He said he had not even thought of the text, but should as soon as we parted. I did not go to hear him,—this was a fault,— but we met in the evening at Bridgewater. The next day we had a long day's walk to Bristol, and sat down, I recollect, by a wellside on the road, to cool ourselves and satisfy our thirst, when Coleridge repeated to me some descriptive lines from his tragedy of Remorse; which I must say became his mouth and that occasion better than they, some years after, did Mr Elliston's and the Drury-lane boards,—

"Oh memory! shield me from the world's poor strife,
And give those scenes thine everlasting life."[2]

I saw no more of him for a year or two, during which period he had been wandering in the Hartz Forest in Germany; and his return was cometary, meteorous, unlike his setting out. It was not till some time after that I knew his friends Lamb and Southey.[3] The last always appears to me (as I first saw him) with a common-place book under his arm, and the first with a *bon-mot* in his mouth. It was at Godwin's that I met with Holcroft[4] and Coleridge, where they were disputing fiercely which was the best—*Man as he was, or man as he is to be.*[5] "Give me," says Lamb, "man as he is *not* to be." This saying was the beginning of a friendship between us, which I believe still continues.—Enough of this for the present.

"But there is matter for another rhyme,
And I to this may add a second tale."[6]

---

present of the Cartoons at Pisa by Buffamalco and others; of one in particular, where Death is seen in the air brandishing his scythe, and the great and mighty of the earth shudder at his approach, while the beggars and the wretched kneel to him as their deliverer. He would of course understand so broad and fine a moral as this at any time." (W.H.) "The Triumph of Death" and other works by Buonamico Buffalmacco (c. 1262–1340) are in the Camposanto in Pisa.

[1] Cf. Coleridge, "The Rime of the Ancient Mariner" 227.

[2] Robert Elliston played Alvar in Coleridge's tragedy, *Remorse*, produced at Drury Lane Theatre, London, in 1813. However, the quotation is not from that play.

[3] Hazlitt's friends the essayist Charles Lamb* and the poet Robert Southey.*

[4] Thomas Holcroft (1745–1809), actor, political activist, and novelist.

[5] Cf. the title of Robert Bage (1720–1801), *Hermsprong, Or Man as He is Not* (1796).

[6] Cf. W. Wordsworth,* "Hart-leap Well" 95–96.

from *The Plain Speaker: Opinions on Books, Men, and Things* (1826)

from *On the Prose-Style of Poets*[1]

It has always appeared to me that the most perfect prose-style, the most powerful, the most dazzling, the most daring, that which went the nearest to the verge of poetry, and yet never fell over, was Burke's.[2] It has the solidity, and sparkling effect of the diamond: all other *fine writing* is like French paste or Bristol-stones[3] in the comparison. Burke's style is airy, flighty, adventurous, but it never loses sight of the subject; nay, is always in contact with, and derives its increased or varying impulse from it. It may be said to pass yawning gulfs "on the unstedfast footing of a spear":[4] still it has an actual resting-place and tangible support under it—it is not suspended on nothing. It differs from poetry, as I conceive, like the chamois from the eagle: it climbs to an almost equal height, touches upon a cloud, overlooks a precipice, is picturesque, sublime—but all the while, instead of soaring through the air, it stands upon a rocky cliff, clambers up by abrupt and intricate ways, and browzes on the roughest bark, or crops the tender flower. The principle which guides his pen is truth, not beauty—not pleasure, but power. He has no choice, no selection of subject to flatter the reader's idle taste, or assist his own fancy: he must take what comes, and make the most of it. He works the most striking effects out of the most unpromising materials, by the mere activity of his mind. He rises with the lofty, descends with the mean, luxuriates in beauty, gloats over deformity. It is all the same to him, so that he loses no particle of the exact, characteristic, extreme impression of the thing he writes about, and that he communicates this to the reader, after exhausting every possible mode of illustration, plain or abstracted, figurative or literal. Whatever stamps the original image more distinctly on the mind, is welcome. The nature of his task precludes continual beauty; but it does not preclude continual ingenuity, force, originality. He had to treat of political questions, mixed modes, abstract ideas, and his fancy (or poetry, if you will) was ingrafted on these artificially, and as it might sometimes be thought, violently, instead of growing naturally out of them, as it would spring of its own accord from individual objects and feelings. There is a resistance in the *matter* to the illustration applied to it—the concrete and abstract are hardly co-ordinate; and therefore it is that, when the first difficulty is overcome, they must agree more closely in the essential qualities, in order that the coincidence may be complete. Otherwise, it is good for nothing; and you justly charge the author's style with being loose, vague, flaccid, and imbecil. The poet has been said

"To make us heirs
Of truth and pure delight in endless lays."[5]

Not so the prose-writer, who always mingles clay with his gold, and often separates truth from mere pleasure. He can only arrive at the last through the first. In poetry, one pleasing or striking image obviously suggests another: the increasing the sense of beauty or grandeur is the principle of composition: in prose, the professed object is to impart conviction, and nothing can be admitted by way of ornament or relief, that does not add new force or clearness to the original conception. The two classes of ideas brought together by the orator or impassioned prose-writer, to wit, the general subject and the particular image, are so far incompatible, and the identity must be more strict, more marked, more determinate, to make them coalesce to any practical purpose. Every word should be a blow: every thought should instantly grapple with its fellow. There must be a weight, a precision, a conformity from association in the tropes and figures of animated prose to fit them to their place in the argument, and make them *tell*, which may be dispensed with in poetry, where there is something much more congenial between the subject-matter and the illustration—

---

[1] The following epigraph from Enfield, *Speaker*, does not appear in the 1826 edition: "Do you read or sing? If you sing, you sing very ill!"

[2] Edmund Burke,* Irish-born statesman and writer.

[3] artificial gems, either glass ("French paste") or made of quartz crystals found near Bristol.

[4] Shakespeare, *1 Henry IV* 1.3.193.

[5] Cf. W. Wordsworth,* "Personal Talk" (1807) 53–54.

"Like beauty making beautiful old rime!"[1] What can be more remote, for instance, and at the same time more apposite, more *the same*, than the following comparison of the English Constitution to "the proud Keep of Windsor," in the celebrated Letter to a Noble Lord?[2]

"Such are *their* ideas; such *their* religion, and such *their* law. But as to *our* country and *our* race, as long as the well-compacted structure of our church and state, the sanctuary, the holy of holies of that ancient law, defended by reverence, defended by power—a fortress at once and a temple[3]—shall stand inviolate on the brow of the British Sion; as long as the British Monarchy—not more limited than fenced by the orders of the State—shall, like the proud Keep of Windsor, rising in the majesty of proportion, and girt with the double belt of its kindred and coeval towers; as long as this awful structure shall oversee and guard the subjected land, so long the mounds and dykes of the low, fat, Bedford level[4] will have nothing to fear from all the pickaxes of all the levellers of France. As long as our Sovereign Lord the King, and his faithful subjects, the Lords and Commons of this realm—the triple cord which no man can break; the solemn, sworn, constitutional frank-pledge of this nation; the firm guarantees of each other's being, and each other's rights; the joint and several securities, each in its place and order, for every kind and every quality of property and of dignity—As long as these endure, so long the Duke of Bedford is safe: and we are all safe together—the high from the blights of envy and the spoliations of rapacity; the low from the iron hand of oppression and the insolent spurn of contempt. Amen! and so be it: and so it will be,

'*Dum domus Æneae Capitoli immobile saxum Accolet; imperiumque pater Romanus habebit.*'"[5]

Nothing can well be more impracticable to a simile than the vague and complicated idea which is here embodied in one; yet how finely, how nobly it stands out, in natural grandeur, in royal state, with double barriers round it to answer for its identity, with "buttress, frieze, and coigne of 'vantage"[6] for the imagination to "make its pendant bed and procreant cradle,"[7] till the idea is confounded with the object representing it—the wonder of a kingdom; and then how striking, how determined the descent, "at one fell swoop,"[8] to the "low, fat, Bedford level!" Poetry would have been bound to maintain a certain decorum, a regular balance between these two ideas; sterling prose throws aside all such idle respect to appearances, and with its pen, like a sword, "sharp and sweet,"[9] lays open the naked truth! The poet's Muse is like a mistress, whom we keep only while she is young and beautiful, *durante bene placito*;[10] the Muse of prose is like a wife, whom we take during life, *for better for worse*. Burke's execution, like that of all good prose, savours of the texture of what he describes, and his pen slides or drags over the ground of his subject, like the painter's pencil. The most rigid fidelity and the most fanciful extravagance meet, and are reconciled in his pages. I never pass Windsor but I think of this passage in Burke, and hardly know to which I am indebted most for enriching my moral sense, that or the fine picturesque stanza in Gray,

"From Windsor's heights the expanse below
Of mead, of lawn, of wood survey," &c.[11]

I might mention that the so much admired description in one of the India speeches, of Hyder Ally's army

---

[1] Shakespeare, Sonnet 106.

[2] See Burke, *Letter to a Noble Lord*, p. 39.

[3] "Templum in modum arcis. ['A temple in the form of a fortress.'] TACITUS of the Temple of Jerusalem." (Burke's note, quoted by Hazlitt)

[4] Burke mocks the Duke of Bedford's obesity as part of a general attack on his political and ideological opponents.

[5] "So long as the house of Aeneas shall dwell on the Capitol's unshaken rock, and the Father of Rome hold sovereign sway" (Virgil, *Aeneid* 9.448–49).

[6] Cf. Shakespeare, *Macbeth* 1.6.6–7.

[7] Cf. Shakespeare, *Macbeth* 1.6.8.

[8] Shakespeare, *Macbeth* 4.3.219.

[9] Cf. Shakespeare, *All's Well That Ends Well* 4.4.33.

[10] "during pleasure"; "at the pleasure of" (L.), a term used in law to describe the term of crown-appointed judges.

[11] Cf. Thomas Gray, "Ode on a Distant Prospect of Eton College" (1747) 6–7.

(I think it is) which "now hung like a cloud upon the mountain, and now burst upon the plain like a thunder-bolt,"[1] would do equally well for poetry or prose. It is a bold and striking illustration of a naturally impressive object. This is not the case with the Abbe Sieyes's far-famed "pigeon-holes,"[2] nor with the comparison of the Duke of Bedford to "the Leviathan, tumbling about his unwieldy bulk in the ocean of royal bounty."[3] Nothing here saves the description but the force of the invective; the startling truth, the vehemence, the remoteness, the aptitude, the perfect peculiarity and coincidence of the allusion. No writer would ever have thought of it but himself; no reader can ever forget it. What is there in common, one might say, between a Peer of the Realm, and "that sea-beast," of those

"Created hugest that swim the ocean-stream?"[4]

Yet Burke has knit the two ideas together, and no man can put them asunder. No matter how slight and precarious the connection, the length of line it is necessary for the fancy to give out in keeping hold of the object on which it has fastened, he seems to have "put his hook in the nostrils"[5] of this enormous creature of the crown, that empurples all its track through the glittering expanse of a profound and restless imagination!

---

[1] A similar passage appears in Burke's speech on the Nabob of Arcoit's Debts, 28 February 1785; Hazlitt is perhaps quoting from memory. Haidar Ali (1722–82) was a Muslim who commanded the army of the Hindu state of Mysore; he was eventually defeated by the British in 1781.

[2] A member of the French National Assembly satirized by Burke in *Letter to a Noble Lord*.*

[3] Following Burke, *Letter to a Noble Lord* (34)* Hazlitt mocks both Bedford's character and his appearance by comparing him to Leviathan, the huge sea-beast of the Bible; see, for example, Job 41.1–10.

[4] Milton, *Paradise Lost* 1.202.

[5] Job 41.1–2.

Sydney Owenson, Lady Morgan
c. 1778 – 1859

The daughter of Jane Mill and the Irish actor Robert Owenson (born Robert MacOwen), Sydney Owenson was baptized in Dublin in 1783; the exact date of her birth is unknown. After her mother's death in 1789, she attended Protestant boarding schools, where she read Shakespeare and became familiar with Irish legends. Employed as a governess, she published *Poems* in 1801 and a novel, *St. Clair*, in 1803. *The Novice of St. Dominick* (1805) was followed by *The Wild Irish Girl* (1806), the novel that made her famous as a champion of Irish culture and political aspiration (in spite of savage criticism in the *Quarterly Review* by the critic J.W. Croker).* She went on to publish *Patriotic Sketches of Ireland* and a collection of ballads, *The Lay of an Irish Harp*, in 1807.

Woman; or, Ida of Athens, inspired by Germaine de Staël's novel, *Corinne* (1807), followed in 1809; then, in 1811, she published *The Missionary*, a novel set in India that inspired Byron,* Percy Bysshe Shelley,* and Moore.* In 1812 she married Sir Thomas Charles Morgan, a surgeon knighted in 1811. Settled in Dublin, she produced a series of "national tales" pursuing radical and nationalistic themes, attacking reactionary regimes in Ireland, England, and America, and satirizing aristocratic life: these included the popular *O'Donnel* (1814), *Florence Macarthy* (1818), *Absenteeism* (1825), and *The O'Briens and the O'Flahertys* (1826). Following the success of *O'Donnel*, the publisher Henry Colburn sent the Morgans to France, where in 1816, Lady Morgan met De Staël: a travel book, *France*, followed in 1817 and another, *Italy*, in 1821.

Lady Morgan's later work included biography (*The Life and Times of Salvator Rosa*, 1824), essays, and fiction, *The Princess, or the Beguine* (1835) and *Luxima, the Prophetess* (1859), an updated version of *The Missionary*. In 1837 she was the first literary woman to receive a pension from the British government. *Woman and Her Master*, published in 1840, was an account of women's contributions to history. After her husband's death in 1843 Lady Morgan worked on her memoirs, a selection of which was published three months before her death in London on 13 April 1859. (A.M.)

from *The Lay of an Irish Harp; or Metrical Fragments* (1807)

The Irish Harp[1]

Fragment I

"Voice of the days of old, let me hear you.—
Awake the soul of song."   OSSIAN[2]

1

Why sleeps the Harp of Erin's pride?
Why with'ring droops its Shamrock wreath?
Why has that song of sweetness died
Which Erin's[3] Harp alone can breathe?

2

5 Oh! 'twas the simplest, wildest thing!
The sighs of *Eve* that faintest flow
O'er airy lyres, did never fling
So sweet, so sad, a song of woe.

3

And yet its sadness seem'd to borrow
10 From love, or joy, a mystic spell;
'Twas doubtful still if *bliss* or *sorrow*
From its melting lapses fell.

4

For if amidst its tone's soft languish
A note of love or joy e'er stream'd,
15 'Twas the plaint of love-sick anguish,
And still the "joy of grief" it seem'd.

5

'Tis said *oppression* taught the lay
To him—(of all the "sons of song"[4]
That bask'd in Erin's brighter day)
20 The *last* of the inspir'd throng;

6

That not in sumptuous hall, or bow'r,
To victor chiefs, on tented plain,
To festive souls, in festal hour,
Did he (sad bard!) pour forth the strain.

7

25 Oh no! for he, opprest, pursued,[5]
Wild, wand'ring, doubtful of his course,
With tears his silent Harp bedew'd,
That drew from *Erin*'s woes their source.

8

It was beneath th'impervious gloom
30 Of some dark forest's deepest dell,
'Twas at some *patriot hero's tomb*,
Or on the drear heath where *he* fell.

9

It was beneath the loneliest cave
That roofs the brow of misery,
35 Or stems the ocean's wildest wave,
Or mocks the sea-blast's keenest sigh.

10

It was through night's most spectral hours,
When reigns the spirit of *dismay*,

---

[1] "With an enthusiasm incidental to my natural and national character, I visited the western part of the province of Connaught in the autumn of 1805, full of many an evident expectation that promised to my feelings, and my taste, a *festival* of national enjoyment. The result of this interesting little pilgrimage has already been given to the world in the story of the "Wild Irish Girl," and in a collection of *Irish Melodies*, learned among those who still "*hum'd the Song of other times.*" But the hope I had long cherished of hearing the *Irish Harp* played in perfection was not only far from being realized, but infinitely disappointed. That encouragement so nutritive to genius, so indispensably necessary to perseverance, no longer stimulates the Irish bard to excellence, nor rewards him when it is attained; and the decline of that tender and impressive instrument, once so dear to Irish enthusiasm, is as visibly rapid, as it is obviously unimpeded by any effort of national pride or national affection." (S.O.) Cf. Ossian, "The War of Caros" and "The Battle of Lora" (from James Macpherson [1736–96], *The Poems of Ossian*, 1773).

[2] unidentified: the poet James Macpherson (1736–96) claimed to have discovered and translated the ancient Scots Gaelic poems of Ossian; actually, they were forgeries.

[3] Ireland's.

[4] Ossian, "Comala, A Dramatic Poem" (1770).

[5] "The persecution begun by the Danes against the Irish bards finished in almost the total extirpation of that sacred order in the reign of Elizabeth." (S.O.) The bards all but disappeared when Elizabeth I dispossessed the Irish nobles who patronized them.

And *terror* views demoniac pow'rs
40 Flit ghastly round in dread array.

11

Such was the time, and such the place,
The bard respir'd *his* song of woe,
To those, who had of Erin's race
Surviv'd their freedom's vital blow.

12

45 Oh, what a lay the minstrel breath'd!
How many bleeding hearts around,
In suff'ring sympathy enwreath'd,
Hung desponding o'er the sound!

13

For still his Harp's wild plaintive tones
50 Gave back their sorrows keener still,
Breath'd *sadder* sighs, heav'd *deeper* moans,
And wilder wak'd *despair's* wild thrill.

14

For still he sung the ills that flow
From dire oppression's ruthless fang,
55 And deepen'd every patriot woe,
And sharpen'd every patriot pang.

15

Yet, ere he ceas'd, a prophet's fire
Sublim'd his lay, and louder rung
The deep-ton'd music of his lyre,
60 And *Erin go brach*[1] he boldly sung.

---

[1] "Ireland for ever!—a national exclamation, and, in less felicitous times, the rallying point to which many an Irish heart revolted from the influence of despair." (S.O.)

---

from *Italy* (1821)

from CHAPTER 2
Passage of the Alps

Savoy,[2] with all its wild variety of soil and scene, its vestiges of extinct volcanos, and sunny vales of pastoral beauty, may be considered as the vestibule of the Alps. As their mightier regions are approached, the country gradually loses its character of civilization; the last stunted vine withers upon the heights of Modane,[3] and culture has ceased to clothe the interstices of rocks with its forced products, ere that acclivity is ascended, where in the midst of "*regions dolorous*,"[4] stand the clustered hovels of the village of Lans-le-bourg.

The exhaustion of a long journey is a species of malady; and the peculiar weariness, physical and moral, which hangs on the close of each day's progress, may be said to be the periodical paroxysm of the disease. The truth of this remark is only to be verified in all its intensity by Continental travellers; and it is never perhaps more strongly illustrated than by those, who like the writer of these pages, reaches the foot of the Alps at the close of a wearisome day, and catches through the deepening shadows of a dreary twilight, and the drifting eddies of a snow shower, the first glimpses of those regions, which appear to the morbid perceptions of exhausted nature—

"An universe of death, which God by curse
Created evil, for evil only good."——MILTON[5]

The dark, narrow, plashy lane of Lans-le-bourg is terminated to the left by a spacious building, which rises directly opposite to the ascent of Mount Cenis. This building includes a barrack, and an inn,[6] built by the

---

[2] a district in the French Alps.

[3] a town in Savoy.

[4] Cf. Milton, *Paradise Lost* 1.65.

[5] Milton, *Paradise Lost* 2.622–23.

[6] "This inn is kept by an English family, and, contrary to general custom, afforded greater accommodation, comfort, and civility, than are usually offered by our emigrating countrymen. Good beds and good fare are peculiarly valuable, and valued, in this dreary spot, where the sudden diminution of temperature which necessarily accompanies

French. All else around was one wild waste of snow; and the murky huts of Lans-le-bourg looked like a Lapland village.

The passage of the Alps, from Hannibal to Napoleon,[1] has been always described as awful and terrific; as something worse

"Than fables yet have feign'd, or fear conceiv'd."[2]

Benvenuto Cellini's journey over them to France, in the sixteenth century; Evelyn's in the seventeenth; and Lady Mary Wortley's, and Horace Walpole's in the eighteenth,[3] are all described in terms which seem to exhaust the details of possible danger. "I intend to set out to-morrow," says the brilliant ambassadress to the Ottoman Porte, "and pass those *dreadful* Alps so much talked of. If I come to the bottom, you shall hear of me." "We began to ascend Mount Cenis, being carried on little seats of twisted osier fixed upon poles, upon men's shoulders."[4]

Horace Walpole's description is still more formidable. "At the foot of Mount Cenis we were obliged to quit our chaise, which was taken to pieces and loaded on mules; and we were carried in low arm-chairs on poles, swathed in beaver bonnets, beaver gloves, beaver stockings, muffs, and bear-skins." "The dexterity and nimbleness of the mountaineers is inconceivable; they run down steeps and frozen precipices."—"We had twelve men and nine mules to carry us."—"On the top of the highest Alps, by the side of a wood of firs, there darted out a young wolf, seized poor dear Tory by the throat; and before we could possibly prevent it, sprung up the side of the rock, and carried him off."[5]

To this perilous mode of passing the Alps Lalande offers an alternative. "*Cela s'appelle se faire ramasser.*"[6] One of the preliminaries of this speedy mode of travelling might be deemed quite sufficient to render it an experiment of rare occurrence; and the whole is sufficiently uninviting, from the first precipitation down the frozen snows of the mountain, till the half-dead traveller is picked up, or "*ramassé*," at the base of his rapid descent.[7]

When, however, the passage of a Piedmontese princess, on her way to some royal bridegroom of France, was expected, the Corvée[8] was exacted in all its terrible rigour; and the whole vassalage of Piedmont and Savoy were put into requisition to clear a path for the traineau of the royal bride.[9] But all under royalty passed, or perished, as it might be.

Impressed with all this perilous imagery, which the last book of travels, looked into over night, had revived in the memory, it was a dreary thing to rise with the dawn, the following morning, and from the window of *Lans-le-bourg* Inn, to behold that "*frozen continent, deep snow and ice, where armies whole have sunk.*"[10] Immediately opposite the door, a black track in the snow was pointed out, as the old line of road over which the shuddering traveller

---

a rapid ascent, leaves the body more susceptible of disagreeable impressions." (S.O.)

[1] The Carthaginian commander Hannibal marched from Spain over the Pyrenees and the Alps into Italy in 218 BC. In 1800 Napoleon crossed the Alps to defeat the Austrians at the battle of Marengo.

[2] Milton, *Paradise Lost* 2.627.

[3] The *Autobiography* of goldsmith and sculptor Benvenuto Cellini (1500–71), recording a journey across the Alps, was first published in 1730; the diarist John Evelyn (1620–1706) recorded his Alpine crossing in his *Diary* (pub. 1818); Lady Mary Wortley Montagu (1689–1762) crossed from Turin to Lyons on her return from Constantinople in 1718; Horace Walpole (1717–97) made the crossing through Savoy to Turin in 1739 as part of a Grand Tour with the poet Thomas Gray (1716–71).

[4] *Turkish Embassy Letters* 52 (12 September 1718).

[5] letter to Richard West, 11 November 1739; Tory was a dog.

[6] "That's called being picked up" (Fr.).

[7] "'This is only practiced on the Savoy side, the Piedmontese mountains not being adapted to the process. For the operation, the traveller is seated on a traineau; and a guide is placed before him, (with iron spikes in his shoes, to stop the machine when it goes too fast,) who throws himself back on the traveller, to prevent the effect of the shock from pitching him out. Thus arranged, the whole are projected down the frozen snow on the side of the mountain, and a quarter of an hour brings them to the foot of Mount Cenis.'—Lalande." (S.O.) See *Voyage d'un français en Italie* (1769), by the French astronomer Joseph-Jérôme Lefrançais de Lalande (1732–1807).

[8] a feudal system of forced labour.

[9] "This was the case in 1775, on the marriage of the present King of France and his brother the Count d'Artois, to the two Princesses of Savoy." (S.O.)

[10] Cf. Milton, *Paradise Lost* 2.587–94.

was borne in osier baskets, on the shoulders of those porters of the Novalese,[1] and of Lans-le-bourg, who were of necessity reduced to the state of beasts of burden; and who frequently were obliged to fortify themselves against the severity of the elements they encountered, by means which sometimes endangered, and sometimes lost the lives of the persons committed to their care.[2] Beaver swathings! reeling porters! frozen precipices! young wolves! and dislocated carriages on mules' backs, were predominating ideas, when, descending to the inn-yard to begin our journey, we found our carriage undisturbed, four post-horses, and two smart postilions, whose impatient "Allons, Monsieur, allons, Madame,"[3] recalled the technical jargon of the first stage from Paris. Their "*vif, vif,*"[4] put the horses into motion; and we ascended in a trot that broad, smooth, magnificent road, which, carried over the mightiest acclivities of the mightiest regions, exceeds the military highways of antiquity, and shames the paved roads of modern France, whose price was the degradation of a nation.[5] The road, indeed, when we passed it, was covered with snow; but the fences on either side, marked its breadth; and the facility of its winding ascent, proved the boldness, ingenuity, and perfection of its design. At certain distances arose the safe asylums (maisons de refuge) against the *tormenta*, or the avalanche: and the Cantonieri[6] presented themselves with their pick-axes and shovels, giving courage where aid was not wanted. A post-house, or a barrack, disputed the site with the *bears* and *wolves*; and the rapidity of the whole passage rendered beaver swathings, or any other extraordinary precautions against cold, unnecessary. All that had been danger, difficulty, and suffering, but twenty years back, was now safe, facile, and enjoyable; secure beyond the chance of accident, sublime beyond the reach of thought. Legitimate princes! divine-righted sovereigns! houses of France! Austria and Savoy! "*which of you have done this?*"[7] There is not one among you, descendants of a Clovis, a Barbarossa, or an Amadeus,[8] but may in safe conscience shake his innocent head, and answer, "*Thou canst not say 'twas I did it!*"[9]—Neither does the world accuse you.

Whoever has wandered far and seen much, has learned to distrust the promises of books; and (in respect of the most splendid efforts of human labour) must have often felt how far the unworn expectation starts beyond its possible accomplishment. But *nature* never disappoints. Neither the memory nor the imagination of authorship can go beyond the fact she dictates, or the image she presents. If general feelings can be measured by individual impressions, Italy, with all her treasures of art, and associations of history, has nothing to exhibit, that strikes the traveller like the Alps which meet his view on his ascent to the summit of Mount Cenis, or of the Semplon.[10] That is a moment in which the imagination feels the real poverty of its resources, the narrow limits of its range. An aspect of the material world then presents itself, which genius, even in its highest exaltation, must leave to original creation, as unimitated and inimitable. The sensation it produces is too strong for pleasure, too intense for enjoyment. There, where all is so new, novelty loses its charm; where all is so safe, conscious security is no proof against "*horrible imaginings*";[11] and those splendid evidences of the science and industry of man, which rise at every step, recede before

---

[1] in Piedmont, Italy.

[2] "'On the very highest precipice of Mount Cenis, the devil of discord, in the similitude of sour wine, had got amongst our Alpine savages, and set them a-fighting with Gray and me in the chairs: they rushed him by me on a crag, where there was scarce room for a doven foot.'—Walpole's Correspondence." (S.O.) Letter to West, 11 November 1739.

[3] "Let's go, Sir; let's go, Madam" (Fr.).

[4] "sharp" or "lively" (Fr.); i.e., the postilions are encouraging the horses.

[5] "The Corvée." (S.O.)

[6] signal-men, guides.

[7] Shakespeare, *Macbeth* 3.4.49.

[8] three rulers and conquerors: Clovis (c. 466–511), a Frankish king who converted to Christianity and eventually established Paris as his capital; Frederick Barbarossa (1123–90), Swabian duke, German king, and Holy Roman Emperor; and Victor Amadeus II (1666–1730), Duke of Savoy (1675–1713), king of Sicily (1713–20), and king of Sardinia (1720–30).

[9] Cf. Shakespeare, *Macbeth* 3.4.50.

[10] William Wordsworth* crossed the Alps by the Simplon Pass in 1792; see W. Wordsworth, *Prelude* 6. Napoleon constructed a road through the pass, 1800–08.

[11] Shakespeare, *Macbeth* 1.3.138.

the terrible possibilities with which they mingle, and which may render the utmost precaution of talent and philanthropy unavailable. It is in vain that the barrier rises and the arch springs; that the gulf is platformed and the precipice skreened—still the eye closes and the breath is suspended, while danger, painted in the unmastered savagery of remote scenes, creates an ideal and proximate peril. Here experience teaches the falsity of the trite maxim, that the mind becomes elevated by the contemplation of nature in the midst of her grandest works, and engenders thoughts "*that wander through eternity.*"[1] The mind in such scenes is not raised. It is stricken back upon its own insignificance. Masses like these sublime deformities, starting out of the ordinary proportions of nature, in their contemplation reduce man to what he is—an atom. In such regions nothing is in conformity with him, all is at variance with his end and being, all is commemorative of those elementary convulsions, which sweep away whatever lives and breathes, in the general wreck of inanimate matter. Engines and agents of the destructive elements that rage around them, these are regions fitted only to raise the storm and to launch the avalanche, to cherish the whirlwind, and attract the bolt; until some convulsive throe within their mystic womb, awakens fiercer contentions: then they heave and shift, and burst and burn, again to subside, cool down, and settle into awful stillness and permanent desolation; at once the wreck and the monument of changes, which scoff at human record, and trace in characters that admit no controversy the fallacy of calculations and the vanity of systems. Well may the countless races of successive ages have left the mysteries of the Alps unexplored, their snows untracked: but immortal glory be the meed of them, the brave, bold spirits, whose unaccommodated natures, in these regions, where "cold performs the effect of fire,"[2] braved dangers in countless forms, to oppose the invading enemies of their country's struggling rights; who climbing where the eagle had not soared, nor the chamois dared to spring, raised the shout of national independence amidst echoes which had never reverberated, save to the howl of the wolf, or the thunder of the avalanche.[3] Gratitude as eternal as the snows of Mount Blanc to them or him, who grappled with obstacles coeval with creation, levelled the pinnacle and blew up the rock, pierced the granite and spanned the torrent, disputing with nature in all her potency her right to separate man from man, and made straight in the desert an highway for progressive civilization![4]

Than such great works as this, one only greater remained—to facilitate the communion of knowledge, and spread the means of civil liberty from pole to pole by their sole omnipotent agent, A FREE PRESS. He who did much, did not this—he who levelled mountains and turned aside torrents, and did more than a thousand ages of feudal patrons could effect, of all his possible performances left this "*greater still behind*";[5] and by that one false calculation, made on the model of examples he derided and of men he had crushed, he fell himself; and now remains "*unrespited, unpitied, unreprieved*,"[6] the victim of the system he revived and of the policy he cherished.

The art of road-making ranks high in the means of civilization; and its utility, better felt than understood in the dark ages, was sufficiently appreciated to render it an object of monopoly to the Church.[7] To build a bridge,

---

[1] Milton, *Paradise Lost* 2.148.

[2] Cf. Milton, *Paradise Lost* 2.595.

[3] "'Les pièces d'artillerie et les caissons sont portés à bras: les grenadiers arrivés au sommet du mont, jettèrent en l'air leurs bonnets ornés de plumets rouges. Un cri de joie s'élève de l'armée, Les Alps sont franchies.'—Campagne d'Italie, 1796." ("The pieces of artillery and the ammunition boxes are carried in their arms; having arrived at the mountain-top, the grenadiers threw into the air their caps decorated with red feathers. A cry of joy goes up from the army: 'The Alps are free!'"). (S.O.) The account is printed verbatim in H. Raisson, *Fastes militaires de France*, vol. 2 (Paris, 1836). We have been unable to establish his source.

[4] Cf. Isaiah 40.3.

[5] Cf. Shakespeare, *Macbeth* 1.3.117.

[6] Milton, *Paradise Lost* 2.185.

[7] "Some remains of the Cantonieri, or *Utricularii*,* established in Gaul under the Romans, were discoverable in the early part of the middle ages in Provence, where they plied in bands on the banks of rivers and marshes. But this living machinery was not always to be trusted; for in undertaking to forward the traveller to another shore, they sometimes sent him to another world." (S.O.)

* "So called from their rafts used in crossing rivers, which were floated on inflated skins." (S.O.) A "utricularius" is a bagpipe-player (L.), a nickname for a mountain guide.

or clear a forest, were deeds of salvation for the next world, as for this; and royal and noble sinners very literally paved their way to heaven, and reached the gates of paradise by causeways made on earth.[1] St. Benedict laid the basis of his own canonization with the first stone of the famous bridge of Avignon;[2] which, says Pope Nicholas the Fifth,[3] was raised by the inspiration of the Holy Ghost. The *Frères Pontifs*[4] by dint of brick and mortar built up a reputation which rendered their order the most opulent as well as the most revered of their day; and the "viceregents of God on earth"[5] could find no higher title to indicate their power than that, borrowed from Roman priests and emperors, of Pontifex Maximus, or chief bridge-builder. But if there is one, by whom this significant epithet is merited more than by all others, it is he who made roads, cleared forests, and built bridges, from the Alps to the Pontine marshes.[6]

We found the plain, which terminates the ascent of Mount Cenis, covered with snow. Its lake, so famous for excellent trout, was a sheet of ice. The windows of the post-house, the inn, the convent, and the barrack, (the colony of this frozen region) were defended by closed shutters. A friar and a few discontented-looking soldiers were loitering about. An old woman offered some scentless lilies for sale, which she called "fiori di Cenisa,"[7] and some little children sat on the steps of the convent up to their knees in snow. The atmosphere was rarefied, and the sky one deep, dark tint of unvaried blue. Even with all that had been done to provide against danger and ensure accommodation, desolation reigned unabated through the scene.

The first step of the descent was not calculated to lessen unpleasant sensations. The winding precipitous road hung suspended for fathoms down, terrace beneath terrace: an arch flung across a gulf, which, when reached, was carelessly trotted across, seemed as it was viewed from on high, scarce passable by the chamois' foot.[8] Here and there blown-up rocks lay scattered in black masses, unfinished excavations yawned, and vestiges of greater projects and bolder facilities than were yet effected, evinced some daring intention suddenly cut short by natural obstacles, or by political change. Torrents of melted snow swelled the stream of the Cenisella; an undulating region of mountains spread round on every side, like the waves of northern seas suddenly frozen in the moment of their stormy fermentation; until gradually the tintless surface of the soil exhibited spots of black earth, a patch of vegetation, a clump of underwood, a tree putting forth its nipped buds, an hut, a sheepfold, a vine. Winter blasts softened into vernal gales, and the doubling of a bold projecting promontory, revealed the sunny plains of Italy:

"To all delight of human sense exposed,
Nature's whole wealth; nay, more—an heaven on earth."[9]

From such a site as this, it is said, Hannibal halted his Carthaginians, and pointed to the recompense of all their arduous undertakings. From such a site as this the

---

[1] "'Pontifices ego à ponte arbitror; nam ab iis sublicius est factus primum, ut restitutus sæpe, cum ideo sacra et uls et cis Tyberim non mediocri ritu fiant.'—['For my part, I think that the name ('pontifices') comes from *pons* 'bridge'; for by them the Bridge-on-Piles was made in the first place, and it was likewise repaired by them, since in that connexion rites are performed on both sides of the Tiber with no small ceremony" (Varro, *De lingua Latina* 5.15.83, trans. Roland G. Kent).]

"It is probable, however, that, in the rude ages of early Roman history, the priests, imported with the religion from more civilized countries, were alone capable of turning an arch. The Gothic architects of the 11th century, who raised our most beautiful cathedrals, were in like manner priests. If this conjecture be just, the term *pontifex* arose from a *general*, and not a particular fact." (S.O.) The title Pontifex Maximus originally applied to the Roman high priest and was adopted by the Church as a title of the pope. It is derived from "pontem faciens," "bridge-builder" (L.), one of the roles of the ancient priesthood—which may have signified not only a literal function but the spiritual function of connecting human beings with the gods. The Bridge-on-Piles was an ancient wooden bridge over the Tiber river in Rome.

[2] St. Benezet (also known as Little Benedict) founded a brotherhood of amateur engineers (the *frères pontifs*) at Avignon in the 12th century to bridge the Rhone.

[3] (1397–1455).

[4] literally, bridge-brothers.

[5] the popes.

[6] a marshy—and therefore potentially unhealthy—area of central Italy, drained by order of Pope Pius VI (1717–99).

[7] "flowers of Cenis" (It.).

[8] Cf. Byron, *Manfred* 1.2.57–59.*

[9] Cf. Milton, *Paradise Lost* 4.206–08.

Lombard Alboin paused amidst his ferocious hosts, to contemplate the paradise of his future conquest, and quaffed from the skull of his enemy his first draught of Italian wine.[1] From such a site as this Napoleon Bonaparte, at the head of an ill-appointed, long suffering, and neglected army, pointed to the plains of Lombardy, and promised victory. His soldiers accepted the pledge,[2] rushed like an Alpine torrent over crags and precipices, and won that Italy, in two brief and splendid campaigns, which had through ages resisted the forces, and witnessed the disasters, of millions of Frenchmen, led on by kings, and organized by experienced generals.[3] Four armies, of the mightiest coalition the world had ever seen united against the independence of a single nation, were swept away, as the snows of Mount Blanc[4] are scattered by its eddying whirlwinds; and the peace dictated at Leoben,[5] attests the military genius of the young commander, who was one day to number more battles gained, and greater triumphs achieved, than any captain of any age can boast since the time of Alexander. But if Bonaparte commanded, it was the *national* army of France that fought and conquered. It was an army of peasants and artisans, and of citizens, who quitting their fertile valleys, their vine-covered hills, and their luxurious cities, ill-appointed, ill-accoutred, traversed the Mount St. Bernard, and struggling against destruction in a thousand forms, marched not

"In perfect phalanx to the Dorian mood
Of lutes and soft recorders,"[6]

but scrambling over the icy crags, or sunk in snowy gulfs, braved the terrors of the season, and the clime, with a gaiety, that no suffering could subdue,—that no interest could sully....[7]

---

[1] "'Secondo i costumi di quei tempi, in un gran convito dei Longobardi, beveva nel cranio de Cunemondo legato in oro.'—Pignotti, vol. ii." (S.O.) "According to the customs of the period, at a great banquet of the Longobards, he drank out of the gold-framed skull of Cunemondo" (Lorenzo Pignotti [1739–1812], *Storia della Toscana* [*History of Tuscany*], 1813–14). Alboin was King of the Lombards from 565–73; in 568 he invaded Italy to establish the Lombard kingdom there.

[2] "Bonaparte, before his departure for this campaign, traced a slight sketch of his intended operations at a private house. In this plan Millissimo is marked, in the confidence of success, as being the first site of the defeat of the enemy. 'Je chasserois,' he says, 'les Autrichiens des gorges du Tyrol'; and he finishes the sketch with these words: 'C'est aux portes de la Vienne que je vous donnerai la paix.' Speaking afterwards of his treaty of Millissimo, he said, 'C'étoit la plus forte sensation de ma vie.'" (S.O.) "I would chase the Austrians from the gullies of the Tyrol"; "It is at the gates of Vienna that I will make peace with you"; "That was the strongest sensation of my life."

[3] "Under Charles VIII., Louis XII., and Francis I.; and in more recent times, under Louis XIII., XIV., and XV." (S.O.) French kings: Charles VIII (1470–98), Louis XII (1462–1515), Francis I (1494–1547), Louis XIII (1601–1643), Louis XIV (1638–1715), Louis XV (1710–74).

[4] Cf. P.B. Shelley, "Mont Blanc."*

[5] In 1797 the Austrian town of Leoben was the site of preliminary peace negotiations between Napoleon and Austrian diplomats.

[6] Cf. Milton, *Paradise Lost* 1.550–51.

[7] "The campaigns of Italy, under the Directory and Consulate, were well worth all the Imperial Battles fought in the days of France's splendid degradation. The pass of Mount St. Bernard stands unrivalled in military history. The artillery was dragged up the heights by sheer strength of arm, by efforts almost superhuman. Pecuniary motives for exertion, proferred by the General, were rejected by the army. The soldiers, one by one, climbed through the crevices of the ice-rock, and in five hours they reached the convent of St. Peter. The descent was yet more perilous. The infantry cut short the difficulty by sliding on their backs down the ice. The First Consul followed their example, and, in the sight of his army, slided down an height of two hundred feet." (S.O.) The Directory was a five-member executive established in France in 1795. It was replaced by the Consulate after a coup in 1799; Napoleon became First Consul for life in 1802.

Thomas Moore
1779 – 1852

Thomas Moore was born in Dublin, the son of John Moore, a grocer, and Anastasia Codd Moore. In 1795 he was one of the first Roman Catholic students admitted to Trinity College, Dublin, where he opposed the Act of Union with England and befriended such revolutionaries as Robert Emmett, hanged for treason in 1803. One of Moore's songs in *Irish Melodies* would be written to Emmet's memory ("Oh! Breathe Not His Name").*

Leaving Trinity in 1799, Moore went to London with the intention of studying law. His translation of odes attributed to the ancient Greek love poet Anacreon (1800) was dedicated to the Prince of Wales. His juvenile love poems appeared in 1801 as *The Poetical Works of Thomas Little Esq.* In 1803, he obtained a government posting in Bermuda. After only a few months, he appointed a deputy and set out on travels in Canada and the eastern United States. Back in England, he recorded his anti-American prejudices in *Epistles, Odes; and Other Poems* (1806), which Francis Jeffrey* attacked in the *Edinburgh Review*. A duel was narrowly averted; eventually Moore and Jeffrey became friends. Byron,* who had attempted to intervene on Moore's behalf, mentioned the fiasco in *English Bards and Scotch Reviewers* (1809).

Moore began writing words for traditional Irish folk melodies, published in ten volumes by the Dublin music publishers William and James Power as *Irish Melodies* (1808–34). He performed both his own songs and traditional Irish songs for his literary and aristocratic friends. Translated into many languages, set to new music by Hector Berlioz, and admired by Byron, Sir Walter Scott,* and Percy Bysshe Shelley,* Moore's lyrics gave him the nickname "Melody" Moore.

In 1811, he married an Irish actress, Elizabeth Dyke. Satirical political poems following the fortunes of the "Fudge family," published in periodicals and in a series of popular volumes, were admired by, among others, Mary Shelley.* By 1814 Moore was working on a new project, an orientalist metrical romance called *Lalla Rookh* after its Persian heroine. However, Moore's success was interrupted when his deputy in Bermuda was discovered to have embezzled £6000. To avoid debtor's prison, Moore went to the Continent, where Byron entrusted him with the manuscript of his memoirs. The Moores lived in France until the debt had been paid in 1822.

Moore's last long poem, *The Loves of the Angels*, was published in 1823. In 1824—the year of Byron's death—encouraged by Lady Byron, Byron's half-sister Augusta Leigh, and Byron's friend John Cam Hobhouse, Byron's publisher John Murray burned Byron's memoirs in spite of Moore's protests. Thereafter, Moore concentrated on prose: biographies of the playwright Richard Brinsley Sheridan (1825), of Byron (1830), and of the Irish rebel and patriot Edward Fitzgerald (1831); and a *History of Ireland* (1835–46). He died on 25 February 1852. (A.M.)

from *The Works of Thomas Moore, Esq., Comprehending All His Melodies, Ballads, etc. Never Before Published Without the Accompanying Music* (1819)

A Canadian Boat-Song.
Written on the River St.-Lawrence[1]

Et remigem cantus hortatur.
Quintilian[2]

Faintly as tolls the evening chime,
Our voices keep tune and our oars keep time.
Soon as the woods on shore look dim,
We'll sing at St. Ann's our parting hymn,[3]
5   Row brothers, row, the stream runs fast,
The Rapids are near and the day-light's past!

Why should we yet our sail unfurl?
There is not a breath the blue wave to curl!
But, when the wind blows off the shore,
10 Oh! sweetly we'll rest our weary oar.
Blow, breezes, blow, the stream runs fast,
The Rapids are near and the day-light's past!

Utawas'[4] tide! this trembling moon,
Shall see us float over thy surges soon.
15 Saint of this green isle! hear our prayers,
Oh! grant us cool heavens and favouring airs.
Blow, breezes, blow, the stream runs fast,
The Rapids are near and the day-light's past.

Written on Passing Deadman's Island,
in the Gulf of St. Lawrence,
Late in the Evening, September, 1804[5]

See you, beneath yon cloud so dark,
Fast gliding along, a gloomy Bark?
Her sails are full, though the wind is still,
And there blows not a breath her sails to fill!

---

[1] "I wrote these words to an air, which our boat-men sung to us very frequently. The wind was so unfavourable, that they were obliged to row all the way, and we were five days in descending the river from Kingston to Montreal, exposed to an intense sun during the day, and at night forced to take shelter from the dews in any miserable hut upon the banks that would receive us. But the magnificent scenery of the St. Lawrence repays all these difficulties.
"Our *Voyageurs* had good voices, and sung perfectly in tune together. The original words of the air, to which I adapted these stanzas, appeared to be a long, incoherent story, of which I could understand but little, from the barbarous pronunciation of the Canadians. It begins,
    Dans mon chemin j'ai rencontré
    Deux cavaliers très-bien montés;
["On my way I met two well-mounted horsemen."]
And the *refrain* to every verse was,
    A l'ombre d'un bois je m'en vais jouer,
    A l'ombre d'un bois je m'en vais danser.
["In the shade of a tree I'm going to play
In the shade of a tree I'm going to dance."]
"I ventured to harmonize this air, and have published it. Without that charm, which association gives to every little memorial of scenes or feelings that are past, the melody may perhaps be thought common and trifling; but I remember when we have entered, at sunset, upon one of those beautiful lakes, into which the St. Lawrence so grandly and unexpectedly opens, I have heard this simple air with a pleasure which the finest compositions of the first masters have never given me, and now, there is not a note of it, which does not recall to my memory the dip of our oars in the St. Lawrence, the flight of our boat down the Rapids, and all those new and fanciful impressions to which my heart was alive, during the whole of this very interesting voyage.
"The above stanzas are supposed to be sung by those voyageurs, who go to the Grande Portage by the Utawas River. For an account of this wonderful undertaking see *Sir Alexander Mackenzie's General History of the Fur Trade*, prefixed to his Journal." (T.M.)

[2] "Song encourages the rower" (Quintilian, *De Institutione Oratoria* 1.10.16).

[3] "'At the Rapid of St. Ann they are obliged to take out part, if not the whole, of their lading. It is from this spot the Canadians consider they take their departure, as it possesses the last church on the island, which is dedicated to the tutelar saint of voyagers.' *Mackenzie's General History of the Fur Trade*." (T.M.)

[4] the Ottawa River.

[5] "This is one of the Magdalen Islands, and, singularly enough, is the property of Sir Isaac Coffin. The above lines were suggested by a superstition very common among sailors, who call this ghost-ship, I think, 'the flying Dutchman.'
"We were thirteen days on our passage from Quebec to Halifax, and I had been so spoiled by the very splendid hospitality, with which my friends of the Phaeton and Boston had treated me, that I was but ill prepared to encounter the miseries of a Canadian ship. The weather however was pleasant, and the scenery along the river delightful. Our passage through the Gut of Canso, with a bright sky and a fair wind, was particularly striking and romantic." (T.M.) The Flying Dutchman was named after the captain of a ship threatened by storm off the Cape of Good Hope. Against reason and the pleas of his sailors, (Continued)

5 Oh! what doth that vessel of darkness bear?
The silent calm of the grave is there,
Save now and again a death-knell rung,
And the flap of the sails with night-fog hung!

There lieth a wreck on the dismal shore
10 Of cold and pitiless Labrador;
Where, under the moon, upon mounts of frost,
Full many a mariner's bones are tost!

Yon shadowy Bark hath been to that wreck,
And the dim blue fire, that lights her deck,
15 Doth play on as pale and livid a crew,
As ever yet drank the church-yard dew!

To Deadman's Isle, in the eye of the blast,
To Deadman's Isle, she speeds her fast;
By skeleton shapes her sails are furl'd,
20 And the hand that steers is not of this world!

Oh! hurry thee on—oh! hurry thee on
Thou terrible Bark! ere the night be gone,
Nor let morning look on so foul a sight
As would blanch for ever her rosy light!

from *Melodies, by Thomas Moore, Esq.* (1821)

Oh! Breathe Not His Name

A<small>IR</small>—*The Brown Maid.*

Oh! breathe not his name—let it sleep in the shade,
Where cold and unhonour'd his relics are laid!
Sad, silent, and dark, be the tears that we shed,
As the night-dew that falls on the grass o'er his head!

5 But the night-dew that falls, though in silence it weeps,
Shall brighten with verdure the grave where he sleeps;
And the tear that we shed, though in secret it rolls,
Shall long keep his memory green in our souls.

The Harp that once through Tara's Halls

A<small>IR</small>—*Gramachree.*

The harp that once through Tara's halls,[1]
The soul of music shed,
Now hangs as mute on Tara's walls
   As if that soul were fled:—
5 So sleeps the pride of former days,
   So glory's thrill is o'er;
And hearts, that once beat high for praise,
   Now feel that pulse no more!

No more to chiefs and ladies bright
10   The harp of Tara swells;
The chord, alone, that breaks at night,
   Its tale of ruin tells:—
Thus Freedom now so seldom wakes,
   The only throb she gives
15 Is when some heart indignant breaks,
   To shew that still she lives!

Believe Me if all those Endearing Young Charms

A<small>IR</small>—*My Lodging is on the cold Ground.*

Believe me if all those endearing young charms,
   Which I gaze on so fondly to-day,
Were to change by to-morrow and fleet in my arms
   Like fairy-gifts fading away—

5 Thou wouldst still be adored, as this moment thou art,
   Let thy loveliness fade as it will;
And around the dear ruin each wish of my heart
   Would entwine itself verdantly still.

It is not while beauty and youth are thine own,
10   And thy cheeks unprofaned by a tear,
That the fervour and faith of a soul can be known
   To which time will but make thee more dear!

---

he kept his course. When he killed a rebel sailor, the dead man's ghost cursed him. The Flying Dutchman is doomed, according to legend, to sail forever, sometimes luring other sailors to their deaths.

[1] Tara's Hall is in Meath, Ireland, where kings, bards, and priests once met to confer on national issues.

Oh! the heart that has truly loved, never forgets,
    But as truly loves on to the close;
As the sun-flower turns on her god, when he sets,
    The same look which she turn'd when he rose!

The Minstrel Boy

Air—The Moreen.

The Minstrel-boy to the war is gone,
    In the ranks of death you'll find him;
His father's sword he has girded on,
    And his wild harp slung behind him.
"Land of song!" said the warrior-bard,
    "Though all the world betrays thee,
One sword, at least, thy rights shall guard,
    One faithful harp shall praise thee!"

The Minstrel fell!—but the foeman's chain
    Could not bring that proud soul under;
The harp he loved ne'er spoke again,
    For he tore its chords asunder;
And said, "No chains shall sully thee,
    Thou soul of love and bravery!
Thy songs were made for the pure and free,
    They shall never sound in slavery."

The Time I've Lost in Wooing

Air—Pease upon a Trencher.

The time I've lost in wooing,
In watching and pursuing
    The light that lies
    In Woman's eyes,
Has been my heart's undoing.
Though Wisdom oft has sought me,
I scorn'd the lore she brought me;
    My only books
    Were Woman's looks,
And Folly's all they've taught me.

Her smile when Beauty granted,
I hung with gaze enchanted,
    Like him the Sprite[1]
    Whom maids by night
Oft meet in glen that's haunted.
Like him, too, Beauty won me,
But, while her eyes were on me,
    If once their ray
    Was turn'd away.
O! winds could not outrun me.

And are those follies going?
And is my proud heart growing
    Too cold or wise
    For brilliant eyes
Again to set it glowing?
No—vain, alas! th' endeavour
From bonds so sweet to sever;—
    Poor Wisdom's chance
    Against a glance
Is now as weak as ever!

---

[1] "This alludes to a kind of Irish fairy, which is to be met with, they say, in the fields, at dusk;—as long as you keep your eyes upon him, he is fixed and in your power; but the moment you look away (and he is ingenious in furnishing some inducement) he vanishes. I had thought that this was the sprite which we call the Leprechaun; but a high authority upon such subjects, Lady MORGAN (in a note upon her national and interesting novel, 'O'Donnel') has given a very different account of that goblin." (T.M.) *O'Donnel*, a popular novel by Sydney Owenson, Lady Morgan,* was published in 1814.

Horace Smith
1779 – 1849

Horatio Smith (he preferred to be called Horace) was born in London on New Year's Eve, 1779, the son of Robert Smith, a lawyer, philanthropist, and antiquarian, and Mary Bogle Smith, a Dissenting minister's daughter. He was educated at Chigwell School and Alfred House Academy and then began work as a clerk; eventually, he became a successful stockbroker. He married twice and had four children. In 1816, he met P.B. Shelley* and they became lifelong friends: Shelley called Smith "the only truly generous person I ever knew, who had money to be generous with"; Smith in return called Shelley "infinitely the most extraordinary character my long life has known."

Encouraged by his father, Smith began writing early; he published his first novel, *A Family Story,* in 1799. His best-known work is *Rejected Addresses* (1812), a book of parodies written in collaboration with his brother James (1775–1839), in which they imagine how famous contemporary poets might have written poetic addresses to commemorate the re-opening of Drury Lane Theatre, after its destruction in a fire. In 1821, Smith retired from business, spent four years in France, and then published over a dozen historical novels in imitation of Scott.* He retired from fiction in 1845 and died in Tunbridge Wells on 12 July 1849. (D.L.M.)

∽∽

from *Amarynthus, the Nympholept: A Pastoral Drama, in Three Acts. With Other Poems* (1821)

On a Stupendous Leg of Granite, Discovered Standing by Itself in the Deserts of Egypt, with the Inscription Inserted Below [1]

In Egypt's sandy silence, all alone,
Stands a gigantic leg, which far off throws
    The only shadow that the desert knows.
"I am great Ozymandias," saith the stone,
5   "The king of kings: this mighty city shows
The wonders of my hand." The city's gone!
    Naught but the leg remaining to disclose
The site of that forgotten Babylon.

We wonder, and some hunter may express
10 Wonder like ours, when thro' the wilderness,
    Where London *stood*, holding the wolf in chace,
He meets some fragment huge, and stops to guess
    What powerful, but unrecorded, race,
Once dwelt in that annihilated place.

---

[1] Smith wrote the poem after visiting the British Museum with P.B. Shelley in 1817; on the same occasion, Shelley wrote "Ozymandias."*

On the Spanish Revolution [2]

O now may I depart in peace![3] for, lo!
    Spain, the priest-ridden and enslaved, hath riven
Her chains asunder; and no rage, no flow
    Of blood, save what the despot, phrensy-driven,
5 Wantonly shed. Did they not crush him? No;
    All with magnanimous mercy was forgiven!
Tyrants, the hour is coming, sure, tho' slow,
    When ye no more can outrage earth and heaven.

As I would joy to see the assassin foil'd
    By his own gun's explosion, so do I
10 Joy, that the oppressor's armies have recoil'd
    Back on themselves; for so shall they rely
On love, not fear, leaving the world o'ertoil'd
    With war and chains, to peace and liberty.

---

[2] Between 1808 and 1813 Spain rose against French domination and, with English help, overthrew Napoleon and the regime of Joseph Buonaparte. When in 1814 the Bourbon king Ferdinand VII was restored to his throne, he abolished the liberal constitution of 1812. The Spanish liberals successfully revolted in 1820 and forced the king to reinstate the constitution. Unfortunately, Ferdinand, with the help of France, later regained his despotic powers.

[3] Cf. Luke 2.29, and Price, *A Discourse on the Love of Our Country* (10).*

William Hone
1780 – 1842

William Hone was born in Bath on 3 June 1780. His father, William Hone, was a legal clerk; his mother was Frances Maria Stawell Hone. The Hones soon moved to London, where Hone was educated by his father and at dame schools. At thirteen, he became a lawyer's copyist. In 1797, he took a step towards radicalism by joining the London Corresponding Society. In July 1800, he married Sarah Johnson; they had twelve children. For the next fifteen years, Hone worked, mostly unsuccessfully, at a variety of jobs. He published the first of his 87 books, pamphlets, and broadsides in 1807, but he did not come to national prominence until 1817, when he published three political parodies of passages from the Anglican *Book of Common Prayer*. He was arrested and charged with blasphemous libel. He defended himself and was acquitted; the three trials (transcripts of which Hone immediately published) are still considered important victories in the struggle for a free press. To protest the Peterloo Massacre in 1819 (see note to line 81), Hone published his most popular pamphlet, *The Political House that Jack Built*; it went through forty editions in 1819 alone and helped to establish the career of George Cruikshank, who illustrated it. The same year, only days after the publication of the first two cantos of Byron's *Don Juan*,* Hone published *Don Juan, Canto the Third!*, in which Juan marries Haidée, moves to London, has twelve children, and becomes a radical publisher. After editing *The Apocryphal New Testament* (1820), which was attacked by the *Quarterly Review*, Hone moved away from political controversy to publish extremely popular almanacs and miscellanies of information: *The Every-Day Book* (1825–27), *The Table Book* (1827–28), and *The Year Book* (1831–32); their success did not save the always-impecunious Hone from going bankrupt in 1827. In the last decade of his life, he moved away from literature altogether: for three years, he ran a coffee-house; then, after converting to Evangelicalism, he worked briefly as the sub-editor of an Evangelical newspaper and even sometimes preached. In 1832, he began to suffer from "paralytic attacks"; he died on 6 November 1842. (D.L.M.)

WILLIAM HONE

The Political House That Jack Built (1819)

"*A straw—thrown up to show which way the wind blows.*"[1]

WITH THIRTEEN CUTS.

The Pen and the Sword

LONDON:
PRINTED BY AND FOR WILLIAM HONE, LUDGATE HILL.

————"Many, whose sequester'd lot
Forbids their interference, looking on,
Anticipate perforce some dire event;
And, seeing the old castle of the state,
That promis'd once more firmness, so assail'd,
That all its tempest-beaten turrets shake,
Stand motionless expectants of its fall."[2]
                                        Cowper.

NOTE.
Each Motto that follows, is from Cowper's "Task."

---

[1] Cf. Byron, *Don Juan** 14.8. The illustration shows the Duke of Wellington throwing his sword onto a scale already bearing three instruments of legal oppression, which are outweighed by a quill pen.

[2] Cowper, *The Task** 5.522–28.

WILLIAM HONE

The Author's Dedication to His Political Godchild.

TO
DOCTOR SLOP,[1]
*in acknowledgment of many public testimonials
of his filial gratitude; and to*
THE NURSERY OF CHILDREN, SIX FEET HIGH,
HIS READERS,
for the delight and instruction of their uninformed minds;
THIS JUVENILE PUBLICATION
is affectionately inscribed, by the Doctor's Political Godfather, THE AUTHOR.

NOTE.—*The Publication wherein the Author of "The Political House that Jack built" conferred upon Dr. Slop the lasting distinction of his name, was a Jeu d'Esprit, entitled "Buonaparte-phobia, or Cursing made easy to the meanest capacity."—it is reprinted, and may be had of the Publisher, Price One Shilling.*

" A distant age asks where the fabric stood."[2]

---

[1] Dr. John Stoddart (1773–1856), former editor of *The Times*. Hone has renamed him after the man-midwife in *Tristram Shandy* (1759–67), by Laurence Sterne (1713–68). Hone had already ridiculed him in the pamphlet (1815) mentioned in his note.

[2] Cowper, *The Task* 5.535.

WILLIAM HONE

THIS IS THE HOUSE THAT JACK BUILT.[1]

———"Not to understand a treasure's worth,
Till time has stolen away the slighted good,
Is cause of half the poverty we feel,
And makes the world the wilderness it is."[2]

THIS IS
THE WEALTH[3]
that lay
5   In the House that Jack built.

———"A race obscene,
Spawn'd in the muddy beds of Nile, came forth,
    Polluting Egypt: gardens, fields and plains,
Were cover'd with the pest;
The croaking nuisance lurk'd in every nook;
Nor palaces, nor even chambers, 'scaped;
And the land stank—so num'rous was the fry."[4]

---

[1] The Commons, King, and Lords were known as the three pillars of the British Constitution. On top of the structure is a statue of Liberty, bearing on her staff the Phrygian cap once associated with the French Revolutionaries and now with reform movements. In this context, "Jack" is John Bull, the stereotypical Englishman.

[2] Cowper, *The Task* 6.50–53.

[3] the Magna Charta (1215); the Bill of Rights (1689); and *habeas corpus* ("you have the body": L.), a protection against arbitrary imprisonment: three guarantees of British liberty.

[4] Cowper, *The Task* 2.826–32.

THESE ARE
THE VERMIN[1]
That Plunder the Wealth,
That lay in the House,
That Jack built.

"Once enslaved, farewell!
  *   *   *   *
Do I forebode impossible events,
And tremble at vain dreams? Heav'n grant I may!"[2]

THIS IS
THE THING,[3]
            that, in spite of new Acts,[4]
And attempts to restrain it,
            by Soldiers or Tax,
Will *poison* the Vermin,
That plunder the Wealth,
That lay in the House,
That Jack built.

---

[1] In the illustration on p. 920, from left to right, a court official, a cavalry officer, a priest/magistrate (probably Charles Ethelston: see note to line 252), another officer, a tax collector, and a lawyer (probably Sir Robert Gifford: see note to line 21).

[2] Cowper, *The Task* 5.477, 491–92.

[3] Hone's own printing press.

[4] The Six Acts, passed after the Peterloo massacre, regulated public meetings, allowed magistrates to seize blasphemous and seditious publications, and extended the Stamp tax to more publications, among other measures.

"The seals of office glitter in his eyes;
He climbs, he pants, he grasps them—
To be a pest where he was useful once."[1]

20   THIS IS
     THE PUBLIC INFORMER,[2]
            who
     Would put down the *Thing*,
            that, in spite of new Acts,
25   And attempts to restrain it,
            by Soldiers and Tax,
Will *poison* the Vermin, that plunder the Wealth,
That lay in the House, that Jack built.

"Ruffians are abroad—
         * * * *
Leviathan is not *so* tamed."[3]

---

[1] Cowper, *The Task* 4.59–60, 657.

[2] Sir Robert Gifford (1779–1826), the Attorney General.

[3] Cowper, *The Task* 4.568, 2.322.

THESE ARE
THE *REASONS* OF LAWLESS POWER[1]
That back the Public Informer,
    who
Would put down the *Thing*,
    that, in spite of new Acts,
And attempts to restrain it,
    by Soldiers or Tax,
Will *poison* the Vermin,
That plunder the Wealth,
That lay in the House,
    That Jack built.

——"Great offices will have Great talents."[2]

---

[1] In the illustration on p. 922, from left to right, a jailor (probably Joseph Nadin [1765–1848], deputy constable of Manchester), an artilleryman standing behind his cannon with his match, a mounted Life Guard, and a grenadier.

[2] Cowper, *The Task* 4.788–89.

This is THE MAN[1]—all shaven and shorn,
All cover'd with Orders—and all forlorn;
THE DANDY OF SIXTY,
      who bows with a grace,
And has *taste* in wigs, collars,
      cuirasses and lace;
Who, to tricksters, and fools,
      leaves the State and its treasure,
And, when Britain's in tears,
      sails about at his pleasure:[2]
Who spurn'd from his presence
      the Friends of his youth,[3]
And now has not one
      who will tell him the truth;
Who took to his counsels,
      in evil hour,
The Friends to the Reasons
      of lawless Power;
That back the Public Informer,
      who
Would put down the *Thing*,
      that, in spite of new Acts,
And attempts to restrain it,
      by Soldiers or Tax,
Will *poison* the Vermin,
That plunder the Wealth,
That lay in the House,
That Jack built.

"Portentous, unexampled, unexplain'd!
———— What man seeing this,

---

[1] the Prince Regent (1762–1830), later George IV.

[2] When the Peterloo massacre occurred, the Prince was on his yacht, the *Royal George*. In 1816, Hone had satirized public spending on it.

[3] As a young man, the Prince had befriended prominent Whigs, who felt betrayed when, as Regent, he favoured the Tories.

And having human feelings, does not blush,
And hang his head, to think himself a man?
———— I cannot rest
A silent witness of the headlong rage,
Or heedless folly, by which thousands die——
Bleed gold for Ministers to sport away."[1]

    THESE ARE
    THE PEOPLE
      all tatter'd and torn,
Who curse the day
      wherein they were born,
On account of Taxation
      too great to be borne,
And pray for relief,
      from night to morn;
Who, in vain, Petition
      in every form,
Who, peaceably Meeting,
      to ask for Reform,[2]
Were sabred by Yeomanry Cavalry,
      who,
Were thank'd by THE MAN,
      all shaven and shorn,
All cover'd with Orders—
      and all forlorn;
THE DANDY OF SIXTY,
      who bows with a grace,
And has *taste* in wigs, collars,
      cuirasses, and lace;
Who, to tricksters, and fools,
      leaves the State and its treasure,
And when Britain's in tears,
      sails about at his pleasure;
Who spurn'd from his presence
      the Friends of his youth,
And now has not one
      who will tell him the truth;

---

[1] Cowper, *The Task* 2.58, 2.26–28,* 3.217–19, 4.508.

[2] On 16 August 1819, sixty thousand people gathered in St. Peter's Fields, Manchester, to demonstrate peacefully for Parliamentary reform. As the illustration shows, the cavalry charged the crowd, killing eleven and injuring hundreds. The Prince approved, praising the cavalry's restraint. The event became known as "Peterloo," after the battle of Waterloo (1815). Cf. P.B. Shelley, *The Masque of Anarchy*.*

100 Who took to his counsels, in evil hour,
The Friends to the Reasons of lawless Power,
That back the Public Informer, who
Would put down the *Thing*, that, in spite of new Acts,
And attempts to restrain it, by Soldiers and Tax,
105 Will *poison* the Vermin, that plunder the Wealth,
That lay in the House, that Jack built.

THE DOCTOR.
"At his last gasp—as if with opium drugg'd."
DERRY-DOWN TRIANGLE
"He that sold his country."
THE SPOUTER OF FROTH
"With merry descants on a nation's woes—
There is a public mischief in his mirth."

THE GUILTY TRIO
"Great skill have they in *palmistry*, and more
To conjure clean away the gold they touch,
Conveying worthless dross into its place;
Loud when they beg, dumb only when they steal.
 * * * *
"Dream after dream ensues;
And still they dream, that they shall still succeed,
And still are disappointed."[1]

---

[1] Cowper, *The Task* 3.807, 4.26, 3.88–89, 4.77, 1.769, 1.570–73, 3.127–29.

This is THE DOCTOR[1]
    of *Circular* fame,
A Driv'ller, a Bigot, a Knave
    without shame:
And *that's* DERRY DOWN TRIANGLE[2]
    by name,
From the Land of mis-rule,
    and half-hanging, and flame:
And *that* is THE SPOUTER OF FROTH
    BY THE HOUR,[3]
The worthless colleague
    of their infamous power;
Who dubb'd *him* "the Doctor"
    whom now he calls "brother,"
And, to get at his Place,
    took a shot at the other;[4]
Who haunts their *Bad House*,
    a base living to earn,
By playing Jack-pudding,[5] and Ruffian,
    in turn;
Who bullies, for those
    whom he bullied before;
Their *Flash*-man, their Bravo,[6]
    a son of a ———;
The hate of the People,
    all tatter'd and torn,

---

[1] Henry Addington, Viscount Sidmouth (1757–1844), the Home Secretary (left, illustration on p. 926). Canning* had mocked him in "Ode to the 'Doctor.'" In 1817, after *habeas corpus* had been suspended, Sidmouth issued a circular letter encouraging prosecutions (like that of Hone) for blasphemous or seditious libel.

[2] Robert Stewart, Viscount Castlereagh (1769–1822) (centre, illustration on p. 926). As Chief Secretary for Ireland, he was largely responsible for suppressing the rebellion of 1798; Hone takes his nickname from the triangular frame onto which rebels were strapped to be flogged. As Foreign Minister (1812–22), he was largely responsible for restoring the pre-Revolutionary order in Europe. As leader of the Commons, he regularly defended repressive measures like Peterloo.

[3] George Canning (right, illustration on p. 926). A famous orator, he was a Member of Parliament, though not a cabinet minister, in 1819.

[4] In 1809, Canning and Castlereagh had fought a duel. Now they are allies.

[5] buffoon.

[6] A flashman is a thieves' accomplice; a bravo is a paid assassin.

Who curse the day
    wherein they were born,[1]
On account of Taxation
    too great to be borne,
And pray for relief
    from night to morn;
Who, in vain, Petition
    in every form,
Who peaceably Meeting,
    to ask for Reform,
Were sabred by Yeomanry Cavalry,
    who,
Were thank'd by THE MAN,
    all shaven and shorn,
All cover'd with Orders—
    and all forlorn;
THE DANDY OF SIXTY,
    who bows with a grace,
And has a *taste* in wigs, collars,
    cuirasses, and lace:
Who to tricksters and fools,
    leaves the State and its treasure,
And, when Britain's in tears,
    sails about at his pleasure:
Who spurn'd from his presence
    the Friends of his youth,
And now has not one
    who will tell him the truth;
Who took to his counsels, in evil hour,
The Friends to the Reasons of lawless Power;
That back the Public Informer, who
Would put down the *Thing*, that, in spite of new Acts,
And attempts to restrain it, by Soldiers and Tax,
Will *poison* the Vermin, that plunder the Wealth,
That lay in the House, that Jack built.

---

[1] Cf. Job 3.3.

    ——"Burghers, men immaculate perhaps
In all their private functions, once combin'd,
Become a loathsome body, only fit
For dissolution.
    ——————— Power usurp'd
Is weakness when oppos'd; conscious of wrong,
'Tis pusillanimous and prone to flight.
    ——————— I could endure
Chains nowhere patiently; and chains at home,
Where I am free by birthright, not at all."[1]

This WORD[2] is the Watchword—
    the talisman word,
That the WATERLOO-MAN'S[3] to crush
    with his sword;
But, if shielded by NORFOLK
    and BEDFORD'S alliance,
It will set both his sword,
    and him, at defiance;

---

[1] Cowper, *The Task* 4.672–75, 5.371–73, 5.477–79.

[2] Before the First Reform Act of 1832, only 400,000 of the 24,000,000 people in Britain could vote; "pocket boroughs" (controlled by landowners or the Crown) and "rotten boroughs" (where the population had declined drastically) returned two Members of Parliament each, while cities like Manchester had no representation.

[3] "Waterloo-Man" was a song critical of Wellington, published in the radical paper *Black Dwarf*, 18 June 1817.

If F<small>ITZWILLIAM</small>, and G<small>ROSVENOR</small>, and
                A<small>LBEMARLE</small> aid it,[1]
And assist its best Champions,
                who then dare invade it?
'Tis the terrible WORD OF FEAR,
                night and morn,
To the *Guilty Trio*,
                all cover'd with scorn;
First, to the Doctor,
                of *Circular* fame,
A Driv'ller, a Bigot, a Knave
                without shame:
And next, Derry Down Triangle
                by name,
From the Land of Mis-rule,
                and Half-hanging, and Flame:
And then, to the Spouter of Froth
                by the hour,
The worthless Colleague
                of their infamous power;
Who dubb'd *him* "the Doctor,"
                whom now he calls "brother,"
And, to get at his Place,
                took a shot at the other;
Who haunts their *Bad House*,
                a base living to earn,
By playing Jack-Pudding, and Ruffian,
                in turn;
Who bullies for those,
                whom he bullied before;
Their *Flash*-man, their Bravo,
                a son of a ———;
The hate of the People,
                all tatter'd and torn,
Who curse the day
                wherein they were born,
On account of Taxation
                too great to be borne,

---

[1] Bernard Edward Howard, Duke of Norfolk (1765–1842), William Wentworth, Earl Fitzwilliam (1748–1833), Richard Grosvenor, later Marquis of Westminster (1795–1869) were sympathetic to the cause of Parliamentary reform. Hone also invokes the memory of Francis Russell, 5th Duke of Bedford (1765–1802), who opposed the suspension of habeas corpus in 1794 (his criticism of Burke's pension provoked Burke's attack on him in *Letter to a Noble Lord*° and Canning and Frere's in "New Morality"*), and George Monck, 1st Duke of Albemarle (1608–70), a strong advocate of the supremacy of civil over military power.

And pray for relief,
    from night to morn,
Who in vain Petition
    in every form,
Who peaceably Meeting
    to ask for Reform,
Were sabred by Yeomanry Cavalry,
    who
Were thank'd by THE MAN,
    all shaven and shorn,
All cover'd with Orders—
    and all forlorn;
THE DANDY OF SIXTY,
    who bows with a grace,
And has *taste* in wigs, collars,
    cuirasses, and lace;
Who, to tricksters, and fools,
    leaves the State and its treasure,
And, when Britain's in tears
    sails about at his pleasure;
Who spurn'd from his presence
    the Friends of his Youth,
And now has not one
    who will tell him the Truth;
Who took to his Counsels,
    in evil hour,
The Friends to the Reasons
    of lawless Power;
That back the Public Informer,
    who
Would put down the Thing,
    that, in spite of new Acts,
And attempts to restrain it
    by Soldiers or Tax,
Will *poison* the Vermin,
That plunder the Wealth,
That lay in the House,
That Jack built.

END OF THE HOUSE THAT JACK BUILT.

WILLIAM HONE

THE CLERICAL MAGISTRATE.[1]

"*The Bishop.* Will you be diligent in Prayers—laying aside the study of the world and the flesh?——*The Priest.* I will.
The Bishop. Will you maintain and set forwards, as much as lieth in you, quietness, peace, and love, among all Christian people? —— *Priest.* I will. The Bishop laying his hand upon the head of him that receiveth the order of Priesthood, shall say, RECEIVE THE HOLY GHOST."
The Form of Ordination for A Priest.[2]................

————"The pulpit (in the sober use
Of its legitimate peculiar pow'rs)
Must stand acknowledg'd, while the world shall stand,
The most important and effectual guard,
Support, and ornament of virtue's cause."

*   *   *   *

Behold the picture! Is it like?[3]

THIS IS A PRIEST,[4]
      made "according to Law,"
Who, on being ordain'd,
      vow'd, by rote, like a daw,

---

[1] a related poem, not quite incorporated into *The Political House that Jack Built*.

[2] the Anglican rule-book for this procedure.

[3] Cowper, *The Task* 2.332–36, 2.408.

[4] Charles Ethelston. As a magistrate, he read the Riot Act before Peterloo; as a priest, he later told his congregation that the massacre was God's will.

That, he felt himself call'd,
        by the Holy Spirit,
To teach men the Kingdom of Heaven
        to merit;
That, to think of the World and the flesh
        he'd cease,
And keep men in quietness,
        love and peace;
And, making thus his profession
        and boast,
Receiv'd, from the Bishop,
        the Holy Ghost:
Then—not having the fear of God
        before him—
Is sworn in a Justice,
        and one of the *Quorum*;[1]
'Gainst his spiritual Oath,
        puts his Oath of the Bench,
And, instead of his Bible,
        examines a wench;
Gets Chairman of Sessions—leaves his flock,
        sick, or dying,
To license Ale-houses—and assist
        in the trying
Of prostitutes, poachers, pickpockets
        and thieves;—
Having *charged* the Grand Jury,
        dines with them, and gives
"CHURCH AND KING without day-light";
        gets *fresh*, and puts in—
To the stocks vulgar people
        who fuddle with gin:
Stage coachmen, and toll-men,
        convicts as he pleases;
And beggars and paupers
        incessantly teazes:
Commits starving vagrants,
        and orders Distress
On the Poor, for their Rates—
        signs warrants to press,
And beats up for names
        to a Loyal Address:

---

[1] the magistracy.

Would indict, for Rebellion,
        those who Petition;
And, all who look peaceable,
        try for Sedition;
If the People were legally Meeting,
        in quiet,
Would pronounce it, decidedly—*sec. Stat.*[1]
        a Riot,
And order the Soldiers
        "to aid and assist,"
That is—kill the helpless,
        Who cannot resist.
He, though vowing "from all worldly studies
        to cease,"
Breaks the Peace of the Church,
        to be Justice of Peace;
Breaks his vows made to Heaven—
        a pander for Power;
A Perjurer—a guide to the People
        no more;
On God turns his back,
        when he turns the State's Agent;
And damns his own Soul,
        to be friends with the ———.

THE END

"'Tis Liberty alone, that gives the flow'r
Of fleeting life its lustre and perfume;
And we are weeds without it."[2]

---

[1] according to the statute" (L.).

[2] Cowper, *The Task* 5.446–48.

John Wilson Croker
1780 – 1857

John Wilson Croker was born on 20 December 1780 in Galway, Ireland, son of the surveyor-general of customs and excise. He was educated at Trinity College, Dublin, and then went to London to study law. He had a successful career as a lawyer. In 1806, he married Rosamond Pennell; they had one child, who died when he was three, breaking their hearts. Also in 1806, Croker was elected to the House of Commons; he had a long and distinguished career as a Tory Member of Parliament (he is said to have coined the term "conservative") and as First Secretary of the Admiralty. He published a number of satires and other works and was active as a scholar, editing Boswell, Pope, and Walpole. But literary history remembers him for the 269 reviews and other articles he published in the *Quarterly Review* between its founding in 1809 and his retirement in 1854, including vitriolic attacks on Hunt,* M.W. Shelley's* *Frankenstein*, Tennyson, and, most notoriously, Keats's *Endymion*.* In the Preface to *Adonais*,* P.B. Shelley states his belief that Keats's distress at this review caused his early death. Shelley was wrong, but Croker's mauling of *Eighteen Hundred and Eleven** does seem to have ended Barbauld's career. Croker got as good as he gave, being satirized by Disraeli, Macaulay, Owenson,* Thackeray, and Hazlitt,* who described him as a "talking potatoe." He died on 10 August 1857. (D.L.M.)

☙☙☙

from the *Quarterly Review* 7 (March and June 1812)

Review of Barbauld's *Eighteen Hundred and Eleven*

Our old acquaintance Mrs. Barbauld turned satirist! The last thing we should have expected, and, now that we have seen her satire, the last thing that we could have desired.

May we (without derogating too much from that reputation of age and gravity of which critics should be so chary) confess that we are yet young enough to have had early obligations to Mrs. Barbauld; and that it really is with no disposition to retaliate on the fair pedagogue of our former life, that on the present occasion, we have called her up to correct her exercise?

But she must excuse us if we think that she has wandered from the course in which she was respectable and useful, and miserably mistaken both her powers and her duty, in exchanging the birchen for the satiric rod,[1] and abandoning the superintendance of the "ovilia"[2] of the nursery, to wage war on the "reluctantes dracones,"[3] statesmen, and warriors, whose misdoings have aroused her indignant muse.

We had hoped, indeed, that the empire might have been saved without the intervention of a lady-author: we even flattered ourselves that the interests of Europe and of humanity would in some degree have swayed our public councils, without the descent of (dea ex machina)[4] Mrs. Anna Letitia Barbauld in a quarto, upon the theatre where the great European tragedy is now performing. Not such, however, is her opinion; an irresistible impulse of public duty—a confident sense of commanding talents—have induced her to dash down her shagreen spectacles[5] and her knitting needles, and to sally forth, hand in hand with her renowned compatriot,[6] in the magnanimous resolution of saving a

---

[1] Schoolteachers (such as Barbauld had been) traditionally beat their students with birchwood canes.

[2] "sheepfolds": Horace, *Odes* 4.4.9.

[3] "struggling serpents": Horace, *Odes* 4.4.11.

[4] "a goddess from the machine" (L.): a feminine version of the "god from the machine" (a stage device) that descended to end some Greek tragedies.

[5] Spectacles were often kept in cases of shagreen, a kind of untanned leather.

[6] See "Art. II." (J.C.). Article 2 in this issue is a review of two tracts on parliamentary reform by William Roscoe (1753–1831), praised in Barbauld's poem and ridiculed later in this review.

sinking state, by the instrumentality of a pamphlet in prose and a pamphlet in verse.

The poem, for so out of courtesy we shall call it, is entitled Eighteen Hundred and Eleven, we suppose, because it was written in the year 1811; but this is a mere conjecture, founded rather on our inability to assign any other reason for the name, than in any particular relation which the poem has to the events of the last year. We do not, we confess, very satisfactorily comprehend the meaning of all the verses which this fatidical spinster has drawn from her poetical distaff; but of what we do understand we very confidently assert that there is not a topic in "Eighteen Hundred and Eleven" which is not quite as applicable to 1810 or 1812, and which, in our opinion, might not, with equal taste and judgment, have been curtailed, or dilated, or transposed, or omitted, without any injustice whatever to the title of the poem, and without producing the slightest discrepancy between the frontispiece and the body of work.

The poem opens with a piece of information, which, though delivered in phraseology somewhat quaint and obscure, we are not disposed to question, namely, that this country is still at war; but it goes on to make ample amends for the flat veracity of this commonplace, by adding a statement, which startled, as much as the former assertion satisfied, our belief. Mrs. Barbauld does not fear to assert, that the year 1811 was one of extraordinary *natural* plenty, but that, with a most perverse taste,

> Man called to Famine, nor invoked in vain.[1]

We had indeed heard that some mad and mischievous partisans had ventured to charge the scarcity which unhappily exists, upon the political measures of government:—but what does Mrs. Barbauld mean? Does she seriously accuse mankind of wishing for a famine, and interceding for starvation? or does she believe that it is in the power of this country, of what remains of independent Europe, nay, of herself, to arrest the progress of war, and, careless of what Buonaparte or his millions may be about, to beckon back peace and plenty, and to diffuse happiness over the reviving world?

But let us select a specimen of her poetry, which shall be also one of her veracity, prophecy, and patriotism. It is the description of the fallen state of this poor realm.

> Thy baseless wealth dissolves in air away,
> Like mists that melt before the morning ray;
> No more in crowded mart or busy street,
> Friends meeting friends with cheerful hurry greet.
>
> Yes, thou must droop; thy Midas dream is o'er,
> The golden tide of commerce leaves thy shore,
> Leaves thee to prove th'alternate ills that haunt
> Enfeebling luxury and ghastly want.—p. 5.[2]

We do not know where Mrs. Anna Letitia now resides, though we can venture to assert that it is not on Parnassus:[3] it must, however, be in some equally unfrequented, though less classical region; for the description just quoted is no more like the scene that is really before our eyes, than Mrs. Barbauld's satire is like her "Lessons for Children," or her "Hymns in Prose."[4]

England, in her prophetic vision, is undone; soon, it seems,

> — to be only known
> By the gray ruin and the mouldering stone.[5]

while America is to go on increasing and improving in arts, in arms, and even, if that be possible, in virtue! Young Americans will cross the Atlantic to visit the sacred ruins of England, just as our young noblemen go to Greece.

> Then the ingenuous youth, whom fancy fires
> With pictured glories of illustrious sires,
> With duteous zeal their pilgrimage shall take,
> From the blue mountains or Ontario's lake—p. 10.[6]

and pay sentimental visits to Cambridge and Stratford-upon-Avon. These "ingenuous" Americans are also to come to London, which they are to find in ruins: however, being of bold and aspiring dispositions,

> They of some broken turret, mined by time,
> The broken stair with perilous step shall climb,

---

[1] Barbauld, *Eighteen Hundred and Eleven* 15.*

[2] Barbauld, *Eighteen Hundred and Eleven* 53–56, 61–64.

[3] a mountain in Greece, sacred to the Muses.

[4] children's books by Barbauld (1787–88, 1781).

[5] Barbauld, *Eighteen Hundred and Eleven* 123–24.

[6] Barbauld, *Eighteen Hundred and Eleven* 127–30.

> Thence stretch their view the wide horizon round,
> By scatter'd hamlets trace its ancient bound,
> And choked no more with fleets, fair Thames survey
> Through reeds and sedge pursue his idle way.[1]

This is a sad prospect! but while all our modern edifices are to be in such a lamentable state of dilapidation, Time is to proceed with so cautious and discriminating a step, that Melrose Abbey, which is now pretty well in ruins, is not to grow a bit older, but to continue a beautiful ruin still; this supernatural longevity is conferred upon it in honour of Mr. Scott.[2]

But let not Mr. Scott be too proud of a distinction which he possesses in a very humble degree, compared with him, to whom

> ———belong
> *The* Roman virtue and the Tuscan song.[3]

Which of the virtues, *the* (κατ᾽ εξοχην)[4] Roman virtue is, Mrs. Barbauld does not condescend to inform us, nor does our acquaintance with Mr. Roscoe enable us to guess any virtue for which he is more particularly famous: so great, however, is to be the enthusiastic reverence which the American youth are to feel for him, that, after visiting the scenes which are to remind them of General Moore, Mr. Clarkson, Lord Chatham, Doctor Davy, Mr. Garrick, and Lord Nelson,[5] they are to pay a visit,

> Where Roscoe, to whose patriot breast belong
> The Roman virtue and the Tuscan song,
> Led Ceres to the black and barren moor,
> Where Ceres never gained a wreath before.—[6]

Or, in other words, (as the note kindly informs us,) to Mr. Roscoe's farm in Derbyshire, where, less we apprehend, by the Roman virtue and the Tuscan song, than by the homely process of drainage and manuring, he has brought some hundred acres of Chatmoss into cultivation. O the unequal dispensations of this poetical providence! Chatham and Nelson empty names! Oxford and Cambridge in ruins! London a desert, and the Thames a sedgy brook! while Mr. Roscoe's barns and piggeries are in excellent repair, and objects not only of curiosity but even of reverence and enthusiasm.

Our readers will be curious to know how these prodigies are to be operated: there is, it seems, a mysterious Spirit or Genius who is to do all this, and a great deal more, as we shall presently see; but who or what he is, or whence he comes, does not very clearly appear, even from the following description:

> There walks a Spirit o'er the peopled earth,
> Secret his progress is, unknown his birth,
> Moody and viewless as the changing wind,
> No force arrests his foot, no chains can bind.—p. 17.[7]

This extraordinary personage is prodigiously wise and potent, but withal a little fickle, and somewhat, we think, for so wise a being, unjust and partial. He has hitherto resided in this country, and chiefly in London; Mrs. Barbauld, however, foresees that he is beginning to be tired of us, and is preparing to go out of town: on his departure that desolation is to take place in reality, which is so often metaphorically ascribed to the secession of some great leader of the ton.[8]

But the same Genius has far more extensive powers even than these;—he "changes nature," he "absorbs the Nile," (we had not heard of the Nile's being absorbed,) and he has of late taken it into his head to travel "northward," among the "Celtic nations," with a mercantile venture of Turkey carpets, of which speculation the immediate effects are, that the "vale of Arno" and the "coast of Baia" are not near so pleasant as the dykes of Batavia; that the Pontine marshes have lately become extremely unwholesome, and that Venice is no longer, as she was a short time since, the mistress of the sea. (p. 20, 21.)[9]

---

[1] Barbauld, *Eighteen Hundred and Eleven* 171–76.

[2] Cf. Barbauld, *Eighteen Hundred and Eleven* 156.

[3] Barbauld, *Eighteen Hundred and Eleven* 147–48.

[4] "pre-eminent" (Gr.).

[5] Cf. Barbauld, *Eighteen Hundred and Eleven* 197–98 (Moore), 143 (Clarkson),* 191 (Chatham), 201–02 (Davy), 192 (Garrick), and 193–96 (Nelson).

[6] Barbauld, *Eighteen Hundred and Eleven* 147–50.

[7] Barbauld, *Eighteen Hundred and Eleven* 215–18.

[8] "fashion" (Fr.).

[9] Cf. Barbauld, *Eighteen Hundred and Eleven* 245 (changing nature), 246-47 (Nile), 261 (northward), 262 (Celtic nations), 266 (Arno), 268 (Baia), 266 (Batavia), 270 (Pontine marshes), and 269 (Venice).

This wonderful person is also so condescending as to assist us in divers little offices, in which we are hardly aware of his interference; he is the real author of Dryden's Virgil and Middleton's Cicero (p. 22,) he dresses "light forms" in "transparent muslins," he "tutors" young ladies "to swell the artful note," and he builds verandas to our balconies; he is, besides, an eminent nursery man, and particularly remarkable for "acacias" and "cedars," and the "chrystal walls" of his hothouses produce the best grapes and pines about London; (p. 23;)[1] in short, there is nothing good, bad, or indifferent that this Genius does not do: but alas! good upon England he intends no longer to confer; our muslins, pines, acacias, and even our forte-pianos are in jeopardy:

> For fairest flowers expand but to decay,
> The worm is in thy core, thy glories fade away;
> Arts, arms, and wealth destroy the fruits they bring,
> Commerce, like beauty, knows no second spring;
> Crime walks the streets, fraud earns her unblest bread,
> O'er want and woe thy gorgeous robe is spread.—p. 24.[2]

Upon this melancholy night, however, a bright day dawns, and all the little sense with which Mrs. Barbauld set out, now dissolves away in blissful visions of American glory. This Genius of her's which "walks the peopled earth," "viewless and secret," suddenly appears walking on the summit of Chimberaço, (which never was nor can be peopled,) displays his "viewless" form on the Andes, and "secretly" arouses, by loud exclamations, all the nations of the western continent.

> Ardent the Genius fans the noble strife,
> And pours through feeble souls a higher life;
> Shouts to the mingled tribes from sea to sea,
> And swears—Thy world, Columbus, shall be free.—p. 25.[3]

And with this oath concludes "Eighteen Hundred and Eleven," upon which we have already wasted too much time. One word, however, we must seriously add. Mrs. Barbauld's former works have been of some utility; her "Lessons for Children," her "Hymns in Prose," her "Selections from the Spectator,"[4] et id genus omne,[5] though they display not much of either taste or talents, are yet something better than harmless: but we must take the liberty of warning her to desist from satire, which indeed is satire on herself alone; and of entreating, with great earnestness, that she will not, for the sake of this ungrateful generation, put herself to the trouble of writing any more party pamphlets in verse. We also assure her, that we should not by any means impute it to want of taste or patriotism on her part, if, for her own country, her fears were less confident, and for America her hopes less ardent; and if she would leave both the victims and the heroes of her political prejudices to the respective judgment which the impartiality of posterity will not fail to pronounce.

from the *Quarterly Review* 19 (April 1818)

Review of Keats's *Endymion: A Poetic Romance*

Reviewers have been sometimes accused of not reading the works which they affected to criticise. On the present occasion we shall anticipate the author's complaint, and honestly confess that we have not read his work. Not that we have been wanting in our duty—far from it—indeed, we have made efforts almost as superhuman as the story itself appears to be, to get through it; but with the fullest stretch of our perseverance, we are forced to confess that we have not been able to struggle beyond the first of the four books of which this Poetic Romance consists. We should extremely lament this want of energy, or whatever it may be, on our parts, were it not for one consolation—namely, that we are no better acquainted

---

[1] Cf. Barbauld, *Eighteen Hundred and Eleven* 288 (Virgil and Cicero), 291 (light forms, muslins), 292 (artful note), 286 (verandahs), 293 (acacias), 294 (cedars), and 295–98 (greenhouses).

[2] Barbauld, *Eighteen Hundred and Eleven* 313–18.

[3] Barbauld, *Eighteen Hundred and Eleven* 331–34.

[4] an edition by Barbauld (1804) of excerpts from the *Spectator* (1711–12), edited and mostly written by Joseph Addison (1672–1719) and Sir Richard Steele (1672–1729), and other eighteenth-century periodicals.

[5] "and everything of that kind": cf. Horace, *Satires* 1.2.2.

with the meaning of the book through which we have so painfully toiled, than we are with that of the three which we have not looked into.

It is not that Mr. Keats, (if that be his real name, for we almost doubt that any man in his senses would put his real name to such a rhapsody,) it is not, we say, that the author has not powers of language, rays of fancy, and gleams of genius—he has all these; but he is unhappily a disciple of the new school of what has been somewhere called Cockney poetry; which may be defined to consist of the most incongruous ideas in the most uncouth language.

Of this school, Mr. Leigh Hunt, as we observed in a former Number, aspires to be the hierophant. Our readers will recollect the pleasant recipes for harmonious and sublime poetry which he gave us in his preface to "Rimini," and the still more facetious instances of his harmony and sublimity in the verses themselves; and they will recollect above all the contempt of Pope, Johnson, and such like poetasters and pseudo-critics, which so forcibly contrasted itself with Mr. Leigh Hunt's self-complacent approbation of

———"all the things itself had wrote,
Of special merit though of little note."[1]

This author is a copyist of Mr. Hunt; but he is more unintelligible, almost as rugged, twice as diffuse, and ten times more tiresome and absurd than his prototype, who, though he impudently presumed to seat himself in the chair of criticism, and to measure his own poetry by his own standard, yet generally had a meaning. But Mr. Keats had advanced no dogmas which he was bound to support by examples; his nonsense therefore is quite gratuitous; he writes it for its own sake, and, being bitten by Mr. Leigh Hunt's insane criticism, more than rivals the insanity of his poetry.

Mr. Keats's preface hints that his poem was produced under peculiar circumstances.

"Knowing within myself (he says) the manner in which this Poem has been produced, it is not without a feeling of regret that I make it public.—What manner I mean, will be *quite clear* to the reader, who must soon perceive great inexperience, immaturity, and every error denoting a feverish attempt, rather than a deed accomplished."—*Preface*, p. vii.

We humbly beg his pardon, but this does not appear to us to be *quite so clear*—we really do not know what he means—but the next passage is more intelligible.

"The two first books, and indeed the two last, I feel sensible are not of such completion as to warrant their passing the press."—*Preface*, p. vii.

Thus "the two first books" are, even in his own judgment, unfit to appear, and "the two last" are, it seems, in the same condition—and as two and two make four, and as that is the whole number of books, we have a clear and, we believe, a very just estimate of the entire work.

Mr. Keats, however, deprecates criticism on this "immature and feverish work" in terms which are themselves sufficiently feverish; and we confess that we should have abstained from inflicting upon him any of the tortures of the "*fierce hell*" of criticism,[2] which terrify his imagination, if he had not begged to be spared in order that he might write more; if we had not observed in him a certain degree of talent which deserves to be put in the right way, or which, at least, ought to be warned of the wrong; and if, finally, he had not told us that he is of an age and temper which imperiously require mental discipline.

Of the story we have been able to make out but little; it seems to be mythological, and probably relates to the loves of Diana and Endymion; but of this, as the scope of the work has altogether escaped us, we cannot speak with any degree of certainty; and must therefore content ourselves with giving some instances of its diction and versification:—and here again we are perplexed and puzzled.—At first it appeared to us, that Mr. Keats had been amusing himself and wearying his readers with an immeasurable game at *bouts-rimés*; but, if we recollect rightly, it is an indispensable condition at this play, that the rhymes when filled up shall have a meaning; and our author, as we have already hinted, has no meaning. He seems to us to write a line at random, and then he follows not the thought excited by this line,

---

[1] Cf. Charles Churchill (1732–64), *The Rosciad* (1761) 155–56.

[2] In his Preface, Keats had written: "there is not a fiercer hell than the failure in a great object. This is not written with the least atom of purpose to forestall criticisms of course."

but that suggested by the *rhyme* with which it concludes. There is hardly a complete couplet inclosing a complete idea in the whole book. He wanders from one subject to another, from the association, not of ideas but of sounds, and the work is composed of hemistichs which, it is quite evident, have forced themselves upon the author by the mere force of the catchwords on which they turn.

We shall select, not as the most striking instance, but as that least liable to suspicion, a passage from the opening of the poem.

> ———"Such the sun, the moon,
> Trees old and young, sprouting a shady boon
> For simple sheep; and such are daffodils
> With the green world they live in; and clear rills
> That for themselves a cooling covert make
> 'Gainst the hot season; the mid forest brake,
> Rich with a sprinkling of fair musk-rose blooms:
> And such too is the grandeur of the dooms
> We have imagined for the mighty dead; &c.
> &c."—pp. 3, 4.[1]

Here it is clear that the word, and not the idea, *moon* produces the simple sheep and their shady *boon*, and that "the *dooms* of the mighty dead" would never have intruded themselves but for the "*fair musk-rose blooms.*"

Again.

> "For 'twas the morn: Apollo's upward fire
> Made every eastern cloud a silvery pyre
> Of brightness so unsullied, that therein
> A melancholy spirit well might win
> Oblivion, and melt out his essence fine
> Into the winds: rain-scented eglantine
> Gave temperate sweets to that well-wooing sun;
> The lark was lost in him; cold springs had run
> To warm their chilliest bubbles in the grass;
> Man's voice was on the mountains; and the mass
> Of nature's lives and wonders puls'd tenfold,
> To feel this sun-rise and its glories old."—p. 8.[2]

Here Apollo's *fire* produces a *pyre*, a silvery pyre of clouds, *wherein* a spirit might *win* oblivion and melt his essence *fine*, and scented *eglantine* gives sweets to the *sun*, and cold springs had *run* into the *grass*, and then the pulse of the *mass* pulsed *tenfold* to feel the glories *old* of the new-born day, &c.

One example more.

> "Be still the unimaginable lodge
> For solitary thinkings; such as dodge
> Conception to the very bourne of heaven,
> Then leave the naked brain: be still the leaven,
> That spreading in this dull and clodded earth
> Gives it a touch ethereal—a new birth."—p. 17.[3]

Lodge, dodge—heaven, leaven—earth, birth; such, in six words, is the sum and substance of six lines.

We come now to the author's taste in versification. He cannot indeed write a sentence, but perhaps he may be able to spin a line. Let us see. The following are specimens of his prosodial notions of our English heroic metre.

> "Dear as the temple's self, so does the moon,
> The passion poesy, glories infinite."—p. 4.
> "So plenteously all weed-hidden roots."—p. 6.
> "Of some strange history, potent to send."—p. 18.
> "Before the deep intoxication."—p. 27.
> "Her scarf into a fluttering pavilion."—p. 33.
> "The stubborn canvass for my voyage
> prepared———."—p. 39.
> "'Endymion! the cave is secreter
> Than the isle of Delos. Echo hence shall stir
> No sighs but sigh-warm kisses, or light noise
> Of thy combing hand, the while it travelling cloys
> And trembles through my labyrinthine
> hair.'"—p. 48.[4]

By this time our readers must be pretty well satisfied as to the meaning of his sentences and the structure of his lines: we now present them with some of the new words with which, in imitation of Mr. Leigh Hunt, he adorns our language.

We are told that "turtles *passion* their voices," (p. 15); that "an arbour was *nested*," (p. 23); and a lady's locks "*gordian'd* up," (p. 32); and to supply the place of the nouns thus verbalized Mr. Keats, with great fecundity, spawns new ones; such as "men-slugs and human *serpentry*," (p. 41); the "*honey-feel* of bliss," (p.

---

[1] *Endymion* 1.13–21.*

[2] *Endymion* 1.95–106.

[3] *Endymion* 1.293–98.

[4] *Endymion* 1.28–29, 65, 324, 502, 628, 772, 965–69.

45); "wives prepare *needments*," (p. 13)—and so forth.[1]

Then he has formed new verbs by the process of cutting off their natural tails, the adverbs, and affixing them to their foreheads; thus, "the wine out-sparkled," (p. 10); the "multitude up-followed," (p. 11); and "night up-took," (p. 29). "The wind up-blows," (p. 32); and the "hours are down-sunken," (p. 36).[2]

But if he sinks some adverbs in the verbs he compensates the language with adverbs and adjectives which he separates from the parent stock. Thus, a lady "whispers *pantingly* and close," makes "*hushing* signs," and steers her skiff into a "*ripply* cove," (p. 23); a shower falls "*refreshfully*," (45); and a vulture has a "*spreaded* tail," (p. 44).[3]

But enough of Mr. Leigh Hunt and his simple neophyte.—If any one should be bold enough to purchase this "Poetic Romance," and so much more patient, than ourselves, as to get beyond the first book, and so much more fortunate as to find a meaning, we entreat him to make us acquainted with his success; we shall then return to the task which we now abandon in despair, and endeavour to make all due amends to Mr. Keats and to our readers.

---

[1] *Endymion* 1.248, 431, 614, 821, 903, 208.

[2] *Endymion* 1.154, 164, 561, 627 ("out-blows"), 708.

[3] *Endymion* 1.407, 409, 430, 898 ("refreshfully"), 867.

Ebenezer Elliott
1781 – 1849

Ebenezer Elliott, sometimes called "The Corn-Law Rhymer," was born in Masborough, Yorkshire, on 17 March 1781. His father, known as "Devil Elliott," was an extreme Calvinist who worked in the iron trade, and his mother, who was frequently ill, gave birth to eleven children, eight of whom lived to adulthood. Elliott was educated at four different schools: he was an indifferent student. When he was five, he contracted smallpox, which left him disfigured and with a desire for solitude. He began to read widely when he was about fourteen. At sixteen, he began working at his father's foundry; at seventeen, he wrote his first poem, "Vernal Walk." Married in 1805 to Frances Gartside, with whom he had thirteen children, he invested his wife's fortune in his father's business, which failed anyway. In 1821, he moved to Sheffield, where he was more successful; in 1842, he settled near Barnsley, where he died on 1 December 1849.

Elliott blamed his own and his family's financial difficulties on the Corn Laws, which imposed a duty on the import of grain to Great Britain. This, combined with poor harvests, raised the price of bread above what poor people could afford. The most recent Law had been passed in 1815; it was not repealed until 1846. *Corn Law Rhymes* (1831) is the collection of poetry for which he is best known. (J.G.)

❦

from *Corn Law Rhymes*, 3rd ed. (1831)

Song

TUNE — *"Robin Adair."*[1]

Child, is thy father dead?
    Father is gone!
Why did they tax his bread?[2]
    God's will be done!
5 Mother has sold her bed;
Better to die than wed!
Where shall she lay her head?
    Home we have none.

Father clamm'd[3] thrice a week,
10   God's will be done!
Long for work did he seek,
    Work he found none:
Tears on his hollow cheek
Told what no tongue could speak:
15 Why did his master break?
    God's will be done!

Doctor said air was best,
    Food we had none;
Father, with panting breast,
20   Groan'd to be gone:
Now he is with the blest!
Mother says death is best!
We have no place of rest!
    Yes, ye have one.

---

[1] A tune originally called "Eileen Aroon" and attributed to Denis Hempson (1694/5?–1807), for which Lady Caroline Keppel (1735–69) wrote new words in the 1750s.

[2] The Corn Laws, also known as "bread taxes," were laws created by Parliament to control the import and export of corn; Parliament was dominated by land owners, who directly benefited from these duties, as they effectively protected their own profits.

[3] "fasted," "starved" (Yorkshire dialect).

Caged Rats

Ye coop us up, and tax our bread,
    And wonder why we pine:
But ye are fat, and round, and red,
    And fill'd with tax-bought wine.
Thus, twelve rats starve while three rats thrive,
    (Like you on mine and me,)
When fifteen rats are caged alive,
    With food for nine and three.

Haste! havoc's torch begins to glow,
    The ending is begun;
Make haste; destruction thinks ye slow;
    Make haste to be undone!

Why are ye call'd "my lord," and "squire,"
    While fed by mine and me,
And wringing food, and clothes, and fire
    From bread-tax'd misery?

Make haste, slow rogues! *prohibit* trade,
    Prohibit honest gain;
Turn all the good that God hath made
    To fear, and hate, and pain;
Till beggars all, assassins all,
    All cannibals we be,
And death shall have no funeral
    From shipless sea to sea.

Lucy Aikin
1781 – 1864

Lucy Aikin was born in Warrington, Lancashire, on 6 November 1781, the fifth child, and only daughter, of John Aikin, M.D. (the brother of Anna Lætitia Barbauld),* and of his cousin Martha Jennings Aikin. Her father encouraged her and was largely responsible for her education; she became proficient in French, Italian, and Latin. She never married but believed she knew "almost every literary woman of celebrity." *Epistles on Women* was her first original book; she also published *Lorimer* (1814), a Gothic novel; histories of the reigns of Elizabeth I, James I, and Charles I; biographies of Joseph Addison and her father; and an edition of Barbauld's works, with a memoir. She was a pioneer of children's literature, publishing versions of *Robinson Crusoe*, *Æsop's Fables*, and other works, in words of one syllable. She died of influenza on 29 January 1864 and was buried in Hampstead Cemetery next to her friend Joanna Baillie.* (D.L.M.)

from *Epistles on women, exemplifying their character and condition in various ages and nations. With miscellaneous poems* (1810)

INTRODUCTION

The poetical epistles occupying the principal part of this volume are presented to the public with all the diffidence and anxiety of a literary novice conscious of a bold and arduous undertaking. As I am not, however, aware of any circumstances in my own case which peculiarly appeal to the indulgence of the reader, I shall decline any further exposure of feelings purely personal, and proceed to the proper business of this introduction,.... to offer such preliminary remarks on the plan of the work as may be necessary to prevent misapprehension.

Let me in the first place disclaim entirely the absurd idea that the two sexes ever can be, or ever ought to be, placed in all respects on a footing of equality. Man when he abuses his power may justly be considered as a tyrant; but his power itself is no tyranny, being founded not on usurpation, but on certain unalterable necessities; ... sanctioned, not by prescription alone, but by the fundamental laws of human nature. As long as the bodily constitution of the species shall remain the same, man must in general assume those public and active offices of life which confer authority, whilst to woman will usually be allotted such domestic and private ones as imply a certain degree of subordination.[1]

Nothing therefore could, in my opinion, be more foolish than the attempt to engage our sex in a struggle for stations that they are physically unable properly to fill; for power of which they must always want the means to possess themselves. No! instead of aspiring to be inferior men, let us content ourselves with becoming noble women:.... but let not sex be carried into every thing. Let the impartial voice of History testify for us, that, when permitted, we have been the worthy associates of the best efforts of the best of men; let the daily observation of mankind bear witness, that no talent, no virtue, is masculine alone; no fault or folly exclusively feminine;.... that there is not an endowment, or propensity, or mental quality of any kind, which may not be derived from her father to the daughter, to the son from his mother. These positions once established, and carried into their consequences, will do every thing for woman. Perceiving that any shaft aimed at her, must strike in its recoil upon some vulnerable part of common human nature, the Juvenals and Popes[2] of future ages will abstain from making her the butt of scorn or malice. Feeling with gratitude of

---

[1] Cf. Wollstonecraft, *A Vindication of the Rights of Woman* (388).*

[2] Cf. Decimus Junius Juvenalis (c. AD 60–136), *Satire* 6; and Alexander Pope, "Of the Characters of Women" (*Moral Essays* 2) (1731–35).

what her heart and mind are capable, the scholars, the sages, and the patriots of coming days will treat her as a sister and a friend.

The politic father will not then leave as a "legacy" to his daughters[1] the injunction to conceal their wit, their learning, and even their good sense, in deference to the "*natural malignity*" with which most men regard every woman of a sound understanding and cultivated mind; nor will even the reputation of our great Milton himself secure him from the charge of a blasphemous presumption in making his Eve address to Adam the acknowledgement, "God is thy head, thou mine"; and in the assertion that the first human pair were formed, "He for God only, she for God in him."[2]

To mark the effect of various codes, institutions, and states of manners, on the virtue and happiness of man, and the concomitant and proportional elevation or depression of woman in the scale of existence, is the general plan of this work.

The historical and biographical authorities from which its facts and many of its sentiments are derived, will easily be recognised by the literary reader, who will know how to estimate my correctness and fidelity: for the use of other readers a few notes are subjoined.

With respect to arrangement, I may remark, that as a strictly chronological one was incompatible with the design of tracing the progress of human society not in one country alone, but in many, I have judged it most advisable to form to myself such an one as seemed best adapted to my own peculiar purposes, moral and poetical. We have no records of any early people in a ruder state than some savage tribes of the present day; and it would be in vain to seek amongst the ancient writers for such distinct and accurate delineations of the customs of Lotophagi and Troglodytes as we now possess of the life and manners of New Hollanders, American Indians and Hottentots.[3] From these latter, therefore, my first descriptions have been borrowed. Of the tribes of ancient Germany, indeed, we possess an unrivaled portraiture; but in the age of Tacitus[4] most of them had already risen far above the lowest stage of human society; and the progenitors of the noblest nations of modern Europe ought not to be classed with families of men whose name has perished from the earth, or wandering hordes of which we do not yet know whether or not they contain a living seed of future greatness.

In the way of explanation I have little more to add. I make no specific claims for my sex. Convinced that it is rather to the policy, or the generosity, of man, than to his justice that we ought to appeal, I have simply endeavoured to point out, that between the two partners of human life, not only the strongest family likeness, but the most complete identity of interest subsists: so that it is impossible for man to degrade his companion without degrading himself, or to elevate her without receiving a proportional accession of dignity and happiness. This is the chief "moral of my song";[5] on this point all my examples are brought to bear. I regard it as the Great Truth to the support of which my pen has devoted itself; and whoever shall rise from the perusal of these epistles deeply impressed with its importance, will afford me the success dearest to my heart,.... the hope of having served, in some small degree, the best interests of the human race.

With respect to the Miscellaneous Poems, I have only to announce, that they comprise such pieces of mine contained in The Athenæum, and the earlier volumes of The Monthly Magazine, as appeared to me in any respect worthy of preservation; and that to these two others have been added.

---

[1] John Gregory (1724–73), *A Father's Legacy to his Daughters* (1774); cf. Mary Wollstonecraft, *A Vindication of the Rights of Woman* (391).*

[2] Milton, *Paradise Lost* 4.637, 4.299.

[3] In Greek mythology, the Lotophagi (lotus eaters) fed upon the lotus, forgetting their homes and friends: see Homer, *Odyssey 9*. The Troglodytes, a legendary prehistoric race of people, lived in caves, dens, and holes. New Hollanders are Australian aborigines. Hottentots are the indigenous African people of the western Cape Colony and the adjoining German territory, so called by colonial rulers.

[4] Roman historian (c. AD 55–after 115) who wrote an early detailed description of the Germans (*De origine et situ Germanorum*) at the end of the first century.

[5] Cf. Spenser, *The Faerie Queene* Introduction 1.9.

EPISTLE 1

ARGUMENT

Subject proposed—the fame of man extended over every period of life—that of woman transient as the beauty on which it is founded—Man renders her a trifler, then despises her, and makes war upon the sex with Juvenal and Pope. A more impartial view of the subject to be attempted. Weakness of woman, and her consequent subserviency. General view of various states of society undertaken. Birth of Eve—Angels prophesy the doom of the sex—description of Adam before he sees her—a joyless, hopeless, indolent creature. Meeting of Adam and Eve—Change produced in both—their mutual happiness and primary equality. Reflections. Conclusion.

Hear, O my friend, my Anna,[1] nor disdain
My sober lyre and moralizing strain!
I sing the Fate of Woman:.... Man to man
Adds praise, and glory lights his mortal span;
5 Creation's lord, he shines from youth to age,
The blooming warrior or the bearded sage;
But she, frail offspring of an April morn,
Poor helpless passenger from love to scorn,
While dimpled youth her sprightly cheek adorns
10 Blooms a sweet rose, a rose amid the thorns;
A few short hours, with faded charms to earth
She sinks, and leaves no vestige of her birth.
E'en while the youth, in love and rapture warm,
Sighs as he hangs upon her beauteous form,
15 Careless and cold he views the beauteous mind,
For virtue, bliss, eternity designed.
"Banish, my fair," he cries, "those studious looks;
Oh! what should beauty learn from crabbed books?
Sweetly to speak and sweetly smile be thine;
20 Beware, nor change that dimple to a line!"

Well pleased she hears, vain triumph lights her eyes;
Well pleased, in prattle and in smiles complies;
But eyes, alas! grow dim, and roses fade,
And man contemns the trifler he has made.
25 The glass reversed by magic power of Spleen,[2]
A wrinkled idiot now the fair is seen;
Then with the sex his headlong rage must cope,
And stab with Juvenal, or sting with Pope.
Be mine, while Truth with calm and artless grace
30 Lifts her clear mirror to the female face,
With steadier hand the pencil's task to guide,
And win a blush from Man's relenting pride.

No Amazon,[3] in frowns and terror drest,
I poise the spear, or nod the threatening crest,
35 Defy the law, arraign the social plan,
Throw down the gauntlet in the face of man,
And, rashly bold, divided empire claim,
Unborrowed honours, and an equal's name:
No, Heaven forbid! I touch no sacred thing,
40 But bow to Right Divine in man and king;[4]
Nature endows him with superior force,
Superior wisdom then I grant, of course;
For who gainsays the despot in his might,
Or when was ever weakness in the right?
45 With passive reverence too I hail the law,
Formed to secure the strong, the weak to awe,
Impartial guardian of unerring sway,
Set up by man for woman to obey.
In vain we pout or argue, rail or chide,
50 He mocks our idle wrath and checks our pride;
Resign we then the club and lion's skin,[5]
And be our sex content to knit and spin;
To bow inglorious to a master's rule,
And good and bad obey, and wise and fool;
55 Here a meek drudge, a listless captive there,
For gold now bartered, now as cheap as air;
Prize of the coward rich or lawless brave,
Scorned and caressed, a plaything and a slave,

---

[1] The *Epistles* are dedicated to Anna (Mrs. Charles Rochemont) Aikin, Aikin's sister-in-law.

[2] Cf. Pope, *The Rape of the Lock* (1714) 4.11–54.

[3] in classical mythology, a race of warrior women.

[4] The Divine Right of Kings stipulated that kings ruled because they were chosen by God to do so and that they were accountable only to God.

[5] manly attributes of Hercules. Under the sway of Omphale, he put them aside and devoted himself to womanly tasks such as spinning.

Yet taught with spaniel soul to kiss the rod,
And worship man as delegate of God.

Ah! what is human life? a narrow span
Eked out with cares and pains to us and man;
A bloody scroll that vice and folly stain,
That blushing Nature blots with tears in vain,
That frowning Wisdom reads with tone severe,
While Pity shudders with averted ear.
Yet will I dare its varying modes to trace
Through many a distant tribe and vanisht race;
The sketch perchance shall touch the ingenuous heart,
And hint its moral with a pleasing art.
Aid me, Historic Muse! unfold thy store
Of rich, of various, never-cloying lore;
Thence Fancy flies with new-born visions fraught,
There old Experience lends his hoards to Thought.

When slumbering Adam pressed the lonely earth,....[1]
Unconscious parent of a wondrous birth,....
As forth to light the infant-woman sprung,
By pitying angels thus her doom was sung:
"Ah! fairest creature! born to changeful skies,
To bliss and agony, to smiles and sighs:
Beauty's frail child, to thee, though doomed to bear
By far the heavier half of human care,
Deceitful Nature's stepdame-love assigned
A form more fragile, and a tenderer mind;
More copious tears from Pity's briny springs,
And, trembling Sympathy! thy finest strings:
While ruder man she prompts, in pride of power,
To bruise, to slay, to ravage, to devour;
On prostrate weakness turn his gory steel,
And point the wounds not all thy tears can heal.
Poor victim! stern the mandate of thy birth,
Ah dote not, smile not, on the things of earth!
Subdue thyself; those rapturous flutterings still!
Armed with meek courage and a patient will,
With thoughtful eye pursue thy destined way,
Adore thy God, and hope a brighter day!"
In solemn notes thus flowed the prescient strain,....
But flowed on Eve's unpractised ear in vain;

In smiling wonder fixt, the new-born bride
Drank the sweet gale, the glowing landscape eyed,
And murmured untried sounds, and gazed on every side.
With look benign the boding angels view
The fearless innocent, and wave adieu:
"Too well thy daughters shall our strain believe;
Too short thy dream of bliss, ill-fated Eve."

Prophetic spirits! that with ken sublime
Sweep the long windings of the flood of time,
Joyless and stern, your deep-toned numbers dwell
On rocks, on whirlpools, and the foaming swell,
But pass unmarked the skiffs that gaily glide
With songs and streamers down the dimpling tide:
Else rapturous notes had floated on the wind,
And hailed the stranger born to bless her kind,
To bear from heaven to earth the golden ties,
Bind willing man, and draw him to the skies.

See where the world's new master roams along,
Vainly intelligent and idly strong;
Mark his long listless step and torpid air,
His brow of densest gloom and fixt infantile stare!
Those sullen lips no mother's lips have prest,
Nor drawn, sweet labour! at her kindly breast;
No mother's voice has touched that slumbering ear,
Nor glistening eye beguiled him of a tear;
Love nursed not him with sweet endearing wiles,
Nor woman taught the sympathy of smiles;
Vacant and sad his rayless glances roll,
Nor hope nor joy illumes his darkling soul;
Ah! hapless world that such a wretch obeys!
Ah! joyless Adam, though a world he sways!

But see!.... they meet,.... they gaze,.... the new-born pair;....
Mark now the wakening youth, the wondering fair:
Sure a new soul that moping idiot warms,
Dilates his stature, and his mien informs!
A brighter crimson tints his glowing cheek;
His broad eye kindles, and his glances speak.
So roll the clouds from some vast mountain's head,
Melt into mist, and down the valleys spread;

---

[1] Cf. Genesis 2.21–23; Milton, *Paradise Lost* 8.460–89.

His crags and caves the bursting sunbeams light,
And burn and blaze upon his topmost height;
140 Broad in full day he lifts his towering crest,
And fire celestial sparkles from his breast.
Eve too, how changed!.... No more with baby grace
The smile runs dimpling o'er her trackless face,
As painted meads invite her roving glance,
145 Or birds with liquid trill her ear intrance:
With downcast look she stands, abasht and meek,
Now pale, now rosy red, her varying cheek;
Now first her fluttering bosom heaves a sigh,
Now first a tear stands trembling in her eye;
150 For hark! the youth, as love and nature teach,
Breathes his full bosom, and breaks forth in *speech*;
His quivering lips the winged accents part,
And pierce, how swift! to Eve's unguarded heart.[1]

Now rose complete the mighty Maker's plan,
155 And Eden opened in the heart of Man;
Kindled by Hope, by gentle Love refined,
Sweet converse cheered him, and a kindred mind;
Nor deem that He, beneficent and just,
In woman's hand who lodged this sacred trust,
160 For man alone her conscious soul informed,
For man alone her tenderer bosom warmed;
Denied to her the cup of joy to sip,
But bade her raise it to his greedy lip,
Poor instrument of bliss, and tool of ease,
165 Born but to serve, existing but to please:....
No;.... hand in hand the happy creatures trod,
Alike the children of no partial God;
Equal they trod till want and guilt arose,
Till savage blood was spilt, and man had foes:[2]
170 Ah! days of happiness,.... with tearful eye
I see you gleam, and fade, and hurry by:
Why should my strain the darkening theme pursue?
Be husht, my plaintive lyre! my listening friend, adieu!

---

[1] Cf. Milton, *Paradise Lost* 4.449–91.

[2] Aikin attributes the fall of humanity not to Eve's eating of the apple (Genesis 3.1–6) but to Cain's murder of Abel (Genesis 4.1–15).

EPISTLE 2

ARGUMENT

The subject resumed. Sketch of savage life in general—The sex oppressed by slaves and barbarians, but held in honour by the good and the brave.—New Holland[3]—brutality of the inhabitants—their courtship. North American Indians—one of their women describes her wretched condition and destroys her female infant. Hardening effect of want on the human mind. Transition to Otaheite[4]—Licentious manners of those islanders— Infanticide. Address to maternal affection—exemplified in the hind—fawns destroyed by the stag. Coast of Guinea—a native sells his son for a slave—agony of the mother—her speech. Pastoral life—Chaldee astronomers[5]—King David.[6] Tartars[7]— removal of a Tartar camp—their gaiety and happy mediocrity of condition relative to the gifts of nature—yet no refined affection between the sexes—female captives and women sent in tribute preferred to the natives—No perfect Arcadia[8] to be found on earth—Caffres and Hottentots[9] sprightly and harmless—but all pastoral and hunting tribes deficient in mental cultivation—hence the weaker sex held by all in some kind of subjection.

Once more my Muse uplifts her drooping eye,
Checks the weak murmur and restrains the sigh;
Once more, my friend, incline thy candid ear,
And grace my numbers with a smile and tear.
5 Not mine the art in solemn garb to dress
The shadowy forms of *delicate distress*;[10]

---

[3] Australia (then a penal colony).

[4] Tahiti.

[5] inhabitants of Chaldea, the country of which Babylon was the capital. The name became associated with a class of learned men ranked with the magicians and astronomers.

[6] the second king of Israel, psalmist and prophet.

[7] Turkish-speaking people living primarily in Russia or any Asian nomadic people.

[8] in Greek mythology, a pastoral and idyllic country inhabited by innocent peoples.

[9] indigenous peoples of southern Africa.

[10] Cf. *The Delicate Distress* (1769), a novel by Elizabeth Griffith (1727–93).

With baleful charms to call from Fancy's bower
Vain shapes of dread to haunt the lonely hour;
In feverish dreams to feed the pampered thought
10 With heavenly bliss.... on earth how vainly sought!
Fan with rash breath the passions' smouldering fire,
Whet the keen wish, the thrilling hope inspire,
Woo the young soul its blossoms to unfold,
Then leave it chilled with more than wintry cold.

15 No;.... rude of hand, with bolder lines I trace
The rugged features of a coarser race:
Fierce on thy view the savage world shall glare,
And all the ills of wretched woman there;
Unknown to her fond love's romantic glow,
20 The graceful throbs of sentimental woe,
The play of passions and the feelings' strife
That weave the web of finely-chequered life.
But thou possest, unspoiled by tyrant art,
Of the large empire of a generous heart,
25 Thou wilt not scorn plain nature's rudest strain,
Nor *homely* misery claim thy sighs in vain.

Come then, my friend; my devious way pursue;
Pierce every clime, and search all ages through;
Stretch wide and wider yet thy liberal mind,
30 And grasp the sisterhood of womankind:
With mingling anger mark, and conscious pride,
The sex by whom exalted or decried;
Crusht by the savage, fettered by the slave,
But served, but honoured, by the good and brave.

35 With daring keel attend yon convict train
To new-found deserts of the Southern Main;
Beasts of strange gait there roam the trackless earth,
And monstrous compounds struggle into birth;
A younger world it seems, abortive, crude,
40 Where untaught Nature sports her fancies rude,
By slow gradations rears her infant plan,
And shows, half-humanized, the monster-man.
Mark the grim ruffian roll his crafty glance,
And crouching, slow, his tiger-step advance,
45 With brandisht club surprise his human prey,
And drag the bleeding victim bride away,
While shouts triumphant wake the orgies dire,
And Rage and Terror trim the nuptial fire.[1]

E'en such is Savage Man, of beasts the worst,
50 In want, in guilt, in lawless rapine nurst.
To the dumb tribes that plod their even life
Unbruised by tyranny, unvext by strife,
Instincts and appetites kind Nature gave,
These just supplying what the others crave;
55 The human brute the headlong passions rule,
While infant Reason flies the moody fool,
Hope, Fear, and Memory play their busy part
And mingle all their chaos in his heart;
Hence Vengeance fires, hence Envy's stings infest,
60 Hence Superstition goads his timorous breast.
O! not for him life's healthful current flows;
An equal stream that murmurs as it goes;
As rage and torpor hold alternate rule,
It roars a flood, or stagnates in a pool,
65 Whose sterile brink no buds of fragrance cheer
By love or pity nurtured with a tear.

What wonder then, the Western wilds among
Where the red Indian's hunter-bow is strung,
(Nature's tough son, whose adamantine frame
70 No pleasures soften and no tortures tame)
If, fiercely pondering in her gloomy mind
The desperate ills that scowl on womankind,
The maddening mother gripes the infant slave,
And forces back the worthless life she gave?[2]

---

[1] "'The courtship' of the savages of New Holland 'consists in watching the lady's retirement, and then knocking her down with repeated blows of a club or wooden sword; after which the truly matrimonial victim is led streaming with blood to her future husband's party, where a scene ensues too shocking to relate.' Collins's Hist. of the Colony in New Holland." (L.A.)

[2] "'In all unpolished nations, it is true, the functions in domestic economy which fall naturally to the share of the women, are so many, that they are subjected to hard labour, and must bear more than their full portion of the common burden. But in America their condition is so peculiarly grievous, and their depression so complete, that servitude is a name too mild to describe their wretched state. A wife, amongst most tribes, is no better than a beast of burden, destined to every office of labour and fatigue. While the men loiter out the day in sloth, or spend it in amusement, the women are condemned to incessant toil. Tasks are imposed upon them without pity, and services (Continued)

75 "Swift, swift," she cries, "receive thy last release;
　 Die, little wretch; die once and be at peace!
　 Why shouldst thou live, in toil, and pain, and strife,
　 To curse the names of mother and of wife?
　 To see at large thy lordly master roam,
80 The beasts his portion and the woods his home;
　 Whilst thou, infirm, the sheltering hut must seek,
　 Poorly dependent, timorously weak,
　 There hush thy babe, with patient love carest,
　 And tearful clasp him to thy milkless breast,
85 Hungry and faint, while feasting on his way
　 Thy reckless hunter wastes the jocund day?[1]
　 Or, harder task, his rapid courses share,
　 With patient back the galling burden bear,
　 While he treads light, and smacks the knotted thong,
90 And goads with taunts his staggering troop along?
　 Enough;.... 'tis love, dear babe, that stops thy breath;
　 'Tis mercy lulls thee to the sleep of death:
　 Ah! would for me, by like indulgent doom,
　 A mother's hand had raised the early tomb!
95 O'er these poor bones the moons had rolled in vain,
　 And brought nor stripes nor famine, toil nor pain;
　 I had not sought in agony the wild,
　 Nor, wretched, frantic mother! killed my child."
　 Want hardens man; by fierce extremes the smart
100 Inflames and chills and indurates his heart,
　 Arms his relentless hand with brutal force,
　 And drives o'er female necks his furious course.

　 Not such his mind where Nature, partial queen,
　 With lavish plenty heaps the bounteous scene;
105 In laughing isles with broad bananas crowned,
　 Where tufted cocoas shade the flowery ground;
　 Here, here at least, where dancing seasons shed
　 Unfading garlands on his sleeping head,
　 Love melts to love, and man's ingenuous mind
110 Feels nature's kindness prompt him to be kind;
　 He acts no tyranny, he knows no strife,
　 One harmless holiday his easy life.
　 Ah cheated hopes!.... see Lawless Love invade
　 The withering scene, and poison every shade;
115 Embruted nations couch beneath his yoke,
　 And infant gore on his dire altars smoke!
　 Lost Otaheite!.... Breathe one parting sigh,
　 Then swift, my friend, we turn the bashful eye.[2]

　 Thrice holy Power, whose fostering, bland embrace
120 Shields the frail scions of each transient race,
　 To whom fair Nature trusts the teeming birth
　 That fills the air, that crowds the peopled earth,
　 Maternal Love! thy watchful glances roll
　 From zone to zone, from pole to distant pole;
125 Cheer the long patience of the brooding hen,
　 Soothe the she-fox that trembles in her den,
　 'Mid Greenland ice-caves warm the female bear,
　 And rouse the tigress from her sultry lair.
　 At thy command, what zeal, what ardour, fires
130 The softer sex! a mightier soul inspires:....
　 Lost to themselves, our melting eyes behold
　 Prudent, the simple, and the timid, bold.

---

are received without complacency or gratitude.
　"'Every circumstance reminds the women of this mortifying inferiority. They must approach their lords with reverence, they must regard them as more exalted beings, and are not permitted to eat in their presence.
　"'There are many districts in America where this dominion is so grievous, and so sensibly felt, that some women, in a wild emotion of maternal tenderness, have destroyed their female children in their infancy, in order to deliver them from that intolerable bondage to which they knew they were doomed.' Robertson's Hist. of America, vol. ii. p. 105.
　"Hearne describes the women of the Northern tribes which he visited, as wading through the snow encumbered with heavy burdens, while the men, themselves carrying nothing, urged them on with blows and threats. He mentions other particulars, also illustrative of the wretched condition of the American females, too numerous and too horrid for poetical narration.
　"Certainly Rousseau did not consult the interests of the weaker sex in his preference of savage life to civilized." (L.A.) See Samuel Hearne, *A Journey from Prince of Wales's Fort in Hudson's Bay, to the Northern Ocean** and Jean-Jacques Rousseau (1712–78), *Discourse on the Origin and Foundations of Inequality* (1755), and cf. Hemans, "Indian Woman's Death-Song."*

[1] Cf. Shakespeare, *Romeo and Juliet* 3.5.9.

[2] "It is supposed that two thirds of the children born in Otaheite are immediately murdered. For the particulars of that dreadful licentiousness which is the consequence of the complete indolence of these islanders, and the countless and nameless evils and enormities which are *its* consequence, see Transactions of the Missionary Society, vol. i." (L.A.)

All own thy sway, save where, on Simoom[1] wing
Triumphant sailing o'er the blasted spring,
135 (Whether in Otaheitan groves accurst,
Or Europe's polisht scenes the fiend be nurst)
Unhallowed Love bids Nature's self depart,
And makes a desert of the female heart.
But O! how oft, their tender bosoms torn
140 By countless shafts, thy noblest votaries mourn!
See the soft hind forsake the dewy lawns
To shroud in thicket-shades her tender fawns;
Fearless for them confront the growling foe,
And aim with hoof and head the desperate blow;
145 Freely for them with new-born courage face
The howling horrors of the deathful chase:
Ah! fond in vain, see fired by furious heat
The jealous stag invade her soft retreat,
Wanton in rage her pleading anguish scorn,
150 And gore his offspring with relentless horn.

Hark to that shriek! from Afric's palmy shore
The yell rolls mingling with the billows' roar:
Grovelling in dust the frantic mother lies;....
"My son, my son, O spare my son!" she cries:
155 "Sell not thy child! Yon dreary ocean crost,
To thee, to me, to all for ever lost,
The white man's slave, no swift-returning oar
Shall homeward urge the wretched captive more,
No tidings reach:.... Who then with kindly care
160 Shall tend our age, and leafy beds prepare?
Who climb for us the cocoa's scaly side,
Or drain the juicy palm?.... who skim the tide,
Or bold in woods with pointed javelin roam,
And bear to us the savoury booty home?
165 Save thine own flesh!.... we must not, will not part....
O save this bleeding, bursting, mother's heart!"

Ah fruitless agony! ah slighted prayer!
That bids the husband and the father spare!
On to the mart the sable tyrant drives
170 His flocks of children and his herds of wives:
For toys, for drams, their kindred blood is sold,
And broken female hearts are paid with gold;
Exulting Avarice gripes his struggling prize,
The savage tenders, and the christian .... *buys.*[2]

175 Shrinkst thou, my startled friend, with feeling tear,
From tints too lively, numbers too sincere?
Swift wouldst thou fly to some unspotted scene
Where love and nature rule the blue serene?
Hail, Pastoral Life; to thy calm scenes belong
180 The lore of sages and the poet's song;
Nurse of rude man, in whose soft lap reclined,
Art, science, dawn upon his wakening mind,
And passion's tender strains, and sentiment refined!

Where cloudless heavens o'er-arch Chaldea's plain,
185 Stretched by his nightly flock, the vacant swain,
His upturned gaze as sportful fancy warmed,
With ready crook the sand-drawn monsters formed;
Thence learn'd, Astronomy, thy studious eye,
To track yon orbs, to sweep yon pathless sky.
190 While still young David roamed the pastoral wild,
The harp, the song, his ardent soul beguiled,
And now to heaven upsoared the ethereal flame,
Now blazed some humble charmer's rustic fame.
E'en now, by Freedom led, see gay Content
195 Stoop from above, to shepherd-wanderers sent;
See o'er the green expanse of pathless plain
The sunburnt Tartars urge the tented wain;
How gay the living prospect! far and wide
Spread flocks and herds, and shouting herdsmen ride;
200 And hark! from youths and maids, a mingled throng,
How full, how joyous, bursts the choral song!

Free are these tribes and blest; a churlish soil
They till not, bowed by tyranny and toil;
Nor troll the deep for life's precarious stay;
205 Nor, beastlike, roam the tangled woods for prey;
Their lot, with sober kindness, gives to share
Labour with plenty, and with freedom, care:
Yet seek not here the boon, all boons above,
The generous intercourse of equal love;

---

[1] a strong dry wind blowing over the desert, supposed to have deleterious effects. Cf. Byron, *The Giaour* 282.*

[2] "These lines were written before the late glorious abolition: but there are still Christian nations to whom they apply with full force." (L.A.) The British Parliament abolished the transatlantic slave trade in 1807.

210　A homely drudge, the Tartar matron knows
　　No eye that kindles and no heart that glows;
　　For foreign charms the faithless husband burns,
　　And clasps in loathed embrace, which fear returns,
　　The captive wife or tributary maid
215　By conquest snatched, or lawless terror paid.[1]

　　No!.... vain the search,.... of warm poetic birth,
　　Arcadian blossoms scorn the fields of earth;
　　No lovelorn swains, to tender griefs a prey,
　　Sigh, sing, and languish through the livelong day;
220　No rapturous husband and enamoured wife,
　　To live and love their only care in life,
　　With crook and scrip on flowery banks reclined
　　Breathe the warm heart and share the answering mind:
　　The sprightly Caffre o'er the moonlight meads
225　In jovial dance his dusky partner leads,
　　And vacant Hottentots, short labour done,
　　Toy, pipe, and carol, in the evening sun;
　　But the high promptings of the conscious soul
　　The weak that elevate, the strong control,
230　Respect, decorum, friendship, ties that bind
　　To woman's form the homage of the mind,
　　Heaven's nobler gifts, to riper ages lent,
　　Disdain the hunter's cave, the shepherd's tent,
　　And *lawless* man, or cold, or fierce, or rude,
　　Proves every mode of female servitude.[2]

---

[1] "An annual tribute of women was exacted by the Tartars, or Huns, from the Chinese; and even the daughters, genuine or adopted, of the eastern emperors were claimed in marriage by the Tanjous as a bond of union between the nations. 'The situation of these unhappy victims is described,' says Gibbon, 'in the verses of a Chinese princess, who laments that she had been condemned by her parents to a distant exile, under a barbarian husband; who complains that sour milk was her only drink, raw flesh her only food, a tent her only palace; and who expresses, in a strain of pathetic simplicity, the natural wish that she were transformed into a bird, to fly back to her dear country, the object of her tender and perpetual regret.' Decline and Fall, vol. iv. p. 363, 8vo edition." (L.A.) Edward Gibbon (1737–94), *The History of the Decline and Fall of the Roman Empire* (1776–88) chap. 26. A Tanjou was a chieftain of the Huns.

[2] The last two epistles deal with the condition of women in Europe, from classical times to Aikin's own.

Charlotte Dacre
1782? – 1825

For reasons which may become clear, we don't know much about Charlotte Dacre's life. She claimed to have been born in 1782, but her obituary suggests 1772. Her father was Jacob Rey, also known as Jonathan King, a political radical but also a usurer and blackmailer; her mother was Deborah Lara King. Jonathan was an abusive and adulterous husband (he was accused of an affair with Mary Robinson),* and the couple was divorced, under Jewish law, in 1785. Both Dacre and her sister Sophia became poets and novelists; together, they published *Trifles of Helicon*, their first book, in 1798. In 1802, Dacre began to publish poems in the *Morning Post* under the name Rosa Matilda. The Italianate surname indicates her affiliation with the Della Cruscan school of Merry ("Della Crusca"),* Cowley ("Anna Matilda"),* and Robinson ("Laura Maria"). It also indicates an interest in *The Monk* (1796), by M.G. Lewis,* in which the hero's demon lover is called first Rosario and then Matilda; Dacre's best-known novel, *Zofloya; or, The Moor* (1806), is a female variation on *The Monk*. She published her first solo book of poems, *Hours of Solitude* (1805), under yet another pseudonym, Charlotte Dacre. The reason may have been that about this time, she became involved with Nicholas Byrne, editor of the *Morning Post*. They had three children but were unable to marry until July 1815, after the death of his first wife. By 1805, the Della Cruscan vogue had passed and *Hours of Solitude* was not well received, but Dacre's four novels got good reviews and sold well. Dacre died on 7 November 1825, "after a long and painful illness, which her purity and sublime greatness of soul enabled her patiently and piously to endure" (*The Times*). Her husband died on 29 June 1833, after being stabbed by a mysterious man in a crape mask. The murder was never solved. (D.L.M.)

༄༅༄༅

from *Hours of Solitude. A Collection of Original Poems, now first published* (1805)

The Poor Negro Sadi

Ah! poor negro Sadi, what sorrows, what anguish
    Oppress the lone victim fate dooms for a slave!
What eye or what heart o'er those sorrows shall
    languish?
    What finger point out the lone African's grave?

5 First torn like a wretch from his innocent dwelling,
    And torn from Abouka, the wife of his soul,
Then forc'd, while his heart was indignantly swelling,
    To bow his proud neck to the despot's controul.

Think not, European, tho' dark his complexion,
10   Dark, dark as the hue of the African's fate,
That his *mind* is devoid of the light of reflexion,
    And knows not distinctions of love or of hate.

And believe, when you see him in agony bending
    Beaneath the hard lash, if he fainting should
    pause,
15 That pure are to heaven his sorrows ascending,
    And dear must you pay for the torture you cause.

Mark, mark the red blood that, so eloquent streaming,
    Appeals to the Godhead thou sayest is thine!
Mark, mark the sunk eye that on heaven is beaming!
20   It calls deep revenge on *oppression* and *crime*.

The poor negro Sadi—what horror befel him,
    To slavery dragg'd in the bloom of his years!
To the food he disdains the vile lash must compel him,
    Ah! food doubly bitter when moisten'd by tears!

25 At length, in a moment of anguish despairing,
    Poor Sadi resolves to escape, or he dies:
He plung'd in the ocean, not knowing nor caring
    If e'er from its waves he was doom'd to arise.

He skims light as down, when at distance espying
    A vessel, its refuge he struggles to gain;
And nearly exhausted, just sinking, just dying,
    Escapes from a grave in the pitiless main.

But vainly preserv'd, sable victim of sorrow!
    An end far more dreadful thine anguish must have;
Tho' a moment from hope it faint lustre may borrow,
    Soon, soon must it sink in the gloom of the grave.

Soft, soft blew the gale, and the green billows swelling,
    Gay sail'd the light vessel for Albion's shore;
Poor Sadi sigh'd deep for his wife and his dwelling,
    That wife and that dwelling he ne'er must see more.

Oh, Britons! so fam'd in the annals of glory,
    The poor negro Sadi is cast on your plains—
Oh, Britons! if just be your fame or your glory,
    The poor negro Sadi shall bless your domains.

As yet see he wanders forlorn and in sadness,
    By many scarce seen, and unpitied by all;
No glance yet his sunk heart has flutter'd with gladness,
    Nor voice sympathetic on him seem'd to call.

In vain, wretched negro! Thou lookest around thee—
    In vain, wretched negro! so lowly dost bend;
Tho' a thousand cold faces for ever surround thee,
    Among them not one is, poor Sadi, thy friend.

Three nights and three days had he wander'd despairing,
    No food nor no shelter the victim had found,
The pangs of keen hunger his bosom were tearing,
    When, o'erpower'd with torture, he sunk on the ground.

He clasp'd his thin hands, now no longer imploring
    The succour which all had so basely denied,
In hopeless submission had finish'd deploring
    The suff'rings he felt must so shortly subside.

On the step of a door his faint body reclining
    Had sought unmolested to yield up its breath,
But hell-born tormentors forbade his resigning
    Within their vile precincts, his sorrows to death.

They dragg'd the lone victim, in misery lying,
    From off the cold stone where he languish'd to rest,
Defenceless they dragg'd him, unpitied—tho' dying,
    His last wretched moments with horror opprest!

Now keen blew the tempest, and keener still blowing,
    His shrunk heart scarce flutter'd, scarce heav'd his faint breath—
His blood was congeal'd, and his tears no more flowing,
    Had froze on his eyelids, now closing in death.

Oh, Heaven! That seest this sad wretch expiring
    By famine's keen tortures, unaided, alone,
Pure, pure to *thy* throne his last sighs are aspiring,
    Tho' sable his skin, tho' *unchristian* his tone!

Oh, poor negro Sadi! what sorrows, what anguish
    Oppress the lone victim fate dooms for a slave!
What eye or what heart for those sorrows shall languish?
    What finger point out the lone African's grave?

The Female Philosopher

You tell me, fair one, that you ne'er can love,
    And seem with scorn to mock the dangerous fire;
But why, then, trait'ress, do you seek to move
    In others what *your* breast can ne'er inspire?

You tell me, you my *friend* alone will be,
    Yet speak of friendship in a voice so sweet,
That, while I struggle to be coldly free,
    I feel my heart with wildest throbbings beat.

Vainly indiff'rence would you bid us feel,
    While so much languor in those eyes appear;
Vainly the stoic's happiness reveal,
    While soft emotion all your features wear.

O, form'd for love! O, wherefore should you fly
    From the seducing charm it spreads around?
O why enshrine your soul with apathy?
    Or wish in frozen fetters to be bound?

Life is a darksome and a dreary day,
    The solitary wretch no pleasure knows;
Love is the star that lights him on his way,
    And guides him on to pleasure and repose.

But oft, forgetful of thy plan severe,
    I've seen thee fondly gaze—I've heard thee sigh;
I've mark'd thy strain of converse, sadly dear,
    While softest rapture lighten'd from thine eye.

Then have I thought some wayward youth employ'd
    Thy secret soul, but left thee to despair,
And oft with pleasing sorrow have enjoy'd
    The task of chasing thy corrosive care.

Yet pride must save me from a dastard love,
    A grov'ling love, that cannot hope return:
A soul like mine was never form'd to prove
    Those viler passions with which some can burn.

Then fear not me; for since it is thy will,
    Adhere with stubborn coolness to thy vow;
Grant me thy philosophic friendship still—
    I'll grant thee *mine* with all the powers I know.

The Apparition

As slow I wander'd o'er yon barren heath,
    Musing on woes to come—on evils past,
    Cursing that fate me in such mould had cast,
I at my side did hear a gentle breath!
When straitway looking down, behold I saw
    A piteous imp—deform'd his limbs appear'd,
    And wither'd quite—while on a stick he rear'd
His wretched weight—on nature's face a flaw!
Pale was his ashy cheek—no hope there beam'd
    From his sunk eye; his matted locks, poor child!
    O'er his misshapen back hung loose and wild,
And conscious of his misery he seem'd.
Loud blew the wind, and shook the slender wight;
    With long, thin hand he grasp'd his stick, and rais'd
    On me his tearful eyes; sadly I gaz'd,
When swift he vanish'd from my troubl'd sight!

Drinking Song

Wine, I Say! I'll Drink to Madness!
Wine's a sov'reign cure for sorrow,
Let's drink to-day, and die to-morrow;
No wonder the bottle should mortals enslave,
Since it snatches the soul from the brink of the grave!
Gentle creature, hither bring,
Wine to soothe my love's despair;
Then in merry accents sing,
Woman false, as she is fair!
Wine, I say! I'll drink to madness!
Wine, my girl, to cure my sadness!
And tell me no more there is folly in drinking,
Can anything equal the folly of thinking?
Magic soother! sparkling wine,
What is nectar, drink divine,
What is nectar to champagne?
Fill the goblet! fill again!
No more, no more of am'rous folly,
From me fly black melancholy;
And tyrant take heed how you come in my view,
Lest in my distraction, your boldness you rue!
Smiling ruin, lovely woman,
Fit companions in our wine;
For in reason surely no man
Comes within your fatal line.
Bring fresh bottles, bring fresh glasses,
From my soul how sorrow passes!
Before my witch'd eyes laughs a gay cover'd plain,
While fancy forms visions that fire my brain!
Then wine, I say! I'll drink to madness!
Wine, my girl, to cure my sadness!
And tell me no more, there's folly in drinking,
    Can any thing equal the folly of thinking!

Jane Taylor
1783 – 1824

Jane Taylor was born on 23 September 1783 in London, one of the six children of Isaac Taylor, an engraver, painter, and Presbyterian minister, and Ann Martin Taylor; the family later moved to Lavenham, and then to Colchester. She was educated at home. Like her older sister Ann, she began to write early; her parents disapproved but allowed them to continue so long as they did not neglect their domestic or religious duties or their education (including training in engraving). Ann published her first poem in 1799; Jane published her first in 1804, winning second prize in a competition (Ann came first). Also in 1804, they published *Original Poetry for Infant Minds*, the first of a series of bestselling collaborative books of poems and hymns for children. It was an extraordinary success and remained in print for a century. Their parents became more indulgent, offering them more time to write and rooms of their own. Jane chose an attic, in which she placed two chairs, one for herself and one for her muse. There she would sit with her eyes shut and imagine a child talking; if the child did not oblige, she would finish the poem herself. Ann married in 1813 and gave up writing for over a decade, but Jane, who never married, published *Display: A Tale for Young People* in 1815 and *Essays in Rhyme, on Morals and Manners*, her own favourite among her books, in 1816; Keats* recommended it to his sister. Then Taylor turned to journalism, contributing essays to *Youth's Magazine*. She died of breast cancer on 12 April 1824. Coleridge's* daughter Sara, later an important Victorian poet, enjoyed her work; and R. Browning, who acknowledged her influence on him, called her poems "the most perfect things of their kind in the English language." (D.L.M.)

※※※

from *Rhymes for the Nursery* (1806)

The Star[1]

Twinkle, twinkle, little star,
How I wonder what you are!
Up above the world so high,
Like a diamond in the sky.

5 When the blazing sun is gone,
When he nothing shines upon,
Then you show your little light,
Twinkle, twinkle, all the night.

Then the trav'ller in the dark,
10 Thanks you for your tiny spark,
He could not see which way to go,
If you did not twinkle so.

In the dark blue sky you keep,
And often thro' my curtains peep,
15 For you never shut your eye,
Till the sun is in the sky.

'Tis your bright and tiny spark,
Lights the trav'ller in the dark:
Tho' I know not what you are,
20 Twinkle, twinkle, little star.

from *Essays in Rhyme, on Morals and Manners*, 3rd ed. (1817)

Recreation

—We took our work,[2] and went, you see,
To take an early cup of tea.
We did so now and then, to pay
The friendly debt, and so did they.

---

[1] Cf. Blake, "The Tyger."*

[2] recreational needlework.

5 Not that our friendship burnt so bright
That all the world could see the light;
'Twas of the ordinary *genus*,[1]
And little love was lost between us:
We lov'd, I think, about as true
10 As such near neighbours mostly do.

　　At first, we all were somewhat dry;
Mamma felt cold, and so did I:
Indeed, that room, sit where you will,
Has draught enough to turn a mill.
15 "I hope you're warm," says Mrs. G.
"O, quite so," says mamma, *says she*;
"I'll take my shawl off by and by."—
"This room is always warm," *says I*.

　　At last the tea came up, and so,
20 With that, our tongues began to go.
Now, in that house you're sure of knowing
The smallest scrap of news that's going;
We find it *there* the wisest way
To take some care of what we say.

25 　　—Says she, "there's dreadful doings still
In that affair about the *will*;
For now the folks in Brewer's Street
Don't speak to *James's*, when they meet.
Poor Mrs. *Sam* sits all alone,
30 And frets herself to skin and bone.
For months she manag'd, she declares,
All the old gentleman's affairs;
And always let him have his way,
And never left him night nor day;
35 Waited and watch'd his every look,
And gave him every drop he took.
Dear Mrs. *Sam*, it was too bad!
He might have left her all he had."

　　"Pray ma'am," says I, "has poor Miss A.
40 Been left as *handsome* as they say?"
"My dear," says she, "'tis no such thing,
She'd nothing but a mourning ring.[2]
But is it not *uncommon* mean
To wear that rusty bombazeen!"[3]
45 "She had," says I, "the very same
Three years ago, for—what's his name?"—
"The Duke of *Brunswick*,—very true,
And has not bought a thread of new,
I'm positive," said Mrs. G.—
50 So then we laugh'd, and drank our tea.

　　"So," says mamma, "I find it's true
What Captain P. intends to do;
To hire that house, or else to buy—"
"Close to the tan-yard, ma'am," says I;
55 "Upon my word it's very strange,
I wish they mayn't repent the change!"
"My dear," says she, "'tis very well
You know, if *they* can bear the smell."

　　"Miss F." says I, "is said to be
60 A sweet young woman, is not she?"
"O, excellent! I hear," she cried;
"O, truly so!" mamma replied.
"How old should you suppose her, pray?
She's older than she looks, they say."
65 "Really," says I, "she seems to me
Not more than twenty-two or three."
"O, then you're wrong," says Mrs. G.
"Their upper servant told our *Jane*,
She'll not see twenty-nine again."
70 "Indeed, so old! I wonder why
She does not marry, then," says I;
"So many thousands to bestow,
And such a beauty, too, you know."
"A beauty! O, my dear Miss B.
75 You must be joking now," says she;
"Her *figure's* rather pretty,"—"Ah!
That's what *I* say," replied mamma.

---

[1] "kind" (L.).

[2] It was customary to wear mourning jewelry, often made from jet (a kind of black lignite found in Yorkshire), in memory of dead friends or relatives, who sometimes left money to buy it.

[3] black silk worn as mourning.

"Miss F." says I, "I've understood,
Spends all her time in doing good:
The people say her coming down
Is quite a blessing to the town."
At that our hostess fetch'd a sigh,
And shook her head; and so, says I,
"It's very kind of her, I'm sure,
To be so generous to the poor."
"No doubt," says she, "'tis very true;
Perhaps there may be *reasons* too:—
You know some people like to pass
For *patrons* with the lower class."

    And here I break my story's thread,
Just to remark, that what she said,
Although I took the other part,
Went like a cordial to my heart.

    Some inuendos more had pass'd,
Till out the scandal came at last.
"Come then, I'll tell you something more,"
Says she,—"Eliza, shut the door.—
I would not trust a creature here,
For all the world, but you, my dear.
Perhaps it's false—I wish it may,
—But let it go no further, pray!"
"O," says mamma, "You need not fear,
We never mention what we hear."
And so, we drew our chairs the nearer,
And whispering, lest the child should hear her,
She told a tale, at least too *long*
To be repeated in a song;
We, panting every breath between,
With curiosity and spleen.
And how we did enjoy the sport!
And echo every faint report,
And answer every candid doubt,
And turn her motives inside out,
And holes in all her virtues pick,
Till we were sated, almost sick.

    —Thus having brought it to a close,
In great good-humour, we arose.
Indeed, 'twas more than time to go,
Our boy had been an hour below.
So, warmly pressing Mrs. G.
To fix a day to come to tea,
We muffled up in cloke and plaid,
And trotted home behind the lad.

Washington Irving
1783 – 1859

Washington Irving was born in New York City on 3 April 1783, youngest of the twelve children of William Irving, a hardware importer, and Sarah Sanders Irving. He was educated in New York and in 1802 began work as a law clerk. At the same time, he published his first essays in the *Morning Chronicle*, a paper edited by his brother Peter. He also fell in love with Matilda Hoffman, his employer's daughter, but their courtship was interrupted by his tour of Europe in 1804–06; she died of tuberculosis in 1809, and Irving never married. He qualified for the law in 1806 but hardly ever practised. In 1809, under the pseudonym Diedrich Knickerbocker, he published a comic *History of New-York, from the Beginning of the World to the End of the Dutch Dynasty*; it was a great success.

In May 1815, after practising a little law, editing a magazine, and serving in the War of 1812, Irving went to England to try to save the Liverpool branch of the family business. He failed, but he would stay in Europe for seventeen years and establish himself there as America's first internationally famous author. In 1819–20, under another pseudonym, he published his most important book, *The Sketch-Book of Geoffrey Crayon, Gent.*, a miscellaneous collection of essays, observations, travel writing, and short stories like "Rip Van Winkle" and "The Legend of Sleepy Hollow." After living in Germany and France and publishing other miscellaneous volumes, in 1826 Irving moved to Spain, where he researched and wrote *A History of the Life and Voyages of Christopher Columbus* (1828)—the first full-length English-language biography of Columbus, and the first book Irving published under his own name—and *A Chronicle of the Conquest of Granada* (1829). *The Alhambra* (1832), a miscellaneous, largely fictional reworking of Spanish themes, is said to have initiated the 19th-century fashion of "Alhambraism." His achievements were recognized by honourary degrees from Columbia, Harvard, and Oxford.

Returning to America in 1832, Irving went on a trip as far west as what is now Oklahoma, and devoted much of the 1830s to a series of books about the exploration of the American West. He then spent four more years (1842–46) in Spain, as American ambassador. In 1848, the publisher G.P. Putnam proposed a collected edition of his works, another landmark for an American author. Irving's last project was a five-volume *Life of George Washington*, which he struggled to complete despite increasing ill health: "I must get through with the work which I have cut out for myself," he declared. "I must weave my web, and then die." The last volume appeared in the middle of 1859; he died on 28 November. He is buried in Sleepy Hollow Cemetery, Tarrytown, New York. (D.L.M.)

❦❦❦

from *The Sketch Book of Geoffrey Crayon, Gent.* (1819)

Rip Van Winkle. A Posthumous Writing of Diedrich Knickerbocker [1]

By Woden, God of Saxons,
From whence comes Wensday, that is Wodensday,
Truth is a thing that ever I will keep
Unto thylke day in which I creep into
My sepulchre——
         CARTWRIGHT [2]

Whoever has made a voyage up the Hudson, must remember the Kaatskill mountains. They are a dismembered branch of the great Appalachian family, and are seen away to the west of the river, swelling up to a noble

---

[1] the pseudonym under which Irving had published his previous book; a brief preface explains that the tale was found among Knickerbocker's papers after his death.

[2] William Cartwright (1611–43), *The Ordinary* (1651) 3.1.1050–54. Woden or Odin was the war-god of the Saxons and other Nordic peoples.

height, and lording it over the surrounding country. Every change of season, every change of weather, indeed, every hour of the day, produces some change in the magical hues and shapes of these mountains, and they are regarded by all the good wives, far and near, as perfect barometers. When the weather is fair and settled, they are clothed in blue and purple, and print their bold outlines on the clear evening sky; but some times, when the rest of the landscape is cloudless, they will gather a hood of gray vapours about their summits, which, in the last rays of the setting sun, will glow and light up like a crown of glory.

At the foot of these fairy mountains, the voyager may have descried the light smoke curling up from a village, whose shingle roofs gleam among the trees, just where the blue tints of the upland melt away into the fresh green of the nearer landscape. It is a little village of great antiquity, having been founded by some of the Dutch colonists, in the early times of the province, just about the beginning of the government of the good Peter Stuyvesant,[1] (may he rest in peace!) and there were some of the houses of the original settlers standing within a few years, with lattice windows, gable fronts surmounted with weathercocks, and built of small yellow bricks brought from Holland.

In that same village, and in one of these very houses, (which, to tell the precise truth, was sadly time worn and weather beaten,) there lived many years since, while the country was yet a province of Great Britain, a simple good natured fellow, of the name of Rip Van Winkle. He was a descendant of the Van Winkles who figured so gallantly in the chivalrous days of Peter Stuyvesant, and accompanied him to the siege of Fort Christina.[2] He inherited, however, but little of the martial character of his ancestors. I have observed that he was a simple good natured man; he was moreover a kind neighbour, and an obedient, henpecked husband. Indeed, to the latter circumstance might be owing that meekness of spirit which gained him such universal popularity; for those men are most apt to be obsequious and conciliating abroad, who are under the discipline of shrews at home. Their tempers, doubtless, are rendered pliant and malleable in the fiery furnace of domestic tribulation, and a curtain lecture is worth all the sermons in the world for teaching the virtues of patience and long suffering. A termagant[3] wife may, therefore, in some respects, be considered a tolerable blessing; and if so, Rip Van Winkle was thrice blessed.

Certain it is, that he was a great favourite among all the good wives of the village, who, as usual with the amiable sex, took his part in all family squabbles, and never failed, whenever they talked those matters over in their evening gossippings, to lay all the blame on Dame Van Winkle. The children of the village, too, would shout with joy whenever he approached. He assisted at their sports, made their playthings, taught them to fly kites and shoot marbles, and told them long stories of ghosts, witches, and Indians. Whenever he went dodging about the village, he was surrounded by a troop of them, hanging on his skirts, clambering on his back, and playing a thousand tricks on him with impunity; and not a dog would bark at him throughout the neighbourhood.

The great error in Rip's composition was an insuperable aversion to all kinds of profitable labour. It could not be for the want of assiduity or perseverance; for he would sit on a wet rock, with a rod as long and heavy as a Tartar's lance, and fish all day without a murmur, even though he should not be encouraged by a single nibble. He would carry a fowling piece on his shoulder, for hours together, trudging through woods and swamps, and up hill and down dale, to shoot a few squirrels or wild pigeons. He would never even refuse to assist a neighbour in the roughest toil, and was a foremost man at all country frolicks for husking Indian corn, or building stone fences; the women of the village, too, used to employ him to run their errands, and to do such little odd jobs as their less obliging husbands would not do for them;—in a word, Rip was ready to attend to any

---

[1] Peter Stuyvesant (1592–1672) was the last Dutch governor of New Amsterdam (1647–64).

[2] In 1655, the Dutch under Stuyvesant captured Fort Christina, on the Delaware River, from the Swedes.

[3] Originally the name of an imaginary, bad-tempered god whom medieval Christians believed Muslims to worship (see the *Chanson de Roland*), "termagant" came to be applied to bad-tempered persons, especially women; cf. Pope, *The Rape of the Lock* (1714) 1.59–60. A "curtain lecture" was a scolding delivered in bed, after the bed-curtains were drawn.

body's business but his own; but as to doing family duty, and keeping his farm in order, it was impossible.

In fact, he declared it was no use to work on his farm; it was the most pestilent little piece of ground in the whole country; every thing about it went wrong, and would go wrong, in spite of him. His fences were continually falling to pieces; his cow would either go astray, or get among the cabbages; weeds were sure to grow quicker in his fields than any where else; the rain always made a point of setting in just as he had some out-door work to do. So that though his patrimonial estate had dwindled away under his management, acre by acre, until there was little more left than a mere patch of Indian corn and potatoes, yet it was the worst conditioned farm in the neighbourhood.

His children, too, were as ragged and wild as if they belonged to nobody. His son Rip, an urchin begotten in his own likeness, promised to inherit the habits, with the old clothes of his father. He was generally seen trooping like a colt at his mother's heels, equipped in a pair of his father's cast-off galligaskins,[1] which he had much ado to hold up with one hand, as a fine lady does her train in bad weather.

Rip Van Winkle, however, was one of those happy mortals, of foolish, well-oiled dispositions, who take the world easy, eat white bread or brown, which ever can be got with least thought or trouble, and would rather starve on a penny than work for a pound. If left to himself, he would have whistled life away, in perfect contentment; but his wife kept continually dinning in his ears about his idleness, his careles[s]ness, and the ruin he was bringing on his family. Morning, noon, and night, her tongue was incessantly going, and every thing he said or did was sure to produce a torrent of household eloquence. Rip had but one way of replying to all lectures of the kind, and that, by frequent use, had grown into a habit. He shrugged his shoulders, shook his head, cast up his eyes, but said nothing. This, however, always provoked a fresh volley from his wife, so that he was fain to draw off his forces, and take to the outside of the house—the only side which, in truth, belongs to a henpecked husband.

Rip's sole domestic adherent was his dog Wolf, who was as much henpecked as his master; for Dame Van Winkle regarded them as companions in idleness, and even looked upon Wolf with an evil eye, as the cause of his master's so often going astray. True it is, in all points of spirit befitting an honourable dog, he was as courageous an animal as ever scoured the woods—but what courage can withstand the ever-during and all-besetting terrors of a woman's tongue? The moment Wolf entered the house, his crest fell, his tail drooped to the ground, or curled between his legs, he sneaked about with a gallows air, casting many a sidelong glance at Dame Van Winkle, and at the least flourish of a broomstick or ladle, would fly to the door with yelping precipitation.

Times grew worse and worse with Rip Van Winkle as years of matrimony rolled on; a tart temper never mellows with age, and a sharp tongue is the only edge tool that grows keener by constant use. For a long while he used to console himself, when driven from home, by frequenting a kind of perpetual club of the sages, philosophers, and other idle personages of the village, that held its sessions on a bench before a small inn, designated by a rubicund portrait of his majesty George the Third.[2] Here they used to sit in the shade, of a long lazy summer's day, talk listlessly over village gossip, or tell endless sleepy stories about nothing. But it would have been worth any statesman's money to have heard the profound discussions that sometimes took place, when by chance an old newspaper fell into their hands, from some passing traveller. How solemnly they would listen to the contents, as drawled out by Derrick Van Bummel, the schoolmaster, a dapper learned little man, who was not to be daunted by the most gigantic word in the dictionary; and how sagely they would deliberate upon public events some months after they had taken place.

The opinions of this junto[3] were completely controlled by Nicholas Vedder, a patriarch of the village, and landlord of the inn, at the door of which he took his seat from morning till night, just moving sufficiently to avoid the sun, and keep in the shade of a large tree; so that the neighbours could tell the hour by his move-

---

[1] breeches.

[2] George III (1738–1820) had come to the throne in 1760.

[3] "junta": "ruling committee" (Sp.).

ments as accurately as by a sun dial. It is true, he was rarely heard to speak, but smoked his pipe incessantly. His adherents, however, (for every great man has his adherents,) perfectly understood him, and knew how to gather his opinions. When any thing that was read or related displeased him, he was observed to smoke his pipe vehemently, and send forth short, frequent, and angry puffs; but when pleased, he would inhale the smoke slowly and tranquilly, and emit it in light and placid clouds, and sometimes taking the pipe from his mouth, and letting the fragrant vapour curl about his nose, would gravely nod his head in token of perfect approbation.

From even this strong hold the unlucky Rip was at length routed by his termagant wife, who would suddenly break in upon the tranquillity of the assemblage, call the members all to nought, nor was that august personage, Nicholas Vedder himself, sacred from the daring tongue of this terrible virago, who charged him outright with encouraging her husband in habits of idleness.

Poor Rip was at last reduced almost to despair; and his only alternative to escape from the labour of the farm and the clamour of his wife, was to take gun in hand, and stroll away into the woods. Here he would sometimes seat himself at the foot of a tree, and share the contents of his wallet[1] with Wolf, with whom he sympathised as a fellow sufferer in persecution. "Poor Wolf," he would say, "thy mistress leads thee a dogs' life of it; but never mind, my lad, while I live thou shalt never want a friend to stand by thee!" Wolf would wag his tail, look wistfully in his master's face, and if dogs can feel pity, I verily believe he reciprocated the sentiment with all his heart.

In a long ramble of the kind on a fine autumnal day, Rip had unconsciously scrambled to one of the highest parts of the Kaatskill mountains. He was after his favourite sport of squirrel shooting, and the still solitudes had echoed and re-echoed with the reports of his gun. Panting and fatigued, he threw himself, late in the afternoon, on a green knoll, covered with mountain herbage, that crowned the brow of a precipice. From an opening between the trees, he could overlook all the lower country for many a mile of rich woodland. He saw at a distance the lordly Hudson, far, far below him, moving on its silent but majestic course, the reflection of a purple cloud, or the sail of a lagging bark, here and there sleeping on its glassy bosom, and at last losing itself in the blue highlands.

On the other side he looked down into a deep mountain glen, wild, lonely, and shagged, the bottom filled with fragments from the impending cliffs, and scarcely lighted by the reflected rays of the setting sun. For some time Rip lay musing on this scene, evening was gradually advancing, the mountains began to throw their long blue shadows over the valleys, he saw that it would be dark long before he could reach the village, and he heaved a heavy sigh when he thought of encountering the terrors of Dame Van Winkle.

As he was about to descend, he heard a voice from a distance, hallooing, "Rip Van Winkle! Rip Van Winkle!" He looked around, but could see nothing but a crow winging its solitary flight across the mountain. He thought his fancy must have deceived him, and turned again to descend, when he heard the same cry ring through the still evening air; "Rip Van Winkle! Rip Van Winkle!"—at the same time Wolf bristled up his back, and giving a low growl, skulked to his master's side, looking fearfully down into the glen. Rip now felt a vague apprehension stealing over him; he looked anxiously in the same direction, and perceived a strange figure slowly toiling up the rocks, and bending under the weight of something he carried on his back. He was surprised to see any human being in this lonely and unfrequented place, but supposing it to be some one of the neighbourhood in need of his assistance, he hastened down to yield it.

On nearer approach, he was still more surprised at the singularity of the stranger's appearance. He was a short square built old fellow, with thick bushy hair, and a grizzled beard. His dress was of the antique Dutch fashion—a cloth jerkin strapped round the waist—several pair of breeches, the outer one of ample volume, decorated with rows of buttons down the sides, and bunches at the knees. He bore on his shoulder a stout keg, that seemed full of liquor, and made signs for Rip

---

[1] pack.

to approach and assist him with the load. Though rather shy and distrustful of this new acquaintance, Rip complied with his usual alacrity, and mutually relieving each other, they clambered up a narrow gully, apparently the dry bed of a mountain torrent. As they ascended, Rip every now and then heard long rolling peals, like distant thunder, that seemed to issue out of a deep ravine, or rather cleft between lofty rocks, toward which their rugged path conducted. He paused for an instant, but supposing it to be the muttering of one of those transient thunder showers which often take place in mountain heights, he proceeded. Passing through the ravine, they came to a hollow, like a small amphitheatre, surrounded by perpendicular precipices, over the brinks of which impending trees shot their branches, so that you only caught glimpses of the azure sky, and the bright evening cloud. During the whole time, Rip and his companion had laboured on in silence; for though the former marvelled greatly what could be the object of carrying a keg of liquor up this wild mountain, yet there was something strange and incomprehensible about the unknown, that inspired awe, and checked familiarity.

On entering the ampitheatre, new objects of wonder presented themselves. On a level spot in the centre was a company of odd-looking personages playing at nine-pins. They were dressed in a quaint, outlandish fashion: some wore short doublets, others jerkins, with long knives in their belts, and most had enormous breeches, of similar style with that of the guide's. Their visages, too, were peculiar: one had a large head, broad face, and small piggish eyes; the face of another seemed to consist entirely of nose, and was surmounted by a white sugarloaf hat, set off with a little red cockstail. They all had beards, of various shapes and colours. There was one who seemed to be the commander. He was a stout old gentleman, with a weather-beaten countenance; he wore a laced doublet, broad belt and hanger, high crowned hat and feather, red stockings, and high heeled shoes, with roses in them. The whole group reminded Rip of the figures in an old Flemish painting, in the parlour of Dominie Van Schaick, the village parson, and which had been brought over from Holland at the time of the settlement.

What seemed particularly odd to Rip, was, that though these folks were evidently amusing themselves, yet they maintained the gravest faces, the most mysterious silence, and were, withal, the most melancholy party of pleasure he had ever witnessed. Nothing interrupted the stillness of the scene, but the noise of the balls, which, whenever they were rolled, echoed along the mountains like rumbling peals of thunder.

As Rip and his companion approached them, they suddenly desisted from their play, and stared at him with such fixed statue-like gaze, and such strange, uncouth, lack lustre countenances, that his heart turned within him, and his knees smote together. His companion now emptied the contents of the keg into large flagons, and made signs to him to wait upon the company. He obeyed with fear and trembling; they quaffed the liquor in profound silence, and then returned to their game.

By degrees, Rip's awe and apprehension subsided. He even ventured, when no eye was fixed upon him, to taste the beverage, which he found had much of the flavour of excellent Hollands.[1] He was naturally a thirsty soul, and was soon tempted to repeat the draught. One taste provoked another, and he reiterated his visits to the flagon so often, that at length his senses were overpowered, his eyes swam in his head, his head gradually declined, and he fell into a deep sleep.

On awakening, he found himself on the green knoll from whence he had first seen the old man of the glen. He rubbed his eyes—it was a bright sunny morning. The birds were hopping and twittering among the bushes, and the eagle was wheeling aloft, and breasting the pure mountain breeze. "Surely," thought Rip, "I have not slept here all night." He recalled the occurrences before he fell asleep. The strange man with the keg of liquor—the mountain ravine—the wild retreat among the rocks—the wo-begone party at nine-pins—the flagon—"Oh! that flagon! that wicked flagon!" thought Rip—"what excuse shall I make to Dame Van Winkle?"

He looked round for his gun, but in place of the clean well-oiled fowling-piece, he found an old firelock

---

[1] Dutch gin.

lying by him, the barrel encrusted with rust, the lock falling off, and the stock worm-eaten. He now suspected that the grave roysters of the mountain had put a trick upon him, and having dosed him with liquor, had robbed him of his gun. Wolf, too, had disappeared, but he might have strayed away after a squirrel or partridge. He whistled after him, shouted his name, but all in vain; the echoes repeated his whistle and shout, but no dog was to be seen.

He determined to revisit the scene of the last evening's gambol, and if he met with any of the party, to demand his dog and gun. As he arose to walk he found himself stiff in the joints, and wanting in his usual activity. "These mountain beds do not agree with me," thought Rip, "and if this frolick should lay me up with a fit of the rheumatism, I shall have a blessed time with Dame Van Winkle." With some difficulty he got down into the glen: he found the gully up which he and his companion had ascended the preceding evening, but to his astonishment a mountain stream was now foaming down it, leaping from rock to rock, and filling the glen with babbling murmurs. He, however, made shift to scramble up its sides, working his toilsome way through thickets of birch, sassafras, and witch hazle, and sometimes tripped up or entangled by the wild grape vines that twisted their coils and tendrils from tree to tree, and spread a kind of network in his path.

At length he reached to where the ravine had opened through the cliffs, to the amphitheatre; but no traces of such opening remained. The rocks presented a high impenetrable wall, over which the torrent came tumbling in a sheet of feathery foam, and fell into a broad deep basin, black from the shadows of the surrounding forest. Here, then, poor Rip was brought to a stand. He again called and whistled after his dog; he was only answered by the cawing of a flock of idle crows, sporting high in air about a dry tree that overhung a sunny precipice; and who, secure in their elevation, seemed to look down and scoff at the poor man's perplexities. What was to be done? the morning was passing away, and Rip felt famished for his breakfast. He grieved to give up his dog and gun; he dreaded to meet his wife; but it would not do to starve among the mountains. He shook his head, shouldered the rusty firelock, and, with a heart full of trouble and anxiety, turned his steps homeward.

As he approached the village, he met a number of people, but none that he knew, which somewhat surprised him, for he had thought himself acquainted with every one in the country round. Their dress, too, was of a different fashion from that to which he was accustomed. They all stared at him with equal marks of surprise, and whenever they cast eyes upon him, invariably stroked their chins. The constant recurrence of this gesture, induced Rip, involuntarily, to do the same, when, to his astonishment, he found his beard had grown a foot long!

He had now entered the skirts of the village. A troop of strange children ran at his heels, hooting after him, and pointing at his gray beard. The dogs, too, not one of which he recognized for his old acquaintances, barked at him as he passed. The very village seemed altered: it was larger and more populous. There were rows of houses which he had never seen before, and those which had been his familiar haunts had disappeared. Strange names were over the doors—strange faces at the windows—every thing was strange. His mind now began to misgive him, that both he and the world around him were bewitched. Surely this was his native village, which he had left but the day before. There stood the Kaatskill mountains—there ran the silver Hudson at a distance—there was every hill and dale precisely as it had always been—Rip was sorely perplexed—"That flagon last night," thought he, "has addled my poor head sadly!"

It was with some difficulty he found the way to his own house, which he approached with silent awe, expecting every moment to hear the shrill voice of Dame Van Winkle. He found the house gone to decay—the roof fallen in, the windows shattered, and the doors off the hinges. A half starved dog that looked like Wolf, was skulking about it. Rip called him by name, but the cur snarled, showed his teeth, and passed on. This was an unkind cut indeed—"My very dog," sighed poor Rip, "has forgotten me!"

He entered the house, which, to tell the truth, Dame Van Winkle had always kept in neat order. It was empty, forlorn, and apparently abandoned. This desolateness overcame all his connubial fears—he called loudly for his wife and children—the lonely chambers rung for a moment with his voice, and then all again was silence.

He now hurried forth, and hastened to his old resort, the little village inn—but it too was gone. A large rickety wooden building stood in its place, with great gaping windows, some of them broken, and mended with old hats and petticoats, and over the door was painted, "The Union Hotel, by Jonathan Doolittle." Instead of the great tree that used to shelter the quiet little Dutch inn of yore, there now was reared a tall naked pole, with something on top that looked like a red night cap,[1] and from it was fluttering a flag, on which was a singular assemblage of stars and stripes—all this was strange and incomprehensible. He recognised on the sign, however, the ruby face of King George, under which he had smoked so many a peaceful pipe, but even this was singularly metamorphosed. The red coat was changed for one of blue and buff, a sword was stuck in the hand instead of a sceptre, the head was decorated with a cocked hat, and underneath was painted in large characters, GENERAL WASHINGTON.

There was, as usual, a crowd of folk about the door, but none that Rip recollected. The very character of the people seemed changed. There was a busy, bustling, disputatious tone about it, instead of the accustomed phlegm and drowsy tranquillity. He looked in vain for the sage Nicholas Vedder, with his broad face, double chin, and fair long pipe, uttering clouds of tobacco smoke instead of idle speeches; or Van Bummel, the schoolmaster, doling forth the contents of an ancient newspaper. In place of these, a lean bilious looking fellow, with his pockets full of handbills, was haranguing vehemently about rights of citizens—elections—members of congress—liberty—Bunker's hill[2]— heroes of seventy-six—and other words, that were a perfect Babylonish jargon[3] to the bewildered Van Winkle.

The appearance of Rip, with his long grizzled beard, his rusty fowling piece, his uncouth dress, and the army of women and children that had gathered at his heels, soon attracted the attention of the tavern politicians. They crowded around him, eyeing him from head to foot, with great curiosity. The orator bustled up to him, and drawing him partly aside, inquired "which side he voted?" Rip stared in vacant stupidity. Another short but busy little fellow pulled him by the arm, and raising on tiptoe, inquired in his ear, "whether he was Federal or Democrat."[4] Rip was equally at a loss to comprehend the question; when a knowing, self-important old gentleman, in a sharp cocked hat, made his way through the crowd, putting them to the right and left with his elbows as he passed, and planting himself before Van Winkle, with one arm akimbo, the other resting on his cane, his keen eyes and sharp hat penetrating, as it were, into his very soul, demanded, in an austere tone, "what brought him to the election with a gun on his shoulder, and a mob at his heels, and whether he meant to breed a riot in the village?" "Alas! gentlemen," cried Rip, somewhat dismayed, "I am a poor quiet man, a native of the place, and a loyal subject of the King, God bless him!"

Here a general shout burst from the bystanders—"A tory![5] a tory! a spy! a refugee! hustle him! away with him!" It was with great difficulty that the self-important man in the cocked hat restored order; and having assumed a tenfold austerity of brow, demanded again of the unknown culprit, what he came there for, and whom he was seeking. The poor man humbly assured him that he meant no harm; but merely came there in search of some of his neighbours, who used to keep about the tavern.

"Well—who are they?—name them."

Rip bethought himself a moment, and inquired, "Where's Nicholas Vedder?"

There was a silence for a little while, when an old man replied, in a thin piping voice, "Nicholas Vedder? why he is dead and gone these eighteen years! There was a wooden tombstone in the church yard that used to tell all about him, but that's rotten and gone too."

---

[1] a Phrygian cap, a symbol of both the American and the French Revolutions.

[2] Bunker Hill, an early British victory (17 June 1775) in the Revolutionary War.

[3] Babel nonsense: Genesis 11.1–9.

[4] the rival political parties in post-Revolutionary America.

[5] British Loyalist.

"Where's Brom Dutcher?"

"Oh he went off to the army in the beginning of the war; some say he was killed at the battle of Stoney-Point—others say he was drowned in a squall, at the foot of Antony's Nose.[1] I don't know—he never came back again."

"Where's Van Bummel, the schoolmaster?"

"He went off to the wars too, was a great militia general, and is now in Congress."

Rip's heart died away, at hearing of these sad changes in his home and friends, and finding himself thus alone in the world. Every answer puzzled him, too, by treating of such enormous lapses of time, and of matters which he could not understand: war—congress—Stoney-Point;—he had no courage to ask after any more friends, but cried out in despair, "does nobody here know Rip Van Winkle?"

"Oh, Rip Van Winkle!" exclaimed two or three, "Oh, to be sure! that's Rip Van Winkle yonder, leaning against the tree."

Rip looked, and beheld a precise counterpart of himself, as he went up the mountain: apparently as lazy, and certainly as ragged. The poor fellow was now completely confounded. He doubted his own identity, and whether he was himself or another man. In the midst of his bewilderment, the man in the cocked hat demanded who he was, and what was his name?

"God knows," exclaimed he, at his wit's end; "I'm not myself—I'm somebody else—that's me yonder— no—that's somebody else, got into my shoes—I was myself last night, but I fell asleep on the mountain, and they've changed my gun, and every thing's changed, and I'm changed, and I can't tell what's my name, or who I am!"

The bystanders began now to look at each other, nod, wink significantly, and tap their fingers against their foreheads. There was a whisper, also, about securing the gun, and keeping the old fellow from doing mischief. At the very suggestion of which, the self-important man in the cocked hat retired with some precipitation. At this critical moment a fresh likely woman pressed through the throng to get a peep at the graybearded man. She had a chubby child in her arms, which, frightened at his looks, began to cry. "Hush, Rip," cried she, "hush, you little fool, the old man wont hurt you." The name of the child, the air of the mother, the tone of her voice, all awakened a train of recollections in his mind. "What is your name, my good woman?" asked he.

"Judith Gardenier."

"And your father's name?"

"Ah, poor man, his name was Rip Van Winkle; it's twenty years since he went away from home with his gun, and never has been heard of since—his dog came home without him; but whether he shot himself, or was carried away by the Indians, nobody can tell. I was then but a little girl."

Rip had but one question more to ask; but he put it with a faltering voice:

"Where's your mother?"

Oh, she too had died but a short time since; she broke a blood vessel in a fit of passion at a New-England pedlar.

There was a drop of comfort, at least, in this intelligence. The honest man could contain himself no longer.—He caught his daughter and her child in his arms.—"I am your father!" cried he—"Young Rip Van Winkle once—old Rip Van Winkle now!—Does nobody know poor Rip Van Winkle!"

All stood amazed, until an old woman, tottering out from among the crowd, put her hand to her brow, and peering under it in his face for a moment, exclaimed, "Sure enough! it is Rip Van Winkle—it is himself. Welcome home again, old neighbour—Why, where have you been these twenty long years?"

Rip's story was soon told, for the whole twenty years had been to him but as one night. The neighbours stared when they heard it; some were seen to wink at each other, and put their tongues in their cheeks; and the self-important man in the cocked hat, who, when the alarm was over, had returned to the field, screwed down the corners of his mouth, and shook his head—upon which there was a general shaking of the head throughout the assemblage.

It was determined, however, to take the opinion of old Peter Vanderdonk, who was seen slowly advancing up the road. He was a descendant of the historian of

---

[1] two strategically important promontories on the Hudson, the sites of battles in 1779 and 1777.

that name,[1] who wrote one of the earliest accounts of the province. Peter was the most ancient inhabitant of the village, and well versed in all the wonderful events and traditions of the neighbourhood. He recollected Rip at once, and corroborated his story in the most satisfactory manner. He assured the company that it was a fact, handed down from his ancestor the historian, that the Kaatskill mountains had always been haunted by strange beings. That it was affirmed that the great Hendrick Hudson,[2] the first discoverer of the river and country, kept a kind of vigil there every twenty years, with his crew of the Half-moon, being permitted in this way to revisit the scenes of his enterprize, and keep a guardian eye upon the river, and the great city called by his name. That his father had once seen them in their old Dutch dresses playing at nine pins in a hollow of the mountain; and that he himself had heard, one summer afternoon, the sound of their balls, like long peals of thunder.

To make a long story short, the company broke up, and returned to the more important concerns of the election. Rip's daughter took him home to live with her; she had a snug, well-furnished house, and a stout cheery farmer for a husband, whom Rip recollected for one of the urchins that used to climb upon his back. As to Rip's son and heir, who was the ditto of himself, seen leaning against the tree, he was employed to work on the farm; but evinced an hereditary disposition to attend to any thing else but his business.

Rip now resumed his old walks and habits; he soon found many of his former cronies, though all rather the worse for the wear and tear of time; and preferred making friends among the rising generation, with whom he soon grew into great favour.

Having nothing to do at home, and being arrived at that happy age when a man can do nothing with impunity, he took his place once more on the bench, at the inn door, and was reverenced as one of the patriarchs of the village, and a chronicle of the old times "before the war." It was some time before he could get into the regular track of gossip, or could be made to comprehend the strange events that had taken place during his torpor. How that there had been a revolutionary war—that the country had thrown off the yoke of old England—and that, instead of being a subject of his Majesty George the Third, he was now a free citizen of the United States. Rip, in fact, was no politician; the changes of states and empires made but little impression on him. But there was one species of despotism under which he had long groaned, and that was—petticoat government. Happily, that was at an end; he had got his neck out of the yoke of matrimony, and could go in and out whenever he pleased, without dreading the tyranny of Dame Van Winkle. Whenever her name was mentioned, however, he shook his head, shrugged his shoulders, and cast up his eyes; which might pass either for an expression of resignation to his fate, or joy at his deliverance.

He used to tell his story to every stranger that arrived at Mr. Doolittle's hotel. He was observed, at first, to vary on some points every time he told it, which was, doubtless, owing to his having so recently awaked. It at last settled down precisely to the tale I have related, and not a man, woman, or child in the neighbourhood, but knew it by heart. Some always pretended to doubt the reality of it, and insisted that Rip had been out of his head, and that this was one point on which he always remained flighty. The old Dutch inhabitants, however, almost universally gave it full credit. Even to this day they never hear a thunder storm of a summer afternoon, about the Kaatskill, but they say Hendrick Hudson and his crew are at their game of nine pins; and it is a common wish of all henpecked husbands in the neighbourhood, when life hangs heavy on their hands, that they might have a quieting draught out of Rip Van Winkle's flagon.[3]

---

[1] Adriaen Van der Donck (1620?–55), author of a history of New Netherland (1655).

[2] Henry Hudson (d. 1611) explored the river now named after him in 1609. In 1611, a mutinous crew set him adrift in Hudson Bay.

[3] In a brief postscript, Irving explains that his story is based on the legend of Frederick Barbarossa (1123–90), Holy Roman Emperor (1152–90), who was supposed to be sleeping in a mountain cave until Germany needed him again.

Leigh Hunt
1784 – 1859

James Henry Leigh Hunt was born on 19 October 1784, the son of Isaac Hunt, a Barbadian lawyer, and Mary Shewell Hunt, daughter of a Philadelphia merchant. Loyalists, they had come to England when the Revolutionary War started, and Isaac became an Anglican preacher; Hunt was their first English-born child. Like Coleridge* and Charles Lamb,* he was educated at Christ's Hospital. He published *Juvenilia*, the first of his forty-odd volumes of verse, criticism, drama, essays, fiction, and memoirs, in 1801. In 1805, he and his brother John founded their first periodical, the *News*. He went on to edit a number of periodicals, of which the most important were the *Examiner*, which he edited from 1808 until 1821, and the *Liberal* (1822–23), a collaborative project with Byron* and P.B. Shelley,* which because of Shelley's untimely death, lasted for only four issues. In July 1809, after courting her for eight years, Hunt married Marianne Kent; they had eleven children. In 1812, Hunt published in the *Examiner* an article on the Prince Regent describing him as, among other things, a fat, fifty-year-old libertine; he and his brother were each sentenced to two years in prison and a fine of £500. Hunt went on editing the *Examiner* in prison and wrote his most important poem, *The Story of Rimini* (1816), there; he even turned his cell into a sort of salon, decorating it beautifully and receiving visits from Jeremy Bentham, Byron, Edgeworth,* Hazlitt,* Charles and Mary Lamb,* James Mill, and Moore.* His later works include *Lord Byron and Some of his Contemporaries* (1828), which was attacked for its unflattering portrayal of Byron; the antiwar poem *Captain Sword and Captain Pen* (1835); and his own favourite among his poems, "Abou Ben Adhem" (1838). His last years were darkened by the deaths of his son Vincent (1852) and of his wife (1857), and by the caricature of him, as Harold Skimpole, in *Bleak House* (1853), by his friend Dickens. He died on 28 August 1859, on a trip to the country. Over a long career as a poet, critic, and editor, he had discovered Keats,* Browning, and Tennyson and supported Lamb, Hazlitt, Shelley, and Dickens. (D.L.M.)

❦

from *The Story of Rimini* (1816)[1]

from Canto 3

One day,—'twas on a summer afternoon,
505 When airs and gurgling brooks are best in tune,
And grasshoppers are loud, and day-work done,
And shades have heavy outlines in the sun,—
The princess came to her accustomed bower
To get her, if she could, a soothing hour,
510 Trying, as she was used, to leave her cares
Without, and slumberously enjoy the airs,
And the low-talking leaves, and that cool light
The vines let in, and all that hushing sight
Of closing wood seen through the opening door,
515 And distant plash of waters tumbling o'er,
And smell of citron blooms, and fifty luxuries more.

She tried, as usual, for the trial's sake,
For even that diminished her heart-ache;
And never yet, how ill soe'er at ease,
520 Came she for nothing 'midst the flowers and trees.
Yet somehow or another, on that day,
She seemed to feel too lightly borne away,—
Too much relieved,—too much inclined to draw
A careless joy from every thing she saw,
525 And looking round her with a new-born eye,
As if some tree of knowledge[2] had been nigh,
To taste of nature, primitive and free,
And bask at ease in her heart's liberty.

---

[1] based on the story of Paolo and Francesca in Dante, *Inferno* 5.121–38, to which this excerpt directly corresponds. Francesca is married to Paolo's brother, son of the lord of Rimini, who discovers the affair and stabs them to death.

[2] Cf. Genesis 2.16–17, 3.1–24.

	Painfully clear those rising thoughts appeared,
530	With something dark at bottom that she feared;
	And snatching from the fields her thoughtful look,
	She reached o'er-head, and took her down a book,
	And fell to reading with as fixed an air,
	As though she had been wrapt since morning there.
535	'Twas Launcelot of the Lake,[1] a bright romance,
	That like a trumpet, made young pulses dance,
	Yet had a softer note that shook still more;—
	She had begun it but the day before,
	And read with a full heart, half sweet, half sad,
540	How old King Ban[2] was spoiled of all he had
	But one fair castle: how one summer's day
	With his fair queen and child he went away
	To ask the great King Arthur for assistance;
	How reaching by himself a hill at distance
545	He turned to give his castle a last look,
	And saw its far white face: and how a smoke,
	As he was looking, burst in volumes forth,
	And good King Ban saw all that he was worth,
	And his fair castle, burning to the ground,
550	So that his wearied pulse felt over-wound,
	And he lay down, and said a prayer apart
	For those he loved, and broke his poor old heart.
	Then read she of the queen with her young child,
	How she came up, and nearly had gone wild,
555	And how in journeying on in her despair,
	She reached a lake and met a lady there,
	Who pitied her, and took the baby sweet
	Into her arms, when lo, with closing feet
	She sprang up all at once, like bird from brake,
560	And vanished with him underneath the lake.
	The mother's feelings we as well may pass:—
	The fairy of the place that lady was,
	And Launcelot (so the boy was called) became
	Her inmate, till in search of knightly fame
565	He went to Arthur's court, and played his part
	So rarely, and displayed so frank a heart,
	That what with all his charms of look and limb,

	The Queen Geneura fell in love with him:—
	And here, with growing interest in her reading,
570	The princess, doubly fixed, was now proceeding.
	Ready she sat with one hand to turn o'er
	The leaf, to which her thoughts ran on before,
	The other propping her white brow, and throwing
	Its ringlets out, under the skylight glowing.
575	So sat she fixed; and so observed was she
	Of one, who at the door stood tenderly,—
	Paulo,—who from a window seeing her
	Go strait across the lawn, and guessing where,
	Had thought she was in tears, and found, that day,
580	His usual efforts vain to keep away.
	"May I come in?" said he:—it made her start,—
	That smiling voice;—she coloured, pressed her heart
	A moment, as for breath, and then with free
	And usual tone said, "O yes,—certainly."
585	There's apt to be, at conscious times like these,
	An affectation of a bright-eyed ease,
	An air of something quite serene and sure,
	As if to seem so, was to be, secure:
	With this the lovers met, with this they spoke,
590	With this they sat down to the self-same book,
	And Paulo, by degrees, gently embraced
	With one permitted arm her lovely waist;
	And both their cheeks, like peaches on a tree,
	Leaned with a touch together, thrillingly;
595	And o'er the book they hung, and nothing said,
	And every lingering page grew longer as they read.
	As thus they sat, and felt with leaps of heart
	Their colour change, they came upon the part
	Where fond Geneura, with her flame long nurst,
600	Smiled upon Launcelot when he kissed her first:—
	That touch, at last, through every fibre slid;
	And Paulo turned, scarce knowing what he did,
	Only he felt he could no more dissemble,
	And kissed her, mouth to mouth, all in a tremble.
605	Sad were those hearts, and sweet was that long kiss:
	Sacred be love from sight, whate'er it is.
	The world was all forgot, the struggle o'er,
	Desperate the joy.—That day they read no more.

---

[1] a medieval romance about Sir Lancelot, the greatest knight in King Arthur's court, but also the lover of his consort, Guinevere (Hunt calls her Geneura).

[2] one of King Arthur's vassals, the king of Benwick, Brittany, and father of Lancelot.

Leigh Hunt

from the *Examiner* (21 September 1817)

Green little vaulter in the sunny grass[1]

Green little vaulter in the sunny grass,
   Catching your heart up at the feel of June,
   Sole voice left stirring midst the lazy noon,
When ev'n the bees lag at the summoning brass;—
5 And you, warm little housekeeper, who class
   With those who think the candles come too soon,
   Loving the fire, and with your tricksome tune
Nick the glad silent moments as they pass;—
O sweet and tiny cousins, that belong,
10   One to the fields, the other to the hearth,
Both have your sunshine; both though small are
     strong
   At your clear hearts; and both were sent on earth
To ring in thoughtful ears this natural song
   —In doors and out,—summer and winter,—Mirth.

from *Foliage* (1818)

To Percy Shelley, on the Degrading Notions of Deity

What wonder, Percy, that with jealous rage
   Men should defame the kindly and the wise,
   When in the midst of the all-beauteous skies,
And all this lovely world, that should engage
5 Their mutual search for the old golden age,
   They seat a phantom, swelled into grim size
   Out of their own passions and bigotries,
And then, for fear, proclaim it meek and sage!

And this they call a light and a revealing!
10   Wise as the clown, who plodding home at night
   In autumn, turns at call of fancied elf,
And sees upon the fog, with ghastly feeling,
   A giant shadow in it's imminent might,
Which his own lanthorn throws up from himself.

---

[1] published together with Keats's "The poetry of earth is never dead"* under the title "Two Sonnets on the Grasshopper and Cricket."

from S.C. Hall, *Book of Gems* (1838)

Abou Ben Adhem and the Angel[2]

Abou Ben Adhem (may his tribe increase!)
 Awoke one night from a deep dream of peace,
And saw, within the moonlight in his room,
Making it rich, and like a lily in bloom,
5 An angel, writing in a book of gold;
Exceeding peace had made Ben Adhem bold:
And to the presence in the room he said,
"What writest thou?" The vision rais'd its head,
And, with a look made of all sweet accord,
10 Answer'd, "The names of those who love the Lord."
"And is mine one?" said Abou. "Nay, not so";
Replied the angel. Abou spoke more low,
But cheerly still; and said, "I pray thee, then,
Write me as one that loves his fellow-men."

15   The angel wrote and vanished. The next night
It came again, with a great wakening light,
And shew'd the names whom love of God had bless'd,
And lo! Ben Adhem's name led all the rest.

from the *Morning Chronicle* 2 (November 1838)

Rondeau[3]

Nelly[4] kiss'd me when we met,
   Jumping from the chair she sat in;
Time, you thief! who love to get
   Sweets into your list, put *that* in.
5 Say I'm jaundic'd, say I'm sad,
   Say that health and wealth have miss'd me,
Say I'm growing old, but add,
   Nelly kiss'd me.

---

[2] based on an anecdote in Barthélémy d'Herbelot (1625–95), *Bibliothèque orientale* (1697).

[3] a French verse form that uses the opening words as a refrain (Hunt's poem is only an approximation of the form).

[4] first published at the end of an essay on Pope in the *Morning Chronicle*. When he reprinted the poem in 1844, Hunt changed "Nelly" to "Jenny." His friend Jane Welsh Carlyle (1801–66) was worried when he became ill during an epidemic of influenza; on his recovery, he went to tell her the good news.

Thomas De Quincey
1785 — 1859

Born in Manchester in 1785 to an affluent linen merchant and his wife, De Quincey was well-educated and earned a reputation as an outstanding student of the classics. At the age of seventeen, however, he ran away from home and spent several months poverty stricken on the streets of London. In 1804, he reconciled with his family and started at Oxford, where he began to experiment with opium, a drug he initially took for neuralgia. By 1813, he was dependent on opium, which he took in the form of laudanum, an inexpensive tincture of alcohol and opium available without a prescription.

After leaving Oxford in 1808 without a degree, De Quincey moved to the Lake District to live near Wordsworth* and Southey,* but he soon lost contact with them. He married Margaret Simpson, the mother of his illegitimate child, in 1816. Between 1818 and 1819, he was editor for the *Westmoreland Magazine* but was dismissed. He then began work for *Blackwood's Edinburgh Magazine* and moved to Edinburgh in the hopes of becoming a regular contributor. However, because of an argument, De Quincey also severed his connections with *Blackwood's*. He left for London and offered to write a piece on his opium experiences for *The London Magazine*; in 1821, the magazine published what would become his best known work, *Confessions of an English Opium Eater*.

Although De Quincey wrote more than two hundred magazine articles, his *Confessions* became an instant success and is the work for which he is most remembered. The success of the autobiography lies, in part, in De Quincey's vivid descriptions of his opium-induced dreams and hallucinations. After the publication of *Confessions*, De Quincey continued to earn a living as a journalist, but he was plagued by financial difficulties and was jailed several times for his debts. He returned to Edinburgh in 1830, becoming still more addicted to opium. Between 1832 and 1837, he lost two of his sons and his wife. *Suspiria de Profundis*, the sequel to *Confessions*, was published in 1845; in 1850, publishers began to release his collected works. He died in Edinburgh in 1859. (J.G.)

❧❧❧

from the *London Magazine* 4 (September 1821)

from *Confessions of an English Opium-Eater: Being an Extract from the Life of a Scholar*

I have often been asked, how I first came to be a regular opium-eater; and have suffered, very unjustly, in the opinion of my acquaintance, from being reputed to have brought upon myself all the sufferings which I shall have to record, by a long course of indulgence in this practice purely for the sake of creating an artificial state of pleasurable excitement. This, however, is a misrepresentation of my case. True it is, that for nearly ten years I did occasionally take opium, for the sake of the exquisite pleasure it gave me: but, so long as I took it with this view, I was effectually protected from all material bad consequences, by the necessity of interposing long intervals between the several acts of indulgence, in order to renew the pleasurable sensations. It was not for the purpose of creating pleasure, but of mitigating pain in the severest degree, that I first began to use opium as an article of daily diet. In the twenty-eighth year of my age, a most painful affection of the stomach, which I had first experienced about ten years before, attacked me in great strength. This affection had originally been caused by extremities of hunger, suffered in my boyish days. During the season of hope and redundant happiness which succeeded (that is, from eighteen to twenty-four) it had slumbered: for the three following years it had revived at intervals: and now, under unfavourable circumstances, from depression of spirits, it attacked me with a violence that yielded to no remedies but opium. As the youthful sufferings, which first produced this derangement of the stomach, were interesting in themselves, and in the circumstances that attended them, I shall here briefly retrace them....

... I contrived, by means which I must omit for want of room, to transfer myself to London. And now began the latter and fiercer stage of my long-sufferings; without using a disproportionate expression I might say, of my agony. For I now suffered, for upwards of sixteen weeks, the physical anguish of hunger in various degrees of intensity; but as bitter, perhaps, as ever any human being can have suffered who has survived it. I would not needlessly harass my reader's feelings, by a detail of all that I endured: for extremities such as these, under any circumstances of heaviest misconduct or guilt, cannot be contemplated, even in description, without a rueful pity that is painful to the natural goodness of the human heart. Let it suffice, at least on this occasion, to say, that a few fragments of bread from the breakfast-table of one individual (who supposed me to be ill, but did not know of my being in utter want), and these at uncertain intervals, constituted my whole support. During the former part of my sufferings (that is, generally in Wales, and always for the first two months in London) I was houseless, and very seldom slept under a roof. To this constant exposure to the open air I ascribe it mainly, that I did not sink under my torments. Latterly, however, when colder and more inclement weather came on, and when, from the length of my sufferings, I had begun to sink into a more languishing condition, it was, no doubt, fortunate for me, that the same person to whose breakfast-table I had access, allowed me to sleep in a large unoccupied house, of which he was tenant. Unoccupied, I call it, for there was no household or establishment in it; nor any furniture, indeed, except a table, and a few chairs. But I found, on taking possession of my new quarters, that the house already contained one single inmate, a poor friendless child, apparently ten years old; but she seemed hunger-bitten; and sufferings of that sort often make children look older than they are. From this forlorn child I learned, that she had slept and lived there alone, for some time before I came: and great joy the poor creature expressed, when she found that I was, in future, to be her companion through the hours of darkness. The house was large; and, from the want of furniture, the noise of the rats made a prodigious echoing on the spacious stair-case and hall; and, amidst the real fleshly ills of cold, and, I fear, hunger, the forsaken child had found leisure to suffer still more (it appeared) from the self-created one of ghosts. I promised her protection against all ghosts whatsoever: but, alas! I could offer her no other assistance. We lay upon the floor, with a bundle of cursed law papers for a pillow: but with no other covering than a sort of large horseman's cloak: afterwards, however, we discovered, in a garret, an old sofa-cover, a small piece of rug, and some fragments of other articles, which added a little to our warmth. The poor child crept close to me for warmth, and for security against her ghostly enemies. When I was not more than usually ill, I took her into my arms, so that, in general, she was tolerably warm, and often slept when I could not: for, during the last two months of my sufferings, I slept much in the daytime, and was apt to fall into transient dozings at all hours. But my sleep distressed me more than my watching: for, besides the tumultuousness of my dreams (which were only not so awful as those which I shall have to describe hereafter as produced by opium), my sleep was never more than what is called *dog-sleep*; so that I could hear myself moaning, and was often, as it seemed to me, wakened suddenly by my own voice; and, about this time, a hideous sensation began to haunt me as soon as I fell into a slumber, which has since returned upon me, at different periods of my life, viz.[1] a sort of twitching (I know not where, but apparently about the region of the stomach), which compelled me violently to throw out my feet for the sake of relieving it. This sensation coming on as soon as I began to sleep, and the effort to relieve it constantly awaking me, at length I slept only from exhaustion; and from increasing weakness (as I said before) I was constantly falling asleep, and constantly awaking. Meantime, the master of the house sometimes came in upon us suddenly, and very early, sometimes not till ten o'clock, sometimes not at all. He was in constant fear of bailiffs: improving on the plan of Cromwell,[2] every night he slept in a different quarter of London; and I observed that he never failed to examine, through a private window, the appearance of those who knocked at the door, before he would allow it to be opened. He breakfasted alone: indeed, his tea equipage would hardly have admitted of his hazarding an invita-

---

[1] short for *videlicet* (L.): "namely."

[2] Oliver Cromwell (1599–1658) led the armies of Parliament against King Charles I in the British Civil War (1642–48); later, he was Lord Protector (dictator) of Britain. As a commander, he was noted for his ability to move his troops rapidly from one location to another.

tion to a second person—any more than the quantity of esculent *matériel* which, for the most part, was little more than a roll, or a few biscuits, which he had bought on his road from the place where he had slept. Or, if he *had* asked a party, as I once learnedly and facetiously observed to him—the several members of it must have *stood* in the relation to each other (not sate in any relation whatever) of succession, as the metaphysicians have it, and not of co-existence; in the relation of the parts of time, and not of the parts of space. During his breakfast, I generally contrived a reason for lounging in; and, with an air of as much indifference as I could assume, took up such fragments as he had left—sometimes, indeed, there were none at all. In doing this, I committed no robbery except upon the man himself, who was thus obliged (I believe) now and then to send out at noon for an extra biscuit; for, as to the poor child, *she* was never admitted into his study (if I may give that name to his chief depository of parchments, law writings, &c.); that room was to her the Blue-beard room[1] of the house, being regularly locked on his departure to dinner, about six o'clock, which usually was his final departure for the night. Whether this child were an illegitimate daughter of Mr. ——, or only a servant, I could not ascertain; she did not herself know; but certainly she was treated altogether as a menial servant. No sooner did Mr. —— make his appearance, than she went below stairs, brushed his shoes, coat, &c.; and, except when she was summoned to run an errand, she never emerged from the dismal Tartarus[2] of the kitchens, &c. to the upper air, until my welcome knock at night called up her little trembling footsteps to the front door. Of her life during the day-time, however, I knew little but what I gathered from her own account at night; for, as soon as the hours of business commenced, I saw that my absence would be acceptable; and, in general, therefore, I went off and sate in the parks, or elsewhere, until night-fall....

This I regret, but another person there was at that time, whom I have since sought to trace with far deeper earnestness, and with far deeper sorrow at my failure.

This person was a young woman, and one of the unhappy class who subsist upon the wages of prostitution. I feel no shame, nor have any reason to feel it, in avowing, that I was then on familiar and friendly terms with many women in that unfortunate condition. The reader needs neither smile at this avowal, nor frown. For, not to remind my classical readers of the old Latin proverb—"*Sine Cerere,*"[3] &c., it may well be supposed that in the existing state of my purse, my connexion with such women could not have been an impure one. But the truth is, that at no time of my life have I been a person to hold myself polluted by the touch or approach of any creature that wore a human shape: on the contrary, from my very earliest youth it has been my pride to converse familiarly, *more Socratico,*[4] with all human beings, man, woman, and child, that chance might fling in my way: a practice which is friendly to the knowledge of human nature, to good feelings, and to that frankness of address which becomes a man who would be thought a philosopher. For a philosopher should not see with the eyes of the poor limitary creature calling himself a man of the world, and filled with narrow and self-regarding prejudices of birth and education, but should look upon himself as a Catholic creature, and as standing in an equal relation to high and low—to educated and uneducated, to the guilty and the innocent. Being myself at that time of necessity a peripatetic, or a walker of the streets, I naturally fell in more frequently with those female peripatetics who are technically called Street-walkers. Many of these women had occasionally taken my part against watchmen who wished to drive me off the steps of houses where I was sitting. But one amongst them, the one on whose account I have at all introduced this subject—yet no! let me not class thee, Oh noble-minded Ann——, with that order of women; let me find, if it be possible, some gentler name to designate the condition of her to whose bounty and compassion, ministering to my necessities when all the world had forsaken me, I owe it that I am at this time alive.—For many weeks I had walked at nights with this

---

[1] In the fairy tale, Bluebeard kept the bodies of his murdered wives in a locked room.

[2] the hell of classical mythology.

[3] The full Latin phrase reads, *Sine Cerere et Libero friget Venus,* which means, "Without food or wine, love grows cold." The line comes from a play, *The Eunuch,* written by the Roman dramatist, Terence (190?–159 BC).

[4] "in the Socratic fashion" (L.).

poor friendless girl up and down Oxford Street, or had rested with her on steps and under the shelter of porticoes. She could not be so old as myself: she told me, indeed, that she had not completed her sixteenth year. By such questions as my interest about her prompted, I had gradually drawn forth her simple history. Hers was a case of ordinary occurrence (as I have since had reason to think), and one in which, if London beneficence had better adapted its arrangements to meet it, the power of the law might oftener be interposed to protect, and to avenge. But the stream of London charity flows in a channel which, though deep and mighty, is yet noiseless and underground; not obvious or readily accessible to poor houseless wanderers: and it cannot be denied that the outside air and frame-work of London society is harsh, cruel, and repulsive. In any case, however, I saw that part of her injuries might easily have been redressed: and I urged her often and earnestly to lay her complaint before a magistrate: friendless as she was, I assured her that she would meet with immediate attention; and that English justice, which was no respecter of persons, would speedily and amply avenge her on the brutal ruffian who had plundered her little property. She promised me often that she would; but she delayed taking the steps I pointed out from time to time: for she was timid and dejected to a degree which showed how deeply sorrow had taken hold of her young heart: and perhaps she thought justly that the most upright judge, and the most righteous tribunals, could do nothing to repair her heaviest wrongs. Something, however, would perhaps have been done: for it had been settled between us at length, but unhappily on the very last time but one that I was ever to see her, that in a day or two we should go together before a magistrate, and that I should speak on her behalf. This little service it was destined, however, that I should never realise. Meantime, that which she rendered to me, and which was greater than I could ever have repaid her, was this:—One night, when we were pacing slowly along Oxford Street, and after a day when I had felt more than usually ill and faint, I requested her to turn off with me into Soho Square: thither we went; and we sate down on the steps of a house, which, to this hour, I never pass without a pang of grief, and an inner act of homage to the spirit of that unhappy girl, in memory of the noble action which she there performed. Suddenly, as we sate, I grew much worse: I had been leaning my head against her bosom; and all at once I sank from her arms and fell backwards on the steps. From the sensations I then had, I felt an inner conviction of the liveliest kind that without some powerful and reviving stimulus, I should either have died on the spot—or should at least have sunk to a point of exhaustion from which all re-ascent under my friendless circumstances would soon have become hopeless. Then it was, at this crisis of my fate, that my poor orphan companion—who had herself met with little but injuries in this world—stretched out a saving hand to me. Uttering a cry of terror, but without a moment's delay, she ran off into Oxford Street, and in less time than could be imagined, returned to me with a glass of port wine and spices, that acted upon my empty stomach (which at that time would have rejected all solid food) with an instantaneous power of restoration: and for this glass the generous girl without a murmur paid out of her own humble purse at a time—be it remembered!—when she had scarcely wherewithal to purchase the bare necessaries of life, and when she could have no reason to expect that I should ever be able to reimburse her.—Oh! youthful benefactress! how often in succeeding years, standing in solitary places, and thinking of thee with grief of heart and perfect love, how often have I wished that, as in ancient times the curse of a father was believed to have a supernatural power, and to pursue its object with a fatal necessity of self-fulfilment,—even so the benediction of a heart oppressed with gratitude, might have a like prerogative; might have power given to it from above to chace—to haunt—to way-lay—to overtake—to pursue thee into the central darkness of a London brothel, or (if it were possible) into the darkness of the grave—there to awaken thee with an authentic message of peace and forgiveness, and of final reconciliation! ...

Meantime, what had become of poor Ann? For her I have reserved my concluding words: according to our agreement, I sought her daily, and waited for her every night, so long as I staid in London, at the corner of Titchfield-street. I inquired for her of every one who was likely to know her; and, during the last hours of my stay in London, I put into activity every means of tracing her that my knowledge of London suggested, and the limited extent of my power made possible. The street where she had lodged I knew, but not the house; and I remembered at last some account which she had given me of ill treatment from her landlord, which made it probable that she had quitted those lodgings before we parted. She had few acquaintance; most people, besides, thought that the earnestness of my inquiries arose from motives which moved their laughter, or their slight regard; and others, thinking I was in chase of a girl who had robbed me of some trifles, were naturally and excusably indisposed to give me any clue to her, if, indeed, they had any to give. Finally, as my despairing resource, on the day I left London I put into the hands of the only person who (I was sure) must know Ann by sight, from having been in company with us once or twice, an address to —— in ——shire, at that time the residence of my family. But, to this hour, I have never heard a syllable about her. This, amongst such troubles as most men meet with in this life, has been my heaviest affliction.—If she lived, doubtless we must have been sometimes in search of each other, at the very same moment, through the mighty labyrinths of London; perhaps, even within a few feet of each other—a barrier no wider in a London street, often amounting in the end to a separation for eternity! During some years, I hoped that she *did* live; and I suppose that, in the literal and unrhetorical use of the word *myriad*, I may say that on my different visits to London, I have looked into many, many myriads of female faces, in the hope of meeting her. I should know her again amongst a thousand, if I saw her for a moment; for, though not handsome, she had a sweet expression of countenance, and a peculiar and graceful carriage of the head.—I sought her, I have said, in hope. So it was for years; but now I should fear to see her; and her cough, which grieved me when I parted with her, is now my consolation. I now wish to see her no longer; but think of her, more gladly, as one long since laid in the grave;— in the grave, I would hope, of a Magdalen;[1] taken away, before injuries and cruelty had blotted out and transfigured her ingenuous nature, or the brutalities of ruffians had completed the ruin they had begun.

---

[1] an asylum for reformed prostitutes, named after St. Mary Magdalene, who was traditionally associated with the woman Christ saved from being stoned for adultery: see John 8.3–11.

from the *London Magazine* 4 (October 1821)

from *Introduction to the Pains of Opium*

Now, then, I was again happy: I now took only 1000 drops[2] of laudanum per day: and what was that? A latter spring had come to close up the season of youth: my brain performed its functions as healthily as ever before: I read Kant[3] again; and again I understood him, or fancied that I did. Again my feelings of pleasure expanded themselves to all around me: and if any man from Oxford or Cambridge, or from neither, had been announced to me in my unpretending cottage, I should have welcomed him with as sumptuous a reception as so poor a man could offer. Whatever else was wanting to a wise man's happiness,—of laudanum I would have given him as much as he wished, and in a golden cup. And, by the way, now that I speak of giving laudanum away, I remember, about this time, a little incident, which I mention, because, trifling as it was, the reader will soon meet it again in my dreams, which it influenced more fearfully than could be imagined. One day a Malay knocked at my door. What business a Malay could have to transact amongst English mountains, I cannot conjecture: but possibly he was on his road to a sea-port about forty miles distant.

The servant who opened the door to him was a young girl born and bred amongst the mountains, who had never seen an Asiatic dress of any sort: his turban, therefore, confounded her not a little: and, as it turned out, that his attainments in English were exactly of the same extent as hers in the Malay, there seemed to be an impassable gulph fixed between all communication of ideas, if either party had happened to possess any. In this dilemma, the girl, recollecting the reputed learning of her master (and, doubtless, giving me credit for a knowledge of all the languages of the earth, besides, perhaps, a few of the lunar ones), came and gave me to understand that there was a sort of demon below, whom she clearly imagined that my art could exorcise from the

---

[2] The size of a drop and the strength of laudanum could vary, but this was certainly a very large daily intake.

[3] Immanuel Kant (1724–1804), a German philosopher notorious for his difficulty.

house. I did not immediately go down: but, when I did, the group which presented itself, arranged as it was by accident, though not very elaborate, took hold of my fancy and my eye in a way that none of the statuesque attitudes exhibited in the ballets at the Opera-House, though so ostentatiously complex, had ever done. In a cottage kitchen, but panelled on the wall with dark wood that from age and rubbing resembled oak, and looking more like a rustic hall of entrance than a kitchen, stood the Malay—his turban and loose trowsers of dingy white relieved upon the dark panelling: he had placed himself nearer to the girl than she seemed to relish; though her native spirit of mountain intrepidity contended with the feeling of simple awe which her countenance expressed as she gazed upon the tiger-cat before her. And a more striking picture there could not be imagined, than the beautiful English face of the girl, and its exquisite fairness, together with her erect and independent attitude, contrasted with the sallow and bilious skin of the Malay, enamelled or veneered with mahogany, by marine air, his small, fierce, restless eyes, thin lips, slavish gestures and adorations. Half-hidden by the ferocious looking Malay, was a little child from a neighbouring cottage who had crept in after him, and was now in the act of reverting its head, and gazing upwards at the turban and the fiery eyes beneath it, whilst with one hand he caught at the dress of the young woman for protection. My knowledge of the Oriental tongues is not remarkably extensive, being indeed confined to two words—the Arabic word for barley, and the Turkish for opium (madjoon), which I have learnt from Anastasius.[1] And, as I had neither a Malay dictionary, nor even Adelung's *Mithridates*,[2] which might have helped me to a few words, I addressed him in some lines from the Iliad; considering that, of such languages as I possessed, Greek, in point of longitude, came geographically nearest to an Oriental one. He worshipped me in a most devout manner, and replied in what I suppose was Malay. In this way I saved my reputation with my neighbours: for the Malay had no means of betraying the secret. He lay down upon the floor for about an hour, and then pursued his journey. On his departure, I presented him with a piece of opium. To him, as an Orientalist, I concluded that opium must be familiar: and the expression of his face convinced me that it was. Nevertheless, I was struck with some little consternation when I saw him suddenly raise his hand to his mouth, and (in the school-boy phrase) bolt the whole, divided into three pieces, at one mouthful. The quantity was enough to kill three dragoons[3] and their horses: and I felt some alarm for the poor creature: but what could be done? I had given him the opium in compassion for his solitary life, on recollecting that if he had travelled on foot from London, it must be nearly three weeks since he could have exchanged a thought with any human being. I could not think of violating the laws of hospitality, by having him seized and drenched with an emetic, and thus frightening him into a notion that we were going to sacrifice him to some English idol. No: there was clearly no help for it:—he took his leave: and for some days I felt anxious: but as I never heard of any Malay being found dead, I became convinced that he was used[4] to opium: and that I must have done him the service I designed, by giving him one night of respite from the pains of wandering.

This incident I have digressed to mention, because this Malay (partly from the picturesque exhibition he assisted to frame, partly from the anxiety I connected with his image for some days) fastened afterwards upon my dreams, and brought other Malays with him worse

---

[1] a novel by Thomas Hope (1808–62).

[2] Johann Christoff Adelung (1732–1806) was a German philologist who, at the time of his death, was working on a book, *Mithridates, or General Linguistics*, which described the relationship between Sanskrit and European languages.

[3] mounted soldiers.

[4] "This, however, is not a necessary conclusion: the varieties of effect produced by opium on different constitutions are infinite. A London Magistrate (Harriott's *Struggles through Life*, vol. iii. p. 391, Third Edition), has recorded that, on the first occasion of his trying laudanum for the gout, he took *forty* drops, the next night *sixty*, and on the fifth night *eighty*, without any effect whatever; and this at an advanced age. I have an anecdote from a country surgeon, however, which sinks Mr. Harriott's case into a trifle; and in my projected medical treatise on opium, which I will publish, provided the College of Surgeons will pay me for enlightening their benighted understandings upon this subject, I will relate it: but it is far too good a story to be published gratis." (T.D.Q.) John Harriott (1745–1817), *Struggles through Life* (1815).

than himself, that ran "a-muck"[1] at me, and led me into a world of troubles....

from *The Pains of Opium*

I now pass to what is the main subject of these latter confessions, to the history and journal of what took place in my dreams; for these were the immediate and proximate cause of my acutest suffering.

The first notice I had of any important change going on in this part of my physical economy, was from the re-awaking of a state of eye generally incident to childhood, or exalted states of irritability. I know not whether my reader is aware that many children, perhaps most, have a power of painting, as it were, upon the darkness, all sorts of phantoms; in some, that power is simply a mechanic affection of the eye; others have a voluntary or a semi-voluntary power to dismiss or to summon them; or, as a child once said to me when I questioned him on this matter, "I can tell them to go, and they go; but sometimes they come, when I don't tell them to come." Whereupon I told him that he had almost as unlimited a command over apparitions, as a Roman centurion over his soldiers.[2]—In the middle of 1817, I think it was, that this faculty became positively distressing to me: at night, when I lay awake in bed, vast processions passed along in mournful pomp; friezes of never-ending stories, that to my feelings were as sad and solemn as if they were stories drawn from times before Œdipus[3] or Priam[4]—before Tyre[5]—before Memphis.[6] And, at the same time, a corresponding change took place in my dreams; a theatre seemed suddenly opened and lighted up within my brain, which presented nightly spectacles of more than earthly splendour. And the four following facts may be mentioned, as noticeable at this time:

1. That, as the creative state of the eye increased, a sympathy seemed to arise between the waking and the dreaming states of the brain in one point—that whatsoever I happened to call up and to trace by a voluntary act upon the darkness was very apt to transfer itself to my dreams; so that I feared to exercise this faculty; for, as Midas turned all things to gold,[7] that yet baffled his hopes and defrauded his human desires, so whatsoever things capable of being visually represented I did but think of in the darkness, immediately shaped themselves into phantoms of the eye; and, by a process apparently no less inevitable, when thus once traced in faint and visionary colours, like writings in sympathetic ink, they were drawn out by the fierce chemistry of my dreams, into insufferable splendour that fretted my heart.

2. For this, and all other changes in my dreams, were accompanied by deep-seated anxiety and gloomy melancholy, such as are wholly incommunicable by words. I seemed every night to descend, not metaphorically, but literally to descend, into chasms and sunless abysses, depths below depths, from which it seemed hopeless that I could ever re-ascend. Nor did I, by waking, feel that I *had* re-ascended. This I do not dwell upon; because the state of gloom which attended these gorgeous spectacles, amounting at last to utter darkness, as of some suicidal despondency, cannot be approached by words.

3. The sense of space, and in the end, the sense of time, were both powerfully affected. Buildings, landscapes, &c. were exhibited in proportions so vast as the bodily eye is not fitted to receive. Space swelled, and was amplified to an extent of unutterable infinity. This, however, did not disturb me so much as the vast expansion of time; I sometimes seemed to have lived for seventy or one hundred years in one night; nay, sometimes had feelings representative of a millennium passed in that time, or, however, of a duration far beyond the limits of any human experience.

4. The minutest incidents of childhood, or forgotten scenes of later years, were often revived: I could not be said to recollect them; for if I had been told of them

---

[1] "See the common accounts in any Eastern traveller or voyager of the frantic excesses committed by Malays who have taken opium, or are reduced to desperation by ill luck at gambling." (T.D.Q.)

[2] See Luke 7.8.

[3] a character in Sophocles's Theban plays, famed for killing his father and marrying his mother.

[4] King of Troy, the city besieged in Homer's *Iliad*.

[5] an ancient city in what is now Lebanon.

[6] ancient capital of Egypt.

[7] See Ovid, *Metamorphoses* 11.

when waking, I should not have been able to acknowledge them as parts of my past experience. But placed as they were before me, in dreams like intuitions, and clothed in all their evanescent circumstances and accompanying feelings, I *recognised* them instantaneously. I was once told by a near relative of mine, that having in her childhood fallen into a river, and being on the very verge of death but for the critical assistance which reached her, she saw in a moment her whole life, in its minutest incidents, arrayed before her simultaneously as in a mirror; and she had a faculty developed as suddenly for comprehending the whole and every part. This, from some opium experiences of mine, I can believe; I have, indeed, seen the same thing asserted twice in modern books, and accompanied by a remark which I am convinced is true; viz. that the dread book of account, which the Scriptures speak of,[1] is, in fact, the mind itself of each individual. Of this at least, I feel assured, that there is no such thing as *forgetting* possible to the mind; a thousand accidents may, and will interpose a veil between our present consciousness and the secret inscriptions on the mind; accidents of the same sort will also rend away this veil; but alike, whether veiled or unveiled, the inscription remains for ever; just as the stars seem to withdraw before the common light of day, whereas, in fact, we all know that it is the light which is drawn over them as a veil—and that they are waiting to be revealed when the obscuring daylight shall have withdrawn....

Many years ago, when I was looking over Piranesi's Antiquities of Rome, Mr. Coleridge, who was standing by, described to me a set of plates by that artist,[2] called his *Dreams*, and which record the scenery of his own visions during the delirium of a fever. Some of them (I describe only from memory of Mr. Coleridge's account) represented vast Gothic halls: on the floor of which stood all sorts of engines and machinery, wheels, cables, pulleys, levers, catapults, &c. &c. expressive of enormous power put forth, and resistance overcome. Creeping along the sides of the walls, you perceived a staircase; and upon it, groping his way upwards, was Piranesi himself: follow the stairs a little further, and you perceive it come to a sudden abrupt termination, without any balustrade, and allowing no step onwards to him who had reached the extremity, except into the depths below. Whatever is to become of poor Piranesi, you suppose, at least, that his labours must in some way terminate here. But raise your eyes, and behold a second flight of stairs still higher: on which again Piranesi is perceived, but this time standing on the very brink of the abyss. Again elevate your eye, and a still more aerial flight of stairs is beheld: and again is poor Piranesi busy on his aspiring labours: and so on, until the unfinished stairs and Piranesi both are lost in the upper gloom of the hall.—With the same power of endless growth and self-reproduction did my architecture proceed in dreams. In the early stage of my malady, the splendours of my dreams were indeed chiefly architectural: and I beheld such pomp of cities and palaces as was never yet beheld by the waking eye, unless in the clouds. From a great modern poet[3] I cite part of a passage which describes, as an appearance actually beheld in the clouds, what in many of its circumstances I saw frequently in sleep:

> The appearance, instantaneously disclosed,
> Was of a mighty city—boldly say
> A wilderness of building, sinking far
> And self-withdrawn into a wondrous depth,
> Far sinking into splendor—without end!
> Fabric it seem'd of diamond, and of gold,
> With alabaster domes, and silver spires,
> And blazing terrace upon terrace, high
> Uplifted; here, serene pavilions bright
> In avenues disposed; there towers begirt
> With battlements that on their restless fronts
> Bore stars—illumination of all gems!
> By earthly nature had the effect been wrought
> Upon the dark materials of the storm
> Now pacified; on them, and on the coves,
> And mountain-steeps and summits, whereunto
> The vapours had receded,—taking there
> Their station under a cerulean sky. &c., &c.[4]

The sublime circumstance—"battlements that on their *restless* fronts bore stars,"—might have been copied from my architectural dreams, for it often occurred.

---

[1] e.g., Revelation 3.5, 5.1–9, 13.8, 17.8, 20.12, 21.27.

[2] engraver Giovanni Battista Piranesi (1720–78).

[3] W. Wordsworth.*

[4] W. Wordsworth, *The Excursion** 2.834–51.

—We hear it reported of Dryden,[1] and of Fuseli[2] in modern times, that they thought proper to eat raw meat for the sake of obtaining splendid dreams: how much better for such a purpose to have eaten opium, which yet I do not remember that any poet is recorded to have done, except the dramatist Shadwell:[3] and in ancient days, Homer is, I think, rightly reputed to have known the virtues of opium.[4]

To my architecture succeeded dreams of lakes—and silvery expanses of water:—these haunted me so much, that I feared (though possibly it will appear ludicrous to a medical man) that some dropsical state or tendency of the brain might thus be making itself (to use a metaphysical word) *objective*; and the sentient organ *project* itself as its own object.—For two months I suffered greatly in my head,—a part of my bodily structure which had hitherto been so clear from all touch or taint of weakness (physically, I mean), that I used to say of it, as the last Lord Orford[5] said of his stomach, that it seemed likely to survive the rest of my person.—Till now I had never felt a head-ach even, or any the slightest pain, except rheumatic pains caused by my own folly. However, I got over this attack, though it must have been verging on something very dangerous.

The waters now changed their character,—from translucent lakes, shining like mirrors, they now became seas and oceans. And now came a tremendous change, which, unfolding itself slowly like a scroll, through many months, promised an abiding torment; and, in fact, it never left me until the winding up of my case. Hitherto the human face had mixed often in my dreams, but not despotically, nor with any special power of tormenting. But now that which I have called the tyranny of the human face began to unfold itself. Perhaps some part of my London life might be answerable for this. Be that as it may, now it was that upon the rocking waters of the ocean the human face began to appear: the sea appeared paved with innumerable faces, upturned to the heavens: faces, imploring, wrathful, despairing, surged upwards by thousands, by myriads, by generations, by centuries:—my agitation was infinite,—my mind tossed—and surged with the ocean.

May, 1818.

The Malay had been a fearful enemy for months. I have been every night, through his means, transported into Asiatic scenes. I know not whether others share in my feelings on this point; but I have often thought that if I were compelled to forego England, and to live in China, and among Chinese manners and modes of life and scenery, I should go mad. The causes of my horror lie deep; and some of them must be common to others. Southern Asia, in general, is the seat of awful images and associations. As the cradle of the human race, it would alone have a dim and reverential feeling connected with it. But there are other reasons. No man can pretend that the wild, barbarous, and capricious superstitions of Africa, or of savage tribes elsewhere, affect him in the way that he is affected by the ancient, monumental, cruel, and elaborate religions of Indostan, &c. The mere antiquity of Asiatic things, of their institutions, histories, modes of faith, &c. is so impressive, that to me the vast age of the race and name overpowers the sense of youth in the individual. A young Chinese seems to me an antediluvian man renewed. Even Englishmen, though not bred in any knowledge of such institutions, cannot but shudder at the mystic sublimity of *castes* that have flowed apart, and refused to mix, through such immemorial tracts of time; nor can any man fail to be awed by the names of the Ganges, or the Euphrates. It contributes much to these feelings, that southern Asia is, and has been for thousands of years, the part of the earth most swarming with human life; the great *officina gentium*.[6] Man is a weed in those regions. The vast empires also, into which the enormous population of Asia has always been cast, give a further sublimity to the feelings associated with all oriental names or images. In

---

[1] John Dryden, English poet and dramatist (1631–1700).

[2] Swiss-born British Romantic painter, Henry Fuseli (1741–1825).

[3] Thomas Shadwell, English poet and dramatist (c. 1642–92).

[4] See *Odyssey* 4.

[5] Horace Walpole (1717–97), author of *The Castle of Otranto* (1764) and *The Mysterious Mother* (1768).

[6] "the workshop of the world" (L.). The full phrase is *officina gentium, vagina nationum*, "the workshop of the world, the mother of nations," and comes from Jordanes, a Romanized Goth, who, in the 6th century, wrote *The Gothic History*, a summary of Cassiodorus's (AD c. 480–575) lost text on the history of the Goths.

China, over and above what it has in common with the rest of southern Asia, I am terrified by the modes of life, by the manners, and the barrier of utter abhorrence, and want of sympathy, placed between us by feelings deeper than I can analyze. I could sooner live with lunatics, or brute animals. All this, and much more than I can say, or have time to say, the reader must enter into before he can comprehend the unimaginable horror which these dreams of oriental imagery, and mythological tortures, impressed upon me. Under the connecting feeling of tropical heat and vertical sun-lights, I brought together all creatures, birds, beasts, reptiles, all trees and plants, usages and appearances, that are found in all tropical regions, and assembled them together in China or Indostan. From kindred feelings, I soon brought Egypt and all her gods under the same law. I was stared at, hooted at, grinned at, chattered at, by monkeys, by paroquets, by cockatoos. I ran into pagodas: and was fixed, for centuries, at the summit, or in secret rooms; I was the idol; I was the priest; I was worshipped; I was sacrificed. I fled from the wrath of Brama[1] through all the forests of Asia: Vishnu hated me: Seeva laid wait for me. I came suddenly upon Isis and Osiris:[2] I had done a deed, they said, which the ibis and the crocodile trembled at. I was buried, for a thousand years, in stone coffins, with mummies and sphinxes, in narrow chambers at the heart of eternal pyramids. I was kissed, with cancerous kisses, by crocodiles; and laid, confounded with all unutterable slimy things, amongst reeds and Nilotic mud.

I thus give the reader some slight abstraction of my oriental dreams, which always filled me with such amazement at the monstrous scenery, that horror seemed absorbed, for a while, in sheer astonishment. Sooner or later, came a reflux of feeling that swallowed up the astonishment, and left me, not so much in terror, as in hatred and abomination of what I saw. Over every form, and threat, and punishment, and dim sightless incarceration, brooded a sense of eternity and infinity that drove me into an oppression as of madness. Into these dreams only, it was, with one or two slight excep-

tions, that any circumstances of physical horror entered. All before had been moral and spiritual terrors. But here the main agents were ugly birds, or snakes, or crocodiles; especially the last. The cursed crocodile became to me the object of more horror than almost all the rest. I was compelled to live with him; and (as was always the case almost in my dreams) for centuries. I escaped sometimes, and found myself in Chinese houses, with cane tables, &c. All the feet of the tables, sofas, &c. soon became instinct with life: the abominable head of the crocodile, and his leering eyes, looked out at me, multiplied into a thousand repetitions: and I stood loathing and fascinated. And so often did this hideous reptile haunt my dreams, that many times the very same dream was broken up in the very same way: I heard gentle voices speaking to me (I hear every thing when I am sleeping); and instantly I awoke: it was broad noon; and my children were standing, hand in hand, at my bed-side; come to show me their coloured shoes, or new frocks, or to let me see them dressed for going out. I protest that so awful was the transition from the damned crocodile, and the other unutterable monsters and abortions of my dreams, to the sight of innocent *human* natures and of infancy, that, in the mighty and sudden revulsion of mind, I wept, and could not forbear it, as I kissed their faces.

June, 1819.

I have had occasion to remark, at various periods of my life, that the deaths of those whom we love, and indeed the contemplation of death generally, is (*cæteris paribus*)[3] more affecting in summer than in any other season of the year. And the reasons are these three, I think: first, that the visible heavens in summer appear far higher, more distant, and (if such a solecism may be excused) more infinite; the clouds, by which chiefly the eye expounds the distance of the blue pavilion stretched over our heads, are in summer more voluminous, massed, and accumulated in far grander and more towering piles: secondly, the light and the appearances of the declining and the setting sun are much more fitted to be types and characters of the Infinite: and, thirdly (which is the main reason) the exuberant and riotous prodigality of life naturally forces the mind more

---

[1] Brama (or Brahma) is the Hindu god who, along with Vishnu and Shiva, make up the Hindu Trinity. Brama is the creator; Vishnu, the preserver; and Shiva (or Seva), the destroyer.

[2] Isis was the Egyptian goddess of fertility, rebirth, creation; her husband Osiris was god of the underworld.

[3] "all other things being equal" (L.).

powerfully upon the antagonist thought of death, and the wintry sterility of the grave. For it may be observed, generally, that wherever two thoughts stand related to each other by a law of antagonism, and exist, as it were, by mutual repulsion, they are apt to suggest each other. On these accounts it is that I find it impossible to banish the thought of death when I am walking alone in the endless days of summer; and any particular death, if not more affecting, at least haunts my mind more obstinately and besiegingly in that season. Perhaps this cause, and a slight incident which I omit, might have been the immediate occasions of the following dream; to which, however, a predisposition must always have existed in my mind; but having been once roused, it never left me, and split into a thousand fantastic varieties, which often suddenly re-united, and composed again the original dream.

I thought that it was a Sunday morning in May, that it was Easter Sunday, and as yet very early in the morning. I was standing, as it seemed to me, at the door of my own cottage. Right before me lay the very scene which could really be commanded from that situation, but exalted, as was usual, and solemnized by the power of dreams. There were the same mountains, and the same lovely valley at their feet; but the mountains were raised to more than Alpine height, and there was interspace far larger between them of meadows and forest lawns; the hedges were rich with white roses; and no living creature was to be seen, excepting that in the green church-yard there were cattle tranquilly reposing upon the verdant graves, and particularly round about the grave of a child whom I had tenderly loved,[1] just as I had really beheld them, a little before sun-rise in the same summer, when that child died. I gazed upon the well-known scene, and I said aloud (as I thought) to myself, "It yet wants much of sun-rise; and it is Easter Sunday; and that is the day on which they celebrate the first fruits of resurrection. I will walk abroad; old griefs shall be forgotten to-day; for the air is cool and still, and the hills are high, and stretch away to Heaven; and the forest-glades are as quiet as the church-yard; and, with the dew, I can wash the fever from my forehead, and then I shall be unhappy no longer." And I turned, as if to open my garden gate; and immediately I saw upon the left a scene far different; but which yet the power of dreams had reconciled into harmony with the other. The scene was an oriental one; and there also it was Easter Sunday, and very early in the morning. And at a vast distance were visible, as a stain upon the horizon, the domes and cupolas of a great city—an image of faint abstraction, caught perhaps in childhood, from some picture of Jerusalem. And not a bow-shot from me, upon a stone, and shaded by Judean palms, there sat a woman; and I looked; and it was—Ann! She fixed her eyes upon me earnestly; and I said to her at length: "So then I have found you at last." I waited: but she answered me not a word. Her face was the same as when I saw it last, and yet again how different! Seventeen years ago, when the lamp-light fell upon her face, as for the last time I kissed her lips (lips, Ann, that to me were not polluted), her eyes were streaming with tears: the tears were now wiped away;[2] she seemed more beautiful than she was at that time, but in all other points the same, and not older. Her looks were tranquil, but with unusual solemnity of expression; and I now gazed upon her with some awe, but suddenly her countenance grew dim, and, turning to the mountains, I perceived vapours rolling between us; in a moment, all had vanished; thick darkness came on; and, in the twinkling of an eye, I was far away from mountains, and by lamp-light in Oxford-street, walking again with Ann—just as we walked seventeen years before, when we were both children.

As a final specimen, I cite one of a different character, from 1820.

The dream commenced with a music which now I often heard in dreams—a music of preparation and of awakening suspense; a music like the opening of the Coronation Anthem,[3] and which, like *that,* gave the feeling of a vast march—of infinite cavalcades filing off—and the tread of innumerable armies. The morning was come of a mighty day—a day of crisis and of final hope for human nature, then suffering some mysterious eclipse, and labouring in some dread extremity. Some-

---

[1] Catherine Wordsworth (1808–12); cf. W. Wordsworth, "Surprized by Joy."*

[2] Cf. Revelation 7.17, 21.4.

[3] composed by George Frederick Handel (1685–1759) for the coronation of George II in 1727.

where, I knew not where—somehow, I knew not how—by some beings, I knew not whom—a battle, a strife, an agony, was conducting,—was evolving like a great drama, or piece of music; with which my sympathy was the more insupportable from my confusion as to its place, its cause, its nature, and its possible issue. I, as is usual in dreams (where, of necessity, we make ourselves central to every movement), had the power, and yet had not the power, to decide it. I had the power, if I could raise myself, to will it; and yet again had not the power, for the weight of twenty Atlantics was upon me, or the oppression of inexpiable guilt. "Deeper than ever plummet sounded,"[1] I lay inactive. Then, like a chorus, the passion deepened. Some greater interest was at stake; some mightier cause than ever yet the sword had pleaded, or trumpet had proclaimed. Then came sudden alarms: hurryings to and fro: trepidations of innumerable fugitives, I knew not whether from the good cause or the bad: darkness and lights: tempest and human faces; and at last, with the sense that all was lost, female forms, and the features that were worth all the world to me, and but a moment allowed,—and clasped hands, and heart-breaking partings, and then—everlasting farewells! and with a sigh, such as the caves of hell sighed when the incestuous mother uttered the abhorred name of death,[2] the sound was reverberated—everlasting farewells! and again, and yet again reverberated—everlasting farewells!

And I awoke in struggles, and cried aloud—"I will sleep no more!"[3] . . .

from the *London Magazine* 8 (October 1823)

On the Knocking at the Gate in Macbeth

From my boyish days I had always felt a great perplexity on one point in Macbeth: it was this: the knocking at the gate,[4] which succeeds to the murder of Duncan, produced to my feelings an effect for which I never could account: the effect was—that it reflected back upon the murder a peculiar awfulness and a depth of solemnity: yet, however obstinately I endeavoured with my understanding to comprehend this, for many years I never could see *why* it should produce such an effect.—

Here I pause for one moment to exhort the reader never to pay any attention to his understanding when it stands in opposition to any other faculty of his mind. The mere understanding, however useful and indispensable, is the meanest faculty in the human mind and the most to be distrusted: and yet the great majority of people trust to nothing else; which may do for ordinary life, but not for philosophic purposes. Of this, out of ten thousand instances that I might produce, I will cite one. Ask of any person whatsoever, who is not previously prepared for the demand by a knowledge of perspective, to draw in the rudest way the commonest appearance which depends upon the laws of that science—as for instance, to represent the effect of two walls standing at right angles to each other, or the appearance of the houses on each side of a street, as seen by a person looking down the street from one extremity. Now in all cases, unless the person has happened to observe in pictures how it is that artists produce these effects, he will be utterly unable to make the smallest approximation to it. Yet why?—For he has actually seen the effect every day of his life. The reason is—that he allows his understanding to overrule his eyes. His understanding, which includes no intuitive knowledge of the laws of vision, can furnish him with no reason why a line which is known and can be proved to be a horizontal line, should not *appear* a horizontal line: a line, that made any angle with the perpendicular less than a right angle, would seem to him to indicate that his houses were all tumbling down together. Accordingly he makes the line of his houses a horizontal line, and fails of course to produce the effect demanded. Here then is one instance out of many, in which not only the understanding is allowed to overrule the eyes, but where the understanding is positively allowed to obliterate the eyes as it were: for not only does the man believe the evidence of his understanding in opposition to that of his eyes, but (which is monstrous!) the idiot is not aware that his eyes ever gave such evidence. He does not know that he has

---

[1] Cf. Shakespeare, *The Tempest* 5.1.56.

[2] Cf. Milton, *Paradise Lost* 2.787–89.

[3] Cf. Shakespeare, *Macbeth* 2.2.34–42.

[4] Shakespeare, *Macbeth* 2.2–2.3.

seen (and therefore *quoad*[1] his consciousness has *not* seen) that which he *has* seen every day of his life. But, to return from this digression,—my understanding could furnish no reason why the knocking at the gate in Macbeth should produce any effect direct or reflected: in fact, my understanding said positively that it could *not* produce any effect. But I knew better: I felt that it did: and I waited and clung to the problem until further knowledge should enable me to solve it.—At length, in 1812, Mr. Williams[2] made his *début* on the stage of Ratcliffe Highway, and executed those unparalleled murders which have procured for him such a brilliant and undying reputation. On which murders, by the way, I must observe, that in one respect they have had an ill effect, by making the connoisseur in murder very fastidious in his taste, and dissatisfied with any thing that has been since done in that line. All other murders look pale by the deep crimson of his: and, as an amateur once said to me in a querulous tone, "There has been absolutely nothing *doing* since his time, or nothing that's worth speaking of." But this is wrong: for it is unreasonable to expect all men to be great artists, and born with the genius of Mr. Williams.—Now it will be remembered that in the first of these murders (that of the Marrs) the same incident (of a knocking at the door soon after the work of extermination was complete) did actually occur which the genius of Shakspeare had invented: and all good judges and the most eminent dilettanti acknowledged the felicity of Shakspeare's suggestion as soon as it was actually realized. Here then was a fresh proof that I had been right in relying on my own feeling in opposition to my understanding; and again I set myself to study the problem: at length I solved it to my own satisfaction; and my solution is this. Murder in ordinary cases, where the sympathy is wholly directed to the case of the murdered person, is an incident of coarse and vulgar horror; and for this reason—that it flings the interest exclusively upon the natural but ignoble instinct by which we cleave to life; an instinct which, as being indispensable to the primal law of self-preservation, is the same in kind (though different in degree) amongst all living creatures; this instinct therefore, because it annihilates all distinctions, and degrades the greatest of men to the level of "the poor beetle that we tread on,"[3] exhibits human nature in its most abject and humiliating attitude. Such an attitude would little suit the purposes of the poet. What then must he do? He must throw the interest on the murderer: our sympathy must be with *him*; (of course I mean a sympathy of comprehension, a sympathy by which we enter into his feelings, and are made to understand them,—not a sympathy[4] of pity or approbation:) in the murdered person all strife of thought, all flux and reflux of passion and of purpose, are crushed by one overwhelming panic: the fear of instant death smites him "with its petrific mace."[5] But in the murderer, such a murderer as a poet will condescend to, there must be raging some great storm of passion,—jealousy, ambition, vengeance, hatred,—which will create a hell within him; and into this hell we are to look. In Macbeth, for the sake of gratifying his own enormous and teeming faculty of creation, Shakspere has introduced two murderers: and, as usual in his hands, they are remarkably discriminated: but, though in Macbeth the strife of mind is greater than in his wife, the tiger spirit not so awake, and his feelings caught chiefly by contagion from her,—yet, as both were finally involved in the guilt of murder, the murderous mind of necessity is finally to be presumed in both. This was to be expressed; and on its own account, as well as to make it a more proportionable antagonist to the unoffending nature of their victim, "the gracious Duncan," and adequately to

---

[1] "also" (L.).

[2] John Williams killed seven people in 1811–12 in what became known as "The Ratcliffe Highway Murders"; Williams hanged himself before he was arrested and was buried with a stake through his heart. De Quincey discusses the case further in "On Murder Considered as One of the Fine Arts" (1827).

[3] Shakespeare, *Measure for Measure* 3.1.79.

[4] "It seems almost ludicrous to guard and explain my use of a word in a situation where it should naturally explain itself. But it has become necessary to do so, in consequence of the unscholarlike use of the word sympathy, at present so general, by which, instead of taking it in its proper sense, as the act of reproducing in our minds the feelings of another, whether for hatred, indignation, love, pity, or approbation, it is made a mere synonyme of the word *pity;* and hence, instead of saying, 'sympathy *with* another,' many writers adopt the monstrous barbarism of 'sympathy *for* another.'" (T.D.Q.)

[5] Cf. Milton, *Paradise Lost* 10.294.

expound "the deep damnation of his taking off";[1] this was to be expressed with peculiar energy. We were to be made to feel that the human nature, *i.e.*, the divine nature of love and mercy, spread through the hearts of all creatures, and seldom utterly withdrawn from man,—was gone, vanished, extinct; and that the fiendish nature had taken its place. And, as this effect is marvellously accomplished in the dialogues and soliloquies themselves, so it is finally consummated by the expedient under consideration; and it is to this that I now solicit the reader's attention. If the reader has ever witnessed a wife, daughter, or sister, in a fainting fit, he may chance to have observed that the most affecting moment in such a spectacle, is *that* in which a sigh and a stirring announce the recommencement of suspended life. Or, if the reader has ever been present in a vast metropolis on the day when some great national idol was carried in funeral pomp to his grave, and chancing to walk near to the course through which it passed, has felt powerfully, in the silence and desertion of the streets and in the stagnation of ordinary business, the deep interest which at that moment was possessing the heart of man,—if all at once he should hear the death-like stillness broken up by the sound of wheels rattling away from the scene, and making known that the transitory vision was dissolved, he will be aware that at no moment was his sense of the complete suspension and pause in ordinary human concerns so full and affecting as at that moment when the suspension ceases, and the goings-on of human life are suddenly resumed. All action in any direction is best expounded, measured, and made apprehensible, by reaction. Now apply this to the case in Macbeth. Here, as I have said, the retiring of the human heart and the entrance of the fiendish heart was to be expressed and made sensible. Another world has stepped in; and the murderers are taken out of the region of human things, human purposes, human desires. They are transfigured: Lady Macbeth is "unsexed";[2] Macbeth has forgot that he was born of woman; both are conformed to the image of devils; and the world of devils is suddenly revealed. But how shall this be conveyed and made palpable? In order that a new world may step in, this world must for a time disappear. The murderers, and the murder, must be insulated—cut off by an immeasurable gulph from the ordinary tide and succession of human affairs—locked up and sequestered in some deep recess: we must be made sensible that the world of ordinary life is suddenly arrested—laid asleep—tranced—racked into a dread armistice: time must be annihilated; relation to things without abolished; and all must pass self-withdrawn into a deep syncope and suspension of earthly passion. Hence it is that when the deed is done—when the work of darkness is perfect, then the world of darkness passes away like a pageantry in the clouds: the knocking at the gate is heard; and it makes known audibly that the reaction has commenced: the human has made its reflux upon the fiendish: the pulses of life are beginning to beat again: and the re-establishment of the goings-on of the world in which we live, first makes us profoundly sensible of the awful parenthesis that had suspended them.

Oh! mighty poet!—Thy works are not as those of other men, simply and merely great works of art; but are also like the phenomena of nature, like the sun and the sea, the stars and the flowers,—like frost and snow, rain and dew, hail-storm and thunder, which are to be studied with entire submission of our own faculties, and in the perfect faith that in them there can be no too much or too little, nothing useless or inert—but that, the further we press in our discoveries, the more we shall see proofs of design and self-supporting arrangement where the careless eye had seen nothing but accident!

N.B. In the above specimen of psychological criticism, I have purposely omitted to notice another use of the knocking at the gate, viz. the opposition and contrast which it produces in the porter's comments to the scenes immediately preceding; because this use is tolerably obvious to all who are accustomed to reflect on what they read. A third use also, subservient to the scenical illusion, has been lately noticed by a critic in the LONDON MAGAZINE: I fully agree with him; but it did not fall in my way to insist on this.

X.Y.Z.[3]

---

[1] Shakespeare, *Macbeth* 3.1.66, 1.7.20.

[2] Cf. Shakespeare, *Macbeth* 1.5.39.

[3] the name under which De Quincey regularly wrote in magazines.

Thomas Love Peacock
1785 – 1866

Thomas Love Peacock was born in Weymouth, England, on 18 October 1785, the son of Samuel Peacock, a glass merchant, and Sarah Love, whose father was a retired master in the Royal Navy. Following his father's death or disappearance, he and his mother lived with her parents; at the age of six Peacock went to school at Englefield Green, where his teacher was John Harris Wicks. His first collection of poems, *Palmyra*, was published in 1805.

Following the break-up of his engagement to Fanny Falkner, whom he would recall in a poem of 1842, "Newark Abbey," Peacock served briefly in the Navy (though he never went to sea). He recorded a walking-tour of the Thames valley in 1808 in an ode, *The Genius of the Thames*, published in 1810. On a subsequent journey to Wales, he met Jane Gryffydh, whom he would marry eight years later.

In 1812 Peacock published another poem, *The Philosophy of Melancholy*; later the same year he met Percy Bysshe Shelley,* a close friend until Shelley's death in 1822. Peacock continued to write: two plays (unpublished during his lifetime), a grammar book for children (*Sir Hornbook*, 1813), an unfinished epic in Spenserian stanzas (*Ahrimanes*), and a satiric attack on Robert Southey* (*Sir Proteus*, 1814). When Shelley eloped with Mary Godwin (later Mary Shelley*) in 1814, he entrusted Peacock with his wife's financial affairs.

Peacock turned to fiction in 1815, publishing his first novel, *Headlong Hall*, a satirical and comic country-house novel of ideas. The success of this novel determined the course of much of his later work, including the novels *Melincourt* (1817), *Nightmare Abbey* (1818), *Crotchet Castle* (1831) and *Gryll Grange* (1860).

Meanwhile, Peacock published his long poem, *Rhododaphne: or the Thessalian Spell* (1818), which resonates with such Romantic works as Shelley's *Alastor** and John Keats's *Endymion*.* He also wrote critical prose ("Essay on Fashionable Literature," 1818; and "The Four Ages of Poetry"—which suggests his reservations about writing verse, and to which Shelley would respond in his "Defence of Poetry").* Peacock's novel *Maid Marian* (1822), based on the legends of Robin Hood, was adapted as an operetta and produced at Covent Garden. Another novel, *The Misfortunes of Elphin*, set in sixth-century Wales, also uses historical and legendary material.

Peacock's wife, Jane, never recovered emotionally from the death of one of her children in 1826. Another child, Mary Ellen, was alienated from her father in 1857 after she left an unhappy marriage (to the novelist George Meredith) to live with another man. During these difficult years Peacock began working on a *Memoir* of Shelley, which he published in instalments in *Fraser's Magazine* between 1858 and 1862. He died on 23 January 1866 and is buried in the New Cemetery, Shepperton. (A.M.)

༄༄༄

from *Ollier's Literary Miscellany* (1820)
from *The Four Ages of Poetry*

Qui inter hæc nutriuntur non magis sapere possunt, quam bene olere qui in culinâ habitant.
                    PETRONIUS[1]

Poetry, like the world, may be said to have four ages, but in a different order: the first age of poetry being the age of iron; the second, of gold; the third, of silver; and the fourth, of brass.[2]

The first, or iron age of poetry, is that in which rude bards celebrate in rough numbers the exploits of ruder chiefs, in days when every man is a warrior, and when the great practical maxim of every form of society, "to

---

[1] "He who is fed on such things can have good taste no more than someone who lives in the kitchen can smell well" (Petronius, *Satyricon* 2).

[2] In classical mythology, the ages occurred in the following order: gold, silver, bronze, iron.

keep what we have and to catch what we can,"[1] is not yet disguised under names of justice and forms of law, but is the naked motto of the naked sword, which is the only judge and jury in every question of *meum* and *tuum*.[2] In these days, the only three trades flourishing (besides that of priest which flourishes always) are those of king, thief, and beggar: the beggar being for the most part a king deject, and the thief a king expectant. The first question asked of a stranger is, whether he is a beggar or a thief:[3] the stranger, in reply, usually assumes the first, and awaits a convenient opportunity to prove his claim to the second appellation.

The natural desire of every man to engross to himself as much power and property as he can acquire by any of the means which might makes right, is accompanied by the no less natural desire of making known to as many people as possible the extent to which he has been a winner in this universal game. The successful warrior becomes a chief; the successful chief becomes a king: his next want is an organ to disseminate the fame of his achievements and the extent of his possessions; and this organ he finds in a bard, who is always ready to celebrate the strength of his arm, being first duly inspired by that of his liquor. This is the origin of poetry, which, like all other trades, takes its rise in the demand for the commodity, and flourishes in proportion to the extent of the market.

Poetry is thus in its origin panegyrical. The first rude songs of all nations appear to be a sort of brief historical notices, in a strain of tumid hyperbole, of the exploits and possessions of a few pre-eminent individuals. . . .

This is the first stage of poetry before the invention of written letters. The numerical modulation is at once useful as a help to memory, and pleasant to the ears of uncultured men, who are easily caught by sound: and from the exceeding flexibility of the yet unformed language, the poet does no violence to his ideas in subjecting them to the fetters of number. The savage indeed lisps in numbers,[4] and all rude and uncivilized people express themselves in the manner which we call poetical.

The scenery by which he is surrounded, and the superstitions which are the creed of his age, form the poet's mind. Rocks, mountains, seas, unsubdued forests, unnavigable rivers, surround him with forms of power and mystery, which ignorance and fear have peopled with spirits, under multifarious names of gods, goddesses, nymphs, genii, and dæmons. Of all these personages marvellous tales are in existence: the nymphs are not indifferent to handsome young men, and the gentlemen-genii are much troubled and very troublesome with a propensity to be rude to pretty maidens: the bard therefore finds no difficulty in tracing the genealogy of his chief to any of the deities in his neighbourhood with whom the said chief may be most desirous of claiming relationship.

In this pursuit, as in all others, some of course will attain a very marked pre-eminence; and these will be held in high honor, like Demodocus in the Odyssey, and will be consequently inflated with boundless vanity, like Thamyris in the Iliad.[5] Poets are as yet the only historians and chroniclers of their time, and the sole depositories of all the knowledge of their age; and though this knowledge is rather a crude congeries of traditional phantasies than a collection of useful truths, yet, such as it is, they have it to themselves. They are observing and thinking, while others are robbing and fighting: and though their object be nothing more than to secure a share of the spoil, yet they accomplish this end by intellectual, not by physical, power: their success excites emulation to the attainment of intellectual eminence: thus they sharpen their own wits and awaken those of others, at the same time that they gratify vanity and amuse curiosity. A skilful display of the little knowledge they have gains them credit for the possession of much more which they have not. Their familiarity with the secret history of gods and genii obtains for them, without much difficulty, the reputation of inspiration; thus they are not only historians but theologians, moralists, and legislators: delivering their oracles *ex cathedrâ*,[6] and being indeed often themselves (as

---

[1] Peacock recycled the maxim in his novel *Maid Marian* (1822).

[2] "mine and yours" (L.).

[3] "See the Odyssey, passim ['throughout' (L.)]: and Thucydides, 1.5." (T.L.P.)

[4] Cf. Pope, *An Epistle to Dr. Arbuthnot* (1735) 128.

[5] Homer's blind bards in *Odyssey* 8 and *Iliad* 2.

[6] "from the throne" (L.); hence, with authority.

Orpheus and Amphion)[1] regarded as portions and emanations of divinity: building cities with a song, and leading brutes with a symphony; which are only metaphors for the faculty of leading multitudes by the nose.

The golden age of poetry finds its materials in the age of iron. This age begins when poetry begins to be retrospective; when something like a more extended system of civil polity is established; when personal strength and courage avail less to the aggrandising of their possessor and to the making and marring of kings and kingdoms, and are checked by organised bodies, social institutions, and hereditary successions. Men also live more in the light of truth and within the interchange of observation; and thus perceive that the agency of gods and genii is not so frequent among themselves as, to judge from the songs and legends of the past time, it was among their ancestors. From these two circumstances, really diminished personal power, and apparently diminished familiarity with gods and genii, they very easily and naturally deduce two conclusions: 1st, That men are degenerated, and 2nd, That they are less in favour with the gods. The people of the petty states and colonies, which have now acquired stability and form, which owed their origin and first prosperity to the talents and courage of a single chief, magnify their founder through the mists of distance and tradition, and perceive him achieving wonders with a god or goddess always at his elbow. They find his name and his exploits thus magnified and accompanied in their traditionary songs, which are their only memorials. All that is said of him is in this character. There is nothing to contradict it. The man and his exploits and his tutelary deities are mixed and blended in one invariable association. The marvellous too is very much like a snow-ball: it grows as it rolls downward, till the little nucleus of truth which began its descent from the summit is hidden in the accumulation of superinduced hyperbole....

...This is the age of Homer, the golden age of poetry. Poetry has now attained its perfection: it has attained the point which it cannot pass: genius therefore seeks new forms for the treatment of the same subjects: hence the lyric poetry of Pindar and Alcæus, and the tragic poetry of Æschylus and Sophocles.[2] The favor of kings, the honour of the Olympic crown, the applause of present multitudes, all that can feed vanity and stimulate rivalry, await the successful cultivator of this art, till its forms become exhausted, and new rivals arise around it in new fields of literature, which gradually acquire more influence as, with the progress of reason and civilization, facts become more interesting than fiction: indeed the maturity of poetry may be considered the infancy of history. The transition from Homer to Herodotus is scarcely more remarkable than that from Herodotus to Thucydides:[3] in the gradual dereliction of fabulous incident and ornamented language, Herodotus is as much a poet in relation to Thucydides as Homer is in relation to Herodotus. The history of Herodotus is half a poem: it was written while the whole field of literature yet belonged to the Muses, and the nine books of which it was composed were therefore of right, as well of courtesy, superinscribed with their nine names....

Then comes the silver age, or the poetry of civilized life. This poetry is of two kinds, imitative and original. The imitative consists in recasting, and giving an exquisite polish to, the poetry of the age of gold: of this Virgil is the most obvious and striking example.[4] The original is chiefly comic, didactic, or satiric: as in Menander, Aristophanes, Horace, and Juvenal.[5] The poetry of this age is characterised by an exquisite and fastidious selection of words, and a laboured and somewhat monotonous harmony of expression: but its monotony consists in this, that experience having exhausted all the varieties of modulation, the civilized

---

[1] Orpheus, whose music was said to make trees and rocks dance, became the focus of a religious cult after he was torn apart by Maenads; Amphion, one of the founders of Thebes, is said to have built the city walls by making the stones move into place with his music.

[2] Greek poets: Pindar (c. 522–443 BC) and Alcæus (fl. c. 600 BC) were lyric poets; Æschylus (525–456 BC) and Sophocles (c. 496–406 BC) were tragic dramatists.

[3] Herodotus (c. 480–425 BC) and Thucydides (c. 460–c. 395 BC) were Greek historians.

[4] Virgil (70–19 BC), who wrote Latin pastorals, georgics, and an epic (the *Aeneid*), adapted the genres and subject-matter of Greek poetry to write about Roman experience and aspirations.

[5] Menander (c. 342–292 BC) and Aristophanes (c. 448–c. 380 BC) were both Athenian comic dramatists, Aristophanes a writer of the satirical Old Comedy and Menander of New Comedy. Horace (65–8 BC) and Juvenal (c. AD 60–c. 136) were both Roman poets and—in different ways—satirists.

poetry selects the most beautiful, and prefers the repetition of these to ranging through the variety of all. But the best expression being that into which the idea naturally falls, it requires the utmost labour and care so to reconcile the inflexibility of civilized language and the laboured polish of versification with the idea intended to be expressed, that sense may not appear to be sacrificed to sound. Hence numerous efforts and rare success.

This state of poetry is however a step towards its extinction. Feeling and passion are best painted in, and roused by, ornamental and figurative language; but the reason and the understanding are best addressed in the simplest and most unvarnished phrase. Pure reason and dispassionate truth would be perfectly ridiculous in verse, as we may judge by versifying one of Euclid's demonstrations.[1] This will be found true of all dispassionate reasoning whatever, and of all reasoning that requires comprehensive views and enlarged combinations. It is only the more tangible points of morality, those which command assent at once, those which have a mirror in every mind, and in which the severity of reason is warmed and rendered palatable by being mixed up with feeling and imagination, that are applicable even to what is called moral poetry: and as the sciences of morals and of mind advance towards perfection, as they become more enlarged and comprehensive in their views, as reason gains the ascendancy in them over imagination and feeling, poetry can no longer accompany them in their progress, but drops into the back ground, and leaves them to advance alone....

Good sense and elegant learning, conveyed in polished and somewhat monotonous verse, are the perfection of the original and imitative poetry of civilized life. Its range is limited, and when exhausted, nothing remains but the *crambe repetita*[2] of common-place, which at length becomes thoroughly wearisome, even to the most indefatigable readers of the newest new nothings.

It is now evident that poetry must either cease to be cultivated, or strike into a new path. The poets of the age of gold have been imitated and repeated till no new imitation will attract notice: the limited range of ethical and didactic poetry is exhausted: the associations of daily life in an advanced state of society are of very dry, methodical, unpoetical matters-of-fact: but there is always a multitude of listless idlers, yawning for amusement, and gaping for novelty: and the poet makes it his glory to be foremost among their purveyors.

Then comes the age of brass, which, by rejecting the polish and the learning of the age of silver, and taking a retrograde stride to the barbarisms and crude traditions of the age of iron, professes to return to nature and revive the age of gold. This is the second childhood of poetry. To the comprehensive energy of the Homeric Muse, which, by giving at once the grand outline of things, presented to the mind a vivid picture in one or two verses, inimitable alike in simplicity and magnificence, is substituted a verbose and minutely-detailed description of thoughts, passions, actions, persons, and things, in that loose rambling style of verse, which any one may write, *stans pede in uno*,[3] at the rate of two hundred lines in an hour. To this age may be referred all the poets who flourished in the decline of the Roman Empire....

Modern poetry has also its four ages: but "it wears its rue with a difference."[4]

To the age of brass in the ancient world succeeded the dark ages, in which the light of the Gospel began to spread over Europe, and in which, by a mysterious and inscrutable dispensation, the darkness thickened with the progress of the light. The tribes that overran the Roman Empire brought back the days of barbarism, but with this difference, that there were many books in the world, many places in which they were preserved, and occasionally some one by whom they were read, who indeed (if he escaped being burned *pour l'amour de Dieu*,)[5] generally lived an object of mysterious fear, with the reputation of magician, alchymist, and astrologer. The emerging of the nations of Europe from this superinduced barbarism, and their settling into new forms of polity, was accompanied, as the first ages of Greece had been, with a wild spirit of adventure, which, co-operating with new manners and new superstitions, raised up a fresh crop of chimæras, not less fruitful,

---

[1] Euclid was a Greek mathematician, fl. 300 BC.

[2] "heated-up cabbage" (L.); i.e. something obvious and over-familiar.

[3] "standing on one foot" (L.).

[4] Cf. Shakespeare, *Hamlet* 4.5.182.

[5] "for the love of God" (Fr.).

though far less beautiful, than those of Greece. The semi-deification of women by the maxims of the age of chivalry, combining with these new fables, produced the romance of the middle ages. The founders of the new line of heroes took the place of the demi-gods of Grecian poetry. Charlemagne and his Paladins, Arthur and his knights of the round table, the heroes of the iron age of chivalrous poetry, were seen through the same magnifying mist of distance, and their exploits were celebrated with even more extravagant hyperbole.[1]

…

From these ingredients of the iron age of modern poetry, dispersed in the rhymes of minstrels and the songs of the troubadours, arose the golden age, in which the scattered materials were harmonized and blended about the time of the revival of learning; but with this peculiar difference, that Greek and Roman literature pervaded all the poetry of the golden age of modern poetry, and hence resulted a heterogeneous compound of all ages and nations in one picture; an infinite licence, which gave to the poet the free range of the whole field of imagination and memory. This was carried very far by Ariosto,[2] but farthest of all by Shakspeare and his contemporaries, who used time and locality merely because they could not do without them, because every action must have its when and where: …

The greatest of English poets, Milton, may be said to stand alone between the ages of gold and silver, combining the excellencies of both; for with all the energy, and power, and freshness of the first, he united all the studied and elaborate magnificence of the second.

The silver age succeeded; beginning with Dryden, coming to perfection with Pope, and ending with Goldsmith, Collins, and Gray.[3]

Cowper[4] divested verse of its exquisite polish; he thought in metre, but paid more attention to his thoughts than his verse. It would be difficult to draw the boundary of prose and blank verse between his letters and his poetry.

The silver age was the reign of authority; but authority now began to be shaken, not only in poetry but in the whole sphere of its dominion. The contemporaries of Gray and Cowper were deep and elaborate thinkers. The subtle scepticism of Hume, the solemn irony of Gibbon, the daring paradoxes of Rousseau, and the biting ridicule of Voltaire,[5] directed the energies of four extraordinary minds to shake every portion of the reign of authority. Enquiry was roused, the activity of intellect was excited, and poetry came in for its share of the general result. The changes had been rung on lovely maid and sylvan shade, summer heat and green retreat, waving trees and sighing breeze, gentle swains and amorous pains, by versifiers who took them on trust, as meaning something very soft and tender, without much caring what: but with this general activity of intellect came a necessity for even poets to appear to know something of what they professed to talk of. Thomson[6] and Cowper looked at the trees and hills which so many ingenious gentlemen had rhymed about so long without looking at them at all, and the effect of the operation on poetry was like the discovery of a new world. Painting shared the influence, and the principles of picturesque beauty were explored by adventurous essayists with indefatigable pertinacity.[7] The success which attended these experiments, and the pleasure which resulted from them, had the usual effect of all new enthusiasms, that of turning the heads of a few unfortunate persons, the patriarchs of the age of brass, who, mistaking the prominent novelty for the all-important totality, seem to have ratiocinated much in the following manner:

---

[1] Charlemagne was celebrated in the early 12th-century French poem *Chanson de Roland*, King Arthur in a number of Middle English poems and in Sir Thomas Malory's prose *Morte D'Arthur* (printed 1485).

[2] Ludovico Ariosto (1474–1533), Italian poet, author of *Orlando Furioso* (1516–32).

[3] the poets Oliver Goldsmith,* William Collins (1721–59), and Thomas Gray (1716–71).

[4] the poet William Cowper.*

[5] the philosophers and historians David Hume (1711–76), Edward Gibbon (1737–94), Jean-Jacques Rousseau (1712–78), and François-Marie Arouet (Voltaire, 1694–1778).

[6] James Thomson (1700–48), author of *The Seasons* (1730, revised 1744, 1746).

[7] such as William Gilpin (*Three Essays: On Picturesque Beauty; On Picturesque Travel; and On Sketching Landscape*, 1792), William Mason (*The English Garden*, 1771–81), William Payne Knight (*The Landscape*, 1794), and Uvedale Price (*Essays on the Picturesque*, 1794). The picturesque refers to a kind of scenery and the aesthetic category that defines its qualities.

"Poetical genius is the finest of all things, and we feel that we have more of it than any one ever had. The way to bring it to perfection is to cultivate poetical impressions exclusively. Poetical impressions can be received only among natural scenes: for all that is artificial is antipoetical. Society is artificial, therefore we will live out of society. The mountains are natural, therefore we will live in the mountains. There we shall be shining models of purity and virtue, passing the whole day in the innocent and amiable occupation of going up and down hill, receiving poetical impressions, and communicating them in immortal verse to admiring generations." To some such perversion of intellect we owe that egregious confraternity of rhymesters, known by the name of the Lake Poets;[1] who certainly did receive and communicate to the world some of the most extraordinary poetical impressions that ever were heard of, and ripened into models of public virtue, too splendid to need illustration. They wrote verses on a new principle; saw rocks and rivers in a new light; and remaining studiously ignorant of history, society, and human nature, cultivated the phantasy only at the expence of the memory and the reason; and contrived, though they had retreated from the world for the express purpose of seeing nature as she was, to see her only as she was not, converting the land they lived in into a sort of fairy-land, which they peopled with mysticisms and chimæras. This gave what is called a new tone to poetry, and conjured up a herd of desperate imitators, who have brought the age of brass prematurely to its dotage.

The descriptive poetry of the present day has been called by its cultivators a return to nature. Nothing is more impertinent than this pretension. Poetry cannot travel out of the regions of its birth, the uncultivated lands of semi-civilized men. Mr. Wordsworth, the great leader of the returners to nature, cannot describe a scene under his own eyes without putting into it the shadow of a Danish boy or the living ghost of Lucy Gray,[2] or some similar phantastical parturition of the moods of his own mind.

In the origin and perfection of poetry, all the associations of life were composed of poetical materials. With us it is decidedly the reverse. We know too that there are no Dryads in Hyde-park nor Naiads in the Regent's-canal.[3] But barbaric manners and supernatural interventions are essential to poetry. Either in the scene, or in the time, or in both, it must be remote from our ordinary perceptions. While the historian and the philosopher are advancing in, and accelerating, the progress of knowledge, the poet is wallowing in the rubbish of departed ignorance, and raking up the ashes of dead savages to find gewgaws and rattles for the grown babies of the age....

These disjointed relics of tradition and fragments of second-hand observation, being woven into a tissue of verse, constructed on what Mr. Coleridge calls a new principle[4] (that is, no principle at all), compose a modern-antique compound of frippery and barbarism, in which the puling sentimentality of the present time is grafted on the misrepresented ruggedness of the past into a heterogeneous congeries of unamalgamating manners, sufficient to impose on the common readers of poetry, over whose understandings the poet of this class possesses that commanding advantage, which, in all circumstances and conditions of life, a man who knows something, however little, always possesses over one who knows nothing.

A poet in our times is a semi-barbarian in a civilized community. He lives in the days that are past. His ideas, thoughts, feelings, associations, are all with barbarous manners, obsolete customs, and exploded superstitions. The march of his intellect is like that of a crab, backward.[5] ... The highest inspirations of poetry are resolvable into three ingredients: the rant of unregulated passion, the whining of exaggerated feeling, and the cant of factitious sentiment: and can therefore serve only to ripen a splendid lunatic like Alexander, a puling drivel-

---

[1] Coleridge,* Southey,* and W. Wordsworth,* all of whom lived in the English Lake District.

[2] characters in two poems first published in the second edition of *Lyrical Ballads*.

[3] classical woodland and water spirits, respectively—here taking up residence in London.

[4] See Coleridge's Preface to *Christabel*.*

[5] Cf. Shakespeare, *Hamlet* 2.2.202.

ler like Werter,[1] or a morbid dreamer like Wordsworth. It can never make a philosopher, nor a statesman, nor in any class of life an useful or rational man. It cannot claim the slightest share in any one of the comforts and utilities of life of which we have witnessed so many and so rapid advances....

... Poetry was the mental rattle that awakened the attention of intellect in the infancy of civil society: but for the maturity of mind to make a serious business of the playthings of its childhood, is as absurd as for a full-grown man to rub his gums with coral,[2] and cry to be charmed to sleep by the jingle of silver bells....

Now when we consider that it is not the thinking and studious, and scientific and philosophical part of the community, not to those whose minds are bent on the pursuit and promotion of permanently useful ends and aims, that poets must address their minstrelsy, but to that much larger portion of the reading public, whose minds are not awakened to the desire of valuable knowledge, and who are indifferent to any thing beyond being charmed, moved, excited, affected, and exalted: charmed by harmony, moved by sentiment, excited by passion, affected by pathos, and exalted by sublimity: harmony, which is language on the rack of Procrustes;[3] sentiment, which is canting egotism in the mask of refined feeling; passion, which is the commotion of a weak and selfish mind; pathos, which is the whining of an unmanly spirit; and sublimity, which is the inflation of an empty head: when we consider that the great and permanent interests of human society become more and more the main spring of intellectual pursuit; that in proportion as they become so, the subordinacy of the ornamental to the useful will be more and more seen and acknowledged; and that therefore the progress of useful art and science, and of moral and political knowledge, will continue more and more to withdraw attention from frivolous and unconducive, to solid and conducive studies: that therefore the poetical audience will not only continually diminish in the proportion of its number to that of the rest of the reading public, but will also sink lower and lower in the comparison of intellectual acquirement: when we consider that the poet must still please his audience, and must therefore continue to sink to their level, while the rest of the community is rising above it: we may easily conceive that the day is not distant, when the degraded state of every species of poetry will be as generally recognized as that of dramatic poetry has long been: and this not from any decrease either of intellectual power, or intellectual acquisition, but because intellectual power and intellectual acquisition have turned themselves into other and better channels, and have abandoned the cultivation and the fate of poetry to the degenerate fry of modern rhymesters, and their olympic judges, the magazine critics, who continue to debate and promulgate oracles about poetry, as if it were still what it was in the Homeric age, the all-in-all of intellectual progression, and as if there were no such things in existence as mathematicians, astronomers, chemists, moralists, metaphysicians, historians, politicians, and political economists, who have built into the upper air of intelligence a pyramid, from the summit of which they see the modern Parnassus far beneath them, and, knowing how small a place it occupies in the comprehensiveness of their prospect, smile at the little ambition and the circumscribed perceptions with which the drivellers and mountebanks upon it are contending for the poetical palm and the critical chair.

---

[1] Perhaps Peacock is referring to Alexander the Great as Dryden depicts him in his poem *Alexander's Feast* (1697). Werther is the melancholy hero of Johann Wolfgang von Goethe's novel *The Sorrows of Young Werther* (1774); he kills himself out of hopeless love.

[2] Infants were given a piece of coral to cut their teeth on.

[3] In classical mythology, the robber Procrustes placed his victims on an iron bed, chopping or stretching to make them fit.

Caroline Lamb
1785 – 1828

Caroline Ponsonby was born in London on 13 November 1785. Her father, Frederick Ponsonby, Earl of Bessborough, was a prominent Whig politician. Because of the ill-health of her mother, Lady Henrietta Spencer, she was raised largely by her aunt, Georgiana Cavendish, Duchess of Devonshire.* At nine, she was sent to a school for young ladies, where she was such a disruptive student that the family doctor declared that she was in a "highly nervous state" because of her over-active brain (in adulthood, she seems to have suffered from manic-depressive illness); he recommended that she should no longer experience any kind of restraint or education, and so she had no more formal education until she was fifteen. In June 1805, she married William Lamb (later, as Lord Melbourne, Prime Minister); she was hysterical at the wedding and soon afterwards suffered a "nervous disorder." They had one son, who was developmentally disabled.

In March 1812, Lamb met Byron.* Despite her initial impression that he was "mad—bad—and dangerous to know," she embarked on a tumultuous affair with him. He tired of her after a few months, but she never got over him. She had a breakdown, stalked him, threatened suicide, and burned copies of all his letters to her, unable to bear parting with the originals. In 1816, she published *Glenarvon*, a novel based on their affair; it was anonymous, but the secret was transparent and it was a great success. In 1819, shortly after the publication of the first two cantos of *Don Juan*,* she published *A New Canto*, a parody of it (the parody was anonymous and its attribution to Lamb is uncertain). Her second novel, *Graham Hamilton* (1822), was designed to "offend nobody" and sold poorly, but her third, *Ada Reis* (1823), another fictionalized critique of Byron and the Byronic hero, did better.

When Byron died in Greece in 1824, Lamb had a nervous breakdown; she had another after she and her husband, out for a drive, happened to encounter Byron's funeral procession. The next year, the Lambs separated; Lamb lived at their country estate while William pursued his political career in London. In December 1827, Lamb began to suffer from dropsy. She died in London on 24 January 1828. (D.L.M.)

༺༻

A New Canto (1819)

1

I'm sick of fame—I'm gorged with it—so full
    I almost could regret the happier hour
When northern oracles proclaimed me dull,[1]
    Grieving my Lord should so mistake his power—
5 E'en they, who now my consequence would lull,
    And vaunt they hail'd and nurs'd the opening flower,
Vile cheats! He knew not, impudent Reviewer,
Clear spring of Helicon[2] from common sewer.

2

'Tis said they killed the gentle soul'd Montgomery[3]—
10   I'll swear, they did not shed for him a tear!
He had not spirit to revenge their mummery,
    Nor lordly purse to print and persevere:
I measured stings with 'em—a method summary—
    Not that I doubt their penitence sincere;
15 And I've a fancy running in my head
They'll like; or so by some it will be said.

3

When doomsday comes, St. Paul's[4] will be on fire—
    I should not wonder if we live to see it—
Of us, proof pickles, Heaven must rather tire,

---

[1] The *Edinburgh Review* panned Byron's first book, *Hours of Idleness* (1807), thus provoking his satire *English Bards and Scotch Reviewers* (1809): see line 13.

[2] a mountain in Greece, sacred to the Muses.

[3] In *English Bards* 418–25 and n., Byron complains about the ill-treatment of James Montgomery (1771–1854) by the *Edinburgh Review* but does not actually say it killed him.

[4] cathedral in London.

And want a reckoning—if so, so be it—
Only about the Cupola, or higher,
   If there's a place unoccupied, give me it—
To catch, before I touch my sinner's salary,[1]
The first grand crackle in the whispering gallery.[2]

4

The ball comes tumbling with a lively crash,
   And splits the pavement up, and shakes the shops,
Teeth chatter, china dances, spreads the flash,
   The omnium[3] falls, the Bank of England stops;
Loyal and radical, discreet and rash,
   Each on his knees in tribulation flops;
The Regent raves (Moore chuckling at his pain)[4]
And sends about for ministers in vain.

5

The roaring streamers flap, red flakes are shot
   This way and that, the town is a volcano—
And yells are heard, like those provoked by Lot,[5]
   Some, of the Smithfield[6] sort, and some *soprano*;
Some holy waster seek, the font is hot,
   And fizzing in a tea-kettle piano.
Now bring your magistrates, with yeomen back'd,
Bawls Belial,[7] and read the *Riot-act*![8]—

6

The Peak of Derbyshire[9] goes to and fro;
   Like drunken sot the Monument[10] is reeling;
Now fierce and fiercer comes the furious glow,
   The planets, like a juggler's ball, are wheeling:
I am a graceless poet, as you know,
   Yet would not wish a proper feeling,
Nor hint you'd hear, from saints in agitation,
The *lapsus linguæ*[11] of an execration.

7

Mark yon bright beauty, in her tragic airs,
   How her clear white the mighty smother tinges!
Delicious chaos! that such beauty bares!—
   And now those eyes outstretch their silken fringes,
Staring bewildered—and anon she tears
   Her raven tresses ere the wide flame singes—
Oh! would she feel as I could do, and cherish
One wild forgetful rapture, ere all perish!—

8

Who would be vain? Fair maids and ugly men
   Together rush, the dainty and the shabby,
(No gallantry will soothe ye, ladies, then)
   High dames, the wandering beggar and her babby,
In motley agony, a desperate train,
   Flocking to holy places like the Abbey,[12]
Till the black volumes, closing o'er them, scowl,
Muffling for ever curse, and shriek, and howl.

9

A woman then may rail, nor would I stint her;
   Her griefs, poor soul, are past redress in law—
And if this matter happen in the winter,
   There'll be at Petersburgh[13] a sudden thaw,
And Alexander's palace, every splinter
   Burn, Christmas like and merry, though the jaw
Of its imperial master take to trembling,
As when the French were quartered in the Cremlin.[14]

---

[1] Cf. Romans 6.23.

[2] a gallery in the dome of St. Paul's, where a whisper on one side of the dome can be heard on the other side.

[3] an index of the stock market.

[4] The Prince of Wales (later George IV) was made Prince Regent when George III became permanently insane in 1811; Moore* had satirized him in *Intercepted Letters; or, The Twopenny Post Bag* (1813).

[5] Cf. Genesis 19.5, 24–25.

[6] a cattle market and slaughterhouse area in London.

[7] Belial was a devil: see Milton, *Paradise Lost* 2.108–17.

[8] A magistrate read the Riot Act to disperse an unlawful assembly.

[9] the Peak District.

[10] a column commemorating the Great Fire of London (1666).

[11] "slip of the tongue" (L.).

[12] Westminster Abbey.

[13] St. Petersburg, the capital of Russia, where Alexander I (1777–1825) was Czar.

[14] French troops under Napoleon occupied Moscow on 14 September 1812. Over the next five days, fires destroyed most of the city. Napoleon began his disastrous retreat on 19 October.

10

Rare doings in the North! as trickle down
    Primeval snows, and white bears swash and caper,
And Bernadotte,[1] that swaggerer of renown,
    To Bonaparte again might hold a taper,
Ay, truckle to him, cap in hand or crown,
    To save his distance from the sturdy vapour.
Napoleon, too, will he look blank and paly?
He hung the citizens of Moscow gaily—

11

He made a gallant youth his darkling prey,
    Nor e'er would massacre or murder mince,
And yet I fear, on this important day
    To see the hero pitifully wince:
Go, yield him up to Beelzebub,[2] and say,
    Pray treat him like a gentleman and prince.
I doubt him thorough-bred, he's not a true one,
A blood hound spaniel-crossed and no Don Juan.

12

Death-watches[3] now, in every baking wall, tick
    Faster and faster, till they tick no more,
And Norway's copper-mines about the Baltic
    Swell, heave, and rumble with their boiling ore,
Like some griped giant's motion peristaltic,
    Then burst, and to the sea vast gutters pour;
And as the waters with the fire stream curl,
Zooks! what a whizzing, roaring, sweltering whirl!

13

Lo! the great deep laid bare, tremendous yawning,
    Its scalding waves retiring from the shore,
Affrighted whales on dry land sudden spawning,
    And small fish fry where fish ne'er fried before.
No Christian eye shall see another dawning—
    The Turkish infidel may now restore
His wives to liberty, and, ere to Hell he go,
Roll to the bottom of the Archipelago![4]

14

And now, ye coward sinners! (I'm a bold one,
    Scorning all here, nor caring for hereafter,
A radical, a stubborn, and an old one)
    Behold! each riding on a burning rafter,
The devils (in my arms I long to fold one)
    Splitting their blue and brazen sides with laughter,
Play at snapdragon,[5] in their merry fits,
O'er some conventicle for hypocrites.

15

Ay, serve the skulkers, with their looks so meek,
    As they've, no doubt, served lobsters in their time,
(Poor *blacks*! no Wilberforce[6] for them can speak,
    Pleading their colour is their only crime,)
Trundle them all to bubble and to squeak—
    No doubt they shut their ears against my rhyme,
Yet sneak, rank elders, fearful of denials,
To pick Susannahs up in Seven-Dials.[7]

16

Brave fiends! for usurers and misers melt
    And make a hell broth of their cursed gold:
On all who mock at want they never felt,
    On all whose consciences are bought and sold,
E'en as on me, be stern damnation dealt,
    And lawyers, damn them all—the blood runs cold,
That man should deal with misery, to mock it,
And filch an only shilling from its pocket.

17

Ay, damn them all, a deep damnation wait
    On all such callous, crooked, hopeless souls!
Ne'er mince the matter to discriminate,
    But let the devil strike them from the Rolls:[8]
'Twill cheer their clients to behold their fate,

---

[1] Jean Baptiste Jules Bernadotte, Crown Prince of Sweden, joined the alliance against Napoleon in 1813.

[2] "Lord of the Flies" (Heb.): a name for Satan.

[3] a kind of beetle; their ticking is an omen of death.

[4] the Greek Archipelago, in the Aegean Sea.

[5] a game in which raisins are snatched from burning brandy.

[6] William Wilberforce (1759–1833), Parliamentary leader of the movement to abolish the slave trade and, by 1819, to emancipate the slaves.

[7] a part of London frequented by prostitutes. For the story of Susanna and the elders, see Daniel 13 (the apocryphal Book of Susanna in some versions of the Bible).

[8] the register of qualified attorneys.

　　　　And round their bonfires dance in merry shoals.
135　Some poor men's tales I've heard upon my journies,
　　　　Would make a bishop long to roast attornies.

18

Perhaps the thing may take another turn,
　　And one smart shock may split the world in two,
And I in Italy, you soon may learn,
140　　On t'other half am reeling far from you.
No doubt 'twould split, where first it ought to burn,
　　Across some city, that its sins should rue,
Some wicked capital, for instance, Paris,
And stop the melodrames from Mr. Harris.[1]

19

145　Save London, none is wickeder, or bigger,
　　　An odious place too, in these modern times,
　　Small incomes, runaways, and swindlers eager
　　　　To fleece and dash; and then their quacks and mimes,
　　Their morals lax, and literary rigour,
150　　Their prim cesuras, and their gendered rhymes,[2]—
　　Mine never could abide their statutes critical,
　　They'd call them neutral or hermaphroditical.

20

True, their poor Play-wrights (truth, I speak with pain)
　　Yield ours a picking, and I beg their pardon—
155　'Tis needless—down must come poor Drury Lane,
　　And, scarcely less poor, down come Covent Garden:[3]
If we must blaze, no squabbles will remain
　　That Actors' hearts against each other harden—
Committees, creditors, all wrapped in flames,
160　That leave no joke for Horace Smith or James.[4]

21

In rebus modus est:[5] whene'er I write
　　I mean to rhapsodize, and nothing more—
If some poor nervous souls my Muse affright,
　　I might a strain of consolation pour,—
165　Talk of the spotless spirits, snowy white,
　　Which, newly clad, refreshing graves restore,
And silvery wreaths of glory round them curl'd,
Serenely rise above the blazing world.

22

Free, bursting from his mound of lively green,
170　　Wing'd light as zephyr of the rosy morn,
The poor man smiling on the proud is seen,
　　With something of a mild, forgiving scorn—
The marbled proud one, haply with the mean,
　　Sole on his prayer of intercession borne:[6]
175　Upward in peal harmonious they move,
Soft as the midnight tide of hallow'd love.

23

The rich humane, who with their common clay
　　Divided graciously, distinguished few;
Good Christians, who had slept their wrongs away,
180　　In peace with this life, and the next in view;
Strugglers with tyrant passion and its prey,
　　Love's single hearted victims, sacred, true,
Who, when dishonour's path alone could save,
Bore a pure pang to an untimely grave—

24

185　Blest they, who wear the vital spirit out,
　　Even thus, degrading not the holy fire,
Nor bear a prostituted sense about,
　　The misery of never quench'd desire,
Still quench'd, still kindling, every thought devout
190　　Lost in the changeful torment—portion dire!—
Return we to our heaven, our fire and smoke,
Though now you may begin to take the joke!

---

[1] Thomas Harris (d. 1820), manager of the Theatre Royal, Covent Garden, and producer of spectacular melodramas.

[2] A monosyllabic rhyme was called masculine; a bisyllabic one, feminine.

[3] the only two theatres in London licensed to present "legitimate" spoken drama. Both burned down regularly.

[4] In 1812, when Drury Lane was rebuilt after a fire, the managers held a competition for a poetic address to commemorate the reopening, but they ended up rejecting all the entries and asking Byron to write an address instead. Horace* and James Smith (1775–1839) then published a parodic book of *Rejected Addresses*, in which they imagined how famous contemporary poets might have undertaken the task.

[5] Cf. Plautus (3rd–2nd c. BC) *Pœnulus* 1.2.28: "In everything the golden mean is best" (tr. Bonnell Thornton).

[6] Cf. Ezekiel 37.12–13, Revelation 20.12.

25

What joke?—My verses—mine, and all beside,
 Wild, foolish tales of Italy and Spain,[1]
The gushing shrieks, the bubbling squeaks, the bride
 Of nature, blue-eyed, black-eyed, and her swain,
Kissing in grottoes, near the moon-lit tide,[2]
 Though to all men of common sense 'tis plain,
Except for rampant and amphibious brute,
Such damp and drizzly places would not suit.

26

Mad world! for fame we rant, call names, and fight—
 I scorn it heartily, yet love to dazzle it,
Dark intellects by day, as shops by night,
 All with a bright, new, speculative gas lit,[3]
Wars the blue vapour with the oil-fed light,
 Hot sputter Blackwood, Jeffrey, Gifford, Hazlitt[4]—
The Muse runs madder, and, as mine may tell,
Like a loose comet, mingles Heaven and Hell.

27

You shall have more of her another time,[5]
 Since gulled you will be with our flights poetic,
Our eight, and ten, and twenty feet sublime,
 Our maudlin, hey-down-derrified pathetic:
For my part, though I'm doom'd to write in rhyme,
 To read it would be worse than an emetic—
But something must be done to cure the spleen,[6]
And keep my name in capitals, like Kean.[7]

---

[1] Byron's *Beppo* (1818) is set in Venice; the first canto of *Don Juan,** in Seville.

[2] Cf. Byron, *Don Juan* 2.184–95.*

[3] Gas lighting was comparatively new in London.

[4] William Blackwood (1776–1834) was the publisher of the Tory *Blackwood's Edinburgh Magazine*; William Gifford (1756–1826), editor of the Tory *Quarterly Review*, Jeffrey* and Hazlitt* were Whig critics.

[5] Cf. Byron, *Don Juan* 1.221.*

[6] melancholy.

[7] Edmund Kean (1787?–1833), the great tragic actor.

---

from *Ada Reis, A Tale* (1823)

Duet

"The kiss that's on thy lip impress'd
 Is cold as parting kiss should be;
And he who clasps thee to his breast
 Again can never feel for thee:
The chain I gave—a true love-token—
 Thou see'st in every link is broken.
Then, since 't is so, 't were best to part;
 I here renounce the oaths I swore;
Correct thy faults, amend thy heart,
 And let us meet no more."

THE ANSWER

"I go: but ere I go from thee,
 Give back what thou hast ta'en from me—
A heart that knew nor care nor guile,
 A parent's fond approving smile,
The hopes which dared aspire to heav'n—
 Give these, and thou shalt be forgiv'n.
Take back the ring, take back the chain;
 Thy gifts, thy oaths, I will resign:
Take back thy heart, since pledged in vain,
 But, oh! restore what once was mine!

"Hope not for this, thy course is run;
 All that is left thee is to die.
The dew drops with the setting sun,
 And see the winds pass scornful by:
So when thou'rt left by me, thou'lt find
 The world as scornful as the wind.
A stamp is set upon thy name,
 A blight clouds o'er thy early fame.
There's nothing now thy fate can save:
 Live scorn'd—or hide thee in the grave!"

from I[saac] Nathan, *Fugitive Pieces and Reminiscences of Lord Byron: containing an entire new edition of the Hebrew Melodies, with the addition of several never before published; ... also some Original Poetry, Letters and Recollections of Lady Caroline Lamb* (1829)

Would I had seen thee dead and cold[1]

Would I had seen thee dead and cold,
   In thy lone grave asleep,
Than live, thy falsehood to behold,
   And penitent to weep:
5 For better, I thy grave could see,
Than know that thou art false to me!

Or rather, would that I had died,
   When happy on thy breast—
My love had then been satisfied,
10   And life's last moments blest,
For they taste bliss without alloy,
Who die in the sweet dream of joy!

But no! I feel the fault was mine,
   To think affection's chain
15 Could thy proud wayward heart confine,
   When *honor's* claim was vain:
Who *robs* the shrine where virtue lies,
Will not the *stolen relic* prize!

---

[1] Cf. Byron, "Stanzas" ("And thou art dead, as young and fair," 1812).

Barron Field
1786 – 1846

Barron Field was born on 23 October 1786, the second son of Henry Field, apothecary to Christ's Hospital, and Esther Barron Field. He was educated at Christ's Hospital, where he befriended Hunt* and Charles Lamb,* an old boy. He also came to know Coleridge,* Hazlitt,* and W. Wordsworth.* While studying law, he published essays in the *Quarterly Review*, Hunt's *Reflector*, and *The Times*. In 1816, he married Jane Cairncross, and shortly afterwards, they left for New South Wales, where he had been appointed judge of the supreme court. In 1819, he published *First Fruits of Australian Poetry*, the first Australian book of poems. A controversial judge, he was recalled in 1824. He later served as chief justice of Gibraltar. After retiring from the law, he continued to write and publish and edited several plays for the Shakspere Society. He died in Torquay on 11 April 1846. (D.L.M.)

☙☙☙

from *First Fruits of Australian Poetry* (1819)

The Kangaroo

—"mixtumque genus, prolesque biformis."
VIRG. Aen. vi.[1]

Kangaroo, Kangaroo!
Thou Spirit of Australia,
That redeems from utter failure,
From perfect desolation,
5   And warrants the creation
Of this fifth part of the Earth,
Which would seem an after-birth,
Not conceiv'd in the Beginning
(For GOD bless'd His work at first,
10   And saw that it was good),
But emerg'd at the first sinning,
When the ground was therefore curst;—
   And hence this barren wood!

Kangaroo, Kangaroo!
15 Tho' at first sight we should say,
In thy nature that there may
Contradiction be involv'd,
Yet, like discord well resolv'd,
It is quickly harmoniz'd.
20 Sphynx or mermaid realiz'd,
Or centaur unfabulous,
Would scarce be more prodigious,
Or Pegasus poetical,
Or hippogriff—chimeras all![2]
25 But, what Nature would compile,
Nature knows to reconcile;
And Wisdom, ever at her side,
Of all her children's justified.

She had made the squirrel fragile;
30 She had made the bounding hart;
But a third so strong and agile
Was beyond ev'n Nature's art;
So she join'd the former two
   In thee, Kangaroo!
35 To describe thee, it is hard:
Converse of the camélopard,[3]
Which beginneth camel-wise,
But endeth of the panther size,
Thy fore half, it would appear,
40 Had belong'd to some "small deer,"[4]
Such as liveth in a tree;
By thy hinder, thou should'st be
A large animal of chace,
Bounding o'er the forest's space;—
45   Join'd by some divine mistake,
None but Nature's hand can make—

---

[1] "and the mongrel breed ... a twiformed offspring" (Virgil, *Aeneid* 6.25; tr. H. Rushton Fairclough). Virgil is describing the Minotaur, half-man, half-bull.

[2] more mythical multiformed animals.

[3] giraffe.

[4] Shakespeare, *King Lear* 3.4.130.

Nature, in her wisdom's play,
On Creation's holiday.

For howsoe'er anomalous,
Thou yet art not incongruous,
Repugnant or preposterous.
Better-proportion'd animal,
More graceful or ethereal,
Was never follow'd by the hound,
With fifty steps to thy one bound.
Thou can'st not be amended: no;
Be as thou art; thou best art so.

When sooty swans are once more rare,
And duck-moles[1] the Museum's care,
Be still the glory of this land,
Happiest Work of finest Hand!

---

[1] "The *cygnus niger* of Juvenal is no *rara avis* in Australia; and time has here given ample proof of the *ornythorinchus paradoxus*." (B.F.) In *Satires* 6.165, Juvenal offers a *cygnus niger* (black swan) as an example of a *rara avis* (rare bird, rarity); they are common in Australia. The *Ornythorhynchus paradoxus* is the duck-billed platypus (Field calls it a duck-mole).

Mary Russell Mitford
1787 – 1855

Mary Mitford was born in Alresford, Hampshire, on 16 December 1787, the only surviving child of Mary Russell, an heiress, and George Mitford, a surgeon who soon spent his wife's fortune. The family was temporarily saved from financial ruin when, in 1797, Mary bought her father a winning lottery ticket. They moved to Reading and Mitford attended the Abbey School in London. However, in 1802 she left school to return home, writing and publishing poetry in part to contribute to the family income. Forced to sell their house outside Reading, the family moved into a cottage in the village of Three Mile Cross. Mitford avoided having to work as a teacher or governess by publishing plays and prose. By 1825 she had written four tragedies. With Macready in the title role, *Julian* was produced at Covent Garden—and attacked by critics—in 1823; *Foscari* (on the same subject as a contemporary play by Byron)* was eventually staged at Covent Garden in 1826. Mitford's most successful play was *Rienzi*, produced at Drury Lane in 1828.

Other plays followed (all were published in two volumes in 1854); but Mitford simultaneously turned to writing prose sketches, four of which were published in Thomas Campbell's* *New Monthly Magazine* in 1821. *Our Village*, her most popular work, began in 1819 with sketches published in the *Lady's Magazine*. By 1824, the first volume was in print; a second followed in 1826. Three more volumes appeared in the next six years, describing village life and picturesque scenes and telling the stories of ordinary people.

Mitford went on to write further sketches—*Belford Regis; or, Sketches of a Country Town* (1835) and *Country Stories* (1837). She became the friend of many writers, including Elizabeth Barrett Browning (with whom she corresponded) and several Americans, including James Greenleaf Whittier, Longfellow,* and Hawthorne.* Hemans* and Harriet Martineau were among her correspondents. In 1837 she was granted a government pension; following her father's death in 1842, friends raised a subscription to pay her considerable debts. *Recollections of a Literary Life* (1852) and *Atherton* (1854) were her last major works. Mitford died following a carriage accident on 10 January 1855. (A.M.)

❧❧❧

from *Our Village: Sketches of Rural Character and Scenery* (1824)

Nutting[1]

September 26th.—One of those delicious autumnal days, when the air, the sky, and the earth seem lulled into a universal calm, softer and milder even than May. We sallied forth for a walk, in a mood congenial to the weather and the season, avoiding, by mutual consent, the bright and sunny common, and the gay high-road, and stealing through shady, unfrequented lanes, where we were not likely to meet any one—not even the pretty family procession which in other years we used to contemplate with so much interest—the father, mother, and children, returning from the wheat-field, the little ones laden with bristling, close-tied bunches of wheat-ears, their own gleanings, or a bottle and a basket which had contained their frugal dinner, while the mother would carry her babe, hushing and lulling it, and the father and an elder child trudged after with the cradle, all seeming weary, and all happy. We shall not see such a procession as this to-day; for the harvest is nearly over, the fields are deserted, the silence may almost be felt. Except the wintry notes of the red-breast, nature herself is mute. But how beautiful, how gentle, how harmonious, how rich! The rain has preserved to the herbage all the freshness and verdure of spring, and the world of leaves has lost nothing of its mid-summer brightness, and the hare-bell is on the banks, and the woodbine in the hedges, and the low furze, which the lambs cropped

---

[1] the process of gathering nuts—in this case, hazelnuts or filberts; cf. the poem of the same title by William Wordsworth.*

in the spring, has burst again into its golden blossoms.

All is beautiful that the eye can see; perhaps the more beautiful for being shut in with a forest-like closeness. We have no prospect in this labyrinth of lanes, cross-roads, mere cart-ways, leading to the innumerable little farms into which this part of the parish is divided. Up-hill or down, these quiet woody lanes scarcely give us a peep at the world, except when, leaning over a gate, we look into one of the small enclosures, hemmed in with hedge-rows, so closely set with growing timber, that the meady opening looks almost like a glade in a wood; or when some cottage, planted at a corner of one of the little greens formed by the meeting of these cross-ways, almost startles us by the unexpected sight of the dwellings of men in such a solitude. But that we have more of hill and dale, and that our cross-roads are excellent in their kind, this side of our parish would resemble the description given of La Vendée, in Madame Laroche-Jacquelin's most interesting book.[1] I am sure, if wood can entitle a country to be called Le Bocage,[2] none can have a better right to the name. Even this pretty, snug farm-house on the hill-side, with its front covered with the rich vine, which goes wreathing up to the very top of the clustered chimney, and its sloping orchard full of fruit—even this pretty, quiet nest can hardly peep out of its leaves. Ah! they are gathering in the orchard harvest. Look at that young rogue in the old mossy apple-tree—that great tree, bending with the weight of its golden-rennets[3]—see how he pelts his little sister beneath with apples as red and as round as her own cheeks, while she, with her outstretched frock, is trying to catch them, and laughing and offering to pelt again as often as one bobs against her; and look at that still younger imp, who, as grave as a judge, is creeping on hands and knees under the tree, picking up the apples as they fall so deedily,[4] and depositing them so honestly in the great basket on the grass, already fixed so firmly and opened so widely, and filled almost to overflowing by the brown rough fruitage of the golden-rennet's next neighbor the russeting; and see that smallest urchin of all, seated apart in infantine state on the turfy bank, with that toothsome piece of deformity, a crumpling, in each hand, now biting from one sweet, hard, juicy morsel and now from another. Is not that a pretty English picture? And then, farther up the orchard, that bold hardy lad, the eldest-born, who has scaled (Heaven knows how!) the tall, straight upper branch of that great pear-tree, and is sitting there as securely and as fearlessly, in as much real safety and apparent danger, as a sailor on the top-mast. Now he shakes the tree with a mighty swing that brings down a pelting shower of stony bergamots,[5] which the father gathers rapidly up, while the mother can hardly assist for her motherly fear—a fear which only spurs the spirited boy to bolder ventures. Is not that a pretty picture? And they are such a handsome family too, the Brookers. I do not know that there is any gipsy blood, but there is the true gipsy complexion, richly brown, with cheeks and lips so deeply red, black hair curling close to their heads in short crisp rings, white shining teeth—and such eyes! That sort of beauty entirely eclipses your mere roses and lilies. Even Lizzy, the prettiest of fair children, would look poor and watery by the side of Willy Brooker, the sober little personage who is picking up the apples with his small chubby hands, and filling the basket so orderly, next to his father the most useful man in the field. "Willy!" He hears without seeing; for we are quite hidden by the high bank, and a spreading hawthorn bush that overtops it, though between the lower branches and the grass we have found a convenient peep-hole.

---

[1] "An almost equally interesting account of that very peculiar and interesting scenery may be found in *The Maid of La Vendée*, an English novel, remarkable for its simplicity and truth of painting, written by Mrs. Le Noir, the daughter of Christopher Smart, an inheritrix of much of his talent. Her words deserve to be better known." (M.M.) In 1793–96, Henri Laroche-Jacquelin led counter-revolutionary troops against the French republican army in La Vendée, a region south of the river Loire; his wife wrote a history of the region. The poet Christopher Smart's daughter, Elizabeth Anne Smart Le Noir (1754–1841), published *The Maid of La Vendée* in 1810. The novel had been first published in 1808 under the title *Clara de Montfier, a Moral Tale*.

[2] "grove, copse" (Fr.).

[3] a variety of apple.

[4] "'Deedily'—I am not quite sure that this word is good English; but it is genuine Hampshire, and is used by the most correct of female writers, Miss Austen. It means (and it is no small merit that it has no exact synonym) any thing done with a profound and plodding attention, an action which engrosses all the powers of mind and body." (M.M.) See Jane Austen,* *Emma* (1815), vol. 2, chap. 10.

[5] a variety of pear.

"Willy!" The voice sounds to him like some fairy dream, and the black eyes are raised from the ground with sudden wonder, the long silky eyelashes thrown back till they rest on the delicate brow, and a deeper blush is burning on those dark cheeks, and a smile is dimpling about those scarlet lips. But the voice is silent now, and the little quiet boy, after a moment's pause, is gone coolly to work again. He is indeed a most lovely child. I think some day or other he must marry Lizzy; I shall propose the match to their respective mammas. At present the parties are rather too young for a wedding—the intended bridegroom being, as I should judge, six, or thereabout, and the fair bride barely five—but at least we might have a betrothment after the royal fashion—there could be no harm in that. Miss Lizzy, I have no doubt, would be as demure and coquettish as if ten winters more had gone over her head, and poor Willy would open his innocent black eyes, and wonder what was going forward. They would be the very Oberon and Titania[1] of the village, the fairy king and queen.

Ah! here is the hedge along which the periwinkle wreathes and twines so profusely, with its evergreen leaves shining like the myrtle, and its starry blue flowers. It is seldom found wild in this part of England; but, when we do meet with it, it is so abundant and so welcome—the very robin-redbreast of flowers, a winter friend.

Unless in those unfrequent frosts which destroy all vegetation, it blossoms from September to June, surviving the last lingering crane's-bill,[2] forerunning the earliest primrose, hardier even than the mountain daisy, peeping out from beneath the snow, looking at itself in the ice, smiling through the tempests of life, and yet welcoming and enjoying the sunbeams. Oh, to be like that flower![3]

The little spring that has been bubbling under the hedge all along the hill-side, begins, now that we have mounted the eminence and are imperceptibly descending, to deviate into a capricious variety of clear deep pools and channels, so narrow and so choked with weeds that a child might overstep them. The hedge has also changed its character. It is no longer the close, compact vegetable wall of hawthorn, and maple, and brier-roses, intertwined with bramble and woodbine, and crowned with large elms or thickly-set saplings. No! the pretty meadow which rises high above us, backed and almost surrounded by a tall coppice, needs no defence on our side but its own steep bank, garnished with tufts of broom, with pollard oaks wreathed with ivy, and here and there with long patches of hazel overhanging the water. "Ah, there are still nuts on that bough!" and in an instant my dear companion, active and eager and delighted as a boy, has hooked down with his walking-stick one of the lissome hazel stalks, and cleared it of its tawny clusters, and in another moment he has mounted the bank; and is in the midst of the nuttery, now transferring the spoil from the lower branches into that vast variety of pockets which gentlemen carry about them, now bending the tall tops into the lane, holding them down by main force so that I might reach them and enjoy the pleasure of collecting some of the plunder myself. A very great pleasure he knew it would be. I doffed my shawl, tucked up my flounces, turned my straw bonnet into a basket, and began gathering and scrambling—for, manage it how you may, nutting is scrambling work; those boughs, however tightly you may grasp them by the young fragrant twigs and the bright green leaves, will recoil and burst away; but there is a pleasure even in that; so on we go, scrambling and gathering with all our might and all our glee. Oh, what an enjoyment! All my life long I have had a passion for that sort of seeking which implies finding (the secret, I believe, of the love of field-sports, which is in man's mind a natural impulse), therefore I love violeting; therefore, when we had a fine garden, I used to love to gather strawberries, and cut asparagus, and, above all, to collect the filberts from the shrubberies; but this hedgerow nutting beats that sport all to nothing. That was a make-believe thing compared with this; there was no surprise, no suspense, no unexpectedness—it was as inferior to this wild nutting as the turning out of a bagfox[4] is to unearthing the fellow, in the eyes of a staunch

---

[1] the king and queen of the fairies in Shakespeare's *A Midsummer Night's Dream*.

[2] wild geranium.

[3] Cf. Robert Burns, "To a Mountain-Daisy."*

[4] a captured fox, set free in order to be hunted.

fox-hunter.

Oh, what enjoyment this nut-gathering is! They are in such abundance that it seems as if there were not a boy in the parish, nor a young man, nor a young woman—for a basket of nuts is the universal tribute of country gallantry: our pretty damsel Harriet has had at least half-a-dozen this season; but no one has found out these. And they are so full, too, we lose half of them from over-ripeness; they drop from the socket at the slightest motion. If we lose, there is one who finds. May is as fond of nuts as a squirrel, and cracks the shell and extracts the kernel with equal dexterity. Her white, glossy head is upturned now to watch them as they fall. See how her neck is thrown back like that of a swan, and how beautifully her folded ears quiver with expectation, and how her quick eye follows the rustling noise, and her light feet dance and pat the ground, and leap up with eagerness, seeming almost sustained in the air, just as I have seen her when Brush is beating a hedge-row, and she knows, from his questing, that there is a hare afoot. See, she has caught that nut just before it touched the water; but the water would have been no defence—she fishes them from the bottom, she delves after them among the matted grass, even my bonnet, how beggingly she looks at that! "Oh, what a pleasure nutting is! Is it not, May? But the pockets are almost full, and so is the basket-bonnet, and that bright watch, the sun, says it is late; and, after all, it is wrong to rob the poor boys, is it not, May?" May shakes her graceful head denyingly, as if she understood the question; "and we must go home now, must we not? But we will come nutting again some time or other—shall we not, my May?"

George Gordon, Lord Byron
1788 – 1824

Byron was born in London on 22 January 1788, the only child of Captain John ("Mad Jack") Byron, a fortune-hunter, and Catherine Gordon Byron, an heiress. The baby had a deformed right foot, which would inconvenience and shame him all his life. Mad Jack had already spent the fortune and broken the heart of one wife, who had borne him a daughter, Augusta, and then died; when he had spent Catherine's fortune and broken her heart, he abandoned his wife and child and moved to France, where he died in 1791. Mrs. Byron took her child to Aberdeen, where sexual abuse by a Calvinist nursemaid left him with a lifelong ambivalence about women and hatred of religious hypocrisy.

In 1798, Byron's great-uncle, the "Wicked Lord" Byron died, and the ten-year-old became the sixth Baron Byron. He was educated at Harrow School and at Trinity College, Cambridge. He fell in love early and often; he also began early to live beyond his means, running up the huge debts with which moneylenders were pleased to accommodate aristocrats. After privately printing a number of his poems, he published his first volume, *Hours of Idleness*, in 1807; a negative review in the *Edinburgh Review* provoked his first major poem, the satire *English Bards, and Scotch Reviewers* (1809).

In 1809, after coming of age and taking his seat in the House of Lords, Byron embarked on a two-year tour of Portugal, Spain, Greece, Albania, and Turkey with his friend John Cam Hobhouse. On this tour (especially after Hobhouse's return to England), he explored the homosexual side of his nature, reporting to another friend that he had had so many boys that he was almost tired of them; he also wrote the first two cantos of *Childe Harold's Pilgrimage* (1812), the poem that would make him famous.

Byron's own return to England was marked by tragedy: the deaths, in rapid succession, of his mother, two college friends, and John Edleston, a Platonic boyfriend. After *Childe Harold* (the first edition, of five hundred copies, sold out in three days), he published a series of narrative poems set in the Near and Middle East; the most successful of these, *The Corsair* (1814), sold ten thousand copies on the day of publication. He had a series of love affairs, notably with the unstable Lady Caroline Lamb,* who not unaptly described Byron himself as "mad—bad—and dangerous to know," and—even more dangerously—with his half-sister, Augusta. In January 1815, apparently in an attempt to redeem himself, he married Annabella Milbanke. The marriage was a disaster: Byron seems to have suffered a psychotic episode, and after enduring a year of abuse, Lady Byron left him, taking their infant daughter, Augusta Ada, in January 1816. Byron never saw either of them again.

Abandoned, bankrupt, his reputation ruined by rumours about his bisexuality and incest, Byron left England, never to return. Before leaving, he had a brief affair with Claire Clairmont (stepsister of Mary Godwin, later Mary Shelley);* she would bear him a daughter, Allegra, in 1817. Byron's first major stop was Geneva, where he met Clairmont, Godwin, and her lover P.B. Shelley,* and began one of the most productive phases of his career, writing the third canto of *Childe Harold* (1816), *Manfred* (1817), and a number of important shorter poems.

Byron spent most of the rest of his life in Italy. After a period of promiscuity, he became the *cavalier servente*, or acknowledged lover, of the Countess Teresa Guiccioli, and after she separated from her husband, they lived together. He took responsibility for his daughter Allegra but then placed her in a convent school, where she died of typhus in 1822, at the age of only five. Later in 1822, P.B. Shelley was drowned; Byron attended his cremation and helped Mary Shelley until she returned to England in 1823. Meanwhile, poetry poured out of him. After writing a fourth canto of *Childe Harold*, he wrote a brief comic tale, *Beppo* (1818), inspired by a comic poem by John Hookham Frere,* and then embarked on his comic epic, *Don Juan* (1819–24). He also wrote a series of plays, ranging from the severely neoclassical *Marino Faliero, Doge of Venice* (1821) to the fantastic—and, many critics alleged, blasphemous—*Cain, A Mystery* (1821).

In his last years, Byron became involved in what he called the "*poetry* of politics." In 1820, he joined the Carbonari, a secret society trying (unsuccessfully) to overthrow Austrian rule in Italy. In July 1823, along with

Pietro Gamba (Countess Guiccioli's brother) and his romantic friend Edward John Trelawny,* Byron sailed to Greece to assist the Greeks in their war of independence against Turkey, which had begun in 1821. His efforts were thoughtful, courageous, and almost completely unsuccessful (Trelawny preferred to defect to a bandit chief with the romantic name Odysseus). After being soaked with rain during a horse ride, Byron came down with fever; he died on 19 April 1824. When news of his death reached London, his friend Hobhouse, his publisher, John Murray, and representatives of his wife and sister burned his memoirs, unread, to protect his reputation—one of the greatest acts of vandalism in literary history. But the news of his death also helped to unite the Greeks in their struggle and to rally European support for them; Greece finally won its independence in 1829. (D.L.M.)

The Giaour.[1] A Fragment of a Turkish Tale (1813)

ADVERTISEMENT

The tale which these disjointed fragments present, is founded upon circumstances now less common in the East than formerly; either because the ladies are more circumspect than in the "olden time"; or because the Christians have better fortune, or less enterprize. The story, when entire, contained the adventures of a female slave, who was thrown, in the Mussulman manner, into the sea for infidelity, and avenged by a young Venetian, her lover, at the time the Seven Islands were possessed by the Republic of Venice,[2] and soon after the Arnauts were beaten back from the Morea, which they had ravaged for some time subsequent to the Russian invasion.[3] The desertion of the Mainotes,[4] on being refused the plunder of Misitra, led to the abandonment of that enterprize, and to the desolation of the Morea, during which the cruelty exercised on all sides was unparalleled even in the annals of the faithful.

No breath of air to break the wave
That rolls below the Athenian's grave,
That tomb[5] which, gleaming o'er the cliff,
First greets the homeward-veering skiff,
5 High o'er the land he saved in vain—
When shall such hero live again?

* * * * *

Fair clime! where every season smiles
Benignant o'er those blessed isles,
Which seen from far Colonna's height,
10 Make glad the heart that hails the sight,
And lend to loneliness delight.
There mildly dimpling—Ocean's cheek
Reflects the tints of many a peak
Caught by the laughing tides that lave
15 These Edens of the eastern wave;
And if at times a transient breeze
Break the blue chrystal of the seas,
Or sweep one blossom from the trees,
How welcome is each gentle air,
20 That wakes and wafts the odours there!
For there—the Rose o'er crag or vale,
Sultana of the Nightingale,[6]
The maid for whom his melody—

---

[1] This text is that of the seventh edition, "with additions" (1816). Byron added to this poem in each new edition: the first edition of 1813 was less than 700 lines in length; the seventh is almost twice as long. The poem is dedicated to Samuel Rogers,* a friend of Byron, whose *Voyage of Columbus* (1812) may have suggested Byron's use of the fragment form.

[2] soon after 1779.

[3] Russia invaded the Morea (or Peloponnesian peninsula) and captured Misithra in 1774.

[4] The inhabitants of Maina were famous for independence and banditry.

[5] "A tomb above the rocks on the promontory, by some supposed the sepulchre of Themistocles." (L.B.) See Plutarch, *Life of Themistocles* 32. Themistocles defeated the Persians at the great naval battle of Salamis, 480 BC: see line 113. The tomb is on the shoreline of the Piraeus, the harbour of Athens. Byron visited it on 18 January 1810.

[6] "The attachment of the nightingale to the rose is a well-known Persian fable—if I mistake not, the 'Bulbul of a thousand tales' is one of his appellations." (L.B.)

His thousand songs are heard on high,
25 Blooms blushing to her lover's tale;
His queen, the garden queen, his Rose,
Unbent by winds, unchill'd by snows,
Far from the winters of the west
By every breeze and season blest,
30 Returns the sweets by nature given
In softest incense back to heaven;
And grateful yields that smiling sky
Her fairest hue and fragrant sigh.
And many a summer flower is there,
35 And many a shade that love might share,
And many a grotto, meant for rest,
That holds the pirate for a guest;
Whose bark in sheltering cove below
Lurks for the passing peaceful prow,
40 Till the gay mariner's guitar[1]
Is heard, and seen the evening star;
Then stealing with the muffled oar,
Far shaded by the rocky shore,
Rush the night-prowlers on the prey,
45 And turn to groans his roundelay.
Strange—that where Nature lov'd to trace,
As if for Gods, a dwelling-place,[2]
And every charm and grace hath mixed
Within the paradise she fixed—
50 There man, enamour'd of distress,
Should mar it into wilderness,
And trample, brute-like, o'er each flower
That tasks not one laborious hour;[3]
Nor claims the culture of his hand
55 To bloom along the fairy land,
But springs as to preclude his care,
And sweetly woos him—but to spare!
Strange—that where all is peace beside
There passion riots in her pride,
60 And lust and rapine wildly reign,
To darken o'er the fair domain.
It is as though the fiends prevail'd

Against the seraphs they assail'd,
And fixed, on heavenly thrones, should dwell
65 The freed inheritors of hell—
So soft the scene, so form'd for joy,
So curst the tyrants that destroy!

He who hath bent him o'er the dead,
Ere the first day of death is fled;
70 The first dark day of nothingness,
The last of danger and distress;
(Before Decay's effacing fingers
Have swept the lines where beauty lingers,)
And mark'd the mild angelic air—
75 The rapture of repose that's there—
The fixed yet tender traits that streak
The languor of the placid cheek,
And—but for that sad shrouded eye,
    That fires not—wins not—weeps not—now—
80   And but for that chill changeless brow,
Where cold Obstruction's apathy[4]
Appals the gazing mourner's heart,
As if to him it could impart
The doom he dreads, yet dwells upon—
85 Yes—but for these and these alone,
Some moments—aye—one treacherous hour,
He still might doubt the tyrant's power,
So fair—so calm—so softly seal'd
The first—last look—by death reveal'd![5]
90 Such is the aspect of this shore—
'Tis Greece—but living Greece no more!
So coldly sweet, so deadly fair,
We start—for soul is wanting there.
Hers is the loveliness in death,
95 That parts not quite with parting breath;

---

[1] "The guitar is the constant amusement of the Greek sailor by night, with a steady fair wind, and during a calm, it is accompanied always by the voice, and often by dancing." (L.B.)

[2] Cf. Milton, *Paradise Lost* 5.69–70.

[3] Cf. Matthew 6.28.

[4] "'Aye, but to die and go we know not where,
To lie in cold obstruction.'
     Measure for Measure [3.1.118–19]." (L.B.)

[5] "I trust that few of my readers have ever had an opportunity of witnessing what is here attempted in description, but those who have will probably retain a painful remembrance of that singular beauty which pervades, with few exceptions, the features of the dead, a few hours, and but for a few hours after 'the spirit is not there.' It is to be remarked in cases of violent death by gun-shot wounds, the expression is always that of languor, whatever the natural energy of the sufferer's character; but in death from a stab the countenance preserves its traits of feeling or ferocity, and the mind its bias, to the last." (L.B.)

But beauty with that fearful bloom,
That hue which haunts it to the tomb—
Expression's last receding ray,
A gilded halo hovering round decay,
The farewell beam of Feeling past away!
Spark of that flame—perchance of heavenly birth—
Which gleams—but warms no more its cherish'd earth!

    Clime of the unforgotten brave!—
Whose land from plain to mountain-cave
Was Freedom's home or Glory's grave—
Shrine of the mighty! can it be,
That this is all remains of thee?
Approach thou craven crouching slave—
Say, is not this Thermopylae?[1]
These waters blue that round you lave
Oh servile offspring of the free—
Pronounce what sea, what shore is this?
The gulf, the rock of Salamis!
These scenes—their story not unknown—
Arise, and make again your own;
Snatch from the ashes of your sires
The embers of their former fires,
And he who in the strife expires
Will add to theirs a name of fear,
That Tyranny shall quake to hear,
And leave his sons a hope, a fame,
They too will rather die than shame;
For Freedom's battle once begun,
Bequeathed by bleeding Sire to Son,
Though baffled oft is ever won.
Bear witness, Greece, thy living page,
Attest it many a deathless age!
While kings in dusty darkness hid,
Have left a nameless pyramid,
Thy heroes—though the general doom
Hath swept the column from their tomb,
A mightier monument command,
The mountains of their native land!
There points thy Muse to stranger's eye,
The graves of those that cannot die!

'Twere long to tell, and sad to trace,
Each step from splendour to disgrace,
Enough—no foreign foe could quell
Thy soul, till from itself it fell,
Yes! Self-abasement pav'd the way
To villain-bonds and despot-sway.

What can he tell who treads thy shore?
    No legend of thine olden time,
No theme on which the muse might soar,
High as thine own in days of yore,
    When man was worthy of thy clime.
The hearts within thy valleys bred,
The fiery souls that might have led
    Thy sons to deeds sublime;
Now crawl from cradle to the grave,
Slaves—nay, the bondsmen of a slave,[2]
    And callous, save to crime;
Stain'd with each evil that pollutes
Mankind, where least above the brutes;
Without even savage virtue blest,
Without one free or valiant breast.
Still to the neighbouring ports they waft
Proverbial wiles, and ancient craft,
In this the subtle Greek is found,
For this, and this alone, renown'd.
In vain might Liberty invoke
The spirit to its bondage broke,
Or raise the neck that courts the yoke:
No more her sorrows I bewail,
Yet this will be a mournful tale,
And they who listen may believe,
Who heard it first had cause to grieve.

          * * * * *

    Far, dark, along the blue sea glancing,
The shadows of the rocks advancing,
Start on the fisher's eye like boat
Of island-pirate or Mainote;
And fearful for his light caique

---

[1] a mountain pass (Gr. "hot gates"), the site of a glorious defeat in 480 BC, when Leonidas of Sparta and a tiny army held off a much larger Persian force for three days, and all died fighting rather than retreat. There were further battles there in 279 and 191 BC.

[2] "Athens is the property of the Kislar Aga, (the slave of the seraglio and guardian of the women), who appoints the Waywode.—A pandar and eunuch—these are not polite yet true appellations—now *governs* the *governor* of Athens!" (L.B.) The Waiwode was the Turkish governor of Athens.

He shuns the near but doubtful creek,
Though worn and weary with his toil,
175 And cumber'd with his scaly spoil,
Slowly, yet strongly, plies the oar,
Till Port Leone's safer shore
Receives him by the lovely light
That best becomes an Eastern night.

* * * * *

180   Who thundering comes on blackest steed?[1]
With slacken'd bit and hoof of speed,
Beneath the clattering iron's sound
The cavern'd echoes wake around
In lash for lash, and bound for bound;
185 The foam that streaks the courser's side,
Seems gather'd from the ocean-tide:
Though weary waves are sunk to rest,
There's none within his rider's breast,
And though to-morrow's tempest lower,
190 'Tis calmer than thy heart, young Giaour![2]
I know thee not, I loathe thy race,
But in thy lineaments I trace
What time shall strengthen, not efface;
Though young and pale, that sallow front
195 Is scath'd by fiery passion's brunt,
Though bent on earth thine evil eye
As meteor like thou glidest by,
Right well I view, and deem thee one
Whom Othman's sons should slay or shun.

200   On—on he hastened—and he drew
My gaze of wonder as he flew:
Though like a demon of the night
He passed and vanished from my sight;
His aspect and his air impressed
205 A troubled memory on my breast;
And long upon my startled ear
Rung his dark courser's hoofs of fear.
He spurs his steed—he nears the steep,
That jutting shadows o'er the deep—
210 He winds around—he hurries by—
The rock relieves him from mine eye—
For well I ween unwelcome he
Whose glance is fixed on those that flee;
And not a star but shines too bright
215 On him who takes such timeless flight.
He wound along—but ere he passed
One glance he snatched—as if his last—
A moment checked his wheeling steed—
A moment breathed him from his speed[3]—
220 A moment on his stirrup stood—
Why looks he o'er the olive wood?—
The crescent glimmers on the hill,
The Mosque's high lamps are quivering still;
Though too remote for sound to wake
225 In echoes of the far tophaike,[4]
The flashes of each joyous peal
Are seen to prove the Moslem's zeal.
To-night—set Rhamazani's sun—
To-night—the Bairam feast's begun—
230 To-night—but who and what art thou
Of foreign garb and fearful brow?
And what are these to thine or thee,
That thou should'st either pause or flee?
He stood—some dread was on his face—
235 Soon Hatred settled in its place—
It rose not with the reddening flush
Of transient Anger's darkening blush,
But pale as marble o'er the tomb,
Whose ghastly whiteness aids its gloom.
240 His brow was bent—his eye was glazed—

He raised his arm, and fiercely raised;
And sternly shook his hand on high,
As doubting to return or fly;—
Impatient of his flight delayed
245 Here loud his raven charger neighed—
Down glanced that hand, and grasped his blade—
That sound had burst his waking dream,

---

[1] The speaker of lines 180–786 is the Turkish fisher described in the previous paragraph.

[2] "Infidel." (L.B.)

[3] Cf. Scott,* *The Lay of the Last Minstrel* (1805) 1.27.1–2.

[4] "'Tophaike,' musquet.—The Bairam is announced by the cannon at sunset; the illumination of the Mosques, and the firing of all kinds of small arms, loaded with *ball*, proclaim it during the night." (L.B.) The Bairam is a three-day festival marking the end of the holy month of Ramadhan.

As Slumber starts at owlet's scream.—
The spur hath lanced his courser's sides—
250 Away—away—for life he rides—
Swift as the hurled on high jerreed,[1]
Springs to the touch his startled steed,
The rock is doubled—and the shore
Shakes with the clattering tramp no more—
255 The crag is won—no more is seen
His Christian crest and haughty mien.—
'Twas but an instant—he restrained
That fiery barb so sternly reined—
'Twas but a moment that he stood,
260 Then sped as if by death pursued;
But in that instant, o'er his soul
Winters of Memory seemed to roll;
And gather in that drop of time
A life of pain, an age of crime.
265 O'er him who loves, or hates, or fears,
Such moment pours the grief of years—
What felt *he* then—at once opprest
By all that most distracts the breast?
That pause—which pondered o'er his fate,
270 Oh, who its dreary length shall date!
Though in Time's record nearly nought,
It was Eternity to Thought![2]
For infinite as boundless space
The thought that Conscience must embrace,
275 Which in itself can comprehend
Woe without name—or hope—or end.—

The hour is past, the Giaour is gone,
And did he fly or fall alone?
Woe to that hour he came or went,
280 The curse for Hassan's sin was sent
To turn a palace to a tomb;

He came, he went, like the Simoom,[3]
That harbinger of fate and gloom,
Beneath whose widely-wasting breath
285 The very cypress droops to death—
Dark tree—still sad, when others' grief is fled,
The only constant mourner o'er the dead!

The steed is vanished from the stall,
No serf is seen in Hassan's hall;
290 The lonely Spider's thin grey pall
Waves slowly widening o'er the wall;
The Bat builds in his Haram bower;
And in the fortress of his power
The Owl usurps the beacon-tower;
295 The wild-dog howls o'er the fountain's brim,
With baffled thirst, and famine, grim,
For the stream has shrunk from its marble bed,
Where the weeds and the desolate dust are spread.
'Twas sweet of yore to see it play
300 And chase the sultriness of day—
As springing high the silver dew
In whirls fantastically flew,
And flung luxurious coolness round
The air, and verdure o'er the ground.—
305 'Twas sweet, when cloudless stars were bright,
To view the wave of watery light,
And hear its melody by night.—
And oft had Hassan's Childhood played
Around the verge of that cascade;
310 And oft upon his mother's breast
That sound had harmonized his rest;
And oft had Hassan's Youth along
Its bank been sooth'd by Beauty's song;
And softer seemed each melting tone
315 Of Music mingled with its own.—
But ne'er shall Hassan's Age repose
Along the brink at Twilight's close—
The stream that filled that font is fled—
The blood that warmed his heart is shed!—
320 And here no more shall human voice
Be heard to rage—regret—rejoice—
The last sad note that swelled the gale

---

[1] "Jerreed, or Djerrid, a blunted Turkish javelin, which is darted from horseback with great force and precision. It is a favourite exercise of the Mussulmans; but I know not if it can be called a *manly* one, since the most expert in the art are the Black Eunuchs of Constantinople.—I think, next to these, a Mamlouk at Smyrna was the most skilful that came within my own observation." (L.B.) Mamlouks were slave-soldiers, originally from Circassia.

[2] Cf. Joseph Addison, *Spectator* 94 (18 June 1711).

[3] "The blast of the desert, fatal to every thing living, and often alluded to in eastern poetry." (L.B.)

Was woman's wildest funeral wail—
That quenched in silence—all is still,
But the lattice that flaps when the wind is shrill—
Though raves the gust, and floods the rain,
No hand shall close its clasp again.
On desert sands 'twere joy to scan
The rudest steps of fellow man,
So here the very voice of Grief
Might wake an Echo like relief—
At least 'twould say, "all are not gone;
There lingers Life, though but in one"—
For many a gilded chamber's there,
Which Solitude might well forbear;
Within that dome as yet Decay
Hath slowly worked her cankering way—
But Gloom is gathered o'er the gate,
Nor there the Fakir's self will wait;
Nor there will wandering Dervise stay,[1]
For Bounty cheers not his delay;
Nor there will weary stranger halt
To bless the sacred "bread and salt."[2]
Alike must Wealth and Poverty
Pass heedless and unheeded by,
For Courtesy and Pity died
With Hassan on the mountain side.—
His roof—that refuge unto men—
Is Desolation's hungry den.—
The guest flies the hall, and the vassal from labour,
Since his turban was cleft by the infidel's sabre![3]

* * * * *

   I hear the sound of coming feet,
But not a voice mine ear to greet—
More near—each turban I can scan,
And silver-sheathed ataghan;[4]
The foremost of the band is seen
An Emir by his garb of green:[5]
"Ho! who art thou?"—"this low salam[6]
Replies of Moslem faith I am."
"The burthen ye so gently bear,
Seems one that claims your utmost care,
And, doubtless, holds some precious freight,
My humble bark would gladly wait."

   "Thou speakest sooth, thy skiff unmoor,
And waft us from the silent shore;
Nay, leave the sail still furl'd, and ply
The nearest oar that's scatter'd by,
And midway to those rocks where sleep
The channel'd waters dark and deep.—
Rest from your task—so—bravely done,
Our course has been right swiftly run,
Yet 'tis the longest voyage, I trow,
That one of"—

* * * * *

   Sullen it plunged, and slowly sank,
The calm wave rippled to the bank;
I watch'd it as it sank, methought
Some motion from the current caught
Bestirr'd it more,—'twas but the beam
That chequer'd o'er the living stream—
I gaz'd, till vanishing from view,
Like lessening pebble it withdrew;
Still less and less, a speck of white
That gemm'd the tide, then mock'd the sight;
And all its hidden secrets sleep,

---

[1] "Fakir" is the Arabic, and "Dervish" is the Turkish, for mendicant.

[2] "To partake of food—to break bread and salt with your host—ensures the safety of the guest, even though an enemy; his person from that moment is sacred." (L.B.)

[3] "I need hardly observe, that Charity and Hospitality are the first duties enjoined by Mahomet; and to say truth, very generally practised by his disciples. The first praise that can be bestowed on a chief, is a panegyric on his bounty; the next, on his valour." (L.B.) Cf. the *Qur'an*, chap. 4.

[4] "The ataghan, a long dagger worn with pistols in the belt, in a metal scabbard, generally of silver; and, among the wealthier, gilt, or of gold." (L.B.)

[5] "Green is the privileged colour of the prophet's numerous pretended descendants; with them, as here, faith (the family inheritance) is supposed to supersede the necessity of good works; they are the worst of a very indifferent brood." (L.B.)

[6] "Salam aleikoum! aleikoum salam! peace be with you; be with you peace—the salutation reserved for the faithful;—to a Christian, 'Urlarula,' a good journey; or saban hiresem, saban serula; good morn, good even; and sometimes, 'may your end be happy'; are the usual salutes." (L.B.)

385 Known but to Genii of the deep,
Which, trembling in their coral caves,
They dare not whisper to the waves.

* * * * *

As rising on its purple wing
The insect-queen[1] of eastern spring,
390 O'er emerald meadows of Kashmeer
Invites the young pursuer near,
And leads him on from flower to flower
A weary chase and wasted hour,
Then leaves him, as it soars on high
395 With panting heart and tearful eye:
So Beauty lures the full-grown child
With hue as bright, and wing as wild;
A chase of idle hopes and fears,
Begun in folly, closed in tears.
400 If won, to equal ills betrayed,
Woe waits the insect and the maid,
A life of pain, the loss of peace,
From infant's play, or man's caprice:
The lovely toy so fiercely sought
405 Has lost its charm by being caught,
For every touch that wooed it's stay
Has brush'd the brightest hues away
Till charm, and hue, and beauty gone,
'Tis left to fly or fall alone.
410 With wounded wing, or bleeding breast,
Ah! where shall either victim rest?
Can this with faded pinion soar
From rose to tulip as before?
Or Beauty, blighted in an hour,
415 Find joy within her broken bower?
No: gayer insects fluttering by
Ne'er droop the wing o'er those that die,
And lovelier things have mercy shewn
To every failing but their own,
420 And every woe a tear can claim
Except an erring sister's shame.

* * * * *

The Mind, that broods o'er guilty woes,

Is like the Scorpion girt by fire,
In circle narrowing as it glows
425 The flames around their captive close,
Till inly search'd by thousand throes,
And maddening in her ire,
One sad and sole relief she knows,
The sting she nourish'd for her foes,
430 Whose venom never yet was vain,
Gives but one pang, and cures all pain,
And darts into her desperate brain.—
So do the dark in soul expire,
Or live like Scorpion girt by fire;[2]
435 So writhes the mind Remorse hath riven,
Unfit for earth, undoom'd for heaven,
Darkness above, despair beneath,
Around it flame, within it death!—

* * * * *

Black Hassan from the Haram flies,
440 Nor bends on woman's form his eyes,
The unwonted chase each hour employs,
Yet shares he not the hunter's joys.
Not thus was Hassan wont to fly
When Leila dwelt in his Serai.
445 Doth Leila there no longer dwell?
That tale can only Hassan tell:
Strange rumours in our city say
Upon that eve she fled away;
When Rhamazan's[3] last sun was set,
450 And flashing from each minaret
Millions of lamps proclaim'd the feast
Of Bairam through the boundless East.
'Twas then she went as to the bath,

---

[1] "The blue-winged butterfly of Kashmeer, the most rare and beautiful of the species." (L.B.)

[2] "Alluding to the dubious suicide of the scorpion, so placed for experiment by gentle philosophers. Some maintain that the position of the sting, when turned towards the head, is merely a convulsive movement; but others have actually brought in the verdict 'Felo de se.' The scorpions are surely interested in a speedy decision of the question; as, if once fairly established as insect Catos, they will probably be allowed to live as long as they think proper, without being martyred for the sake of an hypothesis." (L.B.) "Felo de se" is legal Latin for suicide. Cato the Younger (95–46 BC) committed suicide rather than submit to Julius Caesar. Cf. Landon, "Love's Last Lesson" 95–96.*

[3] "The cannon at sunset close the Rhamazan; see note [to 225]." (L.B.)

Which Hassan vainly search'd in wrath,
But she was flown her master's rage
In likeness of a Georgian page;
And far beyond the Moslem's power
Had wrong'd him with the faithless Giaour.
Somewhat of this had Hassan deem'd,
But still so fond, so fair she seem'd,
Too well he trusted to the slave
Whose treachery deserv'd a grave:
And on that eve had gone to mosque,
And thence to feast in his kiosk.
Such is the tale his Nubians tell,
Who did not watch their charge too well;
But others say, that on that night,
By pale Phingari's[1] trembling light,
The Giaour upon his jet black steed
Was seen—but seen alone to speed
With bloody spur along the shore,
Nor maid nor page behind him bore.

* * * * *

Her eye's dark charm 'twere vain to tell,
But gaze on that of the Gazelle,
It will assist thy fancy well,
As large, as languishingly dark,
But Soul beam'd forth in every spark
That darted from beneath the lid,
Bright as the jewel of Giamschid.[2]
Yea, *Soul*, and should our prophet say
That form was nought but breathing clay,
By Alla! I would answer nay;
Though on Al-Sirat's[3] arch I stood,
Which totters o'er the fiery flood,
With Paradise within my view,
And all his Houris beckoning through.
Oh! who young Leila's glance could read
And keep that portion of his creed[4]
Which saith, that woman is but dust,
A soulless toy for tyrant's lust?
On her might Muftis gaze, and own
That through her eye the Immortal shone—
On her fair cheek's unfading hue,
The young pomegranate's[5] blossoms strew
Their bloom in blushes ever new—
Her hair in hyacinthine[6] flow
When left to roll its folds below;
As midst her handmaids in the hall
She stood superior to them all,
Hath swept the marble where her feet
Gleamed whiter than the mountain sleet
Ere from the cloud that gave it birth,
It fell, and caught one stain of earth.
The cygnet nobly walks the water—
So moved on earth Circassia's daughter—
The loveliest bird of Franguestan![7]
As rears her crest the ruffled Swan,
  And spurns the wave with wings of pride,
When pass the steps of stranger man
  Along the banks that bound her tide;

---

[1] "Phingari, the moon." (L.B.)

[2] "The celebrated fabulous ruby of Sultan Giamschid, the embellisher of Istakhar; from its splendour, named Schebgerag, 'the torch of night'; also the 'cup of the sun,' &c.—In the first editions 'Giamschid' was written as a word of three syllables, so D'Herbelot has it; but I am told Richardson reduces it to a dissyllable, and writes 'Jamshid.' I have left in the text the orthography of the one with the pronunciation of the other." (L.B.) See the articles on "Giamschid" in Barthélémy d'Herbelot (1625–95), *Bibliothèque orientale* (1697); and John Richardson, *Dictionary of Persian, Arabic, and English* (1777).

[3] "Al-Sirat, the bridge of breadth less than the thread of a famished spider, over which the Mussulmans must *skate* into Paradise, to which it is the only entrance; but this is not the worst, the river beneath being hell itself, into which, as may be expected, the unskillful and tender of foot contrive to tumble with a 'facilis descensus Averni,' not very pleasing in prospect to the next passenger. There is a shorter cut downwards for the Jews and Christians." (L.B.) Virgil, *Aeneid* 6.26

[4] "A vulgar error: the Koran allots at least a third of Paradise to well-behaved women; but by far the greater number of Mussulmans interpret the text their own way, and exclude their moieties from heaven. Being enemies to Platonics, they cannot discern 'any fitness of things' in the souls of the other sex, conceiving them to be superseded by the Houris." (L.B.) Cf. George Sale, "Preliminary Discourse," *Koran* (1801) 59; and Henry Fielding, *Tom Jones* 4.4.

[5] "An oriental simile, which may, perhaps, though fairly stolen, be deemed 'plus Arabe qu'en Arabie.'" (L.B.)

[6] "Hyacinthine, in Arabic, 'Sunbul,' as common a thought in the eastern poets as it was among the Greeks." (L.B.) Cf. Milton, *Paradise Lost* 4.301.

[7] "'Franguestan,' Circassia." (L.B.) The women of Circassia were famous for their beauty.

Thus rose fair Leila's whiter neck:—
Thus armed with beauty would she check
Intrusion's glance, till Folly's gaze
Shrunk from the charms it meant to praise.
Thus high and graceful was her gait;
Her heart as tender to her mate—
Her mate—stern Hassan, who was he?
Alas! that name was not for thee!

* * * * *

Stern Hassan hath a journey ta'en
With twenty vassals in his train,
Each arm'd as best becomes a man
With arquebuss and ataghan;
The chief before, as deck'd for war
Bears in his belt the scimitar
Stain'd with the best of Arnaut blood,
When in the pass the rebels stood,
And few return'd to tell the tale
Of what befell in Parne's vale.
The pistols which his girdle bore
Were those that once a pasha wore,
Which still, though gemm'd and boss'd with gold,
Even robbers tremble to behold.—
'Tis said he goes to woo a bride
More true than her who left his side;
The faithless slave that broke her bower,
And, worse than faithless, for a Giaour!—

* * * * *

The sun's last rays are on the hill,
And sparkle in the fountain rill,
Whose welcome waters cool and clear,
Draw blessings from the mountaineer;
Here may the loitering merchant Greek
Find that repose 'twere vain to seek
In cities lodg'd too near his lord,
And trembling for his secret hoard—
Here may he rest where none can see,
In crowds a slave, in deserts free;
And with forbidden wine may stain
The bowl a Moslem must not drain.—

* * * * *

The foremost Tartar's in the gap,
Conspicuous by his yellow cap,
The rest in lengthening line the while
Wind slowly through the long defile;
Above, the mountain rears a peak,
Where vultures whet the thirsty beak,
And their's may be a feast to-night,
Shall tempt them down ere morrow's light.
Beneath, a river's wintry stream
Has shrunk before the summer beam,
And left a channel bleak and bare,
Save shrubs that spring to perish there.
Each side the midway path there lay
Small broken crags of granite gray,
By time or mountain lightning riven,
From summits clad in mists of heaven;
For where is he that hath beheld
The peak of Liakura[1] unveil'd?

* * * * *

They reach the grove of pine at last,
"Bismillah![2] now the peril's past;
For yonder view the opening plain,
And there we'll prick our steeds amain":
The Chiaus[3] spake, and as he said,
A bullet whistled o'er his head;
The foremost Tartar bites the ground!
  Scarce had they time to check the rein
Swift from their steeds the riders bound,
  But three shall never mount again,
Unseen the foes that gave the wound,
  The dying ask revenge in vain.
With steel unsheath'd, and carbine bent,
Some o'er their courser's harness leant,
  Half shelter'd by the steed,
Some fly behind the nearest rock,
And there await the coming shock,
  Nor tamely stand to bleed
Beneath the shaft of foes unseen,
Who dare not quit their craggy screen.

---

[1] Mount Parnassus.

[2] "Bismillah—'In the name of God'; the commencement of all the chapters of the Koran but one, and of prayer and thanksgiving." (L.B.)

[3] a Turkish messenger or attendant.

Stern Hassan only from his horse
Disdains to light, and keeps his course,
Till fiery flashes in the van
590 Proclaim too sure the robber-clan
Have well secur'd the only way
Could now avail the promis'd prey;
Then curl'd his very beard[1] with ire,
And glared his eye with fiercer fire.
595 "Though far and near the bullets hiss,
I've scaped a bloodier hour than this."
And now the foe their covert quit,
And call his vassals to submit;
But Hassan's frown and furious word
600 Are dreaded more than hostile sword,
Nor of his little band a man
Resign'd carbine or ataghan—
Nor raised the craven cry, Amaun![2]
In fuller sight, more near and near,
605 The lately ambush'd foes appear,
And issuing from the grove advance,
Some who on battle charger prance.—
Who leads them on with foreign brand,
Far flashing in his red right hand?[3]
610 "'Tis he—'tis he—I know him now,
I know him by his pallid brow;
I know him by the evil eye[4]
That aids his envious treachery;
I know him by his jet-black barb,
615 Though now array'd in Arnaut garb,
Apostate from his own vile faith,
It shall not save him from the death;
'Tis he, well met in any hour,
Lost Leila's love—accursed Giaour!"
620   As rolls the river into ocean,
In sable torrent wildly streaming;
   As the sea-tide's opposing motion
In azure column proudly gleaming,
Beats back the current many a rood,
625 In curling foam and mingling flood;
While eddying whirl, and breaking wave,
Roused by the blast of winter rave;
Through sparkling spray in thundering clash,
The lightnings of the waters flash
630 In aweful whiteness o'er the shore,
That shines and shakes beneath the roar;
Thus—as the stream and ocean greet,
With waves that madden as they meet—
Thus join the bands whom mutual wrong,
635 And fate and fury drive along.
The bickering sabres' shivering jar
   And pealing wide—or ringing near
   It's echoes on the throbbing ear
The deathshot hissing from afar—
640 The shock—the shout—the groan of war—
   Reverberate along that vale,
   More suited to the shepherd's tale:
Though few the numbers—their's the strife,
That neither spares nor speaks for life!
645 Ah! fondly youthful hearts can press,
To seize and share the dear caress;
But Love itself could never pant
For all that Beauty sighs to grant,
With half the fervour Hate bestows
650 Upon the last embrace of foes,
When grappling in the fight they fold
Those arms that ne'er shall lose their hold;
Friends meet to part—Love laughs at faith;—
True foes, once met, are joined till death!

* * * * *

655 With sabre shiver'd to the hilt,
Yet dripping with the blood he spilt;
Yet strain'd within the sever'd hand
Which quivers round that faithless brand;
His turban far behind him roll'd,

---

[1] "A phenomenon not uncommon with an angry Mussulman. In 1809, the Capitan Pacha's whiskers at a diplomatic audience were no less lively with indignation than a tiger cat's, to the horror of all the dragomans; the portentous mustachios twisted, they stood erect of their own accord, and were expected every moment to change their colour, but at last condescended to subside, which, probably, saved more heads than they contained hairs." (L.B.) A pasha was a high-ranking official in the Ottoman Empire; Byron met Capudan Pasha, the Admiral of the Turkish fleet, in Constantinople on 18 May 1810.

[2] "'Amaun,' quarter, pardon." (L.B.)

[3] Cf. Milton, *Paradise Lost* 2.174.

[4] "The 'evil eye,' a common superstition in the Levant, and of which the imaginary effects are yet very singular on those who conceive themselves affected." (L.B.)

And cleft in twain its firmest fold;
His flowing robe by falchion torn,
And crimson as those clouds of morn
That streak'd with dusky red, portend
The day shall have a stormy end;
A stain on every bush that bore
A fragment of his palampore,[1]
His breast with wounds unnumber'd riven,
His back to earth, his face to heaven,
Fall'n Hassan lies—his unclos'd eye
Yet lowering on his enemy,
As if the hour that seal'd his fate,
Surviving left his quenchless hate;
And o'er him bends that foe with brow
As dark as his that bled below.—

* * * * *

"Yes, Leila sleeps beneath the wave,
But his shall be a redder grave;
Her spirit pointed well the steel
Which taught that felon heart to feel.
He call'd the Prophet, but his power
Was vain against the vengeful Giaour:
He call'd on Alla—but the word
Arose unheeded or unheard.
Thou Paynim fool!—could Leila's prayer
Be pass'd, and thine accorded there?
I watch'd my time, I leagu'd with these,
The traitor in his turn to seize;
My wrath is wreak'd, the deed is done,
And now I go—but go alone."

* * * * *
* * * * *

The browzing camels' bells are tinkling—
His Mother looked from her lattice high,[2]
   She saw the dews of eve besprinkling
The pasture green beneath her eye,
   She saw the planets faintly twinkling,
"'Tis twilight—sure his train is nigh."—
She could not rest in the garden-bower,

---

[1] "The flowered shawls generally worn by persons of rank." (L.B.)

[2] Cf. Judges 5.28.

But gazed through the grate of his steepest tower—
"Why comes he not? his steeds are fleet,
Nor shrink they from the summer heat;
Why sends not the Bridegroom his promised gift,
Is his heart more cold, or his barb less swift?
Oh, false reproach! yon Tartar now
Has gained our nearest mountain's brow,
And warily the steep descends,
And now within the valley bends;
And he bears the gift at his saddle bow—
How could I deem his courser slow?
Right well my largess shall repay
His welcome speed, and weary way."—
The Tartar lighted at the gate,
But scarce upheld his fainting weight;
His swarthy visage spake distress,
But this might be from weariness;
His garb with sanguine spots was dyed,
But these might be from his courser's side;—
He drew the token from his vest—
Angel of Death! 'tis Hassan's cloven crest!
His calpac[3] rent—his caftan red—
"Lady, a fearful bride thy Son hath wed—
Me, not from mercy, did they spare,
But this empurpled pledge to bear.
Peace to the brave! whose blood is spilt—
Woe to the Giaour! for his the guilt."

* * * * *

A turban[4] carv'd in coarsest stone,
A pillar with rank weeds o'ergrown,
Whereon can now be scarcely read
The Koran verse that mourns the dead;
Point out the spot where Hassan fell
A victim in that lonely dell.
There sleeps as true an Osmanlie
As e'er at Mecca bent the knee;

---

[3] "The 'Calpac' is the solid cap or centre part of the head-dress; the shawl is wound round it, and forms the turban." (L.B.)

[4] "The turban—pillar—and inscriptive verse, decorate the tombs of the Osmanlies, whether in the cemetery or the wilderness. In the mountains you frequently pass similar mementos; and on enquiry you are informed that they record some victim of rebellion, plunder, or revenge." (L.B.) Osmanlies are Turks, so named after Osman, first Ottoman Emperor.

As ever scorn'd forbidden wine,
Or pray'd with face towards the shrine,
In orisons resumed anew
At solemn sound of "Alla Hu!"[1]
735 Yet died he by a stranger's hand,
And stranger in his native land—[2]
Yet died he as in arms he stood,
And unaveng'd, at least in blood.
But him the maids of Paradise
740   Impatient to their halls invite,
And the dark Heaven of Houri's eyes
   On him shall glance for ever bright;
They come—their kerchiefs green they wave,[3]
And welcome with a kiss the brave!
745 Who falls in battle 'gainst a Giaour,
Is worthiest an immortal bower.

* * * * *

But thou, false Infidel! shalt writhe
Beneath avenging Monkir's[4] scythe;
And from its torment 'scape alone
750 To wander round lost Eblis'[5] throne;
And fire unquench'd, unquenchable—
Around—within—thy heart shall dwell,
Nor ear can hear, nor tongue can tell[6]
The tortures of that inward hell!—

755 But first, on earth as Vampire[7] sent,
Thy corse shall from its tomb be rent;
Then ghastly haunt thy native place,
And suck the blood of all thy race,
There from thy daughter, sister, wife,
760 At midnight drain the stream of life;
Yet loathe the banquet which perforce
Must feed thy livid living corse;
Thy victims ere they yet expire
Shall know the dæmon for their sire,
765 As cursing thee, thou cursing them,
Thy flowers are wither'd on the stem.
But one that for thy crime must fall—
The youngest—most belov'd of all,
Shall bless thee with a *father's* name—
770 That word shall wrap thy heart in flame!
Yet must thou end thy task, and mark
Her cheek's last tinge, her eye's last spark,
And the last glassy glance must view
Which freezes o'er its lifeless blue;
775 Then with unhallowed hand shalt tear
The tresses of her yellow hair,
Of which in life a lock when shorn,
Affection's fondest pledge was worn;
But now is borne away by thee,
780 Memorial of thine agony!
Wet with thine own best blood shall drip,[8]

---

[1] "'Alla Hu!' the concluding words of the Muezzin's call to prayer from the highest gallery on the exterior of the Minaret. On a still evening, when the Muezzin has a fine voice (which they frequently have) the effect is solemn and beautiful beyond all the bells in Christendom." (L.B.)

[2] Cf. Exodus 2.22.

[3] "The following is part of a battle song of the Turks:—'I see—I see a dark-eyed girl of Paradise, and she waves a handkerchief, a kerchief of green; and cries aloud, Come, kiss me, for I love thee,' &c." (L.B.)

[4] "Monkir and Nekir are the inquisitors of the dead, before whom the corpse undergoes a slight noviciate and preparatory training for damnation. If the answers are none of the clearest, he is hauled up with a scythe and thumped down with a red hot mace till properly seasoned, with a variety of subsidiary probations. The office of these angels is no sinecure; there are but two; and the number of orthodox deceased being in a small proportion to the remainder, their hands are always full." (L.B.)

[5] "Eblis the Oriental Prince of Darkness." (L.B.)

[6] Cf. 1 Corinthians 2.9.

[7] "The Vampire superstition is still general in the Levant. Honest Tournefort tells a long story, which Mr. Southey, in the notes on Thalaba, quotes about these 'Vroucolochas,' as he calls them. The Romaic term is 'Vardoulacha.' I recollect a whole family being terrified by the scream of a child, which they imagined must proceed from such a visitation. The Greeks never mention the word without horror. I find that 'Broucolokas' is an old legitimate Hellenic appellation—at least is so applied to Arsenius, who, according to the Greeks, was after his death animated by the Devil.—The moderns, however, use the word I mention." (L.B.) Joseph Pitton de Tournefort, *Relation d'un voyage du Levant* (1717), quoted in Robert Southey, *Thalaba the Destroyer* (1801), notes to book 8. Arsenius was bishop of Monembasia c. 1530; because he converted to Catholicism, he was excommunicated by the Greek Orthodox church, hence the legend of his becoming a vampire: see the article on him in Pierre Bayle (1647–1706), *Dictionnaire historique et critique* (1697).

[8] "The freshness of the face, and the wetness of the lip with blood, are the never-failing signs of a Vampire. The stories told in Hungary and Greece of these foul feeders are singular, and some of them most *incredibly* attested." (L.B.)

Thy gnashing tooth and haggard lip;
Then stalking to thy sullen grave—
Go—and with Gouls and Afrits rave;
Till these in horror shrink away
From spectre more accursed than they!

* * * * *

"How name ye yon lone Caloyer?[1]
    His features I have scann'd before
In mine own land—'tis many a year,
    Since, dashing by the lonely shore,
I saw him urge as fleet a steed
As ever serv'd a horseman's need.
But once I saw that face—yet then
It was so mark'd with inward pain
I could not pass it by again;
It breathes the same dark spirit now,
As death were stamped upon his brow."

"'Tis twice three years at summer tide
    Since first among our freres he came;
And here it soothes him to abide
    For some dark deed he will not name.
But never at our vesper prayer,
Nor e'er before confession chair
Kneels he, nor recks he when arise
Incense or anthem to the skies,
But broods within his cell alone,
His faith and race alike unknown.
The sea from Paynim land he crost,
And here ascended from the coast,
Yet seems he not of Othman race,
But only Christian in his face:
I'd judge him some stray renegade,
Repentant of the change he made,
Save that he shuns our holy shrine,
Nor tastes the sacred bread and wine.
Great largess to these walls he brought,
And thus our abbot's favour bought;
But were I Prior, not a day
Should brook such stranger's further stay,
Or pent within our penance cell
Should doom him there for aye to dwell.
Much in his visions mutters he

---
[1] "monk" (mod. Gr.).

Of maiden 'whelmed beneath the sea;
Of sabres clashing—foemen flying,
Wrongs aveng'd—and Moslem dying.
On cliff he hath been known to stand,
And rave as to some bloody hand
Fresh sever'd from its parent limb,
Invisible to all but him,
Which beckons onward to his grave,
And lures to leap into the wave."

* * * * *
* * * * *

Dark and unearthly is the scowl
That glares beneath his dusky cowl—
The flash of that dilating eye
Reveals too much of times gone by—
Though varying—indistinct its hue,
Oft will his glance the gazer rue—
For in it lurks that nameless spell
Which speaks—itself unspeakable—
A spirit yet unquelled and high
That claims and keeps ascendancy,
And like the bird whose pinions quake—
But cannot fly the gazing snake—
Will others quail beneath his look,
Nor 'scape the glance they scarce can brook.
From him the half-affrighted Friar
When met alone would fain retire—
As if that eye and bitter smile
Transferred to others fear and guile—
Not oft to smile descendeth he,
And when he doth 'tis sad to see
That he but mocks at Misery.
How that pale lip will curl and quiver!
Then fix once more as if for ever—
As if his sorrow or disdain
Forbade him e'er to smile again.—
Well were it so—such ghastly mirth
From jouaunce ne'er deriv'd its birth.—
But sadder still it were to trace
What once were feelings in that face—
Time hath not yet the features fixed,
But brighter traits with evil mixed—
And there are hues not always faded,
Which speak a mind not all degraded

865 Even by the crimes through which it waded—
The common crowd but see the gloom
Of wayward deeds—and fitting doom—
The close observer can espy
A noble soul, and lineage high.—
870 Alas! though both bestowed in vain,
Which Grief could change—and Guilt could stain—
It was no vulgar tenement
To which such lofty gifts were lent,
And still with little less than dread
875 On such the sight is riveted.—
The roofless cot decayed and rent,
　Will scarce delay the passer by—
The tower by war or tempest bent,
While yet may frown one battlement,
880 　Demands and daunts the stranger's eye—
Each ivied arch—and pillar lone,
Pleads haughtily for glories gone!

"His floating robe around him folding,
　Slow sweeps he through the columned aisle—
885 With dread beheld—with gloom beholding
　The rites that sanctify the pile.
But when the anthem shakes the choir,
And kneel the monks—his steps retire—
By yonder lone and wavering torch
890 His aspect glares within the porch;
There will he pause till all is done—
And hear the prayer—but utter none.
See—by the half-illumin'd wall
His hood fly back—his dark hair fall—
895 That pale brow wildly wreathing round,
As if the Gorgon there had bound
The sablest of the serpent-braid
That o'er her fearful forehead strayed.
For he declines the convent oath,
900 And leaves those locks unhallowed growth—
But wears our garb in all beside;
And—not from piety but pride
Gives wealth to walls that never heard
Of his one holy vow nor word.—
905 Lo!—mark ye—as the harmony
Peals louder praises to the sky—
That livid cheek—that stoney air
Of mixed defiance and despair!

Saint Francis! keep him from the shrine!
910 Else may we dread the wrath divine
Made manifest by awful sign.—
If ever evil angel bore
The form of mortal, such he wore—
By all my hope of sins forgiven
915 Such looks are not of earth nor heaven!"

To love the softest hearts are prone,
But such can ne'er be all his own;
Too timid in his woes to share,
Too meek to meet, or brave despair;
920 And sterner hearts alone may feel
The wound that time can never heal.
The rugged metal of the mine
Must burn before its surface shine,
But plung'd within the furnace-flame,
925 It bends and melts—though still the same;
Then tempered to thy want, or will,
'Twill serve thee to defend or kill;
A breast-plate for thine hour of need,
Or blade to bid thy foeman bleed;
930 But if a dagger's form it bear,
Let those who shape it's edge, beware!
Thus passion's fire, and woman's art,
Can turn and tame the sterner heart;
From these its form and tone are ta'en,
935 And what they make it, must remain,
But break—before it bend again.

　　　* * * * *
　　　* * * * *

If solitude succeed to grief,
Release from pain is slight relief;
The vacant bosom's wilderness
940 Might thank the pang that made it less.
We loathe what none are left to share—
Even bliss—'twere woe alone to bear;
The heart once left thus desolate,
Must fly at last for ease—to hate.
945 It is as if the dead could feel
The icy worm around them steal,
And shudder, as the reptiles creep
To revel o'er their rotting sleep
Without the power to scare away

950 　The cold consumers of their clay!
　　It is as if the desart-bird,[1]
　　　　Whose beak unlocks her bosom's stream
　　　　To still her famish'd nestlings' scream,
　　Nor mourns a life to them transferr'd;
955 　Should rend her rash devoted breast,
　　And find them flown her empty nest.
　　The keenest pangs the wretched find
　　　　Are rapture to the dreary void—
　　The leafless desart of the mind—
960 　　　The waste of feelings unemploy'd—
　　Who would be doom'd to gaze upon
　　A sky without a cloud or sun?
　　Less hideous far the tempest's roar,
　　Than ne'er to brave the billows more—
965 　Thrown, when the war of winds is o'er,
　　A lonely wreck on fortune's shore,
　　'Mid sullen calm, and silent bay,
　　Unseen to drop by dull decay;—
　　Better to sink beneath the shock
970 　Than moulder piecemeal on the rock!

　　　　　　　* * * * *

　　"Father! thy days have pass'd in peace,
　　　'Mid counted beads, and countless prayer;
　　To bid the sins of others cease,
　　Thyself without a crime or care,
975 　Save transient ills that all must bear,
　　Has been thy lot, from youth to age,
　　And thou wilt bless thee from the rage
　　Of passions fierce and uncontroul'd,
　　Such as thy penitents unfold,
980 　Whose secret sins and sorrows rest
　　Within thy pure and pitying breast.
　　My days, though few, have pass'd below
　　In much of joy, but more of woe;
　　Yet still in hours of love or strife,
985 　I've scap'd the weariness of life;
　　Now leagu'd with friends, now girt by foes,
　　I loath'd the languor of repose;
　　Now nothing left to love or hate,
　　No more with hope or pride elate;
990 　I'd rather be the thing that crawls
　　Most noxious o'er a dungeon's walls,[2]
　　Than pass my dull, unvarying days,
　　Condemn'd to meditate and gaze—
　　Yet, lurks a wish within my breast
995 　For rest—but not to feel 'tis rest—
　　Soon shall my fate that wish fulfil;
　　　　And I shall sleep without the dream
　　Of what I was, and would be still,
　　　　Dark as to thee my deeds may seem—
1000 My memory now is but the tomb
　　Of joys long dead—my hope—their doom—
　　Though better to have died with those
　　Than bear a life of lingering woes—
　　My spirit shrunk not to sustain
1005 The searching throes of ceaseless pain;
　　Nor sought the self-accorded grave
　　Of ancient fool, and modern knave:
　　Yet death I have not fear'd to meet,
　　And in the field it had been sweet
1010 Had danger wooed me on to move
　　The slave of glory, not of love.
　　I've brav'd it—not for honour's boast;
　　I smile at laurels won or lost.—
　　To such let others carve their way,
1015 For high renown, or hireling pay;
　　But place again before my eyes
　　Aught that I deem a worthy prize;—
　　The maid I love—the man I hate—
　　And I will hunt the steps of fate,
1020 (To save or slay—as these require)
　　Through rending steel, and rolling fire;
　　Nor need'st thou doubt this speech from one
　　Who would but do—what he *hath* done.
　　Death is but what the haughty brave—
1025 The weak must bear—the wretch must crave—
　　Then let Life go to him who gave:
　　I have not quailed to danger's brow—
　　When high and happy—need I *now*?

　　　　　　　* * * * *
　　　　　　　* * * * *

---

[1] "The pelican is, I believe, the bird so libelled, by the imputation of feeding her chickens with her blood." (L.B.)

[2] Cf. Shakespeare, *Othello* 3.3.270–71.

"I lov'd her, friar! nay, adored—
    But these are words that all can use—
I prov'd it more in deed than word—
There's blood upon that dinted sword—
    A stain it's steel can never lose:
'Twas shed for her, who died for me,
    It warmed the heart of one abhorred:
Nay, start not—no—nor bend thy knee,
    Nor midst my sins such act record,
Thou wilt absolve me from the deed,
For he was hostile to thy creed!
The very name of Nazarene
Was wormwood to his Paynim spleen,
Ungrateful fool! since but for brands,
Well wielded in some hardy hands;
And wounds by Galileans given,
The surest pass to Turkish heav'n;
For him his Houris still might wait
Impatient at the prophet's gate.
I lov'd her—love will find its way
Through paths where wolves would fear to prey,[1]
And if it dares enough, 'twere hard
If passion met not some reward—
No matter how—or where—or why,
I did not vainly seek—nor sigh:
Yet sometimes with remorse in vain
I wish she had not lov'd again.
She died—I dare not tell thee how,
But look—'tis written on my brow!
There read of Cain the curse and crime,[2]
In characters unworn by time:
Still, ere thou dost condemn me—pause—
Not mine the act, though I the cause;
Yet did he but what I had done
Had she been false to more than one;
Faithless to him—he gave the blow,
But true to me—I laid him low;
Howe'er deserv'd her doom might be,
Her treachery was truth to me;
To me she gave her heart, that all
Which tyranny can ne'er enthrall;
And I, alas! too late to save,
Yet all I then could give—I gave—
'Twas some relief—our foe a grave.
His death sits lightly; but her fate
Has made me—what thou well may'st hate.
His doom was seal'd—he knew it well,
Warn'd by the voice of stern Taheer,
Deep in whose darkly boding ear[3]

---

[1] Cf. Pope, *An Essay on Criticism* (1711) 625.

[2] Cf. Genesis 4.15.

[3] "This superstition of a second-hearing (for I never met with downright second-sight in the East) fell once under my own observation.— On my third journey to Cape Colonna early in 1811, as we passed through the defile that leads from the hamlet between Keratia and Colonna, I observed Dervish Tahiri riding rather out of the path, and leaning his head upon his hand, as if in pain.—I rode up and enquired. 'We are in peril,' he answered. 'What peril? we are not now in Albania, nor in the passes to Ephesus, Messalunghi, or Lepanto; there are plenty of us, well armed, and the Choriates have not courage to be thieves'—'True, Affendi, but nevertheless the shot is ringing in my ears.'—'The shot!—not a tophaike has been fired this morning.'—'I hear it notwithstanding—Bom—Bom—as plainly as I hear your voice.'—'Psha.'—'As you please, Affendi; if it is written, so will it be.'—I left this quickeared predestinarian, and rode up to Basili, his Christian compatriot; whose ears, though not at all prophetic, by no means relished the intelligence.—We all arrived at Colonna, remained some hours, and returned leisurely, saying a variety of brilliant things, in more languages than spoiled the building of Babel, upon the mistaken seer. Romaic, Arnaout, Turkish, Italian, and English were all exercised, in various conceits, upon the unfortunate Mussulman. While we were contemplating the beautiful prospect, Dervish was occupied about the columns.—I thought he was deranged into an antiquarian, and asked him if he had become a '*Palao-castro*' man: 'No,' said he, 'but these pillars will be useful in making a stand'; and added other remarks, which at least evinced his own belief in his troublesome faculty of *fore-hearing*.—On our return to Athens we heard from Leoné (a prisoner set ashore some days after) of the intended attack of the Mainotes, mentioned, with the cause of its not taking place, in the notes to Childe Harolde, Canto 2d.—I was at some pains to question the man, and he described the dresses, arms, and marks of the horses of our party so accurately, that with other circumstances, we could not doubt of *his* having been in 'villainous company,' and ourselves in a bad neighbourhood.—Dervish became a soothsayer for life, and I dare say is now hearing more musquetry than ever will be fired, to the great refreshment of the Arnaouts of Berat, and his native mountains.—I shall mention one trait more of this singular race.—In March 1811, a remarkably stout and active Arnaout came (I believe the 50th on the same errand,) to offer himself as an attendant, which was declined: 'Well, Affendi,' quoth he, 'may you live!—you would have found me useful. I shall leave the town for the hills to-morrow; in the winter I return, perhaps you will then receive me.'—Dervish, who was present, remarked as a thing of course, and of no consequence, 'in the mean time he will join the Klephtes,' (robbers), which was true to the letter.—If not cut off, they come

The deathshot peal'd of murder near—
As filed the troop to where they fell!
1080 He died too in the battle broil—
A time that heeds nor pain nor toil—
One cry to Mahomet for aid,
One prayer to Alla—all he made:
He knew and crossed me in the fray—
1085 I gazed upon him where he lay,
And watched his spirit ebb away;
Though pierced like Pard by hunters' steel,
He felt not half that now I feel.
I search'd, but vainly search'd to find,
1090 The workings of a wounded mind;
Each feature of that sullen corse
Betrayed his rage, but no remorse.[1]
Oh, what had Vengeance given to trace
Despair upon his dying face!
1095 The late repentance of that hour,
When Penitence hath lost her power
To tear one terror from the grave—
And will not soothe, and can not save!

* * * * *

"The cold in clime are cold in blood,
1100   Their love can scarce deserve the name;
But mine was like the lava flood
    That boils in Ætna's breast of flame,
I cannot prate in puling strain
Of ladye-love, and beauty's chain;
1105 If changing cheek, and scorching vein—
Lips taught to writhe, but not complain—
If bursting heart, and mad'ning brain—
And daring deed, and vengeful steel—
And all that I have felt—and feel—
1110 Betoken love—that love was mine,
And shewn by many a bitter sign.
'Tis true, I could not whine nor sigh,
I knew but to obtain or die.
I die—but first I have possest,
1115 And come what may, I *have been* blest;
Shall I the doom I sought upbraid?
No—reft of all—yet undismay'd
But for the thought of Leila slain,
Give me the pleasure with the pain,
1120 So would I live and love again.
I grieve, but not, my holy guide!
For him who dies, but her who died;
She sleeps beneath the wandering wave,
Ah! had she but an earthly grave,
1125 This breaking heart and throbbing head
Should seek and share her narrow bed.
She was a form of life and light—
That seen—became a part of sight,
And rose—where'er I turned mine eye—
1130 The Morning-star of Memory!

"Yes, Love indeed is light from heaven—
    A spark of that immortal fire
With angels shar'd—by Alla given,
    To lift from earth our low desire.
1135 Devotion wafts the mind above,
But Heaven itself descends in love—
A feeling from the Godhead caught,
To wean from self each sordid thought—
A Ray of him who form'd the whole—
1140 A Glory circling round the soul!
I grant *my* love imperfect—all
That mortals by the name miscall—
Then deem it evil—what thou wilt—
But say, oh say, *hers* was not guilt!
1145 She was my life's unerring light—
That quench'd—what beam shall break my night?
Oh! would it shone to lead me still,
Although to death or deadliest ill!—
Why marvel ye? if they who lose
1150   This present joy, this future hope,
        No more with sorrow meekly cope—
In phrenzy then their fate accuse—
In madness do those fearful deeds
    That seem to add but guilt to woe.
1155 Alas! the breast that inly bleeds
    Hath nought to dread from outward blow—
Who falls from all he knows of bliss,
Cares little into what abyss.—

---

down in the winter, and pass it unmolested in some town, where they are often as well known as their exploits." (L.B.) "Palao castro" is modern Greek for "ancient fortress." See Byron, *Childe Harold's Pilgrimage* 2 (1812), note to st. 12; and Shakespeare, *1 Henry IV* 3.3.9.

[1] Cf. note to line 89.

Fierce as the gloomy vulture's now
    To thee, old man, my deeds appear—
I read abhorrence on thy brow,
    And this too was I born to bear!
'Tis true, that, like that bird of prey,
With havock have I mark'd my way—
But this was taught me by the dove—
To die—and know no second love.
This lesson yet hath man to learn,
Taught by the thing he dares to spurn—
The bird that sings within the brake,
The swan that swims upon the lake,
One mate, and one alone, will take.
And let the fool still prone to range,
And sneer on all who cannot change—
Partake his jest with boasting boys,
I envy not his varied joys—
But deem such feeble, heartless man,
Less than yon solitary swan—
Far—far beneath the shallow maid
He left believing and betray'd.
Such shame at least was never mine—
Leila—each thought was only thine!—
My good, my guilt, my weal, my woe,
My hope on high—my all below.
Earth holds no other like to thee,
Or if it doth, in vain for me—
For worlds I dare not view the dame
Resembling thee, yet not the same.
The very crimes that mar my youth
This bed of death—attest my truth—
'Tis all too late—thou wert—thou art
The cherished madness of my heart!

"And she was lost—and yet I breathed,
    But not the breath of human life—
A serpent round my heart was wreathed,
    And stung my every thought to strife.—
Alike all time—abhorred all place,
Shuddering I shrunk from Nature's face,
Where every hue that charmed before
The blackness of my bosom wore:—
The rest—thou do'st already know,
And all my sins and half my woe—
    But talk no more of penitence,

Thou see'st I soon shall part from hence—
And if thy holy tale were true—
The deed that's done can'st *thou* undo?
Think me not thankless—but this grief
Looks not to priesthood for relief.[1]
My soul's estate in secret guess—
But would'st thou pity more—say less—
When thou can'st bid my Leila live,
Then will I sue thee to forgive;
Then plead my cause in that high place
Where purchased masses proffer grace—
Go—when the hunter's hand hath wrung
From forest-cave her shrieking young,
And calm the lonely lioness—
But soothe not—mock not *my* distress!

"In earlier days, and calmer hours,
    When heart with heart delights to blend,
Where bloom my native valley's bowers—
    I had—Ah! have I now?—a friend!—
To him this pledge I charge thee send—
Memorial of a youthful vow;
I would remind him of my end,—
    Though souls absorbed like mine allow
Brief thought to distant friendship's claim,
Yet dear to him my blighted name.
'Tis strange—he prophesied my doom,
    And I have smil'd—(I then could smile—)
When Prudence would his voice assume,
    And warn—I reck'd not what—the while—
But now remembrance whispers o'er
Those accents scarcely mark'd before.
Say—that his bodings came to pass,
    And he will start to hear their truth,
And wish his words had not been sooth.
Tell him—unheeding as I was—
    Through many a busy bitter scene
    Of all our golden youth had been—
In pain, my faultering tongue had tried
To bless his memory ere I died;

---

[1] "The monk's sermon is omitted. It seems to have had so little effect upon the patient, that it could have no hopes from the reader. It may be sufficient to say, that it was of a customary length, (as may be perceived from the interruptions and uneasiness of the penitent), and was delivered in the nasal tone of all orthodox preachers." (L.B.) Cf. Byron, *Manfred* 3.1.48–159.*

But heaven in wrath would turn away,
If Guilt should for the guiltless pray.
I do not ask him not to blame—
Too gentle he to wound my name;
And what have I to do with fame?
I do not ask him not to mourn,
Such cold request might sound like scorn;
And what than friendship's manly tear
May better grace a brother's bier?
But bear this ring—his own of old—
And tell him—what thou dost behold!
The wither'd frame, the ruined mind,
The wrack by passion left behind—
A shrivelled scroll, a scatter'd leaf,
Sear'd by the autumn blast of grief!

* * * * *

"Tell me no more of fancy's gleam,
No, father, no, 'twas not a dream;
Alas! the dreamer first must sleep,
I only watch'd, and wish'd to weep;
But could not, for my burning brow
Throbb'd to the very brain as now.
I wish'd but for a single tear,
As something welcome, new, and dear;
I wish'd it then—I wish it still,
Despair is stronger than my will.
Waste not thine orison—despair
Is mightier than thy pious prayer;
I would not, if I might, be blest,
I want no paradise—but rest.
'Twas then, I tell thee, father! then
I saw her—yes—she liv'd again;
And shining in her white symar,[1]
As through yon pale grey cloud—the star
Which now I gaze on, as on her
Who look'd and looks far lovelier;
Dimly I view its trembling spark—
To-morrow's night shall be more dark—
And I—before its rays appear,
That lifeless thing the living fear.
I wander, father! for my soul

Is fleeting towards the final goal;
I saw her, friar! and I rose,
Forgetful of our former woes;
And rushing from my couch, I dart,
And clasp her to my desperate heart;
I clasp—what is it that I clasp?
No breathing form within my grasp,
No heart that beats reply to mine,
Yet, Leila! yet the form is thine!
And art thou, dearest, chang'd so much,
As meet my eye, yet mock my touch?
Ah! were thy beauties e'er so cold,
I care not—so my arms enfold
The all they ever wish'd to hold.
Alas! around a shadow prest,
They shrink upon my lonely breast;
Yet still—'tis there—in silence stands,
And beckons with beseeching hands!
With braided hair, and bright-black eye—
I knew 'twas false—she could not die!
But he is dead—within the dell
I saw him buried where he fell;
He comes not—for he cannot break
From earth—why then art thou awake!
They told me, wild waves roll'd above
The face I view, the form I love;
They told me—'twas a hideous tale!
I'd tell it—but my tongue would fail—
If true—and from thine ocean-cave
Thou com'st to claim a calmer grave;
Oh! pass thy dewy fingers o'er
This brow that then will burn no more;
Or place them on my hopeless heart—
But, shape or shade!—whate'er thou art,
In mercy, ne'er again depart—
Or farther with thee bear my soul,
Than winds can waft—or waters roll!—[2]

* * * * *

"Such is my name, and such my tale,
    Confessor—to thy secret ear,
I breathe the sorrows I bewail,

---

[1] "'Symar'—Shroud." (L.B.) A cymar is actually a long, loose woman's robe.

[2] Cf. Pope, "The Sixth Epistle of the First Book of Horace Imitated" (1738) 70.

GEORGE GORDON, LORD BYRON

  And thank thee for the generous tear
This glazing eye could never shed.
Then lay me with the humblest dead,
And save the cross above my head,
Be neither name nor emblem spread—
By prying stranger to be read,
Or stay the passing pilgrim's tread."

He pass'd—nor of his name and race
Hath left a token or a trace,
Save what the father must not say
Who shrived him on his dying day;
This broken tale was all we knew
Of her he lov'd, or him he slew.[1]

---

[1] "The circumstance to which the above story relates was not very uncommon in Turkey. A few years ago the wife of Muchtar Pacha complained to his father of his son's supposed infidelity; he asked with whom, and she had the barbarity to give in a list of the twelve handsomest women in Yanina. They were seized, fastened up in sacks, and drowned in the lake the same night! One of the guards who was present informed me, that not one of the victims uttered a cry, or shewed a symptom of terror at so sudden a 'wrench from all we know, from all we love.' The fate of Phrosine, the fairest of this sacrifice, is the subject of many a Romaic and Arnaut ditty. The story in the text is one told of a young Venetian many years ago, and now nearly forgotten.—I heard it by accident recited by one of the coffee-house story-tellers who abound in the Levant, and sing or recite their narratives.—The additions and interpolations by the translator will be easily distinguished from the rest by the want of Eastern imagery; and I regret that my memory has retained so few fragments of the original.

"For the contents of some of the notes I am indebted partly to D'Herbelot, and partly to that most eastern, and, as Mr. Webb justly entitles it, 'sublime tale,' the 'Caliph Vathek.' I do not know from what source the author of that singular volume may have drawn his materials; some of his incidents are to be found in the 'Bibliotheque Orientale'; but for correctness of costume, beauty of description, and power of imagination, it far surpasses all European imitations; and bears such marks of originality, that those who have visited the East will find some difficulty in believing it to be more than a translation. As an Eastern tale, even Rasselas must bow before it; his 'Happy Valley' will not bear a comparison with the 'Hall of Eblis.'" (L.B) Mouctar Pasha was the eldest son of Ali Pasha, the Turkish governor of Albania; Byron met them both in Jannina in October 1809. In September 1810, in Athens, Byron rescued a woman from this form of execution: see *Byron's Letters and Journals* 3: 230. See also Henry Weber, *Tales of the East* (1812); William Beckford (1760–1844), *Vathek* (1786); Samuel Johnson (1709–84), *The History of Rasselas, Prince of Abissinia* (1759).

---

from *Hebrew Melodies* (1815)

She Walks in Beauty[2]

1

She walks in beauty, like the night
 Of cloudless climes and starry skies;
And all that's best of dark and bright
 Meet in her aspect and her eyes:
Thus mellow'd to that tender light
 Which heaven to gaudy day denies.

2

One shade the more, one ray the less,
 Had half impair'd the nameless grace
Which waves in every raven tress,
 Or softly lightens o'er her face;
Where thoughts serenely sweet express
 How pure, how dear their dwelling place.

3

And on that cheek, and o'er that brow,
 So soft, so calm, yet eloquent,
The smiles that win, the tints that glow,
 But tell of days in goodness spent,
A mind at peace with all below,
 A heart whose love is innocent!

from *Poems* (1816)

Fare Thee Well![3]

  "Alas! they had been friends in youth;
But whispering tongues can poison truth;
And constancy lives in realms above;
And life is thorny; and youth is vain;

---

[2] Byron met Ann Wilmot (1784–1871), the wife of his cousin Robert John Wilmot, at a party on 11 June 1814. She was in mourning and wore a black dress decorated with spangles.

[3] Lady Byron left her husband on 15 January 1816, after scarcely a year of marriage. She took their infant daughter with her; he never saw either of them again. Their preliminary separation agreement was signed on 17 March, and Byron wrote the first version of "Fare Thee Well!" on the 18th. He sent a copy to his wife a few days later, along with a pathetic note.

George Gordon, Lord Byron

And to be wroth with one we love,
Doth work like madness in the brain;

* * * * *

But never either found another
To free the hollow heart from paining—
They stood aloof, the scars remaining,
Like cliffs which had been rent asunder;
A dreary sea now flows between,
But neither heat, nor frost, nor thunder,
Shall wholly do away, I ween,
The marks of that which once hath been."
                         COLERIDGE's *Christabel*.[1]

Fare thee well! and if for ever—
   Still for ever, fare *thee well*—
Even though unforgiving, never
   'Gainst thee shall my heart rebel.—
5 Would that breast were bared before thee
   Where thy head so oft hath lain,
While that placid sleep came o'er thee
   Which thou ne'er can'st know again:
Would that breast by thee glanc'd over,
10   Every inmost thought could show!
Then, thou would'st at last discover
   'Twas not well to spurn it so—
Though the world for this commend thee—
   Though it smile upon the blow,
15 Even its praises must offend thee,
   Founded on another's woe—
Though my many faults defaced me,
   Could no other arm be found
Than the one which once embraced me,
20   To inflict a cureless wound!
Yet—oh, yet—thyself deceive not—
   Love may sink by slow decay,
But by sudden wrench, believe not,
   Hearts can thus be torn away;
25 Still thine own its life retaineth—
   Still must mine—though bleeding—beat;
And the undying thought which paineth
   Is—that we no more may meet.—
These are words of deeper sorrow
30   Than the wail above the dead;

Both shall live—but every morrow
   Wake us from a widowed bed.—
And when thou wouldst solace gather—
   When our child's first accents flow—
35 Wilt thou teach her to say—"Father!"
   Though his care she must forego?
When her little hands shall press thee—
   When her lip to thine is prest—
Think of him whose prayer shall bless thee—
40   Think of him thy love had blessed.
Should her lineaments resemble
   Those thou never more may'st see—
Then thy heart will softly tremble
   With a pulse yet true to me.—
45 All my faults—perchance thou knowest—
   All my madness—none can know;
All my hopes—where'er thou goest—
   Wither—yet with *thee* they go.—
Every feeling hath been shaken,
50   Pride—which not a world could bow—
Bows to thee—by thee forsaken
   Even my soul forsakes me now.—
But 'tis done—all words are idle—
   Words from me are vainer still;
55 But the thoughts we cannot bridle
   Force their way without the will.—
Fare thee well!—thus disunited—
   Torn from every nearer tie—
Seared in heart—and lone—and blighted—
60   More than this, I scarce can die.

from *The Prisoner of Chillon and Other Poems* (1816)

Darkness[2]

I had a dream, which was not all a dream.
The bright sun was extinguish'd, and the stars

---

[1] lines 401–06, 412–19.*

[2] The dust thrown into the atmosphere by the eruption of Mount Tamboro in 1815 made 1816 the coldest, wettest summer on record, with crop failures across Europe. At the same time, an Italian astronomer was warning that sunspots might lead to the extinguishing of the sun. Byron may also have read *The Last Man; or, Omegarus and Syderia: A Romance in Futurity*, a then-popular novel by Cousin (Continued)

Did wander darkling in the eternal space,
Rayless, and pathless,[1] and the icy earth
Swung blind and blackening in the moonless air;[2]
Morn came, and went—and came, and brought no day,
And men forgot their passions in the dread
Of this their desolation; and all hearts
Were chill'd into a selfish prayer for light:
And they did live by watchfires—and the thrones,
The palaces of crowned kings—the huts,
The habitations of all things which dwell,
Were burnt for beacons; cities were consumed,
And men were gathered round their blazing homes
To look once more into each other's face;
Happy were those who dwelt within the eye
Of the volcanos, and their mountain-torch:
A fearful hope was all the world contain'd;
Forests were set on fire—but hour by hour
They fell and faded—and the crackling trunks
Extinguish'd with a crash—and all was black.
The brows of men by the despairing light
Wore an unearthly aspect, as by fits
The flashes fell upon them; some lay down
And hid their eyes and wept; and some did rest
Their chins upon their clenched hands, and smiled;
And others hurried to and fro, and fed
Their funeral piles with fuel, and looked up
With mad disquietude on the dull sky,
The pall of a past world; and then again
With curses cast them down upon the dust,
And gnash'd their teeth and howl'd:[3] the wild birds shriek'd,
And, terrified, did flutter on the ground,[4]
And flap their useless wings; the wildest brutes
Came tame and tremulous;[5] and vipers crawl'd
And twined themselves among the multitude,
Hissing, but stingless—they were slain for food:[6]
And War, which for a moment was no more,
Did glut himself again;—a meal was bought
With blood, and each sate sullenly apart
Gorging himself in gloom: no love was left;
All earth was but one thought—and that was death,
Immediate and inglorious; and the pang
Of famine fed upon all entrails—men
Died, and their bones were tombless as their flesh;
The meagre by the meagre were devoured,
Even dogs assail'd their masters, all save one,
And he was faithful to a corse, and kept
The birds and beasts and famish'd men at bay,
Till hunger clung them,[7] or the dropping dead
Lured their lank jaws; himself sought out no food,
But with a piteous and perpetual moan
And a quick desolate cry, licking the hand
Which answered not with a caress—he died.
The crowd was famish'd by degrees; but two
Of an enormous city did survive,
And they were enemies; they met beside
The dying embers of an altar-place
Where had been heap'd a mass of holy things
For an unholy usage; they raked up,
And shivering scraped with their cold skeleton hands
The feeble ashes, and their feeble breath
Blew for a little life, and made a flame
Which was a mockery; then they lifted up
Their eyes as it grew lighter, and beheld
Each other's aspects—saw, and shriek'd, and died—
Even of their mutual hideousness they died,
Unknowing who he was upon whose brow
Famine had written Fiend. The world was void,
The populous and the powerful was a lump,
Seasonless, herbless, treeless, manless, lifeless—
A lump of death—a chaos of hard clay.[8]
The rivers, lakes, and ocean all stood still,
And nothing stirred within their silent depths;
Ships sailorless lay rotting on the sea,
And their masts fell down piecemeal; as they dropp'd
They slept on the abyss without a surge—

---

de Grainville (trans. 1806). Cf. Thomas Campbell, "The Last Man";* M.W. Shelley,* *The Last Man* (1826); and Thomas Hood, "The Last Man."*

[1] Cf. Milton, "Il Penseroso" 67–70.

[2] Cf. Ezekiel 32.7–8; Joel 2.31; Revelation 6.12.

[3] Cf. Matthew 25.30.

[4] Cf. Coleridge, "Christabel" 530.*

[5] Cf. Isaiah 11.6.

[6] Cf. Ezekiel 38.20.

[7] Cf. Shakespeare, *Macbeth* 5.5.40.

[8] Cf. Jeremiah 4.23–28.

The waves were dead; the tides were in their grave,
The moon their mistress had expired before;
The winds were withered in the stagnant air,
And the clouds perish'd; Darkness had no need
Of aid from them—She was the universe.[1]

Prometheus[2]

1

Titan! to whose immortal eyes
    The sufferings of mortality,
    Seen in their sad reality,
Were not as things that gods despise;
What was thy pity's recompense?[3]
A silent suffering, and intense;
The rock, the vulture, and the chain,
All that the proud can feel of pain,
The agony they do not show,
The suffocating sense of woe,
    Which speaks but in its loneliness,
And then is jealous lest the sky
Should have a listener, nor will sigh
    Until its voice is echoless.

2

Titan! to thee the strife was given
    Between the suffering and the will,
    Which torture where they cannot kill;
And the inexorable Heaven,[4]
And the deaf tyranny of Fate,
The ruling principle of Hate,
Which for its pleasure doth create
The things it may annihilate,[5]
Refused thee even the boon to die:
The wretched gift eternity
Was thine—and thou hast borne it well.
All that the Thunderer[6] wrung from thee
Was but the menace which flung back
On him the torments of thy rack;
The fate thou didst so well foresee[7]
But would not to appease him tell;
And in thy Silence was his Sentence,
And in his Soul a vain repentance,
And evil dread so ill dissembled
That in his hand the lightnings trembled.

3

Thy Godlike crime was to be kind,[8]
    To render with thy precepts less
    The sum of human wretchedness,
And strengthen Man with his own mind;
But baffled as thou wert from high,
Still in thy patient energy,
In the endurance, and repulse
Of thine impenetrable Spirit,
Which Earth and Heaven could not convulse,
A mighty lesson we inherit:
Thou art a symbol and a sign
To Mortals of their fate and force;
Like thee, Man is in part divine,
A troubled stream from a pure source;
And Man in portions can foresee
His own funereal destiny;
His wretchedness, and his resistance,
And his sad unallied existence:
To which his Spirit may oppose
Itself—an equal to all woes,
And a firm will, and a deep sense,
Which even in torture can descry
Its own concentered recompense,
Triumphant where it dares defy,
And making Death a Victory.

---

[1] Cf. Pope, *The Dunciad* (1742–43) 4.627–56.

[2] The Titan Prometheus stole fire from heaven and gave it to humanity. To punish him, Jupiter (L., Gr.: "Zeus") had him chained to a rock in the Caucasus, where a vulture (in some versions, an eagle) tore at his liver. Cf. M.W. Shelley,* *Frankenstein; or, The Modern Prometheus* (1818); and P.B. Shelley, *Prometheus Unbound.**

[3] Cf. Aeschylus, *Prometheus Bound* 28, 239.

[4] Cf. Aeschylus, *Prometheus Bound* 34, 105.

[5] Cf. Aeschylus, *Prometheus Bound* 779.

[6] Jupiter/Zeus.

[7] Cf. Aeschylus, *Prometheus Bound* 101–02.

[8] Cf. Aeschylus, *Prometheus Bound* 269.

from *Childe Harold's Pilgrimage* (1816)

"Afin que cette application vous forçât de penser à autre chose; il n'y a en vérité de remède que celui-là et le temps."
—*Lettre du Roi de Prusse à D'Alembert,*
Sept. 7, 1776.[1]

from CANTO THE THIRD

1

Is thy face like thy mother's, my fair child!
Ada![2] sole daughter of my house and heart?
When last I saw thy young blue eyes they smil'd,
And then we parted,—not as now we part,[3]
But with a hope.—
          Awaking with a start,
The waters heave around me;[4] and on high
The winds lift up their voices:[5] I depart,
Whither I know not; but the hour's gone by,
When Albion's lessening shores could grieve or glad
   mine eye.

2

Once more[6] upon the waters! yet once more!
And the waves bound beneath me as a steed
That knows his rider.[7] Welcome, to their roar!
Swift be their guidance, wheresoe'er it lead!
Though the strain'd mast should quiver as a reed,
And the rent canvas fluttering strew the gale,
Still must I on; for I am as a weed,
Flung from the rock, on Ocean's foam, to sail
Where'er the surge may sweep, the tempest's breath
   prevail.

3

In my youth's summer I did sing of One,
The wandering outlaw of his own dark mind;
Again I seize the theme then but begun,
And bear it with me, as the rushing wind
Bears the cloud onwards: in that Tale I find
The furrows of long thought, and dried-up tears,
Which, ebbing, leave a sterile track behind,
O'er which all heavily the journeying years
Plod the last sands of life,—where not a flower appears.

4

Since my young days of passion—joy, or pain,
Perchance my heart and harp have lost a string,
And both may jar: it may be, that in vain
I would essay as I have sung to sing.
Yet, though a dreary strain, to this I cling;
So that it wean me from the weary dream
Of selfish grief or gladness—so it fling
Forgetfulness around me—it shall seem
To me, though to none else, a not ungrateful theme.

5

He, who grown aged in this world of woe,
In deeds, not years,[8] piercing the depths of life,
So that no wonder waits him; nor below
Can love, or sorrow, fame, ambition, strife,
Cut to his heart again with the keen knife
Of silent, sharp endurance: he can tell
Why thought seeks refuge in lone caves, yet rife
With airy images, and shapes which dwell
Still unimpair'd, though old, in the soul's haunted cell.

6

'Tis to create, and in creating live
A being more intense, that we endow
With form our fancy, gaining as we give
The life we image, even as I do now.

---

[1] "So that this exercise forces you to think of something else. There is, in truth, no other remedy than that and time." *Oeuvres de Frédéric le Grand* (1846–57) 25: 49–50. Frederick II (the Great) of Prussia recommended "some problem very difficult to solve" as a consolation for Jean le Rond d'Alembert (1717–83), who was in mourning for the death of Claire Françoise, Mlle. l'Espinasse (d. 23 May 1776).

[2] Augusta Ada Byron was born on 10 December 1815. Lady Byron left her husband on 15 January 1816, taking their child with her. Byron never saw either of them again. In 1835, Ada married William King Noel, Baron King (later the Earl of Lovelace). She died in 1852.

[3] Byron left England on 25 April 1816; he never returned.

[4] Byron wrote the first three stanzas while crossing the Channel.

[5] Cf. Isaiah 42.11.

[6] Cf. Shakespeare, *Henry V* 3.1.1.

[7] Cf. Shakespeare, Fletcher, and Massinger, *The Two Noble Kinsmen* 2.1.73–76.

[8] Cf. Byron, *Manfred* 2.1.51–52.*

50   What am I? Nothing; but not so art thou,
       Soul of my thought! with whom I traverse earth,
       Invisible but gazing, as I glow
       Mix'd with thy spirit, blended with thy birth,
       And feeling still with thee in my crush'd feelings' dearth.

                          7
55   Yet must I think less wildly: I *have* thought
       Too long and darkly, till my brain became,
       In its own eddy boiling and o'erwrought,
       A whirling gulf of phantasy and flame:
       And thus, untaught in youth my heart to tame,
60   My springs of life were poison'd.[1] 'Tis too late!
       Yet am I chang'd; though still enough the same
       In strength to bear what time cannot abate,
       And feed on bitter fruits without accusing Fate.

                          8
       Something too much of this:[2]—but now 'tis past,
65   And the spell closes with its silent seal.
       Long absent HAROLD re-appears at last;
       He of the breast which fain no more would feel,
       Wrung with the wounds which kill not, but ne'er heal;
       Yet Time, who changes all, had altered him
70   In soul and aspect as in age: years steal
       Fire from the mind as vigour from the limb;
       And life's enchanted cup but sparkles near the brim.

                          9
       His had been quaff'd too quickly, and he found
       The dregs were wormwood; but he fill'd again,
75   And from a purer fount, on holier ground,
       And deem'd its spring perpetual; but in vain!
       Still round him clung invisibly a chain
       Which gall'd for ever, fettering though unseen,
       And heavy though it clank'd not;[3] worn with pain,
80   Which pin'd although it spoke not, and grew keen,
       Entering with every step, he took, through many a scene.

                          10
       Secure in guarded coldness, he had mix'd
       Again in fancied safety with his kind,
       And deem'd his spirit now so firmly fix'd
85   And sheath'd with an invulnerable mind,
       That, if no joy, no sorrow lurk'd behind;
       And he, as one, might midst the many stand
       Unheeded, searching through the crowd to find
       Fit speculation! such as in strange land[4]
90   He found in wonder-works of God and Nature's hand.

                          11
       But who can view the ripened rose, nor seek
       To wear it? who can curiously behold
       The smoothness and the sheen of beauty's cheek,
       Nor feel the heart can never all grow old?
95   Who can contemplate Fame through clouds unfold
       The star which rises o'er her steep, nor climb?
       Harold, once more within the vortex, roll'd
       On with the giddy circle, chasing Time,
       Yet with a nobler aim than in his youth's fond prime.[5]

                          12
100 But soon he knew himself the most unfit
       Of men to herd with Man; with whom he held
       Little in common; untaught to submit
       His thoughts to others, though his soul was quell'd
       In youth by his own thoughts; still uncompell'd,
105 He would not yield dominion of his mind
       To spirits against whom his own rebell'd;
       Proud though in desolation; which could find
       A life within itself, to breathe without mankind.

                          13
       Where rose the mountains, there to him were friends;
110 Where roll'd the ocean, thereon was his home;
       Where a blue sky, and glowing clime, extends,
       He had the passion and the power to roam;
       The desert, forest, cavern, breaker's foam,
       Were unto him companionship; they spake
115 A mutual language, clearer than the tome
       Of his land's tongue, which he would oft forsake
       For Nature's pages glass'd by sunbeams on the lake.

---

[1] Cf. Samuel Johnson (1709–84), *The Idler* 42.

[2] Cf. Shakespeare, *Hamlet* 3.2.71.

[3] Cf. Byron, *Manfred* 1.1.259.*

[4] Cf. Exodus 2.22.

[5] Cf. Byron, *Manfred* 2.2.50–58.*

14

Like the Chaldean,[1] he could watch the stars,
Till he had peopled them with beings bright
As their own beams; and earth, and earth-born jars,
And human frailties, were forgotten quite:
Could he have kept his spirit to that flight
He had been happy; but this clay will sink
Its spark immortal, envying it the light
To which it mounts, as if to break the link
That keeps us from yon heaven which woos us to its brink.

15

But in Man's dwellings he became a thing
Restless and worn, and stern and wearisome,
Droop'd as a wild-born falcon with clipt wing,
To whom the boundless air alone were home:
Then came his fit again,[2] which to o'ercome,
As eagerly the barr'd-up bird will beat
His breast and beak against his wiry dome
Till the blood tinge his plumage, so the heat
Of his impeded soul would through his bosom eat.

16

Self-exiled Harold wanders forth again,
With nought of hope left, but with less of gloom;
The very knowledge that he lived in vain,
That all was over on this side the tomb,
Had made Despair a smilingness assume,
Which, though 'twere wild—as on the plundered wreck
When mariners would madly meet their doom
With draughts intemperate on the sinking deck,—
Did yet inspire a cheer, which he forbore to check.

17

Stop!—for thy tread is on an Empire's dust!
An Earthquake's spoil is sepulchred below!
Is the spot mark'd with no colossal bust?
Nor column trophied for triumphal show?
None; but the moral's truth tells simpler so,
As the ground was before, thus let it be;—
How that red rain hath made the harvest grow!
And is this all the world has gained by thee,
Thou first and last of fields! king-making Victory?

18

And Harold stands upon this place of skulls,[3]
The grave of France, the deadly Waterloo![4]
How in an hour the power which gave annuls
Its gifts, transferring fame as fleeting too!
In "pride of place"[5] here last the eagle flew,
Then tore with bloody talon the rent plain,
Pierced by the shaft of banded nations through;
Ambition's life and labours all were vain;
He wears the shattered links of the world's broken chain.[6]

19

Fit retribution! Gaul may champ the bit
And foam in fetters;—but is Earth more free?
Did nations combat to make *One* submit;
Or league to teach all kings true sovereignty?
What! shall reviving Thraldom again be
The patched-up idol of enlightened days?
Shall we, who struck the Lion down, shall we
Pay the Wolf homage? proffering lowly gaze
And servile knees to thrones? No; *prove* before ye praise!

20

If not, o'er one fallen despot boast no more!
In vain fair cheeks were furrowed with hot tears
For Europe's flowers long rooted up before

---

[1] a Babylonian—these people were proverbial for their astrological knowledge. Cf. Byron, *Manfred* 3.2.11–14.*

[2] Cf. Shakespeare, *Macbeth* 3.4.21.

[3] Cf. Matthew 27.33.

[4] The British and Prussian armies defeated Napoleon on this battlefield on 18 June 1815. Byron visited the site on 4 May 1816.

[5] "'Pride of place' is a term of falconry, and means the highest pitch of flight.—See *Macbeth*, &c.
  'A Falcon towering in her pride of place
  Was by a mousing Owl hawked at and killed.'"
(L.B.; Shakespeare, *Macbeth* 2.4.12–13.) The eagle was Napoleon's personal emblem.

[6] After his defeat at Waterloo, Napoleon was exiled to St. Helena, where he died.

175   The trampler of her vineyards;[1] in vain years
        Of death, depopulation, bondage, fears,
        Have all been borne, and broken by the accord
        Of roused-up millions: all that most endears
        Glory, is when the myrtle[2] wreathes a sword
180   Such as Harmodius[3] drew on Athens' tyrant lord.

21

        There was a sound of revelry by night,
        And Belgium's capital[4] had gathered then
        Her Beauty and her Chivalry, and bright
        The lamps shone o'er fair women and brave men;
185   A thousand hearts beat happily; and when
        Music arose with its voluptuous swell,
        Soft eyes look'd love to eyes which spake again,
        And all went merry as a marriage-bell;[5]
        But hush! hark! a deep sound strikes like a rising knell!

22

190   Did ye not hear it?—No; 'twas but the wind,
        Or the car rattling o'er the stony street;
        On with the dance! let joy be unconfin'd;
        No sleep till morn, when Youth and Pleasure meet
        To chase the glowing Hours with flying feet—
195   But, hark!—that heavy sound breaks in once more,
        As if the clouds its echo would repeat;
        And nearer, clearer, deadlier than before!
        Arm! Arm! it is—it is—the cannon's opening roar!

23

        Within a windowed niche of that high hall
200   Sate Brunswick's fated chieftain;[6] he did hear
        That sound the first amidst the festival,
        And caught its tone with Death's prophetic ear;
        And when they smil'd because he deem'd it near,
        His heart more truly knew that peal too well
205   Which stretch'd his father[7] on a bloody bier,
        And roused the vengeance blood alone could quell:
        He rush'd into the field, and, foremost fighting, fell.

24

        Ah! then and there was hurrying to and fro,
        And gathering tears, and tremblings of distress,
210   And cheeks all pale, which but an hour ago
        Blush'd at the praise of their own loveliness;
        And there were sudden partings, such as press
        The life from out young hearts, and choking sighs
        Which ne'er might be repeated; who could guess
215   If ever more should meet those mutual eyes,
        Since upon night so sweet such awful morn could rise?

25

        And there was mounting in hot haste: the steed,
        The mustering squadron, and the clattering car,
        Went pouring forward with impetuous speed,
220   And swiftly forming in the ranks of war;
        And the deep thunder peal on peal afar;
        And near, the beat of the alarming drum
        Rous'd up the soldier ere the morning star;
        While throng'd the citizens with terror dumb,
225   Or whispering, with white lips—"The foe! They come! they come!"

---

[1] Cf. Isaiah 63.3.

[2] sacred to Aphrodite/Venus, goddess of love.

[3] "See the famous Song on Harmodius and Aristogiton.—The best English translation is in Bland's Anthology, by Mr. Denman. 'With myrtle my sword will I wreathe,' &c." (L.B.; *Translations Chiefly from the Greek Anthology*, 1806.) Harmodius and Aristogeiton were Athenian patriots who attempted to assassinate the tyrants Hippias and Hipparchus in 514 BC.

[4] Brussels, just south of Waterloo.

[5] "On the night previous to the action, it is said that a ball was given at Brussels." (L.B.) The Duchess of Richmond hosted a ball there on 15 June 1815, the evening before the Waterloo campaign began.

[6] Frederick, Duke of Brunswick (1771–1815), brother of Caroline, Princess of Wales, and nephew of George III, was killed at the battle of Quatre Bras, the first engagement of the Waterloo campaign, 16 June 1815.

[7] Frederick's father, Charles, Duke of Brunswick (1735–1806), was killed at the battle of Auerstädt in 1806.

26

And wild and high the "Cameron's gathering"[1] rose!
The war-note of Lochiel, which Albyn's[2] hills
Have heard, and heard, too, have her Saxon foes:—
How in the noon of night that pibroch[3] thrills,
230 Savage and shrill! But with the breath which fills
Their mountain-pipe, so fill the mountaineers
With the fierce native daring which instils
The stirring memory of a thousand years,
And Evan's, Donald's fame rings in each clansman's ears![4]

27

235 And Ardennes waves above them her green leaves,[5]
Dewy with nature's tear-drops, as they pass,
Grieving, if aught inanimate e'er grieves,
Over the unreturning brave,—alas!
Ere evening to be trodden like the grass
240 Which now beneath them, but above shall grow
In its next verdure, when this fiery mass
Of living valour, rolling on the foe
And burning with high hope, shall moulder cold and low.

28

Last noon beheld them full of lusty life,
245 Last eve in Beauty's circle proudly gay,
The midnight brought the signal-sound of strife,
The morn the marshalling in arms,— the day
Battle's magnificently-stern array!
The thunder-clouds close o'er it, which when rent
250 The earth is covered thick with other clay,
Which her own clay shall cover, heaped and pent,
Rider and horse,—friend, foe,—in one red burial blent! ...[6]

34

There is a very life in our despair,
Vitality of poison,—a quick root
300 Which feeds these deadly branches; for it were
As nothing did we die; but Life will suit
Itself to Sorrow's most detested fruit,
Like to the apples on the Dead Sea's shore,[7]
All ashes to the taste: Did man compute
305 Existence by enjoyment, and count o'er
Such hours 'gainst years of life,—say, would he name three-score?

35

The Psalmist[8] number'd out the years of man:
They are enough; and if thy tale be *true*,
Thou, who didst grudge him even that fleeting span,
310 More than enough, thou fatal Waterloo!
Millions of tongues record thee, and anew
Their children's lips shall echo them, and say—
"Here, where the sword united nations drew,
Our countrymen were warring on that day!"
315 And this is much, and all which will not pass away.[9]

36

There sunk the greatest, nor the worst of men,
Whose spirit antithetically mixt
One moment of the mightiest, and again
On little objects with like firmness fixt,
320 Extreme in all things! hadst thou been betwixt,
Thy throne had still been thine, or never been;
For daring made thy rise as fall: thou seek'st

---

[1] the war song of the Camerons, a Scottish clan.

[2] Gaelic for Scotland.

[3] a warlike bagpipe tune.

[4] "Sir Evan Cameron, and his descendant Donald, the 'gentle Lochiel' of the 'forty-five.'" (L.B.) Sir Evan Cameron (1629–1719) fought against Cromwell, and his grandson Donald Cameron (1695–1748) was a supporter of Charles Stuart, the Young Pretender. His great-great-grandson, John Cameron (1771–1815), was killed at Quatre Bras. (Byron was half-Scottish.)

[5] "The wood of Soignies is supposed to be a remnant of the 'forest of Ardennes,' famous in Boiardo's Orlando, and immortal in Shakespeare's 'As you like it.' It is also celebrated in Tacitus as being the spot of successful defence by the Germans against the Roman encroachments.—I have ventured to adopt the name connected with nobler associations than those of mere slaughter." (L.B.) Cf. Tacitus, *Annals* 1.60 and 3.42; Boiardo, *Orlando Innamorato* 1.2.30. The forest of Ardennes is actually in Luxemburg.

[6] The omitted stanzas lament the death at Waterloo of Byron's cousin Frederick Howard (1785–1815) and meditate on sorrow.

[7] "The (fabled) apples on the brink of the lake Asphaltes were said to be fair without, and within ashes.—Vide Tacitus Histor. 1.5.7." (L.B.) Cf. Deuteronomy 32.32.

[8] King David: see Psalm 90.10.

[9] Cf. Shakespeare, *Henry V* 4.3.41–67.

Even now to re-assume the imperial mien,
And shake again the world, the Thunderer of the scene!

37

325 Conqueror and captive of the earth art thou!
She trembles at thee still, and thy wild name
Was ne'er more bruited in men's minds than now
That thou art nothing, save the jest of Fame,[1]
Who wooed thee once, thy vassal, and became
330 The flatterer of thy fierceness, till thou wert
A god unto thyself; nor less the same
To the astounded kingdoms all inert,
Who deem'd thee for a time whate'er thou didst assert.

38

Oh, more or less than man—in high or low,
335 Battling with nations, flying from the field;
Now making monarchs' necks thy footstool, now
More than thy meanest soldier taught to yield;
An empire thou couldst crush, command, rebuild,
But govern not thy pettiest passion, nor,
340 However deeply in men's spirits skill'd,
Look through thine own, nor curb the lust of war,
Nor learn that tempted Fate will leave the loftiest star.

39

Yet well thy soul hath brook'd the turning tide
With that untaught innate philosophy,
345 Which, be it wisdom, coldness, or deep pride,
Is gall and wormwood[2] to an enemy.
When the whole host of hatred stood hard by,
To watch and mock thee shrinking, thou hast smil'd
With a sedate and all-enduring eye;—
350 When Fortune fled her spoil'd and favourite child,
He stood unbow'd beneath the ills upon him pil'd.

40

Sager than in thy fortunes; for in them
Ambition steel'd thee on too far to show
That just habitual scorn which could contemn
355 Men and their thoughts; 'twas wise to feel, not so
To wear it ever on thy lip and brow,

---

[1] Cf. Pope, *An Essay on Man* (1733–34) 2.18.

[2] Cf. Lamentations 3.19.

And spurn the instruments thou wert to use
Till they were turn'd unto thine overthrow:
'Tis but a worthless world to win or lose;
360 So hath it prov'd to thee, and all such lot who choose.

41

If, like a tower upon a headland rock,
Thou hadst been made to stand or fall alone,
Such scorn of man had help'd to brave the shock;
But men's thoughts were the steps which pav'd thy throne,
365 *Their* admiration thy best weapon shone;
The part of Philip's son[3] was thine, not then
(Unless aside thy purple had been thrown)
Like stern Diogenes to mock at men;
For sceptred cynics earth were far too wide a den.[4]

42

370 But quiet to quick bosoms is a hell,
And *there* hath been thy bane; there is a fire
And motion of the soul which will not dwell
In its own narrow being, but aspire
Beyond the fitting medium of desire;
375 And, but once kindled, quenchless evermore,
Preys upon high adventure, nor can tire
Of aught but rest; a fever at the core,
Fatal to him who bears, to all who ever bore.

43

This makes the madmen who have made men mad

---

[3] Alexander the Great (356–23 BC). He is said to have said that if he had not been a king (kings traditionally wore purple), he would have liked to be a philosopher like Diogenes (the founder of the Cynics). Diogenes is said to have replied that if he had not been a philosopher, he would have liked to be a king like Alexander.

[4] "The great error of Napoleon, 'if we have writ our annals true' [Shakespeare, *Coriolanus* 5.6.112], was a continued obtrusion on mankind of his want of all community of feeling for or with them; perhaps more offensive to human vanity than the active cruelty of more trembling and suspicious tyranny.

"Such were his speeches to public assemblies as well as individuals: and the single expression which he is said to have used on returning to Paris after the Russian winter had destroyed his army, rubbing his hands over a fire, 'This is pleasanter than Moscow,' would probably alienate more favour from his cause than the destruction and reverses which led to the remark." (L.B.)

380 By their contagion; Conquerors and Kings,
Founders of sects and systems, to whom add
Sophists, Bards, Statesmen, all unquiet things
Which stir too strongly the soul's secret springs,
And are themselves the fools to those they fool;
385 Envied, yet how unenviable! what stings
Are theirs! One breast laid open were a school
Which would unteach mankind the lust to shine or
    rule:

44

Their breath is agitation, and their life
A storm whereon they ride, to sink at last,
390 And yet so nurs'd and bigoted to strife,
That should their days, surviving perils past,
Melt to calm twilight, they feel overcast
With sorrow and supineness, and so die;
Even as a flame unfed, which runs to waste
395 With its own flickering, or a sword laid by
Which eats into itself, and rusts ingloriously.

45

He who ascends to mountain-tops, shall find
The loftiest peaks most wrapt in clouds and snow;
He who surpasses or subdues mankind,
400 Must look down on the hate of those below.
Though high *above* the sun of glory glow,
And far *beneath* the earth and ocean spread,
Round him are icy rocks, and loudly blow
Contending tempests on his naked head,
405 And thus reward the toils which to those summits
    led....[1]

68

Lake Leman[2] woos me with its crystal face,
645 The mirror where the stars and mountains view
The stillness of their aspect in each trace
Its clear depth yields of their far height and hue:
There is too much of man here, to look through
With a fit mind the might which I behold;
650 But soon in me shall Loneliness renew
Thoughts hid, but not less cherish'd than of old,
Ere mingling with the herd had penn'd me in their
    fold.

69

To fly from, need not be to hate, mankind;
All are not fit with them to stir and toil,
655 Nor is it discontent to keep the mind
Deep in its fountain, lest it overboil
In the hot throng, where we become the spoil
Of our infection, till too late and long
We may deplore and struggle with the coil,[3]
660 In wretched interchange of wrong for wrong
'Midst a contentious world, striving where none are
    strong.

70

There, in a moment, we may plunge our years
In fatal penitence, and in the blight
Of our own soul, turn all our blood to tears,
665 And colour things to come with hues of Night;
The race of life becomes a hopeless flight
To those that walk in darkness:[4] on the sea,
The boldest steer but where their ports invite,
But there are wanderers o'er Eternity
670 Whose bark drives on and on, and anchored ne'er shall
    be.

71

Is it not better, then, to be alone,
And love Earth only for its earthly sake?
By the blue rushing of the arrowy Rhone,[5]
Or the pure bosom of its nursing lake,
675 Which feeds it as a mother who doth make
A fair but froward infant her own care,
Kissing its cries away as these awake;—
Is it not better thus our lives to wear,
Than join the crushing crowd, doom'd to inflict or
    bear?

---

[1] The omitted stanzas describe Harold's journey up the Rhine to the Alps and include his song "The castled crag of Drachenfels."

[2] Lake Geneva.

[3] Cf. Shakespeare, *Hamlet* 3.1.67.

[4] Cf. Ecclesiastes 2.14; 1 John 2.11.

[5] "The colour of the Rhone at Geneva is *blue*, to a depth of tint which I have never seen equalled in water, salt or fresh, except in the Mediterranean and Archipelago." (L.B.)

72

     I live not in myself, but I become
     Portion of that around me; and to me,
     High mountains are a feeling,[1] but the hum
     Of human cities torture: I can see
     Nothing to loathe in nature, save to be
     A link reluctant in a fleshly chain,
     Class'd among creatures, when the soul can flee,
     And with the sky, the peak, the heaving plain
Of ocean, or the stars, mingle, and not in vain.

73

     And thus I am absorb'd, and this is life:
     I look upon the peopled desart past,
     As on a place of agony and strife,
     Where, for some sin, to Sorrow I was cast,
     To act and suffer, but remount at last
     With a fresh pinion; which I feel to spring,
     Though young, yet waxing vigorous, as the blast
     Which it would cope with, on delighted wing,
Spurning the clay-cold bonds which round our being cling.

74

     And when, at length, the mind shall be all free
     From what it hates in this degraded form,
     Reft of its carnal life, save what shall be
     Existent happier in the fly and worm,—
     When elements to elements conform,
     And dust is as it should be, shall I not
     Feel all I see, less dazzling, but more warm?
     The bodiless thought? the Spirit of each spot?
Of which, even now, I share at times the immortal lot?

75

     Are not the mountains, waves, and skies, a part
     Of me and of my soul, as I of them?
     Is not the love of these deep in my heart
     With a pure passion? should I not contemn
     All objects, if compar'd with these? and stem
     A tide of suffering, rather than forego
     Such feelings for the hard and worldly phlegm
     Of those whose eyes are only turn'd below,
Gazing upon the ground, with thoughts which dare not glow?

76

     But this is not my theme; and I return
     To that which is immediate, and require
     Those who find contemplation in the urn,
     To look on One,[2] whose dust was once all fire,
     A native of the land where I respire
     The clear air for a while—a passing guest,
     Where he became a being,—whose desire
     Was to be glorious; 'twas a foolish quest,
The which to gain and keep, he sacrificed all rest.

77

     Here the self-torturing sophist, wild Rousseau,
     The apostle of affliction, he who threw
     Enchantment over passion, and from woe
     Wrung overwhelming eloquence, first drew
     The breath which made him wretched; yet he knew
     How to make madness beautiful, and cast
     O'er erring deeds and thoughts, a heavenly hue
     Of words, like sunbeams, dazzling as they past
The eyes, which o'er them shed tears feelingly and fast.

78

     His love was passion's essence—as a tree
     On fire by lightning; with ethereal flame
     Kindled he was, and blasted; for to be
     Thus, and enamoured, were in him the same.
     But his was not the love of living dame,
     Nor of the dead who rise upon our dreams,
     But of ideal beauty, which became
     In him existence, and o'erflowing teems
Along his burning page, distempered though it seems.

79

     This breathed itself to life in Júlie, *this*
     Invested her with all that's wild and sweet;

---

[1] Cf. W. Wordsworth, "Tintern Abbey" 77–84.*

[2] Jean-Jacques Rousseau (1712–78), Genevan philosopher and novelist, author of *Le Contrat social* (1762), *Julie; ou, la nouvelle Héloïse* (1761), and *Confessions* (1782–89).

745 This hallowed, too, the memorable kiss[1]
　　Which every morn his fevered lip would greet,
　　From her's, who but with friendship his would meet;
　　But to that gentle touch, through brain and breast
　　Flash'd the thrill'd spirit's love-devouring heat;
750 　In that absorbing sigh perchance more blest,
　　Than vulgar minds may be with all they seek possest.

80

　　His life was one long war with self-sought foes,
　　Or friends by him self-banish'd; for his mind
　　Had grown Suspicion's sanctuary, and chose
755 　For its own cruel sacrifice, the kind,
　　'Gainst whom he raged with fury strange and blind.
　　But he was phrenzied,—wherefore, who may know?
　　Since cause might be which skill could never find;
　　But he was phrenzied by disease or woe,
760 　To that worst pitch of all, which wears a reasoning show.

81

　　For then he was inspired, and from him came,
　　As from the Pythian's mystic cave of yore,[2]
　　Those oracles which set the world in flame,
　　Nor ceased to burn till kingdoms were no more:
765 　Did he not this for France? which lay before
　　Bowed to the inborn tyranny of years?
　　Broken and trembling, to the yoke she bore,
　　Till by the voice of him and his compeers,
　　Roused up to too much wrath which follows o'ergrown fears?

82

770 They made themselves a fearful monument!
　　The wreck of old opinions—things which grew
　　Breathed from the birth of time: the veil they rent,
　　And what behind it lay, all earth shall view.
　　But good with ill they also overthrew,
775 Leaving but ruins, wherewith to rebuild
　　Upon the same foundation, and renew
　　Dungeons and thrones, which the same hour re-fill'd
　　As heretofore, because ambition was self-will'd.

83

　　But this will not endure, nor be endured!
780 Mankind have felt their strength, and made it felt.
　　They might have used it better, but, allured
　　By their new vigour, sternly have they dealt
　　On one another; pity ceased to melt
　　With her once natural charities. But they,
785 Who in oppression's darkness caved had dwelt,
　　They were not eagles, nourish'd with the day;
　　What marvel then, at times, if they mistook their prey?

84

　　What deep wounds ever closed without a scar?
　　The heart's bleed longest, and but heal to wear
790 That which disfigures it; and they who war
　　With their own hopes, and have been vanquish'd, bear
　　Silence, but not submission: in his lair
　　Fix'd Passion holds his breath, until the hour
　　Which shall atone for years; none need despair:
795 It came, it cometh, and will come,—the power
　　To punish or forgive—in *one* we shall be slower.

85

　　Clear, placid Leman! thy contrasted lake,
　　With the wide world I dwelt in, is a thing
　　Which warns me, with its stillness, to forsake
800 Earth's troubled waters for a purer spring.
　　This quiet sail is as a noiseless wing
　　To waft me from distraction; once I loved
　　Torn ocean's roar, but thy soft murmuring
　　Sounds sweet as if a sister's voice reproved,
805 That I with stern delights should e'er have been so moved.

86

　　It is the hush of night, and all between
　　Thy margin and the mountains, dusk, yet clear,

---

[1] "This refers to the account in his 'Confessions' [2.9] of his passion for the Comtesse d'Houdetot (the mistress of St. Lambert) and his long walk every morning for the sake of the single kiss which was the common salutation of French acquaintance.—Rousseau's description of his feelings on this occasion may be considered as the most passionate, yet not impure description and expression of love that ever kindled into words; which after all must be felt, from their very force, to be inadequate to the delineation: a painting can give no sufficient idea of the ocean." (L.B.)

[2] Byron compares Rousseau to the Pythian, the oracle of Apollo at Delphi.

Mellowed and mingling, yet distinctly seen,
Save darken'd Jura,[1] whose capt heights appear
810 Precipitously steep; and drawing near,
There breathes a living fragrance from the shore,
Of flowers yet fresh with childhood; on the ear
Drops the light drip of the suspended oar,[2]
Or chirps the grasshopper one good-night carol more;

87

815 He is an evening reveller, who makes
His life an infancy, and sings his fill;
At intervals, some bird from out the brakes,
Starts into voice a moment, then is still.
There seems a floating whisper on the hill,
820 But that is fancy, for the starlight dews
All silently their tears of love instil,
Weeping themselves away, till they infuse
Deep into Nature's breast the spirit of her hues.

88

Ye stars! which are the poetry of heaven!
825 If in your bright leaves we would read the fate
Of men and empires,—'tis to be forgiven,
That in our aspirations to be great,
Our destinies o'erleap their mortal state,
And claim a kindred with you; for ye are
830 A beauty and a mystery, and create
In us such love and reverence from afar,
That fortune, fame, power, life, have named
themselves a star.[3]

89

All heaven and earth are still—though not in sleep,
But breathless, as we grow when feeling most;
835 And silent, as we stand in thoughts too deep:—[4]
All heaven and earth are still: From the high host
Of stars, to the lull'd lake and mountain-coast,
All is concentered in a life intense
Where not a beam, nor air, nor leaf is lost,
840 But hath a part of being, and a sense
Of that which is of all Creator and defence.

90

Then stirs the feeling infinite, so felt
In solitude, where we are *least* alone;
A truth, which through our being then doth melt
845 And purifies from self: it is a tone,
The soul and source of music, which makes known
Eternal harmony, and sheds a charm
Like to the fabled Cytherea's zone,[5]
Binding all things with beauty;—'twould disarm
850 The spectre Death, had he substantial power to harm.

91

Not vainly did the early Persian make
His altar the high places and the peak
Of earth-o'ergazing mountains, and thus take[6]

---

[1] mountain range north-west of Lake Geneva.

[2] Cf. W. Wordsworth,* "Remembrance of Collins" (1798) 22.

[3] Cf. W. Wordsworth, "Ode" 59.*

[4] Cf. W. Wordsworth, "Ode" 203.*

[5] The zone (girdle, belt) of Venus (Cytherea) made its wearer irresistibly attractive.

[6] "It is to be recollected, that the most beautiful and impressive doctrines of the divine Founder of Christianity were delivered, not in the *Temple*, but on the *Mount* [Matthew 6–7].

"To wave the question of devotion, and turn to human eloquence,—the most effectual and splendid specimens were not pronounced within walls. Demosthenes addressed the public and popular assemblies. Cicero spoke in the forum. That this added to their effect on the mind of both orator and hearers, may be conceived from the difference between what we read of the emotions then and there produced, and those we ourselves experience in the perusal in the closet. It is one thing to read the Iliad at Sigæum and on the tumuli, or by the springs with mount Ida above, and the plain and rivers and Archipelago around you: and another to trim your taper over it in a snug library—*this* I know.

"Were the early and rapid progress of what is called Methodism to be attributed to any cause beyond the enthusiasm excited by its vehement faith and doctrines (the truth or error of which I presume neither to canvas nor to question) I should venture to ascribe it to the practice of preaching in the *fields*, and the unstudied and extemporaneous effusions of its teachers.

"The Mussulmans, whose erroneous devotion (at least in the lower orders) is most sincere, and therefore impressive, are accustomed to repeat their prescribed orisons and prayers where-ever they may be at the stated hours—of course frequently in the open air, kneeling upon a light mat (which they carry for the purpose of a bed or cushion as required); the ceremony lasts some minutes, during which they are totally absorbed, and only living in their supplication; nothing can disturb them. On me the simple and entire sincerity of these men, and the spirit which appeared to be within and upon them, (Continued)

A fit and unwall'd temple, there to seek
855 The Spirit, in whose honour shrines are weak,
Uprear'd of human hands.[1] Come, and compare
Columns and idol-dwellings, Goth or Greek,
With Nature's realms of worship, earth and air,
Nor fix on fond abodes to circumscribe thy prayer!

92

860 The sky is changed!—and such a change! Oh night,[2]
And storm, and darkness, ye are wondrous strong,
Yet lovely in your strength, as is the light
Of a dark eye in woman! Far along,
From peak to peak, the rattling crags among
865 Leaps the live thunder! Not from one lone cloud,
But every mountain now hath found a tongue,
And Jura answers, through her misty shroud,
Back to the joyous Alps, who call to her aloud![3]

93

And this is in the night:—Most glorious night!
870 Thou wert not sent for slumber! let me be
A sharer in thy fierce and far delight,—
A portion of the tempest and of thee!
How the lit lake shines, a phosphoric sea,
And the big rain comes dancing to the earth!
875 And now again 'tis black,—and now, the glee
Of the loud hills shakes with its mountain-mirth,
As if they did rejoice o'er a young earthquake's birth.

94

Now, where the swift Rhone cleaves his way between
Heights which appear as lovers who have parted[4]
880 In hate, whose mining depths so intervene,
That they can meet no more, though broken-hearted;
Though in their souls, which thus each other thwarted,
Love was the very root of the fond rage
Which blighted their life's bloom, and then departed:—
885 Itself expired, but leaving them an age
Of years all winters,—war within themselves to wage.

95

Now, where the quick Rhone thus hath cleft his way,
The mightiest of the storms hath ta'en his stand:
For here, not one, but many, make their play,
890 And fling their thunder-bolts from hand to hand,
Flashing and cast around; of all the band,
The brightest through these parted hills hath fork'd
His lightnings,—as if he did understand,
That in such gaps as desolation work'd,
895 There the hot shaft should blast whatever therein lurk'd.

96

Sky, mountains, river, winds, lake, lightnings! ye!
With night, and clouds, and thunder, and a soul
To make these felt and feeling, well may be
Things that have made me watchful; the far roll
900 Of your departing voices, is the knoll
Of what in me is sleepless,—if I rest.
But where of ye, oh tempests! is the goal?
Are ye like those within the human breast?
Or do ye find, at length, like eagles, some high nest?[5]

97

905 Could I embody and unbosom now
That which is most within me,—could I wreak
My thoughts upon expression, and thus throw
Soul, heart, mind, passions, feelings, strong or weak,
All that I would have sought, and all I seek,
910 Bear, know, feel, and yet breathe—into *one* word,
And that one word were Lightning, I would speak;

---

made a far greater impression than any general rite which was ever performed in places of worship, of which I have seen those of almost every persuasion under the sun: including most of our own sectaries, and the Greek, the Catholic, the Armenian, the Lutheran, the Jewish, and the Mahometan. Many of the negroes, of whom there are numbers in the Turkish empire, are idolaters, and have free exercise of their belief and its rites: some of these I had a distant view of at Patras, and from what I could make out of them, they appeared to be of a truly Pagan description, and not very agreeable to a spectator." (L.B.)

[1] Cf. Acts 7.48.

[2] "The thunder-storms to which these lines refer occurred on the 13th of June, 1816, at midnight. I have seen among the Acroceraunian mountains of Chimari several more terrible, but none more beautiful." (L.B.)

[3] Cf. W. Wordsworth, "To Joanna" (1800) 51–65.

[4] Cf. Coleridge, "Christabel" 411–19.*

[5] Cf. Jeremiah 49.16.

But as it is, I live and die unheard,
With a most voiceless thought, sheathing it as a sword.

98

The morn is up again, the dewy morn,
With breath all incense, and with cheek all bloom,
Laughing the clouds away with playful scorn,
And living as if earth contain'd no tomb,—
And glowing into day: we may resume
The march of our existence: and thus I,
Still on thy shores, fair Leman! may find room
And food for meditation, nor pass by
Much, that may give us pause, if pondered fittingly.....[1]

105

Lausanne! and Ferney! ye have been the abodes
Of names which unto you bequeath'd a name;[2]
Mortals, who sought and found, by dangerous roads,
A path to perpetuity of fame:
They were gigantic minds, and their steep aim,
Was, Titan-like, on daring doubts to pile
Thoughts which should call down thunder, and the flame
Of Heaven, again assail'd,[3] if Heaven the while
On man and man's research could deign do more than smile.

106

The one was fire and fickleness, a child,
Most mutable in wishes, but in mind,
A wit as various,—gay, grave, sage, or wild,—
Historian, bard, philosopher, combined;
He multiplied himself among mankind,
The Proteus[4] of their talents: But his own
Breathed most in ridicule,—which, as the wind,
Blew where it listed,[5] laying all things prone,—
Now to o'erthrow a fool, and now to shake a throne.

107

The other, deep and slow, exhausting thought,
And hiving wisdom with each studious year,
In meditation dwelt, with learning wrought,
And shaped his weapon with an edge severe,
Sapping a solemn creed with solemn sneer;
The lord of irony,—that master-spell,
Which stung his foes to wrath, which grew from fear,
And doom'd him to the zealot's ready Hell,
Which answers to all doubts so eloquently well.

108

Yet, peace be with their ashes,—for by them,
If merited, the penalty is paid;
It is not ours to judge,—far less condemn;
The hour must come when such things shall be made
Known unto all,—or hope and dread allay'd
By slumber, on one pillow,—in the dust,
Which, thus much we are sure, must lie decay'd;
And when it shall revive, as is our trust,
'Twill be to be forgiven, or suffer what is just.

109

But let me quit man's works, again to read
His Maker's, spread around me, and suspend
This page, which from my reveries I feed,
Until it seems prolonging without end.
The clouds above me to the white Alps tend,
And I must pierce them, and survey whate'er
May be permitted, as my steps I bend
To their most great and growing region, where
The earth to her embrace compels the powers of air.

110

Italia! too, Italia! looking on thee,
Full flashes on the soul the light of ages,
Since the fierce Carthaginian[6] almost won thee,

---

[1] The omitted stanzas describe Clarens, the main setting of Rousseau's *Julie*.

[2] "Voltaire and Gibbon." (L.B.) Edward Gibbon (1737–94), author of *The Decline and Fall of the Roman Empire* (1788), lived in Lausanne; Voltaire (1694–1778), author of *Candide* (1759), lived in Ferney.

[3] The Titans piled Mt. Pelion on top of Mt. Ossa in the attempt to reach the top of Mt. Olympus and overthrow the gods: see Virgil, *Georgics* 1.281.

[4] a sea-god, proverbial for shape-shifting; cf. Homer, *Odyssey* 4.

[5] Cf. John 3.8.

[6] Hannibal (247–183 BC), Carthaginian general, crossed the Alps to invade Italy in 218 BC, during the Second Punic War.

1025 To the last halo of the chiefs and sages
Who glorify thy consecrated pages;
Thou wert the throne and grave of empires; still,
The fount at which the panting mind assuages
Her thirst for knowledge, quaffing there her fill,
1030 Flows from the eternal source of Rome's imperial hill.

111

Thus far I have proceeded in a theme
Renew'd with no kind auspices:—to feel
We are not what we have been, and to deem
We are not what we should be,—and to steel
1035 The heart against itself; and to conceal,
With a proud caution, love, or hate, or aught,—
Passion or feeling, purpose, grief or zeal,—
Which is the tyrant spirit of our thought,
Is a stern task of soul:—No matter,—it is taught.

112

1040 And for these words, thus woven into song,
It may be that they are a harmless wile,—
The colouring of the scenes which fleet along,
Which I would seize, in passing, to beguile
My breast, or that of others, for a while.
1045 Fame is the thirst of youth,—but I am not
So young as to regard men's frown or smile,
As loss or guerdon of a glorious lot;
I stood and stand alone,—remember'd or forgot.

113

I have not loved the world, nor the world me;[1]
1050 I have not flatter'd it's rank breath,[2] nor bow'd
To it's idolatries a patient knee,—
Nor coin'd my cheek to smiles,—nor cried aloud
In worship of an echo; in the crowd
They could not deem me one of such; I stood
1055 Among them, but not of them;[3] in a shroud
Of thoughts which were not their thoughts, and
still could,
Had I not filed my mind, which thus itself subdued.[4]

114

I have not loved the world, nor the world me,—
But let us part fair foes; I do believe,
1060 Though I have found them not, that there may be
Words which are things,—hopes which will not
deceive,
And virtues which are merciful, nor weave
Snares for the failing: I would also deem
O'er others' griefs that some sincerely grieve;[5]
1065 That two, or one, are almost what they seem,—
That goodness is no name, and happiness no dream.

115

My daughter! with thy name this song begun—
My daughter! with thy name thus much shall end—
I see thee not,—I hear thee not,—but none
1070 Can be so wrapt in thee; thou art the friend
To whom the shadows of far years extend:
Albeit my brow thou never should'st behold,
My voice shall with thy future visions blend,
And reach into thy heart,—when mine is cold,—
1075 A token and a tone, even from thy father's mould.

116

To aid thy mind's developement,—to watch
Thy dawn of little joys,—to sit and see
Almost thy very growth,—to view thee catch
Knowledge of objects,—wonders yet to thee!
1080 To hold thee lightly on a gentle knee,
And print on thy soft cheek a parent's kiss,—
This, it should seem, was not reserv'd for me;
Yet this was in my nature:—as it is,
I know not what is there, yet something like to this.

117

1085 Yet, though dull Hate as duty should be taught,
I know that thou wilt love me; though my name

---

[1] Cf. 1 John 2.15.

[2] Cf. Shakespeare, *Coriolanus* 3.1.66–67.

[3] Cf. Byron, *Manfred* 2.2.54–57.*

[4] "——————'If it be thus,
For Banquo's issue have I *filed* my mind.' *Macbeth* [3.1.64–65]." (L.B.)

[5] "It is said by Rochefoucault that 'there is *always* something in the misfortunes of men's best friends not displeasing to them.'" (L.B.) François, duc de la Rochefoucauld (1613–80), *Maximes* (1678) 583.

Should be shut from thee, as a spell still fraught
With desolation,—and a broken claim:
Though the grave closed between us,— 'twere the same,
I know that thou wilt love me; though to drain
My blood from out thy being, were an aim,
And an attainment,—all would be in vain,—
Still thou would'st love me, still that more than life retain.

118

The child of love,—though born in bitterness,
And nurtured in convulsion. Of thy sire
These were the elements,—and thine no less.
As yet such are around thee,—but thy fire
Shall be more tempered, and thy hope far higher.
Sweet be thy cradled slumbers! O'er the sea,
And from the mountains where I now respire,
Fain would I waft such blessing upon thee,
As, with a sigh, I deem thou might'st have been to me!

Manfred, A Dramatic Poem (1817)[1]

DRAMATIS PERSONÆ

    MANFRED
    CHAMOIS HUNTER
    ABBOT OF ST. MAURICE
    MANUEL
    HERMAN

    WITCH OF THE ALPS
    ARIMANES
    NEMESIS
    THE DESTINIES

SPIRITS, &c.

The Scene of the Drama is amongst the Higher Alps—partly in the Castle of Manfred, and partly in the Mountains.

---

[1] Byron probably took the name for his hero from the protagonist of Horace Walpole (1717–97), *The Castle of Otranto* (1764). He later added an epigraph from Shakespeare, *Hamlet* 1.5.166–67: "There are more things in heaven and earth, Horatio, / Than are dreamt of in your philosophy."

ACT 1

SCENE 1

MANFRED alone—Scene, a Gothic gallery—Time, Midnight.

MANFRED: The lamp must be replenish'd, but even then
It will not burn so long as I must watch:
My slumbers—if I slumber—are not sleep,
But a continuance of enduring thought,
Which then I can resist not: in my heart
There is a vigil, and these eyes but close
To look within; and yet I live, and bear
The aspect and the form of breathing men.
But grief should be the instructor of the wise;[2]
Sorrow is knowledge: they who know the most
Must mourn the deepest o'er the fatal truth,
The Tree of Knowledge is not that of Life.[3]
Philosophy and science, and the springs
Of wonder, and the wisdom of the world,
I have essayed, and in my mind there is
A power to make these subject to itself—
But they avail not: I have done men good,
And I have met with good even among men—
But this avail'd not: I have had my foes,
And none have baffled, many fallen before me—
But this avail'd not:—Good, or evil, life,
Powers, passions, all I see in other beings,
Have been to me as rain unto the sands,
Since that all-nameless hour. I have no dread,
And feel the curse to have no natural fear,
Nor fluttering throb, that beats with hopes or wishes,
Or lurking love of something on the earth.—[4]

---

[2] Cf. Ecclesiastes 1.18.

[3] See Genesis 2–3.

[4] Cf. Goethe, *Faust* Part 1 (1808) 354–417. Byron resented the suggestion that *Manfred* had been influenced by Goethe's *Faust*, but he had read the account of it in *De l'Allemagne* (1813), by Mme. de Staël; and in August 1816, M.G. Lewis,* who was visiting Geneva, translated part of it orally—"& I was naturally much struck with it" (*Letters and Journals* 7: 113). Goethe himself admired Byron's play and recognized its originality: see E.M. Butler, *Byron and Goethe* (1956).

George Gordon, Lord Byron

Now to my task.—
            Mysterious Agency!
Ye spirits of the unbounded Universe!
Whom I have sought in darkness and in light—
Ye, who do compass earth about, and dwell
In subtler essence—ye, to whom the tops
Of mountains inaccessible are haunts,
And earth's and ocean's caves familiar things—
I call upon ye by the written charm
Which gives me power upon you—Rise! appear!
[*A pause.*]
They come not yet.—Now by the voice of him
Who is the first among you—by this sign,
Which makes you tremble—by the claims of him
Who is undying,—Rise! appear!—Appear!
[*A pause.*]
If it be so.—Spirits of earth and air,
Ye shall not thus elude me: by a power,
Deeper than all yet urged, a tyrant-spell,
Which had its birth-place in a star condemn'd,
The burning wreck of a demolish'd world,
A wandering hell in the eternal space;
By the strong curse which is upon my soul,
The thought which is within me and around me,
I do compel ye to my will.—Appear!
[*A star is seen at the darker end of the gallery; it is stationary; and a voice is heard singing.*][1]

FIRST SPIRIT.

    Mortal! to thy bidding bow'd,
      From my mansion in the cloud,
    Which the breath of twilight builds,
    And the summer's sun-set gilds
      With the azure and vermilion,
    Which is mix'd for my pavilion;
    Though thy quest may be forbidden,
    On a star-beam I have ridden;
    To thine adjuration bow'd,
    Mortal—be thy wish avow'd!

Voice of the SECOND SPIRIT.

Mont Blanc[2] is the monarch of mountains,
    They crowned him long ago
On a throne of rocks, in a robe of clouds,
    With a diadem of snow.
Around his waist are forests braced,
    The Avalanche in his hand;
But ere it fall, that thundering ball
    Must pause for my command.
The Glacier's cold and restless mass
    Moves onward day by day;
But I am he who bids it pass,
    Or with its ice delay.
I am the spirit of the place,
    Could make the mountain bow
And quiver to his cavern'd base—
    And what with me wouldst *Thou*?

Voice of the THIRD SPIRIT.

In the blue depth of the waters,
    Where the wave hath no strife,
Where the wind is a stranger,
    And the sea-snake hath life,
Where the Mermaid is decking
    Her green hair with shells;
Like the storm on the surface
    Came the sound of thy spells;
O'er my calm Hall of Coral
    The deep echo roll'd—
To the Spirit of Ocean
    Thy wishes unfold!

FOURTH SPIRIT.

Where the slumbering earthquake
    Lies pillow'd on fire,
And the lakes of bitumen
    Rise boilingly higher;
Where the roots of the Andes
    Strike deep in the earth,
As their summits to heaven

---

[1] With Manfred's confrontation with the spirits, cf. Goethe, *Faust* 482–517.

[2] the tallest mountain in the Alps; Byron visited it in August-September 1816.

  Shoot soaringly forth;
I have quitted my birth-place,
  Thy bidding to bide—
Thy spell hath subdued me,
  Thy will be my guide!

FIFTH SPIRIT.

I am the Rider of the wind,
  The Stirrer of the storm;
The hurricane I left behind
  Is yet with lightning warm;
To speed to thee, o'er shore and sea
  I swept upon the blast:
The fleet I met sailed well, and yet
  'Twill sink ere night be past.

SIXTH SPIRIT.

My dwelling is the shadow of the night,
Why doth thy magic torture me with light?

SEVENTH SPIRIT.

The star which rules thy destiny,
Was ruled, ere earth began, by me:
It was a world as fresh and fair
As e'er revolved round sun in air;
Its course was free and regular,
Space bosom'd not a lovelier star.
The hour arrived—and it became
A wandering mass of shapeless flame,
A pathless comet, and a curse,
The menace of the universe;
Still rolling on with innate force,
Without a sphere, without a course,
A bright deformity on high,
The monster of the upper sky!
And thou! beneath its influence born—
Thou worm! whom I obey and scorn—
Forced by a power (which is not thine,
And lent thee but to make thee mine)
For this brief moment to descend,
Where these weak spirits round thee bend
And parley with a thing like thee—
What wouldst thou, Child of Clay! with me?

The SEVEN SPIRITS.

Earth, ocean, air, night, mountains, winds, thy star,
  Are at thy beck and bidding, Child of Clay!
Before thee at thy quest their spirits are—
  What wouldst thou with us, son of
    mortals—say?
MANFRED: Forgetfulness—
FIRST SPIRIT: Of what—of whom—
  and why?
MANFRED: Of that which is within me; read it
  there—
Ye know it, and I cannot utter it.
SPIRIT: We can but give thee that which we possess:
Ask of us subjects, sovereignty, the power
  O'er earth, the whole, or portion, or a sign
  Which shall control the elements, whereof
We are the dominators, each and all,
These shall be thine.
MANFRED: Oblivion, self-oblivion—
Can ye not wring from out the hidden realms
  Ye offer so profusely what I ask?
SPIRIT: It is not in our essence, in our skill;
But—thou mayst die.
MANFRED: Will death bestow it on me?
SPIRIT: We are immortal, and do not forget;
We are eternal; and to us the past
  Is, as the future, present. Art thou answered?
MANFRED: Ye mock me—but the power which
    brought ye here
  Hath made you mine. Slaves, scoff not at my will!
  The mind, the spirit, the Promethean spark,
The lightning of my being, is as bright,
  Pervading, and far-darting as your own,
And shall not yield to yours, though coop'd in clay!
Answer, or I will teach you what I am.
SPIRIT: We answer as ye answered; our reply
Is even in thine own words.
MANFRED: Why say ye so?
SPIRIT: If, as thou say'st, thine essence be as ours,
  We have replied in telling thee, the thing
  Mortals call death hath nought to do with us.
MANFRED: I then have call'd ye from your realms in
    vain;
Ye cannot, or ye will not, aid me.

SPIRIT: Say;
What we possess we offer; it is thine:
Bethink ere thou dismiss us, ask again—
Kingdom, and sway, and strength, and length of days—
MANFRED: Accursed! what have I to do with days?
170   They are too long already.—Hence—begone!
SPIRIT: Yet pause: being here, our will would do
            thee service;
Bethink thee, is there then no other gift
Which we can make not worthless in thine eyes?
MANFRED: No, none: yet stay—one moment, ere we
            part—
175   I would behold ye face to face.[1] I hear
Your voices, sweet and melancholy sounds,
As music on the waters;[2] and I see
The steady aspect of a clear large star;
But nothing more. Approach me as ye are,
180   Or one, or all, in your accustom'd forms.
SPIRIT: We have no forms beyond the elements
Of which we are the mind and principle:
But choose a form—in that we will appear.
MANFRED: I have no choice; there is no form on
            earth
185   Hideous or beautiful to me. Let him,
Who is most powerful of ye, take such aspect
As unto him may seem most fitting.—Come!
SEVENTH SPIRIT: [*Appearing in the shape of a beautiful female figure.*]   Behold!
MANFRED: Oh God! if it be thus, and *thou*
Art not a madness and a mockery,
190   I yet might be most happy—I will clasp thee,
And we again will be—   [*The figure vanishes.*]
                      My heart is crushed!
[MANFRED *falls senseless.*]

[*A voice is heard in the Incantation which follows.*]
When the moon is on the wave,
       And the glow-worm in the grass,
And the meteor on the grave,
195   And the wisp on the morass;
When the falling stars are shooting,
And the answer'd owls are hooting,

---

[1] Cf. Exodus 33.11.

[2] Cf. Shakespeare, *The Tempest* 1.2.392.

And the silent leaves are still
In the shadow of the hill,
200   Shall my soul be upon thine,
With a power and with a sign.

Though thy slumber may be deep,
Yet thy spirit shall not sleep,
There are shades which will not vanish,
205   There are thoughts thou canst not banish;
By a power to thee unknown,
Thou canst never be alone;
Thou art wrapt as with a shroud,
Thou art gathered in a cloud;
210   And for ever shalt thou dwell
In the spirit of this spell.

Though thou seest me not pass by,
Thou shalt feel me with thine eye
As a thing that, though unseen,
215   Must be near thee, and hath been;
And when in that secret dread
Thou hast turn'd around thy head,
Thou shalt marvel I am not
As thy shadow on the spot,
220   And the power which thou dost feel
Shall be what thou must conceal.

And a magic voice and verse
Hath baptized thee with a curse;
And a spirit of the air
225   Hath begirt thee with a snare;
In the wind there is a voice
Shall forbid thee to rejoice;
And to thee shall Night deny
All the quiet of her sky;
230   And the day shall have a sun,
Which shall make thee wish it done.

From thy false tears I did distil
An essence which hath strength to kill;
From thy own heart I then did wring
235   The black blood in its blackest spring;
From thy own smile I snatch'd the snake,
For there it coil'd as in a brake;
From thy own lip I drew the charm

Which gave all these their chiefest harm;
In proving every poison known,
I found the strongest was thine own.

By thy cold breast and serpent smile,
By thy unfathom'd gulfs of guile,
By that most seeming virtuous eye,
By thy shut soul's hypocrisy;
By the perfection of thine art
Which pass'd for human thine own heart;
By thy delight in others' pain,
And by thy brotherhood of Cain,[1]
I call upon thee! and compel
Thyself to be thy proper Hell![2]

And on thy head I pour the vial
Which doth devote thee to this trial;
Nor to slumber, nor to die,
Shall be in thy destiny;
Though thy death shall still seem near
To thy wish, but as a fear;
Lo! the spell now works around thee,
And the clankless chain hath bound thee;
O'er thy heart and brain together
Hath the word been pass'd—now wither!

SCENE 2

*The Mountain of the Jungfrau.[3] —Time, Morning.—*MANFRED *alone upon the Cliffs.*

MANFRED: The spirits I have raised abandon me—
The spells which I have studied baffled me—
The remedy I reck'd of tortured me;
I lean no more on super-human aid,
It hath no power upon the past, and for
The future, till the past be gulf'd in darkness,
It is not of my search.—My mother Earth![4]
And thou fresh breaking Day, and you, ye Mountains,
Why are ye beautiful? I cannot love ye.
And thou, the bright eye of the universe,
That openest over all, and unto all
Art a delight—thou shin'st not on my heart.
And you, ye crags, upon whose extreme edge
I stand, and on the torrent's brink beneath
Behold the tall pines dwindled as to shrubs
In dizziness of distance; when a leap,
A stir, a motion, even a breath, would bring
My breast upon its rocky bosom's bed
To rest for ever—wherefore do I pause?
I feel the impulse—yet I do not plunge;
I see the peril—yet do not recede;
And my brain reels—and yet my foot is firm:
There is a power upon me which withholds
And makes it my fatality to live;[5]
If it be life to wear within myself
This barrenness of spirit, and to be
My own soul's sepulchre,[6] for I have ceased
To justify my deeds unto myself—
The last infirmity of evil.[7] Ay,
Thou winged and cloud-cleaving minister,
[*An eagle passes.*]
Whose happy flight is highest into heaven,
Well may'st thou swoop so near me—I should be
Thy prey, and gorge thine eaglets; thou art gone
Where the eye cannot follow thee; but thine
Yet pierces downward, onward, or above
With a pervading vision.—Beautiful!
How beautiful is all this visible world![8]
How glorious in its action and itself!
But we, who name ourselves its sovereigns, we,
Half dust, half deity, alike unfit
To sink or soar, with our mix'd essence make
A conflict of its elements, and breathe
The breath of degradation and of pride,
Contending with low wants and lofty will
Till our mortality predominates,
And men are—what they name not to themselves,

---

[1] See Genesis 4.1–15.

[2] Cf. Milton, *Paradise Lost* 1.254–55 and 4.75.

[3] Byron first saw this mountain on 23 September 1816.

[4] Cf. Aeschylus, *Prometheus Bound* 90.

[5] Cf. Shakespeare, *Hamlet* 3.1.68–76.

[6] Cf. Milton, *Samson Agonistes* 100–02.

[7] Cf. Milton, "Lycidas" 71.

[8] Cf. Shakespeare, *Hamlet* 2.2.294–305.

And trust not to each other. Hark! the note,
[*The Shepherd's pipe in the distance is heard*.]
The natural music of the mountain reed—
For here the patriarchal days are not
50 A pastoral fable—pipes in the liberal air,
Mix'd with the sweet bells of the sauntering herd;[1]
My soul would drink those echoes.—Oh, that I were[2]
The viewless spirit of a lovely sound,
A living voice, a breathing harmony,
55 A bodiless enjoyment—born and dying
With the blessed tone which made me!
[ENTER *from below a* CHAMOIS HUNTER.]
CHAMOIS HUNTER: Even so
This way the chamois leapt: her nimble feet
Have baffled me; my gains to-day will scarce
Repay my break-neck travail.—What is here?
60 Who seems not of my trade, and yet hath reach'd
A height which none even of our mountaineers,
Save our best hunters, may attain: his garb
Is goodly, his mien manly, and his air
Proud as a free-born peasant's, at this distance.—
65 I will approach him nearer.
MANFRED: [*Not perceiving the other.*] To be thus—
Grey-hair'd with anguish, like these blasted pines,
Wrecks of a single winter, barkless, branchless,[3]
A blighted trunk upon a cursed root,
Which but supplies a feeling to decay—
70 And to be thus, eternally but thus,
Having been otherwise! Now furrow'd o'er
With wrinkles, plough'd by moments, not by years;
And hours—all tortured into ages—hours
Which I outlive!—Ye toppling crags of ice!
75 Ye avalanches, whom a breath draws down
In mountainous o'erwhelming, come and crush me!
I hear ye momently above, beneath,
Crash with a frequent conflict; but ye pass,
And only fall on things that still would live;
80 On the young flourishing forest, or the hut
And hamlet of the harmless villager.

CHAMOIS HUNTER: The mists begin to rise from up
    the valley;
I'll warn him to descend, or he may chance
To lose at once his way and life together.
85 MANFRED: The mists boil up around the glaciers;
    clouds
Rise curling fast beneath me, white and sulphury,
Like foam from the roused ocean of deep Hell,[4]
Whose every wave breaks on a living shore,
Heaped with the damn'd like pebbles.—I am giddy.
90 CHAMOIS HUNTER: I must approach him cautiously;
    if near
A sudden step will startle him, and he
Seems tottering already.
MANFRED: Mountains have fallen,
Leaving a gap in the clouds, and with the shock
Rocking their Alpine brethren; filling up
95 The ripe green valleys with destruction's splinters;
Damming the rivers with a sudden dash,
Which crush'd the waters into mist, and made
Their fountains find another channel—thus,
Thus, in its old age, did Mount Rosenberg—[5]
100 Why stood I not beneath it?
CHAMOIS HUNTER: Friend! have a care,
Your next step may be fatal!—for the love
Of him who made you, stand not on that brink!
MANFRED: [*Not hearing him.*]   Such would have
    been for me a fitting tomb;
My bones had then been quiet in their depth;
105 They had not then been strewn upon the rocks
For the wind's pastime—as thus—thus they shall be—
In this one plunge.—Farewell, ye opening heavens!
Look not upon me thus reproachfully—
Ye were not meant for me—Earth! take these atoms![6]
[*As* MANFRED *is in act to spring from the cliff, the*
CHAMOIS HUNTER *seizes and retains him with a sudden
grasp.*]
110 CHAMOIS HUNTER: Hold, madman!—though
    aweary of thy life,

---

[1] Cf. Byron's letter to Augusta Leigh, 19 September 1816.*

[2] Cf. Shakespeare, *Hamlet* 1.2.129–30.

[3] Cf. Byron's letter to Augusta Leigh, 23 September 1816.*

[4] Cf. Byron, *Letters and Journals* 5: 102 (23 September 1816).*

[5] The landslide on Mt. Rossberg, on 2 September 1806, killed over 400 people.

[6] Cf. the suicide attempts in Shakespeare, *King Lear* 4.6.41; and Goethe, *Faust* 686–736.

Stain not our pure vales with thy guilty blood.—
Away with me—I will not quit my hold.
CHAMOIS HUNTER: I am most sick at heart—nay, grasp me not—
I am all feebleness—the mountains whirl
Spinning around me—I grow blind—What art thou?
CHAMOIS HUNTER: I'll answer that anon.—
Away with me!
The clouds grow thicker—there—now lean on me—
Place your foot here—here, take this staff, and cling
A moment to that shrub—now give me your hand,
And hold fast by my girdle—softly—well—
The Chalet will be gained within an hour—
Come on, we'll quickly find a surer footing,
And something like a pathway, which the torrent
Hath wash'd since winter.—Come, 'tis bravely done—
You should have been a hunter.—Follow me.
[*As they descend the rocks with difficulty, the scene closes.*]

ACT 2

SCENE 1

A Cottage among the Bernese Alps.[1]
MANFRED *and the* CHAMOIS HUNTER.

CHAMOIS HUNTER: No, no—yet pause—thou must not yet go forth:
Thy mind and body are alike unfit
To trust each other, for some hours, at least;
When thou art better, I will be thy guide—
But whither?
MANFRED: It imports not: I do know
My route full well, and need no further guidance.
CHAMOIS HUNTER: Thy garb and gait bespeak thee of high lineage—
One of the many chiefs, whose castled crags
Look o'er the lower valleys—which of these
May call thee Lord? I only know their portals;
My way of life leads me but rarely down

To bask by the huge hearths of those old halls,
Carousing with the vassals, but the paths,
Which step from out our mountains to their doors,
I know from childhood—which of these is thine?
MANFRED: No matter.
CHAMOIS HUNTER: Well, sir, pardon me the question,
And be of better cheer. Come, taste my wine;
'Tis of an ancient vintage; many a day
'T has thawed my veins among our glaciers, now
Let it do thus for thine—Come, pledge me fairly.
MANFRED: Away, away! there's blood upon the brim!
Will it then never—never sink in the earth?
CHAMOIS HUNTER: What dost thou mean? thy senses wander from thee.
MANFRED: I say 'tis blood—my blood! the pure warm stream
Which ran in the veins of my fathers, and in ours
When we were in our youth, and had one heart,
And loved each other as we should not love,
And this was shed: but still it rises up,
Colouring the clouds, that shut me out from heaven,
Where thou art not—and I shall never be.
CHAMOIS HUNTER: Man of strange words, and some half-maddening sin,
Which makes thee people vacancy, whate'er
Thy dread and sufferance be, there's comfort yet—
The aid of holy men, and heavenly patience—
MANFRED: Patience and patience! Hence—that word was made
For brutes of burthen, not for birds of prey;
Preach it to mortals of a dust like thine,—
I am not of thine order.
CHAMOIS HUNTER: Thanks to heaven!
I would not be of thine for the free fame
Of William Tell;[2] but whatsoe'er thine ill,
It must be borne, and these wild starts are useless.
MANFRED: Do I not bear it?—Look on me—I live.
CHAMOIS HUNTER: This is convulsion, and no healthful life.

---

[1] Byron travelled through this mountain range in September 1816.

[2] the legendary patriot who helped free Switzerland from Austrian domination in 1308. See Schiller, *Wilhelm Tell* (1804).

MANFRED: I tell thee, man! I have lived many years,
45   Many long years, but they are nothing now
    To those which I must number: ages—ages—
    Space and eternity—and consciousness,
    With the fierce thirst of death—and still unslaked!
  CHAMOIS HUNTER: Why, on thy brow the seal of
      middle age
50   Hath scarce been set; I am thine elder far.
  MANFRED: Think'st thou existence doth depend on
      time?[1]
    It doth; but actions are our epochs: mine
    Have made my days and nights imperishable,
    Endless, and all alike, as sands on the shore,
55   Innumerable atoms; and one desart,
    Barren and cold, on which the wild waves break,
    But nothing rests, save carcases and wrecks,
    Rocks, and the salt-surf weeds of bitterness.
  CHAMOIS HUNTER: Alas! he's mad—but yet I must
      not leave him.
60   MANFRED: I would I were—for then the things I see
    Would be but a distempered dream.
  CHAMOIS HUNTER: What is it
    That thou dost see, or think thou look'st upon?
  MANFRED: Myself, and thee—a peasant of the Alps—
    Thy humble virtues, hospitable home,
65   And spirit patient, pious, proud and free;
    Thy self-respect, grafted on innocent thoughts;
    Thy days of health, and nights of sleep; thy toils,
    By danger dignified, yet guiltless; hopes
    Of cheerful old age and a quiet grave,
70   With cross and garland over its green turf,
    And thy grandchildren's love for epitaph;
    This do I see—and then I look within—
    It matters not—my soul was scorch'd already!
  CHAMOIS HUNTER: And would'st thou then
      exchange thy lot for mine?
75   MANFRED: No, friend! I would not wrong thee,
      nor exchange
    My lot with living being: I can bear—
    However wretchedly, 'tis still to bear—
    In life what others could not brook to dream,
    But perish in their slumber.
  CHAMOIS HUNTER: And with this—
80   This cautious feeling for another's pain,
    Canst thou be black with evil?—say not so.
    Can one of gentle thoughts have wreak'd revenge
    Upon his enemies?
  MANFRED: Oh! no, no, no!
    My injuries came down on those who loved me—
85   On those whom I best loved: I never quell'd
    An enemy, save in my just defence—
    But my embrace was fatal.
  CHAMOIS HUNTER: Heaven give thee rest!
    And penitence restore thee to thyself;
    My prayers shall be for thee.
  MANFRED: I need them not,
90   But can endure thy pity. I depart—
    'Tis time—farewell!—Here's gold, and thanks for
      thee—
    No words—it is thy due. —Follow me not—
    I know my path—the mountain peril's past:—
    And once again, I charge thee, follow not!
                [EXIT MANFRED.]

SCENE 2

A Lower Valley in the Alps.—A Cataract.
Enter MANFRED.

MANFRED: It is not noon—the sunbow's rays[2] still
      arch
    The torrent with the many hues of heaven,
    And roll the sheeted silver's waving column
    O'er the crag's headlong perpendicular,
5   And fling its lines of foaming light along,
    And to and fro, like the pale courser's tail,
    The Giant steed, to be bestrode by Death,
    As told in the Apocalypse.[3] No eyes
    But mine now drink this sight of loveliness;
10   I should be sole in this sweet solitude,
    And with the Spirit of the place divide

---

[1] Cf. Byron, *Childe Harold's Pilgrimage* 3.37–38.*

[2] "This iris is formed by the rays of the sun over the lower part of the Alpine torrents: it is exactly like a rainbow, come down to pay a visit, and so close that you may walk into it:—this effect lasts till noon." (L.B.) Cf. Byron's letter to Augusta Leigh, 23 September 1816.*

[3] Cf. Revelation 6.8; and Byron's letter to Augusta Leigh, 22 September 1816.*

The homage of these waters.—I will call her.
[MANFRED *takes some of the water into the palm of his hand, and flings it in the air, muttering the adjuration. After a pause, the* WITCH OF THE ALPS *rises beneath the arch of the sunbow of the torrent.*]
Beautiful Spirit! with thy hair of light,
And dazzling eyes of glory, in whose form
15 The charms of Earth's least-mortal daughters grow
To an unearthly stature, in an essence
Of purer elements; while the hues of youth,—
Carnation'd like a sleeping infant's cheek,
Rock'd by the beating of her mother's heart,
20 Or the rose tints, which summer's twilight leaves
Upon the lofty glacier's virgin snow,
The blush of earth embracing with her heaven,—
Tinge thy celestial aspect, and make tame
The beauties of the sunbow which bends o'er thee.
25 Beautiful Spirit! in thy calm clear brow,
Wherein is glass'd serenity of soul,
Which of itself shows immortality,
I read that thou wilt pardon to a Son
Of Earth, whom the abstruser powers permit
30 At times to commune with them—if that he
Avail him of his spells—to call thee thus,
And gaze on thee a moment.
WITCH: Son of Earth!
I know thee, and the powers which give thee power;
I know thee for a man of many thoughts,
35 And deeds of good and ill, extreme in both,
Fatal and fated in thy sufferings.
I have expected this—what wouldst thou with me?
MANFRED: To look upon thy beauty—nothing
            further.
The face of the earth hath madden'd me, and I
40 Take refuge in her mysteries, and pierce
To the abodes of those who govern her—
But they can nothing aid me. I have sought
From them what they could not bestow, and now
I search no further.
WITCH: What could be the quest
45 Which is not in the power of the most powerful,
The rulers of the invisible?
MANFRED: A boon;
But why should I repeat it? 'twere in vain.

WITCH: I know not that; let thy lips utter it.
MANFRED: Well, though it torture me, 'tis but the
          same;
50 My pang shall find a voice. From my youth upwards
My spirit walk'd not with the souls of men,
Nor look'd upon the earth with human eyes;
The thirst of their ambition was not mine,
The aim of their existence was not mine;
55 My joys, my griefs, my passions, and my powers,
Made me a stranger; though I wore the form,
I had no sympathy with breathing flesh,
Nor midst the creatures of clay that girded me
Was there but one who—but of her anon.
60 I said, with men, and with the thoughts of men,
I held but slight communion; but instead,
My joy was in the Wilderness, to breathe
The difficult air of the iced mountain's top,
Where the birds dare not build, nor insect's wing
65 Flit o'er the herbless granite; or to plunge
Into the torrent, and to roll along
On the swift whirl of the new breaking wave
Of river-stream, or ocean, in their flow.
In these my early strength exulted; or
70 To follow through the night the moving moon,[1]
The stars and their developement; or catch
The dazzling lightnings till my eyes grew dim;
Or to look, list'ning, on the scattered leaves,
While Autumn winds were at their evening song.
75 These were my pastimes, and to be alone;
For if the beings, of whom I was one,—
Hating to be so,—cross'd me in my path,
I felt myself degraded back to them,
And was all clay again. And then I dived,
80 In my lone wanderings, to the caves of death,
Searching its cause in its effect; and drew
From wither'd bones, and skulls, and heap'd up dust,
Conclusions most forbidden. Then I pass'd
The nights of years in sciences untaught,
85 Save in the old-time; and with time and toil,
And terrible ordeal, and such penance
As in itself hath power upon the air,
And spirits that do compass air and earth,
Space, and the peopled infinite, I made

---

[1] Cf. Coleridge, "The Rime of the Ancyent Marinere" 255.*

      Mine eyes familiar with Eternity,
      Such as, before me, did the Magi, and
      He who from out their fountain dwellings raised
      Eros and Anteros,[1] at Gadara,
      As I do thee;—and with my knowledge grew
95   The thirst of knowledge, and the power and joy
      Of this most bright intelligence, until—
WITCH: Proceed.
MANFRED: Oh! but thus prolonged my words,
      Boasting these idle attributes, because
      As I approach the core of my heart's grief—
100 But to my task. I have not named to thee
      Father or mother, mistress, friend, or being,
      With whom I wore the chain of human ties;
      If I had such, they seem'd not such to me—
      Yet there was one—
WITCH: Spare not thyself—proceed.
105 MANFRED: She was like me in lineaments—her eyes,
      Her hair, her features, all, to the very tone
      Even of her voice, they said were like to mine;
      But soften'd all, and temper'd into beauty;
      She had the same lone thoughts and wanderings,
110 The quest of hidden knowledge, and a mind
      To comprehend the universe: nor these
      Alone, but with them gentler powers than mine,
      Pity, and smiles, and tears—which I had not;
      And tenderness—but that I had for her;
115 Humility—and that I never had.
      Her faults were mine—her virtues were her own—
      I loved her, and destroy'd her!
WITCH: With thy hand?
MANFRED: Not with my hand, but heart—
      which broke her heart—
      It gazed on mine, and withered. I have shed
120 Blood, but not hers—and yet her blood was shed—
      I saw—and could not stanch it.
WITCH: And for this—
      A being of the race thou dost despise,
      The order which thine own would rise above,
      Mingling with us and ours, thou dost forego
125 The gifts of our great knowledge, and shrink'st back

      To recreant mortality—Away!
MANFRED: Daughter of Air! I tell thee, since that
      hour—
      But words are breath—look on me in my sleep,
      Or watch my watchings—Come and sit by me!
130 My solitude is solitude no more,
      But peopled with the Furies;[2]—I have gnash'd
      My teeth in darkness till returning morn,
      Then cursed myself till sunset;—I have pray'd
      For madness as a blessing—'tis denied me.
135 I have affronted death—but in the war
      Of elements the waters shrunk from me,
      And fatal things pass'd harmless—the cold hand
      Of an all-pitiless demon held me back,
      Back by a single hair, which would not break.
140 In phantasy, imagination, all
      The affluence of my soul—which one day was
      A Croesus[3] in creation—I plunged deep,
      But, like an ebbing wave, it dash'd me back
      Into the gulf of my unfathom'd thought.
145 I plunged amidst mankind—Forgetfulness[4]
      I sought in all, save where 'tis to be found,
      And that I have to learn—my sciences,
      My long pursued and super-human art,
      Is mortal here—I dwell in my despair—
150 And live—and live for ever.
WITCH: It may be
      That I can aid thee.
MANFRED: To do this thy power
      Must wake the dead, or lay me low with them.
      Do so—in any shape—in any hour—
      With any torture—so it be the last.
155 WITCH: That is not in my province; but if thou
      Wilt swear obedience to my will, and do
      My bidding, it may help thee to thy wishes.
MANFRED: I will not swear—Obey! and whom?
      the spirits
      Whose presence I command, and be the slave
160 Of those who served me—Never!
WITCH: Is this all?
      Hast thou no gentler answer—Yet bethink thee,

---

[1] "The philosopher Iamblicus. The story of the raising of Eros and Anteros may be found in his life, by Eunapius. It is well told." (L.B.) See *Philostratus and Eunapius: The Lives of the Sophists* (Loeb, 1922).

[2] Greek spirits of vengeance.

[3] king of Lydia (d. 547 BC), proverbial for his wealth.

[4] Cf. Byron's letter to Augusta Leigh, 29 [28] September 1816.*

And pause ere thou rejectest.
MANFRED: I have said it.
WITCH: Enough!—I may retire then—say!
MANFRED: Retire!
[*The* WITCH *disappears.*]
MANFRED: [*Alone.*] We are the fools of time[1] and terror: Days
165 Steal on us and steal from us; yet we live,
Loathing our life, and dreading still to die.
In all the days of this detested yoke—
This vital weight upon the struggling heart,
Which sinks with sorrow, or beats quick with pain,
170 Or joy that ends in agony or faintness—
In all the days of past and future, for
In life there is no present, we can number
How few—how less than few—wherein the soul
Forbears to pant for death, and yet draws back
175 As from a stream in winter, though the chill
Be but a moment's. I have one resource
Still in my science—I can call the dead,
And ask them what it is we dread to be:
The sternest answer can but be the Grave,
180 And that is nothing—if they answer not—
The buried Prophet answered to the Hag
Of Endor;[2] and the Spartan Monarch drew
From the Byzantine maid's unsleeping spirit
An answer and his destiny—he slew
185 That which he loved, unknowing what he slew,
And died unpardon'd—though he call'd in aid
The Phyxian Jove, and in Phigalia roused
The Arcadian Evocators to compel
The indignant shadow to depose her wrath,
190 Or fix her term of vengeance—she replied
In words of dubious import, but fulfill'd.[3]
If I had never lived, that which I love
Had still been living; had I never loved,
That which I love would still be beautiful—
195 Happy and giving happiness. What is she?
What is she now?—a sufferer for my sins—
A thing I dare not think upon—or nothing.
Within few hours I shall not call in vain—
Yet in this hour I dread the thing I dare:
200 Until this hour I never shrunk to gaze
On spirit, good or evil—now I tremble,
And feel a strange cold thaw upon my heart,
But I can act even what I most abhor,
And champion human fears.—The night approaches.
[*EXIT.*]

SCENE 3

The Summit of the Jungfrau Mountain
ENTER FIRST DESTINY.

The moon is rising broad, and round, and bright;
And here on snows, where never human foot[4]
Of common mortal trod, we nightly tread,
And leave no traces; o'er the savage sea,
5 The glassy ocean of the mountain ice,
We skim its rugged breakers, which put on
The aspect of a tumbling tempest's foam,
Frozen in a moment[5]—a dead whirlpool's image;
And this most steep fantastic pinnacle,
10 The fretwork of some earthquake—where the clouds
Pause to repose themselves in passing by—
Is sacred to our revels, or our vigils;
Here do I wait my sisters, on our way
To the Hall of Arimanes, for to-night
15 Is our great festival—'tis strange they come not.
[*A Voice without, singing.*]
    The Captive Usurper,[6]
      Hurl'd down from the throne,
    Lay buried in torpor,
      Forgotten and lone;
20   I broke through his slumbers,

---

[1] Cf. Shakespeare, Sonnet 124.13.

[2] 1 Samuel 28.7–20.

[3] "The story of Pausanias, king of Sparta, (who commanded the Greeks at the battle of Platea, and afterwards perished for an attempt to betray the Lacedemonians) and Cleonice, is told in Plutarch's life of Cimon; and in the Laconica of Pausanias the Sophist in his description of Greece." (L.B.) Cleonice was the "Byzantine maid" whom king Pausanias killed by mistake; her spirit ambiguously foretold his death (cf. 2.4.151). See Plutarch, "Life of Cimon" 6.4–6; and Pausanias (no relation), *Description of Greece* 3.17.7–9.

[4] The Jungfrau was first ascended in 1811.

[5] Cf. Byron's letter to Augusta Leigh, 23 September 1816.*

[6] Napoleon.

   I shivered his chain,
   I leagued him with numbers—
   He's Tyrant again!
With the blood of a million he'll answer my care,
With a nation's destruction—his flight and despair.
    [*Second Voice, without.*]
The ship sail'd on, the ship sail'd fast,
But I left not a sail, and I left not a mast;
There is not a plank of the hull or the deck,
And there is not a wretch to lament o'er his wreck;
Save one, whom I held, as he swam, by the hair,
And he was a subject well worthy my care;
A traitor on land, and a pirate at sea—
But I saved him to wreak further havoc for me!
    [FIRST DESTINY, *answering.*]
   The city lies sleeping;
    The morn, to deplore it,
   May dawn on it weeping:
    Sullenly, slowly,
   The black plague flew o'er it—
    Thousands lie lowly;
   Tens of thousands shall perish—
    The living shall fly from
   The sick they should cherish;
    But nothing can vanquish
   The touch that they die from.
    Sorrow and anguish,
   And evil and dread,
   Envelope a nation—
    The blest are the dead,[1]
   Who see not the sight
    Of their own desolation;
This work of a night—
This wreck of a realm—this deed of my doing—
For ages I've done, and shall still be renewing!
[ENTER *the* SECOND *and* THIRD DESTINIES.]
    The Three
   Our hands contain the hearts of men,
    Our footsteps are their graves;
   We only give to take again
    The spirits of our slaves!

FIRST DESTINY: Welcome!—Where's Nemesis?[2]
SECOND DESTINY: At
 some great work;
But what I know not, for my hands were full.
THIRD DESTINY: Behold she cometh.
[*Enter* NEMESIS.]
FIRST DESTINY: Say, where
 hast thou been?
My sisters and thyself are slow to-night.
NEMESIS: I was detain'd repairing shattered thrones,
Marrying fools, restoring dynasties,[3]
Avenging men upon their enemies,[4]
And making them repent their own revenge;
Goading the wise to madness; from the dull
Shaping out oracles to rule the world
Afresh, for they were waxing out of date,
And mortals dared to ponder for themselves,
To weigh kings in the balance,[5] and to speak
Of freedom, the forbidden fruit.[6]—Away!
We have outstaid the hour—mount we our clouds!
          [EXEUNT.]

SCENE 4

The Hall of ARIMANES.[7]—ARIMANES *on his Throne, a Globe of Fire,*[8] *surrounded by the Spirits.*

Hymn of the SPIRITS.

Hail to our Master!—Prince of Earth and Air!—[9]
 Who walks the clouds and waters—in his hand

---

[1] Cf. Revelation 14.13.

[2] classical goddess of retribution.

[3] e.g., the Bourbons, restored to the throne in the person of Louis XVIII after the fall of Napoleon.

[4] Cf. Isaiah 1.24.

[5] Cf. Daniel 5.27.

[6] Cf. Milton, *Paradise Lost* 1.1–2 and 9.904.

[7] Ahriman, the Zoroastrian principle of evil. Cf. Peacock,* *Ahrimanes* (1812).

[8] Cf. the throne of Eblis in William Beckford (1760–1844), *Vathek* (1786). For the festival of evil spirits, cf. Goethe, *Faust* 3835–4222.

[9] Cf. Ephesians 2.2.

George Gordon, Lord Byron

    The sceptre of the elements, which tear
        Themselves to chaos at his high command!
5 He breatheth—and a tempest shakes the sea;
        He speaketh—and the clouds reply in thunder;
    He gazeth—from his glance the sunbeams flee;
        He moveth—earthquakes rend the world asunder.
    Beneath his footsteps the volcanos rise;
10   His shadow is the Pestilence; his path
    The comets herald through the crackling skies;
        And planets turn to ashes at his wrath.
    To him War offers daily sacrifice;
        To him Death pays his tribute; Life is his,
15 With all its infinite of agonies—
        And his the spirit of whatever is!
    [ENTER the DESTINIES and NEMESIS.]
FIRST DESTINY: Glory to Arimanes! on the earth
    His power increaseth—both my sisters did
    His bidding, nor did I neglect my duty!
20 SECOND DESTINY: Glory to Arimanes! we who bow
    The necks of men, bow down before his throne!
THIRD DESTINY: Glory to Arimanes!—we await
        His nod!
NEMESIS: Sovereign of Sovereigns! we are thine.
    And all that liveth, more or less, is ours,
25 And most things wholly so; still to increase
    Our power increasing thine, demands our care,
    And we are vigilant—Thy late commands
    Have been fulfilled to the utmost.
    [ENTER MANFRED.]
A SPIRIT: What is here?
    A mortal!—Thou most rash and fatal wretch,
30 Bow down and worship!
SECOND SPIRIT: I do know the man—
    A Magian of great power, and fearful skill!
THIRD SPIRIT: Bow down and worship, slave!—
        What, know'st thou not
    Thine and our Sovereign?—Tremble, and obey!
ALL THE SPIRITS: Prostrate thyself, and thy
        condemned clay,
35 Child of the Earth! or dread the worst.
MANFRED: I know it;
    And yet ye see I kneel not.
FOURTH SPIRIT: 'T will be taught thee.
MANFRED: 'Tis taught already;—many a night on the earth,
    On the bare ground, have I bow'd down my face,
    And strew'd my head with ashes;[1] I have known
40 The fulness of humiliation, for
    I sunk before my vain despair, and knelt
    To my own desolation.
FIFTH SPIRIT: Dost thou dare
    Refuse to Arimanes on his throne
    What the whole earth accords, beholding not
45 The terror of his Glory—Crouch! I say.
MANFRED: Bid *him* bow down to that which is above him,
    The overruling Infinite—the Maker
    Who made him not for worship—let him kneel,
    And we will kneel together.
THE SPIRITS: Crush the worm!
50 Tear him in pieces!—
FIRST DESTINY: Hence! Avaunt!—he's mine.
    Prince of the Powers invisible! This man
    Is of no common order, as his port
    And presence here denote; his sufferings
    Have been of an immortal nature, like
55 Our own; his knowledge and his powers and will,
    As far as is compatible with clay,
    Which clogs the etherial essence, have been such
    As clay hath seldom borne; his aspirations
    Have been beyond the dwellers of the earth,
60 And they have only taught him what we know—
    That knowledge is not happiness, and science
    But an exchange of ignorance for that
    Which is another kind of ignorance.
    This is not all—the passions, attributes
65 Of earth and heaven, from which no power, nor being,
    Nor breath from the worm upwards is exempt,
    Have pierced his heart; and in their consequence
    Made him a thing, which I, who pity not,
    Yet pardon those who pity. He is mine,
70 And thine, it may be—be it so, or not,
    No other Spirit in this region hath
    A soul like his—or power upon his soul.
NEMESIS: What doth he here then?

---

[1] Cf. Lamentations 3.16.

FIRST SPIRIT: Let him
     answer that.
MANFRED: Ye know what I have known; and
     without power
75 I could not be amongst ye: but there are
     Powers deeper still beyond—I come in quest
     Of such, to answer unto what I seek.
NEMESIS: What wouldst thou?
MANFRED: Thou canst not
     reply to me.
     Call up the dead—my question is for them.
80 NEMESIS: Great Arimanes, doth thy will avouch
     The wishes of this mortal?
ARIMANES: Yea.
NEMESIS: Whom wouldst thou
     Uncharnel?
MANFRED: One without a tomb[1]—call up
     Astarte.[2]
                     NEMESIS
     Shadow! or Spirit!
85   Whatever thou art,
     Which still doth inherit
        The whole or a part
        Of the form of thy birth,
        Of the mould of thy clay,
90   Which returned to the earth,
        Re-appear to the day!
     Bear what thou borest,
        The heart and the form,
     And the aspect thou worest
95   Redeem from the worm.
     Appear!—Appear!—Appear!
     Who sent thee there requires thee here!
[The Phantom of ASTARTE rises and stands in the midst.]
MANFRED: Can this be death? there's bloom
     upon her cheek;
     But now I see it is no living hue,
100 But a strange hectic—like the unnatural red
     Which Autumn plants upon the perish'd leaf.
     It is the same! Oh, God! that I should dread
     To look upon the same—Astarte!—No,
     I cannot speak to her—but bid her speak—
105 Forgive me or condemn me.
                   NEMESIS
     By the power which hath broken
        The grave which enthrall'd thee,
     Speak to him who hath spoken,
        Or those who have call'd thee!
MANFRED: She is silent,
110 And in that silence I am more than answered.
NEMESIS: My power extends no further. Prince of air!
     It rests with thee alone—command her voice.
ARIMANES: Spirit—obey this sceptre!
NEMESIS: Silent still!
     She is not of our order, but belongs
115 To the other powers. Mortal! thy quest is vain,
     And we are baffled also.
MANFRED: Hear me, hear me—
     Astarte! my beloved! speak to me:
     I have so much endured—so much endure—
     Look on me! the grave hath not changed thee more
120 Than I am changed for thee. Thou lovedst me
     Too much, as I loved thee: we were not made
     To torture thus each other, though it were
     The deadliest sin to love as we have loved.
     Say that thou loath'st me not—that I do bear
125 This punishment for both—that thou wilt be
     One of the blessed—and that I shall die,
     For hitherto all hateful things conspire
     To bind me in existence—in a life
     Which makes me shrink from immortality—
130 A future like the past. I cannot rest.
     I know not what I ask, nor what I seek:
     I feel but what thou art—and what I am;
     And I would hear yet once before I perish
     The voice which was my music—Speak to me!
135 For I have call'd on thee in the still night,
     Startled the slumbering birds from the hush'd boughs,
     And woke the mountain wolves, and made the caves
     Acquainted with thy vainly echoed name,

---

[1] That she has no tomb (i.e., that she has not been buried in consecrated ground) suggests that she has committed suicide.

[2] the classical name (see Cicero, *De Natura Deorum* 3.23; and Lucian, *De Syria Dea* 4) for the Phoenician goddess Milton calls Ashtaroth ("On the Morning of Christ's Nativity" 200–01, *Paradise Lost* 1.422–28). She was both the mother and the bride of Tammuz.

Which answered me—many things answered me—
140 Spirits and men—but thou wert silent all.
Yet speak to me! I have outwatch'd the stars,
And gazed o'er heaven in vain in search of thee.
Speak to me! I have wandered o'er the earth
And never found thy likeness—Speak to me!
145 Look on the fiends around—they feel for me:
I fear them not, and feel for thee alone—
Speak to me! though it be in wrath;—but say—
I reck not what—but let me hear thee once—
This once—once more!
PHANTOM OF ASTARTE: Manfred!
MANFRED: Say on, say on—
150 I live but in the sound—it is thy voice!
PHANTOM: Manfred! To-morrow ends thine earthly ills.
Farewell!
MANFRED: Yet one word more—am I forgiven?
PHANTOM: Farewell!
MANFRED: Say, shall we meet again?
PHANTOM: Farewell!
MANFRED: One word for mercy! Say, thou lovest me.
155 PHANTOM: Manfred!
[*The Spirit of* ASTARTE *departs.*]
NEMESIS: She's gone, and will not be recall'd;
Her words will be fulfill'd. Return to the earth.
A SPIRIT: He is convulsed—This is to be a mortal
And seek the things beyond mortality.
ANOTHER SPIRIT: Yet, see, he mastereth himself, and makes
160 His torture tributary to his will.
Had he been one of us, he would have made
An awful spirit.
NEMESIS: Hast thou further question
Of our great sovereign, or his worshippers?
MANFRED: None.
NEMESIS: Then for a time farewell.
165 MANFRED: We meet then! Where? On the earth?—
Even as thou wilt: and for the grace accorded
I now depart a debtor. Fare ye well!
[*EXIT MANFRED.*]
[*Scene closes.*]

ACT 3

SCENE 1

A Hall in the Castle of MANFRED.
MANFRED *and* HERMAN.

MANFRED: What is the hour?
HERMAN: It wants but one till sunset,
And promises a lovely twilight.
MANFRED: Say,
Are all things so disposed of in the tower
As I directed?
HERMAN: All, my lord, are ready;
5 Here is the key and casket.
MANFRED: It is well:
Thou mayst retire. [*EXIT HERMAN.*]
MANFRED: [*Alone.*] There is a calm upon me—
Inexplicable stillness! which till now
Did not belong to what I knew of life.
If that I did not know philosophy
10 To be of all our vanities the motliest,
The merest word that ever fool'd the ear
From out the schoolman's jargon, I should deem
The golden secret, the sought "Kalon,"[1] found,
And seated in my soul. It will not last,
15 But it is well to have known it, though but once:
It hath enlarged my thoughts with a new sense,
And I within my tablets would note down
That there is such a feeling. Who is there?
[*Re-enter* HERMAN.]
HERMAN: My lord, the abbot of St. Maurice[2] craves
20 To greet your presence.
[ENTER *the* ABBOT OF ST. MAURICE.]
ABBOT: Peace be with Count Manfred!
MANFRED: Thanks, holy father! welcome to these walls;
Thy presence honours them, and blesseth those
Who dwell within them.

---

[1] "moral beauty" (Gr.).

[2] an abbey in the Rhone valley, founded by King Sigismund of Burgundy in the 4th century (Manfred's father was named Sigismund).

ABBOT: Would it were so, Count!—
But I would fain confer with thee alone.
MANFRED: Herman, retire. What would my
      reverend guest?
ABBOT: Thus, without prelude:—Age and zeal, my
      office,
And good intent, must plead my privilege;
Our near, though not acquainted neighbourhood,
May also be my herald. Rumours strange,
And of unholy nature, are abroad,
And busy with thy name; a noble name
For centuries; may he who bears it now
Transmit it unimpair'd!
MANFRED: Proceed,—I listen.
ABBOT: 'Tis said thou holdest converse with the
      things
Which are forbidden to the search of man;
That with the dwellers of the dark abodes,
The many evil and unheavenly spirits
Which walk the valley of the shade of death,[1]
Thou communest. I know that with mankind,
Thy fellows in creation, thou dost rarely
Exchange thy thoughts, and that thy solitude
Is as an anchorite's, were it but holy.
MANFRED: And what are they who do avouch
      these things?
ABBOT: My pious brethren—the scared
      peasantry—
Even thy own vassals—who do look on thee
With most unquiet eyes. Thy life's in peril.
MANFRED: Take it.
ABBOT: I come to save, and not destroy—[2]
I would not pry into thy secret soul;
But if these things be sooth, there still is time
For penitence and pity: reconcile thee
With the true church, and through the church to
      heaven.
MANFRED: I hear thee. This is my reply; whate'er
I may have been, or am, doth rest between
Heaven and myself.— I shall not choose a mortal
To be my mediator.[3] Have I sinn'd
Against your ordinances? prove and punish![4]

---

[1] Cf. Psalm 23.4.

[2] Cf. Matthew 5.17.

[3] Cf. 1 Timothy 2.5.

[4] The original version of the third act of *Manfred* was very different from its final, published form. Byron's publisher, who liked the rest of the play, objected to it; Byron agreed that it was "certainly d—d bad" (*Letters and Journals* 5: 211; 14 April 1817) and rewrote it. The rest of this scene was originally as follows:

  "ABBOT: Then, hear and tremble! For the headstrong wretch
Who in the mail of innate hardihood
Would shield himself, and battle for his sins,
There is the stake on earth—and beyond earth
Eternal—
MANFRED: Charity, most reverend father,
Becomes thy lips so much more than this menace,
That I would call thee back to it: but say,
What would'st thou with me?
ABBOT: It may be there are
Things that would shake thee—but I keep them back,
And give thee till to-morrow to repent.
Then if thou dost not all devote thyself
To penance, and with gift of all thy lands
To the Monastery—
MANFRED: I understand thee,—well!
ABBOT: Expect no mercy; I have warned thee.
MANFRED: Stop— [*Opening the casket.*]
There is a gift for thee within this casket.
[MANFRED *opens the casket, strikes a light, and burns some incense.*]
Ho! Ashtaroth!
[*The* DEMON ASHTAROTH *appears, singing as follows:—*]
    The raven sits
      On the Raven-stone,
  And his black wing flits
      O'er the milk-white bone;
  To and fro, as the night-winds blow,
    The carcass of the assassin swings;
  And there alone, on the Raven-stone,
    The raven flaps his dusky wings.

  The fetters creak—and his ebon beak
    Croaks to the close of the hollow sound;
  And this is the tune, by the light of the Moon,
    To which the Witches dance their round—
Merrily—merrily—cheerily—cheerily—
  Merrily—merrily—speeds the ball:
The dead in their shrouds, and the Demons in clouds,
  Flock to the Witches' Carnival.
ABBOT: I fear thee not—hence—hence—
Avaunt thee, evil One!—help, ho! without there!
MANFRED: Convey this man to the Shreckhorn—to its peak—
To its extremest peak—watch with him there

ABBOT: My son! I did not speak of punishment,
But penitence and pardon;—with thyself
The choice of such remains—and for the last,
Our institutions and our strong belief
Have given me power to smooth the path from sin
To higher hope and better thoughts; the first
I leave to heaven—"Vengeance is mine alone!"
So saith the Lord,[1] and with all humbleness
His servant echoes back the awful word.
MANFRED: Old man! there is no power in holy men,
Nor charm in prayer—nor purifying form
Of penitence—nor outward look—nor fast—
Nor agony—nor, greater than all these,

> From now till sunrise; let him gaze, and know
> He ne'er again will be so near to Heaven.
> But harm him not; and, when the morrow breaks,
> Set him down safe in his cell—away with him!
> ASHTAROTH: Had I not better bring his brethren too,
> Convent and all, to bear him company?
> MANFRED: No, this will serve for the present. Take him up.
> ASHTAROTH: Come, Friar! now an exorcism or two,
> And we shall fly the lighter.
> [ASHTAROTH disappears with the ABBOT, singing as follows:—]
>   A prodigal son, and a maid undone,
>   And a widow re-wedded within the year;
>   And a worldly monk, and a pregnant nun,
>   Are things which every day appear.
> [MANFRED alone.]
> MANFRED: Why would this fool break in on me, and force
> My art to pranks fantastical?—no matter,
> It was not of my seeking. My heart sickens,
> And weighs a fixed foreboding on my soul.
> But it is calm—calm as a sullen sea
> After the hurricane; the winds are still,
> But the cold waves swell high and heavily,
> And there is danger in them. Such a rest
> Is no repose. My life hath been a combat,
> And every thought a wound, till I am scarred
> In the immortal part of me.—What now?
> [Re-enter HERMAN.]"

The action then carries on into the second scene, without a scene change. To the word "Raven-stone" in Ashtaroth's song, Byron added a note: "Raven-stone (Rabenstein), a translation of the German word for the gibbet, which in Germany and Switzerland is permanent, and made of stone." Cf. Goethe, *Faust* 4439–44. For "Ashtaroth," see note to 2.4.83. The ending of this scene recalls that of M.G. Lewis,* *The Monk* (1796).

[1] Cf. Deuteronomy 32.35 and Romans 12.19.

The innate tortures of that deep despair,
Which is remorse without the fear of hell,
But all in all sufficient to itself
Would make a hell of heaven[2]—can exorcise
From out the unbounded spirit, the quick sense
Of its own sins, wrongs, sufferance, and revenge
Upon itself; there is no future pang
Can deal that justice on the self-condemn'd
He deals on his own soul.
ABBOT: All this is well;
For this will pass away, and be succeeded
By an auspicious hope, which shall look up
With calm assurance to that blessed place,
Which all who seek may win, whatever be
Their earthly errors, so they be atoned:
And the commencement of atonement is
The sense of its necessity.—Say on—
And all our church can teach thee shall be taught;
And all we can absolve thee, shall be pardon'd.
MANFRED: When Rome's sixth Emperor was near his last,
The victim of a self-inflicted wound,
To shun the torments of a public death
From senates once his slaves, a certain soldier,
With show of loyal pity, would have staunch'd
The gushing throat with his officious robe;
The dying Roman thrust him back and said—
Some empire still in his expiring glance,
"It is too late—is this fidelity?"[3]
ABBOT: And what of this?
MANFRED: I answer with the Roman—
"It is too late!"
ABBOT: It never can be so,
To reconcile thyself with thy own soul,
And thy own soul with heaven. Hast thou no hope?
'Tis strange—even those who do despair above,
Yet shape themselves some phantasy on earth,
To which frail twig they cling, like drowning men.

[2] Cf. Milton, *Paradise Lost* 1.254–55; and Byron, *The Giaour* 1266–70.*

[3] This is taken from the account of the death of Nero (AD 37–68), Rome's fifth emperor, in Suetonius, *The Lives of the Caesars* 6.49. Otho (AD 32–69), the sixth, also committed suicide.

MANFRED: Ay—father! I have had those earthly
    visions
105 And noble aspirations in my youth,
To make my own the mind of other men,
The enlightener of nations; and to rise
I knew not whither—it might be to fall;
But fall, even as the mountain-cataract,
110 Which having leapt from its more dazzling height,
Even in the foaming strength of its abyss,
(Which casts up misty columns that become
Clouds raining from the re-ascended skies,)
Lies low but mighty still.—But this is past,
115 My thoughts mistook themselves.
ABBOT: And wherefore so?
MANFRED: I could not tame my nature down; for he
Must serve who fain would sway—and soothe—and
    sue—
And watch all time—and pry into all place—
And be a living lie—who would become
120 A mighty thing amongst the mean, and such
The mass are; I disdained to mingle with
A herd, though to be leader—and of wolves.
The lion is alone, and so am I.
ABBOT: And why not live and act with other men?
125 MANFRED: Because my nature was averse from life;
And yet not cruel; for I would not make,
But find a desolation:—like the wind,
The red-hot breath of the most lone Simoom,[1]
Which dwells but in the desart, and sweeps o'er
130 The barren sands which bear no shrubs to blast,
And revels o'er their wild and arid waves,
And seeketh not, so that it is not sought,
But being met is deadly; such hath been
The course of my existence; but there came
135 Things in my path which are no more.
ABBOT: Alas!
I 'gin to fear that thou art past all aid
From me and from my calling; yet so young,
I still would—
MANFRED: Look on me! there is an order
Of mortals on the earth, who do become
140 Old in their youth, and die ere middle age,
Without the violence of warlike death;
Some perishing of pleasure—some of study—
Some worn with toil—some of mere weariness—
Some of disease—and some insanity—
145 And some of withered, or of broken hearts;
For this last is a malady which slays
More than are numbered in the lists of Fate,
Taking all shapes, and bearing many names.
Look upon me! for even of all these things
150 Have I partaken; and of all these things,
One were enough; then wonder not that I
Am what I am, but that I ever was,
Or, having been, that I am still on earth.
ABBOT: Yet, hear me still—
MANFRED: Old man! I do respect
155 Thine order, and revere thine years; I deem
Thy purpose pious, but it is in vain:
Think me not churlish; I would spare thyself,
Far more than me, in shunning at this time
All further colloquy—and so—farewell.
                                   [EXIT MANFRED.]
160 ABBOT: This should have been a noble creature: he
Hath all the energy which would have made
A goodly frame of glorious elements,
Had they been wisely mingled; as it is,
It is an awful chaos—light and darkness—
165 And mind and dust—and passions and pure thoughts,
Mix'd, and contending without end or order,
All dormant or destructive.[2] He will perish,
And yet he must not; I will try once more,
For such are worth redemption; and my duty
170 Is to dare all things for a righteous end.
I'll follow him—but cautiously, though surely.
                                   [EXIT ABBOT.]

SCENE 2

Another Chamber.
MANFRED *and* HERMAN.

HERMAN: My Lord, you bade me wait on you at sunset:
He sinks beyond the mountain.

---

[1] See Byron, *The Giaour* 282–85, and note.*

[2] Cf. Shakespeare, *Hamlet* 3.1.150–60.

MANFRED: Doth he so?
    I will look on him.
    [MANFRED *advances to the Window of the Hall.*]
                    Glorious Orb! the idol
    Of early nature, and the vigorous race
5 Of undiseased mankind, the giant sons[1]
    Of the embrace of angels, with a sex
    More beautiful than they, which did draw down
    The erring spirits who can ne'er return.—
    Most glorious orb! that wert a worship, ere
10 The mystery of thy making was reveal'd!
    Thou earliest minister of the Almighty,
    Which gladden'd, on their mountain tops, the hearts
    Of the Chaldean shepherds,[2] till they pour'd
    Themselves in orisons! Thou material God!
15 And representative of the Unknown—
    Who chose thee for his shadow! Thou chief star!
    Centre of many stars! which mak'st our earth
    Endurable, and temperest the hues
    And hearts of all who walk within thy rays!
20 Sire of the seasons! Monarch of the climes,
    And those who dwell in them! for near or far,
    Our inborn spirits have a tint of thee,
    Even as our outward aspects;—thou dost rise,
    And shine, and set in glory. Fare thee well!
25 I ne'er shall see thee more. As my first glance
    Of love and wonder was for thee, then take
    My latest look: thou wilt not beam on one
    To whom the gifts of life and warmth have been
    Of a more fatal nature. He is gone:
30 I follow.
                              [EXIT MANFRED.]

---

[1] "'That the *Sons of God* saw the daughters of men, that they were fair,' &c. 'There were giants on the earth in those days, and also after that, when the *Sons of God* came in unto the daughters of men: and they bare children to them, the same became mighty men, which were of old, men of renown.'—*Genesis*, ch. vi. verses 2 and 4." (L.B.) Cf. Byron, *Heaven and Earth* (1823).

[2] Cf. Byron, *Childe Harold's Pilgrimage* 3.118 and 3.851–53.*

SCENE 3

The Mountains.—The Castle of MANFRED *at some distance.—A Terrace before a Tower.*[3]*— Time, Twilight.*
HERMAN, MANUEL, *and other Dependants of* MANFRED.

HERMAN: 'Tis strange enough; night after night, for
       years,
    He hath pursued long vigils in this tower,
    Without a witness. I have been within it,—
    So have we all been oft-times; but from it,
5 Or its contents, it were impossible
    To draw conclusions absolute, of aught
    His studies tend to. To be sure, there is
    One chamber where none enter; I would give
    The fee of what I have to come these three years,
10 To pore upon its mysteries.
    MANUEL: 'Twere dangerous;
    Content thyself with what thou knowest already.
    HERMAN: Ah! Manuel! thou art elderly and wise,
    And could'st say much; thou hast dwelt within
       the castle—
    How many years is't?
    MANUEL: Ere Count Manfred's birth,
15 I served his father, whom he nought resembles.
    HERMAN: There be more sons in like predicament.
    But wherein do they differ?
    MANUEL: I speak not
    Of features or of form, but mind and habits:
    Count Sigismund was proud,—but gay and free,—
20 A warrior and a reveller; he dwelt not
    With books and solitude, nor made the night
    A gloomy vigil, but a festal time,
    Merrier than day; he did not walk the rocks
    And forests like a wolf, nor turn aside
25 From men and their delights.
    HERMAN: Beshrew the hour,
    But those were jocund times! I would that such
    Would visit the old walls again; they look
    As if they had forgotten them.

---

[3] Cf. the tower in Beckford, *Vathek*.

MANUEL: These walls
Must change their chieftain first. Oh! I have seen
Some strange things in them, Herman.
HERMAN: Come, be friendly;
Relate me some to while away our watch:
I've heard thee darkly speak of an event
Which happened hereabouts, by this same tower.
MANUEL: That was a night indeed; I do remember
'Twas twilight, as it may be now, and such
Another evening;—yon red cloud, which rests
On Eigher's pinnacle,[1] so rested then,—
So like that it might be the same; the wind
Was faint and gusty, and the mountain snows
Began to glitter with the climbing moon;
Count Manfred was, as now, within his tower,—
How occupied, we knew not, but with him
The sole companion of his wanderings
And watchings—her, whom of all earthly things
That lived, the only thing he seem'd to love,—
As he, indeed, by blood was bound to do,
The Lady Astarte, his—[2]

Hush! who comes here?
[ENTER the ABBOT.]
ABBOT: Where is your master?
HERMAN: Yonder, in the tower.
ABBOT: I must speak with him.
MANUEL: 'Tis impossible;
He is most private, and must not be thus
Intruded on.
ABBOT: Upon myself I take
The forfeit of my fault, if fault there be—
But I must see him.
HERMAN: Thou hast seen him once

---

[1] Byron first saw this mountain on 23 September 1816.

[2] The rest of the act was originally as follows (there was no fourth scene):

"HERMAN: Look—look—the tower—
The tower's on fire. Oh, heavens and earth! what sound,
What dreadful sound is that? [*A crash like thunder.*]
MANUEL: Help, help, there!—to the rescue of the Count,—
The Count's in danger,—what ho! there! approach!
[*The Servants, Vassals, and Peasantry approach stupified with terror.*]
If there be any of you who have heart
And love of human kind, and will to aid
Those in distress—pause not—but follow me—
The portal's open, follow. [MANUEL *goes in.*]
HERMAN: Come—who follows?
What, none of ye?—ye recreants! shiver then
Without. I will not see old MANUEL risk
His few remaining years unaided. [HERMAN *goes in.*]
VASSAL: Hark!
No—all is silent—not a breath—the flame
Which shot forth such a blaze is also gone;
What may this mean? Let's enter!
PEASANT: Faith, not I,—
Not but, if one, or two, or more, will join,
I then will stay behind; but, for my part,
I do not see precisely to what end.

VASSAL: Cease your vain prating—come.
MANUEL: [*Speaking within.*] 'Tis all in vain—
He's dead.
HERMAN: [*Within.*] Not so—even now methought he moved;
But it is dark—so bear him gently out—
Softly—how cold he is! take care of his temples
In winding down the staircase.
[*Re-enter* MANUEL *and* HERMAN, *bearing* MANFRED *in their arms.*]
MANUEL: Hie to the castle, some of ye, and bring
What aid you can. Saddle the barb, and speed
For the leech to the city—quick! some water there!
HERMAN: His cheek is black—but there is a faint beat
Still lingering about the heart. Some water.
[*They sprinkle* MANFRED *with water: after a pause, he gives some signs of life.*]
MANUEL: He seems to strive to speak—come—cheerly, Count!
He moves his lips—canst hear him? I am old,
And cannot catch faint sounds.
[HERMAN *inclining his head and listening.*]
HERMAN: I hear a word
Or two—but indistinctly—what is next?
What's to be done? let's bear him to the castle.
[MANFRED *motions with his hand not to remove him.*]
MANUEL: He disapproves—and 'twere of no avail—
He changes rapidly.
HERMAN: 'Twill soon be over.
MANUEL: Oh! what a death is this! that I should live
To shake my gray hairs over the last chief
Of the house of Sigismund.—And such a death!
Alone—we know not how—unshrived—untended—
With strange accompaniments and fearful signs—
I shudder at the sight—but must not leave him.
MANFRED: [*Speaking faintly and slowly.*] Old man! 'tis not so difficult to die. [MANFRED, *having said this, expires.*]
HERMAN: His eyes are fixed and lifeless.—He is gone.—
MANUEL: Close them.—My old hand quivers.—He departs—
Whither? I dread to think—but he is gone!"

This eve already.
ABBOT: Herman! I command thee,
55 Knock, and apprize the Count of my approach.
HERMAN: We dare not.
ABBOT: Then it seems I must be herald
Of my own purpose.
MANUEL: Reverend father, stop—
I pray you pause.
ABBOT: Why so?
MANUEL: But step this way,
And I will tell you further. [EXEUNT.]

SCENE 4

*Interior of the Tower.
MANFRED alone.*

The stars are forth, the moon above the tops
Of the snow-shining mountains.—Beautiful!
I linger yet with Nature, for the night
Hath been to me a more familiar face
5 Than that of man; and in her starry shade
Of dim and solitary loveliness,
I learn'd the language of another world.
I do remember me, that in my youth,
When I was wandering,—upon such a night[1]
10 I stood within the Coloseum's wall,
'Midst the chief relics of almighty Rome;
The trees which grew along the broken arches
Waved dark in the blue midnight, and the stars
Shone through the rents of ruin; from afar
15 The watchdog bayed beyond the Tiber;[2] and
More near from out the Cæsars' palace came
The owl's long cry, and, interruptedly,
Of distant sentinels the fitful song
Begun and died upon the gentle wind.
20 Some cypresses beyond the time-worn breach
Appeared to skirt the horizon, yet they stood
Within a bowshot—where the Cæsars dwelt,
And dwell the tuneless birds of night, amidst
A grove which springs through levell'd battlements,
25 And twines its roots with the imperial hearths,
Ivy usurps the laurel's place of growth;—
But the gladiators' bloody Circus[3] stands,
A noble wreck in ruinous perfection!
While Cæsar's chambers, and the Augustan halls,
30 Grovel on earth in indistinct decay.—
And thou didst shine, thou rolling moon, upon
All this, and cast a wide and tender light,
Which soften'd down the hoar austerity
Of rugged desolation, and fill'd up,
35 As 'twere, anew, the gaps of centuries;
Leaving that beautiful which still was so,
And making that which was not, till the place
Became religion, and the heart ran o'er
With silent worship of the great of old!—
40 The dead, but sceptred sovereigns, who still rule
Our spirits from their urns.—
'Twas such a night!
'Tis strange that I recall it at this time;
But I have found our thoughts take wildest flight
Even at the moment when they should array
45 Themselves in pensive order.
[ENTER the ABBOT.]
ABBOT: My good Lord!
I crave a second grace for this approach;
But yet let not my humble zeal offend
By its abruptness—all it hath of ill
Recoils on me; its good in the effect
50 May light upon your head—could I say *heart*—
Could I touch *that*, with words or prayers, I should
Recall a noble spirit which hath wandered
But is not yet all lost.
MANFRED: Thou know'st me not;
My days are numbered, and my deeds recorded:
55 Retire, or 'twill be dangerous—Away!
ABBOT: Thou dost not mean to menace me?
MANFRED: Not I;
I simply tell thee peril is at hand,
And would preserve thee.
ABBOT: What dost mean?
MANFRED: Look there!
What dost thou see?

---

[1] Cf. Shakespeare, *The Merchant of Venice* 5.1.1–22.
[2] river flowing through Rome.
[3] the Coliseum.

ABBOT: Nothing.
MANFRED: Look there, I say,
60 And steadfastly;—now tell me what thou seest?
ABBOT: That which should shake me,—but I fear it
    not—
I see a dusk and awful figure rise
Like an infernal god from out the earth;
His face wrapt in a mantle, and his form
65 Robed as with angry clouds; he stands between
Thyself and me—but I do fear him not.
MANFRED: Thou hast no cause—he shall not
    harm thee—but
His sight may shock thine old limbs into palsy.
I say to thee—Retire!
ABBOT: And, I reply—
70 Never—till I have battled with this fiend—
What doth he here?
MANFRED: Why—ay—what doth he here?
I did not send for him,—he is unbidden.
ABBOT: Alas! lost mortal! what with guests like these
Hast thou to do? I tremble for thy sake;
75 Why doth he gaze on thee, and thou on him?
Ah! he unveils his aspect; on his brow
The thunder-scars are graven;[1] from his eye
Glares forth the immortality of hell—
Avaunt!—
MANFRED: Pronounce—what is thy mission?
SPIRIT: Come!
80 ABBOT: What art thou, unknown being? answer!—
    speak!
SPIRIT: The genius of this mortal.—Come! 'tis time.
MANFRED: I am prepared for all things, but deny
The power which summons me. Who sent thee here?
SPIRIT: Thou'lt know anon—Come! come!
MANFRED: I
    have commanded
85 Things of an essence greater far than thine,
And striven with thy masters. Get thee hence![2]
SPIRIT: Mortal! thine hour is come—Away! I say.
MANFRED: I knew, and know my hour is come,
    but not

---

[1] Cf. Milton, *Paradise Lost* 1.600–01.

[2] Cf. Matthew 4.10.

To render up my soul to such as thee:
90 Away! I'll die as I have lived—alone.
SPIRIT: Then I must summon up my brethren.—
    Rise!
[*Other Spirits rise up.*]
ABBOT: Avaunt! ye evil ones!—Avaunt! I say,—
Ye have no power where piety hath power,
And I do charge ye in the name—
SPIRIT: Old man!
95 We know ourselves, our mission, and thine order;
Waste not thy holy words on idle uses,
It were in vain; this man is forfeited.
Once more I summon him—Away! away!
MANFRED: I do defy ye,—though I feel my soul
100 Is ebbing from me, yet I do defy ye;
Nor will I hence, while I have earthly breath
To breathe my scorn upon ye—earthly strength
To wrestle, though with spirits;[3] what ye take
Shall be ta'en limb by limb.
SPIRIT: Reluctant mortal!
105 Is this the Magian who would so pervade
The world invisible, and make himself
Almost our equal?—Can it be that thou
Art thus in love with life? the very life
Which made thee wretched!
MANFRED: Thou false fiend,
    thou liest!
110 My life is in its last hour,—*that* I know,
Nor would redeem a moment of that hour;
I do not combat against death, but thee
And thy surrounding angels;[4] my past power
Was purchased by no compact with thy crew,[5]
115 But by superior science—penance—daring—
And length of watching—strength of mind—and
    skill
In knowledge of our fathers—when the earth
Saw men and spirits walking side by side,
And gave ye no supremacy: I stand

---

[3] Cf. Genesis 32.24–32.

[4] Cf. Ephesians 6.12.

[5] According to the *Malleus Maleficarum* ("The Witches' Hammer," 1484), the witch-hunters' handbook, signing a pact with the devil was the only way for humans to obtain magical powers. Manfred denies this.

120 Upon my strength—I do defy—deny—
Spurn back, and scorn ye!—
SPIRIT: But thy many crimes
Have made thee—
MANFRED: What are they to such as thee?
Must crimes be punish'd but by other crimes,
And greater criminals?—Back to thy hell!
125 Thou hast no power upon me, *that* I feel;
Thou never shalt possess me, *that* I know:
What I have done is done; I bear within:
A torture which could nothing gain from thine:
The mind which is immortal makes itself
130 Requital for its good or evil thoughts—
Is its own origin of ill and end—
And its own place and time[1]—its innate sense,
When stripp'd of this mortality, derives
No colour from the fleeting things without;
135 But is absorb'd in sufferance or in joy,
Born from the knowledge of its own desert.
Thou didst not tempt me, and thou couldst not tempt me;
I have not been thy dupe, nor am thy prey—
But was my own destroyer, and will be
140 My own hereafter.—Back, ye baffled fiends!
The hand of death is on me—but not yours!
[*The Demons disappear.*]
ABBOT: Alas! how pale thou art—thy lips are white—
And thy breast heaves—and in thy gasping throat
The accents rattle—Give thy prayers to heaven—
145 Pray—albeit but in thought,—but die not thus.
MANFRED: 'Tis over—my dull eyes can fix thee not;
But all things swim around me, and the earth
Heaves as it were beneath me. Fare thee well—
Give me thy hand.
ABBOT: Cold—cold—even to the heart—
150 But yet one prayer—alas! how fares it with thee?—
MANFRED: Old man! 'tis not so difficult to die.[2]
[*MANFRED expires.*]

ABBOT: He's gone—his soul hath ta'en its earthless flight—
Whither? I dread to think—but he is gone.

from *Don Juan* (1819)[3]

"Difficile est proprie communia dicere"
                            HOR. *Epist. ad Pison*[4]

DEDICATION[5]

I

Bob Southey! You're a poet—Poet-laureate,
   And representative of all the race,
Although 'tis true that you turn'd out a Tory at
   Last,—yours has lately been a common case,—
5 And now, my Epic Renegade! what are ye at?
   With all the Lakers, in and out of place?
A nest of tuneful persons, to my eye
Like "four and twenty Blackbirds in a pye;[6]

---

[1] Cf. Milton, *Paradise Lost* 1.254–55.

[2] Byron's publisher cut this line from the first edition, to Byron's outrage: "You have destroyed the whole effect & moral of the poem by omitting the last line of Manfred's speaking" (*Letters and Journals* 5: 257; 12 August 1817). It was restored in 1818.

[3] The story of the great seducer was first told by Tirso de Molina (Gabriel Téllez), *El Burlador de Sevilla y convidado di piedra* ("The Trickster of Seville and the Stone Guest," 1616?); it subsequently inspired such masterpieces as Molière, *Dom Juan ou Le Festin de pierre* (1665), Thomas Shadwell, *The Libertine* (1676), and Mozart, *Don Giovanni* (1787). See Oscar Mandel, ed., *The Theatre of Don Juan* (1963), and Ian Watt, *Myths of Modern Individualism* (1996). According to 1.7, Byron first encountered the story in a pantomime, perhaps Charles A. Delpini, *Don Juan; or, The Libertine Destroyed* (1787); two other pantomime versions, both first performed in 1817, may have come to his notice: William Thomas Moncrieff, *Giovanni in London; or, The Libertine Reclaimed*, and Thomas J. Dibdin, *Don Giovanni; or, A Spectre on Horseback!* He had evidently read the discussion of Don Juan in Coleridge, *Biographia Literaria* (chap. 23),* a book he makes fun of in Ded. 13–18.

[4] "It is hard to treat in your own way what is common" (Horace, *Epistola ad Pisones* (*Ars Poetica*) 128, trans. H.R. Fairclough).

[5] Since the first two cantos were published anonymously, Byron asked for the dedication to be omitted: "I won't attack the dog [Southey] so fiercely without putting my name" (*Letters and Journals* 6: 123; 6 May 1819).

[6] Henry James Pye (1745–1813) was appointed Poet Laureate in 1790; Southey was given the position after Pye's death.

2

"Which pye being open'd they began to sing"
    (This old song and new simile holds good),
"A dainty dish to set before the King,"
    Or Regent,[1] who admires such kind of food;—
And Coleridge, too, has lately taken wing,
    But like a hawk encumber'd with his hood,—
Explaining metaphysics to the nation—
I wish he would explain his Explanation.[2]

3

You, Bob! are rather insolent, you know,
    At being disappointed in your wish
To supersede all warblers here below,
    And be the only Blackbird in the dish;
And then you overstrain yourself, or so,
    And tumble downward like the flying fish
Gasping on deck, because you soar too high, Bob,
And fall, for lack of moisture quite a-dry, Bob![3]

4

And Wordsworth, in a rather long "Excursion"[4]
    (I think the quarto holds five hundred pages),
Has given a sample from the vasty version
    Of his new system to perplex the sages;
'Tis poetry—at least by his assertion,
    And may appear so when the dog-star rages—[5]
And he who understands it would be able
To add a story to the Tower of Babel.[6]

5

You—Gentlemen! by dint of long seclusion
    From better company, have kept your own
At Keswick,[7] and, through still continued fusion
    Of one another's minds, at last have grown
To deem as a most logical conclusion,
    That Poesy has wreaths for you alone:
There is a narrowness in such a notion,
Which makes me wish you'd change your lakes for ocean.

6

I would not imitate the petty thought,
    Nor coin my self-love to so base a vice,
For all the glory your conversion brought,
    Since gold alone should not have been its price.
You have your salary; was't for that you wrought?
    And Wordsworth has his place in the Excise.[8]
You're shabby fellows—true—but poets still,
And duly seated on the immortal hill.[9]

7

Your bays may hide the baldness of your brows—[10]
    Perhaps some virtuous blushes;—let them go—
To you I envy neither fruit nor boughs—
    And for the fame you would engross below,
The field is universal, and allows
    Scope to all such as feel the inherent glow:
Scott, Rogers, Campbell, Moore, and Crabbe, will try
'Gainst you the question with posterity.

---

[1] The Prince of Wales (later George IV) was appointed Prince Regent in 1811, after George III had become permanently insane.

[2] Coleridge, *The Statesman's Manual* (1816), *Lay Sermon* (1817), and *Biographia Literaria.**

[3] A "dry-bob" was Regency slang for sex without ejaculation.

[4] W. Wordsworth, *The Excursion.**

[5] Sirius, ascendant during the hottest days of the summer, was once believed to have a maddening influence. Cf. Pope, *An Epistle to Dr. Arbuthnot* (1735) 3–4.

[6] Cf. Genesis 11.1–9.

[7] Of the Lake Poets (or "Lakers": Ded. 6), only Southey lived at Keswick, in the Lake District; Coleridge had moved there with his family in 1800, but he was no longer living there in 1819; Wordsworth lived nearby, at Grasmere.

[8] "Wordsworth's place may be in the Customs—it is, I think, in that or the Excise—besides another at Lord Lonsdale's table, where this poetical charlatan and political parasite licks up the crumbs with a hardened alacrity; the converted Jacobin having long subsided into the clownish sycophant of the worst prejudices of aristocracy." (L.B.) In 1813, Wordsworth had been appointed Distributor of Stamps for Westmoreland (a sinecure), through the influence of his patron Lord Lonsdale. In gratitude, he dedicated *The Excursion* to Lonsdale. (We have added some of Byron's later comments to his sparse notes to the first edition.)

[9] Mount Parnassus, sacred to the Muses.

[10] Bay, or laurel, leaves were awarded both to military heroes and to poets (hence the term "poet laureate"). Julius Caesar was allegedly gratified with his because they hid the fact that he was bald: Suetonius, *Lives of the Caesars* 1.45; and Byron, *Childe Harold's Pilgrimages* 4.1293.

8

For me, who, wandering with pedestrian Muses,[1]
    Contend not with you on the winged steed,
I wish your fate may yield ye, when she chooses,
    The fame you envy, and the skill you need;
And recollect a poet nothing loses
    In giving to his brethren their full meed
Of merit, and complaint of present days
Is not the certain path to future praise.

9

He that reserves his laurels for posterity
    (Who does not often claim the bright reversion)[2]
Has generally no great crop to spare it, he
    Being only injured by his own assertion;
And although here and there some glorious rarity
    Arise like Titan[3] from the sea's immersion,
The major part of such appellants go
To—God knows where—for no one else can know.

10

If, fallen in evil days on evil tongues,[4]
    Milton appeal'd to the Avenger, Time,
If Time, the Avenger, execrates his wrongs,
    And makes the word "Miltonic" mean "*sublime*,"
He deign'd not to belie his soul in songs,
    Nor turn his very talent to a crime;
He did not loathe the Sire to laud the Son,
But closed the tyrant-hater he begun.

11

Think'st thou, could he—the blind Old Man—arise
    Like Samuel from the grave,[5] to freeze once more
The blood of monarchs with his prophecies,
    Or be alive again—again all hoar
With time and trials, and those helpless eyes,
    And heartless daughters—worn—and pale[6]—and poor;
Would *he* adore a sultan? *he* obey
The intellectual eunuch Castlereagh?[7]

12

Cold-blooded, smooth-faced, placid miscreant!
    Dabbling its sleek young hands in Erin's gore,
And thus for wider carnage taught to pant,
    Transferr'd to gorge upon a sister shore,
The vulgarest tool that Tyranny could want,
    With just enough of talent, and no more,
To lengthen fetters by another fix'd,
And offer poison long already mix'd.

13

An orator of such set trash of phrase
    Ineffably—legitimately vile,
That even its grossest flatterers dare not praise,
    Nor foes—all nations—condescend to smile,—
Not even a sprightly blunder's spark can blaze
    From that Ixion grindstone's ceaseless toil,[8]

---

[1] Cf. Horace, *Satires* 2.6.17.

[2] Cf. Pope, *Elegy to the Memory of an Unfortunate Lady* (1717) 9.

[3] the Latin name for Helios, the sun-god.

[4] Cf. Milton, *Paradise Lost* 7.25–26.

[5] 1 Samuel 28.13–14.

[6] "'Pale, but not cadaverous':—Milton's two elder daughters are said to have robbed him of his books, besides cheating and plaguing him in the economy of his house, &c. His feelings on such an outrage, both as a parent and a scholar, must have been singularly painful. Hayley compares him to Lear. See part third, *Life of Milton*, by W. Hayley (or Hailey, as spelt in the edition before me)." (L.B.)

[7] "Or—
    'Would *he* subside into a hackney Laureate—
    A scribbling, self-sold, soul-hired, scorned Iscariot?'
I doubt if 'Laureate' and 'Iscariot' be good rhymes, but must say, as Ben Jonson did to Sylvester, who challenged him to rhyme with—
    'I, John Sylvester,
    Lay with your sister.'
Jonson answered—'I, Ben Jonson, lay with your wife.' Sylvester answered,—'That is not rhyme.'—'No,' said Ben Jonson; 'but it is *true*.'" (L.B.) Coincidentally, Jonson was the first Poet Laureate. Robert Stewart, Viscount Castlereagh (1769–1822), was foreign secretary. Byron despised him for his role in suppressing revolt in his native Ireland, and in the restoration of European monarchies after the fall of Napoleon.

[8] For attempting to rape Hera, Ixion was bound to a wheel that rolled forever through Hades.

That turns and turns to give the world a notion
Of endless torments and perpetual motion.

14

A bungler even in its disgusting trade,
    And botching, patching, leaving still behind
Something of which its masters are afraid,
    States to be curb'd, and thoughts to be confin'd,
Conspiracy or Congress to be made—
    Cobbling at manacles for all mankind—
A tinkering slave-maker, who mends old chains,
With God and man's abhorrence for its gains.

15

If we may judge of matter by the mind,
    Emasculated to the marrow *It*
Hath but two objects, how to serve, and bind,
    Deeming the chain it wears even men may fit,
Eutropius of its many masters,[1]—blind
    To worth as freedom, wisdom as to Wit,
Fearless—because *no* feeling dwells in ice,
Its very courage stagnates to a vice.

16

Where shall I turn me not to *view* its bonds,
    For I will never *feel* them;—Italy!
Thy late reviving Roman soul desponds
    Beneath the lie this State-thing breathed o'er thee—
Thy clanking chain, and Erin's yet green wounds,
    Have voices—tongues to cry aloud for me.
Europe has slaves—allies—kings—armies still,
And Southey lives to sing them very ill.

17

Meantime—Sir Laureate—I proceed to dedicate,
    In honest simple verse, this song to you.
And, if in flattering strains I do not predicate,
    'Tis that I still retain my "buff and blue";[2]
My politics as yet are all to educate:
    Apostasy's so fashionable, too,
To keep *one* creed's a task grown quite Herculean;
Is it not so, my Tory, ultra-Julian?[3]

CANTO 1

1

I want a hero: an uncommon want,
    When every year and month sends forth a new one,
Till, after cloying the gazettes with cant,
    The age discovers he is not the true one;
Of such as these I should not care to vaunt,
    I'll therefore take our ancient friend Don Juan,
We all have seen him in the Pantomime,
Sent to the devil, somewhat ere his time.

2

Vernon, the butcher Cumberland, Wolfe, Hawke,
    Prince Ferdinand, Granby, Burgoyne, Keppel, Howe,
Evil and good, have had their tithe of talk,
    And fill'd their sign-posts then, like Wellesley now;[4]
Each in their turn like Banquo's monarchs stalk,
    Followers of fame, "nine farrow" of that sow:[5]

---

[1] "For the character of Eutropius, the eunuch and minister at the court of Arcadius, see Gibbon." (L.B.) *The Decline and Fall of the Roman Empire*, chap. 32.

[2] the colours of the Whig Club, and of the cover of the leading Whig periodical, the *Edinburgh Review*.

[3] "I allude not to our friend Landor's hero, the traitor Count Julian, but to Gibbon's hero, vulgarly yclept 'The Apostate.'" (L.B.) The Emperor Julian was raised as a Christian, but returned to the worship of the Roman gods before becoming emperor in 361. See Gibbon, *Decline and Fall*, chap. 23; and Landor, *Count Julian* (1812).

[4] Admiral Edward Vernon (1684–1757); William, Duke of Cumberland (1721–65), whose victory over the Young Pretender at Culloden (1746) was marred by ferocity; General James Wolfe (1726–59); Edward, Lord Admiral Hawke (1715–81); Ferdinand, Duke of Brunswick (1721–92); John Manners, Marquess of Granby (1721–90); General John Burgoyne (d. 1792); Augustus, Lord Admiral Keppel (1725–86); Richard, Lord Admiral Howe (1725–99); Arthur Wellesley, Duke of Wellington (1769–1852). Wellington Street and Waterloo Bridge were both opened on the anniversary of Waterloo, in 1817.

[5] Cf. Shakespeare, *Macbeth* 4.1.64–65, 112–24.

15 France, too, had Buonaparté and Dumourier,[1]
Recorded in the Moniteur and Courier.

3

Barnave, Brissot, Condorcet, Mirabeau,
    Petion, Clootz, Danton, Marat, La Fayette,[2]
Were French, and famous people, as we know;
20   And there were others, scarce forgotten yet,
Joubert, Hoche, Marceau, Lannes, Desaix, Moreau[3]
    With many of the military set,
Exceedingly remarkable at times,
But not at all adapted to my rhymes.

4

25 Nelson was once Britannia's god of war,
    And still should be so, but the tide is turn'd;
There's no more to be said of Trafalgar,
    'Tis with our hero quietly inurn'd;
Because the army's grown more popular,
30   At which the naval people are concern'd:
Besides, the Prince is all for the land-service,
Forgetting Duncan, Nelson, Howe, and Jervis.[4]

5

Brave men were living before Agamemnon[5]
    And since, exceeding valorous and sage,
35 A good deal like him too, though quite the same none;
    But then they shone not on the poet's page,
And so have been forgotten:—I condemn none,
    But can't find any in the present age
Fit for my poem (that is, for my new one);
40 So, as I said, I'll take my friend Don Juan.

6

Most epic poets plunge "in medias res,"[6]
    (Horace makes this the heroic turnpike road)
And then your hero tells, whene'er you please,
    What went before—by way of episode,
45 While seated after dinner at his ease,
    Beside his mistress in some soft abode,
Palace, or garden, paradise, or cavern,
Which serves the happy couple for a tavern.

7

That is the usual method, but not mine—
50   My way is to begin with the beginning;
The regularity of my design
    Forbids all wandering as the worst of sinning,
And therefore I shall open with a line
    (Although it cost me half an hour in spinning)
55 Narrating somewhat of Don Juan's father,
And also of his mother, if you'd rather.

8

In Seville was he born, a pleasant city,
    Famous for oranges and women—he
Who has not seen it will be much to pity,
60   So says the proverb—and I quite agree;
Of all the Spanish towns is none more pretty,
    Cadiz perhaps—but that you soon may see:—[7]

---

[1] Charles-François Duperier Dumouriez (1739–1823), French general.

[2] Antoine-Pierre-Joseph Barnave (1761-93), Jean-Pierre Brissot de Warville (1754–93), Marie-Jean-Antoine, marquis de Condorcet (1743–94), Honoré-Gabriel Riquetti, comte de Mirabeau (1749–91), Jérôme Petion de Villeneuve (1753–94), Jean-Baptiste, baron de Clootz (1755–94), Georges-Jacques Danton (1759–94), Jean-Paul Marat (1744–93), Marie-Jean-Paul, marquis de La Fayette (1757–1834), French Revolutionaries. Mirabeau died of natural causes, Marat was assassinated, and La Fayette was still alive; the rest all perished in the Terror. Clootz, who changed his name to Anacharsis Clootz and nominated himself "l'orateur du genre humain," is a clue to Byron's plans for the conclusion of his unfinished epic: on 16 February 1821, he wrote to his publisher: "I meant to take [Don Juan] the tour of Europe—with a proper mixture of siege—battle—and adventure—and to make him finish as *Anacharsis Cloots*—in the French revolution" (*Letters and Journals* 8: 78).*

[3] Barthélemi-Catherine Joubert (1769–99), Lazare Hoche (1768–97), François Sévérin Desgravins Marceau (1769–96), Jean Lannes, duc de Montebello (1769–1809), Louis-Charles-Antoine Desaix de Voygoux (1768–1800), Jean-Victor Moreau (1763–1813), French Revolutionary generals.

[4] Adam, Lord Admiral Duncan (1731–1804), Horatio, Lord Admiral Nelson (1758–1805), killed at Trafalgar (line 27), John, Lord Admiral Jervis (1735–1823); for Howe, see note to line 12.

[5] "'Vixere fortes ante Agamemnona,' &c.—HORACE." (L.B.) *Odes* 4.9.25 (translated in the text). Agamemnon was the leader of the Greek expedition against Troy in Homer, *Iliad*.

[6] "into the middle of things" (L.): see Horace, *Epistola ad Pisones* (*Ars Poetica*) 148–49.

[7] Byron was in Seville from 25 to 29 July, and in Cadiz from 29 July to 3 August 1809.

Don Juan's parents lived beside the river,
A noble stream, and call'd the Guadalquivir.

9

65 His father's name was Jóse—*Don*, of course,
    A true Hidalgo,[1] free from every stain
Of Moor or Hebrew blood, he traced his source
    Through the most Gothic gentlemen of Spain;
A better cavalier ne'er mounted horse,
70   Or, being mounted, e'er got down again,
Than Jóse, who begot our hero, who
Begot—but that's to come—Well, to renew:

10

His mother was a learned lady,[2] famed
    For every branch of every science known—
75 In every christian language ever named,
    With virtues equall'd by her wit alone,
She made the cleverest people quite ashamed,
    And even the good with inward envy groan,
Finding themselves so very much exceeded
80 In their own way by all the things that she did.

11

Her memory was a mine: she knew by heart
    All Calderon and greater part of Lopé,[3]
So that if any actor miss'd his part
    She could have served him for the prompter's copy;
85 For her Feinagle's were an useless art,[4]
    And he himself obliged to shut up shop—he
Could never make a memory so fine as
That which adorn'd the brain of Donna Inez.

12

Her favourite science was the mathematical,
90   Her noblest virtue was her magnanimity,
Her wit (she sometimes tried at wit) was Attic all,
    Her serious sayings darken'd to sublimity;
In short, in all things she was fairly what I call
    A prodigy—her morning dress was dimity,
95 Her evening silk, or, in the summer, muslin,
And other stuffs, with which I won't stay puzzling.

13

She knew the Latin—that is, "the Lord's prayer,"
    And Greek—the alphabet—I'm nearly sure;
She read some French romances here and there,
100   Although her mode of speaking was not pure;
For native Spanish she had no great care,
    At least her conversation was obscure;
Her thoughts were theorems, her words a problem,
As if she deem'd that mystery would ennoble 'em.

14

105 She liked the English and the Hebrew tongue,
    And said there was analogy between 'em;
She proved it somehow out of sacred song,
    But I must leave the proofs to those who've seen 'em,
But this I heard her say, and can't be wrong
110   And all may think which way their judgments lean 'em,
"'Tis strange—the Hebrew noun which means 'I am,'[5]
The English always used to govern d——n."

15

Some women use their tongues—she look'd a lecture,
    Each eye a sermon, and her brow a homily,
115 An all-in-all sufficient self-director,
    Like the lamented late Sir Samuel Romilly,
The Law's expounder, and the State's corrector,
    Whose suicide was almost an anomaly—

---

[1] minor aristocrat.

[2] Despite Byron's denials, Donna Inez is obviously a satirical portrait of his wife.

[3] Calderón de la Barca (1600–81) and Lopé de Vega (1562–1635), Spanish dramatists.

[4] Gregor von Feinagle (1765?–1819) invented a new method of memorization.

[5] Exodus 3.14.

One sad example more, that "All is vanity"[1]
120 (The jury brought their verdict in "Insanity").[2]

16

In short, she was a walking calculation,
    Miss Edgeworth's novels stepping from their
        covers,[3]
Or Mrs. Trimmer's books on education,[4]
    Or "Cœlebs' Wife" set out in quest of lovers,[5]
125 Morality's prim personification,
    In which not Envy's self a flaw discovers,
To others' share let "female errors fall,"[6]
For she had not even one—the worst of all.

17

Oh! she was perfect past all parallel—
130   Of any modern female saint's comparison;
So far above the cunning powers of hell,
    Her guardian angel had given up his garrison;
Even her minutest motions went as well
    As those of the best time-piece made by
        Harrison:[7]
135 In virtues nothing earthly could surpass her,
Save thine "incomparable oil," Macassar![8]

---

[1] Ecclesiastes 1.2.

[2] Sir Samuel Romilly (1757–1818), lawyer and legal reformer, represented Lady Byron during the separation proceedings, despite having previously accepted a retainer from Byron. Byron never forgave him. Romilly's wife died in October 1818, and he committed suicide. This stanza was censored in the first edition and replaced by two rows of asterisks.

[3] Maria Edgeworth,* author of *Moral Tales* (1801) and other fiction.

[4] Sarah Trimmer (1741–1810), author of books for children and publisher of *Guardian to Education* (1802–06).

[5] Hannah More,* *Cœlebs in Search of a Wife* (1809).

[6] Pope, *The Rape of the Lock* 2.17.

[7] John Harrison (1693–1776) invented a chronometer so accurate that it could be used to calculate longitude.

[8] "'Description des *vertus incomparables* de l'Huile de Macassar.'—See the Advertisement." (L.B.) Byron seems to have seen a French advertisement for Alexander Rowland, Jr., *An Historical, Philosophical, and Practical Essay on the Human Hair, with Remarks on the Macassar Oil* (1809).

18

Perfect she was, but as perfection is
    Insipid in this naughty world of ours,
Where our first parents never learn'd to kiss
140   Till they were exiled from their earlier bowers,
Where all was peace, and innocence, and bliss
    (I wonder how they got through the twelve hours)
Don Jóse, like a lineal son of Eve,
Went plucking various fruit without her leave.

19

145 He was a mortal of the careless kind,
    With no great love for learning, or the learn'd,
Who chose to go where'er he had a mind,
    And never dream'd his lady was concern'd:
The world, as usual, wickedly inclined
150   To see a kingdom or a house o'erturn'd,
Whisper'd he had a mistress, some said *two*,
But for domestic quarrels *one* will do.

20

Now Donna Inez had, with all her merit,
    A great opinion of her own good qualities;
155 Neglect, indeed, requires a saint to bear it,
    And such, indeed, she was in her moralities;
But then she had a devil of a spirit,
    And sometimes mix'd up fancies with realities,
And let few opportunities escape
160 Of getting her liege lord into a scrape.

21

This was an easy matter with a man
    Oft in the wrong, and never on his guard;
And even the wisest, do the best they can,
    Have moments, hours, and days, so unprepared,
165 That you might "brain them with their lady's fan";[9]
    And sometimes ladies hit exceeding hard,
And fans turn into falchions in fair hands,
And why and wherefore no one understands.

22

'Tis pity learned virgins ever wed

---

[9] Shakespeare, *1 Henry IV* 2.3.21.

With persons of no sort of education,
Or gentlemen, who, though well-born and bred,
　　Grow tired of scientific conversation:
I don't choose to say much upon this head,
　　I'm a plain man, and in a single station,
But—Oh! ye lords of ladies intellectual,
Inform us truly, have they not hen-peck'd you all?

23

Don Jóse and his lady quarrell'd—why,
　　Not any of the many could divine,
Though several thousand people chose to try,
　　'Twas surely no concern of theirs nor mine;
I loathe that low vice curiosity,
　　But if there's any thing in which I shine
'Tis in arranging all my friends' affairs,
Not having, of my own, domestic cares.

24

And so I interfered, and with the best
　　Intentions, but their treatment was not kind;
I think the foolish people were possess'd,
　　For neither of them could I ever find,
Although their porter afterwards confess'd—
　　But that's no matter, and the worst's behind,
For little Juan o'er me threw, down stairs,
A pail of housemaid's water unawares.

25

A little curly-headed, good-for-nothing,
　　And mischief-making monkey from his birth;
His parents ne'er agreed except in doting
　　Upon the most unquiet imp on earth;
Instead of quarrelling, had they been but both in
　　Their senses, they'd have sent young master forth
To school, or had him soundly whipp'd at home,
To teach him manners for the time to come.

26

Don Jóse and the Donna Inez led
　　For some time an unhappy sort of life,
Wishing each other, not divorced, but dead;
　　They lived respectably as man and wife,
Their conduct was exceedingly well-bred,
　　And gave no outward signs of inward strife,
Until at length the smother'd fire broke out,
And put the business past all kind of doubt.

27

For Inez call'd some druggists and physicians,[1]
　　And tried to prove her loving lord was *mad*,
But as he had some lucid intermissions,
　　She next decided he was only *bad*;
Yet when they ask'd her for her depositions,
　　No sort of explanation could be had,
Save that her duty both to man and God
Required this conduct—which seem'd very odd.

28

She kept a journal, where his faults were noted,
　　And open'd certain trunks of books and letters,
All which might, if occasion served, be quoted;
　　And then she had all Seville for abettors,
Besides her good old grandmother (who doted);
　　The hearers of her case became repeaters,
Then advocates, inquisitors, and judges,
Some for amusement, others for old grudges.

29

And then this best and meekest woman bore
　　With such serenity her husband's woes,
Just as the Spartan ladies did of yore,
　　Who saw their spouses kill'd, and nobly chose
Never to say a word about them more—
　　Calmly she heard each calumny that rose,
And saw *his* agonies with such sublimity,
That all the world exclaim'd, "What magnanimity!"

30

No doubt, this patience, when the world is damning us,
　　Is philosophic in our former friends;
'Tis also pleasant to be deem'd magnanimous,
　　The more so in obtaining our own ends;

---

[1] During the months leading up to their separation, Lady Byron did, or was suspected by her husband of doing, all the things attributed to Inez in these two stanzas.

And what the lawyers call a "*malus animus*"[1]
　　　Conduct like this by no means comprehends:
Revenge in person's certainly no virtue,
But then 'tis not my fault, if *others* hurt you.

31

And if our quarrels should rip up old stories,
　　　And help them with a lie or two additional,
I'm not to blame, as you well know, no more is
　　　Any one else—they were become traditional;
Besides, their resurrection aids our glories
　　　By contrast, which is what we just were wishing all:
And science profits by this resurrection—
Dead scandals form good subjects for dissection.

32

Their friends had tried at reconciliation,
　　　Then their relations, who made matters worse;
('Twere hard to tell upon a like occasion
　　　To whom it may be best to have recourse—
I can't say much for friend or yet relation):
　　　The lawyers did their utmost for divorce,
But scarce a fee was paid on either side
Before, unluckily, Don Jóse died.

33

He died: and most unluckily, because,
　　　According to all hints I could collect
From counsel learned in those kinds of laws
　　　(Although their talk's obscure and circumspect)
His death contrived to spoil a charming cause;
　　　A thousand pities also with respect
To public feeling, which on this occasion
Was manifested in a great sensation.

34

But ah! he died; and buried with him lay
　　　The public feeling and the lawyers' fees:
His house was sold, his servants sent away,
　　　A Jew took one of his two mistresses,
A priest the other—at least so they say:

---

[1] "a bad spirit" (L.).

I ask'd the doctors after his disease,
He died of the slow fever call'd the tertian,
And left his widow to her own aversion.

35

Yet Jóse was an honourable man,[2]
　　　That I must say, who knew him very well;
Therefore his frailties I'll no further scan,
　　　Indeed there were not many more to tell;
And if his passions now and then outran
　　　Discretion, and were not so peaceable
As Numa's (who was also named Pompilius),[3]
He had been ill brought up, and was born bilious.

36

Whate'er might be his worthlessness or worth,
　　　Poor fellow! he had many things to wound him,
Let's own, since it can do no good on earth;
　　　It was a trying moment that which found him
Standing alone beside his desolate hearth,
　　　Where all his household gods lay shiver'd round him;[4]
No choice was left his feelings or his pride,
Save death or Doctors' Commons[5]—so he died.

37

Dying intestate, Juan was sole heir
　　　To a chancery suit, and messuages, and lands,
Which, with a long minority and care,
　　　Promised to turn out well in proper hands:
Inez became sole guardian, which was fair,
　　　And answer'd but to nature's just demands;
An only son left with an only mother
Is brought up much more wisely than another.

38

Sagest of women, even of widows, she
　　　Resolved that Juan should be quite a paragon,
And worthy of the noblest pedigree:

---

[2] Cf. Shakespeare, *Julius Caesar* 3.2.82–99.

[3] the peaceable second king of Rome; see Plutarch, *Parallel Lives*.

[4] Cf. Byron, *Letters and Journals* 6: 69 (19 September 1819).

[5] the divorce courts.

              (His sire was of Castile, his dam from Aragon).
Then for accomplishments of chivalry,
     In case our lord the king should go to war again,
He learn'd the arts of riding, fencing, gunnery,
And how to scale a fortress—or a nunnery.

39

But that which Donna Inez most desired,
     And saw into herself each day before all
The learned tutors whom for him she hired,
     Was, that his breeding should be strictly moral;
Much into all his studies she inquired,
     And so they were submitted first to her, all,
Arts, sciences, no branch was made a mystery
To Juan's eyes, excepting natural history.

40

The languages, especially the dead,
     The sciences, and most of all the abstruse,
The arts, at least all such as could be said
     To be the most remote from common use,
In all these he was much and deeply read;
     But not a page of any thing that's loose,
Or hints continuation of the species,
Was ever suffer'd, lest he should grow vicious.

41

His classic studies made a little puzzle,
     Because of filthy loves of gods and goddesses,
Who in the earlier ages raised a bustle,
     But never put on pantaloons or boddices;
His reverend tutors had at times a tussle,
     And for their Æneids, Iliads, and Odysseys,
Were forced to make an odd sort of apology,
For Donna Inez dreaded the mythology.

42

Ovid's a rake, as half his verses show him,
     Anacreon's morals are a still worse sample,
Catullus scarcely has a decent poem,
     I don't think Sappho's Ode a good example,
Although Longinus tells us there is no hymn
     Where the sublime soars forth on wings more
          ample;[1]
But Virgil's songs are pure, except that horrid one
Beginning with "*Formosum Pastor Corydon.*"[2]

43

Lucretius' irreligion is too strong
     For early stomachs, to prove wholesome food;
I can't help thinking Juvenal was wrong,
     Although no doubt his real intent was good,
For speaking out so plainly in his song,
     So much indeed as to be downright rude;[3]
And then what proper person can be partial
To all those nauseous epigrams of Martial?

44

Juan was taught from out the best edition,
     Expurgated by learned men, who place,
Judiciously, from out the schoolboy's vision,
     The grosser parts; but fearful to deface
Too much their modest bard by this omission,
     And pitying sore his mutilated case,
They only add them all in an appendix,[4]
Which saves, in fact, the trouble of an index;

45

For there we have them all at one fell swoop,[5]
     Instead of being scatter'd through the pages;

---

[1] "See Longinus, Section 10, '(eleven words in Greek: *hina me hen ti peri auten pathos phainetai, pathon de sunodos*).'" (L.B.) See Ovid's *Amores* and *Ars Amatoria*; the erotic lyrics then attributed to Anacreon; the erotic lyrics of Catullus; and the poem by Sappho beginning "To me he seems a peer of the gods," praised by Longinus in *On the Sublime* 10.

[2] "The shepherd Corydon (burned for) fair (Alexis, his master's darling)." Virgil, *Eclogues* 2 (trans. J.W. Mackail). The poem is about homosexual love.

[3] Lucretius, *On the Nature of Things*, a philosophical poem; and Juvenal, *Satires*.

[4] "Fact. There is, or was, such an edition, with all the obnoxious epigrams of Martial placed by themselves at the end." (L.B.) The Delphin edition of Martial (Amsterdam, 1701) has an appendix entitled "Epigrammata Obscaena."

[5] Shakespeare, *Macbeth* 4.3.219.

They stand forth marshall'd in a handsome troop,
    To meet the ingenuous youth of future ages,
Till some less rigid editor shall stoop
    To call them back into their separate cages,
Instead of standing staring altogether,
Like garden gods—and not so decent either.

46

The Missal too (it was the family Missal)
    Was ornamented in a sort of way
Which ancient mass-books often are, and this all
    Kinds of grotesques illumined; and how they,
Who saw those figures on the margin kiss all,
    Could turn their optics to the text and pray
Is more than I know—but Don Juan's mother
Kept this herself, and gave her son another.

47

Sermons he read, and lectures he endured,
    And homilies, and lives of all the saints;
To Jerome and to Chrysostom inured,[1]
    He did not take such studies for restraints;
But how faith is acquired, and then insured,
    So well not one of the aforesaid paints
As Saint Augustine in his fine Confessions,
Which make the reader envy his transgressions.[2]

48

This, too, was a seal'd book to little Juan—
    I can't but say that his mamma was right,
If such an education was the true one.
    She scarcely trusted him from out her sight;
Her maids were old, and if she took a new one
    You might be sure she was a perfect fright,
She did this during even her husband's life—
I recommend as much to every wife.

---

[1] St. Jerome (340?–420), translator of the Bible into Latin, and St. John Chrysostom (347?–407); both were ascetics.

[2] "See his *Confessions*, lib. i. cap. ix. By the representation which Saint Augustine gives of himself in his youth, it is easy to see that he was what we should call a rake. He avoided the school as the plague; he loved nothing but gaming and public shows; he robbed his father of everything he could find; he invented a thousand lies to escape the rod, which they were obliged to make use of to punish his irregularities." (L.B.) See also Augustine, *Confessions* (397–98) 1.10 and 2.2.

49

Young Juan wax'd in goodliness and grace;[3]
    At six a charming child, and at eleven
With all the promise of as fine a face
    As e'er to man's maturer growth was given:
He studied steadily, and grew apace,
    And seem'd, at least, in the right road to heaven,
For half his days were pass'd at church, the other
Between his tutors, confessor, and mother.

50

At six, I said, he was a charming child,
    At twelve he was a fine, but quiet boy;
Although in infancy a little wild,
    They tamed him down amongst them; to destroy
His natural spirit not in vain they toil'd,
    At least it seem'd so; and his mother's joy
Was to declare how sage, and still, and steady,
Her young philosopher was grown already.

51

I had my doubts, perhaps I have them still,
    But what I say is neither here nor there:
I knew his father well, and have some skill
    In character—but it would not be fair
From sire to son to augur good or ill:
    He and his wife were an ill-sorted pair—
But scandal's my aversion—I protest
Against all evil speaking, even in jest.

52

For my part I say nothing—nothing—but
    This I will say—my reasons are my own—
That if I had an only son to put
    To school (as God be praised that I have none)
'Tis not with Donna Inez I would shut
    Him up to learn his catechism alone,
No—no—I'd send him out betimes to college,
For there it was I pick'd up my own knowledge.

53

For there one learns—'tis not for me to boast,

---

[3] Cf. Luke 2.40.

              Though I acquired—but I pass over *that*,
As well as all the Greek I since have lost:
420   I say that there's the place—but "*Verbum sat.*"¹
I think, I pick'd up too, as well as most,
              Knowledge of matters—but no matter *what*—
I never married—but, I think, I know
That sons should not be educated so.

54

425 Young Juan now was sixteen years of age,
              Tall, handsome, slender, but well knit; he seem'd
Active, though not so sprightly, as a page;
              And every body but his mother deem'd
Him almost man; but she flew in a rage,
430   And bit her lips (for else she might have scream'd),
If any said so, for to be precocious
Was in her eyes a thing the most atrocious.

55

Amongst her numerous acquaintance, all
              Selected for discretion and devotion,
435 There was the Donna Julia, whom to call
              Pretty were but to give a feeble notion
Of many charms in her as natural
              As sweetness to the flower, or salt to ocean,
Her zone to Venus, or his bow to Cupid,
440 (But this last simile is trite and stupid.)

56

The darkness of her oriental eye
              Accorded with her Moorish origin;
(Her blood was not all Spanish, by the by;
              In Spain, you know, this is a sort of sin.)
445 When proud Granada fell, and, forced to fly,
              Boabdil² wept, of Donna Julia's kin
Some went to Africa, some staid in Spain,
Her great great grandmamma chose to remain.

57

She married (I forget the pedigree)

---

¹ "A word [to the wise] is enough" (L.).

² Muhammad XI, the last Moorish king of Granada, defeated by the Spanish in 1492.

450   With an Hidalgo, who transmitted down
His blood less noble than such blood should be;
              At such alliances his sires would frown,
In that point so precise in each degree
              That they bred *in and in*, as might be shown,
455 Marrying their cousins—nay, their aunts and nieces,
Which always spoils the breed, if it increases.

58

This heathenish cross restored the breed again,
              Ruin'd its blood, but much improved its flesh;
For, from a root the ugliest in Old Spain
460   Sprung up a branch as beautiful as fresh;
The sons no more were short, the daughters plain:
              But there's a rumour which I fain would hush,
'Tis said that Donna Julia's grandmamma
Produced her Don more heirs at love than law.

59

465 However this might be, the race went on
              Improving still through every generation,
Until it center'd in an only son,
              Who left an only daughter; my narration
May have suggested that this single one
470   Could be but Julia (whom on this occasion
I shall have much to speak about), and she
Was married, charming, chaste, and twenty-three.

60

Her eye (I'm very fond of handsome eyes)
              Was large and dark, suppressing half its fire
475 Until she spoke, then through its soft disguise
              Flash'd an expression more of pride than ire,
And love than either; and there would arise
              A something in them which was not desire,
But would have been, perhaps, but for the soul
480 Which struggled through and chasten'd down the whole.

61

Her glossy hair was cluster'd o'er a brow
              Bright with intelligence, and fair and smooth;
Her eyebrow's shape was like the aerial bow,
              Her cheek all purple with the beam of youth,

Mounting, at times, to a transparent glow,
    As if her veins ran lightning; she, in sooth,
Possess'd an air and grace by no means common:
Her stature tall—I hate a dumpy woman.

62

Wedded she was some years, and to a man
    Of fifty, and such husbands are in plenty;
And yet, I think, instead of such a ONE
    'Twere better to have TWO of five and twenty,
Especially in countries near the sun:
    And now I think on't, "mi vien in mente,"[1]
Ladies even of the most uneasy virtue
Prefer a spouse whose age is short of thirty.

63

'Tis a sad thing, I cannot choose but say,
    And all the fault of that indecent sun,
Who cannot leave alone our helpless clay,
    But will keep baking, broiling, burning on,
That howsoever people fast and pray
    The flesh is frail,[2] and so the soul undone:
What men call gallantry, and gods adultery,
Is much more common where the climate's sultry.

64

Happy the nations of the moral north!
    Where all is virtue, and the winter season
Sends sin, without a rag on, shivering forth;
    ('Twas snow that brought St. Anthony[3] to reason);
Where juries cast up what a wife is worth
    By laying whate'er sum, in mulct, they please on
The lover, who must pay a handsome price,
Because it is a marketable vice.

65

Alfonso was the name of Julia's lord,
    A man well looking for his years, and who
Was neither much beloved, nor yet abhorr'd;
    They lived together as most people do,
Suffering each other's foibles by accord,
    And not exactly either *one* or *two*;
Yet he was jealous, though he did not show it,
For jealousy dislikes the world to know it.

66

Julia was—yet I never could see why—
    With Donna Inez quite a favourite friend;
Between their tastes there was small sympathy,
    For not a line had Julia ever penn'd:
Some people whisper (but, no doubt, they lie,
    For malice still imputes some private end)
That Inez had, ere Don Alfonso's marriage,
Forgot with him her very prudent carriage:

67

And that still keeping up the old connexion,
    Which time had lately render'd much more chaste,
She took his lady also in affection,
    And certainly this course was much the best:
She flatter'd Julia with her sage protection,
    And complimented Don Alfonso's taste;
And if she could not (who can?) silence scandal,
At least she left it a more slender handle.

68

I can't tell whether Julia saw the affair
    With other people's eyes, or if her own
Discoveries made, but none could be aware
    Of this, at least no symptom e'er was shown;
Perhaps she did not know, or did not care,
    Indifferent from the first, or callous grown:
I'm really puzzled what to think or say,
She kept her counsel in so close a way.

69

Juan she saw, and, as a pretty child,
    Caress'd him often, such a thing might be
Quite innocently done, and harmless styled,
    When she had twenty years, and thirteen he;

---

[1] "It comes into my mind" (It.).

[2] Cf. Matthew 26.41.

[3] "For the particulars of St. Anthony's recipe for hot blood in cold weather, see Mr. Alban Butler's *Lives of the Saints*." (L.B.) It was actually St. Francis of Assisi who used to throw himself naked into the snow to counteract the temptations of the flesh.

But I am not so sure I should have smiled
　　　When he was sixteen, Julia twenty-three,
These few short years make wondrous alterations,
Particularly amongst sun-burnt nations.

70
Whate'er the cause might be, they had become
　　　Changed; for the dame grew distant, the youth shy,
Their looks cast down, their greetings almost dumb,
　　　And much embarrassment in either eye;
There surely will be little doubt with some
　　　That Donna Julia knew the reason why,
But as for Juan, he had no more notion
Than he who never saw the sea of ocean.

71
Yet Julia's very coldness still was kind,
　　　And tremulously gentle her small hand
Withdrew itself from his, but left behind
　　　A little pressure, thrilling, and so bland
And slight, so very slight, that to the mind
　　　'Twas but a doubt; but ne'er magician's wand
Wrought change with all Armida's[1] fairy art
Like what this light touch left on Juan's heart.

72
And if she met him, though she smiled no more,
　　　She look'd a sadness sweeter than her smile,
As if her heart had deeper thoughts in store
　　　She must not own, but cherish'd more the while,
For that compression in its burning core;
　　　Even innocence itself has many a wile,
And will not dare to trust itself with truth,
And love is taught hypocrisy from youth.

73
But passion most dissembles yet betrays
　　　Even by its darkness; as the blackest sky
Foretells the heaviest tempest, it displays
　　　Its workings through the vainly guarded eye,
And in whatever aspect it arrays
　　　Itself, 'tis still the same hypocrisy;
Coldness or anger, even disdain or hate,
Are masks it often wears, and still too late.

74
Then there were sighs, the deeper for suppression,
　　　And stolen glances, sweeter for the theft,
And burning blushes, though for no transgression,
　　　Tremblings when met, and restlessness when left;
All these are little preludes to possession,
　　　Of which young Passion cannot be bereft,
And merely tend to show how greatly Love is
Embarrass'd at first starting with a novice.

75
Poor Julia's heart was in an awkward state;
　　　She felt it going, and resolved to make
The noblest efforts for herself and mate,
　　　For honour's, pride's, religion's, virtue's sake;
Her resolutions were most truly great,
　　　And almost might have made a Tarquin[2] quake;
She pray'd the Virgin Mary for her grace,
As being the best judge of a lady's case.

76
She vow'd she never would see Juan more,
　　　And next day paid a visit to his mother,
And look'd extremely at the opening door,
　　　Which, by the Virgin's grace, let in another;
Grateful she was, and yet a little sore—
　　　Again it opens, it can be no other,
'Tis surely Juan now—No! I'm afraid
That night the Virgin was no further pray'd.[3]

77
She now determined that a virtuous woman
　　　Should rather face and overcome temptation,
That flight was base and dastardly, and no man
　　　Should ever give her heart the least sensation;

---

[1] the enchantress in Torquato Tasso (1544–95), *Jerusalem Delivered* (1581).

[2] Sextus Tarquinius raped Lucretia, a Roman matron, who subsequently stabbed herself. See Shakespeare, *The Rape of Lucrece* (1594).

[3] Cf. Dante, *Inferno* 5.138.

That is to say, a thought beyond the common
    Preference, that we must feel upon occasion,
For people who are pleasanter than others,
But then they only seem so many brothers.

78

And even if by chance—and who can tell?
    The devil's so very sly—she should discover
That all within was not so very well,
    And, if still free, that such or such a lover
Might please perhaps, a virtuous wife can quell
    Such thoughts, and be the better when they're over;
And if the man should ask, 'tis but denial:
I recommend young ladies to make trial.

79

And then there are such things as love divine,
    Bright and immaculate, unmix'd and pure,
Such as the angels think so very fine,
    And matrons, who would be no less secure,
Platonic, perfect, "just such love as mine":
    Thus Julia said—and thought so, to be sure,
And so I'd have her think, were I the man
On whom her reveries celestial ran.

80

Such love is innocent, and may exist
    Between young persons without any danger,
A hand may first, and then a lip be kist;
    For my part, to such doings I'm a stranger,
But *hear* these freedoms form the utmost list
    Of all o'er which such love may be a ranger:
If people go beyond, 'tis quite a crime,
But not my fault—I tell them all in time.

81

Love, then, but love within its proper limits,
    Was Julia's innocent determination
In young Don Juan's favour, and to him its
    Exertion might be useful on occasion;
And, lighted at too pure a shrine to dim its
    Etherial lustre, with what sweet persuasion
He might be taught, by love and her together—
I really don't know what, nor Julia either.

82

Fraught with this fine intention, and well fenced
    In mail of proof—her purity of soul,[1]
She, for the future of her strength convinced,
    And that her honour was a rock, or mole,
Exceeding sagely from that hour dispensed
    With any kind of troublesome control;
But whether Julia to the task was equal
Is that which must be mention'd in the sequel.

83

Her plan she deem'd both innocent and feasible,
    And, surely, with a stripling of sixteen
Not scandal's fangs could fix on much that's seizable,
    Or if they did so, satisfied to mean
Nothing but what was good, her breast was peaceable—
    A quiet conscience makes one so serene!
Christians have burnt each other, quite persuaded
That all the Apostles would have done as they did.

84

And if in the mean time her husband died,
    But heaven forbid that such a thought should cross
Her brain, though in a dream! (and then she sigh'd)
    Never could she survive that common loss;
But just suppose that moment should betide,
    I only say suppose it—*inter nos*.
(This should be *entre nous*, for Julia thought
In French, but then the rhyme would go for nought.)

85

I only say suppose this supposition:
    Juan being then grown up to man's estate
Would fully suit a widow of condition,
    Even seven years hence it would not be too late;
And in the interim (to pursue this vision)
    The mischief, after all, could not be great,

---

[1] Cf. Dante, *Inferno* 28.115–17.

For he would learn the rudiments of love,
680 I mean the seraph way of those above.

86

So much for Julia. Now we'll turn to Juan,
    Poor little fellow! he had no idea
Of his own case, and never hit the true one;
    In feelings quick as Ovid's Miss Medea,[1]
685 He puzzled over what he found a new one,
    But not as yet imagined it could be a
Thing quite in course, and not at all alarming,
Which, with a little patience, might grow charming.

87

Silent and pensive, idle, restless, slow,
690   His home deserted for the lonely wood,
Tormented with a wound he could not know,
    His, like all deep grief, plunged in solitude:
I'm fond myself of solitude or so,
    But then, I beg it may be understood,
695 By solitude I mean a sultan's, not
    A hermit's, with a haram for a grot.

88

"Oh Love! in such a wilderness as this,
    Where transport and security entwine,
Here is the empire of thy perfect bliss,
    And here thou art a god indeed divine."[2]
700 The bard I quote from does not sing amiss,
    With the exception of the second line,
For that same twining "transport and security"
Are twisted to a phrase of some obscurity.

89

705 The poet meant, no doubt, and thus appeals
    To the good sense and senses of mankind,
The very thing which every body feels,
    As all have found on trial, or may find,
That no one likes to be disturb'd at meals
710   Or love.—I won't say more about "entwined"
Or "transport," as we knew all that before,
But beg "Security" will bolt the door.

90

Young Juan wander'd by the glassy brooks
    Thinking unutterable things; he threw
715 Himself at length within the leafy nooks
    Where the wild branch of the cork forest grew;
There poets find materials for their books,
    And every now and then we read them through,
So that their plan and prosody are eligible,
720 Unless, like Wordsworth, they prove unintelligible.

91

He, Juan (and not Wordsworth), so pursued
    His self-communion with his own high soul,
Until his mighty heart,[3] in its great mood,
    Had mitigated part, though not the whole
725 Of its disease; he did the best he could
    With things not very subject to control,
And turn'd, without perceiving his condition,
Like Coleridge, into a metaphysician.[4]

92

He thought about himself, and the whole earth,
730   Of man the wonderful, and of the stars,
And how the deuce they ever could have birth;
    And then he thought of earthquakes, and of wars,
How many miles the moon might have in girth,
    Of air-balloons, and of the many bars
735 To perfect knowledge of the boundless skies;
And then he thought of Donna Julia's eyes.

93

In thoughts like these true wisdom may discern
    Longings sublime, and aspirations high,
Which some are born with, but the most part learn
740   To plague themselves withal, they know not why:

---

[1] Cf. Ovid, *Metamorphoses* 7.10–12.

[2] "Campbell's Gertrude of Wyoming, (I think) the opening of Canto II.; but quote from memory." (L.B.) Thomas Campbell,* *Gertrude of Wyoming* (1809) 3.1.1–4.

[3] Cf. W. Wordsworth, "Composed upon Westminster Bridge" 14.*

[4] See Coleridge, "Dejection" 87–93.*

'Twas strange that one so young should thus concern
    His brain about the action of the sky;
If *you* think 'twas philosophy that this did,
    I can't help thinking puberty assisted.

94

745 He pored upon the leaves, and on the flowers,
    And heard a voice in all the winds;[1] and then
He thought of wood nymphs and immortal bowers,
    And how the goddesses came down to men:
He miss'd the pathway, he forgot the hours,
750   And when he look'd upon his watch again,
He found how much old Time had been a winner—
He also found that he had lost his dinner.

95

Sometimes he turn'd to gaze upon his book,
    Boscan, or Garcilasso;[2]—by the wind
755 Even as the page is rustled while we look,
    So by the poesy of his own mind
Over the mystic leaf his soul was shook,
    As if 'twere one whereon magicians bind
Their spells, and give them to the passing gale,
760 According to some good old woman's tale.

96

Thus would he while his lonely hours away
    Dissatisfied, nor knowing what he wanted;
Nor glowing reverie, nor poet's lay,
    Could yield his spirit that for which it panted,
765 A bosom whereon he his head might lay,
    And hear the heart beat with the love it granted,
With—several other things, which I forget,
Or which, at least, I need not mention yet.

97

Those lonely walks, and lengthening reveries,
770   Could not escape the gentle Julia's eyes;
She saw that Juan was not at his ease;
    But that which chiefly may, and must surprise,
Is, that the Donna Inez did not tease
    Her only son with question or surmise;
775 Whether it was she did not see, or would not,
Or, like all very clever people, could not.

98

This may seem strange, but yet 'tis very common;
    For instance—gentlemen, whose ladies take
Leave to o'erstep the written rights of woman,
780   And break the—Which commandment is't they break?[3]
(I have forgot the number, and think no man
    Should rashly quote, for fear of a mistake.)
I say, when these same gentlemen are jealous,
They make some blunder, which their ladies tell us.

99

785 A real husband always is suspicious,
    But still no less suspects in the wrong place,
Jealous of some one who had no such wishes,
    Or pandering blindly to his own disgrace
By harbouring some dear friend extremely vicious;
790   The last indeed's infallibly the case:
And when the spouse and friend are gone off wholly,
He wonders at their vice, and not his folly.

100

Thus parents also are at times short-sighted;
    Though watchful as the lynx, they ne'er discover,
795 The while the wicked world beholds delighted,
    Young Hopeful's mistress, or Miss Fanny's lover,
Till some confounded escapade has blighted
    The plan of twenty years, and all is over;
And then the mother cries, the father swears,
800 And wonders why the devil he got heirs.

101

But Inez was so anxious, and so clear
    Of sight, that I must think, on this occasion,
She had some other motive much more near
    For leaving Juan to this new temptation;

---

[1] Cf. Thomas Gray, "Ode on a Distant Prospect of Eton College" (1742) 39.

[2] Juan Boscán (1500–44) and Garcias Lasso or Garcilaso de la Vega (1503–36), Spanish poets.

[3] the seventh: Exodus 20.14.

805 But what that motive was, I sha'n't say here;
　　Perhaps to finish Juan's education,
Perhaps to open Don Alfonso's eyes,
In case he thought his wife too great a prize.

102

It was upon a day, a summer's day;—
810 　　Summer's indeed a very dangerous season,
And so is spring about the end of May;
　　The sun, no doubt, is the prevailing reason;
But whatsoe'er the cause is, one may say,
　　And stand convicted of more truth than treason,
815 That there are months which nature grows more merry in,
March has its hares, and May must have its heroine.

103

'Twas on a summer's day—the sixth of June:—
　　I like to be particular in dates,
Not only of the age, and year, but moon;
820 　　They are a sort of post-house, where the Fates
Change horses, making history change its tune,
　　Then spur away o'er empires and o'er states,
Leaving at last not much besides chronology,
Excepting the post-obits of theology.

104

825 'Twas on the sixth of June, about the hour
　　Of half-past six—perhaps still nearer seven,
When Julia sate within as pretty a bower
　　As e'er held houri in that heathenish heaven
Described by Mahomet, and Anacreon Moore,[1]
830 　　To whom the lyre and laurels have been given,
With all the trophies of triumphant song—
He won them well, and may he wear them long!

105

She sate, but not alone; I know not well
　　How this same interview had taken place,
835 And even if I knew, I should not tell—
　　People should hold their tongues in any case;
No matter how or why the thing befel,
　　But there were she and Juan, face to face—
When two such faces are so, 'twould be wise,
840 But very difficult, to shut their eyes.

106

How beautiful she look'd! her conscious heart
　　Glow'd in her cheek, and yet she felt no wrong.
Oh Love! how perfect is thy mystic art,
　　Strengthening the weak, and trampling on the strong,
845 How self-deceitful is the sagest part
　　Of mortals whom thy lure hath led along—
The precipice she stood on was immense,
So was her creed in her own innocence.

107

She thought of her own strength, and Juan's youth,
850 　　And of the folly of all prudish fears,
Victorious virtue, and domestic truth,
　　And then of Don Alfonso's fifty years:
I wish these last had not occurr'd, in sooth,
　　Because that number rarely much endears,
855 And through all climes, the snowy and the sunny,
Sounds ill in love, whate'er it may in money.

108

When people say, "I've told you *fifty* times,"
　　They mean to scold, and very often do;
When poets say, "I've written *fifty* rhymes,"
860 　　They make you dread that they'll recite them too;
In gangs of *fifty*, thieves commit their crimes;
　　At *fifty* love for love is rare, 'tis true,
But then, no doubt, it equally as true is,
A good deal may be bought for *fifty* Louis.

109

865 Julia had honour, virtue, truth, and love,
　　For Don Alfonso; and she inly swore,
By all the vows below to powers above,
　　She never would disgrace the ring she wore,
Nor leave a wish which wisdom might reprove;

---

[1] Byron's friend Moore* was known as "Anacreon" Moore because he first became famous for translating the lyric poems then attributed to Anacreon. The reference is to "Paradise and the Peri," one of the tales in Moore's *Lalla Rookh* (1817).

And while she ponder'd this, besides much more,
One hand on Juan's carelessly was thrown,
Quite by mistake—she thought it was her own;

110

Unconsciously she lean'd upon the other,
　Which play'd within the tangles of her hair;[1]
And to contend with thoughts she could not smother,
　She seem'd by the distraction of her air.
'Twas surely very wrong in Juan's mother
　To leave together this imprudent pair,
She who for many years had watch'd her son so—
I'm very certain *mine* would not have done so.

111

The hand which still held Juan's, by degrees
　Gently, but palpably confirm'd its grasp,
As if it said, "detain me, if you please";
　Yet there's no doubt she only meant to clasp
His fingers with a pure Platonic squeeze;
　She would have shrunk as from a toad, or asp,
Had she imagined such a thing could rouse
A feeling dangerous to a prudent spouse.

112

I cannot know what Juan thought of this,
　But what he did, is much what you would do;
His young lip thank'd it with a grateful kiss,
　And then, abash'd at its own joy, withdrew
In deep despair, lest he had done amiss,
　Love is so very timid when 'tis new:
She blush'd, and frown'd not, but she strove to speak,
And held her tongue, her voice was grown so weak.

113

The sun set, and up rose the yellow moon:
　The devil's in the moon for mischief; they
Who call'd her CHASTE, methinks, began too soon
　Their nomenclature; there is not a day,
The longest, not the twenty-first of June,
　Sees half the business in a wicked way
On which three single hours of moonshine smile—
And then she looks so modest all the while.

114

There is a dangerous silence in that hour,
　A stillness, which leaves room for the full soul
To open all itself, without the power
　Of calling wholly back its self-control;
The silver light which, hallowing tree and tower,
　Sheds beauty and deep softness o'er the whole,
Breathes also to the heart, and o'er it throws
A loving languor, which is not repose.

115

And Julia sate with Juan, half embraced
　And half retiring from the glowing arm,
Which trembled like the bosom where 'twas placed;
　Yet still she must have thought there was no harm,
Or else 'twere easy to withdraw her waist;
　But then the situation had its charm,
And then——God knows what next—I can't go on;
I'm almost sorry that I e'er begun.

116

Oh Plato! Plato! you have paved the way,
　With your confounded fantasies, to more
Immoral conduct by the fancied sway
　Your system feigns o'er the controlless core
Of human hearts, than all the long array
　Of poets and romancers:—You're a bore,
A charlatan, a coxcomb—and have been,
At best, no better than a go-between.

117

And Julia's voice was lost, except in sighs,
　Until too late for useful conversation;
The tears were gushing from her gentle eyes,
　I wish, indeed, they had not had occasion,
But who, alas! can love, and then be wise?
　Not that remorse did not oppose temptation,
A little still she strove, and much repented,
And whispering "I will ne'er consent"—consented.

118

'Tis said that Xerxes offer'd a reward

---

[1] Cf. Milton, "Lycidas" 69.

    To those who could invent him a new pleasure;[1]
Methinks, the requisition's rather hard,
    And must have cost his majesty a treasure:
For my part, I'm a moderate-minded bard,
    Fond of a little love (which I call leisure);
I care not for new pleasures, as the old
Are quite enough for me, so they but hold.

119

Oh Pleasure! you're indeed a pleasant thing,
    Although one must be damn'd for you, no doubt;
I make a resolution every spring
    Of reformation, ere the year run out,
But, somehow, this my vestal vow takes wing,
    Yet still, I trust, it may be kept throughout:
I'm very sorry, very much ashamed,
And mean, next winter, to be quite reclaim'd.

120

Here my chaste Muse a liberty must take—
    Start not! still chaster reader—she'll be nice hence—
Forward, and there is no great cause to quake;
    This liberty is a poetic licence,
Which some irregularity may make
    In the design, and as I have a high sense
Of Aristotle and the Rules, 'tis fit
To beg his pardon when I err a bit.

121

This licence is to hope the reader will
    Suppose from June the sixth (the fatal day,
Without whose epoch my poetic skill
    For want of facts would all be thrown away),
But keeping Julia and Don Juan still
    In sight, that several months have pass'd; we'll say
'Twas in November, but I'm not so sure
About the day—the era's more obscure.

122

We'll talk of that anon.—'Tis sweet[2] to hear
    At midnight on the blue and moonlit deep
The song and oar of Adria's gondolier,
    By distance mellow'd, o'er the waters sweep;
'Tis sweet to see the evening star appear;
    'Tis sweet to listen as the night-winds creep
From leaf to leaf; 'tis sweet to view on high
The rainbow, based on ocean, span the sky.

123

'Tis sweet to hear the watch-dog's honest bark
    Bay deep-mouth'd welcome as we draw near home;[3]
'Tis sweet to know there is an eye will mark
    Our coming, and look brighter when we come;
'Tis sweet to be awaken'd by the lark,
    Or lull'd by falling waters; sweet the hum
Of bees, the voice of girls, the song of birds,
The lisp of children, and their earliest words.

124

Sweet is the vintage, when the showering grapes
    In Bacchanal profusion reel to earth
Purple and gushing: sweet are our escapes
    From civic revelry to rural mirth;
Sweet to the miser are his glittering heaps,
    Sweet to the father is his first-born's birth,
Sweet is revenge—especially to women,
Pillage to soldiers, prize-money to seamen.

125

Sweet is a legacy, and passing sweet
    The unexpected death of some old lady
Or gentleman of seventy years complete,
    Who've made "us youth"[4] wait too—too long already
For an estate, or cash, or country-seat,
    Still breaking, but with stamina so steady,

---

[1] Xerxes was king of Persia from 486 to 465 BC. Cf. Cicero, *Tusculan Disputations* 5.7; and Montaigne, "Of Experience" (*Essays* 3.13).

[2] Cf. Lucretius, *On the Nature of Things* 2.1–8.

[3] Cf. Oliver Goldsmith,* *The Vicar of Wakefield*, chap. 22.

[4] Shakespeare, *1 Henry IV* 2.2.79.

That all the Israelites are fit to mob its
Next owner for their double-damn'd post-obits.[1]

126

'Tis sweet to win, no matter how, one's laurels
    By blood or ink; 'tis sweet to put an end
To strife; 'tis sometimes sweet to have our quarrels,
    Particularly with a tiresome friend;
Sweet is old wine in bottles, ale in barrels;
    Dear is the helpless creature we defend
Against the world; and dear the schoolboy spot
We ne'er forget, though there we are forgot.

127

But sweeter still than this, than these, than all,
    Is first and passionate love—it stands alone,
Like Adam's recollection of his fall;
    The tree of knowledge has been pluck'd—all's known—
And life yields nothing further to recall
    Worthy of this ambrosial sin, so shown,
No doubt in fable, as the unforgiven
Fire which Prometheus filch'd for us from heaven.

128

Man's a strange animal, and makes strange use
    Of his own nature, and the various arts,
And likes particularly to produce
    Some new experiment to show his parts;
This is the age of oddities let loose,
    Where different talents find their different marts;
You'd best begin with truth, and when you've lost your
Labour, there's a sure market for imposture.

129

What opposite discoveries we have seen!
    (Signs of true genius, and of empty pockets.)
One makes new noses,[2] one a guillotine,
    One breaks your bones, one sets them in their sockets;
But vaccination certainly has been
    A kind antithesis to Congreve's rockets,[3]
With which the Doctor paid off an old pox,
By borrowing a new one from an ox.[4]

130

Bread has been made (indifferent) from potatoes;
    And galvanism has set some corpses grinning,[5]
But has not answer'd like the apparatus
    Of the Humane Society's beginning[6]
By which men are unsuffocated gratis:
    What wondrous new machines have late been spinning![7]
I said the small-pox has gone out of late;
Perhaps it may be follow'd by the great.[8]

131

'Tis said the great came from America;
    Perhaps it may set out on its return,—
The population there so spreads, they say
    'Tis grown high time to thin it in its turn,
With war, or plague, or famine, any way,
    So that civilisation they may learn;[9]
And which in ravage the more loathsome evil is—
Their real lues, or our pseudo-syphilis?

---

[1] loans repayable after a death; that is, when the borrower comes into an inheritance.

[2] Benjamin Charles Perkins advertised his "metallic tractors" as a "cure for all disorders, [such as] Red Noses."

[3] Sir William Congreve (1772–1828) invented the Congreve rocket (an artillery shell) in 1808.

[4] Edward Jenner (1749–1823) introduced vaccination (inoculation with cowpox) as a preventive for smallpox in 1796. The last two lines of this stanza were censored by the publisher in the first edition and replaced by a double row of asterisks.

[5] Giovanni Aldini, the nephew of Luigi Aldini, published *An Account of the Late Improvements in Galvanism ... Containing the Author's Experiments on the Body of a Malefactor Executed at Newgate* in 1803.

[6] The Royal Humane Society for the rescue and resuscitation of the drowning was founded in 1774.

[7] spinning-jennies, introduced to the textile industry as part of the Industrial Revolution.

[8] syphilis. The last two lines of this stanza and the whole of the next were censored by the publisher and replaced by asterisks in the first edition.

[9] Cf. Malthus, *An Essay on the Principle of Population.**

132

This is the patent age of new inventions
    For killing bodies, and for saving souls,[1]
All propagated with the best intentions;
    Sir Humphry Davy's lantern,[2] by which coals
Are safely mined for in the mode he mentions,
    Tombuctoo travels, voyages to the Poles,[3]
Are ways to benefit mankind, as true,
Perhaps, as shooting them at Waterloo.

133

Man's a phenomenon, one knows not what,
    And wonderful beyond all wondrous measure;
'Tis pity though, in this sublime world, that
    Pleasure's a sin, and sometimes sin's a pleasure;
Few mortals know what end they would be at,
    But whether glory, power, or love, or treasure,
The path is through perplexing ways, and when
The goal is gain'd, we die, you know—and then—

134

What then?—I do not know, no more do you—
    And so good night.—Return we to our story:
'Twas in November, when fine days are few,
    And the far mountains wax a little hoary,
And clap a white cape on their mantles blue;
    And the sea dashes round the promontory,
And the loud breaker boils against the rock,
And sober suns must set at five o'clock.

135

'Twas, as the watchmen say, a cloudy night;
    No moon, no stars, the wind was low or loud
By gusts, and many a sparkling hearth was bright
    With the piled wood, round which the family crowd;
There's something cheerful in that sort of light,
    Even as a summer sky's without a cloud:
I'm fond of fire, and crickets, and all that,
A lobster salad, and champaigne, and chat.

136

'Twas midnight—Donna Julia was in bed,
    Sleeping, most probably,—when at her door
Arose a clatter might awake the dead,
    If they had never been awoke before,
And that they have been so we all have read,
    And are to be so, at the least, once more—
The door was fasten'd, but with voice and fist
First knocks were heard, then "Madam—Madam—hist!

137

"For God's sake, Madam—Madam—here's my master,
    With more than half the city at his back—
Was ever heard of such a curst disaster!
    'Tis not my fault—I kept good watch—Alack!
Do, pray undo the bolt a little faster—
    They're on the stair just now, and in a crack
Will all be here; perhaps he yet may fly—
Surely the window's not so *very* high!"

138

By this time Don Alfonso was arrived,
    With torches, friends, and servants in great number;
The major part of them had long been wived,
    And therefore paused not to disturb the slumber
Of any wicked woman, who contrived
    By stealth her husband's temples to encumber:[4]
Examples of this kind are so contagious,
Were *one* not punish'd, *all* would be outrageous.

139

I can't tell how, or why, or what suspicion
    Could enter into Don Alfonso's head;
But for a cavalier of his condition
    It surely was exceedingly ill-bred,
Without a word of previous admonition,
    To hold a levee round his lady's bed,

---

[1] The British and Foreign Bible Society was founded in 1804.
[2] Sir Humphry Davy (1778–1829) invented the safety lantern in 1815.
[3] e.g., James Grey Jackson, *An Account of the Empire of Marocco* (1809); Sir John Ross (1777–1856), *A Voyage of Discovery … for the Purpose of Exploring Baffin's Bay* (1819).
[4] That is, to give him horns, the traditional symbol of a cuckold.

And summon lackeys, arm'd with fire and sword,
To prove himself the thing he most abhorr'd.

140

Poor Donna Julia! starting as from sleep,
    (Mind—that I do not say—she had not slept)
Began at once to scream, and yawn, and weep;
    Her maid Antonia, who was an adept,
Contrived to fling the bed-clothes in a heap,
    As if she had just now from out them crept:
I can't tell why she should take all this trouble
To prove her mistress had been sleeping double.

141

But Julia mistress, and Antonia maid,
    Appear'd like two poor harmless women, who
Of goblins, but still more of men afraid,
    Had thought one man might be deterr'd by two,
And therefore side by side were gently laid,
    Until the hours of absence should run through,
And truant husband should return, and say,
"My dear, I was the first who came away."

142

Now Julia found at length a voice, and cried,
    "In heaven's name, Don Alfonso, what d'ye mean?
Has madness seized you? would that I had died
    Ere such a monster's victim I had been!
What may this midnight violence betide,
    A sudden fit of drunkenness or spleen?
Dare you suspect me, whom the thought would kill?
Search, then, the room!"—Alfonso said, "I will."

143

He search'd, *they* search'd, and rummaged every where,
    Closet and clothes'-press, chest and window-seat,
And found much linen, lace, and several pair
    Of stockings, slippers, brushes, combs, complete,
With other articles of ladies fair,
    To keep them beautiful, or leave them neat:
Arras they prick'd and curtains with their swords,
And wounded several shutters, and some boards.

144

Under the bed they search'd, and there they found—
    No matter what—it was not that they sought;
They open'd windows, gazing if the ground
    Had signs or footmarks, but the earth said nought;
And then they stared each others' faces round:
    'Tis odd, not one of all these seekers thought,
And seems to me almost a sort of blunder,
Of looking *in* the bed as well as under.

145

During this inquisition, Julia's tongue
    Was not asleep—"Yes, search and search," she cried,
"Insult on insult heap, and wrong on wrong!
    It was for this that I became a bride!
For this in silence I have suffer'd long
    A husband like Alfonso at my side;
But now I'll bear no more, nor here remain,
If there be law, or lawyers, in all Spain.

146

"Yes, Don Alfonso! husband now no more,
    If ever you indeed deserved the name,
Is't worthy of your years?—you have threescore,
    Fifty, or sixty—it is all the same—
Is't wise or fitting causeless to explore
    For facts against a virtuous woman's fame?
Ungrateful, perjured, barbarous Don Alfonso,
How dare you think your lady would go on so?

147

"Is it for this I have disdain'd to hold
    The common privileges of my sex?
That I have chosen a confessor so old
    And deaf, that any other it would vex,
And never once he has had cause to scold,
    But found my very innocence perplex
So much, he always doubted I was married—
How sorry you will be when I've miscarried!

148

"Was it for this that no Cortejo[1] ere
    I yet have chosen from out the youth of Seville?
Is it for this I scarce went any where,
    Except to bull-fights, mass, play, rout, and revel?
Is it for this, whate'er my suitors were,
    I favor'd none—nay, was almost uncivil?
Is it for this that General Count O'Reilly,
Who took Algiers,[2] declares I used him vilely?

149

"Did not the Italian Musico Cazzani
    Sing at my heart six months at least in vain?
Did not his countryman, Count Corniani,[3]
    Call me the only virtuous wife in Spain?
Were there not also Russians, English, many?
    The Count Strongstroganoff I put in pain,
And Lord Mount Coffeehouse, the Irish peer,
Who kill'd himself for love (with wine) last year.

150

"Have I not had two bishops at my feet?
    The Duke of Ichar, and Don Fernan Nunez?
And is it thus a faithful wife you treat?
    I wonder in what quarter now the moon is:
I praise your vast forbearance not to beat
    Me also, since the time so opportune is—
Oh, valiant man! with sword drawn and cock'd trigger,
Now, tell me, don't you cut a pretty figure?

151

"Was it for this you took your sudden journey,
    Under pretence of business indispensible
With that sublime of rascals your attorney,
    Whom I see standing there, and looking sensible

Of having play'd the fool? though both I spurn, he
    Deserves the worst, his conduct's less defensible,
Because, no doubt, 'twas for his dirty fee,
And not from any love to you nor me.

152

"If he comes here to take a deposition,
    By all means let the gentleman proceed;
You've made the apartment in a fit condition:—
    There's pen and ink for you, sir, when you need—
Let every thing be noted with precision,
    I would not you for nothing should be feed—
But, as my maid's undrest, pray turn your spies out."
"Oh!" sobb'd Antonia, "I could tear their eyes out."

153

"There is the closet, there the toilet, there
    The antichamber—search them under, over;
There is the sofa, there the great arm-chair,
    The chimney—which would really hold a lover.
I wish to sleep, and beg you will take care
    And make no further noise, till you discover
The secret cavern of this lurking treasure—
And when 'tis found, let me, too, have that pleasure.

154

"And now, Hidalgo! now that you have thrown
    Doubt upon me, confusion over all,
Pray have the courtesy to make it known
    Who is the man you search for? how d'ye call
Him? what's his lineage? let him but be shown—
    I hope he's young and handsome—is he tall?
Tell me—and be assured, that since you stain
My honour thus, it shall not be in vain.

155

"At least, perhaps, he has not sixty years,
    At that age he would be too old for slaughter,
Or for so young a husband's jealous fears—
    (Antonia! let me have a glass of water.)
I am ashamed of having shed these tears,
    They are unworthy of my father's daughter;
My mother dream'd not in my natal hour
That I should fall into a monster's power.

---

[1] the acknowledged lover of a married woman.

[2] "Donna Julia here made a mistake. Count O'Reilly did not take Algiers—but Algiers very nearly took him: he and his army and fleet retreated with great loss, and not much credit, from before that city in the year 17(75)." (L.B.) Alexander O'Reilly (1722–94), Irish-born Spanish general.

[3] "Musico": "musician" (It.). "Cazzani" is from "cazzo" ("penis"); "Corniani," from "cornuto" ("horned"; i.e., cuckolded).

156

"Perhaps 'tis of Antonia you are jealous,
  You saw that she was sleeping by my side
When you broke in upon us with your fellows:
  Look where you please—we've nothing, sir, to hide;
Only another time, I trust, you'll tell us,
  Or for the sake of decency abide
A moment at the door, that we may be
Drest to receive so much good company.

157

"And now, sir, I have done, and say no more;
  The little I have said may serve to show
The guileless heart in silence may grieve o'er
  The wrongs to whose exposure it is slow:—
I leave you to your conscience as before,
  'Twill one day ask you *why* you used me so?
God grant you feel not then the bitterest grief!
Antonia! where's my pocket-handkerchief?"

158

She ceased, and turn'd upon her pillow; pale
  She lay, her dark eyes flashing through their tears,
Like skies that rain and lighten; as a veil,
  Waved and o'ershading her wan cheek, appears
Her streaming hair; the black curls strive, but fail,
  To hide the glossy shoulder, which uprears
Its snow through all;—her soft lips lie apart,
And louder than her breathing beats her heart.

159

The Senhor Don Alfonso stood confused;
  Antonia bustled round the ransack'd room,
And, turning up her nose, with looks abused
  Her master, and his myrmidons, of whom
Not one, except the attorney, was amused;
  He, like Achates, faithful to the tomb,[1]
So there were quarrels, cared not for the cause,
Knowing they must be settled by the laws.

160

With prying snub-nose, and small eyes, he stood,
  Following Antonia's motions here and there,
With much suspicion in his attitude;
  For reputations he had little care;
So that a suit or action were made good,
  Small pity had he for the young and fair,
And ne'er believed in negatives, till these
Were proved by competent false witnesses.

161

But Don Alfonso stood with downcast looks,
  And, truth to say, he made a foolish figure;
When, after searching in five hundred nooks,
  And treating a young wife with so much rigour,
He gain'd no point, except some self-rebukes,
  Added to those his lady with such vigour
Had pour'd upon him for the last half-hour,
Quick, thick, and heavy—as a thunder-shower.

162

At first he tried to hammer an excuse,
  To which the sole reply was tears and sobs,
And indications of hysterics, whose
  Prologue is always certain throes, and throbs,
Gasps, and whatever else the owners choose:—
  Alfonso saw his wife, and thought of Job's;[2]
He saw too, in perspective, her relations,
And then he tried to muster all his patience.

163

He stood in act to speak, or rather stammer,
  But sage Antonia cut him short before
The anvil of his speech received the hammer,
  With "Pray, sir, leave the room, and say no more,
Or madam dies."—Alfonso mutter'd, "D—n her,"
  But nothing else, the time of words was o'er;
He cast a rueful look or two, and did,
He knew not wherefore, that which he was bid.

---

[1] Æneas's companion, proverbial for faithfulness.

[2] Cf. Job 2.9–10.

164

1305 With him retired his "*posse comitatus*,"[1]
      The attorney last, who linger'd near the door,
Reluctantly, still tarrying there as late as
      Antonia let him—not a little sore
At this most strange and unexplain'd "*hiatus*"
1310   In Don Alfonso's facts, which just now wore
An awkward look; as he revolved the case,
The door was fasten'd in his legal face.

165

No sooner was it bolted, than—Oh shame!
      Oh sin! Oh sorrow! and Oh womankind!
1315 How can you do such things and keep your fame,
      Unless this world, and t'other too, be blind?
Nothing so dear as an unfilch'd good name![2]
      But to proceed—for there is more behind:
With much heart-felt reluctance be it said,
1320 Young Juan slipp'd, half-smother'd, from the bed.

166

He had been hid—I don't pretend to say
      How, nor can I indeed describe the where—
Young, slender, and pack'd easily, he lay,
      No doubt, in little compass, round or square;
1325 But pity him I neither must nor may
      His suffocation by that pretty pair;
'Twere better, sure, to die so, than be shut
With maudlin Clarence in his Malmsey butt.[3]

167

And, secondly, I pity not, because
1330   He had no business to commit a sin,
Forbid by heavenly, fined by human laws,
      At least 'twas rather early to begin;
But at sixteen the conscience rarely gnaws
      So much as when we call our old debts in
1335 At sixty years, and draw the accompts of evil,
And find a deuced balance with the devil.

168

Of his position I can give no notion:
      'Tis written in the Hebrew Chronicle,[4]
How the physicians, leaving pill and potion,
1340   Prescribed, by way of blister, a young belle,
When old King David's blood grew dull in motion,
      And that the medicine answer'd very well;
Perhaps 'twas in a different way applied,
      For David lived, but Juan nearly died.

169

1345 What's to be done? Alfonso will be back
      The moment he has sent his fools away.
Antonia's skill was put upon the rack,
      But no device could be brought into play—
And how to parry the renew'd attack?
1350   Besides, it wanted but few hours of day:
Antonia puzzled; Julia did not speak,
But press'd her bloodless lip to Juan's cheek.

170

He turn'd his lip to hers, and with his hand
      Call'd back the tangles of her wandering hair;
1355 Even then their love they could not all command,
      And half forgot their danger and despair:
Antonia's patience now was at a stand—
      "Come, come, 'tis no time now for fooling there,"
She whisper'd, in great wrath—"I must deposit
1360 This pretty gentleman within the closet.

171

"Pray, keep your nonsense for some luckier night—
      Who can have put my master in this mood?
What will become on't—I'm in such a fright,
      The devil's in the urchin, and no good—
1365 Is this a time for giggling? this a plight?
      Why, don't you know that it may end in blood?
You'll lose your life, and I shall lose my place,
My mistress all, for that half-girlish face.

172

"Had it but been for a stout cavalier
1370   Of twenty-five or thirty—(Come, make haste)

---

[1] "the power of the county" (L.), a group of deputies.
[2] Cf. Shakespeare, *Othello* 3.3.159–61.
[3] See Shakespeare, *Richard III* 1.4.265.
[4] 1 Kings 1.1–4.

But for a child, what piece of work is here![1]
    I really, madam, wonder at your taste—
(Come, sir, get in)—my master must be near.
    There, for the present, at the least he's fast,
And, if we can but till the morning keep
    Our counsel—(Juan, mind, you must not sleep.)"

173

Now, Don Alfonso entering, but alone,
    Closed the oration of the trusty maid:
She loiter'd, and he told her to be gone,
    An order somewhat sullenly obey'd;
However, present remedy was none,
    And no great good seem'd answer'd if she staid:
Regarding both with slow and sidelong view,
She snuff'd the candle, curtsied, and withdrew.

174

Alfonso paused a minute—then begun
    Some strange excuses for his late proceeding;
He would not justify what he had done,
    To say the best, it was extreme ill-breeding;
But there were ample reasons for it, none
    Of which he specified in this his pleading:
His speech was a fine sample, on the whole,
Of rhetoric, which the learn'd call "*rigmarole*."

175

Julia said nought; though all the while there rose
    A ready answer, which at once enables
A matron, who her husband's foible knows,
    By a few timely words to turn the tables,
Which if it does not silence still must pose,
    Even if it should comprise a pack of fables;
'Tis to retort with firmness, and when he
Suspects with *one*, do you reproach with *three*.

176

Julia, in fact, had tolerable grounds,
    Alfonso's loves with Inez were well known;
But whether 'twas that one's own guilt confounds,
    But that can't be, as has been often shown,
A lady with apologies abounds;
    It might be that her silence sprang alone
From delicacy to Don Juan's ear,
To whom she knew his mother's fame was dear.

177

There might be one more motive, which makes two,
    Alfonso ne'er to Juan had alluded,
Mention'd his jealousy, but never who
    Had been the happy lover, he concluded,
Conceal'd amongst his premises; 'tis true,
    His mind the more o'er this its mystery brooded;
To speak of Inez now were, one may say,
Like throwing Juan in Alfonso's way.

178

A hint, in tender cases, is enough;
    Silence is best, besides there is a *tact*
(That modern phrase appears to me sad stuff,
    But it will serve to keep my verse compact)
Which keeps, when push'd by questions rather rough,
    A lady always distant from the fact—
The charming creatures lie with such a grace,
There's nothing so becoming to the face.

179

They blush, and we believe them; at least I
    Have always done so; 'tis of no great use,
In any case, attempting a reply,
    For then their eloquence grows quite profuse;
And when at length they're out of breath, they sigh,
    And cast their languid eyes down, and let loose
A tear or two, and then we make it up;
And then—and then—and then—sit down and sup.

180

Alfonso closed his speech, and begg'd her pardon,
    Which Julia half withheld, and then half granted,
And laid conditions, he thought, very hard on,
    Denying several little things he wanted:
He stood like Adam lingering near his garden,[2]
    With useless penitence perplex'd and haunted,
Beseeching she no further would refuse,
When, lo! he stumbled o'er a pair of shoes.

---

[1] Cf. Shakespeare, *Hamlet* 2.2.300.

[2] Cf. Milton, *Paradise Lost* 12.638.

181

A pair of shoes!—what then? not much, if they
    Are such as fit with lady's feet, but these
(No one can tell how much I grieve to say)
    Were masculine; to see them, and to seize,
Was but a moment's act.—Ah! Well-a-day!
    My teeth begin to chatter, my veins freeze—
Alfonso first examined well their fashion,
And then flew out into another passion.

182

He left the room for his relinquish'd sword,
    And Julia instant to the closet flew.
"Fly, Juan, fly! for heaven's sake—not a word—
    The door is open—you may yet slip through
The passage you so often have explored—
    Here is the garden-key—Fly—fly—Adieu!
Haste—haste!—I hear Alfonso's hurrying feet—
Day has not broke—there's no one in the street."

183

None can say that this was not good advice,
    The only mischief was, it came too late;
Of all experience 'tis the usual price,
    A sort of income-tax laid on by fate:
Juan had reach'd the room-door in a trice,
    And might have done so by the garden-gate,
But met Alfonso in his dressing-gown,
Who threaten'd death—so Juan knock'd him down.

184

Dire was the scuffle, and out went the light,
    Antonia cried out "Rape!" and Julia "Fire!"
But not a servant stirr'd to aid the fight.
    Alfonso, pommell'd to his heart's desire,
Swore lustily he'd be revenged this night;
    And Juan, too, blasphemed an octave higher,
His blood was up; though young, he was a Tartar,
And not at all disposed to prove a martyr.

185

Alfonso's sword had dropp'd ere he could draw it,
    And they continued battling hand to hand,
For Juan very luckily ne'er saw it;
    His temper not being under great command,
If at that moment he had chanced to claw it,
    Alfonso's days had not been in the land
Much longer.—Think of husbands', lovers' lives!
And how ye may be doubly widows—wives!

186

Alfonso grappled to detain the foe,
    And Juan throttled him to get away,
And blood ('twas from the nose) began to flow;
    At last, as they more faintly wrestling lay,
Juan contrived to give an awkward blow,
    And then his only garment quite gave way;
He fled, like Joseph, leaving it; but there,
I doubt, all likeness ends between the pair.[1]

187

Lights came at length, and men, and maids, who found
    An awkward spectacle their eyes before;
Antonia in hysterics, Julia swoon'd,
    Alfonso leaning, breathless, by the door;
Some half-torn drapery scatter'd on the ground,
    Some blood, and several footsteps, but no more:
Juan the gate gain'd, turn'd the key about,
And liking not the inside, lock'd the out.

188

Here ends this canto.—Need I sing, or say,
    How Juan, naked, favour'd by the night,
Who favours what she should not, found his way,
    And reach'd his home in an unseemly plight?
The pleasant scandal which arose next day,
    The nine days' wonder which was brought to light,
And how Alfonso sued for a divorce,
Were in the English newspapers, of course.

189

If you would like to see the whole proceedings,
    The depositions, and the cause at full,
The names of all the witnesses, the pleadings
    Of counsel to nonsuit, or to annul,

---

[1] See the story of Joseph and Potiphar's wife, Genesis 39.7–20.

There's more than one edition, and the readings
    Are various, but they none of them are dull,
The best is that in short-hand ta'en by Gurney,[1]
Who to Madrid on purpose made a journey.

190

But Donna Inez, to divert the train
    Of one of the most circulating scandals
That had for centuries been known in Spain,
    At least since the retirement of the Vandals,
First vow'd (and never had she vow'd in vain)
    To Virgin Mary several pounds of candles;
And then, by the advice of some old ladies,
She sent her son to be shipp'd off from Cadiz.

191

She had resolved that he should travel through
    All European climes, by land or sea,
To mend his former morals, and get new,
    Especially in France and Italy,
(At least this is the thing most people do.)
    Julia was sent into a convent; she
Grieved, but, perhaps, her feelings may be better
Shown in the following copy of her letter:

192

"They tell me 'tis decided; you depart:
    'Tis wise—'tis well, but not the less a pain;
I have no further claim on your young heart,
    Mine is the victim, and would be again;
To love too much has been the only art
    I used;—I write in haste, and if a stain
Be on this sheet, 'tis not what it appears,
My eyeballs burn and throb, but have no tears.

193

"I loved, I love you, for this love have lost
    State, station, heaven, mankind's, my own esteem,
And yet can not regret what it hath cost,
    So dear is still the memory of that dream;
Yet, if I name my guilt, 'tis not to boast,
    None can deem harshlier of me than I deem:
I trace this scrawl because I cannot rest—
I've nothing to reproach, or to request.

194

"Man's love is of man's life a thing apart,
    'Tis woman's whole existence; man may range
The court, camp, church, the vessel, and the mart;
    Sword, gown, gain, glory, offer in exchange
Pride, fame, ambition, to fill up his heart,
    And few there are whom these cannot estrange;
Men have all these resources, we but one,
To love again, and be again undone.

195

"You will proceed in pleasure, and in pride,
    Beloved and loving many; all is o'er
For me on earth, except some years to hide
    My shame and sorrow deep in my heart's core;
These I could bear, but cannot cast aside
    The passion which still rages as before,
And so farewell—forgive me, love me—No,
That word is idle now—but let it go.

196

"My breast has been all weakness, is so yet;
    But still I think I can collect my mind;
My blood still rushes where my spirit's set,
    As roll the waves before the settled wind;
My heart is feminine, nor can forget—
    To all, except one image, madly blind;
So shakes the needle, and so stands the pole,
As vibrates my fond heart to my fix'd soul.

197

"I have no more to say, but linger still,
    And dare not set my seal upon this sheet,
And yet I may as well the task fulfil,
    My misery can scarce be more complete:
I had not lived till now, could sorrow kill;
    Death shuns the wretch who fain the blow would meet,
And I must even survive this last adieu,
And bear with life, to love and pray for you!"

---

[1] William Brodie Gurney (1777–1855), official shorthand writer to the Houses of Parliament, also reported several notorious trials.

198

This note was written upon gilt-edged paper
    With a neat little crow-quill, slight and new:
Her small white hand could hardly reach the taper,
    It trembled as magnetic needles do,
And yet she did not let one tear escape her;
    The seal a sun-flower; "*Elle vous suit partout*,"[1]
The motto, cut upon a white cornelian;
The wax was superfine, its hue vermilion.

199

This was Don Juan's earliest scrape; but whether
    I shall proceed with his adventures is
Dependant on the public altogether;
    We'll see, however, what they say to this,
Their favour in an author's cap's a feather,
    And no great mischief's done by their caprice;
And if their approbation we experience,
Perhaps they'll have some more about a year hence.

200

My poem's epic, and is meant to be
    Divided in twelve books; each book containing,
With love, and war, a heavy gale at sea,
    A list of ships, and captains, and kings reigning,
New characters; the episodes are three:
    A panorama view of hell's in training,
After the style of Virgil and of Homer,
So that my name of Epic's no misnomer.

201

All these things will be specified in time,
    With strict regard to Aristotle's rules,
The *Vade Mecum*[2] of the true sublime,
    Which makes so many poets, and some fools;
Prose poets like blank-verse, I'm fond of rhyme,
    Good workmen never quarrel with their tools;
I've got new mythological machinery,
And very handsome supernatural scenery.

202

There's only one slight difference between
    Me and my epic brethren gone before,
And here the advantage is my own, I ween;
    (Not that I have not several merits more,
But this will more peculiarly be seen)
    They so embellish, that 'tis quite a bore
Their labyrinth of fables to thread through,
Whereas this story's actually true.

203

If any person doubt it, I appeal
    To history, tradition, and to facts,
To newspapers, whose truth all know and feel,
    To plays in five, and operas in three acts;
All these confirm my statement a good deal,
    But that which more completely faith exacts
Is, that myself, and several now in Seville,
Saw Juan's last elopement with the devil.

204

If ever I should condescend to prose,
    I'll write poetical commandments, which
Shall supersede beyond all doubt all those
    That went before; in these I shall enrich
My text with many things that no one knows,
    And carry precept to the highest pitch:
I'll call the work "Longinus o'er a Bottle,
Or, Every Poet his *own* Aristotle."[3]

205

Thou shalt believe in Milton, Dryden, Pope;[4]
    Thou shalt not set up Wordsworth, Coleridge, Southey;
Because the first is crazed beyond all hope,
    The second drunk, the third so quaint and mouthey:
With Crabbe it may be difficult to cope,

---

[1] "She follows you everywhere" (Fr.). Byron himself had a seal with this motto.

[2] handbook.

[3] Longinus, *On the Sublime*, and Aristotle, *Poetics*: two of the most prestigious works of classical literary theory.

[4] Cf. Exodus 20.3–17. Byron's parody of the Ten Commandments caused great offense.

And Campbell's Hippocrene[1] is somewhat
    drouthy:
Thou shalt not steal from Samuel Rogers, nor
Commit—flirtation with the muse of Moore.

206

Thou shalt not covet Mr. Sotheby's Muse,[2]
    His Pegasus, nor any thing that's his;
Thou shalt not bear false witness like "the Blues,"[3]
    (There's one, at least, is very fond of this);
Thou shalt not write, in short, but what I choose:
    This is true criticism, and you may kiss—
Exactly as you please, or not, the rod,
But if you don't, I'll lay it on, by G—d!

207

If any person should presume to assert
    This story is not moral, first, I pray,
That they will not cry out before they're hurt,
    Then that they'll read it o'er again, and say,
(But, doubtless, nobody will be so pert)
    That this is not a moral tale, though gay;
Besides, in canto twelfth, I mean to show
    The very place where wicked people go.

208

If, after all, there should be some so blind
    To their own good this warning to despise,
Led by some tortuosity of mind,
    Not to believe my verse and their own eyes,
And cry that they "the moral cannot find,"
    I tell him, if a clergyman, he lies;
Should captains the remark or critics make,
They also lie too—under a mistake.

209

The public approbation I expect,
    And beg they'll take my word about the moral,
Which I with their amusement will connect,
    (So children cutting teeth receive a coral);
Meantime, they'll doubtless please to recollect
    My epical pretensions to the laurel:
For fear some prudish readers should grow skittish,
I've bribed my grandmother's review—the British.[4]

210

I sent it in a letter to the editor,
    Who thank'd me duly by return of post—
I'm for a handsome article his creditor;
    Yet if my gentle Muse he please to roast,
And break a promise after having made it her,
    Denying the receipt of what it cost,
And smear his page with gall instead of honey,
All I can say is—that he had the money.

211

I think that with this holy new alliance
    I may ensure the public, and defy
All other magazines of art or science,
    Daily, or monthly, or three monthly; I
Have not essay'd to multiply their clients,
    Because they tell me 'twere in vain to try,
And that the Edinburgh Review and Quarterly
Treat a dissenting author very martyrly.

212

"*Non ego hoc ferrem calida juventa
    Consule Planco*,"[5] Horace said, and so
Say I; by which quotation there is meant a
    Hint that some six or seven good years ago
(Long ere I dreamt of dating from the Brenta)[6]
    I was most ready to return a blow,
And would not brook at all this sort of thing
In my hot youth—when George the Third was King.

---

[1] a fountain sacred to the Muses, which started flowing when the winged horse Pegasus (see line 1642) struck the ground with his hoof.

[2] William Sotheby (1757–1833), poet.

[3] bluestockings; i.e., intellectual women. The reference may be to Lady Byron.

[4] William Roberts, editor of the *British Review*, took this accusation seriously and contradicted it in his review of *Don Juan*, prompting Byron to write "Letter to the Editor of my Grandmother's Review" (1822).

[5] "I would not have borne with this in the heat of my youth, when Plancus was consul." Horace, *Odes* 3.14.27–28.

[6] river flowing into the Adriatic at Venice.

213

But now at thirty years my hair is gray—
    (I wonder what it will be like at forty?
I thought of a peruke the other day)
    My heart is not much greener; and, in short, I
Have squander'd my whole summer while 'twas May,
    And feel no more the spirit to retort; I
Have spent my life, both interest and principal,
And deem not, what I deem'd, my soul invincible.

214

No more—no more—Oh! never more on me
    The freshness of the heart can fall like dew,
Which out of all the lovely things we see
    Extracts emotions beautiful and new,
Hived in our bosoms like the bag o' the bee:
    Think'st thou the honey with those objects grew?
Alas! 'twas not in them, but in thy power
To double even the sweetness of a flower.

215

No more—no more—Oh! never more, my heart,
    Canst thou be my sole world, my universe!
Once all in all, but now a thing apart,
    Thou canst not be my blessing or my curse:
The illusion's gone for ever, and thou art
    Insensible, I trust, but none the worse,
And in thy stead I've got a deal of judgment,
Though heaven knows how it ever found a lodgement.

216

My days of love are over, me no more[1]
    The charms of maid, wife, and still less of widow,
Can make the fool of which they made before,
    In short, I must not lead the life I did do;
The credulous hope of mutual minds is o'er,
    The copious use of claret is forbid too,
So for a good old-gentlemanly vice,
I think I must take up with avarice.

217

Ambition was my idol, which was broken
    Before the shrines of Sorrow and of Pleasure;
And the two last have left me many a token
    O'er which reflection may be made at leisure:
Now, like Friar Bacon's brazen head, I've spoken,
    "Time is, Time was, Time's past,"[2]—a chymic treasure
Is glittering youth, which I have spent betimes—
My heart in passion, and my head on rhymes.

218

What is the end of Fame? 'tis but to fill
    A certain portion of uncertain paper:
Some liken it to climbing up a hill,
    Whose summit, like all hills, is lost in vapour;
For this men write, speak, preach, and heroes kill,
    And bards burn what they call their "midnight taper,"
To have, when the original is dust,
A name, a wretched picture, and worse bust.[3]

219

What are the hopes of man? old Egypt's King
    Cheops erected the first pyramid
And largest, thinking it was just the thing
    To keep his memory whole, and mummy hid;
But somebody or other rummaging,
    Burglariously broke his coffin's lid:
Let not a monument give you or me hopes,
Since not a pinch of dust remains of Cheops.[4]

220

But I, being fond of true philosophy,
    Say very often to myself, "Alas!

---

[1] "'Me nec femina, nec puer
Jam, nec spes animi credula mutui,
    Nec certare juvat mero;
Nec vincire novis tempora floribus.'" (L.B.)
Horace, *Odes* 4.1.30: "Now neither a woman nor a boy delights me, nor confident hope of love returned, nor drinking bouts, nor binding my temples with fresh flowers" (trans. C.E. Bennett).

[2] Robert Greene, *Friar Bacon and Friar Bungay* (1594) 11.59.

[3] Bertel Thorwaldsen made a bust of Byron in 1817. Byron didn't like it (*Letters and Journals* 9: 213).

[4] the builder of the Great Pyramid. Cf. *Quarterly Review* 19 (1818): 203.

All things that have been born were born to die,
    And flesh (which Death mows down to hay) is grass;[1]
You've pass'd your youth not so unpleasantly,
    And if you had it o'er again—'twould pass—
So thank your stars that matters are no worse,
And read your Bible, sir, and mind your purse."

221

But for the present, gentle reader! and
    Still gentler purchaser! the bard—that's I—
Must, with permission, shake you by the hand,
    And so your humble servant, and good bye!
We meet again, if we should understand
    Each other; and if not, I shall not try
Your patience further than by this short sample—
'Twere well if others follow'd my example.

222

"Go, little book, from this my solitude!
    I cast thee on the waters—go thy ways!
And if, as I believe, thy vein be good,
    The world will find thee after many days."
When Southey's read, and Wordsworth understood,
    I can't help putting in my claim to praise—
The four first rhymes are Southey's[2] every line:
For God's sake, reader! take them not for mine.

CANTO 2

1

Oh ye! who teach the ingenuous youth of nations,
    Holland, France, England, Germany, or Spain,
I pray ye flog them upon all occasions,
    It mends their morals; never mind the pain:
The best of mothers and of educations
    In Juan's case were but employ'd in vain,
Since in a way, that's rather of the oddest, he
Became divested of his native modesty.

2

Had he but been placed at a public school,
    In the third form, or even in the fourth,
His daily task had kept his fancy cool,
    At least, had he been nurtured in the north;
Spain may prove an exception to the rule,
    But then exceptions always prove its worth—
A lad of sixteen causing a divorce
Puzzled his tutors very much, of course.

3

I can't say that it puzzles me at all,
    If all things be consider'd: first, there was
His lady-mother, mathematical,
    A—never mind; his tutor, an old ass;
A pretty woman—(that's quite natural,
    Or else the thing had hardly come to pass);
A husband rather old, not much in unity
With his young wife—a time, and opportunity.

4

Well—well, the world must turn upon its axis,
    And all mankind turn with it, heads or tails,
And live and die, make love and pay our taxes,
    And as the veering wind shifts, shift our sails;
The king commands us, and the doctor quacks us,
    The priest instructs, and so our life exhales,
A little breath, love, wine, ambition, fame,
Fighting, devotion, dust,—perhaps a name.

5

I said that Juan had been sent to Cadiz—
    A pretty town, I recollect it well—
'Tis there the mart of the colonial trade is,
    (Or was, before Peru learn'd to rebel)[3]
And such sweet girls—I mean, such graceful ladies,
    Their very walk would make your bosom swell;
I can't describe it, though so much it strike,
Nor liken it—I never saw the like:

---

[1] Cf. Isaiah 40.6.

[2] Southey,* *The Lay of the Laureate* (1816), "L'Envoy."

[3] Peru had rebelled against Spain in 1813 and would finally win its independence in 1824.

6

An Arab horse, a stately stag, a barb
    New broke, a camelopard, a gazelle,
No—none of these will do;—and then their garb!
    Their veil and petticoat—Alas! to dwell
Upon such things would very near absorb
    A canto—then their feet and ancles—well,
Thank Heaven I've got no metaphor quite ready,
(And so, my sober Muse—come, let's be steady—

7

Chaste Muse!—well, if you must, you must)—the veil
    Thrown back a moment with the glancing hand,
While the o'erpowering eye, that turns you pale,
    Flashes into the heart:—All sunny land
Of love! when I forget you, may I fail
    To—say my prayers[1]—but never was there plann'd
A dress through which the eyes give such a volley,
Excepting the Venetian Fazzioli.[2]

8

But to our tale: the Donna Inez sent
    Her son to Cadiz only to embark;
To stay there had not answer'd her intent,
    But why?—we leave the reader in the dark—
'Twas for a voyage that the young man was meant,
    As if a Spanish ship were Noah's ark,
To wean him from the wickedness of earth,
And send him like a dove of promise forth.

9

Don Juan bade his valet pack his things
    According to direction, then received
A lecture and some money: for four springs
    He was to travel; and though Inez grieved,
(As every kind of parting has its stings)
    She hoped he would improve—perhaps believed:
A letter, too, she gave (he never read it)
Of good advice—and two or three of credit.

10

In the mean time, to pass her hours away,
    Brave Inez now set up a Sunday school
For naughty children, who would rather play
    (Like truant rogues) the devil, or the fool;
Infants of three years old were taught that day,
    Dunces were whipt, or set upon a stool:
The great success of Juan's education
Spurr'd her to teach another generation.

11

Juan embark'd—the ship got under way,
    The wind was fair, the water passing rough;
A devil of a sea rolls in that Bay,
    As I, who've cross'd it oft, know well enough;
And, standing upon deck, the dashing spray
    Flies in one's face, and makes it weather-tough:
And there he stood to take, and take again,
His first—perhaps his last—farewell of Spain.

12

I can't but say it is an awkward sight
    To see one's native land receding through
The growing waters; it unmans one quite,
    Especially when life is rather new:
I recollect Great Britain's coast looks white,
    But almost every other country's blue,
When gazing on them, mystified by distance,
We enter on our nautical existence.

13

So Juan stood, bewilder'd, on the deck:
    The wind sung, cordage strain'd, and sailors swore,
And the ship creak'd, the town became a speck,
    From which away so fair and fast they bore.
The best of remedies is a beef-steak
    Against sea-sickness; try it, sir, before
You sneer, and I assure you this is true,
For I have found it answer—so may you.

14

Don Juan stood, and, gazing from the stern,
    Beheld his native Spain receding far:

---

[1] Cf. Psalm 137.5.

[2] "*Fazzioli*—literally, little handkerchiefs—the veils most availing of St. Mark." (L.B.)

George Gordon, Lord Byron

First partings form a lesson hard to learn,
    Even nations feel this when they go to war;
There is a sort of unexprest concern,
    A kind of shock that sets one's heart ajar:
At leaving even the most unpleasant people
And places, one keeps looking at the steeple.

15

But Juan had got many things to leave,
    His mother, and a mistress, and no wife,
So that he had much better cause to grieve
    Than many persons more advanced in life;
And if we now and then a sigh must heave
    At quitting even those we quit in strife,
No doubt we weep for those the heart endears—
That is, till deeper griefs congeal our tears.

16

So Juan wept, as wept the captive Jews
    By Babel's waters, still remembering Sion:[1]
I'd weep, but mine is not a weeping Muse,
    And such light griefs are not a thing to die on;
Young men should travel, if but to amuse
    Themselves; and the next time their servants tie on
Behind their carriages their new portmanteau,
Perhaps it may be lined with this my canto.

17

And Juan wept, and much he sigh'd and thought,
    While his salt tears dropp'd into the salt sea,
"Sweets to the sweet"; (I like so much to quote;
    You must excuse this extract, 'tis where she,
The Queen of Denmark, for Ophelia brought
    Flowers to the grave);[2] and, sobbing often, he
Reflected on his present situation,
And seriously resolved on reformation.

18

"Farewell, my Spain! a long farewell!" he cried,
    "Perhaps I may revisit thee no more,
But die, as many an exiled heart hath died,
    Of its own thirst to see again thy shore:
Farewell, where Guadalquivir's waters glide!
    Farewell, my mother! and, since all is o'er,
Farewell, too, dearest Julia!—(Here he drew
Her letter out again, and read it through.)

19

"And, oh! if e'er I should forget, I swear—
    But that's impossible, and cannot be—
Sooner shall this blue ocean melt to air,
    Sooner shall earth resolve itself to sea,
Than I resign thine image, Oh, my fair!
    Or think of any thing excepting thee;
A mind diseased no remedy can physic[3]—
(Here the ship gave a lurch, and he grew sea-sick.)

20

"Sooner shall heaven kiss earth—(here he fell sicker)
    Oh, Julia! what is every other woe?—
(For God's sake let me have a glass of liquor—
    Pedro, Battista, help me down below.)
Julia, my love!—(you rascal, Pedro, quicker)—
    Oh Julia!—(this curst vessel pitches so)—
Beloved Julia, hear me still beseeching!"
(Here he grew inarticulate with retching.)

21

He felt that chilling heaviness of heart,
    Or rather stomach, which, alas! attends,
Beyond the best apothecary's art,
    The loss of love, the treachery of friends,
Or death of those we dote on, when a part
    Of us dies with them as each fond hope ends:
No doubt he would have been much more pathetic,
But the sea acted as a strong emetic.

22

Love's a capricious power; I've known it hold
    Out through a fever caused by its own heat,
But be much puzzled by a cough and cold,
    And find a quinsy very hard to treat;

---

[1] Psalm 137.1.
[2] Shakespeare, *Hamlet* 5.1.230.
[3] Cf. Shakespeare, *Macbeth* 5.3.40.

Against all noble maladies he's bold,
    But vulgar illnesses don't like to meet,
175 Nor that a sneeze should interrupt his sigh,
Nor inflammations redden his blind eye.

23

But worst of all is nausea, or a pain
    About the lower region of the bowels;
Love, who heroically breathes a vein,
180   Shrinks from the application of hot towels,
And purgatives are dangerous to his reign,
    Sea-sickness death: his love was perfect, how else
Could Juan's passion, while the billows roar,
Resist his stomach, ne'er at sea before?

24

185 The ship, call'd the most holy "Trinidada,"
    Was steering duly for the port Leghorn;
For there the Spanish family Moncada
    Were settled long ere Juan's sire was born:
They were relations, and for them he had a
190   Letter of introduction, which the morn
Of his departure had been sent him by
His Spanish friends for those in Italy.

25

His suite consisted of three servants and
    A tutor, the licentiate Pedrillo,
195 Who several languages did understand,
    But now lay sick and speechless on his pillow,
And, rocking in his hammock, long'd for land,
    His headache being increased by every billow;
And the waves oozing through the port-hole made
200 His berth a little damp, and him afraid.

26

'Twas not without some reason, for the wind
    Increased at night, until it blew a gale;
And though 'twas not much to a naval mind,
    Some landsmen would have look'd a little pale,
205 For sailors are, in fact, a different kind:
    At sunset they began to take in sail,
For the sky show'd it would come on to blow,
And carry away, perhaps, a mast or so.

27

At one o'clock the wind with sudden shift
210   Threw the ship right into the trough of the sea,
Which struck her aft, and made an awkward rift,
    Started the stern-post, also shatter'd the
Whole of her stern-frame, and, ere she could lift
    Herself from out her present jeopardy,
215 The rudder tore away: 'twas time to sound
The pumps, and there were four feet water found.[1]

28

One gang of people instantly was put
    Upon the pumps, and the remainder set
To get up part of the cargo, and what not,
220   But they could not come at the leak as yet;
At last they did get at it really, but
    Still their salvation was an even bet:
The water rush'd through in a way quite puzzling,
While they thrust sheets, shirts, jackets, bales of muslin,

29

225 Into the opening; but all such ingredients
    Would have been vain, and they must have gone down,
Despite of all their efforts and expedients,
    But for the pumps: I'm glad to make them known
To all the brother tars who may have need hence,
230   For fifty tons of water were upthrown
By them per hour, and they had all been undone,
But for the maker, Mr. Mann, of London.

30

As day advanced the weather seem'd to abate,
    And then the leak they reckon'd to reduce,
235 And keep the ship afloat, though three feet yet

---

[1] Byron was proud of the verisimilitude of his shipwreck, for which he drew many details from William Bligh, *A Narrative of the Mutiny of the Bounty* (1790); *The Narrative of the Honourable John Byron* (his grandfather; 1768); Sir John G. Dalyell, *Shipwrecks and Disasters at Sea* (1812); and Philip Aubin, *Remarkable Shipwrecks* (1813). See E.H. Coleridge, ed., *The Works of Lord Byron*, vol. 6 (1903); and T.G. Steffan and W.W. Pratt, eds., *Byron's Don Juan: A Variorum Edition* (1957) 4: 61–72.

Kept two hand and one chain-pump still in use.
The wind blew fresh again: as it grew late
  A squall came on, and while some guns broke
    loose,
A gust—which all descriptive power transcends—
Laid with one blast the ship on her beam ends.

31

There she lay motionless, and seem'd upset;
  The water left the hold, and wash'd the decks,
And made a scene men do not soon forget;
  For they remember battles, fires, and wrecks,
Or any other thing that brings regret,
  Or breaks their hopes, or hearts, or heads, or necks:
Thus drownings are much talk'd of by the divers
And swimmers who may chance to be survivors.

32

Immediately the masts were cut away,
  Both main and mizen; first the mizen went,
The main-mast follow'd: but the ship still lay
  Like a mere log, and baffled our intent.
Foremast and bowsprit were cut down, and they
  Eased her at last (although we never meant
To part with all till every hope was blighted),
And then with violence the old ship righted.

33

It may be easily supposed, while this
  Was going on, some people were unquiet,
That passengers would find it much amiss
  To lose their lives as well as spoil their diet;
That even the able seaman, deeming his
  Days nearly o'er, might be disposed to riot,
As upon such occasions tars will ask
For grog, and sometimes drink rum from the cask.

34

There's nought, no doubt, so much the spirit calms
  As rum and true religion; thus it was,
Some plunder'd, some drank spirits, some sung psalms,
  The high wind made the treble, and as bass
The hoarse harsh waves kept time; fright cured the
  qualms
Of all the luckless landsmen's sea-sick maws:
  Strange sounds of wailing, blasphemy, devotion,
Clamour'd in chorus to the roaring ocean.

35

Perhaps more mischief had been done, but for
  Our Juan, who, with sense beyond his years,
Got to the spirit-room, and stood before
  It with a pair of pistols; and their fears,
As if Death were more dreadful by his door
  Of fire than water, spite of oaths and tears,
Kept still aloof the crew, who, ere they sunk,
Thought it would be becoming to die drunk.

36

"Give us more grog," they cried, "for it will be
  All one an hour hence." Juan answer'd, "No!
'Tis true that death awaits both you and me,
  But let us die like men, not sink below
Like brutes";—and thus his dangerous post kept he,
  And none liked to anticipate the blow;
And even Pedrillo, his most reverend tutor,
Was for some rum a disappointed suitor.

37

The good old gentleman was quite aghast,
  And made a loud and pious lamentation;
Repented all his sins, and made a last
  Irrevocable vow of reformation;
Nothing should tempt him more (this peril past)
  To quit his academic occupation,
In cloisters of the classic Salamanca,[1]
To follow Juan's wake, like Sancho Panca.[2]

38

But now there came a flash of hope once more;
  Day broke, and the wind lull'd: the masts were
    gone,
The leak increased; shoals round her, but no shore,
  The vessel swam, yet still she held her own.
They tried the pumps again, and though before

---

[1] Spanish university.

[2] Don Quixote's page, in the novel by Cervantes.

Their desperate efforts seem'd all useless grown,
A glimpse of sunshine set some hands to bale—
The stronger pump'd, the weaker thrumm'd a sail.

39

305 Under the vessel's keel the sail was past,
And for the moment it had some effect;
But with a leak, and not a stick of mast,
Nor rag of canvas, what could they expect?
But still 'tis best to struggle to the last,
310 'Tis never too late to be wholly wreck'd:
And though 'tis true that man can only die once,
'Tis not so pleasant in the Gulf of Lyons.

40

There winds and waves had hurl'd them, and from thence,
Without their will, they carried them away;
315 For they were forced with steering to dispense,
And never had as yet a quiet day
On which they might repose, or even commence
A jurymast or rudder, or could say
The ship would swim an hour, which, by good luck,
320 Still swam—though not exactly like a duck.

41

The wind, in fact, perhaps was rather less,
But the ship labour'd so, they scarce could hope
To weather out much longer; the distress
Was also great with which they had to cope
325 For want of water, and their solid mess
Was scant enough: in vain the telescope
Was used—nor sail nor shore appear'd in sight,
Nought but the heavy sea, and coming night.

42

Again the weather threaten'd,—again blew
330 A gale, and in the fore and after hold
Water appear'd; yet, though the people knew
All this, the most were patient, and some bold,
Until the chains and leathers were worn through
Of all our pumps:—a wreck complete she roll'd,
335 At mercy of the waves, whose mercies are
Like human beings during civil war.

43

Then came the carpenter, at last, with tears
In his rough eyes, and told the captain, he
Could do no more; he was a man in years,
340 And long had voyaged through many a stormy sea,
And if he wept at length, they were not fears
That made his eyelids as a woman's be,
But he, poor fellow, had a wife and children,
Two things for dying people quite bewildering.

44

345 The ship was evidently settling now
Fast by the head; and, all distinction gone,
Some went to prayers again, and made a vow
Of candles to their saints—but there were none
To pay them with; and some look'd o'er the bow;
350 Some hoisted out the boats; and there was one
That begg'd Pedrillo for an absolution,
Who told him to be damn'd—in his confusion.

45

Some lash'd them in their hammocks, some put on
Their best clothes, as if going to a fair;
355 Some cursed the day on which they saw the sun,[1]
And gnash'd their teeth, and, howling, tore their hair;[2]
And others went on as they had begun,
Getting the boats out, being well aware
That a tight boat will live in a rough sea,
360 Unless with breakers close beneath her lee.

46

The worst of all was, that in their condition,
Having been several days in great distress,
'Twas difficult to get out such provision
As now might render their long suffering less:
365 Men, even when dying, dislike inanition;
Their stock was damaged by the weather's stress:
Two casks of biscuit, and a keg of butter,
Were all that could be thrown into the cutter.

---

[1] Cf. Job 3.1–10.
[2] Cf. Jeremiah 20.14; Matthew 8.12; and Dante, *Inferno* 3.100–05.

47

But in the long-boat they contrived to stow
    Some pounds of bread, though injured by the wet;
Water, a twenty-gallon cask or so;
    Six flasks of wine; and they contrived to get
A portion of their beef up from below,
    And with a piece of pork, moreover, met,
But scarce enough to serve them for a luncheon—
Then there was rum, eight gallons in a puncheon.

48

The other boats, the yawl and pinnace, had
    Been stove in the beginning of the gale;
And the long-boat's condition was but bad,
    As there were but two blankets for a sail,
And one oar for a mast, which a young lad
    Threw in by good luck over the ship's rail;
And two boats could not hold, far less be stored,
To save one half the people then on board.

49

'Twas twilight, for the sunless day went down
    Over the waste of waters; like a veil,
Which, if withdrawn, would but disclose the frown
    Of one who hates us, so the night was shown,
And grimly darkled o'er their faces pale,
    And hopeless eyes, which o'er the deep alone
Gazed dim and desolate; twelve days had Fear
Been their familiar, and now Death was here.[1]

50

Some trial had been making at a raft,
    With little hope in such a rolling sea,
A sort of thing at which one would have laugh'd,
    If any laughter at such times could be,
Unless with people who too much have quaff'd,
    And have a kind of wild and horrid glee,
Half epileptical and half hysterical:—
Their preservation would have been a miracle.

51

At half-past eight o'clock, booms, hencoops, spars,
    And all things, for a chance, had been cast loose,
That still could keep afloat the struggling tars,
    For yet they strove, although of no great use:
There was no light in heaven but a few stars,
    The boats put off o'ercrowded with their crews;
She gave a heel, and then a lurch to port,
And, going down head foremost—sunk, in short.

52

Then rose from sea to sky the wild farewell,
    Then shriek'd the timid, and stood still the brave,
Then some leap'd overboard with dreadful yell,
    As eager to anticipate their grave;
And the sea yawn'd around her like a hell,
    And down she suck'd with her the whirling wave,
Like one who grapples with his enemy,
And strives to strangle him before he die.

53

And first one universal shriek there rush'd,
    Louder than the loud ocean, like a crash
Of echoing thunder; and then all was hush'd,
    Save the wild wind and the remorseless dash
Of billows; but at intervals there gush'd,
    Accompanied with a convulsive splash,
A solitary shriek, the bubbling cry
Of some strong swimmer in his agony.

54

The boats, as stated, had got off before,
    And in them crowded several of the crew;
And yet their present hope was hardly more
    Than what it had been, for so strong it blew
There was slight chance of reaching any shore;
    And then they were too many, though so few—
Nine in the cutter, thirty in the boat,
Were counted in them when they got afloat.

55

All the rest perish'd; near two hundred souls
    Had left their bodies; and what's worse, alas!
When over Catholics the ocean rolls,
    They must wait several weeks before a mass

---

[1] Note the mistake in the rhyme scheme, which Byron later corrected.

Takes off one peck of purgatorial coals,
    Because, till people know what's come to pass,
They won't lay out their money on the dead—
440 It costs three francs for every mass that's said.

56

Juan got into the long-boat, and there
    Contrived to help Pedrillo to a place;
It seem'd as if they had exchanged their care,
    For Juan wore the magisterial face
445 Which courage gives, while poor Pedrillo's pair
    Of eyes were crying for their owner's case:
Battista, though, (a name call'd shortly Tita)[1]
Was lost by getting at some aqua-vita.

57

Pedro, his valet, too, he tried to save,
450   But the same cause, conducive to his loss,
Left him so drunk, he jump'd into the wave
    As o'er the cutter's edge he tried to cross,
And so he found a wine-and-watery grave;
    They could not rescue him although so close,
455 Because the sea ran higher every minute,
And for the boat—the crew kept crowding in it.

58

A small old spaniel,—which had been Don Jóse's,
    His father's, whom he loved, as ye may think,
For on such things the memory reposes
460   With tenderness,—stood howling on the brink,
Knowing, (dogs have such intellectual noses!)
    No doubt, the vessel was about to sink;
And Juan caught him up, and ere he stepp'd
Off, threw him in, then after him he leap'd.

59

465 He also stuff'd his money where he could
    About his person, and Pedrillo's too,
Who let him do, in fact, whate'er he would,
    Not knowing what himself to say, or do,
As every rising wave his dread renew'd;
470   But Juan, trusting they might still get through,

---

[1] Byron's own servant Giovanni Battista Lusieri (1798–1874) was nicknamed "Tita."

And deeming there were remedies for any ill,
Thus re-embark'd his tutor and his spaniel.

60

'Twas a rough night, and blew so stiffly yet,
    That the sail was becalm'd between the seas,
475 Though on the wave's high top too much to set,
    They dared not take it in for all the breeze;
Each sea curl'd o'er the stern, and kept them wet,
    And made them bale without a moment's ease,
So that themselves as well as hopes were damp'd,
480 And the poor little cutter quickly swamp'd.

61

Nine souls more went in her: the long-boat still
    Kept above water, with an oar for mast,
Two blankets stitch'd together, answering ill
    Instead of sail, were to the oar made fast:
485 Though every wave roll'd menacing to fill,
    And present peril all before surpass'd,
They grieved for those who perish'd with the cutter,
And also for the biscuit casks and butter.

62

The sun rose red and fiery, a sure sign
490   Of the continuance of the gale: to run
Before the sea, until it should grow fine,
    Was all that for the present could be done:
A few tea-spoonfuls of their rum and wine
    Were served out to the people, who begun
495 To faint, and damaged bread wet through the bags,
And most of them had little clothes but rags.

63

They counted thirty, crowded in a space
    Which left scarce room for motion or exertion;
They did their best to modify their case,
500   One half sate up, though numb'd with the immersion,
While t'other half were laid down in their place,
    At watch and watch; thus, shivering like the tertian
Ague in its cold fit, they fill'd their boat,
With nothing but the sky for a great coat.

64

'Tis very certain the desire of life
    Prolongs it; this is obvious to physicians,
When patients, neither plagued with friends nor wife,
    Survive through very desperate conditions,
Because they still can hope, nor shines the knife
    Nor shears of Atropos[1] before their visions:
Despair of all recovery spoils longevity,
And makes men's miseries of alarming brevity.

65

'Tis said that persons living on annuities
    Are longer lived than others,—God knows why,
Unless to plague the grantors,—yet so true it is,
    That some, I really think, *do* never die;
Of any creditors the worst a Jew it is,
    And *that's* their mode of furnishing supply:
In my young days they lent me cash that way,
Which I found very troublesome to pay.

66

'Tis thus with people in an open boat,
    They live upon the love of life, and bear
More than can be believed, or even thought,
    And stand like rocks the tempest's wear and tear;
And hardship still has been the sailor's lot,
    Since Noah's ark went cruising here and there;
She had a curious crew as well as cargo,
Like the first old Greek privateer, the Argo.[2]

67

But man is a carnivorous production,
    And must have meals, at least one meal a day;
He cannot live, like woodcocks, upon suction,[3]
    But, like the shark and tiger, must have prey:
Although his anatomical construction
    Bears vegetables, in a grumbling way,
Your labouring people think beyond all question,
Beef, veal, and mutton, better for digestion.

68

And thus it was with this our hapless crew;
    For on the third day there came on a calm,
And though at first their strength it might renew,
    And, lying on their weariness like balm,
Lull'd them like turtles sleeping on the blue
    Of ocean, when they woke they felt a qualm,
And fell all ravenously on their provision,
Instead of hoarding it with due precision.

69

The consequence was easily foreseen—
    They ate up all they had, and drank their wine,
In spite of all remonstrances, and then
    On what, in fact, next day were they to dine?
They hoped the wind would rise, these foolish men!
    And carry them to shore; these hopes were fine,
But as they had but one oar, and that brittle,
It would have been more wise to save their victual.

70

The fourth day came, but not a breath of air,
    And Ocean slumber'd like an unwean'd child:
The fifth day, and their boat lay floating there,
    The sea and sky were blue, and clear, and mild—
With their one oar (I wish they had had a pair)
    What could they do? and hunger's rage grew wild:
So Juan's spaniel, spite of his entreating,
Was kill'd, and portion'd out for present eating.

71

On the sixth day they fed upon his hide,
    And Juan, who had still refused, because
The creature was his father's dog that died,
    Now feeling all the vulture in his jaws,
With some remorse received (though first denied)
    As a great favour one of the fore-paws,
Which he divided with Pedrillo, who
Devour'd it, longing for the other too.

---

[1] one of the three Fates: Clotho spun the thread of life, Lachesis measured it, and Atropos ("inflexible") cut it off.

[2] the ship in which Jason and the Argonauts sailed to Colchis to steal the Golden Fleece: see Ovid, *Metamorphoses* 7.

[3] Woodcocks feed by probing the grass with their long bills; they look as if they were sucking.

72

    The seventh day, and no wind—the burning sun
570   Blister'd and scorch'd, and, stagnant on the sea,
    They lay like carcases; and hope was none,
        Save in the breeze that came not; savagely
    They glared upon each other—all was done,
        Water, and wine, and food,—and you might see
575   The longings of the cannibal arise
    (Although they spoke not) in their wolfish eyes.

73

    At length one whisper'd his companion, who
        Whisper'd another, and thus it went round,
    And then into a hoarser murmur grew,
580   An ominous, and wild, and desperate sound,
    And when his comrade's thought each sufferer knew,
        'Twas but his own, suppress'd till now, he found:
    And out they spoke of lots for flesh and blood,
    And who should die to be his fellow's food.

74

585   But ere they came to this, they that day shared
        Some leathern caps, and what remain'd of shoes;
    And then they look'd around them, and despair'd,
        And none to be the sacrifice would choose;
    At length the lots were torn up, and prepared,
590   But of materials that much shock the Muse—
    Having no paper, for the want of better,
    They took by force from Juan Julia's letter.

75

    The lots were made, and mark'd, and mix'd, and handed,
        In silent horror, and their distribution
595   Lull'd even the savage hunger which demanded,
        Like the Promethean vulture, this pollution;
    None in particular had sought or plann'd it,
        'Twas nature gnaw'd them to this resolution,
    By which none were permitted to be neuter—
600   And the lot fell on Juan's luckless tutor.

76

    He but requested to be bled to death:
        The surgeon had his instruments, and bled
    Pedrillo, and so gently ebb'd his breath,
        You hardly could perceive when he was dead.
605   He died as born, a Catholic in faith,
        Like most in the belief in which they're bred,
    And first a little crucifix he kiss'd,
    And then held out his jugular and wrist.

77

    The surgeon, as there was no other fee,
610   Had his first choice of morsels for his pains;
    But being thirstiest at the moment, he
        Preferr'd a draught from the fast-flowing veins:
    Part was divided, part thrown in the sea,
        And such things as the entrails and the brains
615   Regaled two sharks, who follow'd o'er the billow—
    The sailors ate the rest of poor Pedrillo.

78

    The sailors ate him, all save three or four,
        Who were not quite so fond of animal food;
    To these was added Juan, who, before
620   Refusing his own spaniel, hardly could
    Feel now his appetite increased much more;
        'Twas not to be expected that he should,
    Even in extremity of their disaster,
    Dine with them on his pastor and his master.

79

625   'Twas better that he did not; for, in fact,
        The consequence was awful in the extreme:
    For they, who were most ravenous in the act,
        Went raging mad—Lord! how they did blaspheme!
    And foam and roll, with strange convulsions rack'd,
630   Drinking salt water like a mountain-stream,
    Tearing, and grinning, howling, screeching, swearing,
    And, with hyæna laughter, died despairing.

80

    Their numbers were much thinn'd by this infliction,
        And all the rest were thin enough, heaven knows;
635   And some of them had lost their recollection,

Happier than they who still perceived their woes;
But others ponder'd on a new dissection,
　　As if not warn'd sufficiently by those
　　Who had already perish'd, suffering madly,
For having used their appetites so sadly.

81

And next they thought upon the master's mate,
　　As fattest; but he saved himself, because,
Besides being much averse from such a fate,
　　There were some other reasons: the first was,
He had been rather indisposed of late;
　　And that which chiefly proved his saving clause,
Was a small present made to him at Cadiz,
By general subscription of the ladies.

82

Of poor Pedrillo something still remain'd,
　　But was used sparingly,—some were afraid,
And others still their appetites constrain'd,
　　Or but at times a little supper made;
All except Juan, who throughout abstain'd,
　　Chewing a piece of bamboo, and some lead:
At length they caught two boobies, and a noddy,
And then they left off eating the dead body.

83

And if Pedrillo's fate should shocking be,
　　Remember Ugolino condescends
To eat the head of his arch-enemy
　　The moment after he politely ends
His tale;[1] if foes be food in hell, at sea
　　'Tis surely fair to dine upon our friends,
When shipwreck's short allowance grows too scanty,
Without being much more horrible than Dante.

84

And the same night there fell a shower of rain,
　　For which their mouths gaped, like the cracks
　　　of earth
When dried to summer dust; till taught by pain,
　　Men really know not what good water's worth;
If you had been in Turkey or in Spain,
　　Or with a famish'd boat's-crew had your berth,
Or in the desert heard the camel's bell,
You'd wish yourself where Truth is—in a well.[2]

85

It pour'd down torrents, but they were no richer
　　Until they found a ragged piece of sheet,
Which served them as a sort of spongy pitcher,
　　And when they deem'd its moisture was
　　　complete,
They wrung it out, and though a thirsty ditcher
　　Might not have thought the scanty draught so
　　　sweet
As a full pot of porter, to their thinking
They ne'er till now had known the joys of drinking.

86

And their baked lips,[3] with many a bloody crack,
　　Suck'd in the moisture, which like nectar stream'd;
Their throats were ovens, their swoln tongues were
　　black,
　　As the rich man's in hell, who vainly scream'd
To beg the beggar, who could not rain back
　　A drop of dew, when every drop had seem'd
To taste of heaven[4]—If this be true, indeed,
Some Christians have a comfortable creed.

87

There were two fathers in this ghastly crew,[5]
　　And with them their two sons, of whom the one
Was more robust and hardy to the view,
　　But he died early; and when he was gone,
His nearest messmate told his sire, who threw
　　One glance at him, and said, "Heaven's will
　　　be done!
I can do nothing," and he saw him thrown
Into the deep without a tear or groan.

---

[1] Dante, *Inferno* 33.76–78.

[2] The philosopher Democritus said that truth lay at the bottom of a well.

[3] Cf. Coleridge, "The Rime of the Ancyent Marinere" 149.*

[4] Luke 16.19–26.

[5] Cf. Coleridge, "The Rime of the Ancyent Marinere" 332.

88

The other father had a weaklier child,
    Of a soft cheek and aspect delicate;
But the boy bore up long, and with a mild
    And patient spirit held aloof his fate;
Little he said, and now and then he smiled,
    As if to win a part from off the weight
He saw increasing on his father's heart,
With the deep deadly thought, that they must part.

89

And o'er him bent his sire, and never raised
    His eyes from off his face, but wiped the foam
From his pale lips, and ever on him gazed,
    And when the wish'd-for shower at length was come,
And the boy's eyes, which the dull film half glazed,
    Brighten'd, and for a moment seem'd to roam,
He squeezed from out a rag some drops of rain
Into his dying child's mouth—but in vain.

90

The boy expired—the father held the clay,
    And look'd upon it long, and when at last
Death left no doubt, and the dead burthen lay
    Stiff on his heart, and pulse and hope were past,
He watch'd it wistfully, until away
    'Twas borne by the rude wave wherein 'twas cast;
Then he himself sunk down all dumb and shivering,
And gave no sign of life, save his limbs quivering.

91

Now overhead a rainbow, bursting through
    The scattering clouds, shone, spanning the dark sea,
Resting its bright base on the quivering blue;
    And all within its arch appear'd to be
Clearer than that without, and its wide hue
    Wax'd broad and waving, like a banner free,
Then changed like to a bow that's bent, and then
Forsook the dim eyes of these shipwreck'd men.

92

It changed, of course; a heavenly chameleon,
    The airy child of vapour and the sun,
Brought forth in purple, cradled in vermilion,
    Baptized in molten gold, and swathed in dun,
Glittering like crescents o'er a Turk's pavilion,
    And blending every colour into one,
Just like a black eye in a recent scuffle,
(For sometimes we must box without the muffle.)

93

Our shipwreck'd seamen thought it a good omen—
    It is as well to think so, now and then;
'Twas an old custom of the Greek and Roman,
    And may become of great advantage when
Folks are discouraged; and most surely no men
    Had greater need to nerve themselves again
Than these, and so this rainbow look'd like hope—
Quite a celestial kaleidoscope.[1]

94

About this time a beautiful white bird,
    Webfooted, not unlike a dove in size
And plumage, (probably it might have err'd
    Upon its course) pass'd oft before their eyes,
And tried to perch, although it saw and heard
    The men within the boat, and in this guise
It came and went, and flutter'd round them till
Night fell:—this seem'd a better omen still.

95

But in this case I also must remark,
    'Twas well this bird of promise did not perch,
Because the tackle of our shatter'd bark
    Was not so safe for roosting as a church;
And had it been the dove from Noah's ark,
    Returning there from her successful search,
Which in their way that moment chanced to fall,
They would have eat her, olive-branch and all.[2]

---

[1] Sir David Brewster invented the kaleidoscope in 1817. Byron's lawyer, John Hanson, brought him one in November 1818.

[2] Cf. Genesis 8.6–11.

96

With twilight it again came on to blow,
    But not with violence; the stars shone out,
The boat made way; yet now they were so low,
    They knew not where nor what they were about;
Some fancied they saw land, and some said "No!"
    The frequent fog-banks gave them cause to doubt—
Some swore that they heard breakers, others guns,
And all mistook about the latter once.

97

As morning broke the light wind died away,
    When he who had the watch sung out, and swore
If 'twas not land that rose with the sun's ray,
    He wish'd that land he never might see more;
And the rest rubb'd their eyes, and saw a bay,
    Or thought they saw, and shaped their course for shore;
For shore it was, and gradually grew
Distinct, and high, and palpable to view.

98

And then of these some part burst into tears,
    And others, looking with a stupid stare,
Could not yet separate their hopes from fears,
    And seem'd as if they had no further care;
While a few pray'd—(the first time for some years)—
    And at the bottom of the boat three were
Asleep; they shook them by the hand and head,
And tried to awaken them, but found them dead.

99

The day before, fast sleeping on the water,
    They found a turtle of the hawk's-bill kind,
And by good fortune, gliding softly, caught her,
    Which yielded a day's life, and to their mind
Proved even still a more nutritious matter,
    Because it left encouragement behind:
They thought that in such perils, more than chance
Had sent them this for their deliverance.

100

The land appear'd a high and rocky coast,
    And higher grew the mountains as they drew,
Set by a current, toward it: they were lost
    In various conjectures, for none knew
To what part of the earth they had been tost,
    So changeable had been the winds that blew;
Some thought it was Mount Ætna, some the highlands
Of Candia,[1] Cyprus, Rhodes, or other islands.

101

Meantime the current, with a rising gale,
    Still set them onwards to the welcome shore,
Like Charon's bark of spectres, dull and pale:[2]
    Their living freight was now reduced to four,
And three dead, whom their strength could not avail
    To heave into the deep with those before,
Though the two sharks still follow'd them, and dash'd
The spray into their faces as they splash'd.

102

Famine, despair, cold, thirst, and heat, had done
    Their work on them by turns, and thinn'd them to
Such things a mother had not known her son
    Amidst the skeletons of that gaunt crew;
By night chill'd, by day scorch'd, thus one by one
    They perish'd, until wither'd to these few,
But chiefly by a species of self-slaughter,
In washing down Pedrillo with salt water.

103

As they drew nigh the land, which now was seen
    Unequal in its aspect here and there,
They felt the freshness of its growing green,
    That waved in forest-tops, and smooth'd the air,
And fell upon their glazed eyes like a screen
    From glistening waves, and skies so hot and bare—
Lovely seem'd any object that should sweep
Away the vast, salt, dread, eternal deep.

104

The shore look'd wild, without a trace of man,

---

[1] Crete.

[2] Charon ferried the souls of the newly dead across the river Acheron into Hades.

  And girt by formidable waves; but they
Were mad for land, and thus their course they ran,
  Though right ahead the roaring breakers lay:
A reef between them also now began
830   To show its boiling surf and bounding spray,
But finding no place for their landing better,
They ran the boat for shore, and overset her.

105

But in his native stream, the Guadalquivir,
  Juan to lave his youthful limbs was wont;
835 And having learnt to swim in that sweet river,
  Had often turn'd the art to some account:
A better swimmer you could scarce see ever,
  He could, perhaps, have pass'd the Hellespont,
As once (a feat on which ourselves we prided)
840 Leander, Mr. Ekenhead, and I did.[1]

106

So here, though faint, emaciated, and stark,
  He buoy'd his boyish limbs, and strove to ply
With the quick wave, and gain, ere it was dark,
  The beach which lay before him, high and dry:
845 The greatest danger here was from a shark,
  That carried off his neighbour by the thigh;
As for the other two they could not swim,
So nobody arrived on shore but him.

107

Nor yet had he arrived but for the oar,
850   Which, providentially for him, was wash'd
Just as his feeble arms could strike no more,
  And the hard wave o'erwhelm'd him as 'twas dash'd
Within his grasp; he clung to it, and sore
  The waters beat while he thereto was lash'd;
855 At last, with swimming, wading, scrambling, he
Roll'd on the beach, half-senseless, from the sea:

108

There, breathless, with his digging nails he clung
Fast to the sand, lest the returning wave,
From whose reluctant roar his life he wrung,
860   Should suck him back to her insatiate grave:
And there he lay, full length, where he was flung,
  Before the entrance of a cliff-worn cave,
With just enough of life to feel its pain,
And deem that it was saved, perhaps, in vain.

109

865 With slow and staggering effort he arose,
  But sunk again upon his bleeding knee
And quivering hand; and then he look'd for those
  Who long had been his mates upon the sea,
But none of them appear'd to share his woes,
870   Save one, a corpse from out the famish'd three,
Who died two days before, and now had found
An unknown barren beach for burial ground.

110

And as he gazed, his dizzy brain spun fast,
  And down he sunk; and as he sunk, the sand
875 Swam round and round, and all his senses pass'd:
  He fell upon his side, and his stretch'd hand
Droop'd dripping on the oar, (their jury-mast)
  And, like a wither'd lily, on the land
His slender frame and pallid aspect lay,
880 As fair a thing as e'er was form'd of clay.

111

How long in his damp trance young Juan lay[2]
  He knew not, for the earth was gone for him,
And Time had nothing more of night nor day
  For his congealing blood, and senses dim;
885 And how this heavy faintness pass'd away
  He knew not, till each painful pulse and limb,
And tingling vein, seem'd throbbing back to life,
For Death, though vanquish'd, still retired with strife.

112

His eyes he open'd, shut, again unclosed,
890   For all was doubt and dizziness; he thought
He still was in the boat, and had but dozed,

---

[1] In imitation of the classical hero Leander (see Christopher Marlowe, *Hero and Leander*), Byron, accompanied by Lieutenant Ekenhead of the Marines, swam across the Hellespont on 3 May 1810.

[2] Cf. Coleridge, "The Rime of the Ancyent Marinere" 398–99.*

And felt again with his despair o'erwrought,
And wish'd it death in which he had reposed,
 And then once more his feelings back were brought,
And slowly by his swimming eyes was seen
A lovely female face of seventeen.

113

'Twas bending close o'er his, and the small mouth
 Seem'd almost prying into his for breath;
And chafing him, the soft warm hand of youth
 Recall'd his answering spirits back from death;
And, bathing his chill temples, tried to soothe
 Each pulse to animation, till beneath
Its gentle touch and trembling care, a sigh
To these kind efforts made a low reply.

114

Then was the cordial pour'd, and mantle flung
 Around his scarce-clad limbs; and the fair arm
Raised higher the faint head which o'er it hung;
 And her transparent cheek, all pure and warm,
Pillow'd his death-like forehead; then she wrung
 His dewy curls, long drench'd by every storm;
And watch'd with eagerness each throb that drew
A sigh from his heaved bosom—and hers, too.

115

And lifting him with care into the cave,
 The gentle girl and her attendant,—one
Young, yet her elder, and of brow less grave,
 And more robust of figure,—then begun
To kindle fire, and as the new flames gave
 Light to the rocks that roof'd them, which the sun
Had never seen, the maid, or whatsoe'er
She was, appear'd distinct, and tall, and fair.

116

Her brow was overhung with coins of gold,
 That sparkled o'er the auburn of her hair,
Her clustering hair, whose longer locks were roll'd
 In braids behind, and though her stature were
Even of the highest for a female mould,
 They nearly reach'd her heel; and in her air
There was a something which bespoke command,
As one who was a lady in the land.

117

Her hair, I said, was auburn; but her eyes
 Were black as death, their lashes the same hue,
Of downcast length, in whose silk shadow lies
 Deepest attraction, for when to the view
Forth from its raven fringe the full glance flies,
 Ne'er with such force the swiftest arrow flew;
'Tis as the snake late coil'd, who pours his length,
And hurls at once his venom and his strength.

118

Her brow was white and low, her cheek's pure dye
 Like twilight rosy still with the set sun;
Short upper lip—sweet lips! that make us sigh
 Ever to have seen such; for she was one
Fit for the model of a statuary,
 (A race of mere impostors, when all's done—
I've seen much finer women, ripe and real,
Than all the nonsense of their stone ideal.)

119

I'll tell you why I say so, for 'tis just
 One should not rail without a decent cause:
There was an Irish lady, to whose bust
 I ne'er saw justice done, and yet she was
A frequent model;[1] and if e'er she must
 Yield to stern Time and Nature's wrinkling laws,
They will destroy a face which mortal thought
Ne'er compass'd, nor less mortal chisel wrought.

120

And such was she, the lady of the cave:
 Her dress was very different from the Spanish,
Simpler, and yet of colours not so grave;
 For, as you know, the Spanish women banish
Bright hues when out of doors, and yet, while wave
 Around them (what I hope will never vanish)

---

[1] Perhaps Lady Adelaide Forbes (1789–1858), whom Byron had compared to the Apollo Belvedere (*Letters and Journals* 5: 227; 12 May 1817).

The basquiña and the mantilla, they
Seem at the same time mystical and gay.

121
But with our damsel this was not the case:
    Her dress was many-colour'd, finely spun;
Her locks curl'd negligently round her face,
    But through them gold and gems profusely shone;
Her girdle sparkled, and the richest lace
    Flow'd in her veil, and many a precious stone
Flash'd on her little hand; but, what was shocking,
Her small snow feet had slippers, but no stocking.

122
The other female's dress was not unlike,
    But of inferior materials; she
Had not so many ornaments to strike,
    Her hair had silver only, bound to be
Her dowry; and her veil, in form alike,
    Was coarser; and her air, though firm, less free;
Her hair was thicker, but less long; her eyes
As black, but quicker, and of smaller size.

123
And these two tended him, and cheer'd him both
    With food and raiment, and those soft attentions,
Which are (as I must own) of female growth,
    And have ten thousand delicate inventions:
They made a most superior mess of broth,
    A thing which poesy but seldom mentions,
But the best dish that e'er was cook'd since Homer's
Achilles ordered dinner for new comers.[1]

124
I'll tell you who they were, this female pair,
    Lest they should seem princesses in disguise;
Besides, I hate all mystery, and that air
    Of clap-trap, which your recent poets prize;
And so, in short, the girls they really were
    They shall appear before your curious eyes,
Mistress and maid; the first was only daughter
Of an old man, who lived upon the water.

125
A fisherman he had been in his youth,
    And still a sort of fisherman was he;
But other speculations were, in sooth,
    Added to his connexion with the sea,
Perhaps not so respectable, in truth:
    A little smuggling, and some piracy,
Left him, at last, the sole of many masters
Of an ill-gotten million of piastres.

126
A fisher, therefore, was he—though of men,
    Like Peter the Apostle,[2]—and he fish'd
For wandering merchant-vessels, now and then,
    And sometimes caught as many as he wish'd;
The cargoes he confiscated, and gain
    He sought in the slave-market too, and dish'd
Full many a morsel for that Turkish trade,
By which, no doubt, a good deal may be made.

127
He was a Greek, and on his isle had built
    (One of the wild and smaller Cyclades)
A very handsome house from out his guilt,
    And there he lived exceedingly at ease;
Heaven knows what cash he got, or blood he spilt,
    A sad old fellow was he, if you please;
But this I know, it was a spacious building,
Full of barbaric carving, paint, and gilding.

128
He had an only daughter, call'd Haidée,
    The greatest heiress of the Eastern Isles;
Besides, so very beautiful was she,
    Her dowry was as nothing to her smiles:
Still in her teens, and like a lovely tree
    She grew to womanhood, and between whiles
Rejected several suitors, just to learn
How to accept a better in his turn.

---

[1] Homer, *Iliad* 9.

[2] Cf. Matthew 4.18–19.

129

And walking out upon the beach, below
The cliff, towards sunset, on that day she found,
Insensible,—not dead, but nearly so,—
Don Juan, almost famish'd, and half drown'd;
But being naked, she was shock'd, you know,
Yet deem'd herself in common pity bound,
As far as in her lay, "to take him in,
A stranger" dying,[1] with so white a skin.

130

But taking him into her father's house
Was not exactly the best way to save,
But like conveying to the cat the mouse,
Or people in a trance into their grave;
Because the good old man had so much "νους,"[2]
Unlike the honest Arab thieves so brave,
He would have hospitably cured the stranger,
And sold him instantly when out of danger.

131

And therefore, with her maid, she thought it best
(A virgin always on her maid relies)
To place him in the cave for present rest:
And when, at last, he open'd his black eyes,
Their charity increased about their guest;
And their compassion grew to such a size,
It open'd half the turnpike-gates to heaven—
(St. Paul says, 'tis the toll which must be given).[3]

132

They made a fire, but such a fire as they
Upon the moment could contrive with such
Materials as were cast up round the bay,
Some broken planks, and oars, that to the touch
Were nearly tinder, since so long they lay
A mast was almost crumbled to a crutch;
But, by God's grace, here wrecks were in such plenty,
That there was fuel to have furnish'd twenty.

133

He had a bed of furs, and a pelisse,
For Haidee stripped her sables off to make
His couch; and, that he might be more at ease,
And warm, in case by chance he should awake,
They also gave a petticoat apiece,
She and her maid, and promised by day-break
To pay him a fresh visit, with a dish
For breakfast, of eggs, coffee, bread, and fish.

134

And thus they left him to his lone repose:
Juan slept like a top, or like the dead,
Who sleep at last, perhaps, (God only knows)
Just for the present; and in his lull'd head
Not even a vision of his former woes
Throbb'd in accursed dreams, which sometimes spread
Unwelcome visions of our former years,
Till the eye, cheated, opens thick with tears.

135

Young Juan slept all dreamless:—but the maid,
Who smooth'd his pillow, as she left the den
Look'd back upon him, and a moment staid,
And turn'd, believing that he call'd again.
He slumber'd; yet she thought, at least she said,
(The heart will slip even as the tongue and pen)
He had pronounced her name—but she forgot
That at this moment Juan knew it not.

136

And pensive to her father's house she went,
Enjoining silence strict to Zoe, who
Better than her knew what, in fact, she meant,
She being wiser by a year or two:
A year or two's an age when rightly spent,
And Zoe spent hers, as most women do,
In gaining all that useful sort of knowledge
Which is acquired in Nature's good old college.

137

The morn broke, and found Juan slumbering still
Fast in his cave, and nothing clash'd upon

---

[1] Cf. Matthew 25.34–36.

[2] "mind," "intelligence" (Gk.).

[3] Cf. 1 Corinthians 13 and Colossians 3.14.

His rest; the rushing of the neighbouring rill,
    And the young beams of the excluded sun,
Troubled him not, and he might sleep his fill;
    And need he had of slumber yet, for none
1095 Had suffer'd more—his hardships were comparative
To those related in my grand-dad's Narrative.[1]

138

Not so Haidée: she sadly toss'd and tumbled,
    And started from her sleep, and, turning o'er,
Dream'd of a thousand wrecks, o'er which she
    stumbled,
1100   And handsome corpses strew'd upon the shore;
And woke her maid so early that she grumbled,
    And call'd her father's old slaves up, who swore
In several oaths—Armenian, Turk, and Greek—
    They knew not what to think of such a freak.

139

1105 But up she got, and up she made them get,
    With some pretence about the sun, that makes
Sweet skies just when he rises, or is set;
    And 'tis, no doubt, a sight to see when breaks
Bright Phoebus, while the mountains still are wet
1110   With mist, and every bird with him awakes,
And night is flung off like a mourning suit
    Worn for a husband, or some other brute.

140

I say, the sun is a most glorious sight,
    I've seen him rise full oft, indeed of late
1115 I have sat up on purpose all the night,
    Which hastens, as physicians say, one's fate;
And so all ye, who would be in the right
    In health and purse, begin your day to date
From day-break, and when coffin'd at fourscore,
1120 Engrave upon the plate, you rose at four.

141

And Haidée met the morning face to face;
    Her own was freshest, though a feverish flush
Had dyed it with the headlong blood, whose race
From heart to cheek is curb'd into a blush,
1125 Like to a torrent which a mountain's base,
    That overpowers some Alpine river's rush,
Checks to a lake, whose waves in circles spread;
    Or the Red Sea—but the sea is not red.

142

And down the cliff the island virgin came,
1130   And near the cave her quick light footsteps drew,
While the sun smiled on her with his first flame,
    And young Aurora[2] kiss'd her lips with dew,
Taking her for a sister; just the same
    Mistake you would have made on seeing the
    two,
1135 Although the mortal, quite as fresh and fair,
Had all the advantage, too, of not being air.

143

And when into the cavern Haidée stepp'd
    All timidly, yet rapidly, she saw
That like an infant Juan sweetly slept;
1140   And then she stopp'd, and stood as if in awe,
(For sleep is awful) and on tiptoe crept
    And wrapt him closer, lest the air, too raw,
Should reach his blood, then o'er him still as death
Bent, with hush'd lips, that drank his scarce-drawn
    breath.

144

1145 And thus like to an angel o'er the dying
    Who die in righteousness, she lean'd; and there
All tranquilly the shipwreck'd boy was lying,
    As o'er him lay the calm and stirless air:
But Zoe the meantime some eggs was frying,
1150   Since, after all, no doubt the youthful pair
Must breakfast, and betimes—lest they should ask it,
    She drew out her provision from the basket.

145

She knew that the best feelings must have victual,
    And that a shipwreck'd youth would hungry be;
1155 Besides, being less in love, she yawn'd a little,

---

[1] See note to 2.216. John Byron had such bad luck with shipwrecks that he was nicknamed "Foulweather Jack."

[2] goddess of the dawn.

And felt her veins chill'd by the neighbouring sea;
And so, she cook'd their breakfast to a tittle;
I can't say that she gave them any tea,
But there were eggs, fruit, coffee, bread, fish, honey,
With Scio wine,—and all for love, not money.

146

And Zoe, when the eggs were ready, and
The coffee made, would fain have waken'd Juan;
But Haidee stopp'd her with her quick small hand,
And without word, a sign her finger drew on
Her lip, which Zoe needs must understand;
And, the first breakfast spoilt, prepared a new one,
Because her mistress would not let her break
That sleep which seem'd as it would ne'er awake.

147

For still he lay, and on his thin worn cheek
A purple hectic play'd like dying day
On the snow-tops of distant hills; the streak
Of sufferance yet upon his forehead lay,
Where the blue veins look'd shadowy, shrunk, and weak;
And his black curls were dewy with the spray,
Which weigh'd upon them yet, all damp and salt,
Mix'd with the stony vapours of the vault.

148

And she bent o'er him, and he lay beneath,
Hush'd as the babe upon its mother's breast,
Droop'd as the willow when no winds can breathe,
Lull'd like the depth of ocean when at rest,
Fair as the crowning rose of the whole wreath,
Soft as the callow cygnet in its nest;
In short, he was a very pretty fellow,
Although his woes had turn'd him rather yellow.

149

He woke and gazed, and would have slept again,
But the fair face which met his eyes forbade
Those eyes to close, though weariness and pain
Had further sleep a further pleasure made;
For woman's face was never form'd in vain
For Juan, so that even when he pray'd
He turn'd from grisly saints, and martyrs hairy,
To the sweet portraits of the Virgin Mary.

150

And thus upon his elbow he arose,
And look'd upon the lady, in whose cheek
The pale contended with the purple rose,
As with an effort she began to speak;
Her eyes were eloquent, her words would pose,
Although she told him, in good modern Greek,
With an Ionian accent, low and sweet,
That he was faint, and must not talk, but eat.

151

Now Juan could not understand a word,
Being no Grecian; but he had an ear,
And her voice was the warble of a bird,
So soft, so sweet, so delicately clear,
That finer, simpler music ne'er was heard;
The sort of sound we echo with a tear,
Without knowing why—an overpowering tone,
Whence Melody descends as from a throne.

152

And Juan gazed as one who is awoke
By a distant organ, doubting if he be
Not yet a dreamer, till the spell is broke
By the watchman, or some such reality,
Or by one's early valet's cursed knock;
At least it is a heavy sound to me,
Who like a morning slumber—for the night
Shows stars and women in a better light.

153

And Juan, too, was help'd out from his dream,
Or sleep, or whatso'er it was, by feeling
A most prodigious appetite: the steam
Of Zoe's cookery no doubt was stealing
Upon his senses, and the kindling beam
Of the new fire, which Zoe kept up, kneeling
To stir her viands, made him quite awake
And long for food, but chiefly a beef-steak.

154

But beef is rare within these oxless isles;
    Goat's flesh there is, no doubt, and kid, and
        mutton;
And, when a holiday upon them smiles,
    A joint upon their barbarous spits they put on:
But this occurs but seldom, between whiles,
    For some of these are rocks with scarce a hut on;
Others are fair and fertile, among which
This, though not large, was one of the most rich.

155

I say that beef is rare, and can't help thinking
    That the old fable of the Minotaur—
From which our modern morals, rightly shrinking,
    Condemn the royal lady's taste who wore
A cow's shape for a mask—was only (sinking
    The allegory) a mere type, no more,
That Pasiphae promoted breeding cattle,
To make the Cretans bloodier in battle.[1]

156

For we all know that English people are
    Fed upon beef—I won't say much of beer,
Because 'tis liquor only, and being far
    From this my subject, has no business here;
We know, too, they are very fond of war,
    A pleasure—like all pleasures—rather dear;
So were the Cretans—from which I infer
That beef and battles both were owing to her.

157

But to resume. The languid Juan raised
    His head upon his elbow, and he saw
A sight on which he had not lately gazed,
    As all his latter meals had been quite raw,
Three or four things, for which the Lord he praised,
    And, feeling still the famish'd vulture gnaw,
He fell upon whate'er was offer'd, like
A priest, a shark, an alderman, or pike.

158

He ate, and he was well supplied; and she,
    Who watch'd him like a mother, would have fed
Him past all bounds, because she smiled to see
    Such appetite in one she had deem'd dead;
But Zoe, being older than Haidee,
    Knew (by tradition, for she ne'er had read)
That famish'd people must be slowly nurst,
And fed by spoonfuls, else they always burst.

159

And so she took the liberty to state,
    Rather by deeds than words, because the case
Was urgent, that the gentleman, whose fate
    Had made her mistress quit her bed to trace
The sea-shore at this hour, must leave his plate,
    Unless he wish'd to die upon the place—
She snatch'd it, and refused another morsel,
Saying, he had gorged enough to make a horse ill.

160

Next they—he being naked, save a tatter'd
    Pair of scarce decent trowsers—went to work,
And in the fire his recent rags they scatter'd,
    And dress'd him, for the present, like a Turk,
Or Greek—that is, although it not much matter'd,
    Omitting turban, slippers, pistols, dirk,—
They furnish'd him, entire except some stitches,
With a clean shirt, and very spacious breeches.

161

And then fair Haidee tried her tongue at speaking,
    But not a word could Juan comprehend,
Although he listen'd so that the young Greek in
    Her earnestness would ne'er have made an end;
And, as he interrupted not, went eking
    Her speech out to her protegé and friend,
Till pausing at the last her breath to take,
She saw he did not understand Romaic.[2]

162

And then she had recourse to nods, and signs,
    And smiles, and sparkles of the speaking eye,

---

[1] Pasiphaë, queen of Crete, was possessed by lust for a bull sent by Poseidon. She gave birth to the Minotaur, half man and half bull. Her husband Minos imprisoned the monster in a labyrinth built by Daedalus.

[2] modern Greek.

And read (the only book she could) the lines
    Of his fair face, and found, by sympathy,
The answer eloquent, where the soul shines
    And darts in one quick glance a long reply;
And thus in every look she saw exprest
A world of words, and things at which she guess'd.

163

And now, by dint of fingers and of eyes,
    And words repeated after her, he took
A lesson in her tongue; but by surmise,
    No doubt, less of her language than her look:
As he who studies fervently the skies
    Turns oftener to the stars than to his book,
Thus Juan learn'd his alpha beta better
From Haidée's glance than any graven letter.

164

'Tis pleasing to be school'd in a strange tongue
    By female lips and eyes—that is, I mean,
When both the teacher and the taught are young,
    As was the case, at least, where I have been;
They smile so when one's right, and when one's wrong
    They smile still more, and then there intervene
Pressure of hands, perhaps even a chaste kiss;—
I learn'd the little that I know by this:

165

That is, some words of Spanish, Turk, and Greek,
    Italian not at all, having no teachers;
Much English I cannot pretend to speak,
    Learning that language chiefly from its preachers,
Barrow, South, Tillotson, whom every week
    I study, also Blair,[1] the highest reachers
Of eloquence in piety and prose—
I hate your poets, so read none of those.

166

As for the ladies, I have nought to say,
    A wanderer from the British world of fashion,
Where I, like other "dogs, have had my day,"[2]
    Like other men, too, may have had my passion—
But that, like other things, has pass'd away,
    And all her fools whom I *could* lay the lash on,
Foes, friends, men, women, now are nought to me
But dreams of what has been, no more to be.

167

Return we to Don Juan. He begun
    To hear new words, and to repeat them; but
Some feelings, universal as the sun,
    Were such as could not in his breast be shut
More than within the bosom of a nun:
    He was in love,—as you would be, no doubt,
With a young benefactress—so was she,
Just in the way we very often see.

168

And every day by day-break—rather early
    For Juan, who was somewhat fond of rest—
She came into the cave, but it was merely
    To see her bird reposing in his nest;
And she would softly stir his locks so curly,
    Without disturbing her yet slumbering guest,
Breathing all gently o'er his cheek and mouth,
As o'er a bed of roses the sweet south.

169

And every morn his colour freshlier came,
    And every day help'd on his convalescence;
'Twas well, because health in the human frame
    Is pleasant, besides being true love's essence,
For health and idleness to passion's flame
    Are oil and gunpowder; and some good lessons
Are also learnt from Ceres and from Bacchus,
Without whom Venus will not long attack us.[3]

170

While Venus fills the heart (without heart really
    Love, though good always, is not quite so good),

---

[1] Isaac Barrow (1630–77), Robert South (1634–1716), John Tillotson (1630–94), and Hugh Blair (1718-1800), British preachers.

[2] Shakespeare, *Hamlet* 5.1.279.

[3] Cf. Terence, *Eunuchus* 4.5–6. Ceres, or Demeter, was the goddess of agriculture; Bacchus, the god of wine.

1355 Ceres presents a plate of vermicelli,—
    For love must be sustain'd like flesh and blood,—
While Bacchus pours out wine, or hands a jelly:
    Eggs, oysters, too, are amatory food;
But who is their purveyor from above
1360 Heaven knows,—it may be Neptune, Pan, or Jove.

171

When Juan woke he found some good things ready,
    A bath, a breakfast, and the finest eyes
That ever made a youthful heart less steady,
    Besides her maid's, as pretty for their size;
1365 But I have spoken of all this already—
    And repetition's tiresome and unwise,—
Well—Juan, after bathing in the sea,
Came always back to coffee and Haidee.

172

Both were so young, and one so innocent,
1370   That bathing pass'd for nothing; Juan seem'd
To her, as 'twere, the kind of being sent,
    Of whom these two years she had nightly dream'd,
A something to be loved, a creature meant
    To be her happiness, and whom she deem'd
1375 To render happy; all who joy would win
Must share it,—Happiness was born a twin.

173

It was such pleasure to behold him, such
    Enlargement of existence to partake
Nature with him, to thrill beneath his touch,
1380   To watch him slumbering, and to see him wake:
To live with him forever were too much;
    But then the thought of parting made her quake:
He was her own, her ocean-treasure, cast
Like a rich wreck—her first love, and her last.

174

1385 And thus a moon roll'd on, and fair Haidee
    Paid daily visits to her boy, and took
Such plentiful precautions, that still he
    Remain'd unknown within his craggy nook;
At last her father's prows put out to sea,
1390   For certain merchantmen upon the look,

Not as of yore to carry off an Io,[1]
    But three Ragusan vessels, bound for Scio.

175

Then came her freedom, for she had no mother,
    So that, her father being at sea, she was
1395 Free as a married woman, or such other
    Female, as where she likes may freely pass,
Without even the incumbrance of a brother,
    The freest she that ever gazed on glass:
I speak of Christian lands in this comparison,
1400 Where wives, at least, are seldom kept in garrison.

176

Now she prolong'd her visits and her talk
    (For they must talk), and he had learnt to say
So much as to propose to take a walk,—
    For little had he wander'd since the day
1405 On which, like a young flower snapp'd from the stalk,
    Drooping and dewy on the beach he lay,—
And thus they walk'd out in the afternoon,
And saw the sun set opposite the moon.

177

It was a wild and breaker-beaten coast,
1410   With cliffs above, and a broad sandy shore,
Guarded by shoals and rocks as by an host,
    With here and there a creek, whose aspect wore
A better welcome to the tempest-tost;
    And rarely ceased the haughty billow's roar,
1415 Save on the dead long summer days, which make
The outstretch'd ocean glitter like a lake.

178

And the small ripple spilt upon the beach
    Scarcely o'erpass'd the cream of your champaigne,
When o'er the brim the sparkling bumpers reach,
1420   That spring-dew of the spirit! the heart's rain!
Few things surpass old wine; and they may preach

---

[1] sea-nymph raped by Zeus.

Who please,—the more because they preach
  in vain,—
Let us have wine and woman, mirth and laughter,
Sermons and soda-water the day after.

179

Man, being reasonable, must get drunk;
  The best of life is but intoxication:
Glory, the grape, love, gold, in these are sunk
  The hopes of all men, and of every nation;
Without their sap, how branchless were the trunk
  Of life's strange tree, so fruitful on occasion:
But to return,—Get very drunk; and when
You wake with headache, you shall see what then.

180

Ring for your valet—bid him quickly bring
  Some hock and soda-water, then you'll know
A pleasure worthy Xerxes the great king;
  For not the blest sherbet, sublimed with snow,
Nor the first sparkle of the desert-spring,
  Nor Burgundy in all its sunset glow,
After long travel, ennui, love, or slaughter,
Vie with that draught of hock and soda-water.

181

The coast—I think it was the coast that I
  Was just describing—Yes, it *was* the coast—
Lay at this period quiet as the sky,
  The sands untumbled, the blue waves untost,
And all was stillness, save the sea-bird's cry,
  And dolphin's leap, and little billow crost
By some low rock or shelve, that made it fret
Against the boundary it scarcely wet.

182

And forth they wander'd, her sire being gone,
  As I have said, upon an expedition;
And mother, brother, guardian, she had none,
  Save Zoe, who, although with due precision
She waited on her lady with the sun,
  Thought daily service was her only mission,
Bringing warm water, wreathing her long tresses,
And asking now and then for cast-off dresses.

183

It was the cooling hour, just when the rounded
  Red sun sinks down behind the azure hill,
Which then seems as if the whole earth it bounded,
  Circling all nature, hush'd, and dim, and still,
With the far mountain-crescent half surrounded
  On one side, and the deep sea calm and chill
Upon the other, and the rosy sky,
With one star sparkling through it like an eye.

184

And thus they wander'd forth, and hand in hand,
  Over the shining pebbles and the shells,
Glided along the smooth and harden'd sand,
  And in the worn and wild receptacles
Work'd by the storms, yet work'd as it were plann'd,
  In hollow halls, with sparry roofs and cells,
They turn'd to rest; and, each clasp'd by an arm,
Yielded to the deep twilight's purple charm.

185

They look'd up to the sky, whose floating glow
  Spread like a rosy ocean, vast and bright;
They gazed upon the glittering sea below,
  Whence the broad moon rose circling into sight;
They heard the wave's splash, and the wind so low,
  And saw each other's dark eyes darting light
Into each other—and, beholding this,
Their lips drew near, and clung into a kiss;

186

A long, long kiss, a kiss of youth, and love,
  And beauty, all concentrating like rays
Into one focus, kindled from above;
  Such kisses as belong to early days,
Where heart, and soul, and sense, in concert move,
  And the blood's lava, and the pulse a blaze,
Each kiss a heart-quake,—for a kiss's strength,
I think, it must be reckon'd by its length.

187

By length I mean duration; theirs endured
  Heaven knows how long—no doubt they never
    reckon'd;

And if they had, they could not have secured
    The sum of their sensations to a second:
They had not spoken; but they felt allured,
    As if their souls and lips each other beckon'd,
Which, being join'd, like swarming bees they clung—
    Their hearts the flowers from whence the honey sprung.

188

They were alone, but not alone as they
    Who shut in chambers think it loneliness;
The silent ocean, and the starlight bay,
    The twilight glow, which momently grew less,
The voiceless sands, and dropping caves, that lay
    Around them, made them to each other press,
As if there were no life beneath the sky
Save theirs, and that their life could never die.

189

They fear'd no eyes nor ears on that lone beach,
    They felt no terrors from the night, they were
All in all to each other: though their speech
    Was broken words, they *thought* a language there,—
And all the burning tongues the passions teach
    Found in one sigh the best interpreter
Of nature's oracle—first love,—that all
Which Eve has left her daughters since her fall.

190

Haidee spoke not of scruples, ask'd no vows,
    Nor offer'd any; she had never heard
Of plight and promises to be a spouse,
    Or perils by a loving maid incurr'd;
She was all which pure ignorance allows,
    And flew to her young mate like a young bird;
And, never having dreamt of falsehood, she
Had not one word to say of constancy.

191

She loved, and was beloved—she adored,
    And she was worshipp'd; after nature's fashion,
Their intense souls, into each other pour'd,
    If souls could die, had perish'd in that passion,—
But by degrees their senses were restored,
    Again to be o'ercome, again to dash on;
And, beating 'gainst *his* bosom, Haidee's heart
Felt as if never more to beat apart.

192

Alas! they were so young, so beautiful,
    So lonely, loving, helpless, and the hour
Was that in which the heart is always full,
    And, having o'er itself no further power,
Prompts deeds eternity can not annul,
    But pays off moments in an endless shower
Of hell-fire—all prepared for people giving
Pleasure or pain to one another living.

193

Alas! for Juan and Haidee! they were
    So loving and so lovely—till then never,
Excepting our first parents, such a pair
    Had run the risk of being damn'd for ever;
And Haidee, being devout as well as fair,
    Had, doubtless, heard about the Stygian river,[1]
And hell and purgatory—but forgot
Just in the very crisis she should not.

194

They look upon each other, and their eyes
    Gleam in the moonlight; and her white arm clasps
Round Juan's head, and his around her lies
    Half buried in the tresses which it grasps;
She sits upon his knee, and drinks his sighs,
    He hers, until they end in broken gasps;
And thus they form a group that's quite antique,
Half naked, loving, natural, and Greek.

195

And when those deep and burning moments pass'd,
    And Juan sunk to sleep within her arms,
She slept not, but all tenderly, though fast,
    Sustain'd his head upon her bosom's charms;
And now and then her eye to heaven is cast,
    And then on the pale cheek her breast now warms,

---

[1] the river Styx, in Hades, which Byron here identifies with the Christian hell.

Pillow'd on her o'erflowing heart, which pants
With all it granted, and with all it grants.

196

An infant when it gazes on a light,
    A child the moment when it drains the breast,
A devotee when soars the Host[1] in sight,
    An Arab with a stranger for a guest,[2]
A sailor when the prize has struck in fight,[3]
    A miser filling his most hoarded chest,
Feel rapture; but not such true joy are reaping
As they who watch o'er what they love while sleeping.

197

For there it lies so tranquil, so beloved,
    All that it hath of life with us is living;
So gentle, stirless, helpless, and unmoved,
    And all unconscious of the joy 'tis giving;
All it hath felt, inflicted, pass'd, and proved,
    Hush'd into depths beyond the watcher's diving;
There lies the thing we love with all its errors
And all its charms, like death without its terrors.

198

The lady watch'd her lover—and that hour
    Of Love's, and Night's, and Ocean's solitude,
O'erflow'd her soul with their united power;
    Amidst the barren sand and rocks so rude
She and her wave-worn love had made their bower,
    Where nought upon their passion could intrude,
And all the stars that crowded the blue space
Saw nothing happier than her glowing face.

199

Alas! the love of women! it is known
    To be a lovely and a fearful thing;
For all of theirs upon that die is thrown,
    And if 'tis lost, life hath no more to bring
To them but mockeries of the past alone,
    And their revenge is as the tiger's spring,
Deadly, and quick, and crushing; yet, as real
Torture is theirs, what they inflict they feel.

200

They are right; for man, to man so oft unjust,
    Is always so to women; one sole bond
Awaits them, treachery is all their trust;
    Taught to conceal, their bursting hearts despond
Over their idol, till some wealthier lust
    Buys them in marriage—and what rests beyond?
A thankless husband, next a faithless lover,
Then dressing, nursing, praying, and all's over.

201

Some take a lover, some take drams or prayers,
    Some mind their household, others dissipation,
Some run away, and but exchange their cares,
    Losing the advantage of a virtuous station;
Few changes e'er can better their affairs,
    Theirs being an unnatural situation,
From the dull palace to the dirty hovel:
Some play the devil, and then write a novel.[4]

202

Haidee was Nature's bride, and knew not this;
    Haidee was Passion's child, born where the sun
Showers triple light, and scorches even the kiss
    Of his gazelle-eyed daughters; she was one
Made but to love, to feel that she was his
    Who was her chosen: what was said or done
Elsewhere was nothing—She had nought to fear,
Hope, care, nor love beyond, her heart beat *here*.

203

And oh! that quickening of the heart, that beat!
    How much it costs us! yet each rising throb
Is in its cause as its effect so sweet,
    That Wisdom, ever on the watch to rob
Joy of its alchymy, and to repeat
    Fine truths; even Conscience, too, has a tough job

---

[1] the bread or communion wafer consecrated at Mass.

[2] Arabs were famed for their warm hospitality to strangers.

[3] The "prize" is an enemy vessel captured in battle.

[4] Byron's ex-lover, Lady Caroline Lamb,* published *Glenarvon*, a roman-à-clef about their affair, in 1816. She also published a parody of *Don Juan*, entitled *A New Canto*.*

To make us understand each good old maxim,
So good—I wonder Castlereagh don't tax 'em.

204

And now 'twas done—on the lone shore were plighted
    Their hearts; the stars, their nuptial torches, shed
Beauty upon the beautiful they lighted:
    Ocean their witness, and the cave their bed,
By their own feelings hallow'd and united,
    Their priest was Solitude, and they were wed:
And they were happy, for to their young eyes
    Each was an angel, and earth paradise.

205

Oh, Love! of whom great Caesar was the suitor,
    Titus the master, Antony the slave,[1]
Horace, Catullus, scholars, Ovid tutor,[2]
    Sappho the sage blue-stocking, in whose grave
All those may leap who rather would be neuter—
    (Leucadia's rock still overlooks the wave)[3]
Oh, Love! thou art the very god of evil,
For, after all, we cannot call thee devil.

206

Thou mak'st the chaste connubial state precarious,
    And jestest with the brows of mightiest men:
Caesar and Pompey, Mahomet, Belisarius,[4]
    Have much employ'd the muse of history's pen;
Their lives and fortunes were extremely various,
    Such worthies Time will never see again;
Yet to these four in three things the same luck holds,
They all were heroes, conquerors, and cuckolds.

---

[1] Cæsar was Cleopatra's suitor and Mark Antony was her slave. Titus mastered his passion for Berenice, sending her away: see Suetonius, *Life of Titus* 7.1–2.

[2] because of his didactic poem, *Ars Amatoria* ("The Art of Love").

[3] an allusion to Sappho's alleged lesbianism, and to the legend of her suicide: see Robinson, *Sappho and Phaon*.*

[4] Julius Cæsar divorced his third wife, Pompeia, apparently for attempted adultery. Pompey divorced his third wife, Mucia, for committing adultery with Cæsar. Antonina had had several lovers before she married Belisarius, Justinian's great general. Muhammad's favourite wife, Ayesha, was suspected of impropriety, but he received a divine revelation of her purity.

207

Thou mak'st philosophers; there's Epicurus
    And Aristippus, a material crew![5]
Who to immoral courses would allure us
    By theories quite practicable too;
If only from the devil they would insure us,
    How pleasant were the maxim, (not quite new)
"Eat, drink, and love, what can the rest avail us?"
So said the royal sage Sardanapalus.[6]

208

But Juan! had he quite forgotten Julia?
    And should he have forgotten her so soon?
I can't but say it seems to me most truly a
    Perplexing question; but, no doubt, the moon
Does these things for us, and whenever newly a
    Strong palpitation rises, 'tis her boon,
Else how the devil is it that fresh features
Have such a charm for us poor human creatures?

209

I hate inconstancy—I loathe, detest,
    Abhor, condemn, abjure the mortal made
Of such quicksilver clay that in his breast
    No permanent foundation can be laid;
Love, constant love, has been my constant guest,
    And yet last night, being at a masquerade,
I saw the prettiest creature, fresh from Milan,
Which gave me some sensations like a villain.

210

But soon Philosophy came to my aid,
    And whisper'd "think of every sacred tie!"
"I will, my dear Philosophy!" I said,
    "But then her teeth, and then, Oh heaven! her eye!
I'll just inquire if she be wife or maid,
    Or neither—out of curiosity."
"Stop!" cried Philosophy, with air so Grecian,
(Though she was masqued then as a fair Venetian.)

---

[5] Epicurus (342–270 BC), Greek philosopher, and Aristippus (c. 370 BC), pupil of Socrates. Byron thinks of them (unfairly in the case of Epicurus) as advocating the unrestrained pursuit of pleasure.

[6] In 1821, Byron wrote a tragedy about this legendary Assyrian king.

211

"Stop!" so I stopp'd.—But to return: that which
    Men call inconstancy is nothing more
Than admiration due where nature's rich
    Profusion with young beauty covers o'er
Some favour'd object; and as in the niche
    A lovely statue we almost adore,
This sort of adoration of the real
Is but a heightening of the "beau ideal."

212

'Tis the perception of the beautiful,
    A fine extension of the faculties,
Platonic, universal, wonderful,
    Drawn from the stars, and filter'd through the skies,
Without which life would be extremely dull;
    In short, it is the use of our own eyes,
With one or two small senses added, just
To hint that flesh is form'd of fiery dust.

213

Yet 'tis a painful feeling, and unwilling,
    For surely if we always could perceive
In the same object graces quite as killing
    As when she rose upon us like an Eve,
'Twould save us many a heartache, many a shilling,
    (For we must get them any how, or grieve)
Whereas if one sole lady pleased for ever,
How pleasant for the heart, as well as liver!

214

The heart is like the sky, a part of heaven,
    But changes night and day too, like the sky;
Now o'er it clouds and thunder must be driven,
    And darkness and destruction as on high:
But when it hath been scorch'd, and pierced, and riven,
    Its storms expire in water-drops; the eye
Pours forth at last the heart's-blood turn'd to tears,
Which make the English climate of our years.

215

The liver is the lazaret of bile,
    But very rarely executes its function,
For the first passion stays there such a while,
    That all the rest creep in and form a junction,
Like knots of vipers on a dunghill's soil,
    Rage, fear, hate, jealousy, revenge, compunction,
So that all mischiefs spring up from this entrail,
Like earthquakes from the hidden fire call'd "central."

216

In the mean time, without proceeding more
    In this anatomy, I've finish'd now
Two hundred and odd stanzas as before,
    That being about the number I'll allow
Each canto of the twelve, or twenty-four;
    And, laying down my pen, I make my bow,
Leaving Don Juan and Haidee to plead
For them and theirs with all who deign to read.

Letters[1]

To Lady Byron

February 8th. 1816

All I can say seems useless—and all I could say— might be no less unavailing—yet I still cling to the wreck of my hopes—before they sink forever.——Were you then *never* happy with me?—did you never at any time or times express yourself so?—have no marks of affection—of the warmest & most reciprocal attachment passed between us?—or did in fact hardly a day go down without some such on one side and generally on both?—do not mistake me—[two lines crossed out] I have not denied my state of mind—but you know it's causes—& were those deviations from calmness never followed by acknowledgment & repentance?—was not the last which occurred more particularly so?—& had I not—had we not—the days before & on the day when we parted—every reason to believe that we loved each other—that we were to meet again—were not your letters kind?—had I not acknowledged to you all my faults & follies—&

---

[1] Texts are from Leslie A. Marchand, ed., *Byron's Letters and Journals* (1976).

assured you that some had not—& would not be repeated?—I do not require these questions to be answered to me—but to your own heart.———The day before I received your father's letter—I had fixed a day for rejoining you—if I did not write lately—Augusta did—and as you had been my proxy in correspondence with her—so did I imagine—she might be the same for me to you.—Upon your letter to me—this day—I surely may remark—that it's expressions imply a treatment which I am incapable of inflicting—& you of imputing to me—if aware of their latitude—& the extent of the inferences to be drawn from them.—This is not just———but I have no reproaches—nor the wish to find cause for them.——— Will you see me?—when & where you please—in whose presence you please:—the interview shall pledge you to nothing—& I will say & do nothing to agitate either—it is torture to correspond thus—& there are things to be settled & said which cannot be written.———You say "it is my disposition to deem what I *have worthless*"—did I deem *you* so?—did I ever so express myself to you—or of you—to others?———You are much changed within these twenty days or you would never have thus poisoned your own better feelings—and trampled upon mine.———

ever yrs. most truly & affectionately
B

To Augusta Leigh

Clarens.[1] Septr. 18th. 1816

Alpine Journal

Yesterday September 17th. 1816—I set out (with H[obhouse])[2] on an excursion of some days to the Mountains.—I shall keep a short journal of each day's progress for my Sister Augusta—

Sept. 17th.—

Rose at 5.—left Diodati[3] about seven—in one of the country carriages—(a Charaban)[4]—our servants on horseback—weather very fine—the Lake calm and clear—Mont Blanc—and the Aiguille of Argentière both very distinct—the borders of the Lake beautiful—reached Lausanne before Sunset—stopped & slept at Ouchy.—H[obhouse] went to dine with a Mr. Okeden—I remained at our Caravansera (though invited to the house of H's friend—too lazy or tired—or something else to go) and wrote a letter to Augusta—Went to bed at nine—sheets damp—swore and stripped them off & flung them—Heaven knows where—wrapt myself up in the blankets—and slept like a Child of a month's existence—till 5 o Clock of

Septr. 18th.

Called by Berger (my Courier who acts as Valet for a day or two—the learned Fletcher[5] being left in charge of Chattels at Diodati) got up—H[obhouse] walked on before—a mile from Lausanne—the road overflowed by the lake—got on horseback & rode—till within a mile of Vevey—the Colt young but went very well—overtook H. & resumed the carriage which is an open one—stopped at Vevey two hours (the second time I have visited it) walked to the Church—view from the Churchyard superb—within it General Ludlow[6] (the Regicide's) monument—black marble—long inscription—Latin—but simple—particularly the latter part—in which his wife (Margaret de Thomas) records her long—her tried—and unshaken affection—he was an Exile *two and thirty years*—one of the King's (Charles's) Judges—a fine fellow.—I remember reading his memoirs in January 1815 (at Halnaby[7]—) the first part of them is very amusing—the latter less so,—I little thought at the time of their perusal by me of seeing his tomb—near him Broughton[8] (who read King Charles's sentence to Charles Stuart)—is buried with a *queer* and

---

[1] a village on the east shore of Lake Geneva, the main setting of Rousseau's *Julie*.

[2] John Cam Hobhouse (1786–1869), Byron's best friend.

[3] a villa outside Geneva, which Byron had rented for the summer.

[4] a four-wheeled wagon.

[5] William Fletcher, Byron's faithful valet.

[6] Edmund Ludlow (1617?–92) was a member of the court that tried Charles I and signed his death warrant; at the Restoration of Charles II (1660), he fled first to France and then to Switzerland.

[7] an estate in North Yorkshire, belonging to Lady Byron's uncle; the couple spent their honeymoon there.

[8] unidentified.

rather *canting*—but still a Republican epitaph——Ludlow's house shown—it retains still his inscription "Omne Solum forte patria"[1]—Walked down to the Lake side—servants—Carriage—saddle horses—all set off and left us plantés la[2] by some mistake—and we walked on after them towards Clarens—H[obhouse] ran on before and overtook them at last—arrived the second time (1st time was by water) at Clarens beautiful Clarens!—went to Chillon[3] through Scenery worthy of I know not whom—went over the Castle of Chillon again—on our return met an English party in a carriage—a lady in it fast asleep!—fast asleep in the most anti-narcotic spot in the world—excellent—I remember at Chamouni—in the very eyes of Mont Blanc[4]—hearing another woman—English also—exclaim to her party—"did you ever see any thing more *rural*"—as if it was Highgate or Hampstead—or Brompton—or Hayes.[5]— "*Rural*" quotha!—Rocks—pines—torrents—Glaciers—Clouds—and Summits of eternal snow far above them—and "*Rural*!" I did not know the thus exclaiming fair one—but she was a—very good kind of woman.——After a slight & short dinner—we visited the Chateau de Clarens—an English woman has rented it recently—(it was not let when I saw it first) the roses are gone with their Summer—the family out—but the servants desired us to walk over the interior—saw on the table of the saloon—Blair's sermons[6]—and somebody else's (I forgot who's—) sermons—and a set of noisy children— saw all worth seeing and then descended to the "Bosquet de Julie" &c. &c.—our Guide full of *Rousseau*—whom he is eternally confounding with *St. Preux*[7]—and mixing the man and the book—on the steps of a cottage in the village—I saw a young *paysanne*—beautiful as Julie herself—went again as far as Chillon to revisit the little torrent from the hill behind it—Sunset—reflected in the lake—have to get up at 5 tomorrow to cross the mountains on horseback—carriage to be sent round—lodged at my old Cottage—hospitable & comfortable—tired with a longish ride—on the Colt—and the subsequent jolting of the Charaban—and my scramble in the hot sun—shall go to bed—thinking of you dearest Augusta.——Mem.—The Corporal who showed the wonders of Chillon was as drunk as Blucher[8]—and (to my mind) as great a man.—He was *deaf* also—and thinking every one else so—roared out the legends of the Castle so fearfully that H[obhouse] got out of the humour—however we saw all things from the Gallows to the Dungeon (the *Potence* & the *Cachets*) and returned to Clarens with more freedom than belonged to the 15th. Century.——At Clarens the only book (except the Bible) a translation of "*Cecilia*" (Miss Burney's *Cecilia*)[9] and the owner of the Cottage had also called her dog (a fat Pug *ten* years old—and hideous as *Tip*)[10] after Cecilia's (or rather Delville's) dog—Fidde—

Septr. 19th.

Rose at 5—ordered the carriage round.—Crossed the mountains to Montbovon on horseback—and on Mules—and by dint of scrambling on foot also,—the whole route beautiful as a *Dream* and now to me almost as indistinct,—I am so tired—for though healthy I have not the strength I possessed but a few years ago.—At Mont Davant we breakfasted—afterwards on a steep ascent—dismounted—tumbled down & cut a finger open—the baggage also got loose and fell down a ravine, till stopped by a large tree—swore—recovered baggage—horse tired & dropping—mounted Mule—at the approach of the summit of Dent Jamant—dismounted again with H. & all the party.— Arrived at a lake in the very nipple of the bosom of the Mountain.—left our

---

[1] "The whole earth is a brave man's country": Ovid, *Fasti* 1.493.

[2] "abandoned there" (Fr.).

[3] an island in Lake Geneva; the castle there is a prison, described in Byron's *The Prisoner of Chillon* (1816).

[4] Chamonix is at the foot of Mont Blanc and near the great glacier called the Mer de Glace.

[5] suburbs of London.

[6] Hugh Blair (1718–1800) published five volumes of sermons (1777–1801).

[7] the hero of *Julie*.

[8] Gebhard Leberecht von Blücher (1742–1819), the Prussian field marshal whose arrival at Waterloo (1815) helped to defeat Napoleon; Byron may have seen him drunk when he visited England in 1814.

[9] Frances Burney,* *Cecilia* (1782).

[10] Augusta's dog.

quadrupeds with a Shepherd—& ascended further—came to some snow in patches—upon which my forehead's perspiration fell like rain making the same dints as in a sieve—the chill of the wind & the snow turned me giddy—but I scrambled on & upwards—*H.* went to the highest *pinnacle*—I did not—but paused within a few yards (at an opening of the Cliff)—in coming down the Guide tumbled three times—I fell a laughing & tumbled too—the descent luckily soft though steep & slippery—H. also fell—but nobody hurt. The whole of the Mountain superb—the shepherd on a very steep & high cliff playing upon his *pipe*—very different from Arcadia[1]—(where I saw the pastors with a long Musquet instead of a Crook—and pistols in their Girdles)—our Swiss Shepherd's pipe was sweet—& his time agreeable—saw a cow strayed—told that they often break their necks on & over the crags—descended to Montbovon—pretty scraggy village with a wild river—and a wooden bridge.—H. went to fish—caught one—our carriage not come—our horses—mules &c. knocked up—ourselves fatigued—(but so much the better—I shall sleep). The view from the highest point of today's journey comprized on one side the greatest part of Lake Leman—on the other—the valleys & mountains of the Canton Fribourg—and an immense plain with the Lakes of Neufchatel & Morat—and all which the borders of these and of the Lake of Geneva inherit—we had both sides of the Jura before us in one point of view, with Alps in plenty.—In passing a ravine—the Guide recommended strenuously a quickening of pace—as the stones fall with great rapidity & occasional damage—the advice is excellent—but like most good advice impracticable—the road being so rough in this precise point—that neither mules nor mankind—nor horses—can make any violent progress.—Passed without any fractures or menace thereof.—The music of the Cows' bells (for their wealth like the Patriarchs is cattle) in the pastures (which reach to a height far above any mountains in Britain—) and the Shepherds' shouting to us from crag to crag & playing on their reeds where the steeps appeared almost inaccessible, with the surrounding scenery—realized all that I have ever heard or imagined of a pastoral existence—much more so than Greece or Asia Minor—for there we are a little too much of the sabre & musquet order—and if there is a Crook in one hand, you are sure to see a gun in the other—but this was pure and unmixed—solitary—savage and patriarchal[2]—the effect I cannot describe—as we went they played the "Ranz des Vaches"[3] and other airs by way of farewell.—I have lately repeopled my mind with Nature.

Septr. 20th.

Up at 6—off at 8—the whole of this days journey at an average of between from two thousand seven hundred to three thousand feet above the level of the Sea. This valley the longest—narrowest—& considered one of the finest of the Alps——little traversed by travellers—saw the Bridge of La Roche—the bed of the river very low & deep between immense rocks & rapid as anger—a man & mule said to have tumbled over without damage—(the mule was lucky at any rate—unless I knew the *man* I should be loth to pronounce *him* fortunate).—The people looked free & happy and *rich* (which last implies neither of the former) the cows superb—a Bull nearly leapt into the Charaban—"agreeable companion in a postchaise"[4]—Goats & Sheep very thriving—a mountain with enormous Glaciers to the right—the Kletsgerberg—further on—the Hockthorn—nice names—so soft—Hockthorn I believe very lofty & craggy—patched with snow only—no Glaciers on it—but some good epaulettes of clouds.—Past the boundaries—out of Vaud—& into Bern Canton—French exchanged for a bad German—the district famous for Cheese—liberty—property—& no taxes.—H. went to fish—caught none—strolled to river—saw a boy [and] a kid—kid followed him like a dog—kid could not get over a fence & bleated piteously—tried myself to help kid—but nearly overset both self & kid into the river.—Arrived here about six in the evening —nine o clock—going to bed—H. in next room—

---

[1] region in Greece celebrated in pastoral poetry.

[2] Cf. *Manfred* 1.2.47–52.*

[3] "tune of the cows" (Fr.): a folk melody used to call cattle.

[4] Adam Fitz-Adam (Edward Moore, 1712–57), *The World* (1753–56) 6: 119.

knocked his head against the door—and exclaimed of course against doors—not tired today—but hope to sleep nevertheless—women gabbling below—read a French translation of Schiller— Good Night—Dearest Augusta.——

Septr. 21st.

Off early—the valley of Simmenthal as before—entrance to the plain of Thoun very narrow—high rocks—wooded to the top—river—new mountains—with fine Glaciers—Lake of Thoun—extensive plain with a girdle of Alps—walked down to the Chateau de Schadau—view along the lake—crossed the river in a boat rowed by women— *women* [went?] right for the first time in my recollection.—Thoun a pretty town—the whole day's journey Alpine & proud.—

Septr. 22d.

Left Thoun in a boat which carried us the length of the lake in three hours—the lake small—but the banks fine—rocks down to the water's edge.—Landed at Neuhause—passed Interlachen—entered upon a range of scenes beyond all description—or previous conception.—Passed a rock—inscription—2 brothers—one murdered the other—just the place fit for it.—After a variety of windings came to an enormous rock—Girl with fruit—very pretty—blue eyes—good teeth—very fair—long but good features—reminded me of Fy.[1] bought some of her pears—and patted her upon the cheek—the expression of her face very mild—but good—and not at all coquettish.—Arrived at the foot of the Mountain (the Yung-frau—i.e., the Maiden) Glaciers—torrents—one of these torrents *nine hundred feet* in height of visible descent—lodge at the Curate's—set out to see the Valley—heard an Avalanche fall—like thunder—saw Glacier—enormous—Storm came on—thunder—lightning—hail—all in perfection—and beautiful—I was on horseback—Guide wanted to carry my cane—I was going to give it him when I recollected that it was a Swordstick and I thought that the lightning might be attracted towards him—kept it myself—a good deal encumbered with it & my cloak—as it was too heavy for a whip—and the horse was stupid—&

stood still every other peal. Got in—not very wet—the Cloak being staunch—H. wet through—H. took refuge in cottage—sent man— umbrella—& cloak (from the Curate's when I arrived—) after him.—Swiss Curate's house—very good indeed—much better than most English Vicarages—it is immediately opposite the torrent I spoke of—the torrent is in shape curving over the rock—like the *tail* of a white horse streaming in the wind—such as it might be conceived would be that of the "*pale* horse" on which *Death* is mounted in the Apocalypse.[2]—It is neither mist nor water but a something between both—it's immense height (nine hundred feet) gives it a wave—a curve—a spreading here—a condensation there—wonderful—& indescribable.—I think upon the whole—that this day has been better than any of this present excursion.—

Septr. 23d.

Before ascending the mountain—went to the torrent (7 in the morning) again—the Sun upon it forming a *rainbow* of the lower part of all colours—but principally purple and gold—the bow moving as you move—I never saw anything like this—it is only in the Sunshine.——Ascended the Wengren [sic] Mountain. ——at noon reached a valley near the summit—left the horses—took off my coat & went to the summit—7000 feet (English feet) above the level of the *sea*—and about 5000 above the valley we left in the morning—on one side our view comprized the *Yung frau* with all her glaciers—then the *Dent d'Argent*—shining like truth—then the *little Giant* (the Kleiner EIgher) & the great Giant (the Grosser EIgher) and last not least—the Wetterhorn.—The height of the Yung frau is 13000 feet above the sea—and 11000 above the valley—she is the highest of this range,—heard the Avalanches falling every five minutes nearly—as if God was pelting the Devil down from Heaven with snow balls—from where we stood on the *Wengren* [sic] Alp—we had all these in view on one side—on the other the clouds rose from the opposite valley curling up perpendicular precipices—like the foam of the Ocean of Hell during a Springtide —it was white & sulphery—and immeasurably deep in appearance—the side we ascended was (of course) not of

---

[1] Lady Frances ("Fanny") Webster, in whom Byron had once been erotically interested.

[2] Cf. *Manfred* 2.2.1–8.*

so precipitous a nature—but on arriving at the summit we looked down the other side upon a boiling sea of cloud—dashing against the crags on which we stood (these crags on one side quite perpendicular);—staid a quarter of an hour—began to descend—quite clear from cloud on that side of the mountain—in passing the masses of snow—I made a snowball & pelted H. with it—got down to our horses again—eat something—remounted—heard the Avalanches still—came to a morass—H. dismounted—H. got well over—I tried to pass my horse over—the horse sunk up [to] the chin—& of course he & I were in the mud together—bemired all over—but not hurt—laughed and rode on.—Arrived at the Grindenwald—dined—mounted again & rode to the higher Glacier—twilight—but distinct—very fine Glacier—like a *frozen hurricane*[1] — Starlight—beautiful—but a devil of a path—never mind—got safe in—a little lightning—but the whole of the day as fine in point of weather—as the day on which Paradise was made.—Passed *whole woods of withered pines*—*all withered*—trunks stripped & barkless—branches lifeless—done by a single winter— their appearance reminded me of me & my family.[2]—

Septr. 24th.
Set out at seven—up at five—passed the black Glacier—the Mountain Wetterhorn on the right—crossed the Scheideck mountain—came to the Rose Glacier— said to be the largest & finest in Switzerland.— *I* think the Bossons Glacier at Chamouni—as fine—H. does not—came to the Reichenback waterfall—two hundred feet high—halted to rest the horses—arrived in the valley of Oberhasli—rain came on—drenched a little—only 4 hours rain however in 8 days—came to Lake of Brientz—then to town of Brientz—changed—H. hurt his head against door.—In the evening four Swiss Peasant Girls of Oberhasli came & sang the airs of their country—two of the voices beautiful—the tunes also—they sing too that *Tyrolese air* & song which you love—Augusta—because I love it—& I love because you love it—they are still singing—Dearest—you do not know how I should have liked this—were you with me—the airs are so wild & original & at the same time of great sweetness.——The singing is over—but below stairs I hear the notes of a Fiddle which bode no good to my nights rest.—The Lord help us!—I shall go down & see the dancing.—

Septr. 25th.
The whole town of Brientz were apparently gathered together in the rooms below—pretty music—& excellent Waltzing—none but peasants—the dancing much better than in England—the English can't Waltz—never could—nor ever will.—One man with his pipe in his mouth—but danced as well as the others—some other dances in pairs—and in fours—and very good.——I went to bed but the revelry continued below late & early.—Brientz but a village.——Rose early.—Embarked on the Lake of Brientz.—Rowed by women in a long boat—one very young & pretty—seated myself by her—& began to row also—presently we put to shore & another woman jumped in—it seems it is the custom here for the boats to be *manned by women*—for of five men & three women in our bark—all the women took an oar—and but one man.——Got to Interlachen in three hours—pretty Lake—not so large as that of Thoun.—Dined at Interlachen—Girl gave me some flowers—& made me a speech in German—of which I know nothing—I do not know whether the speech was pretty but as the woman was—I hope so.—Saw another—very pretty too—and *tall* which I prefer—I hate short women—for more reasons than one.—Reembarked on the Lake of Thoun—fell asleep part of the way—sent our horses round—found people on the shore blowing up a rock with gunpowder—they blew it up near our boat—only telling us a minute before—mere stupidity—but they might have broke our noddles.—Got to Thoun in the Evening—the weather has been tolerable the whole day—but as the wild part of our tour is finished, it don't matter to us—in all the desirable part—we have been most lucky in warmth & clearness of Atmosphere—for which "Praise we the Lord."——

Septr. 26th.
Being out of the mountains my journal must be as flat as my journey.——From Thoun to Bern good road—hedges—villages—industry—prosperity—and all sorts

---

[1] Cf. *Manfred* 2.3.5–8.*

[2] Cf. *Manfred* 1.2.65–71.*

of tokens of insipid civilization.———From Bern to Fribourg.—Different Canton—Catholics—passed a field of Battle—Swiss beat the French—in one of the late wars against the French Republic.—Bought a dog—a very ugly dog— but "*tres mechant.*"[1] this was his great recommendation in the owner's eyes & mine—for I mean him to watch the carriage—he hath no tail—& is called "Mutz"—which signifies "*Short-tail*"—he is apparently of the Shepherd dog genus!—The greater part of this tour has been on horseback—on foot—and on mule;—the Filly (which is one of two young horses I bought of the Baron de Vincy) carried me very well—she is young and as quiet as anything of her sex can be—very goodtempered—and perpetually neighing—when she wants any thing—which is every five minutes—I have called her *Biche*[2]—because her manners are not unlike a little dog's—but she is a very tame—pretty childish quadruped.—

Septr. 28th. [27th.]

Saw the tree planted in honour of the battle of Morat[3]— 340 years old—a good deal decayed.—Left Fribourg—but first saw the Cathedral—high tower—overtook the baggage of the Nuns of La Trappe who are removing to Normandy from their late abode in the Canton of Fribourg—afterwards a coach with a quantity of Nuns in it—Nuns old—proceeded along the banks of the Lake of Neufchatel—very pleasing & soft—but not so mountainous—at least the Jura not appearing so—after the Bernese Alps—reached Yverdun in the dusk—a long line of large trees on the border of the lake—fine & sombre—the Auberge nearly full—with a German Princess & suite—got rooms—we hope to reach Diodati the day after tomorrow—and I wish for a letter from you my own dearest Sis—May your sleep be soft and your dreams of me.—I am going to bed—good night.—

Septr. 29th. [28th.]

Passed through a fine & flourishing country—but not mountainous—in the evening reached Aubonne (the entrance & bridge something like that of Durham) which commands by far the fairest view of the Lake of Geneva—twilight—the Moon on the Lake—a grove on the height—and of very noble trees.—Here Tavernier (the Eastern traveller) bought (or built) the Chateau because the site resembled and equalled that of *Erivan* (a frontier city of Persia) here he finished his voyages—and I this little excursion—for I am within a few hours of Diodati—& have little more to see—& no more to say.—In the weather for this tour (of 13 days) I have been very fortunate—fortunate in a companion (Mr. H[obhous]e) fortunate in our prospects—and exempt from even the little petty accidents & delays which often render journeys in a less wild country— disappointing.—I was disposed to be pleased—I am a lover of Nature—and an Admirer of Beauty—I can bear fatigue—& welcome privation—and have seen some of the noblest views in the world.—But in all this—the recollections of bitterness—& more especially of recent & more home desolation—which must accompany me through life—have preyed upon me here—and neither the music of the Shepherd—the crashing of the Avalanche—nor the torrent—the mountain—the Glacier—the Forest—nor the Cloud—have for one moment—lightened the weight upon my heart—nor enabled me to lose my own wretched identity in the majesty & the power and the Glory—around—above—& beneath me.—I am past reproaches—and there is a time for all things—I am past the wish of vengeance—and I know of none like for what I have suffered—but the hour will come—when what I feel must be felt—& the——but enough.—— To you— dearest Augusta—I send—and *for* you—I have kept this record of what I have seen & felt.—Love me as you are beloved by me.——

from *To John Murray*

Bologna, 12 August 1819

You are right—Gifford is right—Crabbe is right—Hobhouse is right—you are all right—and I am all wrong—but do pray let me have that pleasure.—Cut me up root and branch—quarter me in the

---

[1] "very vicious" (Fr.).

[2] "doe" (Fr.). "Dog's" in the next line is probably a mistake for "doe's."

[3] a battle between the Swiss and the Burgundians, in 1476.

Quarterly[1]— send round my "disjecti membra poetae"[2] like those of the Levite's Concubine[3]—make—if you will—a spectacle to men and angels[4]—but don't ask me to alter for I can't—I am obstinate and lazy—and there's the truth.—But nevertheless—I will answer your friend C.V.[5] who objects to the quick succession of fun and gravity—as if in that case the gravity did not (in intention at least) heighten the fun.—His metaphor is that "we are never scorched and drenched at the same time!"—Blessings on his experience!—Ask him these questions about "scorching and drenching."—Did he never play at Cricket or walk a mile in hot weather?—did he never spill a dish of tea over his testicles in handing the cup to his charmer to the great shame of his nankeen breeches?—did he never swim in the sea at Noonday with the Sun in his eyes and on his head—which all the foam of ocean could not cool? did he never draw his foot out of a tub of too hot water damning his eyes & his valet's? did he never inject for a Gonorrhea?—or make water through an ulcerated Urethra?—was he ever in a Turkish bath—that marble paradise of sherbet and sodomy?—was he ever in a cauldron of boiling oil like St. John?[6]—or in the sulphureous waves of hell? (where he ought to be for his "scorching and drenching at the same time") did he never tumble into a river or lake fishing—and sit in his wet cloathes in the boat—or on the bank afterwards "scorched and drenched" like a true sportsman?——"Oh for breath to utter"[7]——but make him my compliments—he is a clever fellow for all that—a very clever fellow.——— You ask me for the plan of Donny Johnny—I *have* no plan—I *had* no plan—but I had or have materials—though if like Tony Lumpkin—I am, "to be snubbed so when I am in spirits"[8] the poem will be naught—and the poet turn serious again.—If it don't take I will leave it off where it is with all due respect to the Public—but if continued it must be in my own way—you might as well make Hamlet (or Diggory)[9] "act mad" in a strait waistcoat—as trammel my buffoonery—if I am to be a buffoon—their gestures and my thoughts would only be pitiably absurd—and ludicrously constrained.—Why Man the Soul of such writing is it's licence?—at least the *liberty* of that *licence* if one likes—*not* that one should abuse it—it is like trial by Jury and Peerage—and the Habeas Corpus—a very fine thing—but chiefly in the *reversion*—because no one wishes to be tried for the mere pleasure of proving his possession of the privilege.———But a truce with these reflections;—you are too earnest and eager about a work never intended to be serious;—do you suppose that I could have any intention but to giggle and make giggle?—a playful satire with as little poetry as could be helped—was what I meant—and as to the indecency—do pray read in Boswell—what *Johnson* the sullen moralist—says of *Prior* and Paulo Purgante[10]——....

---

[1] John Murray, who published *Don Juan* 1 and 2 (July 1819) without either his own or Byron's name on the title-page, had established the Tory *Quarterly Review* in 1809. Byron defends his poem against charges of depravity by William Gifford, editor of the *Quarterly* from 1809–24, Crabbe,* a poet whom he admired, and even his close friend John Cam Hobhouse.

[2] "scattered parts of the poet": cf. Horace, *Satires* 1.4.62.

[3] Cf. Judges 19.

[4] Cf. 1 Corinthians 4.9.

[5] In spite of the perplexing initials, Byron here refers to Francis Cohen (later Palgrave), who contributed to the *Quarterly* and to the *Edinburgh Review*.

[6] St. John was alleged to have survived this ordeal; see Tertullian, *de Praescript*, 36.

[7] *1 Henry IV* 2.4.238.

[8] Cf. Tony Lumpkin to his doting mother in Oliver Goldsmith,* *She Stoops to Conquer* (1773) 2.566.

[9] Diggory is a comic servant in *She Stoops to Conquer*; Leslie A. Marchand also notes (*Letters and Journals* 6: 207n) that Diggory plays the role of a madman in a farce by Isaac Jackman, *All the World's a Stage* (1777).

[10] Samuel Johnson defended including Matthew Prior's "Paulo Purgante and his Wife" in his edition of the *English Poets* on the grounds that it was not indecent: see James Boswell, *Life of Johnson* (Monday 22 September 1777).

from *To Douglas Kinnaird*[1]

Venice. Octr. 26th. 1818 [1819]

My dear Douglas—My late expenditure has arisen from living at a distance from Venice and being obliged to keep up two establishments, from frequent journeys—and buying some furniture and books as well as a horse or two—and not from any renewal of the EPICUREAN system as you suspect. I have been faithful to my honest liaison with Countess Guiccioli[2]—and I can assure you that *She* has never cost me directly or indirectly a sixpence—indeed the circumstances of herself and family render this no merit.—I never offered her but one present—a broach of brilliants—and she sent it back to me with her *own hair* in it (I shall *not* say of *what part* but *that* is an Italian custom) and a note to say that she was not in the habit of receiving presents of that value—but hoped that I would not consider her sending it back as an affront—nor the value diminished by the enclosure.—I have not had a whore this half-year— confining myself to the strictest adultery.... —As to "Don Juan"—confess—confess—you dog—and be candid—that it is the sublime of *that there* sort of writing—it may be bawdy—but is it not good English?—it may be profligate—but is it not *life*, is it not *the thing*?—Could any man have written it—who has not lived in the world?—and tooled in a post-chaise? in a hackney coach? in a Gondola? against a wall? in a court carriage? in a vis a vis?—on a table?—and under it?—I have written about a hundred stanzas of a third Canto—but it is damned modest—the outcry has frightened me.—I had such projects for the Don—but the *Cant* is so much stronger than *Cunt*—now a days,—that the benefit of experience in a man who had well weighed the worth of both monosyllables—must be lost to despairing posterity.—After all what stuff this outcry is—Lalla Rookh and Little[3]—are more dangerous than my burlesque poem can be ....

---

[1] Douglas Kinnaird (1788–1830), Byron's friend and banker.

[2] Teresa Gamba Ghiselli (1800–79) married Count Alessandro Guiccioli in 1818; in 1819, she and Byron began a love affair that lasted until his death. She later wrote two memoirs of him.

[3] *Lalla Rookh* (1817) and *Poems of the Late Thomas Little* (1801), poems by Thomas Moore.

from *To John Murray*

Ravenna—Feb[brai]o 16 o 1821

Dear Moray— ... The 5th. is so far from being the last of D.J. that it is hardly the beginning.—I meant to take him the tour of Europe—with a proper mixture of siege—battle—and adventure—and to make him finish as *Anacharsis Cloots*[4]—in the French revolution.—To how many cantos this may extend—I know not—nor whether (even if I live) I shall complete it— but this was my notion.—I meant to have made him a Cavalier Servente[5] in Italy and a cause for a divorce in England—and a Sentimental "Werther-faced man"[6] in Germany—so as to show the different ridicules of the society in each of those countries——and to have displayed him gradually gaté and blasé as he grew older—as is natural.—But I had not quite fixed whether to make him end in Hell—or in an unhappy marriage,—not knowing which would be the severest.—The Spanish tradition says Hell—but it is probably only an Allegory of the other state.——You are now in possession of my notions on the subject.—

... As for News—the Barbarians are marching on Naples——and if they lose a single battle, all Italy will be up.—It will be like the Spanish war if they have any bottom.[7] —"*Letters opened!*" to be sure they are—and that's the reason why I always put in my opinion of the German Austrian Scoundrels;—there is not an Italian who loathes them more than I do—and whatever I could do to scour Italy and the earth of their infamous oppression—would be done "con amore."—

yrs. ever & truly
BYRON

---

[4] Jean-Baptiste Cloots (1755–94), a Prussian sympathizer with the French Revolution, who renamed himself Anacharsis after an ancient philosopher and described himself as the "orator of the human race." He was guillotined in 1794. Cf. note to *Childe Harold's Pilgrimage* 1.3.2.*

[5] the lover of a married woman.

[6] like the hero of Goethe, *The Sorrows of Young Werther* (1774).

[7] Byron sympathized with the Italian movement for independence from Austria and Spain. In 1820, Spanish liberals had revolted against Ferdinand VII and forced him to reinstate the constitution of 1812. France later helped Ferdinand to regain absolute power.

Recollect that the *Hints* must be printed with the *Latin* otherwise there is no sense.—

To Percy Bysshe Shelley

Ravenna, April 26th, 1821

The child[1] continues doing well, and the accounts are regular and favourable. It is gratifying to me that you and Mrs. Shelley do not disapprove of the step which I have taken, which is merely temporary.

I am very sorry to hear what you say of Keats—is it *actually* true? I did not think criticism had been so killing.[2] Though I differ from you essentially in your estimate of his performances, I so much abhor all unnecessary pain, that I would rather he had been seated on the highest peak of Parnassus than have perished in such a manner. Poor fellow! though with such inordinate self-love he would probably have not been very happy. I read the review of "Endymion" in the Quarterly. It was severe,—but surely not so severe as many reviews in that and other journals upon others.

I recollect the effect on me of the Edinburgh on my first poem;[3] it was rage, and resistance, and redress—but not despondency nor despair. I grant that those are not amiable feelings; but, in this world of bustle and broil, and especially in the career of writing, a man should calculate upon his powers of *resistance* before he goes into the arena.

"Expect not life from pain nor danger free,
Nor deem the doom of man reversed for thee."[4]

You know my opinion of *that second-hand* school of poetry. You also know my high opinion of your own poetry,—because it is of *no* school. I read Cenci—but, besides that I think the *subject* essentially *un*-dramatic, I am not an admirer of our old dramatists *as models*. I deny that the English have hitherto had a drama at all. Your Cenci, however, was a work of power, and poetry. As to *my* drama, pray revenge yourself upon it, by being as free as I have been with yours.

I have not yet got your Prometheus, which I long to see. I have heard nothing of mine, and do not know that it is yet published. I have published a pamphlet on the Pope controversy, which you will not like.[5] Had I known that Keats was dead—or that he was alive and so sensitive—I should have omitted some remarks upon his poetry, to which I was provoked by his *attack* upon *Pope*, and my disapprobation of *his own* style of writing.

You want me to undertake a great Poem—I have not the inclination nor the power. As I grow older, the indifference—*not* to life, for we love it by instinct—but to the stimuli of life, increases. Besides, this late failure of the Italians has latterly disappointed me for many reasons,—some public, some personal. My respects to Mrs. S.

Yours ever,
B.

P.S.—Could not you and I contrive to meet this summer? Could not you take a run *alone*?

---

[1] Allegra, Byron's daughter with Mary Shelley's* stepsister, Claire Clairmont. Byron had placed her in a convent, where she died in 1822.

[2] P.B. Shelley believed that Croker's harsh review of *Endymion** had killed Keats; cf. *Adonais.**

[3] The *Edinburgh Review* reviewed Byron's first book harshly; the experience provoked his satire *English Bards and Scotch Reviewers* (1809).

[4] Cf. Samuel Johnson, "The Vanity of Human Wishes" (1755) 155–56.

[5] Byron attacked Keats* in "Some Observations upon an Article in *Blackwood's Edinburgh Magazine*" (1820) and "Letter to John Murray Esq." (1821), because Keats had criticized Pope in "Sleep and Poetry" (1817).

Mary Prince
c. 1788 – after 1833

The daughter of slaves, Mary Prince was born at Brackish Pond, Bermuda, about 1788. Her father was a sawyer, her mother a house-servant in the home of Charles Myners. At Myners' death, Prince was sold to a Captain Williams and made to work for his daughter, Betsey. Hired out to another family at the age of twelve, she was sold again and suffered under an abusive mistress. Sold yet again, in 1806 she was sent to work on Turks Island, where sea water was evaporated to make salt.

In 1818, Prince was sold for $300 to John Wood, a plantation owner in Antigua; there, she worked as a house-servant and laundress. She was taught to read by members of the Moravian church and, in 1826, she married Daniel Jones, a free black carpenter, in the Moravian Chapel: she was beaten by her master when he found out about the marriage.

Prince went to England with the Woods in 1828. There, she ran away and was eventually employed by Thomas Pringle,* Secretary of the Anti-Slavery Society, who introduced Prince to her amanuensis, Susanna Strickland (later Susanna Moodie).* Strickland transcribed the resulting memoir, *The History of Mary Prince, a West Indian Slave*, and arranged in 1831 for its publication. The book was attacked as fabrication by Prince's former owner, John Wood, and other supporters of slavery; but Prince and her publisher sued their detractors for libel and won their case. After 1833, nothing is known about Mary Prince. (A.M.)

∽∽∽

from *The History of Mary Prince, a West Indian Slave. Related by Herself* (1831)[1]

My master ... was a very harsh, selfish man; and we always dreaded his return from sea. His wife was herself much afraid of him; and, during his stay at home, seldom dared to shew her usual kindness to the slaves. He often left her, in the most distressed circumstances, to reside in other female society, at some place in the West Indies of which I have forgot the name. My poor mistress bore his ill-treatment with great patience, and all her slaves loved and pitied her. I was truly attached to her, and, next to my own mother, loved her better than any creature in the world. My obedience to her commands was cheerfully given: it sprung solely from the affection I felt for her, and not from fear of the power which the white people's law had given her over me.

I had scarcely reached my twelfth year when my mistress became too poor to keep so many of us at home; and she hired me out to Mrs. Pruden, a lady who lived about five miles off, in the adjoining parish, in a large house near the sea. I cried bitterly at parting with my dear mistress and Miss Betsey, and when I kissed my mother and brothers and sisters, I thought my young heart would break, it pained me so. But there was no help; I was forced to go. Good Mrs. Williams comforted me by saying that I should still be near the home I was about to quit, and might come over and see her and my kindred whenever I could obtain leave of absence from Mrs. Pruden. A few hours after this I was taken to a strange house, and found myself among strange people. This separation seemed a sore trial to me then; but oh! 'twas light, light to the trials I have since endured!—'twas nothing—nothing to be mentioned with them; but I was a child then, and it was according to my strength.

I knew that Mrs. Williams could no longer maintain me; that she was fain to part with me for my food and clothing; and I tried to submit myself to the change. My new mistress was a passionate woman; but yet she did

---

[1] Prince dictated her story to Susanna Strickland (later Susanna Moodie);* Thomas Pringle,* Secretary to the Anti-Slavery Society, edited it, adding notes and a Supplement explaining the circumstances of the text's publication. This excerpt begins with the fourth paragraph of Prince's *History*: born in Bermuda, she has been bought as a slave for Miss Betsey Williams, a child about her own age; her mother is a household slave in the same family.

not treat me very unkindly. I do not remember her striking me but once, and that was for going to see Mrs. Williams when I heard she was sick, and staying longer than she had given me leave to do. All my employment at this time was nursing a sweet baby, little Master Daniel; and I grew so fond of my nursling that it was my greatest delight to walk out with him by the seashore, accompanied by his brother and sister, Miss Fanny and Master James.—Dear Miss Fanny! She was a sweet, kind young lady, and so fond of me that she wished me to learn all that she knew herself; and her method of teaching me was as follows:—Directly she had said her lessons to her grandmamma, she used to come running to me, and make me repeat them one by one after her; and in a few months I was able not only to say my letters but to spell many small words. But this happy state was not to last long. Those days were too pleasant to last. My heart always softens when I think of them.

At this time Mrs. Williams died. I was told suddenly of her death, and my grief was so great that, forgetting I had the baby in my arms, I ran away directly to my poor mistress's house; but reached it only in time to see the corpse carried out. Oh, that was a day of sorrow,—a heavy day! All the slaves cried. My mother cried and lamented her sore; and I (foolish creature!) vainly entreated them to bring my dear mistress back to life. I knew nothing rightly about death then, and it seemed a hard thing to bear. When I thought about my mistress I felt as if the world was all gone wrong; and for many days and weeks I could think of nothing else. I returned to Mrs. Pruden's; but my sorrow was too great to be comforted, for my own dear mistress was always in my mind. Whether in the house or abroad, my thoughts were always talking to me about her.

I staid at Mrs. Pruden's about three months after this; I was then sent back to Mr. Williams to be sold. Oh, that was a sad sad time! I recollect the day well. Mrs. Pruden came to me and said, "Mary, you will have to go home directly; your master is going to be married, and he means to sell you and two of your sisters to raise money for the wedding." Hearing this I burst out a crying,—though I was then far from being sensible of the full weight of my misfortune, or of the misery that waited for me. Besides, I did not like to leave Mrs. Pruden, and the dear baby, who had grown very fond of me. For some time I could scarcely believe that Mrs. Pruden was in earnest, till I received orders for my immediate return.—Dear Miss Fanny! how she cried at parting with me, whilst I kissed and hugged the baby, thinking I should never see him again. I left Mrs. Pruden's, and walked home with a heart full of sorrow. The idea of being sold away from my mother and Miss Betsey was so frightful, that I dared not trust myself to think about it. We had been bought of Mr. Myners, as I have mentioned, by Miss Betsey's grandfather, and given to her, so that we were by right *her* property, and I never thought we should be separated or sold away from her.

When I reached the house, I went in directly to Miss Betsey. I found her in great distress; and she cried out as soon as she saw me, "Oh, Mary! my father is going to sell you all to raise money to marry that wicked woman. You are *my* slaves, and he has no right to sell you; but it is all to please her." She then told me that my mother was living with her father's sister at a house close by, and I went there to see her. It was a sorrowful meeting; and we lamented with a great and sore crying our unfortunate situation. "Here comes one of my poor picaninnies!"[1] she said, the moment I came in, "one of the poor slave-brood who are to be sold to-morrow."...

The black morning at length came; it came too soon for my poor mother and us. Whilst she was putting on us the new osnaburgs[2] in which we were to be sold, she said, in a sorrowful voice, (I shall never forget it!) "See, I am *shrouding* my poor children; what a task for a mother!"—She then called Miss Betsey to take leave of us. "I am going to carry my little chickens to market," (these were her very words,) "take your last look of them; may be you will see them no more." "Oh, my poor slaves! my own slaves!" said dear Miss Betsey, "you belong to me; and it grieves my heart to part with you."—Miss Betsey kissed us all, and, when she left us, my mother called the rest of the slaves to bid us good

---

[1] from *pequeño*, "little" (Sp.); a term of condescension.

[2] work-clothes made out of heavy cotton (from Osnaburg, a town in Germany where such cloth was originally woven).

bye. One of them, a woman named Moll, came with her infant in her arms. "Ay!" said my mother, seeing her turn away and look at her child with the tears in her eyes, "your turn will come next." The slaves could say nothing to comfort us; they could only weep and lament with us. When I left my dear little brothers and the house in which I had been brought up, I thought my heart would burst.

Our mother, weeping as she went, called me away with the children Hannah and Dinah, and we took the road that led to Hamble Town, which we reached about four o'clock in the afternoon. We followed my mother to the market-place, where she placed us in a row against a large house, with our backs to the wall and our arms folded across our breasts. I, as the eldest, stood first, Hannah next to me, then Dinah; and our mother stood beside, crying over us. My heart throbbed with grief and terror so violently, that I pressed my hands quite tightly across my breast, but I could not keep it still, and it continued to leap as though it would burst out of my body. But who cared for that? Did one of the many by-standers, who were looking at us so carelessly, think of the pain that wrung the hearts of the negro woman and her young ones? No, no! They were not all bad, I dare say, but slavery hardens white people's hearts towards the blacks; and many of them were not slow to make their remarks upon us aloud, without regard to our grief—though their light words fell like cayenne on the fresh wounds of our hearts. Oh those white people have small hearts who can only feel for themselves.

At length the vendue master,[1] who was to offer us for sale like sheep or cattle, arrived, and asked my mother which was the eldest. She said nothing, but pointed to me. He took me by the hand, and led me out into the middle of the street, and, turning me slowly round, exposed me to the view of those who attended the vendue. I was soon surrounded by strange men, who examined and handled me in the same manner that a butcher would a calf or a lamb he was about to purchase, and who talked about my shape and size in like words—as if I could no more understand their meaning than the dumb beasts. I was then put up to sale. The bidding commenced at a few pounds, and gradually rose to fifty-seven,[2] when I was knocked down to the highest bidder; and the people who stood by said that I had fetched a great sum for so young a slave.

I then saw my sisters led forth, and sold to different owners; so that we had not the sad satisfaction of being partners in bondage. When the sale was over, my mother hugged and kissed us, and mourned over us, begging of us to keep up a good heart, and do our duty to our new masters. It was a sad parting; one went one way, one another, and our poor mammy went home with nothing.[3]

My new master was a Captain I——, who lived at Spanish Point. After parting with my mother and sisters,

---

[1] auctioneer; from *vendue*, "sale" (Fr.).

[2] "Bermuda currency; about £38 sterling." (Thomas Pringle,* Prince's editor.)

[3] "Let the reader compare the above affecting account, taken down from the mouth of this negro woman, with the following description of a vendue of slaves at the Cape of Good Hope, published by me in 1826, from the letter of a friend,—and mark their similarity in several characteristic circumstances. The resemblance is easily accounted for: slavery wherever it prevails produces similar effects.—'Having heard that there was to be a sale of cattle, farm stock, &c. by auction, at a Veld-Cornet's in the vicinity, we halted our waggon one day for the purpose of procuring a fresh spann of oxen. Among the stock of the farm sold, was a female slave and her three children. The two eldest children were girls, the one about thirteen years of age, and the other about eleven; the youngest was a boy. The whole family were exhibited together, but they were sold separately, and to different purchasers. The farmers examined them as if they had been so many head of cattle. While the sale was going on, the mother and her children were exhibited on a table, that they might be seen by the company, which was very large. There could not have been a finer subject for an able painter than this unhappy group. The tears, the anxiety, the anguish of the mother, while she met the gaze of the multitude, eyed the different countenances of the bidders, or cast a heart-rending look upon the children; and the simplicity and touching sorrow of the young ones, while they clung to their distracted parent, wiping their eyes, and half concealing their faces,—contrasted with the marked insensibility and jocular countenances of the spectators and purchasers,—furnished a striking commentary on the miseries of slavery, and its debasing effects upon the hearts of its abettors. While the woman was in this distressed situation she was asked, "Can you feed sheep?" Her reply was so indistinct that it escaped me; but it was probably in the negative, for her purchaser rejoined, in a loud and harsh voice, "Then I will teach you with the sjamboc," (a whip made of the rhinoceros' hide). The mother and her three children were sold to three separate purchasers; and they were literally torn from each other.'—*Ed*." (Thomas Pringle.)

I followed him to his store, and he gave me into the charge of his son, a lad about my own age, Master Benjy, who took me to my new home. I did not know where I was going, or what my new master would do with me. My heart was quite broken with grief, and my thoughts went back continually to those from whom I had been so suddenly parted. "Oh, my mother! my mother!" I kept saying to myself, "Oh, my mammy and my sisters and my brothers, shall I never see you again!"
...

Before I entered the house, two slave women, hired from another owner, who were at work in the yard, spoke to me, and asked who I belonged to? I replied, "I am come to live here." "Poor child, poor child!" they both said; "you must keep a good heart, if you are to live here."—When I went in, I stood up crying in a corner. Mrs. I—— came and took off my hat, a little black silk hat Miss Pruden made for me, and said in a rough voice, "You are not come here to stand up in corners and cry, you are come here to work." She then put a child into my arms, and, tired as I was, I was forced instantly to take up my old occupation of a nurse.—I could not bear to look at my mistress, her countenance was so stern. She was a stout tall woman with a very dark complexion, and her brows were always drawn together into a frown. I thought of the words of the two slave women when I saw Mrs. I——, and heard the harsh sound of her voice.

The person I took the most notice of that night was a French Black called Hetty, whom my master took in privateering[1] from another vessel, and made his slave. She was the most active woman I ever saw, and she was tasked to her utmost. A few minutes after my arrival she came in from milking the cows, and put the sweet-potatoes on for supper. She then fetched home the sheep, and penned them in the fold; drove home the cattle, and staked them about the pond side;[2] fed and rubbed down my master's horse, and gave the hog and the fed cow[3] their suppers; prepared the beds, and undressed the children, and laid them to sleep. I liked to look at her and watch all her doings, for her's was the only friendly face I had as yet seen, and I felt glad that she was there. She gave me my supper of potatoes and milk, and a blanket to sleep upon, which she spread for me in the passage before the door of Mrs. I——'s chamber.

I got a sad fright, that night. I was just going to sleep, when I heard a noise in my mistress's room; and she presently called out to inquire if some work was finished that she had ordered Hetty to do. "No, Ma'am, not yet," was Hetty's answer from below. On hearing this, my master started up from his bed, and just as he was, in his shirt, ran down stairs with a long cow-skin[4] in his hand. I heard immediately after, the cracking of the thong, and the house rang to the shrieks of poor Hetty, who kept crying out, "Oh, Massa! Massa! me dead. Massa! have mercy upon me—don't kill me outright."—This was a sad beginning for me. I sat up upon my blanket, trembling with terror, like a frightened hound, and thinking that my turn would come next. At length the house became still, and I forgot for a little while all my sorrows by falling fast asleep.

The next morning my mistress set about instructing me in my tasks. She taught me to do all sorts of household work; to wash and bake, pick cotton and wool, and wash floors, and cook. And she taught me (how can I ever forget it!) more things than these; she caused me to know the exact difference between the smart of the rope, the cart-whip, and the cow-skin, when applied to my naked body by her own cruel hand. And there was scarcely any punishment more dreadful than the blows I received on my face and head from her hard heavy fist. She was a fearful woman, and a savage mistress to her slaves.

There were two little slave boys in the house, on whom she vented her bad temper in a special manner. One of these children was a mulatto, called Cyrus, who

---

[1] the practice of private ships raiding enemy vessels for booty.

[2] "The cattle on a small plantation in Bermuda are, it seems, often thus staked or tethered, both night and day, in situations where grass abounds." (Thomas Pringle.)

[3] "A cow fed for slaughter." (Thomas Pringle.)

[4] "A thong of hard twisted hide, known by this name in the West Indies." (Thomas Pringle.)

had been bought while an infant in his mother's arms; the other, Jack, was an African from the coast of Guinea, whom a sailor had given or sold to my master. Seldom a day passed without these boys receiving the most severe treatment, and often for no fault at all. Both my master and mistress seemed to think that they had a right to ill-use them at their pleasure; and very often accompanied their commands with blows, whether the children were behaving well or ill. I have seen their flesh ragged and raw with licks.—Lick—lick—they were never secure one moment from a blow, and their lives were passed in continual fear. My mistress was not contented with using the whip, but often pinched their cheeks and arms in the most cruel manner. My pity for these poor boys was soon transferred to myself; for I was licked, and flogged, and pinched by her pitiless fingers in the neck and arms, exactly as they were. To strip me naked—to hang me up by the wrists and lay my flesh open with the cow-skin, was an ordinary punishment for even a slight offence. My mistress often robbed me too of the hours that belong to sleep. She used to sit up very late, frequently even until morning; and I had then to stand at a bench and wash during the greater part of the night, or pick wool and cotton; and often I have dropped down overcome by sleep and fatigue, till roused from a state of stupor by the whip, and forced to start up to my tasks.

Poor Hetty, my fellow slave, was very kind to me, and I used to call her my Aunt; but she led a most miserable life, and her death was hastened (at least the slaves all believed and said so,) by the dreadful chastisement she received from my master during her pregnancy. It happened as follows. One of the cows had dragged the rope away from the stake to which Hetty had fastened it, and got loose. My master flew into a terrible passion, and ordered the poor creature to be stripped quite naked, notwithstanding her pregnancy, and to be tied up to a tree in the yard. He then flogged her as hard as he could lick, both with the whip and cow-skin, till she was all over streaming with blood. He rested, and then beat her again and again. Her shrieks were terrible. The consequence was that poor Hetty was brought to bed before her time, and was delivered after severe labour of a dead child. She appeared to recover after her confinement, so far that she was repeatedly flogged by both master and mistress afterwards; but her former strength never returned to her. Ere long her body and limbs swelled to a great size; and she lay on a mat in the kitchen, till the water burst out of her body and she died. All the slaves said that death was a good thing for poor Hetty; but I cried very much for her death. The manner of it filled me with horror. I could not bear to think about it; yet it was always present to my mind for many a day.

After Hetty died all her labours fell upon me, in addition to my own. I had now to milk eleven cows every morning before sunrise, sitting among the damp weeds; to take care of the cattle as well as the children; and to do the work of the house. There was no end to my toils—no end to my blows. I lay down at night and rose up in the morning in fear and sorrow; and often wished that like poor Hetty I could escape from this cruel bondage and be at rest in the grave. But the hand of that God whom then I knew not, was stretched over me; and I was mercifully preserved for better things. It was then, however, my heavy lot to weep, weep, weep, and that for years; to pass from one misery to another, and from one cruel master to a worse. But I must go on with the thread of my story.

One day a heavy squall of wind and rain came on suddenly, and my mistress sent me round the corner of the house to empty a large earthen jar. The jar was already cracked with an old deep crack that divided it in the middle, and in turning it upside down to empty it, it parted in my hand. I could not help the accident, but I was dreadfully frightened, looking forward to a severe punishment. I ran crying to my mistress, "O mistress, the jar has come in two." "You have broken it, have you?" she replied; "come directly here to me." I came trembling: she stripped and flogged me long and severely with the cow-skin; as long as she had strength to use the lash, for she did not give over till she was quite tired.—When my master came home at night, she told him of my fault; and oh, frightful! how he fell a swearing. After abusing me with every ill name he could think of, (too, too bad to speak in England,) and giving me several heavy blows with his hand, he said, "I shall come home to-morrow morning at twelve, on purpose to give you a round hundred." He kept his word—Oh sad for me! I cannot easily forget it. He tied me up upon a ladder, and gave me a hundred lashes with his own hand, and master Benjy stood by to count them for him. When he had licked me for some time he sat down to take breath; then after resting, he beat me again and again, until he was quite wearied, and so hot (for the weather was very sultry), that he sank back in his chair, almost like to faint. While my mistress went to bring him drink, there was a dreadful earthquake. Part of the roof fell down, and every thing in the house went—clatter, clatter, clatter. Oh I thought the end of all things near at hand; and I was so sore with the flogging, that I scarcely cared whether I lived or died. The earth was groaning and shaking; every thing tumbling about; and my mistress and the slaves were shrieking and crying out, "The earthquake! the earthquake!" It was an awful day for us all.

During the confusion I crawled away on my hands and knees, and laid myself down under the steps of the piazza, in front of the house. I was in a dreadful state—my body all blood and bruises, and I could not help moaning piteously. The other slaves, when they saw me, shook their heads and said, "Poor child! poor child!"—I lay there till the morning, careless of what might happen, for life was very weak in me, and I wished more than ever to die. But when we are very young, death always seems a great way off, and it would not come that night to me. The next morning I was forced by my master to rise and go about my usual work, though my body and limbs were so stiff and sore, that I could not move without the greatest pain.—Nevertheless, even after all this severe punishment, I never heard the last of that jar; my mistress was always throwing it in my face.

Some little time after this, one of the cows got loose from the stake, and eat one of the sweet-potatoe slips. I was milking when my master found it out. He came to me, and without any more ado, stooped down, and taking off his heavy boot, he struck me such a severe blow in the small of my back, that I shrieked with agony, and thought I was killed; and I feel a weakness in that part to this day. The cow was frightened at his violence, and kicked down the pail and spilt the milk all about. My master knew that this accident was his own fault, but he was so enraged that he seemed glad of an excuse to go on with his ill usage. I cannot remember how many licks he gave me then, but he beat me till I was unable to stand, and till he himself was weary.

After this I ran away and went to my mother, who was living with Mr. Richard Darrel. My poor mother was both grieved and glad to see me; grieved because I had been so ill used, and glad because she had not seen me for a long, long while. She dared not receive me into the house, but she hid me up in a hole in the rocks near, and brought me food at night, after every body was asleep. My father, who lived at Crow-Lane, over the salt-water channel, at last heard of my being hid up in the cavern, and he came and took me back to my master. Oh I was loth, loth to go back; but as there was no remedy, I was obliged to submit.

When we got home, my poor father said to Capt. I——, "Sir, I am sorry that my child should be forced to run away from her owner; but the treatment she has received is enough to break her heart. The sight of her wounds has nearly broke mine.—I entreat you, for the love of God, to forgive her for running away, and that you will be a kind master to her in future." Capt. I—— said I was used as well as I deserved, and that I ought to be punished for running away. I then took courage and said that I could stand the floggings no longer; that I was weary of my life, and therefore I had run away to my mother; but mothers could only weep and mourn over their children, they could not save them from cruel masters—from the whip, the rope, and the cow-skin. He told me to hold my tongue and go about my work, or he would find a way to settle me. He did not, however, flog me that day....

I think it was about ten years I had worked in the salt ponds at Turk's Island, when my master left off business, and retired to a house he had in Bermuda, leaving his son to succeed him in the island. He took me with him to wait upon his daughters; and I was joyful, for I was sick, sick of Turk's Island, and my heart yearned to see my native place again, my mother, and my kindred.

I had seen my poor mother during the time I was a slave in Turk's Island. One Sunday morning I was on the beach with some of the slaves, and we saw a sloop come in loaded with slaves to work in the salt water. We got a boat and went aboard. When I came upon the deck I asked the black people, "Is there any one here for me?" "Yes," they said, "your mother." I thought they said this in jest—I could scarcely believe them for joy; but when I saw my poor mammy my joy was turned to sorrow, for she had gone from her senses. "Mammy," I said, "is this you?" She did not know me. "Mammy," I said, "what's the matter?" She began to talk foolishly, and said that she had been under the vessel's bottom. They had been overtaken by a violent storm at sea. My poor mother had never been on the sea before, and she was so ill, that she lost her senses, and it was long before she came quite to herself again. She had a sweet child with her—a little sister I had never seen, about four years of age, called Rebecca. I took her on shore with me, for I felt I should love her directly; and I kept her with me a week. Poor little thing! her's has been a sad life, and continues so to this day. My mother worked for some years on the island, but was taken back to Bermuda some time before my master carried me again thither.[1]

After I left Turk's Island, I was told by some negroes that came over from it, that the poor slaves had built up a place with boughs and leaves, where they might meet for prayers, but the white people pulled it down twice, and would not allow them even a shed for prayers. A flood came down soon after and washed away many houses, filled the place with sand, and overflowed the ponds: and I do think that this was for their wickedness; for the Buckra men[2] there were very wicked. I saw and heard much that was very very bad at that place.

I was several years the slave of Mr. D—— after I returned to my native place. Here I worked in the grounds. My work was planting and hoeing sweet-potatoes, Indian corn, plaintains, bananas, cabbages, pumpkins, onions, &c. I did all the household work, and attended upon a horse and cow besides,—going also upon all errands. I had to curry the horse—to clean and feed him—and sometimes to ride him a little. I had more than enough to do—but still it was not so very bad as Turk's Island.

My old master often got drunk, and then he would get in a fury with his daughter, and beat her till she was not fit to be seen. I remember on one occasion, I had gone to fetch water, and when I was coming up the hill I heard a great screaming; I ran as fast as I could to the house, put down the water, and went into the chamber, where I found my master beating Miss D—— dreadfully. I strove with all my strength to get her away from him; for she was all black and blue with bruises. He had beat her with his fist, and almost killed her. The people gave me credit for getting her away. He turned round and began to lick me. Then I said, "Sir, this is not Turk's Island." I can't repeat his answer, the words were too wicked—too bad to say. He wanted to treat me the same in Bermuda as he had done in Turk's Island.

He had an ugly fashion of stripping himself quite naked, and ordering me then to wash him in a tub of water. This was worse to me than all the licks. Sometimes when he called me to wash him I would not come, my eyes were so full of shame. He would then come to beat me. One time I had plates and knives in my hand, and I dropped both plates and knives, and some of the plates were broken. He struck me so severely for this, that at last I defended myself, for I thought it was high time to do so. I then told him I would not live longer with him, for he was a very indecent man—very spiteful, and too indecent; with no shame for his servants, no shame for his own flesh. So I went away to a neighbouring house and sat down and cried till the next morning, when I went home again, not knowing what else to do.

After that I was hired to work at Cedar Hills, and every Saturday night I paid the money to my master. I had plenty of work to do there—plenty of washing; but

---

[1] "Of the subsequent lot of her relatives she can tell but little. She says, her father died while she and her mother were at Turk's Island; and that he had been long dead and buried before any of his children in Bermuda knew of it, they being slaves on other estates. Her mother died after Mary went to Antigua. Of the fate of the rest of her kindred, seven brothers and three sisters, she knows nothing further than this—that the eldest sister, who had several children to her master, was taken by him to Trinidad; and that the youngest, Rebecca, is still alive, and in slavery in Bermuda. Mary herself is now about forty-three years of age.— *Ed*." (Thomas Pringle.)

[2] "Negro term for white people." (Thomas Pringle.)

yet I made myself pretty comfortable. I earned two dollars and a quarter a week, which is twenty pence a day.

During the time I worked there, I heard that Mr. John Wood was going to Antigua. I felt a great wish to go there, and I went to Mr. D——, and asked him to let me go in Mr. Wood's service. Mr. Wood did not then want to purchase me; it was my own fault that I came under him, I was so anxious to go. It was ordained to be, I suppose; God led me there. The truth is, I did not wish to be any longer the slave of my indecent master.

Mr. Wood took me with him to Antigua, to the town of St. John's, where he lived. This was about fifteen years ago. He did not then know whether I was to be sold; but Mrs. Wood found that I could work, and she wanted to buy me. Her husband then wrote to my master to inquire whether I was to be sold? Mr. D—— wrote in reply, "that I should not be sold to any one that would treat me ill." It was strange he should say this, when he had treated me so ill himself. So I was purchased by Mr. Wood for 300 dollars, (or £100 Bermuda currency.)[1]

My work there was to attend the chambers and nurse the child, and to go down to the pond and wash clothes. But I soon fell ill of the rheumatism, and grew so very lame that I was forced to walk with a stick. I got the Saint Anthony's fire,[2] also, in my left leg, and became quite a cripple. No one cared much to come near me, and I was ill a long long time; for several months I could not lift the limb. I had to lie in a little old out-house, that was swarming with bugs and other vermin, which tormented me greatly; but I had no other place to lie in. I got the rheumatism by catching cold at the pond side, from washing in the fresh water; in the salt water I never got cold. The person who lived in next yard, (a Mrs. Greene,) could not bear to hear my cries and groans. She was kind, and used to send an old slave woman to help me, who sometimes brought me a little soup. When the doctor found I was so ill, he said I must be put into a bath of hot water. The old slave got the bark of some bush that was good for the pains, which she boiled in the hot water, and every night she came and put me into the bath, and did what she could for me: I don't know what I should have done, or what would have become of me, had it not been for her.—My mistress, it is true, did send me a little food; but no one from our family came near me but the cook, who used to shove my food in at the door, and say, "Molly, Molly, there's your dinner." My mistress did not care to take any trouble about me; and if the Lord had not put it into the hearts of the neighbours to be kind to me, I must, I really think, have lain and died....

Another time (about five years ago) my mistress got vexed with me, because I fell sick and I could not keep on with my work. She complained to her husband, and he sent me off again to look for an owner. I went to a Mr. Burchell, showed him the note, and asked him to buy me for my own benefit; for I had saved about 100 dollars, and hoped, with a little help, to purchase my freedom. He accordingly went to my master:—"Mr. Wood," he said, "Molly has brought me a note that she wants an owner. If you intend to sell her, I may as well buy her as another." My master put him off and said that he did not mean to sell me. I was very sorry at this, for I had no comfort with Mrs. Wood, and I wished greatly to get my freedom.

The way in which I made my money was this.—When my master and mistress went from home, as they sometimes did, and left me to take care of the house and premises, I had a good deal of time to myself, and made the most of it. I took in washing, and sold coffee and yams and other provisions to the captains of ships. I did not sit still idling during the absence of my owners; for I wanted, by all honest means, to earn money to buy my freedom. Sometimes I bought a hog cheap on board ship, and sold it for double the money on shore; and I also earned a good deal by selling coffee. By this means I by degrees acquired a little cash. A gentleman also lent me some to help to buy my freedom—but when I could not get free he got it back again. His name was Captain Abbot.

My master and mistress went on one occasion into the country, to Date Hill, for change of air, and carried me with them to take charge of the children, and to do the work of the house. While I was in the country, I saw

---

[1] "About £67.10 s. sterling." (Thomas Pringle.)

[2] erysipelas, a streptococcal skin infection.

how the field negroes are worked in Antigua. They are worked very hard and fed but scantily. They are called out to work before daybreak, and come home after dark; and then each has to heave his bundle of grass for the cattle in the pen. Then, on Sunday morning, each slave has to go out and gather a large bundle of grass; and, when they bring it home, they have all to sit at the manager's door and wait till he come out: often have they to wait there till past eleven o'clock, without any breakfast. After that, those that have yams or potatoes, or fire-wood to sell, hasten to market to buy a dog's worth[1] of salt fish, or pork, which is a great treat for them. Some of them buy a little pickle out of the shad barrels, which they call sauce, to season their yams and Indian corn. It is very wrong, I know, to work on Sunday or go to market; but will not God call the Buckra men to answer for this on the great day of judgment—since they will give the slaves no other day?

While we were at Date Hill Christmas came; and the slave woman who had the care of the place (which then belonged to Mr. Roberts the marshal), asked me to go with her to her husband's house, to a Methodist meeting for prayer, at a plantation called Winthorps. I went; and they were the first prayers I ever understood. One woman prayed; and then they all sung a hymn; then there was another prayer and another hymn; and then they all spoke by turns of their own griefs as sinners. The husband of the woman I went with was a black driver. His name was Henry. He confessed that he had treated the slaves very cruelly; but said that he was compelled to obey the orders of his master. He prayed them all to forgive him, and he prayed that God would forgive him. He said it was a horrid thing for a ranger[2] to have sometimes to beat his own wife or sister; but he must do so if ordered by his master.

I felt sorry for my sins also. I cried the whole night, but I was too much ashamed to speak. I prayed God to forgive me. This meeting had a great impression on my mind, and led my spirit to the Moravian church;[3] so that when I got back to town, I went and prayed to have my name put down in the Missionaries' book; and I followed the church earnestly every opportunity. I did not then tell my mistress about it; for I knew that she would not give me leave to go. But I felt I *must* go. Whenever I carried the children their lunch at school, I ran round and went to hear the teachers....

About this time my master and mistress were going to England to put their son to school, and bring their daughters home; and they took me with them to take care of the child. I was willing to come to England: I thought that by going there I should probably get cured of my rheumatism, and should return with my master and mistress, quite well, to my husband. My husband was willing for me to come away, for he had heard that my master would free me,—and I also hoped this might prove true; but it was all a false report.

The steward of the ship was very kind to me. He and my husband[4] were in the same class in the Moravian Church. I was thankful that he was so friendly, for my mistress was not kind to me on the passage; and she told me, when she was angry, that she did not intend to treat me any better in England than in the West Indies—that I need not expect it. And she was as good as her word.

When we drew near to England, the rheumatism seized all my limbs worse than ever, and my body was dreadfully swelled. When we landed at the Tower,[5] I shewed my flesh to my mistress, but she took no great notice of it. We were obliged to stop at the tavern till my master got a house; and a day or two after, my mistress sent me down into the wash-house to learn to wash in the English way. In the West Indies we wash with cold water—in England with hot. I told my mistress I was afraid that putting my hands first into the hot water and then into the cold, would increase the pain in my limbs. The doctor had told my mistress long before I came from the West Indies, that I was a sickly body and the washing did not agree with me. But Mrs. Wood would not release me from the tub, so I was forced to do as I could. I grew worse, and could not stand to wash. I was then forced to sit down with the

---

[1] "A dog is the 72nd part of a dollar." (Thomas Pringle.)

[2] "The head negro of an estate—a person who has the chief superintendence under the manager." (Thomas Pringle.)

[3] an evangelical Protestant sect, founded in 1722.

[4] Prince had married a free black carpenter, Daniel Jones, in 1826.

[5] the Tower of London, on the River Thames.

tub before me, and often through pain and weakness was reduced to kneel or to sit down on the floor, to finish my task. When I complained to my mistress of this, she only got into a passion as usual, and said washing in hot water could not hurt any one;—that I was lazy and insolent, and wanted to be free of my work; but that she would make me do it. I thought her very hard on me, and my heart rose up within me. However I kept still at that time, and went down again to wash the child's things; but the English washerwomen who were at work there, when they saw that I was so ill, had pity upon me and washed them for me.

After that, when we came up to live in Leigh Street, Mrs. Wood sorted out five bags of clothes which we had used at sea, and also such as had been worn since we came on shore, for me and the cook to wash. Elizabeth the cook told her, that she did not think that I was able to stand to the tub, and that she had better hire a woman. I also said myself, that I had come over to nurse the child, and that I was sorry I had come from Antigua, since mistress would work me so hard, without compassion for my rheumatism. Mr. and Mrs. Wood, when they heard this, rose up in a passion against me. They opened the door and bade me get out. But I was a stranger, and did not know one door in the street from another, and was unwilling to go away. They made a dreadful uproar, and from that day they constantly kept cursing and abusing me. I was obliged to wash, though I was very ill. Mrs. Wood, indeed once hired a washerwoman, but she was not well treated, and would come no more.

My master quarrelled with me another time, about one of our great washings, his wife having stirred him up to do so. He said he would compel me to do the whole of the washing given out to me, or if I again refused, he would take a short course with me: he would either send me down to the brig in the river, to carry me back to Antigua, or he would turn me at once out of doors, and let me provide for myself. I said I would willingly go back, if he would let me purchase my own freedom. But this enraged him more than all the rest: he cursed and swore at me dreadfully, and said he would never sell my freedom—if I wished to be free, I was free in England,[1] and I might go and try what freedom would do for me, and be d——d. My heart was very sore with this treatment, but I had to go on. I continued to do my work, and did all I could to give satisfaction, but all would not do.

Shortly after, the cook left them, and then matters went on ten times worse. I always washed the child's clothes without being commanded to do it, and any thing else that was wanted in the family; though still I was very sick—very sick indeed. When the great washing came round, which was every two months, my mistress got together again a great many heavy things, such as bed-ticks, bed-coverlets, &c. for me to wash. I told her I was too ill to wash such heavy things that day. She said, she supposed I thought myself a free woman, but I was not; and if I did not do it directly I should be instantly turned out of doors. I stood a long time before I could answer, for I did not know well what to do. I knew that I was free in England, but I did not know where to go, or how to get my living; and therefore, I did not like to leave the house. But Mr. Wood said he would send for a constable to thrust me out; and at last I took courage and resolved that I would not be longer thus treated, but would go and trust to Providence. This was the fourth time they had threatened to turn me out, and, go where I might, I was determined now to take them at their word; though I thought it very hard, after I had lived with them for thirteen years, and worked for them like a horse, to be driven out in this way, like a beggar. My only fault was being sick, and therefore unable to please my mistress, who thought she never could get work enough out of her slaves; and I told them so: but they only abused me and drove me out. This took place from two to three months, I think, after we came to England.

When I came away, I went to the man (one Mash) who used to black the shoes of the family, and asked his wife to get somebody to go with me to Hatton Garden to the Moravian Missionaries: these were the only persons I knew in England. The woman sent a young girl with me to the mission house, and I saw there a

---

[1] Lord Mansfield's Somerset ruling (1772) was widely interpreted as denying the legal basis for slavery in England. Slavery continued in British colonies, however, until 1833.

gentleman called Mr. Moore. I told him my whole story, and how my owners had treated me, and asked him to take in my trunk with what few clothes I had. The missionaries were very kind to me—they were sorry for my destitute situation, and gave me leave to bring my things to be placed under their care. They were very good people, and they told me to come to the church....

About this time, a woman of the name of Hill told me of the Anti-Slavery Society,[1] and went with me to their office, to inquire if they could do any thing to get me my freedom, and send me back to the West Indies. The gentlemen of the Society took me to a lawyer, who examined very strictly into my case; but told me that the laws of England could do nothing to make me free in Antigua.[2] However they did all they could for me: they gave me a little money from time to time to keep me from want; and some of them went to Mr. Wood to try to persuade him to let me return a free woman to my husband; but though they offered him, as I have heard, a large sum for my freedom, he was sulky and obstinate, and would not consent to let me go free.

This was the first winter I spent in England, and I suffered much from the severe cold, and from the rheumatic pains, which still at times torment me. However, Providence was very good to me, and I got many friends—especially some Quaker ladies,[3] who hearing of my case, came and sought me out, and gave me good warm clothing and money. Thus I had great cause to bless God in my affliction.

When I got better I was anxious to get some work to do, as I was unwilling to eat the bread of idleness. Mrs. Mash, who was a laundress, recommended me to a lady for a charwoman. She paid me very handsomely for what work I did, and I divided the money with Mrs. Mash; for though very poor, they gave me food when my own money was done, and never suffered me to want.

In the spring, I got into service with a lady, who saw me at the house where I sometimes worked as a charwoman. This lady's name was Mrs. Forsyth. She had been in the West Indies, and was accustomed to Blacks, and liked them. I was with her six months, and went with her to Margate. She treated me well, and gave me a good character when she left London.[4]

After Mrs. Forsyth went away, I was again out of place, and went to lodgings, for which I paid two shillings a week, and found coals and candle. After eleven weeks, the money I had saved in service was all gone, and I was forced to go back to the Anti-Slavery office to ask a supply, till I could get another situation. I did not like to go back—I did not like to be idle. I would rather work for my living than get it for nothing. They were very good to give me a supply, but I felt shame at being obliged to apply for relief whilst I had strength to work.

At last I went into the service of Mr. and Mrs. Pringle,[5] where I have been ever since, and am as comfortable as I can be while separated from my dear husband, and away from my own country and all old friends and connections. My dear mistress teaches me daily to read the word of God, and takes great pains to make me understand it. I enjoy the great privilege of being enabled to attend church three times on the Sunday; and I have met with many kind friends since I have been here, both clergymen and others. The Rev. Mr. Young, who lives in the next house, has shown me much kindness, and taken much pains to instruct me, particularly while my master and mistress were absent in Scotland. Nor must I forget, among my friends, the Rev. Mr. Mortimer, the good clergyman of the parish, under whose ministry I have now sat for upwards of twelve months. I trust in God I have profited by what I have heard from him. He never keeps back the truth,

---

[1] Founded in 1823, the Anti-Slavery Society sought to improve the conditions of slaves in the West Indies and to work towards gradual emancipation.

[2] "She came first to the Anti-Slavery Office in Aldermanbury, about the latter end of November 1828; and her case was referred to Mr. George Stephen to be investigated. More of this hereafter.—Ed." (Thomas Pringle.)

[3] members of the Society of Friends (Quakers), a religious group active in the anti-slavery movement.

[4] "She refers to a written certificate which will be inserted afterwards." (Thomas Pringle.)

[5] Thomas Pringle,* a Scottish poet who had lived in South Africa between 1820 and 1826, became secretary of the Anti-Slavery Society in 1827; he and his wife, Margaret Brown Pringle, employed Prince as a domestic servant, and Thomas Pringle edited her memoir.

and I think he has been the means of opening my eyes and ears much better to understand the word of God. Mr. Mortimer tells me that he cannot open the eyes of my heart, but that I must pray to God to change my heart, and make me to know the truth, and the truth will make me free.[1]

I still live in the hope that God will find a way to give me my liberty, and give me back to my husband. I endeavour to keep down my fretting, and to leave all to Him, for he knows what is good for me better than I know myself. Yet, I must confess, I find it a hard and heavy task to do so.

I am often much vexed, and I feel great sorrow when I hear some people in this country say, that the slaves do not need better usage, and do not want to be free.[2] They believe the foreign people,[3] who deceive them, and say slaves are happy. I say, Not so. How can slaves be happy when they have the halter round their neck and the whip upon their back? and are disgraced and thought no more of than beasts?—and are separated from their mothers, and husbands, and children, and sisters, just as cattle are sold and separated? Is it happiness for a driver in the field to take down his wife or sister or child, and strip them, and whip them in such a disgraceful manner?—women that have had children exposed in the open field to shame! There is no modesty or decency shown by the owner to his slaves; men, women, and children are exposed alike. Since I have been here I have often wondered how English people can go out into the West Indies and act in such a beastly manner. But when they go to the West Indies, they forget God and all feeling of shame, I think, since they can see and do such things. They tie up slaves like hogs—moor[4] them up like cattle, and they lick them, so as hogs, or cattle, or horses never were flogged;—and yet they come home and say, and make some good people believe, that slaves don't want to get out of slavery. But they put a cloak about the truth. It is not so. All slaves want to be free—to be free is very sweet. I will say the truth to English people who may read this history that my good friend, Miss S——, is now writing down for me. I have been a slave myself—I know what slaves feel—I can tell by myself what other slaves feel, and by what they have told me. The man that says slaves be quite happy in slavery—that they don't want to be free—that man is either ignorant or a lying person. I never heard a slave say so. I never heard a Buckra man say so, till I heard tell of it in England. Such people ought to be ashamed of themselves. They can't do without slaves, they say. What's the reason they can't do without slaves as well as in England? No slaves here—no whips—no stocks—no punishment, except for wicked people. They hire servants in England; and if they don't like them, they send them away: they can't lick them. Let them work ever so hard in England, they are far better off than slaves. If they get a bad master, they give warning and go hire to another. They have their liberty. That's just what *we* want. We don't mind hard work, if we had proper treatment, and proper wages like English servants, and proper time given in the week to keep us from breaking the Sabbath. But they won't give it: they will have work—work—work, night and day, sick or well, till we are quite done up; and we must not speak up nor look amiss, however much we be abused. And then when we are quite done up, who cares for us, more than for a lame horse? This is slavery. I tell it, to let English people know the truth; and I hope they will never leave off to pray God, and call loud to the great King of England, till all the poor blacks be given free, and slavery done up for evermore.

---

[1] Cf. John 8.32.

[2] "The whole of this paragraph especially, is given as nearly as was possible in Mary's precise words." (Thomas Pringle).

[3] "She means West Indians." (Thomas Pringle).

[4] "A West Indian phrase: to fasten or tie up." (Thomas Pringle).

Thomas Pringle
1789 – 1834

Thomas Pringle was born in Blaiklaw, Teviotdale, Scotland, on 5 January 1789, the son of a farmer. He was disabled as the result of a hip dislocated in infancy. Following three years at grammar school in Kelso, he studied literature at Edinburgh University and then became a clerk in the Register Office, writing poetry in his spare time. In 1816 he contributed to *Albyn's Anthology* and to the *Poetic Mirror*—where he published a poem in imitation of Walter Scott.* In 1817 he launched a new magazine, the *Edinburgh Monthly*: co-contributors included Lockhart,* Wilson, and Hogg.* About the same time, he became editor of another new periodical, *Constable's*, and of the *Star* newspaper. His first collection of poetry, *The Autumnal Collection*, was published in 1817.

The *Edinburgh Monthly Magazine* changed ownership, becoming *Blackwood's*: because of rivalry between *Blackwood's* and *Constable's*, Pringle resigned from *Blackwood's*. Neither the *Star* nor *Constable's* was profitable; and following his marriage to Margaret Brown, Pringle's financial resources were strained. He published a book of poems, *Autumnal Excursion, and Other Poems*; but in 1819 he was forced to return to the Register Office.

In 1820, Pringle and his family emigrated to the Cape, South Africa, to occupy a tract of 20,000 acres which they called Glen-Lynden. Pringle eventually received permission to publish the *South African Journal*, a periodical which appeared in both English and Dutch. At the same time, he worked as editor of a weekly newspaper, *The South African Commercial Advertiser*, and as government librarian. However, in the authoritarian climate of colonial politics, he was forced to give up editorship of the *Advertiser*, and the *Journal* was shut down. Pringle resigned as government librarian; the school he had established failed when he was perceived to have defied the authorities. He and his wife and sister-in-law set sail for London on 7 July 1826, badly in debt and with no means of restitution for their losses.

In London, for a time Pringle edited an annual, *Friendship's Offering*; however, an article on slavery he had contributed to the *New Monthly Magazine* resulted in his appointment as Secretary to the Anti-Slavery Society. In this capacity Pringle introduced the former slave Mary Prince* to her amanuensis, Susanna Strickland (later Susanna Moodie),* and was instrumental in the abolition of slavery (1833). A third collection of poetry, *Ephemerides*, appeared in 1828, and an account of his life in southern Africa, *African Sketches*, was published in 1834. Pringle planned to return to Africa, but he died too soon, on 5 December 1834. (A.M.)

from George Thompson, *Travels and Adventures in Southern Africa, comprising a View of the Present State of the Cape Colony, with Observations on the Progress and Prospects of the British Emigrants* (1827)[1]

Afar in the Desert[2]

Afar in the Desert I love to ride,
With the silent Bush-boy[3] alone by my side:
When the sorrows of life the soul o'ercast,
And, sick of the present, I turn to the past;
5   And the eye is suffused with regretful tears,
From the fond recollections of former years;
And the shadows of things that have long since fled
Flit over the brain, like the ghosts of the dead—
Bright visions of glory, that vanish'd too soon,—
10 Day-dreams that departed ere manhood's noon,—
Attachments by fate or by falsehood reft,—
Companions of early days lost or left,—
And my NATIVE LAND! whose magical name
Thrills to my heart like electric flame;
15 The home of my childhood; the haunts of my prime;
All the passions and scenes of that rapturous time,
When the feelings were young, and the world was new,
Like the fresh bowers of Paradise opening to view!—
All—all now forsaken, forgotten, or gone—
20 And I, a lone exile—remember'd of none—
My high aims abandon'd—and good acts undone—
Aweary of all that is under the sun,—
With that sadness of heart which no stranger may scan,
I fly to the Desert afar from man.

25 Afar in the Desert I love to ride,
With the silent Bush-boy alone by my side:
When the wild turmoil of this wearisome life,
With its scenes of oppression, corruption, and strife;
The proud man's frown, and the base man's fear;
30 And the scorner's laugh, and the sufferer's tear;
And malice, and meanness, and falsehood, and folly,
Dispose me to musing and dark melancholy;
When my bosom is full, and my thoughts are high,
And my soul is sick with the bondman's sigh—
35 Oh, then—there is freedom, and joy, and pride,
Afar in the Desert alone to ride!
There is rapture to vault on the champing steed,
And to bound away with the eagle's speed,
With the death-fraught firelock in my hand,
40 (The only law of the Desert land,)
But 'tis not the innocent to destroy,
For I hate the huntsman's savage joy.

Afar in the Desert I love to ride,
With the silent Bush-boy alone by my side:
45 Away—away from the dwellings of men,
By the wild deer's haunt, and the buffalo's glen;
By vallies remote, where the oribi plays;
Where the gnoo, the gazelle, and the hartebeest graze;
And the gemsbok and eland[4] unhunted recline
50 By the skirts of grey forests o'ergrown with wild vine;
And the elephant browses at peace in his wood;
And the river-horse[5] gambols unscared in the flood;
And the mighty rhinoceros wallows at will
In the *Vley*,[6] where the wild-ass is drinking his fill.

55 Afar in the Desert I love to ride,
With the silent Bush-boy alone by my side:
O'er the brown Karroo,[7] where the bleating cry
Of the springbok's[8] fawn sounds plaintively;
Where the zebra wantonly tosses his mane,

---

[1] first published in the *South African Journal*, 1824. We have added excerpts from Pringle's extensive notes to the version in *African Sketches* (1834).

[2] Samuel Taylor Coleridge* wrote to Pringle, 20 March 1828: "With the omission of about four or at the utmost six lines I do not hesitate to declare ["Afar in the Desert"], among the two or three most perfect lyric Poems in our Language."

[3] Native living in the wilderness.

[4] The oribi, gnu, gazelle, hartebeest, gemsbok, and eland are all members of the antelope family.

[5] hippopotamus.

[6] "meadow" or "swamp" (Afrikaans). Pringle amends to "fen" in 1834.

[7] a dry tableland in southern Africa.

[8] another species of African antelope.

60 In fields seldom freshen'd by moisture or rain;
And the stately koodoo[1] exultingly bounds,
Undisturb'd by the bay of the hunter's hounds;
And the timorous quagha's[2] wild whistling neigh
Is heard by the brak fountain far away;
65 And the fleet-footed ostrich over the waste
Speeds like a horseman who travels in haste;
And the vulture in circles wheels high overhead,
Greedy to scent and to gorge on the dead;
And the grisly wolf, and the shrieking jackal,
70 Howl for their prey at the evening fall;
And the fiend-like laugh of hyænas grim
Fearfully startles the twilight dim.

Afar in the Desert I love to ride,
With the silent Bush-boy alone by my side:
75 Away—away in the wilderness vast,[3]
Where the white man's foot hath never pass'd,
And the quiver'd Koranna or Bechuan[4]
Hath rarely cross'd with his roving clan:
A region of emptiness, howling and drear,
80 Which man hath abandon'd from famine and fear;
Which the snake and the lizard inhabit alone,
And the bat flitting forth from his old hollow stone;
Where grass, nor herb, nor shrub takes root,
Save poisonous thorns that pierce the foot;
85 And the bitter melon, for food and drink,
Is the pilgrim's fare, by the Salt Lake's brink;[5]
A region of drought, where no river glides,
Nor rippling brook with osier'd[6] sides;
Nor reedy pool, nor mossy fountain,
90 Nor shady tree, nor cloud-capp'd mountain,
Are found—to refresh the aching eye:
But the barren earth, and the burning sky,
And the blank horizon round and round,
Without a living sight or sound,
95 Tell to the heart, in its pensive mood,
That this is—NATURE'S SOLITUDE!

And here—while the night-winds round me sigh,
And the stars burn bright in the midnight sky,
As I sit apart by the cavern'd stone,
100 Like Elijah at Horeb's cave[7] alone,
And feel as a moth in the Mighty Hand
That spread the heavens and heaved the land,—
A "still small voice"[8] comes through the wild,
(Like a father consoling his fretful child),
105 Which banishes bitterness, wrath, and fear—
Saying "MAN IS DISTANT, BUT GOD IS NEAR!"

---

[1] yet another antelope: Pringle's notes to the 1834 version carefully distinguish them.

[2] South African equine quadruped, now extinct, related to the ass and zebra. "The cry of the Quagga (pronounced quagha, or quacha) is very different from that of either the horse or ass." (T.P.)

[3] "The Desert of Kalleghanny or Challahenagh, north of the Orange River, and lying between the countries of the Bechuanas and Damards, is said to be for the most part entirely destitute of water, so that the Bechuanas and Corannas in crossing it are forced to subsist on a species of wild water-melon...." (T.P.) See line 85.

[4] "The Corannas, Koras, or Koraquas, are a tribe of independent Hottentots, inhabiting the banks of the Gareep, or Great Orange River" (T.P.); the Bechuana inhabit the country between the Orange and Zambezi rivers in southern Africa, and speak a Bantu language.

[5] "During ... long droughts ..., the water is exhaled, and the dry crystallised salt remains, white as a frozen lake, in the bosom of the dry parched land." (T.P.)

[6] covered with osiers, a type of willow.

[7] 1 Kings 19.9–15.

[8] 1 Kings 19.12.

James Fenimore Cooper
1789 – 1851

James Cooper was born on 15 September 1789, in Burlington, New Jersey, the fifth son of William Cooper, a wealthy landowner, and Elizabeth Fenimore Cooper. When he was one, his family moved to Cooperstown, the frontier settlement founded by his father in upstate New York. He was educated by tutors in Cooperstown, at a boarding school in Albany, and at Yale—until he was expelled in 1805 for a student prank (gunpowder was involved). His father sent him to sea, and he served in the navy for two years. When his father was murdered in 1809, Cooper inherited $50,000. He retired from the navy, and on 1 January 1811, he married Susan De Lancey; they had seven children. He wrote his first novel in 1820, apparently after reading one that was so bad he was sure he could do better; he went on to write thirty-two novels, including *The Last of the Mohicans* (1826) and the four other Leatherstocking Tales, plus a dozen works of non-fiction. In 1826, he took his family on a seven-year trip to Europe; while there, he wrote *Notions of the Americans*, to correct mistaken European notions of America. After his return, he became increasingly alienated from his compatriots; some of his later works are bitterly satirical. In 1848, he began a close study of the Bible, and his last works have religious themes. He was confirmed in the Episcopalian Church in July 1851; he died in Cooperstown on 14 September. (D.L.M.)

---

from *Notions of the Americans, Picked Up by a Travelling Bachelor* (1828)

TO SIR EDWARD WALLER, BART.[1]

&c. &c.

Philadelphia,——.

Since my last letter, I have visited New-Jersey, the eastern parts of Pennsylvania, and Delaware. With the exception of Maine, Illinois, and Indiana, (quite new States,) I have now seen something of all those communities, which, in common parlance, are called the "free States," in contradistinction to those which still encourage the existence of domestic slavery. As respects this material point of policy, the confederation is nearly equally divided in the number of States, thirteen having virtually gotten rid of slavery, and eleven still adhering to the system. The difference between the white population, however, is vastly more in favour of the "free States." We shall not be far out of the way, in stating the whole of the white population of the United States at a little more than ten millions. Of this number, near, if not quite, seven millions are contained in the thirteen northern, middle, and north-western States.

This portion of the Union is governed by the same policy, and its inhabitants seek their prosperity in the same sources of wealth and in the same spirit of improvement. More than half of them are either natives of New-England, or are descended from those who were born in that district of the country. Together, the States I have named cover a surface of little less than 300,000 square miles. If the territory of Michigan be included, (which is not yet sufficiently populous to be a State,) the amount will be swelled to near 330,000. The former will give rather more than twenty-three to the square mile, as the rate of the whole population on the whole surface. But in making the estimate, what I have already said of the vast regions that are not peopled at all, must be kept in view. Perhaps one third of the territory should be excluded from the calculation altogether. This would leave something more than thirty to the square mile, for the average. But even this estimate is necessarily delu-

---

[1] not an actual person. Cooper imagines a club of European gentlemen travelling in America; Sir Edward Waller is a member of the club. "Bart." is an abbreviation of "baronet."

sive, as it is known that in the old States there are sixty and seventy souls to the square mile, and in some parts of them many more.

In the course of reflection on this subject, I have been led to inquire when these republics are to reach that ratio of population which, of necessity, is to compel them to adapt their institutions to the usages of European policy. The result is not quite so conclusive as one might at first be disposed to believe. I find that despotism flourishes with little or no opposition in Russia, a country of about twenty-five to the square mile; in Turkey, one of about fifty;[1] in Spain, one of, say sixty; in Denmark, one of about eighty, &c. &c.; and that liberty is beginning to thrive, or has long thriven, in England, one of more than two hundred; in the Netherlands, one of an equal rate; and, in short, in France, in several of the most populous states of Germany, some of which mount as high as six and nine hundred to the square mile, more particularly the *free* towns!

Here is pretty clear evidence, by that unanswerable argument—fact, that the populousness of a country is not necessarily to control the freedom or despotism of its institutions. But the United States have carried the freedom of their institutions too far, since they go much farther than we have ever found it wise or safe to go in Europe. England herself has stopped short of such excessive freedom. The latter position is certainly much nearer to the truth than the other, and yet if we should assemble even the travelled brethren of our own club, and put the question to them—"How far do you think that liberty and equality of political rights can be carried in a government, without danger to its foundations?"—it would be seen that the replies would smack a little of the early impressions of the different worthies who compose the fraternity. Let us fancy ourselves for a moment in solemn conclave on this knotty point, and we will endeavour to anticipate the different answers. We will begin with the Prince André Kutmynoseandeyesoff.

"I am of opinion," says our accomplished, intelligent, and loyal prince, "that without a vast standing army, a nation can neither secure its frontiers, nor on occasion bring them properly within a ring fence. In what manner is a serf to be made to respect his lord, unless he see that the latter can enforce his rights by having recourse to the bayonet, or in what manner is even rank among ourselves to be regulated, without a common centre whence it must flow? It would be utterly impossible to keep an empire composed of subjects born in the arctic circle and subjects born on the Caspian, men speaking different languages, and worshipping Jesus and Mahomet, together, without such a concentration of power as shall place each in salutary fear of the ruler. It is quite clear that a nation without a vast standing army——"

"I beg pardon for the interruption, mon Prince," cries Professor Jansen: "I agree with you *in toto*, except as to the army. Certainly no spectacle is more beautiful than that of a kind and benevolent monarch, dwelling in the midst of his people like a father in the bosom of a vast family, and at once the source of order and the fountain of honour. Still I can see no great use in an overgrown army, which infallibly leads to a waste of money and a mispending of time. Soldiers are unquestionably necessary to prevent invasion or aggression, and to be in readiness to look down any sudden attempts at revolution; but they are dangerous and extravagant playthings. When a sovereign begins to stir his battalions as he does his chess-men, one can never calculate what move he means to make next; and as to rank, what can be more venerable or more noble than the class of Counts, for instance—["Hear, hear," from Sir Edward Waller]—a set of nobles who hold so happy and so respected an intermediate station between the prince and his people? That is clearly the happiest government in the whole world, where the labour of ruling is devolved on one man: but I shall always protest against the wisdom of a large standing army."

"*Quant à moi*," observes the colonel, making an apologetic bow, "I cannot agree with either the one or the other. An army before all things, but no despot; and, least of all, a despot who does nothing but stay at home and vegetate on his throne. If I must have an absolute

---
[1] "Both in Europe." (J.F.C.)

monarch, King Stork any day to King Log.[1] In my youth, I will confess, certain visions of glory floated before my eyes, and conquest appeared the best good of life; but time and hard service have weakened these impressions, and I can now plainly perceive all the advantages of *La Charte*.[2] In a constitutional monarchy, one can enjoy the advantages of a despotism without any of its disadvantages. You have an army to vindicate the national honour, as ready, as brave, and as efficient, as though the power of its head were unlimited; and yet you have not the constant danger of *lettres de cachet*,[3] bastiles, and monks. By a judicious division of estates, those odious monopolies, which have so fatal a tendency to aristocracy——"

"If you stop there, dear Jules," interrupts a certain Sir Edward Waller, "we shall be in the majority, and the question is our own. Nothing can be more dangerous than a despotism, every one must allow" (though two worthy members had just held the contrary doctrine.) "But you are touching on the very thing now, that must unavoidably prove fatal to your monarchy, *la charte*, and all, since it is clear, that a monarch needs the support of an aristocracy, and an aristocracy is nothing without money.—An enlightened, unpaid, disinterested gentry, who possess all the property——"

"Money!" echoes the colonel, in heat; "it is that money which is the curse of you English. You have it all, and yet you see you are hourly in terror of bankruptcy. Thank God, if the Revolution has done nothing else, it has cut up root and branch all our odious seignories, with their feudal follies; and man now begins to think himself the owner of the soil, and not a plant."

"Nay, my dear Béthizy, keep your temper; you are not now storming the bridge of Lodi.[4] Reflect one moment; what will become of France when her whole territory shall be subdivided in freeholds not bigger than a pocket-handkerchief?"

"And your island! what will the poor devils of paupers do when Lord——shall own the whole island?"

"I think," observes the abbate,[5] perceiving that the argument is likely to wax hot, "that it is a question that will admit of much to be said on both sides, whether a people will leave more lasting and brilliant recollections, if their career has been run under a republican or a monarchical form of government. In Italy, we find arguments to maintain both positions; though at present we are somewhat divided between a hierarchy and such minute geographical divisions as shall insure a close inspection into the interests of all who have any right at all to be consulted in these matters. I can neither agree with the prince, nor with the professor, nor with the Count, nor yet with Sir Edward, though I think all of us must be of opinion that a popular government is a thing quite impracticable."

"Oh! all, all, all, all."

"It is quite certain that your Lazzaroni[6] would scarcely know what to do with political power if they had it," continues the abbate.

"Nor a serf," says the Prince.

"I can see no use in giving it even to a Count," mutters the Dane.

"Nor to a Manchester reformer,"[7] puts in Sir Edward.

"It is quite certain the *canaille*[8] do not know how to use it," adds Jules Béthizy, with a melancholy sigh; and so the question is disposed of.

Now, if my friend Cadwallader were a member of the club (and I hope to live long enough to see the day when he shall become one,) he might give a very different opinion from them all. Let us imagine, for an instant, what would be the nature of his argument. He

---

[1] In Æsop's fable, the frogs ask Jupiter for a king, and he sends them a log. When they ask for a more active king, he sends them a stork, which eats them.

[2] a charter or constitution, one enduring legacy of the French Revolution.

[3] administrative orders, issued by the king, for imprisonment without trial. The Bastille was the state prison whose fall on 14 July 1789 is usually taken to mark the start of the Revolution.

[4] in northern Italy, the site of a major victory by Napoleon on 10 May 1796.

[5] "abbot" (It.).

[6] beggars, so called from the hospital of St. Lazarus, in Naples; cf. Luke 16.19–26.

[7] As a rapidly growing industrial city with no representation in parliament, Manchester was a hotbed of political radicalism.

[8] "rabble" (Fr.).

would probably say, that, "my countrymen have taken care there shall be neither Lazzaroni, nor serf, (he might gag a little at the thought of the blacks,)[1] nor Counts, nor Manchester reformers; and any opinions which may be formed on premises of this nature are, in consequence, utterly inapplicable to us. I dare say the abbate will very willingly admit, that if there were nothing but cardinals in Italy, a popular government would do very well; and perhaps Sir Edward will allow if the English population were all baronets of seven thousand a year, the elective franchise might be extended even in his kingdom without any very imminent danger. It is wonderful how very difficult it is to make men comprehend that a thing can be done by any one else, which they have long been used to consider as exceeding their own ability to perform. This feeling of selfishness, or of vanity, whichever you please, insinuates itself into all our actions, and finally warps our opinions, and obscures our judgments.

"I do not believe it is in the power of man to make a Turk comprehend the nature of English liberty; simply because, when he looks around him, and sees the state of society in which he himself vegetates, he can neither understand the energy of character which requires such latitude for its exertion, nor the state of things which can possibly render it safe. It appears to me, that it is very nearly as difficult to make an Englishman comprehend that it is very possible for a people to prosper under a degree of liberty still greater than that he enjoys. His self-love, his prejudices, and his habits are all opposed to the admission. Experience and fact go for nothing. He is determined there shall be some drawback to all the seeming prosperity of a state of things which exceeds his own notions of the sources whence prosperity ought to flow; and though he may not be sufficiently conversant with the details to lay his finger on the sore spot, he is quite confident there must be one. He swears it is festering, and that by-and-bye we shall hear something of it worth knowing. I remember once to have conversed with a renowned English statesman on this very subject. He was sufficiently complimentary on the institutions of my country, and on the character of my countrymen, but we were neither of us the dupes of such simple courtesy. I believe he did me the justice to see that I understood him, for he very soon took occasion to remark that he should like the government of the United States better if it were a '*Frank Republic*.' Perceiving that I looked surprised, and possibly understanding the expression of my countenance to say how much I wondered that a man of his experience should expect great *frankness* in any government, he went on to explain; 'I mean,' he continued, 'that I should like your government better, if there were no pageant of a head, and if Congress would act for itself directly, without the intervention of a President.'

"This conversation occurred shortly after the Senate of the United States had rejected a treaty with Great Britain, which the President had made (through the public minister), and which the King of Great Britain had previously ratified. '*Hinc illæ lachrymæ.*'[2] I confined my answer to a simple observation, that the actual power of the President was very little, but that we should unnecessarily impede the execution of the laws, and embarrass our intercourse with foreign nations, by abolishing the office, which added greatly to the convenience of the country, without in the slightest degree invading or endangering the liberties of the people.

"Now, what was the amount of the argument which this gifted man agitated in his own mind, on a subject so important to the policy of a great nation? He could understand that a right might exist somewhere to annul the bargain of a minister, for in his proper person he had just before refused to ratify a treaty made by one of his own agents,[3] but he could not understand that this power should, or could, with propriety, be lodged in hands where he was not accustomed to see it. Napoleon would have told him that he himself submitted to a thousand vain and restrictive regulations, which only tended to embarrass his operations and to lessen his influence abroad.

---

[1] "It is manifestly unsafe to found any arguments concerning the political institutions of this country on the existence of slavery, since the slaves have no more to do with government than inanimate objects." (J.F.C.)

[2] "hence those tears" (L.): Terence (190?–159 BC), *Andria* 1.1.99.

[3] "With Mexico." (J.F.C.)

"Again, it is quite common for the American to gather in discourse with Englishmen, either by inuendoes, or direct assertions, that there is little or no religion in his country! Nine times in ten, the former is content to laugh in his sleeve at what he terms the egregious ignorance of his relative; or perhaps he makes a circle of friends merry by enumerating this instance, among fifty others, of the jaundiced views that the folks on the homestead take of the condition of those who have wandered beyond the paternal estate. But should he be tempted to probe the feeling (I will not call it reason) which induces so many warm-hearted, and kindly intentioned individuals in the mother country, to entertain a notion so unjust, not to say so uncharitable, of their fellow-Christians, under another *régime*, he will find that it is in truth bottomed on no other foundation than the circumstance that we have no established church. And yet it is a known fact that the peculiar faith of England,[1] is in America on the comparative increase, and that in England itself, it is on a comparative decrease, one half of the whole population being at this moment, if I am rightly informed, dissenters from the very church they think so necessary to religion, morals, and order. In America, we think the change in the latter country is owing to the establishment itself; and the change in our own, to the fact that men are always willing to acknowledge the merits of any thing which is not too violently obtruded on their notice. We may be wrong, and so may they; but if the fact were only half as well authenticated as is the one that we are competent to maintain our present political institutions, I should consider it a question not worth the trouble of discussion."

That Cadwallader would use some such manner of reply I know, for the anecdote of his conversation with the English statesman (now unhappily no more) I have actually heard him mention. I confess the justice of many of his remarks, for I am perfectly conscious of having been the subject of a great many of these vague and general conjectures on American policy; but a closer observation of the actual state of the country is gradually forcing me to different conclusions. The more candid European will admit that a vast number of our usages and institutions owe their existence, at the present hour, to prejudice. Now, is it not possible that prejudice may have quite as active an agency in keeping down aristocracy, as in keeping it up? It is perfectly absurd to say, that it is an ordering of nature; for nature, so far from decreeing that the inequality of her gifts is to be perpetuated in a direct male line, and in conformity to the rights of primogeniture, is commonly content with visiting a single family with her smiles, at long intervals, and with a very unequal bounty. So far as nature is concerned, then, she is diametrically opposed to the perpetuation of power or consideration in the regular descent. Neither talents, nor physical force, nor courage, nor beauty, is often continued long in any one race. But men do get, and do keep too, the control of things in their own families, in most of the countries of the earth. This is a practical argument, which it will be found difficult to controvert. It is precisely for this reason that I begin to think the people of the United States will not soon part with the power of which they are at present in such absolute possession. But knowledge you will say is power, and knowledge is confined to the few. I am inclined to think, after all, that the degree of knowledge which is necessary to make a man obstinate in the defence of rights which he has been educated to believe inherent, is far from being very profound. It is well known that despots have often failed in attempts on the personal privileges of their subjects. Paul could send a prince to Siberia, but he could not make a Boyar shave.[2] Now, the rights of suffrage, of perfect political equality, of freedom in religion, and of all other political privileges, are the beards of these people. It will be excessively hazardous to attempt to shorten them by a hair. The ornaments of the chin are not more effectually a gift of nature, than are the political privileges of the American his birth-right. Great as is the power of the English aristocracy, there are limits to its exercise, as you very well know, and any man can predict a revolution,

---

[1] the Anglican Church, known in America as the Episcopalian Church.

[2] Paul, Czar of Russia (1754–1801), alienated the boyars, or aristocrats, by his centralizing policies and was assassinated in 1801. His ancestor, Peter the Great (1672–1725), among other modernizing reforms, had cut off the beards of the boyars.

should they attempt to exceed them. I fancy the only difference between the mother and child in this particular is, that the latter, so far as political rights go, has rather a richer inheritance than the former. Time has clearly little to do with the matter beyond the date of our individual existence, since a human life is quite long enough to get thoroughly obstinate opinions on any subject, even though prejudice should be their basis.

From this familiar and obvious manner of reasoning (and I think it will be found to contain a fair proportion of the truth) it would seem to result that there is quite as little likelihood the American will lose any of his extreme liberty, as that the Dutchman, the Frenchman, or the Englishman, will lose any great portion of that which he now enjoys. The question is then narrowed to the use the former will make of his power....

Percy Bysshe Shelley
1792 – 1822

Percy Bysshe Shelley was born at Field Place, Sussex, on 4 August 1792, the oldest son of Timothy Shelley, a landowner and later a Whig Member of Parliament, and Elizabeth Pilfold Shelley. He was educated at Syon House Academy and Eton College, where the regular bullying may have helped to inspire his lifelong hatred of tyranny and violence; and at University College, Oxford, from which, along with his friend Thomas Jefferson Hogg, he was expelled, after less than a year, for publishing a pamphlet entitled *The Necessity of Atheism* (1811). He had already published two Gothic novels and, in collaboration first with his sister Elizabeth and then with Hogg, two volumes of poetry; he would be a prolific writer for the rest of his short life.

The expulsion led to a total and permanent alienation of Shelley from his father, a situation Shelley rapidly made worse by eloping with the sixteen-year-old Harriet Westbrook in August 1811. The elopement initiated two more patterns that remained constant for the rest of his life: travel and experimentation with personal relationships. Shelley and Harriet travelled first to Edinburgh, where Scottish law allowed minors to marry without their parents' consent; then to York, where Hogg joined them and attempted to seduce Harriet; then, accompanied by Eliza Westbrook, to Keswick, where Shelley met Southey;* then to Ireland, where he published pamphlets in favour of Catholic Emancipation and other radical causes; then, accompanied not only by Eliza but also by another of Shelley's soulmates, Elizabeth Hitchener, through Devon and Wales. On trips to London, Shelley met Hunt* and Godwin, whose *Political Justice** had been the most important influence on his political thinking. In the spring of 1813, he published his first major work, *Queen Mab*, a poetical exposition of Godwinian anarchism, pacifism, and vegetarianism; that June, Harriet gave birth to their first child, a girl named Ianthe after the protagonist of the poem.

But Shelley was not happy in his marriage to Harriet, and in 1814, he fell in love with Godwin's daughter Mary. A believer in the Godwinian ideal of free love, he had no qualms about leaving Harriet for Mary; he even invited Harriet to live with them as a sister. When Shelley and Mary eloped on 27 July, they were accompanied instead by Mary's stepsister, Jane (later called Claire) Clairmont. They travelled through France to Switzerland; then, running out of money six weeks later, went back to England. Godwin was not impressed by how literally his disciple had read *Political Justice*; the situation was not improved by the birth of Shelley and Harriet's second child, Charles, in November.

Shelley's grandfather, who died in 1815, left him an annual income of £1000, of which he assigned £200 to Harriet; Godwin, despite not being on speaking terms with him, managed to absorb much of the rest. Also in 1815, Mary gave birth to a premature daughter, who died at the age of only two weeks. It was the first of their family tragedies: their next child, William, born in 1816, would die at the age of three; Clara, born in 1817, at the age of one. There was also a mysterious daughter, either born to or adopted by Shelley in Naples in 1818, who died in infancy. Mary became increasingly depressed. Only their fourth child, Percy Florence, born in 1819, would live to grow up.

In 1816, Clairmont seduced the recently separated Byron,* and at her instigation, the Shelley ménage travelled to Geneva to meet him. The summer they spent together inspired "Hymn to Intellectual Beauty" and "Mont Blanc," several major poems by Byron, and, most famously, *Frankenstein* (1818). In 1817, Clairmont gave birth to a daughter, Allegra.

The ménage went back to England in September 1816, only to be welcomed by more tragedies: the suicides of Mary's half-sister Fanny Imlay and of Harriet. Shelley and Mary married in December, in the hope of gaining custody of Harriet's children; but after a lengthy case, the courts found that Shelley's opinions made him unfit to be a father. Godwin, however, began speaking to him again.

In 1818, the ménage went to Italy, partly for Shelley's health, and partly to take Allegra to Byron, who had agreed to take care of her. (He eventually consigned her to a convent, where she died in 1822.) Over the next four years, they moved restlessly from Bagni di Lucca to Este, to Rome, to Naples, back to Rome, to Livorno, to Florence, to Pisa, back to Livorno, to Bagni di San Giuliano, back to Pisa, back to Bagni di San Giuliano, back to Pisa, and finally to Lerici; the constant travel was probably partly responsible for the deaths of their children. In 1818–19, Shelley wrote his two complementary masterpieces: *Prometheus Unbound*, a utopian vision of a universe transformed by peace and love, and (between writing Acts Three and Four of *Prometheus Unbound*), *The Cenci*, his tragedy of "sad reality." When news of the Peterloo Massacre of 16 August 1819 reached Italy, Shelley wrote *The Masque of Anarchy* and sent it to Hunt, but Hunt thought it was too dangerous to publish until 1832, the year of the first Reform Act. In response to Peacock's "The Four Ages of Poetry,"* Shelley wrote *A Defence of Poetry*; and in response to the death of Keats in Rome, *Adonais*.

In 1822, the Shelleys were living near Lerici with Jane and Edward Williams. Shelley was working on "The Triumph of Life." He had several disturbing visions; in one of them his Doppelgänger asked him: "How long do you mean to be content?" At the end of June, Hunt arrived in Livorno; Shelley and Byron had invited him to Italy to collaborate on a new periodical, *The Liberal*. Shelley and Edward went to see him on Shelley's new boat, the *Don Juan*. On their voyage home, on 8 July, they were lost in a storm. On 18 July, their bodies were found on the beach; Shelley's could be identified because he had a copy of Keats's last book in his pocket. Quarantine laws stipulated that they be buried on the beach, but Byron, Hunt, and their friend Trelawny* arranged for them to be dug up and cremated in a neo-Pagan ceremony devised largely by Trelawny. At a climactic moment, Trelawny snatched Shelley's heart from the burning pyre; Mary took it back to England. In January 1823, Trelawny had Shelley's ashes buried in the Protestant Cemetery in Rome, near Keats and William Shelley. (D.L.M.)

from *Alastor; or, The Spirit of Solitude: and Other Poems* (1816)

PREFACE

The poem entitled "Alastor" may be considered as allegorical of one of the most interesting situations of the human mind. It represents a youth of uncorrupted feelings and adventurous genius led forth by an imagination inflamed and purified through familiarity with all that is excellent and majestic, to the contemplation of the universe. He drinks deep of the fountains of knowledge, and is still insatiate. The magnificence and beauty of the external world sinks profoundly into the frame of his conceptions, and affords to their modifications a variety not to be exhausted. So long as it is possible for his desires to point towards objects thus infinite and unmeasured, he is joyous, and tranquil, and self-possessed. But the period arrives when these objects cease to suffice. His mind is at length suddenly awakened and thirsts for intercourse with an intelligence similar to itself. He images to himself the Being whom he loves. Conversant with speculations of the sublimest and most perfect natures, the vision in which he embodies his own imaginations unites all of wonderful, or wise, or beautiful, which the poet, the philosopher, or the lover could depicture. The intellectual faculties, the imagination, the functions of sense, have their respective requisitions on the sympathy of corresponding powers in other human beings. The Poet is represented as uniting these requisitions, and attaching them to a single image. He seeks in vain for a prototype of his conception. Blasted by his disappointment, he descends to an untimely grave.

The picture is not barren of instruction to actual men. The Poet's self-centred seclusion was avenged by the furies of an irresistible passion pursuing him to speedy ruin. But that Power which strikes the luminaries of the world with sudden darkness and extinction, by awakening them to too exquisite a perception of its influences, dooms to a slow and poisonous decay those meaner spirits that dare to abjure its dominion. Their destiny is more abject and inglorious as their delinquency is more contemptible and pernicious. They who, deluded by no generous error, instigated by no sacred thirst of doubtful knowledge, duped by no illustrious superstition, loving nothing on this earth, and cherishing no hopes beyond, yet keep aloof from sympathies with their kind, rejoicing neither in human joy nor mourning with human grief; these, and such as they, have their apportioned curse. They languish, because none feel with them their common nature. They are morally dead. They are neither friends, nor lovers, nor fathers, nor citizens of the world, nor benefactors of their country. Among those who attempt to exist without human sympathy, the pure and tender-hearted perish through the intensity and passion of their search after its communities, when the vacancy of their spirit suddenly makes itself felt. All else, selfish, blind, and torpid, are those unforeseeing multitudes who constitute, together with their own, the lasting misery and loneliness of the world. Those who love not their fellow-beings, live unfruitful lives, and prepare for their old age a miserable grave.

> "The good die first,
> And those whose hearts are dry as summer dust,
> Burn to the socket!"[1]

The Fragment, entitled "The DÆMON OF THE WORLD,"[2] is a detached part of a poem which the author does not intend for publication. The metre in which it is composed is that of Samson Agonistes[3] and the Italian pastoral drama, and may be considered as the natural measure into which poetical conceptions, expressed in harmonious language, necessarily fall.
December 14, 1815.

---

[1] W. Wordsworth, *The Excursion* 1.529–31.*

[2] a corrected version of parts of Shelley's long poem *Queen Mab* (1813).

[3] Milton's poem (1671) about Samson (Judges 13–16), which uses, in addition to iambic pentameter, rhythms from Greek tragedy, Italian poetry and drama, and the English Bible.

Alastor: Or, The Spirit of Solitude[4]

Nondum amabam, et amare amabam, quærebam quid amarem, amans amare.
Confess. St. August.[5]

Earth, ocean, air, beloved brotherhood!
 If our great Mother has imbued my soul
With aught of natural piety[6] to feel
Your love, and recompense the boon with mine;
5 If dewy morn, and odorous noon, and even,
With sunset and its gorgeous ministers,
And solemn midnight's tingling silentness;
If autumn's hollow sighs in the sere wood,
And winter robing with pure snow and crowns
10 Of starry ice the gray grass and bare boughs;
If spring's voluptuous pantings when she breathes
Her first sweet kisses, have been dear to me;
If no bright bird, insect, or gentle beast
I consciously have injured, but still loved
15 And cherished these my kindred; then forgive
This boast, beloved brethren, and withdraw
No portion of your wonted favour now!
   Mother of this unfathomable world!
Favour my solemn song, for I have loved
20 Thee ever, and thee only; I have watched
Thy shadow, and the darkness of thy steps,
And my heart ever gazes on the depth
Of thy deep mysteries. I have made my bed
In charnels and on coffins, where black death
25 Keeps record of the trophies won from thee,
Hoping to still these obstinate questionings[7]
Of thee and thine, by forcing some lone ghost
Thy messenger, to render up the tale
Of what we are.[8] In lone and silent hours,

---

[4] Shelley's friend Thomas Love Peacock* suggested the title: an *alastor* (Gk.) is a *kakadaimon* or avenging spirit.

[5] "Not yet did I love, yet I was in love with loving; ... I sought what I might love, loving to love" (St. Augustine, *Confessions* 3.1).

[6] Cf. W. Wordsworth, "My Heart Leaps Up" 9.*

[7] Cf. W. Wordsworth, "Ode" 143–44.*

[8] Cf. P.B. Shelley, "Hymn to Intellectual Beauty," 49–52.*

When night makes a weird sound of its own stillness, 30
Like an inspired and desperate alchymist
Staking his very life on some dark hope,
Have I mixed awful talk and asking looks
With my most innocent love, until strange tears
Uniting with those breathless kisses, made 35
Such magic as compels the charmed night
To render up thy charge: ... and, though ne'er yet
Thou hast unveil'd thy inmost sanctuary;
Enough from incommunicable dream,
And twilight phantasms, and deep noonday thought, 40
Has shone within me, that serenely now
And moveless, as a long-forgotten lyre
Suspended in the solitary dome
Of some mysterious and deserted fane,[1]
I wait thy breath, Great Parent, that my strain 45
May modulate with murmurs of the air,
And motions of the forests and the sea,
And voice of living beings, and woven hymns
Of night and day, and the deep heart of man.

    There was a Poet whose untimely tomb 50
No human hands with pious reverence reared,
But the charmed eddies of autumnal winds
Built o'er his mouldering bones a pyramid
Of mouldering leaves in the waste wilderness:—
A lovely youth,—no mourning maiden decked 55
With weeping flowers, or votive cypress wreath,[2]
The lone couch of his everlasting sleep:—
Gentle, and brave, and generous,—no lorn bard
Breathed o'er his dark fate one melodious sigh:
He lived, he died, he sung, in solitude. 60
Strangers have wept to hear his passionate notes,
And virgins, as unknown he past, have pined
And wasted for fond love of his wild eyes.
The fire of those soft orbs has ceased to burn,
And Silence, too enamoured of that voice, 65
Locks its mute music in her rugged cell.

    By solemn vision, and bright silver dream,
His infancy was nurtured. Every sight
And sound from the vast earth and ambient air,
Sent to his heart its choicest impulses. 70
The fountains of divine philosophy
Fled not his thirsting lips, and all of great,
Or good, or lovely, which the sacred past
In truth or fable consecrates, he felt
And knew. When early youth had past, he left 75
His cold fireside and alienated home
To seek strange truths in undiscovered lands.
Many a wide waste and tangled wilderness
Has lured his fearless steps; and he has bought
With his sweet voice and eyes, from savage men, 80
His rest and food. Nature's most secret steps
He like her shadow has pursued, where'er
The red volcano overcanopies
Its fields of snow and pinnacles of ice
With burning smoke, or where bitumen lakes[3] 85
On black bare pointed islets ever beat
With sluggish surge, or where the secret caves
Rugged and dark, winding among the springs
Of fire and poison, inaccessible
To avarice or pride, their starry domes 90
Of diamond and of gold expand above
Numberless and immeasurable halls,
Frequent with crystal column, and clear shrines
Of pearl, and thrones radiant with chrysolite.[4]
Nor had that scene of ampler majesty 95
Than gems or gold, the varying roof of heaven
And the green earth lost in his heart its claims
To love and wonder; he would linger long
In lonesome vales, making the wild his home,
Until the doves and squirrels would partake 100
From his innocuous hand his bloodless food,[5]
Lured by the gentle meaning of his looks,
And the wild antelope, that starts whene'er

---

[1] temple, sanctuary.

[2] a wreath consecrated to the dead, made from the cypress, a tree sacred to mourners.

[3] lakes of mineral pitch, like the "bituminous Lake where *Sodom* flam'd" in Milton, *Paradise Lost* 10.562.

[4] a green or yellow silicate of iron and magnesium, sometimes used as a semi-precious stone (peridot).

[5] Influenced by his friend John Newton's *Defence of Vegetable Regimen*, Shelley was a vegetarian, including this allegorical explanation in a note to *Queen Mab* (1813): "Prometheus (who represents the human race) effected some great change in the condition of his nature, and applied fire to culinary purposes ... From this moment his vitals were devoured by the vulture of disease."

> The dry leaf rustles in the brake, suspend
> Her timid steps to gaze upon a form
> More graceful than her own.
>   His wandering step
> Obedient to high thoughts, has visited
> The awful ruins of the days of old:
> Athens, and Tyre, and Balbec, and the waste
> Where stood Jerusalem, the fallen towers
> Of Babylon, the eternal pyramids,
> Memphis and Thebes, and whatsoe'er of strange
> Sculptured on alabaster obelisk,
> Or jasper tomb, or mutilated sphynx,
> Dark Æthiopia in her desert hills
> Conceals.[1] Among the ruined temples there,
> Stupendous columns, and wild images
> Of more than man, where marble dæmons watch
> The Zodiac's brazen mystery,[2] and dead men
> Hang their mute thoughts on the mute walls around,
> He lingered, poring on memorials
> Of the world's youth, through the long burning day
> Gazed on those speechless shapes, nor, when the moon
> Filled the mysterious halls with floating shades
> Suspended he that task, but ever gazed
> And gazed, till meaning on his vacant mind
> Flashed like strong inspiration, and he saw
> The thrilling secrets of the birth of time.
>   Meanwhile an Arab maiden brought his food,
> Her daily portion, from her father's tent,
> And spread her matting for his couch, and stole
> From duties and repose to tend his steps:—
> Enamoured, yet not daring for deep awe
> To speak her love:—and watched his nightly sleep,
> Sleepless herself, to gaze upon his lips
> Parted in slumber, whence the regular breath
> Of innocent dreams arose: then, when red morn
> Made paler the pale moon, to her cold home
> Wildered, and wan, and panting, she returned.
>
> The Poet wandering on, through Arabie,
> And Persia, and the wild Carmanian waste,
> And o'er the aërial mountains which pour down
> Indus and Oxus from their icy caves,
> In joy and exultation held his way;[3]
> Till in the vale of Cashmire,[4] far within
> Its loneliest dell, where odorous plants entwine
> Beneath the hollow rocks a natural bower,
> Beside a sparkling rivulet he stretched
> His languid limbs. A vision on his sleep
> There came, a dream of hopes that never yet
> Had flushed his cheek. He dreamed a veiled maid
> Sate near him, talking in low solemn tones.
> Her voice was like the voice of his own soul
> Heard in the calm of thought; its music long,
> Like woven sounds of streams and breezes, held
> His inmost sense suspended in its web
> Of many-coloured woof and shifting hues.
> Knowledge and truth and virtue were her theme,
> And lofty hopes of divine liberty,
> Thoughts the most dear to him, and poesy,
> Herself a poet. Soon the solemn mood
> Of her pure mind kindled through all her frame
> A permeating fire: wild numbers then
> She raised, with voice stifled in tremulous sobs
> Subdued by its own pathos: her fair hands
> Were bare alone, sweeping from some strange harp
> Strange symphony, and in their branching veins
> The eloquent blood told an ineffable tale.
> The beating of her heart was heard to fill
> The pauses of her music, and her breath
> Tumultuously accorded with those fits
> Of intermitted song. Sudden she rose,
> As if her heart impatiently endured
> Its bursting burthen: at the sound he turned,
> And saw by the warm light of their own life
> Her glowing limbs beneath the sinuous veil
> Of woven wind, her outspread arms now bare,

---

[1] The poet travels east and then south around the Mediterranean, visiting many of the famous cities and regions of ancient civilizations before arriving in Ethiopia. Shelley uses classical rather than modern place names.

[2] probably the zodiac of Dendera in Egypt, a circular planisphere made famous in Europe following Napoleon's Egyptian campaign of 1798–99.

[3] The Poet travels through Arabia and across the Kermin desert in Persia (Iran). The "aërial mountains" are the Hindu Kush or Indian Caucasus, the fabled source of all the rivers of Asia.

[4] Situated beneath Mt. Caucasus, Cashmire (Kashmir) was thought to be the cradle of civilization. Cf. the "lovely Vale in the Indian Caucasus" in *Prometheus Unbound* 2.1.*

Her dark locks floating in the breath of night,
Her beamy bending eyes, her parted lips
180 Outstretched, and pale, and quivering eagerly.
His strong heart sunk and sickened with excess
Of love. He reared his shuddering limbs and quelled
His gasping breath, and spread his arms to meet
Her panting bosom: ... she drew back a while,
185 Then, yielding to the irresistible joy,
With frantic gesture and short breathless cry
Folded his frame in her dissolving arms.
Now blackness veiled his dizzy eyes, and night
Involved and swallowed up the vision; sleep,
190 Like a dark flood suspended in its course,
Rolled back its impulse on his vacant brain.
  Roused by the shock he started from his trance—
The cold white light of morning, the blue moon
Low in the west, the clear and garish hills,
195 The distinct valley and the vacant woods,
Spread round him where he stood. Whither have fled
The hues of heaven that canopied his bower
Of yesternight? The sounds that soothed his sleep,
The mystery and the majesty of Earth,
200 The joy, the exultation? His wan eyes
Gaze on the empty scene as vacantly
As ocean's moon looks on the moon in heaven.
The spirit of sweet human love has sent
A vision to the sleep of him who spurned
205 Her choicest gifts. He eagerly pursues
Beyond the realms of dream that fleeting shade;
He overleaps the bounds. Alas! alas!
Were limbs, and breath, and being intertwined
Thus treacherously? Lost, lost, for ever lost,
210 In the wide pathless desert of dim sleep,
That beautiful shape! Does the dark gate of death
Conduct to thy mysterious paradise,
O Sleep? Does the bright arch of rainbow clouds,
And pendent mountains seen in the calm lake,
215 Lead only to a black and watery depth,
While death's blue vault, with loathliest vapours hung,
Where every shade which the foul grave exhales
Hides its dead eye from the detested day,
Conducts, O Sleep, to thy delightful realms?
220 This doubt with sudden tide flowed on his heart,
The insatiate hope which it awakened, stung

His brain even like despair.
          While day-light held
The sky, the Poet kept mute conference
With his still soul. At night the passion came,
225 Like the fierce fiend of a distempered dream,
And shook him from his rest, and led him forth
Into the darkness.— As an eagle grasped
In folds of the green serpent, feels her breast
Burn with the poison, and precipitates
230 Through night and day, tempest, and calm, and
    cloud,
Frantic with dizzying anguish, her blind flight
O'er the wide aëry wilderness: thus driven
By the bright shadow of that lovely dream,
Beneath the cold glare of the desolate night,
235 Through tangled swamps and deep precipitous dells,
Startling with careless step the moon-light snake,
He fled. Red morning dawned upon his flight,
Shedding the mockery of its vital hues
Upon his cheek of death. He wandered on
240 Till vast Aornos seen from Petra's steep
Hung o'er the low horizon like a cloud;
Through Balk, and where the desolated tombs
Of Parthian kings scatter to every wind
Their wasting dust, wildly he wandered on,
245 Day after day, a weary waste of hours,
Bearing within his life the brooding care
That ever fed on its decaying flame.[1]
And now his limbs were lean; his scattered hair
Sered by the autumn of strange suffering
250 Sung dirges in the wind; his listless hand
Hung like dead bone within its withered skin;
Life, and the lustre that consumed it, shone
As in a furnace burning secretly
From his dark eyes alone. The cottagers,
255 Who ministered with human charity
His human wants, beheld with wondering awe
Their fleeting visitant. The mountaineer,
Encountering on some dizzy precipice
That spectral form, deemed that the Spirit of wind

---

[1] The Poet wanders through modern Afghanistan into Central Asia: Aornos was a fortress on the Indus River captured by Alexander the Great; Petra is the Sogdian Rock in the Pamir mountain range; Balk is the ancient Persian province of Bactria; Parthia is in modern Iran.

With lightning eyes, and eager breath, and feet
Disturbing not the drifted snow, had paused
In its career: the infant would conceal
His troubled visage in his mother's robe
In terror at the glare of those wild eyes,
To remember their strange light in many a dream
Of after-times; but youthful maidens, taught
By nature, would interpret half the woe
That wasted him, would call him with false names
Brother, and friend, would press his pallid hand
At parting, and watch, dim through tears, the path
Of his departure from their father's door.
    At length upon the lone Chorasmian shore[1]
He paused, a wide and melancholy waste
Of putrid marshes. A strong impulse urged
His steps to the sea-shore. A swan was there,
Beside a sluggish stream among the reeds.
It rose as he approached, and with strong wings
Scaling the upward sky, bent its bright course
High over the immeasurable main.
His eyes pursued its flight.—"Thou hast a home,
Beautiful bird; thou voyagest to thine home,
Where thy sweet mate will twine her downy neck
With thine, and welcome thy return with eyes
Bright in the lustre of their own fond joy.
And what am I that I should linger here,
With voice far sweeter than thy dying notes,
Spirit more vast than thine, frame more attuned
To beauty, wasting these surpassing powers
In the deaf air, to the blind earth, and heaven
That echoes not my thoughts?" A gloomy smile
Of desperate hope wrinkled his quivering lips.
For sleep, he knew, kept most relentlessly
Its precious charge, and silent death exposed,
Faithless perhaps as sleep, a shadowy lure,
With doubtful smile mocking its own strange charms.
    Startled by his own thoughts he looked around.
There was no fair fiend near him, not a sight
Or sound of awe but in his own deep mind.
A little shallop floating near the shore
Caught the impatient wandering of his gaze.
It had been long abandoned, for its sides
Gaped wide with many a rift, and its frail joints
Swayed with the undulations of the tide.
A restless impulse urged him to embark
And meet lone Death on the drear ocean's waste;
For well he knew that mighty Shadow loves
The slimy caverns of the populous deep.
    The day was fair and sunny, sea and sky
Drank its inspiring radiance, and the wind
Swept strongly from the shore, blackening the waves.
Following his eager soul, the wanderer
Leaped in the boat, he spread his cloak aloft
On the bare mast, and took his lonely seat,
And felt the boat speed o'er the tranquil sea
Like a torn cloud before the hurricane.
    As one that in a silver vision floats
Obedient to the sweep of odorous winds
Upon resplendent clouds, so rapidly
Along the dark and ruffled waters fled
The straining boat.—A whirlwind swept it on,
With fierce gusts and precipitating force,
Through the white ridges of the chafed sea.
The waves arose. Higher and higher still
Their fierce necks writhed beneath the tempest's scourge
Like serpents struggling in a vulture's grasp.
Calm and rejoicing in the fearful war
Of wave ruining on wave, and blast on blast
Descending, and black flood on whirlpool driven
With dark obliterating course, he sate:
As if their genii were the ministers
Appointed to conduct him to the light
Of those beloved eyes, the Poet sate
Holding the steady helm. Evening came on,
The beams of sunset hung their rainbow hues
High 'mid the shifting domes of sheeted spray
That canopied his path o'er the waste deep;
Twilight, ascending slowly from the east,
Entwin'd in duskier wreaths her braided locks
O'er the fair front and radiant eyes of day;
Night followed, clad with stars. On every side
More horribly the multitudinous streams
Of ocean's mountainous waste to mutual war
Rushed in dark tumult thundering, as to mock
The calm and spangled sky. The little boat

---

[1] probably the shore of the Aral Sea.

345 Still fled before the storm; still fled, like foam
Down the steep cataract of a wintry river;
Now pausing on the edge of the riven wave;
Now leaving far behind the bursting mass
That fell, convulsing ocean. Safely fled—
350 As if that frail and wasted human form,
Had been an elemental god.
      At midnight
The moon arose: and lo! the etherial cliffs
Of Caucasus,[1] whose icy summits shone
Among the stars like sunlight, and around
355 Whose cavern'd base the whirlpools and the waves
Bursting and eddying irresistibly
Rage and resound for ever.—Who shall save?—
The boat fled on,—the boiling torrent drove,—
The crags closed round with black and jagged arms,
360 The shattered mountain overhung the sea,
And faster still, beyond all human speed,
Suspended on the sweep of the smooth wave,
The little boat was driven. A cavern there
Yawned, and amid its slant and winding depths
365 Ingulphed the rushing sea. The boat fled on
With unrelaxing speed.—"Vision and Love!"
The Poet cried aloud, "I have beheld
The path of thy departure. Sleep and death
Shall not divide us long!"
      The boat pursued
370 The windings of the cavern. Day-light shone
At length upon that gloomy river's flow;
Now, where the fiercest war among the waves
Is calm, on the unfathomable stream
The boat moved slowly. Where the mountain, riven,
375 Exposed those black depths to the azure sky,
Ere yet the flood's enormous volume fell
Even to the base of Caucasus, with sound
That shook the everlasting rocks, the mass
Filled with one whirlpool all that ample chasm;
380 Stair above stair the eddying waters rose,
Circling immeasurably fast, and laved
With alternating dash the knarled roots
Of mighty trees, that stretched their giant arms
In darkness over it. I' the midst was left,
385 Reflecting, yet distorting every cloud,
A pool of treacherous and tremendous calm.
Seized by the sway of the ascending stream,
With dizzy swiftness, round, and round, and round,
Ridge after ridge the straining boat arose,
390 Till on the verge of the extremest curve,
Where, through an opening of the rocky bank,
The waters overflow, and a smooth spot
Of glassy quiet mid those battling tides
Is left, the boat paused shuddering.—Shall it sink
395 Down the abyss? Shall the reverting stress
Of that resistless gulph embosom it?
Now shall it fall?—A wandering stream of wind,
Breathed from the west, has caught the expanded
  sail,
And, lo! with gentle motion, between banks
400 Of mossy slope, and on a placid stream,
Beneath a woven grove it sails, and, hark!
The ghastly torrent mingles its far roar,
With the breeze murmuring in the musical woods.
Where the embowering trees recede, and leave
405 A little space of green expanse, the cove
Is closed by meeting banks, whose yellow flowers[2]
For ever gaze on their own drooping eyes,
Reflected in the crystal calm. The wave
Of the boat's motion marred their pensive task,
410 Which nought but vagrant bird, or wanton wind,
Or falling spear-grass, or their own decay
Had e'er disturbed before. The Poet longed
To deck with their bright hues his withered hair,
But on his heart its solitude returned,
415 And he forbore. Not the strong impulse hid
In those flushed cheeks, bent eyes, and shadowy
  frame,
Had yet performed its ministry: it hung
Upon his life, as lightning in a cloud
Gleams, hovering ere it vanish, ere the floods
420 Of night close over it.
      The noonday sun
Now shone upon the forest, one vast mass

---

[1] The Poet has long since left behind the Indian Caucasus of line 142: this is Mt. Caucasus in Georgia, overlooking the Black Sea. See Stuart Curran, *Shelley's Annus Mirabilis* 64.

[2] narcissi, recalling Ovid's tale of Narcissus, who falls in love with his own reflection (*Metamorphoses* 3).

Of mingling shade, whose brown magnificence
A narrow vale embosoms. There, huge caves,
Scooped in the dark base of their aëry rocks
425 Mocking its moans, respond and roar for ever.
The meeting boughs and implicated leaves
Wove twilight o'er the Poet's path, as led
By love, or dream, or god, or mightier Death,
He sought in Nature's dearest haunt, some bank,
430 Her cradle, and his sepulchre. More dark
And dark the shades accumulate. The oak,
Expanding its immense and knotty arms,
Embraces the light beech. The pyramids
Of the tall cedar overarching, frame
435 Most solemn domes within, and far below,
Like clouds suspended in an emerald sky,
The ash and the acacia floating hang
Tremulous and pale. Like restless serpents, clothed
In rainbow and in fire, the parasites,
440 Starred with ten thousand blossoms, flow around
The gray trunks, and, as gamesome infants' eyes,
With gentle meanings, and most innocent wiles,
Fold their beams round the hearts of those that love,
These twine their tendrils with the wedded boughs
445 Uniting their close union; the woven leaves
Make net-work of the dark blue light of day,
And the night's noontide clearness, mutable
As shapes in the weird clouds. Soft mossy lawns
Beneath these canopies extend their swells,
450 Fragrant with perfumed herbs, and eyed with blooms
Minute yet beautiful. One darkest glen
Sends from its woods of musk-rose, twined with
        jasmine,
A soul-dissolving odour, to invite
To some more lovely mystery. Through the dell,
455 Silence and Twilight here, twin-sisters, keep
Their noonday watch, and sail among the shades,
Like vaporous shapes half seen; beyond, a well,
Dark, gleaming, and of most translucent wave,
Images all the woven boughs above,
460 And each depending leaf, and every speck
Of azure sky, darting between their chasms;
Nor aught else in the liquid mirror laves
Its portraiture, but some inconstant star
Between one foliaged lattice twinkling fair,
465 Or, painted bird, sleeping beneath the moon,
Or gorgeous insect floating motionless,
Unconscious of the day, ere yet his wings
Have spread their glories to the gaze of noon.
    Hither the Poet came. His eyes beheld
470 Their own wan light through the reflected lines
Of his thin hair, distinct in the dark depth
Of that still fountain; as the human heart,
Gazing in dreams over the gloomy grave,
Sees its own treacherous likeness there. He heard
475 The motion of the leaves, the grass that sprung
Startled and glanced and trembled even to feel
An unaccustomed presence, and the sound
Of the sweet brook that from the secret springs
Of that dark fountain rose. A Spirit seemed
480 To stand beside him—clothed in no bright robes
Of shadowy silver or enshrining light,
Borrowed from aught the visible world affords
Of grace, or majesty, or mystery;—
But, undulating woods, and silent well,
485 And leaping rivulet, and evening gloom
Now deepening the dark shades, for speech assuming
Held commune with him, as if he and it
Were all that was,—only ... when his regard
Was raised by intense pensiveness, ... two eyes,
490 Two starry eyes, hung in the gloom of thought,
And seemed with their serene and azure smiles
To beckon him.
            Obedient to the light
That shone within his soul, he went, pursuing
The windings of the dell.—The rivulet
495 Wanton and wild, through many a green ravine
Beneath the forest flowed. Sometimes it fell
Among the moss with hollow harmony
Dark and profound. Now on the polished stones
It danced; like childhood laughing as it went:
500 Then, through the plain in tranquil wanderings crept,
Reflecting every herb and drooping bud
That overhung its quietness.—"O stream!
Whose source is inaccessibly profound,
Whither do thy mysterious waters tend?
505 Thou imagest my life. Thy darksome stillness,
Thy dazzling waves, thy loud and hollow gulphs,
Thy searchless fountain, and invisible course

Have each their type in me: and the wide sky,
And measureless ocean may declare as soon
510 What oozy cavern or what wandering cloud
Contains thy waters, as the universe
Tell where these living thoughts reside, when stretched
Upon thy flowers my bloodless limbs shall waste
I' the passing wind!"
                    Beside the grassy shore
515 Of the small stream he went; he did impress
On the green moss his tremulous step, that caught
Strong shuddering from his burning limbs. As one
Roused by some joyous madness from the couch
Of fever, he did move; yet, not like him,
520 Forgetful of the grave, where, when the flame
Of his frail exultation shall be spent,
He must descend. With rapid steps he went
Beneath the shade of trees, beside the flow
Of the wild babbling rivulet; and now
525 The forest's solemn canopies were changed
For the uniform and lightsome evening sky.
Gray rocks did peep from the spare moss, and stemmed
The struggling brook: tall spires of windlestrae[1]
Threw their thin shadows down the rugged slope,
530 And nought but knarled roots of ancient pines
Branchless and blasted, clenched with grasping roots
The unwilling soil. A gradual change was here,
Yet ghastly. For, as fast years flow away,
The smooth brow gathers, and the hair grows thin
535 And white, and where irradiate dewy eyes
Had shone, gleam stony orbs:—so from his steps
Bright flowers departed, and the beautiful shade
Of the green groves, with all their odorous winds
And musical motions. Calm, he still pursued
540 The stream, that with a larger volume now
Rolled through the labyrinthine dell; and there
Fretted a path through its descending curves
With its wintry speed. On every side now rose
Rocks, which, in unimaginable forms,
545 Lifted their black and barren pinnacles
In the light of evening, and its precipice
Obscuring the ravine, disclosed above,
Mid toppling stones, black gulphs and yawning caves,
Whose windings gave ten thousand various tongues
550 To the loud stream. Lo! where the pass expands
Its stony jaws, the abrupt mountain breaks,
And seems, with its accumulated crags,
To overhang the world: for wide expand
Beneath the wan stars and descending moon
555 Islanded seas, blue mountains, mighty streams,
Dim tracts and vast, robed in the lustrous gloom
Of leaden-coloured even, and fiery hills
Mingling their flames with twilight, on the verge
Of the remote horizon. The near scene,
560 In naked and severe simplicity,
Made contrast with the universe. A pine,
Rock-rooted, stretched athwart the vacancy
Its swinging boughs, to each inconstant blast
Yielding one only response, at each pause
565 In most familiar cadence, with the howl
The thunder and the hiss of homeless streams
Mingling its solemn song, whilst the broad river,
Foaming and hurrying o'er its rugged path,
Fell into that immeasurable void
570 Scattering its waters to the passing winds.
    Yet the gray precipice and solemn pine
And torrent, were not all;—one silent nook
Was there. Even on the edge of that vast mountain,
Upheld by knotty roots and fallen rocks,
575 It overlooked in its serenity
The dark earth, and the bending vault of stars.
It was a tranquil spot, that seemed to smile
Even in the lap of horror. Ivy clasped
The fissured stones with its entwining arms,
580 And did embower with leaves for ever green,
And berries dark, the smooth and even space
Of its inviolated floor, and here
The children of the autumnal whirlwind bore,
In wanton sport, those bright leaves, whose decay,
585 Red, yellow, or etherially pale,
Rivals the pride of summer.[2] 'Tis the haunt
Of every gentle wind, whose breath can teach
The wilds to love tranquillity. One step,
One human step alone, has ever broken

---

[1] dried stalk(s) of grass, also known as "windlestraw" (Sc.).

[2] Cf. Shelley, "Ode to the West Wind" 1–5.*

590   The stillness of its solitude:—one voice
        Alone inspired its echoes;—even that voice
        Which hither came, floating among the winds,
        And led the loveliest among human forms
        To make their wild haunts the depository
595   Of all the grace and beauty that endued
        Its motions, render up its majesty,
        Scatter its music on the unfeeling storm,
        And to the damp leaves and blue cavern mould,
        Nurses of rainbow flowers and branching moss,
600   Commit the colours of that varying cheek,
        That snowy breast, those dark and drooping eyes.
            The dim and horned moon hung low, and poured
        A sea of lustre on the horizon's verge
        That overflowed its mountains. Yellow mist
605   Filled the unbounded atmosphere, and drank
        Wan moonlight even to fullness: not a star
        Shone, not a sound was heard; the very winds,
        Danger's grim playmates, on that precipice
        Slept, clasped in his embrace.—O, storm of death!
610   Whose sightless speed divides this sullen night:
        And thou, colossal Skeleton, that, still
        Guiding its irresistible career
        In thy devastating omnipotence,
        Art king of this frail world, from the red field
615   Of slaughter, from the reeking hospital,
        The patriot's sacred couch, the snowy bed
        Of innocence, the scaffold and the throne,
        A mighty voice invokes thee. Ruin calls
        His brother Death. A rare and regal prey
620   He hath prepared, prowling around the world;
        Glutted with which thou mayst repose, and men
        Go to their graves like flowers or creeping worms,
        Nor ever more offer at thy dark shrine
        The unheeded tribute of a broken heart.
625   When on the threshold of the green recess
        The wanderer's footsteps fell, he knew that death
        Was on him. Yet a little, ere it fled,
        Did he resign his high and holy soul
        To images of the majestic past,
630   That paused within his passive being now,

        Like winds that bear sweet music, when they breathe
        Through some dim latticed chamber. He did place
        His pale lean hand upon the rugged trunk
        Of the old pine. Upon an ivied stone
635   Reclined his languid head, his limbs did rest,
        Diffused and motionless, on the smooth brink
        Of that obscurest chasm;—and thus he lay,
        Surrendering to their final impulses
        The hovering powers of life. Hope and despair,
640   The torturers, slept; no mortal pain or fear
        Marred his repose, the influxes of sense,
        And his own being unalloyed by pain,
        Yet feebler and more feeble, calmly fed
        The stream of thought, till he lay breathing there
645   At peace, and faintly smiling:—his last sight
        Was the great moon, which o'er the western line
        Of the wide world her mighty horn suspended,
        With whose dun beams inwoven darkness seemed
        To mingle. Now upon the jagged hills
650   It rests, and still as the divided frame
        Of the vast meteor sunk, the Poet's blood,
        That ever beat in mystic sympathy
        With nature's ebb and flow, grew feebler still:
        And when two lessening points of light alone
655   Gleamed through the darkness, the alternate gasp
        Of his faint respiration scarce did stir
        The stagnate night:—till the minutest ray
        Was quenched, the pulse yet lingered in his heart.
        It paused—it fluttered. But when heaven remained
660   Utterly black, the murky shades involved
        An image, silent, cold, and motionless,
        As their own voiceless earth and vacant air.
        Even as a vapour fed with golden beams
        That ministered on sunlight, ere the west
665   Eclipses it, was now that wonderous frame—
        No sense, no motion, no divinity—
        A fragile lute, on whose harmonious strings
        The breath of heaven did wander—a bright stream
        Once fed with many-voiced waves—a dream
670   Of youth, which night and time have quenched for
            ever,

Still, dark, and dry, and unremembered now.
    O, for Medea's wondrous alchemy,[1]
Which wheresoe'er it fell made the earth gleam
With bright flowers, and the wintry boughs exhale
675 From vernal blooms fresh fragrance! O, that God,
Profuse of poisons, would concede the chalice
Which but one living man has drained, who now,
Vessel of deathless wrath, a slave that feels
No proud exemption in the blighting curse
680 He bears, over the world wanders for ever,
Lone as incarnate death![2] O, that the dream
Of dark magician in his visioned cave,
Raking the cinders of a crucible
For life and power, even when his feeble hand
685 Shakes in its last decay, were the true law
Of this so lovely world! But thou art fled
Like some frail exhalation; which the dawn
Robes in its golden beams,—ah! thou hast fled!
The brave, the gentle, and the beautiful,
690 The child of grace and genius. Heartless things
Are done and said i' the world, and many worms
And beasts and men live on, and mighty Earth
From sea and mountain, city and wilderness,
In vesper low or joyous orison,
695 Lifts still its solemn voice:—but thou art fled—
Thou canst no longer know or love the shapes
Of this phantasmal scene, who have to thee
Been purest ministers, who are, alas!
Now thou art not. Upon those pallid lips
700 So sweet even in their silence, on those eyes
That image sleep in death, upon that form
Yet safe from the worm's outrage, let no tear
Be shed—not even in thought. Nor, when those hues
Are gone, and those divinest lineaments,
705 Worn by the senseless wind, shall live alone
In the frail pauses of this simple strain,
Let not high verse, mourning the memory
Of that which is no more, or painting's woe
Or sculpture, speak in feeble imagery
710 Their own cold powers. Art and eloquence,
And all the shews o' the world are frail and vain
To weep a loss that turns their lights to shade.
It is a woe too "deep for tears,"[3] when all
Is reft at once, when some surpassing Spirit,
715 Whose light adorned the world around it, leaves
Those who remain behind, not sobs or groans,
The passionate tumult of a clinging hope;
But pale despair and cold tranquillity,
Nature's vast frame, the web of human things,
720 Birth and the grave, that are not as they were.

To Wordsworth

Poet of Nature, thou hast wept to know
That things depart which never may return:
Childhood and youth, friendship and love's first glow,
Have fled like sweet dreams, leaving thee to mourn.
5 These common woes I feel. One loss is mine
Which thou too feel'st, yet I alone deplore.[4]
Thou wert as a lone star, whose light did shine
On some frail bark in winter's midnight roar:
Thou hast like to a rock-built refuge stood
10 Above the blind and battling multitude:
In honoured poverty thy voice did weave
Songs consecrate to truth and liberty,—
Deserting these, thou leavest me to grieve,
Thus having been, that thou shouldst cease to be.

---

[1] Medea the sorceress brewed a magic potion to revive Aeson; when she spilled some of it, grass and flowers sprang up (Ovid, *Metamorphoses* 7).

[2] Ahasuerus, the Wandering Jew of legend and a character in Shelley's *The Wandering Jew* (1810), *Queen Mab*, and *Hellas* (1821). Having rejected Christ on the way to Calvary (John 21.22), he was doomed to wander the earth until the Second Coming.

[3] Cf. W. Wordsworth, "Ode" 205–06.*

[4] W. Wordsworth's increasingly conservative political and religious opinions disillusioned many of his admirers, especially following the publication of *The Excursion*.*

from *History of a Six Weeks' Tour through a Part of France, Switzerland, Germany, and Holland: with Letters Descriptive of a Sail round the Lake of Geneva, and of the Glaciers of Chamouni* (1817)

Mont Blanc
Lines Written in the Vale of Chamouni[1]

1

The everlasting universe of things
Flows through the mind, and rolls its rapid waves,
Now dark—now glittering—now reflecting gloom—
Now lending splendour, where from secret springs
5   The source of human thought its tribute brings
Of waters,—with a sound but half its own,
Such as a feeble brook will oft assume
In the wild woods, among the mountains lone,
Where waterfalls around it leap for ever,
10 Where woods and winds contend, and a vast river
Over its rocks ceaselessly bursts and raves.

2

Thus thou, Ravine of Arve—dark, deep Ravine—
Thou many-coloured, many-voiced vale,
Over whose pines, and crags, and caverns sail
15 Fast cloud shadows and sunbeams: awful scene,
Where Power in likeness of the Arve comes down
From the ice gulphs that gird his secret throne,
Bursting through these dark mountains like the flame
Of lightning thro' the tempest;—thou dost lie,
20 Thy giant brood of pines around thee clinging,
Children of elder time, in whose devotion
The chainless winds still come and ever came
To drink their odours, and their mighty swinging
To hear—an old and solemn harmony;
25 Thine earthly rainbows stretched across the sweep
Of the ethereal waterfall, whose veil
Robes some unsculptured[2] image; the strange sleep
Which when the voices of the desart fail
Wraps all in its own deep eternity;—
30 Thy caverns echoing to the Arve's commotion,
A loud, lone sound no other sound can tame;
Thou art pervaded with that ceaseless motion,
Thou art the path of that unresting sound—
Dizzy Ravine! and when I gaze on thee
35 I seem as in a trance sublime and strange
To muse on my own separate phantasy,
My own, my human mind, which passively
Now renders and receives fast influencings,
Holding an unremitting interchange
40 With the clear universe of things around;
One legion of wild thoughts, whose wandering wings
Now float above thy darkness, and now rest
Where that or thou art no unbidden guest,
In the still cave of the witch Poesy,
45 Seeking among the shadows that pass by
Ghosts of all things that are, some shade of thee,
Some phantom, some faint image; till the breast
From which they fled recalls them, thou art there!

3

Some say that gleams of a remoter world
50 Visit the soul in sleep,—that death is slumber,
And that its shapes the busy thoughts outnumber
Of those who wake and live.—I look on high;
Has some unknown omnipotence unfurled
The veil of life and death? or do I lie
55 In dream, and does the mightier world of sleep
Spread far around and inaccessibly
Its circles? For the very spirit fails,
Driven like a homeless cloud from steep to steep
That vanishes among the viewless[3] gales!
60 Far, far above, piercing the infinite sky,
Mont Blanc appears,—still, snowy, and serene—
Its subject mountains their unearthly forms
Pile around it, ice and rock; broad vales between
Of frozen floods, unfathomable deeps,
65 Blue as the overhanging heaven, that spread

---

[1] The Arve River runs through the valley of Chamouni, now in southeastern France, but in Switzerland when the Shelleys visited in 1816. Mont Blanc is the highest mountain in Europe.

[2] natural, not formed by human hands.

[3] invisible. Cf. Milton, *Paradise Lost* 3.518.

And wind among the accumulated steeps;
A desert peopled by the storms alone,
Save when the eagle brings some hunter's bone,
And the wolf tracks her there—how hideously
70 Its shapes are heaped around! rude, bare, and high,
Ghastly, and scarred, and riven.—Is this the scene
Where the old Earthquake-dæmon[1] taught her young
Ruin? Were these their toys? or did a sea
Of fire, envelope once this silent snow?
75 None can reply—all seems eternal now.
The wilderness has a mysterious tongue
Which teaches awful doubt, or faith so mild,
So solemn, so serene, that man may be
But for such faith[2] with nature reconciled;
80 Thou hast a voice, great Mountain, to repeal
Large codes of fraud and woe; not understood
By all, but which the wise, and great, and good
Interpret, or make felt, or deeply feel.

4

The fields, the lakes, the forests, and the streams,
85 Ocean, and all the living things that dwell
Within the dædal[3] earth; lightning, and rain,
Earthquake, and fiery flood, and hurricane,
The torpor of the year when feeble dreams
Visit the hidden buds, or dreamless sleep
90 Holds every future leaf and flower;—the bound
With which from that detested trance they leap;
The works and ways of man, their death and birth,
And that of him and all that his may be;
All things that move and breathe with toil and sound
95 Are born and die; revolve, subside and swell.
Power dwells apart in its tranquillity
Remote, serene, and inaccessible:
And *this*, the naked countenance of earth,
On which I gaze, even these primæval mountains
100 Teach the adverting mind. The glaciers creep

---

[1] demi-god (not a demon or devil in the usual sense).

[2] "But" may here have the force of "only" or "merely"; manuscript variants of the line include "With such a faith," "In such wise faith," and "In such a faith."

[3] intricately made (like something crafted by Dædalus, who made the Cretan labyrinth and the wings on which he and his son, Icarus, fled Crete); cf. Ovid, *Metamorphoses* 8.

Like snakes that watch their prey, from their far
   fountains,
Slow rolling on; there, many a precipice,
Frost and the Sun in scorn of mortal power
Have piled: dome, pyramid, and pinnacle,
105 A city of death, distinct with many a tower
And wall impregnable of beaming ice.
Yet not a city, but a flood of ruin
Is there, that from the boundaries of the sky
Rolls its perpetual stream; vast pines are strewing
110 Its destined path, or in the mangled soil
Branchless and shattered stand; the rocks, drawn down
From yon remotest waste, have overthrown
The limits of the dead and living world,
Never to be reclaimed. The dwelling-place
115 Of insects, beasts, and birds, becomes its spoil;
Their food and their retreat for ever gone,
So much of life and joy is lost. The race
Of man, flies far in dread; his work and dwelling
Vanish, like smoke before the tempest's stream,
120 And their place is not known.[4] Below, vast caves
Shine in the rushing torrent's restless gleam,
Which from those secret chasms in tumult welling
Meet in the vale, and one majestic River,
The breath and blood of distant lands, for ever
125 Rolls its loud waters to the ocean waves,
Breathes its swift vapours to the circling air.

5

Mont Blanc yet gleams on high:—the power is there,
The still and solemn power of many sights,
And many sounds, and much of life and death.
130 In the calm darkness of the moonless nights,
In the lone glare of day, the snows descend
Upon that Mountain; none beholds them there,
Nor when the flakes burn in the sinking sun,
Or the star-beams dart through them:—Winds
   contend
135 Silently there, and heap the snow with breath
Rapid and strong, but silently! Its home
The voiceless lightning in these solitudes
Keeps innocently, and like vapour broods

---

[4] Cf. Nahum 3.17.

Over the snow. The secret strength of things
140 Which governs thought, and to the infinite dome
Of heaven is as a law, inhabits thee!
And what were thou, and earth, and stars, and sea,
If to the human mind's imaginings
Silence and solitude were vacancy?

from the *Examiner* (19 January 1817)

Hymn to Intellectual Beauty[1]

1

The awful shadow of some unseen Power
    Floats tho' unseen amongst us,—visiting
    This various world with as inconstant wing
As summer winds that creep from flower to flower.—
5 Like moonbeams that behind some piny mountain shower,
    It visits with inconstant glance
    Each human heart and countenance;
Like hues and harmonies of evening,—
    Like clouds in starlight widely spread,—
10   Like memory of music fled,—
    Like aught that for its grace may be
Dear, and yet dearer for its mystery.

2

Spirit of BEAUTY, that dost consecrate
    With thine own hues all thou dost shine upon
15   Of human thought or form,—where art thou gone?
Why dost thou pass away and leave our state,
This dim vast vale of tears, vacant and desolate?
    Ask why the sunlight not forever
    Weaves rainbows o'er yon mountain river,
20 Why aught should fail and fade that once is shewn,
    Why fear and dream and death and birth
    Cast on the daylight of this earth
    Such gloom,—why man has such a scope
For love and hate, despondency and hope?

3

25 No voice from some sublimer world hath ever
    To sage or poet these responses given—
    Therefore the names of Demon, Ghost, and Heaven,
Remain the records of their vain endeavour,
Frail spells—whose uttered charm might not avail to sever,
30   From all we hear and all we see,
    Doubt, chance, and mutability.
Thy light alone—like mist o'er mountains driven,
    Or music by the night wind sent,
    Thro' strings of some still instrument,
35   Or moonlight on a midnight stream,
Gives grace and truth to life's unquiet dream.

4

Love, Hope, and Self-esteem, like clouds depart
    And come, for some uncertain moments lent.
    Man were immortal, and omnipotent,
40 Didst thou, unknown and awful as thou art,
Keep with thy glorious train firm state within his heart.
    Thou messenger of sympathies,
    That wax and wane in lovers' eyes—
Thou—that to human thought art nourishment,
45   Like darkness to a dying flame!
    Depart not as thy shadow came,
    Depart not—lest the grave should be,
Like life and fear, a dark reality.

5

While yet a boy I sought for ghosts, and sped
50   Thro many a listening chamber, cave and ruin,
    And starlight wood, with fearful steps pursuing
Hopes of high talk with the departed dead.
I called on poisonous names with which our youth is fed,[2]
    I was not heard—I saw them not—
55   When musing deeply on the lot
Of life, at that sweet time when winds are wooing
    All vital things that wake to bring
    News of birds and blossoming,—

---

[1] immaterial beauty.

[2] the names associated with conventional religious teaching; cf. line 27.

Sudden, thy shadow fell on me;
I shrieked, and clasped my hands in extacy!

6

I vowed that I would dedicate my powers
   To thee and thine—have I not kept the vow?
     With beating heart and streaming eyes, even now
I call the phantoms of a thousand hours
Each from his voiceless grave: they have in
        visioned bowers
   Of studious zeal or love's delight
     Outwatched with me the envious night—
They know that never joy illumed my brow
     Unlinked with hope that thou wouldst free
   This world from its dark slavery,
     That thou—O awful LOVELINESS,
Wouldst give whate'er these words cannot express.

7

The day becomes more solemn and serene
   When noon is past—there is a harmony
     In autumn, and a lustre in its sky,
Which thro' the summer is not heard or seen,
As if it could not be, as if it had not been!
     Thus let thy power, which like the truth
      Of nature on my passive youth
Descended, to my onward life supply
      Its calm—to one who worships thee,
     And every form containing thee,
   Whom, SPIRIT fair, thy spells did bind
To fear himself, and love all human kind.

from the *Examiner* (11 January 1818)

Ozymandias[1]

I met a Traveller from an antique land,
Who said, "Two vast and trunkless legs of stone
Stand in the desert. Near them, on the sand,
Half sunk, a shattered visage lies, whose frown,
And wrinkled lip, and sneer of cold command,
Tell that its sculptor well those passions read,
Which yet survive, stamped on these lifeless things,
The hand that mocked them, and the heart that fed:
And on the pedestal these words appear:
'My name is OZYMANDIAS, King of Kings.
Look on my works ye Mighty, and despair!'
No thing beside remains. Round the decay
Of that Colossal Wreck, boundless and bare,
The lone and level sands stretch far away."

from *Prometheus Unbound: A Lyrical Drama in Four Acts with Other Poems* (1820)

Prometheus Unbound[2]

PREFACE

The Greek tragic writers, in selecting as their subject any portion of their national history or mythology, employed in their treatment of it a certain arbitrary discretion. They by no means conceived themselves bound to adhere to the common interpretation or to imitate in story as in title their rivals and predecessors. Such a system would have amounted to a resignation of those claims to preference over their competitors which incited the composition. The Agamemnonian story[3] was exhibited on the Athenian theatre with as many varia-

---

[1] the Greek name for the pharaoh Ramses II (1304–1237 BC); cf. Horace Smith, "On a Stupendous Leg of Granite,"* which appeared in the *Examiner* the following month. Shelley's poem was first published under the pseudonym "Glirastes."

[2] Shelley completed most of the first three acts of *Prometheus Unbound* between September 1818 and May 1819, adding Act 4 later in 1819. Mary Shelley's first printed text does not include the following epigraph from Cicero: "Audisne hæc Amphiaræ, sub terram abdite?" ("Do you hear me, Amphiaraus, hidden under the earth?"). When Œdipus' son Eteocles would not give up the throne in favour of his brother Polynices, Amphiaraus was one of the Seven against Thebes, who was swallowed up by the earth as he retreated from battle. He was consulted as an oracle and sometimes worshipped as a god.

[3] The story of Agamemnon, leader of the Greek forces in the Trojan War, husband of Clytemnestra, and father of Iphigenia, Orestes, and Electra, is told in the *Iliad*, in Æschylus (525–456 BC), *Agamemnon* (the first play in the trilogy *Oresteia*, 458 BC), and in Euripides, *Iphigenia in Tauris* (410 BC) and *Iphigenia at Aulis* (c. 406 BC).

tions as dramas.

I have presumed to employ a similar licence. The "Prometheus Unbound" of Æschylus supposed the reconciliation of Jupiter with his victim as the price of the disclosure of the danger threatened to his empire by the consummation of his marriage with Thetis.[1] Thetis, according to this view of the subject, was given in marriage to Peleus, and Prometheus, by the permission of Jupiter, delivered from his captivity by Hercules. Had I framed my story on this model, I should have done no more than have attempted to restore the lost drama of Æschylus; an ambition, which, if my preference to this mode of treating the subject had incited me to cherish, the recollection of the high comparison such an attempt would challenge might well abate. But, in truth, I was averse from a catastrophe so feeble as that of reconciling the Champion with the Oppressor of mankind. The moral interest of the fable, which is so powerfully sustained by the sufferings and endurance of Prometheus, would be annihilated if we could conceive of him as unsaying his high language and quailing before his successful and perfidious adversary. The only imaginary being resembling in any degree Prometheus, is Satan; and Prometheus is, in my judgement, a more poetical character than Satan, because, in addition to courage, and majesty, and firm and patient opposition to omnipotent force, he is susceptible of being described as exempt from the taints of ambition, envy, revenge, and a desire for personal aggrandisement, which, in the Hero of Paradise Lost, interfere with the interest.[2] The character of Satan engenders in the mind a pernicious casuistry which leads us to weigh his faults with his wrongs, and to excuse the former because the latter exceed all measure. In the minds of those who consider that magnificent fiction with a religious feeling it engenders something worse. But Prometheus is, as it were, the type of the highest perfection of moral and intellectual nature, impelled by the purest and the truest motives to the best and noblest ends.

This Poem was chiefly written upon the mountainous ruins of the Baths of Caracalla,[3] among the flowery glades, and thickets of odoriferous blossoming trees, which are extended in ever winding labyrinths upon its immense platforms and dizzy arches suspended in the air. The bright blue sky of Rome, and the effect of the vigorous awakening spring in that divinest climate, and the new life with which it drenches the spirits even to intoxication, were the inspiration of this drama.

The imagery which I have employed will be found, in many instances, to have been drawn from the operations of the human mind, or from those external actions by which they are expressed. This is unusual in modern poetry, although Dante and Shakspeare are full of instances of the same kind: Dante indeed more than any other poet, and with greater success. But the Greek poets, as writers to whom no resource of awakening the sympathy of their contemporaries was unknown, were in the habitual use of this power; and it is the study of their works, (since a higher merit would probably be denied me,) to which I am willing that my readers should impute this singularity.

One word is due in candour to the degree in which the study of contemporary writings may have tinged my composition, for such has been a topic of censure with regard to poems far more popular, and indeed more deservedly popular, than mine. It is impossible that any one who inhabits the same age with such writers as those who stand in the foremost ranks of our own, can conscientiously assure himself that his language and tone of thought may not have been modified by the study of the productions of those extraordinary intellects. It is true, that, not the spirit of their genius, but the forms in which it has manifested itself, are due less to the peculiarities of their own minds than to the peculiarity of the moral and intellectual condition of the minds among which they have been produced. Thus a number of writers possess the form, whilst they want the spirit of those whom, it is alleged, they imitate; because the former is the endowment of the age in which they live, and the latter must be the uncommunicated

---

[1] Æschylus wrote *Prometheus Bound* (c. 430 BC) as the first play in a trilogy. The other two plays, *Prometheus Unbound* and *Prometheus the Firebearer*, are lost.

[2] Shelley shares William Blake's view, in *The Marriage of Heaven and Hell*,* that Satan is the real hero of Milton's epic poem about the fall and redemption of mankind.

[3] See Shelley's letter to Thomas Love Peacock, 23 March 1819.

lightning of their own mind.

The peculiar style of intense and comprehensive imagery which distinguishes the modern literature of England, has not been, as a general power, the product of the imitation of any particular writer. The mass of capabilities remains at every period materially the same; the circumstances which awaken it to action perpetually change. If England were divided into forty republics, each equal in population and extent to Athens, there is no reason to suppose but that, under institutions not more perfect than those of Athens, each would produce philosophers and poets equal to those who (if we except Shakspeare) have never been surpassed. We owe the great writers of the golden age of our literature to that fervid awakening of the public mind which shook to dust the oldest and most oppressive form of the Christian religion.[1] We owe Milton to the progress and developement of the same spirit: the sacred Milton was, let it ever be remembered, a republican, and a bold inquirer into morals and religion. The great writers of our own age are, we have reason to suppose, the companions and forerunners of some unimagined change in our social condition or the opinions which cement it. The cloud of mind is discharging its collected lightning, and the equilibrium between institutions and opinions is now restoring, or is about to be restored.

As to imitation, poetry is a mimetic art.[2] It creates, but it creates by combination and representation. Poetical abstractions are beautiful and new, not because the portions of which they are composed had no previous existence in the mind of man or in nature, but because the whole produced by their combination has some intelligible and beautiful analogy with those sources of emotion and thought, and with the contemporary condition of them: one great poet is a masterpiece of nature which another not only ought to study but must study. He might as wisely and as easily determine that his mind should no longer be the mirror of all that is lovely in the visible universe, as exclude from his contemplation the beautiful which exists in the writings of a great contemporary. The pretence of doing it would be a presumption in any but the greatest; the effect, even in him, would be strained, unnatural, and ineffectual. A poet is the combined product of such internal powers as modify the nature of others; and of such external influences as excite and sustain these powers; he is not one, but both. Every man's mind is, in this respect, modified by all the objects of nature and art; by every word and every suggestion which he ever admitted to act upon his consciousness; it is the mirror upon which all forms are reflected, and in which they compose one form. Poets, not otherwise than philosophers, painters, sculptors, and musicians, are, in one sense, the creators, and, in another, the creations, of their age. From this subjection the loftiest do not escape. There is a similarity between Homer and Hesiod, between Æschylus and Euripides, between Virgil and Horace, between Dante and Petrarch, between Shakspeare and Fletcher, between Dryden and Pope;[3] each has a generic resemblance under which their specific distinctions are arranged. If this similarity be the result of imitation, I am willing to confess that I have imitated.

Let this opportunity be conceded to me of acknowledging that I have, what a Scotch philosopher characteristically terms, "a passion for reforming the world": what passion incited him to write and publish his book, he omits to explain. For my part I had rather be damned with Plato and Lord Bacon, than go to Heaven with Paley and Malthus.[4] But it is a mistake to suppose that

---

[1] the Protestant Reformation and ensuing religious debates and disputes of the sixteenth and seventeenth centuries.

[2] Shelley agrees with Aristotle, *Poetics* 1447a, that art begins in imitation. Cf. "Defence of Poetry."*

[3] Homer (8th century BC), author of the *Iliad* and the *Odyssey*; Hesiod (8th century BC), author of *Theogony* and *Works and Days*; Æschylus (525–456 BC), author of *Prometheus Bound* and the *Oresteia*; Euripides (480–406 BC), Greek tragedian; Virgil (70–19 BC), author of the *Æneid*; Horace (65–8 BC), Roman lyric poet; Dante (1265–1321), author of the *Divine Comedy*; Francesco Petrarca (1304–74), Italian poet; William Shakespeare (1564–1616), English dramatist; John Fletcher (1579–1625), English dramatist; John Dryden (1631–1700), English poet; Alexander Pope (1688–1744), English poet: in each pair but the last, the first writer is usually considered greater than his contemporary.

[4] Francis Bacon (1561–1626), English politician, philosopher, and essayist; William Paley (1743–1805), author of *Natural Theology* (1802), and Thomas Robert Malthus, author of *An Essay on the Principle of Population*.*

I dedicate my poetical compositions solely to the direct enforcement of reform, or that I consider them in any degree as containing a reasoned system on the theory of human life. Didactic poetry is my abhorrence; nothing can be equally well expressed in prose that is not tedious and supererogatory in verse. My purpose has hitherto been simply to familiarize the highly refined imagination of the more select classes of poetical readers with beautiful idealisms of moral excellence; aware that until the mind can love, and admire, and trust, and hope, and endure, reasoned principles of moral conduct are seeds cast upon the highway of life which the unconscious passenger tramples into dust, although they would bear the harvest of his happiness. Should I live to accomplish what I purpose, that is, produce a systematical history of what appear to me to be the genuine elements of human society, let not the advocates of injustice and superstition flatter themselves that I should take Æschylus rather than Plato as my model.

The having spoken of myself with unaffected freedom will need little apology with the candid; and let the uncandid consider that they injure me less than their own hearts and minds by misrepresentation. Whatever talents a person may possess to amuse and instruct others, be they ever so inconsiderable, he is yet bound to exert them: if his attempt be ineffectual, let the punishment of an unaccomplished purpose have been sufficient; let none trouble themselves to heap the dust of oblivion upon his efforts; the pile they raise will betray his grave which might otherwise have been unknown.

DRAMATIS PERSONÆ

PROMETHEUS
DEMOGORGON
JUPITER
THE EARTH
OCEAN
APOLLO
MERCURY
HERCULES
ASIA ⎫
PANTHEA ⎬ *Oceanides*
IONE ⎭
THE PHANTASM OF JUPITER
THE SPIRIT OF THE EARTH
SPIRITS OF THE HOURS

SPIRITS, ECHOES, FAUNS, FURIES

ACT 1

SCENE, a Ravine of Icy Rocks in the Indian Caucasus.[1]
PROMETHEUS is discovered bound to the Precipice.
PANTHEA and IONE are seated at his Feet. Time, Night.
During the Scene, Morning slowly breaks.

PROMETHEUS: Monarch of Gods and Dæmons,[2]
   and all Spirits
But One,[3] who throng those bright and rolling worlds
Which Thou and I alone of living things
Behold with sleepless eyes! regard this Earth
5 Made multitudinous with thy slaves, whom thou
Requitest for knee-worship, prayer, and praise,
And toil, and hecatombs[4] of broken hearts,
With fear and self-contempt and barren hope.
Whilst me, who am thy foe, eyeless in hate,
10 Hast thou made reign and triumph, to thy scorn,
O'er mine own misery and thy vain revenge.
Three thousand years of sleep-unsheltered hours,
And moments aye divided by keen pangs
Till they seemed years, torture and solitude,
15 Scorn and despair,—these are mine empire.
More glorious far than that which thou surveyest
From thine unenvied throne, O, Mighty God!
Almighty, had I deigned to share the shame
Of thine ill tyranny, and hung not here
20 Nailed to this wall of eagle-baffling mountain,
Black, wintry, dead, unmeasured; without herb,

---

[1] The setting is the Indian Caucasus (cf. "Alastor" 144 and n.).

[2] Jupiter, who rules over the other gods and over those intermediary spirits (dæmons) between the human and divine worlds.

[3] Prometheus himself.

[4] originally, sacrifices of a hundred oxen; any large sacrifices.

Insect, or beast, or shape or sound of life.
Ah me! alas, pain, pain ever, for ever!
No change, no pause, no hope! Yet I endure.
I ask the Earth, have not the mountains felt?
I ask yon Heaven, the all-beholding Sun,
Has it not seen? The Sea, in storm or calm,
Heaven's ever-changing Shadow, spread below,
Have its deaf waves not heard my agony?
Ah me! alas, pain, pain ever, for ever!
The crawling glaciers pierce me with the spears
Of their moon-freezing chrystals, the bright chains
Eat with their burning cold into my bones.
Heaven's winged hound, polluting from thy lips
His beak in poison not his own, tears up
My heart; and shapeless sights come wandering by,
The ghastly people of the realm of dream,
Mocking me: and the Earthquake-fiends are charged
To wrench the rivets from my quivering wounds
When the rocks split and close again behind:
While from their loud abysses howling throng
The genii of the storm, urging the rage
Of whirlwind, and afflict me with keen hail.
And yet to me welcome is day and night,
Whether one breaks the hoar frost of the morn,
Or starry, dim, and slow, the other climbs
The leaden-coloured east; for then they lead
The wingless, crawling hours, one among whom
—As some dark Priest hales the reluctant victim—
Shall drag thee, cruel King, to kiss the blood
From these pale feet, which then might trample thee
If they disdained not such a prostrate slave.
Disdain! Ah no! I pity thee. What ruin
Will hunt thee undefended thro' the wide Heaven!
How will thy soul, cloven to its depth with terror,
Gape like a hell within! I speak in grief,
Not exultation, for I hate no more,
As then ere misery made me wise. The curse
Once breathed on thee I would recall. Ye Mountains,
Whose many-voiced Echoes, through the mist
Of cataracts, flung the thunder of that spell!
Ye icy Springs, stagnant with wrinkling frost,
Which vibrated to hear me, and then crept
Shuddering thro' India! Thou serenest Air,
Thro' which the Sun walks burning without beams!
And ye swift Whirlwinds, who on poised wings
Hung mute and moveless o'er yon hushed abyss,
As thunder, louder than your own, made rock
The orbed world! If then my words had power,
Though I am changed so that aught evil wish
Is dead within; although no memory be
Of what is hate, let them not lose it now!
What was that curse? for ye all heard me speak.
FIRST VOICE: [*From the Mountains.*]
Thrice three hundred thousand years
    O'er the Earthquake's couch we stood:
Oft, as men convulsed with fears,
    We trembled in our multitude.
SECOND VOICE: [*From the Springs.*]
Thunder-bolts had parched our water,
    We had been stained with bitter blood,
And had run mute, 'mid shrieks of slaughter,
    Thro' a city and a solitude.
THIRD VOICE: [*From the Air.*]
I had clothed, since Earth uprose,
    Its wastes in colours not their own,
And oft had my serene repose
    Been cloven by many a rending groan.
FOURTH VOICE: [*From the Whirlwinds.*]
We had soared beneath these mountains
    Unresting ages; nor had thunder,
Nor yon volcano's flaming fountains,
    Nor any power above or under
    Ever made us mute with wonder.
FIRST VOICE:
But never bowed our snowy crest
As at the voice of thine unrest.
SECOND VOICE:
Never such a sound before
To the Indian waves we bore.
A pilot asleep on the howling sea
Leaped up from the deck in agony,
And heard, and cried, "Ah, woe is me!"
And died as mad as the wild waves be.
THIRD VOICE:
By such dread words from Earth to Heaven
My still realm was never riven:
When its wound was closed, there stood
Darkness o'er the day like blood.

FOURTH VOICE:
And we shrank back: for dreams of ruin
To frozen caves our flight pursuing
105 Made us keep silence—thus—and thus—
Though silence is a hell to us.
THE EARTH: The tongueless Caverns of the craggy hills
Cried, "Misery!" then; the hollow Heaven replied,
"Misery!" And the Ocean's purple waves,
110 Climbing the land, howled to the lashing winds,
And the pale nations heard it, "Misery!"
PROMETHEUS: I hear a sound of voices: not the voice
Which I gave forth. Mother, thy sons and thou
Scorn him, without whose all-enduring will
115 Beneath the fierce omnipotence of Jove,
Both they and thou had vanished, like thin mist
Unrolled on the morning wind. Know ye not me,
The Titan?[1] He who made his agony
The barrier to your else all-conquering foe?
120 Oh, rock-embosomed lawns, and snow-fed streams,
Now seen athwart frore vapours, deep below,
Thro' whose o'ershadowing woods I wandered once
With Asia, drinking life from her loved eyes;
Why scorns the spirit which informs ye, now
125 To commune with me? me alone, who check'd,
As one who checks a fiend-drawn charioteer,
The falsehood and the force of him who reigns
Supreme, and with the groans of pining slaves
Fills your dim glens and liquid wildernesses:
130 Why answer ye not, still? Brethren!
THE EARTH: They dare not.
PROMETHEUS: Who dares? for I would hear that
    curse again.
Ha, what an awful whisper rises up!
'Tis scarce like sound: it tingles thro' the frame
As lightning tingles, hovering ere it strike.
135 Speak, Spirit! from thine inorganic voice
I only know that thou art moving near
And love. How cursed I him?
THE EARTH: How canst thou hear
Who knowest not the language of the dead?
PROMETHEUS: Thou art a living spirit; speak as they.

---

[1] Prometheus is one of the Titans, the gods who ruled the world before the rise of Jupiter and who have been subsequently imprisoned, oppressed, and subjugated by their successors.

140 THE EARTH: I dare not speak like life, lest Heaven's
    fell King
Should hear, and link me to some wheel of pain
More torturing than the one whereon I roll.
Subtle thou art and good, and tho' the Gods
Hear not this voice, yet thou art more than God
145 Being wise and kind: earnestly hearken now.
PROMETHEUS: Obscurely thro' my brain, like
    shadows dim,
Sweep awful thoughts, rapid and thick. I feel
Faint, like one mingled in entwining love;
Yet 'tis not pleasure.
THE EARTH: No, thou canst not hear:
150 Thou art immortal, and this tongue is known
Only to those who die.
PROMETHEUS: And what art thou,
O, melancholy Voice?
THE EARTH: I am the Earth,
Thy mother; she within whose stony veins,
To the last fibre of the loftiest tree
155 Whose thin leaves trembled in the frozen air,
Joy ran, as blood within a living frame,
When thou didst from her bosom, like a cloud
Of glory, arise, a spirit of keen joy!
And at thy voice her pining sons uplifted
160 Their prostrate brows from the polluting dust,
And our almighty Tyrant with fierce dread
Grew pale, until his thunder chained thee here.
Then, see those million worlds which burn and roll
Around us: their inhabitants beheld
165 My sphered light wane in wide Heaven; the sea
Was lifted by strange tempest, and new fire
From earthquake-rifted mountains of bright snow
Shook its portentous hair beneath Heaven's frown;
Lightning and Inundation vexed the plains;
170 Blue thistles bloomed in cities; foodless toads
Within voluptuous chambers panting crawled:
When Plague had fallen on man, and beast, and worm,
And Famine; and black blight on herb and tree;
And in the corn, and vines, and meadow-grass,
175 Teemed ineradicable poisonous weeds
Draining their growth, for my wan breast was dry
With grief; and the thin air, my breath, was stained
With the contagion of a mother's hate

Breathed on her child's destroyer; aye, I heard
180 Thy curse, the which, if thou rememberest not,
Yet my innumerable seas and streams,
Mountains, and caves, and winds, and yon wide air,
And the inarticulate people of the dead,
Preserve, a treasured spell. We meditate
185 In secret joy and hope those dreadful words
But dare not speak them.
PROMETHEUS: Venerable mother!
All else who live and suffer take from thee
Some comfort; flowers, and fruits, and happy sounds,
And love, though fleeting; these may not be mine.
190 But mine own words, I pray, deny me not.
THE EARTH: They shall be told. Ere Babylon was dust,
The Magus Zoroaster,[1] my dead child,
Met his own image walking in the garden.
That apparition, sole of men, he saw.
195 For know there are two worlds of life and death:
One that which thou beholdest; but the other
Is underneath the grave, where do inhabit
The shadows of all forms that think and live
Till death unite them and they part no more;
200 Dreams and the light imaginings of men,
And all that faith creates or love desires,
Terrible, strange, sublime and beauteous shapes.
There thou art, and dost hang, a writhing shade,
'Mid whirlwind-peopled mountains; all the gods
205 Are there, and all the powers of nameless worlds,
Vast, sceptred phantoms; heroes, men, and beasts;
And Demogorgon,[2] a tremendous gloom;
And he, the supreme Tyrant, on his throne
Of burning gold. Son, one of these shall utter
210 The curse which all remember. Call at will
Thine own ghost, or the ghost of Jupiter,
Hades or Typhon,[3] or what mightier Gods
From all-prolific Evil, since thy ruin
Have sprung, and trampled on my prostrate sons.
215 Ask, and they must reply: so the revenge
Of the Supreme may sweep thro' vacant shades,
As rainy wind thro' the abandoned gate
Of a fallen palace.
PROMETHEUS: Mother, let not aught
Of that which may be evil, pass again
220 My lips, or those of aught resembling me.
Phantasm of Jupiter, arise, appear!
IONE:
My wings are folded o'er mine ears:
My wings are crossed o'er mine eyes:
Yet thro' their silver shade appears,
225 And thro' their lulling plumes arise,
A Shape, a throng of sounds;
May it be no ill to thee
O thou of many wounds!
Near whom, for our sweet sister's sake,
230 Ever thus we watch and wake.
PANTHEA:
The sound is of whirlwind underground,
Earthquake, and fire, and mountains cloven;
The shape is awful like the sound,
Clothed in dark purple, star-inwoven.
235 A sceptre of pale gold
To stay steps proud, o'er the slow cloud
His veined hand doth hold.
Cruel he looks, but calm and strong,
Like one who does, not suffers wrong.
240 PHANTASM OF JUPITER: Why have the secret powers
of this strange world
Driven me, a frail and empty phantom, hither
On direst storms? What unaccustomed sounds
Are hovering on my lips, unlike the voice

---

[1] the founder (6th century BC) of Zoroastrianism, a dualistic religion teaching that two gods, Ormuzd (goodness and light) and Ahriman (evil and darkness) struggle for control of the universe. Cf. Byron, *Manfred* 2.4.*

[2] This mysterious being, who originates in a misreading of "Demiourgos," ("demiurge"), in Plato's *Timæus*, is mentioned in Boccaccio, Spenser, and Milton (*Paradise Lost* 2.965).

[3] Hades or Pluto is the god of the underworld; Typhon, son of the Earth, is a hundred-headed monster who fought the Olympian gods and was imprisoned in Tartarus, the place of punishment in the underworld.

With which our pallid race hold ghastly talk
245 In darkness? And, proud sufferer, who art thou?
PROMETHEUS: Tremendous Image, as thou art must be
He whom thou shadowest forth. I am his foe,
The Titan. Speak the words which I would hear,
Although no thought inform thine empty voice.
250 THE EARTH: Listen! And tho' your echoes must be
    mute,
Grey mountains, and old woods, and haunted springs,
Prophetic caves, and isle-surrounding streams,
Rejoice to hear what yet ye cannot speak.
PHANTASM:
A spirit seizes me and speaks within:
255 It tears me as fire tears a thunder-cloud.
PANTHEA: See, how he lifts his mighty looks, the
    Heaven
Darkens above.
IONE: He speaks! O shelter me!
PROMETHEUS: I see the curse on gestures proud and
    cold,
And looks of firm defiance, and calm hate,
260 And such despair as mocks itself with smiles,
Written as on a scroll: yet speak: Oh, speak!

PHANTASM:
Fiend, I defy thee! with a calm, fixed mind,
    All that thou canst inflict I bid thee do;
Foul Tyrant both of Gods and Human-kind,
265   One only being shalt thou not subdue.
Rain then thy plagues upon me here,
Ghastly disease, and frenzying fear;
And let alternate frost and fire
Eat into me, and be thine ire
270 Lightning, and cutting hail, and legioned forms
Of furies, driving by upon the wounding storms.

Aye, do thy worst. Thou art omnipotent.
    O'er all things but thyself I gave thee power,
And my own will. Be thy swift mischiefs sent
275   To blast mankind, from yon ethereal tower.
Let thy malignant spirit move
In darkness over those I love:
On me and mine I imprecate
The utmost torture of thy hate;
280 And thus devote to sleepless agony,
This undeclining head while thou must reign on high.

But thou, who art the God and Lord: O, thou,
    Who fillest with thy soul this world of woe,
To whom all things of Earth and Heaven do bow
285   In fear and worship: all-prevailing foe!
I curse thee! let a sufferer's curse
Clasp thee, his torturer, like remorse;
'Till thine Infinity shall be
A robe of envenomed agony;
290 And thine Omnipotence a crown of pain,
To cling like burning gold round thy dissolving brain.[1]

Heap on thy soul, by virtue of this Curse,
    Ill deeds, then be thou damned, beholding good;
Both infinite as is the universe,
295   And thou, and thy self-torturing solitude.
An awful image of calm power
Though now thou sittest, let the hour
Come, when thou must appear to be
That which thou art internally.
300 And after many a false and fruitless crime
Scorn track thy lagging fall thro' boundless space and
    time.

PROMETHEUS: Were these my words, O, Parent?
THE EARTH: They were thine.
PROMETHEUS: It doth repent me: words are quick
    and vain;
Grief for awhile is blind, and so was mine.
305 I wish no living thing to suffer pain.
THE EARTH:
Misery, Oh misery to me,
That Jove at length should vanquish thee.
Wail, howl aloud, Land and Sea,
The Earth's rent heart shall answer ye.
310 Howl, Spirits of the living and the dead,
Your refuge, your defence lies fallen and vanquished.

---

[1] an allusion to the death of Hercules, who put on the poisoned shirt of the centaur Nessus, (cf. Sophocles [c. 496–406 BC], *Women of Trachis* [413 BC]) and to Christ's crown of thorns (Matthew 27.28–29, Mark 15.17).

FIRST ECHO:
  Lies fallen and vanquished!
SECOND ECHO: Fallen and vanquished!
IONE:
  Fear not: 'tis but some passing spasm,
    The Titan is unvanquished still.
  But see, where thro' the azure chasm
    Of yon forked and snowy hill
  Trampling the slant winds on high
    With golden-sandalled feet, that glow
  Under plumes of purple dye,
  Like rose-ensanguined ivory,
    A Shape comes now,
  Stretching on high from his right hand
  A serpent-cinctured wand.[1]
PANTHEA: 'Tis Jove's world-wandering herald,
    Mercury.
IONE:
  And who are those with hydra tresses
    And iron wings that climb the wind,
  Whom the frowning God represses
    Like vapours steaming up behind,
  Clanging loud, an endless crowd—
PANTHEA:
    These are Jove's tempest-walking hounds,
  Whom he gluts with groans and blood,
  When charioted on sulphurous cloud
    He bursts Heaven's bounds.
IONE:
  Are they now led, from the thin dead
    On new pangs to be fed?
PANTHEA: The Titan looks as ever, firm, not proud.
FIRST FURY: Ha! I scent life!
SECOND FURY: Let me but look into his
    eyes!
THIRD FURY: The hope of torturing him smells like a
    heap
  Of corpses, to a death-bird after battle.
FIRST FURY: Darest thou delay, O Herald! take cheer,
    Hounds
  Of Hell: what if the Son of Maia[2] soon

---

[1] Mercury's caduceus, the staff wound with a serpent.

[2] Mercury.

Should make us food and sport—who can please long
  The Omnipotent?
MERCURY: Back to your towers of iron,
And gnash beside the streams of fire and wail
  Your foodless teeth. Geryon, arise! and Gorgon,
Chimæra, and thou Sphinx, subtlest of fiends[3]
Who ministered to Thebes Heaven's poisoned wine,
Unnatural love, and more unnatural hate:
These shall perform your task.
FIRST FURY: Oh, mercy! mercy!
We die with our desire: drive us not back!
MERCURY: Crouch then in silence.
                Awful Sufferer
To thee unwilling, most unwillingly
I come, by the great Father's will driven down,
To execute a doom of new revenge.
Alas! I pity thee, and hate myself
That I can do no more: aye from thy sight
Returning, for a season, heaven seems hell,
So thy worn form pursues me night and day,
Smiling reproach. Wise art thou, firm and good,
But vainly wouldst stand forth alone in strife
Against the Omnipotent; as yon clear lamps
That measure and divide the weary years
From which there is no refuge, long have taught,
And long must teach. Even now thy Torturer arms
With the strange might of unimagined pains
The powers who scheme slow agonies in Hell,
And my commission is to lead them here,
Or what more subtle, foul, or savage fiends
People the abyss, and leave them to their task.
Be it not so! there is a secret known
To thee, and to none else of living things,
Which may transfer the sceptre of wide Heaven,
The fear of which perplexes the Supreme:
Clothe it in words, and bid it clasp his throne

---

[3] Geryon was a triple-headed, triple-bodied monster, killed by Hercules; the Gorgons were monstrous women, with snakes for hair, who turned to stone those who looked at them; the Chimæra was a female monster with the head of a lion, the body of a goat, and the tail of a dragon; the Sphinx was a monster with the body of a lion and the head of a woman, who haunted Thebes, killing whoever could not answer her riddle. When Œdipus answered it, causing her death, he went on to kill his father and marry his mother (events alluded to in line 349).

In intercession; bend thy soul in prayer,
And like a suppliant in some gorgeous fane,
Let the will kneel within thy haughty heart:
For benefits and meek submission tame
380 The fiercest and the mightiest.
PROMETHEUS: Evil minds
Change good to their own nature. I gave all
He has; and in return he chains me here
Years, ages, night and day: whether the Sun
Split my parched skin, or in the moony night
385 The chrystal-winged snow cling round my hair:
Whilst my beloved race is trampled down
By his thought-executing ministers.
Such is the tyrants' recompense: 'tis just:
He who is evil can receive no good;
390 And for a world bestowed, or a friend lost,
He can feel hate, fear, shame; not gratitude:
He but requites me for his own misdeed.
Kindness to such is keen reproach, which breaks
With bitter stings the light sleep of Revenge.
395 Submission, thou dost know I cannot try:
For what submission but that fatal word,
The death-seal of mankind's captivity,
Like the Sicilian's hair-suspended sword,[1]
Which trembles o'er his crown, would he accept,
400 Or could I yield? Which yet I will not yield.
Let others flatter Crime, where it sits throned
In brief Omnipotence: secure are they:
For Justice, when triumphant, will weep down
Pity, not punishment, on her own wrongs,
405 Too much avenged by those who err. I wait,
Enduring thus, the retributive hour
Which since we spake is even nearer now.
But hark, the hell-hounds clamour: fear delay:
Behold! Heaven lowers under thy Father's frown.
410 MERCURY: Oh, that we might be spared: I to inflict
And thou to suffer! Once more answer me:
Thou knowest not the period of Jove's power?
PROMETHEUS: I know but this, that it must come.

---

[1] the sword of Damocles. Damocles the flatterer expressed envy of Dionysius the Elder (c. 430–367 BC), wealthy tyrant of Syracuse, in Sicily. To demonstrate the true condition of those in power, Dionysius invited Damocles to a banquet where a sword was suspended by a hair above him.

MERCURY: Alas!
Thou canst not count thy years to come of pain?
415 PROMETHEUS: They last while Jove must reign: nor
     more, nor less
Do I desire or fear.
MERCURY: Yet pause, and plunge
Into Eternity, where recorded time,
Even all that we imagine, age on age,
Seems but a point, and the reluctant mind
420 Flags wearily in its unending flight,
Till it sink, dizzy, blind, lost, shelterless;
Perchance it has not numbered the slow years
Which thou must spend in torture, unreprieved?
PROMETHEUS: Perchance no thought can count
     them, yet they pass.
425 MERCURY: If thou might'st dwell among the Gods the
     while
Lapped in voluptuous joy?
PROMETHEUS: I would not quit
This bleak ravine, these unrepentant pains.
MERCURY: Alas! I wonder at, yet pity thee.
PROMETHEUS: Pity the self-despising slaves of Heaven,
430 Not me, within whose mind sits peace serene,
As light in the sun, throned: how vain is talk!
Call up the fiends.
IONE: O, sister, look! White fire
Has cloven to the roots yon huge snow-loaded cedar;
How fearfully God's thunder howls behind!
435 MERCURY: I must obey his words and thine: alas!
Most heavily remorse hangs at my heart!
PANTHEA: See where the child of Heaven, with
     winged feet,
Runs down the slanted sunlight of the dawn.
IONE: Dear sister, close thy plumes over thine eyes
440 Lest thou behold and die: they come: they come
Blackening the birth of day with countless wings,
And hollow underneath, like death.
FIRST FURY: Prometheus!
SECOND FURY: Immortal Titan!
THIRD FURY: Champion of Heaven's slaves!
PROMETHEUS: He whom some dreadful voice invokes
     is here,
445 Prometheus, the chained Titan. Horrible forms,
What and who are ye? Never yet there came

Phantasms so foul thro' monster-teeming Hell
From the all-miscreative brain of Jove;
Whilst I behold such execrable shapes,
450 Methinks I grow like what I contemplate,
And laugh and stare in loathsome sympathy.
FIRST FURY: We are the ministers of pain, and fear,
And disappointment, and mistrust, and hate,
And clinging crime; and as lean dogs pursue
455 Thro' wood and lake some struck and sobbing fawn,
We track all things that weep, and bleed, and live,
When the great King betrays them to our will.
PROMETHEUS: Oh! many fearful natures in one name,
I know ye; and these lakes and echoes know
460 The darkness and the clangour of your wings.
But why more hideous than your loathed selves
Gather ye up in legions from the deep?
SECOND FURY: We knew not that: Sisters, rejoice, rejoice!
PROMETHEUS: Can aught exult in its deformity?
465 SECOND FURY: The beauty of delight makes lovers glad,
Gazing on one another: so are we.
As from the rose which the pale priestess kneels
To gather for her festal crown of flowers
The aerial crimson falls, flushing her cheek,
470 So from our victim's destined agony
The shade which is our form invests us round,
Else we are shapeless as our mother Night.
PROMETHEUS: I laugh your power, and his who sent you here,
To lowest scorn. Pour forth the cup of pain.
475 FIRST FURY: Thou thinkest we will rend thee bone from bone,
And nerve from nerve, working like fire within?
PROMETHEUS: Pain is my element, as hate is thine;
Ye rend me now: I care not.
SECOND FURY: Dost imagine
We will but laugh into thy lidless eyes?
480 PROMETHEUS: I weigh not what ye do, but what ye suffer,
Being evil. Cruel was the power which called
You, or aught else so wretched, into light.
THIRD FURY: Thou think'st we will live thro' thee, one by one,
Like animal life, and tho' we can obscure not
485 The soul which burns within, that we will dwell
Beside it, like a vain loud multitude
Vexing the self-content of wisest men:
That we will be dread thought beneath thy brain,
And foul desire round thine astonished heart,
490 And blood within thy labyrinthine veins
Crawling like agony.
PROMETHEUS: Why, ye are thus now;
Yet am I king over myself, and rule
The torturing and conflicting throngs within,
As Jove rules you when Hell grows mutinous.
CHORUS OF FURIES:
495 From the ends of the earth, from the ends of the earth,
Where the night has its grave and the morning its birth,
            Come, come, come!
Oh, ye who shake hills with the scream of your mirth,
When cities sink howling in ruin; and ye
500 Who with wingless footsteps trample the sea,
And close upon Shipwreck and Famine's track,
Sit chattering with joy on the foodless wreck;
            Come, come, come!
Leave the bed, low, cold, and red,
505   Strewed beneath a nation dead;
Leave the hatred, as in ashes
    Fire is left for future burning:
It will burst in bloodier flashes
    When ye stir it, soon returning:
510 Leave the self-contempt implanted
In young spirits, sense-enchanted,
    Misery's yet unkindled fuel:
Leave Hell's secrets half unchanted
    To the maniac dreamer; cruel
515 More than ye can be with hate
Is he with fear.
            Come, come, come!
We are steaming up from Hell's wide gate
And we burthen the blasts of the atmosphere,
520 But vainly we toil till ye come here.
IONE: Sister, I hear the thunder of new wings.
PANTHEA: These solid mountains quiver with the sound

Even as the tremulous air: their shadows make
The space within my plumes more black than night.
FIRST FURY:
525 Your call was as a winged car
Driven on whirlwinds fast and far;
It rapt us from red gulphs of war.
SECOND FURY:
From wide cities, famine-wasted;
THIRD FURY:
Groans half heard, and blood untasted;
FOURTH FURY:
530 Kingly conclaves stern and cold,
Where blood with gold is bought and sold;
FIFTH FURY:
From the furnace, white and hot,
In which—
A FURY: Speak not: whisper not:
I know all that ye would tell,
535 But to speak might break the spell
Which must bend the Invincible,
    The stern of thought;
He yet defies the deepest power of Hell.
FURY:
Tear the veil!
ANOTHER FURY:
        It is torn.
CHORUS: The pale stars of the morn
540 Shine on a misery, dire to be borne.
Dost thou faint, mighty Titan? We laugh thee to
   scorn.
Dost thou boast the clear knowledge thou waken'dst
   for man?
Then was kindled within him a thirst which outran
Those perishing waters; a thirst of fierce fever,
545 Hope, love, doubt, desire, which consume him for
   ever.
One[1] came forth of gentle worth
Smiling on the sanguine earth;
His words outlived him, like swift poison
   Withering up truth, peace, and pity.
550 Look! where round the wide horizon
   Many a million-peopled city

Vomits smoke in the bright air.
Mark that outcry of despair!
'Tis his mild and gentle ghost
555   Wailing for the faith he kindled:
Look again, the flames almost
   To a glow-worm's lamp have dwindled:
The survivors round the embers
   Gather in dread.
560   Joy, joy, joy!
Past ages crowd on thee, but each one remembers,
And the future is dark, and the present is spread
Like a pillow of thorns for thy slumberless head.
SEMICHORUS I:
   Drops of bloody agony flow
565 From his white and quivering brow.
Grant a little respite now:
See a disenchanted nation
Springs like day from desolation;[2]
To truth its state is dedicate,
570 And Freedom leads it forth, her mate;
A legioned band of linked brothers
Whom Love calls children—
SEMICHORUS II: 'Tis another's:
See how kindred murder kin:
'Tis the vintage-time for death and sin:
575 Blood, like new wine, bubbles within:
   'Till Despair smothers
The struggling world, which slaves and tyrants win.
[*All the* FURIES *vanish, except one.*]
IONE: Hark, sister! what a low yet dreadful groan
Quite unsuppressed is tearing up the heart
580 Of the good Titan, as storms tear the deep,
And beasts hear the sea moan in inland caves.
Darest thou observe how the fiends torture him?
PANTHEA: Alas! I looked forth twice, but will no
   more.
IONE: What didst thou see?
PANTHEA: A woful sight: a youth
585 With patient looks nailed to a crucifix.
IONE: What next?
PANTHEA: The heaven around, the earth below
Was peopled with thick shapes of human death,

---

[1] Christ.

[2] France, at the time of the Revolution.

All horrible, and wrought by human hands,
And some appeared the work of human hearts,
590 For men were slowly killed by frowns and smiles:
And other sights too foul to speak and live
Were wandering by. Let us not tempt worse fear
By looking forth: those groans are grief enough.
FURY: Behold an emblem: those who do endure
595 Deep wrongs for man, and scorn, and chains, but heap
Thousandfold torment on themselves and him.
PROMETHEUS: Remit the anguish of that lighted stare;
Close those wan lips; let that thorn-wounded brow
Stream not with blood; it mingles with thy tears!
600 Fix, fix those tortured orbs in peace and death,
So thy sick throes shake not that crucifix,
So those pale fingers play not with thy gore.
O, horrible! Thy name I will not speak,
It hath become a curse. I see, I see
605 The wise, the mild, the lofty, and the just,
Whom thy slaves hate for being like to thee,
Some hunted by foul lies from their heart's home,
An early-chosen, late-lamented home;
As hooded ounces[1] cling to the driven hind;
610 Some linked to corpses in unwholesome cells: Some—
Hear I not the multitude laugh loud?—
Impaled in lingering fire: and mighty realms
Float by my feet, like sea-uprooted isles,
Whose sons are kneaded down in common blood
615 By the red light of their own burning homes.
FURY: Blood thou canst see, and fire; and canst hear groans;
Worse things, unheard, unseen, remain behind.
PROMETHEUS: Worse?
FURY: In each human heart terror survives
The ruin it has gorged: the loftiest fear
620 All that they would disdain to think were true:
Hypocrisy and custom make their minds
The fanes of many a worship, now outworn.
They dare not devise good for man's estate,
And yet they know not that they do not dare.
625 The good want power, but to weep barren tears.
The powerful goodness want: worse need for them.
The wise want love; and those who love want wisdom;
And all best things are thus confused to ill.
Many are strong and rich, and would be just,
630 But live among their suffering fellow-men
As if none felt: they know not what they do.[2]
PROMETHEUS: Thy words are like a cloud of winged snakes;
And yet I pity those they torture not.
FURY: Thou pitiest them? I speak no more!
[*Vanishes.*]
PROMETHEUS: Ah woe!
635 Ah woe! Alas! pain, pain ever, for ever!
I close my tearless eyes, but see more clear
Thy works within my woe-illumined mind,
Thou subtle tyrant! Peace is in the grave.
The grave hides all things beautiful and good:
640 I am a God and cannot find it there,
Nor would I seek it: for, though dread revenge,
This is defeat, fierce king, not victory.
The sights with which thou torturest gird my soul
With new endurance, till the hour arrives
645 When they shall be no types of things which are.
PANTHEA: Alas! what sawest thou?
PROMETHEUS: There are two woes;
To speak, and to behold; thou spare me one.
Names are there, Nature's sacred watch-words, they
Were borne aloft in bright emblazonry;
650 The nations thronged around, and cried aloud,
As with one voice, Truth, liberty, and love!
Suddenly fierce confusion fell from heaven
Among them; there was strife, deceit, and fear:
Tyrants rushed in, and did divide the spoil.
655 This was the shadow of the truth I saw.
THE EARTH: I felt thy torture, son, with such mixed joy
As pain and virtue give. To cheer thy state
I bid ascend those subtle and fair spirits,
Whose homes are the dim caves of human thought,
660 And who inhabit, as birds wing the wind,
Its world-surrounding ether: they behold
Beyond that twilight realm, as in a glass,
The future: may they speak comfort to thee!
PANTHEA: Look, sister, where a troop of spirits gather,

---

[1] cheetahs.

[2] See Luke 23.34.

     Like flocks of clouds in spring's delightful weather,
     Thronging in the blue air!
IONE: And see! more come,
Like fountain-vapours when the winds are dumb,
That climb up the ravine in scattered lines.
And, hark? is it the music of the pines?
Is it the lake? Is it the waterfall?
PANTHEA: 'Tis something sadder, sweeter far than all.
CHORUS OF SPIRITS:
      From unremembered ages we
      Gentle guides and guardians be
      Of heaven-oppressed mortality;
      And we breathe, and sicken not,
      The atmosphere of human thought:
      Be it dim, and dank, and grey,
      Like a storm-extinguished day,
      Travelled o'er by dying gleams;
      Be it bright as all between
      Cloudless skies and windless streams,
      Silent, liquid, and serene;
      As the birds within the wind,
      As the fish within the wave,
      As the thoughts of man's own mind
      Float thro' all above the grave;
      We make these our liquid lair,
      Voyaging cloudlike and unpent
      Thro' the boundless element:
      Thence we bear the prophecy
      Which begins and ends in thee!
IONE: More yet come, one by one: the air around them
Looks radiant as the air around a star.
FIRST SPIRIT:
      On a battle-trumpet's blast
      I fled hither, fast, fast, fast,
      'Mid the darkness upward cast.
      From the dust of creeds outworn,
      From the tyrant's banner torn,
      Gathering 'round me, onward borne,
      There was mingled many a cry—
      Freedom! Hope! Death! Victory!
      Till they faded thro' the sky;
      And one sound, above, around,
      One sound beneath, around, above,
      Was moving; 'twas the soul of love;
      'Twas the hope, the prophecy,
      Which begins and ends in thee.
SECOND SPIRIT:
      A rainbow's arch stood on the sea,
      Which rocked beneath, immoveably;
      And the triumphant storm did flee,
      Like a conqueror, swift and proud,
      Between with many a captive cloud,
      A shapeless, dark and rapid crowd,
      Each by lightning riven in half:
      I heard the thunder hoarsely laugh:
      Mighty fleets were strewn like chaff
      And spread beneath a hell of death
      O'er the white waters. I alit
      On a great ship lightning-split,
      And speeded hither on the sigh
      Of one who gave an enemy
      His plank, then plunged aside to die.
THIRD SPIRIT:
      I sate beside a sage's bed,
      And the lamp was burning red
      Near the book where he had fed,
      When a Dream with plumes of flame,
      To his pillow hovering came,
      And I knew it was the same
      Which had kindled long ago
      Pity, eloquence, and woe;
      And the world awhile below
      Wore the shade, its lustre made.
      It has borne me here as fleet
      As Desire's lightning feet:
      I must ride it back ere morrow,
      Or the sage will wake in sorrow.
FOURTH SPIRIT:
      On a poet's lips I slept
      Dreaming like a love-adept
      In the sound his breathing kept;
      Nor seeks nor finds he mortal blisses,
      But feeds on the aerial kisses
      Of shapes that haunt thought's wildernesses.
      He will watch from dawn to gloom
      The lake-reflected sun illume
      The yellow bees in the ivy-bloom,
      Nor heed nor see, what things they be;

      But from these create he can
      Forms more real than living man,
      Nurslings of immortality!
750   One of these awakened me,
      And I sped to succour thee.
   IONE: Behold'st thou not two shapes from the east and west
   Come, as two doves to one beloved nest,
   Twin nurslings of the all-sustaining air
755 On swift still wings glide down the atmosphere?
   And, hark! their sweet, sad voices! 'tis despair
   Mingled with love and then dissolved in sound.
   PANTHEA: Canst thou speak, sister? all my words are drowned.
   IONE: Their beauty gives me voice. See how they float
760 On their sustaining wings of skiey grain,
   Orange and azure deepening into gold:
   Their soft smiles light the air like a star's fire.
   CHORUS OF SPIRITS:
   Hast thou beheld the form of Love?
   FIFTH SPIRIT: As over wide dominions
   I sped, like some swift cloud that wings the wide air's wildernesses,
765 That planet-crested shape swept by on lightning-braided pinions,
   Scattering the liquid joy of life from his ambrosial tresses:
   His footsteps paved the world with light; but as I past 'twas fading,
   And hollow Ruin yawned behind: great sages bound in madness,
   And headless patriots, and pale youths who perished, unupbraiding,
770 Gleamed in the night. I wandered o'er, till thou,
      O King of sadness,
   Turned by thy smile the worst I saw to recollected gladness.
   SIXTH SPIRIT:
   Ah, sister! Desolation is a delicate thing:[1]
   It walks not on the earth, it floats not on the air,
   But treads with silent footstep, and fans with silent wing
775 The tender hopes which in their hearts the best and gentlest bear;
   Who, soothed to false repose by the fanning plumes above
   And the music-stirring motion of its soft and busy feet,
   Dream visions of aërial joy, and call the monster, Love,
   And wake, and find the shadow Pain, as he whom now we greet.
   CHORUS:
780   Tho' Ruin now Love's shadow be,
      Following him, destroyingly,
         On Death's white and winged steed,[2]
      Which the fleetest cannot flee,
      Trampling down both flower and weed,
785 Man and beast, and foul and fair,
      Like a tempest thro' the air;
   Thou shalt quell this horseman grim,
   Woundless though in heart or limb.
   PROMETHEUS: Spirits! how know ye this shall be?
   CHORUS:
790   In the atmosphere we breathe,
   As buds grow red when the snow-storms flee,
     From spring gathering up beneath,
   Whose mild winds shake the elder brake,
   And the wandering herdsmen know
795 That the white-thorn soon will blow:
   Wisdom, Justice, Love, and Peace,
    When they struggle to increase,
      Are to us as soft winds be
      To shepherd boys, the prophecy
800   Which begins and ends in thee.
   IONE: Where are the Spirits fled?
   PANTHEA: Only a sense
   Remains of them, like the omnipotence
   Of music, when the inspired voice and lute
   Languish, ere yet the responses are mute,
805 Which thro' the deep and labyrinthine soul,
   Like echoes thro' long caverns, wind and roll.

---

[1] Cf. Homer, *Iliad* 19.92. "For Homer says, that the goddess Calamity is delicate, and that her feet are tender. 'Her feet are soft,' he says, 'for she treads not upon the ground, but makes her path upon the heads of men!'" (Plato, *Symposium* 195d; tr. P.B.S.)

[2] Cf. Revelation 6.8.

PROMETHEUS: How fair these air-born shapes! and
        yet I feel
    Most vain all hope but love; and thou art far,
    Asia! who, when my being overflowed,
810 Wert like a golden chalice to bright wine
    Which else had sunk into the thirsty dust.
    All things are still: alas! how heavily
    This quiet morning weighs upon my heart;
    Tho' I should dream I could even sleep with grief
815 If slumber were denied not. I would fain
    Be what it is my destiny to be,
    The saviour and the strength of suffering man,
    Or sink into the original gulph of things:
    There is no agony, and no solace left;
820 Earth can console, Heaven can torment no more.
PANTHEA: Hast thou forgotten one who watches thee
    The cold dark night, and never sleeps but when
    The shadow of thy spirit falls on her?
PROMETHEUS: I said all hope was vain but love: thou
        lovest.
825 PANTHEA: Deeply in truth; but the eastern star looks
        white,
    And Asia waits in that far Indian vale
    The scene of her sad exile; rugged once
    And desolate and frozen, like this ravine;
    But now invested with fair flowers and herbs,
830 And haunted by sweet airs and sounds, which flow
    Among the woods and waters, from the ether
    Of her transforming presence, which would fade
    If it were mingled not with thine. Farewell!

ACT 2

SCENE 1

*Morning. A lovely Vale in the Indian Caucasus.
ASIA alone.*

ASIA: From all the blasts of heaven thou hast
        descended:
    Yes, like a spirit, like a thought, which makes
    Unwonted tears throng to the horny eyes,
    And beatings haunt the desolated heart,
5   Which should have learnt repose: thou hast descended
    Cradled in tempests; thou dost wake, O Spring!
    O child of many winds! As suddenly
    Thou comest as the memory of a dream,
    Which now is sad because it hath been sweet;
10 Like genius, or like joy which riseth up
    As from the earth, clothing with golden clouds
    The desert of our life.
    This is the season, this the day, the hour;
    At sunrise thou shouldst come, sweet sister mine,
15 Too long desired, too long delaying, come!
    How like death-worms the wingless moments crawl!
    The point of one white star is quivering still
    Deep in the orange light of widening morn
    Beyond the purple mountains: thro' a chasm
20 Of wind-divided mist the darker lake
    Reflects it: now it wanes: it gleams again
    As the waves fade, and as the burning threads
    Of woven cloud unravel in pale air:
    'Tis lost! and thro' yon peaks of cloudlike snow
25 The roseate sun-light quivers: hear I not
    The Æolian music[1] of her sea-green plumes
    Winnowing the crimson dawn?
    [*PANTHEA ENTERS.*]
                        I feel, I see
    Those eyes which burn thro' smiles that fade in tears,
    Like stars half quenched in mists of silver dew.
30 Beloved and most beautiful, who wearest
    The shadow of that soul by which I live,
    How late thou art! the sphered sun had climbed
    The sea; my heart was sick with hope, before
    The printless air felt thy belated plumes.
35 PANTHEA: Pardon, great Sister! but my wings were
        faint
    With the delight of a remembered dream,
    As are the noon-tide plumes of summer winds
    Satiate with sweet flowers. I was wont to sleep
    Peacefully, and awake refreshed and calm
40 Before the sacred Titan's fall, and thy
    Unhappy love, had made, thro' use and pity,

---

[1] music from an Æolian harp or lyre, an instrument placed in a window so its strings can vibrate in the wind (and named after Æolus, the god of the winds). Cf. Coleridge, "Effusion 35."*

Both love and woe familiar to my heart
As they had grown to thine: erewhile I slept
Under the glaucous caverns of old Ocean
45 Within dim bowers of green and purple moss,
Our young Ione's soft and milky arms
Locked then, as now, behind my dark, moist hair,
While my shut eyes and cheek were pressed within
The folded depth of her life-breathing bosom:
50 But not as now, since I am made the wind
Which fails beneath the music that I bear
Of thy most wordless converse; since dissolved
Into the sense with which love talks, my rest
Was troubled and yet sweet; my waking hours
55 Too full of care and pain.
ASIA: Lift up thine eyes,
And let me read thy dream.
PANTHEA: As I have said
With our sea-sister at his feet I slept.
The mountain mists, condensing at our voice
Under the moon, had spread their snowy flakes,
60 From the keen ice shielding our linked sleep.
Then two dreams came. One, I remember not.
But in the other his pale wound-worn limbs
Fell from Prometheus, and the azure night
Grew radiant with the glory of that form
65 Which lives unchanged within, and his voice fell
Like music which makes giddy the dim brain,
Faint with intoxication of keen joy:
"Sister of her whose footsteps pave the world
With loveliness—more fair than aught but her,
70 Whose shadow thou art—lift thine eyes on me."
I lifted them: the overpowering light
Of that immortal shape was shadowed o'er
By love; which, from his soft and flowing limbs,
And passion-parted lips, and keen, faint eyes,
75 Steamed forth like vaporous fire; an atmosphere
Which wrapt me in its all-dissolving power,
As the warm ether of the morning sun
Wraps ere it drinks some cloud of wandering dew.
I saw not, heard not, moved not, only felt
80 His presence flow and mingle thro' my blood
Till it became his life, and his grew mine,
And I was thus absorb'd, until it past,
And like the vapours when the sun sinks down,

Gathering again in drops upon the pines,
85 And tremulous as they, in the deep night
My being was condensed; and as the rays
Of thought were slowly gathered, I could hear
His voice, whose accents lingered ere they died
Like footsteps of weak melody: thy name
90 Among the many sounds alone I heard
Of what might be articulate; tho' still
I listened through the night when sound was none.
Ione wakened then, and said to me:
"Canst thou divine what troubles me to night?
95 I always knew what I desired before,
Nor ever found delight to wish in vain.
But now I cannot tell thee what I seek;
I know not; something sweet, since it is sweet
Even to desire; it is thy sport, false sister;
100 Thou hast discovered some enchantment old,
Whose spells have stolen my spirit as I slept
And mingled it with thine: for when just now
We kissed, I felt within thy parted lips
The sweet air that sustained me, and the warmth
105 Of the life-blood, for loss of which I faint,
Quivered between our intertwining arms."
I answered not, for the Eastern star grew pale,
But fled to thee.
ASIA: Thou speakest, but thy words
Are as the air: I feel them not: Oh, lift
110 Thine eyes, that I may read his written soul!
PANTHEA: I lift them tho' they droop beneath the load
Of that they would express: what canst thou see
But thine own fairest shadow imaged there?
ASIA: Thine eyes are like the deep, blue, boundless
    heaven
115 Contracted to two circles underneath
Their long, fine lashes; dark, far, measureless,
Orb within orb, and line thro' line inwoven.
PANTHEA: Why lookest thou as if a spirit past?
ASIA: There is a change: beyond their inmost depth
120 I see a shade, a shape: 'tis He, arrayed
In the soft light of his own smiles, which spread
Like radiance from the cloud-surrounded morn.
Prometheus, it is thine! depart not yet!
Say not those smiles that we shall meet again
125 Within that bright pavilion which their beams

Shall build on the waste world? The dream is told.
What shape is that between us? Its rude hair
Roughens the wind that lifts it, its regard
Is wild and quick, yet 'tis a thing of air
130 For thro' its grey robe gleams the golden dew
Whose stars the noon has quench'd not.
DREAM: Follow! Follow!
PANTHEA: It is mine other dream.
ASIA: It disappears.
PANTHEA: It passes now into my mind. Methought
As we sate here, the flower-infolding buds
135 Burst on yon lightning-blasted almond-tree,
When swift from the white Scythian wilderness[1]
A wind swept forth wrinkling the Earth with frost:
I looked, and all the blossoms were blown down;
But on each leaf was stamped, as the blue bells
140 Of Hyacinth tell Apollo's written grief,[2]
O, FOLLOW, FOLLOW!
ASIA: As you speak, your words
Fill, pause by pause, my own forgotten sleep
With shapes. Methought among the lawns together
We wandered, underneath the young grey dawn,
145 And multitudes of dense white fleecy clouds
Were wandering in thick flocks along the mountains
Shepherded by the slow, unwilling wind;
And the white dew on the new bladed grass,
Just piercing the dark earth, hung silently;
150 And there was more which I remember not:
But on the shadows of the morning clouds,
Athwart the purple mountain slope, was written
FOLLOW, O, FOLLOW! As they vanished by,
And on each herb, from which Heaven's dew had
    fallen,
155 The like was stamped, as with a withering fire,
A wind arose among the pines; it shook
The clinging music from their boughs, and then
Low, sweet, faint sounds, like the farewell of ghosts,
Were heard: OH FOLLOW, FOLLOW, FOLLOW ME!

---

[1] Scythia was the classical name for the region north of the Black Sea.

[2] After Hyacinthus died as the result of Zephyrus' jealousy, his lover Apollo turned him into a flower whose petals bore the Greek word *ai*, "alas"; cf. Ovid, *Metamorphoses* 10. The hyacinth we recognize lacks such markings; the flower in the myth may be a small iris with marked petals.

160 And then I said: "Panthea, look on me."
But in the depth of those beloved eyes
Still I saw, FOLLOW, FOLLOW!
ECHO: Follow, follow!
PANTHEA: The crags, this clear spring morning, mock
    our voices
As they were spirit-tongued.
ASIA: It is some being
165 Around the crags. What fine clear sounds! O, list!
ECHOES: [*Unseen.*]
    Echoes we: listen!
  We cannot stay:
    As dew-stars glisten
  Then fade away—
170   Child of Ocean!
ASIA: Hark! Spirits speak. The liquid responses
Of their aerial tongues yet sound.
PANTHEA: I hear.
ECHOES:
  O, follow, follow,
    As our voice recedeth
175 Thro' the caverns hollow,
    Where the forest spreadeth;
[*More distant.*]
  O, follow, follow!
  Thro' the caverns hollow,
    As the song floats thou pursue,
180   Where the wild bee never flew,
  Thro' the noon-tide darkness deep,
  By the odour-breathing sleep
  Of faint night flowers, and the waves
  At the fountain-lighted caves,
185   While our music, wild and sweet,
  Mocks thy gently falling feet,
    Child of Ocean!
ASIA: Shall we pursue the sound? It grows more faint
And distant.
PANTHEA: List! the strain floats nearer now.
ECHOES:
190   In the world unknown
    Sleeps a voice unspoken;
  By thy step alone
    Can its rest be broken;
    Child of Ocean!

195 ASIA: How the notes sink upon the ebbing wind!
ECHOES:
O, follow, follow!
Thro' the caverns hollow,
   As the song floats thou pursue,
   By the woodland noon-tide dew;
200   By the forests, lakes, and fountains
   Thro' the many-folded mountains;
   To the rents, and gulphs, and chasms,
   Where the Earth reposed from spasms,
   On the day when He and thou
205   Parted, to commingle now;
   Child of Ocean!
ASIA: Come, sweet Panthea, link thy hand in mine,
And follow, ere the voices fade away.

SCENE 2

A Forest, intermingled with Rocks and Caverns. ASIA and PANTHEA pass into it. Two young Fauns[1] are sitting on a Rock, listening.

SEMICHORUS I OF SPIRITS:
The path thro' which that lovely twain
   Have past, by cedar, pine, and yew,
   And each dark tree that ever grew,
   Is curtained out from Heaven's wide blue;
5 Nor sun, nor moon, nor wind, nor rain,
   Can pierce its interwoven bowers,
Nor aught, save where some cloud of dew,
Drifted along the earth-creeping breeze,
Between the trunks of the hoar trees,
10   Hangs each a pearl in the pale flowers
   Of the green laurel, blown anew;
And bends, and then fades silently,
One frail and fair anemone:
Or when some star of many a one
15 That climbs and wanders thro' steep night,
Has found the cleft thro' which alone
Beams fall from high those depths upon
Ere it is borne away, away,
By the swift Heavens that cannot stay,
20 It scatters drops of golden light,

Like lines of rain that ne'er unite:
And the gloom divine is all around;
And underneath is the mossy ground.
SEMICHORUS II:
There the voluptuous nightingales,
25   Are awake thro' all the broad noon-day,
When one with bliss or sadness fails,
   And thro' the windless ivy-boughs,
   Sick with sweet love, droops dying away
On its mate's music-panting bosom;
30 Another from the swinging blossom,
   Watching to catch the languid close
   Of the last strain, then lifts on high
   The wings of the weak melody,
'Till some new strain of feeling bear
35   The song, and all the woods are mute;
When there is heard thro' the dim air
The rush of wings, and rising there
   Like many a lake-surrounding flute,
Sounds overflow the listener's brain
40 So sweet, that joy is almost pain.
SEMICHORUS I:
There those enchanted eddies play
   Of echoes, music-tongued, which draw,
   By Demogorgon's mighty law,
   With melting rapture, or sweet awe,
45 All spirits on that secret way;
   As inland boats are driven to Ocean
Down streams made strong with mountain-thaw:
And first there comes a gentle sound
To those in talk or slumber bound,
50   And wakes the destined soft emotion,
Attracts, impels them: those who saw
Say from the breathing earth behind
There steams a plume-uplifting wind
Which drives them on their path, while they
55   Believe their own swift wings and feet
The sweet desires within obey:
And so they float upon their way,
   Until, still sweet, but loud and strong,
   The storm of sound is driven along,
60   Sucked up and hurrying as they fleet
   Behind, its gathering billows meet
And to the fatal mountain bear

---

[1] wood spirits, with human bodies and goat-like legs.

Like clouds amid the yielding air.
FIRST FAUN: Canst thou imagine where those spirits live
65 Which make such delicate music in the woods?
We haunt within the least frequented caves
And closest coverts, and we know these wilds,
Yet never meet them, tho' we hear them oft:
Where may they hide themselves?
SECOND FAUN: 'Tis hard to tell:
70 I have heard those more skilled in spirits say,
The bubbles, which the enchantment of the sun
Sucks from the pale faint water-flowers that pave
The oozy bottom of clear lakes and pools,
Are the pavilions where such dwell and float
75 Under the green and golden atmosphere
Which noon-tide kindles thro' the woven leaves;
And when these burst, and the thin fiery air,
The which they breathed within those lucent domes,
Ascends to flow like meteors thro' the night,
80 They ride on them, and rein their headlong speed,
And bow their burning crests, and glide in fire
Under the waters of the earth again.
FIRST FAUN: If such live thus, have others other lives,
Under pink blossoms or within the bells
85 Of meadow flowers, or folded violets deep,
Or on their dying odours, when they die,
Or on the sunlight of the sphered dew?
SECOND FAUN: Aye, many more which we may well divine.
But, should we stay to speak, noontide would come,
90 And thwart Silenus[1] find his goats undrawn,
And grudge to sing those wise and lovely songs
Of fate, and chance, and God, and Chaos old,
And Love, and the chained Titan's woful dooms,
And how he shall be loosed, and make the earth
95 One brotherhood: delightful strains which cheer
Our solitary twilights, and which charm
To silence the unenvying nightingales.

SCENE 3

A Pinnacle of Rock among Mountains.
ASIA *and* PANTHEA.

PANTHEA: Hither the sound has borne us—to the realm
Of Demogorgon, and the mighty portal,
Like a volcano's meteor-breathing chasm,
Whence the oracular vapour is hurled up
5 Which lonely men drink wandering in their youth,
And call truth, virtue, love, genius, or joy,
That maddening wine of life, whose dregs they drain
To deep intoxication; and uplift,
Like Mænads[2] who cry loud, Evoe! Evoe!
10 The voice which is contagion to the world.
ASIA: Fit throne for such a Power! Magnificent!
How glorious art thou, Earth! And if thou be
The shadow of some spirit lovelier still,
Though evil stain its work, and it should be
15 Like its creation, weak yet beautiful,
I could fall down and worship that and thee.
Even now my heart adoreth: Wonderful!
Look, sister, ere the vapour dim thy brain:
Beneath is a wide plain of billowy mist,
20 As a lake, paving in the morning sky,
With azure waves which burst in silver light,
Some Indian vale. Behold it, rolling on
Under the curdling winds, and islanding
The peak whereon we stand, midway, around,
25 Encinctured by the dark and blooming forests,
Dim twilight-lawns, and stream-illumined caves,
And wind-enchanted shapes of wandering mist;
And far on high the keen sky-cleaving mountains
From icy spires of sun-like radiance fling
30 The dawn, as lifted Ocean's dazzling spray,
From some Atlantic islet scattered up,
Spangles the wind with lamp-like water-drops.
The vale is girdled with their walls, a howl
Of cataracts from their thaw-cloven ravines
35 Satiates the listening wind, continuous, vast,

---

[1] companion of Dionysus (or Bacchus), god of wine; usually depicted as an elderly drunken satyr.

[2] frenzied female worshippers of Bacchus; "evoe" is their ritual cry. Cf. Euripides, *The Bacchæ* (404 BC).

Awful as silence. Hark! the rushing snow!
The sun-awakened avalanche! whose mass,
Thrice sifted by the storm, had gathered there
Flake after flake, in heaven-defying minds
40 As thought by thought is piled, till some great truth
Is loosened, and the nations echo round,
Shaken to their roots, as do the mountains now.
PANTHEA: Look how the gusty sea of mist is breaking
In crimson foam, even at our feet! it rises
45 As Ocean at the enchantment of the moon
Round foodless men wrecked on some oozy isle.
ASIA: The fragments of the cloud are scattered up;
The wind that lifts them disentwines my hair;
Its billows now sweep o'er mine eyes; my brain
50 Grows dizzy; I see thin shapes within the mist.
PANTHEA: A countenance with beckoning smiles:
    there burns
An azure fire within its golden locks!
Another and another: hark! they speak!
SONG OF SPIRITS:
    To the deep, to the deep,
55   Down, down!
    Through the shade of sleep,
    Through the cloudy strife
    Of Death and of Life;
    Through the veil and the bar
60   Of things which seem and are
    Even to the steps of the remotest throne,
      Down, down!

    While the sound whirls around,
      Down, down!
65   As the fawn draws the hound,
    As the lightning the vapour,
    As a weak moth the taper;
    Death, despair; love, sorrow;
    Time both; to day, to morrow;
70   As steel obeys the spirit of the stone,
      Down, down.

    Through the grey, void abysm,
      Down, down!
    Where the air is no prism,
75   And the moon and stars are not,
    And the cavern-crags wear not
    The radiance of Heaven,
    Nor the gloom to Earth given,
    Where there is one pervading, one alone,
80   Down, down!

    In the depth of the deep
      Down, down!
    Like veiled lightning asleep,
    Like the spark nursed in embers,
85   The last look Love remembers,
    Like a diamond, which shines
    On the dark wealth of mines,
    A spell is treasur'd but for thee alone.
      Down, down!

90   We have bound thee, we guide thee;
      Down, down!
    With the bright form beside thee;
    Resist not the weakness,
    Such strength is in meekness
95   That the Eternal, the Immortal,
    Must unloose through life's portal
    The snake-like Doom coiled underneath his throne
      By that alone.

SCENE 4

The Cave of DEMOGORGON. ASIA *and* PANTHEA.

PANTHEA: What veiled form sits on that ebon throne?
ASIA: The veil has fallen.
PANTHEA: I see a mighty darkness
Filling the seat of power, and rays of gloom
Dart round, as light from the meridian sun,
5 Ungazed upon and shapeless; neither limb,
Nor form, nor outline;[1] yet we feel it is
A living Spirit.
DEMOGORGON: Ask what thou wouldst know.
ASIA: What canst thou tell?
DEMOGORGON: All things thou dar'st demand.
ASIA: Who made the living world?

---

[1] Cf. Milton, *Paradise Lost* 2.666–73.

DEMOGORGON: God.
ASIA: Who made all
10   That it contains? thought, passion, reason, will,
     Imagination?
     DEMOGORGON: God: Almighty God.
     ASIA: Who made that sense which, when the winds of
        spring
     In rarest visitation, or the voice
     Of one beloved heard in youth alone,
15   Fills the faint eyes with falling tears which dim
     The radiant looks of unbewailing flowers,
     And leaves this peopled earth a solitude
     When it returns no more?
     DEMOGORGON: Merciful God.
     ASIA: And who made terror, madness, crime, remorse,
20   Which from the links of the great chain of things,
     To every thought within the mind of man
     Sway and drag heavily, and each one reels
     Under the load towards the pit of death;
     Abandoned hope, and love that turns to hate;
25   And self-contempt, bitterer to drink than blood;
     Pain, whose unheeded and familiar speech
     Is howling, and keen shrieks, day after day;
     And Hell, or the sharp fear of Hell?
     DEMOGORGON: He reigns.
     ASIA: Utter his name: a world pining in pain
30   Asks but his name: curses shall drag him down.
     DEMOGORGON: He reigns.
     ASIA: I feel, I know it: who?
     DEMOGORGON: He reigns.
     ASIA: Who reigns? There was the Heaven and Earth at
        first,
     And Light and Love; then Saturn,[1] from whose throne
     Time fell, an envious shadow: such the state
35   Of the earth's primal spirits beneath his sway,
     As the calm joy of flowers and living leaves
     Before the wind or sun has withered them
     And semivital worms; but he refused
     The birthright of their being, knowledge, power,
40   The skill which wields the elements, the thought

Which pierces this dim universe like light,
Self-empire, and the majesty of love;
For thirst of which they fainted. Then Prometheus
Gave wisdom, which is strength, to Jupiter,
45   And with this law alone, "Let man be free,"
Clothed him with the dominion of wide Heaven.
To know nor faith, nor love, nor law; to be
Omnipotent but friendless is to reign;
And Jove now reigned; for on the race of man
50   First famine, and then toil, and then disease,
Strife, wounds, and ghastly death unseen before,
Fell; and the unseasonable seasons drove
With alternating shafts of frost and fire,
Their shelterless, pale tribes to mountain caves:
55   And in their desert hearts fierce wants he sent,
And mad disquietudes, and shadows idle
Of unreal good, which levied mutual war,
So ruining the lair wherein they raged.
Prometheus saw, and waked the legioned hopes
60   Which sleep within folded Elysian flowers,
Nepenthe, Moly, Amaranth,[2] fadeless blooms,
That they might hide with thin and rainbow wings
The shape of Death; and Love he sent to bind
The disunited tendrils of that vine
65   Which bears the wine of life, the human heart;
And he tamed fire which, like some beast of prey,
Most terrible, but lovely, played beneath
The frown of man; and tortured to his will
Iron and gold, the slaves and signs of power,
70   And gems and poisons, and all subtlest forms
Hidden beneath the mountains and the waves.
He gave man speech, and speech created thought,
Which is the measure of the universe;
And Science struck the thrones of earth and heaven,
75   Which shook, but fell not; and the harmonious mind
Poured itself forth in all-prophetic song;
And music lifted up the listening spirit
Until it walked, exempt from mortal care,
Godlike, o'er the clear billows of sweet sound;
80   And human hands first mimicked and then mocked,

---

[1] king of the Titans, the deities who reigned in the Golden Age, before being overthrown by the Olympian gods. Cf. Keats *Hyperion** and *The Fall of Hyperion*.*

[2] Nepenthe was a drug that induced forgetfulness (cf. Homer, *Odyssey* 4); moly was the magical plant that protected Odysseus from the magic of Circe (cf. *Odyssey* 10); amaranth was an unfading flower that bloomed in paradise (cf. Milton, *Paradise Lost* 3.352–59).

With moulded limbs more lovely than its own,
The human form, till marble grew divine;
And mothers, gazing, drank the love men see
Reflected in their race, behold, and perish.
⁸⁵ He told the hidden power of herbs and springs,
And Disease drank and slept. Death grew like sleep.
He taught the implicated orbits woven
Of the wide-wandering stars; and how the sun
Changes his lair, and by what secret spell
⁹⁰ The pale moon is transformed, when her broad eye
Gazes not on the interlunar sea:
He taught to rule, as life directs the limbs,
The tempest-winged chariots of the Ocean,
And the Celt knew the Indian. Cities then
⁹⁵ Were built, and through their snow-like columns flowed
The warm winds, and the azure æther shone,
And the blue sea and shadowy hills were seen.
Such, the alleviations of his state,
Prometheus gave to man, for which he hangs
¹⁰⁰ Withering in destined pain: but who rains down
Evil, the immedicable plague, which, while
Man looks on his creation like a God
And sees that it is glorious, drives him on
The wreck of his own will, the scorn of earth,
¹⁰⁵ The outcast, the abandoned, the alone?
Not Jove: while yet his frown shook heaven, aye when
His adversary from adamantine chains
Cursed him, he trembled like a slave. Declare
Who is his master? Is he too a slave?
¹¹⁰ DEMOGORGON: All spirits are enslaved which serve things evil:
Thou knowest if Jupiter be such or no.
ASIA: Whom called'st thou God?
DEMOGORGON: I spoke but as ye speak,
For Jove is the supreme of living things.
ASIA: Who is the master of the slave?
DEMOGORGON: If the abysm
¹¹⁵ Could vomit forth its secrets. But a voice
Is wanting, the deep truth is imageless;
For what would it avail to bid thee gaze
On the revolving world? What to bid speak
Fate, Time, Occasion, Chance and Change? To these
¹²⁰ All things are subject but eternal Love.

ASIA: So much I asked before, and my heart gave
The response thou hast given; and of such truths
Each to itself must be the oracle.
One more demand; and do thou answer me
¹²⁵ As my own soul would answer, did it know
That which I ask. Prometheus shall arise
Henceforth the sun of this rejoicing world:
When shall the destined hour arrive?
DEMOGORGON: Behold!
ASIA: The rocks are cloven, and through the purple night
¹³⁰ I see cars drawn by rainbow-winged steeds
Which trample the dim winds: in each there stands
A wild-eyed charioteer urging their flight.
Some look behind, as fiends pursued them there,
And yet I see no shapes but the keen stars:
¹³⁵ Others, with burning eyes, lean forth, and drink
With eager lips the wind of their own speed,
As if the thing they loved fled on before,
And now, even now, they clasped it. Their bright locks
Stream like a comet's flashing hair: they all
¹⁴⁰ Sweep onward.
DEMOGORGON: These are the immortal Hours,
Of whom thou didst demand. One waits for thee.
ASIA: A spirit with a dreadful countenance
Checks its dark chariot by the craggy gulph.
Unlike thy brethren, ghastly charioteer,
¹⁴⁵ Who art thou? Whither wouldst thou bear me? Speak!
SPIRIT: I am the shadow of a destiny
More dread than is my aspect: ere yon planet
Has set, the darkness which ascends with me
Shall wrap in lasting night heaven's kingless throne.
¹⁵⁰ ASIA: What meanest thou?
PANTHEA: That terrible shadow floats
Up from its throne, as may the lurid smoke
Of earthquake-ruined cities o'er the sea.
Lo! it ascends the car; the coursers fly
Terrified: watch its path among the stars
¹⁵⁵ Blackening the night!
ASIA: Thus I am answered: strange!
PANTHEA: See, near the verge, another chariot stays;
An ivory shell inlaid with crimson fire,
Which comes and goes within its sculptured rim

    Of delicate strange tracery; the young spirit
160 That guides it has the dove-like eyes of hope;
    How its soft smiles attract the soul! as light
    Lures winged insects thro' the lampless air.
SPIRIT:
    My coursers are fed with the lightning,
        They drink of the whirlwind's stream,
165 And when the red morning is brightning
        They bathe in the fresh sunbeam;
        They have strength for their swiftness I deem,
    Then ascend with me, daughter of Ocean.
    I desire: and their speed makes night kindle;
170   I fear: they outstrip the Typhoon;[1]
    Ere the cloud piled on Atlas[2] can dwindle
        We encircle the earth and the moon:
        We shall rest from long labours at noon:
    Then ascend with me, daughter of Ocean.

SCENE 5

The Car pauses within a Cloud on the Top of a snowy Mountain. ASIA, PANTHEA, *and the* SPIRIT OF THE HOUR.

SPIRIT:
    On the brink of the night and the morning
        My coursers are wont to respire;
    But the Earth has just whispered a warning
        That their flight must be swifter than fire:
5   They shall drink the hot speed of desire!
ASIA: Thou breathest on their nostrils, but my breath
    Would give them swifter speed.
SPIRIT: Alas! it could not.
PANTHEA: Oh Spirit! pause, and tell whence is the light
    Which fills the cloud? the sun is yet unrisen.
10 SPIRIT: The sun will rise not until noon. Apollo[3]
    Is held in heaven by wonder; and the light
    Which fills this vapour, as the aerial hue
    Of fountain-gazing roses fills the water,
    Flows from thy mighty sister.
PANTHEA: Yes, I feel—
15 ASIA: What is it with thee, sister? Thou art pale.
PANTHEA: How thou art changed! I dare not look on thee;
    I feel but see thee not. I scarce endure
    The radiance of thy beauty. Some good change
    Is working in the elements, which suffer
20 Thy presence thus unveiled. The Nereids[4] tell
    That on the day when the clear hyaline[5]
    Was cloven at thy uprise, and thou didst stand
    Within a veined shell, which floated on
    Over the calm floor of the crystal sea,
25 Among the Egean isles, and by the shores
    Which bear thy name; love, like the atmosphere
    Of the sun's fire filling the living world,
    Burst from thee, and illumined earth and heaven
    And the deep ocean and the sunless caves
30 And all that dwells within them; till grief cast
    Eclipse upon the soul from which it came:
    Such art thou now; nor is it I alone,
    Thy sister, thy companion, thine own chosen one,
    But the whole world which seeks thy sympathy.
35 Hearest thou not sounds i' the air which speak the love
    Of all articulate beings? Feelest thou not
    The inanimate winds enamoured of thee? List!
[*Music.*]
ASIA: Thy words are sweeter than aught else but his
    Whose echoes they are: yet all love is sweet,
40 Given or returned. Common as light is love,
    And its familiar voice wearies not ever.
    Like the wide heaven, the all-sustaining air,
    It makes the reptile equal to the God:

---

[1] violent hurricane.

[2] Perseus changed the Titan Atlas, brother of Prometheus, into a mountain so high that Atlas was thought to bear the world on his shoulders.

[3] son of Zeus and Leto, Apollo was the god of medicine, music (and therefore poetry), archery, prophecy, and light; he is sometimes identified with the sun.

[4] sea-nymphs, the fifty daughters of the sea-god Nereus. Asia is identified with the goddess Venus, born of the sea-foam.

[5] transparent or glassy.

They who inspire it most are fortunate,
45 As I am now; but those who feel it most
Are happier still, after long sufferings,
As I shall soon become.
PANTHEA: List! Spirits speak.
VOICE: [*In the Air, singing.*]
Life of Life! thy lips enkindle
　With their love the breath between them;
50 And thy smiles before they dwindle
　Make the cold air fire; then screen them
In those looks, where whoso gazes
　Faints, entangled in their mazes.

Child of Light! thy limbs are burning
55 　Thro' the vest which seems to hide them;
As the radiant lines of morning
　Thro' the clouds ere they divide them;
And this atmosphere divinest
Shrouds thee wheresoe'er thou shinest.

60 Fair are others; none beholds thee,
　But thy voice sounds low and tender
Like the fairest, for it folds thee
　From the sight, that liquid splendour,
And all feel, yet see thee never,
65 As I feel now, lost for ever!

Lamp of Earth! where'er thou movest
　Its dim shapes are clad with brightness
And the souls of whom thou lovest
　Walk upon the winds with lightness,
70 Till they fail, as I am failing,
Dizzy, lost, yet unbewailing!
ASIA:
　My soul is an enchanted boat,
　　Which, like a sleeping swan, doth float
Upon the silver waves of thy sweet singing;
75 　And thine doth like an angel sit
　　Beside the helm conducting it,
Whilst all the winds with melody are ringing.
　It seems to float ever, for ever,
　　Upon that many-winding river,
80 　Between mountains, woods, abysses,
　　A paradise of wildernesses!

Till, like one in slumber bound,
Borne to the ocean, I float down, around,
Into a sea profound, of ever-spreading sound:

85 　Meanwhile thy spirit lifts its pinions
　　In music's most serene dominions;
Catching the winds that fan that happy heaven.
　And we sail on, away, afar,
　　Without a course, without a star,
90 But, by the instinct of sweet music driven;
　Till through Elysian garden islets
　　By thee, most beautiful of pilots,
　Where never mortal pinnace glided,
　　The boat of my desire is guided:
95 Realms where the air we breathe is love,
Which in the winds on the waves doth move,
Harmonizing this earth with what we feel above.

　We have pass'd Age's icy caves,
　　And Manhood's dark and tossing waves,
100 And Youth's smooth ocean, smiling to betray:
　Beyond the glassy gulphs we flee
　　Of shadow-peopled Infancy,
Through Death and Birth, to a diviner day;
　A paradise of vaulted bowers,
105 　Lit by downward-gazing flowers,
　And watery paths that wind between
　　Wildernesses calm and green,
Peopled by shapes too bright to see,
And rest, having beheld; somewhat like thee;
110 Which walk upon the sea, and chaunt melodiously!

ACT 3

SCENE 1

Heaven. JUPITER *on his Throne;* THETIS *and the other Deities assembled.*

JUPITER: Ye congregated powers of heaven, who share
The glory and the strength of him ye serve,
Rejoice! henceforth I am omnipotent.

All else had been subdued to me; alone
5 The soul of man, like unextinguished fire,
   Yet burns towards heaven with fierce reproach, and doubt,
   And lamentation, and reluctant prayer,
   Hurling up insurrection, which might make
   Our antique empire insecure, though built
10 On eldest faith, and hell's coeval, fear;
   And tho' my curses thro' the pendulous air,
   Like snow on herbless peaks, fall flake by flake,
   And cling to it; tho' under my wrath's might
   It climb the crags of life, step after step,
15 Which wound it, as ice wounds unsandalled feet,
   It yet remains supreme o'er misery,
   Aspiring, unrepressed, yet soon to fall:
   Even now have I begotten a strange wonder,
   That fatal child, the terror of the earth,
20 Who waits but till the distant hour arrive,
   Bearing from Demogorgon's vacant throne
   The dreadful might of ever-living limbs
   Which clothed that awful spirit unbeheld,
   To redescend, and trample out the spark.

25 Pour forth heaven's wine, Idæan Ganymede,[1]
   And let it fill the Dædal cups[2] like fire,
   And from the flower-inwoven soil divine
   Ye all-triumphant harmonies arise,
   As dew from earth under the twilight stars:
30 Drink! be the nectar circling thro' your veins
   The soul of joy, ye ever-living Gods,
   Till exultation burst in one wide voice
   Like music from Elysian winds.
                                    And thou
   Ascend beside me, veiled in the light
35 Of the desire which makes thee one with me,
   Thetis, bright image of eternity!
   When thou didst cry, "Insufferable might!
   God! Spare me! I sustain not the quick flames,
   The penetrating presence; all my being,
40 Like him whom the Numidian seps[3] did thaw
   Into a dew with poison, is dissolved,
   Sinking thro' its foundations": even then
   Two mighty spirits, mingling, made a third
   Mightier than either, which, unbodied now,
45 Between us floats, felt, although unbeheld,
   Waiting the incarnation, which ascends,
   (Hear ye the thunder of the fiery wheels
   Griding[4] the winds?) from Demogorgon's throne.
   Victory! victory! Feel'st thou not, O world,
50 The earthquake of his chariot thundering up Olympus?
   [*The Car of the* HOUR *arrives.* DEMOGORGON *descends, and moves towards the Throne of* JUPITER.]
   Awful shape, what art thou? Speak!
   DEMOGORGON: Eternity. Demand no direr name.
   Descend, and follow me down the abyss.
   I am thy child, as thou wert Saturn's child;
55 Mightier than thee: and we must dwell together
   Henceforth in darkness. Lift thy lightnings not.
   The tyranny of heaven none may retain,
   Or reassume, or hold, succeeding thee:
   Yet if thou wilt, as 'tis the destiny
60 Of trodden worms to writhe till they are dead,
   Put forth thy might.
   JUPITER: Detested prodigy!
   Even thus beneath the deep Titanian prisons
   I trample thee! thou lingerest?
                                   Mercy! mercy!
   No pity, no release, no respite! Oh,
65 That thou wouldst make mine enemy my judge,
   Even where he hangs, seared by my long revenge,
   On Caucasus! he would not doom me thus.
   Gentle, and just, and dreadless, is he not
   The monarch of the world? What art thou?
70 No refuge! no appeal!
                         Sink with me then,
   We two will sink on the wide waves of ruin,
   Even as a vulture and a snake outspent
   Drop, twisted in inextricable fight,
   Into a shoreless sea. Let hell unlock
75 Its mounded oceans of tempestuous fire,

---

[1] cupbearer to the gods, carried off by Jupiter, in the shape of an eagle, from Mount Ida, near Troy; see Ovid, *Metamorphoses* 10.

[2] intricately made, as if by Dædalus, the great artificer of Crete; cf. Ovid, *Metamorphoses* 8.

[3] poisonous snake from Numidia, in North Africa.

[4] grating or scraping. Cf. Lucan (AD 39–65), *Pharsalia* 9.

And whelm on them into the bottomless void
This desolated world, and thee, and me,
The conqueror and the conquered, and the wreck
Of that for which they combated.
                                    Ai! Ai!
80 The elements obey me not. I sink
Dizzily down, ever, for ever, down.
And, like a cloud, mine enemy above
Darkens my fall with victory! Ai, Ai!

SCENE 2

The Mouth of a great River in the Island Atlantis.
OCEAN is discovered reclining near the Shore;
APOLLO stands beside him.

OCEAN: He fell, thou sayest, beneath his conqueror's
    frown?
APOLLO: Aye, when the strife was ended which made
    dim
The orb I rule, and shook the solid stars,
The terrors of his eye illumined heaven
5 With sanguine light, through the thick ragged skirts
Of the victorious darkness, as he fell:
Like the last glare of day's red agony,
Which, from a rent among the fiery clouds,
Burns far along the tempest-wrinkled deep.
10 OCEAN: He sunk to the abyss? To the dark void?
APOLLO: An eagle so caught in some bursting cloud
On Caucasus, his thunder-baffled wings
Entangled in the whirlwind, and his eyes
Which gazed on the undazzling sun, now blinded
15 By the white lightning, while the ponderous hail
Beats on his struggling form, which sinks at length
Prone, and the aerial ice clings over it.
OCEAN: Henceforth the fields of Heaven-reflecting sea
Which are my realm, will heave, unstain'd with blood,
20 Beneath the uplifting winds, like plains of corn
Swayed by the summer air; my streams will flow
Round many peopled continents, and round
Fortunate isles; and from their glassy thrones
Blue Proteus[1] and his humid nymphs shall mark

25 The shadow of fair ships, as mortals see
The floating bark of the light laden moon
With that white star, its sightless pilot's crest,
Borne down the rapid sunset's ebbing sea;
Tracking their path no more by blood and groans,
30 And desolation, and the mingled voice
Of slavery and command; but by the light
Of wave-reflected flowers, and floating odours,
And music soft, and mild, free, gentle voices,
That sweetest music, such as spirits love.
35 APOLLO: And I shall gaze not on the deeds which
    make
My mind obscure with sorrow, as eclipse
Darkens the sphere I guide; but list, I hear
The small, clear, silver lute of the young Spirit
That sits on the morning star.
OCEAN: Thou must away;
40 Thy steeds will pause at even, till when farewell:
The loud deep calls me home even now to feed it
With azure calm out of the emerald urns
Which stand for ever full beside my throne.
Behold the Nereids under the green sea,
45 Their wavering limbs borne on the wind-like stream,
Their white arms lifted o'er their streaming hair
With garlands pied and starry sea-flower crowns,
Hastening to grace their mighty sister's joy.
[*A sound of waves is heard.*]
It is the unpastured sea hungering for calm.
Peace, monster; I come now. Farewell.
APOLLO: Farewell.

SCENE 3

Caucasus. PROMETHEUS, HERCULES, IONE, *the* EARTH,
SPIRITS, ASIA, *and* PANTHEA, *borne in the Car with the*
SPIRIT OF THE HOUR. HERCULES *unbinds*
PROMETHEUS, *who descends.*

HERCULES: Most glorious among spirits, thus doth
    strength
To wisdom, courage, and long-suffering love,
And thee, who art the form they animate,
Minister like a slave.

---

[1] a sea-god, the shape-changer; cf. Homer, *Odyssey* 4

PROMETHEUS: Thy gentle words
5 Are sweeter even than freedom long desired
And long delayed.
                     Asia, thou light of life,
Shadow of beauty unbeheld: and ye,
Fair sister nymphs, who made long years of pain
Sweet to remember, thro' your love and care:
10 Henceforth we will not part. There is a cave,
All overgrown with trailing odorous plants,
Which curtain out the day with leaves and flowers,
And paved with veined emerald, and a fountain
Leaps in the midst with an awakening sound.
15 From its curved roof the mountain's frozen tears
Like snow, or silver, or long diamond spires,
Hang downward, raining forth a doubtful light:
And there is heard the ever-moving air,
Whispering without from tree to tree, and birds,
20 And bees; and all around are mossy seats,
And the rough walls are clothed with long soft grass;
A simple dwelling, which shall be our own;
Where we will sit and talk of time and change,
As the world ebbs and flows, ourselves unchanged.
25 What can hide man from mutability?
And if ye sigh, then I will smile; and thou,
Ione, shalt chaunt fragments of sea-music,
Until I weep, when ye shall smile away
The tears she brought, which yet were sweet to shed.
30 We will entangle buds and flowers and beams
Which twinkle on the fountain's brim, and make
Strange combinations out of common things,
Like human babes in their brief innocence;
And we will search, with looks and words of love,
35 For hidden thoughts, each lovelier than the last,
Our unexhausted spirits; and like lutes
Touched by the skill of the enamoured wind,
Weave harmonies divine, yet ever new,
From difference sweet where discord cannot be;
40 And hither come, sped on the charmed winds,
Which meet from all the points of heaven, as bees
From every flower aerial Enna[1] feeds,
At their known island-homes in Himera,[2]
The echoes of the human world, which tell
45 Of the low voice of love, almost unheard,
And dove-eyed pity's murmured pain, and music,
Itself the echo of the heart, and all
That tempers or improves man's life, now free;
And lovely apparitions, dim at first,
50 Then radiant, as the mind, arising bright
From the embrace of beauty, whence the forms
Of which these are the phantoms, casts on them
The gathered rays which are reality,
Shall visit us, the progeny immortal
55 Of Painting, Sculpture, and rapt Poesy,
And arts, tho' unimagined, yet to be.
The wandering voices and the shadows these
Of all that man becomes, the mediators
Of that best worship love, by him and us
60 Given and returned; swift shapes and sounds, which grow
More fair and soft as man grows wise and kind,
And veil by veil, evil and error fall:
Such virtue has the cave and place around.
[*Turning to the* SPIRIT OF THE HOUR.]
For thee, fair Spirit, one toil remains. Ione,
65 Give her that curved shell, which Proteus old
Made Asia's nuptial boon, breathing within it
A voice to be accomplished, and which thou
Didst hide in grass under the hollow rock.
IONE: Thou most desired Hour, more loved and lovely
70 Than all thy sisters, this is the mystic shell;
See the pale azure fading into silver
Lining it with a soft yet glowing light:
Looks it not like lulled music sleeping there?
SPIRIT: It seems in truth the fairest shell of Ocean:
75 Its sound must be at once both sweet and strange.
PROMETHEUS: Go, borne over the cities of mankind
On whirlwind-footed coursers: once again
Outspeed the sun around the orbed world;
And as thy chariot cleaves the kindling air,

---

[1] the Sicilian vale from which Proserpine was abducted by Hades; cf. Ovid, *Metamorphoses* 5 and Milton, *Paradise Lost* 4.268–72.

[2] a city in northern Sicily.

Thou breathe into the many-folded shell, 80
Loosening its mighty music; it shall be
As thunder mingled with clear echoes: then
Return; and thou shalt dwell beside our cave.
And thou, O, Mother Earth!—
THE EARTH: I hear, I feel;
Thy lips are on me, and thy touch runs down 85
Even to the adamantine central gloom
Along these marble nerves; 'tis life, 'tis joy,
And thro' my withered, old, and icy frame
The warmth of an immortal youth shoots down
Circling. Henceforth the many children fair 90
Folded in my sustaining arms; all plants,
And creeping forms, and insects rainbow-winged,
And birds, and beasts, and fish, and human shapes,
Which drew disease and pain from my wan bosom,
Draining the poison of despair, shall take 95
And interchange sweet nutriment; to me
Shall they become like sister-antelopes
By one fair dam, snow-white and swift as wind
Nursed among lilies near a brimming stream.
The dew-mists of my sunless sleep shall float 100
Under the stars like balm: night-folded flowers
Shall suck unwitting[1] hues in their repose:
And men and beasts in happy dreams shall gather
Strength for the coming day, and all its joy:
And death shall be the last embrace of her 105
Who takes the life she gave, even as a mother
Folding her child, says, "Leave me not again."
ASIA: Oh, mother! wherefore speak the name of death?
Cease they to love, and move, and breathe, and speak,
Who die? 110
THE EARTH: It would avail not to reply:
Thou art immortal, and this tongue is known
But to the uncommunicating dead.
Death is the veil which those who live call life:[2]
They sleep, and it is lifted: and meanwhile
In mild variety the seasons mild 115
With rainbow-skirted showers, and odorous winds,
And long blue meteors cleansing the dull night,
And the life-kindling shafts of the keen sun's
All-piercing bow, and the dew-mingled rain
Of the calm moonbeams, a soft influence mild, 120
Shall clothe the forests and the fields, aye, even
The crag-built desarts of the barren deep,
With ever-living leaves, and fruits, and flowers.
And thou! There is a cavern where my spirit
Was panted forth in anguish whilst thy pain 125
Made my heart mad, and those who did inhale it
Became mad too, and built a temple there,
And spoke, and were oracular, and lured
The erring nations round to mutual war,
And faithless faith, such as Jove kept with thee; 130
Which breath now rises, as amongst tall weeds
A violet's exhalation, and it fills
With a serener light and crimson air
Intense, yet soft, the rocks and woods around;
It feeds the quick growth of the serpent vine, 135
And the dark linked ivy tangling wild,
And budding, blown, or odour-faded blooms
Which star the winds with points of coloured light,
As they rain thro' them, and bright golden globes
Of fruit, suspended in their own green heaven, 140
And thro' their veined leaves and amber stems
The flowers whose purple and translucid bowls
Stand ever mantling with aërial dew,
The drink of spirits: and it circles round,
Like the soft waving wings of noonday dreams, 145
Inspiring calm and happy thoughts, like mine,
Now thou art thus restored. This cave is thine.
Arise! Appear!
[*A SPIRIT rises in the likeness of a winged child.*]
                  This is my torch-bearer;
Who let his lamp out in old time with gazing
On eyes from which he kindled it anew 150
With love, which is as fire, sweet daughter mine,
For such is that within thine own. Run, wayward,
And guide this company beyond the peak
Of Bacchic Nysa,[3] Mænad-haunted mountain,
And beyond Indus and its tribute rivers, 155
Trampling the torrent streams and glassy lakes
With feet unwet, unwearied, undelaying,

---

[1] Later editions amend to "unwithering."

[2] Cf. Plato, *Gorgias* 492e and Shelley's sonnet "Lift not the Painted Veil" (1819?).

[3] the mountain where the Mænads nursed Dionysus.

And up the green ravine, across the vale,
Beside the windless and crystalline pool,
160 Where ever lies, on unerasing waves,
The image of a temple, built above,
Distinct with column, arch, and architrave,
And palm-like capital, and over-wrought,
And populous most with living imagery,
165 Praxitelean shapes,[1] whose marble smiles
Fill the hushed air with everlasting love.
It is deserted now, but once it bore
Thy name, Prometheus; there the emulous youths
Bore to thy honour thro' the divine gloom
170 The lamp which was thine emblem; even as those
Who bear the untransmitted torch of hope
Into the grave, across the night of life,
As thou hast borne it most triumphantly
To this far goal of Time. Depart, farewell.
175 Beside that temple is the destined cave.

SCENE 4

A Forest. In the Background a Cave.
PROMETHEUS, ASIA, PANTHEA, IONE, *and the*
SPIRIT OF THE EARTH.

IONE: Sister, it is not earthly: how it glides
Under the leaves! how on its head there burns
A light, like a green star, whose emerald beams
Are twined with its fair hair! how, as it moves,
5 The splendour drops in flakes upon the grass!
Knowest thou it?
PANTHEA: It is the delicate spirit
That guides the earth thro' heaven. From afar
The populous constellations call that light
The loveliest of the planets; and sometimes
10 It floats along the spray of the salt sea,
Or makes its chariot of a foggy cloud,
Or walks thro' fields or cities while men sleep,
Or o'er the mountain tops, or down the rivers,
Or thro' the green waste wilderness, as now,
15 Wondering at all it sees. Before Jove reigned

It loved our sister Asia, and it came
Each leisure hour to drink the liquid light
Out of her eyes, for which it said it thirsted
As one bit by a dipsas,[2] and with her
20 It made its childish confidence, and told her
All it had known or seen, for it saw much,
Yet idly reasoned what it saw; and called her,
For whence it sprung it knew not, nor do I,
Mother, dear mother.
THE SPIRIT OF THE EARTH: [*Running to* ASIA.]
    Mother, dearest mother;
25 May I then talk with thee as I was wont?
May I then hide my eyes in thy soft arms,
After thy looks have made them tired of joy?
May I then play beside thee the long noons,
When work is none in the bright silent air?
30 ASIA: I love thee, gentlest being, and henceforth
Can cherish thee unenvied: speak, I pray:
Thy simple talk once solaced, now delights.
SPIRIT OF THE EARTH: Mother, I am grown wiser,
    though a child
Cannot be wise like thee, within this day;
35 And happier too; happier and wiser both.
Thou knowest that toads, and snakes, and loathly
    worms,
And venomous and malicious beasts, and boughs
That bore ill berries in the woods, were ever
An hindrance to my walks o'er the green world:
40 And that, among the haunts of humankind,
Hard-featured men, or with proud, angry looks,
Or cold, staid gait, or false and hollow smiles,
Or the dull sneer of self-loved ignorance,
Or other such foul masks, with which ill thoughts
45 Hide that fair being whom we spirits call man;
And women too, ugliest of all things evil,
(Tho' fair, even in a world where thou art fair,
When good and kind, free and sincere like thee,)
When false or frowning made me sick at heart
50 To pass them, tho' they slept, and I unseen.
Well, my path lately lay thro' a great city
Into the woody hills surrounding it:

---

[1] like the statues carved by the Greek sculptor Praxiteles (4th century BC).

[2] a poisonous snake. Cf. Lucan, *Pharsalia* 9 and Milton, *Paradise Lost* 10.526.

A sentinel was sleeping at the gate:
When there was heard a sound, so loud, it shook
55 The towers amid the moonlight, yet more sweet
Than any voice but thine, sweetest of all;
A long, long sound, as it would never end:
And all the inhabitants leapt suddenly
Out of their rest, and gathered in the streets,
60 Looking in wonder up to Heaven, while yet
The music pealed along. I hid myself
Within a fountain in the public square,
Where I lay like the reflex of the moon
Seen in a wave under green leaves; and soon
65 Those ugly human shapes and visages
Of which I spoke as having wrought me pain,
Past floating thro' the air, and fading still
Into the winds that scattered them; and those
From whom they past seemed mild and lovely forms
70 After some foul disguise had fallen, and all
Were somewhat changed, and after brief surprise
And greetings of delighted wonder, all
Went to their sleep again: and when the dawn
Came, would'st thou think that toads, and snakes,
  and efts,[1]
75 Could e'er be beautiful? yet so they were,
And that with little change of shape or hue:
All things had put their evil nature off:
I cannot tell my joy, when o'er a lake
Upon a drooping bough with night-shade twined,
80 I saw two azure halcyons[2] clinging downward
And thinning one bright bunch of amber berries,
With quick long beaks, and in the deep there lay
Those lovely forms imaged as in a sky;
So with my thoughts full of these happy changes,
85 We meet again, the happiest change of all.
ASIA: And never will we part, till thy chaste sister
Who guides the frozen and inconstant moon
Will look on thy more warm and equal light
Till her heart thaw like flakes of April snow
And love thee.

90 SPIRIT OF THE EARTH: What; as Asia loves
    Prometheus?
ASIA: Peace, wanton, thou art yet not old enough.
  Think ye by gazing on each other's eyes
  To multiply your lovely selves, and fill
  With sphered fires the interlunar air?
95 SPIRIT OF THE EARTH: Nay, mother, while my sister[3]
    trims her lamp
  'Tis hard I should go darkling.
ASIA: Listen; look!
[*The* SPIRIT OF THE HOUR *ENTERS.*]
PROMETHEUS: We feel what thou hast heard and
    seen: yet speak.
SPIRIT OF THE HOUR: Soon as the sound had ceased
    whose thunder filled
  The abysses of the sky and the wide earth,
100 There was a change: the impalpable thin air
  And the all-circling sunlight were transformed,
  As if the sense of love dissolved in them
  Had folded itself round the sphered world.
  My vision then grew clear, and I could see
105 Into the mysteries of the universe:
  Dizzy as with delight I floated down,
  Winnowing the lightsome air with languid plumes,
  My coursers sought their birth-place in the sun,
  Where they henceforth will live exempt from toil
110 Pasturing flowers of vegetable fire.
  And where my moonlike car will stand within
  A temple, gazed upon by Phidian forms[4]
  Of thee, and Asia, and the Earth, and me,
  And you fair nymphs looking the love we feel;
115 In memory of the tidings it has borne;
  Beneath a dome fretted with graven flowers,
  Poised on twelve columns of resplendent stone,
  And open to the bright and liquid sky.
  Yoked to it by an amphisbenic snake[5]
120 The likeness of those winged steeds will mock
  The flight from which they find repose. Alas,
  Whither has wandered now my partial tongue

---

[1] lizards or newts.

[2] kingfishers: they have now become vegetarians, and deadly nightshade, their food, is no longer poisonous.

[3] Diana, the virginal goddess of the moon.

[4] like those carved by the Greek sculptor Phidias (5th century BC).

[5] a snake with a head at each end.

When all remains untold which ye would hear?
As I have said I floated to the earth:
It was, as it is still, the pain of bliss
To move, to breathe, to be; I wandering went
Among the haunts and dwellings of mankind,
And first was disappointed not to see
Such mighty change as I had felt within
Expressed in outward things; but soon I looked,
And behold, thrones were kingless, and men walked
One with the other even as spirits do,
None fawned, none trampled; hate, disdain, or fear,
Self-love or self-contempt, on human brows
No more inscribed, as o'er the gate of hell,
"All hope abandon ye who enter here";[1]
None frowned, none trembled, none with eager fear
Gazed on another's eye of cold command,
Until the subject of a tyrant's will
Became, worse fate, the abject of his own,
Which spurred him, like an outspent horse, to death.
None wrought his lips in truth-entangling lines
Which smiled the lie his tongue disdained to speak;
None, with firm sneer, trod out in his own heart
The sparks of love and hope till there remained
Those bitter ashes, a soul self-consumed,
And the wretch crept a vampire among men,
Infecting all with his own hideous ill;
None talked that common, false, cold, hollow talk
Which makes the heart deny the *yes* it breathes,
Yet question that unmeant hypocrisy
With such a self-mistrust as has no name.
And women, too, frank, beautiful, and kind
As the free heaven which rains fresh light and dew
On the wide earth, past; gentle radiant forms,
From custom's evil taint exempt and pure;
Speaking the wisdom once they could not think,
Looking emotions once they feared to feel,
And changed to all which once they dared not be,
Yet being now, made earth like heaven; nor pride,
Nor jealousy, nor envy, nor ill shame,
The bitterest of those drops of treasured gall,
Spoilt the sweet taste of the nepenthe,[2] love.

Thrones, altars, judgement-seats, and prisons; wherein,
And beside which, by wretched men were borne
Sceptres, tiaras, swords, and chains, and tomes
Of reasoned wrong, glozed on by ignorance,
Were like those monstrous and barbaric shapes,
The ghosts of a no more remembered fame,
Which, from their unworn obelisks, look forth
In triumph o'er the palaces and tombs
Of those who were their conquerors: mouldering round
Those imaged to the pride of kings and priests,
A dark yet mighty faith, a power as wide
As is the world it wasted, and are now
But an astonishment; even so the tools
And emblems of its last captivity,
Amid the dwellings of the peopled earth,
Stand, not o'erthrown, but unregarded now.
And those foul shapes, abhorred by god and man,
Which, under many a name and many a form
Strange, savage, ghastly, dark, and execrable,
Were Jupiter, the tyrant of the world;
And which the nations, panic-stricken, served
With blood, and hearts broken by long hope, and love
Dragged to his altars soiled and garlandless,
And slain among men's unreclaiming tears,
Flattering the thing they feared, which fear was hate,
Frown, mouldering fast, o'er their abandoned shrines:
The painted veil, by those who were, called life,
Which mimicked, as with colours idly spread,
All men believed and hoped, is torn aside;
The loathsome mask has fallen, the man remains
Sceptreless, free, uncircumscribed, but man
Equal, unclassed, tribeless, and nationless,
Exempt from awe, worship, degree, the king
Over himself; just, gentle, wise: but man
Passionless; no, yet free from guilt or pain,
Which were, for his will made or suffered them,
Nor yet exempt, tho' ruling them like slaves,
From chance, and death, and mutability,
The clogs of that which else might oversoar
The loftiest star of unascended heaven,
Pinnacled dim in the intense inane.

---

[1] the inscription over the gate of hell in Dante, *Inferno* 3.9.

[2] a drug that induced forgetfulness (cf. Homer, *Odyssey* 4).

ACT 4

SCENE 1

*A Part of the Forest near the Cave of PROMETHEUS.
PANTHEA and IONE are sleeping:
they awaken gradually during the first Song.*

VOICE OF UNSEEN SPIRITS:
    The pale stars are gone!
      For the sun, their swift shepherd,
    To their folds them compelling,
      In the depths of the dawn,
5 Hastes, in meteor-eclipsing array, and they flee
      Beyond his blue dwelling,
      As fawns flee the leopard.
But where are ye?
[A Train of dark Forms and Shadows passes by confusedly, singing.]
    Here, oh, here:
10   We bear the bier
Of the Father of many a cancelled year!
    Spectres we
    Of the dead Hours be,
We bear Time to his tomb in eternity.
15   Strew, oh, strew
    Hair, not yew!
Wet the dusty pall with tears, not dew!
    Be the faded flowers
    Of Death's bare bowers
20 Spread on the corpse of the King of Hours!
    Haste, oh, haste!
    As shades are chased,
Trembling, by day, from heaven's blue waste.
    We melt away,
25   Like dissolving spray,
From the children of a diviner day,
    With the lullaby
    Of winds that die
On the bosom of their own harmony!
IONE:
30 What dark forms were they?
PANTHEA:
    The past Hours weak and grey,
    With the spoil which their toil
      Raked together
From the conquest but One could foil.
IONE:
Have they past?
PANTHEA:
35   They have past;
They outspeeded the blast,
While 'tis said, they are fled:
IONE:
Whither, oh, whither?
PANTHEA:
To the dark, to the past, to the dead.
VOICE OF UNSEEN SPIRITS:
40   Bright clouds float in heaven,
    Dew-stars gleam on earth,
  Waves assemble on ocean,
    They are gathered and driven
By the storm of delight, by the panic of glee!
45   They shake with emotion,
    They dance in their mirth.
But where are ye?
    The pine boughs are singing
    Old songs with new gladness,
50   The billows and fountains
    Fresh music are flinging,
Like the notes of a spirit from land and from sea;
    The storms mock the mountains
    With the thunder of gladness.
55 But where are ye?
IONE: What charioteers are these?
PANTHEA: Where are their chariots?
SEMICHORUS OF HOURS:
The voice of the Spirits of Air and of Earth
  Have drawn back the figured curtain of sleep
Which covered our being and darkened our birth
60   In the deep.
A VOICE:
              In the deep?
SEMICHORUS II:
                    Oh, below the deep.
SEMICHORUS I:
An hundred ages we had been kept
  Cradled in visions of hate and care,

And each one who waked as his brother slept,
    Found the truth—
SEMICHORUS II:
                        Worse than his visions were!
SEMICHORUS I:
65 We have heard the lute of Hope in sleep;
    We have known the voice of Love in dreams,
  We have felt the wand of Power, and leap—
SEMICHORUS II:
    As the billows leap in the morning beams!
CHORUS:
  Weave the dance on the floor of the breeze,
70   Pierce with song heaven's silent light,
  Enchant the day that too swiftly flees,
    To check its flight ere the cave of night.
  Once the hungry Hours were hounds
    Which chased the day like a bleeding deer,
75 And it limped and stumbled with many wounds
    Through the nightly dells of the desart year.
  But now, oh weave the mystic measure
    Of music, and dance, and shapes of light,
  Let the Hours, and the spirits of might and pleasure,
80   Like the clouds and sunbeams, unite.
A VOICE: Unite!
PANTHEA: See, where the Spirits of the human mind
  Wrapt in sweet sounds, as in bright veils, approach.
CHORUS OF SPIRITS:
  We join the throng
    Of the dance and the song,
85 By the whirlwind of gladness borne along;
  As the flying-fish leap
    From the Indian deep,
  And mix with the sea-birds, half asleep.
CHORUS OF HOURS:
  Whence come ye, so wild and so fleet,
90 For sandals of lightning are on your feet,
  And your wings are soft and swift as thought,
  And your eyes are as love which is veiled not?
CHORUS OF SPIRITS:
  We come from the mind
    Of human kind
95 Which was late so dusk, and obscene, and blind.
  Now 'tis an ocean
    Of clear emotion,

  A heaven of serene and mighty motion.
  From that deep abyss
100 Of wonder and bliss,
  Whose caverns are crystal palaces;
  From those skiey towers
    Where Thought's crowned powers
  Sit watching your dance, ye happy Hours!
105 From the dim recesses
    Of woven caresses,
  Where lovers catch ye by your loose tresses;
  From the azure isles,
    Where sweet Wisdom smiles,
110 Delaying your ships with her syren wiles.[1]
  From the temples high
    Of Man's ear and eye,
  Roofed over Sculpture and Poesy;
  From the murmurings
115 Of the unsealed springs
  Where Science bedews his Dædal wings.
  Years after years,
  Through blood, and tears,
  And a thick hell of hatreds, and hopes, and fears;
120 We waded and flew,
  And the islets were few
  Where the bud-blighted flowers of happiness grew.
  Our feet now, every palm,
  Are sandalled with calm,
125 And the dew of our wings is a rain of balm;
  And, beyond our eyes,
  The human love lies
  Which makes all it gazes on Paradise.
CHORUS OF SPIRITS AND HOURS:
  Then weave the web of the mystic measure;
130   From the depths of the sky and the ends of the earth,
  Come, swift Spirits of might and of pleasure,
    Fill the dance and the music of mirth,
  As the waves of a thousand streams rush by
  To an ocean of splendour and harmony!
CHORUS OF SPIRITS:
135 Our spoil is won,

---

[1] enticements like those of the Sirens, whose singing was too beautiful to be resisted (Homer *Odyssey* 12).

Our task is done,
We are free to dive, or soar, or run;[1]
Beyond and around,
Or within the bound
140 Which clips the world with darkness round.
We'll pass the eyes
Of the starry skies
Into the hoar deep to colonize:
Death, Chaos, and Night,
145 From the sound of our flight,
Shall flee, like mist from a tempest's might.
And Earth, Air, and Light,
And the Spirit of Might,
Which drives round the stars in their fiery flight;
150 And Love, Thought, and Breath,
The powers that quell Death,
Wherever we soar shall assemble beneath.
And our singing shall build
In the void's loose field
155 A world for the Spirit of Wisdom to wield;
We will take our plan
From the new world of man,
And our work shall be called the Promethean.
CHORUS OF HOURS:
    Break the dance, and scatter the song;
160   Let some depart, and some remain.
SEMICHORUS I:
    We, beyond heaven, are driven along:
SEMICHORUS II:
    Us the enchantments of earth retain:
SEMICHORUS I:
Ceaseless, and rapid, and fierce, and free,
With the Spirits which build a new earth and sea,
165 And a heaven where yet heaven could never be.
SEMICHORUS II:
Solemn, and slow, and serene, and bright,
Leading the Day and outspeeding the Night,
With the powers of a world of perfect light.
SEMICHORUS I:
We whirl, singing loud, round the gathering sphere,
170 Till the trees, and the beasts, and the clouds appear
From its chaos made calm by love, not fear.
SEMICHORUS II:

---

[1] Cf. Milton, *Comus* 1012–17.

We encircle the ocean and mountains of earth,
And the happy forms of its death and birth
Change to the music of our sweet mirth.
CHORUS OF HOURS AND SPIRITS:
175 Break the dance, and scatter the song,
    Let some depart, and some remain,
Wherever we fly we lead along
In leashes, like starbeams, soft yet strong,
    The clouds that are heavy with love's sweet rain.
180 PANTHEA: Ha! they are gone!
IONE: Yet feel you no delight
From the past sweetness?
PANTHEA: As the bare green hill
When some soft cloud vanishes into rain,
Laughs with a thousand drops of sunny water
To the unpavilioned sky!
IONE: Even whilst we speak
185 New notes arise. What is that awful sound?
PANTHEA: 'Tis the deep music of the rolling world
Kindling within the strings of the waved air,
Æolian modulations.
IONE: Listen too,
How every pause is filled with under-notes,
190 Clear, silver, icy, keen awakening tones,
Which pierce the sense, and live within the soul,
As the sharp stars pierce winter's crystal air
And gaze upon themselves within the sea.
PANTHEA: But see where through two openings in
    the forest
195 Which hanging branches overcanopy,
And where two runnels of a rivulet,
Between the close moss violet-inwoven,
Have made their path of melody, like sisters
Who part with sighs that they may meet in smiles,
200 Turning their dear disunion to an isle
Of lovely grief, a wood of sweet sad thoughts;
Two visions of strange radiance float upon
The ocean-like enchantment of strong sound,
Which flows intenser, keener, deeper yet
205 Under the ground and through the windless air.
IONE: I see a chariot like that thinnest boat,
In which the mother of the months is borne
By ebbing night into her western cave,
When she upsprings from interlunar dreams,

210 O'er which is curved an orblike canopy
Of gentle darkness, and the hills and woods
Distinctly seen through that dusk airy veil,
Regard like shapes in an enchanter's glass;
Its wheels are solid clouds, azure and gold,
215 Such as the genii of the thunder-storm,
Pile on the floor of the illumined sea
When the sun rushes under it; they roll
And move and grow as with an inward wind;
Within it sits a winged infant, white
220 Its countenance, like the whiteness of bright snow,
Its plumes are as feathers of sunny frost,
Its limbs gleam white, through the wind-flowing folds
Of its white robe, woof of ætherial pearl.
Its hair is white, the brightness of white light
225 Scattered in strings; yet its two eyes are heavens
Of liquid darkness, which the Deity
Within seems pouring, as a storm is poured
From jagged clouds, out of their arrowy lashes,
Tempering the cold and radiant air around,
230 With fire that is not brightness; in its hand
It sways a quivering moon-beam, from whose point
A guiding power directs the chariot's prow
Over its wheeled clouds, which as they roll
Over the grass, and flowers, and waves, wake sounds,
235 Sweet as a singing rain of silver dew.
PANTHEA: And from the other opening in the wood
Rushes, with loud and whirlwind harmony,
A sphere, which is as many thousand spheres,
Solid as chrystal, yet through all its mass
240 Flow, as through empty space, music and light:
Ten thousand orbs involving and involved,
Purple and azure, white, green, and golden,
Sphere within sphere; and every space between
Peopled with unimaginable shapes,
245 Such as ghosts dream dwell in the lampless deep,
Yet each inter-transpicuous, and they whirl
Over each other with a thousand motions,
Upon a thousand sightless axles spinning,
And with the force of self-destroying swiftness,
250 Intensely, slowly, solemnly roll on,
Kindling with mingled sounds, and many tones,
Intelligible words and music wild.
With mighty whirl the multitudinous orb
Grinds the bright brook into an azure mist
255 Of elemental subtlety, like light;
And the wild odour of the forest flowers,
The music of the living grass and air,
The emerald light of leaf-entangled beams
Round its intense yet self-conflicting speed,
260 Seem kneaded into one aerial mass
Which drowns the sense. Within the orb itself,
Pillowed upon its alabaster arms,
Like to a child o'erwearied with sweet toil,
On its own folded wings, and wavy hair,
265 The Spirit of the Earth is laid asleep,
And you can see its little lips are moving,
Amid the changing light of their own smiles,
Like one who talks of what he loves in dream.
IONE: 'Tis only mocking the orb's harmony.
270 PANTHEA: And from a star upon its forehead, shoot,
Like swords of azure fire, or golden spears
With tyrant-quelling myrtle[1] overtwined,
Embleming heaven and earth united now,
Vast beams like spokes of some invisible wheel
275 Which whirl as the orb whirls, swifter than thought,
Filling the abyss with sun-like lightnings,
And perpendicular now, and now transverse,
Pierce the dark soil, and as they pierce and pass,
Make bare the secrets of the earth's deep heart;
280 Infinite mines of adamant and gold,
Valueless stones, and unimagined gems,
And caverns on crystalline columns poured
With vegetable silver overspread;
Wells of unfathomed fire, and water springs
285 Whence the great sea, even as a child is fed,
Whose vapours clothe earth's monarch mountain-tops
With kingly, ermine snow. The beams flash on
And make appear the melancholy ruins
Of cancelled cycles; anchors, beaks of ships;
290 Planks turned to marble; quivers, helms, and spears,
And gorgon-headed targes,[2] and the wheels
Of scythed chariots, and the emblazonry
Of trophies, standards, and armorial beasts,

---

[1] Myrtle is sacred to Venus, goddess of love.

[2] shields bearing (like that of Athena, or Minerva) the head of a gorgon, the sight of which could turn an enemy to stone.

Round which death laughed, sepulchred emblems
295 Of dead destruction, ruin within ruin!
The wrecks beside of many a city vast,
Whose population which the earth grew over
Was mortal, but not human; see, they lie
Their monstrous works, and uncouth skeletons,
300 Their statues, homes and fanes; prodigious shapes
Huddled in grey annihilation, split,
Jammed in the hard, black deep; and over these,
The anatomies of unknown winged things,
And fishes which were isles of living scale,
305 And serpents, bony chains, twisted around
The iron crags, or within heaps of dust
To which the tortuous strength of their last pangs
Had crushed the iron crags; and over these
The jagged alligator, and the might
310 Of earth-convulsing behemoth,[1] which once
Were monarch beasts, and on the slimy shores,
And weed-overgrown continents of earth,
Increased and multiplied like summer worms
On an abandoned corpse, till the blue globe
315 Wrapt deluge round it like a cloke, and they
Yelled, gasped, and were abolished; or some God
Whose throne was in a comet, past, and cried,
Be not! And like my words they were no more.
THE EARTH:
    The joy, the triumph, the delight, the madness!
320   The boundless, overflowing, bursting gladness,
The vaporous exultation not to be confined!
    Ha! ha! the animation of delight
    Which wraps me, like an atmosphere of light,
And bears me as a cloud is borne by its own wind.
THE MOON:
325   Brother mine, calm wanderer,
    Happy globe of land and air,
Some Spirit is darted like a beam from thee,
    Which penetrates my frozen frame,
    And passes with the warmth of flame,
330 With love, and odour, and deep melody
    Through me, through me!
THE EARTH:
    Ha! ha! the caverns of my hollow mountains,
    My cloven fire-crags, sound-exulting fountains
Laugh with a vast and inextinguishable laughter.
335   The oceans, and the desarts, and the abysses,
    And the deep air's unmeasured wildernesses,
Answer from all their clouds and billows, echoing after.
    They cry aloud as I do. Sceptred curse,
    Who all our green and azure universe
340 Threatenedst to muffle round with black destruction, sending
    A solid cloud to rain hot thunder-stones,
    And splinter and knead down my children's bones
All I bring forth, to one void mass battering and blending.

    Until each crag-like tower, and storied column,
345   Palace, and obelisk, and temple solemn,
My imperial mountains crowned with cloud, and snow, and fire;
    My sea-like forests, every blade and blossom
    Which finds a grave or cradle in my bosom,
Were stamped by thy strong hate into a lifeless mire.

350   How art thou sunk, withdrawn, covered, drunk up
    By thirsty nothing, as the brackish cup
Drained by a desart-troop, a little drop for all;
    And from beneath, around, within, above,
    Filling thy void annihilation, love
355 Bursts in like light on caves cloven by thunder-ball.

THE MOON:
    The snow upon my lifeless mountains
    Is loosened into living fountains,
My solid oceans flow, and sing, and shine:
    A spirit from my heart bursts forth,
360   It clothes with unexpected birth
My cold bare bosom: Oh! it must be thine
    On mine, on mine!

    Gazing on thee I feel, I know
    Green stalks burst forth, and bright flowers grow,
365 And living shapes upon my bosom move:
    Music is in the sea and air,
    Winged clouds soar here and there,
Dark with the rain new buds are dreaming of:
    'Tis love, all love!

---

[1] Cf. Job 40.15–24.

THE EARTH:
370   It interpenetrates my granite mass,
    Through tangled roots and trodden clay doth pass,
Into the utmost leaves and delicatest flowers;
    Upon the winds, among the clouds 'tis spread,
    It wakes a life in the forgotten dead,
375 They breathe a spirit up from their obscurest bowers.

    And like a storm bursting its cloudy prison
    With thunder, and with whirlwind, has arisen
Out of the lampless caves of unimagined being:
    With earthquake shock and swiftness making shiver
380   Thought's stagnant chaos, unremoved for ever,
Till hate, and fear, and pain, light-vanquished shadows, fleeing,

    Leave Man, who was a many-sided mirror,
    Which could distort to many a shape of error,
This true fair world of things, a sea reflecting love;
385   Which over all his kind as the sun's heaven
    Gliding o'er ocean, smooth, serene, and even
Darting from starry depths radiance and light, doth move:

    Leave man, even as a leprous child is left,
    Who follows a sick beast to some warm cleft
390 Of rocks, through which the might of healing springs is poured;
    Then when it wanders home with rosy smile,
    Unconscious, and its mother fears awhile
It is a spirit, then, weeps on her child restored.

    Man, oh, not men! a chain of linked thought,
395   Of love and might to be divided not,
Compelling the elements with adamantine stress;
    As the sun rules, even with a tyrant's gaze,
    The unquiet republic of the maze
Of planets, struggling fierce towards heaven's free wilderness.

400   Man, one harmonious soul of many a soul,
    Whose nature is its own divine controul,
Where all things flow to all, as rivers to the sea;
    Familiar acts are beautiful through love;
    Labour, and pain, and grief, in life's green grove
405 Sport like tame beasts, none knew how gentle they could be!

    His will, with all mean passions, bad delights,
    And selfish cares, its trembling satellites,
A spirit ill to guide, but mighty to obey,
    Is as a tempest-winged ship, whose helm
410   Love rules, through waves which dare not overwhelm,
Forcing life's wildest shores to own its sovereign sway.

    All things confess his strength. Through the cold mass
    Of marble and of colour his dreams pass;
Bright threads whence mothers weave the robes their children wear;
415   Language is a perpetual orphic song,[1]
    Which rules with Dædal harmony a throng
Of thoughts and forms, which else senseless and shapeless were.

    The lightning is his slave; heaven's utmost deep
    Gives up her stars, and like a flock of sheep
420 They pass before his eye, are numbered, and roll on!
    The tempest is his steed, he strides the air;
    And the abyss shouts from her depth laid bare,
Heaven, hast thou secrets? Man unveils me; I have none.

THE MOON:
    The shadow of white death has past
425   From my path in heaven at last,
    A clinging shroud of solid frost and sleep;
    And through my newly-woven bowers,
    Wander happy paramours,
    Less mighty, but as mild as those who keep
430   Thy vales more deep.

THE EARTH:
    As the dissolving warmth of dawn may fold
    A half unfrozen dew-globe, green, and gold,

---

[1] a song like that of Orpheus, which was beautiful enough to move rocks and trees; cf. Ovid, *Metamorphoses* 10.

    And crystalline, till it becomes a winged mist,
       And wanders up the vault of the blue day,
435   Outlives the noon, and on the sun's last ray
    Hangs o'er the sea, a fleece of fire and amethyst.
THE MOON:
        Thou art folded, thou art lying
        In the light which is undying
      Of thine own joy, and heaven's smile divine;
440   All suns and constellations shower
        On thee a light, a life, a power
    Which doth array thy sphere; thou pourest thine
    On mine, on mine!
THE EARTH:
    I spin beneath my pyramid of night,
445   Which points into the heavens dreaming delight,
    Murmuring victorious joy in my enchanted sleep;
      As a youth lulled in love-dreams faintly sighing,
      Under the shadow of his beauty lying,
    Which round his rest a watch of light and warmth
        doth keep.
THE MOON:
450   As in the soft and sweet eclipse,
      When soul meets soul on lovers' lips,
    High hearts are calm, and brightest eyes are dull;
        So when thy shadow falls on me,
        Then am I mute and still, by thee
455   Covered; of thy love, Orb most beautiful,
        Full, oh, too full!
      Thou art speeding round the sun
      Brightest world of many a one;
      Green and azure sphere which shinest
460   With a light which is divinest
      Among all the lamps of Heaven
      To whom life and light is given;
      I, thy crystal paramour
      Borne beside thee by a power
465   Like the polar Paradise,
      Magnet-like of lovers' eyes;
      I, a most enamoured maiden
      Whose weak brain is overladen
      With the pleasure of her love,
470   Maniac-like around thee move
      Gazing, an insatiate bride,
      On thy form from every side
      Like a Mænad, round the cup
      Which Agave lifted up
475   In the weird Cadmæan forest.[1]
    Brother, wheresoe'er thou soarest
    I must hurry, whirl and follow
    Through the heavens wide and hollow,
    Sheltered by the warm embrace
480   Of thy soul from hungry space,
    Drinking from thy sense and sight
    Beauty, majesty, and might,
    As a lover or a cameleon
    Grows like what it looks upon,
485   As a violet's gentle eye
    Gazes on the azure sky
    Until its hue grows like what it beholds,
      As a grey and watery mist
      Glows like solid amethyst
490   Athwart the western mountain it enfolds,
      When the sunset sleeps
        Upon its snow.
THE EARTH:
    And the weak day weeps
      That it should be so.
495 Oh, gentle Moon, the voice of thy delight
    Falls on me like thy clear and tender light
    Soothing the seaman, borne the summer night,
      Through isles for ever calm;
    Oh, gentle Moon, thy crystal accents pierce
500 The caverns of my pride's deep universe,
    Charming the tiger joy, whose tramplings fierce
      Made wounds which need thy balm.
PANTHEA: I rise as from a bath of sparkling water,
    A bath of azure light, among dark rocks,
505 Out of the stream of sound.
    IONE: Ah me! sweet sister,
    The stream of sound has ebbed away from us,
    And you pretend to rise out of its wave,
    Because your words fall like the clear, soft dew
    Shaken from a bathing wood-nymph's limbs and hair.

---

[1] Agave was the daughter of Cadmus, the first king of Thebes, and the mother of Pentheus. When he opposed the introduction of the cult of Bacchus (Dionysus), Agave and the other Mænads tore him to pieces: see Euripides, *The Bacchae*.

PANTHEA: Peace! peace! A mighty Power, which is as
         darkness,
   Is rising out of Earth, and from the sky
   Is showered like night, and from within the air
   Bursts, like eclipse which had been gathered up
   Into the pores of sunlight: the bright visions,
   Wherein the singing spirits rode and shone,
   Gleam like pale meteors through a watery night.
IONE: There is a sense of words upon mine ear.
PANTHEA: An universal sound like words: Oh, list!

DEMOGORGON:
   Thou, Earth, calm empire of a happy soul,
      Sphere of divinest shapes and harmonies,
      Beautiful orb! gathering as thou dost roll
         The love which paves thy path along the skies:
THE EARTH:
   I hear: I am as a drop of dew that dies.

DEMOGORGON:
   Thou, Moon, which gazest on the nightly Earth
      With wonder, as it gazes upon thee;
   Whilst each to men, and beasts, and the swift birth
      Of birds, is beauty, love, calm, harmony:
THE MOON:
   I hear: I am a leaf shaken by thee!

DEMOGORGON:
   Ye kings of suns and stars, Dæmons and Gods,
      Ætherial Dominations, who possess
      Elysian, windless, fortunate abodes
         Beyond Heaven's constellated wilderness:
A VOICE: [*From above.*]
      Our great Republic hears, we are blest, and bless.

DEMOGORGON:
   Ye happy dead, whom beams of brightest verse
      Are clouds to hide, not colours to pourtray,
      Whether your nature is that universe
         Which once ye saw and suffered—
A VOICE: [*From beneath.*]
                                    Or as they
   Whom we have left, we change and pass away.

DEMOGORGON:
   Ye elemental Genii, who have homes
      From man's high mind even to the central stone
      Of sullen lead; from Heaven's star-fretted domes
         To the dull weed some sea-worm battens on:
A CONFUSED VOICE:
      We hear: thy words waken Oblivion.

DEMOGORGON:
   Spirits, whose homes are flesh: ye beasts and birds,
      Ye worms, and fish; ye living leaves and buds;
      Lightning and wind; and ye untameable herds,
         Meteors and mists, which throng air's solitudes:
A VOICE:
      Thy voice to us is wind among still woods.

DEMOGORGON:
   Man, who wert once a despot and a slave;
      A dupe and a deceiver; a decay;
      A traveller from the cradle to the grave
         Through the dim night of this immortal day:
ALL:
      Speak: thy strong words may never pass away.

DEMOGORGON:
   This the day, which down the void abysm
   At the Earth-born's spell yawns for Heaven's despotism,
      And Conquest is dragged captive through the
         deep:
   Love, from its awful throne of patient power
      In the wise heart, from the last giddy hour
      Of dread endurance, from the slippery, steep,
   And narrow verge of crag-like agony, springs
   And folds over the world its healing wings.
   Gentleness, Virtue, Wisdom, and Endurance,
   These are the seals of that most firm assurance
      Which bars the pit over Destruction's strength;
   And if, with infirm hand, Eternity,
   Mother of many acts and hours, should free
      The serpent that would clasp her with his length;
   These are the spells by which to re-assume
   An empire o'er the disentangled doom.
   To suffer woes which Hope thinks infinite;
   To forgive wrongs darker than death or night;

To defy Power, which seems omnipotent;
To love, and bear; to hope till Hope creates
From its own wreck the thing it contemplates;
575   Neither to change, nor faulter,[1] nor repent;[2]
This, like thy glory, Titan, is to be
Good, great and joyous, beautiful and free;
This is alone Life, Joy, Empire, and Victory.

Ode to the West Wind[3]

1

O, wild West Wind, thou breath of Autumn's being,
 Thou, from whose unseen presence the leaves dead
Are driven, like ghosts from an enchanter fleeing,

Yellow, and black, and pale, and hectic red,
5 Pestilence-stricken multitudes: O, thou,
Who chariotest to their dark wintry bed

The winged seeds, where they lie cold and low,
Each like a corpse within its grave, until
Thine azure sister of the spring shall blow

10 Her clarion o'er the dreaming earth, and fill
(Driving sweet buds like flocks to feed in air)
With living hues and odours plain and hill:

Wild Spirit, which art moving every where;
Destroyer and preserver; hear, O, hear!

2

15 Thou on whose stream, 'mid the steep sky's commotion,
Loose clouds like earth's decaying leaves are shed,
Shook from the tangled boughs of Heaven and Ocean,

Angels of rain and lightning: there are spread
On the blue surface of thine airy surge,
20 Like the bright hair uplifted from the head

Of some fierce Mænad,[4] even from the dim verge
Of the horizon to the zenith's height
The locks of the approaching storm. Thou dirge

Of the dying year, to which this closing night
25 Will be the dome of a vast sepulchre,
Vaulted with all thy congregated might

Of vapours, from whose solid atmosphere
Black rain, and fire, and hail will burst: O, hear!

3

Thou who didst waken from his summer dreams
30 The blue Mediterranean, where he lay,
Lulled by the coil of his crystalline streams,

Beside a pumice isle in Baiæ's bay,[5]
And saw in sleep old palaces and towers
Quivering within the wave's intenser day,

35 All overgrown with azure moss and flowers
So sweet, the sense faints picturing them! Thou
For whose path the Atlantic's level powers

Cleave themselves into chasms, while far below
The sea-blooms and the oozy woods which wear
40 The sapless foliage of the ocean, know

Thy voice, and suddenly grow grey with fear,
And tremble and despoil themselves: O, hear!

---

[1] The first ed. reads "flatter."

[2] Cf. Milton, *Paradise Lost* 1.94–96.

[3] "This poem was conceived and chiefly written in a wood that skirts the Arno, near Florence, and on a day when that tempestuous wind, whose temperature is at once mild and animating, was collecting the vapours which pour down the autumnal rains. They began, as I foresaw, at sunset with a violent tempest of hail and rain, attended by that magnificent thunder and lightning peculiar to the Cisalpine regions.
"The phenomenon alluded to at the conclusion of the third stanza is well known to naturalists. The vegetation at the bottom of the sea, of rivers, and of lakes, sympathises with that of the land in the change of seasons, and is consequently influenced by the winds which announce it." (P.B.S.)

[4] a frenzied female worshipper of Bacchus.

[5] Beneath the waters of the Bay of Baiæ, near Naples, Shelley had seen from a boat the ruins of ancient Roman villas: see letter to Thomas Love Peacock, [22] December 1818.*

4

If I were a dead leaf thou mightest bear;
If I were a swift cloud to fly with thee;
A wave to pant beneath thy power, and share

The impulse of thy strength, only less free
Than thou, O, uncontroulable! If even
I were as in my boyhood, and could be

The comrade of thy wanderings over heaven,
As then, when to outstrip thy skiey speed
Scarce seemed a vision; I would ne'er have striven

As thus with thee in prayer in my sore need.
Oh! lift me as a wave, a leaf, a cloud!
I fall upon the thorns of life! I bleed!

A heavy weight of hours has chained and bowed
One too like thee: tameless, and swift, and proud.

5

Make me thy lyre, even as the forest is:
What if my leaves are falling like its own!
The tumult of thy mighty harmonies

Will take from both a deep, autumnal tone,
Sweet though in sadness. Be thou, spirit fierce,
My spirit! Be thou me, impetuous one!

Drive my dead thoughts over the universe
Like withered leaves to quicken a new birth!
And, by the incantation of this verse,

Scatter, as from an unextinguished hearth
Ashes and sparks, my words among mankind!
Be through my lips to unawakened earth

The trumpet of a prophecy! O, wind,
If Winter comes, can Spring be far behind?

To a Skylark

Hail to thee, blithe spirit!
  Bird thou never wert,
    That from heaven, or near it,
      Pourest thy full heart
In profuse strains of unpremeditated art.

    Higher still and higher
      From the earth thou springest
    Like a cloud of fire;
      The blue deep thou wingest,
And singing still dost soar, and soaring ever singest.

    In the golden lightning
      Of the sunken sun,
    O'er which clouds are brightning,
      Thou dost float and run;
Like an unbodied joy whose race is just begun.

    The pale purple even
      Melts around thy flight;
    Like a star of heaven,
      In the broad day-light
Thou art unseen, but yet I hear thy shrill delight,

    Keen as are the arrows
      Of that silver sphere,
    Whose intense lamp narrows
      In the white dawn clear,
Until we hardly see, we feel that it is there.

    All the earth and air
      With thy voice is loud,
    As, when night is bare,
      From one lonely cloud
The moon rains out her beams, and heaven is overflowed.

    What thou art we know not;
      What is most like thee?
    From rainbow clouds there flow not
      Drops so bright to see,
As from thy presence showers a rain of melody.

    Like a poet hidden
      In the light of thought,
    Singing hymns unbidden,

                    Till the world is wrought
40   To sympathy with hopes and fears it heeded not:

                    Like a high-born maiden
                        In a palace tower,
                    Soothing her love-laden
                        Soul in secret hour
45   With music sweet as love, which overflows her bower:

                    Like a glow-worm golden
                        In a dell of dew,
                    Scattering unbeholden
                        Its aërial hue
50   Among the flowers and grass, which screen it from the
                view:

                    Like a rose embowered
                        In its own green leaves,
                    By warm winds deflowered,
                        Till the scent it gives
55   Makes faint with too much sweet these heavy-winged
                thieves:

                    Sound of vernal showers
                        On the twinkling grass,
                    Rain-awakened flowers,
                        All that ever was
60   Joyous, and clear, and fresh, thy music doth surpass:

                    Teach us, sprite or bird,
                        What sweet thoughts are thine:
                    I have never heard,
                        Praise of love or wine
65   That panted forth a flood of rapture so divine.

                    Chorus Hymenæal,[1]
                        Or triumphal chaunt,
                    Matched with thine would be all
                        But an empty vaunt,
70   A thing wherein we feel there is some hidden want.

                    What objects are the fountains
                        Of thy happy strain?
                    What fields, or waves, or mountains?
                        What shapes of sky or plain?
75   What love of thine own kind? what ignorance of pain?

                    With thy clear keen joyance
                        Langour cannot be:
                    Shadow of annoyance
                        Never came near thee:
80   Thou lovest; but ne'er knew love's sad satiety.

                    Waking or asleep,
                        Thou of death must deem
                    Things more true and deep
                        Than we mortals dream,
85   Or how could thy notes flow in such a crystal stream?

                    We look before and after,
                        And pine for what is not:[2]
                    Our sincerest laughter
                        With some pain is fraught;
90   Our sweetest songs are those that tell of saddest
                thought.

                    Yet if we could scorn
                        Hate, and pride, and fear;
                    If we were things born
                        Not to shed a tear,
95   I know not how thy joy we ever should come near.

                    Better than all measures
                        Of delightful sound,
                    Better than all treasures
                        That in books are found,
100   Thy skill to poet were, thou scorner of the ground!

                    Teach me half the gladness
                        That thy brain must know,
                    Such harmonious madness
                        From my lips would flow,
105   The world should listen then, as I am listening now.

---

[1] wedding hymn; Hymen is the god of marriage.

[2] Cf. Shakespeare, *Hamlet* 4.4.36–39.

The Cenci: A Tragedy, in Five Acts (1820)

DEDICATION

To Leigh Hunt, Esq.

My dear Friend,
I inscribe with your name, from a distant country, and after an absence whose months have seemed years, this the latest of my literary efforts.

Those writings which I have hitherto published, have been little else than visions which impersonate my own apprehensions of the beautiful and the just. I can also perceive in them the literary defects incidental to youth and impatience; they are dreams of what ought to be, or may be. The drama which I now present to you is a sad reality. I lay aside the presumptuous attitude of an instructor, and am content to paint, with such colours as my own heart furnishes, that which has been.

Had I known a person more highly endowed than yourself with all that it becomes a man to possess, I had solicited for this work the ornament of his name. One more gentle, honourable, innocent and brave; one of more exalted toleration for all who do and think evil, and yet himself more free from evil; one who knows better how to receive, and how to confer a benefit; though he must ever confer far more than he can receive; one of simpler, and, in the highest sense of the word, of purer life and manners, I never knew; and I had already been fortunate in friendships when your name was added to the list.

In that patient and irreconcilable enmity with domestic and political tyranny and imposture which the tenor of your life has illustrated, and which, had I health and talents, should illustrate mine, let us, comforting each other in our task, live and die.

All happiness attend you!
Your affectionate friend,
PERCY B. SHELLEY.
ROME, *May* 29, 1819.

PREFACE

A Manuscript[1] was communicated to me during my travels in Italy which was copied from the archives of the Cenci Palace at Rome, and contains a detailed account of the horrors which ended in the extinction of one of the noblest and richest families of that city, during the Pontificate of Clement VIII., in the year 1599.[2] The story is, that an old man, having spent his life in debauchery and wickedness, conceived at length an implacable hatred towards his children; which showed itself towards one daughter under the form of an incestuous passion, aggravated by every circumstance of cruelty and violence. This daughter, after long and vain attempts to escape from what she considered a perpetual contamination both of body and mind, at length plotted with her mother-in-law[3] and brother to murder their common tyrant. The young maiden, who was urged to this tremendous deed by an impulse which overpowered its horror, was evidently a most gentle and amiable being; a creature formed to adorn and be admired, and thus violently thwarted from her nature by the necessity of circumstances and opinion. The deed was quickly discovered, and in spite of the most earnest prayers made to the Pope by the highest persons in Rome, the criminals were put to death. The old man had, during his life, repeatedly bought his pardon from the Pope for capital crimes of the most enormous and unspeakable kind, at the price of a hundred thousand crowns; the death therefore of his victims can scarcely be accounted for by the love of justice. The Pope, among other motives for severity, probably felt that whoever killed the Count Cenci, deprived his treasury of a certain and copious source of revenue.[4] Such a story, if

---

[1] Shelley's play, which he tried unsuccessfully to have produced on the London stage, is based on the true story of Beatrice Cenci (1577–99). In May 1818, Mary Shelley* copied a manuscript history of the Cenci family from a copy owned by the Shelleys' friend John Gisborne.

[2] Clement VIII was Pope from 1592–1605.

[3] stepmother.

[4] "The Papal Government formerly took the most extraordinary precautions against the publicity of facts which offer so tragical a demonstration of its own wickedness and weakness; so that the communication of the MS. had become, until very lately, a matter of some difficulty." (P.B.S.)

told so as to present to the reader all the feelings of those who once acted it, their hopes and fears, their confidences and misgivings, their various interests, passions, and opinions, acting upon and with each other, yet all conspiring to one tremendous end, would be as a light to make apparent some of the most dark and secret caverns of the human heart.

On my arrival at Rome, I found that the story of the Cenci was a subject not to be mentioned in Italian society without awakening a deep and breathless interest; and that the feelings of the company never failed to incline to a romantic pity for the wrongs, and a passionate exculpation of the horrible deed to which they urged her, who has been mingled two centuries with the common dust. All ranks of people knew the outlines of this history, and participated in the overwhelming interest which it seems to have the magic of exciting in the human heart. I had a copy of Guido's picture of Beatrice,[1] which is preserved in the Colonna Palace, and my servant instantly recognized it as the portrait of *La Cenci*.

This national and universal interest which the story produces and has produced for two centuries, and among all ranks of people in a great city, where the imagination is kept for ever active and awake, first suggested to me the conception of its fitness for a dramatic purpose. In fact, it is a tragedy which has already received, from its capacity of awakening and sustaining the sympathy of men, approbation and success. Nothing remained, as I imagined, but to clothe it to the apprehensions of my countrymen in such language and action as would bring it home to their hearts. The deepest and the sublimest tragic compositions, King Lear and the two plays in which the tale of Œdipus is told,[2] were stories which already existed in tradition, as matters of popular belief and interest, before Shakspeare and Sophocles made them familiar to the sympathy of all succeeding generations of mankind.

This story of the Cenci is indeed eminently fearful and monstrous: anything like a dry exhibition of it on the stage would be insupportable. The person who would treat such a subject must increase the ideal, and diminish the actual horror of the events, so that the pleasure which arises from the poetry which exists in these tempestuous sufferings and crimes, may mitigate the pain of the contemplation of the moral deformity from which they spring. There must also be nothing attempted to make the exhibition subservient to what is vulgarly termed a moral purpose. The highest moral purpose aimed at in the highest species of the drama, is the teaching of the human heart, through its sympathies and antipathies, the knowledge of itself; in proportion to the possession of which knowledge, every human being is wise, just, sincere, tolerant, and kind. If dogmas can do more, it is well: but a drama is no fit place for the enforcement of them. Undoubtedly no person can be truly dishonoured by the act of another; and the fit return to make to the most enormous injuries is kindness and forbearance, and a resolution to convert the injurer from his dark passions by peace and love. Revenge, retaliation, atonement, are pernicious mistakes. If Beatrice had thought in this manner, she would have been wiser and better; but she would never have been a tragic character: the few whom such an exhibition would have interested, could never have been sufficiently interested for a dramatic purpose, from the want of finding sympathy in their interest among the mass who surround them. It is in the restless and anatomizing casuistry with which men seek the justification of Beatrice, yet feel that she has done what needs justification; it is in the superstitious horror with which they contemplate alike her wrongs and their revenge, that the dramatic character of what she did and suffered consists.

I have endeavoured as nearly as possible to represent the characters as they probably were, and have sought to avoid the error of making them actuated by my own conceptions of right or wrong, false or true: thus under a thin veil converting names and actions of the sixteenth century into cold impersonations of my own mind. They are represented as Catholics, and as Catholics deeply tinged with religion. To a Protestant apprehension there will appear something unnatural in the earnest and perpetual sentiment of the relations between

---

[1] Guido Reni (1575–1642) did not paint the portrait of Beatrice Cenci (in the Galleria Nazionale d'Arte Antica, Rome) once ascribed to him. It may have been painted by Elisabetta Sirani (1638–65), a painter in Guido's circle.

[2] *Œdipus the King* and *Œdipus at Colonus*, two tragedies by Sophocles (496–05 BC).

God and man which pervade the tragedy of the Cenci. It will especially be startled at the combination of an undoubting persuasion of the truth of the popular religion, with a cool and determined perseverance in enormous guilt. But religion in Italy is not, as in Protestant countries, a cloak to be worn on particular days; or a passport which those who do not wish to be railed at carry with them to exhibit; or a gloomy passion for penetrating the impenetrable mysteries of our being, which terrifies its possessor at the darkness of the abyss to the brink of which it has conducted him. Religion co-exists, as it were, in the mind of an Italian Catholic with a faith in that of which all men have the most certain knowledge. It is interwoven with the whole fabric of life. It is adoration, faith, submission, penitence, blind admiration; not a rule for moral conduct. It has no necessary connection with any one virtue. The most atrocious villain may be rigidly devout, and, without any shock to established faith, confess himself to be so. Religion pervades intensely the whole frame of society, and is, according to the temper of the mind which it inhabits, a passion, a persuasion, an excuse, a refuge; never a check. Cenci himself built a chapel in the court of his palace, and dedicated it to St. Thomas the Apostle, and established masses for the peace of his soul. Thus in the first scene of the fourth act, Lucretia's design in exposing herself to the consequences of an expostulation with Cenci after having administered the opiate, was to induce him by a feigned tale to confess himself before death; this being esteemed by Catholics as essential to salvation; and she only relinquishes her purpose when she perceives that her perseverance would expose Beatrice to new outrages.

I have avoided with great care in writing this play the introduction of what is commonly called mere poetry, and I imagine there will scarcely be found a detached simile or a single isolated description, unless Beatrice's description of the chasm appointed for her father's murder should be judged to be of that nature.[1]

In a dramatic composition the imagery and the passion should interpenetrate one another, the former being reserved simply for the full development and illustration of the latter. Imagination is as the immortal God which should assume flesh for the redemption of mortal passion. It is thus that the most remote and the most familiar imagery may alike be fit for dramatic purposes when employed in the illustration of strong feeling, which raises what is low, and levels to the apprehension that which is lofty, casting over all the shadow of its own greatness. In other respects I have written more carelessly; that is, without an overfastidious and learned choice of words. In this respect, I entirely agree with those modern critics who assert, that in order to move men to true sympathy we must use the familiar language of men.[2] And that our great ancestors, the ancient English poets, are the writers, a study of whom might incite us to do that for our own age which they have done for theirs. But it must be the real language of men in general, and not that of any particular class, to whose society the writer happens to belong.[3] So much for what I have attempted: I need not be assured that success is a very different matter; particularly for one whose attention has but newly been awakened to the study of dramatic literature.

I endeavoured whilst at Rome to observe such monuments of this story as might be accessible to a stranger. The portrait of Beatrice at the Colonna Palace is most admirable as a work of art: it was taken by Guido during her confinement in prison. But it is most interesting as a just representation of one of the loveliest specimens of the workmanship of Nature. There is a fixed and pale composure upon the features: she seems sad and stricken down in spirit, yet the despair thus expressed is lightened by the patience of gentleness. Her head is bound with folds of white drapery, from which the yellow strings of her golden hair escape, and fall about her neck. The moulding of her face is exquisitely delicate; the eye-brows are distinct and arched; the lips have that permanent meaning of imagination and sensibility which suffering has not repressed, and which

---

[1] "An idea in this speech was suggested by a most sublime passage in 'El Purgatorio de San Patricio,' ["St. Patrick's Purgatory"] of Calderon: the only plagiarism which I have intentionally committed in the whole piece." (P.B.S.) Pedro Calderón de la Barca (1600–81) was a Spanish dramatist, many of whose plays were on sacred subjects.

[2] Cf. W. Wordsworth, Preface to *Lyrical Ballads* (643).*

[3] Cf. Coleridge, *Biographia Literaria*, chap. 17 (811–12).*

it seems as if death scarcely could extinguish. Her forehead is large and clear; her eyes, which we are told were remarkable for their vivacity, are swollen with weeping and lustreless, but beautifully tender and serene. In the whole mien there is a simplicity and dignity which, united with her exquisite loveliness and deep sorrow, are inexpressibly pathetic. Beatrice Cenci appears to have been one of those rare persons in whom energy and gentleness dwell together without destroying one another: her nature was simple and profound. The crimes and miseries in which she was an actor and a sufferer, are as the mask and the mantle in which circumstances clothed her for her impersonation on the scene of the world.

The Cenci Palace is of great extent; and though in part modernized, there yet remains a vast and gloomy pile of feudal architecture in the same state as during the dreadful scenes which are the subject of this tragedy. The palace is situated in an obscure corner of Rome, near the quarter of the Jews, and from the upper windows you see the immense ruins of Mount Palatine half hidden under their profuse overgrowth of trees. There is a court in one part of the palace (perhaps that in which Cenci built the chapel to St. Thomas), supported by granite columns and adorned with antique friezes of fine workmanship, and built up, according to the ancient Italian fashion, with balcony over balcony of open work. One of the gates of the palace, formed of immense stones and leading through a passage dark and lofty, and opening into gloomy subterranean chambers, struck me particularly.

Of the Castle of Petrella, I could obtain no further information than that which is to be found in the manuscript.

DRAMATIS PERSONÆ

COUNT FRANCESCO CENCI
GIACOMO, BERNARDO, *his Sons*
CARDINAL CAMILLO
ORSINO, *a Prelate*
SAVELLA, *the Pope's Legate*
OLIMPIO, MARZIO, Assassins
ANDREA, *Servant to* CENCI
Nobles, Judges, Guards, Servants

LUCRETIA, *Wife of* CENCI and Stepmother of his children
BEATRICE, *his Daughter*

The SCENE *lies principally in Rome, but changes during the Fourth Act to Petrella, a Castle among the Apulian Apennines.*

TIME.— DURING *the Pontificate of Clement VIII.*

ACT 1

SCENE 1

An Apartment in the Cenci Palace.
ENTER COUNT CENCI *and* CARDINAL CAMILLO.

CAMILLO: That matter of the murder is hushed up
If you consent to yield his Holiness
Your fief that lies beyond the Pincian gate.—[1]
It needed all my interest in the conclave
5   To bend him to this point: he said that you
Bought perilous impunity with your gold;
That crimes like yours if once or twice compounded
Enriched the Church, and respited from hell
An erring soul which might repent and live:
10   But that the glory and the interest
Of the high throne he fills, little consist
With making it a daily mart of guilt
So manifold and hideous as the deeds
Which you scarce hide from men's revolted eyes.
15   CENCI: The third of my possessions—let it go!
Ay, I once heard the nephew[2] of the Pope
Had sent his architect to view the ground,
Meaning to build a villa on my vines
The next time I compounded with his uncle:
20   I little thought he should outwit me so!

---

[1] one of the ancient gates of the city of Rome.

[2] a euphemism for an illegitimate son.

Henceforth no witness—not the lamp—shall see
That which the vassal threatened to divulge,
Whose throat is choked with dust for his reward.
The deed he saw could not have rated higher
Than his most worthless life:—it angers me!
Respited me from Hell!—So may the Devil
Respite their souls from Heaven. No doubt Pope Clement,
And his most charitable nephews, pray
That the Apostle Peter and the saints
Will grant for their sake that I long enjoy
Strength, wealth, and pride, and lust, and length of days
Wherein to act the deeds which are the stewards
Of their revenue.—But much yet remains
To which they show no title.
CAMILLO: Oh, Count Cenci!
So much that thou might'st honourably live,
And reconcile thyself with thine own heart
And with thy God, and with the offended world.
How hideously look deeds of lust and blood
Through those snow white and venerable hairs!
Your children should be sitting round you now,
But that you fear to read upon their looks
The shame and misery you have written there.
Where is your wife? Where is your gentle daughter?
Methinks her sweet looks, which make all things else
Beauteous and glad, might kill the fiend within you.
Why is she barred from all society
But her own strange and uncomplaining wrongs?
Talk with me, Count, you know I mean you well.
I stood beside your dark and fiery youth
Watching its bold and bad career, as men
Watch meteors, but it vanished not—I marked
Your desperate and remorseless manhood; now
Do I behold you, in dishonoured age
Charged with a thousand unrepented crimes.
Yet I have ever hoped you would amend,
And in that hope have saved your life three times.
CENCI: For which Aldobrandino[1] owes you now
My fief beyond the Pincian—Cardinal,
One thing, I pray you, recollect henceforth,
And so we shall converse with less restraint.
A man you knew spoke of my wife and daughter,
He was accustomed to frequent my house;
So the next day *his* wife and daughter came
And asked if I had seen him; and I smiled:
I think they never saw him any more.
CAMILLO: Thou execrable man, beware!—
CENCI: Of thee?
Nay, this is idle:—We should know each other.
As to my character for what men call crime,
Seeing I please my senses as I list,
And vindicate that right with force or guile,
It is a public matter, and I care not
If I discuss it with you. I may speak
Alike to you and my own conscious heart;
For you give out that you have half reformed me,
Therefore strong vanity will keep you silent
If fear should not; both will, I do not doubt.
All men delight in sensual luxury,
All men enjoy revenge; and most exult
Over the tortures they can never feel;
Flattering their secret peace with others' pain.
But I delight in nothing else. I love
The sight of agony, and the sense of joy,
When this shall be another's, and that mine.
And I have no remorse and little fear,
Which are, I think, the checks of other men.
This mood has grown upon me, until now
Any design my captious fancy makes
The picture of its wish, and it forms none
But such as men like you would start to know,
Is as my natural food and rest debarred
Until it be accomplished.
CAMILLO: Art thou not
Most miserable?
CENCI: Why miserable?—
No. I am what your theologians call
Hardened; which they must be in impudence,
So to revile a man's peculiar taste.
True, I was happier than I am, while yet
Manhood remained to act the thing I thought;
While lust was sweeter than revenge; and now
Invention palls; Ay, we must all grow old:
But that there yet remains a deed to act

---

[1] The family name of Pope Clement VIII was Ippolito Aldobrandini.

Whose horror might make sharp an appetite
Duller than mine—I'd do,—I know not what.
When I was young I thought of nothing else
But pleasure; and I fed on honey sweets:
105 Men, by St. Thomas! cannot live like bees,
And I grew tired: yet, till I killed a foe,
And heard his groans, and heard his children's groans,
Knew I not what delight was else on earth,
Which now delights me little. I the rather
110 Look on such pangs as terror ill conceals;
The dry, fixed eye-ball; the pale, quivering lip,
Which tell me that the spirit weeps within
Tears bitterer than the bloody sweat of Christ.
I rarely kill the body, which preserves,
115 Like a strong prison, the soul within my power,
Wherein I feed it with the breath of fear
For hourly pain.
CAMILLO: Hell's most abandoned fiend
Did never, in the drunkenness of guilt,
Speak to his heart as now you speak to me;
120 I thank my God that I believe you not.
[ENTER ANDREA.]
ANDREA: My Lord, a gentleman from Salamanca
Would speak with you.
CENCI: Bid him attend me
In the grand saloon.
                              [EXIT ANDREA.]
CAMILLO: Farewell; and I will pray
Almighty God that thy false, impious words
125 Tempt not his spirit to abandon thee.
                              [EXIT CAMILLO.]
CENCI: The third of my possessions! I must use
Close husbandry, or gold, the old man's sword,
Falls from my withered hand. But yesterday
There came an order from the Pope to make
130 Fourfold provision for my cursed sons;
Whom I have sent from Rome to Salamanca,
Hoping some accident might cut them off;
And meaning, if I could, to starve them there.
I pray thee, God, send some quick death upon them!
135 Bernardo and my wife could not be worse
If dead and damned:—then, as to Beatrice—
[Looking around him suspiciously.]
I think they cannot hear me at that door;
What if they should? And yet I need not speak,
Though the heart triumphs with itself in words.
140 O, thou most silent air, that shall not hear
What now I think! Thou, pavement, which I tread
Towards her chamber,—let your echoes talk
Of my imperious step, scorning surprise,
But not of my intent!—Andrea!
[ENTER ANDREA.]
ANDREA: My lord?
145 CENCI: Bid Beatrice attend me in her chamber
This evening:—no, at midnight, and alone.
                              [EXEUNT.]

SCENE 2

A Garden of the Cenci Palace. ENTER BEATRICE *and*
ORSINO, *as in conversation.*

BEATRICE: Pervert not truth,
Orsino. You remember where we held
That conversation;—nay, we see the spot
Even from this cypress;—two long years are past
5 Since, on an April midnight, underneath
The moon-light ruins of Mount Palatine,
I did confess to you my secret mind.
ORSINO: You said you loved me then.
BEATRICE: You are a priest:
Speak to me not of love.
ORSINO: I may obtain
10 The dispensation of the Pope to marry.
Because I am a priest, do you believe
Your image, as the hunter some struck deer,
Follows me not whether I wake or sleep?
BEATRICE: As I have said, speak to me not of love;
15 Had you a dispensation, I have not;
Nor will I leave this home of misery
Whilst my poor Bernard, and that gentle lady
To whom I owe life, and these virtuous thoughts,
Must suffer what I still have strength to share.
20 Alas, Orsino! All the love that once
I felt for you, is turned to bitter pain.
Ours was a youthful contract, which you first
Broke, by assuming vows no Pope will loose.

And thus I love you still, but holily,
25 Even as a sister or a spirit might;
And so I swear a cold fidelity.
And it is well perhaps we shall not marry.
You have a sly, equivocating vein
That suits me not.—Ah, wretched that I am!
30 Where shall I turn? Even now you look on me
As you were not my friend, and as if you
Discovered that I thought so, with false smiles
Making my true suspicion seem your wrong.
Ah! No, forgive me; sorrow makes me seem
35 Sterner than else my nature might have been;
I have a weight of melancholy thoughts,
And they forebode,—but what can they forebode
Worse than I now endure?
ORSINO: All will be well.
Is the petition yet prepared? You know
40 My zeal for all you wish, sweet Beatrice;
Doubt not but I will use my utmost skill
So that the Pope attend to your complaint.
BEATRICE: Your zeal for all I wish?—Ah me, you are cold!
Your utmost skill—speak but one word—[*Aside.*]
Alas!
45 Weak and deserted creature that I am,
Here I stand bickering with my only friend!
[*To* ORSINO.]
This night my father gives a sumptuous feast,
Orsino; he has heard some happy news
From Salamanca, from my brothers there,
50 And with this outward show of love he mocks
His inward hate. 'Tis bold hypocrisy,
For he would gladlier celebrate their deaths,
Which I have heard him pray for on his knees:
Great God! that such a father should be mine!—
55 But there is mighty preparation made,
And all our kin, the Cenci, will be there,
And all the chief nobility of Rome.
And he has bidden me and my pale mother
Attire ourselves in festival array.
60 Poor lady! She expects some happy change
In his dark spirit from this act; I none.
At supper I will give you the petition:
Till when—farewell.

ORSINO: Farewell.
[EXIT BEATRICE.]
I know the Pope
Will ne'er absolve me from my priestly vow
65 But by absolving me from the revenue
Of many a wealthy see; and, Beatrice,
I think to win thee at an easier rate.
Nor shall he read her eloquent petition:
He might bestow her on some poor relation
70 Of his sixth cousin, as he did her sister,
And I should be debarred from all access.
Then as to what she suffers from her father,
In all this there is much exaggeration:
Old men are testy and will have their way;
75 A man may stab his enemy, or his vassal,
And live a free life as to wine or women,
And with a peevish temper may return
To a dull home, and rate his wife and children;
Daughters and wives call this foul tyranny.
80 I shall be well content, if on my conscience
There rest no heavier sin than what they suffer
From the devices of my love—A net
From which she shall escape not. Yet I fear
Her subtle mind, her awe-inspiring gaze,
85 Whose beams anatomize me, nerve by nerve,
And lay me bare, and make me blush to see
My hidden thoughts.—Ah, no! a friendless girl
Who clings to me, as to her only hope:—
I were a fool, not less than if a panther
90 Were panic-stricken by the antelope's eye,
If she escape me.
[EXIT.]

SCENE 3

A magnificent Hall in the Cenci Palace. A Banquet.
ENTER CENCI, LUCRETIA, BEATRICE, ORSINO, CAMILLO,
NOBLES.

CENCI: Welcome, my friends and kinsmen; welcome ye,
Princes and Cardinals, Pillars of the church,
Whose presence honours our festivity.

I have too long lived like an anchorite,
5 And, in my absence from your merry meetings,
An evil word is gone abroad of me;
But I do hope that you, my noble friends,
When you have shared the entertainment here,
And heard the pious cause for which 'tis given,
10 And we have pledged a health or two together,
Will think me flesh and blood as well as you;
Sinful indeed, for Adam made all so,
But tender-hearted, meek and pitiful.
FIRST GUEST: In truth, my Lord, you seem too light of heart,
15 Too sprightly and companionable a man,
To act the deeds that rumour pins on you.
[*To his companion.*]
I never saw such blithe and open cheer
In any eye!
SECOND GUEST: Some most desired event,
In which we all demand a common joy,
20 Has brought us hither; let us hear it, Count.
CENCI: It is indeed a most desired event.
If, when a parent, from a parent's heart,
Lifts from this earth to the great Father of all
A prayer, both when he lays him down to sleep
25 And when he rises up from dreaming it;
One supplication, one desire, one hope,
That he would grant a wish for his two sons,
Even all that he demands in their regard—
And suddenly, beyond his dearest hope,
30 It is accomplished, he should then rejoice,
And call his friends and kinsmen to a feast,
And task their love to grace his merriment,
Then honour me thus far—for I am he.
BEATRICE: [*To LUCRETIA.*] Great God! How horrible! Some dreadful ill
35 Must have befallen my brothers.
LUCRETIA: Fear not, child,
He speaks too frankly.
BEATRICE: Ah! My blood runs cold.
I fear that wicked laughter round his eye,
Which wrinkles up the skin even to the hair.
CENCI: Here are the letters brought from Salamanca;
40 Beatrice, read them to your mother. God,
I thank thee! In one night didst thou perform,
By ways inscrutable, the thing I sought.
My disobedient and rebellious sons
Are dead!—Why dead!—What means this change of cheer?
45 You hear me not, I tell you they are dead;
And they will need no food or raiment more:
The tapers that did light them the dark way
Are their last cost. The Pope, I think, will not
Expect I should maintain them in their coffins.
50 Rejoice with me—my heart is wondrous glad.
BEATRICE: [*LUCRETIA sinks, half fainting; BEATRICE supports her.*]
It is not true!—Dear Lady, pray look up.
Had it been true, there is a God in Heaven,
He would not live to boast of such a boon.
Unnatural man, thou knowest that it is false.
55 CENCI: Ay, as the word of God; whom here I call
To witness that I speak the sober truth;—
And whose most favouring providence was shown
Even in the manner of their deaths. For Rocco
Was kneeling at the mass, with sixteen others,
60 When the Church fell and crushed him to a mummy,
The rest escaped unhurt. Cristofano
Was stabbed in error by a jealous man,
Whilst she he loved was sleeping with his rival;
All in the self-same hour of the same night;
65 Which shows that Heaven has special care of me.
I beg those friends who love me, that they mark
The day a feast upon their calendars.
It was the twenty-seventh of December:
Ay, read the letters if you doubt my oath.
[*The assembly appears confused; several of the guests rise.*]
70 FIRST GUEST: Oh, horrible! I will depart.—
SECOND GUEST: And I.
THIRD GUEST: No, stay!
I do believe it is some jest; though faith,
'Tis mocking us somewhat too solemnly.
I think his son has married the Infanta,[1]
Or found a mine of gold in El Dorado:[2]

---

[1] Spanish princess.

[2] El Dorado, "the gilded one" (Sp.), was a legendary South American place of immense riches, the elusive goal of sixteenth-century Spanish expeditions. Cf. Voltaire, *Candide* (1759).

75   'Tis but to season some such news; stay, stay!
       I see 'tis only raillery by his smile.
      CENCI: [*Filling a bowl of wine, and lifting it up.*]
       Oh, thou bright wine, whose purple splendour leaps
       And bubbles gaily in this golden bowl
       Under the lamp-light, as my spirits do,
80   To hear the death of my accursed sons!
       Could I believe thou wert their mingled blood,
       Then would I taste thee like a sacrament,
       And pledge with thee the mighty Devil in Hell;
       Who, if a father's curses, as men say,
85   Climb with swift wings after their children's souls,
       And drag them from the very throne of Heaven,
       Now triumphs in my triumph!—But thou art
       Superfluous; I have drunken deep of joy,
       And I will taste no other wine to-night.
90   Here, Andrea! Bear the bowl around.
      A GUEST: [*Rising.*]   Thou wretch!
       Will none among this noble company
       Check the abandoned villain?
      CAMILLO: For God's sake,
       Let me dismiss the guests! You are insane,
       Some ill will come of this.
      SECOND GUEST: Seize, silence him!
95   FIRST GUEST: I will!
      THIRD GUEST: And I!
      CENCI: [*Addressing those who rise with a threatening
       gesture.*]   Who moves? Who speaks?
      [*Turning to the Company.*]
                              'Tis nothing,
       Enjoy yourselves.—Beware! for my revenge
       Is as the sealed commission of a king,
       That kills, and none dare name the murderer.
      [*The Banquet is broken up; several of the Guests are
       departing.*]
      BEATRICE: I do entreat you, go not, noble guests;
100   What although tyranny and impious hate
       Stand sheltered by a father's hoary hair?
       What if 'tis he who clothed us in these limbs
       Who tortures them, and triumphs? What, if we,
       The desolate and the dead, were his own flesh,
105   His children and his wife, whom he is bound
       To love and shelter? Shall we therefore find
       No refuge in this merciless wide world?

       Oh, think what deep wrongs must have blotted out
       First love, then reverence in a child's prone mind,
110   Till it thus vanquish shame and fear! Oh, think!
       I have borne much, and kissed the sacred hand
       Which crushed us to the earth, and thought its stroke
       Was perhaps some paternal chastisement!
       Have excused much, doubted; and when no doubt
115   Remained, have sought by patience, love and tears,
       To soften him; and when this could not be,
       I have knelt down through the long sleepless nights,
       And lifted up to God, the father of all,
       Passionate prayers: and when these were not heard,
120   I have still borne;—until I meet you here,
       Princes and kinsmen, at this hideous feast
       Given at my brothers' deaths. Two yet remain,
       His wife remains and I, whom if ye save not,
       Ye may soon share such merriment again
125   As fathers make over their children's graves.
       Oh! Prince Colonna, thou art our near kinsman;
       Cardinal, thou art the Pope's chamberlain;
       Camillo, thou art chief justiciary;
       Take us away!
      CENCI: [*He has been conversing with CAMILLO during the
       first part of BEATRICE's speech; he hears the conclusion,
       and now advances.*]
                      I hope my good friends here
130   Will think of their own daughters—or perhaps
       Of their own throats—before they lend an ear
       To this wild girl.
      BEATRICE: [*Not noticing the words of CENCI*]
                Dare no one look on me?
       None answer? Can one tyrant overbear
       The sense of many best and wisest men?
135   Or is it that I sue not in some form
       Of scrupulous law, that ye deny my suit?
       Oh, God! that I were buried with my brothers!
       And that the flowers of this departed spring
       Were fading on my grave! and that my father
140   Were celebrating now one feast for all!
      CAMILLO: A bitter wish for one so young and gentle;
       Can we do nothing?—
      COLONNA: Nothing that I see.
       Count Cenci were a dangerous enemy:
       Yet I would second any one.

A CARDINAL: And I.
CENCI: Retire to your chamber, insolent girl!
BEATRICE: Retire thou, impious man! Ay, hide thyself
Where never eye can look upon thee more!
Wouldst thou have honour and obedience
Who art a torturer? Father, never dream,
Though thou mayst overbear this company,
But ill must come of ill.—Frown not on me!
Haste, hide thyself, lest with avenging looks
My brothers' ghosts should hunt thee from thy seat!
Cover thy face from every living eye,
And start if thou but hear a human step:
Seek out some dark and silent corner, there,
Bow thy white head before offended God,
And we will kneel around, and fervently
Pray that he pity both ourselves and thee.
CENCI: My friends, I do lament this insane girl
Has spoilt the mirth of our festivity.
Good night, farewell; I will not make you longer
Spectators of our dull domestic quarrels.
Another time.—
            [EXEUNT all but CENCI and BEATRICE.]
            My brain is swimming round.
Give me a bowl of wine!
[*To* BEATRICE.]
            Thou painted viper!
Beast that thou art! Fair and yet terrible!
I know a charm shall make thee meek and tame,
Now get thee from my sight!
            [*EXIT BEATRICE.*]
            Here, Andrea,
Fill up this goblet with Greek wine. I said
I would not drink this evening, but I must;
For, strange to say, I feel my spirits fail
With thinking what I have decreed to do.
[*Drinking the wine.*]
Be thou the resolution of quick youth
Within my veins, and manhood's purpose stern,
And age's firm, cold, subtle villainy;
As if thou wert indeed my children's blood
Which I did thirst to drink. The charm works well;
It must be done, it shall be done, I swear!
            [*EXIT.*]

ACT 2

SCENE 1

An Apartment in the Cenci Palace.
ENTER LUCRETIA *and* BERNARDO.

LUCRETIA: Weep not, my gentle boy; he struck but me,
Who have borne deeper wrongs. In truth, if he
Had killed me, he had done a kinder deed.
Oh, God Almighty, do thou look upon us,
We have no other friend but only thee!
Yet weep not; though I love you as my own,
I am not your true mother.
BERNARDO: Oh, more, more
Than ever mother was to any child,
That have you been to me! Had he not been
My father, do you think that I should weep?
LUCRETIA: Alas! poor boy, what else couldst thou have done!
[ENTER BEATRICE.]
BEATRICE: [*In a hurried voice.*] Did he pass this way? Have you seen him, brother?
Ah! no, that is his step upon the stairs;
'Tis nearer now; his hand is on the door;
Mother, if I to thee have ever been
A duteous child, now save me! Thou, great God,
Whose image upon earth a father is,
Dost thou indeed abandon me! He comes;
The door is opening now; I see his face;
He frowns on others, but he smiles on me,
Even as he did after the feast last night.
[ENTER *a Servant.*]
Almighty God, how merciful thou art!
'Tis but Orsino's servant.—Well, what news?
SERVANT: My master bids me say, the Holy Father
Has sent back your petition thus unopened.
[*Giving a Paper.*]
And he demands at what hour 'twere secure
To visit you again?

LUCRETIA: At the Ave Mary.[1]
                                [EXIT Servant.]
    So, daughter, our last hope has failed; Ah me,
    How pale you look; you tremble, and you stand
30 Wrapped in some fixed and fearful meditation,
    As if one thought were over strong for you:
    Your eyes have a chill glare; oh, dearest child!
    Are you gone mad? If not, pray speak to me.
BEATRICE: You see I am not mad; I speak to you.
35 LUCRETIA: You talked of something that your
        father did
    After that dreadful feast? Could it be worse
    Than when he smiled, and cried, My sons are dead!
    And every one looked in his neighbour's face
    To see if others were as white as he?
40 At the first word he spoke I felt the blood
    Rush to my heart, and fell into a trance;
    And when it passed I sat all weak and wild;
    Whilst you alone stood up, and with strong words
    Checked his unnatural pride; and I could see
45 The devil was rebuked that lives in him.
    Until this hour thus you have ever stood
    Between us and your father's moody wrath
    Like a protecting presence: your firm mind
    Has been our only refuge and defence:
50 What can have thus subdued it? What can now
    Have given you that cold melancholy look,
    Succeeding to your unaccustomed fear?
BEATRICE: What is it that you say? I was just
        thinking
    'Twere better not to struggle any more.
55 Men, like my father, have been dark and bloody;
    Yet never—O! before worse comes of it,
    'Twere wise to die: it ends in that at last.
LUCRETIA: Oh, talk not so, dear child! Tell me at
        once
    What did your father do or say to you?
60 He stayed not after that accursed feast
    One moment in your chamber.—Speak to me.
BERNARDO: Oh, sister, sister, prithee, speak to us!

BEATRICE: [*Speaking very slowly with a forced
        calmness.*] It was one word, Mother, one little word;
    One look, one smile.
    [*Wildly.*]
                        Oh! he has trampled me
65 Under his feet, and made the blood stream down
    My pallid cheeks. And he has given us all
    Ditch-water, and the fever-stricken flesh
    Of buffaloes, and bade us eat or starve,
    And we have eaten. He has made me look
70 On my beloved Bernardo, when the rust
    Of heavy chains has gangrened his sweet limbs,
    And I have never yet despaired—but now!
    What would I say?
    [*Recovering herself.*]
                        Ah! no, 'tis nothing new.
    The sufferings we all share have made me wild:
75 He only struck and cursed me as he passed;
    He said, he looked, he did,—nothing at all
    Beyond his wont, yet it disordered me.
    Alas! I am forgetful of my duty,
    I should preserve my senses for your sake.
80 LUCRETIA: Nay, Beatrice; have courage, my sweet
        girl.
    If any one despairs it should be I,
    Who loved him once, and now must live with him
    Till God in pity call for him or me.
    For you may, like your sister, find some husband,
85 And smile, years hence, with children round your
        knees;
    Whilst I, then dead, and all this hideous coil,[2]
    Shall be remembered only as a dream.
BEATRICE: Talk not to me, dear lady, of a husband.
    Did you not nurse me when my mother died?
90 Did you not shield me and that dearest boy?
    And had we any other friend but you
    In infancy, with gentle words and looks,
    To win our father not to murder us?
    And shall I now desert you? May the ghost
95 Of my dead mother plead against my soul

---

[1] at the evening hour when church-bells sound to call the faithful to pray to the Virgin.

[2] confusion or turmoil (archaic); cf. Shakespeare, *Hamlet* 3.1.67.

If I abandon her who filled the place
She left, with more even than a mother's love!
BERNARDO: And I am of my sister's mind. Indeed
I would not leave you in this wretchedness,
100 Even though the Pope should make me free to live
In some blithe place, like others of my age,
With sports, and delicate food, and the fresh air.
Oh, never think that I will leave you, mother!
LUCRETIA: My dear, dear children!
[ENTER CENCI, *suddenly*.]
CENCI: What! Beatrice here!
105 Come hither!
[*She shrinks back, and covers her face.*]
Nay, hide not your face, 't is fair;
Look up! Why, yesternight you dared to look
With disobedient insolence upon me,
Bending a stern and an inquiring brow
On what I meant; whilst I then sought to hide
110 That which I came to tell you—but in vain.
BEATRICE: [*Wildly, staggering towards the door.*]
Oh, that the earth would gape! Hide me, Oh God!
CENCI: Then it was I whose inarticulate words
Fell from my lips, who with tottering steps
Fled from your presence, as you now from mine.
115 Stay, I command you: from this day and hour
Never again, I think, with fearless eye,
And brow superior, and unaltered cheek,
And that lip made for tenderness or scorn,
Shalt thou strike dumb the meanest of mankind;
120 Me least of all. Now get thee to thy chamber,
Thou too, loathed image of thy cursed mother,
[*To* BERNARDO.]
Thy milky, meek face makes me sick with hate!
[EXEUNT BEATRICE *and* BERNARDO.]
[*Aside.*] So much has passed between us as must make
Me bold, her fearful.—'Tis an awful thing
125 To touch such mischief as I now conceive:
So men sit shivering on the dewy bank,
And try the chill stream with their feet; once in—
How the delighted spirit pants for joy!
LUCRETIA: [*Advancing timidly towards him.*]
Oh, husband! Pray forgive poor Beatrice,
130 She meant not any ill.
CENCI: Nor you perhaps?

Nor that young imp, whom you have taught by rote
Parricide with his alphabet? nor Giacomo?
Nor those two most unnatural sons, who stirred
Enmity up against me with the Pope?
135 Whom in one night merciful God cut off:
Innocent lambs! They thought not any ill.
You were not here conspiring? You said nothing
Of how I might be dungeoned as a madman;
Or be condemned to death for some offence,
140 And you would be the witnesses?—This failing,
How just it were to hire assassins, or
Put sudden poison in my evening drink?
Or smother me when overcome by wine?
Seeing we had no other judge but God,
145 And he had sentenced me, and there were none
But you to be the executioners
Of his decree enregistered in heaven?
Oh, no! You said not this?
LUCRETIA: So help me God,
I never thought the things you charge me with!
150 CENCI: If you dare speak that wicked lie again,
I'll kill you. What! it was not by your counsel
That Beatrice disturbed the feast last night?
You did not hope to stir some enemies
Against me, and escape, and laugh to scorn
155 What every nerve of you now trembles at?
You judged that men were bolder than they are;
Few dare to stand between their grave and me.
LUCRETIA: Look not so dreadfully! By my salvation
I knew not aught that Beatrice designed;
160 Nor do I think she designed any thing
Until she heard you talk of her dead brothers.
CENCI: Blaspheming liar! You are damned for this!
But I will take you where you may persuade
The stones you tread on to deliver you;
165 For men shall there be none but those who dare
All things; not question that which I command.
On Wednesday next I shall set out: you know
That savage rock, the Castle of Petrella;
'Tis safely walled, and moated round about:
170 Its dungeons under ground, and its thick towers,
Never told tales; though they have heard and seen
What might make dumb things speak. Why do
   you linger?

Make speediest preparation for the journey!
                              [EXIT LUCRETIA.]
The all beholding sun yet shines; I hear
175 A busy stir of men about the streets;
I see the bright sky through the window panes:
It is a garish, broad, and peering day;
Loud, light, suspicious, full of eyes and ears;
And every little corner, nook, and hole,
180 Is penetrated with the insolent light.
Come, darkness! Yet, what is the day to me?
And wherefore should I wish for night, who do
A deed which shall confound both night and day?
'Tis she shall grope through a bewildering mist
185 Of horror: if there be a sun in heaven,
She shall not dare to look upon its beams;
Nor feel its warmth. Let her then wish for night;
The act I think shall soon extinguish all
For me: I bear a darker deadlier gloom
190 Than the earth's shade, or interlunar air,
Or constellations quenched in murkiest cloud,
In which I walk secure and unbeheld
Towards my purpose.—Would that it were done!
                                          [EXIT.]

SCENE 2

A Chamber in the Vatican.
ENTER CAMILLO and GIACOMO, in conversation.

CAMILLO: There is an obsolete and doubtful law,
By which you might obtain a bare provision
Of food and clothing.
GIACOMO: Nothing more? Alas!
Bare must be the provision which strict law
5 Awards, and aged sullen avarice pays.
Why did my father not apprentice me
To some mechanic trade? I should have then
Been trained in no high-born necessities
Which I could meet not by my daily toil.
10 The eldest son of a rich nobleman
Is heir to all his incapacities;
He has wide wants, and narrow powers. If you,
Cardinal Camillo, were reduced at once
From thrice-driven beds of down, and delicate food,
15 An hundred servants, and six palaces,
To that which nature doth indeed require?
CAMILLO: Nay, there is reason in your plea; 'twere hard.
GIACOMO: 'Tis hard for a firm man to bear: but I
Have a dear wife, a lady of high birth,
20 Whose dowry in ill hour I lent my father,
Without a bond or witness to the deed:
And children, who inherit her fine senses,
The fairest creatures in this breathing world;
And she and they reproach me not. Cardinal,
25 Do you not think the Pope would interpose
And stretch authority beyond the law?
CAMILLO: Though your peculiar case is hard, I know
The Pope will not divert the course of law.
After that impious feast the other night
30 I spoke with him, and urged him then to check
Your father's cruel hand; he frowned and said,
"Children are disobedient, and they sting
Their fathers' hearts to madness and despair,
Requiting years of care with contumely.
35 I pity the Count Cenci from my heart;
His outraged love perhaps awakened hate,
And thus he is exasperated to ill.
In the great war between the old and young,
I, who have white hairs and a tottering body,
40 Will keep at least blameless neutrality."
[ENTER ORSINO.]
You, my good lord Orsino, heard those words.
ORSINO: What words?
GIACOMO: Alas, repeat them not again!
There then is no redress for me; at least
None but that which I may achieve myself,
45 Since I am driven to the brink. But, say,
My innocent sister and my only brother
Are dying underneath my father's eye.
The memorable torturers of this land,
Galeaz Visconti, Borgia, Ezzelin,[1]
50 Never inflicted on their meanest slave

---

[1] Galeaz Visconti (1351–1402), Cesare Borgia (1476–1507), and Eccelino da Romano (1194–1259), three medieval tyrants whose careers are featured in Jean-Charles Léonard Simonde de Sismondi's *History of the Italian Republics in the Middle Ages*, 16 vols. (1809–18), which the Shelleys read in 1819.

What these endure; shall they have no protection?
CAMILLO: Why, if they would petition the Pope,
I see not how he could refuse it—yet
He holds it of most dangerous example
In aught to weaken the paternal power,
Being, as 'twere, the shadow of his own.
I pray you now excuse me. I have business
That will not bear delay.
                    [*EXIT CAMILLO.*]
GIACOMO: But you, Orsino,
Have the petition; wherefore not present it?
ORSINO: I have presented it, and backed it with
My earnest prayers, and urgent interest;
It was returned unanswered. I doubt not
But that the strange and execrable deeds
Alleged in it—in truth they might well baffle
Any belief—have turned the Pope's displeasure
Upon the accusers from the criminal:
So I should guess from what Camillo said.
GIACOMO: My friend, that palace-walking devil,
    Gold,
Has whispered silence to his Holiness:
And we are left, as scorpions ringed with fire.
What should we do but strike ourselves to death?[1]
For he who is our murderous persecutor
Is shielded by a father's holy name,
Or I would—
[*Stops abruptly.*]
ORSINO: What? Fear not to speak your
    thought.
Words are but holy as the deeds they cover:
A priest who has forsworn the God he serves;
A judge who makes truth weep at his decree;
A friend who should weave counsel, as I now,
But as the mantle of some selfish guile;
A father who is all a tyrant seems,
Were the profaner for his sacred name.
GIACOMO: Ask me not what I think; the unwilling
    brain
Feigns often what it would not; and we trust
Imagination with such phantasies

As the tongue dares not fashion into words,
Which have no words, their horror makes them dim
To the mind's eye. My heart denies itself
To think what you demand.
ORSINO: But a friend's bosom
Is as the inmost cave of our own mind,
Where we sit shut from the wide gaze of day,
And from the all-communicating air.
You look what I suspected—
GIACOMO: Spare me now!
I am as one lost in a midnight wood,
Who dares not ask some harmless passenger
The path across the wilderness, lest he,
As my thoughts are, should be—a murderer.
I know you are my friend, and all I dare
Speak to my soul that will I trust with thee.
But now my heart is heavy, and would take
Lone counsel from a night of sleepless care.
Pardon me, that I say farewell—farewell!
I would that to my own suspected self
I could address a word so full of peace.
ORSINO: Farewell!—Be your thoughts better or
    more bold.
                    [*EXIT GIACOMO.*]
I had disposed the Cardinal Camillo
To feed his hope with cold encouragement:
It fortunately serves my close designs
That 'tis a trick of this same family
To analyse their own and other minds.
Such self-anatomy shall teach the will
Dangerous secrets: for it tempts our powers,
Knowing what must be thought, and may be done,
Into the depth of darkest purposes:
So Cenci fell into the pit; even I,
Since Beatrice unveiled me to myself,
And made me shrink from what I cannot shun,
Show a poor figure to my own esteem,
To which I grow half reconciled. I'll do
As little mischief as I can; that thought
Shall fee the accuser conscience.
[*After a pause.*]
                    Now what harm
If Cenci should be murdered?—Yet, if murdered,
Wherefore by me? And what if I could take

---

[1] Cf. P.B. Shelley, *Queen Mab* 6.36–38; and Byron, *The Giaour* 422–38.*

The profit, yet omit the sin and peril
In such an action? Of all earthly things
125 I fear a man whose blows outspeed his words;
And such is Cenci: and while Cenci lives
His daughter's dowry were a secret grave
If a priest wins her. Oh, fair Beatrice!
Would that I loved thee not, or, loving thee,
130 Could but despise danger and gold and all
That frowns between my wish and its effect,
Or smiles beyond it! There is no escape:
Her bright form kneels beside me at the altar,
And follows me to the resort of men,
135 And fills my slumber with tumultuous dreams,
So when I wake my blood seems liquid fire;
And if I strike my damp and dizzy head,
My hot palm scorches it: her very name,
But spoken by a stranger, makes my heart
140 Sicken and pant; and thus unprofitably
I clasp the phantom of unfelt delights,
Till weak imagination half possesses
The self-created shadow. Yet much longer
Will I not nurse this life of feverous hours:
145 From the unravelled hopes of Giacomo
I must work out my own dear purposes.
I see, as from a tower, the end of all:
Her father dead; her brother bound to me
By a dark secret, surer than the grave;
150 Her mother scared and unexpostulating
From the dread manner of her wish achieved:
And she!—Once more take courage, my faint heart;
What dares a friendless maiden matched with thee?
I have such foresight as assures success;
155 Some unbeheld divinity doth ever,
When dread events are near, stir up men's minds
To black suggestions; and he prospers best,
Not who becomes the instrument of ill,
But who can flatter the dark spirit, that makes
160 Its empire and its prey of other hearts,
Till it become his slave—as I will do.

[*EXIT.*]

ACT 3

SCENE 1

An Apartment in the Cenci Palace.
LUCRETIA; to her ENTER BEATRICE.

BEATRICE: [*She ENTERS staggering, and speaks wildly.*]
Reach me that handkerchief!—My brain is hurt;
My eyes are full of blood; just wipe them for me—
I see but indistinctly.—
LUCRETIA: My sweet child,
You have no wound; 'tis only a cold dew
5 That starts from your dear brow.—Alas, alas!
What has befallen?
BEATRICE: How comes this hair undone?
Its wandering strings must be what blind me so,
And yet I tied it fast.—O, horrible!
The pavement sinks under my feet! The walls
10 Spin round! I see a woman weeping there,
And standing calm and motionless, whilst I
Slide giddily as the world reels.—My God!
The beautiful blue heaven is flecked with blood!
The sunshine on the floor is black! The air
15 Is changed to vapours such as the dead breathe
In charnel-pits! Pah! I am choked! There creeps
A clinging, black, contaminating mist
About me—'tis substantial, heavy, thick,
I cannot pluck it from me, for it glues
20 My fingers and my limbs to one another,
And eats into my sinews, and dissolves
My flesh to a pollution, poisoning
The subtle, pure, and inmost spirit of life!
My God! I never knew what the mad felt
25 Before; for I am mad beyond all doubt!
[*More wildly.*]
No, I am dead! These putrefying limbs
Shut round and sepulchre the panting soul
Which would burst forth into the wandering air!
[*A pause.*]

What hideous thought was that I had even now?
'Tis gone; and yet its burthen remains here
O'er these dull eyes—upon this weary heart!
O, world! O, life! O, day! O, misery!
LUCRETIA: What ails thee, my poor child? She answers not:
Her spirit apprehends the sense of pain,
But not its cause; suffering has dried away
The source from which it sprung.—
BEATRICE: [*Franticly.*]   Like Parricide—
Misery has killed its father: yet its father
Never like mine—O, God! what thing am I?
LUCRETIA: My dearest child, what has your father done?
BEATRICE: [*Doubtfully.*]   Who art thou, questioner? I have no father.
[*Aside.*]
She is the madhouse nurse who tends on me,
It is a piteous office.
[*To LUCRETIA, in a slow, subdued voice.*]
                              Do you know,
I thought I was that wretched Beatrice
Men speak of, whom her father sometimes hales
From hall to hall by the entangled hair;
At others, pens up naked in damp cells
Where scaly reptiles crawl, and starves her there,
Till she will eat strange flesh. This woful story
So did I overact in my sick dreams,
That I imagined—no, it cannot be!
Horrible things have been in this wild world,
Prodigious mixtures, and confusions strange
Of good and ill; and worse have been conceived
Than ever there was found a heart to do.
But never fancy imaged such a deed
As—
[*Pauses, suddenly recollecting herself.*]
          Who art thou? Swear to me, ere I die
With fearful expectation, that indeed
Thou art not what thou seemest—Mother!
LUCRETIA: Oh!
My sweet child, know you—
BEATRICE: Yet speak it not:
For then if this be truth, that other too
Must be a truth, a firm enduring truth,
Linked with each lasting circumstance of life,
Never to change, never to pass away.
Why so it is. This is the Cenci Palace;
Thou art Lucretia; I am Beatrice.
I have talked some wild words, but will no more.
Mother, come near me: from this point of time,
I am—
[*Her voice dies away faintly.*]
LUCRETIA: Alas! what has befallen thee, child?
What has thy father done?
BEATRICE: What have I done?
Am I not innocent? Is it my crime
That one with white hair, and imperious brow,
Who tortured me from my forgotten years,
As parents only dare, should call himself
My father, yet should be!—Oh, what am I?
What name, what place, what memory shall be mine?
What retrospects, outliving even despair?
LUCRETIA: He is a violent tyrant, surely, child:
We know that death alone can make us free;
His death or ours. But what can he have done
Of deadlier outrage or worse injury?
Thou art unlike thyself; thine eyes shoot forth
A wandering and strange spirit. Speak to me,
Unlock those pallid hands whose fingers twine
With one another.
BEATRICE: 'Tis the restless life
Tortured within them. If I try to speak
I shall go mad. Ay, something must be done;
What, yet I know not—something which shall make
The thing that I have suffered but a shadow
In the dread lightning which avenges it;
Brief, rapid, irreversible, destroying
The consequence of what it cannot cure.
Some such thing is to be endured or done:
When I know what, I shall be still and calm,
And never anything will move me more.
But now!—Oh blood, which art my father's blood,
Circling through these contaminated veins,
If thou, poured forth on the polluted earth,
Could wash away the crime, and punishment
By which I suffer—no, that cannot be!
Many might doubt there were a God above
Who sees and permits evil, and so die:

That faith no agony shall obscure in me.
LUCRETIA: It must indeed have been some bitter
    wrong;
Yet what, I dare not guess. Oh! my lost child,
105 Hide not in proud impenetrable grief
Thy sufferings from my fear.
BEATRICE: I hide them not.
What are the words which you would have me speak?
I, who can feign no image in my mind
Of that which has transformed me. I, whose thought
110 Is like a ghost shrouded and folded up
In its own formless horror. Of all words,
That minister to mortal intercourse,
Which wouldst thou hear? For there is none to tell
My misery: if another ever knew
115 Aught like to it, she died as I will die,
And left it, as I must, without a name.
Death! Death! Our law and our religion call thee
A punishment and a reward. Oh, which
Have I deserved?
LUCRETIA: The peace of innocence;
120 Till in your season you be called to heaven.
Whate'er you may have suffered, you have done
No evil. Death must be the punishment
Of crime, or the reward of trampling down
The thorns which God has strewed upon the path
125 Which leads to immortality.
BEATRICE: Ay, death—
The punishment of crime. I pray thee, God,
Let me not be bewildered while I judge.
If I must live day after day, and keep
These limbs, the unworthy temple of thy spirit,
130 As a foul den from which what thou abhorrest
May mock thee, unavenged—it shall not be!
Self-murder—no that might be no escape,
For thy decree yawns like a Hell between
Our will and it.—Oh! in this mortal world
135 There is no vindication and no law
Which can adjudge and execute the doom
Of that through which I suffer.
[ENTER ORSINO.]
[*She approaches him solemnly.*]
                    Welcome, Friend!
I have to tell you that, since last we met,
I have endured a wrong so great and strange,
140 That neither life or death can give me rest.
Ask me not what it is, for there are deeds
Which have no form, sufferings which have no
    tongue.
ORSINO: And what is he who has thus injured you?
BEATRICE: The man they call my father: a dread
    name.
145 ORSINO: It cannot be—
BEATRICE: What it can be, or not,
Forbear to think. It is, and it has been;
Advise me how it shall not be again.
I thought to die; but a religious awe
Restrains me, and the dread lest death itself
150 Might be no refuge from the consciousness
Of what is yet unexpiated. Oh, speak!
ORSINO: Accuse him of the deed, and let the law
Avenge thee.
BEATRICE: Oh, ice-hearted counsellor!
If I could find a word that might make known
155 The crime of my destroyer; and that done,
My tongue should like a knife tear out the secret
Which cankers my heart's core; ay, lay all bare,
So that my unpolluted fame should be
With vilest gossips a stale mouthed story;
160 A mock, a by-word, an astonishment:—
If this were done, which never shall be done,
Think of the offender's gold, his dreaded hate,
And the strange horror of the accuser's tale,
Baffling belief, and overpowering speech;
165 Scarce whispered, unimaginable, wrapt
In hideous hints—Oh, most assured redress!
ORSINO: You will endure it then?
BEATRICE: Endure!—Orsino,
It seems your counsel is small profit.
[*Turns from him, and speaks half to herself*.]
                    Ay,
All must be suddenly resolved and done.
170 What is this undistinguishable mist
Of thoughts, which rise, like shadow after shadow,
Darkening each other?
ORSINO: Should the offender live?
Triumph in his misdeed? and make, by use,
His crime, whate'er it is, dreadful no doubt,

      Thine element; until thou mayest become
175 Utterly lost; subdued even to the hue
      Of that which thou permittest?
      BEATRICE: [*To herself.*]   Mighty death!
      Thou double-visaged shadow! Only judge!
      Rightfullest arbiter!
      [*She retires absorbed in thought.*]
      LUCRETIA: If the lightning
180 Of God has e'er descended to avenge—
      ORSINO: Blaspheme not! His high Providence commits
      Its glory on this earth, and their own wrongs
      Into the hands of men; if they neglect
      To punish crime—
      LUCRETIA: But if one, like this wretch,
185 Should mock, with gold, opinion, law, and power?
      If there be no appeal to that which makes
      The guiltiest tremble! If, because our wrongs,
      For that they are unnatural, strange and monstrous,
      Exceed all measure of belief? Oh, God!
190 If, for the very reasons which should make
      Redress most swift and sure, our injurer triumphs?
      And we, the victims, bear worse punishment
      Than that appointed for their torturer?
      ORSINO: Think not
      But that there is redress where there is wrong,
195 So we be bold enough to seize it.
      LUCRETIA: How?
      If there were any way to make all sure,
      I know not—but I think it might be good
      To—
      ORSINO: Why, his late outrage to Beatrice;
      For it is such, as I but faintly guess,
200 As makes remorse dishonour, and leaves her
      Only one duty, how she may avenge:
      You, but one refuge from ills ill endured;
      Me, but one counsel—
      LUCRETIA: For we cannot hope
      That aid, or retribution, or resource
205 Will arise thence, where every other one
      Might find them with less need.
      [*BEATRICE advances.*]
      ORSINO: Then—
      BEATRICE: Peace, Orsino!
      And, honoured Lady, while I speak, I pray,
      That you put off, as garments overworn,
      Forbearance and respect, remorse and fear,
210 And all the fit restraints of daily life,
      Which have been borne from childhood, but which now
      Would be a mockery to my holier plea.
      As I have said, I have endured a wrong,
      Which, though it be expressionless, is such
215 As asks atonement, both for what is past,
      And lest I be reserved, day after day,
      To load with crimes an overburthened soul,
      And be—what ye can dream not. I have prayed
      To God, and I have talked with my own heart,
220 And have unravelled my entangled will,
      And have at length determined what is right.
      Art thou my friend, Orsino? False or true?
      Pledge thy salvation ere I speak.
      ORSINO: I swear
      To dedicate my cunning, and my strength,
225 My silence, and whatever else is mine,
      To thy commands.
      LUCRETIA: You think we should devise His death?
      BEATRICE: And execute what is devised,
      And suddenly. We must be brief and bold.
      ORSINO: And yet most cautious.
      LUCRETIA: For the jealous laws
230 Would punish us with death and infamy
      For that which it became themselves to do.
      BEATRICE: Be cautious as ye may, but prompt. Orsino,
      What are the means?
      ORSINO: I know two dull, fierce outlaws,
      Who think man's spirit as a worm's, and they
235 Would trample out, for any slight caprice,
      The meanest or the noblest life. This mood
      Is marketable here in Rome. They sell
      What we now want.
      LUCRETIA: To-morrow, before dawn,
      Cenci will take us to that lonely rock,
240 Petrella, in the Apulian Apennines.
      If he arrive there—
      BEATRICE: He must not arrive.

ORSINO: Will it be dark before you reach the tower?
LUCRETIA: The sun will scarce be set.
BEATRICE: But I remember
Two miles on this side of the fort, the road
245 Crosses a deep ravine; 'tis rough and narrow,
And winds with short turns down the precipice;
And in its depth there is a mighty rock,
Which has, from unimaginable years,
Sustained itself with terror and with toil
250 Over a gulf, and with the agony
With which it clings seems slowly coming down;
Even as a wretched soul hour after hour,
Clings to the mass of life; yet clinging, leans;
And leaning, makes more dark the dread abyss
255 In which it fears to fall: beneath this crag
Huge as despair, as if in weariness,
The melancholy mountain yawns—below,
You hear but see not an impetuous torrent
Raging among the caverns, and a bridge
260 Crosses the chasm; and high above there grow,
With intersecting trunks, from crag to crag,
Cedars, and yews, and pines; whose tangled hair
Is matted in one solid roof of shade
By the dark ivy's twine. At noon-day here
265 'Tis twilight and at sunset blackest night.
ORSINO: Before you reach that bridge make some
    excuse
For spurring on your mules, or loitering
Until—
BEATRICE: What sound is that?
LUCRETIA: Hark! No, it cannot be a servant's step;
270 It must be Cenci, unexpectedly
Returned—Make some excuse for being here.
BEATRICE: [*To* ORSINO *as she goes out.*] That step
    we hear approach must never pass
The bridge of which we spoke.
    [EXEUNT LUCRETIA *and* BEATRICE.]
ORSINO: What shall I do?
Cenci must find me here, and I must bear
275 The imperious inquisition of his looks
As to what brought me hither: let me mask
Mine own in some inane and vacant smile.
[ENTER GIACOMO, *in a hurried manner.*]
How! Have you ventured hither? know you then

That Cenci is from home?
GIACOMO: I sought him here;
280 And now must wait till he returns.
ORSINO: Great God!
Weigh you the danger of this rashness?
GIACOMO: Ay!
Does my destroyer know his danger? We
Are now no more, as once, parent and child,
But man to man; the oppressor to the oppressed;
285 The slanderer to the slandered; foe to foe.
He has cast Nature off, which was his shield,
And Nature casts him off, who is her shame;
And I spurn both. Is it a father's throat
Which I will shake? and say, I ask not gold;
290 I ask not happy years; nor memories
Of tranquil childhood; nor home-sheltered love;
Though all these hast thou torn from me, and more;
But only my fair fame; only one hoard
Of peace, which I thought hidden from thy hate,
295 Under the penury heaped on me by thee;
Or I will—God can understand and pardon,
Why should I speak with man?
ORSINO: Be calm, dear friend.
GIACOMO: Well, I will calmly tell you what he did.
This old Francesco Cenci, as you know,
300 Borrowed the dowry of my wife from me,
And then denied the loan; and left me so
In poverty, the which I sought to mend
By holding a poor office in the state.
It had been promised to me, and already
305 I bought new clothing for my ragged babes,
And my wife smiled; and my heart knew repose;
When Cenci's intercession, as I found,
Conferred this office on a wretch, whom thus
He paid for vilest service. I returned
310 With this ill news, and we sate sad together
Solacing our despondency with tears
Of such affection and unbroken faith
As temper life's worst bitterness; when he,
As he is wont, came to upbraid and curse,
315 Mocking our poverty, and telling us
Such was God's scourge for disobedient sons.
And then, that I might strike him dumb with shame,
I spoke of my wife's dowry; but he coined

A brief yet specious tale, how I had wasted
320 The sum in secret riot; and he saw
My wife was touched, and he went smiling forth.
And when I knew the impression he had made,
And felt my wife insult with silent scorn
My ardent truth, and look averse and cold,
325 I went forth too: but soon returned again;
Yet not so soon but that my wife had taught
My children her harsh thoughts, and they all cried,
"Give us clothes, father! Give us better food!
What you in one night squander were enough
330 For months!" I looked, and saw that home was hell.
And to that hell will I return no more
Until mine enemy has rendered up
Atonement, or, as he gave life to me
I will, reversing nature's law—
ORSINO: Trust me,
335 The compensation which thou seekest here
Will be denied.
GIACOMO: Then—Are you not my friend?
Did you not hint at the alternative,
Upon the brink of which you see I stand,
The other day when we conversed together?
340 My wrongs were then less. That word parricide,
Although I am resolved, haunts me like fear.
ORSINO: It must be fear itself, for the bare word
Is hollow mockery. Mark, how wisest God
Draws to one point the threads of a just doom,
345 So sanctifying it: what you devise
Is, as it were, accomplished.
GIACOMO: Is he dead?
ORSINO: His grave is ready. Know that since we met
Cenci has done an outrage to his daughter.
GIACOMO: What outrage?
ORSINO: That she speaks not, but you may
350 Conceive such half conjectures as I do,
From her fixed paleness, and the lofty grief
Of her stern brow, bent on the idle air,
And her severe unmodulated voice,
Drowning both tenderness and dread; and last
355 From this; that whilst her step-mother and I,

Bewildered in our horror, talked together
With obscure hints; both self-misunderstood,
And darkly guessing, stumbling, in our talk,
Over the truth, and yet to its revenge,
360 She interrupted us, and with a look
Which told before she spoke it, he must die—
GIACOMO: It is enough. My doubts are well appeased;
There is a higher reason for the act
Than mine; there is a holier judge than me,
365 A more unblamed avenger. Beatrice,
Who in the gentleness of thy sweet youth
Hast never trodden on a worm, or bruised
A living flower, but thou hast pitied it
With needless tears! Fair sister, thou in whom
370 Men wondered how such loveliness and wisdom
Did not destroy each other! Is there made
Ravage of thee? O, heart, I ask no more
Justification! Shall I wait, Orsino,
Till he return, and stab him at the door?
375 ORSINO: Not so; some accident might interpose
To rescue him from what is now most sure;
And you are unprovided where to fly,
How to excuse or to conceal. Nay, listen:
All is contrived; success is so assured
380 That—
[ENTER BEATRICE.]
BEATRICE: 'Tis my brother's voice! You know me not?
GIACOMO: My sister, my lost sister!
BEATRICE: Lost indeed!
I see Orsino has talked with you, and
That you conjecture things too horrible
To speak, yet far less than the truth. Now, stay not,
385 He might return: yet kiss me; I shall know
That then thou hast consented to his death.
Farewell, Farewell! Let piety to God,
Brotherly love, justice and clemency,
And all things that make tender hardest hearts,
390 Make thine hard, brother. Answer not—farewell.
                                      [EXEUNT severally.]

SCENE 2

*A mean Apartment in GIACOMO'S House.
GIACOMO alone.*

GIACOMO: 'Tis midnight, and Orsino comes not yet.
[*Thunder, and the sound of a storm.*]
What! can the everlasting elements
Feel with a worm like man? If so, the shaft
Of mercy-winged lightning would not fall
5 On stones and trees. My wife and children sleep:
They are now living in unmeaning dreams:
But I must wake, still doubting if that deed
Be just which was most necessary. O,
Thou unreplenished lamp! whose narrow fire
10 Is shaken by the wind, and on whose edge
Devouring darkness hovers! Thou small flame,
Which, as a dying pulse rises and falls,
Still flickerest up and down, how very soon,
Did I not feed thee, wouldst thou fail and be
15 As thou hadst never been! So wastes and sinks
Even now, perhaps, the life that kindled mine:
But that no power can fill with vital oil
That broken lamp of flesh. Ha! 'tis the blood
Which fed these veins that ebbs till all is cold:
20 It is the form that moulded mine, that sinks
Into the white and yellow spasms of death:
It is the soul by which mine was arrayed
In God's immortal likeness which now stands
Naked before Heaven's judgment-seat!
[*A bell strikes.*]
                              One! Two!
25 The hours crawl on; and when my hairs are white
My son will then perhaps be waiting thus,
Tortured between just hate and vain remorse;
Chiding the tardy messenger of news
Like those which I expect. I almost wish
30 He be not dead, although my wrongs are great;
Yet—'tis Orsino's step—
[ENTER ORSINO.]
                              Speak!
ORSINO: I am come
To say he has escaped.
GIACOMO: Escaped!
ORSINO: And safe
Within Petrella. He passed by the spot
Appointed for the deed an hour too soon.
35 GIACOMO: Are we the fools of such contingencies?
And do we waste in blind misgivings thus
The hours when we should act? Then wind and thunder,
Which seemed to howl his knell, is the loud laughter
With which Heaven mocks our weakness! I henceforth
40 Will ne'er repent of aught designed or done,
But my repentance.
ORSINO: See, the lamp is out.
GIACOMO: If no remorse is ours when the dim air
Has drank this innocent flame, why should we quail
When Cenci's life, that light by which ill spirits
45 See the worst deeds they prompt, shall sink for ever?
No, I am hardened.
ORSINO: Why, what need of this?
Who feared the pale intrusion of remorse
In a just deed? Although our first plan failed,
Doubt not but he will soon be laid to rest.
50 But light the lamp; let us not talk i' the dark.
GIACOMO: [*Lighting the lamp.*]   And yet once quenched I cannot thus relume
My father's life: do you not think his ghost
Might plead that argument with God?
ORSINO: Once gone,
You cannot now recall your sister's peace;
55 Your own extinguished years of youth and hope;
Nor your wife's bitter words; nor all the taunts
Which, from the prosperous, weak misfortune takes;
Nor your dead mother; nor—
GIACOMO: O, speak no more!
I am resolved, although this very hand
60 Must quench the life that animated it.
ORSINO: There is no need of that. Listen: you know
Olimpio, the castellan of Petrella
In old Colonna's[1] time; him whom your father

---

[1] Cenci had complained to Colonna, the powerful owner of Petrella, who had discharged the castle's caretaker, Olimpio.

Degraded from his post? And Marzio,
That desperate wretch, whom he deprived last year
Of a reward of blood, well earned and due?
GIACOMO: I knew Olimpio; and they say he hated
Old Cenci so, that in his silent rage
His lips grew white only to see him pass.
Of Marzio I know nothing.
ORSINO: Marzio's hate
Matches Olimpio's. I have sent these men,
But in your name, and as at your request,
To talk with Beatrice and Lucretia.
GIACOMO: Only to talk?
ORSINO: The moments which even now
Pass onward to to-morrow's midnight hour
May memorise their flight with death: ere then
They must have talked, and may perhaps have done,
And made an end.
GIACOMO: Listen! What sound is that?
ORSINO: The house-dog moans, and the beams
   crack: nought else.
GIACOMO: It is my wife complaining in her sleep:
I doubt not she is saying bitter things
Of me; and all my children round her dreaming
That I deny them sustenance.
ORSINO: Whilst he
Who truly took it from them, and who fills
Their hungry rest with bitterness, now sleeps
Lapped in bad pleasures, and triumphantly
Mocks thee in visions of successful hate
Too like the truth of day.
GIACOMO: If e'er he wakes
Again, I will not trust to hireling hands—
ORSINO: Why, that were well. I must be gone;
   good night!
When next we meet may all be done!
GIACOMO: And all
Forgotten: Oh, that I had never been!
[EXEUNT.]

ACT 4

SCENE 1

An Apartment in the Castle of Petrella. ENTER CENCI.

CENCI: She comes not; yet I left her even now
Vanquished and faint. She knows the penalty
Of her delay; yet what if threats are vain?
Am I not now within Petrella's moat?
Or fear I still the eyes and ears of Rome?
Might I not drag her by the golden hair?
Stamp on her? Keep her sleepless till her brain
Be overworn? Tame her with chains and famine?
Less would suffice. Yet so to leave undone
What I most seek! No, 'tis her stubborn will,
Which, by its own consent, shall stoop as low
As that which drags it down.
[ENTER LUCRETIA.]
                Thou loathed wretch!
Hide thee from my abhorrence; fly, begone!
Yet stay! Bid Beatrice come hither.
LUCRETIA: Oh,
Husband! I pray, for thine own wretched sake,
Heed what thou dost. A man who walks like thee
Through crimes, and through the danger of his crimes,
Each hour may stumble o'er a sudden grave.
And thou art old; thy hairs are hoary grey;
As thou wouldst save thyself from death and hell,
Pity thy daughter; give her to some friend
In marriage: so that she may tempt thee not
To hatred, or worse thoughts, if worse there be.
CENCI: What! like her sister, who has found a home
To mock my hate from with prosperity?
Strange ruin shall destroy both her and thee,
And all that yet remain. My death may be
Rapid, her destiny outspeeds it. Go,
Bid her come hither, and before my mood
Be changed, lest I should drag her by the hair.
LUCRETIA: She sent me to thee, husband. At thy presence

She fell, as thou dost know, into a trance;
And in that trance she heard a voice which said,
"Cenci must die! Let him confess himself!
35 Even now the accusing angel waits to hear
If God, to punish his enormous crimes,
Harden his dying heart!"
CENCI: Why—such things are:
No doubt divine revealings may be made.
'Tis plain I have been favoured from above,
40 For when I cursed my sons, they died.—Aye—so—
As to the right or wrong, that's talk—repentance—
Repentance is an easy moment's work,
And more depends on God than me. Well—well—
I must give up the greater point, which was
45 To poison and corrupt her soul.
[*A pause; LUCRETIA approaches anxiously, and then shrinks back as he speaks.*]
                              One, two;
Ay—Rocco and Cristofano my curse
Strangled: and Giacomo, I think, will find
Life a worse Hell than that beyond the grave:
Beatrice shall, if there be skill in hate,
50 Die in despair, blaspheming: to Bernardo,
He is so innocent, I will bequeath
The memory of these deeds, and make his youth
The sepulchre of hope, where evil thoughts
Shall grow like weeds on a neglected tomb.
55 When all is done, out in the wide Campagna,[1]
I will pile up my silver and my gold;
My costly robes, paintings, and tapestries;
My parchments and all records of my wealth;
And make a bonfire in my joy, and leave
60 Of my possessions nothing but my name;
Which shall be an inheritance to strip
Its wearer bare as infamy. That done,
My soul, which is a scourge, will I resign
Into the hands of him who wielded it;
65 Be it for its own punishment or theirs,
He will not ask it of me till the lash
Be broken in its last and deepest wound;
Until its hate be all inflicted. Yet,
Lest death outspeed my purpose, let me make
70 Short work and sure.
                              [*Going.*]
LUCRETIA: [*Stops him.*]
                        Oh, stay! It was a feint:
She had no vision, and she heard no voice.
I said it but to awe thee.
CENCI: That is well.
Vile palterer with the sacred truth of God,
Be thy soul choked with that blaspheming lie!
75 For Beatrice, worse terrors are in store,
To bend her to my will.
LUCRETIA: Oh! to what will?
What cruel sufferings, more than she has known,
Canst thou inflict?
CENCI: Andrea! go, call my daughter,
And if she comes not, tell her that I come.
80 What sufferings? I will drag her, step by step,
Through infamies unheard of among men:
She shall stand shelterless in the broad noon
Of public scorn, for acts blazoned abroad,
One among which shall be—What? Canst thou guess?
85 She shall become [for what she most abhors
Shall have a fascination to entrap
Her loathing will], to her own conscious self
All she appears to others; and when dead,
As she shall die unshrived and unforgiven,
90 A rebel to her father and her God,
Her corpse shall be abandoned to the hounds;[2]
Her name shall be the terror of the earth;
Her spirit shall approach the throne of God
Plague-spotted with my curses. I will make
95 Body and soul a monstrous lump of ruin.
[ENTER ANDREA.]
ANDREA: The Lady Beatrice—
CENCI: Speak, pale slave! What
  Said she?
ANDREA: My Lord, 'twas what she looked; she said:
"Go tell my father that I see the gulf
Of Hell between us two, which he may pass,
100 I will not."
                              [*EXIT ANDREA.*]
CENCI: Go thou quick, Lucretia,

---

[1] the countryside around Rome, at one time largely deserted.

[2] Cf. the fate of Jezebel, 2 Kings 9.30–37.

Tell her to come; yet let her understand
Her coming is consent: and say, moreover,
That if she come not I will curse her.
                                    [EXIT LUCRETIA.]
                                    Ha!
With what but with a father's curse doth God
105 Panic-strike armed victory, and make pale
Cities in their prosperity? The world's Father
Must grant a parent's prayer against his child,
Be he who asks even what men call me.
Will not the deaths of her rebellious brothers
110 Awe her before I speak? For I on them
Did imprecate quick ruin, and it came.
[ENTER LUCRETIA.]
Well; what? Speak, wretch!
LUCRETIA: She said, "I cannot come;
Go tell my father that I see a torrent
Of his own blood raging between us."
CENCI: [Kneeling.]   God,
115 Hear me! If this most specious mass of flesh,
Which thou hast made my daughter; this my blood,
This particle of my divided being;
Or rather, this my bane and my disease,
Whose sight infects and poisons me; this devil
120 Which sprung from me as from a hell, was meant
To aught good use; if her bright loveliness
Was kindled to illumine this dark world;
If nursed by thy selectest dew of love,
Such virtues blossom in her as should make
125 The peace of life, I pray thee for my sake,
As thou the common God and Father art
Of her, and me, and all; reverse that doom!
Earth, in the name of God, let her food be
Poison, until she be encrusted round
130 With leprous stains! Heaven, rain upon her head
The blistering drops of the Maremma's dew[1]
Till she be speckled like a toad; parch up
Those love-enkindled lips, warp those fine limbs
To loathed lameness! All-beholding sun,
135 Strike in thine envy those life-darting eyes
With thine own blinding beams!

LUCRETIA: Peace! peace!
For thine own sake unsay those dreadful words.
When high God grants, he punishes such prayers.
CENCI: [Leaping up, and throwing his right hand
towards Heaven.]   He does his will, I mine! This
    in addition,
140 That if she have a child—
LUCRETIA: Horrible thought!
CENCI: That if she ever have a child; and thou,
Quick Nature! I adjure thee by thy God,
That thou be fruitful in her, and increase
And multiply,[2] fulfilling his command,
145 And my deep imprecation! May it be
A hideous likeness of herself; that as
From a distorting mirror, she may see
Her image mixed with what she most abhors,
Smiling upon her from her nursing breast.
150 And that the child may from its infancy
Grow, day by day, more wicked and deformed,
Turning her mother's love to misery:
And that both she and it may live, until
It shall repay her care and pain with hate,
155 Or what may else be more unnatural.[3]
So he may hunt her through the clamorous scoffs
Of the loud world to a dishonoured grave.
Shall I revoke this curse? Go, bid her come,
Before my words are chronicled in heaven.
                                    [EXIT LUCRETIA.]
160 I do not feel as if I were a man,
But like a fiend appointed to chastise
The offences of some unremembered world.
My blood is running up and down my veins!
A fearful pleasure makes it prick and tingle:
165 I feel a giddy sickness of strange awe;
My heart is beating with an expectation
Of horrid joy.
[ENTER LUCRETIA.]
                    What? Speak!
LUCRETIA: She bids thee curse;
And if thy curses, as they cannot do,
Could kill her soul—

---

[1] Maremma, a coastal region near Pisa, whose climate was notoriously unwholesome.

[2] Cf. Genesis 1.28.

[3] Cf. Shakespeare, *King Lear* 1.4.281–89.

CENCI: She would not come. 'Tis well,
170 I can do both: first take what I demand,
And then extort concession. To thy chamber!
Fly ere I spurn thee: and beware this night
That thou cross not my footsteps. It were safer
To come between the tiger and his prey.
[EXIT LUCRETIA.]
175 It must be late; mine eyes grow weary dim
With unaccustomed heaviness of sleep.
Conscience! Oh, thou most insolent of lies!
They say that sleep, that healing dew of heaven,
Steeps not in balm the foldings of the brain
180 Which thinks thee an impostor. I will go,
First to belie thee with an hour of rest,
Which will be deep and calm, I feel: and then—
O, multitudinous Hell, the fiends will shake
Thine arches with the laughter of their joy!
185 There shall be lamentation heard in Heaven
As o'er an angel fallen; and upon Earth
All good shall droop and sicken, and ill things
Shall, with a spirit of unnatural life,
Stir and be quickened—even as I am now.
[EXIT.]

SCENE 2

Before the Castle of Petrella. ENTER BEATRICE *and* LUCRETIA *above on the ramparts.*

BEATRICE: They come not yet.
LUCRETIA: 'Tis scarce midnight.
BEATRICE: How slow
Behind the course of thought, even sick with speed,
Lags leaden-footed time!
LUCRETIA: The minutes pass—
If he should wake before the deed is done?
5 BEATRICE: O Mother! He must never wake again.
What thou hast said persuades me that our act
Will but dislodge a spirit of deep hell
Out of a human form.
LUCRETIA: 'Tis true he spoke
Of death and judgment with strange confidence
10 For one so wicked; as a man believing
In God, yet recking not of good or ill.
And yet to die without confession!—
BEATRICE: Oh!
Believe that Heaven is merciful and just,
And will not add our dread necessity
15 To the amount of his offences.
[ENTER OLIMPIO *and* MARZIO, *below.*]
LUCRETIA: See,
They come.
BEATRICE: All mortal things must hasten thus
To their dark end. Let us go down.
[EXEUNT LUCRETIA *and* BEATRICE *from above.*]
OLIMPIO: How feel you to this work?
MARZIO: As one who thinks
A thousand crowns excellent market price
20 For an old murderer's life. Your cheeks are pale.
OLIMPIO: It is the white reflection of your own,
Which you call pale.
MARZIO: Is that their natural hue?
OLIMPIO: Or 'tis my hate, and the deferred desire
To wreak it, which extinguishes their blood.
25 MARZIO: You are inclined then to this business?
OLIMPIO: Ay,
If one should bribe me with a thousand crowns
To kill a serpent which had stung my child,
I could not be more willing.
[ENTER BEATRICE *and* LUCRETIA *below.*]
Noble ladies!
BEATRICE: Are ye resolved?
OLIMPIO: Is he asleep?
MARZIO: Is all
30 Quiet?
LUCRETIA: I mixed an opiate with his drink:
He sleeps so soundly—
BEATRICE: That his death will be
But as a change of sin-chastising dreams,
A dark continuance of the Hell within him,
Which God extinguish! But ye are resolved?
35 Ye know it is a high and holy deed?
OLIMPIO: We are resolved.
MARZIO: As to the how this act
Be warranted, it rests with you.
BEATRICE: Well, follow!
OLIMPIO: Hush! Hark! What noise is that?

MARZIO: Ha!
some one comes!
BEATRICE: Ye conscience-stricken cravens, rock to rest
40 Your baby hearts. It is the iron gate,
Which ye left open, swinging to the wind,
That enters whistling as in scorn. Come, follow!
And be your steps like mine, light, quick, and bold.
[EXEUNT.]

SCENE 3

An Apartment in the Castle.
ENTER BEATRICE and LUCRETIA.

LUCRETIA: They are about it now.
BEATRICE: Nay, it is done.
LUCRETIA: I have not heard him groan.
BEATRICE: He will not groan.
LUCRETIA: What sound is that?
BEATRICE: List! 'tis the tread of feet
About his bed.
LUCRETIA: My God!
5 If he be now a cold stiff corpse—
BEATRICE: O, fear not
What may be done, but what is left undone:
The act seals all.
[ENTER OLIMPIO and MARZIO.]
Is it accomplished?
MARZIO: What?
OLIMPIO: Did you not call?
BEATRICE: When?
OLIMPIO: Now.
BEATRICE: I ask if all is over?
OLIMPIO: We dare not kill an old and sleeping man;
10 His thin gray hair, his stern and reverent brow,
His veined hands crossed on his heaving breast,
And the calm innocent sleep in which he lay,
Quelled me. Indeed, indeed, I cannot do it.
MARZIO: But I was bolder; for I chid Olimpio,
15 And bade him bear his wrongs to his own grave,
And leave me the reward. And now my knife
Touched the loose wrinkled throat, when the old man
Stirred in his sleep, and said, "God! hear, O hear,
A father's curse! What, art thou not our father?"
20 And then he laughed. I knew it was the ghost
Of my dead father speaking through his lips,
And could not kill him.
BEATRICE: Miserable slaves!
Where, if ye dare not kill a sleeping man,
Found ye the boldness to return to me
25 With such a deed undone? Base palterers!
Cowards and traitors! Why, the very conscience
Which ye would sell for gold and for revenge
Is an equivocation: it sleeps over
A thousand daily acts disgracing men;
30 And when a deed where mercy insults heaven—
Why do I talk?
[*Snatching a dagger from one of them and raising it.*]
Hadst thou a tongue to say,
She murdered her own father, I must do it!
But never dream ye shall outlive him long!
OLIMPIO: Stop, for God's sake!
MARZIO: I will go back and kill him.
35 OLIMPIO: Give me the weapon, we must do thy will.
BEATRICE: Take it! Depart! Return!
[EXEUNT OLIMPIO and MARZIO.]
How pale thou art!
We do but that which 'twere a deadly crime
To leave undone.
LUCRETIA: Would it were done!
BEATRICE: Even whilst
That doubt is passing through your mind, the world
40 Is conscious of a change. Darkness and hell
Have swallowed up the vapor they sent forth
To blacken the sweet light of life. My breath
Comes, methinks, lighter, and the jellied blood
Runs freely through my veins. Hark!
[ENTER OLIMPIO and MARZIO.]
He is—
OLIMPIO: Dead!
45 MARZIO: We strangled him, that there might be no blood;

And then we threw his heavy corpse i' the garden
Under the balcony; 'twill seem it fell.
BEATRICE: [*Giving them a bag of coin.*] Here
　　take this gold, and hasten to your homes.
And, Marzio, because thou wast only awed
50 By that which made me tremble, wear thou this!
[*Clothes him in a rich mantle.*]
It was the mantle which my grandfather
Wore in his high prosperity, and men
Envied his state: so may they envy thine.
Thou wert a weapon in the hand of God
55 To a just use. Live long and thrive! And, mark,
If thou hast crimes, repent: this deed is none.
[*A horn is sounded.*]
LUCRETIA: 　Hark, 'tis the castle horn: my God! it sounds
Like the last trump.
BEATRICE: 　　　Some tedious guest is coming.
LUCRETIA: 　The drawbridge is let down; there is a tramp
60 Of horses in the court! fly, hide yourselves!
　　　　　　[*EXEUNT OLIMPIO and MARZIO.*]
BEATRICE: 　Let us retire to counterfeit deep rest;
I scarcely need to counterfeit it now:
The spirit which doth reign within these limbs
Seems strangely undisturbed. I could even sleep
65 Fearless and calm: all ill is surely past.
　　　　　　　　　　[*EXEUNT.*]

SCENE 4

Another Apartment in the Castle. ENTER *on one side the Legate* SAVELLA, *introduced by a Servant, and on the other* LUCRETIA *and* BERNARDO.

SAVELLA: 　Lady, my duty to his Holiness
Be my excuse that thus unseasonably
I break upon your rest. I must speak with
Count Cenci; doth he sleep?
LUCRETIA: 　[*In a hurried and confused manner.*]
　　　　　　　　I think he sleeps;
5 Yet, wake him not, I pray, spare me awhile,
He is a wicked and a wrathful man;
Should he be roused out of his sleep to-night,
Which is, I know, a hell of angry dreams,
It were not well; indeed it were not well.
10 Wait till day break.—
[*Aside.*]
　　　　　　　O, I am deadly sick!
SAVELLA: 　I grieve thus to distress you, but the Count
Must answer charges of the gravest import,
And suddenly; such my commission is.
LUCRETIA: [*With increased agitation.*] I dare not
　　rouse him, I know none who dare;
15 'Twere perilous;—you might as safely waken
A serpent; or a corpse in which some fiend
Were laid to sleep.
SAVELLA: 　　　Lady, my moments here
Are counted. I must rouse him from his sleep,
Since none else dare.
LUCRETIA: 　[*Aside.*] O, terror! O, despair!
[*To BERNARDO.*]
20 Bernardo, conduct you the Lord Legate to
Your father's chamber.
　　　　　　[*EXEUNT SAVELLA and BERNARDO.*]
[*ENTER BEATRICE.*]
BEATRICE: 　　　'Tis a messenger
Come to arrest the culprit who now stands
Before the throne of unappealable God.
Both Earth and Heaven, consenting arbiters,
25 Acquit our deed.
LUCRETIA: 　　　Oh, agony of fear!
Would that he yet might live! Even now I heard
The legate's followers whisper as they passed
They had a warrant for his instant death.
All was prepared by unforbidden means,
30 Which we must pay so dearly, having done.
Even now they search the tower, and find the body;
Now they suspect the truth; now they consult
Before they come to tax us with the fact;
Oh, horrible, 'tis all discovered!
BEATRICE: 　　　　　Mother,
35 What is done wisely, is done well. Be bold
As thou art just. 'Tis like a truant child,
To fear that others know what thou hast done,
Even from thine own strong consciousness, and thus

Write on unsteady eyes and altered cheeks
All thou wouldst hide. Be faithful to thyself, [40]
And fear no other witness but thy fear.
For if, as cannot be, some circumstance
Should rise in accusation, we can blind
Suspicion with such cheap astonishment,
Or overbear it with such guiltless pride, [45]
As murderers cannot feign. The deed is done,
And what may follow now regards not me.
I am as universal as the light;
Free as the earth-surrounding air; as firm
As the world's centre. Consequence, to me, [50]
Is as the wind which strikes the solid rock,
But shakes it not.
    [*A cry within and tumult.*]
VOICES: Murder! Murder! Murder!
[ENTER BERNARDO and SAVELLA.]
SAVELLA: [*To his followers.*]   Go, search the castle
    round; sound the alarm;
    Look to the gates that none escape!
BEATRICE: What now?
BERNARDO: I know not what to say—my father's [55]
    dead.
BEATRICE: How, dead? he only sleeps; you mistake,
    brother.
    His sleep is very calm, very like death;
    'Tis wonderful how well a tyrant sleeps.
    He is not *dead*?
BERNARDO: Dead; murdered!
LUCRETIA: [*With extreme agitation.*]   Oh, no, no,
    He is not murdered, though he may be dead; [60]
    I have alone the keys of those apartments.
SAVELLA: Ha! Is it so?
BEATRICE: My Lord, I pray excuse us;
    We will retire; my mother is not well;
    She seems quite overcome with this strange horror.
            [EXEUNT LUCRETIA and BEATRICE.]
SAVELLA: Can you suspect who may have murdered [65]
    him?
BERNARDO: I know not what to think.
SAVELLA: Can you
    name any
    Who had an interest in his death?
BERNARDO: Alas!
    I can name none who had not, and those most
    Who most lament that such a deed is done;
    My mother, and my sister, and myself. [70]
SAVELLA: 'Tis strange! There were clear marks of
    violence.
    I found the old man's body in the moonlight,
    Hanging beneath the window of his chamber
    Among the branches of a pine: he could not
    Have fallen there, for all his limbs lay heaped [75]
    And effortless; 'tis true there was no blood.—
    Favour me, Sir—it much imports your house
    That all should be made clear—to tell the ladies
    That I request their presence.
                [EXIT BERNARDO.]
[ENTER Guards, bringing in MARZIO.]
GUARD: We have one.
OFFICER: My Lord, we found this ruffian and [80]
    another
    Lurking among the rocks; there is no doubt
    But that they are the murderers of Count Cenci;
    Each had a bag of coin; this fellow wore
    A gold-inwoven robe, which, shining bright
    Under the dark rocks to the glimmering moon, [85]
    Betrayed them to our notice; the other fell
    Desperately fighting.
SAVELLA: What does he confess?
OFFICERS: He keeps firm silence; but these lines
    found on him
    May speak.
SAVELLA: Their language is at least sincere.
[*Reads.*]
    "TO THE LADY BEATRICE: [90]
    That the atonement of what my nature sickens to
    conjecture may soon arrive, I send thee, at thy brother's
    desire, those who will speak and do more than I dare write.
            Thy devoted servant,
                ORSINO."
[ENTER LUCRETIA, BEATRICE, and BERNARDO.]
    Knowest thou this writing, lady? [95]
BEATRICE: No.
SAVELLA: Nor thou?
LUCRETIA: [*Her conduct throughout the scene is marked
    by extreme agitation.*]   Where was it found? What is it?
    It should be

Orsino's hand! It speaks of that strange horror
Which never yet found utterance, but which made
Between that hapless child and her dead father
100 A gulf of obscure hatred.
   SAVELLA: Is it so,
Is it true, Lady, that thy father did
Such outrages as to awaken in thee
Unfilial hate?
   BEATRICE: Not hate, 'twas more than hate;
This is most true, yet wherefore question me?
105   SAVELLA: There is a deed demanding question done;
Thou hast a secret which will answer not.
   BEATRICE: What sayest? My Lord, your words
      are bold and rash.
   SAVELLA: I do arrest all present in the name
Of the Pope's Holiness. You must to Rome.
110   LUCRETIA: O, not to Rome! Indeed we are not
      guilty.
   BEATRICE: Guilty! Who dares talk of guilt? My lord,
I am more innocent of parricide
Than is a child born fatherless. Dear mother,
Your gentleness and patience are no shield
115 For this keen-judging world, this two-edged lie,
Which seems, but is not. What! will human laws,
Rather will ye who are their ministers,
Bar all access to retribution first,
And then, when Heaven doth interpose to do
120 What ye neglect, arming familiar things
To the redress of an unwonted crime,
Make ye the victims who demanded it
Culprits? 'Tis ye are culprits! That poor wretch
Who stands so pale, and trembling, and amazed,
125 If it be true he murdered Cenci, was
A sword in the right hand of justest God.
Wherefore should I have wielded it? unless
The crimes which mortal tongue dare never name,
God therefore scruples to avenge.
   SAVELLA: You own
130 That you desired his death?
   BEATRICE: It would have been
A crime no less than his, if for one moment
That fierce desire had faded in my heart.
'Tis true I did believe, and hope, and pray,
Ay, I even knew—for God is wise and just,

135 That some strange sudden death hung over him.
'Tis true that this did happen, and most true
There was no other rest for me on earth,
No other hope in Heaven;—now what of this?
   SAVELLA: Strange thoughts beget strange deeds;
      and here are both:
140 I judge thee not.
   BEATRICE: And yet, if you arrest me,
You are the judge and executioner
Of that which is the life of life: the breath
Of accusation kills an innocent name,
145 And leaves for lame acquittal the poor life,
Which is a mask without it. 'Tis most false
That I am guilty of foul parricide;
Although I must rejoice, for justest cause,
That other hands have sent my father's soul
150 To ask the mercy he denied to me.
Now leave us free: stain not a noble house
With vague surmises of rejected crime;
Add to our sufferings and your own neglect
No heavier sum; let them have been enough:
Leave us the wreck we have.
   SAVELLA: I dare not, Lady.
155 I pray that you prepare yourselves for Rome:
There the Pope's further pleasure will be known.
   LUCRETIA: O, not to Rome! O, take us not to Rome!
   BEATRICE: Why not to Rome, dear mother?
      There, as here,
Our innocence is as an armed heel
160 To trample accusation. God is there
As here, and with his shadow ever clothes
The innocent, the injured, and the weak;
And such are we. Cheer up, dear Lady, lean
On me; collect your wandering thoughts. My Lord,
165 As soon as you have taken some refreshment,
And had all such examinations made
Upon the spot, as may be necessary
To the full understanding of this matter,
We shall be ready. Mother; will you come?
170   LUCRETIA: Ha! they will bind us to the rack, and
      wrest
Self-accusation from our agony!
Will Giacomo be there? Orsino? Marzio?
All present; all confronted; all demanding

Each from the other's countenance the thing
175 Which is in every heart! O, misery!
   [*She faints, and is borne out.*]
   SAVELLA: She faints; an ill appearance this.
   BEATRICE: My Lord,
   She knows not yet the uses of the world.
   She fears that power is as a beast which grasps
   And loosens not: a snake whose look transmutes
180 All things to guilt which is its nutriment.
   She cannot know how well the supine slaves
   Of blind authority read the truth of things
   When written on a brow of guilelessness:
   She sees not yet triumphant Innocence
185 Stand at the judgment-seat of mortal man,
   A judge and an accuser of the wrong
   Which drags it there. Prepare yourself, My Lord;
   Our suite will join yours in the court below.
                                    [EXEUNT.]

ACT 5

SCENE 1

An Apartment in ORSINO's Palace.
ENTER ORSINO and GIACOMO.

   GIACOMO: Do evil deeds thus quickly come to end?
   O, that the vain remorse which must chastise
   Crimes done, had but as loud a voice to warn
   As its keen sting is mortal to avenge!
5 O, that the hour when present had cast off
   The mantle of its mystery, and shown
   The ghastly form with which it now returns
   When its scared game is roused, cheering the hounds
   Of conscience to their prey! Alas! alas!
10 It was a wicked thought, a piteous deed,
   To kill an old and hoary-headed father.
   ORSINO: It has turned out unluckily, in truth.
   GIACOMO: To violate the sacred doors of sleep;
   To cheat kind nature of the placid death
15 Which she prepares for overwearied age;
   To drag from Heaven an unrepentant soul
   Which might have quenched in reconciling prayers
   A life of burning crimes—
   ORSINO: You cannot say
   I urged you to the deed.
   GIACOMO: O, had I never
20 Found in thy smooth and ready countenance
   The mirror of my darkest thoughts; hadst thou
   Never with hints and questions made me look
   Upon the monster of my thought, until
   It grew familiar to desire—
   ORSINO: 'Tis thus
25 Men cast the blame of their unprosperous acts
   Upon the abettors of their own resolve;
   Or any thing but their weak, guilty selves.
   And yet, confess the truth, it is the peril
   In which you stand that gives you this pale sickness
30 Of penitence; confess, 'tis fear disguised
   From its own shame that takes the mantle now
   Of thin remorse. What if we yet were safe?
   GIACOMO: How can that be? Already Beatrice,
   Lucretia and the murderer, are in prison.
35 I doubt not officers are, whilst we speak,
   Sent to arrest us.
   ORSINO: I have all prepared
   For instant flight. We can escape even now,
   So we take fleet occasion by the hair.
   GIACOMO: Rather expire in tortures, as I may.
40 What! will you cast by self-accusing flight
   Assured conviction upon Beatrice?
   She, who alone in this unnatural work
   Stands like God's angel ministered upon
   By fiends; avenging such a nameless wrong
45 As turns black parricide to piety;
   Whilst we for basest ends—I fear, Orsino,
   While I consider all your words and looks,
   Comparing them with your proposal now,
   That you must be a villain. For what end
50 Could you engage in such a perilous crime,
   Training me on with hints, and signs, and smiles,
   Even to this gulf? Thou art no liar? No,
   Thou art a lie! Traitor and murderer!
   Coward and slave! But no—defend thyself;
   [*Drawing.*]
55 Let the sword speak what the indignant tongue
   Disdains to brand thee with.

ORSINO: Put up your weapon.
　　Is it the desperation of your fear
　　Makes you thus rash and sudden with your friend,
　　Now ruined for your sake? If honest anger
60　Have moved you, know, that what I just proposed
　　Was but to try you. As for me, I think
　　Thankless affection led me to this point,
　　From which, if my firm temper could repent,
　　I cannot now recede. Even whilst we speak
65　The ministers of justice wait below:
　　They grant me these brief moments. Now, if you
　　Have any word of melancholy comfort
　　To speak to your pale wife, 'twere best to pass
　　Out at the postern, and avoid them so.
70　GIACOMO: Oh, generous friend! How canst thou
　　　　　pardon me?
　　Would that my life could purchase thine!
　　ORSINO: That wish
　　Now comes a day too late. Haste; fare thee well!
　　Hear'st thou not steps along the corridor?
　　　　　　　　　　　　　　　[EXIT GIACOMO.]
　　I'm sorry for it; but the guards are waiting
75　At his own gate, and such was my contrivance
　　That I might rid me both of him and them.
　　I thought to act a solemn comedy
　　Upon the painted scene of this new world,
　　And to attain my own peculiar ends
80　By some such plot of mingled good and ill
　　As others weave; but there arose a Power
　　Which grasped and snapped the threads of my
　　　　　device,
　　And turned it to a net of ruin—Ha!
　　[A shout is heard.]
　　Is that my name I hear proclaimed abroad?
85　But I will pass, wrapt in a vile disguise;
　　Rags on my back, and a false innocence
　　Upon my face, through the misdeeming crowd
　　Which judges by what seems. 'Tis easy then
　　For a new name and for a country new,
90　And a new life, fashioned on old desires,
　　To change the honours of abandoned Rome.
　　And these must be the masks of that within,
　　Which must remain unaltered.—Oh, I fear
　　That what is past will never let me rest!

95　Why, when none else is conscious, but myself,
　　Of my misdeeds, should my own heart's contempt
　　Trouble me? Have I not the power to fly
　　My own reproaches? Shall I be the slave
　　Of—what? A word? which those of this false world
100　Employ against each other, not themselves;
　　As men wear daggers not for self-offence.
　　But if I am mistaken, where shall I
　　Find the disguise to hide me from myself,
　　As now I skulk from every other eye?
　　　　　　　　　　　　　　　　　　　　[EXIT.]

SCENE 2

A Hall of Justice. CAMILLO, JUDGES, etc., are discovered seated; MARZIO is led in.

　　FIRST JUDGE: Accused, do you persist in your denial?
　　I ask you, are you innocent, or guilty?
　　I demand who were the participators
　　In your offence? Speak truth, and the whole truth.
5　MARZIO: My God! I did not kill him; I know
　　　　　nothing;
　　Olimpio sold the robe to me from which
　　You would infer my guilt.
　　SECOND JUDGE: Away with him!
　　FIRST JUDGE: Dare you, with lips yet white from
　　　　　the rack's kiss,
　　Speak false? Is it so soft a questioner,
10　That you would bandy lovers' talk with it,
　　Till it wind out your life and soul? Away!
　　MARZIO: Spare me! O, spare! I will confess.
　　FIRST JUDGE: Then
　　　　　speak.
　　MARZIO: I strangled him in his sleep.
　　FIRST JUDGE: Who urged
　　　　　you to it?
　　MARZIO: His own son Giacomo, and the young
　　　　　prelate
15　Orsino sent me to Petrella; there
　　The ladies Beatrice and Lucretia
　　Tempted me with a thousand crowns, and I
　　And my companion forthwith murdered him.

Now let me die.
FIRST JUDGE: This sounds as bad as truth.
   Guards, there,
20 Lead forth the prisoners.
   [ENTER LUCRETIA, BEATRICE, and GIACOMO, guarded.]
                            Look upon this man;
   When did you see him last?
BEATRICE: We never saw him.
MARZIO: You know me too well, Lady Beatrice.
BEATRICE: I know thee! How! where? when?
MARZIO: You
   know 'twas I
   Whom you did urge with menaces and bribes
25 To kill your father. When the thing was done,
   You clothed me in a robe of woven gold
   And bade me thrive: how I have thriven, you see.
   You, my Lord Giacomo, Lady Lucretia,
   You know that what I speak is true.
   [BEATRICE advances towards him; he covers his face, and shrinks back.]
                            Oh, dart
30 The terrible resentment of those eyes
   On the dread earth! Turn them away from me!
   They wound: 'twas torture forced the truth. My Lords,
   Having said this, let me be led to death.
BEATRICE: Poor wretch, I pity thee: yet stay awhile.
35 CAMILLO: Guards, lead him not away.
BEATRICE: Cardinal
   Camillo,
   You have a good repute for gentleness
   And wisdom: can it be that you sit here
   To countenance a wicked farce like this?
   When some obscure and trembling slave is dragged
40 From sufferings which might shake the sternest heart,
   And bade to answer, not as he believes,
   But as those may suspect or do desire,
   Whose questions thence suggest their own reply:
   And that in peril of such hideous torments
45 As merciful God spares even the damned. Speak now
   The thing you surely know, which is, that you,
   If your fine frame were stretched upon that wheel,
   And you were told, "Confess that you did poison
   Your little nephew: that fair blue-eyed child
50 Who was the lode-star of your life"; and though

   All see, since his most swift and piteous death,
   That day and night, and heaven and earth, and time,
   And all the things hoped for or done therein
   Are changed to you, through your exceeding grief,
55 Yet you would say, "I confess anything"—
   And beg from your tormentors, like that slave,
   The refuge of dishonourable death.
   I pray thee, Cardinal, that thou assert
   My innocence.
CAMILLO: [Much moved.]   What shall we think,
   my lords?
60 Shame on these tears! I thought the heart was frozen
   Which is their fountain. I would pledge my soul
   That she is guiltless.
JUDGE: Yet she must be tortured.
CAMILLO: I would as soon have tortured mine own
   nephew;
   [If he now lived, he would be just her age;
65 His hair, too, was her colour, and his eyes
   Like hers in shape, but blue, and not so deep]:
   As that most perfect image of God's love
   That ever came sorrowing upon the earth.
   She is as pure as speechless infancy!
70 JUDGE: Well, be her purity on your head, my lord,
   If you forbid the rack. His Holiness
   Enjoined us to pursue this monstrous crime
   By the severest forms of law; nay even
   To stretch a point against the criminals.
75 The prisoners stand accused of parricide,
   Upon such evidence as justifies
   Torture.
BEATRICE: What evidence? This man's?
JUDGE: Even so.
BEATRICE: [To MARZIO.]   Come near. And who
   art thou, thus chosen forth
   Out of the multitude of living men
80 To kill the innocent?
MARZIO: I am Marzio,
   Thy father's vassal.
BEATRICE: Fix thine eyes on mine;
   Answer to what I ask.
   [Turning to the JUDGES.]
                      I prithee mark
   His countenance: unlike bold calumny

Which sometimes dares not speak the thing it looks,
He dares not look the thing he speaks, but bends
His gaze on the blind earth.
   [*To* MARZIO.]
                     What! wilt thou say
That I did murder my own father?
MARZIO: Oh!
Spare me! My brain swims round—I cannot speak—
It was that horrid torture forced the truth.
Take me away! Let her not look on me!
I am a guilty miserable wretch;
I have said all I know; now, let me die!
BEATRICE: My Lords, if by my nature I had been
So stern, as to have planned the crime alleged,
Which your suspicions dictate to this slave,
And the rack makes him utter, do you think
I should have left this two-edged instrument
Of my misdeed; this man, this bloody knife
With my own name engraven on the heft,
Lying unsheathed amid a world of foes,
For my own death? that with such horrible need
For deepest silence, I should have neglected
So trivial a precaution, as the making
His tomb the keeper of a secret written
On a thief's memory? What is his poor life?
What are a thousand lives? A parricide
Had trampled them like dust; and see, he lives!
   [*Turning to* MARZIO.]
And thou—
MARZIO: Oh, spare me! Speak to me no more!
That stern yet piteous look, those solemn tones,
Wound worse than torture.
   [*To the* JUDGES.]
                  I have told it all;
For pity's sake lead me away to death.
CAMILLO: Guards, lead him nearer the lady Beatrice,
He shrinks from her regard like autumn's leaf
From the keen breath of the serenest north.
BEATRICE: Oh, thou who tremblest on the giddy
      verge
Of life and death, pause ere thou answerest me;
So mayst thou answer God with less dismay:
What evil have we done thee? I, alas!
Have lived but on this earth a few sad years,
And so my lot was ordered, that a father
First turned the moments of awakening life
To drops, each poisoning youth's sweet hope; and then
Stabbed with one blow my everlasting soul,
And my untainted fame; and even that peace
Which sleeps within the core of the heart's heart.
But the wound was not mortal; so my hate
Became the only worship I could lift
To our great Father, who in pity and love,
Armed thee, as thou dost say, to cut him off;
And thus his wrong becomes my accusation:
And art thou the accuser? If thou hopest
Mercy in heaven, show justice upon earth:
Worse than a bloody hand is a hard heart.
If thou hast done murders, made thy life's path
Over the trampled laws of God and man,
Rush not before thy Judge, and say: "My Maker,
I have done this and more; for there was one
Who was most pure and innocent on earth;
And because she endured what never any
Guilty or innocent, endured before;
Because her wrongs could not be told, nor thought;
Because thy hand at length did rescue her;
I with my words killed her and all her kin."
Think, I adjure you, what it is to slay
The reverence living in the minds of men
Towards our ancient house, and stainless fame!
Think what it is to strangle infant pity,
Cradled in the belief of guileless looks,
Till it become a crime to suffer. Think
What 'tis to blot with infamy and blood
All that which shows like innocence, and is,
Hear me, great God! I swear, most innocent,
So that the world lose all discrimination
Between the sly, fierce, wild regard of guilt,
And that which now compels thee to reply
To what I ask: Am I, or am I not
A parricide?
MARZIO: Thou art not!
JUDGE: What is this?
MARZIO: I here declare those whom I did accuse
Are innocent. 'Tis I alone am guilty.
JUDGE: Drag him away to torments; let them be
Subtle and long drawn out, to tear the folds

Of the heart's inmost cell. Unbind him not
Till he confess.
MARZIO: Torture me as ye will:
A keener pain has wrung a higher truth
165 From my last breath. She is most innocent!
Bloodhounds, not men, glut yourselves well with me!
I will not give you that fine piece of nature
To rend and ruin.
                        [*EXIT MARZIO, guarded.*]
CAMILLO: What say ye now, my lords?
JUDGE: Let tortures strain the truth till it be white
170 As snow thrice-sifted by the frozen wind.
CAMILLO: Yet stained with blood.
JUDGE: [*To BEATRICE.*]   Know you
   this paper, lady?
BEATRICE: Entrap me not with questions. Who
   stands here
As my accuser? Ha! wilt thou be he,
Who art my judge? Accuser, witness, judge,
175 What, all in one? Here is Orsino's name;
Where is Orsino? Let his eye meet mine.
What means this scrawl? Alas! ye know not what,
And therefore on the chance that it may be
Some evil, will ye kill us?
[*ENTER an OFFICER.*]
OFFICER: Marzio's dead.
180 JUDGE: What did he say?
OFFICER: Nothing. As soon as we
Had bound him on the wheel, he smiled on us,
As one who baffles a deep adversary;
And holding his breath, died.
JUDGE: There remains nothing
But to apply the question to those prisoners,
185 Who yet remain stubborn.
CAMILLO: I overrule
Further proceedings, and in the behalf
Of these most innocent and noble persons
Will use my interest with the Holy Father.
JUDGE: Let the Pope's pleasure then be done.
   Meanwhile
190 Conduct these culprits each to separate cells;
And be the engines ready: for this night,
If the Pope's resolution be as grave,

Pious, and just as once, I'll wring the truth
Out of those nerves and sinews, groan by groan.
                                 [*EXEUNT.*]

SCENE 3

The Cell of a Prison.
BEATRICE *is discovered asleep on a couch.*
ENTER BERNARDO.

BERNARDO: How gently slumber rests upon her face,
Like the last thoughts of some day sweetly spent
Closing in night and dreams, and so prolonged.
After such torments as she bore last night,
5 How light and soft her breathing comes. Ah, me!
Methinks that I shall never sleep again.
But I must shake the heavenly dew of rest
From this sweet folded flower, thus—wake! awake!
What, sister, canst thou sleep?
BEATRICE: [*Awaking.*]   I was just dreaming
10 That we were all in Paradise. Thou knowest
This cell seems like a kind of Paradise
After our father's presence.
BERNARDO: Dear, dear sister,
Would that thy dream were not a dream! O, God!
How shall I tell?
BEATRICE: What would'st thou tell, sweet brother?
15 BERNARDO: Look not so calm and happy, or, even whilst
I stand considering what I have to say,
My heart will break.
BEATRICE: See now, thou mak'st me weep:
How very friendless thou wouldst be, dear child,
If I were dead. Say what thou hast to say.
20 BERNARDO: They have confessed; they could endure
   no more
The tortures—
BEATRICE: Ha! What was there to confess?
They must have told some weak and wicked lie
To flatter their tormentors. Have they said
That they were guilty? O white innocence,
25 That thou shouldst wear the mask of guilt to hide
Thine awful and serenest countenance
From those who know thee not!

[ENTER JUDGE, with LUCRETIA and GIACOMO, guarded.]
                    Ignoble hearts!
For some brief spasms of pain, which are at least
As mortal as the limbs through which they pass,
Are centuries of high splendour laid in dust?
And that eternal honour which should live
Sunlike, above the reek of mortal fame,
Changed to a mockery and a by-word? What!
Will you give up these bodies to be dragged
At horses' heels, so that our hair should sweep
The footsteps of the vain and senseless crowd,
Who, that they may make our calamity
Their worship and their spectacle, will leave
The churches and the theatres as void
As their own hearts? Shall the light multitude
Fling, at their choice, curses or faded pity,
Sad funeral flowers to deck a living corpse,
Upon us as we pass to pass away,
And leave—what memory of our having been?
Infamy, blood, terror, despair? O thou,
Who wert a mother to the parentless,
Kill not thy child! Let not her wrongs kill thee!
Brother, lie down with me upon the rack,
And let us each be silent as a corpse;
It soon will be as soft as any grave.
'Tis but the falsehood it can wring from fear
Makes the rack cruel.
GIACOMO: They will tear the truth
Even from thee at last, those cruel pains:
For pity's sake say thou art guilty now.
LUCRETIA: O, speak the truth! Let us all quickly die;
And after death, God is our judge, not they;
He will have mercy on us.
BERNARDO: If indeed
It can be true, say so, dear sister mine;
And then the Pope will surely pardon you,
And all be well.
JUDGE: Confess, or I will warp
Your limbs with such keen tortures—
BEATRICE: Tortures!
   Turn
The rack henceforth into a spinning-wheel!
Torture your dog, that he may tell when last
He lapped the blood his master shed—not me!
My pangs are of the mind, and of the heart,
And of the soul; aye, of the inmost soul,
Which weeps within tears as of burning gall
To see, in this ill world where none are true,
My kindred false to their deserted selves.
And with considering all the wretched life
Which I have lived, and its now wretched end,
And the small justice shown by Heaven and Earth
To me or mine; and what a tyrant thou art,
And what slaves these; and what a world we make,
The oppressor and the oppressed—such pangs compel
My answer. What is it thou wouldst with me?
JUDGE: Art thou not guilty of thy father's death?
BEATRICE: Or wilt thou rather tax high-judging God
That he permitted such an act as that
Which I have suffered, and which he beheld;
Made it unutterable, and took from it
All refuge, all revenge, all consequence,
But that which thou hast called my father's death?
Which is or is not what men call a crime,
Which either I have done, or have not done;
Say what ye will. I shall deny no more.
If ye desire it thus, thus let it be,
And so an end of all. Now do your will;
No other pains shall force another word.
JUDGE: She is convicted, but has not confessed.
Be it enough. Until their final sentence
Let none have converse with them. You, young lord,
Linger not here!
BEATRICE: O, tear him not away!
JUDGE: Guards! do your duty.
BERNARDO: [Embracing BEATRICE.]
                                Oh! would ye divide
Body from soul?
OFFICER: That is the headsman's business.
[EXEUNT all but LUCRETIA, BEATRICE, and GIACOMO.]
GIACOMO: Have I confessed? Is it all over now?
No hope! No refuge! O weak, wicked tongue,
Which hast destroyed me, would that thou hadst been
Cut out and thrown to dogs first! To have killed
My father first, and then betrayed my sister;
Ay, thee! the one thing innocent and pure
In this black, guilty world, to that which I
So well deserve! My wife! my little ones!

Destitute, helpless; and I—Father! God!
Canst thou forgive even the unforgiving,
When their full hearts break thus, thus?—
[*Covers his face and weeps.*]
LUCRETIA: O, my child!
To what a dreadful end are we all come!
Why did I yield? Why did I not sustain
Those torments? Oh! that I were all dissolved
Into these fast and unavailing tears,
Which flow and feel not!
BEATRICE: What 'twas weak to do,
'Tis weaker to lament, once being done;
Take cheer! The God who knew my wrong, and made
Our speedy act the angel of his wrath,
Seems, and but seems, to have abandoned us.
Let us not think that we shall die for this.
Brother, sit near me; give me your firm hand,
You had a manly heart. Bear up! bear up!
Oh! dearest Lady, put your gentle head
Upon my lap, and try to sleep awhile:
Your eyes look pale, hollow, and overworn,
With heaviness of watching and slow grief.
Come, I will sing you some low, sleepy tune,
Not cheerful, nor yet sad; some dull old thing,
Some outworn and unused monotony,
Such as our country gossips sing and spin,
Till they almost forget they live: lie down!
So, that will do. Have I forgot the words?
Faith! they are sadder than I thought they were.

                 SONG

False friend, wilt thou smile or weep
When my life is laid asleep?
Little cares for a smile or a tear,
The clay-cold corpse upon the bier!
       Farewell! Heigh ho!
     What is this whispers low?
There is a snake in thy smile, my dear;
And bitter poison within thy tear.
Sweet sleep! were death like to thee,
Or if thou couldst mortal be,
I would close these eyes of pain;
When to wake? Never again.
       O World! farewell!

Listen to the passing bell!
It says, thou and I must part,
With a light and a heavy heart.
[*The scene closes.*]

                SCENE 4

A Hall of the Prison. ENTER CAMILLO *and* BERNARDO.

CAMILLO: The Pope is stern; not to be moved or bent.
He looked as calm and keen as is the engine
Which tortures and which kills, exempt itself
From aught that it inflicts; a marble form,
A rite, a law, a custom; not a man.
He frowned, as if to frown had been the trick
Of his machinery, on the advocates
Presenting the defences, which he tore
And threw behind, muttering with hoarse, harsh voice:
"Which among ye defended their old father
Killed in his sleep?" then to another: "Thou
Dost this in virtue of thy place; 'tis well."
He turned to me then, looking deprecation,
And said these three words, coldly: "They must die."
BERNARDO: And yet you left him not?
CAMILLO: I urged him still;
Pleading, as I could guess, the devilish wrong
Which prompted your unnatural parent's death.
And he replied, "Paolo Santa Croce
Murdered his mother yester evening,
And he is fled. Parricide grows so rife
That soon, for some just cause no doubt, the young
Will strangle us all, dozing in our chairs.
Authority, and power, and hoary hair
Are grown crimes capital. You are my nephew,
You come to ask their pardon; stay a moment;
Here is their sentence; never see me more
Till, to the letter, it be all fulfilled."
BERNARDO: O, God, not so! I did believe indeed
That all you said was but sad preparation
For happy news. O, there are words and looks
To bend the sternest purpose! Once I knew them,
Now I forget them at my dearest need.

What think you if I seek him out, and bathe
His feet and robe with hot and bitter tears?
35 Importune him with prayers, vexing his brain
With my perpetual cries, until in rage
He strike me with his pastoral cross, and trample
Upon my prostrate head, so that my blood
May stain the senseless dust on which he treads,
40 And remorse waken mercy? I will do it!
O, wait till I return!
                                             [*Rushes out.*]
CAMILLO: Alas! poor boy!
A wreck-devoted seaman thus might pray
To the deaf sea.
[ENTER LUCRETIA, BEATRICE, *and* GIACOMO, *guarded.*]
BEATRICE: I hardly dare to fear
That thou bring'st other news than a just pardon.
45 CAMILLO: May God in heaven be less inexorable
To the Pope's prayers, than he has been to mine.
Here is the sentence and the warrant.
BEATRICE: [*Wildly.*]   Oh,
My God! Can it be possible I have
To die so suddenly? So young to go
50 Under the obscure, cold, rotting, wormy ground!
To be nailed down into a narrow place;
To see no more sweet sunshine; hear no more
Blithe voice of living thing; muse not again
Upon familiar thoughts, sad, yet thus lost!
55 How fearful! to be nothing! Or to be—
What? O, where am I? Let me not go mad!
Sweet Heaven, forgive weak thoughts! If there
      should be
No God, no Heaven, no Earth in the void world;
The wide, grey, lampless, deep unpeopled world!
60 If all things then should be—my father's spirit
His eye, his voice, his touch surrounding me;
The atmosphere and breath of my dead life!
If sometimes, as a shape more like himself,
Even the form which tortured me on earth,
65 Masked in grey hairs and wrinkles, he should come
And wind me in his hellish arms, and fix
His eyes on mine, and drag me down, down, down!
For was he not alone omnipotent
On Earth, and ever present? even though dead,
70 Does not his spirit live in all that breathe,

And work for me and mine still the same ruin,
Scorn, pain, despair? Who ever yet returned
To teach the laws of death's untrodden realm?
Unjust perhaps as those which drive us now,
75 O, whither, whither?
LUCRETIA: Trust in God's sweet love,
The tender promises of Christ: ere night
Think we shall be in Paradise.[1]
BEATRICE: 'Tis past!
Whatever comes, my heart shall sink no more.
And yet, I know not why, your words strike chill:
80 How tedious, false, and cold seem all things! I
Have met with much injustice in this world;
No difference has been made by God or man,
Or any power moulding my wretched lot,
'Twixt good or evil, as regarded me.
85 I am cut off from the only world I know,
From light, and life, and love, in youth's sweet prime.
You do well telling me to trust in God,
I hope I do trust in him. In whom else
Can any trust? And yet my heart is cold.
[*During the latter speeches* GIACOMO *has retired conversing
with* CAMILLO, *who now goes out;* GIACOMO *advances.*]
90 GIACOMO: Know you not, mother—sister, know you
          not?
Bernardo even now is gone to implore
The Pope to grant our pardon.
LUCRETIA: Child, perhaps
It will be granted. We may all then live
To make these woes a tale for distant years.
95 O, what a thought! It gushes to my heart
Like the warm blood.
BEATRICE: Yet both will soon be cold:
O, trample out that thought! Worse than despair,
Worse than the bitterness of death, is hope:
It is the only ill which can find place
100 Upon the giddy, sharp, and narrow hour
Tottering beneath us. Plead with the swift frost
That it should spare the eldest flower of spring:
Plead with awakening earthquake, o'er whose couch
Even now a city stands, strong, fair, and free;

---

[1] Cf. Christ's words to one of the thieves crucified with him, Luke 23.43.

105 Now stench and blackness yawns, like death. O, plead
With famine, or wind-walking pestilence,
Blind lightning, or the deaf sea, not with man!
Cruel, cold, formal man; righteous in words,
In deeds a Cain.[1] No, Mother, we must die:
110 Since such is the reward of innocent lives;
Such the alleviation of worst wrongs.
And whilst our murderers live, and hard, cold men,
Smiling and slow, walk through a world of tears
To death as to life's sleep; 'twere just the grave
115 Were some strange joy for us. Come, obscure Death,
And wind me in thine all-embracing arms!
Like a fond mother hide me in thy bosom,
And rock me to the sleep from which none wake.
Live ye, who live, subject to one another
120 As we were once, who now—
[BERNARDO *rushes in.*]
BERNARDO: Oh, horrible!
That tears, that looks, that hope poured forth in
    prayer,
Even till the heart is vacant and despairs,
Should all be vain! The ministers of death
Are waiting round the doors. I thought I saw
125 Blood on the face of one—what if 'twere fancy?
Soon the heart's blood of all I love on earth
Will sprinkle him, and he will wipe it off
As if 'twere only rain. O, life! O, world!
Cover me! let me be no more! To see
130 That perfect mirror of pure innocence
Wherein I gazed, and grew happy and good,
Shivered to dust! To see thee, Beatrice,
Who made all lovely thou didst look upon—
Thee, light of life—dead, dark! while I say, sister,
135 To hear I have no sister; and thou, Mother,
Whose love was a bond to all our loves—
Dead! The sweet bond broken!
[ENTER CAMILLO *and Guards.*]
          They come! Let me
Kiss those warm lips before their crimson leaves
Are blighted—white—cold. Say farewell, before
140 Death chokes that gentle voice! O, let me hear
You speak!
BEATRICE: Farewell, my tender brother. Think
Of our sad fate with gentleness, as now:
And let mild, pitying thoughts lighten for thee
Thy sorrow's load. Err not in harsh despair,
But tears and patience. One thing more, my child,
145 For thine own sake be constant to the love
Thou bearest us; and to the faith that I,
Though wrapt in a strange cloud of crime and shame,
Lived ever holy and unstained. And though
150 Ill tongues shall wound me, and our common name
Be as a mark stamped on thine innocent brow
For men to point at as they pass, do thou
Forbear, and never think a thought unkind
Of those who perhaps love thee in their graves.
155 So mayest thou die as I do; fear and pain
Being subdued. Farewell! Farewell! Farewell!
BERNARDO: I cannot say farewell!
CAMILLO: O, Lady
    Beatrice!
BEATRICE: Give yourself no unnecessary pain,
My dear Lord Cardinal. Here, Mother, tie
160 My girdle for me, and bind up this hair
In any simple knot; aye, that does well.
And yours I see is coming down. How often
Have we done this for one another! now
We shall not do it any more. My Lord,
165 We are quite ready. Well, 'tis very well.

---

[1] a murderer, like Cain in the Bible: see Genesis 4.1–16.

Adonais: An Elegy on the Death of John Keats[1]
(1821)

> Αστήρ πρὶν μὲν ἔλαμπες ενι ζώοισιν εώος.
> Νυν δε θχνῶν, λαμπεις ἕσπερος εν φθίμενοις
> PLATO

> φάρμακον ἦλθε, Βίων, ποτι σον στομα,
>   φάρμακον ἔιδες·
> Πῶς τευ τοὶς χέιλεσσι ποτεδραμε, κοὐκ
>   εγλυκανθη;
> Τις δὲ βροτος τοσσοὖτον ἀνάμερος, ἢ κερασαι τοι,
> Ἢ δοὖναι λαλέοντι το φάρακον; ἔκφυγεν ὠδαν.
> MOSCHUS, EPITAPH. BION.

1

I weep for Adonais—he is dead!
O, weep for Adonais! though our tears
Thaw not the frost which binds so dear a head!
And thou, sad Hour, selected from all years
5 To mourn our loss, rouse thy obscure compeers,
And teach them thine own sorrow, say: with me
Died Adonais; till the Future dares
Forget the Past, his fate and fame shall be
An echo and a light unto eternity!

2

10 Where wert thou mighty Mother, when he lay,
When thy Son lay, pierced by the shaft which flies
In darkness? where was lorn Urania[2]
When Adonais died? With veiled eyes,
'Mid listening Echoes, in her Paradise
15 She sate, while one, with soft enamoured breath,
Rekindled all the fading melodies,
With which, like flowers that mock the corse beneath,
He had adorned and hid the coming bulk of death.

3

O, weep for Adonais—he is dead!
20 Wake, melancholy Mother, wake and weep!
Yet wherefore? Quench within their burning bed
Thy fiery tears, and let thy loud heart keep
Like his, a mute and uncomplaining sleep;
For he is gone, where all things wise and fair
25 Descend;—oh, dream not that the amorous Deep
Will yet restore him to the vital air;
Death feeds on his mute voice, and laughs at our despair.

4

Most musical of mourners, weep again!
Lament anew, Urania!—He died,
30 Who was the Sire of an immortal strain,
Blind, old, and lonely, when his country's pride,
The priest, the slave, and the liberticide,
Trampled and mocked with many a loathed rite
Of lust and blood; he went, unterrified,
35 Into the gulf of death; but his clear Sprite
Yet reigns o'er earth; the third among the sons of light.[3]

5

Most musical of mourners, weep anew!
Not all to that bright station dared to climb;
And happier they their happiness who knew,
40 Whose tapers yet burn through that night of time
In which suns perished; others more sublime,
Struck by the envious wrath of man or God,
Have sunk, extinct in their refulgent prime;
And some yet live, treading the thorny road,

---

[1] The title of Shelley's pastoral elegy for John Keats,* who died of tuberculosis in 1821, alludes to the Greek Adonis (see Ovid, *Metamorphoses* 10) and to the Hebrew word "Adonai," "Lord." Shelley translated the first epigraph, as follows: "Thou wert the morning star among the living, / Ere thy fair light had fled— / Now, having died, thou are as Hesperus, giving / New splendour to the Dead." The second epigraph is from the "Elegy for Bion," usually ascribed to Moschus (fl. c. 150 BC), but probably of later date: "Poison came, Bion, to thy mouth—poison didst thou eat. How could it come to such lips as thine and not be sweetened? What mortal was so cruel as to mix the drug for thee, or to give it to thee, who heard thy voice? He escapes [shall be nameless in] my song." Shelley adopts the position that Keats died as a direct result of negative reviews of his poetry.

[2] In Milton, *Paradise Lost*, Urania is the heavenly muse who inspires the poet.

[3] Homer, Dante, and Milton are the three great epic poets. This stanza celebrates Milton as a champion of liberty during the period following the Restoration of the monarchy in England in 1660.

45   Which leads, through toil and hate, to Fame's
　　　　serene abode.

6

But now, thy youngest, dearest one,[1] has perished
The nursling of thy widowhood, who grew,
Like a pale flower by some sad maiden cherished,
And fed with true love tears, instead of dew;
50   Most musical of mourners, weep anew!
Thy extreme hope, the loveliest and the last,
The bloom, whose petals nipt before they blew
Died on the promise of the fruit, is waste;
The broken lily lies—the storm is overpast.

7

55   To that high Capital, where kingly Death
Keeps his pale court in beauty and decay,
He came; and bought, with price of purest breath,
A grave among the eternal.[2]—Come away!
Haste, while the vault of blue Italian day
60   Is yet his fitting charnel-roof! while still
He lies, as if in dewy sleep he lay;
Awake him not! surely he takes his fill
Of deep and liquid rest, forgetful of all ill.

8

He will awake no more, oh, never more!—
65   Within the twilight chamber spreads apace,
The shadow of white Death, and at the door
Invisible Corruption waits to trace
His extreme way to her dim dwelling-place;
The eternal Hunger sits, but pity and awe
70   Soothe her pale rage, nor dares she to deface
So fair a prey, till darkness, and the law
Of mortal change, shall fill the grave which is her maw.

9

O, weep for Adonais!—The quick Dreams,
The passion-winged Ministers of thought,
75   Who were his flocks, whom near the living streams
Of his young spirit he fed, and whom he taught
The love which was its music, wander not,—
Wander no more, from kindling brain to brain,
But droop there, whence they sprung; and mourn
　　　　their lot
80   Round the cold heart, where, after their sweet pain,
They ne'er will gather strength, or find a home again.

10

And one with trembling hands clasps his cold head,
And fans him with her moonlight wings, and cries;
"Our love, our hope, our sorrow, is not dead;
85   See, on the silken fringe of his faint eyes,
Like dew upon a sleeping flower, there lies
A tear some Dream has loosened from his brain."
Lost Angel of a ruined Paradise!
She knew not 'twas her own; as with no stain
90   She faded, like a cloud which had outwept its rain.

11

One from a lucid urn of starry dew
Washed his light limbs as if embalming them;
Another clipt her profuse locks, and threw
The wreath upon him, like an anadem,[3]
95   Which frozen tears instead of pearls begem;
Another in her wilful grief would break
Her bow and winged reeds, as if to stem
A greater loss with one which was more weak;
And dull the barbed fire against his frozen cheek.

12

100   Another Splendour on his mouth alit,
That mouth, whence it was wont to draw the breath
Which gave it strength to pierce the guarded wit,
And pass into the panting heart beneath
With lightning and with music: the damp death
105   Quenched its caress upon his icy lips;
And, as a dying meteor stains a wreath
Of moonlight vapour, which the cold night clips,
It flushed through his pale limbs, and past to its
　　　　eclipse.

---

[1] Keats is Milton's son in the sense of having been strongly influenced by his great predecessor.

[2] Keats went to Rome hoping that the climate would benefit his health; he was buried in the Protestant cemetery there.

[3] a wreath or garland for the head.

13

And others came … Desires and Adorations,
Winged Persuasions and veiled Destinies,
Splendours, and Glooms, and glimmering Incarnations
Of hopes and fears, and twilight Phantasies;
And Sorrow, with her family of Sighs,
And Pleasure, blind with tears, led by the gleam
Of her own dying smile instead of eyes,
Came in slow pomp;—the moving pomp might seem
Like pageantry of mist on an autumnal stream.[1]

14

All he had loved, and moulded into thought,
From shape, and hue, and odour, and sweet sound,
Lamented Adonais. Morning sought
Her eastern watchtower, and her hair unbound,
Wet with the tears which should adorn the ground,
Dimmed the aerial eyes that kindle day;
Afar the melancholy thunder moaned,
Pale Ocean in unquiet slumber lay,
And the wild winds flew round, sobbing in their dismay.

15

Lost Echo[2] sits amid the voiceless mountains,
And feeds her grief with his remembered lay,
And will no more reply to winds or fountains,
Or amorous birds perched on the young green spray,
Or herdsman's horn, or bell at closing day;
Since she can mimic not his lips, more dear
Than those for whose disdain she pined away
Into a shadow of all sounds:—a drear
Murmur, between their songs, is all the woodmen hear.

16

Grief made the young Spring wild, and she threw down
Her kindling buds, as if she Autumn were,
Or they dead leaves; since her delight is flown
For whom should she have waked the sullen year?
To Phœbus was not Hyacinth so dear
Nor to himself Narcissus,[3] as to both
Thou Adonais: wan they stand and sere
Amid the drooping comrades of their youth,
With dew all turned to tears; odour, to sighing ruth.

17

Thy spirit's sister, the lorn nightingale[4]
Mourns not her mate with such melodious pain;
Not so the eagle, who like thee could scale
Heaven, and could nourish in the sun's domain
Her mighty youth with morning,[5] doth complain,
Soaring and screaming round her empty nest,
As Albion[6] wails for thee: the curse of Cain[7]
Light on his head who pierced thy innocent breast,
And scared the angel soul that was its earthly guest!

18

Ah woe is me! Winter is come and gone,
But grief returns with the revolving year;
The airs and streams renew their joyous tone;
The ants, the bees, the swallows reappear;
Fresh leaves and flowers deck the dead Seasons' bier;
The amorous birds now pair in every brake,
And build their mossy homes in field and brere;
And the green lizard, and the golden snake,
Like unimprisoned flames, out of their trance awake.

19

Through wood and stream and field and hill and Ocean
A quickening life from the Earth's heart has burst
As it has ever done, with change and motion,
From the great morning of the world when first
God dawned on Chaos; in its steam immersed,

---

[1] Cf. Keats, "To Autumn."*

[2] In classical mythology, the nymph Echo mourns for Narcissus, who, in his self-love, rejected her and was transformed into a flower; here, she mourns for the dead Keats, who is "more dear" (132) than Narcissus. See Ovid, *Metamorphoses* 3.

[3] After Hyacinthus died, his lover, Phœbus (or Apollo), turned him into a flower. See Ovid, *Metamorphoses* 10. For Narcissus, see note to line 127.

[4] Cf. Keats, "Ode to a Nightingale."*

[5] The eagle was thought to regain its youth by flying towards the sun; cf. Psalms 103.5.

[6] England.

[7] See Genesis 4.11–12.

The lamps of Heaven flash with a softer light;
All baser things pant with life's sacred thirst;
170 Diffuse themselves; and spend in love's delight,
The beauty and the joy of their renewed might.

20

The leprous corpse touched by this spirit tender
Exhales itself in flowers of gentle breath;
Like incarnations of the stars, when splendour
175 Is changed to fragrance, they illumine death
And mock the merry worm that wakes beneath;
Nought we know, dies. Shall that alone which knows
Be as a sword consumed before the sheath
By sightless lightning?—th'intense atom glows
180 A moment, then is quenched in a most cold repose.

21

Alas! that all we loved of him should be,
But for our grief, as if it had not been,
And grief itself be mortal! Woe is me!
Whence are we, and why are we? of what scene
185 The actors or spectators? Great and mean
Meet massed in death, who lends what life must borrow.
As long as skies are blue, and fields are green,
Evening must usher night, night urge the morrow,
Month follow month with woe, and year wake year to sorrow.

22

190 *He* will awake no more, oh, never more!
"Wake thou," cried Misery, "childless Mother, rise
Out of thy sleep, and slake, in thy heart's core,
A wound more fierce than his with tears and sighs."
And all the Dreams that watched Urania's eyes,
195 And all the Echoes whom their sister's song
Had held in holy silence, cried: "Arise!"
Swift as a Thought by the snake Memory stung,
From her ambrosial rest the fading Splendour[1] sprung.

23

She rose like an autumnal Night, that springs
200 Out of the East, and follows wild and drear
The golden Day, which, on eternal wings,
Even as a ghost abandoning a bier,
Had left the Earth a corpse. Sorrow and fear
So struck, so roused, so rapt Urania;
205 So saddened round her like an atmosphere
Of stormy mist; so swept her on her way
Even to the mournful place where Adonais lay.

24

Out of her secret Paradise she sped,
Through camps and cities rough with stone, and steel,
210 And human hearts, which to her aery tread
Yielding not, wounded the invisible
Palms of her tender feet where'er they fell:
And barbed tongues, and thoughts more sharp than they
Rent the soft Form they never could repel,
215 Whose sacred blood, like the young tears of May,
Paved with eternal flowers that undeserving way.

25

In the death chamber for a moment Death
Shamed by the presence of that living Might
Blushed to annihilation, and the breath
220 Revisited those lips, and life's pale light
Flashed through those limbs, so late her dear delight.
"Leave me not wild and drear and comfortless,
As silent lightning leaves the starless night!
Leave me not!" cried Urania: her distress
225 Roused Death: Death rose and smiled, and met her vain caress.

26

"Stay yet awhile! speak to me once again;
Kiss me, so long but as a kiss may live;
And in my heartless breast and burning brain
That word, that kiss shall all thoughts else survive,
230 With food of saddest memory kept alive,
Now thou art dead, as if it were a part
Of thee, my Adonais! I would give
All that I am to be as thou now art!
But I am chained to Time, and cannot thence depart!

---

[1] I.e. Urania.

27

235 "Oh gentle child, beautiful as thou wert,
Why didst thou leave the trodden paths of men
Too soon, and with weak hands though mighty heart
Dare the unpastured dragon[1] in his den?
Defenceless as thou wert, oh where was then
240 Wisdom the mirrored shield, or scorn the spear?
Or hadst thou waited the full cycle, when
Thy spirit should have filled its crescent sphere,[2]
The monsters of life's waste had fled from thee like deer.

28

"The herded wolves, bold only to pursue;
245 The obscene ravens, clamorous o'er the dead;
The vultures to the conqueror's banner true
Who feed where Desolation first has fed,
And whose wings rain contagion;—how they fled,
When like Apollo, from his golden bow,
250 The Pythian of the age one arrow sped
And smiled!—The spoilers tempt no second blow,
They fawn on the proud feet that spurn them as they go.[3]

29

"The sun comes forth, and many reptiles spawn;
He sets, and each ephemeral insect then
255 Is gathered into death without a dawn,
And the immortal stars awake again;
So is it in the world of living men:
A godlike mind soars forth, in its delight
Making earth bare and veiling heaven, and when
260 It sinks, the swarms that dimmed or shared its light
Leave to its kindred lamps the spirit's awful night."

30

Thus ceased she: and the mountain shepherds came
Their garlands sere, their magic mantles rent;
The Pilgrim of Eternity,[4] whose fame
265 Over his living head like Heaven is bent,
An early but enduring monument,
Came, veiling all the lightnings of his song
In sorrow; from her wilds Ierne[5] sent
The sweetest lyrist of her saddest wrong,[6]
270 And love taught grief to fall like music from his tongue.

31

Midst others of less note, came one frail Form,[7]
A phantom among men; companionless
As the last cloud of an expiring storm
Whose thunder is its knell; he, as I guess,
275 Had gazed on Nature's naked loveliness,
Actæon-like, and now he fled astray
With feeble steps o'er the world's wilderness,
And his own thoughts, along that rugged way,
Pursued, like raging hounds, their father and their
      prey.

32

280 A pardlike[8] Spirit beautiful and swift—
A Love in desolation masked;—a Power
Girt round with weakness;—it can scarce uplift
The weight of the superincumbent hour;
It is a dying lamp, a falling shower,
285 A breaking billow;—even whilst we speak
Is it not broken? On the withering flower
The killing sun smiles brightly: on a cheek
The life can burn in blood, even while the heart may
      break.

33

His head was bound with pansies overblown,
290 And faded violets, white, and pied, and blue;

---

[1] the harsh critic (or critics) who, according to Shelley, had driven Keats to despair and death. Shelley thinks that the anonymous reviewer in the *Quarterly Review* (April 1818)* was Robert Southey;* he was actually John Wilson Croker.

[2] its growing wholeness: Shelley regards Keats's potential as having been unfulfilled.

[3] As Apollo killed the Python, Byron* ("the Pythian of the age") effectively defeated the critics or "spoilers" in his satirical poetry.

[4] Byron, with specific reference to *Childe Harold's Pilgrimage.**

[5] Ireland.

[6] the Irish poet Thomas Moore.*

[7] Shelley himself, who in this stanza compares himself to Actæon, the hunter of classical mythology who was killed by his own hounds. See Ovid, *Metamorphoses* 3.

[8] like a panther or leopard, the animal sacred to Dionysus.

And a light spear topped with a cypress cone,
Round whose rude shaft dark ivy tresses grew
Yet dripping with the forest's noonday dew,
Vibrated, as the ever-beating heart
295 Shook the weak hand that grasped it; of that crew
He came the last, neglected and apart;
A herd-abandoned deer struck by the hunter's dart.

34

All stood aloof, and at his partial[1] moan
Smiled through their tears; well knew that gentle band
300 Who in another's fate now wept his own;
As in the accents of an unknown land,
He sung new sorrow; sad Urania scanned
The Stranger's mien, and murmured: "who art thou?"
He answered not, but with a sudden hand
305 Made bare his branded and ensanguined brow,
Which was like Cain's or Christ's—Oh! that it should
    be so![2]

35

What softer voice is hushed over the dead?
Athwart what brow is that dark mantle thrown?
What form leans sadly o'er the white death-bed,
310 In mockery of monumental stone,
The heavy heart heaving without a moan?
If it be He, who, gentlest of the wise,
Taught, soothed, loved, honoured the departed one;[3]
Let me not vex, with inharmonious sighs
315 The silence of that heart's accepted sacrifice.

36

Our Adonais has drunk poison—oh!
What deaf and viperous murderer could crown
Life's early cup with such a draught of woe?
The nameless worm would now itself disown:
320 It felt, yet could escape the magic tone
Whose prelude held all envy, hate, and wrong,
But what was howling in one breast alone,
Silent with expectation of the song,
Whose master's hand is cold, whose silver lyre unstrung.

37

325 Live thou,[4] whose infamy is not thy fame!
Live! fear no heavier chastisement from me,
Thou noteless blot on a remembered name!
But be thyself, and know thyself to be!
And ever at thy season be thou free
330 To spill the venom when thy fangs o'er flow:
Remorse and Self-contempt shall cling to thee;
Hot Shame shall burn upon thy secret brow,
And like a beaten hound tremble thou shalt—as now.

38

Nor let us weep that our delight is fled
335 Far from these carrion kites that scream below;
He wakes or sleeps with the enduring dead;
Thou canst not soar where he is sitting now.—
Dust to the dust![5] but the pure spirit shall flow
Back to the burning fountain whence it came,
340 A portion of the Eternal, which must glow
Through time and change, unquenchably the same,
Whilst thy cold embers choke the sordid hearth
    of shame.

39

Peace, peace! he is not dead, he doth not sleep—
He hath awakened from the dream of life—
345 'Tis we, who lost in stormy visions, keep
With phantoms an unprofitable strife,
And in mad trance, strike with our spirit's knife
Invulnerable nothings.—*We* decay
Like corpses in a charnel; fear and grief
350 Convulse us and consume us day by day,
And cold hopes swarm like worms within our living
    clay.

---

[1] biased, in this case sympathetic to Keats.

[2] Shelley's forehead is branded, like Cain's (Genesis 4.15), or bloodied, like Christ's when he was crowned with thorns (Matthew 27.29).

[3] Leigh Hunt,* friend of Shelley and champion of Keats.

[4] Shelley continues to address the anonymous reviewer, the one reader whose "envy, hate, and wrong" (321) were not silenced by the "magic tone" (320) of Keats's poetry.

[5] Cf. Genesis 3.19.

40

He has outsoared the shadow of our night;
Envy and calumny and hate and pain,
And that unrest which men miscall delight,
Can touch him not and torture not again;
From the contagion of the world's slow stain
He is secure, and now can never mourn
A heart grown cold, a head grown grey in vain;
Nor, when the spirit's self has ceased to burn,
With sparkless ashes load an unlamented urn.

41

He lives, he wakes—'tis Death is dead, not he;[1]
Mourn not for Adonais.—Thou young Dawn
Turn all thy dew to splendour, for from thee
The spirit thou lamentest is not gone;
Ye caverns and ye forests, cease to moan!
Cease ye faint flowers and fountains, and thou Air
Which like a mourning veil thy scarf hadst thrown
O'er the abandoned Earth, now leave it bare
Even to the joyous stars which smile on it's despair!

42

He is made one with Nature: there is heard
His voice in all her music, from the moan
Of thunder, to the song of night's sweet bird;[2]
He is a presence to be felt and known
In darkness and in light, from herb and stone,
Spreading itself where'er that Power may move
Which has withdrawn his being to its own;
Which wields the world with never wearied love,
Sustains it from beneath, and kindles it above.

43

He is a portion of the loveliness
Which once he made more lovely: he doth bear
His part, while the one Spirit's plastic[3] stress
Sweeps through the dull dense world, compelling
  there,
All new successions to the forms they wear;
Torturing th' unwilling dross that checks it's flight
To it's own likeness, as each mass may bear;
And bursting in it's beauty and it's might
From trees and beasts and men into the Heaven's
  light.

44

The splendours of the firmament of time
May be eclipsed, but are extinguished not;
Like stars to their appointed height they climb
And death is a low mist which cannot blot
The brightness it may veil. When lofty thought
Lifts a young heart above its mortal lair,
And love and life contend in it, for what
Shall be its earthly doom, the dead live there
And move like winds of light on dark and stormy air.

45

The inheritors of unfulfilled renown
Rose from their thrones, built beyond mortal thought,
Far in the Unapparent. Chatterton[4]
Rose pale, his solemn agony had not
Yet faded from him; Sidney,[5] as he fought
And as he fell and as he lived and loved
Sublimely mild, a Spirit without spot,
Arose; and Lucan,[6] by his death approved:
Oblivion as they rose shrank like a thing reproved.

46

And many more, whose names on Earth are dark
But whose transmitted effluence cannot die
So long as fire outlives the parent spark,
Rose, robed in dazzling immortality.
"Thou art become as one of us," they cry,
"It was for thee yon kingless sphere has long
Swung blind in unascended majesty,

---

[1] Cf. 1 Corinthians 15.54 and John Donne, "Death, Be Not Proud" (c. 1615) 14.

[2] the nightingale.

[3] capable of shaping or forming matter.

[4] the young poet Thomas Chatterton,* who committed suicide in poverty and neglect.

[5] the poet Sir Philip Sidney (1554–86), who is said to have given a cup of water to another soldier as he lay dying after battle.

[6] the poet Marcus Annæus Lucanus (AD 39–65), author of the *Pharsalia*, convicted of plotting against the emperor Nero and forced to commit suicide.

Silent alone amid an Heaven of song.
Assume thy winged throne, thou Vesper of our throng!"

47

415 Who mourns for Adonais? oh come forth
Fond wretch! and know thyself and him aright.
Clasp with thy panting soul the pendulous Earth;
As from a centre, dart thy spirit's light
Beyond all worlds, until its spacious might
420 Satiate the void circumference: then shrink
Even to a point within our day and night;
And keep thy heart light lest it make thee sink
When hope has kindled hope, and lured thee to the brink.

48

Or go to Rome, which is the sepulchre
425 O, not of him, but of our joy: 'tis nought
That ages, empires, and religions there
Lie buried in the ravage they have wrought;
For such as he can lend,—they borrow not
Glory from those who made the world their prey;
430 And he is gathered to the kings of thought
Who waged contention with their time's decay,
And of the past are all that cannot pass away.

49

Go thou to Rome,—at once the Paradise,
The grave, the city, and the wilderness;
435 And where its wrecks like shattered mountains rise,
And flowering weeds, and fragrant copses dress
The bones of Desolation's nakedness
Pass, till the Spirit of the spot shall lead
Thy footsteps to a slope of green access
440 Where, like an infant's smile, over the dead,
A light of laughing flowers along the grass is spread.[1]

50

And gray walls moulder round, on which dull Time
Feeds, like slow fire upon a hoary brand;
And one keen pyramid[2] with wedge sublime,
445 Pavilioning the dust of him who planned
This refuge for his memory, doth stand
Like flame transformed to marble; and beneath,
A field is spread, on which a newer band
Have pitched in Heaven's smile their camp of death
450 Welcoming him we lose with scarce extinguished breath.

51

Here pause: these graves are all too young as yet
To have out grown the sorrow which consigned
Its charge to each; and if the seal is set,
Here, on one fountain of a mourning mind,
455 Break it not thou! too surely shalt thou find
Thine own well full, if thou returnest home,
Of tears and gall. From the world's bitter wind
Seek shelter in the shadow of the tomb.
What Adonais is, why fear we to become?

52

460 The One remains, the many change and pass;
Heaven's light forever shines, Earth's shadows fly;
Life, like a dome of many-coloured glass,
Stains the white radiance of Eternity,
Until Death tramples it to fragments.—Die,
465 If thou wouldst be with that which thou dost seek!
Follow where all is fled!—Rome's azure sky,
Flowers, ruins, statues, music, words, are weak
The glory they transfuse with fitting truth to speak.

53

Why linger, why turn back, why shrink, my Heart?
470 Thy hopes are gone before: from all things here
They have departed; thou shouldst now depart!
A light is past from the revolving year,
And man, and woman; and what still is dear
Attracts to crush, repels to make thee wither.
475 The soft sky smiles,—the low wind whispers near:
'Tis Adonais calls! oh, hasten thither,
No more let Life divide what Death can join together.

---

[1] a description of the Protestant cemetery in Rome; the reference to an "infant's smile" reminds the reader that Shelley's eldest child, William, had been buried there in 1819.

[2] the pyramid on the grave of the Roman Caius Cestius, overlooking the Protestant cemetery in Rome. See Shelley's letter to Thomas Love Peacock, [22] December 1818.*

54

That Light whose smile kindles the Universe,
That Beauty in which all things work and move,
480 That Benediction which the eclipsing Curse
Of birth can quench not, that sustaining Love
Which through the web of being blindly wove
By man and beast and earth and air and sea,
Burns bright or dim, as each are mirrors of
485 The fire for which all thirst; now beams on me,
Consuming the last clouds of cold mortality.

55

The breath whose might I have invoked in song
Descends on me; my spirit's bark is driven,
Far from the shore, far from the trembling throng
490 Whose sails were never to the tempest given;
The massy earth and sphered skies are riven!
I am borne darkly, fearfully, afar;
Whilst burning through the inmost veil of Heaven,
The soul of Adonais, like a star,
495 Beacons from the abode where the Eternal are.

from *Posthumous Poems*, ed. M.W. Shelley (1824)

Sonnet IV

Lift not the painted veil which those who live
Call Life: though unreal shapes be pictured there,
And it but mimic all we would believe
With colours idly spread:—behind, lurk Fear
5 And Hope, twin destinies; who ever weave
The shadows, which the world calls substance, there.
I knew one who lifted it—he sought,
For his lost heart was tender, things to love
But found them not, alas! nor was there aught
10 The world contains, the which he could approve.
Through the unheeding many he did move,
A splendour among shadows, a bright blot
Upon this gloomy scene, a Spirit that strove
For truth, and like the Preacher[1] found it not.

---

[1] See Ecclesiastes 1.2.

The Triumph of Life[2]

Swift as a spirit hastening to his task
Of glory and of good, the Sun sprang forth
Rejoicing in his splendour, and the mask

Of darkness fell from the awakened Earth—
5 The smokeless altars of the mountain snows
Flamed above crimson clouds, and at the birth

Of light, the Ocean's orison arose,
To which the birds tempered their matin lay.
All flowers in field or forest which unclose

10 Their trembling eyelids to the kiss of day,
Swinging their censers in the element,
With orient incense lit by the new ray

Burned slow and inconsumably, and sent
Their odorous sighs up to the smiling air;
15 And, in succession due, did continent,

Isle, ocean, and all things that in them wear
The form and character of mortal mould,
Rise as the sun their father rose, to bear

Their portion of the toil, which he of old
20 Took as his own and then imposed on them:
But I, whom thoughts which must remain untold

Had kept as wakeful as the stars that gem
The cone of night, now they were laid asleep
Stretched my faint limbs beneath the hoary stem

25 Which an old chesnut flung athwart the steep
Of a green Apennine: before me fled
The night; behind me rose the day; the deep

---

[2] The text is that of the first publication, edited by Mary Shelley* from a damaged manuscript. Since subsequent editors have done much to decipher portions of the text that Mary Shelley misconstrued or left blank, we note the most significant alternative readings, with reference to the work of G.M. Matthews (1960) and Donald H. Reiman (1965).

Was at my feet, and Heaven above my head,
When a strange trance over my fancy grew
Which was not slumber, for the shade it spread

Was so transparent, that the scene came through
As clear as when a veil of light is drawn
O'er evening hills they glimmer; and I knew

That I had felt the freshness of that dawn,
Bathed in the same cold dew my brow and hair,
And sate as thus upon that slope of lawn

Under the self same bough, and heard as there
The birds, the fountains and the ocean hold
Sweet talk in music through the enamoured air,
And then a vision on my brain was rolled.

*****

As in that trance of wondrous thought I lay,
This was the tenour of my waking dream:—
Methought I sate beside a public way

Thick strewn with summer dust, and a great stream
Of people there was hurrying to and fro,
Numerous as gnats upon the evening gleam,

All hastening onward, yet none seemed to know
Whither he went, or whence he came, or why
He made one of the multitude, and so

Was borne amid the crowd, as through the sky
One of the million leaves of summer's bier;
Old age and youth, manhood and infancy

Mixed in one mighty torrent did appear,
Some flying from the thing they feared, and some
Seeking the object of another's fear;

And others as with steps towards the tomb,
Pored on the trodden worms that crawled beneath,
And others mournfully within the gloom

Of their own shadow walked and called it death;
And some fled from it as it were a ghost,
Half fainting in the affliction of vain breath:

But more with motions, which each other crost,
Pursued or spurned the shadows the clouds threw,
Or birds within the noon-day ether lost,

Upon that path where flowers never grew,
And weary with vain toil and faint for thirst,
Heard not the fountains, whose melodious dew

Out of their mossy cells for ever burst;
Nor felt the breeze which from the forest told
Of grassy paths and wood, lawn-interspersed,[1]

With over-arching elms and caverns cold,
And violet banks where sweet dreams brood, but they
Pursued their serious folly as of old.

And as I gazed, methought that in the way
The throng grew wilder, as the woods of June
When the south wind shakes the extinguished day,

And a cold glare, intenser than the noon,
But icy cold, obscured with [blinding] light[2]
The sun, as he the stars. Like the young moon

When on the sunlit limits of the night
Her white shell trembles amid crimson air,
And whilst the sleeping tempest gathers might,

Doth, as the herald of its coming, bear
The ghost of its dead mother,[3] whose dim frown[4]
Bends in dark ether from her infant's chair,—

---

[1] "wood lawns interspersed" (Reiman).

[2] Reiman comments, "Mrs. Shelley apparently inserted 'blinding' to fill out the meter" (*"The Triumph of Life": A Variorum Edition*, 143).

[3] The shadow of the full moon ("its dead mother") is dimly visible over the crescent new moon. Cf. Coleridge, "Dejection: An Ode,"* and its epigraph from the "Ballad of Sir Patrick Spence."

[4] "whose dim form" (Reiman).

So came a chariot on the silent storm
Of its own rushing splendour, and a Shape
So sate within, as one whom years deform,

Beneath a dusky hood and double cape,
90 Crouching within the shadow of a tomb,
And o'er what seemed the head a cloud-like crape

Was bent, a dun and faint etherial gloom
Tempering the light upon the chariot beam;
A Janus-visaged shadow[1] did assume

95 The guidance of that wonder-winged team;
The shapes which drew in thick lightnings
Were lost:—I heard alone on the air's soft stream

The music of their ever-moving wings.
All the four faces of that charioteer
100 Had their eyes banded; little profit brings

Speed in the van and blindness in the rear,
Nor then avail the beams that quench the sun
Or that with banded eyes could pierce the sphere

Of all that is, has been or will be done;
105 So ill was the car guided—but it past
With solemn speed majestically on.

The crowd gave way, and I arose aghast,
Or seemed to rise, so mighty was the trance,
And saw, like clouds upon the thunders blast,

110 The million with fierce song and maniac dance
Raging around—such seemed the jubilee
As when to meet some conqueror's advance

Imperial Rome poured forth her living sea
From senate house, and forum, and theatre,
115 When [   ] upon the free[2]

Had bound a yoke, which soon they stooped to bear.
Nor wanted here the just similitude
Of a triumphal pageant, for where'er

The chariot rolled, a captive multitude
120 Was driven;—all those who had grown old in power
Or misery,—all who had their age subdued

By action or by suffering, and whose hour
Was drained to its last sand in weal or woe,
So that the trunk survived both fruit and flower;—

125 All those whose fame or infamy must grow
Till the great winter lay the form and name
Of this green earth with them for ever low;—[3]

All but the sacred few who could not tame
Their spirits to the conquerors—but as soon
130 As they had touched the world with living flame,

Fled back like eagles to their native noon,
Or those who put aside the diadem
Of earthly thrones or gems [   ][4]

Were there, of Athens and Jerusalem,[5]
135 Were neither mid the mighty captives seen,
Nor mid the ribald crowd that followed them,

Nor those who went before fierce and obscene.
The wild dance maddens in the van, and those
Who lead it—fleet as shadows on the green,

140 Outspeed the chariot, and without repose
Mix with each other in tempestuous measure
To savage music, wilder as it grows,

They, tortured by their agonizing pleasure,
Convulsed and on the rapid whirlwinds spun
145 Of that fierce spirit, whose unholy leisure

---

[1] shadow with two faces, like Janus, the Roman god of beginnings and endings.

[2] "When Freedom left those who upon the free" (Reiman).

[3] "Of their own earth with them forever low" (Reiman).

[4] "Of earthly thrones or gems till the last one" (Reiman).

[5] "for they of Athens & Jerusalem" (Reiman).

Was soothed by mischief since the world begun,
Throw back their heads and loose their streaming hair;
And in their dance round her who dims the sun,

Maidens and youths fling their wild arms in air
150 As their feet twinkle; they recede, and now
Bending within each other's atmosphere

Kindle invisibly—and as they glow,
Like moths by light attracted and repelled,
Oft to their bright destruction come and go,

155 Till like two clouds into one vale impelled
That shake the mountains when their lightnings mingle
And die in rain—the fiery band which held

Their natures, snaps—the shock still may tingle;[1]
One falls and then another in the path
160 Senseless—nor is the desolation single,

Yet ere I can say *where*—the chariot hath
Past over them—nor other trace I find
But as of foam after the ocean's wrath

Is spent upon the desart shore;—behind,
165 Old men and women foully disarrayed,
Shake their grey hairs in the insulting wind,

To seek, to [   ], to strain with limbs decayed,
Limping to reach the light[2] which leaves them still
Farther behind and deeper in the shade.

170 But not the less with impotence of will
They wheel, though ghastly shadows interpose
Round them and round each other, and fulfil

Their work, and in the dust from whence they rose
Sink, and corruption veils them as they lie,
175 And past in these performs what [   ] in those.[3]

Struck to the heart by this sad pageantry,
Half to myself I said—And what is this?
Whose shape is that within the car? And why—

I would have added—is all here amiss?—
180 But a voice answered—"Life!"—I turned, and knew
(Oh Heaven, have mercy on such wretchedness!)

That what I thought was an old root which grew
To strange distortion out of the hill side,
Was indeed one of those deluded crew,

185 And that the grass, which methought hung so wide
And white, was but his thin discoloured hair,
And that the holes it vainly sought to hide,

Were or had been eyes:—"If thou canst, forbear
To join the dance, which I had well forborne!"
190 Said the grim Feature of my thought: "Aware,[4]

"I will unfold[5] that which to this deep scorn
Led me and my companions, and relate
The progress of the pageant since the morn;

"If thirst of knowledge shall not then abate,
195 Follow it thou even to the night, but I
Am weary."—Then like one who with the weight

Of his own words is staggered, wearily
He paused; and ere he could resume, I cried:
"First, who art thou?"—"Before thy memory,

---

[1] "the shock cease to tingle" (Reiman).

[2] "Limp in the dance & strain with limbs decayed / To reach the car of light" (Reiman).

[3] "And frost in these performs what fire in those" (Reiman).

[4] "Said the grim Feature, of my thought aware" (Reiman).

[5] "I will now tell" (Reiman).

"I feared, loved, hated, suffered, did and died,	200
And if the spark with which Heaven lit my spirit
Had been with purer sentiment supplied,[1]

"Corruption would not now thus much inherit
Of what was once Rousseau,[2]—nor this disguise
Stained that which ought to have disdained to wear it;[3]	205

"If I have been extinguished, yet there rise
A thousand beacons from the spark I bore"—
"And who are those chained to the car?"—"The wise,

"The great, the unforgotten,—they who wore
Mitres and helms and crowns, or wreaths of light,	210
Signs of thought's empire over thought—their lore

"Taught them not this, to know themselves; their might
Could not repress the mystery[4] within,
And for the morn of truth they feigned, deep night

"Caught them ere evening."—"Who is he with chin	215
Upon his breast, and hands crost on his chain?"—
"The Child of a fierce hour; he sought to win

"The world, and lost all that it did contain
Of greatness, in its hope destroyed; and more
Of fame and peace than virtue's self can gain	220

"Without the opportunity which bore
Him on its eagle pinions to the peak
From which a thousand climbers have before

"Fall'n, as Napoleon fell."[5]—I felt my cheek
Alter, to see the shadow pass away	225
Whose grasp had left the giant world so weak,

That every pigmy kicked it as it lay;
And much I grieved to think how power and will
In opposition rule our mortal day,

And why God made irreconcilable	230
Good and the means of good; and for despair
I half disdained mine eyes'[6] desire to fill

With the spent vision of the times that were
And scarce have ceased to be.—"Dost thou behold,"
Said my guide, "those spoilers spoiled, Voltaire,	235

"Frederic, and Paul, Catherine, and Leopold,[7]
And hoary anarchs,[8] demagogues, and sage—
——name the world thinks always old,[9]

"For in the battle, life and they did wage,
She remained conqueror. I was overcome	240
By my own heart alone, which neither age,

"Nor tears, nor infamy, nor now the tomb
Could temper to its object."—"Let them pass,"
I cried, "the world and its mysterious doom

"Is not so much more glorious than it was,	245
That I desire to worship those who drew
New figures on its false and fragile glass

"As the old faded."—"Figures ever new
Rise on the bubble, paint them as you may;
We have but thrown, as those before us threw,	250

---

[1] "Earth had with purer nutriment supplied" (Reiman).

[2] Jean-Jacques Rousseau (1712–78).

[3] "Stained that within which still disdains to wear it.—" (Reiman).

[4] "mutiny" (Reiman).

[5] The French Emperor Napoleon Buonaparte (1769–1821) was defeated by the Prussians and the English at the Battle of Waterloo in 1815.

[6] "eye's" (Reiman).

[7] The "anarchs" of the following line are Frederick II of Prussia (1712–86), Catherine II of Russia (1729–96), and Leopold II (1747–92), Grand Duke of Tuscany and later Holy Roman Emperor. Reiman gives "Kant" for Mary Shelley's "Paul," noting (167) that the word "Kant" is superimposed in the MS on "Pitt." Voltaire (1694–1778), the "demagogue," and (probably) Immanuel Kant (1724–1804), the "sage," inspire the three Enlightenment rulers.

[8] "Chained hoary anarchs" (Reiman).

[9] "Whose name the fresh world thinks already old" (Reiman).

"Our shadows on it as it past away.
But mark how chained to the triumphal chair
The mighty phantoms of an elder day;

"All that is mortal of great Plato there
255 Expiates the joy and woe his master knew not;[1]
The star that ruled his doom was far too fair,[2]

"And life, where long that flower of Heaven grew not,
Conquered that heart by love, which gold, or pain,
Or age, or sloth, or slavery could subdue not.

260 "And near walk the [   ] twain,
The tutor and his pupil,[3] whom Dominion
Followed as tame as vulture in a chain.

"The world was darkened beneath either pinion
Of him whom from the flock of conquerors
265 Fame singled out for her thunder-bearing minion;

"The other long outlived both woes and wars,
Throned in the[4] thoughts of men, and still had kept
The jealous key of truth's eternal doors,

"If Bacon's eagle spirit had not leapt
270 Like lightning out of darkness[5]—he compelled
The Proteus shape of Nature[6] as it slept

"To wake, and lead him to the caves[7] that held
The treasure of the secrets of its reign.
See the great bards of elder time, who quelled[8]

275 "The passions which they sung, as by their strain
May well be known: their living melody
Tempers its own contagion to the vein

"Of those who are infected with it—I
Have suffered what I wrote, or viler pain!
280 And so my words have seeds of misery"—[9]

——he pointed to a company,
Midst whom I quickly recognised the heirs
Of Cæsar's crime, from him to Constantine;
The anarch chiefs,[10] whose force and murderous snares

285 Had founded many a sceptre-bearing line,
And spread the plague of gold and blood abroad:
And Gregory and John,[11] and men divine,

---

[1] "All that is mortal of great Plato there/ Expiates the joy & woe his master knew not" (Reiman).

[2] Plato loved a young man called Aster, whose name is both that of a flower and the word for "star." Cf. P.B. Shelley's first epigraph to *Adonais.*

[3] "And near walk the twain, / The tutor & his pupil" (Reiman). The tutor and his pupil are Aristotle (384–322 BC) and Alexander the Great (356–323 BC).

[4] "Throned in new" (Reiman).

[5] Francis Bacon (1561–1626) introduced the foundation of the scientific method.

[6] See Francis Bacon, *The Wisdom of the Ancients* (1611).

[7] "To wake & to unbar the caves" (Reiman).

[8] "who inly quelled" (Reiman).

[9] After this line, Mary Shelley adds the following note, before resuming the text at the line, "——he pointed to a company":
   "[There is a chasm here in the MS, which it is impossible to fill up. It appears from the context, that other shapes pass, and that Rousseau still stood beside the dreamer, as]—"
   Donald H. Reiman explains how cancelled passages of drafts and fragments intervene in the MS and reconstructs the text as follows (from line 276):
   "…their living melody
Tempers its own contagion to the vein
   "Of those who are infected with it—I
Have suffered what I wrote, or viler pain!—
   "And so my words were seeds of misery—
Even as the deeds of others."—"Not as theirs,"
   I said—he pointed to a company…

[10] These powerful figures, like the "anarchs" of line 237, were hereditary tyrants. Cæsar (100–44 BC) effectively ended the Roman Republic; Constantine (AD 274–337) established Christianity as the Imperial state religion.

[11] Pope Gregory VII (Hildebrand) (c. 1020–85) and many popes called John were powerful figures in the history of the Roman Catholic Church.

Who rose like shadows between man and God;
Till that eclipse, still hanging over heaven,
290 Was worshipped by the world o'er which they strode,

For the true sun it quenched—"Their power was given
But to destroy," replied the leader:—"I
Am one of those who have created, even

"If it be but a world of agony."—
295 "Whence comest thou? and whither goest thou?
How did thy course begin?" I said, "and why?

"Mine eyes are sick of this perpetual flow
Of people, and my heart sick of one sad thought—
Speak!"—"Whence I am,[1] I partly seem to know,

300 "And how and by what paths I have been brought
To this dread pass, methinks even thou mayst guess;—
Why this should be, my mind can compass not;

"Whither the conqueror hurries me, still less;—
But follow thou, and from spectator turn
305 Actor or victim in this wretchedness,

"And what thou wouldst be taught I then may learn
From thee. Now listen:—In the April prime,
When all the forest tips[2] began to burn

"With kindling green, touched by the azure clime
310 Of the young year's dawn, I was laid asleep[3]
Under a mountain, which from unknown time

"Had yawned into a cavern, high and deep;
And from it came a gentle rivulet,
Whose water, like clear air, in its calm sweep

315 "Bent the soft grass, and kept forever wet
The stems of the sweet flowers, and filled the grove
With sounds, which whoso hears[4] must needs forget

"All pleasure and all pain, all hate and love,
Which they had known before that hour of rest;
320 A sleeping mother then would dream not of

"Her only child who died upon her breast
At eventide—a king would mourn no more
The crown of which his brows were dispossest

"When the sun lingered o'er his ocean floor,
325 To gild his rival's new prosperity.
Thou wouldst forget thus vainly to deplore

"Ills, which if ills can find no cure from thee,
The thought of which no other sleep will quell,
Nor other music blot from memory,

330 "So sweet and deep is the oblivious spell;
And whether life had been before that sleep
The heaven which I imagine, or a hell

"Like this harsh world in which I wake to weep,
I know not. I arose, and for a space
335 The scene of woods and waters seemed to keep,

"Though it was now broad day, a gentle trace
Of light diviner than the common sun
Sheds on the common earth,[5] and all the place

"Was filled with magic[6] sounds woven into one
340 Oblivious melody, confusing sense
Amid the gliding waves and shadows dun;

"And, as I looked, the bright omnipresence
Of morning through the orient cavern flowed,
And the sun's image radiantly intense

345 "Burned on the waters of the well that glowed
Like gold, and threaded all the forest's maze
With winding paths of emerald fire; there stood

---

[1] "Whence I came" (Reiman).
[2] "forest tops" (Reiman).
[3] "I found myself asleep" (Reiman).
[4] "With sound which all who hear" (Reiman).

[5] Cf. W. Wordsworth, "Ode" 76.*
[6] "many" (Reiman).

"Amid the sun, as he amid the blaze
Of his own glory, on the vibrating
350 Floor of the fountain, paved with flashing rays,

"A Shape all light, which with one hand did fling
Dew on the earth, as if she were the dawn,
And the invisible rain did ever sing[1]

"A silver music on the mossy lawn;
355 And still before me[2] on the dusky grass,
Iris[3] her many-coloured scarf had drawn:

"In her right hand she bore a crystal glass,
Mantling with bright Nepenthe;[4] the fierce splendour
Fell from her as she moved under the mass

360 "Out of[5] the deep cavern, with palms so tender,
Their tread broke not the mirror of its billow;
She glided along the river, and did bend her

"Head under the dark boughs, till like a willow,
Her fair hair swept the bosom of the stream
365 That whispered with delight to be its pillow.

"As one enamoured is upborne in dream
O'er lily-paven lakes mid silver mist,
To wondrous music, so this shape might seem

"Partly to tread the waves with feet which kissed
370 The dancing foam; partly to glide along
The air which roughened the moist amethyst,[6]

"Or the faint[7] morning beams that fell among
The trees, or the soft shadows of the trees;
And her feet, ever to the ceaseless song

375 "Of leaves, and winds, and waves, and birds, and bees,
And falling drops, moved to a measure new
Yet sweet, as on the summer evening breeze,

"Up from the lake a shape of golden dew
Between two rocks, athwart the rising moon,
380 Dances i' the wind, where never eagle flew;

"And still her feet, no less than the sweet tune
To which they moved, seemed as they moved, to blot
The thoughts of him who gazed on them; and soon

"All that was, seemed as if it had been not;
385 And all[8] the gazer's mind was strewn beneath
Her feet like embers; and she, thought by thought,

"Trampled its sparks into the dust of death;
As day upon the threshold of the east
Treads out the lamps of night, until the breath

390 "Of darkness re-illumine even the least
Of heaven's living eyes—like day she came,
Making the night a dream; and ere she ceased

"To move, as one between desire and shame
Suspended, I said—If, as it doth seem,
395 Thou comest from the realm without a name,

"Into this valley of perpetual dream,
Shew whence I came, and where I am, and why—
Pass not away upon the passing stream.

---

[1] "Whose invisible rain forever seemed to sing" (Reiman).

[2] "And still before her" (Reiman).

[3] the goddess of the rainbow, messenger of the gods.

[4] a drug that induced forgetfulness (cf. Homer, *Odyssey* 4).

[5] "Of the" (Reiman).

[6] the water, which is purple or violet like the semi-precious stone, amethyst.

[7] "slant" (Reiman).

[8] "As if" (Reiman).

"Arise and quench thy thirst, was her reply.
And as a shut lily, stricken by the wand
Of dewy morning's vital alchemy,

"I rose; and, bending at her sweet command,
Touched with faint lips the cup she raised,
And suddenly my brain became as sand

"Where the first wave had more than half erased
The track of deer on desart Labrador;
Whilst the wolf,[1] from which they fled amazed,

"Leaves his stamp visibly upon the shore,
Until the second bursts;—so on my sight
Burst a new vision, never seen before,

"And the fair shape waned in the coming light,
As veil by veil the silent splendour drops
From Lucifer, amid the chrysolite[2]

"Of sun-rise, ere it tinge[3] the mountain tops;
And as the presence of that fairest planet,
Although unseen, is felt by one who hopes

"That his day's path may end as he began it,
In that star's smile, whose light is like the scent
Of a jonquil when evening breezes fan it,

"Or the soft note in which his dear lament
The Brescian shepherd breathes,[4] or the caress
That turned his weary slumber to content;

"So knew I in that light's severe excess
The presence of that shape which on the stream
Moved, as I moved along the wilderness,

"More dimly than a day-appearing dream,
The ghost of a forgotten form of sleep;
A light of heaven, whose half-extinguished beam,

"Through the sick day in which we wake to weep,
Glimmers, for ever sought, for ever lost;
So did that shape its obscure tenour keep

"Beside my path, as silent as a ghost;
But the new Vision, and the cold bright car,
With solemn speed and stunning music,[5] crost

"The forest, and as if from some dread war
Triumphantly returning, the loud million
Fiercely extolled the fortune of her star.

"A moving arch of victory, the vermilion
And green and azure plumes of Iris had
Built high over her wind-winged pavilion,

"And underneath etherial glory clad
The wilderness, and far before her flew
The tempest of the splendour, which forbade

"Shadow to fall from leaf and stone; the crew
Seemed in that light, like atomies to dance[6]
Within a sunbeam;—some upon the new

"Embroidery of flowers, that did enhance
The grassy vesture of the desart, played,
Forgetful of the chariot's swift advance;

"Others stood gazing, till within the shade
Of the great mountain its light left them dim;
Others outspeeded it; and others made

"Circles around it, like the clouds that swim
Round the high moon in a bright sea of air;
And more did follow, with exulting hymn,

---

[1] "Whilst the fierce wolf" (Reiman).

[2] Lucifer, "Light-bearer" (L.), the planet Venus; chrysolite, a semi-precious stone.

[3] "strike" (Reiman).

[4] "The favorite song, 'Stanco di pascolar le peccorelle' ['I am tired of grazing my flock'], is a Brescian national air." (Mary Shelley.) Brescia is a province in the north of Italy.

[5] "With savage music, stunning music" (Reiman).

[6] "atomies that dance" (Reiman).

"The chariot and the captives fettered there:—
But all like bubbles on an eddying flood
Fell into the same track at last, and were

"Borne onward.—I among the multitude
Was swept—me, sweetest flowers delayed not long;
Me, not the shadow nor the solitude;

"Me, not that falling stream's Lethean song;[1]
Me, not the phantom of that early form,
Which moved upon its motion—but among

"The thickest billows of that living storm
I plunged, and bared my bosom to the clime
Of that cold light, whose airs too soon deform.

"Before the chariot had begun to climb
The opposing steep of that mysterious dell,
Behold a wonder worthy of the rhyme

"Of him who from the lowest depths of hell,
Through every paradise and through all glory,
Love led serene, and who returned to tell

"The words of hate and care;[2] the wondrous story
How all things are transfigured except Love;[3]
For deaf as is a sea, which wrath makes hoary,

"The world can hear not the sweet notes that move
The sphere whose light is melody to lovers—
A wonder worthy of his rhyme—the grove

"Grew dense with shadows to its inmost covers,
The earth was grey with phantoms, and the air
Was peopled with dim forms, as when there hovers

"A flock of vampire-bats before the glare
Of the tropic sun, bringing, ere evening,
Strange night upon some Indian vale;[4]—thus were

"Phantoms diffused around; and some did fling
Shadows of shadows, yet unlike themselves,
Behind them; some like eaglets on the wing

"Were lost in the white day;[5] others like elves
Danced in a thousand unimagined shapes
Upon the sunny streams and grassy shelves;

"And others sate chattering like restless apes
On vulgar hands, * * * *[6]
Some made a cradle of the ermined capes

"Of kingly mantles; some across the tire
Of pontiffs rode, like demons;[7] others played
Under the crown which girt with empire

"A baby's or an idiot's brow, and made
Their nests in it. The old anatomies[8]
Sate hatching their bare broods under the shade

"Of demon wings, and laughed from their dead eyes
To reassume the delegated power,
Array'd in which those worms did monarchize,

"Who make this earth their charnel. Others more
Humble, like falcons, sate upon the fist
Of common men, and round their heads did soar;

"Or like small gnats and flies, as thick as mist
On evening marshes, thronged about the brow
Of lawyers, statesmen, priest and theorist:—

"And others, like discoloured flakes of snow
On fairest bosoms and the sunniest hair,
Fell, and were melted by the youthful glow

"Which they extinguished; and, like tears, they were
A veil to those from whose faint lids they rained
In drops of sorrow. I became aware

---

[1] song that induces forgetfulness, like the water of the river Lethe in the classical underworld.

[2] "hate & awe" (Reiman).

[3] Dante ("him" in line 471) told this story in his *Divine Comedy* (early 14th century).

[4] "Indian isle" (Reiman).

[5] "white blaze" (Reiman).

[6] "On vulgar paws and voluble like fire" (Reiman).

[7] "the tiar / Of Pontiffs sate like vultures" (Reiman).

[8] skeletons.

"Of whence those forms proceeded which thus stained
The track in which we moved. After brief space,
From every form the beauty slowly waned;

"From every firmest limb and fairest face
520 The strength and freshness fell like dust, and left
The action and the shape without the grace

"Of life. The marble brow of youth was cleft
With care; and in those eyes where once hope shone,
Desire, like a lioness bereft

525 "Of her last cub, glared ere it died; each one
Of that great crowd sent forth incessantly
These shadows, numerous as the dead leaves blown

"In autumn evening from a poplar tree.
Each like himself and like each other were
530 At first; but some distorted seemed to be

"Obscure clouds, moulded by the casual air;
And of this stuff the car's creative ray
Wrapt[1] all the busy phantoms that were there,

"As the sun shapes the clouds; thus on the way
535 Mask after mask fell from the countenance
And form of all; and long before the day

"Was old, the joy which waked like heaven's glance
The sleepers in the oblivious valley, died;
And some grew weary of the ghastly dance,

540 "And fell, as I have fallen, by the way side;—
Those soonest from whose forms most shadows past,
And least of strength and beauty did abide.

"Then, what is life? I cried."[2]—

---

[1] "Wrought" (Reiman).

[2] Donald H. Reiman adds the following additional lines from MS:
    "Then, what is Life?" I said … the cripple cast
      His eye upon the car which now had rolled
      Onward, as if that look must be the last,

    And answered…. "Happy those for whom the fold
      Of […]"

The Masque of Anarchy. A Poem[3] (1832)

1

As I lay asleep in Italy,
There came a voice from over the sea,
And with great power it forth led me
To walk in the visions of Poesy.

2

5 I met Murder on the way—
He had a mask like Castlereagh[4]—
Very smooth he look'd, yet grim;
Seven bloodhounds followed him:

3

All were fat; and well they might
10 Be in admirable plight,
For one by one, and two by two,
He tossed them human hearts to chew,
Which from his wide cloak he drew.

---

[3] The title-page reads, "Now first published, with a preface by Leigh Hunt,"* and includes the following epigraph from P.B. Shelley's *The Revolt of Islam*:
    "Hope is strong;
    Justice and Truth their winged child have found" (2.13).
On 16 August 1819, a peaceful rally in favour of parliamentary reform was violently suppressed in Manchester. At least six people were killed and at least eighty were wounded. Named the Peterloo Massacre with satiric reference to the place where it occurred (St. Peter's Field) and to the defeat of Napoleon at the Battle of Waterloo, this event angered critics of the Tory government and made parliamentary reform all the more urgent. P.B. Shelley tried to have the poem printed in the *Examiner* in 1819, but its editor, Leigh Hunt, was afraid of strict laws against sedition and did not publish the poem until 1832, by which time the First Reform Bill had been passed. Cf. Hone, *The Political House that Jack Built*.* By "anarchy," Shelley means not lawlessness but the abuse of power: cf. Milton, *Paradise Lost* 2.988; Pope, *The Dunciad* 4.655.

[4] Robert Stewart, Viscount Castlereagh, (1769–1822), Foreign Secretary and Tory house leader. Shelley blames Castlereagh for supporting the reactionary Holy Alliance of 1815, and for Britain's agreement with Austria, France, Russia, Prussia, Portugal, Spain, and Sweden (the "Seven bloodhounds" of line 8) to postpone final abolition of the slave trade.

4

Next came Fraud, and he had on,
Like Lord E—,[1] an ermined gown;
His big tears, for he wept well,
Turned to mill-stones as they fell;

5

And the little children, who
Round his feet played to and fro,
Thinking every tear a gem,
Had their brains knocked out by them.

6

Clothed with the * *[2] as with light,
And the shadows of the night,
Like * * *[3] next, Hypocrisy,
On a crocodile rode by.

7

And many more Destructions played
In this ghastly masquerade,
All disguised, even to the eyes,
Like bishops, lawyers, peers, or spies.[4]

8

Last came Anarchy; he rode
On a white horse, splashed with blood;
He was pale even to the lips,
Like Death in the Apocalypse.[5]

9

And he wore a kingly crown;
And in his grasp a sceptre shone;
And on his brow this mark I saw—
"I am God, and King, and Law!"

10

With a pace stately and fast,
Over English land he past,
Trampling to a mire of blood
The adoring multitude.

11

And a mighty troop around,
With their trampling shook the ground,
Waving each a bloody sword,
For the service of their Lord.

12

And with glorious triumph, they
Rode through England proud and gay,
Drunk as with intoxication
Of the wine of desolation.

13

O'er fields and towns, from sea to sea,
Passed the pageant swift and free,
Tearing up, and trampling down,
Till they came to London town.

14

And each dweller, panic-stricken,
Felt his heart with terror sicken,
Hearing the tempestuous cry
Of the triumph of Anarchy.

---

[1] John Scott, Baron Eldon, who, as Lord Chancellor, had denied Shelley access to his children by his first marriage.

[2] the Bible.

[3] Sidmouth: the Home Secretary, Henry Addington, Viscount Sidmouth (1759–1844).

[4] As Home Secretary, Sidmouth set up a spy system to entrap political activists and had new churches built in industrial towns to distract workers from their misery.

[5] Cf. Revelation 6.8 and Benjamin West's painting, "Death on the Pale Horse" (1817).

15

For with pomp to meet him came,
Clothed in arms like blood and flame,
60 The hired murderers who did sing,
"Thou art God, and Law, and King.

16

"We have waited, weak and lone,
For thy coming, Mighty One!
Our purses are empty, our swords are cold,
65 Give us glory, and blood, and gold."

17

Lawyers and priests, a motley crowd,
To the earth their pale brows bowed;
Like a bad prayer not over loud,
Whispering—"Thou art Law and God."

18

70 Then all cried with one accord,
"Thou art King, and God, and Lord;
Anarchy, to thee we bow,
Be thy name made holy now!"

19

And Anarchy, the skeleton,
75 Bowed and grinned to every one,
As well as if his education,
Had cost ten millions to the nation.

20

For he knew the palaces
Of our kings were nightly his;
80 His the sceptre, crown, and globe,
And the gold-in-woven robe.

21

So he sent his slaves before
To seize upon the Bank and Tower,[1]
And was proceeding with intent
85 To meet his pensioned parliament,

22

When one fled past, a maniac maid,
And her name was Hope, she said:
But she looked more like Despair;
And she cried out in the air;

23

90 "My father, Time, is weak and grey
With waiting for a better day;
See how idiot-like he stands,
Fumbling with his palsied hands!

24

"He has had child after child,
95 And the dust of death is piled
Over every one but me—
Misery! oh, Misery!"

25

Then she lay down in the street,
Right before the horses' feet,
100 Expecting with a patient eye,
Murder, Fraud, and Anarchy.

26

When between her and her foes
A mist, a light, an image rose,
Small at first, and weak and frail
105 Like the vapour of the vale:

27

Till, as clouds grow on the blast,
Like tower-crown'd giants striding fast,
And glare with lightnings as they fly,
And speak in thunder to the sky,

28

110 It grew—a shape arrayed in mail
Brighter than the viper's scale,
And upborne on wings whose grain
Was as the light of sunny rain.

---

[1] the Bank of England and the Tower of London, symbols of governmental and monarchical power.

29

On its helm, seen far away,
A planet, like the morning's, lay;
And those plumes it light rained through,
Like a shower of crimson dew.

30

With step as soft as wind it passed
O'er the heads of men—so fast
That they knew the presence there,
And looked—and all was empty air.

31

As flowers beneath the footstep waken,
As stars from night's loose hair are shaken,
As waves arise when loud winds call,
Thoughts sprung where'er that step did fall.

32

And the prostrate multitude
Looked—and ankle deep in blood,
Hope, that maiden most serene,
Was walking with a quiet mien:

33

And Anarchy, the ghastly birth,
Lay dead earth upon the earth;
The Horse of Death, tameless as wind,
Fled, and with his hoofs did grind
To dust the murderers thronged behind.

34

A rushing light of clouds and splendour,
A sense, awakening and yet tender,
Was heard and felt—and at its close
These words of joy and fear arose:

35

(As if their own indignant earth,
Which gave the sons of England birth,
Had felt their blood upon her brow,
And shuddering with a mother's throe,

36

Had turned every drop of blood,
By which her face had been bedewed,
To an accent unwithstood,
As if her heart had cried aloud:)

37

"Men of England, Heirs of Glory,
Heroes of unwritten story,
Nurslings of one mighty mother,
Hopes of her, and one another,

38

"Rise, like lions after slumber,
In unvanquishable number,
Shake your chains to earth like dew,
Which in sleep had fall'n on you.

39

"What is Freedom? Ye can tell
That which Slavery is too well,
For its very name has grown
To an echo of your own.

40

"'Tis to work, and have such pay
As just keeps life from day to day
In your limbs, as in a cell
For the tyrants' use to dwell:

41

"So that ye for them are made,
Loom, and plough, and sword, and spade;
With or without your own will, bent
To their defence and nourishment.

42

"'Tis to see your children weak
With their mothers pine and peak,
When the winter winds are bleak:—
They are dying whilst I speak.

43

"'Tis to hunger for such diet,
As the rich man in his riot
Casts to the fat dogs that lie
Surfeiting beneath his eye.

44

"'Tis to let the Ghost of Gold[1]
Take from toil a thousand fold,
More than e'er its substance could
In the tyrannies of old:

45

"Paper coin—that forgery
Of the title deeds, which ye
Hold to something of the worth
Of the inheritance of Earth.

46

"'Tis to be a slave in soul,
And to hold no strong controul
Over your own wills, but be
All that others make of ye.

47

"And at length when ye complain,
With a murmur weak and vain,
'Tis to see the tyrant's crew
Ride over your wives and you:—
Blood is on the grass like dew.

48

"Then it is to feel revenge,
Fiercely thirsting to exchange
Blood for blood—and wrong for wrong:
DO NOT THUS, WHEN YE ARE STRONG.

49

"Birds find rest in narrow nest,
When weary of the winged quest;
Beasts find fare in woody lair,
When storm and snow are in the air.

50

"Asses, swine, have litter spread,
And with fitting food are fed;
All things have a home but one:
Thou, oh Englishman, hast none![2]

51

"This is Slavery—savage men,
Or wild beasts within a den,
Would endure not as ye do:
But such ills they never knew.

52

"What art thou, Freedom? Oh! could Slaves
Answer from their living graves
This demand, tyrants would flee
Like a dream's dim imagery.

53

"Thou art not, as impostors say,
A shadow soon to pass away,
A superstition, and a name
Echoing from the caves of Fame.[3]

54

"For the labourer thou art bread,
And a comely table spread,
From his daily labour come,
In a neat and happy home.

55

"Thou art clothes, and fire, and food
For the trampled multitude:
No—in countries that are free
Such starvation cannot be,
As in England now we see.

---

[1] paper currency; cf. Barbauld, *Eighteen Hundred and Eleven* 53–54.*

[2] Cf. Matthew 8.20, Luke 9.58.

[3] Cf. Geoffrey Chaucer (c. 1343–1400), *The House of Fame.*

56

"To the rich thou art a check,
When his foot is on the neck
Of his victim; thou dost make
That he treads upon a snake.[1]

57

"Thou art Justice—ne'er for gold
May thy righteous laws be sold,
As laws are in England:—thou
Shield'st alike the high and low.

58

"Thou art Wisdom—Freedom never
Dreams that God will damn for ever
All who think those things untrue,
Of which priests make such ado.

59

"Thou art Peace—never by thee
Would blood and treasure wasted be,
As tyrants wasted them, when all
Leagued to quench thy flame in Gaul.[2]

60

"What if English toil and blood
Was poured forth, even as a flood!
It availed,—oh Liberty!
To dim—but not extinguish thee.

61

"Thou art Love—the rich have kist
Thy feet, and like him following Christ,[3]
Give their substance to the free,
And through the rough world follow thee.

62

"Oh turn their wealth to arms, and make
War for thy beloved sake,
On wealth *and* war and fraud: whence they
Drew the power which is their prey.

63

"Science, and Poetry, and Thought,
Are thy lamps; they make the lot
Of the dwellers in a cot
So serene, they curse it not.

64

"Spirit, Patience, Gentleness,
All that can adorn and bless,
Art thou: let deeds, not words, express
Thine exceeding loveliness.

65

"Let a great assembly be
Of the fearless, of the free,
On some spot of English ground,
Where the plains stretch wide around.

66

"Let the blue sky overhead,
The green earth, on which ye tread,
All that must eternal be,
Witness the solemnity.

67

"From the corners uttermost
Of the bounds of English coast;
From every hut, village, and town,
Where those who live and suffer, moan
For others' misery and their own:

---

[1] The American Revolutionaries adopted a flag bearing the image of a rattlesnake and the motto "Don't tread on me." Cf. Blake, *America* 7.3.*

[2] the spirit of Revolutionary France, extinguished by reactionary tyranny.

[3] Cf. Matthew 19.21, Mark 10.21.

68

"From the workhouse and the prison,
Where pale as corpses newly risen,
Women, children, young, and old,
Groan for pain, and weep for cold;

69

"From the haunts of daily life,
Where is waged the daily strife
With common wants and common cares,
Which sow the human heart with tares;[1]

70

"Lastly, from the palaces,
Where the murmur of distress
Echoes, like the distant sound
Of a wind alive around;

71

"Those prison-halls of wealth and fashion,
Where some few feel such compassion
For those who groan, and toil, and wail,
As must make their brethren pale;

72

"Ye who suffer woes untold,
Or to feel, or to behold
Your lost country bought and sold
With a price of blood and gold;

73

"Let a vast assembly be,
And with great solemnity
Declare with measured words, that ye
Are, as God has made ye, free!

74

"Be your strong and simple words
Keen to wound as sharpened swords,
And wide as targes let them be,
With their shade to cover ye.

75

"Let the tyrants pour around
With a quick and startling sound,
Like the loosening of a sea,
Troops of armed emblazonry.

76

"Let the charged artillery drive,
Till the dead air seems alive
With the clash of clanging wheels,
And the tramp of horses' heels.

77

"Let the fixed bayonet
Gleam with sharp desire to wet
Its bright point in English blood,
Looking keen as one for food.

78

"Let the horsemen's scimitars
Wheel and flash, like sphereless stars,
Thirsting to eclipse their burning
In a sea of death and mourning.

79

"Stand ye calm and resolute,
Like a forest close and mute,
With folded arms, and looks which are
Weapons of an unvanquished war.

80

"And let Panic, who outspeeds
The career of armed steeds,
Pass, a disregarded shade,
Thro' your phalanx undismay'd.[2]

---

[1] Cf. Matthew 13.24–30.

[2] "The three stanzas next ensuing are printed in italics, not because they are better, or indeed so well written, as some of the rest, but as marking out the sober, lawful, and charitable mode of proceeding advocated and anticipated by this supposed reckless innovator. '*Passive obedience*' he certainly had not; but here follows a picture and a recommendation of '*non-resistance*,' in all its glory. The mingled emotion and dignity of it is admirably expressed in the second line of stanza eighty-five. Let churches militant read it, and blush to call the author no Christian!" (Leigh Hunt.)

81

"Let the laws of your own land,
Good or ill, between ye stand,
Hand to hand, and foot to foot,
Arbiters of the dispute.

82

"The old laws of England—they
Whose reverend heads with age are grey,
Children of a wiser day;
And whose solemn voice must be
Thine own echo—Liberty!

83

"On those who first should violate
Such sacred heralds in their state,
Rest the blood that must ensue,
And it will not rest on you.

84

"And if then the tyrants dare,
Let them ride among you there;
Slash, and stab, and maim, and hew;
What they like, that let them do.

85

"With folded arms and steady eyes,
And little fear and less surprise,
Look upon them as they stay
Till their rage has died away:

86

"Then they will return with shame,
To the place from which they came,
And the blood thus shed will speak
In hot blushes on their cheek:

87

"Every woman in the land
Will point at them as they stand—
They will hardly dare to greet
Their acquaintance in the street:

88

"And the bold, true warriors,
Who have hugged Danger in wars,
Will turn to those who would be free
Ashamed of such base company:

89

"And that slaughter to the nation
Shall steam up like inspiration,
Eloquent, oracular,
A volcano heard afar:

90

"And these words shall then become
Like Oppression's thundered doom,
Ringing through each heart and brain,
Heard again—again—again.

91

"Rise like lions after slumber
In unvanquishable NUMBER!
Shake your chains to earth, like dew
Which in sleep had fall'n on you:
YE ARE MANY—THEY ARE FEW."

from the *Athenæum* 260 (20 October 1832)

With a Guitar[1]

The artist who this idol[2] wrought,
To echo all harmonious thought,

---

[1] This poem was written to accompany a guitar, a gift from P.B. Shelley to the Shelleys' friend, Jane Williams (1798–1884). Jane, her husband Edward (1793–1822), and Shelley himself take on the roles of characters from Shakespeare's *The Tempest*, Miranda, Ferdinand, and the spirit Ariel. Lines 43–90 appeared in the *Athenæum* as a complete poem. The first 42 lines, from Donald H. Reiman and Sharon B. Powers' edition of the Bodleian Library MS. Shelley adds. e.3, (*Shelley's Poetry and Prose* 449–51), are as follows:

    Ariel to Miranda;—Take
    This slave of music for the sake
    Of him who is the slave of thee;
    And teach it all the harmony,
5   In which thou can'st, and only thou,
    Make the delighted spirit glow,
    'Till joy denies itself again
    And too intense is turned to pain;
    For by permission and command
10 Of thine own prince Ferdinand
    Poor Ariel sends this silent token
    Of more than ever can be spoken;
    Your guardian spirit Ariel, who
    From life to life must still pursue
15 Your happiness, for thus alone
    Can Ariel ever find his own;
    From Prospero's enchanted cell,
    As the mighty verses tell,
    To the throne of Naples he
20 Lit you o'er the trackless sea,
    Flitting on, your prow before,
    Like a living meteor.
    When you die, the silent Moon
    In her interlunar swoon
25 Is not sadder in her cell
    Than deserted Ariel;
    When you live again on Earth
    Like an unseen Star of birth
    Ariel guides you o'er the sea
30 Of life from your nativity;
    Many changes have been run
    Since Ferdinand and you begun
    Your course of love, and Ariel still
    Has tracked your steps and served your will;
35 Now, in humbler, happier lot
    This is all remembered not;
    And now, alas! the poor sprite is

    Imprisoned for some fault of his
    In a body like a grave:—
40 From you, he only dares to crave
    For his service and his sorrow
    A smile today, a song tomorrow.

[2] the guitar.

---

45 Felled a tree, while on the steep
    The winds were in their winter sleep,
    Rocked in that repose divine
    On the wind-swept Apennine;
    And dreaming some of Autumn past,
50 And some of Spring approaching fast,
    And some of April buds and showers,
    And some of songs in July bowers,
    And all of love; and so this tree,—
    O that such our death may be!—
55 Died in sleep, and felt no pain,
    To live in happier form again;
    From which, beneath Heaven's fairest star,
    The artist wrought that loved Guitar,
    And taught it justly to reply,
60 To all who question skilfully,
    In language gentle as its own,
    Whispering in enamoured tone
    Sweet oracles of woods and dells,
    And summer winds in sylvan cells;
65 For it had learnt all harmonies
    Of the plains and of the skies,
    Of the forests and the mountains,
    And the many-voiced fountains;
    The clearest echoes of the hills,
70 The softest notes of falling rills,
    The melodies of birds and bees,
    The murmuring of summer seas,
    And pattering rain, and breathing dew,
    And airs of evening; and it knew
75 That seldom-heard mysterious sound,
    Which, driven in its diurnal round,
    As it floats through boundless day,
    Our world enkindles on its way—
    All this it knows, but will not tell
80 To those who cannot question well
    The spirit that inhabits it.
    It talks according to the wit

Of its companions, and no more
Is heard than has been felt before,
To those who tempt it to betray
These secrets of an elder day;—
But sweetly as its answers will
Flatter hands of perfect skill,
It keeps its highest, holiest tone,
For our beloved friend alone.

from *The Poetical Works of Percy Bysshe Shelley*, ed. M.W. Shelley (1839)

England in 1819

An old, mad, blind, despised, and dying king,[1]—
Princes, the dregs of their dull race, who flow
Through public scorn,—mud from a muddy spring—
Rulers, who neither see, nor feel, nor know,
But leech-like to their fainting country cling,
Till they drop, blind in blood, without a blow.
A people starved and stabbed in the untilled field,[2]—
An army, which liberticide and prey
Makes as a two-edged sword to all who wield;
Golden and sanguine laws which tempt and slay;
Religion Christless, Godless—a book sealed;
A Senate,—Time's worst statute unrepealed,—
Are graves, from which a glorious Phantom may
Burst, to illumine our tempestuous day.

---

[1] King George III had been declared insane in 1811; he died in 1820.

[2] St. Peter's Field, Manchester; see *The Masque of Anarchy** and Hone, *The Political House that Jack Built.**

from *Essays, Letters from Abroad, Translations and Fragments*, ed. M.W. Shelley (1840)

from *A Defence of Poetry*[3]

According to one mode of regarding those two classes of mental action, which are called reason and imagination, the former may be considered as mind contemplating the relations borne by one thought to another, however produced; and the latter, as mind acting upon those thoughts so as to colour them with its own light, and composing from them as from elements, other thoughts, each containing within itself the principle of its own integrity. The one is the τὸ ποιειν, or the principle of synthesis, and has for its object those forms which are common to universal nature and existence itself; the other is the τὸ λογιζειν,[4] or principle of analysis, and its action regards the relations of things, simply as relations; considering thoughts, not in their integral unity, but as the algebraical representations which conduct to certain general results. Reason is the enumeration of quantities already known; imagination is the perception of the value of those quantities, both separately and as a whole. Reason respects the differences, and imagination the similitudes of things. Reason is to imagination as the instrument to the agent, as the body to the spirit, as the shadow to the substance.

Poetry, in a general sense, may be defined to be "the expression of the imagination": and poetry is connate with the origin of man. Man is an instrument over which a series of external and internal impressions are driven, like the alternations of an ever-changing wind over an Æolian lyre,[5] which move it by their motion to ever-changing melody. But there is a principle within the human being, and perhaps within all sentient

---

[3] Shelley's essay responds to Thomas Love Peacock's "The Four Ages of Poetry."* We print the first published text, edited by Mary Shelley,* which, except in one footnote, omits explicit references to Peacock's essay.

[4] The distinction is between the Greek terms "poiein," making, and "logizein," reasoning.

[5] an instrument placed in a window, so that its strings can vibrate in the wind. Cf. Coleridge, "Effusion 35"* and "Dejection."*

beings, which acts otherwise than in a lyre, and produces not melody alone, but harmony, by an internal adjustment of the sounds and motions thus excited to the impressions which excite them. It is as if the lyre could accommodate its chords to the motions of that which strikes them, in a determined proportion of sound; even as the musician can accommodate his voice to the sound of the lyre. A child at play by itself will express its delight by its voice and motions; and every inflexion of tone and gesture will bear exact relation to a corresponding antitype in the pleasurable impressions which awakened it; it will be the reflected image of that impression; and as the lyre trembles and sounds after the wind has died away, so the child seeks, by prolonging in its voice and motions the duration of the effect, to prolong also a consciousness of the cause. In relation to the objects which delight a child, these expressions are what poetry is to higher objects. The savage (for the savage is to ages what the child is to years) expresses the emotions produced in him by surrounding objects in a similar manner; and language and gesture, together with plastic or pictorial imitation, become the image of the combined effect of those objects and his apprehension of them. Man in society, with all his passions and his pleasures, next becomes the object of the passions and pleasures of man; an additional class of emotions produces an augmented treasure of expression; and language, gesture, and the imitative arts, become at once the representation and the medium, the pencil and the picture, the chisel and the statue, the chord and the harmony. The social sympathies, or those laws from which as from its elements society results, begin to develop themselves from the moment that two human beings coexist; the future is contained within the present as the plant within the seed; and equality, diversity, unity, contrast, mutual dependence, become the principles alone capable of affording the motives according to which the will of a social being is determined to action, inasmuch as he is social; and constitute pleasure in sensation, virtue in sentiment, beauty in art, truth in reasoning, and love in the intercourse of kind. Hence men, even in the infancy of society, observe a certain order in their words and actions, distinct from that of the objects and the impressions represented by them, all expression being subject to the laws of that from which it proceeds. But let us dismiss those more general considerations which might involve an inquiry into the principles of society itself, and restrict our view to the manner in which the imagination is expressed upon its forms.

In the youth of the world, men dance and sing and imitate natural objects, observing in these actions, as in all others, a certain rhythm or order. And, although all men observe a similar, they observe not the same order, in the motions of the dance, in the melody of the song, in the combinations of language, in the series of their imitations of natural objects. For there is a certain order or rhythm belonging to each of these classes of mimetic representation, from which the hearer and the spectator receive an intenser and purer pleasure than from any other: the sense of an approximation to this order has been called taste by modern writers. Every man in the infancy of art, observes an order which approximates more or less closely to that from which this highest delight results: but the diversity is not sufficiently marked, as that its gradations should be sensible, except in those instances where the predominance of this faculty of approximation to the beautiful (for so we may be permitted to name the relation between this highest pleasure and its cause) is very great. Those in whom it exists to excess are poets, in the most universal sense of the word; and the pleasure resulting from the manner in which they express the influence of society or nature upon their own minds, communicates itself to others, and gathers a sort of reduplication from the community. Their language is vitally metaphorical; that is, it marks the before unapprehended relations of things and perpetuates their apprehension, until words, which represent them, become, through time, signs for portions or classes of thought, instead of pictures of integral thoughts; and then, if no new poets should arise to create afresh the associations which have been thus disorganised, language will be dead to all the nobler purposes of human intercourse. These similitudes or relations are finely said by Lord Bacon to be "the same footsteps of nature impressed upon the various subjects of the world"[1]—and he considers the faculty which perceives them as the storehouse of axioms common to all knowledge. In the infancy of society every author is necessarily a poet, because language itself is poetry; and to be a poet is to apprehend the true and the beautiful, in a word, the good which exists in the relation; subsisting, first between existence and perception, and secondly between perception and expression. Every original language near to its source is in itself the chaos of a cyclic poem: the copiousness of lexicography and the distinctions of grammar are the works of a later age, and are merely the catalogue and the form of the creations of poetry.

But poets, or those who imagine and express this indestructible order, are not only the authors of language and of music, of the dance, and architecture, and statuary, and painting; they are the institutors of laws and the founders of civil society, and the inventors of the arts of life, and the teachers, who draw into a certain propinquity with the beautiful and the true, that partial apprehension of the agencies of the invisible world which is called religion. Hence all original religions are allegorical or susceptible of allegory, and, like Janus,[2] have a double face of false and true. Poets, according to the circumstances of the age and nation in which they appeared, were called, in the earlier epochs of the world, legislators or prophets: a poet essentially comprises and unites both these characters. For he not only beholds intensely the present as it is, and discovers those laws according to which present things ought to be ordered, but he beholds the future in the present, and his thoughts are the germs of the flower and the fruit of latest time. Not that I assert poets to be prophets in the gross sense of the word, or that they can foretell the form as surely as they foreknow the spirit of events: such is the pretence of superstition, which would make poetry an attribute of prophecy, rather than prophecy an attribute of poetry. A poet participates in the eternal, the infinite, and the one; as far as relates to his conceptions, time and place and number are not. The grammatical forms which express the moods of time, and the difference of persons, and the distinction of place, are convertible with respect to the highest poetry without injuring it as poetry; and the choruses of Æschylus, and the book of Job, and Dante's Paradise, would afford, more than any other writings, examples of this fact, if the limits of this essay did not forbid citation. The creations of sculpture, painting, and music, are illustrations still more decisive....

A poem is the very image of life expressed in its eternal truth. There is this difference between a story and a poem, that a story is a catalogue of detached facts, which have no other connexion than time, place, circumstance, cause, and effect; the other is the creation of actions according to the unchangeable forms of human nature, as existing in the mind of the Creator, which is itself the image of all other minds. The one is partial, and applies only to a definite period of time, and a certain combination of events which can never again recur; the other is universal, and contains within itself the germ of a relation to whatever motives or actions have place in the possible varieties of human nature. Time, which destroys the beauty and the use of the story of particular facts, stripped of the poetry which should invest them, augments that of poetry, and for ever develops new and wonderful applications of the eternal truth which it contains. Hence epitomes have been called the moths of just history; they eat out the poetry of it. A story of particular facts is as a mirror which obscures and distorts that which should be beautiful: poetry is a mirror which makes beautiful that which is distorted.

The parts of a composition may be poetical, without the composition as a whole being a poem. A single sentence may be considered as a whole, though it may be found in the midst of a series of unassimilated portions; a single word even may be a spark of inextinguishable thought. And thus all the great historians, Herodotus, Plutarch, Livy, were poets; and although the plan of these writers, especially that of Livy, restrained them from developing this faculty in its highest degree, they made copious and ample amends for their subjection, by filling all the interstices of their subjects with

---

[1] "De Augment. Scient., cap. 1, lib. iii." (note from *Essays, Letters from Abroad, Translations and Fragments*) The reference is to Francis Bacon, *Advancement of Learning* 3.1

[2] the Roman god of beginnings, whose two faces represent his forward- and backward-looking vision.

living images....

... Ethical science arranges the elements which poetry has created, and propounds schemes and proposes examples of civil and domestic life: nor is it for want of admirable doctrines that men hate, and despise, and censure, and deceive, and subjugate one another. But poetry acts in another and diviner manner. It awakens and enlarges the mind itself by rendering it the receptacle of a thousand unapprehended combinations of thought. Poetry lifts the veil from the hidden beauty of the world, and makes familiar objects be as if they were not familiar; it reproduces all that it represents, and the impersonations clothed in its Elysian light stand thenceforward in the minds of those who have once contemplated them, as memorials of that gentle and exalted content which extends itself over all thoughts and actions with which it coexists. The great secret of morals is love; or a going out of our own nature, and an identification of ourselves with the beautiful which exists in thought, action, or person, not our own. A man, to be greatly good, must imagine intensely and comprehensively; he must put himself in the place of another and of many others; the pains and pleasures of his species must become his own. The great instrument of moral good is the imagination; and poetry administers to the effect by acting upon the cause. Poetry enlarges the circumference of the imagination by replenishing it with thoughts of ever new delight, which have the power of attracting and assimilating to their own nature all other thoughts, and which form new intervals and interstices whose void for ever craves fresh food. Poetry strengthens the faculty which is the organ of the moral nature of man, in the same manner as exercise strengthens a limb. A poet therefore would do ill to embody his own conceptions of right and wrong, which are usually those of his place and time, in his poetical creations, which participate in neither. By this assumption of the inferior office of interpreting the effect, in which perhaps after all he might acquit himself but imperfectly, he would resign a glory in the participation of the cause. There was little danger that Homer, or any of the eternal poets, should have so far misunderstood themselves as to have abdicated this throne of their widest dominion. Those in whom the poetical faculty, though great, is less intense, as Euripides, Lucan, Tasso, Spenser,[1] have frequently affected a moral aim, and the effect of their poetry is diminished in exact proportion to the degree in which they compel us to advert to this purpose....

The exertions of Locke, Hume, Gibbon, Voltaire, Rousseau,[2] and their disciples, in favour of oppressed and deluded humanity, are entitled to the gratitude of mankind. Yet it is easy to calculate the degree of moral and intellectual improvement which the world would have exhibited, had they never lived. A little more nonsense would have been talked for a century or two; and perhaps a few more men, women, and children, burnt as heretics. We might not at this moment have been congratulating each other on the abolition of the Inquisition in Spain.[3] But it exceeds all imagination to conceive what would have been the moral condition of the world if neither Dante, Petrarch, Boccacio, Chaucer, Shakspeare, Calderon, Lord Bacon, nor Milton, had

---

[1] Euripides (480–406 BC), Greek tragic dramatist; Marcus Annæus Lucanus (AD 39–65), Roman poet, author of the *Pharsalia*; Torquato Tasso (1544–95), Italian poet, author of the epic poem *Jerusalem Delivered* (1580–81); Edmund Spenser (c. 1552–99), English poet, author of the *Faerie Queene* (1590–96).

[2] "Although Rousseau has been thus classed [by Thomas Love Peacock* in 'The Four Ages of Poetry'], he was essentially a poet. The others, even Voltaire, were mere reasoners." (P.B.S.) Shelley's list includes John Locke (1632–1704), English philosopher, author of the *Essay Concerning Human Understanding* (1690); David Hume (1711–76), philosophical skeptic and historian, author of *Treatise of Human Nature* (1739), *An Enquiry Concerning Human Understanding* (1748), *Dialogues Concerning Natural Religion* (1779), and *History of Great Britain* (1754–62); Edward Gibbon (1737–94), author of *The Decline and Fall of the Roman Empire* (1776–88); Voltaire (François-Marie Arouet, 1694–1778), a central figure of the French Enlightenment, author of *Candide* (1759); and Jean-Jacques Rousseau (1712–78), French philosopher, novelist, autobiographer and educational theorist, author of the *Confessions* (1781–88).

[3] The Inquisition, an ecclesiastical tribunal charged with defending Catholic orthodoxy against heresy, was established in most European countries during the 12th and 13th centuries, exercising its power with particular zeal and fanaticism in Spain. It was abolished by Joseph Buonaparte (1768–1844) in 1808, revived in 1814, and suppressed again in 1820. Revived yet again in 1823, it was finally suppressed in 1834.

ever existed; if Raphael and Michael Angelo[1] had never been born; if the Hebrew poetry had never been translated, if a revival of the study of Greek literature had never taken place; if no monuments of ancient sculpture had been handed down to us; and if the poetry of the religion of the ancient world had been extinguished together with its belief. The human mind could never, except by the intervention of these excitements, have been awakened to the invention of the grosser sciences, and that application of analytical reasoning to the aberrations of society, which it is now attempted to exalt over the direct expression of the inventive and creative faculty itself.

We have more moral, political, and historical wisdom, than we know how to reduce into practice; we have more scientific and economical knowledge than can be accommodated to the just distribution of the produce which it multiplies. The poetry, in these systems of thought, is concealed by the accumulation of facts and calculating processes. There is no want of knowledge respecting what is wisest and best in morals, government, and political economy, or at least what is wiser and better than what men now practise and endure. But we let "*I dare not* wait upon *I would*, like the poor cat in the adage."[2] We want the creative faculty to imagine that which we know; we want the generous impulse to act that which we imagine; we want the poetry of life: our calculations have outrun conception; we have eaten more than we can digest. The cultivation of those sciences which have enlarged the limits of the empire of man over the external world, has, for want of the poetical faculty, proportionally circumscribed those of the internal world; and man, having enslaved the elements, remains himself a slave. To what but a cultivation of the mechanical arts in a degree disproportioned to the presence of the creative faculty, which is the basis of all knowledge, is to be attributed the abuse of all invention for abridging and combining labour, to the exasperation of the inequality of mankind? From what other cause has it arisen that the discoveries which should have lightened, have added a weight to the curse imposed on Adam?[3] Poetry, and the principle of Self, of which money is the visible incarnation, are the God and Mammon[4] of the world.

The functions of the poetical faculty are twofold; by one it creates new materials of knowledge, and power, and pleasure; by the other it engenders in the mind a desire to reproduce and arrange them according to a certain rhythm and order, which may be called the beautiful and the good. The cultivation of poetry is never more to be desired than at periods when, from an excess of the selfish and calculating principle, the accumulation of the materials of external life exceed the quantity of the power of assimilating them to the internal laws of human nature. The body has then become too unwieldy for that which animates it.

Poetry is indeed something divine. It is at once the centre and circumference of knowledge; it is that which comprehends all science, and that to which all science must be referred. It is at the same time the root and blossom of all other systems of thought; it is that from which all spring, and that which adorns all; and that which, if blighted, denies the fruit and the seed, and withholds from the barren world the nourishment and the succession of the scions of the tree of life. It is the perfect and consummate surface and bloom of all things; it is as the odour and the colour of the rose to the texture of the elements which compose it, as the form and splendour of unfaded beauty to the secrets of anatomy and corruption. What were virtue, love, patriotism, friendship,—what were the scenery of this beautiful universe which we inhabit; what were our

---

[1] Humanist and Enlightenment poets, dramatists, philosophers, and artists: Dante Alighieri (1265–1321), author of the *Divine Comedy*; Francesco Petrarca (1304–74), Italian poet; Giovanni Boccaccio (1313–75), Italian poet and humanist, author of *The Decameron* (1349–51); Geoffrey Chaucer (c. 1343–1400), English poet, author of the *Canterbury Tales* (c. 1387–1400); William Shakespeare (1564–1616), English dramatist; Pedro Calderón de la Barca (1600–81), Spanish dramatist; Francis Bacon (1561–1626), philosopher and writer on scientific method, author of *The Advancement of Learning* (1605); John Milton (1608–74), English poet, author of *Paradise Lost* (1667–74); Raffaelo Santi (1483–1520), Italian painter; Michelangelo Buonarotti (1475–1564), Italian sculptor, architect, painter, and poet.

[2] Shakespeare, *Macbeth* 1.7.44–45.

[3] Genesis 3.17–19.

[4] See Matthew 6.24, Luke 16.13.

consolations on this side of the grave—and what were our aspirations beyond it, if poetry did not ascend to bring light and fire from those eternal regions where the owl-winged faculty of calculation dare not ever soar? Poetry is not like reasoning, a power to be exerted according to the determination of the will. A man cannot say, "I will compose poetry." The greatest poet even cannot say it; for the mind in creation is as a fading coal, which some invisible influence, like an inconstant wind, awakens to transitory brightness; this power arises from within, like the colour of a flower which fades and changes as it is developed, and the conscious portions of our nature are unprophetic either of its approach or its departure. Could this influence be durable in its original purity and force, it is impossible to predict the greatness of the results; but when composition begins, inspiration is already on the decline, and the most glorious poetry that has ever been communicated to the world is probably a feeble shadow of the original conceptions of the poet. I appeal to the greatest poets of the present day, whether it is not an error to assert that the finest passages of poetry are produced by labour and study. The toil and the delay recommended by critics, can be justly interpreted to mean no more than a careful observation of the inspired moments, and an artificial connection of the spaces between their suggestions, by the intertexture of conventional expressions; a necessity only imposed by the limitedness of the poetical faculty itself: for Milton conceived the Paradise Lost as a whole before he executed it in portions. We have his own authority also for the muse having "dictated" to him the "unpremeditated song."[1] And let this be an answer to those who would allege the fifty-six various readings of the first line of the Orlando Furioso.[2] Compositions so produced are to poetry what mosaic is to painting. This instinct and intuition of the poetical faculty is still more observable in the plastic and pictorial arts: a great statue or picture grows under the power of the artist as a child in the mother's womb; and the very mind which directs the hands in formation, is incapable of accounting to itself for the origin, the gradations, or the media of the process.

Poetry is the record of the best and happiest moments of the happiest and best minds. We are aware of evanescent visitations of thought and feeling, sometimes associated with place or person, sometimes regarding our own mind alone, and always arising unforeseen and departing unbidden, but elevating and delightful beyond all expression: so that even in the desire and the regret they leave, there cannot but be pleasure, participating as it does in the nature of its object. It is as it were the interpenetration of a diviner nature through our own; but its footsteps are like those of a wind over the sea, which the morning calm erases, and whose traces remain only, as on the wrinkled sand which paves it....

... [T]he literature of England, an energetic developement of which has ever preceded or accompanied a great and free development of the national will, has arisen as it were from a new birth. In spite of the low-thoughted envy which would undervalue contemporary merit, our own will be a memorable age in intellectual achievements, and we live among such philosophers and poets as surpass beyond comparison any who have appeared since the last national struggle for civil and religious liberty. The most unfailing herald, companion, and follower of the awakening of a great people to work a beneficial change in opinion or institution, is poetry. At such periods there is an accumulation of the power of communicating and receiving intense and impassioned conceptions respecting man and nature. The persons in whom this power resides, may often, as far as regards many portions of their nature, have little apparent correspondence with that spirit of good of which they are the ministers. But even whilst they deny and abjure, they are yet compelled to serve, the power which is seated on the throne of their own soul. It is impossible to read the compositions of the most celebrated writers of the present day without being startled with the electric life which burns within their words. They measure the circumference and sound the depths of human nature with a comprehensive and all-penetrating spirit, and they are themselves perhaps the most sincerely astonished at its manifestations; for it is less their spirit than the spirit of the age. Poets are the

---

[1] John Milton, *Paradise Lost* 9.21–24.

[2] a long narrative poem (1516–32) by the Italian poet Ludovico Ariosto (1474–1533).

hierophants of an unapprehended inspiration; the mirrors of the gigantic shadows which futurity casts upon the present; the words which express what they understand not; the trumpets which sing to battle and feel not what they inspire; the influence which is moved not, but moves. Poets are the unacknowledged legislators of the world.

Letters[1]

To Thomas Love Peacock

Naples,
December [22], 1818.[2]

My dear Peacock,

I have received a letter from you here, dated November 1st; you see the reciprocation of letters from the term of our travels is more slow. I entirely agree with what you say about Childe Harold.[3] The spirit in which it is written is, if insane, the most wicked and mischievous insanity that ever was given forth. It is a kind of obstinate and self-willed folly, in which he hardens himself. I remonstrated with him in vain on the tone of mind from which such a view of things alone arises. For its real root is very different from its apparent one. Nothing can be less sublime than the true source of these expressions of contempt and desperation. The fact is, that first, the Italian Women are perhaps the most contemptible of all who exist under the moon—the most ignorant, the most disgusting, the most bigoted, the most filthy; Countesses smell so of garlick that an ordinary Englishman cannot approach them. Well, L.B.[4] is familiar with the lowest sort of these women, the people his gondolieri pick up in the streets. He allows fathers and mothers to bargain with him for their daughters, and though this is common enough in Italy, yet for an Englishman to encourage such sickening vice is a melancholy thing. He associates with wretches who seem almost to have lost the gait and physiognomy of man, and who do not scruple to avow practices which are not only not named, but I believe seldom even conceived in England. He says he disapproves, but he endures. He is not yet an Italian and is heartily and deeply discontented with himself; and contemplating in the distorted mirror of his own thoughts the nature and the destiny of man, what can he behold but objects of contempt and despair? But that he is a great poet, I think the address to ocean[5] proves. And he has a certain degree of candour while you talk to him, but unfortunately it does not outlast your departure. You may think how unwillingly *I* have left my little favourite Alba[6] in a situation where she might fall again under his authority. But I have employed arguments entreaties every thing in vain & when these fail you know I have no longer any right. No, I do not doubt, and, for his sake, I ought to hope, that his present career must end soon in some violent circumstance which must reduce our situation with respect to Alba into its antient tie.

Since I last wrote to you I have seen the ruins of Rome, the Vatican, St. Peter's, and all the miracles of ancient and modern art contained in that majestic city. The impression of it exceeds anything I have ever experienced in my travels. We staied there only a week, intending to return at the end of February, and devote two or three months to its mines of inexhaustible contemplation, to which period I refer you for a minute account of it. We visited the Forum and the ruins of the Coliseum every day.[7] The Coliseum is unlike any work of human hands I ever saw before. It is of enormous height and circuit, and the arches built of massy stones are piled on one another, and jut into the blue air, shattered into the forms of overhanging rocks. It has been changed by time into the image of an amphitheatre

---

[1] from *The Complete Works of Percy Bysshe Shelley*, ed. Roger Ingpen and Walter E. Peck (1909).

[2] Frederick L. Jones, *The Letters of Percy Bysshe Shelley*, dates this letter December [17 or 18], 1818.

[3] Byron,* *Childe Harold's Pilgrimage* 4.

[4] Lord Byron.*

[5] in *Childe Harold's Pilgrimage* 4.179–84.

[6] Allegra (1817–22), the daughter of Claire Clairmont and Byron;* Peacock knew her as Alba.

[7] Cf. Byron, *Manfred* 3.4.9–30* and P.B. Shelley's fragmentary story "The Coliseum," first published in full in Mary Shelley, ed., *Essays, Letters from Abroad* (1840).

of rocky hills overgrown by the wild olive, the myrtle, and the fig tree, and threaded by little paths, which wind among its ruined stairs and immeasurable galleries: the copsewood overshadows you as you wander through its labyrinths, and the wild weeds of this climate of flowers bloom under your feet. The arena is covered with grass, and pierces like the skirts of a natural plain, the chasms of the broken arches around. But a small part of the exterior circumference remains—it is exquisitely light and beautiful; and the effect of the perfection of its architecture, adorned with ranges of Corinthian pilasters, supporting a bold cornice, is such as to diminish the effect of its greatness. The interior is all ruin. I can scarcely believe that when encrusted with Dorian marble and ornamented by columns of Egyptian granite, its effect could have been so sublime and so impressive as in its present state. It is open to the sky, and it was the clear and sunny weather of the end of November in this climate when we visited it, day after day.

Near it is the arch of Constantine, or rather the arch of Trajan; for the servile and avaricious senate of degraded Rome ordered that the monument of his predecessor should be demolished in order to dedicate one to the Christian reptile,[1] who had crept among the blood of his murdered family to the supreme power. It is exquisitely beautiful and perfect. The Forum is a plain in the middle of Rome, a kind of desert full of heaps of stones and pits; and though so near the habitations of men, is the most desolate place you can conceive. The ruins of temples stand in and around it, shattered columns and ranges of others complete, supporting cornices of exquisite workmanship, and vast vaults of shattered domes (laquearis)[2] distinct with the regular compartments, once filled with sculptures of ivory or brass. The temples of Jupiter, and Concord, and Peace, and the Sun, and the Moon, and Vesta,[3] are all within a short distance of this spot. Behold the wrecks of what a great nation once dedicated to the abstractions of the mind! Rome is a city, as it were, of the dead, or rather of those who cannot die, and who survive the puny generations which inhabit and pass over the spot which they have made sacred to eternity. In Rome, at least in the first enthusiasm of your recognitions of ancient time, you see nothing of the Italians. The nature of the city assists the delusion, for its vast and antique walls describe a circumference of sixteen miles, and thus the population is thinly scattered over this space, nearly as great as London. Wide wild fields are enclosed within it, and there are grassy lanes and copses winding among the ruins, and a great green hill, lonely and bare, which overhangs the Tiber.[4] The gardens of the modern palaces are like wild woods of cedar, and cypress, and pine, and the neglected walks are overgrown with weeds. The English burying place is a green slope near the walls, under the pyramidal tomb of Cestius,[5] and is, I think, the most beautiful and solemn cemetery I ever beheld. To see the sun shining on its bright grass, fresh, when we first visited it, with the autumnal dews, and hear the whispering of the wind among the leaves of the trees which have overgrown the tomb of Cestius, and the soil which is stirring in the sun warm earth, and to mark the tombs, mostly of women and young people who were buried there, one might, if one were to die, desire the sleep they seem to sleep. Such is the human mind, and so it peoples with its wishes vacancy and oblivion.

I have told you little about Rome, but I reserve the Pantheon, and St. Peter's, and the Vatican, and Raffael,[6] for my return. About a fortnight ago I left Rome, and Mary and Clare[7] followed in three days; for it was necessary to procure lodgings here without alighting at an Inn. From my peculiar mode of travelling I saw little of the country, but could just observe that the wild beauty of the scenery and the barbarous ferocity of the inhabitants progressively increased. On entering Naples, the first circumstance that engaged my attention was an assassination. A youth ran out of a shop pursued by a woman with a bludgeon, and a man armed with a knife. The man overtook him, and with one blow in the neck laid him dead in the road. On my expressing the emo-

---

[1] the emperor Constantine (AD c. 272–337).

[2] "panelled ceiling" (L.).

[3] the Roman goddess of the hearth.

[4] the river that runs through Rome.

[5] Cf. *Adonais* 433-50 and notes.*

[6] Raffaelo Santi (1483–1520), Italian painter.

[7] Mary Shelley* and her stepsister, Claire Clairmont (1798–1879).

tions of horror and indignation which I felt, a Calabrian[1] priest who travelled with me laughed heartily and attempted to quiz me as what the English call a flat.[2] I never felt such an inclination to beat any one. Heaven knows I have little power, but he saw that I looked extremely displeased, and was silent. This same man, a fellow of gigantic strength and stature, had expressed the most frantic terror of robbers on the road; he cried at the sight of my pistol, and it had been with great difficulty that the joint exertions of myself and the vetturino[3] had quieted his hysterics.

But external nature in these delightful regions contrasts with and compensates for the deformity and degradation of humanity. We have a lodging divided from the sea by the royal gardens, and from our windows we see perpetually the blue waters of the bay, forever changing, yet forever the same, and encompassed by the mountainous island of Capreæ,[4] the lofty peaks which overhang Salerno, and the woody hill of Posilypo, whose promontories hide from us Misenum and the lofty isle Inarime, which, with its divided summit, forms the opposite horn of the bay.[5] From the pleasant walks of the garden we see *Vesuvius*; a smoke by day and a fire by night is seen upon its summit, and the glassy sea often reflects its light or shadow. The climate is delicious. We sit without a fire, with the windows open, and have almost all the productions of an English summer. The weather is usually like what Wordsworth calls "the first fine day of March";[6] sometimes very much warmer, though perhaps it wants that "each minute sweeter than before," which gives an intoxicating sweetness to the awakening of the earth from its winter's sleep in England—We have made two excursions, one to Baiæ and one to Vesuvius, and we propose to visit, successively, the islands, Pæstum, Pompei, and Beneventum.[7]

We set off an hour after sunrise one radiant morning in a little boat, there was not a cloud in the sky nor a wave upon the sea, which was so translucent that you could see the hollow caverns clothed with the glaucous sea-moss, and the leaves and branches of those delicate weeds that pave the unequal bottom of the water.[8] As noon approached, the heat, and especially the light, became intense. We passed Posilipo, and came first to the eastern point of the bay of Puzzoli, which is within the great bay of Naples, and which again incloses that of Baiæ. Here are lofty rocks and craggy islets, with arches and portals of precipice standing in the sea, and enormous caverns, which echoed faintly with the murmur of the languid tide. This is called La Scuola di Virgilio.[9] We then went directly across to the promontory of Misenum, leaving the precipitous islet of Nesida on the right. Here we were conducted to see the Mare Morto,[10] and the Elysian fields; the spot on which Virgil places the scenery of the 6th Æneid.[11] Tho extremely beautiful, as a lake, and woody hills, and this divine sky must make it, I confess my disappointment. The guide showed us an antique cemetery, where the niches used for placing the cinerary urns of the dead yet remain. We then coasted the bay of Baiæ to the left, in which we saw many picturesque and interesting ruins; but I have to remark that we never disembarked but we were disappointed—while from the boat the effect of the scenery was inexpressibly delightful. The colours of the water and the air breathe over all things here the radiance of their own beauty. After passing the Bay of Baiæ, and observing the ruins of its antique grandeur standing

---

[1] from Calabria, the toe of the Italian boot.

[2] a stupid or gullible person.

[3] coachman.

[4] Capri.

[5] the Bay of Naples.

[6] Cf. W. Wordsworth,* "Lines Written at a Small Distance from my House" (*Lyrical Ballads*, 1798) 1–2.

[7] The Bay of Naples is surrounded by volcanic hills, including Vesuvius. The ruins of ancient Pompeii and Herculaneum are on its shore; the Roman resort of Baiæ is submerged beneath its waters. The Shelleys made the excursion to Baiæ on 8 December 1818.

[8] Cf. "Ode to the West Wind" 29–36.*

[9] a complex of ruins thought to have been a school for sorcerers. (The Roman poet Virgil was regarded in the Middle Ages as a magician.)

[10] "dead sea" (It.).

[11] In Virgil, *Æneid* 6, Aeneas enters the Sibyl's cave, finds the golden bough in the forest of Proserpine, and descends to the underworld through the cavern of Avernus. Visitors to the Naples area were (and still are) shown places corresponding to those described by Virgil.

like rocks in the transparent sea under our boat. We landed to visit lake Avernus. We passed thro the cavern of the Sybyl (not Virgil's Sybil)[1] which pierces one of the hills which circumscribe the lake, and came to a calm and lovely basin of water, surrounded by dark woody hills, and profoundly solitary. Some vast ruins of the temple of Pluto stand on a lawny hill on one side of it, and are reflected in its windless mirror. It is far more beautiful than the Elysian fields—but there are all the materials for beauty at the latter, and the Avernus was once a chasm of deadly and pestilential vapours. About ½ mile from Avernus, a high hill, called Monte n[u]ovo was thrown up by volcanic fire.

Passing onward we came to Pozzoli, the ancient Dicæarchea, where there are the columns remaining of a temple to Serapis,[2] and the wreck of an enormous ampitheatre, changed, like the Coliseum, into a natural hill of the overteeming vegetation. Here also is the Solfatara, of which there is a poetical description in the Civil War of Petronius, beginning—Est locus,[3] and in which the verses of the poet are infinitely finer than what he describes, for it is not a very curious place. After seeing these things we returned by moonlight to Naples in our boat. What colours there were in the sky, what radiance in the evening star, and how the moon was encompassed by a light unknown to our regions!

Our next excursion was to Vesuvius. We went to Resina in a carriage, where Mary and I mounted mules and Clare was carried in a chair on the shoulders of four men, much like a member of parliament after he has gained his election, and looking, with less reason, quite as frightened. So we arrived at the hermitage of St Salvador, where an old hermit, belted with rope, set forth the plates for our refreshment.

Vesuvius is, after the glaciers, the most impressive exhibition of the energies of nature I ever saw. It has not the immeasurable greatness, the overpowering magnificence, nor above all, the radiant beauty of the glaciers; but it has all their character of tremendous and irresistible strength. From Resina to the hermitage you wind up the mountain, and cross a vast stream of hardened lava, which is an actual image of the waves of the sea, changed into hard black stone by enchantment. The lines of the boiling fluid seem to hang in the air, and it is difficult to believe that the billows which seem hurrying down upon you are not actually in motion. This plain was once a sea of liquid fire. From the hermitage we crossed another vast stream of lava, and then went on foot up the cone—this is the only part of the ascent in which there is any difficulty, and that difficulty has been much exaggerated. It is composed of rocks of lava, and declivities of ashes; by ascending the former and descending the latter, there is very little fatigue. On the summit is a kind of irregular plain, the most horrible chaos that can be imagined; riven into ghastly chasms, and heaped up with tumuli of great stones and cinders, and enormous rocks blackened and calcined, which had been thrown from the Volcano upon one another in terrible confusion. In the midst stands the conical hill from which the volumes of smoke, and the fountains of liquid fire, are rolled forth forever. The mountain is at present in a slight state of eruption, and a thick heavy white smoke is perpetually rolled out, interrupted by enormous columns of an impenetrable black bituminous vapour, which is hurled up, fold after fold, into the sky with a deep hollow sound, and fiery stones are rained down from its darkness, and a black shower of ashes fall even on where we sate. The lava like the glacier creeps on perpetually, with a crackling sound as of suppressed fire. There are several springs of lava, and in one place it gushes precipitously over a high crag, rolling down the half melted rocks and its own over hanging waves; a cataract of quivering fire. We approached the extremity of one of the rivers of lava; it is about 20 feet in breadth and ten in height; and as the inclined plane was not rapid, its motion was very slow. We saw the masses of its dark exterior surface detach themselves as it moved, and betray the depth of the liquid flame. In the day the fire is but slightly seen; you only observe a tremulous motion in the air, and streams and fountains of white sulphurous smoke. At length we saw the sun sink between Capreæ and

---

[1] Shelley is correct; the actual site of the Cumæan Sibyl's cave was not discovered until 1932.

[2] a Greek-Egyptian god of the underworld.

[3] "There is a place" (L.). The passage is in the *Satyricon* of Petronius, part of a passage thought to be a parody of Lucan's *Civil War*.

Inarime, and, as the darkness increased, the effect of the fire became more beautiful. We were, as it were, surrounded by streams and cataracts of the red and radiant fire, and in the midst from the column of bituminous smoke shot up into the sky, fell the vast masses of rock white with the light of the intense heat, leaving behind them thro the dark vapour trains of splendour. We descended by torch light, and I should have enjoyed the scenery on my return, but that they conducted me, I know not how, to the hermitage in a state of intense bodily suffering, the worst effect of which was spoiling the pleasure of Mary and Clare—Our Guides on the occasion, were complete Savages. You have no idea of the horrible cries which they suddenly utter, no one knows why; the clamour, the vociferation, the tumult. Clare in her palanquin[1] suffered most from it; and when I had gone on before, they threatened to leave her in the middle of the road, which they would have done had not my Italian servant promised them a beating, after which they became very quiet. Nothing, however, can be more picturesque than the gestures and the physiognomies of these savage people. And when, in the darkness of night, they unexpectedly begin to sing in chorus some fragments of their wild but sweet national music, the effect is exceedingly fine.

Since I wrote this, I have seen the museum of this city. Such statues! There is the Venus an ideal shape of the most winning loveliness. A Bacchus, more sublime than any living being. A Satyr making love to a Youth in which the expressed life of the sculpture and the inconceivable beauty of the form of the youth, overcome one's repugnance to the subject. There are multitudes of wonderfully fine statues found in Herculaneum and Pompeii. We are going to see Pompeii the 1st day that the sea is waveless. Herculaneum is almost all filled up; no more excavations are made; the King[2] bought the ground and built a palace upon it.

You don't see much of Hunt.[3] I wish you could contrive to see him when you got to town, and ask him what he means to answer to Lord Byron's invitation. He has now an opportunity, if he likes, of seeing Italy. What do you think of joining his party, and paying us a visit next year; I mean as soon as the reign of winter is dissolved? Write me your thoughts upon this. I cannot express to you the pleasure it would give me to welcome such a party.

I have depression enough of spirits and not good health, though I believe the warm air of Naples does me good. We see absolutely no one here—Adieu.

My dear Peacock,
Affectionately your friend,
P.B.S.

[*Written by Mary Shelley*]

You had better direct all your letters to Livorno & not here—and when you send another parcel I wish you would contrive to get a hair brush and a small tooth comb from Florristen, hairdresser—Germain St. behind [Piccadilly *deleted*] St. James.

To Mary Wollstonecraft Shelley, *Bagni di Pisa*

[Ravenna,
Thursday, August 9, 1821.]

My dearest Mary,

I wrote to you yesterday, and I begin another letter today without knowing exactly when I can send it, as I am told the Post only goes once a week. I dare say the subject of the latter half of my letter gave you pain: but it was necessary to look the affair in the face, and the only satisfactory answer to the calumny must be given by you, and could be given by you, alone. This is evidently the source of the violent denunciations of the Literary Gazette[4]—in themselves contemptible enough, and only to be regarded as effects which show us their cause, which until we put off our mortal nature we never can despise—that is, the belief of persons who have known and seen you, that you are guilty of the most enormous crimes.

A certain degree and a certain kind of infamy is to be borne, and, in fact, is the best compliment which an

---

[1] a conveyance carried on poles; a sedan chair.

[2] Ferdinand IV (1751–1825), deposed during the revolutionary period, was reinstated as King of Naples in 1815.

[3] Byron had invited Leigh Hunt* to stay with him and work on a projected magazine, the *Liberal*.

[4] A weekly journal published by Henry Colburn and edited by William Jerdan, the *Literary Gazette* had negatively reviewed *The Cenci* (1 April 1820) and *Queen Mab* (19 May 1821).

exalted nature can receive from the filthy world of which it is its hell to be a part—but this sort of thing exceeds the measure, and even if it were only for the sake of our dear Percy[1] I would take some pains to suppress it. In fact, it shall be suppressed, even if I am reduced to the disagreeable necessity of prosecuting Elise before the Tuscan tribunals.[2]

After having sent my letter to the Post yesterday, I went out to see some of the antiquities of this place; which appear to be remarkable. This City was once of vast extent, and the traces of its remains are to be found more than four miles from the gate of the modern town. The sea which once came close to it, has now retired to the distance of five miles, leaving a melancholy extent of marshes interspersed with patches of cultivation, and towards the sea shore with pine forests, which have followed the retrocession of the Adriatic and the roots of which are absolutely washed by its waves. The level of the sea and of this tract of country correspond so nearly that a ditch dug to a few feet in depth is immediately filled with sea water. All the antient buildings have been choked up to the height of from five to twenty feet by the deposit of the sea and of the inundations which are frequent in winter. I went in Albe's[3] carriage, first to the Chiesa St Vitale, which is certainly one of the most antient churches in Italy. It is a rotunda, supported upon buttresses and pilasters of white marble; the ill effect of which is somewhat relieved by an interior row of columns. The dome is very high and narrow. The whole church, in spite of the elevation of the soil, is very high for its breadth, and is of a very peculiar and striking construction. In the section of one of the large tables of marble with which the church is lined, they showed me the *perfect figure*, as perfect as if it had been painted, of a Capuchin friar,[4] which resulted merely from the shadings and the position of the stains in the marble. This is what may be called a pure anticipated cognition of a Capuchin.

I then went to the tomb of Theodosius[5] which has now been dedicated to the Virgin, without however any change in its original appearance. It is about a mile from the present city. This building is more than half overwhelmed by the elevated soil, although a portion of the lower story has been excavated and is filled with brackish and stinking waters, and a sort of vaporous darkness, and troops of prodigious frogs. It is a remarkable piece of architecture, and without belonging to a period when the antient taste yet survived, bears nevertheless a certain impression of that taste. It consists of two stories—the lower supported on doric arches and pilasters and a simple entablature; the other, circular within and polygonal outside and roofed with one single mass of ponderous stone, for it is evidently one and Heaven alone knows how they contrived to lift it to that height. It is a sort of flattish dome, rough wrought within by the chisel from which the northern conquerors tore the plates of silver that adorned it; and polished without, with things like handles appended to it which were also wrought out of the solid stone, and to which I suppose the ropes were applied to draw it up. You ascend externally into the second story by a flight of stone steps which are modern.

The next place I went to, was a church called *la chiesa di St Appollinare*, which is a Basilica and built by one, I forget whom, of the Xtian[6] emperors; it is a long church, with a roof like a barn, and supported by twenty-four columns of the finest marble, with an altar of jasper and four columns of jasper and giallo antico, supporting the roof of the tabernacle, which are said to be of immense value. It is something like that church (I forget the name of it) we saw at Rome, fuore delle mura.[7] I suppose the emperor stole these columns, which seem not at all to belong to the place they occupy. Within the city, near the

---

[1] the Shelley's son, Percy Florence (1819–89).

[2] Elise, a servant of the Shelleys, had married Paolo Foggi, who seems to have threatened Shelley with blackmail. A baby girl, registered as Shelley's daughter, was born in Naples on 27 December 1818 and baptized Elena Adelaide Shelley on 27 February. Elena died on 9 June 1820; her mother's identity is unknown. See Richard Holmes, *Shelley: The Pursuit* 465–74. Cf. *The Cenci* 1.3.68.*

[3] Lord Byron's; the nickname is either an abbreviation of "Albanian" (in honour of Byron's Eastern travels) or a vocalization of L.B.

---

[4] a member of an order of Franciscan brothers.

[5] Shelley is perhaps referring to the mausoleum of Theodoric, built in AD 520 by Theodoric the Great as his future tomb.

[6] Christian.

[7] "outside the walls" (It.).

church of St Vitale, there is to be seen the tomb of the Empress Galla Placidia daughter of Theodosius the great, together with those of her husband Constantius, her brother Onorius, and her son Valentinian—all emperors. The tombs are massy cases of marble adorned with rude and tasteless sculpture of lambs, and other Christian emblems with scarcely a trace of the antique. It seems to have been one of the first effects of the Christian religion to destroy the power of producing beauty in art. These tombs are placed in a sort of vaulted chamber, wrought over with rude mosaic which is said to have been built in 1300. I have yet seen no more of Ravenna.

               Friday.

We ride out in the evening through the pine forests which divide this city from the sea. Our way of life is this, and I have accomodated myself to it without much difficulty. L.B. gets up at two, breakfasts—we talk read etc., until six; then we ride, and dine at eight, and after dinner sit talking till four or five in the morning. I get up at 12, and am now devoting the interval between my rising and his, to you.

 L.B. is greatly improved in every respect—in genius in temper in moral views, in health in happiness. The connexion with la Guiccioli[1] has been an inestimable benefit to him. He lives in considerable splendour, but within his income, which is now about 4000 a year:— 1000 of which he devotes to purposes of charity. He has had mischievous passions, but these he seems to have subdued, and is becoming what he should be, a virtuous man. The interest which he took in the politics of Italy, and the actions he performed in consequence of it, are subjects not fit to be *written*, but are such as will delight and surprise you. He is not yet decided to go to Switzerland: a place indeed little fitted for him: the gossip and the cabals of those anglicised coteries would torment him as they did before, and might exasperate him into a relapse of libertinism, which he says he plunged into not from taste but despair. La Guiccioli and her brother[2] (who is Lord B.'s friend and confidant, and acquiesces perfectly in her connexion with him), wish to go to Switzerland; as L.B. says merely from the novelty and pleasure of travelling. L.B. prefers Tuscany or Lucca, and is trying to persuade them to adopt his views. He has made *me* write a long letter to her to engage her to remain—an odd thing enough for an utter stranger to write on subjects of the utmost delicacy to his friend's mistress. But it seems destined that I am always to have some active part in everybody's affairs whom I approach—I have set down in lame Italian the strongest reasons I can think of against the Swiss emigration—to tell you truth I should be very glad to accept as my fee, his establishment in Tuscany. Ravenna is a miserable place; the people are barbarous and wild, and their language the most infernal patois that you can imagine. He would be in every respect better among the Tuscans. I am afraid he would not like Florence on account of the English. What think you of Lucca for him—he would like Pisa better, if it were not for Clare,[3] but I really can hardly recommend him either for his own sake or for hers to come into such close contact with her. Gunpowder and fire ought to be kept at a respectable distance from each other. There is Lucca, Florence, Pisa, Sienna, and I think nothing more. What think you of Prato, or Pistoia, for him—no Englishman approaches those towns; but I fear that no house could be found good enough for him in that region.—I have not yet seen Allegra, but shall tomorrow or next day: as I shall ride over to Bagnacavallo[4] for that purpose.

 He has read to me one of the unpublished cantos of Don Juan,[5] which is astonishingly fine. It sets him not above but far above all the poets of the day: every word is stamped with immortality. I despair of rivalling Lord Byron, as well I may, and there is no other with whom it is worth contending. This canto is in style, but totally, and sustained with incredible ease and power, like the end of the second canto. There is not a word which the most rigid asserter of the dignity of human nature could

---

[1] the Countess Teresa Guiccioli (c. 1800–73), Byron's mistress.

[2] Pietro Count Gamba (1801–27), who later accompanied Byron to Greece.

[3] Mary Shelley's stepsister, Claire Clairmont, who was living with the Shelleys in Pisa.

[4] Where Claire Clairmont and Byron's daughter Allegra had been placed in a convent.

[5] Cantos 3–5 had been published on 8 August.

desire to be cancelled: it fulfills in a certain degree what I have long preached of producing something wholly new and relative to the age, and yet surpassingly beautiful. It may be vanity, but I think I see the trace of my earnest exhortation to him to create something wholly new. He has finished his *life* up to the present time and given it to Moore[1] with liberty for Moore to sell it for the best price he can get, with condition that the bookseller should publish it after his death. Moore has sold it to Murray for *two thousand pounds*. I wish I had been in time to have interceded for a part of it for poor Hunt.[2]—I have spoken to him of Hunt, but not with a direct view of demanding a contribution; and though I am sure that if asked it would not be refused—yet there is something in me that makes it impossible. Lord Byron and I are excellent friends, and were I reduced to poverty, or were I a writer who had no claims to a higher station than I possess—or did I possess a higher than I deserve, we should appear in all things as such, and I would freely ask him any favour. Such is not now the case. The demon of mistrust and of pride lurks between two persons in our situation poisoning the freedom of their intercourse. This is a tax, and a heavy one which we must pay for being human. I think the fault is not on my side nor is it likely, I being the weaker. I hope that in the next world these things will be better managed. What is passing in the heart of another rarely escapes the observation of one who is a strict anatomist of his own.

Write to me at Florence, where I shall remain a day at least and send me letters or news of letters. How is my little darling?[3] And how are you, and how do you get on with your book?[4] Be severe in your corrections, and expect severity from me, your sincere admirer. I flatter myself you have composed something unequalled in its kind, and that, not content with the honours of your birth and your hereditary aristocracy, you will add still higher renown to your name. Expect me at the end of my appointed time. I do not think I shall be detained. Is Clare with you, or is she coming? Have you heard anything of my poor Emilia,[5] from whom I got a letter the day of my departure, saying that her marriage was deferred for a *very short* time, on account of the illness of her sposo?[6] How are the Williams's,[7] and Williams especially? Give my very kindest love to them, and pray take care that they do not want money.

Lord B. has here splendid apartments in the house of his mistress's husband:[8] who is one of the richest men in Italy. *She* is divorced, with an allowance of 1200 crowns a year, a miserable pittance from a man who has 120,000 a year.—Here are two monkies, five cats, eight dogs, and ten horses, all of whom (except the horses), walk about [the] house like the masters of it. *Tita* [the] Venetian is here, and operates as my valet; a fine fellow, with a prodigious black beard, who has stabbed two or three people, and is the most good-natured looking fellow I ever saw.

We have good rumours of the Greeks here, and a Russian war.[9] I hardly wish the Russians to take any part in it. My maxim is with Æschylus:—τὸ δυσσεβὲς—μετὰ μὲν πλείονα τίκτει, σφετέρᾳ δ᾽ εἰκότα γεννᾷ.[10] There is a Greek exercise for you. How should slaves produce any thing but tyranny—even as the seed produces the plant?

Adieu, dear Mary.

Yours affectionately,
S.

This is sent by express to Florence.

---

[1] After Byron's death, the publisher John Murray burned this autobiography is spite of Thomas Moore's* protests.

[2] Leigh Hunt,* editor of the *Liberal*.

[3] Mary and Percy's only surviving child, Percy Florence.

[4] Mary Shelley's novel, *Valperga*, was published in 1823.

[5] Emilia Viviani, a young woman whom the Shelleys befriended in Pisa. She was living in a convent while her father arranged a marriage for her. Cf. Mary Shelley's* satirical short story, "The Bride of Modern Italy."

[6] "spouse" (It.).

[7] the Shelleys' friends, Jane and Edward Williams. P.B. Shelley and Edward were drowned together in 1822.

[8] Count Guiccioli, about 40 years older than Teresa.

[9] In the Greek War of Independence (1821–30), both England and Russia assisted the Greeks against the Ottoman empire.

[10] "The evil deed breeds others after it like to its own race" (*Agamemnon* 759–60).

Edward John Trelawny
1792 – 1881

Edward John Trelawny was born on 13 November 1792, either in London or in Cornwall. His father was Lieutenant-Colonel Charles Trelawny; his mother was Maria Hawkins Trelawny. He was educated at the Royal Fort Boarding School in Bristol and then joined the navy, where he served for seven years. In 1812, he married Caroline Addison, who left him soon afterwards. After the divorce was finalized, he went to Europe, and in 1822, he met Byron* and the Shelleys* in Pisa; he was already telling, as M.W. Shelley recalled, the "strange stories of himself," largely inspired by Byron's early poetry, that would form the basis of his first book, *Adventures of a Younger Son* (1831). When P.B. Shelley was drowned in 1822 (a disaster for which Trelawny was partly responsible, having designed the boat), he presided over the cremation of the body and arranged for the ashes to be buried in the Protestant Cemetery in Rome. In 1823, he went to Greece with Byron, to help the Greeks' struggle for independence from the Ottoman Empire; but Byron's circumspect way of waging war bored him, and he joined a bandit chief, Odysseus Androutzos. He stayed with Androutzos even after the latter had gone over to the Turks, and married his thirteen-year-old sister, Tersitsa. After he had survived an assassination attempt, and after Tersitsa had left him, he returned to England and proposed to both M.W. Shelley and Claire Clairmont, both of whom turned him down. In 1841, he married Augusta Goring; that marriage ended in 1858, the year he published *Recollections of the Last Days of Shelley and Byron*, a factually unreliable book but a major contribution to the Victorian construction of Romanticism; an expanded version appeared in 1878 as *Records of Shelley, Byron, and the Author*. He died on 13 August 1881 and his ashes were buried in Rome, next to Shelley's. (D.L.M.)

༄༅༄

from *Recollections of the Last Days of Shelley and Byron* (1858)

from CHAPTER 12[1]

All things that we love and cherish,
Like ourselves, must fade and perish;
Such is our rude mortal lot,
Love itself would, did they not.

SHELLEY[2]

I got a furnace made at Leghorn, of iron-bars and strong sheet-iron, supported on a stand, and laid in a stock of fuel, and such things as were said to be used by Shelley's much loved Hellenes on their funeral pyres.[3]

On the 13th of August, 1822, I went on board the "Bolivar,"[4] with an English acquaintance, having written to Byron and Hunt to say I would send them word when everything was ready, as they wished to be present. I had previously engaged two large feluccas,[5] with drags and tackling, to go before, and endeavour to find the place where Shelley's boat had foundered; the captain of one of the feluccas having asserted that he was out in the fatal squall, and had seen Shelley's boat go down off Via Reggio, with all sail set. With light and fitful breezes we were eleven hours reaching our destination—the tower of Migliarino, at the Bocca Lericcio, in the Tuscan States.[6] There was a village there, and about two miles

---

[1] Cf. M.W. Shelley, letter to Maria Gisborne, 15 August 1822.*

[2] P.B. Shelley,* "Death" (1820) 12–15.

[3] Homer describes cremation in the *Iliad* 7, 23 and the *Odyssey* 11–12. The Greeks of the Classical period did not practise it.

[4] Byron's boat, named after Simón Bolívar (1783–1830), the South American revolutionary. The English acquaintance was probably Captain Daniel Roberts, who had overseen the building both of the *Bolivar* and of Shelley's boat, the *Don Juan*.

[5] small boats for coastal voyages.

[6] Italy was not yet an independent and unified country. Tuscany was part of the Austrian empire.

from that place Williams[1] was buried. So I anchored, landed, called on the officer in command, a major, and told him my object in coming, of which he was already apprised by his own government. He assured me I should have every aid from him. As it was too late in the day to commence operations, we went to the only inn in the place, and I wrote to Byron to be with us next day at noon. The major sent my letter to Pisa by a dragoon, and made arrangements for the next day. In the morning he was with us early, and gave me a note from Byron, to say he would join us as near noon as he could. At ten we went on board the commandant's boat, with a squad of soldiers in working dresses, armed with mattocks and spades, an officer of the quarantine service,[2] and some of his crew. They had their peculiar tools, so fashioned as to do their work without coming into personal contact with things that might be infectious—long handled tongs, nippers, poles with iron hooks and spikes, and divers others that gave one a lively idea of the implements of torture devised by the holy inquisitors.[3] Thus freighted, we started, my own boat following with the furnace, and the things I had brought from Leghorn. We pulled along the shore for some distance, and landed at a line of strong posts and railings which projected into the sea—forming the boundary dividing the Tuscan and Lucchese States. We walked along the shore to the grave, where Byron and Hunt[4] soon joined us: they, too, had an officer and soldiers from the tower of Migliarino, an officer of the Health Office, and some dismounted dragoons, so we were surrounded by soldiers, but they kept the ground clear, and readily lent their aid. There was a considerable gathering of spectators from the neighbourhood, and many ladies richly dressed were amongst them. The spot where the body lay was marked by the gnarled root of a pine tree.

A rude hut, built of young pine-tree stems, and wattled with their branches, to keep the sun and rain out, and thatched with reeds, stood on the beach to shelter the look-out man on duty. A few yards from this was the grave, which we commenced opening—the Gulf of Spezzia and Leghorn at equal distances of twenty-two miles from us. As to fuel I might have saved myself the trouble of bringing any, for there was an ample supply of broken spars and planks cast on the shore from wrecks, besides the fallen and decaying timber in a stunted pine forest close at hand. The soldiers collected fuel whilst I erected the furnace, and then the men of the Health Office set to work, shovelling away the sand which covered the body, while we gathered round, watching anxiously. The first indication of their having found the body, was the appearance of the end of a black silk handkerchief—I grubbed this out with a stick, for we were not allowed to touch anything with our hands—then some shreds of linen were met with, and a boot with the bone of the leg and the foot in it. On the removal of a layer of brushwood, all that now remained of my lost friend was exposed—a shapeless mass of bones and flesh. The limbs separated from the trunk on being touched.

"Is that a human body?" exclaimed Byron; "why it's more like the carcase of a sheep, or any other animal, than a man: this is a satire on our pride and folly."

I pointed to the letters E.E.W. on the black silk handkerchief.

Byron looking on, muttered, "The entrails of a worm hold together longer than the potter's clay, of which man is made.[5] Hold! let me see the jaw," he added, as they were removing the skull, "I can recognise any one by the teeth, with whom I have talked. I always watch the lips and mouth: they tell what the tongue and eyes try to conceal."

I had a boot of Williams's with me; it exactly corresponded with the one found in the grave. The remains were removed piecemeal into the furnace.

---

[1] P.B. Shelley's friend Edward Williams, who was lost at the same time.

[2] Local quarantine laws prevented people lost at sea from being buried normally; the rest of the chapter explains Trelawny's attempt to overcome this indignity.

[3] The Holy Inquisition, an office of the Catholic church dedicated to fighting heresy, was notorious for its use of torture to obtain confessions.

[4] Leigh Hunt,* who had come to Italy to work with Byron and Shelley on a new periodical, the *Liberal*.

[5] Cf. Romans 9.20–21.

"Don't repeat this with me," said Byron; "let my carcase rot where it falls."

The funereal pyre was now ready; I applied the fire, and the materials being dry and resinous the pine-wood burnt furiously, and drove us back. It was hot enough before, there was no breath of air, and the loose sand scorched our feet. As soon as the flames became clear, and allowed us to approach, we threw frankincense and salt into the furnace, and poured a flask of wine and oil over the body. The Greek oration was omitted, for we had lost our Hellenic bard. It was now so insufferably hot that the officers and soldiers were all seeking shade.

"Let us try the strength of these waters that drowned our friends," said Byron, with his usual audacity. "How far out do you think they were when their boat sank?"

"If you don't wish to be put into the furnace, you had better not try; you are not in condition."

He stripped, and went into the water, and so did I and my companion. Before we got a mile out, Byron was sick, and persuaded to return to the shore. My companion, too, was seized with cramp, and reached the land by my aid. At four o'clock the funereal pyre burnt low, and when we uncovered the furnace, nothing remained in it but dark-coloured ashes, with fragments of the larger bones. Poles were now put under the red-hot furnace, and it was gradually cooled in the sea. I gathered together the human ashes, and placed them in a small oak-box, bearing an inscription on a brass plate, screwed it down, and placed it in Byron's carriage. He returned with Hunt to Pisa, promising to be with us on the following day at Via Reggio. I returned with my party in the same way we came, and supped and slept at the inn. On the following morning we went on board the same boats, with the same things and party, and rowed down the little river near Via Reggio to the sea, pulled along the coast towards Massa, then landed, and began our preparations as before.

Three white wands had been stuck in the sand to mark the Poet's grave, but as they were at some distance from each other, we had to cut a trench thirty yards in length, in the line of the sticks, to ascertain the exact spot, and it was nearly an hour before we came upon the grave.

In the mean time Byron and Leigh Hunt arrived in the carriage, attended by soldiers, and the Health Officer, as before. The lonely and grand scenery that surrounded us so exactly harmonised with Shelley's genius, that I could imagine his spirit soaring over us. The sea, with the islands of Gorgona, Capraji, and Elba, was before us; old battlemented watch-towers stretched along the coast, backed by the marble-crested Apennines glistening in the sun, picturesque from their diversified outlines, and not a human dwelling was in sight. As I thought of the delight Shelley felt in such scenes of loneliness and grandeur whilst living, I felt we were no better than a herd of wolves or a pack of wild dogs, in tearing out his battered and naked body from the pure yellow sand that lay so lightly over it, to drag him back to the light of day; but the dead have no voice, nor had I power to check the sacrilege—the work went on silently in the deep and unresisting sand, not a word was spoken, for the Italians have a touch of sentiment, and their feelings are easily excited into sympathy. Even Byron was silent and thoughtful. We were startled and drawn together by a dull hollow sound that followed the blow of a mattock; the iron had struck a skull, and the body was soon uncovered. Lime had been strewn on it; this, or decomposition, had the effect of staining it of a dark and ghastly indigo colour. Byron asked me to preserve the skull for him; but remembering that he had formerly used one as a drinking-cup,[1] I was determined Shelley's should not be so profaned. The limbs did not separate from the trunk, as in the case of Williams's body, so that the corpse was removed entire into the furnace. I had taken the precaution of having more and larger pieces of timber, in consequence of my experience of the day before of the difficulty of consuming a corpse in the open air with our apparatus. After the fire was well kindled we repeated the ceremony of the previous day; and more wine was poured over Shelley's dead body than he had consumed during his life. This with the oil and salt made the yellow flames glisten and quiver. The heat from the sun and fire was so intense that the atmosphere was tremulous and wavy. The

---

[1] Byron had had a skull found at his family estate, Newstead Abbey, mounted in silver as a cup; see his "Lines Inscribed upon a Cup Formed from a Skull" (1808).

corpse fell open and the heart was laid bare. The frontal bone of the skull, where it had been struck with the mattock, fell off; and, as the back of the head rested on the red-hot bottom bars of the furnace, the brains literally seethed, bubbled, and boiled as in a cauldron, for a very long time.

Byron could not face this scene, he withdrew to the beach and swam off to the "Bolivar." Leigh Hunt remained in the carriage. The fire was so fierce as to produce a white heat on the iron, and to reduce its contents to grey ashes. The only portions that were not consumed were some fragments of bones, the jaw, and the skull, but what surprised us all, was that the heart remained entire. In snatching this relic from the fiery furnace, my hand was severely burnt; and had any one seen me do the act I should have been put into quarantine.

After cooling the iron machine in the sea, I collected the human ashes and placed them in a box, which I took on board the "Bolivar." Byron and Hunt retraced their steps to their home,[1] and the officers and soldiers returned to their quarters. I liberally rewarded the men for the admirable manner in which they behaved during the two days they had been with us.

As I undertook and executed this novel ceremony, I have been thus tediously minute in describing it.

Byron's idle talk during the exhumation of Williams's remains, did not proceed from want of feeling, but from his anxiety to conceal what he felt from others. When confined to his bed and racked by spasms, which threatened his life, I have heard him talk in a much more un-orthodox fashion, the instant he could muster breath to banter. He had been taught during his town-life, that any exhibition of sympathy or feeling was maudlin and unmanly, and that the appearance of daring and indifference, denoted blood and high breeding....

---

[1] Hunt and his family were living in Byron's palace in Pisa.

John Clare
1793 – 1864

John Clare was born in Helpston, Northamptonshire, on 13 July 1793; his twin sister died a few weeks later. His mother, Ann Stimson Clare, a shepherd's daughter, was illiterate; his father, Parker Clare, a thresher, could read the Bible and knew many folk ballads. Between the ages of five and twelve, Clare spent a few months a year first at a local dame school and then at a church school in neighbouring Glinton, where he fell in love with Mary Joyce, a farmer's daughter; nothing came of this love, but he cherished it for the rest of his life and it inspired many of his poems. After the age of twelve, he educated himself while working as a gardener, lime-burner, ploughboy, shoemaker, and thresher, and serving as a volunteer in the militia. Inspired by James Thomson's *Spring*, he began writing poetry at an early age, and his work eventually came to the attention of John Taylor (the publisher of Keats),* who published his *Poems Descriptive of Rural Life and Scenery* in January 1820. It was a great success, selling out four editions in two years. In March 1820, he married Martha ("Patty") Turner; they would have eight children. His second book, *The Village Minstrel* (1821), was also successful, but the other two books published in his lifetime, *The Shepherd's Calendar* (1827) and *The Rural Muse* (1835) were less so, partly because of Taylor's reservations over Clare's use of dialect and earthy subject matter. Clare suffered a breakdown in 1837 and became a patient at a private asylum in Epping Forest. He was treated well and continued to write poetry, but in July 1841 he escaped and walked the eighty miles home, passing through Glinton on the way to look for Mary Joyce, only to find that she had been dead for three years. By December 1841, Patty was no longer able to care for him, and he was confined in the Northampton General Lunatic Asylum for the rest of his life. He continued to write poetry, most of which remained unpublished until the twentieth century. He died on 20 May 1864, after a paralytic seizure.

We have followed our usual policy of presenting the first published versions of Clare's poems, but students should be aware that modern scholarship has sometimes revealed very different versions. (D.L.M.)

༺༻

from *The Rural Muse. Poems by John Clare* (1835)

The Nightingale's Nest[1]

Up this green woodland-ride let's softly rove,
And list the nightingale—she dwells just here.
Hush! let the wood-gate softly clap, for fear
The noise might drive her from her home of love;
5 For here I've heard her many a merry year—
At morn, at eve, nay, all the live-long day,
As though she lived on song. This very spot,
Just where that old-man's-beard[2] all wildly trails
Rude arbours o'er the road, and stops the way—
10 And where that child its blue-bell flowers hath got,
Laughing and creeping through the mossy rails—
There have I hunted like a very boy,
Creeping on hands and knees through matted thorn
To find her nest, and see her feed her young.
15 And vainly did I many hours employ:
All seemed as hidden as a thought unborn.
And where those crimping fern-leaves ramp among
The hazel's under boughs, I've nestled down,
And watched her while she sung; and her renown
20 Hath made me marvel that so famed a bird
Should have no better dress than russet brown.
Her sings would tremble in her ecstasy,[3]
And feathers stand on end, as 'twere with joy,
And mouth wide open to release her heart
25 Of its out-sobbing songs. The happiest part

---
[1] written between 1824 and 1832.

[2] moss.

[3] Here, in 24–25 and in 33, cf. Keats, "Ode to a Nightingale" 57–58.*

Of summer's fame she shared, for so to me
Did happy fancies shapen her employ;
But if I touched a bush, or scarcely stirred,
All in a moment stopt. I watched in vain:
30 The timid bird had left the hazel bush,
And at a distance hid to sing again.
Lost in a wilderness of listening leaves,
Rich Ecstasy would pour its luscious strain,
Till envy spurred the emulating thrush
35 To start less wild and scarce inferior songs;
For while of half the year Care him bereaves,
To damp the ardour of his speckled breast;
The nightingale to summer's life belongs,
And naked trees, and winter's nipping wrongs,
40 Are strangers to her music and her rest.
Her joys are evergreen, her world is wide—
Hark! there she is as usual—let's be hush—
For in this black-thorn clump, if rightly guest,
Her curious house is hidden. Part aside
45 These hazel branches in a gentle way,
And stoop right cautious 'neath the rustling boughs,
For we will have another search to day,
And hunt this fern-strewn thorn-clump round and
      round;
And where this reeded wood-grass idly bows,
50 We'll wade right through, it is a likely nook:
In such like spots, and often on the ground,
They'll build, where rude boys never think to look—
Aye, as I live! her secret nest is here,
Upon this white-thorn stump! I've searched about
55 For hours in vain. There! put that bramble by—
Nay, trample on its branches and get near.
How subtle is the bird! she started out,
And raised a plaintive note of danger nigh,
Ere we were past the brambles; and now, near

60 Her nest, she sudden stops—as choking fear,
That might betray her home. So even now
We'll leave it as we found it: safety's guard
Of pathless solitudes shall keep it still.
See there! she's sitting on the old oak bough,
65 Mute in her fears; our presence doth retard
Her joys, and doubt turns every rapture chill.
Sing on, sweet bird! may no worse hap befall
Thy visions, than the fear that now deceives.
We will not plunder music of its dower,
70 Nor turn this spot of happiness to thrall;
For melody seems hid in every flower,
That blossoms near thy home. These harebells all
Seem bowing with the beautiful in song;
And gaping cuckoo-flower, with spotted leaves,
75 Seems blushing of the singing it has heard.
How curious is the nest; no other bird
Uses such loose materials, or weaves
Its dwelling in such spots: dead oaken leaves
Are placed without, and velvet moss within,
80 And little scraps of grass, and, scant and spare,
What scarcely seem materials, down and hair;
For from men's haunts she nothing seems to win.
Yet Nature is the builder, and contrives
Homes for her children's comfort, even here;
85 Where Solitude's disciples spend their lives
Unseen, save when a wanderer passes near
That loves such pleasant places. Deep adown,
The nest is made a hermit's mossy cell.
Snug lie her curious eggs in number five,
90 Of deadened green, or rather olive brown;
And the old prickly thorn-bush guards them well.
So here we'll leave them, still unknown to wrong,
As the old woodland's legacy of song.

from Frederick Martin, *The Life of John Clare* (1865)

[*I Am*][1]

I am! yet what I am who cares, or knows?
    My friends forsake me like a memory lost.
I am the self-consumer of my woes,
    They rise and vanish, an oblivious host,
5 Shadows of life, whose very soul is lost.
And yet I am—I live—though I am toss'd

Into the nothingness of scorn and noise,
    Into the living sea of waking dream,
Where there is neither sense of life, nor joys,
10   But the huge shipwreck of my own esteem
And all that's dear. Even those I loved the best
Are strange—nay, they are stranger than the rest.

I long for scenes where man has never trod,
    For scenes where woman never smiled or wept;
15 There to abide with my Creator, God,
    And sleep as I in childhood sweetly slept
Full of high thoughts, unborn. So let me lie,
The grass below; above the vaulted sky.

---

[1] written between 1842 and 1846, this poem exists in different versions, one of which was published in the *Bedford Times* (1 January 1848). A sonnet on the same subject exists in MS:
  I feel I am—I only know I am,
  And plod upon the earth, as dull and void:
  Earth's prison chilled my body with its dram
  Of dullness, and my soaring thoughts destroyed,
  I fled to solitudes from passions dream,
  But strife persued—I only know, I am,
  I was a being created in the race
  Of men disdaining bounds of place and time:—
  A spirit that could travel o'er the space
  Of earth and heaven,—like a thought sublime,
  Tracing creation, like my maker, free,—
  A soul unshackled—like eternity,
  Spurning earth's vain and soul debasing thrall
  But now I only know I am,—that's all.
(*The Later Poems of John Clare, 1837–1864*, vol. 1, ed. Eric Robinson and David Powell [1984])

---

from *John Clare: Poems Chiefly from Manuscript*, ed. Edmund Blunden and Alan Porter (1920)

Badger[2]

When midnight comes a host of dogs and men
Go out and track the badger to his den,
And put a sack within the hole, and lie
Till the old grunting badger passes bye.
5 He comes and hears—they let the strongest loose.
The old fox hears the noise and drops the goose.
The poacher shoots and hurries from the cry,
And the old hare half wounded buzzes bye.
They get a forked stick to bear him down
10 And clap the dogs and take him to the town,
And bait him all the day with many dogs,
And laugh and shout and fright the scampering hogs.
He runs along and bites at all he meets:
They shout and hollo down the noisy streets.
15 He turns about to face the loud uproar
And drives the rebels to their very door.
The frequent stone is hurled where eer they go;
When badgers fight, then every one's a foe.
The dogs are clapt and urged to join the fray;
20 The badger turns and drives them all away.
Though scarcely half as big, demure and small,
He fights with dogs for bones and beats them all.
The heavy mastiff, savage in the fray,
Lies down and licks his feet and turns away.
25 The bulldog knows his match and waxes cold,
The badger grins and never leaves his hold.
He drives the crowd and follows at their heels
And bites them through—the drunkard swears and reels.
The frighted women take the boys away,
30 The blackguard laughs and hurries on the fray.
He tries to reach the woods, an awkward race,
But sticks and cudgels quickly stop the chace.
He turns agen and drives the noisy crowd
And beats the many dogs in noises loud.
35 He drives away and beats them every one,

---

[2] written between 1835 and 1837.

And then they loose them all and set them on.
He falls as dead and kicked by boys and men,
Then starts and grins and drives the crowd agen;
Till kicked and torn and beaten out he lies
40 And leaves his hold and cackles, groans, and dies.

Quail's Nest

I wandered out one rainy day
    And heard a bird with merry joys
Cry "wet my foot" for half the way;
    I stood and wondered at the noise,

5 When from my foot a bird did flee—
    The rain flew bouncing from her breast—
I wondered what the bird could be,
    And almost trampled on her nest.

The nest was full of eggs and round—
10   I met a shepherd in the vales,
And stood to tell him what I found.
    He knew and said it was a quail's,

For he himself the nest had found,
    Among the wheat and on the green,
15 When going on his daily round,
    With eggs as many as fifteen.

Among the stranger birds they feed,
    Their summer flight is short and low;
There's very few know where they breed,
20   And scarcely any where they go.

Invitation to Eternity[1]

Say, wilt thou go with me, sweet maid,
Say, maiden, wilt thou go with me
Through the valley-depths of shade,
Of bright and dark obscurity;
5 Where the path has lost its way,
Where the sun forgets the day,
Where there's nor light nor life to see,
Sweet maiden, wilt thou go with me?

Where stones will turn to flooding streams,
10 Where plains will rise like ocean's waves,
Where life will fade like visioned dreams
And darkness darken into caves,
Say, maiden, wilt thou go with me
Through this sad non-identity
15 Where parents live and are forgot,
And sisters live and know us not?

Say, maiden, wilt thou go with me
In this strange death of life to be,
To live in death and be the same,
20 Without this life or home or name,
At once to be and not to be—
That was and is not—yet to see
Things pass like shadows, and the sky
Above, below, around us lie?

25 The land of shadows wilt thou trace,
Nor look nor know each other's face;
The present marred with reason gone,
And past and present both as one?
Say, maiden, can thy life be led
30 To join the living and the dead?
Then trace thy footsteps on with me:
We are wed to one eternity.

Clock-a-Clay[2]

In the cowslip pips I lie,[3]
Hidden from the buzzing fly,
While green grass beneath me lies,
Pearled with dew like fishes' eyes,
5 Here I lie, a clock-a-clay,
Waiting for the time of day.[4]

---

[1] written by 1847.

[2] a lady-bug. The poem was written in about 1848.

[3] Cf. Shakespeare, *The Tempest* 5.1.89.

[4] Children used to tell time by counting how many taps it took to make a lady-bug fly away home.

While the forest quakes surprise,
And the wild wind sobs and sighs,
My home rocks as like to fall,
On its pillar green and tall;
When the pattering rain drives by
Clock-a-clay keeps warm and dry.

Day by day and night by night,
All the week I hide from sight;
In the cowslip pips I lie,
In rain and dew still warm and dry;
Day and night, and night and day,
Red, black-spotted clock-a-clay.

My home shakes in wind and showers,
Pale green pillar topped with flowers,
Bending at the wild wind's breath,
Till I touch the grass beneath;
Here I live, lone clock-a-clay,
Watching for the time of day.

from *The Poems of John Clare*, ed. J.W. Tibble (1935)

Enclosure [*The Mores*][1]

Far spread the moory ground, a level scene
Bespread with rush and one eternal green,
That never felt the rage of blundering plough,
Though centuries wreathed spring blossoms on its brow.
Autumn met plains that stretched them far away
In unchecked shadows of green, brown, and grey.
Unbounded freedom ruled the wandering scene;
No fence of ownership crept in between
To hide the prospect from the gazing eye;
Its only bondage was the circling sky.
A mighty flat, undwarfed by bush and tree,
Spread its faint shadow of immensity,
And lost itself, which seemed to eke its bounds,
In the blue mist the horizon's edge surrounds.

Now this sweet vision of my boyish hours,
Free as spring clouds and wild as forest flowers,
Is faded all—a hope that blossomed free,
And hath been once as it no more shall be.
Enclosure came, and trampled on the grave
Of labour's rights, and left the poor a slave;
And memory's pride, ere want to wealth did bow,
Is both the shadow and the substance now.
The sheep and cows were free to range as then
Where change might prompt, nor felt the bonds of men.
Cows went and came with every morn and night
To the wild pasture as their common right;
And sheep, unfolded with the rising sun,
Heard the swains shout and felt their freedom won,
Tracked the red fallow field and heath and plain,
Or sought the brook to drink, and roamed again;
While the glad shepherd traced their tracks along,
Free as the lark and happy as her song.
But now all's fled, and flats of many a dye
That seemed to lengthen with the following eye,
Moors losing from the sight, far, smooth, and blea,
Where swopt the plover in its pleasure free,
Are banished now with heaths once wild and gay
As poet's visions of life's early day.
Like mighty giants of their limbs bereft,
The skybound wastes in mangled garbs are left,
Fence meeting fence in owner's little bounds
Of field and meadow, large as garden-grounds,
In little parcels little minds to please,
With men and flocks imprisoned, ill at ease.
For with the poor scared freedom bade farewell,
And fortune-hunters totter where they fell;
They dreamed of riches in the rebel scheme
And find too truly that they did but dream.

---

[1] Between 1781 and 1844, Parliament passed some 4,000 acts of enclosure, taking land out of common use—usually for the benefit of large landowners and at the expense of small farmers like Clare. The poem was written between 1821 and 1824. The alternative title, "The Mores," means "the moors."

The Skylark Leaving Her Nest

Right happy bird, so full of mirth,
    Mounting and mounting still more high
    To meet morn's sunshine in the sky
        Ere yet it smiles on earth,

5 How often I delight to stand,
    Listening a minute's length away,
    Where summer spreads her green array
        By wheat or barley land;

To see thee with a sudden start
10   The green and placid herbage leave
    And in mid-air a vision weave
        For joy's delighted heart,

Shedding to heaven a vagrant mirth
    When silence husheth other theme
15   And woods in their dark splendour dream
        Like heaviness on earth.

My mind enjoys the happy sight
    To watch thee to the clear blue sky,
    And when I downward turn my eye
20   Earth glows with lonely light.

Then nearer come thy happy sounds
    And downward drops thy little wing,
    And now the valleys hear thee sing
        And all the dewy grounds

25 Gleam into joy! now from the eye
    Thou'rt dropping sudden as a stone,
    And now thou'rt in the wheat alone,
        And still the circle of the sky.

And absent, like a pleasure gone,
30   Though many come within the way,
    Thy little song to peeping day
        Is still remembered on.

For who that crosses fields of corn
    When skylarks start to meet the day
35   But feels more pleasure on his way
        Upon a summer's morn?

'Tis one of those heart-cheering sights
    In green earth's rural chronicles
    That upon every memory dwells
40   Among home-fed delights.

Felicia Hemans
1793 – 1835

Felicia Dorothea Browne was born in Liverpool on 25 September 1793, the fifth child of George Browne, a wine merchant, and Felicity Wagner Browne. About 1800, her father lost his business and the family moved to North Wales. Educated by her mother, she began to write poems at the age of eight and published the first two of her twenty-two books in 1808, when she was fifteen. One of the subscribers to her first book was Captain Alfred Hemans, a man twice her age; despite the disapproval of her family, they were married in 1812. After a year in Daventry, Northamptonshire, they moved in with her mother in St. Asaph. They had five sons, but in 1818, before the birth of the fifth, Captain Hemans went to Italy, allegedly for health reasons; Hemans never saw him again. Now largely responsible for the support of her mother, sister, and children, she continued to write and publish regularly, becoming one of the most popular and admired poets in Britain. In 1821, her *Dartmoor* won the poetry prize of the National Society of Literature, and her oldest son declared, "Now I am sure mamma is a better poet than Lord Byron!"* Hemans published two tragedies, *The Vespers of Palermo* and *The Siege of Valencia*, in 1823; *The Forest Sanctuary*, her own favourite among her works, in 1825; and *Records of Woman*, her most highly regarded collection, in 1828. But in 1827, her mother died, her sister married, Hemans herself experienced the first symptoms of the heart disease that would kill her, and her Welsh home had to be broken up. She sent her two oldest sons to their father in Italy and moved with the others to a suburb of Liverpool. She was not happy there, but she began to correspond with writers like Baillie,* Mary Howitt, and Maria Jane Jewsbury; through them, she came to know Scott* and the Wordsworths.* In 1831, she moved to Dublin, where her brother had a position with the police, but her health broke down. She published her last book, *Scenes and Hymns of Life*, in 1834, and died on 16 May 1835. (D.L.M.)

☙☙☙

from *Tales, and Historic Scenes, in Verse* (1819)

The Wife of Asdrubal

"This governor,[1] who had braved death when it was at a distance, and protested that the sun should never see him survive Carthage, this fierce Asdrubal, was so mean-spirited, as to come alone, and privately throw himself at the conqueror's feet. The general, pleased to see his proud rival humbled, granted his life, and kept him to grace his triumph. The Carthaginians in the citadel no sooner understood that their commander had abandoned the place, than they threw open the gates, and put the proconsul in possession of Byrsa.[2] The Romans had now no enemy to contend with but the nine hundred deserters, who, being reduced to despair, retired into the temple of Esculapius,[3] which was a second citadel within the first: there the proconsul attacked them; and these unhappy wretches, finding there was no way to escape, set fire to the temple. As the flames spread, they retreated from one part to another, till they got to the roof of the building: there Asdrubal's wife appeared in her best apparel, as if the day of her death had been a day of triumph; and after having uttered the most bitter imprecations against her husband, whom she saw standing below with Emilianus,[4]—'Base coward!' said she, 'the mean things thou hast done to save thy life shall not avail thee; thou shalt die this instant, at least in thy two children.' Having thus spoken, she drew out a dagger, stabbed them both, and

---

[1] Hasdrubal was Governor of Carthage, a North African city and Rome's chief imperial rival, when the Romans finally destroyed it at the end of the Third Punic War (149–46 BC). The surviving Carthaginians were enslaved, and Hasdrubal spent the rest of his life as a state prisoner.

[2] Carthaginian citadel.

[3] a legendary physician, the son of Apollo.

[4] Scipio Africanus Minor (c. 185–129 BC), Roman general.

while they were yet struggling for life, threw them from the top of the temple, and leaped down after them into the flames."—*Ancient Universal History*.[1]

The sun sets brightly—but a ruddier glow
O'er Afric's heaven the flames of Carthage throw;
Her walls have sunk, and pyramids of fire
In lurid splendor from her domes aspire;
5   Sway'd by the wind, they wave—while glares the sky
As when the desert's red Simoom[2] is nigh;
The sculptured altar, and the pillar'd hall,
Shine out in dreadful brightness ere they fall;
Far o'er the seas the light of ruin streams,
10 Rock, wave, and isle, are crimson'd by its beams;
While captive thousands, bound in Roman chains,
Gaze in mute horror on their burning fanes;[3]
And shouts of triumph, echoing far around,
Swell from the victor's tents with ivy crown'd.[4]

15 But mark! from yon fair temple's loftiest height
What towering form bursts wildly on the sight,
All regal in magnificent attire,
And sternly beauteous in terrific ire?
She might be deem'd a Pythia[5] in the hour
20 Of dread communion and delirious power;
A being more than earthly, in whose eye
There dwells a strange and fierce ascendancy.
The flames are gathering round—intensely bright,
Full on her features glares their meteor-light,
25 But a wild courage sits triumphant there,
The stormy grandeur of a proud despair;
A daring spirit, in its woes elate,
Mightier than death, untameable by fate.
The dark profusion of her locks unbound,
30 Waves like a warrior's floating plumage round;
Flush'd is her cheek, inspired her haughty mien,
She seems th' avenging goddess of the scene.

Are those *her* infants, that with suppliant-cry
Cling round her, shrinking as the flame draws nigh,
35 Clasp with their feeble hands her gorgeous vest,
And fain would rush for shelter to her breast?
Is that a mother's glance, where stern disdain,
And passion awfully vindictive, reign?

Fix'd is her eye on Asdrubal, who stands,
40 Ignobly safe, amidst the conquering bands;
On him, who left her to that burning tomb,
Alone to share her children's martyrdom;
Who when his country perish'd, fled the strife,
And knelt to win the worthless boon of life.
45 "Live, traitor, live!" she cries, "since dear to thee,
E'en in thy fetters, can existence be!
Scorn'd and dishonour'd, live!—with blasted name,
The Roman's triumph not to grace, but shame.
O slave in spirit! bitter be thy chain
50 With tenfold anguish to avenge my pain!
Still may the manès[6] of thy children rise
To chase calm slumber from thy wearied eyes;
Still may their voices on the haunted air
In fearful whispers tell thee to despair,
55 Till vain remorse thy wither'd heart consume,
Scourged by relentless shadows of the tomb!
E'en now my sons shall die—and thou, their sire,
In bondage safe, shalt yet in them expire.
Think'st thou I love them not?—'Twas thine to fly—
60 'Tis mine with these to suffer and to die.
Behold their fate!—the arms that cannot save
Have been their cradle, and shall be their grave."

Bright in her hand the lifted dagger gleams,
Swift from her children's hearts the life-blood streams;
65 With frantic laugh she clasps them to the breast
Whose woes and passions soon shall be at rest;
Lifts one appealing, frenzied glance on high,
Then deep midst rolling flames is lost to mortal eye.

---

[1] *Universal History, from the Earliest Account of Time to the Present, Compiled from Original Authors ... The Ancient Part*, 7 vols. (1736–50).

[2] desert wind.

[3] temples.

[4] "It was a Roman custom to adorn the tents of victors with ivy." (F.H.)

[5] priestess and oracle of Apollo at Delphi.

---

[6] "ghosts" (L.).

from *The League of the Alps, The Siege of Valencia, the Vespers of Palermo, and Other Poems* (1826)

Casabianca[1]

The boy stood on the burning deck,
    Whence all but him had fled;
The flame that lit the battle's wreck,
    Shone round him o'er the dead.

5 Yet beautiful and bright he stood,
    As born to rule the storm;
A creature of heroic blood,
    A proud, though child-like form.

The flames roll'd on—he would not go,
10   Without his father's word;
That father, faint in death below,
    His voice no longer heard.

He call'd aloud—"Say, father, say
    If yet my task is done?"
15 He knew not that the chieftain lay
    Unconscious of his son.

"Speak, Father!" once again he cried,
    "If I may yet be gone!"
—And but the booming shots replied,
20   And fast the flames roll'd on.

Upon his brow he felt their breath,
    And in his waving hair;
And look'd from that lone post of death,
    In still, yet brave despair.

25 And shouted but once more aloud,
    "My father! must I stay?"
While o'er him fast, through sail and shroud,
    The wreathing fires made way.

They wrapt the ship in splendor wild,
30   They caught the flag on high,
And stream'd above the gallant child,
    Like banners in the sky.

There came a burst of thunder sound—
    The boy—oh! where was he?
35 —Ask of the winds that far around
    With fragments strew'd the sea!

With mast, and helm, and pennon fair,
    That well had borne their part—
But the noblest thing that perish'd there,
40   Was that young faithful heart.

Evening Prayer at a Girls' School[2]

"Now in thy youth, beseech of Him,
  Who giveth, upbraiding not,
That his light in thy heart become not dim,
  And his love be unforgot;
And thy God, in the darkest of days, will be
Greenness, and beauty, and strength to thee."
                      BERNARD BARTON[3]

Hush! 'tis a holy hour—the quiet room
    Seems like a temple, while yon soft lamp sheds
A faint and starry radiance, through the gloom
    And the sweet stillness, down on bright young heads,
5 With all their clust'ring locks, untouch'd by care,

---

[1] "Young Casabianca, a boy about thirteen years old, son to the admiral of the Orient, remained at his post (in the battle of the Nile), after the ship had taken fire, and all the guns had been abandoned; and perished in the explosion of the vessel, when the flames had reached the powder." (F.H.) The British fleet, commanded by Nelson, defeated Napoleon's fleet, commanded by Louis de Casabianca, at the battle of the Nile, 1 August 1798. Among those killed when the French flagship, *L'Orient*, exploded were the admiral and his son, Giacomo Jocante Casabianca (who in fact was only ten). Hemans's source is probably Southey,* *Life of Horatio, Lord Nelson* (1813). The poem was first published in the *Monthly Magazine* 2 (1826): 164.

[2] The poem was first published in *Forget Me Not; A Christmas and New Year's Present for 1826* (1825) 156–58.

[3] Bernard Barton (1784–1849), "The Ivy, Addressed to a Young Friend" (1825) 43–48.

And bow'd, as flowers are bow'd with night—in
     prayer.

Gaze on,—'tis lovely!—childhood's lip and cheek,
     Mantling beneath its earnest brow of thought—
Gaze—yet what seest thou in those fair, and meek,
     And fragile things, as but for sunshine wrought?
—Thou seest what grief must nurture for the sky,
What death must fashion for eternity!

Oh! joyous creatures, that will sink to rest,
     Lightly, when those pure orisons are done,
As birds with slumber's honey-dew oppress'd,
     'Midst the dim folded leaves, at set of sun—
Lift up your hearts!—though yet no sorrow lies
Dark in the summer-heaven of those clear eyes;

Though fresh within your breasts th'untroubled
          springs
     Of hope make melody where'er ye tread;
And o'er your sleep bright shadows, from the wings
     Of spirits visiting but youth, be spread;
Yet in those flute-like voices, mingling low,
Is woman's tenderness—how soon her woe!

Her lot is on you—silent tears to weep,
     And patient smiles to wear through suffering's
          hour,
And sumless riches, from Affection's deep,
     To pour on broken reeds—a wasted shower!
And to make idols, and to find them clay,[1]
And to bewail that worship—therefore pray!

Her lot is on you—to be found untir'd,
     Watching the stars out by the bed of pain,
With a pale cheek, and yet a brow inspir'd,
     And a true heart of hope, though hope be vain.
Meekly to bear with wrong, to cheer decay,
And oh! to love through all things—therefore pray!

And take the thought of this calm vesper[2] time,
     With its low murmuring sounds and silvery light,
On through the dark days fading from their prime,
     As a sweet dew to keep your souls from blight.
Earth will forsake—oh! happy to have given
Th'unbroken heart's first fragrance unto Heaven!

from *Records of Woman: with Other Poems* (1828)

The Bride of the Greek Isle[3]

Fear!—I'm a Greek, and how should I fear death?
A slave, and wherefore should I dread my freedom?
* * * * * *
I will not live degraded.
                              SARDANAPALUS[4]

Come from the woods with the citron-flowers,[5]
Come with your lyres for the festal hours,
Maids of bright Scio![6] They came, and the breeze
Bore their sweet songs o'er the Grecian seas;—
They came, and Eudora[7] stood rob'd and crown'd,
The bride of the morn, with her train around.
Jewels flash'd out from her braided hair,
Like starry dews midst the roses[8] there;
Pearls on her bosom quivering shone,
Heav'd by her heart thro' its golden zone;
But a brow, as those gems of the ocean pale,

---

[1] Cf. Daniel 2.31–45.

[2] evening prayer.

[3] "Founded on a circumstance related in the Second Series of the Curiosities of Literature, and forming part of a picture in the '*Painted Biography*' there described." (F.H.) D'Israeli, "Of a Biography Painted," *Curiosities of Literature*, 2nd series (1823). The poem was first published in the *New Monthly Magazine* 14 (1825): 370–74.

[4] Byron,* *Sardanapalus* (1821) 1.2.478–80, 1.2.629.

[5] Cf. Byron, *The Bride of Abydos* (1813) 1.9. Orange blossoms are traditionally associated with weddings.

[6] or Chios, a Greek island in the Aegean sea, according to legend the birthplace of Homer. In 1822, forces of the Ottoman empire attacked it, killed 20,000 of the islanders, and enslaved 45,000. Hemans devoted two poems to this event, "Greek Song: The Voice of Scio" (1823) and "The Sisters of Scio" (1830).

[7] "good gift" (Gr.). Her name recalls that of Medora in Byron, *The Corsair* (1814).

[8] Cf. Byron, *The Bride of Abydos* 1.14.

Gleam'd from beneath her transparent veil;
Changeful and faint was her fair cheek's hue,
Tho' clear as a flower which the light looks through;
And the glance of her dark resplendent eye,
For the aspect of woman at times too high,
Lay floating in mists, which the troubled stream
Of the soul sent up o'er its fervid beam.

She look'd on the vine[1] at her father's door,
Like one that is leaving his native shore;
She hung o'er the myrtle[2] once call'd her own,
As it greenly wav'd by the threshold stone;
She turn'd—and her mother's gaze brought back
Each hue of her childhood's faded track.
Oh! hush the song, and let her tears
Flow to the dream of her early years!
Holy and pure are the drops that fall
When the young bride goes from her father's hall;
She goes unto love yet untried and new,
She parts from love which hath still been true;
Mute be the song and the choral strain,
Till her heart's deep well-spring is clear again!
She wept on her mother's faithful breast,
Like a babe that sobs itself to rest;
She wept—yet laid her hand awhile
In *his* that waited her dawning smile,
Her soul's affianced, nor cherish'd less
For the gush of nature's tenderness!
She lifted her graceful head at last—
The choking swell of her heart was past;
And her lovely thoughts from their cells found way
In the sudden flow of a plaintive lay.[3]

---

[1] Cf. Byron, *The Bride of Abydos* 1.5.

[2] Cf. Byron, *The Bride of Abydos* 1.1. The myrtle is sacred to Aphrodite, goddess of love.

[3] "A Greek Bride, on leaving her father's house, takes leave of her friends and relatives frequently in extemporaneous verse.—See Fauriel's Chants Populaires de la Grèce Moderne." (F.H.) Claude Charles Fauriel (1772–1844), *Chants Populaires de la Grèce Moderne* (1824).

THE BRIDE'S FAREWELL

Why do I weep?—to leave the vine
　　Whose clusters o'er me bend,—
The myrtle—yet, oh! call it mine!—
　　The flowers I lov'd to tend.
A thousand thoughts of all things dear,
　　Like shadows o'er me sweep,
I leave my sunny childhood here,
　　Oh, therefore let me weep!

I leave thee, sister! we have play'd
　　Thro' many a joyous hour,
Where the silvery green of the olive shade[4]
　　Hung dim o'er fount and bower.
Yes, thou and I, by stream, by shore,
　　In song, in prayer, in sleep,
Have been as we may be no more—
　　Kind sister, let me weep!

I leave thee, father! Eve's bright moon
　　Must now light other feet,
With the gather'd grapes, and the lyre in tune,
　　Thy homeward step to greet.
Thou in whose voice, to bless thy child,
　　Lay tones of love so deep,
Whose eye o'er all my youth hath smiled—
　　I leave thee! let me weep!

Mother! I leave thee! on thy breast,
　　Pouring out joy and wo,
I have found that holy place of rest
　　Still changeless,—yet I go!
Lips, that have lull'd me with your strain,
　　Eyes, that have watch'd my sleep!
Will earth give love like *yours* again?
　　Sweet mother! let me weep!

And like a slight young tree, that throws
The weight of rain from its drooping boughs,
Once more she wept. But a changeful thing

---

[4] Cf. Byron, *The Bride of Abydos* 1.9.

Is the human heart, as a mountain spring,
That works its way, thro' the torrent's foam,
80 To the bright pool near it, the lily's home!
It is well!—the cloud, on her soul that lay,
Hath melted in glittering drops away.
Wake again, mingle, sweet flute and lyre!
She turns to her lover, she leaves her sire.
85 Mother! on earth it must still be so,
Thou rearest the lovely to see them go!

They are moving onward, the bridal throng,
Ye may track their way by the swells of song;
Ye may catch thro' the foliage their white robes' gleam,
90 Like a swan midst the reeds of a shadowy stream.
Their arms bear up garlands, their gliding tread
Is over the deep-vein'd violet's bed;
They have light leaves around them, blue skies above,
An arch for the triumph of youth and love!

2

95 Still and sweet was the home that stood
In the flowering depths of a Grecian wood,
With the soft green light o'er its low roof spread,
As if from the glow of an emerald shed,
Pouring thro' lime-leaves that mingled on high,
100 Asleep in the silence of noon's clear sky.
Citrons amidst their dark foliage glow'd,
Making a gleam round the lone abode;
Laurels o'erhung it, whose faintest shiver
Scatter'd out rays like a glancing river;
105 Stars of the jasmine its pillars crown'd,
Vine-stalks its lattice and walls had bound,
And brightly before it a fountain's play
Flung showers thro' a thicket of glossy bay,
To a cypress[1] which rose in that flashing rain,
110 Like one tall shaft of some fallen fane.

And thither Ianthis[2] had brought his bride,
And the guests were met by that fountain-side;
They lifted the veil from Eudora's face,
It smiled out softly in pensive grace,
115 With lips of love, and a brow serene,
Meet for the soul of the deep wood-scene.—
Bring wine, bring odours!—the board is spread—
Bring roses! a chaplet for every head!
The wine-cups foam'd, and the rose was shower'd
120 On the young and fair from the world embower'd,
The sun look'd not on them in that sweet shade,
The winds amid scented boughs were laid;
But there came by fits, thro' some wavy tree,
A sound and a gleam of the moaning sea.

125 Hush! be still!—was that no more
Than the murmur from the shore?
Silence!—did thick rain-drops beat
On the grass like trampling feet?—
Fling down the goblet,[3] and draw the sword!
130 The groves are filled with a pirate-horde!
Thro' the dim olives their sabres shine;—
Now must the red blood stream for wine!

The youths from the banquet to battle sprang,
The woods with the shriek of the maidens rang;
135 Under the golden-fruited boughs
There were flashing poniards, and darkening brows,
Footsteps, o'er garland and lyre that fled;
And the dying soon on a greensward bed.

Eudora, Eudora! *thou* dost not fly!—
140 She saw but Ianthis before her lie,
With the blood from his breast in a gushing flow,
Like a child's large tears in its hour of wo,
And a gathering film in his lifted eye,
That sought his young bride out mournfully.—
145 She knelt down beside him, her arms she wound,
Like tendrils, his drooping neck around,

---

[1] Cf. Byron, *The Bride of Abydos* 1.1, 2.665–68. The cypress is a symbol of mourning.

[2] "violet" (Gr.). The violet is a symbol of rebirth and hope. Ianthe (the feminine form) is the name of the heroine of William D'Avenant, *The Siege of Rhodes* (1656); the dedicatee of Byron, *Childe Harold's Pilgrimage* 1–2 (1812); a character in Percy Shelley, *Queen Mab* (1813); Percy Shelley's first daughter (born 1813); a character in Polidori, *The Vampyre* (1819); and one in Landon, "The Improvisatrice."*

[3] Cf. Byron, "The Isles of Greece" (*Don Juan* 3).

As if the passion of that fond grasp
Might chain in life with its ivy-clasp.
But they tore her thence in her wild despair,
The sea's fierce rovers—they left him there;
They left to the fountain a dark-red vein,
And on the wet violets a pile of slain,
And a hush of fear thro' the summer-grove,—
So clos'd the triumph of youth and love!

3

Gloomy lay the shore that night,
When the moon, with sleeping light,
Bath'd each purple Sciote hill,—
Gloomy lay the shore, and still.
O'er the wave no gay guitar
Sent its floating music far;
No glad sound of dancing feet
Woke, the starry hours to greet.
But a voice of mortal wo,
In its changes wild or low,
Thro' the midnight's blue repose,
From the sea-beat rocks arose,
As Eudora's mother stood
Gazing o'er th'Egean flood,
With a fix'd and straining eye—
Oh! was the spoilers' vessel nigh?
Yes! there, becalm'd in silent sleep,
Dark and alone on a breathless deep,
On a sea of molten silver dark,
Brooding it frown'd that evil bark!
There its broad pennon a shadow cast,
Moveless and black from the tall still mast,
And the heavy sound of its flapping sail,
Idly and vainly wooed the gale.
Hush'd was all else—had ocean's breast
Rock'd e'en Eudora that hour to rest?

To rest?—the waves tremble!—what piercing cry
Bursts from the heart of the ship on high?
What light through the heavens, in a sudden spire,
Shoots from the deck up? Fire! 'tis fire!
There are wild forms hurrying to and fro,
Seen darkly clear on that lurid glow;
There are shout, and signal-gun, and call,
And the dashing of water,—but fruitless all!
Man may not fetter, nor ocean tame
The might and wrath of the rushing flame!
It hath twined the mast like a glittering snake,
That coils up a tree from a dusky brake;
It hath touch'd the sails, and their canvass rolls
Away from its breath into shrivell'd scrolls;
It hath taken the flag's high place in air,
And redden'd the stars with its wavy glare,
And sent out bright arrows, and soar'd in glee,
To a burning mount midst the moonlight sea.
The swimmers are plunging from stern and prow—
Eudora, Eudora! where, where art thou?
The slave and his master alike are gone.—
Mother! who stands on the deck alone?
The child of thy bosom!—and lo! a brand
Blazing up high in her lifted hand!
And her veil flung back, and her free dark hair
Sway'd by the flames as they rock and flare;
And her fragile form to its loftiest height
Dilated, as if by the spirit's might,
And her eye with an eagle-gladness fraught,—
Oh! could this work be of woman wrought?
Yes! 'twas her deed!—by that haughty smile
It was her's!—She hath kindled her funeral pile!
Never might shame on that bright head be,
Her blood was the Greek's, and hath made her free.

Proudly she stands, like an Indian bride
On the pyre with the holy dead beside;[1]
But a shriek from her mother hath caught her ear,
As the flames to her marriage-robe draw near,
And starting, she spreads her pale arms in vain
To the form they must never infold again.

One moment more, and her hands are clasp'd,
Fallen is the torch they had wildly grasp'd,
Her sinking knee unto Heaven is bow'd,
And her last look rais'd thro' the smoke's dim shroud,
And her lips as in prayer for her pardon move—
Now the night gathers o'er youth and love![2]

---

[1] a reference to suttee (or "sati," from the Sanskrit for "faithful wife"), the Hindu practice (outlawed by the British in 1829) of immolating a widow on her husband's funeral pyre.

[2] Originally published, as well as several other of these Records, in the *New Monthly Magazine*.

Properzia Rossi[1]

Properzia Rossi, a celebrated female sculptor of Bologna, possessed also of talents for poetry and music, died in consequence of an unrequited attachment.—A painting by Ducis,[2] represents her showing her last work, a basso-relievo of Ariadne,[3] to a Roman Knight, the object of her affection, who regards it with indifference.

> —Tell me no more, no more
> Of my soul's lofty gifts! Are they not vain
> To quench its haunting thirst for happiness?
> Have I not lov'd, and striven, and fail'd to bind
> One true heart unto me, whereon my own
> Might find a resting-place, a home for all
> Its burden of affections? I depart,
> Unknown, tho' Fame goes with me; I must leave
> The earth unknown. Yet it may be that death
> Shall give my name a power to win such tears
> As would have made life precious.[4]

1

One dream of passion and of beauty more!
And in its bright fulfilment let me pour
My soul away! Let earth retain a trace
Of that which lit my being, tho' its race
5   Might have been loftier far.—Yet one more dream!
From my deep spirit one victorious gleam
Ere I depart! For thee alone, for thee!
May this last work, this farewell triumph be,
Thou, lov'd so vainly! I would leave enshrined
10 Something immortal of my heart and mind,
That yet may speak to thee when I am gone,
Shaking thine inmost bosom with a tone
Of lost affection;—something that may prove
What she hath been, whose melancholy love
15 On thee was lavish'd; silent pang and tear,
And fervent song, that gush'd when none were near,
And dream by night, and weary thought by day,
Stealing the brightness from her life away,—
While thou—Awake! not yet within me die,
20 Under the burden and the agony
Of this vain tenderness,—my spirit, wake!
Ev'n for thy sorrowful affection's sake,
Live! in thy work breathe out!—that he may yet,
Feeling sad mastery there, perchance regret
25 Thine unrequited gift.

2

It comes,—the power
Within me born, flows back; my fruitless dower
That could not win me love. Yet once again
I greet it proudly, with its rushing train
Of glorious images:—they throng—they press—
30 A sudden joy lights up my loneliness,—
I shall not perish all![5]
   The bright work grows
Beneath my hand, unfolding, as a rose,
Leaf after leaf, to beauty; line by line,
I fix my thought, heart, soul, to burn, to shine,
35 Thro' the pale marble's veins. It grows—and now
I give my own life's history to thy brow,
Forsaken Ariadne! thou shalt wear
My form, my lineaments; but oh! more fair,
Touch'd into lovelier being by the glow
40   Which in me dwells, as by the summer-light
All things are glorified. From thee my wo
   Shall yet look beautiful to meet his sight,
When I am pass'd away. Thou art the mould
Wherein I pour the fervent thoughts, th'untold,
45 The self-consuming! Speak to him of me,
Thou, the deserted by the lonely sea,
With the soft sadness of thine earnest eye,
Speak to him, lorn one! deeply, mournfully,
Of all my love and grief! Oh! could I throw
50 Into thy frame a voice, a sweet, and low,
And thrilling voice of song! when he came nigh,
To send the passion of its melody

---

[1] Properzia de'Rossi (c.1491–1530), Bolognese sculptor, painter, and poet.

[2] Louis Ducis (1775–1847), *Properzia de'Rossi and her Last Bas-relief* (1812–14).

[3] Cretan princess, who helped Theseus find his way through the labyrinth and kill the Minotaur. They eloped, but he abandoned her on the island of Naxos. See Ovid (43 BC – AD 17), *Heroides* 10.

[4] The epigraph is by Hemans herself.

[5] Horace, *Odes* 3.30.6.

Thro' his pierc'd bosom—on its tones to bear
My life's deep feeling, as the southern air
⁵⁵ Wafts the faint myrtle's breath,—to rise, to swell,
To sink away in accents of farewell,
Winning but one, *one* gush of tears, whose flow
Surely my parted spirit yet might know,
If love be strong as death!

3
      Now fair thou art,
⁶⁰ Thou form, whose life is of my burning heart!
Yet all the vision that within me wrought,
 I cannot make thee! Oh! I might have given
Birth to creations of far nobler thought,
 I might have kindled, with the fire of heaven,
⁶⁵ Things not of such as die! But I have been
Too much alone;[1] a heart whereon to lean,
With all these deep affections, that o'erflow
My aching soul, and find no shore below;
An eye to be my star, a voice to bring
⁷⁰ Hope o'er my path, like sounds that breathe of spring,
These are denied me—dreamt of still in vain,—
Therefore my brief aspirings from the chain,
Are ever but as some wild fitful song,
Rising triumphantly, to die ere long
⁷⁵ In dirge-like echoes.

4
      Yet the world will see
Little of this, my parting work, in thee,
 Thou shalt have fame! Oh, mockery! give the reed
From storms a shelter,—give the drooping vine
Something round which its tendrils may entwine,—
⁸⁰ Give the parch'd flower a rain-drop, and the meed
Of love's kind words to woman! Worthless fame!
That in *his* bosom wins not for my name
Th'abiding place it ask'd! Yet how my heart,
In its own fairy world of song and art,
⁸⁵ Once beat for praise!—Are those high longings o'er?
That which I have been can I be no more?—
Never, oh! never more; tho' still thy sky

Be blue as then, my glorious Italy!
And tho' the music, whose rich breathings fill
⁹⁰ Thine air with soul, be wandering past me still,
And tho' the mantle of thy sunlight streams,
Unchang'd on forms, instinct with poet-dreams;
Never, oh! never more! Where'er I move,
The shadow of this broken-hearted love
⁹⁵ Is on me and around! Too well *they* know,
 Whose life is all within, too soon and well,
When there the blight hath settled;—but I go
 Under the silent wings of peace to dwell;
From the slow wasting, from the lonely pain,
¹⁰⁰ The inward burning of those words—"*in vain*,"
 Sear'd on the heart—I go. 'Twill soon be past.
Sunshine, and song, and bright Italian heaven,
 And thou, oh! thou, on whom my spirit cast
Unvalued wealth,—who know'st not what was given
¹⁰⁵ In that devotedness,—the sad, and deep,
And unrepaid—farewell! If I could weep
Once, only once, belov'd one! on thy breast,
Pouring my heart forth ere I sink to rest!
But that were happiness, and unto me
¹¹⁰ Earth's gift is *fame*. Yet I was form'd to be
So richly blest! With thee to watch the sky,
Speaking not, feeling but that thou wert nigh;
With thee to listen, while the tones of song
Swept ev'n as part of our sweet air along,
¹¹⁵ To listen silently;—with thee to gaze
On forms, the deified of olden days,
This had been joy enough;—and hour by hour,
From its glad well-springs drinking life and power,
How had my spirit soar'd, and made its fame
¹²⁰ A glory for thy brow!—Dreams, dreams!—the fire
Burns faint within me. Yet I leave my name—
 As a deep thrill may linger on the lyre
When its full chords are hush'd—awhile to live,
And one day haply in thy heart revive
¹²⁵ Sad thoughts of me:—I leave it, with a sound,
A spell o'er memory, mournfully profound,
I leave it, on my country's air to dwell,—
Say proudly yet—"'*Twas hers who lov'd me well!*"

---

[1] Cf. Byron, *Mazeppa* (1819) 839.

The Indian City[1]

> What deep wounds ever clos'd without a scar?
> The heart's bleed longest, and but heal to wear
> That which disfigures it.
> Childe Harold.[2]

1

Royal in splendour went down the day
On the plain where an Indian city lay,
With its crown of domes o'er the forest high,
Red as if fused in the burning sky,
5 And its deep groves pierced by the rays which made
A bright stream's way thro' each long arcade,
Till the pillar'd vaults of the Banian[3] stood,
Like torch-lit aisles midst the solemn wood,
And the plantain glitter'd with leaves of gold,
10 As a tree midst the genii-gardens old,
And the cypress lifted a blazing spire,
And the stems of the cocoas were shafts of fire.
Many a white pagoda's gleam
Slept lovely round upon lake and stream,
15 Broken alone by the lotus-flowers,
As they caught the glow of the sun's last hours,
Like rosy wine in their cups, and shed
Its glory forth on their crystal bed.
Many a graceful Hindoo maid,
20 With the water-vase from the palmy shade,
Came gliding light as the desert's roe,
Down marble steps to the tanks below;
And a cool sweet plashing was ever heard,
As the molten glass of the wave was stirr'd;
25 And a murmur, thrilling the scented air,
Told where the Bramin[4] bow'd in prayer.

There wandered a noble Moslem boy
Thro' the scene of beauty in breathless joy;
He gazed where the stately city rose
30 Like a pageant of clouds in its red repose;
He turn'd where birds thro' the gorgeous gloom
Of the woods went glancing on starry plume;
He track'd the brink of the shining lake,
By the tall canes feathered in tuft and brake,
35 Till the path he chose, in its mazes wound
To the very heart of the holy ground.
And there lay the water, as if enshrin'd
In a rocky urn from the sun and wind,
Bearing the hues of the grove on high,
40 Far down thro' its dark still purity.
The flood beyond, to the fiery west
Spread out like a metal-mirror's breast,
But that lone bay, in its dimness deep,
Seem'd made for the swimmer's joyous leap,
45 For the stag athirst from the noontide chase,
For all free things of the wild-wood's race.

Like a falcon's glance on the wide blue sky,
Was the kindling flash of the boy's glad eye,
Like a sea-bird's flight to the foaming wave,
50 From the shadowy bank was the bound he gave;
Dashing the spray-drops, cold and white,
O'er the glossy leaves in his young delight,
And bowing his locks to the waters clear—
Alas! he dreamt not that fate was near.

55 His mother look'd from her tent the while,
O'er heaven and earth with a quiet smile:
She, on her way unto Mecca's fane,[5]
Had stay'd the march of her pilgrim-train,
Calmly to linger a few brief hours,
60 In the Bramin city's glorious bowers;
For the pomp of the forest, the wave's bright fall,
The red gold of sunset—she lov'd them all.

2

The moon rose clear in the splendour given

---

[1] "From a tale in Forbes's Oriental Memoirs." (F.H.) James Forbes (1749–1819), *Oriental Memoirs, Selected and Abridged from a Series of Familiar Letters Written during Seventeen Years' Residence in India*, 4 vols. (1813) 2:337–38. The city is Dhuboy, in Gujurat. The poem was first published in the *New Monthly Magazine* 14 (1825): 574–78.

[2] Byron, *Childe Harold's Pilgrimage* 3.84.*

[3] the banyan or Indian fig (*Ficus bengalensis*). Its branches drop aerial rootlets which, when they reach the ground, take root and form secondary trunks, creating an appearance of "pillar'd vaults."

[4] a member of the highest (priestly) Hindu caste.

[5] Mecca is the birthplace of the prophet Muhammad; Muslims are expected to make a pilgrimage there at least once in their lives.

To the deep-blue night of an Indian heaven;
65　　The boy from the high-arch'd woods came back—
　　　Oh! what had he met in his lonely track?
　　　The serpent's glance, thro' the long reeds bright?
　　　The arrowy spring of the tiger's might?
　　　No!—yet as one by a conflict worn,
70　　With his graceful hair all soil'd and torn,
　　　And a gloom on the lids of his darken'd eye,
　　　And a gash on his bosom—he came to die!
　　　He look'd for the face to his young heart sweet,
　　　And found it, and sank at his mother's feet.

75　　"Speak to me!—whence doth the swift blood run?
　　　What hath befall'n thee, my child, my son?"
　　　The mist of death on his brow lay pale,
　　　But his voice just linger'd to breathe the tale,
　　　Murmuring faintly of wrongs and scorn,
80　　And wounds from the children of Brahma[1] born:
　　　This was the doom for a Moslem found
　　　With foot profane on their holy ground,
　　　This was for sullying the pure waves free
　　　Unto them alone—'twas their God's decree.

85　　A change came o'er his wandering look—
　　　The mother shriek'd not then, nor shook:
　　　Breathless she knelt in her son's young blood,
　　　Rending her mantle to staunch its flood;
　　　But it rush'd like a river which none may stay,
90　　Bearing a flower to the deep away.
　　　That which our love to the earth would chain,
　　　Fearfully striving with Heaven in vain,
　　　That which fades from us, while yet we hold,
　　　Clasp'd to our bosoms, its mortal mould,
95　　Was fleeting before her, afar and fast;
　　　One moment—the soul from the face had pass'd!

　　　Are there no words for that common wo?
　　　—Ask of the thousands, its depths that know!
　　　The boy had breathed, in his dreaming rest,
100　 Like a low-voiced dove, on her gentle breast;
　　　He had stood, when she sorrow'd, beside her knee,
　　　Painfully stilling his quick heart's glee;

　　　He had kiss'd from her cheek the widow's tears,
　　　With the loving lip of his infant years;
105　 He had smil'd o'er her path like a bright spring-day—
　　　Now in his blood on the earth he lay!
　　　Murder'd!—Alas! and we love so well
　　　In a world where anguish like this can dwell!

　　　She bow'd down mutely o'er her dead—
110　 They that stood round her watch'd in dread;
　　　They watch'd—she knew not they were by—
　　　Her soul sat veil'd in its agony.
　　　On the silent lip she press'd no kiss,
　　　Too stern was the grasp of her pangs for this;
115　 She shed no tear as her face bent low,
　　　O'er the shining hair of the lifeless brow;
　　　She look'd but into the half-shut eye,
　　　With a gaze that found there no reply,
　　　And shrieking, mantled her head from sight,
120　 And fell, struck down by her sorrow's might!

　　　And what deep change, what work of power,
　　　Was wrought on her secret soul that hour?
　　　How rose the lonely one?—She rose
　　　Like a prophetess from dark repose!
125　 And proudly flung from her face the veil,
　　　And shook the hair from her forehead pale,
　　　And 'midst her wondering handmaids stood,
　　　With the sudden glance of a dauntless mood.
　　　Ay, lifting up to the midnight sky
130　 A brow in its regal passion high,
　　　With a close and rigid grasp she press'd
　　　The blood-stain'd robe to her heaving breast,
　　　And said—"Not yet—not yet I weep,
　　　Not yet my spirit shall sink or sleep,
135　 Not till yon city, in ruins rent,
　　　Be piled for its victim's monument.
　　　—Cover his dust! bear it on before!
　　　It shall visit those temple-gates once more."

　　　And away in the train of the dead she turn'd,
140　 The strength of her step was the heart that burn'd;
　　　And the Bramin groves in the starlight smil'd,
　　　As the mother pass'd with her slaughter'd child.

---
[1] the creator, one of the three supreme gods of Hinduism.

3

Hark! a wild sound of the desert's horn
Thro' the woods round the Indian city borne,
145 A peal of the cymbal and tambour afar—
War! 'tis the gathering of Moslem war!
The Bramin look'd from the leaguer'd towers—
He saw the wild archer amidst his bowers;
And the lake that flash'd through the plantain shade,
150 As the light of the lances along it play'd;
And the canes that shook as if winds were high,
When the fiery steed of the waste swept by;
And the camp as it lay, like a billowy sea,
Wide round the sheltering Banian tree.

155 There stood one tent from the rest apart—
That was the place of a wounded heart.
—Oh! deep is a wounded heart, and strong
A voice that cries against mighty wrong;
And full of death, as a hot wind's blight,
160 Doth the ire of a crush'd affection light.

Maimuna[1] from realm to realm had pass'd,
And her tale had rung like a trumpet's blast;
There had been words from her pale lips pour'd,
Each one a spell to unsheath the sword.
165 The Tartar had sprung from his steed to hear,
And the dark chief of Araby grasp'd his spear,
Till a chain of long lances begirt the wall,
And a vow was recorded that doom'd its fall.
Back with the dust of her son she came,
170 When her voice had kindled that lightning flame;
She came in the might of a queenly foe,
Banner, and javelin, and bended bow;
But a deeper power on her forehead sate—
There sought the warrior his star of fate;
175 Her eye's wild flash through the tented line
Was hail'd as a spirit and a sign,
And the faintest tone from her lip was caught,
As a Sybil's breath of prophetic thought.

Vain, bitter glory!—the gift of grief,
180 That lights up vengeance to find relief,
Transient and faithless!—it cannot fill
So the deep void of the heart, nor still
The yearning left by a broken tie,
That haunted fever of which we die!

185 Sickening she turn'd from her sad renown,
As a king in death might reject his crown;
Slowly the strength of the walls gave way—
She wither'd faster, from day to day.
All the proud sounds of that banner'd plain,
190 To stay the flight of her soul were vain;
Like an eagle caged, it had striven, and worn
The frail dust ne'er for such conflicts born,
Till the bars were rent, and the hour was come
For its fearful rushing thro' darkness home.

195 The bright sun set in his pomp and pride,
As on that eve when the fair boy died;
She gazed from her couch, and a softness fell
O'er her weary heart with the day's farewell;
She spoke, and her voice in its dying tone
200 Had an echo of feelings that long seem'd flown.
She murmur'd a low sweet cradle song,
Strange midst the din of a warrior throng,
A song of the time when her boy's young cheek
Had glow'd on her breast in its slumber meek;
205 But something which breathed from that mournful strain
Sent a fitful gust o'er her soul again,
And starting as if from a dream, she cried—
"Give him proud burial at my side!
There, by yon lake, where the palm-boughs wave,
210 When the temples are fallen, make there our grave."

And the temples fell, tho' the spirit pass'd,
That stay'd not for victory's voice at last;
When the day was won for the martyr-dead,
For the broken heart, and the bright blood shed.

215 Thro' the gates of the vanquish'd the Tartar steed
Bore in the avenger with foaming speed;
Free swept the flame thro' the idol-fanes,

---

[1] Maimouna is the wise woman in Southey's Islamic epic, *Thalaba the Destroyer* (1801) 8.23ff.

And the streams glow'd red, as from warrior-veins,
And the sword of the Moslem, let loose to slay,
Like the panther leapt on its flying prey,
Till a city of ruin begirt the shade,
Where the boy and his mother at rest were laid.[1]

Palace and tower on that plain were left,
Like fallen trees by the lightning cleft;
The wild vine mantled the stately square,
The Rajah's throne was the serpent's lair,
And the jungle grass o'er the altar sprung—
This was the work of one deep heart wrung!

Indian Woman's Death-Song

An Indian woman, driven to despair by her husband's desertion of her for another wife, entered a canoe with her children, and rowed it down the Mississippi towards a cataract. Her voice was heard from the shore singing a mournful death-song, until overpowered by the sound of the waters in which she perished. The tale is related in Long's Expedition to the source of St Peter's River.[2]

Non, je ne puis vivre avec un coeur brisé. Il faut que je retrouve la joie, et que m'unisse aux esprits libres de l'air.
Bride of Messina,
Translated by Madame de Stael[3]

Let not my child be a girl, for very sad is the life of a woman.
The Prairie[4]

    Down a broad river of the western wilds,
    Piercing thick forest glooms, a light canoe
Swept with the current: fearful was the speed
Of the frail bark, as by a tempest's wing
Borne leaf-like on to where the mist of spray
Rose with the cataract's thunder.[5]—Yet within,
Proudly, and dauntlessly, and all alone,
Save that a babe lay sleeping at her breast,
A woman stood: upon her Indian brow
Sat a strange gladness, and her dark hair wav'd
As if triumphantly. She press'd her child,
In its bright slumber, to her beating heart,
And lifted her sweet voice, that rose awhile
Above the sound of waters, high and clear,
Wafting a wild proud strain, her song of death.

Roll swiftly to the Spirit's land, thou mighty stream and free!
Father of ancient waters,[6] roll! and bear our lives with thee!
The weary bird that storms have toss'd, would seek the sunshine's calm,
And the deer that hath the arrow's hurt,[7] flies to the woods of balm.

Roll on![8]—my warrior's eye hath look'd upon another's face,
And mine hath faded from his soul, as fades a moonbeam's trace;
My shadow comes not o'er his path, my whisper to his dream,
He flings away the broken reed—roll swifter yet, thou stream!

The voice that spoke of other days is hush'd within *his* breast,
But *mine* its lonely music haunts, and will not let me rest;

---

[1] When the poem was first published in the *New Monthly Magazine*, Hemans added a note: "Their tombs are still remaining, according to Forbes, in a grove near the city."

[2] William Hypolitus Keating (1799–1840), *Narrative of an Expedition to the Source of St. Peter's River*, 2 vols. (1824), tells the story of the expedition commanded by Major Stephen Harriman Long (1784–1865). The story of the forsaken Dakota woman is in 1:299–301.

[3] "No, I cannot live with a broken heart. I must find happiness again, and unite myself with the free spirits of the air." Friedrich von Schiller, *Die Braut von Messina* (1803) 2723–27, tr. Germaine de Staël (1766–1817) in *De l'Allemagne* (1810) chap. 19.

[4] James Fenimore Cooper,* *The Prairie* (1827) chap. 26.

[5] Cf. P.B. Shelley, "Alastor" 318–21, 346.*

[6] "'Father of waters,' the Indian name for the Mississippi." (F.H.)

[7] Cf. Cowper, *The Task** 3.108.

[8] Cf. Byron,* *Childe Harold's Pilgrimage* 4.179 (1818).

It sings a low and mournful song of gladness that is
    gone,
I cannot live without that light—Father of waves!
    roll on!

Will he not miss the bounding step that met him from
    the chase?
The heart of love that made his home an ever sunny
    place?
30 The hand that spread the hunter's board, and deck'd his
    couch of yore?—
He will not!—roll, dark foaming stream, on to the
    better shore!

Some blessed fount amidst the woods of that bright
    land must flow,
Whose waters from my soul may lave the memory of
    this wo;
Some gentle wind must whisper there, whose breath
    may waft away
35 The burden of the heavy night, the sadness of the day.

And thou, my babe! tho' born, like me, for woman's
    weary lot,
Smile!—to that wasting of the heart, my own! I leave
    thee not;
Too bright a thing art *thou* to pine in aching love
    away,
Thy mother bears thee far, young Fawn! from sorrow
    and decay.

40 She bears thee to the glorious bowers where none are
    heard to weep,
And where th' unkind one hath no power again to
    trouble sleep;
And where the soul shall find its youth, as wakening
    from a dream,—
One moment, and that realm is ours—On, on, dark
    rolling stream!

Joan of Arc, in Rheims[1]

Jeanne d'Arc avait eu la joie de voir à Chalons quelques amis de son enfance. Une joie plus ineffable encore l'attendait à Rheims, au sein de son triomphe: Jacques d'Arc, son père y se trouva, aussitot que de troupes de Charles VII. y furent entrées; et comme les deux frères de notre Héroine l'avaient accompagnés, elle se vit, pour un instant au milieu de sa famille, dans les bras d'un père vertueux.
                                    Vie de Jeanne d'Arc.[2]

Thou hast a charmed cup, O Fame!
    A draught that mantles high,
And seems to lift this earth-born frame
    Above mortality:
    Away! to me—a woman—bring
Sweet waters from affection's spring.[3]

That was a joyous day in Rheims of old,
When peal on peal of mighty music roll'd
Forth from her throng'd cathedral; while around,
A multitude, whose billows made no sound,
5 Chain'd to a hush of wonder, tho' elate
With victory, listen'd at their temple's gate.
And what was done within?—within, the light
    Thro' the rich gloom of pictured windows flowing,
Tinged with soft awfulness a stately sight,
10 The chivalry of France, their proud heads bowing
In martial vassalage!—while midst that ring,

---

[1] Jeanne d'Arc (c.1412–31), French national hero, was honoured at the coronation of Charles VII in Rheims cathedral, July 1429. The Burgundians captured her and handed her over to the English occupiers in 1430, and the Inquisition tried her for witchcraft in 1431. Eventually, the English convicted her of treason, and she was burned at the stake. Hemans was familiar with Friedrich von Schiller, *Die Jungfrau von Orleans* (1801). Her poem was first published in the *New Monthly Magazine* 17 (1826): 314–16.

[2] "Joan of Arc had had the happiness of seeing several of her childhood friends in Châlons. An even more inexpressible happiness awaited her in Rheims, in the middle of her triumph: Jacques of Arc, her father, arrived there as soon as the troops of Charles VII had entered; and as our Heroine's two brothers had accompanied him, she saw herself, for a moment, in the bosom of her family, in the arms of a virtuous father." "Jeanne d'Arc ou La Pucelle d'Orléans," *Almanach de Gotha pour l'Année 1822.*

[3] Hemans, "Woman and Fame" 1–6.

And shadow'd by ancestral tombs, a king
Receiv'd his birthright's crown. For this, the hymn
    Swell'd out like rushing waters, and the day
15 With the sweet censer's misty breath grew dim,
    As thro' long aisles it floated o'er th'array
Of arms and sweeping stoles. But who, alone
And unapproach'd, beside the altar-stone,
With the white banner, forth like sunshine streaming,
20 And the gold helm, thro' clouds of fragrance gleaming,
    Silent and radiant stood?—the helm was rais'd,
And the fair face reveal'd, that upward gaz'd,
    Intensely worshipping:—a still, clear face,
Youthful, but brightly solemn!—Woman's cheek
25 And brow were there, in deep devotion meek,
    Yet glorified with inspiration's trace
On its pure paleness; while, enthron'd above,
The pictur'd virgin, with her smile of love,
Seem'd bending o'er her votaress.—That slight form!
30 Was that the leader thro' the battle storm?
Had the soft light in that adoring eye,
Guided the warrior where the swords flash'd high?
'Twas so, even so!—and thou, the shepherd's child,
Joanne, the lowly dreamer of the wild!
35 Never before, and never since that hour,
Hath woman, mantled with victorious power,
Stood forth as *thou* beside the shrine didst stand,
Holy amidst the knighthood of the land;
And beautiful with joy and with renown,
40 Lift thy white banner o'er the olden crown,
Ransom'd for France by thee!

                        The rites are done.
Now let the dome with trumpet-notes be shaken,
And bid the echoes of the tombs awaken,
    And come thou forth, that Heaven's rejoicing sun
45 May give thee welcome from thine own blue skies,
    Daughter of victory!—A triumphant strain,
A proud rich stream of warlike melodies,
    Gush'd thro' the portals of the antique fane,
And forth she came.—Then rose a nation's sound—
50 Oh! what a power to bid the quick heart bound,
The wind bears onward with the stormy cheer
Man gives to glory on her high career!
Is there indeed such power?—far deeper dwells
In one kind household voice, to reach the cells
55 Whence happiness flows forth!—The shouts that fill'd
The hollow heaven tempestuously, were still'd
One moment; and in that brief pause, the tone,
As of a breeze that o'er her home had blown,
Sank on the bright maid's heart.—"Joanne!"—
    Who spoke
60 Like those whose childhood with *her* childhood grew
Under one roof?—"Joanne!"—*that* murmur broke
    With sounds of weeping forth!—She turn'd—
    she knew
Beside her, mark'd from all the thousands there,
In the calm beauty of his silver hair,
65 The stately shepherd; and the youth, whose joy
From his dark eye flash'd proudly; and the boy,
The youngest-born, that ever lov'd her best:
"Father! and ye, my brothers!"—On the breast
Of that grey sire she sank—and swiftly back,
70 Ev'n in an instant, to their native track
Her free thoughts flowed.—She saw the pomp no
    more—
The plumes, the banners:—to her cabin-door,
And to the Fairy's fountain in the glade,[1]
Where her young sisters by her side had play'd,
75 And to her hamlet's chapel, where it rose
Hallowing the forest unto deep repose,
Her spirit turn'd.—The very wood-note, sung
    In early spring-time by the bird, which dwelt
Where o'er her father's roof the beech-leaves hung,
80   Was in her heart; a music heard and felt,
Winning her back to nature.—She unbound
    The helm of many battles from her head,[2]
And, with her bright locks bow'd to sweep the ground,
    Lifting her voice up, wept for joy, and said,—
85 "Bless me, my father, bless me! and with thee,
To the still cabin and the beechen-tree,
Let me return!"[3]

---

[1] "A beautiful fountain near Domremi, believed to be haunted by fairies, and a favourite resort of Jeanne d'Arc in her childhood." (F.H.) Domrémy was Jeanne's birthplace.

[2] Cf. Edmund Spenser, *The Faerie Queene* 4.1.12–15.

[3] Cf. the parable of the prodigal son, Luke 15.11–32.

Oh! never did thine eye
Thro' the green haunts of happy infancy
Wander again, Joanne!—too much of fame
90 Had shed its radiance on thy peasant-name;
And bought alone by gifts beyond all price,
The trusting heart's repose, the paradise[1]
Of home with all its loves, doth fate allow
The crown of glory unto woman's brow.

Madeline. A Domestic Tale[2]

> Who should it be?—Where shouldst thou look for
>   kindness?
> When we are sick where can we turn for succour,
> When we are wretched where can we complain;
> And when the world looks cold and surly on us,
> Where can we go to meet a warmer eye
> With such sure confidence as to a mother?
> JOANNA BAILLIE[3]

"My child, my child, thou leav'st me!—I shall hear
The gentle voice no more that blest mine ear
With its first utterance; I shall miss the sound
Of thy light step amidst the flowers around,
5 And thy soft-breathing hymn at twilight's close,
And thy 'Good-night' at parting for repose.
Under the vine-leaves I shall sit alone,
And the low breeze will have a mournful tone
Amidst their tendrils, while I think of thee,
10 My child! and thou, along the moonlight sea,
With a soft sadness haply in thy glance,
Shalt watch thine own, thy pleasant land of France,
Fading to air.—Yet blessings with thee go!
Love guard thee, gentlest! and the exile's wo
15 From thy young heart be far!—And sorrow not
For me, sweet daughter! in my lonely lot,
God shall be with me.—Now farewell, farewell!
Thou that hast been what words may never tell
Unto thy mother's bosom, since the days
20 When thou wert pillow'd there, and wont to raise
In sudden laughter thence thy loving eye
That still sought mine:—those moments are gone by,
Thou too must go, my flower!—Yet with thee dwell
The peace of God!—One, one more gaze—farewell!"

25 This was a mother's parting with her child,
A young meek Bride on whom fair fortune smil'd,
And wooed her with a voice of love away
From childhood's home; yet there, with fond delay
She linger'd on the threshold, heard the note
30 Of her caged bird thro' trellis'd rose-leaves float,
And fell upon her mother's neck, and wept,
Whilst old remembrances, that long had slept,
Gush'd o'er her soul, and many a vanish'd day,
As in one picture traced, before her lay.

35 But the farewell was said; and on the deep,
When its breast heav'd in sunset's golden sleep,
With a calm'd heart, young Madeline ere long
Pour'd forth her own sweet solemn vesper-song,
Breathing of home: thro' stillness heard afar,
40 And duly rising with the first pale star,
That voice was on the waters; till at last
The sounding ocean-solitudes were pass'd,
And the bright land was reach'd, the youthful world
That glows along the West: the sails were furl'd
45 In its clear sunshine, and the gentle bride
Look'd on the home that promis'd hearts untried
A bower of bliss[4] to come.—Alas! we trace
The map of our own paths, and long ere years
With their dull steps the brilliant lines efface,
50 On sweeps the storm, and blots them out with tears.
That home was darken'd soon: the summer breeze
Welcom'd with death the wanderers from the seas,
Death unto one, and anguish how forlorn!
To her, that widow'd in her marriage-morn,
55 Sat in her voiceless dwelling, whence with him,
    Her bosom's first belov'd, her friend and guide,
Joy had gone forth, and left the green earth dim,
    As from the sun shut out on every side,
By the close veil of misery!—Oh! but ill,
60   When with rich hopes o'erfraught, the young
        high heart

---

[1] Cf. Milton, *Paradise Lost* 9.406–07.

[2] "Originally published in the Literary Souvenir for 1828." (F.H.)

[3] Joanna Baillie,* *Rayner: A Tragedy* (1804) 4.2.15–20.

[4] Cf. Spenser, *The Faerie Queene* 2.1.51, 2.12.69–87.

Bears its first blow!—it knows not yet the part
Which life will teach—to suffer and be still,
And with submissive love to count the flowers
Which yet are spared, and thro' the future hours
To send no busy dream!—*She* had not learn'd
Of sorrow till that hour, and therefore turn'd
In weariness from life: then came th'unrest,
The heart-sick yearning of the exile's breast,
The haunting sounds of voices far away,
And household steps; until at last she lay
On her lone couch of sickness, lost in dreams
Of the gay vineyards and blue-rushing streams
In her own sunny land, and murmuring oft
Familiar names, in accents wild, yet soft,
To strangers round that bed, who knew not aught
Of the deep spells wherewith each word was fraught.
To strangers?—Oh! could strangers raise the head
Gently as *hers* was rais'd?—did strangers shed
The kindly tears which bath'd that feverish brow
And wasted cheek with half unconscious flow?
Something was there, that thro' the lingering night
Outwatches patiently the taper's light,
Something that faints not thro' the day's distress,
That fears not toil, that knows not weariness;
Love, true and perfect love!—Whence came that power,
Uprearing thro' the storm the drooping flower?
Whence?—who can ask?—the wild delirium pass'd,
And from her eyes the spirit look'd at last
Into her *mother's* face, and wakening knew
The brow's calm grace, the hair's dear silvery hue,
The kind sweet smile of old!—and had *she* come,
Thus in life's evening, from her distant home,
To save her child?—Ev'n so—nor yet in vain:
In that young heart a light sprung up again,
And lovely still, with so much love to give,
Seem'd this fair world, tho' faded; still to live
Was not to pine forsaken. On the breast
That rock'd her childhood, sinking in soft rest,
"Sweet mother, gentlest mother! can it be?"
The lorn one cried, "and do I look on thee?
Take back thy wanderer from this fatal shore,[1]
Peace shall be ours beneath our vines once more."

---

[1] Cf. W. Wordsworth,* "Laodamia" (1815) 52.

The Grave of a Poetess[2]

"Ne me plaignez pas—si vous saviez
 Combien de peines ce tombeau m'a epargnées!"[3]

I stood beside thy lowly grave;—
 Spring-odours breath'd around,
And music, in the river-wave,
 Pass'd with a lulling sound.

All happy things that love the sun[4]
 In the bright air glanc'd by,
And a glad murmur seem'd to run
 Thro' the soft azure sky.

Fresh leaves were on the ivy-bough
 That fring'd the ruins near;

---

[2] "Extrinsic interest has lately attached to the fine scenery of Woodstock, near Kilkenny, on account of its having been the last residence of the author of Psyche. Her grave is one of many in the church-yard of the village. The river runs smoothly by. The ruins of an ancient abbey that have been partially converted into a church, reverently throw their mantle of tender shadow over it.—*Tales by the O'Hara Family*." (F.H.) John Banim (1798–1842) and Michael Banim (1796–1874), *Tales by the O'Hara Family* (1825). The poem was first published in the *New Monthly Magazine* 20 (1827): 69–70. Hemans would visit the grave of Mary Tighe* in 1831 and describe it as follows: "We went to the tomb, 'the grave of a poetess,' where there is a monument by Flaxman. It consists of a recumbent female figure, with much of the repose, the mysterious sweetness of happy death, which is to me so affecting in monumental sculpture. There is, however, a very small Titania-looking sort of figure with wings, sitting at the head of the sleeper, which I thought interfered with the singleness of effect which the tomb would have produced. Unfortunately, too, the monument is carved in very rough stone, which allows no delicacy of touch. That place of rest made me very thoughtful; I could not but reflect on the many changes which had brought me to the spot I had commemorated three years since, without the slightest idea of ever visiting it; and, though surrounded by attention and the appearance of interest, my heart was envying the repose of her who slept there" (*Works* [1839] 1:238–39). John Flaxman (1755–1826) was a noted sculptor and illustrator. Titania is the queen of the fairies in Shakespeare, *A Midsummer Night's Dream*.

[3] "Do not weep for me—if you only knew / How many pains this tomb has spared me!" Germaine de Staël, *Corinne, ou l'Italie* (1807) 18.3 (the original is in prose).

[4] Cf. William Wordsworth, "Resolution and Independence" 8.*

Young voices were abroad—but thou
    Their sweetness couldst not hear.

And mournful grew my heart for thee,
    Thou in whose woman's mind
15 The ray that brightens earth and sea,
    The light of song was shrined.

Mournful, that thou wert slumbering low,
    With a dread curtain drawn
Between thee and the golden glow
20   Of this world's vernal dawn.

Parted from all the song and bloom
    Thou wouldst have lov'd so well,
To thee the sunshine round thy tomb
    Was but a broken spell.

25 The bird, the insect on the wing,
    In their bright reckless play,
Might feel the flush and life of spring,—
    And thou wert pass'd away!

But then, ev'n then, a nobler thought
30   O'er my vain sadness came;
Th'immortal spirit woke, and wrought
    Within my thrilling frame.

Surely on lovelier things, I said,
    Thou must have look'd ere now,
35 Than all that round our pathway shed
    Odours and hues below.

The shadows of the tomb are here,
    Yet beautiful is earth!
What seest thou then where no dim fear,
40   No haunting dream hath birth?

Here a vain love to passing flowers
    Thou gav'st—but where thou art,
The sway is not with changeful hours,
    There love and death must part.

45 Thou hast left sorrow in thy song,
    A voice not loud, but deep!
The glorious bowers of earth among,
    How often didst thou weep!

Where couldst thou fix on mortal ground
50   Thy tender thoughts and high?—
Now peace the woman's heart hath found,
    And joy the poet's eye.

The Homes of England

> Where's the coward that would not dare
> To fight for such a land?
>   *Marmion*[1]

The stately Homes of England,
    How beautiful they stand!
Amidst their tall ancestral trees,
    O'er all the pleasant land.
5 The deer across their greensward bound
    Thro' shade and sunny gleam,
And the swan glides past them with the sound
    Of some rejoicing stream.

The merry Homes of England!
10   Around their hearths by night,
What gladsome looks of household love
    Meet, in the ruddy light!
There woman's voice flows forth in song,
    Or childhood's tale is told,
15 Or lips move tunefully along
    Some glorious page of old.

---

[1] Walter Scott, *Marmion: A Tale of Flodden Field** 4.30. When first published in *Blackwood's* 21 (1827): 92, the poem had instead an epigraph from Joanna Baillie,* *Ethwald: A Tragedy* (1802) 2.1.2.76–82:
> A land of peace,
> Where yellow fields unspoil'd, and pastures green,
> Mottled with herds and flocks, who crop secure
> Their native herbage, nor have ever known
> A stranger's stall, smile gladly.
> See through its tufted alleys to Heaven's roof
> The curling smoke of quiet dwellings rise.

The blessed Homes of England!
    How softly on their bowers
Is laid the holy quietness
    That breathes from Sabbath-hours!
Solemn, yet sweet, the church-bell's chime
    Floats thro' their woods at morn;
All other sounds, in that still time,
    Of breeze and leaf are born.

The Cottage Homes of England!
    By thousands on her plains,
They are smiling o'er the silvery brooks,
    And round the hamlet-fanes.
Thro' glowing orchards forth they peep,
    Each from its nook of leaves,
And fearless there the lowly sleep,
    As the bird beneath their eaves.

The free, fair Homes of England!
    Long, long, in hut and hall,
May hearts of native proof be rear'd
    To guard each hallow'd wall!
And green for ever be the groves,
    And bright the flowery sod,
Where first the child's glad spirit loves
    Its country and its God![1]

To Wordsworth[2]

Thine is a strain to read among the hills,
    The old and full of voices;—by the source
Of some free stream, whose gladdening presence fills
    The solitude with sound; for in its course
Even such is thy deep song, that seems a part
Of those high scenes, a fountain from their heart.

Or its calm spirit fitly may be taken
    To the still breast, in sunny garden-bowers,
Where vernal winds each tree's low tones awaken,
    And bud and bell with changes mark the hours.
There let thy thoughts be with me, while the day
Sinks with a golden and serene decay.

Or by some hearth where happy faces meet,
    When night hath hush'd the woods, with all their birds,
There, from some gentle voice, that lay were sweet
    As antique music, link'd with household words.
While, in pleased murmurs, woman's lip might move,
And the rais'd eye of childhood shine in love.

Or where the shadows of dark solemn yews
    Brood silently o'er some lone burial-ground,
Thy verse hath power that brightly might diffuse
    A breath, a kindling, as of spring, around;
From its own glow of hope and courage high,
And steadfast faith's victorious constancy.

True bard, and holy!—thou art ev'n as one
    Who, by some secret gift of soul or eye,
In every spot beneath the smiling sun,
    Sees where the springs of living waters lie:
Unseen awhile they sleep—till, touch'd by thee,
Bright healthful waves flow forth to each glad wanderer free.

The Landing of the Pilgrim Fathers in New England[3]

Look now abroad—another race has fill'd
    Those populous borders—wide the wood recedes,
And towns shoot up, and fertile realms are till'd;
    The land is full of harvests and green meads.
                       BRYANT[4]

---

[1] "Originally published in Blackwood's Magazine." (F.H.)

[2] The poem was first published in the *Literary Magnet* ns 1 (1826): 169–70. For W. Wordsworth's remarks on Hemans, see "Extempore Effusion upon the Death of James Hogg" 37–40.*

[3] Of the 102 settlers who landed at Plymouth, Mass. in 1620, 35 were members of the English Separatist Church, a radical Puritan sect, fleeing religious persecution. Hemans was familiar with Daniel Webster (1782–1852), "The Landing of the Pilgrim Fathers in New England" (1820). The poem was first published in the *New Monthly Magazine* 14 (1825): 402.

[4] William Cullen Bryant,* "The Ages" (1821) 280–83. When first published in the *New Monthly Magazine*, the poem had instead an epigraph from another American poet, Robert Treat Paine (1731–1814), "Ode" (1812): (Continued)

The breaking waves dash'd high
    On a stern and rock-bound coast,
And the woods against a stormy sky
    Their giant branches toss'd;

5   And the heavy night hung dark,
        The hills and waters o'er,
    When a band of exiles moor'd their bark
        On the wild New-England shore.

    Not as the conqueror comes,
10   They, the true-hearted came;
    Not with the roll of the stirring drums,
        And the trumpet that sings of fame:

    Not as the flying come,
        In silence and in fear;—
15 They shook the depths of the desert gloom
        With their hymns of lofty cheer.

    Amidst the storm they sang,
        And the stars heard and the sea!
    And the sounding aisles of the dim woods rang
20   To the anthem of the free.

    The ocean-eagle soar'd
        From his nest by the white wave's foam,
    And the rocking pines of the forest roar'd—
        This was their welcome home!

25 There were men with hoary hair,
        Amidst that pilgrim band;—
    Why had *they* come to wither there,
        Away from their childhood's land?

    There was woman's fearless eye,
30   Lit by her deep love's truth;
    There was manhood's brow serenely high,
        And the fiery heart of youth.

    Their dauntless hearts no meteor led
    In terror o'er the ocean;
    From fortune and from fame they fled
    To Heaven and its devotion.

    What sought they thus afar?
        Bright jewels of the mine?
35 The wealth of seas, the spoils of war?—
        They sought a faith's pure shrine!

    Ay, call it holy ground,
        The soil where first they trod!
    They have left unstain'd what there they found—
40   Freedom to worship God.

The Graves of a Household[1]

They grew in beauty, side by side,
    They fill'd one home with glee;—
Their graves are sever'd, far and wide,
    By mount, and stream, and sea.

5   The same fond mother bent at night
        O'er each fair sleeping brow;
    She had each folded flower in sight,—
        Where are those dreamers now?

    One, midst the forests of the west,
10   By a dark stream is laid—[2]
    The Indian knows his place of rest,
        Far in the cedar shade.

    The sea, the blue lone sea, hath one,
        He lies where pearls lie deep;
15 *He* was the lov'd of all, yet none
        O'er his low bed may weep.

    One sleeps where southern vines are drest
        Above the noble slain:
    He wrapt his colours round his breast,
20   On a blood-red field of Spain.[3]

---

[1] The poem was first published in the *New Monthly Magazine* 14 (1825): 534.

[2] Hemans's younger brother, Claude Scott Browne, died in Kingston, Ontario (at the source of the St. Lawrence) in 1821.

[3] Hemans's brothers and her husband, Albert Hemans, served against Napoleon in the Peninsular War (1808–14), which inspired her first long poem, *England and Spain; or, Valour and Patriotism* (1808).

And one—o'er *her* the myrtle showers
    Its leaves, by soft winds fann'd;
She faded midst Italian flowers,—
    The last of that bright band.

25 And parted thus they rest, who play'd
    Beneath the same green tree;
Whose voices mingled as they pray'd
    Around one parent knee!

They that with smiles lit up the hall,
30   And cheer'd with song the hearth,—
Alas! for love, if *thou* wert all,
    And nought beyond, oh earth!

The Image in Lava[1]

Thou thing of years departed!
    What ages have gone by,
Since here the mournful seal was set
    By love and agony!

5 Temple and tower have moulder'd,
    Empires from earth have pass'd,—
And woman's heart hath left a trace
    Those glories to outlast!

And childhood's fragile image
10   Thus fearfully enshrin'd,
Survives the proud memorials rear'd
    By conquerors of mankind.

Babe! wert thou brightly slumbering
    Upon thy mother's breast,
15 When suddenly the fiery tomb
    Shut round each gentle guest?

A strange dark fate o'ertook you,
    Fair babe and loving heart!
One moment of a thousand pangs—
20   Yet better than to part!

Haply of that fond bosom,
    On ashes here impress'd,
Thou wert the only treasure, child!
    Whereon a hope might rest.

25 Perchance all vainly lavish'd,
    Its other love had been,
And where it trusted, nought remain'd
    But thorns on which to lean.

Far better then to perish,
30   Thy form within its clasp,
Than live and lose thee, precious one!
    From that impassion'd grasp.

Oh! I could pass all relics
    Left by the pomps of old,
35 To gaze on this rude monument,
    Cast in affection's mould.

Love, human love! what art thou?
    Thy print upon the dust
Outlives the cities of renown
40   Wherein the mighty trust!

Immortal, oh! immortal
    Thou art, whose earthly glow
Hath given these ashes holiness—
    It must, it *must* be so!

---

[1] "The impression of a woman's form, with an infant clasped to the bosom, found at the uncovering of Herculaneum." (F.H.) Herculaneum and Pompeii were destroyed by the eruption of Vesuvius in AD 79. The image is one of the casts made during the excavations (1763–1820), by pouring plaster into the holes left in the lava by the victims' bodies. The poem was first published in the *New Monthly Magazine* 20 (1827): 255–56.

from *Songs of the Affections* (1830)

The Return

"Hast thou come with the heart of thy childhood back?
    The free, the pure, the kind?"
—So murmur'd the trees in my homeward track,
    As they play'd to the mountain-wind.

"Hath thy soul been true to its early love?"
    Whisper'd my native streams;
"Hath the spirit nursed amidst hill and grove,
    Still revered its first high dreams?"

"Hast thou borne in thy bosom the holy prayer
    Of the child in his parent-halls?"
—Thus breathed a voice on the thrilling air,
    From the old ancestral walls.

"Hast thou kept thy faith with the faithful dead,
    Whose place of rest is nigh?
With the father's blessing o'er thee shed,
    With the mother's trusting eye?"

—Then my tears gush'd forth in sudden rain,
    As I answer'd—"O, ye shades!
I bring not my childhood's heart again
    To the freedom of your glades.

"I have turn'd from my first pure love aside,
    O bright and happy streams!
Light after light, in my soul have died
    The day-spring's glorious dreams.

"And the holy prayer from my thoughts hath pass'd—
    The prayer at my mother's knee;
Darken'd and troubled I come at last,
    Home of my boyish glee!

"But I bear from my childhood a gift of tears,
    To soften and atone;
And oh! ye scenes of those blessed years
    They shall make me again your own."

Woman on the Field of Battle[1]

    Where hath not woman stood,
  Strong in affection's might? a reed, upborne
    By an o'ermastering current![2]

Gentle and lovely form,
    What didst thou here,
When the fierce battle-storm
    Bore down the spear?

Banner and shiver'd crest,
    Beside thee strown,
Tell, that amidst the best,
    Thy work was done!

Yet strangely, sadly fair,
    O'er the wild scene,
Gleams, through its golden hair,
    That brow serene.

Low lies the stately head,—
    Earth-bound the free;
How gave those haughty dead
    A place to thee?

Slumberer! *thine* early bier
    Friends should have crown'd,
Many a flower and tear
    Shedding around.

Soft voices, clear and young,
    Mingling their swell,
Should o'er thy dust have sung
    Earth's last farewell.

Sisters, above the grave
    Of thy repose,
Should have bid violets wave
    With the white rose,

---

[1] The poem was first published in *Blackwood's* 22 (1827): 585–88.

[2] by Hemans; cf. Matthew 11.7.

Now must the trumpet's note,
    Savage and shrill,
For requiem o'er thee float,
    Thou fair and still!

And the swift charger sweep,
    In full career,
Trampling thy place of sleep,—
    Why camest thou here?

Why?—ask the true heart why
    Woman hath been
Ever, where brave men die,
    Unshrinking seen?

Unto this harvest ground
    Proud reapers came,—
Some, for that stirring sound,
    A warrior's name;

Some, for the stormy play
    And joy of strife;
And some, to fling away
    A weary life;—

But thou, pale sleeper, thou,
    With the slight frame,
And the rich locks, whose glow
    Death cannot tame;

Only one thought, one power,
    Thee could have led,
So, through the tempest's hour,
    To lift thy head!

Only the true, the strong,
    The love, whose trust
Woman's deep soul too long
    Pours on the dust!

The Mirror in the Deserted Hall[1]

O, dim, forsaken mirror!
    How many a stately throng
Hath o'er thee gleam'd, in vanish'd hours
    Of the wine-cup and the song!

The song hath left no echo;
    The bright wine hath been quaff'd;
And hush'd is every silvery voice
    That lightly here hath laugh'd.

Oh! mirror, lonely mirror,
    Thou of the silent hall!
Thou hast been flush'd with beauty's bloom—
    Is this, too, vanish'd all?

It is, with the scatter'd garlands
    Of triumphs long ago;
With the melodies of buried lyres;
    With the faded rainbow's glow.

And for all the gorgeous pageants,
    For the glance of gem and plume,
For lamp, and harp, and rosy wreath,
    And vase of rich perfume.

Now, dim, forsaken mirror,
    Thou givest but faintly back
The quiet stars, and the sailing moon,
    On her solitary track.

And thus with man's proud spirit
    Thou tellest me 'twill be,
When the forms and hues of this world fade
    From his memory, as from thee:

And his heart's long-troubled waters
    At last in stillness lie,
Reflecting but the images
    Of the solemn world on high.

---

[1] The poem was first published in the *Literary Souvenir* (1830): 356–57.

Joseph Severn
1793 – 1879

Joseph Severn was born on 7 December 1793 at Hoxton, the eldest of the six children of James Severn, a musician, and his wife, whose family name was Littel. At fourteen he was apprenticed to an engraver, who allowed him to enroll in evening art classes at the Royal Academy Schools, where one of his teachers was Henry Fuseli.

In 1816 Severn met Keats;* in 1818 he painted portraits of all three of the Keats brothers. In 1819 Keats encouraged Severn to enter his oil painting *The Cave of Despair*, based on Spenser's *Faerie Queene* 1.10, in the Royal Academy's student competition for the gold medal in painting; Severn won the prize. In 1820 Severn accompanied Keats, who was ill with tuberculosis, to Italy, in the hope that the climate would improve his health. They set sail on the *Maria Crowther* and settled in Rome at 26 Piazza di Spagna (now the Keats-Shelley House). Severn began work on *The Death of Alcibiades*, which he planned to enter for the Academy's travelling scholarship. But Keats's illness interrupted this project. On 11 January 1821 Severn made a deathbed sketch of Keats, who died in his arms on 23 February 1821. Two years later, Severn had erected at his own expense Keats's headstone inscribed with the epitaph Keats had requested: "Here lies one whose name was writ in water."

After Keats's death, Severn remained in Rome, finished *The Death of Alcibiades*, and won his travelling fellowship. He married Elizabeth Montgomerie in Florence in 1828. The family, which eventually included six children, moved back to England in March 1841, but Severn found it difficult to make a living. Supported by William Gladstone and John Ruskin, he was appointed British Consul in Rome in 1860; but his wife died on the way to Italy. Severn resigned his consulship in 1872, continuing to paint on his pension. He died in Rome on 3 August 1879 and was buried in the new part of the Protestant cemetery; two years later his body was exhumed and reburied beside Keats. His epitaph begins, "To the Memory of Joseph Severn, Devoted Friend and Death-bed Companion of John Keats, Whom He Lived to See Numbered Among the Immortal Poets of England." (A.M.)

સેલ્સ

Letter[1]

To John Taylor[2]

Rome March 6th 182[1]

My dear Sir

I have tried many times to write you—but no—I could not it has been too much for me to think on it—I have been ill from the fatigue and pain I have suffered—the recollection of poor Keats hangs dreadfully upon me—I see him at every glance—I cannot be alone now—my nerves are so shattered.—These brutal Italians have nearly finished their monstrous business[3]—they have burned all the furniture—and are now scraping the walls—making new windows—new door's—and even a new floor—You will see all the miseries [?] attendant on these laws—I verily think I have suffered more from their cursed cruelties—than from all I did for Keats—These wretches have taken the moments when I was suffering in mind and body—they have inraged me day after day—until I trembled at the sound of every voice—I will try now once more to write you on our poor Keats—you will have but little for I can hardly dare to think on it—but I will write at intervals—and pray you to take it as my utmost endeavour—when I am stronger I will send you every word—the remembrance of this

---

[1] from *The Keats Circle: Letters and Papers and More Letters and Poems of the Keats Circle*, 2nd ed., ed. Hyder Edward Rollins (1965).

[2] Keats's publisher, John Taylor, had advanced the money so that Keats could go to Italy. Keats died there on 23 February 1821 and was buried on the 26th.

[3] The Italians had strict quarantine and sanitary laws in cases of communicable disease.

scene of horror will be fresh upon my mind to the end of my days——

Four days previous to his death—the change in him was so great that I passed each moment in dread—not knowing what the next would have—he was calm and firm at its approaches—to a most astonishing degree—he told [me] not to tremble for he did not think that he should be convulsed—he said—"did you ever see any one die" no—"well then I pity you poor Severn—what trouble and danger you have got into for me—now you must be firm for it will not last long—I shall soon be laid in the quiet grave—thank God for the quiet grave—O! I can feel the cold earth upon me—the daisies growing over me—O for this quiet—it will be my first"—when the morning light came and still found him alive—O how bitterly he grieved—I cannot bear his cries—

Each day he would look up in the doctors face to discover how long he should live—he would say—"how long will this posthumous life of mine last"—that look was more than we could ever bear—the extreme brightness of his eyes—with his poor pallid face—were not earthly—<These fo>

These four nights I watch him—each night expecting his death—on the fifth day the doctor prepared me for it—23rd at 4 oclock afternoon—The poor fellow bade me lift him up in bed—he breathed with great difficulty—and seemd to lose the power of coughing up the phlegm—an<d> immense sweat came over him so that my breath felt cold to him—"dont breath on me—it comes like Ice"—he clasped my hand very fast as I held him in my arms—the mucus was boiling within him—it gurgled in his throat—this increased—but yet he seem'd without pain—his eyes look'd upon me with extreme sensibility but without pain—at 11 he died in my arms—The English Nurse had been with me all this da{y—} this was something to me—but I was very bad—n{o} sleep that night—The next day the doctor had me over to his house—I was still the same.—these kind people did every thing to comfort me—I must have sunk under it all—but for them—On the following day a cast was taken[1]—and his death was made known to the brutes here—yet we kept a strong hand over them—we put them off untill the poor fellow was laid in his grave—On Sunday the second day Dr Clark[2] and Dr Luby with an Italian Surgeon—opened the body—they thought it the worst possible Consumption—the lungs were intirely destroyed—the cells were quite gone—but Doctor Clark will write you on this head—This was another night without sleep to me—I felt worse and worse—On the third day Monday 26th the funeral beasts came—many English requested to follow him—those who did so were Dr Clark & Dr Luby Messrs Ewing —Westmacott—Henderson—Pointer—and the Revd Mr Wolf who read the funeral service—he was buried very near to the monument of Caius Cest[i]us[3]—a few yards from Dr Bell and an infant of Mr Shelly's.[4]—The good hearted Doctor made the men put turfs of daisies upon the grave—he said—"this would be poor Keats's wish—could he know it"—I will write again by next post but I am still but in a poor state—farewell

Jos^h Severn

—The expence I fear will be great—perhaps 50£—I owe [?] still on the Doctor—I have not received the 50£ you mention at least Tolonias[5] have had no notice of it—The Doctor pays everything for me and would let me have any money I

---

[1] Plaster casts were made of Keats's face, hand, and foot: a copy of the death mask survives.

[2] Dr. James Clark (1788–1870) was Keats's English doctor in Rome.

[3] the pyramid on the grave of the Roman Caius Cestius, overlooking the Protestant cemetery in Rome. See P.B. Shelley, *Adonais* stanza 50* and Shelley's letter to Thomas Love Peacock, [22] December 1818.*

[4] the Scottish surgeon John Bell (1763–1820) and the three-year-old William Shelley, who died in 1819.

[5] Torlonia was the name of a wealthy family of Roman bankers.

John Lockhart
1794 – 1854

John Gibson Lockhart was born on 12 June 1794, the son of a Scottish Presbyterian minister, John Lockhart, and his second wife, Elizabeth Gibson Lockhart. Educated at Glasgow University and, on a scholarship, at Balliol College, Oxford, Lockhart returned to Scotland to study law and was called to the Scottish bar in 1816. The publisher William Blackwood contracted him in 1817 to translate Friedrich von Schlegel's *Lectures on the History of Literature, Ancient and Modern*. Abandoning law, he began publishing in the Tory magazine, *Blackwood's*, under the pseudonym "Z.," acquiring the nickname "Scorpion" for his satirical pieces and attacking the rival *Edinburgh Review* for its liberal views and Whig politics. In a series of articles in *Blackwood's* between 1818 and 1825, Lockhart (and others) attacked certain writers and their works—including, notoriously, the young John Keats* in 1818. After Keats died in 1821, Percy Bysshe Shelley (in his poem *Adonais*)* accused Lockhart of breaking Keats's heart.

Lockhart met Walter Scott* in 1818 and married his daughter Sophia two years later. Perhaps emulating his father-in law, he published four novels between 1821 and 1824. In the meantime, he also edited *Don Quixote* (with a life of Cervantes) and published a translation of old Spanish ballads. In 1825, he moved to London as editor of the *Quarterly Review*, a position he held until 1853 while continuing to write articles and biographies—including lives of Burns* and, most ambitiously, Scott, whose poetry he also edited. Lockhart died in 1854 while visiting his daughter, Charlotte, at Abbotsford House in Scotland; he was buried near Scott at Dryburgh Abbey. (A.M.)

☙☙☙

from *Blackwood's Edinburgh Magazine* 3 (August 1818)

Cockney School of Poetry. NO. 4[1]

————————Of Keats,
The Muses' son of Promise, and what feats
He yet may do, &c.
            CORNELIUS WEBB[2]

Of all the manias of this mad age, the most incurable, as well as the most common, seems to be no other than the *Metromanie*.[3] The just celebrity of Robert Burns and Miss Baillie[4] has had the melancholy effect of turning the heads of we know not how many farm-servants and unmarried ladies; our very footmen compose tragedies, and there is scarcely a superannuated governess in the island that does not leave a roll of lyrics behind her in her band-box. To witness the disease of any human understanding, however feeble, is distressing; but the spectacle of an able mind reduced to a state of insanity is of course ten times more afflicting. It is with such sorrow as this that we have contemplated the case of Mr John Keats. This young man appears to have received from nature talents of an excellent, perhaps even of a superior order—talents which, devoted to the purposes of any useful profession, must have rendered him a respectable, if not an eminent citizen. His friends, we understand, destined him to the career of medicine, and he was bound apprentice some years ago to a worthy apothecary in town. But all has been undone by a sudden attack of the malady to which we have alluded. Whether Mr John had been sent home with a diuretic or composing draught to some patient far gone in the poetical mania, we have not heard. This much is certain, that he has caught the infection, and that thoroughly. For some time we were in hopes, that he might get off with a violent fit or two; but of late the symptoms are

---

[1] the fourth of Lockhart's essays on the so-called "Cockney" poets, associated with the City of London, and therefore with trade, rather than with Westminster, site of elite political and literary culture.

[2] The epigraph, ascribed to Cornelius Webb (1789?–1848?), is perhaps Lockhart's own (satiric) invention.

[3] "madness for writing verse" (Fr.).

[4] the Scottish writers Robert Burns* and Joanna Baillie.*

terrible. The phrenzy of the "Poems"[1] was bad enough in its way; but it did not alarm us half so seriously as the calm, settled, imperturbable drivelling idiocy of "Endymion."[2] We hope, however, that in so young a person, and with a constitution originally so good, even now the disease is not utterly incurable. Time, firm treatment, and rational restraint, do much for many apparently hopeless invalids; and if Mr Keats should happen, at some interval of reason, to cast his eye upon our pages, he may perhaps be convinced of the existence of his malady, which, in such cases, is often all that is necessary to put the patient in a fair way of being cured.

The readers of the Examiner newspaper were informed, some time ago, by a solemn paragraph, in Mr Hunt's best style, of the appearance of two new stars of glorious magnitude and splendour in the poetical horizon of the land of Cockaigne.[3] One of these turned out, by and by, to be no other than Mr John Keats. This precocious adulation confirmed the wavering apprentice in his desire to quit the gallipots,[4] and at the same time excited in his too susceptible mind a fatal admiration for the character and talents of the most worthless and affected of all the versifiers of our time. One of his first productions was the following sonnet, *"written on the day when Mr Leigh Hunt left prison."* It will be recollected, that the cause of Hunt's confinement was a series of libels against his sovereign, and that its fruit was the odious and incestuous "Story of Rimini."[5]

---

[1] Keats's *Poems* (1817), dedicated to Leigh Hunt.*

[2] Keats's long narrative poem, published in August 1818, based on the classical story of the love of the moon goddess, Diana, for the shepherd, Endymion.

[3] Leigh Hunt, who edited the radical weekly the *Examiner*, praised Keats's early poetry in the 1 December 1816 issue. The Land of Cockaigne was a neverland of medieval romance (with a pun on "Cockney").

[4] medicine pots used by apothecaries; Lockhart is mocking Keats's professional training.

[5] In 1813 Hunt was sentenced to two years in prison for libel against the Prince Regent (later George IV). There he wrote his long poem, *The Story of Rimini* (published in 1816), based on the story of the adulterous lovers Paulo and Francesca in Dante's *Inferno*, canto 5. Lockhart calls their affair "incestuous" because Paulo was Francesca's brother-in-law. Keats's sonnet praising Hunt, which Lockhart goes on to quote, was published in *Poems* (1817).

"What though for shewing truth to flattered state,
   Kind Hunt was shut in prison, yet has he,
   In his immortal spirit been as free
As the sky-searching lark, and as elate.
Minion of grandeur! think you he did wait?
   Think you he nought but prison walls did see,
   Till, so unwilling, thou unturn'dst the key?
Ah, no! far happier, nobler was his fate!
In Spenser's[6] *halls!* he strayed, and bowers fair,
   Culling enchanted flowers; and he flew
With daring Milton! through the fields of air;
   To regions of his own his genius true
Took happy flights. Who shall his fame impair
   When thou art dead, and all thy wretched crew?"

The absurdity of the thought in this sonnet is, however, if possible, surpassed in another, *"addressed to Haydon"* the painter, that clever, but most affected artist, who as little resembles Raphael in genius as he does in person, notwithstanding the foppery of having his hair curled over his shoulders in the old Italian fashion.[7] In this exquisite piece it will be observed, that Mr Keats classes together WORDSWORTH, HUNT AND HAYDON, as the three greatest spirits of the age, and that he alludes to himself, and some others of the rising brood of Cockneys, as likely to attain hereafter an equally honourable elevation. Wordsworth and Hunt! what a juxta-position! The purest, the loftiest, and, we do not fear to say it, the most classical of living English poets, joined together in the same compliment with the meanest, the filthiest, and the most vulgar of Cockney poetasters. No wonder that he who could be guilty of this should class Haydon with Raphael, and himself with Spencer.

"Great spirits now on earth are sojourning;
   He of the cloud, the cataract, the lake,
   Who on Helvellyn's summit, wide awake,
Catches his freshness from Archangel's wing:
He of the rose, the violet, the spring,

---

[6] the poet Edmund Spenser (1552?–99), author of the long allegorical poem *The Faerie Queene* (1589, 1596).

[7] Keats's sonnet, "Great spirits now on earth are sojourning," one of two sonnets addressed to the historical painter Benjamin Robert Haydon (1786–1846), was published in his *Poems* (1817); Haydon was known to his detractors as "the Cockney Raphael," in an unflattering comparison with the Italian painter Raphael (1483–1520).

> *The social smile, the chain for Freedom's sake:*[1]
> *And lo!—whose stedfastness would never take*
> *A meaner sound than Raphael's whispering.*
> *And other spirits there are standing apart*
> *Upon the forehead of the age to come;*
> *These, these will give the world another heart,*
> *And other pulses. Hear ye not the hum*
> *Of mighty workings?*——
> *Listen awhile ye nations, and be dumb."*

The nations are to listen and be dumb! and why, good Johnny Keats? because Leigh Hunt is editor of the Examiner, and Haydon has painted the judgment of Solomon,[2] and you and Cornelius Webb, and a few more city sparks, are pleased to look upon yourselves as so many future Shakspeares and Miltons! The world has really some reason to look to its foundations! Here is a *tempestus in matulâ*[3] with a vengeance. At the period when these sonnets were published, Mr Keats had no hesitation in saying, that he looked on himself as *"not yet a glorious denizen of the wide heaven of poetry,"*[4] but he had many fine soothing visions of coming greatness, and many rare plans of study to prepare him for it … Above all things, it is most pitiably ridiculous to hear men, of whom their country will always have reason to be proud, reviled by uneducated and flimsy striplings, who are not capable of understanding either their merits, or those of any other *men of power*—fanciful dreaming tea-drinkers, who, without logic enough to analyse a single idea, or imagination enough to form one original image, or learning enough to distinguish between the written language of Englishmen and the spoken jargon of Cockneys, presume to talk with contempt of some of the most exquisite spirits the world ever produced, merely because they did not happen to exert their faculties in laborious affected descriptions of flowers seen in window-pots, or cascades heard at Vauxhall;[5] in short, because they chose to be wits, philosophers, patriots, and poets, rather than to found the Cockney school of versification, morality, and politics, a century before its time.…

---

[1] Leigh Hunt,* whom Keats here celebrates for his poetry, his friendship, and his imprisonment for the cause of liberty.

[2] Exhibited in 1814, this was the first of Haydon's large paintings on biblical and historical subjects.

[3] "tempest in a tea-pot" (L.).

[4] Cf. Keats, "Sleep and Poetry" 47–49.

[5] a pleasure-garden in London, site of concerts and other diversions.

Oliver Goldsmith
1794 – 1861

Oliver Goldsmith was born on 6 July 1794 in St. Andrew's, New Brunswick, Canada. His father was Henry Goldsmith, a Loyalist officer and the nephew of Oliver Goldsmith;* his mother was Mary Mason Goldsmith. In 1796, the family moved to Halifax, where Henry worked in the commissariat (the office responsible for meeting the physical needs of the Army). Goldsmith was educated at home and at the Halifax Grammar School. In 1810, he joined his father in the commissariat, where he stayed for 45 years, serving not only in Halifax but also in St. John, St. John's, Corfu, and Hong Kong.

When the Garrison Amateur Theatre was founded in Halifax in 1822, Goldsmith wrote a verse address to commemorate the occasion. He went on to play Tony Lumpkin in his great-uncle's comedy *She Stoops to Conquer*. His most ambitious poem was *The Rising Village* (1825), a response to *The Deserted Village*.* It was not well received, and Goldsmith published only a few other poems. When he retired in 1855, he went to live with his sister in Liverpool, where he died in 1861. (D.L.M.)

೭౩೭౩

from *The Rising Village. A Poem. By Oliver Goldsmith, a Collateral Descendant of the Author of the "Deserted Village"* (1825)[1]

Thou dear companion of my early years,
Partner of all my boyish hopes and fears,
To whom I've oft address'd the youthful strain,
And sought no other praise than thine to gain;
5 Who oft hast bid me emulate the fame
Of him who form'd the glory of our name:
Say, when thou canst, in manhood's ripen'd age,
With judgment scan the more aspiring page,
Wilt thou accept this tribute of my lay,
10 By far too small thy fondness to repay?
Say, dearest Brother, wilt thou now excuse
This bolder flight of my advent'rous muse?

    If, then, adown your cheek a tear should flow,
For Auburn's village[2] and its speechless woe;
15 If, while you weep, you think the "lowly train"[3]
Their early joys can never more regain,
Come, turn with me where happier prospects rise,
Beneath the sternness of our Western skies.
And thou, dear spirit! whose harmonious lay
20 Didst lovely Auburn's piercing woes display,
Do thou to thy fond relative impart
Some portion of thy sweet poetic art;
Like thine, oh! let my verse as gently flow,
While truth and virtue in my numbers glow:
25 And guide my pen with thy bewitching hand,
To paint the Rising Village of the land.

    How chaste and splendid are the scenes that lie
Beneath the circle of Britannia's sky!
What charming prospects there arrest the view,
30 How bright, how varied, and how boundless too!
Cities and plains extending far and wide,
The merchant's glory, and the farmer's pride.[4]
Majestic palaces in pomp display
The wealth and splendour of the regal sway;
35 While the low hamlet and the shepherd's cot,
In peace and freedom, mark the peasant's lot.
There nature's vernal bloom adorns the field,
And Autumn's fruits their rich luxuriance yield.
There men, in bustling crowds, with men combine,
40 That arts may flourish, and fair science shine;

---

[1] We have omitted a Preface by "John Nova Scotia" and Goldsmith's Dedication of the poem to his brother Henry (to whom it is addressed).

[2] the village portrayed in Goldsmith, *The Deserted Village*.*

[3] Goldsmith, *The Deserted Village* 254.

[4] Cf. Goldsmith, *The Traveller* (1764) 35–36.

And thence, to distant climes their labours send,
As o'er the world their widening views extend.
Compar'd with scenes like these, how dark and drear
Did once our desert woods and wilds appear;
45 Where wandering savages, and beasts of prey,
Display'd, by turns, the fury of their sway.[1]

What noble courage must their hearts have fired,
How great the ardour which their souls inspired,
Who leaving far behind, their native plain,
50 Have sought a home beyond the Western main;[2]
And brav'd the perils of the stormy seas,
In search of wealth, of freedom, and of ease!
Oh! none can tell but they who sadly share
The bosom's anguish, and its wild despair,
55 What dire distress awaits the hardy band,
That ventures first to till the desert land.
How great the pain, the danger, and the toil,
Which mark the first rude culture of the soil.
When, looking round, the lonely settler sees
60 His home amid a wilderness of trees:
How sinks his heart in those deep solitudes,
Where not a voice upon his ear intrudes;
Where solemn silence all the waste pervades,
Height'ning the horror of its gloomy shades;
65 Save where the sturdy woodman's strokes resound,
That strew the fallen forest on the ground.
See! from their heights the lofty pines descend,
And crackling, down their pond'rous lengths extend.
Soon, from their boughs, the curling flames arise,
70 Mount into air, and redden all the skies;
And, where the forest late its foliage spread,
The golden corn triumphant waves its head.[3]

How bless'd, did nature's ruggedness appear
The only source of trouble or of fear;
75 How happy, did no hardship meet his view,
No other care his anxious steps pursue;
But, while his labour gains a short repose,
And hope presents a solace for his woes,
New ills arise, new fears his peace annoy,
80 And other dangers all his hopes destroy.
Behold! the savage tribes, in wildest strain,
Approach with death and terror in their train;
No longer silence o'er the forest reigns,
No longer stillness now her pow'r retains;
85 But hideous yells announce the murd'rous band,
Whose bloody footsteps desolate the land;
He hears them oft in sternest mood maintain
Their right to rule the mountain and the plain:
He hears them doom the *white man's* instant death,
90 Shrinks from the sentence, while he gasps for breath;
Then, rousing with one effort all his might,
Darts from his hut, and saves himself by flight.
Yet, what a refuge! Here a host of foes,
On ev'ry side, his trembling steps oppose.
95 Here savage beasts terrific round him howl,
As through the gloomy wood they nightly prowl.
Now morning comes, and all th' appalling roar
Of barb'rous man and beast is heard no more;
The wand'ring Indian turns another way,
100 And brutes avoid the first approach of day.[4]

Yet, though these threat'ning dangers round him
    roll,
Perplex his thoughts, and agitate his soul,
By patient firmness and industrious toil,
He still retains possession of the soil;
105 Around his dwelling scatter'd huts extend,
Whilst ev'ry hut affords another friend.
And now, behold! his bold aggressors fly,
To seek their prey beneath some other sky;
Resign the haunts they can maintain no more,
110 And safety in far distant wilds explore.
His perils vanquish'd, and his fears o'ercome,
Sweet hope portrays a happy peaceful home.

---

[1] Cf. Goldsmith, *The Deserted Village* 357–58.

[2] Cf. Goldsmith, *The Deserted Village* 370.

[3] "The process of clearing land, though simple, is attended with a great deal of labour. The trees are all felled, so as to lie in the same direction; and after the fire has passed over them in that state, whatever may be left is collected into heaps, and reduced to ashes. The grain is then sown between the stumps of the trees, which remain, until the lapse of time, from seven to fifteen years, reduces them to decay." (O.G.)

[4] Cf. Goldsmith, *The Deserted Village* 351–58.

On ev'ry side fair prospects charm his eyes,
And future joys in ev'ry thought arise.
His humble cot, built from the neighb'ring trees,
Affords protection from each chilling breeze;
His rising crops, with rich luxuriance crown'd
In waving softness shed their freshness round;
By nature nourish'd, by her bounty bless'd,
He looks to Heav'n, and lulls his cares to rest.

The arts of culture now extend their sway,
And many a charm of rural life display.
Where once the pine uprear'd its lofty head,
The settlers' humble cottages are spread;
Where the broad firs once shelter'd from the storm,
By slow degrees a neighbourhood they form;
And, as its bounds, each circling year, increase
In social life, prosperity, and peace,
New prospects rise, new objects too appear,
To add more comfort to its lowly sphere.
Where some rude sign or post the spot betrays,
The tavern first its useful front displays.[1]
Here, oft the weary trav'ller at the close
Of ev'ning, finds a snug and safe repose.
The passing stranger here, a welcome guest,
From all his toil enjoys a peaceful rest;
Unless the host, solicitous to please,
With care officious mar his hope of ease,
With flippant questions, to no end confin'd,
Exhaust his patience, and perplex his mind.

Yet, let us not condemn with thoughtless haste,
The hardy settler of the dreary waste,
Who, long within the wilderness immur'd,
In silence and in solitude, endur'd
A banishment from all the busy throng,
And all the pleasures which to life belong;
If, when the stranger comes within his reach,
He long to learn whatever he can teach.
To this, must be ascrib'd in great degree,
That ceaseless, idle curiosity
Which over all the Western world prevails,
And ev'ry breast, or more or less, assails;
Till, by indulgence, so o'erpowering grown,
It sighs to know all business but its own.

Here, oft, when winter's dreary terrors reign,
And cold, and snow, and storm, pervade the plain;
Around the birch-wood blaze the settlers draw,
"To tell of all they felt, and all they saw."[2]
When, thus in peace, are met a happy few,
Sweet are the social pleasures that ensue.
What lively joy each honest bosom feels,
As o'er the past events his mem'ry steals,
And to the list'ners paints the dire distress,
That mark'd his progress in the wilderness;
The danger, trouble, hardship, toil, and strife,
Which chas'd each effort of his struggling life.

In some lone spot of consecrated ground,
Whose silence spreads a holy gloom around,
The village church, in unadorn'd array,
Now lifts her turret to the op'ning day.
How sweet to see the villagers repair
In groups to pay their adoration there;
To view, in homespun dress, each sacred morn,
The old and young her hallow'd seats adorn,
While, grateful for each blessing God has giv'n,
They waft, in pious strains, their thanks to Heav'n.[3]

Oh, heav'n-born faith! sure solace of our woes,
How lost is he who ne'er thy influence knows,
How cold the heart thy charity ne'er fires,
How dead the soul thy spirit ne'er inspires!
When troubles vex and agitate the mind
(By gracious Heav'n for wisest ends design'd),
When dangers threaten, or when fears invade,
Man flies to thee for comfort and for aid;

---

[1] Cf. Goldsmith, *The Deserted Village* 221–22.

[2] Cf. Goldsmith, *The Deserted Village* 94.

[3] "I cannot avoid here stating how much the province of Nova Scotia is indebted to the Society for the Propagation of the Gospel in Foreign Parts. Since the first settlement of the country their funds have been liberally bestowed, to assist in the building of churches, and for the maintenance of Missionaries; there being now not less than thirty in this Province." (O.G.) The first missionaries from the Society for the Propagation of the Gospel in Foreign Parts arrived in Nova Scotia in 1749.

185   The soul, impell'd by thy all-pow'rful laws,
      Seeks safety, only, in a Great First Cause![1]
      If, then, amid the busy scene of life,
      Its joy and pleasure, care, distrust, and strife;
      Man, to his God for help and succour fly,
190   And on the Saviour's pow'r to save, rely;
      If then each thought can force him to confess
      His errors, wants, and utter helplessness;
      How strong must be those feelings which impart
      A sense of all his weakness to his heart,
195   Where not a friend in solitude is nigh,
      His home the wild, his canopy the sky;
      And, far remov'd from ev'ry human arm,
      His God alone can shelter him from harm.

      While now the Rising Village claims a name,
200   Its limits still increase, and still its fame,
      The wand'ring Pedlar, who undaunted trac'd
      His lonely footsteps o'er the silent waste;
      Who travers'd once the cold and snow-clad plain,
      Reckless of danger, trouble, or of pain,
205   To find a market for his little wares,
      The source of all his hopes, and all his cares,
      Establish'd here, his settled home maintains,
      And soon a merchant's higher title gains.

      Around his store on spacious shelves array'd,
210   Behold his great and various stock in trade.
      Here, nails and blankets, side by side, are seen,
      There, horses' collars, and a large tureen;
      Buttons and tumblers, codhooks, spoons and knives,
      Shawls for young damsels, flannels for old wives;
215   Woolcards and stockings, hats for men and boys,
      Mill-saws and fenders, silks, and infants' toys;
      All useful things, and join'd with many more,
      Compose the well assorted country store.[2]

      The half-bred Doctor next here settles down,
220   And hopes the village soon will prove a town.
      No rival here disputes his doubtful skill,
      He cures, by chance, or ends each human ill;
      By turns he physics, or his patient bleeds,
      Uncertain in what case each best succeeds.
225   And if, from friends untimely snatch'd away,
      Some beauty fall a victim to decay;
      If some fine youth, his parents' fond delight,
      Be early hurried to the shades of night,
      Death bears the blame, 'tis his envenom'd dart
230   That strikes the suff'ring mortal to the heart.

      Beneath the shelter[3] of a log-built shed
      The country school-house next erects its head.[4]
      No "man severe,"[5] with learning's bright display,
      Here leads the op'ning blossoms into day:
235   No master here, in ev'ry art refin'd,
      Through fields of science guides th' aspiring mind;
      But some poor wand'rer of the human race,
      Unequal to the task, supplies his place,
      Whose greatest source of knowledge or of skill
240   Consists in reading or in writing ill;[6]
      Whose efforts can no higher merit claim,
      Than spreading Dilworth's[7] great scholastic fame.
      No modest youths surround his awful chair,
      His frowns to deprecate, or smiles to share,[8]
245   But all the terrors of his lawful sway
      The proud despise, the fearless disobey;
      The rugged urchins spurn at all control,
      Which cramps the movements of the freeborn soul,

---

[1] Cf. Pope, *An Essay on Man* (1733–34) 1.145.

[2] "Every shop in America, whether in city or in village, in which the most trifling articles are sold, is dignified with the title of a store." (O.G.)

[3] Cf. James Thomson (1700–48), *Autumn* (1730) 210.

[4] "I must here again express the gratitude that is due to the Society for the Propagation of the Gospel, whose funds are so nobly appropriated to the support of schools in this province. There are, at present, forty schoolmasters, who receive a small salary from the society; twelve scholarships at King's College, and twelve exhibitions at the Collegiate School, in Windsor, to assist the education of persons destined for Holy Orders." (O.G.) Cf. Goldsmith, *The Traveller* (1764) 179–80.

[5] Goldsmith, *The Deserted Village* 199.

[6] Cf. Pope, *An Essay on Criticism* (1711) 1–2; and Goldsmith, *The Deserted Village* 210.

[7] Thomas Dilworth, eighteenth-century English schoolmaster and author of textbooks.

[8] Cf. Goldsmith, *The Deserted Village* 203–06.

Till, in their own conceit so wise they've grown,
They think their knowledge far exceeds his own.[1]

   As thus the Village each successive year
Presents new prospects, and extends its sphere,
While all around its smiling charms expand,
And rural beauties decorate the land.
The humble tenants, who were taught to know
By years of suff'ring, all the weight of woe;
Who felt each hardship nature could endure,
Such pains as time alone could ease or cure,
Relieved from want, in sportive pleasures find
A balm to soften and relax the mind;
And now, forgetful of their former care,
Enjoy each sport, and every pastime share.
Beneath some spreading tree's expanded shade[2]
Here many a manly youth and gentle maid,
With festive dances or with sprightly song
The summer's ev'ning hours in joy prolong,
And as the young their simple sports renew,
The aged witness, and approve them too.[3]
And when the Summer's bloomy charms are fled,
When Autumn's fallen leaves around are spread,
When Winter rules the sad inverted year,[4]
And ice and snow alternately appear,
Sports not less welcome lightly they essay,
To chase the long and tedious hours away.
Here, ranged in joyous groups around the fire,
Gambols and freaks each honest heart inspire:
And if some vent'rous youth obtain a kiss,
The game's reward, and summit of its bliss,
Applauding shouts the victor's prize proclaim,
And ev'ry tongue augments his well earn'd fame;
While all the modest fair one's blushes tell
Success had crown'd his fondest hopes too well.
Dear humble sports, Oh! long may you impart
A guideless pleasure to the youthful heart;
Still may thy joys from year to year increase,
And fill each breast with happiness and peace.
...[5]

   While time thus rolls his rapid years away,[6]
The Village rises gently into day.
How sweet it is, at first approach of morn,
Before the silv'ry dew has left the lawn,
When warring winds are sleeping yet on high,
Or breathe as softly as the bosom's sigh,
To gain some easy hill's ascending height,
Where all the landscape brightens with delight,
And boundless prospects stretch'd on every side,
Proclaim the country's industry and pride.
Here the broad marsh extends its open plain,
Until its limits touch the distant main;
There verdant meads along the uplands spring,
And to the breeze their grateful odours fling;
Here crops of corn in rich luxuriance rise,
And wave their golden riches to the skies;
There smiling orchards interrupt the scene,
Or gardens bounded by some fence of green;
The farmer's cot, deep bosom'd 'mong the trees,
Whose spreading branches shelter from the breeze;
The saw-mill rude, whose clacking all day long
The wilds reecho, and the hills prolong;
The neat white church, beside whose walls are spread
The grass-clod hillocks of the sacred dead,
Where rude cut stones or painted tablets tell,
In labour'd verse, how youth and beauty fell;
How worth and hope were hurried to the grave,
And torn from those who had no power to save.

   Or, when the Summer's dry and sultry sun
Adown the West his fiery course has run;
When o'er the vale his parting rays of light
Just linger, ere they vanish into night,
'Tis sweet to wander round the woodbound lake,
Whose glassy stillness scarce the zephyrs wake;
'Tis sweet to hear the murm'ring of the rill,
As down it gurgles from the distant hill;

---

[1] Cf. Pope, *An Essay on Criticism* 199–200; and Goldsmith, *The Deserted Village* 217–18.

[2] Cf. Goldsmith, *The Deserted Village* 18–19.

[3] Cf. Goldsmith, *The Deserted Village* 20.

[4] Cf. Thomson, *Winter* (1726) 43.

[5] The omitted lines tell the story of Flora, who is driven mad by her lover Albert's desertion of her on their wedding day.

[6] Cf. Goldsmith, *The Traveller* 256.

The note of Whip-poor-Will 'tis sweet to hear,[1]
When sad and slow it breaks upon the ear,
And tells each night, to all the silent vale,
The hopeless sorrows of its mournful tale.
485 Dear lovely spot! Oh may such charms as these,
Sweet tranquil charms, that cannot fail to please,
For ever reign around thee, and impart
Joy, peace, and comfort to each native heart.

    Happy Acadia! though around thy shore
490 Is heard the stormy wind's terrific roar;
Though round thee Winter binds his icy chains,
And his rude tempests sweep along thy plains,
Still Summer comes with her luxuriant band
Of fruits and flowers, to decorate thy land;
495 Still Autumn, smiling o'er thy fertile soil,
With richest gifts repays the lab'rer's toil;
With bounteous hand his varied wants supplies,
And scarce the fruit of other suns denies.
How pleasing, and how glowing with delight,
500 Are now thy budding hopes! How sweetly bright
They rise to view! How full of joy appear
The expectations of each future year!
Not fifty Summers yet have bless'd thy clime
(How short a period in the page of time!)
505 Since savage tribes, with terror in their train,
Rush'd o'er thy fields, and ravag'd all thy plain.
But some few years have roll'd in haste away
Since, through thy vales, the fearless beast of prey,
With dismal yell and loud appalling cry,
510 Proclaim'd their midnight reign of horror nigh.
And now how chang'd the scene![2] The first, afar,
Have fled to wilds beneath the northern star;
The last have learn'd to shun the dreaded eye
Of lordly man, and in their turn to fly.
515 While the poor peasant, whose laborious care
Scarce from the soil could wring his scanty fare;
Now in the peaceful arts of culture skill'd,
Sees his wide barns with ample treasures fill'd;
Now finds his dwelling, as the year goes round,
520 Beyond his hopes, with joy and plenty crown'd.

    And shall not, then, the humble muse display
Though small the tribute, and though poor the lay,
A country's thanks, and strive to bear the fame
To after ages, of Dalhousie's name.[3]
525 He who with heroes oft, through fields of gore,
The standard of his country proudly bore;
Until on Gallia's plain the day was won,
And hosts proclaim'd his task was nobly done.
He who "not less to peaceful arts inclin'd,"[4]
530 Cross'd the deep main to bless the lab'ring hind:
The hardy sons of Scotia's clime to teach[5]
What bounteous Heav'n had plac'd within their
    reach.
He saw the honest uninstructed swain
Exhaust his strength, and till his lands in vain;
535 He call'd fair science to the rustic's aid,[6]
And to his view her gentle path display'd.
His fruitful field with Britain's soil now vies,
And, as to Heav'n his grateful thanks arise,
Thy name, Dalhousie, mixes with his prayers,
540 And the best wishes of the suppliant shares.

---

[1] "The Whip-poor-Will (*Caprimulgus vociferus*) is a native of America. On a summer's evening the wild and mournful cadence of its note is heard at a great distance; and the traveller listens with delight to the repeated tale of its sorrows." (O.G.)

[2] Cf. Thomson, *Summer* (1727) 784.

[3] George Ramsay, 9th Earl of Dalhousie (1770–1838), served with Wellington in Spain and at Waterloo (1815). In 1816, he was appointed Lieutenant-Governor of Nova Scotia. In 1820, he founded Dalhousie College.

[4] Cf. Thomson, *Summer* 875.

[5] "The provinces of Nova Scotia and New Brunswick now comprehend that part of British North America, which was formerly denominated Acadia by the French, and Nova Scotia by the English. I have here used the name of Scotia, as more convenient and applicable to the subject." (O.G.)

[6] "When the Earl of Dalhousie assumed the command of the province of Nova Scotia, its agriculture was in a deplorable state; for though large tracts of land were under cultivation, yet the mode of tillage was so unskilful, and an adherence to old customs so obstinate, that the most fertile soil was often very unproductive.

"Through the influence, and under the patronage of his Lordship, Societies were established for the purpose of diffusing knowledge in agricultural pursuits, and of adopting an approved system of cultivation. These societies have been some time in operation, and the advantages which have been derived from them, and the information which they have afforded, are observable in the improved method of agriculture, now pursued throughout the country." (O.G.)

Nor culture's arts, a nation's noblest friend,
Alone o'er Scotia's field their power extend;
From all her shores, with every gentle gale,
Bright commerce wide expands her swelling sail:[1]
545 And all the land, luxuriant, rich, and gay,
Exulting owns the splendour of their sway.
These are thy blessings, Scotia, and for these,
For wealth, for freedom, happiness, and ease,
Thy grateful thanks to Britain's care are due;
550 Her pow'r protects, her smiles past hopes renew;
Her valour guards thee, and her councils guide;
Then, may thy parent ever be thy pride!

Oh, England! although doubt around thee play'd,
And all thy childhood's years in error stray'd;
555 Matur'd and strong, thou shin'st, in manhood's prime,
The first and brightest star of Europe's clime.
The nurse of science, and the seat of arts,
The home of fairest forms and gentlest hearts;
The land of heroes, generous, free, and brave,
560 The noblest conqu'rors of the field and wave;
Thy flag, on ev'ry sea and shore unfurl'd,
Has spread thy glory, and thy thunder hurl'd.
When, o'er the earth, a tyrant[2] would have thrown
His iron chain, and call'd the world his own,
565 Thine arm preserv'd it, in its darkest hour,
Destroy'd his hopes, and crush'd his dreaded pow'r:
To sinking nations life and freedom gave,
'Twas thine to conquer, as 'twas thine to save.

Then, blest Acadia! ever may thy name,
570 Like hers, be graven on the rolls of fame;
May all thy sons, like hers, be brave and free,
Possessors of her laws and liberty;
Heirs of her splendour, science, pow'r, and skill,
And through succeeding years her children still.
575 Then as the sun, with gentle dawning ray,
From night's dull bosom wakes, and leads the day,
His course majestic keeps, till in the height
He glows one blaze of pure exhaustless light;
So may thy years increase, thy glories rise;
580 To be the wonder of the western skies;
And bliss and peace encircle all thy shore,
Till sun, and moon, and stars shall be no more.[3]

---

[1] Cf. Goldsmith, *The Traveller* 140, and *The Deserted Village* 271–72.

[2] Napoleon.

[3] Cf. Pope, *Windsor-Forest* (1713) 407–08.

William Cullen Bryant
1794 – 1878

William Cullen Bryant was born in Cummington, Massachusetts, on 3 November 1794, second of the seven children of Peter Bryant, a physician, and Sarah Snell Bryant, a direct descendant of the Mayflower pilgrims. With his parents' instruction and encouragement, he began to write poetry at the age of nine. His first book, *The Embargo; or, Sketches of the Times, A Satire; by a Youth of Thirteen*, an attack on Jefferson's mercantile policy, was published in 1808. He was educated at a community school and by private tutors and briefly attended Williams College; then he apprenticed as a lawyer. He was admitted to the bar in 1815 and practised for ten years, but never enjoyed it. In January 1821, he married Frances Fairchild; they had two children. In 1825, he moved to New York and worked as the editor of two unsuccessful literary magazines. In 1826, he became assistant editor of the *New York Evening Post*. In 1829, he became editor-in-chief; he remained so for nearly fifty years. His policy was summed up in the slogan he added to the paper's masthead in 1848: "Free Soil, Free Labor, Free Trade, and Free Speech." Becoming increasingly anti-slavery, he supported Lincoln in the presidential campaign of 1860. As a journalist, Bryant complained: "I have no leisure for poetry," but he continued to write a few poems every year and to publish a new volume every few years. He did have the leisure to travel extensively in the Americas, Europe, and the Middle East, and published two volumes of *Letters of a Traveller* (1850, 1859) and *Letters from the East* (1869). To distract himself from his grief after the death of his wife in 1866, he translated Homer's *Iliad* (1870) and *Odyssey* (1871–72). On 29 May 1878, after making a speech in Central Park, he fell and hit his head. A week later, he suffered a stroke; he died on 12 June. (D.L.M.)

༺༻

from the *North American Review and Miscellaneous Journal* (March 1818)

To a Waterfowl

      Whither, 'midst falling dew,
While glow the heavens with the last steps of day,
Far, through their rosy depths, dost thou pursue
      Thy solitary way?

5   Vainly the fowler's eye
Might mark thy distant flight, to do thee wrong,
As, darkly painted on the crimson sky,
      Thy figure floats along.

      Seek'st thou the plashy brink
10 Of weedy lake, or marge of river wide,
Or where the rocking billows rise and sink
      On the chafed ocean side?

      There is a *Power*, whose care
Teaches thy way along that pathless coast,—
15   The desert and illimitable air,
      Lone wandering, but not lost.

      All day thy wings have fann'd,
At that far height, the cold thin atmosphere;
Yet stoop not, weary, to the welcome land,
20   Though the dark night is near.

      And soon that toil shall end,
Soon shalt thou find a summer home, and rest,
And scream among thy fellows; reeds shall bend,
      Soon, o'er thy sheltered nest.

25   Thou'rt gone, the abyss of heaven
Hath swallowed up thy form, yet, on my heart
Deeply hath sunk the lesson thou hast given,
      And shall not soon depart.

        He, who, from zone to zone,
Guides through the boundless sky thy certain flight,
In the long way that I must trace alone,
        Will lead my steps aright.

from *Poems* (1821)

Thanatopsis[1]

To him who in the love of Nature holds
Communion with her visible forms, she speaks
A various language; for his gayer hours
She has a voice of gladness, and a smile
And eloquence of beauty, and she glides
Into his darker musings, with a mild
And gentle sympathy, that steals away
Their sharpness, ere he is aware. When thoughts
Of the last bitter hour come like a blight
Over thy spirit, and sad images
Of the stern agony, and shroud, and pall,
And breathless darkness, and the narrow house,
Make thee to shudder, and grow sick at heart;—
Go forth under the open sky, and list
To Nature's teachings, while from all around—
Earth and her waters, and the depths of air,—
Comes a still voice[2]—Yet a few days, and thee
The all-beholding sun shall see no more
In all his course; nor yet in the cold ground,
Where thy pale form was laid, with many tears,
Nor in the embrace of ocean shall exist
Thy image. Earth, that nourished thee, shall claim
Thy growth, to be resolv'd to earth again;
And, lost each human trace, surrend'ring up
Thine individual being, shalt thou go
To mix forever with the elements,
To be a brother to th' insensible rock
And to the sluggish clod, which the rude swain
Turns with his share, and treads upon. The oak
Shall send his roots abroad, and pierce thy mould.
Yet not to thy eternal resting place
Shalt thou retire alone—nor couldst thou wish
Couch more magnificent. Thou shalt lie down
With patriarchs of the infant world—with kings
The powerful of the earth—the wise, the good,
Fair forms, and hoary seers of ages past,
All in one mighty sepulchre.—The hills
Rock-ribb'd and ancient as the sun,—the vales
Stretching in pensive quietness between;
The venerable woods—rivers that move
In majesty, and the complaining brooks
That make the meadows green; and pour'd round all,
Old ocean's gray and melancholy waste,—
Are but the solemn decorations all
Of the great tomb of man. The golden sun,
The planets, all the infinite host of heaven,
Are shining on the sad abodes of death,
Through the still lapse of ages. All that tread
The globe are but a handful to the tribes
That slumber in its bosom.—Take the wings
Of morning—and the Barcan desert[3] pierce,
Or lose thyself in the continuous woods
Where rolls the Oregan,[4] and hears no sound,
Save his own dashings—yet—the dead are there,
And millions in those solitudes, since first
The flight of years began, have laid them down
In their last sleep—the dead reign there alone.—
So shalt thou rest—and what if thou shalt fall
Unnoticed by the living—and no friend
Take note of thy departure? All that breathe
Will share thy destiny. The gay will laugh
When thou art gone, the solemn brood of care
Plod on, and each one as before will chase
His favorite phantom; yet all these shall leave
Their mirth and their employments, and shall come,
And make their bed with thee. As the long train
Of ages glide away, the sons of men,

---

[1] "a view of death" (Gr.). An earlier version of the poem was published in *North American Review* 5 (1817): 338–40.

[2] Cf. 1 Kings 19.12.

[3] desert in northeastern Libya.

[4] Native American name for what is now called the Columbia River, which flows from Columbia Lake, BC, through Washington to the Pacific.

The youth in life's green spring, and he who goes
In the full strength of years, matron, and maid,
70 The bow'd with age, the infant in the smiles
And beauty of its innocent age cut off,—
Shall one by one be gathered to thy side,
By those, who in their turn shall follow them.
So live, that when thy summons comes to join
75 The innumerable caravan, that moves
To the pale realms of shade, where each shall take
His chamber in the silent halls of death,
Thou go not, like the quarry-slave at night,
Scourged to his dungeon, but sustain'd and sooth'd
80 By an unfaltering trust, approach thy grave,
Like one who wraps the drapery of his couch
About him, and lies down to pleasant dreams.

John Keats
1795 – 1821

John Keats was born in London on Halloween, 1795, oldest of the four children of Thomas Keats, the manager (and later the owner) of a stable, and Francis Jennings Keats. He and his brothers, George and Tom, were educated at Enfield Academy, where he acquired his love of literature and his Whig politics. When he was only eight, his father was killed in a riding accident. Less than two months later, his mother made a calamitous second marriage; then she disappeared (her husband, of course, kept the stable). She reappeared in 1808, only to die of tuberculosis in March 1809. Her seventy-five-year-old mother, now the head of the family, appointed a tea merchant, Richard Abbey, as trustee. He was a bad trustee; by the time Keats died in 1821, he had been deprived of £2000—the equivalent of a middle-class income for ten or twenty years. The family's finances were further strained by George's expensive decision to emigrate to America in 1818.

In 1811, Keats left Enfield and was apprenticed to a nearby surgeon. (At this time, surgeons and apothecaries, though less highly regarded than university-educated doctors, received a more practical and more up-to-date training.) In 1815, apparently after a disagreement with his master, he went to London and began studying at Guy's Hospital. He was a good student and was soon made a dresser, or nurse and surgeon's assistant. In July 1816, he passed his qualifying examinations. After a summer holiday at Margate, he resumed work as a dresser at Guy's in September.

During his apprenticeship, however, Keats had discovered Spenser's *The Faerie Queene*, a transforming experience for him. He wrote his first poem, "Imitation of Spenser," in 1814. His first published poem, "Solitude," appeared in Leigh Hunt's* *Examiner* in May 1816, and his first great poem, "On First Looking into Chapman's Homer," appeared there in December. That October, he met Hunt, who became his mentor and introduced him to John Hamilton Reynolds, the painter Benjamin Haydon, and P.B. Shelley;* Haydon in turn introduced him to W. Wordsworth* and to Hazlitt, whose "On Gusto"* and lectures on poetry would influence his developing aesthetic theories.

Then—perhaps because of Hunt's literary encouragement, perhaps because of the sheer horror of surgery in the age before anaesthetics or antisepsis—Keats abandoned medicine for poetry. His first book was published in March 1817; it got few reviews and sold poorly. That summer and fall, he wrote *Endymion*, an ambitious 4000-line romance based on Greek mythology; and in November he began to work out his poetics in a series of letters to his brothers and friends.

Endymion was published in April 1818, to viciously negative reviews, especially by Croker* and Lockhart.* In his Preface to *Adonais*,* Shelley later expressed the erroneous but widely held belief that Croker's review had hastened Keats's death. In fact, though Keats was hurt, he soldiered on. After returning from a summer holiday in Scotland to nurse his brother Tom, who had developed tuberculosis, in October he began *Hyperion*, another ambitious treatment of Greek mythology. Tom died in December and Keats abandoned his poem in April 1819, but he had embarked on a year of astonishing creativity, writing "The Eve of St. Agnes," the six Odes, and "Lamia" in quick succession, and then returning to the Hyperion myth in *The Fall of Hyperion* (abandoned September 1819).

He also fell in love. In December 1818, on a visit to Hampstead to see his friend Charles Brown (who would invite him to live with him after Tom's death), Keats met Brown's eighteen-year-old neighbour, Fanny Brawne. They told each other their love on Christmas Day and became engaged in October 1819. By then, however, Keats did not have long to live. In February 1820, he coughed up blood, recognized (thanks to his medical training) that it was arterial, and told Brown: "that drop of blood is my death warrant." *Lamia, Isabella, The Eve of St. Agnes, and Other Poems* appeared in July and received good reviews—especially for the fragmentary *Hyperion*—but it was too late for Keats to enjoy them. For some time the Hunts took care of him, then for a month he stayed with Fanny and her mother. In November, in the desperate hope that the Italian climate would be good for him, he set off for Rome, with his friend the painter Joseph Severn,* who would care for him tenderly until he died on 23 February 1821. He was buried in the Protestant Cemetery in Rome; his tombstone is inscribed, as he had requested, with the words "Here lies one whose name was writ in water." (D.L.M.)

☙☙☙

from the *Examiner* (1 December 1816)

On First Looking into Chapman's Homer[1]

Much have I travel'd in the realms of Gold,
    And many goodly States and Kingdoms seen;
    Round many western Islands have I been,
Which Bards in fealty to Apollo[2] hold;
5 But of one wide expanse had I been told,
    That deep-brow'd Homer ruled as his demesne;
    Yet could I never judge what men could mean,
Till I heard CHAPMAN speak out loud and bold.
Then felt I like some watcher of the skies,
10   When a new planet swims into his ken;[3]
Or like stout CORTEZ,[4] when with eagle eyes
    He stared at the Pacific,—and all his men
Looked at each other with a wild surmise,—
    Silent, upon a peak in Darien.

from the *Examiner* (9 March 1817)

On Seeing the Elgin Marbles[5]

My spirit is too weak—Mortality
    Weighs heavily on me like unwilling sleep,
    And each imagined pinnacle and steep
Of godlike hardship, tells me I must die
5 Like a sick Eagle looking at the sky.
    Yet 'tis a gentle luxury to weep
    That I have not the cloudy winds to keep,
Fresh for the opening of the morning's eye.
Such dim-conceived glories of the brain
10   Bring round the heart an undescribable feud:
So do these wonders a most dizzy pain,
    That mingles Grecian grandeur with the rude
Wasting of old time—with a billowy main—
    A sun—a shadow of a magnitude.

from the *Examiner* (21 September 1817)

The poetry of earth is never dead[6]

The poetry of earth is never dead:
    When all the birds are faint with the hot sun,
    And hide in cooling trees, a voice will run

---

[1] written in October 1816, on the morning after Keats and his friend and mentor Charles Cowden Clarke had stayed up all night reading the translation of Homer (1614) by George Chapman (1559?–1634).

[2] the god of poetry.

[3] William Herschel had discovered Uranus in 1781.

[4] The first European to see the Pacific, from the Isthmus of Darien, in Panama, in 1513, was not actually Hernán Cortez (1485–1547), the conqueror of Mexico, but Vasco Nuñez de Balboa (c. 1475–1519). Keats had read William Robertson (1721–93), *History of America*.

[5] Lord Elgin had brought friezes and other sculptures from the Parthenon, in Athens, to England, in 1806; by 1817, they were in the British Museum (as they still are), and Keats's friend Benjamin Robert Haydon (1786–1846) took him to see them. Cf. "Ode on a Grecian Urn"* and Byron,* *The Curse of Minerva* (1812).

[6] first published in *Poems* (1817); printed in the *Examiner* together with Hunt's "Green little vaulter in the sunny grass."*

From hedge to hedge about the new-mown mead;
That is the Grasshopper's;—he takes the lead
  In summer luxury,—he has never done
    With his delights; for when tired out with fun,
He rests at ease beneath some pleasant weed.
The poetry of earth is ceasing never:
  On a lone winter evening, when the frost
    Has wrought in silence, from the stove there shrills
The Cricket's song, in warmth increasing ever,
  And seems to one, in drowsiness half lost,
    The Grasshopper's among some grassy hills.

from *Endymion* (1818)

from BOOK 1

A thing of beauty is a joy forever:
It's loveliness increases; it will never
Pass into nothingness; but still will keep
A bower quiet for us, and a sleep
Full of sweet dreams, and health, and quiet breathing.
Therefore, on every morrow, are we wreathing
A flowery band to bind us to the earth,
Spite of despondence, of the inhuman dearth
Of noble natures, of the gloomy days,
Of all the unhealthy and o'er-darkened ways
Made for our searching: yes, in spite of all,
Some shape of beauty moves away the pall
From our dark spirits. Such the sun, the moon,
Trees old and young, sprouting a shady boon
For simple sheep; and such are daffodils
With the green world they live in; and clear rills
That for themselves a cooling covert make
'Gainst the hot season; the mid forest brake,
Rich with a sprinkling of fair musk-rose blooms:
And such too is the grandeur of the dooms
We have imagined for the mighty dead;
All lovely tales that we have heard or read:
And endless fountain of immortal drink,
Pouring unto us from the heaven's brink.

Nor do we merely feel these essences
For one short hour; no, even as the trees
That whisper round a temple become soon
Dear as the temple's self, so does the moon,
The passion poesy, glories infinite,
Haunt us till they become a cheering light
Unto our souls, and bound to us so fast,
That, whether there be shine, or gloom o'ercast,
They always must be with us, or we die.

Therefore, 'tis with full happiness that I
Will trace the story of Endymion.
The very music of the name has gone
Into my being, and each pleasant scene
Is growing fresh before me as the green
Of our own vallies: so I will begin
Now while I cannot hear the city's din;
Now while the early budders are just new,
And run in mazes of the youngest hue
About old forests; while the willow trails
Its delicate amber; and the dairy pails
Bring home the increase of milk. And, as the year
Grows lush in juicy stalks, I'll smooth steer
My little boat, for many quiet hours,
With streams that deepen freshly into bowers.
Many and many a verse I hope to write,
Before the daisies, vermeil rimm'd and white,
Hide in deep herbage; and ere yet the bees
Hum about globes of clover and sweet peas,
I must be near the middle of my story.
O may no wintry season, bare and hoary,
See it half finished: but let Autumn bold,
With universal tinge of sober gold,
Be all about me when I make an end.
And now at once, adventuresome, I send
My herald thought into a wilderness:
There let its trumpet blow, and quickly dress
My uncertain path with green, that I may speed
Easily onward, thorough flowers and weed....

"Peona![1] ever have I long'd to slake
My thirst for the world's praises: nothing base,

---

[1] Endymion's sister.

No merely slumberous phantasm, could unlace
The stubborn canvas for my voyage prepar'd—
Though now 'tis tatter'd; leaving my bark bar'd
And sullenly drifting: yet my higher hope
775 Is of too wide, too rainbow-large a scope,
To fret at myriads of earthly wrecks.
Wherein lies happiness? In that which becks
Our ready minds to fellowship divine,
A fellowship with essence; till we shine,
780 Full alchemiz'd, and free of space. Behold
The clear religion of heaven! Fold
A rose leaf round thy finger's taperness,
And soothe thy lips: hist, when the airy stress
Of music's kiss impregnates the free winds,
785 And with a sympathetic touch unbinds
Eolian magic from their lucid wombs:
Then old songs waken from enclouded tombs;
Old ditties sigh above their father's grave;
Ghosts of melodious prophecyings rave
790 Round every spot w[h]ere trod Apollo's foot;
Bronze clarions awake, and faintly bruit,
Where long ago a giant battle was;
And, from the turf, a lullaby doth pass
In every place where infant Orpheus slept.
795 Feel we these things?—that moment have we stept
Into a sort of oneness, and our state
Is like a floating spirit's. But there are
Richer entanglements, enthralments far
More self-destroying, leading, by degrees,
800 To the chief intensity: the crown of these
Is made of love and friendship, and sits high
Upon the forehead of humanity.
All its more ponderous and bulky worth
Is friendship, whence there ever issues forth
805 A steady splendour; but at the tip-top,
There hangs by unseen film, an orbed drop
Of light, and that is love: its influence,
Thrown in our eyes, genders a novel sense,
At which we start and fret; till in the end,
810 Melting into its radiance, we blend,
Mingle, and so become a part of it,—
Nor with aught else can our souls interknit
So wingedly: when we combine therewith,
Life's self is nourish'd by its proper pith,
815 And we are nurtured like a pelican brood.
Aye, so delicious is the unsating food,
That men, who might have tower'd in the van
Of all the congregated world, to fan
And winnow from the coming step of time
820 All chaff of custom, wipe away all slime
Left by men-slugs and human serpentry,
Have been content to let occasion die,
Whilst they did sleep in love's elysium.
And, truly, I would rather be struck dumb,
825 Than speak against this ardent listlessness:
For I have ever thought that it might bless
The world with benefits unknowingly;
As does the nightingale, upperched high,
And cloister'd among cool and bunched leaves—
830 She sings but to her love, nor e'er conceives
How tiptoe Night holds back her dark-grey hood.
Just so my love, although 'tis understood
The mere commingling of passionate breath,
Produce more than our searching witnesseth:
835 What I know not: but who, of men, can tell
That flowers would bloom, or that green fruit would
    swell
To melting pulp, that fish would have bright mail,
The earth its dower of river, wood and vale,
The meadow runnels, runnels pebble-stones,
840 The seed it's harvest, or the lute its tones,
Tones ravishment, or ravishment its sweet,
If human souls did never kiss and greet? ...

from the *Indicator* (10 May 1820)

La Belle Dame Sans Mercy[1]

Ah, what can ail thee, wretched wight,
    Alone and palely loitering;
The sedge is wither'd from the lake,
    And no birds sing.

---

[1] the title of a long poem by Alain Chartier (c. 1385–1433); see Keats, "The Eve of St. Agnes" 292.* Keats wrote his poem 21–28 April 1819, in a letter to his brother and sister-in-law, George and Georgiana Keats. He revised it for publication in the *Indicator*, where it is signed "Caviare." Milnes later published the original version.

5 Ah, what can ail thee, wretched wight,
    So haggard and so woe-begone?
The squirrel's granary is full,
    And the harvest's done.

I see a lily on thy brow,
10   With anguish moist and fever dew;
And on thy cheek a fading rose
    Fast withereth too.

I met a Lady in the meads
    Full beautiful, a fairy's child;
15 Her hair was long, her foot was light,
    And her eyes were wild.

I set her on my pacing steed,
    And nothing else saw all day long;
For sideways would she lean, and sing
20   A fairy's song.

I made a garland for her head,
    And bracelets too, and fragrant zone:[1]
She look'd at me as she did love,
    And made sweet moan.

25 She found me roots of relish sweet,
    And honey wild, and manna dew;[2]
And sure in language strange she said,
    I love thee true.

She took me to her elfin grot,
30   And there she gaz'd and sighed deep,
And there I shut her wild sad eyes—
    So kiss'd to sleep.

And there we slumber'd on the moss,
    And there I dream'd, ah woe betide,
35 The latest dream I ever dream'd
    On the cold hill side.

I saw pale kings, and princes too,
    Pale warriors, death-pale were they all;
Who cried, "La belle Dame sans mercy
40   Hath thee in thrall!"

I saw their starv'd lips in the gloom
    With horrid warning gaped wide,
And I awoke, and found me here
    On the cold hill side.

45 And this is why I sojourn here
    Alone and palely loitering,
Though the sedge is wither'd from the lake,
    And no birds sing.

from *Lamia, Isabella, Eve of St. Agnes, and Other Poems. By John Keats, author of* Endymion (1820)

Lamia[3]

PART 1

Upon a time, before the faery broods
Drove Nymph and Satyr from the prosperous woods,
Before King Oberon's bright diadem,
Sceptre, and mantle, clasp'd with dewy gem,
5 Frighted away the Dryads and the Fauns
From rushes green, and brakes, and cowslip'd lawns,[4]
The ever-smitten Hermes[5] empty left
His golden throne, bent warm on amorous theft:
From high Olympus had he stolen light,
10 On this side of Jove's clouds, to escape the sight
Of his great summoner, and made retreat
Into a forest on the shores of Crete.

---

[1] belt.

[2] Cf. Exodus 16 and Coleridge, "Kubla Khan" 53.*

[3] written in July-August 1819.

[4] that is, before the classical belief in the Olympian gods gave way to the more recent belief in fairies (cf. "Ode to Psyche" 25).* Oberon is the king of the fairies in Shakespeare, *A Midsummer Night's Dream.*

[5] or Mercury (L.), messenger of the gods.

For somewhere in that sacred island[1] dwelt
A nymph, to whom all hoofed Satyrs knelt;
15 At whose white feet the languid Tritons[2] poured
Pearls, while on land they wither'd and adored.
Fast by the springs where she to bathe was wont,
And in those meads where sometime she might haunt,
Were strewn rich gifts, unknown to any Muse,
20 Though Fancy's casket were unlock'd to choose.
Ah, what a world of love was at her feet!
So Hermes thought, and a celestial heat
Burnt from his winged heels to either ear,
That from a whiteness, as the lily clear,
25 Blush'd into roses 'mid his golden hair,
Fallen in jealous curls about his shoulders bare.
From vale to vale, from wood to wood, he flew,
Breathing upon the flowers his passion new,
And wound with many a river to its head,
30 To find where this sweet nymph prepar'd her secret
   bed:
In vain; the sweet nymph might nowhere be found,
And so he rested, on the lonely ground,
Pensive, and full of painful jealousies
Of the Wood-Gods, and even the very trees.
35 There as he stood, he heard a mournful voice,
Such as once heard, in gentle heart, destroys
All pain but pity: thus the lone voice spake:
"When from this wreathed tomb shall I awake!
When move in a sweet body fit for life,
40 And love, and pleasure, and the ruddy strife
Of hearts and lips! Ah, miserable me!"
The God, dove-footed, glided silently
Round bush and tree, soft-brushing, in his speed,
The taller grasses and full-flowering weed,
45 Until he found a palpitating snake,
Bright, and cirque-couchant in a dusky brake.

She was a gordian[3] shape of dazzling hue,
Vermilion-spotted, golden, green, and blue;
Striped like a zebra, freckled like a pard,
50 Eyed like a peacock, and all crimson barr'd;
And full of silver moons, that, as she breathed,
Dissolv'd, or brighter shone, or interwreathed
Their lustres with the gloomier tapestries—
So rainbow-sided, touch'd with miseries,
55 She seem'd, at once, some penanced lady elf,
Some demon's mistress, or the demon's self.
Upon her crest she wore a wannish fire
Sprinkled with stars, like Ariadne's tiar:[4]
Her head was serpent, but ah, bitter-sweet!
60 She had a woman's mouth with all its pearls complete:
And for her eyes: what could such eyes do there
But weep, and weep, that they were born so fair?
As Proserpine still weeps for her Sicilian air.[5]
Her throat was serpent, but the words she spake
65 Came, as through bubbling honey, for Love's sake,
And thus; while Hermes on his pinions lay,
Like a stoop'd falcon ere he takes his prey.

"Fair Hermes, crown'd with feathers, fluttering
   light,
I had a splendid dream of thee last night:
70 I saw thee sitting, on a throne of gold,
Among the Gods, upon Olympus old,
The only sad one; for thou didst not hear
The soft, lute-finger'd Muses chaunting clear,
Nor even Apollo when he sang alone,
75 Deaf to his throbbing throat's long, long melodious
   moan.
I dreamt I saw thee, robed in purple flakes,
Break amorous through the clouds, as morning breaks,
And, swiftly as a bright Phœbean dart,[6]
Strike for the Cretan isle; and here thou art!

---

[1] Crete was the birthplace of Zeus (Gr.) or Jove (L.), king of the Olympians.

[2] sea-gods, usually half-men and half-fish.

[3] knotted, like the Gordian Knot severed by Alexander the Great.

[4] Bacchus gave his bride Ariadne a tiara of seven stars; after she died, it became a constellation.

[5] Hades (Gr.) or Pluto (L.), god of the underworld, carried off Proserpine as she was gathering flowers in the Vale of Enna, in Sicily, and made her his bride. Cf. Ovid, *Metamorphoses* 5 and Milton, *Paradise Lost* 4.268–72.

[6] a sunbeam. Phœbus is Apollo.

80 Too gentle Hermes, hast thou found the maid?"
Whereat the star of Lethe[1] not delay'd
His rosy eloquence, and thus inquired:
"Thou smooth-lipp'd serpent, surely high inspired!
Thou beauteous wreath, with melancholy eyes,
85 Possess whatever bliss thou canst devise,
Telling me only where my nymph is fled,—
Where she doth breathe!" "Bright planet, thou hast said,"
Return'd the snake, "but seal with oaths, fair God!"
"I swear," said Hermes, "by my serpent rod,
90 And by thine eyes, and by thy starry crown!"
Light flew his earnest words, among the blossoms blown.
Then thus again the brilliance feminine:
"Too frail of heart! for this lost nymph of thine,
Free as the air, invisibly, she strays
95 About these thornless wilds; her pleasant days
She tastes unseen; unseen her nimble feet
Leave traces in the grass and flowers sweet;
From weary tendrils, and bow'd branches green,
She plucks the fruit unseen, she bathes unseen:
100 And by my power is her beauty veil'd
To keep it unaffronted, unassail'd
By the love-glances of unlovely eyes,
Of Satyrs, Fauns, and blear'd Silenus' sighs.[2]
Pale grew her immortality, for woe
105 Of all these lovers, and she grieved so
I took compassion on her, bade her steep
Her hair in weïrd syrops, that would keep
Her loveliness invisible, yet free
To wander as she loves, in liberty.
110 Thou shalt behold her, Hermes, thou alone,
If thou wilt, as thou swearest, grant my boon!"
Then, once again, the charmed God began
An oath, and through the serpent's ears it ran
Warm, tremulous, devout, psalterian.[3]

115 Ravish'd, she lifted her Circean head,[4]
Blush'd a live damask, and swift-lisping said,
"I was a woman, let me have once more
A woman's shape, and charming as before.
I love a youth of Corinth—O the bliss!
120 Give me my woman's form, and place me where he is.
Stoop, Hermes, let me breathe upon thy brow,
And thou shalt see thy sweet nymph even now."
The God on half-shut feathers sank serene,
She breath'd upon his eyes, and swift was seen
125 Of both the guarded nymph near-smiling on the green.
It was no dream; or say a dream it was,
Real are the dreams of Gods, and smoothly pass
Their pleasures in a long immortal dream.
One warm, flush'd moment, hovering, it might seem
130 Dash'd by the wood-nymph's beauty, so he burn'd;
Then, lighting on the printless verdure, turn'd
To the swoon'd serpent, and with languid arm,
Delicate, put to proof the lythe Caducean charm.[5]
So done, upon the nymph his eyes he bent
135 Full of adoring tears and blandishment,
And towards her stept: she, like a moon in wane,
Faded before him, cower'd, nor could restrain
Her fearful sobs, self-folding like a flower
That faints into itself at evening hour:
140 But the God fostering her chilled hand,
She felt the warmth, her eyelids open'd bland,
And, like new flowers at morning song of bees,
Bloom'd, and gave up her honey to the lees.
Into the green-recessed woods they flew;
145 Nor grew they pale, as mortal lovers do.

Left to herself, the serpent now began
To change; her elfin blood in madness ran,
Her mouth foam'd, and the grass, therewith besprent,
Wither'd at dew so sweet and virulent;
150 Her eyes in torture fix'd, and anguish drear,
Hot, glaz'd, and wide, with lid-lashes all sear,

---

[1] One of Hermes' duties was to guide the dead to the underworld, in which Lethe is one of the rivers.

[2] Silenus, the foster-father of Bacchus the wine-god, is typically portrayed as drunk.

[3] like the sound of a psaltery (a stringed instrument); or, possibly, like a Psalm.

[4] like that of Circe, the enchantress who turns men into beasts, in Homer, *Odyssey* 10.

[5] Hermes puts a spell on Lamia with his Caduceus, a rod with two "lithe" serpents twined around it.

Flash'd phosphor and sharp sparks, without one
    cooling tear.
The colours all inflam'd throughout her train,
She writh'd about, convuls'd with scarlet pain:
155 A deep volcanian yellow took the place
Of all her milder-mooned body's grace;
And, as the lava ravishes the mead,
Spoilt all her silver mail, and golden brede;
Made gloom of all her frecklings, streaks and bars,
160 Eclips'd her crescents, and lick'd up her stars:
So that, in moments few, she was undrest
Of all her sapphires, greens, and amethyst,
And rubious-argent: of all these bereft,
Nothing but pain and ugliness were left.
165 Still shone her crown; that vanish'd, also she
Melted and disappear'd as suddenly;
And in the air, her new voice luting soft,
Cried, "Lycius! gentle Lycius!"—Borne aloft
With the bright mists about the mountains hoar
170 These words dissolv'd: Crete's forests heard no more.

    Whither fled Lamia, now a lady bright,
A full-born beauty new and exquisite?
She fled into that valley they pass o'er
Who go to Corinth from Cenchreas' shore;[1]
175 And rested at the foot of those wild hills,
The rugged founts of the Peræan rills,
And of that other ridge whose barren back
Stretches, with all its mist and cloudy rack,
South-westward to Cleone.[2] There she stood
180 About a young bird's flutter from a wood,
Fair, on a sloping green of mossy tread,
By a clear pool, wherein she passioned
To see herself escap'd from so sore ills,
While her robes flaunted with the daffodils.

185   Ah, happy Lycius!—for she was a maid
More beautiful than ever twisted braid,
Or sigh'd, or blush'd, or on spring-flowered lea
Spread a green kirtle to the minstrelsy:
A virgin purest lipp'd, yet in the lore

190 Of love deep learned to the red heart's core:
Not one hour old, yet of sciential brain
To unperplex bliss from its neighbour pain;
Define their pettish limits, and estrange
Their points of contact, and swift counterchange;
195 Intrigue with the specious chaos, and dispart
Its most ambiguous atoms with sure art;
As though in Cupid's college she had spent
Sweet days a lovely graduate, still unshent,
And kept his rosy terms in idle languishment.

200   Why this fair creature chose so fairily
By the wayside to linger, we shall see;
But first 'tis fit to tell how she could muse
And dream, when in the serpent prison-house,[3]
Of all she list, strange or magnificent:
205 How, ever, where she will'd, her spirit went;
Whether to faint Elysium,[4] or where
Down through tress-lifting waves the Nereids fair
Wind into Thetis' bower by many a pearly stair;[5]
Or where God Bacchus drains his cups divine,
210 Stretch'd out, at ease, beneath a glutinous pine;
Or where in Pluto's gardens palatine
Mulciber's columns gleam in far piazzian line.[6]
And sometimes into cities she would send
Her dream, with feast and rioting to blend;
215 And once, while among mortals dreaming thus,
She saw the young Corinthian Lycius
Charioting foremost in the envious race,
Like a young Jove with calm uneager face,
And fell into a swooning love of him.
220 Now on the moth-time of that evening dim
He would return that way, as well she knew,
To Corinth from the shore; for freshly blew

---

[1] the harbour of Corinth.

[2] a village between Corinth and Argos.

[3] In a marginal comment on Milton's account of Satan's entering the serpent (*Paradise Lost* 9.179–91), Keats wrote: "Whose head is not dizzy at the possibly [*sic*] speculations of satan in the serpent prison—no passage of poetry can give a greater pain of suffocation" (Wittreich, *The Romantics on Milton* 560).

[4] The Elysian Fields are the paradise of the classical underworld.

[5] Thetis is a Nereid or sea-nymph, the mother of Achilles.

[6] Bacchus is the god of wine; Mulciber, Vulcan (L.), or Hephæstus (Gr.) is the artificer of the gods. Cf. Milton, *Paradise Lost* 1.713–15.

The eastern soft wind, and his galley now
Grated the quaystones with her brazen prow
225 In port Cenchreas, from Egina isle
Fresh anchor'd; whither he had been awhile
To sacrifice to Jove, whose temple there
Waits with high marble doors for blood and incense rare.
Jove heard his vows, and better'd his desire;
230 For by some freakful chance he made retire
From his companions, and set forth to walk,
Perhaps grown wearied of their Corinth talk:
Over the solitary hills he fared,
Thoughtless at first, but ere eve's star appeared
235 His phantasy was lost, where reason fades,
In the calm'd twilight of Platonic shades.[1]
Lamia beheld him coming, near, more near—
Close to her passing, in indifference drear,
His silent sandals swept the mossy green;
240 So neighbour'd to him, and yet so unseen
She stood: he pass'd, shut up in mysteries,
His mind wrapp'd like his mantle, while her eyes
Follow'd his steps, and her neck regal white
Turn'd—syllabling thus, "Ah, Lycius bright,
245 And will you leave me on the hills alone?
Lycius, look back! and be some pity shown."
He did; not with cold wonder fearingly,
But Orpheus-like at an Eurydice;[2]
For so delicious were the words she sung,
250 It seem'd he had lov'd them a whole summer long:
And soon his eyes had drunk her beauty up,
Leaving no drop in the bewildering cup,
And still the cup was full,—while he, afraid
Lest she should vanish ere his lip had paid
255 Due adoration, thus began to adore;
Her soft look growing coy, she saw his chain so sure:
"Leave thee alone! Look back! Ah, Goddess, see
Whether my eyes can ever turn from thee!
For pity do not this sad heart belie—
260 Even as thou vanishest so I shall die.
Stay! though a Naiad of the rivers, stay!

To thy far wishes will thy streams obey:
Stay! though the greenest wood be thy domain,
Alone they can drink up the morning rain:
265 Though a descended Pleiad,[3] will not one
Of thine harmonious sisters keep in tune
Thy spheres, and as thy silver proxy shine?
So sweetly to these ravish'd ears of mine
Came thy sweet greeting, that if thou shouldst fade
270 Thy memory will waste me to a shade:—
For pity do not melt!"—"If I should stay,"
Said Lamia, "here, upon this floor of clay,
And pain my steps upon these flowers too rough,
What canst thou say or do of charm enough
275 To dull the nice remembrance of my home?
Thou canst not ask me with thee here to roam
Over these hills and vales, where no joy is,—
Empty of immortality and bliss!
Thou art a scholar, Lycius, and must know
280 That finer spirits cannot breathe below
In human climes, and live: Alas! poor youth,
What taste of purer air hast thou to soothe
My essence? What serener palaces,
Where I may all my many senses please,
285 And by mysterious sleights a hundred thirsts appease?
It cannot be—Adieu!" So said, she rose
Tiptoe with white arms spread. He, sick to lose
The amorous promise of her lone complain,[4]
Swoon'd, murmuring of love, and pale with pain.
290 The cruel lady, without any show
Of sorrow for her tender favourite's woe,
But rather, if her eyes could brighter be,
With brighter eyes and slow amenity,
Put her new lips to his, and gave afresh
295 The life she had so tangled in her mesh:
And as he from one trance was wakening
Into another, she began to sing,
Happy in beauty, life, and love, and every thing,
A song of love, too sweet for earthly lyres,
300 While, like held breath, the stars drew in their
    panting fires.

---

[1] Cf. the allegory of the cave in Plato, *Republic* 514a–21b.

[2] The poet Orpheus won the right to lead his wife, Eurydice, back from the underworld, on condition that he did not look back at her. Of course he did so and lost her; see Ovid, *Metamorphoses* 10.

[3] The Pleiades are stars, the seven daughters of the Titan Atlas. Cf. Hemans, "The Lost Pleiad."

[4] complaint.

And then she whisper'd in such trembling tone,
As those who, safe together met alone
For the first time through many anguish'd days,
Use other speech than looks; bidding him raise
His drooping head, and clear his soul of doubt, 305
For that she was a woman, and without
Any more subtle fluid in her veins
Than throbbing blood, and that the self-same pains
Inhabited her frail-strung heart as his.
And next she wonder'd how his eyes could miss 310
Her face so long in Corinth, where, she said,
She dwelt but half retir'd, and there had led
Days happy as the gold coin could invent
Without the aid of love; yet in content
Till she saw him, as once she pass'd him by, 315
Where 'gainst a column he leant thoughtfully
At Venus' temple porch, 'mid baskets heap'd
Of amorous herbs and flowers, newly reap'd
Late on that eve, as 'twas the night before
The Adonian feast;[1] whereof she saw no more, 320
But wept alone those days, for why should she adore?
Lycius from death awoke into amaze,
To see her still, and singing so sweet lays;
Then from amaze into delight he fell
To hear her whisper woman's lore so well; 325
And every word she spake entic'd him on
To unperplex'd delight and pleasure known.
Let the mad poets say whate'er they please
Of the sweets of Fairies, Peris,[2] Goddesses,
There is not such a treat among them all, 330
Haunters of cavern, lake, and waterfall,
As a real woman, lineal indeed
From Pyrrha's pebbles[3] or old Adam's seed.
Thus gentle Lamia judg'd, and judg'd aright,
That Lycius could not love in half a fright, 335
So threw the goddess off, and won his heart
More pleasantly by playing woman's part,
With no more awe than what her beauty gave,
That, while it smote, still guaranteed to save.
Lycius to all made eloquent reply, 340
Marrying to every word a twinborn sigh;
And last, pointing to Corinth, ask'd her sweet,
If 'twas too far that night for her soft feet.
The way was short, for Lamia's eagerness
Made, by a spell, the triple league decrease 345
To a few paces; not at all surmised
By blinded Lycius, so in her comprized.
They pass'd the city gates, he knew not how,
So noiseless, and he never thought to know.

    As men talk in a dream, so Corinth all, 350
Throughout her palaces imperial,
And all her populous streets and temples lewd,
Mutter'd, like tempest in the distance brew'd,
To the wide-spreaded night above her towers.
Men, women, rich and poor, in the cool hours, 355
Shuffled their sandals o'er the pavement white,
Companion'd or alone; while many a light
Flared, here and there, from wealthy festivals,
And threw their moving shadows on the walls,
Or found them cluster'd in the corniced shade 360
Of some arch'd temple door, or dusky colonnade.
    Muffling his face, of greeting friends in fear,
Her fingers he press'd hard, as one came near
With curl'd gray beard, sharp eyes, and smooth bald crown,
Slow-stepp'd, and robed in philosophic gown: 365
Lycius shrank closer, as they met and past,
Into his mantle, adding wings to haste,
While hurried Lamia trembled: "Ah," said he,
"Why do you shudder, love, so ruefully?
Why does your tender palm dissolve in dew?"— 370
"I'm wearied," said fair Lamia: "tell me who
Is that old man? I cannot bring to mind
His features:—Lycius! wherefore did you blind
Yourself from his quick eyes?" Lycius replied,
"'Tis Apollonius sage,[4] my trusty guide 375

---

[1] a festival in honour of Adonis, beloved of Venus, killed while hunting a boar. Cf. Ovid, *Metamorphoses* 10, and Shakespeare, *Venus and Adonis*.

[2] superhuman beings in Persian mythology.

[3] In classical myth, Jupiter (like the Jehovah of Genesis) exterminated humanity in a flood. Deucalion and his wife Pyrrha, the only two survivors, repopulated the earth by throwing pebbles, which turned into people; see Ovid, *Metamorphoses* 1.

[4] Apollonius of Tyana (1st century AD); see Keats's endnote.

And good instructor; but to-night he seems
The ghost of folly haunting my sweet dreams."

While yet he spake they had arrived before
A pillar'd porch, with lofty portal door,
[380] Where hung a silver lamp, whose phosphor glow
Reflected in the slabbed steps below,
Mild as a star in water; for so new,
And so unsullied was the marble hue,
So through the crystal polish, liquid fine,
[385] Ran the dark veins, that none but feet divine
Could e'er have touch'd there. Sounds Æolian[1]
Breath'd from the hinges, as the ample span
Of the wide doors disclos'd a place unknown
Some time to any, but those two alone,
[390] And a few Persian mutes, who that same year
Were seen about the markets: none knew where
They could inhabit; the most curious
Were foil'd, who watch'd to trace them to their house:
And but the flitter-winged verse must tell,
[395] For truth's sake, what woe afterwards befel,
'Twould humour many a heart to leave them thus,
Shut from the busy world of more incredulous.

PART 2

Love in a hut, with water and a crust,
Is—Love, forgive us!—cinders, ashes, dust;
Love in a palace is perhaps at last
More grievous torment than a hermit's fast:—
[5] That is a doubtful tale from faery land,
Hard for the non-elect to understand.
Had Lycius liv'd to hand his story down,
He might have given the moral a fresh frown,
Or clench'd it quite: but too short was their bliss
[10] To breed distrust and hate, that make the soft voice hiss.
Besides, there, nightly, with terrific glare,
Love, jealous grown of so complete a pair,
Hover'd and buzz'd his wings, with fearful roar,
Above the lintel of their chamber door,
[15] And down the passage cast a glow upon the floor.

For all this came a ruin: side by side
They were enthroned, in the even tide,
Upon a couch, near to a curtaining
Whose airy texture, from a golden string,
[20] Floated into the room, and let appear
Unveil'd the summer heaven, blue and clear,
Betwixt two marble shafts:—there they reposed,
Where use had made it sweet, with eyelids closed,
Saving a tythe which love still open kept,
[25] That they might see each other while they almost slept;
When from the slope side of a suburb hill,
Deafening the swallow's twitter, came a thrill
Of trumpets—Lycius started—the sounds fled,
But left a thought, a buzzing in his head.
[30] For the first time, since first he harbour'd in
That purple-lined palace of sweet sin,
His spirit pass'd beyond its golden bourn
Into the noisy world almost forsworn.
The lady, ever watchful, penetrant,
[35] Saw this with pain, so arguing a want
Of something more, more than her empery
Of joys; and she began to moan and sigh
Because he mused beyond her, knowing well
That but a moment's thought is passion's passing bell.
[40] "Why do you sigh, fair creature?" whisper'd he:
"Why do you think?" return'd she tenderly:
"You have deserted me;—where am I now?
Not in your heart while care weighs on your brow:
No, no, you have dismiss'd me; and I go
[45] From your breast houseless: ay, it must be so."
He answer'd, bending to her open eyes,
Where he was mirror'd small in paradise,
"My silver planet, both of eve and morn!
Why will you plead yourself so sad forlorn,
[50] While I am striving how to fill my heart
With deeper crimson, and a double smart?
How to entangle, trammel up and snare
Your soul in mine, and labyrinth you there
Like the hid scent in an unbudded rose?
[55] Ay, a sweet kiss—you see your mighty woes.
My thoughts! shall I unveil them? Listen then!

---

[1] like the sound of an æolian harp or wind-harp; cf. Coleridge, "Effusion 35"* and "Dejection."*

What mortal hath a prize, that other men
May be confounded and abash'd withal,
But lets it sometimes pace abroad majestical,
And triumph, as in thee I should rejoice
Amid the hoarse alarm of Corinth's voice.
Let my foes choke, and my friends shout afar,
While through the thronged streets your bridal car
Wheels round its dazzling spokes."—The lady's cheek
Trembled; she nothing said, but, pale and meek,
Arose and knelt before him, wept a rain
Of sorrows at his words; at last with pain
Beseeching him, the while his hand she wrung,
To change his purpose. He thereat was stung,
Perverse, with stronger fancy to reclaim
Her wild and timid nature to his aim:
Besides, for all his love, in self despite,
Against his better self, he took delight
Luxurious in her sorrows, soft and new.
His passion, cruel grown, took on a hue
Fierce and sanguineous as 'twas possible
In one whose brow had no dark veins to swell.
Fine was the mitigated fury, like
Apollo's presence when in act to strike
The serpent[1]—Ha, the serpent! certes, she
Was none. She burnt, she lov'd the tyranny,
And, all subdued, consented to the hour
When to the bridal he should lead his paramour.
Whispering in midnight silence, said the youth,
"Sure some sweet name thou hast, though, by my truth,
I have not ask'd it, ever thinking thee
Not mortal, but of heavenly progeny,
As still I do. Hast any mortal name,
Fit appellation for this dazzling frame?
Or friends or kinsfolk on the citied earth,
To share our marriage feast and nuptial mirth?"
"I have no friends," said Lamia, "no, not one;
My presence in wide Corinth hardly known:
My parents' bones are in their dusty urns
Sepulchred, where no kindled incense burns,
Seeing all their luckless race are dead, save me,

---

[1] Apollo killed a serpent, named Python, at Delphi; when his oracle was established there, the priestess was accordingly known as the Pythian; see Ovid, *Metamorphoses* 1.

And I neglect the holy rite for thee.
Even as you list invite your many guests;
But if, as now it seems, your vision rests
With any pleasure on me, do not bid
Old Apollonius—from him keep me hid."
Lycius, perplex'd at words so blind and blank,
Made close inquiry; from whose touch she shrank,
Feigning a sleep; and he to the dull shade
Of deep sleep in a moment was betray'd.

It was the custom then to bring away
The bride from home at blushing shut of day,
Veil'd, in a chariot, heralded along
By strewn flowers, torches, and a marriage song,
With other pageants: but this fair unknown
Had not a friend. So being left alone,
(Lycius was gone to summon all his kin)
And knowing surely she could never win
His foolish heart from its mad pompousness,
She set herself, high-thoughted, how to dress
The misery in fit magnificence.
She did so, but 'tis doubtful how and whence
Came, and who were her subtle servitors.
About the halls, and to and from the doors,
There was a noise of wings, till in short space
The glowing banquet-room shone with wide-arched grace.
A haunting music, sole perhaps and lone
Supportress of the faery-roof, made moan
Throughout, as fearful the whole charm might fade.
Fresh carved cedar, mimicking a glade
Of palm and plantain, met from either side,
High in the midst, in honour of the bride:
Two palms and then two plantains, and so on,
From either side their stems branch'd one to one
All down the aisled place; and beneath all
There ran a stream of lamps straight on from wall to wall.
So canopied, lay an untasted feast
Teeming with odours. Lamia, regal drest,
Silently paced about, and as she went,
In pale contented sort of discontent,
Mission'd her viewless servants to enrich
The fretted splendour of each nook and niche.

Between the tree-stems, marbled plain at first,
Came jasper pannels; then, anon, there burst
140 Forth creeping imagery of slighter trees,
And with the larger wove in small intricacies.
Approving all, she faded at self-will,
And shut the chamber up, close, hush'd and still,
Complete and ready for the revels rude,
145 When dreadful guests would come to spoil her solitude.

The day appear'd, and all the gossip rout.
O senseless Lycius! Madman! wherefore flout
The silent-blessing fate, warm cloister'd hours,
And show to common eyes these secret bowers?
150 The herd approach'd; each guest, with busy brain,
Arriving at the portal, gaz'd amain,
And enter'd marveling: for they knew the street,
Remember'd it from childhood all complete
Without a gap, yet ne'er before had seen
155 That royal porch, that high-built fair demesne;
So in they hurried all, maz'd, curious and keen:
Save one, who look'd thereon with eye severe,
And with calm-planted steps walk'd in austere;
'Twas Apollonius: something too he laugh'd,
160 As though some knotty problem, that had daft
His patient thought, had now begun to thaw,
And solve and melt:—'twas just as he foresaw.

He met within the murmurous vestibule
His young disciple. "'Tis no common rule,
165 Lycius," said he, "for uninvited guest
To force himself upon you, and infest
With an unbidden presence the bright throng
Of younger friends; yet must I do this wrong,
And you forgive me." Lycius blush'd, and led
170 The old man through the inner doors broad-spread;
With reconciling words and courteous mien
Turning into sweet milk the sophist's spleen.

Of wealthy lustre was the banquet-room,
Fill'd with pervading brilliance and perfume:
175 Before each lucid pannel fuming stood
A censer fed with myrrh and spiced wood,
Each by a sacred tripod held aloft,
Whose slender feet wide-swerv'd upon the soft
Wool-woofed carpets: fifty wreaths of smoke
180 From fifty censers their light voyage took
To the high roof, still mimick'd as they rose
Along the mirror'd walls by twin-clouds odorous.
Twelve sphered tables, by silk seats insphered,
High as the level of a man's breast rear'd
185 On libbard's[1] paws, upheld the heavy gold
Of cups and goblets, and the store thrice told
Of Ceres' horn,[2] and, in huge vessels, wine
Come from the gloomy tun with merry shine.
Thus loaded with a feast the table stood,
190 Each shrining in the midst the image of a God.

When in an antichamber every guest
Had felt the cold full sponge to pleasure press'd,
By minist'ring slaves, upon his hands and feet,
And fragrant oils with ceremony meet
195 Pour'd on his hair, they all mov'd to the feast
In white robes, and themselves in order placed
Around the silken couches, wondering
Whence all this mighty cost and blaze of wealth
    could spring.

Soft went the music the soft air along,
200 While fluent Greek a vowel'd undersong
Kept up among the guests, discoursing low
At first, for scarcely was the wine at flow;
But when the happy vintage touch'd their brains,
Louder they talk, and louder come the strains
205 Of powerful instruments:—the gorgeous dyes,
The space, the splendour of the draperies,
The roof of awful richness, nectarous cheer,
Beautiful slaves, and Lamia's self, appear,
Now, when the wine has done its rosy deed,
210 And every soul from human trammels freed,
No more so strange; for merry wine, sweet wine,
Will make Elysian shades not too fair, too divine.
Soon was God Bacchus at meridian height;
Flush'd were their cheeks, and bright eyes double bright:
215 Garlands of every green, and every scent

---

[1] leopard's.

[2] Ceres (L.) or Demeter (Gr.) is the goddess of the harvest; her horn is the cornucopia.

From vales deflower'd, or forest-trees branch-rent,
In baskets of bright osier'd gold were brought
High as the handles heap'd, to suit the thought
Of every guest; that each, as he did please,
Might fancy-fit his brows, silk-pillow'd at his ease.
    What wreath for Lamia? What for Lycius?
What for the sage, old Apollonius?
Upon her aching forehead be there hung
The leaves of willow and of adder's tongue;
And for the youth, quick, let us strip for him
The thyrsus, that his watching eyes may swim
Into forgetfulness;[1] and, for the sage,
Let spear-grass and the spiteful thistle wage
War on his temples. Do not all charms fly
At the mere touch of cold philosophy?
There was an awful rainbow once in heaven:
We know her woof, her texture; she is given
In the dull catalogue of common things.
Philosophy will clip an Angel's wings,
Conquer all mysteries by rule and line,
Empty the haunted air, and gnomed mine—[2]
Unweave a rainbow,[3] as it erewhile made
The tender-person'd Lamia melt into a shade.

    By her glad Lycius sitting, in chief place,
Scarce saw in all the room another face,
Till, checking his love trance, a cup he took
Full brimm'd, and opposite sent forth a look
'Cross the broad table, to beseech a glance
From his old teacher's wrinkled countenance,
And pledge him. The bald-head philosopher
Had fix'd his eye, without a twinkle or stir
Full on the alarmed beauty of the bride,
Brow-beating her fair form, and troubling her sweet
    pride.
Lycius then press'd her hand, with devout touch,
As pale it lay upon the rosy couch:

'Twas icy, and the cold ran through his veins;
Then sudden it grew hot, and all the pains
Of an unnatural heat shot to his heart.
"Lamia, what means this? Wherefore dost thou start?
Know'st thou that man?" Poor Lamia answer'd not.
He gaz'd into her eyes, and not a jot
Own'd they the lovelorn piteous appeal:
More, more he gaz'd: his human senses reel:
Some hungry spell that loveliness absorbs;
There was no recognition in those orbs.
"Lamia!" he cried—and no soft-toned reply.
The many heard, and the loud revelry
Grew hush; the stately music no more breathes;
The myrtle[4] sicken'd in a thousand wreaths.
By faint degrees, voice, lute, and pleasure ceased;
A deadly silence step by step increased,
Until it seem'd a horrid presence there,
And not a man but felt the terror in his hair.
"Lamia!" he shriek'd; and nothing but the shriek
With its sad echo did the silence break.
"Begone, foul dream!" he cried, gazing again
In the bride's face, where now no azure vein
Wander'd on fair-spaced temples; no soft bloom
Misted the cheek; no passion to illume
The deep-recessed vision:—all was blight;
Lamia, no longer fair, there sat a deadly white.
"Shut, shut those juggling eyes, thou ruthless man!
Turn them aside, wretch! or the righteous ban
Of all the Gods, whose dreadful images
Here represent their shadowy presences,
May pierce them on the sudden with the thorn
Of painful blindness; leaving thee forlorn,
In trembling dotage to the feeblest fright
Of conscience, for their long offended might,
For all thine impious proud-heart sophistries,
Unlawful magic, and enticing lies.
Corinthians! look upon that gray-beard wretch!
Mark how, possess'd, his lashless eyelids stretch
Around his demon eyes! Corinthians, see!
My sweet bride withers at their potency."
"Fool!" said the sophist, in an under-tone
Gruff with contempt; which a death-nighing moan

---

[1] Lamia's wreath should be made of symbols of grief; Lycius's, of the ivy and vine leaves twined around the thyrsus, or wand, of Bacchus, god of wine.

[2] Gnomes were once believed to live in mines.

[3] At a dinner party on 28 December 1817, Keats and Charles Lamb* complained that Newton "had destroyed all the poetry of the rainbow by reducing it to the prismatic colours" (Haydon, *Diary*).

[4] sacred to Venus.

From Lycius answer'd, as heart-struck and lost,
He sank supine beside the aching ghost.
"Fool! Fool!" repeated he, while his eyes still
Relented not, nor mov'd; "from every ill
Of life have I preserv'd thee to this day,
And shall I see thee made a serpent's prey?"
Then Lamia breath'd death breath; the sophist's eye,
Like a sharp spear, went through her utterly,
Keen, cruel, perceant, stinging: she, as well
As her weak hand could any meaning tell,
Motion'd him to be silent; vainly so,
He look'd and look'd again a level—No!
"A Serpent!" echoed he; no sooner said,
Than with a frightful scream she vanished:
And Lycius' arms were empty of delight,
As were his limbs of life, from that same night.
On the high couch he lay!—his friends came round—
Supported him—no pulse, or breath they found,
And, in its marriage robe, the heavy body wound.[1]

---

[1] "'Philostratus, in his fourth book *de Vita Apollonii*, hath a memorable instance in this kind, which I may not omit, of one Menippus Lycius, a young man twenty-five years of age, that going betwixt Cenchreas and Corinth met such a phantasm in the habit of a fair gentlewoman, which taking him by the hand, carried him home to her house, in the suburbs of Corinth, and told him she was a Phœnician by birth, and if he would tarry with her, should hear her sing and play, and drink such wine as never any drank, and no man should molest him; but she, being fair and lovely, would live and die with him, that was fair and lovely to behold. The young man, a philosopher, otherwise staid and discreet, able to moderate his passions, though not this of love, tarried with her a while to his great content, and at last married her, to whose wedding, amongst other guests, came Apollonius; who, by some probable conjectures, found her out to be a serpent, a lamia; and that all her furniture was, like Tantalus' gold, described by Homer, no substance but mere illusions. When she saw herself descried, she wept, and desired Apollonius to be silent, but he would not be moved, and thereupon she, plate, house, and all that was in it, vanished in an instant: many thousands took notice of this fact, for it was done in the midst of Greece.'— Burton's 'Anatomy of Melancholy.' *Part* 3. *Sect.* 2. *Memb.* 1. *Subs.* 1." (J.K.)

The Eve of St. Agnes[2]

1

St. Agnes' Eve—Ah, bitter chill it was!
The owl, for all his feathers, was a-cold;
The hare limp'd trembling through the frozen grass,
And silent was the flock in woolly fold:
Numb were the Beadsman's fingers, while he told
His rosary,[3] and while his frosted breath,
Like pious incense from a censer old,
Seem'd taking flight for heaven, without a death,
Past the sweet Virgin's picture, while his prayer he saith.

2

His prayer he saith, this patient, holy man;
Then takes his lamp, and riseth from his knees,
And back returneth, meagre, barefoot, wan,
Along the chapel aisle by slow degrees:
The sculptur'd dead, on each side, seem to freeze,
Emprison'd in black, purgatorial rails:
Knights, ladies, praying in dumb orat'ries,
He passeth by; and his weak spirit fails
To think how they may ache in icy hoods and mails.

3

Northward he turneth through a little door,
And scarce three steps, ere Music's golden tongue
Flatter'd to tears this aged man and poor;
But no—already had his deathbell rung;
The joys of all his life were said and sung:
His was harsh penance on St. Agnes' Eve:
Another way he went, and soon among
Rough ashes sat he for his soul's reprieve,
And all night kept awake, for sinners' sake to grieve.

---

[2] written January-February 1819. Agnes, a 4th-century Christian martyr, is the patron saint of virgins. Stanza 6 explains how a young woman can obtain a vision of her future husband on 20 January, the night before Agnes's feast-day. The poem also recalls Shakespeare's *Romeo and Juliet*.

[3] A beadsman is paid to pray for others; he "tells" or counts the beads of his rosary, saying a prayer for each one.

4

That ancient Beadsman heard the prelude soft;
And so it chanc'd, for many a door was wide,
From hurry to and fro. Soon, up aloft,
The silver, snarling trumpets 'gan to chide:
The level chambers, ready with their pride,
Were glowing to receive a thousand guests:
The carved angels, ever eager-eyed,
Star'd, where upon their heads the cornice rests,
With hair blown back, and wings put cross-wise on
    their breasts.

5

At length burst in the argent revelry,
With plume, tiara, and all rich array,
Numerous as shadows haunting fairily
The brain, new stuff'd, in youth, with triumphs gay
Of old romance. These let us wish away,
And turn, sole-thoughted, to one Lady there,
Whose heart had brooded, all that wintry day,
On love, and wing'd St. Agnes' saintly care,
As she had heard old dames full many times declare.

6

They told her how, upon St. Agnes' Eve,
Young virgins might have visions of delight,
And soft adorings from their loves receive
Upon the honey'd middle of the night,
If ceremonies due they did aright;
As, supperless to bed they must retire,
And couch supine their beauties, lily white;
Nor look behind, nor sideways, but require
Of Heaven with upward eyes for all that they desire.[1]

7

Full of this whim was thoughtful Madeline:
The music, yearning like a God in pain,
She scarcely heard: her maiden eyes divine,
Fix'd on the floor, saw many a sweeping train
Pass by—she heeded not at all: in vain
Came many a tiptoe, amorous cavalier,
And back retir'd; not cool'd by high disdain,
But she saw not: her heart was otherwhere:
She sigh'd for Agnes' dreams, the sweetest of the year.

8

She danc'd along with vague, regardless eyes,
Anxious her lips, her breathing quick and short:
The hallow'd hour was near at hand: she sighs
Amid the timbrels, and the throng'd resort
Of whisperers in anger, or in sport;
'Mid looks of love, defiance, hate, and scorn,
Hoodwink'd with faery fancy; all amort,
Save to St. Agnes and her lambs unshorn,[2]
And all the bliss to be before to-morrow morn.

9

So, purposing each moment to retire,
She linger'd still. Meantime, across the moors,
Had come young Porphyro, with heart on fire
For Madeline. Beside the portal doors,
Buttress'd from moonlight, stands he, and implores
All saints to give him sight of Madeline,
But for one moment in the tedious hours,
That he might gaze and worship all unseen;
Perchance speak, kneel, touch, kiss—in sooth such
    things have been.

10

He ventures in: let no buzz'd whisper tell:
All eyes be muffled, or a hundred swords
Will storm his heart, Love's fev'rous citadel:
For him, those chambers held barbarian hordes,
Hyena foemen, and hot-blooded lords,
Whose very dogs would execrations howl
Against his lineage: not one breast affords

---

[1] Shortly before the poem was published, Keats made two revisions, which his publisher rejected as indecent. The first was the insertion of a stanza at this point (see also note to line 322):
  'Twas said her future lord would there appear
  Offering, as sacrifice—all in the dream—
  Delicious food, even to her lips brought near,
  Viands, and wine, and fruit, and sugar'd cream,
  To touch her palate with the fine extreme
  Of relish: then soft music heard, and then
  More pleasures follow'd in a dizzy stream
  Palpable almost: then to wake again
  Warm in the virgin morn, no weeping Magdalen.

[2] It was traditional to honour St. Agnes's day with an offering of lambs' wool.

     Him any mercy, in that mansion foul,
90 Save one old beldame, weak in body and in soul.

         11

  Ah, happy chance! the aged creature came,
  Shuffling along with ivory-headed wand,
  To where he stood, hid from the torch's flame,
  Behind a broad hall-pillar, far beyond
95 The sound of merriment and chorus bland:
  He startled her; but soon she knew his face,
  And grasp'd his fingers in her palsied hand,
  Saying, "Mercy, Porphyro! hie thee from this place;
  They are all here to-night, the whole blood-thirsty race!

         12

100 "Get hence! get hence! there's dwarfish Hildebrand;
  He had a fever late, and in the fit
  He cursed thee and thine, both house and land:
  Then there's that old Lord Maurice, not a whit
  More tame for his gray hairs—Alas me! flit!
105 Flit like a ghost away."—"Ah, Gossip dear,
  We're safe enough; here in this arm-chair sit,
  And tell me how"—"Good Saints! not here, not here;
  Follow me, child, or else these stones will be thy bier."

         13

  He follow'd through a lowly arched way,
110 Brushing the cobwebs with his lofty plume,
  And as she mutter'd "Well-a—well-a-day!"[1]
  He found him in a little moonlight room,
  Pale, lattic'd, chill, and silent as a tomb.
  "Now tell me where is Madeline," said he,
115 "O tell me, Angela, by the holy loom
  Which none but secret sisterhood may see,
  When they St. Agnes' wool are weaving piously."

         14

  "St. Agnes! Ah! it is St. Agnes' Eve—
  Yet men will murder upon holy days:
120 Thou must hold water in a witch's sieve,
  And be liege-lord of all the Elves and Fays,
  To venture so: it fills me with amaze
  To see thee, Porphyro!—St. Agnes' Eve!
  God's help! my lady fair the conjuror plays
125 This very night: good angels her deceive!
  But let me laugh awhile, I've mickle time to grieve."

         15

  Feebly she laugheth in the languid moon,
  While Porphyro upon her face doth look,
  Like puzzled urchin on an aged crone
130 Who keepeth clos'd a wond'rous riddle-book,
  As spectacled she sits in chimney nook.
  But soon his eyes grew brilliant, when she told
  His lady's purpose; and he scarce could brook
  Tears, at the thought of those enchantments cold,
135 And Madeline asleep in lap of legends old.

         16

  Sudden a thought came like a full-blown rose,
  Flushing his brow, and in his pained heart
  Made purple riot: then doth he propose
  A strategem, that makes the beldame start:
140 "A cruel man and impious thou art:
  Sweet lady, let her pray, and sleep, and dream
  Alone with her good angels, far apart
  From wicked men like thee. Go, go!—I deem
  Thou canst not surely be the same that thou didst seem."

         17

145 "I will not harm her, by all saints I swear,"
  Quoth Porphyro: "O may I ne'er find grace
  When my weak voice shall whisper its last prayer,
  If one of her soft ringlets I displace,
  Or look with ruffian passion in her face:
150 Good Angela, believe me by these tears;
  Or I will, even in a moment's space,
  Awake, with horrid shout, my foemen's ears,
  And beard them, though they be more fang'd than wolves and bears."

---

[1] Cf. Coleridge, "Christabel" 1.251.*

18

"Ah! why wilt thou affright a feeble soul?
A poor, weak, palsy-stricken, churchyard thing,
Whose passing-bell may ere the midnight toll;
Whose prayers for thee, each morn and evening,
Were never miss'd."—Thus plaining, doth she bring
A gentler speech from burning Porphyro;
So woful, and of such deep sorrowing,
That Angela gives promise she will do
Whatever he shall wish, betide her weal or woe.

19

Which was, to lead him, in close secrecy,
Even to Madeline's chamber, and there hide
Him in a closet, of such privacy
That he might see her beauty unespied,
And win perhaps that night a peerless bride,
While legion'd fairies pac'd the coverlet,
And pale enchantment held her sleepy-eyed.
Never on such a night have lovers met,
Since Merlin paid his Demon all the monstrous debt.[1]

20

"It shall be as thou wishest," said the Dame:
"All cates and dainties shall be stored there
Quickly on this feast-night: by the tambour frame
Her own lute thou wilt see: no time to spare,
For I am slow and feeble, and scarce dare
On such a catering trust my dizzy head.
Wait here, my child, with patience; kneel in prayer
The while: Ah! thou must needs the lady wed,
Or may I never leave my grave among the dead."

21

So saying, she hobbled off with busy fear.
The lover's endless minutes slowly pass'd;
The dame return'd, and whisper'd in his ear
To follow her; with aged eyes aghast
From fright of dim espial. Safe at last,
Through many a dusky gallery, they gain
The maiden's chamber, silken, hush'd, and chaste;
Where Porphyro took covert, pleas'd amain.
His poor guide hurried back with agues in her brain.

22

Her falt'ring hand upon the balustrade,
Old Angela was feeling for the stair,
When Madeline, St. Agnes' charmed maid,
Rose, like a mission'd spirit, unaware:
With silver taper's light, and pious care,
She turn'd, and down the aged gossip led
To a safe level matting. Now prepare,
Young Porphyro, for gazing on that bed;
She comes, she comes again, like ring-dove fray'd and fled.

23

Out went the taper as she hurried in;
Its little smoke, in pallid moonshine, died:
She clos'd the door, she panted, all akin
To spirits of the air, and visions wide:
No uttered syllable, or, woe betide!
But to her heart, her heart was voluble,
Paining with eloquence her balmy side;
As though a tongueless nightingale should swell
Her throat in vain, and die, heart-stifled, in her dell.[2]

24

A casement high and triple-arch'd there was,
All garlanded with carven imag'ries
Of fruits, and flowers, and bunches of knot-grass,
And diamonded with panes of quaint device,
Innumerable of stains and splendid dyes,
As are the tiger-moth's deep-damask'd wings;
And in the midst, 'mong thousand heraldries,
And twilight saints, and dim emblazonings,

---

[1] This obscure line may refer to the episode in which Merlin, the enchanter of Arthurian legend, fell in love with the enchantress Vivien, who trapped him in a cave.

[2] Tereus raped his sister-in-law Philomela and then cut out her tongue so she would not be able to accuse him; eventually, she was turned into a nightingale. See Ovid, *Metamorphoses* 6.

A shielded scutcheon blush'd with blood of queens
    and kings.[1]

25

Full on this casement shone the wintry moon,
And threw warm gules on Madeline's fair breast,
As down she knelt for heaven's grace and boon;
Rose-bloom fell on her hands, together prest,
And on her silver cross soft amethyst,
And on her hair a glory, like a saint:
She seem'd a splendid angel, newly drest,
Save wings, for heaven:—Porphyro grew faint:
She knelt, so pure a thing, so free from mortal taint.

26

Anon his heart revives: her vespers done,
Of all its wreathed pearls her hair she frees;
Unclasps her warmed jewels one by one;
Loosens her fragrant boddice; by degrees
Her rich attire creeps rustling to her knees:
Half-hidden, like a mermaid in sea-weed,
Pensive awhile she dreams awake, and sees,
In fancy, fair St. Agnes in her bed,
But dares not look behind, or all the charm is fled.

27

Soon, trembling in her soft and chilly nest,
In sort of wakeful swoon, perplex'd she lay,
Until the poppied warmth of sleep oppress'd
Her soothed limbs, and soul fatigued away;
Flown, like a thought, until the morrow-day;
Blissfully haven'd both from joy and pain;
Clasp'd like a missal where swart Paynims pray;[2]
Blinded alike from sunshine and from rain,
As though a rose should shut, and be a bud again.

28

Stol'n to this paradise, and so entranced,
Porphyro gazed upon her empty dress,
And listen'd to her breathing, if it chanced
To wake into a slumberous tenderness;
Which when he heard, that minute did he bless,
And breath'd himself: then from the closet crept,
Noiseless as fear in a wide wilderness,
And over the hush'd carpet, silent, stept,
And 'tween the curtains peep'd, where, lo!—how
    fast she slept.

29

Then by the bed-side, where the faded moon
Made a dim, silver twilight, soft he set
A table, and, half anguish'd, threw thereon
A cloth of woven crimson, gold, and jet:—
O for some drowsy Morphean amulet![3]
The boisterous, midnight, festive clarion,
The kettle-drum, and far-heard clarionet,
Affray his ears, though but in dying tone:—
The hall door shuts again, and all the noise is gone.

30

And still she slept an azure-lidded sleep,
In blanched linen, smooth, and lavender'd,
While he from forth the closet brought a heap
Of candied apple, quince, and plum, and gourd;
With jellies soother than the creamy curd,
And lucent syrops, tinct with cinnamon;
Manna[4] and dates, in argosy transferr'd
From Fez; and spiced dainties, every one,
From silken Samarcand to cedar'd Lebanon.[5]

31

These delicates he heap'd with glowing hand
On golden dishes and in baskets bright
Of wreathed silver: sumptuous they stand
In the retired quiet of the night,
Filling the chilly room with perfume light.—
"And now, my love, my seraph fair, awake!
Thou art my heaven, and I thine eremite:

---

[1] The heraldic shield in Madeline's stained-glass window indicates that she is of royal blood.

[2] shut up like a Christian prayer-book in a country of dark-skinned non-Christians.

[3] Morpheus is the classical god of sleep.

[4] See Exodus 16.

[5] Fez is in Morocco; Samarcand, in Persia (Iran). Lebanon was famous for its cedars: see Psalm 104.16.

                    Open thine eyes, for meek St. Agnes' sake,
                    Or I shall drowse beside thee, so my soul doth ache."

                                          32
280   Thus whispering, his warm, unnerved arm
                    Sank in her pillow. Shaded was her dream
                    By the dusk curtains:—'twas a midnight charm
                    Impossible to melt as iced stream:
                    The lustrous salvers in the moonlight gleam;
285   Broad golden fringe upon the carpet lies:
                    It seem'd he never, never could redeem
                    From such a stedfast spell his lady's eyes;
                So mus'd awhile, entoil'd in woofed phantasies.

                                          33
                    Awakening up, he took her hollow lute,—
290   Tumultuous,—and, in chords that tenderest be,
                    He play'd an ancient ditty, long since mute,
                    In Provence call'd, "La belle dame sans mercy":[1]
                    Close to her ear touching the melody;—
                    Wherewith disturb'd, she utter'd a soft moan:
295   He ceased—she panted quick—and suddenly
                    Her blue affrayed eyes wide open shone:
                Upon his knees he sank, pale as smooth-sculptured
                        stone.

                                          34
                    Her eyes were open, but she still beheld,
300   Now wide awake, the vision of her sleep:
                    There was a painful change, that nigh expell'd
                    The blisses of her dream so pure and deep
                    At which fair Madeline began to weep,
                    And moan forth witless words with many a sigh;
305   While still her gaze on Porphyro would keep;
                    Who knelt, with joined hands and piteous eye,
                Fearing to move or speak, she look'd so dreamingly.

                                          35
                    "Ah, Porphyro!" said she, "but even now
                    Thy voice was at sweet tremble in mine ear,
                    Made tuneable with every sweetest vow;
310   And those sad eyes were spiritual and clear:

---

[1] the title of a long poem by Alain Chartier (c.1385–1433); Keats had not yet written his own poem with this title.*

                    How chang'd thou art! how pallid, chill, and
                        drear!
                    Give me that voice again, my Porphyro,
                    Those looks immortal, those complainings dear!
                    Oh leave me not in this eternal woe,
315   For if thou diest, my Love, I know not where to go."

                                          36
                    Beyond a mortal man impassion'd far
                    At these voluptuous accents, he arose,
                    Ethereal, flush'd, and like a throbbing star
                    Seen mid the sapphire heaven's deep repose;
320   Into her dream he melted, as the rose
                    Blendeth its odour with the violet,—
                    Solution sweet: meantime the frost-wind blows[2]
                    Like Love's alarum pattering the sharp sleet
                Against the window-panes; St. Agnes' moon hath set.

                                          37
325   'Tis dark: quick pattereth the flaw-blown sleet:
                    "This is no dream, my bride, my Madeline!"
                    'Tis dark: the iced gusts still rave and beat:
                    "No dream, alas! alas! and woe is mine!
                    Porphyro will leave me here to fade and pine.—
330   Cruel! what traitor could thee hither bring?
                    I curse not, for my heart is lost in thine,
                    Though thou forsakest a deceived thing;—
                A dove forlorn and lost with sick unpruned wing."

                                          38
                    "My Madeline! sweet dreamer! lovely bride!
335   Say, may I be for aye thy vassal blest?

---

[2] Keats's second rejected revision (see note to line 54) was to replace lines 314–22:
    See, while she speaks his arms encroaching slow,
    Have zoned her, heart to heart,—loud, loud the dark winds blow!

    For on the midnight came a tempest fell;
    More sooth, for that his quick rejoinder flows
    Into her burning ear: and still the spell
    Unbroken guards her in serene repose.
    With her wild dream he mingled, as a rose
    Marrieth its odour to a violet.
    Still, still she dreams, louder the frost wind blows,

Thy beauty's shield, heart-shap'd and vermeil
    dyed?
Ah, silver shrine, here will I take my rest
After so many hours of toil and quest,
A famish'd pilgrim,—saved by miracle.
Though I have found, I will not rob thy nest
Saving of thy sweet self; if thou think'st well
To trust, fair Madeline, to no rude infidel.

39

"Hark! 'tis an elfin-storm from faery land,
Of haggard seeming, but a boon indeed:
Arise—arise! the morning is at hand;—
The bloated wassaillers will never heed:—
Let us away, my love, with happy speed;
There are no ears to hear, or eyes to see,—
Drown'd all in Rhenish and the sleepy mead:
Awake! arise! my love, and fearless be,
For o'er the southern moors I have a home for thee."

40

She hurried at his words, beset with fears,
For there were sleeping dragons all around,
At glaring watch, perhaps, with ready spears—
Down the wide stairs a darkling way they found.—
In all the house was heard no human sound.
A chain-droop'd lamp was flickering by each door;
The arras, rich with horseman, hawk, and hound,
Flutter'd in the besieging wind's uproar;
And the long carpets rose along the gusty floor.

41

They glide, like phantoms, into the wide hall;
Like phantoms, to the iron porch, they glide;
Where lay the Porter, in uneasy sprawl,
With a huge empty flaggon by his side:
The wakeful bloodhound rose, and shook his hide,
But his sagacious eye an inmate owns:
By one, and one, the bolts full easy slide:—
The chains lie silent on the footworn stones;—
The key turns, and the door upon its hinges groans.

42

And they are gone: ay, ages long ago
These lovers fled away into the storm.
That night the Baron dreamt of many a woe,
And all his warrior-guests, with shade and form
Of witch, and demon, and large coffin-worm,
Were long be-nightmar'd. Angela the old
Died palsy-twitch'd, with meagre face deform;
The Beadsman, after thousand aves told,
For aye unsought for slept among his ashes cold.

Ode to a Nightingale[1]

1

My heart aches, and a drowsy numbness pains
    My sense, as though of hemlock[2] I had drunk,
Or emptied some dull opiate to the drains
    One minute past, and Lethe-wards[3] had sunk:
'Tis not through envy of thy happy lot,
    But being too happy in thine happiness,—
        That thou, light-winged Dryad of the trees,
        In some melodious plot
Of beechen green, and shadows numberless,
    Singest of summer in full-throated ease.

2

O, for a draught of vintage! that hath been
    Cool'd a long age in the deep-delved earth,
Tasting of Flora[4] and the country green,

---

[1] written about 1 May 1819. Twenty years later, Keats's friend and housemate Charles Armitage Brown remembered the composition of the poem: "In the spring of 1819 a nightingale had built her nest near my house. Keats felt a tranquil and continual joy in her song; and one morning he took his chair from the breakfast-table to the grass-plot under a plum-tree, where he sat for two or three hours. When he came into the house, I perceived he had some scraps of paper in his hand, and these he was quietly thrusting behind the books. On enquiry, I found those scraps, four or five in number, contained his poetic feeling on the song of our nightingale" (*The Keats Circle* 2: 65).

[2] the poison used to execute Socrates.

[3] Lethe is the river of forgetfulness in the classical underworld.

[4] Roman goddess of flowers.

      Dance, and Provençal song,[1] and sunburnt mirth!
15 O for a beaker full of the warm South,
      Full of the true, the blushful Hippocrene,[2]
         With beaded bubbles winking at the brim,
         And purple-stained mouth;
      That I might drink, and leave the world unseen,
20   And with thee fade away into the forest dim:

3

Fade far away, dissolve, and quite forget
      What thou among the leaves hast never known,
The weariness, the fever, and the fret[3]
      Here, where men sit and hear each other groan;
25 Where palsy shakes a few, sad, last gray hairs,
      Where youth grows pale, and spectre-thin, and
         dies;[4]
      Where but to think is to be full of sorrow
         And leaden-eyed despairs,
      Where Beauty cannot keep her lustrous eyes,
30   Or new Love pine at them beyond to-morrow.

4

Away! away! for I will fly to thee,
      Not charioted by Bacchus and his pards,[5]
But on the viewless wings of Poesy,
      Though the dull brain perplexes and retards:
35 Already with thee! tender is the night,
      And haply the Queen-Moon is on her throne,
         Cluster'd around by all her starry Fays;
         But here there is no light,
      Save what from heaven is with the breezes blown
40   Through verdurous glooms and winding
         mossy ways.

5

I cannot see what flowers are at my feet,
      Nor what soft incense hangs upon the boughs,
But, in enbalmed darkness, guess each sweet
      Wherewith the seasonable month endows
45 The grass, the thicket, and the fruit-tree wild;
      White hawthorn, and the pastoral eglantine;
         Fast fading violets cover'd up in leaves;
         And mid-May's eldest child,
      The coming musk-rose, full of dewy wine,
50   The murmurous haunt of flies on summer eves.[6]

6

Darkling I listen; and, for many a time
      I have been half in love with easeful Death,
Call'd him soft names in many a mused rhyme,
      To take into the air my quiet breath;
55 Now more than ever seems it rich to die,
      To cease upon the midnight with no pain,
         While thou art pouring forth thy soul abroad
         In such an ecstasy!
      Still wouldst thou sing, and I have ears in vain—
60   To thy high requiem become a sod.

7

Thou wast not born for death, immortal Bird!
      No hungry generations tread thee down;
The voice I hear this passing night was heard
      In ancient days by emperor and clown:
65 Perhaps the self-same song that found a path
      Through the sad heart of Ruth, when, sick for
         home,
         She stood in tears amid the alien corn;[7]
         The same that oft-times hath
      Charm'd magic casements, opening on the foam
70   Of perilous seas, in faery lands forlorn.

8

Forlorn! the very word is like a bell
      To toll me back from thee to my sole self!
Adieu! the fancy cannot cheat so well

---

[1] Provence, in southern France, was famous for the poetry of the troubadours.

[2] a fountain on Mt. Helicon, sacred to the Muses.

[3] Cf. Shakespeare, *Macbeth* 3.2.23, and W. Wordsworth, "Tintern Abbey" 26–28, 52–55.*

[4] Tom Keats had died of consumption on 1 December 1818. Cf. W. Wordsworth,* *The Excursion* 4.760.

[5] The chariot of Bacchus, or Dionysus, god of wine, was drawn by leopards.

---

[6] Cf. Shakespeare, *A Midsummer Night's Dream* 2.1.249–52.

[7] See Ruth 1–2.

As she is fam'd to do, deceiving elf.
75 Adieu! adieu!¹ thy plaintive anthem fades
    Past the near meadows, over the still stream,
       Up the hill-side; and now 'tis buried deep
         In the next valley-glades:
    Was it a vision, or a waking dream?
80   Fled is that music:—Do I wake or sleep?²

Ode on a Grecian Urn³

1

Thou still unravish'd bride of quietness,
   Thou foster-child of silence and slow time,
Sylvan historian, who canst thus express
   A flowery tale more sweetly than our rhyme:
5 What leaf-fring'd legend haunts about thy shape
   Of deities or mortals, or of both,
      In Tempe or the dales of Arcady?⁴
   What men or gods are these? What maidens loth?
What mad pursuit? What struggle to escape?
10   What pipes and timbrels? What wild ecstasy?

2

Heard melodies are sweet, but those unheard
   Are sweeter; therefore, ye soft pipes, play on;
Not to the sensual ear, but, more endear'd,
   Pipe to the spirit ditties of no tone:
15 Fair youth, beneath the trees, thou canst not leave
   Thy song, nor ever can those trees be bare;
      Bold Lover, never, never canst thou kiss,
   Though winning near the goal—yet, do not grieve;
She cannot fade, though thou hast not thy bliss,
20   For ever wilt thou love, and she be fair!

3

Ah, happy, happy boughs! that cannot shed
   Your leaves, nor ever bid the Spring adieu;
And, happy melodist, unwearied,
   For ever piping songs for ever new;
25 More happy love! more happy, happy love!
   For ever warm and still to be enjoy'd,
      For ever panting, and for ever young;
All breathing human passion far above,⁵
   That leaves a heart high-sorrowful and cloy'd,
30   A burning forehead, and a parching tongue.

4

Who are these coming to the sacrifice?
   To what green altar, O mysterious priest,
Lead'st thou that heifer lowing at the skies,
   And all her silken flanks with garlands drest?
35 What little town by river or sea shore,
   Or mountain-built with peaceful citadel,
      Is emptied of this folk, this pious morn?
And, little town, thy streets for evermore
   Will silent be; and not a soul to tell
40   Why thou art desolate, can e'er return.

5

O Attic shape!⁶ Fair attitude! with brede
   Of marble men and maidens overwrought,
With forest branches and the trodden weed;
   Thou, silent form, dost tease us out of thought
45 As doth eternity: Cold Pastoral!
   When old age shall this generation waste,
      Thou shalt remain, in midst of other woe
Than ours, a friend to man, to whom thou say'st,
   "Beauty is truth, truth beauty,"⁷—that is all
50   Ye know on earth, and all ye need to know.

---

[1] Cf. C. Smith, "On the Departure of the Nightingale."*

[2] Cf. Spenser, *Amoretti* 77, Shakespeare, *A Midsummer Night's Dream* 4.1.191–93, and Keats, "Ode to Psyche" 5–6.*

[3] written early in May 1819.

[4] beautiful, pastoral regions of Greece.

[5] Cf. Hazlitt, "Of Gusto."*

[6] Athens is in the Greek province of Attica.

[7] Cf. Keats's letter to Benjamin Bailey, 22 November 1817.* In the first publication of the poem (*Annals of the Fine Arts*, January 1820), these words are not in quotation marks.

Ode to Psyche[1]

O Goddess! hear these tuneless numbers, wrung
    By sweet enforcement and remembrance dear,
And pardon that thy secrets should be sung
    Even into thine own soft-conched ear:
5 Surely I dreamt to-day, or did I see
    The winged Psyche with awaken'd eyes?[2]
I wander'd in a forest thoughtlessly,
    And, on the sudden, fainting with surprise,
Saw two fair creatures, couched side by side
10   In deepest grass, beneath the whisp'ring roof
    Of leaves and trembled blossoms, where there ran
        A brooklet, scarce espied:[3]

'Mid hush'd, cool-rooted flowers, fragrant-eyed,
    Blue, silver-white, and budded Tyrian,[4]
15 They lay calm-breathing on the bedded grass;
    Their arms embraced, and their pinions too;
    Their lips touch'd not, but had not bade adieu
As if disjoined by soft-handed slumber,
And ready still past kisses to outnumber
20   At tender eye-dawn of aurorean love:[5]
        The winged boy I knew;
    But who wast thou, O happy, happy dove?
        His Psyche true!

O latest born and loveliest vision far
25   Of all Olympus' faded hierarchy![6]
Fairer than Phœbe's sapphire-region'd star,[7]
Or Vesper, amorous glow-worm of the sky;[8]
Fairer than these, though temple thou hast none,
    Nor altar heap'd with flowers;
30 Nor virgin-choir to make delicious moan
    Upon the midnight hours;
No voice, no lute, no pipe, no incense sweet
    From chain-swung censer teeming;
No shrine, no grove, no oracle, no heat
35   Of pale-mouth'd prophet dreaming.[9]

O brightest! though too late for antique vows,
    Too, too late for the fond believing lyre,
When holy were the haunted forest boughs,
    Holy the air, the water, and the fire;
40 Yet even in these days so far retir'd
    From happy pieties, thy lucent fans,
        Fluttering among the faint Olympians,
I see, and sing, by my own eyes inspired.
So let me be thy choir, and make a moan
45   Upon the midnight hours;
Thy voice, thy lute, thy pipe, thy incense sweet
    From swinged censer teeming;
Thy shrine, thy grove, thy oracle, thy heat
    Of pale-mouth'd prophet dreaming.

50 Yes, I will be thy priest, and build a fane
    In some untrodden region of my mind,[10]
Where branched thoughts, new grown with pleasant
        pain,
    Instead of pines shall murmur in the wind:
Far, far around shall those dark-cluster'd trees
55   Fledge the wild-ridged mountains steep by steep;
And there by zephyrs, streams, and birds, and bees,
    The moss-lain Dryads shall be lull'd to sleep;
And in the midst of this wide quietness
A rosy sanctuary will I dress
60 With the wreath'd trellis of a working brain,
    With buds, and bells, and stars without a name,
With all the gardener Fancy e'er could feign,

---

[1] Keats commented on this poem in a letter to his brother and sister-in-law, George and Georgiana Keats, 14 February–4 May 1819 (*Letters* 2: 105–06). It draws on the story of Cupid and Psyche in *The Golden Ass*, by Apuleius (c.120–c.180). Cf. Tighe, *Psyche*,* which Keats had read.

[2] Cf. "Ode to a Nightingale" 79–80* and *The Fall of Hyperion* 1.1–18.*

[3] Cf. Milton, *Paradise Lost* 4.741–43 and 4.790–91.

[4] purple, like the dye made from the murex (a shellfish) at Tyre.

[5] Aurora is the classical goddess of dawn.

[6] The gods of classical mythology, superseded by Christianity.

[7] Phoebe, Artemis (Gr.), or Diana (L.), is the goddess of the moon.

[8] Vesper, the evening star, is the planet Venus; in Apuleius's story, Venus is Cupid's mother.

[9] Cf. Milton, "On the Morning of Christ's Nativity" (1629) 173–80.

[10] Cf. Spenser, *Amoretti* 22.

Who breeding flowers, will never breed the same:
And there shall be for thee all soft delight
　　That shadowy thought can win,
A bright torch, and a casement ope at night,
　　To let the warm Love in!

To Autumn[1]

1

Season of mists and mellow fruitfulness,
　　Close bosom-friend of the maturing sun;
Conspiring with him how to load and bless
　　With fruit the vines that round the thatch-eves run;
To bend with apples the moss'd cottage-trees,
　　And fill all fruit with ripeness to the core;
　　　　To swell the gourd, and plump the hazel shells
With a sweet kernel; to set budding more,
And still more, later flowers for the bees,
　　Until they think warm days will never cease,
　　　　For Summer has o'er-brimm'd their clammy cells.

2

Who hath not seen thee oft amid thy store?
　　Sometimes whoever seeks abroad may find
Thee sitting careless on a granary floor,
　　Thy hair soft-lifted by the winnowing wind;
Or on a half-reap'd furrow sound asleep,
　　Drows'd with the fume of poppies, while thy hook
　　　　Spares the next swath and all its twined flowers:
And sometimes like a gleaner thou dost keep
　　Steady thy laden head across a brook;
　　Or by a cyder-press, with patient look,
　　　　Thou watchest the last oozings hours by hours.

3

Where are the songs of Spring? Ay, where are they?[2]
　　Think not of them, thou hast thy music too,—
While barred clouds bloom the soft-dying day,
　　And touch the stubble-plains with rosy hue;
Then in a wailful choir the small gnats mourn
　　Among the river sallows, borne aloft
　　　　Or sinking as the light wind lives or dies;
And full-grown lambs loud bleat from hilly bourn;
　　Hedge-crickets sing; and now with treble soft
　　The red-breast whistles from a garden-croft;
　　　　And gathering swallows twitter in the skies.

Ode on Melancholy[3]

1

No, no, go not to Lethe, neither twist
　　Wolf's-bane,[4] tight-rooted, for its poisonous wine;
Nor suffer thy pale forehead to be kiss'd
　　By nightshade,[5] ruby grape of Proserpine;[6]
Make not your rosary of yew-berries,[7]
　　Nor let the beetle, nor the death-moth be
　　　　Your mournful Psyche,[8] nor the downy owl
A partner in your sorrow's mysteries;
　　For shade to shade will come too drowsily,
　　And drown the wakeful anguish of the soul.

---

[1] Keats described the inspiration for this poem in a letter to John Hamilton Reynolds, 21 September 1819, two days after he wrote it (*Letters* 2: 167).

[2] Cf. W. Wordsworth, "Ode," stanza 4.*

[3] Cf. C. Smith, "To Melancholy."* Keats wrote, and then discarded, a stanza to precede the first one of the printed poem:
　　Though you should build a bark of dead men's bones,
　　　　And rear a phantom gibbet for a mast,
　　Stitch creeds together for a sail, with groans
　　　　To fill it out, bloodstained and aghast;
　　Although your rudder be a Dragon's tail,
　　　　Long sever'd, yet still hard with agony,
　　　　　　Your cordage large uprootings from the skull
　　Of bald Medusa; certes you would fail
　　　　To find the Melancholy, whether she
　　　　Dreameth in any isle of Lethe dull.
Medusa was one of the Gorgons; she had snakes for hair. Lethe was the river of forgetfulness in the underworld.

[4] *Aconitum lycoctonum*, a poisonous plant.

[5] *Atropa belladonna*, a plant with poisonous berries.

[6] Hades (Gr.) or Pluto (L.), ruler of the underworld, abducted Proserpine (L.) or Persephone (Gr.) and made her his wife. Cf. Ovid, *Metamorphoses* 5, and Milton, *Paradise Lost* 4.268–72.

[7] Yews commonly grow in graveyards.

[8] "Psyche" is the Greek word for "butterfly" as well as for "soul."

2

But when the melancholy fit shall fall
    Sudden from heaven like a weeping cloud,
That fosters the droop-headed flowers all,
    And hides the green hill in an April shroud;
15 Then glut thy sorrow on a morning rose,
    Or on the rainbow of the salt sand-wave,
    Or on the wealth of globed peonies;
Or if thy mistress some rich anger shows,
    Emprison her soft hand, and let her rave,
20   And feed deep, deep upon her peerless eyes.

3

She dwells with Beauty—Beauty that must die;
    And Joy, whose hand is ever at his lips
Bidding adieu; and aching Pleasure nigh,
    Turning to poison while the bee-mouth sips:
25 Ay, in the very temple of Delight
    Veil'd Melancholy has her sovran shrine,[1]
        Though seen of none save him whose
            strenuous tongue
    Can burst Joy's grape against his palate fine;
His soul shall taste the sadness of her might,
30   And be among her cloudy trophies hung.[2]

Hyperion

BOOK 1

Deep in the shady sadness of a vale
Far sunken from the healthy breath of morn,
Far from the fiery noon, and eve's one star,
Sat gray-hair'd Saturn,[3] quiet as a stone,
5 Still as the silence round about his lair;
Forest on forest hung about his head
Like cloud on cloud. No stir of air was there,
Not so much life as on a summer's day
Robs not one light seed from the feather'd grass,
10 But where the dead leaf fell, there did it rest.
A stream went voiceless by, still deadened more
By reason of his fallen divinity
Spreading a shade: the Naiad[4] 'mid her reeds
Press'd her cold finger closer to her lips.

15 Along the margin-sand large foot-marks went,
No further than to where his feet had stray'd,
And slept there since. Upon the sodden ground
His old right hand lay nerveless, listless, dead,
Unsceptred; and his realmless eyes were closed;
20 While his bow'd head seem'd list'ning to the Earth,
His ancient mother, for some comfort yet.

It seem'd no force could wake him from his place;
But there came one,[5] who with a kindred hand
Touch'd his wide shoulders, after bending low
25 With reverence, though to one who knew it not.
She was a Goddess of the infant world;
By her in stature the tall Amazon
Had stood a pigmy's height: she would have ta'en
Achilles[6] by the hair and bent his neck;
30 Or with a finger stay'd Ixion's wheel.[7]
Her face was large as that of Memphian sphinx,[8]
Pedestal'd haply in a palace court,
When sages look'd to Egypt for their lore.
But oh! how unlike[9] marble was that face:
35 How beautiful, if sorrow had not made
Sorrow more beautiful than Beauty's self.
There was a listening fear in her regard,
As if calamity had but begun;
As if the vanward clouds of evil days
40 Had spent their malice, and the sullen rear

---

[1] Cf. Hazlitt,* "On Poetry in General."

[2] Trophies were hung in Greek and Roman temples. Cf. Shakespeare, Sonnet 31, line 10.

[3] the king of the Titans, the race of gods overthrown by the Olympians; the brother of Hyperion (the Titan of the sun), and the father of Jupiter, king of the Olympians, who overthrew him.

[4] a river-nymph.

[5] Thea, the sister and consort of Hyperion.

[6] the hero of Homer's *Iliad*.

[7] For attempting to rape Juno, the consort of Jupiter, Ixion was bound to an eternally turning wheel in the underworld. Cf. Ovid, *Metamorphoses* 4.

[8] Memphis was the Lower Egyptian capital; the pyramids and the Great Sphinx are nearby.

[9] Cf. Milton, *Paradise Lost* 1.75.

Was with its stored thunder labouring up.
One hand she press'd upon that aching spot
Where beats the human heart, as if just there,
Though an immortal, she felt cruel pain:
45 The other upon Saturn's bended neck
She laid, and to the level of his ear
Leaning with parted lips, some words she spake
In solemn tenour and deep organ tone:
Some mourning words, which in our feeble tongue
50 Would come in these like accents; O how frail
To that large utterance of the early Gods!
"Saturn, look up!—though wherefore, poor old King?[1]
I have no comfort for thee, no not one:
I cannot say, 'O wherefore sleepest thou?'
55 For heaven is parted from thee, and the earth
Knows thee not, thus afflicted, for a God;
And ocean too, with all its solemn noise,
Has from thy sceptre pass'd; and all the air
Is emptied of thine hoary majesty.
60 Thy thunder, conscious of the new command,
Rumbles reluctant[2] o'er our fallen house;
And thy sharp lightning in unpractised hands
Scorches and burns our once serene domain.
O aching time! O moments big as years!
65 All as ye pass swell out the monstrous truth,
And press it so upon our weary griefs
That unbelief has not a space to breathe.
Saturn, sleep on:—O thoughtless, why did I
Thus violate thy slumbrous solitude?
70 Why should I ope thy melancholy eyes?
Saturn, sleep on! while at thy feet I weep."

As when, upon a tranced summer-night,
Those green-rob'd senators of mighty woods,
Tall oaks, branch-charmed by the earnest stars,
75 Dream, and so dream all night without a stir,
Save from one gradual solitary gust
Which comes upon the silence, and dies off,
As if the ebbing air had but one wave;

---

[1] Cf. Shakespeare, *King Lear*.

[2] Cf. Milton, *Paradise Lost* 6.58–59. Keats underlined this passage and commented on the "powerful effect" of "reluctant" in his copy of Milton (Wittreich, *The Romantics on Milton* 559).

So came these words and went; the while in tears
80 She touch'd her fair large forehead to the ground,
Just where her falling hair might be outspread
A soft and silken mat for Saturn's feet.
One moon, with alteration slow, had shed
Her silver seasons four upon the night,
85 And still these two were postured motionless,
Like natural sculpture in cathedral cavern;
The frozen God still couchant on the earth,
And the sad Goddess weeping at his feet:
Until at length old Saturn lifted up
90 His faded eyes, and saw his kingdom gone,
And all the gloom and sorrow of the place,
And that fair kneeling Goddess; and then spake,
As with a palsied tongue, and while his beard
Shook horrid with such aspen-malady:
95 "O tender spouse of gold Hyperion,
Thea, I feel thee ere I see thy face;
Look up, and let me see our doom in it;
Look up, and tell me if this feeble shape
Is Saturn's; tell me, if thou hear'st the voice
100 Of Saturn; tell me, if this wrinkling brow,
Naked and bare of its great diadem,
Peers like the front of Saturn. Who had power
To make me desolate? whence came the strength?
How was it nurtur'd to such bursting forth,
105 While Fate seem'd strangled in my nervous grasp?
But it is so; and I am smother'd up,
And buried from all godlike exercise
Of influence benign on planets pale,
Of admonitions to the winds and seas,
110 Of peaceful sway above man's harvesting,
And all those acts which Deity supreme
Doth ease its heart of love in.—I am gone
Away from my own bosom: I have left
My strong identity, my real self,
115 Somewhere between the throne, and where I sit
Here on this spot of earth. Search, Thea, search!
Open thine eyes eterne, and sphere them round
Upon all space: space starr'd, and lorn of light;
Space region'd with life-air; and barren void;
120 Spaces of fire, and all the yawn of hell.—
Search, Thea, search! and tell me, if thou seest
A certain shape or shadow, making way

With wings or chariot fierce to repossess
A heaven he lost erewhile: it must—it must
Be of ripe progress—Saturn must be King.
Yes, there must be a golden victory;
There must be Gods thrown down, and trumpets
    blown
Of triumph calm, and hymns of festival
Upon the gold clouds metropolitan,
Voices of soft proclaim, and silver stir
Of strings in hollow shells; and there shall be
Beautiful things made new, for the surprise
Of the sky-children; I will give command:
Thea! Thea! Thea! where is Saturn?"

    This passion lifted him upon his feet,
And made his hands to struggle in the air,
His Druid locks to shake and ooze with sweat,
His eyes to fever out, his voice to cease.
He stood, and heard not Thea's sobbing deep;
A little time, and then again he snatch'd
Utterance thus.—"But cannot I create?
Cannot I form? Cannot I fashion forth
Another world, another universe,
To overbear and crumble this to nought?
Where is another chaos? Where?"—That word
Found way unto Olympus, and made quake
The rebel three.[1]—Thea was startled up,
And in her bearing was a sort of hope,
As thus she quick-voic'd spake, yet full of awe.

    "This cheers our fallen house: come to our friends,
O Saturn! come away, and give them heart;
I know the covert, for thence came I hither."
Thus brief; then with beseeching eyes she went
With backward footing through the shade a space:
He follow'd, and she turn'd to lead the way
Through aged boughs, that yielded like the mist
Which eagles cleave upmounting from their nest.

    Meanwhile in other realms big tears were shed,
More sorrow like to this, and such like woe,
Too huge for mortal tongue or pen of scribe:
The Titans fierce, self-hid, or prison-bound,
Groan'd for the old allegiance once more,
And listen'd in sharp pain for Saturn's voice.
But one of the whole mammoth-brood still kept
His sov'reignty, and rule, and majesty;—
Blazing Hyperion on his orbed fire
Still sat, still snuff'd the incense, teeming up
From man to the sun's God; yet unsecure:
For as among us mortals omens drear
Fright and perplex, so also shuddered he—
Not at dog's howl, or gloom-bird's hated screech,
Or the familiar visiting of one
Upon the first toll of his passing-bell,
Or prophesyings of the midnight lamp;
But horrors, portion'd to a giant nerve,
Oft made Hyperion ache. His palace bright
Bastion'd with pyramids of glowing gold,
And touch'd with shade of bronzed obelisks,
Glar'd a blood-red through all its thousand courts,
Arches, and domes, and fiery galleries;
And all its curtains of Aurorian clouds[2]
Flush'd angerly:[3] while sometimes eagle's wings,
Unseen before by Gods or wondering men,
Darken'd the place; and neighing steeds were heard,[4]
Not heard before by Gods or wondering men.
Also, when he would taste the spicy wreaths
Of incense, breath'd aloft from sacred hills,
Instead of sweets, his ample palate took
Savour of poisonous brass and metal sick:
And so, when harbour'd in the sleepy west,
After the full completion of fair day,—
For rest divine upon exalted couch
And slumber in the arms of melody,
He pac'd away the pleasant hours of ease
With stride colossal, on from hall to hall;
While far within each aisle and deep recess,
His winged minions in close clusters stood,
Amaz'd and full of fear; like anxious men
Who on wide plains gather in panting troops,

---

[1] the three supreme Olympians: Jupiter, Neptune, and Pluto, Saturn's sons.

[2] Aurora is the goddess of the dawn.

[3] Cf. W. Wordsworth,* *The Excursion* 2.852–81.

[4] Cf. Shakespeare, *Julius Caesar* 2.2.23.

When earthquakes jar their battlements and towers.
Even now, while Saturn, rous'd from icy trance,
Went step for step with Thea through the woods,
Hyperion, leaving twilight in the rear,
Came slope upon the threshold of the west;
Then, as was wont, his palace-door flew ope
In smoothest silence, save what solemn tubes,
Blown by the serious Zephyrs,[1] gave of sweet
And wandering sounds, slow-breathed melodies;
And like a rose in vermeil tint and shape,
In fragrance soft, and coolness to the eye,
That inlet to severe magnificence
Stood full blown, for the God to enter in.

    He enter'd, but he enter'd full of wrath;
His flaming robes stream'd out beyond his heels,
And gave a roar, as if of earthly fire,
That scar'd away the meek ethereal Hours[2]
And made their dove-wings tremble. On he flared,
From stately nave to nave, from vault to vault,
Through bowers of fragrant and enwreathed light,
And diamond-paved lustrous long arcades,
Until he reach'd the great main cupola;
There standing fierce beneath, he stampt his foot,
And from the basements deep to the high towers
Jarr'd his own golden region; and before
The quavering thunder thereupon had ceas'd,
His voice leapt out, despite of godlike curb,
To this result: "O dreams of day and night!
O monstrous forms! O effigies of pain!
O spectres busy in a cold, cold gloom!
O lank-eared Phantoms of black-weeded pools!
Why do I know ye? why have I seen ye? why
Is my eternal essence thus distraught
To see and to behold these horrors new?
Saturn is fallen, am I too to fall?
Am I to leave this haven of my rest,
This cradle of my glory, this soft clime,
This calm luxuriance of blissful light,
These crystalline pavilions, and pure fanes,
Of all my lucent empire? It is left
Deserted, void, nor any haunt of mine.
The blaze, the splendor, and the symmetry,
I cannot see—but darkness, death and darkness.
Even here, into my centre of repose,
The shady visions come to domineer,
Insult, and blind, and stifle up my pomp.—
Fall!—No, by Tellus[3] and her briny robes!
Over the fiery frontier of my realms
I will advance a terrible right arm
Shall scare that infant thunderer, rebel Jove,
And bid old Saturn take his throne again."—
He spake, and ceas'd, the while a heavier threat
Held struggle with his throat but came not forth;
For as in theatres of crowded men
Hubbub increases more they call out "Hush!"
So at Hyperion's words the Phantoms pale
Bestirr'd themselves, thrice horrible and cold;
And from the mirror'd level where he stood
A mist arose, as from a scummy marsh.
At this, through all his bulk an agony
Crept gradual, from the feet unto the crown,
Like a lithe serpent vast and muscular
Making slow way, with head and neck convuls'd
From over-strained might. Releas'd, he fled
To the eastern gates, and full six dewy hours
Before the dawn in season due should blush,
He breath'd fierce breath against the sleepy portals,
Clear'd them of heavy vapours, burst them wide
Suddenly on the ocean's chilly streams.
The planet orb of fire, whereon he rode
Each day from east to west the heavens through,
Spun round in sable curtaining of clouds;
Not therefore veiled quite, blindfold, and hid,
But ever and anon the glancing spheres,
Circles, and arcs, and broad-belting colure,[4]
Glow'd through, and wrought upon the muffling dark
Sweet-shaped lightnings from the nadir[5] deep

---

[1] west winds.

[2] the Horæ, twelve nymphs who attend on the Sun.

[3] the Earth, the mother of the Titans.

[4] one of two imaginary circles that intersect at right angles at the poles, dividing the sky into four equal parts at the equinoctial and solstitial points on the ecliptic. Cf. Milton, *Paradise Lost* 9.66.

[5] the point in the heavens directly under the observer—the opposite of the zenith.

Up to the zenith,—hieroglyphics old,
Which sages and keen-eyed astrologers
Then living on the earth, with labouring thought
Won from the gaze of many centuries:
Now lost, save what we find on remnants huge
Of stone, or marble swart; their import gone,
Their wisdom long since fled.—Two wings this orb
Possess'd for glory, two fair argent wings,
Ever exalted at the God's approach:
And now, from forth the gloom their plumes immense
Rose, one by one, till all outspreaded were;
While still the dazzling globe maintain'd eclipse,
Awaiting for Hyperion's command.
Fain would he have commanded, fain took throne
And bid the day begin, if but for change.
He might not:—No, though a primeval God:
The sacred seasons might not be disturb'd.
Therefore the operations of the dawn
Stay'd in their birth, even as here 'tis told.
Those silver wings expanded sisterly,
Eager to sail their orb; the porches wide
Open'd upon the dusk demesnes of night;
And the bright Titan, phrenzied with new woes,
Unus'd to bend, by hard compulsion bent
His spirit to the sorrow of the time;
And all along a dismal rack of clouds,
Upon the boundaries of day and night,
He stretch'd himself in grief and radiance faint.
There as he lay, the Heaven with its stars
Look'd down on him with pity, and the voice
Of Cœlus,[1] from the universal space,
Thus whisper'd low and solemn in his ear.
"O brightest of my children dear, earth-born
And sky-engendered, Son of Mysteries
All unrevealed even to the powers
Which met at thy creating; at whose joys
And palpitations sweet, and pleasures soft,
I, Cœlus, wonder, how they came and whence;
And at the fruits thereof what shapes they be,
Distinct, and visible; symbols divine,
Manifestations of that beauteous life
Diffus'd unseen throughout eternal space:
Of these new-form'd art thou, oh brightest child!
Of these, thy brethren and the Goddesses!
There is sad feud among ye, and rebellion
Of son against his sire. I saw him fall,
I saw my first-born[2] tumbled from his throne!
To me his arms were spread, to me his voice
Found way from forth the thunders round his head!
Pale wox[3] I, and in vapours hid my face.
Art thou, too, near such doom? vague fear there is:
For I have seen my sons most unlike Gods.
Divine ye were created, and divine
In sad demeanour, solemn, undisturb'd,
Unruffled, like high Gods, ye liv'd and ruled:
Now I behold in you fear, hope, and wrath;
Actions of rage and passion; even as
I see them, on the mortal world beneath,
In men who die.—This is the grief, O Son!
Sad sign of ruin, sudden dismay, and fall!
Yet do thou strive; as thou art capable,
As thou canst move about, an evident God;
And canst oppose to each malignant hour
Ethereal presence:—I am but a voice;
My life is but the life of winds and tides,
No more than winds and tides can I avail:—
But thou canst.—Be thou therefore in the van
Of circumstance; yea, seize the arrow's barb
Before the tense string murmur.—To the earth!
For there thou wilt find Saturn, and his woes.
Meantime I will keep watch on thy bright sun,
And of thy seasons be a careful nurse."—
Ere half this region-whisper had come down,
Hyperion arose, and on the stars
Lifted his curved lids, and kept them wide
Until it ceas'd; and still he kept them wide:
And still they were the same bright, patient stars.
Then with a slow incline of his broad breast,
Like to a diver in the pearly seas,
Forward he stoop'd over the airy shore,
And plung'd all noiseless into the deep night.

---

[1] Uranus, the Sky, the father of the Titans.

[2] Saturn.

[3] waxed, became.

BOOK 2

Just at the self-same beat of Time's wide wings
Hyperion slid into the rustled air,
And Saturn gain'd with Thea that sad place
Where Cybele[1] and the bruised Titans mourn'd.
5 It was a den where no insulting light
Could glimmer on their tears; where their own groans
They felt, but heard not, for the solid roar
Of thunderous waterfalls and torrents hoarse,
Pouring a constant bulk, uncertain where.
10 Crag jutting forth to crag, and rocks that seem'd
Ever as if just rising from a sleep,
Forehead to forehead held their monstrous horns;
And thus in thousand hugest phantasies
Made a fit roofing to this nest of woe.
15 Instead of thrones, hard flint they sat upon,
Couches of rugged stone, and slaty ridge
Stubborn'd with iron. All were not assembled:
Some chain'd in torture, and some wandering.
Cœus, and Gyges, and Briareüs,
20 Typhon, and Dolor, and Porphyrion,[2]
With many more, the brawniest in assault,
Were pent in regions of laborious breath;
Dungeon'd in opaque element, to keep
Their clenched teeth still clench'd, and all their limbs
25 Lock'd up like veins of metal, crampt and screw'd;
Without a motion, save of their big hearts
Heaving in pain, and horribly convuls'd
With sanguine feverous boiling gurge of pulse.
Mnemosyne[3] was straying in the world;
30 Far from her moon had Phœbe wandered;
And many else, were free to roam abroad,
But for the main, here found they covert drear.
Scarce images of life, one here, one there,
Lay vast and edgeways; like a dismal cirque
35 Of Druid stones,[4] upon a forlorn moor,

When the chill rain begins at shut of eve,
In dull November, and their chancel vault,
The Heaven itself, is blinded throughout night.
Each one kept shroud, nor to his neighbour gave
40 Or word, or look, or action of despair.
Creüs was one; his ponderous iron mace
Lay by him, and a shatter'd rib of rock
Told of his rage, ere he thus sank and pined.
Iäpetus another; in his grasp,
45 A serpent's plashy neck; its barbed tongue
Squeez'd from the gorge, and all its uncurl'd length
Dead; and because the creature could not spit
Its poison in the eyes of conquering Jove.
Next Cottus: prone he lay, chin uppermost,
50 As though in pain; for still upon the flint
He ground severe his skull, with open mouth
And eyes at horrid working. Nearest him
Asia, born of most enormous Caf,[5]
Who cost her mother Tellus keener pangs,
55 Though feminine, than any of her sons:
More thought than woe was in her dusky face,
For she was prophesying of her glory;
And in her wide imagination stood
Palm-shaded temples, and high rival fanes,
60 By Oxus or in Ganges'[6] sacred isles.
Even as Hope upon her anchor leans,[7]
So leant she, not so fair, upon a tusk
Shed from the broadest of her elephants.
Above her, on a crag's uneasy shelve,
65 Upon his elbow rais'd, all prostrate else,
Shadow'd Enceladus; once tame and mild
As grazing ox unworried in the meads;
Now tiger-passion'd, lion-thoughted, wroth,
He meditated, plotted, and even now
70 Was hurling mountains in that second war,
Not long delay'd, that scar'd the younger Gods
To hide themselves in forms of beast and bird.
Not far hence Atlas; and beside him prone
Phorcus, the sire of Gorgons. Neighbour'd close
75 Oceanus, and Tethys, in whose lap

---

[1] consort of Saturn and mother of the Olympians; she is called Ops in 2.78 and 2.113.

[2] more Titans.

[3] "Memory" (Gr.), the mother of the Muses.

[4] a stone circle, such as Stonehenge. The Druids were ancient British priests.

[5] more Titans.

[6] sacred rivers in Afghanistan and India.

[7] Cf. Hebrews 6.19.

Sobb'd Clymene among her tangled hair.[1]
In midst of all lay Themis, at the feet
Of Ops the queen all clouded round from sight;
No shape distinguishable, more than when
80 Thick night confounds the pine-tops with the clouds:
And many else whose names may not be told.
For when the Muse's wings are air-ward spread,
Who shall delay her flight? And she must chaunt
Of Saturn, and his guide, who now had climb'd
85 With damp and slippery footing from a depth
More horrid still. Above a sombre cliff
Their heads appear'd, and up their stature grew
Till on the level height their steps found ease:
Then Thea spread abroad her trembling arms
90 Upon the precincts of this nest of pain,
And sidelong fix'd her eye on Saturn's face:
There saw she direst strife; the supreme God
At war with all the frailty of grief,
Of rage, of fear, anxiety, revenge,
95 Remorse, spleen, hope, but most of all despair.
Against these plagues he strove in vain; for Fate
Had pour'd a mortal oil upon his head,
A disanointing poison:[2] so that Thea,
Affrighted, kept her still, and let him pass
100 First onwards in, among the fallen tribe.

    As with us mortal men, the laden heart
Is persecuted more, and fever'd more,
When it is nighing to the mournful house
Where other hearts are sick of the same bruise;
105 So Saturn, as he walk'd into the midst,
Felt faint, and would have sunk among the rest,
But that he met Enceladus's eye,
Whose mightiness, and awe of him, at once
Came like an inspiration; and he shouted,
110 "Titans, behold your God!" at which some groan'd;
Some started on their feet; some also shouted;
Some wept, some wail'd, all bow'd with reverence;
And Ops, uplifting her black folded veil,
Show'd her pale cheeks, and all her forehead wan,
115 Her eye-brows thin and jet, and hollow eyes.
There is a roaring in the bleak-grown pines
When Winter lifts his voice; there is a noise
Among immortals when a God gives sign,
With hushing finger, how he means to load
120 His tongue with the full weight of utterless thought,
With thunder, and with music, and with pomp:
Such noise is like the roar of bleak-grown pines;
Which, when it ceases in this mountain'd world,
No other sound succeeds; but ceasing here,
125 Among these fallen, Saturn's voice therefrom
Grew up like organ, that begins anew
Its strain, when other harmonies, stopt short,
Leave the dinn'd air vibrating silverly.
Thus grew it up—"Not in my own sad breast,
130 Which is its own great judge and searcher out,
Can I find reason why ye should be thus:
Not in the legends of the first of days,
Studied from that old spirit-leaved book
Which starry Uranus with finger bright
135 Sav'd from the shores of darkness, when the waves
Low-ebb'd still hid it up in shallow gloom;—
And the which book ye know I ever kept
For my firm-based footstool:—Ah, infirm!
Not there, nor in sign, symbol, or portent
140 Of element, earth, water, air, and fire,—
At war, at peace, or inter-quarreling
One against one, or two, or three, or all
Each several one against the other three,
As fire with air loud warring when rain-floods
145 Drown both, and press them both against earth's face,
Where, finding sulphur, a quadruple wrath
Unhinges the poor world;—not in that strife.
Wherefrom I take strange lore, and read it deep,
Can I find reason why ye should be thus:
150 No, no-where can unriddle, though I search,
And pore on Nature's universal scroll
Even to swooning, why ye, Divinities,
The first-born of all shap'd and palpable Gods,
Should cower beneath what, in comparison,
155 Is untremendous might. Yet ye are here,
O'erwhelm'd, and spurn'd, and batter'd, ye are here!
O Titans, shall I say 'Arise!'—Ye groan:
Shall I say 'Crouch!'—Ye groan. What can I then?

---

[1] Cf. Milton, "Lycidas" 69.

[2] The "mortal oil" has undone the anointment that is part of the coronation of a monarch. Cf. Shakespeare, *Hamlet*, 1.5.61–62, 77.

O Heaven wide! O unseen parent dear!
What can I? Tell me, all ye brethren Gods,
How we can war, how engine our great wrath!
O speak your counsel now, for Saturn's ear
Is all a-hunger'd. Thou, Oceanus,
Ponderest high and deep; and in thy face
I see, astonied, that severe content
Which comes of thought and musing: give us help!"

So ended Saturn; and the God of the Sea,
Sophist and sage, from no Athenian grove,
But cogitation in his watery shades,
Arose, with locks not oozy,[1] and began,
In murmurs, which his first-endeavouring tongue
Caught infant-like from the far-foamed sands.
"O ye, whom wrath consumes! who, passion-stung,
Writhe at defeat, and nurse your agonies!
Shut up your senses, stifle up your ears,
My voice is not a bellows unto ire.
Yet listen, ye who will, whilst I bring proof
How ye, perforce, must be content to stoop:
And in the proof much comfort will I give,
If ye will take that comfort in its truth.
We fall by course of Nature's law, not force
Of thunder, or of Jove. Great Saturn, thou
Hast sifted well the atom-universe;[2]
But for this reason, that thou art the King,
And only blind from sheer supremacy,
One avenue was shaded from thine eyes,
Through which I wandered to eternal truth.
And first, as thou wast not the first of powers,
So art thou not the last; it cannot be:
Thou art not the beginning nor the end.[3]
From chaos and parental darkness came
Light, the first fruits of that intestine broil,
That sullen ferment, which for wondrous ends
Was ripening in itself. The ripe hour came,
And with it light, and light, engendering
Upon its own producer, forthwith touch'd
The whole enormous matter into life.

Upon that very hour, our parentage,
The Heavens and the Earth, were manifest:
Then thou first-born, and we the giant-race,
Found ourselves ruling new and beauteous realms.
Now comes the pain of truth, to whom 'tis pain;
O folly! for to bear all naked truths,
And to envisage circumstance, all calm,
That is the top of sovereignty. Mark well!
As Heaven and Earth are fairer, fairer far
Than Chaos and blank Darkness, though once chiefs;
And as we show beyond that Heaven and Earth
In form and shape compact and beautiful,
In will, in action free, companionship,
And thousand other signs of purer life;
So on our heels a fresh perfection treads,
A power more strong in beauty, born of us
And fated to excel us, as we pass
In glory that old Darkness: nor are we
Thereby more conquer'd, than by us the rule
Of shapeless Chaos. Say, doth the dull soil
Quarrel with the proud forests it hath fed,
And feedeth still, more comely than itself?
Can it deny the chiefdom of green groves?
Or shall the tree be envious of the dove
Because it cooeth, and hath snowy wings
To wander wherewithal and find its joys?
We are such forest-trees, and our fair boughs
Have bred forth, not pale solitary doves,
But eagles golden-feather'd, who do tower
Above us in their beauty, and must reign
In right thereof; for 'tis the eternal law
That first in beauty should be first in might:
Yea, by that law, another race may drive
Our conquerors to mourn as we do now.
Have ye beheld the young God of the Seas,[4]
My dispossessor? Have ye seen his face?
Have ye beheld his chariot, foam'd along
By noble winged creatures he hath made?
I saw him on the calmed waters scud,
With such a glow of beauty in his eyes,
That it enforc'd me to bid sad farewell
To all my empire: farewell sad I took,

---

[1] Cf. Milton, "Lycidas" 175.
[2] Cf. Milton, *Paradise Lost* 2.900.
[3] Cf. Revelation 1.8.
[4] Neptune.

240 And hither came, to see how dolorous fate
　　Had wrought upon ye; and how I might best
　　Give consolation in this woe extreme.
　　Receive the truth, and let it be your balm."

　　　　Whether through poz'd conviction, or disdain,
245 They guarded silence, when Oceanus
　　Left murmuring, what deepest thought can tell?
　　But so it was, none answer'd for a space,
　　Save one whom none regarded, Clymene;
　　And yet she answer'd not, only complain'd,
250 With hectic lips, and eyes up-looking mild,
　　Thus wording timidly among the fierce:
　　"O Father,[1] I am here the simplest voice,
　　And all my knowledge is that joy is gone,
　　And this thing woe crept in among our hearts,
255 There to remain for ever, as I fear:
　　I would not bode of evil, if I thought
　　So weak a creature could turn off the help
　　Which by just right should come of mighty Gods;
　　Yet let me tell my sorrow, let me tell
260 Of what I heard, and how it made me weep,
　　And know that we had parted from all hope.
　　I stood upon a shore, a pleasant shore,
　　Where a sweet clime was breathed from a land
　　Of fragrance, quietness, and trees, and flowers.
265 Full of calm joy it was, as I of grief;
　　Too full of joy and soft delicious warmth;
　　So that I felt a movement in my heart
　　To chide, and to reproach that solitude
　　With songs of misery, music of our woes;
270 And sat me down, and took a mouthed shell
　　And murmur'd into it, and made melody—
　　O melody no more! for while I sang,
　　And with poor skill let pass into the breeze
　　The dull shell's echo, from a bowery strand
275 Just opposite, an island of the sea,
　　There came enchantment with the shifting wind,
　　That did both drown and keep alive my ears.
　　I threw my shell away upon the sand,
　　And a wave fill'd it, as my sense was fill'd
280 With that new blissful golden melody.

---

[1] Clymene is Oceanus's daughter.

　　A living death was in each gush of sounds,
　　Each family of rapturous hurried notes,
　　That fell, one after one, yet all at once,
　　Like pearl beads dropping sudden from their string:
285 And then another, then another strain,
　　Each like a dove leaving its olive perch,
　　With music wing'd instead of silent plumes,
　　To hover round my head, and make me sick
　　Of joy and grief at once. Grief overcame,
290 And I was stopping up my frantic ears,
　　When, past all hindrance of my trembling hands,
　　A voice came sweeter, sweeter than all tune,
　　And still it cried, 'Apollo! young Apollo!
　　The morning-bright Apollo! young Apollo!'
295 I fled, it follow'd me, and cried 'Apollo!'
　　O Father, and O Brethren, had ye felt
　　Those pains of mine; O Saturn, hadst thou felt,
　　Ye would not call this too indulged tongue
　　Presumptuous, in thus venturing to be heard."

300 　　So far her voice flow'd on, like timorous brook
　　That, lingering along a pebbled coast,
　　Doth fear to meet the sea: but sea it met,
　　And shudder'd; for the overwhelming voice
　　Of huge Enceladus swallow'd it in wrath:
305 The ponderous syllables, like sullen waves
　　In the half-glutted hollows of reef-rocks,
　　Came booming thus, while still upon his arm
　　He lean'd; not rising, from supreme contempt.
　　"Or shall we listen to the over-wise,
310 Or to the over-foolish giant, Gods?
　　Not thunderbolt on thunderbolt, till all
　　That rebel Jove's whole armoury were spent,
　　Not world on world upon these shoulders piled,
　　Could agonize me more than baby-words
315 In midst of this dethronement horrible.
　　Speak! roar! shout! yell! ye sleepy Titans all.
　　Do ye forget the blows, the buffets vile?
　　Are ye not smitten by a youngling arm?
　　Dost thou forget, sham Monarch of the Waves,
320 Thy scalding in the seas? What, have I rous'd
　　Your spleens with so few simple words as these?
　　O joy! for now I see ye are not lost:
　　O joy! for now I see a thousand eyes

Wide glaring for revenge!"—As this he said,
325　He lifted up his stature vast, and stood,
　　　Still without intermission speaking thus:
　　　"Now ye are flames, I'll tell you how to burn,
　　　And purge the ether of our enemies;
　　　How to feed fierce the crooked stings of fire,
330　And singe away the swollen clouds of Jove,
　　　Stifling that puny essence in its tent.
　　　O let him feel the evil he hath done;
　　　For though I scorn Oceanus's lore,
　　　Much pain have I for more than loss of realms:
335　The days of peace and slumberous calm are fled;
　　　Those days, all innocent of scathing war,
　　　When all the fair Existences of heaven
　　　Came open-eyed to guess what we would speak:—
　　　That was before our brows were taught to frown,
340　Before our lips knew else but solemn sounds;
　　　That was before we knew the winged thing,
　　　Victory, might be lost, or might be won.
　　　And be ye mindful that Hyperion,
　　　Our brightest brother, still is undisgraced—
345　Hyperion, lo! his radiance is here!"

　　　　All eyes were on Enceladus's face,
　　　And they beheld, while still Hyperion's name
　　　Flew from his lips up to the vaulted rocks,
　　　A pallid gleam across his features stern:
350　Not savage, for he saw full many a God
　　　Wroth as himself. He look'd upon them all,
　　　And in each face he saw a gleam of light,
　　　But splendider in Saturn's, whose hoar locks
　　　Shone like the bubbling foam about a keel
355　When the prow sweeps into a midnight cove.
　　　In pale and silver silence they remain'd,
　　　Till suddenly a splendour, like the morn,
　　　Pervaded all the beetling gloomy steeps,
　　　All the sad spaces of oblivion,
360　And every gulf, and every chasm old,
　　　And every height, and every sullen depth,
　　　Voiceless, or hoarse with loud tormented streams:
　　　And all the everlasting cataracts,
　　　And all the headlong torrents far and near,
365　Mantled before in darkness and huge shade,
　　　Now saw the light and made it terrible.

　　　It was Hyperion:—a granite peak
　　　His bright feet touch'd, and there he stay'd to view
　　　The misery his brilliance had betray'd
370　To the most hateful seeing of itself.
　　　Golden his hair of short Numidian curl,[1]
　　　Regal his shape majestic, a vast shade
　　　In midst of his own brightness, like the bulk
　　　Of Memnon's image at the set of sun
375　To one who travels from the dusking East:
　　　Sighs, too, as mournful as that Memnon's harp[2]
　　　He utter'd, while his hands contemplative
　　　He press'd together, and in silence stood.
　　　Despondence seiz'd again the fallen Gods
380　At sight of the dejected King of Day,
　　　And many hid their faces from the light:
　　　But fierce Enceladus sent forth his eyes
　　　Among the brotherhood; and, at their glare,
　　　Uprose Iäpetus, and Creüs too,
385　And Phorcus, sea-born, and together strode
　　　To where he towered on his eminence.
　　　There those four shouted forth old Saturn's name;
　　　Hyperion from the peak loud answered, "Saturn!"
　　　Saturn sat near the Mother of the Gods,
390　In whose face was no joy, though all the Gods
　　　Gave from their hollow throats the name of "Saturn!"

BOOK 3

　　　Thus in alternate uproar and sad peace,
　　　Amazed were those Titans utterly.
　　　O leave them, Muse! O leave them to their woes;
　　　For thou art weak to sing such tumults dire:
5　　A solitary sorrow best befits
　　　Thy lips, and antheming a lonely grief.
　　　Leave them, O Muse! for thou anon wilt find
　　　Many a fallen old Divinity
　　　Wandering in vain about bewildered shores.
10　Meantime touch piously the Delphic harp,[3]
　　　And not a wind of heaven but will breathe

---

[1] Numidia is a region in the Sahara.

[2] According to legend, the statue of Memnon made a melodious sound at sunrise and a mournful one at sunset.

[3] one inspired by Apollo, like the Delphic oracle.

In aid soft warble from the Dorian flute;[1]
For lo! 'tis for the Father of all verse.
Flush every thing that hath a vermeil hue,
Let the rose glow intense and warm the air,
And let the clouds of even and of morn
Float in voluptuous fleeces o'er the hills;
Let the red wine within the goblet boil,
Cold as a bubbling well; let faint-lipp'd shells,
On sands, or in great deeps, vermilion turn
Through all their labyrinths; and let the maid
Blush keenly, as with some warm kiss surpris'd.
Chief isle of the embowered Cyclades,
Rejoice, O Delos,[2] with thine olives green,
And poplars, and lawn-shading palms, and beech,
In which the Zephyr breathes the loudest song,
And hazels thick, dark-stemm'd beneath the shade:
Apollo is once more the golden theme!
Where was he, when the Giant of the Sun
Stood bright, amid the sorrow of his peers?
Together had he left his mother fair
And his twin-sister[3] sleeping in their bower,
And in the morning twilight wandered forth
Beside the osiers of a rivulet,
Full ankle-deep in lilies of the vale.
The nightingale had ceas'd, and a few stars
Were lingering in the heavens, while the thrush
Began calm-throated. Throughout all the isle
There was no covert, no retired cave
Unhaunted by the murmurous noise of waves,
Though scarcely heard in many a green recess.
He listen'd, and he wept, and his bright tears
Went trickling down the golden bow he held.
Thus with half-shut suffused eyes he stood,
While from beneath some cumbrous boughs hard by
With solemn step an awful Goddess came,
And there was purport in her looks for him,
Which he with eager guess began to read
Perplex'd, the while melodiously he said:

"How cam'st thou over the unfooted sea?
Or hath that antique mien and robed form
Mov'd in these vales invisible till now?
Sure I have heard those vestments sweeping o'er
The fallen leaves, when I have sat alone
In cool mid-forest. Surely I have traced
The rustle of those ample skirts about
These grassy solitudes, and seen the flowers
Lift up their heads, as still the whisper pass'd.
Goddess! I have beheld those eyes before,
And their eternal calm, and all that face,
Or I have dream'd."—"Yes," said the supreme shape,
"Thou hast dream'd of me; and awaking up
Didst find a lyre all golden by thy side,
Whose strings touch'd by thy fingers, all the vast
Unwearied ear of the whole universe
Listen'd in pain and pleasure at the birth
Of such new tuneful wonder. Is't not strange
That thou shouldst weep, so gifted? Tell me, youth,
What sorrow thou canst feel; for I am sad
When thou dost shed a tear: explain thy griefs
To one who in this lonely isle hath been
The watcher of thy sleep and hours of life,
From the young day when first thy infant hand
Pluck'd witless the weak flowers, till thine arm
Could bend that bow heroic to all times.
Show thy heart's secret to an ancient Power
Who hath forsaken old and sacred thrones
For prophecies of thee, and for the sake
Of loveliness new born."—Apollo then,
With sudden scrutiny and gloomless eyes,
Thus answer'd, while his white melodious throat
Throbb'd with the syllables.—"Mnemosyne!
Thy name is on my tongue, I know not how;
Why should I tell thee what thou so well seest?
Why should I strive to show what from thy lips
Would come no mystery? For me, dark, dark,[4]
And painful vile oblivion seals my eyes:
I strive to search wherefore I am so sad,
Until a melancholy numbs my limbs;
And then upon the grass I sit, and moan,
Like one who once had wings.—O why should I

---

[1] Music in the Dorian mode was supposed to inspire courage. Cf. Milton, *Paradise Lost* 1.550–51. Keats marked these lines in his copy of Milton (Wittreich, *The Romantics on Milton* 555).

[2] the birthplace of Apollo, an island in the Cyclades, an Ægean archipelago.

[3] Apollo's mother, Latona, and his sister, Diana.

[4] Cf. Milton, *Samson Agonistes* 80.

Feel curs'd and thwarted, when the liegeless air
Yields to my step aspirant? why should I
Spurn the green turf as hateful to my feet?
95 Goddess benign, point forth some unknown thing:
Are there not other regions than this isle?
What are the stars? There is the sun, the sun!

And the most patient brilliance of the moon!
And stars by thousands! Point me out the way
100 To any one particular beauteous star,
And I will flit into it with my lyre,
And make its silvery splendour pant with bliss.
I have heard the cloudy thunder: Where is power?
Whose hand, whose essence, what divinity
105 Makes this alarum in the elements,
While I here idle listen on the shores
In fearless yet in aching ignorance?
O tell me, lonely Goddess, by thy harp,
That waileth every morn and eventide,
110 Tell me why thus I rave, about these groves!
Mute thou remainest—Mute! yet I can read
A wondrous lesson in thy silent face:
Knowledge enormous makes a God of me.
Names, deeds, gray legends, dire events, rebellions,
115 Majesties, sovran voices, agonies,
Creations and destroyings, all at once
Pour into the wide hollows of my brain,
And deify me, as if some blithe wine
Or bright elixir peerless I had drunk,
120 And so become immortal."—Thus the God,
While his enkindled eyes, with level glance
Beneath his white soft temples, stedfast kept
Trembling with light upon Mnemosyne.
Soon wild commotions shook him, and made flush
125 All the immortal fairness of his limbs;
Most like the struggle at the gate of death;
Or liker still to one who should take leave
Of pale immortal death, and with a pang
As hot as death's is chill, with fierce convulse
130 Die into life: so young Apollo anguish'd:
His very hair, his golden tresses famed
Kept undulation round his eager neck.
During the pain Mnemosyne upheld
Her arms as one who prophesied.—At length
135 Apollo shriek'd;—and lo! from all his limbs
Celestial. . . .

from the *Indicator* (28 June 1820)

A Dream
After Reading Dante's Episode of
Paulo and Francesca[1]

As Hermes once took to his feathers light,
 When lulled Argus, baffled, swoon'd and slept,
So on a Delphic reed my idle spright
So play'd, so charm'd, so conquer'd, so bereft
5 The dragon world of all its hundred eyes;
And, seeing it asleep, so fled away—
Not unto Ida with its snow-cold skies,
Nor unto Tempe where Jove griev'd a day;
But to that second circle of sad hell,
10 Where 'mid the gust, the world-wind, and the flaw
Of rain and hailstones, lovers need not tell
Their sorrows. Pale were the sweet lips I saw,
Pale were the lips I kiss'd, and fair the form
I floated with about that melancholy storm.[2]

from the *Plymouth and Devonport Weekly Journal* (1838)

On Sitting Down to Read King Lear Once Again[3]

O golden tongued Romance, with serene lute!
 Fair plumed Syren, Queen of far-away!
Leave melodizing on this wintry day,

---

[1] Keats described the dream, and copied out the poem, in a letter to George and Georgiana, April 1819 (*Letters* 2: 91). For a version of the story of Paolo and Francesca, see Leigh Hunt, *The Story of Rimini* 3.504–608.*

[2] signed "Caviare."

[3] written on 22 January 1818, while revising *Endymion: A Poetic Romance* (cf. line 1). Keats described the writing of the poem in letters to Benjamin Bailey, 23 January 1818 (*Letters* 1: 212), and to his brothers, 23–24 January 1818 (*Letters* 1: 214).

Shut up thine olden pages, and be mute:
Adieu! for, once again, the fierce dispute
    Betwixt damnation and impassion'd clay
    Must I burn through; once more humbly assay
The bitter-sweet of this Shakesperian fruit:
Chief Poet! and ye clouds of Albion,[1]
    Begetters of our deep eternal theme!
When through the old oak Forest I am gone,
    Let me not wander in a barren dream,
But, when I am consumed in the fire,
Give me new Phœnix[2] wings to fly at my desire.

Bright star, would I were stedfast as thou art[3]

Bright star, would I were stedfast as thou art—[4]
    Not in lone splendour hung aloft the night
And watching, with eternal lids apart,[5]
    Like nature's patient, sleepless Eremite,
The moving waters at their priestlike task
    Of pure ablution round earth's human shores,
Or gazing on the new soft-fallen mask
    Of snow upon the mountains and the moors—
No—yet still stedfast, still unchangeable,
    Pillow'd upon my fair love's ripening breast,
To feel for ever its soft fall and swell,
    Awake for ever in a sweet unrest,
Still, still to hear her tender-taken breath,
And so live ever—or else swoon to death.

---

[1] England.

[2] a mythical Egyptian bird which is consumed by fire, and then reborn, once every 500 years.

[3] written in 1819.

[4] Cf. Shakespeare, *Julius Cæsar* 3.1.58–62.

[5] In 1818, Keats had remarked that the scenery of the Lake District "refine[s] one's sensual vision into a sort of north star which can never cease to be open lidded and stedfast over the wonders of the great Power" (*Letters* 1: 299).

from *Life, Letters, and Literary Remains of John Keats*, ed. Richard Monkton Milnes (1848)

Ode on Indolence[6]

"They toil not, neither do they spin."[7]

1

One morn before me were three figures seen,
    With bowed necks, and joined hands, side-faced;
And one behind the other stepp'd serene,
    In placid sandals, and in white robes graced;
They pass'd, like figures on a marble urn,
    When shifted round to see the other side;
        They came again; as when the urn once more
Is shifted round, the first seen shades return;
    And they were strange to me, as may betide
        With vases, to one deep in Phidian lore.[8]

2

How is it, Shadows! that I knew ye not?
    How came ye muffled in so hush a mask?
Was it a silent deep-disguised plot
    To steal away, and leave without a task
My idle days? Ripe was the drowsy hour;
    The blissful cloud of summer-indolence
        Benumb'd my eyes; my pulse grew less and less;
Pain had no sting, and pleasure's wreath no flower:
    O, why did ye not melt, and leave my sense
        Unhaunted quite of all but—nothingness?

3

A third time pass'd they by, and, passing, turn'd
    Each one the face a moment whiles to me;
Then faded, and to follow them I burn'd
    And ached for wings, because I knew the three;
The first was a fair Maid, and Love her name;

---

[6] Keats described the mood of indolence that inspired this poem in a letter to George and Georgiana, 19 March 1819 (*Letters* 2: 78–79), in which he also mentioned James Thomson's *The Castle of Indolence* (1748).

[7] Matthew 6.28–29.

[8] Phidias was the 5th-century Athenian sculptor who designed the Elgin marbles.

The second was Ambition, pale of cheek,
    And ever watchful with fatigued eye;
The last, whom I love more, the more of blame
    Is heap'd upon her, maiden most unmeek,—
        I knew to be my demon Poesy.

4

They faded, and, forsooth! I wanted wings:
    O folly! What is Love? and where is it?
And for that poor Ambition! it springs
    From a man's little heart's short fever-fit;[1]
For Poesy!—no,—she has not a joy,—
    At least for me,—so sweet as drowsy noons,
        And evenings steep'd in honied indolence;
O, for an age so shelter'd from annoy,
    That I may never know how change the moons,
        Or hear the voice of busy common-sense!

5

And once more came they by;—alas! wherefore?
    My sleep had been embroider'd with dim dreams;
My soul had been a lawn besprinkled o'er
    With flowers, and stirring shades, and baffled beams:
The morn was clouded, but no shower fell,
    Tho' in her lids hung the sweet tears of May;
        The open casement press'd a new-leaved vine,
Let in the budding warmth and throstle's lay;
    O Shadows! 'twas a time to bid farewell!
        Upon your skirts had fallen no tears of mine.

6

So, ye three Ghosts, adieu! Ye cannot raise
    My head cool-bedded in the flowery grass;
For I would not be dieted with praise,
    A pet-lamb in a sentimental farce![2]
Fade softly from my eyes, and be once more
    In masque-like figures on the dreamy urn;
        Farewell! I yet have visions for the night,
And for the day faint visions there is store;
    Vanish, ye Phantoms! from my idle spright,
        Into the clouds, and never more return!

[1] Cf. Shakespeare, *Macbeth* 3.2.23.
[2] Cf. Keats's letter to Sarah Jeffrey, 9 June 1819 (*Letters* 2: 116).

When I Have Fears That I May Cease To Be[3]

When I have fears that I may cease to be[4]
    Before my pen has glean'd my teeming brain,
Before high piled books, in charact'ry,
    Hold like rich garners the full-ripen'd grain;
When I behold, upon the night's starr'd face,
    Huge cloudy symbols of a high romance,
And think that I may never live to trace
    Their shadows, with the magic hand of chance;
And when I feel, fair creature of an hour![5]
    That I shall never look upon thee more,
Never have relish in the faery power
    Of unreflecting love!—then on the shore
Of the wide world I stand alone, and think
Till Love and Fame to nothingness do sink.

from *Miscellanies of the Philobiblon Society* (1856)

Hyperion, A Vision[6]

CANTO 1

Fanatics have their dreams, wherewith they weave
A paradise for a sect; the savage, too,
From forth the loftiest fashion of his sleep
Guesses at heaven; pity these have not
Traced upon vellum or wild Indian leaf
The shadows of melodious utterance,
But bare of laurel they live, dream, and die;

[3] written in January 1818.

[4] Cf. Milton, "When I consider how my light is spent"; W. Wordsworth, "Song" ("She dwelt among the untrodden ways");* and P.B. Shelley, "To Wordsworth."*

[5] According to Richard Woodhouse, this is the (otherwise unidentified) "Lady whom [Keats] saw for some few moments at Vauxhall" (a London pleasure garden), described in "Fill for me a brimming bowl" (August 1814), and addressed in "Time's sea hath been five years at its slow ebb" (4 February 1818).

[6] begun in July 1819 and abandoned by 21 September 1819; now called "The Fall of Hyperion."

For Poesy alone can tell her dreams,—
With the fine spell of words alone can save
Imagination from the sable chain
And dumb enchantment. Who alive can say,
"Thou art no Poet—may'st not tell thy dreams?"
Since every man whose soul is not a clod
Hath visions and would speak, if he had loved,
And been well nurtured in his mother tongue.
Whether the dream now purposed to rehearse
Be poet's or fanatic's will be known
When this warm scribe, my hand, is in the grave.
    Methought I stood where trees of every clime,
Palm, myrtle, oak, and sycamore, and beech,
With plantane and spice-blossoms, made a screen,
In neighbourhood of fountains (by the noise
Soft-showering in mine ears), and (by the touch
Of scent) not far from roses. Twining round
I saw an arbour with a drooping roof
Of trellis vines, and bells, and larger blooms,
Like floral censers, swinging high in air;
Before its wreathed doorway, on a mound
Of moss, was spread a feast of summer fruits,
Which, nearer seen, seem'd refuse of a meal
By angel tasted or our Mother Eve;[1]
For empty shells were scatter'd on the grass,
And grapestalks but half-bare, and remnants more
Sweet-smelling, whose pure kinds I could not know.
Still was more plenty than the fabled horn[2]
Thrice emptied could pour forth at banqueting,
For Proserpine return'd to her own fields,
Where the white heifers low. And appetite,
More yearning than on earth I ever felt,
Growing within, I ate deliciously,—
And, after not long, thirsted; for thereby
Stood a cool vessel of transparent juice
Sipp'd by the wander'd bee, the which I took,
And pledging all the mortals of the world,
And all the dead whose names are in our lips,
Drank. That full draught is parent of my theme.

No Asian poppy nor elixir fine
Of the soon-fading, jealous, Caliphat,
No poison gender'd in close monkish cell,
To thin the scarlet conclave of old men,[3]
Could so have rapt unwilling life away.
Among the fragrant husks and berries crush'd
Upon the grass, I struggled hard against
The domineering potion, but in vain.
The cloudy swoon came on, and down I sank,
Like a Silenus[4] on an antique vase.
How long I slumber'd 'tis a chance to guess.
When sense of life return'd, I started up
As if with wings; but the fair trees were gone,
The mossy mound and arbour were no more:
I look'd around upon the curved sides
Of an old sanctuary, with roof august,
Builded so high, it seem'd that filmed clouds
Might spread beneath as o'er the stars of heaven.
So old the place was, I remember'd none
The like upon the earth: what I had seen
Of gray cathedrals, buttress'd walls, rent towers,
The superannuations of sunk realms,
Or Nature's rocks toil'd hard in waves and winds,
Seem'd but the faulture of decrepit things
To that eternal domed monument.
Upon the marble at my feet there lay
Store of strange vessels and large draperies,
Which needs had been of dyed asbestos wove,
Or in that place the moth could not corrupt,[5]
So white the linen, so, in some, distinct
Ran imageries from a sombre loom.
All in a mingled heap confused there lay
Robes, golden tongs, censer and chafing-dish,
Girdles, and chains, and holy jewelries.
    Turning from these with awe, once more I raised
My eyes to fathom the space every way:
The emboss'd roof, the silent massy range
Of columns north and south, ending in mist

---

[1] Milton, *Paradise Lost* 5.303–07, 326–28.

[2] the cornucopia of Demeter (Gr.) or Ceres (L.), mother of Proserpine (line 37), who as the bride of Hades spends half the year in the underworld. Cf. Ovid, *Metamorphoses* 5.

[3] Keats considers Muslim rulers (the "Caliphat") and Catholic monks especially prone to use poison. The "scarlet conclave" is the college of cardinals, who elect the Pope.

[4] a drunken satyr, a companion of Bacchus the wine-god.

[5] Cf. Matthew 6.19–20.

85 Of nothing; then to eastward, where black gates
Were shut against the sunrise evermore;
Then to the west I looked, and saw far off
An image, huge of feature as a cloud,
At level of whose feet an altar slept,
90 To be approach'd on either side by steps
And marble balustrade, and patient travail
To count with toil the innumerable degrees.
Towards the altar sober-paced I went,
Repressing haste as too unholy there;
95 And, coming nearer, saw beside the shrine
One ministering; and there arose a flame.
As in midday the sickening east-wind
Shifts sudden to the south, the small warm rain
Melts out the frozen incense from all flowers,
100 And fills the air with so much pleasant health
That even the dying man forgets his shroud;—
Even so that lofty sacrificial fire,
Sending forth Maian[1] incense, spread around
Forgetfulness of everything but bliss,
105 And clouded all the altar with soft smoke;
From whose white fragrant curtains thus I heard
Language pronounced: "If thou canst not ascend
These steps,[2] die on that marble where thou art.
Thy flesh, near cousin to the common dust,
110 Will parch for lack of nutriment; thy bones
Will wither in few years, and vanish so
That not the quickest eye could find a grain
Of what thou now art on that pavement cold.
The sands of thy short life are spent this hour,
115 And no hand in the universe can turn
Thy hourglass, if these gumm'd leaves be burnt
Ere thou canst mount up these immortal steps."
I heard, I look'd: two senses both at once,
So fine, so subtle, felt the tyranny
120 Of that fierce threat and the hard task proposed.
Prodigious seem'd the toil; the leaves were yet
Burning, when suddenly a palsied chill
Struck from the paved level up my limbs,
And was ascending quick to put cold grasp
125 Upon those streams that pulse beside the throat.
I shriek'd, and the sharp anguish of my shriek
Stung my own ears; I strove hard to escape
The numbness, strove to gain the lowest step.
Slow, heavy, deadly was my pace: the cold
130 Grew stifling, suffocating at the heart;
And when I clasp'd my hands I felt them not.
One minute before death my iced foot touch'd
The lowest stair; and, as it touch'd, life seem'd
To pour in at the toes; I mounted up
135 As once fair angels on a ladder flew
From the green turf to heaven.[3] "Holy Power,"
Cried I, approaching near the horned shrine,[4]
"What am I that should so be saved from death?
What am I that another death come not
140 To choke my utterance, sacrilegious, here?"
Then said the veiled shadow: "Thou hast felt
What 'tis to die and live again before
Thy fated hour; that thou hadst power to do so
Is thine own safety; thou hast dated on
145 Thy doom." "High prophetess," said I, "purge off,
Benign, if so it please thee, my mind's film."[5]
"None can usurp this height," return'd that shade,
"But those to whom the miseries of the world
Are misery, and will not let them rest.
150 All else who find a haven in the world,
Where they may thoughtless sleep away their days,
If by a chance into this fane they come,
Rot on the pavement where thou rottedst half."
"Are there not thousands in the world," said I,
155 Encouraged by the sooth voice of the shade,
"Who love their fellows even to the death,
Who feel the giant agony of the world,
And more, like slaves to poor humanity,
Labour for mortal good? I sure should see
160 Other men here, but I am here alone."
"Those whom thou spakest of are no visionaries,"
Rejoin'd that voice; "they are no dreamers weak;
They seek no wonder but the human face,
No music but a happy-noted voice:

---

[1] like the perfume of May-flowers, or (possibly) appropriate for Maia, the mother of Mercury. Cf. Dante, *Purgatorio* 24.145–50.

[2] Cf. Dante, *Purgatorio* 4, 9, 12–13.

[3] Genesis 28.12. Cf. Milton, *Paradise Lost* 3.510–11.

[4] Cf. Exodus 27.2.

[5] Cf. Milton, *Paradise Lost* 3.51–55.

165 They come not here, they have no thought to come;
And thou art here, for thou art less than they.
What benefit canst thou do, or all thy tribe,
To the great world? thou art a dreaming thing,
A fever of thyself: think of the earth;
170 What bliss, even in hope, is there for thee?
What haven? every creature hath its home,
Every sole man hath days of joy and pain,
Whether his labours be sublime or low—
The pain alone, the joy alone, distinct:
175 Only the dreamer venoms all his days,
Bearing more woe than all his sins deserve.
Therefore, that happiness be somewhat shared,
Such things as thou art are admitted oft
Into like gardens thou didst pass erewhile,
180 And suffer'd in these temples: for that cause
Thou standest safe beneath this statue's knees."
"That I am favour'd for unworthiness,
By such propitious parley medicined
In sickness not ignoble, I rejoice,
185 Aye, and could weep for love of such award."
So answer'd I, continuing, "If it please,[1]
Majestic shadow, tell me where I am,
Whose altar this, for whom this incense curls;
What image this whose face I cannot see
190 For the broad marble knees; and who thou art,
Of accent feminine, so courteous?"
    Then the tall shade, in drooping linen veil'd,
Spoke out, so much more earnest, that her breath
Stirr'd the thin folds of gauze that drooping hung
195 About a golden censer from her hand
Pendent; and by her voice I knew she shed
Long-treasured tears. "This temple, sad and lone,
Is all spared from the thunder of a war
Foughten long since by giant hierarchy
200 Against rebellion: this old image here,
Whose carved features wrinkled as he fell,
Is Saturn's; I, Moneta,[2] left supreme,
Sole goddess of this desolation."
I had no words to answer, for my tongue,
205 Useless, could find about its roofed home
No syllable of a fit majesty
To make rejoinder to Moneta's mourn:
There was a silence, while the altar's blaze
Was fainting for sweet food. I look'd thereon,
210 And on the paved floor, where nigh were piled
Faggots of cinnamon, and many heaps
Of other crisped spicewood: then again
I look'd upon the altar, and its horns
Whiten'd with ashes, and its languorous flame,
215 And then upon the offerings again;
And so, by turns, till sad Moneta cried:
"The sacrifice is done, but not the less
Will I be kind to thee for thy good will.
My power, which to me is still a curse,
220 Shall be to thee a wonder; for the scenes
Still swooning vivid through my globed brain,

---

[1] Between lines 186 and 187 the manuscript contains the following twenty-four lines, cancelled (apparently in accordance with Keats's wishes) in the first publication:
    Majestic shadow, tell me: sure not all
    Those melodies sung into the world's ear
    Are useless: sure a poet is a sage;
    A humanist, physician to all men.
    That I am none I feel, as vultures feel
    They are no birds when eagles are abroad.
    What am I then? Thou spakest of my tribe:
    What tribe?"—The tall shade veil'd in drooping white
    Then spake, so much more earnest, that the breath
    Mov'd the thin linen folds that drooping hung
    About a golden censer from the hand
    Pendent.—"Art thou not of the dreamer tribe?
    The poet and the dreamer are distinct,
    Diverse, sheer opposite, antipodes.
    The one pours out a balm upon the world,
    The other vexes it." Then shouted I
    Spite of myself, and with a Pythia's spleen,
    "Apollo! faded, far flown Apollo!
    Where is thy misty pestilence to creep
    Into the dwellings, through the door crannies,
    Of all mock lyrists, large self worshipers,
    And careless hectorers in proud bad verse.
    Though I breathe death with them it will be life
    To see them sprawl before me into graves.
The Pythia or Pythian was the priestess of Apollo, who, as the god of medicine as well as of poetry, could punish humanity with pestilences (he does so in the *Iliad*). The last lines are usually read as an attack on Hunt,* W. Wordsworth,* and Byron,* respectively.

[2] the mother of the Muses. The name is also a surname of Juno; it means "she who warns" or "she who admonishes." The character is also called Mnemosyne (Gr. "Memory") 1.307, 2.51. Saturn, the king of the Titans, was overthrown by his son Jupiter.

With an electral changing misery,
Thou shalt with these dull mortal eyes behold
Free from all pain, if wonder pain thee not."
225 As near as an immortal's sphered words
Could to a mother's soften were these last:
And yet I had a terror of her robes,
And chiefly of the veils that from her brow
Hung pale, and curtain'd her in mysteries,
230 That made my heart too small to hold its blood.
This saw that Goddess, and with sacred hand
Parted the veils. Then saw I a wan face,
Not pined by human sorrows, but bright-blanch'd
By an immortal sickness which kills not;
235 It works a constant change, which happy death
Can put no end to; deathwards progressing
To no death was that visage; it had past
The lily and the snow; and beyond these
I must not think now, though I saw that face.
240 But for her eyes I should have fled away;
They held me back with a benignant light,
Soft, mitigated by divinest lids
Half-closed, and visionless entire they seem'd
Of all external things; they saw me not,
245 But in blank splendour beam'd, like the mild moon,
Who comforts those she sees not, who knows not
What eyes are upward cast. As I had found
A grain of gold upon a mountain's side,
And, twinged with avarice, strain'd out my eyes
250 To search its sullen entrails rich with ore,
So, at the view of sad Moneta's brow,
I asked to see what things the hollow brow
Behind environed: what high tragedy
In the dark secret chambers of her skull
255 Was acting, that could give so dread a stress
To her cold lips, and fill with such a light
Her planetary eyes, and touch her voice
With such a sorrow? "Shade of Memory!"
Cried I, with act adorant at her feet,
260 "By all the gloom hung round thy fallen house,
By this last temple, by the golden age,
By great Apollo, thy dear foster-child,
And by thyself, forlorn divinity,
The pale Omega[1] of a wither'd race,
265 Let me behold, according as thou saidst,
What in thy brain so ferments to and fro!"
No sooner had this conjuration past
My devout lips, than side by side we stood
(Like a stunt bramble by a solemn pine)
270 Deep in the shady sadness of a vale[2]
Far sunken from the healthy breath of morn,
Far from the fiery noon and eve's one star.
Onward I look'd beneath the gloomy boughs,
And saw what first I thought an image huge,
275 Like to the image pedestall'd so high
In Saturn's temple; then Moneta's voice
Came brief upon mine ear. "So Saturn sat
When he had lost his realms"; whereon there grew
A power within me of enormous ken
280 To see as a god sees, and take the depth
Of things as nimbly as the outward eye
Can size and shape pervade. The lofty theme
Of those few words hung vast before my mind
With half-unravell'd web. I sat myself
285 Upon an eagle's watch, that I might see,
And seeing ne'er forget. No stir of life
Was in this shrouded vale,—not so much air
As in the zoning of a summer's day
Robs not one light seed from the feathered grass;
290 But where the dead leaf fell there did it rest.
A stream went noiseless by, still deaden'd more
By reason of the fallen divinity
Spreading more shade; the Naiad[3] 'mid her reeds
Prest her cold finger closer to her lips.
295 　Along the margin-sand large foot-marks went
No further than to where old Saturn's feet
Had rested, and there slept how long a sleep!
Degraded, cold, upon the sodden ground
His old right hand lay nerveless, listless, dead,
300 Unsceptred, and his realmless eyes were closed;
While his bowed head seem'd listening to the Earth,
His ancient mother, for some comfort yet.[4]

---

[1] the final letter in the Greek alphabet.

[2] the first line of *Hyperion*,* of which the rest of the poem is a revision.

[3] a river-nymph.

[4] Heaven was the father and Earth was the mother of the Titans.

It seem'd no force could wake him from his place;
But there came one who, with a kindred hand,
305 Touch'd his wide shoulders, after bending low
With reverence, though to one who knew it not.
Then came the griev'd voice of Mnemosyne,
And griev'd I hearken'd. "That divinity
Whom thou saw'st step from yon forlornest wood,
310 And with slow pace approach our fallen king,
Is Thea,[1] softest-natured of our brood."
I mark'd the Goddess, in fair statuary[2]
Surpassing wan Moneta by the head,
And in her sorrow nearer woman's tears.
315 There was a list'ning fear in her regard,
As if calamity had but begun;
As if the venom'd clouds of evil days
Had spent their malice, and the sullen rear
Was with its stored thunder labouring up.
320 One hand she press'd upon that aching spot
Where beats the human heart, as if just there,
Though an immortal, she felt cruel pain;
The other upon Saturn's bended neck
She laid, and to the level of his ear
325 Leaning, with parted lips some words she spoke
In solemn tenour and deep organ-tone;
Some mourning words, which in our feeble tongue
Would come in this like accenting; how frail
To that large utterance of the early gods!
330 "Saturn, look up! And for what, poor lost king?
I have no comfort for thee; no, not one;
I cannot say, wherefore thus sleepest thou?[3]
For Heaven is parted from thee, and the Earth
Knows thee not, so afflicted, for a god.
335 The Ocean, too, with all its solemn noise,
Has from thy scepter pass'd; and all the air
Is emptied of thy hoary majesty.
Thy thunder, captious at the new command,
Rumbles reluctant o'er our fallen house;
340 And thy sharp lightning, in unpracticed hands,
Scourges and burns our once serene domain.
With such remorseless speed still come new woes,

That unbelief has not a space to breathe.
Saturn! sleep on: me thoughtless, why should I
345 Thus violate thy slumber's solitude?
Why should I ope thy melancholy eyes?
Saturn! sleep on, while at thy feet I weep."
As when upon a tranced summer-night
Forests, branch-charmed by the earnest stars,
350 Dream, and so dream all night without a noise,
Save from one gradual solitary gust
Swelling upon the silence, dying off,
As if the ebbing air had but one wave,
So came these words and went; the while in tears
355 She prest her fair large forehead to the earth,
Just where her fallen hair might spread in curls
A soft and silken net for Saturn's feet.
Long, long these two were postured motionless,
Like sculpture builded-up upon the grave
360 Of their own power. A long awful time
I look'd upon them: still they were the same;
The frozen God still bending to the earth,
And the sad Goddess weeping at his feet;
Moneta silent. Without stay or prop
365 But my own weak mortality, I bore
The load of this eternal quietude,
The unchanging gloom and the three fixed shapes
Ponderous upon my senses, a whole moon;
For by my burning brain I measured sure
370 Her silver seasons shedded on the night,
And every day by day methought I grew
More gaunt and ghostly. Oftentimes I pray'd
Intense, that death would take me from the vale
And all its burthens; gasping with despair
375 Of change, hour after hour I cursed myself,
Until old Saturn raised his faded eyes,
And look'd around and saw his kingdom gone,
And all the gloom and sorrow of the place,
And that fair kneeling goddess at his feet.
380 As the moist scent of flowers, and grass, and leaves,
Fills forest-dells with a pervading air,
Known to the woodland nostril, so the words
Of Saturn fill'd the mossy glooms around,
Even to the hollows of time-eaten oaks,
385 And to the windings of the foxes' hole,
With sad, low tones, while thus he spoke, and sent

---

[1] the sister and consort of Hyperion.

[2] height, statuesqueness.

[3] Cf. Milton, *Paradise Lost* 5.38.

Strange moanings to the solitary Pan.
"Moan, brethren, moan, for we are swallow'd up
And buried from all godlike exercise
Of influence benign on planets pale, 390
And peaceful sway upon man's harvesting,
And all those acts which Deity supreme
Doth ease its heart of love in. Moan and wail;
Moan, brethren, moan; for lo, the rebel spheres
Spin round; the stars their ancient courses keep; 395
Clouds still with shadowy moisture haunt the earth,
Still suck their fill of light from sun and moon;
Still buds the tree, and still the seashores murmur;
There is no death in all the universe,
No smell of death.—There shall be death. Moan, moan; 400
Moan, Cybele,[1] moan; for thy pernicious babes
Have changed a god into an aching palsy.
Moan, brethren, moan, for I have no strength left;
Weak as the reed, weak, feeble as my voice.
Oh! Oh! the pain, the pain of feebleness; 405
Moan, moan, for still I thaw; or give me help;
Throw down those imps, and give me victory.
Let me hear other groans, and trumpets blown
Of triumph calm, and hymns of festival,
From the gold peaks of heaven's high-piled clouds; 410
Voices of soft proclaim, and silver stir
Of strings in hollow shells; and there shall be
Beautiful things made new, for the surprise
Of the sky-children." So he feebly ceased,
With such a poor and sickly-sounding pause, 415
Methought I heard some old man of the earth
Bewailing earthly loss; nor could my eyes
And ears act with that unison of sense
Which marries sweet sound with the grace of form,
And dolorous accent from a tragic harp 420
With large-limb'd visions. More I scrutiniz'd.
Still fixt he sat beneath the sable trees,
Whose arms spread straggling in wild serpent forms,
With leaves all hush'd; his awful presence there
(Now all was silent) gave a deadly lie 425
  To what I erewhile heard: only his lips
Trembled amid the white curls of his beard;
They told the truth, though round the snowy locks
Hung nobly, as upon the face of heaven
A mid-day fleece of clouds. Thea arose, 430
And stretcht her white arm through the hollow dark,
Pointing some whither: whereat he too rose,
Like a vast giant, seen by men at sea
To grow pale from the waves at dull midnight.
They melted from my sight into the woods; 435
Ere I could turn, Moneta cried, "These twain
Are speeding to the families of grief,
Where, rooft in by black rocks, they waste in pain
And darkness, for no hope." And she spake on,
As ye may read who can unwearied pass 440
Onward from the antechamber of this dream,
Where, even at the open doors, awhile
I must delay, and glean my memory
Of her high phrase—perhaps no further dare.

CANTO 2

"Mortal, that thou mayst understand aright,
I humanize my sayings to thine ear,
Making comparisons of earthly things;[2]
Or thou mightst better listen to the wind,
Whose language is to thee a barren noise, 5
Though it blows legend-laden thro' the trees.
In melancholy realms big tears are shed,
More sorrow like to this, and such like woe,
Too huge for mortal tongue or pen of scribe.
The Titans fierce, reef-hid or prison-bound, 10
Groan for the old allegiance once more,
Listening in their doom for Saturn's voice.
But one of the whole eagle-brood still keeps
His sovereignty, and rule, and majesty:
Blazing Hyperion on his orbed fire 15
Still sits, still snuffs the incense teeming up
From Man to the Sun's God—yet insecure.
For as upon the earth drear prodigies
Fright and perplex,[3] so also shudders he;
Not at dog's howl or gloom-bird's hated screech, 20
Or the familiar visiting of one

---

[1] the consort of Saturn and mother of the Olympian gods ("pernicious babes").

[2] Cf. Milton, *Paradise Lost* 5.571–76.

[3] Cf. Milton, *Paradise Lost* 1.594–600.

Upon the first toll of his passing bell,
Or prophesyings of the midnight lamp;
But horrors, portioned to a giant nerve,
25 Make great Hyperion ache. His palace bright,
Bastioned with pyramids of shining gold,
And touched with shade of bronzed obelisks,
Glares a blood-red thro' all the thousand courts,
Arches, and domes, and fiery galleries;
30 And all its curtains of Aurorian clouds[1]
Flash angerly;[2] when he would taste the wreaths
Of incense breathed aloft from sacred hills
Instead of sweets, his ample palate takes
Savour of poisonous brass and metal rich;
35 Wherefore when harbour'd in the sleepy West,
After the full completion of fair day,
For rest divine upon exalted couch,
And slumber in the arms of melody,
He paces through the pleasant hours of ease,
40 With strides colossal,[3] on from hall to hall,
While far within each aisle and deep recess
His winged minions in close clusters stand
Amazed, and full of fear; like anxious men,
Who on a wide plain gather in sad troops,
45 When earthquakes jar their battlements and towers.
Even now where Saturn, roused from icy trance,
Goes step for step with Thea from yon woods,
Hyperion, leaving twilight in the rear,
Is sloping to the threshold of the West.
50 Thither we tend." Now in clear light I stood,
Relieved from the dusk vale. Mnemosyne
Was sitting on a square-edg'd polish'd stone,
That in its lucid depth reflected pure
Her priestess' garments.[4] My quick eye ran on
55 From stately nave to nave, from vault to vault,
Through bow'rs of fragrant and enwreathed light,
And diamond-paned lustrous long arcades.

Anon rush'd by the bright Hyperion,
His flaming robes stream'd out beyond his heels,
60 And gave a river as if of earthly fire,
That scared away the meek ethereal hours,
And made their dove-wings tremble. On he flared[5]

from *Poetical Works of John Keats* (1898)

This living hand, now warm and capable[6]

This living hand, now warm and capable
Of earnest grasping, would, if it were cold
And in the icy silence of the tomb,
So haunt thy days and chill thy dreaming nights
5 That thou would wish thine own heart dry of blood,
So in my veins red life might stream again,
And thou be conscience-calm'd. See, here it is—
I hold it towards you.

Letters[7]

To Benjamin Bailey[8]

22 November 1817

My dear Bailey,
I will get over the first part of this (*unsaid*)[9] Letter as soon as possible for it relates to the affair of poor Crips[10]—To a Man of your nature, such a letter as Haydon's must have been extremely cutting—What occasions the greater part of the World's Quarrels? Simply this, two Minds meet and do not understand each other time enough to p[r]aevent any shock or surprise at the

---

[1] dawn clouds, from Aurora, goddess of the dawn.

[2] Cf. W. Wordsworth, *The Excursion** 2.834–81.

[3] The Colossus, a statue of the sun-god Helios which bestrode the harbour of Rhodes, was one of the seven wonders of the classical world. Cf. Shakespeare, *Julius Cæsar* 1.2.135–36, and P.B. Shelley, "Ozymandias."*

[4] Cf. Dante, *Purgatorio* 9.94–96.

[5] Cf. Milton, *Paradise Lost* 2.940.

[6] written in November or December 1819.

[7] from *The Letters of John Keats*, ed. Hyder Edward Rollins (1958).

[8] Keats met Bailey (1791–1853) in spring 1817, when the latter was studying divinity at Oxford.

[9] a play on the legal use of "said."

[10] Charles Cripps (b. 1796), a pupil of Keats's friend Benjamin Robert Haydon (1786–1846), a painter.

conduct of either party—As soon as I had known Haydon three days I had got enough of his character not to have been surp[r]ised at such a Letter as he has hurt you with. Nor when I knew it was it a principle with me to drop his acquaintance although with you it would have been an imperious feeling. I wish you knew all that I think about Genius and the Heart—and yet I think you are thoroughly acquainted with my innermost breast in that respect or you could not have known me even thus long and still hold me worthy to be your dear friend. In passing however I must say of one thing that has pressed upon me lately and encreased my Humility and capability of submission and that is this truth— Men of Genius are great as certain ethereal Chemicals operating on the Mass of neutral intellect—by [*for* but] they have not any individuality, any determined Character. I would call the top and head of those who have a proper self Men of Power—

But I am running my head into a Subject which I am certain I could not do justice to under five years s[t]udy and 3 vols octavo—and moreover long to be talking about the Imagination—so my dear Bailey do not think of this unpleasant affair if possible—do not—I defy any ha[r]m to come of it—I defy—I'll shall write to Crips this Week and reque[s]t him to tell me all his goings on from time to time by Letter wherever I may be—it will all go on well—so don't because you have suddenly discover'd a Coldness in Haydon suffer yourself to be teased. Do not my dear fellow. O I wish I was as certain of the end of all your troubles as that of your momentary start about the authenticity of the Imagination. I am certain of nothing but of the holiness of the Heart's affections and the truth of Imagination—What the imagination seizes as Beauty must be truth[1]—whether it existed before or not—for I have the same Idea of all our Passions as of Love they are all in their sublime, creative of essential Beauty—In a Word, you may know my favorite Speculation by my first Book and the little song I sent in my last[2]—which is a representation from the fancy of the probable mode of operating in these Matters—The Imagination may be compared to Adam's dream—he awoke and found it truth.[3] I am the more zealous in this affair, because I have never yet been able to perceive how any thing can be known for truth by consequitive reasoning—and yet it must be—Can it be that even the greatest Philosopher ever arrived at his goal without putting aside numerous objections—However it may be, O for a Life of Sensations rather than of Thoughts! It is 'a Vision in the form of Youth' a Shadow of reality to come—and this consideration has further conv[i]nced me for it has come as auxiliary to another favorite Speculation of mine, that we shall enjoy ourselves here after by having what we called happiness on Earth repeated in a finer tone and so repeated—And yet such a fate can only befall those who delight in sensation rather than hunger as you do after Truth—Adam's dream will do here and seems to be a conviction that Imagination and its empyreal reflection is the same as human Life and its spiritual repetition. But as I was saying—the simple imaginative Mind may have its rewards in the repeti[ti]on of its own silent Working coming continually on the spirit with a fine suddenness—to compare great things with small[4]—have you never by being surprised with an old Melody—in a delicious place—by a delicious voice, fe[l]t over again your very speculations and surmises at the time it first operated on your soul—do you not remember forming to yourself the singer's face more beautiful that [*for* than] it was possible and yet with the elevation of the Moment you did not think so—even then you were mounted on the Wings of Imagination so high—that the Prototype must be here after—that delicious face you will see—What a time! I am continually running away from the subject—sure this cannot be exactly the case with a complex Mind—one that is imaginative and at the same time careful of its fruits—who would exist partly on sensation partly on thought—to whom it is necessary that years should bring the philosophic Mind[5]—such an one I consider your's and therefore it is necessary to your eternal Happiness that you not only

---

[1] Cf. "Ode on a Grecian Urn" 49.*

[2] The song is "O Sorrow" (*Endymion* * 4.146–81).

[3] Cf. Genesis 2.21-22 and Milton, *Paradise Lost* 8.283–311 and 8.452–90.

[4] Cf. Milton, *Paradise Lost* 2.921–22.

[5] Cf. W. Wordsworth, "Ode" 189.*

have drink this old Wine of Heaven which I shall call the redigestion of our most ethereal Musings on Earth; but also increase in knowledge and know all things. I am glad to hear you are in a fair Way for Easter—you will soon get through your unpleasant reading and then!—but the world is full of troubles and I have not much reason to think myself pesterd with many—I think Jane or Marianne has a better opinion of me than I deserve—for really and truly I do not think my Brothers illness connected with mine[1]—you know more of the real Cause than they do—nor have I any chance of being rack'd as you have been—you perhaps at one time thought there was such a thing as Worldly Happiness to be arrived at, at certain periods of time marked out—you have of necessity from your disposition been thus led away—I scarcely remember counting upon any Happiness—I look not for it if it be not in the present hour—nothing startles me beyond the Moment. The setting sun will always set me to rights—or if a Sparrow come before my Window I take part in its existence and pick about the Gravel. The first thing that strikes me on hea[r]ing a Misfortune having befallen another is this. 'Well it cannot be helped.—he will have the pleasure of trying the resources of his spirit, and I beg now my dear Bailey that hereafter should you observe any thing cold in me not to but [*for* put] it to the account of heartlessness but abstraction—for I assure you I sometimes feel not the influence of a Passion or Affection during a whole week—and so long this sometimes continues I begin to suspect myself and the genuiness of my feelings at other times—thinking them a few barren Tragedy-tears—My Brother Tom is much improved—he is going to Devonshire—whither I shall follow him—at present I am just arrived at Dorking to change the Scene—change the Air and give me a spur to wind up my Poem.[2] Of which there are wanting 500 Lines. I should have been here a day sooner but the Reynoldses persuaded me to stop in Town to meet your friend Christie—There were Rice and Martin—we talked about Ghosts—I will have some talk with Taylor and let you know—when please God I come down a[t] Christmas—I will find that Examiner if possible. My best regards to Gleig—My Brothers to you and Mrs Bentley

      Your affectionate friend
        John Keats

I want to say much more to you—a few hints will set me going
  Direct Burford Bridge near Dorking

To J.H. Reynolds[3]

        22 November 1817
        Saturday

My Dear Reynolds,
There are two things which tease me here—one of them Crips—and the other that I cannot go with Tom into Devonshire—however I hope to do my duty to myself in a week or so; and then Ill try what I can do for my neighbour—now is not this virtuous? on returning to Town—Ill damn all Idleness—indeed, in superabundance of employment, I must not be content to run here and there on little two penny errands—but turn Rakehell i e go a *making* or Bailey will think me just as great a Promise keeper as *he* thinks you—for my self I do not,—and do not remember above one Complaint against you for matter o' that—Bailey writes so abominable a hand, to give his Letter a fair reading requires a little time; so I had not seen when I saw you last, his invitation to Oxford at Christmas—I'll go with you—You know how poorly Rice[4] was—I do not think it was all corporeal—bodily pain was not used to keep him silent. Ill tell you what; he was hurt at what your Sisters said about his joking with your Mother he was, smoothly to sain—It will all blow over. God knows, my Dear Reynolds, I should not talk any sorrow to you—you must have enough vexations—so I won't any more. If I ever start a rueful subject in a Letter to you—blow me! Why dont you—Now I was going to ask a very silly

---

[1] Jane and Marianne Reynolds, Keats's friends, were afraid that he was developing consumption, like his brother Tom (1799–1818). Keats probably contracted the illness while nursing Tom.

[2] *Endymion.*

[3] John Hamilton Reynolds (1794–1852), Keats's friend, a lawyer and poet.

[4] Keats's friend James Rice (1792–1832), a lawyer. He had consumption.

Question neither you nor any body else could answer, under a folio, or at least a Pamphlet—you shall judge—Why dont you, as I do, look unconcerned at what may be called more particularly Heart-vexations? They never surprize me—lord! a man should have the fine point of his soul taken off to become fit for this world—I like this place very much—There is Hill & Dale and a little River—I went up Box hill this Evening after the Moon—you a' seen the Moon—came down—and wrote some lines. Whenever I am separated from you, and not engaged in a continued Poem—every Letter shall bring you a lyric—but I am too anxious for you to enjoy the whole, to send you a particle. One of the three Books I have with me is Shakespear's Poems: I neer found so many beauties in the sonnets—they seem to be full of fine things said unintentionally—in the intensity of working out conceits—Is this to be borne? Hark ye!

> When lofty trees I see barren of leaves
> Which erst from heat did canopy the herd,
> And Summer's green all girded up in sheaves,
> Borne on the bier with white and bristly beard.[1]

He has left nothing to say about nothing or any thing: for look at Snails, you know what he says about Snails, you know where he talks about "cockled snails"[2]—well, in one of these sonnets, he says—the chap slips into—no! I lie! This is in the Venus and Adonis: the Simile brought it to my Mind.

> Audi[3]—As the snail, whose tender horns being hit,
>   Shrinks back into his shelly cave with pain,
>   And there all smothered up in shade doth sit,
>   Long after fearing to put forth again:
>   So at his blody view her eyes are fled,
>   Into the deep dark Cabins of her head.[4]

He overwhelms a genuine Lover of Poesy with all manner of abuse, talking about—

> "a poets rage
> And stretched metre of an antique song"—[5]

Which by the by will be a capital Motto for my Poem—wont it?—He speaks too of "Time's antique pen"—and "aprils first born flowers"—and "deaths eternal cold"[6]—By the Whim King! I'll give you a Stanza, because it is not material in connection and when I wrote it I wanted you to——give your vote, pro or con.—

> Christalline Brother of the Belt of Heaven,
> Aquarius! To whom King Jove ha'th given
> Two liquid pulse streams! s'tead of feather'd wings—
> Two fan like fountains—thine illuminings
> For Dian play:
> Dissolve the frozen purity of air;
> Let thy white shoulders silvery and bare
> Show cold through watery pinions: make more bright
> The Star-Queen's Crescent on her marriage night:
> Haste Haste away!—[7]

Now I hope I shall not fall off in the winding up,—as the Woman said to the——I mean up and down. I see there is an advertizement in the chronicle to Poets—he is so overloaded with poems on the late Princess.[8]—I suppose you do not lack—send me a few—lend me thy hand to laugh a little—send me a little pullet sperm, a few finch eggs[9]—and remember me to each of our Card playing Club—when you die you will all be turned into Dice, and be put in pawn with the Devil—for Cards they crumple up like any King[10]—I mean John in the stage play what pertains Prince Arthur—I rest

                Your affectionate friend
                John Keats

Give my love to both houses—hinc atque illinc.[11]

---

[1] Shakespeare, Sonnet 12, lines 5–8.

[2] Shakespeare, *Love's Labours Lost* 4.3.333.

[3] "Hear" (L.).

[4] Shakespeare, *Venus and Adonis* 1033–38.

[5] Shakespeare, Sonnet 17, lines 11–12. Keats used line 12 as the epigraph for *Endymion.**

[6] Shakespeare, Sonnet 19, line 10; Sonnet 21, line 7; Sonnet 13, line 12.

[7] *Endymion* 4.581–90.

[8] Princess Charlotte, the only child of the Prince of Wales, had died in childbirth on 6 November (the child was stillborn). The event led to nationwide mourning (e.g., Byron,* *Childe Harold's Pilgrimage* 4.167–72).

[9] Cf. Shakespeare, *1 Henry IV* 2.4.1–2, *The Merry Wives of Windsor* 3.5.27, *Troilus and Cressida* 5.1.35.

[10] Shakespeare, *King John* 5.7.31.

[11] "on this side and on that" (L.). Cf. Shakespeare, *Romeo and Juliet* 3.1.89, 97–98, 104, 106; Virgil, *Georgics* 3.257.

To George and Tom Keats[1]

21, 27 (?) December 1817
Hampstead Sunday
22 December 1818[2]

My dear Brothers

I must crave your pardon for not having written ere this & & I saw Kean[3] return to the public in Richard III, & finely he did it, & at the request of Reynolds I went to criticise his Luke in Riches—the critique is in todays champion,[4] which I send you with the Examiner in which you will find very proper lamentation on the obsoletion of christmas Gambols & pastimes:[5] but it was mixed up with so much egotism of that drivelling nature that pleasure is entirely lost. Hone the publisher's trial, you must find very amusing; & as Englishmen very encouraging—his *Not Guilty* is a thing, which not to have been, would have dulled still more Liberty's Emblazoning—Lord Ellenborough has been paid in his own coin—Wooler & Hone have done us an essential service[6]—I have had two very pleasant evenings with Dilke[7] yesterday & today; & am at this moment just come from him & feel in the humour to go on with this, began in the morning, & from which he came to fetch me. I spent Friday evening with Wells[8] & went the next morning to see *Death on the Pale horse*.[9] It is a wonderful picture, when West's age is considered; But there is nothing to be intense upon; no women one feels mad to kiss; no face swelling into reality. the excellence of every Art is its intensity, capable of making all disagreeables evaporate, from their being in close relationship with Beauty & Truth—Examine King Lear & you will find this examplified throughout; but in this picture we have unpleasantness without any momentous depth of speculation excited, in which to bury its repulsiveness—The picture is larger than Christ rejected[10]—I dined with Haydon the sunday after you left, & had a very pleasant day, I dined too (for I have been out too much lately) with Horace Smith & met his two brothers[11] with Hill & Kingston & one Du Bois, they only served to convince me, how superior humour is to wit in respect to enjoyment—These men say things which make one start, without making one feel, they are all alike; their manners are alike; they all know fashionables; they have a mannerism in their very eating & drinking, in their mere handling a Decanter—They talked of Kean & his low company—Would I were with that company instead of yours said I to myself! I know such like acquaintance will never do for me & yet I am going to Reynolds, on wednesday—Brown[12] & Dilke walked with me & back from the Christmas pantomime.[13] I had not a dispute but a disquisition with Dilke, on various subjects; several things dovetailed in my mind, & at once it struck me, what quality went to form a Man of Achievement especially in Literature & which Shakespeare posessed so enormously—I mean *Negative Capability*, that is when man is capable of being in uncertainties, Mysteries, doubts, without any irritable reaching after fact & reason—Coleridge, for instance, would let go by a fine isolated verisimilitude

---

[1] Keats's brothers George (1797–1841) and Tom (1799–1818) had been living together since 1816.

[2] probably misdated by the copyist.

[3] Edmund Kean (1787–1833), Shakespearean actor. Among his famous roles were the lead in Shakespeare's *Richard III* and Luke in *Riches*, an adaptation of Massinger's *The City Madam*.

[4] The *Champion* was a newspaper, for which Keats reviewed Kean's performance on 21 December 1817.

[5] Leigh Hunt,* "Christmas and Other Old National Merry-Makings Considered." Hunt was editor of the *Examiner*.

[6] Hone* and Thomas Wooler (1786?–1853) were radical publishers who had recently been acquitted of blasphemous libel. The conservative Lord Chief Justice Ellenborough (1750–1818) had presided over Hone's trials, which were popularly believed to have killed him.

[7] Charles Wentworth Dilke (1789–1864), Keats's friend, a civil servant.

[8] Charles Jeremiah Wells (c. 1800–79), Tom's former schoolmate and Keats's friend.

[9] a painting by the American Benjamin West (1738–1820), based on the vision of Death in Revelation 6.8.

[10] a painting exhibited by West in 1814.

[11] Horace Smith* and his brothers James (1775–1839) and Leonard (1778–1837).

[12] Charles Armitage Brown (1787–1842), Keats's friend and housemate.

[13] *Harlequin's Vision; or, The Feast of the Statue*.

caught from the Penetralium[1] of mystery, from being incapable of remaining content with half knowledge. This pursued through Volumes would perhaps take us no further than this, that with a great poet the sense of Beauty overcomes every other consideration, or rather obliterates all consideration.

Shelley's poem is out & there are words about its being objected too, as much as Queen Mab was.[2] Poor Shelley I think he has his Quota of good qualities, in sooth la!![3] Write soon to your most sincere friend & affectionate Brother

John

To J.H. Reynolds

3 February 1818
Hampstead Tuesday.

My dear Reynolds,

I thank you for your dish of Filberts[4]—Would I could get a basket of them by way of desert every day for the sum of two pence—Would we were a sort of ethereal Pigs, & turn'd loose to feed upon spiritual Mast & Acorns—which would be merely being a squirrel & feed upon filberts. For what is a squirrel but an airy pig, or a filbert but a sort of archangelical acorn. About the nuts being worth cracking, all I can say is that where there are a throng of delightful Images ready drawn simplicity is the only thing. The first is the best on account of the first line, and the "arrow—foil'd of its antler'd food"— and moreover (and this is the only word or two I find fault with, the more because I have had so much reason to shun it as a quicksand) the last has "tender and true"—We must cut this, and not be rattlesnaked into any more of the like—It may be said that we ought to read our Contemporaries. that Wordsworth &c should have their due from us. but for the sake of a few fine imaginative or domestic passages, are we to be bullied into a certain Philosophy engendered in the whims of an Egotist—Every man has his speculations, but every man does not brood and peacock over them till he makes a false coinage and deceives himself—Many a man can travel to the very bourne of Heaven,[5] and yet want confidence to put down his halfseeing. Sancho[6] will invent a Journey heavenward as well as any body. We hate poetry that has a palpable design upon us—and if we do not agree, seems to put its hand in its breeches pocket. Poetry should be great & unobtrusive, a thing which enters into one's soul, and does not startle it or amaze it with itself but with its subject.—How beautiful are the retired flowers! how they would lose their beauty were they to throng into the highway crying out, "admire me I am a violet! dote upon me I am a primrose! Modern poets differ from the Elizabethans in this. Each of the moderns like an Elector of Hanover governs his petty state, & knows how many straws are swept daily from the Causeways in all his dominions & has a continual itching that all the Housewives should have their coppers well scoured: the antients were Emperors of vast Provinces, they had only heard of the remote ones and scarcely cared to visit them.—I will cut all this—I will have no more of Wordsworth or Hunt in particular—Why should we be of the tribe of Manasseh when we can wander with Esau?[7] why should we kick against the Pricks,[8] when we can walk on Roses? Why

---

[1] the innermost part of a building, especially a temple (L.); the word is usually used in the plural, "penetralia."

[2] P.B. Shelley* was forced to expurgate the treatment of sibling incest in *Laon and Cythna* (1817); the expurgated version is entitled *The Revolt of Islam*. His earlier epic *Queen Mab* (1813) was unpublishable because of its outspoken atheism and republicanism.

[3] Cf. Shakespeare, *Antony and Cleopatra* 4.4.8.

[4] Reynolds had sent Keats two sonnets on Robin Hood, by the twopenny post.

[5] Cf. Shakespeare, *Hamlet* 3.1.79–80.

[6] Sancho Panza, the practical squire of Cervantes' *Don Quixote*.

[7] For Manasseh, see Judges 6.15 and 7.23; for Esau, Genesis 25.29–34.

[8] Cf. Acts 9.5 and 26.14.

should we be owls, when we can be Eagles? Why be teased with "nice Eyed wagtails,"[1] when we have in sight "the Cherub Contemplation"?[2]—Why with Wordsworths "Matthew with a bough of wilding in his hand"[3] when we can have Jacques "under an oak &c"[4]—The secret of the Bough of Wilding will run through your head faster than I can write it—Old Matthew spoke to him some years ago on some nothing, & because he happens in an Evening Walk to imagine the figure of the old man—he must stamp it down in black & white, and it is henceforth sacred—I don't mean to deny Wordsworth's grandeur & Hunt's merit, but I mean to say we need not be teased with grandeur & merit—when we can have them uncontaminated & unobtrusive. Let us have the old Poets, & robin Hood Your letter and its sonnets gave me more pleasure than will the 4th Book of Childe Harold & the whole of any body's life & opinions.[5] In return for your dish of filberts, I have gathered a few Catkins, I hope they'll look pretty.

 To J.H.R. In answer to his Robin Hood Sonnets.
  "No those days are gone away &c"—[6]
I hope you will like them they are at least written in the Spirit of Outlawry.—Here are the Mermaid lines
  "Souls of Poets dead & gone, &c"—
I will call on you at 4 tomorrow, and we will trudge together for it is not the thing to be a stranger in the Land of Harpsicols.[7] I hope also to bring you my 2ᵈ book—In the hope that these Scribblings will be some amusement for you this Evening—I remain copying on the Hill

    Yʳ sincere friend and Coscribbler
      John Keats.

---

[1] Leigh Hunt, *The Nymphs* (1818) 2.169–71.

[2] Milton, "Il Penseroso" 54.

[3] W. Wordsworth, "The Two April Mornings" 59–60.*

[4] Shakespeare, *As You Like It* 2.1.30–32.

[5] The fourth canto of Byron's* *Childe Harold's Pilgrimage* was due out in April 1818.

[6] Keats included two poems ("Robin Hood" and "Lines on the Mermaid Tavern") in his letter to Reynolds; when Richard Woodhouse (our only source for the text) copied out the letter, he included only the first lines.

[7] Keats and Reynolds would be going to a musical evening.

To J.H. Reynolds

3 May 1818
Teignmouth May 3ᵈ

My dear Reynolds.
What I complain of is that I have been in so an uneasy a state of Mind as not to be fit to write to an invalid. I cannot write to any length under a disguised feeling. I should have loaded you with an addition of gloom, which I am sure you do not want. I am now thank God in a humour to give you a good groats worth—for Tom, after a Night without a Wink of sleep, and overburdened with fever, has got up after a refreshing day sleep and is better than he has been for a long time; and you I trust have been again round the Common without any effect but refreshment.—As to the Matter I hope I can say with Sir Andrew "I have matter enough in my head" in your favor[8] And now, in the second place, for I reckon that I have finished my Imprimis, I am glad you blow up the weather—all through your letter there is a leaning towards a climate-curse, and you know what a delicate satisfaction there is in having a vexation anathematized: one would think there has been growing up for these last four thousand years, a grandchild Scion of the old forbidden tree, and that some modern Eve had just violated it; and that there was come with double charge, "Notus and Afer black with thunderous clouds from Sierra-leona"[9]—I shall breathe worsted stockings sooner than I thought for.[10] Tom wants to be in Town—we will have some such days upon the heath like that of last summer and why not with the same book: or what say you to a black Letter Chaucer printed in 1596: aye I've got one huzza! I shall have it bounden gothique a nice somber binding—it will go a little way to unmodernize. And also I see no reason, because I have been away this last month, why I should not have a peep at your Spencerian[11]—notwithstanding you speak of your

---

[8] Cf. Shakespeare, *The Merry Wives of Windsor* 1.1.112 (Keats misattributes the line to Sir Andrew Aguecheek, in *Twelfth Night*).

[9] Milton, *Paradise Lost* 10.702–03.

[10] Keats would be returning to his house in London, where he felt oppressed by the proximity of his landlord's children.

[11] Reynolds's poem "The Romance of Youth."

office, in my thought a little too early, for I do not see why a Mind like yours is not capable of harbouring and digesting the whole Mystery of Law as easily as Parson Hugh does Pepins—which did not hinder him from his poetic Canary[1]—Were I to study physic or rather Medicine again,—I feel it would not make the least difference in my Poetry; when the Mind is in its infancy a Bias is in reality a Bias, but when we have acquired more strength, a Bias becomes no Bias. Every department of knowledge we see excellent and calculated towards a great whole. I am so convinced of this, that I am glad at not having given away my medical Books, which I shall again look over to keep alive the little I know thitherwards; and moreover intend through you and Rice to become a sort of Pip-civilian.[2] An extensive knowledge is needful to thinking people—it takes away the heat and fever; and helps, by widening speculation, to ease the Burden of the Mystery:[3] a thing I begin to understand a little, and which weighed upon you in the most gloomy and true sentence in your Letter. The difference of high Sensations with and without knowledge appears to me this—in the latter case we are falling continually ten thousand fathoms deep and being blown up again[4] without wings and with all [the] horror of a bare shoulderd Creature—in the former case, our shoulders are fledge,[5] and we go thro' the same air and space without fear. This is running one's rigs on the score of abstracted benefit—when we come to human Life and the affections it is impossible how a parallel of breast and head can be drawn—(you will forgive me for thus privately treading out [of] my depth and take it for treading as schoolboys tread the water)—it is impossible to know how far knowledge will console us for the death of a friend and the ill "that flesh is heir to"[6]—With respect to the affections and Poetry you must know by a sympathy my thoughts that way; and I dare say these few lines will be but a ratification: I wrote them on May-day—and intend to finish the ode all in good time.—

    Mother of Hermes! And still youthful Maia!
        May I sing to thee
    As thou wast hymned on the shores of Baiae?
        Or may I woo thee
    In earlier Sicilian? or thy smiles
    Seek as they once were sought, in Grecian isles,
    By Bards who died content in pleasant sward,
    Leaving great verse unto a little clan?
    O give me their old vigour, and unheard,
    Save of the quiet Primrose, and the span
    Of Heaven, and few ears
    Rounded by thee my song should die away
    Content as theirs
    Rich in the simple worship of a day.—

You may be anxious to know for fact to what sentence in your Letter I allude. You say "I fear there is little chance of any thing else in this life." You seem by that to have been going through with a more painful and acute zest the same labyrinth that I have—I have come to the same conclusion thus far. My Branchings out therefrom have been numerous: one of them is the consideration of Wordsworth's genius and as a help, in the manner of gold being the meridian Line of worldly wealth,—how he differs from Milton.—And here I have nothing but surmises, from an uncertainty whether Miltons apparently less anxiety for Humanity proceeds from his seeing further or no than Wordsworth: And whether Wordsworth has in truth epic passion, and martyrs himself to the human heart, the main region of his song[7]—In regard to his genius alone—we find what he says true as far as we have experienced and we can judge no further but by larger experience—for axioms in philosophy are not axioms until they are proved upon our pulses: We read fine—— things but never feel them to thee full until we have gone the same step as the Author.—I know this is not plain; you will know exactly my meaning when I say, that now I shall relish Hamlet more than I ever have done—Or, better—You are sensible no man can set down Venery as a bestial or

---

[1] Cf. Shakespeare, *The Merry Wives of Windsor* 1.2.11 and 2.2.57, 59.

[2] A pip is a seed and a "civilian" is an expert in civil law: with the help of Rice and Reynolds, Keats will become an embryonic lawyer.

[3] W. Wordsworth, "Tintern Abbey" 39.*

[4] Cf. Milton, *Paradise Lost* 2.933–38.

[5] Cf. Milton, *Paradise Lost* 3.627.

[6] Shakespeare, *Hamlet* 3.1.63.

[7] W. Wordsworth, "Prospectus" (1814) 40–41.

joyless thing until he is sick of it and therefore all philosophizing on it would be mere wording. Until we are sick, we understand not;—in fine, as Byron says, "Knowledge is Sorrow";[1] and I go on to say that "Sorrow is Wisdom"—and further for aught we can know for certainty! "Wisdom is folly"[2]—So you see how I have run away from Wordsworth, and Milton; and shall still run away from what was in my head, to observe, that some kind of letters are good squares others handsome ovals, and others some orbicular, others spheroid—and why should there not be another species with two rough edges like a Rat-trap? I hope you will find all my long letters of that species, and all will be well; for by merely touching the spring delicately and ethereally, the rough edged will fly immediately into a proper compactness, and thus you may make a good wholesome loaf, with your own leven in it, of my fragments—If you cannot find this said Rat-trap sufficiently tractable—alas for me, it being an impossibility in grain for my ink to stain otherwise: If I scribble long letters I must play my vagaries. I must be too heavy, or too light, for whole pages—I must be quaint and free of Tropes and figures—I must play my draughts as I please, and for my advantage and your erudition, crown a white with a black, or a black with a white, and move into black or white, far and near as I please—I must go from Hazlitt to Patmore, and make Wordsworth and Coleman play at leap-frog—or keep one of them down a whole half holiday at fly the garter[3]—"From Gray to Gay, from Little to Shakespeare"[4]—Also as a long cause requires two or more sittings of the Court, so a long letter will require two or more sittings of the Breech wherefore I shall resume after dinner.—

Have you not seen a Gull, an orc, a sea Mew,[5] or any thing to bring this Line to a proper length, and also fill up this clear part; that like the Gull I may *dip*—I hope, not out of sight—and also, like a Gull, I hope to be lucky in a good sized fish—This crossing a letter[6] is not without its association—for chequer work leads us naturally to a Milkmaid,[7] a Milkmaid to Hogarth to Shakespeare Shakespear to Hazlitt—Hazlitt to Shakespeare and thus by merely pulling an apron string we set a pretty peal of Chimes at work—Let them chime on while, with your patience,—I will return to Wordsworth—whether or no he has an extended vision or a circumscribed grandeur—whether he is an eagle in his nest, or on the wing—And to be more explicit and to show you how tall I stand by the giant, I will put down a simile of human life as far as I now perceive it; that is, to the point to which I say we both have arrived at— 'Well—I compare human life to a large Mansion of Many Apartments,[8] two of which I can only describe, the doors of the rest being as yet shut upon me—The first we step into we call the infant or thoughtless Chamber, in which we remain as long as we do not think—We remain there a long while, and notwithstanding the doors of the second Chamber remain wide open, showing a bright appearance, we care not to hasten to it; but are at length imperceptibly impelled by the awakening of the thinking principle—within us—we no sooner get into the second Chamber, which I shall call the Chamber of Maiden-Thought, than we become intoxicated with the light and the atmosphere, we see nothing but pleasant wonders, and think of delaying there for ever in delight: However among the effects this breathing is father of is that tremendous one of sharpening one's vision into the heart and nature of Man—of convincing ones nerves that the World is full of Misery and Heartbreak, Pain, Sickness and oppression—whereby This Chamber of Maiden Thought becomes gradually darken'd and at the same time on all

---

[1] Cf. Byron, *Manfred* 1.1.10.*

[2] Cf. Thomas Gray (1716–71), "Ode on a Distant Prospect of Eton College" (1747) 100.

[3] P.G. Patmore (1786–1855) was an author and the friend of Charles Lamb* and Hazlitt;* George Colman the Younger (1762–1836), a playwright. Leap-frog and fly-the-garter are children's games.

[4] Cf. Pope, *An Essay on Man* (1733–34) 4.380. "Thomas Little" was a pseudonym of Thomas Moore.*

[5] Cf. Milton, *Paradise Lost* 11.835.

[6] Keats has crossed his letter: after filling the page, he has turned it ninety degrees and is writing on it the other way, to save paper and postage.

[7] Cf. Milton, "L'Allegro" 65, 96.

[8] Cf. John 14.2 and W. Wordsworth, "Tintern Abbey" 139–41.*

sides of it many doors are set open—but all dark—all leading to dark passages—We see not the ballance of good and evil.[1] We are in a Mist—*We* are now in that state—We feel the "burden of the Mystery," To this point was Wordsworth come, as far as I can conceive when he wrote 'Tintern Abbey' and it seems to me that his Genius is explorative of those dark Passages. Now if we live, and go on thinking, we too shall explore them. He is a Genius and superior [to] us, in so far as he can, more than we, make discoveries, and shed a light in them—Here I must think Wordsworth is deeper than Milton—though I think it has depended more upon the general and gregarious advance of intellect, than individual greatness of Mind—From the Paradise Lost and the other Works of Milton, I hope it is not too presuming, even between ourselves to say, his Philosophy, human and divine, may be tolerably understood by one not much advanced in years, In his time englishmen were just emancipated from a great superstition[2]—and Men had got hold of certain points and resting places in reasoning which were too newly born to be doubted, and too much opposed by the Mass of Europe not to be thought ethereal and authentically divine—who could gainsay his ideas on virtue, vice, and Chastity in Comus,[3] just at the time of the dismissal of Cod-pieces and a hundred other disgraces? Who would not rest satisfied with his hintings at good and evil in the Paradise Lost, when just free from the inquisition and burning in Smithfield?[4] The Reformation produced such immediate and great benefits, that Protestantism was considered under the immediate eye of heaven, and its own remaining Dogmas and superstitions, then, as it were, regenerated, constituted those resting places and seeming sure points of Reasoning—from that I have mentioned, Milton, whatever he may have thought in the sequel, appears to have been content with these by his writings—He did not think into the human heart, as Wordsworth has done—Yet Milton as a Philosopher, had sure as great powers as Wordsworth—What is then to be inferr'd? O many things—It proves there is really a grand march of intellect—, It proves that a mighty providence subdues the mightiest Minds to the service of the time being, whether it be in human Knowledge or Religion—I have often pitied a Tutor who has to hear "Nom^e: Musa"[5]—so often dinn'd into his ears—I hope you may not have the same pain in this scribbling—I may have read these things before, but I never had even a thus dim perception of them: and moreover I like to say my lesson to one who will endure my tediousness for my own sake—After all there is certainly something real in the World—Moore's present to Hazlitt is real—I like that Moore, and am glad I saw him at the Theatre just before I left Town. Tom has spit a leetle blood this afternoon, and that is rather a damper—but I know—the truth is there is something real in the World Your third Chamber of Life shall be a lucky and gentle one—stored with the wine of love—and the Bread of Friendship—When you see George if he should not have reced a letter from me tell him he will find one at home most likely—tell Bailey I hope soon to see him—Remember me to all The leaves have been out here for MONY a day—I have written to George for the first stanzas of my Isabel[6]—I shall have them soon and will copy the whole out for you.

Your affectionate friend
John Keats.

---

[1] Cf. W. Wordsworth, "Prospectus" 8–9.

[2] Catholicism.

[3] Milton's *Comus* (1634) is a masque about an unsuccessful attempt to tempt a Lady into unchastity. Codpieces were pouches for the male genitals, attached to the front of the breeches; they had gone out of fashion by Milton's day.

[4] The Inquisition was a papal judicial institution dedicated to combating heresy (such as Protestantism), witchcraft, and other offenses. Smithfield was a public place of execution, north-west of London; during the reign of Mary I, a Catholic, Protestants were executed there.

[5] "Nominative case: 'musa'" ("muse"): a phrase a Latin teacher would often hear his pupils repeat.

[6] "Isabella; or, The Pot of Basil," a narrative poem based on a tale by Giovanni Boccaccio (1313–75). Keats published it in 1820.

To Richard Woodhouse[1]

27 October 1818

My dear Woodhouse,
Your Letter gave me a great satisfaction; more on account of its friendliness, than any relish of that matter in it which is accounted so acceptable in the 'genus irritabile'[2] The best answer I can give you is in a clerk-like manner to make some observations on two principle points, which seem to point like indices into the midst of the whole pro and con, about genius, and views and atchievements and ambition and cœtera. 1st As to the poetical Character itself, (I mean that sort of which, if I am any thing, I am a Member; that sort distinguished from the wordsworthian or egotistical sublime; which is a thing per se and stands alone)[3] it is not itself—it has no self—it is every thing and nothing—It has no character—it enjoys light and shade; it lives in gusto,[4] be it foul or fair, high or low, rich or poor, mean or elevated—It has as much delight in conceiving an Iago as an Imogen.[5] What shocks the virtuous philosop[h]er, delights the camelion Poet. It does no harm from its relish of the dark side of things any more than from its taste for the bright one; because they both end in speculation. A Poet is the most unpoetical of any thing in existence; because he has no Identity—he is continually in for—and filling some other Body—The Sun, the Moon, the Sea and Men and Women who are creatures of impulse are poetical and have about them an unchangeable attribute—the poet has none; no identity—he is certainly the most unpoetical of all God's Creatures. If then he has no self, and if I am a Poet, where is the Wonder that I should say I would ~~right~~ write no more? Might I not at that very instant [have] been cogitating on the Characters of saturn and Ops?[6] It is a wretched thing to confess; but is a very fact that not one word I ever utter can be taken for granted as an opinion growing out of my identical nature—how can it, when I have no nature? When I am in a room with People if I ever am free from speculating on creations of my own brain, then not myself goes home to myself:[7] but the identity of every one in the room begins to [for so] to press upon me that, I am in a very little time an[ni]hilated—not only among Men; it would be the same in a Nursery of children: I know not whether I make myself wholly understood: I hope enough so to let you see that no dependence is to be placed on what I said that day. In the second place I will speak of my views, and of the life I purpose to myself—I am ambitious of doing the world some good: if I should be spared that may be the work of maturer years—in the interval I will assay to reach to as high a summit in Poetry as the nerve bestowed upon me will suffer. The faint conceptions I have of Poems to come brings the blood frequently into my forehead—All I hope is that I may not lose all interest in human affairs—that the solitary indifference I feel for applause even from the finest Spirits, will not blunt any acuteness of vision I may have. I do not think it will—I feel assured I should write from the mere yearning and fondness I have for the Beautiful even if my night's labours should be burnt every morning and no eye ever shine upon them. But even now I am perhaps not speaking from myself; but from some character in whose soul I now live. I am sure however that this next sentence is from myself. I feel your anxiety, good opinion and friendliness in the highest degree, and am

Your's most sincerely
John Keats

---

[1] Richard Woodhouse (1788–1834), a lawyer. He was also one of the readers for Taylor and Hessey, Keats's publishers.

[2] "the irritable race" (L.) of poets (Horace, *Epistles* 2.2.102). Woodhouse had written to Keats after reading Croker's negative review* of *Endymion* in the *Quarterly Review*.

[3] Cf. Shakespeare, *Troilus and Cressida* 1.2.15–16.

[4] Cf. Hazlitt, "On Gusto."*

[5] Iago is the villain of Shakespeare's tragedy *Othello*; Imogen, the heroine of his late romance *Cymbeline*.

[6] Saturn was the king of the Titans; his consort, Cybele or Ops, was the Titaness of the harvest. See *Hyperion*,* on which Keats was working at this time.

[7] Cf. Shakespeare, *Troilus and Cressida* 3.3.105–07.

To Percy Bysshe Shelley

16 August 1820
Hampstead August 16th

My dear Shelley,
I am very much gratified that you, in a foreign country, and with a mind almost over occupied, should write to me in the strain of the Letter beside me. If I do not take advantage of your invitation it will be prevented by a circumstance I have very much at heart to prophesy[1]— There is no doubt that an english winter would put an end to me, and do so in a lingering hateful manner, therefore I must either voyage or journey to Italy as a soldier marches up to a battery. My nerves at present are the worst part of me, yet they feel soothed when I think that come what extreme may, I shall not be destined to remain in one spot long enough to take a hatred of any four particular bed-posts. I am glad you take any pleasure in my poor Poem;— which I would willingly take the trouble to unwrite, if possible, did I care so much as I have done about Reputation.[2] I received a copy of the Cenci, as from yourself from Hunt. There is only one part of it I am judge of; the Poetry, and dramatic effect, which by many spirits now a days is considered the mammon. A modern work it is said must have a purpose,[3] which may be the God—*an artist* must serve Mammon[4]—he must have "self concentration" selfishness perhaps. You I am sure will forgive me for sincerely remarking that you might curb your magnanimity and be more of an artist, and 'load every rift' of your subject with ore.[5] The thought of such discipline must fall like cold chains upon you, who perhaps never sat with your wings furl'd for six Months together. And is not this extraordina[r]y talk for the writer of Endymion? whose mind was like a pack of scattered cards—I am pick'd up and sorted to a pip. My Imagination is a Monastery and I am its Monk—you must explain my metap^{cs} [*for* metaphysics] to yourself. I am in expectation of Prometheus[6] every day. Could I have my own wish for its interest effected you would have it still in manuscript—or be but now putting an end to the second act. I remember you advising me not to publish my first-blights, on Hampstead heath—I am returning advice upon your hands. Most of the Poems in the volume[7] I send you have been written above two years, and would never have been publish'd but from a hope of gain; so you see I am inclined enough to take your advice now. I must exp[r]ess once more my deep sense of your kindness, adding my sincere thanks and respects for Mrs Shelley. In the hope of soon seeing you <I> remain
most sincerely <yours,>
John Keats—

---

[1] P.B. Shelley had learned of Keats's consumption and invited Keats to spend the winter in Italy (*Letters* 2: 220–21). The "circumstance" that might have prevented Keats from accepting the invitation was his death. Keats did accept the invitation; he died in Rome.

[2] Shelley had praised *Endymion* (1818), which had been harshly reviewed. Shelley later wrote *Adonais** in the belief that these reviews had caused Keats's death.

[3] Cf. W. Wordsworth, Preface to *Lyrical Ballads* (642).*

[4] Cf. Matthew 6.24 and Luke 16.13.

[5] Cf. Spenser, *The Faerie Queene* 2.7.28.

[6] *Prometheus Unbound.** Shelley had instructed his publisher to send Keats all his books.

[7] *Lamia, Isabella, Eve of St. Agnes, and Other Poems* (1820).

John Richardson
1796 – 1852

John Richardson was born at Queenston, Upper Canada (Ontario), in 1796. His father was a medical officer; his mother was the daughter of John Askin, a fur-trader who was probably of Native descent. At fifteen he enlisted in the British army and fought against the Americans in the War of 1812; he was imprisoned in Kentucky for a year and spent 1816–1818 in the British garrisons in the West Indies. Accounts in his later writing of forest warfare, slavery, and military discipline and excess were based on these personal experiences. In 1818 he moved to England; he lived in Paris for a while and, in 1825, married his first wife Jane Marsh (she died a few years later). In 1826, Richardson began a writing career with an anonymous account of his war experiences in the *New Monthly Magazine*. A novel, *Wacousta; or, The Prophecy: a Tale of the Canadas* (1832) remains his best-known and most successful work.

Richardson married his second wife, Maria Caroline Drayson, in 1832. In 1835 he went to Spain to fight with the British Legion (a mercenary force) on the royalist side of a civil conflict. He returned to Canada as foreign correspondent for the London *Times* in 1838, but he was fired for his support of Lord Durham's reform policies. He then published a sequel to *Wacousta* entitled *The Canadian Brothers; or, The Prophecy Fulfilled* (1840), which makes use of his experience as a prisoner-of-war. He started a weekly paper in Brockville (1841–42), in which he published his "Recollection of the West Indies" and a serialized account of his experiences in the War of 1812. When that venture failed, he launched a new journal in Kingston, *The Canadian Loyalist and Spirit of 1812* (1843–44). That too failed. Richardson was then appointed in 1845 as superintendent of police on the Welland Canal: his men were insubordinate and the force had to be disbanded. His wife died in 1846; Richardson's last years in Canada were unhappy and unsettled. He moved to New York about 1850, where he continued to write and publish novels, attempted to adapt *The Canadian Brothers* for an American readership, and died impoverished in 1852. Richardson was the first Canadian-born novelist to achieve international recognition. *Wacousta* was adapted for the stage in the mid-nineteenth century and again in 1979 by the Canadian poet and playwright James Reaney. (A.M.)

JOHN RICHARDSON

from *Tecumseh; or, The Warrior of the West: A Poem, in Four Cantos, with Notes* (1828)[1]

CANTO 1

1

In truth it is as fair and sweet a day
As ever dawn'd on Erie's silvery lake;
And wanton sunbeams on its surface play,
Which slightest breeze nor rippling currents break:
Yet Devastation's voice her fiends obey,
And stern Bellona[2] loves, e'en here, to slake
Her quenchless thirst in seas of human gore,
Which soon must dye that lake and distant shore.

2

And there is many a proud and stately bark
Emerging from the sombre mists of night;
And many a sturdy tar and gallant spark
Awaiting there the coming hour of fight:
The streamers gaily float in air—and hark,
The boatswain pipes—when soon with fingers light
The active crews unfurl the snow-white sail,
Which vainly falls, to woo the slumbering gale.

3

And who are they[3] who, fierce defying, dare
To range their prows along th'adjacent shore,
To seek the angry lion[4] in his lair,
And boldly brave the sea-god's[5] savage roar?
A haughty and an upstart band they are,
Nor seen, nor known, nor understood before;[6]
Yet not unworthy to contend in arms
With foemen best inur'd to war's alarms.

4

Well charg'd each gun—unsheath'd each pond'rous glaive,—
They come in strength their deadly foe to find,
Resolv'd to win, or meet a watery grave;
And favour'd by the light and partial wind
Bear onward now—now gaily turn and brave
The raging fury of the fleet behind,[7]

---

[1] Richardson's poem, which he claimed to have written in 1823, focuses on the Shawnee leader and warrior Tecumseh or Tecumthe (1768–1813), who opposed white settlement in the Ohio Valley, refusing to make treaties with the Americans and encouraging an alliance of aboriginal resistance. During the War of 1812 between the Americans and the British in Canada, Tecumseh supported the British; canto 1 of Richardson's poem describes an important American naval victory on Lake Erie on 10 September 1813 (the Battle of Lake Erie or the Battle of Put-in-Bay). Following this British defeat, in October Tecumseh pressured Major General Henry Proctor either to fight the Americans under William Henry Harrison or to surrender arms to the Natives. Proctor agreed to fight alongside the Natives; but at the Battle of Moraviantown, also known as the Battle of the Thames, near Chatham, Ontario (then called Upper Canada), the British put up only a token fight before fleeing. Tecumseh was killed; General Proctor was court-martialed for his conduct. At this same battle, Richardson himself was taken prisoner by the Americans; he claimed to have shaken hands with Tecumseh before the battle. A much-revised version of *Tecumseh* was published in 1842.

[2] the Roman goddess of war.

[3] the Americans.

[4] The lion is a heraldic emblem of Britain, opposed in this poem to the American eagle.

[5] Neptune or Poseidon.

[6] "It is a fact well known to those who composed the right division of the army of Upper Canada, that a few months previous to this unfortunate engagement, the trees of which the American flotilla was formed were actually standing in their native forests. The whole of their naval force had been captured late in the preceding year, at the reduction of Detroit: of the few vessels which composed it, however, one was subsequently burnt, another retaken. Although it could not be presumed the enemy were inactive, no inconsiderable degree of surprise was excited, when a squadron of nine sail suddenly appeared off the harbour of Amherstburg, at the head of Lake Erie. Our own force had only been increased by the addition of the Detroit, which was at that moment in an unfinished state, and consisted of six barks, two of which alone were of any magnitude. The superiority was therefore decidedly in favour of the enemy, who sailed triumphantly near the port, and, fully prepared for the event, awaited the moment when, urged by the increasing necessities of the garrison, Captain Barclay was compelled to weigh anchor, and attempt a communication with the second division. This could only be effected by an action, unfavourable, under every circumstance, to the little band of martyrs. They fell, certainly—but, God knows, not without a struggle; nor was it until after two hours and a half of incessant cannonading, that the British flag was replaced by the eagles of America." (J.R.)

[7] the British fleet, hindered from leaving Fort Amherstburg harbour by the wind.

Whose crews with deep complainings rend the air,
And murmur cursings—earnest of despair!

5

But now the breeze is up—the anchor weigh'd—
The swelling canvass bends before the gale;
Each towering ship, in battle-pomp array'd,
In distance answers to the chieftain's hail:[1]
Each warrior-brow is clear'd—nor gloom, nor shade,
Nor disappointed feelings now prevail:
All hearts are light—the chase is full in view—
They pant for combat, and forthwith pursue.

6

Nor long they follow—nor a coward foe,
Nor one unus'd, unskill'd in naval war;
Their sails are instant clew'd[2]—their course is slow—
Each bark awaits her rival from afar;
While with a secret, and exulting glow
They count the little fleet who cross the bar,[3]
And reckless of their weakness dare engage,
And with superior force the contest wage.

7

The clarion shrilly sounds—the warlike drum
In rolling murmurs breaks upon the ear;
The boatswain's whistle, and the busy hum
Of order, rise in echoes long and clear.
In firm array and dauntless front they come,
And with one loud and universal cheer
Bear nobly down upon th'assembled fleet,
Who with loud cries of war their presence greet.

8

And now the thick sulphureous mists[4] ascend,
And Murder opens all her mouths of blood;
While streams of light with curling volumes blend,
And dart along the surface of the flood,
Which, startled at the cries of foe and friend,
Shrinks back, and seems as 'twere to brood
O'er scenes of fearful death, which darkly stain
The spotless bosom of her silvery plain!

9

And oh! by Heaven, it is a glorious day—
A contest worthy of two rival foes
Whom fame and vengeance urg'd to deadly fray;
While in gigantic grasp they boldly close,
And hide the noonday sun's refulgent ray,
Which never yet with greater splendour rose
Upon the surface of the dark smooth wave,
Now furrow'd first to form a human grave.

10

Who, that had heard the thunder of that hour,
The fierce incessant roll of murderous war,
Had sworn that Jove, all dreadful in his power,
Had shap'd to earth his high, imperial car,
And bade destruction o'er creation lower,
Winging stern havoc through the realms afar,
And filling nature with one general cry
Of hate and blood, despair and agony.

11

But hark! what shout was that? What joyous sound
Now bursts amid the deafening din of arms—
Can aught than horror or dire rage be found
Amid the reign of carnage and alarms?
Loud, and more loud it grows—but now 'tis drown'd
In thundering peals—and now again it warms
Still louder;—'tis the wild and harrowing scream
Which conquest swells upon the battle's gleam.

12

And who are they who, thus exulting, wake
Each spring of action in that lengthened shout?
Whose the wild sounds which too delusive break
Upon the wond'ring ear, and eking out

---

[1] The British chieftain is Robert Heriot Barclay (1786–1837), a veteran of the Battle of Trafalgar (1805).

[2] unfurled.

[3] the sandbar in the harbour's mouth.

[4] Sulphur was used in the manufacture of gunpowder.

In distance ring along the troubled lake,
Startling the storm-bird in its wonted route,
And, e'en amid the cannon's ceaseless roar,
Is heard in echo on the distant shore?

13

It is the lion-band,[1] who fondly deem
That hour arriv'd so pleasing to the brave;
Already Victory hath appeared to beam
Upon their brows,—for many a watery grave
Their foes have found, and in the flattering dream
Of hope they reck of little left to crave:
The eagle standard from the chieftain's prow[2]
Is dash'd below, and triumph hovers now.

14

Fallacious thought! for many a bark is there
Unhurt by Havoc's devastating hand;
And now their engines vomit from afar
Destruction, carnage, and the flaming brand—
While yet more deadly grows the furious war,
And murder's glaive, which desolates the land,
Is steep'd in torrents of the slime, and gore
Which stain the deck, and from the bulwarks pour.

15

And thou too, Barclay, like a branchless trunk,[3]
Lay blasted, bleeding, mid the death-fraught
    scene,
Writhing and faint, ere cruel Slaughter drunk
With the rich dye of life, with haggard mien,
Deep, and more deep, in wild destruction sunk
Each sanguine hope—who then, alas! had seen
Thy flashing eye, had read not suffering there,
But burning indignation, and despair.

16

Each gallant ship floats now a stubborn wreck,[4]
A shapeless, useless, and unwieldy womb;
The towering masts are gone—the groaning deck
Is cover'd with dismounted guns, and gloom,
And sternest rage prevail—they little reck
Of aught beyond an honourable tomb
Within the bosom of the dark-green deep,
Where many a tar already sleeps his sleep.

17

And every leader too has nobly bled,
And fallen in the fierce, convulsive war;
Some deeply gash'd, some number'd with the
    dead,
But one exempt from honourable scar:[5]
Yet there exists a greater, surer dread—

---

[1] the British.

[2] "The Detroit, on which Captain Barclay had hoisted his flag, was, in default of the usual ship-guns, indiscriminately armed with those taken from the forts for the occasion, and were of various calibers—two twenty-four pounders, eighteens, twelves, nines, and, if I mistake not, even sixes. They were all long guns, and so well served, that, soon after the engagement commenced, the American commodore, to whom Captain Barclay found himself immediately opposed, was compelled to strike, having only eighteen effective men left. The boats of the fleet were so much injured, however, that it was found impossible to take possession of the prize." (J.R.)

[3] "This gallant, but unfortunate commander, had already lost one limb in fighting the battles of his country. Soon after the Saint Lawrence struck, he received a severe wound in his only remaining arm, which disabled him during the rest of the action." (J.R.) Barclay had critically injured his left arm in battle against the French in 1809.

[4] "Having myself fallen into the hands of the Americans, three weeks after this unfortunate affair, I was conducted to the harbour in which the united and shattered fleets still lay, in the same state as at the close of the engagement. Being permitted to visit my friends on board, I had an opportunity of witnessing the devastation of that sanguinary day. The decks were literally filled with wounded sufferers—every mast of the Detroit had been carried away—half the guns were dismounted, and the bulwarks completely shattered—nay, it was absolutely impossible to place the hand upon that side which had been exposed to the enemy's fire, without covering part of a fracture, either from grape, canister, round, or chain-shot. In fact, it would be difficult to conceive a more desperate spirit of defence or conquest than that which must have actuated the contending parties." (J.R.) Richardson was taken prisoner by the Americans at the Battle of the Thames, October 1813.

[5] "There was, in truth, but one commander who escaped the fury of the adverse fire. Captain Finnes, who commanded the Queen Charlotte, and Lieutenant Garden, a fine, promising young officer, of the Newfoundland regiment, (a part of which were acting on board the different ships as marines), were both killed by the same ball: the spot was pointed out to me on the bulwarks, on which the blood of the one, and the brains of the other, were mingled together in one melancholy and undistinguishable mass." (J.R.)

        A risk more imminent and cruel far!
135 The leading ships no more the helm obey,—[1]
        They fall aboard, and all is dire dismay!

18

        What man can compass, or what mortal dare,
        To wring hard conquest from a mightier foe,
        Was done in vain. Alas! a day so fair
140 Was doom'd to close in agony, and woe;
        And many a generous seaman, in despair,
        Felt the hot tear of indignation flow
  Upon his dark and furrow'd cheek, where Shame
  Stamp'd her first empire in the flush of flame.

19

145   For now they mark the hostile chief ascend[2]
        A deck unstain'd, uninjur'd in the fray;
        His standard rais'd, the crew their efforts blend,
        And through the mastless fleet pursue their way:
        While thund'ring broadsides on the wrecks
            descend,

20

150 Whose fainter lightnings on the victors play,
      And leave the weakness of a band reveal'd
      Too few to conquer, yet too proud to yield.

      But what, alas! can courage these avail
      Against the tide of fortune and of power?
155 A force untouch'd the floating barks assail,
      And from their massive bulwarks fiercely shower
      New deaths which fly and hiss along the gale,
      And seek in fury whom they may devour.[3]
      The fatal word is passed—down sinks each eye—
160 Proud Albion's[4] flag has ceas'd to wave on high!

21

      Now all is still, and up the mountain height
      A thousand native warriors wildly spring,
      And gaze around, and strain their aching sight,
      As though the fev'rish glance alone could bring
165 Conviction to their hopes—but all is night
      Where late the battle's roar was heard to ring,
  And friends and foes one universal cloud
  Enwraps and veils, as in a silvery shroud.

22

      Oh, hour of dark uncertainty! when most
170 We fondly covet what we dread to know;
      When secret doubting mingles with the boast
      Of strength and firmness to resist the blow
      Of adverse fortune, and the mighty host
      Of warring thoughts more wild and painful
          grow;—
175 Too soon, indeed, thou, short-liv'd hour, wert pass'd—
  One fond, delusive vision and the last.

23

      For soon, too soon, stern rage and terror broke
      Upon each heart, as now the fresh'ning breeze
      Dispers'd the columns of sulphureous smoke,
180 Which gradual rising o'er the rippling seas,
      Disclos'd the valiant bent beneath a yoke

---

[1] "It was at this critical period of the action, when the different commanders were either killed or disabled, that the two principal ships, the Detroit and Queen Charlotte, rendered unmanageable from the injury sustained in their rigging, fell foul of each other; and although every attempt was made by the surviving officers to remedy the evil, and bring the opposite broadsides to bear upon the enemy, exertion proved vain; and the God of battles seemed, for once, to have opposed himself to the successes of those who had so often ranged themselves beneath his protecting arm." (J.R.)

[2] "While those two ships, in which were centered the hopes of the little squadron, lay in this unfavourable position, using every possible means to extricate themselves, and fighting the few remaining serviceable guns with a resolution worthy of a better fate, Commodore Perry, who had finally abandoned the Saint Lawrence, and hoisted his flag on board the Niagara (a vessel of the same force, armed also with thirty-two pounders, and scarcely touched in the action), now bore up, under an easy press of sail, and discharged his battery with effect into the unfortunate wrecks. Waring immediately, a second and equally destructive broadside followed, and rendered further resistance unavailing. The guns were nearly now all unserviceable—those at least of the only battery which could be brought to bear; the different barks lay like logs on the water, and the helplessness of the crews could only be surpassed by the gloom which obscured each brow, when the inevitable order was given to strike." (J.R.) Commodore Oliver Hazard Perry (1785–1819) commanded the American navy in this battle. After he was forced to move from the Lawrence to the Niagara, the American fleet rallied and forced the British forces to surrender.

[3] Cf. 1 Peter 5.8.

[4] England's.

Accurs'd, and following where the victors please.
Then shriek'd, as from the inmost depths of hell,
The savage war-cry and the deafening yell!

24

Still there's a hope which lingers in the mind
When every fairer dream of joy is past;
There is a solace vague, and undefin'd
E'en when life's sun is wholly overcast,
Which cheers the drooping spirits of mankind,
And wakes the soul to expectation vast,
If but a glimmering of false light appear
To check the current of each maddening fear.

25

While yet the anxious far-strain'd eye could trace
The various movements of the hostile crews,
A wild expression beam'd upon each face
Half hope, half terror—cherish'd to abuse—
For hope, alas! could find no resting place,
Yet, so it is, the human heart pursues
Each cheating shade, to which it fondly clings,
And comfort from its very anguish wrings.

26

But soon the sombre wings of night confound
The wounded squadrons in one common veil—
Late rival, now in sad alliance bound—
While the full breeze swells faint the shatter'd sail,
And bears them slowly to the hostile ground:
Oh! then how felt the sickening heart to fail,
As the sad crowds receded from the shore
To mourn in secret, and their friends deplore.

27

Say, who that towering warrior[1] who reclines
His godlike form against the craggy steep,
And, like some spirit of the mountain, shines
Pre-eminent, above the rolling deep
A monument of strength—while, o'er the lines
Of his severe, and war-worn features creep
Those burning thoughts which mark the soul of flame,
Fever'd, and restless in its lust of fame?

28

No sound escapes him, yet his lip is pale—
And, thro' his earnest fixedness of gaze,
There beams anon a fire beneath the veil
Of his dark brow, which like a meteor blaze,
A moment shines, and dies along the gale;
While, turn'd to where the sunbeam dips his rays,
His eagle vision with each thought keeps pace,
And seems to dart beyond the realms of space.

29

So, when victorious near the dark Wabash,[2]
His mighty arm achiev'd a world's repose,
That eye with blasting fire was seen to flash,
And with its very glance confound his foes,
As, darting through the waves with fearful splash,
He like a demon of the waters rose,
And carried death among the lawless band,
The ruthless wasters of his native land.

---

[1] Tecumseh.

[2] "The success with which Tecumseh combated their encroachments on the borders of the Wabash, is well known to, nor can be denied by, the Americans. General Harrison, to whom he was almost constantly opposed, was candid enough to ascribe to him talents and feelings worthy a more enlightened people; and I have repeatedly heard him render that tribute to his personal intrepidity, which the really brave and liberal-minded soldier is ever ready to accord his foe. Nothing could testify in favour of the true character of the warrior in a greater degree, than the dread in which he was universally held by the various forces employed at different periods against him." (J.R.) In spite of Tecumseh's efforts and opposition, by the treaty of Fort Wayne, 1809, the Natives ceded their lands along the Wabash River, which flows from Ohio into Indiana. Harrison, then Governor of Indiana, defeated Tecumseh at the Battle of Tippecanoe in 1811.

30

Not the wild mammoth of Ohio's banks[1]
Dash'd fiercer splashing through the foaming flood,
When his huge form press'd low the groaning ranks
Of giant oaks which deck'd his native wood,
Than rag'd Tecumseh through the deep phalanx
Of deadliest enemies soon bath'd in blood,
Whose quivering scalps, half-crimson'd in their gore,
The reeking warrior from the spoilers bore.

31

Blood of the Prophet![2] and of giant mould,
Undaunted leader of a dauntless band,
Vain were each effort of thy foes most bold
To stay the arm of slaughter, or withstand
The vivid lightnings of that eye where roll'd
Deep vengeance for the sufferings of a land
Long doom'd the partage of a numerous horde,
Whom lawless rapine o'er its vallies pour'd.

32

Nor yet, (though terrible in warlike rage,
And, like the panther, bounding on his prey
When the fierce war-cry prov'd the battle's gage,
And death, and desolation mark'd his way)
Less bright in wisdom he, the gen'rous sage,
Whose prudent counsels shed a partial ray
Of gladness o'er that too-devoted realm
Which craft, and Christians leagued to overwhelm.

33

Though dearer to his soul than the young cry
Of infant weakness to a mother's ear;
Though sweeter than the first-awaken'd sigh
Of virgin love—the war-whoop long and clear;
Though nurs'd in camps, and living but to die,
Or check Oppression in her wide career—
'Twas he first caused those scenes of blood to cease,
And deign'd the vanquish'd what they sued for—peace!

34

E'en mid the wilds which echo'd back the shout
Of conquering nations fighting in his train;
E'en near the waves, still crimson'd in the route
Of bleeding foes fast flying from the plain,
Was sign'd the glorious armistice which doubt[3]
And apprehension wrung from those who fain
Had dash'd the laurel from that warrior brow,
Which frown'd defiance on their faithless vow.

35

Nor wrong the chieftain of the snow-white crest:[4]
For scarce ten moons had dipp'd in silvery dew
The verdant beauties of the glowing West,
When now a mighty mass of foemen threw
Their lengthen'd columns o'er the soil, and press'd
The spot where first the generous warrior drew
The rich warm breath of sacred liberty,
And swore to fall, or set his country free.

---

[1] "The tradition handed down among the Indians, and faithfully reported by Mr. Jefferson, in his Notes on Virginia, is as follows:—'That in ancient times, a herd of these tremendous animals came to the Bickbone-licks, and began a universal destruction of the bear, deer, elk, buffalo, and other animals, which had been created for the use of the Indians; that the Great Man above, looking down and seeing this, was so enraged that he seized his lightnings, descended on the earth, seated himself on a neighbouring mountain, on a rock, on which his seat and the prints of his feet are still to be seen, and hurled his bolts among them till the whole were slaughtered except the big bull, who, presenting his forehead to the shafts, shook them off as they fell; but missing one at length, it wounded him in the side! whereon, springing round, he bounded over the Ohio, over the Wabash, the Illinois, and finally over the great lakes, where he is living at this day.'—JEFFERSON'S *Notes on Virginia*." (J.R.) Thomas Jefferson,* *Notes on the State of Virginia*, was first published in 1782.

[2] Tecumseh's younger brother Tenskwatawa (1775–1836), whose religious visions inspired the Native opposition to settlement.

[3] "After various and unsuccessful attempts to bring this expedition to a favourable issue, General Harrison was glad to enter into terms highly advantageous to the Indians, and securing to those persecuted people a momentary respite from oppression. Tecumseh, however, attached little faith to treaties so repeatedly violated on the slightest pretext. The event fully justified his expectation." (J.R.)

[4] "During the latter part of his life, Tecumseh was generally distinguished by a large plume of ostrich feathers, the whiteness of which, contrasted with the darkness of his complexion, and the brilliancy of his black and piercing eye, gave a singularly wild and terrific expression to his features;—it was evident that he could be terrible." (J.R.)

36

'Twas then that, like a mighty avalanche,
His arm gigantic with his wrath kept pace,
And, rear'd on high, like some vast towering
   branch
Of a tall pine, dealt vengeance for a race
Whose bleeding wounds the warrior swore to
   stanch
With the deep groans of those he pledg'd to chase
Like the fierce monsters of his native wood,
Till gorg'd with victims and with human blood.

37

How well that purpose of his soul he kept,
Whole hecatombs[1] of bleaching bones and clay,
O'er which nor sorrowing spouse nor sire e'er
   wept,
Too well attest; no burial rite had they—
No tomb in which their ashes hallowed slept;
But, torn by vultures, and by beasts of prey,
E'en fertilized the bosom of that soil
They came with savage fury to despoil.

38

Still red with recent slaughter was the hand
On which the warrior's burning brow reclin'd,
As stern he gaz'd upon the captive band,
Whose crippled barks eve's fast reviving wind
Bore now in triumph to the hostile strand,
Leaving despair and harrowing grief behind,
And tears, and desolation, and fell hate,
And vain repinings at th'award of fate.

39

It was a scene of sorrowing and wo
Beyond all thought—all language to relate:
Yet none, I ween, more keenly felt the blow
Than *he* who, in his anger fiercely great,
Swore by the life-blood of each fallen foe,
Which stain'd his fast-clench'd hand, to immolate
Fresh ranks, in vengeance for those hapless brave,
Whom more than human valour could not save.

40

He swore, but secret—for no sound betrays[2]
The maddening, burning agony of soul
Which o'er his brow and o'er each feature plays.
Deeply he feels—but, feeling, can control
The hell which on his quivering being preys,
While the hot fires of hatred seem to roll
In boiling floods throughout each tortur'd vein,
And rack the fibres of his burning brain.

41

His eyes inflam'd within their orbits roll'd,
Whence flash'd the fury of the lightning's blast:
Oh! Could he grapple in one deadly fold
Of vengeful hate, unutterable, vast—
Could he but reach the victor in his hold,
Then were he paid for all his sufferings past—
Then were his own and country's wrongs forgiven
In the hot life-blood smoking up to heaven!

42

But hold! what shadow moves along the night,
And bears him cautious to the chieftain's side?
'Tis youthful Uncas,[3] foremost in the fight,
His father's sole born, and his nation's pride;
He too hath mark'd, and sicken'd at the sight,—
He too hath seen the foe triumphant ride,

---

[1] in ancient Greece, an offering of one hundred oxen to the gods.

[2] "It would be difficult to describe, or even to comprehend, the feelings of the warrior, when the absolute conviction of defeat was impressed on his mind:—his natural antipathy to the Americans—the various and important consequences attached to an event so replete with advantages to the enemy, to whom the command of the lake now afforded every facility of inundating the country with troops—and the strong interest excited for the fate of the heroic, but unfortunate commander, added to the sentiment of actual veneration with which the generous though unavailing gallantry of the whole fleet inspired him,—called up all the more powerful and impetuous passions of this child of nature. The struggle was internal—not manifested by ignoble and unavailing complaint;—his was one of those countenances which require not the aid of words to divulge the emotions of the soul. He swore to avenge them, or to fall; and he fulfilled the purport of his oath to the very letter." (J.R.)

[3] in this poem, Tecumseh's son. The historical Tecumseh did not have a son named Uncas: Richardson appropriates the name of a 17th-century Mohegan leader, who also inspires a character in James Fenimore Cooper's *The Last of the Mohicans* (1826). Uncas is killed in Canto 2 of Richardson's poem.

And spread their Eagles o'er the liquid plain,
In all the insolence of proud disdain.

43

He turn'd in speechless anguish to his sire,
And to his lips that sinewy hand uprais'd,
Encrust' in blood, and trembling with the fire
Which o'er the warrior's features wildly blaz'd:—
Ne'er had young Uncas known his Father's ire
So vast, so terrible as now he gaz'd,
And, with emotion sad and undefin'd,
Watch'd the dark conflict of his tortur'd mind.

44

Uncertain if to speak—th' intruder stood
Wrapp'd in his mantle near the suffering chief;
While but the measur'd splashing of the flood
Broke on the silence of his stubborn grief;
Or fainter night-breeze, whispering through the wood,
Call'd forth those plaintive sounds from rustling leaf,
Which, in the boundless forests of the West,
So frequent woo the wearied soul to rest.

45

There was a certain wildness in the scene,
The hour, and in the chieftain's towering height,
As his tall plumage wav'd the rocks between,
Which made him as the genius of the night
Appear; while the dull beams of evening's queen
Cast o'er the whole that dense and hazy light
Which lends colossal grandeur to each form,
When the charg'd skies proclaim a coming storm.

46

The fond youth shudder'd, yet he knew not why;
He would have spoken, but a secret dread,
A dark foreboding of deep agony,
Hung o'er his fainting soul, and fiercely fed
The grief within. Oh! was it but to die
For him, that much-lov'd sire whose throbbing head
Now lean'd in anguish 'gainst the rugged rock,
How would he fly to meet death's rudest shock!

47

Sudden, on the stillness of the night there broke
The lonely murmuring of a distant drum;
So faint, so indistinct, each dying stroke
Fell on the listening organ like the hum
Of the lake insect—but the sound awoke
The gloomy chieftain from his trance. "They come,"
He cried; "the foe eternal of this land—
Yet deem they not Tecumseh is at hand."

48

'Twas then his dark and lowering brow grew bright
With some deep purpose, confident and fell:
"Haste thee, my Uncas, with the roe-buck's flight,[1]
And seek our slumbering Warriors in the dell;
Bid them arm quickly,—ere to-morrow's light
Shall piercing shrieks fast mingle with our yell,
And ring in echo through the fatal wood,
The dire precursors of revenge and blood.

49

"In caution, and in silence, lead the band
To where yon jutting rock our barks conceal;
There let them launch them instant from the strand,
And calmly o'er the drifting current steal;
Thy sire will go before;—a lighted brand
Shall mark the spot where ye may bend each keel,
And fall securely on our slumbering prey—
Haste thee, my boy, nor linger on the way."

50

He said, and bounded to the water's side,
Quick as the chamois of his native grove:
The light canoe soon floated on the tide,
And noiseless skimm'd the rippling waves above;
So frail, it seem'd the hand-work of some bride,
To bear a spirit to his earthly love:
But now 'tis vanish'd, and the tall white plume
Is lost in distance and increasing gloom.

---

[1] the North American white-tailed deer.

Mary Wollstonecraft Shelley
1797 – 1851

Mary Wollstonecraft Godwin was born in London, on 30 August 1797, the daughter of William Godwin* and the second daughter of Mary Wollstonecraft.* Her mother died of puerperal fever eleven days after her birth, and Godwin undertook to raise the baby along with Wollstonecraft's first child, Fanny Imlay Godwin, born in 1794. When in 1801 he married Mary Jane Clairmont (née Vail), her two children Charles Gaulis Clairmont and Clara Mary Jane (Claire) Clairmont joined the family. Mary's half-brother William Godwin Jr. was born in 1803.

Mary Godwin was mainly educated at home, where she studied ancient and modern history, mythology, literature, the Bible, French, Latin, and art. Over her lifetime she became fluent in Italian and French, learned Greek as well as Latin, and read Spanish. James Opie's portrait of her mother hung in the house; her stepmother, with whom she had a difficult relationship, was a writer and publisher of children's books. Visitors to the Godwin home during her childhood included Coleridge* and Charles and Mary Lamb.*

In June 1812 Mary Godwin was sent to Scotland to stay with the family of William Baxter, one of Godwin's admirers. During a visit back to London in November, she met Percy Bysshe Shelley* and his wife Harriet Shelley. In March 1814 she returned home from Scotland and encountered Shelley again; meeting at Wollstonecraft's grave in St. Pancras churchyard, they fell in love. Early in the morning of 28 July 1814, Mary Godwin, accompanied by her stepsister Claire Clairmont, eloped with Shelley to the continent.

The lovers kept a journal of their tour, which developed into Mary's own journal. Her first book, *History of a Six Weeks' Tour of France, Switzerland, and Germany* (1817) included P.B. Shelley's "Mont Blanc."* She and Percy Shelley returned to England in September 1814; Mary was pregnant, but the baby, born in February 1815, died twelve days later. From August 1815 until April 1816 the couple lived at Bishopsgate, in Windsor Great Park, where, in January 1816, their son William was born.

In May 1816 Mary Godwin travelled to Geneva, Switzerland with P.B. Shelley, who was in poor health, their four-month-old son, and Claire Clairmont. Clairmont, who had earlier initiated an affair with Lord Byron,* was pregnant and anxious to see Byron again. In her introduction to the 1831 revised edition of *Frankenstein*, Mary Shelley tells how that book, first published in 1818, came to be written. The aftermath of the Geneva summer was tragic, however: on 9 October Fanny Imlay Godwin committed suicide at Swansea; on 9 November P.B. Shelley's wife Harriet drowned herself. On 30 December, shortly after the discovery of Harriet's body, the Shelleys were married at St. Mildred's Church, London.

In March 1817 they moved to Albion House, Marlow. The court of chancery refused P.B. Shelley's efforts to gain custody of his and Harriet's children, Ianthe and Charles. Mary Shelley's second daughter, Clara Everina Shelley, was born at Bishopsgate on 2 September 1817. In March 1818 the family, including Claire Clairmont and her daughter Clara Allegra Byron, travelled to Italy for P.B. Shelley's health. At Leghorn Mary Shelley became reacquainted with Maria (Reveley) Gisborne (who had cared for her as a newborn baby) and her husband, John Gisborne. From Leghorn, the Shelleys moved to Bagni di Lucca, where Mary did research into the life of Castruccio Castracani, the subject of her next novel, *Valperga* (1823). From there, they moved to Venice and Este, so that Claire Clairmont could visit Allegra, by now in Byron's custody. Clara Shelley, already ill before the journey, died of dysentery at Venice on 24 September 1818. The Shelleys spent the winter at Naples and travelled to Rome in April 1819; there, on 7 June, William died of malaria. Grieving the loss of two children and pregnant with another, Mary Shelley appears to have suffered a severe depression.

At Leghorn from June until October 1819, P.B. Shelley wrote his tragedy *The Cenci*;* Mary Shelley translated the original source into English. During the same period, Mary wrote *Mathilda*, a fictional account of a father's incestuous love for his daughter. Godwin withheld the novella from publication; it was eventually published in 1959. From Leghorn, the Shelleys went to Florence, where their only surviving child, Percy Florence Shelley, was born on 12 November 1819. In January 1820, however, they moved to Pisa; in May 1822 they and their friends Edward and Jane Williams moved to Casa Magni at San Terenzo for the summer. There, in June, Mary Shelley suffered a near-fatal miscarriage. On 8 July, P.B. Shelley and Edward Williams, returning in their boat the *Don Juan* from welcoming Leigh and Marianne Hunt* to Italy, drowned in a squall in the gulf of Spezia.

Following P.B. Shelley's death, Mary Shelley was determined to edit and publish his works. Within a year, she also began to publish short stories and essays (in periodicals and in the popular annuals of the times). Sir Timothy Shelley, P.B. Shelley's father, would not consider supporting Percy Florence unless he was raised in England; Shelley and her son consequently returned to England in August 1823. There she formed new friendships with such writers as Frances Wright, Thomas Moore,* Lady Morgan,* Caroline Norton, and John Howard Payne. She continued her friendship with the Lambs and Peacock* and renewed her childhood friendship with Isabella Baxter Booth. She rejected offers of marriage from Payne and Trelawny* and appears to have been attracted to Washington Irving.*

After Mary's publication of P.B. Shelley's *Posthumous Poems* (1824), Sir Timothy Shelley stopped the allowance for Percy Florence to discourage Mary from bringing the family name to public attention. She negotiated for a reasonable allowance, but she also wrote and published her own work to raise money. Her third published novel, *The Last Man*, appeared in 1826; *The Fortunes of Perkin Warbeck*, set in the fifteenth century, appeared in 1830. Her last two novels, *Lodore* (1835) and *Falkner* (1837), have contemporary settings and characters. Between 1832 and 1839, she wrote most of the essays in the five volumes of Dionysius Lardner's *Cabinet of Biography*. In 1839 Edward Moxon published her edition of the *Poetical Works of Percy Bysshe Shelley* (4 vols.) and *Essays, Letters from Abroad, Translations and Fragments by Percy Bysshe Shelley* (2 vols.). Her one-volume edition of P.B. Shelley's poetical works appeared in 1840. In an effort to include biographical information without offending Sir Timothy Shelley, she added contextual notes to the poems.

Rambles in Germany and Italy, in 1840, 1842, and 1843 (1844), Shelley's last book, is based on letters written during journeys to the continent with her son and his friends. In 1844 Sir Timothy Shelley died, leaving the Shelley estate and title to Percy Florence. Four years later, Percy Florence married Jane Gibson St. John, who became Mary's literary executor. On 1 February 1851, Mary Shelley died of a brain tumour at her home in London. Sir Percy Florence and Lady Jane Shelley buried her with her parents, whose graves had been moved from St. Pancras churchyard to St. Peter's Church, Bournemouth, near Boscombe, the Shelleys' home. (A.M.)

∽∽∽

from *The Liberal: Verse and Prose from the South*[1] 4 (1823)

from *Giovanni Villani*[2]

Among the many accusations that have been made against modern writers by the exclusive lovers of ancient literature, none has been more frequently repeated than the want of art manifested in the conception of their works, and of unity in the execution. They compare the Greek temples to Gothic churches,[3] and bidding us remark the sublime simplicity of the one, and the overcharged ornament of the other, they tell us, that such is the perfection of antiquity compared with the monstrous distortions of modern times. These arguments and views, followed up in all their details, have given rise to volumes concerning the Classic and the Romantic, a difference much dwelt on by German

---

[1] Leigh Hunt,* P.B. Shelley,* and Byron* edited four numbers of this short-lived periodical in 1822–23.

[2] Giovanni Villani (c. 1275–1348), author of the *Florentine Chronicles* (*Cronica* or *Storia Fiorentina*, c. 1308), was one of the authors Mary Shelley had read while researching her novel *Valperga* (published in February 1823).

[3] as, for example, Joseph Addison does in his comparison between the Pantheon and a Gothic cathedral in *Spectator* 415 (June 1712).

writers, and treated at length by Madame de Staël in her "L'Allemagne."[1] All readers, who happen at the same time to be thinkers, must have formed their own opinion of this question; but assuredly the most reasonable is that which would lead us to admire the beauties of all, referring those beauties to the standard of excellence that must decide on all merit in the highest resort, without reference to narrow systems and arbitrary rules. Methinks it is both presumptuous and sacrilegious to pretend to give the law to genius. We are too far removed from the point of perfection to judge with accuracy of what ought to be, and it is sufficient if we understand and feel what is. The fixed stars appear to aberrate; but it is we that move, not they. The regular planets make various excursions into the heavens, and we are told that some among them never return to the point whence they departed, and by no chance ever retrace the same path in the pathless sky. Let us, applying the rules which appertain to the sublimest objects in nature, to the sublimest work of God, a Man of Genius,—let us, I say, conclude, that though one of this species appear to err, the failure is in our understandings, not in his course; and though lines and rules, "centric and eccentric scribbled o'er,"[2] have been marked out for the wise to pursue, that these in fact have generally been the leading-strings and go-carts of mediocrity, and have never been constituted the guides of those superior minds which are themselves the law, and whose innate impulses are the fiats, of intellectual creation.

But zeal for the cause of genius has carried me further than I intended. Let us again recur to the charges brought against modern writers, and instead of cavilling at their demerits, let me be pardoned if I endeavour to discover that which is beautiful even in their defects, and to point out the benefits we may reap in the study of the human mind from this capital one—the want of unity and system.

It is a frequent fault among modern authors, and peculiarly among those of the present day, to introduce themselves, their failings and opinions, into the midst of works dedicated to objects sufficiently removed, as one might think, from any danger of such an incursion. This has sometimes the effect of a play-house anecdote I once heard, of a man missing his way behind the scenes, in passing from one part of the house to the other, and suddenly appearing in his hat and unpicturesque costume, stalking amidst the waves of a frightful storm, much to the annoyance of the highly-wrought feelings of the spectators of the impending catastrophe of a disastrous melodrame. Thus the Poet, in propriâ personâ,[3] will elbow his way between the despairing fair one and her agitated lover; he will cause a murderer's arm to be uplifted till it ought to ache, and his own hobby will sometimes displace the more majestic quadruped that just before occupied the scene.

These are the glaring defects of the intrusion of self in a work of art. But well-managed, there are few subjects, especially in poetry, that excite stronger interest or elicit more beautiful lines. To sit down for the purpose of talking of oneself, will sometimes freeze the warmth of inspiration; but, when elevated and carried away by the subject in hand, some similitude or contrast may awaken a chord which else had slept, and the whole mind will pour itself into the sound; and he must be a critic such as Sterne describes,[4] his stop-watch in his hand, who would arrest the lengthened echo of the deepest music of the soul. Let each man lay his hand on his heart and say, if Milton's reference to his own blindness and personal circumstances[5] does not throw an interest over Paradise Lost, which they would not lose to render the work as much no man's or any man's production as the Æneid—supposing *Ille ego*[6] to be an interpolation, which I fondly trust it is not.

---

[1] In 1815 Mary Shelley had read *De L'Allemagne* (*On Germany*, 1810), by the critic and novelist Anne-Louise-Germaine de Staël (1766–1817).

[2] Milton, *Paradise Lost* 8.83.

[3] "in his own person" (L.).

[4] Cf. Laurence Sterne (1713–68), *Tristram Shandy* (1759–67), vol. 3, chap. 12.

[5] See Milton, *Paradise Lost* 3.1–55, 7.23–31.

[6] "I am he," the opening words of the four-line introduction to Virgil's *Aeneid*, probably not written by Virgil himself.

This habit of self-analysis and display has also caused many men of genius to undertake works where the individual feeling of the author embues the whole subject with a peculiar hue. I have frequently remarked, that these books are often the peculiar favourites among men of imagination and sensibility. Such persons turn to the human heart as the undiscovered country.[1] They visit and revisit their own; endeavour to understand its workings, to fathom its depths, and to leave no lurking thought or disguised feeling in the hiding places where so many thoughts and feelings, for fear of shocking the tender consciences of those inexpert in the task of self-examination, delight to seclude themselves. As a help to the science of self-knowledge, and also as a continuance of it, they wish to study the minds of others, and particularly of those of the greatest merit. The sight of land was not more welcome to Columbus, than are these traces of individual feeling, chequering their more formal works of art, to the voyagers in the noblest of terræ incognitæ,[2] the soul of man. Sometimes, despairing to attain to a knowledge of the secrets of the best and wisest, they are pleased to trace human feeling wherever it is artlessly and truly pourtrayed. No book perhaps has been oftener the vade-mecum[3] of men of wit and sensibility than Burton's Anatomy of Melancholy;[4] the zest with which it is read being heightened by the proof the author gave in his death of his entire initiation into the arcana of his science.[5] The essential attributes of such a book must be truth; for else the fiction is more tame than any other; and thus Sterne may become this friend to the reading man, but his imitators never can; for affectation is easily detected and deservedly despised. Montaigne[6] is another great favourite; his pages are referred to as his conversation would be, if indeed his conversation was half so instructive, half so amusing, or contained half so vivid a picture of his internal spirit as his essays. Rousseau's Confessions,[7] written in a more liberal and even prodigal spirit of intellectual candour, is to be ranked as an inestimable acquisition to this class of production. Boswell's Life of Johnson[8] has the merit of carrying light into the recesses not of his own, but another's peculiar mind. Spence's Anecdotes[9] is a book of the same nature, but less perfect in its kind. Half the beauty of Lady Mary Montague's Letters[10] consists in the *I* that adorns them; and this *I*, this sensitive, imaginative, suffering, enthusiastic pronoun, spreads an inexpressible charm over Mary Wollstonecraft's Letters from Norway.[11]

An historian is perhaps to be held least excusable, if he intrude personally on his readers. Yet they might well follow the example of Gibbon, who, while he left the pages of his Decline and Fall[12] unstained by any thing that is not applicable to the times of which he treated, has yet, through the medium of his Life and Letters,[13] given a double interest to his history and opinions. Yet an author of Memoirs, or a History of his own Times, must necessarily appear sometimes upon the scene. Mr. Hyde gives greater interest to Lord Clarendon's History

---

[1] Shakespeare, *Hamlet* 3.1.79.

[2] "unknown lands" (L.).

[3] a book for ready reference; literally, "go with me" (L.).

[4] Robert Burton (1577–1640), *The Anatomy of Melancholy* (1621).

[5] Burton was rumoured to have committed suicide to avoid being caught making a false prediction about the date of his own death.

[6] Michel de Montaigne (1533–92), *Essais* (1580, 1588, 1595).

[7] Jean-Jacques Rousseau (1712–78), *Confessions* (1781–88).

[8] James Boswell (1740–95), *The Life of Samuel Johnson* (1791).

[9] Joseph Spence (1699–1768), *Anecdotes, Observations, and Characters, of Books and Men* (published posthumously in 1820).

[10] Lady Mary Wortley Montagu (1689–1762), *Letters … Written, during her Travels in Europe, Asia and Africa* (1763).

[11] "I cannot help here alluding to the papers of 'Elia,' which have lately appeared in a periodical publication. When collected together, they must rank among the most beautiful and highly valued specimens of the kind of writing spoken of in the text." (M.W.S.) See *Letters Written during a Short Residence in Sweden, Norway, and Denmark,** by Mary Shelley's mother Mary Wollstonecraft. Shelley's note refers to Charles Lamb's* essays, published in the *London Magazine* (1820–23) under the pseudonym "Elia."

[12] Edward Gibbon (1737–94), *The Decline and Fall of the Roman Empire* (1776–88), which Mary Shelley read at various times from 1815–18.

[13] published in *Miscellaneous Works* (1796), which Mary Shelley read in 1815.

of the Rebellion,[1] though I have often regretted that a quiet *I* had not been inserted in its room.

And now drawing the lines of this reasoning together, it may be conjectured why I like, and how I would excuse, the dear, rambling, old fashioned pages of Giovanni Villani, the author of the Croniche Fiorentine;[2] the writer who makes the persons of Dante's Spirits familiar to us; who guides us through the unfinished streets and growing edifices of Firenze la bella,[3] and who in short transports us back to the superstitions, party spirit, companionship, and wars of the thirteenth and fourteenth centuries. Dante's commentators had made me familiar with the name of Villani, and I became desirous of obtaining what appeared to be the key of the mysterious allusions of the Divina Comedia. There is something venerable and endearing in the very appearance of this folio of the sixteenth century. The Italian is old and delightfully ill-spelt: I say delightfully, for it is spelt for Italian ears, and the mistakes let one into the secret of the pronunciation of Dante and Petrarch[4] better than the regular orthography of the present day. The abbreviations are many, and the stops in every instance misplaced; the ink is black, the words thickly set, so that the most seems to have been made of every page. It requires a little habit to read it with the same fluency as another book, but when this difficulty is vanquished, it acquires additional charms from the very labour that has been bestowed.

I know that in describing the outward appearance of my friend, I perform a thankless office, since few will sympathise in an affection which arises from a number of associations in which they cannot participate. But in developing the spirit that animates him, I undertake a more grateful task, although, by stripping him of his original garb and dressing him in a foreign habiliment, I divest him of one of his greatest beauties. Though in some respects rather old fashioned, his Italian is still received as a model of style; and those Italians who wish to purify their language from Gallicisms, and restore to it some of its pristine strength and simplicity, recur with delight to his pages. All this is lost in the English; but even thus I trust that his facts will interest, his simplicity charm, and his real talent be appreciated....

from *London Magazine* 9 (March 1824)

On Ghosts

I look for ghosts—but none will force
Their way to me; 'tis falsely said
That there was ever intercourse
Between the living and the dead.—*Wordsworth.*[5]

What a different earth do we inhabit from that on which our forefathers dwelt! The antediluvian world, strode over by mammoths, preyed upon by the megatherion,[6] and peopled by the offspring of the Sons of God,[7] is a better type of the earth of Homer, Herodotus, and Plato, than the hedged-in cornfields and measured hills of the present day. The globe was then encircled by a wall which paled in the bodies of men, whilst their feathered thoughts soared over the boundary; it had a brink, and in the deep profound which it overhung, men's imaginations, eagle-winged, dived and flew, and brought home strange tales to their believing auditors. Deep caverns harboured giants; cloudlike birds cast their shadows upon the plains; while far out at sea lay islands of bliss, the fair paradise of Atlantis or El Dorado[8]

---

[1] Edward Hyde, 1st Earl of Clarendon (1609–74), *The True Historical Narrative of the Rebellion and Civil Wars in England* (1702–04).

[2] Shelley is interested in Villani's influence on the poet Dante Alighieri (1265–1321), a fellow Florentine and author of *The Divine Comedy* (finished shortly before Dante's death). Villani's *Chronicles* (c. 1308) contain the earliest account of Dante's life and works.

[3] "Florence the beautiful" (It.).

[4] the Italian poet and humanist Francesco Petrarca or Petrarch (1304–74).

[5] William Wordsworth,* "The Affliction of Margaret" 57–60, from *Poems in Two Volumes* (1807).

[6] "huge beast" (Gr.). In 1796 the French anatomist Georges Cuvier (1769–1832) had argued that the fossil remains of the mammoth and the giant ground sloth were those of extinct species.

[7] See Genesis 6.1–4, where the offspring of the sons of God and the daughters of men are giants.

[8] places of the imagination: Plato mentions a lost island civilization called Atlantis in the *Timæus* and the *Critias*; "El Dorado" ("the gilded man") originated in Spanish accounts of a Native   (Continued)

sparkling with untold jewels. Where are they now? The Fortunate Isles[1] have lost the glory that spread a halo round them; for who deems himself nearer to the golden age, because he touches at the Canaries[2] on his voyage to India? Our only riddle is the rise of the Niger; the interior of New Holland,[3] our only terra incognita; and our sole mare incognitum,[4] the north-west passage. But these are tame wonders, lions in leash; we do not invest Mungo Park,[5] or the Captain of the Hecla,[6] with divine attributes; no one fancies that the waters of the unknown river bubble up from hell's fountains, no strange and weird power is supposed to guide the iceberg, nor do we fable that a stray pick-pocket from Botany Bay[7] has found the gardens of the Hesperides within the circuit of the Blue Mountains.[8] What have we left to dream about? The clouds are no longer the charioted servants of the sun, nor does he any more bathe his glowing brow in the bath of Thetis;[9] the rainbow has ceased to be the messenger of the Gods, and thunder is no longer their awful voice, warning man of that which is to come. We have the sun which has been weighed and measured, but not understood; we have the assemblage of the planets, the congregation of the stars, and the yet unshackled ministration of the winds:—such is the list of our ignorance.

Nor is the empire of the imagination less bounded in its own proper creations, than in those which were bestowed on it by the poor blind eyes of our ancestors. What has become of enchantresses with their palaces of crystal and dungeons of palpable darkness? What of fairies and their wands? What of witches and their familiars? and, last, what of ghosts, with beckoning hands and fleeting shapes, which quelled the soldier's brave heart, and made the murderer disclose to the astonished noon the veiled work of midnight? These which were realities to our forefathers, in our wiser age—

——Characterless are grated
To dusty nothing.[10]

Yet is it true that we do not believe in ghosts? There used to be several traditional tales repeated, with their authorities, enough to stagger us when we consigned them to that place where that is which "is as though it had never been."[11] But these are gone out of fashion. Brutus's dream[12] has become a deception of his overheated brain, Lord Lyttleton's vision[13] is called a cheat; and one by one these inhabitants of deserted houses, moonlight glades, misty mountain tops, and midnight church-yards, have been ejected from their immemorial seats, and small thrill is felt when the dead majesty of Denmark blanches the cheek and unsettles the reason of his philosophic son.[14]

---

ceremony offering gold and jewels to the gods, and gave rise to the legend of a South American place of unimaginable riches. Cf. Voltaire, *Candide* (1759).

[1] in classical and Celtic legend, islands in the Western Ocean where the souls of the blest live happily in a paradise.

[2] The Canary Islands are in the Atlantic Ocean off the coast of Spain; they have sometimes been identified as the Fortunate Isles of mythology.

[3] Australia.

[4] "unknown sea" (L.).

[5] Mungo Park (1771–1806) was a Scottish explorer of the African continent, the first European to explore the Niger River.

[6] Sir William Edward Parry (1790–1855), who returned in 1820 from a voyage of discovery to find the Northwest Passage between Greenland and Bering Strait.

[7] in southeast Australia south of Sydney; a British penal colony was established there in 1788.

[8] a region of Australia west of Sydney.

[9] a sea-nymph, mother of Achilles; here, simply the sea.

[10] Shakespeare, *Troilus and Cressida* 3.2.195–96.

[11] Matteo Villani (d. 1363) was Giovanni Villani's brother and continued his *Chronicles*. This is his comment on the response of survivors to the Black Death.

[12] At the Battle of Philippi, according to Plutarch and Suetonius, Brutus was afflicted by dreams of Cæsar, whom he had conspired to assassinate; in Shakespeare's *Julius Cæsar* 4.3, Cæsar's ghost appears to Brutus the night before the battle.

[13] Thomas, 2nd Baron Lyttleton (1744–79) was alleged to have predicted the exact time of his own death: see Boswell, *Life of Johnson* (1791) 2:505 (1784). In 1816, P.B. Shelley* recorded two of Matthew Gregory Lewis's ghostly anecdotes of Lyttleton in Mary Shelley's *Journal*.

[14] Shakespeare, *Hamlet* 1.1.4.

But do none of us believe in ghosts? If this question be read at noon-day, when—

> Every little corner, nook, and hole,
> Is penetrated with the insolent light—[1]

at such a time derision is seated on the features of my reader. But let it be twelve at night in a lone house; take up, I beseech you, the story of the Bleeding Nun;[2] or of the Statue, to which the bridegroom gave the wedding ring, and she came in the dead of night to claim him, tall, white, and cold; or of the Grandsire,[3] who with shadowy form and breathless lips stood over the couch and kissed the foreheads of his sleeping grandchildren, and thus doomed them to their fated death; and let all these details be assisted by solitude, flapping curtains, rushing wind, a long and dusky passage, an half open door—O, then truly, another answer may be given, and many will request leave to sleep upon it, before they decide whether there be such a thing as a ghost in the world, or out of the world, if that phraseology be more spiritual. What is the meaning of this feeling?

For my own part, I never saw a ghost except once in a dream. I feared it in my sleep; I awoke trembling, and lights and the speech of others could hardly dissipate my fear. Some years ago I lost a friend, and a few months afterwards visited the house where I had last seen him. It was deserted, and though in the midst of a city, its vast halls and spacious apartments occasioned the same sense of loneliness as if it had been situated on an uninhabited heath. I walked through the vacant chambers by twilight, and none save I awakened the echoes of their pavement. The far mountains (visible from the upper windows) had lost their tinge of sunset; the tranquil atmosphere grew leaden coloured as the golden stars appeared in the firmament; no wind ruffled the shrunk-up river which crawled lazily through the deepest channel of its wide and empty bed; the chimes of the Ave Maria had ceased, and the bell hung moveless in the open belfry: beauty invested a reposing world, and awe was inspired by beauty only. I walked through the rooms filled with sensations of the most poignant grief. He had been there; his living frame had been caged by those walls, his breath had mingled with that atmosphere, his step had been on those stones, I thought:—the earth is a tomb, the gaudy sky a vault, we but walking corpses. The wind rising in the east rushed through the open casements, making them shake;—methought, I heard, I felt—I know not what—but I trembled. To have seen him but for a moment, I would have knelt until the stones had been worn by the impress, so I told myself, and so I knew a moment after, but then I trembled, awe-struck and fearful. Wherefore? There is something beyond us of which we are ignorant. The sun drawing up the vaporous air makes a void, and the wind rushes in to fill it,—thus beyond our soul's ken there is an empty space; and our hopes and fears, in gentle gales or terrific whirlwinds, occupy the vacuum; and if it does no more, it bestows on the feeling heart a belief that influences do exist to watch and guard us, though they be impalpable to the coarser faculties.

I have heard that when Coleridge was asked if he believed in ghosts,—he replied that he had seen too many to put any trust in their reality; and the person of the most lively imagination that I ever knew echoed this reply. But these were not real ghosts (pardon, unbelievers, my mode of speech) that they saw; they were shadows, phantoms unreal; that while they appalled the senses, yet carried no other feeling to the mind of others than delusion, and were viewed as we might view an optical deception which we see to be true with our eyes, and know to be false with our understandings. I speak of other shapes. The returning bride, who claims the fidelity of her betrothed; the murdered man who shakes to remorse the murderer's heart; ghosts that lift the curtains at the foot of your bed as the clock chimes one; who rise all pale and ghastly from the church-yard and haunt their ancient abodes; who, spoken to, reply; and whose cold unearthly touch makes the hair stand stark upon the head; the true old-fashioned, foretelling, flitting, gliding ghost,—who has seen such a one?

I have known two persons who at broad daylight have owned that they believed in ghosts, for that they had seen one. One of these was an Englishman, and the

---

[1] P.B. Shelley, *The Cenci* 2.1.179–80.*

[2] See M.G. Lewis,* *The Monk* (1796), chap. 4.

[3] from "The Family Portraits," in *Fantasmagoriana* (1812, trans. into English as *Tales of the Dead*); see also Mary Shelley's Introduction to the 1831 edition of *Frankenstein*.

other an Italian. The former had lost a friend he dearly loved, who for a while appeared to him nightly, gently stroking his cheek and spreading a serene calm over his mind. He did not fear the appearance, although he was somewhat awe-stricken as each night it glided into his chamber, and,

> Ponsi del letto in su la sponda manca.[1]

This visitation continued for several weeks, when by some accident he altered his residence, and then he saw it no more. Such a tale may easily be explained away;—but several years had passed, and he, a man of strong and virile intellect, said that "he had seen a ghost."

The Italian[2] was a noble, a soldier, and by no means addicted to superstition: he had served in Napoleon's armies from early youth, and had been to Russia, had fought and bled, and been rewarded, and he unhesitatingly, and with deep belief, recounted his story.

This Chevalier, a young, and (somewhat a miraculous incident) a gallant Italian, was engaged in a duel with a brother officer, and wounded him in the arm. The subject of the duel was frivolous; and distressed therefore at its consequences he attended on his youthful adversary during his consequent illness, so that when the latter recovered they became firm and dear friends. They were quartered together at Milan, where the youth fell desperately in love with the wife of a musician, who disdained his passion, so that it preyed on his spirits and his health; he absented himself from all amusements, avoided all his brother officers, and his only consolation was to pour his love-sick plaints into the ear of the Chevalier, who strove in vain to inspire him either with indifference towards the fair disdainer, or to inculcate lessons of fortitude and heroism. As a last resource he urged him to ask leave of absence; and to seek, either in change of scene, or the amusement of hunting, some diversion to his passion. One evening the youth came to the Chevalier, and said, "Well, I have asked leave of absence, and am to have it early to-morrow morning, so lend me your fowling-piece and cartridges, for I shall go to hunt for a fortnight." The Chevalier gave him what he asked; among the shot there were a few bullets. "I will take these also," said the youth, "to secure myself against the attack of any wolf, for I mean to bury myself in the woods."

Although he had obtained that for which he came, the youth still lingered. He talked of the cruelty of his lady, lamented that she would not even permit him a hopeless attendance, but that she inexorably banished him from her sight, "so that," said he, "I have no hope but in oblivion." At length he rose to depart. He took the Chevalier's hand and said, "You will see her to-morrow, you will speak to her, and hear her speak; tell her, I entreat you, that our conversation to-night has been concerning her, and that her name was the last that I spoke." "Yes, yes," cried the Chevalier, "I will say any thing you please; but you must not talk of her any more, you must forget her." The youth embraced his friend with warmth, but the latter saw nothing more in it than the effects of his affection, combined with his melancholy at absenting himself from his mistress, whose name, joined to a tender farewell, was the last sound that he uttered.

When the Chevalier was on guard that night, he heard the report of a gun. He was at first troubled and agitated by it, but afterwards thought no more of it, and when relieved from guard went to bed, although he passed a restless, sleepless night. Early in the morning some one knocked at his door. It was a soldier, who said that he had got the young officer's leave of absence, and had taken it to his house; a servant had admitted him, and he had gone up stairs, but the room door of the officer was locked, and no one answered to his knocking, but something oozed through from under the door that looked like blood. The Chevalier, agitated and frightened at this account, hurried to his friend's house, burst open the door, and found him stretched on the ground—he had blown out his brains, and the body lay a headless trunk, cold, and stiff.

The shock and grief which the Chevalier experienced in consequence of this catastrophe produced a fever which lasted for some days. When he got well, he obtained leave of absence, and went into the country to try to divert his mind. One evening at moonlight, he

---

[1] "It puts itself on the left side of the bed" (It.). Petrarch, *Canzoniere* 359.

[2] His name was Angelo Mengaldo: see Mary Shelley, *Journals* 1: 231–32 (20 October 1818).

was returning home from a walk, and passed through a lane with a hedge on both sides, so high that he could not see over them. The night was balmy; the bushes gleamed with fireflies, brighter than the stars which the moon had veiled with her silver light. Suddenly he heard a rustling near him, and the figure of his friend issued from the hedge and stood before him, mutilated as he had seen him after his death. This figure he saw several times, always in the same place. It was impalpable to the touch, motionless, except in its advance, and made no sign when it was addressed. Once the Chevalier took a friend with him to the spot. The same rustling was heard, the same shadow stept forth, his companion fled in horror, but the Chevalier staid, vainly endeavouring to discover what called his friend from his quiet tomb, and if any act of his might give repose to the restless shade.

Such are my two stories, and I record them the more willingly, since they occurred to men, and to individuals distinguished the one for courage and the other for sagacity. I will conclude my "modern instances," with a story told by M.G. Lewis,[1] not probably so authentic as these, but perhaps more amusing. I relate it as nearly as possible in his own words.

"A gentleman journeying towards the house of a friend, who lived on the skirts of an extensive forest, in the east of Germany, lost his way. He wandered for some time among the trees, when he saw a light at a distance. On approaching it he was surprised to observe that it proceeded from the interior of a ruined monastery. Before he knocked at the gate he thought it proper to look through the window. He saw a number of cats assembled round a small grave, four of whom were at that moment letting down a coffin with a crown upon it. The gentleman startled at this unusual sight, and, imagining that he had arrived at the retreats of fiends or witches, mounted his horse and rode away with the utmost precipitation. He arrived at his friend's house at a late hour, who sate up waiting for him. On his arrival his friend questioned him as to the cause of the traces of agitation visible in his face. He began to recount his adventures after much hesitation, knowing that it was scarcely possible that his friend should give faith to his relation. No sooner had he mentioned the coffin with the crown upon it, than his friend's cat, who seemed to have been lying asleep before the fire, leaped up, crying out, 'Then I am king of the cats'; and then scrambled up the chimney, and was never seen more."

from *The Keepsake* (1831)[2]

Transformation

Forthwith this frame of mine was wrench'd
    With a woful agony,
Which forced me to begin my tale,
    And then it set me free.

Since then, at an uncertain hour,
    That agony returns;
And till my ghastly tale is told
    This heart within me burns.
        COLERIDGE'S ANCIENT MARINER.[3]

I have heard it said, that, when any strange, supernatural, and necromantic adventure has occurred to a human being, that being, however desirous he may be to conceal the same, feels at certain periods torn up as it were by an intellectual earthquake, and is forced to bare the inner depths of his spirit to another. I am a witness of the truth of this. I have dearly sworn to myself never to reveal to human ears the horrors to which I once, in excess of fiendly pride, delivered myself over. The holy man who heard my confession, and reconciled me to the church, is dead. None knows that once——

Why should it not be thus? Why tell a tale of impious tempting of Providence, and soul-subduing humiliation? Why? answer me, ye who are wise in the secrets of human nature! I only know that so it is; and in spite of strong resolve—of a pride that too much

---

[1] In 1816, P.B. Shelley records hearing this story from M.G. Lewis;* see Mary Shelley, *Journals* 1: 129.

[2] *The Keepsake* was one of the foremost of the English literary annuals, perhaps the most widely read venue for poetry and short fiction in the second quarter of the nineteenth century.

[3] "The Rime of the Ancient Mariner" (1817) 578–85.*

masters me—of shame, and even of fear, so to render myself odious to my species—I must speak.

Genoa! my birth-place—proud city! looking upon the blue waves of the Mediterranean sea—dost thou remember me in my boyhood, when thy cliffs and promontories, thy bright sky and gay vineyards, were my world? Happy time! when to the young heart the narrow-bounded universe, which leaves, by its very limitation, free scope to the imagination, enchains our physical energies, and, sole period in our lives, innocence and enjoyment are united. Yet, who can look back to childhood, and not remember its sorrows and its harrowing fears? I was born with the most imperious, haughty, tameless spirit, with which ever mortal was gifted. I quailed before my father only; and he, generous and noble, but capricious and tyrannical, at once fostered and checked the wild impetuosity of my character, making obedience necessary, but inspiring no respect for the motives which guided his commands. To be a man, free, independent; or, in better words, insolent and domineering, was the hope and prayer of my rebel heart.

My father had one friend, a wealthy Genoese noble, who in a political tumult was suddenly sentenced to banishment, and his property confiscated. The Marchese Torella went into exile alone. Like my father, he was a widower: he had one child, the almost infant Juliet, who was left under my father's guardianship. I should certainly have been an unkind master to the lovely girl, but that I was forced by my position to become her protector. A variety of childish incidents all tended to one point,—to make Juliet see in me a rock of refuge; I in her, one, who must perish through the soft sensibility of her nature too rudely visited, but for my guardian care. We grew up together. The opening rose in May was not more sweet than this dear girl. An irradiation of beauty was spread over her face. Her form, her step, her voice—my heart weeps even now, to think of all of relying, gentle, loving, and pure, that was enshrined in that celestial tenement. When I was eleven and Juliet eight years of age, a cousin of mine, much older than either—he seemed to us a man—took great notice of my playmate; he called her his bride, and asked her to marry him. She refused, and he insisted, drawing her unwillingly towards him. With the countenance and emotions of a maniac I threw myself on him—I strove to draw his sword—I clung to his neck with the ferocious resolve to strangle him: he was obliged to call for assistance to disengage himself from me. On that night I led Juliet to the chapel of our house: I made her touch the sacred relics—I harrowed her child's heart, and profaned her child's lips with an oath, that she would be mine, and mine only.

Well, those days passed away. Torella returned in a few years, and became wealthier and more prosperous than ever. When I was seventeen, my father died; he had been magnificent to prodigality; Torella rejoiced that my minority would afford an opportunity for repairing my fortunes. Juliet and I had been affianced beside my father's deathbed—Torella was to be a second parent to me.

I desired to see the world, and I was indulged. I went to Florence, to Rome, to Naples; thence I passed to Toulon, and at length reached what had long been the bourne of my wishes, Paris. There was wild work in Paris then. The poor king, Charles the Sixth,[1] now sane, now mad, now a monarch, now an abject slave, was the very mockery of humanity. The queen, the dauphin, the Duke of Burgundy, alternately friends and foes—now meeting in prodigal feasts, now shedding blood in rivalry—were blind to the miserable state of their country, and the dangers that impended over it, and gave themselves wholly up to dissolute enjoyment or savage strife. My character still followed me. I was arrogant and self-willed; I loved display, and above all, I threw all control far from me. Who could control me in Paris? My young friends were eager to foster passions which furnished them with pleasures. I was deemed handsome—I was master of every knightly accomplishment. I was disconnected with any political party. I grew a favourite with all: my presumption and arrogance was pardoned in one so young: I became a spoiled child. Who could control me? not the letters and advice of Torella—only strong necessity visiting me in the abhorred shape of an empty purse. But there were means

---

[1] Charles VI (1368–1422) became king of France in 1380. He suffered from frequent attacks of insanity, and his reign was marked by anarchy.

to refill this void. Acre after acre, estate after estate, I sold. My dress, my jewels, my horses and their caparisons, were almost unrivalled in gorgeous Paris, while the lands of my inheritance passed into possession of others.

The Duke of Orleans was waylaid and murdered by the Duke of Burgundy. Fear and terror possessed all Paris. The dauphin and the queen shut themselves up; every pleasure was suspended. I grew weary of this state of things, and my heart yearned for my boyhood's haunts. I was nearly a beggar, yet still I would go there, claim my bride, and rebuild my fortunes. A few happy ventures as a merchant would make me rich again. Nevertheless, I would not return in humble guise. My last act was to dispose of my remaining estate near Albaro for half its worth, for ready money. Then I despatched all kinds of artificers, arras, furniture of regal splendour, to fit up the last relic of my inheritance, my palace in Genoa. I lingered a little longer yet, ashamed at the part of the prodigal[1] returned, which I feared I should play. I sent my horses. One matchless Spanish jennet I despatched to my promised bride; its caparisons flamed with jewels and cloth of gold. In every part I caused to be entwined the initials of Juliet and her Guido. My present found favour in hers and in her father's eyes.

Still to return a proclaimed spendthrift, the mark of impertinent wonder, perhaps of scorn, and to encounter singly the reproaches or taunts of my fellow-citizens, was no alluring prospect. As a shield between me and censure, I invited some few of the most reckless of my comrades to accompany me: thus I went armed against the world, hiding a rankling feeling, half fear and half penitence, by bravado and an insolent display of satisfied vanity.

I arrived in Genoa. I trod the pavement of my ancestral palace. My proud step was no interpreter of my heart, for I deeply felt that, though surrounded by every luxury, I was a beggar. The first step I took in claiming Juliet must widely declare me such. I read contempt or pity in the looks of all. I fancied, so apt is conscience to imagine what it deserves, that rich and poor, young and old, all regarded me with derision. Torella came not near me. No wonder that my second father should expect a son's deference from me in waiting first on him. But, galled and stung by a sense of my follies and demerit, I strove to throw the blame on others. We kept nightly orgies in Palazzo Carega. To sleepless, riotous nights, followed listless, supine mornings. At the Ave Maria[2] we showed our dainty persons in the streets, scoffing at the sober citizens, casting insolent glances on the shrinking women. Juliet was not among them—no, no; if she had been there, shame would have driven me away, if love had not brought me to her feet.

I grew tired of this. Suddenly I paid the Marchese a visit. He was at his villa, one among the many which deck the suburb of San Pietro d'Arena. It was the month of May—a month of May in that garden of the world—the blossoms of the fruit trees were fading among thick, green foliage; the vines were shooting forth; the ground strewed with the fallen olive blooms; the fire-fly was in the myrtle hedge; heaven and earth wore a mantle of surpassing beauty. Torella welcomed me kindly, though seriously; and even his shade of displeasure soon wore away. Some resemblance to my father—some look and tone of youthful ingenuousness, lurking still in spite of my misdeeds, softened the good old man's heart. He sent for his daughter—he presented me to her as her betrothed. The chamber became hallowed by a holy light as she entered. Hers was that cherub look, those large, soft eyes, full dimpled cheeks, and mouth of infantine sweetness, that expresses the rare union of happiness and love. Admiration first possessed me; she is mine! was the second proud emotion, and my lips curled with haughty triumph. I had not been the *enfant gâté*[3] of the beauties of France not to have learnt the art of pleasing the soft heart of woman. If towards men I was overbearing, the deference I paid to them was the more in contrast. I commenced my courtship by the display of a thousand gallantries to Juliet, who, vowed to me from infancy, had never admitted the devotion of others; and who, though accustomed to expressions of admiration, was uninitiated in the language of lovers.

---

[1] See Luke 15.11–32.

[2] prayers to the Virgin Mary, signaled by the Angelus bell in the evening.

[3] "spoiled child" (Fr.).

For a few days all went well. Torella never alluded to my extravagance; he treated me as a favourite son. But the time came, as we discussed the preliminaries to my union with his daughter, when this fair face of things should be overcast. A contract had been drawn up in my father's lifetime. I had rendered this, in fact, void, by having squandered the whole of the wealth which was to have been shared by Juliet and myself. Torella, in consequence, chose to consider this bond as cancelled, and proposed another, in which, though the wealth he bestowed was immeasurably increased, there were so many restrictions as to the mode of spending it, that I, who saw independence only in free career being given to my own imperious will, taunted him as taking advantage of my situation, and refused utterly to subscribe to his conditions. The old man mildly strove to recall me to reason. Roused pride became the tyrant of my thought: I listened with indignation—I repelled him with disdain.

"Juliet, thou art mine! Did we not interchange vows in our innocent childhood? are we not one in the sight of God? and shall thy cold-hearted, cold-blooded father divide us? Be generous, my love, be just; take not away a gift, last treasure of thy Guido—retract not thy vows—let us defy the world, and setting at nought the calculations of age, find in our mutual affection a refuge from every ill."

Fiend I must have been, with such sophistry to endeavour to poison that sanctuary of holy thought and tender love. Juliet shrank from me affrighted. Her father was the best and kindest of men, and she strove to show me how, in obeying him, every good would follow. He would receive my tardy submission with warm affection; and generous pardon would follow my repentance. Profitless words for a young and gentle daughter to use to a man accustomed to make his will, law; and to feel in his own heart a despot so terrible and stern, that he could yield obedience to nought save his own imperious desires! My resentment grew with resistance; my wild companions were ready to add fuel to the flame. We laid a plan to carry off Juliet. At first it appeared to be crowned with success. Midway, on our return, we were overtaken by the agonized father and his attendants. A conflict ensued. Before the city guard came to decide the victory in favour of our antagonists, two of Torella's servitors were dangerously wounded.

This portion of my history weighs most heavily with me. Changed man as I am, I abhor myself in the recollection. May none who hear this tale ever have felt as I. A horse driven to fury by a rider armed with barbed spurs, was not more a slave than I, to the violent tyranny of my temper. A fiend possessed my soul, irritating it to madness. I felt the voice of conscience within me; but if I yielded to it for a brief interval, it was only to be a moment after torn, as by a whirlwind, away—borne along on the stream of desperate rage—the plaything of the storms engendered by pride. I was imprisoned, and, at the instance of Torella, set free. Again I returned to carry off both him and his child to France; which hapless country, then preyed on by freebooters and gangs of lawless soldiery, offered a grateful refuge to a criminal like me. Our plots were discovered. I was sentenced to banishment; and, as my debts were already enormous, my remaining property was put in the hands of commissioners for their payment. Torella again offered his mediation, requiring only my promise not to renew my abortive attempts on himself and his daughter. I spurned his offers, and fancied that I triumphed when I was thrust out from Genoa, a solitary and penniless exile. My companions were gone: they had been dismissed the city some weeks before, and were already in France. I was alone—friendless; with nor sword at my side, nor ducat in my purse.

I wandered along the sea-shore, a whirlwind of passion possessing and tearing my soul. It was as if a live coal had been set burning in my breast. At first I meditated on what *I should do*. I would join a band of freebooters. Revenge!—the word seemed balm to me:—I hugged it—caressed it—till, like a serpent, it stung me. Then again I would abjure and despise Genoa, that little corner of the world. I would return to Paris, where so many of my friends swarmed; where my services would be eagerly accepted; where I would carve out fortune with my sword, and might, through success, make my paltry birth-place, and the false Torella, rue the day when they drove me, a new Coriolanus,[1] from her walls. I would return to Paris—thus, on foot—a beggar—and present myself in my poverty to those I had formerly entertained sumptuously? There was gall in the mere thought of it.

The reality of things began to dawn upon my mind, bringing despair in its train. For several months I had been a prisoner: the evils of my dungeon had whipped my soul to madness, but they had subdued my corporeal frame. I was weak and wan. Torella had used a thousand artifices to administer to my comfort; I had detected and scorned them all—and I reaped the harvest of my obduracy. What was to be done?—Should I crouch before my foe, and sue for forgiveness?—Die rather ten thousand deaths!—Never should they obtain that victory! Hate—I swore eternal hate! Hate from whom? — to whom?—From a wandering outcast—to a mighty noble. I and my feelings were nothing to them: already had they forgotten one so unworthy. And Juliet!—her angel-face and sylph-like form gleamed among the clouds of my despair with vain beauty; for I had lost her—the glory and flower of the world! Another will call her his!—that smile of paradise will bless another!

Even now my heart fails within me when I recur to this rout of grim-visaged ideas. Now subdued almost to tears, now raving in my agony, still I wandered along the rocky shore, which grew at each step wilder and more desolate. Hanging rocks and hoar precipices overlooked the tideless ocean; black caverns yawned; and for ever, among the seaworn recesses, murmured and dashed the unfruitful waters. Now my way was almost barred by an abrupt promontory, now rendered nearly impracticable by fragments fallen from the cliff. Evening was at hand, when, seaward, arose, as if on the waving of a wizard's wand, a murky web of clouds, blotting the late azure sky, and darkening and disturbing the till now placid deep. The clouds had strange fantastic shapes; and they changed, and mingled, and seemed to be driven about by a mighty spell. The waves raised their white crests; the thunder first muttered, then roared from across the waste of waters, which took a deep purple dye, flecked with foam. The spot where I stood, looked, on one side, to the wide-spread ocean; on the other, it was barred by a rugged promontory. Round this cape suddenly came, driven by the wind, a vessel. In vain the mariners tried to force a path for her to the open sea—the gale drove her on the rocks. It will perish!—all on board will perish!—Would I were among them! And to my young heart the idea of death came for the first time blended with that of joy. It was an awful sight to behold that vessel struggling with her fate. Hardly could I discern the sailors, but I heard them. It was soon all over!—A rock, just covered by the tossing waves, and so unperceived, lay in wait for its prey. A crash of thunder broke over my head at the moment that, with a frightful shock, the skiff dashed upon her unseen enemy. In a brief space of time she went to pieces. There I stood in safety; and there were my fellow-creatures, battling, how hopelessly, with annihilation. Methought I saw them struggling—too truly did I hear their shrieks, conquering the barking surges in their shrill agony. The dark breakers threw hither and thither the fragments of the wreck: soon it disappeared. I had been fascinated to gaze till the end: at last I sank on my knees—I covered my face with my hands: I again looked up; something was floating on the billows towards the shore. It neared and neared. Was that a human form?—It grew more distinct; and at last a mighty wave, lifting the whole freight, lodged it upon a rock. A human being bestriding a sea-chest!—A human being!—Yet was it one? Surely never such had existed before—a misshapen dwarf, with squinting eyes, distorted features, and body deformed, till it became a horror to behold. My blood, lately warming towards a fellow-being so snatched from a watery tomb, froze in my heart. The dwarf got off his chest; he tossed his straight, straggling hair from his odious visage:

"By St. Beelzebub!"[2] he exclaimed, "I have been well bested." He looked round and saw me. "Oh, by the fiend! here is another ally of the mighty one. To what saint did you offer prayers, friend—if not to mine? Yet I remember you not on board."

---

[1] the arrogant Roman general Coriolanus was banished for his temper; see Shakespeare, *Coriolanus* 3.3.

[2] Beelzebub, not a saint but one of the devils ("lord of the flies"; the name appears to be a Hebrew and Aramaic compound); cf. Matthew 12.24–29, Luke 11.15–22.

I shrank from the monster and his blasphemy. Again he questioned me, and I muttered some inaudible reply. He continued:—

"Your voice is drowned by this dissonant roar. What a noise the big ocean makes! Schoolboys bursting from their prison are not louder than these waves set free to play. They disturb me. I will no more of their ill-timed brawling.—Silence, hoary One!—Winds, avaunt!—to your homes!—Clouds, fly to the antipodes, and leave our heaven clear!"

As he spoke, he stretched out his two long lank arms, that looked like spider's claws, and seemed to embrace with them the expanse before him. Was it a miracle? The clouds became broken, and fled; the azure sky first peeped out, and then was spread a calm field of blue above us; the stormy gale was exchanged to the softly breathing west; the sea grew calm; the waves dwindled to riplets.[1]

"I like obedience even in these stupid elements," said the dwarf. "How much more in the tameless mind of man! It was a well got up storm, you must allow—and all of my own making."

It was tempting Providence to interchange talk with this magician. But *Power*, in all its shapes, is venerable to man. Awe, curiosity, a clinging fascination, drew me towards him.

"Come, don't be frightened, friend," said the wretch: "I am good-humoured when pleased; and something does please me in your well-proportioned body and handsome face, though you look a little woebegone. You have suffered a land—I, a sea wreck. Perhaps I can allay the tempest of your fortunes as I did my own. Shall we be friends?"—And he held out his hand; I could not touch it. "Well, then, companions—that will do as well. And now, while I rest after the buffeting I underwent just now, tell me why, young and gallant as you seem, you wander thus alone and downcast on this wild sea-shore."

The voice of the wretch was screeching and horrid, and his contortions as he spoke were frightful to behold. Yet he did gain a kind of influence over me, which I could not master, and I told him my tale. When it was ended, he laughed long and loud: the rocks echoed back the sound: hell seemed yelling around me.

"Oh, thou cousin of Lucifer!" said he; "so thou too hast fallen through thy pride; and, though bright as the son of Morning,[2] thou art ready to give up thy good looks, thy bride, and thy well-being, rather than submit thee to the tyranny of good. I honour thy choice, by my soul!—So thou hast fled, and yield the day; and mean to starve on these rocks, and to let the birds peck out thy dead eyes, while thy enemy and thy betrothed rejoice in thy ruin. Thy pride is strangely akin to humility, methinks."

As he spoke, a thousand fanged thoughts stung me to the heart.

"What would you that I should do?" I cried.

"I!—Oh, nothing, but lie down and say your prayers before you die. But, were I you, I know the deed that should be done."

I drew near him. His supernatural powers made him an oracle in my eyes; yet a strange unearthly thrill quivered through my frame as I said—"Speak!—teach me—what act do you advise?"

"Revenge thyself, man!—humble thy enemies!—set thy foot on the old man's neck, and possess thyself of his daughter!"

"To the east and west I turn," cried I, "and see no means! Had I gold, much could I achieve; but, poor and single, I am powerless."

The dwarf had been seated on his chest as he listened to my story. Now he got off; he touched a spring; it flew open!—What a mine of wealth—of blazing jewels, beaming gold, and pale silver—was displayed therein. A mad desire to possess this treasure was born within me.

"Doubtless," I said, "one so powerful as you could do all things."

"Nay," said the monster, humbly, "I am less omnipotent than I seem. Some things I possess which you may covet; but I would give them all for a small share, or even for a loan of what is yours."

"My possessions are at your service," I replied, bitterly—"my poverty, my exile, my disgrace—I make

---

[1] Cf. Mark 4.35–41.

[2] Cf. Isaiah 14.12.

a free gift of them all."

"Good! I thank you. Add one other thing to your gift, and my treasure is yours."

"As nothing is my sole inheritance, what besides nothing would you have?"

"Your comely face and well-made limbs."

I shivered. Would this all-powerful monster murder me? I had no dagger. I forgot to pray—but I grew pale.

"I ask for a loan, not a gift," said the frightful thing: "lend me your body for three days—you shall have mine to cage your soul the while, and, in payment, my chest. What say you to the bargain?—Three short days."

We are told that it is dangerous to hold unlawful talk; and well do I prove the same. Tamely written down, it may seem incredible that I should lend any ear to this proposition; but, in spite of his unnatural ugliness, there was something fascinating in a being whose voice could govern earth, air, and sea. I felt a keen desire to comply; for with that chest I could command the world. My only hesitation resulted from a fear that he would not be true to his bargain. Then, I thought, I shall soon die here on these lonely sands, and the limbs he covets will be mine no more:—it is worth the chance. And, besides, I knew that, by all the rules of art-magic, there were formula and oaths which none of its practisers dared break. I hesitated to reply; and he went on, now displaying his wealth, now speaking of the petty price he demanded, till it seemed madness to refuse. Thus is it: place our bark in the current of the stream, and down, over fall and cataract it is hurried; give up our conduct to the wild torrent of passion, and we are away, we know not whither.

He swore many an oath, and I adjured him by many a sacred name; till I saw this wonder of power, this ruler of the elements, shiver like an autumn leaf before my words; and as if the spirit spake unwillingly and per force within him, at last, he, with broken voice, revealed the spell whereby he might be obliged, did he wish to play me false, to render up the unlawful spoil. Our warm life-blood must mingle to make and to mar the charm.

Enough of this unholy theme. I was persuaded—the thing was done. The morrow dawned upon me as I lay upon the shingles, and I knew not my own shadow as it fell from me. I felt myself changed to a shape of horror, and cursed my easy faith and blind credulity. The chest was there—there the gold and precious stones for which I had sold the frame of flesh which nature had given me. The sight a little stilled my emotions: three days would soon be gone.

They did pass. The dwarf had supplied me with a plenteous store of food. At first I could hardly walk, so strange and out of joint were all my limbs; and my voice—it was that of the fiend. But I kept silent, and turned my face to the sun, that I might not see my shadow, and counted the hours, and ruminated on my future conduct. To bring Torella to my feet—to possess my Juliet in spite of him—all this my wealth could easily achieve. During dark night I slept, and dreamt of the accomplishment of my desires. Two suns had set—the third dawned. I was agitated, fearful. Oh expectation, what a frightful thing art thou, when kindled more by fear than hope! How dost thou twist thyself round the heart, torturing its pulsations! How dost thou dart unknown pangs all through our feeble mechanism, now seeming to shiver us like broken glass, to nothingness—now giving us a fresh strength, which can *do* nothing, and so torments us by a sensation, such as the strong man must feel who cannot break his fetters, though they bend in his grasp. Slowly paced the bright, bright orb up the eastern sky; long it lingered in the zenith, and still more slowly wandered down the west: it touched the horizon's verge—it was lost! Its glories were on the summits of the cliff—they grew dun and gray. The evening star shone bright. He will soon be here.

He came not!—By the living heavens, he came not!—and night dragged out its weary length, and, in its decaying age, "day began to grizzle its dark hair";[1] and the sun rose again on the most miserable wretch that ever upbraided its light. Three days thus I passed. The jewels and the gold—oh, how I abhorred them!

Well, well—I will not blacken these pages with demoniac ravings. All too terrible were the thoughts, the raging tumult of ideas that filled my soul. At the end of that time I slept; I had not before since the third sunset;

---

[1] Byron,* *Werner* 3.4.152–53.

and I dreamt that I was at Juliet's feet, and she smiled, and then she shrieked—for she saw my trans-formation—and again she smiled, for still her beautiful lover knelt before her. But it was not I—it was he, the fiend, arrayed in my limbs, speaking with my voice, winning her with my looks of love. I strove to warn her, but my tongue refused its office; I strove to tear him from her, but I was rooted to the ground—I awoke with the agony. There were the solitary hoar precipices—there the plashing sea, the quiet strand, and the blue sky over all. What did it mean? was my dream but a mirror of the truth? was he wooing and winning my betrothed? I would on the instant back to Genoa—but I was banished. I laughed—the dwarf's yell burst from my lips—*I* banished! O, no! they had not exiled the foul limbs I wore; I might with these enter, without fear of incurring the threatened penalty of death, my own, my native city.

I began to walk towards Genoa. I was somewhat accustomed to my distorted limbs; none were ever so ill adapted for a straight-forward movement; it was with infinite difficulty that I proceeded. Then, too, I desired to avoid all the hamlets strewed here and there on the sea-beach, for I was unwilling to make a display of my hideousness. I was not quite sure that, if seen, the mere boys would not stone me to death as I passed, for a monster: some ungentle salutations I did receive from the few peasants or fishermen I chanced to meet. But it was dark night before I approached Genoa. The weather was so balmy and sweet that it struck me that the Marchese and his daughter would very probably have quitted the city for their country retreat. It was from Villa Torella that I had attempted to carry off Juliet; I had spent many an hour reconnoitring the spot, and knew each inch of ground in its vicinity. It was beautifully situated, embosomed in trees, on the margin of a stream. As I drew near, it became evident that my conjecture was right; nay, moreover, that the hours were being then devoted to feasting and merriment. For the house was lighted up; strains of soft and gay music were wafted towards me by the breeze. My heart sank within me. Such was the generous kindness of Torella's heart that I felt sure that he would not have indulged in public manifestations of rejoicing just after my unfortunate banishment, but for a cause I dared not dwell upon.

The country people were all alive and flocking about; it became necessary that I should study to conceal myself; and yet I longed to address some one, or to hear others discourse, or in any way to gain intelligence of what was really going on. At length, entering the walks that were in immediate vicinity to the mansion, I found one dark enough to veil my excessive frightfulness; and yet others as well as I were loitering in its shade. I soon gathered all I wanted to know—all that first made my very heart die with horror, and then boil with indignation. To-morrow Juliet was to be given to the penitent, reformed, beloved Guido—to-morrow my bride was to pledge her vows to a fiend from hell! And I did this!—my accursed pride—my demoniac violence and wicked self-idolatry had caused this act. For if I had acted as the wretch who had stolen my form had acted—if, with a mien at once yielding and dignified, I had presented myself to Torella, saying, I have done wrong, forgive me; I am unworthy of your angel-child, but permit me to claim her hereafter, when my altered conduct shall manifest that I abjure my vices, and endeavour to become in some sort worthy of her. I go to serve against the infidels; and when my zeal for religion and my true penitence for the past shall appear to you to cancel my crimes, permit me again to call myself your son. Thus had he spoken; and the penitent was welcomed even as the prodigal son of scripture: the fatted calf was killed for him; and he, still pursuing the same path, displayed such open-hearted regret for his follies, so humble a concession of all his rights, and so ardent a resolve to reacquire them by a life of contrition and virtue, that he quickly conquered the kind, old man; and full pardon, and the gift of his lovely child, followed in swift succession.

O! had an angel from Paradise whispered to me to act thus! But now, what would be the innocent Juliet's fate? Would God permit the foul union—or, some prodigy destroying it, link the dishonoured name of Carega with the worst of crimes? To-morrow at dawn they were to be married: there was but one way to prevent this—to meet mine enemy, and to enforce the ratification of our agreement. I felt that this could only be done by a mortal struggle. I had no sword—if indeed my distorted arms could wield a soldier's weapon—but I had a dagger, and in that lay my every hope. There was no time for pondering or balancing nicely the question: I might die in the attempt; but besides the burning jealousy and despair of my own heart, honour, mere humanity, demanded that I should fall rather than not destroy the machinations of the fiend.

The guests departed—the lights began to disappear; it was evident that the inhabitants of the villa were seeking repose. I hid myself among the trees—the garden grew desert—the gates were closed—I wandered round and came under a window—ah! well did I know the same!—a soft twilight glimmered in the room—the curtains were half withdrawn. It was the temple of innocence and beauty. Its magnificence was tempered, as it were, by the slight disarrangements occasioned by its being dwelt in, and all the objects scattered around displayed the taste of her who hallowed it by her presence. I saw her enter with a quick light step—I saw her approach the window—she drew back the curtain yet further, and looked out into the night. Its breezy freshness played among her ringlets, and wafted them from the transparent marble of her brow. She clasped her hands, she raised her eyes to Heaven. I heard her voice. Guido! she softly murmured, Mine own Guido! and then, as if overcome by the fulness of her own heart, she sank on her knees:—her upraised eyes—her negligent but graceful attitude—the beaming thankfulness that lighted up her face—oh, these are tame words! Heart of mine, thou imagest ever, though thou canst not pourtray, the celestial beauty of that child of light and love.

I heard a step—a quick firm step along the shady avenue. Soon I saw a cavalier, richly dressed, young and, methought, graceful to look on, advance.—I hid myself yet closer.—The youth approached; he paused beneath the window. She arose, and again looking out she saw him, and said—I cannot, no, at this distant time I cannot record her terms of soft silver tenderness; to me they were spoken, but they were replied to by him.

"I will not go," he cried: "here where you have been, where your memory glides like some Heaven-visiting ghost, I will pass the long hours till we meet, never, my Juliet, again, day or night, to part. But do thou, my love, retire; the cold morn and fitful breeze will make thy cheek pale, and fill with langour thy love-lighted eyes. Ah, sweetest! could I press one kiss upon them, I could, methinks, repose."

And then he approached still nearer, and methought he was about to clamber into her chamber. I had hesitated, not to terrify her; now I was no longer master of myself. I rushed forward—I threw myself on him—I tore him away—I cried, "O loathsome and foul-shaped wretch!"

I need not repeat epithets, all tending, as it appeared, to rail at a person I at present feel some partiality for. A shriek rose from Juliet's lips. I neither heard nor saw—I *felt* only mine enemy, whose throat I grasped, and my dagger's hilt; he struggled, but could not escape: at length hoarsely he breathed these words: "Do!—strike home! destroy this body—you will still live: may your life be long and merry!"

The descending dagger was arrested at the word, and he, feeling my hold relax, extricated himself and drew his sword, while the uproar in the house, and flying of torches from one room to the other, showed that soon we should be separated—and I—oh! far better die: so that he did not survive, I cared not. In the midst of my frenzy there was much calculation:—fall I might, and so that he did not survive, I cared not for the death-blow I might deal against myself. While still, therefore, he thought I paused, and while I saw the villanous resolve to take advantage of my hesitation, in the sudden thrust he made at me, I threw myself on his sword, and at the same moment plunged my dagger, with a true desperate aim, in his side. We fell together, rolling over each other, and the tide of blood that flowed from the gaping wound of each mingled on the grass. More I know not—I fainted.

Again I returned to life: weak almost to death, I found myself stretched upon a bed—Juliet was kneeling beside it. Strange! my first broken request was for a mirror. I was so wan and ghastly, that my poor girl hesitated, as she told me afterwards; but, by the mass! I thought myself a right proper youth when I saw the dear reflection of my own well-known features. I confess it is a weakness, but I avow it, I do entertain a considerable affection for the countenance and limbs I behold, whenever I look at a glass; and have more mirrors in my house, and consult them oftener than any beauty in Venice. Before you too much condemn me, permit me to say that no one better knows than I the value of his own body; no one, probably, except myself, ever having had it stolen from him.

Incoherently I at first talked of the dwarf and his crimes, and reproached Juliet for her too easy admission of his love. She thought me raving, as well she might, and yet it was some time before I could prevail on myself to admit that the Guido whose penitence had won her back for me was myself; and while I cursed bitterly the monstrous dwarf, and blest the well-directed blow that had deprived him of life, I suddenly checked myself when I heard her say—Amen! knowing that him whom she reviled was my very self. A little reflection taught me silence—a little practice enabled me to speak of that frightful night without any very excessive blunder. The wound I had given myself was no mockery of one—it was long before I recovered—and as the benevolent and generous Torella sat beside me, talking such wisdom as might win friends to repentance, and mine own dear Juliet hovered near me, administering to my wants, and cheering me by her smiles, the work of my bodily cure and mental reform went on together. I have never, indeed, wholly recovered my strength—my cheek is paler since—my person a little bent. Juliet sometimes ventures to allude bitterly to the malice that caused this change, but I kiss her on the moment, and tell her all is for the best. I am a fonder and more faithful husband—and true is this—but for that wound, never had I called her mine.

I did not revisit the sea-shore, nor seek for the fiend's treasure; yet, while I ponder on the past, I often think, and my confessor was not backward in favouring the idea, that it might be a good rather than an evil spirit, sent by my guardian angel, to show me the folly and misery of pride. So well at least did I learn this lesson, roughly taught as I was, that I am known now by all my friends and fellow-citizens by the name of Guido il Cortese.[1]

---

[1] "Guido the Courteous or the Kind" (It.).

Absence

Ah! he is gone—and I alone!—
    How dark and dreary seems the time!
'Tis thus, when the glad sun is flown,
    Night rushes o'er the Indian clime.

5 Is there no star to cheer this night?
    No soothing twilight for the breast?
Yes, Memory sheds her fairy light,
    Pleasing as sunset's golden west.

And hope of dawn—oh! brighter far
10   Than clouds that in the orient burn;
More welcome than the morning star
    Is the dear thought—he will return!

A Dirge[2]

This morn, thy gallant bark, love,
    Sail'd on the sunny sea;
'Tis noon, and tempests dark, love,
    Have wreck'd it on the lee.
5   Ah, woe! ah, woe! ah, woe!
    By spirits of the deep
    He's cradled on the billow,
    To his unwaking sleep!

Thou liest upon the shore, love,
10   Beside the swelling surge;
But sea-nymphs ever more, love,
    Shall sadly chant thy dirge.
    O come! O come! O come!
    Ye spirits of the deep!
15   While near his sea-weed pillow,
    My lonely watch I keep.

From far across the sea, love,
    I hear a wild lament,
By Echo's voice, for thee, love,
20   From Ocean's caverns sent:—

---

[2] Mary Shelley later included this poem in her notes to Percy Bysshe Shelley's poems of 1822 (the year of his death by drowning).

O list! O list! O list!
  The spirits of the deep—
Loud sounds their wail of sorrow,
  While I for ever weep!

from *The Keepsake* (1839)

Stanzas[1]

How like a star you rose upon my life,
  Shedding fair radiance o'er my darkened hour!
At your uprise swift fled the turbid strife
  Of grief and fear,—so mighty was your power!
5 And I must weep that you now disappear,
  Casting eclipse upon my cheerless night—
My heaven deserting for another sphere,
  Shedding elsewhere your aye-regretted light.

An Hesperus no more to gild my eve,
10   You glad the morning of another heart;
And my fond soul must mutely learn to grieve,
  While thus from every joy it swells apart.
Yet I may worship still those gentle beams,
  Though not on me they shed their silver rain;
15 And thought of you may linger in my dreams,
  And Memory pour balm upon my pain.

Stanzas

O, come to me in dreams, my love!
  I will not ask a dearer bliss;
Come with the starry beams, my love,
  And press mine eyelids with thy kiss.
5 'Twas thus, as ancient fables tell,
  Love visited a Grecian maid,
Till she disturbed the sacred spell,
  And woke to find her hopes betrayed.[2]

But gentle sleep shall veil my sight,
10   And Psyche's lamp shall darkling be,
When, in the visions of the night,
  Thou dost renew thy vows to me.

Then come to me in dreams, my love,
  I will not ask a dearer bliss;
15 Come with the starry beams, my love,
  And press mine eyelids with thy kiss.

Letter[3]

To Maria Gisborne[4]

Pisa August 15th 1822[5]

I said in a letter to Peacock,[6] my dear Mrs Gisborne, that I would send you some account of the last miserable months of my disastrous life. From day to day I have put this off, but I will now endeavour to fulfill my design. The scene of my existence is closed & though there be no pleasure in retracing the scenes that have preceded the event which has crushed my hopes yet there seems to be a necessity in doing so, and I obey the impulse that urges me. I wrote to you either at the end

---

[1] probably based on the same epigram, attributed to Plato, that P.B. Shelley uses as an epigraph for *Adonais*.* His translation is as follows: "Thou wert the morning star among the living, / Ere thy fair light had fled— / Now, having died, thou are as Hesperus, giving / New splendour to the Dead." Hesperus is the evening star.

[2] Psyche loves Cupid, but she is forbidden to look at his face; when she disobeys and a drop of hot oil from her lamp awakens him, he leaves her in anger: see Apuleius (AD c. 125–after 170), *The Golden Ass*, and Mary Tighe, *Psyche; or, The Legend of Love*.*

[3] from *The Letters of Mary Wollstonecraft Shelley*, ed. Betty T. Bennett (1980).

[4] a friend of Shelley's parents (Godwin* had unsuccessfully proposed to her after Wollstonecraft's* death in 1797), and of both the Shelleys during their residence in Italy.

[5] a few weeks after Percy Bysshe Shelley's death by drowning, 8 July 1822. Shortly afterwards, Mary Shelley went to Pisa with Jane Williams, whose husband Edward had drowned along with Shelley, and Claire Clairmont, her step-sister; she stayed there until 11 September.

[6] the Shelleys' friend Thomas Love Peacock;* the letter in question does not survive.

of May or the beginning of June. I described to you the place we were living in:[1]—Our desolate house, the beauty yet strangeness of the scenery and the delight Shelley took in all this—he never was in better health or spirits than during this time. I was not well in body or mind. My nerves were wound up to the utmost irritation, and the sense of misfortune hung over my spirits. No words can tell you how I hated our house & the country about it. Shelley reproached me for this—his health was good & the place was quite after his own heart—What could I answer—that the people were wild & hateful, that though the country was beautiful yet I liked a more <u>countryfied</u> place, that there was great difficulty in living—that all our Tuscans would leave us, & that the very jargon of these <u>Genovese</u> was disgusting—This was all I had to say but no words could describe my feelings—the beauty of the woods made me weep & shudder—so vehement was my feeling of dislike that I used to rejoice when the winds & waves permitted me to go out in the boat so that I was not obliged to take my usual walk among tree shaded paths, allies of vine festooned trees—all that before I doated on—& that now weighed on me. My only moments of peace were on board that unhappy boat, when lying down with my head on his knee I shut my eyes & felt the wind & our swift motion alone. My ill health might account for much of this—bathing in the sea somewhat relieved me—but on the 8th of June (I think it was) I was threatened with a miscarriage, & after a week of great ill health on sunday the 16th this took place at eight in the morning. I was so ill that for seven hours I lay nearly lifeless—kept from fainting by brandy, vinegar eau de Cologne &c—at length ice was brought to our solitude—it came before the doctor so Claire & Jane were afraid of using it but Shelley overruled them & by an unsparing application of it I was restored. They all thought & so did I at one time that I was about to die—I hardly wish that I had, my own Shelley could

---

[1] On 30 April the Shelleys had moved to Casa Magni, San Terenzo, a mile from Lerici on the Gulf of Spezia in northwestern Italy; there they lived with their son, Percy Florence, their friends Jane and Edward Williams, who had been unable to find a suitable house nearby, and—for part of the time—Claire Clairmont (who had just lost her child, Allegra).

never have lived without me, the sense of eternal misfortune would have pressed to heavily upon him, & what would have become of my poor babe?[2] My convalescence was slow and during it a strange occurence happened to retard it. But first I must describe our house to you. The floor on which we lived was thus

1 is a terrace that went the whole length of our house & was precipitous to the sea. 2 the large dining hall—3, a private staircase. 4 my bedroom 5 M^{rs} [*Williams's*] bedroom, 6 Shelleys & 7 the entrance from the great staircase. Now to return. As I said Shelley was at first in perfect health but having over fatigued himself one day, & then the fright my illness gave him caused a return of nervous sensations & visions as bad as in his worst times. I think it was the saturday after my illness while yet unable to walk I was confined to my bed—in the middle of the night I was awoke by hearing him scream & come rushing into my room; I was sure that he was asleep & tried to waken him by calling on him, but he continued to scream which inspired me with such a panic that I jumped out of bed & ran across the hall to M^{rs} W's room where I fell through weakness, though I was so frightened that I got up again immediately—she let me in & Williams went to S. who had been awakened by my getting out of bed—he said that he had not been alseep & that it was a vision that he saw that had frightened him—But as he declared that he had not screamed it was certainly a dream & no waking vision—What had frightened him was this—He dreamt that lying as he did in bed Edward & Jane came into him, they were in the most horrible condition, their bodies lacerated—their bones starting through their skin, the faces pale yet stained with blood, they could hardly walk, but Edward was the weakest & Jane was supporting him—Edward said—Get up, Shelley, the sea is flooding the house & it is all coming down." S. got

---

[2] Percy Florence Shelley, her only surviving child, born November 1819.

up, he thought, & went to the his window that looked on the terrace & the sea & thought he saw the sea rushing in. Suddenly his vision changed & he saw the figure of himself strangling me, that had made him rush into my room, yet fearful of frightening me he dared not approch the bed, when my jumping out awoke him, or as he phrased it caused his vision to vanish. All this was frightful enough, & talking it over the next morning he told me that he had had many visions lately—he had seen the figure of himself which met him as he walked on the terrace & said to him—"How long do you mean to be content"—No very terrific words & certainly not prophetic of what has occurred. But Shelley had often seen these figures when ill; but the strangest thing is that Mrs W. saw him. Now Jane though a woman of sensibility, has not much imagination & is not in the slightest degree nervous—neither in dreams or otherwise. She was standing one day, the day before I was taken ill, at a window that looked on the Terrace with Trelawny—it was day—she saw as she thought Shelley pass by the window, as he often was then, without a coat or jacket—he passed again—now as he passed both times the same way—and as from the side towards which he went each time there was no way to get back except past the window again (except over a wall twenty feet from the ground) she was struck at seeing him pass twice thus & looked out & seeing him no more she cried—"Good God can Shelley have leapt from the wall? Where can he be gone?" Shelley, said Trelawny—"No Shelley has past—What do you mean?" Trelawny says that she trembled exceedingly when she heard this & it proved indeed that Shelley had never been on the terrace & was far off at the time she saw him. Well we thought {no} more of these things & I slowly got better. Having heard from Hunt[1] that he had sailed from Genoa, on Monday July 1st S., Edward & Captain Roberts[2] (the Gent. who built our boat) departed in our boat for Leghorn to receive him—I was then just better, had begun to crawl from my bedroom to the terrace; but bad spirits succeded to ill health, and this departure of Shelley's seemed to add insuferably to my misery. I could not endure that he should go—I called him back two or three times, & told him that if I did not see him soon I would go to Pisa with the child—I cried bitterly when he went away. They went & Jane, Claire & I remained alone with the children—I could not walk out, & though I gradually gathered strength it was slowly & my ill spirits encreased; in my letters to him I entreated him to return—"the feeling that some misfortune would happen," I said, "haunted me": I feared for the child, for the idea of danger connected with him never struck me—When Jane & Claire took their evening walk I used to patrole the terrace, oppressed with wretchedness, yet gazing on the most beautiful scene in the world. This Gulph of Spezia is subdivided into many small bays of which ours was far the most beautiful—the two horns of the bay (so to express myself) were wood covered promontories crowned with castles—at the foot of these on the furthest was Lerici on the nearest San^t Arenzo—Lerici being above a mile by land from us & San Arenzo about a hundred or two yards—trees covered the hills that enclosed this bay & then beautiful groups were picturesquely contrasted with the rocks the castle on [and] the town—the sea lay far extended in front while to the west we saw the promontory & islands which formed one of the extreme boundarys of the Gulph—to see the sun set upon this scene, the stars shine & the moon rise was a sight of wondrous beauty, but to me it added only to my wretchedness—I repeated to myself all that another would have said to console me, & told myself the tale of love peace & competence which I enjoyed—but I answered myself by tears—did not my William die?[3] & did I hold my Percy[4] by a firmer tenure?—Yet I thought when he, when my Shelley returns I shall be happy—he will comfort me, if my boy be ill he will restore him & encourage me. I had a letter or two from Shelley mentioning the difficulties he had in establishing the Hunts, & that he was unable to fix the time of his return. Thus a week past. On Monday

---

[1] The Shelleys' friend Leigh Hunt;* the Hunts had arrived in the port city of Genoa from England, and were now on their way to Pisa, where they would live on a floor of Byron's* house, Casa Lanfranchi.

[2] Edward Williams and Daniel Roberts, a Royal Navy Commander on half pay during non-active service.

[3] The Shelleys' son William died of malaria in Rome, 7 June 1819.

[4] her child, Percy Florence.

8th Jane had a letter from Edward, dated saturday, he said that he waited at Leghorn for S. who was at Pisa   That S's return was certain, "but" he continued, "if he should not come by monday I will come in a felucca,[1] & you may expect me teusday evening at furthest." This was monday, the fatal monday, but with us it was stormy all day & we did not at all suppose that they could put to sea. At twelve at night we had a thunderstorm; Teusday it rained all day & was calm—the sky wept on their graves—on Wednesday—the wind was fair from Leghorn & in the evening several felucca's arrived thence—one brought word that they had sailed monday, but we did not believe them—thursday was another day of fair wind & when twelve at night came & we did not see the tall sails of the little boat double the promontory before us we began to fear not the truth, but some illness—some disagreeable news for their detention. Jane got so uneasy that she determined to proceed the next day to Leghorn in a boat to see what was the matter—friday came & with it a heavy sea & bad wind—Jane however resolved to be rowed to Leghorn (since no boat could sail) and busied herself in preparations—I wished her to wait for letters, since friday was letter day—she would not—but the sea detained her, the swell rose so that no boat would venture out—At 12 at noon our letters came— there was one from Hunt to Shelley, it said—"pray write to tell us how you got home, for they say that you had bad weather after you sailed monday & we are anxious"—the paper fell from me—I trembled all over—Jane read it—"Then it is all over!" she said. "No, my dear Jane," I cried, "it is not all over, but this suspense is dreadful—come with me, we will go to Leghorn, we will post to be swift & learn our fate." We crossed to Lerici, despair in our hearts; they raised our spirits there by telling us that no accident had been heard of & that it must have been known &c—but still our fear was great—& without resting we posted to Pisa It must have been fearful to see us—two poor, wild, aghast creatures —driving (like Matilda)[2] towards the <u>sea</u> to learn if we were to be for ever doomed to misery. I knew that Hunt was at Pisa at Lord Byrons' house but I thought that L.B. was at Leghorn. I settled that we should drive to Casa Lanfranchi[3] that I should get out & ask the fearful question of Hunt, "do you know any thing of Shelley?" On entering Pisa the idea of seeing Hunt for the first time for four years under such circumstances, & asking him such a question was so terrific to me that it was with difficulty that I prevented myself from going into convulsions—my struggles were dreadful—they knocked at the door & some one called out "Chi è?"[4] it was the Guiccioli's[5] maid L.B. was in Pisa—Hunt was in bed, so I was to see L.B. instead of him—This was a great relief to me; I staggered up stairs—the Guiccioli came to meet me smiling while I could hardly say—"Where is he—Sapete alcuna cosa di Shelley"[6] —They knew nothing—he had left Pisa on sunday—on Monday he had sailed—there had been bad weather monday afternoon—more they knew not. Both LB & the lady have told me since—that on that terrific evening I looked more like a ghost than a woman—light seemed to emanate from my features, my face was very white I looked like marble—Alas. I had risen almost from a bed of sickness for this journey—I had travelled all day—it was now 12 at night—& we, refusing to rest, proceeded to Leghorn—not in despair—no, for then we must have died; but with sufficient hope to keep up the agitation of the spirits which was all my life. It was past two in the morning when we arrived—They took us to the wrong

---

[1] a fast narrow Mediterranean sailing ship.

[2] The heroine of Shelley's novella *Mathilda*, unpublished until edited by Elizabeth Nitchie in 1959, drives towards the sea in the hope of preventing her guilt-ridden father, obsessed by incestuous desire, from drowning himself. The manuscript of *Mathilda* was at this time in Godwin's* possession: he would neither get it published nor return it to its author.

[3] Byron's house in Pisa.

[4] "Who's there?" (It.).

[5] Countess Teresa Gamba Guiccioli (c. 1800–73), married to a man forty years her senior, was Byron's* lover from 1819 until his death in 1824.

[6] "What do you know about Shelley?" (It.).

inn—neither Trelawny[1] or Cap[n] Roberts were there nor did we exactly know where they were so we were obliged to wait until daylight. We threw ourselves drest on our beds & slept a little but at 6 o'clock we went to one or two inns to ask for one or the other of these gentlemen. We found Roberts at the Globe. He came down to us with a face which seemed to tell us that the worst was true, and here we learned all that had occurred during the week they had been absent from us, & under what circumstances they had departed on their return.———Shelley had past most of the time a[t] Pisa—arranging the affairs of the Hunts—& skrewing LB's mind to the sticking place[2] about the journal.[3] He had found this a difficult task at first but at length he had succeeded to his heart's content with both points. M[rs] Mason[4] said that she saw him in better health and spirits than she had ever known him, when he took leave of her sunday July 7th   His face burnt by the sun, & his heart light that he had succeeded in rendering the Hunts' tolerably comfortable. Edward had remained at Leghorn. On Monday July 8th during the morning they were employed in buying many things—eatables &c for our solitude. There had been a thunderstorm early but about noon the weather was fine & the wind right fair for Lerici—They were impatient to be gone. Roberts said, "Stay until tomorrow to see if the weather is settled; & S. might have staid but Edward was in so great an anxiety to reach home—saying they would get there in seven hours with that wind—that they sailed! S. being in one of those extravagant fits of good spirits in which you have sometimes seen him. Roberts went out to the end of the mole & watched them out of sight—they sailed at one & went off at the rate of about 7 knots[5]—About three—Roberts, who was still on the mole—saw wind coming from the Gulph—or rather what the Italians call a temporale[6] anxious to know how the boat w[d] weather the storm, he got leave to go up the tower & with the glass discovered them about ten miles out at sea, off Via Reggio, they were taking in their topsails—"The haze of the storm," he said, "hid them from me & I saw them no more—when the storm cleared I looked again fancying that I should see them on their return to us—but there was no boat on the sea."—This then was all we knew, yet we did not despair—they might have been driven over to Corsica & not knowing the coast & Gone god knows where. Reports favoured this belief.—it was even said that they had been seen in the Gulph—We resolved to return with all possible speed—We sent a courier to go from tower to tower along the coast to know if any thing had been seen or found, & at 9 AM. we quitted Leghorn—stopped but one moment at Pisa & proceeded towards Lerici. When at 2 miles from Via Reggio we rode down to that town to know if they knew any thing—here our calamity first began to break on us—a little boat & a water cask had been found five miles off—they had manufactured a piccolissima lancia[7] of thin planks stiched by a shoemaker just to let them run on shore without wetting themselves as our boat drew 4 feet water.—the description of that found tallied with this—but then this boat was very cumbersome & in bad weather they might have been easily led to throw it overboard—the cask frightened me most—but the same reason might in some sort be given for that. I must tell you that Jane & I were not now alone—Trelawny accompanied us back to our home. We journied on & reached the Magra[8] about ½ past ten P.M. I cannot describe to you what I felt in the first moment when, fording this river, I felt the water splash about our wheels—I was suffocated—I gasped for breath—I thought I should have gone into convulsions, & I

---

[1] Edward John Trelawny, whom the Shelleys met in January 1822 and who wrote about the acquaintance in *Recollections of the Last Days of Shelley and Byron** and *Records of Shelley, Byron, and the Author* (1878).

[2] Shakespeare, *Macbeth* 1.7.60.

[3] *The Liberal*, a collaborative venture of Byron, Hunt, and Percy Shelley, appeared in four parts in 1822–23.

[4] Margaret King Moore, Countess of Mount Cashel (1773–1835), a former pupil of Wollstonecraft,* had left her husband to live in Italy with George William Tighe; the couple was known as Mr. and Mrs. Mason.

[5] seven nautical miles (about 13 km) an hour.

[6] "thunderstorm" (It.).

[7] "tiniest boat" (It.).

[8] a river flowing into the sea south of Lerici.

struggled violently that Jane might not perceive it—looking down the river I saw the two great lights burning at the foce[1]—A voice from within me seemed to cry aloud that is his grave. After passing the river I gradually recovered. Arriving at Lerici we [were] obliged to cross our little bay in a boat—San Arenzo was illuminated for a festa—what a scene—the roaring sea—the scirocco wind[2]—the lights of the town towards which we rowed—& our own desolate hearts—that coloured all with a shroud—we landed; nothing had been heard of them. This was saturday July 13. & thus we waited until Thursday July 25th thrown about by hope & fear. We sent messengers along the coast towards Genoa & to Via Reggio—nothing had been found more than the lancetta; reports were brought us—we hoped—& yet to tell you all the agony we endured during those 12 days would be to make you conceive a universe of pain[3]—each moment intolerable & giving place to one still worse. The people of the country too added to one's discomfort—they are like wild savages—on festa's the men & women & children in different bands—the sexes always separate—pass the whole night in dancing on the sands close to our door running into the sea then back again & screaming all the time one perpetuel air—the most detestable in the world—then the scirocco perpetually blew & the sea for ever moaned their dirge. On Thursday 25th Trelawny left us to go to Leghorn to see what was doing or what could be done. On friday I was very ill but as evening came on I said to Jane—"If any thing had been found on the coast Trelawny would have returned to let us know. He has not returned so I hope." About 7 o'clock P.M. he did return—all was over—all was quiet now, they had been found washed on shore—Well all this was to be endured.

Well what more have I to say? The next day we returned to Pisa   And here we are still—days pass away—one after another—& we live thus. We are all together—we shall quit Italy together. Jane must proceed to London—if letters do not alter my views I shall remain in Paris.—Thus we live—Seeing the Hunts now & then. Poor Hunt has suffered terribly as you may guess. Lord Byron is very kind to me & comes with the Guiccioli to see me often.

Today—this day—the sun shining in the sky—they are gone to the desolate sea coast to perform the last offices to their earthly remains. Hunt, LB. & Trelawny. The quarantine laws would not permit us to remove them sooner—& now only on condition that we burn them to ashes. That I do not dislike—His rest shall be at Rome beside my child—where one day I also shall join them[4]—Adonais is not Keats's it is his own elegy—he bids you there go to Rome.[5]—I have seen the spot where he now lies—the sticks that mark the spot where the sands cover him—he shall not be there it is too nea[r] Via Reggio—They are now about this fearful office—& I live!

One more circumstance I will mention. As I said he took leave of Mrs Mason in high spirits on sunday—"Never," said she, "did I see him look happier than the last glance I had of his countenance." On Monday he was lost—on monday night she dreamt—that she was somewhere—she knew not where & he came looking very pale & fearfully melancholy—she said to him—"You look ill, you are tired, sit down & eat." "No," he replied, "I shall never eat more; I have not a soldo[6] left in the world."—"Nonsense," said she, "this is no inn—you need not pay—"—"Perhaps, he answered, "it is the worse for that." Then she awoke & going to sleep again she dreamt that my Percy was dead & she awoke crying bitterly (so bitterly th) & felt so miserable—that she said to herself—"why if the little boy should die I should not feel it in this manner." She [was] so struck with these dreams that she mentioned them to her servant the next day—saying she hoped all was well with us.

Well here is my story—the last story I shall have to tell—all that might have been bright in my life is now despoiled—I shall live to improve myself, to take care of

---

[1] "mouth of the river" (It.).

[2] sultry south-east wind, traditionally considered unhealthy.

[3] Cf. Milton, *Paradise Lost* 2.622.

[4] Percy Bysshe Shelley* was buried in the Protestant Cemetery, Rome, near the site of William's grave (the supposed gravesite turned out to contain the remains of an adult). Mary Shelley died in England and was buried in St. Peter's Churchyard, Bournemouth, with her parents.

[5] See P.B. Shelley's poem *Adonais: An Elegy on the Death of John Keats*, 424, 433.*

[6] "penny" (It.).

my child, & render myself worthy to join him. soon my weary pilgrimage will begin—I rest now—but soon I must leave Italy—& then—there is an end of all despair. Adieu   I hope you are well & happy. I have an idea that while he was at Pisa that he received a letter from you that I have never seen—so not knowing where to direct I shall send this letter to Peacock—I shall send it open—he may be glad to read it—

                    Your's ever truly Mary WS.—Pisa I shall probably write to you soon again.

I have left out a material circumstance—A Fishing boat saw them go down—It was about 4 in the afternoon—they saw the boy at mast head, when baffling winds struck the sails, they had looked away a moment & looking again the boat was gone—This is their story but there is little down [*doubt*] that these men might have saved them, at least Edward who could swim. They c^d not they said get near her—but 3 quarters of an hour after passed over the spot where they had seen her—they protested no wreck of her was visible, but Roberts going on board their boat found several spars belonging to her.—perhaps they let them perish to obtain these. Trelawny thinks he can get her up, since another fisherman things [*thinks*] that he has found the spot where she lies, having drifted near shore. T. does this to know perhaps the cause of her wreck—but I care little about it

Journal[1]

                    May 14th [1824][2]

This then is my English life! And thus I am to drag on existence! No—I must make up my made mind to break through my servitude and go—I cannot—cannot live here. Of what use am I? confined in my prison-room—friendless—Each day I string me to task; I endeavour to read & write—my ideas a [*for* are] stagnate and my understanding refuses to follow the words I read—day after day passes while torrents fall from the dark clouds, and my mind is as gloomy as this odious sky—without human friends I must attach myself to natural objects—but though I talk of the country what difference shall I find in this miserable climate—

Italy—dear Italy—murdress of those I love & of all my happiness—one word of your soft language coming unawares upon me has drowned me in bitterest tears—When shall shall I hear it again spoken? when see your sky your trees your streams—Never in good spirits, the imprisonment attendant on a succession of rainy days has quite overcome me—God knows I strive to be content—but in vain—

Amidst all the depressing circumstances that weigh on me—none sinks deeper than the failure of my intellectual powers—Nothing I write pleases me. Whether I am just in this, or whether the want of Shelleys (oh my loved Shelley—it is some alleviation only to write your name, drowned though I am the while in tears) encouragement—I can hardly tell but it seems to me as if the lovely and sublime objects of nature were ↑ had been ↓* my best inspirers & wanting these I am lost. Although so utterly miserable at Genoa, yet what reveries were mine as I walked on the road and looked on the changing aspect of the ravine—the sunny deep & its boats—the promontories clothed in purple light—the starry heavens—the fireflies—the uprising of spring—then I could think—and my imagination could invent & combine, and self become absorbed in the grandeur of the universe I created—Now my mind is a blank—a gulph filled with formless mist—

The last man! Yes I may well describe that solitary being's feelings, feeling myself as the last relic of a beloved race, my companions, extinct before me—[3]

And thus has the accumulating sorrows of days & weeks been forced to find a voice, because the word <u>lucerna</u>[4] met my eyes and the idea of lost Italy sprung in

---

[1] from *The Journals of Mary Shelley 1814–1844*, ed. Paula R. Feldman and Diana Scott-Kilvert (1987).

[2] Shelley and her son Percy Florence left Italy for England in 1823. There, she attempted (unsuccessfully) to arrange an adequate allowance from the Shelley family while she continued writing to support herself and her child.

[3] Shelley had begun work on her novel *The Last Man*, which would be published in 1826; her hero, Lionel Verney, becomes the sole survivor of a plague that kills all other human beings.

[4] "oil lamp" (It.).

* ↑ Word ↓ indicates an authorial insertion.

my mind—what graceful lamps those are, though of bare construction and vulgar use—I thought of bringing one with me—I am glad I did not—I will go back only to have a <u>lucerna</u>—if I told people so they would think me mad— & yet not madder than they seem to do now when I say that the blue skies and verdure clad earth of that dear land is necessary to my existence.—

If there be a kind spirit attendant on me, in compensation for these miserable days, let me only dream to night that I am in Italy! Mine own Shelley—what a horror you had (fully sympathized by me) of returning to this miserable country—To be here without ↑ you ↓ is to be doubly exiled—to be away from Italy, is to lose you twice—Dearest—why cannot I study & become worthy of you? Why is my spirit thus losing all energy?—indeed, indeed, I must go back, or your poor utterly lost Mary will never dare think herself worthy to visit you beyond the grave.

I do not remember ever having been so completely miserable as I am tonight—

May 15th

This then was the "coming event" that cast its shadow on my last night's miserable thoughts. Byron has become ↑ one ↓ of the people of the grave[1]—that innumerable conclave to which the beings I best loved belong. I knew him in the bright days of youth, when neither care or fear had visited me: before death had made me feel my mortality and the earth was the scene of my hopes—Can I forget our evening visits to Diodati—our excursions of the lake when he sang the Tyrolese hymn—and his voice was harmonized with winds and waves?[2]—Can I forget his attentions & consolations to me during my deepest misery?—Never.

Beauty sat on his countenance and power beamed from his eye—his faults being for the most part weaknesses induced one readily to pardon them. Albe[3]—the dear capricious fascinating Albe has left this desart world

What do I do here? Why and am I doomed to live on seeing all expire before me? God grant I may die young—A new race is springing about me—At the age of twenty six I am in the condition of an aged person—all my old friends are gone—I have no wish to form new—I cling to the few remaining—but they slide away & my heart fails when I think by how few ties I hold to the world—Albe, dearest Albe, was knit by long associations—Each day I repeat with bitterer feelings "Life is the desart and the solitude—how populous the grave."[4] and that regions its its ↑ to the ↓ dearer and best beloved beings which ↑ it ↓ has torn from me, now adds that resplendent Spirit, whom I loved whose departure leaves the dull earth still darker as midnight

---

[1] Byron* died at Missolonghi, Greece, on 19 April 1824; the news reached England on 14 May.

[2] Shelley is remembering the summer of 1816, when Byron stayed at the Villa Diodati on Lake Geneva and the Shelleys stayed across the lake at Belle Rive; the Tyrolese hymn is a Swiss song of liberty.

[3] Byron's nickname, perhaps a version of "L.B.," perhaps short for "Albanian," with reference to Byron's travels.

[4] Cf. Edward Young (1683–1765), *The Complaint: or Night Thoughts* (1742–45) 1.111–16.

William Apess
1798 – 1839

William Apess was born in the forest near Colrain, Massachusetts, on 31 January 1798. His father, William Apes, of mixed European and Pequot background, was a shoemaker; his mother, whose name may have been Candace, was of uncertain background; she was either an indentured servant or a slave (she was freed in 1805). When Apess was three, his parents separated, and he and two brothers and two sisters were placed in the care of his maternal grandparents. Both grandparents were alcoholic and abusive, and after a brutal beating, Apess was indentured to a succession of white families. He began attending the meetings of the Methodists, who welcomed Native Americans and other oppressed groups. In 1813, after his last master forbade him to do so, he ran away and joined the New York militia, to serve in the War of 1812. After the war, he wandered the North-East, supporting himself as a bartender, bookseller, cook, and farm labourer. He was baptized in 1818 and soon began preaching. In 1821, he married Mary Wood; they had at least three children. He was ordained a Methodist minister in 1829. His first book, *A Son of the Forest* (1829), the first full-length Native American autobiography, has been compared to Equiano's *Interesting Narrative.** He went on to publish a sermon, an essay arguing that Native Americans were descendants of the ten lost tribes of Israel, and a collection of biographical portraits of Christian Pequots, including himself and his wife. In 1833, he went to live in the Native community of Mashpee, Massachusetts, where he assisted the inhabitants in the struggle for the rights to control their natural resources and appoint a minister of their choice. He was arrested on 4 July 1833, sentenced to thirty days in jail, and fined $100, but the struggle was largely successful; *Indian Nullification of the Unconstitutional Laws of Massachusetts* (1835) is his documentary account of it. His last work was *Eulogy on King Philip* (1836), in praise of Metacomet, or King Philip (d. 1676), seventeenth-century chief of the Wampanoag. In his last years, Apess appears to have succumbed to the alcoholism against which he had struggled all his life; he died in New York City in April or May of 1839. (D.L.M.)

☙❦❧

from *A Son of the Forest* (1829)

CHAPTER 3

After I had been some time on the island,[1] I took much comfort in beating on an old drum; this was my business, as I was enlisted for a drummer. About this time I was greatly alarmed on account of the execution of a soldier who was shot on Governor's Island for mutiny. I cannot tell how I felt when I saw the soldiers parade, and the condemned clothed in white with bibles in their hands, come forward. The band then struck up the dead march, and the procession moved with a mournful and measured tread to the place of execution, where the poor creatures were compelled to kneel on their coffins, which were along side their newly dug graves. While in this position the chaplain went forward and conversed with them—after he had retired a soldier went up and drew their caps over their faces; thus blindfolded he led one of them some distance from the other. An officer then advanced, and raised his handkerchief as a signal to the platoon to prepare to fire—he then made another for them to aim at the wretch who had been left kneeling on his coffin, and at a third signal the platoon fired, and the immortal essence of the offender in an instant was in the spirit-land. To me this was an awful day—my heart seemed to leap into my throat. Death never appeared so awful. But what must have been the feelings of the unhappy man, who had so narrowly escaped the grave? He was completely overcome, and wept like a child, and it was found necessary to help him back to his quarters. This spectacle made me serious; but it wore off in a few days.

---

[1] Governor's Island, in New York Bay, south of Manhattan. In 1813, Apess enlisted in the United States Army for the War of 1812.

Shortly after this we were ordered to Staten Island, where we remained about two months.—Then we were ordered to join the army destined to conquer Canada. As the soldiers were tired of the island, this news animated them very much. They thought it a great thing to march through the country and assist in taking the enemy's land. As soon as our things were ready we embarked on board a sloop for Albany, and then went on to Greenbush, where we were quartered. In the mean time I had been transferred to the ranks. This I did not like; to carry a musket was too fatiguing, and I had a positive objection to being placed on the guard, especially at night.[1] As I had only enlisted for a drummer, I thought that this change by the officer was contrary to law, and as the bond was broken, liberty was granted me; therefore being heartily tired of a soldier's life, and having a desire to see my father once more, I went off very deliberately; I had no idea that they had a lawful claim on me, and was greatly surprised as well as alarmed, when arrested as a deserter from the army. Well, I was taken up and carried back to the camp, where the officers put me under guard. We shortly after marched for Canada, and during this dreary march the officers tormented me by telling me that it was their intention to make a fire in the woods, stick my skin full of pine splinters, and after having an Indian pow-wow over me, burn me to death. Thus they tormented me day after day.

We halted for some time at Burlington: but resumed our march and went into winter quarters at Plattsburgh.[2] All this time God was very good to me, as I had not a sick day. I had by this time become very bad. I had previously learned to drink rum, play cards and commit other acts of wickedness, but it was here that I first took the name of the Lord in vain, and oh, what a sting it left behind. We continued here until the ensuing fall, when we received orders to join the main army under Gen. Hampton.[3] Another change now took place,—we had several pieces of heavy artillery with us, and of course horses were necessary to drag them, and I was taken from the ranks and ordered to take charge of one team. This made my situation rather better. I now had the privilege of riding. The soldiers were badly off, as the officers were very cruel to them, and for every little offence they would have them flogged. One day the officer of our company got angry at me, and pricked my ear with the point of his sword.

We soon joined the main army, and pitched our tents with them. It was now very cold, and we had nothing but straw to lay on. There was also a scarcity of provisions, and we were not allowed to draw our full rations. Money would not procure food—and when any thing was to be obtained the officers had always the preference, and they, poor souls, always wanted the whole for themselves. The people generally, have no idea of the extreme sufferings of the soldiers on the frontiers during the last war; they were indescribable, the soldiers eat with the utmost greediness raw corn and every thing eatable that fell in their way. In the midst of our afflictions, our valiant general ordered us to march forward to subdue the country in a trice. The pioneers had great difficulty in clearing the way—the enemy retreated burning every thing as they fled. They destroyed every thing, so that we could not find forage for the horses. We were now cutting our way through a wilderness, and were very often benumbed with the cold. Our sufferings now for the want of food were extreme—the officers too began to feel it, and one of them offered me two dollars for a little flour, but I did not take his money, and he did not get my flour; I would not have given it to *him* for fifty dollars. The soldiers united their flour and baked unleavened bread, of this we made a delicious repast.

After we had proceeded about thirty miles, we fell in with a body of Canadians and Indians—the woods fairly resounded with their yells. Our "brave and chivalrous" general ordered a picked troop to disperse them; we fired but one cannon and a retreat was sounded to the

---

[1] Apess was only 15 (his enlistment was actually illegal), and only 155 cm (5' 2") tall.

[2] Burlington (VT) and Plattsburgh (NY) are both on the shore of Lake Champlain, which, surrounded by New York, Vermont, and Québec, was one of the crucial theatres of the war.

[3] General Wade Hampton (c. 1752–1835) commanded the American army stationed near Lake Champlain in 1813. He was widely regarded as incompetent and resigned in 1814.

great mortification of the soldiers, who were ready and willing to fight. But as our general did not fancy the smell of gunpowder, he thought it best to close the campaign, by retreating with seven thousand men, before a "host" of seven hundred. Thus were many a poor fellow's hopes of conquest and glory blasted by the timidity of one man. This little brush with an enemy that we could have crushed in a single moment cost us several men in killed and wounded.[1] The army now fell back on Plattsburgh, where we remained during the winter; we suffered greatly for the want of barracks, having to encamp in the open fields a good part of the time. My health, through the goodness of God, was preserved, notwithstanding many of the poor soldiers sickened and died. So fast did they go off, that it appeared to me as if the plague was raging among them.

When the spring opened, we were employed in building forts. We erected three in a very short time. We soon received orders to march, and joined the army under Gen. Wilkinson, to reduce Montreal. We marched to Odletown in great splendor, "Heads up and eyes right,"[2] with a noble commander at our head, and the splendid city of Montreal in our view. The city no doubt presented a scene of the wildest uproar and confusion; the people were greatly alarmed as we moved on with all the pomp and glory of an army flushed with many victories. But when we reached Odletown, John Bull met us with a picked troop. They soon retreated, and some took refuge in an old fortified mill, which we pelted with a goodly number of cannon balls. It appeared as if we were determined to sweep every thing before us. It was really amusing to see our feminine general with his night-cap on his head and a dishcloth tied round his precious body, crying out to his men, "Come on, my brave boys, we will give John Bull a bloody nose." We did not succeed in taking the mill, and the British kept up an incessant cannonade from the fort. Some of the balls cut down the trees, so that we had frequently to spring out of their way when falling.

I thought it was a hard time, and I had reason too, as I was in the front of the battle, assisting in working a twelve pounder, and the British aimed directly at us. Their balls whistled around us, and hurried a good many of the soldiers into the eternal world, while others were most horribly mangled. Indeed they were so hot upon us, that we had not time to remove the dead as they fell. The horribly disfigured bodies of the dead—the piercing groans of the wounded and the dying—the cries of help and succour from those who could not help themselves—were most appalling. I can never forget it. We continued fighting till near sundown, when a retreat was sounded along our line, and instead of marching forward to Montreal, we wheeled about, and having once set our faces toward Plattsburgh, and turned our backs ingloriously on the enemy, we hurried off with all possible speed. We carried our dead and wounded with us. Oh, it was a dreadful sight to behold so many brave men sacrificed in this manner. In this way our campaign closed. During the whole of this time the Lord was merciful to me, as I was not suffered to be hurt. We once more reached Plattsburgh, and pitched our tents in the neighbourhood. While here, intelligence of the capture of Washington was received.[3] Now, says the orderly sergeant, the British have burnt up all the papers at Washington, and our enlistment for the war among them, we had better give in our names as having enlisted for five years.

We were again under marching orders, as the enemy it was thought, contemplated an attack on Plattsburgh. Thither we moved without delay, and were posted in one of the forts. By the time we were ready for them, the enemy made his appearance on Lake Champlain, with his vessels of war. It was a fine thing to see their noble vessels moving like things of life upon this mimic sea, with their streamers floating in the wind. This armament was intended to co-operate with the army, which numbered fourteen thousand men, under the command of the captain general of Canada,[4] and at that very time in view of our troops. They presented a very

---

[1] In November 1813, in a battle about 145 km (90 miles) from Montréal, an American army of 8,000, commanded by General James Wilkinson (1757–1825), was defeated by a British force of only 800. Wilkinson was relieved of his command.

[2] a disciplined manner of marching, drilled into the troops.

[3] The British captured and burned Washington on 24–25 August 1814.

[4] General Sir George Prevost (1767–1816).

imposing aspect. Their red uniform, and the instruments of death which they bore in their hands, glittered in the sun beams of heaven, like so many sparkling diamonds. Very fortunately for us and for the country, a brave and noble commander had placed himself at the head of the army.[1] It was not an easy task to frighten him. For notwithstanding his men were inferior in point of number to those of the enemy, say as one to seven, yet relying on the bravery of his men, he determined to fight to the last extremity. The enemy in all the pomp and pride of war, had sat down before the town and its slender fortifications, and he commenced a cannonade, which we returned without much ceremony. Congreve rockets,[2] bomb shells, and cannon balls, poured upon us like a hail storm. There was scarcely any intermission, and for six days and nights we did not leave our guns, and during that time the work of death paused not, as every day some shot took effect. During the engagement, I had charge of a small magazine. All this time our fleet, under the command of the gallant M'Donough,[3] was lying on the peaceful waters of Champlain. But this little fleet was to be taken, or destroyed: it was necessary, in the accomplishment of their plans. Accordingly the British commander bore down on our vessels in gallant style. As soon as the enemy showed fight, our men flew to their guns. Then the work of death and carnage commenced. The adjacent shores resounded with the alternate shouts of the sons of liberty, and the groans of their parting spirits. A cloud of smoke mantled the heavens, shutting out the light of day—while the continual roar of artillery, added to the sublime horrors of the scene. At length the boasted valour of the haughty Britons failed them—they quailed before the incessant and well directed fire of our brave and hardy tars, and after a hard fought battle, surrendered to that foe they had been sent to crush. On land the battle raged pretty fiercely. On our side the Green mountain boys[4] behaved with the greatest bravery. As soon as the British commander had seen the fleet fall into the hands of the Americans, his boasted courage forsook him, and he ordered his army of heroes, fourteen thousand strong, to retreat before a handful of militia.

This was indeed a proud day for our country. We had met a superior force on the Lake, and "they were ours."[5] On land we had compelled the enemy to seek safety in flight. Our army did not lose many men, but on the lake many a brave man fell—fell in the defence of his country's rights. The British moved off about sundown.

We remained in Plattsburgh until the peace. As soon as it was known that the war had terminated, and the army disbanded, the soldiers were clamorous for their discharge, but it was concluded to retain our company in the service—I, however, obtained my release. Now, according to the act of enlistment, I was entitled to forty dollars bounty money, and one hundred and sixty acres of land. The government also owed me for fifteen months pay. I have not seen any thing of bounty money, land, or arrearages, from that day to this. I am not, however, alone in this—hundreds were served in the same manner. But I could never think that the government acted right toward the "*Natives*," not merely in refusing to pay us, but in claiming our services in cases of perilous emergency, and still deny us the right of citizenship; and as long as our nation is debarred the privilege of voting for civil officers, I shall believe that the government has no claim on our services.[6]

---

[1] General Alexander Macomb (1782–1841) assumed command at Plattsburgh at the end of August and drove back a greatly superior British force on 11 September.

[2] Invented by Sir William Congreve (1772–1828) in 1805, these had a range of over 2500 m (2700 yards) and could weigh between 3.5 and 19 kilos (8–40 lbs).

[3] Captain Thomas Macdonough (1783–1825), whose naval victory on 11 September forced the British to retreat and gave the Americans control of the lake.

[4] militiamen from the Green Mountains, a part of the Appalachian range in central Vermont.

[5] Cf. the famous dispatch of Oliver Hazard Perry (1785–1819) to General William Henry Harrison (1773–1841) after the battle of Lake Erie (10 September 1813): "We have met the enemy and they are ours." Cf. Richardson, *Tecumseh*,* n. 1.

[6] The Treaty of Ghent, which ended the War of 1812, was signed on 24 December 1814 and ratified by the Senate on 17 February 1815. According to Apess's army records, he deserted by 14 September 1815.

CHAPTER 4

I believe that there are many good people in the United States, who would not trample upon the rights of the poor, but there are many others who are willing to roll in their coaches upon the tears and blood of the poor and unoffending natives—those who are ready at all times to speculate on the indians and cheat them out of their rightful possessions. Let the poor indian attempt to resist the encroachments of his white neighbours, what a hue and cry is instantly raised against him. It has been considered as a trifling thing for the whites to make war on the indians for the purpose of driving them from their country, and taking possession thereof. This was, in their estimation, all right, as it helped to extend the territory, and enriched some individuals. But let the thing be changed. Suppose an overwhelming army should march into the United States, for the purpose of subduing it, and enslaving the citizens. How quick would they fly to arms, gather in multitudes around the tree of liberty, and contend for their rights with the last drop of their blood. And should the enemy succeed, would they not eventually rise and endeavour to regain liberty? And who would blame them for it?

When I left the army, I had not a shilling in my pocket. I depended upon the precarious bounty of the inhabitants, until I reached the place where some of my brethren[1] dwelt. I tarried with them but a short time, and then set off for Montreal. I was anxious, in some degree, to become steady, and went to learn the business of a baker. My bad habits now overcome my good intentions. I was addicted to drinking rum, and would sometimes get quite intoxicated. As it was my place to carry out the bread, I frequently fell in company, and one day, being in liquor, I met one of the king's soldiers, and after abusing him with my tongue, I gave him a sound flogging. In the course of the affair I broke a pitcher which the soldier had, and as I had to pay for it, I was wicked enough to take my master's money, without his knowledge, for that purpose. My master liked me, but he thought if I acted so once, I would a second time, and he therefore discharged me. I was now placed in a bad situation—by my misconduct, I had lost a good home! I went and hired myself to a farmer, for four dollars per month. After serving him two months, he paid me, and with the money I bought some decent clothes. By spells, I was hired as a servant, but this kind of life did not suit me, and I wished to return to my brethren. My mind changed, and I went up the St. Lawrence to Kingston, where I obtained a situation on board of a sloop, in the capacity of a cook, at twelve dollars per month. I was on board the vessel some time, and when we settled, the captain cheated me out of twelve dollars. My next move was in the country; I agreed to serve a merchant faithfully, and he promised to give me twelve dollars a month. Every thing went on smooth for a season; at last I became negligent and careless, in consequence of his giving me a pint of rum every day, which was the allowance he made for each person in his employment.

While at this place, I attended a Methodist meeting—at the time I felt very much affected, as it brought up before my mind the great and indescribable enjoyments I had found in the house of prayer, when I was endeavoring to serve the Lord. It soon wore off, and I relapsed into my former bad habits.

I now went again into the country, and stayed with a farmer, for one month; he paid me five dollars. Then I shifted my quarters to another place and agreed with a Dutch farmer to stay with him all winter at five dollars a month. With this situation I was much pleased. My work was light—I had very little to do except procuring firewood. I often went with them on hunting excursions, besides, my brethren were all around me, and it therefore seemed like home. I was now in the bay of Quinty,[2] the scenery was diversified. There were also some natural curiosities. On the very top of a high mountain in the neighbourhood there was a large pond of water, to which there was no visible outlet;—this pond was unfathomable. It was very surprising to me that so great a body of water should be found so far above the common level of the earth. There was also in

---

[1] Apess always uses this word to refer to other Native Americans. These were probably Mohawks.

[2] on the north shore of Lake Ontario. The brethren Apess met there were probably Mohawks or Mississauga.

the neighbourhood a rock, that had the appearance of being hollowed out by the hand of a skilful artificer; through this rock wound a narrow stream of water: it had a most beautiful and romantic appearance, and I could not but admire the wisdom of God in the order, regularity and beauty of creation; I then turned my eyes to the forest and it appeared alive with its sons and daughters. There appeared to be the utmost order and regularity in their encampment and they held all things in common.

Oh what a pity that this state of things should change. How much better would it be if the whites would act like a civilized people, and instead of giving my brethren of the woods "rum!" in exchange for their furs, give them food and clothing for themselves and children. If this course were pursued, I believe that God would bless both the whites and natives three fold. I am bold to aver that the minds of the natives were turned against the gospel and soured toward the whites because *some* of the missionaries have joined the unholy brethren in speculations to the advantage of themselves, regardless of the rights, feelings and interests of the untutored sons of the forest. If a good missionary goes amongst them, and preaches the pure doctrine of the gospel, he must necessarily tell them that they must "love God and their neighbour as themselves—to love men, deal justly, and walk humbly."[1] They would naturally reply, your doctrine is very good, but the whole course of your conduct is decidedly at variance with your profession—we think the whites need fully as much religious instruction as we do. In this way many a good man's path is hedged up, and he is prevented from being useful among the natives, in consequence of the bad conduct of those who are, properly speaking only "wolves in sheep's clothing."[2] However, the natives are on the whole willing to receive the gospel, and of late, through the instrumentality of *pious missionaries*, much good has been done—many of them have been reclaimed from the most abandoned and degrading practices, and brought to a knowledge of the truth as it is in Jesus!

---

[1] Cf. Luke 10.27 and Micah 6.8.

[2] Cf. Matthew 7.15.

Thomas Hood
1799 – 1845

Thomas Hood was born in London on 23 May 1799, one of the six surviving children of Thomas Hood, a Scottish publisher and bookseller, and Elizabeth Sands Hood, whose father and brother were prominent engravers. After attending several schools, at the age of fifteen he began studying engraving with his uncle. Soon, however, Hood, who had had scarlet fever in childhood, had to take an extended trip to Dundee for his health. There he began writing. He suffered from precarious health for the rest of his life, but he did not let it interfere with his productivity: "no gentleman alive," he later claimed, "has written so much Comic and spitten so much blood." Back in London, he resumed engraving and kept on writing. In 1821, he became sub-editor of the *London Magazine*, where he began to publish his work. He met such contributors as De Quincey,* Hazlitt,* and Charles Lamb,* and also Keats's* friend John Hamilton Reynolds; his first book (1825) was written in collaboration with Reynolds. In May 1825, he and Reynolds's sister Jane were married; they had two children. He came into his own as a comic writer with *Whims and Oddities, in Prose and Verse* (1826). Starting in 1828, he threw himself into editing a series of comic periodicals and annuals, doing much of the writing and illustrating himself. He also published serious poetry, including *The Plea of the Midsummer Fairies* (1827) and *The Dream of Eugene Aram* (1831), and two novels, *Tylney Hall* (1834) and *Up the Rhine* (1840). Near the end of his life, he wrote a group of powerful poems of social protest, of which the most spectacularly successful was "The Song of the Shirt" (1843), a denunciation of sweatshop labour. He died on 3 May 1845. (D.L.M.)

☙❧

from *Whims and Oddities*, 3rd ed. (1828)[1]

The Last Man[2]

'Twas in the year two thousand and one,
A pleasant morning of May,
I sat on the gallows-tree all alone,
A chaunting a merry lay,—
5   To think how the pest had spared my life,
To sing with the larks that day!

When up the heath came a jolly knave,
Like a scarecrow, all in rags:
It made me crow to see his old duds
10   All abroad in the wind, like flags:—
So up he came to the timbers' foot
And pitch'd down his greasy bags.—

Good Lord! how blithe the old beggar was!
At pulling out his scraps,—
15   The very sight of his broken orts
Made a work in his wrinkled chaps:
"Come down," says he, "you Newgate[3]-bird,
And have a taste of my snaps!"—

Then down the rope, like a tar from the mast,
20   I slided, and by him stood:
But I wished myself on the gallows again
When I smelt that beggar's food,
A foul beef-bone and a mouldy crust;
"Oh!" quoth he, "the heavens are good!"

25   Then after this grace he cast him down:
Says I, "You'll get sweeter air
A pace or two off, on the windward side,"
For the felons' bones lay there.

---

[1] first ed. published 1826.

[2] a response to Byron's "Darkness," * Campbell's "The Last Man",* and especially M.W. Shelley's* novel *The Last Man* (1826).

[3] prison in London.

But he only laugh'd at the empty skulls,
And offered them part of his fare.

"I never harm'd *them*, and they won't harm me:
Let the proud and the rich be cravens!"
I did not like that strange beggar man,
He look'd so up at the heavens.
Anon he shook out his empty old poke;
"There's the crumbs," saith he, "for the ravens!"

It made me angry to see his face,
It had such a jesting look;
But while I made up my mind to speak,
A small case-bottle he took:
Quoth he, "though I gather the green water-cress,
My drink is not of the brook!"

Full manners-like he tender'd the dram;
Oh it came of a dainty cask!
But, whenever it came to his turn to pull,
"Your leave, good sir, I must ask;
But I always wipe the brim with my sleeve,
When a hangman sups at my flask!"

And then he laugh'd so loudly and long,
The churl was quite out of breath;
I thought the very Old One[1] was come
To mock me before my death,
And wish'd I had buried the dead men's bones
That were lying about the heath!

But the beggar gave me a jolly clap—
"Come, let us pledge each other,
For all the wide world is dead beside,
And we are brother and brother—
I've a yearning for thee in my heart,
As if we had come of one mother."

"I've a yearning for thee in my heart
That almost makes me weep,
For as I pass'd from town to town
The folks were all stone-asleep,—

But when I saw thee sitting aloft,
It made me both laugh and leap!"

Now a curse (I thought) be on his love,
And a curse upon his mirth,—
An' it were not for that beggar man
I'd be the King of the earth,—
But I promis'd myself, an hour should come
To make him rue his birth—

So down we sat and bous'd again
Till the sun was in mid-sky,
When, just when the gentle west-wind came,
We hearken'd a dismal cry:
"Up, up, on the tree," quoth the beggar man,
"Till these horrible dogs go by!"

And, lo! from the forest's far-off skirts,
They came all yelling for gore,
A hundred hounds pursuing at once,
And a panting hart before,
Till he sunk adown at the gallows' foot
And there his haunches they tore!

His haunches they tore, without a horn
To tell when the chase was done;
And there was not a single scarlet coat[2]
To flaunt it in the sun!—
I turn'd, and look'd at the beggar man,
And his tears dropt one by one!

And with curses sore he chid at the hounds,
Till the last dropt out of sight,
Anon saith he, "let's down again,
And ramble for our delight,
For the world's all free, and we may choose
A right cozie barn for to-night!"

With that, he set up his staff on end,
And it fell with the point due West;
So we far'd that way to a city great,
Where the folks had died of the pest—

---

[1] the Devil.

[2] worn by hunters.

It was fine to enter in house and hall,
Wherever it liked me best;—

For the porters all were stiff and cold,
And could not lift their heads;
105 And when he came where their masters lay,
The rats leapt out of the beds:
The grandest palaces in the land
Were as free as workhouse sheds.

But the beggar man made a mumping face,
110 And knocked at every gate:
It made me curse to hear how he whined,
So our fellowship turn'd to hate,
And I bade him walk the world by himself,
For I scorn'd so humble a mate!

115 So *he* turn'd right and *I* turn'd left,
As if we had never met;
And I chose a fair stone house for myself,
For the city was all to let;
And for three brave holydays drank my fill
120 Of the choicest that I could get.

And because my jerkin was coarse and worn,
I got me a properer vest;
It was purple velvet, stitch'd o'er with gold,
And a shining star at the breast!—
125 'Twas enough to fetch old Joan from her grave
To see me so purely drest!—

But Joan was dead and under the mould,
And every buxom lass;
In vain I watch'd, at the window pane,
130 For a Christian soul to pass!
But sheep and kine wander'd up the street,
And browz'd on the new-come grass.—

When lo! I spied the old beggar man,
And lustily he did sing!—
135 His rags were lapp'd in a scarlet cloak,
And a crown he had like a King;
So he stept right up before my gate
And danc'd me a saucy fling!

Heaven mend us all!— but, within my mind,
140 I had kill'd him then and there;
To see him lording so braggart-like
That was born to his beggar's fare,
And how he had stolen the royal crown
His betters were meant to wear.

145 But God forbid that a thief should die
Without his share of the laws!
So I nimbly whipt my tackle out,
And soon tied up his claws,—
I was judge, myself, and jury, and all,
150 And solemnly tried the cause.

But the beggar man would not plead, but cried
Like a babe without its corals,
For he knew how hard it is apt to go
When the law and a thief have quarrels,—
155 There was not a Christian soul alive
To speak a word for his morals.

Oh, how gaily I doff'd my costly gear,
And put on my work-day clothes;
I was tired of such a long Sunday life,—
160 And never was one of the sloths;
But the beggar man grumbled a weary deal,
And made many crooked mouths.

So I haul'd him off to the gallows' foot,
And blinded him in his bags;
165 'Twas a weary job to heave him up,
For a doom'd man always lags;
But by ten of the clock he was off his legs
In the wind, and airing his rags!

So there he hung, and there I stood,
170 The LAST MAN left alive,
To have my own will of all the earth:
Quoth I, now I shall thrive!
But when was ever honey made
With one bee in a hive!

175 My conscience began to gnaw my heart
Before the day was done,

For other men's lives had all gone out,
　　　　Like candles in the sun!—
　　　But it seem'd as if I had broke, at last,
180　　A thousand necks in one!

　　　So I went and cut his body down
　　　　To bury it decentlie;—
　　　God send there were any good soul alive
　　　　To do the like by me!
185　　But the wild dogs came with terrible speed,
　　　　And bade me up the tree!

　　　My sight was like a drunkard's sight,
　　　　And my head began to swim,
　　　To see their jaws all white with foam,
190　　Like the ravenous ocean brim;—
　　　But when the wild dogs trotted away
　　　　Their jaws were bloody and grim!

　　　Their jaws were bloody and grim, good Lord!
　　　　But the beggar man, where was he?—
195　　There was nought of him but some ribbons of rags
　　　　Below the gallows' tree!—
　　　I know the Devil, when I am dead,
　　　　Will send his hounds for me!—

　　　I've buried my babies one by one,
200　　And dug the deep hole for Joan,
　　　And covered the faces of kith and kin,
　　　　And felt the old churchyard stone
　　　Go cold to my heart, full many a time,
　　　　But I never felt so lone!

205　　For the lion and Adam were company,
　　　　And the tiger him beguiled;
　　　But the simple kine are foes to my life,
　　　　And the household brutes are wild.
　　　If the veriest cur would lick my hand,
210　　　I could love it like a child!

　　　And the beggar man's ghost besets my dreams,
　　　　At night, to make madder,—
　　　And my wretched conscience, within my breast,
　　　　Is like a stinging adder;—

215　　I sigh when I pass the gallows' foot,
　　　　And look at the rope and ladder!—

　　　For hanging looks sweet,—but, alas! in vain
　　　　My desperate fancy begs,—
　　　I must turn my cup of sorrows quite up,
220　　And drink it to the dregs,—
　　　For there is not another man alive,
　　　　In the world, to pull my legs!

　　　　Faithless Nelly Gray
　　　　　A Pathetic Ballad

　　　Ben Battle was a soldier bold,
　　　　And used to war's alarms;
　　　But a cannon-ball took off his legs,
　　　　So he laid down his arms!

5　　　Now as they bore him off the field,
　　　　Said he, "Let others shoot,
　　　For here I leave my second leg,
　　　　And the Forty-second Foot!"[1]

　　　The army-surgeons made him limbs:
10　　　Said he,—"They're only pegs:
　　　But there's as wooden members quite,
　　　　As represent my legs!"

　　　Now Ben he loved a pretty maid,
　　　　Her name was Nelly Gray;
15　　So he went to pay her his devours,[2]
　　　　When he'd devour'd his pay!

　　　But when he called on Nelly Gray,
　　　　She made him quite a scoff;
　　　And when she saw his wooden legs,
20　　　Began to take them off!

　　　"O, Nelly Gray! O, Nelly Gray!
　　　　Is this your love so warm?

---

[1] an infantry regiment, the Black Watch, now known as the Royal Highlanders.

[2] "*devoirs*" (Fr.): "respects."

  The love that loves a scarlet coat,
   Should be more uniform!"

25 Said she, "I loved a soldier once,
   For he was blythe and brave;
  But I will never have a man
   With both legs in the grave!

  "Before you had those timber toes,
30 Your love I did allow,
  But then, you know, you stand upon
   Another footing now!"

  "O, Nelly Gray! O, Nelly Gray!
   For all your jeering speeches,
35 At duty's call, I left my legs
   In Badajos's[1] *breaches*!"

  "Why, then," said she, "you've lost the feet
   Of legs in war's alarms,
  And now you cannot wear your shoes
40 Upon your feats of arms!"

  "O, false and fickle Nelly Gray!
   I know why you refuse:—
  Though I've no feet—some other man
   Is standing in my shoes!

45 "I wish I ne'er had seen your face;
   But, now, a long farewell!

  For you will be my death:—alas!
   You will not be my *Nell*!"

  Now when he went from Nelly Gray,
50 His heart so heavy got—
  And life was such a burthen grown,
   It made him take a knot!

  So round his melancholy neck,
   A rope he did entwine,
55 And, for his second time in life,
   Enlisted in the Line![2]

  One end he tied around a beam,
   And then removed his pegs,
  And, as his legs were off,—of course,
60 He soon was off his legs!

  And there he hung, till he was dead
   As any nail in town,—
  For though distress had cut him up,
   It could not cut him down!

65 A dozen men sat on his corpse,
   To find out why he died—
  And they buried Ben in four cross-roads,
   With a *stake* in his inside![3]

---

[1] The British army under Wellington captured the Spanish city of Badajos in 1812, during the Peninsular War.

[2] the front-line army.

[3] This traditional form of burial for suicides persisted until at least 1823.

Peter Jones
1802 – 1856

Peter Jones, a member of the Ojibwa nation, was born Kahkewaquonaby ("Sacred Feathers") on 1 January 1802 near what is now Hamilton, Ontario. He was the second son of Augustus Jones, a retired surveyor. His mother, Tuhbenahneequay (Sarah Henry), was the daughter of a Mississauga chief. Jones was raised by his mother, who taught him the ways of her people. In 1816, his father recognized that his sons' band was deteriorating; he took charge of them, sending Kahkewaquonaby to a school near his farm, where the young boy learned to read and write English and became known as Peter.

In 1817, Augustus moved with his Iroquois family to the region of the Grand River and took Peter, now fifteen, with him. In June 1823, Peter and his half-sister Polly went to a five-day meeting of the Methodist Episcopal Church; he became a convert and began a fairly successful campaign to convert the Mississaugas to the Methodist church. In January 1829, the Credit Band elected Jones as one of their three chiefs. He began numerous missionary tours in Upper Canada and the northern United States; in 1831, he sailed to Britain on another successful missionary tour. There he met Eliza Field, a devout Englishwoman, who came to North America to be Peter's wife. He became a fully ordained Methodist minister on 6 October 1833. He served the Credit Band in various ways: as an educator, translator, and minister. In the 1840s, his health began to deteriorate, though he continued to work for his people and his faith. He died on 29 June 1856. (J.G.)

♾

from *History of the Ojebway Indians; with Especial Reference to Their Conversion to Christianity* (1861)

Letter to John Jones[1]

The following is the opinion The Author formed of England and its inhabitants on his first visit, in the year 1831 (extracted from a letter to his brother, Mr. John Jones, dated London, December 30th, 1831):—

I have thought you would be pleased to hear my remarks, as an Indian traveller, on the customs and manners of the English people, and therefore send you the following, made from actual observation:—

"The English, in general, are a noble, generous-minded people—free to act and free to think; they very much pride themselves on their civil and religious privileges; in their learning, generosity, manufactures, and commerce; and they think that no other nation is equal to them.

"I have found them very open and friendly, always ready to relieve the wants of the poor and needy when properly brought before them. No nation, I think, can be more fond of novelties than the English; they will gaze upon a foreigner as if he had just dropped down from the moon; and I have often been amused in seeing what a large number of people a *monkey riding* upon a *dog* will collect, where such things may be seen almost every day. When my Indian name, *Kahkewaquonaby*,[2] is announced to attend any public meeting, so great is the curiosity, the place is sure to be filled. They are truly industrious, and in general very honest and upright. Their close attention to business produces, I think, too much worldly-mindedness, and hence they forget to think enough about their souls and their God; their motto seems to be 'Money, money; get money, get rich, and be a gentleman.' With this sentiment they fly about in every direction, like a swarm of bees, in search of the treasure which lies so near their hearts. These remarks refer to the men of the world, and of such there are not a few.

---

[1] John Jones (1798–1847) is Peter's elder brother.

[2] He also had a Mohawk name, Desagondensta, translated as "he stands people on their feet."

"The English are very fond of good living, and many who live on roast beef, plum pudding, and turtle soup, get very fat, and round as a toad. They eat four times in a day. Breakfast at eight or nine, which consists of coffee or tea, bread, and butter, and sometimes a little fried bacon, fish, or eggs. Dinner at about two, P.M., when everything that is good is spread before the eater; which winds up with fruit, nuts, and a few glasses of wine. Tea at six, with bread and butter, toast, and sometimes sweet cake. Supper about nine or ten, when the leavings of the dinner again make their appearance, upon which John Bull[1] makes a hearty meal to go to bed upon at midnight.

"The fashion in dress varies so much, I am unable to describe it. I will only say, that the ladies of fashion wear very curious bonnets, which look something like a farmer's scoop-shovel; and when they walk in the tiptoe style they put me in mind of the little snipes that run along the shores of the lakes in Canada. They also wear sleeves as big as bushel bags, which make them appear as if they had three bodies with one head. Yet, with all their big bonnets and sleeves, the English ladies, I think, are the best of women …

"P. Jones."

---

[1] a personification of the national character of England, invented by John Arbuthnot (1667–1735) in his satirical political pamphlets.

Catherine Parr Traill
1802 – 1899

Catherine Parr Traill was born in Kent on 9 January 1802, one of the five daughters of Thomas and Elizabeth Homer Strickland; one of her sisters grew up to be Susanna Moodie.* Thomas Strickland, who died when Catherine was sixteen, taught his daughters such subjects as mathematics and geography, at that time deemed inappropriate for girls. Four of the five sisters grew up to be writers; several were painters. After her father's death, Catherine wrote and published stories for children.

In 1832, she met and married a widower and retired army officer, Lt. Thomas Traill, a good friend of J.W.D. Moodie, her sister Susanna's husband. Within a week of Catherine and Thomas's wedding, they emigrated to Canada, settling north of what is now Cobourg, Ontario. The two eventually had eleven children, two of whom died as infants.

Their first pioneering years are detailed in Catherine's letters home, which became her best-known work, *The Backwoods of Canada: Being Letters from the Wife of an Emigrant Officer*, published in 1836 and subsequently translated into German and French. Besides *The Backwoods of Canada*, she is known for her books for children and her botanical writing.

For financial reasons, the Traills had to sell their farm in 1839. They then lived in Peterborough and the surrounding area until 1846, when they moved to Rice Lake. However, their home burned in 1857. Following her husband's death in 1859, Catherine moved to Lakefield to be closer to family. She continued to publish botanical texts and children's literature until a few years before her death in 1899. (J.G.)

❧❧❧

from *The Young Emigrants; or, Pictures of Canada, Calculated to Amuse and Instruct the Minds of Youth* (1826)

LETTER 5
Agnes to Ellen

Roselands, June 22.

After a silence of some months, I again sit down to write to my beloved sister, assured that a letter from her absent Agnes will be welcomed with delight. With what joy should I hail the day that made us once more inmates of the same dwelling. I think I should then be quite happy, and not have a thought or wish beyond the home I now inhabit, which is becoming dearer to me every day....

Once a week we bake. This is my busy day, and I find enough to employ me. The household-bread is made with a mixture of rye and maize-flour, with new milk; and it is far nicer, and more delicate, than the best English bread I ever tasted. My cakes and puddings gain me great credit. I also make all the pastry. I intend preserving a great deal of fruit this summer, such as cranberries, raspberries, and strawberries. This we can do with very little expense, as we have a plentiful store of maple-sugar, having made nearly six hundred weight[1] this spring.

Papa engaged a party of Indians to make the sugar for us, as they far excel the settlers in the art of refining it. The method practised round us, is to top the maples when the sap rises, and place a trough under them; but this is very wasteful, as it kills the tree. The Indian plan is much better: with a hollow knife they scoop out a piece from the trunk of the tree, at a certain distance from the ground; into this incision they insert a spout or tube of elder-wood, through which the sap flows into the troughs below. Every day the liquor is collected into one great vessel. A fire is lighted round it, and the sap is kept boiling till the watery particles have evaporated: it

---

[1] A hundredweight is 112 lb or about 51 kg.

is then purified with eggs, and kept stirred with an iron ladle. Two gallons of sap are reckoned to produce one pound of sugar. From two hundred and sixty maple-trees, the Indians produced six hundred weight of sugar, and a quantity of molasses: a goodly stock, you will say, for such a small household as ours.

I used often to walk with papa and mamma into the woods, to visit the Indians, while they were making the sugar. Their picturesque figures, dresses, attitudes, and employments, contrasted with the ruddy glare of the fires, and the dark trees of the forest above them, would have formed a subject worthy of the pencil of a West or a Salvator Rosa.[1]

Some of the men were tending the fires, stirring the liquor in the boiling kettles, or purifying it: others collecting the fresh sap, tapping the trees, or binding up the wounds in those that had ceased to flow. Here a group of Indian children were seated on their fathers' blankets, round the fires, weaving baskets or mats, or scooping the tubes of elder-wood: there a party were dancing the Indian dance, or singing, in wild, irregular cadence, the songs of their native tribes; while some, more industrious, were employed in collecting wood and supplying the fires with fuel.

Among the Indians there was one old man, for whom I contracted quite a friendship. He used to lift me over the fallen timbers, and place me near the fire at which he was at work, spreading his blanket on a block or trunk of wood, for my accommodation. This old Indian told me he was called Hawk-head by his own people, but that he had been baptized into the Christian church by a white missionary, who came from a distant country and preached the word of God in their village. But this was many years ago, when he was in the pride of his strength; and he had forgotten much of his duty since that time. He said, in excuse for it, "Young lady! the Hawk-head has grown old, and his memory has faded, and his eyes have waxed dim, since he heard the words of missionary John. He has seen his children, to the third generation, rise up before him, ready to fill his place; and he expects soon to be called away to the land of spirits."

I was much interested by the conversation of this venerable man, and hoped to improve the good seed that the missionary had sown in his heart. I explained to him many points of faith, of which he was anxious to be informed; and I also mentioned to him my intention of opening an evening-school, for the instruction of the children of his tribe in the knowledge of God and of their Saviour. The old man said, "Hawk-head would be glad to see his children taught that which is right and good"; and he promised to speak to his children on the subject. I found my Indian proselyte a powerful auxiliary, as he possessed great influence over the minds of the tribe of which he was the chief. I have now fourteen Indian children under my tuition, who are making great improvement in their moral conduct. Several Indian mothers came to our school, a short time since, and entreated that they also might be taught what was good, as well as their children.

At first our school opened under very unpromising auspices: few of the labourers would allow their children to attend it, and we had but four little Indians, who had been prevailed upon by my friend the Hawk-head to attend. But, in spite of this disappointment, we resolved not to be discouraged; and in the course of another month we had gained ten more Indians, and several of the children of the Irish peasants. The school has only been established since the beginning of last March, and we have now twenty-five regular scholars; and I am happy to say that a considerable alteration has already taken place in the manners and behaviour of the inhabitants of the village, which, when we first settled here, was a sad, wicked, disorderly place.

Besides our constant attendance at the school, we have some who only come occasionally; (perhaps once a week;) but these are idle, and of irregular habits, and do not like to observe the necessary restraints which we are forced to exact. Some few come from motives of curiosity, or to pass away a dull hour; but we do not exclude any. And I trust that not unfrequently it happens, that

---

[1] Benjamin West (1738–1820), American painter and president of the Royal Academy; Salvator Rosa (1615–73), Italian Baroque painter.

"Those who came to scoff remain'd to pray."[1]

You do not know, my dear Ellen, what real and heartfelt pleasure we feel in instructing these children in their moral duties, and teaching them the knowledge of God and the advantages of religion....

Papa intends making potash this year; likewise building a saw-mill, which can be worked by the little stream of water that flows through our grounds. He will then ship timber for Montreal, which he hopes will answer well.

The settlers who make potash, clear the land by firing the woods, or setting fire to the timber, after they are piled in heaps. You will see twenty or thirty acres, chopped into lengths and heaped together, all blazing at once. Of a night, the effect is very grand. But it is a dangerous practice; for if the weather is dry and warm, there is a great chance of the flames communicating from the woods to the corn-fields and fences, and from thence to the out-buildings and the homesteads.

Last summer, the woods near us caught fire, owing to the extreme dryness of the season, and occasioned considerable damage to the farmer on whose land it commenced, scorching up one hundred and twenty acres of meadow land. We had one acre of wheat in the ear destroyed; and we were beginning to entertain great fears for the safety of our corn and cattle, when a very heavy shower of rain falling, (which seemed as if by the interposition of the Almighty himself,) extinguished the flames.

When the forests take fire, which not unfrequently happens, they present a most awful and imposing spectacle. The flames rush to the tops of the trees, roaring, crackling, crashing, and filling the air with glowing sparkles and burning splinters, as the trees sink beneath the wasting effects of the devouring element; wreaths of red and yellow smoke hover and wave above the burning woods, while the surrounding atmosphere becomes tinged with a lurid and angry redness. When the flames are extinguished, the scene presents an appearance of desolation, dreary beyond description. Instead of waving woods of green, once so charming to the eye, you behold only the trunks of black and branchless trees: white ashes (beneath which the fire still lingers) strew the once-verdant and flowery ground: all is dark and dismal, that was lately so fresh and lovely. Such, my dear Ellen, is the appearance of a Canadian forest on fire. But even this (which in many respects might be considered as a calamity) is not without its benefits; the earth being freed, in the course of a few hours, from a superfluity of timber, which would take the settler at least many weeks, or even months, to accomplish; and the wood-ashes which strew his land, render it fruitful to a most astonishing degree. Thus, in nature, we often see that which we at first rashly accounted an evil, become, through the superintending providence of an all-wise and merciful God, a positive blessing and benefit to mankind....

---

[1] Cf. Goldsmith, *The Deserted Village* 180.*

Letitia Elizabeth Landon
1802 – 1838

Letitia Elizabeth Landon was born on 14 August 1802 in London. Her parents, John Landon (a former African explorer) and Catherine Bishop Landon, were well off. She was educated at a day school and then at home. In 1814, her father lost much of his money, and soon afterwards Landon, who had already begun writing for the amusement of her family, came to wonder whether she could help to support it. Her mother consulted William Jerdan, editor of the *Literary Gazette*, and Landon's first published poem appeared in the *Literary Gazette* in 1818, under the signature "L."; soon, her signature "L.E.L." would be famous. Her first book of poems, *The Fate of Adelaide*, appeared in 1821. Her father died in 1824, and Landon moved from the family home to a boarding house, but she continued to support her mother and brother. She published five more collections of poetry—*The Improvisatrice* (1824), *The Troubadour* (1825), *The Golden Violet* (1827), *The Venetian Bracelet* (1829), and *The Vow of the Peacock* (1835)—and four works of prose fiction: *Romance and Reality* (1831); a historical novel, *Francesca Carrara* (1834); a collection of stories for children, *Traits and Trials of Early Life* (1836); and *Ethel Churchill* (1837); most of these books were critical and commercial successes. She regularly published poetry and criticism in the *Literary Gazette*, the *New Monthly Magazine*, and elsewhere. And she contributed to and edited a number of the annuals that were then such an important part of the literary marketplace. Jerdan later estimated that she earned an impressive £2585 from her writing—but at a great personal cost: "What is my life?" she asked rhetorically: "One day of drudgery after another"; she longed for "oblivion, and five hundred a year!"

As she came to prominence, Landon befriended such writers as Edward Bulwer-Lytton, Anna Maria Hall, Maria Jane Jewsbury, Mitford,* Jane Porter, Emma Roberts, and Agnes Strickland. But as a single woman in a man's profession, she was vulnerable to rumours of sexual misconduct. In 1834, these rumours forced her to break off her engagement with John Forster, the friend and later the biographer of Dickens. Depressed, Landon became engaged to George Maclean, the governor of Cape Coast Castle on the Gold Coast (now Ghana), who was home on leave. They were married (with her brother as the priest) on 7 June 1838 and left for the Gold Coast on 5 July; they arrived on 11 August. On 15 October, Landon was found dead in her bedroom, with an empty bottle of cyanide in her hand. The same day, she was buried in unconsecrated ground. The coroner's jury ruled that the death was accidental. (D.L.M.)

ഌഌ

from *The Improvisatrice and Other Poems* (1824)

The Improvisatrice[1]

ADVERTISEMENT

Poetry needs no Preface: if it do not speak for itself, no comment can render it explicit. I have only, therefore, to state that *The Improvisatrice* is an attempt to illustrate that species of inspiration common in Italy, where the mind is warmed from earliest childhood by all that is beautiful in Nature and glorious in Art. The character depicted is entirely Italian,—a young female with all the loveliness, vivid feeling, and genius of her own impassioned land. She is supposed to relate her own history; with which are intermixed the tales and episodes which various circumstances call forth.

Some of the minor poems have appeared in *The Literary Gazette*.

L.E.L.

---

[1] a poet who improvised verses in public; cf. Hemans,* "Corinne at the Capitol" (1830).

I am a daughter of that land,
Where the poet's lip and the painter's hand
Are most divine,—where earth and sky
Are picture both and poetry—
5 I am of Florence. 'Mid the chill
Of hope and feeling, oh! I still
Am proud to think to where I owe
My birth, though but the dawn of woe!

    My childhood passed 'mid radiant things,
10 Glorious as Hope's imaginings;
Statues but known from shapes of the earth,
By being too lovely for mortal birth;
Paintings whose colours of life were caught
From the fairy tints in the rainbow wrought;
15 Music whose sighs had a spell like those
That float on the sea at the evening's close;
Language so silvery, that every word
Was like the lute's awakening chord;
Skies half sunshine, and half starlight;
20 Flowers whose lives were a breath of delight;
Leaves whose green pomp knew no withering;
Fountains bright as the skies of our Spring;
And songs whose wild and passionate line
Suited a soul of romance like mine.

25   My power was but a woman's power;
Yet, in that great and glorious dower
Which Genius gives, I had my part:
I poured my full and burning heart
In song, and on the canvass made
30   My dreams of beauty visible;
I know not which I loved the most—
    Pencil[1] or lute,—both loved so well.

    Oh, yet my pulse throbs to recall,
When first upon the gallery's wall
35 Picture of mine was placed, to share
Wonder and praise from each one there.
Sad were my shades; methinks they had
    Almost a tone of prophecy—
I ever had, from earliest youth,
40   A feeling what my fate would be.
My first was of a gorgeous hall,
Lighted up for festival;
Braided tresses, and cheeks of bloom,
Diamond agraff,[2] and foam-white plume;
45 Censers of roses, vases of light
Like what the moon sheds on a summer night.
Youths and maidens with linked hands,
Joined in the graceful sarabands,
Smiled on the canvass; but apart
50 Was one who leant in silent mood,
As revelry to his sick heart
    Were worse than veriest solitude.
Pale, dark-eyed, beautiful, and young,
    Such as he had shone o'er my slumbers,
55 When I had only slept to dream
    Over again his magic numbers.

    Divinest Petrarch![3] he whose lyre,
Like morning light, half dew, half fire,
To Laura and to love was vowed—
60 He looked on one, who with the crowd
Mingled, but mixed not; on whose cheek
    There was a blush, as if she knew
Whose look was fixed on her's. Her eye,
    Of a spring sky's delicious blue,
65 Had not the language of that bloom,
But mingling tears, and light, and gloom,
Was raised abstractedly to Heaven:—
No sign was to her lover given.
I painted her with golden tresses,
70 Such as float on the wind's caresses
When the laburnums wildly fling
Their sunny blossoms to the spring.
A cheek which had the crimson hue
    Upon the sun-touched nectarine;
75 A lip of perfume and of dew;
    A brow like twilight's darkened line.

---

[1] paintbrush.

[2] a kind of clasp.

[3] Francesco Petrarca (1304–74), Italian poet and humanist, known especially for his sonnets expressing his love for Laura (d. 1348). Landon was familiar with Jacques François Paul Aldonce de Sade, *The Life of Petrarch* (1775).

I strove to catch each charm that long
Has lived,—thanks to her lover's song!
Each grace he numbered one by one,
80   That shone in her of Avignon.[1]

   I ever thought that poet's fate
   Utterly lone and desolate.
   It is the spirit's bitterest pain
   To love, to be beloved again;
85   And yet between a gulf which ever
   The hearts that burn to meet must sever.
   And he was vowed to one sweet star,
   Bright yet to him, but bright afar.

   O'er some, Love's shadow may but pass
90   As passes the breath stain o'er glass;
   And pleasures, cares, and pride combined,
   Fill up the blank Love leaves behind.
   But there are some whose love is high,
   Entire, and sole idolatry;
95   Who, turning from a heartless world,
      Ask some dear thing which may renew
   Affection's severed links, and be
      As true as they themselves are true.
   But Love's bright fount is never pure;
100   And all his pilgrims must endure
   All passion's mighty suffering
   Ere they may reach the blessed spring.
   And some who waste their lives to find
      A prize which they may never win:
105   Like those who search for Irem's groves,[2]
      Which found, they may not enter in.
   Where is the sorrow but appears
   In Love's long catalogue of tears?
   And some there are who leave the path
110   In agony and fierce disdain;
   But bear upon each cankered breast
      The scar that never heals again.

   My next was of a minstrel too,[3]
   Who proved what woman's hand might do,
115   When, true to the heart pulse, it woke
      The harp. Her head was bending down,
   As if in weariness, and near,
      But unworn, was a laurel crown.[4]
   She was not beautiful, if bloom
120   And smiles form beauty; for, like death,
   Her brow was ghastly; and her lip
   Was parched, as fever were its breath.
   There was a shade upon her dark,
   Large, floating eyes, as if each spark
125   Of minstrel ecstacy was fled,
   Yet, leaving them no tears to shed;
   Fixed in their hopelessness of care,
   And reckless in their great despair.
   She sat beneath a cypress tree,[5]
130   A little fountain ran beside,
   And, in the distance, one dark rock
      Threw its long shadow o'er the tide;
   And to the west, where the nightfall
   Was darkening day's gemm'd coronal,
135   Its white shafts crimsoning in the sky,
   Arose the sun-god's sanctuary.
   I deemed, that of lyre, life, and love
      She was a long, last farewell taking;—
   That, from her pale and parched lips,
140   Her latest, wildest song was breaking.

SAPPHO'S SONG

FAREWELL, my lute!—and would that I
   Had never waked thy burning chords!
Poison has been upon thy sigh,
   And fever has breathed in thy words.

---

[1] the city in southeastern France where Petrarch first saw Laura, in 1327.

[2] Irem is one of the paradises described in the Qur'an.

[3] Sappho was a Greek poet, who lived on the island of Lesbos in the 7th century BC. According to legend, she killed herself for love of Phaon, a ferryman, by throwing herself from the rock of Leucata, a promontory on the coast of Epirus; cf. Robinson, *Sappho and Phaon.*

[4] sacred to Apollo, god of poetry.

[5] symbolic of mourning.

145 Yet wherefore, wherefore should I blame
       Thy power, thy spell, my gentlest lute?
   I should have been the wretch I am,
       Had every chord of thine been mute.

   It was my evil star above,
150   Not my sweet lute, that wrought me wrong;
   It was not song that taught me love,
       But it was love that taught me song.

   If song be past, and hope undone,
       And pulse, and head, and heart, are flame;
155 It is thy work, thou faithless one!
       But, no!—I will not name thy name!

   Sun-god, lute, wreath, are vowed to thee!
       Long be their light upon my grave—
   My glorious grave—yon deep blue sea:
160   I shall sleep calm beneath its wave!

   ———

   FLORENCE! with what idolatry
       I've lingered in thy radiant halls,
   Worshipping, till my dizzy eye
       Grew dim with gazing on those walls,
165 Where time had spared each glorious gift
   By Genius unto Memory left!
   And when seen by the pale moonlight,
   More pure, more perfect, though less bright,
   What dreams of song flashed on my brain,
170 Till each shade seemed to live again;
   And then the beautiful, the grand,
   The glorious of my native land,
   In every flower that threw its veil
   Aside, when wooed by the spring gale;
175 In every vineyard, where the sun,
   His task of summer ripening done,
   Shone on their clusters, and a song
   Came lightly from the peasant throng;—
   In the dim loveliness of night,
180 In fountains with their diamond light,
   In aged temple, ruined shrine,
   And its green wreath of ivy twine;—
   In every change of earth and sky,
   Breathed the deep soul of poesy.

185 As yet I loved not;—but each wild,
   High thought I nourished raised a pyre
   For love to light; and lighted once
   By love, it would be like the fire
   The burning lava floods that dwell
190 In Etna's[1] cave unquenchable.

   One evening in the lovely June,
       Over the Arno's[2] waters gliding,
   I had been watching the fair moon
       Amid her court of white clouds riding;—
195 I had been listening to the gale,
       Which wafted music from around,
   (For scarce a lover, at that hour,
       But waked his mandolin's light sound),—
   And odour was upon the breeze,
200 Sweet thefts from rose and lemon trees.
   They stole me from my lulling dream,
       And said they knew that such an hour
   Had ever influence on my soul,
       And raised my sweetest minstrel power.
205 I took my lute,—my eye had been
   Wandering round the lovely scene,
   Filled with those melancholy tears,
   Which come when all most bright appears,
   And hold their strange and secret power,
210 Even on pleasure's golden hour.
   I had been looking on the river,
   Half-marvelling to think that ever
   Wind, wave, or sky, could darken where
   All seemed so gentle and so fair:
215 And mingled with these thoughts there came
       A tale, just one that Memory keeps—
   Forgotten music, till some chance
       Vibrate the chord whereon it sleeps!

   A MOORISH ROMANCE

   SOFTLY through the pomegranate groves
220 Came the gentle song of the doves;
   Shone the fruit in the evening light,

   ———

   [1] a volcano in Sicily.
   [2] the river running through Florence.

    Like Indian rubies, blood-red and bright;
    Shook the date-trees each tufted head,
    As the passing wind their green nuts shed;
225 And, like dark columns, amid the sky
    The giant palms ascended on high;
    And the mosque's gilded minaret
    Glistened and glanced as the daylight set.
    Over the town a crimson haze
230 Gathered and hung of the evening's rays;
    And far beyond, like molten gold,
    The burning sands of the desert rolled.
    Far to the left, the sky and sea
    Mingled their gray immensity;
235 And with flapping sail and idle prow
    The vessels threw their shades below.
    Far down the beach, where a cypress grove
    Casts its shade round a little cove,
    Darkling and green, with just a space
240 For the stars to shine on the water's face,
    A small bark lay, waiting for night
    And its breeze to waft and hide its flight.
    Sweet is the burthen, and lovely the freight,
    For which those furled-up sails await,
245 To a garden, fair as those
    Where the glory of the rose
    Blushes, charmed from the decay
    That wastes other blooms away;
    Gardens of the fairy tale
250 Told, till the wood-fire grows pale,
    By the Arab tribes, when night,
    With its dim and lovely light,
    And its silence, suiteth well
    With the magic tales they tell.
255 Through that cypress avenue,
    Such a garden meets the view,
    Filled with flowers—flowers that seem
    Lighted up by the sunbeam;
    Fruits of gold and gems, and leaves
260 Green as Hope before it grieves
    O'er the false and broken-hearted,
    All with which its youth has parted,
    Never to return again,
    Save in memories of pain!

265 There is a white rose in yon bower,
    But holds it a yet fairer flower:
    And music from that cage is breathing,
    Round which a jasmine braid is wreathing,
    A low song from a lonely dove,
270 A song such exiles sing and love,
    Breathing of fresh fields, summer skies—
    Now to be breathed of but in sighs!
    But fairer smile and sweeter sigh
    Are near when LEILA's[1] step is nigh!
275 With eyes dark as the midnight time,
    Yet lighted like a summer clime
    With sun-rays from within; yet now
    Lingers a cloud upon that brow,—
    Though never lovelier brow was given
280 To Houri[2] of an Eastern heaven!
    Her eye is dwelling on that bower,
    As every leaf and every flower
    Were being numbered in her heart;—
        There are no looks like those which dwell
285 On long remembered things, which soon
        Must take our first and last farewell!

        Day fades apace; another day,
    That maiden will be far away,
    A wanderer o'er the dark-blue sea,
290 And bound for lovely Italy,
    Her mother's land! Hence, on her breast
    The cross beneath a Moorish vest;
    And hence those sweetest sounds, that seem
    Like music murmuring in a dream,
295 When in our sleeping ear is ringing
    The song the nightingale is singing;
    When by that white and funeral stone,
        Half hidden by the cypress gloom,
    The hymn the mother taught her child
300   Is sung each evening at her tomb.[3]
    But quick the twilight time has past,

---

[1] also the name of the main female character in Byron, *The Giaour*.*

[2] one of the beautiful maidens believed by some Muslims to be available in paradise for the enjoyment of the faithful (from the Arabic for "black-eyed").

[3] Cf. the story of Safie and her mother in M.W. Shelley,* *Frankenstein* (1818) 2.6.

Like one of those sweet calms that last
A moment and no more, to cheer
The turmoil of our pathway here.

305   The bark is waiting in the bay,
Night darkens round:—LEILA away!
Far, ere tomorrow, o'er the tide,
Or wait and be—ABDALLA's bride!

    She touched her lute—never again
310 Her ear will listen to its strain!
She took her cage, first kissed the breast—
    Then freed the white dove prisoned there:
It paused one moment on her hand,
    Then spread its glad wings to the air.
315 She drank the breath, as it were health,
    That sighed from every scented blossom;
And, taking from each one a leaf,
    Hid them, like spells, upon her bosom.
Then sought the secret path again
320   She once before had traced, when lay
A Christian in her father's chain;
    And gave him gold, and taught the way
To fly. She thought upon the night,
When, like an angel of the light,
325 She stood before the prisoner's sight,
And led him to the cypress grove,
And showed the bark and hidden cove;
And bade the wandering captive flee,
In words he knew from infancy!
330 And then she thought how for her love
    He had braved slavery and death,
That he might only breathe the air
    Made sweet and sacred by her breath.
She reached the grove of cypresses,—
335   Another step is by her side:
Another moment, and the bark
    Bears the fair Moor across the tide!

    'Twas beautiful, by the pale moonlight,
To mark her eyes,—now dark, now bright,
340 As now they met, now shrank away,
From the gaze that watched and worshipped their day.
They stood on the deck, and the midnight gale

Just waved the maiden's silver veil—
Just lifted a curl, as if to show
345 The cheek of rose that was burning below:
And never spread a sky of blue
More clear for the stars to wander through!
And never could their mirror be
A calmer or a lovelier sea!
350 For every wave was a diamond gleam:
And that light vessel well might seem
A fairy ship, and that graceful pair
Young Genii,[1] whose home was of light and air!

    Another evening came, but dark;
355 The storm clouds hovered round the bark
Of misery:—they just could see
The distant shore of Italy,
As the dim moon through vapours shone—
A few short rays, her light was gone.
360 O'er head a sullen scream was heard,
As sought the land the white sea-bird,
Her pale wings like a meteor streaming.
Upon the waves a light is gleaming—
Ill-omened brightness, sent by Death
365 To light the night-black depths beneath.
The vessel rolled amid the surge;
The winds howled round it, like a dirge
Sung by some savage race. Then came
The rush of thunder and of flame:
370 It showed two forms upon the deck,—
One clasped around the other's neck,
As there she could not dream of fear—
In her lover's arms could danger be near?
He stood and watched her with the eye
375 Of fixed and silent agony.
The waves swept on: he felt her heart
    Beat close and closer yet to his!
They burst upon the ship!—the sea
    Has closed upon their dream of bliss!

380 Surely theirs is a pleasant sleep,
    Beneath that ancient cedar tree,
Whose solitary stem has stood
    For years alone beside the sea!

---

[1] elemental spirits; in this context, possibly genies or djinns.

    The last of a most noble race,
385 That once had there their dwelling-place,
    Long past away! Beneath its shade,
    A soft green couch the turf had made:—
    And glad the morning sun is shining
    On those beneath the boughs reclining.
390 Nearer the fisher drew. He saw
        The dark hair of the Moorish maid,
    Like a veil, floating o'er the breast,
        Where tenderly her head was laid;—
    And yet her lover's arm was placed
395 Clasping around the graceful waist!
    But then he marked the youth's black curls
        Were dripping wet with foam and blood;
    And that the maiden's tresses dark
        Were heavy with the briny flood!
400 Woe for the wind!—woe for the wave!
    They sleep the slumber of the grave!
    They buried them beneath that tree;
        It long had been a sacred spot.
    Soon it was planted round with flowers
405   By many who had not forgot;
    Or yet lived in those dreams of truth,
    The Eden birds of early youth,
    That make the loveliness of love:
    And called the place "THE MAIDEN'S COVE,"—
410 That she who perished in the sea
    Might thus be kept in memory.

———

FROM many a lip came sounds of praise,
    Like music from sweet voices ringing;
For many a boat had gathered round,
415   To list the song I had been singing.
There are some moments in our fate
    That stamp the colour of our days;
As, till then, life had not been felt,—
    And mine was sealed in the slight gaze
420 Which fixed my eye, and fired my brain,
And bowed my heart beneath the chain.
'Twas a dark and flashing eye,
Shadows, too, that tenderly,
With almost female softness, came
425 O'er its mingled gloom and flame.
His cheek was pale; or toil, or care,
Or midnight study, had been there,
Making its young colours dull,
Yet leaving it most beautiful.
430 Raven curls their shadow threw,
Like the twilight's darkening hue,
O'er the pure and mountain snow
Of his high and haughty brow;
Lighted by a smile, whose spell
435 Words are powerless to tell.
Such a lip!—oh, poured from thence
Lava floods of eloquence
Would come with fiery energy,
Like those words that cannot die.
440 Words the Grecian warrior spoke
When the Persian's chain he broke;[1]
Or that low and honey tone,
Making woman's heart his own;
Such as should be heard at night,
445 In the dim and sweet starlight;
Sounds that haunt a beauty's sleep,
Treasures for her heart to keep.
Like the pine of summer tall,
Apollo, on his pedestal
450 In our own gallery, never bent
More graceful, more magnificent;
Ne'er looked the hero, or the king,
    More nobly than the youth who now,
As if soul-centred in my song,
455   Was leaning on a galley's prow.
He spoke not when the others spoke,
    His heart was all too full for praise;
But his dark eyes kept fixed on mine,
    Which sank beneath their burning gaze.
460 Mine sank—but yet I felt the thrill
Of that look burning on me still.
I heard no word that others said—
    Heard nothing, save one low-breathed sigh.
My hand kept wandering on my lute,
465   In music, but unconsciously:

---

[1] a reference to the Persian Wars (500–449 BC). The Grecian warrior is probably either Miltiades, Athenian commander at the battle of Marathon (490), or Themistocles, commander at the battle of Salamis (480), the two most famous Greek victories.

My pulses throbbed, my heart beat high,
A flush of dizzy ecstasy
    Crimsoned my cheek; I felt warm tears
Dimming my sight, yet was it sweet,
470 My wild heart's most bewildering beat,
    Consciousness, without hopes or fears,
Of a new power within me waking,
Like light before the morn's full breaking.
I left the boat—the crowd: my mood
475 Made my soul pant for solitude.

    Amid my palace halls was one,
The most peculiarly my own:
The roof was blue and fretted gold,
The floor was of the Parian stone,[1]
480 Shining like snow, as only meet
For the light tread of fairy feet;
And in the midst, beneath a shade
Of clustered rose, a fountain played,
Sprinkling its scented waters round,
485 With a sweet and lulling sound,—
O'er oranges, like Eastern gold,
Half hidden by the dark green fold
Of their large leaves;—o'er hyacinth bells,
Where every summer odour dwells.
490 And, nestled in the midst, a pair
Of white wood-doves, whose home was there:
And, like an echo to their song,
At times a murmur past along;
A dying tone, a plaining fall,
495 So sad, so wild, so musical—
As the wind swept across the wire,
And waked my lone Æolian lyre,[2]
Which lay upon the casement, where
The lattice wooed the cold night air,
500 Half hidden by a bridal twine
Of jasmine with the emerald vine.
And ever as the curtains made
A varying light, a changeful shade;
As the breeze waved them to and fro,
505 Came on the eye the glorious show
Of pictured walls, where landscape wild
Of wood, and stream, or mountain piled,
Or sunny vale, or twilight grove,
Or shapes whose every look was love;
510 Saints, whose diviner glance seemed caught
From Heaven,—some whose earthlier thought
Was yet more lovely,—shone like gleams
Of Beauty's spirit seen in dreams.

I threw me on a couch to rest,
515   Loosely I flung my long black hair;
It seemed to soothe my troubled breast
    To drink the quiet evening air.
I look'd upon the deep-blue sky,
And it was all hope and harmony.
520 Afar I could see the Arno's stream
Glorying in the clear moonbeam;
And the shadowy city met my gaze,
Like the dim memory of other days;
And the distant wood's black coronal
525 Was like oblivion, that covereth all.
I know not why my soul felt sad;
    I touched my lute,—it would not waken,
Save to old songs of sorrowing—
    Of hope betrayed—of hearts forsaken:
530 Each lay of lighter feeling slept,
I sang, but, as I sang, I wept.

THE CHARMED CUP

AND fondly round his neck she clung;
Her long black tresses round him flung,
Love-chains, which would not let him part;
535 And he could feel her beating heart,
The pulses of her small white hand,
The tears she could no more command,
The lip which trembled, though near his,
The sigh that mingled with her kiss;—
540 Yet parted he from that embrace.
He cast one glance upon her face:
His very soul felt sick to see

---

[1] a kind of fine white marble, from the island of Paros.

[2] a stringed instrument that is not played but placed in a window, where the wind can cause its strings to vibrate (called a "wind-lute" in line 1370); cf. Coleridge, "Effusion 35"* and "Dejection."*

Its look of utter misery;
Yet turned he not: one moment's grief,
545 One pang, like lightning, fierce and brief,
One thought, half pity, half remorse,
Pass'd o'er him. On he urged his horse;
Hill, ford, and valley spurred he by,
And when his castle gate was nigh,
550 White foam was on his 'broider'd rein,
And each spur had a blood-red stain.
But soon he entered that fair hall:
His laugh was loudest there of all;
And the cup that wont one name to bless,
555 Was drained for its forgetfulness.
The ring, once next his heart, was broken;
The gold chain kept another token.
Where is the curl he used to wear—
The raven tress of silken hair?
560 The winds have scattered it. A braid,
Of the first Spring day's golden shade
Waves with the dark plumes on his crest.
Fresh colours are upon his breast;
The slight blue scarf, of simplest fold,
565 Is changed for one of woven gold.
And he is by a maiden's side,
Whose gems of price, and robes of pride,
Would suit the daughter of a king;
And diamonds are glistening
570 Upon her arm. There's not one curl
Unfastened by a loop of pearl.
And he is whispering in her ear
Soft words that ladies love to hear.

    Alas!—the tale is quickly told—
575 His love hath felt the curse of gold!
And he is bartering his heart
For that in which it hath no part.
There's many an ill that clings to love;
But this is one all else above;—
580 For love to bow before the name
Of this world's treasure: shame! oh, shame!
Love, be thy wings as light as those
That waft the zephyr from the rose,—
This may be pardoned—something rare
585 In loveliness has been thy snare!

But how, fair Love, canst thou become
A thing of mines—a sordid gnome?[1]

    And she whom JULIAN left—she stood
A cold white statue; as the blood
590 Had, when in vain her last wild prayer,
Flown to her heart and frozen there.
Upon her temple, each dark vein
Swelled in its agony of pain.
Chill, heavy damps were on her brow;
595 Her arms were stretched at length, though now
Their clasp was on the empty air:
A funeral pall—her long black hair
Fell over her; herself the tomb
Of her own youth, and breath, and bloom.

600   Alas! that man should ever win
So sweet a shrine to shame and sin
As woman's heart!—and deeper woe
For her fond weakness, not to know
That yielding all but breaks the chain
605 That never reunites again!

    It was a dark and tempest night—
No pleasant moon, no blest starlight;
But meteors[2] glancing o'er the way,
Only to dazzle and betray.
610 And who is she, that 'mid the storm,
Wraps her slight mantle round her form?
Her hair is wet with rain and sleet,
And blood is on her small snow feet.
She has been forced a way to make
615 Through prickly weed and thorned brake,
Up rousing from its coil the snake;
And stirring from their damp abode
The slimy worm and loathsome toad:
And shuddered as she heard the gale
620 Shriek like an evil spirit's wail;
When followed, like a curse, the crash

---

[1] In folklore, gnomes were tiny, misshapen subterranean creatures associated with mines; they were believed to be guardians of hidden treasure.

[2] the *ignis fatuus* or will-o'-the-wisp, fires caused by the spontaneous combustion of marsh gas.

Of the pines in the lightning flash:—
A place of evil and of fear—
Oh! what can JULIAN's love do here?

625   On, on the pale girl went. At last
The gloomy forest depths are past,
And she has reached the wizard's den,
Accursed by God and shunned by men.
And never had a ban been laid
630 Upon a more unwholesome shade.
There grew dank elders, and the yew
Its thick sepulchral shadow threw;
And brooded there each bird most foul,
The gloomy bat and sullen owl.

635   But IDA entered in the cell,
Where dwelt the wizard of the dell.
Her heart lay dead, her life-blood froze
To look upon the shape which rose
To bar her entrance. On that face
640 Was scarcely left a single trace
Of human likeness: the parched skin
Shewed each discoloured bone within;
And but for the most evil stare
Of the wild eyes' unearthly glare,
645 It was a corpse, you would have said,
From which life's freshness long had fled.
Yet IDA knelt her down and prayed
To that dark sorcerer for his aid.
He heard her prayer with withering look;
650 Then from unholy herbs he took
A drug, and said it would recover
The lost heart of her faithless lover.
She trembled as she turned to see
His demon sneer's malignity;
655 And every step was winged with dread,
To hear the curse howled as she fled.

    It is the purple twilight hour,
And JULIAN is in IDA's bower.
He has brought gold, as gold could bless
660 His work of utter desolateness!
He has brought gems, as if Despair
Had any pride in being fair!

But IDA only wept, and wreathed
Her white arms round his neck; then breathed
665 Those passionate complaints that wring
A woman's heart, yet never bring
Redress. She called upon each tree
To witness her lone constancy!
She called upon the silent boughs,
670 The temple of her JULIAN's vows
Of happiness too dearly bought!
Then wept again. At length she thought
Upon the forest sorcerer's gift—
The last, lone hope that love had left!
675 She took the cup, and kissed the brim;
Mixed the dark spell, and gave it him
To pledge his once dear IDA's name!
He drank it. Instantly the flame
Ran through his veins: one fiery throb
680 Of bitter pain—one gasping sob
Of agony—the cold death sweat
Is on his face—his teeth are set—
His bursting eyes are glazed and still:
The drug has done its work of ill.
685 Alas! for her who watched each breath,
The cup her love had mixed bore—death!

———

    LORENZO!—when next morning came,
For the first time I heard thy name!
LORENZO!—how each ear-pulse drank
690   The more than music of that tone!
LORENZO!—how I sighed that name,
As breathing it, made it mine own!
I sought the gallery: I was wont
    To pass the noontide there, and trace
695 Some Statue's shape of loveliness—
    Some Saint, some Nymph, or Muse's face.
There in my rapture I could throw
    My pencil and its hues aside,
And, as the vision past me, pour
700   My song of passion, joy, and pride.
And he was there,—LORENZO there!
    How soon the morning past away,
With finding beauties in each thing
    Neither had seen before that day!

705 Spirit of Love! soon thy rose-plumes wear
The weight and the sully of canker and care:
Falsehood is round thee; Hope leads thee on,
Till every hue from thy pinion is gone.
But one bright moment is all thine own,
710 The one ere thy visible presence is known;
When, like the wind of the South, thy power,
Sunning the heavens, sweetening the flower,
Is felt, but not seen. Thou art sweet and calm
As the sleep of a child, as the dew-fall of balm.
715 Fear has not darkened thee; Hope has not made
The blossoms expand, it but opens to fade.
Nothing is known of those wearing fears
Which will shadow the light of thy after-years.
Then art thou bliss:—but once throw by
720 The veil which shrouds thy divinity;
Stand confessed,—and thy quiet is fled!
Wild flashes of rapture may come instead,
But pain will be with them. What may restore
The gentle happiness known before?
725 I owned not to myself I loved,—
   No word of love LORENZO breathed;
But I lived in a magic ring,
   Of every pleasant flower wreathed.
A brighter blue was on the sky,
730 A sweeter breath in music's sigh;
The orange shrubs all seemed to bear
Fruit more rich, and buds more fair.
There was a glory on the noon,
A beauty in the crescent moon,
735 A lulling stillness in the night,
A feeling in the pale starlight.
There was a charmed note on the wind,
   A spell in Poetry's deep store—
Heart-uttered words, passionate thoughts,
740   Which I had never marked before.
'Twas as my heart's full happiness
Poured over all its own excess.
One night there was a gorgeous feast
   For maskers in COUNT LEON's hall;
745 And all of gallant, fair, and young,
   Were bidden to the festival.
I went, garb'd as a Hindoo girl;
   Upon each arm an amulet,
And by my side a little lute
750   Of sandal-wood with gold beset.
And shall I own that I was proud
To hear, amid the gazing crowd,
A murmur of delight, when first
   My mask and veil aside I threw?
755 For well my conscious cheek betrayed
   Whose eye was gazing on me too!
And never yet had praise been dear,
As on that evening, to mine ear.
LORENZO! I was proud to be
760 Worshipped and flattered but for thee!

THE HINDOO GIRL'S SONG

PLAYFUL and wild as the fire-flies' light,
This moment hidden, the next moment bright;
Like the foam on the dark-green sea,
Is the spell that is laid on my lover by me.
765 Were your sigh as sweet as the sumbal's[1] sigh,
When the wind of the evening is nigh;
Were your smile like that glorious light,
Seen when the stars gem the deep midnight;
Were that sigh and that smile for ever the same—
770 They were shadows, not fuel, to love's dull'd flame.

   Love once formed an amulet,
With pearls, and a rainbow, and rose-leaves set.
The pearls were pure as pearls could be,
And white as maiden purity;
775 The rose had the beauty and breath of soul,
And the rainbow-changes crowned the whole.
Frown on your lover one little while,
Dearer will be the light of your smile;
Let your blush, laugh, and sigh ever mingle together,
780 Like the bloom, sun, and clouds of the sweet spring weather.
Love never must sleep in security,
Or most calm and cold will his waking be.

———

   And as that light strain died away,
   Again I swept the breathing strings:

---

[1] or *sumbul* (Arabic), a medicinal plant with a proverbially sweet smell.

But now the notes I waked were sad,
As those the pining wood-dove sings.

THE INDIAN BRIDE

SHE has lighted her lamp, and crowned it with flowers,
The sweetest that breathed of the summer hours:
Red and white roses linked in a band,
Like a maiden's blush or a maiden's hand;
Jasmines,—some like silver spray,
Some like gold in the morning ray;
Fragrant stars,—and favourites they,
When Indian girls, on a festival-day,
Braid their dark tresses: and over all weaves
The rosy bower of lotus leaves—
Canopy suiting the lamp-lighted bark,
Love's own flowers and Love's own ark.

She watched the sky, the sunset grew dim;
She raised to CAMDEO[1] her evening hymn.
The scent of the night-flowers came on the air;
And then, like a bird escaped from the snare,
She flew to the river—(no moon was bright,
But the stars and the fire-flies gave her their light);
She stood beneath the mangoes' shade,
Half delighted and half afraid;
She trimmed the lamp, and breathed on each bloom,
(Oh, that breath was sweeter than all their perfume!)
Threw spices and oil on the spire of flame,
Called thrice on her absent lover's name;
And every pulse throbbed as she gave
Her little boat to the Ganges'[2] wave.

There are a thousand fanciful things
Linked round the young heart's imaginings.
In its first love-dream, a leaf or a flower
Is gifted then with a spell and a power:
A shade is an omen, a dream is a sign,
From which the maiden can well divine
Passion's whole history. Those only can tell
Who have loved as young hearts can love so well,
How the pulses will beat, and the cheek will be dyed,
When they have some love augury tried.
Oh, it is not for those whose feelings are cold,
Withered by care, or blunted by gold;
Whose brows have darkened with many years,
To feel again youth's hopes and fears—
What they now might blush to confess,
Yet what made their spring-day's happiness!

ZAIDE watched her flower-built vessel glide,
Mirror'd beneath on the deep-blue tide;
Lovely and lonely, scented and bright,
Like Hope's own bark, all bloom and light.
There's not one breath of wind on the air,
The Heavens are cloudless, the waters are fair,
No dew is falling; yet woe to that shade!
The maiden is weeping—her lamp has decayed.

Hark to the ring of the cymetar!
It tells that the soldier returns from afar.
Down from the mountains the warriors come:
Hark to the thunder-roll of the drum!—
To the startling voice of the trumpet's call!—
To the cymbal's clash!—to the atabal![3]
The banners of crimson float in the sun,
The warfare is ended, the battle is won.
The mother hath taken the child from her breast,
And raised it to look on its father's crest.
The pathway is lined, as the bands pass along,
With maidens, who meet them with flowers and song.
And ZAIDE hath forgotten in AZIM's arms
All her so false lamp's falser alarms.

This looks not a bridal,—the singers are mute,
Still is the mandore,[4] and breathless the lute;
Yet there the bride sits. Her dark hair is bound,
And the robe of her marriage floats white on the ground.
Oh! where is the lover, the bridegroom?—oh! where?
Look under yon black pall—the bridegroom is there!
Yet the guests are all bidden, the feast is the same,

---

[1] possibly Kamadhenu, a name for Devi, the major Hindu goddess.

[2] or Ganga, a river in northern India, sacred in Hinduism.

[3] an Arabian kettledrum (Sp., from Arabic).

[4] a three-stringed lute (Fr.).

And the bride plights her troth amid smoke and 'mid
    flame!¹
They have raised the death-pyre of sweet-scented
    wood,
860 And sprinkled it o'er with the sacred flood
Of the Ganges. The priests are assembled:—their song
Sinks deep on the ear as they bear her along,
That bride of the dead. Ay, is not this love?—
That one pure, wild feeling all others above:
865 Vowed to the living, and kept to the tomb! —
The same in its blight as it was in its bloom.
With no tear in her eye, and no change in her smile,
Young ZAIDE had come nigh to the funeral pile.
The bells of the dancing-girls ceased from their sound;
870 Silent they stood by that holiest mound.
From a crowd like the sea-waves there came not a
    breath,
When the maiden stood by the place of death!
One moment was given—the last she might spare!
To the mother, who stood in her weeping there.
875 She took the jewels that shone on her hand;
She took from her dark hair its flowery band,
And scattered them round. At once they raise
The hymn of rejoicing and love in her praise.
A prayer is muttered, a blessing said,—
880 Her torch is raised!—she is by the dead.
She has fired the pile! At once there came
A mingled rush of smoke and of flame:
The wind swept it off. They saw the bride,—
Laid by her AZIM, side by side.
885 The breeze had spread the long curls of her hair:
Like a banner of fire they played on the air.
The smoke and the flame gathered round as before,
Then cleared;—but the bride was seen no more!

———

I heard the words of praise, but not
    The one voice that I paused to hear;
890 And other sounds to me were like
    A tale poured in a sleeper's ear.

Where was LORENZO?—He had stood
    Spell-bound: but when I closed the lay,
895 As if the charm ceased with the song,
    He darted hurriedly away.
I masqued again and wandered on
    Through many a gay and gorgeous room
What with sweet waters, sweeter flowers,
900   The air was heavy with perfume.

The harp was echoing the lute,
Soft voices answered to the flute,
And, like rills in the noontide clear,
Beneath the flame-hung gondolier,
905 Shone mirrors peopled with the shades
Of stately youths and radiant maids;
And on the ear in whispers came
Those winged words of soul and flame,
Breathed in the dark-eyed beauty's ear
910 By some young love-touched cavalier;
Or mixed at times some sound more gay,
Of dance, or laugh, or roundelay.
Oh, it is sickness to the heart
To bear in revelry its part,
915 And yet feel bursting:—not one thing
Which has part in its suffering,—
The laugh as glad, the step as light,
The song as sweet, the glance as bright;
As the laugh, step, and glance and song,
920 Did to young happiness belong.

I turned me from the crowd, and reached
    A spot which seemed unsought by all—
An alcove filled with shrubs and flowers,
    But lighted by the distant hall,
925 With one or two fair statues placed,
    Like deities of the sweet shrine.
That human art should ever frame
    Such shapes so utterly divine!
A deep sigh breathed,—I knew the tone;
930   My cheek blushed warm, my heart beat high;—
One moment more I too was known,—
    I shrank before LORENZO's eye.
He leant beside a pedestal.
    The glorious brow, of Parian stone,

———

¹ a reference to suttee (or "sati" from the Sanskrit for "faithful wife"), the Hindu practice (outlawed by the British in 1829) of immolating a widow on her husband's funeral pyre. Cf. Raja Rammohun Roy, "Abstract of the Arguments regarding the Burning of Widows."*

935 Of the Antinous,[1] by his side,
    Was not more noble than his own!
They were alike: he had the same
    Thick-clustering curls the Roman wore—
The fixed and melancholy eye—
940   The smile which past like lightning o'er
The curved lip. We did not speak,
But the heart breathed upon each cheek;
We looked round with those wandering looks,
    Which seek some object for their gaze,
945 As if each other's glance was like
    The too much light of morning's rays.
I saw a youth beside me kneel;
I heard my name in music steal;
I felt my hand trembling in his;—
950 Another moment, and his kiss
Had burnt upon it; when like thought,
    So swift it past, my hand was thrown
Away, as if in sudden pain.
    LORENZO like a dream had flown!
955 We did not meet again:—he seemed
    To shun each spot where I might be;
And, it was said, another claimed
    The heart—more than the world to me!

I loved him as young Genius loves,
960   When its own wild and radiant heaven
Of starry thought burns with the light,
    The love, the life, by passion given.
I loved him, too, as woman loves—
    Reckless of sorrow, sin, or scorn;
965 Life had no evil destiny
    That, with him, I could not have borne!
I had been nurst in palaces;
    Yet earth had not a spot so drear,
That I should not have thought a home
970   In Paradise, had he been near!
How sweet it would have been to dwell,
Apart from all, in some green dell
Of sunny beauty, leaves and flowers;
And nestling birds to sing the hours!
975 Our home, beneath some chesnut's shade,

But of the woven branches made:
Our vesper hymn, the low lone wail
The rose hears from the nightingale;
And waked at morning by the call
980 Of music from a waterfall.
But not alone in dreams like this,
Breathed in the very hope of bliss,
I loved: my love had been the same
In hushed despair, in open shame.
985 I would have rather been a slave,
    In tears, in bondage, by his side,
Than shared in all, if wanting him,
    This world had power to give beside!
My heart was withered,—and my heart
990   Had ever been the world to me;
And love had been the first fond dream,
    Whose life was in reality.
I had sprung from my solitude
    Like a young bird upon the wing
995 To meet the arrow; so I met
    My poisoned shaft of suffering.
And as that bird, with drooping crest
And broken wing, will seek his nest,
But seek in vain; so vain I sought
1000 My pleasant home of song and thought.
There was one spell upon my brain,
Upon my pencil, on my strain;
But one face to my colours came;
My chords replied but to one name—
1005 LORENZO!—all seemed vowed to thee,
To passion, and to misery!
I had no interest in the things
    That once had been like life, or light;
No tale was pleasant to mine ear,
1010   No song was sweet, no picture bright.
I was wild with my great distress,
My lone, my utter hopelessness!
I would sit hours by the side
Of some clear rill, and mark it glide,
1015 Bearing my tears along, till night
Came with dark hours; and soft starlight
Watch o'er its shadowy beauty keeping,
    Till I grew calm:—then I would take
The lute, which had all day been sleeping

---

[1] Antinous (AD 110–30), the lover of the emperor Hadrian, was famous for his beauty.

Upon a cypress tree, and wake
The echoes of the midnight air
With words that love wrung from despair.

SONG

FAREWELL!—we shall not meet again!
　　As we are parting now,
I must my beating heart restrain—
　　Must veil my burning brow!
Oh, I must coldly learn to hide
　　One thought, all else above—
Must call upon my woman's pride
　　To hide my woman's love!
Check dreams I never may avow;
　　Be free, be careless, cold as thou!
Oh! those are tears of bitterness,
　　Wrung from the breaking heart,
When two, blest in their tenderness,
　　Must learn to live—apart!
But what are they to that lone sigh,
　　That cold and fixed despair,
That weight of wasting agony
　　It must be mine to bear?
Methinks I should not thus repine,
If I had but one vow of thine.
I could forgive inconstancy,
To be one moment loved by thee!
With me the hope of life is gone,
　　The sun of joy is set;
One wish my soul still dwells upon—
　　The wish it could forget.
I would forget that look, that tone,
My heart hath all too dearly known.
But who could ever yet efface
From memory love's enduring trace?
All may revolt, all may complain—
But who is there may break the chain?
Farewell!—I shall not be to thee
　　More than a passing thought;
But every time and place will be
　　With thy remembrance fraught!
Farewell! we have not often met,—
　　We may not meet again;

But on my heart the seal is set
　　Love never sets in vain!
Fruitless as constancy may be,
No chance, no change, may turn from thee
One who has loved thee wildly, well,—
But whose first love-vow breathed—farewell!

And lays which only told of love
　　In all its varied sorrowing,
The echoes of the broken heart,
　　Were all the songs I now could sing.
Legends of olden times in Greece
　　When not a flower but had its tale;
When spirits haunted each green oak;
　　When voices spoke in every gale;
When not a star shone in the sky
　　Without its own love history.
Amid its many songs was one
　　That suited well with my sick mind.
I sang it when the breath of flowers
　　Came sweet upon the midnight wind.

LEADES AND CYDIPPE[1]

SHE sat her in her twilight bower,
A temple formed of leaf and flower;
Rose and myrtle[2] framed the roof,
To a shower of April proof;
And primroses, pale gems of Spring,
Lay on the green turf glistening
Close by the violet, whose breath
Is so sweet in a dewy wreath.
And oh, that myrtle! how green it grew!
With flowers as white as the pearls of dew
That shone beside; and the glorious rose
Lay, like a beauty in warm repose,
Blushing in slumber. The air was bright
With the spirit and glow of its crimson light.

---

[1] Cydippe is the name of the heroine of Ovid (43 BC–AD 17), *Heroides* 20.

[2] sacred to Aphrodite.

1095   CYDIPPE had turned from her columned hall,
Where, the queen of the feast, she was worshipped by all;
Where the vases were burning with spices and flowers,
And the odorous waters were playing in showers
And lamps were blazing—those lamps of perfume
1100 Which shed such a charm of light over the bloom
Of woman, when Pleasure a spell has thrown
Over one night-hour and made it her own.
And the ruby wine-cup shone with a ray,
As the gems of the East had there melted away;
1105 And the bards were singing those songs of fire,
That bright eyes and the goblet so well inspire;—
While she, the glory and pride of the hour,
Sat silent and sad in her secret bower!

There is a grief that wastes the heart,
1110 Like mildew on a tulip's dyes,—
When hope, deferred but to depart,
Loses its smiles, but keeps its sighs;
When love's bark, with its anchor gone,
Clings to a straw, and still trusts on.
1115 Oh, more than all!—methinks that Love
    Should pray that it might ever be
Beside the burning shrine which had
    Its young heart's fond idolatry.
Oh, absence is the night of love!
1120   Lovers are very children then;
Fancying ten thousand feverish shapes,
    Until their light returns again.
A look, a word, is then recalled,
    And thought upon until it wears,
1125 What is, perhaps, a very shade,
    The tone and aspect of our fears.
And this was what was withering now
The radiance of CYDIPPE's brow.
She watched until her cheek grew pale;
1130 The green wave bore no bounding sail:
Her sight grew dim; 'mid the blue air
No snowy dove came floating there,
The dear scroll hid beneath his wing,
With plume and soft eye glistening,
1135 To seek again, in leafy dome,
The nest of its accustomed home!

Still far away, o'er land and seas,
Lingered the faithless LEADES.

    She thought on the spring days, when she had been,
1140 Lonely and lovely, a maiden queen;
When passion to her was a storm at sea,
Heard 'mid the green land's tranquillity.
But a stately warrior came from afar;
He bore on his bosom the glorious scar,
1145 So worshipped by woman—the death-seal of war.
And the maiden's heart was an easy prize,
When valour and faith were her sacrifice.

    Methinks might that sweet season last,
In which our first love-dream is past;
1150 Ere doubts and cares, and jealous pain,
Are flaws in the heart's diamond-chain;—
Men might forget to think on Heaven,
And yet have the sweet sin forgiven.

But ere the marriage feast was spread,
1155   LEADES said that he must brook
To part awhile from that best light,
    Those eyes which fixed his every look.
Just press again his native shore,
    And then he would that shore resign
1160 For her dear sake, who was to him
    His household-god!—his spirit's shrine!

    He came not! Then the heart's decay
Wasted her silently away:—
A sweet fount, which the mid-day sun
1165 Has all too hotly looked upon!

    It is most sad to watch the fall
Of autumn leaves!—but worst of all
It is to watch the flower of spring
Faded in its fresh blossoming!
1170 To see the once so clear blue orb
    Its summer light and warmth forget;
Darkening, beneath its tearful lid,
    Like a rain-beaten violet!

To watch the banner-rose of health
    Pass from the cheek!—to mark how plain,
Upon the wan and sunken brow,
    Become the wanderings of each vein!
The shadowy hand, so thin, so pale!
    The languid step!—the drooping head!
The long wreaths of neglected hair!
    The lip, whence red and smile are fled!
And having watched thus day by day,
Light, life, and colour, pass away!
To see, at length, the glassy eye
Fix dull in dread mortality;
Mark the last ray, catch the last breath,
Till the grave sets its sign of death!

    This was CYDIPPE's fate!—They laid
The maiden underneath the shade
Of a green cypress,—and that hour
    The tree was withered, and stood bare!
The spring brought leaves to other trees,
    But never other leaf grew there!
It stood, 'mid others flourishing,
A blighted, solitary thing.

    The summer sun shone on that tree,
When shot a vessel o'er the sea—
When sprang a warrior from the prow—
LEADES! by the stately brow.
Forgotten toil, forgotten care,
All his worn heart has had to bear.
That heart is full! He hears the sigh
That breathed "Farewell!" so tenderly.
If even then it was most sweet,
What will it be that now they meet?
Alas! alas! Hope's fair deceit!
He spurred o'er land, has cut the wave,
To look but on CYDIPPE's grave.

It has blossomed in beauty, that lone tree,
    LEADES' kiss restored its bloom;
For wild he kissed the withered stem—
    It grew upon CYDIPPE's tomb!
And there he dwelt. The hottest ray,
Still dew upon the branches lay
Like constant tears. The winter came;
But still the green tree stood the same.
And it was said, at evening's close,
A sound of whispered music rose;
That 'twas the trace of viewless feet
Made the flowers more than flowers sweet.
At length LEADES died. That day,
Bark and green foliage past away
From the lone tree,—again a thing
Of wonder and of perishing!

    One evening I had roamed beside
The winding of the Arno's tide;
The sky was flooded with moonlight;
Below were waters azure bright,
Pallazzos with their marble halls,
Green gardens, silver waterfalls,
And orange groves and citron shades,
And cavaliers and dark-eyed maids;
Sweet voices singing, echoes sent
From many a rich-toned instrument.
I could not bear this loveliness!
    It was on such a night as this
That love had lighted up my dream
    Of long despair and short-lived bliss.
I sought the city; wandering on,
    Unconscious where my steps might be;
My heart was deep in other thoughts;
    All places were alike to me:—
At length I stopp'd beneath the walls
Of San Mark's old cathedral[1] halls.
I entered:—and, beneath the roof,
Ten thousand wax-lights burnt on high;
And incense on the censers fumed
As for some great solemnity.
The white-robed choristers were singing;
Their cheerful peal the bells were ringing:
Then deep-voiced music floated round,
As the far arches sent forth sound—
The stately organ:—and fair bands
Of young girls strewed, with lavish hands,

---

[1] The cathedral in Florence is actually Santa Maria del Fiore, but there is a famous convent of St. Mark in the city.

<pre>
1255   Violets o'er the mosaic floor;
       And sang while scattering the sweet store.

       I turned me to a distant aisle,
           Where but a feeble glimmering came
       (Itself in darkness) of the smile
1260   Sent from the tapers' perfumed flame;
       And coloured as each pictured pane
       Shed o'er the blaze its crimson stain:—
       While, from the window o'er my head,
       A dim and sickly gleam was shed
1265   From the young moon,—enough to shew
       That tomb and tablet lay below.
       I leant upon one monument,—
           'Twas sacred to unhappy love:
       On it were carved a blighted pine—
1270   A broken ring—a wounded dove.
       And two or three brief words told all
           Her history who lay beneath:—
       "The flowers—at morn her bridal flowers,—
           Formed, ere the eve, her funeral wreath."

1275   I could but envy her. I thought
           How sweet it must be thus to die!
       Your last looks watched,—your last sigh caught,
           As life or Heaven were in that sigh!
       Passing in loveliness and light;
1280   Your heart as pure,—your cheek as bright
       As the spring-rose, whose petals shut,
       By sun unscorched, by shower unwet;
       Leaving behind a memory
       Shrined in love's fond eternity.

1285   But I was wakened from this dream
           By a burst of light—a gush of song—
       A welcome, as the stately doors
           Poured in a gay and gorgeous throng.
       I could see all from where I stood.
1290   And first I looked upon the bride;
       She was a pale and lovely girl:—
           But, oh God! who was by her side?—
       LORENZO! No, I did not speak;
       My heart beat high, but could not break.
1295   I shrieked not, wept not; but stood there
</pre>

       Motionless in my still despair;
       As I were forced by some strange thrall,
       To bear with and to look on all,—
       I heard the hymn, I heard the vow;
1300   (Mine ear throbs with them even now!)
       I saw the young bride's timid cheek
           Blushing beneath her silver veil.
       I saw LORENZO kneel! Methought
           ('Twas but a thought!) he too was pale.
1305   But when it ended, and his lip
           Was prest to her's—I saw no more!
       My heart grew cold,—my brain swam round,—
           I sank upon the cloister floor!

       I lived,—if that may be called life,
1310   From which each charm of life has fled—
       Happiness gone, with hope and love,—
           In all but breath already dead.

       Rust gathered on the silent chords
           Of my neglected lyre,—the breeze
1315   Was now its mistress: music brought
           For me too bitter memories!
       The ivy darkened o'er my bower;
       Around, the weeds choked every flower.
       I pleased me in this desolateness,
1320   As each thing bore my fate's impress.

       At length I made myself a task—
           To paint that Cretan maiden's fate,[1]
       Whom Love taught such deep happiness,
           And whom Love left so desolate.
1325   I drew her on a rocky shore:—
       Her black hair loose, and sprinkled o'er
       With white sea-foam;—her arms were bare,
       Flung upwards in their last despair.
       Her naked feet the pebbles prest;
1330   The tempest wind sang in her vest:
       A wild stare in her glassy eyes;
       White lips, as parched by their hot sighs;

---

[1] Ariadne, a Cretan princess, helped Theseus find his way through the labyrinth and kill the Minotaur. They eloped, but he abandoned her on the island of Naxos. See Ovid, *Heroides* 10.

And cheek more pallid than the spray,
Which, cold and colourless, on it lay:—
Just such a statue as should be
    Placed ever, Love! beside thy shrine;
Warning thy victims of what ills—
    What burning tears, false god! are thine.
Before her was the darkling sea;
    Behind, the barren mountains rose—
A fit home for the broken heart
    To weep away life, wrongs, and woes!

I had now but one hope:—that when
    The hand that traced these tints was cold—
Its pulse but in their passion seen,—
    LORENZO might these tints behold,
And find my grief;—think—see—feel all
I felt, in this memorial!

It was one evening,—the rose-light
    Was o'er each green veranda shining;
Spring was just breaking, and white buds
    Were 'mid the darker ivy twining.
My hall was filled with the perfume
Sent from the early orange bloom:
The fountain, in the midst, was fraught
With rich hues from the sunset caught;—
And the first song came from the dove,
Nestling in the shrub alcove.
But why pause on my happiness?—
    Another step was with mine there!
Another sigh than mine made sweet
    With its dear breath the scented air!
LORENZO! could it be my hand
    That now was trembling in thine own?
LORENZO! could it be mine ear
    That drank the music of thy tone?

We sat us by a lattice, where
    Came in the soothing evening breeze,
Rich with the gifts of early flowers,
    And the soft wind-lute's symphonies.
And in the twilight's vesper-hour,
Beneath the hanging jasmine-shower,

I heard a tale,—as fond, as dear
As e'er was poured in woman's ear!

LORENZO'S HISTORY

I WAS betrothed from earliest youth
    To a fair orphan, who was left
Beneath my father's roof and care,—
    Of every other friend bereft:
An heiress, with her fertile vales,
    Caskets of Indian gold and pearl;
Yet meek as poverty itself,
    And timid as a peasant girl:
A delicate frail thing,—but made
For spring sunshine, or summer shade;—
A slender flower, unmeet to bear
One April shower,—so slight, so fair.

I loved her as a brother loves
    His favourite sister:—and when war
First called me from our long-shared home
    To bear my father's sword afar,
I parted from her,—not as one
    Whose life and soul are wrung by parting:
With death-cold brow and throbbing pulse,
    And burning tears like life-blood starting.
Lost in war-dreams, I scarcely heard
    The prayer that bore my name above:
The "Farewell!" that kissed off her tears,
    Had more of pity than of love!
I thought of her not with that deep,
Intensest memory love will keep
More tenderly than life. To me
    She was but as a dream of home,—
One of those calm and pleasant thoughts
    That o'er the soldier's spirit come;
Remembering him, when battle lours,
Of twilight walks and fireside hours.

I came to thy bright FLORENCE when
    The task of blood was done:
I saw thee! Had I lived before?
    Oh, no! my life but then begun.

Ay, by that blush! the summer rose
    Has not more luxury of light!
Ay, by those eyes! whose language is
    Like what the clear stars speak at night,
1415 Thy first look was a fever spell!—
Thy first word was an oracle
Which seal'd my fate! I worshipped thee,
My beautiful, bright deity!
Worshipped thee as a sacred thing
1420 Of Genius' high imagining;—
But loved thee for thy sweet revealing
Of woman's own most gentle feeling.
I might have broken from the chain
    Thy power, thy glory round me flung;
1425 But never might forget thy blush—
    The smile which on thy sweet lips hung!
I lived but in thy sight! One night
    From thy hair fell a myrtle blossom;
It was a relic that breathed of thee:—
1430   Look! it has withered in my bosom!
Yet was I wretched, though I dwelt
    In the sweet sight of Paradise:
A curse lay on me. But not now,
    Thus smiled upon by those dear eyes,
1435 Will I think over thoughts of pain.
I'll only tell thee that the line
    That ever told Love's misery,
    Ne'er told of misery like mine!
I wedded.—I could not have borne
1440   To see the young IANTHE[1] blighted
By that worst blight the spring can know—
    Trusting affection ill requited!
Oh, was it that she was too fair,
    Too innocent for this damp earth;
1445 And that her native star above
    Reclaimed again its gentle birth?
She faded. Oh, my peerless queen,
    I need not pray thee pardon me
For owning that my heart then felt

---

[1] Ianthe is also the name of the heroine of William D'Avenant, *The Siege of Rhodes* (1656), the dedicatee of Byron,* *Childe Harold's Pilgrimage* 1–2 (1812), a character in Percy Bysshe Shelley, *Queen Mab* (1813), Shelley's first daughter (born 1813), and a character in John Polidori, *The Vampyre* (1819).

1450 For any other than for thee!
I bore her to those azure isles
    Where health dwells by the side of spring;
And deemed their green and sunny vales,
    And calm and fragrant airs, might bring
1455 Warmth to the cheek, light to the eye,
Of her who was too young to die.
It was in vain!—and, day by day,
The gentle creature died away.
As parts the odour from the rose,—
1460 As fades the sky at twilight's close,—
She past so tender and so fair;
    So patient, though she knew each breath
Might be her last; her own mild smile
    Parted her placid lips in death.
1465 Her grave is under southern skies;
Green turf and flowers o'er it rise.
Oh! nothing but a pale spring wreath
Would fade o'er her who lies beneath!
I gave her prayers—I gave her tears—
1470   I staid awhile beside her grave;
Then led by Hope, and led by Love,
    Again I cut the azure wave.
What have I more to say, my life!
    But just to pray one smile of thine,
1475 Telling I have not loved in vain—
    That thou dost join these hopes of mine?
Yes, smile, sweet love! our life will be
    As radiant as a fairy tale!
Glad as the sky-lark's earliest song—
1480   Sweet as the sigh of the spring gale!
All, all that life will ever be,
Shone o'er, divinest love! by thee.

Oh, mockery of happiness!
    Love now was all too late to save.
1485 False Love! oh, what had you to do
    With one you had led to the grave?
A little time I had been glad
    To mark the paleness on my cheek;
To feel how, day by day, my step
1490   Grew fainter, and my hand more weak;
To know the fever of my soul

      Was also preying on my frame:
      But now I would have given worlds
          To change the crimson hectic's flame[1]
1495 For the pure rose of health; to live
      For the dear life that Love could give.
      Oh, youth may sicken at its bloom,
      And wealth and fame pray for the tomb;—
      But can Love bear from Love to part,
1500 And not cling to that one dear heart?
      I shrank away from death,—my tears
      Had been unwept in other years:—
      But thus, in Love's first ecstasy,
      Was it not worse than death to die?
1505 LORENZO! I would live for thee!
      But thou wilt have to weep for me!
      That sun has kissed the morning dews,—
          I shall not see its twilight close!
      That rose is fading in the noon,
1510   And I shall not outlive that rose!
      Come, let me lean upon thy breast,
      My last, best place of happiest rest!
      Once more let me breathe thy sighs—
      Look once more in those watching eyes!
1515 Oh! but for thee, and grief of thine,
      And parting, I should not repine!
      It is deep happiness to die,
      Yet live in Love's dear memory.
      Thou wilt remember me,—my name
1520 Is linked with beauty and with fame.
      The summer airs, the summer sky,
      The soothing spell of Music's sigh,—
      Stars in their poetry of night,
      The silver silence of moonlight,—
1525 The dim blush of the twilight hours,
      The fragrance of the bee-kissed flowers;—
      But, more than all, sweet songs will be
      Thrice sacred unto Love and me.
      LORENZO! be this kiss a spell!
1530 My first!—my last! FAREWELL!—FAREWELL!

      THERE is a lone and stately hall,—
      Its master dwells apart from all.
      A wanderer through Italia's land,
          One night a refuge there I found.
1535 The lightning flash rolled o'er the sky,

          The torrent rain was sweeping round:—
      These won me entrance. He was young,
          The castle's lord, but pale like age;
      His brow, as sculpture beautiful,
1540   Was wan as Grief's corroded page.
      He had no words, he had no smiles,
          No hopes:—his sole employ to brood
      Silently over his sick heart
          In sorrow and in solitude.
1545 I saw the hall where, day by day,
      He mused his weary life away;—
      It scarcely seemed a place for woe,
          But rather like a genie's home.
      Around were graceful statues ranged,
1550   And pictures shone around the dome.
      But there was one—a loveliest one!—
          One picture brightest of all there!
      Oh! never did the painter's dream
          Shape thing so gloriously fair!
1555 It was a face!—the summer day
          Is not more radiant in its light!
      Dark flashing eyes, like the deep stars
          Lighting the azure brow of night;
      A blush like sunrise o'er the rose;
1560   A cloud of raven hair, whose shade
      Was sweet as evening's, and whose curls
          Clustered beneath a laurel braid.
      She leant upon a harp:—one hand
          Wandered, like snow, amid the chords;
1565 The lips were opening with such life,
          You almost heard the silvery words.
      She looked a form of light and life,—
          All soul, all passion, and all fire;
      A priestess of Apollo's, when
1570   The morning beam falls on her lyre;
      A Sappho, or ere love had turned
      The heart to stone where once it burned.
      But by the picture's side was placed
      A funeral urn, on which was traced
1575 The heart's recorded wretchedness;—

---

[1] a symptom of consumption.

And on a tablet, hung above,
Was 'graved one tribute of sad words—
"Lorenzo to his Minstrel Love."

Home

I left my home;—'twas in a little vale,
Sheltered from snow-storms by the stately pines;
A small clear river wandered quietly,
Its smooth waves only cut by the light barks
5 Of fishers, and but darkened by the shade
The willows flung, when to the southern wind
They threw their long green tresses. On the slope
Were five or six white cottages, whose roofs
Reached not to the laburnum's height, whose boughs
10 Shook over them bright showers of golden bloom.
Sweet silence reigned around:—no other sound
Came on the air, than when the shepherd made
The reed-pipe rudely musical, or notes
From the wild birds, or children in their play
15 Sending forth shouts or laughter. Strangers came
Rarely or never near the lonely place....
I went into far countries. Years past by,
But still that vale in silent beauty dwelt
Within my memory. Home I came at last.
20 I stood upon a mountain height, and looked
Into the vale below; and smoke arose,
And heavy sounds; and through the thick dim air
Shot blackened turrets, and brick walls, and roofs
Of the red tile. I entered in the streets:
25 There were ten thousand hurrying to and fro;
And masted vessels stood upon the river,
And barges sullied the once dew-clear stream.
Where were the willows, where the cottages?
I sought my home; I sought and found a city,
30 Alas! for the green valley!

from *The Troubadour, Catalogue of Pictures, and Historical Sketches* (1825)

The Proud Ladye[1]

Oh, what could the ladye's beauty match,
    An it were not the ladye's pride;
An hundred knights from far and near
    Woo'd at that ladye's side.

5 The rose of the summer slept on her cheek,
    Its lily upon her breast,
And her eye shone forth like the glorious star
    That rises the first in the west.

There were some that woo'd for her land and gold,
10   And some for her noble name,
And more that woo'd for her loveliness;
    But her answer was still the same.

"There is a steep and lofty wall,
    Where my warders trembling stand,
15 He who at speed shall ride round its height,
    For him shall be my hand."

Many turn'd away from the deed,
    The hope of their wooing o'er;
But many a young knight mounted the steed
20   He never mounted more.

At last there came a youthful knight,
    From a strange and far countrie,
The steed that he rode was white as the foam
    Upon a stormy sea.

25 And she who had scorn'd the name of love,
    Now bow'd before its might,
And the ladye grew meek as if disdain
    Were not made for that stranger knight.

---

[1] "This ballad is also taken, with some slight change, from a legend in Russell's Germany." (L.E.L.) John Russell, *A Tour of Germany* (1824) chap. 11. Landon's ballad is included in her "The Troubadour," canto 4.

    She sought at first to steal his soul
30   By dance, song, and festival;
    At length on bended knee she pray'd
        He would not ride the wall.

    But gaily the young knight laugh'd at her fears,
        And flung him on his steed,—
35   There was not a saint in the calendar
        That she pray'd not to in her need.

    She dared not raise her eyes to see
        If heaven had granted her prayer,
    Till she heard a light step bound to her side,—
40   The gallant knight stood there!

    And took the ladye ADELINE
        From her hair a jewell'd band,
    But the knight repell'd the offer'd gift,
        And turn'd from the offer'd hand.

45   And deemest thou that I dared this deed,
        Ladye, for love of thee;
    The honour that guides the soldier's lance
        Is mistress enough for me.

    Enough for me to ride the ring,
50   The victor's crown to wear;
    But not in honour of the eyes
        Of any ladye there.

    I had a brother whom I lost
        Through thy proud crueltie,
55   And far more was to me his love,
        Than woman's love can be.

    I came to triumph o'er the pride
        Through which that brother fell,
    I laugh to scorn thy love and thee,
60   And now, proud dame, farewell!

    And from that hour the ladye pined,
        For love was in her heart,
    And on her slumber there came dreams
        She could not bid depart.

65   Her eye lost all its starry light,
        Her cheek grew wan and pale,
    Till she hid her faded loveliness
        Beneath the sacred veil.

    And she cut off her long dark hair,
70   And bade the world farewell,
    And she now dwells a veiled nun
        In Saint Marie's cell.

from *The Golden Violet, with its tales of Romance and Chivalry: and Other Poems* (1827)

Love's Last Lesson

Teach it me, if you can,—forgetfulness![1]
I surely shall forget, if you can bid me;
I who have worshipp'd thee, my god on earth,
I who have bow'd me at thy lightest word.
5   Your last command, "Forget me," will it not
Sink deeply down within my inmost soul?
Forget thee!—ay, forgetfulness will be
A mercy to me. By the many nights
When I have wept for that I dared not sleep,—
10 A dream had made me live my woes again,
Acting my wretchedness, without the hope
My foolish heart still clings to, though that hope
Is like the opiate which may lull a while,
Then wake to double torture; by the days
15 Pass'd in lone watching and in anxious fears,
When a breath sent the crimson to my cheek,
Like the red gushing of a sudden wound;
By all the careless looks and careless words
Which have to me been like the scorpion's stinging;
20 By happiness blighted, and by thee, for ever;
By thy eternal work of wretchedness;
By all my wither'd feelings, ruin'd health,
Crush'd hopes, and rifled heart, I will forget thee![2]
Alas! my words are vanity. Forget thee!

---

[1] Cf. Byron, *Manfred* 1.1.135–36.*

[2] Cf. *Manfred* 1.1.242–51.*

25 Thy work of wasting is too surely done.
The April shower may pass and be forgotten,
The rose fall and one fresh spring in its place,
And thus it may be with light summer love.
It was not thus with mine: it did not spring,
30 Like the bright colour on an evening cloud,
Into a moment's life, brief, beautiful;
Not amid lighted halls, when flatteries
Steal on the ear like dew upon the rose,
As soft, as soon dispersed, as quickly pass'd;
35 But you first call'd my woman's feelings forth,
And taught me love ere I had dream'd love's name.
I loved unconsciously: your name was all
That seem'd in language, and to me the world
Was only made for you; in solitude,
40 When passions hold their interchange together,
Your image was the shadow of my thought;
Never did slave, before his Eastern lord,
Tremble as I did when I met your eye,
And yet each look was counted as a prize;
45 I laid your words up in my heart like pearls
Hid in the ocean's treasure-cave. At last
I learn'd my heart's deep secret: for I hoped,
I dream'd you loved me; wonder, fear, delight,
Swept my heart like a storm; my soul, my life,
50 Seem'd all too little for your happiness;
Had I been mistress of the starry worlds
That light the midnight, they had all been yours,
And I had deem'd such boon but poverty.
As it was, I gave all I could—my love,
55 My deep, my true, my fervent, faithful love;
And now you bid me learn forgetfulness:
It is a lesson that I soon shall learn.
There is a home of quiet for the wretched,
A somewhat dark, and cold, and silent rest,
60 But still it is rest,—for it is the grave.

She flung aside the scroll, as it had part
In her great misery. Why should she write?
What could she write? Her woman's pride forbade
To let him look upon her heart, and see
65 It was an utter ruin;—and cold words,
And scorn and slight, that may repay his own,
Were as a foreign language, to whose sound

She might not frame her utterance. Down she bent
Her head upon an arm so white that tears
70 Seem'd but the natural melting of its snow,
Touch'd by the flush'd cheek's crimson; yet life-blood
Less wrings in shedding than such tears as those.

And this then is love's ending! It is like
The history of some fair southern clime.
75 Hot fires are in the bosom of the earth,
And the warm'd soil puts forth its thousand flowers,
Its fruits of gold, summer's regality,
And sleep and odours float upon the air:
At length the subterranean element
80 Breaks from its secret dwelling-place, and lays
All waste before it; the red lava stream
Sweeps like the pestilence; and that which was
A garden in its colours and its breath,
Fit for the princess of a fairy tale,
85 Is as a desert, in whose burning sands,
And ashy waters, who is there can trace
A sign, a memory of its former beauty?[1]
It is thus with the heart; love lights it up
With hopes like young companions, and with joys
90 Dreaming deliciously of their sweet selves.

This is at first; but what is the result?
Hopes that lie mute in their own sullenness,
For they have quarrell'd even with themselves;
And joys indeed like birds of Paradise:[2]
95 And in their stead despair coils scorpion-like
Stinging itself;[3] and the heart, burnt and crush'd
With passion's earthquake, scorch'd and wither'd up,
Lies in its desolation,—this is love.

What is the tale that I would tell? Not one
100 Of strange adventure, but a common tale
Of woman's wretchedness; one to be read
Daily in many a young and blighted heart.

---

[1] Cf. Byron, *Manfred* 1.1.110–23, 2.1.52–58,* and *Childe Harold's Pilgrimage* 4.120 (1818).

[2] "In Eastern tales, the bird of Paradise never rests on the earth." (L.E.L.) Cf. Coleridge, "Effusion 35" 24–25.*

[3] Cf. Byron, *The Giaour* 422–38.*

The lady whom I spake of rose again
From the red fever's couch, to careless eyes
Perchance the same as she had ever been.
But oh, how alter'd to herself! She felt
That bird-like pining for some gentle home
To which affection might attach itself,
That weariness which hath but outward part
In what the world calls pleasure, and that chill
Which makes life taste the bitterness of death.

And he she loved so well,—what opiate
Lull'd consciousness into its selfish sleep?—
He said he loved her not; that never vow
Or passionate pleading won her soul for him;
And that he guess'd not her deep tenderness.

Are words, then, only false? are there no looks,
Mute but most eloquent; no gentle cares
That win so much upon the fair weak things
They seem to guard? And had he not long read
Her heart's hush'd secret in the soft dark eye
Lighted at his approach, and on the cheek
Colouring all crimson at his lightest look?
This is the truth; his spirit wholly turn'd
To stern ambition's dream, to that fierce strife
Which leads to life's high places, and reck'd not
What lovely flowers might perish in his path.

And here at length is somewhat of revenge:
For man's most golden dreams of pride and power
Are vain as any woman dreams of love;
Both end in weary brow and wither'd heart,
And the grave closes over those whose hopes
Have lain there long before.

Erinna

INTRODUCTORY NOTICE

Among the obligations I owe to "The Brides of Florence,"[1] and to the information contained in its interesting notes, I must refer particularly for the origin of the present poem. In one of those notes is the first, indeed the only account I ever met with of Erinna. The following short quotation is sufficient for my present purpose:—"Erinna was a poetess from her cradle, and she only lived to the completion of her eighteenth year.—Of Erinna very little is known; there is in the Grecian Anthology a sepulchral epigram by Antipater[2] on this young poetess." A poem of the present kind had long floated on my imagination; and this gave it a local habitation and a name.[3] There seemed to me just enough known of Erinna to interest; and I have not attempted to write a classical fiction; feelings are what I wish to narrate, not incidents:[4] my aim has been to draw the portrait and trace the changes of a highly poetical mind, too sensitive perhaps of the chill and bitterness belonging even to success. The feelings which constitute poetry are the same in all ages, they are acted upon by similar causes. Erinna is an ideal not a historical picture, and as such I submit it less to the judgment than to the kindness of my friends.

Was she of spirit race, or was she one
Of earth's least earthly daughters, one to whom
A gift of loveliness and soul is given,
Only to make them wretched?

There is an antique gem, on which her brow
Retains its graven beauty even now.
Her hair is braided, but one curl behind
Floats as enamour'd of the summer wind;
The rest is simple. Is she not too fair

---

[1] W. Fraser [Randolph Fitz-Eustace], *The Brides of Florence: a play, in five acts: illustrative of the Manners of the Middle Ages, with Historical notes, and Minor Poems* (1824) 230–33.

[2] Antipater of Sidon, 2nd century BC. For his epigram about Erinna, see the *Greek Anthology* 7.713.

[3] Shakespeare, *A Midsummer Night's Dream* 5.1.17.

[4] Cf. W. Wordsworth, Preface to *Lyrical Ballads*.*

Even to think of maiden's sweetest care?
The mouth and brow are contrasts. One so fraught
With pride, the melancholy pride of thought
Conscious of power, and yet forced to know
How little way such power as that can go;
Regretting, while too proud of the fine mind,
Which raises but to part it from its kind:
But the sweet mouth had nothing of all this;
It was a mouth the rose had lean'd to kiss
For her young sister, telling, now though mute,
How soft an echo it was to the lute.
The one spoke genius, in it high revealing;
The other smiled a woman's gentle feeling.
It was a lovely face: the Greek outline
Flowing, yet delicate and feminine;
The glorious lightning of the kindled eye,
Raised, as it communed with its native sky.
A lovely face, the spirit's fitting shrine;
The one almost, the other quite divine.[1]

My hand is on the lyre, which never more
With its sweet commerce, like a bosom friend,
Will share the deeper thoughts which I could trust
Only to music and to solitude.
5 It is the very grove, the olive grove,
Where first I laid my laurel crown[2] aside,
And bathed my fever'd brow in the cold stream;
As if that I could wash away the fire
Which from that moment kindled in my heart.
10 I well remember how I flung myself,
Like a young goddess, on a purple cloud
Of light and odour—the rich violets
Were so ethereal in bloom and breath:
And I,—I felt immortal, for my brain
15 Was drunk and mad with its first draught of fame.
'Tis strange there was one only cypress tree,[3]
And then, as now, I lay beneath its shade.
The night had seen me pace my lonely room,
Clasping the lyre I had no heart to wake,
20 Impatient for the day: yet its first dawn
Came cold as death; for every pulse sank down,
Until the very presence of my hope
Became to me a fear. The sun rose up;
I stood alone mid thousands: but I felt
25 Mine inspiration; and, as the last sweep
Of my song died away amid the hills,
My heart reverberate the shout which bore
To the blue mountains and the distant heaven
ERINNA's name, and on my bended knee,
30 Olympus,[4] I received thy laurel crown.

And twice new birth of violets have sprung,
Since they were first my pillow, since I sought
In the deep silence of the olive grove
The dreamy happiness which solitude
35 Brings to the soul o'erfill'd with its delight:
For I was like some young and sudden heir
Of a rich palace heap'd with gems and gold,
Whose pleasure doubles as he sums his wealth
And forms a thousand plans of festival;
40 Such were my myriad visions of delight.
The lute, which hitherto in Delphian shades[5]
Had been my twilight's solitary joy,
Would henceforth be a sweet and breathing bond
Between me and my kind. Orphan unloved,
45 I had been lonely from my childhood's hour,
Childhood whose very happiness is love:
But that was over now; my lyre would be
My own heart's true interpreter, and those
To whom my song was dear, would they not bless
50 The hand that waken'd it? I should be loved
For the so gentle sake of those soft chords
Which mingled others' feelings with mine own.

Vow'd I that song to meek and gentle thoughts.
To tales that told of sorrow and of love,
55 To all our nature's finest touches, all
That wakens sympathy: and I should be
Alone no longer; every wind that bore,

---

[1] The epigraphs or prologues are by Landon.

[2] Laurel was sacred to Apollo, god of poetry; laurel crowns were awarded to the winners of athletic or poetic competitions.

[3] symbolic of mourning.

[4] the highest mountain in Greece; its summit was the home of the gods.

[5] The town of Delphi, at the foot of Mount Parnassus, was the home of the Delphic oracle.

And every lip that breathed one strain of mine,
Henceforth partake in all my joy and grief.
60 Oh! glorious is the gifted poet's lot,
And touching more than glorious: 'tis to be
Companion of the heart's least earthly hour;
The voice of love and sadness, calling forth
Tears from their silent fountain: 'tis to have
65 Share in all nature's loveliness; giving flowers
A life as sweet, more lasting than their own;
And catching from green wood and lofty pine
Language mysterious as musical;
Making the thoughts, which else had only been
70 Like colours on the morning's earliest hour,
Immortal, and worth immortality;
Yielding the hero that eternal name
For which he fought; making the patriot's deed
A stirring record for long after time;
75 Cherishing tender thoughts, which else had pass'd
Away like tears; and saving the loved dead
From death's worst part—its deep forgetfulness.

From the first moment when a falling leaf,
Or opening bud, or streak of rose-touch'd sky,
80 Waken'd in me the flush and flow of song,
I gave my soul entire unto the gift
I deem'd mine own, direct from heaven; it was
The hope, the bliss, the energy of life;
I had no hope that dwelt not with my lyre,
85 No bliss whose being grew not from my lyre,
No energy undevoted to my lyre.
It was my other self, that had a power;
Mine, but o'er which I had not a control.
At times it was not with me, and I felt
90 A wonder how it ever had been mine:
And then a word, a look of loveliness,
A tone of music, call'd it into life;
And song came gushing, like the natural tears,
To check whose current does not rest with us.

95 Had I lived ever in the savage woods,
Or in some distant island, which the sea
With wind and wave guards in deep loneliness;
Had my eye never on the beauty dwelt

Of human face, and my ear never drank
100 The music of a human voice; I feel
My spirit would have pour'd itself in song,
Have learn'd a language from the rustling leaves,
The singing of the birds, and of the tide.
Perchance, then, happy had I never known
105 Another thought could be attach'd to song
Than of its own delight. Oh! let me pause
Over this earlier period, when my heart
Mingled its being with its pleasures, fill'd
With rich enthusiasm, which once flung
110 Its purple colouring o'er all things of earth,
And without which our utmost power of thought
But sharpens arrows that will drink our blood.
Like woman's soothing influence o'er man,
Enthusiasm is upon the mind;
115 Softening and beautifying that which is
Too harsh and sullen in itself. How much
I loved the painter's glorious art, which forms
A world like, but more beautiful than this;
Just catching nature in her happiest mood!
120 How drank I in fine poetry, which makes
The hearing passionate, fill'd with memories
Which steal from out the past like rays from clouds!
And then the sweet songs of my native vale,
Whose sweetness and whose softness call'd to mind
125 The perfume of the flowers, the purity
Of the blue sky; oh, how they stirr'd my soul!—
Amid the many golden gifts which heaven
Has left, like portions of its light, on earth,
None hath such influence as music hath.
130 The painter's hues stand visible before us
In power and beauty; we can trace the thoughts
Which are the workings of the poet's mind:
But music is a mystery, and viewless
Even when present, and is less man's act,
135 And less within his order; for the hand
That can call forth the tones, yet cannot tell
Whither they go, or if they live or die,
When floated once beyond his feeble ear;
And then, as if it were an unreal thing,
140 The wind will sweep from the neglected strings
As rich a swell as ever minstrel drew.

		A poet's word, a painter's touch, will reach
		The innermost recesses of the heart,
		Making the pulses throb in unison
145		With joy or grief, which we can analyse;
		There is the cause for pleasure and for pain:
		But music moves us, and we know not why;
		We feel the tears, but cannot trace their source.
		Is it the language of some other state,
150		Born of its memory? For what can wake
		The soul's strong instinct of another world,
		Like music? Well with sadness doth it suit,
		To hear the melancholy sounds decay,
		And think (for thoughts are life's great human links,
155		And mingle with our feelings,) even so
		Will the heart's wildest pulses sink to rest.

		    How have I loved, when the red evening fill'd
		Our temple with its glory, first, to gaze
		On the strange contrast of the crimson air,
160		Lighted as if with passion, and flung back,
		From silver vase and tripod rich with gems,
		To the pale statues round, where human life
		Was not, but beauty was, which seemed to have
		Apart existence from humanity:
165		Then, to go forth where the tall waving pines
		Seem'd as behind them roll'd a golden sea,
		Immortal and eternal; and the boughs,
		That darkly swept between me and its light,
		Were fitting emblems of the worldly cares
170		That are the boundary between us and heaven;
		Meanwhile, the wind, a wilful messenger
		Lingering amid the flowers on his way,
		At intervals swept past in melody,
		The lutes and voices of the choral hymn
175		Contending with the rose-breath on his wing!
		Perhaps it is these pleasures' chiefest charm,
		They are so indefinable, so vague.
		From earliest childhood all too well aware
		Of the uncertain nature of our joys,
180		It is delicious to enjoy, yet know
		No after consequence will be to weep.
		Pride misers with enjoyment, when we have
		Delight in things that are but of the mind:
		But half humility when we partake

185		Pleasures that are half wants, the spirit pines
		And struggles in its fetters, and disdains
		The low base clay to which it is allied.
		But here our rapture raises us: we feel
		What glorious power is given to man, and find
190		Our nature's nobleness and attributes,
		Whose heaven is intellect; and we are proud
		To think how we can love those things of earth
		Which are least earthly; and the soul grows pure
		In this high communing, and more divine.
195		 This time of dreaming happiness pass'd by,
		Another spirit was within my heart;
		I drank the maddening cup of praise, which grew
		Henceforth the fountain of my life; I lived
		Only in others' breath; a word, a look,
200		Were of all influence on my destiny:
		If praise they spoke, 'twas sunlight to my soul;
		Or censure, it was like the scorpion's sting.

		    And a yet darker lesson was to learn—
		The hollowness of each: that praise, which is
205		But base exchange of flattery; that blame,
		Given by cautious coldness, which still deems
		'Tis safest to depress; that mockery,
		Flinging shafts but to show its own keen aim;
		That carelessness, whose very censure's chance;
210		And, worst of all, the earthly judgment pass'd
		By minds whose native clay is unredeem'd
		By aught of heaven, whose every thought falls foul
		Plague spot on beauty which they cannot feel,
		Tainting all that it touches with itself.
215		O dream of fame, what hast thou been to me
		But the destroyer of life's calm content!
		I feel so more than ever, that thy sway
		Is weaken'd over me. Once I could find
		A deep and dangerous delight in thee;
220		But that is gone. I am too much awake.
		Light has burst o'er me, but not morning's light;
		'Tis such light as will burst upon the tomb,
		When all but judgment's over. Can it be,
		That these fine impulses, these lofty thoughts,
225		Burning with their own beauty, are but given
		To make me the low slave of vanity,
		Heartless and humbled? O my own sweet power,

Surely thy songs were made for more than this!
What a worst waste of feeling and of life
230 Have been the imprints on my roll of time,
Too much, too long! To what use have I turn'd
The golden gifts in which I pride myself?
They are profaned; with their pure ore I made
A temple resting only on the breath
235 Of heedless worshippers. Alas! that ever
Praise should have been what it has been to me—
The opiate of my heart. Yet I have dream'd
Of things which cannot be; the bright, the pure,
That all of which the heart may only dream;
240 And I have mused upon my gift of song,
And deeply felt its beauty, and disdain'd
The pettiness of praise to which at times
My soul has bow'd; and I have scorn'd myself
For that my cheek could burn, my pulses beat
245 At idle words. And yet, it is in vain
For the full heart to press back every throb
Wholly upon itself. Ay, fair as are
The visions of a poet's solitude,
There must be something more for happiness;
250 They seek communion. It had seem'd to me
A miser's selfishness, had I not sought
To share with others those impassion'd thoughts,
Like light, or hope, or love, in their effects.
When I have watch'd the stars write on the sky
255 In characters of light, have seen the moon
Come like a veiled priestess from the east,
While, like a hymn, the wind swell'd on mine ear,
Telling soft tidings of eve's thousand flowers,
Has it not been the transport of my lute
260 To find its best delight in sympathy?
Alas! the idols which our hopes set up,
They are Chaldean[1] ones, half gold, half clay;
We trust, we are deceived, we hope, we fear,
Alike without foundation; day by day
265 Some new illusion is destroyed, and life
Gets cold and colder on towards its close.
Just like the years which make it, some are check'd
By sudden blights in spring; some are dried up
By fiery summers; others waste away
270 In calm monotony of quiet skies,
And peradventure these may be the best:
They know no hurricanes, no floods that sweep
As a God's vengeance were upon each wave;
But then they have no ruby fruits, no flowers
275 Shining in purple, and no lighted mines
Of gold and diamond. Which is the best,—
Beauty and glory, in a southern clime,
Mingled with thunder, tempest; or the calm
Of skies that scarcely change, which, at the least,
280 If much of shine they have not, have no storms?
I know not: but I know fair earth or sky
Are self-consuming in their loveliness,
And the too radiant sun and fertile soil
In their luxuriance run themselves to waste,
285 And the green valley and the silver stream
Become a sandy desert. Oh! the mind,
Too vivid in its lighted energies,
May read its fate in sunny Araby.
How lives its beauty in each Eastern tale,
290 Its growth of spices, and its groves of balm!
They are exhausted; and what is it now?
A wild and burning wilderness. Alas!
For such similitude. Too much this is
The fate of this world's loveliest and best.

295 Is there not a far people, who possess
Mysterious oracles of olden time,
Who say that this earth labours with a curse,
That it is fallen from its first estate,
And is now but the shade of what it was?[2]
300 I do believe the tale. I feel its truth
In my vain aspirations, in the dreams
That are revealings of another world,
More pure, more perfect than our weary one,
Where day is darkness to the starry soul.

305 O heart of mine! my once sweet paradise
Of love and hope! how changed thou art to me!
I cannot count thy changes: thou hast lost
Interest in the once idols of thy being;

---

[1] Babylonian (the Chaldeans were the dominant people of ancient Babylonia); the reference is to the dream of Nebuchadnezzar, Daniel 2.31–45.

[2] Erinna is thinking of the Israelites and their story of the Fall, Genesis 3.

They have departed, even as if wings
310 Had borne away their morning; they have left
Weariness, turning pleasure into pain,
And too sure knowledge of their hollowness.

    And that too is gone from me; that which was
My solitude's delight! I can no more
315 Make real existence of a shadowy world.
Time was, the poet's song, the ancient tale,
Were to me fountains of deep happiness,
For they grew visible in my lonely hours,
As things in which I had a deed and part;
320 Their actual presence had not been more true:
But these are bubbling sparkles, that are found
But at the spring's first source. Ah! years may bring
The mind to its perfection, but no more
Will those young visions live in their own light;
325 Life's troubles stir life's waters all too much,
Passions chase fancies, and, though still we dream,
The colouring is from reality.

    Farewell, my lyre! thou hast not been to me
All I once hoped. What is the gift of mind,
330 But as a barrier to so much that makes
Our life endurable,—companionship,
Mingling affection, calm and gentle peace,
Till the vex'd spirit seals with discontent
A league of sorrow and of vanity,
335 Built on a future which will never be!

    And yet I would resign the praise that now
Makes my cheek crimson, and my pulses beat,
Could I but deem that when my hand is cold,
And my lip passionless, my songs would be
340 Number'd mid the young poet's first delights;
Read by the dark-eyed maiden in an hour
Of moonlight, till her cheek shone with its tears;
And murmur'd by the lover when his suit
Calls upon poetry to breathe of love.
345 I do not hope a sunshine burst of fame,
My lyre asks but a wreath of fragile flowers.
I have told passionate tales of breaking hearts,
Of young cheeks fading even before the rose;
My songs have been the mournful history
350 Of woman's tenderness and woman's tears;
I have touch'd but the spirit's gentlest chords,—
Surely the fittest for my maiden hand;—
And in their truth my immortality.

    Thou lovely and lone star, whose silver light,
355 Like music o'er the waters, steals along
The soften'd atmosphere; pale star, to thee
I dedicate the lyre, whose influence
I would have sink upon the heart like thine.

    In such an hour as this, the bosom turns
360 Back to its early feelings; man forgets
His stern ambition and his worldly cares,
And woman loathes the petty vanities
That mar her nature's beauty; like the dew,
Shedding its sweetness o'er the sleeping flowers
365 Till all their morning freshness is revived,
Kindly affections, sad, but yet sweet thoughts
Melt the cold eyes, long, long unused to weep.
O lute of mine, that I shall wake no more!
Such tearful music linger on thy strings,
370 Consecrate unto sorrow and to love;
Thy truth, thy tenderness, be all thy fame!

from *The Venetian Bracelet, The Lost Pleiad, A History of the Lyre, and Other Poems* (1829)

Revenge

Ay, gaze upon her rose-wreathed hair,
    And gaze upon her smile;
Seem as you drank the very air
    Her breath perfumed the while:

5 And wake for her the gifted line,
    That wild and witching lay,
And swear your heart is as a shrine,
    That only owns her sway.

'Tis well: I am revenged at last,—
10   Mark you that scornful cheek,—

    The eye averted as you pass'd,
        Spoke more than words could speak.

    Ay, now by all the bitter tears
        That I have shed for thee,—
15 The racking doubts, the burning fears,—
        Avenged they well may be—

    By the nights pass'd in sleepless care,
        The days of endless woe;
    All that you taught my heart to bear,
20   All that yourself will know.

    I would not wish to see you laid
        Within an early tomb;
    I should forget how you betray'd,
        And only weep your doom:

25 But this is fitting punishment,
        To live and love in vain,—
    Oh my wrung heart, be thou content,
        And feed upon his pain.

    Go thou and watch her lightest sigh,—
30   Thine own it will not be;
    And bask beneath her sunny eye,—
        It will not turn on thee.

    'Tis well: the rack, the chain, the wheel,
        Far better had'st thou proved;
35 Ev'n I could almost pity feel,
        For thou art not beloved.

Lines of Life[1]

    Orphan in my first years, I early learnt
    To make my heart suffice itself, and seek
    Support and sympathy in its own depths.[2]

    Well, read my cheek, and watch my eye,—
        Too strictly school'd are they,

    One secret of my soul to show,
        One hidden thought betray.

5   I never knew the time my heart
        Look'd freely from my brow;
    It once was check'd by timidness,
        'Tis taught by caution now.

    I live among the cold, the false,
10   And I must seem like them;
    And such I am, for I am false
        As those I most condemn.

    I teach my lip its sweetest smile,
        My tongue its softest tone;
15 I borrow others' likeness, till
        Almost I lose my own.

    I pass through flattery's gilded sieve,
        Whatever I would say;
    In social life, all, like the blind,
20   Must learn to feel their way.

    I check my thoughts like curbed steeds
        That struggle with the rein;
    I bid my feelings sleep, like wrecks
        In the unfathom'd main.

25 I hear them speak of love, the deep,
        The true, and mock the name;
    Mock at all high and early truth,
        And I too do the same.

    I hear them tell some touching tale,
30   I swallow down the tear;
    I hear them name some generous deed,
        And I have learnt to sneer.

    I hear the spiritual, the kind,
        The pure, but named in mirth;
35 Till all of good, ay, even hope,
        Seems exiled from our earth.

---

[1] Shakespeare, Sonnet 16, line 9.

[2] The epigraph or prologue is by Landon.

    And one fear, withering ridicule,
        Is all that I can dread;
    A sword hung by a single hair
40   For ever o'er the head.[1]

    We bow to a most servile faith,
        In a most servile fear;
    While none among us dares to say
        What none will choose to hear.

45   And if we dream of loftier thoughts,
        In weakness they are gone;
    And indolence and vanity
        Rivet our fetters on.

    Surely I was not born for this!
50   I feel a loftier mood
    Of generous impulse, high resolve,
        Steal o'er my solitude!

    I gaze upon the thousand stars
        That fill the midnight sky;
55   And wish, so passionately wish,
        A light like theirs on high.

    I have such eagerness of hope
        To benefit my kind;
    And feel as if immortal power
60   Were given to my mind.

    I think on that eternal fame,
        The sun of earthly gloom,
    Which makes the gloriousness of death,
        The future of the tomb—

65   That earthly future, the faint sign
        Of a more heavenly one;

    —A step, a word, a voice, a look,—
        Alas! my dream is done.

    And earth, and earth's debasing stain,
70   Again is on my soul;
    And I am but a nameless part
        Of a most worthless whole.

    Why write I this? because my heart
        Towards the future springs,
75   That future where it loves to soar
        On more than eagle wings.

    The present, it is but a speck
        In that eternal time,
    In which my lost hopes find a home,
80   My spirit knows its clime.

    Oh! not myself,—for what am I?—
        The worthless and the weak,
    Whose every thought of self should raise
        A blush to burn my cheek.

85   But song has touch'd my lips with fire,
        And made my heart a shrine;
    For what, although alloy'd, debased,
        Is in itself divine.

    I am myself but a vile link
90   Amid life's weary chain;
    But I have spoken hallow'd words,
        Oh do not say in vain!

    My first, my last, my only wish,
        Say will my charmed chords
95   Wake to the morning light of fame,
        And breathe again my words?

    Will the young maiden, when her tears
        Alone in moonlight shine—
    Tears for the absent and the loved—
100   Murmur some song of mine?

---

[1] According to legend, Damocles envied the luxurious lifestyle of Dionysius the Elder, tyrant of Syracuse (a Greek colony in Sicily), so Dionysius invited him to a banquet. When Damocles took his place at the table, he saw above him a sword suspended by a single hair; he was too terrified to move or eat. The "sword of Damocles" is proverbial for any impending evil.

Will the pale youth by his dim lamp,
   Himself a dying flame,
From many an antique scroll beside,
   Choose that which bears my name?

Let music make less terrible
   The silence of the dead;
I care not, so my spirit last
   Long after life has fled.

from the *New Monthly Magazine* 35 (1832)

On the Ancient and Modern Influence of Poetry[1]

It is curious to observe how little one period resembles another. Centuries are the children of one mighty family, but there is no family-likeness between them. We ourselves are standing on the threshold of a new era, and we are already hastening to make as wide a space, mark as vast a difference as possible, between our own age and its predecessor. Whatever follies we may go back upon, whatever opinions we may re-adopt, they are never those which have gone *immediately* before us. Already there is a wide gulph between the last century and the present. In religion, in philosophy, in politics, in manners, there has passed a great change; but in none has been worked a greater change than in poetry, whether as it regards the art itself, or the general feeling towards it. The decline and fall of that Roman empire of the mind seems now advanced as an historical fact; while we are equally ready to admit that some twenty years since the republic was in its plenitude of power. In the meantime a new set of aspirants have arisen, and a new set of opinions are to be won. But it is from the past that we best judge of the present; and perhaps we shall more accurately say what poetry is by referring to what it has been.

Poetry in every country has had its origin in three sources, connected with the strongest feelings belonging to the human mind—Religion, War, and Love. The mysteries of the present; the still greater mysteries of the future; the confession of some superior power so deeply felt; higher impulses speaking so strongly of some spiritual influence of a purer order than those of our common wants and wishes;—these all found words and existence in poetry. The vainest fictions of mythology were the strongest possible evidence how necessary to the ignorance of humanity was the belief of a superior power; so entire was the interior conviction, that sooner than believe in nothing no belief was too absurd for adoption. The imagination, which is the source of poetry, has in every country been the beginning as well as the ornament of civilization. It civilizes because it refines. A general view of its influence in the various quarters of the globe will place this in the most striking point of view.

Africa is the least civilized quarter of the globe, not so much from its savage as from its apathetic state; one could almost believe that it had been formed from the dregs of the other parts. Now, the distinguishing mark of its deficiency in that soil of mind wherewith the intellect works, is its total want of imagination. It is the only great portion of the world which is not emphatically made known to us by its own peculiar religion. Her mythology was the earthly immortality of Greece. Greece is indelibly linked with the idea of civilization; but all those fine and graceful beliefs which made its springs holy places, and haunted the fragrant life of every flower and leaf, were the creations of its earliest time. Look from thence to the fierce regions of the North,—how full is the Scandinavian faith of the wild and wonderful! or to the East, how gorgeous their tales of enchantment, with their delicate Peris,[2] and the fallen and fearful spirits in their subterranean caverns!—again, the faith of Brahma,[3] with its thousand deities. Or, to cross the wide Atlantic, there are the vestiges of a terrible creed yet touched with something of spiritual loveliness, in their singing-birds bringing tidings of the departed,

---

[1] This essay was published anonymously, and its attribution to Landon has been questioned.

[2] originally beautiful but malevolent spirits in Persian mythology; later delicate, fairy-like beings; cf. Thomas Moore,* "Paradise and the Peri," in *Lalla Rookh* (1817).

[3] the creator, one of the three supreme gods of Hinduism.

and in the green hunting-grounds which made their future hope. Each and all these creeds are the work and wonder of the imagination—but in these Africa has no part. No august belief fills with beauty or terror the depths of her forests, and no fallen temple makes its site sacred though in ruins. Her creeds have neither beauty nor grandeur. The Devil is their principal Deity, and their devotion is born of physical fear. Other nations have had their various faiths, created and coloured by the scenes which gave them birth. The religion of Greece was beautiful as her own myrtle and olive groves. The Scandinavian was like its own wild mountains and snowy wastes, with just gleams of beauty from its starry nights and meteors. The Arabian was glowing and magnificent as the summer earth and radiant sky of its believers; while that of the American Indian was terrible as the huge serpents and the interminable forests which gave shelter to its mysteries. But in Africa the sunny sky, the noble rivers, the woods, splendid in size and foliage, have been without their wonted effect. Slaves from the earliest period, the very superstitions of her sable sons are mean fears caught from their masters; all about them is earthly, utterly unredeemed by those spiritual awakenings which are as lights from another world. We might believe that some great original curse has been said over them, and that they are given over into the hand of man and not of God.[1] And in simple truth that curse has been slavery. The Helots[2] even of Greece were uninspired. "A slave cannot be eloquent," said Longinus;[3] nor poetical either—the wells of his enthusiasm are dried up. What some ancient writer says of iron may be applied to Poetry—its use is the first step to civilization, and civilization is freedom.

Next to Religion War was the great source of poetry; and the deeds of the brave were sung in that spirit of encouragement which one man will ever receive from the praise bestowed on the deeds of another, when he meditates similar achievements of his own. And here we may be permitted a few words on what we cannot but consider an unjust and erroneous opinion, now much insisted upon,—that poets and conquerors have been equal enemies of the human race—the one but acting what the other praised; and that the sin of encouragement was equal, if not greater, than that of commission. In answer to this we must observe that it is not fair to judge of former actions by our present standard. Our first view of society is always the same: we see the human race dwelling in small dispersed sets, with rude habits, the results of hardships and of dangers. A more favourable situation, or, more commonly, the influence of some superior mind, which from the wonderful effects produced by a single man is often a nation's history: these or similar causes first placed some of the tribes in positions of comparative comfort and advancement. This position would of course be envied by their savage and starving neighbours, who would consider brute force the only means of sharing their advantages. Single motives never last: ambition, aggrandisement, conquest with a view to security, soon gave a thousand motives to warfare that had originally began in want and self-defence. It has required centuries so to consolidate kingdoms that now a breathing space is allowed for reflection on the sin of sacrificing man's most valuable possession—life. But what part has the poet taken in these scenes of bloodshed? One certainly of amelioration. If he has sung of conquerors, the qualities held up to admiration were those of magnanimity and generosity. He has spoken of the love of liberty as holding light the love of life; and the highest eulogium of a warrior was that he died in defence of his native country. But to give our assertion the support of an example.—Perhaps the spirit which animates, the desire which excites, the power which supports, a conqueror, were never more entirely personified than in Xerxes.[4] He possessed to the utmost that grasping ambition, that carelessness of human blood, which characterize the mere conqueror; yet with all the purple pomp of his power, we are not aware of his having been held up otherwise than in reprobation, while the whole world has been filled with

---

[1] Landon is thinking of the curse of Canaan, Genesis 9.25. Africans were sometimes believed to be the descendants of Canaan.

[2] a people enslaved by the Spartans, who also made them proverbial for moral degeneracy.

[3] *On the Sublime* 9.3–4.

[4] Persian emperor (r. 485–65 BC). It was actually his father, Darius, whom the Athenians defeated at Marathon (490 BC); Xerxes himself suffered defeat at Salamis (480).

the fame of his brave opposers; and the names of those who fell at Marathon are still the watchwords of freedom. Again, in the days of chivalry, what were the qualities the minstrel lauded in the knight?—his valour, certainly, but still more his courtesy, his protection of the weak against the strong, his devotion, his truth;—till the "ungentle knight" was almost as much a phrase of disgrace as that of the "recreant."

Love was the third great fountain of poetry's inspiration; and who that has ever loved will deny the necessity of a language, beyond the working-day tongue of our ordinary run of hopes and fears, to express feelings which have so little in common with them. What has been the most popular love-poetry in all countries?—that which gave expression to its spiritual and better part—constancy kept like a holy thing—blessings on the beloved one, though in that blessing we have ourselves no share; or sad and affectionate regrets in whose communion our own nature grows more kindly from its sympathy. We are always the better for entering into other's sorrow or other's joy.

The whole origin and use of poetry may be expressed in a few brief words: it originates in that idea of superior beauty and excellence inherent in every nature—and it is employed to keep that idea alive; and the very belief in excellence is one cause of its existence. When we speak of poetry as the fountain whence youth draws enthusiasm for its hopes,—where the warrior strengthens his courage, and the lover his faith,—the treasury where the noblest thoughts are garnered,—the archives where the noblest deeds are recorded,—we but express an old belief. One of our great reviews—the "Westminster"—in speaking of the fine arts, &c. says, "The aristocracy do well to encourage poetry: it is by fiction themselves exist—and what is poetry but fiction?" We deny that poetry is fiction; its merit and its power lie alike in its truth: to one heart the aspiring and elevated will come home; to another the simple and natural: the keynote to one will be the voice of memory, which brings back young affections—early confidence,—hill and valley yet glad with the buoyant step which once past over them,—flowers thrice lovely from thoughts indelibly associated with their leaf or breath: such as these are touched by all that restores, while it recalls, days whose enjoyment would have been happiness, could they but have had the knowledge of experience without its weariness. To another, poetry will be a vision and a delight, because the virtue of which he dreams is there realized—and because the "love which his spirit has painted"[1] is to be found in its pages. But in each and all cases the deep well of sympathy is only to be found when the hazel rod is poised by the hand of truth. And, till some moral steam is discovered as potent as that now so active in the physical world, vain will be the effort to regulate mankind like machinery: there will ever be spiritual awakenings, and deep and tender thoughts, to turn away from the hurry and highways of life, and whose place of refuge will still be the green paths and pleasant waters of poesy. That tribes of worse than idle followers have crowded the temple, and cast the dust they brought around the soiled altar,—that many have profaned their high gift to base use—that poetry has often turned aside from its divine origin and diviner end,—is what must be equally admitted and lamented; but who will deny that our best and most popular (indeed in this case best and popular are equivalent terms) poetry makes its appeal to the higher and better feelings of our nature, and not a poet but owes his fame to that which best deserves it? What a code of pure and beautiful morality, applicable to almost every circumstance, might be drawn from Shakspeare!

The influence of poetry has two eras,—first as it tends to civilize; secondly as it tends to prevent that very civilization from growing too cold and too selfish. Its first is its period of action; its second is that of feeling and reflection: it is that second period which at present exists. On the mere principle of utility, in our wide and weary world, with its many sorrows and more cares, how anxiously we ought to keep open every source of happiness! and who among us does not recollect some hour when a favourite poet spread before us a page like that of a magician's; when some expression has seemed like the very echo of our feelings; how often and with what a sensation of pleasure have long-remembered passages sprang to our lips; how every natural beauty has caught a fresh charm from being linked with some associate verse! Who that has these or similar recollections but would keep the ear open, and the heart alive, to the

---

[1] Byron,* "Stanzas to Augusta" (1816) 7.

"song that lightens the languid way!"[1]

Why one age should be more productive in poetry than another is one of those questions—a calculation of the mental longitude—likely to remain unanswered. That peculiar circumstances do not create the poet is proved by the fact, that only one individual is so affected: if it were mere circumstance, it would affect alike all who are brought within its contact. What confirmation of this theory (if theory it be) is to be found in the history of all poets!—where are we to seek the cause which made them such, if not in their own minds? We daily see men living amid beautiful scenery; and scenery is much dwelt upon by the advocates of circumstance. Switzerland is a most beautiful country, yet what great poet has it ever produced? The spirit which in ancient days peopled grove and mountain with Dryad and Oread,[2] or, in modern times, with associations, must be in him who sees, not in the object seen. How many there are, leading a life of literary leisure, living in a romantic country, and writing poetry all their days, who yet go down to their unremembered graves no more poets than if they had never turned a stanza! While, on the other hand, we see men with every obstacle before them, with little leisure and less encouragement, yet force their upward way, make their voice heard, and leave their memory in imperishable song. Take Burns for an example: much stress has been laid on the legendary ballads he was accustomed to hear from infancy; but if these were so potent, why did they not inspire his brother as well as himself? Mr. Gilbert Burns[3] is recorded, by every biographer, to have been a sensible, and even a superior man; he dwelt in the same country—he heard the same songs—why was he not a poet too? There can be but one answer,—there was not that inherent quality in his mind which there was in his brother's. Many young men are born to a higher name than fortune—many spend their youth amid the most exciting scenes—yet why do none of these turn out a Byron, but for some innate first cause? What made Milton in old age,—in sickness, in poverty—depressed by all that would have weighed to the very dust an ordinary man—without one of man's ordinary encouragements,—what could have made him turn to the future as to a home, collect his glorious energies, and finish a work, the noblest aid ever given to the immortality of a language? What, but that indefinable spirit, whose enthusiasm is nature's own gift to the poet. *Poeta nascitur non fit*[4] is, like many other old truths, the very truth after all.

We cannot but consider that, though some be still among us, our own great poets belong to another age. Their fame is established, and their horde of imitators have dispersed; those wearying followers who, to use the happy expression of a contemporary writer, "think that breaking the string is bending the bow of Ulysses."[5] We hear daily complaints of the want of present taste and talent for poetry: we are more prepared to admit the latter than the former. In the most sterile times of the imagination, love of poetry has never been lacking; the taste may have been bad, but still the taste existed. Wordsworth truly says, "that, with the young, poetry is a passion";[6] and there will always be youth in the world to indulge the hopes, and feel the warm and fresh emotions, which their fathers have found to be vain, or have utterly exhausted. To these, poetry will ever be a natural language; and it is the young who make the reputation of a poet. We soon lose that keen delight, which marvels if others share not in it: the faculty of appreciation is the first which leaves us. It is tact rather than feeling which enables experience to foresee the popularity of a new poet. As to the alleged want of taste, we only refer to the editions of established authors which still find purchasers: one has just appeared of Scott, another of Byron. With what enthusiasm do some set up Wordsworth for an idol, and others Shelley! But this taste is quite another feeling to that which creates; and the little now written possesses beauty not originality. The writers do not set their own mark on their

---

[1] Thomas Moore,* "Boat Glee" (1811) 1, 14.

[2] A Dryad is a tree nymph; an Oread is a mountain nymph.

[3] the younger brother of poet Robert Burns.*

[4] "A poet is born, not made" (L.): proverbial, after Lucius Annæus Florus (fl. AD 125), *De Qualitate Vitæ*.

[5] Penelope, besieged by suitors during the absence of her husband Odysseus (L. Ulysses), agrees to marry whichever of them can string his bow and shoot an arrow through twelve axes (Homer, *Odyssey* 19); only Odysseus, who has returned home in disguise, is able to do so (21).

[6] "Essay, Supplementary to the Preface" of *Lyrical Ballads* (1815).

property: one might have put forth the work of the other, or it might be that of their predecessors. This was not the case some few years ago. Who could have mistaken the picturesque and chivalric page of Scott for the impassioned one of Byron? or who could for a moment have hesitated as to whether a poem was marked with the actual and benevolent philosophy of Wordsworth, or the beautiful but ideal theory of Shelley? We are now producing no great or original (the words are synonymous) poet. We have graceful singing in the bower, but no voice that startles us into wonder, and hurries us forth to see whose trumpet is awakening the land. We know that when the snow has long lain, warming and fertilizing the ground, and when the late summer comes, hot and clear, the rich harvest will be abundant under such genial influences. Perhaps poetry too may have its atmosphere; and a long cold winter may be needed for its glad and glorious summer. The soil of song, like that of earth, may need rest for renewal. Again we repeat, that though the taste be not, the spirit of the day is, adverse to the production of poetry. Selfishness is its principle, indifference its affectation, and ridicule its commonplace. We allow no appeals save to our reason, or to our fear of laughter. We must either be convinced or sneered into things. Neither calculation nor sarcasm are the elements for poetry. A remark made by Scott to one of his great compeers shows how he knew the age in which he was fated to end his glorious career: —"Ah—it is well that we have made our reputation!" The personal is the destroyer of the spiritual; and to the former everything is now referred. We talk of the author's self more than his works, and we know his name rather than his writings. There is a base macadamizing spirit in literature; we seek to level all the high places of old. But till we can deny that fine "farther looking hope"[1] which gives such a charm to Shakspeare's confessional sonnets; till we can deny that "The Paradise Lost" was the work of old age, poverty, and neglect, roused into delightful exertion by a bright futurity; till we can deny the existence of those redeemers of humanity—we must admit, also, the existence of a higher, more prophetic, more devoted and self-relying spirit than is to be accounted for on the principles either of vanity or of lucre: we shall be compelled to admit that its inspiration is, indeed,

"A heavenly breath
Along an earthly lyre."[2]

Methinks there are some mysteries in the soul on whose precincts it were well to "tread with unsandalled foot."[3] Poetry like religion requires faith, and we are the better and happier for yielding it. The imagination is to the mind what life is to the body—its vivifying and active part. In antiquity, poetry had to create, it now has to preserve. Its first effort was against barbarism, its last is against selfishness. A world of generous emotions, of kindly awakenings, those

"Which bid the perished pleasures move
In mournful mockery o'er the soul of love";[4]

a world of thought and feeling, now lies in the guardianship of the poet. These are they who sit in the gate called the beautiful, which leads to the temple. Its meanest priests should feel that their office is sacred. Enthusiasm is no passion of the drawing-room, or of the pence-table: its home is the heart, and its hope is afar. This is too little the creed of our generation; yet, without such creed, poetry has neither present life nor future immortality. As Whitehead finely says in his poem of "The Solitary,"—

"Not for herself, not for the wealth she brings,
Is the muse wooed and won, but for the deep,
Occult, profound, unfathomable things,—
The engine of our tears whene'er we weep,
The impulse of our dreams whene'er we sleep,
The mysteries that our sad hearts possess,
Which, and the keys whereof, the Muse doth keep,—
Oh! to kindle soft humanity, to raise,
With gentle strength infused, the spirit bowed;
To pour a second sunlight on our days,
And draw the restless lightning from our cloud;
To cheer the humble and to dash the proud.
Besought in peace to live, in peace to die,—

---

[1] W. Wordsworth,* "The Force of Prayer; or, The Founding of Boulton Priory: A Tradition" (1815) 47.

[2] Laman Blanchard (1803–45), "The Spirit of Poesy" 5–6.

[3] Cf. Cowper,* "To an Afflicted Protestant Lady in France" 16; Hogg,* "Mador of the Moor" 4.32–33.

[4] Coleridge,* "Lines: On an Autumnal Evening" (1793) 7–8; cf. Moore,* "The Veiled Prophet of Khorassan" 227, from *Lalla Rookh* (1817).

The poet's task is done—Oh, Immortality!"[1]
He is only a true poet, who can say, in the words of
Coleridge, "My task has been my delight; I have not
looked either to guerdon or praise, and to me Poetry is
its own exceeding great reward."[2]

from *Fisher's Drawing Room Scrap Book* (1836)

Immolation of a Hindoo Widow[3]

Gather her raven hair in one rich cluster,
Let the white champac light it, as a star
Gives to the dusky night a sudden lustre,
    Shining afar.

5 Shed fragrant oils upon her fragrant bosom,
Until the breathing air around grows sweet;
Scatter the languid jasmine's yellow blossom
    Beneath her feet.

Those small white feet are bare—too soft are they
10 To tread on aught but flowers; and there is roll'd
Round the slight ankle, meet for such display,
    The band of gold.

Chains and bright stones are on her arms and neck;
What pleasant vanities are linked with them,
15 Of happy hours, which youth delights to deck
    With gold and gem.

She comes! So comes the Moon, when she has found
A silvery path wherein thro' heaven to glide.
Fling the white veil—a summer cloud—around;
20   She is a bride!

And yet the crowd that gather at her side
Are pale, and every gazer holds his breath.
Eyes fill with tears unbidden, for the bride—
    The bride of Death!

25 She gives away the garland from her hair,
She gives the gems that she will wear no more;
All the affections, whose love-signs they were,
    Are gone before.

The red pile blazes—let the bride ascend,
30 And lay her head upon her husband's heart,
Now in a perfect unison to blend—
    No more to part.

from *The Zenana and Minor Poems of L.E.L.* (1839)

Felicia Hemans[4]

No more, no more—oh, never more[5] returning,
    Will thy beloved presence gladden earth;
No more wilt thou with sad, yet anxious yearning
    Cling to those hopes which have no mortal birth.
5 Thou art gone from us, and with thee departed,
    How many lovely things have vanished too:
Deep thoughts[6] that at thy will to being started,
    And feelings, teaching us our own were true.
Thou hast been round us, like a viewless spirit,
10   Known only by the music on the air;
The leaf or flowers which thou hast named inherit
    A beauty known but from thy breathing there:
For thou didst on them fling thy strong emotion,
    The likeness from itself the fond heart gave;
15 As planets from afar look down on ocean,
    And give their own sweet image to the wave.

---

[1] Charles Whitehead (1804–62), *The Solitary* 2.406–12, 415–19, 422–23.

[2] Preface, *The Poetical Works of S.T. Coleridge* (1828).

[3] Cf. "The Improvisatrice" 851–88.*

[4] first published in *Fisher's Drawing Room Scrap Book* (1838). Earlier, Landon had published "Stanzas on the Death of Mrs. Hemans," *New Monthly Magazine* 44 (1835): 286–88.

[5] Cf. Byron, *Don Juan* 1.214.*

[6] Cf. Wordsworth, "Ode" 206.*

And thou didst bring from foreign lands their treasures,[1]
    As floats thy various melody along;
We know the softness of Italian measures,
20   And the grave cadence of Castilian song.
A general bond of union is the poet,
    By its immortal verse is language known,
And for the sake of song do others know it—
    One glorious poet makes the world his own.
25 And thou—how far thy gentle sway extended!
    The heart's sweet empire over land and sea;
Many a stranger and far flower was blended
    In the soft wreath that glory bound for thee.
The echoes of the Susquehanna's[2] waters
30   Paused in the pine-woods words of thine to hear;
And to the wide Atlantic's younger daughters
    Thy name was lovely, and thy song was dear.

Was not this purchased all too dearly?—never
    Can fame atone for all that fame hath cost.
35 We see the goal, but know not the endeavour,
    Nor what fond hopes have on the way been lost.
What do we know of the unquiet pillow,
    By the worn cheek and tearful eyelid prest,
When thoughts chase thoughts, like the tumultuous
      billow,
40   Whose very light and foam reveals unrest?
We say, the song is sorrowful, but know not
    What may have left that sorrow on the song;
However mournful words may be, they show not
    The whole extent of wretchedness and wrong.
45 They cannot paint the long sad hours, passed only
    In vain regrets o'er what we feel we are.
Alas! the kingdom of the lute is lonely—
    Cold is the worship coming from afar.

Yet what is mind in woman, but revealing
50   In sweet clear light the hidden world below,
By quicker fancies and a keener feeling
    Than those around, the cold and careless, know?

What is to feed such feeling, but to culture
    A soil whence pain will never more depart?
55 The fable of Prometheus and the vulture[3]
    Reveals the poet's and the woman's heart.
Unkindly are they judged—unkindly treated—
    By careless tongues and by ungenerous words;
While cruel sneer, and hard reproach, repeated,
60   Jar the fine music of the spirit's chords.
Wert thou not weary—thou whose soothing numbers[4]
    Gave other lips the joy thine own had not?
Didst thou not welcome thankfully the slumbers
    Which closed around thy mourning human lot?

65 What on this earth could answer thy requiring,
    For earnest faith—for love, the deep and true,
The beautiful, which was thy soul's desiring,
    But only from thyself its being drew.
How is the warm and loving heart requited
70   In this harsh world, where it awhile must dwell.
Its best affections wronged, betrayed, and slighted—
    Such is the doom of those who love too well.
Better the weary dove should close its pinion,
    Fold up its golden wings and be at peace;
75 Enter, O ladye, that serene dominion
    Where earthly cares and earthly sorrows cease.
Fame's troubled hour has cleared, and now replying,
    A thousand hearts their music ask of thine.
Sleep with a light, the lovely and undying
80   Around thy grave—a grave which is a shrine.

On Wordsworth's Cottage, near Grasmere Lake

Not for the glory on their heads
    Those stately hill-tops wear,
Although the summer sunset sheds
    Its constant crimson there.

---

[1] a reference to Hemans, *Translations from Camoens, and Other Poets, with Original Poetry* (1818), *Lays of Many Lands* (1826), and the many poems with foreign subjects included in her other volumes.

[2] a river flowing through New York and Pennsylvania.

[3] As a punishment for stealing fire and giving it to humanity, the Titan Prometheus was nailed to a crag in the Caucasus, where a vulture (or, in some versions of the myth, an eagle) tore at his liver (which healed every night, only to be torn again the next day). Cf. Byron, "Prometheus,"* Percy Bysshe Shelley, *Prometheus Unbound.**

[4] verses.

5 Not for the gleaming lights that break
 The purple of the twilight lake,
  Half dusky and half fair,
 Does that sweet valley seem to be
 A sacred place on earth to me.

10 The influence of a moral spell
  Is found around the scene,
 Giving new shadows to the dell,
  New verdure to the green.
 With every mountain-top is wrought
15 The presence of associate thought,
  A music that has been;
 Calling that loveliness to life,
 With which the inward world is rife.

 His home—our English poet's home—[1]
20 Amid these hills is made;
 Here, with the morning hath he come,
  There, with the night delayed.
 On all things is his memory cast,
 For every place wherein he past,
25 Is with his mind arrayed,
 That, wandering in a summer hour,
 Asked wisdom of the leaf and flower.

 Great poet, if I dare to throw
  My homage at thy feet,
30 'Tis thankfulness for hours which thou
  Hast made serene and sweet;
 As wayfarers have insense thrown
 Upon some mighty altar-stone
  Unworthy, and yet meet,
35 The human spirit longs to prove
 The truth of its uplooking love.

 Until thy hand unlocked its store,
  What glorious music slept!
 Music that can be hushed no more
40 Was from our knowledge kept.
 But the great Mother gave to thee
 The poet's universal key,

 And forth the fountains swept—
  A gushing melody for ever,
45 The witness of thy high endeavour.

 Rough is the road which we are sent,
  Rough with long toil and pain;
 And when upon the steep ascent,
  A little way we gain,
50 Vexed with our own perpetual care,
 Little we heed what sweet things are
  Around our pathway blent;
 With anxious steps we hurry on,
 The very sense of pleasure gone.

55 But thou dost in this feverish dream
  Awake a better mood,
 With voices from the mountain stream,
  With voices from the wood.[2]
 And with their music dost impart
60 Their freshness to the world-worn heart,
  Whose fever is subdued
 By memories sweet with other years,
 By gentle hopes, and soothing tears.

 A solemn creed is thine, and high,
65 Yet simple as a child,
 Who looketh hopeful to yon sky
  With eyes yet undefiled[3]
 By all the glitter and the glare
 This life's deceits and follies wear,
70 Exalted, and yet mild,
 Conscious of those diviner powers
 Brought from a better world than ours.[4]

 Thou hast not chosen to rehearse
  The old heroic themes;
75 Thou hast not given to thy verse
  The heart's impassioned dreams.
 Forth flows thy song as waters flow,
 So bright above—so calm below,

---

[1] Cf. W. Wordsworth,* *Home at Grasmere* (1888).

[2] Cf. Wordsworth, "The Tables Turned" 21–24.*

[3] Cf. Wordsworth, "My Heart Leaps Up."*

[4] Cf. Wordsworth, "Ode" 58–65.*

                    Wherein the heaven seems
80   Eternal as the golden shade
                Its sunshine on the stream hath laid.

                The glory which thy spirit hath
                    Is round life's common things,
                And flingeth round our common path,
85   As from an angel's wings,
                A light that is not of our sphere,[1]
                Yet lovelier for being here,
                    Beneath whose presence springs
                A beauty never mark'd before,
90   Yet once known, vanishing no more.

                How often with the present sad,
                    And weary with the past,
                A sunny respite have we had,
                    By but a chance look cast
95   Upon some word of thine that made
                The sullenness forsake the shade,
                    Till shade itself was past:
                For Hope divine, serene and strong,
                Perpetual lives within thy song.

100   Eternal as the hills thy name,
                    Eternal as thy strain;
                So long as ministers of Fame
                    Shall Love and Hope remain.
                The crowded city in its streets,
105   The valley, in its green retreats,
                    Alike thy words retain.
                What need hast thou of sculptured stone?—
                Thy temple, is thy name alone.

from *Life and Literary Remains of L.E.L.*, ed.
Laman Blanchard (1841)

A Poet's Love

Faint and more faint amid the world of dreams,
That which was once my all, thy image seems,
Pale as a star that in the morning gleams.

Long time that sweet face was my guiding star,
5   Bringing me visions of the fair and far,
Remote from this world's toil and this world's jar.

Around it was an atmosphere of light,
Deep with the tranquil loveliness of night,
Subdued and shadowy, yet serenely bright.

10   Like to a spirit did it dwell apart,
Hushed in the sweetest silence of my heart,
Lifting me to the heaven from whence thou art.

Too soon the day broke on that haunted hour,
Loosing its spell, and weakening its power,
15   All that had been imagination's dower.

The noontide quenched that once enchanted ray,
Care, labour, sorrow, gathered on the day;
Toil was upon my steps, dust on my way.

They melted down to earth my upward wings;[2]
20   I half forgot the higher, better things—
The hope which yet again thy image brings.

Would I were worthier of thee! I am fain,
Amid my life of bitterness and pain,
To dream once more my early dreams again.

Influence of Poetry

This is the charm of poetry: it comes
On sad perturbed moments: and its thoughts,
Like pearls amid the troubled waters, gleam.
That which we garnered in our eager youth,
5   Becomes a long delight in after years:
The mind is strengthened and the heart refreshed
By some old memory of gifted words,
That bring sweet feelings, answering to our own.
Or dreams that waken some more lofty mood
10   Than dwelleth with the commonplace of life.

---

[1] Cf. Wordsworth, "Elegiac Stanzas" 15–16.*

[2] So that he and his son, Icarus, could escape from the island of Crete, Daedalus made pairs of wings out of feathers held together with wax. Despite his father's warning, Icarus flew too close to the sun; the wax melted, and he crashed into the sea: see Ovid, *Metamorphoses* 8.

Changes in London[1]

The presence of perpetual change
    Is ever on the earth;
To-day is only as the soil
    That gives to-morrow birth.

5 Where stood the tower there grows the weed;
    Where stood the weed the tower:
No present hour its likeness leaves
    To any future hour.

Of each imperial city built
10   Far on the eastern plains,
A desert waste of tomb and sand
    Is all that now remains.

Our own fair city filled with life,
    Has yet a future day,
15 When power, and might, and majesty,
    Will yet have passed away.

---

[1] first published in Landon, *Ethel Churchill; or, The Two Brides* (1837).

Thomas Lovell Beddoes
1803 – 1849

Thomas Lovell Beddoes was born in Clifton, Shropshire, on 30 June 1803. His father, Thomas Beddoes, was a famous radical, physician, and scientist; his mother, Anna Edgeworth Beddoes, was the sister of Maria Edgeworth.* Beddoes was educated at Charterhouse School and Oxford; after graduating in 1825, he went to Göttingen, Germany, to study medicine. In 1829, he seems to have attempted suicide; he was also expelled from Göttingen for drunkenness. He earned his M.D. from Würzburg in 1831 but was deported the following year for the radical politics that were to get him into trouble for the rest of his life. He lived in Baden, Berlin, Frankfurt, and Zürich, rarely returning to England. His first play, *The Brides' Tragedy* (1822) was well received; an early version of his morbid masterpiece, *Death's Jest-Book; or, The Fool's Tragedy*, was finished by 1829, but Beddoes was advised not to publish it and kept on revising and expanding it for the next twenty years. In Basel, in 1848, he lost a leg after an accident during an operation; on 26 January 1849 he poisoned himself, complaining in his suicide note that "Life was too great a bore on one peg & that a bad one." *Death's Jest-Book* was finally published in 1850. (D.L.M.)

---

from *Poems Chiefly from Outidana* (composed 1823–25)[1]

Lines Written in a Blank Leaf of the "Prometheus Unbound"

Write it in gold—a Spirit of the sun,
An Intellect ablaze with heavenly thoughts,
A Soul with all the dews of pathos shining,
Odorous with love, and sweet to silent woe
5 With the dark glories of concentrate song,
Was sphered in mortal earth. Angelic sounds
Alive with panting thoughts sunned the dim world.
The bright creations of an human heart
Wrought magic in the bosoms of mankind.
10 A flooding summer burst on Poetry;
Of which the crowning sun, the night of beauty,
The dancing showers, the birds whose anthems wild
Note after note unbind the enchanted leaves
Of breaking buds, eve, and the flow of dawn,
15 Were centred and condensed in his one name
As in a providence—and that was SHELLEY.
—OXFORD, 1822.

from *Torrismond* (composed 1824)

Song[2]

How many times do I love thee, dear?
   Tell me how many thoughts there be
     In the atmosphere
     Of a new-fall'n year,
5 Whose white and sable hours appear
   The latest flake of Eternity:
So many times do I love thee, dear.

How many times do I love again?
   Tell me how many beads there are
10   In a silver chain
     Of evening rain,
Unravelled from the tumbling main,
   And threading the eye of a yellow star:
So many times do I love again.

---

[1] Our texts are all from *The Works of Thomas Lovell Beddoes*, ed. H.W. Donner (1935).

[2] from the drama *Torrismond* 1.3.15–28.

from *Death's Jest-Book* (1825–28)

Dirge[1]

If thou wilt ease thine heart
Of love and all its smart,
    Then sleep, dear, sleep;
And not a sorrow
5   Hang any tear on your eyelashes;
    Lie still and deep,
Sad soul, until the sea-wave washes
The rim o' th' sun to-morrow,
    In eastern sky.

10 But wilt thou cure thy heart
Of love and all its smart,
    Then die, dear, die;
'Tis deeper, sweeter,
Than on a rose bank to lie dreaming
15   With folded eye;
And then alone, amid the beaming
Of love's stars, thou'lt meet her
    In eastern sky.

Song[2]

A cypress-bough, and a rose-wreath sweet,
A wedding-robe, and a winding-sheet,
    A bridal-bed and a bier.
Thine be the kisses, maid,
5   And smiling Love's alarms;
And thou, pale youth, be laid
In the grave's cold arms.
Each in his own charms,
    Death and Hymen[3] both are here;
10   So up with scythe and torch,
    And to the old church porch,
While all the bells ring clear:
And rosy, rosy the bed shall bloom,
And earthy, earthy heap up the tomb.

15 Now tremble dimples on your cheek,
Sweet be your lips to taste and speak,
    For he who kisses is near:
For her the bridegroom fair,
In youthful power and force;
20 For him the grizard bare,
Pale knight on a pale horse,[4]
To woo him to a corpse.
    Death and Hymen both are here;
    So up with scythe and torch,
25   And to the old church porch,
While all the bells ring clear:
And rosy, rosy the bed shall bloom,
And earthy, earthy heap up the tomb.

Song[5]

Old Adam, the carrion crow,
    The old crow of Cairo;
He sat in the shower, and let it flow
Under his tail and over his crest;
5   And through every feather
    Leaked the wet weather;
And the bough swung under his nest;
For his beak it was heavy with marrow.
    Is that the wind dying? O no;
10   It's only two devils, that blow
Through a murderer's bones, to and fro,
    In the ghosts' moonshine.

2

Ho! Eve, my grey carrion wife,
    When we have supped on kings' marrow,
15 Where shall we drink and make merry our life?
Our nest it is queen Cleopatra's scull,[6]
    'Tis cloven and cracked,
    And battered and hacked,
But with tears of blue eyes it is full:

---

[1] *Death's Jest Book* 2.2.1–18.

[2] 4.3.230–57.

[3] Greek god of marriage.

[4] death; cf. Revelation 6.8.

[5] 5.4.95–118.

[6] Cleopatra (69–30 BC), Queen of Egypt. Cf. Shakespeare, *Antony and Cleopatra*.

20 Let us drink then, my raven of Cairo.
    Is that the wind dying? O no;
    It's only two devils, that blow
    Through a murderer's bones, to and fro,
        In the ghosts' moonshine.

from *Death's Jest Book* (revised, 1829–49)

Song from the Waters[1]

The swallow leaves her nest,
The soul my weary breast;
But therefore let the rain
    On my grave
5 Fall pure; for why complain?
Since both will come again
    O'er the wave.

The wind dead leaves and snow
Doth hurry to and fro;
10 And, once, a day shall break
    O'er the wave,
When a storm of ghosts shall shake
The dead, until they wake
    In the grave.

Dream-Pedlary[2]

1

If there were dreams to sell,
    What would you buy?
Some cost a passing bell;
    Some a light sigh,
5 That shakes from Life's fresh crown
    Only a roseleaf down.
If there were dreams to sell,
Merry and sad to tell,
And the crier rung the bell,
10   What would you buy?

2

A cottage lone and still,
    With bowers nigh,
Shadowy, my woes to still,
    Until I die.
15 Such pearl from Life's fresh crown
Fain would I shake me down.
Were dreams to have at will,
This would best heal my ill,
    This would I buy.

3

20 But there were dreams to sell,
    Ill didst thou buy;
Life is a dream, they tell,
    Waking, to die.
Dreaming a dream to prize,
25 Is wishing ghosts to rise;
And, if I had the spell
To call the buried, well,
    Which one would I?

4

If there are ghosts to raise,
30   What shall I call,
Out of hell's murky haze,
    Heaven's blue hall?
Raise my loved longlost boy
To lead me to his joy.
35 There are no ghosts to raise;
Out of death lead no ways;
    Vain is the call.

5

Know'st thou not ghosts to sue?
    No love thou hast.
40 Else lie, as I will do,
    And breathe thy last.
So out of Life's fresh crown
Fall like a rose-leaf down.
Thus are the ghosts to woo;
45 Thus are all dreams made true,
    Ever to last!

---

[1] 1.4.259–72.

[2] This poem was part of the *Death's Jest-Book* project, but Beddoes did not include it in the final version of the play.

Susanna Moodie
1803 – 1885

Susanna Strickland was born near Bungay, Suffolk, on 6 December 1803, the sixth daughter of Thomas Strickland, retired manager of the Greenland Dock on the Thames, and Elizabeth Homer Strickland. In 1808 the family moved to Reydon Hall in Suffolk; they also had a house in Norwich. The Strickland sisters were raised in relative isolation, with access to their father's library: Agnes and Elizabeth became well known for *Lives of the Queens of England* (1840–48) and other popular biographies.

At the Congregational Chapel at Wrentham, Susanna underwent a religious conversion; *Enthusiasm, and Other Poems* (1831) consists largely of poems on religious subjects. Other influences on her later writing included Mary Russell Mitford,* with whom Strickland corresponded and whose rural sketches she imitated, Suffolk folklore, and the literary and humanitarian circle of Thomas Pringle,* poet and secretary of the Anti-Slavery Society. Strickland's "Sketches from the Country" (in *La Belle Assemblée* 1827, 1828, 1829) and the slavery narratives she transcribed for Pringle (*The History of Mary Prince** and *Negro Slavery Described by ... Ashton Warner*, both in 1831) influenced the style and content of her later work.

Through Pringle, she met John Wedderburn Dunbar Moodie, whom she married in 1831. In July 1832, they sailed for Canada, settling first near Cobourg in Upper Canada (Ontario) and then in the woods north of Peterborough. John Moodie served in the militia during the Mackenzie Rebellion in 1837; the family moved to Belleville in 1840. During this period, the Moodies had seven children, two of whom died. From 1838 until 1851, Susanna contributed novels, poems, and sketches to the *Literary Garland* in Montréal. She and her husband also edited and wrote for the *Victoria Magazine*—to which her siblings Catharine Parr Traill,* Samuel Strickland, and Agnes Strickland also contributed. Her best-known work, the settlement narrative *Roughing It in the Bush; or, Life in Canada* (1852), developed out of sketches in the *Literary Garland*; published by Richard Bentley in London, it was well received and went through three English and three American editions in the 1850s. *Life in the Clearings* followed in 1853, at Bentley's request. Of several novels, the best-known is the autobiographical *Flora Lyndsay; or, Passages in an Eventful Life* (1854). Moodie lived the rest of her life in Canada, writing less as the years went by. Following her husband's death in 1869, she lived with her children in Toronto, where she died on 8 April 1885. (A.M.)

༄༅༄

from *Enthusiasm; and Other Poems* (1831)

The Dream

Methought last night I saw thee lowly laid,
    Thy pallid cheek yet paler, on the bier;
And scattered round thee many a lovely braid
    Of flowers, the brightest of the closing year;
5 Whilst on thy lips the placid smile that played,
    Proved thy soul's exit to a happier sphere,
In silent eloquence reproaching those
Who watched in agony thy last repose.

A pensive, wandering, melancholy light
10   The moon's pale radiance on thy features cast,
Which, through the awful stillness of the night,
    Gleamed like some lovely vision of the past,
Recalling hopes once beautiful and bright,
    Now, like that struggling beam, receding fast,
15 Which o'er the scene a softening glory shed,
And kissed the brow of the unconscious dead.

Yes—it was thou!—and we were doomed to part,
    Never in this wide world to meet again.
The blow that levelled thee was in my heart,
20   And thrilled my breast with more than mortal pain.

Despair forbade the gathering tears to start;
    But soon the gushing torrents fell like rain
O'er thy pale form, as free and unrepressed
As the rash shower that rocks the storm to rest.

25 For all this goodly earth contained for me,
    Of bright or beautiful, lay withering there:
What were its gayest scenes bereft of thee—
    What were its joys in which thou couldst now share?
While memory recalled each spot, where we
30   Had twined together many a garland fair,

Of hope's own wreathing, and the summer hours
Smiled not on happier, gayer hearts than ours.

Hearts, chilled and silent, as the pensive beam,
    Whose shadowy glory resting on the pall,
35 Casts on the dead a sad portentous gleam,
    And serves past hours of rapture to recall,
Till the soul roused herself with one wild scream,
    As shuddering nature felt the powerful call,
And I awoke in ecstasy to find
40 'Twas but a fleeting phantom of the mind!

Nathaniel Hawthorne
1804 – 1864

Nathaniel Hawthorne was born on 4 July 1804 in Salem, Massachusetts. His father, Nathaniel Hathorne (our Nathaniel added the *w* later), a sea captain, was the descendant of one of the oldest families in Massachusetts; one of his ancestors had been a judge at the Salem witch trials of 1692. His mother, Elizabeth Manning Hathorne, was also from an old Massachusetts family. When Hawthorne was four, his father died of yellow fever in Surinam and his mother took her three children to live with her family. The Mannings arranged for him to be educated privately and at Bowdoin College, where his friends included Henry Wadsworth Longfellow and Franklin Pierce; they also supported him during his long literary apprenticeship. Hawthorne published a romance, *Fanshawe*, in 1828, but became dissatisfied with it and destroyed all the copies he could. Soon, however, he began publishing stories in the *Salem Gazette*; in an annual, *The Token*; and elsewhere; in 1837, he published a selection of these, *Twice-Told Tales*. In 1839, he was given a position in the Boston customs house, where he worked for two years; at the same time, he proposed marriage to Sophia Peabody. Through Sophia and her sisters, he became interested in the Transcendentalist movement, and in April 1841, he moved to the utopian community of Brook Farm, but he found conditions there not conducive to his writing, and he left in October. He married Sophia in July 1842; they had three children. They rented the Old Manse at Concord, where their neighbours included Amos Bronson Alcott, Emerson, Margaret Fuller, and Thoreau. In 1846, Hawthorne published his second collection of stories, *Mosses from an Old Manse*.

In April 1846, Hawthorne was given another customs job, in Salem; but in June 1849, after the Whig election victory, he was dismissed. He describes the experience in "The Custom House," the prologue to his first romance, *The Scarlet Letter* (1850). That April, he moved to Lenox, Massachusetts, where Melville was his neighbour. He published his second romance (he did not think of them as novels), *The House of the Seven Gables*, in 1851, and his third, *The Blithedale Romance* (based on his experiences at Brook Farm), in 1852.

When his friend Pierce was nominated Democratic candidate for President, Hawthorne wrote a campaign biography; after Pierce won, Hawthorne was made American consul at Liverpool. He served there until 1857 and then travelled extensively in Italy, where he met the Brownings. He left Italy in May 1859 and lived for a year in England, where he wrote *The Marble Faun* (1860). He returned to America in June 1860 and settled again in Concord. The outbreak of the Civil War distressed him terribly, and in 1862, his health began to fail. He died on 19 May 1864, in Plymouth, New Hampshire, while travelling for his health. He is one of America's major novelists and an important influence on Melville, James, Howells, Mary Jane Wilkins Freeman, Jewett, Faulkner, and O'Connor. (D.L.M.)

☙❧

from *Mosses from an Old Manse* (1846)

Roger Malvin's Burial[1]

One of the few incidents of Indian warfare, naturally susceptible of the moonlight of romance, was that expedition, undertaken for the defence of the frontiers in the year 1725, which resulted in the well-remembered "Lovell's Fight."[2] Imagination, by casting certain circumstances judiciously into the shade, may see much

---

[1] first published in *The Token* (1832).

[2] In May 1725, Captain John Lovewell, who had recently lost several family members to Native attacks and who had been promised a bounty of £100 for every scalp he could bring back to Boston, led 46 men against the Pequawket of southwestern Maine. They were outnumbered and defeated and had to retreat, abandoning three wounded men.

to admire in the heroism of a little band, who gave battle to twice their number in the heart of the enemy's country. The open bravery displayed by both parties was in accordance with civilized ideas of valor, and chivalry itself might not blush to record the deeds of one or two individuals. The battle, though so fatal to those who fought, was not unfortunate in its consequences to the country; for it broke the strength of a tribe, and conduced to the peace which subsisted during several ensuing years. History and tradition are unusually minute in their memorials of this affair; and the captain of a scouting party of frontier-men has acquired as actual a military renown, as many a victorious leader of thousands. Some of the incidents contained in the following pages will be recognized, notwithstanding the substitution of fictitious names, by such as have heard, from old men's lips, the fate of the few combatants who were in a condition to retreat after "Lovell's Fight."

* * * * *

The early sunbeams hovered cheerfully upon the tree-tops, beneath which two weary and wounded men had stretched their limbs the night before. Their bed of withered oak-leaves was strewn upon the small level space, at the foot of a rock, situated near the summit of one of the gentle swells, by which the face of the country is there diversified. The mass of granite, rearing its smooth, flat surface, fifteen or twenty feet above their heads, was not unlike a gigantic grave-stone, upon which the veins seemed to form an inscription in forgotten characters. On a tract of several acres around this rock, oaks and other hard-wood trees had supplied the place of the pines, which were the usual growth of the land; and a young and vigorous sapling stood close beside the travellers.

The severe wound of the elder man had probably deprived him of sleep; for, so soon as the first ray of sunshine rested on the top of the highest tree, he reared himself painfully from his recumbent posture and sat erect. The deep lines of his countenance, and the scattered grey of his hair, marked him as past the middle age; but his muscular frame would, but for the effects of his wound, have been as capable of sustaining fatigue, as in the early vigor of life. Languor and exhaustion now sat upon his haggard features, and the despairing glance which he sent forward through the depths of the forest, proved his own conviction that his pilgrimage was at an end. He next turned his eyes to the companion who reclined by his side. The youth, for he had scarcely attained the years of manhood, lay, with his head upon his arm, in the embrace of an unquiet sleep, which a thrill of pain from his wounds seemed each moment on the point of breaking. His right hand grasped a musket, and to judge from the violent action of his features, his slumbers were bringing back a vision of the conflict, of which he was one of the few survivors. A shout,—deep and loud in his dreaming fancy,—found its way in an imperfect murmur to his lips, and, starting even at the slight sound of his own voice, he suddenly awoke. The first act of reviving recollection was to make anxious inquiries respecting the condition of his wounded fellow-traveller. The latter shook his head.

"Reuben,[1] my boy," said he, "this rock, beneath which we sit, will serve for an old hunter's grave-stone. There is many and many a long mile of howling wilderness before us yet; nor would it avail me anything, if the smoke of my own chimney were but on the other side of that swell of land. The Indian bullet was deadlier than I thought."

"You are weary with our three days' travel," replied the youth, "and a little longer rest will recruit you. Sit you here, while I search the woods for the herbs and roots that must be our sustenance; and having eaten, you shall lean on me, and we will turn our faces homeward. I doubt not, that, with my help, you can attain to some one of the frontier garrisons."

"There is not two days' life in me, Reuben," said the other, calmly, "and I will no longer burthen you with my useless body, when you can scarcely support your own. Your wounds are deep, and your strength is failing fast; yet, if you hasten onward alone, you may be preserved. For me there is no hope; and I will await death here."

"If it must be so, I will remain and watch by you," said Reuben, resolutely.

---

[1] Reuben, the first-born son of Jacob, persuades his brothers not to kill their half-brother Joseph but to abandon him in a pit in the wilderness: Genesis 37.21–22.

"No, my son, no," rejoined his companion. "Let the wish of a dying man have weight with you; give me one grasp of your hand, and get you hence. Think you that my last moments will be eased by the thought, that I leave you to die a more lingering death? I have loved you like a father, Reuben, and at a time like this, I should have something of a father's authority. I charge you to be gone, that I may die in peace."

"And because you have been a father to me, should I therefore leave you to perish, and to lie unburied in the wilderness?" exclaimed the youth. "No; if your end be in truth approaching, I will watch by you, and receive your parting words. I will dig a grave here by the rock, in which, if my weakness overcome me, we will rest together; or, if Heaven gives me strength, I will seek my way home."

"In the cities, and wherever men dwell," replied the other, "they bury their dead in the earth; they hide them from the sight of the living; but here, where no step may pass, perhaps for a hundred years, wherefore should I not rest beneath the open sky, covered only by the oak-leaves, when the autumn winds shall strew them? And for a monument, here is this grey rock, on which my dying hand shall carve the name of Roger Malvin; and the traveller in days to come will know, that here sleeps a hunter and a warrior. Tarry not, then, for a folly like this, but hasten away, if not for your own sake, for hers who will else be desolate."

Malvin spoke the last few words in a faltering voice, and their effect upon his companion was strongly visible. They reminded him that there were other, and less questionable duties, than that of sharing the fate of a man whom his death could not benefit. Nor can it be affirmed that no selfish feeling strove to enter Reuben's heart, though the consciousness made him more earnestly resist his companion's entreaties.

"How terrible, to wait the slow approach of death in this solitude!" exclaimed he. "A brave man does not shrink in the battle, and, when friends stand round the bed, even women may die composedly; but here"—

"I shall not shrink, even here, Reuben Bourne," interrupted Malvin: "I am a man of no weak heart; and, if I were, there is a surer support than that of earthly friends. You are young, and life is dear to you. Your last moments will need comfort far more than mine; and when you have laid me in the earth, and are alone, and night is settling on the forest, you will feel all the bitterness of the death that may now be escaped. But I will urge no selfish motive to your generous nature. Leave me for my sake; that, having said a prayer for your safety, I may have space to settle my account, undisturbed by worldly sorrows."

"And your daughter! How shall I dare to meet her eye!" exclaimed Reuben. "She will ask the fate of her father, whose life I vowed to defend with my own. Must I tell her, that he travelled three days' march with me from the field of battle, and that then I left him to perish in the wilderness? Were it not better to lie down and die by your side, than to return safe, and say this to Dorcas?"

"Tell my daughter," said Roger Malvin, "that, though yourself sore wounded, and weak, and weary, you led my tottering footsteps many a mile, and left me only at my earnest entreaty, because I would not have your blood upon my soul. Tell her, that through pain and danger you were faithful, and that, if your life-blood could have saved me, it would have flowed to its last drop. And tell her, that you will be something dearer than a father, and that my blessing is with you both, and that my dying eyes can see a long and pleasant path, in which you will journey together."

As Malvin spoke, he almost raised himself from the ground, and the energy of his concluding words seemed to fill the wild and lonely forest with a vision of happiness. But when he sank exhausted upon his bed of oak-leaves, the light, which had kindled in Reuben's eye, was quenched. He felt as if it were both sin and folly to think of happiness at such a moment. His companion watched his changing countenance, and sought, with generous art, to wile him to his own good.

"Perhaps I deceive myself in regard to the time I have to live," he resumed. "It may be, that, with speedy assistance, I might recover of my wound. The former fugitives must, ere this, have carried tidings of our fatal battle to the frontiers, and parties will be out to succor those in like condition with ourselves. Should you meet

---

[1] Cf. Acts 9.36, 39.

one of these, and guide them hither, who can tell but that I may sit by my own fireside again?"

A mournful smile strayed across the features of the dying man, as he insinuated that unfounded hope; which, however, was not without its effect on Reuben. No merely selfish motive, nor even the desolate condition of Dorcas, could have induced him to desert his companion, at such a moment. But his wishes seized upon the thought, that Malvin's life might be preserved, and his sanguine nature heightened, almost to certainty, the remote possibility of procuring human aid.

"Surely there is reason, weighty reason, to hope that friends are not far distant"; he said, half aloud. "There fled one coward, unwounded, in the beginning of the fight, and most probably he made good speed. Every true man on the frontier would shoulder his musket, at the news; and though no party may range so far into the woods as this, I shall perhaps encounter them in one day's march. Counsel me faithfully," he added, turning to Malvin, in distrust of his own motives. "Were your situation mine, would you desert me while life remained?"

"It is now twenty years," replied Roger Malvin, sighing, however, as he secretly acknowledged the wide dissimilarity between the two cases,—"it is now twenty years, since I escaped, with one dear friend, from Indian captivity, near Montreal. We journeyed many days through the woods, till at length, overcome with hunger and weariness, my friend lay down, and besought me to leave him; for he knew that, if I remained, we both must perish. And, with but little hope of obtaining succor, I heaped a pillow of dry leaves beneath his head, and hastened on."

"And did you return in time to save him?" asked Reuben, hanging on Malvin's words, as if they were to be prophetic of his own success.

"I did," answered the other, "I came upon the camp of a hunting-party, before sunset of the same day. I guided them to the spot where my comrade was expecting death; and he is now a hale and hearty man, upon his own farm, far within the frontiers, while I lie wounded here, in the depths of the wilderness."

This example, powerful in effecting Reuben's decision, was aided, unconsciously to himself, by the hidden strength of many another motive. Roger Malvin perceived that the victory was nearly won.

"Now go, my son, and Heaven prosper you!" he said. "Turn not back with your friends, when you meet them, lest your wounds and weariness overcome you; but send hitherward two or three, that may be spared, to search for me. And believe me, Reuben, my heart will be lighter with every step you take towards home." Yet there was perhaps a change, both in his countenance and voice, as he spoke thus; for, after all, it was a ghastly fate, to be left expiring in the wilderness.

Reuben Bourne, but half convinced that he was acting rightly, at length raised himself from the ground, and prepared for his departure. And first, though contrary to Malvin's wishes, he collected a stock of roots and herbs, which had been their only food during the last two days. This useless supply he placed within reach of the dying man, for whom, also, he swept together a fresh bed of dry oak-leaves. Then climbing to the summit of the rock, which on one side was rough and broken, he bent the oak-sapling downward, and bound his handkerchief to the topmost branch. This precaution was not unnecessary, to direct any who might come in search of Malvin; for every part of the rock, except its broad smooth front, was concealed, at a little distance, by the dense undergrowth of the forest. The handkerchief had been the bandage of a wound upon Reuben's arm; and, as he bound it to the tree, he vowed, by the blood that stained it, that he would return, either to save his companion's life, or to lay his body in the grave. He then descended, and stood, with downcast eyes, to receive Roger Malvin's parting words.

The experience of the latter suggested much and minute advice, respecting the youth's journey through the trackless forest. Upon this subject he spoke with calm earnestness, as if he were sending Reuben to the battle or the chase, while he himself remained secure at home; and not as if the human countenance that was about to leave him, were the last he would ever behold. But his firmness was shaken before he concluded.

"Carry my blessing to Dorcas, and say that my last prayer shall be for her and you. Bid her to have no hard thoughts because you left me here"—Reuben's heart smote him—"for that your life would not have weighed with you, if its sacrifice could have done me good. She will marry you, after she has mourned a little while for her father; and Heaven grant you long and happy days! and may your children's children stand round your death-bed! And, Reuben," added he, as the weakness of mortality made its way at last, "return, when your wounds are healed and your weariness refreshed, return to this wild rock, and lay my bones in the grave, and say a prayer over them."

An almost superstitious regard, arising perhaps from the customs of the Indians, whose war was with the dead, as well as the living, was paid by the frontier inhabitants to the rites of sepulture; and there are many instances of the sacrifice of life, in the attempt to bury those who had fallen by the "sword of the wilderness."[1] Reuben, therefore, felt the full importance of the promise, which he most solemnly made, to return, and perform Roger Malvin's obsequies. It was remarkable, that the latter, speaking his whole heart in his parting words, no longer endeavored to persuade the youth, that even the speediest succor might avail to the preservation of his life. Reuben was internally convinced that he should see Malvin's living face no more. His generous nature would fain have delayed him, at whatever risk, till the dying scene were past; but the desire of existence and the hope of happiness had strengthened in his heart, and he was unable to resist them.

"It is enough," said Roger Malvin, having listened to Reuben's promise. "Go, and God speed you!"

The youth pressed his hand in silence, turned, and was departing. His slow and faltering steps, however, had borne him but a little way, before Malvin's voice recalled him.

"Reuben, Reuben," said he, faintly; and Reuben returned and knelt down by the dying man.

"Raise me, and let me lean against the rock," was his last request. "My face will be turned towards home, and I shall see you a moment longer, as you pass among the trees."

Reuben, having made the desired alteration in his companion's posture, again began his solitary pilgrimage. He walked more hastily at first than was consistent with his strength; for a sort of guilty feeling, which sometimes torments men in their most justifiable acts, caused him to seek concealment from Malvin's eyes. But, after he had trodden far upon the rustling forest-leaves, he crept back, impelled by a wild and painful curiosity, and, sheltered by the earthy roots of an uptorn tree, gazed earnestly at the desolate man. The morning sun was unclouded, and the trees and shrubs imbibed the sweet air of the month of May; yet there seemed a gloom on Nature's face, as if she sympathized with mortal pain and sorrow. Roger Malvin's hands were uplifted in a fervent prayer, some of the words of which stole through the stillness of the woods, and entered Reuben's heart, torturing it with an unutterable pang. They were the broken accents of a petition for his own happiness and that of Dorcas; and, as the youth listened, conscience, or something in its similitude, pleaded strongly with him to return, and lie down again by the rock. He felt how hard was the doom of the kind and generous being whom he had deserted in his extremity. Death would come, like the slow approach of a corpse, stealing gradually towards him through the forest, and showing its ghastly and motionless features from behind a nearer, and yet a nearer tree. But such must have been Reuben's own fate, had he tarried another sunset; and who shall impute blame to him, if he shrink from so useless a sacrifice? As he gave a parting look, a breeze waved the little banner upon the sapling-oak, and reminded Reuben of his vow.

Many circumstances contributed to retard the wounded traveller in his way to the frontiers. On the second day, the clouds, gathering densely over the sky, precluded the possibility of regulating his course by the position of the sun; and he knew not but that every effort of his almost exhausted strength was removing him farther from the home he sought. His scanty sustenance was supplied by the berries, and other spontaneous products of the forest. Herds of deer, it is true, sometimes bounded past him, and partridges frequently whirred up before his foot-steps; but his ammunition had been expended in the fight, and he had no means of slaying them. His wounds, irritated by

---

[1] Lamentations 5.9.

the constant exertion in which lay the only hope of life, wore away his strength, and at intervals confused his reason. But, even in the wanderings of intellect, Reuben's young heart clung strongly to existence, and it was only through absolute incapacity of motion, that he at last sank down beneath a tree, compelled there to await death.

In this situation he was discovered by a party, who, upon the first intelligence of the fight, had been despatched to the relief of the survivors. They conveyed him to the nearest settlement, which chanced to be that of his own residence.

Dorcas, in the simplicity of the olden time, watched by the bed-side of her wounded lover, and administered all those comforts that are in the sole gift of woman's heart and hand. During several days, Reuben's recollection strayed drowsily among the perils and hardships through which he had passed, and he was incapable of returning definite answers to the inquiries, with which many were eager to harass him. No authentic particulars of the battle had yet been circulated; nor could mothers, wives, and children tell, whether their loved ones were detained by captivity, or by the stronger chain of death. Dorcas nourished her apprehensions in silence, till one afternoon, when Reuben awoke from an unquiet sleep, and seemed to recognize her more perfectly than at any previous time. She saw that his intellect had become composed, and she could no longer restrain her filial anxiety.

"My father, Reuben?" she began; but the change in her lover's countenance made her pause.

The youth shrank, as if with a bitter pain, and the blood gushed vividly into his wan and hollow cheeks. His first impulse was to cover his face; but, apparently with a desperate effort, he half raised himself, and spoke vehemently, defending himself against an imaginary accusation.

"Your father was sore wounded in the battle, Dorcas, and he bade me not burthen myself with him, but only to lead him to the lake-side, that he might quench his thirst and die. But I would not desert the old man in his extremity, and, though bleeding myself, I supported him; I gave him half my strength, and led him away with me. For three days we journeyed on together, and your father was sustained beyond my hopes; but, awaking at sunrise on the fourth day, I found him faint and exhausted,— he was unable to proceed,— his life had ebbed away fast,— and"—

"He died!" exclaimed Dorcas, faintly.

Reuben felt it impossible to acknowledge that his selfish love of life had hurried him away, before her father's fate was decided. He spoke not; he only bowed his head; and, between shame and exhaustion, sank back and hid his face in the pillow. Dorcas wept, when her fears were thus confirmed; but the shock, as it had been long anticipated, was on that account the less violent.

"You dug a grave for my poor father in the wilderness, Reuben?" was the question by which her filial piety manifested itself.

"My hands were weak, but I did what I could," replied the youth in a smothered tone. "There stands a noble tomb-stone above his head, and I would to Heaven I slept as soundly as he!"

Dorcas, perceiving the wildness of his latter words, inquired no farther at that time; but her heart found ease in the thought, that Roger Malvin had not lacked such funeral rites as it was possible to bestow. The tale of Reuben's courage and fidelity lost nothing when she communicated it to her friends; and the poor youth, tottering from his sick chamber to breathe the sunny air, experienced from every tongue the miserable and humiliating torture of unmerited praise. All acknowledged that he might worthily demand the hand of the fair maiden, to whose father he had been "faithful unto death";[1] and, as my tale is not of love, it shall suffice to say, that, in the space of two years, Reuben became the husband of Dorcas Malvin. During the marriage ceremony, the bride was covered with blushes, but the bridegroom's face was pale.

There was now in the breast of Reuben Bourne an incommunicable thought; something which he was to conceal most heedfully from her whom he most loved and trusted. He regretted, deeply and bitterly, the moral cowardice that had restrained his words, when he was about to disclose the truth to Dorcas; but pride, the fear of losing her affection, the dread of universal scorn,

---

[1] Revelation 2.10.

forbade him to rectify this falsehood. He felt, that, for leaving Roger Malvin, he deserved no censure. His presence, the gratuitous sacrifice of his own life, would have added only another, and a needless agony, to the last moments of the dying man. But concealment had imparted to a justifiable act, much of the secret effect of guilt; and Reuben, while reason told him that he had done right, experienced, in no small degree, the mental horrors, which punish the perpetrator of undiscovered crime. By a certain association of ideas, he at times almost imagined himself a murderer. For years, also, a thought would occasionally recur, which, though he perceived all its folly and extravagance, he had not power to banish from his mind; it was a haunting and torturing fancy, that his father-in-law was yet sitting at the foot of the rock, on the withered forest-leaves, alive, and awaiting his pledged assistance. These mental deceptions, however, came and went, nor did he ever mistake them for realities; but in the calmest and clearest moods of his mind, he was conscious that he had a deep vow unredeemed, and that an unburied corpse was calling to him out of the wilderness. Yet such was the consequence of his prevarication that he could not obey the call. It was now too late to require the assistance of Roger Malvin's friends, in performing his long-deferred sepulture; and superstitious fears, of which none were more susceptible than the people of the outward settlements, forbade Reuben to go alone. Neither did he know where, in the pathless and illimitable forest, to seek that smooth and lettered rock, at the base of which the body lay; his remembrance of every portion of his travel thence was indistinct, and the latter part had left no impression upon his mind. There was, however, a continual impulse, a voice audible only to himself, commanding him to go forth and redeem his vow; and he had a strange impression that, were he to make the trial, he would be led straight to Malvin's bones. But, year after year, that summons, unheard but felt, was disobeyed. His one secret thought became like a chain, binding down his spirit, and, like a serpent, gnawing into his heart; and he was transformed into a sad and downcast, yet irritable man.

In the course of a few years after their marriage, changes began to be visible in the external prosperity of Reuben and Dorcas. The only riches of the former had been his stout heart and strong arm; but the latter, her father's sole heiress, had made her husband master of a farm, under older cultivation, larger, and better stocked than most of the frontier establishments. Reuben Bourne, however, was a neglectful husbandman; and while the lands of the other settlers became annually more fruitful, his deteriorated in the same proportion. The discouragements to agriculture were greatly lessened by the cessation of Indian war, during which men held the plough in one hand, and the musket in the other; and were fortunate if the products of their dangerous labor were not destroyed, either in the field or in the barn, by the savage enemy. But Reuben did not profit by the altered condition of the country; nor can it be denied, that his intervals of industrious attention to his affairs were but scantily rewarded with success. The irritability, by which he had recently become distinguished, was another cause of his declining prosperity, as it occasioned frequent quarrels, in his unavoidable intercourse with the neighboring settlers. The results of these were innumerable lawsuits; for the people of New England, in the earliest stages and wildest circumstances of the country, adopted, whenever attainable, the legal mode of deciding their differences. To be brief, the world did not go well with Reuben Bourne, and, though not till many years after his marriage, he was finally a ruined man, with but one remaining expedient against the evil fate that had pursued him. He was to throw sunlight into some deep recess of the forest, and seek subsistence from the virgin bosom of the wilderness.

The only child of Reuben and Dorcas was a son, now arrived at the age of fifteen years, beautiful in youth, and giving promise of a glorious manhood. He was peculiarly qualified for, and already began to excel in, the wild accomplishments of frontier life. His foot was fleet, his aim true, his apprehension quick, his heart glad and high; and all, who anticipated the return of Indian war, spoke of Cyrus[1] Bourne as a future leader in the land. The boy was loved by his father with a deep and silent

---

[1] Isaiah 44.28–45.1 celebrates the Persian emperor Cyrus as the redeemer of Israel.

strength, as if whatever was good and happy in his own nature had been transferred to his child, carrying his affections with it. Even Dorcas, though loving and beloved, was far less dear to him; for Reuben's secret thoughts and insulated emotions had gradually made him a selfish man; and he could no longer love deeply, except where he saw, or imagined, some reflection or likeness of his own mind. In Cyrus he recognized what he had himself been in other days; and at intervals he seemed to partake of the boy's spirit, and to be revived with a fresh and happy life. Reuben was accompanied by his son in the expedition, for the purpose of selecting a tract of land, and felling and burning the timber, which necessarily preceded the removal of the household gods. Two months of autumn were thus occupied; after which Reuben Bourne and his young hunter returned, to spend their last winter in the settlements.

. . . .

It was early in the month of May, that the little family snapped asunder whatever tendrils of affections had clung to inanimate objects, and bade farewell to the few, who, in the blight of fortune, called themselves their friends. The sadness of the parting moment had, to each of the pilgrims, its peculiar alleviations. Reuben, a moody man, and misanthropic because unhappy, strode onward, with his usual stern brow and downcast eye, feeling few regrets, and disdaining to acknowledge any. Dorcas, while she wept abundantly over the broken ties by which her simple and affectionate nature had bound itself to everything, felt that the inhabitants of her inmost heart moved on with her, and that all else would be supplied wherever she might go. And the boy dashed one tear-drop from his eye, and thought of the adventurous pleasures of the untrodden forest. Oh! who, in the enthusiasm of a day-dream, has not wished that he were a wanderer in a world of summer wilderness, with one fair and gentle being hanging lightly on his arm? In youth, his free and exulting step would know no barrier but the rolling ocean or the snow-topt mountains; calmer manhood would choose a home, where Nature had strewn a double wealth, in the vale of some transparent stream; and when hoary age, after long, long years of that pure life, stole on and found him there, it would find him the father of a race, the patriarch of a people, the founder of a mighty nation yet to be. When death, like the sweet sleep which we welcome after a day of happiness, came over him, his far descendants would mourn over the venerated dust. Enveloped by tradition in mysterious attributes, the men of future generations would call him godlike; and remote posterity would see him standing, dimly glorious, far up the valley of a hundred centuries!

The tangled and gloomy forest, through which the personages of my tale were wandering, differed widely from the dreamer's Land of Fantasie; yet there was something in their way of life that Nature asserted as her own; and the gnawing cares, which went with them from the world, were all that now obstructed their happiness. One stout and shaggy steed, the bearer of all their wealth, did not shrink from the added weight of Dorcas; although her hardy breeding sustained her, during the larger part of each day's journey, by her husband's side. Reuben and his son, their muskets on their shoulders, and their axes slung behind them, kept an unwearied pace, each watching with a hunter's eye for the game that supplied their food. When hunger bade, they halted and prepared their meal on the bank of some unpolluted forest-brook, which, as they knelt down with thirsty lips to drink, murmured a sweet unwillingness, like a maiden at love's first kiss. They slept beneath a hut of branches, and awoke at peep of light, refreshed for the toils of another day. Dorcas and the boy went on joyously, and even Reuben's spirit shone at intervals with an outward gladness; but inwardly there was a cold, cold sorrow, which he compared to the snow-drifts, lying deep in the glens and hollows of the rivulets, while the leaves were brightly green above.

Cyrus Bourne was sufficiently skilled in the travel of the woods, to observe that his father did not adhere to the course they had pursued in their expedition of the preceding autumn. They were now keeping farther to the north, striking out more directly from the settlements, and into a region, of which savage beasts and savage men were as yet the sole possessors. The boy sometimes hinted his opinions upon the subject, and Reuben listened attentively, and once or twice altered the direction of their march in accordance with his son's counsel. But having so done, he seemed ill at ease. His quick and wandering glances were sent forward, apparently in search of enemies lurking behind the tree-trunks; and seeing nothing there, he would cast his eyes backwards, as if in fear of some pursuer. Cyrus, perceiving that his father gradually resumed the old direction, forbore to interfere; nor, though something began to weigh upon his heart, did his adventurous nature permit him to regret the increased length and the mystery of their way.

On the afternoon of the fifth day, they halted and made their simple encampment nearly an hour before sunset. The face of the country, for the last few miles, had been diversified by swells of land, resembling huge waves of a petrified sea; and in one of the corresponding hollows, a wild and romantic spot, had the family reared their hut, and kindled their fire. There is something chilling, and yet heart-warming, in the thought of three, united by strong bands of love, and insulated from all that breathe beside. The dark and gloomy pines looked down upon them, and, as the wind swept through their tops, a pitying sound was heard in the forest; or did those old trees groan, in fear that men were come to lay the axe to their roots at last? Reuben and his son, while Dorcas made ready their meal, proposed to wander out in search of game, of which that day's march had afforded no supply. The boy, promising not to quit the vicinity of the encampment, bounded off with a step as light and elastic as that of the deer he hoped to slay; while his father, feeling a transient happiness as he gazed after him, was about to pursue an opposite direction. Dorcas, in the meanwhile, had seated herself near their fire of fallen branches, upon the moss-grown and mouldering trunk of a tree, uprooted years before. Her employment, diversified by an occasional glance at the pot, now beginning to simmer over the blaze, was the perusal of the current year's Massachusetts' Almanac, which, with the exception of an old black-letter Bible, comprised all the literary wealth of the family. None pay a greater regard to arbitrary divisions of time, than those who are excluded from society; and Dorcas mentioned, as if the information were of importance, that it was now the twelfth of May. Her husband started.

"The twelfth of May! I should remember it well," muttered he, while many thoughts occasioned a momentary confusion in his mind. "Where am I? Whither am I wandering? Where did I leave him?"

Dorcas, too well accustomed to her husband's wayward moods to note any peculiarity of demeanor, now laid aside the Almanac, and addressed him in that mournful tone, which the tender-hearted appropriate to griefs long cold and dead.

"It was near this time of the month, eighteen years ago, that my poor father left this world for a better. He had a kind arm to hold his head, and a kind voice to cheer him, Reuben, in his last moments; and the thought of the faithful care you took of him, has comforted me many a time since. Oh! death would have been awful to a solitary man, in a wild place like this!"

"Pray Heaven, Dorcas," said Reuben, in a broken voice, "pray Heaven that neither of us three dies solitary, and lies unburied, in this howling wilderness!" And he hastened away, leaving her to watch the fire, beneath the gloomy pines.

Reuben Bourne's rapid pace gradually slackened, as the pang, unintentionally inflicted by the words of Dorcas, became less acute. Many strange reflections, however, thronged upon him; and, straying onward, rather like a sleep-walker than a hunter, it was attributable to no care of his own, that his devious course kept him in the vicinity of the encampment. His steps were imperceptibly led almost in a circle, nor did he observe that he was on the verge of a tract of land heavily timbered, but not with pine trees. The place of the latter was here supplied by oaks, and other of the harder woods; and around their roots clustered a dense and bushy undergrowth, leaving, however, barren spaces between the trees, thick-strewn with withered leaves. Whenever the rustling of the branches, or the creaking of the trunks, made a sound, as if the forest were waking from slumber, Reuben instinctively raised the musket that rested on his arm, and cast a quick, sharp glance on every side; but, convinced by a partial observation that no animal was near, he would again give himself up to his thoughts. He was musing on the strange influence that had led him away from his premeditated course, and so far into the depths of the wilderness. Unable to penetrate to the secret place of his soul, where his motives lay hidden, he believed that a supernatural voice had called him onward, and that a supernatural power had obstructed his retreat. He trusted that it was Heaven's intent to afford him an opportunity of expiating his sin; he hoped that he might find the bones, so long unburied; and that, having laid the earth over them, peace would throw its sunlight into the sepulchre of his heart. From these thoughts he was aroused by a rustling in the forest, at some distance from the spot to which he had wandered. Perceiving the motion of some object behind a thick veil of undergrowth, he fired, with the instinct of a hunter, and the aim of a practised marksman. A low moan, which told his success, and by which even animals can express their dying agony, was unheeded by Reuben Bourne. What were the recollections now breaking upon him?

The thicket into which Reuben had fired, was near the summit of a swell of land, and was clustered around the base of a rock, which, in the shape and smoothness of one of its surfaces, was not unlike a gigantic gravestone. As if reflected in a mirror, its likeness was in Reuben's memory. He even recognized the veins which seemed to form an inscription in forgotten characters; everything remained the same, except that a thick covert of bushes shrouded the lower part of the rock, and would have hidden Roger Malvin, had he still been sitting there. Yet, in the next moment, Reuben's eye was caught by another change, that time had effected, since he last stood, where he was now standing again, behind the earthy roots of the uptorn tree. The sapling, to which he had bound the blood-stained symbol of his vow, had increased and strengthened into an oak, far indeed from its maturity, but with no mean spread of shadowy branches. There was one singularity observable in this tree, which made Reuben tremble. The middle and lower branches were in luxuriant life, and an excess of vegetation had fringed the trunk, almost to the ground; but a blight had apparently stricken the upper part of the oak, and the very topmost bough was withered, sapless, and utterly dead. Reuben remembered how the little banner had fluttered on that topmost bough, when it was green and lovely, eighteen years before. Whose guilt had blasted it?

. . . .

Dorcas, after the departure of the two hunters, continued her preparations for their evening repast. Her sylvan table was the moss-covered trunk of a large fallen tree, on the broadest part of which she had spread a snow-white cloth, and arranged what were left of the bright pewter vessels that had been her pride in the settlements. It had a strange aspect—that one little spot of homely comfort, in the desolate heart of Nature. The sunshine yet lingered upon the higher branches of the trees that grew on rising ground; but the shadows of evening had deepened into the hollow, where the encampment was made; and the fire-light began to redden as it gleamed up the tall trunks of the pines, or hovered on the dense and obscure mass of foliage that circled round the spot. The heart of Dorcas was not sad; for she felt it was better to journey in the wilderness, with two whom she loved, than to be a lonely woman in a crowd that cared not for her. As she busied herself in arranging seats of mouldering wood, covered with leaves, for Reuben and her son, her voice danced through the gloomy forest, in the measure of a song that she had learned in youth. The rude melody, the production of a bard who won no name, was descriptive of a winter evening in a frontier cottage, when, secured from savage inroad by the high-piled snow-drifts, the family rejoiced by their own fire-side. The whole song possessed that nameless charm, peculiar to unborrowed thought; but four continually-recurring lines shone out from the rest, like the blaze of the hearth whose joys they celebrated. Into them, working magic with a few simple words, the poet had instilled the very essence of domestic love and household happiness, and they were poetry and picture joined in one. As Dorcas sang, the walls of her forsaken home seemed to encircle her; she no longer saw the gloomy pines; nor heard the wind, which still, as she began each verse, sent a heavy breath through the branches, and died away in a hollow moan, from the burthen of the song. She was aroused by the report of a gun, in the vicinity of the encampment; and either the sudden sound, or her loneliness by the glowing fire, caused her to tremble violently. The next moment, she laughed in the pride of a mother's heart.

"My beautiful young hunter! my boy has slain a deer!" she exclaimed, recollecting that, in the direction whence the shot proceeded, Cyrus had gone to the chase.

She waited a reasonable time, to hear her son's light step bounding over the rustling leaves, to tell of his success. But he did not immediately appear, and she sent her cheerful voice among the trees in search of him.

"Cyrus! Cyrus!"

His coming was still delayed, and she determined, as the report of the gun had apparently been very near, to seek for him in person. Her assistance, also, might be necessary in bringing home the venison, which she flattered herself he had obtained. She therefore set forward, directing her steps by the long-past sound, and singing as she went, in order that the boy might be aware of her approach, and run to meet her. From behind the trunk of every tree, and from every hiding place in the thick foliage of the undergrowth, she hoped to discover the countenance of her son, laughing with the sportive mischief that is born of affection. The sun was now beneath the horizon, and the light that came down among the trees was sufficiently dim to create many illusions in her expecting fancy. Several times she seemed indistinctly to see his face gazing out from among the leaves; and once she imagined that he stood beckoning to her, at the base of a craggy rock. Keeping her eyes on this object, however, it proved to be no more than the trunk of an oak, fringed to the very ground with little branches, one of which, thrust out farther than the rest, was shaken by the breeze. Making her way round the foot of the rock, she suddenly found herself close to her husband, who had approached in another direction. Leaning upon the butt of his gun, the muzzle of which rested upon the withered leaves, he was apparently absorbed in the contemplation of some object at his feet.

"How is this, Reuben? Have you slain the deer, and fallen asleep over him?" exclaimed Dorcas, laughing cheerfully, on her first slight observation of his posture and appearance.

He stirred not, neither did he turn his eyes towards her; and a cold, shuddering fear, indefinite in its source and object, began to creep into her blood. She now perceived that her husband's face was ghastly pale, and his features were rigid, as if incapable of assuming any other expression than the strong despair which had hardened upon them. He gave not the slightest evidence that he was aware of her approach.

"For the love of Heaven, Reuben, speak to me!" cried Dorcas, and the strange sound of her own voice affrighted her even more than the dead silence.

Her husband started, stared into her face; drew her to the front of the rock, and pointed with his finger.

Oh! there lay the boy, asleep, but dreamless, upon the fallen forest-leaves! His cheek rested upon his arm, his curled locks were thrown back from his brow, his limbs were slightly relaxed. Had a sudden weariness overcome the youthful hunter? Would his mother's voice arouse him? She knew that it was death.

"This broad rock is the grave-stone of your near kindred, Dorcas," said her husband. "Your tears will fall at once over your father and your son."

She heard him not. With one wild shriek that seemed to force its way from the sufferer's inmost soul, she sank insensible by the side of her dead boy. At that moment the withered topmost bough of the oak loosened itself in the stilly air, and fell in soft, light fragments upon the rock, upon the leaves, upon Reuben, upon his wife and child, and upon Roger Malvin's bones. Then Reuben's heart was stricken, and the tears gushed out like water from a rock.[1] The vow that the wounded youth had made, the blighted man had come to redeem. His sin was expiated, the curse was gone from him; and in the hour when he had shed blood dearer to him than his own, a prayer, the first for years, went up to Heaven from the lips of Reuben Bourne.

---

[1] Cf. Isaiah 48.21.

Henry Wadsworth Longfellow
1807 – 1882

Henry Wadsworth Longfellow was born on 27 February 1807, in Portland, Maine, the son of Stephen Longfellow, a lawyer and congressman, and Zilpah Longfellow, whose ancestor John Alden had come to America on the Mayflower. His first poem appeared in the *Portland Gazette* when he was fourteen. After graduating from Bowdoin College in 1825, Longfellow travelled and studied in Italy, France, and Spain for several years, returning to Bowdoin as a professor of languages and a librarian. In 1831 he married Mary Storer Potter, with whom he again travelled to Europe. There he studied Swedish, Danish, Finnish, and Dutch languages and literatures and was influenced by German Romanticism. Mary Longfellow died following a miscarriage at Rotterdam in 1835.

In 1839 Longfellow published his novel *Hyperion* and a collection of poems, *Voices of The Night*. From 1839–1854, he was Professor of Modern Languages at Harvard, the colleague of Oliver Wendell Holmes and James Russell Lowell. His long poem *Evangeline*, about the exile of the Acadians from Nova Scotia, was published in 1847; his most famous and popular narrative poem, *The Song of Hiawatha*, appeared in 1855.

Longfellow and his second wife, Frances, had five surviving children; however, in 1861 she died of severe burns following a tragic accident. Thereafter Longfellow settled into a more retired life of writing. Among his later works are *Tales of a Wayside Inn* (1863), which includes "Paul Revere's Ride"; a translation of Dante's *The Divine Comedy* (1865–67); and *Christus: A Mystery* (1872), a trilogy on the history of Christianity. He died in Cambridge, Massachusetts, on 24 March 1882 and was the first American to be honoured by a bust to his memory in Poets' Corner, Westminster Abbey. (A.M.)

രുള

from *Ballads and Other Poems* (1842)

The Wreck of the Hesperus

It was the schooner Hesperus,
    That sailed the wintry sea;
And the skipper had taken his little daughter,
    To bear him company.

5 Blue were her eyes as the fairy-flax,
    Her cheeks like the dawn of day,
And her bosom white as the hawthorn buds,
    That ope in the month of May.

The skipper he stood beside the helm,
10   With his pipe in his mouth,
And watched how the veering flaw did blow
    The smoke now West, now South.

Then up and spake an old Sailòr,
    Had sailed the Spanish Main,
15 "I pray thee, put into yonder port,
    For I fear a hurricane.

"Last night, the moon had a golden ring,
    And to-night no moon we see!"
The skipper, he blew a whiff from his pipe,
20   And a scornful laugh laughed he.[1]

Colder and louder blew the wind,
    A gale from the Northeast;
The snow fell hissing in the brine,
    And the billows frothed like yeast.

25 Down came the storm, and smote amain,
    The vessel in its strength;
She shuddered and paused, like a frighted steed,
    Then leaped her cable's length.

---

[1] Cf. the ballad "Sir Patrick Spens," 5–16, and Coleridge's epigraph to "Dejection."*

"Come hither! come hither! my little daughtèr,
    And do not tremble so;
For I can weather the roughest gale,
    That ever wind did blow."

He wrapped her warm in his seaman's coat
    Against the stinging blast;
He cut a rope from a broken spar,
    And bound her to the mast.

"O father! I hear the church-bells ring,
    O say, what may it be?"
"'Tis a fog-bell on a rock-bound coast!"—
    And he steered for the open sea.

"O father! I hear the sound of guns,
    O say, what may it be?"
"Some ship in distress, that cannot live
    In such an angry sea!"

"O father! I see a gleaming light,
    O say, what may it be?"
But the father answered never a word,
    A frozen corpse was he.

Lashed to the helm, all stiff and stark,
    With his face to the skies,
The lantern gleamed through the gleaming snow
    On his fixed and glassy eyes.

Then the maiden clasped her hands and prayed
    That savèd she might be;
And she thought of Christ, who stilled the wave,
    On the Lake of Galilee.[1]

And fast through the midnight dark and drear,
    Through the whistling sleet and snow,
Like a sheeted ghost, the vessel swept
    Towards the reef of Norman's Woe.[2]

And ever the fitful gusts between
    A sound came from the land;
It was the sound of the trampling surf,
    On the rocks and the hard sea-sand.

The breakers were right beneath her bows,
    She drifted a dreary wreck,
And a whooping billow swept the crew
    Like icicles from her deck.

She struck where the white and fleecy waves
    Looked soft as carded wool,
But the cruel rocks, they gored her side
    Like the horns of an angry bull.

Her rattling shrouds, all sheathed in ice,
    With the masts went by the board;
Like a vessel of glass, she stove and sank,
    Ho! ho! the breakers roared!

At daybreak, on the bleak sea-beach,
    A fisherman stood aghast,
To see the form of a maiden fair,
    Lashed close to a drifting mast.

The salt sea was frozen on her breast,
    The salt tears in her eyes;
And he saw her hair, like the brown sea-weed,
    On the billows fall and rise.

Such was the wreck of the Hesperus,
    In the midnight and the snow!
Christ save us all from a death like this,
    On the reef of Norman's Woe!

The Village Blacksmith

Under a spreading chestnut tree
    The village smithy stands;
The smith, a mighty man is he,
    With large and sinewy hands;
And the muscles of his brawny arms
    Are strong as iron bands.

---

[1] Mark 4.39.

[2] near Cape Ann in Massachusetts.

His hair is crisp, and black, and long,
    His face is like the tan;
His brow is wet with honest sweat,
    He earns whate'er he can,
And looks the whole world in the face,
    For he owes not any man.

Week in, week out, from morn till night,
    You can hear his bellows blow;
You can hear him swing his heavy sledge,
    With measured beat and slow,
Like a sexton ringing the village bell,
    When the evening sun is low.

And children coming home from school
    Look in at the open door;
They love to see the flaming forge,
    And hear the bellows roar,
And catch the burning sparks that fly
    Like chaff from a threshing floor.

He goes on Sunday to the church,
    And sits among his boys;
He hears the parson pray and preach,
    He hears his daughter's voice,
Singing in the village choir,
    And it makes his heart rejoice.

It sounds to him like her mother's voice,
    Singing in Paradise!
He needs must think of her once more,
    How in the grave she lies;
And with his hard, rough hand he wipes
    A tear out of his eyes.

Toiling,—rejoicing,—sorrowing,
    Onward through life he goes;
Each morning sees some task begin,
    Each evening sees it close;
Something attempted, something done,
    Has earned a night's repose.

Thanks, thanks to thee, my worthy friend,
    For the lesson thou hast taught!

Thus at the flaming forge of life
    Our fortunes must be wrought;
Thus on its sounding anvil shaped
    Each burning deed and thought!

Excelsior[1]

The shades of night were falling fast,
As through an Alpine village passed
A youth, who bore, 'mid snow and ice,
A banner with the strange device
    Excelsior!

His brow was sad; his eye beneath,
Flashed like a faulchion[2] from its sheath,
And like a silver clarion rung
The accents of that unknown tongue,
    Excelsior!

In happy homes he saw the light
Of household fires gleam warm and bright;
Above, the spectral glaciers shone,
And from his lips escaped a groan,
    Excelsior!

"Try not the Pass!" the old man said;
"Dark lowers the tempest overhead,
The roaring torrent is deep and wide!"
And loud that clarion voice replied
    Excelsior!

"O stay," the maiden said, "and rest
Thy weary head upon this breast!"
A tear stood in his bright blue eye,
But still he answered, with a sigh,
    Excelsior!

"Beware the pine-tree's withered branch!
Beware the awful avalanche!"
This was the peasant's last Good-night,

---

[1] "Higher!" (L.)

[2] a falchion, a sword with a short, curved blade.

A voice replied, far up the height,
  Excelsior!

At break of day, as heavenward
The pious monks of Saint Bernard[1]
Uttered the oft-repeated prayer,
A voice cried through the startled air
  Excelsior!

A traveller, by the faithful hound,
Half-buried in the snow was found,
Still grasping in his hand of ice
That banner with the strange device
  Excelsior!

There in the twilight cold and gray,
Lifeless, but beautiful, he lay,
And from the sky, serene and far,
A voice fell, like a falling star,
  Excelsior!

from *Poems on Slavery* (1842)

The Slave's Dream

Beside the ungathered rice he lay,
  His sickle in his hand;
His breast was bare, his matted hair
  Was buried in the sand.
Again, in the mist and shadow of sleep,
  He saw his Native Land.

Wide through the landscape of his dreams
  The lordly Niger flowed;
Beneath the palm-trees on the plain
  Once more a king he strode;
And heard the tinkling caravans
  Descend the mountain-road.

He saw once more his dark-eyed queen
  Among her children stand;
They clasped his neck, they kissed his cheeks,
  They held him by the hand!—
A tear burst from the sleeper's lids
  And fell into the sand.

And then at furious speed he rode
  Along the Niger's bank;
His bridle-reins were golden chains,
  And, with a martial clank,
At each leap he could feel his scabbard of steel
  Smiting his stallion's flank.

Before him, like a blood-red flag,
  The bright flamingoes flew;
From morn till night he followed their flight,
  O'er plains where the tamarind grew,
Till he saw the roofs of Caffre[2] huts,
  And the ocean rose to view.

At night he heard the lion roar,
  And the hyæna scream,
And the river-horse,[3] as he crushed the reeds
  Beside some hidden stream;
And it passed, like a glorious roll of drums,
  Through the triumph of his dream.

The forests, with their myriad tongues,
  Shouted of liberty;
And the Blast of the Desert cried aloud,
  With a voice so wild and free,
That he started in his sleep and smiled
  At their tempestuous glee.

He did not feel the driver's whip,
  Nor the burning heat of day;
For Death had illumined the Land of Sleep,
  And his lifeless body lay
A worn-out fetter, that the soul
  Had broken and thrown away!

---

[1] the monks who operate a hospice in the St. Bernard Pass, Switzerland.

[2] or Kaffir (from the Arabic word for infidel): South-African Bantu.

[3] a literal translation of "hippopotamus."

Edgar Allan Poe
1809 – 1849

Edgar Allan Poe was born in Boston, Massachusetts, on 19 January 1809, son of two actors, Elizabeth Arnold Poe and David Poe, who abandoned the family in 1810. Following his mother's death in Richmond, Virginia, when he was only two, Poe was raised by John and Frances Allan, a prosperous couple who had no children of their own but who never formally adopted their foster son. He went to England with the Allans in 1815, returning to Richmond in 1820 when Allan's attempt to establish an English branch of his import-export business failed. In 1826 he entered the University of Virginia, studying ancient and modern languages. When John Allan refused to pay his gambling debts or continue to support him at the university, Poe enlisted in the United States Army. In 1830 he entered the Military Academy at West Point to train as an officer, but following Frances Allan's death and John Allan's remarriage, he refused to obey orders and was dismissed.

By this time Poe had published his first book, *Tamerlane and Other Poems* (1827), which shows the influence of Byron;* by 1831, when he went to live with his grandmother, aunt, and cousins in Baltimore, he had published two other volumes of verse (*Al Aaraaf, Tamerlane, and Minor Poems*, 1829, and *Poems. Second Edition*, 1831). The following year he published five tales, including "Metzengerstein,"* in the *Courier*. His story "MS. Found in a Bottle" won first prize in a fiction contest in 1833.

In 1836, Poe married his thirteen-year-old cousin, Virginia Clemm. Forced to support himself and his family, he produced a series of tales of terror and comic burlesques for various periodicals and took on editorial positions with the *Southern Literary Messenger* in Richmond (in 1835), and *Burton's Gentleman's Magazine* in Philadelphia (in 1838), which became *Graham's Magazine* in 1840: many of his tales were first published in these magazines; his critical essay "The Philosophy of Composition" was published in *Graham's* in 1846. From 1842–44 he worked as a freelance writer in Philadelphia, settling in New York in 1844 to work for the *Evening Mirror*—where he published his most famous poem, "The Raven" (1845). In 1847, Virginia Poe died of tuberculosis. In spite of his grief and the heavy drinking that accompanied it, Poe continued to lecture, write, and visit friends. Following a trip to Richmond, he was found delirious outside a polling station in Baltimore on election day, and died four days later, on 7 October 1849. (A.M.)

                ぐっか

from *Tamerlane and Other Poems* (1827)

Visit of the Dead

. . . .

Thy soul shall find itself alone—
Alone of all on earth—unknown
The cause—but none are near to pry
Into thine hour of secrecy.
5 Be silent in that solitude,
Which is not loneliness—for then
The spirits of the dead, who stood
In life before thee, are again
In death around thee, and their will
10 Shall then o'ershadow thee—be still:
For the night, tho' clear, shall frown:
And the stars shall look not down
From their thrones, in the dark heav'n;
With light like Hope to mortals giv'n,
15 But their red orbs, without beam,
To thy withering heart shall seem
As a burning, and a fever
Which would cling to thee forever.
But 'twill leave thee, as each star
20 In the morning light afar

Will fly thee—and vanish:
—But its *thought* thou can'st not banish.
The breath of God will be still;
And the wish upon the hill
By that summer breeze unbrok'n
Shall charm thee—as a token,
And a symbol which shall be
Secrecy in thee.

from *Al Aaraaf, Tamerlane, and Minor Poems* (1829)

Sonnet—To Science[1]

Science! meet daughter of old Time thou art
   Who alterest all things with thy peering eyes!
Why prey'st thou thus upon the poet's heart,
   Vulture! whose wings are dull realities!
How should he love thee—or how deem thee wise
   Who woulds't not leave him, in his wandering,
To seek for treasure in the jewell'd skies
   Albeit, he soar with an undaunted wing?
Hast thou not dragg'd Diana[2] from her car,
   And driv'n the Hamadryad[3] from the wood
To seek a shelter in some happier star?
   The gentle Naiad[4] from her fountain-flood?
The elfin from the green grass? and from me
The summer dream beneath the shrubbery?

---

[1] This sonnet was originally printed just before Poe's long poem, "Al Aaraaf," with which it is connected thematically. The title poem of the book, "Al Aaraaf," was inspired by Tycho Brahe's discovery in 1572 of a comet given the name of the Muslim space between heaven and hell, Al Aaraaf. Nesace, the deity who rules Poe's Al Aaraaf, has been commissioned by God to spread the powers of creative imagination throughout the universe; Ligeia, goddess of harmony, is her messenger in this task. Angelo, the earthly lover of the nymph Ianthe, joins her in Al Aaraaf; but he introduces disharmony in opposition to the work of Nesace. Poe intended to write four parts; he completed only the first two.

[2] virgin goddess of the moon, associated also with hunting.

[3] tree nymph; cf. Nesace in "Al Aaraaf."

[4] water nymph.

from *Poems by Edgar A. Poe*, 2nd ed. (1831)

Letter to Mr. ———[5]

                West Point, ——— 1831.

DEAR B———.

.   .   .   .

Believing only a portion of my former volume to be worthy a second edition—that small portion I thought it as well to include in the present book as to republish by itself. I have, therefore, herein combined Al Aaraaf and Tamerlane with other Poems hitherto unprinted. Nor have I hesitated to insert from the "Minor Poems," now omitted, whole lines, and even passages, to the end that being placed in a fairer light, and the trash shaken from them in which they were imbedded, they may have some chance of being seen by posterity.

.   .   .   .

It has been said, that a good critique on a poem may be written by one who is no poet himself. This, according to *your* idea and *mine* of poetry, I feel to be false—the less poetical the critic, the less just the critique, and the converse. On this account, and because there are but few B———s in the world, I would be as much ashamed of the world's good opinion as proud of your own. Another than yourself might here observe "Shakspeare is in possession of the world's good opinion, and yet Shakspeare is the greatest of poets. It appears then that the world judge correctly, why should you be ashamed of their favorable judgment?" The difficulty lies in the interpretation of the word "judgment" or "opinion." The opinion is the world's, truly, but it may be called theirs as a man would call a book his, having bought it: he did not write the book, but it is his; they did not originate the opinion, but it is theirs. A fool, for example, thinks Shakspeare a great poet—yet the fool has

---

[5] Poe revised this essay, the Preface to *Poems* (1831), and reprinted it as "Letter to B———" in the *Southern Literary Messenger*, July 1836, commenting that "we shall not be called upon to endorse all the writer's opinions." "B." might be Elam Bliss, who published the 1831 *Poems* (and also published William Bryant's* 1832 *Poems*).

never read Shakspeare. But the fool's neighbor, who is a step higher on the Andes of the mind, whose head (that is to say his more exalted thought) is too far above the fool to be seen or understood, but whose feet (by which I mean his every day actions) are sufficiently near to be discerned, and by means of which that superiority is ascertained, which *but* for them would never have been discovered—this neighbor asserts that Shakspeare is a great poet—the fool believes him, and it is henceforward his *opinion*. This neighbor's own opinion has, in like manner, been adopted from one above *him*, and so, ascendingly, to a few gifted individuals, who kneel around the summit, beholding, face to face, the master spirit who stands upon the pinnacle. * * *

You are aware of the great barrier in the path of an American writer. He is read, if at all, in reference to the combined and established wit of the world. I say established; for it is with literature as with law or empire—an established name is an estate in tenure, or a throne in possession. Besides, one might suppose that books, like their authors, improve by travel—their having crossed the sea is, with us, so great a distinction. Our antiquaries abandon time for distance; our very fops glance from the binding to the bottom of the title-page, where the mystic characters which spell London, Paris, or Genoa, are precisely so many letters of recommendation.

* * * * *

I mentioned just now a vulgar error as regards criticism. I think the notion that no poet can form a correct estimate of his own writings is another. I remarked before, that in proportion to the poetical talent, would be the justice of a critique upon poetry. Therefore, a bad poet would, I grant, make a false critique, and his self-love would infallibly bias his little judgment in his favor; but a poet, who is indeed a poet, could not, I think, fail of making a just critique. Whatever should be deducted on the score of self-love, might be replaced on account of his intimate acquaintance with the subject; in short, we have more instances of false criticism than of just, where one's own writings are the test, simply because we have more bad poets than good. There are of course many objections to what I say: Milton is a great example of the contrary; but his opinion with respect to the Paradise Regained,[1] is by no means fairly ascertained. By what trivial circumstances men are often led to assert what they do not really believe! Perhaps an inadvertent word has descended to posterity. But, in fact, the Paradise Regained is little, if at all, inferior to the Paradise Lost, and is only supposed so to be because men do not like epics, whatever they may say to the contrary, and reading those of Milton in their natural order, are too much wearied with the first to derive any pleasure from the second.

I dare say Milton preferred Comus[2] to either—if so—justly. * * * * * * * * * * * * * *

As I am speaking of poetry, it will not be amiss to touch slightly upon the most singular heresy in its modern history—the heresy of what is called very foolishly, the Lake School.[3] Some years ago I might have been induced, by an occasion like the present, to attempt a formal refutation of their doctrine; at present it would be a work of supererogation. The wise must bow to the wisdom of such men as Coleridge and Southey, but being wise, have laughed at poetical theories so prosaically exemplified.

Aristotle, with singular assurance, has declared poetry the most philosophical of all writing[4]—but it required a Wordsworth to pronounce it the most metaphysical. He seems to think that the end of poetry is, or should be, instruction—yet it is a truism that the end of our existence is happiness; if so, the end of every separate part of our existence—every thing connected with our existence should be still happiness. Therefore

---

[1] Milton's four-book sequel to *Paradise Lost*, published in 1671; the poem focuses on Christ's temptation in the wilderness and on his successful resistance to Satan.

[2] a pastoral entertainment with songs and dances, representing the victory of chastity over the seductions and temptations of Comus; first performed in 1634.

[3] the writers Coleridge,* Southey,* William Wordsworth,* and sometimes De Quincey,* all of whom lived in the English Lake District.

[4] "Spoudiotaton kai philosophikotaton genos." (E.A.P.); inaccurately quoted from *Poetics* 9.3: "Poetry, therefore, is a more philosophical and a higher thing than history." Aristotle continues: "for poetry tends to express the universal, history the particular"; cf. Wordsworth, Preface to *Lyrical Ballads* (1802 text).

the end of instruction should be happiness; and happiness is another name for pleasure;—therefore the end of instruction should be pleasure: yet we see the above mentioned opinion implies precisely the reverse.

To proceed: ceteris paribus,[1] he who pleases, is of more importance to his fellow men than he who instructs, since utility is happiness, and pleasure is the end already obtained which instruction is merely the means of obtaining.

I see no reason, then, why our metaphysical poets should plume themselves so much on the utility of their works, unless indeed they refer to instruction with eternity in view; in which case, sincere respect for their piety would not allow me to express my contempt for their judgment; contempt which it would be difficult to conceal, since their writings are professedly to be understood by the few, and it is the many who stand in need of salvation. In such case I should no doubt be tempted to think of the devil in Melmoth,[2] who labors indefatigably through three octavo volumes, to accomplish the destruction of one or two souls, while any common devil would have demolished one or two thousand.

* * * * *

Against the subtleties which would make poetry a study—not a passion—it becomes the metaphysician to reason—but the poet to protest. Yet Wordsworth and Coleridge are men in years; the one imbued in contemplation from his childhood, the other a giant in intellect and learning. The diffidence, then, with which I venture to dispute their authority would be overwhelming, did I not feel, from the bottom of my heart, that learning has little to do with the imagination—intellect with the passions—or age with poetry. * * * * *

"Trifles, like straws, upon the surface flow,
He who would search for pearls must dive below,"[3]
are lines which have done much mischief. As regards the greater truths, men oftener err by seeking them at the bottom than at the top; the depth lies in the huge abysses where wisdom is sought—not in the palpable palaces where she is found. The ancients were not always right in hiding the goddess in a well:[4] witness the light which Bacon[5] has thrown upon philosophy; witness the principles of our divine faith—that moral mechanism by which the simplicity of a child may overbalance the wisdom of a man.[6]

Poetry, above all things, is a beautiful painting whose tints, to minute inspection, are confusion worse confounded, but start boldly out to the cursory glance of the connoisseur.

We see an instance of Coleridge's liability to err in his Biographia Litteraria—professedly his literary life and opinions, but, in fact, a treatise *de omni scibili et quibusdam aliis.*[7] He goes wrong by reason of his very profundity, and of his error we have a natural type in the contemplation of a star. He who regards it directly and intensely sees, it is true, the star, but it is the star without a ray—while he who surveys it less inquisitively is conscious of all for which the star is useful to us below—its brilliancy and its beauty.

* * * * *

As to Wordsworth, I have no faith in him: That he had, in youth, the feelings of a poet, I believe—for there are glimpses of extreme delicacy in his writings—(and delicacy is the poet's own kingdom—his *El Dorado*)[8]— but they have the appearance of a better day recollected; and glimpses, at best, are little evidence of present poetic fire—we know that a few straggling flowers spring up daily in the crevices of the Avalanche.

---

[1] "other things being equal" (L.).

[2] In Charles Maturin (1782–1834), *Melmoth the Wanderer* (1820), the main character in each of a succession of stories is offered relief or rescue as part of a pact with the devil.

[3] Cf. John Dryden, Prologue to *All for Love* (1678) 25–26.

[4] Cf. Plato, *Theaetetus* 174a–175e.

[5] Sir Francis Bacon (1561–1626), one of the first thinkers to advocate observation of nature, rather than reiteration of the views of the ancients, as the basis for knowledge.

[6] See Matthew 18.1–5, Luke 18.15–17.

[7] "of everything that can be known—and some other things" (L.); the first part of this quotation, *de omni scibili*, was the title of one of the proposed 900 theses of the Italian philosopher Pico della Mirandola (1463–94).

[8] an imaginary land of gold and jewels, sought for by Spanish explorers of South America. Cf. Voltaire, *Candide* (1759).

He was to blame in wearing away his youth in contemplation with the end of poetizing in his manhood. With the increase of his judgment the light which should make it apparent has faded away. His judgment consequently is too correct. This may not be understood, but the old Goths of Germany would have understood it, who used to debate matters of importance to their State twice, once when drunk, and once when sober—sober that they might not be deficient in formality—drunk lest they should be destitute of vigor.

The long wordy discussions by which he tries to reason us into admiration of his poetry, speak very little in his favor: they are full of such assertions as this—(I have opened one of his volumes at random) "Of genius the only proof is the act of doing well what is worthy to be done, and what was never done before"[1]—indeed! then it follows that in doing what is *un*worthy to be done, or what *has* been done before, no genius can be evinced: yet the picking of pockets is an unworthy act, pockets have been picked time immemorial, and Barrington, the pickpocket,[2] in point of genius, would have thought hard of a comparison with William Wordsworth, the poet.

Again—in estimating the merit of certain poems, whether they be Ossian's or M'Pherson's,[3] can surely be of little consequence, yet, in order to prove their worthlessness, Mr. W. has expended many pages in the controversy. *Tantæne animis?*[4] Can great minds descend to such absurdity? But worse still: that he may bear down every argument in favor of these poems, he triumphantly drags forward a passage in his abomination of which he expects the reader to sympathize. It is the beginning of the epic poem "*Temora*."[5] "The blue waves of Ullin roll in light; the green hills are covered with day; trees shake their dusky heads in the breeze." And this—this gorgeous, yet simple imagery—where all is alive and panting with immortality—than which earth has nothing more grand, nor paradise more beautiful—this—William Wordsworth, the author of Peter Bell,[6] has *selected* to dignify with his imperial contempt. We shall see what better he, in his own person, has to offer. Imprimis:

"And now she's at the poney's head,
And now she's at the poney's tail,
On that side now, and now on this,
And almost stifled her with bliss—
A few sad tears does Betty shed,
She pats the poney where or when
She knows not: happy Betty Foy!
O Johnny! never mind the Doctor!"[7]

Secondly:

"The dew was falling fast, the—stars began to blink,
 I heard a voice, it said—— drink, pretty creature, drink;
 And looking o'er the hedge, before me I espied
 A snow-white mountain lamb with a—maiden at its side.
 No other sheep were near, the lamb was all alone,
 And by a slender cord was—tether'd to a stone."[8]

Now we have no doubt this is all true; we *will* believe it, indeed we will, Mr. W. Is it sympathy for the sheep you wish to excite? I love a sheep from the bottom of my heart.

* * * * *

But there *are* occasions, dear B——, there are occasions when even Wordsworth is reasonable. Even Stamboul,[9] it is said, shall have an end, and the most unlucky blunders must come to a conclusion. Here is an extract from his preface.

"Those who have been accustomed to the phraseology of modern writers, if they persist in reading this book to a conclusion (*impossible!*) will, no doubt, have to struggle with feelings of awkwardness; (ha! ha! ha!)

---

[1] "Essay, Supplementary to the Preface" (1815).

[2] George Barrington (1755–c.1804), a professional pickpocket sentenced in 1790 to transportation to Australia.

[3] The poet James Macpherson (1736–96) claimed to have discovered and translated the ancient Scots Gaelic poems of Ossian; in fact, they were forgeries.

[4] Cf. Virgil, *Aeneid* 1.11: "Do heavenly spirits know such rage?"

[5] one of the Ossian poems (1763); in his "Essay, Supplementary to the Preface" Wordsworth describes Ossian as a phantom "begotten by the snug embrace of an impudent Highlander upon a cloud of tradition."

[6] a much-parodied poem by William Wordsworth (1798).

[7] Cf. William Wordsworth, "The Idiot Boy" 392–96, 402–03, 407.*

[8] Cf. Wordsworth, "The Pet Lamb" 1–6; Poe has added the dashes.

[9] Constantinople (now called Istanbul).

they will look round for poetry (ha! ha! ha! ha!) and will be induced to inquire by what species of courtesy these attempts have been permitted to assume that title."[1] Ha! ha! ha! ha! ha!

Yet let not Mr. W. despair; he has given immortality to a wagon, and the bee Sophocles has eternalized a sore toe, and dignified a tragedy with a chorus of turkeys.[2]

* * * * *

Of Coleridge I cannot speak but with reverence. His towering intellect! his gigantic power! To use an author quoted by himself, "Jai trouve souvent que la plupart des sectes ont raison dans une bonne partie de ce quelles avancent, mais non pas en ce quelles nient,"[3] and, to employ his own language, he has imprisoned his own conceptions by the barrier he has erected against those of others. It is lamentable to think that such a mind should be buried in metaphysics, and, like the Nyctanthes,[4] waste its perfume upon the night alone. In reading that man's poetry I tremble, like one who stands upon a volcano, conscious, from the very darkness bursting from the crater, of the fire and the light that are weltering below.

* * * * *

What is Poetry? Poetry! that Proteus-like[5] idea, with as many appellations as the nine-titled Corcyra![6] Give me, I demanded of a scholar some time ago, give me a definition of poetry? "Tres volontiers,"[7]—and he proceeded to his library, brought me a Dr. Johnson,[8] and overwhelmed me with a definition. Shade of the immortal Shakspeare! I imagined to myself the scowl of your spiritual eye upon the profanity of that scurrilous Ursa Major.[9] Think of poetry, dear B——, think of poetry, and then think of—Dr. Samuel Johnson! Think of all that is airy and fairy-like, and then of all that is hideous and unwieldy; think of his huge bulk, the Elephant! and then—and then think of the Tempest—the Midsummer Night's Dream—Prospero—Oberon—and Titania![10]

* * * * *

A poem, in my opinion, is opposed to a work of science by having, for its *immediate* object, pleasure, not truth;[11] to romance, by having for its object an *indefinite* instead of a *definite* pleasure, being a poem only so far as this object is attained: romance presenting perceptible images with definite, poetry with *in*definite sensations, to which end music is an *essential,* since the comprehension of sweet sound is our most indefinite conception. Music, when combined with a pleasurable idea, is poetry; music without the idea is simply music; the idea without the music is prose from its very definitiveness.

What was meant by the invective against him who had no music in his soul?[12]

* * * * *

To sum up this long rigmarole, I have, dear B——, what you no doubt perceive, for the metaphysical poets, *as* poets, the most sovereign contempt. That they have followers proves nothing—

> No Indian prince has to his palace
> More followers than a thief to the gallows.[13]

---

[1] from Preface to *Lyrical Ballads* (1800)—with Poe's interpolations.

[2] Wordsworth's poem *Benjamin the Waggoner* was published in 1819; the tragic poet Sophocles (c. 496–406 BC) was known as the "Attic bee" because of his industry; "sore toe" is a loose translation of Oedipus, the name of Sophocles' most famous hero.

[3] "I have found that most sects are right about most of what they affirm, but not about what they deny" (Fr.); see Coleridge,* *Biographia Literaria* 12; the passage is quoted from Leibniz, *Trois Lettres à M. Remond de Mont-Mort* (1741).

[4] a species of flower that blooms only at night.

[5] changeable, like Proteus, a sea god who assumed different shapes.

[6] the Greek island of Korfu, which has been called by many names over a history reaching back to Homeric times.

[7] "very willingly" (Fr.).

[8] I.e., a copy of Samuel Johnson's *Dictionary of the English Language* (1755).

[9] the Great Bear, the most conspicuous constellation in the northern sky (here referring to Johnson).

[10] Prospero is the magician in Shakespeare's *The Tempest,* Oberon and Titania are the king and queen of the fairies in *A Midsummer Night's Dream.*

[11] Cf. Coleridge, *Biographia Literaria,* chapter 14.*

[12] Cf. Shakespeare, *The Merchant of Venice* 5.1.91.

[13] Samuel Butler, *Hudibras* (1663–80) 2.1.272–73.

To Helen[1]

Helen, thy beauty is to me
Like those Nicean[2] barks of yore,
That gently, o'er a perfum'd sea,
    The weary way-worn wanderer bore
5   To his own native shore.

On desperate seas long wont to roam,
    Thy hyacinth hair,[3] thy classic face,
Thy Naiad airs have brought me home
    To the beauty of fair Greece,
10 And the grandeur of old Rome.

Lo! in that little window-niche
    How statue-like I see thee stand!
    The folded scroll within thy hand—
A Psyche[4] from the regions which
15   Are Holy land!

The Doomed City[5]

Lo! Death hath rear'd himself a throne
In a strange city, all alone,
Far down within the dim west—
And the good, and the bad, and the worst, and the best,
Have gone to their eternal rest.

5 There shrines, and palaces, and towers
Are—not like any thing of ours—
O! no—O! no—*ours* never loom
To heaven with that ungodly gloom!
Time-eaten towers that tremble not!
10 Around, by lifting winds forgot,
Resignedly beneath the sky
The melancholy waters lie.

A heaven that God doth not contemn
With stars is like a diadem—
15 We liken our ladies' eyes to them—
But there! that everlasting pall!
It would be mockery to call
Such dreariness a heaven at all.

Yet tho' no holy rays come down
20 On the long night-time of that town,
Light from the lurid, deep sea
Streams up the turrets silently—
Up thrones—up long-forgotten bowers
Of sculptur'd ivy and stone flowers—
25 Up domes—up spires—up kingly halls—
Up fanes—up Babylon-like[6] walls—
Up many a melancholy shrine
Whose entablatures intertwine
The mask—the viol[7]—and the vine.

30 There open temples—open graves
Are on a level with the waves—
But not the riches there that lie
In each idol's diamond eye.
Not the gaily-jewell'd dead
35 Tempt the waters from their bed:
For no ripples curl, alas!
Along that wilderness of glass—
No swellings hint that winds may be
Upon a far-off happier sea:
40 So blend the turrets and shadows there
That all seem pendulous in air,
While from the high towers of the town
Death looks gigantically down.

But lo! a stir is in the air!
45 The wave! there is a ripple there!

---

[1] "Helen" is Sarah Helen Whitman, a poet to whom Poe was briefly engaged in 1845.

[2] Perhaps Poe alludes to the ancient town of Nicæa, now Nice; perhaps he is thinking of Milton's "Nyseian isle" (*Paradise Lost* 4.275).

[3] dark curled hair like that of the beautiful youth Hyacinthus; see Ovid, *Metamorphoses* 10.

[4] a beautiful maiden, Cupid's lover, whose name means "breath" or "soul." Cf. Tighe, *Psyche.**

[5] The title was later changed, first to "The City of Sin" (1836) and then to "The City in the Sea. A Prophecy" (1845).

[6] Babylon was one of the great cities of the ancient pagan world: see also Rev. 16.18–19.

[7] a stringed instrument; see Isaiah 14.11.

As if the towers had thrown aside,
In slightly sinking, the dull tide—
As if the turret-tops had given
A vacuum in the filmy heaven:
50 The waves have now a redder glow—
The very hours are breathing low—
And when, amid no earthly moans,
Down, down that town shall settle hence,
Hell rising from a thousand thrones
55 Shall do it reverence,
And Death to some more happy clime
Shall give his undivided time.

from the *Saturday Courier* (14 January 1832)

Metzengerstein

"Pestis eram vivus, moriens tua mors ero."
MARTIN LUTHER[1]

Horror and fatality have been stalking abroad in all ages. Why then give a date to the story I have to tell? I will not. Besides I have other reasons for concealment. Let it suffice to say that, at the period of which I speak, there existed, in the interior of Hungary, a settled although hidden belief in the doctrines of the Metempsychosis.[2] Of the doctrines themselves—that is, of their falsity, or probability—I say nothing. I assert, however, that much of our incredulity (as La Bruyere observes of all our unhappiness,) *vient de ne pouvoir etre seuls.*[3]

But there were some points in the Hungarian superstition (the Roman term was religio,) which were fast verging to absurdity. They, the Hungarians, differed essentially from the Eastern authorities. For example—"The soul," said the former, (I give the words of an acute, and intelligent Parisian,) "*ne demeure, qu'un seul fois, dans un corps sensible—au reste—ce quon croit d'etre un cheval—un chien—un homme—n'est que le resemblance peu tangible de ces animaux.*"[4]

The families of Berlifitzing, and Metzengerstein had been at variance for centuries. Never, before, were two houses so illustrious mutually embittered by hostility so deadly. Indeed, at the era of this history, it was remarked by an old crone of haggard, and sinister appearance, that fire and water might sooner mingle, than a Berlifitzing clasp the hand of a Metzengerstein. The origin of this enmity seems to be found in the words of an ancient prophecy. "A lofty name shall have a fearful fall, when, like the rider over his horse, the mortality of Metzengerstein shall triumph over the immortality of Berlifitzing."

To be sure, the words themselves had little or no meaning—but more trivial causes have given rise (and that no long while ago,) to consequences equally eventful. Besides, the estates, which were contiguous, had long exercised a rival influence, in the affairs of a busy government. Moreover, near neighbors are seldom friends, and the inmates of the Castle Berlifitzing might look, from their lofty buttresses, into the very windows of the Chateau Metzengerstein; and least of all was the more than feudal magnificence thus discovered, calculated to allay the irritable feelings of the less ancient, and less wealthy Berlifitzings. What wonder then, that the words, however silly, of that prediction, should have succeeded in setting, and keeping at variance, two families, already predisposed to quarrel, by every instigation of hereditary jealousy? The words of the prophecy implied, if they implied any thing, a final triumph on the part of the already more powerful house, and were, of course, remembered, with the more bitter animosity, on the side of the weaker, and less influential.

Wilhelm, Count Berlifitzing, although honourably, and loftily descended, was, at the epoch of this narrative, an infirm, and doting old man, remarkable for nothing but an inordinate, and inveterate personal antipathy to the family of his rival, and so passionate a love of horses, and of hunting, that neither bodily decrepitude, great age, nor mental incapacity, prevented his daily participa-

---

[1] "Living, I was your plague; dying, I will be your death" (L.); from the letters of the German religious reformer Martin Luther (1483–1546).

[2] transmigration of the soul into another body at death.

[3] Jean de La Bruyère (1645–96); the quotation means "comes from not being able to be alone" (Fr.).

[4] "lives only once in a palpable body; otherwise, what we believe to be a horse—a dog—a man—is only a scarcely tangible resemblance of those animals" (Fr.).

tion in the dangers of the chace.

Frederick, Baron Metzengerstein, was, on the other hand, not yet of age. His father, the Minister G——, died young. His mother, the Lady Mary, followed quickly after. Frederick was, at that time, in his fifteenth year. In a city fifteen years are no long period—a child may be still a child in his third lustrum. But in a wilderness—in so magnificent a wilderness as that old principality, fifteen years have a far deeper meaning.

The beautiful Lady Mary!—how could she die?—and of consumption! But it is a path I have prayed to follow. I would wish all I love to perish of that gentle disease. How glorious! to depart in the hey-day of the young blood—the heart all passion—the imagination all fire—amid the remembrances of happier days—in the fall of the year, and so be buried up forever in the gorgeous, autumnal leaves. Thus died the Lady Mary. The young Baron Frederick stood, without a living relative, by the coffin of his dead mother. He laid his hand upon her placid forehead. No shudder came over his delicate frame—no sigh from his gentle bosom—no curl upon his kingly lip. Heartless, self-willed, and impetuous from his childhood, he had arrived at the age of which I speak, through a career of unfeeling, wanton, and reckless dissipation, and a barrier had long since arisen in the channel of all holy thoughts, and gentle recollections.

From some peculiar circumstances attending the administration of his father, the young Baron, at the decease of the former, entered immediately upon his vast possessions. Such estates were, never before, held by a nobleman of Hungary. His castles were without number—of these, the chief, in point of splendor and extent, was the Chateau Metzengerstein. The boundary line of his dominions was never clearly defined, but his principal park embraced a circuit of one hundred and fifty miles.

Upon the succession of a proprietor so young, with a character so well known, to a fortune so unparalleled, little speculation was afloat in regard to his probable course of conduct. And, indeed, for the space of three days, the behavior of the heir, out-heroded Herod,[1] and fairly surpassed the expectations of his most enthusiastic admirers. Shameful debaucheries—flagrant treacheries—unheard-of atrocities, gave his trembling vassals quickly to understand, that no servile submission on their part—no punctilios of conscience on his own were, thenceforward, to prove any protection against the bloodthirsty and remorseless fangs of a petty Caligula.[2] On the night of the fourth day, the stables of the Castle Berlifitzing were discovered to be on fire—and the neighbourhood unanimously added the crime of the incendiary, to the already frightful list of the Baron's misdemeanors and enormities. But, during the tumult occasioned by this occurrence, the young nobleman, himself, sat, apparently buried in meditation, in a vast, and desolate upper apartment of his family palace of Metzengerstein. The rich, although faded tapestry hangings which swung gloomily upon the walls, represented the majestic, and shadowy forms of a thousand illustrious ancestors. Here rich-ermined priests, and pontifical dignitaries, familiarly seated with the autocrat, and the sovereign, put a veto on the wishes of some temporal king, or restrained, with the fiat of papal supremacy, the rebellious sceptre of the Arch-Enemy. Here the dark, tall statures of the Princes Metzengerstein—their muscular war coursers plunging over the carcass of a fallen foe—startled the firmest nerves with their vigorous expression—and here, the voluptuous, and swan-like figures of the dames of days gone by, floated away, in the mazes of an unreal dance, to the strains of imaginary melody.

But as the Baron listened, or affected to listen, to the rapidly increasing uproar in the stables of the Castle Berlifitzing, or perhaps pondered, like Nero,[3] upon some more decided audacity, his eyes were unwittingly rivetted to the figure of an enormous and unnaturally coloured horse, represented, in the tapestry, as belonging to a Saracen[4] ancestor of the family of his rival. The horse, itself, in the foreground of the design, stood

---

[1] acted the role of an angry tyrant even better than the biblical King Herod (as represented in a medieval mystery play).

[2] The Roman emperor Caligula (AD 12–41) was known for his extravagance and cruelty.

[3] Roman emperor from AD 54–68, Nero was alleged to have set Rome on fire for the pleasure of seeing it burn.

[4] an Arab or Muslim of the time of the Crusades.

motionless, and statue-like; while, farther back, its discomfited rider perished by the dagger of a Metzengerstein. There was a fiendish expression on the lip of the young Frederick, as he became aware of the direction which his glance had, thus, without his consciousness, assumed. But he did not remove it. On the contrary, the longer he gazed, the more impossible did it appear that he might ever withdraw his vision from the fascination of that tapestry. It was with difficulty that he could reconcile his dreamy and incoherent feelings, with the certainty of being awake. He could, by no means, account for the singular, intense, and overwhelming anxiety which appeared falling, like a shroud, upon his senses. But the tumult without, becoming, suddenly, more violent, with a kind of compulsory, and desperate exertion, he diverted his attention to the glare of ruddy light thrown full by the flaming stables upon the windows of the apartment. The action was but momentary: his gaze returned mechanically to the wall. To his extreme horror and surprise, the head of the gigantic steed had, in the meantime, altered its position. The neck of the animal, before arched, as if in compassion, over the prostrate body of its lord, was now extended at full length, in the direction of the Baron. The eyes, before invisible, now wore an energetic, and human expression, while they gleamed with a fiery, and unusual red, and the distended lips of the apparently enraged horse left in full view his sepulchral and disgusting teeth.

Stupified with terror, the young nobleman tottered to the door. As he threw it open, a flash of red light, streaming far into the chamber, flung his shadow, with a clear, decided outline, against the quivering tapestry: and he shuddered to perceive that shadow, as he staggered, for a moment, upon the threshold, assuming the exact position, and precisely filling up the contour of the relentless, and triumphant murderer of the Saracen Berlifitzing.

With a view of lightening the oppression of his spirits, the Baron hurried into the open air. At the principal gate of the Chateau he encountered three equerries. With much difficulty, and, at the imminent peril of their lives, they were restraining the unnatural, and convulsive plunges of a gigantic, and fiery-coloured horse.

"Whose horse is that? Where did you get him?" demanded the youth, in a querulous, and husky tone of voice, as he became instantly aware that the mysterious steed, in the tapestried chamber, was the very counterpart of the furious animal before his eyes.

"He is your own property, Sire," replied one of the equerries—"at least, he is claimed by no other owner. We caught him, just now, flying all smoking, and foaming with rage, from the burning stables of the Castle Berlifitzing. Supposing him to have belonged to the old Count's stud of foreign horses, we led him back as an estray. But the grooms there disclaim any title to the creature, which is singular, since he bears evident marks of a narrow escape from the flames"——

"The letters W.V.B. are, moreover, branded very distinctly upon his forehead," interrupted a second equerry. "We, at first, supposed them to be the initials of William Von Berlifitzing."

"Extremely singular!" said the young Baron, with a musing air, apparently unconscious of the meaning of his words. "He is, as you say, a remarkable horse—a prodigious horse! Although, as you very justly observe, of a suspicious and untractable character. Let him be mine, however," added he, after a pause, "perhaps a rider, like Frederick of Metzengerstein, may tame even the devil, from the stables of Berlifitzing."

"You appear to be mistaken, my lord, the horse (as I think we mentioned) is *not* from the stables of the Count. If such were the case, we know our duty better than to bring him in the presence of a noble of your name."

"True!" observed the Baron, dryly, and, at that instant, a page of the bed-chamber came from the Chateau with a heightened colour, and precipitate step. He whispered into his master's ear, an account of the miraculous, and sudden disappearance of a small portion of the tapestry in an apartment which he designated—entering, at the same time, into particulars of a minute, and circumstantial character, but, from the low tone of voice in which these latter were communicated, nothing escaped to gratify the excited curiosity of the equerries.

The young Frederick, however, during the conference, seemed agitated by a variety of emotions. He soon, however, recovered his composure, and an expression of determined malignancy settled upon his countenance, as he gave peremptory orders that a certain chamber should be immediately locked up, and the key placed, forthwith, in his own possession.

. . . .

"Have you heard of the unhappy death of the hunter Berlifitzing?" said one of his vassals to the Baron, as, after the affair of the page, the huge and mysterious steed, which that nobleman had adopted as his own, plunged, and curvetted with redoubled, and supernatural fury down the long avenue which extended from the Chateau to the stables of Metzengerstein.

"No!" said the Baron, turning abruptly towards the speaker, "dead! say you?"

"It is true, my lord, and is no unwelcome intelligence, I imagine, to a noble of your family?"

A rapid smile, of a peculiar and unintelligible meaning, shot over the beautiful countenance of the listener—"How died he?"

"In his great exertions to rescue a favourite portion of his hunting-stud, he has, himself, perished miserably in the flames."

"I-n-d-e-e-d!" ejaculated the Baron, as if slowly, and deliberately impressed with the truth of some exciting idea.

"Indeed," repeated the vassal.

"Shocking!" said the youth, calmly, and returned into the Chateau.

From this date, a marked alteration took place in the outward demeanour of the dissolute young Baron, Frederick, of Metzengerstein. Indeed, the behaviour of the heir disappointed every expectation, and proved little in accordance with the views of many a manœuvering mamma, while his habits and manners, still less than formerly, offered any thing congenial with those of the neighbouring aristocracy. He was seldom to be seen at all; never beyond the limits of his own domain. There are few, in this social world, who are utterly companionless, yet so seemed he; unless, indeed, that unnatural, impetuous, and fiery-coloured horse which he thenceforward continually bestrode, had any mysterious right to the title of his friend. Numerous invitations on the part of the neighbourhood for a long time, however, continually flocked in. "Will the Baron attend our excursions? Will the Baron honour our festivals with his presence?"—"Baron Frederick does not hunt—Baron Frederick will not attend," were the haughty, and laconic answers. These repeated insults were not to be endured by an imperious nobility. Such invitations became less cordial—less frequent. In time they ceased altogether. The widow of the unfortunate Count Berlifitzing, was even heard to express a hope "that the Baron might be at home, when he did not choose to be at home, since he disdained the company of his equals—and ride when he did not wish to ride, since he preferred the society of a horse." This, to be sure, was a very silly explosion of hereditary pique, and merely proved how singularly unmeaning our sayings are apt to become, when we desire to be unusually energetic.

The charitable, nevertheless, attributed the alteration in the conduct of the young nobleman, to the natural sorrow of a son for the untimely loss of his parents; forgetting, however, his atrocious, and reckless behaviour, during the short period immediately succeeding that bereavement. Some there were, indeed, who suggested a too haughty idea of self-consequence and dignity. Others again, among whom may be mentioned the family physician, did not hesitate in speaking of morbid melancholy, and hereditary ill health; while dark hints of a more equivocal nature, were current among the multitude.

Indeed the Baron's perverse attachment to his lately acquired charger, an attachment which seemed to attain new strength from every fresh example of the brute's ferocious, and demon-like propensities; at length became, in the eyes of all reasonable men, a hideous, and unnatural fervour. In the glare of noon, at the dead hour of night, in sickness or in health, in calm or in tempest, in moonlight or in shadow, the young Metzengerstein seemed rivetted to the saddle of that colossal horse, whose untractable audacities so well accorded with the spirit of his own. There were circumstances, moreover, which, coupled with late events, gave an unearthly, and portentous character to the mania of the rider, and the capabilities of the steed. The space passed over in a single leap, had been accurately measured, and was found to exceed, by an incalculable distance, the wildest expectations of the most imaginative; while the red lightning, itself, was declared to have been outridden in many a long-continued, and impetuous career. The Baron, besides, had no particular name for the animal, although all the rest of his extensive collection, were distinguished by characteristic appellations. Its stable was appointed at a distance from the others, and with regard to grooming, and other necessary offices, none but the owner, in person, had ever ventured to officiate, or even to enter the enclosure of that particular stall. It was also to be observed, that although the three grooms who had caught the horse, as he fled from the conflagration at Berlifitzing, had succeeded in arresting his course, by means of a chain-bridle and noose, yet no one of the three could, with any certainty affirm, that he had, during that dangerous struggle, or at any period thereafter, actually placed his hand upon the body of the beast.

Among all the retinue of the Baron, however, none were found to doubt the ardour of that extraordinary affection which existed, on the part of the young nobleman, for the fiery qualities of his horse; at least, none but an insignificant, and misshapen little page, whose deformities were in every body's way, and whose opinions were of the least possible importance. He, if his ideas are worth mentioning at all, had the effrontery to assert, that his master never vaulted into the saddle without an unaccountable, and almost imperceptible shudder, and that upon his return from every habitual ride, during which his panting and bleeding brute was never known to pause in his impetuosity, although he, himself, evinced no appearance of exhaustion, yet an expression of triumphant malignity distorted every muscle in his countenance.

These ominous circumstances portended in the opinion of all people, some awful, and impending calamity. Accordingly one tempestuous night, the Baron descended, like a maniac, from his bed-chamber, and, mounting in great haste, bounded away into the mazes of the forest.

An occurrence so common attracted no particular attention, but his return was looked for with intense anxiety on the part of his domestics, when, after some hours absence, the stupendous, and magnificent battlements of the Chateau Metzengerstein were discovered crackling, and rocking to their very foundation, under the influence of a dense, and livid mass of ungovernable fire. As the flames, when first seen, had already made so terrible a progress, that all efforts to save any portion of the building were evidently futile, the astonished neighbourhood stood idly around in silent, and apathetic wonder. But a new, and fearful object soon rivetted the attention of the multitude, and proved the vast superiority of excitement which the sight of human agony exercises in the feelings of a crowd, above the most appalling spectacles of inanimate matter.

Up the long avenue of aged oaks, which led from the forest to the main entrance of the Chateau Metzengerstein, a steed bearing an unbonnetted, and disordered rider, was seen leaping with an impetuosity which outstripped the very demon of the tempest, and called forth from every beholder an ejaculation of "Azrael!"[1]

The career of the horseman was, indisputably on his own part, uncontrollable. The agony of his countenance, the convulsive struggling of his frame gave evidence of superhuman exertion; but no sound, save a solitary shriek, escaped from his lacerated lips, which were bitten through and through, in the intensity of terror. One instant, and the clattering of hoofs resounded sharply, and shrilly, above the roaring of the flames, and the shrieking of the winds—another, and clearing, at a single plunge, the gateway, and the moat, the animal bounded, with its rider, far up the tottering staircase of the palace, and was lost in the whirlwind of hissing, and chaotic fire.

The fury of the storm immediately died away, and a dead calm suddenly succeeded. A white flame still enveloped the building, like a shroud, and streaming far away into the quiet atmosphere, shot forth a glare of preternatural light, while a cloud of wreathing smoke settled heavily over the battlements, and slowly, but distinctly assumed the appearance of a motionless and colossal horse.

Frederick, Baron Metzengerstein, was the last of a long line of princes. His family name is no longer to be found among the Hungarian aristocracy.

---

[1] the angel of death.

Henry Louis Vivian Derozio
1809 – 1831

Henry Louis Vivian Derozio, who has been called the first Anglo-Indian poet, was born in Calcutta on 18 April 1809. His father, Francis Derozio, was a Christian Indian office worker; his mother, Sophia Johnson Derozio, was English. At six, Derozio went to David Drummond's Academy in Calcutta; at fourteen, he was taken out of school to work, first in his father's office and then in his English uncle's indigo factory in Behar. While in Behar, Derozio began to submit poems to the *India Gazette*. In 1827, impressed by his talent, the editor, John Grant, offered to publish a book of his work and invited him to come back to Calcutta. Soon, Grant had made him assistant editor, he was publishing in a variety of Calcutta periodicals, and he had founded his own paper, the *Calcutta Gazette*. His many poems include *The Fakeer of Jungheera* (1828), an eighty-page narrative in the manner of Byron's* Turkish Tales or Landon's "The Improvisatrice."* Before he was nineteen, he was appointed Professor of English Literature and History at the Hindu College founded in 1817. "To the Pupils of the Hindu College" makes clear his devotion to his students, and he was by all accounts an inspiring teacher, but his encouragement of wide-ranging and open discussion of religious issues troubled conservative parents, and he was dismissed in April 1831. Undeterred, he started a new paper, the *East Indian*, the first to address issues of concern to his mixed-race community. He died of cholera on 26 December 1831. (D.L.M.)

※※※

from *Poems* (1827)

The Harp of India[1]

Why hang'st thou lonely on yon withered bough?
    Unstrung, for ever, must thou there remain?
Thy music once was sweet—who hears it now?
    Why doth the breeze sigh over thee in vain?—
    Silence hath bound thee with her fatal chain;
5 Neglected, mute, and desolate art thou,
    Like ruined monument on desert plain!—
O! many a hand more worthy far than mine
    Once thy harmonious chords to sweetness gave,
And many a wreath for them did Fame entwine
10   Of flowers still blooming on the minstrel's grave:
Those hands are cold—but if thy notes divine
    May be by mortal wakened once again,
Harp of my country, let me strike the strain!

March, 1827

from *The Fakeer of Jungheera: A Metrical Tale and Other Poems* (1828)

My country! in thy days of glory past

My country! in thy days of glory past
A beauteous halo circled round thy brow,
And worshipped as a deity thou wast—
Where is that glory, where that reverence now?
5 Thy eagle pinion is chained down at last,
And grovelling in the lowly dust art thou:
Thy minstrel hath no wreath to weave for thee
Save the sad story of thy misery!—
Well—let me dive into the depths of time,
And bring from out the ages that have rolled
10 A few small fragments of these wrecks sublime,
Which human eye may never more behold;
And let the guerdon of my labour be
My fallen country! one kind wish for thee!

---

[1] This is the first poem in the volume, which has an epigraph from Thomas Moore,* "The Harp of Erin" (1807).

from *The Fakeer of Jungheera*

from CANTO 2

The Legend of the Shushan[1]

O! Love is strong, and its hopes 'twill build
    Where nothing beside would dare;
O! Love is bright, and its beams will gild
    The desert dark, and bare.

---

[1] "A student of that excellent institution, the Hindu College, once brought me a translation of the Betal Puncheesa, and the following fragment of a tale having struck me for its wildness, I thought of writing a ballad, the subject of which should be strictly Indian. The Shushan is a place to which the dead are conveyed, to be burnt. In conformity with the practice of eastern story tellers, who frequently repeat the burden or moral of the song, have I introduced the 'O Love is strong,' &c. wherever an opportunity offered:—

"'Thereupon, he took the Jogee aside, and said, "O Gosayn! you have given me many rubies, but have never even once eaten in my house: I am therefore much ashamed, so pray tell me what it is that you want?" "Great King," replied the Jogee, "On the banks of the river Godavurry is a Shushan, where all I wish for will be gained by Muntra. Seven-eighths of what I want have been already obtained, and I now seek at your hands the remaining portion. You must therefore stay with me one whole night." "Agreed," replied the King, "appoint the day." "On the evening of the fourteenth day of the month Bhader, come to me armed." "Go," returned the Raja "and I promise to be with you on the day you have fixed." With this promise the Devotee took leave of the King, and proceeded to the Shushan. The Raja was lost in meditation, till the time appointed stole upon him, and then having armed himself, he went alone in the evening to the Jogee.

"'"Come in and sit down my son," said the Devotee; and the Raja complied with his request, while at the same time he, unalarmed, beheld demons, ghosts, witches, and malignant spirits, dancing around him, and changing their forms. "Now," said the Raja, "What are your commands?" "Four miles south of this," replied the Jogee, "is a Shushan, where, on a tree, hangs a corpse; bring me that corpse, while I pray." Having now sent the King away, the Jogee sat himself down, and commenced his devotions. The dark night frowned upon him; and such a storm with rain come on, as if the heavens would have exhausted themselves, and never have rained again, while the demons, and evil spirits set up a howl that might have daunted the stoutest heart. But the King held on his way, and though snakes came wreathing round his legs, he got free of them by repeating a charm. At last overcoming all opposition, he reached the cemetery, where he saw demons beating human beings, witches gnawing the livers of children, and tigers and elephants roaring. As he cast his eyes upon a Serus tree, he saw it root and branch in flames, and heard these words sounding from all quarters, "strike, strike! seize, seize! take care that none escape." "Come what will," said he then to himself, "this undoubtedly

And youth is the time, the joyful time
    When visions of bliss are before us;
But alas! when gone, in our sober prime
    We sigh for the days flown o'er us.

For youth and love their hopes will build
    Where nothing beside would dare;
And they both are bright, and their beams will gild
    The desert dark, and bare.

The rain fell fast, and the midnight blast
    Its horrible chaunt did sing,
And it howled and raved as it madly past
    Like a demon on wildest wing.

The precipitous lightning beamed all bright,
    As it flashed from the dark, dark sky,
Like the beautiful glance (which kills with its light)
    Of a woman's large black eye.

It hissed through the air, and it dipped in the wave,
    And it madly plunged into earth,
Then pursued the wind to its desolate cave,
    And hurried to its home in the north;

---

is the Jogee of whom the Dev made mention to me." So saying, he went up to the tree, where he saw a corpse hanging with its head downwards. "Now," cried he, "my labour is at an end," then fearlessly climbing the tree, he made a cut with his sword at the rope, that suspended the corpse, which as soon as it fell began to cry. The King hearing its voice, was pleased at the thought that it must have been a living being; then having descended, "who are you?" said he to it. To his great astonishment, the corpse only laughed, and without any reply, climbed the tree. The King followed it, and having brought it down in his arms, repeated his question. But receiving no answer, he thought that it might have been the oilman, who the Dev had said had been kept in the cemetery by the Jogee; then having bound it in his cloak, began to bring it away.

"'"He who greatly ventures, will greatly win. "Who are you," said Betal, the corpse, to the Raja, "and where are you taking me?" "I am Raja Vicrom," said the King, "and I am taking you to the Jogee." "Let it be agreed between us," replied Betal, "that if you speak while we are on the road I shall return." To this the Raja consented, and proceeded with the corpse. While they were on the way, "O King," said Betal, "the learned and the wise spend their time in songs and study, and the indolent and ignorant, in frivolity and sleep. It therefore behoves us to make an easy journey of it with pleasant conversation. Hear then what I now tell thee."'" (H.L.V.D.)

Some spirit had charmed each gathered cloud
    Till the mystic spell it broke;
And then uprising, oft' and loud
    The heavens in thunder spoke.

And sooth it seemed as if save that gleam
    All nature had lost her light—
The moon had concealed her beautiful beam;
    'Twas a fearful, fearful night.

On the wings of the storm each star had past
    To its home of rest far away,
As if in the blast there could not last
    Of radiance even a ray;

As if like hope and joy they ne'er
    Too long should brightly shine,
Lest if on earth they for ever were,
    Existence might be divine!

'Twas a dismal night; and the tempest sang
    As it rushed o'er flood and fell;
And loud the laugh of spirits rang
    With the demon's midnight yell.

And the shriek and cry rose wild and high
    From many an earthless form;
And roar and shout cut through the sky,
    And mixed with the voice of the storm.

But Love is strong, and its hopes 'twill build
    Where nothing beside would dare;
And Love is bright, and its beams will gild
    The desert dark, and bare

And youth is the time, the joyful time
    When visions of bliss are before us;
But alas! gone, in our sober prime
    We sigh for the days flown o'er us.

For love and youth their hopes will build
    Where nothing beside would dare;
And they both are bright, and their beams will gild
    The desert dark, and bare.

O! why at this hour in the dark Shushan
    Is the Prince Jogindra sighing?
Sure that cannot be a dwelling for man
    Where the loathsome dead are lying.

Unearthly dogs are barking there
    As to break the dead sleeper's dream;
And the grey wolf howls—'tis his dismal lair—
    And the owl glints by with a scream.

The night wind moans, like a sick man's groans
    When he fevered gasps on his bed—
Then why is the Prince here all alone?—
    Ah! Radhika fair is dead!

The wind may moan like a sick man's groan
    When he fevered gasps on his bed—
But why is the Prince here all alone
    Though Radhika fair be dead?

Her spirit is gone to some region blest
    Unhurt by the storm and the strife—
She will not wake from her dreamless rest;
    And who shall charm her to life?

But there was a man, and a holy man,
    A gifted Sunyasee,[1]
Who bade him dwell in the dark Shushan
    For days and black nights three.

"There demons shall come and bid thee do
    Full many a fearful deed;
But if thou quail or shrink, thou'lt rue,
    And death shall be thy meed.

"Each night three trials must be past,
    Of earthly pain severest;
And thou, if true, shalt win at last
    Thy Radhika fairest, dearest!

"*But there's one deed thou shalt not do
    Though a spirit bright bids thee—*

---

[1] "A Sunyasee is a devotee who lives in the desert—
    'The moss his bed, the cave his humble cell,
    His food the fruits, his drink the crystal well.'" (H.L.V.D.)
Thomas Parnell (1679–1718), "The Hermit" (1722) 3–4.

           Yet if thou dare, that deed thou'lt rue";
95   Said the sainted Sunyasee.

       "Now name that deed, thou holy man!"
           Cried the Prince all eagerly;
       "And I shall dwell in the dark Shushan
           For days and black nights three."

100   "It may not be," said the Sunyasee;
           "Thy faith must yet be tried;
       And if great thy love and thy wisdom be,
           Thou Prince! shalt win thy bride.

       "But all unarmed, that home of the dead
105   And heedless of friend or foe,
       With feet unshod must Jogindra tread"—
           Said the Prince—"With joy I go."

       For Love is strong, and its hopes 'twill build
           Where nothing beside would dare;
110   And Love is bright, and its beams will gild
           The desert dark and bare.

       And youth is the time, the joyful time
           When visions of bliss are before us;
       But alas! when gone, in our sober prime
115   We sigh for the days flown o'er us.

       For love and youth their hopes will build
           Where nothing beside would dare;
       And they both are bright, and their beams will gild
           The desert dark and bare.

120   Three days are done, and two nights gone
           In painful trials past;
       This night remains, and the bride is won,
           If strong he be to the last.

       He sat on a stone, all mute and lone,
125   By the corpse of his Radhika fair,
       When the lightning flashed, and the wind made moan,
           And a beautiful spirit stood there!

       Her eyes seemed made of the pure star-light,
           And her face was mild and sweet;

130   Her neck was white as the flower of night,
           And her tresses kissed her feet.

       Her form was like to the cypress tree,
           And her cheek, it was young love's bed;
       Her fairy step, was light and free,
135   Her lip like the lotus red.

       Her voice was sweet as when ripplets meet
           And sigh o'er a pebbled strand;
       So soft was her song, it seemed to belong
           To a happy, heavenly land.

           The Spirit's Song

       Oh! now do not leave me
           Since false friends have flown;
       Dear Love! do not grieve me,
           I've thought thee mine own.
145   'Mid tempest and storm, love!
           Mid good and mid ill,
       Thy form, thy bright form, love!
           My star hath been still.
       Though prospects before me
150   Were darksome, and drear,
       Though clouds gathered o'er me
           Still, still thou wast near!
       My visions have faded,
           The tear fills mine eye,
155   My hopes are degraded,
           They're hurled from on high.
       Like thoughts that are straying
           Where darkness should be,
       Bright moon beams are playing
160   Above the green sea.
       Now clouds are concealing
           The face of the moon—
       As onward she's wheeling,
           She's darkened, too soon!
165   O! thus on my sorrow
           There shone silver beams;
       Alas! ere the morrow
           They vanished like dreams!
       My bird was the sweetest

          That ever did sing,
170	 But ah! 'twas the fleetest,
            And wild was its wing.
        But sweeter, far sweeter
            Did hope weave her lay,
175   And ah me! much fleeter
            She flew far away.
        I've found thee, I've found thee—
            My griefs would be done
        If love's chain had bound thee,
180   And made us but one.
        Then oh! do not leave me,
            Or wretched I'll be—
        For now what could grieve me
            But parting from thee?

185   Her dawning smile breaks pensively;
            With supplicating hands,
        And sad yet soft beseeching eye
            That fairy vision stands.

        Jogindra's glance upon her dwelt,
190   As there were magic in her form;
        He gazed, he sighed, he almost felt
            His heart within him warm.

        "But no!" he cried, "for constancy
            Is every charm above;
195   And I shall still be true to thee,
            My Radhika! my Love!"

        The storm is hushed, and the moon her light
            Has softly flung o'er all,
        And the dark Shushan is a palace bright
200   With lamps on each crystal wall.

        'Mid a glittering throng the sound of song
            Now floats on the scented air,
        As minstrel seraphs glad and young
            Were waking their music there!

205   From heavenliest bowers they've gathered flowers,
            Red roses, and jasmines white;
        On the wings of joy swift fly the hours,
            For the night is a bridal night!
        And high on a throne of azure, and gold
210   Jogindra in princely pride
        All smiling sits,—on his arm behold
            Leans Radhika fair his bride!

        O! Love is strong, and its hopes 'twill build
            Where nothing beside would dare;
215   O! Love is bright and its beams will gild
            The desert dark and bare.

        And youth is the time, the joyful time
            When visions of bliss are before us;
        But alas! when gone, in our sober prime
220   We sigh for the days flown o'er us.

        For love and youth their hopes will build
            Where nothing beside would dare;
        And they both are bright, and their beams will gild
            The desert dark and bare.

from *The Poetical Works of Henry Louis Vivian Derozio*, ed. B.B. Shah (1907)

To the Pupils of the Hindu College

Expanding like the petals of young flowers
    I watch the gentle opening of your minds
And the sweet loosening of the spell that binds
    Your intellectual energies and powers
5   That stretch (like young birds in soft summer hours,)
    Their wings to try their strength. O! how the winds
Of circumstance, and freshening April showers
    Of early knowledge, and unnumbered kinds
Of new perceptions shed their influence;
10 And how you worship truth's omnipotence!
What joyance rains upon me, when I see
Fame in the mirror of futurity,
Weaving the chaplets you have yet to gain,
And then I feel I have not lived in vain.

Bibliography

Anthologies

Stillinger, Jack, and Deirdre Shauna Lynch, eds. *The Norton Anthology of English Literature: The Romantic Period.* 8th ed. Vol. D. New York: Norton, 2006.

Bloom, Harold, and Lionel Trilling, eds. *Romantic Poetry and Prose.* New York: Oxford UP, 1973.

Breen, Jennifer, ed. *Women Romantic Poets 1785–1832: An Anthology.* London: Dent, 1992.

Feldman, Paula R., ed. *British Women Poets of the Romantic Era: An Anthology.* Baltimore: Johns Hopkins UP, 1997.

McGann, Jerome J., ed. *The New Oxford Book of Romantic Period Verse.* Oxford: Oxford UP, 1993.

Mellor, Anne K., and Richard E. Matlak, eds. *British Literature, 1780–1830.* Fort Worth: Harcourt Brace, 1996.

Newman, Lance, Joel Pace, and Chris Koenig-Woodyard, eds. *Transatlantic Romanticism: An Anthology of British, American, and Canadian Literature 1767–1867.* New York: Pearson/Longman, 2006.

Perkins, David, ed. *English Romantic Writers.* Rev. ed. Fort Worth: Harcourt Brace, 1995.

Perkins, George, and Barbara Perkins, eds. *The American Tradition in Literature.* Shorter 9th ed. Boston: McGraw-Hill, 1999.

Wolfson, Susan, and Peter Manning, eds. *The Longman Anthology of British Literature. Volume 2A: The Romantics and Their Contemporaries.* New York: Longman, 1999.

Wu, Duncan, ed. *Romanticism: An Anthology.* 2nd ed. Oxford: Blackwell, 1998.

—, ed. *Romantic Women Poets: An Anthology.* Oxford: Blackwell, 1997.

General Studies

Abrams, M.H. *The Correspondent Breeze: Essays on English Romanticism.* New York: Norton, 1984.

—. *The Milk of Paradise: The Effect of Opium Visions on the Works of De Quincey, Crabbe, Francis Thompson and Coleridge.* Rev. ed. New York: Harper & Row, 1970.

—. *The Mirror and the Lamp: Romantic Theory and the Critical Tradition.* New York: Norton, 1953.

—. *Natural Supernaturalism: Tradition and Revolution in Romantic Literature.* New York: Norton, 1973.

—. "Structure and Style in the Greater Romantic Lyric." *From Sensibility to Romanticism: Essays Presented to Frederick A. Pottle.* Ed. Frederick W. Hilles and Harold Bloom. Oxford: Oxford UP, 1965. 527–60.

Almeida, Joselyn. "The Sight of a New World: Discovery and Romanticism." *Wordsworth Circle* 32 (2001): 148–51.

Bainbridge, Simon. *Napoleon and English Romanticism.* Cambridge: Cambridge UP, 1995.

Balfour, Ian. *The Rhetoric of Romantic Prophecy.* Stanford: Stanford UP, 2002.

Barker-Benfield, J.G. *The Culture of Sensibility: Sex and Society in Eighteenth-Century Britain.* Chicago: U of Chicago P, 1992.

Barrell, John. *The Dark Side of the Landscape: The Rural Poor in English Painting, 1730–1840.* Cambridge: Cambridge UP, 1980.

Bate, Walter Jackson. *From Classic to Romantic: Premises of Taste in Eighteenth-Century England.* 1946. Rpt. New York: Harper Torchbooks, 1961.

Baum, Joan. *Mind-Forg'd Manacles: Slavery and the English Romantic Poets.* North Haven CT: Archon, 1994.

Beer, John, ed. *Questioning Romanticism.* Baltimore: Johns Hopkins UP, 1995.

Behrendt, Stephen C., and Harriet Kramer Linkin, eds. *Approaches to Teaching British Women Poets of the Romantic Period.* New York: MLA, 1997.

Bewell, Alan. *Romanticism and Colonial Disease.* Baltimore: Johns Hopkins UP, 1999.

Bloom, Harold. *The Visionary Company: A Reading of English Romantic Poetry.* Garden City NY: Doubleday, 1961.

Bostetter, Edward E. *The Romantic Ventriloquists: Wordsworth, Coleridge, Keats, Shelley, Byron.* Seattle: U of Washington P, 1963.

Bush, Douglas. *Mythology and the Romantic Tradition in English Poetry.* New York: Norton, 1963.

Butler, Marilyn. *Romantics, Rebels and Reactionaries: English Literature and its Background 1760–1830.* Oxford: Oxford UP, 1981.

—, ed. *Burke, Paine, Godwin, and the Revolution Controversy*. Cambridge: Cambridge UP, 1984.

Chai, Leon. *The Romantic Foundations of the American Renaissance*. Ithaca, NY: Cornell UP, 1987.

Chandler, James. *England in 1819: The Politics of Literary Culture and the Case of Romantic Historicism*. Chicago: U of Chicago P, 1998.

—, and Kevin Gilmartin, eds. *Romantic Metropolis: The Urban Scene of British Culture, 1780–1840*. Cambridge: Cambridge UP, 2005.

Christensen, Jerome. *Romanticism at the End of History*. Baltimore: Johns Hopkins UP, 2000.

Cook, Elizabeth Heckendorn. *Epistolary Bodies: Gender and Genre in the Eighteenth-Century Republic of Letters*. Stanford: Stanford UP, 1996.

Crossley, Ceri, and Ian Small, eds. *The French Revolution and British Culture*. New York: Oxford UP, 1989.

Curran, Stuart. *Poetic Form and British Romanticism*. New York: Oxford UP, 1986.

—. "Romantic Poetry: The I Altered." *Romanticism and Feminism*. Ed. Anne K. Mellor. Bloomington: Indiana UP, 1988. 185–207.

Davidoff, Leonore, and Catherine Hall. *Family Fortunes: Men and Women of the English Middle Class, 1780–1850*. Chicago: U of Chicago P, 1987.

Davis, David Brion. *The Problem of Slavery in the Age of Revolution, 1770–1823*. Ithaca, NY: Cornell UP, 1975.

—. *The Problem of Slavery in Western Culture*. Ithaca, NY: Cornell UP, 1966.

Davis, Leith. *Acts of Union: Scotland and the Literary Negotiation of the British Nation, 1707–1830*. Stanford: Stanford UP, 1998.

De Man, Paul. *The Rhetoric of Romanticism*. New York: Columbia UP, 1984.

—. "The Rhetoric of Temporality." *Blindness and Insight: Essays in the Rhetoric of Contemporary Criticism*. New York: Oxford UP, 1971. 187–228.

Edwards, Paul, and David Dabydeen, eds. *Black Writers in Britain, 1760–1890*. Edinburgh: Edinburgh UP, 1991.

Eger, Elizabeth, Charlotte Grant, Cliona O. Gallchoir, and Penny Warburton, eds. *Women, Writing and the Public Sphere, 1700–1830*. Cambridge: Cambridge UP, 2001.

Engell, James. *The Creative Imagination, Enlightenment to Romanticism*. Cambridge, MA: Harvard UP, 1981.

Erickson, Lee. *The Economy of Literary Form: English Literature and the Industrialization of Publishing, 1800–1850*. Baltimore: Johns Hopkins UP, 1996.

Favret, Mary A., and Nicola J. Watson, eds. *At the Limits of Romanticism: Essays in Cultural, Feminist, and Materialist Criticism*. Bloomington: Indiana UP, 1994.

Feldman, Paula R., and Theresa M. Kelley, eds. *Romantic Women Writers: Voices and Counter-Voices*. Hanover, NH: UP of New England, 1995.

Ferguson, Moira. *Subject to Others: British Women Writers and Colonial Slavery, 1670–1834*. New York: Routledge, 1992.

Ferris, Ina. "Writing on the Border: The National Tale, Female Writing, and the Public Sphere." *Romanticism, History and the Possibilities of Genre: Re-Forming Literature, 1789–1837*. Ed. Tilottama Rajan and Julia M. Wright. Cambridge: Cambridge UP, 1998. 86–106.

Frye, Northrop. *A Study of English Romanticism*. New York: Random House, 1968.

Fulford, Tim, and Peter J. Kitson, eds. *Romanticism and Colonialism: Writing and Empire, 1780–1830*. Cambridge: Cambridge UP, 1998.

Gamer, Michael. *Romanticism and the Gothic: Genre, Reception, and Canon Formation*. Cambridge: Cambridge UP, 2000.

Gaull, Marilyn. *English Romanticism: The Human Context*. New York: Norton, 1988.

Gilbert, Sandra M., and Susan Gubar. *The Madwoman in the Attic: The Woman Writer and the Nineteenth-Century Literary Imagination*. New Haven: Yale UP, 1979.

Gilmartin, Kevin. *Print Politics: The Press and Radical Opposition in Early Nineteenth-Century England*. Cambridge: Cambridge UP, 1996.

Gilroy, Amanda, ed. *Romantic Geographies: Discourses of Travel 1775–1844*. Manchester: Manchester UP, 2000.

Graff, Gerald. *Professing Literature: An Institutional History*. Chicago: U of Chicago P, 1987.

Guillory, John. *Cultural Capital: The Problem of Literary Canon Formation*. Chicago: U of Chicago P, 1993.

Hartman, Geoffrey H. *Beyond Formalism: Literary Essays, 1958–1970*. New Haven: Yale UP, 1970.

Hayter, Alethea. *Opium and the Romantic Imagination*. London: Faber, 1968.

Hofkosh, Sonia, and Alan Richardson, eds. *Romanticism, Race and Imperial Culture, 1780–1834*. Bloomington: Indiana UP, 1996.

Homans, Margaret. *Bearing the Word: Language and Female Experience in Nineteenth-Century Women's Writing*. Chicago: U of Chicago P, 1986.

Jackson, J.R. de J. *Poetry of the Romantic Period*. London:

Routledge and Kegan Paul, 1980.

—. *Romantic Poetry by Women: A Bibliography, 1770–1835*. Oxford: Clarendon P, 1993.

Jamison, Kay Redfield. *Touched with Fire: Manic-Depressive Illness and the Artistic Temperament*. New York: Free P, 1993.

Johnson, Claudia L. *Equivocal Beings: Politics, Gender, and Sentimentality in the 1790s: Wollstonecraft, Radcliffe, Burney, Austen*. Chicago: U of Chicago P, 1995.

Johnson, C.R. *Provincial Poetry, 1789–1839. British Verse Printed in the Provinces: The Romantic Background*. Otley: Smith Settle for the Jed P, 1992.

Jones, Howard Mumford. *Revolution and Romanticism*. Cambridge MA: Harvard UP/Belknap P, 1974.

Keach, William. "A Transatlantic Romantic Century." *European Romantic Review* 11.1 (2000): 31–34.

Kelly, Gary. *Women, Writing, and Revolution, 1790–1827*. Oxford: Clarendon P, 1993.

Klancher, Jon P. *The Making of English Reading Audiences 1790–1832*. Madison: U of Wisconsin P, 1987.

Landry, Donna. *The Muses of Resistance: Labouring-Class Women's Poetry in Britain, 1739–1796*. Cambridge: Cambridge UP, 1990.

Leask, Nigel. *British Romantic Writers and the East: Anxieties of Empire*. Cambridge: Cambridge UP, 1992.

Lee, Debbie. *Slavery and the Romantic Imagination*. Philadelphia: U of Pennsylvania P, 2002.

Lovejoy, Arthur O. "On the Discrimination of Romanticisms." *PMLA* 39.2 (1924): 229–53.

—. *The Great Chain of Being: A Study of the History of an Idea*. 1936. Rpt. Cambridge: Harvard UP, 1936.

Mahoney, Charles. *Romantics and Renegades: The Poetics of Political Reaction*. Basingstoke: Palgrave Macmillan, 2003.

Maier, Pauline. *American Scripture: Making the Declaration of Independence*. New York: Knopf, 1997.

Makdisi, Saree. *Romantic Imperialism: Universal Empire and the Culture of Modernity*. Cambridge: Cambridge UP, 1998.

Manning, Peter. *Reading Romantics: Texts and Contexts*. New York: Oxford UP, 1990.

Mazzeo, Tilar J. "The Impossibility of Being Anglo-American: The Rhetoric of Emigration and Transatlanticism in British Romantic Culture, 1791–1831." *European Romantic Review* 16.1 (2005): 59–78.

McFarland, Thomas. *Romantic Cruxes: The English Essayists and the Spirit of the Age*. Oxford: Clarendon P, 1987.

—. *Romanticism and the Forms of Ruin: Wordsworth, Coleridge, and Modalities of Fragmentation*. Princeton: Princeton UP, 1981.

McGann, Jerome J. *The Beauty of Inflections: Literary Investigations in Historical Method and Theory*. Oxford: Clarendon P, 1985.

—. *The Poetics of Sensibility: A Revolution in Literary Style*. Oxford: Clarendon P, 1985.

—. *The Romantic Ideology: A Critical Investigation*. Chicago: U of Chicago P, 1983.

McKusick, James C. *Green Writing: Romanticism and Ecology*. New York: St. Martin's P, 2000.

Mellor, Anne K. *English Romantic Irony*. Cambridge, MA: Harvard UP, 1980.

—. "English Women Writers and the French Revolution." *Rebel Daughters: Women and the French Revolution*. Ed. Sara E. Melzer and Leslie W. Rabine. New York: Oxford UP, 1992. 255–72.

—. *Mothers of the Nation: Women's Political Writing in English, 1780–1830*. Bloomington: Indiana UP, 2000.

—, ed. *Romanticism and Feminism*. Bloomington: Indiana UP, 1988.

—. *Romanticism and Gender*. New York: Routledge, 1993.

Midgeley, Clare. *Women against Slavery: The British Campaigns, 1780–1870*. London: Routledge, 1992.

Miller, J. Hillis. "English Romanticism, American Romanticism: What's the Difference?" *Theory Now and Then*. Durham: Duke UP, 1991.

Pace, Joel, Chris Koenig-Woodyard, and Lance Newman, eds. "Introducing Transatlantic Romanticism." *Romanticism on the Net* 38–39 (May 2005): n.p. <http://www.erudit.org/revue/ron/2005/v/n38–39/011666ar.html>.

Pascoe, Judith. *Romantic Theatricality: Gender, Poetry, and Spectatorship*. Ithaca, NY: Cornell UP, 1997.

Patterson, Orlando. *Slavery and Social Death: A Comparative Study*. Cambridge, MA: Harvard UP, 1982.

Paulson, Ronald. *Representations of Revolution, 1789–1820*. New Haven: Yale UP, 1983.

Pfau, Thomas, and Robert F. Gleckner, eds. *Lessons of Romanticism: A Critical Companion*. Durham, NC: Duke UP, 1998.

Philp, Mark, ed. *The French Revolution and British Popular Politics*. Cambridge: Cambridge UP, 1991.

Plasa, Carl. *Textual Politics from Slavery to Postcolonialism: Race and Identification*. New York: St. Martin's P, 2000.

Poovey, Mary. *The Proper Lady and the Woman Writer: Ideology as Style in the Works of Mary Wollstonecraft, Mary Shelley, and Jane Austen*. Chicago: U of Chicago P, 1984.

Porte, Joel. *In Respect to Egotism: Studies in American Romantic Writing*. Cambridge: Cambridge UP, 1991.

Potkay, Adam, and Sandra Burr, eds. *Black Atlantic Writers of the Eighteenth Century: Living the New Exodus in England and the Americas*. New York: St. Martin's P, 1995.

Praz, Mario. *The Romantic Agony*. 2nd ed. Trans. Angus Davidson. Introd. Frank Kermode. London: Oxford UP, 1970.

Pyle, Forest. *The Ideology of Imagination: Subject and Society in the Discourse of Romanticism*. Stanford: Stanford UP, 1995.

Rajan, Tilottama. *Dark Interpreter: The Discourse of Romanticism*. Ithaca NY: Cornell UP, 1980.

—. *The Supplement of Reading: Figures of Understanding in Romantic Theory and Practice*. Ithaca NY: Cornell UP, 1990.

Redfield, Marc. *The Politics of Aesthetics: Nationalism, Gender, Romanticism*. Stanford: Stanford UP, 2003.

Reiman, Donald H., ed. *The Romantics Reviewed: Contemporary Reviews of British Romantic Writers*. 9 vols. New York: Garland, 1972.

Richardson, Alan, and Sonia Hofkosh, eds. *Romanticism, Race, and Imperial Culture, 1780–1834*. Bloomington: Indiana UP, 1996.

Richardson, Alan. *Literature, Education, and Romanticism: Reading as Social Practice, 1780–1832*. Cambridge: Cambridge UP, 1994.

—. *A Mental Theater: Poetic Drama and Consciousness in the Romantic Age*. University Park: Penn State UP, 1988.

Ross, Marlon B. *The Contours of Masculine Desire: Romanticism and the Rise of Women's Poetry*. New York: Oxford UP, 1989.

Ruttenburg, Nancy. *Democratic Personality: Popular Voice and the Trial of American Authorship*. Stanford: Stanford UP, 1998.

Ryan, Robert M. *The Romantic Reformation: Religious Politics in English Literature, 1789–1824*. Cambridge: Cambridge UP, 1997.

Rzepka, Charles J. *The Self as Mind: Vision and Identity in Wordsworth, Coleridge, and Keats*. Cambridge, MA: Harvard UP, 1986.

Schock, Peter A. *Romantic Satanism: Myth and the Historical Moment in Blake, Shelley and Byron*. New York: Palgrave Macmillan, 2003.

Scrivener, Michael. *Poetry and Reform: Periodical Verse from the English Democratic Press, 1792–1824*. Detroit: Wayne State UP, 1992.

Simpson, David. *Romanticism, Nationalism, and the Revolt against Theory*. Chicago: U of Chicago P, 1993.

Siskin, Clifford. *The Historicity of Romantic Discourse*. New York: Oxford UP, 1988.

—. *The Work of Writing: Literature and Social Change in Britain, 1700–1830*. Baltimore: Johns Hopkins UP, 1998.

Smith, Hilda L., and Carole Pateman, eds. *Women Writers and the Early Modern British Political Tradition*. Cambridge: Cambridge UP, 1998.

Smith, Olivia. *The Politics of Language, 1791–1819*. Oxford: Clarendon P, 1984.

Sorensen, Janet. *The Grammar of Empire in Eighteenth-Century British Writing*. Cambridge: Cambridge UP, 2000.

Spacks, Patricia M. *Imagining a Self: Autobiography and Novel in Eighteenth-Century England*. Cambridge, MA: Harvard UP, 1976.

Steinman, Lisa M. "Transatlantic Cultures: Godwin, Brown, and Mary Shelley." *Wordsworth Circle* 32 (2001): 126–30.

Tanner, Tony. "Notes for a Comparison between American and European Romanticism." *Journal of American Studies* 2 (1968): 83–103.

Taylor, Clare. *British and American Abolitionists: An Episode in Transatlantic Understanding*. Edinburgh: Edinburgh UP, 1974.

Thomas, Helen. *Romanticism and Slave Narratives: Transatlantic Testimonies*. Cambridge: Cambridge UP, 2000.

Thompson, E.P. *Customs in Common*. New York: New Press, 1991.

—. *The Making of the English Working Class*. 1963. London: Gollancz, 1980.

Todd, Janet. *Sensibility: An Introduction*. London: Methuen, 1986.

—. *Women's Friendship in Literature*. New York: Columbia UP, 1980.

Ty, Eleanor. *Empowering the Feminine: The Narratives of Mary Robinson, Jane West, and Amelia Opie, 1796–1812*. Toronto: U of Toronto P, 1998.

—. *Unsex'd Revolutionaries: Five Women Novelists of the 1790s*. Toronto: U of Toronto P, 1993.

Verhoeven, W.M. *Revolutionary Histories: Transatlantic Cultural Nationalism, 1775–1815*. New York: Palgrave, 2002.

Voller, Jack G. *The Supernatural Sublime: The Metaphysics of Terror in Anglo-American Romanticism*. Dekalb: Northern Illinois UP, 1994.

Weiskel, Thomas. *The Romantic Sublime: Studies in the Structure and Psychology of Transcendence*. Baltimore: Johns Hopkins UP, 1976.

Wellek, René. "The Concept of 'Romanticism' in Literary History." *Comparative Literature* 1 (Winter 1949): 1–23.

—. *A History of Modern Criticism, 1750–1950*. Vol. 2: *The Romantic Age*. Cambridge: Cambridge UP, 1955.

Whale, John. *Imagination under Pressure, 1789–1832: Aesthetics, Politics and Utility*. Cambridge: Cambridge UP, 2000.

Wilkie, Brian. *Romantic Poets and Epic Tradition*. Madison: U of Wisconsin P, 1965.

Williams, Eric. *Capitalism and Slavery*. Chapel Hill: U of North Carolina P, 1945.

Williams, Raymond. *The Country and the City*. London: Chatto & Windus, 1973.

—. *Culture and Society, 1780–1950*. London: Chatto & Windus, 1958.

Wilson, Carol Shiner, and Joel Haefner, eds. *Re-Visioning Romanticism: British Women Writers, 1776–1837*. Philadelphia: U of Pennsylvania P, 1994.

Wolfson, Susan J. *Formal Charges: The Shaping of Poetry in British Romanticism*. Stanford: Stanford UP, 1997.

Adams and Adams

EDITIONS:

Butterfield, L.H., et al., eds. *Adams Family Correspondence*. 7 vols. Cambridge, MA: Harvard UP/Belknap P, 1963–73.

Adams Family Papers: an Electronic Archive. <http://www.masshist.org/digitaladams/aea/letter/>.

Butterfield, L.H., Marc Friedlaender, and Mary-Jo Kline, eds. *The Book of Abigail and John: Selected Letters of the Adams Family, 1762–1784*. Cambridge, MA: Harvard UP, 1975.

STUDIES:

Ellis, Joseph J. *Passionate Sage: The Character and Legacy of John Adams*. New York: Norton, 1993.

Levin, Phyllis Lee. *Abigail Adams: A Biography*. New York: St. Martin's P, 1987.

See also Vidal, Wilstach, under JEFFERSON.

Aikin

STUDY:

Summerfield, Geoffrey. *Fantasy and Reason: Children's Literature in the Eighteenth Century*. Athens: U of Georgia P, 1985.

See also Behrendt & Linkin, in General Bibliography.

Apess

EDITION:

O'Connell, Barry, ed. *On Our Own Ground: The Complete Writings of William Apess, a Pequot*. Amherst: U of Massachusetts P, 1992.

STUDY:

Haynes, Carolyn. "'A Mark for Them All to … Hiss At': The Formation of Methodist and Pequot Identity in the Conversion Narrative of William Apess." *Early American Literature* 31 (1996): 25–44.

Krupat, Arnold. *Ethnocriticism: Ethnography, History, Literature*. Berkeley: U of California P, 1992.

—. *The Voice in the Margin: Native American Literature and the Canon*. Berkeley: U of California P, 1989.

Ruoff, A. LaVonne Brown. "Three Nineteenth-Century American Indian Autobiographies." *Redefining American Literary History*. Ed. Ruoff and Jerry W. Ward, Jr. New York: MLA, 1990. 251–69.

Tiro, Karim M. "Denominated '*SAVAGE*': Methodism, Writing, and Identity in the Works of William Apess, A Pequot." *American Quarterly* 48.4 (1996): 653–79.

Austen

EDITIONS:

Chapman, Robert W., ed. *Jane Austen's Letters to her Sister Cassandra and Others*. 2nd ed. Oxford: Oxford UP, 1959.

—. *The Works of Jane Austen*. 6 vols. Rev. B.C. Southam. Oxford: Oxford UP, 1967.

Doody, Margaret Anne, and Douglas Murray, eds. *Catharine and Other Writings*. Oxford: Oxford UP, 1993.

Southam, B.C., ed. *Jane Austen: The Critical Heritage*. London and New York, Routledge & K. Paul, 1968.

STUDIES:

Auerbach, Nina. *Communities of Women: An Idea in Fiction*. Cambridge MA: Harvard UP, 1978.

Butler, Marilyn. *Jane Austen and the War of Ideas*. Oxford: Clarendon P, 1975.

Epstein, Julia. "Jane Austen's Juvenilia and the Female Epistolary Tradition." *Papers on Language and Literature* 21.4 (Fall 1985): 399–416.

Grey, J. David, ed. *Jane Austen's Beginnings: The Juvenilia and Lady Susan*. Ann Arbor: UMI Research P, 1989.

Harding, D.W. "Regulated Hatred: An Aspect of the Work of Jane Austen." *Scrutiny* 9 (1940): 346–62.

Johnson, Claudia L. *Jane Austen: Women, Politics, and the Novel*. Chicago: U of Chicago P, 1988.

McMaster, Juliet, ed. *Jane Austen's Achievement: Papers Delivered at the Jane Austen Bicentennial Conference, University of Alberta*. London: Macmillan, 1976.

Shields, Carol. *Jane Austen*. Toronto: Viking, 2001.

Tanner, Tony. *Jane Austen*. London: Macmillan, 1986.

Tomalin, Claire. *Jane Austen: A Life*. Rev. ed. London: Penguin, 2000.

See also Claudia L. Johnson, Poovey, in General Bibliography; Jones, under DACRE; Cottom, under RADCLIFFE.

Baillie

EDITIONS:

Breen, Jennifer, ed. *The Selected Poems of Joanna Baillie, 1762–1851*. Manchester: Manchester UP, 1999.

Cox, Jeffrey N., ed. and introd. *Seven Gothic Dramas, 1789–1825*. Athens: Ohio UP, 1992.

Duthie, Peter, ed. *Plays on the Passions (1798 edition)*. Peterborough: Broadview, 2001.

Slagle, Judith Bailey, ed. *The Collected Letters of Joanna Baillie*. Vol. 1. Madison, NJ: Fairleigh Dickinson UP, 1999.

The Dramatic and Poetical Works of Joanna Baillie. London: Longman, Brown, Green, and Longmans, 1851. Rpt. Hildesheim and New York: Georg Olms Verlag, 1976.

STUDIES:

Brewer, William D. "Joanna Baillie and Lord Byron." *Keats-Shelley Journal* 44 (1995): 165–81.

Burroughs, Catherine B. *Closet Stages: Joanna Baillie and the Theater Theory of British Romantic Women Writers*. Philadelphia: U of Pennsylvania P, 1997.

Henderson, Andrea. "Passion and Fashion in Joanna Baillie's 'Introductory Discourse.'" *PMLA* 112.2 (March 1997): 198–213.

Mellor, Anne K. "Joanna Baillie and the Counter-Public Sphere." *Studies in Romanticism* 33 (Winter 1994): 559–67.

Slagle, Judith Bailey. *Joanna Baillie: A Literary Life*. Madison, NJ: Fairleigh Dickinson UP, 2002.

Watkins, Daniel P. *A Materialist Critique of English Romantic Drama*. Gainesville: UP of Florida, 1993. Chap. 3.

See also Favret & Watson, Feldman & Kelley, Wilson & Haefner, in General Bibliography.

Barbauld

EDITIONS:

McCarthy, William, and Elizabeth Kraft, eds. *Anna Letitia Barbauld: Selected Poetry and Prose*. Peterborough: Broadview, 2002.

—, eds. *The Poems of Anna Letitia Barbauld*. Athens: U of Georgia P, 1994.

STUDIES:

Bellanca, Mary Ellen. "Science, Animal Sympathy, and Anna Barbauld's 'The Mouse's Petition.'" *Eighteenth-Century Studies* 37 (2003): 47–67.

Bradshaw, Penny. "Dystopian Futures: Time-Travel and Millenarian Visions in the Poetry of Anna Barbauld and Charlotte Smith." *Romanticism on the Net* 21 (February 2001): n.p. <http://www.erudit.org/revue/ron/2001/v/n21/005959ar.html>.

Curran, Stuart. "Dynamics of Female Friendship in the Later Eighteenth Century." *Nineteenth-Century Contexts* 23 (2001): 221–39.

Keach, William. "A Regency Prophecy and the End of Anna Barbauld's Career." *Studies in Romanticism* 33 (Winter 1994): 569–77.
Kraft, Elizabeth. "Anna Letitia Barbauld's 'Washing-Day' and the Montgolfier Balloon." *Literature and History* 4 (1995): 25–41.
Levasseur, Susan J. "'All Monstrous, All Prodigious Things': Anna Barbauld's 'The Rights of Woman' and Mary Wollstonecraft's Revolution in Female Manners." *Nineteenth-Century Feminisms* 5 (2001): 10–36.

See also Feldman & Kelley, Wilson & Haefner, in General Bibliography.

Barlow

EDITION:

The Political Writings of Joel Barlow, new edition with Joel Barlow: A Bibliographical List, prepared by Division of Bibliography, Library of Congress. New York: Burt Franklin, 1971.

STUDIES:

Arner, Robert D. "Joel Barlow's Poetics: 'Advice to a Raven in Russia.'" *Connecticut Review* 5 (1972): 38–43.
Lemay, J.A. Leo. "The Contexts and Themes of 'The Hasty-Pudding.'" *Early American Literature* 17 (1982): 3–23.
Woodress, James. *A Yankee's Odyssey: The Life of Joel Barlow*. Philadelphia: Lippincott, 1958.
Zatar, Rafia. "The Proof of the Pudding: Of Haggis, Hasty Pudding, and Transatlantic Influence." *Early American Literature* 31 (1996): 133–49.

Beddoes

EDITIONS:

Donner, H.W., ed. *The Works of Thomas Lovell Beddoes*. London: Oxford UP, 1935.
—. *The Letters of Thomas Lovell Beddoes*. London: Elkin Mathews and John Lane, 1894.

STUDIES:

Donner, H.W. *Thomas Lovell Beddoes: The Making of a Poet*. Oxford: Blackwell, 1935.
Ricks, Christopher. "I. Thomas Lovell Beddoes" and "II. Pilgrim Misery: Thomas Lovell Beddoes." *Grand Street* 1 (1982): 32–48 and 3 (1984): 90–102.

See also Reeves, Wolfson, under HOOD.

Blake

EDITIONS:

Bentley, Gerald E., Jr., ed. *William Blake: The Critical Heritage*. London: Routledge, 1975.
—, ed. *William Blake's Writings*. Oxford: Clarendon P, 1978.
Erdman, David V., gen. ed. *Blake's Illuminated Books*. 6 vols. London/Princeton: The William Blake Trust/Princeton UP, 1991–95. Available (without notes) in one volume as *William Blake: The Complete Illuminated Books*. New York: Thames and Hudson, 2001.
—, ed. *The Complete Poetry and Prose of William Blake*. Commentary by Harold Bloom. Rev. ed. Berkeley: U of California P, 1982.
—, ed. *The Notebook of William Blake: A Photographic and Typographic Facsimile*. New York: Readex, 1977.
Johnson, Mary Lynn, and John E. Grant, eds. *Blake's Poetry and Designs: Authoritative Texts, Illuminations in Color and Monochrome, Related Prose, Criticism*. New York: Norton, 1979.

STUDIES:

Behrendt, Stephen C. *Reading William Blake*. New York: St. Martin's P, 1992.
Bentley, G.E. *Blake Books: Annotated Catalogues of William Blake's Writings*. Oxford: Oxford UP, 1977.
—. *The Stranger from Paradise: A Biography of William Blake*. New Haven: Yale UP, 2001.
Bindman, David. *Blake as an Artist*. Oxford: Phaidon, 1977.
Blake, David, and Elliott Gruner. "Redeeming Captivity: The Negative Revolution of Blake's *Visions of the Daughters of Albion*." *Symbiosis* 1 (1997): 21–34.
Curran, Stuart, and Joseph Anthony Wittreich Jr., eds. *Blake's Sublime Allegory: Essays on* The Four Zoas, Milton, Jerusalem. Madison: U of Wisconsin P, 1973.
Damon, S. Foster. *A Blake Dictionary: The Ideas and Symbols of William Blake*. Rev. ed. Hanover, NH: UP of New England, 1988.
—. *William Blake: His Philosophy and Symbols*. Boston: Houghton Mifflin, 1924.
Damrosch, Leopold, Jr. *Symbol and Truth in Blake's Myth*. Princeton: Princeton UP, 1980.
De Luca, V.A. *Words of Eternity: Blake and the Poetics of the Sublime*. Princeton: Princeton UP, 1991.
Eaves, Morris. *The Counter-Arts Conspiracy: Art and Industry in the Age of Blake*. Ithaca: Cornell UP, 1992.
—. *William Blake's Theory of Art*. Princeton: Princeton UP, 1982.

Erdman, David V. *Blake, Prophet against Empire: A Poet's Interpretation of the History of his own Times*. Rev. ed. Princeton: Princeton UP, 1969.

—, et al., eds. *A Concordance to the Writings of William Blake*. Ithaca: Cornell UP, 1967.

Essick, Robert N. *William Blake and the Language of Adam*. Oxford: Clarendon P, 1989.

—. *William Blake, Printmaker*. Princeton: Princeton UP, 1980.

Frosch, Thomas R. *The Awakening of Albion: The Renovation of the Body in the Poetry of William Blake*. Ithaca: Cornell UP, 1974.

Frye, Northrop. *Fearful Symmetry: A Study of William Blake*. Princeton: Princeton UP, 1947.

Hilton, Nelson. *Literal Imagination: Blake's Vision of Words*. Berkeley: U of California P, 1983.

King, James. *William Blake: His Life*. New York: St. Martin's P, 1991.

Mellor, Anne K. *Blake's Human Form Divine*. Berkeley: U of California P, 1974.

Mitchell, W.J.T. *Blake's Composite Art: A Study of the Illuminated Poetry*. Princeton: Princeton UP, 1978.

Moskal, Jeanne. *Blake, Ethics and Forgiveness*. Tuscaloosa: U of Alabama P, 1994.

Nurmi, Martin K. *William Blake*. Kent, OH: Kent State UP, 1976.

Paley, Morton D. *The Continuing City: William Blake's Jerusalem*. Oxford: Clarendon P, 1983.

—. *Energy and the Imagination: A Study of the Development of Blake's Thought*. Oxford: Clarendon P, 1970.

—. *William Blake*. Oxford: Phaidon, 1978.

Raine, Kathleen. *William Blake*. New York: Praeger, 1971.

Thompson, E.P. *Witness against the Beast: William Blake and the Moral Law*. New York: New Press, 1993.

Viscomi, Joseph. *Blake and the Idea of the Book*. Princeton: Princeton UP, 1993.

Wilkie, Brian. *Blake's Thel and Oothoon*. English Literary Studies. Victoria, BC: U of Victoria, 1990.

Wittreich, Joseph Anthony, Jr. *Angel of Apocalypse: Blake's Idea of Milton*. Madison: U of Wisconsin P, 1975.

See also Schock, in General Bibliography; and Harrison, under PAINE.

Blamire

EDITION:

Lonsdale, Henry, ed. *The Poetical Works of Miss Susanna Blamire, "The Muse of Cumberland."* Preface, memoir, and notes by Patrick Maxwell. Edinburgh: John Menzies, 1842. Rpt. Oxford: Woodstock, 1994.

STUDY:

Wordsworth, Jonathan. *Susanna Blamire: Poet of Friendship, 1747–1794*. Privately published, 1995.

See also Behrendt & Linkin, in General Bibliography.

Bloomfield

EDITIONS:

Collected Poems (1800–1822). Rpt. introd. Jonathan N. Lawson. Gainesville: Scholars' Facsimiles and Reprints, 1971.

The Farmer's Boy, Rural Tales, Good Tidings, with An Essay on War. Rpt. with introd. Donald H. Reiman. New York: Garland, 1977.

Hart, W.H., ed. *Selections from the Correspondence of Robert Bloomfield, The Suffolk Poet*. London: Spottiswoode, 1870. Rpt. Redhill, Surrey: Commercial Lithographic Company, 1969.

STUDIES:

Lucas, John. "Bloomfield and Clare." *The Independent Spirit: John Clare and the Self-Taught Tradition*. Ed. John Goodridge. Helpston: John Clare Society/Margaret Grainger Memorial Trust, 1994. 55–68.

Wickett, William, and Nicholas Duval. *The Farmer's Boy: The Story of a Suffolk Poet*. Lavenham: Terence Dalton, 1971.

Zimmerman, Donald Mark. "The Medium of Antipastoral: Protest between the Lines of Bloomfield's *The Farmer's Boy*." *ANQ: A Quarterly Journal of Short Articles, Notes, and Reviews* 17 (2004): 35–39.

Bowles

EDITIONS:

Bowles, William Lisle. *Fourteen Sonnets, Elegiac and Descriptive. Written during a Tour*. 1789. Rpt. with nine other books. Introd. Donald H. Reiman. New York: Garland, 1978.

Greever, Garland, ed. *A Wiltshire Parson and his Friends: The Correspondence of William Lisle Bowles.* Boston: Houghton Mifflin, 1926.

STUDIES:

Fairbanks, A. Harris. "'Dear Native Brook': Coleridge, Bowles, and Thomas Warton, the Younger." *Wordsworth Circle* 6.4 (Autumn 1975): 313–15.

Ruddick, Bill. "'Genius of the Sacred Fountain of Tears': A Bicentenary Tribute to the Sonnets of William Lisle Bowles." *Charles Lamb Bulletin* ns 72 (1990): 276–84.

Brooke

EDITION:

Brooke, Charlotte. *Reliques of Irish Poetry.* 1789. Rpt. with *A Memoir of Miss Brooke* (1816), by Aaron Crossley Hobart Seymour. Introd. Leonard R.N. Ashley. Gainesville: Scholars' Facsimiles and Reprints, 1970.

STUDIES:

Davis, Leith. "Birth of the Nation: Gender and Writing in the Work of Henry and Charlotte Brooke." *Eighteenth-Century Life* 18 (1994): 27–47.

MacCraith, Mícheál. "Charlotte Brooke and James Macpherson." *Litteraria Pragensia: Studies in Literature and Culture* 10 (2000): 5–17.

Wright, Julia M. "'Sons of Song': Irish Literature in the Age of Nationalism." *Romantic Poetry.* Ed. Angela Esterhammer. Amsterdam: Benjamins, 2002. 333–53.

Brown

EDITION:

Krause, Sidney J., S.W. Reid, and Donald A. Ringe, eds. *The Novels and Related Works of Charles Brockden Brown: Bicentennial Edition.* 6 vols. Kent, OH: Kent State UP, 1977–1986.

STUDIES:

Axelrod, Alan. *Charles Brockden Brown: An American Tale.* Austin: U of Texas P, 1983.

Grabo, Norman S. *The Coincidental Art of Charles Brockden Brown.* Chapel Hill: U of North Carolina P, 1981.

See also Steinman, in General Bibliography; Clemit, under GODWIN.

Bryant

EDITIONS:

Bryant, William Cullen II, and Thomas G. Voss, eds. *The Letters of William Cullen Bryant.* 4 vols. New York: Fordham UP, 1975–84.

Bryant, W.C. II, ed. *Power for Sanity: Selected Editorials of William Cullen Bryant, 1829–1861.* 1994.

Godwin, Parke, ed. *Poetical Works of William Cullen Bryant.* New York: Russell & Russell, 1967.

STUDIES:

Brown, Charles Henry. *William Cullen Bryant.* New York: Scribner, 1971.

Krapf, Norbert, ed. *Under Open Sky: Poets on William Cullen Bryant.* New York: Fordham UP, 1986.

Burke

EDITIONS:

Copeland, Thomas W., et al., eds. *The Correspondence of Edmund Burke.* 10 vols. Chicago: U of Chicago P, 1958–78.

Langford, Paul, gen. ed. *The Writings and Speeches of Edmund Burke.* 8 vols. to date. Oxford: Clarendon P, 1981—.

STUDIES:

Boulton, James T. *The Language of Politics in the Age of Wilkes and Burke.* London: Routledge and Kegan Paul, 1963.

De Bruyn, Frans. *The Literary Genres of Edmund Burke: The Political Uses of Literary Form.* Oxford: Clarendon P, 1996.

Kramnick, Isaac. *The Rage of Edmund Burke: Portrait of an Ambivalent Conservative.* New York: Basic Books, 1977.

O'Brien, Conor Cruise. *The Great Melody: A Thematic Biography and Commented Anthology of Edmund Burke.* Chicago: U of Chicago P, 1992.

See also Butler, in General Bibliography.

Burney

EDITIONS:

Bloom, Edward A., ed. *Evelina; or, the History of a Young Lady's Entrance into the World.* Oxford: Oxford UP, 1968.

—, and Lillian D. Bloom, eds. *Camilla; or, A Picture of Youth.* Oxford: Oxford UP, 1972.

Doody, Margaret Anne, et al., eds. *The Wanderer; or, Female Difficulties.* Oxford: Oxford UP, 1991.

Hemlow, Joyce, et al., eds. *The Journals and Letters of Fanny Burney (Madame d'Arblay).* 12 vols. Oxford: Clarendon P, 1972–84.

STUDIES:
Doody, Margaret Anne. *Frances Burney: The Life in the Works*. New Brunswick, NJ: Rutgers UP, 1988.
Rogers, Katharine M. *Frances Burney: The World of "Female Difficulties."* New York: Harvester Wheatsheaf, 1990.
Straub, Kristina. *Divided Fictions: Fanny Burney and Feminine Strategy*. Lexington: UP of Kentucky, 1987.

See also Claudia L. Johnson, Todd, in General Bibliography.

Burns

EDITIONS:
Ferguson, J. De Lancey, and G. Ross Roy, eds. *The Letters of Robert Burns*. 2 vols. Oxford: Clarendon P, 1985.
Kinsley, James, ed. *The Poems and Songs of Robert Burns*. 3 vols. Oxford: Clarendon P, 1968.
Low, Donald A. *Robert Burns: The Critical Heritage*. London: Routledge, 1974.
—, ed. *The Songs of Robert Burns*. London: Routledge, 1993.

STUDIES:
Brown, Mary Ellen. *Burns and Tradition*. London: MacMillan, 1984.
Crawford, Robert, ed. *Robert Burns and Cultural Authority*. Edinburgh: Edinburgh UP, 1997.
Douglas, Hugh. *Robert Burns: The Tinder Heart*. Herndon, VA: Sutton, 1996.
Fowler, R.H. *Robert Burns*. London: Routledge, 1988.
McIlvanney, Liam. *Burns the Radical: Poetry and Politics in Late Eighteenth-Century Scotland*. East Linton: Tuckwell, 2002.
McIntyre, Ian. *Robert Burns: A Life*. London: Penguin, 2001.

See also Feldman & Kelley, in General Bibliography.

Byron

EDITIONS:
Lovell, Ernest J., Jr., ed. *His Very Self and Voice: Collected Conversations of Lord Byron*. New York: Macmillan, 1954.
—, ed. *Lady Blessington's Conversations of Lord Byron*. Princeton: Princeton UP, 1969.
—, ed. *Medwin's Conversations of Lord Byron*. Princeton: Princeton UP, 1966.
Marchand, Leslie A., ed. *Byron's Letters and Journals*. 12 vols. London: John Murray, 1973–82.
McGann, Jerome J., ed. *Lord Byron: The Complete Poetical Works*. 7 vols. Oxford: Clarendon P, 1980–93.
Rutherford, Andrew, ed. *Byron: The Critical Heritage*. London: Routledge and Kegan Paul, 1970.
Steffan, Truman Guy, E. Steffan, and Willis W. Pratt, eds. *Don Juan*. 1957. Rev. ed. London: Penguin, 1982.

STUDIES:
Beaty, Frederick L. *Byron the Satirist*. Dekalb: Northern Illinois UP, 1985.
Christensen, Jerome. *Lord Byron's Strength: Romantic Writing and Commercial Society*. Baltimore: Johns Hopkins UP, 1993.
Crompton, Louis. *Byron and Greek Love: Homophobia in 19th-Century England*. Berkeley: U of California P, 1985.
Franklin, Caroline. *Byron's Heroines*. Oxford: Clarendon, 1992.
Garber, Frederick. *Self, Text, and Romantic Irony: The Example of Byron*. Princeton: Princeton UP, 1988.
Graham, Peter W. *Don Juan and Regency England*. Charlottesville: UP of Virginia, 1990.
Haslett, Moyra. *Byron's Don Juan and the Don Juan Legend*. Oxford: Clarendon, 1997.
Levine, Alice, and Robert N. Keane, eds. *Rereading Byron: Essays Selected from Hofstra University's Byron Bicentennial Conference*. New York: Garland, 1993.
Manning, Peter J. *Byron and his Fictions*. Detroit: Wayne State UP, 1978.
Marchand, Leslie A. *Byron: A Biography*. 3 vols. New York: Knopf, 1957. Condensed as *Byron: A Portrait*. New York: Knopf, 1970.
McGann, Jerome J. *Byron and Romanticism*. Ed. James Soderholm. New York: Cambridge UP, 2002.
—. *Don Juan in Context*. London: J. Murray, 1976.
—. *Fiery Dust: Byron's Poetical Development*. Chicago: U of Chicago P, 1968.
—. "'My Brain is Feminine': Byron and the Poetry of Deception." *Byron: Augustan and Romantic*. Ed. Andrew Rutherford. Basingstoke: Macmillan, 1990. 26–51.
Moore, Doris Langley. *The Late Lord Byron: Posthumous Dramas*. Rev. ed. London: John Murray, 1976.
—. *Lord Byron: Accounts Rendered*. London: John Murray, 1974.
Robinson, Charles E. *Shelley and Byron: The Snake and Eagle Wreathed in Fight*. Baltimore: Johns Hopkins UP, 1976.
Roessel, David E. *In Byron's Shadow: Modern Greece in the English and American Imagination*. Oxford: Oxford UP, 2002.

Shilstone, Frederick W., ed. *Approaches to Teaching Byron's Poetry*. New York: MLA, 1991.
Storey, Mark. *Byron and the Eye of Appetite*. Basingstoke: Macmillan, 1986.
Thorslev, Peter L., Jr. *The Byronic Hero: Types and Prototypes*. Minneapolis: U of Minnesota P, 1962.
Watkins, Daniel P. *Social Relations in Byron's Eastern Tales*. Rutherford, NJ: Fairleigh Dickinson UP, 1987.

See also Bostetter, Favret & Watson, Jamison, Mellor, Richardson, Schock, in General Bibliography; Brewer, under BAILLIE; Paley, under CAMPBELL; Crane, under TRELAWNY.

Campbell

EDITIONS:
Beattie, William. *Life and Letters of Thomas Campbell*. 3 vols. London: Moxon, 1849.
Robertson, J. Logie, ed. *The Complete Poetical Works of Thomas Campbell*. London: Oxford UP, 1907.

STUDY:
Paley, Morton D. "Envisioning Lastness: Byron's 'Darkness,' Campbell's 'The Last Man,' and the Critical Aftermath." *Romanticism* 1 (1995): 1.14.

Canning and Frere

EDITIONS:
Canning, George. *Ulm and Trafalgar; The Poetical Works*. Rpt. with four books by William Gifford. Introd. Donald H. Reiman. New York: Garland, 1978.
Frere, Sir Bartle, and William Edward Frere, eds. *The Works of the Right Honourable John Hookham Frere in Verse and Prose*. Memoir by Sir Bartle Frere. 2nd ed. 3 vols. London: B.M. Pickering, 1874.
Frere, John Hookham. *Prospectus and Specimen of an Intended National Work*. 1817–18. Rpt. Introd. Donald H. Reiman. New York: Garland, 1978.
Morley, Henry, ed. *Parodies and Other Burlesque Pieces by George Canning, George Ellis, and John Hookham Frere, with the Whole Poetry of the Anti-Jacobin*. London: Routledge, 1890.

STUDIES:
Edgecombe, Rodney Stenning. "*Little Dorrit* and Canning's 'New Morality.'" *Modern Philology* 95 (1998): 484–89.
Hinde, Wendy. *George Canning*. New York: St. Martin's P, 1973.

Cary

EDITION:
Bentley, D.M.R., ed. *Abram's Plains: A Poem. By Thomas Cary*. London, ON: Canadian Poetry P, 1986.

STUDIES:
Bentley, D.M.R. "Thomas Cary's *Abram's Plains* and its Preface." *Canadian Poetry* 5 (1979): 1–28.
Glickman, Susan. "Canadian Prospects: *Abram's Plains* in Context." *University of Toronto Quarterly* 59 (1990): 498–515.

Cavendish

EDITION:
Foster, Vere, ed. *The Two Duchesses: Georgiana Duchess of Devonshire, Elizabeth Duchess of Devonshire: Family Correspondence of and relating to Georgiana, Duchess of Devonshire, Elizabeth, Duchess of Devonshire ... and others, 1777–1859*. 1898. Rpt. Bath: C. Chivers, 1972.

STUDIES:
Foreman, Amanda. *Georgiana, Duchess of Devonshire*. New York: Random House, 1998.
Stott, Anne. "'Female Patriotism': Georgiana, Duchess of Devonshire, and the Westminster Election of 1784." *Eighteenth-Century Life* 17 (1993): 60–84.

Chatterton

EDITION:
Taylor, Donald S., and Benjamin B. Hoover, eds. *The Complete Works of Thomas Chatterton: A Bicentenary Edition*. 2 vols. Oxford: Clarendon P, 1971.

STUDIES:
Groom, Nick, ed. *Thomas Chatterton and Romantic Culture*. Foreword by Peter Ackroyd. New York: St. Martin's P, 1999.
Haywood, Ian. *The Making of History: A Study of the Literary Forgeries of James Macpherson and Thomas Chatterton in Relation to Eighteenth-Century Ideas of History and Fiction*. Rutherford, NJ: Fairleigh Dickinson UP, 1986.
Kaplan, Louise J. *The Family Romance of the Impostor-Poet Thomas Chatterton*. New York: Atheneum, 1988.
Kelly, Linda. *The Marvellous Boy: The Life and Myth of Thomas Chatterton*. London: Weidenfeld and Nicolson, 1971.

Clare

EDITIONS:

John Clare: Poems Chiefly from Manuscript. London: R. Cobden-Sanderson, 1920.

Robinson, Eric, et al., eds. *The Early Poems of John Clare, 1804–1822.* 2 vols. Oxford: Clarendon P, 1989.

—, et al., eds. *The Later Poems of John Clare, 1837–1864.* 2 vols. Oxford: Oxford UP, 1984.

—, David Powell, and P.M.S. Dawson, eds. *Poems of the Middle Period, 1822–1837.* 5 vols. Oxford: Clarendon P, 1996—.

—, and David Powell, eds. *John Clare.* Oxford Standard Authors. New York: Oxford UP, 1984.

Robinson, Eric, and Geoffrey Summerfield, eds. *The Shepherd's Calendar.* London: Oxford UP, 1973.

Storey, Mark, ed. *The Letters of John Clare.* Oxford: Clarendon P, 1985.

Tibble, J.W., and Anne Tibble, eds. *The Prose of John Clare.* London: Routledge, 1951.

Williams, Merryn, and Raymond, eds. *John Clare: Selected Poetry and Prose.* London: Methuen, 1986.

STUDIES:

Barrell, John. *The Idea of Landscape and the Sense of Place, 1730–1840: An Approach to the Poetry of John Clare.* Cambridge: Cambridge UP, 1972.

Bate, Jonathan. *John Clare: A Biography.* London: Picador, 2003.

Haughton, Hugh, Adam Phillips, and Geoffrey Summerfield, eds. *John Clare in Context.* Cambridge: Cambridge UP, 1994.

Perkins, David. "Sweet Helpston! John Clare on Badger Baiting." *Studies in Romanticism* 38 (Fall 1999): 387–407.

Todd, Janet M. *In Adam's Garden: A Study of John Clare's Pre-Asylum Poetry.* Gainesville: U of Florida P, 1973.

See also Lucas, under BLOOMFIELD.

Clarkson

EDITIONS:

Clarkson, Thomas. *An Essay on the Slavery and Commerce of the Human Species, particularly the African.* 1786. Rpt. Miami: Mnemosyne, 1969.

—. *The History of the Rise, Progress, and Accomplishment of the Abolition of the African Slave-Trade by the British Parliament.* 1808. Rpt. London: Frank Cass, 1968.

Griggs, Earl Leslie, and Clifford H. Prator, eds. *Henry Christophe and Thomas Clarkson: A Correspondence.* Berkeley: U of California P, 1952.

STUDY:

Wilson, Ellen Gibson. *Thomas Clarkson: A Biography.* York: William Sessions, 1989.

Cobbett

STUDIES:

Spater, George. *William Cobbett: The Poor Man's Friend.* 2 vols. Cambridge: Cambridge UP, 1982.

Ulrich, John McAllister. *Signs of their Times: History, Labor, and the Body in Cobbett, Carlyle, and Disraeli.* Athens: Ohio UP, 2002.

Williams, Raymond. *Cobbett.* Oxford: Oxford UP, 1983.

Wilson, David A. *Paine and Cobbett: The Trans-Atlantic Connection.* Kingston: McGill-Queen's UP, 1988.

Coleridge

EDITIONS:

Coburn, Kathleen, gen. ed. *The Collected Works of Samuel Taylor Coleridge.* 16 vols. in 31. Princeton: Princeton UP, 1969–2001.

—, ed. *The Notebooks of Samuel Taylor Coleridge.* 3 vols. in 8. New York: Pantheon, 1957–83.

Engell, James, and W. Jackson Bate, eds. *Biographia Literaria.* Vol. 7 of Coburn, ed. *Collected Works.* 2 vols. 1983.

Griggs, Earl Leslie, ed. *Collected Letters of Samuel Taylor Coleridge.* 6 vols. Oxford: Clarendon P, 1956–73.

Jackson, J.R. de J., ed. *Coleridge: The Critical Heritage.* 2 vols. London: Routledge and Kegan Paul, 1970.

STUDIES:

Barfield, Owen. *What Coleridge Thought.* London: Oxford UP, 1972.

Bate, Walter Jackson. *Coleridge.* New York: Macmillan, 1968.

Burwick, Frederick, ed. *Coleridge's* Biographia Literaria: *Text and Meaning.* Columbus: Ohio State UP, 1989.

Christensen, Jerome. *Coleridge's Blessed Machine of Language.* Ithaca: Cornell UP, 1981.

Everest, Kelvin. *Coleridge's Secret Ministry: The Context of the Conversation Poems, 1795–1798.* New York: Barnes & Noble, 1979.

Ford, Jennifer. *Coleridge on Dreaming: Romanticism, Dreams, and the Medical Imagination.* Cambridge: Cambridge UP, 1998.

Holmes, Richard. *Coleridge: Early Visions*. London: Hodder and Stoughton, 1989.

—. *Coleridge: Darker Reflections*: London: Harper Collins, 1998.

Keane, Patrick J. *Coleridge's Submerged Politics: The Ancient Mariner and Robinson Crusoe*. Columbia: U of Missouri P, 1994.

Lefebure, Molly. *The Bondage of Love: A Life of Mrs. Samuel Taylor Coleridge*. London: Gollancz, 1986.

—. *Samuel Taylor Coleridge, A Bondage of Opium*. London: Gollancz, 1974.

Levere, Trevor H. *Poetry Realized in Nature: Samuel Taylor Coleridge and Early Nineteenth-Century Science*. Cambridge: Cambridge UP, 1981.

Lockridge, Laurence S. *Coleridge the Moralist*. Ithaca: Cornell UP, 1977.

Lowes, John Livingston. *The Road to Xanadu: A Study in the Ways of the Imagination*. Boston: Houghton Mifflin, 1927.

Magnuson, Paul A. *Coleridge's Nightmare Poetry*. Charlottesville: UP of Virginia, 1974.

McFarland, Thomas. *Coleridge and the Pantheist Tradition*. Oxford: Clarendon P, 1969.

McKusick, James C. *Coleridge's Philosophy of Language*. New Haven: Yale UP, 1986.

Morrow, John. *Coleridge's Political Thought: Property, Morality and the Limits of Traditional Discourse*. New York: St. Martin's P, 1990.

Paley, Morton D. *Coleridge's Later Poetry*. Oxford: Clarendon P, 1996.

Parker, Reeve. *Coleridge's Meditative Art*. Ithaca: Cornell UP, 1975.

Perry, Seamus, ed. *S.T. Coleridge: Interviews and Recollections*. New York: Palgrave, 2000.

Richards, I.A. *Coleridge on Imagination*. London: K. Paul, Trench, Trubner, 1934.

Roe, Nicholas. *Wordsworth and Coleridge: The Radical Years*. Oxford: Clarendon P, 1988.

Ruoff, Gene W. *Wordsworth and Coleridge: The Making of the Major Lyrics, 1802–1804*. New Brunswick, NJ: Rutgers UP, 1989.

Wallace, Catherine Miles. *The Design of Biographia Literaria*. London: Allen & Unwin, 1983.

Warren, Robert Penn. Introduction to "The Rime of the Ancient Mariner." New York: Reynal & Hitchcock, 1946.

Wheeler, Kathleen M. *Sources, Processes and Methods in Coleridge's Biographia Literaria*. Cambridge: Cambridge UP, 1980.

Willey, Basil. *Samuel Taylor Coleridge*. New York: Norton, 1973.

See also Abrams (*The Correspondent Breeze*, *The Milk of Paradise*), Bostetter, Hayter, McFarland (*Romanticism and the Forms of Ruin*), McGann, Rzepka, in General Bibliography; Fairbanks, under BOWLES; Matheson, under COWPER; Griggs, under PRINGLE; Vargo, under ROBINSON; Morton, under TAYLOR; Ros, Thompson, under THELWALL; Magnuson, Newlyn, under WORDSWORTH.

Cooper

EDITIONS:

Beard, James Franklin, ed. *Letters and Journals of James Fenimore Cooper*. 6 vols. Cambridge, MA: Harvard UP, 1960–68.

Cooper, James Fenimore. *Cooper's Novels*. 32 vols. New York: W.A. Townsend, 1859–61.

Dekker, George, and John P. McWilliams, eds. *Fenimore Cooper: The Critical Heritage*. London: Routledge and Kegan Paul, 1973.

STUDIES:

Adams, Charles Hansforth. *The Guardian of the Law: Authority and Identity in James Fenimore Cooper*. University Park: Penn State UP, 1990.

McWilliams, John. *Political Justice in a Republic: James Fenimore Cooper's America*. Berkeley: U of California P, 1972.

Railton, Stephen. *Fenimore Cooper: A Study of His Life and Imagination*. Princeton: Princeton UP, 1978.

Tompkins, Jane. *Sensational Designs: The Cultural Work of American Fiction, 1790–1860*. New York: Oxford UP, 1985.

Cowley

EDITION:

Link, Frederick M., ed. *The Plays of Hannah Cowley*. 2 vols. New York: Garland, 1979.

STUDY:

Elfenbein, Andrew. "Lesbian Aestheticism on the Eighteenth-Century Stage." *Eighteenth-Century Life* 25.1 (Winter 2001): 1–16.

See also entries under MERRY.

Cowper

EDITIONS:

Baird, John D., and Charles Ryskamp, eds. *The Poems of William Cowper.* 2 vols. Oxford: Clarendon P, 1980–95.

King, James, and Charles Ryskamp, eds. *The Letters and Prose Writings of William Cowper.* 5 vols. Oxford: Clarendon P, 1979–86.

STUDIES:

Hutchings, Bill. *The Poetry of William Cowper.* London: Croom Helm, 1983.

King, James. *William Cowper: A Biography.* Durham: Duke UP, 1986.

Matheson, Ann. "The Influence of Cowper's *The Task* on Coleridge's Conversation Poems." *New Approaches to Coleridge: Biographical and Critical Essays.* Ed. Donald Sultana. Totowa, NJ: Barnes and Noble, 1981. 137–50.

Crabbe

EDITIONS:

Dalrymple-Champneys, Norma, and Arthur Pollard, eds. *George Crabbe: The Complete Poetical Works.* 3 vols. Oxford: Clarendon P, 1988.

Edwards, Gavin, ed. *George Crabbe: Selected Poems.* London: Penguin, 1991.

Faulkner, Thomas C., ed., with the assistance of Rhonda L. Blair. *Selected Letters and Journals of George Crabbe.* Oxford: Clarendon P, 1985.

Pollard, Arthur, ed. *Crabbe: The Critical Heritage.* London: Routledge and Kegan Paul, 1972.

STUDIES:

Hatch, Ronald B. *Crabbe's Arabesque: Social Drama in the Poetry of George Crabbe.* Montreal: McGill-Queen's UP, 1976.

Powell, Neil. *George Crabbe: An English Life, 1754–1832.* London: Pimlico, 2004.

See also Abrams (*The Milk of Paradise*), Barrell, Williams, in General Bibliography; and Winborn, under MALTHUS.

Crèvecoeur

EDITIONS:

Adams, Percy G., ed. and trans. *Eighteenth-Century Travels in Pennsylvania and New York.* Lexington: U of Kentucky P, 1961.

Blake, Warren Barton, ed. *Letters from an American Farmer, and Sketches of Eighteenth-Century America: More Letters from an American Farmer.* London: Dent, 1962.

Moore, Dennis D. *More Letters from the American Farmer: An Edition of the Essays in English Left Unpublished by Crèvecoeur.* Athens: U of Georgia P, 1995.

STUDIES:

Allen, Gay Wilson, and Roger Asselineau. *St. John de Crèvecoeur: The Life of an American Farmer.* New York: Viking, 1987.

Cook, Elizabeth Heckendorn. *Epistolary Bodies: Gender and Genre in the Eighteenth-Century Republic of Letters.* Stanford: Stanford UP, 1996. 140–72.

Raban, Jonathan. *Hunting Mister Heartbreak: A Discovery of America.* New York: Edward Burlingame, 1991.

Ruttenburg, Nancy. *Democratic Personality: Popular Voice and the Trial of American Authorship.* Stanford: Stanford UP, 1998.

Cristall

EDITION:

Wu, Duncan, ed. *Romantic Women Poets: An Anthology.* Oxford: Blackwell, 1997. Contains the whole of *Poetical Sketches.*

STUDY:

See McGann, in General Bibliography.

Croker

EDITION:

Pool, Bernard, ed. *The Croker Papers: 1808–1857: New and Abridged Edition.* London: Batsford, 1967.

STUDIES:

Brightfield, Myron Franklin. *John Wilson Croker.* Berkeley: U of California P, 1940.

Morgan, Peter F. "Croker as Literary Critic in the *Quarterly Review.*" *Wordsworth Circle* 8 (1977): 62–68.

Riley, Paul. "John Wilson Croker and Keats' *Endymion.*" *Studies in the Humanities* 5.2 (1976): 32–37.

Cugoano

EDITION:

Cugoano, Ottobah. *Thoughts and Sentiments on the Evil of Slavery.* 1787. Rpt. Introd. Paul Edwards. London: Dawsons, 1969.

STUDIES:

Edwards, Paul. "Three West-African Writers of the 1780s." *The Slave's Narrative.* Ed. Charles T. Davis and Henry Louis Gates, Jr. Oxford: Oxford UP, 1985. 175–98.

Sandiford, Keith A. *Measuring the Moment: Strategies of Protest in Eighteenth-Century Afro-English Writing.* Selinsgrove, PA: Susquehanna UP, 1988.

See also Paul Edwards & David Dabydeen, in General Bibliography.

Dacre

EDITIONS:

Craciun, Adriana, ed. *Zofloya; or, The Moor: A Romance of the Fifteenth Century.* Peterborough: Broadview, 1997.

Dacre, Charlotte. *Hours of Solitude.* 1805. Rpt. Introd. Donald H. Reiman. New York: Garland, 1978.

STUDIES:

Craciun, Adriana. "'I hasten to be disembodied': Charlotte Dacre, the Demon Lover, and Representations of the Body." *European Romantic Review* 6 (1995): 75–97.

Jones, Ann H. *Ideas and Innovations: Best Sellers of Jane Austen's Age.* New York: AMS, 1986.

McGann, Jerome J. "'My Brain is Feminine': Byron and the Poetry of Deception." *Byron: Augustan and Romantic.* Ed. Andrew Rutherford. New York: St. Martin's P, 1990. 26–51.

Darwin

EDITIONS:

Darwin, Erasmus. *The Botanic Garden.* 1791. 2 vols. in 1. Rpt. Menston: Scolar, 1973.

—. *The Temple of Nature.* 1803. Rpt. Menston: Scolar, 1973.

King-Hele, Desmond, ed. *The Letters of Erasmus Darwin.* Cambridge: Cambridge UP, 1981.

STUDIES:

King-Hele, Desmond. *Erasmus Darwin: A Life of Unequalled Achievement.* London: DLM, 1999.

—. *Erasmus Darwin and the Romantic Poets.* London: Macmillan, 1986.

De Quincey

EDITIONS:

De Quincey, Thomas. *Confessions of an English Opium-Eater.* 1822. Oxford: Woodstock, 1989.

Jordan, John E., ed. *De Quincey as Critic.* London: Routledge and Kegan Paul, 1973.

Lindop, Grevel, gen. ed. *The Works of Thomas De Quincey.* 21 vols. London: Pickering and Chatto, 2000–02.

STUDIES:

Barrell, John. *The Infection of Thomas De Quincey: A Psychopathology of Imperialism.* New Haven: Yale UP, 1991.

Baxter, Edmund. *De Quincey's Art of Autobiography.* Edinburgh: Edinburgh UP, 1990.

Clej, Alina. *A Genealogy of the Modern Self: Thomas De Quincey and the Intoxication of Writing.* Stanford: Stanford UP, 1995.

De Luca, V.A. *Thomas De Quincey: The Prose of Vision.* Toronto: U of Toronto P, 1980.

Devlin, D.D. *De Quincey, Wordsworth, and the Art of Prose.* London: Macmillan, 1983.

Karbiener, Karen. "Cross-Cultural Confessions: America Passes Judgment on Thomas De Quincey." *Symbiosis* 3 (1999): 119–30.

Lindop, Grevel. *The Opium-Eater: A Life of Thomas De Quincey.* London: Dent, 1981.

Miller, J. Hillis. *The Disappearance of God: Five Nineteenth-Century Writers.* Cambridge MA: Harvard UP/Belknap P, 1963.

Rzepka, Charles J. *Sacramental Commodities: Gift, Text, and the Sublime in De Quincey.* Amherst: U of Massachussetts P, 1995.

Russett, Margaret. *De Quincey's Romanticism: Canonical Minority and the Forms of Transmission.* Cambridge: Cambridge UP, 1997.

See also Abrams (*The Milk of Paradise*), Hayter, Leask, McFarland (*Romantic Cruxes*), in General Bibliography.

Derozio

EDITIONS:

Mukhopadhyay, Abirlal, et al., eds. *Song of the Stormy Petrel: Complete Works of Henry Louis Vivian Derozio.* Calcutta: Progressive Publishers, 2001.

Poems of Henry Louis Vivian Derozio: A Forgotten Anglo-Indian Poet. Introd. F.B. Bradley-Birt. Oxford: Humphrey Milford/Oxford UP, 1923.

STUDIES:

Mukherji, Sajni Kripalani. "The Hindu College: Henry Derozio and Michael Madhusudan Dutt." *A History of Indian Literature in English.* Ed. Arvind Krishna Mehrotra. New York: Columbia UP, 2003. 41–52.

Nair, K.R. Ramachandran. *Three Indo-Anglian Poets: Henry Derozio, Toru Dutt and Sarojini Naidu.* New Delhi: Sterling, 1987.

Edgeworth

EDITION:

Butler, Marilyn, and W.J. McCormack, eds. *The Works of Maria Edgeworth*. 12 vols. London: Pickering & Chatto, 1996.

STUDIES:

Butler, Marilyn. *Maria Edgeworth: A Literary Biography*. Oxford: Oxford UP, 1972.

Kelly, Gary. "Amelia Opie, Lady Caroline Lamb, and Maria Edgeworth: Official and Unofficial Ideology." *ARIEL: A Review of International English Literature* 12/4 (October 1981): 3–24.

Kowaleski-Wallace, Elizabeth. *Their Fathers' Daughters: Hannah More, Maria Edgeworth, and Patriarchal Complicity*. New York: Oxford UP, 1991.

Lane, Maggie. *Literary Daughters*. New York: St. Martin's P, 1989.

See also Feldman & Kelley, Ferguson, in General Bibliography.

Elliott

EDITION:

Elliott, Edwin, ed. *The Poetical Works of Ebenezer Elliott: A New and Revised Edition*. 2 vols. London: Henry S. King & Co., 1876.

STUDY:

Morris, K., and Ray Hearne. *Ebenezer Elliott: Corn Law Rhymer and Poet of the Poor*. Rotherham: Rotherwood, 2002.

Equiano

EDITIONS:

Allison, Robert J., ed. *The Interesting Narrative of the Life of Olaudah Equiano*. Boston: Bedford/St. Martin's P, 1995.

Costanzo, Angelo, ed. *The Interesting Narrative of the Life of Olaudah Equiano, or Gustavus Vassa, the African. Written by Himself*. Peterborough: Broadview, 2001.

STUDIES:

Carretta, Vincent. *Equiano, the African: Biography of a Self-Made Man*. Athens: U of Georgia P, 2005.

Costanzo, Angelo. *Surprizing Narrative: Olaudah Equiano and the Beginnings of Black Autobiography*. New York: Greenwood, 1987.

Edwards, Paul. "Three West African Writers of the 1780s." *The Slave's Narrative*. Ed. Charles T. Davis and Henry Louis Gates, Jr. Oxford: Oxford UP, 1985. 175–98.

Plasa, Carl. *Textual Politics from Slavery to Postcolonialism: Race and Identification*. New York: St. Martin's P, 2000.

Walvin, James. *An African's Life: The Life and Times of Olaudah Equiano, 1745–1797*. New York: Cassell, 1998.

See also Gates, under PRINCE; and Edwards, under SANCHO.

Fanshawe

EDITION:

The Literary Remains of Catherine Maria Fanshawe, with Notes by the Reverend William Harness. London: B.M. Pickering, 1876.

Field

EDITION:

Edwards, Richard, ed. *First Fruits of Australian Poetry: Correctly reprinted from the rare first edition of 1819 with three poems included in the second edition of 1823*. Sydney: Barn on the Hill, 1941.

STUDIES:

Bishop, T.G. "Ceremonies of Separation in Australian Literature." *Kentucky Review* 12 (1995): 19–39.

Cousins, A.D. "Barron Field and the Translation of Romanticism to Colonial Australia." *Southerly* 58.4 (Summer 1998): 157–74.

Franklin

EDITIONS:

Bell, Whitfield J., Jr., ed. *The Complete Poor Richard Almanacks, published by Benjamin Franklin*. Barre, MA: Imprint Society, 1970.

Isaacson, Walter, ed. *A Benjamin Franklin Reader*. New York: Simon and Schuster, 2003.

Labaree, Leonard W., and William Bradford Willcox, eds. *The Papers of Benjamin Franklin*. 37 vols. New Haven: Yale UP, 1960–99.

Labaree, Leonard W., et al., eds. *The Autobiography of Benjamin Franklin*. New Haven: Yale UP, 1964.

STUDIES:

Blair, Walter, and Hamlin Hill. *America's Humor: From Poor Richard to Doonesbury*. New York: Oxford UP, 1978.

Isaacson, Walter. *Benjamin Franklin: An American Life*. New York: Simon and Schuster, 2003.

Lemay, J.A. Leo, ed. *Reappraising Benjamin Franklin; A Bicentennial Perspective*. Cranbury, NJ: Associated UP, 1993.

Freneau

EDITIONS:

Clark, Harry Hayden, ed. *Letters on Various Interesting and Important Subjects*. 1943.

—, ed. *Poems of Freneau*. 1929. Rpt. New York: Hafner, 1960.

Hiltner, Judith R., ed. *The Newspaper Verse of Philip Freneau: An Edition and Bibliographical Survey*. Troy, NY: Whitston, 1986.

Marsh, Philip M., ed. *The Prose of Philip Freneau*. New Brunswick, NJ: Scarecrow, 1955.

Pattee, Fred Lewis, ed. *The Poems of Philip Freneau, Poet of the American Revolution*. 3 vols. Princeton: Princeton University Library, 1902–07.

STUDIES:

Marsh, Philip M. *The Works of Philip Freneau: A Critical Study*. Metuchen, NJ: Scarecrow, 1968.

Vitzthum, Richard C. *Land and Sea: The Lyric Poems of Philip Freneau*. Minneapolis: U of Minnesota P, 1978.

Godwin

EDITIONS:

Clemit, Pamela, and Gina Luria Walker, eds. *Memoirs of the Author of* A Vindication of the Rights of Woman. Peterborough: Broadview, 2001.

Handwerk, Gary, and A.A. Markley, eds. *Caleb Williams*. Peterborough: Broadview, 2000.

Holmes, Richard, ed. *Mary Wollstonecraft:* A Short Residence in Sweden, Norway and Denmark *and William Godwin:* Memoirs of the Author of "The Rights of Woman." London: Penguin, 1987.

Philp, Mark, Pamela Clemit, and Martin Fitzpatrick, eds. *Political and Philosophical Writings of William Godwin*. 7 vols. London: Pickering, 1993.

Philp, Mark, Pamela Clemit, and Maurice Hindle, eds. *Collected Novels and Memoirs of William Godwin*. 8 vols. London: Pickering, 1992.

Priestley, F.E.L., ed. *Enquiry concerning Political Justice and its Influence on Morals and Happiness*. 3rd ed. 2 vols. Toronto: U of Toronto P, 1946.

Wardle, Ralph M., ed. *Godwin and Mary: Letters of William Godwin and Mary Wollstonecraft*. Lawrence: Kansas UP, 1966.

STUDIES:

Clemit, Pamela. *The Godwinian Novel: The Rational Fictions of Godwin, Brockden Brown, Mary Shelley*. Oxford: Clarendon P, 1993.

Kelly, Gary. *The English Jacobin Novel, 1780–1805*. Oxford: Clarendon P, 1976.

St. Clair, William. *The Godwins and the Shelleys: The Biography of a Family*. London: Faber, 1989.

Woodcock, George. "Things as they Might Be, Things as they Are: Notes on the Novels of William Godwin." *Dalhousie Review* 54 (Winter 1974–75): 685–97.

See also Butler, Steinman, in General Bibliography.

Goldsmith (1)

EDITIONS:

Balderston, Katharine C., ed. *The Collected Letters of Oliver Goldsmith*. 1928. Rpt. Folcroft, PA: Folcroft Library Editions, 1969.

Friedman, Arthur, ed. *Collected Works of Oliver Goldsmith*. 5 vols. Oxford: Clarendon P, 1966.

Rousseau, G.S., ed. *Goldsmith: The Critical Heritage*. London: Routledge and Kegan Paul, 1974.

STUDIES:

Ginger, John. *The Notable Man: The Life and Times of Oliver Goldsmith*. London: Hamish Hamilton, 1977.

Newey, Vincent. "Goldsmith's 'Pensive Plain': Re-Viewing *The Deserted Village*." *Early Romantics: Perspectives in British Poetry from Pope to Wordsworth*. Ed. Thomas Woodman. New York: St. Martin's P, 1998. 93–116.

Goldsmith (2)

EDITIONS:

Lynch, Gerald, ed. *The Rising Village*. London, ON: Canadian Poetry Press, 1989.

Myatt, Wilfrid E., ed. *Autobiography of Oliver Goldsmith: A Chapter in Canada's Literary History*. Foreword by Phyllis R. Blakeley. 2nd ed. Hantsport, NS: Lancelot, 1985.

STUDIES:

Keith, W.J. "*The Rising Village* Again." *Canadian Poetry* 3 (1978): 1–13.

Lynch, Gerald. "Oliver Goldsmith's *The Rising Village*: Controlling Nature." *Canadian Poetry* 6 (1980): 35–49.

Grant

EDITION:

Grant, J.P. *Memoir and Correspondence of Mrs. Grant of Laggan.* 3 vols. London: Longman, Brown, Green, and Longmans, 1844.

Hands

EDITION:

The Death of Amnon. A Poem. With an Appendix: containing Pastorals, and other Poetical Pieces. 1789. Rpt. with *The Rural Lyre*, by Ann Yearsley. Introd. Caroline Franklin. London: Routledge/Thoemmes, 1996.

STUDY:

Dereli, Cynthia. "In Search of a Poet: The Life and Work of Elizabeth Hands." *Women's Writing* 8.1 (March 2001): 169–82.

See also Landry, in General Bibliography.

Hawthorne

EDITIONS:

Charvat, William, Fredson Bowers, et al., gen. eds. *The Centenary Edition of the Works of Nathaniel Hawthorne.* 20 vols. to date. Columbus: Ohio State UP, 1962—.

McIntosh, James, ed. *Nathaniel Hawthorne's Tales: Authoritative Texts, Backgrounds, Criticism.* New York: Norton, 1987.

Myerson, Joel, ed. *Selected Letters of Nathaniel Hawthorne.* Columbus: Ohio State UP, 2002.

Pearce, Roy Harvey, ed. *Nathaniel Hawthorne: Tales and Sketches.* New York: Library of America, 1982.

STUDIES:

Bercovitch, Sacvan. *The Office of The Scarlet Letter.* Baltimore: Johns Hopkins UP, 1991.

Crews, Frederick. *The Sins of the Fathers: Hawthorne's Psychological Themes, with a New Afterword.* Berkeley: U of California P, 1989.

James, Henry. *Hawthorne.* New York: Harper, 1879.

Levin, Harry. *The Power of Blackness: Hawthorne, Poe, Melville.* New York: Knopf, 1958.

Miller, J. Hillis. *Hawthorne and History: Defacing It.* Cambridge: Blackwell, 1991.

Valenti, Patricia Dunlavy. *Sophia Peabody Hawthorne: A Life.* Columbia: U of Missouri P, 2004.

Hays

EDITIONS:

Appeal to the Men of Great Britain in Behalf of the Women. 1798. Rpt. Introd. Gina Luria. New York: Garland, 1974.

Brookes, Marilyn L., ed. *Memoirs of Emma Courtney.* Peterborough: Broadview, 2000.

Ty, Eleanor, ed. *The Victim of Prejudice.* 2nd ed. Peterborough: Broadview, 1998.

Wedd, A.F., ed. *The Fate of the Fenwicks: Letters to Mary Hays (1796–1828).* London: Methuen, 1927.

—, ed. *The Love-Letters of Mary Hays (1779–1780).* London: Methuen, 1925.

STUDIES:

Rajan, Tilottama. "Autonarration and Genotext in Mary Hays' *Memoirs of Emma Courtney.*" *Studies in Romanticism* 32 (Summer 1993): 149–76.

Waters, Mary A. "'The First of a New Genus': Mary Wollstonecraft as a Literary Critic and Mentor to Mary Hays." *Eighteenth-Century Studies* 37.3 (Spring 2004): 415–34.

See also Kelly (*Women, Writing and Revolution*) and Ty, in General Bibliography.

Hazlitt

EDITIONS:

Bonner, William Hallam, and Gerald Lahey, eds. *The Letters of William Hazlitt.* London: Macmillan, 1979.

Howe, P.P., ed. *The Complete Works of William Hazlitt.* 21 vols. London: Dent, 1930–34.

The Spirit of the Age. Introd. Robert Woof. Foreword by Michael Foot. Grasmere: Wordsworth Trust, 2004.

STUDIES:

Bromwich, David. *Hazlitt: The Mind of a Critic.* New York: Oxford UP, 1983.

Grayling, A.C. *The Quarrel of the Age: The Life and Times of William Hazlitt.* London: Weidenfeld and Nicolson, 2000.

Jones, Stanley. *Hazlitt, a Life: From Winterslow to Frith Street.* Oxford: Clarendon P, 1989.

Kinnaird, John. *William Hazlitt, Critic of Power.* New York: Columbia UP, 1978.

Mahoney, Charles. *Romantics and Renegades: The Poetics of Political Reaction.* Basingstoke: Palgrave/Macmillan, 2003.

See also McFarland (*Romantic Cruxes*) and Wellek, in General Bibliography.

Hearne

EDITION:

Glover, Richard, ed. *A Journey from Prince of Wales's Fort in Hudson's Bay to the Northern Ocean 1769, 1770, 1771, 1772.* Toronto: Macmillan, 1958.

Hemans

EDITIONS:

Feldman, Paula R., ed. *Records of Woman, with other poems.* Lexington: UP of Kentucky, 1999.

Kelly, Gary, ed. *Felicia Hemans: Selected Poems, Prose, and Letters.* Peterborough: Broadview, 2002.

Wolfson, Susan J., ed. *Felicia Hemans: Selected Poems, Letters, Reception Materials.* Princeton: Princeton UP, 2000.

—, and Elizabeth Fay, eds. *The Siege of Valencia: A Parallel Text Edition.* Peterborough: Broadview, 2002.

STUDIES:

Armstrong, Isobel. *Victorian Poetry: Poetry, Poetics and Politics.* New York: Routledge, 1993. Chap. 12.

Clarke, Norma. *Ambitious Heights: Writing, Friendship, Love: The Jewsbury Sisters, Felicia Hemans, and Jane Welsh Carlyle.* London: Routledge, 1990.

Leighton, Angela. *Victorian Women Poets: Writing against the Heart.* Charlottesville: U of Virginia P, 1992.

Sweet, Nanora, and Julie Melnyk, eds. *Felicia Hemans: Reimagining Poetry in the Nineteenth Century.* Foreword by Marlon B. Ross. New York: Palgrave, 2001.

See also Favret & Watson, Feldman & Kelley, Wilson & Haefner, McGann (*Poetics of Sensibility*), and Mellor (*Romanticism and Gender*), in General Bibliography.

Hogg

EDITIONS:

Carey, John, ed. *The Private Memoirs and Confessions of a Justified Sinner.* Oxford: Oxford UP, 1981.

Groves, David, ed. *Selected Poems and Songs.* Edinburgh: Scottish Academic P, 1986.

—, Antony Hasler, and Douglas S. Mack, eds. *The Three Perils of Woman; or, Love, Leasing, and Jealousy: A Series of Domestic Scottish Tales.* Edinburgh: Edinburgh UP, 1995.

Mack, Douglas S., ed. *The Collected Works of James Hogg.* 13 vols. to date. Edinburgh: Edinburgh UP, 1995—.

STUDY:

Gifford, Douglas. *James Hogg.* Edinburgh: Ramsay Head, 1976.

Hone

EDITIONS:

Kent, David A., and D.R. Ewen, eds. *Regency Radical: Selected Writings of William Hone.* Detroit: Wayne State UP, 2003.

Rickword, Edgell, ed. *Radical Squibs & Loyal Ripostes: Satirical Pamphlets of the Regency Period, 1819–1821.* Illustrated by George Cruikshank and Others. New York: Barnes and Noble, 1971.

STUDY:

Wood, Marcus. *Radical Satire and Print Culture, 1790–1822.* Oxford: Clarendon P, 1994.

See also Olivia Smith, in General Bibliography.

Hood

EDITIONS:

Clubbe, John, ed. *Selected Poems of Thomas Hood.* Cambridge MA: Harvard UP, 1970.

Jerrold, Walter, ed. *The Complete Poetical Works of Thomas Hood.* London: Oxford UP, 1920.

Morgan, Peter F., ed. *The Letters of Thomas Hood.* Toronto: U of Toronto P, 1973.

STUDIES:

Clubbe, John. *Victorian Forerunner: The Later Career of Thomas Hood.* Durham, NC: Duke UP, 1968.

Reeves, James. *Five Late Romantic Poets: George Darley, Hartley Coleridge, Thomas Hood, Thomas Lovell Beddoes, Emily Brontë.* London: Heinemann, 1974.

Wolfson, Susan J. "Representing Some Late Romantic-Era, Non-Canonical Male Poets: Thomas Hood, Winthrop Mackworth Praed, Thomas Lovell Beddoes." *Romanticism on the Net* 19 (August 2000): n.p. <http://www.erudit.org/revue/ron/2000/v/n19/005932ar.html>.

Hunt

EDITIONS:

Gates, Eleanor M., ed. *Leigh Hunt: A Life in Letters, together with some Correspondence of William Hazlitt.* Essex, CT: Falls River, 1998.

Milford, H.S., ed. *The Poetical Works of Leigh Hunt*. 1923. Rpt. New York: AMS, 1978.

STUDIES:

Blainey, Ann. *Immortal Boy: A Portrait of Leigh Hunt*. New York: St. Martin's P, 1985.

Mizukoshi, Ayumi. *Keats, Hunt, and the Aesthetics of Pleasure*. New York: Palgrave, 2001.

Turley, Richard Marggraf. *The Politics of Language in Romantic Literature*. New York: Palgrave Macmillan, 2002.

Inchbald

EDITIONS:

Backscheider, Paula R., ed. *The Plays of Elizabeth Inchbald*. 2 vols. New York: Garland, 1980.

Manvell, Roger, ed. *Selected Comedies*. Lanham, MD: UP of America, 1987.

Tompkins, J.M.S., ed. *A Simple Story*. London: Oxford UP, 1967.

STUDIES:

Jenkins, Annibel. *I'll Tell You What: The Life of Elizabeth Inchbald*. Lexington: UP of Kentucky, 2003.

Manvell, Roger. *Elizabeth Inchbald: England's Principal Woman Dramatist and Independent Woman of Letters in 18th-Century London: A Biographical Study*. Lanham, MD: UP of America, 1987.

See also Kelly (*The English Jacobin Novel*), in General Bibliography.

Irving

EDITIONS:

Pochmann, Henry A., Richard Dilworth Rust, and Herbert L. Kleinfeld, eds. *The Complete Works of Washington Irving*. 30 vols. Madison: U of Wisconsin P/Boston: Twayne, 1969–89.

Tuttleton, James W., ed. *History, Tales, and Sketches*. New York: Library of America, 1983.

STUDIES:

Antelyes, Peter. *Tales of Adventurous Enterprise: Washington Irving and the Poetics of Western Expansion*. New York: Columbia UP, 1990.

Johnston, Johanna. *The Heart that would not Hold: A Biography of Washington Irving*. New York: Evans, 1971.

Roth, Martin. *Comedy and America: The Lost World of Washington Irving*. Port Washington, NY: Kennikat, 1976.

Rubin-Dorsky, Jeffrey. *Adrift in the Old World: The Psychological Pilgrimage of Washington Irving*. Chicago: U of Chicago P, 1988.

Jefferson

EDITIONS:

Appleby, Joyce, and Terence Ball, eds. *Thomas Jefferson: Political Writings*. Cambridge: Cambridge UP, 1999.

Boyd, Julian P., ed. *The Declaration of Independence: The Evolution of the Text*. Washington and Charlottesville: Library of Congress in association with the Thomas Jefferson Memorial Foundation, 1999.

Peterson, Merrill D., ed. *Writings:* Autobiography, Notes on the State of Virginia, *Public and Private Papers, Addresses, Letters*. New York: Library of America, 1984.

Wilstach, Paul, ed. *Correspondence between John Adams and Thomas Jefferson (1812–1826)*. Indianapolis: Bobbs Merrill, 1925.

STUDIES:

Bernstein, R.B. *Thomas Jefferson*. New York: Oxford UP, 2003.

Ellis, Joseph J. *American Sphinx: The Character of Thomas Jefferson*. New York: Knopf, 1997.

Vidal, Gore. *Inventing a Nation: Washington, Adams, Jefferson*. New Haven: Yale UP, 2003.

Wills, Garry. *Inventing America: Jefferson's Declaration of Independence*. Garden City, NY: Doubleday, 1978.

See also Maier, in General Bibliography.

Jeffrey

EDITIONS:

Morgan, Peter F., ed. *Jeffrey's Criticism: A Selection*. Edinburgh: Scottish Academic, 1983.

Wordsworth, Jonathan, ed. *Francis Jeffrey: On the Lake Poets*. Poole: Woodstock, 1998.

STUDY:

Flynn, Philip. *Francis Jeffrey*. Newark: U of Delaware P, 1977.

Keats

EDITIONS:

Matthews, G.M., ed. *Keats: The Critical Heritage*. London: Routledge and K. Paul, 1971.

Rollins, Hyder Edward, ed. *The Keats Circle: Letters and Papers and More Letters and Papers of the Keats Circle*. Rev. ed. 2 vols. Cambridge, MA: Harvard UP, 1965.

—, ed. *The Letters of John Keats*. 2 vols. Cambridge, MA: Harvard UP, 1958.

Stillinger, Jack, ed. *The Poems of John Keats*. Cambridge, MA: Harvard UP/ Belknap P, 1978.

STUDIES:

Bate, W. Jackson. *John Keats*. 1963. New York: Oxford UP, 1966.

Brooks, Cleanth. *The Well-Wrought Urn: Studies in the Structure of Poetry*. 1947. New York: Harcourt, 1975.

Bush, Douglas. *John Keats: His Life and Writings*. New York: Macmillan, 1966.

De Almeida, Hermione. *Romantic Medicine and John Keats*. New York: Oxford UP, 1991.

Goellnicht, Donald C. *The Poet Physician: Keats and Medical Science*. Pittsbrgh, PA: Pittsburgh UP, 1984.

Levinson, Marjorie. *Keats's Life of Allegory: The Origins of a Style*. Oxford: Blackwell, 1988.

McFarland, Thomas. *The Masks of Keats: The Endeavour of a Poet*. Oxford: Oxford UP, 2000.

Motion, Andrew. *Keats*. London: Faber, 1997.

Ricks, Christopher. *Keats and Embarrassment*. Oxford: Clarendon P, 1974.

Roe, Nicholas. *John Keats and the Culture of Dissent*. New York: Clarendon P, 1997.

Ryan, Robert M. *Keats: The Religious Sense*. Princeton: Princeton UP, 1976.

Sperry, Stuart. *Keats the Poet*. 1973. Princeton: Princeton UP, 1994.

Stillinger, Jack. *The Hoodwinking of Madeline, and Other Essays on Keats's Poems*. Urbana: U of Illinois P, 1971.

—. *Reading "The Eve of St. Agnes": The Multiples of Complex Literary Transaction*. New York: Oxford UP, 1999.

—. *The Texts of Keats' Poems*. Cambridge, MA: Harvard UP, 1974.

Vendler, Helen. *The Odes of John Keats*. Cambridge, MA: Harvard UP, 1983.

Waldoff, Leon. *Keats and the Silent Work of Imagination*. Urbana: U of Illinois P, 1985.

Ward, Aileen. *John Keats: The Making of a Poet*. Rev. ed. New York: Farrar, Straus, and Giroux, 1986.

Wasserman, Earl. *The Finer Tone: Keats' Major Poems*. Baltimore: Johns Hopkins UP, 1953.

Watkins, Daniel P. *Keats's Poetry and the Politics of Imagination*. Rutherford, NJ: Fairleigh Dickinson UP, 1989.

Wolfson, Susan J. *The Questioning Presence: Wordsworth, Keats, and the Interrogative Mode in Romantic Poetry*. Ithaca: Cornell UP, 1986.

See also Bostetter, Perkins, Rajan, Rzepka, in General Bibliography; Riley, under CROKER; Mizukoshi, under HUNT.

Caroline Lamb

EDITION:

Wilson, Frances, ed. *Glenarvon*. London: Everyman, 1995.

STUDIES:

Blyth, Henry. *Caro: The Fatal Passion*. New York: Coward, McCann and Geoghegan, 1973.

Kelsall, Malcolm. "The Byronic Hero and Revolution in Ireland: The Politics of *Glenarvon*." *The Byron Journal* 19 (1991): 53–68.

Wu, Duncan. "Appropriating Byron: Lady Caroline Lamb's *A New Canto*." *Wordsworth Circle* 26.3 (1995): 140–46.

See also Kelly, under EDGEWORTH.

Mary and Charles Lamb

EDITIONS:

Lopate, Phillip, ed. *Essays of Elia*. Iowa City: U of Iowa P, 2003.

Lucas, E.V., ed. *The Works of Charles and Mary Lamb*. 7 vols. London: Methuen, 1903–05.

Marrs, Edwin W., Jr., ed. *The Letters of Charles and Mary Anne Lamb*. 3 vols. Ithaca: Cornell UP, 1975–78.

STUDIES:

Aaron, Jane. *A Double Singleness: Gender and the Writings of Charles and Mary Lamb*. Oxford: Clarendon P, 1991.

Burton, Sarah. *A Double Life: A Biography of Charles and Mary Lamb*. London: Viking, 2003.

Courtney, Winifred F. *Young Charles Lamb, 1775–1802*. London: Macmillan, 1982.

Hussey, Cyril C. "Fresh Light on the Poems of Mary Lamb." *Charles Lamb Bulletin* Supplement, 1972.

Pollin, Burton R. "Charles Lamb and Charles Lloyd as Jacobins and Anti-Jacobins." *Studies in Romanticism* 12 (Summer 1973): 633–47.

Polowetzky, Michael. *Prominent Sisters: Mary Lamb, Dorothy Wordsworth, and Sarah Disraeli*. Westport, CT: Praeger, 1996.

Randel, Fred V. *The World of Elia: Charles Lamb's Essayistic Romanticism*. Port Washington, NY: Kennikat, 1975.

See also McFarland (*Romantic Cruxes*), in General Bibliography; and entries under LLOYD.

Landon

EDITIONS:

McGann, Jerome J., and Daniel Riess, eds. *Letitia Elizabeth Landon: Selected Writings*. Peterborough: Broadview, 1997.

Wordsworth, Jonathan, introd. *The Improvisatrice*. Poole: Woodstock, 1996.

STUDIES:

Armstrong, Isobel. *Victorian Poetry: Poetry, Poetics, and Politics*. London: Routledge, 1993. Chap. 12.

Greer, Germaine. *Slip-Shod Sibyls: Recognition, Rejection and the Woman Poet*. London: Viking, 1995.

Leighton, Angela. *Victorian Women Poets: Writing against the Heart.* Charlottesville: U of Virginia P, 1993. Chap. 2.

Linkin, Harriet K. "Romantic Aesthetics in Mary Tighe and Letitia Landon: How Women Poets Recuperate the Gaze." *European Romantic Review* 7 (Winter 1997): 159–88.

Stephenson, Glennis. *Letitia Landon: The Woman behind L.E.L.* Manchester: Manchester UP, 1995.

See also Mellor (*Romanticism and Gender*), Pascoe, Ross, in General Bibliography.

Landor

EDITIONS:

De Selincourt, Ernest, ed. *Imaginary Conversations*. London: Humphrey Milford, 1928.

Hanley, Keith, ed. *Walter Savage Landor: Selected Poetry and Prose*. Manchester: Carcanet, 1981.

Proudfit, Charles L., ed. *Landor as Critic*. London: Routledge and Kegan Paul, 1979.

Welby, T. Earle, and Stephen Wheeler, eds. *The Complete Works of Walter Savage Landor*. 16 vols. London: Chapman and Hall, 1927–36.

STUDIES:

Elwin, Malcolm. *Landor: A Replevin*. London: Macdonald, 1958.

Pinsky, Robert. *Landor's Poetry*. Chicago: U of Chicago P, 1968.

Super, R.H. *Walter Savage Landor: A Biography*. New York: New York UP, 1954.

See also Bush (chap. 7), in General Bibliography.

Lee

EDITIONS:

Alliston, April, ed. *The Recess; or, A Tale of Other Times*. Lexington: UP of Kentucky, 2000.

Lee, Sophia, and Harriet Lee. *Canterbury Tales*. 2 vols. 1832. Rpt. New York: AMS, 1978.

Lewis

EDITIONS:

Cox, Jeffrey N., ed. *Seven Gothic Dramas, 1789–1825.* [Includes *The Castle Spectre* and *The Captive*.] Athens OH: Ohio UP, 1992.

Macdonald, D.L., and Kathleen Scherf, eds. *The Monk: A Romance*. Peterborough: Broadview, 2004.

Peck, Louis F., ed. "Letters." Appended to *A Life of Matthew Gregory Lewis*. Cambridge MA: Harvard UP, 1961.

STUDIES:

Conger, Syndy M. *Matthew Lewis, Charles Maturin, and the Germans: An Interpretative Study of the Influence of German Literature on Two Gothic Novels*. Salzburg: Universität Salzburg, 1977.

Macdonald, D.L. *Monk Lewis: A Critical Biography*. Toronto: U of Toronto P, 2000.

Lindsay

EDITIONS:

Lenta, Margaret, and Basil Le Cordeur, eds. *The Cape Diaries of Lady Anne Barnard, 1799–1800*. 2 vols. Cape Town: Van Riebeeck Society, 1999.

Robinson, A.M. Lewin, ed. *The Letters of Lady Anne Barnard to Henry Dundas, from the Cape and Elsewhere, 1793–1803, Together with her Journal of a Tour into the Interior, and Certain Other Letters*. Cape Town: Balkema, 1973.

—, with Margaret Lenta and Dorothy Driver, eds. *The Cape Journals of Lady Anne Barnard, 1797–1798*. Cape Town: Van Riebeeck Society, 1994.

Scott, Sir Walter. *Auld Robin Gray*. Edinburgh: Ballantyne, 1825. Rpt. New York: AMS Press, 1971.

STUDIES:

Driver, Dorothy. "Lady Anne Barnard's Cape Journals and the Concept of Self-Othering." *Pretexts: Studies in Writing and Culture* 5.1–2 (1995): 46–65.

Hunter, Andy. "The Peregrinations of 'Auld Robin Gray' and 'Eugénie Grandet.'" *Etudes Ecossaises* 7 (2001): 183–93.

Little

See Feldman & Kelley, in General Bibliography.

Lloyd

EDITIONS:

Poems on Various Subjects [1795]; *Blank Verse* [with Charles Lamb, 1798]; *Poetical Essays on the Character of Pope; Poems* [1797]. Rpt. Introd. Donald H. Reiman. New York: Garland, 1978.

Desultory Thoughts in London. Introd. Donald H. Reiman. New York: Garland, 1978.

Nugae Canorae. 1819. Rpt. Introd. Donald H. Reiman. New York: Garland, 1977.

STUDIES:

Fairer, David. "Baby Language and Revolution: The Early Poetry of Charles Lloyd and Charles Lamb." *Charles Lamb Bulletin* 74 (April 1991): 33–52.

Pratt, Lynda. "'Perilous Acquaintance'? Lloyd, Coleridge and Southey in the 1790's: Five Unpublished Letters." *Romanticism: The Journal of Romantic Culture and Criticism* 6.1 (2000): 98–115.

See also entries under CHARLES LAMB.

Longfellow

EDITIONS:

Hilen, Andrew, ed. *The Letters of Henry Wadsworth Longfellow.* 6 vols. Cambridge, MA: Belknap, 1966–82.

Scudder, H.E., ed. *The Complete Poetical Works of Henry Wadsworth Longfellow.* Boston: Houghton Mifflin, 1922.

STUDIES:

Frank, Armin Paul, and Christel-Maria Maas. *Transnational Longfellow: A Project of American National Poetry.* Frankfurt: Peter Lang, 2005.

Wagenknecht, Edward. *Henry Wadsworth Longfellow: His Poetry and Prose.* New York: Ungar, 1986.

Macaulay

EDITION:

Letters on Education. 1790. Rpt. Oxford and New York: Woodstock Books, 1994.

STUDY:

Hill, Bridget. *The Republican Virago: The Life and Times of Catharine Macaulay, Historian.* Oxford: Clarendon P, 1992.

See also Eger, Grant et al., in General Bibliography.

Malthus

EDITION:

Appleman, Philip, ed. *An Essay on the Principle of Population.* New York: Norton, 2004.

STUDY:

Winborn, Colin, "George Crabbe, Thomas Malthus, and the 'Bounds of Necessity.'" *Romanticism: The Journal of Romantic Culture and Criticism* 8.1 (2002): 75–89.

Marcet

STUDY:

Hollis, Hilda. "The Rhetoric of Jane Marcet's Popularizing Political Economy." *Nineteenth-Century Contexts* 24.4 (2002): 379–96.

Merry

STUDY:

Labbe, Jacqueline M. "The Anthologized Romance of Della Crusca and Anna Matilda." *Romanticism on the Net: An Electronic Journal Devoted to Romantic Studies* 18 (May 2000). n.p. <http://www.erudit.org/revue/ron/2005/v/n38-39/011666ar.html>.

See also McGann (*Poetics of Sensibility*), in General Bibliography; see also entries under COWLEY.

Mitford

EDITION:

Recollections of a Literary Life; or, Books, Places, and People. New York: Harper, 1852. Rpt. New York: AMS, 1975.

STUDY:

Owen, J.C. "Utopia in Little: Mary Russell Mitford and Our Village." *Studies in Short Fiction* 5 (1968): 245–56.

Moodie

See Gray, under TRAILL.

Moore

EDITIONS:

Dowden, Wilfred S., ed., Barbara Bartholomew and Joy L. Linsley, assoc. eds. *The Journal of Thomas Moore.* 6 vols. Newark: U of Delaware P, 1983.

—ed. *Letters.* 2 vols. Oxford: Clarendon P, 1964.

Godley, A.D., ed. *The Poetical Works of Thomas Moore.* London: H. Frowde, 1910.

STUDIES:
Jones, Howard Mumford. *The Harp That Once: A Chronicle of the Life of Thomas Moore*. New York: Holt, 1937.
White, Terence De Vere. *Tom Moore: The Irish Poet*. London: Hamish Hamilton, 1977.
Wright, Julia M. "'Sons of Song': Irish Literature in the Age of Nationalism." *Romantic Poetry*. Ed. Angela Esterhammer. Amsterdam: Benjamins, 2002. 333–53.

More

EDITIONS:
The Works of Hannah More. 18 vols. London: T. Cadell and W. Davies, 1818.
Hole, Robert, ed. *Selected Writings of Hannah More*. London: Pickering and Chatto, 1996.

STUDIES:
Collingwood, Jeremy, and Margaret Collingwood. *Hannah More*. Oxford: Lion, 1990.
Myers, Mitzi. "Reform or Ruin: 'A Revolution in Female Manners.'" *Studies in Eighteenth-Century Culture* 11 (1982): 199–216.
Myers, Sylvia Harcstark. *The Bluestocking Circle: Women, Friendship, and the Life of the Mind in Eighteenth-Century England*. Oxford: Clarendon P, 1990.

See also Wilson & Haefner, in General Bibliography; and Kowaleski-Wallace, under EDGEWORTH.

Nairne

EDITIONS:
Rogers, Charles, ed. *Life and Songs of the Baroness Nairne, with a Memoir and Poems of Caroline Oliphant the Younger*. Edinburgh: Grant, 1896.
The Songs of Lady Nairne. London: Foulis, 1911.

Opie

EDITIONS:
King, Shelley, and John B. Pierce, eds. The Father and Daughter *with* Dangers of Coquetry. Peterborough: Broadview, 2003.
King, Shelley, and John B. Pierce, eds. *Adeline Mowbray*. Oxford: Oxford UP, 1999.
Poems. London, 1802. Rpt. New York: Garland, 1978.

STUDIES:
Brightwell, Cecilia Lucy. *Memorials of the Life of Amelia Opie*. Norwich: Fletcher and Alexander, 1854.
Eberle, Roxanne. "Amelia Opie's *Adeline Mowbray*: Diverting the Libertine Gaze; or, The Vindication of a Fallen Woman." *Studies in the Novel* 26 (1994): 121–52.
Kelly, Gary. "Discharging Debts: The Moral Economy of Amelia Opie's Fiction." *Wordsworth Circle* 11 (1980): 198–203.
Thame, David. "Amelia Opie's Maniacs." *Women's Writing* 7.2 (2000): 309–26.
Wake, Ann Frank. "Indirect Dissent: 'Landscaping' Female Agency in Amelia Alderson Opie's Poems of the 1790s." *Rebellious Hearts: British Women Writers and the French Revolution*. Ed. Adriana Craciun, Kari E. Lokke, and Madelyn Gotwirth. Albany: SUNY P, 2001.

See also Ty (*Empowering the Feminine*), in General Bibliography; Jones, under DACRE; and Kelly, under EDGEWORTH.

Owenson

EDITIONS:
The O'Briens and the O'Flahertys: A National Tale. Introd. Mary Campbell. London: Pandora, 1988.
The Wild Irish Girl. London: R. Phillips, 1806. Rpt. London: Pandora, 1986.
Wright, Julia M., ed. *The Missionary: An Indian Tale*. Peterborough: Broadview, 2002.

STUDIES:
Campbell, Mary. *Lady Morgan: The Life and Times of Sydney Owenson*. London: Pandora, 1988.
Newcomer, James. *Lady Morgan the Novelist*. Lewisburg: Bucknell UP, 1990.
O'Brien, Anne E. "Lady Morgan's Travel Writing on Italy: A Novel Approach." *Cross-Cultural Travel: Papers from the Royal Irish Academy Symposium on Literature and Travel*. Ed. Jane Conroy. New York: Peter Lang, 2003.

See also Favret & Watson, Feldman & Kelley, in General Bibliography.

Paine

EDITION:

Foner, Eric, ed. *Thomas Paine: Collected Writings:* Common Sense; The Crisis; and Other Pamphlets, Articles and Letters; Rights of Man; The Age of Reason. New York: Library of America, 1995.

STUDIES:

Ayer, A.J. *Thomas Paine.* London: Secker & Warburg, 1988.

Harrison, John R. "'Empire Is No More': William Blake, Tom Paine and the American Revolution." *Literature and History* 7.1 (Spring 1998): 16–32.

Keane, John. *Tom Paine: A Political Life.* Boston: Little, Brown, 1995.

See also Butler, in General Bibliography; Wilson, under COBBETT.

Peacock

EDITIONS:

Brett-Smith, Herbert F.B., and C.E. Jones, eds. *The Works of Thomas Love Peacock.* 10 vols. 1924–34. Rpt. New York: AMS, 1967.

Garnett, Richard, ed. *Thomas Love Peacock: Letters to Edward Hookham and Percy B. Shelley.* Boston: Bibliophile Society, 1910.

STUDY:

Butler, Marilyn. *Peacock Displayed: A Satirist in His Context.* Boston: Routledge and Kegan Paul, 1979.

Poe

EDITIONS:

Mabbott, Thomas Olive, with the assistance of E.D. Kewer and M.C. Mabbott, ed. *Collected Works of Edgar Allan Poe.* 3 vols. Cambridge, MA: Belknap P of Harvard UP, 1969.

Ostrom, John Ward, ed. *The Letters of Edgar Allan Poe.* 2 vols. 1948. Rpt. New York: Gordian, 1966.

Quinn, Patrick F., ed. *Poetry and Tales.* New York: Library of America, 1984.

Thompson, G.R., ed. *Essays and Reviews.* New York: Library of America, 1984.

STUDIES:

Hoffman, Daniel. *Poe Poe Poe Poe Poe Poe Poe.* Garden City, NY: Doubleday, 1972.

Kennedy, J. Gerald, and Liliane Weissberg, eds. *Romancing the Shadow: Poe and Race.* Oxford and New York: Oxford UP, 2001.

Meyers, Jeffery. *Edgar Allan Poe: His Life and Legacy.* New York: Charles Scribner's Sons, 1992.

Silverman, Kenneth. *Edgar Allan Poe: Mournful and Never-Ending Remembrance.* New York: Harper Collins, 1991.

Symons, Julian. *The Tell-Tale Heart: The Life and Works of Edgar Allan Poe.* New York: Harper & Row, 1978.

Wagenknecht, Edward. *Edgar Allan Poe: The Man behind the Legend.* New York: Oxford UP, 1963.

See also Levin, under HAWTHORNE.

Price

EDITIONS:

Peach, Bernard, ed. *Richard Price and the Ethical Foundations of the American Revolution: Selections from his Pamphlets, with Appendices.* Durham: Duke UP, 1979.

Thomas, D.O., ed. *Political Writings.* Cambridge: Cambridge UP, 1991.

STUDIES:

Laboucheix, Henri. *Richard Price as Moral Philosopher and Political Theorist.* Oxford: Voltaire Foundation, 1982.

Thomas, D.O. *The Honest Mind: The Thought and Work of Richard Price.* Oxford: Clarendon P, 1972.

Prince

EDITIONS:

Ferguson, Moira, ed. *The History of Mary Prince, a West Indian Slave, Related by Herself.* London: Pandora, 1987.

Gates, Henry Louis, Jr., ed. *The Classic Slave Narratives.* New York: Signet Classic, 1987. 183–242.

STUDIES:

Ferguson, Moira. *Subject to Others: British Women Writers and Colonial Slavery, 1670–1834.* New York: Routledge, 1992. Chap. 13.

Pacquet, Sandra Puochet. "The Heartbeat of a West Indian Slave: *The History of Mary Prince.*" *African American Review* 26 (1992): 131–46.

Pringle

EDITIONS:

Pereira, Ernest, and Michael Chapman, eds. *African Poems of Thomas Pringle*. Pietermaritzburg: U of Natal P, 1989.

Wahl, John Robert, ed. *Poems Illustrative of South Africa: African Sketches: Part One*. Cape Town: C. Struik, 1970.

STUDY:

Griggs, Earl Leslie. "Samuel Taylor Coleridge and Thomas Pringle." *Quarterly Bulletin of the South African Library* 6.1 (September 1951).

Radcliffe

EDITION:

Dobrée, Donamy, ed. *The Mysteries of Udolpho*. Introd. and notes by Terry Castle. London: Oxford UP, 1966, 1998.

STUDIES:

Cottom, Daniel. *The Civilised Imagination: A Study of Ann Radcliffe, Jane Austen, and Sir Walter Scott*. Cambridge and New York: Cambridge UP, 1985.

Miles, Robert. *Ann Radcliffe: The Great Enchantress*. Manchester: Manchester UP, 1995.

Norton, Rictor. *Mistress of Udolpho: The Life of Ann Radcliffe*. London and New York: Leicester UP, 1999.

Rogers, Deborah D., ed. *The Critical Response to Ann Radcliffe*. Westport, CT: Greenwood P, 1994.

—. *Ann Radcliffe: A Bio-Bibliography*. Westport, CT: Greenwood P, 1996.

See also Claudia L. Johnson, in General Bibliography.

Rammohun Roy

EDITIONS:

The English Works of Raja Rammohun Roy: with an English translation of Tuhfatul Muwahhiddin. New York: AMS P, 1978.

Robertson, Bruce Carlisle, ed. *The Essential Writings of Raja Rammohan Ray*. Delhi: Oxford UP, 1999.

Reeve

EDITIONS:

Plans of Education. 1792. Rpt. New York: Garland, 1974.

The Progress of Romance through Times, Countries, and Manners. 1785. Rpt. New York: Garland, 1970.

Trainer, James, ed. with introd. *The Old English Baron: A Gothic Story*. London: Oxford UP, 1967.

Reynolds

EDITION:

Wark, Robert R., ed. *Discourses on Art*. Rev. Ed. New Haven and London: Published for the Paul Mellon Centre for Studies in British Art by Yale UP, 1975.

Robinson

EDITIONS:

Levy, M.J., ed. *Perdita: The Memoirs of Mary Robinson*. London & Chester Springs: Peter Owen, 1994.

Pascoe, Judith, ed. *Mary Robinson: Selected Poems*. Peterborough: Broadview, 2000.

STUDIES:

Labbe, Jacqueline. "Selling One's Sorrows: Charlotte Smith, Mary Robinson, and the Marketing of Poetry." *Wordsworth Circle* 25 (1994): 68–71.

McGann, Jerome J. "Mary Robinson and the Myth of Sappho." *Modern Language Quarterly* 56 (1995): 55–76.

Pascoe, Judith. "The Spectacular Flâneuse: Mary Robinson and the City of London." *Wordsworth Circle* 23 (1992): 165–71.

Ty, Eleanor. "Engendering a Female Subject: Mary Robinson's (Re)Presentations of the Self." *English Studies in Canada* 21 (1995): 407–31.

Vargo, Lisa. "The Claims of 'Real Life and Manners': Coleridge and Mary Robinson." *Wordsworth Circle* 26 (1995): 134–37.

See also Feldman & Kelley, eds., McGann (*Poetics of Sensibility*), Pascoe, Ty (*Empowering the Feminine*), Wilson & Haefner, eds., in General Bibliography.

Sancho

EDITIONS:

Carretta, Vincent, and Philip Gould, eds. *Genius in Bondage: Literature of the Early Black Atlantic*. Lexington: UP of Kentucky, 2001.

Edwards, Paul, and Polly Rewt, eds. *The Letters of Ignatius Sancho*. Edinburgh: Edinburgh UP, 1994.

STUDY:

Edwards, Paul. *Unreconciled Strivings and Ironic Strategies: Three Afro-British Authors of the Georgian Era: Ignatius Sancho, Olaudah Equiano, Robert Wedderburn*. Edinburgh: U of Edinburgh Centre for African Studies, 1992.

Scott

EDITIONS:

Anderson, W.E.K., ed. *The Journals of Sir Walter Scott*. Oxford: Clarendon P, 1972.

Grierson, H.J.C., et al., eds. *The Letters of Sir Walter Scott*. 12 vols. London: Constable, 1932–37.

Hewitt, David, et al., eds. *The Waverley Novels*. 10 vols. to date. Edinburgh: Edinburgh UP, 1993—.

Robertson, J.L., ed. *Poetical Works of Sir Walter Scott*. 1904. Rpt. London: Oxford UP, 1964.

STUDIES:

Ferris, Ina. *The Achievement of Literary Authority: Gender, History, and the Waverley Novels*. Ithaca: Cornell UP, 1991.

Goslee, Nancy Moore. *Scott the Rhymer*. Lexington: UP of Kentucky, 1988.

Johnson, Edgar. *Sir Walter Scott: The Great Unknown*. 2 vols. New York: Macmillan, 1970.

Lukács, Georg. *The Historical Novel*. 1937. Trans. Hannah and Stanley Mitchell. London: Merlin, 1962.

Millgate, Jane. *Walter Scott: The Making of the Novelist*. Toronto: U of Toronto P, 1984.

Sutherland, John. *The Life of Walter Scott*. Oxford: Blackwell, 1995.

See also Cottom, under RADCLIFFE.

Severn

EDITION:

Rollins, Hyder Edward, ed. *The Keats Circle: Letters and Papers and More Letters and Poems of the Keats Circle*. 2nd ed. 2 vols. Cambridge, MA: Harvard UP, 1965.

Seward

STUDIES:

Ashmun, Margaret Eliza. *The Singing Swan: An Account of Anna Seward and her Acquaintance with Dr. Johnson, Boswell, & Others of their Time*. 1931. Rpt. New York: Greenwood, 1968.

Curran, Stuart. "Dynamics of Female Friendship in the Later Eighteenth Century." *Nineteenth-Century Contexts* 23 (2001): 221–39.

See also Robinson, under C. SMITH.

Mary Shelley

EDITIONS:

Bennett, Betty T., and Charles E. Robinson, eds. *The Mary Shelley Reader, Containing* Frankenstein, Mathilda, *Tales and Stories, Essays and Reviews, and Letters*. New York: Oxford UP, 1990.

Bennett, Betty T., ed. *The Letters of Mary Wollstonecraft Shelley*. 3 vols. Baltimore: Johns Hopkins UP, 1980–88.

Crook, Nora, gen. ed. *Mary Shelley's Literary Lives and Other Writings*. 4 vols. London: Pickering & Chatto, 2002.

Crook, Nora, ed., with Pamela Clemit. *The Novels and Selected Works of Mary Shelley*. 8 vols. London: Pickering & Chatto, 1996.

Feldman, Paula R., and Diana Scott-Kilvert, eds. *The Journals of Mary Shelley, 1814–1844*. 2 vols. Oxford: Clarendon P, 1987.

Macdonald, D.L., and Kathleen Scherf, eds. *Frankenstein, or The Modern Prometheus*. 2nd ed. Peterborough: Broadview, 1999.

McWhir, Anne, ed. *The Last Man*. Peterborough: Broadview, 1996.

Nitchie, Elizabeth, ed. *Mathilda*. Chapel Hill: U of North Carolina P, 1959.

Rajan, Tillotoma, ed. *Valperga; or, The Life and Adventures of Castruccio, Prince of Lucca*. Peterborough: Broadview, 1998.

Robinson, Charles E., ed. *Mary Shelley: Collected Tales and Stories*. Baltimore: Johns Hopkins UP, 1976.

—, ed. *The* Frankenstein *Notebooks*. 2 vols. New York: Garland, 1996.

Vargo, Lisa, ed. *Lodore*. Peterborough: Broadview, 1997.

STUDIES:

Baldick, Chris. *In Frankenstein's Shadow: Myth, Monstrosity, and Nineteenth-Century Writing*. Oxford: Clarendon P, 1987.

Buss, Helen M., D.L. Macdonald, and Anne McWhir, eds. *Mary Wollstonecraft and Mary Shelley: Writing Lives*. Waterloo: Wilfrid Laurier UP, 2001.

Cantor, Paul A. *Creature and Creator: Myth-making and English Romanticism*. Cambridge: Cambridge UP, 1984.

Conger, Syndy M., Frederick S. Frank, and Gregory O'Dea, eds.; assistant editor, Jennifer Yocum. *Iconoclastic Departures: Mary Shelley after* Frankenstein: *Essays in Honor of the Bicentenary of Mary Shelley's Birth*. Madison, NJ: Fairleigh Dickinson UP, 1997.

Fisch, Audrey A., Anne K. Mellor, and Esther H. Schor, eds. *The Other Mary Shelley: Beyond* Frankenstein. New York: Oxford UP, 1993.

Garrett, Martin. *A Mary Shelley Chronology*. Houndmills, Basingstoke: Palgrave, 2002.

Levine, George, and U.C. Knoepflmacher, eds. *The Endurance of* Frankenstein: *Essays on Mary Shelley's Novel*. Berkeley: U of California P, 1979.

Mellor, Anne K. *Mary Shelley: Her Life, Her Fiction, Her Monsters*. New York: Methuen, 1988.

Spark, Muriel. *Mary Shelley*. Rev. ed. New York: New American Library, 1987.

Sunstein, Emily W. *Mary Shelley: Romance and Reality*. Boston: Little, Brown, 1989.

Veeder, William R. *Mary Shelley &* Frankenstein: *The Fate of Androgyny*. Chicago: U of Chicago P, 1986.

Williams, John. *Mary Shelley: A Literary Life*. Houndmills, Basingstoke: Macmillan, 2000.

See also Feldman & Kelley, Gilbert & Gubar, Poovey, Steinman, in General Bibliography; Clemit, under GODWIN; and Alexander, under D. WORDSWORTH.

P. B. Shelley

EDITIONS:

Barcus, James E., ed. *Shelley: The Critical Heritage*. London: Routledge & Kegan Paul, 1975.

Behrendt, Stephen C., ed. Zastrozzi *and* St. Irvyne; or, The Rosicrucian. Peterborough: Broadview, 2002.

Cameron, Kenneth Neill, Donald H. Reiman, and Doucet Devin Fischer, eds. *Shelley and his Circle, 1773–1822*. 10 vols. Cambridge, MA: Harvard UP, 1961–86.

Hutchinson, Thomas, ed. *Shelley: Poetical Works*. Rev. ed. G.M. Matthews. London: Oxford UP, 1970.

Jones, Frederick L., ed. *The Letters of Percy Bysshe Shelley*. 2 vols. Oxford: Clarendon P, 1964.

Lauritsen, John, ed. *Plato: The Banquet*. Translated by Percy Bysshe Shelley. Provincetown: Pagan P, 2001.

Massey, Irving, ed. *Posthumous Poems of Shelley*. Montréal: McGill-Queen's UP, 1969.

Notopoulos, James, ed. "Shelley's Translations from Plato: A Critical Edition." In *The Platonism of Shelley: A Study of Platonism and the Poetic Mind*. Durham: Duke UP, 1949. Rpt. New York: Octagon, 1969.

Reiman, Donald H., and Neil Freistat, eds. *Shelley's Poetry and Prose*. 2nd ed. New York: Norton, 2002.

—, eds. *The Complete Poetry of Percy Shelley*. 2 vols. to date. Baltimore: Johns Hopkins UP, 2000—.

Zillman, Lawrence John, ed. *Shelley's* Prometheus Unbound: *The Text and the Drafts*. New Haven: Yale UP, 1968.

STUDIES:

Behrendt, Stephen C. *Shelley and his Audiences*. Lincoln: U of Nebraska P, 1989.

Bieri, James. *Percy Bysshe Shelley: A Biography*. 2 vols. Newark: U of Delaware P, 2004–05.

Brown, Nathaniel. *Sexuality and Feminism in Shelley*. Cambridge, MA: Harvard UP, 1979.

Cameron, Kenneth Neill. *Shelley: The Golden Years*. Cambridge, MA: Harvard UP, 1974.

—. *The Young Shelley: Genesis of a Radical*. 1950. Rpt. New York: Octagon, 1973.

Chernaik, Judith. *The Lyrics of Shelley*. Cleveland: P of Case Western Reserve U, 1972.

Crook, Nora, and Derek Guiton. *Shelley's Venomed Melody*. Cambridge: Cambridge UP, 1986.

Curran, Stuart. *Shelley's Annus Mirabilis: The Maturing of an Epic Vision*. San Marino, CA: Huntington Library, 1975.

—. *Shelley's* Cenci: *Scorpions Ringed with Fire*. Princeton: Princeton UP, 1970.

Duffy, Edward. *Rousseau in England: The Context for Shelley's Critique of the Enlightenment*. Berkeley: U of California P, 1979.

Foot, Paul. *Red Shelley*. London: Sidgwick and Jackson, 1980.

Gelpi, Barbara Charlesworth. *Shelley's Goddess: Maternity, Language, Subjectivity*. New York: Oxford UP, 1992.

Hogle, Jerrold E. *Shelley's Process: Radical Transference and the Development of his Major Works*. New York: Oxford UP, 1988.

Holmes, Richard. *Shelley: The Pursuit*. London: Weidenfeld and Nicolson, 1974.

Keach, William. *Shelley's Style*. New York: Methuen, 1984.

King-Hele, Desmond. *Shelley: His Thought and Work*. 3rd ed. London: Macmillan, 1984.

Leighton, Angela. *Shelley and the Sublime: An Interpretation of the Major Poems*. Cambridge: Cambridge UP, 1984.

Peterfreund, Stuart. *Shelley among Others: The Play of the Intertext and the Idea of Language*. Baltimore: Johns Hopkins UP, 2002.

Pulos, C.E. *The Deep Truth: A Study of Shelley's Skepticism*. Lincoln: U of Nebraska P, 1954.

Reiman, Donald H. *Percy Bysshe Shelley.* 1969. Rev. ed. Boston: Twayne, 1989.

Roberts, Hugh. *Shelley and the Chaos of History: A New Politics of Poetry.* University Park: Pennsylvania State UP, 1997.

Scrivener, Michael Henry. *Radical Shelley: The Philosophical Anarchism and Utopian Thought of Percy Bysshe Shelley.* Princeton: Princeton UP, 1982.

Wasserman, Earl R. *Shelley: A Critical Reading.* Baltimore: Johns Hopkins UP, 1971.

See also Bostetter, Perkins, Schock, Wolfson, in General Bibliography; Robinson, under BYRON.

Charlotte Smith

EDITIONS:

Curran, Stuart M., gen. ed. *Collected Works of Charlotte Smith.* 14 vols. London: Pickering & Chatto, 2005–07.

—, ed. *The Poems of Charlotte Smith.* New York: Oxford UP, 1993.

Fletcher, Loraine, ed. *Emmeline, the Orphan of the Castle.* Peterborough: Broadview, 2003.

—, ed. *Celestina.* Peterborough: Broadview, 2004.

Todd, Janet, and Antje Blank. *Desmond.* Peterborough: Broadview, 2001.

Labbe, Jacqueline, ed. *The Old Manor House.* Peterborough: Broadview, 2002.

STUDIES:

Curran, Stuart. "Charlotte Smith and British Romanticism." *South Central Review* 11 (1999): 66–78.

Fletcher, Loraine. *Charlotte Smith: A Critical Biography.* Houndmills, Basingstoke: Macmillan, 1998.

Labbe, Jacqueline M. *Charlotte Smith: Romanticism, Poetry, and the Culture of Gender.* Manchester: Manchester UP, 2003.

Robinson, Daniel. "Reviving the Sonnet: Women Romantic Poets and the Sonnet Claim." *European Romantic Review* 6 (1995): 98–127.

See also Curran ("Romantic Poetry"), Wilson & Haefner, in General Bibliography; Bradshaw, under BARBAULD; Labbe, under ROBINSON.

Horace Smith

EDITIONS:

Amarynthus, the Nympholet: A Pastoral Drama, in Three Acts. With Other Poems. 1821. Rpt. Introd. Donald H. Reiman. New York: Garland, 1977.

Rejected Addresses and *Horace in London.* 1812–13. Rpt. Introd. Donald H. Reiman. New York: Garland, 1977.

STUDY:

Beavan, Arthur H. *James and Horace Smith: A Family Narrative: Based upon hitherto unpublished private diaries, letters, and other documents.* London: Hurst and Blackett, 1899.

Southey

EDITIONS:

Fitzgerald, Maurice H., ed. *Letters of Robert Southey: A Selection.* London: H. Frowde, Oxford UP, 1912.

Fulford, Tim, and Daniel Roberts, eds. *Robert Southey: Poetical Works 1793–1810.* 5 vols. London: Pickering and Chatto, 2004.

—, and Lynda Pratt, eds. *Robert Southey: Later Poetical Works, 1811–1838.* 4 vols. London: Pickering and Chatto, forthcoming.

Madden, Lionel, ed. *Robert Southey: The Critical Heritage.* London: Routledge and Kegan Paul, 1972.

Simmons, Jack, ed. *Letters from England.* London: Cresset, 1951.

Zeitlin, Jacob, ed. *Selected Prose of Robert Southey.* New York: Macmillan, 1916.

STUDIES:

Bernhardt-Kabisch, Ernest. *Robert Southey.* Boston: Twayne, 1977.

Storey, Mark. *Robert Southey: A Life.* Oxford: Oxford UP, 1997.

Taylor

EDITIONS:

The Authoress: A Tale. 1819. Rpt. Introd. Rainer Schowerling. Stuttgart: Besler, 1988.

Barry, F.V., ed. *Jane Taylor: Prose and Poetry.* London: Humphrey Milford, 1924.

Original Poems for Infant Minds. 2 vols. 1804–05. *Rhymes for the Nursery.* 1806. Rpt. Pref. Christina Duff Stewart. New York: Garland, 1976.

STUDIES:

Morton, Timothy. "'Twinkle, Twinkle, Little Star' as an Ambient Poem: A Study of a Dialectical Image, with Some Remarks on Coleridge and Wordsworth." *Romanticism & Ecology*. Ed. James McKusick. College Park: U of Maryland, 2001. Unpaginated.

Smulders, Sharon. "The Good Mother: Language, Gender, and Power in Ann and Jane Taylor's Poetry for Children." *Children's Literature Association Quarterly* 27 (2002): 4–15.

See also Curran ("Romantic Poetry"), Davidoff & Hall, in General Bibliography.

Thelwall

EDITIONS:

Ode to Science. 1791. *John Gilpin's Ghost*. 1795. *Poems Chiefly Written in Retirement*. 1801. *The Trident of Albion*. 1805. Rpt. Introd. Donald H. Reiman. New York: Garland, 1978.

The Peripatetic. 1793. Rpt. Introd. Donald H. Reiman. 3 vols. in 2. New York: Garland, 1978.

Poems Chiefly Written in Retirement. 1801. Rpt. Oxford: Woodstock, 1989.

STUDIES:

Ros, Nicolas. *Wordsworth and Coleridge:* Lyrical Ballads*: The Radical Years*. Oxford: Clarendon P, 1988.

Scrivener, Michael. *Seditious Allegories: John Thelwall and Jacobin Writing*. University Park: Pennsylvania State UP, 2001.

Thompson, Judith. "An Autumnal Blast, a Killing Frost: Coleridge's Poetic Conversation with John Thelwall." *Studies in Romanticism* 36 (1997): 427–56.

Tighe

EDITIONS:

Linkin, Harriet Kramer, ed. *The Collected Poems and Journals of Mary Tighe*. Lexington: UP of Kentucky, 2005.

Psyche, or, The Legend of Love. 1805. Rpt. Introd. Donald H. Reiman. New York: Garland, 1978.

STUDIES:

Linkin, Harriet Kramer. "Romanticism and Mary Tighe's Psyche: Peering at the Hem of Her Blue Stockings." *Studies in Romanticism* 35 (1996): 55–72.

Weller, Earle Vonard. *Keats and Mary Tighe: The Poems of Mary Tighe with Parallel Passages from the Work of John Keats*. New York: Century, 1928.

See also Ross, in General Bibliography; and Linkin, under LANDON.

Traill

EDITIONS:

The Female Emigrant's Guide, and Hints on Canadian Housekeeping. Toronto: Maclear, 1854–55. (Later published as *The Canadian Settler's Guide*. Rpt. 1974.)

Peterman, Michael, ed. *The Backwoods of Canada*. Ottawa: Carleton UP, 1997.

STUDIES:

Ballstadt, Carl. *Catharine Parr Traill and Her Works*. Downsview: ECWP, 1989.

Gray, Charlotte. *Sisters in the Wilderness: The Lives of Susanna Moodie and Catherine Parr Traill*. Toronto: Viking, 1999.

Trelawny

EDITIONS:

Forman, H. Buxton, ed. *The Letters of Edward John Trelawny*. New York: H. Frowde, Oxford UP, 1910.

Recollections of the Last Days of Shelley and Byron. Introd. David Crane. London: Robinson, 2000.

Records of Shelley, Byron, and the Author. Introd. Anne Barton. New York: New York Review Books, 2000.

St Clair, William, ed. *Adventures of a Younger Son*. London: Oxford UP, 1974.

STUDIES:

Crane, David. *Lord Byron's Jackal: The Life of Edward John Trelawny*. London: HarperCollins, 1998.

St Clair, William. *Trelawny: The Incurable Romancer*. London: John Murray, 1977.

Wakefield

EDITIONS:

Reflections on the Present Condition of the Female Sex, with Suggestions for its Improvement. 1798. Rpt. Introd. Gina Luria. New York: Garland, 1974.

Shteir, Ann B., ed. *Mental Improvement*. East Lansing, MI: Colleagues, 1995.

STUDIES:

Dougal, Theresa A. "Teaching Conduct or Telling a New Tale? Priscilla Wakefield and the Juvenile Travellers." *Eighteenth-Century Women: Studies in their Lives, Work, and Culture* 1 (2001): 299–319.

Hill, Bridget. "Priscilla Wakefield as a Writer of Children's Educational Books." *Women's Writing* 4 (1997): 3–14.

Wheatley

EDITIONS:

Caretta, Vincent, ed. *Complete Writings*. London: Penguin, 2001.

Mason, Julian D., Jr., ed. *The Poems of Phillis Wheatley*. Rev. ed. Chapel Hill: U of North Carolina P, 1989.

Shields, John, ed. *The Collected Works of Phillis Wheatley*. New York: Oxford UP, 1988.

STUDIES:

Baker, Houston A., Jr. *Workings of the Spirit: The Poetics of Afro-American Women's Writings*. Chicago: U of Chicago P, 1991.

Connor, Kimberly Rae. *Conversions and Visions in the Writings of African-American Women*. Knoxville: U of Tennessee P, 1994.

Foster, Frances Smith. *Written by Herself: Literary Production by African-American Women, 1746–1892*. Bloomington: Indiana UP, 1993.

Gates, Henry Louis, Jr. *The Signifying Monkey: A Theory of African-American Literary Criticism*. New York: Oxford UP, 1988.

Williams

EDITIONS:

Julia: A Novel. 1790. Rpt. Introd. Gina Luria. New York: Garland, 1974.

Letters Written in France, in the Summer 1790, to a friend in England, containing various anecdotes relative to the French Revolution. Rpt. Oxford: Woodstock, 1989.

Poems. 1786. Rpt. Oxford: Woodstock, 1994.

Todd, Janet, ed. *Letters from France. 1795, 1796*. 8 vols. Delmar, NY: Scholar's Facsimiles and Reprints, 1975.

STUDIES:

Favret, Mary A. *Romantic Correspondence: Women, Politics, and the Fiction of Letters*. Cambridge: Cambridge UP, 1993. Chap. 3.

Jones, Chris. "Helen Maria Williams and Radical Sensibility." *Prose Studies* 12 (1989): 3–24.

Jones, Vivien. "Femininity, Nationalism, and Romanticism: The Politics of Gender in the Revolution Controversy." *History of European Ideas* 16 (1993): 299–305.

Mellor, Anne K. "English Women Writers and the French Revolution." In *Rebel Daughter: Women and the French Revolution*. Ed. Sara E. Melzer and Leslie W. Rabine. New York: Oxford UP, 1992. 255–72.

Watson, Nicola J. *Revolution and the Form of the English Novel, 1790–1825: Intercepted Letters, Interrupted Seductions*. Oxford: Clarendon P, 1994.

See also Favret & Watson, Kelly, Feldman & Kelley, in General Bibliography.

Wollstonecraft

EDITIONS:

The Female Reader. 1789. Rpt. Introd. Moira Ferguson. Delmar: Scholar's Facsimiles & Reprints, 1979.

Godwin, William, ed. *Posthumous Works of the Author of* A Vindication of the Rights of Woman. 4 vols. 1798. Rpt. Introd. Gina Luria. New York: Garland, 1974.

Holmes, Richard, ed. *Mary Wollstonecraft:* A Short Residence in Sweden, Norway and Denmark *and William Godwin:* Memoirs of the Author of "The Rights of Woman." London: Penguin, 1987.

Kelly, Gary, ed. Mary *and* The Wrongs of Woman. Oxford: Oxford UP, 1976.

Macdonald, D.L., and Kathleen Scherf, eds. *The Vindications:* A Vindication of the Rights of Men, A Vindication of the Rights of Woman. Peterborough: Broadview, 1997.

Poston, Carol H., ed. *Letters Written During a Short Residence in Sweden, Norway, and Denmark*. Lincoln: U of Nebraska P, 1976.

—, ed. *A Vindication of the Rights of Woman*. 2nd ed. New York: Norton, 1988.

Todd, Janet, ed. *The Collected Letters of Mary Wollstonecraft*. London: Allen Lane, 2003.

—, ed. *Mary Wollstonecraft: Political Writings*. Toronto: U of Toronto P, 1993.

Todd, Janet, and Marilyn Butler, eds., assistant ed., Emma Rees-Mogg. *The Works of Mary Wollstonecraft*. 7 vols. London: Pickering and Chatto, 1989.

STUDIES:

Conger, Syndy M. *Mary Wollstonecraft and the Language of Sensibility*. Rutherford, NJ: Fairleigh Dickinson UP, 1994.

Falco, Mario, ed. *Feminist Interpretations of Mary Wollstonecraft*. University Park: Pennsylvania State UP, 1996.

Ferguson, Moira, and Janet Todd. *Mary Wollstonecraft*. Boston: Twayne, 1984.

Gunther-Canada, Wendy. *Rebel Writer: Mary Wollstonecraft and Enlightenment Politics*. DeKalb: Northern Illinois UP, 2001.

Johnson, Claudia L., ed. *The Cambridge Companion to Mary Wollstonecraft*. Cambridge: Cambridge UP, 2002.

Kelly, Gary. *Revolutionary Feminism: The Mind and Career of Mary Wollstonecraft*. London: Macmillan, 1992.

Lorch, Jennifer. *Mary Wollstonecraft: The Making of a Revolutionary Feminist*. New York: Berg, 1990.

Myers, Mitzi. "Mary Wollstonecraft's *Letters Written ... in Sweden*: Toward Romantic Autobiography." *Studies in Eighteenth-Century Culture* 8 (1979): 165–85.

—. "Reform or Ruin: 'A Revolution in Female Manners.'" *Studies in Eighteenth-Century Culture* 11 (1982): 119–216.

Sapiro, Virginia. *A Vindication of Political Virtue: The Political Theory of Mary Wollstonecraft*. Chicago: U of Chicago P, 1992.

Sunstein, Emily. *A Different Face: The Life of Mary Wollstonecraft*. New York: Harper & Row, 1975.

Tomalin, Claire. *The Life and Death of Mary Wollstonecraft*. London: Weidenfeld and Nicolson, 1974.

See also Claudia L. Johnson, Mellor (*Romanticism and Gender*), Poovey, Ty, in General Bibliography; Levasseur, under BARBAULD; St Clair, under GODWIN; Waters, under HAYS; Buss, et al., under M. SHELLEY; and Alexander, under D. WORDSWORTH.

Dorothy Wordsworth

EDITIONS:

De Selincourt, Ernest, ed. *Journals of Dorothy Wordsworth*. 2 vols. London: Macmillan, 1941.

De Selincourt, Ernest, et al., eds. *The Letters of William and Dorothy Wordsworth*. 2nd ed. Rev. C.L. Shaver, Mary Moorman, and Alan G. Hill. 8 vols. Oxford: Clarendon P, 1967–93.

Hill, Alan G., ed. *Letters of Dorothy Wordsworth: A Selection*. Oxford: Clarendon, 1985.

Levin, Susan, ed. "The Collected Poems of Dorothy Wordsworth." In *Dorothy Wordsworth & Romanticism*. By Susan Levin. New Brunswick, NJ: Rutgers UP, 1987.

Moorman, Mary, ed. *The Journals of Dorothy Wordsworth*. 2nd ed. Oxford: Oxford UP, 1971.

Woof, Pamela, ed. *The Grasmere and Alfoxden Journals*. Oxford: Oxford UP, 2002.

STUDIES:

Gittings, Robert, and Jo Manton. *Dorothy Wordsworth*. Oxford: Clarendon P, 1985.

Hardwick, Elizabeth. *Seduction and Betrayal: Women and Literature*. Rpt. Introd. Joan Didion. New York: New York Review Books, 2001.

Homans, Margaret. *Women Writers and Poetic Identity: Dorothy Wordsworth, Emily Brontë, and Emily Dickinson*. Princeton: Princeton UP, 1980.

Levin, Susan. *Dorothy Wordsworth & Romanticism*. New Brunswick, NJ: Rutgers UP, 1987.

Mellor, Anne K. "Writing the Self/Self Writing: William Wordsworth's *Prelude*/Dorothy Wordsworth's Journals." *Romanticism and Gender*. New York: Routledge, 1993. 144–69.

Wordsworth Circle 9 (1978) [special issue on Dorothy Wordsworth].

See also Homans, in General Bibliography.

William Wordsworth

EDITIONS:

Brett, R.L., and A.R. Jones, eds. *Lyrical Ballads: Wordsworth and Coleridge*. Rev. ed. London: Methuen, 1968.

Curtis, Jared, ed. *The Fenwick Notes of William Wordsworth*. London: Bristol Classical P, 1993.

Darlington, Beth, ed. *The Love Letters of William and Mary Wordsworth*. Ithaca: Cornell UP, 1981.

Gill, Stephen, ed. *William Wordsworth*. Oxford: Oxford UP, 1984.

Hayden, John O., ed. *Selected Prose*. Harmondsworth: Penguin, 1988.

—, ed. *William Wordsworth: Poems*. 2 vols. London: Penguin, 1977.

Maxwell, J.C., ed. *The Prelude: A Parallel Text*. London: Penguin, 1971.

Owen, W.J.B., and Jane Worthington Smyser, eds. *The Prose Works of William Wordsworth*. 3 vols. Oxford: Clarendon P, 1974.

Parrish, Stephen, gen. ed. *The Cornell Wordsworth*. Ithaca: Cornell UP, 1975–.

Wordsworth, Jonathan, M.H. Abrams, and Stephen Gill, eds. *The Prelude: 1799, 1805, 1850*. New York: Norton, 1979.

STUDIES:

Averill, James H. *Wordsworth and the Poetry of Human Suffering*. Ithaca: Cornell UP, 1980.

Bibliography

Bate, Jonathan. *Romantic Ecology: Wordsworth and the Environmental Tradition*. London and New York: Routledge, 1991.

Bewell, Alan. *Wordsworth and the Enlightenment: Nature, Man, and Society in the Experimental Poetry*. New Haven: Yale UP, 1989.

Bialostosky, Don H. *Making Tales: The Poetics of Wordsworth's Narrative Experiments*. Chicago: U of Chicago P, 1984.

Chandler, James K. *Wordsworth's Second Nature: A Study of the Poetry and Politics*. Chicago: U of Chicago P, 1984.

Galperin, William H. *Revision and Authority in Wordsworth: The Interpretation of a Career*. Philadelphia: U of Pennsylvania P, 1989.

Gill, Stephen. *William Wordsworth: A Life*. Oxford: Clarendon P, 1989.

—, ed. *The Cambridge Companion to Wordsworth*. Cambridge: Cambridge UP, 2003.

Hartman, Geoffrey. *The Unremarkable Wordsworth*. Minneapolis: U of Minnesota P, 1987.

—. *Wordsworth's Poetry 1787–1814*. 1964. Rpt. New Haven: Yale UP, 1971.

Heffernan, James A.W. *Wordsworth's Theory of Poetry, 1797–1814*. Lincoln: U of Nebraska P, 1980.

Jacobus, Mary. *Romanticism, Writing, and Sexual Difference: Essays on* The Prelude. Oxford: Clarendon P, 1989.

—. *Tradition and Experiment in Wordsworth's* Lyrical Ballads, *1798*. Oxford: Clarendon, 1976.

Johnston, Kenneth R., and Gene W. Ruoff, eds. *The Age of William Wordsworth: Critical Essays on the Romantic Tradition*. New Brunswick: Rutgers UP, 1987.

Johnston, Kenneth R. *The Hidden Wordsworth: Poet, Lover, Rebel, Spy*. New York: Norton, 1998.

—. *Wordsworth and* The Recluse. New Haven: Yale UP, 1984.

Kelley, Theresa M. *Wordsworth's Revisionary Aesthetics*. Cambridge: Cambridge UP, 1988.

Kneale, Douglas J. *Monumental Writing: Aspects of Rhetoric in Wordsworth's Poetry*. Lincoln: U of Nebraska P, 1988.

Levinson, Marjorie. *Wordsworth's Great Period Poems: Four Essays*. Cambridge: Cambridge UP, 1986.

Lindenberger, Herbert. *On Wordsworth's* Prelude. Princeton: Princeton UP, 1963.

Liu, Alan. *Wordsworth: The Sense of History*. Stanford: Stanford UP, 1989.

Magnuson, Paul. *Coleridge and Wordsworth: A Lyrical Dialogue*. Princeton: Princeton UP, 1988.

Mahoney, John. *Wordsworth and the Critics: The Development of a Critical Reputation*. Rochester: Camden House, 2001.

McFarland, Thomas, ed. *William Wordsworth: Intensity and Achievement*. Oxford: Clarendon P, 1992.

Newlyn, Lucy. *Coleridge, Wordsworth, and the Language of Allusion*. Oxford: Clarendon P, 1986.

Onorato, Richard J. *The Character of the Poet: Wordsworth in* The Prelude. Princeton: Princeton UP, 1971.

Pace, Joel, and Matthew Scott, eds. *Wordsworth in American Literary Culture*. Houndmills, Basingstoke: Macmillan, 2005.

Page, Judith W. *Wordsworth and the Cultivation of Women*. Berkeley: U of California P, 1994.

Parrish, Stephen M. *The Art of the* Lyrical Ballads. Cambridge, MA: Harvard UP, 1973.

Perkins, David. *Wordsworth and the Poetry of Sincerity*. Cambridge, MA: Belknap P of Harvard UP, 1964.

Reed, Mark L. *Wordsworth: The Chronology of the Early Years, 1770–1799*. Cambridge, MA: Harvard UP, 1967.

—. *Wordsworth: The Chronology of the Middle Years, 1800–1815*. Cambridge, MA: Harvard UP, 1975.

Sheats, Paul D. *The Making of Wordsworth's Poetry, 1785–1798*. Cambridge, MA: Harvard UP, 1973.

Simpson, David. *Wordsworth and the Figurings of the Real*. London: Macmillan, 1982.

—. *Wordsworth's Historical Imagination: The Poetry of Displacement*. New York: Methuen, 1987.

Wolfson, Susan J. *The Questioning Presence: Wordsworth, Keats, and the Interrogative Mode in Romantic Poetry*. Ithaca: Cornell UP, 1986.

Wordsworth, Jonathan. *William Wordsworth: The Borders of Vision*. Oxford: Clarendon P, 1982.

Wordsworth, Jonathan, Michael C. Jaye, and Robert Woof, asst. Peter Funnell. *William Wordsworth and the Age of English Romanticism*. Foreword by M.H. Abrams. New Brunswick: Rutgers UP, 1987.

Wu, Duncan. *Wordsworth's Reading, 1770–1799*. Cambridge: Cambridge UP, 1993.

—. *Wordsworth's Reading, 1800–1815*. Cambridge: Cambridge UP, 1995.

See also Bostetter, Manning, McFarland (*Romanticism and the Forms of Ruin*), Perkins, Rzepka, in General Bibliography; Margoliouth, Roe, Ruoff, under COLERIDGE; Devlin, under DE QUINCEY; Morton, under TAYLOR; Ros, under THELWALL; and Mellor, under D. WORDSWORTH.

Yearsley

EDITIONS:

Poems on Various Subjects. London: G.G.S. and J. Robinson, 1787. Rpt. Oxford: Woodstock, 1999.

The Royal Captives: A Fragment of Secret History Copied from an Old Manuscript. 4 vols. 1795. Rpt. Introd. Gina Luria, New York: Garland, 1974.

STUDIES:

Doody, Margaret Anne. *The Daring Muse: Augustan Poetry Reconsidered*. Cambridge: Cambridge UP, 1985.

Ferguson, Moira. *Eighteenth-Century Women Poets: Nation, Class, and Gender*. Albany: SUNY P, 1995.

—. "Resistance and Power in the Life and Writings of Ann Yearsley." *The Eighteenth Century: Theory and Interpretation* 27 (1986): 246–68.

—. "The Unpublished Poems of Ann Yearsley." *Tulsa Studies in Women's Literature* 12 (1993): 13–46.

Landry, Donna. *The Muses of Resistance: Laboring-class Women's Poetry in Britain, 1739–1796*. Cambridge: Cambridge UP, 1990.

Richardson, Alan. "Darkness Visible: Race and Representation in Bristol Abolitionist Poetry, 1770–1810." *Wordsworth Circle* 27 (1996): 67–72.

See also McGann (*Poetics of Sensibility*), in General Bibliography.

Index of Authors, Titles, and First Lines

A Creole Boy from the West Indies brought 849
A cypress-bough, and a rose-wreath sweet 1488
A dinner party, coffee, tea 850
A flower was offerd to me 296
A green and silent spot amid the hills! 749
A little black thing among the snow 295
A Pause of Sorrow hangs upon the World 223
A simple child, dear brother Jim 623
A slumber did my spirit seal 652
A thing of beauty is a joy forever 1339
A trader I am to the African shore 57
A warrior so bold and a virgin so bright 863
Abou Ben Adhem (may his tribe increase!) 970
Abou Ben Adhem and the Angel 970
Abram's Plains: A Poem 192
Absence 1420
Abstract of the Arguments regarding the Burning of Widows 826
ADAMS, ABIGAIL 161
ADAMS, JOHN 161
Address to a Child During a Boisterous Winter Evening 726
Address to the Opposers of the Repeal of the Corporation and Test Acts, An Adieu and Recall to Love, The 241
Adonais 1248
Advertisement to *Lyrical Ballads* 618
Advice to a Raven in Russia 229
Ae Fond Kiss, And Then We Sever 370
Afar in the Desert 1144
Age of Reason, The 72
Ah Sun-flower! weary of time 297
Ah what avails the sceptred race 846
Ah! he is gone—and I alone! 1420
Ah! poor negro Sadi, what sorrows, what anguish 953
Ah, what can ail thee, wretched wight 1340
AIKIN, LUCY 944
Alas, alas for thee 77
Alastor: Or, The Spirit of Solitude 1153
Alien Boy, The 346
All the night in woe 295
All wordly shapes shall melt in gloom 884
Alonzo the Brave and Fair Imogine 863

America a Prophecy (Preludium) 284
An old, mad, blind, despised, and dying king 1275
And did those feet in ancient time 298
And has the remnant of my life 729
And this place our forefathers made for man! 779
Anecdote for Fathers 622
Anent a brooklette as I laie reclynd 209
Annotations to the *Works of Sir Joshua Reynolds* 302
Annotations to Thornton's *The Lord's Prayer, Newly Translated* 305
Annotations to Wordsworth's Preface to *The Excursion* 304
Anti-Jacobin, The 610
APESS, WILLIAM 1429
Apparition, The 955
Appeal to the Men of Great Britain ("What Women Are") 476
Arachne! Poor degraded maid! 190
As Hermes once took to his feathers light 1373
As I lay asleep in Italy 1266
As late on Skiddaw mount I lay supine 781
As slow I wander'd o'er yon barren heath 955
Auguries of Innocence 301
Auld Lang Syne 371
Auld Robin Gray 187
AUSTEN, JANE 867
Ay, gaze upon her rose-wreathed hair 1474
Badger 1295
BAILLIE, JOANNA 493
BARBAULD, ANNA LAETITIA 90
BARLOW, JOEL 227
Battle of Blenheim, The 839
BEDDOES, THOMAS LOVELL 1487
Before I see another day 637
Before Twilight. Eyezion 597
Beggars 663
Behold her, single in the field 667
Believe Me if all those Endearing Young Charms 914
BELLAMY, THOMAS 130
Ben Battle was a soldier bold 1438
Benevolent Planters, The 130
Beside the ungathered rice he lay 1506
Biographia Literaria 798

1559

Index of Authors, Titles, and First Lines

Birth-Day, The 354
Bishop Bruno 843
Bishop Bruno awoke in the dead midnight 844
Black fool, why winter here? These frozen skies 229
BLAKE, WILLIAM 264
BLAMIRE, SUSANNA 152
Blest as the Gods! Sicilian Maid is he 340
BLOOMFIELD, ROBERT 573
Bob Southey! You're a poet—Poet-laureate 1063
Bonny Kilmeny gaed up the glen 711
Borough, The (Letter 22) 231
BOWLES, WILLIAM 555
Boy of Egremond, The 561
Breakfast 850
Bride of the Greek Isle, The 1302
Bright star, would I were stedfast as thou art 1374
Bring, bring to deck my brow, ye Sylvan girls 336
BROOKE, CHARLOTTE 77
BROWN, CHARLES BROCKDEN 717
BRYANT, WILLIAM CULLEN 1334
BURKE, EDMUND 22
BURNEY, FRANCES 202
BURNS, ROBERT 360
By the same [Werther] 163
By the Same. Just before His Death 163
BYRON, GEORGE GORDON, LORD 1004
Caged Rats 943
Caller Herrin' 584
Camp, The 348
CAMPBELL, THOMAS 884
Can'st thou forget, O! Idol of my Soul! 338
Canadian Boat-Song. Written on the River
    St.-Lawrence, A 913
CANNING, GEORGE 610
Captive, The 865
CARY, THOMAS 192
Casabianca 1301
Cast-Away, The 58
Cataract of Lodore, The 842
CAVENDISH, GEORGIANA 261
Cease, Wilberforce, to urge thy generous aim! 102
Cenci, The 1210
Changes in London 1486
CHATTERTON, THOMAS 208
Child of distress, who meet'st the bitter scorn 113
Child to His Sick Grand-Father, A 500
Child, is thy father dead? 942

Childe Harold's Pilgrimage (canto 3) 1028
Chimney Sweeper, The (Songs of Experience) 295
Chimney Sweeper, The (Songs of Innocence) 266
Choosing a Profession 849
Christabel 782
CLARE, JOHN 1293
Clarkson! it was an obstinate Hill to climb 668
CLARKSON, THOMAS 472
Clock-a-Clay 1296
Clod & the Pebble, The 293
COBBETT, WILLIAM 556
Cockney School of Poetry 1324
Cold blew the freezing Northern blast 861
Cold was the night wind, drifting fast the snows 836
COLERIDGE, SAMUEL TAYLOR 746
Come from the woods with the citron-flowers 1302
Come, Reason, come! each nerve rebellious bind 335
Come, soft Æolian harp, while zephyr plays 336
Come, sportive Fancy! Come with me, and trace 349
Comin' thro' the Rye 371
Complaint of a Forsaken Indian Woman, The 637
Composed upon Westminster Bridge 665
Confessions of an English Opium-Eater 971
Conquest of Prejudice 851
Constancy to an Ideal Object 820
Conversations on Political Economy (10, On the Condition
    of the Poor) 604
COOPER, JAMES FENIMORE 1146
COWLEY, HANNAH 85
COWPER, WILLIAM 55
CRABBE, GEORGE 231
CRISTALL, ANN BATTEN 597
CROKER, JOHN WILSON 935
Crystal Cabinet, The 300
CUGOANO, OTTOBAH 322
DACRE, CHARLOTTE 953
Dang'rous to hear, is that melodious tongue 335
Dark was the dawn, and o'er the deep 344
Darkness 1025
DARWIN, ERASMUS 59
Dawn had not streak'd the spacious veil of night 597
DE CRÈVECOEUR, J. HECTOR ST. JOHN 64
De Monfort 515
DE QUINCEY, THOMAS 971
Dear Beatrice, with pleasure I read your kind letter 237
Declaration of Independence, The 87
Deep in the shady sadness of a vale 1362

Index of Authors, Titles, and First Lines

Defence of Poetry, A 1275
Dejection: An Ode 796
Delusive Hope! more transient than the ray 336
DEROZIO, HENRY LOUIS VIVIAN 1519
Deserted Village, The 46
Dialogue between Jack Anvil the Blacksmith, and Tom Hod the Mason, A 120
Dirge (Beddoes) 1488
Dirge, A (M.W. Shelley) 1420
Discourse on the Love of our Country, A 5
Discourse, Delivered to the Students of the Royal Academy, A 11
Divine Image, The 267
Do you see the OLD BEGGAR who sits at yon gate 355
Don Juan 1063
Doomed City, The 1513
DORSET, CATHERINE ANN 190
Down a broad river of the western wilds 1311
Dream After Reading Dante's Episode of Paulo and Francesca, A 1373
Dream, A 266
Dream, The 1490
Dream-Children; A Reverie 851
Dream-Pedlary 1489
Drinking Song 955
Duet 996
Dungeon, The 779
Earth has not any thing to shew more fair 665
Earth rais'd up her head 293
Earth, ocean, air, beloved brotherhood! 1154
Earth's Answer 293
Ecchoing Green, The 265
EDGEWORTH, MARIA 586
Effusion 35 747
Eighteen Hundred and Eleven, A Poem 105
Elegiac Sonnets 162
Elegiac Stanzas, Suggested by a Picture of Peele Castle 669
ELLIOTT, EBENEZER 942
Emigrants, The 166
Enclosure [The Mores] 1297
Endymion (from Book 1) 1339
England in 1819 1275
Enquiry Concerning Political Justice, An (from Book 2, chapter 2; from Book 8, chapter 8) 246
Epistle to William Wilberforce 102
Epistles on women 944

EQUIANO, OLAUDAH 140
Ere on my bed my limbs I lay 793
Erinna 1469
Essay on the Principle of Population, An (from Chapter 10) 577
Essay on the Slavery and Commerce of the Human Species, An (The Slavery of the Africans in the European Colonies) 472
Ettrick Shepherd, The 692
Eve of St. Agnes, The 1351
Evening 716
Evening Prayer at a Girls' School 1301
Evening. Gertrude 601
Excelsior 1505
Excursions in North America (Letter 32) 180
Excursion, The 675
Excuse me, STELLA, sunk in humble state 221
Expanding like the petals of young flowers 1523
Expostulation and Reply 635
Exulting BEAUTY,—phantom of an hour 326
Eyam 82
Faint and more faint amid the world of dreams 1485
Faintly as tolls the evening chime 913
Fair flower, that dost so comely grow 199
Faithless Nelly Gray 1438
Familiar Epistle to a Friend, A 237
Fanatics have their dreams, wherewith they weave 1375
FANSHAWE, CATHERINE MARIA 572
Far o'er the waves my lofty bark shall glide 340
Far spread the moory ground, a level scene 1297
Fare Thee Well! 1024
Farewell, for Two Years, to England, A 487
Farewell, ye coral caves, ye pearly sands 337
Farewell, ye tow'ring Cedars, in whose shade 339
Farmer's Boy, The (Spring) 573
Favour'd by Heav'n are those, ordain'd to taste 333
Fears In Solitude 749
Felicia Hemans 1482
Female Philosopher, The 954
FIELD, BARRON 998
Fire, Famine, and Slaughter 748
First Fire, The 114
Five years have passed; five summers, with the length 638
Floating Island 727
Fly, The 296
For one short week I leave, with anxious heart 82

Index of Authors, Titles, and First Lines

Forced from home and all its pleasures 56
Four Ages of Poetry, The 985
France. An Ode 752
FRANKLIN, BENJAMIN 1
FRENEAU, PHILIP 198
FRERE, JOHN HOOKHAM 610
From the thirteenth cantata of Metastasio 163
Frost at Midnight 754
Garden of Love, The 297
Gather her raven hair in one rich cluster 1482
Gentle and lovely form 1320
George The Third's Soliloquy 199
Germ of new life, whose powers expanding slow 113
Giaour, The 1005
Giovanni Villani 1404
Given to a Lady Who Asked Me to Write A Poem 465
Go, cruel tyrant of the human breast! 163
Go, idle Boy! I quit thy pow'r 241
GODWIN, WILLIAM 245
GOLDSMITH, OLIVER (1730?-1774) 46
GOLDSMITH, OLIVER (1794-1861) 1327
Goody Blake, and Harry Gill 619
Go—you may call it madness, folly 562
Grand-dad, they say your old and frail 500
GRANT, ANNE 237
Grasmere Journal 730
Grasmere—A Fragment 728
Grateful Negro, The 586
Grave of a Poetess, The 1315
Graves of a Household, The 1318
Green little vaulter in the sunny grass 970
Ha, old acquaintance! many a month has past 114
Ha! whaur ye gaun, ye crowlin ferlie! 362
Hail, happy day, when, smiling like the morn 219
Hail to thee, blithe spirit! 1208
HANDS, ELIZABETH 149
Harmonious Powers with Nature work 727
Harp of India, The 1519
Harp that once through Tara's Halls, The 914
Hast thou come with the heart of thy childhood back? 1320
Hasty-Pudding, The (Canto 1) 227
Haunted Beach, The 343
Have you heard of a Collier of honest renown 125
HAWTHORNE, NATHANIEL 1492
HAYS, MARY 476
HAZLITT, WILLIAM 886

He stopt,—it surely was a groan 837
Hear the voice of the Bard! 293
HEARNE, SAMUEL 135
Heccar and Gaira. An African Eclogue 212
Helen, thy beauty is to me 1513
HEMANS, FELICIA 1299
Here bounds the gaudy gilded chair 354
Here droops the muse! while from her glowing mind 343
Here, from the Castle's terraced site 565
High on a rock, coæval with the skies 334
History of Mary Prince, The 1131
History of the Ojebway Indians (Letter to John Jones) 1440
History of the Rise, Progress and Accomplishment of the Abolition of the African Slave-trade (illustration) 475
HOGG, JAMES 711
Holy Thursday (*Songs of Experience*) 294
Holy Thursday (*Songs of Innocence*) 267
Holy Willie's Prayer 368
Home 1466
Home at Grasmere 673
Homes of England, The 1316
HONE, WILLIAM 917
Honora, shou'd that cruel time arrive 84
HOOD, THOMAS 1435
How like a star you rose upon my life 1421
How many times do I love thee, dear? 1487
Human Abstract, The 297
HUNT, LEIGH 968
Hush! 'tis a holy hour—the quiet room 1301
Hymn to Intellectual Beauty 1166
Hyperion 1362
Hyperion, A Vision [The Fall of Hyperion] 1375
I Am 1295
I am a daughter of that land 1445
I am! yet what I am who cares, or knows? 1295
I hate that drum's discordant sound 45
I hate the Elegiac lay 85
I have a boy of five years old 622
I have no name 268
I heard a thousand blended notes 624
I left my home;—'twas in a little vale 1466
I loved Theotormon 277
I met a Traveler from an antique land 1167
I saw a boy with eager eye 850
I stood beside thy lowly grave 1315
I traveld thro' a Land of Men 299
I travell'd among unknown Men 662

Index of Authors, Titles, and First Lines

I wake! delusive phantoms hence, away! 340
I wander thro' each charter'd street 297
I wandered lonely as a Cloud 668
I wandered out one rainy day 1296
I want a hero: an uncommon want 1066
I was angry with my friend 298
I was thy Neighbour once, thou rugged Pile! 669
I weep for Adonais—he is dead! 1248
I went to the Garden of Love 297
I'm sick of fame—I'm gorg'd with it—so full 992
I'm wearin' awa', John 583
I've sent my empty pot again 829
I've watched you now a full half hour 668
Idiot Boy, The 629
Idiot, The 836
If from the public way you turn your steps 656
If Heaven has into being deign'd to call 116
If there exists a HELL—the case is clear 200
If there were dreams to sell 1489
If thou wilt ease thine heart 1488
If you go to the field where the Reapers now bind 849
Image in Lava, The 1319
Immolation of a Hindoo Widow 1482
Improvisatrice, The 1445
In clouds drew on the evening's close 601
In Congress, July 4, 1776 [Declaration of Independence] 87
In early youth's unclouded scene 165
In Egypt's sandy silence, all alone 916
In futurity 294
In royal Anna's golden days 465
In SENSIBILITY's lov'd praise 490
In spite of all the learn'd have said 198
In the cowslip pips I lie 1296
In the sweet shire of Cardigan 621
In truth it is as fair and sweet a day 1395
In Xanadu did KUBLA KHAN 792
INCHBALD, ELIZABETH 215
Indian Burying-Ground, The 198
Indian City, The 1308
Indian Woman's Death-Song 1311
Infant Joy 268
Infant Sorrow 298
Influence of Poetry 1485
Inscription for an Ice-House 112

Interesting Narrative of the Life of Olaudah Equiano, The 140
Interview, The 243
Introduction (*Songs of Experience*) 293
Introduction (*Songs of Innocence*) 265
Introductory Discourse to *A Series of Plays* 500
Invitation to Eternity 1296
Irish Harp, The 905
IRVING, WASHINGTON 959
Is it in mansions rich and gay 355
Is it to love, to fix the tender gaze 334
Is there, for honest poverty 369
Is this a holy thing to see 294
Is thy face like thy mother's, my fair child! 1028
It had pleas'd God to form poor Ned 836
It is a beauteous Evening, calm and free 666
It is an ancient Mariner 757
It is an ancient Marinere 756
It seems a day 655
It was a Summer evening 839
It was the schooner Hesperus 1503
Italy (chapter 2, Passage of the Alps) 906
Itchin, when I behold thy banks again 555
January, 1795 327
JEFFERSON, THOMAS 87
JEFFREY, FRANCIS 830
Joan of Arc, in Rheims 1312
John Barleycorn 363
JONES, PETER 1440
Journals, 14 and 15 May 1824 (M.W. Shelley) 1427
Journey from Prince of Wales's Fort in Hudson's Bay to the Northern Ocean, A 135
Just at the self-same beat of Time's wide wings 1367
Kangaroo, Kangaroo! 998
Kangaroo, The 998
KEATS, JOHN 1337
Kentish Journal (from *Cobbett's Weekly Register*) 558
Kilmeny 711
Kubla Khan 792
La Belle Dame Sans Mercy 1340
Laird o' Cockpen, The 584
LAMB, CAROLINE 992
LAMB, CHARLES 848
LAMB, MARY 848
Lamb, The 265

Lamentation of Cucullin, The 77
Lamia 1341
Land o' the Leal, The 583
Landing of the Pilgrim Fathers in New England,
    The 1317
LANDON, LETITIA ELIZABETH 1445
LANDOR, WALTER SAVAGE 846
Last Man, The (Campbell) 884
Last Man, The (Hood) 1435
Lead me, Sicilian Maids, to haunted bow'rs 341
LEE, HARRIET 309
Legend of the Shushan, The 1520
LEIGH, HELEN 462
Let not the rugged brow the rhymes accuse 736
Let not the title of my verse offend 462
Let others boast the golden spoil 463
Letter from Abigail to John Adams, 31 March 1776 61
Letter from John to Abigail Adams, 14 April 1776 62
*Letter from the Right Honourable Edmund Burke to a
    Noble Lord*, A 33
Letter to Augusta Leigh, September 1816 [Alpine Journal]
    (Byron) 1122
Letter to Benjamin Bailey, 22 November 1817
    (Keats) 1382
Letter to Charles James Fox, 14 January 1801 (W.
    Wordsworth) 706
Letter to Douglas Kinnaird, 26 October [1819]
    (Byron) 1129
Letter to Esther Burney, 22 March-June 1812
    (Burney) 202
Letter to George and Tom Keats, December 1817
    (Keats) 1386
Letter to Gilbert Imlay, [March 1796]
    (Wollstonecraft) 460
Letter to Gilbert Imlay, 19 August [1794]
    (Wollstonecraft) 458
Letter to Gilbert Imlay, 9 February [1795]
    (Wollstonecraft) 459
Letter to J.H. Reynolds, 22 November 1817 (Keats) 1384
Letter to J.H. Reynolds 3 February 1818 (Keats) 1387
Letter to J.H. Reynolds, 3 May 1818 (Keats) 1388
Letter to John Jones (Peter Jones) 1440
Letter to John Murray, 12 August 1819 (Byron) 1127
Letter to John Murray, 16 February 1821 (Byron) 1129
Letter to John Taylor, 6 March 1821 (Severn) 1322
Letter to Joseph Cottle, 26 April 1814 (Coleridge) 820

Letter to Joseph Johnson, 26 December 1792
    (Wollstonecraft) 458
Letter to Lady Byron, 8 February 1816 (Byron) 1121
Letter to M.W. Shelley, 9 August 1821
    (P.B. Shelley) 1285
Letter to Maria Gisborne, 15 August 1822
    (M.W. Shelley) 1422
Letter to Mary Wordsworth, 11 August [1810]
    (W. Wordsworth) 708
Letter to Mr. ⸺ (Poe) 1508
Letter to P.B. Shelley, 16 August 1820 (Keats) 1393
Letter to P.B. Shelley, 26 April 1821 (Byron) 1130
Letter to Rev^d Dr Trusler, 23 August 1799 (Blake) 305
Letter to Richard Woodhouse, 27 October 1818
    (Keats) 1392
Letter to S.T. Coleridge, 27 September 1796
    (Charles Lamb) 854
Letter to Thomas Butts, 22 November 1802 (Blake) 307
Letter to Thomas Love Peacock, [22] December 1818
    (P.B. Shelley) 1281
Letter to Thomas Manning, 15 February 1801
    (Charles Lamb) 856
Letter to William Godwin, [17 August 1796]
    (Wollstonecraft) 461
Letter to William Godwin, 17 August 1796
    (Wollstonecraft) 460
Letter to William Wordsworth, 30 January 1801
    (Charles Lamb) 854
Letters from an American Farmer (Letter 12) 64
Letters from England (Letter 55) 840
Letters of the Late Ignatius Sancho (Letter 36) 43
Letters on Education (Part 1, Letter 24) 52
*Letters Written During a Short Residence in Sweden, Norway,
    and Denmark* (Letters 1, 6, 7, 8, 15) 428
Letters Written in France (Letters 4, 11) 483
LEWIS, MATTHEW GREGORY 863
Lift not the painted veil which those who live 1256
LINDSAY, LADY ANNE 186
Lines of Life 1475
Lines to Mary Wollstonecraft Godwin 858
Lines Written a Few Miles Above Tintern Abbey 638
Lines Written in a Blank Leaf of the "Prometheus
    Unbound" 1487
Lines Written in Early Spring 624
Little Black Boy, The 266
Little Fly 296

Index of Authors, Titles, and First Lines

Little Girl Found, The 295
Little Girl Lost, The 294
Little Lamb who made thee 265
LITTLE, JANET 465
LLOYD, CHARLES 858
Lo! Death hath rear'd himself a throne 1513
Lochinvar. Lady Heron's Song 724
LOCKHART, JOHN 1324
LOGAN, MARIA 463
London 297
London Summer Morning, A 349
London, 1802 666
Long wintry months are past; the Moon that now 173
LONGFELLOW, HENRY WADSWORTH 1503
Lord Randal 723
Love and Freindship 867
Love in a hut, with water and a crust 1347
Love seeketh not Itself to please 293
Love steals unheeded o'er the tranquil mind 337
Love's Last Lesson 1467
Lucy Gray 653
MACAULAY, CATHARINE 52
Madeline. A Domestic Tale 1314
Maie Selynesse on erthes boundes bee hadde? 212
MALTHUS, THOMAS ROBERT 577
Manfred, A Dramatic Poem 1041
Man's a Man, for a' That: A Song, A 369
MARCET, JANE 604
Marriage of Heaven and Hell, The 268
Mary, I've trod the turf, beneath whose damp 859
Masque of Anarchy, The 1266
Memoirs of the Author of A Vindication of the Rights of Woman (from Chapters 6, 9, and 10) 250
Memorial to the Supreme Court 822
Mental Traveller, The 299
MERRY, ROBERT 241
Methought last night I saw thee lowly laid 1490
Metzengerstein 1514
Michael, A Pastoral Poem 656
Midway the hill of science, after steep 105
MILNE, CHRISTIAN 829
Milton 298
Milton! thou should'st be living at this hour 666
Minstrel Boy, The 915
Mirror in the Deserted Hall, The 1321
MITFORD, MARY RUSSELL 1000

Mont Blanc 1164
MOODIE, SUSANNA 1490
MOORE, THOMAS 912
MORE, HANNAH 115
Morning. Rosamonde 599
Mother to Her Waking Infant, A 499
Mother, I Cannot Mind My Wheel 846
Mouse's Petition, The 91
Much have I travel'd in the realms of Gold 1338
My child, my child, thou leav'st me!—I shall hear 1314
My country! in thy days of glory past 1519
My Days Among the Dead Are Passed 845
My First Acquaintance with Poets 889
My hand is on the lyre, which never more 1470
My heart aches, and a drowsy numbness pains 1357
My heart leaps up when I behold 667
My mother bore me in the southern wild 266
My mother groand! my father wept 298
My pensive Sara! thy soft cheek reclin'd 747
My Pretty Rose Tree 296
My spirit is too weak—Mortality 1338
NAIRNE, CAROLINA OLIPHANT, LADY 583
Natural Child, The 462
Needy Knife-grinder! whither are you going? 610
Negro Girl, The 344
Negro's Complaint, The 56
Nelly kiss'd me when we met 970
New Canto, A 992
New Morality, The 611
Night 603
Nightingale, The 778
Nightingale's Nest, The 1293
No breath of air to break the wave 1005
No cloud, no relique of the sunken day 778
No more, no more—oh, never more returning 1482
No, no, go not to Lethe, neither twist 1361
Noon. Lysander 599
Northanger Abbey (from Chapter 5) 883
Not for the glory on their heads 1483
Not for the promise of the labor'd field 358
Notions of the Americans, Picked Up by a Travelling Bachelor 1146
Now in thy dazzling half-op'd eye 499
Now, o'er the tessellated pavement strew 336
Now, round my favour'd grot let roses rise 336
Nurse's Song 268

Index of Authors, Titles, and First Lines

Nutting (Mitford) 1000
Nutting (W. Wordsworth) 655
Nymph of the rock! whose dauntless spirit braves 164
O come, blest Spirit! Whatsoe'er thou art 573
O, dim, forsaken mirror! 1321
O Goddess! hear these tuneless numbers, wrung 1360
O golden tongued Romance, with serene lute! 1373
O happy time of youthful lovers 688
O my Luve's like a red, red rose 370
O now may I depart in peace! for, lo! 916
O Rose thou art sick 296
O thou! meek Orb! that stealing o'er the dale 338
O Thou, who in the heavens dost dwell 368
O we have met, and now I call 243
O where hae ye been, lord Randal, my son? 723
O! Love is strong, and its hopes 'twill build 1520
O! How can LOVE exulting Reason quell! 334
O! Reason! vaunted Sov'reign of the mind! 335
O! seize again thy golden quill 85
O, come to me in dreams, my love! 1421
O, dim, forsaken mirror! 1321
O, wild West Wind, thou breath of Autumn's being 1207
O, young Lochinvar is come out of the west 724
O'er the tall cliff that bounds the billowy main 339
O'NEILL, HENRIETTA 358
Obscurest night involv'd the sky 58
Ode [Intimations of Immortality] 670
Ode 13 45
Ode on a Grecian Urn 1359
Ode on Indolence 1374
Ode on Melancholy 1361
Ode to a Nightingale 1357
Ode to Beauty 326
Ode to Psyche 1360
Ode to the Poppy 358
Ode to the West Wind 1207
Of warres glum pleasaunce doe I chaunte mie laie 214
Oft had I heard of Lucy Gray 653
Oh Sigh! thou steal'st, the herald of the breast 341
Oh ye! who teach the ingenuous youth of nations 1095
Oh! Breathe Not His Name 914
Oh! can'st thou bear to see this faded frame 342
Oh! for a lodge in some vast wilderness 55
Oh! hear a pensive captive's prayer 91
Oh! I could toil for thee o'er burning plains 337
Oh! pleasant exercise of hope and joy! 673
Oh! what's the matter? what's the matter? 619

Oh! ye bright Stars! that on the Ebon fields 339
Oh, what could the ladye's beauty match 1466
Old Adam, the carrion crow 1488
Old Beggar, The 355
Old Familiar Faces, The 849
Old Man Travelling 636
Old *Peter Grimes* made Fishing his employ 232
Old Woman's Tale. Lothaire, The 309
On a Stupendous Leg of Granite 916
On Being Brought from Africa to America 218
On De Monfort; a Tragedy, in Five Acts 215
On Dover Cliffs. July 20, 1787 555
On First Looking into Chapman's Homer 1338
On Ghosts 1407
On Gusto 886
On Happienesse 212
On Lovers' Vows; A Play in Five Acts 216
On Man, on Nature, and on Human life 673
On Mrs. Montagu 222
On Poetry, and Our Relish for the Beauties of Nature 455
On Receiving a Branch of Mezereon 744
On Seeing the Elgin Marbles 1338
On Sitting Down to Read King Lear Once Again 1373
On The Ancient and Modern Influence of Poetry 1477
On the Death of the Rev. Mr. George Whitefield 218
On the departure of the nightingale 162
On the Knocking at the Gate in Macbeth 982
On the low margin of a murm'ring stream 342
On the Prose-Style of Poets 901
On the Spanish Revolution 916
On the Standard of Taste 717
On the Supernatural in Poetry 566
On these white cliffs, that calm above the flood 555
On thy grey bark, in witness of my flame 163
On Wordsworth's Cottage 1483
Once a dream did weave a shade 266
One day—'twas on a summer afternoon 968
One dream of passion and of beauty more! 1306
One morn before me were three figures seen 1374
OPIE, AMELIA 608
OWENSON, SYDNEY, LADY MORGAN 904
Ozymandias 1167
PAINE, THOMAS 72
Pains of Opium, The 977
Pains of Sleep, The 793
Passage of the Mountain of Saint Gothard, The 261
Past ruin'd Ilion Helen lives 847

Index of Authors, Titles, and First Lines

Pathway of light! o'er thy empurpled zone 492
Patient Joe; or, the Newcastle Collier 125
Pavement slip'ry; People sneezing 327
Peaceful our valley, fair and green 728
PEACOCK, THOMAS LOVE 985
Piping down the valleys wild 265
Pity would be no more 297
POE, EDGAR ALLAN 1507
Poem, On the Supposition of an Advertisement, A 149
Poem, On the Supposition of the Book Having Been Published and Read, A 150
Poet of Nature, thou hast wept to know 1163
Poet's Garret, The 349
Poet's Love, A 1485
Poetry of earth is never dead, The 1338
Poison Tree, A 298
Political House That Jack Built, The 918
POLWHELE, RICHARD 467
Poor melancholy bird—that all night long 162
Poor Negro Sadi, The 953
Poor of the Borough, The (Peter Grimes) 231
Preface to *Lyrical Ballads* 640
Prepare your wreaths, Aonian maids divine 342
Press'd by the Moon, mute arbitress of tides 165
PRICE, RICHARD 5
PRINCE, MARY 1131
PRINGLE, THOMAS 1143
Progress of Romance, The (Evening 7) 16
Prometheus 1027
Prometheus Unbound 1167
Properzia Rossi 1306
Proud Ladye, The 1466
Psyche; or, The Legend of Love 735
Quail's Nest 1296
Queen of the silver bow!—by thy pale beam 162
RADCLIFFE, ANN 563
Rainbow, The 861
Rapt in the visionary theme! 351
Reaper's Child, The 849
Recollections of the Last Days of Shelley and Byron (from Chapter 12) 1289
Recreation 956
Red, Red Rose, A 370
Redbreast, The 861
REEVE, CLARA 16
Reflections on the Death of Louis XVI 223

Reflections on the Revolution in France 22
Remarks Concerning the Savages of North-America 1
Resolution and Independence 663
Return, blest years!—when not the jocund Spring 83
Return, The 1320
Revenge 1474
Review of Barbauld's *Eighteen Hundred and Eleven* 935
Review of Keats's *Endymion* 938
Review of *The Excursion* 830
REYNOLDS, SIR JOSHUA 11
RICHARDSON, CHARLOTTE 861
RICHARDSON, JOHN 1394
Riddle, A 572
Right happy bird, so full of mirth 1298
Rights of Woman, The (Barbauld) 111
Rights of Woman—Spoken by Miss Fontenelle, The 371
Rime of the Ancient Mariner, The (1817) 757
Rime of the Ancyent Marinere, The (1798) 756
Rintrah roars & shakes his fires in the burden'd air 268
Rip Van Winkle 959
Rising Village. A Poem, The 1327
Robert Bruce's March To Bannockburn 372
ROBINSON, MARY 325
Roger Malvin's Burial 1492
ROGERS, SAMUEL 561
Rondeau ["Soft as yon silver ray"] 564
Rondeau ["Nelly kissed me"] 970
Rose Aylmer 846
ROY, RAJA RAMMOHUN 822
Royal in splendour went down the day 1308
Sailor, Who Had Served in the Slave-Trade, The 837
SANCHO, IGNATIUS 43
Sapphics 610
Sappho and Phaon 328
Savage of Aveyron, The 352
Say, what remains when Hope is fled? 561
Say, wilt thou go with me, sweet maid 1296
Scene on the Northern Shore of Sicily 565
Science! meet daughter of old Time thou art 1508
Scorn not the Sonnet; Critic, you have frowned 691
Scots, wha hae wi' Wallace bled 372
SCOTT, JOHN 45
SCOTT, SIR WALTER 722
Season of mists and mellow fruitfulness 1361
See you, beneath yon cloud so dark 913
Sent with a Flower Pot, Begging a Slip of Geranium 829

Index of Authors, Titles, and First Lines

SEVERN, JOSEPH 1322
SEWARD, ANNA 82
She dwelt among th'untrodden ways 652
She had a tall Man's height, or more 663
She Walks in Beauty 1024
SHELLEY, MARY WOLLSTONECRAFT 1403
SHELLEY, PERCY BYSSHE 1152
Short is perhaps our date of life 570
Should auld acquaintance be forgot 371
Sick Rose, The 296
Sighing I see yon little troop at play 164
Simon Lee, the old Huntsman 621
Since all, that beat about in Nature's range 820
Skylark Leaving Her Nest, The 1298
Slave's Dream, The 1506
Slavery, A Poem 116
Slow in the Wintry Morn, the struggling light 167
SMITH, CHARLOTTE 161
SMITH, HORACE 916
Soft as yon silver ray, that sleeps 564
Soft falls the show'r, the thunders cease! 861
Soldier's Wife, The 836
Solitary Reaper, The 667
Son of the Forest, A 1429
Song ["She dwelt among th'untrodden ways"] 652
Song ["A cypress-bough, and a rose-wreath sweet"] 1488
Song ["Child, is thy father dead?"] 942
Song ["How many times do I love thee, dear?"] 1487
Song ["Old Adam, the carrion crow"] 1488
Song ["Where shall the lover rest"] 723
Song from the Waters 1489
Song of a Hindustani Girl 608
Song, Woo'd and Married and A' 553
Song. For Mable Kelly. By Carolan 79
Sonnet 10. To Honora Sneyd 84
Sonnet 71. To the Poppy 84
Sonnet IV ["Lift not the painted veil"] 1256
Sonnet, to William Wilberforce, Esq. 57
Sonnet: To the Torrid Zone 492
Sonnet—To Science 1508
SOUTHEY, ROBERT 835
Spider, The 190
Spirit of love and sorrow—hail! 565
Spirit of strength! to whom in wrath 'tis given 552
St. Agnes' Eve—Ah, bitter chill it was! 1351
Stanzas ["O, come to me in dreams, my love!"] 1421

Stanzas ["How like a star you rose upon my life"] 421
Stanzas On Hearing for Certainty That We Were to be Tried for High Treason 570
Star, The 956
Stay, gaoler, stay, and hear my woe! 865
Stay near me—do not take thy flight! 667
Still the loud death drum, thundering from afar 105
Stoklewath Or, The Cumbrian Village 152
Storie of William Canynge, The 209
Storied Sonnet 564
Story of Rimini, The (from Canto 3) 968
Strange fits of passion I have known 652
Stranger Minstrel, A 781
Stranger, approach! within this iron door 112
Strictures on the Modern System of Female Education (Chapter 4) 127
Summer Evening's Meditation, A 92
Sun upon the Weirdlaw Hill, The 725
Supposed to be written by Werter 163
Surprized by Joy—impatient as the Wind 687
Sweet Auburn, loveliest village of the plain 46
Sweet Autumn! how thy melancholy grace 564
Sweet Babe! that, on thy mother's guardian breast 571
Sweet Meat Has Sour Sauce: or, The Slave-Trader in the Dumps 57
Sweet poet of the woods—a long adieu! 162
Sweet Spring! while others hail thy op'ning flowers 487
Swift as a spirit hastening to his task 1256
Tables Turned, The 636
Tam O'Shanter. A Tale 364
Task, The (from Book 2, The Time-Piece) 55
TAYLOR, JANE 956
Teach it me, if you can,—forgetfulness! 1467
Tecumseh; or, The Warrior of the West 1395
Temple of Nature, The (from Canto 4) 59
Tents, *marquees*, and baggage wagons 348
Thanatopsis 1335
That was a joyous day in Rheims of old 1312
The artist who this idol wrought 1274
The boy stood on the burning deck 1301
The breaking waves dash'd high 1318
The bride she is winsome and bonny 553
The cock, warm roosting 'midst his feather'd dames 493
The dinner was over, the table-cloth gone 150
The everlasting universe of things 1164
The Frost performs it's secret ministry 754

Index of Authors, Titles, and First Lines

The Harp that once through Tara's Halls 914
The kiss that's on thy lip impress'd 996
The laid o' Cockpen, he's proud an' he's great 584
The lilly cheek, the "purple light of love" 835
The little hedge-row birds 636
The Maiden caught me in the Wild 300
The Minstrel-boy to the war is gone 915
The Muses are turned gossips; they have lost 104
The partial Muse, has from my earliest hours 162
The poetry of earth is never dead 1338
The presence of perpetual change 1486
The shades of night were falling fast 1505
The shadowy daughter of Urthona stood before red Orc 284
The stately Homes of England 1316
The Sun does arise 265
The sun had thrown its noontide ray 599
The sun sets brightly—but a ruddier glow 1300
The sun upon the Weirdlaw hill 725
The swallow leaves her nest 1490
The tea-kettle bubbled, the tea things were set 149
The Time I've lost in Wooing 915
The unremitting voice of nightly streams 693
The weary traveler, who, all night long 564
The wolf, escorted by his milk-drawn dam 59
The world is too much with us; late and soon 666
The youth whom fav'ring Heaven's decree 79
THELWALL, JOHN 570
There is a thorn; it looks so old 625
There was a Boy, ye knew him well, ye Cliffs 651
There was a roaring in the wind all night 663
There was a time when meadow, grove, and stream 670
There was a time! that time the Muse bewails 464
There was a time, poor phrensied maid 609
There was three kings into the east 363
They grew in beauty, side by side 1317
Thine is a strain to read among the hills 1317
Thirty-Eight. Address'd to Mrs. H——Y 165
This is the charm of poetry: it comes 1485
This is the Wealth 920
This Lime-Tree Bower My Prison 780
This living hand, now warm and capable 1382
This morn, thy gallant bark, love 1420
Thorn, The 625
Thou dear companion of my early years 1327
Thou still unravish'd bride of quietness 1359
Thou thing of years departed! 1319

Thou, who with all the poet's genuine rage 467
Thoughts and Sentiments on the Evil and Wicked Traffic of the Slavery and Commerce of the Human Species 322
Thoughts on my Sick-bed 729
Three years she grew in sun and shower 655
Thunder (1790) 497
Thunder (1840) 552
Thus in alternate uproar and sad peace 1371
Thy country, Wilberforce, with just disdain 57
Thy Plains, O *Abram*! and thy pleasing views 192
Thy soul shall find itself alone 1507
TIGHE, MARY 735
'Tis eight o'clock,—a clear March night 629
'Tis past! The sultry tyrant of the south 92
'Tis the middle of night by the castle clock 783
'Tis thy will, and I must leave thee 608
Titan! to whose immortal eyes 1027
To —— 562
To a Butterfly ["I've watched you now"] 668
To a Butterfly ["Stay near me"] 667
To a Gentleman 794
To a Lady, Who Said It Was Sinful to Read Novels 829
To a Little Invisible Being 113
To A Louse, On Seeing one on a Lady's Bonnet 362
To A Maniac 609
To A Mountain-Daisy, On turning one down, with the Plough 361
To a Mouse, On turning her up in her Nest 360
To a nightingale 162
To a Skylark 1208
To a Waterfowl 1334
To Ætna's scorching sands my Phaon flies! 338
To Afric's torrid clime, where every day 130
To Anna Matilda 242
To Autumn ["Season of mists and mellow fruitfulness"] 1361
To Autumn ["Sweet Autumn! how thy melancholy grace"] 564
To Della Crusca ["I hate the Elegiac lay"] 85
To Della Crusca. The Pen 85
To fortitude 164
To Helen 1513
To him who in the love of Nature holds 1335
To love these Books, and harmless Tea 829
To Mary Wollstonecraft 835
To Melancholy 565
To Melancholy. Written on the banks of the Arun 164

Index of Authors, Titles, and First Lines

To Mercy Pity peace and Love 267
To Mira, on the Care of Her Infant 224
To Mr. Alderman Wood, On the Subject of Teaching the Children of the Poor to Read 556
To Mr. C——ge 105
To Opium 463
To Percy Shelley, on the Degrading Notions of Deity 970
To S.M. a Young African Painter, on Seeing His Works 220
To see a World in a Grain of Sand 301
To Sensibility 490
To show the lab'ring bosom's deep intent 220
To Sir Toby, a Sugar-Planter in the Interior Parts of Jamaica 200
To the Infant Hampden 571
To the moon 162
To the Poet Coleridge 351
To the Poor 113
To the Pupils of the Hindu College 1523
To the Right Honourable William, Earl of Dartmouth 219
To the River Itchin, Near Winton 555
To the Same [Stella] 221
To Thomas Clarkson 668
To Time Past. Written Dec. 1772 83
To Toussaint L'Ouverture 666
To Wordsworth (Hemans) 1317
To Wordsworth (P.B. Shelley) 1163
Toussaint, the most unhappy Man of Men! 666
TRAILL, CATHERINE PARR 1442
Transformation 1411
TRELAWNY, EDWARD JOHN 1289
Triumph of Life, The 1256
Turn to yon vale beneath, whose tangled shade 334
Twas on a Holy Thursday their innocent faces clean 267
'Twas in heaven pronounced, and 'twas muttered in hell 572
'Twas in the mazes of a wood 352
'Twas in the year two thousand and one 1435
'Twas mercy brought me from my *Pagan* land 218
'Twas on a Mountain, near the Western Main 346
'Twas summer, and the sun had mounted high 675
Twinkle, twinkle, little star 956
Two April Mornings, The 654
Two Boys, The 850
Two-Part Prelude of 1799, The 693

Tyger, The 296
Tyger Tyger, burning bright 296
Under a spreading chestnut tree 1504
Unsex'd Females, The 467
Unto a Yorkshire school was sent 851
Up this green woodland-ride let's softly rove 1293
Up! up! My friend, and clear your looks 636
Upon a lonely desert Beach 343
Upon a time, before the faery broods 1341
Vaudracour and Julia 688
Venus! to thee, the Lesbian Muse shall sing 341
Verses On Hearing That an Airy and Pleasant Situation ... Was Surrounded with New Buildings 464
Village Blacksmith, The 1504
Vindication of the Rights of Men, A 375
Vindication of the Rights of Woman, A 385
Visions of the Daughters of Albion 277
Visit of the Dead 1507
WAKEFIELD, PRISCILLA 180
Wanderer, The 675
Warre, The 214
Was it for this 693
Washing-Day 103
We are Seven 623
We took our work, and went, you see 956
We walk'd along, while bright and red 654
Weak is the sophistry, and vain the art 339
Weary way-wanderer languid and sick at heart 836
Wee, modest, crimson-tipped flow'r 361
Wee, sleekit, cowrin, tim'rous *beastie* 360
Well! If the Bard was weather-wise, who made 796
Well, read my cheek, and watch my eye 1475
Well, they are gone, and here must I remain 780
Wha'll buy my caller herrin' 584
What mean these dreams, and hideous forms that rise 199
What means the mist opake that veils these eyes 341
What way does the Wind come? What way does he go? 726
What Women Are 476
What wonder, Percy, that with jealous rage 970
WHEATLEY, PHILLIS 218
When chapmen billies leave the street 364
When first, descending from the Moorlands 692
When I Have Fears That I May Cease To Be 1375
When latest Autumn spreads her evening veil 164
When midnight comes a host of dogs and men 1295

1570

Index of Authors, Titles, and First Lines

When my mother died I was very young 266
When summer smil'd, and birds on ev'ry spray 151
When the sheep are in the fauld, when the cows com hame 187
When the voices of children are heard on the green 268
When, in the gloomy mansion of the dead 341
Where antique woods o'er-hang the mountain's crest 339
Where are they gone, the old familiar faces? 849
Where shall the lover rest 723
While Europe's eye is fixed on mighty things 371
While from the dizzy precipice I gaze 343
While Summer Roses all their glory yield 84
Whilst war, destruction, crimes that fiends delight 224
Whither, 'midst falling dew 1334
Who has not wak'd to list the busy sounds 349
Why art thou chang'd? O Phaon! tell me why? 337
Why boast, O arrogant, imperious man 222
Why do I live to loath the cheerful day 337
Why hang'st thou lonely on yon withered bough? 1519
Why should I wish to hold in this low sphere 163
Why sleeps the Harp of Erin's pride? 905
Why William, on that old grey stone 635
Why, through each aching vein, with lazy pace 335
Why, when I gaze on Phaon's beauteous eyes 334
Widow, The 836
Wife of Asdrubal, The 1299
Wild Honey Suckle, The 199
Wild is the foaming Sea! The surges roar! 338
Wild midst the teeming buds of opening May 599
WILLIAMS, HELEN MARIA 483

Wine, I Say! I'll Drink to Madness! 955
Winter Day, A 493
Wintry Day, The 355
With a Guitar 1274
With happiness stretchd across the hills 307
WOLLSTONECRAFT, MARY 374
Woman on the Field of Battle 1320
WORDSWORTH, DOROTHY 726
WORDSWORTH, WILLIAM 617
Would I had seen thee dead and cold 997
Wreck of the Hesperus, The 1503
Write it in gold—a Spirit of the sun 1487
Written in the Church Yard at Middleton in Sussex 165
Written on Passing Deadman's Island, in the Gulf of St. Lawrence 913
Written, Originally Extempore, on Seeing a Mad Heifer Run through the Village Where the Author Lives 151
Wrongs of Woman: or Maria. A Fragment, The (Chapter 5) 446
Ye Alps audacious, thro' the Heavens that rise 227
Ye Clouds, that far above me float and pause 752
Ye coop us up, and tax our bread 943
Ye plains, where three fold harvests press the ground 261
Ye, who in alleys green and leafy bow'rs 335
YEARSLEY, ANN 221
Yes, I will go, where circling whirlwinds rise 342
Yes, injured Woman! rise, assert thy right! 111
You tell me, fair one, that you ne'er can love 954
Young Emigrants, The (Letter 5) 1442